# PHILIP'S

# ATLAS
## OF THE
# WORLD

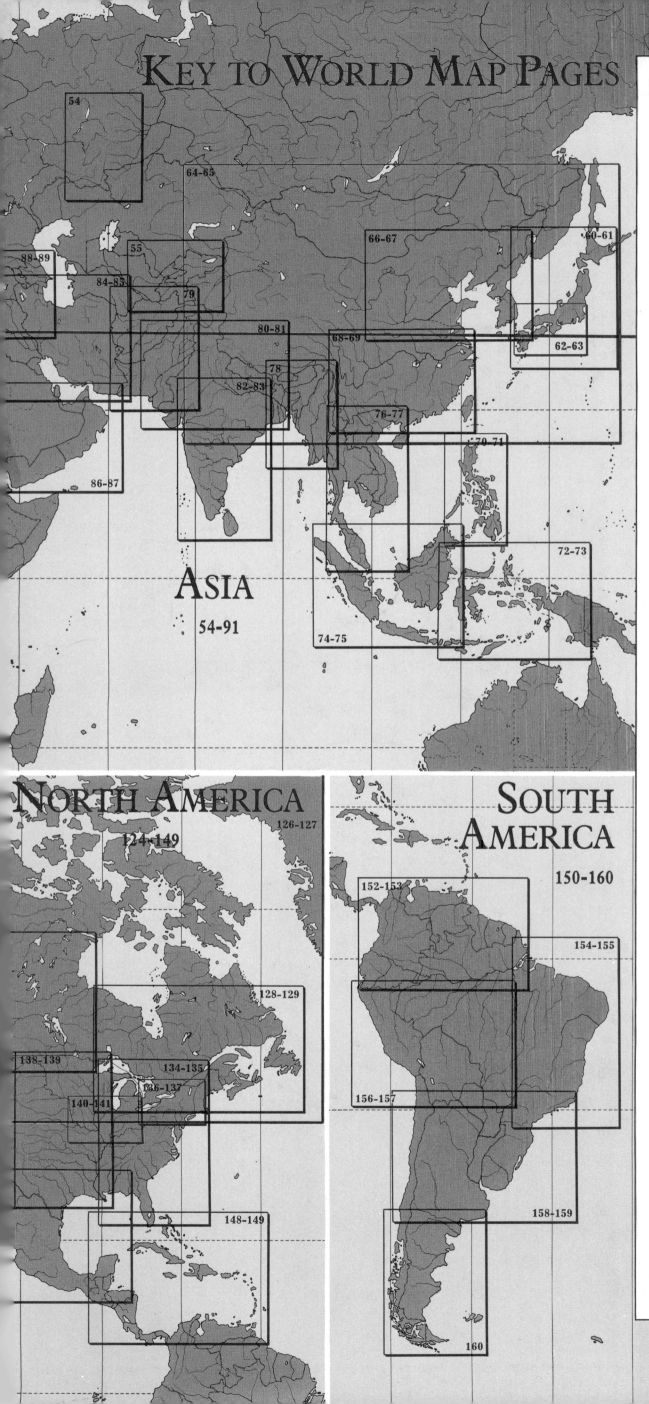

# KEY TO WORLD MAP PAGES

ASIA
54-91

NORTH AMERICA
124-149

SOUTH AMERICA
150-160

# COUNTRY INDEX

# PHILIP'S

# ATLAS
## OF THE
# WORLD

Published by George Philip Limited
59 Grosvenor Street, London W1X 9DA

ISBN 0-540-05686-3

© 1992 George Philip Limited

Printed in Hong Kong

# PHILIP'S WORLD MAPS

The reference maps which form the main body of this atlas have been prepared in accordance with the highest standards of international cartography to provide an accurate and detailed representation of the earth. The scales and projections used have been carefully chosen to give balanced coverage of the world, while emphasizing the most densely populated and economically significant regions. A hallmark of Philip's mapping is the use of hill shading and relief colouring to create a graphic impression of landforms: this makes the maps exceptionally easy to read. However, knowledge of the key features employed in the construction and presentation of the maps will enable the reader to derive the fullest benefit from the atlas.

## Map sequence

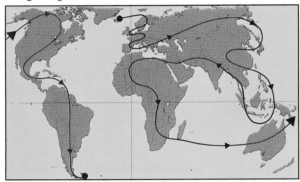

The atlas covers the earth continent by continent: first Europe; then its land neighbour Asia (mapped north before south, in a clockwise sequence), then Africa, Australia and Oceania, North America and South America. This is the classic arrangement adopted by most cartographers since the 16th century. For each continent, there are maps at a variety of scales. First, physical relief and political maps of the whole continent. Then a series of larger-scale maps of the regions within the continent, each followed, where required, by still larger-scale maps of the most important or densely populated areas. The governing principle is that by turning the pages of the atlas, the reader moves steadily from north to south through each continent, with each map overlapping its neighbours. A key map showing this sequence, and the area covered by each map, can be found on the endpapers of the atlas.

## Map presentation

With very few exceptions (eg for the Arctic and Antarctic), the maps are drawn with north at the top, regardless of whether they are presented upright or sideways on the page. In the borders will be found the map title; a locator diagram showing the area covered and the page numbers for maps of adjacent areas; the scale; the projection used; the degrees of latitude and longitude; and the letters and figures used in the index for locating place names and geographical features. Physical relief maps also have a height reference panel identifying the colours used for each layer of contouring.

## Map symbols

Each map contains a vast amount of detail which can only be conveyed clearly and accurately by the use of symbols. Points and circles of varying sizes locate and identify the relative importance of towns and cities; different styles of type are employed for administrative, geographical and regional place names. A variety of pictorial symbols denote landscape features such as glaciers, marshes and reefs, and man-made structures including roads, railways, airports, canals and dams. International borders are shown by red lines. Where neighbouring countries are in dispute, for example in the Middle East, the maps show the *de facto* boundary between nations, regardless of the legal or historical situation. The symbols are explained on the first page of the World Maps section of the atlas.

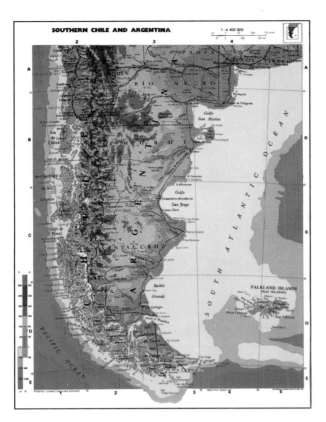

## Map scales

| 1: 16 000 000 |
|---|
| 1 inch = 252 statute miles |

The scale of each map is given in the numerical form known as the 'representative fraction'. The first figure is always one, signifying one unit of distance on the map; the second figure, usually in millions, is the number by which the map unit must be multiplied to give the equivalent distance on the earth's surface. Calculations can easily be made in centimetres and kilometres, by dividing the earth units figure by 100 000 (ie deleting the last five 0s). Thus 1:1 000 000 means 1 cm = 10 km. The calculation for inches and miles is more laborious, but 1 000 000 divided by 63 360 (the number of inches in a mile) shows that 1:1 000 000 means approximately 1 inch = 16 miles. The table below provides distance equivalents for scales down to 1:50 000 000.

| LARGE SCALE | | |
|---|---|---|
| 1: 1 000 000 | 1 cm = 10 km | 1 inch = 16 miles |
| 1: 2 500 000 | 1 cm = 25 km | 1 inch = 39.5 miles |
| 1: 5 000 000 | 1 cm = 50 km | 1 inch = 79 miles |
| 1: 6 000 000 | 1 cm = 60 km | 1 inch = 95 miles |
| 1: 8 000 000 | 1 cm = 80 km | 1 inch = 126 miles |
| 1: 10 000 000 | 1 cm = 100 km | 1 inch = 158 miles |
| 1: 15 000 000 | 1 cm = 150 km | 1 inch = 237 miles |
| 1: 20 000 000 | 1 cm = 200 km | 1 inch = 316 miles |
| 1: 50 000 000 | 1 cm = 500 km | 1 inch = 790 miles |
| SMALL SCALE | | |

## Measuring distances

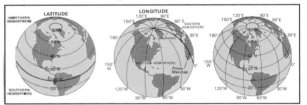

Although each map is accompanied by a scale bar, distances cannot always be measured with confidence because of the distortions involved in portraying the curved surface of the earth on a flat page. As a general rule, the larger the map scale (ie the lower the number of earth units in the representative fraction), the more accurate and reliable will be the distance measured. On small-scale maps such as those of the world and of entire continents, measurement may only be accurate along the 'standard parallels', or central axes, and should not be attempted without considering the map projection.

## Map projections

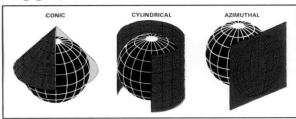

Unlike a globe, no flat map can give a true scale representation of the world in terms of area, shape and position of every region. Each of the numerous systems that have been devised for projecting the curved surface of the earth on to a flat page involves the sacrifice of accuracy in one or more of these elements. The variations in shape and position of landmasses such as Alaska, Greenland and Australia, for example, can be quite dramatic when different projections are compared.

For this atlas, the guiding principle has been to select projections that involve the least distortion of size and distance. The projection used for each map is noted in the border. Most fall into one of three categories - conic, cylindrical or azimuthal - whose basic concepts are shown above. Each involves plotting the forms of the earth's surface on a grid of latitude and longitude lines, which may be shown as parallels, curves or radiating spokes.

## Latitude and longitude

Accurate positioning of individual points on the earth's surface is made possible by reference to the geometrical system of latitude and longitude. Latitude *parallels* are drawn west-east around the earth and numbered by degrees north and south of the Equator, which is designated 0° of latitude. Longitude *meridians* are drawn north-south and numbered by degrees east and west of the *prime meridian*, 0° of longitude, which passes through Greenwich in England. By referring to these co-ordinates and their sub-divisions of minutes (1/60th of a degree) and seconds (1/60th of a minute), any place on earth can be located to within a few hundred yards. Latitude and longitude are indicated by blue lines on the maps; they are straight or curved according to the projection employed. Reference to these lines is the easiest way of determining the relative positions of places on different maps, and for plotting compass directions.

## Name forms

For ease of reference, both English and local name forms appear in the atlas. Oceans, seas and countries are shown in English throughout the atlas; country names may be abbreviated to their commonly accepted form (eg Germany, not Federal Republic of Germany). Conventional English forms are also used for place names on the smaller-scale maps of the continents. However, local name forms are used on all large-scale and regional maps, with the English form given in brackets only for important cities - the large-scale map of European Russia thus shows Moskva (Moscow). For countries which do not use a Roman script, place names have been transcribed according to the systems adopted by the British and US Geographic Names Authorities. For China, the Pin Yin system has been used, with some more widely known forms appearing in brackets, as with Beijing (Peking). Both English and local names appear in the index, the English form being cross-referenced to the local form.

V

# CONTENTS

NOTE
The titles to the World Maps
list the main countries, states
and provinces covered by
each map. A name given in
*italics* indicates that only part
of the country is shown on
the map.

**Netherlands, Belgium and Luxembourg**
1:1 000 000

**20-21**

**Northern France**
1:2 000 000

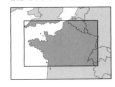

**22-23**

**Southern France**
1:2 000 000
Corsica, Monaco

**24-25**

**Germany**  1:2 000 000

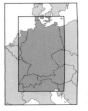

**26-27**

**Switzerland**  1:800 000
Liechtenstein

**28-29**

**Austria, Czechoslovakia and Hungary**  1:2 000 000
*Poland*

**30-31**

**Malta, Crete, Corfu, Rhodes and Cyprus**
1:800 000 - 1:1 040 000

**32**

**Balearics, Canaries and Madeira**  1:800 000 - 1:1 600 000
Mallorca, Menorca, Ibiza

**33**

**Eastern Spain**  1:2 000 000
Andorra

**34-35**

**Western Spain and Portugal**  1:2 000 000

**36-37**

**Northern Italy, Slovenia and Croatia**
1:2 000 000
San Marino, Slovenia, *Croatia*

**38-39**

**Southern Italy**  1:2 000 000
Sardinia, Sicily

**40-41**

**The Lower Danube**
1:2 000 000

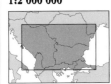

**42-43**

**Greece and Albania**
1:2 000 000

**44-45**

**Romania**  1:2 000 000

**46**

**Poland**  1:2 000 000

**47**

**Eastern Europe and Turkey**
1:8 000 000

**48-49**

**Western Russia, Belorussia and the Baltic States**  1:4 000 000
*Russian Fed.*, Estonia, Latvia, Lithuania, Belorussia, *Ukraine*

**50-51**

**Ukraine, Moldavia and the Caucasus**  1:4 000 000
*Russian Fed.*, Ukraine, Georgia, *Armenia*, *Azerbaijan*, Moldavia

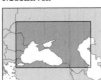

**52-53**

# ASIA

**Southern Urals**  1:4 000 000
*Russian Fed.*

**54**

**Central Asia**  1:4 000 000
*Kazakhstan*, **Kirghizia**, **Tajikistan**, *Uzbekistan*

**55**

**Russia and Central Asia**
1:16 000 000
Russian Fed., Kazakhstan, Turkmenistan, Uzbekistan

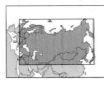

**56-57**

**Asia: Physical**
1:40 000 000
**58**

**Asia: Political**
1:40 000 000
**59**

**Japan**  1:4 000 000
Ryukyu Islands

**60-61**

**Southern Japan**  1:2 000 000

**62-63**

**China**  1:12 000 000
Mongolia

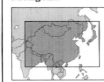

**64-65**

**Northern China and Korea**  1:4 800 000
North Korea, South Korea

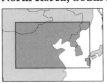

**66-67**

**Southern China**  1:4 800 000
Hong Kong, Taiwan, Macau

**68-69**

**Philippines**  1:3 200 000

**70-71**

**Eastern Indonesia**
1:5 600 000

**72-73**

**Western Indonesia**
1:5 600 000
Malaysia, Singapore, Brunei

**74-75**

**Mainland South-East Asia**  1:4 800 000
Thailand, Vietnam, Cambodia, Laos

**76-77**

**Bangladesh, North-Eastern India and Burma**
1:4 800 000
Bhutan

**78**

**Afghanistan and Pakistan**
1:5 600 000

**79**

**The Indo-Gangetic Plain**
1:4 800 000
*India*, Nepal, *Pakistan*, Kashmir

**80-81**

**Southern India and Sri Lanka**  1:4 800 000

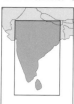
**82-83**

**The Middle East**  1:5 600 000
Iran, Iraq, *Saudi Arabia*, Kuwait

**84-85**

**Southern Arabian Peninsula**  1:5 600 000
*Saudi Arabia*, Yemen, United Arab Emirates, Oman, Qatar

**86-87**

**Turkey**  1:4 000 000
Syria

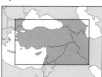
**88-89**

**Arabia and the Horn of Africa**  1:12 000 000
Saudi Arabia, Oman, Yemen, *Somalia*, Ethiopia, Djibouti

**90**

**The Near East**  1:2 000 000
Israel, Lebanon, *Jordan*

**91**

# AFRICA

**Africa: Physical**
1:32 000 000
**92**

**Africa: Political**
1:32 000 000
**93**

**The Nile Valley**  1:6 400 000
Egypt, Sudan, *Ethiopia*
The Nile Delta  1:3 200 000

**94-95**

**Central North Africa**
1:6 400 000
Libya, Chad, *Niger*

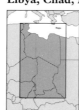
**96-97**

**North-West Africa**
1:6 400 000
Algeria, Morocco, Tunisia, *Mauritania*, *Niger*, *Mali*

**98-99**

**West Africa**  1:6 400 000
Nigeria, Ivory Coast, Ghana, Senegal, Guinea, Burkina Faso

**100-101**

**Central Africa**  1:6 400 000
*Zaïre*, Angola, Cameroon, Congo, Gabon, Central African Republic

**102-103**

**Southern Africa**  1:6 400 000
South Africa, Zimbabwe, Madagascar, *Mozambique*, Botswana, Namibia

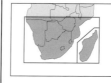
**104-105**

**East Africa**  1:6 400 000
Kenya, Tanzania, Zambia, Uganda, Malawi

**106-107**

**Horn of Africa**  1:6 400 000
Somalia, *Ethiopia*, Djibouti

**108**

**Indian Ocean**  1:40 000 000
Mauritius, Réunion, Seychelles, Maldives
**109**

# AUSTRALIA AND OCEANIA

**Australia and Oceania: Physical and Political**
1:16 000 000
**110-111**

**Western Australia**
1:6 400 000
*Northern Territory*

**112-113**

**Eastern Australia**
1:6 400 000
Queensland, Tasmania, New South Wales

**114-115**

**South-East Australia**
1:3 200 000
*New South Wales*, Victoria, *South Australia*

**116-117**

**New Zealand - North Island**  1:2 800 000

**118**

**New Zealand - South Island**  1:2 800 000

**119**

**Papua New Guinea**
1:5 200 000

**120**

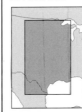
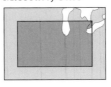

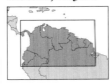

IX

# World Statistics: Countries

This alphabetical list includes all the countries and territories of the world. If a territory is not completely independent, then the country it is associated with is named. The area figures give the total area of land, inland water and ice. Units for areas and populations are thousands. The annual income is the Gross National Product per capita in US dollars. The figures are the latest available, usually 1989-91.

| Country/Territory | Area km² Thousands | Area miles² Thousands | Population Thousands | Capital | Annual Income US $ |
|---|---|---|---|---|---|
| Adélie Land (Fr) | 432 | 167 | 0.03 | - | |
| Afghanistan | 652 | 25 | 16,433 | Kabul | 450 |
| Albania | 28.8 | 11.1 | 3,250 | Tiranë | 1,000 |
| Algeria | 2,382 | 920 | 24,960 | Algiers | 2,060 |
| American Samoa (US) | 0.20 | 0.08 | 39 | Pago Pago | 6,000 |
| Amsterdam Is. (Fr) | 0.05 | 0.02 | 0.03 | - | |
| Andorra (Fr/Spain) | 0.45 | 0.17 | 52 | Andorre-la-Vella | |
| Angola | 1,247 | 481 | 10,020 | Luanda | 620 |
| Anguilla (UK) | 0.40 | 0.09 | 8 | The Valley | |
| Antigua & Barbuda | 0.44 | 0.17 | 77 | St. John's | 4,600 |
| Argentina | 2,767 | 1,068 | 32,322 | Buenos Aires | 2,370 |
| Armenia | 29.8 | 11.5 | 3,300 | Yerevan | |
| Aruba (Neths) | 0.19 | 0.07 | 60 | Oranjestad | 6,000 |
| Ascension Is. (UK) | 0.09 | 0.03 | 1.5 | Georgetown | |
| Australia | 7,687 | 2,968 | 17,086 | Canberra | 17,080 |
| Austral. Antarc. Terr. | 6,120 | 2,363 | 0 | - | |
| Austria | 83.9 | 32.4 | 7,712 | Vienna | 19,240 |
| Azerbaijan | 86.6 | 33.4 | 7,000 | Baku | |
| Azores (Port) | 2.2 | 0.87 | 260 | Ponta Delgada | |
| Bahamas | 13.9 | 5.4 | 253 | Nassau | 11,510 |
| Bahrain | 0.68 | 0.26 | 503 | Manama | 6,500 |
| Bangladesh | 144 | 56 | 115,594 | Dacca | 200 |
| Barbados | 0.43 | 0.17 | 255 | Bridgetown | 6,540 |
| Belau (US) | 0.46 | 0.18 | 15 | Koror | |
| Belgium | 30.5 | 11.8 | 9,845 | Brussels | 15,440 |
| Belize | 23.0 | 8.9 | 188 | Belmopan | 1,970 |
| Belorussia | 207.6 | 80.1 | 10,200 | Minsk | |
| Benin | 113 | 43 | 4,736 | Porto-Novo | 360 |
| Bermuda (UK) | 0.05 | 0.02 | 61 | Hamilton | 25,000 |
| Bhutan (India) | 47.0 | 18.1 | 1,517 | Thimphu | 190 |
| Bolivia | 1,099 | 424 | 7,400 | La Paz/Sucre | 620 |
| Botswana | 582 | 225 | 1,291 | Gaborone | 2,040 |
| Bouvet Is. (Nor) | 0.05 | 0.02 | 0.02 | - | |
| Brazil | 8,512 | 3,286 | 153,322 | Brasilia | 2,680 |
| Brit. Antarctic Terr. (UK) | 1,709 | 660 | 0.3 | Stanley | |
| Brit. Ind. Oc. Terr. (UK) | 0.08 | 0.03 | 3 | - | |
| Brunei | 5.8 | 2.2 | 266 | Bandar Seri Begawan | 6,000 |
| Bulgaria | 111 | 43 | 9,011 | Sofia | 2,210 |
| Burkina Faso | 274 | 106 | 9,001 | Ouagadougou | 330 |
| Burma (Myanmar) | 677 | 261 | 41,675 | Rangoon | 500 |
| Burundi | 27.8 | 10.7 | 5,438 | Bujumbura | 210 |
| Cambodia | 181 | 70 | 8,246 | Phnom Penh | 300 |
| Cameroon | 475 | 184 | 11,834 | Yaoundé | 940 |
| Canada | 9,976 | 3,852 | 26,522 | Ottawa | 20,450 |
| Canary Is. (Spain) | 7.3 | 2.8 | 1,700 | Las Palmas/S.Cruz | |
| Cape Verde Is. | 4.0 | 1.6 | 370 | Praia | 890 |
| Cayman Is. (UK) | 0.26 | 0.10 | 27 | Georgetown | |
| Cent. African Rep. | 623 | 241 | 3,039 | Bangui | 390 |
| Chad | 1,284 | 496 | 5,679 | Ndjamena | 190 |
| Chatham Is. (NZ) | 0.96 | 0.37 | 0.05 | Waitangi | |
| Chile | 757 | 292 | 13,386 | Santiago | 1,940 |
| China | 9,597 | 3,682 | 1,139,060 | Beijing | 370 |
| Christmas Is. (Aus) | 0.14 | 0.05 | 2.3 | The Settlement | |
| Cocos (Keeling) Is. (Aus) | 0.01 | 0.005 | 0.70 | - | |
| Colombia | 1,139 | 440 | 32,987 | Bogotá | 1,240 |
| Comoros | 2.2 | 0.86 | 551 | Moroni | 480 |
| Congo | 342 | 132 | 2,271 | Brazzaville | 1,010 |
| Cook Is. (NZ) | 0.24 | 0.11 | 18 | Avarua | 900 |
| Costa Rica | 51.1 | 19.7 | 2,994 | San José | 1,910 |
| Croatia | 56.5 | 21.8 | 4,680 | Zagreb | |
| Crozet Is. (Fr) | 0.51 | 0.19 | 35 | - | |
| Cuba | 111 | 43 | 10,609 | Havana | 3,000 |
| Cyprus | 9.3 | 3.6 | 702 | Nicosia | 8,040 |
| Czechoslovakia | 128 | 49 | 15,678 | Prague | 3,140 |
| Denmark | 43.1 | 16.6 | 5,140 | Copenhagen | 22,090 |
| Djibouti | 23.2 | 9.0 | 409 | Djibouti | 1,000 |
| Dominica | 0.75 | 0.29 | 83 | Roseau | 1,940 |
| Dominican Rep. | 48.7 | 18.8 | 7,170 | Santo Domingo | 820 |
| Ecuador | 284 | 109 | 10,782 | Quito | 960 |
| Egypt | 1,001 | 387 | 53,153 | Cairo | 600 |
| El Salvador | 21.0 | 8.1 | 5,252 | San Salvador | 1,100 |
| Equatorial Guinea | 28.1 | 10.8 | 348 | Malabo | 330 |
| Estonia | 44.7 | 17.4 | 1,600 | Tallinn | |
| Ethiopia | 1,222 | 472 | 50,974 | Addis Ababa | 120 |
| Falkland Is. (UK) | 12.2 | 4.7 | 2 | Stanley | |
| Faroe Is. (Den) | 1.4 | 0.54 | 47 | Tórshavn | 22,090 |
| Fiji | 18.3 | 7.1 | 765 | Suva | 1,770 |
| Finland | 338 | 131 | 4,986 | Helsinki | 26,070 |
| France | 552 | 213 | 56,440 | Paris | 19,480 |
| French Guiana (Fr) | 90.0 | 34.7 | 99 | Cayenne | 2,500 |
| French Polynesia (Fr) | 4.0 | 1.5 | 206 | Papeete | 6,000 |
| Gabon | 268 | 103 | 1,172 | Libreville | 3,220 |
| Gambia, The | 11.3 | 4.4 | 861 | Banjul | 260 |
| Georgia | 69.7 | 26.9 | 5,500 | Tbilisi | |
| Germany | 357 | 138 | 79,479 | Berlin/Bonn | 17,000 |
| Ghana | 239 | 92 | 15,028 | Accra | 390 |
| Gibraltar (UK) | 0.007 | 0.003 | 31 | - | 4,000 |
| Greece | 132 | 51 | 10,269 | Athens | 6,000 |
| Greenland (Den) | 2,176 | 840 | 60 | Godthåb | 6,000 |
| Grenada | 0.34 | 0.13 | 85 | St. George's | 2,120 |
| Guadeloupe (Fr) | 1.7 | 0.66 | 344 | Basse-Terre | 7,000 |
| Guam (US) | 0.55 | 0.21 | 119 | Agana | 6,000 |
| Guatemala | 109 | 42 | 9,197 | Guatemala City | 900 |
| Guinea | 246 | 95 | 5,756 | Conakry | 480 |
| Guinea-Bissau | 36.1 | 13.9 | 965 | Bissau | 180 |
| Guyana | 215 | 83 | 796 | Georgetown | 370 |
| Haiti | 27.8 | 10.7 | 6,486 | Port-au-Prince | 370 |
| Honduras | 112 | 43 | 5,105 | Tegucigalpa | 590 |
| Hong Kong (UK) | 1.1 | 0.40 | 5,801 | - | 11,540 |
| Hungary | 93.0 | 35.9 | 10,344 | Budapest | 2,780 |
| Iceland | 103 | 40 | 255 | Reykjavik | 21,150 |
| India | 3,288 | 1,269 | 843,931 | Delhi | 350 |
| Indonesia | 1,905 | 735 | 179,300 | Jakarta | 560 |
| Iran | 1,648 | 636 | 58,031 | Tehran | 2,450 |
| Iraq | 438 | 169 | 18,920 | Baghdad | 2,000 |
| Ireland | 70.3 | 27.1 | 3,523 | Dublin | 9,550 |
| Israel | 27.0 | 10.4 | 4,659 | Jerusalem | 10,970 |
| Italy | 301 | 116 | 57,663 | Rome | 16,850 |
| Ivory Coast | 322 | 125 | 11,998 | Abidjan | 730 |
| Jamaica | 11.0 | 4.2 | 2,420 | Kingston | 1,510 |
| Jan Mayen Is. (Nor) | 0.38 | 0.15 | 0.06 | - | |
| Japan | 378 | 146 | 123,537 | Tokyo | 25,430 |
| Johnston Is. (US) | 0.002 | 0.0009 | 0.30 | - | |
| Jordan | 89.2 | 34.4 | 4,009 | Amman | 1,240 |
| Kazakhstan | 2,717 | 1,049 | 16,500 | Alma Ata | |
| Kenya | 580 | 224 | 24,032 | Nairobi | 370 |
| Kerguelen Is. (Fr) | 7.2 | 2.8 | 0 | - | |
| Kermadec Is. (NZ) | 0.03 | 0.01 | 0 | - | |
| Kirghizia | 199 | 76.5 | 4,300 | Bishkek | |
| Kiribati | 0.72 | 0.28 | 66 | Tarawa | 760 |
| Korea, North | 121 | 47 | 21,773 | Pyongyang | 900 |
| Korea, South | 99.0 | 38.2 | 43,302 | Seoul | 5,400 |
| Kuwait | 17.8 | 6.9 | 2,143 | Kuwait City | 16,380 |
| Laos | 237 | 91 | 4,139 | Vientiane | 200 |
| Latvia | 63.1 | 24.6 | 2,700 | Riga | |
| Lebanon | 10.4 | 4.0 | 2,701 | Beirut | 2,000 |
| Lesotho | 30.4 | 11.7 | 1,774 | Maseru | 470 |
| Liberia | 111 | 43 | 2,607 | Monrovia | 500 |
| Libya | 1,760 | 679 | 4,545 | Tripoli | 5,800 |
| Liechtenstein | 0.16 | 0.06 | 29 | Vaduz | 33,000 |
| Lithuania | 65.2 | 25.4 | 3,751 | Vilnius | |
| Luxembourg | 2.6 | 1.0 | 384 | Luxembourg | 28,770 |
| Macau (Port) | 0.02 | 0.006 | 479 | - | 2,000 |
| Madagascar | 587 | 227 | 11,197 | Antananarivo | 230 |
| Madeira (Port) | 0.81 | 0.31 | 280 | Funchal | |
| Malawi | 118 | 46 | 8,556 | Lilongwe | 200 |
| Malaysia | 330 | 127 | 17,861 | Kuala Lumpur | 2,340 |
| Maldives | 0.30 | 0.12 | 215 | Malé | 440 |
| Mali | 1,240 | 479 | 8,156 | Bamako | 270 |
| Malta | 0.32 | 0.12 | 354 | Valletta | 6,630 |
| Mariana Is. (US) | 0.48 | 0.18 | 22 | Saipan | |
| Marshall Is. (US) | 0.18 | 0.07 | 42 | Majuro | |
| Martinique (Fr) | 1.1 | 0.42 | 341 | Fort-de-France | 4,000 |
| Mauritania | 1,025 | 396 | 2,050 | Nouakchott | 500 |
| Mauritius | 1.9 | 0.72 | 1,075 | Port Louis | 2,250 |
| Mayotte (Fr) | 0.37 | 0.14 | 84 | Mamoundzou | |
| Mexico | 1,958 | 756 | 86,154 | Mexico City | 2,490 |
| Micronesia, Fed. Stat (US) | 0.70 | 0.27 | 103 | Kolonia | |
| Midway Is. (US) | 0.005 | 0.002 | 0.45 | - | |
| Moldavia | 33.7 | 13.0 | 4,300 | Kishinev | |
| Monaco | 0.002 | 0.0001 | 29 | - | 20,000 |
| Mongolia | 1,567 | 605 | 2,190 | Ulan Bator | 400 |
| Montserrat (UK) | 0.10 | 0.04 | 13 | Plymouth | |
| Morocco | 447 | 172 | 25,061 | Rabat | 950 |
| Mozambique | 802 | 309 | 15,656 | Maputo | 80 |
| Namibia | 824 | 318 | 1,781 | Windhoek | 1,000 |
| Nauru | 0.02 | 0.008 | 10 | Domaneab | |
| Nepal | 141 | 54 | 18,916 | Katmandu | 170 |
| Netherlands | 41.9 | 16.2 | 15,019 | Amsterdam | 17,330 |
| Neths. Antilles (Neths) | 0.99 | 0.38 | 189 | Willemstad | 6,000 |
| New Caledonia (Fr) | 19.0 | 7.3 | 168 | Nouméa | 4,000 |
| New Zealand | 269 | 104 | 3,429 | Wellington | 12,680 |
| Nicaragua | 130 | 50 | 3,871 | Managua | 800 |
| Niger | 1,267 | 489 | 7,732 | Niamey | 310 |
| Nigeria | 924 | 357 | 108,542 | Lagos (Abuja) | 270 |
| Niue (NZ) | 0.26 | 0.10 | 3 | Alofi | |
| Norfolk Is. (Aus) | 0.03 | 0.01 | 2 | Kingston | |
| Norway | 324 | 125 | 4,242 | Oslo | 23,120 |
| Oman | 212 | 82 | 1,502 | Muscat | 5,220 |
| Pakistan | 796 | 307 | 112,050 | Islamabad | 380 |
| Panama | 77.1 | 29.8 | 2,418 | Panama City | 1,830 |
| Papua New Guinea | 463 | 179 | 3,699 | Port Moresby | 860 |
| Paraguay | 407 | 157 | 4,277 | Asunción | 1,110 |
| Peru | 1,285 | 496 | 22,332 | Lima | 1,160 |
| Peter 1st Is. (Nor) | 0.18 | 0.07 | 0 | - | |
| Philippines | 300 | 116 | 61,480 | Manila | 730 |
| Pitcairn Is. (UK) | 0.03 | 0.01 | 0.06 | Adamstown | |
| Poland | 313 | 121 | 38,180 | Warsaw | 1,700 |
| Portugal | 92.4 | 35.7 | 10,525 | Lisbon | 4,890 |
| Puerto Rico (US) | 8.9 | 3.4 | 3,599 | San Juan | 6,470 |
| Qatar | 11.0 | 4.2 | 368 | Doha | 15,860 |
| Queen Maud Land (Nor) | 2,800 | 1,081 | 0 | - | |
| Réunion (Fr) | 2.5 | 0.97 | 599 | St.-Denis | 4,000 |
| Romania | 238 | 92 | 23,200 | Bucharest | 1,640 |
| Ross Dependency (NZ) | 435 | 168 | 0 | - | |
| Russia | 17,075 | 6,591 | 147,400 | Moscow | |
| Rwanda | 26.3 | 10.2 | 7,181 | Kigali | 310 |
| St. Christopher/Nevis | 0.36 | 0.14 | 44 | Basseterre | 3,300 |
| St. Helena (UK) | 0.31 | 0.12 | 7 | Jamestown | |
| St. Lucia | 0.62 | 0.24 | 151 | Castries | 1,900 |
| St. Paul Is. (Fr) | 0.007 | 0.003 | 0 | - | |
| St. Pierre & Miquelon (Fr) | 0.24 | 0.09 | 6 | St. Pierre | |
| St. Vincent/Grenadines | 0.39 | 0.15 | 116 | Kingstown | 1,610 |
| San Marino | 0.06 | 0.02 | 24 | San Marino | |
| São Tomé & Príncipe | 0.96 | 0.37 | 121 | São Tomé | 380 |
| Saudi Arabia | 2,150 | 830 | 14,870 | Riyadh | 6,230 |
| Senegal | 197 | 76 | 7,327 | Dakar | 710 |
| Seychelles | 0.28 | 0.11 | 67 | Victoria | 4,670 |
| Sierra Leone | 71.7 | 27.7 | 4,151 | Freetown | 240 |
| Singapore | 0.62 | 0.24 | 3,003 | Singapore | 12,310 |
| Slovenia | 20.3 | 7.8 | 1,940 | Ljubljana | |
| Solomon Is. | 28.9 | 11.2 | 321 | Honiara | 580 |
| Somalia | 638 | 246 | 7,497 | Mogadishu | 150 |
| South Africa | 1,221 | 471 | 35,282 | Pretoria | 2,520 |
| South Georgia (UK) | 3.8 | 1.4 | 0.05 | - | |
| South Sandwich Is. (UK) | 0.38 | 0.15 | 0 | - | |
| Spain | 505 | 195 | 38,959 | Madrid | 10,920 |
| Sri Lanka | 65.6 | 25.3 | 16,993 | Colombo | 470 |
| Sudan | 2,506 | 967 | 25,204 | Khartoum | 450 |
| Surinam | 163 | 63 | 422 | Paramaribo | 3,050 |
| Svalbard (Nor) | 62.0 | 23.9 | 4 | Longyearbyen | |
| Swaziland | 17.4 | 6.7 | 768 | Mbabane | 820 |
| Sweden | 450 | 174 | 8,618 | Stockholm | 23,680 |
| Switzerland | 41.3 | 15.9 | 6,712 | Bern | 32,790 |
| Syria | 185 | 71 | 12,116 | Damascus | 990 |
| Taiwan | 36.0 | 13.9 | 20,300 | Taipei | 6,600 |
| Tajikistan | 143 | 55.2 | 5,100 | Dushanbe | |
| Tanzania | 945 | 365 | 25,635 | Dar es Salaam | 120 |
| Thailand | 513 | 198 | 57,196 | Bangkok | 1,420 |
| Togo | 56.8 | 21.9 | 3,531 | Lome | 410 |
| Tokelau (NZ) | 0.01 | 0.005 | 2 | Nukunonu | |
| Tonga | 0.75 | 0.29 | 95 | Nuku'alofa | 1,010 |
| Trinidad & Tobago | 5.1 | 2.0 | 1,227 | Port of Spain | 3,470 |
| Tristan da Cunha (UK) | 0.11 | 0.04 | 0.33 | Edinburgh | |
| Tunisia | 164 | 63 | 8,180 | Tunis | 1,420 |
| Turkey | 779 | 301 | 57,326 | Ankara | 1,630 |
| Turkmenistan | 488 | 186 | 3,500 | Ashkhabad | |
| Turks & Caicos Is. (UK) | 0.43 | 0.17 | 10 | Grand Turk | |
| Tuvalu | 0.03 | 0.01 | 10 | Funafuti | 600 |
| Uganda | 236 | 91 | 18,795 | Kampala | 220 |
| Ukraine | 604 | 232 | 51,700 | Kiev | |
| United Arab Emirates | 83.6 | 32.3 | 1,589 | Abu Dhabi | 19,860 |
| United Kingdom | 244 | 94 | 57,405 | London | 16,070 |
| United States | 9,373 | 3,619 | 249,928 | Washington | 21,700 |
| Uruguay | 177 | 68 | 3,094 | Montevideo | 2,560 |
| Uzbekistan | 447 | 173 | 19,900 | Tashkent | |
| Vanuatu | 12.2 | 4.7 | 147 | Port Vila | 1,060 |
| Vatican City | 0.0004 | 0.0002 | 1.0 | - | |
| Venezuela | 912 | 352 | 19,735 | Caracas | 2,560 |
| Vietnam | 332 | 127 | 66,200 | Hanoi | 300 |
| Virgin Is. (UK) | 0.15 | 0.06 | 13 | Road Town | |
| Virgin Is. (US) | 0.34 | 0.13 | 117 | Charlotte Amalie | 12,000 |
| Wake Is. | 0.008 | 0.003 | 0.30 | - | |
| Wallis & Futuna Is. (Fr) | 0.20 | 0.08 | 18 | Mata-Utu | |
| Western Sahara (Mor) | 266 | 103 | 179 | El Aiun | |
| Western Samoa | 2.8 | 1.1 | 164 | Apia | 730 |
| Yemen | 528 | 204 | 11,282 | San'a | 640 |
| Yugoslavia | 179 | 69.4 | 17,144 | Belgrade | 3,060 |
| Zaire | 2,345 | 906 | 35,562 | Kinshasa | 230 |
| Zambia | 753 | 291 | 8,073 | Lusaka | 420 |
| Zimbabwe | 391 | 151 | 9,369 | Harare | 640 |

# WORLD STATISTICS: CITIES

This list shows the principal cities with more than 500,000 inhabitants (for China only cities with more than 1 million are included). The figures are taken from the most recent census or estimate available, and as far as possible are the population of the metropolitan area, eg greater New York, Mexico or London. All the figures are in thousands. The top 20 world cities are indicated with their rank in brackets following the name.

**Afghanistan**
Kabul 1,127
**Algeria**
Algiers 1,722
Oran 664
**Angola**
Luanda 1,200
**Argentina**
Buenos Aires [8] 10,728
Cordoba 1,055
Rosario 1,016
Mendoza 668
La Plata 611
San Miguel Tucuman 571
**Armenia**
Yerevan 1,199
**Australia**
Sydney 3,531
Melbourne 2,965
Brisbane 1,215
Perth 1,083
Adelaide 1,013
**Austria**
Vienna 1,483
**Azerbaijan**
Baku 1,757
**Bangladesh**
Dacca 4,770
Chittagong 1,840
Khulna 860
Rajshahi 430
**Belgium**
Brussels 970
Antwerp 500
**Belorussia**
Minsk 1,589
Gomel 500
**Bolivia**
La Paz 993
**Brazil**
São Paulo [3] 16,832
Rio de Janeiro [7] 11,141
Belo Horizonte 3,446
Recife 2,945
Pôrto Alegre 2,924
Salvador 2,362
Fortaleza 2,169
Çuritiba 1,926
Brasilia 1,557
Nova Iguaçu 1,325
Belem 1,296
Santos 1,200
Goiâna 928
Campinas 845
Manaus 834
São Gonçalo 731
Guarulhos 718
Duque de Caxias 666
Santo Andre 637
Osasco 594
São Bernado do Campo 566
São Luis 564
Natal 512
**Bulgaria**
Sofia 1,129
**Burma**
Rangoon 2,459
Mandalay 533
**Cambodia**
Phnom Penh 500
**Cameroon**
Douala 1,030
Yaoundé 654
**Central African Rep.**
Bangui 597
**Chad**
Ndjamena 512
**Canada**
Toronto 3,427
Montréal 2,921
Vancouver 1,381
Ottawa-Hull 819
Edmonton 785
Calgary 671
Winnipeg 623
Québec 603
Hamilton 557

**Chile**
Santiago 4,858
**China**
Shanghai [5] 12,320
Beijing [10] 9,750
Tianjin 5,459
Shenyang 4,285
Wuhan 3,493
Canton 3,359
Chongqing 2,832
Harbin 2,668
Chengdu 2,642
Xi'an 2,387
Zibo 2,329
Nanjing 2,290
Nanchang 2,289
Lupanshui 2,247
Taiyuan 1,929
Changchun 1,908
Dalian 1,682
Zhaozhuang 1,612
Zhengzhou 1,610
Kunming 1,516
Jinan 1,464
Tangshan 1,410
Guiyang 1,403
Lanzhou 1,391
Linyi 1,385
Pingxiang 1,305
Qiqihar 1,301
Anshan 1,298
Qingdao 1,273
Xintao 1,272
Hangzhou 1,271
Fushun 1,270
Yangcheng 1,265
Yulin 1,255
Dongguang 1,230
Chao'an 1,227
Xiaogan 1,219
Fuzhou 1,205
Suining 1,195
Changsha 1,193
Shijiazhuang 1,187
Jilin 1,169
Xintai 1,167
Puyang 1,125
Baotou 1,119
Bozhou 1,112
Zhongshan 1,073
Luoyang 1,063
Laiwu 1,054
Leshan 1,039
Urumchi 1,038
Ningbo 1,033
Datong 1,020
Huainan 1,019
Heze 1,017
Handan 1,014
Linhai 1,012
Macheng 1,010
Changshu 1,004
**Colombia**
Bogotá 4,185
Medellin 1,506
Cali 1,397
Barranquilla 920
Cartagena 560
**Congo**
Brazzaville 596
**Croatia**
Zagreb 1,175
**Cuba**
Havana 2,059
**Czechoslovakia**
Prague 1,194
**Denmark**
Copenhagen 1,339
**Dominican Rep.**
Santo Domingo 1,313
**Ecuador**
Guayaquil 1,301
Quito 1,110
**Egypt**
Cairo [18] 6,325
Alexandria 2,893
El Giza 1,858
Shubra el Kheima 711
**El Salvador**
San Salvador 973

**Ethiopia**
Addis Ababa 1,686
**Finland**
Helsinki 987
**France**
Paris [13] 8,510
Lyons 1,170
Marseilles 1,080
Lille 935
Bordeaux 628
Toulouse 523
**Georgia**
Tbilisi 1,194
**Germany**
Berlin 3,301
Hamburg 1,594
Munich 1,189
Cologne 928
Essen 623
Frankfurt 619
Dortmund 584
Düsseldorf 563
Stuttgart 552
Leipzig 545
Bremen 533
Duisburg 525
Dresden 518
Hanover 500
**Ghana**
Accra 965
**Greece**
Athens 3,027
Thessalonika 872
**Guatemala**
Guatemala 2,000
**Guinea**
Conakry 705
**Haiti**
Port-au-Prince 1,144
**Honduras**
Tegucigalpa 605
**Hong Kong**
Kowloon 2,302
Hong Kong 1,176
Tsuen Wan 690
**Hungary**
Budapest 2,115
**India**
Calcutta [11] 9,194
Bombay [14] 8,243
Delhi 5,729
Madras 4,289
Bangalore 2,922
Ahmadabad 2,548
Hyderabad 2,546
Poona 1,686
Kanpur 1,639
Nagpur 1,302
Jaipur 1,015
Lucknow 1,008
Coimbatore 920
Patna 919
Surat 914
Madurai 908
Indore 829
Varanasi 797
Jabalpur 757
Agra 747
Vadodara 744
Cochin 686
Dhanbad 678
Bhopal 671
Jamshedpur 670
Allahabad 650
Ulhasnagar 649
Tiruchchirappalli 610
Ludhiana 606
Srinagar 606
Vishakhapatnam 604
Amritsar 595
Gwalior 556
Calicut 546
Vijayawada 543
Meerut 537
Dharwad 527
Trivandrum 520
Salem 519
Solapur 515
Jodhpur 506
Ranchi 503

**Indonesia**
Jakarta [17] 7,348
Surabaya 2,224
Medán 1,806
Bandung 1,567
Semarang 1,026
Palembang 787
Ujung Pandang 709
Malang 512
**Iran**
Tehran [19] 6,043
Mashhad 1,464
Esfahan 987
Tabriz 971
Shiraz 848
Ahvaz 580
Bakhtaran 561
Qom 543
**Iraq**
Baghdad 4,649
Basra 617
Mosul 571
**Ireland**
Dublin 921
**Italy**
Rome 2,817
Milan 1,464
Naples 1,203
Turin 1,012
Palermo 731
Genoa 712
**Ivory Coast**
Abidjan 1,850
Bouaké 640
**Jamaica**
Kingston 525
**Japan**
Tokyo [6] 11,829
Yokohama 2,993
Osaka 2,636
Nagoya 2,116
Sapporo 1,543
Kyoto 1,479
Kobe 1,411
Fukuoka 1,160
Kawasaki 1,089
Kitakyushu 1,056
Hiroshima 1,044
Sakai 818
Chiba 789
Sendai 700
Okayama 572
Kumamoto 556
Kagoshima 531
Higashiosaka 523
Hamamatsu 514
Amagasaki 509
Funabashi 507
**Jordan**
Amman 1,160
Irbid 680
**Kazakhstan**
Alma Ata 1,108
Karaganda 614
Astrakhan 509
**Kenya**
Nairobi 1,429
Mombasa 500
**Kirghizia**
Bishkek 616
**Korea, North**
Pyongyang 2,639
Hamhung 775
Chongjin 754
Chinnampo 691
Sinuiju 500
**Korea, South**
Seoul [9] 10,513
Pusan 3,754
Taegu 2,206
Inchon 1,604
Kwangju 1,165
Taejon 866
Ulsan 551

**Latvia**
Riga 915
**Lebanon**
Beirut 702
**Libya**
Tripoli 980
Benghazi 650
**Lithuania**
Vilnius 582
**Madagascar**
Antananarivo 703
**Malaysia**
Kuala Lumpur 1,103
**Mali**
Bamako 646
**Mauritania**
Nouakchott 500
**Mexico**
Mexico City [1] 18,748
Guadalajara 2,587
Monterrey 2,335
Puebla 1,218
León 947
Torreón 730
San Luis Potosi 602
Ciudad Juárez 596
Mérida 580
Culiacán Rosales 560
Mexicali 511
**Moldavia**
Kishinev 565
**Mongolia**
Ulan Bator 500
**Morocco**
Casablanca 2,158
Rabat-Salé 893
Fès 548
**Mozambique**
Maputo 1,070
**Netherlands**
Rotterdam 1,040
Amsterdam 1,038
The Hague 684
Utrecht 526
**New Zealand**
Auckland 851
**Nicaragua**
Managua 682
**Nigeria**
Lagos 1,097
Ibadan 1,060
Ogbomosho 527
**Norway**
Oslo 643
**Pakistan**
Karachi 5,208
Lahore 2,953
Faisalabad 1,104
Rawalpindi 795
Hyderabad 752
Multan 722
Gujranwala 659
Peshawar 556
**Panama**
Panama City 625
**Paraguay**
Asunción 708
**Peru**
Lima-Callao 4,605
Arequipa 592
**Philippines**
Manila 1,728
Quezon City 1,326
Cebu 552
Caloocan 524
**Poland**
Warsaw 1,671
Lodz 852
Krakow 744
Wroclaw 640
Poznan 586
**Portugal**
Lisbon 1,612
Oporto 1,315
**Puerto Rico**
San Juan 1,816
**Romania**
Bucharest 2,014
**Russia**
Moscow [12] 8,967
St Petersburg 5,020
Nizhniy Novgorod 1,438
Novosibirsk 1,436
Yekaterinburg 1,367
Samara 1,257
Chelyabinsk 1,179

Omsk 1,148
Kazan 1,094
Perm 1,091
Ufa 1,083
Rostov 1,020
Volgograd 999
Krasnoyarsk 912
Saratov 905
Voronezh 887
Vladivostok 648
Izhevsk 635
Yaroslavl 633
Togliatti 630
Irkutsk 626
Simbirsk 625
Krasnodar 620
Barnaul 602
Khaborovsk 601
Novokuznetsk 600
Orenburg 547
Penza 543
Tula 540
Kemerovo 520
Ryazan 515
Tomsk 502
Naberezhniye-Chelni 501
**Saudi Arabia**
Riyadh 2,000
Jedda 1,400
Mecca 618
Medina 500
**Senegal**
Dakar 1,382
**Singapore**
Singapore 2,600
**Somali Rep.**
Mogadishu 1,000
**South Africa**
Cape Town 1,912
Johannesburg 1,762
East Rand 1,038
Durban 982
Pretoria 823
Port Elizabeth 652
West Rand 647
Vereeniging 540
**Spain**
Madrid 3,123
Barcelona 1,694
Valencia 739
Seville 668
Zaragoza 596
Malaga 595
**Sri Lanka**
Colombo 1,412
**Sudan**
Omdurman 600
Khartoum 510
**Sweden**
Stockholm 1,471
Gothenburg 720
Malmö 500
**Switzerland**
Zurich 839
**Syria**
Damascus 1,361
Aleppo 1,308
**Taiwan**
Taipei 2,680
Kaohsiung 1,343
Taichung 715
Tainan 657
Panchiao 506
**Tajikistan**
Dushanbe 595
**Tanzania**
Dar es Salaam 1,100
**Thailand**
Bangkok 5,609
**Tunisia**
Tunis 774
**Turkey**
Istanbul 5,495
Ankara 2,252
Izmir 1,490
Adana 776
Bursa 614
**Uganda**
Kampala 500

**Ukraine**
Kiev 2,587
Kharkhov 1,611
Dnepropetrovsk 1,179
Odessa 1,115
Donetsk 1,110
Zaporozhye 884
Lvov 790
Krivoy Rog 713
Mariupol 529
Lugansk 509
Nikolayev 503
**United Kingdom**
London [17] 6,378
Manchester 1,669
Birmingham 1,400
Liverpool 1,060
Glasgow 730
Newcastle 617
**Uruguay**
Montevideo 1,248
**United States**
New York [2] 18,120
Los Angeles [4] 13,770
Chicago [15] 8,181
San Francisco [20] 6,042
Philadelphia 5,963
Detroit 4,620
Dallas 3,766
Boston 3,736
Washington 3,734
Houston 3,642
Miami 3,001
Cleveland 2,769
Atlanta 2,737
Saint Louis 2,467
Seattle 2,421
Minneapolis-SP. 2,388
San Diego 2,370
Baltimore 2,343
Pittsburgh 2,284
Phoenix 2,030
Tampa 1,995
Denver 1,858
Cincinnati 1,729
Kansas City 1,575
Milwaukee 1,572
Portland 1,414
Sacramento 1,385
Norfolk 1,380
Columbus 1,344
San Antonio 1,323
New Orleans 1,307
Indianapolis 1,237
Buffalo 1,176
Providence 1,118
Charlotte 1,112
Hartford 1,108
Salt Lake City 1,065
San Jose 712
Memphis 653
Jacksonville 610
**Uzbekistan**
Tashkent 2,073
**Venezuela**
Caracas 3,247
Maracaibo 1,295
Valencia 1,135
Maracay 857
Barquisimeto 718
**Vietnam**
Ho Chi Minh 3,900
Hanoi 3,100
Haiphong 1,279
Da-Nang 500
**Yemen**
San'a 500
**Yugoslavia**
Belgrade 1,470
Skopje 505
**Zaïre**
Kinshasa 2,654
Lubumbashi 543
**Zambia**
Lusaka 900
**Zimbabwe**
Harare 681
Bulawayo 500

# WORLD STATISTICS: DISTANCES

The table shows air distances in miles and kilometres between thirty major cities. Known as 'Great Circle' distances, these measure the shortest routes between the cities, which aircraft use where possible. The maps show the world centred on six individual cities, and illustrate, for example, why direct flights from Japan to northern America and Europe are across the Arctic regions, and Singapore is on the direct line route from Europe to Australia. The maps have been constructed on an Azimuthal Equidistant projection, on which all distances measured through the centre point are true to scale. The circular lines are drawn at 5,000, 10,000 and 15,000 km from the central city.

Distances below and to the left of the diagonal are in **Kms**; those above and to the right of the diagonal are in **Miles**.

| | Berlin | Bombay | Buenos Aires | Cairo | Calcutta | Caracas | Chicago | Copenhagen | Darwin | Hong Kong | Honolulu | Johannesburg | Lagos | Lisbon | London | Los Angeles | Mexico City | Moscow | Nairobi | New York | Paris | Peking | Reykjavik | Rio de Janeiro | Rome | Singapore | Sydney | Tokyo | Toronto | Wellington |
|---|---|---|---|---|---|---|---|---|---|---|---|---|---|---|---|---|---|---|---|---|---|---|---|---|---|---|---|---|---|---|
| **Berlin** | | 3907 | 7400 | 1795 | 4370 | 5241 | 4402 | 222 | 8044 | 5440 | 7310 | 5511 | 3230 | 1436 | 557 | 5785 | 6047 | 1000 | 3958 | 3967 | 545 | 4860 | 1482 | 6230 | 734 | 6179 | 10002 | 5545 | 4037 | 11272 |
| **Bombay** | 6288 | | 9275 | 2706 | 1034 | 9024 | 8048 | 3990 | 4510 | 2683 | 8024 | 4334 | 4730 | 4982 | 4467 | 8700 | 9728 | 3126 | 2816 | 7793 | 4356 | 2956 | 5179 | 8332 | 3837 | 2432 | 6313 | 4189 | 7760 | 7686 |
| **Buenos Aires** | 11909 | 14925 | | 7341 | 10268 | 3167 | 5599 | 7498 | 9130 | 11481 | 7558 | 5025 | 4919 | 5964 | 6917 | 6122 | 4591 | 8374 | 6463 | 5298 | 6867 | 11972 | 7106 | 1214 | 6929 | 9867 | 7332 | 11410 | 5650 | 6202 |
| **Cairo** | 2890 | 4355 | 11814 | | 3541 | 6340 | 6127 | 1992 | 7216 | 5064 | 8838 | 3894 | 2432 | 2358 | 2180 | 7580 | 7687 | 1803 | 2197 | 5605 | 1994 | 4688 | 3272 | 6149 | 1325 | 5137 | 8959 | 5947 | 5737 | 10268 |
| **Calcutta** | 7033 | 1664 | 16524 | 5699 | | 9609 | 7978 | 4395 | 3758 | 1653 | 7048 | 5256 | 5727 | 5639 | 4946 | 8152 | 9494 | 3438 | 3839 | 7921 | 4883 | 2031 | 5398 | 9366 | 4486 | 1800 | 5678 | 3195 | 7805 | 7055 |
| **Caracas** | 8435 | 14522 | 5096 | 10203 | 15464 | | 2502 | 5215 | 11221 | 10166 | 6009 | 6847 | 4810 | 4044 | 4664 | 3612 | 2228 | 6175 | 7173 | 2131 | 4738 | 8947 | 4297 | 2825 | 5196 | 11407 | 9534 | 8801 | 2406 | 8154 |
| **Chicago** | 7084 | 12953 | 9011 | 3206 | 12839 | 4027 | | 4250 | 9361 | 7783 | 4247 | 8689 | 5973 | 3992 | 3949 | 1742 | 1694 | 4971 | 8005 | 711 | 4132 | 6588 | 2956 | 5311 | 4809 | 9369 | 9243 | 6299 | 435 | 8358 |
| **Copenhagen** | 357 | 6422 | 12067 | 9860 | 7072 | 8392 | 6840 | | 8017 | 5388 | 7088 | 5732 | 3436 | 1540 | 592 | 5594 | 5912 | 970 | 4167 | 3845 | 638 | 4475 | 1306 | 6345 | 951 | 6195 | 9968 | 5403 | 3892 | 11160 |
| **Darwin** | 12946 | 7257 | 14693 | 11612 | 6047 | 18059 | 15065 | 12903 | | 2654 | 5369 | 6611 | 8837 | 9391 | 8605 | 7888 | 9091 | 7053 | 6472 | 9971 | 8582 | 3735 | 8632 | 9948 | 8243 | 2081 | 1957 | 3375 | 9630 | 3309 |
| **Hong Kong** | 8754 | 4317 | 18478 | 8150 | 2659 | 16360 | 12526 | 8671 | 4271 | | 5543 | 6669 | 7360 | 6853 | 5980 | 7232 | 8775 | 4439 | 5453 | 8047 | 5984 | 1220 | 6015 | 11001 | 5769 | 1615 | 4582 | 1786 | 7810 | 5857 |
| **Honolulu** | 11764 | 12914 | 12164 | 14223 | 11343 | 9670 | 6836 | 11407 | 8640 | 8921 | | 11934 | 10133 | 7821 | 7228 | 2558 | 3781 | 7036 | 10739 | 4958 | 7437 | 5070 | 6081 | 8290 | 8026 | 6721 | 5075 | 3854 | 4638 | 4669 |
| **Johannesburg** | 8870 | 6974 | 8088 | 6267 | 8459 | 11019 | 13984 | 9225 | 10639 | 10732 | 19206 | | 2799 | 5089 | 5637 | 10362 | 9063 | 5692 | 1818 | 7979 | 5426 | 7276 | 6797 | 4420 | 4811 | 5381 | 6860 | 8418 | 8310 | 7308 |
| **Lagos** | 5198 | 7612 | 7916 | 3915 | 9216 | 7741 | 9612 | 5530 | 14222 | 11845 | 16308 | 4505 | | 2360 | 3118 | 7713 | 6879 | 3886 | 2366 | 5268 | 2929 | 7119 | 4175 | 3750 | 2510 | 6925 | 9643 | 8376 | 5560 | 9973 |
| **Lisbon** | 2311 | 8018 | 9600 | 3794 | 9075 | 6501 | 6424 | 2478 | 15114 | 11028 | 12587 | 8191 | 3799 | | 987 | 5668 | 5391 | 2427 | 4015 | 3369 | 903 | 6007 | 1832 | 4805 | 1157 | 7385 | 11295 | 6928 | 3565 | 12163 |
| **London** | 928 | 7190 | 11131 | 3508 | 7961 | 7507 | 6356 | 952 | 13848 | 9623 | 11632 | 9071 | 5017 | 1588 | | 5442 | 5552 | 1552 | 4237 | 3463 | 212 | 5057 | 1172 | 5778 | 889 | 6743 | 10558 | 5942 | 3545 | 11691 |
| **Los Angeles** | 9311 | 14000 | 9852 | 12200 | 13120 | 5812 | 2804 | 9003 | 12695 | 11639 | 4117 | 16676 | 12414 | 9122 | 8758 | | 1549 | 9659 | 2446 | 5645 | 6251 | 4310 | 6310 | 6331 | 8776 | 7502 | 5475 | 2170 | 6719 | |
| **Mexico City** | 9732 | 15656 | 7389 | 12372 | 15280 | 3586 | 2726 | 9514 | 14631 | 14122 | 6085 | 14585 | 11071 | 8676 | 8936 | 2493 | | 6664 | 9207 | 2090 | 5717 | 7742 | 4635 | 4780 | 6365 | 10321 | 8058 | 7024 | 2018 | 6897 |
| **Moscow** | 1610 | 5031 | 13477 | 2902 | 5534 | 9938 | 8000 | 1561 | 11350 | 7144 | 11323 | 9161 | 6254 | 3906 | 2498 | 9769 | 10724 | | 3942 | 4666 | 1545 | 3600 | 2053 | 7184 | 1477 | 5237 | 9008 | 4651 | 4637 | 10283 |
| **Nairobi** | 6370 | 4532 | 10402 | 3536 | 6179 | 11544 | 12883 | 6706 | 10415 | 8776 | 17282 | 2927 | 3807 | 6461 | 6819 | 15544 | 14818 | 6344 | | 7358 | 4029 | 5727 | 5395 | 5548 | 3350 | 4635 | 7552 | 6996 | 7570 | 8490 |
| **New York** | 6385 | 12541 | 8526 | 9020 | 12747 | 3430 | 1145 | 6188 | 16047 | 12950 | 7980 | 12841 | 8477 | 5422 | 5572 | 3936 | 3364 | 7510 | 11842 | | 3626 | 6828 | 2613 | 4832 | 4280 | 9531 | 9935 | 6741 | 356 | 8951 |
| **Paris** | 876 | 7010 | 11051 | 3210 | 7858 | 6650 | 6650 | 1026 | 13812 | 9630 | 11098 | 8732 | 4714 | 1454 | 342 | 9085 | 9200 | 2486 | 6485 | 5836 | | 5106 | 1384 | 5708 | 687 | 6671 | 10539 | 6038 | 3738 | 11798 |
| **Peking** | 7822 | 4757 | 19268 | 7544 | 3269 | 14399 | 10603 | 7202 | 6011 | 1963 | 8160 | 11710 | 11457 | 9668 | 8138 | 10060 | 12460 | 5794 | 9216 | 10988 | 8217 | | 4897 | 10773 | 5049 | 2783 | 5561 | 1304 | 6557 | 6700 |
| **Reykjavik** | 2385 | 8335 | 11437 | 5266 | 8687 | 6915 | 4757 | 2103 | 13892 | 9681 | 9787 | 10938 | 6718 | 2948 | 1887 | 6936 | 7460 | 3304 | 8683 | 4206 | 2228 | 7882 | | 6135 | 2048 | 7155 | 10325 | 5469 | 2600 | 10725 |
| **Rio de Janeiro** | 10025 | 13409 | 1953 | 9896 | 15073 | 4546 | 8547 | 10211 | 16011 | 17704 | 13342 | 7113 | 6035 | 7734 | 9299 | 10155 | 7693 | 11562 | 8928 | 7777 | 9187 | 17338 | 9874 | | 5725 | 9763 | 8389 | 11551 | 5180 | 7367 |
| **Rome** | 1180 | 6175 | 11151 | 2133 | 7219 | 8363 | 7739 | 1531 | 13265 | 9284 | 12916 | 7743 | 4039 | 1861 | 1431 | 10188 | 10243 | 2376 | 5391 | 6888 | 1105 | 8126 | 3297 | 9214 | | 6229 | 10143 | 6127 | 4399 | 11523 |
| **Singapore** | 9944 | 3914 | 15879 | 8267 | 2897 | 18359 | 15078 | 9969 | 3349 | 2599 | 10816 | 8660 | 11145 | 11886 | 10852 | 14123 | 16610 | 8428 | 7460 | 15339 | 10737 | 4478 | 11514 | 15712 | 10025 | | 3915 | 3306 | 9350 | 5298 |
| **Sydney** | 16096 | 10160 | 11800 | 14418 | 9138 | 15343 | 14875 | 16042 | 3150 | 7374 | 8168 | 11040 | 15519 | 18178 | 16992 | 12073 | 12969 | 14497 | 12153 | 15989 | 16962 | 8949 | 16617 | 13501 | 16324 | 6300 | | 4861 | 9800 | 1383 |
| **Tokyo** | 8924 | 6742 | 18362 | 9571 | 5141 | 14164 | 10137 | 8696 | 5431 | 2874 | 6202 | 13547 | 13480 | 11149 | 9562 | 8811 | 11304 | 7485 | 11260 | 10849 | 9718 | 2099 | 8802 | 18589 | 9861 | 5321 | 7823 | | 6410 | 5762 |
| **Toronto** | 6497 | 12488 | 9093 | 9233 | 12561 | 3873 | 700 | 6265 | 15498 | 12569 | 7465 | 13374 | 8948 | 5737 | 5704 | 3492 | 3247 | 7462 | 12183 | 574 | 6015 | 10552 | 4184 | 8336 | 7080 | 15047 | 15772 | 10316 | | 8820 |
| **Wellington** | 18140 | 12370 | 9981 | 16524 | 11354 | 13122 | 13451 | 17961 | 5325 | 9427 | 7513 | 11761 | 16050 | 19575 | 18814 | 10814 | 11100 | 16549 | 13664 | 14405 | 18987 | 10782 | 17260 | 11855 | 18545 | 8526 | 2226 | 9273 | 14194 | |

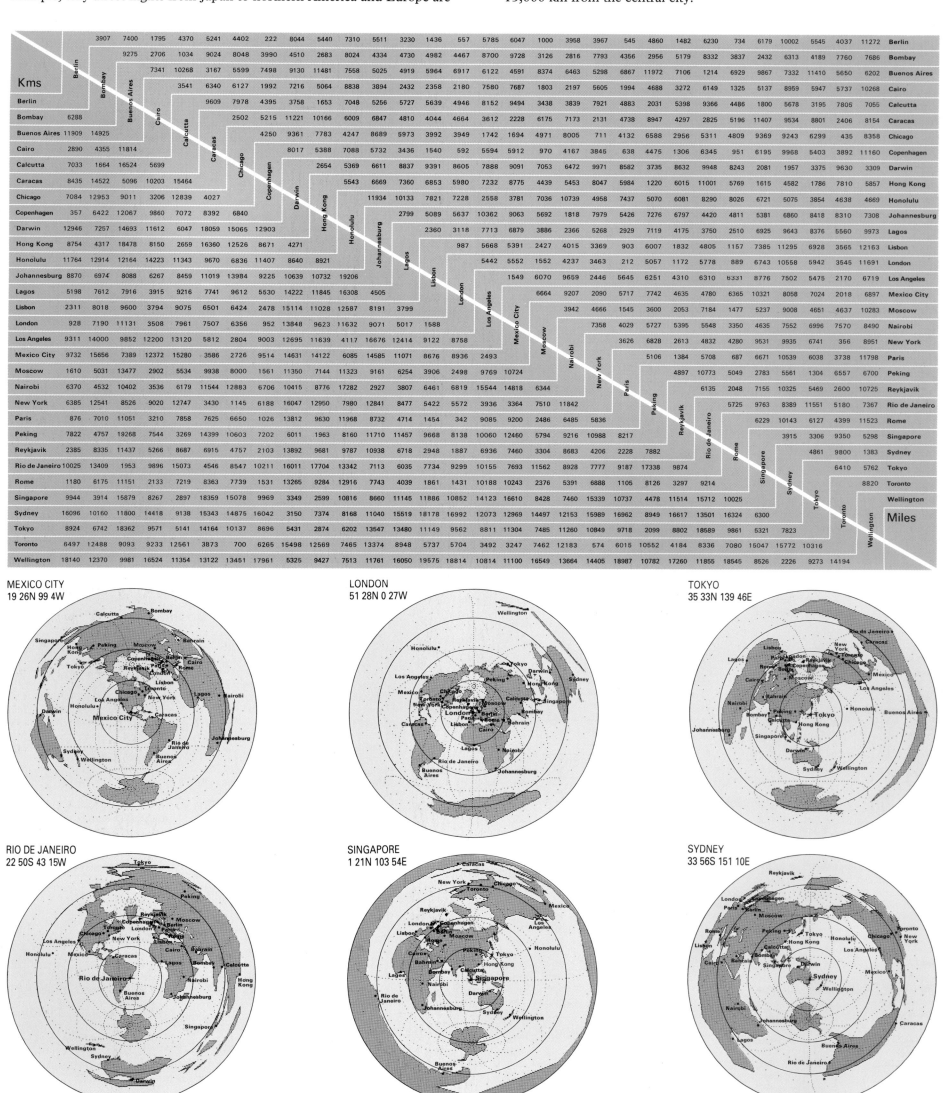

**MEXICO CITY**
19 26N 99 4W

**LONDON**
51 28N 0 27W

**TOKYO**
35 33N 139 46E

**RIO DE JANEIRO**
22 50S 43 15W

**SINGAPORE**
1 21N 103 54E

**SYDNEY**
33 56S 151 10E

# World Statistics: Climate

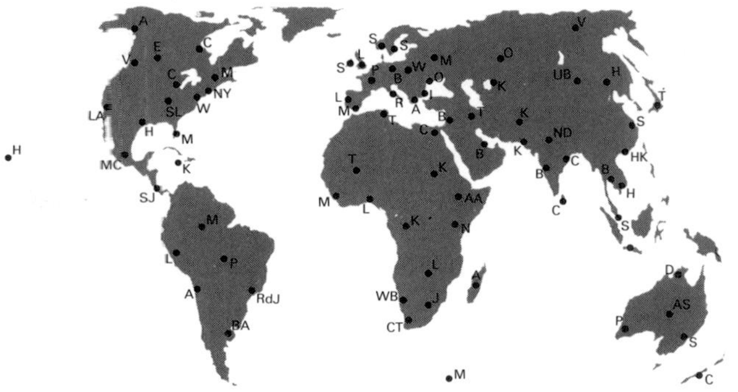

Rainfall and temperature figures are provided for more than 70 cities around the world. As climate is affected by altitude, the height of each city is shown in metres beneath its name. For each month, the figures in red show average temperature in degrees Celsius or centigrade, and in blue the total rainfall or snow in millimetres; the average annual temperature and total annual rainfall are at the end of the rows.

| EUROPE | Jan. | Feb. | Mar. | Apr. | May | June | July | Aug. | Sept. | Oct. | Nov. | Dec. | Year |
|---|---|---|---|---|---|---|---|---|---|---|---|---|---|
| **Athens, Greece** | 62 | 37 | 37 | 23 | 23 | 14 | 6 | 7 | 15 | 51 | 56 | 71 | 402 |
| 107 m | 10 | 10 | 12 | 16 | 20 | 25 | 28 | 28 | 24 | 20 | 15 | 11 | 18 |
| **Berlin, Germany** | 46 | 40 | 33 | 42 | 49 | 65 | 73 | 69 | 48 | 49 | 46 | 43 | 603 |
| 55 m | -1 | 0 | 4 | 9 | 14 | 17 | 19 | 18 | 15 | 9 | 5 | 1 | 9 |
| **Istanbul, Turkey** | 109 | 92 | 72 | 46 | 38 | 34 | 34 | 30 | 58 | 81 | 103 | 119 | 816 |
| 114 m | 5 | 6 | 7 | 11 | 16 | 20 | 23 | 23 | 20 | 16 | 12 | 8 | 14 |
| **Lisbon, Portugal** | 111 | 76 | 109 | 54 | 44 | 16 | 3 | 4 | 33 | 62 | 93 | 103 | 708 |
| 77 m | 11 | 12 | 14 | 16 | 17 | 20 | 22 | 23 | 21 | 18 | 14 | 12 | 17 |
| **London, UK** | 54 | 40 | 37 | 37 | 46 | 45 | 57 | 59 | 49 | 57 | 64 | 48 | 593 |
| 5 m | 4 | 5 | 7 | 9 | 12 | 16 | 18 | 17 | 15 | 11 | 8 | 5 | 11 |
| **Málaga, Spain** | 61 | 51 | 62 | 46 | 26 | 5 | 1 | 3 | 29 | 64 | 64 | 62 | 474 |
| 33 m | 12 | 13 | 16 | 17 | 19 | 29 | 25 | 26 | 23 | 20 | 16 | 13 | 18 |
| **Moscow, Russia** | 39 | 38 | 36 | 37 | 53 | 58 | 88 | 71 | 58 | 45 | 47 | 54 | 624 |
| 156 m | -13 | -10 | -4 | 6 | 13 | 16 | 18 | 17 | 12 | 6 | -1 | -7 | 4 |
| **Odessa, Ukraine** | 57 | 62 | 30 | 21 | 34 | 34 | 42 | 37 | 37 | 13 | 35 | 71 | 473 |
| 64 m | -3 | -1 | 2 | 9 | 15 | 20 | 22 | 22 | 18 | 12 | 9 | 1 | 10 |
| **Paris, France** | 56 | 46 | 35 | 42 | 57 | 54 | 59 | 64 | 55 | 50 | 51 | 50 | 619 |
| 75 m | 3 | 4 | 8 | 11 | 15 | 18 | 20 | 19 | 17 | 12 | 7 | 4 | 12 |
| **Rome, Italy** | 71 | 62 | 57 | 51 | 46 | 37 | 15 | 21 | 63 | 99 | 129 | 93 | 744 |
| 17 m | 8 | 9 | 11 | 14 | 18 | 22 | 25 | 25 | 22 | 17 | 13 | 10 | 16 |
| **Shannon, Irish Republic** | 94 | 67 | 56 | 53 | 61 | 57 | 77 | 79 | 86 | 86 | 96 | 117 | 929 |
| 2 m | 5 | 5 | 7 | 9 | 12 | 14 | 16 | 16 | 14 | 11 | 8 | 6 | 10 |
| **Stockholm, Sweden** | 43 | 30 | 25 | 31 | 34 | 45 | 61 | 76 | 60 | 48 | 53 | 48 | 554 |
| 44 m | -3 | -3 | -1 | 5 | 10 | 15 | 18 | 17 | 12 | 7 | 3 | 0 | 7 |
| **ASIA** | | | | | | | | | | | | | |
| **Bahrain** | 8 | 18 | 13 | 8 | <3 | 0 | 0 | 0 | 0 | 0 | 18 | 18 | 81 |
| 5 m | 17 | 18 | 21 | 25 | 29 | 32 | 33 | 34 | 31 | 28 | 24 | 19 | 26 |
| **Bangkok, Thailand** | 8 | 20 | 36 | 58 | 198 | 160 | 160 | 175 | 305 | 206 | 66 | 5 | 1,397 |
| 2 m | 26 | 28 | 29 | 30 | 29 | 29 | 28 | 28 | 28 | 28 | 26 | 25 | 28 |
| **Beirut, Lebanon** | 191 | 158 | 94 | 53 | 18 | 3 | <3 | <3 | 5 | 51 | 132 | 185 | 892 |
| 34 m | 14 | 14 | 16 | 18 | 22 | 24 | 27 | 28 | 26 | 24 | 19 | 16 | 21 |
| **Bombay, India** | 3 | 3 | 3 | <3 | 18 | 485 | 617 | 340 | 264 | 64 | 13 | 3 | 1,809 |
| 11 m | 24 | 24 | 26 | 28 | 30 | 29 | 27 | 27 | 27 | 28 | 27 | 26 | 27 |
| **Calcutta, India** | 10 | 31 | 36 | 43 | 140 | 297 | 325 | 328 | 252 | 114 | 20 | 5 | 1,600 |
| 6 m | 20 | 22 | 27 | 30 | 30 | 30 | 29 | 29 | 29 | 28 | 23 | 19 | 26 |
| **Colombo, Sri Lanka** | 89 | 69 | 147 | 231 | 371 | 224 | 135 | 109 | 160 | 348 | 315 | 147 | 2,365 |
| 7 m | 26 | 26 | 27 | 28 | 28 | 27 | 27 | 27 | 27 | 27 | 26 | 26 | 27 |
| **Harbin, China** | 6 | 5 | 10 | 23 | 43 | 94 | 112 | 104 | 46 | 33 | 8 | 5 | 488 |
| 160 m | -18 | -15 | -5 | 6 | 13 | 19 | 22 | 21 | 14 | 4 | -6 | -16 | 3 |
| **Ho Chi Minh, Vietnam** | 15 | 3 | 13 | 43 | 221 | 330 | 315 | 269 | 335 | 269 | 114 | 56 | 1,984 |
| 9 m | 26 | 27 | 29 | 30 | 29 | 28 | 28 | 28 | 27 | 27 | 27 | 26 | 28 |
| **Hong Kong** | 33 | 46 | 74 | 137 | 292 | 394 | 381 | 361 | 257 | 114 | 43 | 31 | 2,162 |
| 33 m | 16 | 15 | 18 | 22 | 26 | 28 | 28 | 28 | 27 | 25 | 21 | 18 | 23 |
| **Jakarta, Indonesia** | 300 | 300 | 211 | 147 | 114 | 97 | 64 | 43 | 66 | 112 | 142 | 203 | 1,798 |
| 8 m | 26 | 26 | 27 | 27 | 27 | 27 | 27 | 27 | 27 | 27 | 27 | 26 | 27 |
| **Kabul, Afghanistan** | 31 | 36 | 94 | 102 | 20 | 5 | 3 | 3 | <3 | 15 | 20 | 10 | 338 |
| 1,815 m | -3 | -1 | 6 | 13 | 18 | 22 | 25 | 24 | 20 | 14 | 7 | 3 | 12 |
| **Karachi, Pakistan** | 13 | 10 | 8 | 3 | 3 | 18 | 81 | 41 | 13 | <3 | 3 | 5 | 196 |
| 4 m | 19 | 20 | 24 | 28 | 30 | 31 | 30 | 29 | 28 | 28 | 24 | 20 | 26 |
| **Kazalinsk, Kazakhstan** | 10 | 10 | 13 | 13 | 15 | 5 | 5 | 8 | 8 | 10 | 13 | 15 | 125 |
| 63 m | -12 | -11 | -3 | 6 | 18 | 23 | 25 | 23 | 16 | 8 | -1 | -7 | 7 |
| **New Delhi, India** | 23 | 18 | 13 | 8 | 13 | 74 | 180 | 172 | 117 | 10 | 3 | 10 | 640 |
| 218 m | 14 | 17 | 23 | 28 | 33 | 34 | 31 | 30 | 29 | 26 | 20 | 15 | 25 |
| **Omsk, Russia** | 15 | 8 | 8 | 13 | 31 | 51 | 51 | 51 | 28 | 25 | 18 | 20 | 318 |
| 85 m | -22 | -19 | -12 | -1 | 10 | 16 | 18 | 16 | 10 | 1 | -11 | -18 | -1 |
| **Shanghai, China** | 48 | 58 | 84 | 94 | 94 | 180 | 147 | 142 | 130 | 71 | 51 | 36 | 1,135 |
| 7 m | 4 | 5 | 9 | 14 | 20 | 24 | 28 | 28 | 23 | 19 | 12 | 7 | 16 |
| **Singapore** | 252 | 173 | 193 | 188 | 173 | 173 | 170 | 196 | 178 | 208 | 254 | 257 | 2,413 |
| 10 m | 26 | 27 | 28 | 28 | 28 | 28 | 28 | 27 | 27 | 27 | 27 | 27 | 27 |
| **Tehran, Iran** | 46 | 38 | 46 | 36 | 13 | 3 | 3 | 3 | 3 | 8 | 20 | 31 | 246 |
| 1,220 m | 2 | 5 | 9 | 16 | 21 | 26 | 30 | 29 | 25 | 18 | 12 | 6 | 17 |
| **Tokyo, Japan** | 48 | 74 | 107 | 135 | 147 | 165 | 142 | 152 | 234 | 208 | 97 | 56 | 1,565 |
| 6 m | 3 | 4 | 7 | 13 | 17 | 21 | 25 | 26 | 23 | 17 | 11 | 6 | 14 |
| **Ulan Bator, Mongolia** | <3 | <3 | 3 | 5 | 10 | 28 | 76 | 51 | 23 | 5 | 5 | 3 | 208 |
| 1,325 m | -26 | -21 | -13 | -1 | 6 | 14 | 16 | 14 | 8 | -1 | -13 | -22 | -3 |
| **Verkhoyansk, Russia** | 5 | 5 | 3 | 5 | 8 | 23 | 28 | 25 | 13 | 8 | 8 | 5 | 134 |
| 100 m | -50 | -45 | -32 | -15 | 0 | 12 | 14 | 9 | 2 | -15 | -38 | -48 | -17 |
| **AFRICA** | | | | | | | | | | | | | |
| **Addis Ababa, Ethiopia** | <3 | 3 | 25 | 135 | 213 | 201 | 206 | 239 | 102 | 28 | <3 | 0 | 1,151 |
| 2,450 m | 19 | 20 | 20 | 20 | 19 | 18 | 18 | 19 | 21 | 22 | 21 | 20 | 20 |
| **Antananarivo, Madagas.** | 300 | 279 | 178 | 53 | 18 | 8 | 8 | 10 | 18 | 61 | 135 | 287 | 1,356 |
| 1,372 m | 21 | 21 | 21 | 19 | 18 | 15 | 14 | 15 | 17 | 19 | 21 | 21 | 19 |
| **Cairo, Egypt** | 5 | 5 | 5 | 3 | 3 | <3 | 0 | 0 | <3 | <3 | 3 | 5 | 28 |
| 116 m | 13 | 15 | 18 | 21 | 25 | 28 | 28 | 28 | 26 | 24 | 20 | 15 | 22 |
| **Cape Town, South Africa** | 15 | 8 | 18 | 48 | 79 | 84 | 89 | 66 | 43 | 31 | 18 | 10 | 508 |
| 17 m | 21 | 21 | 20 | 17 | 14 | 13 | 12 | 13 | 14 | 16 | 18 | 19 | 17 |
| **Johannesburg, S. Africa** | 114 | 109 | 89 | 38 | 25 | 8 | 8 | 8 | 23 | 56 | 107 | 125 | 709 |
| 1,665 m | 20 | 20 | 18 | 16 | 13 | 10 | 11 | 13 | 16 | 18 | 19 | 20 | 16 |

| | Jan. | Feb. | Mar. | Apr. | May | June | July | Aug. | Sept. | Oct. | Nov. | Dec. | Year |
|---|---|---|---|---|---|---|---|---|---|---|---|---|---|
| **Khartoum, Sudan** | <3 | <3 | <3 | <3 | 3 | 8 | 53 | 71 | 18 | 5 | <3 | 0 | 158 |
| 390 m | 24 | 25 | 28 | 31 | 33 | 34 | 32 | 31 | 32 | 32 | 28 | 25 | 29 |
| **Kinshasa, Zaïre** | 135 | 145 | 196 | 196 | 158 | 8 | 3 | 3 | 31 | 119 | 221 | 142 | 1,354 |
| 325 m | 26 | 26 | 27 | 27 | 26 | 24 | 23 | 24 | 25 | 26 | 26 | 26 | 25 |
| **Lagos, Nigeria** | 28 | 46 | 102 | 150 | 269 | 460 | 279 | 64 | 140 | 206 | 69 | 25 | 1,836 |
| 3 m | 27 | 28 | 29 | 28 | 28 | 26 | 26 | 25 | 26 | 26 | 28 | 28 | 27 |
| **Lusaka, Zambia** | 231 | 191 | 142 | 18 | 3 | <3 | <3 | 0 | <3 | 10 | 91 | 150 | 836 |
| 1,277 m | 21 | 22 | 21 | 21 | 19 | 16 | 16 | 18 | 22 | 24 | 23 | 22 | 21 |
| **Monrovia, Liberia** | 31 | 56 | 97 | 216 | 516 | 973 | 996 | 373 | 744 | 772 | 236 | 130 | 5,138 |
| 23 m | 26 | 26 | 27 | 27 | 26 | 25 | 24 | 25 | 25 | 25 | 26 | 26 | 26 |
| **Nairobi, Kenya** | 38 | 64 | 125 | 211 | 158 | 46 | 15 | 23 | 31 | 53 | 109 | 86 | 958 |
| 1,820 m | 19 | 19 | 19 | 19 | 18 | 16 | 16 | 16 | 18 | 19 | 18 | 18 | 18 |
| **Timbuktu, Mali** | <3 | <3 | 3 | <3 | 5 | 23 | 79 | 81 | 38 | 3 | <3 | <3 | 231 |
| 301 m | 22 | 24 | 28 | 32 | 34 | 35 | 32 | 30 | 32 | 31 | 28 | 23 | 29 |
| **Tunis, Tunisia** | 64 | 51 | 41 | 36 | 18 | 8 | 3 | 8 | 33 | 51 | 48 | 61 | 419 |
| 66 m | 10 | 11 | 13 | 16 | 19 | 23 | 26 | 27 | 25 | 20 | 16 | 11 | 18 |
| **Walvis Bay, South Africa** | <3 | 5 | 8 | 3 | 3 | <3 | <3 | 3 | <3 | <3 | <3 | <3 | 23 |
| 7 m | 19 | 19 | 19 | 18 | 17 | 16 | 15 | 14 | 14 | 15 | 17 | 18 | 18 |
| **AUSTRALIA, NEW ZEALAND AND ANTARCTICA** | | | | | | | | | | | | | |
| **Alice Springs, Australia** | 43 | 33 | 28 | 10 | 15 | 13 | 8 | 8 | 8 | 18 | 31 | 38 | 252 |
| 579 m | 29 | 28 | 25 | 20 | 15 | 12 | 12 | 14 | 18 | 23 | 26 | 28 | 21 |
| **Christchurch, N. Zealand** | 56 | 43 | 48 | 48 | 66 | 66 | 69 | 48 | 46 | 43 | 48 | 56 | 638 |
| 10 m | 16 | 16 | 14 | 12 | 9 | 6 | 6 | 7 | 9 | 12 | 14 | 16 | 11 |
| **Darwin, Australia** | 386 | 312 | 254 | 97 | 15 | 3 | <3 | 3 | 13 | 51 | 119 | 239 | 1,491 |
| 30 m | 29 | 29 | 29 | 29 | 28 | 26 | 25 | 26 | 28 | 29 | 30 | 29 | 28 |
| **Mawson, Antarctica** | 11 | 30 | 20 | 10 | 44 | 180 | 4 | 40 | 3 | 20 | 0 | 0 | 362 |
| 14 m | 0 | -5 | -10 | -14 | -15 | -16 | -18 | -18 | -19 | -13 | -5 | -1 | -11 |
| **Perth, Australia** | 8 | 10 | 20 | 43 | 130 | 180 | 170 | 149 | 86 | 56 | 20 | 13 | 881 |
| 60 m | 23 | 23 | 22 | 19 | 16 | 14 | 13 | 13 | 15 | 16 | 19 | 22 | 18 |
| **Sydney, Australia** | 89 | 102 | 127 | 135 | 127 | 117 | 117 | 76 | 73 | 71 | 73 | 73 | 1,181 |
| 42 m | 22 | 22 | 21 | 18 | 15 | 13 | 12 | 13 | 15 | 18 | 19 | 21 | 17 |
| **NORTH AMERICA** | | | | | | | | | | | | | |
| **Anchorage, Alaska, USA** | 20 | 18 | 15 | 10 | 13 | 18 | 41 | 66 | 66 | 56 | 25 | 23 | 371 |
| 40 m | -11 | -8 | -5 | 2 | 7 | 12 | 14 | 13 | 9 | 2 | -5 | -11 | 2 |
| **Chicago, Ill., USA** | 51 | 51 | 66 | 71 | 86 | 89 | 84 | 81 | 79 | 66 | 61 | 51 | 836 |
| 251 m | -4 | -3 | 2 | 9 | 14 | 20 | 23 | 22 | 19 | 12 | 5 | -1 | 10 |
| **Churchill, Man., Canada** | 15 | 13 | 18 | 23 | 32 | 44 | 46 | 58 | 51 | 43 | 39 | 21 | 402 |
| 13 m | -28 | -26 | -20 | -10 | -2 | 6 | 12 | 11 | 5 | -2 | -12 | -22 | -7 |
| **Edmonton, Alta., Canada** | 25 | 19 | 19 | 22 | 43 | 77 | 89 | 78 | 39 | 17 | 16 | 25 | 466 |
| 676 m | -15 | -10 | -5 | 4 | 11 | 15 | 17 | 16 | 11 | 6 | -4 | -10 | 3 |
| **Honolulu, Hawaii, USA** | 104 | 66 | 79 | 48 | 25 | 18 | 23 | 28 | 36 | 48 | 64 | 104 | 643 |
| 12 m | 23 | 18 | 19 | 20 | 22 | 24 | 25 | 26 | 26 | 24 | 22 | 19 | 22 |
| **Houston, Tex., USA** | 89 | 76 | 84 | 91 | 119 | 117 | 99 | 99 | 104 | 94 | 89 | 109 | 1,171 |
| 12 m | 12 | 13 | 17 | 21 | 24 | 27 | 28 | 29 | 26 | 22 | 16 | 12 | 21 |
| **Kingston, Jamaica** | 23 | 15 | 23 | 31 | 102 | 89 | 38 | 91 | 99 | 180 | 74 | 36 | 800 |
| 34 m | 25 | 25 | 25 | 26 | 26 | 28 | 28 | 28 | 27 | 27 | 26 | 26 | 26 |
| **Los Angeles, Calif., USA** | 79 | 76 | 71 | 25 | 10 | 3 | <3 | <3 | 5 | 15 | 31 | 66 | 381 |
| 95 m | 13 | 14 | 14 | 16 | 17 | 19 | 21 | 22 | 21 | 18 | 16 | 14 | 17 |
| **Mexico City, Mexico** | 13 | 5 | 10 | 20 | 53 | 119 | 170 | 152 | 130 | 51 | 18 | 8 | 747 |
| 2,309 m | 12 | 13 | 16 | 18 | 19 | 19 | 17 | 18 | 18 | 16 | 14 | 13 | 16 |
| **Miami, Fla., USA** | 71 | 53 | 64 | 81 | 173 | 178 | 155 | 160 | 203 | 234 | 71 | 51 | 1,516 |
| 8 m | 20 | 20 | 22 | 23 | 25 | 27 | 28 | 28 | 27 | 25 | 22 | 21 | 24 |
| **Montréal, Que., Canada** | 72 | 65 | 74 | 74 | 66 | 82 | 90 | 92 | 88 | 76 | 81 | 87 | 946 |
| 57 m | -10 | -9 | -3 | 6 | 13 | 18 | 21 | 20 | 15 | 9 | 2 | -7 | 6 |
| **New York, N.Y., USA** | 94 | 97 | 91 | 81 | 81 | 84 | 107 | 109 | 86 | 89 | 76 | 91 | 1,092 |
| 96 m | -1 | -1 | 3 | 10 | 16 | 20 | 23 | 23 | 21 | 15 | 7 | 2 | 11 |
| **St Louis, Mo., USA** | 58 | 64 | 89 | 97 | 114 | 114 | 89 | 86 | 81 | 74 | 71 | 64 | 1,001 |
| 173 m | 0 | 1 | 7 | 13 | 19 | 24 | 26 | 26 | 22 | 15 | 8 | 2 | 14 |
| **San José, Costa Rica** | 15 | 5 | 20 | 46 | 229 | 241 | 211 | 241 | 305 | 300 | 145 | 41 | 1,798 |
| 1,146 m | 19 | 19 | 21 | 21 | 22 | 21 | 21 | 21 | 21 | 20 | 20 | 19 | 20 |
| **Vancouver, B.C., Canada** | 154 | 115 | 101 | 60 | 52 | 45 | 32 | 41 | 67 | 114 | 150 | 182 | 1,113 |
| 14 m | 3 | 5 | 6 | 9 | 12 | 15 | 17 | 17 | 14 | 10 | 6 | 4 | 10 |
| **Washington, D.C., USA** | 86 | 76 | 91 | 84 | 94 | 99 | 112 | 109 | 94 | 74 | 66 | 79 | 1,064 |
| 22 m | 1 | 2 | 7 | 12 | 18 | 23 | 25 | 24 | 20 | 14 | 8 | 3 | 13 |
| **SOUTH AMERICA** | | | | | | | | | | | | | |
| **Antofagasta, Chile** | 0 | 0 | 0 | <3 | <3 | 3 | 5 | 3 | <3 | 3 | <3 | 0 | 13 |
| 94 m | 21 | 21 | 20 | 18 | 16 | 15 | 14 | 14 | 15 | 16 | 18 | 19 | 17 |
| **Buenos Aires, Argentina** | 79 | 71 | 109 | 89 | 76 | 61 | 56 | 61 | 79 | 86 | 84 | 99 | 950 |
| 27 m | 23 | 23 | 21 | 17 | 13 | 9 | 10 | 11 | 13 | 15 | 19 | 22 | 16 |
| **Lima, Peru** | 3 | <3 | <3 | <3 | 5 | 5 | 8 | 8 | 8 | 3 | 3 | <3 | 41 |
| 120 m | 23 | 24 | 24 | 22 | 19 | 17 | 17 | 16 | 17 | 18 | 19 | 21 | 20 |
| **Manaus, Brazil** | 249 | 231 | 262 | 221 | 170 | 84 | 58 | 38 | 46 | 107 | 142 | 203 | 1,811 |
| 44 m | 28 | 28 | 28 | 27 | 28 | 28 | 28 | 28 | 29 | 29 | 29 | 28 | 28 |
| **Paraná, Brazil** | 287 | 236 | 239 | 102 | 13 | <3 | 3 | 5 | 28 | 127 | 231 | 310 | 1,582 |
| 260 m | 23 | 23 | 23 | 23 | 23 | 21 | 21 | 22 | 24 | 24 | 24 | 23 | 23 |
| **Rio de Janeiro, Brazil** | 125 | 122 | 130 | 107 | 79 | 53 | 41 | 43 | 66 | 79 | 104 | 137 | 1,082 |
| 61 m | 26 | 26 | 25 | 24 | 22 | 21 | 21 | 21 | 21 | 22 | 23 | 25 | 23 |

# WORLD STATISTICS: PHYSICAL DIMENSIONS

Each topic list is divided into continents and within a continent the items are listed in size order. The order of the continents is as in the atlas, Europe through to South America. Certain lists down to this mark > are complete; below they are selective. The world top ten are shown in square brackets; in the case of mountains this has not been done because the world top thirty are all in Asia. The figures are rounded as appropriate.

## WORLD, CONTINENTS, OCEANS

|  | km² | miles² | % |
|---|---|---|---|
| The World | 509,450,000 | 196,672,000 |  |
| Land | 149,450,000 | 57,688,000 | 29.3 |
| Water | 360,000,000 | 138,984,000 | 70.7 |
|  |  |  |  |
| Asia | 44,500,000 | 17,177,000 | 29.8 |
| Africa | 30,302,000 | 11,697,000 | 20.3 |
| North America | 24,241,000 | 9,357,000 | 16.2 |
| South America | 17,793,000 | 6,868,000 | 11.9 |
| Antarctica | 14,100,000 | 5,443,000 | 9.4 |
| Europe | 9,957,000 | 3,843,000 | 6.7 |
| Australia & Oceania | 8,557,000 | 3,303,000 | 5.7 |
|  |  |  |  |
| Pacific Ocean | 179,679,000 | 69,356,000 | 49.9 |
| Atlantic Ocean | 92,373,000 | 35,657,000 | 25.7 |
| Indian Ocean | 73,917,000 | 28,532,000 | 20.5 |
| Arctic Ocean | 14,090,000 | 5,439,000 | 3.9 |

## SEAS

| Pacific | km² | miles² |
|---|---|---|
| South China Sea | 2,318,000 | 895,000 |
| Bering Sea | 2,268,000 | 875,000 |
| Sea of Okhotsk | 1,528,000 | 590,000 |
| East China & Yellow | 1,249,000 | 482,000 |
| Sea of Japan | 1,008,000 | 389,000 |
| Gulf of California | 162,000 | 62,500 |
| Bass Strait | 75,000 | 29,000 |

| Atlantic | km² | miles² |
|---|---|---|
| Caribbean Sea | 2,766,000 | 1,068,000 |
| Mediterranaen Sea | 2,516,000 | 971,000 |
| Gulf of Mexico | 1,543,000 | 596,000 |
| Hudson Bay | 1,232,000 | 476,000 |
| North Sea | 575,000 | 223,000 |
| Black Sea | 452,000 | 174,000 |
| Baltic Sea | 397,000 | 153,000 |
| Gulf of St. Lawrence | 238,000 | 92,000 |

| Indian | km² | miles² |
|---|---|---|
| Red Sea | 438,000 | 169,000 |
| The Gulf | 239,000 | 92,000 |

## MOUNTAINS

| Europe |  | m | ft |
|---|---|---|---|
| Mont Blanc | France/Italy | 4,807 | 15,771 |
| Monte Rosa | Italy/Switzerland | 4,634 | 15,203 |
| Dom | Switzerland | 4,545 | 14,911 |
| Weisshorn | Switzerland | 4,505 | 14,780 |
| Matterhorn/Cervino | Italy/Switzerland | 4,478 | 14,691 |
| Mt. Maudit | France/Italy | 4,465 | 14,649 |
| Finsteraarhorn | Switzerland | 4,275 | 14,025 |
| Aletschhorn | Switzerland | 4,182 | 13,720 |
| Jungfrau | Switzerland | 4,158 | 13,642 |
| Barre des Ecrins | France | 4,103 | 13,461 |
| Gran Paradiso | Italy | 4,061 | 13,323 |
| Piz Bernina | Italy/Switzerland | 4,052 | 13,294 |
| Ortles | Italy | 3,899 | 12,792 |
| Monte Viso | Italy | 3,841 | 12,602 |
| Grossglockner | Austria | 3,797 | 12,457 |
| Wildspitze | Austria | 3,774 | 12,382 |
| Weisskügel | Austria/Italy | 3,736 | 12,257 |
| Dammastock | Switzerland | 3,640 | 11,942 |
| Tödi | Switzerland | 3,623 | 11,886 |
| Presanella | Italy | 3,556 | 11,667 |
| Monte Adamello | Italy | 3,554 | 11,660 |
| Mulhacén | Spain | 3,478 | 11,411 |
| Pico de Aneto | Spain | 3,404 | 11,168 |
| Marmolada | Italy | 3,342 | 10,964 |
| > Etna | Italy | 3,340 | 10,958 |
| Musala | Bulgaria | 2,925 | 9,596 |
| Olympus | Greece | 2,917 | 9,570 |
| Gerlach | Czechoslovakia | 2,655 | 8,711 |
| Galdhöpiggen | Norway | 2,469 | 8,100 |
| Pietrosul | Romania | 2,305 | 7,562 |
| Hvannadalshnúkur | Iceland | 2,119 | 6,952 |
| Narodnaya | Russia | 1,894 | 6,214 |
| Ben Nevis | UK | 1,343 | 4,406 |

| Asia |  | m | ft |
|---|---|---|---|
| Everest | China/Nepal | 8,848 | 29,029 |
| Godwin Austen (K2) | China/Kashmir | 8,611 | 28,251 |
| Kanchenjunga | India/Nepal | 8,598 | 28,208 |
| Lhotse | China/Nepal | 8,516 | 27,939 |
| Makalu | China/Nepal | 8,481 | 27,824 |
| Cho Oyu | China/Nepal | 8,201 | 26,906 |
| Dhaulagiri | Nepal | 8,172 | 26,811 |
| Manaslu | Nepal | 8,156 | 26,758 |
| Nanga Parbat | Kashmir | 8,126 | 26,660 |
| Annapurna | Nepal | 8,078 | 26,502 |
| Gasherbrum | China/Kashmir | 8,068 | 26,469 |
| Broad Peak | India | 8,051 | 26,414 |
| Gosainthan | China | 8,012 | 26,286 |
| Disteghil Sar | Kashmir | 7,885 | 25,869 |
| Nuptse | Nepal | 7,879 | 25,849 |
| Masherbrum | Kashmir | 7,826 | 25,676 |
| Nanda Devi | India | 7,817 | 25,646 |
| Rakaposhi | Kashmir | 7,788 | 25,551 |
| Kamet | India | 7,756 | 25,446 |
| Namcha Barwa | China | 7,756 | 25,446 |
| Gurla Mandhata | China | 7,728 | 25,354 |
| Muztag | China | 7,723 | 25,338 |
| Kongur Shan | China | 7,719 | 25,324 |
| Tirich Mir | Pakistan | 7,690 | 25,229 |
| > Saser | Kashmir | 7,672 | 25,170 |
| Pik Kommunizma | Tajikistan | 7,495 | 24,590 |
| Aling Gangri | China | 7,315 | 23,999 |
| Elbrus | Russia | 5,633 | 18,481 |
| Demavand | Iran | 5,604 | 18,386 |
| Ararat | Turkey | 5,165 | 16,945 |
| Gunong Kinabalu | Malaysia (Borneo) | 4,101 | 13,455 |
| Yu Shan | Taiwan | 3,997 | 13,113 |
| Fuji-san | Japan | 3,776 | 12,388 |
| Rinjani | Indonesia | 3,726 | 12,224 |
| Mt. Rajang | Philippines | 3,364 | 11,037 |
| Pidurutalagala | Sri Lanka | 2,524 | 8,281 |

| Africa |  | m | ft |
|---|---|---|---|
| Kilimanjaro | Tanzania | 5,895 | 19,340 |
| Mt. Kenya | Kenya | 5,199 | 17,057 |
| Ruwenzori | Uganda/Zaïre | 5,109 | 16,762 |
| Ras Dashan | Ethiopia | 4,620 | 15,157 |
| Meru | Tanzania | 4,565 | 14,977 |
| Karisimbi | Rwanda/Zaïre | 4,507 | 14,787 |
| Mt. Elgon | Kenya/Uganda | 4,321 | 14,176 |
| Batu | Ethiopia | 4,307 | 14,130 |
| Gughe | Ethiopia | 4,200 | 13,779 |
| Toubkal | Morocco | 4,165 | 13,665 |
| Irhil Mgoun | Morocco | 4,071 | 13,356 |
| Mt. Cameroon | Cameroon | 4,070 | 13,353 |
| Teide | Spain (Tenerife) | 3,718 | 12,198 |
| Thabana Ntlenyana | Lesotho | 3,482 | 11,424 |
| > Emi Kussi | Chad | 3,415 | 11,204 |
| Mt. aux Sources | Lesotho/S. Africa | 3,282 | 10,768 |
| Mt. Piton | Réunion | 3,069 | 10,069 |

| Oceania |  | m | ft |
|---|---|---|---|
| Puncak Jaya | Indonesia | 5,029 | 16,499 |
| Puncak Mandala | Indonesia | 4,760 | 15,617 |
| Puncak Trikora | Indonesia | 4,750 | 15,584 |
| Mt. Wilhelm | Papua New Guinea | 4,508 | 14,790 |
| > Mauna Kea | USA (Hawaii) | 4,208 | 13,806 |
| Mauna Loa | USA (Hawaii) | 4,169 | 13,678 |
| Mt. Cook | New Zealand | 3,753 | 12,313 |
| Mt. Balbi | Solomon Is. | 2,743 | 8,999 |
| Orohena | Tahiti | 2,241 | 7,352 |
| Kosciusko | Australia | 2,230 | 7,316 |

| North America |  | m | ft |
|---|---|---|---|
| Mt. McKinley | USA (Alaska) | 6,194 | 20,321 |
| Mt. Logan | Canada | 6,050 | 19,849 |
| Citlaltepetl | Mexico | 5,700 | 18,701 |
| Mt. St.Elias | USA/Canada | 5,489 | 18,008 |
| Popocatepetl | Mexico | 5,452 | 17,887 |
| Mt. Foraker | USA (Alaska) | 5,304 | 17,401 |
| Ixtaccihuatl | Mexico | 5,286 | 17,342 |
| Lucania | USA (Alaska) | 5,226 | 17,145 |
| Mt. Steele | Canada | 5,011 | 16,440 |
| Mt. Bona | USA (Alaska) | 5,005 | 16,420 |
| Mt. Blackburn | USA (Alaska) | 4,996 | 16,391 |
| Mt. Sanford | USA (Alaska) | 4,949 | 16,237 |
| Mt. Wood | Canada | 4,848 | 15,905 |
| Nev. de Toluca | Mexico | 4,670 | 15,321 |
| Mt. Fairweather | USA (Alaska) | 4,663 | 15,298 |
| Mt. Whitney | USA | 4,418 | 14,495 |
| Mt. Elbert | USA | 4,399 | 14,432 |
| Mt. Harvard | USA | 4,395 | 14,419 |
| Mt. Rainier | USA | 4,392 | 14,409 |
| Blanca Peak | USA | 4,364 | 14,317 |
| Long's Peak | USA | 4,345 | 14,255 |
| Nev. de Colima | Mexico | 4,339 | 14,235 |
| Mt. Shasta | USA | 4,317 | 14,163 |
| Tajumulco | Guatemala | 4,217 | 13,835 |
| > Gannett Peak | USA | 4,202 | 13,786 |
| Mt. Waddington | Canada | 3,994 | 13,104 |
| Mt. Robson | Canada | 3,954 | 12,972 |
| Ch. Grande | Costa Rica | 3,837 | 12,589 |
| Loma Tinta | Haiti | 3,175 | 10,417 |

| South America |  | m | ft |
|---|---|---|---|
| Aconcagua | Argentina | 6,960 | 22,834 |
| Illimani | Bolivia | 6,882 | 22,578 |
| Bonete | Argentina | 6,872 | 22,546 |
| Ojos del Salado | Argentina/Chile | 6,863 | 22,516 |
| Tupungato | Argentina/Chile | 6,800 | 22,309 |
| Pissis | Argentina | 6,779 | 22,241 |
| Mercedario | Argentina/Chile | 6,770 | 22,211 |
| Huascaran | Peru | 6,768 | 22,204 |
| Llullaillaco | Argentina/Chile | 6,723 | 22,057 |
| Nudo de Cachi | Argentina | 6,720 | 22,047 |
| Yerupaja | Peru | 6,632 | 21,758 |
| N. de Tres Cruces | Argentina/Chile | 6,620 | 21,719 |
| Incahuasi | Argentina/Chile | 6,601 | 21,657 |
| Ancohuma | Bolivia | 6,550 | 21,489 |
| Sajama | Bolivia | 6,520 | 21,391 |
| Coropuna | Peru | 6,425 | 21,079 |
| Ausangate | Peru | 6,384 | 20,945 |
| Cerro del Toro | Argentina | 6,380 | 20,932 |
| Ampato | Peru | 6,310 | 20,702 |
| Chimborasso | Ecuador | 6,267 | 20,561 |
| > Cotopaxi | Ecuador | 5,897 | 19,347 |
| Cayambe | Ecuador | 5,796 | 19,016 |
| S. Nev.de S. Marta | Colombia | 5,775 | 18,947 |
| Pico Bolivar | Venezuela | 5,007 | 16,427 |

| Antarctica |  | m | ft |
|---|---|---|---|
| Vinson Massif |  | 4,897 | 16,066 |
| Mt. Kirkpatrick |  | 4,528 | 14,855 |
| Mt. Markham |  | 4,349 | 14,268 |

## OCEAN DEPTHS

| Atlantic Ocean | m | ft |  |
|---|---|---|---|
| Puerto Rico (Milwaukee) Deep | 9,200 | 30,183 | [7] |
| Cayman Trench | 7,680 | 25,197 | [10] |
| Gulf of Mexico | 5,203 | 17,070 |  |
| Mediterranean | 5,121 | 16,801 |  |
| Black Sea | 2,211 | 7,254 |  |
| North Sea | 310 | 1,017 |  |
| Baltic Sea | 294 | 965 |  |
| Hudson Bay | 111 | 364 |  |

| Indian Ocean | m | ft |
|---|---|---|
| Java Trench | 7,450 | 24,442 |
| Red Sea | 2,266 | 7,434 |
| Persian Gulf | 73 | 239 |

| Pacific Ocean | m | ft |  |
|---|---|---|---|
| Mariana Trench | 11,022 | 36,161 | [1] |
| Tonga Trench | 10,822 | 35,505 | [2] |
| Japan Trench | 10,554 | 34,626 | [3] |
| Kuril Trench | 10,542 | 34,586 | [4] |
| Mindanao Trench | 10,497 | 34,439 | [5] |
| Kermadec Trench | 10,047 | 32,962 | [6] |
| Peru-Chile Trench | 8,050 | 26,410 | [8] |
| Aleutian Trench | 7,822 | 25,662 | [9] |
| Middle American Trench | 6,662 | 21,857 |  |

| Arctic Ocean | m | ft |
|---|---|---|
| Molloy Deep | 5,608 | 18,399 |

## LAND LOWS

|  |  | m | ft |
|---|---|---|---|
| Caspian Sea | Europe | -28 | -92 |
| Dead Sea | Asia | -400 | -1,312 |
| Lake Assal | Africa | -156 | -512 |
| Lake Eyre North | Oceania | -16 | -52 |
| Death Valley | N. America | -86 | -282 |
| Valdés Peninsula | S. America | -40 | -131 |

## RIVERS

### Europe

| | | km | miles | |
|---|---|---|---|---|
| Volga | Caspian Sea | 3,700 | 2,300 | |
| Danube | Black Sea | 2,850 | 1,770 | |
| Ural | Caspian Sea | 2,535 | 1,574 | |
| Dnieper | Volga | 2,285 | 1,420 | |
| Kama | Volga | 2,030 | 1,260 | |
| Don | Volga | 1,990 | 1,240 | |
| Petchora | Arctic | 1,790 | 1,110 | |
| Oka | Volga | 1,480 | 920 | |
| Belaya | Kama | 1,420 | 880 | |
| Dniester | Black Sea | 1,400 | 870 | |
| Vyatka | Kama | 1,370 | 850 | |
| Rhine | North Sea | 1,320 | 820 | |
| N. Dvina | Arctic | 1,290 | 800 | |
| Desna | Dnieper | 1,190 | 740 | |
| Elbe | North Sea | 1,145 | 710 | |
| Vistula | Baltic Sea | 1,090 | 675 | |
| Loire | Atlantic | 1,020 | 635 | |
| Thames | North Sea | 335 | 210 | |

### Asia

| | | km | miles | |
|---|---|---|---|---|
| Yangtse | Pacific | 6,380 | 3,960 | [3] |
| Yenisei-Angara | Arctic | 5,550 | 3,445 | [5] |
| Ob-Irtysh | Arctic | 5,410 | 3,360 | [6] |
| Hwang Ho | Pacific | 4,840 | 3,005 | [7] |
| Amur | Pacific | 4,510 | 2,800 | [9] |
| Mekong | Pacific | 4,500 | 2,795 | [10] |
| Lena | Arctic | 4,400 | 2,730 | |
| Irtysh | Ob | 4,250 | 2,640 | |
| Yenisei | Arctic | 4,090 | 2,540 | |
| Ob | Arctic | 3,680 | 2,285 | |
| Indus | Indian | 3,100 | 1,925 | |
| Brahmaputra | Indian | 2,900 | 1,800 | |
| Syr Darya | Aral Sea | 2,860 | 1,775 | |
| Salween | Indian | 2,800 | 1,740 | |
| Euphrates | Indian | 2,700 | 1,675 | |
| Vilyuy | Lena | 2,650 | 1,645 | |
| Kolyma | Arctic | 2,600 | 1,615 | |
| Amu Darya | Aral Sea | 2,540 | 1,575 | |
| Ural | Caspian Sea | 2,535 | 1,575 | |
| Ganges | Indian | 2,510 | 1,560 | |
| Si Kiang | Pacific | 2,100 | 1,305 | |
| Irrawaddy | Indian | 2,010 | 1,250 | |
| Tarim-Yarkand | Lop Nor | 2,000 | 1,240 | |
| Tigris | Indian | 1,900 | 1,180 | |
| Angara | Yenisei | 1,830 | 1,135 | |
| Godavari | Indian | 1,470 | 915 | |
| Sutlej | Indian | 1,450 | 900 | |
| Yamuna | Indian | 1,400 | 870 | |

### Africa

| | | km | miles | |
|---|---|---|---|---|
| Nile | Mediterranean | 6,670 | 4,140 | [1] |
| Zaïre/Congo | Atlantic | 4,670 | 2,900 | [8] |
| Niger | Atlantic | 4,180 | 2,595 | |
| Zambezi | Indian | 2,740 | 1,700 | |
| Oubangi/Uele | Zaïre | 2,250 | 1,400 | |
| Kasai | Zaïre | 1,950 | 1,210 | |
| Shaballe | Indian | 1,930 | 1,200 | |
| Orange | Atlantic | 1,860 | 1,155 | |
| Cubango | Okavango Swamps | 1,800 | 1,120 | |
| Limpopo | Indian | 1,600 | 995 | |
| Senegal | Atlantic | 1,600 | 995 | |
| Volta | Atlantic | 1,500 | 930 | |
| Benue | Niger | 1,350 | 840 | |

### Australia

| | | km | miles | |
|---|---|---|---|---|
| Murray-Darling | Indian | 3,720 | 2,310 | |
| Darling | Murray | 3,070 | 1,905 | |
| Murray | Indian | 2,575 | 1,600 | |
| Murrumbidgee | Murray | 1,690 | 1,050 | |

### North America

| | | km | miles | |
|---|---|---|---|---|
| Mississippi-Missouri | Gulf of Mexico | 6,020 | 3,740 | [4] |
| Mackenzie | Arctic | 4,240 | 2,630 | |
| Mississippi | Gulf of Mexico | 3,780 | 2,350 | |
| Missouri | Mississippi | 3,725 | 2,310 | |
| Yukon | Pacific | 3,185 | 1,980 | |
| Rio Grande | Gulf of Mexico | 3,030 | 1,880 | |
| Arkansas | Mississippi | 2,340 | 1,450 | |
| Colorado | Pacific | 2,330 | 1,445 | |
| Red | Mississippi | 2,040 | 1,270 | |
| Columbia | Pacific | 1,950 | 1,210 | |
| Saskatchewan | L Winnipeg | 1,940 | 1,205 | |
| Snake | Columbia | 1,670 | 1,040 | |
| Churchill | Hudson Bay | 1,600 | 990 | |
| Ohio | Mississippi | 1,580 | 980 | |
| Brazos | Gulf of Mexico | 1,400 | 870 | |
| St Lawrence | Atlantic | 1,170 | 730 | |

### South America

| | | km | miles | |
|---|---|---|---|---|
| Amazon | Atlantic | 6,430 | 3,990 | [2] |
| Paraná-Plate | Atlantic | 4,000 | 2,480 | |
| Purus | Amazon | 3,350 | 2,080 | |
| Madeira | Amazon | 3,200 | 1,990 | |
| São Francisco | Atlantic | 2,900 | 1,800 | |
| Paraná | Plate | 2,800 | 1,740 | |
| Tocantins | Atlantic | 2,640 | 1,640 | |
| Paraguay | Paraná | 2,550 | 1,580 | |
| Orinoco | Atlantic | 2,500 | 1,550 | |
| Pilcomayo | Paraná | 2,500 | 1,550 | |
| Araguaia | Tocantins | 2,250 | 1,400 | |
| Juruá | Amazon | 2,000 | 1,240 | |
| Xingu | Amazon | 1,980 | 1,230 | |
| Ucayali | Amazon | 1,900 | 1,180 | |
| Marañón | Amazon | 1,600 | 990 | |
| Uruguay | Plate | 1,600 | 990 | |
| Magdalena | Caribbean | 1,540 | 960 | |

## LAKES

### Europe

| | | km² | miles² | |
|---|---|---|---|---|
| Lake Ladoga | Russia | 18,400 | 7,100 | |
| Lake Onega | Russia | 9,700 | 3,700 | |
| Saimaa system | Finland | 8,000 | 3,100 | |
| Vänern | Sweden | 5,500 | 2,100 | |
| Rybinsk Res. | Russia | 4,700 | 1,800 | |

### Asia

| | | km² | miles² | |
|---|---|---|---|---|
| Caspian Sea | Asia | 371,000 | 143,000 | [1] |
| Aral Sea | Kazakh/Uzbek | 36,000 | 13,900 | [6] |
| Lake Baikal | Russia | 31,500 | 12,200 | [9] |
| Tonlé Sap | Cambodia | 20,000 | 7,700 | |
| Lake Balkhash | Kazakhstan | 18,500 | 7,100 | |
| Dongting Hu | China | 12,000 | 4,600 | |
| Issyk Kul | Kirghizia | 6,200 | 2,400 | |
| Lake Urmia | Iran | 5,900 | 2,300 | |
| Koko Nur | China | 5,700 | 2,200 | |
| Poyang Hu | China | 5,000 | 1,900 | |
| Lake Khanka | China/Russia | 4,400 | 1,700 | |
| Lake Van | Turkey | 3,500 | 1,400 | |
| Ubsa Nur | China | 3,400 | 1,300 | |

### Africa

| | | km² | miles² | |
|---|---|---|---|---|
| Lake Victoria | E. Africa | 68,000 | 26,000 | [3] |
| Lake Tanganyika | C. Africa | 33,000 | 13,000 | [7] |
| Lake Malawi/Nyasa | E. Africa | 29,000 | 11,000 | [10] |
| Lake Chad | C. Africa | 25,000 | 9,700 | |
| Lake Turkana | Ethiopia/Kenya | 8,500 | 3,300 | |
| Lake Volta | Ghana | 8,500 | 3,300 | |
| Lake Bangweulu | Zambia | 8,000 | 3,100 | |
| Lake Rukwa | Tanzania | 7,000 | 2,700 | |
| Lake Mai-Ndombe | Zaïre | 6,500 | 2,500 | |
| Lake Kariba | Zambia/Zimbabwe | 5,300 | 2,000 | |
| Lake Mobutu | Uganda/Zaïre | 5,300 | 2,000 | |
| Lake Nasser | Egypt/Sudan | 5,200 | 2,000 | |
| Lake Mweru | Zambia/Zaïre | 4,900 | 1,900 | |
| Lake Cabora Bassa | S. Africa | 4,500 | 1,700 | |
| Lake Kyoga | Uganda | 4,400 | 1,700 | |
| Lake Tana | Ethiopia | 3,630 | 1,400 | |
| Lake Kivu | Rwanda/Zaïre | 2,650 | 1,000 | |
| Lake Edward | Uganda/Zaïre | 2,200 | 850 | |

### Australia

| | | km² | miles² | |
|---|---|---|---|---|
| Lake Eyre | Australia | 9,000 | 3,500 | |
| Lake Torrens | Australia | 5,800 | 2,200 | |
| Lake Gairdner | Australia | 4,800 | 1,900 | |

### North America

| | | km² | miles² | |
|---|---|---|---|---|
| Lake Superior | Canada/USA | 82,200 | 31,700 | [2] |
| Lake Huron | Canada/USA | 59,600 | 23,000 | [4] |
| Lake Michigan | USA | 58,000 | 22,400 | [5] |
| Great Bear Lake | Canada | 31,500 | 12,200 | [8] |
| Great Slave Lake | Canada | 28,700 | 11,100 | |
| Lake Erie | Canada/USA | 25,700 | 9,900 | |
| Lake Winnipeg | Canada | 24,400 | 9,400 | |
| Lake Ontario | Canada/USA | 19,500 | 7,500 | |
| Lake Nicaragua | Nicaragua | 8,200 | 3,200 | |
| Lake Athabasca | Canada | 8,000 | 3,100 | |
| Smallwood Res. | Canada | 6,530 | 2,520 | |
| Reindeer Lake | Canada | 6,400 | 2,500 | |
| Lake Winnipegosis | Canada | 5,400 | 2,100 | |
| Nettilling Lake | Canada | 5,500 | 2,100 | |
| Lake Nipigon | Canada | 4,850 | 1,900 | |
| Lake Manitoba | Canada | 4,700 | 1,800 | |

### South America

| | | km² | miles² | |
|---|---|---|---|---|
| Lake Titicaca | Bolivia/Peru | 8,200 | 3,200 | |
| Lake Poopo | Peru | 2,800 | 1,100 | |

## ISLANDS

### Europe

| | | km² | miles² | |
|---|---|---|---|---|
| Great Britain | UK | 229,880 | 88,700 | [8] |
| Iceland | Atlantic Ocean | 103,000 | 39,800 | |
| Ireland | Ireland/UK | 84,400 | 32,600 | |
| Novaya Zemlya (N) | Russia | 48,200 | 18,600 | |
| W. Spitzbergen | Norway | 39,000 | 15,100 | |
| Novaya Zemlya (S) | Russia | 33,200 | 12,800 | |
| Sicily | Italy | 25,500 | 9,800 | |
| Sardinia | Italy | 24,000 | 9,300 | |
| NE.Spitzbergen | Norway | 15,000 | 5,600 | |
| Corsica | France | 8,700 | 3,400 | |
| Crete | Greece | 8,350 | 3,200 | |
| Zealand | Denmark | 6,850 | 2,600 | |

### Asia

| | | km² | miles² | |
|---|---|---|---|---|
| Borneo | S E. Asia | 737,000 | 284,000 | [3] |
| Sumatra | Indonesia | 425,000 | 164,000 | [6] |
| Honshu | Japan | 230,000 | 88,800 | [7] |
| Celebes | Indonesia | 189,000 | 73,000 | |
| Java | Indonesia | 126,700 | 48,900 | |
| Luzon | Philippines | 104,700 | 40,400 | |
| Mindanao | Philippines | 95,000 | 36,700 | |
| Hokkaido | Japan | 78,400 | 30,300 | |
| Sakhalin | Russia | 76,400 | 29,500 | |
| Sri Lanka | Indian Ocean | 65,600 | 25,300 | |
| Taiwan | Pacific Ocean | 36,000 | 13,900 | |
| Kyushu | Japan | 35,700 | 13,800 | |
| Hainan | China | 34,000 | 13,100 | |
| Timor | Indonesia | 33,600 | 13,000 | |
| Shikoku | Japan | 18,800 | 7,300 | |
| Halmahera | Indonesia | 18,000 | 6,900 | |
| Ceram | Indonesia | 17,150 | 6,600 | |
| Sumbawa | Indonesia | 15,450 | 6,000 | |
| Flores | Indonesia | 15,200 | 5,900 | |
| Samar | Philippines | 13,100 | 5,100 | |
| Negros | Philippines | 12,700 | 4,900 | |
| Bangka | Indonesia | 12,000 | 4,600 | |
| Palawan | Philippines | 12,000 | 4,600 | |
| Panay | Philippines | 11,500 | 4,400 | |
| Sumba | Indonesia | 11,100 | 4,300 | |
| Mindoro | Philippines | 9,750 | 3,800 | |
| Buru | Indonesia | 9,500 | 3,700 | |
| Bali | Indonesia | 5,600 | 2,200 | |
| Cyprus | Mediterranean | 3,570 | 1,400 | |
| Wrangel I. | Russia | 2,800 | 1,100 | |

### Africa

| | | km² | miles² | |
|---|---|---|---|---|
| Madagascar | Indian Ocean | 587,000 | 226,600 | [4] |
| Socotra | Indian Ocean | 3,600 | 1,400 | |
| Réunion | Indian Ocean | 2,500 | 965 | |
| Tenerife | Atlantic Ocean | 2,350 | 900 | |
| Mauritius | Indian Ocean | 1,865 | 720 | |

### Oceania

| | | km² | miles² | |
|---|---|---|---|---|
| New Guinea | Indon./Pap. NG | 780,000 | 301,080 | [2] |
| New Zealand (S) | New Zealand | 150,500 | 58,100 | |
| New Zealand (N) | New Zealand | 114,400 | 44,200 | |
| Tasmania | Australia | 67,800 | 26,200 | |
| New Britain | Papua NG | 37,800 | 14,600 | |
| New Caledonia | Pacific Ocean | 16,100 | 6,200 | |
| Viti Levu | Fiji | 10,500 | 4,100 | |
| Hawaii | Pacific Ocean | 10,450 | 4,000 | |
| Bougainville | Papua NG | 9,600 | 3,700 | |
| Guadalcanal | Solomon Is | 6,500 | 2,500 | |
| Vanua Levu | Fiji | 5,550 | 2,100 | |
| New Ireland | Papua NG | 3,200 | 1,200 | |

### North America

| | | km² | miles² | |
|---|---|---|---|---|
| Greenland | Greenland | 2,175,600 | 839,800 | [1] |
| Baffin I. | Canada | 508,000 | 196,100 | [5] |
| Victoria I. | Canada | 212,200 | 81,900 | [9] |
| Ellesmere I. | Canada | 212,000 | 81,800 | [10] |
| Cuba | Cuba | 114,500 | 44,200 | |
| Newfoundland | Canada | 96,000 | 37,100 | |
| Hispaniola | Atlantic Ocean | 76,200 | 29,400 | |
| Banks I. | Canada | 67,000 | 25,900 | |
| Devon I. | Canada | 54,500 | 21,000 | |
| Melville I. | Canada | 42,400 | 16,400 | |
| Vancouver I. | Canada | 32,150 | 12,400 | |
| Somerset I. | Canada | 24,300 | 9,400 | |
| Jamaica | Caribbean | 11,400 | 4,400 | |
| Puerto Rico | Atlantic Ocean | 8,900 | 3,400 | |
| Cape Breton I. | Canada | 4,000 | 1,500 | |

### South America

| | | km² | miles² | |
|---|---|---|---|---|
| Tierra del Fuego | Argentina/Chile | 47,000 | 18,100 | |
| Falkland I. (E.) | Atlantic Ocean | 6,800 | 2,600 | |
| South Georgia | Atlantic Ocean | 4,200 | 1,600 | |
| Galapagos (Isabela) | Pacific Ocean | 2,250 | 870 | |

XV

# INTRODUCTION TO
# WORLD
# GEOGRAPHY

# THE UNIVERSE

About 15 billion years ago, time and space began with the most colossal explosion in cosmic history: the 'Big Bang' that initiated the universe. According to current theory, in the first millionth of a second of its existence it expanded from a dimensionless point of infinite mass and density into a fireball about 30 billion kilometres across; and it has been expanding ever since.

It took almost a million years for the primal fireball to cool enough for atoms to form. They were mostly hydrogen, still the most abundant material in the universe. But the new matter was not evenly distributed around the young universe, and a few billion years later atoms in relatively dense regions began to cling together under the influence of gravity, forming distinct masses of gas separated by vast expanses of empty space. These first proto-galaxies, to begin with, were dark places: the universe had cooled. But gravitational attraction continued its work, condensing matter into coherent lumps inside the galactic gas clouds. About three billion years later, some of these masses had contracted so much that internal pressure produced the high temperatures necessary to bring about nuclear fusion: the first stars were born.

There were several generations of stars, each feeding on the wreckage of its extinct predecessors as well as the original galactic gas swirls. With each new generation, progressively larger atoms were forged in stellar furnaces and the galaxy's range of elements, once restricted to hydrogen, grew larger. About ten billion years after the Big Bang, a star formed on the outskirts of our galaxy with enough matter left over to create a retinue of planets. Some 4.7 billion years after that, a few planetary atoms had evolved into structures of complex molecules that lived, breathed and eventually pointed telescopes at the sky.

They found that their Sun is just one of more than 100 billion stars in the home galaxy alone. Our galaxy, in turn, forms part of a local group of 25 or so similar structures, some much larger than our own; there are at least 100 million other galaxies in the universe as a whole. The most distant ever observed, a highly energetic galactic core known only as Quasar PKS 2000-330, lies about 15 billion light-years away.

## LIFE OF A STAR

For most of its existence, a star produces energy by the nuclear fusion of hydrogen into helium at its core. The duration of this hydrogen-burning period – known as the main sequence – depends on the star's mass; the greater the mass, the higher the core temperatures and the sooner the star's supply of hydrogen is exhausted. Dim, dwarf stars consume their hydrogen slowly, eking it out over a thousand billion years or more. The Sun, like other stars of its mass, should spend about 10 billion years on the main sequence; since it was formed less than five billion years ago, it still has half its life left.

Once all a star's core hydrogen has been fused into helium, nuclear activity moves outward into layers of unconsumed hydrogen. For a time, energy production sharply increases: the star grows hotter and expands enormously, turning into a so-called red giant. Its energy output will increase a thousandfold, and it will swell to a hundred times its present diameter.

After a few hundred million years, helium in the core will become sufficiently compressed to initiate a new cycle of nuclear fusion: from helium to carbon. The star will contract somewhat, before beginning its last expansion, in the Sun's case engulfing the Earth and perhaps Mars. In this bloated condition, the Sun's outer layers will break off into space, leaving a tiny inner core, mainly of carbon, that shrinks progressively under the force of its own gravity: dwarf stars can attain a density more than 10,000 times that of normal matter, with crushing surface gravities to match. Gradually, the nuclear fires will die down, and the Sun will reach its terminal stage: a black dwarf, emitting insignificant amounts of energy.

However, stars more massive than the Sun may undergo another transformation. The additional mass allows gravitational collapse to continue indefinitely: eventually, all the star's remaining matter shrinks to a point, and its density approaches infinity – a state that will not permit even sub-atomic structures to survive.

The star has become a black hole: an anomalous 'singularity' in the fabric of space and time. Although vast coruscations of radiation will be emitted by any matter falling into its grasp, the singularity itself has an escape velocity that exceeds the speed of light, and nothing can ever be released from it. Within the boundaries of the black hole, the laws of physics are suspended, but no physicist can ever observe the extraordinary events that may occur.

## THE END OF THE UNIVERSE

The likely fate of the universe is disputed. One theory (top) dictates that the expansion begun at the time of the Big Bang will continue 'indefinitely', with ageing galaxies moving farther and farther apart in an immense, dark graveyard. Alternately, (bottom) gravity may overcome the expansion. Galaxies will fall back together until everything is again concentrated at a single point, followed by a new Big Bang and a new expansion, in an endlessly repeated cycle. The first theory is supported by the amount of visible matter in the universe; the second assumes there is enough dark material to bring about the gravitational collapse.

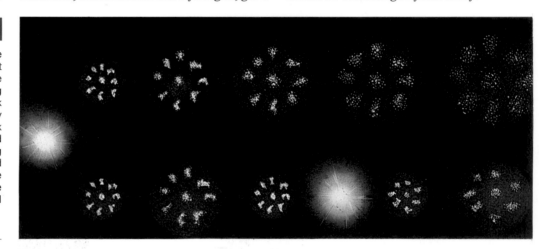

## GALACTIC STRUCTURES

The universe's 100 million galaxies show clear structural patterns, originally classified by the American astronomer Edwin Hubble in 1925. Spiral galaxies like our own (top row) have a central, almost spherical bulge and a surrounding disc composed of spiral arms. Barred spirals (bottom row) have a central bar of stars across the nucleus, with spiral arms trailing from the ends of the bar. Elliptical galaxies (far left) have a uniform appearance, ranging from a flattened disc to a near sphere. So-called SO galaxies (left row, right) have a central bulge, but no spiral arms. A few have no discernible structure at all. Galaxies also vary enormously in size, from dwarfs only 2,000 light-years across to great assemblies of stars 80 or more times larger.

## THE HOME GALAXY

The Sun and its planets are located in one of the spiral arms, a little less than 30,000 light-years from the galactic centre and orbiting around it in a period of more than 200 million years. The centre is invisible from the Earth, masked by vast, light-absorbing clouds of interstellar dust. The galaxy is probably around 12 billion years old and, like other spiral galaxies, has three distinct regions. The central bulge is about 30,000 light-years in diameter. The disc in which the Sun is located is not much more than 1,000 light-years thick but 100,000 light-years from end to end. Around the galaxy is the halo, a spherical zone 150,000 light-years across studded with globular star-clusters and sprinkled with individual suns.

Globular clusters

Bulge

Disc

Solar System

Star charts are drawn as projections of a vast, hollow sphere with the observer in the middle. Each circle below represents one hemisphere, centred on the north and south celestial poles respectively – projections of the Earth's poles in the heavens. At the present era, the north pole is marked by the star Polaris; the south pole has no such convenient reference point. The rectangular map shows the stars immediately above and below the celestial equator.

Astronomical coordinates are normally given in terms of 'Right Ascension' for longitude and 'Declination' for latitude or altitude. Since the stars appear to rotate around the Earth once every 24 hours, Right Ascension is measured eastward – anti-clockwise – in hours and minutes. One hour is equivalent to 15 angular degrees; zero on the scale is the point at which the Sun crosses the celestial equator at the spring equinox, known to astronomers as the First Point in Aries. Unlike the Sun, stars always rise and set at the same point on the horizon. Declination measures (in degrees) a star's angular distance above or below the celestial equator.

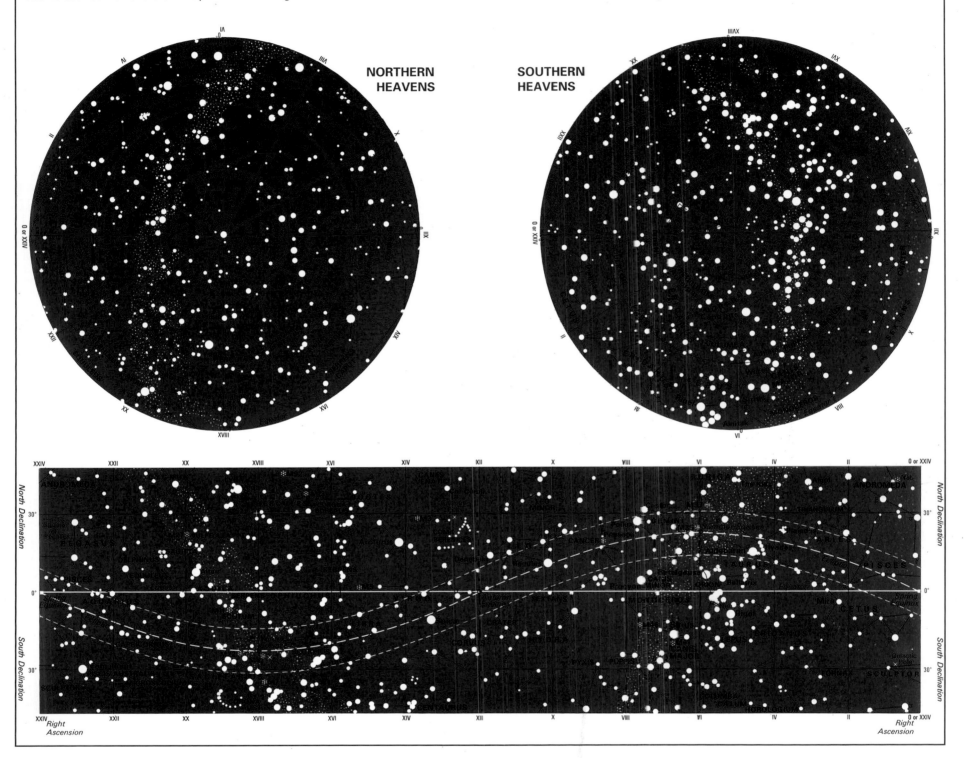

NORTHERN HEAVENS

SOUTHERN HEAVENS

North Declination

South Declination

Right Ascension

North Declination

South Declination

Right Ascension

The constellations and their English names

| | | | | | | | |
|---|---|---|---|---|---|---|---|
| Andromeda | Andromeda | Circinus | Compasses | Lacerta | Lizard | Piscis Austrinus | Southern Fish |
| Antila | Air Pump | Columba | Dove | Leo | Lion | Puppis | Ship's Stern |
| Apus | Bird of Paradise | Coma Berenices | Berenice's Hair | Leo Minor | Little Lion | Pyxis | Mariner's Compass |
| Aquarius | Water-carrier | Corona Australis | Southern Crown | Lepus | Hare | Reticulum | Net |
| Aquila | Eagle | Corona Borealis | Northern Crown | Libra | Scales | Sagitta | Arrow |
| Ara | Altar | Corvus | Crow | Lupus | Wolf | Sagittarius | Archer |
| Aries | Ram | Crater | Cup | Lynx | Lynx | Scorpius | Scorpion |
| Auriga | Charioteer | Crux | Southern Cross | Lyra | Harp | Sculptor | Sculptor |
| Boötes | Herdsman | Cygnus | Swan | Mensa | Table | Scutum | Shield |
| Caelum | Chisel | Delphinus | Dolphin | Microscopium | Microscope | Serpens | Serpent |
| Camelopardalis | Giraffe | Dorado | Swordfish | Monoceros | Unicorn | Sextans | Sextant |
| Cancer | Crab | Draco | Dragon | Musca | Fly | Taurus | Bull |
| Canes Venatici | Hunting Dogs | Equuleus | Little House | Norma | Level | Telescopium | Telescope |
| Canis Major | Great Dog | Eridanus | Eridanus | Octans | Octant | Triangulum | Triangle |
| Canis Minor | Little Dog | Fornax | Furnace | Ophiuchus | Serpent Bearer | Triangulum Australe | Southern Triangle |
| Capricornus | Goat | Gemini | Twins | Orion | Orion | Tucana | Toucan |
| Carina | Keel | Grus | Crane | Pavo | Peacock | Ursa Major | Great Bear |
| Cassiopeia | Cassiopeia | Hercules | Hercules | Pegasus | Winged Horse | Ursa Minor | Little Bear |
| Centaurus | Centaur | Horologium | Clock | Perseus | Perseus | Vela | Sails |
| Cepheus | Cepheus | Hydra | Water Snake | Phoenix | Phoenix | Virgo | Virgin |
| Cetus | Whale | Hydrus | Sea Serpent | Pictor | Easel | Volans | Flying Fish |
| Chamaeleon | Chameleon | Indus | Indian | Pisces | Fishes | Vulpecula | Fox |

The 20 nearest stars, excluding the Sun, with their distance from Earth in light-years*

| | |
|---|---|
| Proxima Centauri | 4.3 |
| Alpha Centauri A | 4.3 |
| Alpha Centauri B | 4.3 |
| Barnard's Star | 6.0 |
| Wolf 359 | 8.1 |
| Lal 21185 | 8.2 |
| Sirius A | 8.7 |
| Sirius B | 8.7 |
| UV Ceti A | 9.0 |
| UV Citi B | 9.0 |
| Ross 154 | 9.3 |
| Ross 248 | 10.3 |
| Epsilon Eridani | 10.8 |
| L 789-6 | 11.1 |
| Ross 128 | 11.1 |
| 61 Cygni A | 11.2 |
| 61 Cygni B | 11.2 |
| Procyon A | 11.3 |
| Procyon B | 11.3 |
| Epsilon Indi | 11.4 |

Many of the nearest stars, like Alpha Centauri A and B, are doubles, orbiting about the common centre of gravity and to all intents and purposes equidistant from Earth. Many of them are dim objects, with no name other than the designation given by the astronomers who investigated them. However, they include Sirius, the brightest star in the sky, and Procyon, the seventh brightest. Both are far larger than the Sun: of the nearest stars only Epsilon Eridani is similar in size and luminosity.

* A light-year equals approx. 9,500,000,000,000 kilometres

# THE SOLAR SYSTEM

Lying 27,000 light years from the centre of one of billions of galaxies that comprise the observable universe, our solar system contains nine planets and their moons, innumerable asteroids and comets and a miscellany of dust and gas, all tethered by the immense gravitational field of the Sun, the middling-sized star whose thermonuclear furnaces provide them all with heat and light. The solar system was probably formed about 4.6 billion years ago, when a spinning cloud of gas, mostly hydrogen but seeded with other, heavier elements, condensed enough to ignite a nuclear reaction and create a star. The Sun still accounts for almost 99.9% of the system's total mass; one planet, Jupiter, contains most of the remainder.

By composition as well as distance, the planetary array divides quite neatly in two: an inner system of four small, solid planets, including the Earth, and an outer system, from Jupiter to Neptune, of four huge gas giants. Between the two groups lies a scattering of asteroids, perhaps as many as 40,000; possibly the remains of a planet destroyed by some unexplained catastrophe, they are more likely to be debris left over from the solar system's formation, prevented by the gravity of massive Jupiter from coalescing into a larger body. The ninth planet, Pluto, seems to be a world of the inner system type: small, rocky and something of an anomaly.

By the 1990s, the solar system also included some newer anomalies: several thousand spacecraft. Most were in orbit around the Earth, but some had probed far and wide around the system. The information beamed back by these robotic investigators has transformed our knowledge of our celestial environment.

Much of the early history of science is the story of people trying to make sense of the errant points of light that were all they knew of the planets. Now, people have themselves stood on the Earth's Moon; probes have landed on Mars and Venus and orbiting radars have mapped far distant landscapes with astonishing accuracy. In the 1980s, the US Voyagers skimmed all four major planets of the outer system, bringing new revelations with each close approach. Only Pluto, inscrutably distant in an orbit that takes it 50 times the Earth's distance from the Sun, remains unvisited by our messengers.

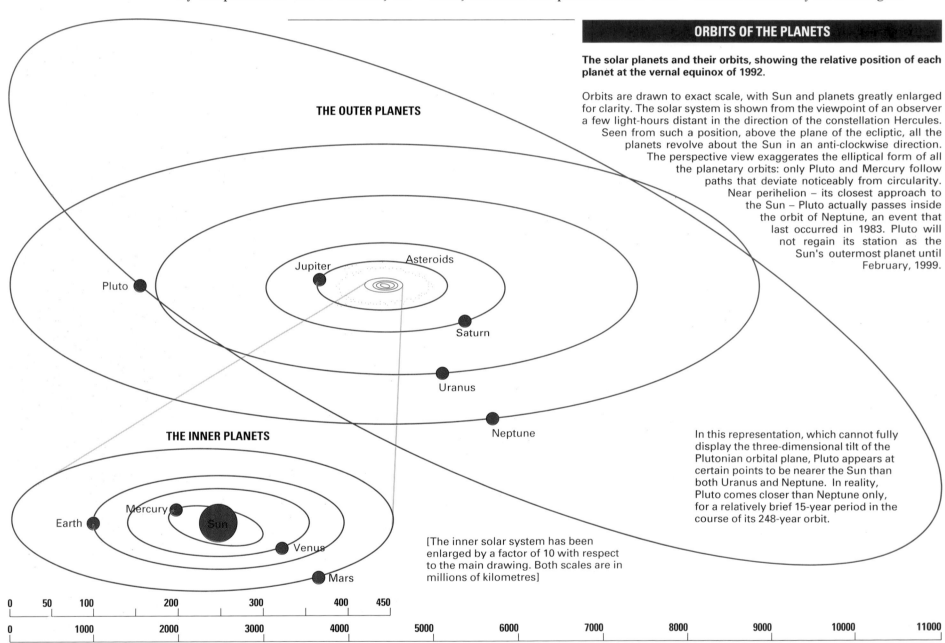

**THE OUTER PLANETS**

**THE INNER PLANETS**

Pluto · Jupiter · Asteroids · Saturn · Uranus · Neptune · Mercury · Earth · Sun · Venus · Mars

[The inner solar system has been enlarged by a factor of 10 with respect to the main drawing. Both scales are in millions of kilometres]

## ORBITS OF THE PLANETS

**The solar planets and their orbits, showing the relative position of each planet at the vernal equinox of 1992.**

Orbits are drawn to exact scale, with Sun and planets greatly enlarged for clarity. The solar system is shown from the viewpoint of an observer a few light-hours distant in the direction of the constellation Hercules. Seen from such a position, above the plane of the ecliptic, all the planets revolve about the Sun in an anti-clockwise direction. The perspective view exaggerates the elliptical form of all the planetary orbits: only Pluto and Mercury follow paths that deviate noticeably from circularity. Near perihelion – its closest approach to the Sun – Pluto actually passes inside the orbit of Neptune, an event that last occurred in 1983. Pluto will not regain its station as the Sun's outermost planet until February, 1999.

In this representation, which cannot fully display the three-dimensional tilt of the Plutonian orbital plane, Pluto appears at certain points to be nearer the Sun than both Uranus and Neptune. In reality, Pluto comes closer than Neptune only, for a relatively brief 15-year period in the course of its 248-year orbit.

| PLANETARY DATA | | | | | | | | | |
|---|---|---|---|---|---|---|---|---|---|
| | Mean distance from Sun (million km) | Mass (Earth = 1) | Period of orbit (Earth years) | Period of rotation (Earth days) | Equatorial diameter (km) | Average density (water = 1) | Surface gravity (Earth = 1) | Escape velocity (km/sec) | Number of known satellites |
| *Sun* | - | 332,946 | - | 25.38 | 1,392,000 | 1.41 | 27.9 | 617.5 | - |
| **Mercury** | 58.3 | 0.06 | 0.241 | 58.67 | 4,878 | 5.5 | 0.38 | 4.27 | 0 |
| **Venus** | 107.7 | 0.8 | 0.615 | 243 | 12,104 | 5.25 | 0.90 | 10.36 | 0 |
| **Earth** | 149.6 | 1.0 | 1.00 | 0.99 | 12,756 | 5.52 | 1.00 | 11.18 | 1 |
| **Mars** | 227.3 | 0.1 | 1.88 | 1.02 | 6,794 | 3.94 | 0.38 | 5.03 | 2 |
| **Jupiter** | 777.9 | 317.8 | 11.86 | 0.41 | 142,800 | 1.33 | 2.64 | 60.22 | 16 |
| **Saturn** | 1,427.1 | 95.2 | 29.63 | 0.42 | 120,000 | 0.706 | 1.16 | 36.25 | 17 |
| **Uranus** | 2,872.3 | 14.5 | 83.97 | 0.45 | 52,000 | 1.70 | 1.11 | 22.4 | 15 |
| **Neptune** | 4,502.7 | 17.2 | 164.8 | 0.67 | 48,400 | 1.77 | 1.21 | 23.9 | 8 |
| **Pluto** | 5,894.2 | 0.002 | 248.63 | 6.38 | 3,000 | 5.50 | 0.47 | 5.1 | 1 |

Planetary days are given in sidereal time -- that is, with respect to the stars rather than the Sun. Most of the information in the table was confirmed by spacecraft and often obtained from photographs and other data transmitted back to the Earth. In the case of Pluto, however, only earthbound observations have been made, and no spacecraft can hope to encounter it until well into the next century. Given the planet's small size and great distance, figures for its diameter and rotation period cannot be definitive.

Since Pluto does not appear to be massive enough to account for the perturbations in the orbits of Uranus and Neptune that led to its 1930 discovery, it is quite possible that a tenth and even more distant planet may exist. Once Pluto's own 248-year orbit has been observed for long enough, further discrepancies may give a clue as to any tenth planet's whereabouts. Even so, distance alone would make it very difficult to locate, especially since telescopes powerful enough to find it are normally engaged in galactic study.

## THE PLANETS

**Mercury** is the closest planet to the Sun and hence the fastest-moving. It has no significant atmosphere and a cratered, wrinkled surface very similar to that of Earth's moon.

**Venus** has much the same physical dimensions as Earth. However, its carbon dioxide atmosphere is 90 times as dense, accounting for a runaway greenhouse effect that makes the Venusian surface, at 475°C, the hottest of all the planets. Radar mapping shows relatively level land with volcanic regions whose sulphurous discharges explain the sulphuric acid rains reported by soft-landing space probes before they succumbed to Venus's fierce climate.

**Earth** seen from space is easily the most beautiful of the inner planets; it is also, and more objectively, the largest, as well the only home of known life. Living things are the main reason why the Earth is able to retain a substantial proportion of corrosive and highly reactive oxygen in its atmosphere, a state of affairs that contradicts the laws of chemical equilibrium; the oxygen in turn supports the life that constantly regenerates it.

**Mars** was once considered the likeliest of the other planets to share Earth's cargo of life: seasonal expansion of dark patches strongly suggested vegetation and the planet's apparent icecaps indicated the vital presence of water. But close inspection by spacecraft brought disappointment: chemical reactions account for the seeming vegetation, the icecaps are mainly frozen carbon dioxide and whatever oxygen the planet once possessed is now locked up in the iron-bearing rock that covers its cratered surface and gives it its characteristic red hue.

**Jupiter** masses almost three times as much as all the other planets together; had it scooped up a little more matter during its formation, it might have evolved into a small companion star for the Sun. The planet is mostly gas, under intense pressure in the lower atmosphere above a core of fiercely compressed hydrogen and helium. The upper layers form strikingly-coloured rotating belts, the outward sign of the intense storms created by Jupiter's rapid diurnal rotation. Close approaches by spacecraft have shown an orbiting ring system, and discovered several previously unknown moons: Jupiter has at least 16.

**Saturn** is structurally similar to Jupiter, rotating fast enough to produce an obvious bulge at its equator. Ever since the invention of the telescope, however, Saturn's rings have been the feature that has attracted most observers. Voyager probes in 1980 and 1981 sent back detailed pictures that showed them to be composed of thousands of separate ringlets, each in turn made up of tiny icy particles, interacting in a complex dance that may serve as a model for the study of galactic and even larger structures.

**Uranus** was unknown to the ancients: although it is faintly visible to the naked eye, it was not discovered until 1781. Its composition is broadly similar to Jupiter and Saturn, though its distance from the Sun ensures an even colder surface temperature. Observations in 1977 suggested the presence of a faint ring system, amply confirmed when Voyager 2 swung past the planet in 1986.

**Neptune** is always more than 4,000 million Km from Earth, and despite its diameter of almost 50,000 km it can only be seen by telescope. Its 1846 discovery was the result of mathematical predictions by astronomers seeking to explain irregularities in the orbit of Uranus, but until Voyager 2 closed with the planet in 1989 little was known of it. Like Uranus, it has a ring system; Voyager's photographs revealed a total of eight moons.

**Pluto** is the most mysterious of the solar planets, if only because even the most powerful telescopes can scarcely resolve it from a point of light to a disc. It was discovered as recently as 1930, like Neptune as the result of perturbations in the orbits of the two then outermost planets. Its small size as well as its eccentric and highly tilted orbit have led to suggestions that it is a former satellite of Neptune, somehow liberated from its primary. In 1978 Pluto was found to have a moon of its own, Charon, apparently half the size of Pluto itself.

Mars

Jupiter

Uranus — 2,872.3

Saturn

Uranus

Neptune — 4,502.7

Neptune

Pluto

Pluto — 5,894.2

# THE EARTH: TIME & MOTION

The basic unit of time measurement is the day, one rotation of the Earth on its axis. The subdivision of the day into hours, minutes and seconds is arbitrary and simply for our convenience. Our present calendar is based on the solar year of 365.24 days, the time taken by the Earth to orbit the Sun. As the Earth rotates from west to east, the Sun appears to rise in the east and set in the west. When the Sun is setting in Shanghai, on the opposite side of the world New York is just emerging into sunlight. Noon, when the

sun is directly overhead, is coincident at all places on the same meridian, with shadows pointing directly toward the poles.

Calendars based on the movements of the Sun and Moon have been used since ancient times. The Julian Calendar, with its leap year, introduced by Julius Caesar, fixed the average length of the year at 365.25 days, which was about 11 minutes too long (the Earth completes its orbit in 365 days, 5 hours, 48 minutes and 46 seconds of mean solar time). The cumulative error was

rectified by the Gregorian Calendar, introduced by Pope Gregory XIII in 1582, when he decreed that the day following October 4 was October 15, and that century years do not count as leap years unless divisible by 400. England did not adopt the reformed calendar until 1752, when it found itself 11 days behind the continent.

Britain imposed the Gregorian Calendar on all its possessions, including the American colonies. All dates preceding September 2 were marked O.S., for Old Style.

## EARTH DATA

Maximum distance from the Sun (Aphelion): 152,007,016 km.
Minimum distance from Sun (Perihelion): 147,000,830 km.
Obliquity of the ecliptic: 23° 27' 08".
Length of year - solar tropical (equinox to equinox): 365.24 days
Length of year - sidereal (fixed star to fixed star): 365.26 days
Length of day - mean solar day: 24h, 03m, 56s.
Length of day - mean sidereal day: 23h, 56m, 04s.

Superficial area: 510,000,000 sq. km.
Land surface: 149,000,000 sq. km. (29.2%)
Water surface: 361,000,000 sq. km. (70.8%)
Equatorial circumference: 40,077 km.
Meridional circumference: 40,009 km.
Equatorial diameter: 12,756.8 km.
Polar diameter: 12,713.8 km.
Equatorial radius: 6,378.4 km.
Polar radius: 6,356.9 km.
Volume of the Earth: $1,083,230 \times 10^6$ cu. km.
Mass of the Earth: $5.9 \times 10^{21}$ tonnes

## THE SEASONS

The Earth revolves around the Sun once a year in an 'anti-clockwise' direction, tilted at a constant angle, $66\frac{1}{2}°$. In June, the northern hemisphere is tilted towards the Sun: as a result it receives more hours of sunshine in a day and therefore has its warmest season, summer. By December, the Earth has rotated halfway round the Sun so that the southern hemisphere that is tilted towards the Sun and has its summer; the hemisphere that is tilted away from the Sun has winter. On 21 June the Sun is directly overhead at the Tropic of Cancer ($23\frac{1}{2}°$ N), and this is midsummer in the northern hemisphere. Midsummer in the southern hemisphere occurs on 21 December, when the Sun is overhead at the Tropic of Capricorn ($23\frac{1}{2}°$ S).

## DAY & NIGHT

The Sun appears to rise in the east, reach its highest point at noon, and then set in the west, to be followed by night. In reality it is not the Sun that is moving but the Earth revolving from west to east.

At the summer solstice in the northern hemisphere (21 June), the Arctic has total daylight and the Antarctic total darkness. The opposite occurs at the winter solstice (21 December). At the equator, the length of day and night are almost equal all year.

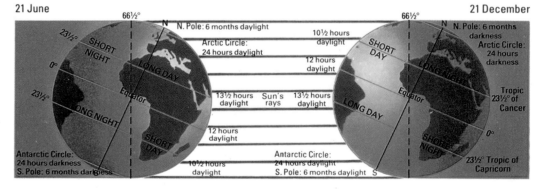

## THE SUN'S PATH

The diagrams on the left illustrate the apparent path of the Sun at (A) the equator, (B) in mid-latitude (45°), (C) at the Arctic Circle ($66\frac{1}{2}°$) and (D) at the North Pole, where there are six months of continuous daylight and six months of continuous night.

## MEASUREMENTS OF TIME

Astronomers distinguish between solar time and sidereal time. Solar time derives from the period taken by the Earth to rotate on its axis: one rotation defines a solar day. But the speed of the Earth along its orbit around the Sun is not constant. The length of day - or 'apparent solar day' - as defined by the apparent successive transits of the Sun - is irregular because the Earth must complete more than one rotation before the Sun returns to the same meridian. The constant sidereal day is defined as the interval between two successive apparent transits of a star, or the first point of Aries, across the same meridian. If the Sun is at the equinox and overhead at a meridian one day, then the next day it will be to the east by approximately 1°. Thus the Sun will not cross the meridian until four minutes after the sidereal noon.

*From the diagrams on the right it is possible to discover the time of sunrise or sunset on a given date and for latitudes between 60°N and 60°S.*

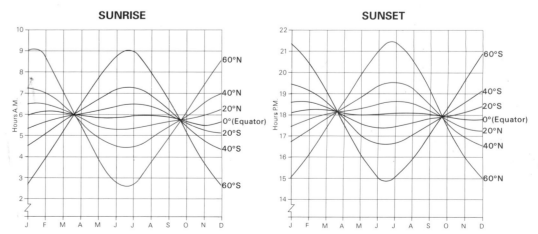

# THE MOON

## PHASES OF THE MOON

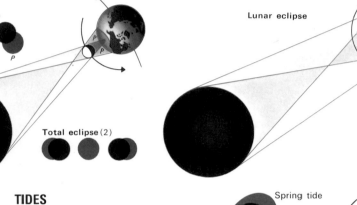

New moon · Crescent moon · Half moon, first quarter · Gibbous moon · Full moon · Waning moon · Half moon, third quarter · Old moon

The Moon rotates more slowly than the Earth, making one complete turn on its axis in just over 27 days. Since this corresponds to its period of revolution around the Earth, the Moon always presents the same hemisphere or face to us, and we never see 'the dark side'. The interval between one full Moon and the next (and between new Moons) is about 29½ days - a lunar month. The apparent changes in the shape of the Moon are caused by its changing position in relation to the Earth; like the planets, it produces no light of its own and shines only by reflecting the rays of the Sun.

Partial eclipse (1)

Lunar eclipse

Total eclipse (2)

## TIDES

The daily rise and fall of the ocean's tides are the result of the gravitational pull of the Moon and that of the Sun, though the effect of the latter is only 46.6% as strong as that of the Moon. This effect is greatest on the hemisphere facing the Moon and causes a tidal 'bulge'. When lunar and solar forces pull together, with Sun, Earth and Moon in line (near new and full Moons), higher 'spring tides' (and lower low tides) occur; when lunar and solar forces are least coincidental with the Sun and Moon at an angle (near the Moon's first and third quarters), 'neap tides' occur, which have a small tidal range.

Spring tide · Neap tide · Last quarter · New moon · Spring tide · Full moon · Neap tide · First quarter · Gravitational pull by Sun and Moon

## ECLIPSES

When the Moon passes between the Sun and the Earth it causes a partial eclipse of the Sun (1) if the Earth passes through the Moon's outer shadow (P), or a total eclipse (2) if the inner cone shadow crosses the Earth's surface. In a lunar eclipse, the Earth's shadow crosses the Moon and, again, provides either a partial or total eclipse. Eclipses of the Sun and the Moon do not occur every month because of the 5° difference between the plane of the Moon's orbit and the plane in which the Earth moves. In the 1990s only 14 lunar eclipses are possible, for example, seven partial and seven total; each is visible only from certain, and variable, parts of the world. The same period witnesses 13 solar eclipses - six partial (or annular) and seven total.

## MOON DATA

**Distance from Earth:** The Moon orbits at a mean distance of 384,199.1 km, at an average speed of 3,683 km/h in relation to the Earth.

**Size & mass:** The average diameter of the Moon is 3,475.1 km. It is 400 times smaller than the Sun but is about 400 times closer to the Earth, so we see them as the same size. The Moon has a mass of 7.348 x 10$^{19}$ tonnes, with a density 3.344 times that of water.

**Visibility:** Only 59% of the Moon's surface is directly visible from Earth. Reflected light takes 1.25 seconds to reach Earth - compared to 8 minutes 27.3 seconds for light from the Sun.

**Temperature:** With the Sun overhead the temperature on the lunar equator can reach 117.2°C [243°F]. At night it can sink to -162.7°C [-261°F].

---

## STANDARD TIME ZONES

Zones using Greenwich Mean Time (GMT)
Zones slow of Greenwich Mean Time
Zones fast of Greenwich Mean Time
10 Hours fast or slow of Greenwich Mean Time
Half-hour zones
- - - International boundaries
Time zone boundaries, sometimes coinciding with international boundaries

Projection: Mercator

COPYRIGHT GEORGE PHILIP LTD.

Theoretically a time zone extends for 15° of longitude (360° ÷ 24 hours = 15°) so that the sun is overhead at noon in each zone. Zone boundaries are rarely lines of longitude, but are adjusted to follow international boundaries or to avoid separating cities and towns from neighbours by a time difference. Countries such as U.S.A. and Canada, the U.S.S.R. and Australia which stretch through many degrees of longitude have a number of time zones. To relate work and leisure, normally planned with clock time, more closely to sun time or daylight, the standard zone time can be adjusted for part of the year; Summer Time is an example of this.

Actual solar time when it is noon at Greenwich is shown along the top of the map

## TIME ZONES

The Earth rotates through 360° in 24 hours, and therefore it moves 15° every hour. The world is divided into 24 standard time zones, each centred on lines of longitude at 15° intervals, so that every country falls within one or more agreed zones. The Greenwich meridian, based on the location of the Royal Observatory in London, lies at the centre of the first zone. All places to the west of Greenwich are one hour behind for every 15° of longitude; places to the east are ahead by one hour for every 15°.

When it is 12 noon at the Greenwich meridian, 180° east it is midnight of the same day – while 180° west the day is only just beginning. To overcome this the International Date Line was established, approximately following the 180° meridian. Thus if you travelled eastwards from Japan (140° East) to Samoa (170° West) you would pass from Sunday night into Sunday morning.

# THE EARTH: GEOLOGY

The origin of the Earth is still open to conjecture, although the most widely accepted theory is that it was formed from a solar cloud consisting mainly of hydrogen 4,600 million years ago. The cloud condensed, forming the planets. The lighter elements floated to the surface of the Earth, where they cooled to form a crust; the inner material remained hot and molten. The first rocks were formed over 3,500 million years ago, but the Earth's surface has since been constantly altered.

The crust consists of a brittle, low-density material varying from 5 to 50 kilometres deep beneath the continents, consisting predominately of silica and aluminium: hence its name, sial . Below the sial is a basaltic layer known as sima , comprising mainly silica and magnesium. The crust accounts for only 1.5 per cent of the Earth s volume.

Immediately below the crust the mantle begins, with a distinct change in density and chemical properties. The rock is rich in iron and magnesium silicates, and temperatures reach 1,600°C. The rigid upper mantle extends down to a depth of about 1,000 kilometres, below which is a more viscous lower mantle about 1,900 kilometres thick.

The outer core, measuring about 2,100 kilometres thick, consists of molten iron and nickel at 2,100°C to 5,000°C, possibly separated from the less dense mantle by an oxidized shell. About 5,000 kilometres below the surface is a liquid transition zone, below which is the solid inner core, a sphere of about 2,700 kilometres diameter where rock is three times as dense as in the crust. The temperature at the centre of the Earth is probably about 5,000°C.

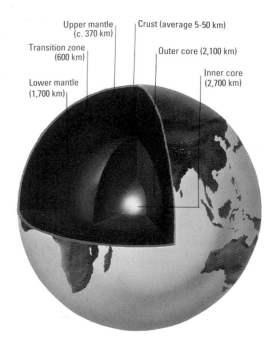

The complementary, almost jigsaw-puzzle fit of the Atlantic coasts led to Alfred Wegener's proposition of continental drift in Germany (1915). His theory suggested that an ancient super-continent, which he called Pangaea, incorporating all the Earth's land masses, gradually split up to form the continents we know today. By 180 million years ago Pangaea had divided into two major groups and the southern part, Gondwanaland, had itself begun to break up with India and Antarctica-Australia becoming isolated. By 135 million years ago the widening of the splits in the North Atlantic and Indian Oceans persisted, a South Atlantic gap had appeared and India continued to move 'north' towards Asia. By 65 million years ago South America had completely split from Africa.
To form today's pattern India 'collided' with Asia (crumpling up sediments to form the Himalayas); South America rotated and moved west to connect with North America; Australia separated from Antarctica and moved north; and the familiar gap developed between Greenland and Europe.

## CONTINENTAL DRIFT

About 200 million years ago the original Pangaea land mass began to split into two continental groups, which further separated over time to produce the present day configuration.

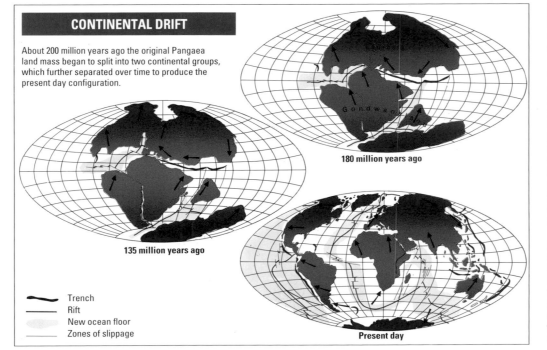

180 million years ago

135 million years ago

Present day

⌇ Trench
— Rift
▒ New ocean floor
⌇ Zones of slippage

## PLATE TECTONICS

The original debate about the drift theory of Wegener and others formed a long prelude to a more radical idea: plate tectonics. The discovery that the continents are carried along on the top of slowly-moving crustal plates (which float on heavier liquid material – the lower mantle – much as icebergs do on water) provided the mechanism for the drift theories to work. The plates converge and diverge along margins marked by seismic and volcanic activity. Plates diverge from mid-ocean ridges where molten lava pushes up and forces the plates apart at a rate of up to 40 mm a year; converging plates form either a trench (where the oceanic plates sink below the lighter continental rock) or mountain ranges (where two continents collide).

The debate about plate tectonics is not over, however. In addition to abiding questions such as what force actually moves the plates (massive convection currents in the Earth's interior is the most popular explanation), and why many volcanoes and earthquakes occur in mid-plate (such as Hawaii and central China), evidence began to emerge in the early 1990s that, with more sophisticated equipment and models, the whole theory might be in doubt.

## EARTHQUAKES

Earthquake magnitude is usually rated according to either the Richter or the Modified Mercalli scale, both devised by seismologists in the 1930s. The Richter scale measures absolute earthquake power with mathematical precision: each step upwards represents a ten-fold increase in shockwave amplitude. Theoretically, there is no upper limit, but the largest earthquakes measured have been rated at between 8.8 and 8.9. The 12–point Mercalli scale, based on observed effects, is often more meaningful, ranging from I (earthquakes noticed only by seismographs) to XII (total destruction); intermediate points include V (people awakened at night; unstable objects overturned), VII (collapse of ordinary buildings; chimneys and monuments fall); and IX (conspicuous cracks in ground; serious damage to reservoirs).

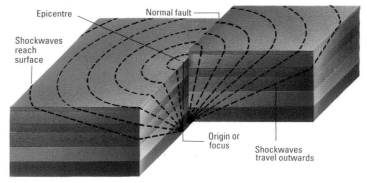

## DISTRIBUTION

### NOTABLE EARTHQUAKES SINCE 1900

| Year | Location | Mag. | Deaths |
|---|---|---|---|
| 1906 | San Francisco, USA | 8.3 | 503 |
| 1906 | Valparaiso, Chile | 8.6 | 22,000 |
| 1908 | Messina, Italy | 7.5 | 83,000 |
| 1915 | Avezzano, Italy | 7.5 | 30,000 |
| 1920 | Gansu, China | 8.6 | 180,000 |
| 1923 | Yokohama, Japan | 8.3 | 143,000 |
| 1927 | Nan Shan, China | 8.3 | 200,000 |
| 1932 | Gansu, China | 7.6 | 70,000 |
| 1934 | Bihar, India/Nepal | 8.4 | 10,700 |
| 1935 | Quetta, India* | 7.5 | 60,000 |
| 1939 | Chillan, Chile | 8.3 | 28,000 |
| 1939 | Erzincan, Turkey | 7.9 | 30,000 |
| 1960 | Agadir, Morocco | 5.8 | 12,000 |
| 1962 | Khorasan, Iran | 7.1 | 12,230 |
| 1963 | Skopje, Yugoslavia | 6.0 | 1,000 |
| 1964 | Anchorage, Alaska | 8.4 | 131 |
| 1968 | N. E. Iran | 7.4 | 12,000 |
| 1970 | N. Peru | 7.7 | 66,794 |
| 1972 | Managua, Nicaragua | 6.2 | 5,000 |
| 1974 | N. Pakistan | 6.3 | 5,200 |
| 1976 | Guatemala | 7.5 | 22,778 |
| 1976 | Tangshan, China | 8.2 | 650,000 |
| 1978 | Tabas, Iran | 7.7 | 25,000 |
| 1980 | El Asnam, Algeria | 7.3 | 20,000 |
| 1980 | S. Italy | 7.2 | 4,800 |
| 1985 | Mexico City, Mexico | 8.1 | 4,200 |
| 1988 | N.W. Armenia, USSR | 6.8 | 55,000 |
| 1990 | N. Iran | 7.7 | 36,000 |

The highest magnitude recorded on the Richter scale is 8.9, in Japan on 2 March 1933 (2,990 deaths). The most devastating quake ever was at Shaanxi (Shensi), central China, on 24 January 1566, when an estimated 830,000 people were killed.

* now Pakistan

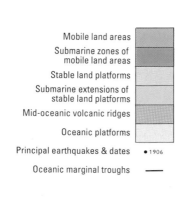

Mobile land areas
Submarine zones of mobile land areas
Stable land platforms
Submarine extensions of stable land platforms
Mid-oceanic volcanic ridges
Oceanic platforms
Principal earthquakes & dates  •1906
Oceanic marginal troughs  —

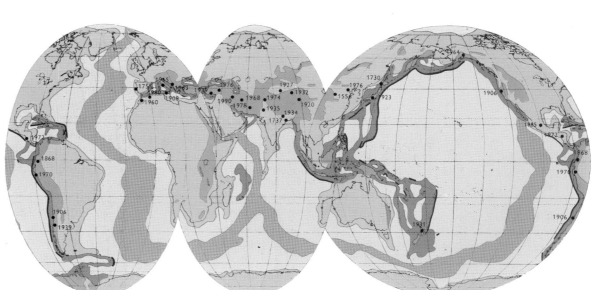

Earthquakes are a series of rapid vibrations originating from the the slipping or faulting of parts of the Earth's crust when stresses within build to breaking point, and usually occur at depths between 8 and 30 kilometres.

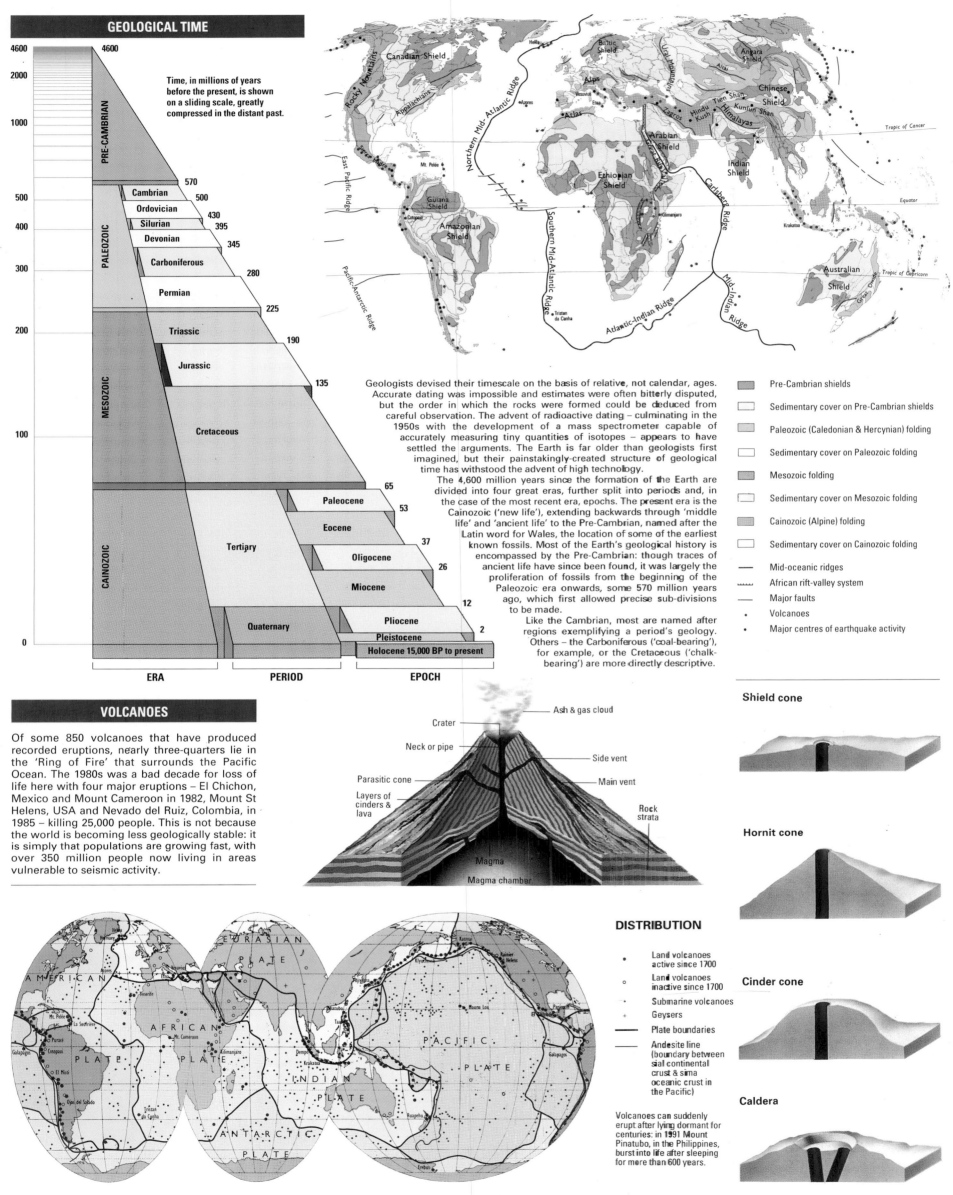

## GEOLOGICAL TIME

4600

2000

1000

500

400

300

200

100

0

Time, in millions of years before the present, is shown on a sliding scale, greatly compressed in the distant past.

**PRE-CAMBRIAN** — 4600

**PALEOZOIC**
- Cambrian — 570
- Ordovician — 500
- Silurian — 430
- Devonian — 395
- Carboniferous — 345
- Permian — 280

**MESOZOIC**
- Triassic — 225
- Jurassic — 190
- Cretaceous — 135

**CAINOZOIC**
- Tertiary
  - Paleocene — 65
  - Eocene — 53
  - Oligocene — 37
  - Miocene — 26
  - Pliocene — 12
- Quaternary
  - Pleistocene — 2
  - Holocene 15,000 BP to present

ERA     PERIOD     EPOCH

Geologists devised their timescale on the basis of relative, not calendar, ages. Accurate dating was impossible and estimates were often bitterly disputed, but the order in which the rocks were formed could be deduced from careful observation. The advent of radioactive dating – culminating in the 1950s with the development of a mass spectrometer capable of accurately measuring tiny quantities of isotopes – appears to have settled the arguments. The Earth is far older than geologists first imagined, but their painstakingly-created structure of geological time has withstood the advent of high technology.

The 4,600 million years since the formation of the Earth are divided into four great eras, further split into periods and, in the case of the most recent era, epochs. The present era is the Cainozoic ('new life'), extending backwards through 'middle life' and 'ancient life' to the Pre-Cambrian, named after the Latin word for Wales, the location of some of the earliest known fossils. Most of the Earth's geological history is encompassed by the Pre-Cambrian: though traces of ancient life have since been found, it was largely the proliferation of fossils from the beginning of the Paleozoic era onwards, some 570 million years ago, which first allowed precise sub-divisions to be made.

Like the Cambrian, most are named after regions exemplifying a period's geology. Others – the Carboniferous ('coal-bearing'), for example, or the Cretaceous ('chalk-bearing') are more directly descriptive.

- ▨ Pre-Cambrian shields
- ☐ Sedimentary cover on Pre-Cambrian shields
- ▨ Paleozoic (Caledonian & Hercynian) folding
- ☐ Sedimentary cover on Paleozoic folding
- ▨ Mesozoic folding
- ☐ Sedimentary cover on Mesozoic folding
- ▨ Cainozoic (Alpine) folding
- ☐ Sedimentary cover on Cainozoic folding
- — Mid-oceanic ridges
- ⋯ African rift-valley system
- — Major faults
- • Volcanoes
- • Major centres of earthquake activity

## VOLCANOES

Of some 850 volcanoes that have produced recorded eruptions, nearly three-quarters lie in the 'Ring of Fire' that surrounds the Pacific Ocean. The 1980s was a bad decade for loss of life here with four major eruptions – El Chichon, Mexico and Mount Cameroon in 1982, Mount St Helens, USA and Nevado del Ruiz, Colombia, in 1985 – killing 25,000 people. This is not because the world is becoming less geologically stable: it is simply that populations are growing fast, with over 350 million people now living in areas vulnerable to seismic activity.

Ash & gas cloud
Crater
Neck or pipe
Side vent
Parasitic cone
Main vent
Layers of cinders & lava
Rock strata
Magma
Magma chamber

**Shield cone**

**Hornit cone**

**Cinder cone**

**Caldera**

### DISTRIBUTION

- • Land volcanoes active since 1700
- ○ Land volcanoes inactive since 1700
- - Submarine volcanoes
- + Geysers
- ▬ Plate boundaries
- — Andesite line (boundary between sial continental crust & sima oceanic crust in the Pacific)

Volcanoes can suddenly erupt after lying dormant for centuries: in 1991 Mount Pinatubo, in the Philippines, burst into life after sleeping for more than 600 years.

AMERICAN PLATE
EURASIAN PLATE
AFRICAN PLATE
INDIAN PLATE
ANTARCTIC PLATE
PACIFIC PLATE

9

# THE EARTH: OCEANS

The Earth is a misnamed planet: almost 71% of its total surface area – 360,059,000 square kilometres – is covered by its oceans and seas. This great cloak of liquid water gives the planet its characteristic blue appearance from space, and is one of two obvious differences between the Earth and its near-neighbours in space, Mars and Venus. The other difference is the presence of life, and the two are closely linked.

In a strict geographical sense, the Earth has only three oceans: the Atlantic, the Pacific and the Indian. Sub-divided vertically instead of horizontally, however, there are many more. The most active is the sunlit upper layer, home of most sea-life and the vital interface between air and water. In this surface zone, huge energies are exchanged between the oceans and the atmosphere above; it is also a kind of membrane through which the ocean breathes, absorbing enormous quantities of carbon dioxide and partially exchanging them for oxygen, largely through the phytoplankton, tiny plants that photosynthesize solar energy and provide the food base for all other marine life.

As depth increases, light and colour fade away, the longer wavelengths dying first. At 50 metres, the ocean is a world of green and blue and violet; at 100 metres, only blue remains; by 200 metres, there is only a dim twilight. The temperature falls away with the light until some time before 1,000 metres – the precise depth varies – there occurs a temperature change almost as abrupt as the transition between air and water far above.

Below this thermocline, at a near-stable 3°C, the waters are forever unmoved by the winds of the upper world and are stirred only by the slow action of deep ocean currents. The pressure is crushing, touching 1,000 atmospheres in the deepest trenches: a force of one tonne bearing down on every square centimetre.

Yet even here the oceans support life, and not only the handful of strange, deep-sea creatures that find a living in the near-empty abyss. The deep ocean serves as a gigantic storehouse both for heat and for assorted atmospheric chemicals, regulating and balancing the proportions of various trace compounds and elements and ensuring a large measure of stability for both the climate and the ecology that depend on it.

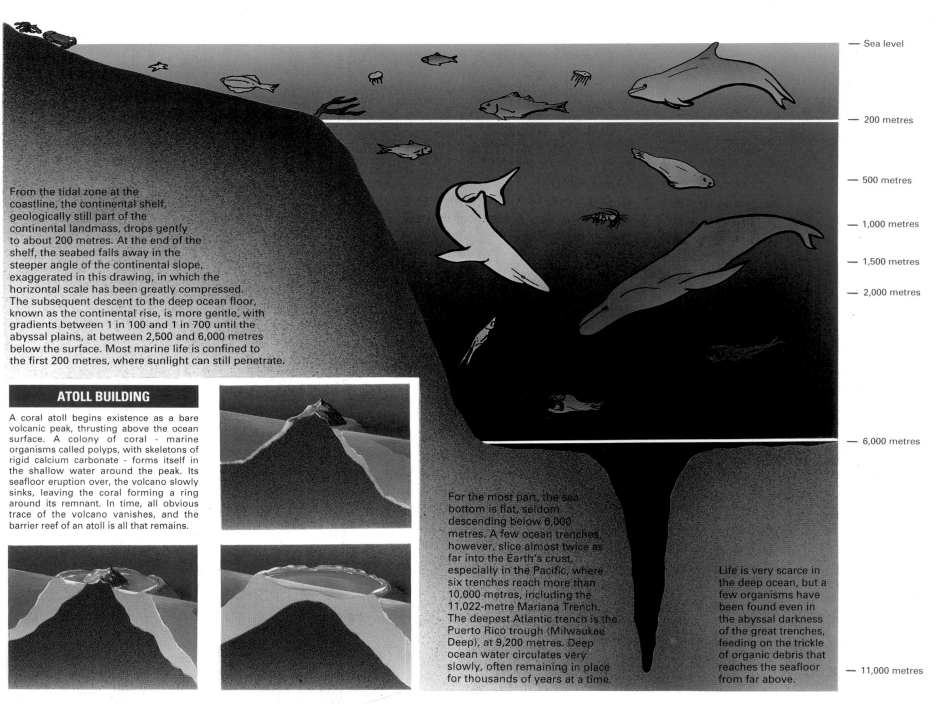

— Sea level

— 200 metres

— 500 metres

— 1,000 metres

— 1,500 metres

— 2,000 metres

— 6,000 metres

— 11,000 metres

From the tidal zone at the coastline, the continental shelf, geologically still part of the continental landmass, drops gently to about 200 metres. At the end of the shelf, the seabed falls away in the steeper angle of the continental slope, exaggerated in this drawing, in which the horizontal scale has been greatly compressed. The subsequent descent to the deep ocean floor, known as the continental rise, is more gentle, with gradients between 1 in 100 and 1 in 700 until the abyssal plains, at between 2,500 and 6,000 metres below the surface. Most marine life is confined to the first 200 metres, where sunlight can still penetrate.

## ATOLL BUILDING

A coral atoll begins existence as a bare volcanic peak, thrusting above the ocean surface. A colony of coral - marine organisms called polyps, with skeletons of rigid calcium carbonate - forms itself in the shallow water around the peak. Its seafloor eruption over, the volcano slowly sinks, leaving the coral forming a ring around its remnant. In time, all obvious trace of the volcano vanishes, and the barrier reef of an atoll is all that remains.

For the most part, the sea bottom is flat, seldom descending below 6,000 metres. A few ocean trenches, however, slice almost twice as far into the Earth's crust, especially in the Pacific, where six trenches reach more than 10,000 metres, including the 11,022-metre Mariana Trench. The deepest Atlantic trench is the Puerto Rico trough (Milwaukee Deep), at 9,200 metres. Deep ocean water circulates very slowly, often remaining in place for thousands of years at a time.

Life is very scarce in the deep ocean, but a few organisms have been found even in the abyssal darkness of the great trenches, feeding on the trickle of organic debris that reaches the seafloor from far above.

## PROFILE OF AN OCEAN

The deep ocean floor is no more uniform than the surface of the continents, although it was not until the development of effective sonar equipment that it was possible to examine submarine contours in detail. The Atlantic (right) and the Pacific show similar patterns. Off-shore comes the continental shelf, sliding downwards to the continental slope and the steeper continental rise, after which the seabed rolls onward into the abyssal plains. In the wide Pacific, these are interrupted by gently-rising abyssal hills; in both oceans, the plains extend all the way to the mid-oceanic ridges, where the upwelling of new crustal material is constantly forcing the oceans wider. Volcanic activity is responsible for the formation of seamounts and tablemounts or guyots, their flat-topped equivalents. In this cross-section, only the Azores are high enough to break the surface and become islands.

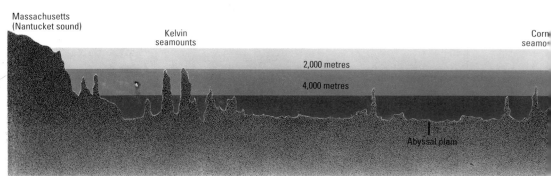

Massachusetts
(Nantucket sound)

Kelvin
seamounts

Corn
seamo

2,000 metres

4,000 metres

Abyssal plain

# OCEAN CURRENTS

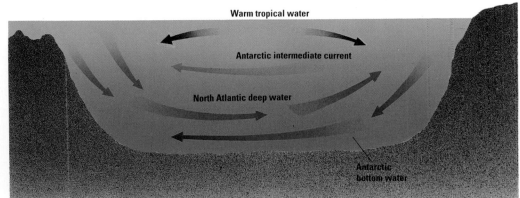

NORTH

Arctic

Atlantic Ocean

SOUTH

Antarctic

Warm tropical water

Antarctic intermediate current

North Atlantic deep water

Antarctic bottom water

Moving immense quantities of energy as well as billions of tonnes of water every hour, the ocean currents are a vital part of the great heat engine that drives the Earth's climate. They themselves are produced by a twofold mechanism. At the surface, winds push huge masses of water before them; in the deep ocean, below an abrupt temperature gradient that separates the churning surface waters from the still depths, density variations cause slow vertical movements.

The pattern of circulation of the great surface currents is determined by the displacement known as the Coriolis effect. As the Earth turns beneath a moving object - whether it is a tennis ball or a vast mass of water - it appears to be deflected to one side. The deflection is most obvious near the equator, where the Earth's surface is spinning eastward at 1700 km/h; currents moving poleward are curved clockwise in the northern hemisphere and anti-clockwise in the southern.

The result is a system of spinning circles known as gyres. The Coriolis effect piles up water on the left of each gyre, creating a narrow, fast-moving stream that is matched by a slower, broader returning current on the right. North and south of the equator, the fastest currents are located in the west and in the east respectively. In each case, warm water moves from the equator and cold water returns to it. Cold currents often bring an upwelling of nutrients with them, supporting the world's most economically important fisheries.

Depending on the prevailing winds, some currents on or near the equator may reverse their direction in the course of the year - a seasonal variation on which Asian monsoon rains depend, and whose occasional failure can bring disaster to millions of people.

## CURRENTS & TEMPERATURES

(Northern Hemisphere: winter)

← Warm Current
← Cold Current

## CURRENTS & TEMPERATURES

(Northern Hemisphere: summer)

← Warm Current
← Cold Current

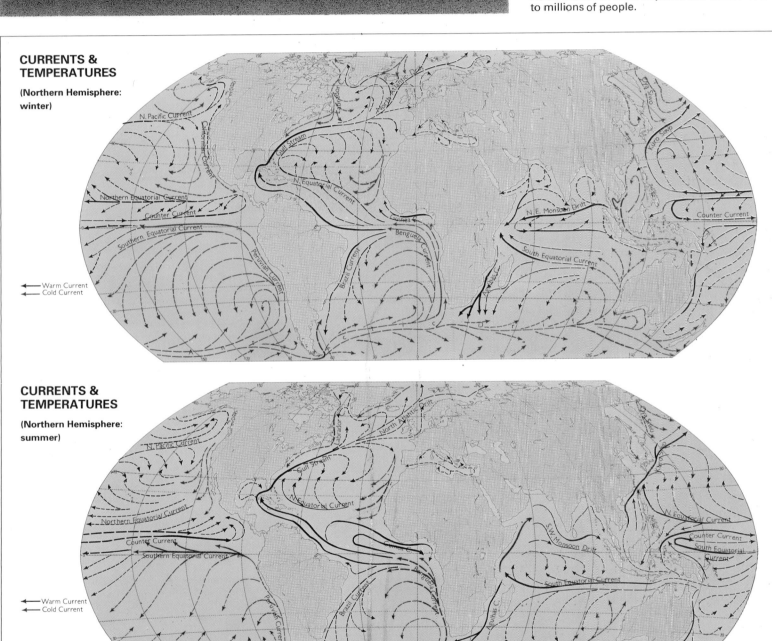

## SEAWATER

The chemical composition of the sea, in grams per tonne of seawater, excluding the elements of water itself

| | |
|---|---|
| Chlorine | 19400 |
| Sodium | 10800 |
| Magnesium | 1290 |
| Sulphur | 904 |
| Calcium | 411 |
| Potassium | 392 |
| Bromine | 67 |
| Strontium | 8.1 |
| Boron | 4.5 |
| Fluorine | 1.3 |
| Lithium | 0.17 |
| Rubidium | 0.12 |
| Phosphorus | 0.09 |
| Iodine | 0.06 |
| Barium | 0.02 |
| Arsenic | 0.003 |
| Cesium | 0.0003 |

Seawater also contains virtually every other element, although the quantities involved are too small for reliable measurement. In natural conditions, its composition is broadly consistent across the world's seas and oceans; but especially in coastal areas, variations, sometimes substantial, may be caused by the presence of industrial waste and sewage sludge.

Mid-Atlantic ridge

Atlantic seamount

Azores

Josephine seamounts

Gettysburg seamounts

Gibraltar

# THE EARTH: ATMOSPHERE

Extending from the surface far into space, the atmosphere is a meteor shield, a radiation deflector, a thermal blanket and a source of chemical energy for the Earth's diverse inhabitants. Five-sixths of its mass is found in the first 15 kilometres, the troposphere, no thicker in relative terms than the skin of an onion. Clouds, cyclonic winds, precipitation and virtually all the phenomena we call weather occur in this narrow layer. Above, a thin layer of ozone blocks ultra-violet radiation. Beyond 100 kilometres, atmospheric density is lower than most laboratory vacuums, yet these tenuous outer reaches, composed largely of hydrogen and helium, trap cosmic debris and incoming high-energy particles alike.

## CIRCULATION OF THE AIR

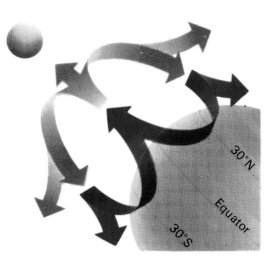

30°N

Equator

30°S

## STRUCTURE OF ATMOSPHERE

## TEMPERATURE

## PRESSURE

10⁻⁵³mb

900 km

10⁻⁴⁷mb

800

10⁻⁴¹mb

700

10⁻³⁵mb

600

10⁻²⁸mb

500

10⁻²²mb

400

ca. 1 500 °C

10⁻¹⁶mb

300

10⁻¹⁰mb

200

−58 °C

100

10⁻³mb

−91 °C
−93 °C
−33 °C
−8 °C
−12 °C
−38 °C
−53 °C

15 °C

0

Mesosphere
Ozone layer
Tropopause

10³mb

## CHEMICAL STRUCTURE

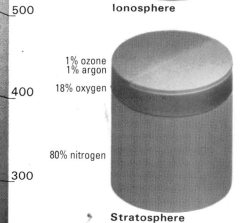

Inner:
50% helium
50% hydrogen

Middle:
25% helium
75% hydrogen

Outer:
100% hydrogen

**Exosphere**

15% helium

15% oxygen
& atomic
oxygen

70% nitrogen

**Ionosphere**

1% ozone
1% argon

18% oxygen

80% nitrogen

**Stratosphere**

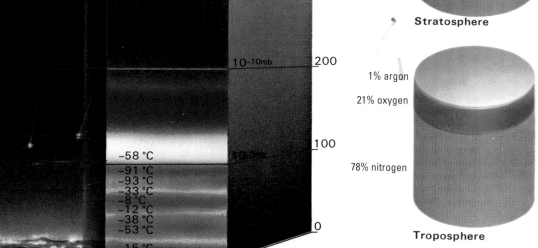

1% argon

21% oxygen

78% nitrogen

**Troposphere**

### Exosphere
The atmosphere's upper layer has no clear outer boundary, merging imperceptibly with interplanetary space. Its lower boundary, at an altitude of approximately 600 kilometres, is almost equally vague. The exosphere is mainly composed of hydrogen and helium in changing proportions, with a small quantity of atomic oxygen up to 600 kilometres. Helium vanishes with increasing altitude, and above 2,400 kilometres the exosphere is almost entirely hydrogen.

### Ionosphere
Gas molecules in the ionosphere, mainly helium, oxygen and nitrogen, are electrically charged - ionized - by the Sun's radiation. Within the ionosphere's range of 50 to 600 kilometres in altitude, they group themselves into four layers, known conventionally as D, E, F1 and F2, all of which can reflect radio waves of differing frequencies. The high energy of ionospheric gas gives it a notional temperature of more than 2,000°C, although its density is negligible. The auroras - aurora borealis and its southern counterpart, aurora australis - occur in the ionosphere when charged particles from the Sun interact with the Earth's magnetic fields, at their strongest near the poles.

### Stratosphere
Separated at its upper and lower limits by the distinct thresholds of the stratopause and the tropopause, the stratosphere is a remarkably stable layer between 50 kilometres and about 15 kilometres. Its temperature rises from -55°C at its lower extent to approximately 0°C near the stratopause, where a thin layer of ozone absorbs ultra-violet radiation. "Mother-of-pearl" or nacreous cloud occurs at about 25 kilometres' altitude. Stratospheric air contains enough ozone to make it poisonous, although it is in any case far too rarified to breathe.

### Troposphere
The narrowest of all the atmospheric layers, the troposphere extends up to 15 kilometres at the equator but only 8 kilometres at the poles. Since this thin region contains about 85% of the atmosphere's total mass and almost all of its water vapour, it is also the realm of the Earth's weather. Temperatures fall steadily with increasing height by about 1°C for every 100 metres above sea level.

Heated by the relatively high surface temperatures near the Earth's equator, air expands and rises to create a belt of low pressure. Moving northward towards the poles, it gradually cools, sinking once more and producing high pressure belts at about latitudes 30° North and South. Water vapour carried with the air falls as rain, releasing vast quantities of energy as well as liquid water when it condenses.

The high and low pressure belts are both areas of comparative calm, but between them, blowing from high to low pressure areas, are the prevailing winds. The atmospheric circulatory system is enormously complicated by the Coriolis effect brought about by the spinning Earth: winds are deflected to the right in the northern hemisphere and to the left in the southern, giving rise to the typically cyclonic pattern of swirling clouds carried by the moving masses of air.

Although clouds appear in an almost infinite variety of shapes and sizes, there are recognizable features that form the basis of a classification first put forward by Luke Howard, a London chemist, in 1803 and later modified by the World Meteorological Organization. The system derives from the altitude of clouds and whether they form hairlike filaments ('cirrus'), heaps or piles ('cumulus') or layers ('stratus'). Each characteristic carries some kind of message – not always a clear one – to forecasters about the weather to come.

## CLASSIFICATION OF CLOUDS

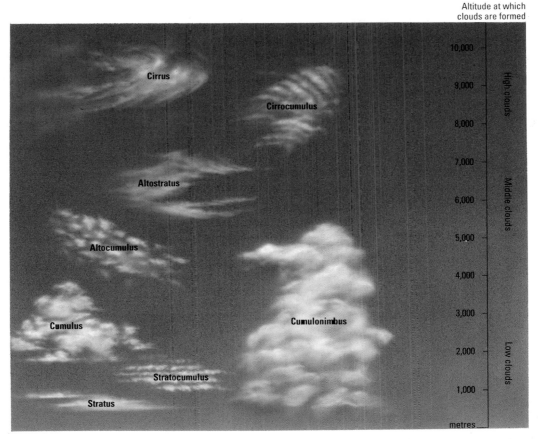

Altitude at which clouds are formed

High clouds
10,000
9,000
8,000

Cirrus
Cirrocumulus

7,000

Altostratus

Middle clouds
6,000

5,000

Altocumulus

4,000

Cumulonimbus

3,000
Cumulus

Low clouds
2,000

Stratocumulus
1,000

Stratus

metres

Clouds form when damp, usually rising, air is cooled. Thus they form when a wind rises to cross hills or mountains; when a mass of air rises over, or is pushed up by, another mass of denser air; or when local heating of the ground causes convection currents. The types of clouds are classified according to altitude as high, middle, or low. The high ones, composed of ice crystals, are cirrus, cirrostratus and cirrocumulus. The middle clouds are altostratus, a grey or bluish striated, fibrous, or uniform sheet producing light drizzle, and altocumulus, a thicker and fluffier version of cirrocumulus. The low clouds include nimbostratus, a dark grey layer that brings almost continuous rain or snow; cumulus, a detached 'heap' – brilliant white in sunlight but dark and flat at the base; and stratus, which forms dull, overcast skies at low altitudes. Cumulonimbus, associated with storms and rains, heavy and dense with flat base and a high, fluffy outline, can be tall enough to occupy middle as well as low altitudes.

## PRESSURE & WINDS

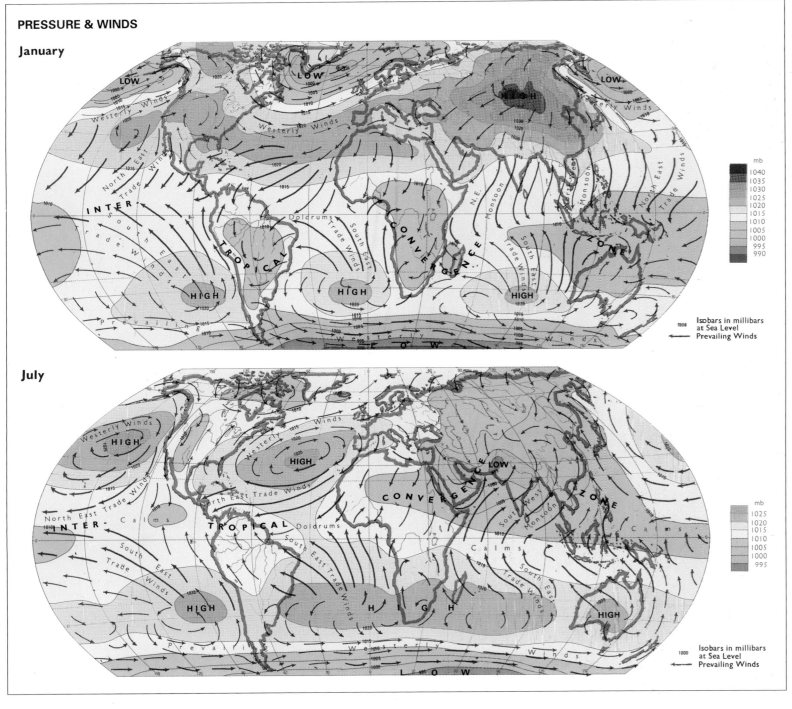

January

July

Isobars in millibars at Sea Level
Prevailing Winds

mb
1040
1035
1030
1025
1020
1015
1010
1005
1000
995
990

mb
1025
1020
1015
1010
1005
1000
995

Isobars in millibars at Sea Level
Prevailing Winds

## CLIMATE RECORDS

### Pressure & Winds

Highest barometric pressure: Agata, Siberia, USSR, 1,083.8 mb [32 in] at altitude 262 m [862 ft], 31 Dec. 1968.

Lowest barometric pressure: Typhoon Tip, 480 km [300 mls] west of Guam, Pacific Ocean, 870 mb [25.69 in], 12 Oct. 1979.

Highest recorded windspeed: Mt Washington, New Hampshire, USA 371 kph [231 mph], 12 Apr. 1934. This is three times as strong as hurricane force on the Beaufort Scale.

Windiest place: Commonwealth Bay, George V Coast, Antarctica, where gales frequently reach over 320 kph [200 mph].

Worst recorded storm: Bangladesh (then East Pakistan) cyclone*, 13 Nov. 1970 – over 300,000 dead or missing. The 1991 cyclone, Bangladesh's and the world's second worst in terms of loss of life, killed an estimated 138,000.

Worst recorded tornado: Missouri/Illinois/Indiana, USA, 18 Mar. 1925 – 792 deaths. The tornado was only 275 m (300 yds) wide.

* Tropical cyclones are known as hurricanes in Central and North America and as typhoons in the Far East

# THE EARTH: CLIMATE

Climate is weather in the long term: the seasonal pattern of hot and cold, wet and dry, averaged over time. At the simplest level, it is caused by the uneven heating of the Earth. Surplus heat at the equator passes towards the poles, levelling out the energy differential. Its passage is marked by a ceaseless churning of the atmosphere and the oceans, further agitated by the the Earth's diurnal spin and the motion it imparts to moving air and water. The heat's means of transport – by winds and ocean currents, by the continual evaporation and recondensation of water molecules – is the weather itself.

There are four basic types of climate, each open to considerable sub-division: tropical, desert, temperate and polar. But

although latitude is obviously a critical factor, it is not the only determinant. The differential heating of land and sea, the funnelling and interruption of winds and ocean currents by landmasses and mountain ranges, and the transpiration of vegetation: all combine to add complexity. New York, Naples and the Gobi Desert share almost the same latitude, for example, but their climates are very different. And although the sheer intricacy of the weather system often defies day-to-day prediction in these or any other places – despite the satellites and number-crunching supercomputers with which present-day meteorologists are equipped – their climatic patterns retain a year-on-year stability.

They are not indefinitely stable, however. The planet regularly passes through long,

cool periods of around 100,000 years: these are the ice ages, probably caused by recurring long-term oscillations in the Earth's orbital path and fluctuations in the Sun's energy output. In the present era, the Earth is nearest to the Sun in the middle of the northern hemisphere's winter; 11,000 years ago, at the end of the last ice age, the northern winter fell with the Sun at its most distant.

Left to its own devices, the climate even now should be drifting towards another glacial period. But global warming caused by increasing carbon dioxide levels in the atmosphere, largely the result of 20th-century fuel-burning and deforestation, may well precipitate change far faster than the great, slow cycles of the solar system.

| 11: | OCEAN CURRENTS |
| 12: | CIRCULATION OF THE AIR |
| 13: | CLASSIFICATION OF CLOUDS PRESSURE & WINDS |
| 16: | HYDROLOGICAL CYCLE |
| 17: | NATURAL VEGETATION |
| 21: | GREENHOUSE EFFECT |
| 30: | LAND USE |
| 46: | GLOBAL WARMING |

## CLIMATE REGIONS

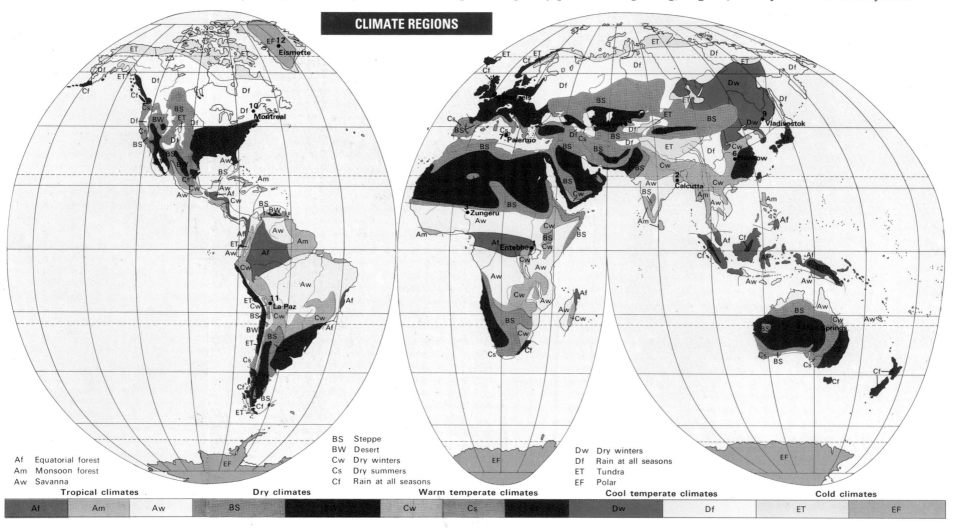

Af Equatorial forest
Am Monsoon forest
Aw Savanna
**Tropical climates**

BS Steppe
BW Desert
Cw Dry winters
Cs Dry summers
Cf Rain at all seasons
**Dry climates** — **Warm temperate climates**

Dw Dry winters
Df Rain at all seasons
ET Tundra
EF Polar
**Cool temperate climates** — **Cold climates**

| Af | Am | Aw | BS | BW | Cw | Cs | Dw | Df | ET | EF |

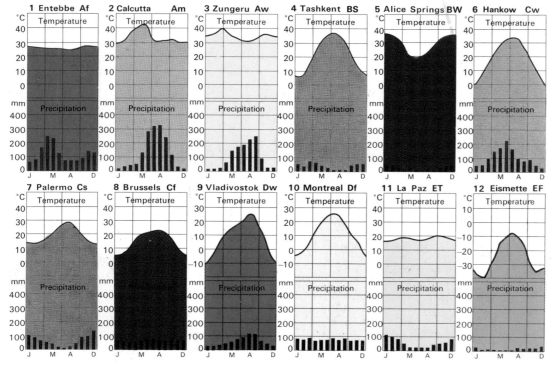

## CLIMATE & WEATHER TERMS

**Absolute humidity:** amount of water vapour contained in a given volume of air.
**Cloud cover:** amount of cloud in the sky; measured in oktas (from 1 - 8), with 0 clear, & 8 total cover.
**Condensation:** the conversion of water vapour, or moisture in the air into liquid.
**Cyclone:** violent storm resultinig from counter clockwise rotation of winds in the northern hemisphere & clockwise in the southern: called hurricane in N. America, typhoon in the Far East.
**Depression:** approximately circular area of low pressure.
**Dew:** water droplets condensed out of the air after the ground has cooled at night.
**Dew point:** temperature at which air becomes saturated (reaches a relative humidity of 100%) at a constant pressure.
**Drizzle:** precipitation where drops are less than 0.5 mm (0.02 in) in diameter.
**Evaporation:** conversion of water from liquid into vapour, or moisture in the air.
**Frost:** dew that has frozen when the air temperature falls below freezing point.
**Hail:** frozen rain; small balls of ice, often falling during thunder storms.
**Hoar frost:** formed on objects when the dew point is below freezing point.
**Humidity:** amount of moisture in the air.
**Isobar:** cartographic line connecting places of equal atmospheric pressure.
**Isotherm:** cartographic line connecting places of equal temperature.
**Lightning:** massive electrical discharge released in thunderstorm from cloud to cloud or cloud to ground, the result of the tip becoming positively charged & the bottom negatively charged.
**Precipitation:** measurable rain, snow, sleet or hail.
**Prevailing wind:** most common direction of wind at a given location.
**Rain:** precipitation of liquid particles with diameter larger than 0.5 mm (0.02 in).
**Relative humidity:** amount of water vapour contained in a given volume of air at a given temperature.
**Sleet:** translucent or transparent ice-pellets (partially melted snow).
**Snow:** formed when water vapour condenses below freezing point.
**Thunder:** sound produced by the rapid expansion of air heated by lightning.
**Tidal wave:** giant ocean wave generated by earthquakes (tsunami) or cyclonic winds.
**Tornado:** severe funnel-shaped storm that twists as hot air spins vertically (waterspout at sea).
**Whirlwind:** rapidly rotating column of air, only a few metres across made visible by dust.

COPYRIGHT GEORGE PHILIP LTD

## WINDCHILL FACTOR

In sub-zero weather, even moderate winds significantly reduce effective temperatures. The chart below shows the windchill effect across a range of speeds. Figures in the pink zone are not dangerous to well-clad people; in the blue zone, the risk of serious frostbite is acute.

|  | Wind speed (km/h) | | | | |
|---|---|---|---|---|---|
|  | 16 | 32 | 48 | 64 | 80 |
| 0°C | -8 | -14 | -17 | -19 | -20 |
| -5°C | -14 | -21 | -25 | -27 | -28 |
| -10°C | -20 | -28 | -33 | -35 | -36 |
| -15°C | -26 | -36 | -40 | -43 | -44 |
| -20°C | -32 | -42 | -48 | -51 | -52 |
| -25°C | -38 | -49 | -56 | -59 | -60 |
| -30°C | -44 | -57 | -63 | -66 | -68 |
| -35°C | -51 | -64 | -72 | -74 | -76 |
| -40°C | -57 | -71 | -78 | -82 | -84 |
| -45°C | -63 | -78 | -86 | -90 | -92 |
| -50°C | -69 | -85 | -94 | -98 | -100 |

## BEAUFORT WIND SCALE

Named for the 19th-century British naval officer who devised it, the Beaufort Scale assesses wind speed according to its effects. It was originally designed as an aid for sailors, but has since been adapted for use on land.

| Scale | Wind speed kph | mph | Effect |
|---|---|---|---|
| 0 | 0-1 | 0-1 | **Calm** Smoke rises vertically |
| 1 | 1-5 | 1-3 | **Light air** Wind direction shown only by smoke drift |
| 2 | 6-11 | 4-7 | **Light breeze** Wind felt on face; leaves rustle; vanes moved by wind |
| 3 | 12-19 | 8-12 | **Gentle breeze** Leaves and small twigs in constant motion; wind extend small flag |
| 4 | 20-28 | 13-18 | **Moderate** Raises dust and loose paper; small branches move |
| 5 | 29-38 | 19-24 | **Fresh** Small trees in leaf sway; crested wavelets on inland waters |
| 6 | 39-49 | 25-31 | **Strong** Large branches move; difficult to use umbrellas; overhead wires whistle |
| 7 | 50-61 | 32-38 | **Near gale** Whole trees in motion; difficult to walk against wind |
| 8 | 62-74 | 39-46 | **Gale** Twigs break from trees; walking very difficult |
| 9 | 75-88 | 47-54 | **Strong gale** Slight structural damage |
| 10 | 89-102 | 55-63 | **Storm** Trees uprooted; serious structural damage |
| 11 | 103-117 | 64-72 | **Violent Storm** Widespread damage |
| 12 | 118+ | 73+ | **Hurricane** |

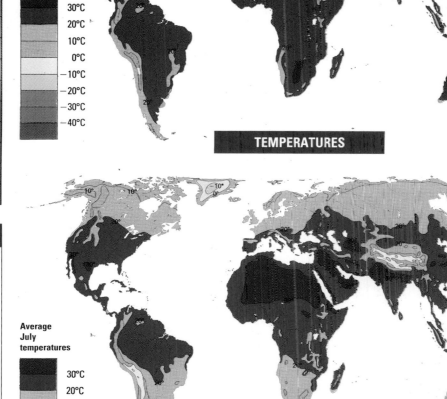

**Average January temperatures**

- 30°C
- 20°C
- 10°C
- 0°C
- −10°C
- −20°C
- −30°C
- −40°C

**TEMPERATURES**

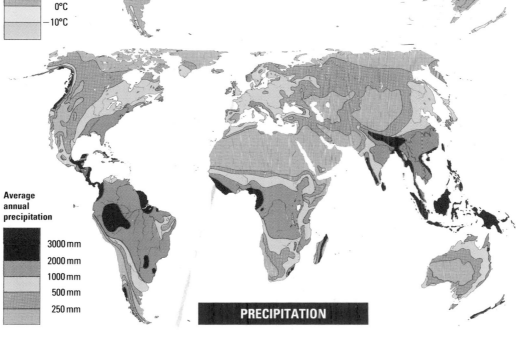

**Average July temperatures**

- 30°C
- 20°C
- 10°C
- 0°C
- −10°C

**Average annual precipitation**

- 3000 mm
- 2000 mm
- 1000 mm
- 500 mm
- 250 mm

**PRECIPITATION**

## CLIMATE RECORDS

### Temperature

Highest recorded temperature: Al Aziziyah, Libya, 58°C [136.4°F], 13 Sep. 1922.

Highest mean annual temperature: Dallol, Ethiopia, 34.4°C [94°F], 1960-66.

Longest heatwave: Marble Bar, W. Australia, 162 days over 38°C [100°F], 23 Oct. 1923 - 7 Apr. 1924.

Lowest recorded temperature (outside poles): Verkhoyansk, Siberia, USSR -68°C [-90°F], 6 Feb. 1933. Verkhoyansk also registered the greatest annual range of temperature: - 70°C to 37°C [-94°F to 98°F].

Lowest mean annual temperature: Polus Nedostupnosti, Pole of Cold, Antarctica, -57.8°C [-72°F].

### Precipitation

Driest place: Arica, N. Chile, 0.8mm [0.3 in] per year (60-year average).

Longest drought: Calama, N. Chile: no recorded rainfall in 400 years to 1971.

Wettest place (average): Tututendo, Colombia: mean annual rainfall 11,770 mm [463.4 in].

Wettest place (12 months): Cherrapunji, Meghalaya, N.E. India, 26,470 mm [1,040 in], Aug. 1860 to Aug. 1861. Cherrapunji also holds the record for rainfall in one month: 930 mm [37 in] July 1861.

Wettest place (24 hours): Cilaos, Réunion, Indian Ocean, 1,870 mm [73.6 in], 15-16 Mar. 1952.

Heaviest hailstones: Gopalganj, Bangladesh, up to 1.02 kg [2.25 lb], 14 Apr. 1986 (killed 92 people).

Heaviest snowfall (continuous): Bessans, Savoie, France, 1730 mm [68 in] in 19 hours, 5-6 Apr. 1969.

Heaviest snowfall (season/year): Paradise Ranger Station, Mt Rainier, Washington, USA, 31,102 mm [1,224.5 in], 19 Feb. 1971 to 18 Feb. 1972.

A weak anticyclone in Northern India gives clear skies and North-Easterly winds.

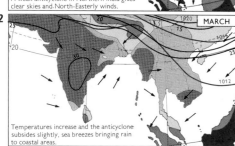

Temperatures increase and the anticyclone subsides slightly, sea breezes bringing rain to coastal areas.

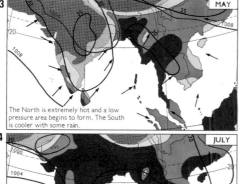

The North is extremely hot and a low pressure area begins to form. The South is cooler with some rain.

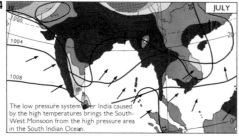

The low pressure system over India caused by the high temperatures brings the South-West Monsoon from the high pressure area in the South Indian Ocean.

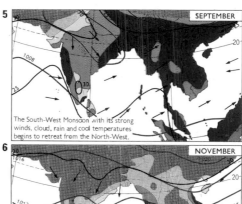

The South-West Monsoon with its strong winds, cloud, rain and cool temperatures begins to retreat from the North-West.

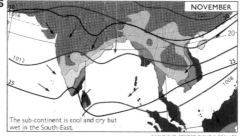

The sub-continent is cool and dry but wet in the South-East.

COPYRIGHT. GEORGE PHILIP & SON. LTD.

## THE MONSOON

While it is crucial to the agriculture of South Asia, the monsoon that follows the dry months is unpredictable - in duration as well as intensity. A season of very heavy rainfall, causing disastrous floods, can be succeeded by years of low precipitation, leading to serious drought.

**Monthly rainfall**

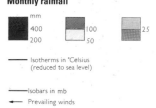

mm
400
200
100
50
25

Isotherms in °Celsius (reduced to sea level)

Isobars in mb

Prevailing winds

# THE EARTH: WATER

Fresh water is essential to all terrestrial life, from the humblest bacterium to the most advanced technological society. Yet freshwater resources form a minute fraction of the Earth's 1.41 billion cubic kilometres of water: most human needs must be met from the 2,000 cubic kilometres circulating in rivers at any one time. Agriculture accounts for huge quantities: without large-scale irrigation, most of the world's people would starve. And since fresh water is just as essential for most industrial processes – smelting a tonne of nickel, for example, requires about 4,000 tonnes of water – the combination of growing population and advancing industry has put water supplies under strain.

Fortunately water is seldom used up: the planet's hydrological cycle circulates it with benign efficiency, at least on a global scale. More locally, though, human activity can cause severe shortages: water for industry and agriculture is being withdrawn from many river basins and underground aquifers faster than natural recirculation can replace it.

## THE HYDROLOGICAL CYCLE

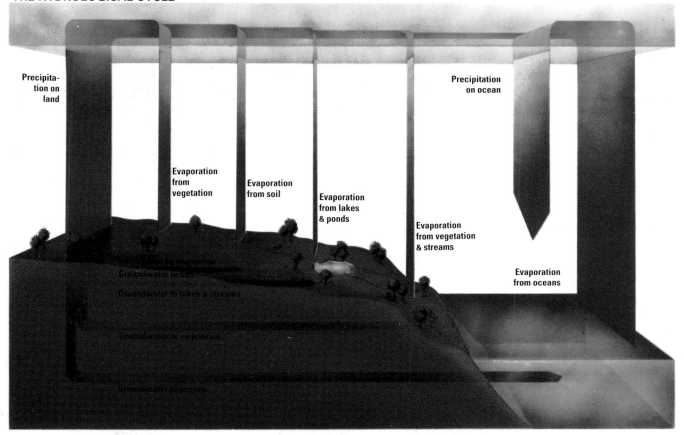

Precipitation on land

Precipitation on ocean

Evaporation from vegetation

Evaporation from soil

Evaporation from lakes & ponds

Evaporation from vegetation & streams

Evaporation from oceans

Interception by vegetation
Groundwater in soil
Groundwater to lakes & streams
Groundwater to vegetation
Groundwater to oceans

Water vapour is constantly drawn into the air from the Earth's rivers, lakes, seas and plant transpiration. In the atmosphere, it circulates around the planet, transporting energy as well as water itself. When the vapour cools it falls as rain or snow, and returns to the surface to evaporate once more. The whole cycle is driven by the Sun.

## WATER DISTRIBUTION

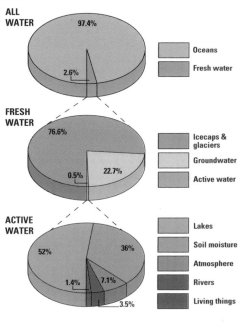

The distribution of planetary water, by percentage. Oceans and icecaps together account for more than 99% of the total; the breakdown of the remainder is estimated.

ALL WATER
97.4% — 2.6%
Oceans
Fresh water

FRESH WATER
76.6% — 0.5% — 22.7%
Icecaps & glaciers
Groundwater
Active water

ACTIVE WATER
52% — 1.4% — 7.1% — 3.5% — 36%
Lakes
Soil moisture
Atmosphere
Rivers
Living things

Almost all the world's water is 3,000 million years old, and all of it cycles endlessly through the hydrosphere, though at different rates. Water vapour circulates over days, even hours, deep ocean water circulates over millenia and ice-cap water remains solid for millions of years.

## WATER RUNOFF

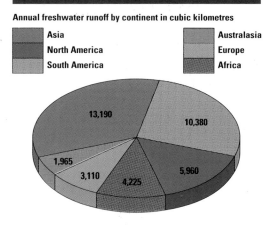

**Annual freshwater runoff by continent in cubic kilometres**

Asia
North America
South America

Australasia
Europe
Africa

13,190
10,380
1,965
3,110
4,225
5,960

## WATER UTILIZATION

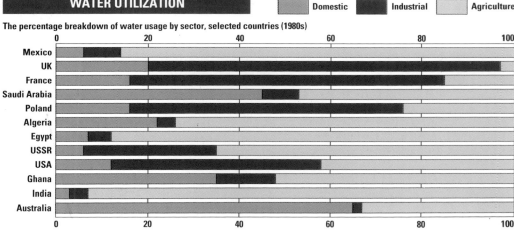

Domestic   Industrial   Agriculture

The percentage breakdown of water usage by sector, selected countries (1980s)

Mexico
UK
France
Saudi Arabia
Poland
Algeria
Egypt
USSR
USA
Ghana
India
Australia

0   20   40   60   80   100

## WATER SUPPLY

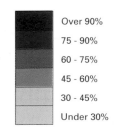

Percentage of total population with access to safe drinking water (latest available year, 1980s)

Over 90%
75 - 90%
60 - 75%
45 - 60%
30 - 45%
Under 30%

**Least well provided countries (rural areas only):**

| | | | |
|---|---|---|---|
| Paraguay | 8% | Guinea | 15% |
| Mozambique | 12% | Mauritania | 17% |
| Uganda | 12% | Malawi | 17% |
| Angola | 15% | Morocco | 17% |

## WHERE THE RIVERS RUN

- Pacific Ocean
- Indian Ocean
- Arctic Ocean
- Atlantic Ocean
- Caribbean Sea
- Mediterranean Sea
- Inland basins

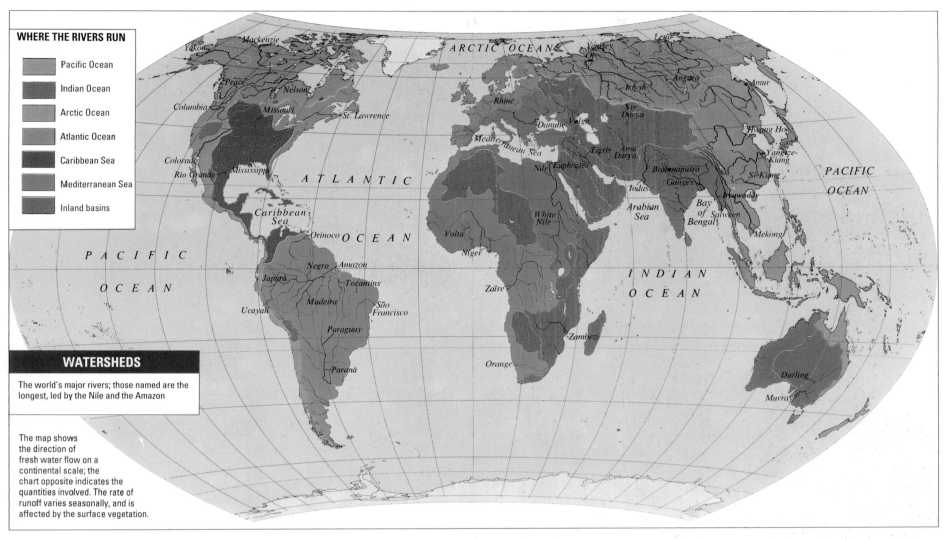

## WATERSHEDS

The world's major rivers; those named are the longest, led by the Nile and the Amazon

The map shows the direction of fresh water flow on a continental scale; the chart opposite indicates the quantities involved. The rate of runoff varies seasonally, and is affected by the surface vegetation.

## LAND USE BY CONTINENT

- Forest
- Permanent pasture & rough grazing
- Permanent crops & plantations
- Arable
- Non-productive

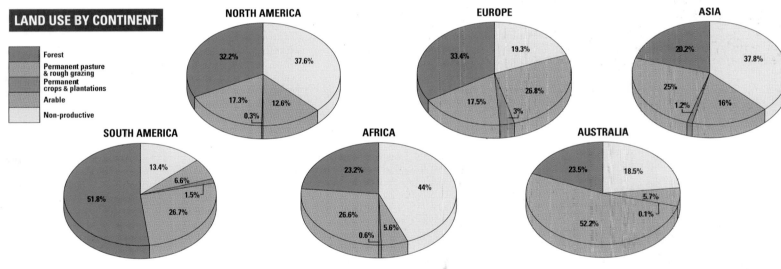

**NORTH AMERICA**
32.2%, 37.6%, 17.3%, 0.3%, 12.6%

**EUROPE**
33.4%, 19.3%, 17.5%, 3%, 26.8%

**ASIA**
20.2%, 37.8%, 25%, 1.2%, 16%

**SOUTH AMERICA**
13.4%, 6.6%, 1.5%, 51.8%, 26.7%

**AFRICA**
23.2%, 44%, 26.6%, 0.6%, 5.6%

**AUSTRALIA**
23.5%, 18.5%, 5.7%, 52.2%, 0.1%

The proportion of productive land has reached its upper limit in Europe, and in Asia more than 80% of potential cropland is already under cultivation. Elsewhere, any increase is often matched by corresponding losses due to desertification and erosion; projections for 2025 show a decline in cropland per capita for all continents, most notably in Africa.

## NATURAL VEGETATION

### Regional variation in vegetation

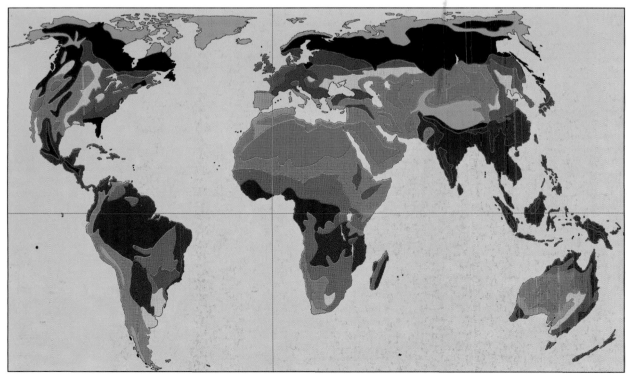

- Tundra & mountain vegetation
- Needleleaf evergreen forest
- Mixed needleleaf evergreen & broadleaf deciduous trees
- Broadleaf deciduous woodland
- Mid-latitude grassland
- Evergreen broadleaf & deciduous trees & shrubs
- Semi-desert scrub
- Desert
- Tropical grassland (savanna)
- Tropical broadleaf rainforest & monsoon forest
- Sub-tropical broadleaf & needleleaf forest

The map illustrates the natural climax vegetation of a region, as dictated by its climate and topography. In most cases, human agricultural activity has drastically altered the vegetation pattern. Western Europe, for example, lost most of its broadleaf forest many centuries ago, and irrigation has turned some natural semi-desert into productive land.

17

COPYRIGHT GEORGE PHILIP LTDCOPYRIGHT GEORGE PHILIP LTD

# THE EARTH: LANDSCAPE

Above and below the surface of the oceans, the features of the Earth's crust are constantly changing. The phenomenal forces generated by convection currents in the molten core of our planet carry the vast segments or 'plates' of the crust across the globe in an endless cycle of creation and destruction. New crust emerges along the central depths of the oceans, where molten magma flows from the margins of neighbouring plates to form the massive mid-ocean ridges. The sea floor spreads, and where ocean plates meet continental plates, they dip back into the earth's core to melt once again into magma.

Less dense, the continental plates 'float' among the oceans, drifting into and apart from each other at a rate which is almost imperceptibly slow. A continent may travel little more than 25 millimetres per year – in an average lifetime, Europe will move no more than a man's height – yet in the vast span of geological time, this process throws up giant mountain ranges and opens massive rifts in the land's surface.

The world's greatest mountain ranges have been formed in this way – the Himalayas by the collision of the Indo-Australian and Eurasian plates, the Andes by the meeting of the Nazca and South American plates. The Himalayas are a classic example of 'fold mountains', formed by the crumpling of the Earth's surface where two land masses have been driven together. The coastal range of the Andes, by contrast, was formed by the upsurge of molten volcanic rock created by the friction of the continent 'overriding' the ocean plate.

Destruction of the landscape, however, begins as soon as it is formed. Wind, water, ice and sea, the main agents of erosion, mount a constant assault that even the hardest rocks cannot withstand. Mountain peaks may dwindle by as little as a few millimetres each year, but if they are not uplifted by further movements of the crust they will eventually be reduced to rubble. Water is the most powerful destroyer – it has been estimated that 100 billion tonnes of rock is washed into the oceans every year.

When water freezes, its volume increases by about nine per cent, and no rock is strong enough to resist this pressure. Where water has penetrated tiny fissures or seeped into softer rock, a severe freeze followed by a thaw may result in rockfalls or earth-slides, creating major destruction in a few minutes. Over much longer periods, acidity in rainwater breaks down the chemical composition of porous rocks like limestone, eating away the rock to form deep caves and tunnels. Chemical decomposition also occurs in riverbeds and glacier valleys, hastening the process of mechanical erosion.

Rivers and glaciers, like the sea itself, generate much of their effect through abrasion – pounding the landscape with the debris they carry with them. But as well as destroying they also create new landscapes, many of them spectacular : vast deltas, as at the mouth of the Mississippi or the Nile; cliffs, rock arches and stacks, as on the south coast of Australia; and the fjords cut by long-melted glaciers in British Columbia, Norway and New Zealand.

The vast ridges that divide the Earth's crust beneath each of the world's major oceans mark the boundaries between tectonic plates which are moving very gradually in opposite directions. As the plates shift apart, molten magma rises from the Earth's core to seal the rift and the sea floor slowly spreads towards the continental landmasses. The rate of sea floor spreading has been calculated by magnetic analysis of the rock – at about 40 mm [1.5 in] a year in the North Atlantic. Near the ocean shore, underwater volcanoes mark the line where the continental rise begins. As the plates meet, much of the denser ocean crust dips beneath the continental plate and is melted back into the magma.

## THE SPREADING EARTH

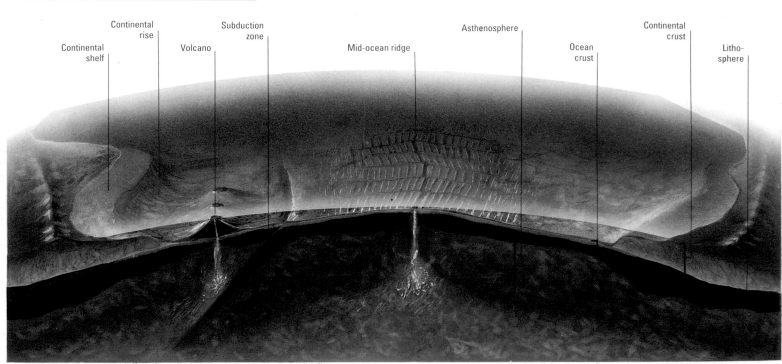

Continental shelf · Continental rise · Volcano · Subduction zone · Mid-ocean ridge · Asthenosphere · Ocean crust · Continental crust · Litho-sphere

## TYPES OF ROCK

Rocks are divided into three types, according to the way in which they are formed:

**Igneous rocks**, including granite and basalt, are formed by the cooling of magma from within the Earth's crust.

**Metamorphic rocks**, such as slate, marble and quartzite, are formed below the Earth's surface by the compression or baking of existing rocks.

**Sedimentary rocks**, like sandstone and limestone, are formed on the surface of the Earth from the remains of living organisms and eroded fragments of older rocks.

## MOUNTAIN BUILDING

Mountains are formed when pressures on the Earth's crust caused by continental drift become so intense that the surface buckles or cracks. This happens most dramatically where two tectonic plates collide : the Rockies, Andes, Alps, Urals and Himalayas resulted from such impacts. These are all known as fold mountains, because they were formed by the compression of the rocks, forcing the surface to bend and fold like a crumpled rug.

The other main building process is when the crust fractures to create faults, allowing rock to be forced upwards in large blocks; or when the pressure of magma within the crust forces the surface to bulge into a dome, or erupts to form a volcano. Large mountain ranges may reveal a combination of those features; the Alps, for example, have been compressed so violently that the folds are fragmented by numerous faults and intrusions of molten rock.

Over millions of years, even the greatest mountain ranges can be reduced by erosion to a rugged landscape known as a peneplain.

**Types of fold:** Geographers give different names to the degrees of fold that result from continuing pressure on the rock strata. A simple fold may be symmetric, with even slopes on either side, but as the pressure builds up, one slope becomes steeper and the fold becomes asymmetric. Later, the ridge or 'anticline' at the top of the fold may slide over the lower ground or 'syncline' to form a recumbent fold. Eventually, the rock strata may break under the pressure to form an overthrust and finally a nappe fold.

Symmetric · Asymmetric · Recumbent · Overthrust · Nappe

**Types of fault:** Faults are classified by the direction in which the blocks of rock have moved. A normal fault results when a vertical movement causes the surface to break apart; compression causes a reverse fault. Sideways movement causes shearing, known as a strike-slip fault. When the rock breaks in two places, the central block may be pushed up in a horst fault, or sink in a graben fault.

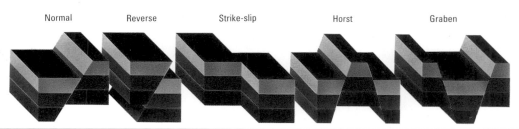

Normal · Reverse · Strike-slip · Horst · Graben

## MOULDING THE LAND

While hidden forces of extraordinary power are moving the continents from below the Earth's crust, the more familiar elements of wind and water, heat and cold combine to sculpt the surface of the landscape. Erosion by weathering is seen in desert regions, where rocks degrade imperceptibly into sand through the effects of changing temperatures and strong winds.

The power of water is fiercer still. Coastlines change faster than most landscape features, both by erosion and by the build-up of sand and pebbles carried by the sea. In severe storms, giant waves pound the shoreline with rocks and boulders, and frequently destroy concrete coastal defences; but even in quieter conditions, the sea steadily erodes cliffs and headlands and creates new land in the form of sand-dunes, spits and salt-marshes.

Rivers, too, are incessantly at work shaping the landscape on their way to join the sea. In highland regions, where the flow is rapid, they cut deep gorges and V-shaped valleys. As they reach more gentle slopes, rivers release some of the debris they have carried downstream, broadening out and raising levees along their banks by depositing mud and sand. In the lowland plains, they may drift into meanders, depositing more sediment and even building deltas when they finally approach the sea.

Ice has created some of the world's dramatic landscapes. As glaciers move slowly downhill, they scrape away rock from the mountains and valley sides, creating spectacular landscape features.

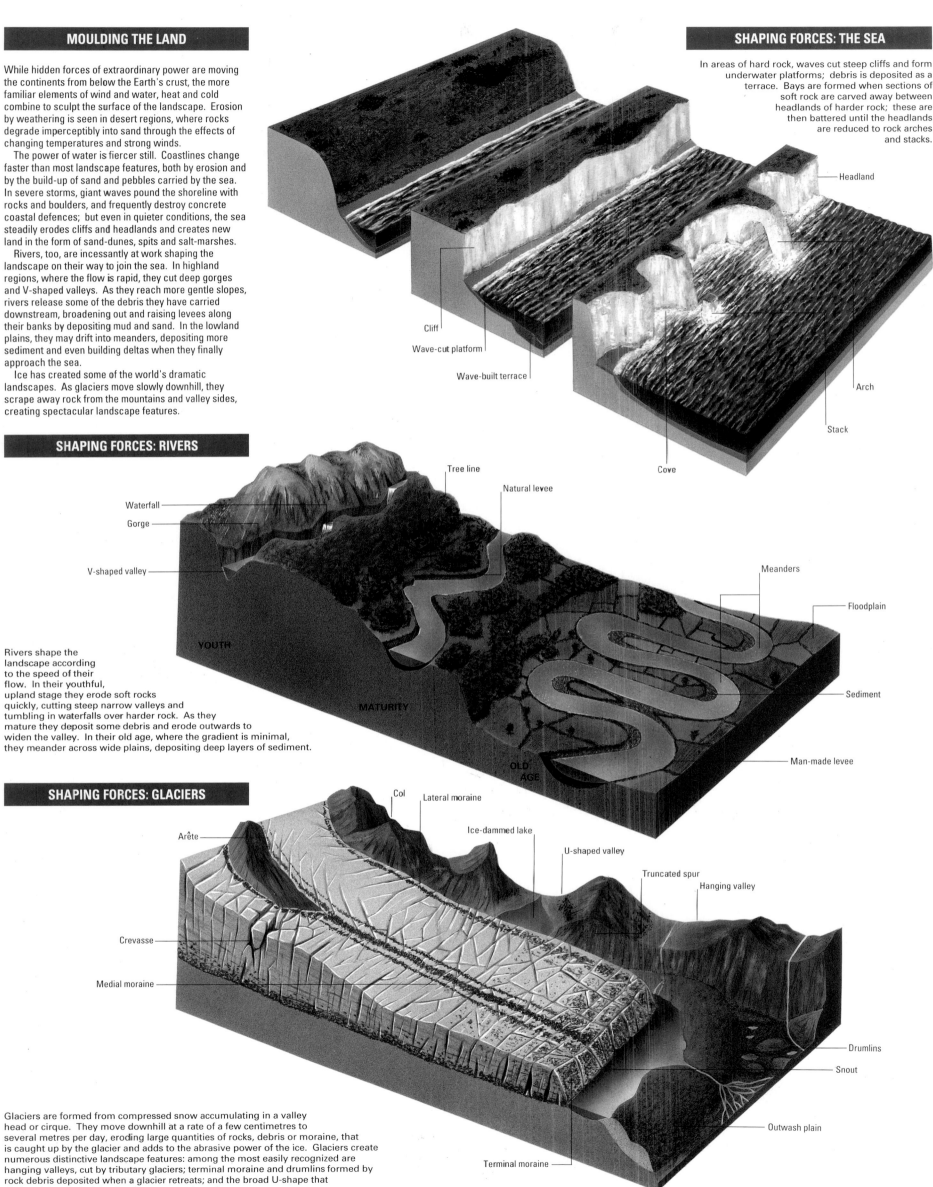

## SHAPING FORCES: THE SEA

In areas of hard rock, waves cut steep cliffs and form underwater platforms; debris is deposited as a terrace. Bays are formed when sections of soft rock are carved away between headlands of harder rock; these are then battered until the headlands are reduced to rock arches and stacks.

Headland

Cliff

Wave-cut platform

Wave-built terrace

Arch

Stack

Cove

## SHAPING FORCES: RIVERS

Rivers shape the landscape according to the speed of their flow. In their youthful, upland stage they erode soft rocks quickly, cutting steep narrow valleys and tumbling in waterfalls over harder rock. As they mature they deposit some debris and erode outwards to widen the valley. In their old age, where the gradient is minimal, they meander across wide plains, depositing deep layers of sediment.

Waterfall

Gorge

V-shaped valley

Tree line

Natural levee

Meanders

Floodplain

Sediment

Man-made levee

YOUTH

MATURITY

OLD AGE

## SHAPING FORCES: GLACIERS

Glaciers are formed from compressed snow accumulating in a valley head or cirque. They move downhill at a rate of a few centimetres to several metres per day, eroding large quantities of rocks, debris or moraine, that is caught up by the glacier and adds to the abrasive power of the ice. Glaciers create numerous distinctive landscape features; among the most easily recognized are hanging valleys, cut by tributary glaciers; terminal moraine and drumlins formed by rock debris deposited when a glacier retreats; and the broad U-shape that distinguishes a glacial valley from one cut by a river.

Arête

Crevasse

Medial moraine

Col

Lateral moraine

Ice-dammed lake

U-shaped valley

Truncated spur

Hanging valley

Drumlins

Snout

Outwash plain

Terminal moraine

# THE EARTH: ENVIRONMENT

Unique among the planets, the Earth has been the home of living creatures for most of its existence. Precisely how these improbable assemblies of self-replicating chemicals ever began remains a matter of conjecture, but the planet and its passengers have matured together for a very long time. Over three billion years, life has not only adapted to its environment: it has also slowly changed that environment to suit itself.

The planet and its biosphere – the entirety of its living things – function like a single organism. The British scientist James Lovelock, who first stated this 'Gaia hypothesis' in the 1970s, went further: the planet, he declared, actually was a living organism, equipped on a colossal scale with the same sort of stability-seeking

mechanisms used by lesser lifeforms like bacteria and humans to keep themselves running at optimum efficiency.

Lovelock's theory was inspired by a study of the Earth's atmosphere, whose constituents he noted are very far from the state of chemical equilibrium observed elsewhere in the solar system. The atmosphere has contained a substantial amount of free oxygen for the last two billion years; yet without constant renewal, the oxygen molecules would soon be locked permanently in oxides. The nitrogen, too, would find chemical stability, probably in nitrates (accounting for some of the oxygen). Without living plants and algae to remove it, carbon dioxide would steadily increase from its present-day 0.03%; in a few million

years, it would form a thick blanket similar to the atmosphere of lifeless Venus, where surface temperatures reach 475°C.

It is not enough, however, for the biosphere simply to produce oxygen. While falling concentrations would be first uncomfortable and ultimately fatal for most contemporary life, at levels above the current 21% even moist vegetation is highly inflammable, and a massive conflagration becomes almost inevitable – a violent form of negative feedback to set the atmosphere on the path back to sterile equilibrium.

Fortunately, the biosphere has evolved over eons into a subtle and complex control system, sensing changes and reacting to them quickly but gently, tending always to maintain the balance it has achieved.

**Air-sea interface**

The ocean surface is the location of most of the great systems of heat exchange that keep the Earth functioning properly. In addition, the ocean absorbs and circulates critical atmospheric gases.

**The high atmosphere**

On the edge of space, the ionized outer atmosphere shields the Earth from meteors and high-energy solar particles. Below, a layer of ozone traps ultra-violet radiation.

**Tropical vegetation**

The lush growth of rainforest and other vegetation in the Earth's tropical zones is one of the most important oxygen generators on the planet. Large-scale transpiration influences rainfall and climate patterns both locally and far afield.

**Continental shelves**

The warm, shallow fringes amount to 21% of the Earth's total ocean area but contain a far higher proportion of its plant and animal life. Vulnerable to coastal and marine pollution, plankton and other plants in these waters are key elements in the carbon and oxygen cycles upon which all life depends.

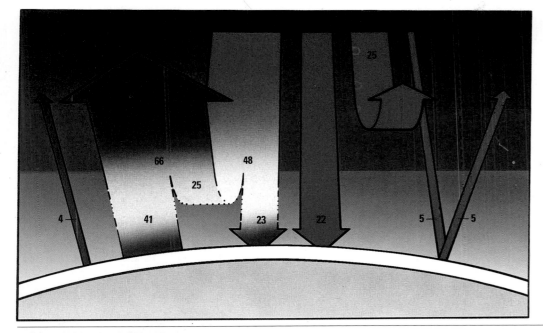

## THE EARTH'S ENERGY BALANCE

Apart from a modest quantity of internal heat from its molten core, the Earth receives all its energy from the Sun. If the planet is to remain at a constant temperature, it must re-radiate exactly as much as it receives. Even a minute surplus would lead to a warmer Earth, a deficit to a cooler one; because the planetary energy budget is constantly audited by the laws of physics, which do not permit juggling, it must balance with absolute precision. The temperature at which thermal equilibrium is reached depends on a multitude of interconnected factors. Two of the most important are the relative brightness of the Earth – its index of reflectivity, called the albedo – and the heat-trapping capacity of the atmosphere – the celebrated 'greenhouse effect'.

Because the Sun is very hot, most of its energy arrives in the form of relatively short-wave radiation: the shorter the waves, the more energy they carry. Some of the incoming energy is reflected straight back into space, exactly as it arrived; some is absorbed by the atmosphere on its way towards the surface; some is absorbed by the earth itself. Absorbed energy heats the Earth and its atmosphere alike. But since its temperature is very much lower than that of the Sun, outgoing energy is emitted at much longer infra-red wavelengths. Some of the outgoing radiation escapes directly into outer space; some of it is reabsorbed by the atmosphere. Atmospheric energy eventually finds its way back into space, too, after a complex series of interactions. These include the air movements we call the weather and, almost incidentally, the maintenance of life on Earth.

This diagram does not attempt to illustrate the actual mechanisms of heat exchange, but gives a reasonable account (in percentages) of what happens to 100 energy 'units'. Short-wave radiation is shown in yellow, long-wave in red.

## THE CARBON CYCLE

Most of the constituents of the atmosphere are kept in constant balance by complex cycles in which life plays an essential and indeed a dominant part. The control of carbon dioxide, which left to its own devices would be the dominant atmospheric gas, is possibly the most important, although since all the Earth's biological and geophysical cycles interact and interlock, it is hard to separate them even in theory and quite impossible in practice.

The Earth has a huge supply of carbon, only a small quantity of which is in the form of carbon dioxide. Of that, around 98% is dissolved in the sea; the fraction circulating in the air amounts to only 340 parts per million of the atmosphere, where its capacity as a greenhouse gas is the key regulator of the planetary temperature. In turn, life regulates the regulator, keeping carbon dioxide concentrations below danger level.

If all life were to vanish tomorrow from the Earth, the atmosphere would begin the process of change immediately, although it might take several million years to achieve a new, inorganic stability. First, the oxygen content would begin to fall away; with no more assistance than a little solar radiation, a few electrical storms and its own high chemical potential, oxygen would steadily combine with atmospheric nitrogen and volcanic outgassing. In doing so, it would yield sufficient acid to react with carbonaceous rocks such as limestone, releasing carbon dioxide. Once carbon dioxide levels exceeded about 1%, its greenhouse power would increase disproportionately. Rising temperatures – well above the boiling point of water would speed chemical reactions; in time, the Earth's atmosphere would consist of little more than carbon dioxide and superheated water vapour.

Living things, however, circulate carbon. They do so first by simply existing: after all, the carbon atom is the basic building block of living matter. During life, plants absorb atmospheric carbon dioxide, incorporating the carbon itself into their structure – leaves and trunks in the case of land plants, shells

in the case of plankton and the tiny creatures that feed on it. The oxygen thereby freed is added to the atmosphere, at least for a time. Most plant carbon is returned to circulation when the plants die and decay, combining once more with the oxygen released during life. However, a small proportion – about one part in 1000 – is removed almost permanently, buried beneath mud on land, at sea sinking as dead matter to the ocean floor. In time, it is slowly compressed into sedimentary rocks such as limestone and chalk.

But in the evolution of the Earth, nothing is quite permanent. On an even longer timescale, the planet's crustal movements force new rock upward in mid-ocean ridges. Limestone deposits are

moved, and sea levels change; ancient limestone is exposed to weathering, and a little of its carbon is released to be fixed in turn by the current generation of plants.

The carbon cycle has continued quietly for an immensely long time, and without gross disturbance there is no reason why it would not continue almost indefinitely in the future. However, human beings have found a way to release fixed carbon at a rate far faster than existing global systems can recirculate it. Oil and coal deposits represent the work of millions of years of carbon accumulation; but it has taken only a few human generations of high-energy scavenging to endanger the entire complex regulatory cycle.

**Organic decay, animal respiration & burning**

**AIR**

**Plankton photosynthesis**

**Absorption by living plants**

**Plankton respiration**

**LAND**

**Mineral washout**

**SEA**

**Sea shells to sedimentary rock**

**[98% of existing carbon dioxide held in solution in the sea]**

## THE GREENHOUSE EFFECT

Constituting barely 0.03% of the atmosphere, carbon dioxide has a hugely disproportionate effect on the Earth's climate and even its habitability. Like the glass panes in a greenhouse, it is transparent to most incoming short-wave radiation, which passes freely to heat the planet beneath. But when the warmed earth re-transmits that energy, in the form of longer-wave infra-red radiation, the carbon dioxide functions as an opaque shield, so that the planetary surface (like the interior of a greenhouse) stays relatively hot.

Recent increases in CO$_2$ levels are causing alarm: global warming associated with a runaway greenhouse effect could bring disaster. But a serious reduction would be just as damaging, with surface temperatures falling dramatically; during the last ice age, for example, the carbon dioxide concentration was around 180 parts per million, and a total absence of the gas would likely leave the planet a ball of ice, or at best frozen tundra.

The diagram shows incoming sunlight as yellow; high-energy ultra-violet (blue) is trapped by the ozone layer while outgoing heat from the warmed Earth (red) is partially retained by carbon dioxide.

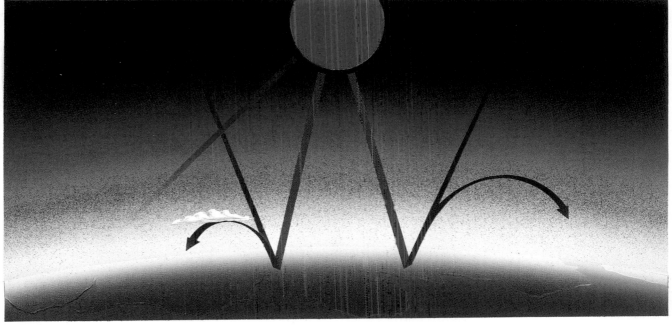

# PEOPLE: DEMOGRAPHY

As the 20th century draws to its close, the Earth's population increases by nearly 10,000 every hour – enough to fill a new major city every week. The growth is almost entirely confined to the developing world, which accounted for 67% of total population in 1950 and is set to reach 84% by 2025. In developed countries, populations are almost static, and in some places, such as Germany, are actually falling. In fact, there is a clear correlation between wealth and low fertility: as incomes rise, reproduction rates drop.

The decline is already apparent. With the exception of Africa, the actual rates of increase are falling nearly everywhere. The structure of populations, however, ensures that human numbers will continue to rise even as fertility diminishes. Developed nations, like the UK, have an even spread across ages, and usually a growing proportion of elderly people: the over-75s often outnumber the under-5s, and women of child-bearing age form only a modest part of the total. Developing nations fall into a pattern somewhere between that of Kenya and Brazil: the great majority of their people are in the younger age groups, about to enter their most fertile years. In time, even Kenya's population profile should resemble the developed model, but the transition will come about only after a few more generations' growth.

It remains to be seen whether the planet will tolerate the population growth that seems inevitable before stability is reached. More people consume more resources, increasing the strain on an already troubled environment. However, more people should mean a greater supply of human ingenuity – the only commodity likely to resolve the crisis .

## LARGEST NATIONS

The world's most populous nations, in millions (1989)

1. China        1120
2. India        812
3. USA          250
4. Indonesia    179
5. Brazil       147
6. Russia       147
7. Japan        123
8. Nigeria      109
9. Pakistan     109
10. Bangladesh  107
11. Mexico      84
12. Germany     79
13. Vietnam     66
14. Philippines 60
15. Italy       58
16. UK          57
17. Turkey      57
18. France      56
19. Thailand    55
20. Iran        55
21. Egypt       53
22. Ukraine     52
23. Ethiopia    51
24. S. Korea    43
25. Burma       41

## CROWDED NATIONS

Population per square kilometre (1989), exc. nations of less than one million

1. Hong Kong         5826.2
2. Singapore         4401.6
3. Bangladesh        795.4
4. Mauritius         577.3
5. Taiwan            554.2
6. Netherlands       439.0
7. S. Korea          432.3
8. Puerto Rico       412.9
9. Belgium           328.5
10. Japan            327.0
11. Lebanon          283.2
12. Rwanda           280.1
13. India            273.1
14. Sri Lanka        259.6
15. El Salvador      251.3
16. Trinidad & Tobago 246.2
17. UK               236.8
18. Germany          224.9
19. Israel           224.6
20. Jamaica          219.3

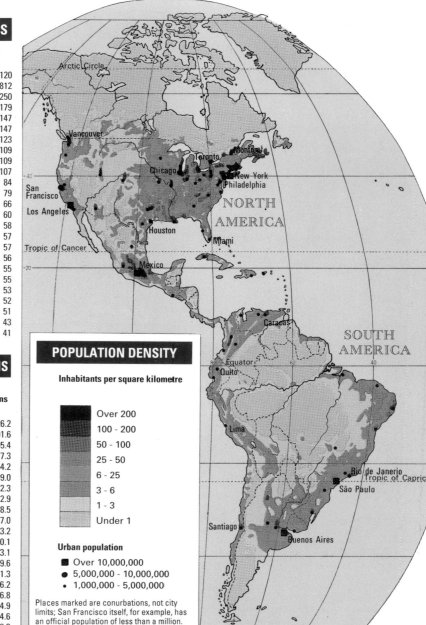

### POPULATION DENSITY

Inhabitants per square kilometre

- Over 200
- 100 - 200
- 50 - 100
- 25 - 50
- 6 - 25
- 3 - 6
- 1 - 3
- Under 1

Urban population
- ■ Over 10,000,000
- ● 5,000,000 - 10,000,000
- • 1,000,000 - 5,000,000

Places marked are conurbations, not city limits; San Francisco itself, for example, has an official population of less than a million.

Projection : Mollweide's Interrupted Homolographic

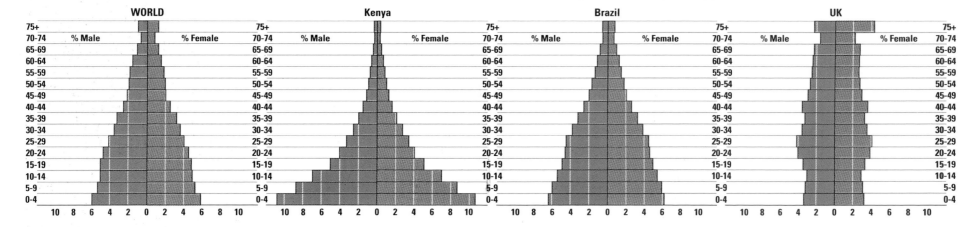

WORLD | Kenya | Brazil | UK

## RATES OF GROWTH

Apparently small rates of population growth lead to dramatic increases over two or three generations. The table below translates annual percentage growth into the number of years required to double a population.

| % change | Doubling time |
|----------|---------------|
| 0.5 | 139.0 |
| 1.0 | 69.7 |
| 1.5 | 46.6 |
| 2.0 | 35.0 |
| 2.5 | 28.1 |
| 3.0 | 23.4 |
| 3.5 | 20.1 |
| 4.0 | 17.7 |

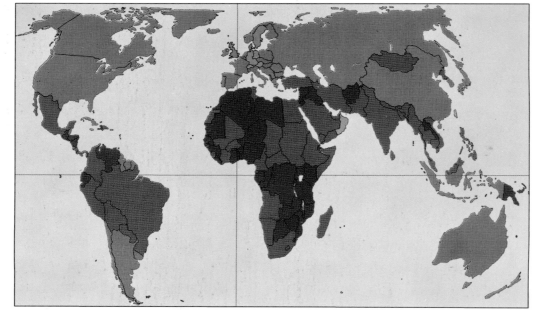

## POPULATION CHANGE

Estimated percentage change in total population, 1988-2000

- Over 60%
- 40 - 60%
- 20 - 40%
- 0 - 20%        [USA 0.8%]
- Loss or no change  [UK 0.3%]

| Highest expected gain* | Lowest expected gain |
|---|---|
| Haiti +84% | Andorra -15% |
| Kenya +82% | Switzerland -10% |
| El Salvador +77% | Oman -5% |
| Jordan +75% | Sweden -4% |
| Tanzania +74% | Germany -2% |

* India (191 million), China (187), Nigeria (49), Pakistan (48), Indonesia (38), Bangladesh (36) & Brazil (34) are expected to gain most in total population over the same period

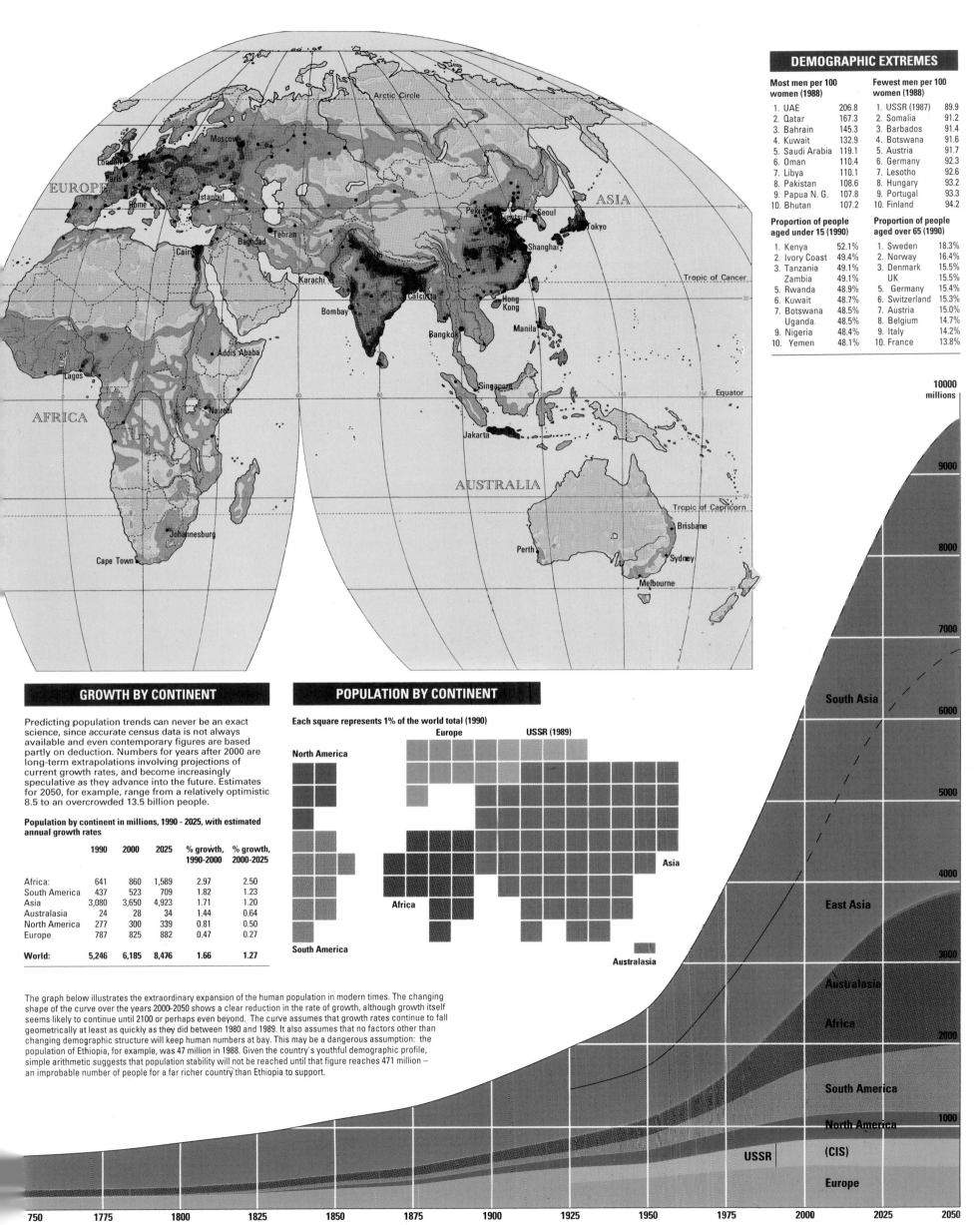

**EUROPE**

London
Paris
Rome
Moscow
Istanbul
Baghdad
Tehran
Cairo
Karachi
Bombay
Calcutta
Peking (Tentsin)
Seoul
Tokyo
Shanghai
Hong Kong
Manila
Bangkok
Singapore
Jakarta

**ASIA**

**AFRICA**

Lagos
Addis Ababa
Nairobi
Johannesburg
Cape Town

**AUSTRALIA**

Brisbane
Perth
Sydney
Melbourne

Arctic Circle
Tropic of Cancer
Equator
Tropic of Capricorn

## DEMOGRAPHIC EXTREMES

| Most men per 100 women (1988) | | Fewest men per 100 women (1988) | |
|---|---|---|---|
| 1. UAE | 206.8 | 1. USSR (1987) | 89.9 |
| 2. Qatar | 167.3 | 2. Somalia | 91.2 |
| 3. Bahrain | 145.3 | 3. Barbados | 91.4 |
| 4. Kuwait | 132.9 | 4. Botswana | 91.6 |
| 5. Saudi Arabia | 119.1 | 5. Austria | 91.7 |
| 6. Oman | 110.4 | 6. Germany | 92.3 |
| 7. Libya | 110.1 | 7. Lesotho | 92.6 |
| 8. Pakistan | 108.6 | 8. Hungary | 93.2 |
| 9. Papua N. G. | 107.8 | 9. Portugal | 93.3 |
| 10. Bhutan | 107.2 | 10. Finland | 94.2 |

| Proportion of people aged under 15 (1990) | | Proportion of people aged over 65 (1990) | |
|---|---|---|---|
| 1. Kenya | 52.1% | 1. Sweden | 18.3% |
| 2. Ivory Coast | 49.4% | 2. Norway | 16.4% |
| 3. Tanzania | 49.1% | 3. Denmark | 15.5% |
| Zambia | 49.1% | UK | 15.5% |
| 5. Rwanda | 48.9% | 5. Germany | 15.4% |
| 6. Kuwait | 48.7% | 6. Switzerland | 15.3% |
| 7. Botswana | 48.5% | 7. Austria | 15.0% |
| Uganda | 48.5% | 8. Belgium | 14.7% |
| 9. Nigeria | 48.4% | 9. Italy | 14.2% |
| 10. Yemen | 48.1% | 10. France | 13.8% |

## GROWTH BY CONTINENT

Predicting population trends can never be an exact science, since accurate census data is not always available and even contemporary figures are based partly on deduction. Numbers for years after 2000 are long-term extrapolations involving projections of current growth rates, and become increasingly speculative as they advance into the future. Estimates for 2050, for example, range from a relatively optimistic 8.5 to an overcrowded 13.5 billion people.

**Population by continent in millions, 1990 - 2025, with estimated annual growth rates**

| | 1990 | 2000 | 2025 | % growth, 1990-2000 | % growth, 2000-2025 |
|---|---|---|---|---|---|
| Africa: | 641 | 860 | 1,589 | 2.97 | 2.50 |
| South America | 437 | 523 | 709 | 1.82 | 1.23 |
| Asia | 3,080 | 3,650 | 4,923 | 1.71 | 1.20 |
| Australasia | 24 | 28 | 34 | 1.44 | 0.64 |
| North America | 277 | 300 | 339 | 0.81 | 0.50 |
| Europe | 787 | 825 | 882 | 0.47 | 0.27 |
| **World:** | **5,246** | **6,185** | **8,476** | **1.66** | **1.27** |

The graph below illustrates the extraordinary expansion of the human population in modern times. The changing shape of the curve over the years 2000-2050 shows a clear reduction in the rate of growth, although growth itself seems likely to continue until 2100 or perhaps even beyond. The curve assumes that growth rates continue to fall geometrically at least as quickly as they did between 1980 and 1989. It also assumes that no factors other than changing demographic structure will keep human numbers at bay. This may be a dangerous assumption: the population of Ethiopia, for example, was 47 million in 1988. Given the country's youthful demographic profile, simple arithmetic suggests that population stability will not be reached until that figure reaches 471 million – an improbable number of people for a far richer country than Ethiopia to support.

## POPULATION BY CONTINENT

Each square represents 1% of the world total (1990)

North America
Europe
USSR (1989)
Asia
Africa
South America
Australasia

**10000 millions**

9000
8000
7000

South Asia

6000
5000
4000

East Asia

3000

Australasia
Africa

2000

South America

1000

North America
USSR
(CIS)
Europe

750   1775   1800   1825   1850   1875   1900   1925   1950   1975   2000   2025   2050

23

# PEOPLE: CITIES

In 1750, barely three humans in every hundred lived in a city; by 2000, more than half of a vastly greater world population will find a home in some kind of urban area. In 1850, only London and Paris had more than a million inhabitants; by 2000, at least 24 cities will each contain over ten million people. The increase is concentrated in the Third World, if only because levels of urbanization in most developed countries - more than 90% in the UK and Belgium, and almost 75% in the USA, despite that country's great open spaces - have already reached practical limits.

Such large-scale concentration is relatively new to the human race. Although city life has always attracted country-dwellers in search of trade, employment or simply human contact, until modern times they paid a high price. Crowding and poor sanitation ensured high death rates, and until about 1850, most cities needed a steady flow of incomers simply to maintain their populations: there were 600,000 more deaths than births in 18th-century London, for example, and some other large cities showed an even worse imbalance.

With improved public health, cities could grow from their own human resources, and large-scale urban living became a commonplace in the developed world. Since about 1950, the pattern has been global. Like their counterparts in 19th-century Europe and the USA, the great new cities are driven into rapid growth by a kind of push-pull mechanism. The push is generated by agricultural overcrowding: only so many people can live from a single plot of land, and population pressure drives many into towns. The pull comes from the possibilities of economic improvement, an irresistible lure to the world's rural hopefuls.

Such improvement is not always obvious: the typical Third World city, with millions of people living (often illegally) in shanty towns and many thousands existing homeless on the ill-made streets, does not present a great image of prosperity. Yet modern shanty towns are healthier than industrializing Pittsburgh or Manchester in the last century, and these human ant-hills teem with industry as well as squalor: throughout the world, above-average rates of urbanization have gone hand-in-hand with above-average economic growth. Surveys consistently demonstrate that Third World city-dwellers are generally better off than their rural counterparts, whose poverty is less concentrated but often more desperate. This only serves to increase the attraction of the city for the rural poor.

However, the sheer speed of the urbanization process threatens to overwhelm the limited abilities of city authorities to provide even rudimentary services and administration. The 24 million people expected to live in Mexico City by 2000, for example, would swamp a more efficient local government than Mexico can provide. Improvements are often swallowed up by the relentless rise in urban population: although safe drinking water should reach 75% of Third World city-dwellers by the end of the century - a considerable achievement - population growth will add 100 million to the list of those without it.

## THE URBANIZATION OF THE EARTH

City-building, 1850-2000; each white spot represents a city of at least one million inhabitants.

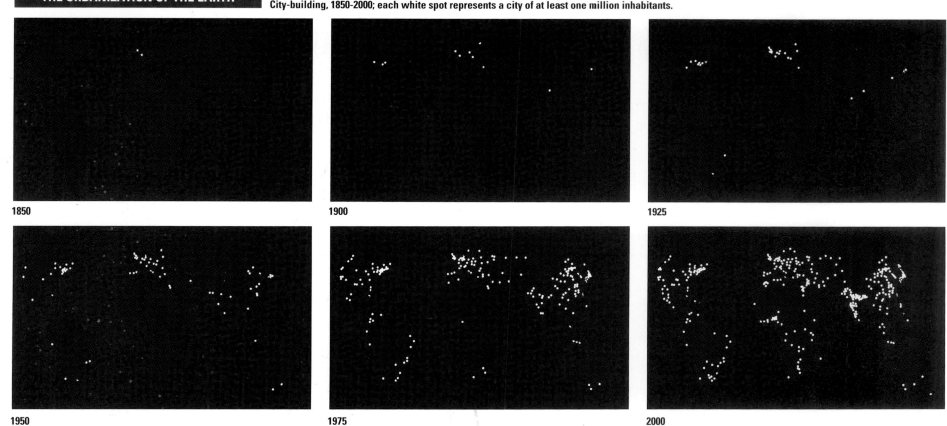

1850

1900

1925

1950

1975

2000

## URBAN POPULATION

Percentage of total population living in towns & cities (1990)

[UK 92.5%]

[USA 74.0 %]

| | |
|---|---|
| Over 75% | |
| 50 - 75% | |
| 25 - 50% | |
| 10 - 25% | |
| Under 10% | |

| Highest urban population* | | Lowest urban population | |
|---|---|---|---|
| Macau | 98.7% | Bhutan | 5.3% |
| Belgium | 96.9% | Burundi | 7.3% |
| Kuwait | 95.6% | Rwanda | 7.7% |
| Hong Kong | 93.2% | Burkina Faso | 9.0% |
| UK | 92.5% | Nepal | 9.6% |
| Israel | 91.6% | Uganda | 10.4% |
| Iceland | 90.5% | Oman | 10.0% |

* Several countries, including Bermuda, Monaco, Singapore & Vatican City, are designated as '100% urban'

## EXPANDING CITIES

**The growth of the world's largest cities, 1950-2000. Intermediate rings indicate relative size in 1970 & 1985.**

### New York
1950: 14.83 million
2000: 16.10 million
Average annual growth: 0.16%

### London
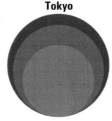
1950: 8.35 million
2000: 10.79 million
Average annual growth: 0.51%

### Tokyo
1950: 6.25 million
2000: 21.32 million
Average annual growth: 2.5%

### Buenos Aires

1950: 5.25 million
2000: 13.05 million
Average annual growth: 1.8%

### Calcutta

1950: 4.45 million
2000: 15.94 million
Average annual growth: 2.6%

### Mexico City
1950: 2.97 million
2000: 24.44 million
Average annual growth: 4.3%

### Shanghai

1950: 4.3 million
2000: 14.69 million
Average annual growth: 2.5%

### Rio de Janeiro

1950: 2.94 million
2000: 13.0 million
Average annual growth: 3.0%

### São Paulo

1950: 2.28 million
2000: 23.6 million
Average annual growth: 4.8%

### Seoul

1950: 1.45 million
2000: 12.97 million
Average annual growth: 4.5%

Each set of circles illustrates a city's size in 1950, 1970, 1985 and 2000. In most cases, expansion has been steady and, often, explosive. New York and London, however, went through patches of negative growth during the period. In New York, the world's largest city in 1950, population reached a peak around 1970. London shrank slightly between 1970 and 1985 before resuming a very modest rate of increase. In both cases, the divergence from world trends can be explained in part by counting methods: each is at the centre of a great agglomeration, and definitions of where 'city limits' lie may vary over time. But their relative decline also matches a pattern often seen in mature cities in the developed world, where urbanization, already at a very high level, has reached a plateau.

## CITIES IN DANGER

As the 1980s advanced, most industrial countries, alarmed by acid rain and urban smog, took significant steps to limit air pollution. These controls, however, are expensive to install and difficult to enforce, and clean air remains a luxury most developed as well as developing cities must live without.

Those taking part in the United Nations' Global Environment Monitoring System (right) frequently show dangerous levels of pollutants ranging from soot to sulphur dioxide and photo-chemical smog; air in the majority of cities without such sampling equipment is likely to be at least as bad.

## URBAN AIR POLLUTION

**The world's most polluted cities: number of days each year when sulphur dioxide levels exceeded the WHO threshold of 150 micrograms per cubic metre (average over 4 to 15 years, 1970s - 1980s)**

Sulphur dioxide is the main pollutant associated with industrial cities. According to the World Health Organization, more than seven days in a year above 150 µg per cubic metre bring a serious risk of respiratory disease: at least 600 million people live in urban areas where $SO_2$ concentrations regularly reach damaging levels.

## LARGEST CITIES

The world's most populous cities, in millions of inhabitants, based on estimates for the year 2000*

| | | |
|---|---|---|
| 1. | Mexico City | 24.4 |
| 2. | São Paulo | 23.6 |
| 3. | Tokyo-Yokohama | 21.3 |
| 4. | New York | 16.1 |
| 5. | Calcutta | 15.9 |
| 6. | Bombay | 15.4 |
| 7. | Shanghai | 14.7 |
| 8. | Tehran | 13.7 |
| 9. | Jakarta | 13.2 |
| 10. | Buenos Aires | 13.1 |
| 11. | Rio de Janeiro | 13.0 |
| 12. | Seoul | 13.0 |
| 13. | Delhi | 12.8 |
| 14. | Lagos | 12.4 |
| 15. | Cairo-Giza | 11.8 |
| 16. | Karachi | 11.6 |
| 17. | Manila-Quezon | 11.5 |
| 18. | Peking (Beijing) | 11.5 |
| 19. | Dhaka | 11.3 |
| 20. | Osaka-Kobe | 11.2 |
| 21. | Los Angeles | 10.9 |
| 22. | London | 10.8 |
| 23. | Bangkok | 10.3 |
| 24. | Moscow | 10.1 |
| 25. | Tientsin (Tianjin) | 10.0 |
| 26. | Lima-Callao | 8.8 |
| 27. | Paris | 8.8 |
| 28. | Milan | 8.7 |
| 29. | Madras | 7.8 |
| 30. | Baghdad | 7.7 |
| 31. | Chicago | 7.0 |
| 32. | Bogotá | 6.9 |
| 33. | Hong Kong | 6.1 |
| 34. | Leningrad | 5.8 |
| 35. | Pusan | 5.8 |
| 36. | Santiago | 5.6 |
| 37. | Shenyang | 5.5 |
| 38. | Madrid | 5.4 |
| 39. | Naples | 4.5 |
| 40. | Philadelphia | 4.3 |

[City populations are based on urban agglomerations rather than legal city limits. In some cases, such as Tokyo-Yokohama and Cairo-Giza, where two adjacent cities have merged into one concentration, they have been regarded as a single unit]

* For list of largest cities in 1990, see page XI

## INFORMAL CITIZENS

**Proportion of population living in squatter settlements, selected cities in the developing world (1980s)**

Urbanization in most Third World countries has been coming about far faster than local governments can provide services and accommodation for the new city-dwellers. Many – in some cities, most – find their homes in improvized squatter settlements, often unconnected to power, water and sanitation networks. Yet despite their ramshackle housing and marginal legality, these communities are often the most dynamic part of a city economy. They are also growing in size; and given the squatters' reluctance to be counted by tax-demanding authorities, the percentages shown here are likely to be underestimates.

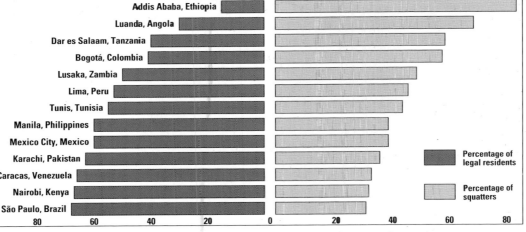

Percentage of legal residents

Percentage of squatters

## URBAN ADVANTAGES

Despite overcrowding and poor housing, living standards in the developing world's cities are almost invariably better than in the surrounding countryside. Resources - financial, material and administrative - are concentrated in the towns, which are usually also the centres of political activity and pressure. Governments - frequently unstable, and rarely established on a solid democratic base - are usually more responsive to urban discontent than rural misery. In many countries, especially in Africa, food prices are often kept artificially low, appeasing underemployed urban masses at the expense of agricultural development. The imbalance encourages further cityward migration, helping to account for the astonishing rate of post-1950 urbanization and putting great strain on the ability of many nations to provide even modest improvements for their people.

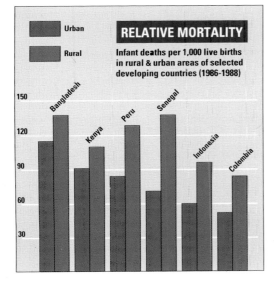

**RELATIVE MORTALITY**
Urban / Rural
Infant deaths per 1,000 live births in rural & urban areas of selected developing countries (1986-1988)

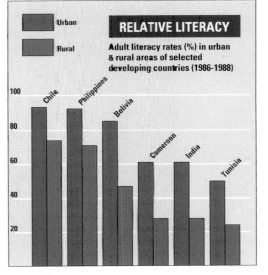

**RELATIVE LITERACY**
Urban / Rural
Adult literacy rates (%) in urban & rural areas of selected developing countries (1986-1988)

# PEOPLE: THE HUMAN FAMILY

Strictly speaking, all human beings belong to a single race: *Homo sapiens* has no sub-species. But although all humans are inter-fertile, anthropologists and geneticists distinguish three main racial types, whose differences reflect not so much evolutionary origin as long periods of separation.

Racial affinities are not always obvious. The Caucasoid group stems from Europe, North Africa and India, but still includes Australian aboriginals within its broad type; Mongoloid peoples comprise American Indians and Eskimos as well as most Chinese, central Asians and Malays; Negroids are mostly of African origin, but also include the Papuan peoples of New Guinea.

Migration in modern times has mingled racial groups to an unprecedented extent, and most nations now have some degree of racially mixed population.

Language is almost the definition of a particular human culture; the world has well over 5,000, most of them with only a few hundred thousand speakers. In one important sense, all languages are equal: although different vocabularies and linguistic structures greatly influence patterns of thought, all true human languages can carry virtually unlimited information. But even if there is no theoretical difference in the communicative power of English and one of the 500 or more tribal languages of Papua New Guinea, for example, an English speaker has access to very much more of the global culture than a Papuan who knows no other tongue.

Like language, religion encourages the internal cohesion of a single human group at the expense of creating gulfs of incomprehension between different groups. All religions satisfy a deep-seated human need, assigning men and women to a comprehensible place in what most of them still consider a divinely ordered world. But religion is also a means by which a culture can assert its individuality: the startling rise of Islam in the late 20th century is partly a response by large sections of the developing world to the secular, Western-inspired world order from which many non-Western peoples feel excluded. Like uncounted millions of human beings before them, they find in their religion not only a personal faith but a powerful group identity.

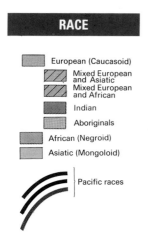

### RACE

- European (Caucasoid)
- Mixed European and Asiatic
- Mixed European and African
- Indian
- Aboriginals
- African (Negroid)
- Asiatic (Mongoloid)
- Pacific races

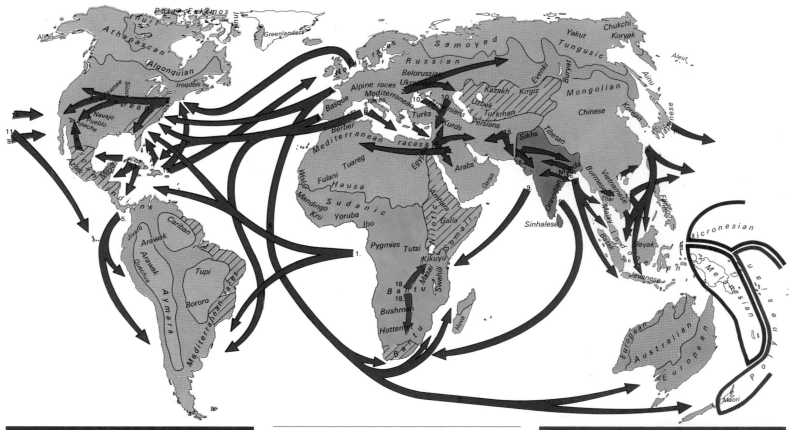

## MOVEMENTS OF POPULATION

1. Africa to America (slaves), c. 1500-1860
2. Western Russia to Siberia, c. 1850-1950
3. W., E. & N. Europe to N. America, c. 1850-1900
4. From East Coast N. America, c. 1860-1960
5. Southern Europe to America, c. 1880-1920
6. Europe to S., E. & Central Africa, c. 1880-1950
7. Europe to Australia & N. Zealand, c. 1840-1950
8. China to S-E Asia & N. America, c. 1900-1950
9. India to Africa & South-East Asia, c. 1860-1910

**Major migrations of peoples since 600 AD**

10. European & N. American Jews to Israel, 1948-
11. Japan to N. & S. America, c. 1870-1910
12. Arabs to North Africa, 7th-9th centuries
13. C. America to N. America & Europe, c. 1950-1970
14. Migration in the Middle East, c. 1950-
15. Refugees from Afghanistan, 1979-
16. Migration in India, 1946-
17. Migration in & from South-East Asia, c. 1960-
18. Spread of the Bantu peoples, c. 1700-1900

## BUILDING THE USA

**U.S. Immigration 1820-1990**

'Give me your tired, your poor/Your huddled masses yearning to breathe free....'

So starts Emma Lazarus's poem *The New Colossus*, inscribed on the Statue of Liberty. For decades the USA was the magnet that attracted millions of immigrants, notably from Central and Eastern Europe, the flow peaking in the early years of this century.

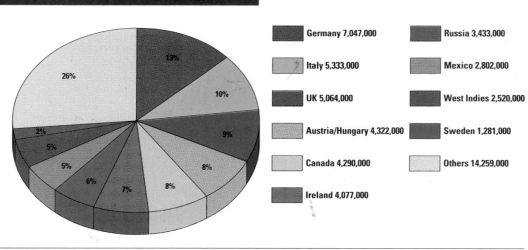

- Germany 7,047,000
- Italy 5,333,000
- UK 5,064,000
- Austria/Hungary 4,322,000
- Canada 4,290,000
- Ireland 4,077,000
- Russia 3,433,000
- Mexico 2,802,000
- West Indies 2,520,000
- Sweden 1,281,000
- Others 14,259,000

## MIGRATION

**The movement of migrants in thousands (1985-1990)**

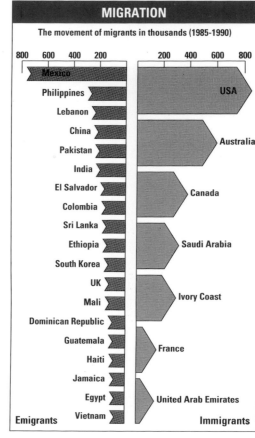

Emigrants — Immigrants

Mexico — USA
Philippines — Australia
Lebanon — Canada
China — Saudi Arabia
Pakistan — Ivory Coast
India — France
El Salvador — United Arab Emirates
Colombia
Sri Lanka
Ethiopia
South Korea
UK
Mali
Dominican Republic
Guatemala
Haiti
Jamaica
Egypt
Vietnam

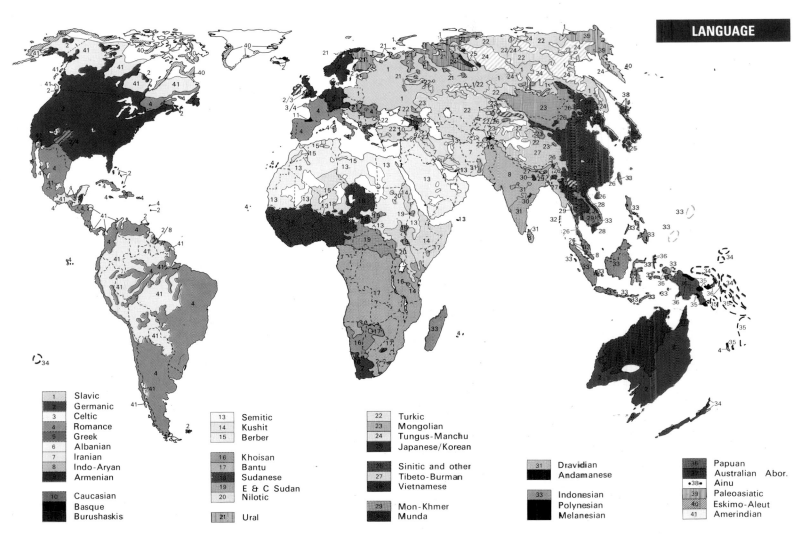

| | |
|---|---|
| 1 | Slavic |
| 2 | Germanic |
| 3 | Celtic |
| 4 | Romance |
| 5 | Greek |
| 6 | Albanian |
| 7 | Iranian |
| 8 | Indo-Aryan |
| 9 | Armenian |
| 10 | Caucasian |
| 11 | Basque |
| 12 | Burushaskis |

| | |
|---|---|
| 13 | Semitic |
| 14 | Kushit |
| 15 | Berber |
| 16 | Khoisan |
| 17 | Bantu |
| 18 | Sudanese |
| 19 | E & C Sudan |
| 20 | Nilotic |
| 21 | Ural |

| | |
|---|---|
| 22 | Turkic |
| 23 | Mongolian |
| 24 | Tungus-Manchu |
| 25 | Japanese/Korean |
| 26 | Sinitic and other |
| 27 | Tibeto-Burman |
| 28 | Vietnamese |
| 29 | Mon-Khmer |
| 30 | Munda |

| | |
|---|---|
| 31 | Dravidian |
| 32 | Andamanese |
| 33 | Indonesian |
| 34 | Polynesian |
| 35 | Melanesian |

| | |
|---|---|
| 36 | Papuan |
| 37 | Australian Abor. |
| 38 | Ainu |
| 39 | Paleoasiatic |
| 40 | Eskimo-Aleut |
| 41 | Amerindian |

**Languages** form a kind of tree of development, splitting from a few ancient proto-tongues into branches that have grown apart and further divided with the passage of time. English and Hindi, for example, both belong to the great Indo-European family, although the relationship is only apparent after much analysis and comparison with non-Indo-European languages such as Chinese or Arabic; Hindi is part of the Indo-Aryan subgroup; English is a member of Indo-European's Germanic branch; French, another Indo-European tongue, traces its descent through the Latin, or Romance, branch. A few languages – Basque is one example – have no apparent links with any other, living or dead. Most modern languages, of course, have acquired enormous quantities of vocabulary from each other.

**MOTHER TONGUES**

Native speakers of the major languages, in millions (1989)

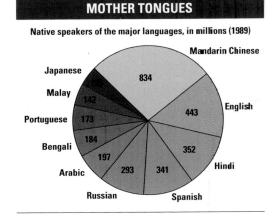

| | |
|---|---|
| Mandarin Chinese | 834 |
| English | 443 |
| Hindi | 352 |
| Spanish | 341 |
| Russian | 293 |
| Arabic | 197 |
| Bengali | 184 |
| Portuguese | 173 |
| Malay | 142 |
| Japanese | 125 |

**Religions** are not as easily mapped as the physical contours of landscape. Divisions are often blurred and frequently overlapping: most nations include people of many different faiths – or no faith at all. Some religions, like Islam and Christianity, have proselytes worldwide; others, like Hinduism and Confucianism, are restricted to a particular area, though modern migrations have taken some Indians and Chinese very far from their cultural origins. It is also difficult to show the degree to which religion exercises control over daily life: Christian Western Europe, for example, is nowadays far less dominated by its religion than are the Islamic nations of the Middle East. Similarly, figures for the major faiths' adherents make no distinction between nominal believers enrolled at birth and those for whom religion is a vital part of existence.

| | RELIGION |
|---|---|

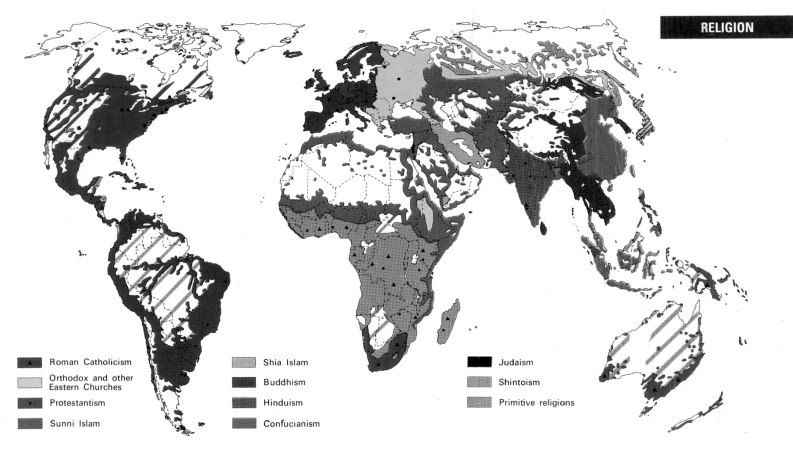

| | |
|---|---|
| ▲ | Roman Catholicism |
| | Orthodox and other Eastern Churches |
| • | Protestantism |
| | Sunni Islam |
| | Shia Islam |
| | Buddhism |
| | Hinduism |
| | Confucianism |
| | Judaism |
| | Shintoism |
| | Primitive religions |

# PEOPLE: CONFLICT & COOPERATION

Humans are social animals, rarely functioning well except in groups. Evolution has made them so: hunter-gatherers in cooperative bands were far more effective than animals that prowled alone. Agriculture, the building of cities and industrialization are all developments that depended on human cooperative ability – and in turn increased the need for it.

Unfortunately, human groups do not always cooperate so well with other human groups, and friction between them sometimes leads to cooperatively organized violence. War is itself a very human activity, with no real equivalent in any other species. It is an extreme form of social coercion

generally used by the strong against the weak. The colonization of the Americas and Australia, for example, was in effect the waging of aggressive war by well-armed Europeans against indigenous peoples incapable of offering a serious defense.

Most often, war achieves little but death and ruin. The great 20th-century wars accomplished nothing for the nations involved in them, although the world paid a price of between 50 and 100 million dead as well as immense material damage. The relative peace in the postwar developed world is at least partly due to the nuclear weapons with which rival powers have armed themselves – weapons so powerful that their

use would leave a scarcely habitable planet with no meaningful distinction between victor and vanquished.

Yet warfare remains endemic: the second half of the 20th century was one of the bloodiest periods in history, and death by organized violence remains unhappily common. The map below attempts to show the serious conflicts that have scarred the Earth since 1945. Most are civil wars in poor countries, rather than international conflicts between rich ones; some of them are still unresolved, while others, like apparently extinct volcanoes, may erupt again at intervals, adding to the world's miserable population of refugees.

## THE WORLD'S REFUGEES

Refugees and their national origin; the host nations and the relative size of their refugee populations (1991)

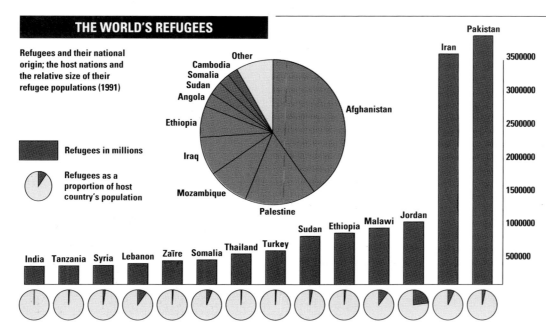

■ Refugees in millions

◔ Refugees as a proportion of host country's population

The pie-chart shows the origins of the world's refugees, the bar-chart their destinations. According to the United Nations High Commissioner for Refugees in 1990, there were almost 15 million of them, a number that continued to increase and was almost certain to be amplified during the decade. Some have fled from climatic change, some from economic disaster and others from political persecution; the great majority are the victims of war.
All but a few who make it overseas seek asylum in neighbouring countries, which are often the least equipped to deal with them and where they are rarely welcome. Lacking any rights or power, they frequently become an embarrassment and a burden to their reluctant hosts.
Usually, the best any refugee can hope for is rudimentary food and shelter in temporary camps that all to often become semi-permanent, with little prospect of assimilation by host populations: many Palestinians, for example, have been forced to live in camps since 1948.

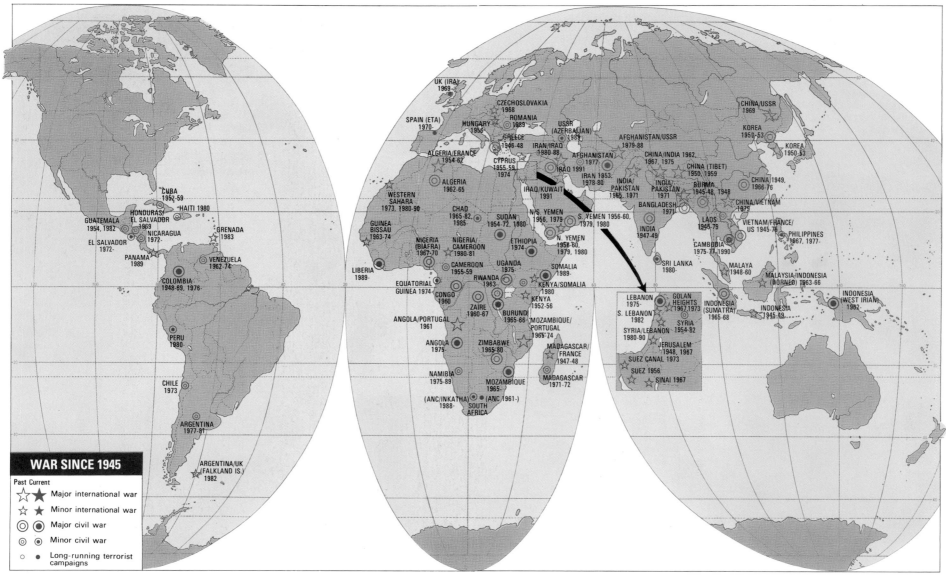

## WAR SINCE 1945

Past  Current
☆  ★  Major international war
☆  ★  Minor international war
◎  ◉  Major civil war
⊙  ⦿  Minor civil war
○  ●  Long-running terrorist campaigns

# UNITED NATIONS

The United Nations Organization was born as World War II drew to its conclusion. Six years of strife had strengthened the world's desire for peace, but an effective international organization was needed to help achieve it. That body would replace the League of Nations which, since its inception in 1920, had signally failed to curb the aggression of at least some of its member nations. At the United Nations Conference on International Organization held in San Francisco, the United Nations Charter was drawn up. Ratified by the Security Council and signed by 51 nations, it came into effect on 24 October 1945.

The Charter set out the aims of the organization: to maintain peace and security, and develop friendly relations between nations; to achieve international cooperation in solving economic, social, cultural and humanitarian problems; to promote respect for human rights and fundamental freedoms; and to harmonize the activities of nations in order to achieve these common goals.

By 1992, the UN had expanded to more than 160 member countries; it is the largest international political organization, employing 23,000 people worldwide; its headquarters in New York accounts for 7,000 staff and it also has major offices in Rome, Geneva and Vienna.

The United Nations has six principal organs:

## The General Assembly

The forum at which member nations discuss moral and political issues affecting world development, peace and security meets annually in September, under a newly-elected President whose tenure lasts one year. Any member can bring business to the agenda, and each member nation has one vote. Decisions are made by simple majority, save for matters of very great importance, when a two-thirds majority is required. While the General Assembly has no powers of enforcement, its recommendations to member nations are regarded as persuasive and it is empowered to instruct UN organs or agencies to implement its decisions.

## The Security Council

A legislative and executive body, the Security Council is the primary instrument for establishing and maintaining international peace by attempting to settle disputes between nations. It has the power to dispatch UN forces to stop aggression, and member nations undertake to make armed forces, assistance and facilities available as required. The Security Council has ten temporary members elected by the General Assembly for two-year terms, and five permanent members - China, France, Russia, UK and USA. On questions of substance, the vote of each of the permanent members is required within the necessary nine-vote majority.

## The Economic and Social Council

By far the largest United Nations executive, the Council operates as a conduit between the General Assembly and the many United Nations agencies it instructs to implement Assembly decisions, and whose work it coordinates. The Council also sets up commissions to examine economic conditions, collects data and issues studies and reports, and may make recommendations to the Assembly. The Council's overall aim is to help the peoples of the world with education, health and human rights. It has 54 member countries, elected by the General Assembly to three-year terms.

## The Secretariat

This is the staff of the United Nations, and its task is to administer the policies and programmes of the UN and its organs, and assist and advise the Head of the Secretariat, the Secretary-General – a full-time, non-political, appointment made by the General Assembly.

## The Trusteeship Council

The Council administers trust territories with the aim of promoting their advancement. Only one remains - the Trust Territory of the Pacific Is. (Palau), administered by the USA.

## The International Court of Justice (the World Court)

The World Court is the judicial organ of the United Nations. It deals only with United Nations disputes and all members are subject to its jurisdiction, which includes both cases submitted to it by member nations and matters especially provided for in the Charter or in treaties. The Court's decisions are only binding in respect of a particular dispute; failure to heed a judgement may involve recourse to the Security Council. There are 15 judges, elected for nine-year terms by the General Assembly and the Security Council. The Court sits in The Hague.

United Nations agencies and programmes, and inter-governmental agencies coordinated by the UN, contribute to harmonious world development. Social and humanitarian operations include:

**United Nations Development Programme (UNDP):** plans and funds projects to help developing countries make better use of resources. Voluntary pledges of $1.3 billion were made for 1990, to fund almost 7,000 projects in 152 countries.

**United Nations International Childrens' Fund (UNICEF):** created at the General Assembly's first session in 1945 to help children in the aftermath of World War II, it now provides basic healthcare and aid worldwide. Voluntarily funded, three-quarters of its income is derived from government donations.

**United Nations Fund for Population Activities (UNFPA):** promotes awareness of population issues and family planning, providing appropriate assistance.

**Food & Agriculture Organization (FAO):** aims to raise living standards and nutrition levels in rural areas by improving food production and distribution.

**United Nations Educational, Scientific & Cultural Organization (UNESCO):** promotes international cooperation through broader and better education.

**World Health Organization (WHO):** promotes and provides for better health care, public and environmental health and medical research.

**Membership:** There are 13 independent states who are not members of the UN – Andorra, Kiribati, Liechtenstein, N. Korea, S. Korea, Monaco, Nauru, San Marino, Switzerland, Taiwan, Tonga, Tuvalu and Vatican City. By 1992, the successor states of the former USSR had either joined or were planning to join. There were 51 members in 1945. Official languages are Chinese, English, French, Russian, Spanish and (a recent addition) Arabic.

**Funding:** The UN budget for 1988-1989 was US $ 1,788,746,000. Contributions are assessed by members' ability to pay, with the maximum 25% of the total, the minimum 0.01%. Contributions for 1988-1989 were: USA 25%, Japan 11.38%, USSR 9.99%, W. Germany 8.08%, France 6.25%, UK 4.86%, Italy 3.99%, Canada 3.09%, Spain 1.95%, Netherlands 1.65% (others 23.75%).

**Peacekeeping:** The UN has been involved in 18 peacekeeping operations worldwide since 1945, five of which (Afghanistan/Pakistan, Iran/Iraq, Angola, Namibia and Honduras) were initiated in 1988-1989. In June 1991 UN personnel totalling over 11,000 were working in eight separate areas.

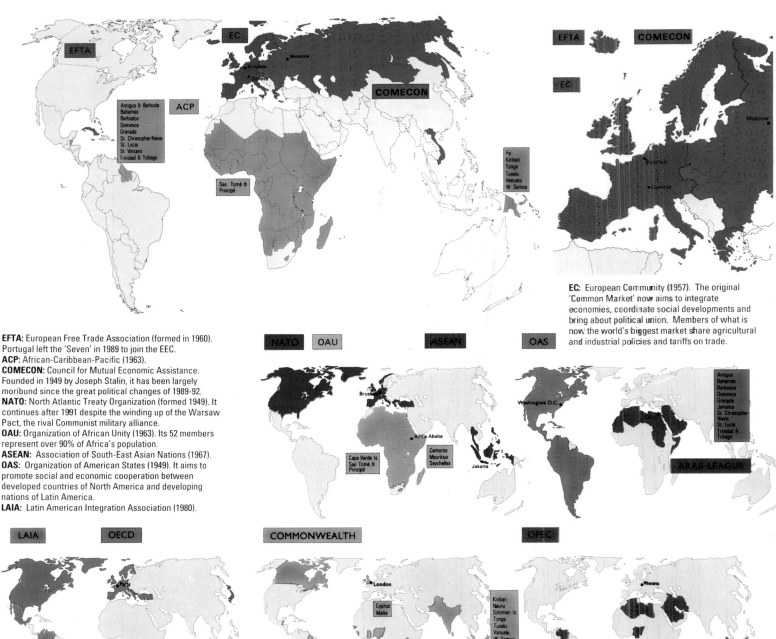

United Nations agencies are involved in many aspects of international trade, safety and security:

**General Agreement on Tariffs and Trade (GATT):** sponsors international trade negotiations and advocates a common code of conduct.

**International Maritime Organization (IMO):** promotes unity amongst merchant shipping, especially in regard to safety, marine pollution and standardization.

**International Labour Organization (ILO):** seeks to improve labour conditions and promote productive employment to raise living standards.

**World Meteorological Organization (WMO):** promotes cooperation in weather observation, reporting and forecasting.

**World Intellectual Property Organization (WIPO):** seeks to protect intellectual property such as artistic copyright, scientific patents and trademarks.

**Disarmament Commission:** considers and makes recommendations to the General Assembly on disarmament issues.

**International Atomic Energy Agency (IAEA):** fosters development of peaceful uses for nuclear energy, establishes safety standards and monitors the destruction of nuclear material designed for military use.

**The World Bank** comprises three United Nations agencies:

**International Monetary Fund (IMF):** cultivates international monetary cooperation and expansion of trade.

**International Bank for Reconstruction & Development (IBRD):** provides funds and technical assistance to developing countries.

**International Finance Corporation (IFC):** Encourages the growth of productive private enterprise in less developed countries.

**EC:** European Community (1957). The original 'Common Market' now aims to integrate economies, coordinate social developments and bring about political union. Members of what is now the world's biggest market share agricultural and industrial policies and tariffs on trade.

**EFTA:** European Free Trade Association (formed in 1960). Portugal left the 'Seven' in 1989 to join the EEC.
**ACP:** African-Caribbean-Pacific (1963).
**COMECON:** Council for Mutual Economic Assistance. Founded in 1949 by Joseph Stalin, it has been largely moribund since the great political changes of 1989-92.
**NATO:** North Atlantic Treaty Organization (formed 1949). It continues after 1991 despite the winding up of the Warsaw Pact, the rival Communist military alliance.
**OAU:** Organization of African Unity (1963). Its 52 members represent over 90% of Africa's population.
**ASEAN:** Association of South-East Asian Nations (1967).
**OAS:** Organization of American States (1949). It aims to promote social and economic cooperation between developed countries of North America and developing nations of Latin America.
**LAIA:** Latin American Integration Association (1980).

**OECD:** Organization for Economic Cooperation and Development (1961). The 24 major Western free-market economies plus Yugoslavia as an associate member. 'G7' is its 'inner group' of USA, Canada, Japan, UK, Germany, Italy and France.
**COMMONWEALTH:** The Commonwealth of Nations evolved from the British Empire; it comprises 18 nations recognizing the British monarch as head of state and 32 nations with their own heads of state.
**OPEC:** Organization of Petroleum Exporting Countries (1960). It controls three-quarters of the world's oil supply.

# PRODUCTION: AGRICULTURE

The invention of agriculture transformed human existence more than any other development, though it may not have seemed much of an improvement to its first practitioners. Primitive farming required brutally hard work, and it tied men and women to a patch of land, highly vulnerable to local weather patterns and to predators, especially human predators – drawbacks still apparent in much of the world today. It is difficult to imagine early humans being interested in such an existence while there were still animals around to hunt and wild seeds and berries to gather. Probably the spur was population pressure, with consequent overhunting and scarcity.

Despite its difficulties, the new life-style had a few overwhelming advantages. It supported far larger populations, eventually including substantial cities, with all the varied cultural and economic activities they allowed. Later still, it furnished the surpluses that allowed industrialization, another enormous step in human development.

Machines relieved many farmers of their burden of endless toil, and made it possible for relatively small numbers to provide food for more than five billion people.

Then as now, the whole business of farming involves the creation of a severely simplified ecology, under the tutelage and for the benefit of the farmer. Natural plant life is divided into crops, to be protected and nurtured, and weeds, the rest, to be destroyed. From the earliest days, crops were selectively bred to increase their food yield, usually at the expense of their ability to survive, which became the farmer's responsibility; 20th-century plant geneticists have carried the technique to highly productive extremes. Due mainly to new varieties of rice and wheat, world grain production has increased by 70% since 1965, more than doubling in the developing countries, although such high yields demand equally high consumption of fertilizers and pesticides to maintain them. Mechanized farmers in North America and Europe

continue to turn out huge surpluses, although not without environmental costs.

Where production is inadequate, the reasons are as likely to be political as agricultural. Africa, the only continent where food production per capita is actually falling, suffers acutely from economic mis-management, as well as from the perennial problems of war and banditry. Dismal harvests in the USSR, despite its excellent farmland, helped bring about the collapse of the Soviet system.

There are other limits to progress. Increasing population puts relentless pressure on farmers not only to maintain high yields but also to increase them. Most of the world's potential cropland is already under the plough. The over-working of marginal land is one of the prime causes of desertification; new farmlands burned out of former rainforests are seldom fertile for long. Human numbers may yet outrun the land's ability to feed them, as they did almost 10,000 years ago.

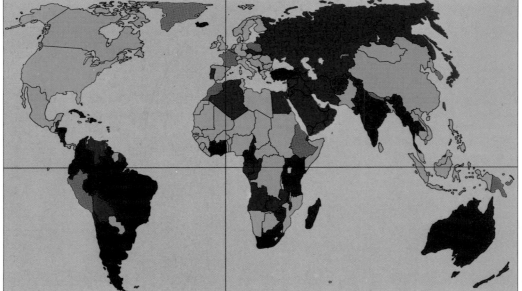

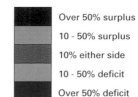

## SELF-SUFFICIENCY IN FOOD

Balance of trade in food products as a percentage of total trade in food products (1988)

- Over 50% surplus
- 10 - 50% surplus
- 10% either side
- 10 - 50% deficit
- Over 50% deficit

| Most self-sufficient | | Least self-sufficient | |
|---|---|---|---|
| Uganda | 93% | Algeria | -97% |
| Argentina | 92% | Saudi Arabia | -95% |
| Burma | 86% | Czechoslovakia | -92% |
| Chile | 82% | Venezuela | -92% |
| Iceland | 82% | Gabon | -88% |
| Uruguay | 82% | Oman | -88% |
| Kenya | 80% | Syria | -88% |
| New Zealand | 80% | Egypt | -86% |
| Costa Rica | 79% | Japan | -85% |

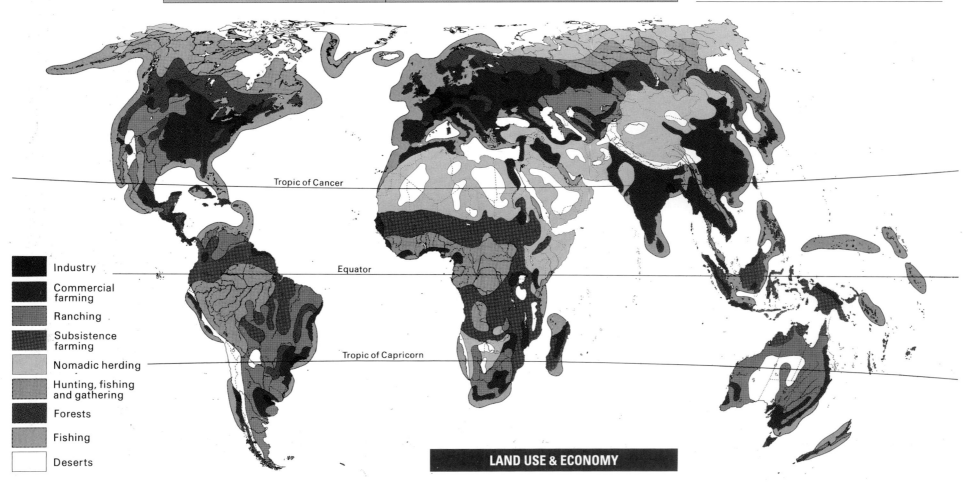

- Industry
- Commercial farming
- Ranching
- Subsistence farming
- Nomadic herding
- Hunting, fishing and gathering
- Forests
- Fishing
- Deserts

Tropic of Cancer

Equator

Tropic of Capricorn

### LAND USE & ECONOMY

## STAPLE CROPS

**Separate figures for Russia, Ukraine and the other successors of the defunct USSR are not yet available**

**Wheat:** Grown in a range of climates, with most varieties - including the highest-quality bread wheats - requiring temperate conditions. Mainly used in baking, it is also used for pasta and breakfast cereals.

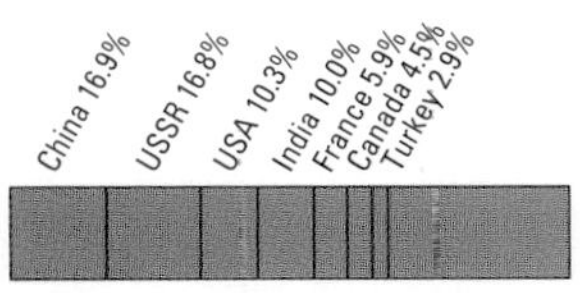
China 16.9%
USSR 16.8%
USA 10.3%
India 10.0%
France 5.9%
Canada 4.5%
Turkey 2.9%

World total (1989): 538,056,000 tonnes

**Maize:** Originating in the New World and still an important human food in Africa and Latin America, in the developed world it is processed into breakfast cereals, oil, starches and adhesives. It is also used for animal feed.

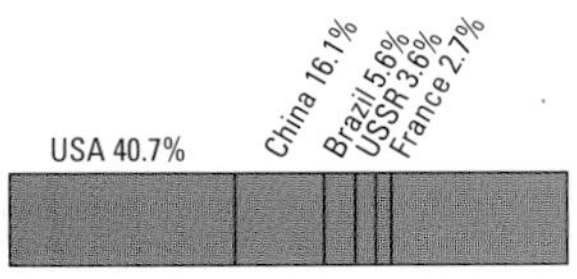
USA 40.7%
China 16.1%
Brazil 5.6%
USSR 3.6%
France 2.7%

World total (1989): 470,318,000 tonnes

**Oats:** Most widely used to feed livestock, but eaten by humans as oatmeal or porridge. Oats have a beneficial effect on the cardio-vascular system, and human consumption is likely to increase.

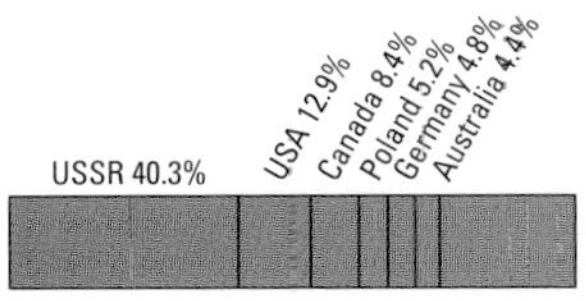
USSR 40.3%
USA 12.9%
Canada 8.4%
Poland 5.2%
Germany 4.8%
Australia 4.4%

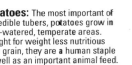

World total (1989): 42,197,000 tonnes

**Millet:** The name covers a number of small grained cereals, members of the grass family with a short growing season. Used to produce flour and meal, animal feed and fermented to make beer, especially in Africa.

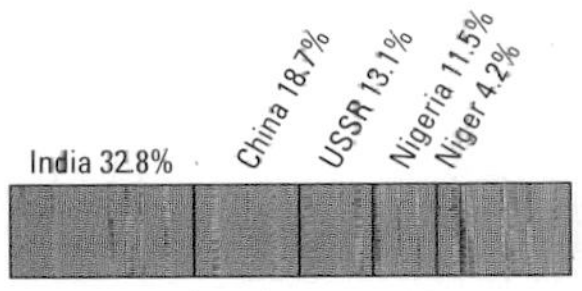
India 32.8%
China 18.7%
USSR 13.1%
Nigeria 11.5%
Niger 4.2%

World total (1989): 30,512,000 tonnes

**Cassava:** A tropical shrub that needs high rainfall (over 1000 mm annually) and a 10 - 30 month growing season to produce its large, edible tubers. Used as flour by humans, as cattle feed and in industrial starches.

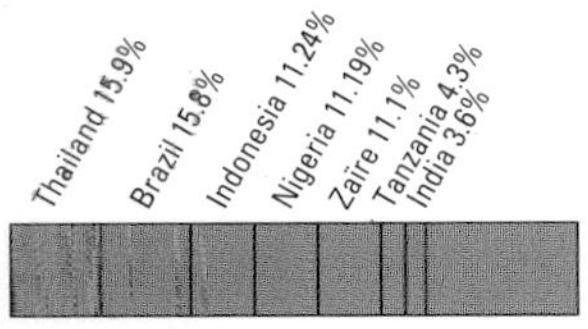
Thailand 15.9%
Brazil 15.8%
Indonesia 11.24%
Nigeria 11.19%
Zaïre 11.1%
Tanzania 4.3%
India 3.6%

World total (1989): 147,500,000 tonnes

**Rice:** Thrives on the high humidity and temperatures of the Far East, where it is the traditional staple food of half the human race. Usually grown standing in water, rice responds well to continuous cultivation, with three or four crops annually.

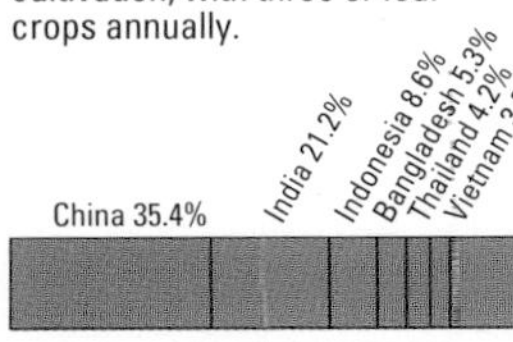
China 35.4%
India 21.2%
Indonesia 8.6%
Bangladesh 5.3%
Thailand 4.2%
Vietnam 3.6%

World total (1989): 506,291,000 tonnes

**Barley:** Primarily used as animal feed, but widely eaten by humans in Africa and Asia. Elsewhere, malted barley furnishes beer and spirits. Able to withstand the dry heat of sub-arid tropics, its growing season is only 80 days.

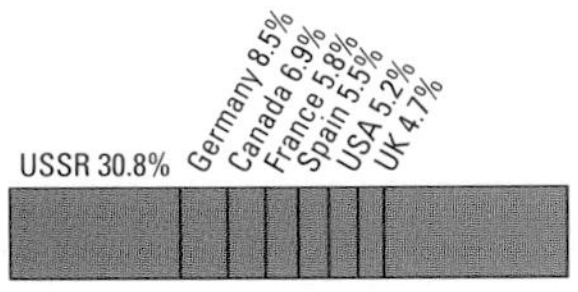
USSR 30.8%
Germany 8.5%
Canada 6.9%
France 5.8%
Spain 5.5%
USA 5.2%
UK 4.7%

World total (1989): 168,964,000 tonnes

**Rye:** Hardy and tolerant of poor and sandy soils, it is an important foodstuff and animal feed in Central and Eastern Europe and the USSR. Rye produces a dark, heavy bread as well as alcoholic drinks.

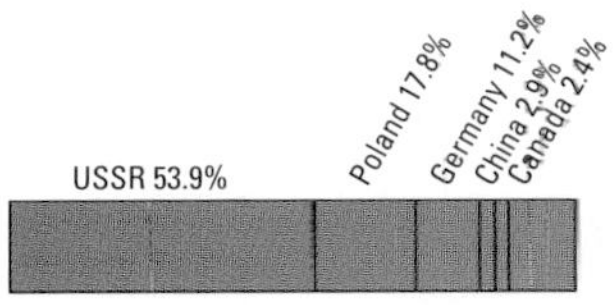
USSR 53.9%
Poland 17.8%
Germany 11.2%
China 2.9%
Canada 2.4%

World total (1989): 34,893,000 tonnes

**Potatoes:** The most important of the edible tubers, potatoes grow in well-watered, temperate areas. Weight for weight less nutritious than grain, they are a human staple as well as an important animal feed.

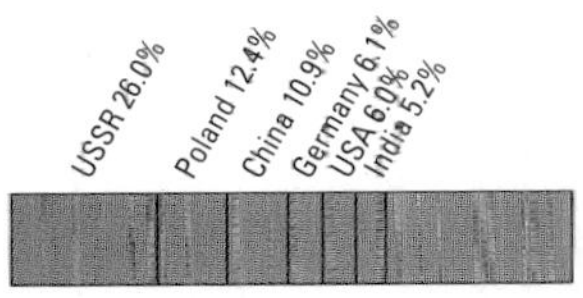
USSR 26.0%
Poland 12.4%
China 10.9%
Germany 6.1%
USA 6.0%
India 5.2%

World total (1989): 276,740,000 tonnes

**Soya:** Beans from soya bushes are very high - 30-40% - in protein. Most are processed into oil and proprietary protein foods. Consumption since 1950 has tripled, mainly due to the health-conscious developed world.

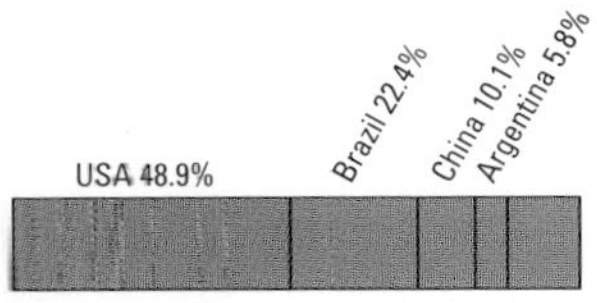
USA 48.9%
Brazil 22.4%
China 10.1%
Argentina 5.8%

World total (1989): 107,350,000 tonnes

Cereals are grasses with starchy, edible seeds; every important civilization has depended on them as a source of food. The major cereal grains contain about 10% protein and 75% carbohydrate; grain is easy to store, handle and transport, and contributes more than any other group of foods to the energy and protein content of human diet. If all the cereals were consumed directly by man, there would be no shortage of food in the world, but a considerable proportion of the total output is used as animal feed.

Starchy tuber crops or root crops, represented here by potatoes and cassava, are second in importance only to cereals as staple foods; easily cultivated, they provide high yields for little effort and store well – potatoes for up to six months, cassava for up to a year in the ground. Protein content is low (2% or less), and starch content high; some minerals and vitamins are present, but populations that rely heavily on these crops may suffer from malnutrition.

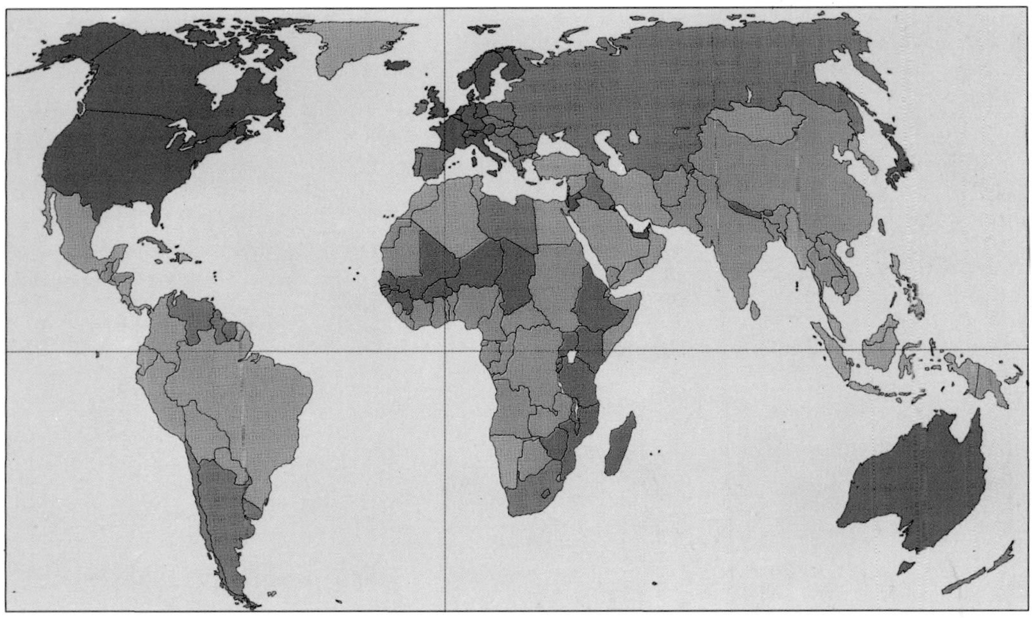

## IMPORTANCE OF AGRICULTURE

**Percentage of the total population dependent on agriculture (1989)**

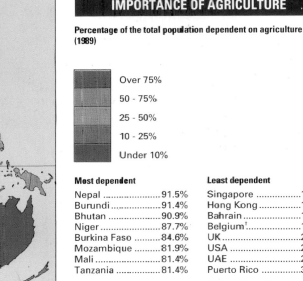

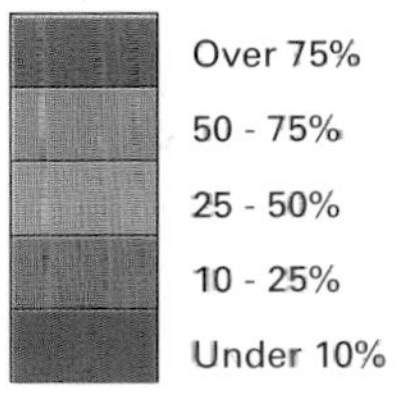
Over 75%
50 - 75%
25 - 50%
10 - 25%
Under 10%

| Most dependent | | Least dependent | |
|---|---|---|---|
| Nepal | 91.5% | Singapore | 1.0% |
| Burundi | 91.4% | Hong Kong | 1.3% |
| Bhutan | 90.9% | Bahrain | 1.8% |
| Niger | 87.7% | Belgium[†] | 1.9% |
| Burkina Faso | 84.6% | UK | 2.0% |
| Mozambique | 81.9% | USA | 2.4% |
| Mali | 81.4% | UAE | 2.7% |
| Tanzania | 81.4% | Puerto Rico | 3.0% |

[†] includes Luxembourg

## FOOD & POPULATION

**Comparison of food production and population by continent (1989). The left column indicates percentage shares of total world food production; the right shows population in proportion.**

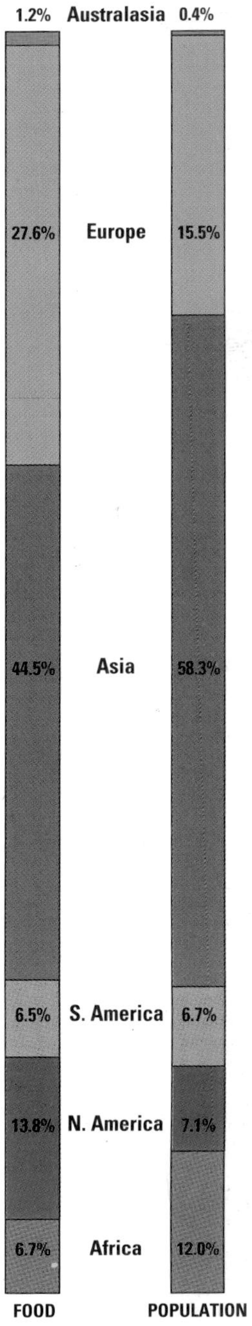
1.2% Australasia 0.4%
27.6% Europe 15.5%
44.5% Asia 58.3%
6.5% S. America 6.7%
13.8% N. America 7.1%
6.7% Africa 12.0%
FOOD
POPULATION

## ANIMAL PRODUCTS

**Separate figures for Russia, Ukraine and the other successors of the defunct USSR are not yet available**

Traditionally, food animals subsisted on land unsuitable for cultivation, supporting agricultural production with their fertilizing dung. But free-ranging animals grow slowly and yield less meat than those more intensively reared; the demands of urban markets in the developed world have encouraged the growth of factory-like production methods. A large proportion of staple crops, especially cereals, are fed to animals, an inefficient way to produce protein but one likely to continue as long as people value meat and dairy products in their diet.

**Cheese:** Least perishable of all dairy products, cheese is milk fermented with selected bacterial strains to produce a foodstuff with a potentially immense range of flavours and textures. The vast majority of cheeses are made from cow's milk, although sheep and goat cheeses are highly prized.

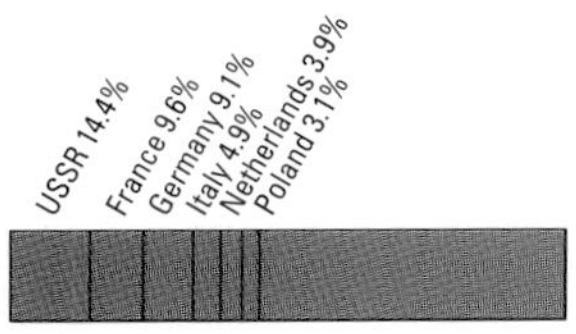
USSR 14.4%
France 9.6%
Germany 9.1%
Italy 4.9%
Netherlands 3.9%
Poland 3.1%

World total (1989): 14,475,276 tonnes

**Lamb & Mutton:** Sheep are the least demanding of domestic animals. Although unsuited to intensive rearing, they can thrive on marginal pastureland incapable of supporting beef cattle on a commercial scale. Sheep are raised as much for their valuable wool as for the meat that they provide, with Australia the world leader.

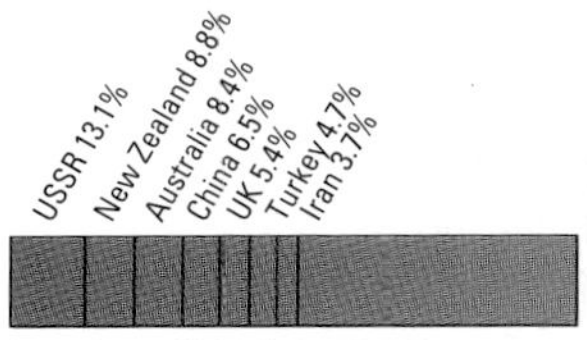
USSR 13.1%
New Zealand 8.8%
Australia 8.4%
China 6.5%
UK 5.4%
Turkey 4.7%
Iran 3.7%

World total (1989): 6,473,000 tonnes

**Beef & Veal:** Most beef and veal is reared for home markets, and the top five producers are also the biggest consumers. The USA produces nearly a quarter of the world's beef and eats even more. Australia, with its small domestic market, is by far the largest exporter.

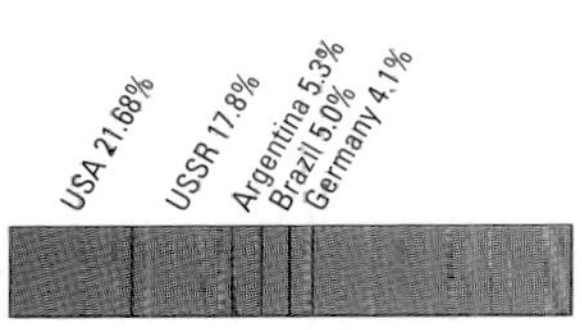
USA 21.68%
USSR 17.8%
Argentina 5.3%
Brazil 5.0%
Germany 4.1%

World total (1989): 49,436,000 tonnes

**Milk:** Many human groups, including most Asians, find raw milk indigestible after infancy, and it is often only the starting point for other dairy products such as butter, cheese and yoghurt. Most world production comes from cows, but sheep's milk and goats' milk are also important.

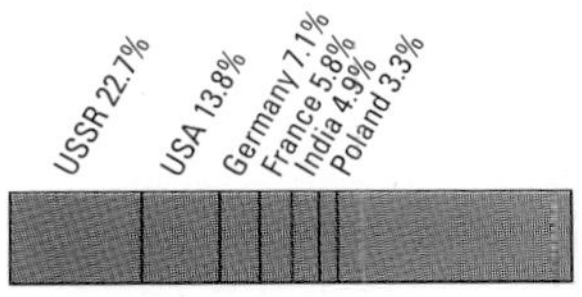
USSR 22.7%
USA 13.8%
Germany 7.1%
France 5.8%
India 4.9%
Poland 3.3%

World total (1989): 474,020,000 tonnes

**Butter:** A traditional source of vitamin A as well as calories, butter has lost much popularity in the developed world for health reasons, although it remains a valuable food. Most butter from India, the world's second-largest producer, is clarified into ghee, which has religious as well as nutritional importance.

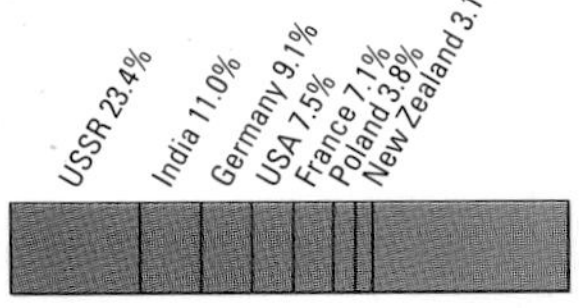
USSR 23.4%
India 11.0%
Germany 9.1%
USA 7.5%
France 7.1%
Poland 3.8%
New Zealand 3.1%

World total (1989): 7,611,826 tonnes

**Pork:** Although pork is forbidden to many millions, notably Muslims, on religious grounds, more is produced than any other meat in the world, mainly because it is the cheapest. It accounts for about 90% of China's meat output, although per capita meat consumption is relatively low.

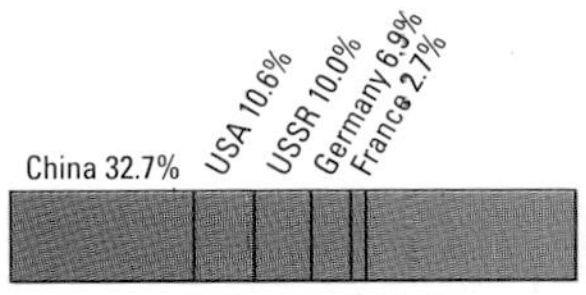
China 32.7%
USA 10.6%
USSR 10.0%
Germany 6.9%
France 2.7%

World total (1989): 67,460,000 tonnes

**Fish:** Commercial fishing requires large shoals of fish, often of only one species, within easy reach of markets. Although the great majority are caught wild in the sea, fish-farming of both marine and freshwater species is assuming increasing importance, especially as natural stocks become depleted.

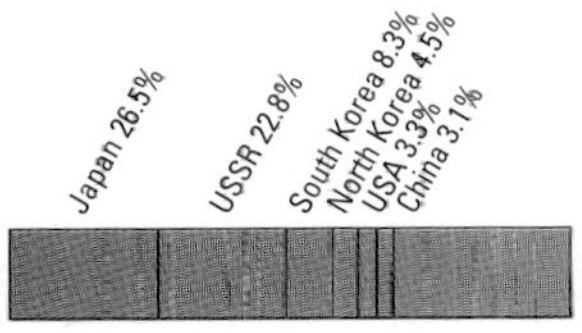
Japan 26.5%
USSR 22.8%
South Korea 8.3%
North Korea 4.5%
USA 3.3%
China 3.1%

World total (1989): 14,143,923 tonnes

## SUGARS

**Sugar cane:** Confined to tropical regions, cane sugar accounts for the bulk of international trade in the commodity. Most is produced as a foodstuff, but some countries, notably Brazil and South Africa, distill sugar cane and use the resulting ethyl alcohol to make motor fuels.

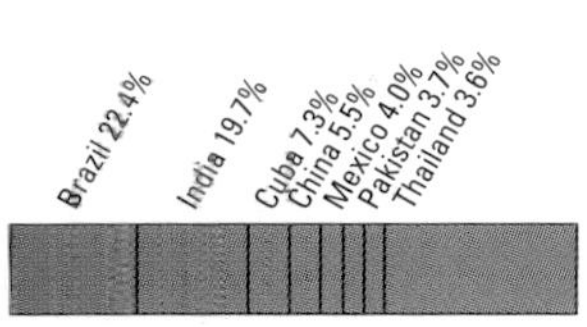
Brazil 22.4%
India 19.7%
Cuba 7.3%
China 5.5%
Mexico 4.0%
Pakistan 3.7%
Thailand 3.6%

World total (1989): 1,007,184,000 tonnes

**Sugar beet:** A temperate crop closely related to the humble beetroot, sugar beet's yield after processing is indistinguishable from cane sugar. Sugar beet is steadily replacing sugar cane imports in Europe, to the detriment of the developing countries that rely on it as a major cash crop.

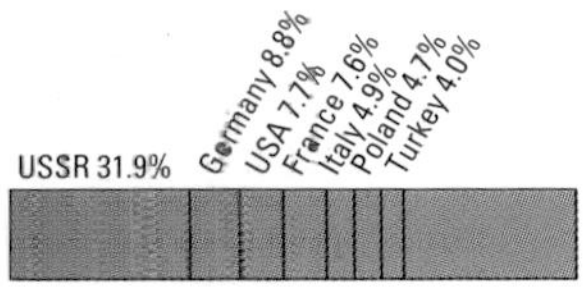
USSR 31.9%
Germany 8.8%
USA 7.7%
France 7.6%
Italy 4.9%
Poland 4.7%
Turkey 4.0%

World total (1989): 305,882,000 tonnes

# PRODUCTION: ENERGY

We live in a high-energy civilization. While vast discrepancies exist between rich and poor – a North American consumes 13 times as much energy as a Chinese, for example – even developing nations have more power at their disposal than was imaginable a century ago. Abundant energy supplies keep us warm or cool, fuel our industries and our transport systems, even feed us: high-intensity agriculture, with its fertilizers, pesticides and machinery, is heavily energy-dependent.

Unfortunately, most of the world's energy comes from fossil fuels: coal, oil and gas deposits laid down over many millions of years. These are the Earth's capital, not its income, and we are consuming that capital at an alarming rate. New discoveries have persistently extended the known reserves: in 1989, the reserves-to-production ratio for oil assured over 45 years' supply, an improvement of almost a decade on the 1970 situation. But despite the effort and ingenuity of prospectors, stocks are clearly limited. They are also very unequally distributed, with the Middle East accounting for most oil reserves, and the CIS, especially Russia, possessing an even higher proportion of the world's natural gas. Coal reserves are more evenly shared, and also more plentiful: coal will outlast oil and gas by a very wide margin.

It is possible to reduce energy demand by improving efficiency: most industrial nations have dramatically increased output since the 1970s without a matching rise in energy consumption. But as fossil stocks continue to diminish, renewable energy sources – solar, wave and wind power, as well as more conventional hydro-electricity – must take on steadily greater importance.

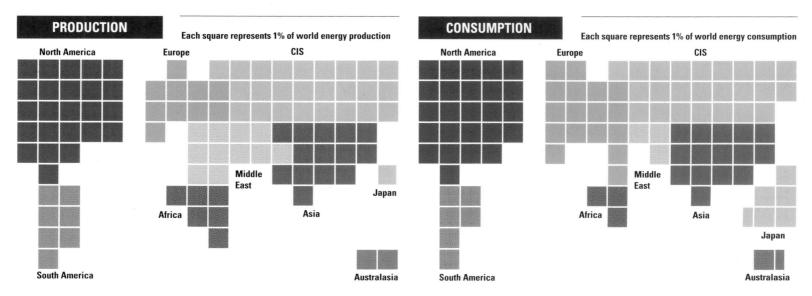

**PRODUCTION** — Each square represents 1% of world energy production

North America · Europe · CIS · Middle East · Japan · Africa · Asia · South America

**CONSUMPTION** — Each square represents 1% of world energy consumption

North America · Europe · CIS · Middle East · Japan · Africa · Asia · South America · Australasia

## CONVERSIONS

For historical reasons, oil is still traded in 'barrels'. The weight and volume equivalents shown below are all based on average density 'Arabian light' crude oil, and should be considered approximate.

The energy equivalents given for a tonne of oil are also somewhat imprecise: oil and coal of different qualities will have varying energy contents, a fact usually reflected in their price on world markets.

**1 barrel:**

- 0.136 tonnes
- 159 litres
- 35 Imperial gallons
- 42 US gallons

**1 tonne:**

- 7.33 barrels
- 1185 litres
- 256 Imperial gallons
- 261 US gallons

**1 tonne oil:**

- 1.5 tonnes hard coal
- 3.0 tonnes lignite
- 12,000 kWh

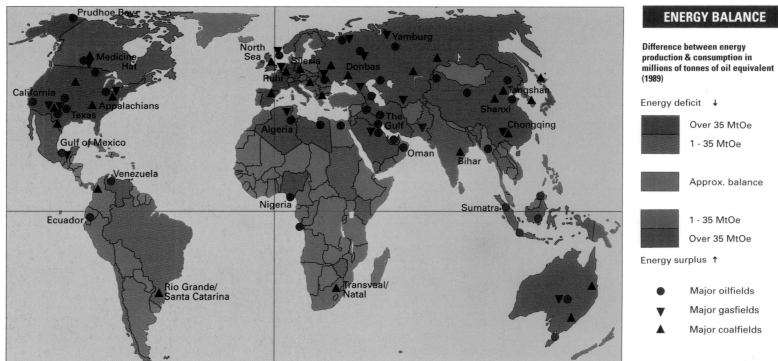

Map labels: Prudhoe Bay, Medicine Hat, California, Appalachians, Texas, Gulf of Mexico, Venezuela, Ecuador, Rio Grande/Santa Catarina, North Sea, Ruhr, Silesia, Donbas, Algeria, Nigeria, The Gulf, Oman, Bihar, Transvaal/Natal, Yamburg, Tangshan, Shanxi, Chongqing, Sumatra

### ENERGY BALANCE

Difference between energy production & consumption in millions of tonnes of oil equivalent (1989)

Energy deficit ↓

- Over 35 MtOe
- 1 - 35 MtOe
- Approx. balance
- 1 - 35 MtOe
- Over 35 MtOe

Energy surplus ↑

- ● Major oilfields
- ▼ Major gasfields
- ▲ Major coalfields

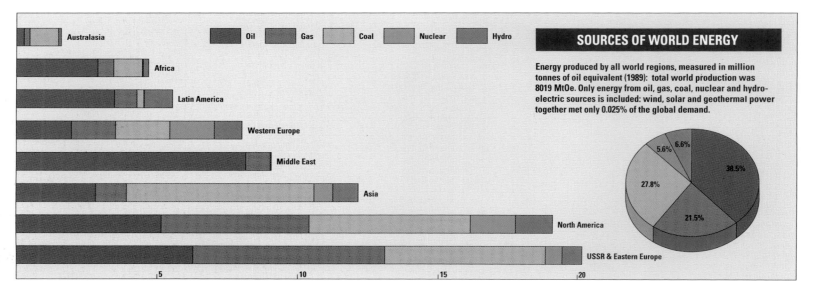

Legend: Oil · Gas · Coal · Nuclear · Hydro

Australasia · Africa · Latin America · Western Europe · Middle East · Asia · North America · USSR & Eastern Europe

5 · 10 · 15 · 20

### SOURCES OF WORLD ENERGY

Energy produced by all world regions, measured in million tonnes of oil equivalent (1989): total world production was 8019 MtOe. Only energy from oil, gas, coal, nuclear and hydro-electric sources is included: wind, solar and geothermal power together met only 0.025% of the global demand.

Pie chart: 38.5%, 21.5%, 27.8%, 5.6%, 6.6%

## FOSSIL FUEL RESERVES

Known world reserves in years as a multiple of annual production, 1970, 1980 and 1989

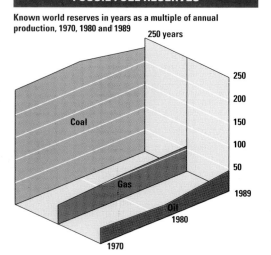

250 years

## ENERGY AND OUTPUT

Tonnes of oil equivalent consumed to produce US $1000 of GDP, four industrial nations (1973-89)

Intensity of energy use is a rough indicator of efficiency: the 1973-4 oil crisis caused a dramatic improvement in each of the countries illustrated, though the USA remains relatively profligate. Exactly comparable figures for communist economies are not available, but estimates suggest that for equivalent production, the USSR and China use between two and four times as much energy as the USA.

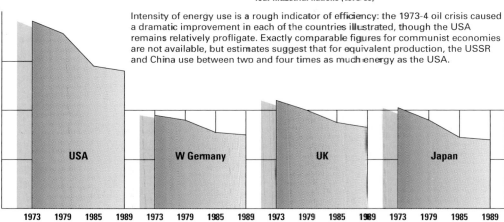

## COAL RESERVES

World coal reserves by region & country, thousand million tonnes (1988)

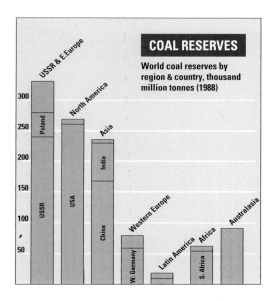

## GAS RESERVES

World natural gas reserves by region & country, thousand million tonnes (1988)

Ca: Canada
In: Indonesia
Ma: Malaysia
AD: Abu Dhabi
SA: Saudi Arabia
Qa: Qatar
Iq: Iraq
No: Norway
Ne: Netherlands
Ve: Venezuela
Mx: Mexico
Al: Algeria
Ni: Nigeria

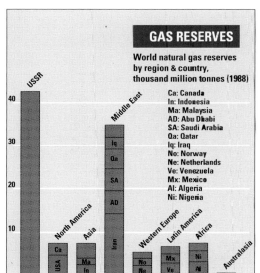

## OIL RESERVES

World oil reserves by region & country, thousand million tonnes (1988)

AD: Abu Dhabi
Ve: Venezuela
Mx: Mexico

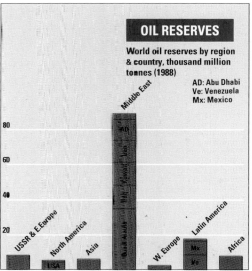

## OIL MOVEMENTS

Major world movements of oil in millions of tonnes (1989)

| | |
|---|---:|
| Middle East to Western Europe | 195.5 |
| Middle East to Japan | 150.0 |
| Middle East to Asia (exc. Japan and China) | 127.5 |
| Latin America to USA | 126.1 |
| Middle East to USA | 94.1 |
| USSR to Western Europe | 78.1 |
| North Africa to Western Europe | 93.5 |
| West Africa to Western Europe | 39.6 |
| West Africa to USA | 59.8 |
| Canada to USA | 45.0 |
| South-East Asia to Japan | 42.2 |
| Latin America to Western Europe | 28.7 |
| Western Europe to USA | 28.7 |
| Middle East to Latin America | 20.5 |

**Total world movements: 1577 million tonnes**

Only inter-regional movements in excess of 20 million tonnes are shown. Other Middle Eastern oil shipments throughout the world totalled 47.4 million tonnes; miscellaneous USSR oil exports amounted to 88.8 million tonnes.

## FUEL EXPORTS

Fuels as a percentage of total value of all exports (1986)

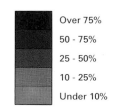

Over 75%
50 - 75%
25 - 50%
10 - 25%
Under 10%

**Direction of trade**

Coal
Oil

Arrows show the major trade direction of selected fuels, & are proportional to export value

## NUCLEAR POWER

Percentage of electricity generated by nuclear power stations, leading nations (1988)

| | | |
|---|---|---|
| 1. France ............... 70% | 11. W. Germany ...... 34% |
| 2. Belgium ............. 66% | 12. Japan ................ 28% |
| 3. Hungary ............. 49% | 13. Czechoslovakia.. 27% |
| 4. South Korea ...... 47% | 14. UK .................... 18% |
| 5. Sweden ............. 46% | 15. USA ................. 17% |
| 6. Taiwan .............. 41% | 16. Canada ........... 16% |
| 7. Switzerland ....... 37% | 17. Argentina ......... 12% |
| 8. Finland .............. 36% | 18. USSR ............... 11% |
| 9. Spain ................. 36% | 19. Yugoslavia ........ 6% |
| 10. Bulgaria ............. 36% | 20. Netherlands ...... 5% |

The decade 1980-1990 was a bad time for the nuclear power industry. Major projects regularly ran vastly over-budget, and fears of long-term environmental damage were heavily reinforced by the 1986 Soviet disaster at Chernobyl. Although the number of reactors in service continued to increase throughout the period, orders for new plant shrank dramatically, and most countries cut back on their nuclear programmes.

## HYDRO-ELECTRICITY

Percentage of electricity generated by hydro-electrical power stations, leading nations (1988)

| | |
|---|---|
| 1. Paraguay ......... 99.9% | 11. Laos ................ 95.5% |
| 2. Zambia ........... 99.6% | 12. Nepal .............. 95.2% |
| 3. Norway............ 99.5% | 13. Iceland ............ 94.0% |
| 4. Congo .............. 99.1% | 14. Uruguay .......... 93.0% |
| 5. Costa Rica ...... 98.3% | 15. Brazil................ 91.7% |
| 6. Uganda ........... 98.3% | 16. Albania ........... 87.2% |
| 7. Rwanda ........... 97.7% | 17. Fiji ................... 81.4% |
| 8. Malawi ........... 97.6% | 18. Ecuador .......... 80.7% |
| 9. Zaïre ............... 97.4% | 19. C. African Rep. 80.4% |
| 10. Cameroon ....... 97.2% | 20. Sri Lanka ......... 80.4% |

Countries heavily reliant on hydro-electricity are usually small and non-industrial: a high proportion of hydro-electric power more often reflects a modest energy budget than vast hydro-electric resources. The USA, for instance, produces only 8% of power requirements from hydro-electricity; yet that 8% amounts to more than three times the hydro-power generated by all of Africa.

## ALTERNATIVE ENERGY SOURCES

**Solar:** Each year the sun bestows upon the Earth almost a million times as much energy as is locked up in all the planet's oil reserves, but only an insignificant fraction is trapped and used commercially. In some experimental installations, mirrors focus the sun's rays on to boilers, whose steam generates electricity by spinning turbines. Solar cells turn the sunlight into electricity directly, and although efficiencies are still low, advancing technology offers some prospect of using the sun as the main world electricity source by 2100.

**Wind:** Caused by uneven heating of the Earth, winds are themselves a form of solar energy. Windmills have been used for centuries to turn wind power into mechanical work; recent models, often arranged in banks on gust-swept high ground, usually generate electricity.

**Tidal:** The energy from tides is potentially enormous, although only a few installations have been built to exploit it. In theory at least, waves and currents could also provide almost unimaginable power, and the thermal differences in the ocean depths are another huge well of potential energy. But work on extracting it is still in the experimental stage.

**Geothermal:** The Earth's temperature rises by 1°C for every 30 metres' descent, with much steeper temperature gradients in geologically active areas. El Salvador, for example, produces 39% of its electricity from geothermal power stations. More than 130 are operating worldwide.

**Biomass:** The oldest of human fuels ranges from animal dung, still burned in cooking fires in much of North Africa and elsewhere, to sugar cane plantations feeding high-technology distilleries to produce ethanol for motor vehicle engines. In Brazil and South Africa, plant ethanol provides up to 25% of motor fuel. Throughout the developing world most biomass energy comes from firewood: although accurate figures are impossible to obtain, it may yield as much as 10% of the world's total energy consumption.

33

# PRODUCTION: MINERALS

Even during the Stone Age, when humans often settled near the outcrops of flint on which their technology depended, mineral resources have attracted human exploiters. Their descendants have learned how to make use of almost every known element. These elements can be found, in one form or another, somewhere in the Earth's bountiful crust. Iron remains the most important, but modern industrial civilization has a voracious appetite for virtually all of them.

Mineral deposits once dictated the site of new industries; today, most industrial countries are heavily dependent on imports for many of their key materials. Most mining, and much refining of raw ores, is done in developing countries, where labour is cheap.

The main map below shows the richest sources of the most important minerals at present; some reserves – lead and mercury, for example – are running very low. The map takes no account of undersea deposits, most of which are considered inaccessible. Growing shortages, though, may encourage submarine mining: plans have already been made to recover the nodules of manganese found widely scattered on ocean floors.

## MINERAL EXPORTS

**Minerals & metals as a percentage of total exports (1986)**

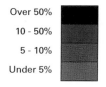

- Over 50%
- 10 - 50%
- 5 - 10%
- Under 5%

**Direction of trade**

- Copper
- Iron
- Bauxite (Aluminium)

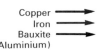

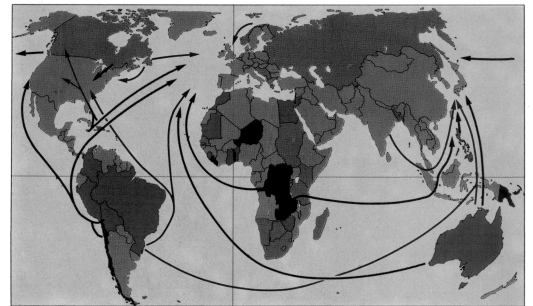

## URANIUM

In its pure state, uranium is an immensely heavy, white metal; but although spent uranium is employed as projectiles in anti-missile cannon, where its mass ensures a lethal punch, its main use is as a fuel in nuclear reactors, and in nuclear weaponry. Uranium is very scarce: the main source is the rare ore pitchblende, which itself contains only 0.2% uranium oxide. Only a minute fraction of that is the radioactive $U^{235}$ isotope, though so-called breeder reactors can transmute the more common $U^{238}$ into highly radioactive plutonium.

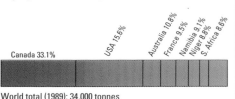

Canada 33.1% | USA 15.6% | Australia 10.8% | France 9.5% | Namibia 9.1% | Niger 8.9% | S. Africa 8.6%

World total (1989): 34,000 tonnes

## METALS

Separate figures for Russia, Ukraine and the other successors of the defunct USSR are not as yet available

**Aluminium:** Produced mainly from its oxide, bauxite, which yields 25% of its weight in aluminium. The cost of refining and production is often too high for producer-countries to bear, so bauxite is largely exported. Lightweight and corrosion resistant, aluminium alloys are widely used in aircraft, vehicles, cans and packaging.

USA 22.4% | USSR 13.2% | Canada 8.6% | Australia 6.9% | Brazil 4.9% | Norway 4.8% | Germany 4.%

World total (1989): 18,000,000 tonnes *

**Copper:** Derived from low-yielding sulphide ores, copper is an important export for several developing countries. An excellent conductor of heat and electricity, it forms part of most electrical items, and is used in the manufacture of brass and bronze. Major importers include Japan and Germany.

Chile 17.7% | USA 16.5% | USSR 10.4% | Canada 8.1% | Zambia 5.5% | Zaïre 4.9% | Poland 4.4% | China 4.2%

World total (1989): 9,100,000 tonnes *

**Lead:** A soft metal, obtained mainly from galena (lead sulphide), which occurs in veins associated with iron, zinc and silver sulphides. Its use in vehicle batteries accounts for the USA's prime consumer status; lead is also made into sheeting and piping. Its use as an additive to paints and petrol is decreasing.

USSR 14.7% | Australia 14.6% | USA 12.3% | China 10.1% | Canada 8.1% | Peru 5.7% | Mexico 4.8%

World total (1989): 3,400,000 tonnes *

**Mercury:** The only metal that is liquid at normal temperatures, most is derived from its sulphide, cinnabar, found only in small quantities in volcanic areas. Apart from its value in thermometers and other instruments, most mercury production is used in anti-fungal and anti-fouling preparations, and to make detonators.

USSR 27.3% | China 18.2% | Spain 17.6% | Algeria 12% | USA 7.8% | Mexico 6.3% | Turkey 3.7%

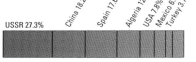

World total (1989): 5,500,000 kilograms *

**Tin:** Soft, pliable and non-toxic, used to coat 'tin' (tin-plated steel) cans, in the manufacture of foils and in alloys. The principal tin-bearing mineral is cassiterite ($SnO_2$), found in ore formed from molten rock. Producers and refiners were hit by a price collapse in 1991.

Brazil 22.5% | China 14.9% | Malaysia 14.4% | Indonesia 14.2% | Bolivia 7.1% | Thailand 6.6% | USSR 6.3%

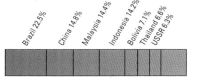

World total (1989): 223,000 tonnes *

**Zinc:** Often found in association with lead ores, zinc is highly resistant to corrosion, and about 40% of the refined metal is used to plate sheet steel, particularly vehicle bodies – a process known as galvanizing. Zinc is also used in dry batteries, paints and dyes.

Canada 16.6% | USSR 12.9% | Australia 11.0% | China 8.5% | Peru 8.2% | USA 4.0% | Mexico 3.9%

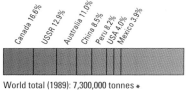

World total (1989): 7,300,000 tonnes *

## DIAMOND

Most diamond is found in kimberlite, or "blue ground", a basic peridotite rock; erosion may wash the diamond from its kimberlite matrix and deposit it with sand or gravel on river beds. Only a small proportion of the world's diamond, the most flawless, is cut into gemstones - "diamonds"; most is used in industry, where the material's remarkable hardness and abrasion resistance finds a use in cutting tools, drills and dies, as well as in styluses. Australia, not among the top 12 producers at the beginning of the 1980s, had by 1986 become world leader and by 1989 was the source of 37.5% of world production. The other main producers were Zaïre (18.9%), Botswana (16.3%), the then USSR (11.8%) and South Africa (9.7%). Between them, these five nations accounted for over 94% of the world total of 96,600,000 carats - at 0.2 grams per carat, almost one tonne.

**Gold:** Regarded for centuries as the most valuable metal in the world and used to make coins, gold is still recognized as the monetary standard. A soft metal, it is alloyed to make jewellery; the electronics industry values its corrosion resistance and conductivity.

S. Africa 29.9% | USSR 14.1% | USA 13.1% | Australia 10.0% | Canada 7.9% | China 4.2% | Brazil 2.4%

World total (1989): 2,026,000 kilograms *

**Silver:** Most silver comes from ores mined and processed for other metals (including lead and copper). Pure or alloyed with harder metals, it is used for jewellery and ornaments. Industrial use includes dentistry, electronics, photography and as a chemical catalyst.

Mexico 15.5% | USA 13.5% | Peru 12.4% | USSR 10.1% | Canada 8.8% | Australia 7.2% | Poland 6.7%

World total (1989): 14,896,000 kilograms *

*Figures for aluminium are for refined metal, all other figures refer to ore production.*

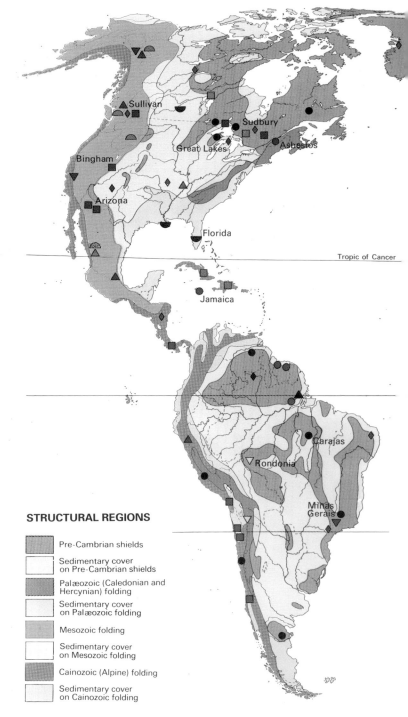

Tropic of Cancer

### STRUCTURAL REGIONS

- Pre-Cambrian shields
- Sedimentary cover on Pre-Cambrian shields
- Palæozoic (Caledonian and Hercynian) folding
- Sedimentary cover on Palæozoic folding
- Mesozoic folding
- Sedimentary cover on Mesozoic folding
- Cainozoic (Alpine) folding
- Sedimentary cover on Cainozoic folding

## IRON & FERRO-ALLOYS

Ever since the art of high-temperature smelting was discovered, some time in the second millennium BC, iron has been by far the most important metal known to man. The earliest iron ploughs transformed primitive agriculture and led to the first human population explosion, while iron weapons - or the lack of them - ensured the rise or fall of entire cultures.

Widely distributed around the world, iron ores usually contain 25-60% iron; blast furnaces process the raw product into pig-iron, which is then alloyed with carbon other minerals to produce steels of various qualities. From the time of the Industrial Revolution steel has been almost literally the backbone of modern civilization, the prime structural material on which all else is built.

Iron-smelting usually developed close to sources of ore and, later, to the coalfields that fueled the furnaces. Today, most ore comes from a few richly-endowed locations where large-scale mining is possible. Iron and steel plants are generally built at coastal sites so that giant ore carriers, which account for a sizeable proportion of the world's merchant fleet, can easily discharge their cargoes.

World production of pig iron and ferro-alloys (1988). All countries with an annual output of more than one million tonnes are shown

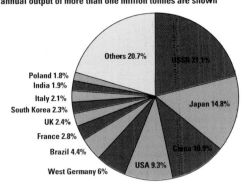

Others 20.7%
USSR 21.1%
Japan 14.8%
Poland 1.8%
India 1.9%
Italy 2.1%
South Korea 2.3%
UK 2.4%
France 2.8%
Brazil 4.4%
China 10.9%
West Germany 6%
USA 9.3%

**Total world production: 545 million tonnes**

Development of world production of pig iron and ferro-alloys (1945-1988) in million tonnes

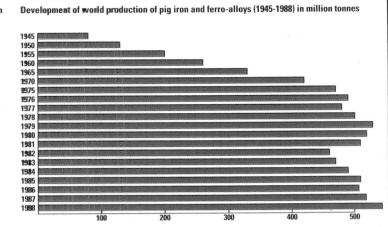

**Chromium:** Most of the world's chromium production is alloyed with iron and other metals to produce steels with various different properties. Combined with iron, nickel, cobalt and tungsten, chromium produces an exceptionally hard steel, resistant to heat; chrome steels are used for many household items where utility must be matched with appearance - cutlery, for example. Chromium is also used in production of refractory bricks, and its salts for tanning and dyeing leather and cloth.

**Manganese:** In its pure state, manganese is a hard, brittle metal. Alloyed with chrome, iron and nickel, it produces abrasion-resistant steels; manganese-aluminium alloys are light but tough. Found in batteries and inks, manganese is also used in glass production. Manganese ores are frequently found in the same location as sedimentary iron ores. Pyrolusite ($MnO_2$) and psilomelane are the main economically-exploitable sources.

**Nickel:** Combined with chrome and iron, nickel produces stainless and high-strength steels; similar alloys go to make magnets and electrical heating elements. Nickel combined with copper is widely used to make coins; cupro-nickel alloy is very resistant to corrosion. Its ores yield only modest quantities of nickel - 0.5 to 3.0% - but also contain copper, iron and small amounts of precious metals. Japan, the USA, the UK, Germany and France are the principal importers.

USSR 24.4% | China 17.2% | Brazil 15.5% | Australia 10.7% | USA 5.8% | India 5.2% | Canada 4.1% | South Africa 3.0% | Sweden 2.2%

World total production of iron ore (1989): 989,000,000 tonnes

S. Africa 33.7% | USSR 28.9% | India 7.9% | Turkey 6.7% | Albania 5.5% | Zimbabwe 4.9% | Finland 3.3%

World total (1989): 12,700,000 tonnes

USSR 36.7% | S. Africa 15.1% | China 11.3% | Gabon 9.7% | Australia 8.9% | India 5.6%

World total (1989): 24,000,000 tonnes

USSR 23.1% | Canada 22.3% | New Caledonia 10.6% | Australia 7.1% | Indonesia 6.6% | Cuba 4.9% | S. Africa 3.7%

World total (1989): 910,000 tonnes

## DISTRIBUTION

### Base metals
- ■ Copper
- ▲ Lead
- ⏚ Mercury
- ▽ Tin
- ◆ Zinc

### Iron and ferro-alloys
- ● Iron
- ⏚ Chrome
- ▣ Nickel
- ▲ Manganese

### Light metals
- ● Bauxite

### Rare metals
- ◆ Uranium

### Precious metals
- ▼ Gold
- ⏚ Silver

### Precious stones
- ◆ Diamonds

### Mineral fertilizers
- ⏚ Phosphates

### Industrial minerals
- ● Asbestos

Map labels: Murmansk, Norilsk, Mirnyy, Urals, Nikopol, Krivoy Rog, Almadén, Kounradskiy, Hebei, Central Morocco, Agadez, Yunnan, Bihar, Goa, Philippines, Guinea, Malaysia, Belitung, Bakwanga, Ok Tedi, Copperbelt, Gove, Weipa, Argyle, Great Dyke, Hamersley Range, Mt. Isa, New Caledonia, Orapa, Witwatersrand, Kimberley, Kalgoorlie, Roxby Downs, Broken Hill

ic of Capricorn

# PRODUCTION: MANUFACTURING

In its broadest sense, manufacturing is the application of energy, labour and skill to raw materials in order to transform them into finished goods with a higher value than the various elements used in production.

Since the early days of the Industrial Revolution, manufacturing has implied the use of an organized workforce harnessed to some form of machine. The tendency has consistently been for increasingly expensive human labour to be replaced by increasingly complex machinery, which has evolved over time from water-powered looms to fully-integrated robotic plants.

Obviously, not all industries – or manufacturing countries - have reached the same level. Textiles, for example, the foundation of the early industrial revolution in the West, can be mass-produced with fairly modest technology; today, they are usually produced in developing countries, mostly in Asia, where low labour costs compensate for the large workforce the relatively simple machinery requires. Nevertheless, the trend towards high-technology production, however uneven, seems inexorable. Gains in efficiency make up for the staggering cost of the equipment itself, and the outcome is that fewer and fewer people are employed to produce more and more goods.

One paradoxical result of the increase in industrial efficiency is a relative decline in the importance of the industrial sector of a nation's economy. The economy has already passed through one transition, generations past, when workers were drawn from the land into factories. The second transition releases labour into what is called the service sector of the economy: a diffuse but vital concept that includes not only such obvious services as transport and administration, but also finance, insurance and activities as diverse as fashion design or the writing of computer software.

The process is far advanced in the mature economies of the West, with Japan not far behind. Almost two-thirds of US wealth, for example, is now generated in the service sector, and less than half of Japanese Gross National Product comes from industry. The shrinkage, though, is only relative: between them, these two industrial giants produce almost twice as much manufactured goods as the rest of the world put together. And it is on the solid base of production that the rest of their prosperity rests.

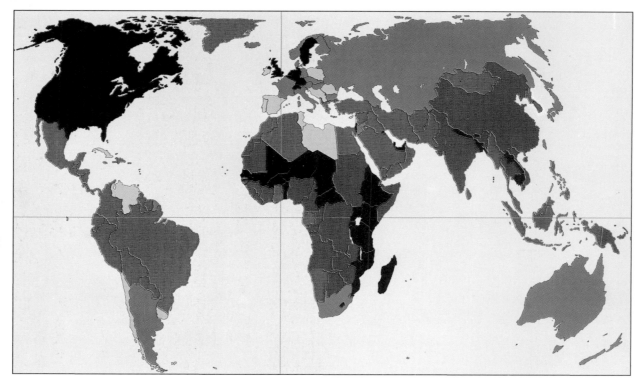

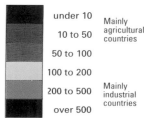

## EMPLOYMENT

The number of workers employed in manufacturing for every 100 workers engaged in agriculture

| | | |
|---|---|---|
| | under 10 | Mainly agricultural countries |
| | 10 to 50 | |
| | 50 to 100 | |
| | 100 to 200 | |
| | 200 to 500 | Mainly industrial countries |
| | over 500 | |

Selected countries
(latest available figure, 1986-1989)

| | |
|---|---|
| Singapore | 6,166 |
| Hong Kong | 2,632 |
| UK | 912 |
| Belgium | 751 |
| Germany (W) | 749 |
| USA | 641 |
| Sweden | 615 |
| France | 331 |
| Japan | 320 |
| Czechoslovakia | 286 |

## DIVISION OF EMPLOYMENT

Distribution of workers between agriculture, industry and services, selected countries (late 1980s)

The six countries selected illustrate the usual stages of economic development, from dependence on agriculture through industrial growth to the expansion of the services sector.

- Agriculture
- Industry
- Services

Nepal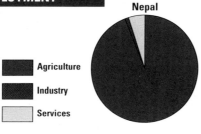

Nigeria

Pakistan

Brazil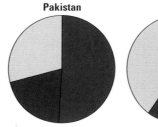

Hong Kong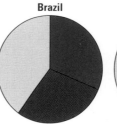

USA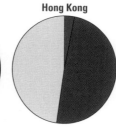

## THE WORKFORCE

Percentages of men and women between 15 and 64 in employment, selected countries (late 1980s)

The figures include employees and self-employed, who in developing countries are often subsistence farmers. People in full-time education are excluded. Because of the population age structure in developing countries, the employed population has to support a far larger number of non-workers than its industrial equivalent. For example, more than 52% of Kenya's people are under 15, an age group that makes up less than a tenth of the UK population.

Men  Women

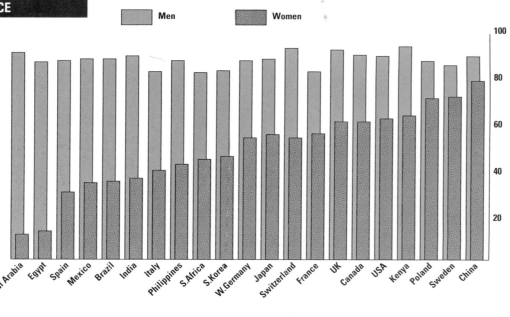

## WEALTH CREATION

The Gross National Product (GNP) of the world's largest economies, US $ billion (1989)

| | | | | | |
|---|---|---|---|---|---|
| 1. | USA | 5,237,707 | 21. | Denmark | 105,263 |
| 2. | Japan | 2,920,310 | 22. | Norway | 92,097 |
| 3. | Germany | 1,272,959 | 23. | Saudi Arabia | 89,986 |
| 4. | France | 1,000,866 | 24. | Indonesia | 87,936 |
| 5. | Italy | 871,955 | 25. | South Africa | 86,029 |
| 6. | UK | 834,166 | 26. | Turkey | 74,731 |
| 7. | Canada | 500,337 | 27. | Argentina | 68,780 |
| 8. | China | 393,006 | 28. | Poland | 66,974 |
| 9. | Brazil | 375,146 | 29. | Thailand | 64,437 |
| 10. | Spain | 358,352 | 30. | Hong Kong | 59,202 |
| 11. | India | 287,383 | 31. | Yugoslavia | 59,080 |
| 12. | Australia | 242,131 | 32. | Greece | 53,626 |
| 13. | Netherlands | 237,451 | 33. | Algeria | 53,116 |
| 14. | Switzerland | 197,984 | 34. | Venezuela | 47,164 |
| 15. | South Korea | 186,467 | 35. | Israel | 44,131 |
| 16. | Sweden | 184,230 | 36. | Portugal | 44,058 |
| 17. | Mexico | 170,053 | 37. | Philippines | 42,754 |
| 18. | Belgium | 162,026 | 38. | Pakistan | 40,134 |
| 19. | Austria | 131,899 | 39. | New Zealand | 39,437 |
| 20. | Finland | 109,705 | 40. | Colombia | 38,607 |

There are no accurate figures available for either the USSR or its successor nations.

## PATTERNS OF PRODUCTION

Breakdown of industrial output by value, selected countries (1987)

| | Food & agriculture | Textiles & clothing | Machinery & transport | Chemicals | Other |
|---|---|---|---|---|---|
| Algeria | 26% | 20% | 11% | 1% | 41% |
| Argentina | 24% | 10% | 16% | 12% | 37% |
| Australia | 18% | 7% | 21% | 8% | 45% |
| Austria | 17% | 8% | 25% | 6% | 43% |
| Belgium | 19% | 8% | 23% | 13% | 36% |
| Brazil | 15% | 12% | 24% | 9% | 40% |
| Burkina Faso | 62% | 18% | 2% | 1% | 17% |
| Canada | 15% | 7% | 25% | 9% | 44% |
| Denmark | 22% | 6% | 23% | 10% | 39% |
| Egypt | 20% | 27% | 13% | 10% | 31% |
| Finland | 13% | 6% | 24% | 7% | 50% |
| France | 18% | 7% | 33% | 9% | 33% |
| Greece | 20% | 22% | 14% | 7% | 38% |
| Hong Kong | 6% | 40% | 20% | 2% | 33% |
| Hungary | 6% | 11% | 37% | 11% | 35% |
| India | 11% | 16% | 26% | 15% | 32% |
| Indonesia | 23% | 11% | 10% | 10% | 47% |
| Iran | 13% | 22% | 22% | 7% | 36% |
| Israel | 13% | 10% | 28% | 8% | 42% |
| Ireland | 28% | 7% | 20% | 15% | 28% |
| Italy | 7% | 13% | 32% | 10% | 38% |
| Japan | 10% | 6% | 38% | 10% | 37% |
| Kenya | 35% | 12% | 14% | 9% | 29% |
| Malaysia | 21% | 5% | 23% | 14% | 37% |
| Mexico | 24% | 12% | 14% | 12% | 39% |
| Netherlands | 19% | 4% | 28% | 11% | 38% |
| New Zealand | 26% | 10% | 16% | 6% | 43% |
| Norway | 21% | 3% | 26% | 7% | 44% |
| Pakistan | 34% | 21% | 8% | 12% | 25% |
| Philippines | 40% | 7% | 7% | 10% | 35% |
| Poland | 15% | 16% | 30% | 6% | 33% |
| Portugal | 17% | 22% | 16% | 8% | 38% |
| Singapore | 6% | 5% | 46% | 8% | 36% |
| South Africa | 14% | 8% | 17% | 11% | 49% |
| South Korea | 15% | 17% | 24% | 9% | 35% |
| Spain | 17% | 9% | 22% | 9% | 43% |
| Sweden | 10% | 2% | 35% | 8% | 44% |
| Thailand | 30% | 17% | 14% | 6% | 33% |
| Turkey | 20% | 14% | 15% | 8% | 43% |
| UK | 14% | 6% | 32% | 11% | 36% |
| USA | 12% | 5% | 35% | 10% | 38% |
| Venezuela | 23% | 8% | 9% | 11% | 49% |
| W.Germany | 12% | 5% | 38% | 10% | 36% |
| Yugoslavia | 13% | 17% | 25% | 6% | 39% |

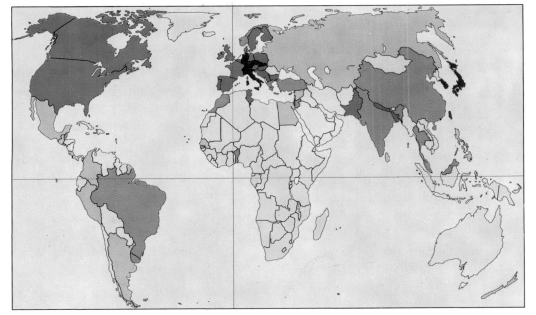

## INDUSTRY & TRADE

Manufactured goods as a percentage of total exports (1989)

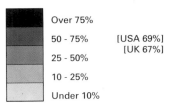

- Over 75%
- 50 - 75%    [USA 69%]
- 25 - 50%    [UK 67%]
- 10 - 25%
- Under 10%

The Far East & South-East Asia (Japan 99.5%, Macau 98.5%, Taiwan 96.8%, Hong Kong 96.1%, S. Korea 95.9%) is most dominant, but many countries in Europe (eg Austria 98.4%) are also heavily dependent on manufactured goods.

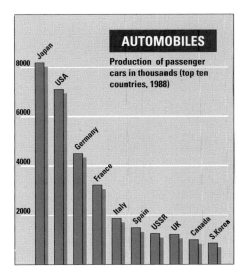

### AUTOMOBILES
Production of passenger cars in thousands (top ten countries, 1988)

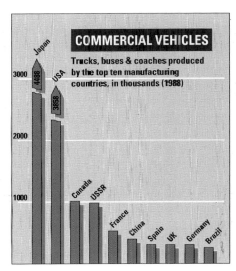

### COMMERCIAL VEHICLES
Trucks, buses & coaches produced by the top ten manufacturing countries, in thousands (1988)

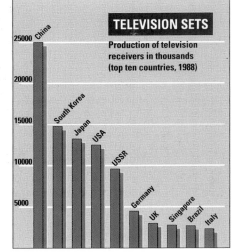

### TELEVISION SETS
Production of television receivers in thousands (top ten countries, 1988)

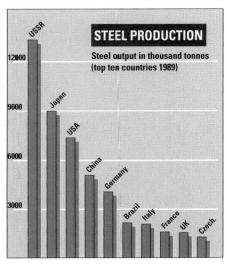

### STEEL PRODUCTION
Steel output in thousand tonnes (top ten countries 1989)

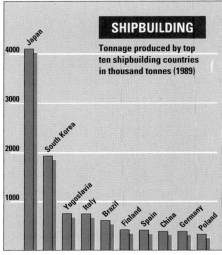

### SHIPBUILDING
Tonnage produced by top ten shipbuilding countries in thousand tonnes (1989)

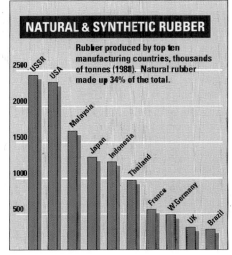

### NATURAL & SYNTHETIC RUBBER
Rubber produced by top ten manufacturing countries, thousands of tonnes (1988). Natural rubber made up 34% of the total.

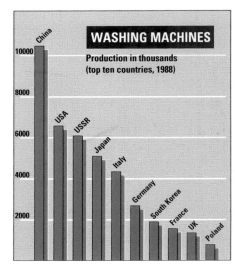

### WASHING MACHINES
Production in thousands (top ten countries, 1988)

## INDUSTRIAL POWER

Industrial output (mining, manufacturing, construction, energy & water production), top 40 nations, US $ billion (1988)

| | | | | | |
|---|---|---|---|---|---|
| 1. USA | 1,249.54 | | 21. Austria | 50.63 |
| 2. Japan | 1,155.41 | | 22. Belgium | 46.88 |
| 3. Germany | 479.69 | | 23. Poland | 39.52 |
| 4. USSR | 326.54 | | 24. Finland | 35.50 |
| 5. France | 304.95 | | 25. South Africa | 35.46 |
| 6. UK | 295.00 | | 26. Saudi Arabia | 33.36 |
| 7. Italy | 286.00 | | 27. Denmark | 30.79 |
| 8. China | 174.05 | | 28. Iraq | 30.27 |
| 9. Canada | 171.06 | | 29. Czechoslovakia | 30.18 |
| 10. Spain | 126.60 | | 30. Yugoslavia | 29.32 |
| 11. Brazil | 116.13 | | 31. Indonesia | 29.03 |
| 12. Netherlands | 76.48 | | 32. Norway | 28.74 |
| 13. Sweden | 75.17 | | 33. Argentina | 26.27 |
| 14. South Korea | 74.00 | | 34. Turkey | 26.07 |
| 15. India | 72.69 | | 35. Israel | 24.15 |
| 16. Australia | 72.63 | | 36. Algeria | 22.88 |
| 17. E. Germany | 64.66 | | 37. Venezuela | 22.70 |
| 18. Switzerland | 63.37 | | 38. Romania | 22.19 |
| 19. Mexico | 61.57 | | 39. Iran | 19.90 |
| 20. Taiwan | 54.81 | | 40. Thailand | 18.62 |

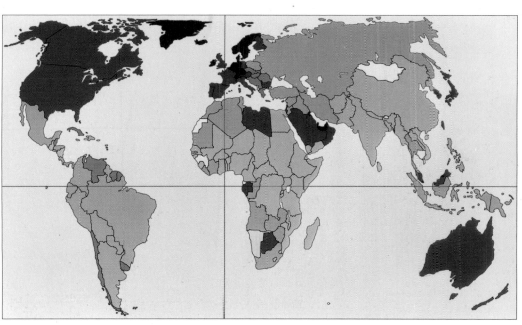

## EXPORTS PER CAPITA

Value of exports in US $, divided by total population (1988)

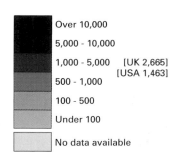

- Over 10,000
- 5,000 - 10,000
- 1,000 - 5,000    [UK 2,665]
- 500 - 1,000    [USA 1,463]
- 100 - 500
- Under 100
- No data available

**Highest per capita**

| | |
|---|---|
| Singapore | 16,671 |
| Hong Kong | 12,676 |
| UAE | 10,217 |
| Belgium | 10,200 |
| Bahamas | 8,580 |
| Qatar | 8,431 |

# PRODUCTION: TRADE

Thriving international trade is the outward sign of a healthy world economy – the obvious indicator that some countries have goods to sell and others the wherewithal to buy them. Despite local fluctuations, trade throughout the 1980s grew consistently faster than output, increasing in value by almost 50% in the decade 1979-89. It remains dominated by the wealthy, industrialized countries of the Organization for Economic Development: between them, the 24 OECD members account for almost 75% of world imports and exports in most years. OECD dominance is just as marked in the trade in 'invisibles' - a column in the balance sheet that includes, among other headings, the export of services, interest payments on overseas investments, tourism and even remittances from migrant workers abroad. In the UK, 'invisibles' account for more than half all trading income.

However, the size of these great trading economies means that imports and exports usually comprise a fraction of their total wealth: in the case of the export-conscious Japanese, trade in goods and services amounts to less than 18% of GDP. In poorer countries, trade - often in a single commodity - may amount to 50% GDP or more. And there are oddities: import-export figures for the entrepôt economy of Singapore, for example, the transit point for much Asian trade, are almost double that small nation's total earnings.

## WORLD TRADE

**Percentage of total world exports by value (1989)**

- Over 10%
- 5 - 10%
- 1 - 5%
- 0.5 - 1%
- 0.25 - 0.5%
- Under 0.25%

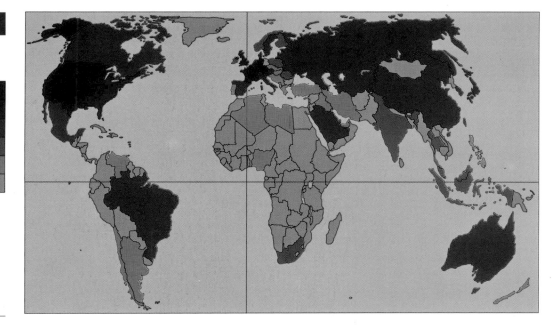

[USA 15.7%]  [UK 6.3%]

## THE GREAT TRADING NATIONS

The imports and exports of the top ten trading nations as a percentage of world trade (1989). Each country's trade in manufactured goods is shown in orange.

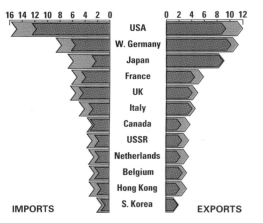

USA
W. Germany
Japan
France
UK
Italy
Canada
USSR
Netherlands
Belgium
Hong Kong
S. Korea

IMPORTS     EXPORTS

## MAJOR EXPORTS

Leading manufactured items and their exporters, by percentage of world total in US dollars (late 1980s)

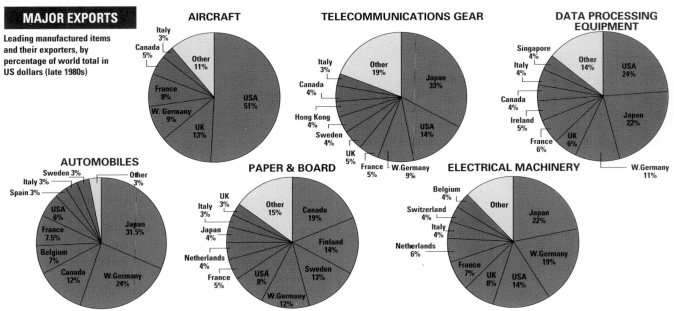

**AIRCRAFT**
- Italy 3%
- Canada 5%
- France 8%
- W. Germany 9%
- UK 13%
- USA 51%
- Other 11%

**TELECOMMUNICATIONS GEAR**
- Italy 3%
- Canada 4%
- Hong Kong 4%
- Sweden 4%
- UK 5%
- France 5%
- W.Germany 9%
- USA 14%
- Japan 33%
- Other 19%

**DATA PROCESSING EQUIPMENT**
- Singapore 4%
- Italy 4%
- Canada 4%
- Ireland 5%
- France 6%
- UK 6%
- W. Germany 11%
- Japan 22%
- USA 24%
- Other 14%

**AUTOMOBILES**
- Sweden 3%
- Italy 3%
- Spain 3%
- USA 6%
- France 7.5%
- Belgium 7%
- Canada 12%
- W.Germany 24%
- Japan 31.5%
- Other 3%

**PAPER & BOARD**
- UK 3%
- Italy 3%
- Japan 4%
- Netherlands 4%
- France 5%
- USA 8%
- W.Germany 12%
- Sweden 13%
- Finland 14%
- Canada 19%
- Other 15%

**ELECTRICAL MACHINERY**
- Belgium 4%
- Switzerland 4%
- Italy 4%
- Netherlands 6%
- France 7%
- UK 8%
- USA 14%
- W.Germany 19%
- Japan 22%
- Other

## TRADED PRODUCTS

Top ten manufactures traded, by value in billions of US $ (late 1980s)

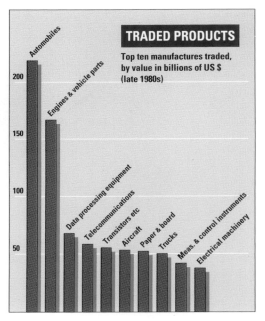

- Automobiles
- Engines & vehicle parts
- Data processing equipment
- Telecommunications
- Transistors etc
- Aircraft
- Paper & board
- Trucks
- Meas. & control instruments
- Electrical machinery

## DEPENDENCE ON TRADE

Value of exports as a percentage of Gross Domestic Product (1988)

- Over 50%
- 40 - 50%
- 30 - 40%
- 20 - 30%          [UK 21%]
- 10 - 20%          [USA 6.5%]
- Under 10%

- • Most dependent on industrial exports (over 75% of total exports)
- • Most dependent on fuel exports (over 75% of total exports)
- ○ Most dependent on mineral & metal exports (over 75% of total exports)

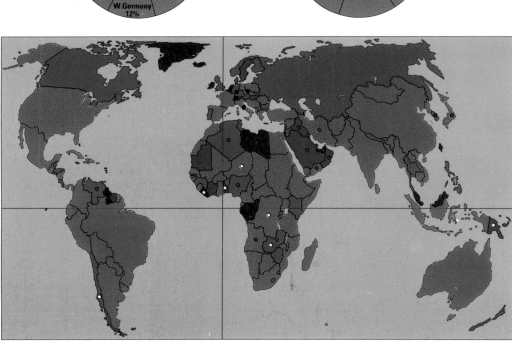

## WORLD SHIPPING

While ocean passenger traffic is now relatively modest, sea transport still carries most of world trade. Oil and bulk carriers make up the majority of the world fleet, although the general cargo category was the fastest growing in 1989, a year in which total tonnage increased by 1.5%.

Almost 30% of world shipping sails under a 'flag of convenience', whereby owners take advantage of low taxes by registering their vessels in a foreign country the ships will never see, notably Panama and Liberia.

### MERCHANT FLEETS

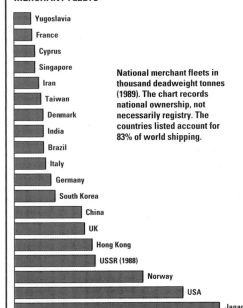

National merchant fleets in thousand deadweight tonnes (1989). The chart records national ownership, not necessarily registry. The countries listed account for 83% of world shipping.

Yugoslavia
France
Cyprus
Singapore
Iran
Taiwan
Denmark
India
Brazil
Italy
Germany
South Korea
China
UK
Hong Kong
USSR (1988)
Norway
USA
Japan
Greece

20,000    40,000    60,000    80,000

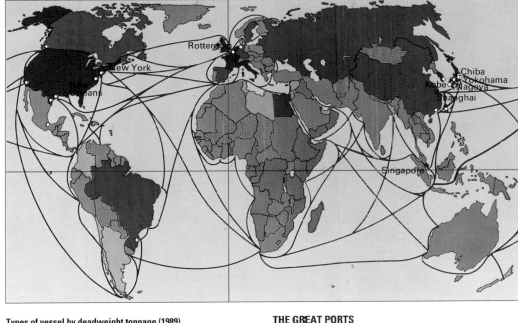

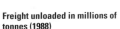
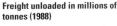

Freight unloaded in millions of tonnes (1988)

Over 100
50 - 100
10 - 50
5 - 10
Under 5
Land-locked countries

Major seaports

● Over 100 million tonnes per year
◐ 50-100 million tonnes per year

### Types of vessel by deadweight tonnage (1989)

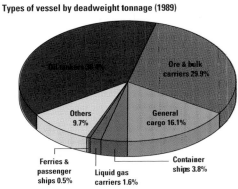

Oil tankers 38.4%
Ore & bulk carriers 29.9%
General cargo 16.1%
Others 9.7%
Ferries & passenger ships 0.5%
Liquid gas carriers 1.6%
Container ships 3.8%

### THE GREAT PORTS

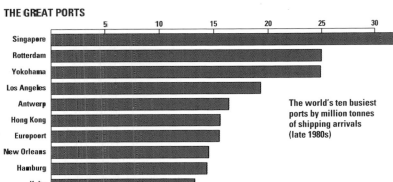

5    10    15    20    25    30

Singapore
Rotterdam
Yokohama
Los Angeles
Antwerp
Hong Kong
Europoort
New Orleans
Hamburg
Kobe

The world's ten busiest ports by million tonnes of shipping arrivals (late 1980s)

## TRADE IN PRIMARY PRODUCTS

Exports in primary products (excluding fuels, minerals & metals) as a percentage of total exports (1988)

Over 75%
50 - 75%
25 - 50%
10 - 25%        [USA 17.6%]
Under 10%       [UK 9%]

### Direction of trade

➡ Major movements of wheat
➡ Major movements of coffee
➡ Major movements of hardwoods

Arrows show the major trade direction of selected primary products, & are proportional to export value

## BALANCE OF TRADE

Value of exports in proportion to the value of imports (1988)

Exports exceed imports by:
  More than 50%
  10 - 50%
10% either side
Imports exceed exports by:
  10 - 50%
  More than 50%

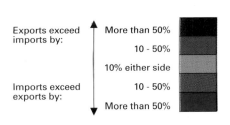

The total world trade balance should amount to zero, since exports must equal imports on a global scale. In practice, at least $100 billions in exports go unrecorded, leaving the world with an apparent deficit and many countries in a better position than public accounting reveals. However, a favourable trade balance is not necessarily a sign of prosperity: many poorer countries must maintain a high surplus in order to service debts, and do so by restricting imports below their real requirements.

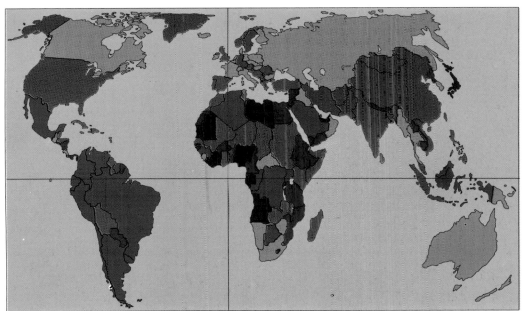

# QUALITY OF LIFE: WEALTH

Throughout the 1980s, most of the world became at least slightly richer. There were exceptions: in Africa, the poorest of the continents, many incomes actually fell, and the upheavals in Eastern Europe in 1989 left whole populations awash with political freedom but worse off financially in economies still teetering towards capitalism.

Most of the improvements, however, came to those who were already, in world terms, extremely affluent: the gap between rich and poor grew steadily wider. And in those developing countries that showed significant statistical progress, advances were often confined to a few favoured areas while conditions in other, usually rural, districts went from bad to worse.

The pattern of world poverty varies from region to region. In most of Asia, the process of recognized development is generally under way, with production increases outpacing population growth. By 2000, less than 10% of the Chinese population should be officially rated 'poor': without the means to buy either adequate food or the basic necessities required to take a full part in everyday life. Even India's lower growth rate should be enough to reduce the burden of poverty for at least some of its people. In Latin America, average per capita production is high enough for most countries to be considered 'middle income' in world rankings. But although adequate resources exist, Latin American wealth is distributed with startling inequality. According to a 1990 World Bank report, a tax of only 2% on the richest fifth would raise enough money to pull every one of the continent's 437 million people above the poverty line.

In Africa, solutions will be harder to find. The bane of high population growth has often been aggravated by incompetent administration, a succession of natural disasters and war. Population is the crux of the problem: numbers are growing anything up to twice as fast as the economies that try to support them. Aid from the developed world is only a partial solution; although Africa receives more than any other continent, much has been wasted on over-ambitious projects or lost in webs of inexperienced or corrupt bureaucracy. Yet without aid, Africa seems doomed to permanent crisis.

The rich countries can afford to increase their spending. The 24 members of the Organization for Economic Cooperation and Development comprise only 16% of the world's population, yet between them the nations accounted for almost 80% of total world production in 1988, a share that is likely to increase as 2000 approaches.

## CURRENCIES

**Currency units of the world's most powerful economies**

1. USA: US Dollar($,US$) = 100 cents
2. Japan: Yen (Y,¥) = 100 sen
3. Germany: Deutsche Mark (DM) = 100 Pfennige
4. France: French Franc (Fr) = 100 centimes
5. Italy: Italian Lira (L, £, Lit) = 100 centesimi
6. UK: Pound Sterling (£) = 100 pence
7. Canada: Canadian Dollar (C$, Can$) = 100 cents
8. China: Renminbi Yuan (RMBY, $, Y) = 10 jiao = 100 fen
9. Brazil: Cruzado (Cr$) = 100 centavos
10. Spain: Peseta (Pta, Pa) = 100 céntimos
11. India: Indian Rupee (Re, Rs) = 100 paisa
12. Australia: Australian Dollar ($A) = 100 cents
13. Netherlands: Guilder, Florin (Gld, f) = 100 centimes
14. Switzerland: Swiss Franc (SFr, SwF) = 100 centimes
15. South Korea: Won (W) = 100 Chon
16. Sweden: Swedish Krona (SKr) = 100 öre
17. Mexico: Mexican Pesos (Mex$) = 100 centavos
18. Belgium: Belgian Franc (BFr) = 100 centimes
19. Austria: Schilling (S, Sch) = 100 groschen
20. Finland: Markka (FMk) = 100 penni
21. Denmark: Danish Krone (DKr) = 100 öre
22. Norway: Norwegian Krone (NKr) = 100 öre
23. Saudi Arabia: Riyal (SAR, SRI$) = 100 halalah
24. Indonesia: Rupiah (Rp) = 100 sen
25. South Africa: Rand (R) = 100 cents

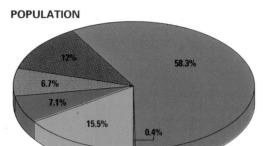

## CONTINENTAL SHARES

Shares of population and of wealth (GNP) by continent

Generalized continental figures show the startling difference between rich and poor but mask the successes or failures of individual countries. Japan, for example, with less than 4% of Asia's population, produces almost 70% of the continent's output.

**POPULATION**

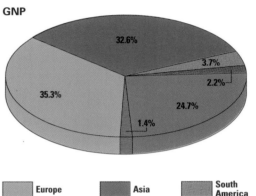

58.3%
12%
6.7%
7.1%
15.5%
0.4%

**GNP**

32.6%
3.7%
2.2%
24.7%
1.4%
35.3%

Europe | Asia | South America
Australia | Africa | North America

## INDICATORS

The gap between the world's rich and poor is now so great that it is difficult to illustrate it on a single graph. Car ownership in the USA, for example, is almost 2,000 times as common as it is in Bangladesh. Within each income group, however, comparisons have some meaning: the affluent Japanese on their overcrowded island have far fewer cars than the Americans; the Chinese, perhaps because of propaganda value, have more television sets than the Indians, whose per capita income is similar, while Nigerians prefer to spend their money on vehicles.

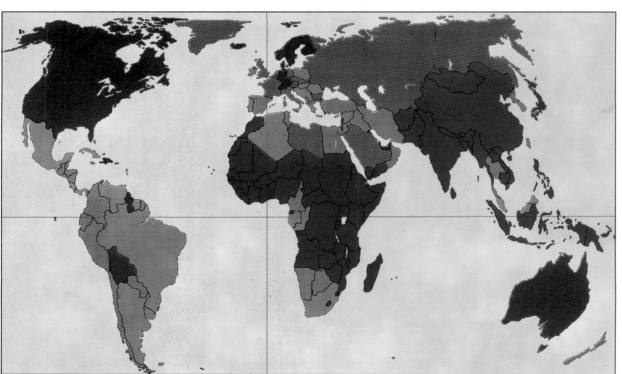

## LEVELS OF INCOME

**Gross National Product per capita: the value of total production divided by population (1986)**

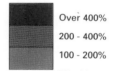

Over 400%
200 - 400%
100 - 200%

[World average wealth per person US $2,940]

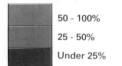

50 - 100%
25 - 50%
Under 25%

[Gross National Product (GNP) is the value of a nation's total production plus or minus the net balance of foreign financial transactions – including investments, banking and insurance]

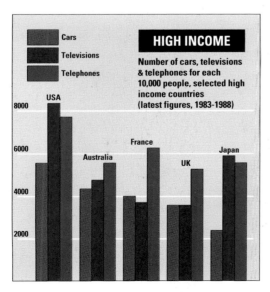

**HIGH INCOME**

Number of cars, televisions & telephones for each 10,000 people, selected high income countries (latest figures, 1983-1988)

Cars
Televisions
Telephones

USA
France
Australia
UK
Japan

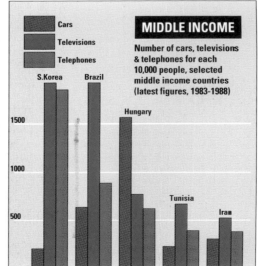

**MIDDLE INCOME**

Number of cars, televisions & telephones for each 10,000 people, selected middle income countries (latest figures, 1983-1988)

Cars
Televisions
Telephones

S.Korea
Brazil
Hungary
Tunisia
Iran

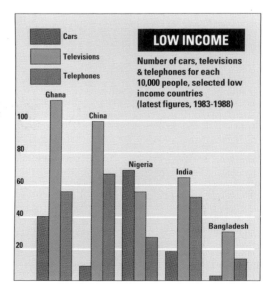

**LOW INCOME**

Number of cars, televisions & telephones for each 10,000 people, selected low income countries (latest figures, 1983-1988)

Cars
Televisions
Telephones

Ghana
China
Nigeria
India
Bangladesh

## DEBT & AID

**International debtors and the development aid they receive (1989)**

■ Debt, $ per capita

■ Aid, $ per capita

Although aid grants make a vital contribution to many of the world's poorer countries, they are usually dwarfed by the burden of debt that developing economies are expected to repay. In the case of Mozambique, aid amounted to more than 70% of GNP. In 1990, the World Bank rated Mozambique as the world's poorest country; yet debt interest payments came to almost 75 times its entire export earnings.

## AID DONORS

**Development aid by donor country, in millions of US$ and as a percentage of donor's GNP (1988)**

Not all aid is given in cash grants: much is delivered in the form of cheap loans or technical assistance. Since the 1970s, OECD countries belonging to the Development Assistance Committee (DAC) have agreed in principle to give 0.7% of their GNP, but most have failed to meet their commitment. Aid often comes with political or cultural strings attached: Saudi Arabia, in GNP terms by far the largest giver, supports only Arab and Islamic causes; Soviet aid goes mostly to allies and most Western nations have biases of their own.

■ AID in US$

■ % GNP

— DAC threshold

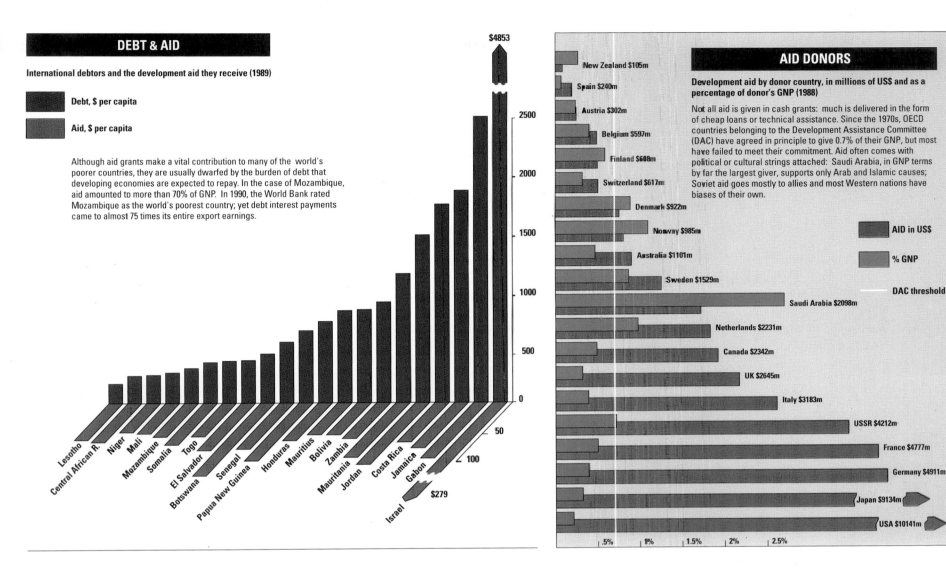

Inflation (right) is an excellent index of a country's financial stability, and usually its prosperity or at least its prospects. Inflation rates above 20% are generally matched by slow or even negative growth; above 50%, an economy is left reeling. Most advanced countries during the 1980s had to wrestle with inflation that occasionally touched or even exceeded 10%; in Japan, the growth leader, price increases averaged only 1.8% between 1980 and 1988.

Government spending (below right) is more difficult to interpret. Obviously, very low levels indicate a weak state, and high levels a strong one; but in poor countries, the 10-20% absorbed by the government may well amount to most of the liquid cash available, whereas in rich countries most of the 35-50% typically in government hands is returned in services.

GNP per capita figures (below) should also be compared with caution. They do not reveal the vast differences in living costs between different countries: the equivalent of US $100 is worth considerably more in poorer nations than it is in the USA itself.

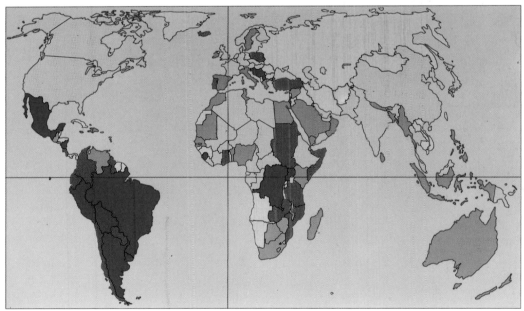

## INFLATION

**Average annual rate of inflation (1980-1988)**

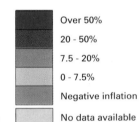

■ Over 50%
■ 20 - 50%
■ 7.5 - 20%
■ 0 - 7.5%
■ Negative inflation
☐ No data available

**Highest inflation**
Bolivia .......................... 483%
Argentina ...................... 291%
Brazil ............................. 189%
**Lowest inflation**
Oman ........................... -6.5%
Saudi Arabia ................. -4.2%
Kuwait .......................... -3.9%
[UK 5.7%] [USA 4.0%]

## THE WEALTH GAP

**The world's richest & poorest countries, by Gross National Product per capita in US $ (1989)**

| | | | | | |
|---|---|---|---|---|---|
| 1. | Liechtenstein | 33,000 | 1. | Mozambique | 80 |
| 2. | Switzerland | 30,270 | 2. | Ethiopia | 120 |
| 3. | Bermuda | 25,000 | 3. | Tanzania | 120 |
| 4. | Luxembourg | 24,860 | 4. | Laos | 170 |
| 5. | Japan | 23,730 | 5. | Nepal | 170 |
| 6. | Finland | 22,060 | 6. | Somalia | 170 |
| 7. | Norway | 21,850 | 7. | Bangladesh | 180 |
| 8. | Sweden | 21,710 | 8. | Malawi | 180 |
| 9. | Iceland | 21,240 | 9. | Bhutan | 190 |
| 10. | USA | 21,100 | 10. | Chad | 190 |
| 11. | Denmark | 20,510 | 11. | Sierra Leone | 200 |
| 12. | Canada | 19,020 | 12. | Burundi | 220 |
| 13. | UAE | 18,430 | 13. | Gambia | 230 |
| 14. | France | 17,830 | 14. | Madagascar | 230 |
| 15. | Austria | 17,360 | 15. | Nigeria | 250 |
| 16. | Germany | 16,500 | 16. | Uganda | 250 |
| 17. | Belgium | 16,390 | 17. | Mali | 260 |
| 18. | Kuwait | 16,380 | 18. | Zaïre | 260 |
| 19. | Netherlands | 16,010 | 19. | Niger | 290 |
| 20. | Italy | 15,150 | 20. | Burkina Faso | 310 |

GNP per capita is calculated by dividing a country's Gross National Product by its population. The UK ranks 21st, with US $14,570.

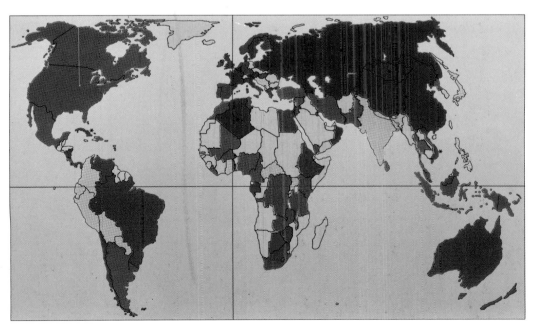

## STATE REVENUE

**Central government revenue as a percentage of GNP (1988) [* estimate]**

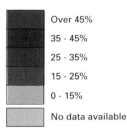

■ Over 45%
■ 35 - 45%
■ 25 - 35%
■ 15 - 25%
■ 0 - 15%
☐ No data available

**Highest proportion**
Botswana .........................74%
Hungary ...........................58%
Kuwait ..............................52%
Netherlands .....................51%
Gabon ..............................47%

[UK 36.4%] [USA 19.7%]

# QUALITY OF LIFE: STANDARDS

At first sight, most international contrasts are swamped by differences in wealth. The rich not only have more money, they have more of everything, including years of life. Those with only a little money are obliged to spend most of it on food and clothing, the basic maintenance costs of existence; air travel and tourism are unlikely to feature on the lists of their expenditure. However, poverty and wealth are both relative: slum-dwellers living on social security payments in an affluent industrial country have far more resources at their disposal than an average African peasant, but feel their own poverty none the less acutely. A middle-class Indian lawyer cannot command a fraction of the earnings of a counterpart in New York, London or Rome; nevertheless, he rightly sees himself as prosperous.

In 1990 the United Nations Development Programme published its first Human Development Index, an attempt to construct a comparative scale by which at least a simplified form of well-being might be measured. The index, running from 1 to 100, combined figures for life expectancy and literacy with a wealth scale that matched incomes against the official poverty lines of a group of industrialized nations. National scores ranged from a startling 98.7 for Sweden to a miserable 11.6 for Niger, reflecting the all too familiar gap between rich and poor.

Comparisons between nations with similar incomes are more interesting, showing the effect of government policies. For example, Sri Lanka was awarded 78.9 against 43.9 for its only slightly poorer neighbour, India; Zimbabwe, at 57.6, had more than double the score of Senegal, despite no apparent disparities in average income. Some development indicators may be interpreted in two ways. There is a very clear correlation, for example, between the wealth of a nation and the level of education that its people enjoy. Education helps create wealth, of course; but are rich countries wealthy because they are educated, or well-educated because they are rich? Women's fertility rates appear to fall almost in direct proportion to the amount of secondary education they receive; but high levels of female education are associated with rich countries, where fertility is already low.

Not everything, though, is married to wealth. The countries cited on these pages have been chosen, representatively, to give a range covering different cultures as well as different economic power, revealing disparities among rich and among poor as well as between the two obvious groups.

Income distribution, for example, shows that in Brazil (following the general pattern of Latin America) most national wealth is concentrated in a few hands; Bangladesh is much poorer, but what little wealth there is, is more evenly spread.

Among the developed countries the USA, with its poorest 20% sharing less than 5% of the national cake, has a noticeably less even distribution than Japan, where despite massive industrialization traditional values act as a brake against poverty. Hungary, still enmeshed in Communism when these statistics were compiled, shows the most even distribution of all, which certainly matches with Socialist theory. However, the inequalities in Communist societies, a contributing factor in the demise of most of them in the late 1980s, are not easily measured in money terms: Communist élites are less often rewarded with cash than with power and privilege, commodities not easily expressed statistically.

There are other limits to statistical analysis. Even without taking account of such imponderables as personal satisfaction, it will always be more difficult to measure a reasonable standard of living than a nation's income or its productivity. Lack of money certainly brings misery, but its presence does not guarantee contentment.

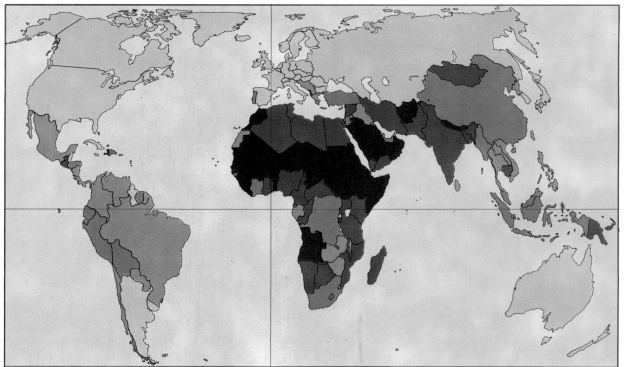

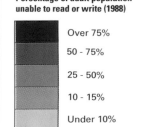

**LITERACY**

Percentage of adult population unable to read or write (1988)

Over 75%

50 - 75%

25 - 50%

10 - 15%

Under 10%

Highest rates of illiteracy
Somalia ................................. 88%
Burkina Faso ......................... 87%
Niger ..................................... 86%
Mali ....................................... 83%
Mauritania ............................ 83%
Chad ...................................... 78%
Benin ..................................... 76%
Nepal ..................................... 76%
Guinea ................................... 75%

[UK 4.86%]  [USA 4%]

## EDUCATION

The developing countries made great efforts in the 1970s and 1980s to bring at least a basic education to their people. Primary school enrolments rose above 60% in all but the poorest nations. Figures often include teenagers or young adults, however, and there are still an estimated 300 million children worldwide who receive no schooling at all. Secondary and higher education are expanding far more slowly, and the gap between rich and poor is probably even larger than it appears from the charts here, while the bare statistics provide no real reflection of educational quality.

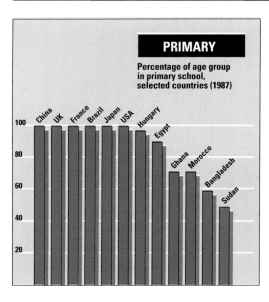

**PRIMARY**
Percentage of age group in primary school, selected countries (1987)

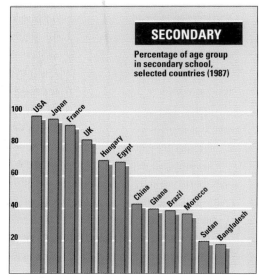

**SECONDARY**
Percentage of age group in secondary school, selected countries (1987)

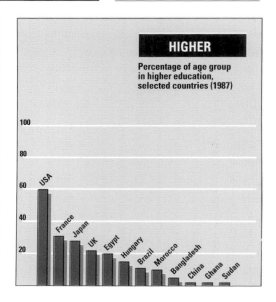

**HIGHER**
Percentage of age group in higher education, selected countries (1987)

## DISTRIBUTION OF SPENDING

**Percentage share of household spending, (1989)**

- ■ Food
- ■ Medicine & Education
- ■ Clothing
- ■ Transport
- ■ Energy & Housing
- ■ Other

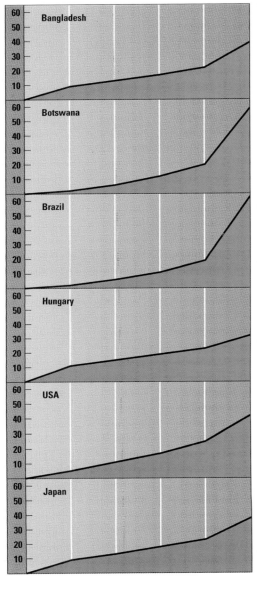

UK  USA  Japan  Hungary  Brazil  Egypt  Nigeria  B'desh

## DISTRIBUTION OF INCOME

**Percentage share of household income from poorest fifth to richest fifth, selected countries (1989)**

Bangladesh
Botswana
Brazil
Hungary
USA
Japan

## FERTILITY & EDUCATION

- ■ Fertility rate: average number of children borne per woman
- ■ Percentage of female age group in secondary education

**Fertility rates compared with female education, selected countries (1988)**

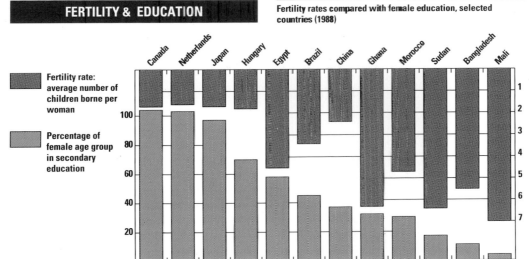

Canada  Netherlands  Japan  Hungary  Egypt  Brazil  China  Ghana  Morocco  Sudan  Bangladesh  Mali

## TOURIST SPENDING

**Countries spending the most on overseas tourism US $ million (1987)**

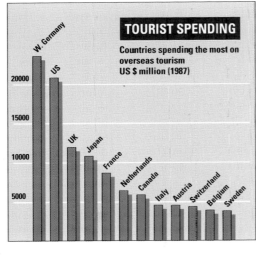

W. Germany  US  UK  Japan  France  Netherlands  Canada  Italy  Austria  Switzerland  Belgium  Sweden

## TOURIST EARNING

**Countries receiving the most from overseas tourism US $ million (1987)**

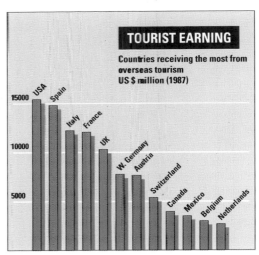

USA  Spain  Italy  France  UK  W. Germany  Austria  Switzerland  Canada  Mexico  Belgium  Netherlands

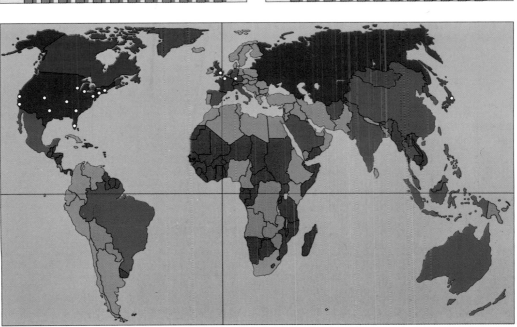

Since the age group for secondary schooling is usually defined as 12 to 17 years, percentages for countries with a significant number of 11- or 18-year-olds in secondary school may actually exceed 100. A high proportion of employed women may indicate either an advanced, industrial economy where female opportunities are high, or a poor country where many women's lives are dominated by agricultural toil. The lowest rates are found in Islamic nations, whose religious precepts often exclude women even from field-work.

## WOMEN AT WORK

**Women in paid employment as a percentage of the total workforce (1989)**

- ■ Over 40%
- ■ 30 - 40%
- ■ 20 - 30%
- ■ 10 - 20%
- ■ Under 10%

**Highest proportion**
Burundi ............................ 53%
Ghana ............................... 51%
Mozambique ................... 48%

**Lowest proportion**
UAE ..................................... 6%
Saudi Arabia ..................... 7%
Bangladesh ....................... 7%

[UK 42%]   [USA 44%]

Small economies in attractive areas are often completely dominated by tourism: in some West Indian islands, tourist spending provides over 90% of total income. In cash terms the USA is the world leader: its 1987 earnings exceeded 15 billion dollars, though that sum amounted to only 0.4% of its GDP.

## AIR TRAVEL

**Millions of passenger km [number carried, international & domestic, multiplied by distance flown by each from airport of origin] (1988)**

- ■ Over 100,000
- ■ 50,000 - 100,000
- ■ 10,000 - 50,000
- ■ 1,000 - 10,000
- ■ 500 - 1,000
- ■ Under 500

○ Major airports (over 20 million passengers a year)

The world's busiest airport in terms of total passengers is Chicago's O'Hare; the busiest international airport is Heathrow, the largest of London's airports.

# QUALITY OF LIFE: HEALTH

According to statistics gathered in the late 1980s and early 1990s, a third of the world's population has no access to safe drinking water: malaria is on the increase; cholera, thought vanquished, is reappearing in South America; an epidemic of the terrifying AIDS virus is gathering force in Africa; and few developing countries can stretch their health care budgets beyond US $2 per person per year.

Yet human beings, by every statistical index, have never been healthier. In the richest nations, where food is plentiful, the demands of daily work are rarely onerous and medical care is both readily available and highly advanced, the average life expectancy is often more than 75 years – approaching the perceived limits for human longevity. In middle-income nations such as Brazil and the Philippines, life expectancy usually extends at least to the mid-60s; in China, it has already reached 70. Even in poverty-stricken Ethiopia and Chad, lifespans are close to 50. Despite economic crisis, drought, famine and even war, every country in the world reported an increase between 1965 and 1990.

It was not always so, even in countries then considered rich. By comparison, in 1880 the life expectancy of an average Berliner was under 30 years and infant mortality in the United Kingdom, then the wealthiest nation, stood at 144 per thousand births – a grim toll exceeded today only by three of the poorest African countries (Mali, Sierra Leone and Guinea). Even by 1910, European death rates were almost twice as high as the world average less than 80 years later; infant mortality in Norway, Europe's healthiest country, was then higher than in present-day Indonesia. In far less than a century, human prospects have improved beyond recognition.

In global terms, the transformation is less the result of high technology medicine – still too expensive for all but a minority, even in rich countries – than of improvements in agriculture and hence nutrition, matched by the widespread diffusion of the basic concepts of disease and public health. One obvious consequence, as death rates everywhere continue to fall, is sustained population growth. Another is the rising expectation of continued improvement felt by both rich and poor nations alike.

In some ways, the task is easier for developing countries, striving with limited resources to attain health levels to which the industrialized world has only recently become accustomed. As the tables below illustrate, infectious disease is rare among the richer nations, while ailments such as cancer, which tend to kill in advanced years, do not seriously impinge on populations with shorter lifespans.

Yet infectious disease is relatively cheap to eliminate, or at least reduce, and it is likely to be easier to raise life expectancy from 60 to 70 than from 75 to 85. The ills of the developed world and its ageing population are more expensive to treat – though most poor countries would be happy to suffer from the problems of the affluent. Western nations regularly spend more money on campaigns to educate their citizens out of over-eating and other bad habits than many developing countries can devote to an entire health budget – an irony that marks the dimensions of the rich-poor divide.

Indeed, wealth itself may be the most reliable indicator of longevity. Harmful habits are usually the province of the rich; yet curiously, though the dangerous effects of tobacco have been proved beyond doubt, the affluent Japanese combine very high cigarette consumption with the longest life expectancy of all the major nations. Similarly, heavy alcohol consumption seems to have no effect on longevity: the French, world leaders in 1988 and in most previous surveys, outlive the more moderate British by a year, and the abstemious Indians by almost two decades.

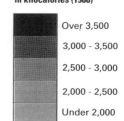

## FOOD CONSUMPTION

**Average daily food intake per person in kilocalories (1988)**

| | |
|---|---|
| ■ | Over 3,500 |
| ■ | 3,000 - 3,500 |
| ■ | 2,500 - 3,000 |
| ■ | 2,000 - 2,500 |
| ■ | Under 2,000 |

**Highest intake**
East Germany......................3,814
UAE .....................................3,733
Greece ................................3,688
USA .....................................3,645
Bulgaria ..............................3,642

**Lowest intake**
Mozambique .......................1,595
Chad....................................1,717
Ethiopia ..............................1,749
Ghana .................................1,759
Guinea ................................1,776

[USA 3,645]  [UK 3,256]

## CAUSES OF DEATH

The rich not only live longer, on average, than the poor; they also die from different causes. Infectious and parasitic diseases, all but eliminated in the developed world, remain a scourge in poorer countries. On the other hand, more than two-thirds of the populations of OECD nations eventually succumb to cancer or circulatory disease; the proportion in Latin America is only about 45%. In addition to the three major diseases shown here, respiratory infection and injury also claim more lives in developing nations, which lack the drugs and medical skills required to treat them.

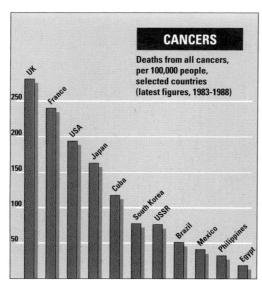

**CANCERS**

Deaths from all cancers, per 100,000 people, selected countries (latest figures, 1983-1988)

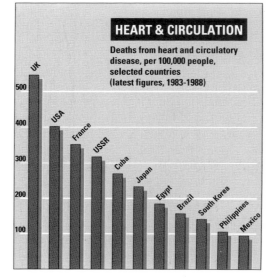

**HEART & CIRCULATION**

Deaths from heart and circulatory disease, per 100,000 people, selected countries (latest figures, 1983-1988)

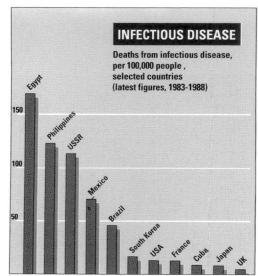

**INFECTIOUS DISEASE**

Deaths from infectious disease, per 100,000 people , selected countries (latest figures, 1983-1988)

## LIFE EXPECTANCY

**Years of life expectancy at birth, selected countries (1988-1989)**

The chart shows combined data for both sexes. On average, women live longer than men worldwide, even in developing countries with high maternal mortality rates. Overall, life expectancy is steadily rising, though the difference between rich and poor nations remains dramatic.

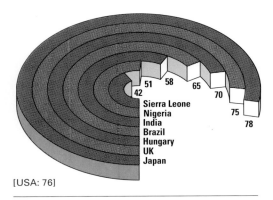

51 58 65 70 75 78
42
Sierra Leone
Nigeria
India
Brazil
Hungary
UK
Japan

[USA: 76]

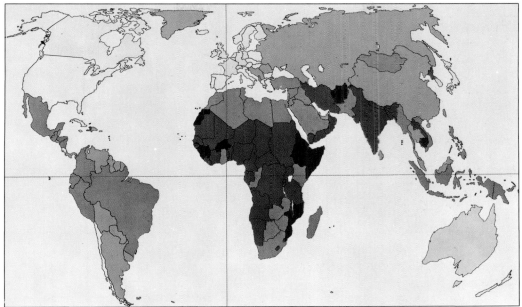

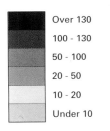

## INFANT MORTALITY

**Number of babies who die before the age of one year, per thousand live births (1988)**

| | |
|---|---|
| | Over 130 |
| | 100 - 130 |
| | 50 - 100 |
| | 20 - 50 |
| | 10 - 20 |
| | Under 10 |

**Highest infant mortality**
Afghanistan ........................172
Ethiopia .............................154

**Lowest infant mortality**
Iceland .................................3
Japan ...................................5

[USA 10]  [UK 9]

## HOSPITAL CAPACITY

**Hospital beds available for each 1,000 people (1983-1988)**

| Highest capacity | | Lowest capacity | |
|---|---|---|---|
| Finland | 14.9 | Bangladesh | 0.2 |
| Sweden | 13.2 | Nepal | 0.2 |
| France | 12.9 | Ethiopia | 0.3 |
| USSR | 12.8 | Mauritania | 0.4 |
| Netherlands | 12.0 | Mali | 0.5 |
| North Korea | 11.7 | Burkina Faso | 0.6 |
| Switzerland | 11.3 | Pakistan | 0.6 |
| Austria | 10.4 | Niger | 0.7 |
| Czechoslovakia | 10.1 | Haiti | 0.8 |
| Hungary | 9.1 | Chad | 0.8 |

[ UK 8] [USA 5.9]

The availability of a bed can mean anything from a private room in a well-equipped Californian teaching hospital to a place in the overcrowded annexe of a rural African clinic. In the Third World especially, quality of treatment can vary enormously from place to place within the same country.

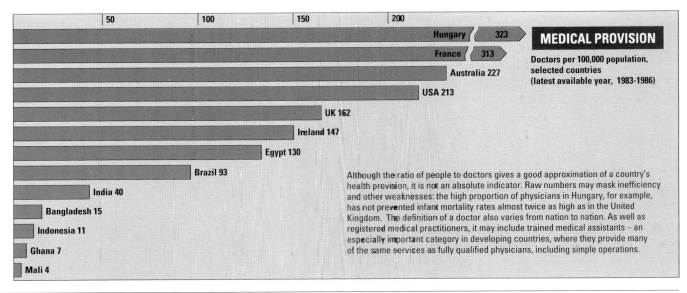

50     100     150     200

Hungary 323
France 313
Australia 227
USA 213
UK 162
Ireland 147
Egypt 130
Brazil 93
India 40
Bangladesh 15
Indonesia 11
Ghana 7
Mali 4

## MEDICAL PROVISION

**Doctors per 100,000 population, selected countries (latest available year, 1983-1986)**

Although the ratio of people to doctors gives a good approximation of a country's health provision, it is not an absolute indicator. Raw numbers may mask inefficiency and other weaknesses: the high proportion of physicians in Hungary, for example, has not prevented infant mortality rates almost twice as high as in the United Kingdom. The definition of a doctor also varies from nation to nation. As well as registered medical practitioners, it may include trained medical assistants – an especially important category in developing countries, where they provide many of the same services as fully qualified physicians, including simple operations.

## THE AIDS CRISIS

The Acquired Immune Deficiency Syndrome was first identified in 1981, when American doctors found otherwise healthy young men succumbing to rare infections. By 1984, the cause had been traced to the Human Immunodeficiency Virus (HIV), which can remain dormant for many years and perhaps indefinitely: only half of those known to carry the virus in 1981 had developed AIDS ten years later.

By 1991 the World Health Organization knew of more than 250,000 AIDS cases worldwide and suspected the true number to be at least four times as high. In Western countries in the early 1990s, most AIDS deaths were among male homosexuals or needle-sharing drug-users. However, the disease is spreading fastest among heterosexual men and women, which is its usual vector in the Third World, where most of its victims live. Africa is the most severely hit: a 1992 UN report estimated that 2 million African children will die of AIDS before the year 2000 – and some 10 million will be orphaned.

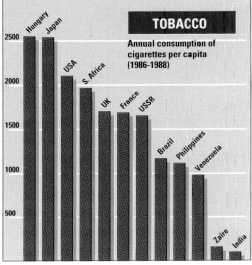

## TOBACCO

**Annual consumption of cigarettes per capita (1986-1988)**

Hungary  Japan  USA  S. Africa  UK  France  USSR  Brazil  Philippines  Venezuela  Zaire  India

## CRIME & PUNISHMENT

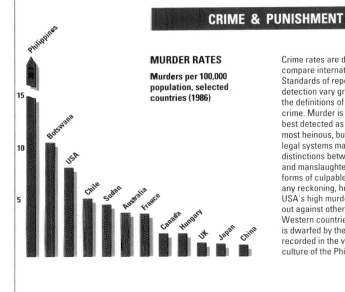

### MURDER RATES

**Murders per 100,000 population, selected countries (1986)**

Philippines  Botswana  USA  Chile  Sudan  Australia  France  Canada  Hungary  UK  Japan  China

Crime rates are difficult to compare internationally. Standards of reporting and detection vary greatly, as do the definitions of many types of crime. Murder is probably the best detected as well as the most heinous, but different legal systems make different distinctions between murder and manslaughter or other forms of culpable homicide. By any reckoning, however, the USA's high murder rate stands out against otherwise similar Western countries, although it is dwarfed by the killings recorded in the very different culture of the Philippines.

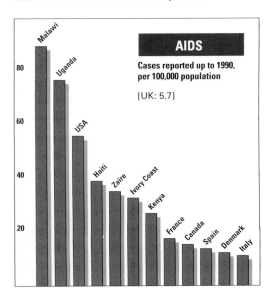

## AIDS

**Cases reported up to 1990, per 100,000 population**

[UK: 5.7]

Malawi  Uganda  USA  Haiti  Zaire  Ivory Coast  Kenya  France  Canada  Spain  Denmark  Italy

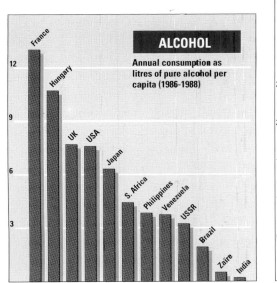

## ALCOHOL

**Annual consumption as litres of pure alcohol per capita (1986-1988)**

France  Hungary  UK  USA  Japan  S. Africa  Philippines  Venezuela  USSR  Brazil  Zaire  India

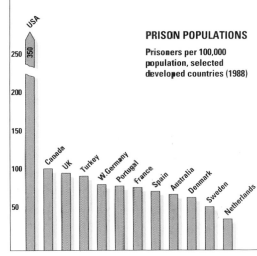

### PRISON POPULATIONS

**Prisoners per 100,000 population, selected developed countries (1988)**

USA 350  Canada  UK  Turkey  W. Germany  Portugal  France  Spain  Australia  Denmark  Sweden  Netherlands

Differences in prison population reflect penal policies as much as the relative honesty or otherwise of different nations, and by no means all governments publish accurate figures. In more than 50 countries, people are still regularly imprisoned without trial, in 60 torture is a normal part of interrogation, and some 130 retain the death penalty, often administered for political crimes and in secret. Over 2,000 executions were recorded in 1990 by the civil rights organization Amnesty International; the real figure, as Amnesty itself maintains, was almost certainly much higher.

# QUALITY OF LIFE: ENVIRONMENT

Humans have always had a dramatic effect on their environment, at least since the invention of agriculture almost 10,000 years ago. Generally, the Earth has accepted human interference without obvious ill effects: the complex systems that regulate the global environment have absorbed substantial damage while maintaining a stable and comfortable home for the planet's trillions of lifeforms. But advancing human technology and the rapidly expanding populations it supports are now threatening to overwhelm the Earth's ability to cope.

Industrial wastes, acid rainfall, expanding deserts and large-scale deforestation all combine to create environmental change at a rate far faster than the Earth can accommodate. Equipped with chain-saws and flame-throwers, humans can now destroy more forest in a day than their ancestors could in a century, upsetting the balance between plant and animal, carbon dioxide and oxygen, on which all life ultimately depends. The fossil fuels that power industrial civilization have pumped enough carbon dioxide and other green~house gases into the atmosphere to make climatic change a near-certainty. Chlorofluorocarbons (CFCs) and other man-made chemicals are rapidly eroding the ozone layer, the planet's screen against ultra-violet radiation.

As a result, the Earth's average temperature has risen by approximately 0.5°C since the beginning of this century. Further rises seem inevitable, with 1990 marked as the hottest year worldwide since records began. A warmer Earth probably means a wetter Earth, with melting icecaps raising sea levels and causing severe flooding in some of the world's most densely populated regions. Other climatic models suggest an alternative doom: rising temperatures could increase cloud cover, reflecting more solar energy back into space and causing a new ice age.

Either way, the consequences for humans could be disastrous – perhaps the Earth's own way of restoring ecological balance over the next few thousand years. Fortunately, there is a far faster mechanism available. Human ingenuity has provoked the present crisis; but human ingenuity, inspired if need be by fear, can respond to it. Production of CFCs is already almost at a standstill, and the first faltering steps towards stabilization and ultimately reduction of carbon dioxide have been taken, with Denmark pioneering the way by taxing emissions in 1991.

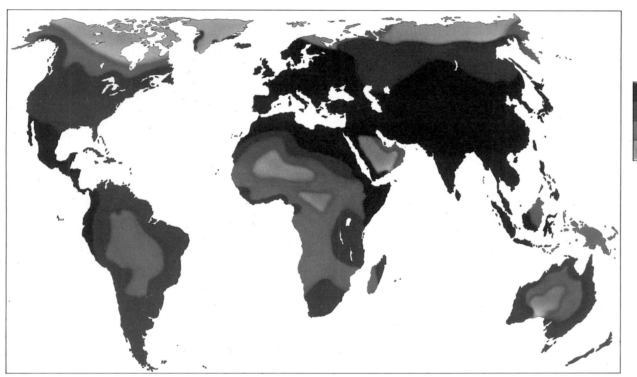

## THE HISTORY OF HUMAN EXPANSION

The growth of ecological control: areas where human activity dominates the environment, from primitive times to the year 2000

- By 1500 AD
- By 1900 AD
- By 2000 AD
- Areas not dominated by human activity

## THE RISE IN CARBON DIOXIDE

Emissions of carbon dioxide in millions of tonnes, 1950-1991

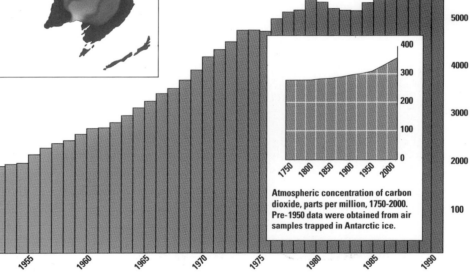

Atmospheric concentration of carbon dioxide, parts per million, 1750-2000. Pre-1950 data were obtained from air samples trapped in Antarctic ice.

Since the beginning of the Industrial Revolution, human activity has pumped steadily more carbon dioxide into the atmosphere. Most was quietly absorbed by the oceans, whose immense 'sink' capacity meant that 170 years were needed for levels to increase from the pre-industrial 280 parts per million to 300 (inset graph). But the vast increase in fuel-burning since 1950 (main graph) has overwhelmed even the oceanic sink. Atmospheric concentrations are now rising almost as steeply as carbon dioxide emissions themselves.

## GREENHOUSE POWER

Relative contributions to the greenhouse effect by the major heat-absorbing gases in the atmosphere

The chart combines greenhouse potency and volume. Carbon dioxide has a greenhouse potential of only 1 but its concentration of 350 parts per million, makes it predominate. CFC 12 , with 25,000 times the absorption capacity of CO$_2$, is present only as 0.00044 ppm.

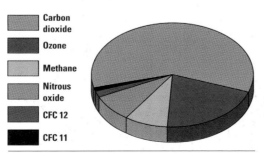

- Carbon dioxide
- Ozone
- Methane
- Nitrous oxide
- CFC 12
- CFC 11

## CARBON DIOXIDE

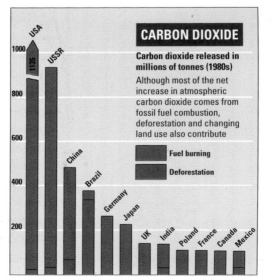

Carbon dioxide released in millions of tonnes (1980s)

Although most of the net increase in atmospheric carbon dioxide comes from fossil fuel combustion, deforestation and changing land use also contribute

- Fuel burning
- Deforestation

## GLOBAL WARMING

The rise in average temperatures caused by carbon dioxide and other greenhouse gases (1960-2020)

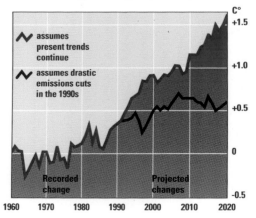

- assumes present trends continue
- assumes drastic emissions cuts in the 1990s

Recorded change

Projected changes

## ACID RAIN

### Acid rainfall & sources of acidic emissions (1980s)

Acid rain is caused when sulphur & nitrogen oxides in the air combine with water vapour to form sulphuric, nitric & other acids.

■ Regions where sulphur and nitrogen oxides are released in high concentrations, mainly from fossil fuel combustion.

● Major cities with high levels of air pollution (including nitrogen & sulphur emissions)

### Areas of heavy acid deposition

pH numbers indicate acidity, decreasing from a neutral 7. Normal rain, slightly acid from dissolved carbon dioxide, never exceeds a pH of 5.6.

■ pH less than 4.0 (most acidic)
■ pH 4.0 to 4.5
■ pH 4.5 to 5.0

⌐ ¬ Areas where acid rain is a potential danger

## THE ANTARCTIC

The vast Antarctic ice-sheet, containing some 70% of the Earth's fresh water, plays a crucial role in the circulation of atmosphere and oceans and hence in determining the planetary climate. The frozen southern continent is also the last remaining wilderness – the largest area to remain free from human colonization.

Ever since Amundsen and Scott raced for the South Pole in 1911, various countries have pressed territorial claims over sections of Antarctica, spurred in recent years by its known and suspected mineral wealth: enough iron ore to supply the world at present levels for 200 years, large oil reserves and, probably, the biggest coal deposits on Earth.

However, the 1961 Antarctic Treaty set aside the area for peaceful uses only, guaranteeing freedom of scientific investigation, banning waste disposal and nuclear testing, and suspending the issue of territorial rights. By 1990, the original 12 signatories had grown to 25, with a further 15 nations granted observer status in subsequent deliberations. However, the Treaty itself was threatened by wrangles between different countries, government agencies and international pressure groups.

Finally, in July, 1991, the belated agreement of the UK and the US assured unanimity on a new accord to ban all mineral exploration for a further 50 years. The ban can only be rescinded if all present signatories, plus a majority of any future adherents, agree. While the treaty has always lacked a formal mechanism for enforcement, it is firmly underwritten by public concern generated by the efforts of environmental pressure groups such as Greenpeace, foremost in the campaign to have Antarctica declared a 'World Park'.

It seems likely that the virtually uninhabited continent will remain untouched by tourism, nuclear-free and dedicated to peaceful scientific research.

## DESERTIFICATION

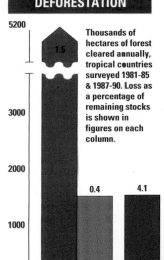

■ Existing deserts
■ Areas with a high risk of desertification
■ Areas with a moderate risk of desertification
■ Former areas of rainforest
■ Existing rainforest

## DEFORESTATION

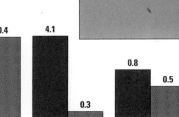

**Thousands of hectares of forest cleared annually, tropical countries surveyed 1981-85 & 1987-90. Loss as a percentage of remaining stocks is shown in figures on each column.**

| | Brazil | India | Indonesia | Burma | Thailand | Vietnam | Philippines | Costa Rica | Cameroon |
|---|---|---|---|---|---|---|---|---|---|
| 1987-90 | 1.5 | 4.1 | 0.8 | 2.1 | 2.5 | 2.0 | 1.5 | 7.6 | 0.6 |
| 1981-85 | 0.4 | 0.3 | 0.5 | 0.3 | 2.4 | 0.7 | 1.0 | 4.0 | 0.4 |

 1987-90  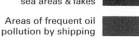 1981-85

## WATER POLLUTION

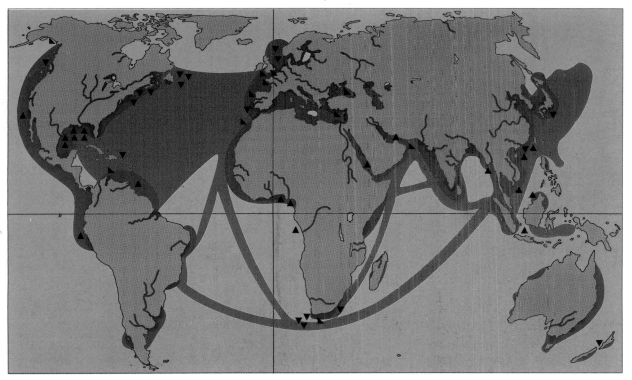

■ Severely polluted sea areas & lakes
■ Less polluted sea areas & lakes
■ Areas of frequent oil pollution by shipping

◣ Major oil tanker spills
▲ Major oil rig blow outs
▼ Offshore dumpsites for industrial & municipal waste
— Severely polluted rivers & estuaries

Poisoned rivers, domestic sewage and oil spillage have combined in recent years to reduce the world's oceans to a sorry state of contamination, notably near the crowded coasts of industrialized nations. Shipping routes, too, are constantly affected by tanker discharges. Oil spills of all kinds, however, declined significantly during the 1980s, from a peak of 750,000 tonnes in 1979 to under 50,000 tonnes in 1990. The most notorious tanker spill of that period – when the *Exxon Valdez* (94,999 gross registered tonnes) ran aground in Prince William Sound, Alaska, in March 1989 – released only 267,000 barrels, a relatively small amount compared to the results of blow-outs and war damage (see table). The worst tanker accident in history occurred in July 1979, when the *Atlantic Empress* and the *Aegean Captain* collided off Trinidad.

# CITY MAPS

Oslo, Copenhagen 2, Helsinki, Stockholm 3, London 4, Paris 5, The Ruhr 6, Berlin, Hamburg, Munich 7, Madrid, Barcelona, Lisbon, Athens 8, Turin, Milan, Rome, Naples 9, Prague, Warsaw, Vienna, Budapest 10, Moscow, St Petersburg 11, Osaka, Hong Kong, Seoul 12, Tokyo 13, Peking, Shanghai, Tientsin, Canton 14, Bangkok, Manila, Singapore, Jakarta 15, Delhi, Bombay, Calcutta 16, Istanbul, Tehran, Baghdad, Karachi 17, Lagos, Cairo, Johannesburg 18, Sydney, Melbourne 19, Montréal, Toronto 20, Boston 21, New York 22, Philadelphia 24, Washington, Baltimore 25, Chicago 26, San Francisco 27, Los Angeles 28, Mexico City 29, Havana, Caracas, Lima, Santiago 30, Rio de Janeiro, São Paulo 31, Buenos Aires 32

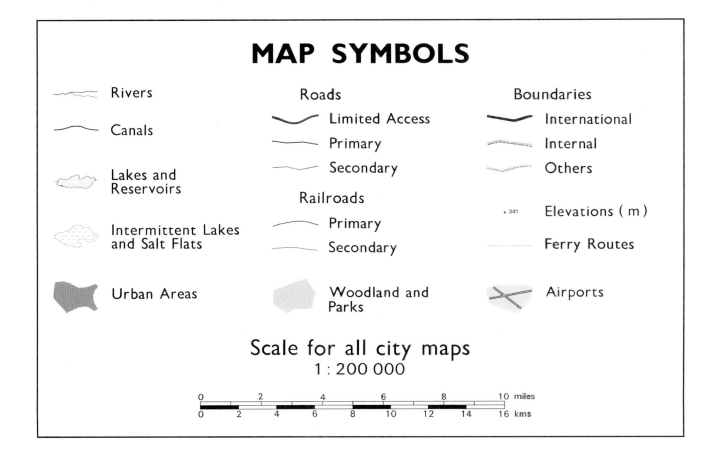

## MAP SYMBOLS

| | | | | | |
|---|---|---|---|---|---|
| Rivers | | Roads | | Boundaries | |
| Canals | | Limited Access | | International | |
| | | Primary | | Internal | |
| Lakes and Reservoirs | | Secondary | | Others | |
| | | Railroads | | | |
| Intermittent Lakes and Salt Flats | | Primary | | ▲ 341 Elevations (m) | |
| | | Secondary | | Ferry Routes | |
| Urban Areas | | Woodland and Parks | | Airports | |

### Scale for all city maps
### 1 : 200 000

| 0 | 2 | 4 | 6 | 8 | 10 miles |
|---|---|---|---|---|---|
| 0 | 2  4  6  8  10  12  14 | | | | 16 kms |

1: 200 000

5 miles
8 km

1  2  3  4  5  6

**A**

Utvika  Br_løkka  Heggelielva  Venner  Sørkedalen  Slakteren  Turter  Sandermosen  451  Slattum  Nittedal  Huseby  Glosli  Fro

N o r d m a r k a

Homledal  Trvvass-høgda  531  Maridalen  Maridalsvatnet  407  Skytta  Skedsmo

60

Sollihøgda  OSLO AKERSHUS FYLKE  Burudvatn  Bogstadvatnet  418  Sognsvatn  Holmenkollen  Kjelsås  Alnsjøen  Vestli  Kjeller

**B**

Bærums Verk  Ila  Røa  Ris  Ulleval  Grorud  Stovner  Strømmen  Rud  Lillestrøm  Ber

Rustad  Smestad  Bryn  Kolsås  379  Lilleaker  OSLO  Sagene  Grefsen  Alnabru  E6

Toverud  Skui  Haslum  Skøyen  Universitet  Tøyen  Østre Aker  363  Lørenskog  Øyeren

Sylling  Tanum  Bærum  Lysaker  Bygdøy  Hovedøya  Gamlebyen  Ekeberg  Lutvatn  Nordre Elvåga  Arnes

Stabekk  Stovivatn  Hovik  Sandvika  Fornebu  Lindøya  Ormøya  Bekkelaget  Lambert Seter  Nordstrand  Oppsal  Bøler  Nøklevatn  Rælingen

Stependen  Snarøya  Fornebu  Malmøya  Ljan  Skullerud  Sondre Elvåga  Ramstalltsjøen

Sandangen  Nesøya  Ostøya  NESODDTANGEN  Østmark-kapellet  Losby

Semsvatn  Hvalstad  Brønnøya  Flaskebekk  Oksval  Skokefall  Haukelo  Østmark-kapellet  Nordbysjøen

**C**

Sørsdal  Hvalstrand  Bonnefjorden  Klemetsrud  Sandbakken  Tonekollen 368  Mosjøen

59 50  Lierskogen  Asker  Oslofjorden  215  Sørby  Kolbotn  Krokhøl  Siggerud  Vardåsen 374  59

Tranby  Blakstad  Nesodden  Oppegård  Myrvoll  Bru  Børtervatna

Skogen  Dikemark  Vollen  Fjellstrand  Svestad  Hasle  Gjersjøen  Binningsvatna

Lier  Gjellumvatn  E18/E6  Oppegård  134  Oppegård  Langen

Frogner  Reistad  Nærsnes  Slemmestad  Blylaget  Garder

1  2  3  East from Greenwich  4  5  6

Gerlev  7  Snostrup  Ølstykke  8  Farum  Stavnsholt  9  Overød  Jægersborg  Søllerød  Nærum  Skodsborg  11

12  Skuldelev  Lille Rørbæk  Ganløse Orned  Farum Sø  Lille Værløse  Holte  Ørholm  Lundtofte  10

Lille  Svestrup  Ganløse  Furesø  Virum  Brede  Hjortekær  Jægersborg Dyrehave  Tårbæk

Østby  Jyllinge  Stenløse  Jonstrup  Sønderup  Store Hareskov 42  Bagsværd Sø  Kongens Lyngby  Klampenborg

Sønderby  Værebro Å  Smørumnedre  Måløv  Hareskovby  Bagsværd  Vangede  Jægersborg  Ordrup  Skovshoved

**D**

Roskilde Fjord  Pederstrup  Hjortespring  Gladsakse  Buddinge  Gentofte  Hellerup  Charlottenlund

Agerup  Ledøje  Ballerup  Herlev  Søborg  Svanemøllen

Bognæs  Hove Å  Nybølle  Skovlunde  Husum  Bispebjerg  Trekroner

Kattinge Vig  Risby  KØBENHAVN  Brønshøj  Fælled parken  Refshaleøen

Sengeløse  Vestskoven  Islev  Vanløse  Lillehavn

Vasby  Herstedøster  Rødovre  Frederiksberg  Christianshavn

55 40  Store Kattingeso  Glostrup  Brøndbyøster  Valby  Sundbyerne

**E**

Svogerslev  Roskilde  Hedehusene  Albertslund  Tåstrup  Hvidovre  Kastrup  Saltholm

Vallensbæk  Avedøre  Tårnby  Kastrup Lufthavn

Sterkende  Tranemde  Brøndbyvester  Ishøj Strand  Brøndby Strand  Vallensbæk Strand  Store Magleby  Dragør

Gadstrup  Hundige  Hundige Strand  Greve Strand  Mosede  Mosede Strand  Kongelunden  Ullerup  Søvang  Sydstranden

Viby  Havdrup  Snoldelev  Karlslunde Strand  K ø g e   B u g t  AFLANDSHAGE

Ø r e s u n d  D r o g d e n  A m a g e r

Travemünde  Helsinki  Swinoujście  Rønne

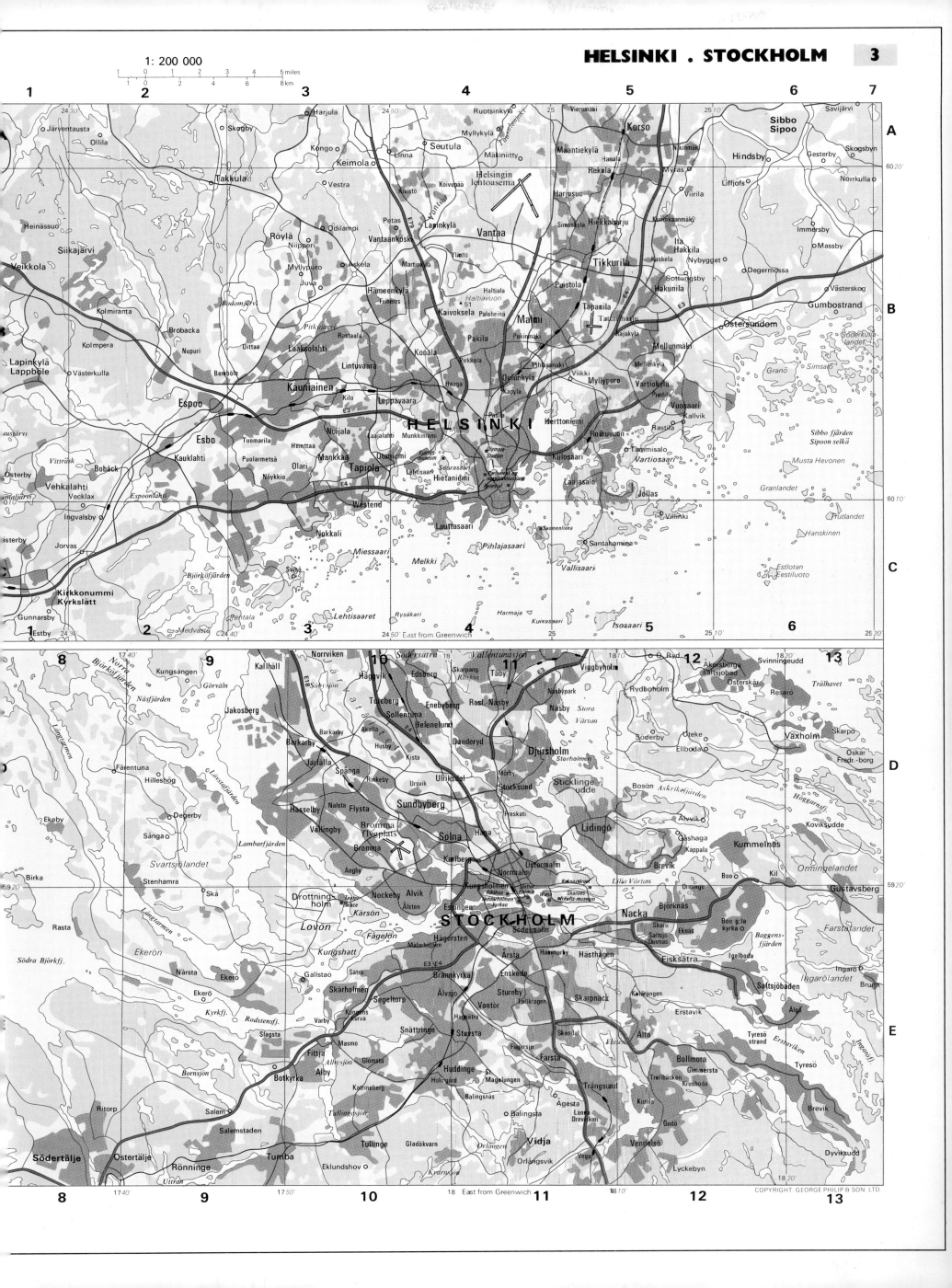

1 : 200 000

1: 200 000

0  1  2  3  4  5 miles
0  2  4  6  8 km

**Brentwood** · Shenfield · **Chipping Ongar** · Brook Street · Pilgrims Hatch · Upminster · Hornchurch · Romford · Havering · **Dagenham** · **Barking** · **Ilford** · Redbridge · **Woodford** · **Chigwell** · **Loughton** · Waltham Abbey · **Epping** · Theydon Bois · **Cheshunt** · **Enfield** · **Potters Bar** · **Barnet** · Finchley · Southgate · Wood Green · **Tottenham** · Walthamstow · **Chingford** · **Stratford** · **Hackney** · Stoke Newington · Islington · **Camden** · **Hampstead** · **Hendon** · **Edgware** · **Stanmore** · **Harrow** · **Wembley** · Willesden · Cricklewood · Kilburn · **Westminster** · Kensington · **Hammersmith** · **Chelsea** · **Fulham** · **Putney** · **Wandsworth** · **Ealing** · **Acton** · **Chiswick** · **Brentford** · **Southall** · **Hayes** · **Hillingdon** · **Uxbridge** · **Ruislip** · **Pinner** · **Hounslow** · **Twickenham** · **Richmond** · **Kingston upon Thames** · **Surbiton** · **Wimbledon** · **Mitcham** · **Merton** · **Sutton** · **Banstead** · **Epsom** · **Esher** · **Weybridge** · Walton on Thames · East Molesey · Thames Ditton · Long Ditton · Claygate · **Staines** · **Ashford** · Sunbury · Shepperton · Chertsey · Byfleet · Ripley

**Greenwich** · **Woolwich** · **Lewisham** · **Catford** · **Bromley** · **Beckenham** · **Croydon** · Thornton Heath · Streatham · **Clapham** · **Lambeth** · **Southwark** · **Camberwell** · **Peckham** · **Deptford** · **Eltham** · **Bexley** · Bexleyheath · **Erith** · **Dartford** · Swanley · **Sidcup** · **Orpington** · Chislehurst · Petts Wood · Purley · Coulsdon · Caterham · Warlingham · Woldingham · Westerham · Oxted · **Sevenoaks** · Otford · Eynsford · Riverhead · Borough Green · Wrotham · West Kingsdown · New Ash Green · **Swanscombe** · Greenhithe · Stone · **Tilbury** · **Grays** · West Thurrock · Northfleet · Purfleet · Aveley · South Ockendon · North Stifford · Chadwell St. Mary · Little Thurrock · **Isstead Rise** · Meopham · Culverstone Green · Stansted · Trottiscliffe · Kemsing · Kingsdown · Farningham · Horton Kirby · South Darenth · Sutton at Hone · Wilmington · Hextable

River Thames · River Darent · River Cray · River Roding · River Lee · River Brent · River Mole · River Wey · River Colne · Epping Forest · Weald Park · Hainault Forest · Wimbledon Common · Richmond Park · Bushy Park · Hampton Court Palace · Hatfield · Watford · Rickmansworth · Bricket Wood · Borehamwood · Radlett · Shenley · Abbots Langley · Croxley Green · Cassiobury Park · Chorleywood · Chipperfield · Denham Green · Iver · West Drayton · Heathrow Airport · Yiewsley · Cowley

East from Greenwich · West from Greenwich · GREATER LONDON

1: 200 000

5 miles
8 km

PARIS

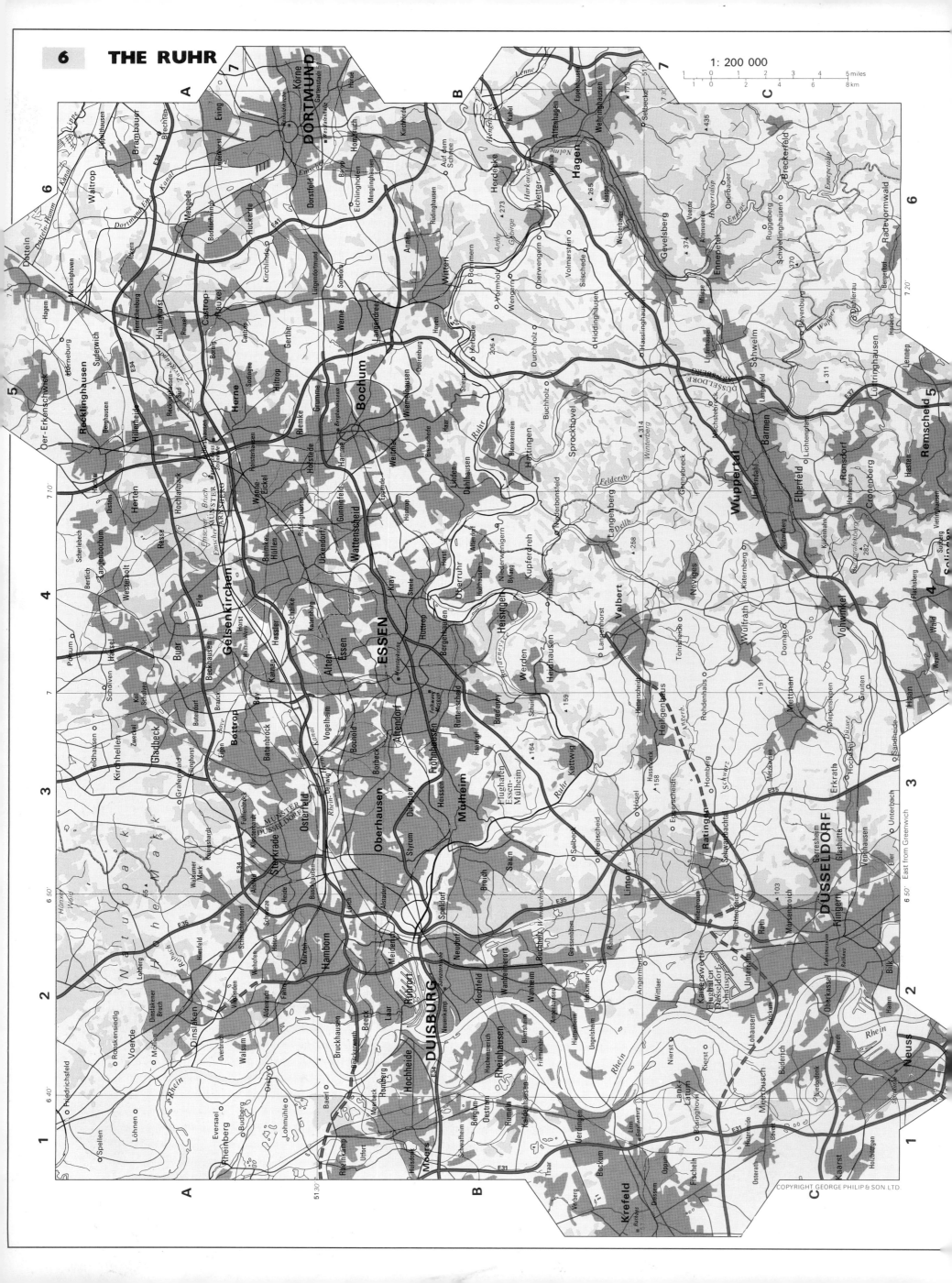

1 : 200 000

COPYRIGHT GEORGE PHILIP & SON LTD

1: 200 000

5 miles
8 km

BERLIN

HAMBURG

MÜNCHEN

East from Greenwich

COPYRIGHT GEORGE PHILIP AND SON LTD.

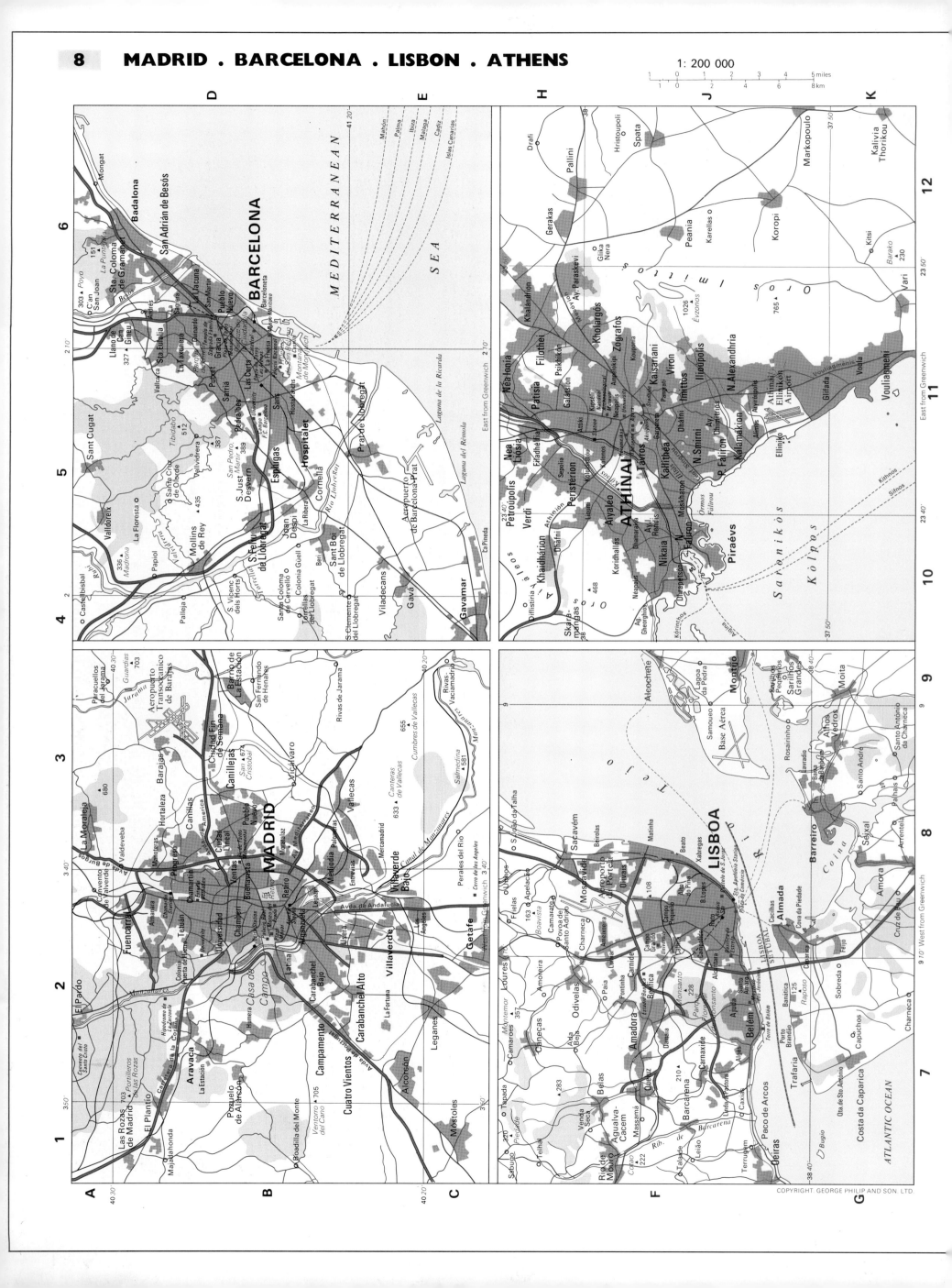

1 : 200 000

1 : 200 000

5 miles
8 km

WARSZAWA

BUDAPEST

PRAHA

WIEN

East from Greenwich

1: 200 000

5 miles
8 km

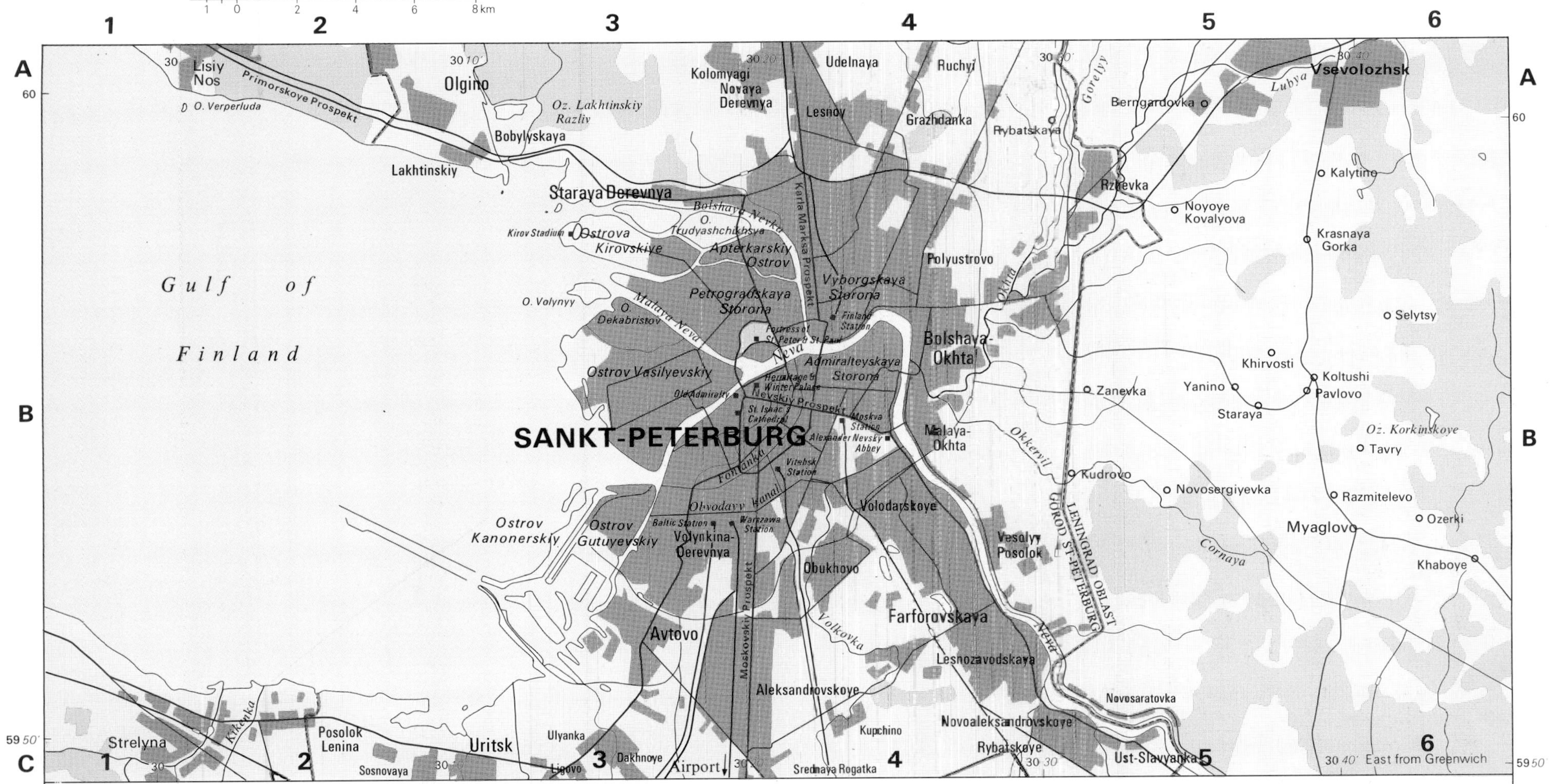

**Gulf of Finland**

**SANKT-PETERBURG**

Lisiy Nos
Olgino
Udelnaya
Ruchyi
Vsevolozhsk
Kolomyagi
Novaya Derevnya
Lesnoy
Grazhdanka
Rybatskaya
Berngardovka
Lubya
O. Verperluda
Primorskoye Prospekt
Lakhtinskiy
Staraya Derevnya
Bolshaya Nevka
Rzhevka
Kalytino
Noyoye Kovalyova
Krasnaya Gorka
Oz. Lakhtinskiy Razliv
Bobylyskaya
Kirov Stadium
Ostrova Kirovskive
Iudyashchobsya
Apterkarskiy Ostrov
Vyborgskaya Storona
Polyustrovo
Selytsy
Petrogradskaya Storona
O. Volynyy
Finland Station
Khirvosti
Koltushi
O. Dekabristov
Malaya Neva
Admiralteyskaya Storona
Bolshaya-Okhta
Zanevka
Yanino
Pavlovo
Ostrov Vasilyevskiy
Staraya
Oz. Korkinskoye
St. Isaac Cathedral
Moskva
Malaya-Okhta
Kudrovo
Tavry
Old Admiralty Winter Palace
Alexander Nevsky Abbey
Razmitelevo
Ozerki
Fontanka
Vitebsk Station
Okkervil
Myaglovo
Ostrov Kanonerskiy
Obvodny Kanal
Volodarskoye
Vesolyy Posolok
Khaboye
Gornaya
Ostrov Gutuyevskiy
Baltic Station
Warzawa Station
Volynkina-Derevnya
Obukhovo
Farforovskaya
LENINGRAD OBLAST
GOROD ST-PETERBURG
Avtovo
Moskovsky Prospekt
Volkovka
Lesnozavodskaya
Novosaratovka
Aleksandrovskoye
Strelyna
Posolok Lenina
Uritsk
Ulyanka
Ligovo
Dakhnoye
Airport
Srednaya Rogatka
Kupchino
Novoaleksandrovskoye
Rybatskoye
Ust-Slavyanka
Sosnovaya
East from Greenwich

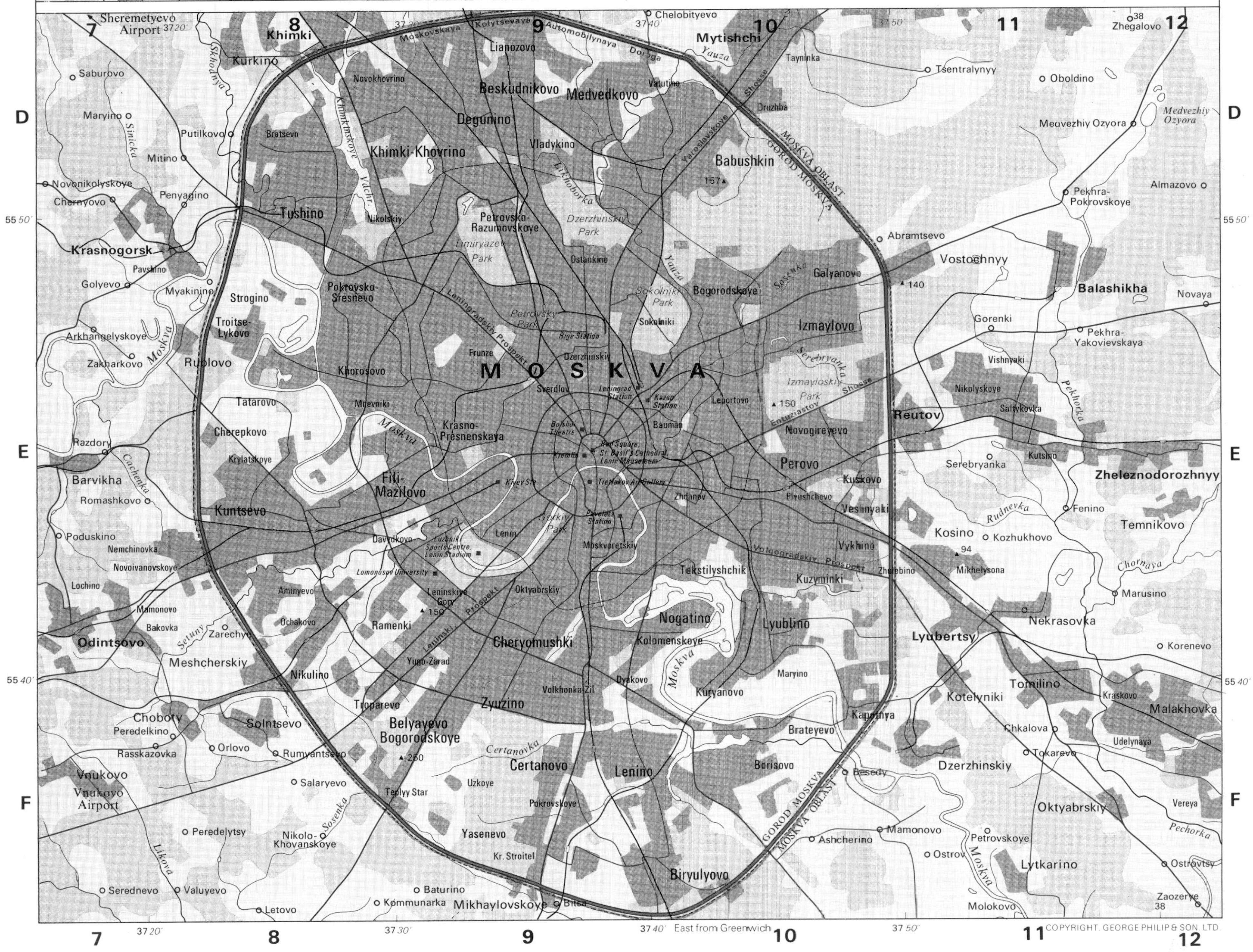

**MOSKVA**

Sheremetyevo Airport
Khimki
Moskovskaya
Kolytsevaya
Lianozovo
Automobilnaya Doroga
Chelobityevo
Mytishchi
Zhegalovo
Saburovo
Kurkino
Novokhovrino
Beskudnikovo
Medvedkovo
Vatutino
Yauza
Tayninka
Tsentralnyy
Oboldino
Maryino
Sinicka
Putilkovo
Bratsevo
Degunino
Druzhba
Medvezhiy Ozora
Medvezhiy Ozora
Mitino
Khimki-Khovrino
Vladykino
Ukhtomka
MOSKVA GOROD MOSKVA OBLAST
Pekhra-Pokrovskoye
Almazovo
Novonikolyskoye
Penyagino
Tushino
Nikolskiy
Petrovsko-Razumovskoye
Babushkin
Abramtsevo
Vostochnyy
Chernyovo
Vachka
Timiryazev Park
Dzerzhinskiy Park
Gorenki
Balashikha
Novaya
Krasnogorsk
Pavshino
Strogino
Ostankino
Yauza
Sokolniki Park
Bogorodskoye
Galyanovo
Vishnyaki
Nikolyskiy
Pekhra-Yakovievskaya
Golyevo
Myakinino
Troitse-Lykovo
Petrovsky Park
Rige Station
Sokolniki
Izmaylovo
Arkhangelskoye
Zakharkovo
Rublovo
Khorosovo
Frunze
Dzerzhinskiy
Serebryanka
Izmaylovski Park
Reutov
Tatarovo
Mnevniki
Sverdlov
Kazan Station
Leningrad Station
Leportovo
Salyykovka
Zheleznodorozhnyy
Razdory
Cherepkovo
Krasno-Presnenskaya
Bolshoi Theatre
Bauman
Novogireyevo
Perovo
Serebryanka
Barvikha
Krylatskoye
Kremlin
Red Square, St. Basil's Cathedral, Lenin Mausoleum
Kuskovo
Kutsino
Romashkovo
Fili-Mazilovo
Kuntsevo
Kiev St.
Tretyakov Art Gallery
Zhdanov
Plyushchevo
Vesnyaki
Kosino
Kozhukhovo
Temnikovo
Poduskino
Nemchinovka
Davidkovo
Kurskaya Sports Centre Lenin Stadium
Lenin
Paveletz Station
Gorky Park
Moskvaretskiy
Vykhino
Kuzyminki
Zhelebino
Mikhelysona
Novoivanovskoye
Lomonosov University
Leninskiy Gori
Tekstilyshchik
Marusino
Lochino
Aminyevo
Uchakova
Ramenki
Leninskiy Prospekt
Oktyabrskiy
Nogatina
Lyublino
Nekrasovka
Korenevo
Odintsovo
Bakovka
Zarechy
Setuny
Yugo-Zarad
Cheryomushki
Kolomenskoye
Maryino
Lyubertsy
Meshcherskiy
Nikulino
Dyakovo
Moskva
Kuryanovo
Kotelyniki
Troparevo
Volkhonka Zil
Zyuzino
Kapmtna
Kraskovo
Malakhovka
Choboty
Peredelkino
Solntsevo
Orlovo
Rumyantsevo
Belyayevo Bogorodskoye
Certanovka
Lenino
Borisovo
Besedy
Tokarevo
Udelnaya
Dzerzhinskiy
Rasskazovo
Certanovo
Salaryevo
Uzkoye
Pokrovskoye
GOROD MOSKVA MOSKVA OBLAST
Oktyabrskiy
Vereya
Vnukovo
Vnukovo Airport
Teplyy Star
Yasenevo
Kr. Stroitel
Ashcherino
Lytkarino
Pechorka
Serednevo
Valuyevo
Likena
Peredelytsy
Nikolo-Khovanskoye
Baturino
Kommunarka
Mikhaylovskoye
Bitsa
Biryulyovo
Mamonovo
Petrovskoe
Ostrov
Ostrovtsy
Letovo
Molokovo
Zaozerye
East from Greenwich

1: 200 000

5 miles
8 km

## Osaka map

1  2  3  4

A  34 50'  34 50'  A

Dōjō  403  552  Tadain  Meizino-Meri-Minō National Park  294  Hattori
Najio  Yamaguchi  Shukunoshō  Takatsuki
Nose  Kawanishi  Minō  Hanchō  Tonda
Ogo Ogo  Maitani  Ikeda  Senri  EXPO 70 Site  Ibaraki  Hirakata
509  Funasaka  Takarazuka  Osaka International Airport  Toyonaka  Kori
Arima  462  Senriyama  Yamada  Settsu  Neyegawa
Karato  722  Rokko-Zan  932  Kwansei Gakuin University  Itami  Swita  Kadoma
596  Iwazono  Hirota  Higashiyodogawa  Asahi  Moriguchi  Shijōnawate
Tanigami  Nishinomiya  Muko  Jūsō  Byodo  Miyakojima  Jōtō  Dāitō
Obu-tōge  365  Akiya  Naruo  Amagasaki  Umeda  Higashi  Kōnoike
Maya-Zan  699  Kōbe University  Okamoto  Ashiya  Kanzaki  Station Kita  Minami  Higashinari  Shikiri
403  Nada  Higashinada  Nishiyodogawa  Fukushima  Aji  Nishi  Ikuno  ŌSAKA  Higashiōsaka
Fukiai  KŌBE  Rokkō Island  Konohana  Nanwa  Stadium  Tennōji  Abeno  Kyūhōji  Yamamoto
Ikuta  Kōbe Harbour  Minato  Taishō  Kizuri  Yao
Nagata  Nishinari  Higashisumiyoshi  Tainaka  Yao Airport  Onchi
Suma  Osaka Harbour  Sumiyoshi  Ikeuchi  Kashiwara
Sakai Harbour  Matsubara  Fujidera

### Osaka Bay

Sakai  Kanaoka  Mozu  Tomb of Niatoko  Habikino

East from Greenwich

## Hong Kong map

5  6

New Territories

Shan Mei  Chuen Lung  Shing  Shan Liu  Wong  Shek Hang
Sheng Fa Shan  578  Lo Wai  Wo Yi Hop  Fo Tan  Chuk Yeung  Chuk Wan
Shek Lung Kung  474  Pak Tim Pa  532  Needle Hill  Sha Tin  Sha Kok Mei  Inner Sai Kung  Port Shelter
Chai Wan Kok  Tsuen Wan  Kwai Chung  Che Kung Miu  Sha Tin Wai  Wong Ngua Shan  603  Pak Kong  Kiu Tsui
Ting Kau  Tai Wo Hau  Keng Hau  Tai Lo Shan  Ho Chung  Ma Nam Wat  Sharp Island
Ngua Kok  Tsing Yi  Kowloon Res.  Beacon Hill  Tsz Wan  Kowloon Peak  Chuk Kok  Port Shelter
Nan Wan  Cheung Sha Wan  Shek Mei  Wong Ngau Chi Wan  602  432  Tai Po Tsai  Shelter Island
Sham Shui Po  San Po Kong  Tsang  Lan Shue  Razor Hill  Yau Yue Wan
Ngong Shuen Chau  Mong Kok  Kowloon City  Hong Kong  Siu Mau  Ma Yau Tong  Hang Hou  Mang Kung Uk
KOWLOON  Yau Ma Tei  Kwai Wan  Kwun Tong  Lam Tin  Rennie's Mill
HONG KONG  Royal Observatory  Tsim Sha Tsui  Hung Hom  Cha Kwo Ling  Yau Tong  High Junk Peak  344
Sai Ying Pun  Sheung Wan  Tung Lo  North Pt  Sai Wan Ho  Lei Yue Mun  Tai Tan Wau  Sheung Lau Wan
Kau Yi Chau  Green Island  Kennedy Town  Central  Wan Chai  Tai Hang  Shau Kei Wan  Po Toi
VICTORIA  Jardine's  Happy Valley  528  Chai Wan  Tei  Tong Tsui
Pok Fu Lam  Hong Kong Island  Mt. 430  Pak ka Shan  Tit Cham Chau  Tung Lung I.
Kong Sin Wan  Nichols  433  Tai Tam  TATHONG PT
Wong Chuk  Violet Hill  Tai Tam Tuk Res.
BOULDER PT.  Aberdeen  Stanley Mound  386  Shek O
Yung Shue Wan  Ap Lei Chau  Middle I.  Stanley
Lamma  George Island  Round Island  Tai Tam Bay  Kau Pei Chau  HOK TSUI
Lo So Shing  Sok Kwu Wan  Stanley Peninsula  Sung Kong
Island  Tung O  353  BLUFF HEAD  Lo Chau  Po Toi Island

114 10 East from Greenwich

## Seoul map

7  8

F  37 40'  37 40'  F

Dobong San  719  Surag Sap  638
GYEONG GI  SEOUL  Dobong  Banghag  Sangye  Bulam San  507
Galyeon  Eun Pyeong  Bughan San  841  Do Bong  Suyu  Gongneung
Haengju Castle  Pyeongchang  Mia Dong  Seoggwan  Hoegi  Jungwha
Yeogchon  Hongeun  Eungam  Seong Bug  Samseon  Jegi
Gimpo International Airport  Susaeg  National Museum  Jong Ro  Secret Garden  Dong Dae Mun  Abba San  348
Seo Dae Mun  Namgajha  Jung  City Hall Station  Hawangsibri  Dabsibri
Mangweon  Deungchon  Hwagog  Mog  Chenchean  Namdaemun  Namsan Park  Seoul Tower  Seong Dong
Gang Seo  Haewoen  Ma Po  Yong San  Donhingoe  Race Course Seongsu  Cheonho
Yeong Dung Po  Yeoido  Seobingo  Sinsa  Jayang  Gang Dong
Seoul-Incheon Expressway  Siheon  Donghingoe  Site of 1988 Olympic Games
Gu Ro  Gocheog  Noryangjin  Jamweon  Seocho  Gang Nam
Gaebong  Daebang  Dong Jag  Sadang  Bangbae  Daechi  Jamsil
Dogsan  Sinrim  Gwan Ag  Garibong  Tangjae  291
Siheung  629  Guryong San  Gwanag San  Seoul National University  Gyeong Busan Expressway

East from Greenwich  127

COPYRIGHT. GEORGE PHILIP AND SON. LTD.

1: 200 000

0 1 2 3 4 5 miles
0 2 4 6 8 km

**1** **2** **3** **4**

**A**

Kujiai
Kawagoe
Kitain Temple
Fukuyakami
Omiya
Ofukuro-Shinden
Shimo-okudomi
Fukuoka
Tsuruma
Uran
Kushiki
Kashi-Hazaki
Yamazaki
Matsubushi
Toyofuta
Koshigaya
Yoshikawa
Nagareyama
Kashiwa
Yono
Urawa
Dōjō
Saido
Ōmagi
Daimon
Angyō
Higashi-kaizoka
Shioha
Ohirodo
Yokosuka
Nazukari
Kogane
Kanegasaku
Halchōbori

**35°50'**

Shimotomi
Ōi
Fujimi
Mizuko
Harigaya
Fujikubo
Kami-tomi
Ūwada
Sakanoshita
Shiro
Adachi
Chikumazawa
Miyato
Nobudome
Tajima
Numakage
Matsumotoshinden
Shimo-sasome
Bijoki
Todamachi
Toda
Warabi
Hatogaya
Yanagishima
Maeda
Sōka
Yashio
Takenotsuka
Mabashi
Higurashi
Misato
Kamishiki

Tokorozawa
Niiza
Kiyose
Sugasawa
Kami-kiyoto
Kamiyama
Kurihara
Maesawa
Asaka
Shirako
Yamato
Momote
Shimura
Akabane
Kawaguchi
Adachi-Ku
Nishi-arai
Ōyada
Mizumoto
Kanamachi
Matsudo

**B**

Higashimurayama
Ogawa
Nonakashinden
Suzuki-shinden
Shimosato
Kurume
Hōya
Tanashi
Shimo-shakujii
Itabashi-Ku
Kami-Itabashi
Kasuga
Yahara
Ōyama
Tabata
Senju
Katsushika-Ku
Takasago
Kokonoji Temple
Ichikawa

Kodaira
Musashino
Nerima
Nagasaki
Toshimaen
Numabukuro
Ochiai
Ikebukuro
Zōshigaya
Ōtsuka
Komagome
Nippori
Honden
Arakawa-Ku
Taitō-Ku
Mukojima
Shirokiwa
Edogawa
Nakayama

Kokubunji
Koganei
Ogikubo
Asagaya
Nakano-Ku
Toshima-Ku
Mejiro
Ushigome
Bunkyō
University
Ueno
Asakusa
Sumida
Kameido
Takagi
Karaki

**35°40'**

Kunitachi
Mitaka
Suginami-Ku
Shimo-ogikubo
Shinjuku-Ku
Ichigaya
Yotsuya
Nihonbashi
Funabori
Mizue
Hon-cyotoku

Yaho
Fuchu
Takaido
Kamikitazawa
Honcho
Shinjuku Shrine
National Stadium
Toyoma Park
Kitazawa
Aoyama
Akasaka
Kasumigaseki
Ginza
Chūō-Ku
Kōtō-Ku
Kasai
Urayasu

Shimogawara
Koremasa
Chōfu
Tamaden
Shibuya-Ku
Sangenjaya
Ebisu
Azabu
Minato-Ku
Shiba
Tōkyō Harbour
Harumi
Tōkyō Disneyland

Tama
Inagi
Suge
Komae
Setagaya-Ku
Komazawa
Meguro-Ku
Ōsaki
Shirogane
Shinagawa-Ku
**TŌKYŌ**

**C**

Tsurumi
Okura
Hosoyama
Ikuta
Takaishi
Mampukuji
Mizonokuchi
Kodanaka
Ōokayama
Jiyūgaoka
Ōimachi
*Shinagawa Bay*

Machida
Sugō
Maginu
Arima
Kamoshida
Ēda
Ōdana
Chitose
Yamada
Kosugi
Matuko
Ikegami
Ōta-Ku
Ōmori
*Tokyo Bay*

Nagatsuta
Ichgao
Takeshita
Kachida
Minami-tsunashima
Hiyoshi
Saiwai
Kamata
Haneda
Tōkyō-Haneda International Airport
Hamano

Kanamori
Kawawa
Ikebe
Nippa
Kikuna
Ōsone
Kamimukō
Kawasaki
Kawasaki Harbour
Tokyo Bay Bridge

Kamitsuruma
Tōkaichiba
Saedo
Kamoi
Kōzukue
Tsurumi-Ku
Seiji Temple
*Bay*

**35°30'**

Shimotsuruma
Yamato
Kawai
Imajuku
Kami-sugata
Kanagawa-Ku
Land under reclamation
Nakajima

Fukami
Seyu
Futatsubashi
Furugamine
Kami-hoshikawa
Sakuragi
Ohitsu
Nakano
Narawa
Sodegaura

**D**

Ayase
Izumi
Nakada
Okazu
Akuwa
Hodogaya-Ku
Futamatagawa
Nishi
Yokohama Harbour
Egawa
BANZU-HANA
Takayanagi

Shimo-tsuchidana
Fukatani
Kashio
Naka-Ku
Honmoku
**Yokohama**
Minami-Ku
Isogo-Ku
HONMOKU-MISAKI
Nakasato
Nishiyama
Nagasuga

Harajuku
Totsuka-Ku
Kōnan
Sasashita
Hino
Negishi Bay
Sugita
**Kisarazu**

Kami-nakazato
Tomioka

**1** **2** East from Greenwich **3** **4**

1: 200 000

COPYRIGHT. GEORGE PHILIP AND SON. LTD.

1 : 200 000

5 miles
8 km

**MANILA**

Quezon City
San Juan del Monte
Mandaluyong
Makati
Rizal
Pasay
Caloocan
Navotas
Malabon

Antipolo
Taytay
Cainta
Angono
Tayuman
Binangonan
Guping
Lunsad
Darangan
Bilbiran
Calumpangan

*Laguna de Bay*

*Manila Bay*

Cavite
Las Pinas
Paranaque
Parañaque
Bacoor

Manila International Airport

**BANGKOK**

To Don Muang Airport
Nontha Buri
Bang Khen
Bang Kapi
Bang Lat Phrao
Khlong Lat Phrao
Bang Na
Phra Khanong
Phra Pradaeng
Samrong
Samut Prakan
Thon Buri
Bangkok Yai
Khlongsan
Rat Burana
Khun Thian
Taling Chan
Pathumwan
Dusit
Bangrak

*Chao Phraya*

**JAKARTA**

Jakarta
Tanjung Priok
Koja Utara
Cilincing
Pulo Gadung
Kemayoran Airport
Cempaka Putih
Kramat Jati
Jatinegara
Halim Perdanakusuma International Airport
Kota
Kebayoran Baru
Kebayoran Lama
Pondok Indah
Cilandak
Pasar Minggu
Tebet

*Teluk Jakarta*

JAKARTA JAWA BARAT

**SINGAPORE**

MALAYSIA
SINGAPORE
Changi Airport
Woodlands New Town
Sembawang
Jurong
Queenstown
Toa Payoh
Ang Mo Kio
Bedok
Tampines New Town
Bukit Timah
Holland Village
Buona Vista
Sentosa

*Straits of Singapore*

East from Greenwich

COPYRIGHT GEORGE PHILIP AND SON LTD.

1: 200 000

CALCUTTA

DELHI

New Delhi

Delhi Cantonment

BOMBAY

ARABIAN SEA

1: 200 000

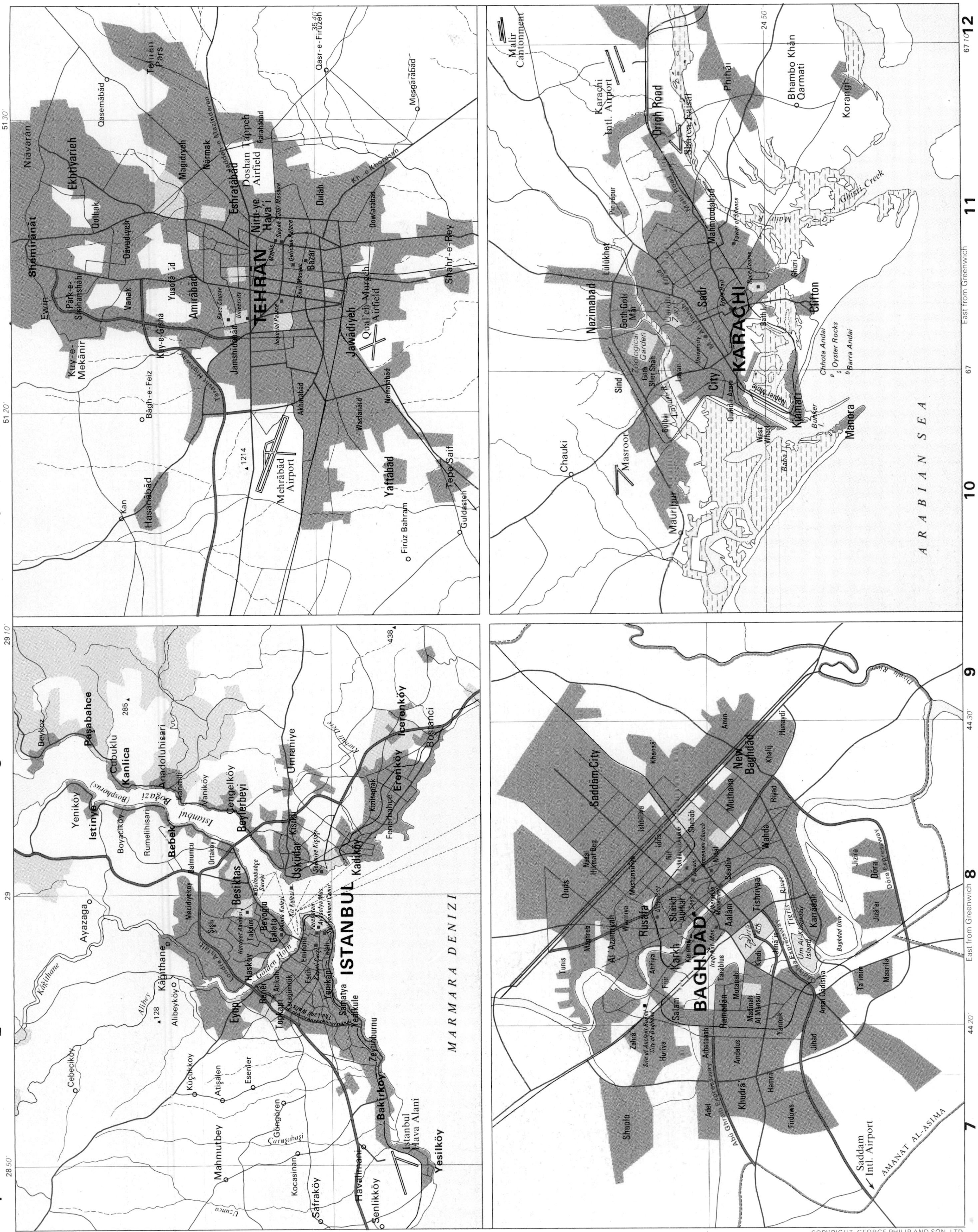

miles
km

**TEHRAN**

Tehrān Pars
Qasr-e-Firūzeh
Qasemābād
Mesgarābād
Niāvarān
Ekhtīyarīeh
Doshan Tappeh Airfield
Farahābād
Shemīrānat
Dolhak
Magidiyeh
Narmak
Eshratābād
Nīrū-ye Hava'ī
Dūlāb
Darvūdiyeh
Shahr-e Rey
Qual'eh-Morghī Airfield
Jawādiyeh
Ewin
Park-e Shahanshāh
Vanak
Yusūfā'd
Amīrābād
Jamshīdābād
Bāzār
Gulistān Palace
Imperial Palace
Kūy-e Gūshā
Kūy-e Mekānir
Bāgh-e-Feiz
Akbarābād
Wastaniard
Namghābād
Kan
Hasanābād
Mehrābād Airport
Yaffābād
Tepe Saif
Guldasteh
Firūz Bahrām

**ISTANBUL**

Beykoz
Peşabahce
Çubuklu
Kanlıca
Anadoluhisari
Yeniköy
Istinye
Rumelihisari
Vaniköy
Çengelköy
Beylerbeyi
Üsküdar
Kadıköy
Erenköy
İçerenköy
Bostancı
Kızıltoprak
Ayazaga
Kâğıthane
Alibey
Beşiktaş
Meçidiyeköy
Şişli
Taksim
Beyoğlu
Galata
Eyüp
Haskóy
Golden Horn
Fatih
Topkapı
Sanatya
Yedikule
Zeytinburnu
Bakırköy
Yesilköy
İstanbul Hava Alani
Mahmutbey
Kocasinan
Safraköy
Senlıköy
Havutlağı

MARMARA DENIZI

**KARACHI**

Malir Cantonment
Karachi Intl. Airport
Drigh Road
Sohrab Goth
Phihai
Bhambo Khân Qarmati
Korangi
Nazimabad
Luiūkhet
Sadr
Mahmudabad
Gothi Golī Mār
Goth Garden
Zoological Garden
Sher Shah
Clifton
Sind
Masroor
City
Chhota Andai
Oyster Rocks
Barra Andai
Chauki
Kiamari
Manora
West Wharf
Mauripur
Ghizri Creek

ARABIAN SEA

**BAGHDAD**

Saddām City
New Baghdad
Amin
Khansa
Muthaṇe
Husayni
Riyadh
Oujis
Hikmat Beg
Istihbarat
Idris
Shebab
Jizira
Rusāfa
Shaikh
Wahda
Dora
Al Azamīyah
Waziriya
Mustansiriya
Saadun
Karrādah
Dora Expressway
Tunis
Maghreb
Kifah
Baghdad Univ.
Al Mansūr
Salam
Fikr
Tababus
Ta'mim
Zahra
Madinat Al Mansūr
Ramadan
Andalus
Mutanabi
Hūrīa
'Andalus
Ataf Qadisiya
Khudrā
Jihad
Hamra
Ma'arifa
Shoala
Adel
Abu Ghraib Expressway
Firdows
Saddam Intl. Airport
AMANAT AL-ASIMA

East from Greenwich

COPYRIGHT. GEORGE PHILIP AND SON. LTD

1 : 200 000

1 0 1 2 3 4 5 miles
1 0 1 2 3 4 6 8 km

## CAIRO

Cairo International Airport
Almaza Airport
Masr el Gedida (Heliopolis)
El Qâhira
EL QÂHIRA
EL GÎZA
Masr el Qadîma (Old Cairo)
Imbâba
El Zamâlik
Shabrâmant
Gebel el Muqattam
Gebel et Tura
EL BAHR EL AHMAR
EL QÂHIRA
El Ma'âdi
Hilmiya
El Matariya
El Zeitûn
El Waili el Kubrâ
El Daher
El Basâtîya
Shubrâ EL QÂHIRA
El Kheima
Bâsûs
Basûs
Gezîrat
Warrâq Muhammad el-Hadf
Warrâq el 'Arab
Warrâq el Hadr
Geziret
el Dhahab
Bûlaq
El Munâ
Ghurîya
Madînet Nasr
Birak el Khalifa
El Basâtîn
El Basâlîn
Saft el Ahmah
El Kôm el Ahmah
El Bîraghi
El Baragh
El Talibîya
El Duqqi
El Awkaf
University
Garden City
Nâhia
Kirdâsa
Abû en Nuprus
Minshât el Bekkari
Tirsâ
Abû Musallam
Zâwiyet Abû Musallam
Sphinx
Pyramids
Cheops
Khafra
Myceninus
Bahr el Lubeini
El Mahit Idku il el Gharbi
Burtus
Ausîm
Hakim
256
204
198
178
83
Wâdî el Nahdein
Wâdî el Labibhi
Gebel el Ahmar
Helîopolis
Musturud
Bâhtim
East from Greenwich
31 20
31 10
30 N
6 30 N

## LAGOS

LAGOS
Lagos Lagoon
Bight of Benin
IKORODU
LAGOS MUNICIPALITY
Victoria Island
Iddo Island
Lagos Island
Free Commerce Creek
Oba's Palace
University of Lagos
Ebute-Metta
Shomolu
Yaba
Mushin
Ijebu
Idi-Oro
Apapa
Ajegunle
Agege
Ikeja
Lagos-Ikeja Airport
Oshodi
Isolo
Coker
Oworonsoki
Somolu
Agboyi Creek
Ebute-Ikorodu
Gbogbo
Gbagbo
Maiekete
Oreta
Igbopa
Aron
Ason
Ofin
Osorun
Ibese
Moba
Ogoyo
Alaguntan
Iboju
Iganmu
Ijora
Okokomaiko
Porto Novo Creek
Badagri Creek
Ogogoro
Okeogbe
Tarqua Bay
Lagos State
National Stadium
Ojota
Onisigun
Ogudu
Erunkan
Eregun
Ejigbo
Okunola
Cardoso
Idimu
Arida
Ikotun
Iseri-Osun
Jiesa-Tedo
Kirikiri
Amuwo
Olute
Agboju
Imore
Isunba
Ikeeta
Isagatedo
Evu
Shogunle
Shogunle
6 30 N
7 30
7 20
A
B

## JOHANNESBURG

JOHANNESBURG
Springs
Kwa-Thema
Brakpan
Benoni
Boksburg
Germiston
Alberton
Kempton Park
Modderfontein
Edenvale
Bedfordview
Kensington
Sandton
Sandown
Morningside
Randburg
Ferndale
Fontainebleau
Blackheath
Maraisburg
Roodepoort
Discovery
Florida
Meadowlands
Soweto
Moroka
Mofolo
Orlando East
Orlando West
Nancefield
Diepkloof Airfield
Baragwanath
Turffontein
Mondeor
Klipriviersberg
Krugersdorp
Lewisham
Jan Smuts Airport
Rand Airport
Wifield
Isando
Davegton
Daveyton
Geduld Dam
Modderfontein Deep Levels
Van Ryn Dam
New Modder
Petit
Springs
Bredell
Rietfontein
Rusville
Brentwood Park
Lakefield
Benoni South
Boksburg North
Boksburg South
Elsburg
Elspark
Wadeville
Roodekop
Alrode
New Redruth
Florentia
Verwoerdpark
Southcrest
Meyersdal
Moffat Park
Regents Park
Rosettenville
Robertsham
South Hills
La Rochelle
Booysens
Turffontein
Kenilworth
Ophirton
Newlands
Fairland
Northcliff
Windsor
Linden
Blairgowrie
Craighall
Hyde Park
Parkhurst
Greenside
Parkview
Westcliff
Saxonwold
Houghton
Observatory
Yeoville
Bellevue
Bertrams
Doornfontein
Bramley
Highlands North
Orange Grove
Norwood
Sydenham
Alexandra
Kelvin
Lombardy East
Sunningdale
Primrose
Simmer and Jack Mines
Victoria Lake
Elandsfontein
Sunnyridge
Delville
Parkhill Gardens
Lamboton
Cinderella Dam
Cinderella
Finaalspan
Dalview
Bornero
Rhodesfield
Allengrove
Eden
Creslawn
Lindropark
Lakeside
Modderfontein
Thornhill
Dunvegan
Eastleigh
Edenvale
The Wilds
Westdene
Crosby
Auckland Park
Rossmore
Melville
Brixton
Vrededorp
Mayfair
Fordsburg
Jukskei River
Rabie Park
Emmarentia
Greenhills
Melville Koppies
Montgomery Park
Rand Leases Gold Mines
Durban Roodepoort Deep Gold Mines
Kloofendal
Honeydew
Fleurhof
Weltevreden Park Ext
New Canada Dam
Klipspruit
Orlando Dam
Jabulani
Zola
Emdeni
Chiawelo
Molapo
Naledi
Dube
Mapetla
Moletsane
Poortview
Luipaardsvlei
Witpoortjie
Silverfields
Roodepoort Res
Kenmare
Kagiso
Coronationville
Newclare
Westbury
Pageview
Main Reef Road
Nasrec
Nancefield
1818
East from Greenwich
27 50
28
28 10
28 20
26 10 S

COPYRIGHT. GEORGE PHILIP AND SON. LTD.

1 : 200 000

0 1 2 3 4 5 miles
0 2 4 6 8 km

**Sydney (top map)**

1 2 3 4

A — Doonside, Blacktown, Winston Hills, Epping, Pennant Hills Park, Gordon, Killara, Forestville, Manly Warringah War Memorial Park, Dee Why, DEE WHY HEAD
Rooty Hill, Great Western Highway, Prospect, Severn Hills, Carlingford, Marsfield, Macquarie University, Lindfield, Chatswood, Middle Harbour, North Manly, Allambie Heights, Queenscliffe
Wallgrove, Western Freeway, Northmead, Eastwood, North Ryde, Lane Cove National Park, Willoughby, Middle Cove, Seaforth, Clontarf, Balgowlah, Manly
Prospect Reservoir, Greystanes, Wentworthville, Parramatta North, Dundas, Rydalmere, Ryde, Lane Cove, Chatswood, Northbridge, Balgowlah Heights, NORTH POINT

33°50' — Horsley Park, Parramatta, Granville, Parramatta River, Ermington, Gore Hill, Crows Nest, Mosman, MIDDLE HEAD, NORTH HEAD
Merrylands, North Auburn, Rhodes, Gladesville, Hunters Hill, Greenwich, North Sydney, St Leonards, MIDDLE HEAD, SOUTH HEAD
Auburn, Mortlake, Drummoyne, Balmain, Sydney Harbour Bridge, Taronga Zoological Park, Watsons Bay, Port Jackson

B — Cecil Park, Fairfield, Villawood, Regents Park, Flemington, Strathfield, Burwood, Concord, Five Dock, Observatory, Government House, Royal Botanic Gardens, Rose Bay, Double Bay, Dover Heights
Bossley Park, Bonnyrigg, Cabramatta, Carramar, Bass Hill, Hume Highway, Chullora, Enfield, Ashfield, SYDNEY, Leichhardt, Univ. of Sydney, Darling Harbour, Kings Cross, Paddington, Woollahra, Bondi
Hoxton Park Aerodrome, Green Valley, Liverpool, Moorebank, Georges Hall, Yagoona, Bankstown, Belmore, Campsie, Canterbury, Marrickville, Erskineville, S. Peters, Waterloo, Kensington, Randwick, Clovelly
West Hoxton, Hoxton Park, Lurnea, Milperra, Revesby, Padstow, Punchbowl, Lakemba, Earlwood, Rosebery, Univ. of N.S.W., Kingsford, Coogee
Warwick Farm Race Track, Bankstown Aerodrome, East Hills, Beverley Hills, Arncliffe, Mascot, Botany, Maroubra

34° — Glenfield, Macquarie Fields, Ingleburn, Military Reserve, Riverwood, Peakhurst, Bexley, Rockdale, Brighton le Sands, Sydney Airport, Banksmeadow, Pagewood, Malabar
Hurstville, Kogarah, Beverly Park, Ramsgate, San Souci, Phillip Bay, Long Bay, Little Bay
Minto, Menai, Woronora, Como, Oyster Bay, Blakehurst, Georges River Bridge, Sylvania, Captain Cook Bridge, Kurnell, La Perouse, Captain Cook Landing Place Park, CAPE BANKS

C — Botany Bay, Woolooware Bay, TOWRA POINT, SOUTH PACIFIC OCEAN
Sutherland, East from Greenwich, Jannali, Gymea, Miranda, Woolooware Bay, POTTER POINT

151°20'

---

**Melbourne (bottom map)**

5 6 7 8 9

D 37°40' — Westmeadows, Epping, Wattle Glen, Watsons Creek, Little Sugarloaf 271
Broadmeadows, Lalor, Mill Park, Plenty, Diamond Creek, Kangaroo Ground
Melbourne Airport, Tullamarine, Campbellfield, Thomastown, Greensborough, Maroondah, Research, Mt Lofty
Keilor, Glenroy, Fawkner, Reservoir, Bundoora Park, Bundoora, Watsonia, Eltham, Warrandyte, Wonga Park
Airport West, Pascoe Vale, Edwards Lake, Latrobe Uni., Heidelberg West, Macleod, Lower Plenty, Warrandyte Park

E — Keilor East, Niddrie, Essendon Airport, Coburg, Preston, Rosanna, Heidelberg, Bulleen, View Bank, Templestowe, Warrandyte South, Lilydale
Avondale Heights, Essendon, Moonee Ponds, Brunswick, Thornbury, Northcote, Ivanhoe, Templestowe Lower, Doncaster East, Park Orchards, Chirnside Park
Braybrook, Ascot Vale, Moonee Valley Racecourse, Royal Park, Zoo, Carlton, Fairfield, Bulleen, Balwyn North, Doncaster, Donvale, Warranwood, Croydon North, Mooroolbark
Maidstone, Flemington Racecourse, Yarra Bend, Eastern Freeway, Box Hill, Blackburn, Ringwood, Croydon

F 37°50' — Sunshine, Tottenham, Footscray, MELBOURNE, Kew, Balwyn, Box Hill, Nunawading, Mitcham, East Ringwood, Kilsyth, Mt Dandenong 633
Brooklyn, Fishermans Bend, Richmond, Canterbury, Surrey Hills, Box Hill South, Vermont, Heathmont, Montrose
Altona North, Newport, Spotswood, Albert Park, South Yarra, Camberwell, Burwood, Blackburn South, Forest Hill, Vermont Sth, Bayswater, Dongala Forest Res.
Williamstown, Port Melbourne, Middle Park, Toorak, Malvern, Glen Iris, Burwood Highway, Burwood East, Wantirna, Boronia, The Basin, Olinda
Altona, Hobsons Bay, St. Kilda, Armadale, Ashburton, Ashwood, Mt Waverley, Syndal, Glen Waverley, One Tree Hill 562, Ferntree Gully, Sassafras
Altona Bay, Caulfield, Elsternwick, Chadstone, Glen Iris, Caribbean Gardens, Ferntree Gully N.P., Tremont
Elwood, Glenhuntly, Carnegie, Murrumbeena, Oakleigh, Wheelers Hill, Scoresby, Knoxfield, Upper Ferntree Gully, Upwey, Belgrave
Brighton, McKinnon, Bentleigh, Bentleigh East, Clayton, Notting Hill, Mulgrave, Rowville, Tecoma

144°50' 145° East from Greenwich 145°10' 145°20'

COPYRIGHT. GEORGE PHILIP AND SON. LTD.

1: 200 000

5 miles
8 km

1    2    3    4    5

**MONTREAL · TORONTO Map**

Lorraine
Ste-Thérèse
St.-Augustin
Ste-Thérèse Ouest
Ste-Rose
Auteuil
Chicot
Chicot
Vimont
St Vincent de Paul
Pointe-Aux-Trembles
R. des Prairies
Rivière-des-Prairies
Montréal-Est
St.-Eustache
Fabreville
Ville de Laval
Duvernay
Montréal Nord
Anjou
Longue Point
Île de Boucherville
Boucherville
La Fresnière
St.-Martin
Pont-Viau
St-Léonard
St-Jean-de-dieu
Deux-Montagnes
Laval-Ouest
Laval-des-Rapides
St-Michel
Parc Maisonneuve
St-Joseph-du-Lac
Laval-sur-le-Lac
Ste-Dorothée
Chomedey
Abord à Plouffe
Ahuntsic
Boul. Pie-IX Olympique
Maisonneuve
Ste-Marthe-sur-le-Lac
Roxboro
Aéroport de Cartierville
MONTRÉAL
Chambly
Jacques Cartier
Longueuil
Le Trappe
Pointe-Calumet
Île Bizard
Dollard-des-Ormeaux
St.-Laurent
Mont Royal
Outremont
Parc Mont-Royal
Île Ste Hélène
Mackayville
Île Bizard
Ste-Geneviève
Dollard Des Ormeaux
Univ. McGill
Terre des Hommes
St.-Hubert
Pierrefonds
Aéroport de Dorval
Westmount
Hampstead
Côte-St-Luc
Forum
Pont Victoria
Lemoyne
Préville
Greenfield Park
Lac des Deux Montagnes
Beaconsfield
Pointe-Claire
Kirkland
Côte-St-Luc
St-Pierre
Verdun
Île des Soeurs
Pont Champlain
Notre-Dame
Île-Cadieux
Baie-d'Urfé
Dorval
Lachine
Lasalle
Brossard
Vaudreuil-sur-le-Lac
Senneville
Ste-Anne de Bellevue
Île aux Herons
St. Jacques
Canal de la Rive Sud
La Prairie
Vaudreuil
Terrasse-Vaudreuil
Île Perrot
Lac Saint - Louis
Caughnawaga
Sainte-Catherine
La Prairie
Dorion
Ile-Perrot
Notre-Dame-de-L'Île-Perrot
MONTREAL VAUDREUIL
West from Greenwich
Candiac

Maple
Richvale
Richmond Hill
Buttonville
Cherrywood
Kleinburg
Langstaff
Armadale
DURHAM
Dunbarton
Coleraine
East Don
Milliken
Markham
YORK TORONTO
Brown
Rouge
Fairport
Thornhill
Concord
Newton Brook
Agincourt
Malvern
Port Union
Woodbridge
Pine Grove
Edgeley
Fisherville
Willowdale
Northmount
MacDonald
Morningside Park
Highland Creek
West Rouge
Rouge Hill
Humber Summit
G. Ross Lord Park
York University
North York
Lansing
York Mills
Wexford
Scarborough
West Hill
Beaumonte Heights
Black Creek Pioneer Village
Canada Forces Base
Armour Heights
Don Mills
Bendale
Thistletown
Downsview Dells Park
Wilket Creek Park
Cliffside
Scarborough
Kipling Heights
West Don
Ontario Science Centre
Highland Creek
Rexdale
Downsview
Lawrence Heights
Leaside
Danforth
Malton
Weston
Humbermea
Thorncliffe
Dentonia Park
Oakdale
Forest Hill
York
East York
Birch Cliff
Toronto International Airport (Lester B. Pearson)
Humber Valley Village
Mount Dennis
Danforth Ave
Key Gardens
Hanlon
Lambton Mills
Swansea
University of Toronto
Parliament Buildings
Riverdale
Etobicoke
Humber Valley Park
High Park
Bloor
CN Tower
Islington
Kingsway
Parkdale
Gardiner Expressway
TORONTO
Markland Wood
Humber Bay
Exhibition Stadium
Toronto Harbour
Burnhamthorpe
Summerville
The Queensway
Humber Bay
Ontario Place
Toronto Island
Island Park
Browns Line
Mimico
GIBRALTAR POINT
Cooksville
Mississauga
Long Branch
Lakeview
New Toronto
West from Greenwich
Lake Ontario

COPYRIGHT GEORGE PHILIP AND SON LTD.

6    7    8    9    10

1: 200 000

miles / km

1  0  1  2  3  4  5 miles
1  0  2  4  6  8 km

**1**  **2**  **3**  **4**

**A**

NEW HAMPSHIRE
MASSACHUSETTS

Seavey Hill
Peters Pond
**Methuen**
**Lawrence**
West Boxford
Baldpate Hill
Baldpate Pond
Rowley
Chaplinville
▲65
Long Pond
Colinsville
South Lawrence
**North Andover**
Town Farm Hill
87
Georgetown
Rowley
**Ipswich**
Mascoptic Lake
Lowell Dracut State Forest
Kenwood
West Andover
Shawsheen Village
**Andover**
Woodchuck Hill
Boston Hill
Boxford State Forest
Lowe Pond
State Forest Hood Pond
Willowdale State Forest
Turner Hill
81
42 40'

**North Chelmsford**

42 40'

**B**

**Lowell**
North Tewksbury
111
Haggetts Pond
Harold
Bald Hill
75
Topsfield
Putnamville Res.
**Wenham**
**South Hamilton**
**West Chelmsford**
Ballardvale
Parker State Forest
Salem Turnpike
ESSEX
MIDDLESEX
**Danvers**
Wenham Lake
**North Beverly**
**Chelmsford**
North Billerica
East Billerica
Tewksbury
Fosters Pond
Martins Pond
Middleton
Middleton Pond
Beverly Municipal Airport
Davensport
**Beverly**
124
Warren Hill
South Chelmsford
Manning State
**N. Reading**
North Wilmington
Ubrans Hill
Beverley Harbor

**C**

Heart Pond
River Pines
**Billerica**
**Pinehurst**
Silver Lake
**Wilmington**
**Reading**
Reading Highlands
Suntaug Lake
**Peabody**
Witch House
Salem Maritime Nat. Hist. Site
**Salem**
Salem Harbor
Rail Tree Hill
Riverside
Nutting Lake
L. Quannapowitt
South Lynnfield
South Peabody
**Marblehead**
Carlisle
**Burlington**
North Woburn
Route 128
Mishawum Lake
**Wakefield**
North Saugus
Spring Pond
Clifton
North Acton
**Bedford**
**Woburn**
Wynnmere
Stoneham
Saugus R. Greenwood
**Saugus**
Brenls Pond
**Lynn**
**Swampscott**
National Wildlife Refuge
Horn Pond
Breakheart Reservation
West Lynn
Nahant Bay
East Acton
Old Manse
**Concord**
Laurence G. Hanscom Field
North Lexington
North Res.
Middlesex Fells Reservation
Split Pond
**Melrose**
Mt. Hood Mem. Park
Lynn Harbor
**Nahant**

42 30'

42 30'

West Concord
Minute Man Natural History Park
114
**Winchester**
South Res.
**Malden**
EAST POINT
Nahant Harbor
Fairhaven Hill
Sandy Pond
**Lexington**
Arlington Heights
East Lexington
Mystic Lakes
West Medford
**Revere**
Beachmont
Broad Sound
ESSEX
SUFFOLK
Fairhaven Bay
Lincoln
Cambridge Reservoir
South Lincoln
Concord
**Arlington**
**Medford**
**Everett**
**Chelsea**
Orient Hts.
Farrar Pond
North Sudbury
69
**Belmont**
**Somerville**
Charlestown
East Boston
**Winthrop**
Boston Bay
Cat Rock Hill
146 Prospect Hill
**Waltham**
Park
Waverley
N. Cambridge
Harvard University
Logan International Airport
Deer Island
**Sudbury**
Goodman Hill
**Weston**
**Watertown**
**Cambridge**
Bunker Hill Mon.
Old North Church
Outer Brewster Island
South Sudbury
Heard Pond
Reeves Hill 124
Wayland
Weston Reservoir
Auburndale
North Brighton
**Allston**
Mass. Inst. of Tech.
Old State House
**BOSTON**
Boston Harbor
Calf Island
Middle Brewster Island

42 20'

42 20'

Hultman Aqueduct
Cochituate
Norumbega Reservoir
Massachusetts Tpk.
**Newton**
Newton Highlands
Chestnut Hill
John F. Kennedy Nat. Hist. Site
Museum of Fine Arts
**South Boston**
Old Harbor
Spectacle Island
Great Brewster Island
Saxonville
**Framingham**
Wellesley Fells
Wellesley Hills
**Brookline**
Boylston St.
**Roxbury**
Blake House
Grove Hall
Fields Corner
Dorchester Bay
Thompson Island
**Hull**
POINT ALLERTON
Morses Pond
Oak Hill Park
Arnold Arboretum
Jamaica Plain
Franklin Park
Squantum
Long Island
Peddocks Island
Hingham Bay
**Wellesley**
Needham Heights
Roslindale
W. Roxbury
**Dorchester**
**Wollaston**
Grape Island
Nantasket Beach
North Cohasset
**Natick**
L. Waban
**Needham**
SUFFOLK NORFOLK
**Mattapan**
Milton Village
Quincy Bay
Houghs Neck
Hingham Harbor
**Hingham**
Lake Cochituate
Stony Brook Res.
Hyde Park
**Quincy**
Adams Nat. Hist. Site
North Weymouth
Brush Hill 121
125
**Dedham**
Dover
Strawberry Hill 118
Fowl Meadow Res.
Blue Hills Reservation
**Milton**
South Quincy
East Braintree
**Weymouth**
East Weymouth
South Hingham

42 10'

East Holliston
Sherborn
Karns Pond
**Westwood**
Islington
158
Gt. Blue Hill 194
Route 128
**Braintree**
South Braintree
Whitmans Pond
Pilgrims Hy.
Liberty Plain
Harding
**Norwood**
North Randolph
Ponkapog
Ponkapog Pond
Great Pond
South Weymouth
Accord
Millis
MIDDLESEX NORFOLK
**Medfield**
Willett Pond
**Norwood Memorial Airport**
**Canton**
Reservoir Pond
**Randolph**
South Braintree
NORFOLK PLYMOUTH
Accord Pond

71 20'
71 10'
West from Greenwich
71

**1**  **2**  **3**  **4**

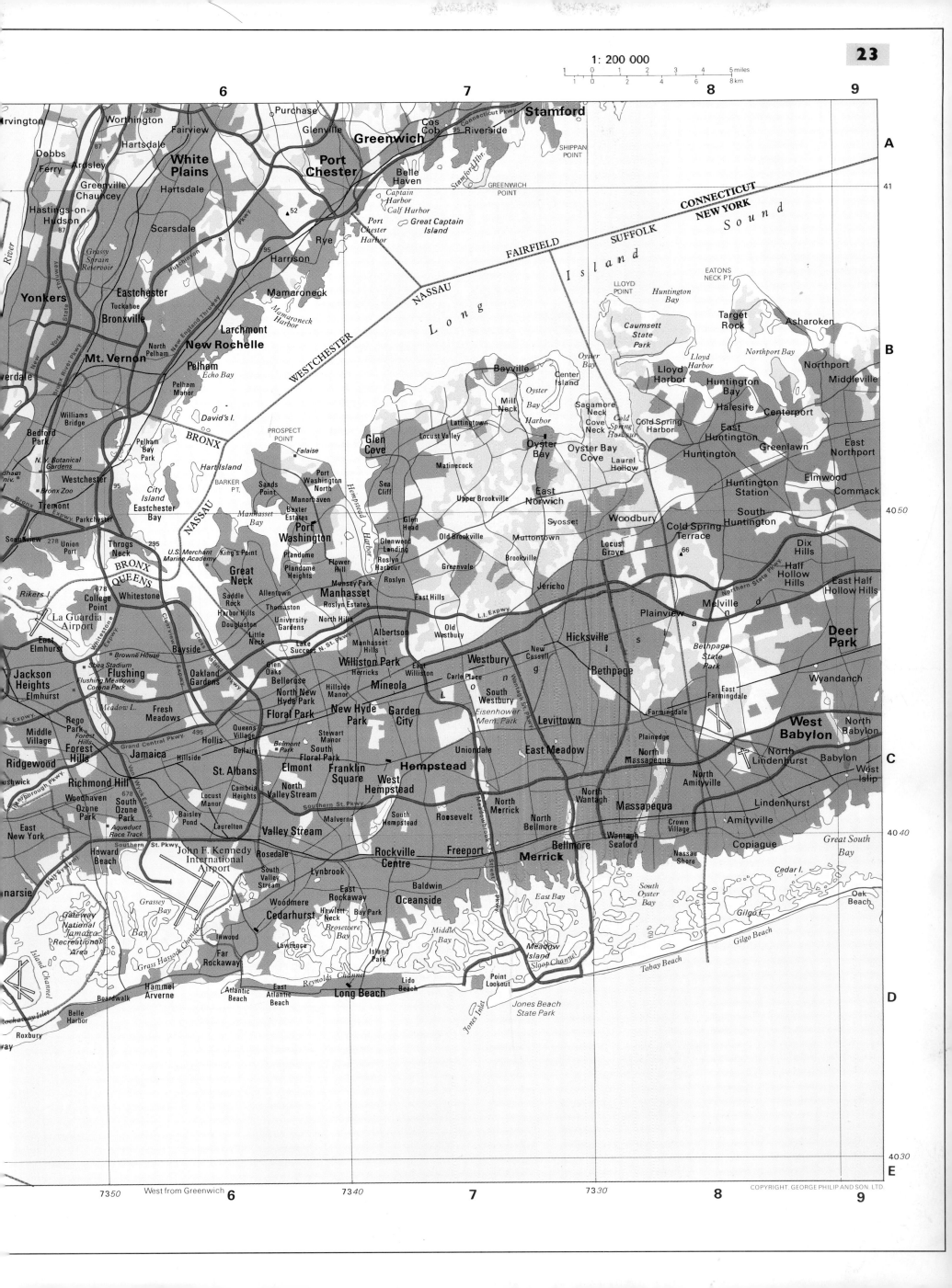

1: 200 000

5 miles
8 km

6                    7                    8                    9

**A**                                                                          41

**B**

Irvington    Worthington    Fairview    Purchase    Glenville    Cos Cob    Riverside    **Stamford**
Dobbs Ferry    Hartsdale        **Greenwich**                    SHIPPAN POINT
Ardsley    287                                                    Belle Haven    GREENWICH POINT
Greenville Chauncey    Hartsdale    White Plains    Port Chester    Captain Harbor    Calf Harbor
Hastings-on-Hudson    87    Scarsdale    52    Rye    Great Captain Island
                                                            CONNECTICUT
                                                            NEW YORK

**Yonkers**    Eastchester    95    Harrison    FAIRFIELD    SUFFOLK    Long    Island    Sound
Tuckahoe    Mamaroneck    NASSAU    LLOYD POINT    EATONS NECK PT.
Bronxville    Larchmont    Mamaroneck Harbor    WESTCHESTER    Huntington Bay
Mt. Vernon    New Rochelle    Caumsett State Park    Target Rock    Asharoken
Pelham    Echo Bay    Northport Bay    Northport
riverdale    Pelham Manor    David's I.    Bayville    Center Island    Lloyd Harbor    Huntington Bay    Middleville
Bedford Park    BRONX    Falaise    PROSPECT POINT    Glen Cove    Oyster Bay    Sagamore Neck    Cold Spring Harbor    Halesite    Centerport
N.Y. Botanical Gardens    Pelham Bay Park    HART ISLAND    Port Washington North    Matinecock    Oyster Bay    Oyster Bay Cove    Laurel Hollow    East Huntington    Greenlawn    East Northport
Westchester    BARKER PT.    Sands Point    Sea Cliff    Upper Brookville    East Norwich    Huntington    Huntington Station    Elmwood    Commack
Tremont    95    City Island    Manorhaven    Baxter Estates    Glen Head    Old Brookville    Woodbury    Cold Spring Terrace    South Huntington    Dix Hills
Union Port    278    Eastchester Bay    Port Washington    Glenwood Landing    Syosset    Muttontown    Locust Grove    66    Half Hollow Hills
Throgs Neck    295    Manhasset Bay    Plandome    Roslyn Harbour    Greenvale    Brookville    Jericho    Melville    East Half Hollow Hills
BRONX QUEENS    U.S. Merchant Marine Academy    Plandome Heights    Roslyn    East Hills    Plainview    Northern State Pkwy.    **Deer Park**
Rikers I.    678    King's Point    Great Neck    Saddle Rock    Thomaston    Manhasset    North Hills    Old Westbury    Hicksville    Bethpage State Park
College Point    Whitestone    Harbor Hills    University Gardens    Manhasset Hills    Albertson    New Cassell    Westbury    Bethpage
La Guardia Airport    Douglaston    Little Neck    Lake Success    Williston Park    East Williston    Carle Place    South Westbury    Farmingdale    East Farmingdale    Wyandanch
East Elmhurst    Bayside    Glen Oaks    Herricks    Mineola    Eisenhower Mem. Park    Levittown    Plainedge    **West Babylon**    North Babylon
Jackson Heights    Flushing    Oakland Gardens    Bellerose    Hillside Manor    New Hyde Park    Garden City    Uniondale    East Meadow    North Massapequa    North Lindenhurst    Babylon    West Islip
Elmhurst    Flushing Meadows Corona Park    North New Hyde Park    Floral Park    Franklin Square    **Hempstead**    North Merrick    Massapequa    North Amityville    Lindenhurst
Rego Park    Fresh Meadows    Queens Village    Stewart Manor    Elmont    West Hempstead    Roosevelt    North Bellmore    North Wantagh    Amityville
Middle Village    Forest Hills    Hollis    Bellaire    New Hyde Park    South Floral Park    South Hempstead    North Merrick    Crown Village    Copiague
Forest Hills    Jamaica    Hillside    Belmont Park    Cambria Heights    North Valley Stream    Malverne    Bellmore    Nassau Shore    Great South Bay
Ridgewood    Richmond Hill    Locust Manor    Valley Stream    South Valley Stream    Rockville Centre    Freeport    **Merrick**    Wantagh Seaford    Cedar I.
Woodhaven South Ozone Park    Baisley Pond    Laurelton    Rosedale    Lynbrook    Baldwin    East Bay    South Oyster Bay    Gilgo I.    Oak Beach
East New York    Aqueduct Race Track    Howard Beach    John F. Kennedy International Airport    East Rockaway    Oceanside    Hewlett Neck    Bay Park    Island Park    Gilgo Beach
narsie    Gateway National Recreational Area    Grassey Bay    Cedarhurst    Brosewere Bay    Middle Bay    Meadow Island    Tobay Beach
Jamaica Bay    Grass Hassock Channel    Inwood    Lawrence    Reynolds Channel    Lido Beach    Point Lookout    Jones Beach State Park
Boardwalk    Hammel Arverne    Atlantic Beach    East Atlantic Beach    Long Beach    Jones Inlet
Belle Harbor    Roxbury

**C**                                                                          40 40

**D**

**E**                                                                          40 30

West from Greenwich    6            7            8            9
73 50                73 40        73 30

COPYRIGHT GEORGE PHILIP AND SON LTD.

1 : 200 000

5 miles
8 km

# PHILADELPHIA

Bristol
Burlington
Willingboro
Palmyra
Pennsauken
Camden
Cherry Hill
Haddonfield
West Berlin
Berlin
Albion
Florence

Willow Grove
Abington
Jenkintown
Germantown
Gloucester City
Woodbury
Pitman

Norristown
Conshohocken
King of Prussia
Bryn Mawr
Ardmore
Upper Darby
Havertown
Drexel Hill
Darby
Lansdowne
Yeadon
Collingdale
Swarthmore
Media
Broomall
Newtown Square
Wayne
Paoli
Malvern

Phoenixville
Valley Forge
Audubon
Oaks

West Chester
Dulworthtown
Wilmington

Delaware River
Schuylkill River
Pennypack Creek

PENNSYLVANIA
NEW JERSEY
DELAWARE

Philadelphia International Airport
Philadelphia Airport

West from Greenwich

COPYRIGHT. GEORGE PHILIP AND SON. LTD.

1:200 000

Owings Mills

1    2    3    4

**Towson**

Lutherville
Timonium

Providence

Riderwood

Ruxton

Parkville

Perry
Hall

Germantown

Joppatowne

Loreley

Carney

White Marsh

Harrisonville

Pikesville

BALTIMORE
CITY OF BALTIMORE

Rodgers
Forge

Loch Raven Village

Middle
River

Bird River
Harewood Park

HARFORD
BALTIMORE

Harewood
Hts.

Randallstown

Woodmore

Rockdale

Milford

Lochearn

Fullerton

Putty Hill

Overlea

Elmwood

Rossville

Kenwood

Middleborough

Martin State
Nat'l Airport

Carroll
Island

Granite

Hobbville

Rosedale

Woodstock

Woodlawn

Daniels
Patapsco
State Park

Catonsville
Manor

West
Edmondale

John Hopkins Univ.
& Art Museum

Druid Hill
Park

Druid Lake

North Ave.

Chesaco
Park

Essex

Miller
Island

Baltimore National Pike

Valley
Mede

Normandy
Heights

**BALTIMORE**

Eastpoint

North Point

Buck River

Pine
Orchard

Ellicott City

Columbia
Hills

Oella

**Catonsville**

Bloomsbury

Arbutus

Carroll
Park

Fort McHenry Nat.
Mon. & Hist. Shrine

Patapsco
River

**Dundalk**

Inverness

Edgemere

Hart Island

Oakland
Mills

Worthington

Jonestown

**Halethorpe**

Ilchester

**Lansdowne**

Baltimore
Highlands

Turner

Francis Scott Key Bridge

Sparrows
Point

Bethlehem
Steel Plant

Bay Shore
Park

Chesapeake
Bay

**Columbia**

Elkridge

**Linthicum Heights**

Shipley

Pumphrey

Arundel
Gardens

**Brooklyn**

Arundel
Village

Curtis Bay

Fort Howard

Old
Road Bay

BALTIMORE
ANNE ARUNDEL

Baltimore Washington
Int'l Airport

Ferndale

Rippling
Ridge

Foremans Corner

5    6    7    8    9

Travilah

Rockville

Foxhall

Fairland

Muirkirk

Montpelier

Randolph
Hills

Glenmont

Meadowood

Calverton

The Glen

Montrose

Wheaton
Regional Park

**Wheaton**

White
Oak

Beltsville

Shady Oak

Cabin John
Regional Park

Kensington

Kemp Mill

Oak View

Beltsville
Airport

Dranesville

Great Falls

**Potomac**

Chevy Chase
View

Adelphi

**Greenbelt**

Great Falls
Park

**Bethesda**

**Chevy
Chase**

Woodmont

**Silver Spring**

Langley Park

**College
Park**

Univ. of Maryland

Lanham

Seabrook

**Reston**

Glen Echo

Cabin John

Somerset

Takoma
Park

Chillum

University
Park

Greenbelt
Park

East
Pines

**New
Carrollton**

Dulles Airport Access Rd.

Langley

Brookmont

Rock Creek
Park

Brightwood

**Hyattsville**

Mt. Rainier

Riverdale

John Hanson Hwy.

Edmonston

**McLean**

American
University

Glenarden

Hunters
Valley

Franklin
Park

**WASHINGTON**

Georgetown

Bladensburg

Landover
Hills

**Vienna**

Pimmit
Hills

Dunn
Loring

The White
House

Trinidad

Cheverly

Palmer
Park

Fairmount Heights

**Arlington**

Rosslyn

Lincoln Memorial

The Mall

Library of
Congress

**Seat
Pleasant**

Kettering

**Falls
Church**

Seven Corners

Hillwood

Arlington Nat'l
Cemetery

Pentagon

Ft. du Pont
Park

Capitol
Hts.

Millwood

Ritchie

District Hts.

Broyhill
Park

ARLINGTON
FAIRFAX

East Arlington

G. Mason Mem. Br.
East
Potomac
Park

Oakland

Coral
Hills

**Fairfax**

Annalee Hts.

Holmes
Acres

L. Barcroft

Baileys
Crossroads

Parklawn

Washington
Nat'l Airport

Anacostia

PRINCE GEORGES

**Suitland**

**Forestville**

**Annandale**

Fairfax Station

Kings Park

North
Springfield

**Alexandria**

Glassmanor

Forest
Heights

**Hillcrest
Hts.**

**Silver Hill**

Morningside

Andrews
Air Force
Base

West Springfield

**Springfield**

Franconia

Rose Hill

Groveton

Huntington

Belle
Haven

Fort Foote
Village

South
Lawn

Oxon Hill

Temple
Hills Park

Camp
Springs

Oaklawn

5    6    7    8    9

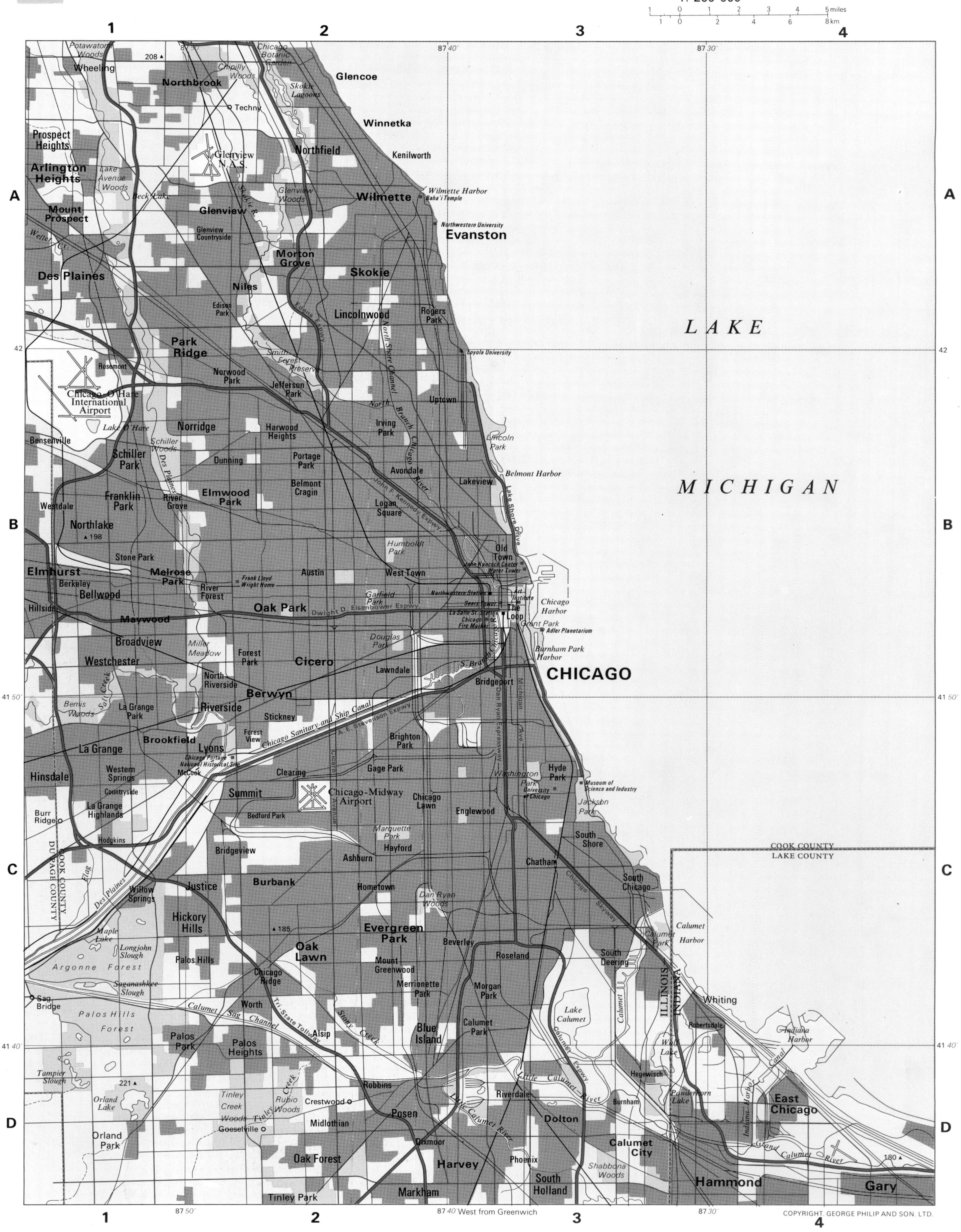

1: 200 000

1    2    3    4

A    A

B    B

C    C

D    D

1    2    3    4

LAKE

MICHIGAN

Potawatomi Woods
Wheeling
208 ▲
Northbrook
Chipilly Woods
Chicago Botanic Garden
Glencoe
Techny
Skokie Lagoons
Winnetka
Prospect Heights
Glenview N.A.S.
Northfield
Kenilworth
Arlington Heights
Lake Avenue Woods
Glenview Woods
Wilmette Harbor
Baha'i Temple
Wilmette
Mount Prospect
Beck Lake
Glenview
Glenview Countryside
Morton Grove
Northwestern University
Evanston
Des Plaines
Niles
Skokie
Weller Cr.
Edison Park
Evans Expy.
Lincolnwood
Rogers Park
42    42
Park Ridge
Norwood Park
Smith Forest Preserve
North Shore Channel
Loyola University
Chicago O'Hare International Airport
Resmont
Jefferson Park
North Branch Chicago River
Uptown
Bensenville
Lake O'Hare
Schiller Woods
Des Plaines R.
Dunning
Harwood Heights
Irving Park
Lincoln Park
Schiller Park
Norridge
Portage Park
Avondale
John F. Kennedy Expwy.
Lakeview
Belmont Harbor
Westdale
Franklin Park
River Grove
Elmwood Park
Belmont Cragin
Logan Square
Lake Shore Drive
Northlake
▲198
Stone Park
Humboldt Park
Old Town
John Hancock Center Water Tower
B    B
Elmhurst
Melrose Park
River Forest
Austin
West Town
Frank Lloyd Wright Home
Northwestern Station
Art Institute
Chicago Harbor
Berkeley
Garfield Park
Sears Tower
Bellwood
Oak Park
Dwight D. Eisenhower Expwy.
La Salle St. Station
The Loop
Grant Park
Hillside
Maywood
Chicago Fire Marker
Adler Planetarium
Broadview
Miller Meadow
Forest Park
Cicero
Douglas Park
Lawndale
S. Branch
Burnham Park Harbor
Westchester
North Riverside
Berwyn
Bridgeport
CHICAGO
41 50    41 50
Bemis Woods
Salt Creek
La Grange Park
Riverside
Stickney
Forest View
Chicago Sanitary and Ship Canal
Brighton Park
Michigan Ave.
La Grange
Brookfield
Lyons
A. E. Stevenson Expwy.
Gage Park
Hyde Park
Washington Park
Hinsdale
Western Springs
McCook
Clearing
Cicero Avenue
Chicago-Midway Airport
Chicago Lawn
University of Chicago
Museum of Science and Industry
Countryside
La Grange Highlands
Summit
Bedford Park
Englewood
Jackson Park
Dan Ryan Expressway
Burr Ridge
Hodgkins
Bridgeview
Ashburn
Hayford
Marquette Park
South Shore
C    C
Des Plaines R.
Willow Springs
Justice
Burbank
Hometown
Chatham
Dan Ryan Woods
South Chicago
COOK COUNTY / LAKE COUNTY
Hickory Hills
Chicago Ridge
Oak Lawn
Evergreen Park
Beverley
Chicago Skyway
Calumet Park
Calumet Harbor
Maple Lake
Argonne Forest
Longjohn Slough
▲185
Palos Hills
Mount Greenwood
Roseland
South Deering
ILLINOIS / INDIANA
Sag Bridge
Saganashkee Slough
Worth
Merrionette Park
Morgan Park
Lake Calumet
Calumet Expy.
Whiting
Palos Hills Forest
Calumet Sag Channel
Alsip
Blue Island
Calumet Park
Robertsdale
Indiana Harbor
41 40    41 40
Tampier Slough
221 ▲
Palos Park
Palos Heights
Stony Creek
Little Calumet River
Wolf Lake
Hegewisch
Powderhorn Lake
180 ▲
Orland Lake
Tinley Creek Woods
Rubio Woods
Crestwood
Robbins
Riverdale
Burnham
Grand Calumet River
East Chicago
Orland Park
Goeselville
Midlothian
Posen
Dolton
Shabbona Woods
Indiana Harbor Canal
Oxmoor
Harvey
Phoenix
Calumet City
Hammond
Gary
Tinley Park
Markham
South Holland

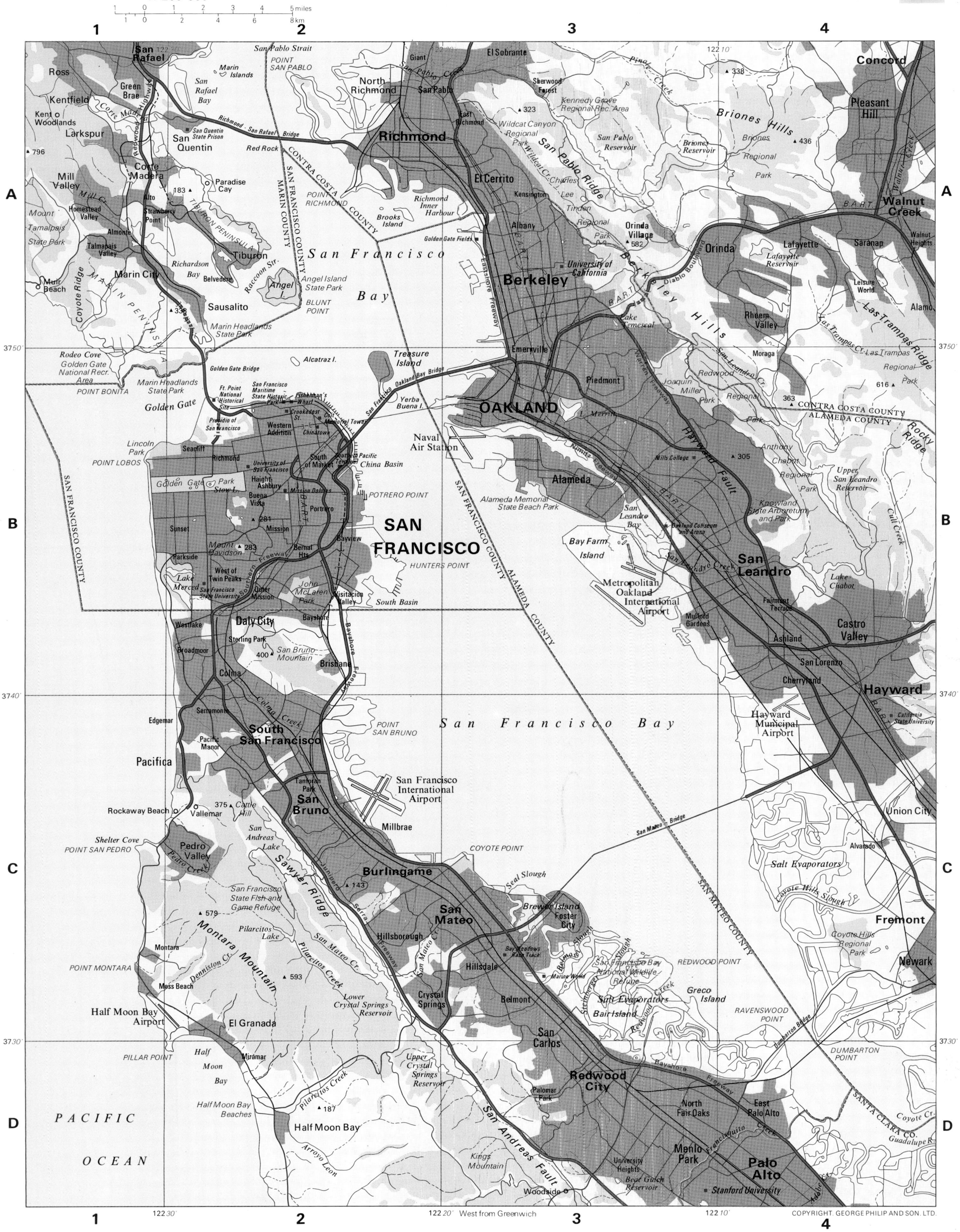

1: 200 000

0 1 2 3 4 5 miles
0 2 4 6 8 km

**SAN FRANCISCO**

**OAKLAND**

**Berkeley**

**Richmond**

San Rafael

Ross
Kentfield
Kent o Woodlands
Larkspur
Green Brae
Mill Valley
Corte Madera
San Quentin
San Quentin State Prison
Almonte
Talmalpais Valley
Tiburon
Belvedere
Mount Tamalpais State Park
Marin City
Muir Beach
Sausalito

San Rafael Bay
San Pablo Strait
POINT SAN PABLO
Marin Islands
North Richmond
San Pablo
El Sobrante
Giant
Sherwood Forest
Kennedy Grove Regional Rec. Area
Concord
Pleasant Hill
Briones Hills
Briones Reservoir
Briones Regional Park
Walnut Creek

Richmond Inner Harbour
Brooks Island
Richmond San Rafael Bridge
Red Rock
Point Richmond
El Cerrito
Albany
Kensington
Tilden Regional Park
Orinda Village
Orinda
Lafayette
Lafayette Reservoir
Saranap
Walnut Heights

Golden Gate Fields
University of California
Berkeley Hills
Rheem Valley
Moraga
Leisure World
Alamo

San Francisco Bay
Emeryville
Piedmont
Lake Temescal
Redwood Regional Park
Joaquin Miller Park

Treasure Island
Oakland Bay Bridge
Yerba Buena I.
Alcatraz I.
Angel Island State Park
BLUNT POINT
Angel

Golden Gate Bridge
Ft. Point National Historical Site
San Francisco Maritime State Historical Park
Fisherman's Wharf
Crookedest St.
Telegraph Tower
Western Addition
Chinatown
South of Market
Pacific
China Basin
Naval Air Station
Alameda
Mills College
Anthony Chabot Regional Park
Upper San Leandro Reservoir
Rocky Ridge

Golden Gate
Presidio of San Francisco
Lincoln Park
POINT LOBOS
Seacliff
Richmond
University of San Francisco
Haight Ashbury
Buena Vista
Mission Dolores
Potrero
POTRERO POINT
San Leandro Bay
Oakland Coliseum and Arena
San Leandro
Lake Chabot

Golden Gate Park
Stow L.
Sunset
Mount Davidson
Bernal Hts.
Bayview
HUNTERS POINT
Bay Farm Island
Metropolitan Oakland International Airport
Mulford Gardens
Fairmont Terrace
Ashland
Castro Valley
San Lorenzo
Cherryland

Parkside
West of Twin Peaks
Lake Merced
San Francisco State University
Outer Mission
John McLaren Park
Visitacion Valley
South Basin
Hayward
California State University

Westlake
Daly City
Bayshore
Broadmoor
Sterling Park
San Bruno Mountain
Brisbane
Colma
Colma Creek
Serramonte
Edgemar
Pacific Manor
South San Francisco
Point San Bruno
San Francisco Bay
Hayward Municipal Airport

Pacifica
Tanforan Park
San Bruno
San Francisco International Airport
Millbrae
Union City
Alvarado
Salt Evaporators
Coyote Hills Regional Park

Rockaway Beach
Vallemar
Cattle Hill
San Andreas Lake
Pedro Valley
Pedro Creek
POINT SAN PEDRO
Shelter Cove
San Francisco State Fish and Game Refuge
Montara
Burlingame
Hillsborough
San Mateo
Coyote Point
Seal Slough
Brewer Island
Foster City
San Francisco Bay National Wildlife Refuge
Redwood Point
Greco Island
Fremont
Coyote Hills Regional Park
Newark

Moss Beach
Half Moon Bay Airport
El Granada
Montara Mountain
Pilarcitos Lake
Pilarcitos Creek
Lower Crystal Springs Reservoir
Hillsdale
Marine World
Bay Meadows Race Track
Bair Island
Salt Evaporators
RAVENSWOOD POINT

PILLAR POINT
Half Moon Bay
Miramar
Crystal Springs
Belmont
San Carlos
Redwood City
Palomar Park
North Fair Oaks
East Palo Alto
DUMBARTON POINT

PACIFIC OCEAN
Half Moon Bay Beaches
Upper Crystal Springs Reservoir
San Andreas Fault
Menlo Park
Palo Alto
University Heights
Stanford University
Woodside
Kings Mountain

SAN FRANCISCO COUNTY
CONTRA COSTA COUNTY
ALAMEDA COUNTY
SAN MATEO COUNTY
SANTA CLARA CO.

796
183
338
323
582
436
616
363
338
305
400
375
143
579
593
187
281
283

3750'  3740'  3730'
122 30'   122 20'  West from Greenwich   122 10'

1: 200 000

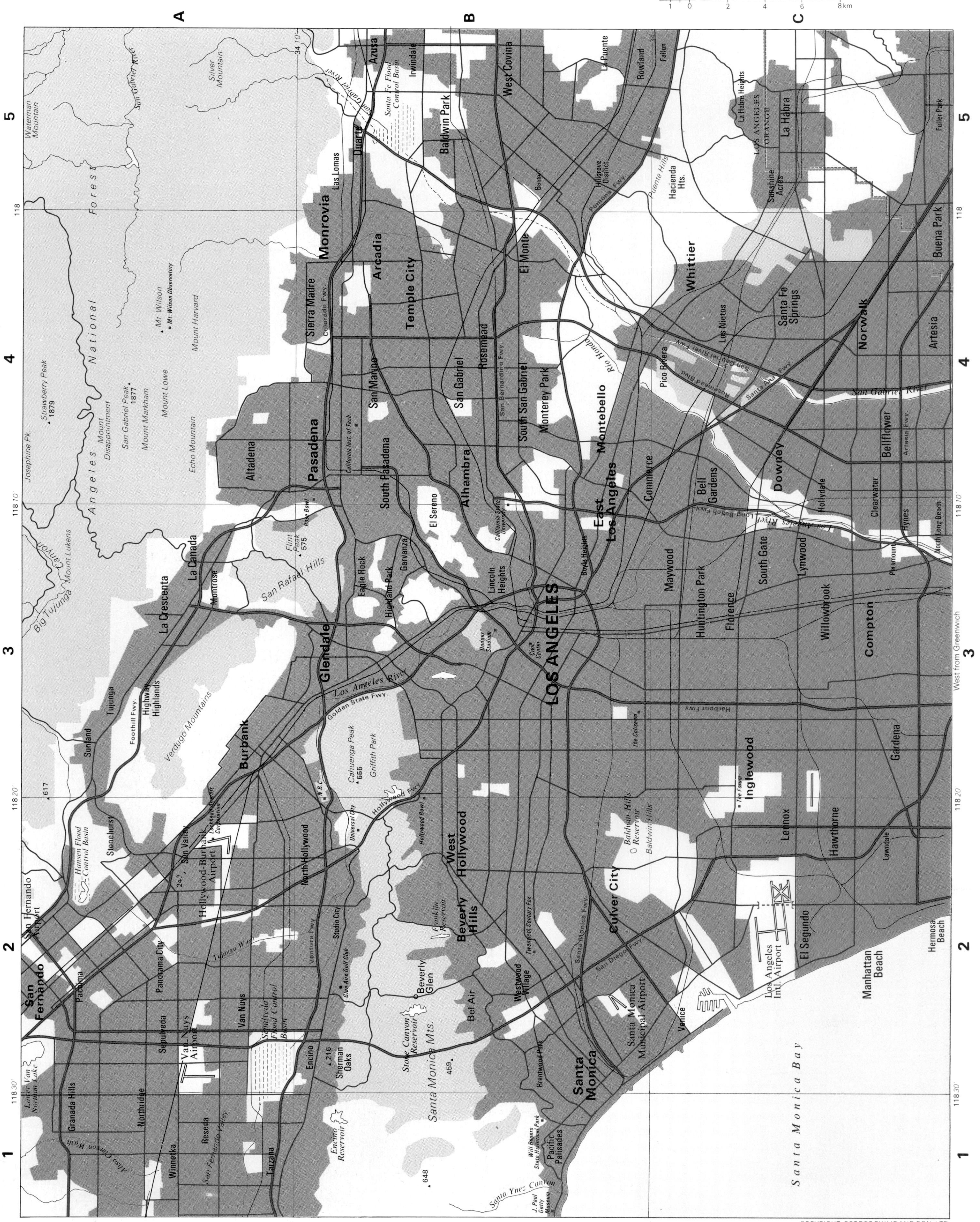

5 miles
8 km

**LOS ANGELES**

Waterman Mountain
Silver Mountain
San Gabriel River
Angeles National Forest
Josephine Pk.
Strawberry Peak 1879
Mount Disappointment
San Gabriel Peak 1877
Mount Markham
Mount Lowe
Mount Harvard
Mr. Wilson
Mt. Wilson Observatory
Echo Mountain
Las Lomas
Azusa
Irwindale
Duarte
Santa Fe Flood Control Basin
West Covina
La Puente
Rowland
Fallon
LOS ANGELES ORANGE
La Habra Heights
La Habra
Fuller Park
Monrovia
Baldwin Park
Bassett
Hilgrove District
Puente Hills
Hacienda Hts.
Buena Park
Sierra Madre
Arcadia
Colorado Fwy
El Monte
Whittier
Sunshine Acres
Temple City
San Marino
San Gabriel
South San Gabriel
Monterey Park
Santa Fe Springs
Big Tujunga Canyon
Mount Lukens
Altadena
Pasadena
South Pasadena
California Inst. of Tech.
Rosemead
San Bernardino Fwy
East Los Angeles
Montebello
Pico Rivera
Los Nietos
San Gabriel River
Norwalk
Artesia
Rio Hondo
Santa Ana Fwy
Tujunga
La Crescenta
La Canada
Montrose
San Rafael Hills
Eagle Rock
Highland Park
Garvanza
El Sereno
Alhambra
Lincoln Heights
Commerce
Downey
Clearwater
Bellflower
Artesia Fwy
Flint Peak 575
Rose Bowl
Boyle Heights
Civic Center
Maywood
Bell Gardens
Hollydale
Highway Highlands
Foothill Fwy
Verdugo Mountains
617
Glendale
Los Angeles River
Los Angeles Fwy
Dodger Stadium
Huntington Park
Florence
South Gate
Lynwood
Hynes
North Long Beach
Sunland
Burbank
Golden State Fwy
Cahuenga Peak 666
Griffith Park
Harbour Fwy
The Coliseum
Willowbrook
Compton
Paramount
Los Angeles River
Long Beach Fwy
Stonehurst
N.B.C.
Hollywood
Hollywood Fwy
Hollywood Bowl
West Hollywood
Baldwin Hills Reservoir
Baldwin Hills
Inglewood
Gardena
Lockheed Aircraft Company
24.2
North Hollywood
Universal City
Beverly Hills
The Fox
Lennox
Hawthorne
Lawndale
San Fernando
San Fernando Airport
Hollywood-Burbank Airport
San Valley
Studio City
Ventura Fwy
Franklin Reservoir
Twentieth Century Fox
Santa Monica Fwy
Culver City
Baldwin Hills
El Segundo
Los Angeles Intl. Airport
Pacoima
Panorama City
Tujunga Wash
Beverly Glen
Bel Air
Westwood Village
San Diego Fwy
Santa Monica Municipal Airport
Manhattan Beach
Hermosa Beach
Sepulveda
Van Nuys Airport
Van Nuys
Sepulveda Flood Control Basin
Cine Aire Golf Club
Stone Canyon Reservoir
Santa Monica Mts.
Brentwood Park
Santa Monica
Venice
Lower Van Norman Lake
Granada Hills
Northridge
Reseda
216
Encino
Sherman Oaks
459
Will Rogers State Historical Park
Pacific Palisades
Santa Monica Bay
Winnetka
Tarzana
Encino Reservoir
648
Santa Ynez Canyon
J. Paul Getty Museum
San Fernando Valley
Arroyo Calabasas Wash
San Diego Fwy

West from Greenwich

1: 200 000

1 0 1 2 3 4 5 miles
1 0 2 4 6 8 km

1  2  3  4

99 20'  99 10'  99

Hila  La Colmena
San Mateo Tecoloapan
Barrientos
Cuautepec El Alto
Ecatepec de Morelos
Santa María Tulpetlac
Santa Isabel Ixtapan
Planta de Evaporación
Río Nextipayac

Ciudad López Mateos
San Andrés Atenco
Cuautepec de Madero
Santa Cecilia
Santa Clara
Río Los Morales
Gran Canal

A

San Nicolás Viejo
Tlalnepantla
Pirámide de Tenayuca
La Loma
Ticomán
San Pedro Zacatenco
Juan González Romero
Ciudad Azteca

San Juan Ixtacala
Progreso Nacional

Ciudad Satélite
Reynosa Tamaulipas

Presa de Rancho Colorado
Río Tlalnepantla
Indios Verdes
Nueva Azcapotzalco

19 30'
Azcapotzalco
Villa Gustavo A. Madero
Villa de Guadalupe
Bosque de Guadalupe
San Juan de Aragón
Lago de Texcoco
19 30'

Santiago Tepatlaxco
Naucalpan de Juárez
San Juan Toltotepec
Presa Tenantongo
Parque Nacional de los Remedios

**CIUDAD DE MÉXICO**

Zedizore
Nueva Tenochtitlán
Parque San Juan de Aragón

San Francisco Chimalpa
Río Sn. Lorenzo
130
San Rafael Chamapa
El Toreo
Tacuba
Central Station
Río Consulado
VENUSTIANO CARRANZA

Hipódromo de las Américas
Colonial
Tenochtitlán
Palacio Nacional

San José Río Hondo
Lomas Chapultepec
Bellas Artes
Ciudadela
Tlaxcoaque
Aeropuerto Internacional

Paseo de la Reforma
Bosque de Chapultepec
Castillo de Chapultepec

La Magdalena Chichicaspa
Tecamachalco
Pantitlán
Chimalhuacán
San Pablo
Xochitenco
San Pedro
Xochiaca

B
Presa Los Jazmines
Lomas Reforma
Tacubaya
Viaducto Presidente Miguel Alemán
Ciudad Deportiva
Netzahualcóyotl
Los Pirules
San Lorenzo Chimalco
B

San Bartolomé Coatepec
Unidad Santa Fe
Av. Constituyentes
Ciudad de los Deportes
Juan Escutia
Agrícola Oriental
San Agustín Atlapulco

Santa Cruz Ayotusco
Iztacalco
Tepalcates
ESTADO DE MÉXICO
DISTRITO FEDERAL

Dos Ríos
Olivar del Conde
Mixcoac
IZTACALCO IZTAPALAPA
La Magdalena Atlipac

Huixquilucan
Molino de Rosas
Héroes de Churubusco
Santa Martha Acatitla
Los Reyes

Chimalpa
Presa Tarango
Olivar de los Padres
Universidad Iberoamericana
Santa María Aztahuacán
Tecamachalco

Cuajimalpa
Río Cañada de los Helechos
Presa Mixcoac
Av. Río Churubusco
Iztapalapa

General Ignacio Allende
Contadero
Lomas de San Ángel Inn
Villa Obregón
San Ángel
Prado Churubusco
Parque Nacional
Santa Cruz Meyehualco

19 20'
Tlaltenango
Coyoacán
Los Reyes
2460 Cerro de la Estrella
Tlalpizáhuac
19 20'

San Lorenzo Acopilco
Santa Rosa Xochiac
San Bartolo Ameyalco
Estadio Olímpico
Rosedal La Candelaria
Ciudad Universitaria
San Francisco Culhuacán

La Marquesa
Parque Nacional Desierto de los Leones
San Jerónimo Lidice
Jardines del Pedregal de San Ángel
El Reloj
San Lorenzo Tezonco
IZTAPALAPA
TLAHUAC

Parque Nacional del Insurgente Miguel Hidalgo
La Magdalena Contreras
TLALPAN
Pirámide de Cuicuilco
El Vergel
Zapotitlán

Estadio Azteca
La Nopalera
Tlaltenco

San Nicolás Totolapan
Tlalpan
Las Fuentes Brotantes
Tepepan
Lago de Xochimilco
Jardines Flotantes
Tlahuac
Gran Canal
Cerro Xico 2346

Santa Úrsula Xitla
San Pedro Mártir
Tulyehualco

Xitle
Xochitepec
San Lucas Xochimanca
Xochimilco
San Gregorio Atlapulco
XOCHIMILCO TLAHUAC

C
Cerro Xitle 3128
San Andrés Totoltepec
Santiago Tepalcatlalpan
Natívitas
San Juan Ixtayopan
C

La Magdalena Petlalco
San Miguel Xicalco
San Mateo Xalpa
Santa Cruz Alcapixca
Mixquic

San Miguel Ajusco
San Andrés Ahuayucan
San Antonio Tecómitl
Tetelco

Parque Nacional de Ajusco
Cerro Ajusco 3937
Santa Cecilia Tepetlapa
San Francisco Tecoxpa
San Jerónimo Miacatlán
San Juan y San Pedro Tezompa

Topilejo
San Pedro Actopan
San Augustín Ohtenco
Milpa Alta

San Francisco Tlalnepantla
San Salvador Cuauhtenco
San Pablo Ostotepec
Santa Ana Tlacotenco

San Lorenzo Tlacoyucan

19 10'
Aserradero
Cerro Pelado 3620
Cerro Cuautzin 3497
Cerro Tláloc 3690
19 10'

El Guarda Parres
TLALPAN MILPA ALTA

D
DISTRITO FEDERAL
ESTADO DE MORELOS
Cerro Chichinautzin 3476
DISTRITO FEDERAL
ESTADO DE MORELOS
D

Parque Nacional de las Lagunas de Zempoala
Tres Marías
Parque Nacional del Tepozteco

1  2  3  4

1 : 200 000

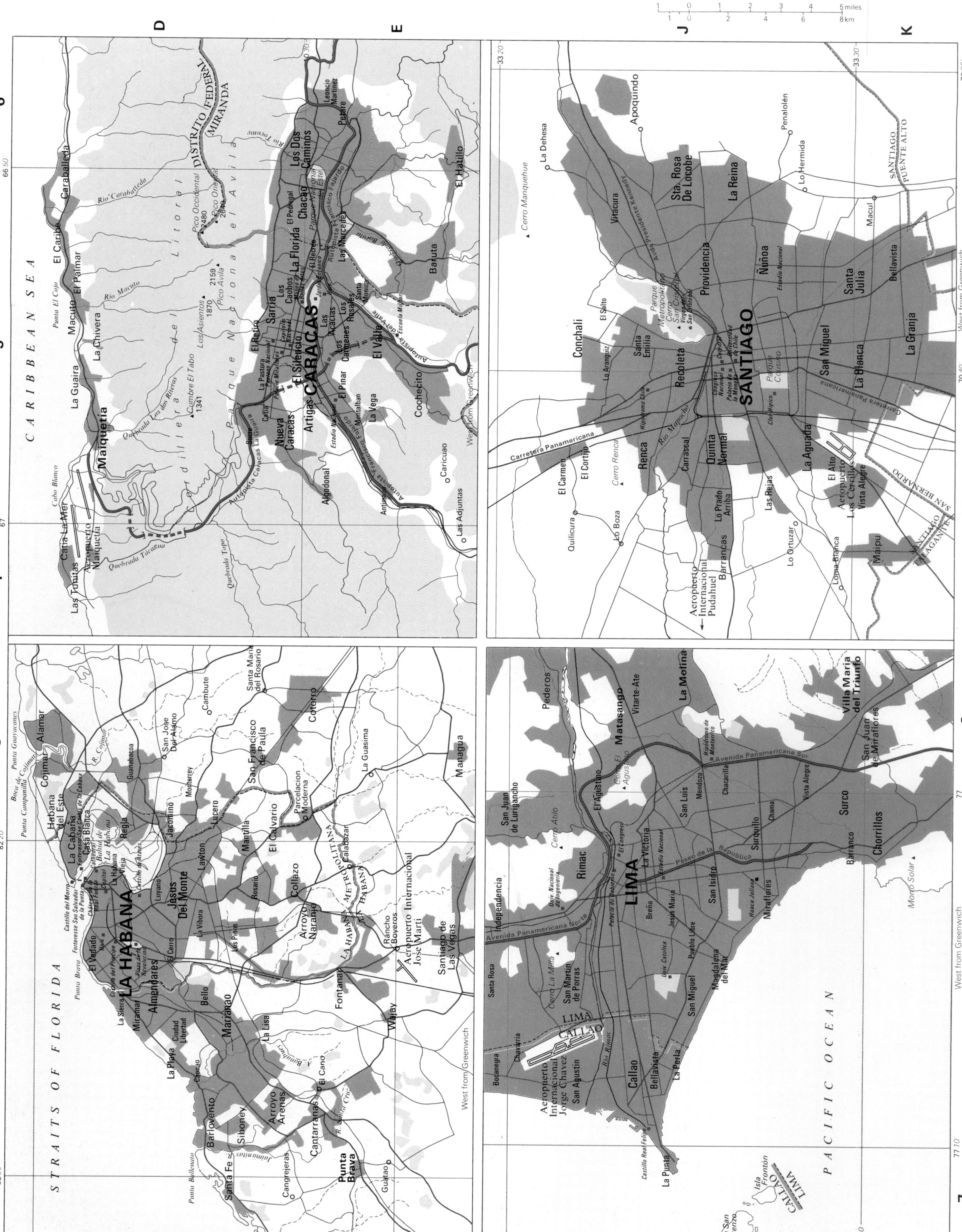

1 2 3 4 5 miles
1 2 4 6 8 km

# CARACAS

CARIBBEAN SEA

DISTRITO FEDERAL
MIRANDA

Río Caraballeda
Caraballeda
El Caribe
Carballeda
Río Carabaleta
Pico Occidental 2480
Pico Oriental 2640
Litoral
Los Dos Caminos
Leoncio Martínez
Padre
Chacao
El Pedregal
Parque Nacional del Este
La Florida
El Recreo
Las Mercedes
El Hatillo
Parque Nacional el Ávila
2159
1870 2398
Los Asientos
Pico Ávila
La Chivera
Río Macuto
Macuto El Palmar
Punta El Cojo
El Retiro
Sarría
Los Caobos
Las Acacias
Baruta
La Guaira
Maiquetía
Punta El Tabo
Cumbre El Tabo
Las Palmas
El Silencio
CARACAS
Artigas
Los Rosales
Los Cármenes
El Valle
Bello Monte
Cochecito
Quebrada Las dos Rieras
Nueva Caracas
La Pastora
El Pinar
Montalbán
La Vega
Cumbre Los dos Rieras 1341
Catia
Algodonal
Antímano
Caricuao
Autopista Caracas La Guaira
Las Adjuntas
Quebrada Tacagua
Las Tehuitas
Cabo Blanco
Caña La Mar
Aeropuerto Maiquetía
Santa Fe

# SANTIAGO

Apoquindo
La Dehesa
Cerro Manquehue
Vitacura
Sta. Rosa De Locobe
La Reina
Peñalolén
Lo Hermida
SANTIAGO PUENTE ALTO
Macul
Ñuñoa
Providencia
Santa Julia
Bellavista
Conchalí
El Salto
Parque Metropolitano
Cerro San Cristóbal
Recoleta
SANTIAGO
San Miguel
La Granja
La Blanca
La Aranguiz
Santa Emilia
Parque Cousiño
Carrera Panamericana
El Carmen
El Cortijo
Cerro Renca
Renca
Río Mapocho
Carrascal
Quinta Normal
Las Rejas
La Aguada
El Alto
Aeropuerto Los Cerrillos
Quilicura
Lo Boza
Lo Ortuzar
Lo Prado Arriba
Barrancas
Loma Blanca
Vista Alegre
Maipú
PORTEZUELO
SAN BERNARDO
Aeropuerto Internacional Pudahuel

# LA HABANA

STRAITS OF FLORIDA
Santa María del Rosario
Cambute
Cotorro
Boca de Cojímar
Punta Guayacanes
Cojímar Alamar
Habana del Este
Punta Campanilla
La Cabaña
Casa Blanca
Regla
San José De Alamo
Guanabacoa
San Francisco de Paula
Monterrey
La Guásima
Managua
Castillo del Morro
Castillo San Salvador de la Punta
Fortaleza San Salvador
La Habana Vieja
Luyanó
Jacomino
Lucero
Parcelacion Moderna
LA HABANA
El Vedado
Cerro
Jesús Del Monte
Lawton
Mantilla
El Calvario
Punta Brava
La Sierra
Miramar
Almendares
Bello
Rosario
Collazo
Arroyo Naranjo
La HABANA METROPOLITANA
La Playa
Ciudad Libertad
Mariano
La Lisa
Las Piñas
La Víbora
Calabazar
Rancho Boyeros
Aeropuerto Internacional José Martí
Santiago de Las Vegas
Espada
Barlovento
Siboney
Arroyo Arenas
El Cano
Wajay
Fontanar
Punta Brava
Cangrejeras
Guatao
Santa Cruz
Punta Bullones

# LIMA

Pederos
La Molina
Villa María del Triunfo
Vitarte-Ate
Matasango
Hipódromo de Monterrico
San Juan de Lurigancho
San Juan de Miraflores
El Agustino
Cerro El Agustino
San Luis
Surco
Cerro Alto
Mendoza
Chacarilla
Vista Alegre
Chorrillos
Rímac
LIMA
La Victoria
San Isidro
Surquillo
Barranco
Independencia
Breña
Jesús María
Chama
Paseo de la República
Avenida Panamericana Sur
Avenida Panamericana Norte
Santa Rosa
San Martín de Porras
San Miguel
Pueblo Libre
Magdalena del Mar
Miraflores
LIMA
CALLAO
Río Rímac
Callao
Bellavista
La Perla
Bocanegra
Chacarria
Aeropuerto Internacional Jorge Chávez
San Agustín
La Punta
Castillo Real Felipe
CALLAO
Isla Frontón
Isla San Lorenzo
PACIFIC OCEAN
Morro Solar

COPYRIGHT GEORGE PHILIP AND SON LTD

1 : 200 000

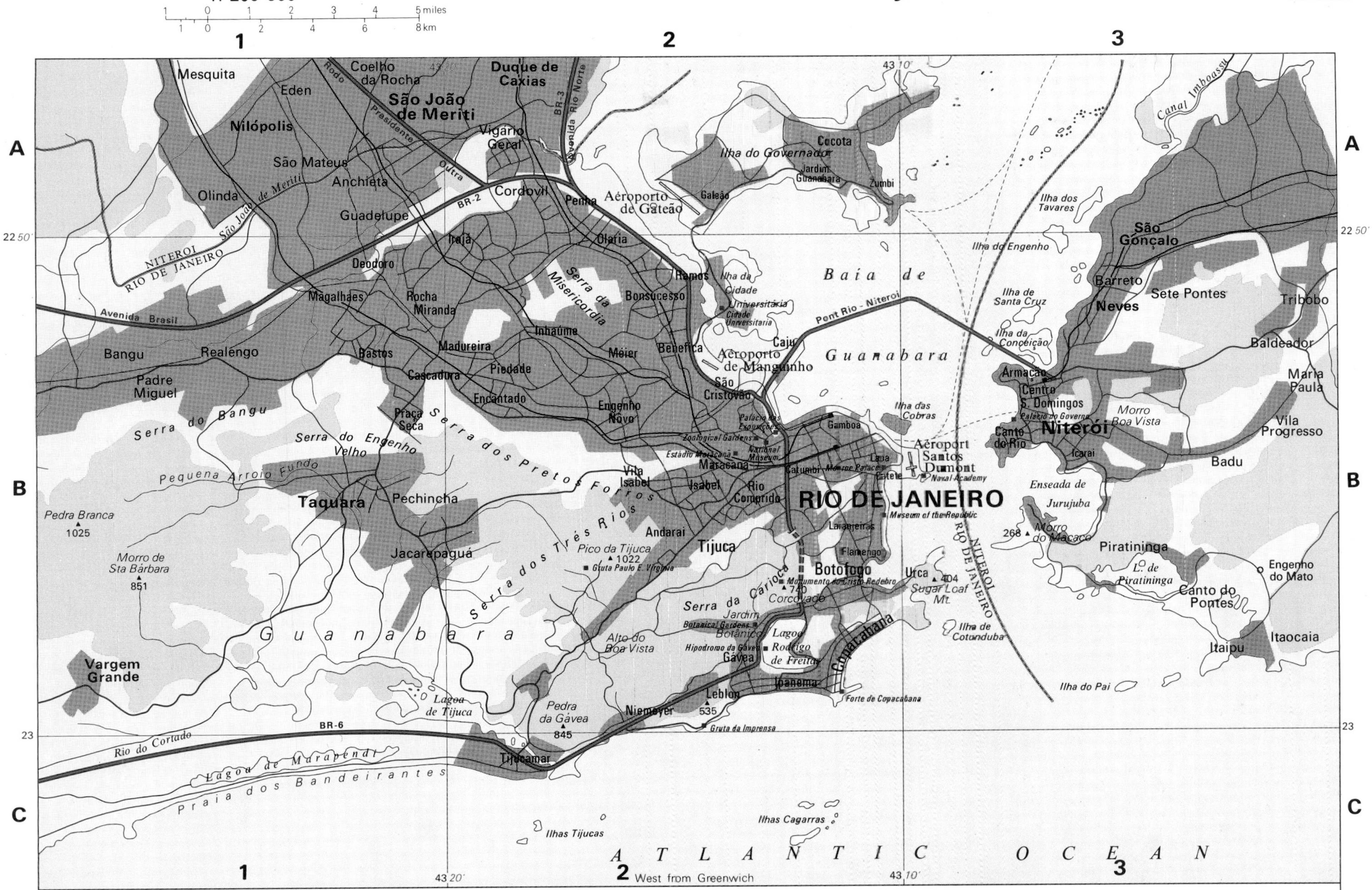

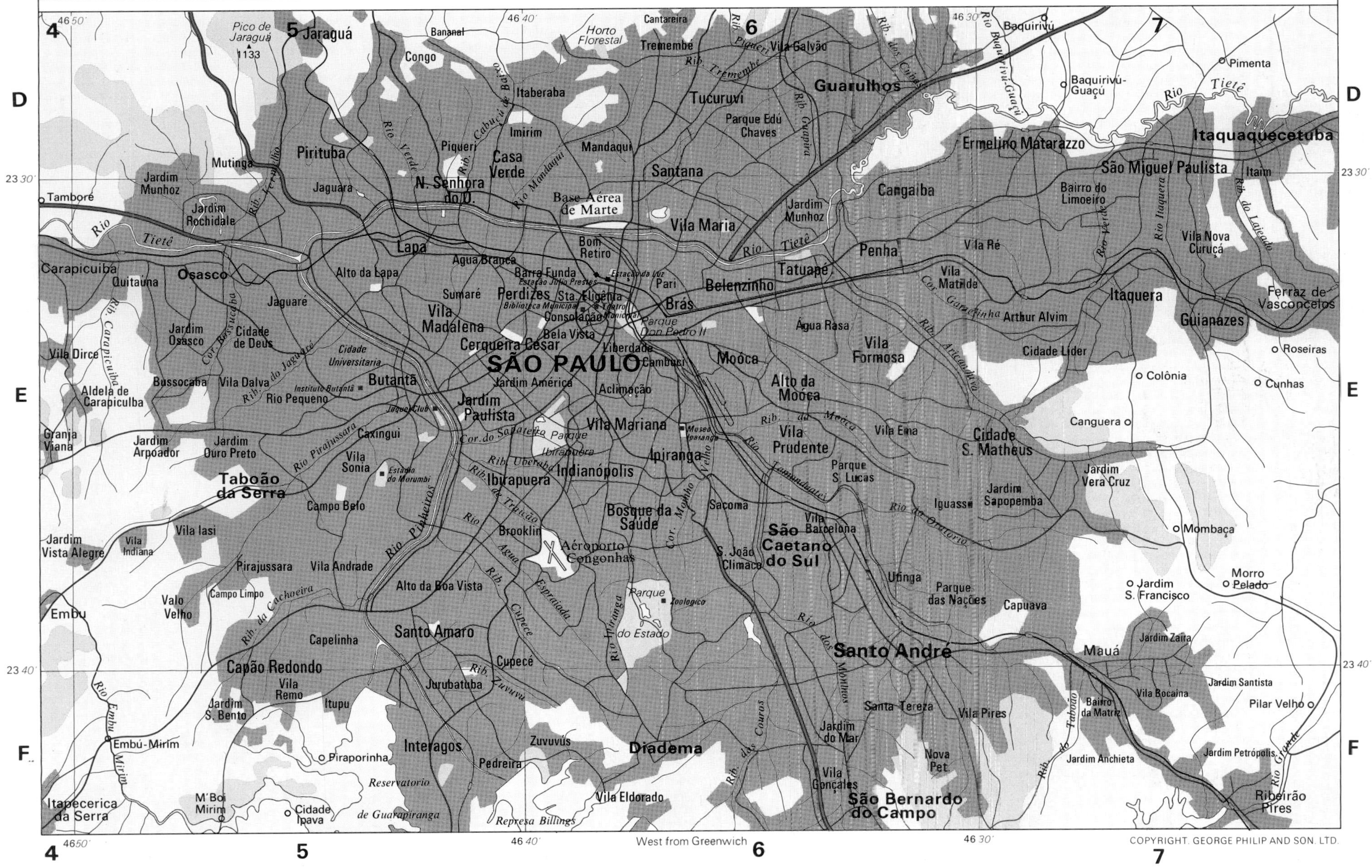

0 1 2 3 4 5 miles
1 0 2 4 6 8 km

**1**     **2**     **3**

Mesquita
Coelho da Rocha
Eden
São João de Meriti
Duque de Caxias
Nilópolis
São Mateus
Anchieta
Vigário Geral
Olinda
Guadelupe
Cordovil
Penha
Aéroporto de Galeão
Ilha do Governador
Cocota
Jardim Guanabara
Zumbi
São Gonçalo
Deodoro
Olaria
Ilha dos Tavares
Magalhães
Rocha Miranda
Bonsucesso
Ilha da Cidade
Baía de
Ilha do Engenho
Bangu
Realengo
Madureira
Piedade
Meier
Benfica
Cidade Universitaria
Ilha de Santa Cruz
Barreto
Sete Pontes
Tribobo
Padre Miguel
Cascadura
Engenho Novo
São Cristovão
Caju
Guanabara
Ilha da Conceição
Armação
Centro
S. Domingos
Baldeador
Serra do Bangu
Encantado
Gamboa
Ilha das Cobras
Niterói
Maria Paula
Praça Seca
Vila Isabel
Isabel
Rio Comprido
RIO DE JANEIRO
Aéroport Santos Dumont
Canto do Rio
Icaraí
Morro Boa Vista
Vila Progresso
Taquara
Pechincha
Andaraí
Tijuca
Lagoa
Enseada de Jurujuba
Badu
Jacarepaguá
Pico da Tijuca 1022
Gruta Paulo E. Virgínia
Serra da Carioca
Corcovado
Museum of the Republic
Piratininga
Lº de Piratininga
Guanabara
Alto da Boa Vista
Jardim Botánica Gardens
Lagoa Rodrigo de Freitas
Urca
Sugar Loaf Mt.
Morro do Macaco
Canto do Pontes
Engenho do Mato
Vargem Grande
Pedra da Gávea 845
Niemeyer 535
Leblon
Ipanema
Copacabana
Forte de Copacabana
Ilha de Cotonduba
Itaocaia
Itaipu
Lagoa de Tijuca
Gruta da Imprensa
Ilha do Pai
BR-6
Tijucamar
Rio do Cortado
Lagoa de Marapendi
Praia dos Bandeirantes
Ilhas Tijucas
Ilhas Cagarras

ATLANTIC OCEAN

West from Greenwich

**4**    **5**    **6**    **7**

Pico de Jaraguá 1133
Jaraguá
Bananal
Cantareira
Horto Florestal
Tremembé
Vila Galvão
Baquirivú
Pimenta
Congo
Itaberaba
Tucuruvi
Guarulhos
Baquirivú-Guaçú
Piqueri
Casa Verde
Mandaqui
Parque Edú Chaves
Ermelino Matarazzo
Itaquaquecetuba
Pirituba
Imirim
Santana
Cangaíba
São Miguel Paulista
Itaim
Mutinga
N. Senhora do Ó
Base Aérea de Marte
Jardim Munhoz
Bairro do Limoeiro
Vila Nova Curuçá
Jardim Munhoz
Jardim Rochidale
Jaguara
Lapa
Vila Maria
Penha
Vila Ré
Jaguaré
Tamboré
Rio Tietê
Alto da Lapa
Agua Branca
Bom Retiro
Pari
Tatuapé
Vila Matilde
Itaquera
Carapicuiba
Osasco
Barra Funda
Belenzinho
Arthur Alvim
Ferraz de Vasconcelos
Vila Dirce
Quitauna
Sumaré
Perdizes
Sta. Eficenia
Brás
Agua Rasa
Cidade Lider
Guianázes
Bussocaba
Vila Dalva
Vila Madalena
Consolação
Bela Vista
Mooca
Roseiras
Jardim Osasco
Cidade de Deus
Cerqueira Cesar
Liberdade
Cambuci
Vila Formosa
Colônia
Cunhas
Aldeia de Carapiculba
Cidade Universitaria
SÃO PAULO
Alto da Mooca
Butantã
Jardim América
Aclimação
Vila Ema
Canguera
Granja Viana
Jardim Arpoador
Jardim Ouro Preto
Jardim Paulista
Vila Mariana
Vila Prudente
Cidade S. Matheus
Caxingui
Vila Sonia
Indianópolis
Ipiranga
Parque S. Lucas
Jardim Vera Cruz
Taboão da Serra
Campo Belo
Ibirapuera
São Caetano do Sul
Jardim Sapopemba
Mombaça
Jardim Vista Alegre
Vila Iasi
Vila Indiana
Brooklin
Bosque da Saúde
Sacomã
Vila Barcelona
Jardim Zaira
Pirajussara
Vila Andrade
Aéroporto Congonhas
S. João Climaco
Iguassú
Morro Pelado
Valo Velho
Campo Limpo
Alto da Boa Vista
Parque das Nações
Capuava
Jardim S. Francisco
Embu
Capelinha
Santo Amaro
Parque Zoologico
Santo André
Mauá
Jardim Santista
Capão Redondo
Cupecê
Santa Tereza
Vila Pires
Vila Bocaina
Pilar Velho
Jardim S. Bento
Vila Remo
Itupu
Jurubatuba
Jardim do Mar
Nova Pet
Jardim Anchieta
Jardim Petrópolis
Itapecerica da Serra
M'Boi Mirim
Cidade Ipava
Interlagos
Piraporinha
Pedreira
Diadema
Vila Gonçales
São Bernardo do Campo
Ribeirão Pires
Reservatorio
Represa Billings
Vila Eldorado

West from Greenwich

1: 200 000

5 miles
8 km

# BUENOS AIRES

Rio de la Plata

West from Greenwich

Quilmes
Espeleta
Berazategui
Villa Augusta
Villa D. Sobral
Villa San Francisco
Espéoia
Ranelagh
Bosques
Don Bosco
Bernal
Gdor. Monteverde
Florencio Varela
Wilde
Villa Dominico
Sarandi
Avellaneda
Villa Barilari
San Francisco Solano
Cleypole
Rafael Calzada
Villa C. Colón
Gerli
Villa D. Colón
Monte Chingolo
Temperley
José Mármol
Almirante Brown
Burzaco
Ministro Rivadavia
La Boca
Barracas
Villa Alsina
Diamante
Caraza
Lanús
Remedios de Escalada
Banfield
Lomas de Zamora
Turdera
Santa Catalina
Llavallol
San Telmo
Almagro
Cabecito
Nueva Pompeya
Villa Lugano
Fiorito
Ingr. Budge
La Salada
Villa Hogar Alemán
Luis Guillón
Monte Grande
Esteban Echeverría
Ezeiza
Aeroparque de la Ciudad de Buenos Aires
Porto Nuevo
Retiro
Av. Entre Rios
Once Station
Congreso
Plaza de Mayo
Government House
Palermo
La Paternal
Belgrano
Flores
Parques
Floresta
Nueva Chicago
Versailles
Villa Devoto
Liniers
DISTRITO FEDERAL
BUENOS AIRES
Villa Madero
Tapiales
San Justo
Tablada
Aldo Bonzi
Ciudad General Belgrano
Aeropuerto Ezeiza
Nuñez
Olivos
I. Anchorena
Las Barrancas
Florida
Saavedra
Vicente López
La Lucila
Martínez
Munro
General Urquiza
Acassuso
Villa Lynch
General San Martín
Villa Bosch
Lourdes
Saenz Peña
Ciudadela
Ramos Mejía
M. J. Haedo
Villa Luzuriaga
Ituzaingó
San Isidro
Beccar
Victoria
Villa Adelina
Boulogne
Carapachay
San Andres
Villa Ballester
Santos Lugares
Caseros
Villa Alianza
Villa D.F. Sarmiento
Villa Basso
San Fernando
Tigre
Las Conchas
General Pacheco
Don Torcuato
Billinghurst
El Palomar
Hurlingham
Morón
Castelar
San Antonio de Padua
Villa Reichembach
Libertad
Merlo
Moreno
Paso del Rey
Francisco Alvarez
La Reja
El Talar de Pacheco
Los Polvorines
Villa de Mayo
Campo de Mayo
Muñiz
José C. Paz
General Sarmiento
San Miguel
Bella Vista
Villa Leloir
Villa Ariza
Villa León
Villa Altube
Villa Iglesias
Grand Bourg
Igr. P. Nogues
Tortuguitas
Del Viso
Benavidez
Garin
Villa Rosa
Toro
Pinazo
Presidente Derqui
Piñero
Mariano Acosta
Pontevedra
20 de Junio
Marcos Paz
Gonzalez Catán
Laferrere
Isidro Casanova
Rafael Castillo
Lujan
Nirevex
Catupa
R. Reconquista
R. Reconquista
R. Puente Cascallares
A. Morales
A. La Horqueta
Villa Maipú
Av. General Paz
Av. N.S. Martin
Av. Rivadavia
Riachuelo
G. Brown
Matanza

# INDEX TO CITY MAPS

Place names in this index are given a letter-figure reference to a map square made from the lines of latitude and longitude that appear on the city maps. The full geographic reference is provided in the border of each map. The letter-figure reference will take the reader directly to the square, and by using the geographical co-ordinates the place sought can be pinpointed within that square.

The location given is the city or suburban centre, and not necessarily the name. Lakes, airports and other features having a large area are given co-ordinates for their centres. Rivers that enter the sea, lake or main stream within the map area have the co-ordinates of that entrance. If the river flows through the map, then the co-ordinates are given to the name. The same rule applies to canals. A river carries the symbol → after its name.

As an aid to identification, every place name is followed by the city map name or its abbreviation; for example, Oakland in California will be followed by S.F. Some of the place names so described will be completely independent of the main city.

An explanation of the alphabetical order rules is to be found at the beginning of the World Map Index.

## ABBREVIATIONS USED IN THE INDEX

*Ath.* – Athinai (Athens)
*B.* – Baie, Bahía, Bay, Bucht
*B.A.* – Buenos Aires
*Bagd.* – Baghdad
*Balt.* – Baltimore
*Bangk.* – Bangkok
*Barc.* – Barcelona
*Beij.* – Beijing (Peking)
*Berl.* – Berlin
*Bomb.* – Bombay
*Bost.* – Boston
*Bud.* – Budapest
*C.* – Cabo, Cap, Cape
*Calc.* – Calcutta
*Car.* – Caracas
*Chan.* – Channel
*Chic.* – Chicago
*Cr.* – Creek
*E.* – East
*El Qâ.* – El Qâhira (Cairo)
*G.* – Golfe, Golfo, Gulf, Guba
*Gzh.* – Guangzhou (Canton)
*H.K.* – Hong Kong
*Hbg.* – Hamburg
*Hd.* – Head
*Hels.* – Helsinki
*Hts.* – Heights
*I.(s)* – Île, Ilha, Insel, Isla, Island, Isle
*Ist.* – Istanbul
*J.* – Jabal, Jebel
*Jak.* – Jakarta
*Jobg.* – Johannesburg
*K.* – Kap, Kapp
*Kar.* – Karachi
*Kep.* – Kepulauan
*Købn.* – København (Copenhagen)
*L.* – Lac, Lacul, Lago, Lagoa, Lake
*L.A.* – Los Angeles
*La Hab.* – La Habana (Havana)
*Lisb.* – Lisboa (Lisbon)
*Lon.* – London
*Mdrd.* – Madrid
*Melb.* – Melbourne
*Méx.* – México
*Mil.* – Milano
*Mos.* – Moskva (Moscow)
*Mt. (e)* – Mont, Monte, Monti, Montaña, Mountain
*Mtrl.* – Montréal
*Mün.* – München (Munich)
*N.* – Nord, Norte, North, Northern, Nouveau
*Nápl.* – Nápoli (Naples)
*N.Y.* – New York City
*Os.* – Ostrov
*Oz.* – Ozero
*Pen.* – Peninsula, Peninsule
*Phil.* – Philadelphia
*Pk.* – Park, Peak
*Pra.* – Praha (Prague)
*Pt.* – Point
*Pta.* – Ponta, Punta
*Pte.* – Pointe
*R.* – Rio, River
*Ra. (s)* – Range(s)
*Res.* – Reserve, Reservoir
*Rio J.* – Rio de Janeiro
*S.* – San, South
*S.F.* – San Francisco
*S. Pau.* – São Paulo
*Sa.* – Serra, Sierra
*Sd.* – Sound
*Shang.* – Shanghai
*Sing.* – Singapore
*St.* – Saint, Sankt, Sint
*St-Pet.* – St-Petersburg
*Sta.* – Santa, Station
*Ste.* – Sainte
*Stgo.* – Santiago
*Sto.* – Santo
*Stock.* – Stockholm
*Str.* – Strait, Stretto
*Syd.* – Sydney
*Tehr.* – Tehran
*Tianj.* – Tianjin (Tientsin)
*Tori.* – Torino (Turin)
*Trto.* – Toronto
*W.* – West
*Wash.* – Washington
*Wsaw.* – Warszawa (Warsaw)

## A


Aalām, *Bagd.* **17 F8** 33 19N 44 23 E
Abada, *Calc.* **16 E5** 22 32N 88 13 E
Abbadia di Stura, *Tori.* **9 B3** 45 7N 7 44 E
Abbey Wood, *Lon.* **4 C5** 51 29N 0 7 E
Abbots Langley, *Lon.* **4 A2** 51 42N 0 25W
Abeno, *Ōsaka* **12 C4** 34 38N 135 31 E
Aberdeen, *H.K.* **12 E6** 22 14N 114 8 E
Abfanggraben, *Mün.* **7 F11** 48 10N 11 41 E
Abington, *Phil.* **24 A4** 40 7N 75 7W
Ablon-sur-Seine, *Paris* **5 C4** 48 43N 2 25 E
Abord à Plouffe, *Mtrl.* **20 A3** 43 32N 73 43W
Abramtsevo, *Mos.* **11 E10** 55 49N 37 49 E
Abridge, *Lon.* **4 B5** 51 38N 0 7 E
Abû en Numrus, *El Qâ.* **18 D5** 29 57N 31 12 E
Acassuso, *B.A.* **32 A3** 34 29 S 58 30W
Accord, *Bost.* **21 D4** 42 10N 70 52W
Accord Pond, *Bost.* **21 D4** 42 10N 70 53W
Accotink Cr. →, *Wash.* **25 D6** 38 51N 77 15W
Acerra, *Nápl.* **9 H13** 40 56N 14 22 E
Acha San, *Sŏul* **12 G8** 37 33N 127 5 E
Acheres, *Paris* **5 B2** 48 57N 2 3 E
Acília, *Rome* **9 G9** 41 47N 12 21 E
Aclimação, *S. Pau.* **31 E6** 23 34 S 46 37W
Acostia →, *Wash.* **25 D8** 38 51N 77 1W
Acton, *Lon.* **4 B3** 51 30N 0 16W
Açúcar, Pão de, *Rio J.* **31 B3** 22 56 S 43 9W
Ada Beja, *Lisb.* **8 F7** 38 47N 9 13W
Adabe Cr. →, *S.F.* **27 D4** 37 26N 122 6W
Adachi, *Tōkyō* **13 B2** 35 49N 139 34 E
Adachi-Ku, *Tōkyō* **13 B3** 35 47N 139 47 E
Adams Nat. Hist. Site, *Bost.* **21 D4** 42 15N 71 0W
Addington, *Lon.* **4 C4** 51 21N 0 1W
Addiscombe, *Lon.* **4 C4** 51 22N 0 4W
Adel, *Bagd.* **17 E7** 33 20N 44 17 E
Adelphi, *Wash.* **25 C8** 39 0N 76 58W
Aderklaa, *Wien* **10 G11** 48 17N 16 32 E
Admiralteyskaya Storona, *St-Pet.* **11 B4** 59 56N 30 20 E
Áffori, *Mil.* **9 D6** 45 31N 9 10 E
Aflandshage, *Købn.* **2 E10** 55 33N 12 35 E
Afragola, *Nápl.* **9 H12** 40 55N 14 18 E
Aganpur, *Delhi* **16 B3** 28 33N 77 20 E
Agboju, *Lagos* **18 B1** 6 27N 7 16 E
Agboyi Cr. →, *Lagos* **18 A2** 6 33N 7 24 E
Ågerup, *Købn.* **2 D8** 55 43N 12 19 E
Ågesta, *Stock.* **3 E11** 59 12N 18 6 E
Agincourt, *Trto.* **20 D9** 43 47N 79 16W
Agnano Terme, *Nápl.* **9 J12** 40 49N 14 10 E
Agora, *Ath.* **8 J11** 37 57N 23 43 E
Agra Canal, *Delhi* **16 B2** 28 33N 77 17 E
Agricola Oriental, *Méx.* **29 B3** 19 23N 99 4W
Agro Romano, *Rome* **9 F8** 41 56N 12 17 E
Agua Branca, *S. Pau.* **31 E5** 23 31 S 46 40W
Agua Espraiada →, *S. Pau.* **31 E6** 23 36 S 46 41W
Água Rasa, *S. Pau.* **31 E6** 23 32 S 46 33W
Agualva-Cacem, *Lisb.* **8 F7** 38 46N 9 15W
Agustino, Cerro El, *Lima* **30 G8** 12 3 S 76 59W
Ahrensfelde, *Berl.* **7 A4** 52 34N 13 34 E
Ahuntsic, *Mtrl.* **20 A3** 43 32N 73 41W
Ai →, *Ōsaka* **12 B4** 34 46N 135 35 E
Aigremont, *Paris* **5 B2** 48 54N 2 1 E
Airport West, *Melb.* **19 E6** 37 42 S 144 52 E
Aiyaleo, *Ath.* **8 J11** 37 59N 23 40 E
Ajegunle, *Lagos* **18 B2** 6 26N 7 20 E
Aji, *Ōsaka* **12 B3** 34 40N 135 27 E
Ajuda, *Lisb.* **8 F7** 38 42N 9 12W
Ajusco, Parque Nacional de, *Méx.* **29 C2** 19 12N 99 15W
Akabane, *Tōkyō* **13 B3** 35 46N 139 42 E
Akalla, *Stock.* **3 D10** 59 24N 17 55 E
Akasaka, *Tōkyō* **13 B3** 35 40N 139 43 E
Akbarābād, *Tehr.* **17 C5** 35 40N 51 20 E
Åkersberga Saltsjobad, *Stock.* **3 D12** 59 26N 18 15 E
Akerselva →, *Oslo* **2 B4** 59 54N 10 45 E
Akrópolis, *Ath.* **8 J11** 37 57N 23 43 E
Akuwa, *Tōkyō* **13 D2** 35 26N 139 30 E
Al 'Azamiyah, *Bagd.* **17 E8** 33 22N 44 22 E
Alaguntan, *Lagos* **18 B2** 6 25N 7 29 E
Alamar, *La Hab.* **30 B3** 23 9N 82 16W
Alameda, *S.F.* **27 B3** 37 46N 122 15W
Alameda Memorial State Beach Park, *S.F.* **27 B3** 37 45N 122 16W
Alamo, *S.F.* **27 A4** 37 51N 122 2W
Albany, *S.F.* **27 A3** 37 53N 122 17W
Alberante, *Jobg.* **18 F9** 26 16 S 28 7 E
Albern, *Wien* **10 H10** 48 9N 16 29 E
Albert Hall, *Lon.* **4 C3** 51 29N 0 10W
Albert Park, *Melb.* **19 F6** 37 51 S 144 58 E
Albertfalva, *Bud.* **10 K13** 47 26N 19 3 E
Alberton, *Jobg.* **18 F9** 26 15 S 28 7 E
Albertslund, *Købn.* **2 E9** 55 39N 12 21 E
Albertson, *N.Y.* **23 C7** 40 46N 73 38W
Albertville, *Jobg.* **18 E8** 26 9 S 27 58 E
Albion, *Phil.* **24 C5** 39 46N 74 57W
Alby, *Stock.* **3 E10** 59 14N 17 51 E
Albysjön, *Stock.* **3 E10** 59 14N 17 52 E
Alcantara, *Lisb.* **8 F7** 38 43N 9 10W
Alcatraz I., *S.F.* **27 B2** 37 49N 122 25W
Alcochete, *Lisb.* **8 F9** 38 45N 8 58W
Alcorcón, *Mdrd.* **8 B2** 40 20N 3 48W
Aldan, *Phil.* **24 B3** 39 55N 75 17W
Aldela de Carapiculba, *S. Pau.* **31 E5** 23 34 S 46 49W
Aldene, *N.Y.* **22 D3** 40 39N 74 17W
Aldenrade, *Ruhr* **6 A2** 51 31N 6 44 E
Alder Planetarium, *Chic.* **26 B3** 41 5N 87 36W
Aldershof, *Berl.* **7 B4** 52 26N 13 33 E
Aldo Bonzi, *B.A.* **32 C3** 34 42 S 58 31W
Aleksandrovskoye, *St-Pet.* **11 B4** 59 51N 30 20 E
Aleksandrów, *Wsaw.* **10 E8** 52 10N 21 14 E
Alexander Nevsky Abbey, *St-Pet.* **11 B4** 59 54N 30 23 E
Alexandra, *Jobg.* **18 E9** 26 6 S 28 5 E
Alexandra, *Sing.* **15 G7** 1 17N 103 49 E
Alexandria, *Wash.* **25 E7** 38 49N 77 5W
Alfortville, *Paris* **5 C4** 48 48N 2 24 E
Algés, *Lisb.* **8 F7** 38 42N 9 13W
Älgo, *Stock.* **3 E13** 59 16N 18 20 E
Algodonal, *Car.* **30 E5** 10 29N 66 58W
Alhambra, *L.A.* **28 B4** 34 5N 118 7W
Alhos Vedros, *Lisb.* **8 G8** 38 39N 9 1W
Alibey →, *Ist.* **17 A2** 41 3N 28 56 E
Alibeyköy, *Ist.* **17 A2** 41 4N 28 56 E
Alima, *Manila* **15 E3** 14 27N 120 55 E
Alimos, *Ath.* **8 J11** 37 52N 23 43 E
Aliperti, *Nápl.* **9 H13** 40 53N 14 28 E
Alipore, *Calc.* **16 E6** 22 31N 88 20 E
Alipur, *Calc.* **16 D5** 22 43N 88 12 E
Aliso Canyon Wash →, *L.A.* **28 A1** 34 15N 118 31W
Allach, *Mün.* **7 F9** 48 11N 11 27 E
Allambie Heights, *Syd.* **19 A4** 33 46 S 151 15 E
Allendale, *N.Y.* **22 A4** 41 1N 74 9W
Allengrove, *Jobg.* **18 E10** 26 5 S 28 14 E
Allentown, *N.Y.* **23 C6** 40 47N 73 43W
Allermohe, *Hbg.* **7 E8** 53 29N 10 7 E
Allerton, Pt., *Bost.* **21 D4** 42 18N 70 52W
Allston, *Bost.* **21 C3** 42 21N 71 7W
Alluets, Forêt des, *Paris* **5 B1** 48 56N 1 55 E
Almada, *Lisb.* **8 F8** 38 41N 9 8W
Almagro, *B.A.* **32 B4** 34 38 S 58 24W
Almanara, *Mdrd.* **8 B2** 40 28N 3 41W
Almaza Airport, *El Qâ.* **18 C6** 30 5N 31 21 E
Almazovo, *Mos.* **11 D12** 55 50N 38 3 E
Almendares, *La Hab.* **30 B2** 23 6N 82 23W
Almendares →, *La Hab.* **30 B2** 23 7N 82 24W
Almirante Brown, *B.A.* **32 C4** 34 48 S 58 23W
Almirante G. Brown, Parques, *B.A.* **32 C4** 34 40 S 58 28W
Almonesson, *Phil.* **24 C4** 39 48N 75 5W
Almonte, *S.F.* **27 A1** 37 53N 122 31W
Alnabru, *Oslo* **2 B5** 59 55N 10 50 E
Alnsjøen, *Oslo* **2 B5** 59 57N 10 51 E
Alperton, *Lon.* **4 B3** 51 32N 0 17W
Alpignano, *Tori.* **9 B1** 45 6N 7 31 E
Alpine, *N.Y.* **22 B5** 40 57N 73 57W
Alpur, *Calc.* **16 C6** 22 50N 88 23 E
Alrode, *Jobg.* **18 F9** 26 17 S 28 7 E
Alsergrund, *Wien* **10 G10** 48 13N 16 21 E
Alsfeld, *Ruhr* **6 A3** 51 31N 6 50 E
Alsip, *Chic.* **26 C2** 41 40N 87 44W
Alstaden, *Ruhr* **6 B2** 51 28N 6 49 E
Ålsten, *Stock.* **3 E10** 59 19N 17 57 E
Alster →, *Hbg.* **7 D8** 53 38N 10 4 E
Alsterdorf, *Hbg.* **7 D8** 53 36N 10 0 E
Älta, *Stock.* **3 E12** 59 15N 18 11 E
Altadena, *L.A.* **28 A4** 34 11N 118 8W
Alte-Donau →, *Wien* **10 G10** 48 14N 16 25 E
Alte Süderelbe, *Hbg.* **7 D7** 53 31N 9 52 E
Alten-Essen, *Ruhr* **6 B4** 51 29N 7 1 E
Altendorf, *Ruhr* **6 B3** 51 27N 6 58 E
Altenhagen, *Ruhr* **6 B6** 51 22N 7 27 E
Altenvoerde, *Ruhr* **6 C6** 51 18N 7 22 E
Altenwerder, *Hbg.* **7 D7** 53 30N 9 55 E
Alter Finkenkrug, *Berl.* **7 A1** 52 35N 13 3 E
Altglenicke, *Berl.* **7 B4** 52 25N 13 32 E
Altlandsberg Nord, *Berl.* **7 A5** 52 34N 13 43 E
Altmannsdorf, *Wien* **10 H9** 48 9N 16 18 E
Alto, *S.F.* **27 A1** 37 54N 122 30W
Alto da Boa Vista, *S. Pau.* **31 E5** 23 38 S 46 42W
Alto da Lapa, *S. Pau.* **31 E5** 23 31 S 46 43W
Alto da Moóca, *S. Pau.* **31 E6** 23 34 S 46 33W
Alto do Pina, *Lisb.* **8 F8** 38 44N 9 7W
Altona, *Hbg.* **7 D7** 53 32N 9 56 E
Altona, *Melb.* **19 F5** 37 51 S 144 49 E
Altona B., *Melb.* **19 F6** 37 52 S 144 51 E
Altona North, *Melb.* **19 F5** 37 50 S 144 49 E
Altona Sports Park, *Melb.* **19 F6** 37 51 S 144 51 E
Altstadt, *Hbg.* **7 D8** 53 32N 10 0 E
Alvarado, *S.F.* **27 C4** 37 35N 122 4W
Alvik, *Stock.* **3 E10** 59 19N 17 58 E
Älvsjo, *Stock.* **3 E11** 59 16N 18 0 E
Älvvik, *Stock.* **3 D12** 59 21N 18 15 E
Am Hasenbergl, *Mün.* **7 F10** 48 12N 11 33 E
Am Steinhof, *Wien* **10 G9** 48 12N 16 17 E
Am Wald, *Mün.* **7 G10** 48 3N 11 36 E
Ama Keng, *Sing.* **15 F7** 1 23N 103 41 E
Amadora, *Lisb.* **8 F7** 38 45N 9 13W
Amagasaki, *Ōsaka* **12 B3** 34 42N 135 23 E
Amager, *Købn.* **2 E10** 55 36N 12 35 E
Amāl Qādisiya, *Bagd.* **17 F8** 33 16N 44 20 E
Amalienborg Slott, *Købn.* **2 D10** 55 41N 12 35 E
Amata, *Mil.* **9 D5** 45 34N 9 8 E
Ambler, *Phil.* **24 A3** 40 9N 75 13W
Ambrose Channel, *N.Y.* **22 D5** 40 31N 73 50W
Ameixoeira, *Lisb.* **8 F8** 38 46N 9 8W
Ames Hill, *Bost.* **21 B2** 42 38N 71 13W
Amin, *Bagd.* **17 F8** 33 19N 44 29 E
Aminyevo, *Mos.* **11 E8** 55 41N 37 25 E
Amirābād, *Tehr.* **17 C5** 35 43N 51 24 E
Amityville, *N.Y.* **23 C8** 40 40N 73 23W
Ammersbek →, *Hbg.* **7 C8** 53 42N 10 7 E
Amora, *Lisb.* **8 G8** 38 37N 9 6W
Amoreira, *Lisb.* **8 F7** 38 48N 9 11W
Amorosa, *Jobg.* **18 E8** 26 5 S 27 52 E
Ampelokipi, *Ath.* **8 J11** 37 58N 23 47 E
Amper →, *Mün.* **7 F9** 48 14N 11 25 E
Amselhain, *Berl.* **7 A5** 52 38N 13 43 E
Amuwo, *Lagos* **18 B1** 6 28N 7 18 E
Anacostia, *Wash.* **25 D8** 38 51N 76 59W
Anacostia River Park, *Wash.* **25 D8** 38 54N 76 57W
Anadoluhisari, *Ist.* **17 A3** 41 4N 29 3 E
Anandanagar, *Calc.* **16 C5** 22 51N 88 16 E
Anchieta, *Rio J.* **31 A1** 22 48 S 43 21W
Ancol, *Jak.* **15 H9** 6 7 S 106 49 E
Andalus, *Bagd.* **17 F7** 33 19N 44 18 E
Andalusia, *Phil.* **24 A5** 40 4N 74 58W
Andarai, *Rio J.* **31 B2** 22 56 S 43 14W
Andeli Beijie, *Beij.* **14 B3** 39 57N 116 21 E
Anderson Cr. →, *Melb.* **19 E8** 37 44 S 145 12 E
Andilly, *Paris* **5 A3** 49 0N 2 17 E
Andingmen, *Beij.* **14 B3** 39 55N 116 23 E
Andover, *Bost.* **21 B3** 42 39N 71 7W
Andrésy, *Paris* **5 B2** 48 58N 2 3 E
Andrews Air Force Base, *Wash.* **25 E8** 38 48N 76 52W
Ang Mo Kio, *Sing.* **15 F8** 1 22N 103 50 E
Ängby, *Stock.* **3 D10** 59 20N 17 53 E
Angel I., *S.F.* **27 A2** 37 52N 122 25W
Angel Island State Park, *S.F.* **27 A2** 37 52N 122 25W
Angerbruch →, *Ruhr* **6 C3** 51 18N 6 59 E
Angerhausen, *Ruhr* **6 B2** 51 22N 6 43 E
Angermund, *Ruhr* **6 C2** 51 19N 6 46 E
Angke, Kali →, *Jak.* **15 H9** 6 6 S 106 46 E
Angono, *Manila* **15 D4** 14 31N 121 8 E
Angyalföld, *Bud.* **10 J13** 47 32N 19 5 E
Angyō, *Tōkyō* **13 A3** 35 50N 139 45 E
Aniene →, *Rome* **9 F10** 41 56N 12 35 E
Anik, *Bomb.* **16 G8** 19 1N 72 53 E
Anin, *Wsaw.* **10 E7** 52 13N 21 9 E
Anjou, *Mtrl.* **20 A4** 43 36N 73 33W
Annadale, *N.Y.* **22 D3** 40 32N 74 10W
Annalee Heights, *Wash.* **25 D6** 38 51N 77 10W
Annandale, *Wash.* **25 D6** 38 50N 77 11W
Annen, *Ruhr* **6 B6** 51 27N 7 22 E
Annet-sur-Marne, *Paris* **5 B6** 48 55N 2 43 E
Anthony Chabot Regional Park, *S.F.* **27 B4** 37 46N 122 7W
Antignano, *Nápl.* **9 H12** 40 51N 14 13 E
Antimano, *Car.* **30 E5** 10 27N 66 59W
Antipolo, *Manila* **15 D5** 14 35N 121 10 E
Antony, *Paris* **5 C3** 48 44N 2 17 E
Antwerp, *Jobg.* **18 E9** 26 5 S 28 9 E
Aoyama, *Tōkyō* **13 C3** 35 39N 139 42 E
Ap Lei Chau, *H.K.* **12 E5** 22 14N 114 9 E
Apapa, *Lagos* **18 B2** 6 26N 7 21 E
Apelacão, *Lisb.* **8 F8** 38 48N 9 7W
Apoquindo, *Stgo* **30 J11** 33 23 S 70 30W
Apshawa, *N.Y.* **22 A2** 41 1N 74 22W
Apterkarskiy Os., *St-Pet.* **11 B4** 59 57N 30 20 E
Aquincum, *Bud.* **10 J13** 47 33N 19 3 E
Ara →, *Tōkyō* **13 B4** 35 41N 139 50 E
Arakawa-Ku, *Tōkyō* **13 B3** 35 44N 139 48 E
Arakpur, *Delhi* **16 B2** 28 35N 77 11 E
Arany-hegyi-patak →, *Bud.* **10 J13** 47 34N 19 4 E
Aravaca, *Mdrd.* **8 B2** 40 27N 3 47W
Arbataash, *Bagd.* **17 E7** 33 20N 44 19 E
Arbutus, *Balt.* **25 B2** 39 15N 76 41W
Arc de Triomphe, *Paris* **5 B3** 48 52N 2 17 E
Arcadia, *L.A.* **28 B4** 34 7N 118 1W
Arceuil, *Paris* **5 C3** 48 48N 2 19 E
Arden, *Phil.* **24 C2** 39 48N 75 29W
Ardey Gebirge, *Ruhr* **6 B6** 51 24N 7 23 E
Ardmore, *Phil.* **24 A3** 40 0N 75 17W
Ardsley, *N.Y.* **23 A5** 41 0N 73 50W
Arese, *Mil.* **9 D5** 45 32N 9 4 E
Arganzuela, *Mdrd.* **8 B2** 40 23N 3 42W
Argenteuil, *Paris* **5 B3** 48 56N 2 15 E
Argonne Forest, *Chic.* **26 C1** 41 42N 87 53W
Ariadana, *Calc.* **16 E6** 22 39N 88 22 E
Aricanduva →, *S. Pau.* **31 E6** 23 31 S 46 33W
Arida, *Lagos* **18 A1** 6 33N 7 16 E
Arima, *Ōsaka* **12 B2** 34 47N 135 15 E
Arima, *Tōkyō* **13 C2** 35 33N 139 33 E
Arima →, *Ōsaka* **12 A2** 34 50N 135 14 E
Arkhangelyskoye, *Mos.* **11 E7** 55 47N 37 17 E
Arkley, *Lon.* **4 B3** 51 38N 0 13W
Arlington, *Bost.* **21 C2** 42 24N 71 10W
Arlington, *Wash.* **25 D7** 38 53N 77 7W
Arlington Heights, *Bost.* **21 C2** 42 25N 71 10W
Arlington Heights, *Chic.* **26 A1** 42 5N 87 55W
Arlington Nat. Cemetery, *Wash.* **25 D7** 38 52N 77 4W
Armação, *Rio J.* **31 B3** 22 52 S 43 6W
Armadale, *Melb.* **19 F7** 37 51 S 145 0 E
Armadale, *Trto.* **20 C9** 43 50N 79 14W
Armainvilliers, Forêt d', *Paris* **5 C6** 48 46N 2 42 E
Armour Heights, *Trto.* **20 D8** 43 45N 79 25W
Arncliffe, *Syd.* **19 B3** 33 56 S 151 8 E
Arnold Arboretum, *Bost.* **21 D3** 42 18N 71 8W
Arnouville-les-Gonesse, *Paris* **5 B4** 48 59N 2 24 E
Arrentela, *Lisb.* **8 G8** 38 37N 9 6W
Arrone →, *Rome* **9 F8** 41 55N 12 16 E
Arroyo Arenas, *La Hab.* **30 B2** 23 3N 82 27W
Arroyo Cr. →, *S.F.* **26 D2** 37 27N 122 25W
Arroyo Naranjo, *La Hab.* **30 B2** 23 2N 82 21W
Årsta, *Stock.* **3 E11** 59 17N 18 3 E
Artesia, *L.A.* **28 C4** 33 51N 118 4W
Arthur Alvim, *S. Pau.* **31 E7** 23 32 S 46 28W
Arthur Kill →, *N.Y.* **22 D3** 40 32N 74 15W
Artigas, *Car.* **30 E5** 10 29N 66 56W
Arundel Gardens, *Balt.* **25 B3** 39 12N 76 37W
Arundel Village, *Balt.* **25 B3** 39 13N 76 35W
Aryiróupolis, *Ath.* **8 J11** 37 52N 23 44 E
Arzano, *Nápl.* **9 H12** 40 54N 14 16 E
Asagaya, *Tōkyō* **13 B2** 35 41N 139 38 E
Asahi, *Ōsaka* **12 B4** 34 43N 135 31 E
Asaka, *Tōkyō* **13 B2** 35 47N 139 35 E
Asakusa, *Tōkyō* **13 B3** 35 42N 139 47 E
Asalatpur, *Delhi* **16 B1** 28 37N 77 4 E
Asati, *Calc.* **16 F5** 22 28N 88 15 E
Aschheim, *Mün.* **7 F11** 48 10N 11 42 E
Ascot Vale, *Melb.* **19 E6** 37 46 S 144 53 E
Aserradero, *Méx.* **29 D2** 19 10N 99 16W
Asharoken, *N.Y.* **23 B8** 40 55N 73 21W
Ashburn, *Chic.* **26 C2** 41 45N 87 43W
Ashburton, *Melb.* **19 F7** 37 51 S 145 4 E

34 Ashburton, L.


Ashburton, L., Balt. 25 B2 39 19N 76 40W
Ashchherino, Mos. 11 F10 55 36N 37 46 E
Ashfield, Syd. 19 B3 33 53 S 151 7 E
Ashford, Lon. 4 C2 51 25N 0 26W
Ashiya, Ōsaka 12 B2 34 43N 135 18 E
Ashiya →, Ōsaka 12 B2 34 42N 135 18 E
Ashland, S.F. 27 B4 37 41N 122 7W
Ashstead, Lon. 4 D3 51 18N 0 17W
Ashwood, Melb. 19 F7 37 52 S 145 5 E
Asker, Oslo 2 B2 59 50N 10 25 E
Askisto, Hels. 3 B3 60 16N 24 47 E
Askrikefjärden, Stock. 3 D12 59 22N 18 13 E
Asnieres, Paris 5 B3 48 54N 2 16 E
Ason, Lagos 18 A3 6 34N 7 31 E
Aspern, Wien 10 G10 48 13N 16 29 E
Aspern, Flugplatz, Wien 10 G11 48 13N 16 30 E
Assiano, Mil. 9 E5 45 27N 9 3 E
Aston Mills, Phil. 24 B2 39 52N 75 26W
Astoria, N.Y. 22 C5 40 46N 73 55W
Atares, Castillo de, La Hab. 30 B2 23 7N 82 21W
Atco, Phil. 24 C5 39 46N 74 53W
Atghara, Calc. 16 E6 22 37N 88 26 E
Athens = Athínai, Ath. 8 J11 37 58N 23 43 E
Athínai, Ath. 8 J11 37 58N 23 43 E
Athinai-Ellinikón Airport, Ath. 8 J2 37 51N 23 44 E
Athis-Mons, Paris 5 C4 48 42N 2 23 E
Atīfīya, Bagd. 17 E8 33 21N 44 21 E
Atikali, Ist. 17 A2 41 1N 28 56 E
Atilo, Cerro, Lima 30 G8 12 2 S 77 2W
Atişalen, Ist. 17 A2 41 3N 28 52 E
Atlandsberg, Berl. 7 A5 52 33N 13 43 E
Atlantic Beach, N.Y. 23 D6 40 35N 73 44W
Atta, Delhi 16 B2 28 34N 77 19 E
Attiki, Ath. 8 H11 38 0N 23 43 E
Atzalpur, Delhi 16 A3 28 43N 77 20 E
Atzgersdorf, Wien 10 H9 48 8N 16 18 E
Aubervilliers, Paris 5 B4 48 54N 2 22 E
Aubing, Mün. 7 G9 48 9N 11 25 E
Auburn, Syd. 19 B3 33 51 S 151 1 E
Auburndale, Bost. 21 C2 42 20N 71 14W
Auckland Park, Jobg. 18 F9 26 11 S 28 0 E
Audubon, Phil. 24 A2 40 7N 75 25W
Auf-dem-Schnee, Ruhr 6 B6 51 26N 7 25 E
Auffargis, Paris 5 C1 48 42N 1 53 E
Augustówka, Wsaw. 10 E7 52 11N 21 5 E
Aulnay-sous-Bois, Paris 5 B4 48 56N 2 29 E
Aurelio, Rome 9 F9 51 54N 12 26 E
Ausîm, El Qâ. 18 C4 30 7N 31 8 E
Aussen Alster, Hbg. 7 D8 53 33N 10 0 E
Austerlitz, Gare d', Paris 5 B4 48 50N 2 22 E
Austin, Chic. 26 B2 41 53N 87 45W
Auteuil, Mtrl. 20 A3 43 37N 73 44W
Avedøre, Købn. 2 E9 55 37N 12 27 E
Aveley, Lon. 4 C6 51 29N 0 15 E
Avellaneda, B.A. 32 C4 34 40 S 58 22W
Avenel, N.Y. 22 D3 40 34N 74 16W
Avenel, Wash. 25 D8 38 59N 76 59W
Avila, Parque National el, Car. 30 D5 10 31N 66 52W
Avila, Pico, Car. 30 D5 10 32N 66 52W
Avini, Nápl. 9 J13 40 48N 14 28 E
Avondale, Chic. 26 B2 41 56N 87 41W
Avondale Heights, Melb. 19 E6 37 45 S 144 52 E
Avtovo, St-Pet. 11 B3 59 51N 30 16 E
Ayase, Tōkyō 13 D1 35 25N 139 26 E
Ayase →, Tōkyō 13 A3 35 52N 139 45 E
Ayazaga, Ist. 17 A2 41 6N 28 59 E
Ayer Chawan, P., Sing. 15 G7 1 16N 103 41 E
Ayer Merbau, P., Sing. 15 G7 1 16N 103 42 E
Ayía Paraskevi, Ath. 8 H11 38 1N 23 49 E
Áyios Dhimitrios, Ath. 8 J11 37 53N 23 44 E
Áyios Ioánnis Rendis, Ath. 8 J10 37 57N 23 39 E
Azabu, Tōkyō 13 C3 35 39N 139 43 E
Azadpur, Delhi 16 A2 28 42N 77 10 E
Azcapotzalco, Méx. 29 B2 19 28N 99 10W
Azteca, Estadia, Méx. 29 C3 19 8N 99 9W
Azusa, L.A. 28 B5 34 7N 117 54W


# B


Ba He →, Beij. 14 B3 39 57N 116 27 E
Baba I., Kar. 17 H10 24 49N 66 57 E
Babarpur, Delhi 16 A2 28 41N 77 16 E
Babelsberg, Berl. 7 B1 52 22N 13 7 E
Babushkin, Mos. 11 D10 55 51N 37 42 E
Babylon, N.Y. 23 C9 40 42N 73 19W
Back →, Balt. 25 B4 39 17N 76 27W
Back B., Bomb. 16 H7 18 56N 72 48 E
Bacoor, Manila 15 E3 14 27N 120 56 E
Bacoor B., Manila 15 E3 14 27N 120 54 E
Badagri Cr. →, Lagos 18 B1 6 24N 7 17 E
Badahela, Delhi 16 B1 28 38N 77 4 E
Badalona, Barc. 8 D6 41 26N 2 14 E
Badersfeld, Mün. 7 F10 48 15N 11 31 E
Badgers Mt., Lon. 4 C5 51 20N 0 8 E
Badi, Delhi 16 A1 28 44N 77 8 E
Badinan, Calc. 16 C5 22 53N 88 14 E
Badu, Rio J. 31 B3 22 54 S 43 3W
Baerl, Ruhr 6 B2 51 29N 6 40 E
Bærum, Oslo 2 B3 59 54N 10 36 E
Bærums Verk, Oslo 2 B2 59 56N 10 28 E
Baggensfjärden, Stock. 3 E12 59 18N 18 19 E
Bággio, Mil. 9 E5 45 27N 9 6 E
Bāgh-e-Feiz, Tehr. 17 C4 35 44N 51 19 E
Baghdād, Bagd. 17 E8 33 20N 44 23 E
Bagmari, Calc. 16 E6 22 34N 88 23 E
Bagneux, Paris 5 C3 48 47N 2 18 E
Bagnolet, Paris 5 B4 48 52N 2 25 E
Bagnoli, Nápl. 9 J11 40 48N 14 9 E
Bagraula, Delhi 16 B1 28 34N 77 4 E
Bagsværd, Købn. 2 D9 55 45N 12 27 E
Bagsværd Sø, Købn. 2 D9 55 46N 12 28 E
Baguiati, Calc. 16 E6 22 36N 88 25 E
Bagumbayan, Manila 15 E4 14 28N 121 3 E
Baha'i Temple, Chic. 26 A2 42 4N 87 41W
Bahrenfeld, Hbg. 7 D7 53 34N 9 55 E
Bahtîm, El Qâ. 18 C5 30 8N 31 16 E
Bahu Bheri, Calc. 16 C5 22 50N 88 14 E
Baidyabati, Calc. 16 D5 22 46N 88 19 E
Baie-d'Urfé, Mtrl. 20 B2 43 25N 73 53W
Baierbrunn, Mün. 7 G10 48 1N 11 29 E
Baijala, Calc. 16 C5 22 51N 88 16 E
Baileys Crossroads, Wash. 25 D7 38 50N 77 6W
Bailly, Paris 5 B2 48 50N 2 4 E
Bainchipota, Calc. 16 C5 22 51N 88 16 E
Bair I., S.F. 27 C3 37 30N 122 13W
Bairro da Matriz, S. Pau. 31 F7 23 40 S 46 27W
Bairro do Limoeiro, S. Pau. 31 E7 23 30 S 46 27W
Baisha, Gzh. 14 G8 23 8N 113 11 E
Baisley Pond, N.Y. 23 C6 40 40N 73 47W
Baixa da Banheira, Lisb. 8 G8 38 39N 9 2W
Baiyun Shan, Gzh. 14 G8 23 8N 113 15 E
Baj Baj, Calc. 16 F5 22 28N 88 11 E
Bakirkoy, Ist. 17 B2 40 58N 28 52 E
Bakovka, Mos. 11 E8 55 40N 37 19 E
Bala-Cynwyd, Phil. 24 A3 40 0N 75 15W
Balagarh, Calc. 16 D6 22 44N 88 27 E
Balara, Manila 15 D4 14 39N 121 3 E
Balarambati, Calc. 16 D5 22 48N 88 12 E
Balashikha, Mos. 11 E11 55 48N 37 58 E
Bald Hill, Bost. 21 B3 42 38N 71 0W
Baldeador, Rio J. 31 B3 22 51 S 43 1W
Baldeneysee, Ruhr 6 B4 51 24N 7 1 E
Baldissero Torinese, Tori. 9 B3 45 4N 7 48 E
Baldpate Hill, Bost. 21 A3 42 42N 71 0W
Baldpate Pond, Bost. 21 A3 42 41N 71 0W
Baldwin, N.Y. 23 D7 40 38N 73 37W
Baldwin Hills, L.A. 28 B2 34 0N 118 21W
Baldwin Hills Res., L.A. 28 B2 34 0N 118 21W
Baldwin Park, L.A. 28 B5 34 5N 117 57W
Bal'etan →, Gzh. 14 G8 23 5N 113 14 E
Balgowlah, Syd. 19 A4 33 47 S 151 16 E
Balgowlah Heights, Syd. 19 A4 33 48 S 151 16 E
Balham, Lon. 4 C4 51 26N 0 8W
Balihati, Calc. 16 D5 22 44N 88 18 E
Balingsnäs, Stock. 3 E11 59 13N 18 0 E
Balingsta, Stock. 3 E11 59 12N 18 3 E
Balintawak, Manila 15 D3 14 39N 120 59 E
Balitai, Tianj. 14 E6 39 5N 117 11 E
Balizhuang, Beij. 14 B3 39 53N 116 28 E
Ballabhpur, Calc. 16 D6 22 44N 88 20 E
Ballainvilliers, Paris 5 C3 48 40N 2 17 E
Ballardvale, Bost. 21 B3 42 37N 71 9W
Ballenato, Pta., La Hab. 30 B2 23 55N 82 28W
Ballerup, Købn. 2 D9 55 43N 12 21 E
Bally, Calc. 16 E6 22 38N 88 20 E
Ballygunge, Calc. 16 E6 22 31N 88 21 E
Balmain, Syd. 19 B4 33 51 S 151 11 E
Balmumcu, Ist. 17 A3 41 3N 29 2 E
Balongbato, Manila 15 D3 14 39N 120 59 E
Baltikri, Calc. 16 E5 22 36N 88 18 E
Baltimore, Balt. 25 B3 39 17N 76 37W
Baltimore Highlands, Balt. 25 B3 39 14N 76 38W
Baltimore-Washington Int. Airport, Balt. 25 B3 39 11N 76 39W
Baluhati, Calc. 16 E5 22 39N 88 15 E
Balwyn, Melb. 19 E7 37 48 S 145 4 E
Balwyn North, Melb. 19 E7 37 47 S 145 4 E
Bambang, Manila 15 D4 14 31N 121 4 E
Bamondongri, Bomb. 16 H9 18 58N 73 1 E
Ban Baan Phichit, Bangk. 15 B2 13 49N 100 37 E
Ban Hugli, Calc. 16 E6 22 38N 88 22 E
Ban Lat Phrao, Bangk. 15 B2 13 47N 100 35 E
Banabuey →, La Hab. 30 B2 23 5N 82 27W
Bananal, S. Pau. 31 D5 23 27 S 46 41W
Banática, Lisb. 8 F7 38 40N 9 11W
Bandeirantes, Praia dos, Rio J. 31 C1 23 0 S 43 23W
Bandipur, Calc. 16 D6 22 43N 88 26 E
Bandipur, Calc. 16 C4 22 50N 88 9 E
Bandra, Bomb. 16 G7 19 3N 72 49 E
Bandra Pt., Bomb. 16 G7 19 2N 72 49 E
Banfield, B.A. 32 C4 34 44 S 58 24W
Bang Kapi, Bangk. 15 B2 13 45N 100 38 E
Bang Khen, Bangk. 15 A2 13 52N 100 35 E
Bang Na, Bangk. 15 B2 13 40N 100 36 E
Bang Su, Khlong →, Bangk. 15 B2 13 47N 100 31 E
Bangbae, Sŏul 12 H7 37 29N 126 59 E
Banghag, Sŏul 12 G8 37 38N 127 1 E
Bangka, Jak. 15 J9 6 15 S 106 48 E
Bangkok, Bangk. 15 B2 13 44N 100 30 E
Bangkok Noi, Khlong →, Bangk. 15 B1 13 45N 100 29 E
Bangkok Yai, Bangk. 15 B1 13 43N 100 29 E
Bangkok Yai, Khlong →, Bangk. 15 B1 13 44N 100 29 E
Banglo, Calc. 16 E5 22 31N 88 14 E
Bangrak, Bangk. 15 B2 13 43N 100 31 E
Bangu, Rio J. 31 B1 22 52 S 43 26W
Bangu, Sa. do, Rio J. 31 B1 22 53 S 43 24W
Bankipur, Calc. 16 D5 22 47N 88 13 E
Bankra, Calc. 16 E5 22 36N 88 17 E
Banks, C., Syd. 19 C4 34 0 S 151 16 E
Bankstown, Syd. 19 B3 33 55 S 151 2 E
Bankstown Aerodrome, Syd. 19 B2 33 55 S 150 59 E
Banna →, Tori. 9 A3 45 12N 7 42 E
Banstala, Calc. 16 E6 22 31N 88 24 E
Banstead, Lon. 4 D3 51 18N 0 12W
Bantra, Calc. 16 E5 22 35N 88 18 E
Banyule Flats Res., Melb. 19 E7 37 44 S 145 5 E
Baquirivú, S. Pau. 31 D7 23 26 S 46 28W
Baquirivú-Guaçu, S. Pau. 31 D7 23 28 S 46 28W
Bara, Calc. 16 D5 22 45N 88 16 E
Baragwanath Airfield, Jobg. 18 F8 26 14 S 27 58 E
Barai, Calc. 16 C6 22 52N 88 22 E
Barajas, Mdrd. 8 B3 40 28N 3 34W
Barajas, Aeropuerto Transoceanico de, Mdrd. 8 B3 40 28N 3 33W
Barakpur, Calc. 16 D6 22 47N 88 21 E
Baranagar, Calc. 16 E6 22 38N 88 22 E
Barbaiana, Mil. 9 D5 45 32N 9 1 E
Barca, Tori. 9 B3 45 6N 7 43 E
Barcarena, Lisb. 8 F7 38 43N 9 16W
Barcarena →, Lisb. 8 F7 38 41N 9 16W
Barcelona, Barc. 8 D6 41 22N 2 10 E
Barcelona-Prat, Aeropuerta de, Barc. 8 E5 41 17N 2 5 E
Barceloneta, Barc. 8 D6 41 22N 2 11 E
Barcroft, L., Wash. 25 D6 38 50N 77 9W
Baréggio, Mil. 9 E5 45 28N 9 0 E
Bariti Bil, Calc. 16 D6 22 48N 88 25 E
Barkarby, Stock. 3 D10 59 24N 17 52 E
Barker Pt., N.Y. 23 B6 40 50N 73 44W
Barking, Lon. 4 B5 51 32N 0 5 E
Barkingside, Lon. 4 B5 51 35N 0 4 E
Barlovento, La Hab. 30 B2 23 5N 82 28W
Barmbek, Hbg. 7 D8 53 34N 10 1 E
Barmen, Ruhr 6 C5 51 16N 7 12 E
Barneau, Paris 5 D6 48 38N 2 43 E
Barnes, Lon. 4 C3 51 28N 0 14W
Barnet, Lon. 4 B3 51 39N 0 11W
Barnsboro, Phil. 24 C4 39 45N 75 9W
Baronia Park, Syd. 19 A3 33 49 S 151 8 E
Barop, Ruhr 6 B6 51 29N 7 25 E
Barra, Nápl. 9 H12 40 50N 14 19 E
Barra Andai, Kar. 17 H11 24 47N 66 59 E
Barra Funda, S. Pau. 31 E6 23 31 S 46 39W
Barracas, B.A. 32 B4 34 39 S 58 24W
Barrackpore Airport, Calc. 16 D6 22 46N 88 21 E
Barrancas, Stgo 30 J10 33 26 S 70 44W
Barranco, Lima 30 G8 12 9 S 77 2W
Barreiro, Lisb. 8 G8 38 39N 9 5W
Barreto, Rio J. 31 B3 22 50 S 43 5W
Barrientos, Méx. 29 A2 19 34N 99 11W
Barrington, Phil. 24 B4 39 52N 75 3W
Barrio de La Estación, Mdrd. 8 B3 40 26N 3 32W
Bartala, Calc. 16 E5 22 32N 88 15 E
Barton Park, Syd. 19 B3 33 56 S 151 9 E
Bartyki, Wsaw. 10 F7 52 10N 21 6 E
Baru, Kali →, Jak. 15 J10 6 12 S 106 51 E
Baruipara, Calc. 16 D5 22 45N 88 13 E
Baruta, Car. 30 E5 10 26N 66 52W
Barvikha, Mos. 11 E7 55 44N 37 16 E
Basai Darapur, Delhi 16 B1 28 38N 77 6 E
Bass Hill, Syd. 19 B3 33 54 S 151 0 E
Bassett, L.A. 28 B5 34 3N 117 59W
Bastille, Place de la, Paris 5 B4 48 51N 2 22 E
Bastos, Rio J. 31 B1 22 52 S 43 21W
Basudebpur, Calc. 16 D6 22 49N 88 24 E
Basus, El Qâ. 18 C5 30 7N 31 12 E
Batanagar, Calc. 16 E5 22 31N 88 15 E
Batenbrock, Ruhr 6 A3 51 31N 6 57 E
Bath Beach, N.Y. 22 D4 40 36N 74 0W
Bath I., Kar. 17 H11 24 49N 67 1 E
Batok, Bukit, Sing. 15 F7 1 21N 103 46 E
Battersea, Lon. 4 C4 51 28N 0 9W
Baturino, Mos. 11 F9 55 35N 37 30 E
Bauman, Mos. 11 E10 55 45N 37 40 E
Baumgarten, Wien 10 G9 48 12N 16 17 E
Bauria, Calc. 16 E5 22 30N 88 10 E
Baxter Estates, N.Y. 23 B6 40 50N 73 42W
Bay Farm I., S.F. 27 B3 37 44N 122 14W
Bay Meadows Race Track, S.F. 27 C3 37 32N 122 17W
Bay Park, N.Y. 23 D7 40 37N 73 39W
Bay Ridge, N.Y. 22 D4 40 37N 74 1W
Bay Ridge Channel, N.Y. 22 D4 40 39N 74 1W
Bay Shore Park, Balt. 25 B4 39 13N 76 25W
Baykoz, Ist. 17 A3 41 7N 29 7 E
Bayonne, N.Y. 22 C4 40 40N 74 6W
Bayshore, S.F. 27 B3 37 42N 122 24W
Bayside, N.Y. 23 C6 40 45N 73 46W
Bayswater, Lon. 4 B3 51 30N 0 10W
Bayswater, Melb. 19 F8 37 50 S 145 17 E
Bayview, S.F. 27 B2 37 44N 122 23W
Bayville, N.Y. 23 B7 40 54N 73 33W
Bāzār, Tehr. 17 C5 35 40N 51 25 E
Beachmont, Bost. 21 C4 42 23N 70 59W
Beacon Hill, H.K. 12 D6 22 21N 114 10 E
Beaconsfield, Mtrl. 20 B2 43 25N 73 53W
Beacontree Heath, Lon. 4 B5 51 33N 0 9 E
Beam →, Lon. 4 B6 51 30N 0 10 E
Bear Cr. →, Balt. 25 B3 39 13N 76 30W
Bear Gulch Res., S.F. 27 D3 37 26N 122 13W
Beato, Lisb. 8 F8 38 44N 9 5W
Beauchamp, Paris 5 A3 49 0N 2 11 E
Beaumonte Heights, Trto. 20 D7 43 45N 79 34W
Beaverdam Cr. →, Wash. 25 C8 39 0N 76 5W
Bebek, Ist. 17 A3 41 4N 29 2 E
Beccar, B.A. 32 A3 34 27 S 58 32W
Běchovice, Pra. 10 B3 50 4N 14 36 E
Beck L., Chic. 26 A1 42 4N 87 52W
Beckenham, Lon. 4 C4 51 24N 0 1W
Beckhausen, Ruhr 6 A4 51 33N 7 1 E
Beckton, Lon. 4 B5 51 30N 0 4 E
Beddington, Lon. 4 C4 51 21N 0 8W
Beddington Corner, Lon. 4 C4 51 23N 0 9W
Bedford, Bost. 21 C2 42 27N 71 15W
Bedford Park, Chic. 26 C2 41 46N 87 46W
Bedford Park, N.Y. 23 B5 40 52N 73 52W
Bedford Stuyvesant, N.Y. 22 C5 40 41N 73 56W
Bedford View, Jobg. 18 F9 26 10 S 28 7 E
Bedok, Sing. 15 G8 1 19N 103 56 E
Beeck, Ruhr 6 B2 51 28N 6 44 E
Beeckerwerth, Ruhr 6 B2 51 28N 6 42 E
Behala, Calc. 16 E5 22 30N 88 18 E
Bei Hai, Beij. 14 B3 39 54N 116 21 E
Beicai, Shang. 14 J12 31 11N 121 32 E
Beicang, Tianj. 14 D5 39 13N 117 7 E
Beigai, Tianj. 14 E6 39 9N 117 10 E
Beijiaoshichang, Beij. 14 B2 39 57N 116 19 E
Beijing, Beij. 14 B2 39 53N 116 21 E
Beinasco, Tori. 9 B2 45 1N 7 34 E
Beirolas, Lisb. 8 F8 38 46N 9 5W
Beitsun, Gzh. 14 G8 23 7N 113 10 E
Békásmegyer, Bud. 10 J13 47 35N 19 3 E
Bekkelaget, Oslo 2 B4 59 53N 10 47 E
Bel Air, L.A. 28 B2 34 4N 118 27W
Bela Vista, S. Pau. 31 E6 23 33 S 46 38W
Bélanger, Mtrl. 20 A3 43 35N 73 42W
Belas, Lisb. 8 F7 38 46N 9 17W
Belém, Lisb. 8 F7 38 41N 9 12W
Belém, Torre de, Lisb. 8 F7 38 41N 9 12W
Belenzinho, S. Pau. 31 E6 23 32 S 46 34W
Belfield, Syd. 19 B3 33 53 S 151 6 E
Belgachi, Calc. 16 E5 22 36N 88 18 E
Belgharia, Calc. 16 E6 22 39N 88 22 E
Belgrano, B.A. 32 B4 34 33 S 58 27W
Belgrave, Melb. 19 F9 37 54 S 145 21 E
Bell Gardens, L.A. 28 C4 33 58N 118 9W
Bella Vista, B.A. 32 B2 34 34 S 58 41W
Bellaire, N.Y. 23 C6 40 42N 73 44W
Bellavista, Lima 30 G8 12 4 S 77 8W
Bellavista, Stgo 30 K11 33 31 S 70 35W
Belle Harbour, N.Y. 23 D5 40 34N 73 51W
Belle Haven, N.Y. 23 A7 41 0N 73 37W
Belle Haven, Wash. 25 E7 38 46N 77 3W
Bellefonte, Phil. 24 C1 39 45N 75 30W
Bellerose, N.Y. 23 C6 40 44N 73 42W
Belleview, Wash. 25 D6 38 57N 77 14W
Belleville, N.Y. 22 C4 40 48N 74 8W
Bellflower, L.A. 28 C4 33 53N 118 7W
Bellingham, Lon. 4 C4 51 25N 0 1W
Bellmawr, Phil. 24 B4 39 52N 75 5W
Bellmore, N.Y. 23 D7 40 39N 73 31W
Bello, La Hab. 30 B2 23 5N 82 24W
Bells Lake, Phil. 24 C4 39 45N 75 3W
Bellwood, Chic. 26 B1 41 52N 87 53W
Belmont, Bost. 21 C2 42 23N 71 10W
Belmont, Lon. 4 B3 51 36N 0 18W
Belmont, S.F. 27 C3 37 31N 122 17W
Belmont Cragin, Chic. 26 B2 41 56N 87 45W
Belmont Harbor, Chic. 26 B3 41 56N 87 38W
Belmont Hills, Phil. 24 A3 40 1N 75 15W
Belmont Slough, S.F. 27 C3 37 32N 122 15W
Belmore, Syd. 19 B3 33 55 S 151 5 E
Belopurpada, Bomb. 16 G9 19 0N 73 1 E
Beltsville, Wash. 25 C8 39 2N 76 54W
Beltsville Airport, Wash. 25 C9 39 1N 76 49W
Belur, Calc. 16 E6 22 37N 88 21 E
Belvedere, Lon. 4 C5 51 29N 0 9 E
Belvedere, S.F. 27 A2 37 52N 122 27W
Belyayevo Bogorodskoye, Mos. 11 F9 55 39N 37 31 E
Bemböle, Hels. 3 B2 60 13N 24 39 E
Bemis Woods, Chic. 26 C1 41 49N 87 54W
Bemowo, Wsaw. 10 E6 52 15N 20 53 E
Benavidez, B.A. 32 A2 34 24 S 58 41W
Bendale, Trto. 20 D9 43 45N 79 13W
Bendungan Hilir, Jak. 15 J9 6 12 S 106 48 E
Benefica, Rio J. 31 B2 22 52 S 43 14W
Benfica, Lisb. 8 F7 38 45N 9 11W
Benin B., Lagos 18 B2 6 24N 7 28 E
Benjamin Franklin Br., Phil. 24 B4 39 57N 75 8W
Benoni, Jobg. 18 F10 26 11 S 28 18 E
Benoni South, Jobg. 18 F10 26 12 S 28 17 E
Bensenville, Chic. 26 B1 41 57N 87 56W
Bensonhurst, N.Y. 22 D5 40 35N 73 59W
Bentleigh, Melb. 19 F7 37 54 S 145 2 E
Bentleigh East, Melb. 19 F7 37 54 S 145 4 E
Beraberi, Calc. 16 D6 22 46N 88 27 E
Berario, Jobg. 18 E8 26 7 S 27 57 E
Berazategui, B.A. 32 C5 34 45 S 58 15W
Berea, Jobg. 18 F9 26 10 S 28 3 E
Berg am Laim, Mün. 7 G10 48 7N 11 38 E
Bergbaumuseum, Ruhr 6 B5 51 29N 7 13 E
Bergenfield, N.Y. 22 B5 40 55N 73 59W
Berger, Oslo 2 B6 59 56N 11 7 E
Bergerhausen, Ruhr 6 B4 51 26N 7 2 E
Bergerhof, Ruhr 6 C6 51 12N 7 21 E
Bergham, Mün. 7 G10 48 2N 11 37 E
Berghausen, Ruhr 6 A5 51 36N 7 12 E
Berghm-Oestrum, Ruhr 6 B1 51 25N 6 39 E
Bergstedt, Hbg. 7 C8 53 40N 10 7 E
Beri, Barc. 8 D5 41 20N 2 1 E
Berih, Sungei →, Sing. 15 F7 1 22N 103 40 E
Berkeley, Chic. 26 B1 41 53N 87 54W
Berkeley, S.F. 27 A3 37 51N 122 16W
Berkeley Heights, N.Y. 22 C2 40 40N 74 26W
Berkeley Hills, S.F. 27 A3 37 51N 122 11W
Berlin, Berl. 7 A3 52 31N 13 23 E
Berlin, Phil. 24 C5 39 47N 74 55W
Bermondsey, Lon. 4 C4 51 29N 0 3W
Bernabeu, Estadio, Mdrd. 8 B2 40 27N 3 41W
Bernal, B.A. 32 C5 34 43 S 58 17W
Bernal Heights, S.F. 27 B2 37 44N 122 24W
Berne, Hbg. 7 D8 53 38N 10 8 E
Berngardovka, St-Pet. 11 A5 60 0N 30 34 E
Berthpage, N.Y. 23 C8 40 45N 73 29W
Bertlich, Ruhr 6 A4 51 36N 7 4 E
Bertolla Barca, Tori. 9 B3 45 6N 7 44 E
Berwyn, Chic. 26 B2 41 50N 87 47W
Berwyn, Phil. 24 A2 40 2N 75 26W
Berwyn Heights, Wash. 25 D8 38 59N 76 55W
Besedy, Mos. 11 F10 55 38N 37 47 E
Besiktas, Ist. 17 A3 41 2N 29 0 E
Beskudnikovo, Mos. 11 D9 55 52N 37 34 E
Besós →, Barc. 8 D6 41 24N 2 13 E
Bessancourt, Paris 5 A3 49 2N 2 12 E
Bestazzo, Mil. 9 E5 45 25N 9 0 E
Bethayres, Phil. 24 A4 40 7N 75 3W
Bethesda, Wash. 25 D7 38 59N 77 6W
Bethlehem Steel Plant, Balt. 25 B4 39 13N 76 29W
Bethnal Green, Lon. 4 B4 51 31N 0 2W
Bethpage State Park, N.Y. 23 C8 40 45N 73 25W
Betor, Calc. 16 E5 22 34N 88 17 E
Beuvronne →, Paris 5 B6 48 59N 2 40 E
Beverley, Chic. 26 C3 41 42N 87 39W
Beverley Hills, Syd. 19 B3 33 56 S 151 5 E
Beverley Park, Syd. 19 B3 33 58 S 151 8 E
Beverly, Bost. 21 B4 42 34N 70 53W
Beverly, Phil. 24 A5 40 3N 74 55W
Beverly Glen, L.A. 28 B2 34 6N 118 26W
Beverly Harbor, Bost. 21 B4 42 32N 70 51W
Beverly Hills, L.A. 28 B2 34 5N 118 24W
Beverly Municipal Airport, Bost. 21 B4 42 36N 70 55W
Bexley, Lon. 4 C5 51 26N 0 8 E
Bexley, Syd. 19 B3 33 56 S 151 7 E
Bexleyheath, Lon. 4 C5 51 27N 0 8 E
Beyenburg, Ruhr 6 C5 51 15N 7 19 E
Beylerbeyi, Ist. 17 A3 41 2N 29 2 E
Beyoğlu, Ist. 17 A2 41 1N 28 58 E
Bezons, Paris 5 B3 48 56N 2 13 E
Bhadrakali, Calc. 16 D6 22 40N 88 20 E
Bhadreswar, Calc. 16 D5 22 49N 88 22 E
Bhadua, Calc. 16 D5 22 40N 88 12 E
Bhalswa, Delhi 16 A2 28 44N 77 10 E
Bhambo Khān Qarmati, Kar. 17 H11 24 49N 67 7 E
Bhandardaha, Calc. 16 E5 22 37N 88 12 E
Bhatpara, Calc. 16 C6 22 52N 88 25 E
Bhatpur, Calc. 16 D6 22 43N 88 25 E
Bhatsala, Calc. 16 E5 22 30N 88 16 E
Bhawanipore, Calc. 16 E6 22 32N 88 21 E
Bhopura, Delhi 16 A2 28 41N 77 19 E
Białołeka Dworska, Wsaw. 10 E7 52 19N 21 1 E
Bickley, Lon. 4 C5 51 23N 0 3 E
Bicutan, Manila 15 D4 14 30N 121 3 E
Bidyadharpur, Calc. 16 C6 22 50N 88 24 E
Bielany, Wsaw. 10 E6 52 17N 20 57 E
Biesdorf, Berl. 7 A4 52 30N 13 33 E
Bièvre →, Paris 5 C2 48 44N 2 9 E
Bièvres, Paris 5 C3 48 45N 2 13 E
Big Timber Cr. →, Phil. 24 B4 39 52N 75 7W
Big Tujunga Canyon →, L.A. 28 A3 34 16N 118 12W
Biggin Hill, Lon. 4 D5 51 18N 0 1 E
Bijoki, Tōkyō 13 B2 35 49N 139 38 E
Bilibiran, Manila 15 E5 14 29N 121 10 E
Bilk, Ruhr 6 C2 51 12N 6 46 E
Billbrook, Hbg. 7 D8 53 31N 10 4 E
Bille →, Hbg. 7 D8 53 32N 10 4 E
Billerica, Bost. 21 B2 42 33N 71 16W
Billinghurst, B.A. 32 B3 34 34 S 58 37W
Billings, Represa, S. Pau. 31 F6 23 42 S 46 39W
Billstedt, Hbg. 7 D8 53 32N 10 6 E
Billwerder, Hbg. 7 D8 53 30N 10 7 E
Billwerder B., Hbg. 7 D8 53 31N 10 3 E
Binacayan, Manila 15 E3 14 27N 120 55 E
Binangonan, Manila 15 E5 14 28N 121 10 E
Binaria, Jak. 15 H10 6 7 S 106 51 E
Bingzhoubao, Gzh. 14 G8 23 2N 113 11 E
Binningsvatna, Oslo 2 C6 50 46N 11 3 E
Binondo, Manila 15 D3 14 36N 120 58 E
Binzago, Mil. 9 D5 45 37N 9 8 E
Birak el Kiyam, El Qâ. 18 C4 30 2N 31 9 E
Birch Cliff, Trto. 20 D9 43 41N 79 16W
Bird →, Balt. 25 A4 39 22N 76 22W
Birka, Stock. 3 D8 59 20N 17 33 E
Birkenhöhe, Berl. 7 A4 52 38N 13 36 E
Birkenstein, Berl. 7 A5 52 31N 13 40 E
Birkholz, Berl. 7 A4 52 37N 13 34 E
Birkholzaue, Berl. 7 A4 52 38N 13 36 E
Biryulyovo, Mos. 11 F10 55 35N 37 40 E
Bisamberg, Wien 10 G10 48 19N 16 21 E
Bispebjerg, Købn. 2 D10 55 42N 12 31 E
Bitsa, Mos. 11 F9 55 35N 37 36 E
Biwon Secret Garden, Sŏul 12 G7 37 34N 126 59 E
Bizard, Î., Mtrl. 20 B2 43 29N 73 53W
Björknas, Stock. 3 E12 59 19N 18 12 E
Björköfjärden, Hels. 3 C2 60 7N 24 38 E
Black Cr. →, Trto. 20 D8 43 40N 79 30W
Blackburn, Melb. 19 E7 37 48 S 145 9 E
Blackburn L., Melb. 19 E7 37 49 S 145 9 E
Blackburn South, Melb. 19 F7 37 50 S 145 9 E
Blackfen, Lon. 4 C5 51 26N 0 6 E
Blackheath, Jobg. 18 E8 26 8 S 27 57 E
Blackheath, Lon. 4 C5 51 28N 0 0 E
Blackmore, Lon. 4 A6 51 41N 0 19 E
Blacktown, Syd. 19 A2 33 46 S 150 56 E
Blackwall, Lon. 4 B4 51 30N 0 0 E
Blackwood, Phil. 24 C4 39 47N 75 4W
Bladensburg, Wash. 25 D8 38 55N 76 55W
Blairgowrie, Jobg. 18 E9 26 6 S 28 0 E
Blakehurst, Syd. 19 B3 33 59 S 151 6 E
Blakstad, Oslo 2 C2 50 49N 10 28 E
Blanco, C., Car. 30 D5 10 36N 66 59W
Blankenburg, Berl. 7 A3 52 35N 13 27 E
Blankenese, Hbg. 7 D6 53 33N 9 48 E
Blankenfelde, Berl. 7 A3 52 37N 13 23 E
Blankenstein, Ruhr 6 B5 51 24N 7 11 E
Blenheim, Phil. 24 C4 39 48N 75 4W
Bliersheim, Ruhr 6 B2 51 23N 6 42 E
Blind Cr. →, Melb. 19 F8 37 53 S 145 12 E
Blizne, Wsaw. 10 E6 52 14N 20 52 E
Bloomfield, N.Y. 22 C3 40 48N 74 12W
Bloomingdale, N.Y. 22 A3 41 0N 74 19W
Bloomsbury, Balt. 25 B2 39 15N 76 44W
Błota, Wsaw. 10 F8 52 9N 21 11 E
Bloubosspruit →, Jobg. 18 F9 26 16 S 28 0 E
Blue Hills Reservation, Bost. 21 D3 42 13N 71 5W
Blue Island, Chic. 26 C2 41 40N 87 40W
Bluff Hd., H.K. 12 E6 22 11N 114 12 E
Blumberg, Berl. 7 A4 52 36N 13 39 E
Blunt Pt., S.F. 27 A2 37 51N 122 25W
Blutenberg, Mün. 7 G9 48 9N 11 27 E
Blylaget, Oslo 2 C4 59 46N 10 41 E
Boa Vista, Alto do, Rio J. 31 B2 22 58 S 43 16W
Boa Vista, Morro, Rio J. 31 B3 22 53 S 43 5W
Boadilla del Monte, Mdrd. 8 B1 40 24N 3 52W
Boardwalk, N.Y. 23 D6 40 34N 73 49W
Boavista, Lisb. 8 F8 38 48N 9 8W
Bobäck, Hels. 3 B2 60 10N 24 31 E
Boberg, Hbg. 7 D8 53 30N 10 9 E
Bobigny, Paris 5 B4 48 54N 2 26 E
Bobylyskaya, St-Pet. 11 B3 59 59N 30 10 E
Bocanegra, Lima 30 F8 11 59 S 77 7W
Boccea, Rome 9 F8 41 57N 12 19 E
Bochold, Ruhr 6 B3 51 28N 6 57 E
Bochum, Ruhr 6 B5 51 28N 7 13 E
Bockum, Ruhr 6 B1 51 21N 6 37 E
Bodelschwingh, Ruhr 6 A6 51 33N 7 22 E
Bodomjärvi, Hels. 3 B3 60 15N 24 40 E
Bogenhausen, Mün. 7 G10 48 8N 11 36 E
Bognæs, Købn. 2 D7 55 41N 12 1 E
Bogorodskoye, Mos. 11 E10 55 48N 37 42 E
Bogota, N.Y. 22 B4 40 52N 74 2W
Bogstadvatnet, Oslo 2 B3 59 58N 10 37 E
Bohaidalu, Tianj. 14 E6 39 7N 117 12 E
Bohnsdorf, Berl. 7 B4 52 23N 13 34 E
Bois-Colombes, Paris 5 B3 48 55N 2 16 E
Bois-d'Arcy, Paris 5 C2 48 48N 2 1 E
Boisement, Paris 5 A2 49 1N 2 0 E
Boissy-St.-Léger, Paris 5 C5 48 44N 2 31 E
Boksburg, Jobg. 18 F10 26 12 S 28 15 E
Boksburg North, Jobg. 18 F10 26 12 S 28 15 E
Boksburg South, Jobg. 18 F10 26 13 S 28 16 E
Boldinasco, Mil. 9 E5 45 29N 9 8 E
Bøler, Oslo 2 B5 59 53N 10 50 E
Bollate, Mil. 9 D5 45 32N 9 7 E
Bollensdorf, Berl. 7 A5 52 30N 13 42 E
Bollmora, Stock. 3 E12 59 14N 18 14 E
Bolshaya Nevka, St-Pet. 11 B3 59 58N 30 18 E
Bolshaya-Okhta, St-Pet. 11 B4 59 56N 30 26 E
Bolshoi Theatre, Mos. 11 E9 55 45N 37 37 E
Bom Retiro, S. Pau. 31 E6 23 31 S 46 38W
Bombay, Bomb. 16 H8 18 56N 72 50 E
Bombay Harbour, Bomb. 16 H8 18 58N 72 55 E
Bombay Univ., Bomb. 16 H7 18 55N 72 49 E
Bommern, Ruhr 6 B6 51 25N 7 20 E
Bonaero Park, Jobg. 18 E10 26 7 S 28 15 E
Bondi, Syd. 19 B4 33 53 S 151 16 E
Bondoufle, Paris 5 D4 48 36N 2 22 E
Bondy, Paris 5 B4 48 54N 2 28 E
Bondy, Forêt de, Paris 5 B5 48 54N 2 33 E
Bonifacio Monument, Manila 15 D3 14 38N 120 58 E
Bonifica di Maccarese, Rome 9 F8 41 50N 12 15 E
Bonifica di Porto, Rome 9 G8 41 48N 12 16 E
Bonita, Pt., S.F. 27 B1 37 48N 122 31W
Bonnelles, Paris 5 D2 48 37N 2 1 E
Bonneuil-sur-Marne, Paris 5 C5 48 46N 2 30 E
Bönningstedt, Hbg. 7 C7 53 40N 9 54 E
Bonnyrigg, Syd. 19 B2 33 53 S 150 54 E
Bonsari, Bomb. 16 G9 19 4N 73 1 E
Bonsucesso, Rio J. 31 B2 22 51 S 43 15W
Boo, Stock. 3 D12 59 20N 18 16 E
Boonton, N.Y. 22 B2 40 54N 74 24W
Boonton Res., N.Y. 22 B2 40 53N 74 24W
Booth Corner, Phil. 24 B2 39 50N 75 29W
Boothwyn, Phil. 24 C2 39 49N 75 26W
Borbeck, Ruhr 6 B3 51 28N 6 56 E
Bordeaux, Jobg. 18 E9 26 5 S 28 1 E
Bordeaux, Mtrl. 20 A3 43 31N 73 43W
Borehamwood, Lon. 4 B3 51 39N 0 15W
Borgaretto, Tori. 9 B2 45 0N 7 35 E
Bórgaro Torinese, Tori. 9 B2 45 9N 7 39 E
Borghese, Villa, Rome 9 F9 41 54N 12 29 E
Borisovo, Mos. 11 F10 55 38N 37 44 E
Borle, Bomb. 16 G8 19 2N 72 54 E
Bornig, Ruhr 6 A5 51 33N 7 16 E
Bornsjön, Stock. 3 E9 59 14N 17 44 E
Boronia, Melb. 19 F8 37 51 S 145 17 E
Borough Green, Lon. 4 D6 51 17N 0 18 E
Borough Park, N.Y. 22 D5 40 38N 73 59W
Børtervatna, Oslo 2 C6 50 46N 11 3 E
Boscoreale, Nápl. 9 J13 40 46N 14 28 E
Boscotrecase, Nápl. 9 J13 40 46N 14 27 E
Bösinghovn, Ruhr 6 C1 51 18N 6 38 E
Bosmont, Jobg. 18 F8 26 10 S 27 57 E
Bosön, Stock. 3 D12 59 22N 18 11 E
Bosporus = Istanbul Boğazi, Ist. 17 A3 41 5N 29 3 E
Bosque da Saúde, S. Pau. 31 E6 23 36 S 46 37W
Bosques, B.A. 32 C5 34 48 S 58 15W
Bossley Park, Syd. 19 B2 33 51 S 150 53 E
Bossucaba →, S. Pau. 31 E5 23 31 S 46 46W
Bostanci, Ist. 17 B3 40 57N 29 5 E
Bostelbek, Hbg. 7 E7 53 28N 9 55 E
Boston, Bost. 21 C3 42 21N 71 3W
Boston B., Bost. 21 C4 42 22N 70 55W
Boston Harbor, Bost. 21 C4 42 20N 70 58W
Boston Hill, Bost. 21 B3 42 38N 71 5W
Botany, Syd. 19 B4 33 56 S 151 12 E
Botany B., Lon. 4 A4 51 40N 0 7W
Botany B., Syd. 19 B4 33 58 S 151 11 E
Botič →, Pra. 10 B3 50 4N 14 26 E
Botkyrka, Stock. 3 E9 59 15N 17 49 E
Botofogo, Rio J. 31 B2 22 56 S 43 10W
Bottrop, Ruhr 6 A3 51 32N 6 57 E
Bötzow, Berl. 7 A1 52 39N 13 8 E
Bouafle, Paris 5 B1 48 57N 1 54 E
Boucherville, Mtrl. 20 A5 43 36N 73 28W
Boucherville, Îs. de, Mtrl. 20 A5 43 36N 73 28W
Bougival, Paris 5 B2 48 51N 2 8 E
Boulder Pt., H.K. 12 E5 22 14N 114 6 E

Choisy-le-Roi 35

Boullay-les-Troux, Paris 5 C2 48 40N 2 2 E
Boulogne, B.A. 32 B3 34 30 S 58 33W
Boulogne, Bois de, Paris 5 B3 48 51N 2 14 E
Boulogne-Billancourt, Paris 5 B3 48 50N 2 14 E
Bouqueval, Paris 5 A4 49 1N 2 25 E
Bourg-la-Reine, Paris 5 C3 48 46N 2 19 E
Boussy-St.-Antoine, Paris 5 C5 48 41N 2 33 E
Bouviers, Paris 5 C2 48 46N 2 4 E
Bovert, Ruhr 6 C1 51 16N 6 37 E
Bovisa, Mil. 9 D6 45 30N 9 10 E
Bovisio-Masciago, Mil. 9 D5 45 36N 9 8 E
Bow, Lon. 4 B4 51 31N 0 1W
Bowleys Quarters, Balt. 25 A4 39 20N 76 24W
Box Hill, Melb. 19 E7 37 48 S 145 6 E
Boxford State Forest, Bost. 21 B3 42 39N 71 2W
Boy, Ruhr 6 A3 51 31N 7 0 E
Boyaciköy, Ist. 17 A3 41 5N 29 2 E
Boye →, Ruhr 6 A3 51 30N 6 59 E
Boyle Heights, L.A. 28 B3 34 1N 118 12 E
Braddell Heights, Sing. 15 F8 1 20N 103 51 E
Brahmanpur, Bomb. 16 G8 19 5N 72 52 E
Braintree, Bost. 21 D3 42 12N 71 0W
Brakpan, Jobg. 18 F11 26 14 S 28 20 E
Brambauer, Ruhr 6 A6 51 35N 7 26 E
Bramfeld, Hbg. 7 D8 53 36N 10 5 E
Bramley, Jobg. 18 E9 26 7 S 28 4 E
Brande, Hbg. 7 D6 53 37N 9 49 E
Brandenburg Gate, Berl. 7 A3 52 30N 13 21 E
Brandizzo, Tori. 9 A3 45 10N 7 49 E
Brands Hatch, Lon. 4 C6 51 21N 0 15 E
Brandýs nad Labem, Pra. 10 A3 50 10N 14 39 E
Brandywine, Phil. 24 C1 39 49N 75 32W
Brandywine Cr. →, Phil. 24 C1 39 43N 75 31W
Brani, P., Sing. 15 G8 1 15N 103 50 E
Branik, Pra. 10 B2 50 1N 14 25 E
Brännkyrka, Stock. 3 E11 59 17N 18 0 E
Brás, S. Pau. 31 E6 23 32 S 46 36W
Brateyevo, Mos. 11 F10 55 39N 37 45 E
Bratsevo, Mos. 11 D8 55 51N 37 24 E
Brauck, Ruhr 6 A3 51 32N 7 0 E
Brava, Pta., La Hab. 30 B2 23 8N 82 23W
Braybrook, Melb. 19 E6 37 46 S 144 51 E
Brázdim, Pra. 10 A3 50 10N 14 35 E
Breakheart Reservation, Bost. 21 C3 42 28N 71 1W
Brechten, Ruhr 6 A6 51 34N 7 27 E
Breckerfeld, Ruhr 6 C6 51 15N 7 28 E
Brede, Købn. 2 D10 55 47N 12 30 E
Bredeney, Ruhr 6 B3 51 24N 6 59 E
Breeds Pond, Bost. 21 C4 42 28N 70 58W
Breezy Pt., N.Y. 22 D5 40 33N 73 56W
Breitenlee, Wien 10 G11 48 15N 16 30 E
Breitscheid, Ruhr 6 B3 51 21N 6 51 E
Breña, Lima 30 G8 12 3 S 77 3W
Brenschede, Ruhr 6 B5 51 26N 7 12 E
Brent, Lon. 4 B3 51 33N 0 15W
Brent →, Lon. 4 B2 51 30N 0 20W
Brent Res., Lon. 4 B3 51 34N 0 14W
Brentford, Lon. 4 C3 51 28N 0 18W
Brenthurst, Jobg. 18 F11 26 15 S 28 21 E
Brentwood, Lon. 4 B6 51 36N 0 18 E
Brentwood Park, Jobg. 18 E10 26 7 S 28 17 E
Brentwood Park, L.A. 28 B2 34 3N 118 29W
Brera, Mil. 9 E6 45 28N 9 11 E
Bresso, Mil. 9 D6 45 32N 9 11 E
Brétigny-sur-Orge, Paris 5 D3 48 36N 2 18 E
Brevik, Stock. 3 D12 59 20N 18 12 E
Břevnov, Pra. 10 B2 50 4N 14 22 E
Brewer I., S.F. 27 C3 37 33N 122 16W
Bricket Wood, Lon. 4 A2 51 42N 0 21W
Bridesburg, Phil. 24 B4 39 59N 75 4W
Bridgeport, Chic. 26 B3 41 50N 87 38W
Bridgeport, Phil. 24 A2 40 6N 75 21W
Bridgeview, Chic. 26 C2 41 45N 87 48W
Brie-Comte-Robert, Paris 5 C5 48 41N 2 36 E
Brighton, Melb. 19 F6 37 55 S 144 59 E
Brighton le Sands, Syd. 19 B3 33 57 S 151 9 E
Brighton Park, Chic. 26 C2 41 48N 87 41W
Brightwood, Wash. 25 D7 38 57N 77 1W
Brigittenau, Wien 10 G10 48 14N 16 22 E
Briis-sous-Forges, Paris 5 D2 48 37N 2 7 E
Brimbank Park, Melb. 19 E6 37 43 S 144 50 E
Brimsdown, Lon. 4 B4 51 39N 0 0 E
Brione, Tori. 9 B1 45 8N 7 28 E
Briones Hills, S.F. 27 A4 37 56N 122 8W
Briones Regional Park, S.F. 27 A4 37 55N 122 8W
Briones Res., S.F. 27 A3 37 55N 122 11W
Brisbane, S.F. 27 B2 37 40N 122 23W
Bristol, Phil. 24 A5 40 6N 74 53W
Britz, Berl. 7 B3 52 26N 13 27 E
Brixton, Lon. 4 C4 51 27N 0 8W
Broad Axe, Phil. 24 A3 40 8N 75 14W
Broad Sd., Bost. 21 C4 42 23N 70 56W
Broadmeadows, Melb. 19 E6 37 40 S 144 55 E
Broadmoor, S.F. 27 B2 37 41N 122 29W
Broadview, Chic. 26 B1 41 51N 87 52W
Brobacka, Hels. 3 B2 60 15N 24 36 E
Brockley, Lon. 4 C4 51 27N 0 2W
Bródno, Wsaw. 10 E7 52 17N 21 1 E
Bródnowski, Kanal, Wsaw. 10 E7 52 17N 21 3 E
Broich, Ruhr 6 B3 51 25N 6 50 E
Bromley, Lon. 4 C5 51 24N 0 0 E
Bromley-by-Bow, Lon. 4 B4 51 31N 0 0 E
Bromley Common, Lon. 4 C5 51 22N 0 2 E
Bromma, Stock. 3 D10 59 21N 17 55 E
Bromma flygplats, Stock. 3 D10 59 21N 17 56 E
Brompton, Lon. 4 C3 51 29N 0 10W
Brøndby Strand, Købn. 2 E9 55 36N 12 25 E
Brøndbyøster, Købn. 2 E9 55 39N 12 26 E
Brøndbyvester, Købn. 2 E9 55 37N 12 23 E
Brondesbury, Lon. 4 B3 51 32N 0 12W
Brønnøya, Oslo 2 B3 59 51N 10 32 E
Brønshøj, Købn. 2 D9 55 41N 12 29 E
Bronx Zoo, N.Y. 23 B5 40 50N 73 51W
Bronxville, N.Y. 23 B6 40 56N 73 49W
Brook Street, Lon. 4 B6 51 36N 0 17 E
Brookfield, Chic. 26 C1 41 48N 87 50W
Brookhaven, Phil. 24 B2 39 52N 75 23W
Brooklandville, Balt. 25 A2 39 25N 76 40W
Brooklin, S. Pau. 31 E6 23 37 S 46 39W
Brookline, Bost. 21 D3 42 19N 71 8W
Brooklyn, Balt. 25 B3 39 13N 76 36W
Brooklyn, Melb. 19 E5 37 49 S 144 49 E
Brooklyn, N.Y. 22 D5 40 37N 73 57W
Brookmont, Wash. 25 D7 38 57N 77 7W
Brooks I., S.F. 27 A2 37 53N 122 21W
Brookville, N.Y. 23 C7 40 48N 73 33W
Broomall, Phil. 24 B2 39 58N 75 22W
Brosewere B., N.Y. 23 D6 40 37N 73 40W
Brossard, Mtrl. 20 B5 43 27N 73 28W
Brou-sur-Chantereine, Paris 5 B5 48 53N 2 37 E
Brown, Trto. 20 D9 43 48N 79 14W
Browns Line, Trto. 20 E7 43 36N 79 32W
Broyhill Park, Wash. 25 D6 38 52N 77 12W
Bru, Oslo 2 C5 59 47N 10 54 E
Bruckhausen, Ruhr 6 B2 51 29N 6 43 E
Brughério, Mil. 9 D6 45 33N 9 17 E
Bruino, Tori. 9 B1 45 1N 7 27 E
Bruløkka, Oslo 2 A2 60 1N 10 22 E
Brunn, Stock. 3 E13 59 17N 18 25 E
Brunnthal, Mün. 7 G11 48 0N 11 41 E
Brunoy, Paris 5 C4 48 41N 2 29 E
Brunswick, Melb. 19 E6 37 45 S 144 57 E
Brusciano, Nápl. 9 H13 40 55N 14 25 E
Brush Hill, Bost. 21 D1 42 15N 71 22W
Bruzzano, Mil. 9 D6 45 31N 9 10 E
Bry-sur-Marne, Paris 5 B5 48 50N 2 32 E
Bryn, Oslo 2 B2 59 55N 10 27 E
Bryn Athyn, Phil. 24 A4 40 8N 75 3W
Bryn Mawr, Phil. 24 A3 40 1N 75 19W
Brzeziny, Wsaw. 10 E7 52 19N 21 2 E
Bubeneč, Pra. 10 B2 50 6N 14 24 E
Buc, Paris 5 C2 48 46N 2 7 E
Buch, Berl. 7 A3 52 38N 13 29 E
Buchburg, Wien 10 G9 48 13N 16 11 E
Buchenhain, Mün. 7 G9 48 1N 11 29 E
Buchholz, Berl. 7 A3 52 36N 13 25 E
Buchholz, Ruhr 6 B2 51 23N 6 46 E
Buckhurst Hill, Lon. 4 B5 51 37N 0 2 E
Buckingham Palace, Lon. 4 B4 51 30N 0 8W
Buckow, Berl. 7 B3 52 25N 13 26 E
Buda, Bud. 10 J13 47 30N 19 2 E
Budafok, Bud. 10 K13 47 25N 19 2 E
Budakeszi, Bud. 10 J12 47 30N 18 56 E
Budaörs, Bud. 10 K12 47 27N 18 57 E
Budapest, Bud. 10 K13 47 29N 19 3 E
Budatétény, Bud. 10 K13 47 25N 19 1 E
Budberg, Ruhr 6 A1 51 32N 6 38 E
Buddinge, Købn. 2 D10 55 44N 12 30 E
Büderich, Ruhr 6 C2 51 15N 6 41 E
Buena Park, L.A. 28 C4 33 51N 118 1W
Buena Vista, S.F. 27 B2 37 45N 122 26W
Buenavista, Mdrd. 8 B2 40 25N 3 40W
Buenos Aires, B.A. 32 B4 34 36 S 58 22W
Buenos Aires, Aeroparque de la Ciudad de, B.A. 32 B4 34 34 S 58 25W
Buer, Ruhr 6 A4 51 34N 7 2 E
Bufalotta, Rome 9 F10 41 59N 12 33 E
Buggajha, Sŏul 12 G7 37 34N 126 55 E
Bughan San, Sŏul 12 G7 37 38N 126 58 E
Bugio, Lisb. 8 G7 38 39N 9 18W
Bukit Panjang, Sing. 15 F7 1 22N 103 45 E
Bukit Timah, Sing. 15 F7 1 20N 103 47 E
Bulam San, Sŏul 12 G8 37 38N 127 4 E
Bûlâq, El Qâ. 18 C5 30 3N 31 14 E
Bulacao, Manila 15 D3 14 29N 120 54 E
Bule, Manila 15 E4 14 26N 121 2 E
Bulim, Sing. 15 F7 1 22N 103 43 E
Bull Brook →, Bost. 21 A4 42 41N 70 52W
Bulleen, Melb. 19 E7 37 46 S 145 4 E
Bullen Park, Melb. 19 E7 37 46 S 145 4 E
Bullion, Paris 5 D1 48 37N 1 59 E
Bulmke-Hüllen, Ruhr 6 A4 51 31N 7 7 E
Bulphan, Lon. 4 B7 51 32N 0 21 E
Bundoora, Melb. 19 E7 37 41 S 145 2 E
Bundoora Park, Melb. 19 E7 37 42 S 145 2 E
Bunker I., Kar. 17 H10 24 48N 66 57 E
Bunkyo, Tōkyō 13 B3 35 42N 139 45 E
Bunnefjorden, Oslo 2 B4 59 50N 10 44 E
Buona Vista, Sing. 15 G7 1 16N 103 47 E
Buquirivú-Guaçu →, S. Pau. 31 D7 23 28 S 46 28W
Burbank, Chic. 26 C2 41 44N 87 46W
Burbank, L.A. 28 A3 34 12N 118 18W
Bures, Paris 5 B1 48 56N 1 57 E
Bures-sur-Yvette, Paris 5 C2 48 41N 2 9 E
Burggrafenberg, Ruhr 6 C4 51 13N 7 7 E
Burgh Heath, Lon. 4 D3 51 18N 0 13W
Burlingame, S.F. 27 C2 37 34N 122 20W
Burlington, Bost. 21 B2 42 30N 71 13W
Burlington, Phil. 24 A5 40 4N 74 53W
Burnham, Chic. 26 D3 41 38N 87 33W
Burnham Park Harbor, Chic. 26 B3 41 51N 87 36W
Burnhamthorpe, Trto. 20 E7 43 37N 79 35W
Burnt Oak, Lon. 4 B3 51 36N 0 15W
Burr Ridge, Chic. 26 C1 41 46N 87 54W
Burtus, El Qâ. 18 C4 30 8N 31 8 E
Burudvatn, Oslo 2 B3 59 58N 10 35 E
Burwood, Melb. 19 F7 37 50 S 145 6 E
Burwood, Syd. 19 B3 33 52 S 151 5 E
Burwood East, Melb. 19 F7 37 51 S 145 8 E
Burzaco, B.A. 32 C4 34 49 S 58 23W
Buschhausen, Ruhr 6 A3 51 30N 6 50 E
Bush Hill Park, Lon. 4 B4 51 38N 0 4W
Bushey, Lon. 4 B2 51 38N 0 22W
Bushwick, N.Y. 23 C5 40 41N 73 54W
Bushy Cr. →, Melb. 19 E8 37 42 S 145 17 E
Bushy Park, Lon. 4 C2 51 24N 0 20W
Bussocaba, S. Pau. 31 E5 23 34 S 46 47W
Bussy-St.-Georges, Paris 5 B6 48 50N 2 41 E
Bussy-St.-Martin, Paris 5 B6 48 50N 2 41 E
Bustleton, Phil. 24 A4 40 4N 75 2W
Butantã, S. Pau. 31 E5 23 34 S 46 42W
Butcher I., Bomb. 16 H8 18 57N 72 53 E
Butendorf, Ruhr 6 A3 51 33N 6 59 E
Butler, N.Y. 22 B2 40 59N 74 20W
Buttonville, Trto. 20 C8 43 51N 79 20W
Butts Corner, Wash. 25 E6 38 46N 77 19W
Byculla, Bomb. 16 H8 18 58N 72 50 E
Byberry, Phil. 24 A5 40 6N 74 59W
Byfang, Ruhr 6 B4 51 24N 7 5 E
Byfleet, Lon. 4 D2 51 19N 0 28W
Bygdøy, Oslo 2 B4 59 54N 10 40 E

## C

C.N. Tower, Trto. 20 E8 43 38N 79 23W
Caballito, B.A. 32 B4 34 37 S 58 25W
Cabin John, Wash. 25 D6 38 58N 77 10W
Cabin John Cr. →, Wash. 25 C7 39 2N 77 8W
Cabin John Regional Park, Wash. 25 C6 39 0N 77 10W
Cabramatta, Syd. 19 B2 33 53 S 150 56 E
Cabuçú de Baixo →, S. Pau. 31 D5 23 30 S 46 40W
Cachan, Paris 5 C3 48 47N 2 19 E
Cachenka →, Mos. 11 E7 55 46N 37 17 E
Cachoeira →, S. Pau. 31 E5 23 38 S 46 43W
Cacilhas, Lisb. 8 F8 38 41N 9 8W
Cadieux, Î., Mtrl. 20 B1 43 25N 74 1W
Cagarras, Is., Rio J. 31 C2 23 1 S 43 12W
Cahuenga Pk., L.A. 28 B3 34 8N 118 19 E
Cainta, Manila 15 D4 14 34N 121 6 E
Cairo = El Qâhira, El Qâ. 18 C5 30 2N 31 13 E
Cairo Int. Airport, El Qâ. 18 C6 30 7N 31 23 E
Caivano, Nápl. 9 H12 40 57N 14 18 E
Caju, Rio J. 31 B2 22 52 S 43 12W
Čakovice, Pra. 10 B3 50 9N 14 31 E
Calabazar, La Hab. 30 B2 23 1N 82 20W
Calcutta, Calc. 16 E6 22 34N 88 21 E
Caldwell, N.Y. 22 B3 40 50N 74 19W
Calf Harbour, N.Y. 23 B7 40 59N 73 37W
Calf I., Bost. 21 C4 42 20N 70 53W
Calhua, Lisb. 8 F8 38 44N 9 9W
California, Univ. of, S.F. 27 A3 37 52N 122 16W
California Inst. of Tech., L.A. 28 B4 34 8N 118 8W
California State Univ., L.A. 28 B3 34 4N 118 10W
California State Univ., S.F. 27 C4 37 39N 122 6W
Callao, Lima 30 G8 12 3 S 77 8W
Caloocan, Manila 15 D3 14 39N 120 58 E
Calumet →, Chic. 26 C3 41 43N 87 31W
Calumet, L., Chic. 26 C3 41 40N 87 35W
Calumet City, Chic. 26 D3 41 36N 87 32W
Calumet Harbor, Chic. 26 C3 41 43N 87 30W
Calumet Park, Chic. 26 C3 41 40N 87 39W
Calumet Sag Channel →, Chic. 26 C2 41 40N 87 47W
Calumpang, Manila 15 D4 14 37N 121 5 E
Calvairate, Mil. 9 E6 45 27N 9 13 E
Calverton, Wash. 25 C8 39 3N 76 56W
Calvizzano, Nápl. 9 H12 40 54N 14 11 E
Calzada, Manila 15 D4 14 32N 121 4 E
Camarate, Lisb. 8 F8 38 48N 9 7W
Camaroes, Lisb. 8 F7 38 49N 9 14W
Camberwell, Lon. 4 C4 51 28N 0 5W
Camberwell, Melb. 19 F7 37 50 S 145 5 E
Cambria Heights, N.Y. 23 C6 40 41N 73 44W
Cambridge, Bost. 21 C3 42 23N 71 7W
Cambridge Res., Bost. 21 C2 42 24N 71 16W
Cambuci, S. Pau. 31 E6 23 33 S 46 47W
Cambute, La Hab. 30 B3 23 5N 82 16W
Camden, Lon. 4 B4 51 32N 0 8W
Camden, Phil. 24 B4 39 56N 75 7W
Camp Springs, Wash. 25 E8 38 48N 76 55W
Campamento, Mdrd. 8 B2 40 23N 3 46W
Campanilla, Pta., La Hab. 30 A3 23 10N 82 18W
Campbellfield, Melb. 19 E6 37 40 S 144 57 E
Camperdown, Syd. 19 B4 33 53 S 151 11 E
Campi Flegrei, Nápl. 9 H11 40 50N 14 9 E
Campo, Casa de, Mdrd. 8 B2 40 25N 3 45W
Campo Belo, S. Pau. 31 E5 23 36 S 46 44W
Campo de Mayo, B.A. 32 B2 34 32 S 58 40W
Campo Grande, Lisb. 8 F8 38 45N 9 9W
Campo Limpo, S. Pau. 31 E5 23 38 S 46 46W
Campo Pequeño, Lisb. 8 F8 38 44N 9 8W
Campolide, Lisb. 8 F8 38 43N 9 9W
Campsie, Syd. 19 B3 33 54 S 151 6 E
C'an San Joan, Barc. 8 D6 41 28N 2 11 E
Canacao, Manila 15 E3 14 29N 120 54 E
Canacao B., Manila 15 E3 14 29N 120 54 E
Cañada de los Helechos →, Méx. 29 B2 19 21N 99 15W
Canarsie, N.Y. 23 D5 40 38N 73 53W
Candiac, Mtrl. 20 B5 43 23N 73 29W
Caneças, Lisb. 8 F7 38 48N 9 13W
Cangaiba, S. Pau. 31 E6 23 30 S 46 31W
Cangrejeras, La Hab. 30 B1 23 3N 82 30W
Canguera, S. Pau. 31 E7 23 34 S 46 26W
Canillas, Mdrd. 8 B3 40 27N 3 38W
Canillejas, Mdrd. 8 B3 40 26N 3 36W
Cann Hall, Lon. 4 B5 51 33N 0 0 E
Canning Town, Lon. 4 B5 51 30N 0 1 E
Canoe Grove Res., N.Y. 22 C2 40 45N 74 21W
Cantalupo, Mil. 9 D4 45 34N 8 58 E
Cantareira, S. Pau. 31 D6 23 26 S 46 36W
Cantarranas, La Hab. 30 B2 23 2N 82 28W
Canteras de Vallecas, Mdrd. 8 B3 40 20N 3 37W
Canterbury, Melb. 19 E7 37 49 S 145 4 E
Canterbury, Syd. 19 B3 33 55 S 151 7 E
Canto do Rio, Rio J. 31 B3 22 54 S 43 7W
Canton, Bost. 21 D3 42 10N 71 8W
Caohe, Shang. 14 J11 31 10N 121 24 E
Caonao, La Hab. 30 B2 23 5N 82 24W
Capão Redondo, S. Pau. 31 E5 23 39 S 46 45W
Caparica, Lisb. 8 F8 38 40N 9 9W
Caparica, Costa da, Lisb. 8 G7 38 38N 9 15W
Capelinha, S. Pau. 31 E5 23 39 S 46 44W
Capitol Heights, Wash. 25 D8 38 52N 76 55W
Capodichino, Aeroporto di, Nápl. 9 H12 40 52N 14 17 E
Capodimonte, Nápl. 9 H12 40 52N 14 14 E
Capodimonte, Bosco di, Nápl. 9 H12 40 40N 14 15 E
Captain Cook Bridge, Syd. 19 C3 34 0 S 151 7 E
Captain Cook Landing Place Park, Syd. 19 C4 34 1 S 151 14 E
Captain Harbour, N.Y. 23 B7 40 59N 73 37W
Capuava, S. Pau. 31 E7 23 38 S 46 28W
Capuchos, Lisb. 8 G7 38 38N 9 16W
Caraballeda, Car. 30 D5 10 36N 66 50W
Carabanchel Alto, Mdrd. 8 B2 40 22N 3 44W
Carabanchel Bajo, Mdrd. 8 B2 40 23N 3 44W
Carabatteda →, Car. 30 D5 10 37N 66 51W
Caracas, Car. 30 E5 10 30N 66 54W
Carapachay, B.A. 32 B3 34 31 S 58 32W
Carapicuiba, S. Pau. 31 E5 23 31 S 46 49W
Carapicuiba →, S. Pau. 31 E5 23 31 S 46 49W
Caravita, Nápl. 9 H13 40 52N 14 21 E
Caraza, B.A. 32 C4 34 41 S 58 25W
Cardito, Nápl. 9 H12 40 56N 14 17 E
Cardoso, Lagos 18 A1 6 34N 7 16 E
Caribbean Gardens, Melb. 19 F8 37 54 S 145 12 E
Caricuao, Car. 30 E5 10 25N 66 58W
Caridad, Manila 15 E3 14 28N 120 53 E
Carioca, Sa. da, Rio J. 31 B2 22 57 S 43 13W
Carle Place, N.Y. 23 C7 40 44N 73 35W
Carlingford, Syd. 19 A3 33 46 S 151 3 E
Carlisle, Bost. 21 B1 42 31N 71 20W
Carlshof, Mün. 7 F11 48 15N 11 41 E
Carlstadt, N.Y. 22 B4 40 50N 74 6W
Carlton, Melb. 19 E6 37 47 S 144 57 E
Carnaxide, Lisb. 8 F7 38 43N 9 14W
Carnegie, Melb. 19 F7 37 53 S 145 3 E
Carnegie Hall, N.Y. 22 C5 40 45N 73 59W
Carnetin, Paris 5 B6 48 54N 2 42 E
Carney, Balt. 25 A3 39 23N 76 31W
Carnide, Lisb. 8 F7 38 45N 9 11W
Caronno Pert, Mil. 9 D5 45 35N 9 2 E
Carramar, Syd. 19 B2 33 51 S 150 58 E
Carrascal, Stgo 30 J10 33 25 S 70 42W
Carrières-sous-Bois, Paris 5 B2 48 55N 2 6 E
Carrières-sous-Poissy, Paris 5 B2 48 56N 2 2 E
Carrières-sur-Seine, Paris 5 B3 48 55N 2 11 E
Carroll I., Balt. 25 B4 39 19N 76 20W
Carroll Park, Balt. 25 B3 39 16N 76 38W
Carshalton, Lon. 4 C3 51 22N 0 10W
Carshalton on the Hill, Lon. 4 C4 51 20N 0 9W
Carteret, N.Y. 22 D3 40 34N 74 13W
Cartierville, Aéroport de, Mtrl. 20 A3 43 31N 73 42 E
Carugate, Mil. 9 D6 45 32N 9 20 E
Carupa, B.A. 32 A3 34 25 S 58 33W
Casa Blanca, La Hab. 30 B3 23 8N 82 19W
Casa Verde, S. Pau. 31 D5 23 29 S 46 40W
Casalnuovo di Nápoli, Nápl. 9 H12 40 54N 14 20 E
Casalotti, Rome 9 F9 41 54N 12 22 E
Casandrino, Nápl. 9 H12 40 56N 14 15 E
Casavatore, Nápl. 9 H12 40 53N 14 15 E
Cascadura, Rio J. 31 B2 22 52 S 43 19W
Caselette, Tori. 9 B1 45 6N 7 28 E
Caselette, Laghi di, Tori. 9 B1 45 7N 7 29 E
Caselle Torinese, Tori. 9 A3 45 10N 7 38 E
Caseros, B.A. 32 B3 34 36 S 58 34W
Casória, Nápl. 9 H12 40 54N 14 17 E
Cassignanica, Mil. 9 E7 45 27N 9 20 E
Cassiobury Park, Lon. 4 B2 51 39N 0 25W
Castel di Camerletto, Tori. 9 B1 45 6N 7 27 E
Castel di Guido, Rome 9 F8 41 53N 12 17 E
Castel Malnome, Rome 9 F8 41 50N 12 19 E
Castel San Cristina, Tori. 9 B3 45 8N 7 40 E
Castel Sant'Angelo, Rome 9 F9 41 54N 12 27 E
Castelar, B.A. 32 B3 34 39 S 58 39W
Castellbisbal, Barc. 8 D4 41 28N 1 58 E
Castello di Cisterna, Nápl. 9 H13 40 54N 14 24 E
Castelvécchio, Tori. 9 B3 45 1N 7 46 E
Castiglione Torinese, Tori. 9 B3 45 6N 7 48 E
Castleton Corners, N.Y. 22 D4 40 36N 74 8W
Castro Valley, S.F. 27 B4 37 41N 122 5W
Castrop, Ruhr 6 A5 51 32N 7 18 E
Castrop-Rauxel, Ruhr 6 A5 51 33N 7 18 E
Cat Rock Hill, Bost. 21 C2 42 23N 71 18W
Caterham, Lon. 4 D4 51 16N 0 5W
Catete, Rio J. 31 B2 22 54 S 43 10W
Catford, Lon. 4 C4 51 26N 0 1W
Catia, Car. 30 D5 10 31N 66 56W
Catia La Mer, Car. 30 D4 10 36N 67 0W
Catonsville, Balt. 25 B2 39 16N 76 43W
Catonsville Manor, Balt. 25 B2 39 17N 76 44W
Cattle Hill, S.F. 27 C2 37 36N 122 27W
Catumbi, Rio J. 31 B2 22 54 S 43 12W
Caughnawaga, Mtrl. 20 B3 43 24N 73 40W
Caulfield, Melb. 19 F7 37 52 S 145 1 E
Caulfield Racecourse, Melb. 19 F7 37 53 S 145 4 E
Caumsett State Park, N.Y. 23 B8 40 55N 73 27W
Cavite, Manila 15 E3 14 29N 120 54 E
Cavoretto, Tori. 9 B3 45 1N 7 41 E
Caxias, Lisb. 8 F7 38 42N 9 16W
Caxingui, S. Pau. 31 E5 23 35 S 46 43W
Cebeciköy, Ist. 17 A2 41 7N 28 53 E
Cecchignola, Rome 9 G10 41 48N 12 29 E
Cecil Park, Syd. 19 B2 33 52 S 150 51 E
Cecilienhof, Berl. 7 B1 52 35N 13 5 E
Cedar Grove, N.Y. 22 B3 40 50N 74 13W
Cedar Grove Res., N.Y. 22 B3 40 51N 74 12W
Cedar I., N.Y. 23 D8 40 38N 73 22W
Cedar Knolls, N.Y. 22 B2 40 49N 74 27W
Cedarhurst, N.Y. 23 D6 40 37N 73 43W
Cedarvale, Trto. 20 D8 43 41N 79 26W
Celle →, Paris 5 D1 48 36N 1 59 E
Cempaka Putih, Jak. 15 J10 6 10 S 106 51 E
Çengelköy, Ist. 17 A3 41 2N 29 3 E
Centennial Park, Syd. 19 B4 33 53 S 151 14 E
Center Square, Phil. 24 C2 39 46N 75 22W
Centerport, N.Y. 23 B8 40 53N 73 22W
Centerton, Phil. 24 B5 39 59N 74 53W
Centocelle, Rome 9 F10 41 52N 12 34 E
Central Park, N.Y. 22 C5 40 46N 73 58W
Central Park, Sing. 15 G8 1 17N 103 50 E
Centre City, Phil. 24 C3 39 46N 75 11W
Centre I., N.Y. 23 B7 40 54N 73 31W
Cércola, Nápl. 9 H13 40 51N 14 21 E
Cergy-Pontoise, Paris 5 A2 49 1N 2 4 E
Cernay-la-Ville, Paris 5 C1 48 40N 1 58 E
Cernusco sul Naviglio, Mil. 9 D6 45 31N 9 19 E
Cerqueira Cesar, S. Pau. 31 E5 23 33 S 46 40W
Cerro Ajusco, Méx. 29 C2 19 12N 99 15W
Cerro de la Estrella, Méx. 29 B3 19 20N 99 5W
Cerro de los Angeles, Mdrd. 8 C2 40 18N 3 41W
Cerro el Piacho, Méx. 29 A3 19 35N 99 6W
Cerro Maggiore, Mil. 9 D4 45 35N 8 57 E
Certanovka →, Mos. 11 F9 55 38N 37 48 E
Certanovo, Mos. 11 F9 55 38N 37 36 E
Cesano Boscone, Mil. 9 E5 45 26N 9 5 E
Cesate, Mil. 9 D5 45 35N 9 4 E
Cha Kwo Ling, H.K. 12 E6 22 18N 114 13 E
Chabot, L., S.F. 27 B4 37 43N 122 6W
Chacao, Car. 30 D5 10 30N 66 50W
Chacarilla, Lima 30 G9 12 6 S 76 59W
Chadds Ford, Phil. 24 B1 39 52N 75 35W
Chadstone, Melb. 19 F7 37 52 S 145 5 E
Chadwell Heath, Lon. 4 B5 51 34N 0 8 E
Chadwell St. Mary, Lon. 4 C7 51 29N 0 20 E
Chai Wan, H.K. 12 E6 22 16N 114 14 E
Chai Wan Kok, H.K. 12 D5 22 22N 114 6 E
Chakdaha, Calc. 16 F5 22 28N 88 19 E
Chama, Lima 30 G8 12 7 S 77 0W
Chamartin, Mdrd. 8 B2 40 27N 3 40W
Chamberi, Mdrd. 8 B2 40 26N 3 42W
Chambourcy, Paris 5 B2 48 54N 2 2 E
Champdani, Calc. 16 D5 22 48N 88 19 E
Champigny-sur-Marne, Paris 5 C5 48 49N 2 30 E
Champlain, Pont, Mtrl. 20 B4 43 28N 73 31W
Champlan, Paris 5 D3 48 42N 2 16 E
Champrosay, Paris 5 C4 48 39N 2 25 E
Champs-sur-Marne, Paris 5 B5 48 50N 2 34 E
Chamrail, Calc. 16 E5 22 38N 88 17 E
Chancheon, Sŏul 12 G7 37 33N 126 56 E
Chandernagore, Calc. 16 C6 22 51N 88 21 E
Chanditala, Calc. 16 D5 22 41N 88 15 E
Changi, Sing. 15 F8 1 23N 103 59 E
Changi Airport, Sing. 15 F8 1 21N 103 59 E
Changning, Shang. 14 J11 31 13N 121 24 E
Changpu Gongyuan, Shang. 14 J12 31 17N 121 31 E
Chanteloup-les-Vignes, Paris 5 B2 48 58N 2 1 E
Chantereine, Paris 5 B5 48 53N 2 37 E
Chantian, Gzh. 14 F8 23 13N 113 15 E
Chao Phraya →, Bangk. 15 B2 13 40N 100 31 E
Chaoyang, Beij. 14 B3 39 53N 116 26 E
Chaoyang Gongyuan, Beij. 14 B3 39 54N 116 28 E
Chaoyangmen, Beij. 14 B3 39 54N 116 23 E
Chapel End, Lon. 4 B4 51 35N 0 1W
Chapet, Paris 5 B1 48 58N 1 55 E
Chaplinville, Bost. 21 A4 42 42N 70 54W
Chapultepec, Bosque de, Méx. 29 B2 19 25N 99 11W
Chapultepec, Castillo de, Méx. 29 B2 19 25N 99 10W
Charenton-le-Pont, Paris 5 C4 48 49N 2 25 E
Charles-de-Gaulle, Aéroport, Paris 5 A5 49 0N 2 33 E
Charles Lee Tinden Regional Park, S.F. 27 A3 37 53N 122 14W
Charleston, N.Y. 22 D3 40 32N 74 14W
Charlestown, Bost. 21 C3 42 22N 71 4W
Charlottenburg, Berl. 7 A2 52 31N 13 14 E
Charlottenburg, Schloss, Berl. 7 A2 52 31N 13 18 E
Charlottenlund, Købn. 2 D10 55 44N 12 35 E
Charlton, Lon. 4 C5 51 29N 0 1 E
Charneca, Lisb. 8 F8 38 47N 9 8W
Charneca, Lisb. 8 G7 38 37N 9 12W
Chase Side, Lon. 4 B4 51 39N 0 4W
Châteaufort, Paris 5 C2 48 44N 2 5 E
Châtenay-Malabry, Paris 5 C3 48 46N 2 16 E
Chatham, Chic. 26 C3 41 45N 87 36W
Chatham, N.Y. 22 C2 40 44N 74 23W
Châtillon, Paris 5 C3 48 48N 2 17 E
Chatou, Paris 5 B2 48 53N 2 9 E
Chatpur, Calc. 16 E6 22 36N 88 22 E
Chatra, Calc. 16 D5 22 45N 88 19 E
Chatswood, Syd. 19 A4 33 47 S 151 11 E
Chauki, Kar. 17 G10 24 55N 66 56 E
Chavarria, Lima 30 G8 12 0 S 77 7W
Chavenay, Paris 5 B1 48 51N 1 59 E
Chavenay-Villepreux, Aérodrôme de, Paris 5 B1 48 50N 1 58 E
Chaville, Paris 5 C3 48 48N 2 11 E
Che Kung Miu, H.K. 12 D6 22 22N 114 10 E
Cheam, Lon. 4 C3 51 21N 0 12W
Chelles, Paris 5 B5 48 53N 2 35 E
Chelles, Canal de, Paris 5 B5 48 51N 2 35 E
Chells-le-Pin, Aérodrome, Paris 5 B5 48 53N 2 36 E
Chelmsford, Bost. 21 B1 42 35N 71 20W
Chelobityevo, Mos. 11 D10 55 54N 37 40 E
Chelsea, Bost. 21 C3 42 23N 71 1W
Chelsea, Lon. 4 C3 51 29N 0 10W
Chelsea, Phil. 24 B2 39 51N 75 27W
Chelsfield Village, Lon. 4 C5 51 21N 0 6 E
Cheltenham, Phil. 24 A4 40 3N 75 6W
Chembur, Bomb. 16 G8 19 3N 72 53 E
Chennevières, Paris 5 A2 49 0N 2 6 E
Chennevières-sur-Marne, Paris 5 C5 48 47N 2 31 E
Cheongdam, Sŏul 12 G8 37 31N 127 2 E
Cheonho, Sŏul 12 G8 37 32N 127 6 E
Cheops, El Qâ. 18 D4 29 58N 31 8 E
Chepo, Gzh. 14 G9 23 7N 113 23 E
Cherepkovo, Mos. 11 E8 55 45N 37 21 E
Chernyovo, Mos. 11 D7 55 50N 37 17 E
Cherry Hill, Phil. 24 B4 39 54N 75 1W
Cherry L., Melb. 19 F5 37 51 S 144 49 E
Cherryland, S.F. 27 B4 37 40N 122 7W
Cherrywood, Trto. 20 C10 43 51N 79 8W
Chertsey, Lon. 4 C2 51 23N 0 29W
Cheryomushki, Mos. 11 E9 55 40N 37 33 E
Chesaco Park, Balt. 25 B3 39 18N 76 30W
Chesapeake B., Balt. 25 B4 39 12N 76 22W
Cheshunt, Lon. 4 A4 51 42N 0 0 E
Chess →, Lon. 4 B2 51 38N 0 27W
Chessington, Lon. 4 C3 51 21N 0 18W
Chessington Zoo, Lon. 4 C3 51 20N 0 19W
Chester, Phil. 24 B2 39 50N 75 23W
Chester Cr. →, Phil. 24 B2 39 50N 75 21W
Chester Heights, Phil. 24 B2 39 53N 75 27W
Chestnut, Phil. 24 A3 40 4N 75 13W
Chestnut Hill, Bost. 21 D2 42 19N 71 10W
Cheung Sha Wan, H.K. 12 D5 22 20N 114 8 E
Cheverly, Wash. 25 D8 38 55N 76 54W
Chevilly-Larue, Paris 5 C4 48 46N 2 21 E
Chevreuse, Paris 5 C2 48 42N 2 2 E
Chevry-Cossigny, Paris 5 C5 48 43N 2 39 E
Chevy Chase, Wash. 25 D7 38 59N 77 4W
Chevy Chase View, Wash. 25 C7 39 0N 77 4W
Cheyney, Phil. 24 B1 39 55N 75 31W
Chhalera Bangar, Delhi 16 B2 28 33N 77 17 E
Chhinamor, Calc. 16 D5 22 48N 88 17 E
Chhota Andai, Kar. 17 H11 24 48N 66 59 E
Chia Keng, Sing. 15 F8 1 21N 103 52 E
Chiaiano, Nápl. 9 H12 40 53N 14 13 E
Chiaravalle Milanese, Mil. 9 E6 45 24N 9 16 E
Chiawelo, Jobg. 18 F8 26 17 S 27 51 E
Chicago, Chic. 26 B3 41 52N 87 38W
Chicago, Univ. of, Chic. 26 C3 41 47N 87 35W
Chicago Harbor, Chic. 26 B3 41 52N 87 36W
Chicago Lawn, Chic. 26 C2 41 47N 87 40W
Chicago-Midway Airport, Chic. 26 C2 41 47N 87 45W
Chicago-O'Hare Int. Airport, Chic. 26 B1 41 58N 87 53W
Chicago Ridge, Chic. 26 C2 41 41N 87 46W
Chicago Sanitary and Ship Canal, Chic. 26 C2 41 49N 87 45W
Chichinautzin, Cerro, Méx. 29 D3 19 6N 99 8W
Chicot, Mtrl. 20 A2 43 35N 73 56W
Chicot →, Mtrl. 20 A2 43 34N 73 51W
Chienzui, Gzh. 14 F9 23 12N 113 22 E
Chieri, Tori. 9 B3 45 0N 7 49 E
Chigwell, Lon. 4 B5 51 36N 0 6 E
Chigwell Row, Lon. 4 B5 51 37N 0 7 E
Chik Sha, H.K. 12 E6 22 17N 114 16 E
Chikumazawa, Tōkyō 13 B2 35 49N 139 32 E
Childs Hill, Lon. 4 B3 51 33N 0 12W
Chilla Saroda, Delhi 16 B2 28 35N 77 18 E
Chillum, Wash. 25 D8 38 57N 76 58W
Chilly-Mazarin, Paris 5 C3 48 42N 2 17 E
Chimalhuacán, Méx. 29 B4 19 25N 89 57 E
Chimalpa, Méx. 29 B1 19 21N 99 19W
China, Tg., Sing. 15 G8 1 14N 103 50 E
China Basin, S.F. 27 B2 37 46N 122 22W
Chingford, Lon. 4 B5 51 37N 0 0 E
Chinguopota, Calc. 16 F5 22 29N 88 14 E
Chipilly Woods, Chic. 26 A2 42 8N 87 48W
Chipperfield, Lon. 4 A2 51 42N 0 29W
Chipping Ongar, Lon. 4 A6 51 41N 0 15 E
Chipstead, Lon. 4 D4 51 17N 0 8W
Chirle, Bomb. 16 H9 18 55N 73 2 E
Chirnside Park, Melb. 19 E8 37 45 S 145 18 E
Chislehurst, Lon. 4 C5 51 24N 0 6 E
Chislehurst West, Lon. 4 C5 51 25N 0 4 E
Chiswick, Lon. 4 C3 51 29N 0 16W
Chiswick House, Lon. 4 C3 51 28N 0 15W
Chitlade Palace, Bangk. 15 B2 13 45N 100 31 E
Chitose, Tōkyō 13 C2 35 39N 139 37 E
Chiyoda-Ku, Tōkyō 13 B3 35 41N 139 44 E
Chkalova, Mos. 11 F11 55 39N 37 56 E
Choa Chu Kang, Sing. 15 F7 1 22N 103 40 E
Choboty, Mos. 11 F8 55 39N 37 21 E
Chodov u Prahy, Pra. 10 B3 50 1N 14 30 E
Chōfu, Tōkyō 13 C2 35 38N 139 32 E
Choisel, Paris 5 C2 48 41N 2 1 E
Choisy-le-Roi, Paris 5 C4 48 46N 2 24 E

36 Chomedey


Chomedey, Mtrl. 20 A3 43 32N 73 45W
Chong Nonsi, Khlong —►, Bangk. 15 B2 13 42N 100 32 E
Chong Pang, Sing. 15 F7 1 26N 103 49 E
Chongwen, Beij. 14 B3 39 52N 116 23 E
Chongwenmen, Beij. 14 B3 39 52N 116 22 E
Chorleywood, Lon. 4 B2 51 39N 0 29W
Chornaya —►, Mos. 11 E12 55 41N 38 0 E
Chorrillos, Lima 30 H8 12 10 S 77 1W
Christianshavn, Købn. 2 D10 55 40N 12 35 E
Chrome, N.Y. 22 D3 40 34N 74 13W
Chrzanów, Wsaw. 10 E6 52 13N 20 53 E
Chuen Lung, H.K. 12 D5 22 23N 114 6 E
Chuk Kok, H.K. 12 D6 22 20N 114 15 E
Chulalongkon Univ., Bangk. 15 B2 13 44N 100 31 E
Chullora, Syd. 19 B3 33 54 S 151 5 E
Chunchura, Calc. 16 C6 22 53N 88 23 E
Chuō-Ku, Tōkyō 13 B3 35 40N 139 46 E
Church End, Lon. 4 B3 51 35N 0 11W
Chvaly, Pra. 10 B3 50 6N 14 35 E
Chye Kay, Sing. 15 F7 1 25N 103 49 E
Ciampino, Rome 9 G10 41 47N 12 36 E
Ciampino, Aeroporto di, Rome 9 G10 41 47N 12 35 E
Cicero, Chic. 26 B2 41 51N 87 44W
Cidade, I. da, Rio J. 31 B2 22 51 S 43 13W
Cidade de Deus, S. Pau. 31 E5 23 33 S 46 45W
Cidade Ipava, S. Pau. 31 F5 23 42 S 46 45W
Cidade Lider, S. Pau. 31 E7 23 33 S 46 27W
Cidade São Matheus, S. Pau. 31 E7 23 35 S 46 29W
Cidena, Kali —►, Jak. 15 H9 6 5 S 106 48 E
Cilandak, Jak. 15 J9 6 17 S 106 47 E
Cilincing, Jak. 15 H10 6 6 S 106 54 E
Ciliwung —►, Jak. 15 J10 6 6 S 106 47 E
Čimice, Pra. 10 B2 50 8N 14 25 E
Cinderella, Jobg. 18 F10 26 14 S 28 15 E
Cinderella Dam, Jobg. 18 F10 26 14 S 28 14 E
Cinecittà, Rome 9 F10 41 51N 12 34 E
Cinisello Bálsamo, Mil. 9 D6 45 33N 9 13 E
Cinkota, Bud. 10 J14 47 31N 19 14 E
Cinnaminson, Phil. 24 B5 39 59N 74 59W
Cipete, Jak. 15 J9 6 15 S 106 47 E
Cipresso, Tori. 9 B3 45 2N 7 48 E
Cisliano, Mil. 9 E4 45 26N 8 59 E
Citta degli Studi, Mil. 9 E6 45 28N 9 12 E
Città del Vaticano, Rome 9 F9 41 54N 12 26 E
City I., N.Y. 23 B6 40 50N 73 47W
Ciudad Azteca, Méx. 29 A3 19 32N 99 1W
Ciudad Fin de Semana, Mdrd. 8 B3 40 26N 3 34W
Ciudad General Belgrano, B.A. 32 C3 34 43 S 58 33W
Ciudad Libertad, La Hab. 30 B2 23 5N 82 25W
Ciudad Lineál, Mdrd. 8 B3 40 26N 3 38W
Ciudad López Mateos, Méx. 29 A2 19 33N 99 16W
Ciudad Satélite, Méx. 29 A2 19 30N 99 13W
Ciudad Universitaria, Méx. 29 C2 19 9N 99 10W
Ciudadela, B.A. 32 B3 34 38 S 58 32W
Ciudadela, Parque de la, Barc. 8 D6 41 23N 2 11 E
Clairefontaine, Paris 5 D1 48 36N 1 54 E
Clamart, Paris 5 C3 48 48N 2 15 E
Clapham, Lon. 4 C4 51 27N 0 8W
Clapton, Lon. 4 B4 51 33N 0 3W
Clark, N.Y. 22 D3 40 38N 74 18W
Clarksboro, Phil. 24 C3 39 48N 75 13W
Claye-Souilly, Paris 5 B6 48 56N 2 41 E
Claygate, Lon. 4 C3 51 21N 0 19W
Clayhall, Lon. 4 B5 51 35N 0 3 E
Clayhill, Lon. 4 A4 51 40N 0 5W
Claymont, Phil. 24 C2 39 48N 75 27W
Claypole, B.A. 32 C4 34 48 S 58 20W
Clayton, Melb. 19 F7 37 55 S 145 7 E
Clearing, Chic. 26 C2 41 47N 87 45W
Clearwater, L.A. 28 C3 33 52N 118 10W
Clement, Sing. 15 G7 1 18N 103 46 E
Clementon, Phil. 24 C5 39 48N 74 59W
Clichy, Paris 5 B3 48 54N 2 18 E
Clichy-sous-Bois, Paris 5 B5 48 54N 2 32 E
Cliffside, Trto. 20 D9 43 44N 79 14W
Cliffside Park, N.Y. 22 C5 40 49N 73 59W
Clifton, Bost. 21 C4 42 29N 70 52W
Clifton, Kar. 17 H11 24 48N 67 1 E
Clifton, N.Y. 22 D4 40 37N 74 4W
Clifton, N.Y. 22 B4 40 51N 74 7W
Clifton, L., Balt. 25 B3 39 19N 76 35W
Clifton Heights, Phil. 24 B3 39 55N 75 17W
Clifton Park, Balt. 25 A3 39 20N 76 35W
Clontarf, Syd. 19 A4 33 48 S 151 16 E
Closter, N.Y. 22 B5 40 58N 73 57W
Clovelly, Syd. 19 B4 33 54 S 151 15 E
Cobbin's Brook —►, Lon. 4 A5 51 40N 0 0 E
Cobbs Cr. —►, Phil. 24 B3 39 58N 75 18W
Cobham, Lon. 4 C2 51 19N 0 23W
Cobras, I. das, Rio J. 31 B3 22 53 S 43 9W
Coburg, Melb. 19 E6 37 44 S 144 56 E
Cochecito, Car. 30 E5 10 26N 66 55W
Cochichewick, L., Bost. 21 A3 42 42N 71 5W
Cochituate, Bost. 21 C1 42 20N 71 21W
Cochituate, L., Bost. 21 D1 42 16N 71 21W
Cockfosters, Lon. 4 B4 51 39N 0 8W
Cocota, Rio J. 31 A2 22 48 S 43 11W
Coelho da Rocha, Rio J. 31 A1 22 46 S 43 21W
Couilly, Paris 5 C5 48 48N 2 32 E
Coignières, Paris 5 C1 48 44N 1 55 E
Coina, Lisb. 8 G8 38 39N 9 5W
Cojimar, La Hab. 30 B3 23 9N 82 17W
Cojimar —►, La Hab. 30 B3 23 9N 82 17W
Cojimar, Boca de, La Hab. 30 A3 23 10N 82 17W
Coker, Lagos 18 B2 6 28N 7 20 E
Colaba, Bomb. 16 H7 18 53N 72 48 E
Colaba Pt., Bomb. 16 H7 18 53N 72 48 E
Cold Spring Harbor, N.Y. 23 B8 40 52N 73 27W
Cold Spring Terrace, N.Y. 23 C8 40 49N 73 25W
Coleraine, Trto. 20 D6 43 49N 79 40W
Colindale, Lon. 4 B3 51 35N 0 15W
Collazo, La Hab. 30 B2 23 2N 82 21W
College Park, Wash. 25 D8 38 59N 76 55W
College Point, N.Y. 23 C5 40 47N 73 50W
Collégien, Paris 5 B6 48 50N 2 41 E
Collegno, Tori. 9 B2 45 5N 7 34 E
Collier Row, Lon. 4 B5 51 35N 0 10 E
Colliers Wood, Lon. 4 C3 51 24N 0 10W
Collingdale, Phil. 24 B3 39 54N 75 17W
Collingswood, Phil. 24 B4 39 55N 75 5W
Collinsville, Bost. 21 A1 42 40N 71 20W
Collinsville, N.Y. 22 C2 40 48N 74 26W
Colma, S.F. 27 B2 37 40N 122 27W
Colma Cr. —►, S.F. 27 C2 37 38N 122 23W
Colney Hatch, Lon. 4 B4 51 36N 0 9W
Cologno Monzese, Mil. 9 D6 45 31N 9 16 E
Colombes, Paris 5 B3 48 55N 2 15 E
Colonia, N.Y. 22 D3 40 35N 74 18W
Colônia, S. Pau. 31 E7 23 33 S 46 27W
Colonia Güell, Barc. 8 D5 41 21N 2 2 E
Colonia Puerta de Hierro, Mdrd. 8 B2 40 27N 3 43W
Colonial Manor, Phil. 24 B4 39 51N 75 9W
Colorado —►, Méx. 29 B4 19 23N 89 58 E
Colosseo, Rome 9 F9 41 53N 12 29 E
Columbia, Balt. 25 B1 39 12N 76 50W
Columbia Hills, Balt. 25 B1 39 14N 76 51W
Columbia Univ., N.Y. 22 C5 40 48N 73 58W
Colwyn, Phil. 24 B3 39 54N 75 14W
Combault, Paris 5 C5 48 48N 2 37 E
Combs-la-Ville, Paris 5 D5 48 39N 2 33 E
Comércio, Praça do, Lisb. 8 F8 38 41N 9 9W
Commack, N.Y. 23 B9 40 50N 73 19W
Commerce, L.A. 28 B4 34 0N 118 9W
Como, Syd. 19 C3 34 0 S 151 4 E
Compans, Paris 5 B5 48 59N 2 39 E
Compton, L.A. 28 C3 33 53N 118 14W
Conceição, I. da, Rio J. 31 B3 22 52 S 43 6W
Concepcion, Manila 15 D4 14 39N 121 6 E
Conchali, Stgo 30 J11 33 22 S 70 39W
Concord, Bost. 21 C1 42 27N 71 20W
Concord, S.F. 27 A4 37 58N 122 3W
Concord, Syd. 19 B3 33 52 S 151 6 E
Concord, Trto. 20 D8 43 48N 79 29W
Concordville, Phil. 24 B1 39 53N 75 31W
Concorezzo, Mil. 9 D6 45 35N 9 19 E
Condécourt, Paris 5 A1 49 2N 1 56 E
Coney Island, N.Y. 22 D4 40 34N 74 0W
Conflans-Ste.-Honorine, Paris 5 B2 48 59N 2 5 E
Congo, S. Pau. 31 D5 23 27 S 46 42W
Congonhas, Aéroporto, S. Pau. 31 E6 23 38 S 46 39W
Conshohocken, Phil. 24 A3 40 4N 75 18W
Contadero, Méx. 29 B2 19 20N 99 17W
Convento de Valverde, Mdrd. 8 A2 40 30N 3 40W
Coogee, Syd. 19 B4 33 55 S 151 16 E
Cooksville, Trto. 20 E7 43 35N 79 38W
Cooper —►, Phil. 24 B4 39 57N 75 6W
Copacabana, Rio J. 31 B2 22 58 S 43 11W
Copenhagen = København, Købn. 2 D9 55 40N 12 26 E
Copiague, N.Y. 23 D8 40 39N 73 23W
Coral Hills, Wash. 25 D8 38 51N 76 55W
Corbeil-Essonnes, Paris 5 D4 48 36N 2 29 E
Corbets Tey, Lon. 4 B6 51 32N 0 15 E
Corbiglia, Tori. 9 B1 45 3N 7 29 E
Corcovado, Rio J. 31 B2 22 57 S 43 12W
Cordon, Paris 5 D6 48 39N 2 41 E
Córdova, Tori. 9 B3 45 5N 7 48 E
Cordovil, Rio J. 31 A2 22 49 S 43 18W
Cormano, Mil. 9 D6 45 32N 9 10 E
Cormeilles-en-Parisis, Paris 5 B3 48 58N 2 11 E
Cornaredo, Mil. 9 D5 45 30N 9 1 E
Cornaya —►, St-Pet. 11 B5 59 53N 30 35 E
Cornellá, Barc. 8 D5 41 21N 2 4 E
Cornwells Heights, Phil. 24 A5 40 4N 74 57W
Coróglio, Nápl. 9 J12 40 48N 14 10 E
Coronation Memorial, Delhi 16 A2 28 42N 77 12 E
Córsico, Mil. 9 E5 45 25N 9 6 E
Corte Madera, S.F. 27 A1 37 55N 122 30W
Corte Madera —►, S.F. 27 A1 37 55N 122 30W
Corviale, Rome 9 F9 41 51N 12 25 E
Cos Cob, N.Y. 23 A7 41 1N 73 36W
Cossigny, Paris 5 C6 48 43N 2 40 E
Cossipore, Calc. 16 E6 22 37N 88 22 E
Cotao, Lisb. 8 F7 38 45N 9 17W
Côte St.-Luc, Mtrl. 20 B4 43 28N 73 39W
Cotorro, La Hab. 30 B3 23 2N 82 15W
Cotunduba, I. de, Rio J. 31 B3 22 57 S 43 8W
Coubert, Paris 5 C6 48 40N 2 41 E
Coubron, Paris 5 B5 48 54N 2 34 E
Coulsdon, Lon. 4 D4 51 18N 0 7W
Countryside, Chic. 26 C1 41 47N 87 52W
Courbevoie, Paris 5 B3 48 53N 2 14 E
Courcouronnes, Paris 5 D4 48 37N 2 24 E
Courdimanche, Paris 5 A1 49 2N 2 0 E
Courcelle, Paris 5 C2 48 43N 2 7 E
Couros —►, S. Pau. 31 F6 23 37 S 46 34W
Courtry, Paris 5 B5 48 55N 2 35 E
Cousino, Parque, Stgo 30 J11 33 27 S 70 40W
Cove Neck, N.Y. 23 B8 40 52N 73 29W
Cowley, Lon. 4 B2 51 31N 0 28W
Coyoacan, Méx. 29 B3 19 21N 99 9W
Coyote Cr. —►, S.F. 27 D4 37 28N 122 4W
Coyote Hills Regional Park, S.F. 27 C4 37 32N 122 7W
Coyote Hills Slough, S.F. 27 C4 37 33N 122 7W
Coyote Pt., S.F. 27 C3 37 35N 122 18W
Coyote Ridge, S.F. 27 A1 37 51N 122 33W
Craighall Park, Jobg. 18 E9 26 7 S 28 1 E
Crane —►, Lon. 4 C2 51 29N 0 29W
Cranford, Lon. 4 C2 51 29N 0 25W
Cranford, N.Y. 22 D3 40 39N 74 19W
Cranham, Lon. 4 B6 51 33N 0 16 E
Cray —►, Lon. 4 C5 51 28N 0 10 E
Crayford, Lon. 4 C5 51 27N 0 11 E
Creekmouth, Lon. 4 B5 51 31N 0 6 E
Cresskill, N.Y. 22 B5 40 56N 73 57W
Crescenzago, Mil. 9 D6 45 30N 9 14 E
Crespières, Paris 5 B1 48 52N 1 55 E
Cressely, Paris 5 C2 48 44N 2 6 E
Cresslawn, Jobg. 18 E10 26 6 S 28 13 E
Crestwood, Chic. 26 D2 41 38N 87 43W
Creteil, Paris 5 C4 48 47N 2 27 E
Cricklewood, Lon. 4 B3 51 33N 0 13W
Crispano, Nápl. 9 H12 40 57N 14 17 E
Cristo Redebro, Monumento do, Rio J. 31 B2 22 56 S 43 12W
Crockenhill, Lon. 4 C5 51 22N 0 9 E
Croissy-Beaubourg, Paris 5 C5 48 49N 2 39 E
Croissy-sur-Seine, Paris 5 B2 48 52N 2 8 E
Cronenberg, Ruhr 6 C4 51 12N 7 9 E
Crosby, Jobg. 18 F8 26 11 S 27 59 E
Crosne, Paris 5 C4 48 43N 2 27 E
Cross I., Bomb. 16 H8 18 56N 72 51 E
Crouch End, Lon. 4 B4 51 34N 0 7W
Croud —►, Paris 5 B4 48 57N 2 24 E
Crown Gardens, Jobg. 18 F8 26 15 S 28 0 E
Crown Mines, Jobg. 18 F9 26 12 S 27 58 E
Crown Village, N.Y. 23 C8 40 40N 73 26W
Crows Nest, Syd. 19 A3 33 49 S 151 12 E
Croxley Green, Lon. 4 B2 51 38N 0 26W
Croydon, Lon. 4 C4 51 22N 0 5W
Croydon, Melb. 19 E8 37 48 S 145 17 E
Croydon, Phil. 24 A5 40 5N 74 54W
Croydon North, Melb. 19 E8 37 46 S 145 16 E
Cruz de Pau, Lisb. 8 G8 38 37N 9 7W
Crystal Palace, Lon. 4 C4 51 25N 0 4W
Crystal Springs, S.F. 27 C2 37 31N 122 20W
Csepel, Bud. 10 K13 47 25N 19 4 E
Csepelsziget, Bud. 10 K13 47 22N 19 4 E
Csillaghegy, Bud. 10 J13 47 35N 19 2 E
Csillagtelep, Bud. 10 K13 47 24N 19 8 E
Cski-hegyek, Bud. 10 K12 47 30N 18 57 E
Csömör, Bud. 10 J14 47 33N 19 14 E
Cuajimalpa, Méx. 29 B2 19 21N 99 17W
Cuatro Vientos, Mdrd. 8 B2 40 22N 3 47W
Cuautepec de Madero, Méx. 29 A3 19 32N 99 8W
Cuautepec El Alto, Méx. 29 A3 19 33N 99 7W
Cuautzin, Cerro, Méx. 29 D3 19 10N 99 8W
Cubao, Manila 15 D4 14 37N 121 3 E
Cubas —►, S. Pau. 31 D6 23 28 S 46 31W
Cubuklu, Ist. 17 A3 41 5N 29 4 E
Cudham, Lon. 4 D5 51 19N 0 4 E
Cuffley, Lon. 4 A4 51 42N 0 6W
Cuicuilco, Pirámido de, Méx. 29 C2 19 17N 99 10W
Culembeeck, Jobg. 18 E7 26 9 S 27 49 E
Culiculi, Manila 15 D4 14 33N 121 0 E
Cull Creek, S.F. 27 B4 37 45N 122 2W
Culver City, L.A. 28 B2 34 1N 118 24W
Culverstone Green, Lon. 4 C7 51 20N 0 20 E
Cumbre El Tabo, Car. 30 D5 10 33N 66 56W
Cumbres de Vallecas, Mdrd. 8 B3 40 20N 3 33W
Cunhas, S. Pau. 31 E7 23 34 S 46 23W
Cupecé, S. Pau. 31 E5 23 39 S 46 40W
Cupece —►, S. Pau. 31 E6 23 37 S 46 42W
Curtis B., Balt. 25 B3 39 13N 76 34W
Curtis Cr. —►, Balt. 25 B3 39 12N 76 34W
Cusago, Mil. 9 E5 45 26N 9 1 E
Cusano Milanese, Mil. 9 D6 45 33N 9 11 E
Çuvuşabaşi —►, Ist. 17 A2 40 58N 28 51 E
Cyrildene, Jobg. 18 F9 26 10 S 28 6 E
Czernrakow, Wsaw. 10 E7 52 11N 21 3 E
Czyste, Wsaw. 10 E6 52 13N 20 57 E


# D


Da Yunhe —►, Tianj. 14 D5 39 19N 117 10 E
Dabizhuang, Tianj. 14 D6 39 11N 117 16 E
Ďáblice, Pra. 10 B2 50 8N 14 29 E
Dabsibri, Sŏul 12 G8 37 33N 127 2 E
Dachang, Shang. 14 J11 31 17N 121 24 E
Dachau, Mün. 7 F9 48 15N 11 27 E
Dachau-Ost, Mün. 7 F9 48 15N 11 27 E
Dachauer Moos, Mün. 7 F9 48 13N 11 27 E
Daebang, Sŏul 12 G7 37 30N 126 55 E
Daechi, Sŏul 12 G8 37 30N 127 2 E
Dagenham, Lon. 4 B5 51 32N 0 8 E
Daglfing, Mün. 7 G10 48 8N 11 39 E
Dahirpur, Delhi 16 A2 28 43N 77 11 E
Dahlem, Berl. 7 B2 52 27N 13 16 E
Dahlerau, Ruhr 6 C5 51 13N 7 18 E
Dahlwitz-Hoppegarten, Berl. 7 A5 52 30N 13 41 E
Dahongmen, Beij. 14 C3 39 48N 116 21 E
Daiman, Tōkyō 13 A3 35 53N 139 44 E
Daitō, Ōsaka 12 B4 34 42N 135 38 E
Dajiaoting, Beij. 14 B3 39 51N 116 27 E
Dajingcun, Beij. 14 B3 39 50N 116 13 E
Dakhnoye, St-Pet. 11 C3 59 49N 30 15 E
Dalar, Bomb. 16 G7 19 0N 72 49 E
Dalejsky —►, Pra. 10 B2 50 2N 14 24 E
Dalibia, Gzh. 14 G7 23 2N 113 6 E
Dallgow, Berl. 7 A1 52 32N 13 5 E
Dalston, Lon. 4 B4 51 32N 0 4W
Dalview, Jobg. 18 F11 26 14 S 28 20 E
Daly City, S.F. 27 B2 37 42N 122 27W
Damaia, Lisb. 8 F7 38 44N 9 12W
Dämeritzsee, Berl. 7 B5 52 34N 13 43 E
Damiette, Paris 5 C2 48 41N 2 7 E
Dampierre, Paris 5 C1 48 42N 1 59 E
Dan Neramit, Bangk. 15 B2 13 48N 100 34 E
Dan Ryan Woods, Chic. 26 C2 41 44N 87 40W
Dandenong, Mt., Melb. 19 E9 37 49 S 145 21 E
Danderyd, Stock. 3 D11 59 24N 18 1 E
Danforth, Trto. 20 D9 43 43N 79 16W
Daniels, Balt. 25 B2 39 19N 76 48W
Danvers, Bost. 21 B4 42 34N 70 56W
Dapharpur, Calc. 16 E5 22 38N 88 14 E
Darangan, Manila 15 E5 14 29N 121 10 E
Darave, Bomb. 16 G9 19 1N 73 1 E
Darby, Phil. 24 B3 39 55N 75 15W
Darby Cr. —►, Phil. 24 B3 39 54N 75 15W
Darent —►, Lon. 4 C6 51 21N 0 12 E
Darling, Phil. 24 B2 39 54N 75 28W
Darlington Corners, Phil. 24 B1 39 55N 75 34W
Dartford, Lon. 4 C6 51 26N 0 13 E
Dashi, Gzh. 14 G8 23 1N 113 17 E
Dashimae, Tōkyō 13 B3 35 46N 139 46 E
Datteln, Ruhr 6 A6 51 39N 7 20 E
Datteln-Hamm Kanal, Ruhr 6 A6 51 38N 7 28 E
Datun, Beij. 14 A3 40 0N 116 23 E
Dauko, Calc. 16 E5 22 31N 88 12 E
Daulatpur, Delhi 16 A1 28 44N 77 6 E
Davenport, Bost. 21 B4 42 33N 70 54W
Daveyton, Jobg. 18 E11 26 9 S 28 24 E
Davidkovo, Mos. 11 E8 55 43N 37 29 E
David's I., N.Y. 23 B6 40 53N 73 46W
Davidson, Mt., S.F. 27 B2 37 44N 122 27W
Davron, Paris 5 B1 48 52N 1 56 E
Dāvudiyeh, Tehr. 17 C5 35 45N 51 25 E
Dawidy, Wsaw. 10 F6 52 8N 20 58 E
Dayap, Manila 15 D4 14 35N 121 4 E
Dayuange, Gzh. 14 F7 23 11N 113 7 E
Dead Run —►, Balt. 25 B2 39 18N 76 41W
Dedham, Bost. 21 D2 42 15N 71 10W
Dee Why, Syd. 19 A4 33 46 S 151 17 E
Deer I., Bost. 21 C4 42 21N 70 57W
Deer Park, N.Y. 23 C9 40 46N 73 19W
Degerby, Stock. 3 D9 59 22N 17 42 E
Degermossa, Hels. 3 B6 60 17N 25 12 E
Degunino, Mos. 11 D9 55 52N 37 33 E
Deisenhofen, Mün. 7 G10 48 0N 11 35 E
Dejvice, Pra. 10 B2 50 6N 14 23 E
Dekabristov, Os., St-Pet. 11 B3 59 56N 30 15 E
Del Viso, B.A. 32 A2 34 27 S 58 47W
Delanco, Phil. 24 A5 40 2N 74 57W
Delaware —►, Phil. 24 A4 40 1N 75 0W
Delbruch, Ruhr 6 B4 51 22N 7 8 E
Delhi, Delhi 16 B2 28 39N 77 13 E
Delhi Cantonment, Delhi 16 B1 28 35N 77 7 E
Delhi Univ., Delhi 16 A2 28 41N 77 12 E
Dellwig, Ruhr 6 B3 51 29N 6 55 E
Delran, Phil. 24 A5 40 0N 74 57W
Delville, Jobg. 18 F10 26 11 S 28 13 E
Demarest, N.Y. 22 B5 40 57N 73 57W
Denham, Lon. 4 B2 51 35N 0 30W
Denham Green, Lon. 4 B2 51 34N 0 29W
Denniston Cr. —►, S.F. 27 C2 37 30N 122 29W
Dentonia Park, Trto. 20 D9 43 42N 79 17W
Denville, N.Y. 22 B2 40 53N 74 28W
Deodoro, Rio J. 31 B1 22 51 S 43 22W
Depgsu Palace, Sŏul 12 G7 37 34N 126 58 E
Deptford, Lon. 4 C4 51 28N 0 1W
Der Sarai, Delhi 16 B2 28 33N 77 10 E
Des Plaines, Chic. 26 A1 42 2N 87 54W
Des Plaines —►, Chic. 26 B1 41 48N 87 49W
Deshengmen, Beij. 14 B3 39 56N 116 21 E
Desierto de los Leones, Parque Nacional, Méx. 29 C2 19 18N 99 18W
Desio, Mil. 9 D6 45 36N 9 12 E
Deuil-la-Barre, Paris 5 B3 48 58N 2 19 E
Deulpur, Calc. 16 E5 22 36N 88 10 E
Deungchon, Sŏul 12 G7 37 33N 126 52 E
Deutsch-Wagram, Wien 10 G11 48 17N 16 33 E
Deutsche Oper, Berl. 7 A2 52 30N 13 19 E
Deutscher Museum, Mün. 7 G10 48 7N 11 35 E
Deux-Montagnes, Mtrl. 20 A2 43 32N 73 53W
Deux Montagnes, L. des, Mtrl. 20 B2 43 27N 73 59W
Devault, Phil. 24 A1 40 4N 75 32W
Dháfni, Ath. 8 J11 37 55N 23 44 E
Dhakuria, Calc. 16 E6 22 30N 88 22 E
Dhakuria L., Calc. 16 E6 22 30N 88 21 E
Dhamarakia, Ath. 8 J10 37 58N 23 39 E
Dharava, Bomb. 16 G8 19 1N 72 51 E
Dhrapersón, Ath. 8 J10 37 56N 23 37 E
Dhutumkhar, Bomb. 16 H9 18 54N 73 1 E
Dia Deva, Bomb. 16 H8 18 57N 72 53 E
Diadema, S. Pau. 31 F6 23 41 S 46 37W
Diamante, B.A. 32 C4 34 41 S 58 25W
Diamond Cr. —►, Melb. 19 E7 37 44 S 145 9 E
Diamond Creek, Melb. 19 E8 37 40 S 145 10 E
Didaowai, Tianj. 14 E6 39 8N 117 12 E
Diepensiepen, Ruhr 6 C3 51 14N 6 58 E
Diepkloof, Jobg. 18 F8 26 14 S 27 57 E
Diessem, Ruhr 6 C1 51 19N 6 34 E
Difficult Run —►, Wash. 25 D6 38 55N 77 18W
Digla, W. —►, El Qâ. 18 D6 29 58N 31 22 E
Digra, Calc. 16 D5 22 49N 88 19 E
Dikemark, Oslo 2 C2 59 48N 10 22 E
Dilerpur, Calc. 16 C5 22 51N 88 10 E
Dinslaken, Ruhr 6 A2 51 33N 6 43 E
Dinslakener Bruch, Ruhr 6 A2 51 34N 6 44 E
Dinwiddie, Jobg. 18 F9 26 16 S 28 9 E
Diósd, Bud. 10 K12 47 24N 18 57 E
Dirnismaning, Mün. 7 F10 48 13N 11 38 E
Disappointment, Mt., L.A. 28 A4 34 15N 118 7W
Discovery, Jobg. 18 E8 26 8 S 27 54 E
Disteln, Ruhr 6 A4 51 36N 7 9 E
District Heights, Wash. 25 D8 38 51N 76 53W
Ditan Gongyuan, Beij. 14 B3 39 56N 116 23 E
Dix Hills, N.Y. 23 C8 40 48N 73 21W
Dixmoor, Chic. 26 D2 41 37N 87 40W
Diyala —►, Bagd. 17 F9 33 13N 44 30 E
Djakarta = Jakarta, Jak. 15 H10 6 9 S 106 52 E
Djursholm, Stock. 3 D11 59 24N 18 5 E
Do Bong, Sŏul 12 G8 37 37N 127 1 E
Dobbs, N.Y. 23 A5 41 1N 73 52W
Döberitz, Berl. 7 A1 52 32N 13 3 E
Döbling, Wien 10 G10 48 14N 16 20 E
Dobong, Sŏul 12 G8 37 39N 127 2 E
Dobong San, Sŏul 12 F8 37 40N 127 0 E
Dōbrowa, Wsaw. 10 E6 52 19N 20 52 E
Doddinghurst, Lon. 4 A6 51 40N 0 18 E
Dodger Stadium, L.A. 28 B3 34 4N 118 14W
Dogsan, Sŏul 12 H7 37 28N 126 54 E
Doirone, Tori. 9 B2 45 3N 7 32 E
Dōjō, Ōsaka 12 A2 34 51N 135 14 E
Dōjō, Tōkyō 13 A2 35 51N 139 37 E
Dollard-des-Ormeaux, Mtrl. 20 B3 43 29N 73 49W
Dollis Hill, Lon. 4 B3 51 33N 0 13W
Dolni, Pra. 10 B3 50 3N 14 33 E
Dolni Chabry, Pra. 10 B2 50 8N 14 26 E
Dolni Počernice, Pra. 10 B3 50 5N 14 34 E
Dolton, Chic. 26 D3 41 37N 87 35W
Domont, Paris 5 A3 49 2N 2 19 E
Don Bosco, B.A. 32 C5 34 42 S 58 17W
Don Mills, Trto. 20 D8 43 44N 79 21W
Don Pedro II, Parque, S. Pau. 31 E6 23 33 S 46 36W
Don Torcuato, B.A. 32 A3 34 29 S 58 38W
Donau —►, Bud. 10 J13 47 33N 19 4 E
Donau-Oder Kanal, Wien 10 G11 48 12N 16 32 E
Donaufeld, Wien 10 G10 48 15N 16 24 E
Donaukanal, Wien 10 G10 48 10N 16 27 E
Donaupark, Wien 10 G10 48 14N 16 24 E
Donaustadt, Wien 10 G10 48 13N 16 29 E
Doncaster, Melb. 19 E7 37 47 S 145 8 E
Doncaster East, Melb. 19 E7 37 46 S 145 8 E
Dong Dae Mun, Sŏul 12 G8 37 34N 127 2 E
Dong Jag, Sŏul 12 G7 37 30N 126 56 E
Dongala Forest Reserve, Melb. 19 F9 37 50 S 145 20 E
Dongan Hills, N.Y. 22 D4 40 35N 74 5W
Dongbinggo, Sŏul 12 G7 37 31N 126 58 E
Dongcheng, Beij. 14 B3 39 54N 116 23 E
Dongfeng Nongchang, Beij. 14 B3 39 57N 116 28 E
Dongjiao, Gzh. 14 G8 23 5N 113 12 E
Dongjuzi, Tianj. 14 E6 39 7N 117 14 E
Dongkou, Shang. 14 J12 31 17N 121 33 E
Dongmenwai, Tianj. 14 E6 39 8N 117 11 E
Dongri, Bomb. 16 H8 18 53N 72 57 E
Dongwuyuan, Beij. 14 B2 39 55N 116 18 E
Dongzhimen, Beij. 14 B3 39 55N 116 24 E
Donvale, Melb. 19 E8 37 47 S 145 11 E
Doonside, Syd. 19 A2 33 46 S 150 51 E
Doornfontein, Jobg. 18 F9 26 11 S 28 3 E
Dōra, Bagd. 17 F8 33 15N 44 25 E
Dora Riparia —►, Tori. 9 B2 45 4N 7 38 E
Dorchester, Bost. 21 D3 42 17N 71 4W
Dorchester B., Bost. 21 D3 42 18N 71 1W
Dorchester Heights Nat. Hist. Site, Bost. 21 D3 42 19N 71 2W
Dorion, Mtrl. 20 B1 43 23N 74 1W
Dornach, Mün. 7 G11 48 9N 11 41 E
Dornap, Ruhr 6 C4 51 15N 7 3 E
Dornbach, Wien 10 G9 48 13N 16 18 E
Dorsey Run —►, Balt. 25 B2 39 11N 76 47W
Dorstfeld, Ruhr 6 A6 51 30N 7 24 E
Dortmund, Ruhr 6 A6 51 30N 7 28 E
Dorval, Mtrl. 20 B3 43 26N 73 44W
Dorval, Aéroport de, Mtrl. 20 B3 43 28N 73 44W
Dos Rios, Méx. 29 B1 19 22N 99 20W
Doshan Tappeh Airport, Tehr. 17 C5 35 41N 51 28 E
Dotmund-Ems Kanal, Ruhr 6 A6 51 35N 7 24 E
Double B., Syd. 19 B4 33 52 S 151 15 E
Douglas Park, Chic. 26 B2 41 51N 87 42W
Douglaston, N.Y. 23 C6 40 46N 73 44W
Dove Elbe —►, Hbg. 7 E8 53 28N 10 7 E
Dover, Bost. 21 D2 42 14N 71 16W
Dover Heights, Syd. 19 B4 33 52 S 151 16 E
Dowlatābād, Tehr. 17 D5 35 38N 51 27 E
Downe, Lon. 4 C5 51 20N 0 3 E
Downey, L.A. 28 C4 33 56N 118 9W
Downsview, Trto. 20 D7 43 43N 79 30W
Downsview Dells Park, Trto. 20 D7 43 44N 79 30W
Dracut, Bost. 21 A2 42 40N 71 17W
Dragør, Købn. 2 E10 55 35N 12 38 E
Drancy, Paris 5 B4 48 55N 2 26 E
Dranesville, Wash. 25 C5 39 0N 77 20W
Draveil, Paris 5 C4 48 41N 2 23 E
Drayton Green, Lon. 4 B3 51 30N 0 19W
Dreilinden, Berl. 7 B2 52 24N 13 10 E
Dresher, Phil. 24 A4 40 9N 75 9W
Drewnica, Wsaw. 10 E7 52 18N 21 6 E
Drexel Hill, Phil. 24 B3 39 56N 75 18W
Drexel Inst. of Technology, Phil. 24 B3 39 57N 75 11W
Drigh Road, Kar. 17 G11 24 52N 67 7 E
Drogden, Købn. 2 E11 55 37N 12 42 E
Drottningholm, Stock. 3 E10 59 19N 17 53 E
Druento, Tori. 9 B2 45 8N 7 34 E
Druid Hill Park, Balt. 25 B3 39 19N 76 38W
Druid Lake, Balt. 25 B3 39 19N 76 38W
Drummoyne, Syd. 19 B3 33 51 S 151 8 E
Druzhba, Mos. 11 D10 55 52N 37 44 E
Duarte, L.A. 28 B5 34 8N 117 57W
Dubeč, Pra. 10 B3 50 3N 14 35 E
Dubi Bheri, Calc. 16 C5 22 52N 88 16 E
Duffryn Mawr, Phil. 24 A2 40 2N 75 27W
Dugnano, Mil. 9 D6 45 33N 9 11 E
Dugny, Paris 5 B4 48 57N 2 24 E
Duiha, Calc. 16 E5 22 34N 88 15 E
Duisburg, Ruhr 6 B2 51 26N 6 45 E
Dulāb, Tehr. 17 D5 35 39N 51 27 E
Dulworthtown, Phil. 24 B1 39 54N 75 33W
Dum Dum, Calc. 16 E6 22 38N 88 25 E
Dum Dum Int. Airport, Calc. 16 E6 22 38N 88 26 E
Dumbarton Pt., S.F. 27 D4 37 29N 122 6W
Dumjor, Calc. 16 E5 22 37N 88 13 E
Dumont, N.Y. 22 B5 40 56N 73 59W
Dümpten, Ruhr 6 B3 51 27N 6 54 E
Duna —►, Bud. 10 J13 47 33N 19 4 E
Dunbarton, Trto. 20 C10 43 50N 79 6W
Dundalk, Balt. 25 B3 39 17N 76 31W
Dundas, Syd. 19 A3 33 47 S 151 3 E
Dunearn, Sing. 15 G7 1 19N 103 49 E
Dunellen, N.Y. 22 D2 40 35N 74 26W
Dunn Loring, Wash. 25 D6 38 54N 77 13W
Dunning, Chic. 26 B2 41 56N 87 48W
Dunton Green, Lon. 4 D6 51 17N 0 11 E
Dunvegan, Jobg. 18 E9 26 9 S 28 8 E
Duomo, Mil. 9 E6 45 28N 9 11 E
Duomo, Nápl. 9 H12 40 51N 14 15 E
Duomo, Tori. 9 B3 45 4N 7 45 E
Duque de Caxias, Rio J. 31 A2 22 46 S 43 18W
Durban Roodepoort Deep Gold Mines, Jobg. 18 F8 26 11 S 27 52 E
Durchholz, Ruhr 6 B5 51 23N 7 18 E
Düssel —►, Ruhr 6 C3 51 13N 6 58 E
Düsseldorf, Ruhr 6 C2 51 13N 6 46 E
Düsseldorf-Lohausen, Flughafen, Ruhr 6 C2 51 17N 6 45 E
Duvenstedt, Hbg. 7 C8 53 42N 10 6 E
Duvenstedter Brook, Hbg. 7 C8 53 43N 10 8 E
Duvernay, Mtrl. 20 A3 43 35N 73 40W
Dyakovo, Mos. 11 E9 55 40N 37 39 E
Dyviksudd, Stock. 3 E13 59 11N 18 23 E
Dzerzhinskiy, Mos. 11 F11 55 38N 37 51 E
Dzerzhinskiy, Mos. 11 E9 55 47N 37 37 E
Dzerzhinskiy Park, Mos. 11 E9 55 50N 37 37 E


# E


Eagle Rock, L.A. 28 B3 34 8N 118 12 E
Ealing, Lon. 4 B3 51 30N 0 18W
Earls Court, Lon. 4 C3 51 29N 0 11W
Earlsfield, Lon. 4 C3 51 26N 0 10W
Earlwood, Syd. 19 B3 33 55 S 151 8 E
East Acton, Bost. 21 C1 42 28N 71 24W
East Acton, Lon. 4 B3 51 30N 0 14W
East Arlington, Wash. 25 D7 38 51N 77 4W
East Atlantic Beach, N.Y. 23 D6 40 35N 73 43W
East B., N.Y. 22 D5 40 38N 73 32W
East Barnet, Lon. 4 B4 51 38N 0 9W
East Bedfont, Lon. 4 C2 51 26N 0 28W
East Billerica, Bost. 21 B2 42 35N 71 13W
East Boston, Bost. 21 C3 42 22N 71 1W
East Braintree, Bost. 21 D3 42 13N 70 58W
East Chicago, Chic. 26 D4 41 38N 87 26W
East Don —►, Trto. 20 D8 43 48N 79 25W
East Dulwich, Lon. 4 C4 51 26N 0 4W
East Elmhurst, N.Y. 23 C5 40 45N 73 52W
East Farmingdale, N.Y. 23 C8 40 44N 73 25W
East Finchley, Lon. 4 B3 51 35N 0 10W
East Half Hollow Hills, N.Y. 23 C9 40 47N 73 19W
East Ham, Lon. 4 B5 51 32N 0 3 E
East Hanover, N.Y. 22 C2 40 49N 74 21W
East Hills, N.Y. 23 C7 40 47N 73 37W
East Hills, Syd. 19 B2 33 57 S 150 59 E
East Holliston, Bost. 21 D1 42 12N 71 25W
East Horsley, Lon. 4 D2 51 16N 0 25W
East Humber —►, Trto. 20 D7 43 47N 79 35W
East Huntington, N.Y. 23 B8 40 52N 73 24W
East Lamma Channel, H.K. 12 E5 22 13N 114 9 E
East Lexington, Bost. 21 C2 42 25N 71 12W
East Los Angeles, L.A. 28 B3 34 1N 118 10 E
East Meadow, N.Y. 23 C7 40 42N 73 31W
East Molesey, Lon. 4 C2 51 24N 0 21W
East New York, N.Y. 23 C5 40 40N 73 53W
East Newark, N.Y. 22 C3 40 45N 74 10W
East Northport, N.Y. 23 B9 40 52N 73 18W
East Norwich, N.Y. 23 B7 40 50N 73 31W
East Orange, N.Y. 22 C3 40 46N 74 11W
East Palo Alto, S.F. 27 D4 37 28N 122 8W
East Paterson, N.Y. 22 B4 40 53N 74 8W
East Pines, Wash. 25 D8 38 57N 76 54W
East Point, Bost. 21 C4 42 25N 70 54W
East Potomac Park, Wash. 25 D7 38 52N 77 1W
East Richmond, S.F. 27 A3 37 56N 122 19W
East Ringwood, Melb. 19 E8 37 48 S 145 15 E
East River —►, N.Y. 22 C5 40 44N 73 58W
East Rockaway, N.Y. 23 D6 40 38N 73 40W
East Rutherford, N.Y. 22 B4 40 50N 74 5W
East Sheen, Lon. 4 C3 51 27N 0 16W
East View Garden, Sing. 15 F8 1 20N 103 57 E
East Weymouth, Bost. 21 D4 42 13N 70 55W
East Wickham, Lon. 4 C5 51 28N 0 5 E
East Williston, N.Y. 23 C7 40 45N 73 37W
East York, Trto. 20 D8 43 40N 79 22W
Eastchester, N.Y. 23 B6 40 56N 73 49W
Eastchester B., N.Y. 23 B6 40 50N 73 48W
Eastcote, Lon. 4 B2 51 34N 0 23W
Eastleigh, Jobg. 18 E9 26 7 S 28 9 E
Eastpoint, Balt. 25 B3 39 17N 76 34W
Eastwood, Syd. 19 A3 33 47 S 151 4 E
Eatons Neck Pt., N.Y. 23 B8 40 57N 73 24W
Eaubonne, Paris 5 B3 49 0N 2 16 E
Ebara, Tōkyō 13 C3 35 36N 139 42 E
Ebisu, Tōkyō 13 C3 35 38N 139 42 E
Ebute-Ikorodu, Lagos 18 A2 6 35N 7 29 E

Gerthe 37


Ebute-Metta, *Lagos* 18 B2 6 28N 7 23 E
Ecatepec de Morelos, *Méx.* 29 A3 19 35N 99 2W
Echo B., *N.Y.* 23 B6 40 54N 73 45W
Echo Mt., *L.A.* 28 A4 34 12N 118 8W
Écouen, *Paris* 5 A4 49 1N 2 22 E
Ecquevilly, *Paris* 5 B1 48 57N 1 55 E
Ecser, *Bud.* 10 K14 47 26N 19 19 E
Eda, *Tōkyō* 13 C2 35 33N 139 33 E
Eddington, *Phil.* 24 A5 40 5N 74 55W
Eddystone, *Phil.* 24 B2 39 51N 75 20W
Eden, *Rio J.* 31 A1 22 47 S 43 23W
Edendale, *Jobg.* 18 E9 26 8 S 28 9 E
Edenvale, *Jobg.* 18 E9 26 8 S 28 9 E
Edgars Cr. →, *Melb.* 19 E6 37 43 S 144 58 E
Edge Hill, *Phil.* 24 A4 40 7N 75 9W
Edgeley, *Trto.* 20 D7 43 47N 79 31W
Edgemar, *S.F.* 27 C2 37 39N 122 29W
Edgemere, *Balt.* 25 B4 39 14N 76 26W
Edgemont, *Phil.* 24 B2 39 58N 75 26W
Edgewater Park, *Phil.* 24 A5 40 3N 74 54W
Edgware, *Lon.* 4 B3 51 36N 0 15W
Edison, *N.Y.* 22 D2 40 31N 74 23W
Edison Park, *Chic.* 26 A2 42 1N 87 48W
Edleen, *Jobg.* 18 E10 26 5 S 28 12 E
Edmondston, *Wash.* 25 D8 38 56N 76 54W
Edo →, *Tōkyō* 13 C4 35 38N 139 52 E
Edogawa, *Tōkyō* 13 B4 35 43N 139 52 E
Edsberg, *Stock.* 3 D10 59 26N 17 57 E
Edwards L., *Melb.* 19 E6 37 42 S 144 59 E
Eestiluoto, *Hels.* 3 C6 60 7N 25 13 E
Egawa, *Tōkyō* 13 D4 35 22N 139 54 E
Egenbüttel, *Hbg.* 7 D7 53 39N 9 51 E
Eggerscheidt, *Ruhr* 6 C3 51 19N 6 53 E
Egham, *Lon.* 4 C1 51 25N 0 30W
Eiche, *Berl.* 7 A4 52 33N 13 35 E
Eiche Sud, *Berl.* 7 A4 52 33N 13 35 E
Eichlinghofen, *Ruhr* 6 B6 51 29N 7 24 E
Eichwalde, *Berl.* 7 B4 52 22N 13 37 E
Eidelstedt, *Hbg.* 7 D7 53 36N 9 54 E
Eiffel, Tour, *Paris* 5 B3 48 51N 2 17 E
Eigen, *Ruhr* 6 A3 51 32N 6 56 E
Eilbek, *Hbg.* 7 D8 53 34N 10 2 E
Eimsbüttel, *Hbg.* 7 D7 53 34N 9 57 E
Eissendorf, *Hbg.* 7 E7 53 27N 9 57 E
Ejby, *Købn.* 2 D9 55 41N 12 24 E
Ejigbo, *Lagos* 18 A1 6 33N 7 18 E
Ekeberg, *Oslo* 2 B4 59 53N 10 46 E
Ekeby, *Stock.* 3 D8 59 21N 17 35 E
Ekerö, *Stock.* 3 E9 59 17N 17 46 E
Ekerön, *Stock.* 3 E9 59 18N 17 41 E
Ekhtiyarieh, *Tehr.* 17 C5 35 46N 51 28 E
Eklundshov, *Stock.* 3 E10 59 11N 17 54 E
Eknäs, *Stock.* 3 E12 59 18N 18 13 E
El 'Abbasiya, *El Qâ.* 18 C5 30 3N 31 16 E
El Agustino, *Lima* 30 G8 12 2 S 77 0W
El Alto, *Stgo* 30 J10 33 29 S 70 42W
El Awkal, *El Qâ.* 18 C5 30 2N 31 12 E
El Baragil, *El Qâ.* 18 C4 30 4N 31 9 E
El Basâtîn, *El Qâ.* 18 D5 29 58N 31 16 E
El Calvario, *La Hab.* 30 B3 23 3N 82 19W
El Cano, *La Hab.* 30 B2 23 2N 82 27W
El Caribe, *Car.* 30 D5 10 36N 66 52W
El Carmen, *Stgo* 30 J10 33 22 S 70 43W
El Cerrito, *S.F.* 27 A3 37 54N 122 18W
El Cerro, *La Hab.* 30 B2 23 6N 82 23W
El Cojo, Pta., *Car.* 30 D5 10 36N 66 53W
El Cortijo, *Stgo* 30 J10 33 22 S 70 42W
El Duqqi, *El Qâ.* 18 C5 30 2N 31 12 E
El Gamâliya, *El Qâ.* 18 C5 30 2N 31 15 E
El Ghurîya, *El Qâ.* 18 C5 30 2N 31 15 E
El Gîza, *El Qâ.* 18 C5 30 0N 31 12 E
El Granada, *S.F.* 27 C2 37 30N 122 27W
El Guarda Parres, *Méx.* 29 D2 19 9N 99 11W
El Hatillo, *Car.* 30 E6 10 25N 66 49W
El Khalîfa, *El Qâ.* 18 C5 30 0N 31 15 E
El Kôm el Ahmar, *El Qâ.* 18 C5 30 6N 31 10 E
El Ma'âdi, *El Qâ.* 18 D5 29 57N 31 15 E
El Matarîya, *El Qâ.* 18 C5 30 7N 31 18 E
El Monte, *L.A.* 28 B4 34 3N 118 1W
El Muhît Idkû el Gharbî →, *El Qâ.* 18 C4 30 6N 31 6 E
El Mûski, *El Qâ.* 18 C5 30 3N 31 15 E
El Palmar, *Car.* 30 D5 10 36N 66 53W
El Palomar, *B.A.* 32 B3 34 36 S 58 37W
El Pardo, *Mdrd.* 8 A2 40 30N 3 46W
El Pedregal, *Car.* 30 D5 10 30N 66 51W
El Pinar, *Car.* 30 E5 10 28N 66 56W
El Plantio, *Mdrd.* 8 B1 40 28N 3 51W
El Qâhira, *El Qâ.* 18 C5 30 2N 31 13 E
El Qubba, *El Qâ.* 18 C5 30 4N 31 16 E
El Recreo, *Car.* 30 E5 10 29N 66 52W
El Reloj, *Méx.* 29 C3 19 19N 99 9W
El Retiro, *Car.* 30 D5 10 31N 66 54W
El Salto, *Stgo* 30 J11 33 22 S 70 38W
El Segundo, *L.A.* 28 C2 33 55N 118 24W
El Sereno, *L.A.* 28 B3 34 6N 118 10 E
El Silencio, *Car.* 30 D5 10 30N 66 55W
El Sobrante, *S.F.* 27 A3 37 58N 122 17W
El Talar de Pacheco, *B.A.* 32 A3 34 27 S 58 38W
El Talibîya, *El Qâ.* 18 D5 29 59N 31 10 E
El Valle, *Car.* 30 E5 10 29N 66 54W
El Vedado, *La Hab.* 30 B2 23 8N 82 23W
El Vergel, *Méx.* 29 C3 19 18N 99 5W
El Wâyli el Kubra, *El Qâ.* 18 C5 30 5N 31 17 E
El Zamalik, *El Qâ.* 18 C5 30 3N 31 12 E
Elam, *Phil.* 24 B1 39 51N 75 32W
Élancourt, *Paris* 5 C1 48 47N 1 57 E
Elandsfontein, *Jobg.* 18 E10 26 9 S 28 13 E
Elbe →, *Hbg.* 7 D6 53 32N 9 49 E
Elberfeld, *Ruhr* 6 C4 51 15N 7 9 E
Elephanta Caves, *Bomb.* 16 H8 18 57N 72 57 E
Elephanta I., *Bomb.* 16 H8 18 57N 72 56 E
Elisenau, *Berl.* 7 A4 52 38N 13 37 E
Elizabeth, *N.Y.* 22 D3 40 39N 74 13W
Elkins Park, *Phil.* 24 A4 40 4N 75 8W
Elkridge, *Balt.* 25 B2 39 13N 76 42W
Ellboda, *Stock.* 3 D12 59 24N 18 15 E
Eller, *Ruhr* 6 C3 51 12N 6 51 E
Ellerbek, *Hbg.* 7 D7 53 39N 9 52 E
Ellicott City, *Balt.* 25 B2 39 15N 76 49W
Ellinghorst, *Ruhr* 6 A3 51 33N 6 57 E
Ellinikón, *Ath.* 8 J11 37 50N 23 45 E
Ellis I., *N.Y.* 22 C4 40 41N 74 2W
Elm Park, *Lon.* 4 B6 51 32N 0 12 E
Elmers End, *Lon.* 4 C4 51 23N 0 2W
Elmhurst, *Chic.* 26 B1 41 53N 87 55W
Elmhurst, *N.Y.* 23 C5 40 44N 73 53W
Elmont, *N.Y.* 23 C6 40 42N 73 42W
Elmstead, *Lon.* 4 C5 51 24N 0 2 E
Elmwood, *Balt.* 25 A3 39 20N 76 31W
Elmwood, *N.Y.* 23 B8 40 51N 73 20W
Elmwood Park, *Chic.* 26 B2 41 55N 87 48W
Elmwood Park, *N.Y.* 22 B4 40 54N 74 7W
Elsburg, *Jobg.* 18 F10 26 15 S 28 13 E
Elsburgspruit →, *Jobg.* 18 F10 26 16 S 28 12 E
Elsmere, *Phil.* 24 C1 39 44N 75 35W
Elspark, *Jobg.* 18 F10 26 15 S 28 13 E
Elsternwick, *Melb.* 19 F7 37 52 S 145 0 E
Eltham, *Lon.* 4 C5 51 27N 0 3 E
Eltham, *Melb.* 19 E7 37 42 S 145 9 E
Elthorn Heights, *Lon.* 4 B2 51 31N 0 20W
Eltingrille, *N.Y.* 22 D4 40 32N 74 9W
Elwood, *Melb.* 19 F6 37 53 S 144 59 E
Élysée, *Paris* 5 B3 48 52N 2 19 E
Embu, *S. Pau.* 31 E4 23 38 S 46 50W
Embu-Mirim, *S. Pau.* 31 F5 23 41 S 46 49W
Embu Mirim →, *S. Pau.* 31 F5 23 43 S 46 47W
Emdeni, *Jobg.* 18 F7 26 14 S 27 49 E
Émerainville, *Paris* 5 C5 48 48N 2 37 E
Emerson, *N.Y.* 22 B4 40 57N 74 2W
Emerson Park, *Lon.* 4 B6 51 34N 0 13 E
Emeryville, *S.F.* 27 B3 37 49N 122 17W
Eminonu, *Ist.* 17 A2 41 0N 28 57 E
Emmarentia, *Jobg.* 18 E9 26 9 S 28 0 E
Emperor's Palace, *Tōkyō* 13 B3 35 40N 139 45 E
Empire State Building, *N.Y.* 22 C5 40 44N 73 59W
Emscher →, *Ruhr* 6 A6 51 30N 7 26 E
Emscher Bruch, *Ruhr* 6 A4 51 33N 7 8 E
Emscher Zweigkanal, *Ruhr* 6 A4 51 33N 7 9 E
Encantado, *Rio J.* 31 B2 22 53 S 43 19W
Encino, *L.A.* 28 B2 34 9N 118 28W
Encino Res., *L.A.* 28 B1 34 8N 118 30W
Enebyberg, *Stock.* 3 D10 59 25N 17 59 E
Enfield, *Lon.* 4 B4 51 39N 0 4W
Enfield, *Phil.* 24 A3 40 6N 75 11W
Enfield, *Syd.* 19 B3 33 53 S 151 6 E
Enfield Chase, *Lon.* 4 A4 51 40N 0 8W
Enfield Highway, *Lon.* 4 B4 51 39N 0 3W
Enfield Lock, *Lon.* 4 A4 51 40N 0 1W
Enfield Wash, *Lon.* 4 B4 51 39N 0 2W
Eng Khong Gardens, *Sing.* 15 F7 1 20N 103 46 E
Engenho, I. do, *Rio J.* 31 B3 22 50 S 43 6W
Engenho Nôvo, *Rio J.* 31 B2 22 53 S 43 17W
Engenho Velho, Sa. do, *Rio J.* 31 B1 22 54 S 43 21W
Engenno do Mato, *Rio J.* 31 B3 22 56 S 43 2W
Enghein-les-Bains, *Paris* 5 B3 48 58N 2 18 E
Englewood, *Chic.* 26 C3 41 46N 87 38W
Englewood, *N.Y.* 22 B5 40 53N 73 58W
Englewood Cliffs, *N.Y.* 22 B5 40 53N 73 59W
Englischer Garten, *Mün.* 7 G10 48 9N 11 35 E
Enmore, *Syd.* 19 B4 33 54 S 151 10 E
Ennepe →, *Ruhr* 6 C6 51 17N 7 23 E
Ennepetal, *Ruhr* 6 C6 51 17N 7 21 E
Ennepetalsp →, *Ruhr* 6 C6 51 14N 7 24 E
Enskede, *Stock.* 3 E11 59 17N 18 4 E
Entrevias, *Mdrd.* 8 B2 40 22N 3 40W
Épiais-les-Louvres, *Paris* 5 A5 49 1N 2 33 E
Epinay, *Paris* 5 B3 48 57N 2 19 E
Epinay-sous-Sénart, *Paris* 5 C5 48 41N 2 30 E
Epinay-sur-Orge, *Paris* 5 C3 48 40N 2 19 E
Eppende, *Ruhr* 6 B4 51 28N 7 9 E
Eppenhausen, *Ruhr* 6 B6 51 22N 7 29 E
Epping, *Lon.* 4 A5 51 41N 0 6 E
Epping, *Melb.* 19 D7 37 39 S 145 1 E
Epping, *Syd.* 19 A3 33 46 S 151 5 E
Epping Forest, *Lon.* 4 B5 51 39N 0 2 E
Epsom, *Lon.* 4 D3 51 19N 0 15W
Epsom Racecourse, *Lon.* 4 D3 51 18N 0 15W
Éragny, *Paris* 5 A2 49 1N 2 5 E
Ercolano, *Nápl.* 9 J13 40 48N 14 21 E
Érd, *Bud.* 10 K12 47 23N 18 56 E
Erdenheim, *Phil.* 24 A3 40 5N 75 12W
Eregun, *Lagos* 18 A2 6 35N 7 22 E
Erenköy, *Ist.* 17 B3 40 58N 29 3 E
Ergal, *Paris* 5 C1 48 47N 1 55 E
Erial, *Phil.* 24 C4 39 46N 75 0W
Erith, *Lon.* 4 C6 51 28N 0 11 E
Erkner, *Berl.* 7 B5 52 25N 13 44 E
Erkrath, *Ruhr* 6 C3 51 13N 6 54 E
Erlaa, *Wien* 10 H9 48 9N 16 19 E
Erle, *Ruhr* 6 A4 51 33N 7 4 E
Ermelino Matarazzo, *S. Pau.* 31 D7 23 29 S 46 28W
Ermington, *Syd.* 19 A3 33 48 S 151 4 E
Ermont, *Paris* 5 B3 48 59N 2 15 E
Ersébet-Telep, *Bud.* 10 K14 47 27N 19 10 E
Ershatou, *Gzh.* 14 G8 23 6N 113 18 E
Erskineville, *Syd.* 19 B4 33 54 S 151 12 E
Erstavik, *Stock.* 3 E12 59 16N 18 14 E
Erstaviken, *Stock.* 3 E12 59 16N 18 20 E
Erunkan, *Lagos* 18 A2 6 36N 7 23 E
Eschenried, *Mün.* 7 F9 48 13N 11 24 E
Esenler, *Ist.* 17 A2 41 1N 28 52 E
Esher, *Lon.* 4 C2 51 22N 0 20W
Eshratābād, *Tehr.* 17 C5 35 42N 51 27 E
España, *B.A.* 32 C5 34 46 S 58 14W
Espeleta, *B.A.* 32 C5 34 45 S 58 15W
Esplugas, *Barc.* 8 D5 41 22N 2 5 E
Espoo, *Hels.* 3 B2 60 13N 24 38 E
Espoonlahti, *Hels.* 3 B2 60 9N 24 31 E
Esposizione Univ. di Roma (E.U.R.), *Rome* 9 G9 41 49N 12 28 E
Essen, *Ruhr* 6 B4 51 27N 7 0 E
Essen-Mülheim, Flughafen, *Ruhr* 6 B3 51 24N 6 56 E
Essendon, *Melb.* 19 E6 37 44 S 144 55 E
Essendon Airport, *Melb.* 19 E6 37 43 S 144 54 E
Essex, *Balt.* 25 B4 39 18N 76 28W
Essex Falls, *N.Y.* 22 C3 40 49N 74 16W
Essingen, *Stock.* 3 E10 59 19N 17 59 E
Essling, *Wien* 10 G11 48 12N 16 30 E
Est, Gare de l', *Paris* 5 B4 48 52N 2 21 E
Estado, Parque do, *S. Pau.* 31 E6 23 38 S 46 38W
Estby, *Hels.* 3 C1 60 5N 24 27W
Este, Parque Nacional del, *Car.* 30 E5 10 29N 66 50W
Esteban Echeverria, *B.A.* 32 C4 34 48 S 58 29W
Estlotan, *Hels.* 3 C6 60 7N 25 13 E
Estrela, Basilica da, *Lisb.* 8 F8 38 42N 9 9W
Étiolles, *Paris* 5 D4 48 38N 2 28 E
Etobicoke, *Trto.* 20 E7 43 39N 79 34W
Etobicoke Cr. →, *Trto.* 20 E7 43 35N 79 32W
Etzenhauzen, *Mün.* 7 F9 48 16N 11 27 E
Eun Pyeong, *Sŏul* 12 G7 37 36N 126 56 E
Eungam, *Sŏul* 12 G7 37 34N 126 55 E
Evanston, *Chic.* 26 A2 42 3N 87 40W
Évecquemont, *Paris* 5 A1 49 0N 1 56 E
Everett, *Bost.* 21 C3 42 24N 71 3W
Evergreen Park, *Chic.* 26 C2 41 43N 87 42W
Eversael, *Ruhr* 6 A1 51 32N 6 39 E
Evesboro, *Phil.* 24 B5 39 54N 74 55W
Eving, *Ruhr* 6 A6 51 33N 7 28 E
Evry, *Paris* 5 D4 48 38N 2 26 E
Évry-les-Châteaux, *Paris* 5 D5 48 39N 2 38 E
Évzonos, *Ath.* 8 J11 37 55N 23 49 E
Ewin, *Tehr.* 17 C5 35 47N 51 23 E
Ewu, *Lagos* 18 A1 6 33N 7 19 E
Exelberg, *Wien* 10 G9 48 14N 16 15 E
Eynsford, *Lon.* 4 C6 51 21N 0 12 E
Eyup, *Ist.* 17 A2 41 2N 28 55 E
Ez Zeitûn, *El Qâ.* 18 C5 30 6N 31 18 E
Ézanville, *Paris* 5 A4 49 1N 2 21 E
Ezeiza, *B.A.* 32 D3 34 50 S 58 31W
Ezeiza, Aeropuerto, *B.A.* 32 C3 34 48 S 58 32W


# F


Fabreville, *Mtrl.* 20 A2 43 33N 73 51W
Fælledparken, *Købn.* 2 D10 55 42N 12 34 E
Fågelön, *Stock.* 3 E10 59 18N 17 55 E
Fagersjo, *Stock.* 3 E11 59 14N 18 4 E
Fagnano, *Mil.* 9 E4 45 24N 8 59 E
Fahrn, *Ruhr* 6 A2 51 30N 6 45 E
Faibano, *Nápl.* 9 H13 40 55N 14 27 E
Fair Lawn, *N.Y.* 22 B4 40 55N 74 7W
Fairfax, *Phil.* 24 C1 39 47N 75 33W
Fairfax, *Wash.* 25 D6 38 50N 77 19W
Fairfax Station, *Wash.* 25 E6 38 48N 77 19W
Fairfield, *Melb.* 19 E7 37 46 S 145 2 E
Fairfield, *N.Y.* 22 B3 40 53N 74 17W
Fairfield, *Syd.* 19 B2 33 52 S 150 56 E
Fairhaven B., *Bost.* 21 C1 42 25N 71 21W
Fairhaven Hill, *Bost.* 21 C1 42 26N 71 21W
Fairland, *Jobg.* 18 E8 26 8 S 27 57 E
Fairland, *Wash.* 25 C8 39 4N 76 57W
Fairmont Terrace, *S.F.* 27 B4 37 42N 122 7W
Fairmount Heights, *Wash.* 25 D8 38 54N 76 54W
Fairmount Park, *Phil.* 24 A3 40 3N 75 13W
Fairport, *Trto.* 20 D10 43 49N 79 4W
Fairview, *N.Y.* 22 C5 40 48N 73 59W
Fairview, *N.Y.* 23 A6 41 1N 73 46W
Falenica, *Wsaw.* 10 F8 52 9N 21 12 E
Falenty, *Wsaw.* 10 F6 52 8N 20 55 E
Falkenburg, *Berl.* 7 A4 52 34N 13 32 E
Falkenhagen, *Berl.* 7 A1 52 34N 13 5 E
Falkensee, *Berl.* 7 A1 52 34N 13 4 E
Fallon, *L.A.* 28 C5 33 59N 117 54W
Falls Church, *Wash.* 25 D6 38 53N 77 12W
Falls Run →, *Balt.* 25 A1 39 21N 76 52W
Falomo, *Lagos* 18 B2 6 26N 7 26 E
Fangcun, *Gzh.* 14 G8 23 6N 113 13 E
Fanwood, *N.Y.* 22 D2 40 37N 74 23W
Far Rockaway, *N.Y.* 23 D6 40 36N 73 45W
Farahābād, *Tehr.* 17 C5 35 41N 51 29 E
Färentuna, *Stock.* 3 D8 59 23N 17 39 E
Farforovskaya, *St-Pet.* 11 B4 59 52N 30 27 E
Farm Pond, *Bost.* 21 D2 42 13N 71 20W
Farmingdale, *N.Y.* 23 C8 40 43N 73 27W
Farmsen, *Hbg.* 7 D8 53 36N 10 8 E
Farnborough, *Lon.* 4 C5 51 21N 0 3 E
Farningham, *Lon.* 4 C6 51 23N 0 12 E
Farrar Pond, *Bost.* 21 C1 42 24N 71 21W
Farrarmere, *Jobg.* 18 E10 26 9 S 28 18 E
Farsta, *Stock.* 3 E11 59 14N 18 5 E
Farstalandet, *Stock.* 3 E13 59 18N 18 23 E
Farum, *Købn.* 2 D8 55 48N 12 21 E
Farum Sø, *Købn.* 2 D9 55 48N 12 21 E
Fasanerie-Nord, *Mün.* 7 F10 48 11N 11 32 E
Fasangarten, *Mün.* 7 G10 48 5N 11 36 E
Fat Tau Chau, *H.K.* 12 E6 22 16N 114 16 E
Fatih, *Ist.* 17 A2 41 0N 28 56 E
Favoriten, *Wien* 10 H10 48 9N 16 23 E
Fawkner, *Melb.* 19 E6 37 42 S 144 56 E
Fawkner Park, *Melb.* 19 F6 37 50 S 144 58 E
Feasterville, *Phil.* 24 A4 40 9N 75 0W
Febrero, Parque de, *B.A.* 32 B4 34 36 S 58 25W
Feijó, *Lisb.* 8 G8 38 39N 9 9W
Feldersbruch →, *Ruhr* 6 B5 51 23N 7 4 E
Feldhausen, *Ruhr* 6 A3 51 36N 6 58 E
Feldkirchen, *Mün.* 7 G11 48 8N 11 43 E
Feldmoching, *Mün.* 7 F10 48 14N 11 32 E
Fellowship, *Phil.* 24 B5 39 56N 74 57W
Feltham, *Lon.* 4 C2 51 26N 0 24W
Feltonville, *Phil.* 24 A4 40 1N 75 8W
Fenerbahce, *Ist.* 17 B3 40 58N 29 2 E
Fengtai, *Beij.* 14 C2 39 49N 116 14 E
Fenino, *Mos.* 11 E11 55 43N 37 56 E
Ferencváros, *Bud.* 10 K13 47 29N 19 5 E
Ferihegyi Airport, *Bud.* 10 K14 47 26N 19 14 E
Ferndale, *Balt.* 25 B3 39 11N 76 38W
Ferndale, *Jobg.* 18 E9 26 5 S 28 0 E
Ferntree Gully, *Melb.* 19 F8 37 52 S 145 17 E
Ferntree Gully Nat. Park, *Melb.* 19 F8 37 52 S 145 19 E
Ferny Cr. →, *Melb.* 19 F8 37 54 S 145 16 E
Férolles-Attilly, *Paris* 5 C5 48 44N 2 37 E
Ferraz de Vasconcelos, *S. Pau.* 31 E7 23 32 S 46 22W
Ferrières-en-Brie, *Paris* 5 C6 48 49N 2 42 E
Ferry, *N.Y.* 23 A5 41 0N 73 52W
Fetcham, *Lon.* 4 D2 51 17N 0 21W
Feucherolles, *Paris* 5 B1 48 52N 1 58 E
Fichtenau, *Berl.* 7 B5 52 27N 13 42 E
Fields Corner, *Bost.* 21 D3 42 18N 71 3W
Fiera Camp, *Mil.* 9 E5 45 28N 9 9 E
Figino, *Mil.* 9 E5 45 29N 9 4 E
Fijir, *Bagd.* 17 E8 33 21N 44 21 E
Filadhélfia, *Ath.* 8 H11 38 2N 23 43 E
Fili-Masilovo, *Mos.* 11 E8 55 44N 37 29 E
Filothei, *Ath.* 8 H11 38 2N 23 46 E
Finaalspan, *Jobg.* 18 F10 26 16 S 28 16 E
Finchley, *Lon.* 4 B3 51 36N 0 10W
Finkenkrug, *Berl.* 7 A1 52 33N 13 3 E
Finkenwerder, *Hbg.* 7 D7 53 32N 9 51 E
Finsbury, *Lon.* 4 B4 51 31N 0 6W
Finsbury Park, *Lon.* 4 B4 51 34N 0 6W
Fiorito, *B.A.* 32 C4 34 42 S 58 26W
Firdows, *Bagd.* 17 F7 33 17N 44 17 E
Firōz Bahram, *Tehr.* 17 D4 35 37N 51 14 E
Fischeln, *Ruhr* 6 C1 51 18N 6 35 E
Fish Brook →, *Bost.* 21 B3 42 39N 71 1W
Fishermans Bend, *Melb.* 19 E6 37 49 S 144 55 E
Fisher's Hill, *Jobg.* 18 F10 26 10 S 28 10 E
Fisherville, *Trto.* 20 D8 43 46N 79 28W
Fisksätra, *Stock.* 3 E12 59 17N 18 13 E
Fittja, *Stock.* 3 E10 59 14N 17 51 E
Fitzroy Gardens, *Melb.* 19 E7 37 48 S 144 58 E
Five Cowrie Cr. →, *Lagos* 18 B2 6 26N 7 25 E
Five Dock, *Syd.* 19 B3 33 52 S 151 8 E
Fjellstrand, *Oslo* 2 C3 59 47N 10 36 E
Flachsberg, *Ruhr* 6 C4 51 11N 7 4 E
Flag →, *Chic.* 26 C1 41 43N 87 55W
Flamengo, *Rio J.* 31 B2 22 56 S 43 11W
Flaminio, *Rome* 9 F9 41 55N 12 28 E
Flaskebekk, *Oslo* 2 B3 59 51N 10 39 E
Flatbush, *N.Y.* 22 D5 40 39N 73 56W
Flaten, *Stock.* 3 E11 59 15N 18 9 E
Flemington, *Syd.* 19 B3 33 53 S 151 4 E
Flemington Racecourse, *Melb.* 19 E6 37 47 S 144 54 E
Fleury-Mérogis, *Paris* 5 D4 48 37N 2 21 E
Flingern, *Ruhr* 6 C2 51 13N 6 48 E
Flint Pk., *L.A.* 28 B3 34 9N 118 11 E
Floral Park, *N.Y.* 23 C6 40 43N 73 42W
Florence, *L.A.* 28 C3 33 57N 118 14W
Florence, *Phil.* 24 C5 39 44N 74 55W
Florence Bloom Bird Sanctuary, *Jobg.* 18 E9 26 7 S 28 0 E
Florencio Varela, *B.A.* 32 C5 34 49 S 58 18W
Florentia, *Jobg.* 18 F9 26 16 S 28 8 E
Flores, *B.A.* 32 B4 34 38 S 58 27W
Floresta, *B.A.* 32 B4 34 37 S 58 27W
Florham Park, *N.Y.* 22 C2 40 46N 74 23W
Florida, *B.A.* 32 B4 34 31 S 58 28W
Florida, *Jobg.* 18 F8 26 10 S 27 55 E
Florida L., *Jobg.* 18 F8 26 10 S 27 54 E
Floridsdorf, *Wien* 10 G10 48 15N 16 26 E
Flourtown, *Phil.* 24 A3 40 6N 75 13W
Flower Hill, *N.Y.* 23 C6 40 48N 73 40W
Flushing, *N.Y.* 23 C6 40 45N 73 49W
Flushing Meadows Corona Park, *N.Y.* 23 C5 40 44N 73 50W
Flysta, *Stock.* 3 D10 59 22N 17 54 E
Fo Tan, *H.K.* 12 D6 22 23N 114 11 E
Föhrenhain, *Wien* 10 G10 48 19N 16 26 E
Folcroft, *Phil.* 24 B3 39 53N 75 16W
Folsom, *Phil.* 24 B3 39 53N 75 19W
Fontainebleau, *Jobg.* 18 E8 26 6 S 27 57 E
Fontana, *La Hab.* 30 B2 23 1N 82 24W
Fontanka, *St-Pet.* 11 B3 59 54N 30 16 E
Fontenay-aux-Roses, *Paris* 5 C3 48 47N 2 17 E
Fontenay-le-Fleury, *Paris* 5 C2 48 48N 2 2 E
Fontenay-lès-Briis, *Paris* 5 D2 48 37N 2 9 E
Fontenay-sous-Bois, *Paris* 5 B4 48 51N 2 28 E
Foots Cray, *Lon.* 4 C5 51 24N 0 7 E
Footscray, *Melb.* 19 E6 37 48 S 144 56 E
Forbidden City, *Beij.* 14 B3 39 53N 116 21 E
Fordham Univ., *N.Y.* 23 B5 40 51N 73 51W
Fords, *N.Y.* 22 D3 40 31N 74 19W
Fordsburg, *Jobg.* 18 F9 26 12 S 28 2 E
Foremans Corner, *Balt.* 25 B3 39 11N 76 33W
Forest Gate, *Lon.* 4 B5 51 32N 0 1 E
Forest Heights, *Wash.* 25 E7 38 48N 77 0W
Forest Hill, *Lon.* 4 C4 51 26N 0 2W
Forest Hill, *Melb.* 19 F8 37 50 S 145 10 E
Forest Hill, *Trto.* 20 D8 43 41N 79 25W
Forest Hills, *N.Y.* 23 C5 40 42N 73 51W
Forest Park, *Chic.* 26 B2 41 51N 87 47W
Forest View, *Chic.* 26 C2 41 48N 87 47W
Forestville, *Syd.* 19 A4 33 46 S 151 12 E
Forestville, *Wash.* 25 D8 38 50N 76 52W
Forges-les-Bains, *Paris* 5 D2 48 37N 2 5 E
Fornacino, *Tori.* 9 B3 45 9N 7 44 E
Fornebu, *Oslo* 2 B3 59 53N 10 36 E
Fornebu Airport, *Oslo* 2 B3 59 56N 10 37 E
Foro Italico, *Rome* 9 F9 41 56N 12 26 E
Foro Romano, *Rome* 9 F9 41 53N 12 29 E
Forst Rantzau, *Hbg.* 7 C6 53 43N 9 49 E
Forstenried, *Mün.* 7 G9 48 5N 11 29 E
Forstenrieder Park, *Mün.* 7 G9 48 3N 11 27 E
Fort du Pont Park, *Wash.* 25 D8 38 52N 76 56W
Fort Foote Village, *Wash.* 25 E7 38 46N 77 1W
Fort Howard, *Balt.* 25 B4 39 12N 76 26W
Fort Lee, *N.Y.* 22 B5 40 50N 73 58W
Fort McHenry Nat. Mon., *Balt.* 25 B3 35 15N 76 35W
Fort Washington, *Phil.* 24 A3 40 8N 75 13W
Fort William, *Calc.* 16 E6 22 33N 88 20 E
Fosters Pond, *Bost.* 21 B3 42 36N 71 8W
Fourcherolle, *Paris* 5 C1 48 42N 1 58 E
Fourmile Run →, *Wash.* 25 D7 38 50N 77 2W
Fourqueux, *Paris* 5 B2 48 53N 2 3 E
Fowl Meadow Res., *Bost.* 21 D3 42 13N 71 8W
Fox Chase, *Phil.* 24 A4 40 4N 75 5W
Foxhall, *Wash.* 25 C7 39 4N 77 3W
Framingham, *Bost.* 21 D1 42 18N 71 24W
Francisco Alvarez, *B.A.* 32 B1 34 38 S 58 50W
Francisquito Cr. →, *S.F.* 27 D4 37 27N 122 9W
Franconia, *Wash.* 25 E7 38 47N 77 7W
Franconville, *Paris* 5 A3 48 59N 2 13 E
Francop, *Hbg.* 7 D7 53 30N 9 51 E
Frankel, *Sing.* 15 G8 1 18N 103 55 E
Frankford, *Phil.* 24 A4 40 1N 75 5W
Franklin L., *N.Y.* 22 B3 40 59N 74 13W
Franklin Lakes, *N.Y.* 22 B3 40 59N 74 13W
Franklin Park, *Bost.* 21 D3 42 18N 71 5W
Franklin Park, *Chic.* 26 B1 41 55N 87 52W
Franklin Park, *Wash.* 25 D7 38 55N 77 9W
Franklin Res., *L.A.* 28 B2 34 5N 118 24W
Franklin Roosevelt Park, *Jobg.* 18 E8 26 8 S 27 59 E
Franklin Roosevelt Park, *Phil.* 24 B3 39 54N 75 10W
Franklin Square, *N.Y.* 23 C6 40 42N 73 40W
Frattamaggiore, *Nápl.* 9 H12 40 56N 14 16 E
Frauenkirche, *Mün.* 7 G10 48 8N 11 34 E
Frederiksberg, *Købn.* 2 D10 55 40N 12 33 E
Frederiksdal, *Købn.* 2 D9 55 46N 12 25 E
Fredersdorf, *Berl.* 7 A5 52 31N 13 45 E
Fredersdorf Nord, *Berl.* 7 A5 52 32N 13 45 E
Freeport, *N.Y.* 23 D7 40 39N 73 35W
Freidrichshain, Volkspark, *Berl.* 7 A3 52 31N 13 25 E
Freiham, *Mün.* 7 G9 48 8N 11 25 E
Freimann, *Mün.* 7 F10 48 11N 11 37 E
Fremont, *S.F.* 27 C4 37 33N 122 2W
Fresh Meadows, *N.Y.* 23 C6 40 44N 73 47W
Fresh Pond, *Bost.* 21 C3 42 22N 71 8W
Freskati, *Stock.* 3 D11 59 22N 18 3 E
Fresnes, *Paris* 5 C3 48 45N 2 18 E
Fretay, *Paris* 5 D3 48 39N 2 15 E
Freudenau, *Wien* 10 G10 48 11N 16 25 E
Friedenau, *Berl.* 7 B3 52 28N 13 20 E
Friederikenhof, *Berl.* 7 B3 52 23N 13 21 E
Friedrichsfeld, *Ruhr* 6 A1 51 37N 6 39 E
Friedrichsfelde, *Berl.* 7 B4 52 29N 13 33 E
Friedrichshagen, *Berl.* 7 B4 52 27N 13 37 E
Friedrichshain, *Berl.* 7 A3 52 31N 13 25 E
Friedrichshulde, *Hbg.* 7 D7 53 36N 9 51 E
Friedrichslust, *Berl.* 7 A5 52 33N 13 43 E
Frielas, *Lisb.* 8 F8 38 49N 9 7W
Friemersheim, *Ruhr* 6 B2 51 23N 6 42 E
Friern Barnet, *Lon.* 4 B4 51 37N 0 9W
Friherrs, *Hels.* 3 B3 60 16N 24 49 E
Frogner, *Oslo* 2 A6 60 1N 11 6 E
Frohnau, *Berl.* 7 A2 52 38N 13 16 E
Frohnhausen, *Ruhr* 6 B3 51 26N 6 56 E
Frontón, I., *Lima* 30 G7 12 7 S 77 11W
Frunze, *Mos.* 11 E9 55 47N 37 33 E
Fuchū, *Tōkyō* 13 B1 35 40N 139 29 E
Fuencarral, *Mdrd.* 8 B2 40 29N 3 42W
Fuhlenbrock, *Ruhr* 6 A3 51 32N 6 54 E
Fuhlsbüttel, *Hbg.* 7 D8 53 37N 10 1 E
Fujidera, *Ōsaka* 12 C4 34 34N 135 36 E
Fujikubo, *Tōkyō* 13 B2 35 49N 139 31 E
Fujimi, *Tōkyō* 13 B2 35 50N 139 33 E
Fukagawa, *Tōkyō* 13 C3 35 39N 139 48 E
Fukami, *Tōkyō* 13 D1 35 28N 139 27 E
Fukiai, *Ōsaka* 12 B2 34 42N 135 12 E
Fukuoka, *Tōkyō* 13 A2 35 52N 139 31 E
Fukushima, *Ōsaka* 12 B3 34 41N 135 28 E
Fulatani, *Tōkyō* 13 D1 35 22N 139 30 E
Fulham, *Lon.* 4 C3 51 28N 0 12W
Fuller Park, *L.A.* 28 C5 33 51N 117 56W
Fullerton, *Balt.* 25 A3 39 22N 76 30W
Funabori, *Tōkyō* 13 B4 35 41N 139 52 E
Funasaka, *Ōsaka* 12 B2 34 48N 135 16 E
Fünfhaus, *Wien* 10 G10 48 11N 16 20 E
Fünfhausen, *Hbg.* 7 E8 53 27N 10 2 E
Furesø, *Købn.* 2 D9 55 47N 12 25 E
Fürstenried, *Mün.* 7 G9 48 5N 11 28 E
Furth, *Mün.* 7 G10 48 2N 11 35 E
Furu →, *Tōkyō* 13 A3 35 54N 139 49 E
Furuyakami, *Tōkyō* 13 A2 35 54N 139 31 E
Futago-tamagawaen, *Tōkyō* 13 C2 35 36N 139 39 E
Futamatagawa, *Tōkyō* 13 D2 35 27N 139 31 E
Futatsubashi, *Tōkyō* 13 D1 35 28N 139 27 E
Fuxing Dao, *Shang.* 14 J12 31 16N 121 33 E
Fuxing Gongyuan, *Shang.* 14 J11 31 13N 121 27 E
Fuxinglu, *Beij.* 14 B2 39 52N 116 16 E
Fuxingmen, *Beij.* 14 B2 39 53N 116 19 E


# G


Gadstrup, *Købn.* 2 E7 55 34N 12 5 E
Gaebong, *Sŏul* 12 H7 37 29N 126 52 E
Gage Park, *Chic.* 26 C2 41 47N 87 42W
Gagny, *Paris* 5 B5 48 53N 2 32 E
Gaillon, *Paris* 5 A1 49 1N 1 53 E
Galata, *Ist.* 17 A2 41 1N 28 58 E
Galátsion, *Ath.* 8 H11 38 1N 23 45 E
Galeão, *Rio J.* 31 A2 22 49 S 43 14W
Galéria →, *Rome* 9 F9 41 57N 12 20 E
Gallows Corner, *Lon.* 4 B6 51 35N 0 13 E
Gällstaö, *Stock.* 3 E10 59 17N 17 51 E
Galyanovo, *Mos.* 11 E10 55 48N 37 47 E
Galyeon, *Sŏul* 12 G7 37 36N 126 55 E
Gambir, *Jak.* 15 H9 6 9 S 106 48 E
Gamboa, *Rio J.* 31 B2 22 53 S 43 11W
Gambolóita, *Mil.* 9 E6 45 26N 9 13 E
Gamelinha →, *S. Pau.* 31 E6 23 31 S 46 31W
Gamlebyen, *Oslo* 2 B4 59 54N 10 46 E
Gamlebyen, *Shang.* 14 J11 31 13N 121 29 E
Gamō, *Tōkyō* 13 A3 35 52N 139 48 E
Gang Dong, *Sŏul* 12 G8 37 30N 127 5 E
Gang Nam, *Sŏul* 12 G7 37 30N 126 59 E
Gang Sea, *Sŏul* 12 G7 37 32N 126 51 E
Gangadharpur, *Calc.* 16 E5 22 45N 88 11 E
Gangtou, *Gzh.* 14 F7 23 12N 113 8 E
Gangwei, *Gzh.* 14 G8 23 4N 113 11 E
Ganløse, *Købn.* 2 D8 55 47N 12 15 E
Ganløse Orned, *Købn.* 2 D8 55 48N 12 18 E
Ganshi, *Gzh.* 14 F7 23 10N 113 8 E
Gants Hill, *Lon.* 4 B5 51 34N 0 4 E
Gaoqiao, *Shang.* 14 H12 31 21N 121 34 E
Garbagnate Milanese, *Mil.* 9 D5 45 34N 9 4 E
Garbatella, *Rome* 9 F10 41 51N 12 30 E
Garches, *Paris* 5 B2 48 50N 2 11 E
Garching, *Mün.* 7 F11 48 14N 11 39 E
Garden City, *El Qâ.* 18 C5 30 2N 31 14 E
Garden City, *N.Y.* 23 C7 40 43N 73 38W
Garden Reach, *Calc.* 16 E5 22 33N 88 15 E
Gardena, *L.A.* 28 C3 33 53N 118 18W
Garder, *Oslo* 2 C3 59 45N 10 38 E
Garfield, *N.Y.* 22 B4 40 52N 74 7W
Garfield Park, *Chic.* 26 B2 41 52N 87 42W
Gargareta, *Ath.* 8 J11 37 57N 23 43 E
Garges-lès-Gonesse, *Paris* 5 B4 48 58N 2 25 E
Garhi Naraina, *Delhi* 16 B1 28 37N 77 8 E
Garibong, *Sŏul* 12 H7 37 29N 126 54 E
Garin, *B.A.* 32 A2 34 25 S 58 44W
Gariya, *Calc.* 16 F6 22 28N 88 23 E
Garji, *Calc.* 16 C5 22 50N 88 19 E
Garne, *Paris* 5 C1 48 41N 1 58 E
Garrison, *Balt.* 25 A2 39 24N 76 45W
Garstedt, *Hbg.* 7 C7 53 40N 9 59 E
Gartenstadt, *Ruhr* 6 B6 51 30N 7 30 E
Garulia, *Calc.* 16 C6 22 48N 88 22 E
Garvanza, *L.A.* 28 B3 34 6N 118 11 E
Garwood, *N.Y.* 22 D3 40 38N 74 18W
Gary, *Chic.* 26 D4 41 35N 87 23W
Gåshaga, *Stock.* 3 D12 59 21N 18 13 E
Gássino Torinese, *Tori.* 9 B3 45 7N 7 49 E
Gästerby, *Hels.* 3 C1 60 8N 24 27 E
Gateão, Aeroporto de, *Rio J.* 31 A2 22 49 S 43 15W
Gateway of India, *Bomb.* 16 H8 18 55N 72 50 E
Gatow, *Berl.* 7 B1 52 29N 13 11 E
Gaurhati, *Calc.* 16 D6 22 48N 88 21 E
Gauripur, *Calc.* 16 D6 22 53N 88 25 E
Gavá, *Barc.* 8 E4 41 18N 2 0 E
Gavamar, *Barc.* 8 E4 41 16N 1 58 E
Gavanpada, *Bomb.* 16 H9 18 57N 73 0 E
Gávea, *Rio J.* 31 B2 22 58 S 43 13W
Gávea, Pedra da, *Rio J.* 31 B2 22 59 S 43 18W
Gbogbo, *Lagos* 18 A3 6 35N 7 31 E
Gebel el Ahmar, *El Qâ.* 18 C5 30 2N 31 19 E
Gebel el Muqattam, *El Qâ.* 18 C5 30 1N 31 17 E
Gebel et Tura, *El Qâ.* 18 D5 29 56N 31 15 E
Geduld Dam, *Jobg.* 18 F11 26 12 S 28 24 E
Geiselgasteig, *Mün.* 7 G10 48 3N 11 33 E
Geist Res., *Phil.* 24 C1 39 50N 75 24W
Gellért hegy, *Bud.* 10 K13 47 29N 19 3 E
Gelsenkirchen, *Ruhr* 6 A4 51 32N 7 2 E
General Ignacio Allende, *Méx.* 29 B1 19 20N 99 21W
General Pacheco, *B.A.* 32 A3 34 27 S 58 36W
General San Martin, *B.A.* 32 B3 34 35 S 58 32W
General Sarmiento, *B.A.* 32 B2 34 32 S 58 43W
General Urquiza, *B.A.* 32 B4 34 34 S 58 28W
Gennebreck, *Ruhr* 6 C5 51 18N 7 12 E
Gennevilliers, *Paris* 5 B3 48 56N 2 17 E
Gentilly, *Paris* 5 C4 48 48N 2 21 E
Gentofte, *Købn.* 2 D10 55 44N 12 32 E
Georges →, *Syd.* 19 B2 33 56 S 150 55 E
Georges Hall, *Syd.* 19 B2 33 54 S 150 59 E
Georges I., *Bost.* 21 D4 42 19N 70 55W
Georges River Bridge, *Syd.* 19 C3 34 0 S 151 6 E
Georgetown, *Wash.* 25 D7 38 54N 77 3W
Georgetown Rowley State Forest, *Bost.* 21 A4 42 41N 70 56W
Georgswerder, *Hbg.* 7 D8 53 30N 10 1 E
Gerasdorf bei Wein, *Wien* 10 G10 48 17N 16 28 E
Gerberau, *Mün.* 7 F9 48 12N 11 27 E
Gérbido, *Tori.* 9 B2 45 2N 7 36 E
Gerlev, *Købn.* 2 D7 55 49N 12 0 E
Gerli, *B.A.* 32 C4 34 41 S 58 22W
Germantown, *Balt.* 25 A4 39 24N 76 33W
Germantown, *Phil.* 24 A3 40 2N 75 11W
Germiston, *Jobg.* 18 F9 26 13 S 28 10 E
Gerresheim, *Ruhr* 6 C3 51 14N 6 51 E
Gerstdhof, *Wien* 10 G9 48 14N 16 18 E
Gerthe, *Ruhr* 6 A5 51 31N 7 16 E

38 Gesîrat el Rauda


Gesîrat el Rauda, *El Qâ.* 18 C5 30 1N 31 13 E
Gesîrat Muhammad, *El Qâ.* 18 C5 30 6N 31 11 E
Gesterby, *Hels.* 3 A6 60 20N 25 17 E
Getafe, *Mdrd.* 8 C2 40 18N 3 43W
Gevelsberg, *Ruhr* 6 C6 51 19N 7 21 E
Geylang, *Sing.* 15 G8 1 18N 103 53 E
Geylang →, *Sing.* 15 G8 1 18N 103 52 E
Geylang Serai, *Sing.* 15 G8 1 19N 103 53 E
Gezîrat edn Dhahab, *El Qâ.* 18 D5 29 59N 31 13 E
Gezîrat Warrâq el Hadar, *El Qâ.* 18 C5 30 6N 31 13 E
Gharapuri, *Bomb.* 16 H8 18 57N 72 57 E
Ghatkopar, *Bomb.* 16 G8 19 4N 72 54 E
Ghazipur, *Delhi* 16 B2 28 37N 77 19 E
Ghizri, *Kar.* 17 H11 24 49N 67 2 E
Ghizri Cr. →, *Kar.* 17 H11 24 47N 67 5 E
Ghonda, *Delhi* 16 A2 28 41N 77 16 E
Ghushuri, *Calc.* 16 E6 22 37N 88 21 E
Gianicolense, *Rome* 9 F9 51 53N 12 28 E
Giant, *S.F.* 27 A2 37 58N 122 20W
Gibbsboro, *Phil.* 24 B5 39 50N 74 57W
Gibbstown, *Phil.* 24 C3 39 49N 75 17W
Gibraltar Pt., *Trto.* 20 E8 43 36N 79 23W
Gidea Park, *Lon.* 4 B6 51 35N 0 11 E
Giesing, *Mün.* 7 G10 48 6N 11 35 E
Gif-sur-Yvette, *Paris* 5 C2 48 42N 2 8 E
Gilgo Beach, *N.Y.* 23 D8 40 36N 73 24W
Gilgo I., *N.Y.* 23 D8 40 37N 73 23W
Gillette, *N.Y.* 22 C2 40 40N 74 29W
Gimmersta, *Stock.* 3 E12 59 14N 18 14 E
Ginza, *Tōkyō* 13 C3 35 39N 139 46 E
Girgaum, *Bomb.* 16 H8 18 57N 72 50 E
Giugliano in Campània, *Nápl.* 9 H12 40 55N 14 12 E
Givoletto, *Tori.* 9 B1 45 9N 7 29 E
Gjellumvatn, *Oslo* 2 C2 59 47N 10 26 E
Gjersjøen, *Oslo* 2 C4 59 47N 10 47 E
Glacier Hills, *N.Y.* 22 B2 40 51N 74 28W
Gladbeck, *Ruhr* 6 A3 51 34N 6 58 E
Gladesville, *Syd.* 19 B3 33 50 S 151 8 E
Gladökvarn, *Stock.* 3 E10 59 11N 17 59 E
Gladsakse, *Købn.* 2 D9 55 45N 12 25 E
Glashutte, *Hbg.* 7 C8 53 41N 10 2 E
Glashütte, *Ruhr* 6 C3 51 13N 6 51 E
Glasmoor, *Hbg.* 7 C8 53 42N 10 1 E
Glassmanor, *Wash.* 25 E7 38 49N 77 0W
Glen Cove, *N.Y.* 23 B7 40 52N 73 38W
Glen Echo, *Wash.* 25 D7 38 58N 77 8W
Glen Hd., *N.Y.* 23 C7 40 49N 73 37W
Glen Iris, *Melb.* 19 F7 37 51 S 145 3 E
Glen Mills, *Phil.* 24 B2 39 55N 75 29W
Glen Oaks, *N.Y.* 23 C6 40 45N 73 43W
Glen Riddle, *Phil.* 24 B2 39 53N 75 26W
Glen Ridge, *N.Y.* 22 C3 40 48N 74 12W
Glen Rock, *N.Y.* 22 B4 40 57N 74 7W
Glen Waverley, *Melb.* 19 F8 37 52 S 145 10 E
Glenardon, *Wash.* 25 D8 38 56N 76 51W
Glencoe, *Chic.* 26 A2 42 7N 87 44W
Glendale, *L.A.* 28 B3 34 9N 118 15 E
Glendora, *Phil.* 24 B4 39 50N 75 4W
Glenfield, *Syd.* 19 B2 33 58 S 150 53 E
Glenhazel, *Jobg.* 18 E9 26 8 S 28 6 E
Glenhuntly, *Melb.* 19 F7 37 52 S 145 1 E
Glenmont, *Wash.* 25 C7 39 3N 77 4W
Glenolden, *Phil.* 24 B3 39 54N 75 17W
Glenroy, *Melb.* 19 E6 37 42 S 144 55 E
Glenside, *Phil.* 24 A4 40 6N 75 9W
Glenview, *Chic.* 26 A2 42 3N 87 48W
Glenview Countryside, *Chic.* 26 A2 42 3N 87 49W
Glenview Woods, *Chic.* 26 A2 42 4N 87 46W
Glenville, *N.Y.* 23 A6 41 1N 73 41W
Glenvista, *Jobg.* 18 F9 26 17 S 28 3 E
Glenwood Landing, *N.Y.* 23 C7 40 48N 73 38W
Glienicke, *Berl.* 7 A2 52 38N 13 18 E
Glömsta, *Stock.* 3 E10 59 14N 17 55 E
Glosli, *Oslo* 2 A5 60 1N 10 55 E
Glostrup, *Købn.* 2 E9 55 39N 12 23 E
Gloucester City, *Phil.* 24 B4 39 53N 75 7W
Gocheog, *Sŏul* 12 G7 37 30N 126 52 E
Goclawek, *Wsaw.* 10 E7 52 14N 21 7 E
Goeselville, *Chic.* 26 D2 41 37N 87 46W
Goetjensort, *Hbg.* 7 E8 53 29N 10 2 E
Golabari, *Calc.* 16 E6 22 35N 88 20 E
Golabki, *Wsaw.* 10 E6 52 12N 20 52 E
Golden Gate, *S.F.* 27 B2 37 48N 122 29W
Golden Gate Bridge, *S.F.* 27 B2 37 49N 122 28W
Golden Gate National Recreation Area, *S.F.* 27 B1 37 49N 122 31W
Golden Gate Park, *S.F.* 27 B2 37 46N 122 28W
Golden Horn, *Ist.* 17 A2 41 1N 28 57 E
Golders Green, *Lon.* 4 B3 51 34N 0 11W
Golyevo, *Mos.* 11 E7 55 48N 37 18 E
Gometz-la-Ville, *Paris* 5 C2 48 40N 2 7 E
Gometz-le-Châtel, *Paris* 5 C2 48 40N 2 8 E
Gondangdra, *Jak.* 15 J9 6 11 S 106 49 E
Gonesse, *Paris* 5 B4 48 59N 2 26 E
Gongreung, *Sŏul* 12 G8 37 36N 127 3 E
González Catán, *B.A.* 32 C3 34 46 S 58 38W
Goodman Hill, *Bost.* 21 C1 42 22N 71 23W
Goodmayes, *Lon.* 4 B5 51 33N 0 6 E
Gopalnagar, *Calc.* 16 C5 22 50N 88 13 E
Gopalpur, *Calc.* 16 E6 22 38N 88 26 E
Górce, *Wsaw.* 10 E6 52 15N 20 55 E
Gordon, *Syd.* 19 A3 33 46 S 151 8 E
Gore Hill, *Syd.* 19 A4 33 49 S 151 10 E
Gorelyy →, *St-Pet.* 11 A5 60 1N 30 30 E
Gorenki, *Mos.* 11 E11 55 47N 37 53 E
Gorkiy Park, *Mos.* 11 E9 55 43N 37 36 E
Görväln, *Stock.* 3 D9 59 26N 17 45 E
Gose Elbe →, *Hbg.* 7 E8 53 28N 10 6 E
Gosen, *Berl.* 7 B5 52 23N 13 43 E
Gosener kanal, *Berl.* 7 B5 52 24N 13 42 E
Goshenville, *Phil.* 24 B1 39 59N 75 32W
Gospel Oak, *Lon.* 4 B4 51 32N 0 9W
Gotanda, *Tōkyō* 13 C3 35 37N 139 43 E
Gotanno, *Tōkyō* 13 B3 35 45N 139 49 E
Goth Goli Mār, *Kar.* 17 G11 24 53N 67 1 E
Goth Sher Shāh, *Kar.* 17 G10 24 53N 66 59 E
Gournay-sur-Marne, *Paris* 5 B5 48 51N 2 34 E
Goussainville, *Paris* 5 A4 49 1N 2 27 E
Gouvernes, *Paris* 5 B6 48 51N 2 41 E
Governador, I. do, *Rio J.* 31 A2 22 48 S 43 13W
Governor's I., *N.Y.* 22 C4 40 41N 74 1W
Grabicz, *Wsaw.* 10 E8 52 19N 21 12 E
Grabów, *Wsaw.* 10 F6 52 8N 20 59 E
Gracia, *Barc.* 8 D6 41 24N 2 10 E
Gradyville, *Phil.* 24 B2 39 56N 75 27W
Gräfelfing, *Mün.* 7 G9 48 7N 11 25 E
Grafenwald, *Ruhr* 6 A3 51 34N 6 54 E
Graham Memorial Park, *Balt.* 25 A4 39 25N 76 29W
Gran Canal, *Méx.* 29 A3 19 34N 99 1W
Granada Hills, *L.A.* 28 A1 34 16N 118 30W
Grand Bourg, *B.A.* 32 A2 34 29 S 58 42W
Grand Calumet →, *Chic.* 26 D4 41 37N 87 28W
Grand Union Canal, *Lon.* 4 A2 51 42N 0 26W
Grande →, *S. Pau.* 31 F7 23 43 S 46 24W
Grange, *Tori.* 9 B1 45 7N 7 29 E
Grange Hill, *Lon.* 4 B5 51 36N 0 5 E
Granite, *Balt.* 25 A1 39 20N 76 51W
Graniteville, *N.Y.* 22 D3 40 37N 74 10W
Granja Viana, *S. Pau.* 31 E4 23 35 S 46 50W
Granlandet, *Hels.* 3 B6 60 10N 25 15 E
Granö, *Hels.* 3 B6 60 13N 25 14 E
Grant Park, *Chic.* 26 B3 41 52N 87 37W
Granville, *Syd.* 19 A3 33 49 S 151 1 E
Grape I., *Bost.* 21 D4 42 16N 70 55W
Grass Hassock Channel, *N.Y.* 23 D6 40 36N 73 47W
Grassy B., *N.Y.* 23 D6 40 36N 73 47W
Grassy Sprain Res., *N.Y.* 23 B5 40 58N 73 50W
Gratosóglio, *Mil.* 9 E6 45 24N 9 1 E
Gratzwalde, *Berl.* 7 B5 52 28N 13 42 E
Gravesend, *N.Y.* 22 D5 40 36N 73 56W
Grays, *Lon.* 4 C6 51 28N 0 19 E
Grazhdanka, *St-Pet.* 11 B4 59 59N 30 24 E
Great Blue Hill, *Bost.* 21 D3 42 12N 71 4W
Great Bookham, *Lon.* 4 D2 51 16N 0 21W
Great Brewster I., *Bost.* 21 C4 42 19N 70 53W
Great Captain I., *N.Y.* 23 B7 40 59N 73 37W
Great Falls, *Wash.* 25 D6 38 59N 77 17W
Great Falls Park, *Wash.* 25 D6 38 59N 77 14W
Great Kills, *N.Y.* 22 D4 40 32N 74 9W
Great Kills Harbour, *N.Y.* 22 D4 40 32N 74 8W
Great Neck, *N.Y.* 23 C6 40 48N 73 44W
Great Pond, *Bost.* 21 D3 42 11N 71 2W
Great South B., *N.Y.* 23 D9 40 39N 73 19W
Greco, *Mil.* 9 D6 45 30N 9 12 E
Greco I., *S.F.* 27 C3 37 30N 122 10W
Green Brae, *S.F.* 27 A1 37 57N 122 31W
Green Brook, *N.Y.* 22 D2 40 35N 74 26W
Green I., *H.K.* 12 E5 22 17N 114 6 E
Green Land, *Jak.* 15 J9 6 17 S 106 46 E
Green Pond, *N.Y.* 22 A2 41 1N 74 29W
Green Street, *Lon.* 4 A3 51 40N 0 16W
Green Street Green, *Lon.* 4 C5 51 21N 0 5 E
Green Valley, *Syd.* 19 B2 33 54 S 150 53 E
Green Village, *N.Y.* 22 C2 40 44N 74 27W
Greenbelt, *Wash.* 25 C8 39 0N 76 52W
Greenbelt Park, *Wash.* 25 D8 38 58N 76 53W
Greenfield Park, *Mtrl.* 20 B5 43 29N 73 28W
Greenfields Village, *Phil.* 24 C4 39 49N 75 9W
Greenford, *Lon.* 4 B2 51 31N 0 21W
Greenhithe, *Lon.* 4 C6 51 27N 0 17 E
Greenlawn, *N.Y.* 23 B8 40 52N 73 22W
Greenpoint, *N.Y.* 22 C5 40 43N 73 57W
Greensborough, *Melb.* 19 E7 37 41 S 145 5 E
Greenside, *Jobg.* 18 E9 26 8 S 28 1 E
Greenvale, *N.Y.* 23 C7 40 48N 73 35W
Greenville Chauncey, *N.Y.* 23 B5 40 59N 73 50W
Greenwich, *Lon.* 4 C4 51 28N 0 0 E
Greenwich, *N.Y.* 23 A7 41 1N 73 37W
Greenwich, *Syd.* 19 B4 33 50 S 151 11 E
Greenwich Observatory, *Lon.* 4 C4 51 28N 0 0 E
Greenwich Pt., *N.Y.* 23 A7 41 0N 73 34W
Greenwich Village, *N.Y.* 22 C5 40 44N 73 59W
Greenwood, *Bost.* 21 C3 42 29N 71 2W
Grefsen, *Oslo* 2 B4 59 56N 10 47 E
Grégy-sur-Yerres, *Paris* 5 C5 48 40N 2 37 E
Greiffenburg, *Ruhr* 6 B1 51 20N 6 37 E
Gressy, *Paris* 5 B6 48 58N 2 40 E
Greve Strand, *Købn.* 2 E8 55 34N 12 18 E
Greystanes, *Syd.* 19 A2 33 49 S 150 58 E
Griebnitzsee, *Berl.* 7 B1 52 23N 13 8 E
Griffith Park, *L.A.* 28 B3 34 7N 118 18 E
Grignon, *Paris* 5 B1 48 50N 1 56 E
Grigny, *Paris* 5 D4 48 39N 2 23 E
Grinzing, *Wien* 10 G10 48 15N 16 20 E
Grisy-Suisnes, *Paris* 5 C6 48 41N 2 40 E
Gröbenried, *Mün.* 7 F9 48 13N 11 25 E
Grochów, *Wsaw.* 10 E7 52 15N 21 5 E
Grodzisk, *Wsaw.* 10 E7 52 19N 21 4 E
Grogol, *Jak.* 15 H9 6 9 S 106 47 E
Grogol, Kali →, *Jak.* 15 J9 6 11 S 106 47 E
Gronsdorf, *Mün.* 7 G11 48 7N 11 42 E
Grorud, *Oslo* 2 B5 59 57N 10 52 E
Gross Borstel, *Hbg.* 7 D7 53 36N 9 58 E
Gross Flottbek, *Hbg.* 7 D7 53 33N 9 53 E
Gross Glienicke, *Berl.* 7 B1 52 28N 13 6 E
Gross-Hadern, *Mün.* 7 G9 48 6N 11 29 E
Gross-Lappen, *Mün.* 7 F10 48 11N 11 35 E
Grosse Krampe, *Berl.* 7 B5 52 23N 13 40 E
Grosse Müggelsee, *Berl.* 7 B4 52 26N 13 38 E
Grossenbaum, *Ruhr* 6 B2 51 22N 6 46 E
Grossenzersdorf, *Wien* 10 G11 48 12N 16 33 E
Grossenzersdorfer Arm →, *Wien* 10 G11 48 12N 16 31 E
Grosser Biberhaufen, *Wien* 10 G10 48 12N 16 28 E
Grosser Wannsee, *Berl.* 7 B2 52 25N 13 10 E
Grossfeld-Siedlung, *Wien* 10 G10 48 16N 16 26 E
Grosshesselohe, *Mün.* 7 G10 48 4N 11 32 E
Grossjedlersdorf, *Wien* 10 G10 48 16N 16 23 E
Grossziethen, *Berl.* 7 B3 52 23N 13 26 E
Groszówka, *Wsaw.* 10 E8 52 14N 21 13 E
Grove Hall, *Bost.* 21 D3 42 18N 71 4W
Grove Park, *Lon.* 4 C5 51 25N 0 1 E
Grove Park, *Lon.* 4 C3 51 29N 0 15W
Groveton, *Wash.* 25 E7 38 46N 77 6W
Grugliasco, *Tori.* 9 B2 45 4N 7 34 E
Gruiten, *Ruhr* 6 C4 51 12N 7 0 E
Grume, *Ruhr* 6 B5 51 30N 7 15 E
Grumo Nevano, *Nápl.* 9 H12 40 56N 14 15 E
Grünau, *Berl.* 7 B4 52 25N 13 34 E
Grunewald, *Berl.* 7 B2 52 28N 13 15 E
Grünwald, *Mün.* 7 G10 48 2N 11 31 E
Grünwalder Forst, *Mün.* 7 G10 48 2N 11 33 E
Grymes Hill, *N.Y.* 22 D4 40 36N 74 6W
Gu Ro, *Sŏul* 12 G7 37 30N 126 51 E
Guadalupe, *Manila* 15 D4 14 34N 121 2 E
Guadalupe →, *S.F.* 27 D4 37 28N 122 4W
Guadalupe, Basilica de, *Méx.* 29 B3 19 29N 99 7W
Guadelupe, *Rio J.* 31 A1 22 49 S 43 20W
Guanabacoa, *La Hab.* 30 B3 23 7N 82 17W
Guanabara, *Rio J.* 31 B1 22 57 S 43 20W
Guanabara, B. de, *Rio J.* 31 B2 22 52 S 43 10W
Guanabara, Jardim, *Rio J.* 31 A2 22 48 S 43 11W
Guang'anmen, *Beij.* 14 B2 39 51N 116 18 E
Guangminglou, *Beij.* 14 B3 39 51N 116 23 E
Guangqumen, *Beij.* 14 B3 39 52N 116 25 E
Guangzhou, *Gzh.* 14 G8 23 6N 113 13 E
Guanshuo, *Gzh.* 14 G9 23 4N 113 22 E
Guantai, *Nápl.* 9 H12 40 52N 14 11 E
Guapira →, *S. Pau.* 31 D6 23 30 S 46 33W
Guarapiranga, Res. de, *S. Pau.* 31 F5 23 43 S 46 43W
Guardias, *Mdrd.* 8 B3 40 29N 3 31W
Guarulhos, *S. Pau.* 31 D6 23 28 S 46 32W
Guatao, *La Hab.* 30 B2 23 0N 82 29W
Guayacanes, Pta., *La Hab.* 30 A3 23 10N 82 16W
Gubernador Monteverde, *B.A.* 32 C5 34 47 S 58 16W
Gudö, *Stock.* 3 E12 59 12N 18 12 E
Güell, Parque de, *Barc.* 8 D6 41 24N 2 10 E
Guermantes, *Paris* 5 B6 48 51N 2 42 E
Gugging, *Wien* 10 G9 48 18N 16 15 E
Guianazes, *S. Pau.* 31 E7 23 32 S 46 24W
Guildford, *Syd.* 19 B2 33 51 S 150 59 E
Guinardó, *Barc.* 8 D6 41 24N 2 10 E
Gujiazhai, *Shang.* 14 H11 31 21N 121 23 E
Gulbāi, *Kar.* 17 G10 24 52N 66 58 E
Guldasteh, *Tehr.* 17 D4 35 36N 51 15 E
Gulistan Palace, *Tehr.* 17 C5 35 40N 51 24 E
Gulph Mills, *Phil.* 24 A2 40 4N 75 20W
Gumbostrand, *Hels.* 3 B6 60 15N 25 17 E
Güngören, *Ist.* 17 A2 41 1N 28 52 E
Gunnarsby, *Hels.* 3 C1 60 6N 24 28W
Gunnersbury, *Lon.* 4 C3 51 29N 0 17W
Gunnigfeld, *Ruhr* 6 B4 51 29N 7 8 E
Gunpowder Falls →, *Balt.* 25 A4 39 23N 76 36W
Gunung Sahari, *Jak.* 15 H9 6 9 S 106 49 E
Gupiing, *Manila* 15 E5 14 27N 121 12 E
Guryong San, *Sŏul* 12 H8 37 28N 127 3 E
Gustavsberg, *Stock.* 3 E13 59 19N 18 23 E
Guttenberg, *N.Y.* 22 C4 40 48N 74 0W
Gutuyevskiy, Os., *St-Pet.* 11 B3 59 53N 30 15 E
Guyancourt, *Paris* 5 C2 48 46N 2 4 E
Guyancourt, Aérodrome de, *Paris* 5 C2 48 45N 2 3 E
Gvali-patak →, *Bud.* 10 K13 47 23N 19 7 E
Gwan Ag, *Sŏul* 12 H7 37 29N 126 57 E
Gwanag San, *Sŏul* 12 H7 37 27N 126 58 E
Gwynns Falls →, *Balt.* 25 B2 39 19N 76 42W
Gyál, *Bud.* 10 K14 47 23N 19 13 E
Gyeongbong Palace, *Sŏul* 12 G7 37 34N 126 58 E
Gynea, *Syd.* 19 C3 34 1 S 151 5 E


# H


Haaga, *Hels.* 3 B4 60 13N 24 53 E
Haan, *Ruhr* 6 C3 51 11N 6 59 E
Haar, *Mün.* 7 G11 48 6N 11 43 E
Haar, *Ruhr* 6 B5 51 26N 7 13 E
Haarzopf, *Ruhr* 6 B3 51 25N 6 57 E
Habana del Este, *La Hab.* 30 B3 23 9N 82 19W
Habay, *Manila* 15 E3 14 27N 120 56 E
Habikino, *Ōsaka* 12 C4 34 33N 135 36 E
Habinghorst, *Ruhr* 6 A5 51 34N 7 18 E
Hacienda Heights, *L.A.* 28 C5 33 59N 117 59W
Hackbridge, *Lon.* 4 C4 51 23N 0 9W
Hackensack, *N.Y.* 22 B4 40 52N 74 4W
Hackney, *Lon.* 4 B4 51 32N 0 3W
Hackney Wick, *Lon.* 4 B4 51 32N 0 1W
Haddon Heights, *Phil.* 24 B4 39 53N 75 3W
Haddonfield, *Phil.* 24 B4 39 53N 75 3W
Hadersdorf, *Wien* 10 G9 48 12N 16 14 E
Hadley Wood, *Lon.* 4 B3 51 39N 0 10W
Haga, *Stock.* 3 D11 59 21N 18 1 E
Hagem, *Ruhr* 6 A5 51 38N 7 19 E
Hagen, *Ruhr* 6 B6 51 21N 7 27 E
Hägersten, *Stock.* 3 E10 59 18N 17 59 E
Haggetts Pond, *Bost.* 21 B2 42 39N 71 11W
Häggvik, *Stock.* 3 D10 59 26N 17 56 E
Hagonoy, *Manila* 15 D4 14 30N 121 4 E
Hagsätra, *Stock.* 3 E11 59 15N 18 0 E
Hahipur, *Calc.* 16 D5 22 47N 88 10 E
Hahnerberg, *Ruhr* 6 C4 51 12N 7 9 E
Hai He →, *Tianj.* 14 E6 39 4N 117 17 E
Haidarpur, *Delhi* 16 A1 28 43N 77 8 E
Haidhausen, *Mün.* 7 G10 48 7N 11 36 E
Haidian, *Beij.* 14 B2 39 59N 116 16 E
Haight-Ashbury, *S.F.* 27 B2 37 46N 122 26W
Haiguangsi, *Tianj.* 14 E6 39 7N 117 11 E
Hainault, *Lon.* 4 B5 51 36N 0 6 E
Haizhu Guangchang, *Gzh.* 14 G8 23 6N 113 16 E
Hakim, *El Qâ.* 18 C4 30 4N 31 7 E
Hakunila, *Hels.* 3 B5 60 16N 25 6 E
Halchōbori, *Tōkyō* 13 B4 35 48N 139 55 E
Haledon, *N.Y.* 22 B3 40 57N 74 11W
Halesite, *N.Y.* 23 B8 40 53N 73 24W
Halethorpe, *Balt.* 25 B2 39 14N 76 41W
Half Hollow Hills, *N.Y.* 23 C8 40 48N 73 21W
Half Moon B., *S.F.* 26 D2 37 27N 122 25W
Half Moon Bay Airport, *S.F.* 27 C1 37 31N 122 30W
Half Moon Bay Beaches, *S.F.* 26 D2 37 28N 122 26W
Halim, *Jak.* 15 J10 6 15 S 106 53 E
Halim Perdanakusuma Airport, *Jak.* 15 J10 6 16 S 106 53 E
Halstead, *Lon.* 4 D5 51 19N 0 8 E
Halstenbeck, *Hbg.* 7 D7 53 38N 9 50 E
Haltiala, *Hels.* 3 B4 60 16N 24 57 E
Haltiavuori, *Hels.* 3 B4 60 16N 24 56 E
Ham, *Lon.* 4 C3 51 25N 0 18W
Ham, *Paris* 5 A2 49 1N 2 3 E
Hamberg, *Jobg.* 18 E8 26 9 S 27 54 E
Hamborn, *Ruhr* 6 B2 51 29N 6 46 E
Hamburg, *Hbg.* 7 D8 53 33N 10 0 E
Hamburg Flughafen, *Hbg.* 7 D7 53 38N 9 59 E
Hämeenkylä, *Hels.* 3 B3 60 16N 24 48 E
Hamm, *Hbg.* 7 D8 53 33N 10 3 E
Hamm, *Ruhr* 6 C2 51 12N 6 44 E
Hammarby, *Stock.* 3 E11 59 17N 18 5 E
Hamme, *Ruhr* 6 B5 51 29N 7 12 E
Hammel Arverne, *N.Y.* 23 D6 40 35N 73 48W
Hammerbrook, *Hbg.* 7 D8 53 32N 10 1 E
Hammersmith, *Lon.* 4 C3 51 29N 0 14W
Hammond, *Chic.* 26 D4 41 36N 87 29W
Hampstead, *Lon.* 4 B3 51 33N 0 10W
Hampstead, *Mtrl.* 20 B4 43 28N 73 37W
Hampstead Garden Suburb, *Lon.* 4 B3 51 34N 0 11W
Hampstead Heath, *Lon.* 4 B3 51 33N 0 10W
Hampton Court Palace, *Lon.* 4 C2 51 24N 0 20W
Hampton Hill, *Lon.* 4 C2 51 25N 0 21W
Hampton Wick, *Lon.* 4 C3 51 24N 0 18W
Hamrā, *Bagd.* 17 F7 33 18N 44 18 E
Han Gang →, *Sŏul* 12 G7 37 32N 126 55 E
Hanakuri, *Tōkyō* 13 A3 35 50N 139 47 E
Hanala, *Hels.* 3 A5 60 20N 25 4 E
Hancho, *Ōsaka* 12 B3 34 48N 135 28 E
Haneda, *Tōkyō* 13 C3 35 32N 139 44 E
Hang Hau, *H.K.* 12 E6 22 19N 114 16 E
Hanjiashu, *Tianj.* 14 D5 39 11N 117 4 E
Hanlon, *Trto.* 20 E7 43 38N 79 39W
Hansen Flood Control Basin, *L.A.* 28 A2 34 15N 118 23W
Hansha, *Calc.* 16 D6 22 48N 88 24 E
Hanskinen, *Hels.* 3 C6 60 8N 25 16 E
Hanwell, *Lon.* 4 B2 51 30N 0 20W
Hanworth, *Lon.* 4 C2 51 26N 0 23W
Haora, *Calc.* 16 E5 22 34N 88 18 E
Happy Valley, *H.K.* 12 E6 22 16N 114 10 E
Harajuku, *Tōkyō* 13 D2 35 22N 139 20 E
Haraki, *Tōkyō* 13 B4 35 42N 139 56 E
Harat, *Calc.* 16 C5 22 52N 88 11 E
Harbor Hills, *N.Y.* 23 C6 40 46N 73 44W
Harburg, *Hbg.* 7 E7 53 27N 9 59 E
Harding, *Bost.* 21 D2 42 12N 71 19W
Hardricourt, *Paris* 5 A1 49 0N 1 53 E
Harefield, *Lon.* 4 B2 51 36N 0 28W
Hareskovby, *Købn.* 2 D9 55 45N 12 23 E
Harewood Park, *Balt.* 25 A4 39 22N 76 21W
Harigaya, *Tōkyō* 13 B2 35 49N 139 33 E
Haringey, *Lon.* 4 B4 51 34N 0 4W
Haripur, *Calc.* 16 D5 22 42N 88 10 E
Harjula, *Hels.* 3 A3 60 21N 24 45 E
Harjusuo, *Hels.* 3 B5 60 19N 25 0 E
Harkortsee, *Ruhr* 6 B6 51 23N 7 24 E
Harksheide, *Hbg.* 7 C8 53 43N 10 0 E
Harlaching, *Mün.* 7 G10 48 5N 11 33 E
Harlem, *N.Y.* 22 C5 40 48N 73 56W
Harlesden, *Lon.* 4 B3 51 32N 0 14W
Harlington, *Lon.* 4 C2 51 29N 0 25W
Harmaja, *Hels.* 3 C4 60 6N 24 58 E
Harmashatar hegy, *Bud.* 10 J13 47 33N 19 0 E
Harmondsworth, *Lon.* 4 C2 51 29N 0 29W
Harmonville, *Phil.* 24 A3 40 5N 75 18W
Harold Hill, *Lon.* 4 B6 51 36N 0 14 E
Harold Parker State Forest, *Bost.* 21 B3 42 37N 71 4W
Harold Wood, *Lon.* 4 B6 51 35N 0 14 E
Harrington Park, *N.Y.* 22 B5 40 59N 73 59W
Harrison, *N.Y.* 22 C4 40 44N 74 9W
Harrison, *N.Y.* 23 B6 40 57N 73 42W
Harrisonville, *Balt.* 25 A2 39 22N 76 49W
Harrow, *Lon.* 4 B2 51 34N 0 20W
Harrow on the Hill, *Lon.* 4 B2 51 34N 0 21W
Harrow School, *Lon.* 4 B2 51 34N 0 20W
Harrow Weald, *Lon.* 4 B2 51 36N 0 20W
Hart I., *Balt.* 25 B4 39 14N 76 23W
Hart I., *N.Y.* 23 B6 40 51N 73 46W
Hartford, *Phil.* 24 B5 39 58N 74 53W
Hartley, *Lon.* 4 C6 51 22N 0 18 E
Hartsdale, *N.Y.* 23 A6 41 1N 73 48W
Harumi, *Tōkyō* 13 C3 35 38N 139 47 E
Harvard, Mt., *L.A.* 28 A4 34 12N 118 4W
Harvard Univ., *Bost.* 21 C3 42 23N 71 7W
Harvestehude, *Hbg.* 7 D7 53 34N 9 58 E
Harvey, *Chic.* 26 D3 41 36N 87 39W
Harwood Heights, *Chic.* 26 B2 41 57N 87 46W
Hasanābād, *Tehr.* 17 C4 35 44N 51 16 E
Hasbrouck Heights, *N.Y.* 22 B4 40 51N 74 6W
Haselbach, *Wien* 10 G9 48 18N 16 14 E
Haselhorst, *Berl.* 7 A2 52 33N 13 14 E
Hasköy, *Ist.* 17 A2 41 2N 28 57 E
Hasle, *Oslo* 2 C3 59 46N 10 38 E
Hasloh, *Hbg.* 7 C7 53 41N 9 54 E
Haslohfeld, *Hbg.* 7 C7 53 41N 9 56 E
Haslum, *Oslo* 2 B3 59 55N 10 34 E
Haspe, *Ruhr* 6 B6 51 21N 7 25 E
Haspertalsp, *Ruhr* 6 C6 51 17N 7 24 E
Hasselbeck, *Ruhr* 6 C3 51 19N 6 56 E
Hässelby, *Stock.* 3 D10 59 22N 17 50 E
Hasslinghausen, *Ruhr* 6 C5 51 20N 7 16 E
Hasten, *Ruhr* 6 C5 51 11N 7 11 E
Hästhagen, *Stock.* 3 E11 59 18N 18 9 E
Hastings-on-Hudson, *N.Y.* 23 B5 40 59N 73 51W
Hatch End, *Lon.* 4 B2 51 36N 0 22W
Hatiara, *Calc.* 16 E6 22 36N 88 26 E
Hatogaya, *Tōkyō* 13 B3 35 49N 139 44 E
Hattingen, *Ruhr* 6 B5 51 23N 7 11 E
Hatton, *Lon.* 4 C2 51 28N 0 25W
Hattori, *Ōsaka* 12 A4 34 51N 135 36 E
Hauketo, *Oslo* 2 B4 59 50N 10 48 E
Hauldres →, *Paris* 5 D5 48 37N 2 37 E
Hausbruch, *Hbg.* 7 E7 53 28N 9 53 E
Havalimani, *Ist.* 17 B2 40 59N 28 50 E
Havana = La Habana, *La Hab.* 30 B2 23 7N 82 21W
Havdrup, *Købn.* 2 E7 55 33N 12 7 E
Havel →, *Berl.* 7 A2 52 37N 13 11 E
Havelkanal, *Berl.* 7 A2 52 36N 13 10 E
Haverford, *Phil.* 24 A3 40 0N 75 18W
Havering, *Lon.* 4 B6 51 33N 0 13 E
Havering-atte-Bower, *Lon.* 4 B6 51 37N 0 11 E
Havertown, *Phil.* 24 B3 39 58N 75 18W
Hawangsibri, *Sŏul* 12 G8 37 33N 127 1 E
Haweolgog, *Sŏul* 12 G8 37 35N 127 1 E
Haworth, *N.Y.* 22 B5 40 57N 73 59W
Hawthorne, *L.A.* 28 C2 33 54N 118 21W
Hawthorne, *N.Y.* 22 B4 40 57N 74 8W
Hayes, *Lon.* 4 C5 51 22N 0 0 E
Hayes, *Lon.* 4 B2 51 31N 0 25W
Hayes End, *Lon.* 4 B2 51 31N 0 26W
Hayford, *Chic.* 26 C2 41 45N 87 42W
Hayward, *S.F.* 27 B4 37 40N 122 4W
Hayward Fault, *S.F.* 27 B3 37 46N 122 10W
Haywood Municipal Airport, *S.F.* 27 C4 32 39N 122 9W
Headley, *Lon.* 4 D3 51 16N 0 16W
Headstone, *Lon.* 4 B2 51 35N 0 21W
Heard Pond, *Bost.* 21 C1 42 20N 71 23W
Heart Pond, *Bost.* 21 B1 42 33N 71 23W
Heath Park, *Lon.* 4 B6 51 34N 0 12 E
Heathmont, *Melb.* 19 E8 37 49 S 145 14 E
Heathrow Airport, *Lon.* 4 C2 51 28N 0 27W
Hebbville, *Balt.* 25 A2 39 20N 76 45W
Hebe Haven, *H.K.* 12 D6 22 21N 114 15 E
Hebei, *Tianj.* 14 E6 39 9N 117 11 E
Hedehusene, *Købn.* 2 E8 55 39N 12 11 E
Hedong, *Gzh.* 14 G8 23 5N 113 14 E
Hedong, *Tianj.* 14 E6 39 7N 117 11 E
Heerdt, *Ruhr* 6 C2 51 13N 6 42 E
Hegewisch, *Chic.* 26 D3 41 39N 87 32W
Heggelielva →, *Oslo* 2 A3 60 1N 10 36 E
Heidelberg, *Melb.* 19 E7 37 45 S 145 4 E
Heidelberg West, *Melb.* 19 E7 37 43 S 145 2 E
Heidemühle, *Berl.* 7 B5 52 29N 13 40 E
Heidhausen, *Ruhr* 6 B4 51 22N 7 1 E
Heiligenhaus, *Ruhr* 6 C3 51 19N 6 57 E
Heiligensee, *Berl.* 7 A2 52 36N 13 13 E
Heiligenstadt, *Wien* 10 G10 48 14N 16 21 E
Heimfeld, *Hbg.* 7 E7 53 28N 9 57 E
Heinäsuo, *Hels.* 3 B1 60 18N 24 27 E
Heinersdorf, *Berl.* 7 A3 52 34N 13 26 E
Heisingen, *Ruhr* 6 B4 51 24N 7 3 E
Heissen, *Ruhr* 6 B3 51 26N 6 54 E
Helderkruin, *Jobg.* 18 E8 26 7 S 27 51 E
Helenelund, *Stock.* 3 D10 59 24N 17 58 E
Heliopolis, *El Qâ.* 18 C5 30 5N 31 19 E
Hellersdorf, *Berl.* 7 A4 52 32N 13 35 E
Hellerup, *Købn.* 2 D10 55 44N 12 33 E
Helmahof, *Wien* 10 G11 48 18N 16 34 E
Helsingfors = Helsinki, *Hels.* 3 B4 60 10N 24 55 E
Helsinki, *Hels.* 3 B4 60 10N 24 55 E
Helsinki Airport, *Hels.* 3 B4 60 10N 24 58 E
Hempstead, *N.Y.* 23 C7 40 42N 73 37W
Hempstead Harbor, *N.Y.* 23 B7 40 50N 73 39W
Henan, *Gzh.* 14 G8 23 5N 113 15 E
Hendon, *Lon.* 4 B3 51 35N 0 14W
Hengsha, *Gzh.* 14 G8 23 9N 113 12 E
Hengsteysee, *Ruhr* 6 B6 51 24N 7 27 E
Hennigsdorf, *Berl.* 7 A2 52 38N 13 12 E
Henrichenburg, *Ruhr* 6 A5 51 35N 7 19 E
Henriville, *Paris* 5 C1 48 44N 1 56 E
Henrykow, *Wsaw.* 10 E6 52 19N 20 58 E
Henson Cr. →, *Wash.* 25 E8 38 47N 76 58W
Henttaa, *Hels.* 3 B3 60 11N 24 45 E
Heping, *Tianj.* 14 E6 39 7N 117 11 E
Heping Gongyuan, *Shang.* 14 J12 31 16N 121 30 E
Hepingli, *Beij.* 14 B3 39 57N 116 23 E
Herbeck, *Ruhr* 6 C5 51 12N 7 18 E
Herbede, *Ruhr* 6 B5 51 25N 7 16 E
Herblay, *Paris* 5 B2 48 59N 2 9 E
Herdecke, *Ruhr* 6 B6 51 24N 7 25 E
Herlev, *Købn.* 2 D9 55 43N 12 27 E
Hermannskogel, *Wien* 10 G9 48 16N 16 17 E
Hermitage and Winter Palace, *St-Pet.* 11 B3 59 55N 30 19 E
Hermosa Beach, *L.A.* 28 C2 33 51N 118 23W
Hermsdorf, *Berl.* 7 A2 52 37N 13 18 E
Hernals, *Wien* 10 G10 48 13N 16 20 E
Herne, *Ruhr* 6 A5 51 32N 7 13 E
Herne Hill, *Lon.* 4 C4 51 27N 0 6W
Hernwood Heights, *Balt.* 25 A2 39 22N 76 49W
Héroes de Churubusco, *Méx.* 29 B3 19 21N 99 6W
Herongate, *Lon.* 4 B7 51 35N 0 21 E
Herons, Î. aux, *Mtrl.* 20 B4 43 25N 73 34W
Herricks, *N.Y.* 23 C7 40 45N 73 39W
Herring Run →, *Balt.* 25 B3 39 18N 76 30W
Hersham, *Lon.* 4 C2 51 21N 0 22W
Herstedøster, *Købn.* 2 D9 55 40N 12 22 E
Herten, *Ruhr* 6 A4 51 35N 7 8 E
Herttoniemi, *Hels.* 3 B5 60 12N 25 2 E
Hessler, *Ruhr* 6 A4 51 31N 7 3 E
Heston, *Lon.* 4 C2 51 28N 0 22W
Hetterscheidt, *Ruhr* 6 B3 51 20N 6 56 E
Hetzendorf, *Wien* 10 H9 48 9N 16 17 E
Heuberg, *Wien* 10 G9 48 13N 16 16 E
Heven, *Ruhr* 6 B5 51 26N 7 18 E
Hewlett Neck, *N.Y.* 23 D6 40 37N 73 41W
Hexi, *Tianj.* 14 E5 39 8N 117 9 E
Hexingcun, *Tianj.* 14 E6 39 6N 117 10 E
Hextable, *Lon.* 4 C6 51 24N 0 10 E
Heybridge, *Lon.* 4 B7 51 39N 0 22 E
Hibernia, *N.Y.* 22 B2 40 57N 74 29W
Hickory Hills, *Chic.* 26 C2 41 43N 87 49W
Hicksville, *N.Y.* 23 C7 40 46N 73 30W
Hiddinghausen, *Ruhr* 6 B5 51 21N 7 17 E
Hiekkaharju, *Hels.* 3 B5 60 18N 25 2 E
Hiesfeld, *Ruhr* 6 A2 51 33N 6 46 E
Hietaniemi, *Hels.* 3 B4 60 10N 24 54 E
Hietzing, *Wien* 10 G9 48 10N 16 17 E
Higashi, *Ōsaka* 12 B4 34 41N 135 30 E
Higashi-kaizuka, *Tōkyō* 13 A3 35 50N 139 46 E
Higashimonzen, *Tōkyō* 13 A3 35 55N 139 40 E
Higashimurayama, *Tōkyō* 13 B1 35 45N 139 26 E
Higashinada, *Ōsaka* 12 B2 34 42N 135 15 E
Higashinari, *Ōsaka* 12 B4 34 40N 135 32 E
Higashiōsaka, *Ōsaka* 12 C4 34 39N 135 37 E
Higashisumiyoshi, *Ōsaka* 12 C4 34 37N 135 31 E
Higashiyodogawa, *Ōsaka* 12 B3 34 44N 135 28 E
High Beach, *Lon.* 4 B5 51 39N 0 1 E
High Junk Pk., *H.K.* 12 E6 22 17N 114 17 E
High Park, *Trto.* 20 E8 43 38N 79 27W
Higham Hill, *Lon.* 4 B4 51 35N 0 2W
Highbury, *Lon.* 4 B4 51 33N 0 6W
Highgate, *Lon.* 4 B4 51 34N 0 8W
Highland Cr. →, *Trto.* 20 D9 43 45N 79 13W
Highland Creek, *Trto.* 20 D9 43 46N 79 8W
Highland Park, *L.A.* 28 B3 34 7N 118 13 E
Highland Park, *N.Y.* 22 D2 40 30N 74 25W
Highlands North, *Jobg.* 18 E9 26 8 S 28 5 E
Highway Highlands, *L.A.* 28 A3 34 14N 118 16W
Higurashi, *Tōkyō* 13 A2 35 47N 139 55 E
Hila, *Méx.* 29 A2 19 35N 99 17W
Hillcrest Heights, *Wash.* 25 E8 38 49N 76 57W
Hillerheide, *Ruhr* 6 A5 51 35N 7 12 E
Hilleshög, *Stock.* 3 D9 59 23N 17 42 E
Hillgrove District, *L.A.* 28 B5 34 1N 117 58W
Hillingdon, *Lon.* 4 B2 51 32N 0 27W
Hillingdon Heath, *Lon.* 4 B2 51 31N 0 26W
Hillsborough, *S.F.* 27 C2 37 32N 122 21W
Hillsdale, *N.Y.* 22 A4 41 0N 74 1W
Hillsdale, *S.F.* 27 C3 37 32N 122 18W
Hillsdale Manor, *N.Y.* 22 A4 41 1N 74 3W
Hillside, *Chic.* 26 B1 41 52N 87 55W
Hillside, *N.Y.* 23 C5 40 42N 73 46W
Hillside Manor, *N.Y.* 23 C6 40 44N 73 40W
Hilltop, *Phil.* 24 C4 39 49N 75 4W
Hillwood, *Wash.* 25 D7 38 52N 77 9W
Hilmīya, *El Qâ.* 18 C5 30 6N 31 19 E
Hiltrop, *Ruhr* 6 A5 51 31N 7 15 E
Hindsby, *Hels.* 3 A6 60 20N 25 13 E
Hingham, *Bost.* 21 D4 42 14N 70 54W
Hingham B., *Bost.* 21 D4 42 17N 70 56W
Hingham Harbor, *Bost.* 21 D4 42 15N 70 53W
Hino, *Tōkyō* 13 D2 35 23N 139 35 E
Hinsbeck, *Ruhr* 6 B4 51 22N 7 4 E
Hinschenfelde, *Hbg.* 7 D8 53 35N 10 0 E
Hinsdale, *Chic.* 26 C1 41 47N 87 55W
Hinterhainbach, *Wien* 10 G9 48 14N 16 13 E
Hintersdorf, *Wien* 10 G9 48 18N 16 13 E
Hirakata, *Ōsaka* 12 B4 34 48N 135 38 E
Hirota, *Ōsaka* 12 B2 34 44N 135 20 E
Hirschstetten, *Wien* 10 G10 48 14N 16 27 E
Hither Green, *Lon.* 4 C4 51 26N 0 0 E
Hiyoshi, *Tōkyō* 13 C2 35 32N 139 38 E
Hjortekær, *Købn.* 2 D10 55 47N 12 32 E
Hjortespring, *Købn.* 2 D9 55 44N 12 25 E
Hlubočepy, *Pra.* 10 B2 50 2N 14 23 E
Ho Chung, *H.K.* 12 D6 22 21N 114 14 E
Ho Man Tin, *H.K.* 12 E6 22 19N 114 11 E
Hoboken, *N.Y.* 22 C4 40 44N 74 3W
Hobsons B., *Melb.* 19 F6 37 51 S 144 55 E
Hochbrück, *Mün.* 7 F10 48 14N 11 37 E
Hochdahl, *Ruhr* 6 C3 51 13N 6 55 E
Hochemmerich, *Ruhr* 6 B2 51 24N 6 42 E
Hochfeld, *Ruhr* 6 B2 51 25N 6 45 E
Hochheide, *Ruhr* 6 B2 51 27N 6 40 E
Hochlar, *Ruhr* 6 A5 51 36N 7 11 E
Hochlarmark, *Ruhr* 6 A5 51 34N 7 11 E
Hodgkins, *Chic.* 26 C1 41 46N 87 53W
Hodogaya-Ku, *Tōkyō* 13 D2 35 26N 139 35 E
Hoegi, *Sŏul* 12 G8 37 35N 127 3 E
Hofberg, *Wien* 10 G10 48 12N 16 21 E
Hoffman I., *N.Y.* 22 D4 40 34N 74 3W
Hofstede, *Ruhr* 6 A5 51 30N 7 11 E
Höggarnsfjärden, *Stock.* 3 D13 59 22N 18 22 E
Hohe Mark, Naturpark, *Ruhr* 6 A2 51 35N 6 49 E
Hohe Schaar, *Hbg.* 7 E7 53 29N 9 58 E
Hohenbrunn, *Mün.* 7 G11 48 2N 11 42 E
Hohenfelde, *Hbg.* 7 D8 53 33N 10 1 E
Höhenkirchen, *Mün.* 7 G11 48 1N 11 42 E
Hohenraden, *Hbg.* 7 C6 53 41N 9 49 E
Hohenschönhausen, *Berl.* 7 A4 52 33N 13 30 E
Hohenwisch, *Hbg.* 7 E7 53 29N 9 53 E

Kennedy Grove Regional Rec. Area 39

Hohokus, *N.Y.* 22 **A4** 41 0N 74 5W
Hok Tsui, *H.K.* 12 **E6** 22 12N 114 15 E
Holborn, *Lon.* 4 **B4** 51 31N 0 7W
Holečovice, *Pra.* 10 **B2** 50 6N 14 28 E
Holland Village, *Sing.* 15 **G7** 1 18N 103 47 E
Hollis, *N.Y.* 23 **C6** 40 42N 73 45W
Höllriegelskreuth, *Mün.* 7 **G9** 48 2N 11 30 E
Holly Oak, *Phil.* 24 **C2** 39 47N 75 27W
Hollydale, *L.A.* 28 **C4** 33 55N 118 10W
Hollywood Bowl, *L.A.* 28 **B2** 34 6N 118 21W
Hollywood-Burbank Airport, *L.A.* 28 **A2** 34 11N 118 21W
Holmenkollen, *Oslo* 2 **B4** 59 57N 10 41 E
Holmes, *Phil.* 24 **B3** 39 53N 75 18W
Holmes Acres, *Wash.* 25 **D6** 38 51N 77 13W
Holmes Run →, *Wash.* 25 **E7** 38 48N 77 6W
Holmesburg, *Phil.* 24 **A4** 40 2N 75 2W
Holmgård, *Stock.* 3 **E10** 59 14N 18 0 E
Holsfjorden, *Oslo* 2 **B1** 59 58N 10 17 E
Holsterhausen, *Ruhr* 6 **A5** 51 32N 7 11 E
Holte, *Købn.* 2 **D9** 55 48N 12 27 E
Holten, *Ruhr* 6 **A2** 51 31N 6 47 E
Holthausen, *Ruhr* 6 **B4** 51 25N 7 5 E
Holzbüttgen, *Ruhr* 6 **C1** 51 13N 6 37 E
Homberg, *Ruhr* 6 **B2** 51 27N 6 41 E
Hombruch, *Ruhr* 6 **B6** 51 28N 7 27 E
Homerton, *Lon.* 4 **B4** 51 32N 0 2W
Homestead Lake, *Jobg.* 18 **F10** 26 10 S 28 17 E
Homestead Valley, *S.F.* 27 **A1** 37 53N 122 32W
Hometown, *Chic.* 26 **C2** 41 44N 87 42W
Homledal, *Oslo* 2 **B1** 59 59N 10 18 E
Homówek, *Wsaw.* 10 **E5** 52 17N 20 48 E
Hon-gyōtoku, *Tōkyō* 13 **B4** 35 41N 139 57 E
Hōnanchō, *Tōkyō* 13 **B2** 35 40N 139 39 E
Honcho, *Tōkyō* 13 **B3** 35 40N 139 41 E
Honden, *Tōkyō* 13 **B4** 35 43N 139 50 E
Honeydew, *Jobg.* 18 **E8** 26 4 S 27 55 E
Hong Kah, *Sing.* 15 **F7** 1 21N 103 43 E
Hong Kong, *H.K.* 12 **E5** 22 17N 114 11 E
Hong Kong, Univ. of, *H.K.* 12 **E5** 22 16N 114 8 E
Hong Kong Airport, *H.K.* 12 **E6** 22 19N 114 11 E
Hong Kong I., *H.K.* 12 **E6** 22 16N 114 11 E
Hong Lim Park, *Sing.* 15 **G8** 1 17N 103 50 E
Hongeun, *Sŏul* 12 **G7** 37 35N 126 56 E
Honggiao, *Shang.* 14 **J11** 31 12N 121 22 E
Honggou, *Shang.* 14 **J11** 31 16N 121 29 E
Hongkou Gongyuan, *Shang.* 14 **J11** 31 17N 121 28 E
Hongmiao, *Beij.* 14 **B3** 39 54N 116 26 E
Hongqiao, *Tianj.* 14 **E5** 39 8N 117 9 E
Hongqiao Airport, *Shang.* 14 **J10** 31 12N 121 19 E
Honjyo, *Tōkyō* 13 **B3** 35 41N 139 48 E
Honmoku, *Tōkyō* 13 **D2** 35 24N 139 39 E
Hönow, *Berl.* 7 **A4** 52 32N 13 38 E
Höntrop, *Ruhr* 6 **B4** 51 27N 7 9 E
Hood Pond, *Bost.* 21 **A4** 42 40N 70 57W
Hooghly →, *Calc.* 16 **D6** 22 41N 88 21 E
Hook, *Lon.* 4 **C3** 51 22N 0 17W
Hopelawn, *N.Y.* 22 **D3** 40 31N 74 17W
Hörde, *Ruhr* 6 **B7** 51 29N 7 30 E
Horikiri, *Tōkyō* 13 **B4** 35 44N 139 50 E
Horn, *Hbg.* 7 **D8** 53 33N 10 5 E
Horn Pond, *Bost.* 21 **C2** 42 28N 71 9W
Hornchurch, *Lon.* 4 **B6** 51 33N 0 14 E
Horneburg, *Ruhr* 6 **A5** 51 37N 7 17 E
Horni, *Pra.* 10 **B3** 50 2N 14 33 E
Horni Počernice, *Pra.* 10 **B3** 50 6N 14 36 E
Hornsey, *Lon.* 4 **B4** 51 35N 0 7W
Horoměřice, *Pra.* 10 **B1** 50 8N 14 20 E
Horsley Park, *Syd.* 19 **B2** 33 50 S 150 51 E
Horst, *Ruhr* 6 **B4** 51 26N 7 6 E
Horsthausen, *Ruhr* 6 **A5** 51 33N 7 12 E
Hortaleza, *Mdrd.* 8 **B3** 40 28N 3 38W
Horto Florestal, *S. Pau.* 31 **D6** 23 27 S 46 38W
Horton Kirby, *Lon.* 4 **C6** 51 23N 0 14 E
Hösel, *Ruhr* 6 **B3** 51 20N 6 53 E
Hosoyama, *Tōkyō* 13 **C2** 35 36N 139 31 E
Hospitalet, *Barc.* 8 **D5** 41 21N 2 6 E
Hostafranchs, *Barc.* 8 **D5** 41 21N 2 8 E
Hoterheide, *Ruhr* 6 **C1** 51 16N 6 37 E
Houbetin, *Pra.* 10 **B3** 50 6N 14 33 E
Houghs Neck, *Bost.* 21 **D4** 42 15N 70 57W
Houghton, *Jobg.* 18 **F9** 26 10 S 28 3 E
Houilles, *Paris* 5 **B3** 48 56N 2 11 E
Hounslow, *Lon.* 4 **C2** 51 28N 0 21W
Houses of Parliament, *Lon.* 4 **C4** 51 29N 0 7W
Hove Å →, *Købn.* 2 **D8** 55 43N 12 7 E
Hovedøya, *Oslo* 2 **B4** 59 53N 10 43 E
Høvik, *Oslo* 2 **B3** 59 54N 10 34 E
Hovorčovice, *Pra.* 10 **A3** 50 10N 14 31 E
Howard Beach, *N.Y.* 23 **D5** 40 39N 73 50W
Hoxton Park, *Syd.* 19 **B2** 33 55 S 150 51 E
Hoxton Park Aerodrome, *Syd.* 19 **B2** 33 54 S 150 50 E
Hōya, *Tōkyō* 13 **B2** 35 44N 139 34 E
Høybråten, *Oslo* 2 **B5** 59 56N 10 55 E
Hradčany, *Pra.* 10 **B2** 50 5N 14 24 E
Hsiya, *Gzh.* 14 **G7** 23 9N 113 6 E
Huangpu, *Gzh.* 14 **G9** 23 5N 113 23 E
Huangpu, *Shang.* 14 **J12** 31 14N 121 30 E
Huangpu Gongyuan, *Shang.* 14 **J11** 31 14N 121 29 E
Huangpu Jiang →, *Shang.* 14 **J11** 31 11N 121 29 E
Huangtugang, *Beij.* 14 **C2** 39 49N 116 15 E
Huat Choe, *Sing.* 15 **F7** 1 20N 103 41 E
Huckarde, *Ruhr* 6 **A6** 51 32N 7 24 E
Huckingen, *Ruhr* 6 **B2** 51 21N 6 44 E
Huddinge, *Stock.* 3 **E11** 59 14N 18 0 E
Hudson →, *N.Y.* 22 **B5** 40 43N 73 6W
Huertas de San Beltran, *Barc.* 8 **D5** 41 22N 2 9 E
Huguenot, *N.Y.* 22 **D3** 40 32N 74 13W
Huguenot Park, *N.Y.* 22 **D3** 40 31N 74 12W
Huidui, *Tianj.* 14 **E6** 39 4N 117 16 E
Huisquilucan →, *Méx.* 29 **B2** 19 24N 99 17W
Huixquilucan, *Méx.* 29 **B1** 19 21N 99 21W
Hull, *Bost.* 21 **D4** 42 18N 70 54W
Hulman Aqueduct, *Bost.* 21 **C1** 42 20N 71 23W
Hulmeville, *Phil.* 24 **A5** 40 8N 74 55W
Hulsdonk, *Ruhr* 6 **B1** 51 27N 6 36 E
Humaljärvi, *Hels.* 3 **B1** 60 10N 24 26 E
Humber →, *Trto.* 20 **D7** 43 47N 79 38W
Humber B., *Trto.* 20 **E8** 43 37N 79 27W
Humber Bay, *Trto.* 20 **E8** 43 38N 79 29W
Humber Summit, *Trto.* 20 **D7** 43 45N 79 32W
Humber Valley Park, *Trto.* 20 **E8** 43 39N 79 29W
Humber Valley Village, *Trto.* 20 **D7** 43 40N 79 31W
Humberlea, *Trto.* 20 **D7** 43 43N 79 31W
Humboldt Park, *Chic.* 26 **B2** 41 54N 87 42W
Humera, *Mdrd.* 8 **B2** 40 25N 3 46W
Hummelsbüttel, *Hbg.* 7 **D8** 53 39N 10 4 E
Hun Yeang, *Sing.* 15 **F8** 1 21N 103 55 E
Hunaydī, *Bagd.* 17 **F8** 33 18N 44 29 E
Hundige, *Købn.* 2 **E8** 55 35N 12 18 E
Hundige Strand, *Købn.* 2 **E9** 55 35N 12 20 E
Hung Hom, *H.K.* 12 **E6** 22 18N 114 11 E
Hunters Hill, *Syd.* 19 **B3** 33 50 S 151 9 E
Hunters Pt., *S.F.* 27 **B2** 37 43N 122 21W
Hunters Valley, *Wash.* 25 **D6** 38 54N 77 17W
Huntington, *N.Y.* 23 **B8** 40 51N 73 25W
Huntington, *Wash.* 25 **E7** 38 47N 77 4W
Huntington B., *N.Y.* 23 **B8** 40 54N 73 24W
Huntington Bay, *N.Y.* 23 **B8** 40 56N 73 26W
Huntington Park, *L.A.* 28 **C3** 33 58N 118 13W
Huntington Station, *N.Y.* 23 **B8** 40 50N 73 23W
Hünxer Wald, *Ruhr* 6 **A2** 51 37N 6 49 E
Hurffville, *Phil.* 24 **C4** 39 45N 75 6W
Hurīya, *Bagd.* 17 **E7** 33 21N 44 19 E
Hurlingham, *B.A.* 32 **B3** 34 35 S 58 37W
Hurlingham, *Jobg.* 18 **E9** 26 6 S 28 2 E
Hurstville, *Syd.* 19 **B3** 33 57 S 151 6 E
Husby, *Stock.* 3 **D10** 59 24N 17 56 E
Huseby, *Oslo* 2 **A6** 60 0N 11 1 E
Hustivař, *Pra.* 10 **B3** 50 3N 14 31 E
Husum, *Købn.* 2 **D9** 55 42N 12 27 E
Hütteldorf, *Wien* 10 **G9** 48 12N 16 15 E
Hüttenheim, *Ruhr* 6 **B2** 51 21N 6 43 E
Huttrop, *Ruhr* 6 **B4** 51 26N 7 3 E
Hüvösvölgy, *Bud.* 10 **J13** 47 32N 19 0 E
Hvalstad, *Oslo* 2 **B2** 59 51N 10 27 E
Hvalstrand, *Oslo* 2 **B3** 59 50N 10 30 E
Hvidovre, *Købn.* 2 **E9** 55 38N 12 27 E
Hwagog, *Sŏul* 12 **G7** 37 32N 126 51 E
Hyattsville, *Wash.* 25 **D8** 38 57N 76 57W
Hyde Park, *Bost.* 21 **D3** 42 15N 71 7W
Hyde Park, *Chic.* 26 **C3** 41 47N 87 35W
Hyde Park, *Jobg.* 18 **E9** 26 6 S 28 2 E
Hyde Park, *Lon.* 4 **B3** 51 30N 0 10W
Hyde Park, *Syd.* 19 **B4** 33 52 S 151 12 E
Hynes, *L.A.* 28 **C3** 33 52N 118 10W

# I

Ibaraki, *Ōsaka* 12 **B4** 34 48N 135 34 E
Ibayo Tipas, *Manila* 15 **D4** 14 32N 121 4 E
Ibese, *Lagos* 18 **A2** 6 33N 7 28 E
Ibirapuera, *S. Pau.* 31 **E5** 23 36 S 46 40W
Ibirapuera, Parque, *S. Pau.* 31 **E6** 23 35 S 46 38W
Iboju, *Lagos* 18 **B3** 6 25N 7 31 E
Icarai, *Rio J.* 31 **B3** 22 54 S 43 6W
Icerenköy, *Ist.* 17 **B3** 40 58N 29 6 E
Ichapur, *Calc.* 16 **D6** 22 48N 88 22 E
Ichgao, *Tōkyō* 13 **C2** 35 32N 139 32 E
Ichigaya, *Tōkyō* 13 **B3** 35 41N 139 43 E
Ichikawa, *Tōkyō* 13 **B4** 35 43N 139 54 E
Ickenham, *Lon.* 4 **B2** 51 33N 0 26W
Ickern, *Ruhr* 6 **A6** 51 35N 7 21 E
Iddo, *Lagos* 18 **B2** 6 28N 7 22 E
Idi-Oro, *Lagos* 18 **A2** 6 31N 7 21 E
Idimu, *Lagos* 18 **A1** 6 34N 7 17 E
Idrīs, *Bagd.* 17 **E8** 33 22N 44 27 E
Iganmu, *Lagos* 18 **B2** 6 28N 7 22 E
Igbobi, *Lagos* 18 **A2** 6 31N 7 22 E
Igbologun, *Lagos* 18 **B1** 6 24N 7 19 E
Igbopa, *Lagos* 18 **A3** 6 32N 7 31 E
Igelboda, *Stock.* 3 **E12** 59 17N 18 17 E
Igny, *Paris* 5 **C3** 48 44N 2 13 E
Iguassú, *S. Pau.* 31 **E6** 23 36 S 46 30W
Ijesa-Tedo, *Lagos* 18 **B1** 6 29N 7 19 E
Ijora, *Lagos* 18 **B2** 6 27N 7 22 E
Ikebe, *Tōkyō* 13 **C2** 35 31N 139 34 E
Ikebukuro, *Tōkyō* 13 **B3** 35 43N 139 42 E
Ikeda, *Ōsaka* 12 **B3** 34 48N 135 25 E
Ikegami, *Tōkyō* 13 **C3** 35 33N 139 42 E
Ikeja, *Lagos* 18 **A2** 6 35N 7 20 E
Ikeuchi, *Ōsaka* 12 **C4** 34 35N 135 32 E
Ikotun, *Lagos* 18 **A1** 6 32N 7 16 E
Ikoyi, *Lagos* 18 **B2** 6 27N 7 26 E
Ikuata, *Lagos* 18 **B2** 6 24N 7 21 E
Ikuno, *Ōsaka* 12 **B4** 34 40N 135 30 E
Ikuta, *Ōsaka* 12 **B2** 34 41N 135 10 E
Ikuta, *Tōkyō* 13 **C2** 35 36N 139 32 E
Ila, *Oslo* 2 **B3** 59 57N 10 35 E
Ilchester, *Balt.* 25 **B2** 39 14N 76 46W
Ilford, *Lon.* 4 **B5** 51 33N 0 4 E
Ilioúpolis, *Ath.* 8 **J11** 37 54N 23 47 E
Illovo, *Jobg.* 18 **E9** 26 7 S 28 3 E
Ilsós →, *Ath.* 8 **J11** 37 55N 23 41 E
Imajuku, *Tōkyō* 13 **D2** 35 28N 139 32 E
Imbâba, *El Qâ.* 18 **C5** 30 3N 31 12 E
Imielin, *Wsaw.* 10 **F7** 52 9N 21 0 E
Imirim, *S. Pau.* 31 **D6** 23 29 S 46 39W
Imittós, *Ath.* 8 **J11** 37 55N 23 45 E
Immersby, *Hels.* 3 **B6** 60 18N 25 16 E
Imore, *Lagos* 18 **B1** 6 25N 7 17 E
Imperial Palace, *Tōkyō* 13 **B3** 35 41N 139 45 E
Ina →, *Ōsaka* 12 **B3** 34 48N 135 27 E
Inagi, *Tōkyō* 13 **C2** 35 38N 139 31 E
Incirano, *Mil.* 9 **D5** 45 34N 9 9 E
Independencia, *Lima* 30 **F8** 11 59 S 77 3W
Indian Gabe, *Delhi* 16 **B2** 28 36N 77 13 E
Indian Museum, *Calc.* 16 **E6** 22 33N 88 21 E
Indiana Harbor, *Chic.* 26 **C4** 41 40N 87 26W
Indiana Harbor Canal, *Chic.* 26 **D4** 41 39N 87 26W
Indianópolis, *S. Pau.* 31 **E6** 23 35 S 46 38W
Indios Verdes, *Méx.* 29 **B3** 19 29N 99 6W
Ingarö, *Stock.* 3 **E13** 59 17N 18 24 E
Ingaröfjärden, *Stock.* 3 **E13** 59 14N 18 25 E
Ingarölandet, *Stock.* 3 **E13** 59 17N 18 22 E
Ingenieur Budge, *B.A.* 32 **C4** 34 43 S 58 27W
Ingierstrand, *Oslo* 2 **C4** 59 49N 10 46 E
Ingleburn, *Syd.* 19 **C2** 34 0 S 150 52 E
Inglewood, *L.A.* 28 **C3** 33 57N 118 19W
Ingrave, *Lon.* 4 **B7** 51 35N 0 20 E
Ingvalsby, *Hels.* 3 **C2** 60 9N 24 32 E
Inhaúme, *Rio J.* 31 **B2** 22 51 S 43 17W
Inner Port Shelter, *H.K.* 12 **D6** 22 22N 114 17 E
Interagos, *S. Pau.* 31 **F5** 23 41 S 46 42W
Intramuros, *Manila* 15 **D3** 14 35N 120 57 E
Invalides, *Paris* 5 **B3** 48 51N 2 18 E
Inverness, *Balt.* 25 **B4** 39 15N 76 29W
Inwood, *N.Y.* 23 **D6** 40 36N 73 45W
Inzersdorf, *Wien* 10 **H10** 48 8N 16 21 E
Ipanema, *Rio J.* 31 **B2** 22 59 S 43 12W
Ipiranga, *S. Pau.* 31 **E6** 23 35 S 46 36W
Ipiranga →, *S. Pau.* 31 **E6** 23 37 S 46 37W
Iponri, *Lagos* 18 **B2** 6 28N 7 22 E
Ipswich, *Bost.* 21 **A4** 42 41N 70 50W
Ipswich →, *Bost.* 21 **B4** 42 39N 70 53W
Irajá, *Rio J.* 31 **B2** 22 50 S 43 19W
Irving Park, *Chic.* 26 **B2** 41 57N 87 42W
Irvington, *N.Y.* 23 **A5** 41 2N 73 52W
Irwindale, *L.A.* 28 **B5** 34 6N 117 54W
Isabel, *Rio J.* 31 **B2** 22 55 S 43 14W
Isagatedo, *Lagos* 18 **A1** 6 31N 7 19 E
Isando, *Jobg.* 18 **E10** 26 8 S 28 12 E
Isar →, *Mün.* 7 **F11** 48 15N 11 41 E
Iselin, *N.Y.* 22 **D3** 40 34N 74 19W
Iserbrook, *Hbg.* 7 **D6** 53 34N 9 49 E
Iseri-Osun, *Lagos* 18 **A1** 6 30N 7 16 E
Ishbīlīya, *Bagd.* 17 **E8** 33 21N 44 26 E
Isheri-Olofin, *Lagos* 18 **A1** 6 34N 7 16 E
Ishi →, *Ōsaka* 12 **C4** 34 34N 135 37 E
Ishikiri, *Ōsaka* 12 **B4** 34 40N 135 39 E
Ishizu →, *Ōsaka* 12 **C3** 34 33N 135 26 E
Ishøj Strand, *Købn.* 2 **E9** 55 36N 12 20 E
Isidro Casanova, *B.A.* 32 **C3** 34 42 S 58 36W
Island Channel, *N.Y.* 23 **D5** 40 35N 73 52W
Island Park, *N.Y.* 23 **D7** 40 36N 73 38W
Island Park, *Trto.* 20 **E8** 43 37N 79 22W
Islev, *Købn.* 2 **D9** 55 41N 12 27 E
Isleworth, *Lon.* 4 **C3** 51 28N 0 19W
Islington, *Bost.* 21 **D2** 42 13N 71 13W
Islington, *Lon.* 4 **B4** 51 32N 0 6W
Islington, *Trto.* 20 **E7** 43 38N 79 30W
Ismaning, *Mün.* 7 **F11** 48 13N 11 40 E
Ismayloskiypark, *Mos.* 11 **E10** 55 46N 37 46 E
Isogo-Ku, *Tōkyō* 13 **D2** 35 23N 139 37 E
Isolo, *Lagos* 18 **A1** 6 31N 7 19 E
Isosaari, *Hels.* 3 **C5** 60 6N 25 3 E
Issy-les-Moulineaux, *Paris* 5 **C3** 48 49N 2 15 E
Istanbul, *Ist.* 17 **B2** 41 0N 28 58 E
Istanbul Boğazi, *Ist.* 17 **A3** 41 5N 29 3 E
Istanbul Hava Alani, *Ist.* 17 **B2** 40 58N 28 50 E
Istead Rise, *Lon.* 4 **C7** 51 24N 0 21 E
Istinye, *Ist.* 17 **A3** 41 6N 29 3 E
Isunba, *Lagos* 18 **B1** 6 25N 7 17 E
Itä Hakkila, *Hels.* 3 **B5** 60 17N 25 7 E
Itabashi-Ku, *Tōkyō* 13 **B2** 35 46N 139 38 E
Itaberaba, *S. Pau.* 31 **D6** 23 28 S 46 39W
Itaeweon, *Sŏul* 12 **G7** 37 32N 126 58 E
Itaim, *S. Pau.* 31 **D7** 23 29 S 46 23W
Itaipu, *Rio J.* 31 **B3** 22 58 S 43 2W
Italie, Place d', *Paris* 5 **C4** 48 49N 2 22 E
Itami, *Ōsaka* 12 **B3** 34 46N 135 24 E
Itaocaia, *Rio J.* 31 **B3** 22 58 S 43 2W
Itapecerica da Serra, *S. Pau.* 31 **F5** 23 42 S 46 50W
Itaquaquecetuba, *S. Pau.* 31 **D7** 23 29 S 46 23W
Itaquera, *S. Pau.* 31 **E7** 23 32 S 46 27W
Itaquera →, *S. Pau.* 31 **E7** 23 28 S 46 26W
Ithan, *Phil.* 24 **A2** 40 1N 75 21W
Itupu, *S. Pau.* 31 **F5** 23 40 S 46 43W
Ituzaingo, *B.A.* 32 **B3** 34 39 S 58 38W
Ivanhoe, *Melb.* 19 **E7** 37 45 S 145 3 E
Iver, *Lon.* 4 **B1** 51 32N 0 30W
Ivry-sur-Seine, *Paris* 5 **C4** 48 49N 2 22 E
Iwazono, *Ōsaka* 12 **B2** 34 45N 135 18 E
Izabelin, *Wsaw.* 10 **E5** 52 17N 20 48 E
Izmaylovo, *Mos.* 11 **E10** 55 47N 37 47 E
Iztacalco, *Méx.* 29 **B3** 19 23N 99 6W
Iztapalapa, *Méx.* 29 **B3** 19 21N 99 6W
Izumi, *Tōkyō* 13 **D1** 35 25N 139 29 E

# J

J. G. Strijdom Post Office Tower, *Jobg.* 18 **F9** 26 11 S 28 2 E
J. Paul Getty Museum, *L.A.* 28 **B1** 34 2N 118 33W
Jabavu, *Jobg.* 18 **F8** 26 14 S 27 52 E
Jabulani, *Jobg.* 18 **F8** 26 14 S 27 51 E
Jacarepaguá, *Rio J.* 31 **B1** 22 56 S 43 20W
Jackson Heights, *N.Y.* 23 **C5** 40 44N 73 53W
Jackson Park, *Chic.* 26 **C3** 41 46N 87 34W
Jacksonville, *N.Y.* 22 **B3** 40 57N 74 18W
Jacomino, *La Hab.* 30 **B3** 23 6N 82 19W
Jacques Cartier, *Mtrl.* 20 **A5** 43 31N 73 27W
Jægersborg, *Købn.* 2 **D10** 55 45N 12 31 E
Jægersborg Dyrehave, *Købn.* 2 **D10** 55 46N 12 33 E
Jægersborg Hegn, *Købn.* 2 **D10** 55 49N 12 33 E
Jafarpur, *Calc.* 16 **D6** 22 45N 88 22 E
Jagacha, *Calc.* 16 **E5** 22 35N 88 17 E
Jagannathpur, *Calc.* 16 **D5** 22 43N 88 18 E
Jagatdal, *Calc.* 16 **C6** 22 51N 88 23 E
Jagatmagar, *Calc.* 16 **D5** 22 46N 88 13 E
Jagatpur, *Delhi* 16 **A2** 28 44N 77 13 E
Jagdispur, *Calc.* 16 **E5** 22 39N 88 17 E
Jaguara, *S. Pau.* 31 **E5** 23 30 S 46 45W
Jaguaré, *S. Pau.* 31 **E5** 23 32 S 46 45W
Jaguaré →, *S. Pau.* 31 **E5** 23 32 S 46 45W
Jahangirpur, *Delhi* 16 **A2** 28 43N 77 12 E
Jaimanitas →, *La Hab.* 30 **B2** 23 5N 82 29W
Jakarta, *Jak.* 15 **H10** 6 9 S 106 52 E
Jakarta, Teluk, *Jak.* 15 **H9** 6 5 S 106 50 E
Jakosberg, *Stock.* 3 **D9** 59 25N 17 47 E
Jalan Kayu, *Sing.* 15 **F8** 1 24N 103 52 E
Jamaica, *N.Y.* 23 **C6** 40 42N 73 48W
Jamaica B., *N.Y.* 23 **D6** 40 36N 73 49W
Jamaica Plain, *Bost.* 21 **D3** 42 18N 71 6W
Jamshīdābād, *Tehr.* 17 **C5** 35 42N 51 22 E
Jamsil, *Sŏul* 12 **G8** 37 30N 127 4 E
Jamweon, *Sŏul* 12 **G8** 37 30N 127 0 E
Jan Smuts Airport, *Jobg.* 18 **E10** 26 7 S 28 14 E
Janai, *Calc.* 16 **D5** 22 43N 88 15 E
Janā'in, *Bagd.* 17 **F8** 33 18N 44 22 E
Janki, *Wsaw.* 10 **F6** 52 8N 20 52 E
Jannali, *Syd.* 19 **C3** 34 0 S 151 4 E
Jánoshegy, *Bud.* 10 **J12** 47 31N 18 57 E
Janów, *Wsaw.* 10 **E6** 52 16N 20 50 E
Janvry, *Paris* 5 **D2** 48 38N 2 9 E
Jaraguá, *S. Pau.* 31 **D5** 23 27 S 46 44W
Jaraguá, Pico de, *S. Pau.* 31 **D5** 23 27 S 46 46W
Jarama →, *Mdrd.* 8 **B3** 40 29N 3 32W
Jardim América, *S. Pau.* 31 **E6** 23 34 S 46 39W
Jardim Anchieta, *S. Pau.* 31 **F7** 23 41 S 46 27W
Jardim Arpoador, *S. Pau.* 31 **E5** 23 35 S 46 48W
Jardim do Mar, *S. Pau.* 31 **F6** 23 41 S 46 33W
Jardim Munhoz, *S. Pau.* 31 **E6** 23 30 S 46 33W
Jardim Osasco, *S. Pau.* 31 **E5** 23 33 S 46 47W
Jardim Ouro Preto, *S. Pau.* 31 **E5** 23 35 S 46 46W
Jardim Paulista, *S. Pau.* 31 **E5** 23 34 S 46 41W
Jardim Petrópolis, *S. Pau.* 31 **F7** 23 41 S 46 23W
Jardim Rochidale, *S. Pau.* 31 **E5** 23 30 S 46 46W
Jardim Santista, *S. Pau.* 31 **F7** 23 40 S 46 24W
Jardim São Bento, *S. Pau.* 31 **F5** 23 40 S 46 46W
Jardim São Francisco, *S. Pau.* 31 **E7** 23 38 S 46 26W
Jardim Sapopemba, *S. Pau.* 31 **E7** 23 36 S 46 29W
Jardim Vera Cruz, *S. Pau.* 31 **E7** 23 35 S 46 27W
Jardim Vista Alegre, *S. Pau.* 31 **E5** 23 37 S 46 49W
Jardim Zaira, *S. Pau.* 31 **E7** 23 39 S 46 25W
Jardines Flotantes, *Méx.* 29 **C3** 19 16N 99 6W
Jardine's Lookout, *H.K.* 12 **E6** 22 16N 114 11 E
Järfälla, *Stock.* 3 **D10** 59 23N 17 51 E
Järvafältet, *Stock.* 3 **D10** 59 25N 17 54 E
Järventausta, *Hels.* 3 **A1** 60 21N 24 28 E
Jasai, *Bomb.* 16 **H9** 18 56N 73 1 E
Jaskhar, *Bomb.* 16 **H8** 18 54N 72 58 E
Jatinegara, *Jak.* 15 **J10** 6 13 S 106 52 E
Jauli, *Delhi* 16 **A3** 28 44N 77 20 E
Jawādiyeh, *Tehr.* 17 **D5** 35 39N 51 22 E
Jaworowa, *Wsaw.* 10 **F6** 52 9N 20 56 E
Jayang, *Sŏul* 12 **G8** 37 32N 127 3 E
Jedlesee, *Wien* 10 **G10** 48 15N 16 23 E
Jefferson, *Phil.* 24 **C3** 39 45N 75 12W
Jefferson Park, *Chic.* 26 **B2** 41 58N 87 46W
Jeffersonville, *Phil.* 24 **A2** 40 8N 75 23W
Jegi, *Sŏul* 12 **G8** 37 34N 127 1 E
Jells Park, *Melb.* 19 **F8** 37 53 S 145 11 E
Jelonki, *Wsaw.* 10 **E6** 52 14N 20 54 E
Jenfeld, *Hbg.* 7 **D8** 53 34N 10 8 E
Jenkintown, *Phil.* 24 **A4** 40 6N 75 8W
Jeongreung, *Sŏul* 12 **G8** 37 35N 127 0 E
Jericho, *N.Y.* 23 **C7** 40 47N 73 32W
Jerónimes, Mosteiro dos, *Lisb.* 8 **F7** 38 41N 9 11W
Jersey City, *N.Y.* 22 **C4** 40 42N 74 4W
Jésus, Î., *Mtrl.* 20 **A3** 43 36N 73 44W
Jesus Del Monte, *La Hab.* 30 **B2** 23 6N 82 21W
Jesús Maria, *Lima* 30 **G8** 12 4 S 77 3W
Jhenkari, *Calc.* 16 **D5** 22 45N 88 18 E
Jhil Kuranga, *Delhi* 16 **B2** 28 39N 77 14 E
Jiangqiao, *Shang.* 14 **J11** 31 15N 121 20 E
Jiangtai, *Beij.* 14 **B3** 39 57N 116 28 E
Jianguomen, *Beij.* 14 **B3** 39 53N 116 24 E
Jiangwan, *Shang.* 14 **J11** 31 18N 121 28 E
Jianshan Gongyuan, *Tianj.* 14 **E6** 39 5N 117 12 E
Jihād, *Bagd.* 17 **F7** 33 17N 44 19 E
Jingan, *Shang.* 14 **J11** 31 14N 121 25 E
Jinočany, *Pra.* 10 **B1** 50 2N 14 16 E
Jinonice, *Pra.* 10 **B2** 50 3N 14 22 E
Jirny, *Pra.* 10 **B4** 50 7N 14 41 E
Jiuxianqiao, *Beij.* 14 **B3** 39 58N 116 28 E
Jiyźgaoka, *Tōkyō* 13 **C3** 35 35N 139 40 E
Jizā'er, *Bagd.* 17 **F8** 33 15N 44 23 E
Jizīra, *Bagd.* 17 **F8** 33 15N 44 25 E
Joan Despi, *Barc.* 8 **D5** 41 22N 2 2 E
Joaquin Miller Park, *S.F.* 27 **B3** 37 48N 122 11W
Johannesburg, *Jobg.* 18 **F9** 26 11 S 28 2 E
Johanneskirchen, *Mün.* 7 **F10** 48 10N 11 38 E
Johannesstift, *Berl.* 7 **A2** 52 34N 13 12 E
Johannisthal, *Berl.* 7 **B4** 52 26N 13 30 E
John F. Kennedy Int. Airport, *N.Y.* 23 **D6** 40 39N 73 45W
John F. Kennedy Nat. Hist. Site, *Bost.* 21 **C3** 42 20N 71 7W
John Hancock Center, *Chic.* 26 **B3** 41 53N 87 37W
John Hopkins Univ., *Balt.* 25 **B3** 39 19N 76 37W
John McLaren Park, *S.F.* 27 **B2** 37 43N 122 24W
Joinville-le-Pont, *Paris* 5 **C4** 48 49N 2 27 E
Jollas, *Hels.* 3 **B5** 60 10N 25 5 E
Jones Beach State Park, *N.Y.* 23 **D7** 40 35N 73 32W
Jones Falls →, *Balt.* 25 **B3** 39 20N 76 36W
Jones Inlet, *N.Y.* 23 **D7** 40 34N 73 34W
Jonestown, *Balt.* 25 **B2** 39 13N 76 48W
Jong Ro, *Sŏul* 12 **G7** 37 34N 126 58 E
Jongmyo Royal Shrine, *Sŏul* 12 **G7** 37 34N 126 59 E
Jonstrup, *Købn.* 2 **D9** 55 45N 12 20 E
Joppatowne, *Balt.* 25 **A4** 39 24N 76 20W
Jordan Valley, *H.K.* 12 **D6** 22 20N 114 12 E
Jorge Chavez, Aeropuerto Int., *Lima* 30 **G8** 12 2 S 77 8W
Jorvas, *Hels.* 3 **C2** 60 8N 24 30 E
José C. Paz, *B.A.* 32 **B2** 34 31 S 58 44W
José L. Suárez, *B.A.* 32 **B3** 34 32 S 58 34W
José Mármol, *B.A.* 32 **C4** 34 47 S 58 22W
Jose Marti, Aeropuerto Int., *La Hab.* 30 **C2** 22 59N 82 22W
Josephine Pk., *L.A.* 28 **A4** 34 17N 118 7W
Jōsō, *Ōsaka* 12 **B3** 34 42N 135 27 E
Jōtō, *Ōsaka* 12 **B4** 34 42N 135 33 E
Jouars-Pontchartrain, *Paris* 5 **C1** 48 47N 1 53 E
Jouy-en-Josas, *Paris* 5 **C3** 48 46N 2 10 E
Jouy-le-Moutier, *Paris* 5 **A2** 49 0N 2 2 E
Józefów, *Wsaw.* 10 **F8** 52 8N 21 13 E
Juan Escutia, *Méx.* 29 **B3** 19 23N 99 3W
Juan González Romero, *Méx.* 29 **A3** 19 30N 99 3W
Juhu, *Bomb.* 16 **G9** 19 5N 73 0 E
Juilly, *Paris* 5 **A6** 49 0N 2 42 E
Jūjā, *Tōkyō* 13 **B3** 35 45N 139 43 E
Jukskeirivier →, *Jobg.* 18 **E9** 26 5 S 28 6 E
Julianów, *Wsaw.* 10 **E7** 52 10N 21 9 E
Jung, *Sŏul* 12 **G7** 37 33N 126 59 E
Jungfernheide, Volkspark, *Berl.* 7 **A2** 52 32N 13 18 E
Jungfernsee, *Berl.* 7 **B1** 52 25N 13 6 E
Jungwha, *Sŏul* 12 **G8** 37 35N 127 3 E
Junk B., *H.K.* 12 **E6** 22 17N 114 15 E
Jurong, *Sing.* 15 **G7** 1 19N 103 40 E
Jurong, Selat, *Sing.* 15 **G7** 1 17N 103 42 E
Jurong, Sungei →, *Sing.* 15 **G7** 1 17N 103 45 E
Jurubatuba, *S. Pau.* 31 **F5** 23 40 S 46 41W
Jurujuba, Enseada de, *Rio J.* 31 **B3** 22 54 S 43 6W
Justice, *Chic.* 26 **C2** 41 44N 87 49W
Juusjärvi, *Hels.* 3 **B1** 60 12N 24 26 E
Juva, *Hels.* 3 **B3** 60 16N 24 45 E
Juvisy-sur-Orge, *Paris* 5 **C4** 48 41N 2 21 E
Jwalahari, *Delhi* 16 **B1** 28 40N 77 6 E
Jyllinge, *Købn.* 2 **D7** 55 45N 12 6 E

# K

Kaarst, *Ruhr* 6 **C1** 51 13N 6 36 E
Kabaty, *Wsaw.* 10 **F7** 52 8N 21 4 E
Kabel, *Ruhr* 6 **B6** 51 24N 7 28 E
Kadiköy, *Ist.* 17 **B3** 40 59N 29 1 E
Kadoma, *Ōsaka* 12 **B4** 34 44N 135 35 E
Kafr es Sammân, *El Qâ.* 18 **D4** 29 58N 31 8 E
Kâğithane, *Ist.* 17 **A2** 41 4N 28 58 E
Kâğithane →, *Ist.* 17 **A2** 41 9N 28 56 E
Kagran, *Wien* 10 **G10** 48 14N 16 26 E
Kahlenberg, *Wien* 10 **G9** 48 16N 16 19 E
Kai Tak, *H.K.* 12 **D6** 22 20N 114 11 E
Kaisariani, *Ath.* 8 **J11** 37 57N 23 46 E
Kaiser-Mühlen, *Wien* 10 **G10** 48 13N 16 25 E
Kaiserebersdorf, *Wien* 10 **H10** 48 9N 16 26 E
Kaiserswerth, *Ruhr* 6 **C2** 51 18N 6 44 E
Kaivoksela, *Hels.* 3 **B4** 60 15N 24 53 E
Kakukk-hegy, *Bud.* 10 **K12** 47 29N 18 57 E
Kalachhara, *Calc.* 16 **D5** 22 42N 88 15 E
Kalamákion, *Ath.* 8 **J11** 37 52N 23 43 E
Kaldenhausen, *Ruhr* 6 **B1** 51 23N 6 39 E
Kalipur, *Calc.* 16 **D5** 22 40N 88 17 E
Kalkaji, *Delhi* 16 **B2** 28 32N 77 12 E
Kalksburg, *Wien* 10 **H9** 48 8N 16 15 E
Kallang →, *Sing.* 15 **F8** 1 21N 103 51 E
Kallhäll, *Stock.* 3 **D9** 59 26N 17 48 E
Kallithéa, *Ath.* 8 **J11** 37 56N 23 43 E
Kallvik, *Hels.* 3 **B5** 60 12N 25 8 E
Kaltbründsberg, *Wien* 10 **G9** 48 10N 16 13 E
Kaltenleutgeben, *Wien* 10 **H9** 48 7N 16 11 E
Kalveboderne, *Købn.* 2 **E10** 55 37N 12 31 E
Kalytino, *St-Pet.* 11 **B5** 59 59N 30 39 E
Kamaraerdö, *Bud.* 10 **K12** 47 26N 18 59 E
Kamarhati, *Calc.* 16 **D6** 22 40N 88 23 E
Kamarkunda, *Calc.* 16 **D5** 22 49N 88 12 E
Kamata, *Tōkyō* 13 **C3** 35 33N 139 43 E
Kamdebpur, *Calc.* 16 **C5** 22 53N 88 19 E
Kameari, *Tōkyō* 13 **B4** 35 45N 139 50 E
Kameido, *Tōkyō* 13 **B4** 35 42N 139 50 E
Kami-hoshikawa, *Tōkyō* 13 **D2** 35 27N 139 35 E
Kami-Itabashi, *Tōkyō* 13 **B3** 35 45N 139 40 E
Kami-nakazato, *Tōkyō* 13 **D2** 35 22N 139 36 E
Kami-saruyama, *Tōkyō* 13 **C2** 35 30N 139 31 E
Kami-sugata, *Tōkyō* 13 **D2** 35 28N 139 34 E
Kami-tomi, *Tōkyō* 13 **B1** 35 48N 139 29 E
Kamikitazawa, *Tōkyō* 13 **C2** 35 39N 139 36 E
Kamikiyoto, *Tōkyō* 13 **B2** 35 45N 139 30 E
Kamishiki, *Tōkyō* 13 **B4** 35 46N 139 57 E
Kamitsuruma, *Tōkyō* 13 **C1** 35 30N 139 26 E
Kamiyama, *Tōkyō* 13 **B2** 35 46N 139 32 E
Kamoi, *Tōkyō* 13 **C2** 35 30N 139 34 E
Kamoshida, *Tōkyō* 13 **C2** 35 33N 139 31 E
Kampong Batak, *Sing.* 15 **F8** 1 20N 103 54 E
Kampong Mandai Kechil, *Sing.* 15 **F7** 1 26N 103 46 E
Kampong Pachitan, *Sing.* 15 **G8** 1 19N 103 54 E
Kampong Potong Pasir, *Sing.* 15 **F8** 1 20N 103 52 E
Kampong Reteh, *Sing.* 15 **G8** 1 19N 103 53 E
Kampong Tengah, *Sing.* 15 **F7** 1 22N 103 42 E
Kampong Ulu Jurong, *Sing.* 15 **F7** 1 20N 103 42 E
Kampung Ambon, *Jak.* 15 **J10** 6 11 S 106 53 E
Kampung Bali, *Jak.* 15 **J9** 6 11 S 106 48 E
Kan, *Tehr.* 17 **C4** 35 45N 51 16 E
Kanagawa-Ku, *Tōkyō* 13 **D2** 35 29N 139 38 E
Kanamachi, *Tōkyō* 13 **B4** 35 46N 139 52 E
Kanamori, *Tōkyō* 13 **C1** 35 31N 139 27 E
Kanda, *Tōkyō* 13 **B3** 35 41N 139 45 E
Kandang Kerbau, *Sing.* 15 **G8** 1 18N 103 51 E
Kandilli, *Ist.* 17 **A3** 41 4N 29 3 E
Kanegasaku, *Tōkyō* 13 **B4** 35 48N 139 56 E
Kangaroo Ground, *Melb.* 19 **E8** 37 41 S 145 13 E
Kankinara, *Calc.* 16 **C6** 22 51N 88 24 E
Kankurgachi, *Calc.* 16 **E6** 22 34N 88 23 E
Kanlica, *Ist.* 17 **A3** 41 5N 29 3 E
Kanoaka, *Ōsaka* 12 **C4** 34 33N 135 31 E
Kanonerskiy, Os., *St-Pet.* 11 **B3** 59 53N 30 13 E
Kanzaki →, *Ōsaka* 12 **B3** 34 41N 135 24 E
Kapellerfeld, *Wien* 10 **G10** 48 18N 16 29 E
Kapotnya, *Mos.* 11 **F10** 55 39N 37 48 E
Käppala, *Stock.* 3 **D12** 59 21N 18 13 E
Käpylä, *Hels.* 3 **B4** 60 13N 24 57 E
Karachi, *Kar.* 17 **G11** 24 50N 67 0 E
Karachi Int. Airport, *Kar.* 17 **G11** 24 5N 67 9 E
Karachi Univ., *Kar.* 17 **G11** 24 51N 67 0 E
Karagümrük, *Ist.* 17 **A2** 41 1N 28 56 E
Karāma, *Bagd.* 17 **E8** 33 20N 44 22 E
Karato, *Ōsaka* 12 **B2** 34 46N 135 12 E
Karave, *Bomb.* 16 **G9** 19 0N 73 0 E
Karet, *Jak.* 15 **J9** 6 12 S 106 49 E
Karkar Duman, *Delhi* 16 **B2** 28 39N 77 18 E
Karkh, *Bagd.* 17 **E8** 33 20N 44 22 E
Karlberg, *Stock.* 3 **D11** 59 20N 18 1 E
Karlin, *Pra.* 10 **B2** 50 5N 14 26 E
Karlsfeld, *Mün.* 7 **F9** 48 13N 11 28 E
Karlshorst, *Berl.* 7 **B4** 52 29N 13 31 E
Karlslunde Strand, *Købn.* 2 **E8** 55 33N 12 15 E
Karnap, *Ruhr* 6 **A4** 51 31N 7 0 E
Karolinenhof, *Berl.* 7 **B4** 52 23N 13 38 E
Karow, *Berl.* 7 **A3** 52 36N 13 29 E
Karrādah, *Bagd.* 17 **F8** 33 17N 44 23 E
Kärsön, *Stock.* 3 **E10** 59 19N 17 54 E
Kasai, *Tōkyō* 13 **C4** 35 39N 139 52 E
Kasetsart, *Bangk.* 15 **A2** 13 50N 100 34 E
Kashi-Hazaki, *Tōkyō* 13 **A3** 35 54N 139 42 E
Kashio, *Tōkyō* 13 **D2** 35 24N 139 34 E
Kashiwa, *Tōkyō* 13 **A4** 35 51N 139 57 E
Kashiwara, *Ōsaka* 12 **C4** 34 34N 135 37 E
Kaskela, *Hels.* 3 **B5** 60 17N 25 6 E
Kastrup, *Købn.* 2 **E10** 55 38N 12 39 E
Kastrup Lufthavn, *Købn.* 2 **E11** 55 37N 12 14 E
Kasuga, *Tōkyō* 13 **B2** 35 45N 139 38 E
Kasuge, *Tōkyō* 13 **B3** 35 45N 139 49 E
Kasumigasek, *Tōkyō* 13 **C3** 35 40N 139 46 E
Katabira →, *Tōkyō* 13 **D2** 35 27N 139 38 E
Katernberg, *Ruhr* 6 **A4** 51 30N 7 4 E
Katong Park, *Sing.* 15 **G8** 1 18N 103 53 E
Katrineberg, *Stock.* 3 **E10** 59 13N 17 54 E
Katsushika-Ku, *Tōkyō* 13 **B4** 35 44N 139 51 E
Kattinge Vig, *Købn.* 2 **D7** 55 40N 12 1 E
Kau Pei Chau, *H.K.* 12 **E6** 22 12N 114 15 E
Kau Yi Chau, *H.K.* 12 **E5** 22 17N 114 4 E
Kauklahti, *Hels.* 3 **B2** 60 11N 24 36 E
Kaulsdorf, *Berl.* 7 **B4** 52 29N 13 34 E
Kauniainen, *Hels.* 3 **B3** 60 13N 24 44 E
Kawagoe, *Tōkyō* 13 **A1** 35 54N 139 29 E
Kawaguchi, *Tōkyō* 13 **B3** 35 47N 139 43 E
Kawai, *Tōkyō* 13 **D2** 35 29N 139 31 E
Kawamukō, *Tōkyō* 13 **C2** 35 30N 139 34 E
Kawanishi, *Ōsaka* 12 **B3** 34 49N 135 24 E
Kawasaki, *Tōkyō* 13 **C3** 35 31N 139 43 E
Kawasaki Harbour, *Tōkyō* 13 **D3** 35 30N 139 47 E
Kawawa, *Tōkyō* 13 **C2** 35 31N 139 33 E
Kawęczyn, *Wsaw.* 10 **E7** 52 16N 21 5 E
Kayu Putih, *Jak.* 15 **J10** 6 10 S 106 53 E
Kbely, *Pra.* 10 **B3** 50 8N 14 32 E
Kearny, *N.Y.* 22 **C4** 40 45N 74 8W
Kebayoran Baru, *Jak.* 15 **J9** 6 14 S 106 47 E
Kebayoran Lama, *Jak.* 15 **J9** 6 13 S 106 46 E
Kebon Jeruk, *Jak.* 15 **J9** 6 11 S 106 46 E
Keferloh, *Mün.* 7 **G11** 48 5N 11 43 E
Keilor, *Melb.* 19 **E6** 37 42 S 144 50 E
Keilor East, *Melb.* 19 **E6** 37 44 S 144 51 E
Keimola, *Hels.* 3 **A3** 60 20N 24 49 E
Kelenföld, *Bud.* 10 **K13** 47 27N 19 2 E
Kelvedon Hatch, *Lon.* 4 **A6** 51 40N 0 16 E
Kelvin, *Jobg.* 18 **E9** 26 4 S 28 5 E
Kemang, *Jak.* 15 **J9** 6 15 S 106 48 E
Kemayoran, *Jak.* 15 **J10** 6 10 S 106 51 E
Kemayoran Airport, *Jak.* 15 **H10** 6 8 S 106 50 E
Kemp Mill, *Wash.* 25 **C7** 39 0N 77 1W
Kempton Park, *Jobg.* 18 **E10** 26 5 S 28 14 E
Kempton Racecourse, *Lon.* 4 **C2** 51 24N 0 23W
Kemsing, *Lon.* 4 **D6** 51 18N 0 12 E
Kendall Green, *Bost.* 21 **C2** 42 22N 71 16W
Kendua, *Calc.* 16 **E5** 22 34N 88 10 E
Keng Hau, *H.K.* 12 **D6** 22 22N 114 10 E
Kenilworth, *Chic.* 26 **A2** 42 5N 87 42W
Kenilworth, *N.Y.* 22 **C3** 40 40N 74 16W
Kenley, *Lon.* 4 **D4** 51 19N 0 6W
Kenmare, *Jobg.* 18 **E7** 26 6 S 27 48 E
Kennedy Grove Regional Rec. Area, *S.F.* 27 **A3** 37 56N 122 14W

40 Kennedy Town


Kennedy Town, *H.K.* 12 E5 22 16N 114 6 E
Kensal Green, *Lon.* 4 B3 51 32N 0 13W
Kensington, *Jobg.* 18 F9 26 11 S 28 6 E
Kensington, *Lon.* 4 C3 51 29N 0 10W
Kensington, *N.Y.* 22 D5 40 38N 73 57W
Kensington, *Phil.* 24 B4 39 59N 75 6W
Kensington, *S.F.* 27 A3 37 54N 122 17W
Kensington, *Syd.* 19 B4 33 54 S 151 13 E
Kensington, *Wash.* 25 C7 39 1N 77 4W
Kensington Palace, *Lon.* 4 B3 51 30N 0 11W
Kent Woodlands, *S.F.* 27 A1 37 56N 122 34W
Kentfield, *S.F.* 27 A1 37 57N 122 33W
Kentish Town, *Lon.* 4 B4 51 32N 0 8W
Kentland, *Wash.* 25 D8 38 55N 76 53W
Kenton, *Lon.* 4 B3 51 34N 0 17W
Kenwood, *Balt.* 25 A4 39 20N 76 30W
Kenwood, *Bost.* 21 B2 42 40N 71 14W
Kenwood House, *Lon.* 4 B4 51 34N 0 9W
Kepa, *Wsaw.* 10 E7 52 13N 21 3 E
Keppel Harbour, *Sing.* 15 G7 1 15N 103 49 E
Kerameikos, *Ath.* 8 J11 37 58N 23 42 E
Kerepes, *Bud.* 10 J14 47 33N 19 17 E
Keston, *Lon.* 4 C5 51 21N 0 1 E
Keston Mark, *Lon.* 4 C5 51 21N 0 2 E
Keth Wara, *Delhi* 16 A2 28 40N 77 13 E
Kettering, *Wash.* 25 D9 38 53N 76 49W
Kettwig, *Ruhr* 6 B3 51 22N 6 56 E
Kew, *Jobg.* 18 E9 26 7 S 28 5 E
Kew, *Lon.* 4 C3 51 28N 0 17W
Kew, *Melb.* 19 E7 37 48 S 145 2 E
Kew Gardens, *Lon.* 4 C3 51 28N 0 17W
Key Gardens, *Trto.* 20 E9 43 39N 79 18W
Khaboye, *St-Pet.* 11 B6 59 53N 30 44 E
Khaidhárion, *Ath.* 8 H10 38 2N 23 38 E
Khairna, *Bomb.* 16 G9 19 5N 73 0 E
Khalándrion, *Ath.* 8 H11 38 3N 23 48 E
Khalīj, *Bagd.* 17 F8 33 18N 44 28 E
Khansā, *Bagd.* 17 E8 33 21N 44 28 E
Kharavli, *Bomb.* 16 H8 18 54N 72 55 E
Khardah, *Calc.* 16 D6 22 43N 88 22 E
Khayala, *Delhi* 16 B1 28 39N 77 6 E
Khefren, *El Qâ.* 18 D4 29 58N 31 8 E
Khichripur, *Delhi* 16 B2 28 37N 77 18 E
Khimki, *Mos.* 11 D8 55 53N 37 24 E
Khimki-Khovrino, *Mos.* 11 D9 55 51N 37 31 E
Khimkinskoye Vdkr., *Mos.* 11 D8 55 51N 37 27 E
Khirvosti, *St-Pet.* 11 B5 59 56N 30 37 E
Khlongsan, *Bangk.* 15 B1 13 43N 100 29 E
Kholargós, *Ath.* 8 J11 37 59N 23 48 E
Khorel, *Calc.* 16 D5 22 41N 88 18 E
Khorosovo, *Mos.* 11 E8 55 46N 37 27 E
Khudrā, *Bagd.* 17 F7 33 19N 44 17 E
Khun Thian, *Bangk.* 15 B1 13 41N 100 27 E
Khuraiji Khas, *Delhi* 16 B2 28 38N 77 16 E
Khurigachi, *Calc.* 16 D5 22 48N 88 21 E
Kiamari, *Kar.* 17 H10 24 49N 66 58 E
Kidderpore, *Calc.* 16 E5 22 32N 88 19 E
Kienwerder, *Berl.* 7 B2 52 22N 13 11 E
Kierling, *Wien* 10 G9 48 18N 16 16 E
Kierlingbach →, *Wien* 10 G9 48 18N 16 19 E
Kierlinger Forst, *Wien* 10 G9 48 17N 16 14 E
Kierst, *Ruhr* 6 C2 51 18N 6 42 E
Kifisós →, *Ath.* 8 J11 37 58N 23 42 E
Kikenka →, *St-Pet.* 11 B2 59 50N 30 3 E
Kikuna, *Tōkyō* 13 C2 35 30N 139 37 E
Kil, *Stock.* 3 D12 59 20N 18 19 E
Kilburn, *Lon.* 4 B3 51 32N 0 11W
Killara, *Syd.* 19 A4 33 46 S 151 10 E
Kilo, *Hels.* 3 B3 60 13N 24 47 E
Kilokri, *Delhi* 16 B2 28 34N 77 15 E
Kilsyth, *Melb.* 19 E8 37 48 S 145 18 E
Kimberton, *Phil.* 24 A1 40 7N 75 34W
Kimlin Park, *Sing.* 15 G7 1 18N 103 49 E
Kindi, *Bagd.* 17 F8 33 18N 44 22 E
King of Prussia, *Phil.* 24 A2 40 5N 75 22W
Kings Cross, *Syd.* 19 B4 33 52 S 151 12 E
Kings Domain, *Melb.* 19 E6 37 49 S 144 58 E
Kings Mt., *S.F.* 27 D3 37 27N 122 19W
King's Park, *H.K.* 12 E6 22 18N 114 10 E
Kings Park, *Wash.* 25 E6 38 48N 77 17W
King's Point, *N.Y.* 23 C6 40 48N 73 45W
Kingsbury, *Lon.* 4 B3 51 34N 0 15W
Kingsford, *Syd.* 19 B4 33 55 S 151 14 E
Kingston upon Thames, *Lon.* 4 C3 51 24N 0 17W
Kingston Vale, *Lon.* 4 C3 51 25N 0 25W
Kingsway, *Trto.* 20 E7 43 38N 79 32W
Kingswood, *Lon.* 4 D3 51 17N 0 12W
Kinnelon, *N.Y.* 22 B2 40 59N 74 23W
Kipling Heights, *Trto.* 20 D7 43 43N 79 34W
Kipséli, *Ath.* 8 J11 37 59N 23 45 E
Kirchhellen, *Ruhr* 6 A3 51 36N 6 56 E
Kirchhörde, *Ruhr* 6 B6 51 27N 7 27 E
Kirchlinde, *Ruhr* 6 A6 51 31N 7 22 E
Kirchof, *Hbg.* 7 E8 53 29N 10 1 E
Kirchsteinbek, *Hbg.* 7 D8 53 31N 10 7 E
Kirchstockbach, *Mün.* 7 G11 48 1N 11 40 E
Kirchtrudering, *Mün.* 7 G11 48 7N 11 40 E
Kirdasa, *El Qâ.* 18 C4 30 2N 31 6 E
Kirikiri, *Lagos* 18 B1 6 26N 7 18 E
Kirkkonummi, *Hels.* 3 C1 60 6N 24 28W
Kirkland, *Mtrl.* 20 B2 43 26N 73 51W
Kirovskiye, Os., *St-Pet.* 11 B3 59 57N 30 14 E
Kisarazu, *Tōkyō* 13 D4 35 21N 139 54 E
Kisikli, *Ist.* 17 A3 41 1N 29 2 E
Kispest, *Bud.* 10 K13 47 27N 19 8 E
Kista, *Stock.* 3 D10 59 24N 17 57 E
Kistarcsa, *Bud.* 10 J14 47 32N 19 16 E
Kita, *Ōsaka* 12 B4 34 41N 135 30 E
Kita-Ku, *Tōkyō* 13 B3 35 44N 139 44 E
Kitain-Temple, *Tōkyō* 13 A1 35 54N 139 29 E
Kitazawa, *Tōkyō* 13 C3 35 39N 139 40 E
Kiu Tsiu, *H.K.* 12 D6 22 22N 114 17 E
Kivistö, *Hels.* 3 B4 60 18N 24 50 E
Kiyose, *Tōkyō* 13 B2 35 46N 139 31 E
Kiziltoprak, *Ist.* 17 B3 40 58N 29 3 E
Kizu →, *Ōsaka* 12 C3 34 37N 135 27 E
Kizuri, *Ōsaka* 12 C4 34 38N 135 34 E
Kjeller, *Oslo* 2 B6 59 58N 11 1 E
Kjelsås, *Oslo* 2 B4 59 57N 10 47 E
Kladow, *Berl.* 7 B1 52 27N 13 9 E
Klampenborg, *Købn.* 2 D10 55 46N 12 35 E
Klánovice, *Pra.* 10 B3 50 5N 14 40 E
Klaudyń, *Wsaw.* 10 E6 52 17N 20 50 E
Klecany, *Pra.* 10 A2 50 10N 14 24 E
Kledering, *Wien* 10 H10 48 8N 16 26 E
Klein Gleinicke, *Berl.* 7 B1 52 23N 13 5 E
Klein-Hadern, *Mün.* 7 G9 48 7N 11 28 E
Klein Jukskei →, *Jobg.* 18 E8 26 6 S 27 57 E
Kleinburg, *Trto.* 20 C7 43 51N 79 37W
Kleine Grasbrook, *Hbg.* 7 D7 53 31N 9 59 E
Kleinmachnow, *Berl.* 7 B2 52 24N 13 14 E
Kleinschönebeck, *Berl.* 7 B5 52 29N 13 42 E
Kleinziethen, *Berl.* 7 B3 52 22N 13 26 E
Klemetsrud, *Oslo* 2 B5 59 50N 10 51 E
Klender, *Jak.* 15 J10 6 12 S 106 53 E
Klippoortje, *Jobg.* 18 F10 26 14 S 28 10 E
Klipriviersberg, *Jobg.* 18 F9 26 16 S 28 2 E
Klipspruit →, *Jobg.* 18 F8 26 14 S 27 53 E
Kloofendal, *Jobg.* 18 E8 26 8 S 27 52 E
Klosterhardt, *Ruhr* 6 A3 51 32N 6 52 E
Klosterneuburg, *Wien* 10 G9 48 18N 16 19 E
Knockholt Pound, *Lon.* 4 D5 51 18N 0 7 E
Knowland State Arboretum and Park, *S.F.* 27 B4 37 45N 122 7W
Knox Park, *Melb.* 19 F8 37 54 S 145 15 E
Knoxville, *Melb.* 19 F8 37 53 S 145 14 E
Köbanya, *Bud.* 10 K13 47 28N 19 9 E
Kobe, *Ōsaka* 12 B2 34 41N 135 13 E
Kōbe Harbour, *Ōsaka* 12 C2 34 39N 135 11 E
København, *Købn.* 2 D9 55 40N 12 26 E
Kobylisy, *Pra.* 10 B2 50 7N 14 26 E
Kobyłka, *Wsaw.* 10 D8 52 20N 21 10 E
Kocasinan, *Ist.* 17 A2 41 1N 28 50 E
Kočife, *Pra.* 10 B2 50 3N 14 21 E
Kodaira, *Tōkyō* 13 B1 35 43N 139 28 E
Kodanaka, *Tōkyō* 13 C2 35 34N 139 37 E
Kogane, *Tōkyō* 13 B4 35 49N 139 55 E
Koganei, *Tōkyō* 13 B2 35 42N 139 31 E
Kogarah, *Syd.* 19 B3 33 57 S 151 8 E
Køge Bugt, *Købn.* 2 E9 55 34N 12 24 E
Köhlbrand Rethe, *Hbg.* 7 D7 53 31N 9 56 E
Köhlfleet, *Hbg.* 7 D7 53 32N 9 53 E
Koivupää, *Hels.* 3 B4 60 18N 24 53 E
Koja, *Jak.* 15 H10 6 8 S 106 52 E
Koja Utara, *Jak.* 15 H10 6 5 S 106 53 E
Kokobunji, *Tōkyō* 13 B1 35 42N 139 27 E
Kokobunji-Temple, *Tōkyō* 13 B4 35 44N 139 55 E
Kol Scholven, *Ruhr* 6 A3 51 35N 6 59 E
Kolarängen, *Stock.* 3 E12 59 16N 18 10 E
Kolbotn, *Oslo* 2 C4 59 48N 10 48 E
Kole Kalyan, *Bomb.* 16 G8 19 5N 72 50 E
Kolmiranta, *Hels.* 3 B2 60 15N 24 31 E
Kolmperä, *Hels.* 3 B2 60 15N 24 32 E
Koło, *Wsaw.* 10 E6 52 14N 20 56 E
Kolodeje, *Pra.* 10 B3 50 3N 14 38 E
Kolokinthou, *Ath.* 8 J11 38 0N 23 42 E
Kolomenskoye, *Mos.* 11 E10 55 40N 37 40 E
Kolomyagi, *St-Pet.* 11 A3 60 0N 30 19 E
Kolónos, *Ath.* 8 J11 37 59N 23 43 E
Kolovraty, *Pra.* 10 B3 50 0N 14 37 E
Kolsås, *Oslo* 2 B3 59 55N 10 30 E
Koltushi, *St-Pet.* 11 B5 59 55N 30 38 E
Komae, *Tōkyō* 13 C2 35 37N 139 34 E
Komagome, *Tōkyō* 13 B3 35 43N 139 45 E
Komazawa, *Tōkyō* 13 C3 35 37N 139 40 E
Komdhara, *Calc.* 16 C5 22 52N 88 14 E
Kommunarka, *Mos.* 11 F8 55 35N 37 29 E
Komorów, *Wsaw.* 10 F5 52 9N 20 48 E
Kona, *Calc.* 16 E5 22 37N 88 18 E
Konala, *Hels.* 3 B4 60 14N 24 52 E
Kōnan, *Tōkyō* 13 D2 35 23N 139 35 E
Kondli, *Delhi* 16 B2 28 36N 77 19 E
Kong Sin Wan, *H.K.* 12 E5 22 15N 114 7 E
Kongelunden, *Købn.* 2 E10 55 34N 12 34 E
Kongens Lyngby, *Købn.* 2 D10 55 46N 12 30 E
Kongo, *Hels.* 3 A3 60 20N 24 47 E
Königshardt, *Ruhr* 6 A3 51 33N 6 51 E
Konnagar, *Calc.* 16 D6 22 42N 88 21 E
Konohana, *Ōsaka* 12 B3 34 40N 135 26 E
Kōnoike, *Ōsaka* 12 B4 34 42N 135 37 E
Konradshöhe, *Berl.* 7 A2 52 35N 13 13 E
Koonung Cr. →, *Melb.* 19 E7 37 46 S 145 4 E
Kopanina, *Pra.* 10 B1 50 3N 14 17 E
Koparkhairna, *Bomb.* 16 G8 19 6N 72 59 E
Köpenick, *Berl.* 7 B4 52 26N 13 35 E
Korangi, *Kar.* 17 H11 24 47N 67 8 E
Koremasa, *Tōkyō* 13 C1 35 39N 139 29 E
Korenevo, *Mos.* 11 E12 55 40N 38 0 E
Kori, *Ōsaka* 12 B4 34 47N 135 38 E
Koridhallós, *Ath.* 8 J10 37 59N 23 39 E
Korkinskoye, Oz., *St-Pet.* 11 B6 59 55N 30 42 E
Körne, *Ruhr* 6 A7 51 30N 7 30 E
Korso, *Hels.* 3 A5 60 21N 25 5 E
Koshigaya, *Tōkyō* 13 A3 35 53N 139 47 E
Kosino, *Mos.* 11 E11 55 43N 37 50 E
Kosugi, *Tōkyō* 13 C2 35 34N 139 39 E
Kota, *Jak.* 15 H9 6 7 S 106 48 E
Kotelyniki, *Mos.* 11 F11 55 39N 37 52 E
Kōtō-Ku, *Tōkyō* 13 B3 35 40N 139 48 E
Kotrang, *Calc.* 16 D6 22 41N 88 20 E
Kouponia, *Ath.* 8 J11 37 57N 23 47 E
Koviksudde, *Stock.* 3 D13 59 21N 18 21 E
Kowloon, *H.K.* 12 E5 22 18N 114 10 E
Kowloon City, *H.K.* 12 E6 22 19N 114 11 E
Kowloon Pk., *H.K.* 12 D6 22 20N 114 13 E
Kowloon Res., *H.K.* 12 D5 22 21N 114 9 E
Kowloon Tong, *H.K.* 12 D6 22 20N 114 10 E
Kozhukhovo, *Mos.* 11 E11 55 43N 37 53 E
Kozukue, *Tōkyō* 13 C2 35 30N 139 35 E
Krailling, *Mün.* 7 G9 48 5N 11 25 E
Kramat Jati, *Jak.* 15 J10 6 15 S 106 51 E
Krampnitz, *Berl.* 7 B1 52 27N 13 3 E
Krampnitzsee, *Berl.* 7 B1 52 27N 13 3 E
Kranji, *Sing.* 15 F7 1 26N 103 45 E
Kranji, Sungei →, *Sing.* 15 F7 1 26N 103 44 E
Kranji Dam, *Sing.* 15 F7 1 26N 103 44 E
Kraskovo, *Mos.* 11 F11 55 39N 37 58 E
Krasnaya Gorka, *St-Pet.* 11 B5 59 58N 30 38 E
Krasno-Presnenskaya, *Mos.* 11 E9 55 45N 37 32 E
Krasnogorsk, *Mos.* 11 E7 55 49N 37 18 E
Krasnyj Stroitel, *Mos.* 11 F9 55 36N 37 35 E
Kray, *Ruhr* 6 B4 51 27N 7 4 E
Krč, *Pra.* 10 B2 50 2N 14 26 E
Krefeld, *Ruhr* 6 B1 51 20N 6 33 E
Kremlin, *Mos.* 11 E9 55 45N 37 38 E
Kresson, *Phil.* 24 B5 39 51N 74 54W
Kreuzberg, *Berl.* 7 A3 52 30N 13 24 E
Krishnarampur, *Calc.* 16 D5 22 43N 88 13 E
Kritzendorf, *Wien* 10 G9 48 19N 16 18 E
Krokhol, *Oslo* 2 C5 59 48N 10 55 E
Krugersdorp, *Jobg.* 18 E7 26 6 S 27 48 E
Krukut, Kali →, *Jak.* 15 J9 6 13 S 106 48 E
Krumme Lanke, *Berl.* 7 B2 52 27N 13 14 E
Krummensee, *Berl.* 7 A5 52 35N 13 41 E
Krupunder, *Hbg.* 7 D7 53 37N 9 53 E
Krusboda, *Stock.* 3 E12 59 13N 18 14 E
Krylatskoye, *Mos.* 11 E8 55 44N 37 23 E
Küçúkkoy, *Ist.* 17 A2 41 3N 28 52 E
Kudrovo, *St-Pet.* 11 B5 59 54N 30 30 E
Kuivasaari, *Hels.* 3 C5 60 6N 25 0 E
Kujiai, *Tōkyō* 13 A1 35 57N 139 26 E
Küllenhahn, *Ruhr* 6 C4 51 14N 7 8 E
Kulosaari, *Hels.* 3 B5 60 11N 25 0 E
Kulturpalasset, *Wsaw.* 10 E7 52 14N 21 0 E
Kumla, *Stock.* 3 E12 59 13N 18 11 E
Kummelnäs, *Stock.* 3 D12 59 21N 18 16 E
Kungens kurva, *Stock.* 3 E10 59 15N 17 53 E
Kungsängen, *Stock.* 3 D9 59 26N 17 43 E
Kungshatt, *Stock.* 3 E10 59 17N 17 53 E
Kungsholmen, *Stock.* 3 D11 59 20N 18 2 E
Kuningan, *Jak.* 15 J9 6 13 S 106 49 E
Kuninkaanmäki, *Hels.* 3 B5 60 18N 25 7 E
Kunitachi, *Tōkyō* 13 B1 35 41N 139 27 E
Kunming Hu, *Beij.* 14 B2 39 59N 116 13 E
Kunratice, *Pra.* 10 B2 50 0N 14 28 E
Kunratický →, *Pra.* 10 B2 50 2N 14 24 E
Kunsthalle, *Hbg.* 7 D8 53 33N 10 0 E
Kuntsevo, *Mos.* 11 E8 55 43N 37 23 E
Kupchino, *St-Pet.* 11 B4 59 50N 30 23 E
Kupferdreh, *Ruhr* 6 B4 51 23N 7 5 E
Kurbali Dere →, *Ist.* 17 B3 40 58N 29 1 E
Kurihara, *Tōkyō* 13 B2 35 45N 139 34 E
Kurkino, *Mos.* 11 D8 55 53N 37 22 E
Kurla, *Bomb.* 16 G8 19 4N 72 52 E
Kurmuri, *Bomb.* 16 G8 19 4N 72 53 E
Kurnell, *Syd.* 19 C4 34 0 S 151 10 E
Kurume, *Tōkyō* 13 B2 35 45N 139 31 E
Kuryanovo, *Mos.* 11 F10 55 39N 37 42 E
Kushihiki, *Tōkyō* 13 A2 35 54N 139 36 E
Kushtia, *Calc.* 16 E6 22 31N 88 23 E
Kuskovo, *Mos.* 11 E10 55 44N 37 48 E
Kutsino, *Mos.* 11 E11 55 44N 37 55 E
Kuy-e-Gishā, *Tehr.* 17 C5 35 44N 51 23 E
Kuy-e-Mekānir, *Tehr.* 17 C5 35 46N 51 22 E
Kuzyminki, *Mos.* 11 E10 55 42N 37 46 E
Kvarnsjön, *Stock.* 3 E10 59 11N 17 58 E
Kwa-Thema, *Jobg.* 18 F11 26 17 S 28 23 E
Kwai Chung, *H.K.* 12 D5 22 22N 114 7 E
Kwitang, *Jak.* 15 J10 6 11 S 106 50 E
Kwun Tong, *H.K.* 12 E6 22 18N 114 13 E
Kyje, *Pra.* 10 B3 50 6N 14 33 E
Kyōhōji, *Ōsaka* 12 C4 34 38N 135 33 E
Kyrkfjärden, *Stock.* 3 E9 59 16N 17 45 E
Kyrkslätt, *Hels.* 3 C1 60 6N 24 28W


## L


La Aguada, *Stgo* 30 J10 33 28 S 70 40W
La Blanca, *Stgo* 30 K11 33 30 S 70 40W
La Boca, *B.A.* 32 B4 34 38 S 58 22W
La Bottáccia, *Rome* 9 F8 41 54N 12 18 E
La Bretèche, *Paris* 5 B2 48 51N 2 1 E
La Brosse, *Paris* 5 C1 48 43N 1 20 E
La Cabana, *La Hab.* 30 B3 23 8N 82 20W
La Canada, *L.A.* 28 A3 34 12N 118 12W
La Cassa, *Tori.* 9 A2 45 11N 7 30 E
La Celle-les-Bordes, *Paris* 5 D1 48 38N 1 57 E
La Celle-St.-Cloud, *Paris* 5 B2 48 50N 2 9 E
La Chivera, *Car.* 30 D5 10 35N 66 54W
La Colmena, *Méx.* 29 A2 19 35N 99 16W
La Courneuve, *Paris* 5 B4 48 55N 2 22 E
La Crescenta, *L.A.* 28 A3 34 13N 118 14W
La Défense, *Paris* 5 B3 48 53N 2 12 E
La Dehesa, *Stgo* 30 J11 33 21 S 70 33W
La Estación, *Mdrd.* 8 B2 40 27N 3 48W
La Floresta, *Barc.* 8 D5 41 26N 2 3 E
La Florida, *Car.* 30 D5 10 30N 66 52W
La Fortuna, *Mdrd.* 8 B2 40 21N 3 46W
La Fransa, *Barc.* 8 D5 41 22N 2 9 E
La Fresnière, *Mtrl.* 20 A2 43 33N 73 58W
La Frette-sur-Seine, *Paris* 5 B3 48 58N 2 11 E
La Garenne-Colombes, *Paris* 5 B3 48 54N 2 15 E
La Giustiniana, *Rome* 9 F9 41 59N 12 24 E
La Grange, *Chic.* 26 C1 41 48N 87 53W
La Grange des Noues, *Paris* 5 A4 49 1N 2 28 E
La Grange Highlands, *Chic.* 26 C1 41 46N 87 53W
La Grange Park, *Chic.* 26 C1 41 49N 87 51W
La Granja, *Stgo* 30 K11 33 31 S 70 38W
La Guaira, *Car.* 30 D5 10 36N 66 55W
La Guardia Airport, *N.Y.* 23 C5 40 46N 73 52W
La Guasima, *La Hab.* 30 B3 23 0N 82 17W
La Habana, *La Hab.* 30 B2 23 7N 82 21W
La habana, B. de, *La Hab.* 30 B3 23 7N 82 20W
La Habana Vieia, *La Hab.* 30 B2 23 7N 82 20W
La Habra, *L.A.* 28 C5 33 56N 117 57W
La Habre Heights, *L.A.* 28 C5 33 59N 117 56W
La Horqueta →, *B.A.* 32 C1 34 43 S 58 51W
La Lisa, *La Hab.* 30 B2 23 3N 82 25W
La Llacuna, *Barc.* 8 D6 41 24N 2 12 E
La Loma, *Méx.* 29 A2 19 31N 99 11W
La Lucila, *B.A.* 32 B4 34 30 S 58 29W
La Magdalena Atlipac, *Méx.* 29 B4 19 22N 89 56 E
La Magdalena Chichicaspa, *Méx.* 29 B2 19 24N 99 18W
La Magdalena Contreras, *Méx.* 29 C2 19 17N 99 13W
La Magdalena Petlalco, *Méx.* 29 C2 19 13N 99 10W
La Maison Blanche, *Paris* 5 C1 48 44N 1 54 E
La Maladrerie, *Paris* 5 B2 48 54N 2 1 E
La Marquesa, *Méx.* 29 C1 19 18N 99 22W
La Milla, Cerro, *Lima* 30 G8 12 2 S 77 5W
La Molina, *Lima* 30 G9 12 4 S 76 56W
La Monachina, *Rome* 9 F9 41 53N 12 21 E
La Moraleja, *Mdrd.* 8 A3 40 30N 30 38W
La Nopalera, *Méx.* 29 C3 19 18N 99 5W
La Pastora, *Car.* 30 D5 10 31N 66 55W
La Paterna, *B.A.* 32 B4 34 35 S 58 26W
La Patte-d'Oie, *Paris* 5 A3 49 0N 2 10 E
La Perla, *Lima* 30 G8 12 4 S 77 7W
La Perouse, *Syd.* 19 B4 33 59 S 151 14 E
La Pineda, *Barc.* 8 E5 41 15N 2 1 E
La Pisana, *Rome* 9 F9 41 51N 12 23 E
La Playa, *La Hab.* 30 B2 23 6N 82 26W
La Prairie, *Mtrl.* 20 B5 43 25N 73 29W
La Puente, *L.A.* 28 B5 34 1N 117 54W
La Punta, *Lima* 30 G7 12 4 S 77 10W
La Puntigala, *Barc.* 8 D6 41 27N 2 13 E
La Queue-en-Brie, *Paris* 5 C5 48 47N 2 34 E
La Reina, *Stgo* 30 J11 33 26 S 70 33W
La Reja, *B.A.* 32 B2 34 38 S 58 48W
La Ribera, *Barc.* 8 D5 41 21N 2 4 E
La Romanie, *Paris* 5 C1 48 43N 1 53 E
La Rústica, *Rome* 9 F10 41 54N 12 36 E
La Sagrera, *Barc.* 8 D6 41 25N 2 11 E
La Salada, *B.A.* 32 C4 34 43 S 58 28W
La Scala, *Mil.* 9 E6 45 28N 9 11 E
La Selce, *Rome* 9 F9 41 53N 12 20 E
La Sierra, *La Hab.* 30 B2 23 7N 82 24W
La Taxonera, *Barc.* 8 D6 41 25N 2 10 E
La Vega, *Car.* 30 E5 10 28N 66 56W
La Verrière, *Paris* 5 C1 48 45N 1 57 E
La Vibora, *La Hab.* 30 B2 23 5N 82 22W
La Victoria, *Lima* 30 G8 12 3 S 77 2W
La Ville-du-Bois, *Paris* 5 D3 48 39N 2 16 E
Laab im Walde, *Wien* 10 H9 48 9N 16 10 E
Laaer Berg, *Wien* 10 H10 48 9N 16 24 E
Laajalahti, *Hels.* 3 B3 60 11N 24 48 E
Laajasalo, *Hels.* 3 B5 60 10N 25 1 E
Laaksolahti, *Hels.* 3 B3 60 14N 24 45 E
Laar, *Ruhr* 6 B2 51 27N 6 44 E
Lablâba, W. el →, *El Qâ.* 18 C5 30 1N 31 19 E
Lachine, *Mtrl.* 20 B3 43 26N 73 42W
Ládvi, *Pra.* 10 B2 50 8N 14 27 E
Łady, *Wsaw.* 10 F6 52 8N 20 57 E
Lafayette, *S.F.* 27 A4 37 52N 122 6W
Lafayette Hill, *Phil.* 24 A3 40 5N 75 15W
Lafayette Res., *S.F.* 27 A4 37 52N 122 8W
Laferrere, *B.A.* 32 C3 34 45 S 58 35W
Lagny, *Paris* 5 B6 48 52N 2 42 E
Lagoa da Pedra, *Lisb.* 8 F9 38 43N 8 58W
Lagos, *Lagos* 18 B2 6 27N 7 23 E
Lagos Harbour, *Lagos* 18 B2 6 26N 7 23 E
Lagos-Ikeja Airport, *Lagos* 18 A1 6 34N 7 19 E
Lagos Island, *Lagos* 18 B2 6 26N 7 23 E
Lagos Lagoon, *Lagos* 18 B2 6 30N 7 28 E
Laguna de B., *Manila* 15 E4 14 29N 121 6 E
Laim, *Mün.* 7 G10 48 7N 11 30 E
Lainate, *Mil.* 9 D5 45 34N 9 1 E
Lainz, *Wien* 10 H9 48 10N 16 16 E
Lainzer Tiergarten, *Wien* 10 G9 48 10N 16 13 E
Lajeado →, *S. Pau.* 31 E7 23 28 S 46 24W
Lake Avenue Woods, *Chic.* 26 A1 42 4N 87 53W
Lake Hiawatha, *N.Y.* 22 B2 40 52N 74 23W
Lakefield, *Jobg.* 18 F10 26 11 S 28 17 E
Lakemba, *Syd.* 19 B3 33 55 S 151 5 E
Lakeside, *Jobg.* 18 E9 26 5 S 28 8 E
Lakeview, *Chic.* 26 B3 41 56N 87 38W
Lakeview, *Trto.* 20 E7 43 35N 79 32W
Lakhtinskiy, *St-Pet.* 11 B2 59 59N 30 9 E
Lakhtinskiy Razliv, Oz., *St-Pet.* 11 B3 59 59N 30 12 E
Lakshmanpur, *Calc.* 16 E5 22 38N 88 16 E
Laleham, *Lon.* 4 C2 51 24N 0 29W
Lâleli, *Ist.* 17 A2 41 0N 28 57 E
Lalor, *Melb.* 19 E6 37 40 S 144 59 E
Lam San, *Sing.* 15 F7 1 22N 103 43 E
Lam Tin, *H.K.* 12 E6 22 18N 114 14 E
Lambarfjärden, *Stock.* 3 D9 59 21N 17 48 E
Lambert, *Oslo* 2 B4 59 52N 10 48 E
Lambeth, *Lon.* 4 C4 51 28N 0 6W
Lambrate, *Mil.* 9 E6 45 28N 9 16 E
Lambro →, *Mil.* 9 E6 45 24N 9 17 E
Lambro, Parco, *Mil.* 9 E6 45 29N 9 14 E
Lambton, *Jobg.* 18 F10 26 14 S 28 10 E
Lambton Hills, *Trto.* 20 E7 43 39N 79 30W
Lamma I., *H.K.* 12 E5 22 12N 114 7 E
Lampton, *Lon.* 4 C2 51 28N 0 21W
Landianchang, *Beij.* 14 B2 39 57N 116 13 E
Landover Hills, *Wash.* 25 D8 38 56N 76 54W
Landstrasse, *Wien* 10 G10 48 12N 16 23 E
Landwehr kanal, *Berl.* 7 B3 52 29N 13 24 E
Lane Cove, *Syd.* 19 A3 33 48 S 151 9 E
Lane Cove National Park, *Syd.* 19 A3 33 47 S 151 8 E
Langen, *Oslo* 2 C5 59 44N 10 57 E
Langenberg, *Ruhr* 6 B4 51 20N 7 7 E
Langenbochum, *Ruhr* 6 A4 51 36N 7 7 E
Langendreer, *Ruhr* 6 B5 51 28N 7 18 E
Langenhorn, *Hbg.* 7 D7 53 39N 9 59 E
Langenhorst, *Ruhr* 6 B4 51 21N 7 1 E
Langenzersdorf, *Wien* 10 G10 48 18N 16 21 E
Langer See, *Berl.* 7 B4 52 24N 13 37 E
Langerfeld, *Ruhr* 6 C5 51 16N 7 14 E
Langley, *Wash.* 25 D6 38 57N 77 11W
Langley Park, *Wash.* 25 D8 38 59N 76 58W
Langstaff, *Trto.* 20 C8 43 50N 79 26W
Längtarmen, *Stock.* 3 D8 59 24N 17 36 E
Langwald, *Mün.* 7 F9 48 10N 11 25 E
Lanham, *Wash.* 25 D8 38 59N 76 51W
Lank-Latum, *Ruhr* 6 C2 51 18N 6 40 E
Lankwitz, *Berl.* 7 B3 52 25N 13 21 E
Länna Drevviken, *Stock.* 3 E11 59 12N 18 8 E
L'Annunziatella, *Rome* 9 G10 41 49N 12 33 E
Lansdowne, *Balt.* 25 B3 39 14N 76 38W
Lansdowne, *Phil.* 24 B3 39 56N 75 16W
Lansing, *Trto.* 20 D8 43 45N 79 24W
Lanús, *B.A.* 32 C4 34 42 S 58 23W
Lapa, *Rio J.* 31 B2 22 54 S 43 10W
Lapa, *S. Pau.* 31 E5 23 31 S 46 42W
Lapangan Merdeka, *Jak.* 15 J9 6 10 S 106 49 E
Lapinkylä, *Hels.* 3 B4 60 18N 24 51 E
Lapinkylä, *Hels.* 3 B1 60 13N 24 27 E
Lappböle, *Hels.* 3 B1 60 13N 24 27 E
Laranjeiras, *Rio J.* 31 B2 22 55 S 43 10W
Larchmont, *N.Y.* 23 B6 40 55N 73 44W
Larkspur, *S.F.* 27 A1 37 55N 122 31W
Las, *Wsaw.* 10 E7 52 13N 21 6 E
Las Acacias, *Car.* 30 E5 10 29N 66 54W
Las Adjuntas, *Car.* 30 E4 10 25N 67 0W
Las Barrancas, *B.A.* 32 A4 34 28 S 58 29W
Las Conchas, *B.A.* 32 A3 34 25 S 58 34W
Las Corts, *Barc.* 8 D5 41 23N 2 9 E
Las Fuentes Brotantes, *Méx.* 29 C2 19 16N 99 11W
Las Kabacki, *Wsaw.* 10 F7 52 7N 21 2 E
Las Lomas, *L.A.* 28 B5 34 8N 117 59W
Las Mercedes, *Car.* 30 E5 10 28N 66 51W
Las Pinas, *Manila* 15 E3 14 29N 120 58 E
Las Rejas, *Stgo* 30 J10 33 27 S 70 42W
Las Rozas de Madrid, *Mdrd.* 8 B1 40 29N 3 52W
Las Trampas Cr. →, *S.F.* 27 A4 37 53N 122 6W
Las Trampas Regional Park, *S.F.* 27 B4 37 49N 122 3W
Las Trampas Ridge, *S.F.* 27 A4 37 50N 122 3W
Las Tunitas, *Car.* 30 D4 10 36N 67 1W
Lasalle, *Mtrl.* 20 B4 43 26N 73 37W
Lasek Bielański, *Wsaw.* 10 E6 52 17N 20 57 E
Lasek Na Kole, *Wsaw.* 10 E6 52 15N 20 56 E
Laski, *Wsaw.* 10 E6 52 18N 20 50 E
Latina, *Mdrd.* 8 B2 40 24N 3 44W
Latrobe Univ., *Melb.* 19 E7 37 43 S 145 3 E
Lattingtown, *N.Y.* 23 B7 40 52N 73 34W
Laufzorn, *Mün.* 7 G10 48 0N 11 33 E
Laurel Hollow, *N.Y.* 23 B8 40 51N 73 28W
Laurel Springs, *Phil.* 24 C4 39 49N 75 0W
Laurelton, *N.Y.* 23 C6 40 40N 73 45W
Laurence Hanscom Field, *Bost.* 21 C2 42 28N 71 16W
Lausdomini, *Nápl.* 9 H13 40 55N 14 26 E
Lauttasaari, *Hels.* 3 C4 60 9N 24 53 E
Lava Nuova, *Nápl.* 9 J13 40 47N 14 23 E
Laval-des-Rapides, *Mtrl.* 20 A3 43 33N 73 41W
Laval-Ouest, *Mtrl.* 20 A2 43 32N 73 52W
Laval-sur-le-Lac, *Mtrl.* 20 A2 43 31N 73 52W
Lavradio, *Lisb.* 8 F8 38 40N 9 2W
Lawndale, *Chic.* 26 B2 41 50N 87 42W
Lawndale, *L.A.* 28 C2 33 52N 118 22W
Lawndale, *Phil.* 24 A4 40 3N 75 5W
Lawnside, *Phil.* 24 B4 39 51N 75 1W
Lawrence, *Bost.* 21 A3 42 43N 71 7W
Lawrence, *N.Y.* 23 D6 40 36N 73 43W
Lawrence Heights, *Trto.* 20 D8 43 43N 79 25W
Lawrence Park, *Phil.* 24 B2 39 57N 75 20W
Lawton, *La Hab.* 30 B2 23 5N 82 20W
Layāri, *Kar.* 17 G11 24 52N 67 0 E
Layāri →, *Kar.* 17 G10 24 52N 66 58 E
Lazienkowski Park, *Wsaw.* 10 E7 52 13N 21 1 E
Le Blanc-Mesnil, *Paris* 5 B4 48 56N 2 27 E
Le Bourget, *Paris* 5 B4 48 56N 2 25 E
Le Chesnay, *Paris* 5 C2 48 49N 2 8 E
Le Christ de Saclay, *Paris* 5 C3 48 43N 1 59 E
Le Kremlin-Bicêtre, *Paris* 5 C4 48 48N 2 21 E
Le Mesnil-Amelot, *Paris* 5 A5 49 1N 2 35 E
Le Mesnil-le-Roi, *Paris* 5 B2 48 56N 2 7 E
Le Mesnil-St.-Denis, *Paris* 5 C1 48 44N 1 57 E
Le Pecq, *Paris* 5 B2 48 53N 2 6 E
Le Perreux, *Paris* 5 B4 48 50N 2 29 E
Le Pin, *Paris* 5 B5 48 54N 2 37 E
Le Plessis-Bouchard, *Paris* 5 A3 49 0N 2 14 E
Le Plessis-Gassot, *Paris* 5 A4 49 2N 2 24 E
Le Plessis-Pâté, *Paris* 5 D3 48 36N 2 19 E
Le Plessis-Robinson, *Paris* 5 C3 48 47N 2 15 E
Le Plessis-Trévise, *Paris* 5 C5 48 48N 2 34 E
Le Port-Marly, *Paris* 5 B2 48 52N 2 6 E
Le Pré-St.-Gervais, *Paris* 5 B4 48 53N 2 23 E
Le Raincy, *Paris* 5 B5 48 53N 2 31 E
Le Thillay, *Paris* 5 A4 49 0N 2 28 E
Le Trappe, *Mtrl.* 20 B1 43 30N 74 1W
Le Val d'Enfer, *Paris* 5 C3 48 45N 2 11 E
Le Vésinet, *Paris* 5 B2 48 54N 2 8 E
Lea →, *Lon.* 4 B4 51 30N 0 2W
Lea Bridge, *Lon.* 4 B4 51 33N 0 2W
Leakin Park, *Balt.* 25 B2 39 18N 76 41W
Leaside, *Trto.* 20 D8 43 42N 79 22W
Leatherhead, *Lon.* 4 D3 51 17N 0 19W
Leaves Green, *Lon.* 4 D5 51 19N 0 1 E
Leblon, *Rio J.* 31 B2 22 59 S 43 14W
Léchelle, Forêt de la, *Paris* 5 C6 48 43N 2 41 E
Ledøje, *Købn.* 2 D8 55 42N 12 18 E
Lee, *Lon.* 4 C5 51 27N 0 0 E
Leeupan, *Jobg.* 18 F10 26 13 S 28 18 E
Leganes, *Mdrd.* 8 C2 40 19N 3 45W
Legazpi, *Mdrd.* 8 B2 40 23N 3 41W
Legoa, Kali →, *Jak.* 15 H10 6 6 S 106 52 E
Lehtisaaret, *Hels.* 3 C3 60 6N 24 46 E
Lehtisaari, *Hels.* 3 B4 60 10N 24 51 E
Lei Yue Mun, *H.K.* 12 E6 22 17N 114 14 E
Leião, *Lisb.* 8 F7 38 43N 9 17W
Leichhardt, *Syd.* 19 B3 33 53 S 151 9 E
Leigang, *Gzh.* 14 G7 23 2N 113 6 E
Léini, *Tori.* 9 A3 45 11N 7 42 E
Leisure World, *S.F.* 27 A4 37 51N 122 4W
Lemoyne, *Mtrl.* 20 B5 43 29N 73 29W
Lemsahl, *Hbg.* 7 C8 53 41N 10 5 E
Lenin, *Mos.* 11 E9 55 43N 37 34 E
Leningrad = St. Petersburg, *St-Pet.* 11 B3 59 55N 30 15 E
Lenino, *Mos.* 11 F9 55 38N 37 39 E
Leninskiye Gory, *Mos.* 11 E9 55 41N 37 32 E
Lenne →, *Ruhr* 6 B7 51 25N 7 30 E
Lennep, *Ruhr* 6 C5 51 11N 7 15 E
Lenni, *Phil.* 24 B2 39 53N 75 27W
Lennox, *L.A.* 28 C2 33 56N 118 20W
Leonardo da Vinci, Aeroporto Int., *Rome* 9 G8 41 47N 12 15 E
Leoncio Martinez, *Car.* 30 E6 10 29N 66 48W
Leonia, *N.Y.* 22 B5 40 51N 73 59W
Leopard, *Phil.* 24 A2 40 1N 75 26W
Leopardi, *Nápl.* 9 J13 40 45N 14 24 E
Leopoldau, *Wien* 10 G10 48 15N 16 26 E
Leopoldstadt, *Wien* 10 G10 48 13N 16 22 E
Leportovo, *Mos.* 11 E10 55 46N 37 43 E
Leppävaara, *Hels.* 3 B3 60 13N 24 49 E
Lera, Mte., *Tori.* 9 A1 45 10N 7 27 E
L'Éremo, *Tori.* 9 B3 45 2N 7 44 E
Les Alluets-le-Roi, *Paris* 5 B1 48 54N 1 55 E
Les Clayes-sous-Bois, *Paris* 5 C1 48 49N 1 59 E
Les Essarts-le-Roi, *Paris* 5 C1 48 42N 1 53 E
Les Gâtines, *Paris* 5 C1 48 48N 1 58 E
Les Grésillons, *Paris* 5 B2 48 56N 2 1 E
Les Layes, *Paris* 5 C1 48 43N 1 55 E
Les Lilas, *Paris* 5 B4 48 52N 2 25 E
Les Loges-en-Josas, *Paris* 5 C2 48 45N 2 8 E
Les Molières, *Paris* 5 C2 48 40N 2 4 E
Les Mureaux, *Paris* 5 B1 48 59N 1 54 E
Les Pavillons-sous-Bois, *Paris* 5 B5 48 54N 2 30 E
Les Vaux de Cernay →, *Paris* 5 C1 48 41N 1 59 E
Lésigny, *Paris* 5 C5 48 44N 2 37 E
Lesnosavodskaya, *St-Pet.* 11 B4 59 51N 30 29 E
Lesnoy, *St-Pet.* 11 B4 59 59N 30 22 E
Lester B. Pearson Int. Airport, *Trto.* 20 D7 43 40N 79 38 E
L'Étang-la-Ville, *Paris* 5 B2 48 52N 2 4 E
Letná, *Pra.* 10 B2 50 0 S 14 26 E
Letňany, *Pra.* 10 B3 50 8N 14 30 E
Letovo, *Mos.* 11 F8 55 34N 37 24 E
Leuville-sur-Orge, *Paris* 5 D3 48 36N 2 15 E
Levallois-Perret, *Paris* 5 B3 48 53N 2 16 E
Lévis St.-Nom, *Paris* 5 C1 48 43N 1 57 E
Levittown, *N.Y.* 23 C7 40 43N 73 31W
Lewisdale, *Wash.* 25 D8 38 58N 76 59W
Lewisham, *Jobg.* 18 E7 26 7 S 27 49 E
Lewisham, *Lon.* 4 C4 51 27N 0 1W
Lexington, *Bost.* 21 C2 42 25N 71 12W
Leyton, *Lon.* 4 B4 51 33N 0 1W
Leytonstone, *Lon.* 4 B5 51 34N 0 0 E
L'Hautil, *Paris* 5 A2 49 0N 2 0 E
L'Hay-les-Roses, *Paris* 5 C4 48 46N 2 20 E
Lhotka, *Pra.* 10 B2 50 1N 14 26 E
Liangshui He →, *Beij.* 14 C3 39 48N 116 23 E
Lianhua Chi, *Beij.* 14 B2 39 52N 116 16 E
Lianhua He →, *Beij.* 14 B2 39 52N 116 13 E
Lianozovo, *Mos.* 11 D9 55 53N 37 34 E
Libčice nad Vitavou, *Pra.* 10 A2 50 11N 14 22 E
Liben, *Pra.* 10 B2 50 6N 14 27 E
Liberdade, *S. Pau.* 31 E6 23 33 S 46 37W
Libertad, *B.A.* 32 C2 34 41 S 58 41W
Liberty I., *N.Y.* 22 C4 40 41N 74 2W
Liberty Plain, *Bost.* 21 D4 42 11N 70 52W
Liberty Res., *Balt.* 25 A1 39 23N 76 52W
Libeznice, *Pra.* 10 A2 50 11N 14 29 E
Library of Congress, *Wash.* 25 D7 38 53N 77 0W
Libuč, *Pra.* 10 B2 50 0N 14 27 E
Lichiao, *Gzh.* 14 G8 23 3N 113 18 E
Lichtenbroich, *Ruhr* 6 C2 51 17N 6 49 E
Lichtenburg, *Berl.* 7 A4 52 31N 13 30 E
Lichtenplatz, *Ruhr* 6 C5 51 14N 7 11 E
Lichtenrade, *Berl.* 7 B3 52 23N 13 24 E
Lichterfelde, *Berl.* 7 B2 52 25N 13 19 E
Licignano di Nápoli, *Nápl.* 9 H13 40 54N 14 21 E
Lidcombe, *Syd.* 19 B3 33 52 S 151 3 E
Lidingö, *Stock.* 3 D11 59 21N 18 8 E
Lido Beach, *N.Y.* 23 D7 40 35N 73 37W
Lier, *Oslo* 2 C1 59 47N 10 13 E
Lierskogen, *Oslo* 2 C1 59 49N 10 15 E
Lieshi Lingyuan, *Gzh.* 14 G8 23 7N 113 16 E
Liesing, *Wien* 10 H9 48 8N 16 17 E
Liesing →, *Wien* 10 H10 48 8N 16 28 E
Lieusant, *Paris* 5 D5 48 38N 2 33 E
Liffjofs, *Hels.* 3 B6 60 19N 25 12 E
Ligovo, *St-Pet.* 11 C3 59 49N 30 10 E
Lijordet, *Oslo* 2 B3 59 56N 10 36 E
Likhoborka →, *Mos.* 11 D9 55 50N 37 37 E
Likova →, *Mos.* 11 F8 55 36N 37 20 E
Lilla Värtan, *Stock.* 3 D12 59 20N 18 11 E
Lille Rørbæk, *Købn.* 2 D7 55 47N 12 6 E

Midland Park 41


Lille Værløse, Købn. 2 D9 55 47N 12 22 E
Lillehavfrue, Købn. 2 D10 55 42N 12 35 E
Lillestrøm, Oslo 2 B6 59 57N 11 3 E
Liluah, Calc. 16 E5 22 37N 88 19 E
Lilydale, Melb. 19 E9 37 45 S 145 21 E
Lima, Lima 30 G8 12 3 S 77 2W
Lima, Phil. 24 B2 39 55N 75 26W
Limbiate, Mil. 9 D5 45 35N 9 7 E
Limehouse, Lon. 4 B4 51 30N 0 1W
Limeil-Brévannes, Paris 5 C4 48 44N 2 29 E
Limito, Mil. 9 E6 45 28N 9 19 E
Limoges-Fourches, Paris 5 D5 48 37N 2 39 E
Limours, Paris 5 D2 48 38N 2 4 E
Linas, Paris 5 D3 48 37N 2 16 E
Linate, Mil. 9 E6 45 26N 9 16 E
Linate, Aeroporto Internazionale di, Mil. 9 E6 45 26N 9 16 E
Linbigh, Balt. 25 A3 39 21N 76 31W
Linbropark, Jobg. 18 E9 26 5 S 28 7 E
Lincoln, Bost. 21 C2 42 25N 71 18W
Lincoln Center, N.Y. 22 C5 40 46N 43 59W
Lincoln Heights, L.A. 28 B3 34 4N 118 12 E
Lincoln Memorial, Wash. 25 D7 38 53N 77 2W
Lincoln Park, Chic. 26 B3 41 57N 87 38W
Lincoln Park, N.Y. 22 B3 40 56N 74 18W
Lincoln Park, S.F. 27 B1 37 47N 122 30W
Lincolnwood, Chic. 26 A2 42 1N 87 43W
Linda-a-Pastora, Lisb. 8 F7 38 42N 9 15W
Linden, Jobg. 18 E9 26 8 S 28 0 E
Linden, N.Y. 22 D3 40 38N 74 14W
Linden-Dahlhausen, Ruhr 6 B5 51 25N 7 10 E
Lindenberg, Berl. 7 A4 52 36N 13 31 E
Lindenhorst, Ruhr 6 A6 51 33N 7 27 E
Lindenhurst, N.Y. 23 C8 40 40N 73 22W
Lindenwold, Phil. 24 C5 39 49N 74 59W
Linderhausen, Ruhr 6 C5 51 17N 7 17 E
Lindfield, Syd. 19 A3 33 46 S 151 9 E
Lindøya, Oslo 2 B4 59 53N 10 42 E
Lingotto, Tori. 9 B2 45 1N 7 39 E
Liniers, B.A. 32 B3 34 39 S 58 30W
Linksfield, Jobg. 18 E9 26 9 S 28 6 E
Linmeyer, Jobg. 18 F9 26 15 S 28 4 E
Linn, Ruhr 6 B1 51 20N 6 38 E
Linna, Hels. 3 A4 60 20N 24 50 E
Linthicum Heights, Balt. 25 B2 39 12N 76 47W
Lintorf, Ruhr 6 B3 51 20N 6 50 E
Lintuvaara, Hels. 3 B3 60 14N 24 49 E
Linwood, Phil. 24 C2 39 49N 75 25W
Lioúmi, Ath. 8 J11 38 0N 23 40 E
Lipków, Wsaw. 10 E5 52 16N 20 48 E
Lippalthausen, Ruhr 6 A6 51 36N 7 26 E
Liqizhuang, Tianj. 14 E6 39 4N 117 10 E
Lirich, Ruhr 6 B2 51 29N 6 49 E
Lisboa, Lisb. 8 F8 38 42N 9 8W
Lisbon = Lisboa, Lisb. 8 F8 38 42N 9 8W
Lishui, Gzh. 14 F7 23 12N 113 9 E
Lisiy Nos, St-Pet. 11 A2 60 1N 30 0 E
Lissone, Mil. 9 D6 45 36N 9 14 E
Lissy, Paris 5 D6 48 38N 2 42 E
Litoral, Cord. del, Car. 30 D5 10 33N 66 54W
Little B., Syd. 19 B4 33 58 S 151 15 E
Little Calumet →, Chic. 26 D3 41 39N 87 34W
Little Falls, N.Y. 22 B3 40 52N 74 14W
Little Ferry, N.Y. 22 B4 40 50N 74 2W
Little Neck, N.Y. 23 C6 40 46N 73 43W
Little Paint Br. →, Wash. 25 C8 39 0N 76 55W
Little Patuxent →, Balt. 25 B1 39 13N 76 51W
Little Rouge →, Trto. 20 C9 43 45N 79 11W
Little Sugarloaf, Melb. 19 E8 37 40 S 145 18 E
Little Thurrock, Lon. 4 C7 51 29N 0 20 E
Liuhang, Shang. 14 H11 31 21N 121 21 E
Liuhuahu Gongyuan, Gzh. 14 G8 23 8N 113 14 E
Liverpool, Syd. 19 B2 33 55 S 150 55 E
Livingstone, N.Y. 22 C3 40 47N 74 19W
Livry-Gargan, Paris 5 B5 48 55N 2 31 E
Liwanhu Gongyuan, Gzh. 14 G8 23 7N 113 13 E
Lizhuang, Gzh. 14 G7 23 6N 113 7 E
Ljan, Oslo 2 B4 59 51N 10 48 E
Llano de Can Gineu, Barc. 8 D6 41 27N 2 10 E
Llavallol, B.A. 32 C4 34 48 S 58 25W
Llobregat →, Barc. 8 D5 41 19N 2 5 E
Lloyd Harbor, N.Y. 23 B8 40 54N 73 26W
Lloyd Pt., N.Y. 23 B8 40 56N 73 29W
Lo Aranguiz, Stgo 30 J11 33 23 S 70 40W
Lo Boza, Stgo 30 J10 33 23 S 70 43W
Lo Chau, H.K. 12 E6 22 11N 114 15 E
Lo Hermida, Stgo 30 J11 33 28 S 70 33W
Lo Ortuzar, Stgo 30 J10 33 28 S 70 43W
Lo Prado Arriba, Stgo 30 J10 33 26 S 70 42W
Lo So Shing, H.K. 12 E5 22 12N 114 7 E
Lo Wai, H.K. 12 D5 22 22N 114 8 E
Lobau, Wien 10 G11 48 10N 16 31 E
Lobos, Pt., S.F. 27 B1 37 46N 122 30W
Loch Raven Village, Balt. 25 A3 39 23N 76 34W
Locham, Mün. 7 G9 48 7N 11 26 E
Lochearn, Balt. 25 A2 39 20N 76 43W
Lochino, Mos. 11 E7 55 41N 37 17 E
Lochkov, Pra. 10 B2 50 0N 14 21 E
Lockhausen, Mün. 7 F9 48 10N 11 24 E
Locksbottom, Lon. 4 C5 51 21N 0 3 E
Locust Grove, N.Y. 23 C8 40 48N 73 29W
Locust Manor, N.Y. 23 C6 40 41N 73 45W
Locust Valley, N.Y. 23 B7 40 52N 73 36W
Lodi, N.Y. 22 B4 40 52N 74 5W
Lofty, Mt., Melb. 19 E8 37 42 S 145 17 E
Logan, Phil. 24 A4 40 2N 75 8W
Logan Int. Airport, Bost. 21 C4 42 22N 71 0W
Logan Square, Chic. 26 B2 41 55N 87 42W
Lognes-Émerainville, Aérodrome de, Paris 5 C5 48 49N 2 37 E
Lohausen, Ruhr 6 C2 51 16N 6 44 E
Lohberg, Ruhr 6 A2 51 34N 6 45 E
Lohme, Berl. 7 A5 52 37N 13 40 E
Lohmühle, Ruhr 6 A1 51 30N 6 39 E
Löhnen, Ruhr 6 A1 51 35N 6 39 E
Lokstedt, Hbg. 7 D7 53 36N 9 56 E
Lokyang, Sing. 15 G7 1 19N 103 40 E
Lölökhet, Kar. 17 G11 24 54N 67 2 E
Loma Blanca, Stgo 30 J10 33 29 S 70 43W
Lomas Chapultepec, Méx. 29 B2 19 25N 99 12W
Lomas de San Angel Inn, Méx. 29 B2 19 20N 99 13W
Lomas de Zamora, B.A. 32 C4 34 45 S 58 24W
Lombardy East, Jobg. 18 E9 26 6 S 28 7 E
Lomomosov Univ., Mos. 11 E9 55 42N 37 31 E
Lomus Reforma, Méx. 29 B2 19 24N 99 14W
London, Lon. 4 B4 51 30N 0 6W
London, City of, Lon. 4 B4 51 30N 0 6W
London, Tower of, Lon. 4 B4 51 30N 0 4W
London Zoo, Lon. 4 B4 51 31N 0 9W
Long B., Syd. 19 B4 33 59 S 151 15 E
Long Beach, N.Y. 23 D7 40 35N 73 39W
Long Branch, Trto. 20 E7 43 35N 79 31W
Long Brook →, Wash. 25 E6 38 49N 77 15W
Long Ditton, Lon. 4 C3 51 22N 0 19W
Long I., Bost. 21 D4 42 19N 70 59W
Long I., N.Y. 23 C7 40 45N 73 30W
Long Island City, N.Y. 22 C5 40 45N 73 56W
Long Island Sd., N.Y. 23 B7 40 57N 73 30W
Long Pond, Bost. 21 A1 42 41N 71 22W
Longchamp, Hippodrôme de, Paris 5 B3 48 51N 2 13 E
Longchêne, Paris 5 D2 48 38N 2 0 E
Longhua Gongyuan, Shang. 14 J11 31 10N 121 26 E
Longjohn Slough, Chic. 26 C1 41 42N 87 52W
Longjumeau, Paris 5 C3 48 41N 2 17 E
Longlands, Lon. 4 C5 51 25N 0 5 E
Longpont-sur-Orge, Paris 5 D3 48 38N 2 17 E
Longtan Hu →, Beij. 14 B3 39 51N 116 24 E
Longue Point, Mtrl. 20 A4 43 35N 73 31W
Longueuil, Mtrl. 20 A5 43 31N 73 29W
Loni, Delhi 16 A2 28 45N 77 17 E
Lord's Cricket Ground, Lon. 4 B3 51 31N 0 10W
Loreley, Balt. 25 A4 39 23N 76 24W
Lørenskog, Oslo 2 B5 59 55N 10 59 E
Loreto, Mil. 9 E6 45 29N 9 12 E
Lorraine, Mtrl. 20 A3 43 39N 73 46W
Los Angeles, L.A. 28 B3 34 3N 118 14 E
Los Angeles, Mdrd. 8 B2 40 20N 3 41W
Los Angeles →, L.A. 28 C3 33 55N 118 10W
Los Angeles Int. Airport, L.A. 28 C2 33 56N 118 23W
Los Asientos, Car. 30 D5 10 32N 66 53W
Los Caobos, Car. 30 D5 10 30N 66 53W
Los Carmenes, Car. 30 E5 10 28N 66 54W
Los Cerrillas, Aeroporto, Stgo 30 J10 33 29 S 70 42W
Los Dos Caminos, Car. 30 D6 10 30N 66 49W
Los dos Riteras →, Car. 30 D5 10 35N 66 57W
Los Jazmines, Presa, Méx. 29 B2 19 25N 99 15W
Los Nietos, L.A. 28 C4 33 57N 118 4W
Los Pinos, La Hab. 30 B2 23 4N 82 22W
Los Pirules, Méx. 29 B3 19 24N 99 2W
Los Polvorines, B.A. 32 B2 34 30 S 58 41W
Los Remedios →, Méx. 29 B2 19 28N 99 13W
Los Remedios, Parque Nacional de, Méx. 29 B2 19 27N 99 15W
Los Reyes, Méx. 29 B4 19 21N 99 6W
Los Rosales, Car. 30 E5 10 28N 66 53W
Losby, Oslo 2 B5 59 53N 10 59 E
Loughton, Lon. 4 B5 51 38N 0 4 E
Loures, Lisb. 8 F7 38 49N 9 10W
Louveciennes, Paris 5 B2 48 51N 2 8 E
Louvres, Paris 5 A5 49 2N 2 30 E
Lovön, Stock. 3 E10 59 18N 17 51 E
Lövstafjärden, Stock. 3 D9 59 23N 17 46 E
Lowe, Mt., L.A. 28 A4 34 13N 118 5W
Lowe Pond, Bost. 21 A3 42 41N 71 0W
Lowell, Bost. 21 B2 42 38N 71 16W
Lowell Dracut State Forest, Bost. 21 B1 42 39N 71 22W
Lower Crystal Springs Res., S.F. 27 C2 37 31N 122 21W
Lower Edmonton, Lon. 4 B4 51 37N 0 3W
Lower Montville, N.Y. 22 B2 40 53N 74 21W
Lower New York B., N.Y. 22 D4 40 32N 74 5W
Lower Plenty, Melb. 19 E7 37 44 S 145 7 E
Lower Shing Mun Res., H.K. 12 D5 22 22N 114 9 E
Lower Sydenham, Lon. 4 C4 51 25N 0 2W
Lower Van Norman L., L.A. 28 A2 34 17N 118 28W
Lübars, Berl. 7 A3 52 37N 13 21 E
Lubeinī, Bahr el →, El Qâ. 18 C4 30 1N 31 5 E
Lubya →, St-Pet. 11 A5 60 1N 30 39 E
Lucento, Tori. 9 B2 45 5N 7 39 E
Lucero, La Hab. 30 B3 23 5N 82 19W
Ludwigsfeld, Mün. 7 F9 48 12N 11 27 E
Lugarno, Syd. 19 B3 33 59 S 151 2 E
Lugouqiao, Beij. 14 C2 39 49N 116 10 E
Luhu, Gzh. 14 G8 23 9N 113 16 E
Luipaardsvei, Jobg. 18 E7 26 6 S 27 49 E
Luis Guillón, B.A. 32 C4 34 48 S 58 26W
Lujia, Shang. 14 J12 31 15N 121 37 E
Lukens, Mt., L.A. 28 A3 34 16N 118 12W
Lumiar, Lisb. 8 F8 38 4N 9 10W
Lundtofte, Købn. 2 D10 55 47N 12 32 E
Lung Mei, H.K. 12 D6 22 23N 114 15 E
Lunsad, Manila 15 E5 14 27N 121 11 E
Luojiang, Gzh. 14 G8 23 5N 113 17 E
Lura →, Mil. 9 D5 45 34N 9 5 E
Lurnea, Syd. 19 B2 33 56 S 150 54 E
Lurup, Hbg. 7 D7 53 35N 9 54 E
Lustheim, Mün. 7 F10 48 14N 11 34 E
Lütgendortmund, Ruhr 6 A6 51 30N 7 20 E
Lutherville-Timonium, Balt. 25 A3 39 25N 76 36W
Lüttringhausen, Ruhr 6 C5 51 12N 7 14 E
Lutvatn, Oslo 2 B5 59 54N 10 52 E
Luwan, Shang. 14 J11 31 12N 121 27 E
Luyano, La Hab. 30 B2 23 6N 82 20W
Luzhniki Sports Centre, Mos. 11 E9 55 43N 37 31 E
Lyckebyn, Stock. 3 E12 59 11N 18 13 E
Lynbrook, N.Y. 23 D6 40 38N 73 41W
Lyndhurst, Jobg. 18 E9 26 7 S 28 6 E
Lyndhurst, N.Y. 22 C4 40 49N 74 7W
Lynn, Bost. 21 C4 42 28N 70 57W
Lynn Harbor, Bost. 21 C4 42 26N 70 56W
Lynnfield, Bost. 21 B3 42 32N 71 2W
Lynwood, L.A. 28 C3 33 55N 118 11W
Lyon, Gare de, Paris 5 B4 48 50N 2 22 E
Lyons, Chic. 26 C2 41 48N 87 49W
Lyonsville, N.Y. 22 C4 40 57N 74 26W
Lysaker, Oslo 2 B3 59 54N 10 38 E
Lysakerselva →, Oslo 2 B3 59 54N 10 38 E
Lysolaje, Pra. 10 B2 50 8N 14 22 E
Lytkarino, Mos. 11 F11 55 35N 37 55 E
Lyubertsy, Mos. 11 E11 55 40N 37 51 E
Lyublino, Mos. 11 E10 55 41N 37 44 E


# M


Ma Nam Wat, H.K. 12 D6 22 21N 114 16 E
Ma Po, Sŏul 12 G7 37 32N 126 56 E
Ma Tsz Keng, H.K. 12 D5 22 21N 114 7 E
Ma Yau Tong, H.K. 12 E6 22 19N 114 14 E
Maantiekylä, Hels. 3 A5 60 20N 25 0 E
Maarifa, Bagd. 17 F8 33 15N 44 21 E
Mabashi, Tōkyō 13 B4 35 48N 139 55 E
Mabato Pt., Manila 15 E4 14 29N 121 3 E
Mabolo, Manila 15 E3 14 26N 120 56 E
Macaco, Morro do, Rio J. 31 B3 22 56 S 43 6W
McCook, Chic. 26 C2 41 47N 87 49W
McGill Univ., Mtrl. 20 A4 43 30N 73 35W
Machida, Tōkyō 13 C1 35 32N 139 26 E
Macierzysz, Wsaw. 10 E6 52 13N 20 50 E
Maciołki, Wsaw. 10 E7 52 19N 21 9 E
Mackayville, Mtrl. 20 A5 43 30N 73 26W
McKinnon, Melb. 19 F7 37 54 S 145 1 E
Mclean, Wash. 25 D6 38 56N 77 10W
Macleod, Melb. 19 E7 37 43 S 145 4 E
Macopocho →, Stgo 30 J10 33 24 S 70 40W
Macquarie Fields, Syd. 19 B2 33 59 S 150 53 E
Macquarie Univ., Syd. 19 A3 33 46 S 151 7 E
MacRitchie Res., Sing. 15 F7 1 20N 103 49 E
Macul, Stgo 30 K11 33 30 S 70 35W
Macuto, Car. 30 D5 10 36N 66 53W
Macuto →, Car. 30 D5 10 36N 66 53W
Madatpur, Calc. 16 C6 22 53N 88 27 E
Maddalena, Colle della, Tori. 9 B3 45 2N 7 43 E
Madhudaha, Calc. 16 E6 22 30N 88 24 E
Madhyamgram, Calc. 16 D6 22 41N 88 26 E
Madīnah Al Mansōr, Bagd. 17 F8 33 18N 44 20 E
Mâdinet el Muqattam, El Qâ. 18 C5 30 1N 31 15 E
Mâdinet Nasr, El Qâ. 18 C5 30 4N 31 18 E
Madipur, Delhi 16 B1 28 40N 77 8 E
Madison, N.Y. 22 C2 40 45N 74 24W
Madonna della Scala, Tori. 9 B3 44 59N 7 46 E
Madonna dell'Arco, Nápl. 9 H13 40 52N 14 23 E
Madrid, Mdrd. 8 B2 40 24N 3 42W
Madrona, Barc. 8 D5 41 27N 2 1 E
Madureira, Rio J. 31 B2 22 52 S 43 19W
Maeda, Tōkyō 13 B3 35 48N 139 45 E
Maesawa, Tōkyō 13 B2 35 44N 139 31 E
Magalhaes, Rio J. 31 B1 22 51 S 43 22W
Magdalena del Mar, Lima 30 G8 12 5 S 77 5W
Magholpur, Delhi 16 A1 28 41N 77 6 E
Maghreb, Bagd. 17 E8 33 23N 44 22 E
Magidiyeh, Tehr. 17 C5 35 43N 51 28 E
Maginu, Tōkyō 13 C2 35 34N 139 34 E
Magliana, Rome 9 F9 41 50N 12 26 E
Maglód, Bud. 10 K14 47 27N 19 18 E
Magnolia, Phil. 24 B4 39 51N 75 1W
Magny-les-Hameaux, Paris 5 C2 48 44N 2 3 E
Maharajpur, Delhi 16 B2 28 39N 77 19 E
Maheshtala, Calc. 16 F5 22 29N 88 15 E
Mahiari, Calc. 16 E5 22 35N 88 14 E
Mahikpur, Calc. 16 E5 22 32N 88 13 E
Mahim, Bomb. 16 G8 19 2N 72 50 E
Mahim B., Bomb. 16 G7 19 2N 72 49 E
Mahishdanga, Calc. 16 C5 22 53N 88 11 E
Mahlsdorf, Berl. 7 A4 52 30N 13 37 E
Mahmoodabad, Kar. 17 G11 24 51N 67 4 E
Mahmutbey, Ist. 17 A1 41 2N 28 49 E
Mahpar, Jak. 15 H9 6 9 S 106 49 E
Mahul, Bomb. 16 G8 19 0N 72 53 E
Maida Vale, Lon. 4 B3 51 31N 0 11W
Maidstone, Melb. 19 E6 37 47 S 144 52 E
Maincourt-sur-Yvette, Paris 5 C1 48 42N 1 58 E
Maipu, Stgo 30 K10 33 30 S 70 45W
Maiquetia, Car. 30 D5 10 35N 66 57W
Maiquetia Aeropuerto, Car. 30 D4 10 36N 67 0W
Maisons-Alfort, Paris 5 C4 48 48N 2 26 E
Maisons-Laffitte, Paris 5 B2 48 57N 2 8 E
Maissoneuve, Mtrl. 20 A4 43 32N 73 33W
Maitani, Ōsaka 12 B3 34 48N 135 22 E
Majadahonda, Mdrd. 8 B1 40 28N 3 52W
Majlis, Tehr. 17 C5 35 41N 51 25 E
Makati, Manila 15 D4 14 33N 121 7 E
Mäkiniitty, Hels. 3 A4 60 20N 24 58 E
Mala Straná, Pra. 10 B2 50 4N 14 24 E
Malabar, Syd. 19 B4 33 58 S 151 14 E
Malabar Hill, Bomb. 16 H7 18 57N 72 48 E
Malabon, Manila 15 D3 14 39N 120 56 E
Malacanang Palace, Manila 15 D3 14 35N 120 59 E
Malagrotta, Rome 9 F9 41 52N 12 20 E
Malakhovka, Mos. 11 F12 55 39N 38 0 E
Malakoff, Paris 5 C3 48 49N 2 18 E
Malakpur, Delhi 16 A2 28 42N 77 12 E
Malanday, Manila 15 D4 14 38N 121 5 E
Malanghero, Tori. 9 A2 45 12N 7 39 E
Mälarhöjaen, Stock. 3 E10 59 18N 17 58 E
Malaspina, L., Mil. 9 E6 45 28N 9 18 E
Malassis, Paris 5 D2 48 37N 2 3 E
Malate, Manila 15 D3 14 34N 120 59 E
Malaya Neva, St-Pet. 11 B3 59 56N 30 16 E
Malaya-Okhta, St-Pet. 11 B4 59 55N 30 25 E
Malchow, Berl. 7 A3 52 34N 13 29 E
Malden, Bost. 21 C3 42 26N 71 3W
Malden, Lon. 4 C3 51 23N 0 15W
Malešice, Pra. 10 B3 50 5N 14 30 E
Malekete, Lagos 18 A3 6 33N 7 32 E
Malir →, Kar. 17 H11 24 49N 67 4 E
Malir Cantonment, Kar. 17 G12 24 58N 67 10 E
Malmi, Hels. 3 B4 60 15N 24 59 E
Malmøya, Oslo 2 B4 59 52N 10 45 E
Måløv, Købn. 2 D9 55 44N 12 20 E
Malton, Trto. 20 D7 43 42N 79 38W
Malvern, Jobg. 18 F9 26 11 S 28 5 E
Malvern, Melb. 19 F7 37 50 S 145 2 E
Malvern, Phil. 24 A1 40 2N 75 31W
Malvern, Trto. 20 D9 43 47N 79 13W
Malvern East, Jobg. 18 F9 26 11 S 28 7 E
Malverne, N.Y. 23 C6 40 40N 73 40W
Mamaroneck, N.Y. 23 B6 40 56N 73 43W
Mamaroneck Harbour, N.Y. 23 B6 40 56N 73 42W
Mamonovo, Mos. 11 F10 55 36N 37 49 E
Mamonovo, Mos. 11 E8 55 41N 37 18 E
Mampong Prapatan, Jak. 15 J9 6 15 S 106 49 E
Mampukuji, Tōkyō 13 C2 35 36N 139 31 E
Man Budrukh, Bomb. 16 G8 19 2N 72 55 E
Man Khurd, Bomb. 16 G8 19 3N 72 55 E
Managua, La Hab. 30 C3 22 58N 82 17W
Manayunk, Phil. 24 A3 40 1N 75 12W
Mandaluyong, Manila 15 D4 14 35N 121 1 E
Mandaoli, Delhi 16 B2 28 37N 77 17 E
Mandaqui, S. Pau. 31 D6 23 29 S 46 37W
Mandaqui →, S. Pau. 31 D6 23 30 S 46 40W
Mandres-les-Roses, Paris 5 C5 48 42N 2 32 E
Mandvi, Bomb. 16 H8 18 56N 72 50 E
Mang Kung Uk, H.K. 12 E6 22 18N 114 16 E
Manggarai, Jak. 15 J10 6 12 S 106 50 E
Manguinho, Aéroporto de, Rio J. 31 B2 22 52 S 43 14W
Mangweon, Sŏul 12 G7 37 33N 126 55 E
Manhasset, N.Y. 23 C6 40 47N 73 40W
Manhasset B., N.Y. 23 C6 40 49N 73 43W
Manhasset Hills, N.Y. 23 C7 40 45N 73 41W
Manhattan, N.Y. 22 C5 40 48N 73 57W
Manhattan Beach, L.A. 28 C2 33 53N 118 24W
Manhatten, N.Y. 22 D5 40 34N 73 56W
Manila, Manila 15 D3 14 35N 120 58 E
Manila B., Manila 15 D3 14 32N 120 56 E
Manila Int. Airport, Manila 15 D4 14 31N 121 0 E
Mankkaa, Hels. 3 B3 60 11N 24 47 E
Mankunda, Calc. 16 C6 22 50N 88 22 E
Manly, Syd. 19 A4 33 47 S 151 17 E
Manly Warringah War Memorial Park, Syd. 19 A4 33 46 S 151 15 E
Manning State Park, Bost. 21 B4 42 34N 71 20W
Mannsworth, Wien 10 H11 48 8N 16 30 E
Manoa, Phil. 24 B3 39 58N 75 18W
Manor Park, Lon. 4 B5 51 32N 0 1 E
Manora, Kar. 17 H10 24 47N 66 58 E
Manorhaven, N.Y. 23 B6 40 50N 73 41W
Manoteras, Mdrd. 8 B3 40 28N 3 39W
Manquehue, Cerro, Stgo 30 J11 33 21 S 70 35W
Mantegazza, Mil. 9 D4 45 30N 8 58 E
Mantilla, La Hab. 30 B3 23 4N 82 20W
Mantua, Phil. 24 C3 39 47N 75 10W
Mantua Cr. →, Phil. 24 C3 39 47N 75 13W
Manufacta, Jobg. 18 E8 26 9 S 27 51 E
Manzanares, Canal de, Mdrd. 8 C3 40 19N 3 38W
Mapetla, Jobg. 18 F8 26 16 S 27 51 E
Maple, Trto. 20 C7 43 51N 79 30W
Maple L., Chic. 26 C1 41 43N 87 53W
Maple Shade, Phil. 24 B4 39 57N 75 0W
Maplewood, N.Y. 22 C3 40 43N 74 16W
Maracana, Rio J. 31 B2 22 54 S 43 13W
Maraisburg, Jobg. 18 F8 26 10 S 27 57 E
Marano di Nàpoli, Nápl. 9 H12 40 53N 14 11 E
Maraoli, Bomb. 16 G8 19 2N 72 53 E
Marapendi, L. de, Rio J. 31 C1 23 0 S 43 23W
Marblehead, Bost. 21 C4 42 29N 70 51W
Marcelin, Wsaw. 10 E6 52 19N 20 59 E
Marcella, N.Y. 22 B2 40 59N 74 29W
Marcos Paz, B.A. 32 C2 34 46 S 58 49W
Marcoussis, Paris 5 D3 48 38N 2 13 E
Marcus Hook, Phil. 24 C2 39 49N 75 25W
Marcus Hook Cr. →, Phil. 24 B2 39 49N 75 24W
Marechiaro, Nápl. 9 J12 40 48N 14 12 E
Mareil-Marly, Paris 5 B2 48 52N 2 4 E
Margareten, Wien 10 G10 48 11N 16 20 E
Margency, Paris 5 A3 49 0N 2 17 E
Margitsziget, Bud. 10 J13 47 31N 19 2 E
Maria, Wien 10 G10 48 11N 16 21 E
Maria Paula, Rio J. 31 B3 22 53 S 43 1W
Marianao, La Hab. 30 B2 23 4N 82 25W
Marianella, Nápl. 9 H12 40 53N 14 13 E
Mariano Acosta, B.A. 32 C2 34 42 S 58 47W
Mariano J. Haedo, B.A. 32 B3 34 39 S 58 35W
Maridalen, Oslo 2 B4 59 59N 10 45 E
Maridalsvatnet, Oslo 2 B4 59 59N 10 46 E
Mariendorf, Berl. 7 B3 52 26N 13 23 E
Marienfelde, Berl. 7 B3 52 24N 13 23 E
Marienthal, Hbg. 7 D8 53 34N 10 4 E
Miriglianella, Nápl. 9 H13 40 55N 14 26 E
Marigliano, Nápl. 9 H13 40 55N 14 27 E
Marikina, Manila 15 D4 14 38N 121 5 E
Marikina →, Manila 15 D4 14 33N 121 4 E
Marin City, S.F. 27 A1 37 52N 122 30W
Marin Headlands State Park, S.F. 27 A2 37 50N 122 28W
Marin Is., S.F. 27 A2 37 57N 122 27W
Marin Pen., S.F. 27 A1 37 50N 122 30W
Marine World, S.F. 27 C3 37 32N 122 16W
Mariners Harbour, N.Y. 22 D3 40 38N 74 10W
Mario, Mt., Rome 9 F9 41 55N 12 27 E
Markham, Chic. 26 D2 41 35N 87 40W
Markham, Phil. 24 B1 39 53N 75 30W
Markham, Trto. 20 D8 43 49N 79 22W
Markham, Mt., L.A. 28 A4 34 14N 118 6W
Marki, Wsaw. 10 E7 52 19N 21 6 E
Markland Wood, Trto. 20 E7 43 38N 79 34W
Marlton, Phil. 24 B5 39 53N 74 55W
Marly, Forêt de, Paris 5 B2 48 52N 2 2 E
Marly-le-Roi, Paris 5 B2 48 52N 2 5 E
Marne →, Paris 5 C4 48 47N 2 29 E
Marne-la-Vallée, Paris 5 B5 48 50N 2 37 E
Marolles-en-Brie, Paris 5 C5 48 44N 2 33 E
Maroonda Aquaduct, Melb. 19 E7 37 40 S 145 9 E
Maroubra, Syd. 19 B4 33 56 S 151 16 E
Marple, Phil. 24 B2 39 56N 75 20W
Marquette Park, Chic. 26 C2 41 46N 87 42W
Marrickville, Syd. 19 B3 33 54 S 151 9 E
Marschlande, Hbg. 7 E8 53 27N 10 6 E
Marsfield, Syd. 19 A3 33 46 S 151 7 E
Marte, Base Aérea de, S. Pau. 31 E6 23 30 S 46 38W
Martesana, Naviglio della, Mil. 9 D6 45 31N 9 17 E
Martin State Nat. Airport, Balt. 25 B4 39 19N 76 24W
Martinez, B.A. 32 A3 34 29 S 58 31W
Martinkylä, Hels. 3 B4 60 17N 24 51 E
Martins Pond, Bost. 21 B3 42 35N 71 7W
Martinsried, Mün. 7 G9 48 6N 11 27 E
Maruko, Tōkyō 13 C3 35 33N 139 40 E
Marusino, Mos. 11 E11 55 41N 37 58 E
Marxloh, Ruhr 6 A2 51 30N 6 47 E
Maryino, Mos. 11 E10 55 40N 37 45 E
Maryland, Sing. 15 G7 1 19N 103 47 E
Maryland, Univ. of, Wash. 25 D8 39 58N 76 56W
Marylebone, Lon. 4 B4 51 31N 0 9W
Marymont, Wsaw. 10 E6 52 16N 20 58 E
Marysin Wawerski, Wsaw. 10 E7 52 14N 21 9 E
Marzahn, Berl. 7 A4 52 32N 13 34 E
Masambong, Manila 15 D4 14 38N 121 0 E
Mascot, Syd. 19 B4 33 55 S 151 12 E
Mascuppic L., Bost. 21 A2 42 39N 71 23W
Mashamba, Stock. 3 E10 59 15N 17 48 E
Maspeth, N.Y. 22 C5 40 43N 73 55W
Masr el Gedida, El Qâ. 18 C5 30 5N 31 19 E
Masr el Qadîma, El Qâ. 18 C5 30 0N 31 14 E
Masroor Airport, Kar. 17 G10 24 53N 66 56 E
Massa di Somma, Nápl. 9 H13 40 50N 14 22 E
Massachusetts B., Bost. 21 C4 42 25N 70 50W
Massachusetts Inst. of Tech., Bost. 21 C3 42 22N 71 6W
Massamá, Lisb. 8 F7 38 45N 9 16W
Massapequa, N.Y. 23 C8 40 40N 73 28W
Massby, Hels. 3 B6 60 17N 25 16 E
Massey →, Trto. 20 D9 43 42N 79 19W
Massy, Paris 5 C3 48 43N 2 16 E
Matarza →, B.A. 32 C3 34 47 S 58 35W
Matasango, Lima 30 G9 12 3 S 76 58W
Mathle, Calc. 16 E5 22 34N 88 13 E
Matihutong, Beij. 14 B2 39 56N 116 19 E
Matinecock, N.Y. 23 B7 40 51N 73 36W
Matinha, Lisb. 8 F8 38 45N 9 5W
Matraman, Jak. 15 J10 6 12 S 106 51 E
Matsubara, Ōsaka 12 C4 34 34N 135 33 E
Matsubushi, Tōkyō 13 A3 35 55N 139 49 E
Matsudo, Tōkyō 13 B4 35 46N 139 54 E
Matsumoloshinden, Tōkyō 13 B2 35 50N 139 36 E
Mattapan, Bost. 21 D3 42 16N 71 6W
Mátyásföld, Bud. 10 J14 47 30N 19 12 E
Mau Tso Ngam, H.K. 12 D6 22 22N 114 13 E
Mauá, S. Pau. 31 E7 23 39 S 46 27W
Mauer, Wien 10 H9 48 9N 16 16 E
Mauerbach →, Wien 10 G9 48 12N 16 13 E
Mauldre, Paris 5 C1 48 54N 1 53 E
Maurecourt, Paris 5 B2 48 59N 2 3 E
Mauregard, Paris 5 A5 49 2N 2 34 E
Maurepas, Paris 5 C1 48 46N 1 55 E
Mauripur, Kar. 17 G10 24 52N 66 55 E
Maxhof, Mün. 7 G9 48 4N 11 29 E
Maya-Zan, Ōsaka 12 B2 34 43N 135 12 E
Maybunga, Manila 15 D4 14 34N 121 4 E
Mayfair, Jobg. 18 F9 26 11 S 28 0 E
Mayfair, Phil. 24 A4 40 2N 75 3W
Maypajo, Manila 15 D3 14 38N 120 58 E
Maytubig, Manila 15 D3 14 33N 120 59 E
Maywood, Chic. 26 B1 41 52N 87 51W
Maywood, L.A. 28 C3 33 59N 118 12W
Maywood, N.Y. 22 B4 40 53N 74 3W
Mazagaon, Bomb. 16 H8 18 57N 72 50 E
M'Boi Mirim, S. Pau. 31 F5 23 42 S 46 46W
Meadow I., N.Y. 23 D7 40 36N 73 32W
Meadow L., N.Y. 23 C5 40 44N 73 50W
Meadowlands, Jobg. 18 F8 26 12 S 27 53 E
Meadowood, Wash. 25 C7 39 4N 77 0W
Měcholupy, Pra. 10 B3 50 3N 14 32 E
Měčice, Pra. 10 A3 50 11N 14 31 E
Mecidiyekoy, Ist. 17 A3 41 4N 29 0 E
Meckinghoven, Ruhr 6 A5 51 37N 7 19 E
Médan, Paris 5 B1 48 57N 1 59 E
Medfield, Bost. 21 D2 42 11N 71 18W
Medford, Bost. 21 C3 42 25N 71 7W
Media, Phil. 24 B2 39 55N 75 23W
Mediodia, Mdrd. 8 B3 40 22N 3 39W
Medvastö, Hels. 3 C2 60 5N 24 38 E
Medvedkovo, Mos. 11 D9 55 52N 37 37 E
Medvezhiy Ozyora, Mos. 11 D11 55 52N 37 59 E
Meerbeck, Ruhr 6 B1 51 28N 6 38 E
Meerbusch, Ruhr 6 C2 51 16N 6 40 E
Meguro →, Tōkyō 13 C3 35 37N 139 45 E
Meguro-Ku, Tōkyō 13 C3 35 37N 139 42 E
Mehpalpur, Delhi 16 B1 28 32N 77 7 E
Mehrābād Airport, Tehr. 17 C4 35 41N 51 18 E
Mehram Nagar, Delhi 16 B1 28 34N 77 8 E
Mehrow, Berl. 7 A4 52 34N 13 37 E
Meiderich, Ruhr 6 B2 51 27N 6 47 E
Meidling, Wien 10 G10 48 10N 16 20 E
Meiendorf, Hbg. 7 D8 53 37N 10 8 E
Méier, Rio J. 31 B2 22 52 S 43 15W
Meiji Shrine, Tōkyō 13 B3 35 41N 139 41 E
Meizino-Mori-Minō National Park, Ōsaka 12 A3 34 51N 135 28 E
Mejiro, Tōkyō 13 B3 35 43N 139 43 E
Melbourne, Melb. 19 E6 37 48 S 144 58 E
Melbourne Airport, Melb. 19 E6 37 40 S 144 50 E
Melbourne Univ., Melb. 19 E6 37 47 S 144 57 E
Melito di Nápoli, Nápl. 9 H12 40 55N 14 13 E
Melkki, Hels. 3 C4 60 8N 24 53 E
Mellingstedt, Hbg. 7 C8 53 40N 10 6 E
Mellunkylä, Hels. 3 B5 60 14N 25 6 E
Mellunmäki, Hels. 3 B5 60 14N 25 6 E
Melrose, Bost. 21 C3 42 27N 71 2W
Melrose, N.Y. 22 C5 40 49N 73 55W
Melrose Park, Chic. 26 B1 41 53N 87 50W
Melun-Sénart, Paris 5 D5 48 37N 2 31 E
Melun-Villaroche, Aérodrome de, Paris 5 D6 48 37N 2 41 E
Melville, N.Y. 23 C8 40 47N 73 24W
Menai, Syd. 19 C3 34 1 S 151 1 E
Menandon, Paris 5 A2 49 2N 2 3 E
Mendoza, Lima 30 G9 12 5 S 76 59W
Mengede, Ruhr 6 A6 51 34N 7 23 E
Mengjiazhai, Shang. 14 J11 31 19N 121 27 E
Menglinghausen, Ruhr 6 B6 51 28N 7 25 E
Menlo Park, S.F. 27 D3 37 27N 122 11W
Menlo Park Terrace, N.Y. 22 D3 40 34N 74 18W
Mentang, Jak. 15 J9 6 11 S 106 49 E
Menucourt, Paris 5 A1 49 1N 1 59 E
Meopham, Lon. 4 C7 51 22N 0 21 E
Mérantaise →, Paris 5 C2 48 42N 2 8 E
Mercamadrid, Mdrd. 8 B3 40 21N 3 39W
Merced, L., S.F. 27 B2 37 43N 122 29W
Merchantville, Phil. 24 B4 39 56N 75 3W
Mercier, Pont, Mtrl. 20 B3 43 24N 73 39W
Merdeka Palace, Jak. 15 J9 6 10 S 106 49 E
Meredale, Jobg. 18 F8 26 16 S 27 58 E
Mergellina, Nápl. 9 J12 40 49N 14 13 E
Meriden, N.Y. 22 B2 40 56N 74 27W
Merion Station, Phil. 24 B3 39 59N 75 15W
Merlimau, Sing. 15 G7 1 17N 103 42 E
Merlimau, P., Sing. 15 G7 1 17N 103 42 E
Merlo, B.A. 32 B2 34 39 S 58 43W
Merri Cr. →, Melb. 19 E6 37 47 S 144 59 E
Merrick, N.Y. 23 D7 40 39N 73 32W
Merrionette Park, Chic. 26 C2 41 41N 87 40W
Merritt, L., S.F. 27 B3 37 48N 122 15W
Merrylands, Syd. 19 A3 33 50 S 150 59 E
Merton, Lon. 4 C3 51 24N 0 11W
Mesgarābād, Tehr. 17 D6 35 27N 51 30 E
Meshcherskiy, Mos. 11 E8 55 40N 37 23 E
Mesquita, Rio J. 31 A1 22 46 S 43 25W
Messe, Wien 10 G10 48 13N 16 24 E
Messy, Paris 5 B6 48 58N 2 42 E
Metanópoli, Mil. 9 E6 45 24N 9 15 E
Methuen, Bost. 21 A2 42 42N 71 12W
Metropolitan Opera, N.Y. 22 C5 40 46N 74 59W
Mettman, Ruhr 6 C3 51 15N 6 58 E
Metuchen, N.Y. 22 D2 40 32N 74 21W
Metzkausen, Ruhr 6 C3 51 16N 6 57 E
Meudon, Paris 5 C3 48 48N 2 14 E
Meulan, Paris 5 A1 49 0N 1 54 E
México, Aeropuerto Int. de, Méx. 29 B3 19 25N 99 4W
México, Ciudad de, Méx. 29 B2 19 25N 99 7W
Mezzate, Mil. 9 E6 45 26N 9 17 E
Mia Dong, Sŏul 12 G8 37 36N 127 0 E
Miano, Nápl. 9 H12 40 53N 14 15 E
Miasto, Wsaw. 10 E7 52 15N 21 0 E
Michalin, Wsaw. 10 F8 52 9N 21 13 E
Michałowice, Wsaw. 10 E5 52 10N 20 52 E
Michle, Pra. 10 B2 50 3N 14 28 E
Mickleton, Phil. 24 C3 39 47N 75 14W
Middle →, Balt. 25 B4 39 18N 76 24W
Middle B., N.Y. 23 D7 40 36N 73 36W
Middle Branch →, Balt. 25 B3 39 15N 76 37W
Middle Brewster I., Bost. 21 C4 42 20N 70 51W
Middle Cove, Syd. 19 A4 33 48 S 151 13 E
Middle Harbour, Syd. 19 A4 33 47 S 151 14 E
Middle Hd., Syd. 19 A4 33 49 S 151 14 E
Middle I., H.K. 12 E6 22 16N 114 10 E
Middle Park, Melb. 19 F6 37 50 S 144 57 E
Middle River, Balt. 25 A4 39 20N 76 26W
Middle Village, N.Y. 23 C5 40 43N 73 52W
Middleborough, Balt. 25 B4 39 18N 76 24W
Middlesex, N.Y. 22 D2 40 34N 74 27W
Middlesex Fells Reservation, Bost. 21 C3 42 27N 71 6W
Middlesex Res., N.Y. 22 D3 40 37N 74 19W
Middleton, Bost. 21 B3 42 35N 71 0W
Middleton Pond, Bost. 21 B3 42 35N 71 1W
Middleville, N.Y. 23 B9 40 54N 73 19W
Midland Beach, N.Y. 22 D4 40 34N 74 6W
Midland Park, N.Y. 22 B4 40 59N 74 9W

Pitampura Kalan 43

North Springfield, *Wash.* **25 E6** 38 48N 77 11W
North Stifford, *Lon.* **4 B6** 51 30N 0 18 E
North Sudbury, *Bost.* **21 C1** 42 24N 71 24W
North Sydney, *Syd.* **19 B4** 33 50 S 151 13 E
North Tewksbury, *Bost.* **21 B2** 42 38N 71 14W
North Valley Stream, *N.Y.* **23 C6** 40 41N 73 42W
North Wantagh, *N.Y.* **23 C7** 40 41N 73 30W
North Weymouth, *Bost.* **21 D4** 42 14N 70 56W
North Wilmington, *Bost.* **21 B3** 42 34N 71 9W
North Woburn, *Bost.* **21 B2** 42 30N 71 10W
North Woolwich, *Lon.* **4 B5** 51 30N 0 3 E
North York, *Trto.* **20 D8** 43 45N 79 27W
Northaw, *Lon.* **4 A4** 51 42N 0 8W
Northbridge, *Syd.* **19 A4** 33 49 S 151 15 E
Northbrook, *Chic.* **26 A1** 42 7N 87 50W
Northcliff, *Jobg.* **18 E8** 26 8 S 27 58 E
Northcote, *Melb.* **19 E7** 37 46 S 145 0 E
Northeastern Univ., *Bost.* **21 C3** 42 20N 71 4W
Northfield, *Chic.* **26 A2** 42 5N 87 45W
Northfleet, *Lon.* **4 C7** 51 26N 0 21 E
Northlake, *Chic.* **26 B1** 41 54N 87 53W
Northmead, *Jobg.* **18 E10** 26 9 S 28 19 E
Northmead, *Syd.* **19 A3** 33 47 S 151 0 E
Northmount, *Trto.* **20 D8** 43 46N 79 23W
Northolt, *Lon.* **4 B2** 51 32N 0 22W
Northport, *N.Y.* **23 B8** 40 54N 73 20W
Northport B., *N.Y.* **23 B8** 40 54N 73 22W
Northridge, *L.A.* **28 A1** 34 14N 118 30W
Northumberland Heath, *Lon.* **4 C6** 51 28N 0 10 E
Northvale, *N.Y.* **22 A5** 41 0N 73 59W
Northwest Branch →, *Balt.* **25 B3** 39 16N 76 35W
Northwest Branch →, *Wash.* **25 C8** 39 2N 76 56W
Northwestern Univ., *Chic.* **26 A2** 42 3N 87 40W
Northwood, *Lon.* **4 B2** 51 36N 0 25W
Norumbega Res., *Bost.* **21 D2** 42 19N 71 17W
Norwalk, *L.A.* **28 C4** 33 53N 118 4W
Norwood, *Bost.* **21 D2** 42 11N 71 13W
Norwood, *Jobg.* **18 E9** 26 9 S 28 4 E
Norwood, *N.Y.* **22 B5** 40 59N 73 57W
Norwood, *Phil.* **24 B3** 39 53N 75 17W
Norwood Memorial Airport, *Bost.* **21 D3** 42 11N 71 9W
Norwood Park, *Chic.* **26 B2** 41 59N 87 48W
Noryangjin, *Sŏul* **12 G7** 37 30N 126 56 E
Nose, *Ōsaka* **12 B2** 34 49N 135 10 E
Nossa Senhora do Ó, *S. Pau.* **31 E5** 23 30 S 46 41W
Notre-Dame, *Mtrl.* **20 B5** 43 28N 73 28W
Notre-Dame, *Paris* **5 B4** 48 51N 2 21 E
Notre-Dame, Bois, *Paris* **5 C5** 48 45N 2 34 E
Notre Dame de L'Île Perrot, *Mtrl.* **20 B2** 43 23N 73 53W
Notting Hill, *Lon.* **4 B3** 51 30N 0 12W
Notting Hill, *Melb.* **19 F7** 37 54 S 145 9 E
Nottingham, *Phil.* **24 A5** 40 7N 74 58W
Nova Milanese, *Mil.* **9 D6** 45 35N 9 12 E
Novate Milanese, *Mil.* **9 D5** 45 30N 9 8 E
Novaya Derevnya, *St-Pet.* **11 A3** 60 0N 30 19 E
Nové Mesto, *Pra.* **10 B2** 50 4N 14 25 E
Novoaleksandrovskoye, *St-Pet.* **11 B4** 59 50N 30 31 E
Novogireyevo, *Mos.* **11 E10** 55 45N 37 46 E
Novoivanovskoye, *Mos.* **11 E7** 55 42N 37 21 E
Novokhovrino, *Mos.* **11 D8** 55 53N 37 27 E
Novonikolyskoye, *Mos.* **11 D7** 55 50N 37 14 E
Novosaratovka, *St-Pet.* **11 B5** 59 50N 30 32 E
Novosergiyevka, *St-Pet.* **11 B5** 59 54N 30 34 E
Nowe-Babice, *Wsaw.* **10 E6** 52 15N 20 51 E
Nöykkiö, *Hels.* **3 B3** 60 10N 24 42 E
Noyoye Kovalyova, *St-Pet.* **11 B5** 59 58N 30 34 E
Nozay, *Paris* **5 D3** 48 39N 2 14 E
Nueva Atzacoalco, *Méx.* **29 B3** 19 29N 99 4W
Nueva Caracas, *Car.* **30 D5** 10 30N 66 57W
Nueva Chicago, *B.A.* **32 B4** 34 39 S 58 29W
Nueva Pompeya, *B.A.* **32 C4** 34 40 S 58 25W
Nueva Tenochtitlán, *Méx.* **29 B3** 19 27N 99 5W
Nuijala, *Hels.* **3 B3** 60 12N 24 46 E
Numabukuro, *Tōkyō* **13 B2** 35 43N 139 39 E
Numakage, *Tōkyō* **13 A2** 35 50N 139 37 E
Numata, *Tōkyō* **13 B3** 35 45N 139 46 E
Nunawading, *Melb.* **19 E8** 37 49 S 145 10 E
Nunez, *B.A.* **32 B4** 34 32 S 58 27W
Nunhead, *Lon.* **4 C4** 51 27N 0 3W
Ñuñoa, *Stgo* **30 J11** 33 27 S 70 35W
Nupuri, *Hels.* **3 B2** 60 14N 24 36 E
Nusle, *Pra.* **10 B2** 50 3N 14 26 E
Nussdorf, *Wien* **10 G10** 48 15N 16 21 E
Nuthe →, *Berl.* **7 B1** 52 22N 13 5 E
Nutley, *N.Y.* **22 C4** 40 49N 74 9W
Nutting L., *Bost.* **21 B2** 42 32N 71 16W
Nützenberg, *Ruhr* **6 C4** 51 15N 7 8 E
Nybølle, *Købn.* **2 D8** 55 42N 12 15 E
Nybygget, *Hels.* **3 B6** 60 17N 25 11 E
Nymphenburg, *Mün.* **7 G10** 48 9N 11 30 E
Nymphenburg, Schloss, *Mün.* **7 G10** 48 9N 11 30 E

# O

Oak Beach, *N.Y.* **23 D9** 40 38N 73 19W
Oak Forest, *Chic.* **26 D2** 41 36N 87 44W
Oak Hill Park, *Bost.* **21 D2** 42 17N 71 11W
Oak Lane, *Phil.* **24 A4** 40 3N 75 8W
Oak Lawn, *Chic.* **26 C2** 41 42N 87 45W
Oak Park, *Chic.* **26 B2** 41 52N 87 47W
Oak Ridge, *N.Y.* **22 A2** 41 2N 74 28W
Oak Valley, *Phil.* **24 C4** 39 48N 75 9W
Oak View, *Wash.* **25 C8** 39 1N 76 58W
Oakland, *N.Y.* **22 A3** 41 1N 74 13W
Oakland, *S.F.* **27 B3** 37 48N 122 18W
Oakland, *Wash.* **25 D8** 38 52N 76 54W
Oakland Coliseum, *S.F.* **27 B3** 37 44N 122 11W
Oakland Gardens, *N.Y.* **23 C6** 40 45N 73 46W
Oakland Int. Airport, *S.F.* **27 B3** 37 43N 122 12W
Oakland Mills, *Balt.* **25 B2** 39 13N 76 49W
Oakland Naval Air Station, *S.F.* **27 B3** 37 47N 122 19W
Oaklands, *Jobg.* **18 E9** 26 8 S 28 4 E
Oaklawn, *Wash.* **25 E8** 38 46N 76 56W
Oakleigh, *Melb.* **19 F7** 37 54 S 145 5 E
Oaks, *Phil.* **24 A2** 40 8N 75 26W
Oakwood, *N.Y.* **22 D4** 40 34N 74 7W
Oakwood Beach, *N.Y.* **22 D4** 40 33N 74 7W
Oatley, *Syd.* **19 B3** 33 59 S 151 4 E
Obalende, *Lagos* **18 B2** 6 26N 7 25 E
Oba's Palace, *Lagos* **18 B2** 6 26N 7 22 E
Oberbauer, *Ruhr* **6 C6** 51 17N 7 25 E
Oberföhring, *Mün.* **7 G10** 48 10N 11 37 E
Oberhaching, *Mün.* **7 G10** 48 1N 11 35 E
Oberhausen, *Ruhr* **6 B3** 51 28N 6 54 E
Oberhausen, *Wien* **10 G11** 48 10N 16 34 E
Oberkassel, *Ruhr* **6 C2** 51 14N 6 45 E
Oberkirchbach, *Wien* **10 G9** 48 17N 16 12 E
Oberlaa, *Wien* **10 H10** 48 8N 16 24 E
Oberlisse, *Wien* **10 G10** 48 17N 16 26 E
Obermenzing, *Mün.* **7 F9** 48 10N 11 28 E
Obermoos Schwaige, *Mün.* **7 F9** 48 14N 11 27 E
Oberschleissheim, *Mün.* **7 F10** 48 15N 11 33 E
Oberschöneweide, *Berl.* **7 B4** 52 27N 13 31 E
Oberwengern, *Ruhr* **6 B6** 51 23N 7 22 E
Obitsu →, *Tōkyō* **13 D4** 35 25N 139 56 E
Oboldino, *Mos.* **11 D11** 55 53N 37 56 E
Observatory, *Jobg.* **18 F9** 26 10 S 28 4 E
Ōbu, *Ōsaka* **12 B1** 34 43N 135 8 E
Obu-tōge, *Ōsaka* **12 B1** 34 44N 135 9 E
Óbuda, *Bud.* **10 J13** 47 33N 19 2 E
Obudaisziget, *Bud.* **10 J13** 47 33N 19 3 E
Obukhovo, *St-Pet.* **11 B4** 59 53N 30 22 E
Occidental, Pico, *Car.* **30 D5** 10 32N 66 51W
Oceanside, *N.Y.* **23 D7** 40 38N 73 37W
Ochakovo, *Mos.* **11 E8** 55 41N 37 26 E
Ochiai, *Tōkyō* **13 B3** 35 43N 139 42 E
Ochota, *Wsaw.* **10 E6** 52 13N 20 58 E
Ochsenwerder, *Hbg.* **7 E8** 53 28N 10 4 E
Ochsenzoll, *Hbg.* **7 C8** 53 41N 10 0 E
Odana, *Tōkyō* **13 C2** 35 33N 139 35 E
Oden-Stockach, *Mün.* **7 G11** 48 5N 11 41 E
Odilampi, *Hels.* **3 B3** 60 18N 24 45 E
Odintsovo, *Mos.* **11 E7** 55 40N 37 16 E
Odivelas, *Lisb.* **8 F7** 38 47N 9 10W
Odolany, *Wsaw.* **10 E6** 52 13N 20 55 E
Oeiras, *Lisb.* **8 F7** 38 41N 9 18W
Oella, *Balt.* **25 B2** 39 16N 76 46W
Oer-Erkenschwick, *Ruhr* **6 A5** 51 38N 7 15 E
Oern, *Mün.* **7 G10** 48 10N 11 32 E
Ofin, *Lagos* **18 A3** 6 32N 7 30 E
Ofukuro-shinden, *Tōkyō* **13 A1** 35 53N 139 28 E
Ogawa, *Tōkyō* **13 B1** 35 44N 139 28 E
Ogden, *Phil.* **24 C2** 39 49N 75 27W
Ogikubo, *Tōkyō* **13 B2** 35 42N 139 37 E
Ogo Ogo, *Ōsaka* **12 B1** 34 49N 135 8 E
Ogogoro, *Lagos* **18 B2** 6 25N 7 24 E
Ogongo, *Manila* **15 D4** 14 35N 121 4 E
Ogoyo, *Lagos* **18 B2** 6 25N 7 29 E
Ogudu, *Lagos* **18 A2** 6 34N 7 24 E
O'Hare, L., *Chic.* **26 B1** 41 57N 87 53W
Ōhirodo, *Tōkyō* **13 A4** 35 50N 139 53 E
Ohlsdorf, *Hbg.* **7 D8** 53 37N 10 3 E
Ōi, *Tōkyō* **13 A2** 35 51N 139 31 E
Ōimachi, *Tōkyō* **13 C3** 35 35N 139 43 E
Oise →, *Paris* **5 A2** 49 2N 2 5 E
Oittaa, *Hels.* **3 B3** 60 15N 24 42 E
Ojota, *Lagos* **18 A2** 6 35N 7 23 E
Okamoto, *Ōsaka* **12 B2** 34 43N 135 15 E
Okazu, *Tōkyō* **13 D2** 35 25N 139 31 E
Okęcie, *Wsaw.* **10 E6** 52 11N 20 56 E
Okęcie Airport, *Wsaw.* **10 E6** 52 10N 20 57 E
Okelra, *Lagos* **18 B2** 6 29N 7 22 E
Okeogbe, *Lagos* **18 B2** 6 24N 7 23 E
Okhla, *Delhi* **16 B2** 28 33N 77 16 E
Okhta →, *St-Pet.* **11 B4** 59 56N 30 25 E
Okkervil →, *St-Pet.* **11 B4** 59 56N 30 30 E
Okrzeszyn, *Wsaw.* **10 F7** 52 8N 21 8 E
Oksval, *Oslo* **2 B4** 59 51N 10 40 E
Oktyabrskiy, *Mos.* **11 F11** 55 37N 37 58 E
Oktyabrskiy, *Mos.* **11 E9** 55 41N 37 35 E
Okubo, *Tōkyō* **13 B3** 35 41N 139 42 E
Okunola, *Lagos* **18 A1** 6 35N 7 17 E
Ōkura, *Tōkyō* **13 C1** 35 35N 139 27 E
Olari, *Hels.* **3 B3** 60 10N 24 44 E
Olaria, *Rio J.* **31 B2** 22 50 S 43 16W
Old Brookville, *N.Y.* **23 C7** 40 49N 73 35W
Old Cairo, *El Qâ.* **18 C5** 30 0N 31 14 E
Old Coulsdon, *Lon.* **4 D4** 51 17N 0 6W
Old Forge Village, *N.Y.* **22 C2** 40 48N 74 29W
Old Harbor, *Bost.* **21 D3** 42 19N 71 1W
Old Road B., *Balt.* **25 B4** 39 12N 76 27W
Old Tappan, *N.Y.* **22 A5** 41 0N 73 59W
Old Town, *Chic.* **26 B3** 41 54N 87 37W
Old Westbury, *N.Y.* **23 C7** 40 46N 73 35W
Oldmans Cr. →, *Phil.* **24 C2** 39 47N 75 26W
Olgino, *St-Pet.* **11 A3** 60 0N 30 10 E
Olimpico, Estadio, *Méx.* **29 C2** 19 19N 99 11W
Olinda, *Melb.* **19 F9** 37 51 S 145 21 E
Olinda, *Rio J.* **31 A1** 22 49 S 43 25W
Olivais, *Lisb.* **8 F8** 38 45N 9 7W
Olivar de los Padres, *Méx.* **29 B2** 19 21N 99 14W
Olivar del Conde, *Méx.* **29 B2** 19 22N 99 12W
Olivos, *B.A.* **32 B4** 34 30 S 58 28W
Ollila, *Hels.* **3 A2** 60 20N 24 32 E
Olney, *Phil.* **24 A4** 40 2N 75 8W
Olona →, *Mil.* **9 E5** 45 29N 9 6 E
Ølstykke, *Købn.* **2 D7** 55 47N 12 8 E
Olute, *Lagos* **18 B1** 6 27N 7 17 E
Olympia-Stadion, *Hels.* **3 B4** 60 11N 24 55 E
Olympique Parc, *Mtrl.* **20 A4** 43 33N 73 33W
Ōmagi, *Tōkyō* **13 A3** 35 52N 139 43 E
Ōmiya, *Tōkyō* **13 A2** 35 54N 139 37 E
Ōmori, *Tōkyō* **13 C3** 35 34N 139 43 E
Ōnari, *Tōkyō* **13 A2** 35 55N 139 36 E
Once, *B.A.* **32 B4** 34 37 S 58 24W
Onchi, *Ōsaka* **12 C4** 34 36N 135 38 E
Onchi →, *Ōsaka* **12 C4** 34 38N 135 37 E
One Tree Hill, *Melb.* **19 F8** 37 52 S 145 19 E
Onisigun, *Lagos* **18 A2** 6 35N 7 24 E
Ōokayama, *Tōkyō* **13 C3** 35 36N 139 40 E
Opacz, *Wsaw.* **10 E6** 52 10N 20 53 E
Ophirton, *Jobg.* **18 F9** 26 13 S 28 1 E
Oppegård, *Oslo* **2 C4** 59 45N 10 49 E
Oppsal, *Oslo* **2 B5** 59 53N 10 50 E
Oppum, *Ruhr* **6 C1** 51 19N 6 36 E
Oradell, *N.Y.* **22 B4** 40 57N 74 2W
Oradell Res., *N.Y.* **22 B4** 40 58N 74 0W
Orange, *N.Y.* **22 C3** 40 46N 74 15W
Orange Grove, *Jobg.* **18 E9** 26 9 S 28 5 E
Oratorio →, *S. Pau.* **31 E6** 23 36 S 46 32W
Orbassano, *Tori.* **9 B2** 45 0N 7 31 E
Orchards, *Jobg.* **18 E9** 26 9 S 28 4 E
Ordrup, *Købn.* **2 D10** 55 45N 12 34 E
Orech, *Pra.* **10 B1** 50 1N 14 17 E
Øresund, *Købn.* **2 D11** 55 45N 12 40 E
Oreta, *Lagos* **18 A3** 6 31N 7 31 E
Orge →, *Paris* **5 D3** 48 36N 2 17 E
Orgeval, *Paris* **5 B1** 48 55N 1 58 E
Orhølm, *Købn.* **2 D10** 55 48N 12 30 E
Orient Heights, *Bost.* **21 C4** 42 23N 70 59W
Oriental, Pico, *Car.* **30 D5** 10 32N 66 51W
Origgio, *Mil.* **9 D5** 45 35N 9 1 E
Orinda, *S.F.* **27 A3** 37 52N 122 10W
Orinda Village, *S.F.* **27 A3** 37 53N 122 12W
Orland L., *Chic.* **26 D1** 41 38N 87 52W
Orland Park, *Chic.* **26 D1** 41 37N 87 52W
Orlando Dam, *Jobg.* **18 F8** 26 15 S 27 55 E
Orlando East, *Jobg.* **18 F8** 26 14 S 27 55 E
Orlando West, *Jobg.* **18 F8** 26 13 S 27 54 E
Orlången, *Stock.* **3 E11** 59 11N 18 2 E
Orlångsvik, *Stock.* **3 E11** 59 11N 18 3 E
Orlovo, *Mos.* **11 F8** 55 38N 37 22 E
Orly, *Paris* **5 C4** 48 45N 2 23 E
Ormesson-sur-Marne, *Paris* **5 C5** 48 47N 2 32 E
Orminge, *Stock.* **3 E12** 59 19N 18 14 E
Ormingelandet, *Stock.* **3 D13** 59 20N 18 22 E
Ormond, *Melb.* **19 F7** 37 54 S 145 1 E
Órmos Fálirou, *Ath.* **8 J11** 37 54N 23 40 E
Ormøya, *Oslo* **2 B4** 59 52N 10 45 E
Oros Aiyáleos, *Ath.* **8 J10** 38 0N 23 36 E
Oros Imittoś, *Ath.* **8 J11** 37 53N 23 48 E
Örpadfold, *Bud.* **10 J14** 47 32N 19 12 E
Orpington, *Lon.* **4 C5** 51 22N 0 6 E
Orsay, *Paris* **5 C3** 48 41N 2 11 E
Orsby, *Ruhr* **6 A2** 51 31N 6 41 E
Orsett, *Lon.* **4 B7** 51 30N 0 22 E
Ortaköy, *Ist.* **17 A3** 41 3N 29 1 E
Ortica, *Mil.* **9 E6** 45 28N 9 16 E
Oruba, *Lagos* **18 A2** 6 34N 7 24 E
Ōsaka, *Ōsaka* **12 C4** 34 42N 135 30 E
Ōsaka B., *Ōsaka* **12 C2** 34 35N 135 18 E
Ōsaka Castle, *Ōsaka* **12 B4** 34 41N 135 30 E
Ōsaka Harbour, *Ōsaka* **12 C3** 34 38N 135 25 E
Ōsaka Univ., *Ōsaka* **12 B3** 34 41N 135 29 E
Ōsaki, *Tōkyō* **13 C3** 35 36N 139 42 E
Osasco, *S. Pau.* **31 E5** 23 31 S 46 46W
Osdorf, *Berl.* **7 B3** 52 24N 13 20 E
Osdorf, *Hbg.* **7 D7** 53 34N 9 50 E
Oshodi, *Lagos* **18 A2** 6 33N 7 21 E
Oskar Frederikborg, *Stock.* **3 D13** 59 24N 18 24 E
Oslo, *Oslo* **2 B4** 59 54N 10 43 E
Oslofjorden, *Oslo* **2 C3** 59 40N 10 35 E
Ōsone, *Tōkyō* **13 C2** 35 31N 139 37 E
Osorun, *Lagos* **18 A2** 6 33N 7 29 E
Ospiate, *Mil.* **9 D5** 45 32N 9 6 E
Ossów, *Wsaw.* **10 E8** 52 18N 21 12 E
Ostankino, *Mos.* **11 E9** 55 49N 37 37 E
Østby, *Købn.* **2 D7** 55 45N 12 2 E
Osterath, *Ruhr* **6 C1** 51 16N 6 36 E
Österby, *Hels.* **3 B1** 60 10N 24 25 E
Osterfeld, *Ruhr* **6 A3** 51 30N 6 53 E
Osterley, *Lon.* **4 C2** 51 28N 0 21W
Osterley Park, *Lon.* **4 C2** 51 29N 0 21W
Östermalm, *Stock.* **3 D11** 59 20N 18 4 E
Österskär, *Stock.* **3 D12** 59 26N 18 16 E
Östersundom, *Hels.* **3 B6** 60 15N 25 10 E
Ostertälje, *Stock.* **3 E8** 59 11N 17 39 E
Ostiense, *Rome* **9 F9** 41 51N 12 29 E
Østmarkkapellet, *Oslo* **2 B5** 59 52N 10 51 E
Ostøya, *Oslo* **2 B3** 59 52N 10 34 E
Östra Ryd, *Stock.* **3 D12** 59 27N 18 11 E
Østre Aker, *Oslo* **2 B4** 59 54N 10 49 E
Ostrov, *Mos.* **11 F11** 55 36N 37 50 E
Ostrovtsy, *Mos.* **11 F12** 55 36N 38 0 E
Ōta-Ku, *Tōkyō* **13 C3** 35 34N 139 41 E
Otaniemi, *Hels.* **3 B3** 60 11N 24 49 E
Otford, *Lon.* **4 D6** 51 18N 0 11 E
Othmarschen, *Hbg.* **7 D7** 53 33N 9 53 E
Otsuka, *Tōkyō* **13 B3** 35 43N 139 44 E
Ottakring, *Wien* **10 G9** 48 12N 16 18 E
Ottávia, *Rome* **9 F9** 41 57N 12 24 E
Ottaviano, *Nápl.* **9 H13** 40 50N 14 28 E
Ottensen, *Hbg.* **7 D7** 53 33N 9 55 E
Ottobrunn, *Mün.* **7 G11** 48 3N 11 40 E
Ottocalli, *Nápl.* **9 H12** 40 52N 14 17 E
Otwock, *Wsaw.* **10 F8** 52 8N 21 13 E
Ouerenburg, *Ruhr* **6 B5** 51 27N 7 16 E
Ouiapo, *Manila* **15 D3** 14 35N 120 59 E
Oulunkylä, *Hels.* **3 B4** 60 13N 24 58 E
Ourcq, Canal de l', *Paris* **5 B4** 48 54N 2 28 E
Ousit, *Bangk.* **15 B2** 13 47N 100 31 E
Outer Brewster I., *Bost.* **21 C4** 42 20N 70 52W
Outer Mission, *S.F.* **27 B2** 37 43N 122 26W
Outremont, *Mtrl.* **20 A4** 43 31N 73 36W
Overbruch, *Ruhr* **6 A2** 51 32N 6 43 E
Overlea, *Balt.* **25 A3** 39 21N 76 32W
Øverød, *Købn.* **2 D9** 55 48N 12 28 E
Ōwada, *Tōkyō* **13 B2** 35 48N 139 31 E
Owings Mills, *Balt.* **25 A2** 39 25N 76 47W
Oworonsoki, *Lagos* **18 A2** 6 32N 7 24 E
Oxon Hill, *Wash.* **25 E8** 38 48N 76 59W
Oxshott, *Lon.* **4 D2** 51 19N 0 21W
Oyada, *Tōkyō* **13 B4** 35 46N 139 50 E
Ōyama, *Tōkyō* **13 B3** 35 44N 139 42 E
Øyeren, *Oslo* **2 B6** 59 55N 11 6 E
Oyodo, *Ōsaka* **12 B3** 34 42N 135 29 E
Oyster B., *N.Y.* **23 B7** 40 52N 73 31W
Oyster B., *Syd.* **19 C3** 34 0 S 151 5 E
Oyster Bay Cove, *N.Y.* **23 B8** 40 51N 73 29W
Oyster Bay Harbour, *N.Y.* **23 B7** 40 53N 73 32W
Oyster Rock, *Bomb.* **16 H7** 18 54N 72 49 E
Oyster Rocks, *Kar.* **17 H11** 24 48N 66 59 E
Ozarów-Franciszków, *Wsaw.* **10 E5** 52 13N 20 48 E
Ozerki, *St-Pet.* **11 B6** 59 53N 30 42 E
Ozoir-la-Ferrière, *Paris* **5 C6** 48 46N 2 40 E
Ozone Park, *N.Y.* **23 C5** 40 40N 73 50W

# P

Pacific Manor, *S.F.* **27 C2** 37 38N 122 27W
Pacific Palisades, *L.A.* **28 B1** 34 2N 118 32W
Pacifica, *S.F.* **27 C2** 37 37N 122 27W
Packanack L., *N.Y.* **22 B3** 40 56N 74 15W
Paco, *Manila* **15 D3** 14 35N 120 59 E
Paco de Arcos, *Lisb.* **8 F7** 38 41N 9 17W
Paddington, *Lon.* **4 B3** 51 30N 0 10W
Paddington, *Syd.* **19 B4** 33 53 S 151 14 E
Pademangan, *Jak.* **15 H9** 6 7 S 106 49 E
Paderno, *Mil.* **9 D5** 45 33N 9 9 E
Padre Miguel, *Rio J.* **31 B1** 22 52 S 43 25W
Padstow, *Syd.* **19 B3** 33 57 S 151 2 E
Pagewood, *Syd.* **19 B4** 33 56 S 151 14 E
Pagote, *Bomb.* **16 H8** 18 53N 72 59 E
Pai, I. do, *Rio J.* **31 B3** 22 59 S 43 5W
Paia, *Lisb.* **8 F7** 38 46N 9 11W
Paikpara, *Calc.* **16 E6** 22 36N 88 23 E
Paint Br. →, *Wash.* **25 C8** 38 57N 76 55W
Paiyun Airport, *Gzh.* **14 F8** 23 10N 113 15 E
Pak ka Shan, *H.K.* **12 E6** 22 16N 114 13 E
Pak Kong, *H.K.* **12 D6** 22 22N 114 15 E
Pak Tim Pa, *H.K.* **12 D5** 22 22N 114 7 E
Pakila, *Hels.* **3 B4** 60 15N 24 55 E
Palace Museum, *Beij.* **14 B3** 39 54N 116 21 E
Palaión Fáliron, *Ath.* **8 J11** 37 53N 23 42 E
Palaiseau, *Paris* **5 C3** 48 42N 2 14 E
Palam, *Delhi* **16 B1** 28 35N 77 4 E
Palam Int. Airport, *Delhi* **16 B1** 28 32N 77 8 E
Palazzo Reale, *Nápl.* **9 H12** 40 50N 14 15 E
Palazzo Reale, *Tori.* **9 B3** 45 4N 7 40 E
Palazzolo, *Mil.* **9 D5** 45 34N 9 9 E
Palazzuolo, *Nápl.* **9 H13** 40 54N 14 28 E
Palermo, *B.A.* **32 B4** 34 35 S 58 24W
Palhais, *Lisb.* **8 G8** 38 37N 9 2W
Palisades, *N.Y.* **22 A5** 41 1N 73 57W
Palisades Park, *N.Y.* **22 B4** 40 50N 74 1W
Palleja, *Barc.* **8 D5** 41 25N 2 0 E
Palmer Park, *Wash.* **25 D8** 38 55N 76 52W
Palmers Green, *Lon.* **4 B4** 51 36N 0 6W
Palmyra, *Phil.* **24 A4** 40 0N 75 1W
Palo Alto, *S.F.* **27 D4** 37 27N 122 8W
Paloheinä, *Hels.* **3 B4** 60 15N 24 56 E
Palomar Park, *S.F.* **27 D3** 37 29N 122 16W
Palomeras, *Mdrd.* **8 B3** 40 22N 3 39W
Palos Heights, *Chic.* **26 D2** 41 39N 87 47W
Palos Hills, *Chic.* **26 C2** 41 42N 87 49W
Palos Hills Forest, *Chic.* **26 C1** 41 40N 87 52W
Palos Park, *Chic.* **26 C1** 41 40N 87 50W
Palota-Üjfalu, *Bud.* **10 J13** 47 33N 19 7 E
Palpara, *Calc.* **16 E6** 22 38N 88 22 E
Palta, *Calc.* **16 D6** 22 46N 88 23 E
Pamplona, *Manila* **15 E3** 14 27N 120 58 E
Panayaan, *Manila* **15 E3** 14 27N 120 57 E
Panchghara, *Calc.* **16 D5** 22 44N 88 16 E
Panchur, *Calc.* **16 E5** 22 32N 88 16 E
Pancoran, *Jak.* **15 J9** 6 14 S 106 49 E
Pandan, Selat, *Sing.* **15 G7** 1 16N 103 45 E
Pandan, Sungei →, *Sing.* **15 G7** 1 18N 103 43 E
Pandan Res., *Sing.* **15 G7** 1 18N 103 44 E
Panehpara, *Calc.* **16 E5** 22 34N 88 15 E
Pangrati, *Ath.* **8 J11** 37 56N 23 45 E
Pangsua, Sungei →, *Sing.* **15 F7** 1 25N 103 45 E
Panihati, *Calc.* **16 D6** 22 41N 88 22 E
Panjang, Bukit, *Sing.* **15 F7** 1 22N 103 45 E
Panje, *Bomb.* **16 H8** 18 54N 72 57 E
Panke →, *Berl.* **7 A3** 52 31N 13 22 E
Pankow, *Berl.* **7 A3** 52 34N 13 23 E
Panorama City, *L.A.* **28 A2** 34 13N 118 26W
Panpur, *Calc.* **16 C6** 22 51N 88 26 E
Pantheon, *Rome* **9 F9** 41 53N 12 28 E
Pantin, *Paris* **5 B4** 48 53N 2 24 E
Pantitlán, *Méx.* **29 B3** 19 24N 99 4W
Panuacan, *Manila* **15 D4** 14 35N 121 0 E
Panvel Cr. →, *Bomb.* **16 H9** 18 59N 73 0 E
Paoli, *Phil.* **24 A2** 40 2N 75 28W
Papiol, *Barc.* **8 D5** 41 25N 2 0 E
Paracuellos del Jarama, *Mdrd.* **8 A3** 40 30N 3 31W
Paradise Cay, *S.F.* **27 A2** 37 54N 122 28W
Paramount, *L.A.* **28 C3** 33 53N 118 11W
Paramus, *N.Y.* **22 B4** 40 56N 74 2W
Paranaque, *Manila* **15 D3** 14 30N 120 59 E
Paray-Vieille-Poste, *Paris* **5 C4** 48 42N 2 20 E
Parbasdorf, *Wien* **10 G11** 48 16N 16 35 E
Parbatipur, *Calc.* **16 E5** 22 39N 88 13 E
Parcelacion Moderna, *La Hab.* **30 B3** 23 2N 82 19W
Parco Regionale, *Mil.* **9 D5** 45 35N 9 5 E
Parel, *Bomb.* **16 H7** 18 59N 72 49 E
Pari, *S. Pau.* **31 E6** 23 32 S 46 36W
Parioli, *Rome* **9 F9** 41 55N 12 29 E
Paris, *Paris* **5 B4** 48 53N 2 20 E
Paris-Le Bourget, Aéroport de, *Paris* **5 B4** 48 58N 2 26 E
Paris-Orly, Aéroport de, *Paris* **5 C4** 48 43N 2 22 E
Pārk-e-Shahānshāh, *Tehr.* **17 C5** 35 46N 51 24 E
Park Orchards, *Melb.* **19 E8** 37 46 S 145 13 E
Park Ridge, *Chic.* **26 A1** 42 0N 87 50W
Park Ridge, *N.Y.* **22 A4** 41 2N 74 2W
Park Royal, *Lon.* **4 B3** 51 31N 0 16W
Parkchester, *N.Y.* **23 C5** 40 49N 73 50W
Parkdale, *Trto.* **20 E8** 43 38N 79 25W
Parkdene, *Jobg.* **18 F10** 26 11 S 28 15 E
Parkhafen, *Hbg.* **7 D7** 53 32N 9 54 E
Parkhill Gardens, *Jobg.* **18 F10** 26 14 S 28 11 E
Parkhurst, *Jobg.* **18 E9** 26 8 S 28 1 E
Parklawn, *Wash.* **25 D7** 38 50N 77 7W
Parkmore, *Jobg.* **18 E9** 26 5 S 28 2 E
Parkside, *S.F.* **27 B2** 37 44N 122 29W
Parktown, *Jobg.* **18 F9** 26 10 S 28 2 E
Parktown North, *Jobg.* **18 E9** 26 8 S 28 2 E
Parkview, *Jobg.* **18 E9** 26 9 S 28 1 E
Parkville, *Balt.* **25 A3** 39 23N 76 34W
Parkville, *N.Y.* **22 D5** 40 38N 73 57W
Parkwood, *Jobg.* **18 E9** 26 9 S 28 2 E
Parque Edú Chaves, *S. Pau.* **31 D6** 23 29 S 46 34W
Parramatta, *Syd.* **19 A2** 33 49 S 150 59 E
Parramatta →, *Syd.* **19 A3** 33 49 S 151 3 E
Parramatta North, *Syd.* **19 A3** 33 48 S 151 0 E
Parramatta Park, *Syd.* **19 A3** 33 48 S 151 0 E
Parsippany, *N.Y.* **22 B2** 40 51N 74 26W
Paşabahce, *Ist.* **17 A3** 41 6N 29 5 E
Pasadena, *L.A.* **28 B4** 34 9N 118 8W
Pasar Minggu, *Jak.* **15 J9** 6 16 S 106 49 E
Pasay, *Manila* **15 D3** 14 32N 120 59 E
Pascoe Vale, *Melb.* **19 E6** 37 43 S 144 55 E
Pasig, *Manila* **15 D4** 14 33N 121 4 E
Pasig →, *Manila* **15 D4** 14 31N 121 6 E
Pasila, *Hels.* **3 B4** 60 12N 24 56 E
Pasing, *Mün.* **7 G9** 48 8N 11 28 E
Pasir Panjang, *Sing.* **15 G7** 1 17N 103 46 E
Pasir Ris Beach, *Sing.* **15 F8** 1 22N 103 56 E
Paso del Rey, *B.A.* **32 B2** 34 39 S 58 45W
Passaic, *N.Y.* **22 B4** 40 51N 74 9W
Passaic →, *N.Y.* **22 B3** 40 42N 74 10W
Passirana, *Mil.* **9 D5** 45 32N 9 2 E
Patapsco →, *Balt.* **25 B2** 39 19N 76 49W
Patapsco State Park, *Balt.* **25 B2** 39 18N 76 47W
Pateres, *Manila* **15 D4** 14 32N 121 3 E
Paterson, *N.Y.* **22 B4** 40 54N 74 9W
Pathumwan, *Bangk.* **15 B2** 13 44N 100 31 E
Patipukun, *Calc.* **16 E6** 22 36N 88 24 E
Patisia, *Ath.* **8 H11** 38 2N 23 45 E
Patterson Park, *Balt.* **25 B3** 39 17N 76 34W
Patul, *Calc.* **16 D4** 22 45N 88 9 E
Paulo E. Virginia, Gruta, *Rio J.* **31 B2** 22 56 S 43 16W
Paulsboro, *Phil.* **24 C3** 39 49N 75 14W
Paulshof, *Berl.* **7 A5** 52 34N 13 42 E
Pausin, *Berl.* **7 A1** 52 38N 13 2 E
Pavarolo, *Tori.* **9 B3** 45 4N 7 49 E
Pavlovo, *St-Pet.* **11 B5** 59 55N 30 38 E
Pavne, *Bomb.* **16 G9** 19 5N 73 1 E
Pavshino, *Mos.* **11 E7** 55 49N 37 20 E
Paya Lebar, *Sing.* **15 F8** 1 21N 103 52 E
Paylampur, *Calc.* **16 D5** 22 46N 88 15 E
Peabody, *Bost.* **21 B4** 42 32N 70 57W
Peabody Inst., *Balt.* **25 B3** 39 17N 76 37W
Peakhurst, *Syd.* **19 B3** 33 57 S 151 3 E
Pécel, *Bud.* **10 K14** 47 29N 19 20 E
Pecetto Torinese, *Tori.* **9 B3** 45 1N 7 44 E
Pechincha, *Rio J.* **31 B1** 22 55 S 43 20W
Pechorka →, *Mos.* **11 F12** 55 37N 38 2 E
Peckham, *Lon.* **4 C4** 51 28N 0 3W
Pecqueuse, *Paris* **5 D2** 48 38N 2 3 E
Peddocks I., *Bost.* **21 D4** 42 17N 70 56W
Pederstrup, *Købn.* **2 D9** 55 44N 12 20 E
Pedra Branca, *Rio J.* **31 B1** 22 55 S 43 26W
Pedralbes, *Barc.* **8 D5** 41 23N 2 7 E
Pedregal de San Angel, Jardines del, *Méx.* **29 C2** 19 19N 99 12W
Pedreira, *S. Pau.* **31 F5** 23 41 S 46 40W
Pedreros, *Lima* **30 G8** 12 2 S 76 57W
Pedricktown, *Phil.* **24 C2** 39 45N 75 24W
Pedro Cr. →, *S.F.* **27 C2** 37 35N 122 31W
Pedro Valley, *S.F.* **27 C2** 37 35N 122 29W
Peirce Res., *Sing.* **15 F7** 1 22N 103 49 E
Pekhra-Pokrovskoye, *Mos.* **11 D11** 55 50N 37 56 E
Pekhra-Yakovlevskaya, *Mos.* **11 E11** 55 47N 37 57 E
Peking = Beijing, *Beij.* **14 B2** 39 53N 116 21 E
Pelado, Cerro, *Méx.* **29 D2** 19 10N 99 14W
Pelcowizna, *Wsaw.* **10 E7** 52 17N 21 0 E
Pelham, *N.Y.* **23 B6** 40 54N 73 46W
Pelham B. Park, *N.Y.* **23 B6** 40 52N 73 48W
Pelham Manor, *N.Y.* **23 B6** 40 53N 73 46W
Penalolén, *Stgo* **30 J11** 33 28 S 70 30W
Peng Siang →, *Sing.* **15 F7** 1 24N 103 43 E
Penge, *Lon.* **4 C4** 51 24N 0 3W
Penha, *Rio J.* **31 A2** 22 49 S 43 17W
Penha, *S. Pau.* **31 E6** 23 31 S 46 32W
Penjaringan, *Jak.* **15 H9** 6 7 S 106 48 E
Penn Square, *Phil.* **24 A3** 40 8N 75 19W
Penn Wynne, *Phil.* **24 B3** 39 59N 75 16W
Pennant Hills Park, *Syd.* **19 A3** 33 46 S 151 6 E
Penndel, *Phil.* **24 A5** 40 9N 74 54W
Penns Grove, *Phil.* **24 C2** 39 44N 75 27W
Pennsauken, *Phil.* **24 B4** 39 57N 75 5W
Pennsauken Cr. →, *Phil.* **24 B4** 39 59N 75 3W
Pennsylvania, Univ. of, *Phil.* **24 B3** 39 51N 75 11W
Pennypack Cr. →, *Phil.* **24 A4** 40 0N 75 3W
Pentala, *Hels.* **3 C3** 60 6N 24 40 E
Penyagino, *Mos.* **11 D8** 55 50N 37 20 E
Penzing, *Wien* **10 G9** 48 11N 16 18 E
Pequannock, *N.Y.* **22 B3** 40 57N 74 17W
Pequena Arroio Fundo →, *Rio J.* **31 B1** 22 58 S 43 21W
Perales del Rio, *Mdrd.* **8 C3** 40 18N 3 38W
Perchtoldsdorf, *Wien* **10 H9** 48 7N 16 17 E
Perdizes, *S. Pau.* **31 E6** 23 32 S 46 39W
Peredelkino, *Mos.* **11 F8** 55 38N 37 20 E
Peredelytsy, *Mos.* **11 F8** 55 36N 37 21 E
Peristérion, *Ath.* **8 H11** 38 1N 23 42 E
Perivale, *Lon.* **4 B3** 51 31N 0 18W
Perlach, *Mün.* **7 G10** 48 5N 11 37 E
Perlacher Forst, *Mün.* **7 G10** 48 4N 11 34 E
Pero, *Mil.* **9 D5** 45 30N 9 5 E
Peropok, Bukit, *Sing.* **15 G7** 1 19N 103 42 E
Perovo, *Mos.* **11 E10** 55 44N 37 45 E
Perrot, Î., *Mtrl.* **20 B2** 43 23N 73 56W
Perry Hall, *Balt.* **25 A4** 39 24N 76 28W
Perth Amboy, *N.Y.* **22 D3** 40 30N 74 16W
Pertusella, *Mil.* **9 D5** 45 35N 9 3 E
Pesanggrahag, Kali →, *Jak.* **15 J9** 6 10 S 106 44 E
Peschiera Borromeo, *Mil.* **9 E6** 45 26N 9 19 E
Pesek, P., *Sing.* **15 G7** 1 17N 103 41 E
Pest, *Bud.* **10 K13** 47 29N 19 4 E
Pesterzsébet, *Bud.* **10 K13** 47 26N 19 6 E
Pesthidegkút, *Bud.* **10 J12** 47 33N 18 57 E
Pestimre, *Bud.* **10 K14** 47 24N 19 11 E
Pestlörinc, *Bud.* **10 K14** 47 26N 19 11 E
Pestujhely, *Bud.* **10 J13** 47 32N 19 7 E
Petare, *Car.* **30 E6** 10 29N 66 48W
Petas, *Hels.* **3 B4** 60 15N 24 50 E
Peters Pond, *Bost.* **21 A2** 42 43N 71 15W
Petit, *Jobg.* **18 E11** 26 6 S 28 22 E
Petit-Brûlé, *Mtrl.* **20 A1** 43 35N 74 2W
Petojo Selatan, *Jak.* **15 J9** 6 10 S 106 48 E
Petrograd = St. Petersburg, *St-Pet.* **11 B3** 59 55N 30 15 E
Petrogradskaya Storona, *St-Pet.* **11 B4** 59 56N 30 20 E
Petroúpolis, *Ath.* **8 H11** 38 3N 23 40 E
Petrovice, *Pra.* **10 B3** 50 2N 14 33 E
Petrovsko-Rasumovskoye, *Mos.* **11 E9** 55 49N 37 34 E
Petrovskoye, *Mos.* **11 F11** 55 36N 37 53 E
Petrovsky Park, *Mos.* **11 E9** 55 47N 37 34 E
Pfaueninsel, *Berl.* **7 B1** 52 26N 13 7 E
Phihāi, *Kar.* **17 G11** 24 50N 67 8 E
Philadelphia, *Phil.* **24 B3** 39 57N 75 11W
Philadelphia Airport, *Phil.* **24 A5** 40 4N 75 0W
Philadelphia Int. Airport, *Phil.* **24 B3** 39 52N 75 16W
Phillip B., *Syd.* **19 B4** 33 58 S 151 14 E
Phinga, *Calc.* **16 D6** 22 41N 88 25 E
Phoenix, *Chic.* **26 D3** 41 36N 87 37W
Phoenixville, *Phil.* **24 A1** 40 7N 75 31W
Phra Khanong, *Bangk.* **15 B2** 13 40N 100 36 E
Phra Pradaeng, *Bangk.* **15 C2** 13 39N 100 33 E
Phranakhon, *Bangk.* **15 B1** 13 44N 100 29 E
Pianezza, *Tori.* **9 B2** 45 6N 7 32 E
Pianura, *Nápl.* **9 H11** 40 51N 14 10 E
Piaslów, *Wsaw.* **10 E5** 52 11N 20 49 E
Pico Rivera, *L.A.* **28 C4** 33 59N 118 5W
Piedade, *Lisb.* **8 F7** 38 49N 9 16W
Piedade, *Rio J.* **31 B2** 22 52 S 43 18W
Piedade, Cova da, *Lisb.* **8 F8** 38 40N 9 8W
Piedmont, *S.F.* **27 B3** 37 49N 122 14W
Pierrefitte, *Paris* **5 B4** 48 58N 2 21 E
Pierrefonds, *Mtrl.* **20 B2** 43 27N 73 52W
Pierrelaye, *Paris* **5 A2** 49 1N 2 8 E
Pietralata, *Rome* **9 F10** 41 55N 12 33 E
Pihlajamäki, *Hels.* **3 B4** 60 14N 24 58 E
Pihlajasaari, *Hels.* **3 C4** 60 8N 24 55 E
Pikesville, *Balt.* **25 A2** 39 22N 76 42W
Pilar Velho, *S. Pau.* **31 F7** 23 40 S 46 22W
Pilarcitos Cr. →, *S.F.* **27 C2** 37 33N 122 24W
Pilarcitos L., *S.F.* **27 C2** 37 33N 122 25W
Pilgrim Corner, *Phil.* **24 B3** 39 57N 75 19W
Pilgrims Hatch, *Lon.* **4 B6** 51 37N 0 17 E
Pillar Pt., *S.F.* **26 D2** 37 29N 122 30W
Pimenta, *S. Pau.* **31 D7** 23 27 S 46 24W
Pimlico, *Lon.* **4 C4** 51 29N 0 8W
Pimmit Hills, *Wash.* **25 D6** 38 54N 77 12W
Pimville, *Jobg.* **18 F8** 26 16 S 27 54 E
Pinazo →, *B.A.* **32 A2** 34 29 S 58 49W
Pine Brook, *N.Y.* **22 B3** 40 51N 74 18W
Pine Grove, *Trto.* **20 D7** 43 47N 79 34W
Pine Hill, *Phil.* **24 C5** 39 47N 74 59W
Pine Orchard, *Balt.* **25 B1** 39 16N 76 52W
Pinehurst, *Bost.* **21 B2** 42 31N 71 12W
Piñero, *B.A.* **32 B2** 34 31 S 58 46W
Pines Lake, *N.Y.* **22 B3** 40 59N 74 15W
Piney Run →, *Wash.* **25 D6** 38 58N 77 14W
Pinganli, *Beij.* **14 B3** 39 56N 116 20 E
Pinheiros →, *S. Pau.* **31 E5** 23 37 S 46 44W
Pinjrāpur, *Kar.* **17 G11** 24 53N 67 4 E
Pinn →, *Lon.* **4 B2** 51 30N 0 28W
Pinnau →, *Hbg.* **7 C6** 53 40N 9 49 E
Pinneberg, *Hbg.* **7 C6** 53 40N 9 48 E
Pinner, *Lon.* **4 B2** 51 35N 0 22W
Pinner Green, *Lon.* **4 B2** 51 35N 0 23W
Pino Torinese, *Tori.* **9 B3** 45 2N 7 46 E
Pinole Cr. →, *S.F.* **27 A3** 37 58N 122 12W
Pioltello, *Mil.* **9 D6** 45 30N 9 19 E
Piossasco, *Tori.* **9 C1** 44 59N 7 27 E
Piqueri, *S. Pau.* **31 D5** 23 29 S 46 41W
Piqueri →, *S. Pau.* **31 D6** 23 27 S 46 34W
Pira, *Delhi* **16 A1** 28 40N 77 7 E
Piraévs, *Ath.* **8 J10** 37 54N 23 39 E
Pirajussara, *S. Pau.* **31 E5** 23 37 S 46 46W
Pirajussara →, *S. Pau.* **31 E5** 23 33 S 46 42W
Piraporinha, *S. Pau.* **31 F5** 23 41 S 46 44W
Piratininga, *Rio J.* **31 B3** 22 56 S 43 4W
Piratininga, L. de, *Rio J.* **31 B3** 22 56 S 43 4W
Pirituba, *S. Pau.* **31 D5** 23 29 S 46 44W
Pirkkola, *Hels.* **3 B4** 60 14N 24 55 E
Pisangan, *Jak.* **15 J10** 6 12 S 106 52 E
Piscataway, *N.Y.* **22 D2** 40 34N 74 27W
Pisnice, *Pra.* **10 C2** 49 59N 14 28 E
Pitampura Kalan, *Delhi* **16 A1** 28 41N 77 7 E

44 Pitkäjärvi


Pitkäjärvi, Hels. 3 B3 60 15N 24 45 E
Pitman, Phil. 24 C4 39 44N 75 7W
Plainedge, N.Y. 23 C8 40 43N 73 27W
Plainfield, N.Y. 22 D2 40 36N 74 23W
Plainview, N.Y. 23 C8 40 46N 73 27W
Plaisir, Paris 5 C1 48 49N 1 56 E
Plandome, N.Y. 23 C6 40 48N 73 42W
Plandome Heights, N.Y. 23 C6 40 48N 73 42W
Planegg, Mün. 7 G9 48 6N 11 25 E
Plazo Mayor, Mdrd. 8 B2 40 25N 3 43W
Pleasant Hill, S.F. 27 A4 37 56N 122 4W
Plenty, Melb. 19 E7 37 40 S 145 5 E
Pluit, Jak. 15 H9 6 7 S 106 47 E
Plumsock, Phil. 24 B2 39 58N 75 28W
Plumstead, Lon. 4 C5 51 29N 0 5 E
Plymouth Meeting, Phil. 24 A3 40 6N 75 16W
Plyushchevo, Mos. 11 E10 55 44N 37 45 E
Po →, Tori. 9 B3 45 7N 7 46 E
Po Toi, H.K. 12 E6 22 16N 114 17 E
Po Toi I., H.K. 12 E6 22 10N 114 15 E
Podbaba, Pra. 10 B2 50 7N 14 22 E
Podoli, Pra. 10 B2 50 2N 14 25 E
Podra, Calc. 16 E5 22 33N 88 16 E
Poduskino, Mos. 11 E7 55 43N 37 15 E
Poggioreale, Nápl. 9 H12 40 51N 14 17 E
Pogliano Milanese, Mil. 9 D4 45 32N 8 59 E
Pohick Cr. →, Wash. 25 E6 38 47N 77 16W
Point Breeze, Phil. 24 B3 39 54N 75 13W
Point Lookout, N.Y. 23 D7 40 35N 73 34W
Point View Res., N.Y. 22 B3 40 58N 74 14W
Pointe-Aux-Trembles, Mtrl. 20 A4 43 38N 73 30W
Pointe-Calumet, Mtrl. 20 B2 43 29N 73 58W
Pointe-Claire, Mtrl. 20 B3 43 27N 73 48W
Poissy, Paris 5 B2 48 55N 2 2 E
Pok Fu Lam, H.K. 12 E5 22 16N 114 7 E
Pokrovsko-Sresnevo, Mos. 11 E8 55 48N 37 27 E
Pokrovskoye, Mos. 11 F9 55 37N 37 36 E
Pöllena, Nápl. 9 H13 40 51N 14 22 E
Polsum, Ruhr 6 A4 51 37N 7 2 E
Polyustrovo, St-Pet. 11 B4 59 57N 30 25 E
Pomigliano d'Arco, Nápl. 9 H13 40 54N 14 23 E
Pompei, Nápl. 9 J13 40 45N 14 29 E
Pomponne, Paris 5 B6 48 52N 2 40 E
Pomprap, Bangk. 15 B2 13 44N 100 30 E
Pompton →, N.Y. 22 B3 40 53N 74 16W
Pompton Lakes, N.Y. 22 A3 41 0N 74 15W
Pompton Plains, N.Y. 22 B3 40 58N 74 18W
Ponders End, Lon. 4 B4 51 38N 0 2W
Pondok Indah, Jak. 15 J9 6 16 S 106 46 E
Ponkapog, Bost. 21 D3 42 11N 71 4W
Ponkapog Pond, Bost. 21 D3 42 11N 71 5W
Pont-Viau, Mtrl. 20 A3 43 34N 73 41W
Pontault-Combault, Paris 5 C5 48 47N 2 36 E
Pontcarré, Paris 5 C6 48 47N 2 42 E
Pontchartrain, Paris 5 C1 48 48N 1 54 E
Ponte Galéria, Rome 9 G8 41 48N 12 19 E
Pontes, Canto do, Rio J. 31 B3 22 56 S 43 3W
Pontevedra, B.A. 32 C2 34 44 S 58 41W
Ponticelli, Nápl. 9 H12 40 51N 14 19 E
Pontinha, Lisb. 8 F7 38 45N 9 11W
Pontoise, Paris 5 A2 49 2N 2 4 E
Poortview, Jobg. 18 E8 26 5 S 27 51 E
Poplar, Lon. 4 B4 51 30N 0 0 E
Poppenbüttel, Hbg. 7 D8 53 39N 10 4 E
Port Chester, N.Y. 23 A6 41 0N 73 40W
Port Chester Harbour, N.Y. 23 B7 40 58N 73 38W
Port Jackson, Syd. 19 B4 33 51 S 151 14 E
Port Kennedy, Phil. 24 A2 40 6N 75 25W
Port Melbourne, Melb. 19 F6 37 50 S 144 54 E
Port Newark, N.Y. 22 C4 40 41N 74 9W
Port Reading, N.Y. 22 D3 40 34N 74 13W
Port Richmond, N.Y. 22 D4 40 38N 74 7W
Port Shelter, H.K. 12 D6 22 20N 114 17 E
Port Union, Trto. 20 D10 43 47N 79 7W
Port Washington, N.Y. 23 C6 40 49N 73 42W
Port Washington North, N.Y. 23 B6 40 50N 73 41W
Portage Park, Chic. 26 B2 41 56N 87 45W
Portela, Aeroporto da, Lisb. 8 F8 38 46N 9 7W
Pórtici, Nápl. 9 J12 40 48N 14 19 E
Porto Brandão, Lisb. 8 F7 38 40N 9 12W
Porto Novo Cr. →, Lagos 18 B2 6 25N 7 22 E
Porto Nuevo, B.A. 32 B4 34 35 S 58 22W
Portrero, S.F. 27 B2 37 46N 122 25W
Posen, Chic. 26 D2 41 38N 87 41W
Posillipo, Nápl. 9 J12 40 49N 14 13 E
Posillipo, C. di, Nápl. 9 J12 40 48N 14 12 E
Posolok Lenina, St-Pet. 11 C2 59 50N 30 5 E
Potawatomi Woods, Chic. 26 A1 42 8N 87 53W
Potomac, Wash. 25 D6 38 59N 77 13W
Potomac →, Wash. 25 D7 38 58N 77 9W
Potrero Pt., S.F. 27 B2 37 45N 122 22W
Potsdam, Berl. 7 B1 52 23N 13 3 E
Potter Pt., Syd. 19 C4 34 2 S 151 13 E
Potters Bar, Lon. 4 A4 51 41N 0 10W
Potzham, Mün. 7 G10 48 1N 11 36 E
Pötzleinsdorf, Wien 10 G9 48 14N 16 17 E
Povoa de Santo Adriao, Lisb. 8 F8 38 47N 9 9W
Powderhorn L., Chic. 26 D3 41 38N 87 31W
Powiśle, Wsaw. 10 E7 52 14N 21 1 E
Powózki, Wsaw. 10 E6 52 15N 20 58 E
Powsin, Wsaw. 10 F7 52 8N 21 6 E
Powsinek, Wsaw. 10 F7 52 9N 21 6 E
Poyo, Barc. 8 D6 41 28N 2 12 E
Pozuelo de Alarcón, Mdrd. 8 B2 40 25N 3 48W
Praça Seca, Rio J. 31 B1 22 53 S 43 20W
Prado, Museo del, Mdrd. 8 B2 40 25N 3 42W
Prado Churubusco, Méx. 29 B3 19 20N 99 8W
Praga, Wsaw. 10 E7 52 15N 21 2 E
Prague = Praha, Pra. 10 B2 50 4N 14 25 E
Praha, Pra. 10 B2 50 4N 14 25 E
Praha-Ruzyně Airport, Pra. 10 B1 50 6N 14 16 E
Praires, R. des →, Mtrl. 20 A4 43 38N 73 36W
Prat de Llobregat, Barc. 8 E5 41 19N 2 5 E
Prater, Wien 10 G10 48 12N 16 25 E
Pratts Bottom, Lon. 4 C5 51 20N 0 7 E
Prawet Buri Rom, Khlong →, Bangk. 15 B2 13 43N 100 38 E
Preakness, N.Y. 22 B3 40 56N 74 12W
Precotto, Mil. 9 D6 45 30N 9 13 E
Prédecelles →, Paris 5 D2 48 36N 2 7 E
Pregnana Milanese, Mil. 9 D4 45 30N 9 0 E
Prem Prachakan, Khlong →, Bangk. 15 B2 13 46N 100 35 E
Prenestino Labicano, Rome 9 F10 41 53N 12 33 E
Prenzlauerberg, Berl. 7 A3 52 32N 13 24 E
Presidente Derqui, B.A. 32 A1 34 29 S 58 50W
Presidente Outra, Rodo, Rio J. 31 A1 22 47 S 43 21W
Preston, Melb. 19 E6 37 44 S 144 59 E
Pretos Forros, Sa. dos, Rio J. 31 B2 22 54 S 43 17W
Préville, Mtrl. 20 B5 43 28N 73 29W
Přezletice, Pra. 10 B3 50 9N 14 34 E
Primavalle, Rome 9 F9 41 55N 12 25 E
Primrose, Jobg. 18 F9 26 11 S 28 9 E
Princes B., N.Y. 22 D3 40 30N 74 12W
Princess Elizabeth Park, Sing. 15 F7 1 21N 103 45 E
Progreso, Mdrd. 8 B3 40 27N 3 39W
Progreso Nacional, Méx. 29 A3 19 30N 99 9W
Prosek, Pra. 10 B3 50 7N 14 30 E
Prospect, Syd. 19 A2 33 48 S 150 55 E
Prospect Heights, Chic. 26 A1 42 5N 87 55W
Prospect Hill Park, Bost. 21 C2 42 23N 71 13W
Prospect Park, N.Y. 22 B3 40 55N 74 10W
Prospect Park, Phil. 24 B3 39 53N 75 18W
Prospect Pt., N.Y. 23 B6 40 52N 73 42W
Prospect Res., Syd. 19 A2 33 49 S 150 53 E
Providence, Balt. 25 A3 39 25N 76 34W
Providencia, Stgo 30 J11 33 25 S 70 36W
Průhonice, Pra. 10 C3 50 0N 14 33 E
Pruszków, Wsaw. 10 E5 52 10N 20 48 E
Psikhikón, Ath. 8 H11 38 1N 23 46 E
Pudong, Shang. 14 J12 31 13N 121 30 E
Puduo, Shang. 14 J11 31 15N 121 24 E
Pueblo Libre, Lima 30 G8 12 5 S 77 4W
Pueblo Nuevo, Barc. 8 D6 41 23N 2 11 E
Pueblo Nuevo, Mdrd. 8 B3 40 25N 3 37W
Puente Cascallares, B.A. 32 C2 34 41 S 58 48W
Puente Hills, L.A. 28 C5 33 59N 117 59W
Puffing Billy Station, Melb. 19 F9 37 54 S 145 20 E
Puhuangyu, Beij. 14 B3 39 50N 116 22 E
Puistola, Hels. 3 B5 60 16N 25 2 E
Pukinmäki, Hels. 3 B4 60 15N 24 57 E
Pullach, Mün. 7 G9 48 3N 11 31 E
Pulo, Manila 15 D4 14 34N 121 4 E
Pulo Gadung, Jak. 15 J10 6 11 S 106 54 E
Pumphrey, Balt. 25 B3 39 13N 76 39W
Punchbowl, Syd. 19 B3 33 55 S 151 3 E
Punde, Bomb. 16 H8 18 53N 72 57 E
Punggol, Sing. 15 F8 1 23N 103 54 E
Punggol, Sungei →, Sing. 15 F8 1 24N 103 54 E
Punggol Pt., Sing. 15 F8 1 24N 103 54 E
Punta Brava, La Hab. 30 B2 23 1N 82 29W
Puolarmetsä, Hels. 3 B3 60 11N 24 41 E
Puotila, Hels. 3 B5 60 13N 25 6 E
Purchase, N.Y. 23 A6 41 2N 73 43W
Purfleet, Lon. 4 C6 51 29N 0 14 E
Purkersdorf, Wien 10 G8 48 12N 16 11 E
Purley, Lon. 4 C4 51 20N 0 6W
Puteaux, Paris 5 B3 48 53N 2 14 E
Puth Kalan, Delhi 16 A1 28 42N 77 4 E
Putilkovo, Mos. 11 D8 55 51N 37 22 E
Putnamville Res., Bost. 21 B4 42 36N 70 56W
Putney, Lon. 4 C3 51 27N 0 13W
Putty Hill, Balt. 25 A3 39 22N 76 30W
Putxet, Barc. 8 D5 41 24N 2 8 E
Putzbrunn, Mün. 7 G11 48 4N 11 42 E
Pyeongchang, Sŏul 12 G7 37 35N 126 57 E
Pyramids, El Qâ. 18 D4 29 58N 31 7 E
Pyry, Wsaw. 10 F6 52 8N 21 0 E


# Q


Qanât el Ismâ'iliya, El Qâ. 18 C5 30 7N 31 17 E
Qasemābād, Tehr. 17 C6 35 4N 51 3 E
Qasr-e-Firōzeh, Tehr. 17 D6 35 29N 51 31 E
Qianmen, Beij. 14 B3 39 51N 116 21 E
Qibao, Shang. 14 K11 31 9N 121 20 E
Qingguang, Tianj. 14 D5 39 11N 117 2 E
Qinghua Univ., Beij. 14 A2 40 0N 116 17 E
Qinghuayuan, Beij. 14 B2 39 59N 116 19 E
Qingningsi, Shang. 14 J12 31 16N 121 33 E
Qolhak, Tehr. 17 C5 35 45N 51 26 E
Quadraro, Rome 9 F10 41 51N 12 33 E
Quaid-i-Azam, Kar. 17 G10 24 50N 66 59 E
Qual'eh Murgeh Airport, Tehr. 17 D5 35 38N 51 22 E
Qualiano, Nápl. 9 H11 40 55N 14 9 E
Quannapowitt, L., Bost. 21 B3 42 30N 71 4W
Quartiere Zingone, Mil. 9 E5 45 25N 9 3 E
Quarto, Nápl. 9 H11 40 52N 14 8 E
Quds, Bagd. 17 E8 33 23N 44 24 E
Quebrada Baruta →, Car. 30 E5 10 29N 66 53W
Quebrada Tácagua →, Car. 30 D4 10 36N 67 1W
Quebrada Topo →, Car. 30 D4 10 32N 67 0W
Queen Mary Res., Lon. 4 C2 51 24N 0 27W
Queens Village, N.Y. 23 C6 40 43N 73 44W
Queensbury, Lon. 4 B3 51 35N 0 16W
Queenscliffe, Syd. 19 A4 33 47 S 151 17 E
Queenstown, Sing. 15 G7 1 18N 103 48 E
Quellerina, Jobg. 18 E8 26 9 S 27 56 E
Queluz, Lisb. 8 F7 38 45N 9 14W
Quezon City, Manila 15 D4 14 37N 121 2 E
Quickborn, Hbg. 7 C7 53 43N 9 54 E
Quilicura, Stgo 30 J10 33 22 S 70 43W
Quilmes, B.A. 32 C5 34 43 S 58 15W
Quincy, Bost. 21 D3 42 14N 71 0W
Quincy B., Bost. 21 D4 42 16N 70 59W
Quincy-sous-Sénart, Paris 5 C5 48 40N 2 32 E
Quinta Normal, Stgo 30 J10 33 26 S 70 40W
Quinto Romano, Mil. 9 E5 45 28N 9 7 E
Quirinale, Rome 9 F9 41 53N 12 29 E
Quitaúna, S. Pau. 31 E5 23 31 S 46 48W


# R


Raasdorf, Wien 10 G11 48 14N 16 33 E
Raccoon Cr. →, Phil. 24 C3 39 48N 75 21W
Raccoon Str., S.F. 27 A2 37 52N 122 26W
Radevormwald, Ruhr 6 C6 51 12N 7 22 E
Radlett, Lon. 4 A3 51 41N 0 19W
Radlice, Pra. 10 B2 50 3N 14 23 E
Radnor, Phil. 24 A2 40 2N 75 21W
Radonice, Pra. 10 B3 50 8N 14 36 E
Radotin, Pra. 10 C2 49 59N 14 21 E
Rælingen, Oslo 2 B6 59 53N 11 5 E
Rafael Calzada, B.A. 32 C4 34 47 S 58 21W
Rafael Castillo, B.A. 32 C3 34 42 S 58 36W
Raffles Park, Sing. 15 G7 1 19N 103 48 E
Raghunathpur, Calc. 16 D5 22 41N 88 16 E
Rahlstedt, Hbg. 7 D8 53 35N 10 7 E
Rahm, Ruhr 6 B2 51 21N 6 47 E
Rahnsdorf, Berl. 7 B5 52 25N 13 41 E
Rahway, N.Y. 22 D3 40 36N 74 17W
Rail Tree Hill, Bost. 21 B2 42 36N 71 22W
Rainbow Lakes, N.Y. 22 B3 40 53N 74 27W
Rainham, Lon. 4 B6 51 31N 0 11 E
Rainier, Mt., Wash. 25 D8 38 56N 76 57W
Raj Bhawan, Calc. 16 E6 22 33N 88 20 E
Rajakylä, Hels. 3 B5 60 15N 25 5 E
Rajapur, Calc. 16 E5 22 39N 88 11 E
Rajganj, Calc. 16 E5 22 34N 88 14 E
Rajpur, Delhi 16 A2 28 41N 77 12 E
Rákos-patak →, Bud. 10 K14 47 29N 19 12 E
Rákoscsaba, Bud. 10 K14 47 28N 19 17 E
Rákoshegy, Bud. 10 K14 47 27N 19 14 E
Rákosker, Bud. 10 K14 47 28N 19 14 E
Rákoskert, Bud. 10 K14 47 27N 19 18 E
Rákosliget, Bud. 10 K14 47 29N 19 16 E
Rákospalota, Bud. 10 J13 47 34N 19 7 E
Rákosszentmihály, Bud. 10 J13 47 31N 19 8 E
Raków, Wsaw. 10 E6 52 11N 20 56 E
Rakowiec, Wsaw. 10 E6 52 12N 20 58 E
Ramadân, Bagd. 17 F8 33 19N 44 20 E
Ramanathpur, Calc. 16 D5 22 41N 88 14 E
Rambler Channel, H.K. 12 D5 22 21N 114 6 E
Ramblewood, Phil. 24 B5 39 55N 74 56W
Ramenki, Mos. 11 E8 55 41N 37 28 E
Ramersdorf, Mün. 7 G10 48 6N 11 35 E
Ramnathpur, Calc. 16 E5 22 35N 88 18 E
Ramos, Rio J. 31 B2 22 50 S 43 14W
Ramos Mejia, B.A. 32 B3 34 39 S 58 33W
Rampur, Delhi 16 A2 28 44N 77 18 E
Ramsgate, Syd. 19 B3 33 58 S 151 8 E
Ramstadjøen, Oslo 2 B6 59 53N 11 3 E
Rancho Boyeros, La Hab. 30 C2 22 59N 82 22W
Rancho Colorado, Presa de, Méx. 29 B2 19 29N 99 16W
Rancocas Cr. →, Phil. 24 A5 40 2N 74 58W
Rand Afrikaans Univ., Jobg. 18 F9 26 11 S 28 0 E
Rand Airport, Jobg. 18 F9 26 14 S 28 8 E
Randallstown, Balt. 25 A2 39 21N 76 46W
Randburg, Jobg. 18 E8 26 5 S 27 57 E
Randhart, Jobg. 18 F9 26 16 S 28 7 E
Randolph, Bost. 21 D3 42 10N 71 3W
Randolph Hills, Wash. 25 C7 39 3N 77 6W
Randpark, Jobg. 18 E8 26 6 S 27 58 E
Randwick, Syd. 19 B4 33 54 S 151 14 E
Ranelagh, B.A. 32 C5 34 47 S 58 14W
Rannersdorf, Wien 10 H10 48 7N 16 27 E
Raparkrif, Jobg. 18 E8 26 5 S 27 57 E
Raposo, Lisb. 8 F7 38 40N 9 11W
Raritan →, N.Y. 22 D2 40 30N 74 27W
Raritan B., N.Y. 22 E3 40 29N 74 12W
Rasskazovka, Mos. 11 F8 55 38N 37 20 E
Rasta, Stock. 3 E8 59 18N 17 37 E
Rastaala, Hels. 3 B3 60 15N 24 47 E
Rastila, Hels. 3 B5 60 12N 25 7 E
Raszyn, Wsaw. 10 F6 52 9N 20 54 E
Rat Burana, Bangk. 15 B2 13 40N 100 30 E
Ratanpur, Calc. 16 D5 22 49N 88 14 E
Rath, Ruhr 6 C2 51 16N 6 49 E
Ratingen, Ruhr 6 C3 51 18N 6 52 E
Rato, Lisb. 8 F8 38 43N 9 8W
Rauxel, Ruhr 6 A5 51 34N 7 18 E
Ravenswood Pt., S.F. 27 C4 37 30N 122 8W
Rawamangun, Jak. 15 J10 6 11 S 106 52 E
Rayners Lane, Lon. 4 B2 51 34N 0 23W
Raynes Park, Lon. 4 C3 51 24N 0 12W
Raypur, Calc. 16 F6 22 28N 88 22 E
Razdory, Mos. 11 E7 55 44N 37 17 E
Razmitelevo, St-Pet. 11 B5 59 54N 30 39 E
Razor Hill, H.K. 12 D6 22 20N 114 15 E
Reading, Bost. 21 B3 42 31N 71 5W
Reading Highlands, Bost. 21 B3 42 31N 71 5W
Reáglie, Tori. 9 B3 45 3N 7 44 E
Real, Palacio, Mdrd. 8 B2 40 25N 3 43W
Real Felipe, Castillo, Lima 30 G8 12 4 S 77 9W
Real Fuerta, Château de la, La Hab. 30 B2 23 8N 82 20W
Realengo, Rio J. 31 B1 22 52 S 43 24W
Réau, Paris 5 D5 48 36N 2 37 E
Recklinghausen, Ruhr 6 A5 51 37N 7 12 E
Recklinghausen-Süd, Ruhr 6 A5 51 34N 7 14 E
Recoleta, Stgo 30 J11 33 25 S 70 40W
Reconquista →, B.A. 32 B3 34 33 S 58 35W
Red Bank Battle Mon., Phil. 24 B3 39 52N 75 11W
Red Fort, Delhi 16 B2 28 39N 77 14 E
Red Rock, S.F. 27 A2 37 55N 122 25W
Red Square, Mos. 11 E9 55 45N 37 37 E
Redbridge, Lon. 4 B5 51 34N 0 3 E
Redwood City, S.F. 27 D3 37 29N 122 14W
Redwood Cr. →, S.F. 27 D3 37 31N 122 11W
Redwood Pt., S.F. 27 C3 37 32N 122 11W
Redwood Regional Park, S.F. 27 B4 37 48N 122 8W
Reeves Hill, Bost. 21 C1 42 20N 71 20W
Refshaleøen, Købn. 2 D10 55 41N 12 36 E
Regents Park, Jobg. 18 F9 26 14 S 28 4 E
Regents Park, Lon. 4 B4 51 31N 0 9W
Regents Park, Syd. 19 B3 33 52 S 151 1 E
Regi Lagni →, Nápl. 9 H13 40 56N 14 23 E
Regina Margherita, Tori. 9 B2 45 4N 7 34 E
Regla, La Hab. 30 B3 23 7N 82 19W
Rego Park, N.Y. 23 C5 40 43N 73 51W
Reiherstieg, Hbg. 7 D7 53 30N 9 58 E
Reinickendorf, Berl. 7 A3 52 34N 13 22 E
Reinoldikirche, Ruhr 6 A6 51 30N 7 28 E
Reistad, Oslo 2 C1 59 46N 10 16 E
Reitbrook, Hbg. 7 E8 53 28N 10 8 E
Rekola, Hels. 3 B5 60 19N 25 4 E
Rellingen, Hbg. 7 D7 53 39N 9 50 E
Rembertów, Wsaw. 10 E7 52 15N 21 9 E
Remedios de Escalada, B.A. 32 C4 34 43 S 58 24W
Rémola, Laguna del, Barc. 8 E5 41 16N 2 4 E
Remscheid, Ruhr 6 C5 51 11N 7 11 E
Renca, Stgo 30 J10 33 24 S 70 42W
Renca, Cerro, Stgo 30 J10 33 23 S 70 40W
Rener, Ist. 17 A2 41 1N 28 56 E
Renmin Gongyuan, Tianj. 14 E6 39 6N 117 12 E
Rennemoulin, Paris 5 B2 48 50N 2 2 E
Rennie's Mill, H.K. 12 E6 22 18N 114 15 E
Renzel, Hbg. 7 C7 53 43N 9 52 E
Repaupo, Phil. 24 C3 39 48N 75 18W
Repaupo Cr. →, Phil. 24 C3 39 49N 75 20W
Řeporyje, Pra. 10 B1 50 1N 14 18 E
République, Place de la, Paris 5 B4 48 52N 2 22 E
Repy, Pra. 10 B2 50 4N 14 17 E
Resarö, Stock. 3 D13 59 25N 18 20 E
Rescaldina, Mil. 9 D4 45 36N 8 57 E
Research, Melb. 19 E8 37 42 S 145 10 E
Reseda, L.A. 28 A1 34 12N 118 31W
Reservoir, Melb. 19 E7 37 42 S 145 1 E
Reservoir Pond, Bost. 21 D3 42 10N 71 7W
Residenz, Mün. 7 G10 48 8N 11 34 E
Resse, Ruhr 6 A4 51 34N 7 6 E
Reston, Wash. 25 D6 38 57N 77 20W
Retiro, B.A. 32 B4 34 35 S 58 22W
Retiro, Mdrd. 8 B2 40 24N 3 40W
Reutov, Mos. 11 E11 55 45N 37 50 E
Réveillon →, Paris 5 C5 48 42N 2 30 E
Revere, Bost. 21 C3 42 25N 71 0W
Revesby, Syd. 19 B3 33 57 S 151 0 E
Revolucion, Plaza de la, La Hab. 30 B2 23 7N 82 23W
Rexdale, Trto. 20 D7 43 43N 79 35W
Reynolds Channel, N.Y. 23 D6 40 35N 73 41W
Reynosa Tamaulipas, Méx. 29 A2 19 30N 99 10W
Rheem Valley, S.F. 27 A4 37 50N 122 8W
Rhein-Herne Kanal, Ruhr 6 B3 51 29N 6 59 E
Rheinberg, Ruhr 6 A1 51 32N 6 37 E
Rheinhausen, Ruhr 6 B2 51 24N 6 43 E
Rheinkamp, Ruhr 6 B1 51 29N 6 36 E
Rho, Mil. 9 D5 45 31N 9 2 E
Rhodes, Syd. 19 A3 33 49 S 151 6 E
Rhodesfield, Jobg. 18 E10 26 6 S 28 14 E
Rhodon, Paris 5 C2 48 42N 2 3 E
Rhodon →, Paris 5 C2 48 42N 2 4 E
Rhu, Tg., Sing. 15 G8 1 17N 103 51 E
Ribeirão Pires, S. Pau. 31 F7 23 42 S 46 23W
Ričanský →, Pra. 10 B3 50 5N 14 36 E
Říčany, Pra. 10 C3 49 59N 14 39 E
Ricarda, Laguna de la, Barc. 8 E5 41 17N 2 6 E
Richardson B., S.F. 27 A2 37 52N 122 29W
Richmond, Lon. 4 C3 51 27N 0 17W
Richmond, Melb. 19 E7 37 48 S 145 0 E
Richmond, S.F. 27 B2 37 46N 122 27W
Richmond, S.F. 27 A2 37 56N 122 21W
Richmond →, N.Y. 22 D3 40 34N 74 11W
Richmond, Pt., S.F. 27 A2 37 54N 122 23W
Richmond Hill, N.Y. 23 C5 40 41N 73 51W
Richmond Hill, Trto. 20 C8 43 51N 79 24W
Richmond Inner Harbour, S.F. 27 A2 37 54N 122 20W
Richmond Park, Lon. 4 C3 51 26N 0 16W
Richmond Valley, N.Y. 22 D3 40 31N 74 13W
Richvale, Trto. 20 C8 43 51N 79 26W
Rickers I., N.Y. 23 C5 40 47N 73 53W
Rickmansworth, Lon. 4 B2 51 38N 0 28W
Riddel Cr. →, Melb. 19 F8 37 52 S 145 13 E
Riderwood, Balt. 25 A3 39 24N 76 37W
Ridgefield, N.Y. 22 C4 40 49N 74 0W
Ridgefield Park, N.Y. 22 B4 40 52N 74 1W
Ridgewood, N.Y. 23 C5 40 42N 73 53W
Ridley Cr. →, Phil. 24 B2 39 51N 75 20W
Ridley Creek State Park, Phil. 24 B2 39 57N 75 26W
Ridley Park, Phil. 24 B3 39 52N 75 19W
Riedmoos, Mün. 7 F10 48 16N 11 32 E
Riem, Mün. 7 G11 48 8N 11 41 E
Riemke, Ruhr 6 A5 51 30N 7 12 E
Rimac, Lima 30 G8 12 2 S 77 2W
Rimau, Tg., Sing. 15 G7 1 15N 103 48 E
Ringwood, Melb. 19 E8 37 48 S 145 4 E
Rinkeby, Stock. 3 D10 59 23N 17 55 E
Rio Comprido, Rio J. 31 B2 22 55 S 43 12W
Rio de Janeiro, Rio J. 31 B2 22 54 S 43 12W
Rio de Mouro, Lisb. 8 F7 38 46N 9 15W
Rio Hondo →, L.A. 28 B4 34 2N 118 15W
Rio Pequeno, S. Pau. 31 E5 23 34 S 46 44W
Rione Trieste, Nápl. 9 H13 40 52N 14 27 E
Ripley, Lon. 4 D2 51 17N 0 29W
Rippling Ridge, Balt. 25 B3 39 11N 76 37W
Ris, Oslo 2 B4 59 56N 10 41 E
Ris-Orangis, Paris 5 D4 48 38N 2 24 E
Risby, Købn. 2 D8 55 41N 12 19 E
Rishra, Calc. 16 D6 22 42N 88 20 E
Ritan Gongyuan, Beij. 14 B3 39 53N 116 24 E
Ritchie, Wash. 25 D8 38 52N 76 51W
Rithala, Delhi 16 A1 28 43N 77 6 E
Ritorp, Stock. 3 E8 59 12N 17 38 E
Rivalta di Torino, Tori. 9 B1 45 2N 7 31 E
Rivas de Jarama, Mdrd. 8 B3 40 22N 3 31W
Rivas-Vaciamadrio, Mdrd. 8 C3 40 19N 3 30W
Rivasacco, Tori. 9 A1 45 10N 7 29 E
Rive Sud, Canal de la, Mtrl. 20 B4 43 24N 73 31W
River Edge, N.Y. 22 B4 40 56N 74 1W
River Forest, Chic. 26 B2 41 53N 87 49W
River Grove, Chic. 26 B1 41 55N 87 50W
River Pines, Bost. 21 B2 42 33N 71 17W
River Vale, N.Y. 22 B4 40 59N 74 1W
Riverdale, Chic. 26 D3 41 38N 87 37W
Riverdale, N.Y. 22 B3 40 59N 74 17W
Riverdale, Trto. 20 E8 43 39N 79 21W
Riverdale, Wash. 25 D8 38 57N 76 54W
Riverdale Park, Trto. 20 D8 43 40N 79 21W
Riverhead, Lon. 4 D6 51 16N 0 10 E
Riverlea, Jobg. 18 F8 26 12 S 27 58 E
Riverside, Bost. 21 C2 42 32N 71 18W
Riverside, Chic. 26 C2 41 49N 87 49W
Riverside, N.Y. 23 B5 40 54N 73 54W
Riverside, N.Y. 23 A7 41 1N 73 34W
Riverside, Phil. 24 A5 40 2N 74 57W
Riverton, Phil. 24 A4 40 2N 75 0W
Riverwood, Syd. 19 B3 33 57 S 151 3 E
Rivière-des-Praires, Mtrl. 20 A4 43 38N 73 34W
Rivodora, Tori. 9 B3 45 5N 7 47 E
Rivoli, Tori. 9 B1 45 4N 7 30 E
Riyad, Bagd. 17 F8 33 18N 44 27 E
Rizal, Manila 15 D4 14 33N 121 0 E
Rizal Park, Manila 15 D3 14 35N 120 58 E
Rizel Stadium, Manila 15 D3 14 34N 120 59 E
Røa, Oslo 2 B3 59 57N 10 39 E
Robassomero, Tori. 9 A2 45 11N 7 34 E
Robbins, Chic. 26 D2 41 38N 87 42W
Robert E. Lee Memorial Park, Balt. 25 A3 39 23N 76 40 E
Robertsdale, Chic. 26 C3 41 40N 87 30W
Robertsham, Jobg. 18 F9 26 15 S 28 1 E
Robin Hills, Jobg. 18 E8 26 5 S 27 58 E
Rocha Miranda, Rio J. 31 B1 22 51 S 43 20W
Rochar →, Sing. 15 G8 1 18N 103 52 E
Rochelle Park, N.Y. 22 B4 40 54N 74 4W
Rock Cr. →, Wash. 25 D7 38 54N 77 3W
Rock Creek Park, Wash. 25 D7 38 56N 77 2W
Rockaway, N.Y. 23 D6 40 32N 73 56W
Rockaway Beach, S.F. 27 C2 37 36N 122 29W
Rockaway Islet, N.Y. 23 D5 40 34N 73 53W
Rockaway Neck, N.Y. 22 B2 40 50N 74 22W
Rockaway Point, N.Y. 23 D5 40 33N 73 54W
Rockburn Branch →, Balt. 25 B2 39 13N 76 43W
Rockdale, Balt. 25 A2 39 21N 76 46W
Rockdale, Syd. 19 B3 33 57 S 151 8 E
Rockland, Phil. 24 C1 39 47N 75 34W
Rocklege, Phil. 24 A4 40 4N 75 5W
Rockleigh, N.Y. 22 A5 41 0N 73 55W
Rockville, Wash. 25 C6 39 4N 77 10W
Rockville Centre, N.Y. 23 D7 40 39N 73 38W
Rocky Hill, Phil. 24 B1 39 58N 75 32W
Rocky Ridge, S.F. 27 B4 37 47N 122 3W
Rocky Run →, Wash. 25 D6 38 58N 77 14W
Rodaon, Wien 10 H9 48 8N 16 12 E
Rodeo Cove, S.F. 27 B1 37 49N 122 32W
Rodgers Forge, Balt. 25 A3 39 22N 76 37W
Roding →, Lon. 4 B5 51 30N 0 5 E
Rodość, Wsaw. 10 E6 52 11N 20 55 E
Rødovre, Købn. 2 D9 55 40N 12 26 E
Rodrigo de Freitas, L., Rio J. 31 B2 22 58 S 43 12W
Rodstensfjärden, Stock. 3 E9 59 16N 17 48 E
Roehampton, Lon. 4 C3 51 27N 0 15W
Rogers Park, Chic. 26 A2 42 0N 87 40W
Rohdenhaus, Ruhr 6 C4 51 18N 7 0 E
Röhlinghausen, Ruhr 6 A4 51 30N 7 9 E
Roihuvuori, Hels. 3 B5 60 11N 25 2 E
Roissy, Paris 5 C5 48 47N 2 39 E
Roissy-en-France, Paris 5 A5 49 0N 2 30 E
Rokkō Sanchi, Ōsaka 12 B2 34 44N 135 13 E
Rokko-Zan, Ōsaka 12 B2 34 46N 135 16 E
Rokytka →, Pra. 10 B3 50 6N 14 27 E
Roland Lake, Balt. 25 A3 39 23N 76 38W
Roland Park, Balt. 25 A3 39 20N 76 39W
Roma, Rome 9 F9 41 54N 12 28 E
Római-Fürdő, Bud. 10 J13 47 34N 19 4 E
Romainville, Paris 5 B4 48 52N 2 26 E
Romani, Nápl. 9 H13 40 52N 14 22 E
Romano Banco, Mil. 9 E5 45 25N 9 6 E
Romashkovo, Mos. 11 E7 55 43N 37 19 E
Rome = Roma, Rome 9 F9 41 54N 12 28 E
Romford, Lon. 4 B6 51 34N 0 11 E
Roncáglia, Tori. 9 B1 45 2N 7 29 E
Rönninge, Stock. 3 E9 59 12N 17 45 E
Ronsdorf, Ruhr 6 C5 51 13N 7 11 E
Ronskensiedig, Ruhr 6 A2 51 36N 6 41 E
Rontgental, Berl. 7 A4 52 38N 13 31 E
Roodekop, Jobg. 18 F10 26 17 S 28 11 E
Roodepoort, Jobg. 18 E8 26 9 S 27 53 E
Roodepoort-Wes, Jobg. 18 E8 26 8 S 27 51 E
Roosevelt, N.Y. 23 C7 40 40N 73 35W
Rooty Hill, Syd. 19 A2 33 46 S 150 50 E
Roppongi, Tōkyō 13 C3 35 39N 139 44 E
Rosairinho, Lisb. 8 F8 38 40N 9 0W
Rosanna, Melb. 19 E7 37 44 S 145 4 E
Rosario, La Hab. 30 B2 23 3N 82 21W
Rosario, Manila 15 D4 14 35N 121 4 E
Rose B., Syd. 19 B4 33 51 S 151 16 E
Rose Hill, Wash. 25 E7 38 47N 77 6W
Rose Tree, Phil. 24 B2 39 56N 75 23W
Rosebank, N.Y. 22 D4 40 36N 74 4W
Rosebery, Syd. 19 B4 33 55 S 151 12 E
Rosedal La Candelaria, Méx. 29 B3 19 20N 99 10W
Rosedale, Balt. 25 B3 39 19N 76 31W
Rosedale, N.Y. 23 D6 40 39N 73 43W
Roseiras, S. Pau. 31 E7 23 33 S 46 23W
Roseland, Chic. 26 C3 41 42N 87 37W
Roseland, N.Y. 22 C3 40 49N 74 17W
Roselle, N.Y. 22 D3 40 39N 74 15W
Roselle Park, N.Y. 22 D3 40 39N 74 16W
Rosemead, L.A. 28 B4 34 4N 118 4W
Rosemere, Mtrl. 20 A2 43 34N 73 50W
Rosemont, Chic. 26 B1 41 59N 87 52W
Rosemont, Phil. 24 A3 40 1N 75 19W
Rosenborg Have, Købn. 2 D10 55 41N 12 33 E
Rosengarten, Hbg. 7 D6 53 31N 9 49 E
Rosenthal, Berl. 7 A3 52 35N 13 22 E
Rosettenville, Jobg. 18 F9 26 15 S 28 3 E
Rosherville Dam, Jobg. 18 F9 26 13 S 28 6 E
Rósio, Mil. 9 E4 45 25N 8 57 E
Rösjön, Stock. 3 D11 59 26N 18 0 E
Roskilde, Købn. 2 E7 55 38N 12 5 E
Roskilde Fjord, Købn. 2 D7 55 45N 12 4 E
Roslags-Näsby, Stock. 3 D11 59 25N 18 2 E
Roslindale, Bost. 21 D3 42 17N 71 7W
Roslyn, N.Y. 23 C7 40 47N 73 38W
Roslyn, Phil. 24 A4 40 7N 75 8W
Roslyn Estates, N.Y. 23 C7 40 47N 73 40W
Roslyn Harbour, N.Y. 23 C7 40 48N 73 38W
Rosne →, Paris 5 B4 48 58N 2 25 E
Rosny-sous-Bois, Paris 5 B5 48 52N 2 30 E
Ross, S.F. 27 A1 37 57N 122 33W
Rosslyn, Wash. 25 D7 38 53N 77 4W
Rossville, Balt. 25 A4 39 20N 76 28W
Rossville, N.Y. 22 D3 40 33N 74 12W
Rosta, Tori. 9 B1 45 4N 7 27 E
Rotbach →, Ruhr 6 A2 51 34N 6 41 E
Rothenburgsort, Hbg. 7 D8 53 32N 10 2 E
Rotherbaum, Hbg. 7 D7 53 33N 9 58 E
Rotherhithe, Lon. 4 C4 51 29N 0 2W
Rothneusiedl, Wien 10 H10 48 8N 16 23 E
Rothschmaige, Mün. 7 F9 48 14N 11 27 E
Rouge →, Trto. 20 D9 43 47N 79 12W
Rouge Hill, Trto. 20 D10 43 48N 79 6W
Round I., H.K. 12 E6 22 13N 114 12 E
Roundshaw, Lon. 4 C4 51 20N 0 7W
Roussigny, Paris 5 D2 48 38N 2 6 E
Rowland, L.A. 28 B5 34 0N 117 55W
Rowley, Bost. 21 A4 42 43N 70 52W
Rowville, Melb. 19 F8 37 55 S 145 14 E
Roxboro, Mtrl. 20 A3 43 31N 73 48W
Roxborough, Phil. 24 A3 40 1N 75 13W
Roxbury, Bost. 21 D3 42 19N 71 5W
Roxbury, N.Y. 23 D5 40 33N 73 53W
Roxeth, Lon. 4 B2 51 33N 0 20W
Royal Observatory, H.K. 12 E6 22 18N 114 10 E
Royal Park, Melb. 19 E6 37 46 S 144 57 E
Röylä, Hels. 3 B3 60 18N 24 42 E
Royston Park, Lon. 4 B2 51 36N 0 22W
Rozas, Portilleros de las, Mdrd. 8 B2 40 29N 3 49W
Roztoky, Pra. 10 B2 50 9N 14 23 E
Rubbianetta, Tori. 9 B2 45 9N 7 34 E
Rubi →, Barc. 8 D5 41 26N 2 0 E
Rubio Woods, Chic. 26 D2 41 38N 87 45W
Rublovo, Mos. 11 E8 55 47N 37 21 E
Ruchyi, St-Pet. 11 A4 60 0N 30 25 E
Rud, Oslo 2 B6 59 56N 11 0 E
Rüdinghausen, Ruhr 6 B6 51 26N 7 24 E
Rudnevka →, Mos. 11 E11 55 43N 37 56 E
Rudolfsheim, Wien 10 G10 48 12N 16 20 E
Rudolfshöhe, Berl. 7 A5 52 37N 13 44 E
Rudow, Berl. 7 B4 52 25N 13 29 E
Rueil-Malmaison, Paris 5 B3 48 52N 2 11 E
Ruffys Cr. →, Melb. 19 E7 37 45 S 145 7 E
Ruggeberg, Ruhr 6 C6 51 16N 7 23 E
Ruhlsdorf, Berl. 7 B3 52 23N 13 15 E
Ruhr →, Ruhr 6 B3 51 27N 6 56 E
Ruhrort, Ruhr 6 B2 51 27N 6 44 E
Ruislip, Lon. 4 B2 51 34N 0 24W
Rumelihisari, Ist. 17 A3 41 4N 29 2 E
Rumeln, Ruhr 6 B2 51 23N 6 41 E
Rumyantsevo, Mos. 11 F8 55 38N 37 25 E
Rungis, Paris 5 C4 48 44N 2 21 E
Runnemede, Phil. 24 B4 39 50N 75 4W
Ruotsinkylä, Hels. 3 A4 60 21N 24 59 E
Rusāfa, Bagd. 17 E8 33 21N 44 23 E
Rush Green, Lon. 4 B6 51 33N 0 10 E
Russa, Calc. 16 F6 22 29N 88 21 E
Russell Lea, Syd. 19 B3 33 51 S 151 10 E
Rustad, Oslo 2 B2 59 56N 10 24 E
Rustenfeld, Wien 10 H10 48 7N 16 23 E
Rusville, Jobg. 18 E10 26 9 S 28 18 E
Rutherford, N.Y. 22 C4 40 49N 74 6W
Rüttenscheid, Ruhr 6 B3 51 25N 6 58 E
Ruxton, Balt. 25 A3 39 23N 76 38W
Ruzyně, Pra. 10 B1 50 5N 14 17 E
Rybatskaya, St-Pet. 11 B5 59 49N 30 30 E
Rybatskoye, St-Pet. 11 B4 59 50N 30 29 E
Rydalmere, Syd. 19 A3 33 48 S 151 2 E
Rydboholm, Stock. 3 D12 59 26N 18 12 E
Ryde, Syd. 19 A3 33 48 S 151 6 E
Rye, N.Y. 23 B7 40 58N 73 40W
Rynfield, Jobg. 18 E10 26 9 S 28 19 E
Ryogoku, Tōkyō 13 B3 35 40N 139 48 E
Rysäkari, Hels. 3 C4 60 6N 24 50 E
Rzhevka, St-Pet. 11 B5 59 59N 30 31 E

# S

Saadõn, *Bagd.* — 17 F8 33 19N 44 25 E
Saarn, *Ruhr* — 6 B3 51 24N 6 51 E
Saavedra, *B.A.* — 32 B4 34 33 S 58 29W
Saboli, *Delhi* — 16 A2 28 42N 77 18 E
Sabugo, *Lisb.* — 8 F7 38 49N 9 17W
Saburovo, *Mos.* — 11 D7 55 53N 37 15 E
Sãbysjön, *Stock.* — 3 D10 59 26N 17 52 E
Sabzi Mandi, *Delhi* — 16 A2 28 40N 77 12 E
Sacavém, *Lisb.* — 8 F8 38 47N 9 5W
Saclay, *Paris* — 5 C3 48 43N 2 10 E
Saclay, Étang de, *Paris* — 5 C2 48 44N 2 9 E
Sacoma, *S. Pau.* — 31 E6 23 36 S 46 35W
Sacré-Coeur, *Paris* — 5 B4 48 53N 2 20 E
Sacrow, *Berl.* — 7 B1 52 25N 13 6 E
Sacrower See, *Berl.* — 7 B1 52 25N 13 6 E
Sadang, *Sŏul* — 12 H7 37 29N 126 58 E
Sadar Bazar, *Delhi* — 16 B2 28 39N 77 11 E
Saddãm City, *Bagd.* — 17 E8 33 23N 44 27 E
Saddle Brook, *N.Y.* — 22 B4 40 53N 74 5W
Saddle River, *N.Y.* — 22 A4 41 1N 74 6W
Saddle Rock, *N.Y.* — 23 C6 40 47N 73 45W
Sadr, *Kar.* — 17 G11 24 51N 67 2 E
Sadyba, *Wsaw.* — 10 E7 52 11N 21 3 E
Saedo, *Tōkyō* — 13 C2 35 30N 139 33 E
Saensaep, Khlong →, *Bangk.* — 15 B2 13 44N 100 32 E
Sáenz Pena, *B.A.* — 32 B3 34 37 S 58 32W
Safdar Jang Airport, *Delhi* — 16 B2 28 35N 77 12 E
Safdar Jangs Tomb, *Delhi* — 16 B2 28 35N 77 12 E
Safrakõy, *Ist.* — 17 A1 41 0N 28 48 E
Saft el Laban, *El Qâ.* — 18 C5 30 1N 31 10 E
Sag Bridge, *Chic.* — 26 C1 41 41N 87 55W
Sagamore Neck, *N.Y.* — 23 B8 40 53N 73 29W
Saganashkee Slough, *Chic.* — 26 C1 41 41N 87 53W
Sagene, *Oslo* — 2 B4 59 55N 10 46 E
Sagrada Família, Temple de, *Barc.* — 8 D6 41 24N 2 10 E
Sahapur, *Calc.* — 16 E5 22 31N 88 11 E
Sahibabad, *Delhi* — 16 A1 28 41N 77 4 E
Sai Kung, *H.K.* — 12 D6 22 23N 114 16 E
Sai Wan Ho, *H.K.* — 12 E6 22 17N 114 12 E
Sai Ying Pun, *H.K.* — 12 E5 22 17N 114 9 E
Saido, *Tōkyō* — 13 A2 35 52N 139 39 E
Sailmouille →, *Paris* — 5 D3 48 37N 2 17 E
St. Albans, *N.Y.* — 23 C6 40 42N 73 44W
St. Andrä, *Wien* — 10 G9 48 19N 16 12 E
St. Andrews, *Jobg.* — 18 E9 26 9 S 28 7 E
St. Aubin, *Paris* — 5 C2 48 44N 2 8 E
St. Augustin, *Mtrl.* — 20 A2 43 37N 73 58W
St. Basil's Cathedral, *Mos.* — 11 E9 55 45N 37 38 E
St.-Benoit, *Paris* — 5 C1 48 40N 1 54 E
St.-Brice-sous-Forêt, *Paris* — 5 A4 49 0N 2 21 E
St.-Cloud, *Paris* — 5 B3 48 50N 2 13 E
St.-Cyr-l'École, *Paris* — 5 C2 48 47N 2 4 E
St.-Cyr-l'École, Aérodrome de, *Paris* — 5 C2 48 48N 2 4 E
St. Davids, *Phil.* — 24 A2 40 2N 75 23W
St.-Denis, *Paris* — 5 B4 48 56N 2 20 E
St. Eustache, *Mtrl.* — 20 A2 43 33N 73 54W
St.-Forget, *Paris* — 5 C2 48 43N 2 1 E
St. Georg, *Hbg.* — 7 D8 53 33N 10 1 E
St.-Germain, Forêt de, *Paris* — 5 B2 48 57N 2 5 E
St. Germain-en-Laye, *Paris* — 5 B2 48 53N 2 4 E
St.-Germain-lès-Corbeil, *Paris* — 5 D4 48 37N 2 29 E
St.-Gratien, *Paris* — 5 B4 48 58N 2 17 E
St. Helier, *Lon.* — 4 C3 51 23N 0 11W
St.-Hubert, *Mtrl.* — 20 B5 43 29N 73 25W
St. Isaac's Cathedral, *St-Pet.* — 11 B3 59 55N 30 19 E
St. Jacques →, *Mtrl.* — 20 B5 43 26N 73 29W
St.-Jean-de-Beauregard, *Paris* — 5 D3 48 39N 2 10 E
St.-Jean-de-dieu, *Mtrl.* — 20 A4 43 34N 73 31W
St.-Joseph-du-Lac, *Mtrl.* — 20 A1 43 32N 74 0W
St. Katherine's Dock, *Lon.* — 4 B4 51 30N 0 5W
St. Kilda, *Melb.* — 19 F6 37 51 S 144 58 E
St. Lambert, *Mtrl.* — 20 A5 43 30N 73 29W
St.-Lambert, *Paris* — 5 C2 48 43N 2 1 E
St.-Laurent, *Mtrl.* — 20 A3 43 30N 73 43W
St. Lawrence, *Mtrl.* — 20 A5 43 26N 73 29W
St.-Lazare, Gare, *Paris* — 5 B3 48 52N 2 19 E
St.-Léonard, *Mtrl.* — 20 A4 43 35N 73 34W
St. Leonards, *Syd.* — 19 B4 33 50 S 151 12 E
St. Leu-la-Forêt, *Paris* — 5 A3 49 1N 2 14 E
St.-Louis, L., *Mtrl.* — 20 B3 43 24N 73 48W
St. Magelungen, *Stock.* — 3 E11 59 13N 18 4 E
St.-Mandé, *Paris* — 5 B4 48 50N 2 24 E
St.-Mard, *Paris* — 5 A6 49 2N 2 41 E
St.-Martin, *Mtrl.* — 20 A3 43 33N 73 45W
St.-Martin, Bois, *Paris* — 5 C5 48 48N 2 35 E
St. Mary Cray, *Lon.* — 4 C5 51 23N 0 7 E
St.-Maur-des-Fossés, *Paris* — 5 C4 48 48N 2 29 E
St.-Maurice, *Paris* — 5 C4 48 49N 2 24 E
St.-Mesmes, *Paris* — 5 B6 48 59N 2 41 E
St. Michaeliskirche, *Hbg.* — 7 D7 53 32N 9 59 E
St. Michael's, *Sing.* — 15 G8 1 19N 103 51 E
St.-Michel, *Mtrl.* — 20 A4 43 34N 73 37W
St.-Michel-sur-Orge, *Paris* — 5 D3 48 38N 2 18 E
St. Nikolaus-Kirken, *Pra.* — 10 B2 50 5N 14 23 E
St. Nom-la-Bretèche, *Paris* — 5 B2 48 51N 2 1 E
St.-Ouen, *Paris* — 5 B4 48 56N 2 20 E
St. Ouen-l'Aumône, *Paris* — 5 A2 49 2N 2 6 E
St. Pauli, *Hbg.* — 7 D7 53 33N 9 57 E
St. Pauls Cathedral, *Lon.* — 4 B4 51 30N 0 5W
St. Paul's Cray, *Lon.* — 4 C5 51 23N 0 6 E
St. Petersburg, *St-Pet.* — 11 B3 59 55N 30 15 E
St.-Pierre, *Mtrl.* — 20 B4 43 27N 73 38W
St. Prix, *Paris* — 5 A3 49 0N 2 15 E
St.-Quentin, Étang de, *Paris* — 5 C2 48 47N 2 0 E
St.-Quentin-en-Yvelines, *Paris* — 5 C1 48 46N 1 57 E
St.-Rémy-lès-Chevreuse, *Paris* — 5 D2 48 42N 2 4 E
St.-Thibault-des-Vignes, *Paris* — 5 B6 48 51N 2 41 E
St. Veit, *Wien* — 10 G9 48 11N 16 16 E
St.-Vincent-de-Paul, *Mtrl.* — 20 A4 43 36N 73 39W
Ste.-Anne-de-Bellevue, *Mtrl.* — 20 B2 43 24N 73 55W
Ste.-Catherine, *Mtrl.* — 20 B4 43 24N 73 31W
Ste.-Dorothée, *Mtrl.* — 20 A3 43 31N 73 48W
Ste.-Gemme, *Paris* — 5 B4 48 52N 1 59 E
Ste.-Geneviève, *Mtrl.* — 20 B2 43 28N 73 51W

Ste.-Geneviève-des-Bois, *Paris* — 5 D3 48 38N 2 19 E
Ste.-Hélène, Î., *Mtrl.* — 20 A4 43 31N 73 32W
Ste. Marthe-sur-le-Lac, *Mtrl.* — 20 A2 43 31N 73 56W
Ste.-Rose, *Mtrl.* — 20 A3 43 37N 73 46W
Ste. Thérèse, *Mtrl.* — 20 A3 43 38N 73 49W
Ste. Thérèse-Ouest, *Mtrl.* — 20 A2 43 36N 73 50W
Saiwai, *Tōkyō* — 13 C3 35 32N 139 41 E
Sakai, *Ōsaka* — 12 C3 34 34N 135 27 E
Sakai →, *Tōkyō* — 13 D1 35 27N 139 29 E
Sakai Harbour, *Ōsaka* — 12 C3 34 36N 135 26 E
Sakanoshita, *Tōkyō* — 13 B2 35 48N 139 30 E
Sakra, P., *Sing.* — 15 G7 1 15N 103 41 E
Sakuragi, *Tōkyō* — 13 B2 35 28N 139 38 E
Salam, *Bagd.* — 17 E8 33 20N 44 20 E
Salaryevo, *Mos.* — 11 F8 55 37N 37 25 E
Salem, *Bost.* — 21 B4 42 30N 70 54W
Salem, *Stock.* — 3 E9 59 13N 17 46 E
Salem Harbor, *Bost.* — 21 B4 42 30N 70 52W
Salem Maritime Nat. Hist. Site, *Bost.* — 21 B4 42 31N 70 52W
Salemstaden, *Stock.* — 3 E9 59 13N 17 46 E
Salkhia, *Calc.* — 16 E6 22 36N 88 21 E
Salmannsdorf, *Wien* — 10 G9 48 14N 16 14 E
Salmdorf, *Mün.* — 7 G11 48 7N 11 43 E
Salmedina, *Mdrd.* — 8 C3 40 18N 3 35W
Salomea, *Wsaw.* — 10 E7 52 11N 20 55 E
Salsette I., *Bomb.* — 16 G8 19 2N 72 53 E
Salt Cr. →, *Chic.* — 26 C1 41 51N 87 54W
Salt Cr. →, *Melb.* — 19 E7 37 45 S 145 4 E
Salt Water L., *Calc.* — 16 E6 22 33N 88 26 E
Saltholm, *Køben.* — 2 E11 55 38N 12 46 E
Saltsjö-Duvnäs, *Stock.* — 3 E12 59 18N 18 12 E
Saltsjöbaden, *Stock.* — 3 E12 59 16N 18 18 E
Saltykovka, *Mos.* — 11 E11 55 45N 37 54 E
Salvatorkirche, *Ruhr* — 6 B2 51 26N 6 45 E
Sam Sen, Khlong →, *Bangk.* — 15 B2 13 45N 100 33 E
Samatya, *Ist.* — 17 B2 40 59N 28 55 E
Samoueo, *Lisb.* — 8 F8 38 43N 8 59W
Sampaloc, *Manila* — 15 D3 14 36N 120 59 E
Samphanthawong, *Bangk.* — 15 B2 13 44N 100 31 E
Samrong, *Bangk.* — 15 C2 13 39N 100 35 E
Samseon, *Sŏul* — 12 G8 37 34N 127 0 E
San Agustin, *Sŏul* — 30 G8 12 1 S 77 9W
San Agustin Atlapulco, *Méx.* — 29 B4 19 23N 89 57 E
San Andreas Fault, *S.F.* — 27 B2 37 23N 122 18W
San Andreas L., *S.F.* — 27 C2 37 35N 122 25W
San Andrés, *B.A.* — 32 B3 34 34 S 58 33W
San Andrés, *Barc.* — 8 D6 41 26N 2 11 E
San Andrés Ahuayucan, *Méx.* — 29 C3 19 13N 99 7W
San Andrés Atenco, *Méx.* — 29 A2 19 32N 99 13W
San Andrés Totoltepec, *Méx.* — 29 C2 19 16N 99 10W
San Andrián de Besós, *Barc.* — 8 D6 41 25N 2 13 E
San Angel, *Méx.* — 29 B2 19 20N 99 11W
San Antonio, *Manila* — 15 E3 14 29N 120 53 E
San Antonio de Padua, *B.A.* — 32 C2 34 40 S 58 42W
San Agustin Ohtenco, *Méx.* — 29 C3 19 14N 99 0W
San Bartolo Ameyalco, *Méx.* — 29 C2 19 19N 99 16W
San Bartolomé Coatepec, *Méx.* — 29 B2 19 23N 99 18W
San Basilio, *Rome* — 9 F10 41 56N 12 35 E
San Bóvio, *Mil.* — 9 E6 45 27N 9 18 E
San Bruno, *S.F.* — 27 C2 37 36N 122 24W
San Bruno, Pt., *S.F.* — 27 C2 37 39N 122 22W
San Bruno Mt., *S.F.* — 27 C3 37 41N 122 26W
San Carlos, *S.F.* — 27 C3 37 30N 122 16W
San Carlos de la Cabana, Forteresse, — 30 B2 23 8N 82 20W
San Clemente del Llobregat, *Barc.* — 8 E4 41 19N 1 59 E
San Cristobal, *Mdrd.* — 8 B3 40 25N 3 35W
San Cristobal, Cerro, *Stgo* — 30 J11 33 25 S 70 38W
San Donato Milanese, *Mil.* — 9 E5 45 24N 9 16 E
San Felice, *Mil.* — 9 B3 45 1N 7 46 E
San Feliu de Llobregat, *Barc.* — 8 D5 41 22N 2 2 E
San Fernando, *B.A.* — 32 A3 34 26 S 58 32W
San Fernando, *L.A.* — 28 A2 34 17N 118 26W
San Fernando Airport, *L.A.* — 28 A2 34 17N 118 25W
San Fernando de Henares, *Mdrd.* — 8 B3 40 25N 3 31W
San Fernando Valley, *L.A.* — 28 A1 34 12N 118 31W
San Francisco, *S.F.* — 27 B2 37 46N 122 23W
San Francisco, Univ. of, *S.F.* — 27 B2 37 47N 122 27W
San Francisco Chimalpa, *Méx.* — 29 B1 19 26N 99 20W
San Francisco Culhuacán, *Méx.* — 29 C3 19 19N 99 6W
San Francisco de Paula, *La Hab.* — 30 B3 23 3N 82 17W
San Francisco Int. Airport, *S.F.* — 27 C2 37 37N 122 22W
San Francisco Solano, *B.A.* — 32 C5 34 46 S 58 19W
San Francisco State Univ., *S.F.* — 27 B2 37 43N 122 28W
San Francisco Tecoxpa, *Méx.* — 29 C3 19 12N 99 0W
San Francisco Tlalnepantla, *Méx.* — 29 C3 19 12N 99 0W
San Fruttuoso, *Mil.* — 9 D6 45 34N 9 14 E
San Gabriel, *L.A.* — 28 B4 34 5N 118 5W
San Gabriel Pk., *L.A.* — 28 A4 34 14N 118 5W
San Giacomo, *Tori.* — 9 A2 45 11N 7 36 E
San Gillio, *Tori.* — 9 B2 45 8N 7 32 E
San Giórgio a Crem., *Nápl.* — 9 J13 40 50N 14 20 E
San Giovanni a Teduccio, *Nápl.* — 9 J12 40 49N 14 18 E
San Giuseppe Vesuviano, *Nápl.* — 9 H13 40 50N 14 29 E
San Gregorio Atlapulco, *Méx.* — 29 C3 19 15N 99 4W
San Isidro, *B.A.* — 32 A3 34 28 S 58 30W
San Isidro, *Lima* — 30 G8 12 5 S 77 2W
San Isidro, *Manila* — 15 D4 14 38N 121 5 E
San Jerónimo Lidice, *Méx.* — 29 C2 19 19N 99 14W
San Jerónimo Miacatlán, *Méx.* — 29 C4 19 12N 98 59W
San Jorge, Castelo de, *Lisb.* — 8 F8 38 42N 9 8W
San Jose Del Alamo, *La Háb.* — 30 B3 23 6N 82 17W

San José Rio Hondo, *Barc.* — 29 B2 19 26N 99 14W
San Juan →, *Manila* — 15 D4 14 35N 121 0 E
San Juan de Aragón, *Méx.* — 29 B3 19 28N 99 4W
San Juan de Aragón, Parque, *Méx.* — 29 B3 19 27N 99 4W
San Juan de Lurigancho, *Lima* — 30 F8 11 59 S 77 0W
San Juan de Miraflores, *Lima* — 30 H9 12 10 S 76 58W
San Juan del Monte, *Manila* — 15 D4 14 36N 121 1 E
San Juan Ixtacala, *Méx.* — 29 A2 19 31N 99 10W
San Juan Ixtayopan, *Méx.* — 29 C4 19 14N 98 59W
San Juan Toltotepec, *Méx.* — 29 B2 19 28N 99 15W
San Juan y San Pedro Tezompa, *Méx.* — 29 C4 19 12N 98 57W
San Just Desvern, *Barc.* — 8 D5 41 22N 2 4 E
San Justo, *B.A.* — 32 C3 34 40 S 58 33W
San Leandro, *S.F.* — 27 B4 37 43N 122 9W
San Leandro B., *S.F.* — 27 B3 37 45N 122 13W
San Leandro Cr. →, *S.F.* — 27 B3 37 44N 122 12W
San Lorenzo, *Mil.* — 9 D4 45 34N 8 57 E
San Lorenzo, *S.F.* — 27 B4 37 41N 122 6W
San Lorenzo, *Méx.* — 29 C4 19 19N 99 4W
San Lorenzo, I., *Lima* — 30 G7 12 6 S 77 12W
San Lorenzo Acopilco, *Méx.* — 29 C1 19 19N 99 20 E
San Lorenzo Chimalco, *Méx.* — 29 B4 19 24N 89 58 E
San Lorenzo Tezonco, *Méx.* — 29 C3 19 19N 99 3W
San Lorenzo Tlacoyucan, *Méx.* — 29 C3 19 10N 99 2W
San Lucas Xochimanca, *Méx.* — 29 C3 19 16N 99 3W
San Luis, *Lima* — 30 G8 12 4 S 77 0W
San Luis Tlaxialtemako, *Méx.* — 29 C3 19 16N 99 2W
San Marino, *L.A.* — 28 B4 34 7N 118 6W
San Martín, *Barc.* — 8 D6 41 24N 2 11 E
San Martín de Porras, *Lima* — 30 G8 12 1 S 77 5W
San Martino, *S.F.* — 9 B3 45 6N 7 47 E
San Mateo, *S.F.* — 27 C3 37 33N 122 19W
San Mateo Cr. →, *S.F.* — 27 C2 37 31N 122 27W
San Mateo Tecoloapan, *Méx.* — 29 A2 19 35N 99 14W
San Mateo Xalpa, *Méx.* — 29 C3 19 15N 99 4W
San Máuro Torinese, *Tori.* — 9 B3 45 6N 7 45 E
San Miguel, *Lima* — 30 G8 12 5 S 77 6W
San Miguel, *Manila* — 15 D4 14 36N 120 59 E
San Miguel, *Stgo* — 30 J11 33 29 S 70 39W
San Miguel Ajusco, *Méx.* — 29 C2 19 13N 99 11W
San Miguel Xicalco, *Méx.* — 29 C3 19 13N 99 9W
San Nicholas, *Manila* — 15 D3 14 36N 120 57 E
San Nicola, *Rome* — 9 F9 41 58N 12 21 E
San Nicolás Totolapan, *Méx.* — 29 C2 19 16N 99 16W
San Nicolás Viejo, *Méx.* — 29 A1 19 35N 99 23W
San Onófrio, *Rome* — 9 F9 41 57N 12 25 E
San Pablo, *Méx.* — 29 B4 19 25N 89 56 E
San Pablo, *S.F.* — 27 A2 37 57N 122 20W
San Pablo, Pt., *S.F.* — 27 A2 37 58N 122 25W
San Pablo Cr. →, *S.F.* — 27 A2 37 58N 122 22W
San Pablo Ostotepec, *Méx.* — 29 C3 19 11N 99 5W
San Pablo Res., *S.F.* — 27 A3 37 55N 122 14W
San Pablo Ridge, *S.F.* — 27 A3 37 55N 122 16W
San Pablo Str., *S.F.* — 27 A2 37 58N 122 25W
San Pancrázio, *Tori.* — 9 B2 45 6N 7 32 E
San Pedro, *Méx.* — 29 B3 19 24N 89 56 E
San Pedro, Pt., *S.F.* — 27 C1 37 35N 122 31W
San Pedro Actopan, *Méx.* — 29 C3 19 12N 99 0W
San Pedro Martir, *Barc.* — 8 D5 41 23N 2 6 E
San Pedro Martir, *Méx.* — 29 C2 19 16N 99 10W
San Pedro Zacatenco, *Méx.* — 29 B3 19 30N 99 6W
San Pietro, *Rome* — 9 F9 41 53N 12 27 E
San Pietro, *Tori.* — 9 B3 45 1N 7 45 E
San Pietro a Patierno, *Nápl.* — 9 H12 40 53N 14 17 E
San Pietro all'Olmo, *Mil.* — 9 E5 45 29N 9 0 E
San Po Kong, *H.K.* — 12 D6 22 20N 114 11 E
San Quentin, *S.F.* — 27 A2 37 56N 122 27W
San Rafael, *S.F.* — 27 A2 37 57N 122 28W
San Rafael B., *S.F.* — 27 A2 37 57N 122 28W
San Rafael Chamapa, *Méx.* — 29 B2 19 27N 99 15W
San Rafael Hills, *L.A.* — 28 A3 34 10N 118 12W
San Roque, *Manila* — 15 D4 14 37N 121 5 E
San Salvador Cuauhtenco, *Méx.* — 29 C3 19 11N 99 8W
San Salvador de la Punta, Forteresse, *La Hab.* — 30 B2 23 8N 82 21W
San Sebastiano al Vesúvio, *Nápl.* — 9 H13 40 50N 14 22 E
San Siro, *Mil.* — 9 E5 45 28N 9 7 E
San Souci, *Syd.* — 19 B3 33 59 S 151 8 E
San Telmo, *B.A.* — 32 B4 34 37 S 58 23W
San Vicenc dels Horts, *Barc.* — 8 D5 41 23N 2 0 E
San Vitaliano, *Nápl.* — 9 H13 40 55N 14 28 E
San Vito, *Mil.* — 9 B5 45 24N 9 0 E
San Vito, *Nápl.* — 9 J13 40 49N 14 22 E
San Vito, *Tori.* — 9 B3 45 2N 7 41 E
Sandbakken, *Oslo* — 2 C5 59 49N 10 54 E
Sandermoen, *Oslo* — 2 A4 60 0N 10 48 E
Sanderstead, *Lon.* — 4 D4 51 19N 0 4W
Sandheide, *Ruhr* — 6 B2 51 12N 6 56 E
Sandhurst, *Jobg.* — 18 E9 26 6 S 28 3 E
Sandown, *Jobg.* — 18 E9 26 5 S 28 4 E
Sandown Racecourse, *Lon.* — 4 C2 51 22N 0 21W
Sands Point, *N.Y.* — 23 B6 40 50N 73 43W
Sandton, *Jobg.* — 18 E9 26 5 S 28 4 E
Sandungen, *Oslo* — 2 B2 59 52N 10 21 E
Sandvika, *Oslo* — 2 B3 59 53N 10 32 E
Sandy Pond, *Bost.* — 21 C2 42 26N 71 18W
Sangano, *Tori.* — 9 B1 45 1N 7 26 E
Sangenjaya, *Tōkyō* — 13 C2 35 38N 139 39 E
Sangley Pt., *Manila* — 15 E3 14 29N 120 54 E
Sangye, *Sŏul* — 12 G8 37 38N 127 3 E
Sankrail, *Calc.* — 16 E5 22 33N 88 13 E
Sanlihe, *Beij.* — 14 B2 39 53N 116 18 E
Sanlintang, *Shang.* — 14 K11 31 7N 121 29 E
Sanpada, *Bomb.* — 16 G9 19 3N 73 0 E
Sans, *Barc.* — 8 D5 41 22N 2 7 E
Sant Ambrogio, Basilica di, *Mil.* — 9 E6 45 28N 9 10 E

Sant Boi de Llobregat, *Barc.* — 8 D5 41 20N 2 2 E
Sant Cugat, *Barc.* — 8 D5 41 28N 2 5 E
Santa Ana, *Manila* — 15 D4 14 34N 121 0 E
Santa Ana Tlacotenco, *Méx.* — 29 C4 19 11N 98 58W
Santa Bárbara, Morro de, *Rio J.* — 31 B1 22 56 S 43 26W
Santa Catalina, *B.A.* — 32 C4 34 47 S 58 24W
Santa Cecilia Tepetlapa, *Méx.* — 29 C3 19 13N 99 5W
Santa Clara, *S.F.* — 29 A3 19 33N 99 3W
Santa Coloma de Cervelló, *Barc.* — 8 D5 41 21N 2 0 E
Santa Coloma de Gramanet, *Barc.* — 8 D6 41 27N 2 13 E
Santa Cruz →, *La Hab.* — 30 B2 23 4N 82 29W
Santa Cruz, Ilhe de, *Rio J.* — 31 B3 22 51 S 43 7W
Santa Cruz Aleapixca, *Méx.* — 29 C3 19 14N 99 4W
Santa Cruz Ayotoxco, *Méx.* — 29 C3 19 14N 99 21W
Santa Cruz de Olorde, *Barc.* — 8 D5 41 25N 2 3 E
Santa Cruz Int. Airport, *Bomb.* — 16 G8 19 5N 72 51 E
Santa Cruz Meyehualco, *Méx.* — 29 B3 19 20N 99 2W
Santa Elena, *Manila* — 15 D4 14 38N 121 5 E
Santa Eligênia Consolação, *S. Pau.* — 30 J11 33 25 S 46 38W
Santa Emilia, *Stgo* — 30 J11 33 25 S 70 39W
Santa Eulalia, *Barc.* — 8 D6 41 25N 2 10 E
Santa Fe, *La Hab.* — 30 B2 23 4N 82 30W
Santa Fe Flood Control Basin, *L.A.* — 28 B5 34 7N 117 57W
Santa Fe Springs, *L.A.* — 28 C4 33 56N 118 3W
Santa Isabel Ixtapan, *Méx.* — 29 A4 19 35N 89 57W
Santa Julia, *Stgo* — 30 K11 33 30 S 70 35W
Santa Lucia, *Stgo* — 1 J11 33 26N 99 13W
Santa Margherita, *Tori.* — 9 B3 45 3N 7 43 E
Santa Maria Aztahuacán, *Méx.* — 29 B3 19 21N 99 2W
Santa Maria del Rosario, *La Hab.* — 30 B3 23 3N 82 15W
Santa Maria Tulpetlac, *Méx.* — 29 A3 19 34N 99 3W
Santa Martha Acatitla, *Méx.* — 29 B3 19 20N 99 2W
Santa Monica, *L.A.* — 30 E5 10 28N 66 53W
Santa Monica, *L.A.* — 28 B2 34 1N 118 29W
Santa Monica B., *L.A.* — 28 C1 33 58N 118 30W
Santa Monica Mt., *L.A.* — 28 B2 34 3N 118 35W
Santa Rosa, *Lima* — 30 F8 11 59 S 77 5W
Santa Rosa De Locobe, *Stgo* — 30 J11 33 25 S 70 33W
Santa Rosa Xochiac, *Méx.* — 29 C2 19 19N 99 17W
Santa Úrsula Xitla, *Méx.* — 31 E6 23 40 S 46 33W
Santa Ynez Canyon →, *L.A.* — 28 B1 34 2N 118 33W
Santahamina, *Hels.* — 3 C5 60 8N 25 2 E
Santana, *S. Pau.* — 31 E6 23 32 S 46 38W
Sant'Anastasia, *Nápl.* — 9 H13 40 51N 14 24 E
Sant'Antimo, *Nápl.* — 9 H12 40 56N 14 16 E
Santeny, *Paris* — 5 C5 48 43N 2 34 E
Santiago, *Stgo* — 30 J11 33 26 S 70 40W
Santiago Acahualtepec, *Méx.* — 29 B3 19 20N 99 0W
Santiago de Las Vegas, *La Hab.* — 30 C2 22 58N 82 22W
Santiago Tepatcatlalpan, *Méx.* — 29 C3 19 14N 99 8W
Santiago Tepatlaxco, *Méx.* — 29 B1 19 28N 99 20W
Sant'Ilário, *Mil.* — 9 D4 45 34N 8 54 E
Santo Amaro, *Lisb.* — 8 F7 38 42N 9 11W
Santo Amaro, *S. Pau.* — 31 E5 23 39 S 46 42W
Santo Andre, *Lisb.* — 31 E6 23 38 S 46 41W
Santo António, Qta. de, *Lisb.* — 8 F7 38 39N 9 15W
Santo António da Charneca, *Lisb.* — 8 G8 38 37N 9 1W
Santo Niño, *Manila* — 15 D4 14 38N 121 5 E
Santo Rosario, *Manila* — 15 D4 14 33N 121 4 E
Santo Tomas, Univ. of, *Manila* — 15 D3 14 36N 120 59 E
Santo Tomas, *Manila* — 15 D4 14 33N 121 4 E
Santol, *Manila* — 15 D4 14 36N 121 1 E
Santos Dumont, Aéroport, *Rio J.* — 31 B3 22 54 S 43 9W
Santos Lugares, *B.A.* — 32 B3 34 35 S 58 33W
Santoshpur, *Calc.* — 16 E5 22 31N 88 16 E
Santragachi, *Calc.* — 16 E5 22 36N 88 15 E
Sanyuanli, *Gzh.* — 14 G8 8 8N 113 14 E
São Bernardo do Campo, *S. Pau.* — 31 F6 23 42 S 46 33W
São Caetano do Sul, *S. Pau.* — 31 E6 23 37 S 46 34W
São Domingos, Centro, *Rio J.* — 31 B3 22 53 S 43 6W
São Gonçalo, *Rio J.* — 31 A3 22 49 S 43 4W
São João Climaco, *S. Pau.* — 31 E6 23 37 S 46 35W
São João da Talha, *Lisb.* — 8 F8 38 49N 9 5W
São João de Meriti, *Rio J.* — 31 A1 22 47 S 43 18W
São Lucas, Paque, *S. Pau.* — 31 E6 23 35 S 43 33W
São Mateus, *Rio J.* — 31 A1 22 48 S 43 22W
São Miguel Paulista, *S. Pau.* — 31 D7 23 29 S 46 26W
São Paulo, *Pau.* — 31 E6 23 32 S 46 38W
Sapa, *Calc.* — 16 E5 22 30N 88 15 E
Sapang Baho →, *Manila* — 15 D4 14 33N 121 4 E
Sapopemba, *S. Pau.* — 31 E6 23 35 S 46 41W
Sarandi, *B.A.* — 32 C4 34 40 S 58 20W
Saraswati →, *Calc.* — 16 D5 22 41N 88 12 E
Sarcelles, *Paris* — 5 B4 48 59N 2 22 E
Sarecky, *Pra.* — 10 B2 50 5N 14 21 E
Sarenga, *Calc.* — 16 E5 22 31N 88 12 E
Sarilhos Grandes, *Lisb.* — 8 F9 38 40N 8 58W
Sarilhos Pequenos, *Lisb.* — 8 F9 38 40N 8 58W
Sariá, *Barc.* — 8 D5 41 24N 2 7 E
Saronikós Kólpos, *Ath.* — 8 J10 37 52N 23 38 E
Sarriá, *Car.* — 30 D5 10 30N 66 53W
Sarsol, *Bomb.* — 16 G9 19 2N 72 59 E
Sartrouville, *Paris* — 5 B3 48 56N 2 10 E
Sasad, *Bud.* — 10 J13 47 28N 19 1 E
Sashalom, *Bud.* — 10 J14 47 30N 19 10 E
Saska, *Wsaw.* — 10 E7 52 14N 21 3 E
Sassafras, *Melb.* — 19 F9 37 52 S 145 20 E

Satalice, *Pra.* — 10 B3 50 7N 14 34 E
Satgachi, *Calc.* — 16 E6 22 37N 88 25 E
Satghara, *Calc.* — 16 D6 22 43N 88 21 E
Satpukur, *Calc.* — 16 E6 22 37N 88 24 E
Sätra, *Stock.* — 3 E10 59 17N 17 54 E
Satsuna, *Calc.* — 16 F5 22 28N 88 17 E
Sau Mau Ping, *H.K.* — 12 E6 22 19N 114 13 E
Saugus, *Bost.* — 21 C3 42 28N 71 0W
Saugus →, *Bost.* — 21 C3 42 27N 70 58W
Saulx-les-Chartreux, *Paris* — 5 C3 48 41N 2 16 E
Sausalito, *S.F.* — 27 A2 37 51N 122 28W
Sausset →, *Paris* — 5 B5 48 56N 2 28 E
Savigny-sur-Orge, *Paris* — 5 C4 48 40N 2 21 E
Savijärvi, *Hels.* — 3 A5 60 20N 25 19 E
Savonera, *Tori.* — 9 B2 45 7N 7 36 E
Sawah Besar, *Jak.* — 15 H9 6 8 S 43 8 E
Sawyer Ridge, *S.F.* — 27 C2 37 33N 122 24W
Saxonville, *Bost.* — 21 D2 42 19N 71 24W
Saxonwold, *Jobg.* — 18 E9 26 9 S 28 2 E
Scarborough, *Trto.* — 20 D9 43 44N 79 14W
Scarsdale, *N.Y.* — 23 B6 40 58N 73 47W
Sceaux, *Paris* — 5 C3 48 46N 2 17 E
Schalke, *Ruhr* — 6 A4 51 33N 7 4 E
Schapenrust, *Jobg.* — 18 F11 26 15 S 28 30 E
Scharfenberg, *Berl.* — 7 A2 52 35N 13 15 E
Scheiblingstein, *Wien* — 10 G9 48 16N 16 15 E
Schenefeld, *Hbg.* — 7 D7 53 36N 9 52 E
Scherlebech, *Ruhr* — 6 A4 51 37N 7 8 E
Schildow, *Berl.* — 7 A3 52 38N 13 22 E
Schiller Park, *Chic.* — 26 B1 41 56N 87 52W
Schiller Woods, *Chic.* — 26 B1 41 57N 87 51W
Schlachtensee, *Berl.* — 7 B2 52 26N 13 13 E
Schlossgarten, *Berl.* — 7 A2 52 31N 13 18 E
Schmachtendorf, *Ruhr* — 6 A2 51 32N 6 48 E
Schmargendorf, *Berl.* — 7 B2 52 28N 13 17 E
Schmöckwitz, *Berl.* — 7 B4 52 23N 13 38 E
Schmelsen, *Hbg.* — 7 D7 53 38N 9 54 E
Scholven, *Ruhr* — 6 A4 51 36N 7 0 E
Schönblick, *Berl.* — 7 B5 52 27N 13 43 E
Schönbrunn, Schloss, *Wien* — 10 G9 48 10N 16 19 E
Schöneberg, *Berl.* — 7 B3 52 29N 13 21 E
Schönefeld, *Berl.* — 7 B4 52 23N 13 30 E
Schöneiche, *Berl.* — 7 B5 52 27N 13 41 E
Schönwalde, *Berl.* — 7 A1 52 37N 13 7 E
Schottenwald, *Wien* — 10 G9 48 13N 16 16 E
Schuir, *Ruhr* — 6 B3 51 23N 6 59 E
Schulzendorf, *Berl.* — 7 A2 52 36N 13 16 E
Schuylkill →, *Phil.* — 24 B3 39 53N 75 11W
Schwabing, *Mün.* — 7 G10 48 10N 11 35 E
Schwafheim, *Ruhr* — 6 B1 52 25N 6 36 E
Schwanebeck, *Berl.* — 7 A4 52 37N 13 32 E
Schwanenwerder, *Berl.* — 7 B2 52 25N 13 10 E
Schwarz, *Ruhr* — 6 C3 51 19N 6 44 E
Schwarzbachtal, *Ruhr* — 6 C3 51 17N 6 51 E
Schwarze, *Ruhr* — 6 A2 51 37N 6 48 E
Schwarze Berge, *Ruhr* — 6 C3 51 27N 9 6 E
Schwarzlackenau, *Wien* — 10 G10 48 16N 16 23 E
Schwechat, *Wien* — 10 H10 48 7N 16 29 E
Schwelflinghäusen, *Ruhr* — 6 C6 51 15N 7 24 E
Schwelm, *Ruhr* — 6 C5 51 16N 7 16 E
Sciciano, *Nápl.* — 9 H13 40 54N 14 28 E
Scoresby, *Melb.* — 19 F8 37 54 S 145 14 E
Scotch Plains, *N.Y.* — 22 D2 40 39N 74 22W
Scotts Level Br. →, *Balt.* — 25 A2 39 23N 76 45W
Sea Cliff, *N.Y.* — 23 B7 40 50N 73 38W
Seabrook, *Wash.* — 25 D9 38 58N 76 49W
Seacliff, *S.F.* — 27 B2 37 47N 122 28W
Seaforth, *Syd.* — 19 A4 33 48 S 151 15 E
Seagate, *N.Y.* — 23 D4 40 34N 74 0W
Seal Slough, *S.F.* — 27 C3 37 34N 122 18W
Sears Tower, *Chic.* — 26 B3 41 52N 87 38W
Seat Pleasant, *Wash.* — 25 D8 38 53N 76 53W
Seavey Hill, *Bost.* — 21 A1 42 42N 71 23W
Šeberov, *Pra.* — 10 B3 50 0N 14 30 E
Secaucus, *N.Y.* — 22 C4 40 47N 74 3W
Secondigliano, *Nápl.* — 9 H12 40 53N 14 15 E
Seddinsee, *Berl.* — 7 B5 52 23N 13 41 E
Sedgefield, *N.Y.* — 22 B2 40 51N 74 26W
Sedriano, *Mil.* — 9 E4 45 29N 8 58 E
Seeberg, *Berl.* — 7 A5 52 30N 13 7 E
Seeburg, *Berl.* — 7 A1 52 30N 13 7 E
Seefeld, *Berl.* — 7 A5 52 37N 13 40 E
Seegefeld, *Berl.* — 7 B2 52 24N 13 7 E
Seehof, *Berl.* — 7 B2 52 24N 13 17 E
Segeltorp, *Stock.* — 3 E10 59 16N 17 56 E
Segrate, *Mil.* — 9 E6 45 29N 9 16 E
Seguro, *Mil.* — 9 B3 45 28N 13 7 E
Seine →, *Paris* — 5 C4 48 48N 2 25 E
Seixal, *Lisb.* — 8 G8 38 38N 9 5W
Selby, *Jobg.* — 18 F9 26 12 S 28 2 E
Seletar, P., *Sing.* — 15 F8 1 26N 103 49 E
Seletar, Sungei →, *Sing.* — 15 F8 1 25N 103 51 E
Seletar Hills, *Sing.* — 15 F8 1 22N 103 48 E
Seletar Res., *Sing.* — 15 F8 1 24N 103 48 E
Selhurst, *Lon.* — 4 C4 51 23N 0 5W
Selsdon, *Lon.* — 4 D4 51 20N 0 4W
Selytsy, *St-Pet.* — 11 B6 59 56N 30 42 E
Sembawang →, *Sing.* — 15 F7 1 26N 103 49 E
Sembawang, *Sing.* — 15 F7 1 27N 103 48 E
Sembawang Hill, *Sing.* — 15 F7 1 22N 103 49 E
Semsvatn, *Oslo* — 2 B2 59 51N 10 25 E
Senago, *Mil.* — 9 D5 45 34N 9 7 E
Senan, *Jak.* — 15 J10 6 13 S 106 50 E
Sénart, Forêt de, *Paris* — 5 D4 48 40N 2 28 E
Senayan Sports Centre, *Jak.* — 15 J9 6 13 S 106 47 E
Sendling, *Mün.* — 7 G10 48 7N 11 31 E
Sengeløse, *Køben.* — 2 D8 55 40N 12 14 E
Senju, *Tōkyō* — 13 B3 35 44N 139 48 E
Senlikköy, *Ist.* — 17 B1 40 58N 28 47 E
Senlisse, *Paris* — 5 C1 48 41N 1 59 E
Sennevière, *Mtrl.* — 20 B2 43 24N 73 57W
Senri, *Ōsaka* — 12 B4 34 49N 135 30 E
Senriyama, *Ōsaka* — 12 B4 34 47N 135 30 E
Sentosa, *Sing.* — 15 G7 1 15N 103 49 E
Seo Dae Mun, *Sŏul* — 12 G7 37 34N 126 56 E
Seobinggo, *Sŏul* — 12 G7 37 31N 126 58 E
Seoggwan, *Sŏul* — 12 G8 37 35N 127 2 E
Seong Bug, *Sŏul* — 12 G8 37 35N 127 2 E
Seong Dong, *Sŏul* — 12 G8 37 33N 127 1 E
Seoul = Sŏul, *Sŏul* — 12 G8 37 34N 127 51 E
Seoul National Univ., *Sŏul* — 12 H7 37 28N 126 57 E
Seoul Tower, *Sŏul* — 12 G7 37 28N 126 59 E
Sepah Salar Mosque, *Tehr.* — 17 C5 35 40N 51 25 E
Sepolia, *Ath.* — 8 H11 38 1N 23 42 E
Sepulveda, *B.A.* — 28 A2 34 10N 118 28W
Sepulveda Flood Control Basin, *L.A.* — 28 A2 34 10N 118 28W
Serangoon →, *Sing.* — 15 F8 1 23N 103 55 E
Serangoon, Sungei →, *Sing.* — 15 F8 1 23N 103 55 E
Serangoon Garden, *Sing.* — 15 F8 1 21N 103 51 E

**46** Serangoon Harbour


Serangoon Harbour, *Sing.* **15 F8** 1 23N 103 57 E
Seraya, P., *Sing.* **15 G7** 1 16N 103 43 E
Serebryanka, *Mos.* **11 E11** 55 44N 37 53 E
Serebryanka →, *Mos.* **11 E10** 55 47N 37 44 E
Serednevo, *Mos.* **11 F7** 55 35N 37 18 E
Serramonte, *S.F.* **27 C2** 37 39N 122 28W
Servon, *Paris* **5 C5** 48 43N 2 35 E
Šestajovice, *Pra.* **10 B3** 50 6N 14 40 E
Sesto San Giovanni, *Mil.* **9 D6** 45 31N 9 13 E
Seta Budi, *Jak.* **15 J9** 6 12 S 106 49 E
Setagaya-Ku, *Tōkyō* **13 C2** 35 37N 139 36 E
Sete Pontes, *Rio J.* **31 B3** 22 50 S 43 4W
Seter, *Oslo* **2 B4** 59 52N 10 47 E
Séttimo Milanese, *Mil.* **9 E5** 45 28N 9 3 E
Séttimo Torinese, *Tori.* **9 B3** 45 8N 7 46 E
Settsu, *Ōsaka* **12 B4** 34 47N 135 33 E
Setuny →, *Mos.* **11 E8** 55 43N 37 21 E
Seurasaari, *Hels.* **3 B4** 60 11N 24 53 E
Seutula, *Hels.* **3 A4** 60 20N 24 52 E
Seven Corners, *Wash.* **25 D7** 38 53N 77 9W
Seven Kings, *Lon.* **4 B5** 51 33N 0 5 E
Sevenoaks, *Lon.* **4 D6** 51 16N 0 11 E
Severn Hills, *Syd.* **19 A2** 33 46 S 150 57 E
Sévesco →, *Mil.* **9 D5** 45 35N 9 9 E
Sevran, *Paris* **5 B5** 48 56N 2 31 E
Sèvres, *Paris* **5 C3** 48 49N 2 13 E
Sewaren, *N.Y.* **22 D3** 40 33N 74 15W
Sewell, *Phil.* **24 C4** 39 46N 75 8W
Sewri, *Bomb.* **16 H8** 18 59N 72 50 E
Seya, *Tōkyō* **13 D1** 35 28N 139 28 E
Sforzesso, Castello, *Mil.* **9 E6** 45 28N 9 10 E
Sha Kok Mei, *H.K.* **12 D6** 22 23N 114 16 E
Sha Tin, *H.K.* **12 D6** 22 23N 114 11 E
Sha Tin Wai, *H.K.* **12 D6** 22 22N 114 11 E
Shaala, *Bagd.* **17 E7** 33 22N 44 16 E
Shabanzhuang, *Beij.* **14 B3** 39 51N 116 25 E
Shabbona Woods, *Chic.* **26 D3** 41 36N 87 33W
Shabrâmant, *El Qâ.* **18 D5** 29 56N 31 11 E
Shadipur, *Delhi* **16 B2** 28 38N 77 11 E
Shady Oak, *Wash.* **25 C6** 39 1N 77 17W
Shahabad, *Bomb.* **16 G9** 19 0N 73 2 E
Shahar, *Bomb.* **16 G8** 19 5N 72 52 E
Shahdara, *Delhi* **16 A2** 28 40N 77 18 E
Shahe, *Gzh.* **14 G8** 23 9N 113 19 E
Shahpur Jel, *Delhi* **16 B2** 28 33N 77 12 E
Shahr-e-Rey, *Tehr.* **17 D5** 35 36N 51 25 E
Shaikh Aomar, *Bagd.* **17 E8** 33 20N 44 23 E
Shakarpor Khas, *Delhi* **16 B2** 28 37N 77 14 E
Shakurpur, *Delhi* **16 A1** 28 40N 77 8 E
Sham Shui Po, *H.K.* **12 E5** 22 19N 114 9 E
Shamepur, *Delhi* **16 A1** 28 44N 77 8 E
Shamian, *Gzh.* **14 G8** 23 6N 113 13 E
Shamspur, *Delhi* **16 B2** 28 36N 77 17 E
Shan Liu, *H.K.* **12 D6** 22 23N 114 16 E
Shan Mei, *H.K.* **12 D6** 22 24N 114 10 E
Shanghai, *Shang.* **14 J12** 31 14N 121 28 E
Shanghetou, *Tianj.* **14 D5** 39 11N 117 0 E
Shanjing, *Gzh.* **14 G9** 23 4N 113 23 E
Sharea Faisal, *Kar.* **17 G11** 24 52N 67 8 E
Sharon Hill, *Phil.* **24 B3** 39 54N 75 16W
Sharp I., *H.K.* **12 D6** 22 21N 114 17 E
Sharp Park, *S.F.* **27 C2** 37 38N 122 29W
Shau Kei Wan, *H.K.* **12 E6** 22 16N 114 13 E
Shawocun, *Beij.* **14 B2** 39 53N 116 13 E
Shawsheen Village, *Bost.* **21 A3** 42 40N 71 7W
Shea Stadium, *N.Y.* **23 C5** 40 45N 73 50W
Sheakhala, *Calc.* **16 D5** 22 45N 88 10 E
Shebāb, *Bagd.* **17 E8** 33 20N 44 26 E
Sheepshead B., *N.Y.* **22 D5** 40 35N 73 55W
Shek Hang, *H.K.* **12 D6** 22 24N 114 17 E
Shek Kip Mei, *H.K.* **12 D5** 22 20N 114 9 E
Shek Lung Kung, *H.K.* **12 D5** 22 23N 114 5 E
Shek O, *H.K.* **12 E6** 22 13N 114 15 E
Shellpot Cr. →, *Phil.* **24 C1** 39 44N 75 30W
Shelter Cove, *S.F.* **27 C1** 37 35N 122 30W
Shelter I., *H.K.* **12 E6** 22 19N 114 17 E
Shemirānāt, *Tehr.* **17 C5** 35 47N 51 25 E
Shenfield, *Lon.* **4 B6** 51 37N 0 19 E
Sheng Fa Shan, *H.K.* **12 D5** 22 23N 114 5 E
Shenley, *Lon.* **4 A3** 51 41N 0 16W
Shepherds Bush, *Lon.* **4 B3** 51 30N 0 13W
Shepperton, *Lon.* **4 C2** 51 23N 0 26W
Sherborn, *Bost.* **21 D1** 42 14N 71 22W
Sherman Oaks, *L.A.* **28 B2** 34 8N 118 29W
Sherwood Forest, *S.F.* **27 A3** 37 57N 122 16W
Shet Bandar, *Bomb.* **16 H8** 18 57N 72 55 E
Sheung Lau Wan, *H.K.* **12 E6** 22 16N 114 16 E
Sheung Wan, *H.K.* **12 E5** 22 16N 114 9 E
Sheva, *Bomb.* **16 H8** 18 56N 72 57 E
Sheva Nhava, *Bomb.* **16 H8** 18 57N 72 57 E
Shiba, *Tōkyō* **13 C3** 35 38N 139 45 E
Shiba →, *Tōkyō* **13 A3** 35 50N 139 44 E
Shibuya-Ku, *Tōkyō* **13 C3** 35 39N 139 41 E
Shijōnawate, *Ōsaka* **12 B4** 34 44N 135 37 E
Shimo-okudomi, *Tōkyō* **13 A1** 35 52N 139 27 E
Shimo-tsuchidana, *Tōkyō* **13 D1** 35 24N 139 27 E
Shimogawara, *Tōkyō* **13 C1** 35 39N 139 27 E
Shimosalo, *Tōkyō* **13 B2** 35 45N 139 31 E
Shimosasame, *Tōkyō* **13 B2** 35 48N 139 37 E
Shimoshakujii, *Tōkyō* **13 B2** 35 43N 139 35 E
Shimotomi, *Tōkyō* **13 B1** 35 49N 139 27 E
Shimotsuruma, *Tōkyō* **13 D1** 35 29N 139 26 E
Shimura, *Tōkyō* **13 B3** 35 46N 139 41 E
Shinagawa B., *Tōkyō* **13 C3** 35 35N 139 48 E
Shinagawa-Ku, *Tōkyō* **13 C3** 35 36N 139 44 E
Shing Mun Res., *H.K.* **12 D5** 22 23N 114 8 E
Shinjuku-Ku, *Tōkyō* **13 B3** 35 41N 139 42 E
Shinkoiwa, *Tōkyō* **13 B4** 35 43N 139 51 E
Shinnakano, *Tōkyō* **13 B3** 35 41N 139 40 E
Shinoha, *Tōkyō* **13 A3** 35 50N 139 49 E
Shipai, *Gzh.* **14 G9** 23 8N 113 20 E
Shipley, *Balt.* **25 B3** 39 12N 76 39W
Shippan Pt., *N.Y.* **23 A7** 41 1N 73 31W
Shirako, *Tōkyō* **13 B2** 35 47N 139 36 E
Shiraone, *Bomb.* **16 G9** 19 2N 73 1 E
Shirinashi →, *Ōsaka* **12 C3** 34 38N 135 27 E
Shirley, *Lon.* **4 C4** 51 22N 0 2W
Shiro, *Tōkyō* **13 B2** 35 48N 139 30 E
Shirogane, *Tōkyō* **13 C3** 35 37N 139 44 E
Shisha Hai, *Beij.* **14 B3** 39 55N 116 21 E
Shitou, *Gzh.* **14 G9** 23 1N 113 23 E
Shiweitang, *Gzh.* **14 G8** 23 6N 113 12 E
Shogunle, *Lagos* **18 A2** 6 34N 7 20 E
Shomolu, *Lagos* **18 A2** 6 32N 7 22 E
Shooters Hill, *Lon.* **4 C5** 51 28N 0 4 E
Shoreditch, *Lon.* **4 B4** 51 31N 0 4W
Shoreham, *Lon.* **4 D6** 51 19N 0 10 E
Short Hills, *N.Y.* **22 C2** 40 44N 74 21W
Shortlands, *Lon.* **4 C5** 51 23N 0 0 E
Shrirampur, *Calc.* **16 D5** 22 45N 88 21 E
Shuangkou, *Tianj.* **14 D5** 39 14N 117 2 E
Shuangtuo, *Tianj.* **14 D6** 39 13N 117 19 E
Shubrâ el Kheima, *El Qâ.* **18 C5** 30 6N 31 14 E
Shuikuo, *Gzh.* **14 F8** 23 10N 113 10 E
Shuishang Gongyuan, *Tianj.* **14 E5** 39 5N 117 9 E
Shukunoshō, *Ōsaka* **12 A4** 34 50N 135 31 E
Sibbo, *Hels.* **3 A6** 60 21N 25 14 E
Sibbo fjärden, *Hels.* **3 B6** 60 11N 25 17 E
Siboney, *La Hab.* **30 B2** 23 4N 82 28W
Sibpur, *Calc.* **16 E5** 22 34N 88 19 E
Sibřina, *Pra.* **10 B4** 50 3N 14 40 E
Sidcup, *Lon.* **4 C5** 51 25N 0 6 E
Siebenhirten, *Wien* **10 H9** 48 8N 16 17 E
Siedlung, *Berl.* **7 A1** 52 35N 13 7 E
Siekierki, *Wsaw.* **10 E7** 52 12N 21 4 E
Sielce, *Wsaw.* **10 E7** 52 12N 21 2 E
Siemensstadt, *Berl.* **7 A2** 52 32N 13 16 E
Sieraków, *Wsaw.* **10 E5** 52 19N 20 48 E
Sierra Madre, *L.A.* **28 B4** 34 9N 118 3W
Sievering, *Wien* **10 G10** 48 15N 16 20 E
Siggerud, *Oslo* **2 C5** 59 47N 10 52 E
Siheung, *Sŏul* **12 H7** 37 28N 126 54 E
Siikajärvi, *Hels.* **3 B2** 60 17N 24 31 E
Sikátorpuszta, *Bud.* **10 J14** 47 34N 19 10 E
Silampur, *Delhi* **16 B2** 28 39N 77 16 E
Silschede, *Ruhr* **6 B6** 51 21N 7 22 E
Silver Hill, *Wash.* **25 E8** 38 49N 76 55W
Silver L., *Bost.* **21 B3** 42 33N 71 9W
Silver Mt., *L.A.* **28 A5** 34 12N 117 55W
Silver Spring, *Wash.* **25 D7** 38 59N 77 2W
Silverfields, *Jobg.* **18 E7** 26 7 S 27 49 E
Silvertown, *Lon.* **4 C5** 51 29N 0 1 E
Simla, *Calc.* **16 E6** 22 35N 88 22 E
Simmer and Jack Mines, *Jobg.* **18 F9** 26 12 S 28 8 E
Simmering, *Wien* **10 G10** 48 10N 16 24 E
Simmering Heide, *Wien* **10 G10** 48 10N 16 26 E
Simonkylä, *Hels.* **3 B5** 60 18N 25 1 E
Simpang Bedok, *Sing.* **15 G8** 1 19N 103 56 E
Simsalö, *Hels.* **3 B6** 60 14N 25 17 E
Singao, *N.Y.* **22 B3** 40 53N 74 14W
Singapore, *Sing.* **15 G8** 1 17N 103 51 E
Singapore →, *Sing.* **15 G8** 1 17N 103 51 E
Singapore, Univ. of, *Sing.* **15 G7** 1 19N 103 49 E
Singapore Airport, *Sing.* **15 F8** 1 21N 103 54 E
Singlewell, *Lon.* **4 C7** 51 25N 0 21 E
Singur, *Calc.* **16 D5** 22 48N 88 13 E
Sinicka →, *Mos.* **11 D7** 55 52N 37 18 E
Sinki, Selat, *Sing.* **15 G7** 1 15N 103 42 E
Sinrim, *Sŏul* **12 H7** 37 28N 126 56 E
Sinsa, *Sŏul* **12 G8** 37 31N 127 0 E
Sinthi, *Calc.* **16 E6** 22 37N 88 23 E
Sinweol, *Sŏul* **12 G7** 37 31N 126 51 E
Sipoo, *Hels.* **3 A6** 60 21N 25 14 E
Sipoon selkä, *Hels.* **3 B6** 60 11N 25 17 E
Sipson, *Lon.* **4 C2** 51 29N 0 26W
Siqeil, *El Qâ.* **18 C4** 30 7N 31 10 E
Şişli, *Ist.* **17 A2** 41 3N 28 58 E
Skå, *Stock.* **3 E9** 59 19N 17 44 E
Skärholmen, *Stock.* **3 E10** 59 16N 17 53 E
Skarpäng, *Stock.* **3 D11** 59 26N 18 0 E
Skarpnäck, *Stock.* **3 E11** 59 16N 18 7 E
Skarpö, *Stock.* **3 D13** 59 24N 18 22 E
Skedsmo, *Oslo* **2 B6** 59 59N 11 2 E
Skhodnya →, *Mos.* **11 D8** 55 53N 37 23 E
Skodsborg, *Købn.* **2 D10** 55 49N 12 34 E
Skogby, *Hels.* **3 A2** 60 21N 24 40 F
Skogen, *Oslo* **2 C1** 59 48N 10 18 E
Skogsbyn, *Hels.* **3 A6** 60 20N 25 18 E
Skokie, *Chic.* **26 A2** 42 2N 87 43W
Skokie →, *Chic.* **26 A2** 42 3N 87 46W
Skokie Lagoons, *Chic.* **26 A2** 42 7N 87 46W
Skoklefall, *Oslo* **2 B4** 59 50N 10 40 E
Sköndal, *Stock.* **3 E11** 59 15N 18 6 E
Skovlunde, *Købn.* **2 D9** 55 42N 12 25 E
Skovshoved, *Købn.* **2 D10** 55 45N 12 35 E
Skøyen, *Oslo* **2 B4** 59 55N 10 40 E
Skui, *Oslo* **2 B2** 59 55N 10 25 E
Skuldelev, *Købn.* **2 D7** 55 46N 12 1 E
Skullerud, *Oslo* **2 B5** 59 51N 10 50 E
Skuru, *Stock.* **3 E12** 59 18N 18 12 E
Skytta, *Oslo* **2 B5** 59 59N 10 54 E
Slade Green, *Lon.* **4 C6** 51 27N 0 11 E
Slagsta, *Stock.* **3 E9** 59 15N 17 48 E
Slakteren, *Oslo* **2 A4** 60 1N 10 40 E
Slattum, *Oslo* **2 A5** 60 0N 10 55 E
Slemmestad, *Oslo* **2 C2** 59 46N 10 29 E
Slependen, *Oslo* **2 B3** 59 52N 10 30 E
Sligo Cr. →, *Wash.* **25 C7** 39 0N 77 1W
Slipi, *Jak.* **15 J9** 6 11 S 106 47 E
Slipi Orchard Garden, *Jak.* **15 J9** 6 10 S 106 46 E
Slivenec, *Pra.* **10 B2** 50 1N 14 21 E
Slone Canyon Res., *L.A.* **28 B2** 34 6N 118 27W
Sloop Channel, *N.Y.* **23 D7** 40 36N 73 31W
Sluhy, *Pra.* **10 A3** 50 11N 14 33 E
Służew, *Wsaw.* **10 E7** 52 10N 21 1 E
Służewiec, *Wsaw.* **10 E7** 52 10N 21 0 E
Smalleytown, *N.Y.* **22 D2** 40 39N 74 28W
Smestad, *Oslo* **2 B2** 59 55N 10 25 E
Smichov, *Pra.* **10 B2** 50 4N 14 23 E
Smith Forest Preserve, *Chic.* **26 B2** 41 59N 87 45W
Smith Mills, *N.Y.* **22 A2** 41 0N 74 23W
Smithfield, *Syd.* **19 B2** 33 51 S 150 56 E
Smoke Rise, *N.Y.* **22 A2** 41 0N 74 24W
Smørumnedre, *Købn.* **2 D8** 55 44N 12 7 E
Snakeden Br. →, *Wash.* **25 D6** 38 58N 77 17W
Snarøya, *Oslo* **2 B3** 59 52N 10 33 E
Snättringe, *Stock.* **3 E10** 59 15N 17 58 E
Snoldelev, *Købn.* **2 E8** 55 33N 12 10 E
Snostrup, *Købn.* **2 D7** 55 48N 12 7 E
Søborg, *Købn.* **2 D9** 55 43N 12 29 E
Sobreda, *Lisb.* **8 G7** 38 39N 9 11W
Soccavo, *Nápl.* **9 H12** 40 50N 14 11 E
Sodegaura, *Tōkyō* **13 D4** 35 24N 139 57 E
Söderby, *Stock.* **3 D12** 59 24N 18 12 E
Söderkullalandet, *Hels.* **3 B6** 60 14N 25 19 E
Södermalm, *Stock.* **3 E11** 59 18N 18 4 E
Södersätra, *Stock.* **3 D10** 59 27N 17 56 E
Södertälje, *Stock.* **3 E8** 59 11N 17 36 E
Sodingen, *Ruhr* **6 A5** 51 32N 7 15 E
Sodpur, *Calc.* **16 D6** 22 42N 88 24 E
Södra Björkfjärden, *Stock.* **3 E8** 59 17N 17 34 E
Soeurs, Î. des, *Mtrl.* **20 B4** 43 27N 73 32W
Sognsvatn, *Oslo* **2 B4** 59 58N 10 43 E
Soignolles-en-Brie, *Paris* **5 D6** 48 39N 2 43 E
Soisy-sous-Montmorency, *Paris* **5 B3** 48 59N 2 17 E
Soisy-sur-Seine, *Paris* **5 D4** 48 39N 2 27 E
Sojiji Temple, *Tōkyō* **13 D3** 35 29N 139 40 E
Sok Kwu Wan, *H.K.* **12 E5** 22 12N 114 7 E
Sōka, *Tōkyō* **13 B3** 35 49N 139 48 E
Sokolniki, *Mos.* **11 E10** 55 47N 37 40 E
Sokolniki Park, *Mos.* **11 E10** 55 48N 37 40 E
Sokołów, *Wsaw.* **10 F6** 52 9N 20 51 E
Solalinden, *Mün.* **7 G11** 48 5N 11 42 E
Solaro, *Mil.* **9 D5** 45 36N 9 6 E
Solers, *Paris* **5 D6** 48 39N 2 43 E
Solingen, *Ruhr* **6 C4** 51 10N 7 5 E
Sollentuna, *Stock.* **3 D10** 59 25N 17 56 E
Søllerød, *Købn.* **2 D9** 55 48N 12 29 E
Sollihøgda, *Oslo* **2 B2** 59 58N 10 21 E
Solln, *Mün.* **7 G10** 48 4N 11 31 E
Solna, *Stock.* **3 D10** 59 21N 17 59 E
Solntsevo, *Mos.* **11 F8** 55 39N 37 24 E
Solymár, *Bud.* **10 J12** 47 35N 18 56 E
Somapah Changi, *Sing.* **15 F8** 1 20N 103 57 E
Somapan Serangoon, *Sing.* **15 F8** 1 21N 103 53 E
Somborn, *Ruhr* **6 B6** 51 29N 7 20 E
Somerdale, *Phil.* **24 B4** 39 50N 75 1W
Somerset, *Wash.* **25 D7** 38 57N 77 5W
Somerton, *Phil.* **24 A4** 40 7N 75 1W
Somerville, *Bost.* **21 C3** 42 22N 71 5W
Somma, Mte., *Nápl.* **9 H13** 40 50N 14 25 E
Somma Vesuviana, *Nápl.* **9 H13** 40 52N 14 26 E
Sonari, *Bomb.* **16 H8** 18 54N 72 59 E
Sønderby, *Købn.* **2 D7** 55 44N 12 2 E
Søndersø, *Købn.* **2 D9** 55 46N 12 21 E
Sondre Elvåga, *Oslo* **2 B5** 59 51N 10 54 E
Sonnberg, *Wien* **10 G9** 48 19N 16 15 E
Sørby, *Oslo* **2 C4** 59 49N 10 41 E
Sørkedalen, *Oslo* **2 A3** 60 1N 10 37 E
Soroksár, *Bud.* **10 K13** 47 24N 19 7 E
Soroksár-Újtelep, *Bud.* **10 K13** 47 25N 19 7 E
Soroksari Duna →, *Bud.* **10 K13** 47 25N 19 5 E
Sørsdal, *Oslo* **2 B1** 59 50N 10 16 E
Sosenka →, *Mos.* **11 E10** 55 46N 37 42 E
Sosnovaya, *St-Pet.* **11 C2** 59 49N 30 8 E
Sottungsby, *Hels.* **3 B5** 60 16N 25 8 E
Sŏul, *Sŏul* **12 G8** 37 34N 127 51 E
Soundview, *N.Y.* **23 C5** 40 49N 73 53W
South Basin, *S.F.* **27 B2** 37 42N 122 22W
South Beach, *N.Y.* **22 D4** 40 35N 74 4W
South Boston, *Bost.* **21 C3** 42 20N 71 2W
South Braintree, *Bost.* **21 D4** 42 11N 70 59W
South Branch →, *Phil.* **24 C4** 39 50N 75 5W
South Brooklyn, *N.Y.* **22 C5** 40 41N 73 59W
South Chelmsford, *Bost.* **21 B1** 42 34N 71 22W
South Chicago, *Chic.* **26 C3** 41 44N 87 32W
South Darenth, *Lon.* **4 C6** 51 23N 0 15 E
South Deering, *Chic.* **26 C3** 41 42N 87 33W
South Floral Park, *N.Y.* **23 C6** 40 42N 73 41W
South Gate, *L.A.* **28 C3** 33 56N 118 12W
South Germiston, *Jobg.* **18 F10** 26 11 S 28 13 E
South Hackensack, *N.Y.* **22 B4** 40 51N 74 2W
South Hamilton, *Bost.* **21 B4** 42 36N 70 52W
South Harbour, *Manila* **15 D3** 14 34N 120 58 E
South Harrow, *Lon.* **4 B2** 51 33N 0 21W
South Hd., *Syd.* **19 B4** 33 50 S 151 16 E
South Hempstead, *N.Y.* **23 C7** 40 40N 73 37W
South Hills, *Jobg.* **18 F9** 26 14 S 28 5 E
South Hingham, *Bost.* **21 D4** 42 12N 70 53W
South Holland, *Chic.* **26 D3** 41 36N 87 35W
South Hornchurch, *Lon.* **4 B6** 51 32N 0 11 E
South Huntington, *N.Y.* **23 C8** 40 49N 73 23W
South Lawn, *Wash.* **25 E7** 38 47N 77 0W
South Lawrence, *Bost.* **21 A3** 42 41N 71 9W
South Lincoln, *Bost.* **21 C2** 42 24N 71 19W
South Lynnfield, *Bost.* **21 B4** 42 30N 70 59W
South Norwood, *Lon.* **4 C4** 51 23N 0 3W
South Ockendon, *Lon.* **4 B6** 51 30N 0 16 E
South of Market, *S.F.* **27 B2** 37 46N 122 24W
South Orange, *N.Y.* **22 C3** 40 45N 74 14W
South Oxley, *Lon.* **4 B2** 51 37N 0 23W
South Oyster B., *N.Y.* **23 D8** 40 38N 73 27W
South Ozone Park, *N.Y.* **23 C6** 40 41N 73 49W
South Pasadena, *L.A.* **28 B4** 34 7N 118 8W
South Peabody, *Bost.* **21 B4** 42 30N 70 57W
South Peters, *Syd.* **19 B4** 33 54 S 151 11 E
South Plainfield, *N.Y.* **22 D2** 40 35N 74 24W
South Quincy, *Bost.* **21 D3** 42 13N 71 0W
South Res., *Bost.* **21 C3** 42 26N 71 6W
South San Francisco, *S.F.* **27 C2** 37 38N 122 26W
South San Gabriel, *L.A.* **28 B4** 34 3N 118 6W
South Shore, *Chic.* **26 C3** 41 45N 87 34W
South Sudbury, *Bost.* **21 C1** 42 21N 71 24W
South Valley Stream, *N.Y.* **23 D6** 40 38N 73 43W
South Westbury, *N.Y.* **23 C7** 40 44N 73 34W
South Weymouth, *Bost.* **21 D4** 42 10N 70 56W
South Wimbledon, *Lon.* **4 C3** 51 24N 0 11W
South Yarra, *Melb.* **19 F6** 37 50 S 144 59 E
Southall, *Lon.* **4 B2** 51 30N 0 22W
Southborough, *Lon.* **4 C5** 51 23N 0 3 E
Southcrest, *Jobg.* **18 F9** 26 15 S 28 5 E
Southend, *Lon.* **4 C4** 51 25N 0 0 E
Southfields, *Lon.* **4 C3** 51 26N 0 11W
Southgate, *Lon.* **4 B4** 51 38N 0 7W
Southwark, *Lon.* **4 C4** 51 29N 0 5W
Søvang, *Købn.* **2 E10** 55 34N 12 37 E
Soweto, *Jobg.* **18 F8** 26 14 S 27 52 E
Soya, *Tōkyō* **13 B4** 35 44N 139 55 E
Spadenland, *Hbg.* **7 E8** 53 28N 10 3 E
Spandau, *Berl.* **7 A1** 52 33N 13 9 E
Spånga, *Stock.* **3 D10** 59 23N 17 53 E
Sparkhill, *N.Y.* **22 A5** 41 1N 73 55W
Sparrows Point, *Balt.* **25 B4** 39 13N 76 29W
Spectacle I., *Bost.* **21 C4** 42 19N 70 59W
Speicher-See, *Mün.* **7 F11** 48 12N 11 42 E
Speising, *Wien* **10 H9** 48 10N 16 17 E
Speldorf, *Ruhr* **6 B2** 51 26N 6 49 E
Spellen, *Ruhr* **6 A1** 51 36N 6 36 E
Sphinx, *El Qâ.* **18 D4** 29 58N 31 8 E
Spinaceto, *Rome* **9 G9** 41 47N 12 27 E
Splitrock Res., *N.Y.* **22 B2** 40 58N 74 26W
Spořilov, *Pra.* **10 B3** 50 2N 14 29 E
Spot Pond, *Bost.* **21 C3** 42 26N 71 4W
Spotswood, *Melb.* **19 F6** 37 50 S 144 52 E
Spree →, *Berl.* **7 A2** 52 32N 13 12 E
Spreehafen, *Hbg.* **7 D7** 53 31N 9 59 E
Spring Pond, *Bost.* **21 C4** 42 29N 70 56W
Springeberg, *Berl.* **7 B5** 52 26N 13 43 E
Springfield, *N.Y.* **22 C3** 40 42N 74 18W
Springfield, *Phil.* **24 B3** 39 56N 75 19W
Springfield, *Wash.* **25 E6** 38 46N 77 10W
Springs, *Jobg.* **18 F11** 26 15 S 28 23 E
Sprockhövel, *Ruhr* **6 B5** 51 22N 7 14 E
Squantum, *Bost.* **21 D3** 42 17N 71 0W
Squirrel's Heath, *Lon.* **4 B6** 51 34N 0 12 E
Srednaya Rogatka, *St-Pet.* **11 C4** 59 49N 30 22 E
Sródmieĉcie, *Wsaw.* **10 E7** 52 13N 21 0 E
Staaken, *Berl.* **7 A1** 52 31N 13 8 E
Staatsoper, *Wien* **10 G10** 48 12N 16 21 E
Stabekk, *Oslo* **2 B3** 59 54N 10 36 E
Stadlau, *Wien* **10 G10** 48 13N 16 27 E
Stahnsdorf, *Berl.* **7 B2** 52 23N 13 12 E
Staines, *Lon.* **4 C2** 51 26N 0 29W
Stains, *Paris* **5 B4** 48 57N 2 22 E
Stamford, *N.Y.* **23 A7** 41 2N 73 32W
Stamford Harbor, *N.Y.* **23 A7** 41 0N 73 34W
Stamford Hill, *Lon.* **4 B4** 51 34N 0 4W
Stammersdorf, *Wien* **10 G10** 48 18N 16 24 E
Stanford Univ., *S.F.* **27 D4** 37 26N 122 10W
Stanley, *H.K.* **12 E6** 22 13N 114 12 E
Stanley Mound, *H.K.* **12 E6** 22 13N 114 12 E
Stanley Pen., *H.K.* **12 E6** 22 12N 114 12 E
Stanmore, *Lon.* **4 B3** 51 37N 0 18W
Stansted, *Lon.* **4 C6** 51 20N 0 18 E
Stapleford Abbotts, *Lon.* **4 B6** 51 37N 0 10 E
Stapleton, *N.Y.* **22 D4** 40 36N 74 5W
Stará Boleslav, *Pra.* **10 A3** 50 11N 14 39 E
Stara Milosna, *Wsaw.* **10 E8** 52 15N 21 12 E
Staraya, *St-Pet.* **11 B5** 59 55N 30 37 E
Staraya Derevnya, *St-Pet.* **11 B3** 59 58N 30 15 E
Stare, *Wsaw.* **10 E7** 52 15N 21 0 E
Stare Babice, *Wsaw.* **10 E5** 52 15N 20 49 E
Staré Mesto, *Pra.* **10 B2** 50 5N 14 25 E
State House, *Lagos* **18 B2** 6 26N 7 24 E
Staten, *N.Y.* **22 D4** 40 34N 74 7W
Staten Island Zoo, *N.Y.* **22 D4** 40 38N 74 6W
Statenice, *Pra.* **10 B1** 50 9N 14 19 E
Stavnsholt, *Købn.* **2 D9** 55 48N 12 24 E
Steele, *Ruhr* **6 B4** 51 27N 7 4 E
Steele Creek, *Melb.* **19 E6** 37 44 S 144 52 E
Steglitz, *Berl.* **7 B2** 52 27N 13 19 E
Stehstücken, *Berl.* **7 B1** 52 23N 13 7 E
Steilshoop, *Hbg.* **7 D8** 53 36N 10 2 E
Steinberger Slough, *S.F.* **27 C3** 37 32N 122 13W
Steinriegel, *Wien* **10 G9** 48 16N 16 12 E
Steinstücken, *Berl.* **7 B1** 52 21N 13 7 E
Steinwerder, *Hbg.* **7 D7** 53 32N 9 57 E
Stellingen, *Hbg.* **7 D7** 53 35N 9 56 E
Stenhamra, *Stock.* **3 D9** 59 20N 17 40 E
Stenløse, *Købn.* **2 D8** 55 46N 12 11 E
Stephansdom, *Wien* **10 G10** 48 12N 16 21 E
Stepney, *Lon.* **4 B4** 51 30N 0 3W
Sterkende, *Købn.* **2 E8** 55 36N 12 10 E
Sterkrade, *Ruhr* **6 A3** 51 31N 6 52 E
Sterling Park, *S.F.* **27 B2** 37 41N 122 27W
Stevenson, *Balt.* **25 A2** 39 24N 76 42W
Stewart Manor, *N.Y.* **23 C6** 40 43N 73 40W
Sticklinge udde, *Stock.* **3 D11** 59 23N 18 6 E
Stickney, *Chic.* **26 C2** 41 49N 87 46W
Stienitzaue, *Berl.* **7 A5** 52 38N 13 44 E
Stiepel, *Ruhr* **6 B5** 51 25N 7 14 E
Stiftskirche, *Ruhr* **6 C2** 51 12N 6 41 E
Still Run →, *Phil.* **24 C3** 39 47N 75 16W
Stockholm, *Stock.* **3 E11** 59 19N 18 4 E
Stocksund, *Stock.* **3 D11** 59 23N 18 3 E
Stockum, *Ruhr* **6 C2** 51 16N 6 44 E
Stodůlky, *Pra.* **10 B1** 50 3N 14 19 E
Stoke D'Abernon, *Lon.* **4 D2** 51 19N 0 23W
Stoke Newington, *Lon.* **4 B4** 51 33N 0 4W
Stolpe-Süd, *Berl.* **7 A2** 52 37N 13 14 E
Stone, *Lon.* **4 C6** 51 26N 0 16 E
Stone Grove, *Lon.* **4 B3** 51 37N 0 16W
Stone Park, *Chic.* **26 B1** 41 53N 87 52W
Stonebridge, *Lon.* **4 B3** 51 32N 0 16W
Stoneham, *Bost.* **21 C3** 42 29N 71 5W
Stonehurst, *L.A.* **28 A2** 34 15N 118 21W
Stony Brook Res., *Bost.* **21 D3** 42 15N 71 8W
Stony Cr. →, *Chic.* **26 C2** 41 40N 87 45W
Stony Cr. →, *Melb.* **19 E6** 37 49 S 144 53 E
Stora Värtan, *Stock.* **3 D11** 59 25N 18 7 E
Store Hareskov, *Købn.* **2 D9** 55 46N 12 23 E
Store Kattingesø, *Købn.* **2 E7** 55 39N 12 0 E
Store Magleby, *Købn.* **2 E10** 55 35N 12 35 E
Storholmen, *Stock.* **3 D11** 59 23N 18 8 E
Stovivatn, *Oslo* **2 B2** 59 54N 10 26 E
Stovner, *Oslo* **2 B5** 59 57N 10 55 E
Stow L., *S.F.* **27 B2** 37 46N 122 28W
Stračnice, *Pra.* **10 B2** 50 4N 14 28 E
Strandbad Gansehäufe, *Wien* **10 G10** 48 13N 16 26 E
Strasslach, *Mün.* **7 G10** 48 0N 11 30 E
Strasstrudering, *Mün.* **7 G11** 48 6N 11 41 E
Stratford, *Lon.* **4 B5** 51 33N 0 0 E
Stratford, *Phil.* **24 C4** 39 49N 75 0W
Strathfield, *Syd.* **19 B3** 33 52 S 151 5 E
Strawberry Hill, *Bost.* **21 D2** 42 14N 71 15W
Strawberry Pk., *L.A.* **28 A4** 34 16N 118 7W
Strawberry Pt., *S.F.* **27 A1** 37 53N 122 30W
Streatham, *Lon.* **4 C4** 51 25N 0 7W
Streatham Vale, *Lon.* **4 C4** 51 24N 0 8W
Strebersdorf, *Wien* **10 G10** 48 17N 16 23 E
Střečovice, *Pra.* **10 B2** 50 5N 14 23 E
Strelyna, *St-Pet.* **11 C1** 59 49N 30 0 E
Střížkov, *Pra.* **10 B2** 50 7N 14 28 E
Strogino, *Mos.* **11 E8** 55 48N 37 24 E
Strømmen, *Oslo* **2 B5** 59 56N 10 59 E
Stromovka, *Pra.* **10 B2** 50 6N 14 25 E
Strunkede Wasserschloss, *Ruhr* **6 A5** 51 33N 7 12 E
Studio City, *L.A.* **28 B2** 34 8N 118 24W
Stupinigi, *Tori.* **9 C2** 44 59N 7 36 E
Stura di Lanzo →, *Tori.* **9 A2** 45 11N 7 47 E
Stureby, *Stock.* **3 E11** 59 15N 18 4 E
Stuvsta, *Stock.* **3 E11** 59 15N 18 0 E
Styrum, *Ruhr* **6 B3** 51 27N 6 52 E
Subhepur, *Delhi* **16 A2** 28 44N 77 15 E
Sucat, *Manila* **15 E4** 14 27N 121 2 E
Success, L., *N.Y.* **23 C6** 40 45N 73 42W
Suchdol, *Pra.* **10 B2** 50 8N 14 22 E
Sucre, *Car.* **30 D5** 10 31N 66 57W
Sucy-en-Brie, *Paris* **5 C5** 48 46N 2 31 E
Sudberg, *Ruhr* **6 C4** 51 10N 7 6 E
Sudbury, *Bost.* **21 C1** 42 22N 71 24W
Suderelbe →, *Hbg.* **7 E7** 53 28N 9 58 E
Suderwich, *Ruhr* **6 A5** 51 36N 7 16 E
Sugamo, *Tōkyō* **13 B3** 35 44N 139 43 E
Sugar Loaf Mt. = Açúcar, Pão de, *Rio J.* **31 B3** 22 56 S 43 9W
Sugartown, *Phil.* **24 B1** 39 59N 75 30W
Sugasawa, *Tōkyō* **13 B2** 35 46N 139 32 E
Suge, *Tōkyō* **13 C2** 35 37N 139 32 E
Suginami-Ku, *Tōkyō* **13 B2** 35 41N 139 37 E
Sugita, *Tōkyō* **13 D2** 35 22N 139 37 E
Sugō, *Tōkyō* **13 C2** 35 34N 139 33 E
Suitland, *Wash.* **25 D8** 38 50N 76 55W
Sukchar, *Calc.* **16 D6** 22 42N 88 22 E
Sulejówek, *Wsaw.* **10 E8** 52 14N 21 14 E
Sulldorf, *Hbg.* **7 D6** 53 34N 9 49 E
Sultan Mosque, *Sing.* **15 G8** 1 18N 103 51 E
Suma, *Ōsaka* **12 C1** 34 38N 135 8 E
Sumaré, *S. Pau.* **31 E5** 23 32 S 46 41W
Sumida, *Tōkyō* **13 B3** 35 42N 139 49 E
Sumida →, *Tōkyō* **13 B3** 35 39N 139 45 E
Sumiyoshi, *Ōsaka* **12 C4** 34 36N 135 30 E
Summer Palace, *Beij.* **14 B2** 39 59N 116 13 E
Summerville, *Trto.* **20 E7** 43 37N 79 33W
Summit, *Chic.* **26 C2** 41 47N 87 47W
Summit, *N.Y.* **22 C2** 40 43N 74 22W
Sun Valley, *L.A.* **28 A2** 34 13N 118 21W
Sunamachi, *Tōkyō* **13 B4** 35 40N 139 50 E
Sunashinden, *Tōkyō* **13 A2** 35 53N 139 30 E
Sunbury, *Lon.* **4 C2** 51 25N 0 26W
Sunda Kelapa, *Jak.* **15 H9** 6 6 S 106 48 E
Sundbyberg, *Stock.* **3 D10** 59 22N 17 57 E
Sundbyerne, *Købn.* **2 E10** 55 39N 12 36 E
Sung Kong, *H.K.* **12 E6** 22 11N 114 17 E
Sungai Bambu, *Jak.* **15 H10** 6 6 S 106 53 E
Sungai Buloh, *Sing.* **15 F7** 1 25N 103 42 E
Sungei Simpang, *Sing.* **15 F7** 1 26N 103 49 E
Sunland, *L.A.* **28 A3** 34 15N 118 18W
Sunnyridge, *Jobg.* **18 F10** 26 10 S 28 10 E
Sunset, *S.F.* **27 B2** 37 44N 122 29W
Sunshine, *Melb.* **19 E5** 37 48 S 144 49 E
Sunshine Acres, *L.A.* **28 C5** 33 56N 117 59W
Suntaug L., *Bost.* **21 B3** 42 31N 71 0W
Sunter, *Jak.* **15 H10** 6 7 S 106 51 E
Sunter, Kali, *Jak.* **15 J10** 6 10 S 106 53 E
Suomenlinna, *Hels.* **3 C4** 60 9N 24 59 E
Superga, *Tori.* **9 B3** 45 4N 7 46 E
Superga, Basilica di, *Tori.* **9 B3** 45 5N 7 45 E
Sura, *Calc.* **16 E6** 22 33N 88 24 E
Surag San, *Sŏul* **12 F8** 37 40N 127 4 E
Surbiton, *Lon.* **4 C3** 51 23N 0 17W
Surco, *Lima* **30 G8** 12 9 S 77 0W
Suresnes, *Paris* **5 B3** 48 52N 2 13 E
Surquillo, *Lima* **30 G8** 12 6 S 77 1W
Surrey Hills, *Melb.* **19 F7** 37 50 S 145 5 E
Surrey Hills, *Syd.* **19 B4** 33 53 S 151 13 E
Surrey Park, *Melb.* **19 E7** 37 49 S 145 6 E
Susaeg, *Sŏul* **12 G7** 37 34N 126 54 E
Süssenbrunn, *Wien* **10 G10** 48 16N 16 29 E
Sutherland, *Syd.* **19 C3** 34 2 S 151 3 E
Sutton, *Lon.* **4 C3** 51 21N 0 11W
Sutton at Hone, *Lon.* **4 C6** 51 24N 0 14 E
Suyu, *Sŏul* **12 G8** 37 37N 127 0 E
Suzukishinden, *Tōkyō* **13 B2** 35 43N 139 31 E
Svanemøllen, *Købn.* **2 D10** 55 43N 12 34 E
Svartsjölandet, *Stock.* **3 D9** 59 20N 17 43 E
Sverdlov, *Mos.* **11 E9** 55 46N 37 36 E
Svestad, *Oslo* **2 C3** 59 46N 10 36 E
Svestrup, *Købn.* **2 D7** 55 46N 12 8 E
Svinningeudd, *Stock.* **3 D12** 59 26N 18 17 E
Svinö, *Hels.* **3 C3** 60 7N 24 44 E
Svogerslev, *Købn.* **2 E7** 55 38N 12 0 E
Swampscott, *Bost.* **21 C4** 42 28N 70 53W
Swanley, *Lon.* **4 C5** 51 23N 0 9 E
Swanscombe, *Lon.* **4 C6** 51 26N 0 18 E
Swansea, *Trto.* **20 E8** 43 39N 79 27W
Swarthmore, *Phil.* **24 B2** 39 54N 75 22W
Swedesboro, *Phil.* **24 C3** 39 45N 75 17W
Swedesburg, *Phil.* **24 A3** 40 5N 75 19W
Swinburne I., *N.Y.* **22 D4** 40 33N 74 3W
Swita, *Ōsaka* **12 B4** 34 45N 135 30 E
Syampur, *Calc.* **16 F5** 22 28N 88 12 E
Sycamore Mills, *Phil.* **24 B2** 39 57N 75 25W
Sydenham, *Jobg.* **18 E9** 26 9 S 28 5 E
Sydney, *Syd.* **19 B4** 33 52 S 151 12 E
Sydney, Univ. of, *Syd.* **19 B4** 33 54 S 151 11 E
Sydney Airport, *Syd.* **19 B4** 33 56 S 151 10 E
Sydney Harbour Bridge, *Syd.* **19 B4** 33 51 S 151 12 E
Sydstranden, *Købn.* **2 E10** 55 34N 12 38 E
Sylling, *Oslo* **2 B1** 59 54N 10 16 E
Sylvania, *Syd.* **19 C3** 34 0 S 151 7 E
Syndal, *Melb.* **19 F7** 37 52 S 145 9 E
Syon House, *Lon.* **4 C3** 51 28N 0 18W
Syosset, *N.Y.* **23 C7** 40 49N 73 30W
Szabadság-hegy, *Bud.* **10 J12** 47 30N 18 59 E
Szczęsliwice, *Wsaw.* **10 E6** 52 12N 20 57 E
Szemere-Telep, *Bud.* **10 K14** 47 26N 19 13 E
Széphalom, *Bud.* **10 J12** 47 34N 18 57 E
Szilasliget, *Bud.* **10 J14** 47 34N 19 16 E


# T


Tabata, *Tōkyō* **13 B3** 35 44N 139 46 E
Tablada, *B.A.* **32 C3** 34 41 S 58 32W
Taboão →, *S. Pau.* **31 F7** 23 40 S 46 27W
Taboão da Serra, *S. Pau.* **31 E5** 23 36 S 46 45W
Tabor, *N.Y.* **22 B2** 40 52N 74 28W
Täby, *Stock.* **3 D11** 59 26N 18 2 E
Tacony, *Phil.* **24 A4** 40 1N 75 2W
Tacuba, *Méx.* **29 B2** 19 26N 99 11W
Tacubaya, *Méx.* **29 B2** 19 24N 99 10W
Tadain, *Ōsaka* **12 A3** 34 51N 135 24 E
Tadworth, *Lon.* **4 D3** 51 17N 0 14W
Tagig, *Manila* **15 D4** 14 31N 121 4 E
Tagig →, *Manila* **15 D4** 14 31N 121 5 E
Tai Hang, *H.K.* **12 E6** 22 16N 114 11 E
Tai Lo Shan, *H.K.* **12 D6** 22 21N 114 13 E
Tai Po Tsai, *H.K.* **12 D6** 22 20N 114 15 E
Tai Seng, *Sing.* **15 F8** 1 20N 103 53 E
Tai Shui Hang, *H.K.* **12 D6** 22 24N 114 13 E
Tai Tam B., *H.K.* **12 E6** 22 12N 114 13 E
Tai Tam Tuk Res., *H.K.* **12 E6** 22 14N 114 13 E
Tai Wan Tau, *H.K.* **12 E6** 22 17N 114 17 E
Tai Wo Hau, *H.K.* **12 D5** 22 21N 114 7 E
Tai Wo Ping, *H.K.* **12 D5** 22 20N 114 9 E
Ta'imim, *Bagd.* **17 F8** 33 15N 44 21 E
Tainaka, *Ōsaka* **12 C4** 34 36N 135 35 E
Taishō, *Ōsaka* **12 C3** 34 38N 135 27 E
Taitō-Ku, *Tōkyō* **13 B3** 35 43N 139 47 E
Tajima, *Tōkyō* **13 B2** 35 48N 139 36 E
Tajpur, *Calc.* **16 D5** 22 44N 88 15 E
Takaido, *Tōkyō* **13 B2** 35 40N 139 37 E
Takaishi, *Tōkyō* **13 C2** 35 36N 139 31 E
Takarazuka, *Ōsaka* **12 B2** 34 47N 135 20 E
Takasago, *Tōkyō* **13 B4** 35 44N 139 52 E
Takatsuki, *Ōsaka* **12 A4** 34 50N 135 37 E
Takayanagi, *Tōkyō* **13 D4** 35 23N 139 57 E
Takegahana, *Tōkyō* **13 B4** 35 47N 139 54 E
Takenotsuka, *Tōkyō* **13 B3** 35 47N 139 47 E
Takeshita, *Tōkyō* **13 C2** 35 33N 139 32 E
Takinegawa, *Tōkyō* **13 B3** 35 45N 139 44 E
Takkula, *Hels.* **3 B2** 60 19N 24 38 E
Takoma Park, *Wash.* **25 D7** 38 58N 77 0W
Taksim, *Ist.* **17 A2** 41 2N 28 58 E
Talaide, *Lisb.* **8 F7** 38 44N 9 18W
Talampas, *Manila* **15 D4** 14 36N 121 4 E
Taling Chan, *Bangk.* **15 B1** 13 46N 100 27 E
Talleyville, *Phil.* **24 C1** 39 48N 75 32W
Tallkrogen, *Stock.* **3 E11** 59 16N 18 4 E
Talmapais Valley, *S.F.* **27 A1** 37 52N 122 32W
Tama, *Tōkyō* **13 C1** 35 38N 139 26 E
Tama →, *Tōkyō* **13 C2** 35 32N 139 39 E
Tama Kyźryō, *Tōkyō* **13 C2** 35 34N 139 30 E
Tamaden, *Tōkyō* **13 C2** 35 39N 139 38 E
Tamagawa-josui →, *Tōkyō* **13 B1** 35 41N 139 47 E
Taman Sari, *Jak.* **15 H9** 6 8 S 106 48 E
Tamanduatei →, *S. Pau.* **31 E6** 23 37 S 46 38W
Tambora, *Jak.* **15 H9** 6 8 S 106 47 E
Tamboré, *S. Pau.* **31 E4** 23 30 S 46 50W
Tammisalo, *Hels.* **3 B5** 60 11N 25 5 E
Tammûh, *El Qâ.* **18 D5** 29 55N 31 15 E
Tampier Slough, *Chic.* **26 D1** 41 39N 87 54W
Tan Tock Seng, *Sing.* **15 G8** 1 19N 103 50 E
Tanah Abang, *Jak.* **15 J9** 6 12 S 106 48 E
Tanashi, *Tōkyō* **13 B2** 35 43N 139 32 E
Tanforan Park, *S.F.* **27 C2** 37 37N 122 24W
Tangjae, *Sŏul* **12 H8** 37 29N 127 2 E
Tanglin, *Sing.* **15 G7** 1 18N 103 47 E
Tangstedt, *Hbg.* **7 C7** 53 40N 9 51 E
Tangstedter Forst, *Hbg.* **7 C8** 53 43N 10 3 E
Tanigami, *Ōsaka* **12 B2** 34 45N 135 10 E
Tanjung Duren, *Jak.* **15 J9** 6 10 S 106 46 E
Tanjung Priok, *Jak.* **15 H10** 6 6 S 106 52 E
Tanum, *Oslo* **2 B2** 59 53N 10 28 E
Taoranting Gongyuan, *Beij.* **14 B3** 39 51N 116 20 E
Taoranting Hu, *Beij.* **14 B3** 39 50N 116 20 E
Tapada, *Lisb.* **8 F7** 38 49N 9 16W
Tapanila, *Hels.* **3 B5** 60 15N 25 2 E
Tapiales, *B.A.* **32 C3** 34 42 S 58 30W
Tapiola, *Hels.* **3 B3** 60 10N 24 48 E
Tappan, *N.Y.* **22 A5** 41 1N 73 57W
Tappan, L., *N.Y.* **22 A5** 41 1N 73 59W
Tappeh, *Tehr.* **17 C5** 35 41N 51 29 E
Tapsia, *Calc.* **16 E6** 22 32N 88 23 E
Taquara, *Rio J.* **31 B1** 22 55 S 43 21W
Tara, *Bomb.* **16 G7** 19 5N 72 49 E
Tarāblus, *Bagd.* **17 F8** 33 19N 44 21 E
Tarango, Presa, *Méx.* **29 B2** 19 21N 99 12W
Tårbæk, *Købn.* **2 D10** 55 46N 12 35 E
Tarchomin, *Wsaw.* **10 E6** 52 19N 20 58 E
Tardeo, *Bomb.* **16 H7** 18 57N 72 48 E
Target Rock, *N.Y.* **23 B8** 40 55N 73 24W
Targówek, *Wsaw.* **10 E7** 52 16N 21 3 E
Tårnby, *Købn.* **2 E10** 55 37N 12 35 E

Villecresnes 47


Taronga Zoo. Park, Syd. 19 B4 33 50 S 151 14 E
Tarqua B., Lagos 18 B2 6 24N 7 23 E
Tarzana, L.A. 28 A1 34 10N 118 32W
Tåstrup, Købn. 2 E8 55 39N 12 18 E
Tatarovo, Mos. 11 E8 55 45N 37 24 E
Tatarpur, Delhi 16 B1 28 38N 77 9 E
Tatenberg, Hbg. 7 E8 53 29N 10 3 E
Tathong Channel, H.K. 12 E6 22 15N 114 16 E
Tathong Pt., H.K. 12 E6 22 14N 114 17 E
Tatsfield, Lon. 4 D5 51 17N 0 1 E
Tattariharju, Hels. 3 B5 60 15N 25 2 E
Tatuapé, S. Pau. 31 E6 23 31 S 46 33W
Taufkirchen, Mün. 7 G10 48 2N 11 36 E
Tavares, I. dos, Rio J. 31 A3 22 49 S 43 6W
Tavernanova, Nápl. 9 H13 40 54N 14 21 E
Taverny, Paris 5 A3 49 1N 2 13 E
Távros, Ath. 8 J11 37 57N 23 43 E
Tavry, St-Pet. 11 B6 59 54N 30 40 E
Taylortown, N.Y. 22 B2 40 56N 74 23W
Tayninka, Mos. 11 D10 55 53N 37 45 E
Taytay, Manila 15 D4 14 34N 121 7 E
Tayuman, Manila 15 D4 14 31N 121 9 E
Teaneck, N.Y. 22 B4 40 52N 74 1W
Teatro Colón, B.A. 32 B4 34 36 S 58 23 E
Teban Gardens, Sing. 15 G7 1 19N 103 44 E
Tebet, Jak. 15 J10 6 14 S 106 50 E
Tecamachaleo, Méx. 29 B2 19 25N 99 14W
Techny, Chic. 26 A2 42 6N 87 48W
Teck Hock, Sing. 15 F8 1 21N 103 54 E
Tecoma, Melb. 19 F9 37 54 S 145 20 E
Teddington, Lon. 4 C2 51 25N 0 20W
Tegel, Berl. 7 A2 52 34N 13 16 E
Tegel, Flughafen, Berl. 7 A2 52 35N 13 15 E
Tegeler Fliess →, Berl. 7 A3 52 37N 13 21 E
Tegeler See, Berl. 7 A2 52 34N 13 15 E
Tegelort, Berl. 7 A2 52 34N 13 13 E
Tehar, Delhi 16 B1 28 37N 77 7 E
Tehrān, Tehr. 17 C5 35 41N 51 25 E
Tehrān Pars, Tehr. 17 C6 35 44N 51 32 E
Tei Tong Tsui, H.K. 12 E6 22 16N 114 17 E
Tejo →, Lisb. 8 F8 38 45N 9 3W
Tekstilyshchik, Mos. 11 E10 55 42N 37 41 E
Tela, Delhi 16 A2 28 43N 77 19 E
Telhal, Lisb. 8 F7 38 48N 9 18W
Telinipara, Calc. 16 D6 22 46N 88 23 E
Telok Blangah, Sing. 15 G7 1 17N 103 49 E
Teltow, Berl. 7 B2 52 23N 13 17 E
Teltow kanal, Berl. 7 B3 52 26N 13 29 E
Temescal, L., S.F. 27 A3 37 50N 122 13W
Temnikovo, Mos. 11 E12 55 43N 38 1 E
Tempelhof, Berl. 7 B3 52 27N 13 23 E
Tempelhof, Flughafen, Berl. 7 B3 52 28N 13 27 E
Temperley, B.A. 32 C4 34 46 S 58 22W
Temple City, L.A. 28 B4 34 6N 118 3W
Temple Hills Park, Wash. 25 E8 38 48N 76 56W
Templestowe, Melb. 19 E7 37 45 S 145 8 E
Templestowe Lower, Melb. 19 E7 37 45 S 145 6 E
Tenafly, N.Y. 22 B5 40 54N 73 58W
Tenantongo, Presa, Méx. 29 B2 19 28N 99 15W
Tengah →, Sing. 15 F7 1 23N 103 43 E
Tengeh, Sungei →, Sing. 15 F6 1 20N 103 39 E
Tennoji, Ōsaka 12 C4 34 39N 135 30 E
Tenochtitlán, Méx. 29 B3 19 26N 99 7W
Tepalcates, Méx. 29 B3 19 23N 99 3W
Tepe Saif, Tehr. 17 D4 35 36N 51 17 E
Tepepan, Méx. 29 C3 19 16N 99 9W
Teplyy Star, Mos. 11 F9 55 37N 37 30 E
Tepozteco, Parque Nac. del, Méx. 29 D3 19 3N 99 5W
Terrasse Vaudreuil, Mtrl. 20 B2 43 23N 73 59W
Terrazzano, Mil. 9 D5 45 32N 9 4 E
Terrugem, Lisb. 8 F7 38 41N 9 17W
Terusan Banjir, Jak. 15 H9 6 7 S 106 46 E
Terzigno, Nápl. 9 J13 40 48N 14 29 E
Tessancourt-sur-Aubette, Paris 5 A1 49 1N 1 55 E
Testona, Tori. 9 C3 44 59N 7 42 E
Tetelco, Méx. 29 C4 19 12N 98 57W
Tetreauville, Mtrl. 20 A4 43 35N 73 32W
Tetti Neirotti, Tori. 9 B2 45 3N 7 32 E
Tetuán, Mdrd. 8 B2 40 27N 3 42W
Teufelsberg, Berl. 7 B2 52 29N 13 14 E
Tévere →, Rome 9 F9 41 56N 12 27 E
Tewksbury, Bost. 21 B2 42 37N 71 12W
Texcoco, L. de, Méx. 29 B4 19 30N 89 58 E
Thalkirchen, Mün. 7 G10 48 6N 11 32 E
Thames Ditton, Lon. 4 C2 51 23N 0 20W
Thamesmead, Lon. 4 B5 51 30N 0 7 E
Thana Cr. →, Bomb. 16 G8 19 4N 72 54 E
The Basin, Melb. 19 F8 37 51 S 145 19 E
The Glen, Wash. 25 C6 39 2N 77 12W
The Loop, Chic. 26 B3 41 52N 87 37W
The Narrows, N.Y. 22 D4 40 37N 74 3W
The Ridge, Delhi 16 B2 28 37N 77 10 E
The White House, Wash. 25 D7 38 53N 77 1W
The Wilds, Jobg. 18 F9 26 10 S 28 2 E
Theseión, Ath. 8 J11 37 57N 23 43 E
Theydon Bois, Lon. 4 A5 51 40N 0 6 E
Thiais, Paris 5 C4 48 46N 2 23 E
Thieux, Paris 5 A6 49 0N 2 40 E
Thistletown, Trto. 20 D7 43 44N 79 34W
Thiverval-Grignon, Paris 5 B1 48 51N 1 55 E
Thomaston, N.Y. 23 C6 40 47N 73 43W
Thomastown, Melb. 19 E7 37 40 S 145 2 E
Thompson I., Bost. 21 D4 42 19N 70 59W
Thomson, Sing. 15 F8 1 20N 103 50 E
Thon Buri, Bangk. 15 B1 13 45N 100 29 E
Thong Hoe, Sing. 15 F7 1 25N 103 42 E
Thorigny-sur-Marne, Paris 5 B6 48 53N 2 41 E
Thornbury, Melb. 19 E7 37 44 S 145 1 E
Thorncliffe, Trto. 20 D8 43 42N 79 20W
Thornhill, Jobg. 18 E9 26 6 S 28 9 E
Thornhill, Trto. 20 D8 43 48N 79 25W
Thornton, Phil. 24 B1 39 54N 75 31W
Thornton Heath, Lon. 4 C4 51 23N 0 6W
Thorofare, Phil. 24 B3 39 50N 75 11W
Throgs Neck, N.Y. 23 C6 40 48N 73 49W
Tian Guan, Sing. 15 F7 1 21N 103 49 E
Tian'anmen, Beij. 14 B3 39 53N 116 21 E
Tiancun, Beij. 14 B2 39 54N 116 12 E
Tianjin, Tianj. 14 E5 39 7N 117 12 E
Tiantan Gongyuan, Beij. 14 B3 39 51N 116 22 E
Tiateloco, Méx. 29 B3 19 27N 99 8W
Tibidabo, Barc. 8 D5 41 25N 2 6 E
Tiburon, S.F. 27 A2 37 52N 122 27W
Tiburon Pen., S.F. 27 A2 37 53N 122 28W
Tiburtino, Rome 9 F10 41 53N 12 30 E
Ticomán, Méx. 29 A3 19 31N 99 8W
Tiefenbroich, Ruhr 6 C2 51 18N 6 49 E
Tiefersee, Berl. 7 B1 52 24N 13 5 E
Tiejiangyin, Beij. 14 C3 39 49N 116 23 E
Tientsin = Tianjin, Tianj. 14 E5 39 7N 117 12 E
Tiergarten, Berl. 7 A3 52 31N 13 20 E
Tietê →, S. Pau. 31 D7 23 28 S 46 24W
Tigery, Paris 5 D5 48 38N 2 30 E
Tigre, B.A. 32 A3 34 25 S 58 34W
Tigris →, Bagd. 17 F8 33 17N 44 23 E
Tijuca, Rio J. 31 B2 22 56 S 43 13W
Tijuca, L. de, Rio J. 31 B2 22 59 S 43 20W
Tijuca, Pico da, Rio J. 31 B2 22 56 S 43 15W
Tijucamar, Rio J. 31 C2 23 0 S 43 18W
Tijucas, Is., Rio J. 31 C2 23 1 S 43 17W
Tikkurila, Hels. 3 B5 60 17N 25 2 E
Tilanqiao, Shang. 14 J11 31 15N 121 29 E
Tilbury, Lon. 4 C7 51 27N 0 21 E
Timah, Bukit, Sing. 15 F7 1 21N 103 46 E
Timiryazev Park, Mos. 11 E9 55 49N 37 33 E
Ting Kau, H.K. 12 D5 22 22N 114 4 E
Tinley Cr. →, Chic. 26 D2 41 39N 87 45W
Tinley Creek Woods, Chic. 26 D2 41 38N 87 48W
Tinley Park, Chic. 26 D2 41 35N 87 46W
Tipas, Manila 15 D4 14 32N 121 4 E
Tirsa, El Qâ. 18 D5 29 57N 31 12 E
Tishrīyaa, Bagd. 17 F8 33 18N 44 24 E
Tit Cham Chau, H.K. 12 E6 22 15N 114 17 E
Titagarh, Calc. 16 D6 22 44N 88 22 E
Tivoli, Købn. 2 D10 55 40N 12 35 E
Tizapán, Méx. 29 C2 19 19N 99 13W
Tlalnepantla, Méx. 29 A2 19 32N 99 11W
Tlalnepantla →, Méx. 29 A2 19 30N 99 18W
Tláloc, Cerro, Méx. 29 D3 19 7N 99 3W
Tlalpan, Méx. 29 C2 19 17N 99 10W
Tlalpitzáhuac, Méx. 29 C4 19 19N 98 56W
Tlaltenango, Méx. 29 B2 19 20N 99 17W
Tlaltenco, Méx. 29 C3 19 19N 99 0W
Tlaxcoaque, Méx. 29 B3 19 25N 99 8W
To Kwai Wan, H.K. 12 E6 22 18N 114 11 E
Toa Payoh, Sing. 15 F8 1 20N 103 50 E
Tobay Beach, N.Y. 23 D8 40 36N 73 26W
Točná, Pra. 10 C2 49 58N 14 25 E
Tocome →, Car. 30 D6 10 28N 66 49W
Toda, Tōkyō 13 A3 35 50N 139 40 E
Todamachī, Tōkyō 13 B2 35 48N 139 39 E
Todt Hill, N.Y. 22 D4 40 36N 74 6W
Toei, Khlong →, Bangk. 15 B2 13 43N 100 32 E
Togasaki, Tōkyō 13 B4 35 47N 139 51 E
Tōkagi, Tōkyō 13 B4 35 42N 139 55 E
Tōkaichiba, Tōkyō 13 C2 35 31N 139 30 E
Tokarevo, Mos. 11 F11 55 38N 37 54 E
Tokorozawa, Tōkyō 13 B1 35 47N 139 28 E
Tōkyō, Tōkyō 13 C3 35 43N 139 45 E
Tōkyō B., Tōkyō 13 C4 35 33N 139 53 E
Tōkyō-Haneda Int. Airport, Tōkyō 13 C3 35 33N 139 45 E
Tōkyō Harbour, Tōkyō 13 C3 35 38N 139 46 E
Tokyo Univ., Tōkyō 13 B3 35 42N 139 46 E
Tollygunge, Calc. 16 F6 22 29N 88 21 E
Tolly's Nala, Calc. 16 E6 22 33N 88 19 E
Tolworth, Lon. 4 C3 51 22N 0 17W
Tomang, Jak. 15 J9 6 10 S 106 47 E
Tomba di Nerone, Rome 9 F9 41 58N 12 26 E
Tomilino, Mos. 11 F11 55 39N 37 55 E
Tomioka, Tōkyō 13 D2 35 22N 139 37 E
Tonda, Ōsaka 12 B4 34 49N 135 35 E
Tondo, Manila 15 D3 14 36N 120 57 E
Tone-unga →, Tōkyō 13 A4 35 55N 139 56 E
Tonekollen, Oslo 2 C6 50 49N 11 0 E
Tong Kang, Sungei →, Sing. 15 F8 1 23N 103 53 E
Tonghui He →, Beij. 14 B3 39 53N 116 28 E
Tönisheide, Ruhr 6 C4 51 18N 7 3 E
Tonndorf, Hbg. 7 D8 53 35N 10 8 E
Toorak, Melb. 19 F7 37 50 S 145 1 E
Toot Hill, Lon. 4 A6 51 41N 0 11 E
Topilejo, Méx. 29 C3 19 12N 99 9W
Topkapi, Ist. 17 A2 41 1N 28 55 E
Topsfield, Bost. 21 B4 42 38N 70 57W
Tor di Quinto, Rome 9 F9 41 56N 12 27 E
Tor Pignattara, Rome 9 F10 41 52N 12 31 E
Tor Sapienza, Rome 9 F10 41 53N 12 35 E
Torcy, Paris 5 B5 48 51N 2 39 E
Torino, Tori. 9 B2 45 5N 7 39 E
Toro, B.A. 32 B1 34 30 S 58 50W
Toronto, Trto. 20 E9 43 39N 79 13W
Toronto, Univ. of, Trto. 20 E8 43 39N 79 23W
Toronto Harbour, Trto. 20 E8 43 38N 79 21W
Toronto I., Trto. 20 E8 43 37N 79 23W
Toronto Int. Airport, Trto. 20 D7 43 40N 79 38 E
Torre Annunziata, Nápl. 9 J13 40 45N 14 26 E
Torre Cervara, Rome 9 F10 41 55N 12 35 E
Torre del Greco, Nápl. 9 J13 40 47N 14 21 E
Torre Novo, Rome 9 F10 41 51N 12 36 E
Torrellas →, Barc. 8 D5 41 23N 2 1 E
Torrellas del Llobregat, Barc. 8 D4 41 20N 1 59 E
Torresdale, Phil. 24 A5 40 3N 74 59W
Torrevécchia, Rome 9 F9 41 55N 12 25 E
Tortuguitas, B.A. 32 A2 34 28 S 58 44W
Toshima-Ku, Tōkyō 13 B3 35 43N 139 43 E
Toshimaen, Tōkyō 13 B2 35 43N 139 38 E
Totowa, N.Y. 22 B3 40 54N 74 13W
Totsuka-Ku, Tōkyō 13 D2 35 23N 139 32 E
Tottenham, Lon. 4 B4 51 35N 0 4W
Tottenham, Melb. 19 E6 37 48 S 144 51 E
Tottenville, N.Y. 22 D3 40 30N 74 14W
Totteridge, Lon. 4 B3 51 37N 0 11W
Toussus-le-Noble, Paris 5 C2 48 44N 2 6 E
Toussus-le-Noble, Aérodrome de, Paris 5 C2 48 44N 2 6 E
Toverud, Oslo 2 B2 59 55N 10 20 E
Towaco, N.Y. 22 B3 40 55N 74 18W
Tower Hamlets, Lon. 4 B4 51 31N 0 2W
Town Farm Hill, Bost. 21 A3 42 40N 71 3W
Townley, N.Y. 22 C3 40 41N 74 14W
Towra Pt., Syd. 19 C4 34 0 S 151 10 E
Towson, Balt. 25 A3 39 24N 76 36W
Tøyen, Oslo 2 B4 59 55N 10 47 E
Toyofuta, Tōkyō 13 A4 35 54N 139 55 E
Toyonaka, Ōsaka 12 B3 34 46N 135 28 E
Traar, Ruhr 6 B1 51 22N 6 36 E
Trafaria, Lisb. 8 F7 38 40N 9 13W
Tragliata, Rome 9 F8 41 58N 12 14 E
Traicão →, S. Pau. 31 E6 23 35 S 46 41W
Trälhavet, Stock. 3 D13 59 26N 18 22 E
Tranby, Oslo 2 C1 59 49N 10 14 E
Tranegilde, Købn. 2 E9 55 37N 12 20 E
Trångsund, Stock. 3 E11 59 13N 18 8 E
Trappenfelde, Berl. 7 A4 52 34N 13 39 E
Trappes, Paris 5 C1 48 46N 1 59 E
Trastévere, Rome 9 F9 51 53N 12 28 E
Travilah, Wash. 25 C6 39 4N 77 15W
Travilah Regional Park, Wash. 25 C6 39 4N 77 17W
Travis, N.Y. 22 D3 40 35N 74 11W
Treasure I., S.F. 27 B2 37 49N 122 22W
Třeboradice, Pra. 10 B3 50 9N 14 31 E
Třebotov, Pra. 10 C1 49 58N 14 17 E
Trecase, Nápl. 9 J13 40 46N 14 26 E
Trekroner, Købn. 2 D10 55 42N 12 36 E
Tremblay-lès-Gonesse, Paris 5 B5 48 58N 2 30 E
Tremembé, S. Pau. 31 D6 23 27 S 46 36W
Tremembe →, S. Pau. 31 D6 23 27 S 46 34W
Tremont, Melb. 19 F9 37 53 S 145 20 E
Tremont, N.Y. 23 B5 40 50N 73 52W
Trenno, Mil. 9 E5 45 29N 9 6 E
Treptow, Berl. 7 B3 52 29N 13 27 E
Tres Marias, Méx. 29 D2 19 3N 99 15W
Trés Rios, Sa. dos, Rio J. 31 B2 22 56 S 43 17W
Tretiakov Art Gallery, Mos. 11 E9 55 44N 37 38 E
Trevose, Phil. 24 A5 40 8N 74 59W
Trezzano sul Navíglio, Mil. 9 E5 45 24N 9 4 E
Tribobo, Rio J. 31 B3 22 50 S 43 0W
Triel-sur-Seine, Paris 5 B2 48 58N 2 0 E
Trieste, Rome 9 F10 41 55N 12 30 E
Trinidad, Wash. 25 D8 38 54N 76 59W
Triome, Jobg. 18 F8 26 10 S 27 58 E
Trionfale, Rome 9 F9 41 54N 12 26 E
Triulzo, Mil. 9 E6 45 25N 9 16 E
Trócchia, Nápl. 9 H13 40 51N 14 23 E
Troitse-Lykovo, Mos. 11 E8 55 47N 37 23 E
Troja, Pra. 10 B2 50 7N 14 25 E
Trollbäcken, Stock. 3 E12 59 14N 18 12 E
Trombay, Bomb. 16 G8 19 2N 72 56 E
Troparevo, Mos. 11 F8 55 39N 37 29 E
Trottiscliffe, Lon. 4 D7 51 18N 0 21 E
Troy Hills, N.Y. 22 B2 40 50N 74 23W
Troyeville, Jobg. 18 F9 26 11 S 28 4 E
Truc di Miola, Tori. 9 A2 45 11N 7 30 E
Trudyashchikhsya, Os., St-Pet. 11 B3 59 58N 30 18 E
Trutlandet, Hels. 3 C6 60 9N 25 17 E
Tryvasshøgda, Oslo 2 B4 59 59N 10 40 E
Tseng Lan Shue, H.K. 12 D6 22 20N 114 14 E
Tsentralynyy, Mos. 11 D11 55 53N 37 51 E
Tsim Sha Tsui, H.K. 12 E6 22 17N 114 10 E
Tsing Yi, H.K. 12 D5 22 21N 114 6 E
Tsuen Wan, H.K. 12 D5 22 22N 114 7 E
Tsurugamine, Tōkyō 13 D2 35 28N 139 33 E
Tsuruma, Tōkyō 13 A2 35 52N 139 31 E
Tsurumi →, Tōkyō 13 C3 35 32N 139 40 E
Tsurumi-Ku, Tōkyō 13 D3 35 30N 139 41 E
Tsz Wan Shan, H.K. 12 D6 22 20N 114 11 E
Tua Kang Lye, Sing. 15 G7 1 18N 103 46 E
Tuas, Sing. 15 G6 1 19N 103 39 E
Tuchoměřice, Pra. 10 B1 50 7N 14 16 E
Tuckahoe, N.Y. 23 B6 40 56N 73 49W
Tucuruvi, S. Pau. 31 D6 23 28 S 46 35W
Tufello, Rome 9 F10 41 56N 12 32 E
Tufnell Park, Lon. 4 B4 51 33N 0 8W
Tujunga, L.A. 28 A3 34 15N 118 16W
Tujunga Wash →, L.A. 28 A2 34 12N 118 23W
Tullamarine, Melb. 19 E6 37 41 S 144 50 E
Tullinge, Stock. 3 E10 59 12N 17 54 E
Tullingesjön, Stock. 3 E10 59 12N 17 52 E
Tulse Hill, Lon. 4 C4 51 26N 0 6W
Tulyehualco, Méx. 29 C3 19 15N 99 0W
Tumba, Stock. 3 E9 59 12N 17 49 E
Tune, Købn. 2 E8 55 35N 12 10 E
Tung Lo Wan, H.K. 12 E6 22 17N 114 11 E
Tung Lung I., H.K. 12 E6 22 15N 114 17 E
Tung O, H.K. 12 E5 22 11N 114 8 E
Tunis, Bagd. 17 E8 33 23N 44 21 E
Tuomarila, Hels. 3 B3 60 11N 24 41 E
Tura, El Qâ. 18 D5 29 55N 31 16 E
Turambhe, Bomb. 16 G9 19 4N 73 0 E
Turdera, B.A. 32 C4 34 48 S 58 26W
Tureberg, Stock. 3 D10 59 25N 17 55 E
Turffontein, Jobg. 18 F9 26 14 S 28 2 E
Turin = Torino, Tori. 9 B2 45 5N 7 39 E
Turner, Balt. 25 B3 39 14N 76 31W
Turner Hill, Bost. 21 A4 42 40N 70 53W
Turnersville, Phil. 24 C4 39 46N 75 3W
Turnham Green, Lon. 4 C3 51 29N 0 16W
Turów, Wsaw. 10 E8 52 19N 21 11 E
Turter, Oslo 2 A4 60 0N 10 46 E
Tuscolano, Rome 9 F10 41 52N 12 31 E
Tushino, Mos. 11 D8 55 50N 37 24 E
Tuusulanjoki →, Hels. 3 A4 60 20N 24 54 E
Twickenham, Lon. 4 C2 51 26N 0 20W
Twickenham Rugby Ground, Lon. 4 C2 51 27N 0 20W
Twin Oaks, Phil. 24 B2 39 50N 75 25W
Twórki, Wsaw. 10 E5 52 10N 20 49 E
Tyresö, Stock. 3 E13 59 14N 18 20 E
Tyresö strand, Stock. 3 E12 59 15N 18 17 E


# U


Uberaba →, S. Pau. 31 E6 23 35 S 46 41W
Uberruhr, Ruhr 6 B4 51 25N 7 4 E
Ubin, P., Sing. 15 F8 1 24N 103 57 E
Uboldo, Mil. 9 D5 45 36N 9 0 E
Uckendorf, Ruhr 6 B4 51 29N 7 7 E
Udelnaya, St-Pet. 11 A4 60 0N 30 21 E
Udelynaya, Mos. 11 F11 55 38N 37 59 E
Udlding, Mün. 7 F9 48 15N 11 25 E
Uellendahl, Ruhr 6 C5 51 16N 7 10 E
Ueno, Tōkyō 13 B3 35 42N 139 46 E
Uerdingen, Ruhr 6 B1 51 21N 6 38 E
Uhlenhorst, Hbg. 7 D8 53 34N 10 1 E
Üholičky, Pra. 10 B1 50 9N 14 19 E
Uhřiněves, Pra. 10 B3 50 2N 14 35 E
Újezd nad Lesy, Pra. 10 B3 50 4N 14 39 E
Újpalota, Bud. 10 J13 47 32N 19 8 E
Újpest, Bud. 10 J13 47 35N 19 4 E
Ukita, Tōkyō 13 B4 35 40N 139 51 E
Ullerup, Købn. 2 E10 55 34N 12 36 E
Ullevål, Oslo 2 B4 59 56N 10 46 E
Üllo, Bud. 10 K14 47 23N 19 20 E
Ulriksdal, Stock. 3 D10 59 23N 17 59 E
Ulu Bedok, Sing. 15 G8 1 19N 103 55 E
Ulu Pandan →, Sing. 15 G7 1 19N 103 45 E
Ulyanka, St-Pet. 11 B3 59 50N 30 14 E
Um Al-Khanazir, Bagd. 17 F8 33 17N 44 22 E
Umeda, Ōsaka 12 B3 34 41N 135 29 E
Umejima, Tōkyō 13 B3 35 46N 139 48 E
Umraniye, Ist. 17 A3 41 1N 29 4 E
Unětický →, Pra. 10 B2 50 9N 14 24 E
Ungelsheim, Ruhr 6 B2 51 21N 6 43 E
Unhos, Lisb. 8 F8 38 49N 9 7W
Unidad Santa Fe, Méx. 29 B2 19 23N 99 13W
Union, N.Y. 22 C3 40 42N 74 16W
Union City, N.Y. 22 C4 40 45N 74 2W
Union City, S.F. 27 C4 37 36N 122 2W
Union Port, N.Y. 23 C5 40 48N 73 51W
Uniondale, N.Y. 23 C7 40 42N 73 35W
United Nations H.Q., N.Y. 22 C5 40 45N 73 59W
Universal City, L.A. 28 B2 34 8N 118 21W
Universidad de Chila, Stgo 30 J11 33 26 S 70 39W
University Gardens, N.Y. 23 C6 40 46N 73 42W
University Heights, S.F. 27 D3 37 26N 122 13W
University Park, Wash. 25 D8 38 58N 76 56W
Unsani, Calc. 16 E5 22 35N 88 15 E
Unterbach, Ruhr 6 C3 51 12N 6 53 E
Unterbiberg, Mün. 7 G10 48 6N 11 38 E
Unterföhring, Mün. 7 F11 48 11N 11 38 E
Unterhaching, Mün. 7 G10 48 3N 11 37 E
Unterkirchbach, Wien 10 G9 48 17N 16 12 E
Unterlaa, Wien 10 H10 48 8N 16 24 E
Untermauerbach, Wien 10 G9 48 14N 16 11 E
Untermenzing, Mün. 7 F9 48 10N 11 28 E
Unterrath, Ruhr 6 C2 51 16N 6 45 E
Unterschleissheim, Mün. 7 F10 48 16N 11 35 E
Upminster, Lon. 4 B6 51 33N 0 14 E
Upper Brookville, N.Y. 23 B7 40 50N 73 35W
Upper Crystal Springs Res., S.F. 26 D2 37 28N 122 20W
Upper Darby, Phil. 24 B3 39 57N 75 16W
Upper Edmonton, Lon. 4 B4 51 36N 0 3W
Upper Elmers End, Lon. 4 C4 51 23N 0 1W
Upper Fern Tree Gully, Melb. 19 F8 37 53 S 145 18 E
Upper New York B., N.Y. 22 D4 40 39N 74 3W
Upper Norwood, Lon. 4 C4 51 24N 0 6W
Upper Peirce Res., Sing. 15 F7 1 22N 103 47 E
Upper San Leandro Res., S.F. 27 B4 37 46N 122 6W
Upper Sydenham, Lon. 4 C4 51 26N 0 4W
Upper Tooting, Lon. 4 C4 51 25N 0 9W
Upton, Lon. 4 B5 51 32N 0 1 E
Uptons Hill, Bost. 21 B3 42 33N 71 0W
Uptown, Chic. 26 B2 41 58N 87 40W
Upwey, Melb. 19 F9 37 53 S 145 20 E
Urawa, Tōkyō 13 A2 35 51N 139 39 E
Urayasu, Tōkyō 13 C4 35 39N 139 53 E
Urbe, Aeroporto d', Rome 9 F10 41 57N 12 30 E
Urca, Rio J. 31 B3 22 56 S 43 9W
Uritsk, St-Pet. 11 C3 59 49N 30 10 E
Üröm, Bud. 10 J13 47 35N 19 1 E
Ursus, Wsaw. 10 E6 52 11N 20 52 E
Ursvik, Stock. 3 D10 59 23N 17 57 E
Usera, Mdrd. 8 B2 40 22N 3 42W
Ushigome, Tōkyō 13 B3 35 42N 139 44 E
Usküdar, Ist. 17 A3 41 1N 29 0 E
Ust-Slavyanka, St-Pet. 11 C5 59 51N 30 32 E
Uteke, Stock. 3 D12 59 24N 18 15 E
Utfort, Ruhr 6 B1 51 28N 6 37 E
Utinga, S. Pau. 31 E6 23 38 S 46 31W
Utrata, Wsaw. 10 E7 52 15N 21 4 E
Uttarpara, Calc. 16 E5 22 39N 88 21 E
Utterslev Mose, Købn. 2 D9 55 42N 12 29 E
Uttran, Stock. 3 E9 59 12N 17 43 E
Utvika, Oslo 2 A1 60 2N 10 15 E
Uxbridge, Lon. 4 B2 51 32N 0 28W
Uzkoye, Mos. 11 F9 55 37N 37 32 E
Uzunca →, Ist. 17 A1 41 54N 28 50 E


# V


Vadaul, Bomb. 16 G8 19 2N 72 55 E
Værebro Å →, Købn. 2 D8 55 47N 12 7 E
Vahal, Bomb. 16 H9 18 58N 73 2 E
Vaires-sur-Marne, Paris 5 B5 48 52N 2 38 E
Val della Torre, Tori. 9 B1 45 8N 7 27 E
Valby, Købn. 2 E9 55 39N 12 29 E
Valcannuta, Rome 9 F9 41 52N 12 25 E
Valdeveba, Mdrd. 8 B3 40 29N 3 39W
Vale, Wash. 25 D5 38 55N 77 20W
Valentino, Parco del, Tori. 9 B3 45 3N 7 41 E
Valenton, Paris 5 C4 48 44N 2 27 E
Valera, Mil. 9 D5 45 33N 9 3 E
Vallcarca, Barc. 8 D5 41 25N 2 9 E
Valldoreix, Barc. 8 D5 41 27N 2 3 E
Vallecas, Mdrd. 8 B3 40 22N 3 37W
Vallemar, S.F. 27 C2 37 36N 122 28W
Vallensbæk, Købn. 2 E9 55 38N 12 21 E
Vallensbæk Strand, Købn. 2 E9 55 36N 12 23 E
Vallentunasjön, Stock. 3 D11 59 27N 18 1 E
Valleranello, Rome 9 G9 41 46N 12 29 E
Valley Forge, Phil. 24 A2 40 5N 75 27W
Valley Forge Hist. State Park, Phil. 24 A2 40 5N 75 27W
Valley Mede, Balt. 25 B1 39 16N 76 50W
Valley Stream, N.Y. 23 C6 40 40N 73 43W
Vällingby, Stock. 3 D10 59 21N 17 52 E
Vallisaari, Hels. 3 C5 60 7N 25 0 E
Vallvidrera, Barc. 8 D5 41 24N 2 6 E
Valo Velho, S. Pau. 31 E5 23 38 S 46 47W
Valuyevo, Mos. 11 F8 55 30N 37 21 E
Valvidrera →, Barc. 8 D5 41 25N 2 0 E
Van Dyks Park, Jobg. 18 F10 26 15 S 28 18 E
Van Nuys, L.A. 28 A2 34 11N 118 27W
Van Nuys Airport, L.A. 28 A2 34 12N 118 29W
Van Ryn Dam, Jobg. 18 E11 26 8 S 28 21 E
Vanak, Tehr. 17 C5 35 45N 51 23 E
Vangede, Købn. 2 D10 55 45N 12 30 E
Vaniköy, Ist. 17 A3 41 3N 29 3 E
Vanløse, Købn. 2 D9 55 41N 12 28 E
Vantaa, Hels. 3 B4 60 18N 24 56 E
Vantaa →, Hels. 3 B4 60 13N 24 53 E
Vantaankoski, Hels. 3 B4 60 18N 24 50 E
Vantör, Stock. 3 E11 59 16N 18 2 E
Vanves, Paris 5 C3 48 49N 2 17 E
Vanzago, Mil. 9 D4 45 31N 8 59 E
Värby, Stock. 3 E10 59 15N 17 52 E
Vardåsen, Oslo 2 C6 50 48N 11 6 E
Varedo, Mil. 9 D5 45 35N 9 8 E
Varennes-Jarcy, Paris 5 C5 48 40N 2 33 E
Vargem Grande, Rio J. 31 B1 22 58 S 43 27W
Városliget, Bud. 10 J13 47 30N 19 5 E
Vartiokylä, Hels. 3 B5 60 13N 25 6 E
Vartiosaari, Hels. 3 B5 60 11N 25 5 E
Vasby, Købn. 2 D8 55 40N 12 12 E
Vashi, Bomb. 16 G8 19 4N 72 59 E
Vasilyevskiy, Os., St-Pet. 11 B3 59 55N 30 16 E
Västerkulla, Hels. 3 B2 60 16N 24 31 E
Västerskog, Hels. 3 B6 60 16N 25 17 E
Vasto, Nápl. 9 H12 40 51N 14 16 E
Vatutino, Mos. 11 D10 55 52N 37 40 E
Vaucresson, Paris 5 B2 48 50N 2 9 E
Vaudreuil, Mtrl. 20 B1 43 24N 74 1W
Vaudreuil-sur-le Lac, Mtrl. 20 B1 43 25N 74 1W
Vauhallan, Paris 5 C3 48 44N 2 12 E
Vaujours, Paris 5 B5 48 56N 2 34 E
Vauréal, Paris 5 A2 49 2N 2 1 E
Vaux-sur-Seine, Paris 5 A1 49 0N 1 57 E
Vauxhall, Lon. 4 C4 51 29N 0 7W
Vaxholm, Stock. 3 D13 59 24N 18 20 E
Vecklax, Hels. 3 B2 60 10N 24 31 E
Vecsés, Bud. 10 K14 47 24N 19 16 E
Vedano al Lissone, Mil. 9 D6 45 36N 9 16 E
Veddel, Hbg. 7 D8 53 31N 10 2 E
Vega, Stock. 3 E11 59 11N 18 8 E
Vehkalahti, Hels. 3 B2 60 11N 24 30 E
Veikkola, Hels. 3 B1 60 17N 24 26 E
Velbert, Ruhr 6 B4 51 21N 7 1 E
Veleň, Pra. 10 A3 50 10N 14 33 E
Veleslavin, Pra. 10 B2 50 5N 14 21 E
Vélizy-Villacoublay, Paris 5 C3 48 47N 2 11 E
Velka-Chuchle, Pra. 10 B2 50 0N 14 23 E
Venaria, Tori. 9 B2 45 8N 7 37 E
Venda Seca, Lisb. 8 F7 38 46N 9 15W
Vendelsö, Stock. 3 E12 59 12N 18 11 E
Venice, L.A. 28 C2 33 59N 118 27W
Venner, Oslo 2 A3 60 1N 10 36 E
Vennhausen, Ruhr 6 C3 51 13N 6 51 E
Ventas, Mdrd. 8 B2 40 26N 3 40W
Ventorro del Cano, Mdrd. 8 B2 40 23N 3 49W
Verberg, Ruhr 6 B1 51 21N 6 34 E
Verde →, S. Pau. 31 E7 23 29 S 46 27W
Verdi, Ath. 8 H11 38 2N 23 40 E
Verdugo Mt., L.A. 28 A3 34 12N 118 17W
Verdun, Mtrl. 20 B4 43 27N 73 35W
Vereya, Mos. 11 F12 55 37N 38 2 E
Vérhalom, Bud. 10 J13 47 31N 19 1 E
Vermelho →, S. Pau. 31 E5 23 30 S 46 46W
Vermont, Melb. 19 F8 37 50 S 145 12 E
Vermont South, Melb. 19 F8 37 51 S 145 11 E
Verneuil-sur-Seine, Paris 5 B1 48 58N 1 59 E
Vernouillet, Paris 5 B1 48 58N 1 56 E
Verona, N.Y. 22 C3 40 49N 74 15W
Verperluda, Os., St-Pet. 11 B2 59 59N 30 0 E
Verrières-le-Buisson, Paris 5 C3 48 44N 2 16 E
Versailles, B.A. 32 B3 34 38 S 58 31W
Versailles, Paris 5 C2 48 48N 2 7 E
Veshnyaki, Mos. 11 E10 55 43N 37 48 E
Vesolyy Posolok, St-Pet. 11 B4 59 53N 30 28 E
Vestli, Oslo 2 B5 59 58N 10 55 E
Vestra, Hels. 3 B3 60 19N 24 46 E
Vestskoven, Købn. 2 D9 55 41N 12 23 E
Vesuvio, Nápl. 9 J13 40 49N 14 25 E
Vets Stadium, Phil. 24 B3 39 54N 75 10W
Viby, Købn. 2 E7 55 33N 12 1 E
Vicálvaro, Mdrd. 8 B3 40 24N 3 36W
Vicente Lopez, B.A. 32 B4 34 31 S 58 30W
Victoria, B.A. 32 A3 34 27 S 58 32W
Victoria, H.K. 12 E6 22 17N 114 11 E
Victoria, Pont, Mtrl. 20 B4 43 29N 73 32W
Victoria Gardens, Bomb. 16 H8 18 58N 72 50 E
Victoria Harbour, H.K. 12 E5 22 17N 114 10 E
Victoria Island, Lagos 18 B2 6 25N 7 25 E
Victoria L., Jobg. 18 F9 26 13 S 28 9 E
Victoria Lawn Tennis Courts, Melb. 19 F7 37 50 S 145 1 E
Victoria Park, H.K. 12 E5 22 16N 114 8 E
Vidja, Stock. 3 E11 59 12N 18 4 E
Vidrholec, Pra. 10 B3 50 5N 14 39 E
Vienna = Wien, Wien 10 G10 48 12N 16 22 E
Vienna, Wash. 25 D6 38 54N 77 16W
Vieringhausen, Ruhr 6 C4 51 10N 7 9 E
Vierlinden, Ruhr 6 A2 51 32N 6 45 E
Vierumäki, Hels. 3 A5 60 21N 25 2 E
Vierzigstücken, Hbg. 7 D6 53 30N 9 49 E
View Bank, Melb. 19 E7 37 43 S 145 6 E
Vigárío Geral, Rio J. 31 A2 22 48 S 43 18W
Vigentino, Mil. 9 E6 45 26N 9 13 E
Viggbyholm, Stock. 3 D11 59 26N 18 7 E
Vighignolo, Mil. 9 E5 45 29N 9 2 E
Vigneux-sur-Seine, Paris 5 C4 48 42N 2 24 E
Viikki, Hels. 3 B5 60 13N 25 1 E
Viirilä, Hels. 3 B5 60 19N 25 8 E
Vila Andrade, S. Pau. 31 E5 23 37 S 46 44W
Vila Barcelona, S. Pau. 31 E6 23 37 S 46 33W
Vila Bocaina, S. Pau. 31 F7 23 40 S 46 26W
Vila Dalva, S. Pau. 31 E5 23 34 S 46 46W
Vila Dirce, S. Pau. 31 E4 23 33 S 46 50W
Vila Eldorado, S. Pau. 31 F6 23 42 S 46 38W
Vila Ema, S. Pau. 31 E6 23 35 S 46 31W
Vila Formosa, S. Pau. 31 E6 23 36 S 46 44W
Vila Galvão, S. Pau. 31 D6 23 27 S 46 34W
Vila Gonçales, S. Pau. 31 F6 23 42 S 46 33W
Vila Iasi, S. Pau. 31 E5 23 37 S 46 47W
Vila Indiana, S. Pau. 31 E5 23 37 S 46 48W
Vila Isabel, Rio J. 31 B2 22 54 S 43 15W
Vila Madalena, S. Pau. 31 E5 23 32 S 46 41W
Vila Maria, S. Pau. 31 E6 23 31 S 46 36W
Vila Mariana, S. Pau. 31 E6 23 34 S 46 36W
Vila Matilde, S. Pau. 31 E6 23 31 S 46 30W
Vila Nova Curuçá, S. Pau. 31 E7 23 31 S 46 25W
Vila Pires, S. Pau. 31 F6 23 41 S 46 30W
Vila Progresso, Rio J. 31 B3 22 53 S 43 1W
Vila Prudente, S. Pau. 31 E6 23 35 S 46 33W
Vila Ré, S. Pau. 31 E7 23 31 S 46 29W
Vila Remo, S. Pau. 31 F5 23 40 S 46 45W
Vila Sonia, S. Pau. 31 E5 23 35 S 46 43W
Viladecans, Barc. 8 E5 41 18N 2 1 E
Villa Ada, Rome 9 F10 41 55N 12 30 E
Villa Adelina, B.A. 32 B3 34 31 S 58 33W
Villa Alianza, B.A. 32 B3 34 37 S 58 33W
Villa Alsina, B.A. 32 C4 34 40 S 58 24W
Villa Altube, B.A. 32 B2 34 31 S 58 45W
Villa Ariza, B.A. 32 B3 34 38 S 58 39W
Villa Augusta, B.A. 32 C5 34 45 S 58 15W
Villa Ballester, B.A. 32 B3 34 33 S 58 33W
Villa Barilari, B.A. 32 C4 34 42 S 58 20W
Villa Basso, B.A. 32 B3 34 38 S 58 36W
Villa Bosch, B.A. 32 B3 34 35 S 58 33W
Villa C. Colon, B.A. 32 C4 34 41 S 58 21W
Villa D. F. Sarmiento, B.A. 32 B3 34 38 S 58 35W
Villa D. Sobral, B.A. 32 C5 34 45 S 58 15W
Villa de Guadalupe, Méx. 29 B3 19 29N 99 6W
Villa de Mayo, B.A. 32 B2 34 30 S 58 40W
Villa Devoto, B.A. 32 B3 34 36 S 58 31W
Villa Dominico, B.A. 32 C5 34 41 S 58 19W
Villa Giambruno, B.A. 32 C5 34 48 S 58 15W
Villa Gustavo A. Madero, Méx. 29 B3 19 29N 99 8W
Villa Hogar Alemán, B.A. 32 C4 34 49 S 58 26W
Villa Iglesias, B.A. 32 B2 34 30 S 58 45W
Villa Leloir, B.A. 32 B2 34 36 S 58 41W
Villa Leon, B.A. 32 B2 34 38 S 58 41W
Villa Lugano, B.A. 32 C4 34 41 S 58 27W
Villa Luzuriago, B.A. 32 C3 34 40 S 58 34W
Villa Lynch, B.A. 32 B3 34 35 S 58 31W
Villa Madero, B.A. 32 C3 34 41 S 58 30W
Villa Maria del Triunfo, Lima 30 G9 12 9 S 76 57W
Villa Obregon, Méx. 29 B2 19 20N 99 12W
Villa Reichembach, B.A. 32 B2 34 39 S 58 40W
Villa Rosa, B.A. 32 A1 34 25 S 58 5W
Villa San Francisco, B.A. 32 C5 34 46 S 58 15W
Villacoublay, Aérodrome de, Paris 5 C3 48 46N 2 12 E
Village Green, Phil. 24 B2 39 52N 75 26W
Villanova, Phil. 24 A2 40 1N 75 20W
Villarbasse, Tori. 9 B1 45 2N 7 27 E
Villaretto, Tori. 9 B3 45 8N 7 41 E
Villaricca, Nápl. 9 H12 40 55N 14 11 E
Villaroche, Paris 5 D5 48 37N 2 39 E
Villaroy, Paris 5 C2 48 46N 2 5 E
Villasanta, Mil. 9 D6 45 36N 9 18 E
Villastanza, Mil. 9 D4 45 32N 8 57 E
Villaverde, Mdrd. 8 B2 40 21N 3 42W
Villaverde Bajo, Mdrd. 8 B2 40 20N 3 40W
Villawood, Syd. 19 B2 33 52 S 150 58 E
Ville-d'Avray, Paris 5 C3 48 49N 2 11 E
Ville de Laval, Mtrl. 20 A3 43 34N 73 43W
Villebon-sur-Yvette, Paris 5 C3 48 41N 2 14 E
Villecresnes, Paris 5 C5 48 43N 2 31 E

48 Villejuif


Villejuif, *Paris* 5 C4 48 47N 2 21 E
Villejust, *Paris* 5 C3 48 41N 2 15 E
Villemoisson-sur-Orge, *Paris* 5 C3 48 40N 2 19 E
Villemomble, *Paris* 5 B5 48 52N 2 30 E
Villeneuve-la-Garenne, *Paris* 5 B3 48 56N 2 19 E
Villeneuve-le-Roi, *Paris* 5 C4 48 43N 2 24 E
Villeneuve-St.-Georges, *Paris* 5 C4 48 43N 2 27 E
Villeneuve-sous-Dammartin, *Paris* 5 A5 49 2N 2 38 E
Villennes-sur-Seine, *Paris* 5 B1 48 56N 2 0 E
Villeparisis, *Paris* 5 B5 48 56N 2 36 E
Villepinte, *Paris* 5 B5 48 57N 2 30 E
Villepreux, *Paris* 5 C1 48 49N 1 59 E
Villevaudé, *Paris* 5 B5 48 55N 2 39 E
Villeziers, *Paris* 5 C3 48 40N 2 10 E
Villiers-le-Bâcle, *Paris* 5 C2 48 44N 2 8 E
Villiers-le-Bel, *Paris* 5 A4 49 0N 2 23 E
Villiers-St. Frédéric, *Paris* 5 C1 48 49N 1 53 E
Villiers-sur-Marne, *Paris* 5 C5 48 49N 2 32 E
Villiers-sur-Orge, *Paris* 5 D3 48 39N 2 18 E
Villinki, *Hels.* 3 C5 60 9N 25 6 E
Villoresi, Canale, *Mil.* 9 D4 45 33N 8 59 E
Vimodrone, *Mil.* 9 D6 45 30N 9 16 E
Vimont, *Mtrl.* 20 A3 43 36N 73 43W
Vincennes, *Paris* 5 B4 48 51N 2 26 E
Vincennes, Bois de, *Paris* 5 C4 48 49N 2 26 E
Vinohrady, *Pra.* 10 B2 50 4N 14 26 E
Vinoř, *Pra.* 10 B3 50 8N 14 34 E
Vinořský →, *Pra.* 10 A3 50 11N 14 39 E
Violet Hill, *H.K.* 12 E6 22 15N 114 11 E
Virányos, *Bud.* 10 J12 47 31N 18 59 E
Virgeo del San Cristóbal, *Stgo* 30 J11 33 25 S 70 38W
Viroflay, *Paris* 5 C3 48 48N 2 10 E
Viron, *Ath.* 8 J11 37 55N 23 46 E
Virreyes, *B.A.* 32 A3 34 27 S 58 33W
Virum, *Købn.* 2 D9 55 47N 12 27 E
Viry-Châtillon, *Paris* 5 C4 48 40N 2 21 E
Vishnyaki, *Mos.* 11 E11 55 46N 37 53 E
Visitacion Valley, *S.F.* 27 B2 37 42N 122 23W
Vista Alegre, *Lima* 30 G9 12 8 S 76 59W
Vista Alegre, *Stgo* 30 K10 33 30 S 70 43W
Vitacura, *Stgo* 30 J11 33 23 S 70 35W
Vitarte-Ate, *Lima* 30 G9 12 3 S 76 57W
Vitinia, *Rome* 9 G9 41 47N 12 24 E
Vitry-sur-Seine, *Paris* 5 C4 48 47N 2 23 E
Vitträsk, *Hels.* 3 B1 60 11N 24 29 E
Vittuone, *Mil.* 9 E4 45 28N 8 57 E
Vladykino, *Mos.* 11 D9 55 51N 37 35 E
Vltava →, *Pra.* 10 A2 50 10N 14 2 E
Vnukovo, *Mos.* 11 F7 55 37N 37 17 E
Voerde, *Ruhr* 6 C6 51 18N 7 23 E
Voerde, *Ruhr* 6 A2 51 35N 6 42 E
Vogelheim, *Ruhr* 6 B3 51 29N 6 59 E
Vohwinkel, *Ruhr* 6 C4 51 13N 7 4 E
Voisins-le-Bretonneux, *Paris* 5 C2 48 45N 2 3 E
Vokovice, *Pra.* 10 B2 50 5N 14 21 E
Volgelsdorf, *Berl.* 7 B5 52 30N 13 44 E
Volkhonka-Zil, *Mos.* 11 F9 55 39N 37 37 E
Volkovka →, *St-Pet.* 11 B4 59 54N 30 25 E
Volksdorf, *Hbg.* 7 D8 53 39N 10 8 E
Volla, *Nápl.* 9 H13 40 52N 14 20 E
Vollen, *Oslo* 2 C2 59 48N 10 27 E
Volmarstein, *Ruhr* 6 B6 51 22N 7 22 E
Volodarskoye, *St-Pet.* 11 B4 59 54N 30 23 E
Volpiano, *Tori.* 9 A3 45 12N 7 46 E
Volynkina-Derevnya, *St-Pet.* 11 B3 59 53N 30 18 E
Volynyy, Os., *St-Pet.* 11 B3 59 57N 30 14 E
Võmero, *Nápl.* 9 H12 40 50N 14 13 E
Vorderhainbach, *Wien* 10 G9 48 13N 16 12 E
Vorhalle, *Ruhr* 6 B6 51 23N 7 26 E
Vormholz, *Ruhr* 6 B5 51 24N 7 19 E
Vösendorf, *Wien* 10 H10 48 7N 16 20 E
Vostochnyy, *Mos.* 11 E11 55 49N 37 51 E
Vouliagmeni, *Ath.* 8 K11 37 50N 23 46 E
Vrčovice, *Pra.* 10 B2 50 4N 14 28 E
Vsevolozhsk, *St-Pet.* 11 A5 60 0N 30 39 E
Vuosaari, *Hels.* 3 B5 60 13N 25 8 E
Vyborgskaya Storona, *St-Pet.* 11 B4 59 57N 30 22 E
Vyčehrad, *Pra.* 10 B2 50 3N 14 25 E
Vykhino, *Mos.* 11 E10 55 42N 37 48 E
Vysočany, *Pra.* 10 B2 50 6N 14 29 E


# W


Waban, L., *Bost.* 21 D2 42 17N 71 18W
Wachterhof, *Mün.* 7 G11 48 2N 11 42 E
Waddington, *Lon.* 4 D4 51 18N 0 7W
Wadeville, *Jobg.* 18 F10 26 15 S 28 11 E
Wahda, *Bagd.* 17 F8 33 18N 44 26 E
Währing, *Wien* 10 G10 48 14N 16 20 E
Waidmannslust, *Berl.* 7 A3 52 36N 13 20 E
Wajay, *La Hab.* 30 B2 23 0N 82 25W
Wakefield, *Bost.* 21 B3 42 30N 71 5W
Wald, *Ruhr* 6 C4 51 11N 7 3 E
Waldesruh, *Berl.* 7 B4 52 28N 13 37 E
Waldheim, *Berl.* 7 A1 52 34N 13 3 E
Waldperlach, *Mün.* 7 G11 48 4N 11 40 E
Waldtrudering, *Mün.* 7 G11 48 6N 11 42 E
Waldwick, *N.Y.* 22 A4 41 1N 74 5W
Wall Street, *N.Y.* 22 C4 40 42N 74 0W
Wallgrove, *Syd.* 19 A2 33 47 S 150 51 E
Wallington, *Lon.* 4 C4 51 21N 0 8W
Wallington, *N.Y.* 22 B4 40 50N 74 8W
Walnut Cr. →, *S.F.* 27 A4 37 55N 122 3W
Walnut Creek, *S.F.* 27 A4 37 53N 122 3W
Walnut Heights, *S.F.* 27 A4 37 52N 122 2W
Walsum, *Ruhr* 6 A2 51 32N 6 42 E
Walsumer Mark, *Ruhr* 6 A3 51 33N 6 50 E
Walt Whitman Br., *Phil.* 24 B4 39 4N 75 9W
Waltershof, *Hbg.* 7 D7 53 31N 9 54 E
Waltham, *Bost.* 21 C2 42 23N 71 14W
Waltham Abbey, *Lon.* 4 A5 51 41N 0 1 E
Waltham Forest, *Lon.* 4 B4 51 36N 0 0 E
Walthamstow, *Lon.* 4 B4 51 34N 0 1W
Walton on Thames, *Lon.* 4 C2 51 22N 0 23W
Walton on the Hill, *Lon.* 4 D3 51 16N 0 14W
Waltrop, *Ruhr* 6 A6 51 36N 7 25 E
Walworth, *Lon.* 4 C4 51 29N 0 5W
Wambachsee, *Ruhr* 6 B2 51 23N 6 47 E
Wan Chai, *H.K.* 12 E6 22 16N 114 10 E
Wanaque, *N.Y.* 22 A3 41 1N 74 17W
Wandezhuang, *Tianj.* 14 E5 39 6N 117 10 E
Wandle →, *Lon.* 4 C3 51 27N 0 11W
Wandsbek, *Hbg.* 7 D8 53 34N 10 4 E
Wandsworth, *Lon.* 4 C3 51 27N 0 11W
Wang Hin, Khlong →, *Bangk.* 15 A2 13 50N 100 35 E
Wanheim, *Ruhr* 6 B2 51 23N 6 45 E
Wanheimerort, *Ruhr* 6 B2 51 24N 6 45 E
Wanne-Eickel, *Ruhr* 6 A4 51 31N 7 9 E
Wannsee, *Berl.* 7 B1 52 25N 13 9 E
Wansdorf, *Berl.* 7 A1 52 38N 13 5 E
Wanstead, *Lon.* 4 B5 51 34N 0 1 E
Wantagh Seaford, *N.Y.* 23 D8 40 39N 73 28W
Wantirna, *Melb.* 19 F8 37 50 S 145 14 E
Wapping, *Lon.* 4 B4 51 30N 0 3W
Warabi, *Tōkyō* 13 B3 35 49N 139 42 E
Ward, *Phil.* 24 B1 39 52N 75 30W
Warlingham, *Lon.* 4 D4 51 18N 0 2W
Warnberg, *Mün.* 7 G10 48 4N 11 31 E
Warngal Park, *Melb.* 19 E7 37 45 S 145 4 E
Warrandyte, *Melb.* 19 E8 37 43 S 145 13 E
Warrandyte Park, *Melb.* 19 E8 37 44 S 145 14 E
Warrandyte South, *Melb.* 19 E8 37 44 S 145 14 E
Warranwood, *Melb.* 19 E8 37 46 S 145 14 E
Warrâq el 'Arab, *El Qâ.* 18 C5 30 4N 31 11 E
Warrâq el Hadf, *El Qâ.* 18 C5 30 5N 31 12 E
Warren Hill, *Bost.* 21 B1 42 35N 71 21W
Warsaw = Warszawa, *Wsaw.* 10 E7 52 14N 21 0 E
Warszawa, *Wsaw.* 10 E7 52 14N 21 0 E
Wartenberg, *Berl.* 7 A4 52 34N 13 31 E
Warwick Farm Racetrack, *Syd.* 19 B2 33 54 S 150 56 E
Wasa, *Stock.* 3 E11 59 19N 18 5 E
Wasfanārd, *Tehr.* 17 D5 35 38N 51 20 E
Washington, *Wash.* 25 D7 38 53N 77 2W
Washington Heights, *N.Y.* 22 B5 40 51N 73 56W
Washington Memorial Museum, *Phil.* 24 A2 40 5N 75 26W
Washington Nat. Airport, *Wash.* 25 D7 38 51N 77 2W
Washington Park, *Chic.* 26 C3 41 47N 87 36W
Washington Square, *Phil.* 24 A3 40 9N 75 19W
Washington Township, *N.Y.* 22 A4 41 0N 74 3W
Wasserschloss, *Ruhr* 6 A4 51 32N 7 1 E
Watching Mts., *N.Y.* 22 C2 40 43N 74 20W
Watchung, *N.Y.* 22 D2 40 38N 74 29W
Waterloo, *Syd.* 19 B4 33 53 S 151 12 E
Waterman Mt., *L.A.* 28 A5 34 14N 117 56W
Watertown, *Bost.* 21 C2 42 22N 71 10W
Watford, *Lon.* 4 A2 51 40N 0 27W
Watkins Island, *Wash.* 25 C6 39 2N 77 15W
Watsonia, *Melb.* 19 E7 37 43 S 145 6 E
Watsons B., *Syd.* 19 B4 33 50 S 151 18 E
Watsons Creek, *Melb.* 19 E8 37 40 S 145 13 E
Wattenscheid, *Ruhr* 6 B4 51 28N 7 8 E
Wattle Glen, *Melb.* 19 D8 37 39 S 145 11 E
Wattle Park, *Melb.* 19 F7 37 50 S 145 6 E
Watts →, *Wash.* 25 C6 39 2N 77 15W
Waverley, *Bost.* 21 C2 42 23N 71 10W
Waverley, *Jobg.* 18 E9 26 7 S 28 4 E
Waverley, *Syd.* 19 B4 33 53 S 151 15 E
Wawer, *Wsaw.* 10 E7 52 13N 21 8 E
Wawrzyszew, *Wsaw.* 10 E6 52 17N 20 53 E
Wayland, *Bost.* 21 C1 42 21N 71 20W
Wayne, *N.Y.* 22 B3 40 55N 74 15W
Wayne, *Phil.* 24 A2 40 2N 75 24W
Wazirabad, *Delhi* 16 A2 28 43N 77 13 E
Wazīrīya, *Bagd.* 17 E8 33 22N 44 23 E
Wazirpur, *Delhi* 16 A2 28 41N 77 10 E
Weald Park, *Lon.* 4 B6 51 37N 0 16 E
Wedding, *Berl.* 7 A3 52 32N 13 21 E
Weehawken, *N.Y.* 22 C4 40 45N 74 2W
Wegendorf, *Berl.* 7 A5 52 36N 13 45 E
Wehofen, *Ruhr* 6 A2 51 31N 6 46 E
Wehringhausen, *Ruhr* 6 B6 51 21N 7 28 E
Weidling, *Wien* 10 G9 48 17N 16 18 E
Weidling →, *Wien* 10 G9 48 17N 16 19 E
Weidlingbach, *Wien* 10 G9 48 16N 16 15 E
Weigongcum, *Beij.* 14 B2 39 57N 116 16 E
Weijin He →, *Tianj.* 14 E6 39 3N 117 12 E
Weissensee, *Berl.* 7 A3 52 33N 13 27 E
Weitmar, *Ruhr* 6 B5 51 27N 7 11 E
Welcome Monument, *Jak.* 15 J9 6 12N 106 49 E
Weller Creek, *Chic.* 26 A1 42 2N 87 52W
Wellesley, *Bost.* 21 D2 42 17N 71 17W
Wellesley Fells, *Bost.* 21 D2 42 18N 71 18W
Wellesley Hills, *Bost.* 21 D2 42 18N 71 16W
Welling, *Lon.* 4 C5 51 27N 0 6 E
Wellingsbüttel, *Hbg.* 7 D8 53 38N 10 6 E
Weltevreden Park Extension, *Jobg.* 18 E8 26 7 S 27 56 E
Wembley, *Lon.* 4 B3 51 33N 0 17W
Wembley Stadium, *Jobg.* 18 F9 26 13 S 28 1 E
Wembley Stadium, *Lon.* 4 B3 51 33N 0 16W
Wemmer Pan, *Jobg.* 18 F9 26 13 S 28 3 E
Wendenschloss, *Berl.* 7 B4 52 24N 13 35 E
Wengern, *Ruhr* 6 B6 51 24N 7 20 E
Wenham, *Bost.* 21 B4 42 36N 70 53W
Wenham L., *Bost.* 21 B4 42 35N 70 53W
Wenhuagong, *Tianj.* 14 E6 39 5N 117 14 E
Wennington, *Lon.* 4 B6 51 30N 0 12 E
Wenonah, *Phil.* 24 C4 39 47N 75 9W
Wentworthville, *Syd.* 19 A2 33 48 S 150 58 E
Werden, *Ruhr* 6 B4 51 23N 7 1 E
Werne, *Ruhr* 6 B5 51 29N 7 18 E
Werneuchen, *Berl.* 7 A5 52 38N 13 44 E
Wesoła, *Wsaw.* 10 E8 52 15N 21 13 E
West Andover, *Bost.* 21 B2 42 39N 71 10W
West Babylon, *N.Y.* 23 C8 40 43N 73 21W
West Bedford, *Bost.* 21 C2 42 28N 71 18W
West Berlin, *Phil.* 24 C5 39 48N 74 56W
West Boxford, *Bost.* 21 A3 42 42N 71 3W
West Caldwell, *N.Y.* 22 B3 40 51N 74 16W
West Chelmsford, *Bost.* 21 B1 42 36N 71 23W
West Chester, *Phil.* 24 B1 39 57N 75 35W
West Concord, *Bost.* 21 C1 42 27N 71 24W
West Covina, *L.A.* 28 B5 34 4N 117 55W
West Don →, *Trto.* 20 D8 43 44N 79 24W
West Drayton, *Lon.* 4 B2 51 30N 0 28W
West Dulwich, *Lon.* 4 C4 51 26N 0 5W
West Edmondale, *Balt.* 25 B2 39 17N 76 42W
West Ham, *Lon.* 4 B5 51 31N 0 1 E
West Harrow, *Lon.* 4 B2 51 34N 0 21W
West Heath, *Lon.* 4 C5 51 29N 0 7 E
West Hempstead, *N.Y.* 23 C7 40 41N 73 38W
West Hill, *Trto.* 20 D9 43 46N 79 10W
West Hollywood, *L.A.* 28 B2 34 5N 118 21W
West Hoxton, *Syd.* 19 B1 33 55 S 150 49 E
West Islip, *N.Y.* 23 C9 40 41N 73 18W
West Kingsdown, *Lon.* 4 C6 51 20N 0 15 E
West Lamma Channel, *H.K.* 12 E5 22 14N 114 4 E
West Lynn, *Bost.* 21 C4 42 27N 70 58W
West Medford, *Bost.* 21 C3 42 25N 71 7W
West New York, *N.Y.* 22 C4 40 46N 74 1W
West Norwood, *N.Y.* 22 B5 40 59N 73 58W
West of Twin Peaks, *S.F.* 27 B2 37 43N 122 27W
West Orange, *N.Y.* 22 C3 40 46N 74 15W
West Park, *Jobg.* 18 E8 26 9 S 27 59 E
West Paterson, *N.Y.* 22 B3 40 54N 74 11W
West Rouge, *Trto.* 20 D10 43 48N 79 7W
West Roxbury, *Bost.* 21 D3 42 16N 71 9W
West Springfield, *Wash.* 25 E6 38 47N 77 13W
West Thurrock, *Lon.* 4 C6 51 28N 0 16 E
West Town, *Chic.* 26 B2 41 53N 87 42W
West Wharf, *Kar.* 17 H10 24 49N 66 58 E
West Wickham, *Lon.* 4 C4 51 22N 0 0 E
Westbury, *N.Y.* 23 C7 40 45N 73 34W
Westchester, *Chic.* 26 B1 41 51N 87 53W
Westchester, *N.Y.* 23 B5 40 51N 73 51W
Westcliff, *Jobg.* 18 F9 26 10 S 28 1 E
Westdale, *Chic.* 26 B1 41 55N 87 54W
Westdene, *Jobg.* 18 F8 26 10 S 27 59 E
Westend, *Hels.* 3 C3 60 9N 24 48 E
Westerbauer, *Ruhr* 6 B6 51 20N 7 23 E
Westerham, *Lon.* 4 D5 51 16N 0 4 E
Westerham, *Mün.* 7 G10 48 3N 11 36 E
Westerholt, *Ruhr* 6 A4 51 36N 7 5 E
Westerleigh, *N.Y.* 22 D4 40 37N 74 7W
Western Addition, *S.F.* 27 B2 37 47N 122 25W
Western Run →, *Balt.* 25 A2 39 22N 76 39W
Western Springs, *Chic.* 26 C1 41 47N 87 52W
Westfalenhalle, *Ruhr* 6 B6 51 29N 7 27 E
Westfield, *N.Y.* 22 D2 40 39N 74 21W
Westlake, *S.F.* 27 B2 37 42N 122 29W
Westmeadows, *Melb.* 19 D6 37 39 S 144 55 E
Westminster, *Lon.* 4 B4 51 30N 0 7W
Westminster Abbey, *Lon.* 4 C4 51 29N 0 7W
Westmont, *Phil.* 24 B4 39 54N 75 3W
Westmount, *Mtrl.* 20 B4 43 29N 73 35W
Weston, *Bost.* 21 C2 42 22N 71 16W
Weston, *Trto.* 20 D7 43 42N 79 30W
Weston Res., *Bost.* 21 C2 42 20N 71 11W
Westover Hills, *Phil.* 24 C1 39 45N 75 35W
Westtown, *Phil.* 24 B1 39 56N 75 32W
Westville, *Phil.* 24 B4 39 52N 75 7W
Westville Grove, *Phil.* 24 B4 39 51N 75 7W
Westwood, *Bost.* 21 D2 42 12N 71 14W
Westwood, *N.Y.* 22 B4 40 59N 74 3W
Westwood Village, *L.A.* 28 B2 34 3N 118 26W
Wetter, *Ruhr* 6 B6 51 23N 7 23 E
Wexford, *Trto.* 20 D9 43 45N 79 18W
Wey →, *Lon.* 4 D2 51 18N 0 27W
Weybridge, *Lon.* 4 C2 51 22N 0 27W
Weyer, *Ruhr* 6 C4 51 10N 7 1 E
Weymouth, *Bost.* 21 D4 42 12N 70 57W
Whampoa, Sungei →, *Sing.* 15 G8 1 18N 103 52 E
Wheaton, *Wash.* 25 C7 39 2N 77 2W
Wheaton Regional Park, *Wash.* 25 C7 39 3N 77 1W
Wheelers Hill, *Melb.* 19 F8 37 53 S 145 10 E
Wheeling, *Chic.* 26 A1 42 8N 87 54W
Whetstone, *Lon.* 4 B3 51 37N 0 10W
Whippany, *N.Y.* 22 B2 40 49N 74 24W
Whippany →, *N.Y.* 22 B2 40 50N 74 20W
White Marsh, *Balt.* 25 A4 39 23N 76 28W
White Meadow L., *N.Y.* 22 B1 40 55N 74 30W
White Oak, *Wash.* 25 C8 39 2N 76 59W
White Plains, *N.Y.* 23 A6 41 0N 73 46W
Whitechapel, *Lon.* 4 B4 51 31N 0 3W
Whitehorse, *Phil.* 24 B2 39 59N 75 28W
Whiteley Village, *Lon.* 4 C2 51 21N 0 25W
Whitemarsh →, *Balt.* 25 A4 39 22N 76 29W
Whitestone, *N.Y.* 23 C6 40 47N 73 48W
Whiting, *Chic.* 26 C4 41 41N 87 30W
Whitmans Pond, *Bost.* 21 D4 42 12N 70 55W
Whittier, *L.A.* 28 C4 33 58N 118 2W
Whitton, *Lon.* 4 C2 51 27N 0 21W
Whyteleafe, *Lon.* 4 D4 51 18N 0 5W
Wieden, *Wien* 10 G10 48 11N 16 22 E
Wiemelhausen, *Ruhr* 6 B5 51 27N 7 13 E
Wien, *Wien* 10 G10 48 12N 16 22 E
Wien-Schwechat, Flughafen, *Wien* 10 H11 48 6N 16 34 E
Wiener Berg, *Wien* 10 H10 48 9N 16 21 E
Wiener Wald, *Wien* 10 G9 48 16N 16 14 E
Wieruchów, *Wsaw.* 10 E5 52 14N 20 49 E
Wierzbno, *Wsaw.* 10 E7 52 11N 21 1 E
Wilanów, *Wsaw.* 10 E7 52 10N 21 4 E
Wilanówka →, *Wsaw.* 10 F7 52 13N 21 6 E
Wildcat Canyon Regional Park, *S.F.* 27 A3 37 56N 122 17W
Wildcat Cr. →, *S.F.* 27 A3 37 57N 122 15W
Wilde, *B.A.* 32 C5 34 24 S 58 18W
Wilhelmsburg, *Hbg.* 7 E7 53 29N 9 59 E
Wilhelmshagen, *Berl.* 7 B5 52 26N 13 42 E
Wilket Creek Park, *Trto.* 20 D8 43 43N 79 21W
Willesden, *Lon.* 4 B3 51 32N 0 15W
Willesden Green, *Lon.* 4 B3 51 32N 0 13W
Willett Pond, *Bost.* 21 D2 42 10N 71 14W
William Girling Res., *Lon.* 4 B4 51 38N 0 1W
Williams Bridge, *N.Y.* 23 B5 40 52N 73 51W
Williamsburg, *N.Y.* 22 C5 40 42N 73 56W
Williamstown, *Melb.* 19 F6 37 51 S 144 52 E
Williamstown Junction, *Phil.* 24 C5 39 45N 74 56W
Willingboro, *Phil.* 24 A5 40 2N 74 53W
Williston Park, *N.Y.* 23 C7 40 45N 73 38W
Willoughby, *Syd.* 19 A4 33 48 S 151 12 E
Willow Grove, *Phil.* 24 A4 40 8N 75 7W
Willow Springs, *Chic.* 26 C1 41 44N 87 51W
Willowbrook, *L.A.* 28 C3 33 54N 118 13W
Willowbrook, *N.Y.* 22 D4 40 35N 74 8W
Willowdale, *Phil.* 24 B5 39 52N 74 58W
Willowdale, *Trto.* 20 D8 43 46N 79 25W
Willowdale State Forest, *Bost.* 21 B4 42 39N 70 54W
Wilmette, *Chic.* 26 A2 42 4N 87 42W
Wilmette Harbor, *Chic.* 26 A2 42 4N 87 41W
Wilmington, *Bost.* 21 B3 42 33N 71 9W
Wilmington, *Lon.* 4 C6 51 25N 0 12 E
Wilmington, *Phil.* 24 C1 39 44N 75 33W
Wilson, Mt., *L.A.* 28 A4 34 13N 118 4W
Wimbledon, *Lon.* 4 C3 51 25N 0 13W
Wimbledon Common, *Lon.* 4 C3 51 26N 0 14W
Wimbledon Park, *Lon.* 4 C3 51 25N 0 11W
Wimbledon Tennis Ground, *Lon.* 4 C3 51 25N 0 12W
Winchester, *Bost.* 21 C3 42 26N 71 8W
Winchmore Hill, *Lon.* 4 B4 51 38N 0 5W
Windsor Cresta, *Jobg.* 18 E8 26 7 S 27 59 E
Winfield, *N.Y.* 22 D3 40 38N 74 16W
Winnetka, *Chic.* 26 A2 42 6N 87 43W
Winnetka, *L.A.* 28 A1 34 10N 118 32W
Winning, *Mün.* 7 G10 48 2N 11 37 E
Winston Hills, *Syd.* 19 A2 33 46 S 150 57 E
Winterberg, *Ruhr* 6 C5 51 19N 7 12 E
Winterhude, *Hbg.* 7 D8 53 35N 10 0 E
Winterthur, *Phil.* 24 C1 39 48N 75 35W
Winthrop, *Bost.* 21 C4 42 22N 70 58W
Winzeldorf, *Hbg.* 7 C7 53 40N 9 54 E
Wisley Gardens, *Lon.* 4 D2 51 18N 0 28W
Wiśniowa Góra, *Wsaw.* 10 E8 52 13N 21 12 E
Wissahickon Cr. →, *Phil.* 24 A3 40 0N 75 12W
Wissinoming, *Phil.* 24 A4 40 1N 75 4W
Wissous, *Paris* 5 C3 48 44N 2 19 E
Witch House, *Bost.* 21 B4 42 31N 70 54W
Witfield, *Jobg.* 18 F10 26 11 S 28 12 E
Witpoortjie, *Jobg.* 18 E8 26 8 S 27 50 E
Witten, *Ruhr* 6 B6 51 26N 7 20 E
Wittenau, *Berl.* 7 A2 52 35N 13 19 E
Wittlaer, *Ruhr* 6 C2 51 19N 6 44 E
Witwatersrand, Univ. of, *Jobg.* 18 F9 26 11 S 28 1 E
Włochy, *Wsaw.* 10 E6 52 12N 20 54 E
Wo Mei, *H.K.* 12 D6 22 21N 114 15 E
Wo Yi Hop, *H.K.* 12 D5 22 23N 114 8 E
Woburn, *Bost.* 21 C3 42 29N 71 9W
Woburn, *Trto.* 20 D9 43 46N 79 12W
Wohldorf-Ohlstedt, *Hbg.* 7 C8 53 41N 10 7 E
Wola, *Wsaw.* 10 E6 52 14N 20 57 E
Woldingham, *Lon.* 4 D4 51 16N 0 1W
Wolf Lake, *Chic.* 26 D3 41 39N 87 31W
Wolf Trap Farm Park, *Wash.* 25 D6 38 56N 77 17W
Wolfpassing, *Wien* 10 G9 48 18N 16 10 E
Wolica, *Wsaw.* 10 F7 52 9N 21 3 E
Wolica, *Wsaw.* 10 F6 52 7N 20 51 E
Wólka Węglowa, *Wsaw.* 10 E6 52 18N 20 52 E
Wollaston, *Bost.* 21 D3 42 15N 71 2W
Wołomin, *Wsaw.* 10 D8 52 20N 21 12 E
Woltersdorf, *Berl.* 7 B5 52 27N 13 44 E
Wong Chuk Hang, *H.K.* 12 E6 22 15N 114 10 E
Wong Chuk Wan, *H.K.* 12 D6 22 23N 114 17 E
Wong Chuk Yeung, *H.K.* 12 D6 22 24N 114 15 E
Wong Ngua Shan, *H.K.* 12 D6 22 22N 114 14 E
Wong Tai Sin, *H.K.* 12 D6 22 20N 114 11 E
Wonga Park, *Melb.* 19 E8 37 44 S 145 17 E
Wood End, *Lon.* 4 B2 51 33N 0 21W
Wood Green, *Lon.* 4 B4 51 36N 0 6W
Wood Hill, *Bost.* 21 B2 42 39N 71 11W
Woodbridge, *N.Y.* 22 D3 40 33N 74 16W
Woodbridge, *Trto.* 20 D7 43 47N 79 35W
Woodbridge Cr. →, *N.Y.* 22 D3 40 32N 74 15W
Woodbury, *N.Y.* 23 C8 40 49N 73 28W
Woodbury, *Phil.* 24 B4 39 50N 75 9W
Woodbury Cr. →, *Phil.* 24 B4 39 51N 75 11W
Woodbury Heights, *Phil.* 24 C4 39 49N 75 7W
Woodchuck Hill, *Bost.* 21 B3 42 39N 71 4W
Woodcliff Lake, *N.Y.* 22 A4 41 1N 74 2W
Woodford, *Lon.* 4 B5 51 36N 0 1 E
Woodford Bridge, *Lon.* 4 B5 51 36N 0 3 E
Woodford Green, *Lon.* 4 B5 51 36N 0 1 E
Woodford Wells, *Lon.* 4 B5 51 37N 0 1 E
Woodhaven, *N.Y.* 23 C5 40 41N 73 51W
Woodlands, *Sing.* 15 F7 1 26N 103 46 E
Woodlawn, *Balt.* 25 B2 39 19N 76 44W
Woodlyn, *Phil.* 24 B2 39 52N 75 21W
Woodlynne, *Phil.* 24 B4 39 54N 75 6W
Woodmere, *N.Y.* 23 D6 40 38N 73 43W
Woodmont, *Wash.* 25 D7 38 59N 77 5W
Woodmore, *Balt.* 25 A2 39 22N 76 47W
Woodridge, *N.Y.* 22 B4 40 50N 74 4W
Woodrow, *N.Y.* 22 D3 40 32N 74 11W
Woodside, *Lon.* 4 C4 51 23N 0 4W
Woodside, *N.Y.* 23 C5 40 44N 73 54W
Woodside, *S.F.* 27 D3 37 26N 122 16W
Woodstock, *Balt.* 25 B1 39 19N 76 52W
Woodstream, *Phil.* 24 B5 39 54N 74 57W
Woollahra, *Syd.* 19 B4 33 53 S 151 15 E
Woolooware B., *Syd.* 19 C3 34 1 S 151 8 E
Woolwich, *Lon.* 4 C5 51 29N 0 4 E
Wördern, *Wien* 10 G9 48 19N 16 12 E
World Trade Center, *N.Y.* 22 C4 40 42N 74 0W
Worli, *Bomb.* 16 G7 19 1N 72 49 E
Woronora, *Syd.* 19 C3 34 1 S 151 2 E
Worth, *Chic.* 26 C2 41 41N 87 47W
Worthington, *Balt.* 25 B2 39 14N 76 47W
Worthington, *N.Y.* 23 A6 41 2N 73 49W
Wrotham, *Lon.* 4 D6 51 18N 0 18 E
Wrotham Park, *Lon.* 4 A3 51 40N 0 10W
Wuhlgarten, *Berl.* 7 A4 52 31N 13 34 E
Wujiaochang, *Shang.* 14 J12 31 18N 121 31 E
Wülfrath, *Ruhr* 6 C4 51 16N 7 2 E
Wulfsmühle, *Hbg.* 7 C7 53 41N 9 51 E
Wulksfelde, *Hbg.* 7 C8 53 42N 10 6 E
Wupper →, *Ruhr* 6 C5 51 14N 7 18 E
Wuppertal, *Ruhr* 6 C5 51 17N 7 10 E
Würm →, *Mün.* 7 G9 48 8N 11 27 E
Würm-kanal, *Mün.* 7 F9 48 13N 11 29 E
Wusong, *Shang.* 14 H11 31 22N 121 29 E
Wusong Jiang →, *Shang.* 14 J11 31 15N 121 29 E
Wyandanch, *N.Y.* 23 C8 40 44N 73 20W
Wyckoff, *N.Y.* 22 A3 41 0N 74 10W
Wyczółki, *Wsaw.* 10 F6 52 9N 20 59 E
Wygoda, *Wsaw.* 10 E7 52 15N 21 7 E
Wyncote, *Phil.* 24 A4 40 5N 75 8W
Wynnewood, *Phil.* 24 A3 40 0N 75 17W
Wynnmere, *Bost.* 21 C3 42 29N 71 9W
Wyola, *Phil.* 24 A2 40 0N 75 24W


# X


Xabregas, *Lisb.* 8 F8 38 43N 9 6W
Xiaodianzhuang, *Tianj.* 14 D6 39 14N 117 14 E
Xiaoping, *Gzh.* 14 F8 23 12N 113 13 E
Xiasha chong, *Gzh.* 14 G7 23 8N 113 9 E
Xicheng, *Beij.* 14 B2 39 54N 116 19 E
Xico, Cerro, *Méx.* 29 C4 19 15N 98 56W
Xicun, *Gzh.* 14 G8 23 8N 113 13 E
Xidan, *Beij.* 14 B3 39 52N 116 20 E
Xigu Gongyuan, *Tianj.* 14 D6 39 10N 117 10 E
Xigucun, *Tianj.* 14 D5 39 10N 117 9 E
Xijiao Airport, *Beij.* 14 B2 39 57N 116 12 E
Xikeng, *Gzh.* 14 F7 23 11N 113 6 E
Xilou, *Tianj.* 14 E6 39 5N 117 12 E
Ximenwai, *Tianj.* 14 E5 39 8N 117 9 E
Xingfusancun, *Beij.* 14 B3 39 55N 116 25 E
Xinhua, *Tianj.* 14 E6 39 6N 117 12 E
Xinkai He →, *Tianj.* 14 D6 39 12N 117 15 E
Xintang, *Gzh.* 14 G9 23 9N 113 24 E
Xitle, *Méx.* 29 C2 19 15N 99 12W
Xitle, Cerro, *Méx.* 29 C2 19 14N 99 12W
Xiyuan, *Beij.* 14 B2 39 59N 116 14 E
Xizhimen, *Beij.* 14 B2 39 55N 116 19 E
Xochiaca, *Méx.* 29 B4 19 24N 89 58 E
Xochimilco, *Méx.* 29 C3 19 15N 99 5W
Xochimilco, L. de, *Méx.* 29 C3 19 16N 99 7W
Xochitenco, *Méx.* 29 B4 19 24N 89 58 E
Xochitepec, *Méx.* 29 C3 19 15N 99 9W
Xuanwu, *Beij.* 14 B2 39 52N 116 19 E
Xuhui, *Shang.* 14 J11 31 11N 121 26 E


# Y


Yaba, *Lagos* 18 A2 6 30N 7 22 E
Yadun Shui, *Gzh.* 14 G8 23 5N 113 15 E
Yaftābād, *Tehr.* 17 D4 35 37N 51 17 E
Yagoona, *Syd.* 19 B3 33 54 S 151 2 E
Yahara, *Tōkyō* 13 B2 35 44N 139 37 E
Yaho, *Tōkyō* 13 B1 35 40N 139 26 E
Yakire, *Tōkyō* 13 B4 35 45N 139 54 E
Yamada, *Ōsaka* 12 B4 34 47N 135 32 E
Yamada, *Tōkyō* 13 C2 35 33N 139 37 E
Yamada →, *Ōsaka* 12 B2 34 45N 135 10 E
Yamaguchi, *Ōsaka* 12 B2 34 49N 135 14 E
Yamamoto, *Ōsaka* 12 C4 34 38N 135 37 E
Yamato, *Tōkyō* 13 B2 35 46N 139 36 E
Yamato, *Tōkyō* 13 D1 35 29N 139 27 E
Yamato →, *Ōsaka* 12 C3 34 36N 135 26 E
Yamazaki, *Tōkyō* 13 A4 35 55N 139 53 E
Yamuna →, *Delhi* 16 B2 28 37N 77 15 E
Yan Kit, *Sing.* 15 F8 1 21N 103 58 E
Yanagishima, *Tōkyō* 13 B3 35 49N 139 45 E
Yanbu, *Gzh.* 14 G7 23 5N 113 9 E
Yanghuayuan, *Beij.* 14 C2 39 49N 116 18 E
Yangjiazhuang, *Shang.* 14 H11 31 22N 121 25 E
Yangliuqing, *Tianj.* 14 E5 39 8N 117 0 E
Yangpu, *Shang.* 14 J12 31 16N 121 32 E
Yanino, *St-Pet.* 11 B5 59 55N 30 36 E
Yao, *Ōsaka* 12 C4 34 37N 135 36 E
Yao Airport, *Ōsaka* 12 C4 34 35N 135 36 E
Yarmōk, *Bagd.* 17 F7 33 18N 44 19 E
Yarra →, *Melb.* 19 E6 37 51 S 144 53 E
Yarra Bend Nat. Park, *Melb.* 19 E7 37 47 S 145 0 E
Yarraville, *Melb.* 19 E6 37 48 S 144 53 E
Yasenevo, *Mos.* 11 F9 55 36N 37 21 E
Yashio, *Tōkyō* 13 B3 35 48N 139 49 E
Yau Ma Tei, *H.K.* 12 E5 22 18N 114 10 E
Yau Tong, *H.K.* 12 E6 22 17N 114 14 E
Yau Yue Wan, *H.K.* 12 E6 22 19N 114 15 E
Yauza →, *Mos.* 11 D10 55 54N 37 43 E
Yeading, *Lon.* 4 B2 51 31N 0 23W
Yeadon, *Phil.* 24 B3 39 55N 75 15W
Yedikule, *Ist.* 17 B2 40 59N 28 55 E
Yenikapi, *Ist.* 17 A2 41 0N 28 56 E
Yeniköy, *Ist.* 17 A3 41 6N 29 3 E
Yennora, *Syd.* 19 B2 33 51 S 150 58 E
Yeogchon, *Sŏul* 12 G7 37 35N 126 55 E
Yeoido, *Sŏul* 12 G7 37 31N 126 55 E
Yeong Dung Po, *Sŏul* 12 G7 37 31N 126 54 E
Yeongdong, *Sŏul* 12 G8 37 30N 127 1 E
Yerba Buena I., *S.F.* 27 B2 37 48N 122 21W
Yerres, *Paris* 5 C5 48 43N 2 30 E
Yerres →, *Paris* 5 C5 48 43N 2 26 E
Yesilköy, *Ist.* 17 B2 40 57N 28 50 E
Yew Tee, *Sing.* 15 F7 1 23N 103 45 E
Yiewsley, *Lon.* 4 B2 51 31N 0 27W
Yiheyuan, *Beij.* 14 A2 40 0N 116 14 E
Yinhangzhen, *Shang.* 14 H12 31 20N 121 31 E
Yio Chu Kang, *Sing.* 15 F8 1 23N 103 51 E
Yixingbu, *Tianj.* 14 D6 39 11N 117 12 E
Ylästö, *Hels.* 3 B4 60 17N 24 35 E
Yodo →, *Ōsaka* 12 B4 34 45N 135 35 E
Yokohama, *Tōkyō* 13 D3 35 26N 139 41 E
Yokohama Harbour, *Tōkyō* 13 D2 35 27N 139 39 E
Yokosuka, *Tōkyō* 13 A4 35 50N 139 54 E
Yong San, *Sŏul* 12 G7 37 32N 126 58 E
Yongding He →, *Beij.* 14 C1 39 49N 116 10 E
Yongdingmen, *Beij.* 14 B3 39 50N 116 20 E
Yongfucun, *Gzh.* 14 G8 23 8N 113 17 E
Yonkers, *N.Y.* 23 B5 40 56N 73 52W
Yono, *Tōkyō* 13 A2 35 52N 139 37 E
York, *Trto.* 20 D8 43 40N 79 26W
York Mills, *Trto.* 20 D8 43 45N 79 22W
Yoshikawa, *Tōkyō* 13 A4 35 53N 139 50 E
Yotsuga, *Tōkyō* 13 B3 35 40N 139 44 E
You'anmen, *Beij.* 14 B2 39 51N 116 19 E
Yoyogi Park, *Tōkyō* 13 C3 35 40N 139 41 E
Yuanxiatian, *Gzh.* 14 F8 23 12N 113 17 E
Yuexiu Gongyuan, *Gzh.* 14 G8 23 8N 113 16 E
Yugo-Zarad, *Mos.* 11 E9 55 40N 37 30 E
Yung Shue Wan, *H.K.* 12 E5 22 13N 114 6 E
Yuquanshan, *Beij.* 14 A2 40 0N 116 13 E
Yusofābād, *Tehr.* 17 C5 35 43N 51 24 E
Yuyuan Tan, *Beij.* 14 B2 39 53N 116 16 E
Yuyuantan Gongyuan, *Beij.* 14 B2 39 54N 116 16 E
Yvelines, Forêt des, *Paris* 5 D1 48 38N 1 53 E
Yvette →, *Paris* 5 C1 48 43N 1 57 E


# Z


Záběhlice, *Pra.* 10 B2 50 3N 14 29 E
Żacisze, *Wsaw.* 10 E7 52 17N 21 4 E
Zahrā, *Bagd.* 17 E7 33 22N 44 19 E
Zakharkovo, *Mos.* 11 E7 55 46N 37 18 E
Żalov, *Pra.* 10 A2 50 10N 14 22 E
Załuski, *Wsaw.* 10 F6 52 9N 20 55 E
Zamdorf, *Mün.* 7 G10 48 8N 11 35 E
Zanevka, *St-Pet.* 11 B5 59 55N 30 31 E
Zaozerye, *Mos.* 11 F12 55 35N 38 1 E
Zapote, *Manila* 15 E3 14 27N 120 56 E
Zapotitlán, *Méx.* 29 C3 19 18N 99 2W
Zápy, *Pra.* 10 B4 50 9N 14 40 E
Zarechye, *Mos.* 11 E8 55 41N 37 22 E
Zawady, *Wsaw.* 10 E7 52 10N 21 6 E
Zâwiyet Abû Musallam, *El Qâ.* 18 D4 29 56N 31 9 E
Zawrā Park, *Bagd.* 17 F8 33 18N 44 23 E
Zbójna Góra, *Wsaw.* 10 E8 52 11N 21 13 E
Zbraslav, *Pra.* 10 C2 49 58N 14 23 E
Zbuzany, *Pra.* 10 B1 50 1N 14 17 E
Zdiby, *Pra.* 10 B2 50 9N 14 27 E
Zehlendorf, *Berl.* 7 B2 52 26N 13 16 E
Zeleneč, *Pra.* 10 B3 50 8N 14 39 E
Zempoala, Parque Nac. de las Lagunas de, *Méx.* 29 D2 19 5N 99 18W
Zepernick, *Berl.* 7 A4 52 38N 13 33 E
Żerań, *Wsaw.* 10 E6 52 18N 20 58 E
Zerzeń, *Wsaw.* 10 E7 52 12N 21 7 E
Zeytinburnu, *Ist.* 17 B2 40 58N 28 53 E
Zhabei, *Shang.* 14 J11 31 16N 121 26 E
Zhangguizhuang, *Tianj.* 14 E6 39 7N 117 19 E
Zhangxingzhuang, *Tianj.* 14 D6 39 10N 117 12 E
Zhdanov, *Mos.* 11 E10 55 44N 37 41 E
Zhegalovo, *Mos.* 11 D11 55 54N 37 59 E
Zheleznodorozhnyy, *Mos.* 11 E12 55 45N 38 0 E
Zhenru, *Shang.* 14 J11 31 16N 121 22 E
Zhicun, *Gzh.* 14 G8 23 0N 113 18 E
Zhongshan Gongyuan, *Shang.* 14 J11 31 13N 121 24 E
Zhoucun, *Gzh.* 14 F8 23 11N 113 11 E
Zhoujiadu, *Shang.* 14 J11 31 11N 121 29 E
Zhoujiazhen, *Shang.* 14 J12 31 16N 121 33 E
Zhu Jiang →, *Gzh.* 14 G9 23 6N 113 20 E
Zhulebino, *Mos.* 11 E11 55 42N 37 50 E
Zhushadi, *Gzh.* 14 F9 23 11N 113 22 E
Zielona, *Wsaw.* 10 E8 52 14N 21 11 E
Zielonka, *Wsaw.* 10 E7 52 18N 21 9 E
Zitadella, *Berl.* 7 A2 52 31N 13 11 E
Zizhuyuan Gongyuan, *Beij.* 14 B2 39 55N 116 17 E
Žižkov, *Pra.* 10 B2 50 5N 14 28 E
Zličin, *Pra.* 10 B1 50 3N 14 17 E
Zōbki, *Wsaw.* 10 E7 52 17N 21 6 E
Zografos, *Ath.* 8 J11 37 58N 23 47 E
Żoliborz, *Wsaw.* 10 E6 52 16N 20 57 E
Zugliget, *Bud.* 10 K12 47 30N 18 59 E
Zugló, *Bud.* 10 J13 47 31N 19 8 E
Zumbi, *Rio J.* 31 A2 22 49 S 43 10W
Zuvuvu →, *S. Pau.* 31 F5 23 40 S 46 42W
Zuvuvus, *S. Pau.* 31 F6 23 41 S 46 39W
Zweckel, *Ruhr* 6 A3 51 35N 6 57 E
Zyuzino, *Mos.* 11 F9 55 39N 37 34 E

# WORLD MAPS

## MAP SYMBOLS

### SETTLEMENTS

| ◨ PARIS | ■ Berne | ◉ Livorno | ◉ Brugge | ⊙ Algeciras | ⊙ Frèjus | ○ Oberammergau | ∘ Thira |
|---------|---------|-----------|----------|-------------|----------|----------------|---------|

Settlement symbols and type styles vary according to the scale of each map and indicate the importance of towns on the map rather than specific population figures

∴   Ruins or Archæological Sites      ᵛ   Wells in Desert

### ADMINISTRATION

**Boundaries**

——— International

— — — International (Undefined or Disputed)

·········· Internal

**National Parks**

International boundaries show the *de facto* situation where there are rival claims to territory.

**Country Names**
NICARAGUA

**Administrative Areas**
KENT
CALABRIA

### COMMUNICATIONS

**Roads**

——— Primary

⌢ Secondary

⌢·— Trails and Seasonal

**Railroads**

⌢ Primary

⌢ Secondary

·····— Under Construction

✧ Airfields

⌣ Passes

⊣---⊢ Railroad Tunnels

·········· Principal Canals

### PHYSICAL FEATURES

⌢ Perennial Streams

········· Intermittent Streams

⬮ Perennial Lakes

⬭ Intermittent Lakes

⬮ Swamps and Marshes

▭ Permanent Ice and Glaciers

▲ 2259 Elevations (m)

▼ 2604 Sea Depths (m)

*408* Elevation of Lake Surface Above Sea Level (m)

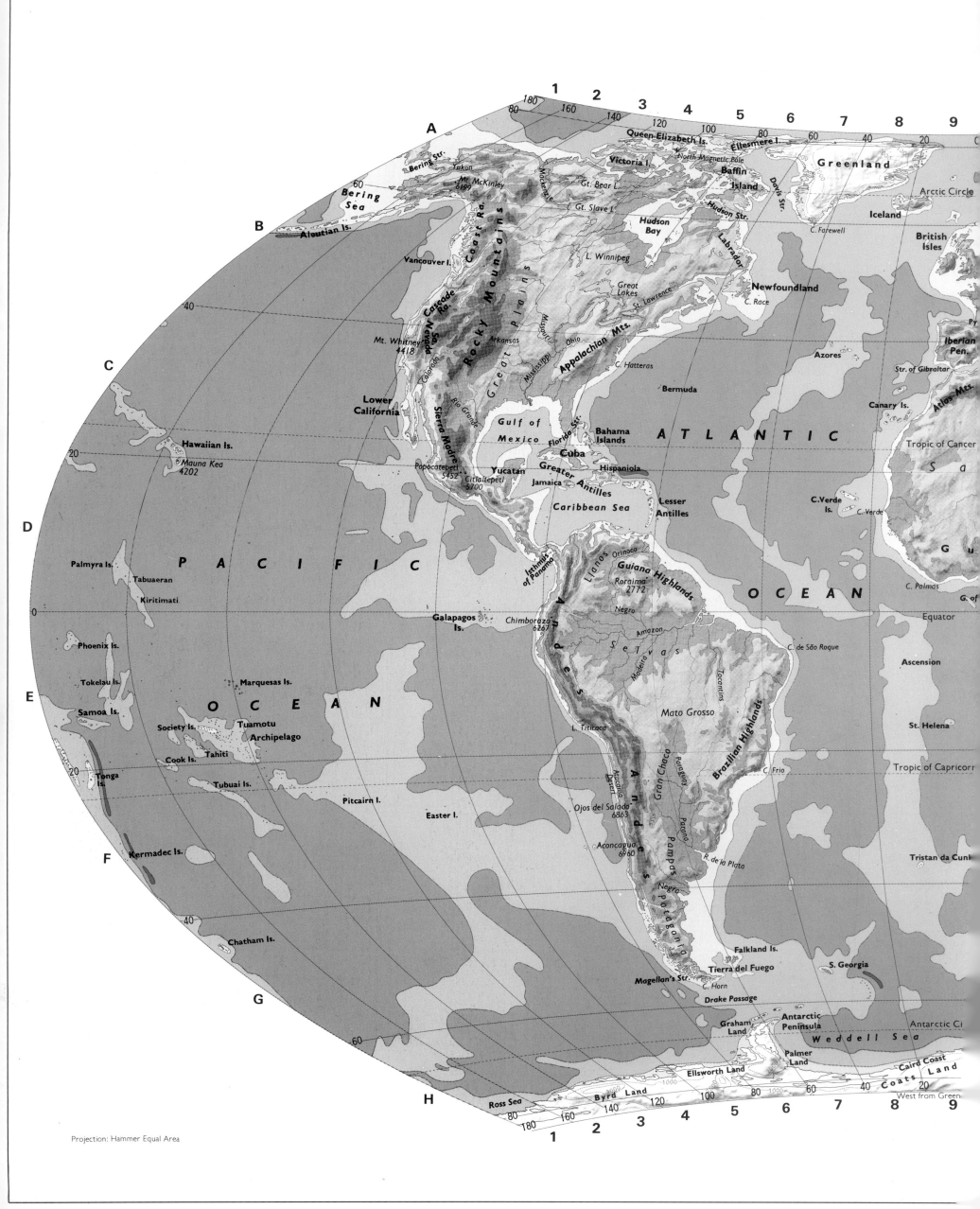

Projection: Hammer Equal Area

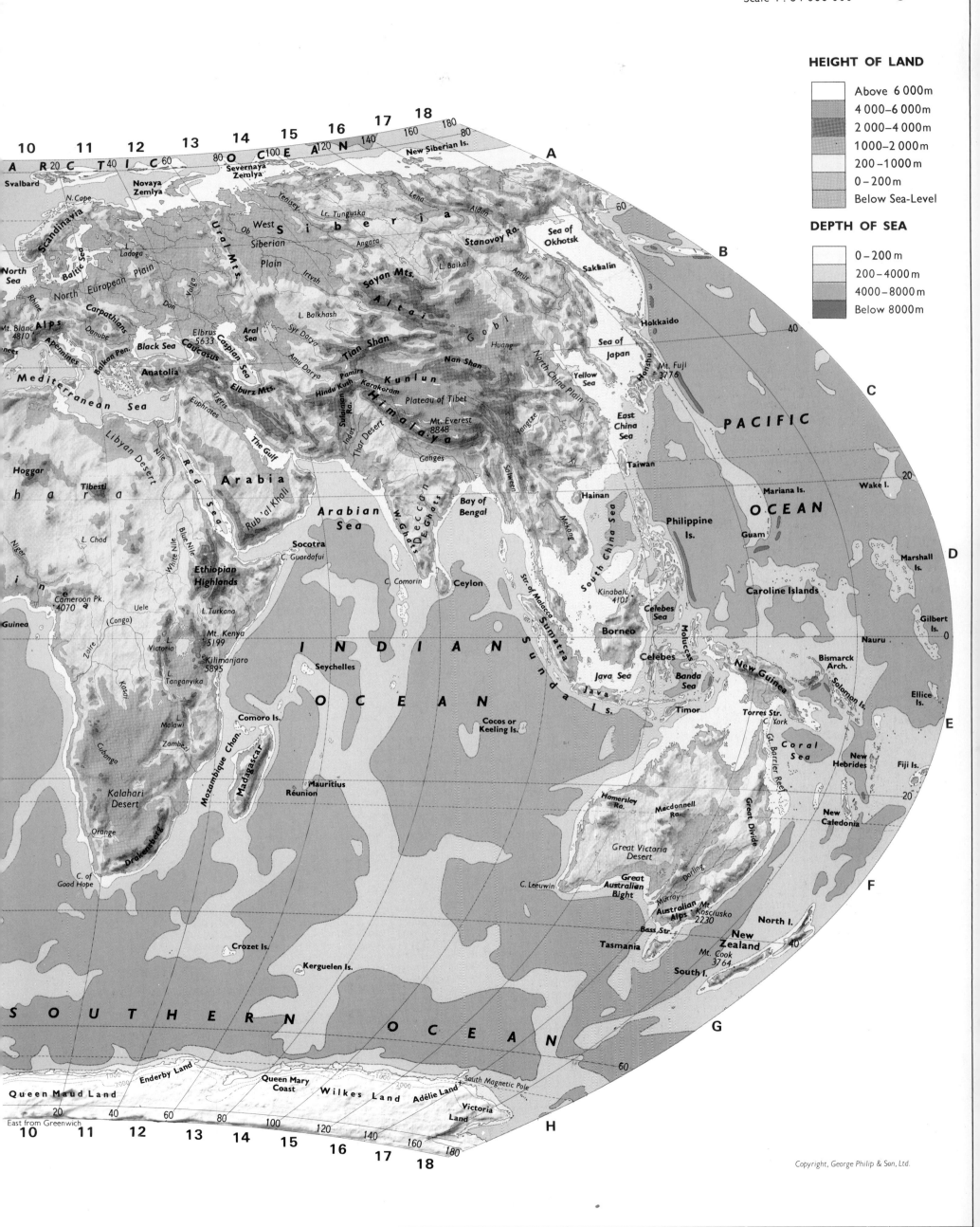

**HEIGHT OF LAND**

Above 6 000m
4 000–6 000m
2 000–4 000m
1000–2 000m
200–1000m
0–200m
Below Sea-Level

**DEPTH OF SEA**

0–200 m
200–4000m
4000–8000m
Below 8000m

A R C T I C   O C E A N

Svalbard
N. Cape
Novaya Zemlya
Severnaya Zemlya
New Siberian Is.
Scandinavia
Baltic Sea
North Sea
North European Plain
Rhine
Ladoga
Ural Mts.
West Siberian Plain
Ob
Yenisey
Lr. Tunguska
S i b e r i a
Lena
Aldon
Stanovoy Ra.
Sea of Okhotsk
Angara
Irtysh
L. Baikal
Amur
Sakhalin
Hokkaido
Sea of Japan
Honshu
Mt. Fuji 3776
Volga
Don
Danube
Carpathians
Alps
Mt. Blanc 4810
Apennines
Balkan Pen.
Black Sea
Anatolia
Caucasus
Caspian Sea
Elbrus 5633
Aral Sea
Syr Darya
L. Balkhash
Altai
Sayan Mts.
Tian Shan
Gobi
Huang
Nan Shan
Kunlun
North China Plain
Yellow Sea
East China Sea
Taiwan
Mediterranean Sea
Libyan Desert
Nile
Amu Darya
Pamir
Hindu Kush
Karakoram
Plateau of Tibet
H i m a l a y a
Mt. Everest 8848
Ganges
Yangtze
Salween
Mekong
Elburz Mts.
Tigris
Euphrates
The Gulf
Sulaiman Ra.
Indus
Thar Desert
Hainan
PACIFIC OCEAN
Mariana Is.
Wake I.
Hoggar
Tibesti
L. Chad
S a h a r a
Arabia
Red Sea
Rub 'al Khali
Socotra
C. Guardafui
Arabian Sea
Deccan
W. Ghats
E. Ghats
Bay of Bengal
Philippine Is.
Guam
Marshall Is.
Niger
Guinea
Cameroon Pk. 4070
Uele
(Congo)
White Nile
Blue Nile
Ethiopian Highlands
L. Turkana
C. Comorin
Ceylon
South China Sea
Kinabalu 4101
Borneo
Celebes Sea
Moluccas
Caroline Islands
Gilbert Is.
Nauru
Zaire
L. Victoria
Mt. Kenya 5199
Kilimanjaro 5895
L. Tanganyika
Seychelles
I N D I A N
O C E A N
Sumatra
S u n d a   I s.
Java Sea
Celebes
Banda Sea
New Guinea
Bismarck Arch.
Solomon Is.
Ellice Is.
Str. of Malacca
Kosai
L. Malawi
Zambezi
Comoro Is.
Madagascar
Mozambique Chan.
Cocos or Keeling Is.
Java
Timor
Torres Str.
C. York
Coral Sea
Gr. Barrier Reef
New Hebrides
Fiji Is.
Cubango
Kalahari Desert
Orange
Mauritius
Réunion
Hamersley Ra.
Macdonnell Ra.
Great Divide
New Caledonia
Drakensberg
Great Victoria Desert
C. of Good Hope
Crozet Is.
C. Leeuwin
Great Australian Bight
Darling
Murray
Australian Alps
Mt. Kosciusko 2230
North I.
Kerguelen Is.
Tasmania
Bass Str.
New Zealand
Mt. Cook 3764
South I.
S O U T H E R N   O C E A N
Queen Maud Land
East from Greenwich
Enderby Land
Queen Mary Coast
Wilkes Land
Adélie Land
South Magnetic Pole
Victoria Land

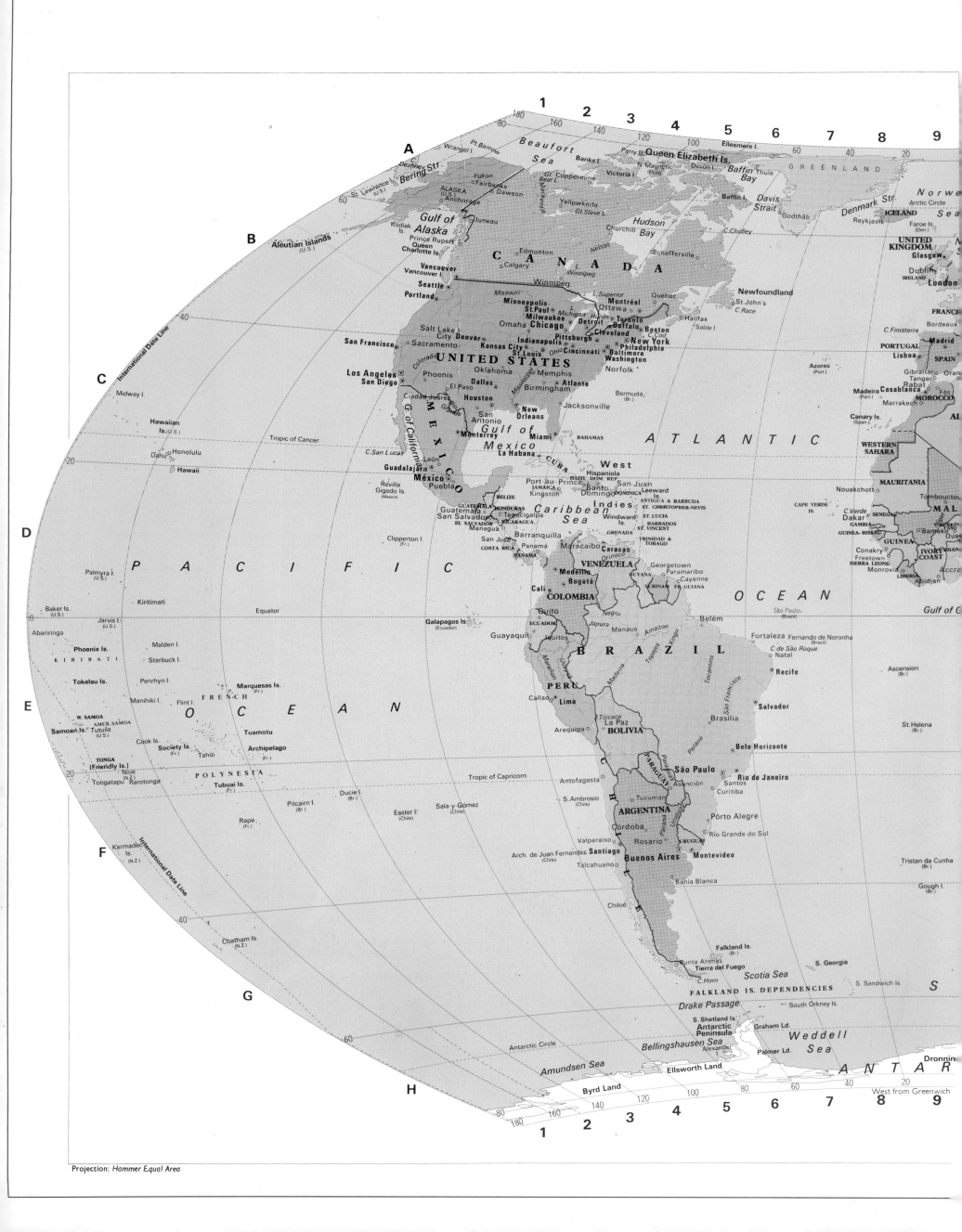

Projection: *Hammer Equal Area*

10   11   12   13   14   15   16   17   18

ARCTIC  OCEAN

Svalbard
(Norway)
Zemlya Frantsa Iosifa
Novaya Zemlya
Severnaya Zemlya
Laptev Sea
New Siberian Is.
East Siberian Sea
**A**

Nord Kapp
Narvik
Barents Sea
Kara Sea
Tiksi
Verkhoyansk
Nizhne-Kolymsk
Arctic Circle
Anadyr

NORWAY
SWEDEN
FINLAND
Arkhangelsk
Murmansk
Salekhard
Ob
Yenisey
Lena
Vilyuysk
Yakutsk
Okhotsk
Bering Sea
Kamchatka
Petropavlovsk-Kamchatskiy
**B**

Oslo
Helsinki
St. Peterburg
**RUSSIA**
Perm
Tomsk
Krasnoyarsk
L. Baykal
Sea of Okhotsk
Sakhalin
C. Lopatka

Stockholm
EST.
Yaroslavl
Kazan
**Yekaterinburg**
**Novosibirsk**
Omsk
Novokuznetsk
Irkutsk
Ulan Ude
Amur
Komsomolsk
Khabarovsk
Kuril Is.

København
DENMARK
LATVIA
LITH.
BELO.
Minsk
**Moskva**
Samara
Ufa
Chelyabinsk
Barnaul
Ulaanbaatar
Vladivostok
Sapporo
Hakodate

Hamburg
Berlin
POLAND
Warsza
RUSSIA
Voronezh
Orenburg
Karaganda
**MONGOLIA**
Harbin
Changchun
Shenyang
N.KOREA
Sea of Japan
**JAPAN**
Tōkyō

russel
Paris
Praha
CZECH
Lvov
**Kharkov**
Rostov
Volga
Volgograd
Irtysh
Beijing
Tianjin
Dalian
Sŏul
S.KOREA
Kyoto
Yokohama

Milano
Budapest
ROMANIA
**UKRAINE**
Saratov
Astrakhan
**KAZAKHSTAN**
L. Balkhash
Alma Ata
Taiyuan
Jinan
Qingdao
Pusan
Kōbe
Nagoya
Osaka

Torino
Beograd
Bucuresti
Black Sea
Grozny
Tbilisi
Aral Sea
Caspian Sea
Lanzhou
Xi'an
Huang
**CHINA**
Kitakyūshū
**C**

Marseille
Roma
Sofiya
Istanbul
Yerevan
Baku
GEO.
UZBEKISTAN
Samarkand
Tashkent
KIRGHIZIA
Nanjing
Wuhan
**Shanghai**
East China Sea

Barcelona
Napoli
Sardinia
BULGARIA
Izmir
TURKEY
Ankara
ARM.
AZ.
Tabriz
TURKMENISTAN
Ashkhabad
Dushanbe
TAJ.
Chengdu
Chongqing
Changsha
Fuzhou
PACIFIC

Valencia
Sicily
Athinai
GREECE
Halab
SYRIA
Dimashq
Baghdad
Tehrān
Mashhad
AFGHANISTAN
Kabul
Rawalpindi
Srinagar
XIZANG
(TIBET)
Lhasa
Kunming
Guangzhou
Taibei
TAIWAN
Tropic of Cancer

Alger
Tunis
MALTA
Crete
CYPRUS
LEB.
Bayrūt
Amman
IRAQ
Eşfahān
**IRAN**
Shiraz
Lahore
Delhi
NEPAL
Katmandu
Hong Kong
Wake I.
(U.S.)

GERIA
Tarābulus
Banghāzī
Tel Aviv-Yafo
El Iskandariya
JORDAN
Jerusalem
ISR.
Abādān
Būshehr
**PAKISTAN**
Agra
Kanpur
Lucknow
BANGLA
DESH
Dhaka
BURMA
Mandalay
Hainan
South China Sea
NORTHERN MARIANAS
20

Ain Salah
**LIBYA**
El Qâhira
Ar Riyād
QATAR
BAHRAIN
U.A.E.
Karachi
**INDIA**
Ganga
Calcutta
Hanoi
VIET.
OCEAN
Guam
(U.S.)

**EGYPT**
Aswān
Makkah
SAUDI ARABIA
OMAN
The Gulf
KUWAIT
Ahmadabad
Nagpur
Bay of Bengal
MYANMAR
Rangoon
Vientiane
NAM.
Manila
PHILIPPINES

**NIGER**
**CHAD**
Omdurmân
El Khartûm
YEMEN
Arabian Sea
Bombay
Pune
Hyderabad
THAILAND
Bangkok
CAMBODIA
Cebu
FEDERATED STATES
**D**

Niamey
Kano
L.Chad
Ndjamena
SUDAN
Blue Nile
Asmera
Aden
Gulf of Aden
Socotra
(Yemen)
Bangalore
**Madras**
Andaman Is.
(India)
Phanh Bho
Ho Chi Minh
Phnom Penh
Yap
Truk
Caroline Is.
Ponape
OF MICRONESIA

adougou
**NIGERIA**
Ibadan
CENTRAL AFRICAN REPUBLIC
Addis Abeba
**ETHIOPIA**
DJIBOUTI
SOMALI REP.
Lakshadweep Is.
Nicobar Is.
(India)
Colombo
SRI LANKA
(CEYLON)
Dondra Hd.
MALAYSIA
SABAH
BELAU
MARSHALL IS.
Gilbert Is.

Lagos
Douala
Yaounde
Bangui
White Nile
L. Turkana
MALDIVES
Medan
Kuala Lumpur
PEN. MALAYSIA
BRUNEI
KUCHING
SARAWAK
NAURU

QUATORIAL GUINEA
inea
Libreville
SÃO TOMÉ
AND PRINCIPE
GABON
CONGO
**ZAÏRE**
(CONGO)
Zaire
(Congo)
Kisangani
UGANDA
Kampala
**KENYA**
Nairobi
SEYCHELLES
Chagos Arch.
(Br.)
Equator
Singapore
Borneo
Palembang
Banjarmasin
Sulawesi
Maluku
Irian Jaya
PAPUA
New Ireland
KIRIBATI

Brazzaville
Kinshasa
Kananga
(Kasai)
Victoria
RW.
BUR.
Mombasa
Zanzibar
Dar es Salaam
Amirante Is.
Diego Garcia
(Br.)
**INDONESIA**
Jakarta
Bandung
Jawa
Surabaya
Ujung Pandang
Timor
Rabaul
NEW GUINEA
New Britain
SOLOMON IS.
Santa Cruz Is.
TUVALU
**E**

Luanda
**ANGOLA**
Benguela
Lubumbashi
TANZANIA
L. Tanganyika
Aldabra
COMORO IS.
Sunda Islands
Arafura Sea
Timor Sea
Port Moresby
C York
Louisiade Arch.

ZAMBIA
Lusaka
MALAWI
Christmas I.
(Australia)
Cocos
(Keeling Is.)
(Australia)
Darwin
Cairns
VANUATU
Vanua Levu
Viti Levu
FIJI
Suva

**NAMIBIA**
Harare
ZIMBABWE
MOZAMBIQUE
MADAGASCAR
Antananarivo
Rodriguez
MAURITIUS
Réunion
(Fr.)
Tropic of Capricorn
North West C.
WESTERN
NORTHERN TERRITORY
Townsville
Alice Springs
QUEENSLAND
New Caledonia
(Fr.)
20

Bulawayo
Windhoek
**BOTSWANA**
Gaborone
Pretoria
SWAZ.
Maputo
Mozambique Chan.
**AUSTRALIA**
Rockhampton
Norfolk I.
(Australia)
**F**

SOUTH WEST AFRICA
Johannesburg
LES.
Durban
AUSTRALIA
SOUTH
AUSTRALIA
Brisbane
NEW SOUTH WALES
Lord Howe I.
(Australia)

**SOUTH AFRICA**
Cape Town
C.of Good Hope
Port Elizabeth
Perth
Fremantle
Kalgoorlie-Boulder
C. Leeuwin
Great Australian Bight
Adelaide
Darling
Newcastle
**Sydney**
Canberra
North C.
Auckland
North I.

Amsterdam
(Fr.)
St.Paul
(Fr.)
VICTORIA
**Melbourne**
Tasman Sea
NEW ZEALAND
Wellington
40

Pr.Edward Is.
(South Africa)
Crozet Is.
(Fr.)
TASMANIA
Hobart
C.Farewell
Christchurch
South I.
Dunedin

Kerguelen
(Fr.)
Stewart I.
Bounty Is.
(N.Z.)
Antipodes Is.
(N.Z.)

Bouvet I.
(Norway)
McDonald I.
(Australia)
Heard I.
(Australia)
Campbell I.
(N.Z.)
Auckland Is.
(N.Z.)
**G**

OUTHERN  OCEAN
Macquarie I.
(Australia)
Balleny Is.

Antarctic Circle

aud Land
Enderby Land
Wilkes Land
S Magnetic Pole
Ross Sea
**H**

CTICA
East from Greenwich

10   11   12   13   14   15   16   17   18

1 : 28 000 000

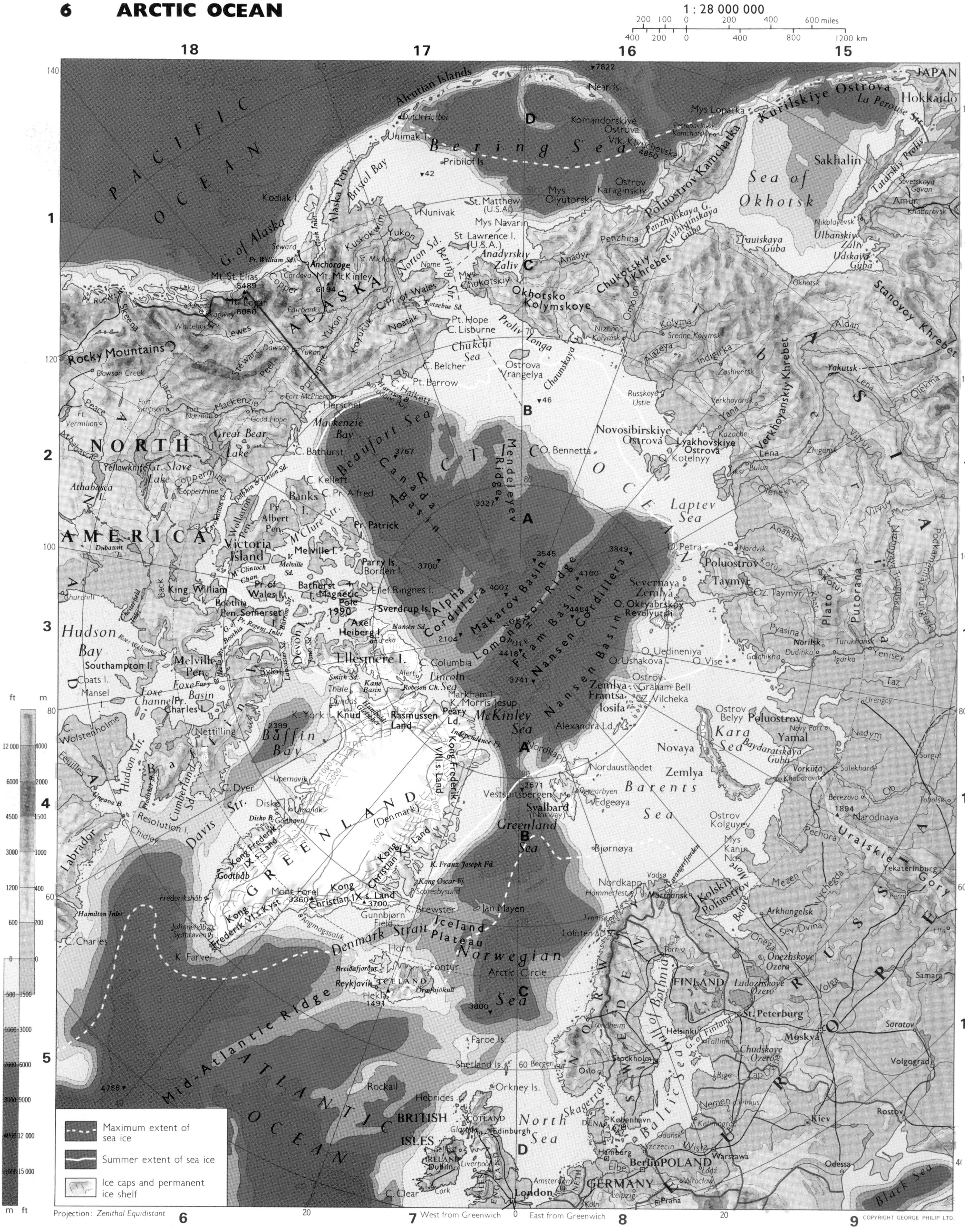

200 100 0 200 400 600 miles
400 200 0 400 800 1200 km

18 17 16 15

**Legend:**
- - - - Maximum extent of sea ice
——— Summer extent of sea ice
Ice caps and permanent ice shelf

Projection: Zenithal Equidistant

6 7 West from Greenwich 0 East from Greenwich 8 9 COPYRIGHT GEORGE PHILIP LTD.

**Elevation scale (ft / m):**
ft / m
12 000 / 4000
6000 / 2000
4500 / 1500
3000 / 1000
1200 / 400
600 / 200
0 / 0
500 / 1500
1000 / 3000
2000 / 6000
4000 / 12 000
5000 / 15 000
m / ft

PACIFIC OCEAN
ATLANTIC OCEAN
ARCTIC OCEAN

NORTH AMERICA
ASIA
EUROPE
RUSSIA
JAPAN

Bering Sea
Sea of Okhotsk
Beaufort Sea
Chukchi Sea
Laptev Sea
Kara Sea
Barents Sea
Greenland Sea
Norwegian Sea
Iceland Sea
Baffin Bay
Hudson Bay
Davis Str.
Denmark Strait
North Sea
Baltic Sea
Black Sea
G. of Alaska
Bristol Bay

Greenland (Denmark)
Iceland
ALASKA
Svalbard (Norway)
Novaya Zemlya
Severnaya Zemlya
Novosibirskiye Ostrova
Victoria Island
Banks I.
Melville I.
Ellesmere I.
Baffin I.
Southampton I.
Victoria Island
Kodiak I.
Aleutian Islands
Kuril'skiye Ostrova
Sakhalin
Hokkaido
Franz Josef Ld.
Jan Mayen
Faroe Is.
BRITISH ISLES
IRELAND

Rocky Mountains
Mid-Atlantic Ridge
Mendeleyev Ridge
Lomonosov Ridge
Alpha Cordillera
Nansen Cordillera
Makarov Basin
Nansen Basin
Fram Basin
Iceland Plateau

NORTH POLE
Magnetic Pole 1990

Mt. St. Elias 5489
Mt. McKinley 6194
Mt. Logan 6050
Hekla 1491

FINLAND
SWEDEN
NORWAY
DENMARK
GERMANY
POLAND

Moskvá
St. Peterburg
Arkhangelsk
Murmansk
Berlin
London
Dublin
Reykjavik
Oslo
Stockholm
Helsinki
Kiev
Warszawa

Yukon
Mackenzie
Lena
Yenisey
Ob
Volga

Arctic Circle

Great Bear Lake
Great Slave Lake
Lake Athabasca
Hudson Bay

1 : 28 000 000

200 100 0 200 400 600 miles
400 200 0 400 800 1200 km

**1**   **2** West from Greenwich East from Greenwich   **3**   **4**

ATLANTIC OCEAN

INDIAN OCEAN

SOUTHERN

Atlantic - Indian Basin

S O U T H E R N

Antarctic Circle

▼8265
Zavodovski I.
Visokoi I.
Leskov I.
Saunders I. Candlemas I.
Montagu I. S. Sandwich Is.
Bristol I.

South Georgia
Bird I. (U.K.)

Bases on
King George Island:
Jubany (Argentina)
Com. Ferraz (Brazil)
Ten. Rodolfo Marsh (Chile)
Great Wall (China)
King Sejong (Korea)
Arctowski (Poland)
Artigas (Uruguay)
Bellingshausen (Russia)

▼5552
Orcadas (Arg.)
Signy I. (U.K.) South
Coronation I. Orkney Is.

Stanley (U.K.)
Falkland Is.

Scotia Sea

Drake Passage

Falkland Is. Dependencies

6739 ▼

Georg Forster
(Germany)
Sande (S.Afr.) 70 Dakshin Gangotri
(India)
Georg von Prinsesse Astrid Kyst Riiser-
Neumayer Prinsesse Ragnhild Larsen-halvøya
(Germany) Kyst
Müllig Hofmann fjell Lützow-Holmbukta
Kronprinsesse Martha 2717 3630 Kyst Syowa (Japan)
Kyst Sør-Rondane Kronprins
Mizuho Olav Kyst Molodezhnaya
(Japan) (Russia)
Queen Maud Land Enderby Ld
3212 Kemp 2260
3039 Land
3318 Mawson
2990 (Austr.)
Mac- 2645 Stefansson B.
Robertson
Land C. Darnley
3556 5355 Prince Charles Mts.
2600 Amery
Lambert Ice Shelf
2311 Glacier Prydz Bay
1431 80 American Zhongshan (China)
Highland Davis (Austr.)
East 1800
Antarctica West
4030 Ice Shelf
1040 Wilhelm II
Queen Coast
Mary Drygalski I.
3030 Mirnyy Davis Sea
2570 (Russia) Masson I.
3488 Vostok (Russia) Land Shackleton
3700 Ice Shelf
Denman Gl.
Scott Gl. Mill I.
2407 Bowman I.
3087 Knox Coast
Casey (Austr.)
Budd C. Poinsett
Coast
Banzare Sabrina Totten Glacier
Coast Dalton Iceberg
2216 2435 Tongue
2798 4776 Porpoise Bay
Clarie Blodgett Iceberg
Coast Tongue
Terre Dumont d'Urville (Fr.)
Adélie
George V
Land Magnetic Pole 1990
Oates Land Commonwealth B.
Leningradskaya (Russia) Freshfields

Weddell Sea

Elephant I.
Clarence I.
Gen. Bernardo
O'Higgins (Chile)
Joinville I.
Esperanza (Arg.)
Marambio (Arg.)
James Ross I.
Robertson I.
Antarctic
Peninsula
Halley Bay
(U.K.)

South Shetland Is.
Kg. George I.
Capitan Arturo Prat (Chile)
Deception I.
Palmer Arch.
Graham Land
Palmer (U.S.A.)
Faraday (U.K.)
Anvers I.
Biscoe Is.
Adelaide I.
Rothera (Arg.)

Alexander
I. 2987
Charcot I.

Peter I Øy
(Nor.)

Ronne Ice Shelf

Berkner
975 I.
158 Filchner Ice Shelf
1312
Pensacola
Mountains 3657

Vahsel Bay
Belgrano II
(Arg.)

Coats Land

Caird Coast

Transantarctic Mountains

2000

3556
2600

4030
1040

SOUTH
Amundsen-Scott POLE
2773 (U.S.A.)
2407

Thiel
Mts.
Horlick Mts.
1797 3022
4335
3810
4176
3488
4628
Queen
Maud Mts.
Queen
Alexandra Ra.
Mt. Markham
4349
Beardmore Glacier

2801
3491

2407
3087

Ellsworth Land
Ellsworth Mts.
4897 Vinson
Massif

2896

West
Antarctica

Marie Byrd
Land
Rockefeller
Plateau
Mt. Sidley 666
4181 2080
8109
3496 Edward VII
Getz Land
Ice Shelf

Siple (U.S.A.)

Kohler
Ra.

Bellingshausen Sea

C. Byrd
Thurston I.
Hudson Mts.
Walgreen
C. Flying Fish
Abbot
Ice Shelf
Dart

Amundsen Sea

Shirase
Ice Shelf
C. Colbeck
Bay of Whales
Roosevelt I. 80

Ross Ice Shelf

Shackleton Inlet

Mt. Lister
4023
Mt. Erebus McMurdo
3743 Scott (N.Z.)
Ross McMurdo
I. (U.S.A.)
Victoria Pr. Albert Mts.
Mt.
Franklin Land
Mt.
Coulman I. Murchison
3802
Ross Possession I. 3719
Sea C. Adare
D

Ross Sea

Pacific Basin

Southeast Pacific Basin

Ross Basin

Wilkes Land

Balleny Is.
Scott I.
Antarctic Circle

Southeast Indian Rise

PACIFIC OCEAN
Antarctic Ridge

Southwestern Basin
Pacific

▼6240

Macquarie I.
(Austr.)

Tasman Plat.

Campbell I.
(N.Z.)
Auckland Is.
(N.Z.)

Tasman Sea

Tasmania
Hobart
Bass Strait
Melbourne
AUSTRALIA

Antipodes Is.
90
Campbell
Plateau
Bounty Is. Stewart I.
Dunedin NEW ZEALAND

Tierra
del
Fuego
Estrecho
de la Maire
C. de Hornos
Hoste I.
CHILE
ARGENTINA

Ice cap

Permanent ice shelf

Maximum extent of
sea ice

March (Summer) extent
of sea ice

▲3488 Surface elevation and
3700 depth of ice

Stanley Permanent bases
(U.K.)

Projection: Zenithal Equidistant

COPYRIGHT GEORGE PHILIP LTD.

The Antarctic Treaty was signed in Washington in
1959 so that scientific and technical research could
continue unhampered by international politics.

All territorial claims covering land areas south
of latitude 60°S have been suspended. Those
claims were :

| | |
|---|---|
| Norwegian claim | 45°E - 20°W |
| Australian claims | { 45°E - 136°E |
| | { 142°E - 160°E } |
| French claim | 136°E - 142°E |
| New Zealand claim | 160°E - 150°W |
| Chilean claim | 90°W - 53°W |
| British claim | 80°W - 20°W |
| Argentine claim | 74°W - 53°W |

ft m
12 000 4000
6000 2000
4500 1500
3000 1000
1200 400
600 200
0 0
500 1500
1000 3000
2000 6000
3000 9000
4000 12 000
5000 15 000
m ft

**13**   **12**   **11**   **10**

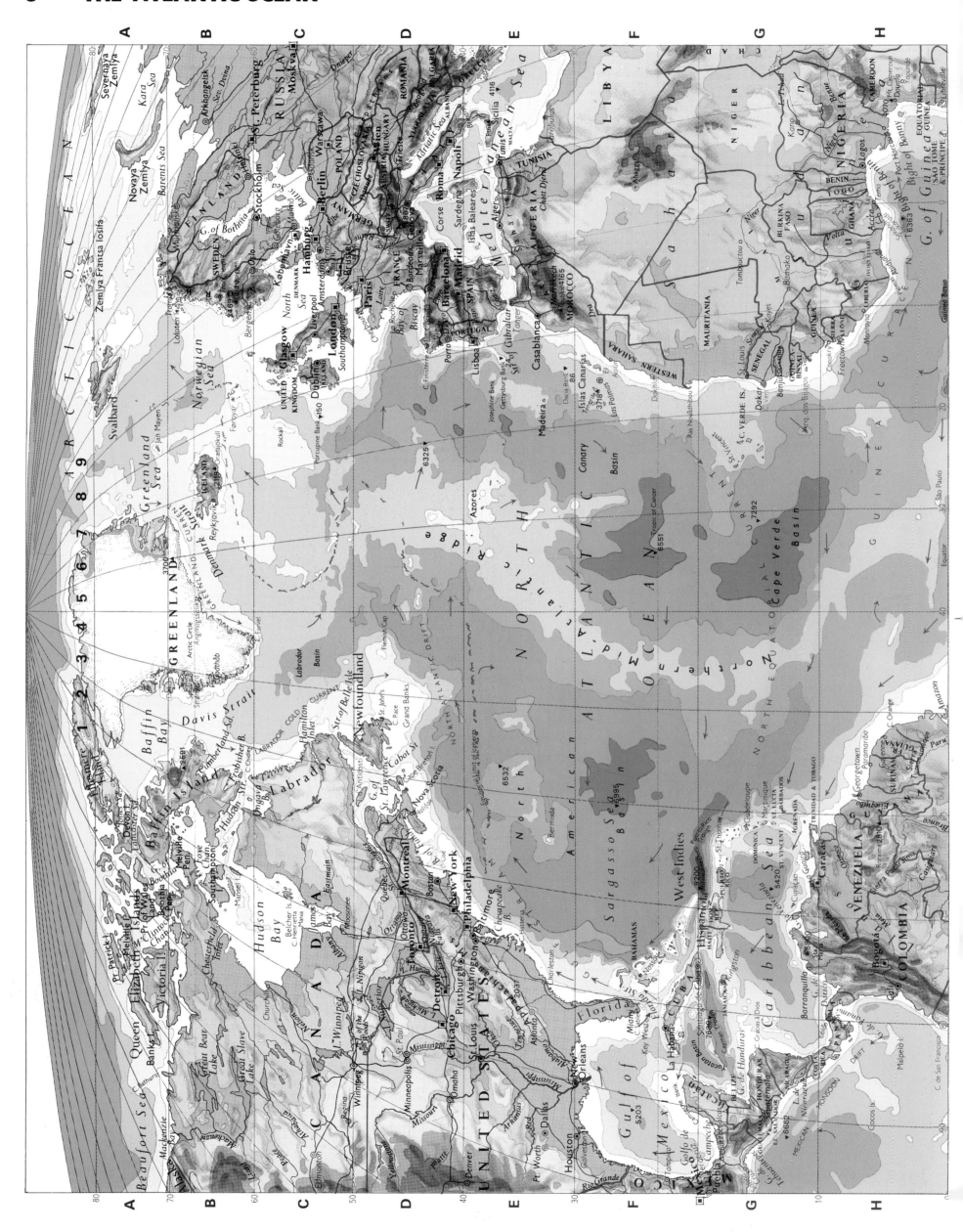

1 : 36 000 000

Projection: Moliweide

COPYRIGHT: GEORGE PHILIP & SON LTD.

→ Direction of Currents

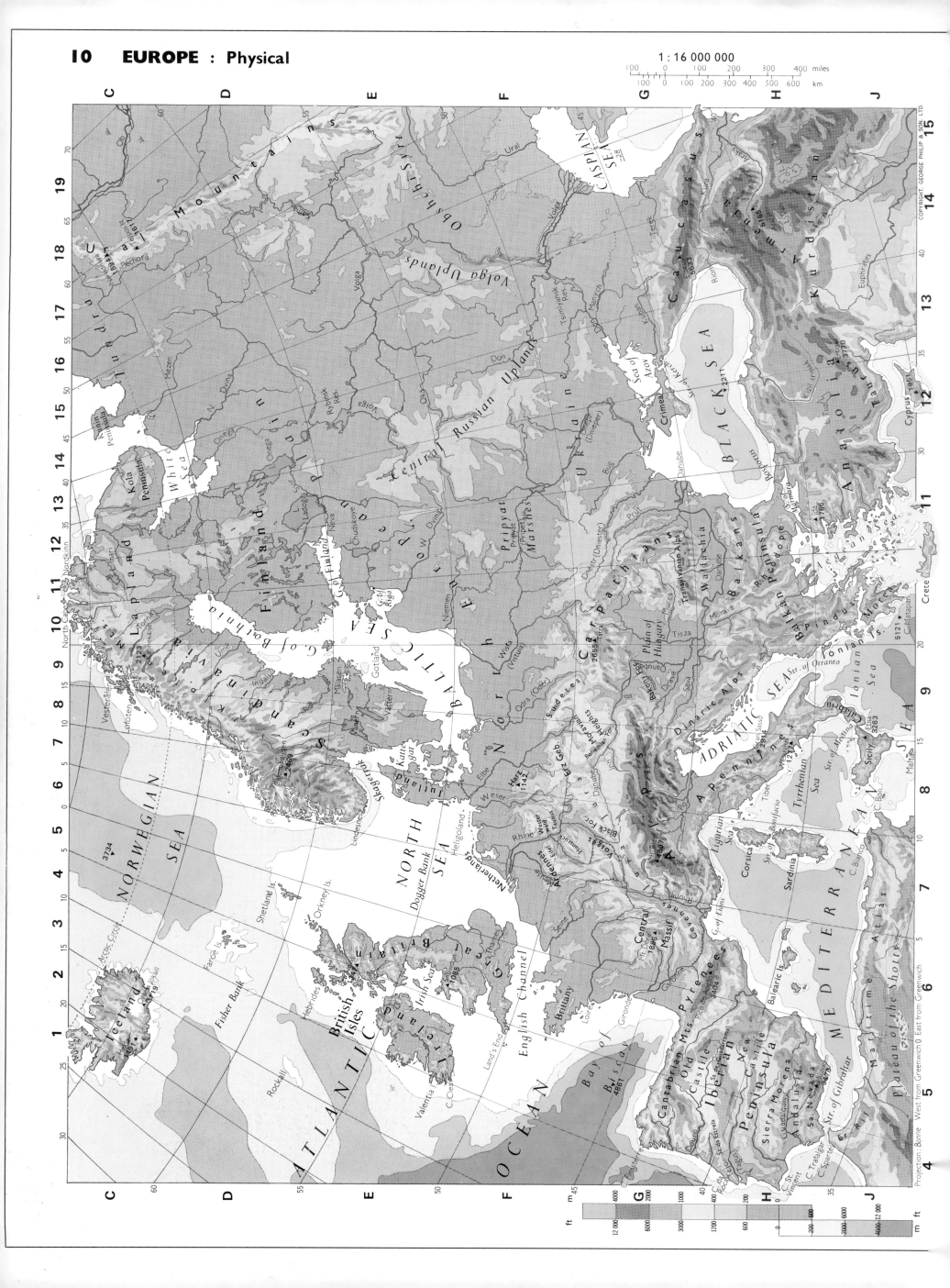

1 : 16 000 000

COPYRIGHT. GEORGE PHILIP & SON, LTD.

Projection: Bonne    West from Greenwich 0 East from Greenwich

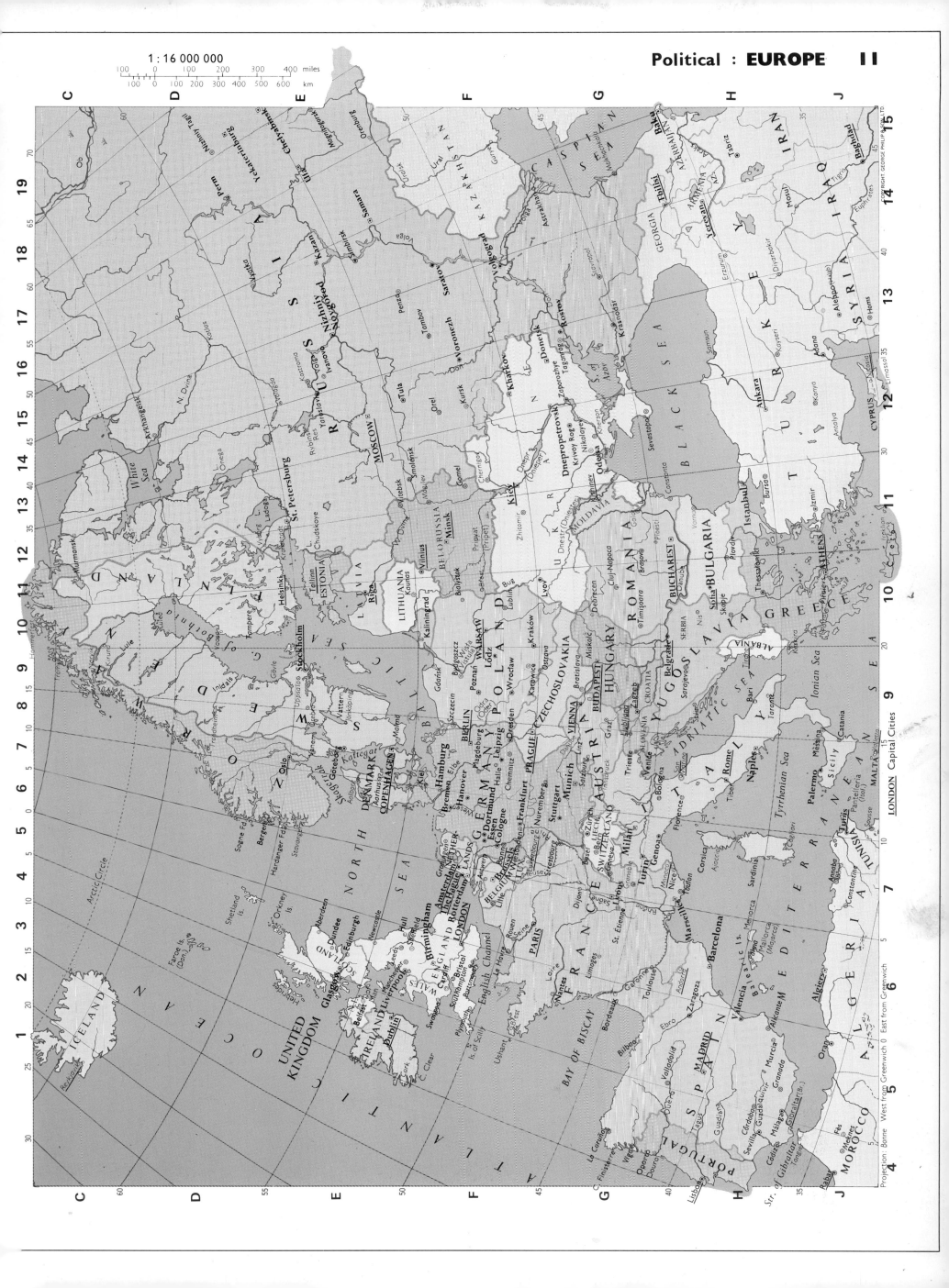

1 : 16 000 000

100   0   100   200   300   400 miles
100   0   200   300   400   500   600 km

LONDON Capital Cities

Projection : Bonne   West from Greenwich 0   East from Greenwich

COPYRIGHT GEORGE PHILIP & SON LTD.

ICELAND
on the same scale
as general map

NORWEGIAN SEA

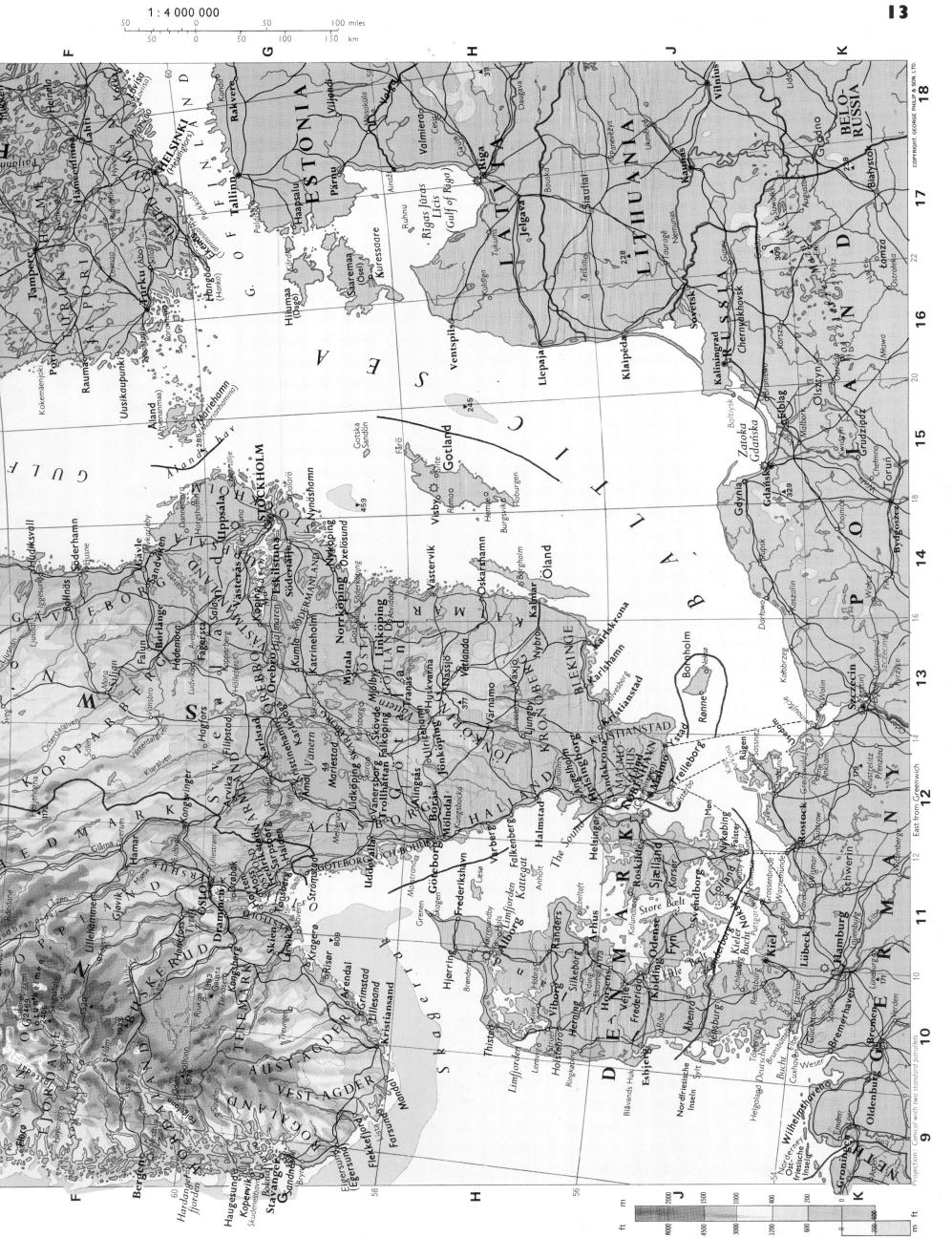

1 : 4 000 000

50    50    100 miles
50    0    50    100    150 km

18

F    G    H    J    K

Mikkeli    Lovisa    Kunda    Rakvere    Volga    Viljandi    Vilnius    BELO-
Lahti    HELSINKI    (Helsingfors)    ESTONIA    Daugava    RUSSIA
TUR UN-PORI    FINLAND    Tallinn    Valmiera    Riga    LITHUANIA    Vilnius    17
Tampere    Turku (Åbo)    Hungö (Hanko)    Haapsalu    Pärnu    LATVIA    Jelgava    Šiaulai    Kaunas    Gardno    Blalystok
Pori    Rauma    Uusikaupunki    Hiiumaa (Dag)    Saaremaa (Ösel)    Kuressaare    Rigas Jūras Lícis (Gulf of Riga)    Bauska    RUSSIA    Chernyakhovsk    16
Åland (Åvenanmaa)    Mariehamn (Maarianhamina)    Gotska Sandön    Gotland    Ruhnu    Ventspils    Klaipeda    Kaliningrad    POLAND

GULF    BALTIC    SEA    Liepaja    Zatoka Gdańska    Gdynia    Olsztyn    15
Hudiksvall    Söderhamn    Gävle    Sandviken    Stockholm    Uppsala    Nynäshamn    Oxelösund    Visby    Gotland    Borholm    Gdańsk    Torun    Bydgoszcz    14
GÄVLEBORG    KOPPARBERG    Borlänge    Falun    Avesta    Västerås    Eskilstuna    Södertälje    Norrköping    Oskarshamn    Öland    Karlskrona    Szczecin    POLAND    13
Mora    Orebro    Katrineholm    Linköping    Motala    Mjölby    Nässjö    Vetlanda    Kalmar    BLEKINGE    Karlshamn    Rönne    Kolobrzeg    12
HEDMARK    Karlstad    Kristinehamn    Jönköping    Huskvarna    Växjö    KRONOBERG    Kristianstad    Ystad    Rügen    Rostock    GERMANY
Hamar    Arvika    Skövde    Trollhättan    Vänersborg    Borås    HALLAND    Halmstad    Helsingborg    MALMÖ    KØBENHAVN    Trelleborg    Greifswald    Schwerin
Kongsvinger    GÖTEBORG OCH BOHUS    Göteborg    Varberg    Falkenberg    Kungsbacka    The Sound    Roskilde    Sjælland    Korsør    Nykøbing    Lübeck    Hamburg
OSLO    Drammen    Fredrikstad    Halden    Strömstad    Frederikshavn    Kattegat    Aalborg    Randers    Århus    Odense    Fyn    Kiel    Bremen
BUSKERUD    TELEMARK    Arendal    Grimstad    Lillesand    Kristiansand    Skagerrak    Thisted    Viborg    Silkeborg    Herning    Vejle    Kolding    DENMARK    Flensburg    Oldenburg
AUST-AGDER    VEST-AGDER    Farsund    Mandal    Esbjerg    Ribe    Åbenrå    Nordfriesische Inseln    Sylt    Helgoland    Wilhelmshaven    Bremerhaven
SOGN OG    HORDALAND    Bergen    Haugesund    Stavanger    ROGALAND    Egersund    Flekkefjord

Projection. Conical with two standard parallels

ft m
6000    2000
4500    1500
3000    1000
1200    400
600    200
0
m ft

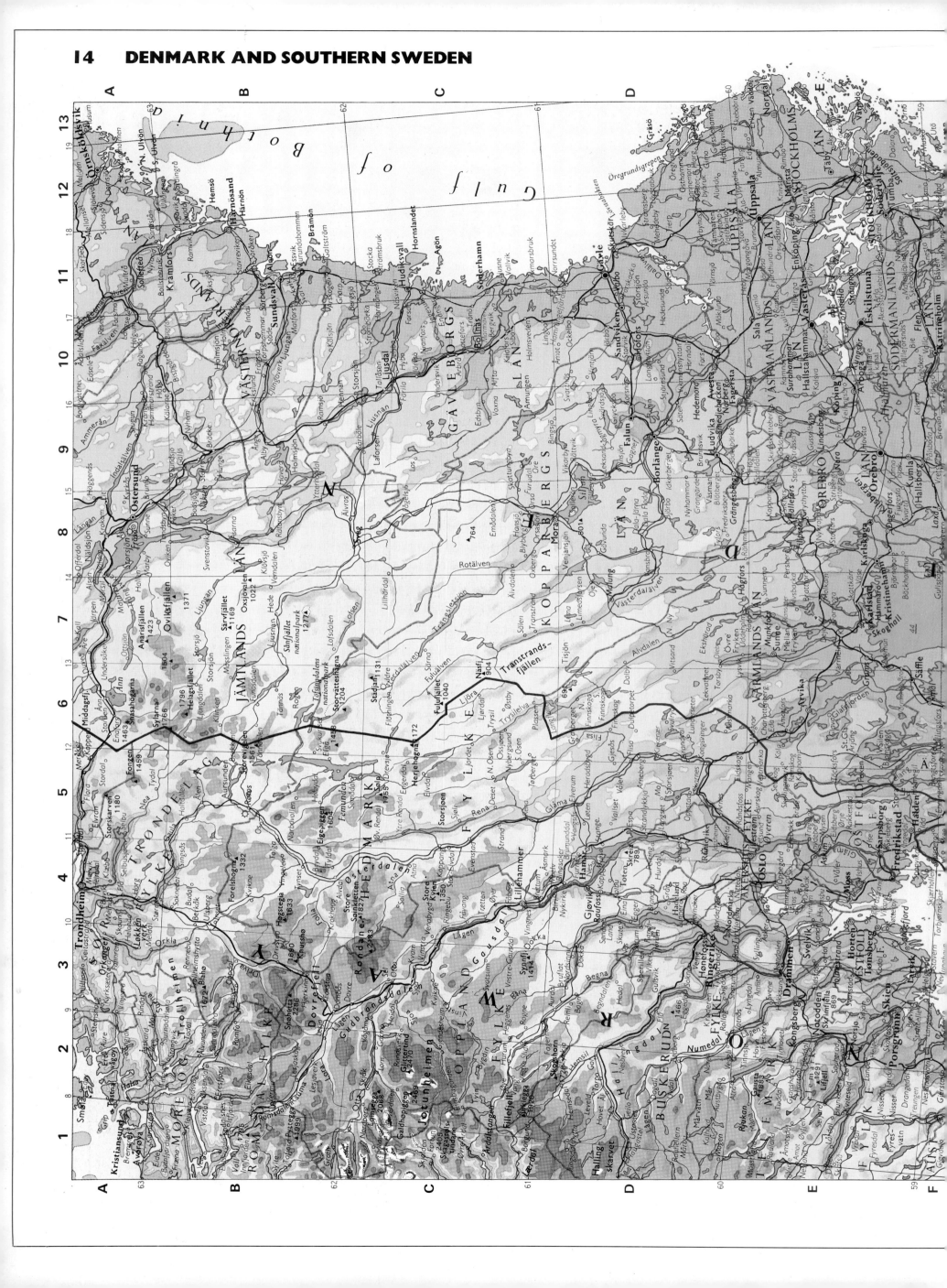

1 : 2 000 000

10 0 10 20 30 40 50 miles
10 0 10 20 30 40 50 60 70 80 km

G    H    J    K

POLAND

BALTIC SEA

Gotland
Visby
Öland
Kalmar
Karlskrona
Bornholm
Rönne
Nexö

KALMAR LÄN
JÖNKÖPINGS LÄN
KRONOBERGS LÄN
BLEKINGE LÄN
ÖSTERGÖTLANDS LÄN
SKARABORGS LÄN
HALLANDS LÄN
MALMÖHUS LÄN
KRISTIANSTADS LÄN

Norrköping
Oxelösund
Linköping
Motala
Mjölby
Nässjö
Jönköping
Huskvarna
Värnamo
Växjö
Kalmar
Nybro
Oskarshamn
Västervik
Karlskrona
Ronneby
Karlshamn
Kristianstad
Simrishamn
Ystad
Trelleborg
Malmö
Lund
Landskrona
Helsingborg
Ängelholm
Halmstad
Falkenberg
Varberg
Kungsbacka
Mölndal
Göteborg
Borås
Alingsås
Trollhättan
Uddevalla
Lidköping
Mariestad
Skövde
Falköping

GERMANY
Kiel
Flensburg
Rügen
Hiddensee
Rostock
Fehmarn
Arkona

Kattegat
Skagerrak

Skagen
Frederikshavn
Hjørring
Ålborg
Ålborg Bugt
NORDJYLLANDS AMT
Randers
Århus
Djursland
Viborg
Holstebro
Herning
Silkeborg
Horsens
Vejle
Kolding
Fredericia
Esbjerg
Ribe
Tønder
Haderslev
Åbenrå
Sønderborg

DENMARK

JYLLAND
FYN
Odense
Svendborg
Middelfart
Nyborg
Assens

SJÆLLAND
KØBENHAVN
Roskilde
Køge
Helsingør
Hillerød
Frederikssund
Slagelse
Næstved
Vordingborg
Korsør
Kalundborg
Holbæk

LOLLAND
FALSTER
Nykøbing
Nakskov
Maribo

Møn

Bornholm

Poland
Słupsk
Łeba

Projection: Conical with two standard parallels
East from Greenwich
COPYRIGHT GEORGE PHILIP & SON, LTD.

m / ft
6000 4500 3000 1200 600 200 0

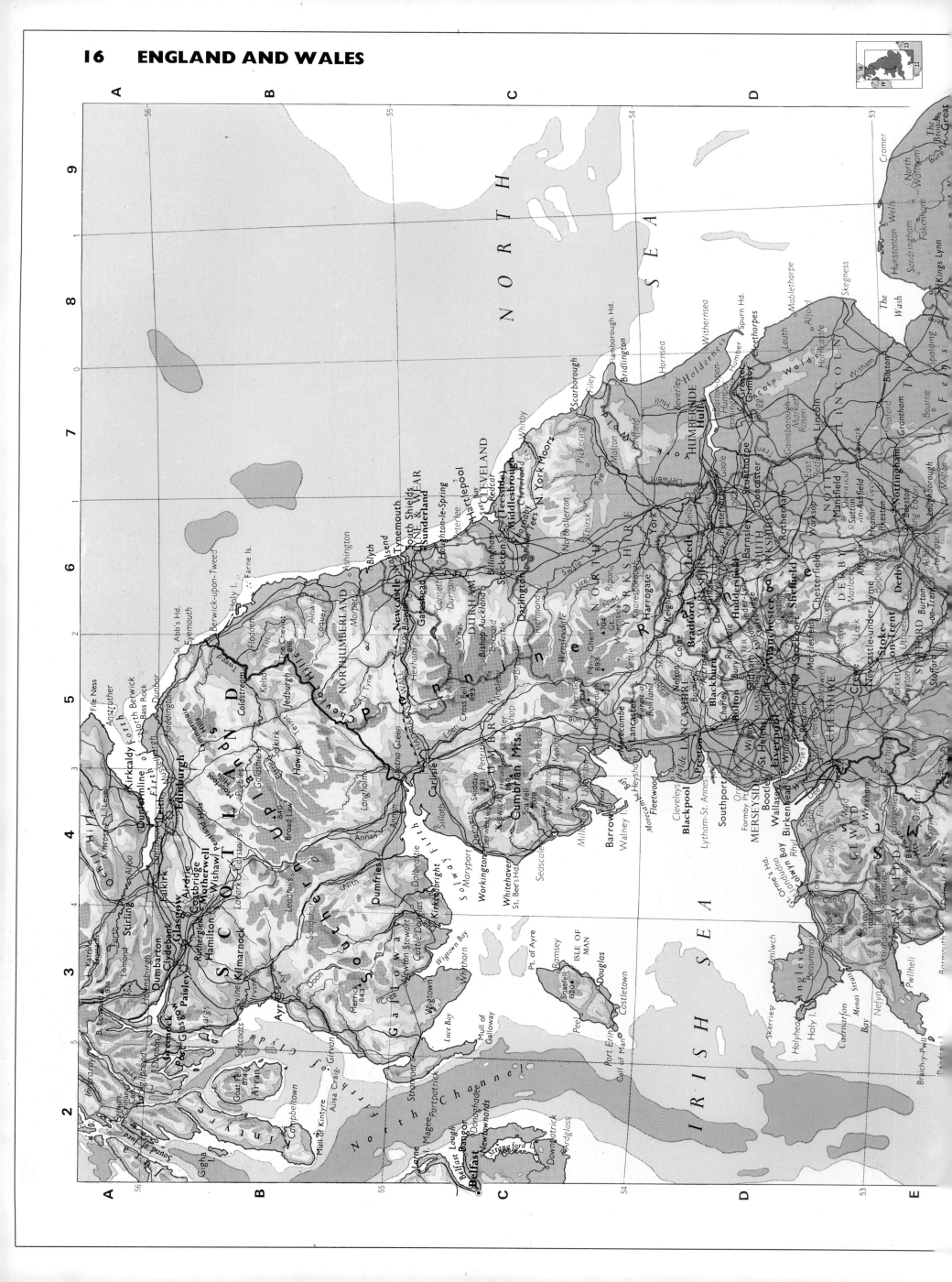

1 : 1 600 000

SCILLY ISLES
On same Scale

Projection: Conical with two standard parallels.

East from Greenwich COPYRIGHT GEORGE PHILIP & SON, LTD.

ENGLISH CHANNEL

FRANCE

Channel Islands

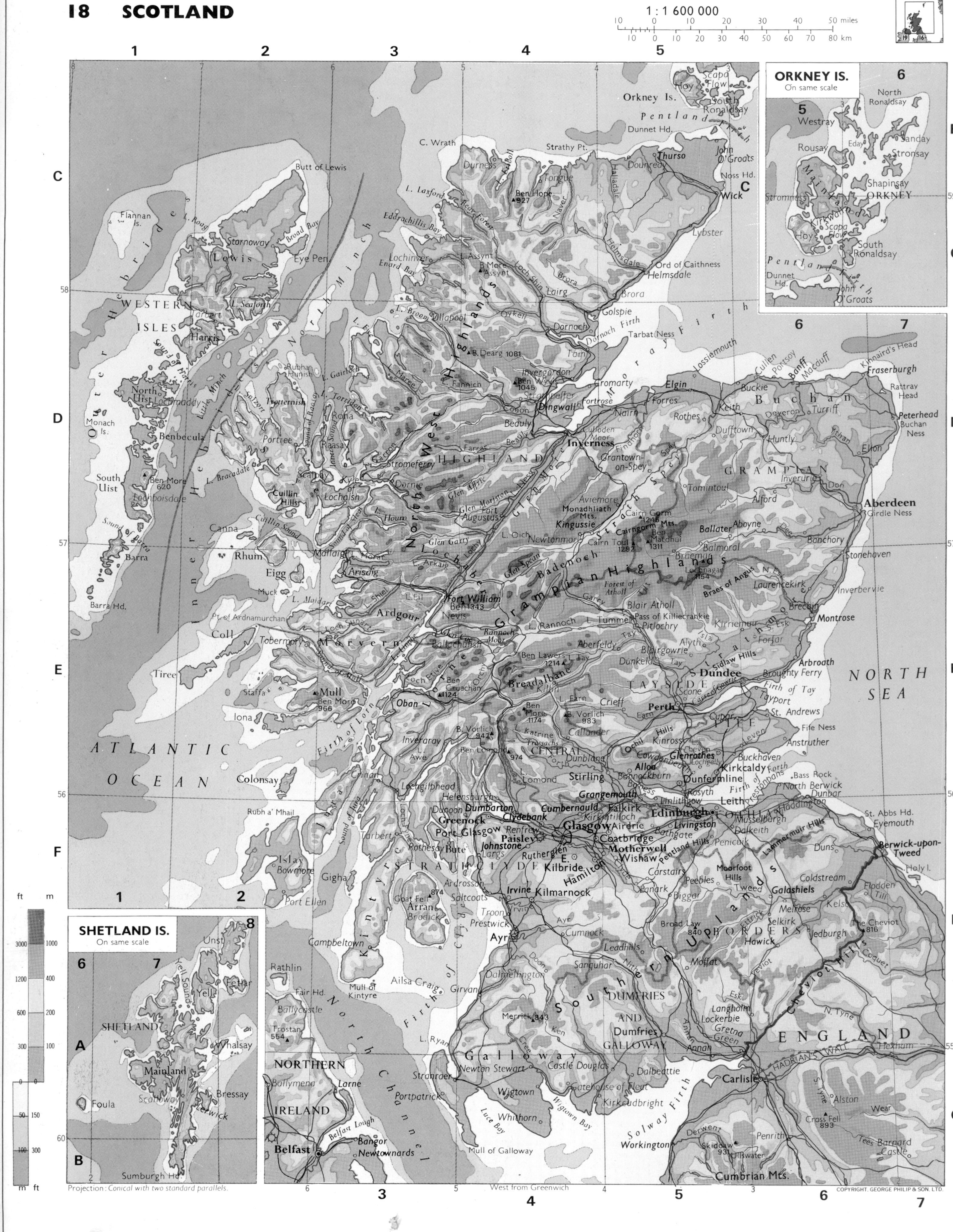

# 18 SCOTLAND

1 : 1 600 000

Scale: miles 10 0 10 20 30 40 50 miles; km 10 0 10 20 30 40 50 60 70 80 km

## ORKNEY IS.
On same scale

Scapa Flow, Hoy, South Ronaldsay, Westray, Rousay, Eday, Sanday, Stronsay, Shapinsay, ORKNEY, Stromness, Mainland, Kirkwall, Scapa Flow, South Ronaldsay, Dunnet Hd., Pentland Firth, John O'Groats

## SHETLAND IS.
On same scale

Unst, Yell, Fetlar, SHETLAND, Mainland, Whalsay, Scalloway, Bressay, Lerwick, Foula, Sumburgh Hd.

## Main map labels

Orkney Is., Pentland Firth, C. Wrath, Strathy Pt., Dunnet Hd., John O'Groats, Noss Hd., Thurso, Wick, Lybster, Butt of Lewis, Broad Bay, Stornoway, Lewis, Eye Pen., Durness, Tongue, Ben Hope 927, Halladale, Reay Forest, Eddrachillis Bay, Lochinver, Enard Bay, B. More Assynt, Loch Shin, Lairg, Brora, Golspie, Ord of Caithness, Helmsdale, Western Isles, Harris, Tarbert, L. Seaforth, Ullapool, L. Broom, Oykell, Dornoch, Dornoch Firth, Tarbat Ness, Moray Firth, North Uist, Lochmaddy, Benbecula, Monach Is., South Uist, Lochboisdale, Ben More 620, Barra, Barra Hd., Canna, Rhum, Eigg, Muck, Coll, Tiree, Staffa, Iona, Mull, Ben More 966, Tobermory, Morvern, Ardgour, Pt. of Ardnamurchan, Gairloch, Trotternish, Portree, Raasay, Scalpay, Cuillin Sound, Cuillin Hills, Kyle of Lochalsh, Dornie, Glenelg, Knoydart, Mallaig, Arisaig, Glen Garry, Loch Lochy, Fort Augustus, West Highlands, Invergarry, Glen Affric, Glen Moriston, Stromeferry, Torridon, L. Maree, Fannich, B. Dearg 1081, Dingwall, Beauly, Conon, Farrar, Strathpeffer, Invergordon, Ben Wyvis 1045, Cromarty, Fortrose, Nairn, Forres, Elgin, Lossiemouth, Buckie, Cullen, Portsoy, Banff, Macduff, Fraserburgh, Kinnaird's Head, Rattray Head, Peterhead, Buchan Ness, Buchan, Deveron, Turriff, Ellon, Inverness, Culloden Moor, Grantown-on-Spey, Findhorn, Dufftown, Huntly, Keith, Rothes, Alford, Inverurie, Aberdeen, Girdle Ness, Grampian, Aviemore, Monadhliath Mts., Cairn Gorm 1245, Cairngorm Mts., Cairn Toul 1292, Ben Macdhui 1311, Braemar, Balmoral, Ballater, Aboyne, Banchory, Stonehaven, Kingussie, Newtonmore, Grampian Highlands, Spean, Fort William, Ben Nevis 1343, Loch Linnhe, Glencoe, Ballachulish, Rannoch Moor, Loch Rannoch, L. Tummel, Forest of Atholl, Blair Atholl, Pass of Killiecrankie, Pitlochry, Kirriemuir, Braes of Angus, Lochnagar 1154, Laurencekirk, Inverbervie, Brechin, Montrose, Arbroath, Broughty Ferry, Sound of Mull, Loch Etive, Ben Cruachan 1124, Oban, Loch Awe, Inveraray, Ben Lawers 1214, Breadalbane, Aberfeldy, Dunkeld, Blairgowrie, Alyth, Forfar, Sidlaw Hills, Dundee, Firth of Tay, Tayport, St. Andrews, Fife Ness, Perth, Crieff, Comrie, Callander, Trossachs, L. Katrine, Ben Lomond 974, B. Vorlich 942, Ben Vorlich 985, Loch Lomond, Aberfeldy, Firth of Lorn, Colonsay, Crinan, Lochgilphead, Helensburgh, Dumbarton, Clydebank, Greenock, Port Glasgow, Dunoon, Rothesay, Bute, Paisley, Johnstone, Largs, Glasgow, Rutherglen, E. Kilbride, Hamilton, Motherwell, Wishaw, Coatbridge, Airdrie, Falkirk, Kirkintilloch, Cumbernauld, Grangemouth, Linlithgow, Bathgate, Livingston, Edinburgh, Leith, Musselburgh, Dalkeith, Penicuik, Pentland Hills, Moorfoot Hills, Lammermuir Hills, Haddington, Dunbar, North Berwick, Bass Rock, St. Abbs Hd., Eyemouth, Berwick-upon-Tweed, Holy I., Duns, Coldstream, Flodden, Till, The Cheviot 816, Jedburgh, Cheviot Hills, Kelso, Melrose, Galashiels, Selkirk, Hawick, Peebles, Bigger, Lanark, Carstairs, Carluke, Kilmarnock, Irvine, Troon, Prestwick, Ayr, Saltcoats, Ardrossan, Brodick, Arran, Goat Fell 874, Kintyre, Campbeltown, Mull of Kintyre, Islay, Bowmore, Port Ellen, Gigha, Jura, Sound of Jura, Tarbert, Rubh a' Mhail, Ailsa Craig, Firth of Clyde, Girvan, Cumnock, Dalmellington, Sanquhar, Leadhills, Moffat, Broad Law 840, Southern Uplands, Borders, Merrick 843, Trostan 554, Newton Stewart, Wigtown, Whithorn, Mull of Galloway, Wigtown Bay, Luce Bay, L. Ryan, Stranraer, Portpatrick, Galloway, Dumfries and Galloway, Dumfries, Castle Douglas, Dalbeattie, Kirkcudbright, Gatehouse of Fleet, Langholm, Lockerbie, Gretna Green, Annan, Solway Firth, Carlisle, Hadrian's Wall, Hexham, England, Alston, Cross Fell 893, Skiddaw 931, Workington, Penrith, Ullswater, Cumbrian Mts., Tees, Barnard Castle, Wear, North Sea, Atlantic Ocean, North Channel, Northern Ireland, Belfast, Belfast Lough, Newtownards, Bangor, Larne, Ballymena, Rathlin, Fair Hd., Ballycastle, Dunvegan, West from Greenwich

Elevation key (ft / m): 3000 / 1000, 1200 / 400, 600 / 200, 300 / 100, 0 / 0, 150 / 50, 300 / 100

Projection: Conical with two standard parallels.

COPYRIGHT. GEORGE PHILIP & SON. LTD.

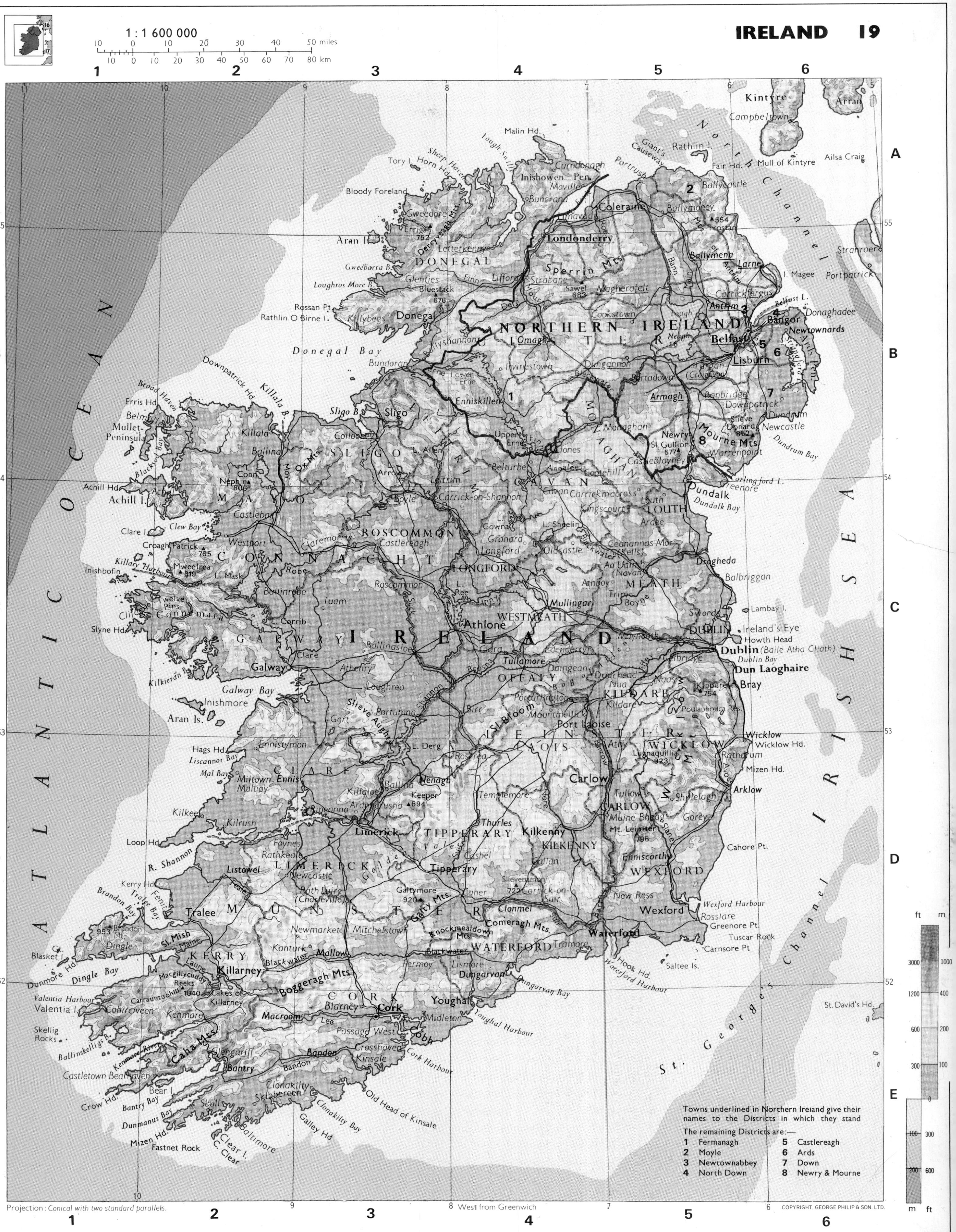

1 : 1 600 000

10    0    10    20    30    40    50 miles
10    0   10   20   30   40   50   60   70   80 km

1    2    3    4    5    6

**ATLANTIC OCEAN**

**NORTH CHANNEL**

**IRISH SEA**

**St. George's Channel**

Kintyre
Campbeltown
Arran
Mull of Kintyre
Ailsa Craig
Stranraer
Portpatrick

Malin Hd.
Tory I.
Horn Hd.
Sheep Haven
Lough Swilly
Bloody Foreland
Gweedore
Errigal 752
Aran I.
Letterkenny
**DONEGAL**
Gweebarra B.
Glenties
Bluestack 676
Loughros More B.
Rossan Pt.
Rathlin O'Birne I.
Killybegs
Donegal

Carndonagh
Inishowen Pen.
Moville
Buncrana
Limavady
Coleraine
**Londonderry**
Sperrin Mts.
Strabane
Sawel 883
Magherafelt
Cookstown
**NORTHERN IRELAND**
Omagh
Dungannon
Portadown
Craigavon
**Armagh**
Banbridge

Giant's Causeway
Portrush
Rathlin I.
Fair Hd.
Ballycastle
**Ballymoney**
554 Trostan
**Ballymena**
Antrim
Larne
Carrickfergus
**Belfast**
**Lisburn**
Bangor
Newtownards
Donaghadee
Ards Pen.
Downpatrick
Slieve Donard 852
**Mourne Mts.**
St. Gullion 577
Warrenpoint
Newcastle
Dundrum
Dundrum Bay

Donegal Bay
Bundoran
Ballyshannon
Lower L. Erne
Enniskillen
Irvinestown
Upper L. Erne
Belturbet

Broad Haven
Erris Hd.
Belmullet
Mullet Peninsula
Downpatrick Hd.
Killala B.
Sligo B.
Sligo
Collooney
Ballina
Killala
**MAYO**
Nephin 806
Conn
Achill Hd.
Achill I.
Clare I.
Clew Bay
Castlebar
**SLIGO**
Ox Mts.
Moy
Arrow
L. Allen
L. Gill
Carrick-on-Shannon
**LEITRIM**
**CAVAN**
Cavan
Carrickmacross
Kingscourt
Ardee
**LOUTH**
Dundalk
Dundalk Bay
Carlingford L.
Greenore

Croagh Patrick 765
Mweelrea 819
Killary Harbour
Inishbofin
Twelve Pins
**CONNEMARA**
Slyne Hd.
Clifden
**GALWAY**
**CONNACHT**
**ROSCOMMON**
Castlereagh
Boyle
Roscommon
Robe
Ballinrobe
L. Mask
L. Corrib
Tuam
Claremorris
**LONGFORD**
Longford
Granard
L. Sheelin
Oldcastle
Ceanannas Mor (Kells)
**MEATH**
An Uaimh (Navan)
Trim
Athboy
Drogheda
Balbriggan

Inishmore
Aran Is.
Galway Bay
Kilkieran
Galway
Clare
Athenry
Loughrea
Ballinasloe
**IRELAND**
Ballinasloe
Shannon
Clara
Tullamore
**OFFALY**
Edenderry
Maynooth
**DUBLIN**
**Dublin** (Baile Átha Cliath)
Dublin Bay
**Dun Laoghaire**
Ireland's Eye
Howth Head
Lambay I.
Swords

Slieve Aughty
Gort
L. Derg
Ennistymon
Lisdoonvarna
Mal Bay
**CLARE**
Miltown Malbay
Ennis
Killaloe
Scarriff
Nenagh
Ardnacrusha
Keeper 694
Birr
Roscrea
Templemore
**LAOIS**
Port Laoise
Mountmellick
Portarlington
Slieve Bloom
**KILDARE**
Kildare
Kippure 754
Poulaphouca Res.
Athy
**LEINSTER**
Naas
Bray
Wicklow
Wicklow Hd.
Lugnaquillia 923
**WICKLOW**
Rathdrum
Mizen Hd.
Arklow

Loop Hd.
Kilkee
Kilrush
Foynes
Rathkeale
Listowel
Newcastle
Rathluirc (Charleville)
**LIMERICK**
Limerick
**TIPPERARY**
Tipperary
Cashel
Caher
Thurles
**Kilkenny**
**KILKENNY**
Slievenamon 722
Carrick-on-Suir
Callan
Clonmel
Carlow
**CARLOW**
Tullow
Muine Bheag
Mt. Leinster 795
Gorey
Shillelagh
Cahore Pt.

Kerry Hd.
Brandon Hd.
Brandon 953
Mt. Brandon
Tralee Bay
Fenit
Tralee
Sl. Mish
Dingle
Dingle Bay
Blasket I.
Dunmore Hd.
**KERRY**
Castleisland
Killarney
Macgillycuddy Reeks
Carrauntoohill 1040
Lakes of Killarney
Kenmare
Valentia Harbour
Valentia I.
Cahirciveen
Skellig Rocks
Ballinskelligs B.
Kenmare River
Caha Mts.
Glengariff
Bantry
Bear I.
Castletown Bearhaven
Bantry Bay
Crow Hd.
Dunmanus Bay
Mizen Hd.
Clear I.
C. Clear
Fastnet Rock
Baltimore
Skull
Galley Hd.
Clonakilty Bay
Skibbereen
Clonakilty
Old Head of Kinsale

Newmarket
Kanturk
Mallow
Blackwater
Newcastle
Galtymore 920
Galty Mts.
Mitchelstown
Knockmealdown Mts.
Comeragh Mts.
Dungarvan
Dungarvan Bay
Lismore
Fermoy
**Blackwater**
**WATERFORD**
**Waterford**
Tramore
New Ross
**Wexford**
Rosslare
Wexford Harbour
Greenore Pt.
Tuscar Rock
Carnsore Pt.
Saltee Is.
Hook Hd.
Wexford Harbour
**WEXFORD**
Enniscorthy
**MUNSTER**

Boggeragh Mts.
**CORK**
Blarney
**Cork**
Macroom
Lee
Bandon
Bandon
Kinsale
Crosshaven
Passage West
Cobh
Cork Harbour
Midleton
Youghal
Youghal Harbour

St. David's Hd.

Towns underlined in Northern Ireland give their names to the Districts in which they stand
The remaining Districts are:—

1  Fermanagh          5  Castlereagh
2  Moyle              6  Ards
3  Newtownabbey       7  Down
4  North Down         8  Newry & Mourne

ft    m
3000
1200
600
300
100
m    ft

Projection: Conical with two standard parallels.

West from Greenwich

COPYRIGHT. GEORGE PHILIP & SON. LTD.

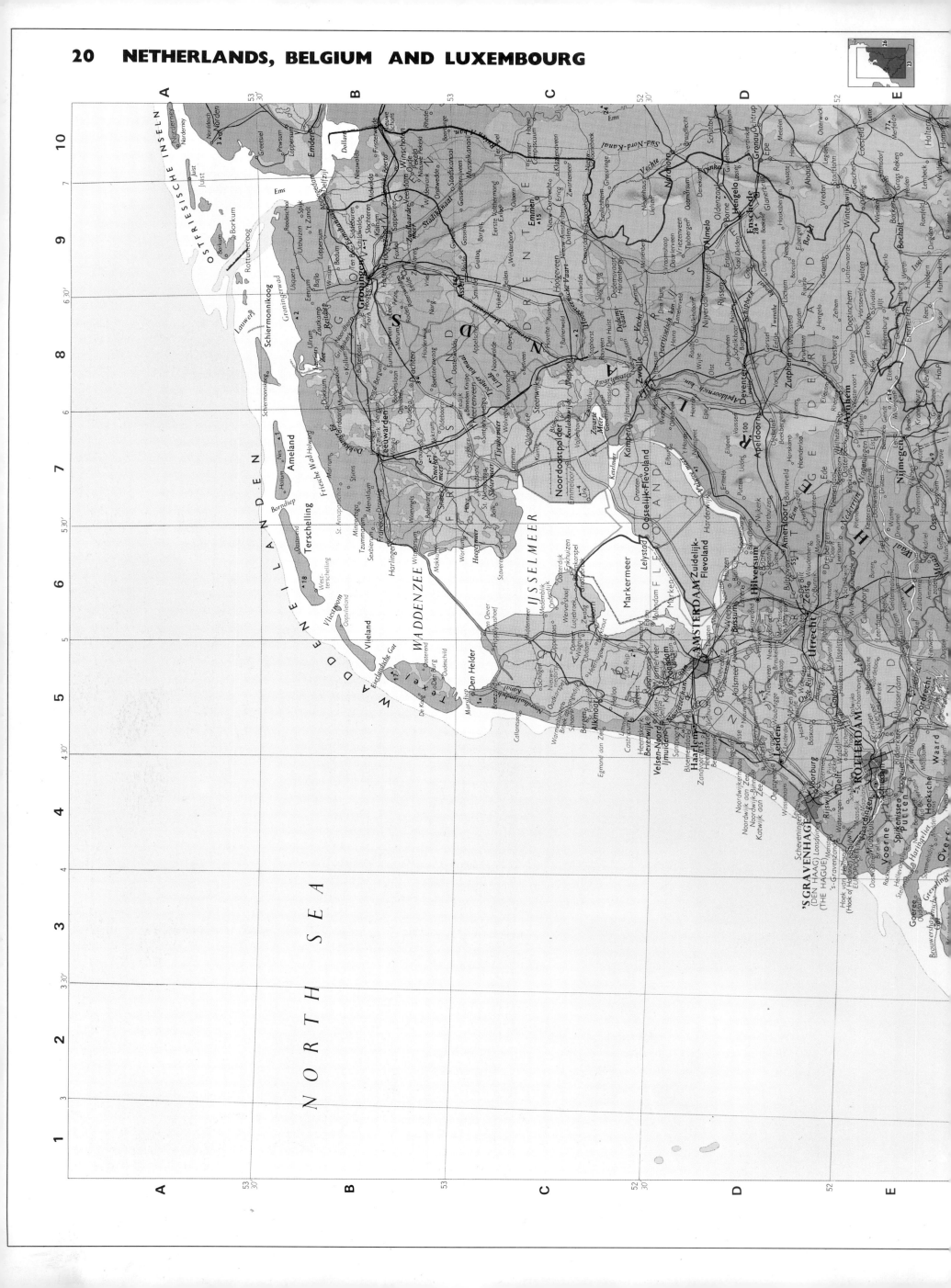

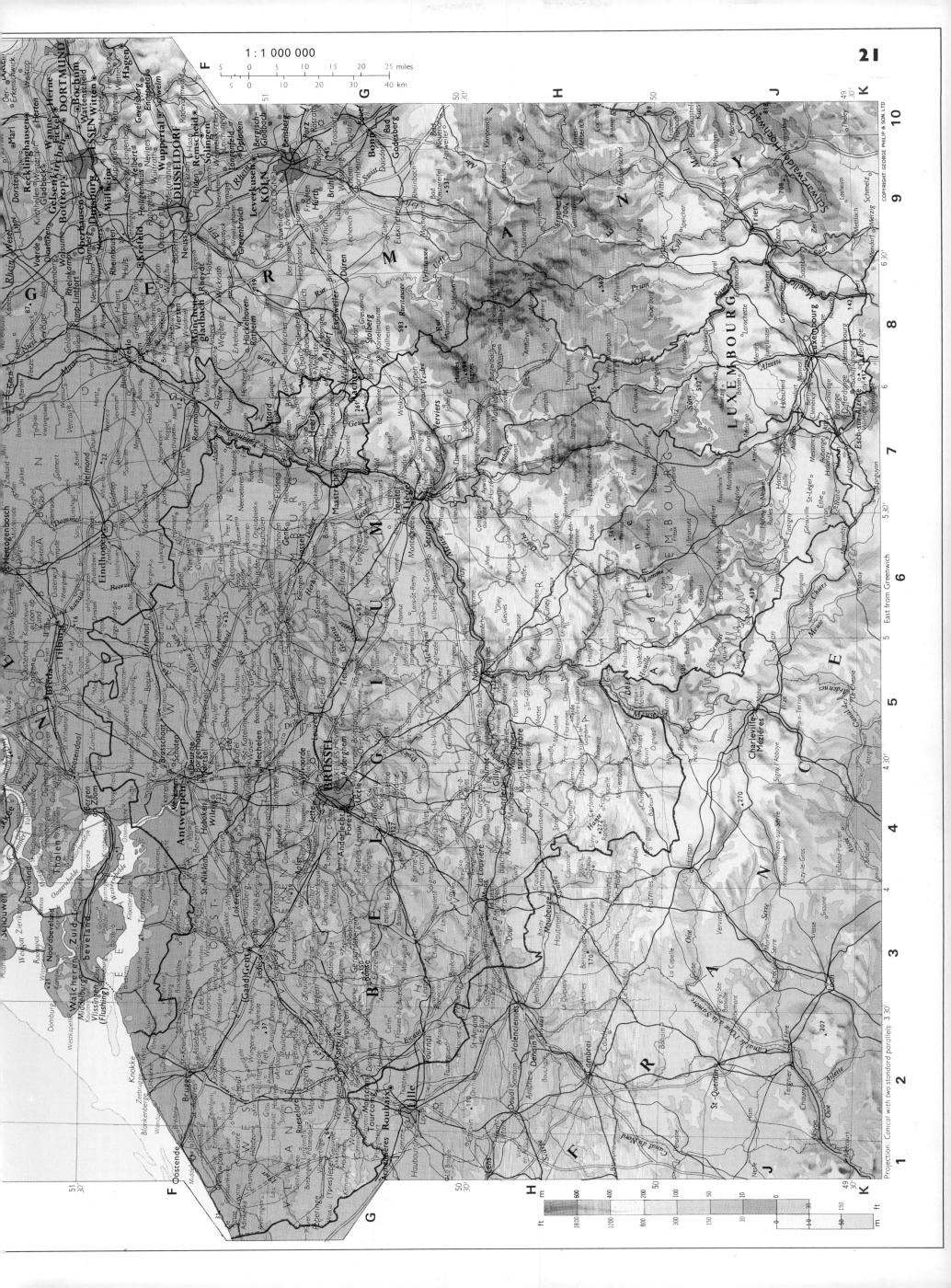

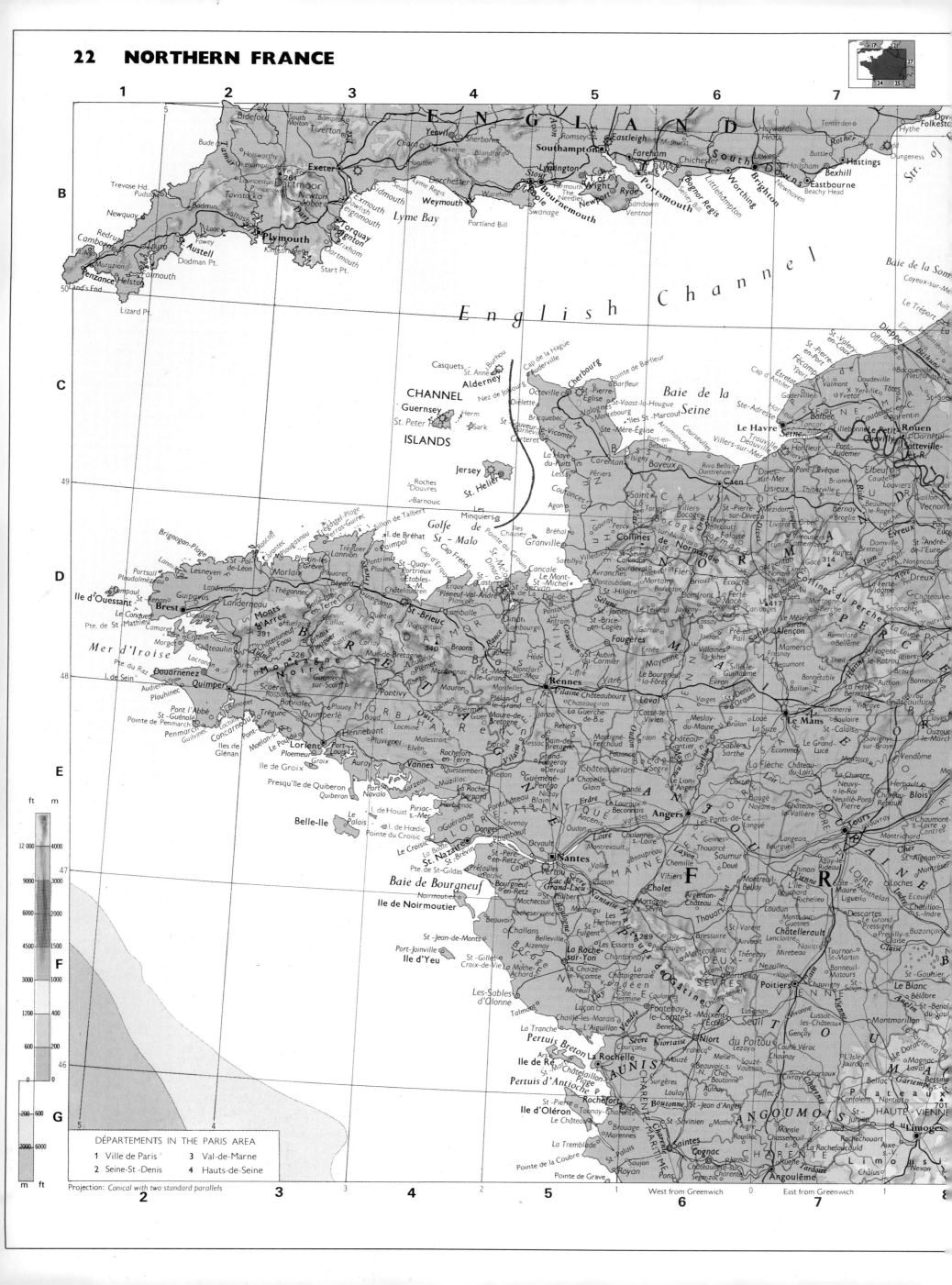

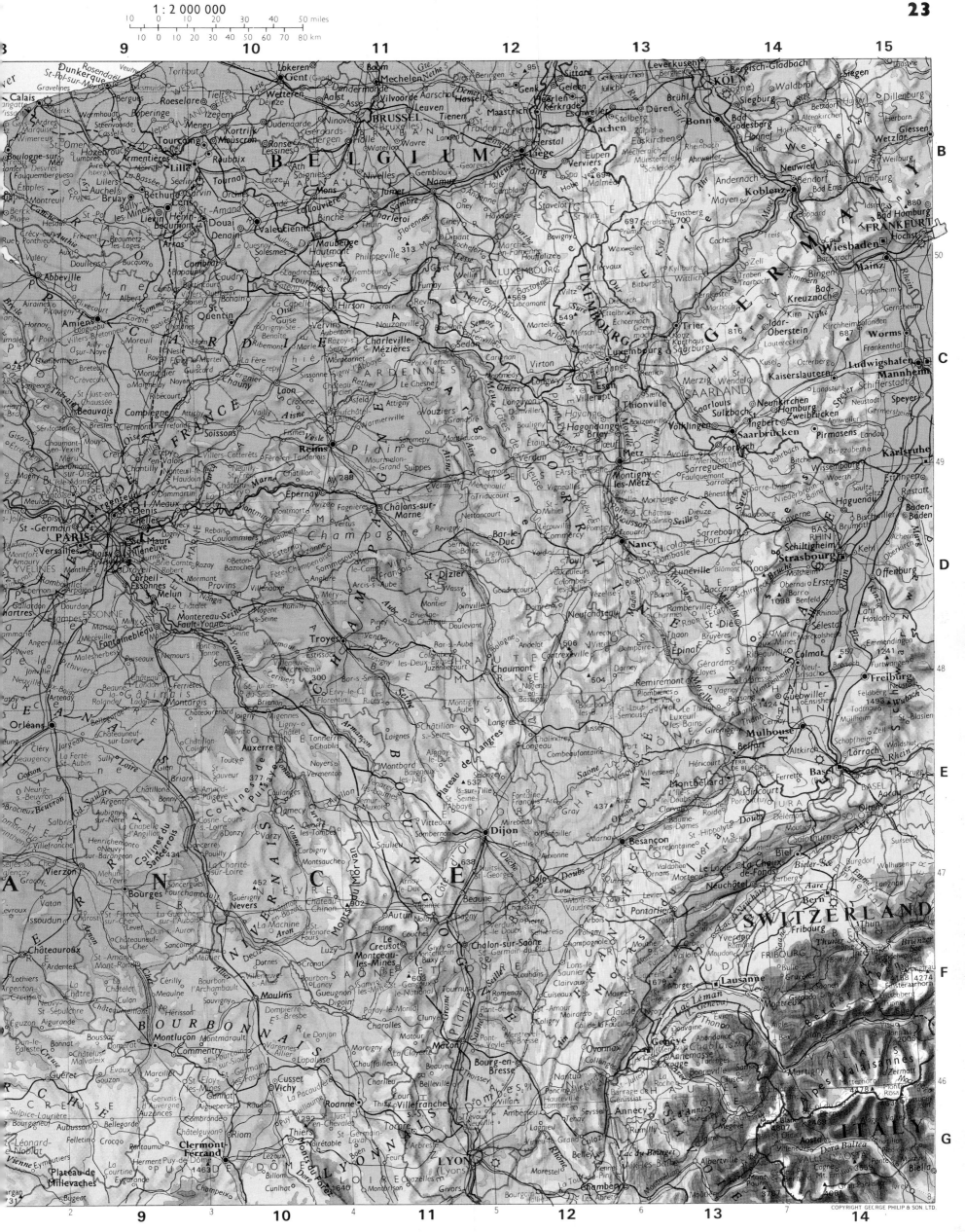

1 : 2 000 000

10 0 10 20 30 40 50 miles
10 0 10 20 30 40 50 60 70 80 km

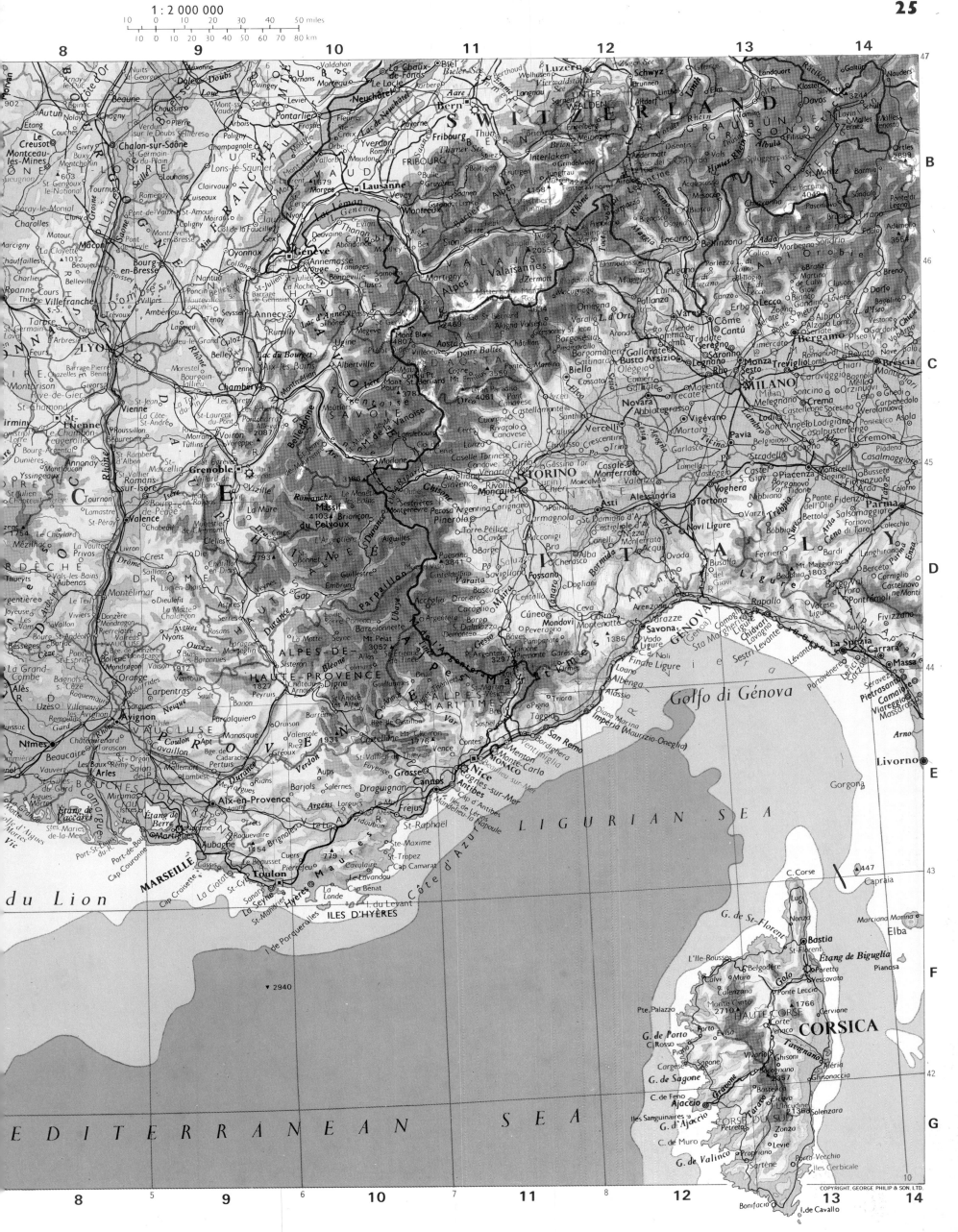

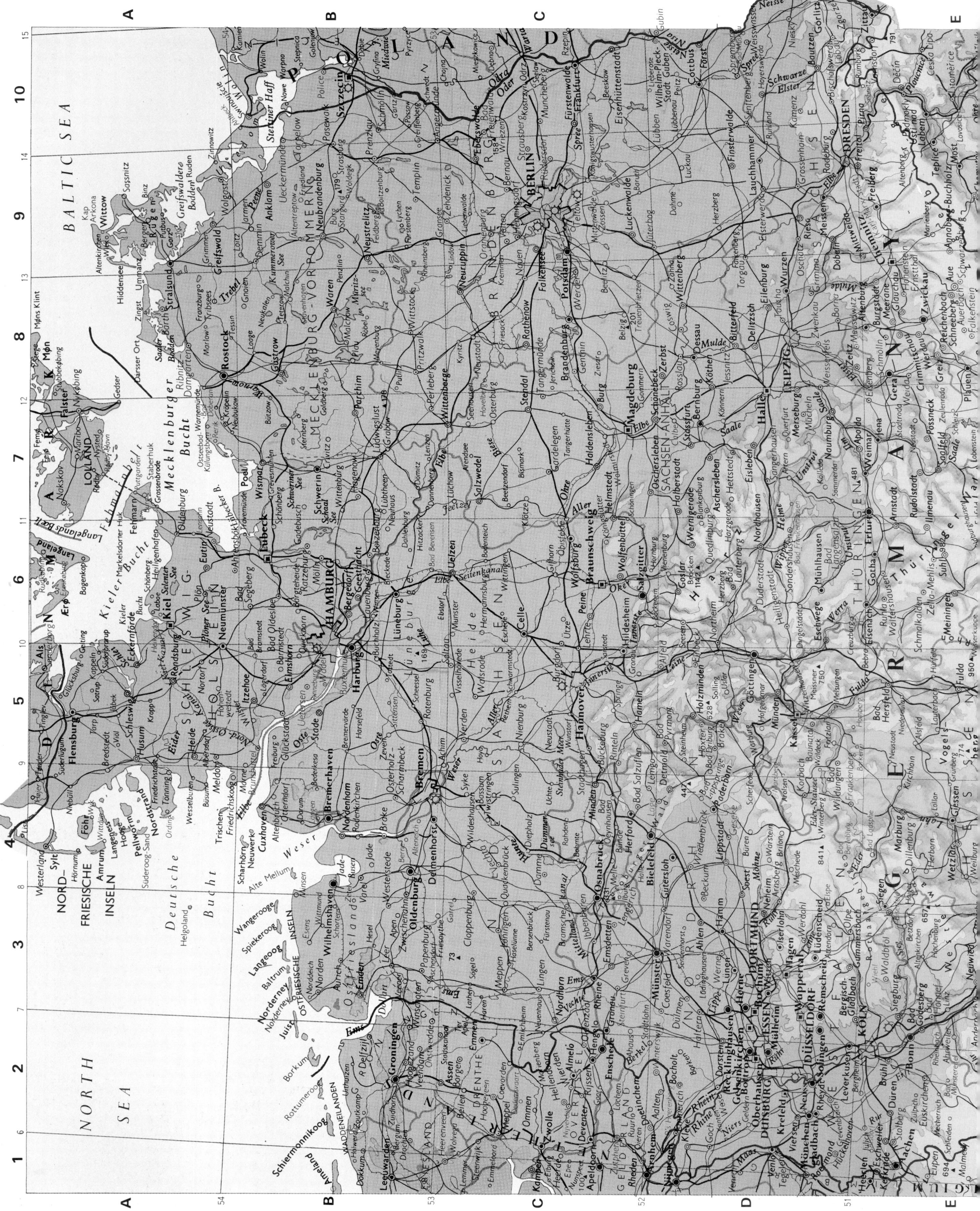

BALTIC SEA

NORTH SEA

POLAND

BERLIN

HAMBURG

Bremen

Rostock

Lübeck

Kiel

Flensburg

Schwerin

Magdeburg

Potsdam

LEIPZIG

DRESDEN

Halle

Hannover

Braunschweig

Osnabrück

Münster

DORTMUND

ESSEN

DÜSSELDORF

KÖLN

Bonn

Wilhelmshaven

Oldenburg

MECKLENBURG-VORPOMMERN

BRANDENBURG

SACHSEN-ANHALT

SACHSEN

THÜRINGEN

NIEDERSACHSEN

SCHLESWIG-HOLSTEIN

NORDFRIESISCHE INSELN

OSTFRIESISCHE INSELN

DEUTSCHLAND

NEDERLAND

GELDERLAND

OVERIJSSEL

DRENTHE

FRIESLAND

Groningen

Stralsund

Greifswald

RÜGEN

Stettiner Haff

Cuxhaven

Bremerhaven

Lüneburg

Celle

Göttingen

Bielefeld

Kassel

Erfurt

Weimar

Jena

Gera

Zwickau

Chemnitz

Görlitz

Cottbus

Frankfurt

Neubrandenburg

Güstrow

Wismar

Neumünster

Emden

Siegen

Marburg

Gießen

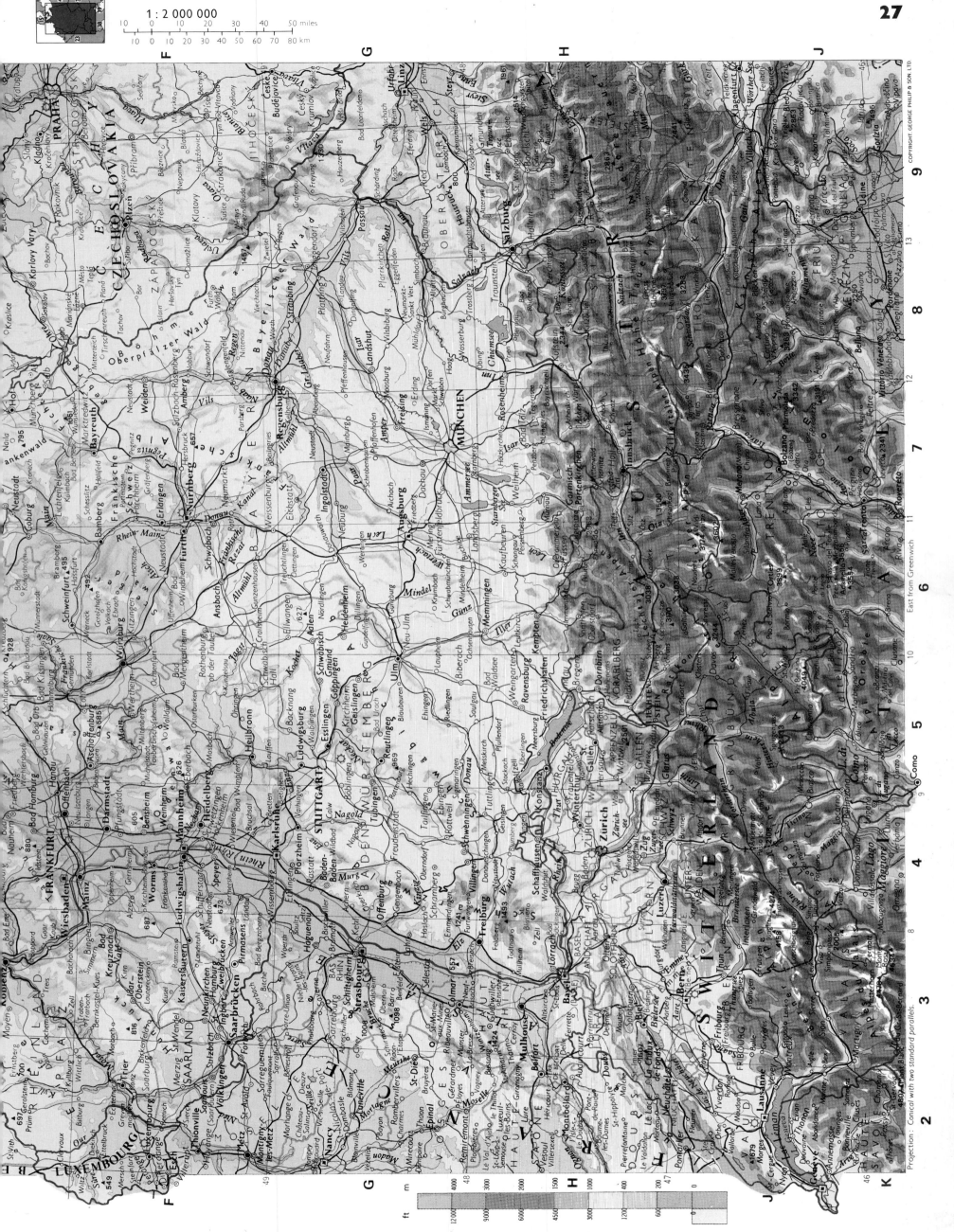

1 : 2 000 000

East from Greenwich

Projection: Conical with two standard parallels.

Projection: *Conical with two standard parallels*

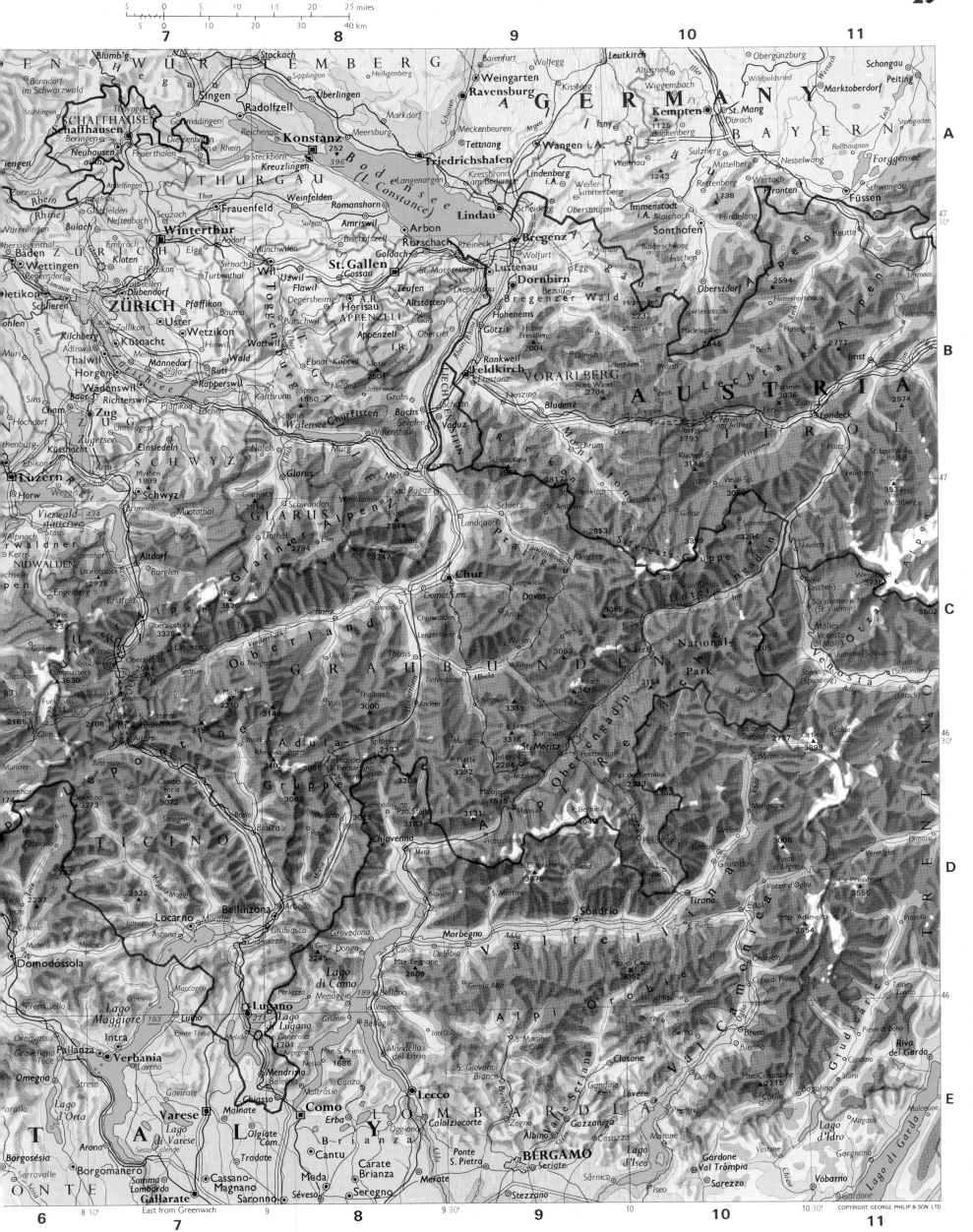

1 : 800 000

5   0   5   10   15   20   25 miles
5   0   10   20   30   40 km

7          8          9          10          11

**Germany**

Blumb'g.   Schwenningen   Stockach   Baienfurt   Wolfegg   Leutkirch   Obergünzburg   Schongau
Bonndorf im Schwarzwald   Singen   Sipplingen   Heiligenberg   Wangen   Kisslegg   Wiggensbach   Wildpoldsried   Marktoberdorf   Peiting
Stühlingen   Radolfzell   Überlingen   Markdorf   Meckenbeuren   Isny   Altusried   Kempten   Durach   St. Mang   Nesselwang

**Schaffhausen**
Beringen   **Konstanz**   252   Meersburg   Friedrichshafen   Tettnang   Wangen i.A.   Sulzberg   Rettenberg   Pfronten   Forggensee
Neuhausen a.Rh.   Feuerthalen   Steckborn   396   Kreuzlingen   Kressbronn am Bodensee   Lindenberg i.A.   Immenstadt   Hindelang   Füssen

**Thurgau**   Bodensee (L. Constance)   Lindau   Bregenz   Sonthofen   Oberstdorf

**Winterthur**   St. Gallen   Rorschach   Dornbirn   Bregenzer Wald   2594

**Zürich**   Appenzell   Feldkirch   **Vorarlberg**   **Austria**

**Graubünden**

**Chur**   Davos   National-Park

**Ticino**   **Adula-Gruppe**   St. Moritz   Ober-Engadin

**Bellinzona**   Chiavenna   Sondrio   Tirano

**Locarno**   **Lombardia**

**Lugano**   Lago di Como   Lecco   **Bergamo**

Varese   Como   Lago d'Iseo   Lago di Garda

**Italy**

East from Greenwich

6          7          8          9          10          11

COPYRIGHT. GEORGE. PHILIP & SON. LTD.

Countries and regions: HESSEN, THÜRINGEN, SACHSEN, BAYERN, BADEN-WÜRTTEMBERG, VORARLBERG, LIECHTENSTEIN, SWITZERLAND, ITALY, AUSTRIA, SLOVENIA, ZÁPADOČESKÝ, STŘEDOČESKÝ, JIHOČESKÝ, SEVEROČESKÝ, VÝCHODOČES, NIEDERÖST, OBERÖSTERR, TIROL, KÄRNTEN, STEIERMARK, FRIULI, VENEZIA GIULIA, TRENTINO, ALTO ADIGE, LOMBARDIA, GRAUBÜNDEN

Major cities: DRESDEN, PRAHA (PRAGUE), Chemnitz (Karl-Marx-Stadt), STUTTGART, MÜNCHEN (Munich), Nürnberg, Regensburg, Augsburg, Salzburg, Linz, Graz, Klagenfurt, Ljubljana, Zagreb, Trieste, Bergamo, Brescia, Verona, Vicenza, Bolzano, Trento, Innsbruck, Würzburg, Bayreuth, Plzeň, Liberec, Erfurt, Weimar, Jena, Gera, Zwickau, Plauen, Hof, Karlovy Vary, Ústí nad Labem, Kladno, České Budějovice, Maribor

Rivers: Main, Donau (Danube), Inn, Lech, Isar, Elbe (Labe), Vltava, Drau, Mur, Enns

Scale bar:
ft / m
12 000 / 4000
9000 / 3000
6000 / 2000
4500 / 1500
3000 / 1000
1200 / 400
600 / 200
0 / 0

Projection: Conical with two standard parallels

1 : 2 000 000

East from Greenwich

COPYRIGHT. GEORGE PHILIP & SON. LTD.

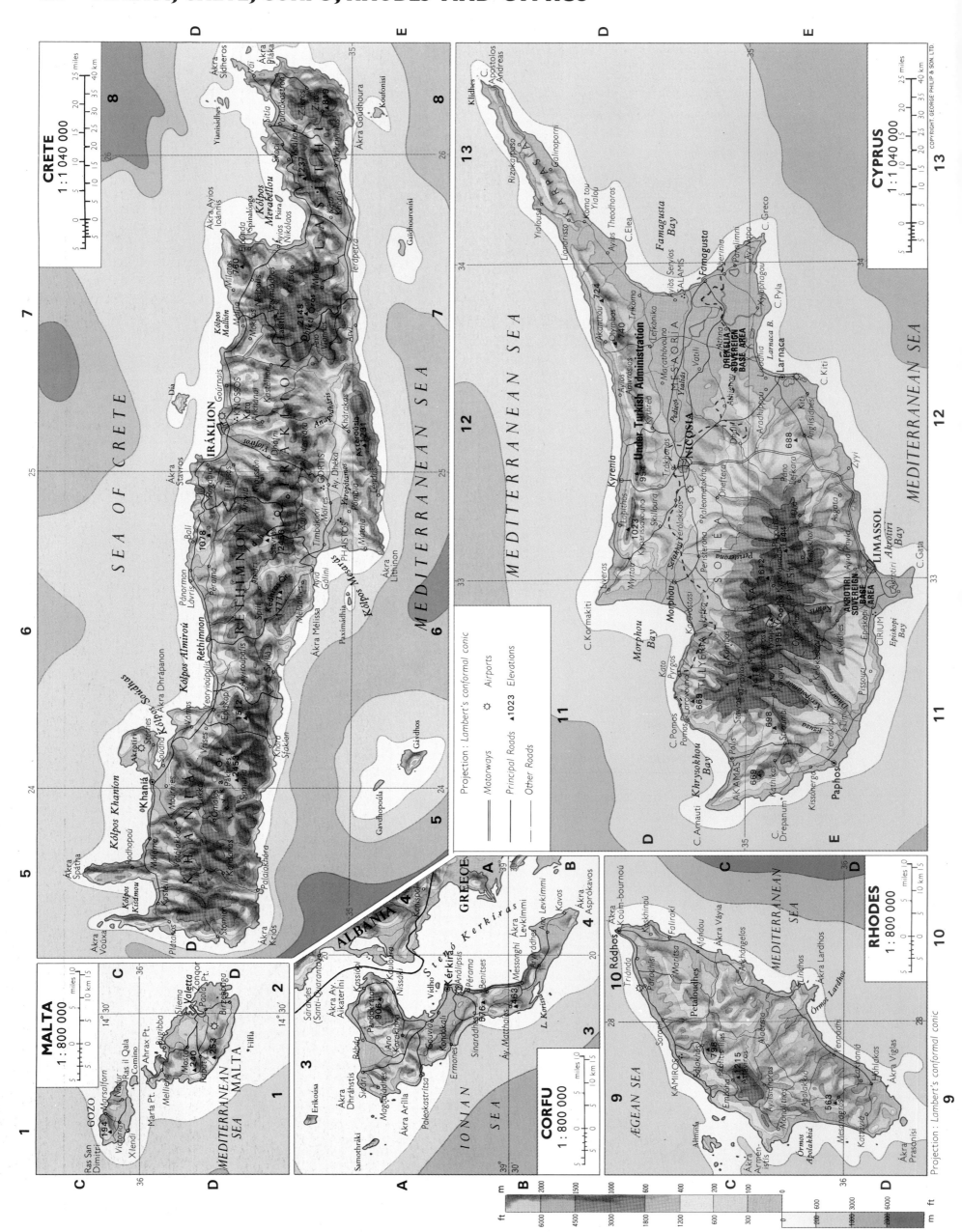

**CRETE**
1:1 040 000

**MALTA**
1:800 000

**CORFU**
1:800 000

**RHODES**
1:800 000

**CYPRUS**
1:1 040 000

Projection : Lambert's conformal conic

Motorways
Principal Roads
Other Roads
Airports
▲1023 Elevations

COPYRIGHT GEORGE PHILIP & SON, LTD.

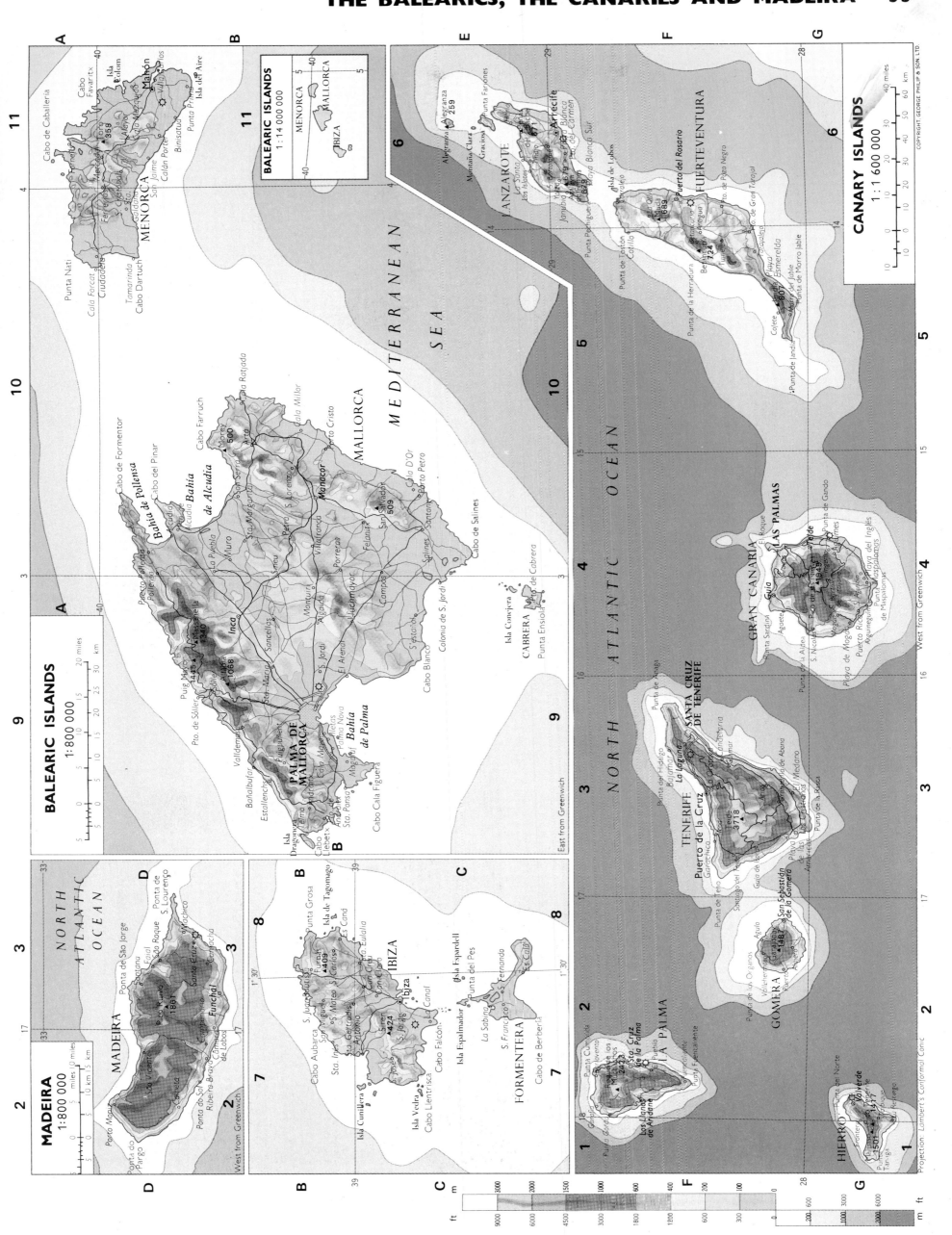

## MENORCA

Cabo de Caballeria
Punta Nati
Cala Forcat
Ciudadela
Tamarinda
Cabo Dartuch
Binisatud
San Jaime
Cala Porter
Punta Prima
Isla del Aire
Cabo Favaritx
Isla Colom
Villa Carlos
Mahón
Monte Toro 358
Mercadal
Alayor
Sta. Galdana
Ferrerias

### BALEARIC ISLANDS
1:14 000 000

MENORCA
MALLORCA
IBIZA

## BALEARIC ISLANDS
1:800 000

## MEDITERRANEAN SEA

## MALLORCA

Cabo de Formentor
Cabo de Pollensa
Cabo del Pinar
Bahía de Pollensa
Puerto Pollensa
Pollensa
Pto. de Sóller
Sóller
Puig Mayor 1445
Lluch 1340
Alaró
Inca
La Puebla
Muro
Sta. Margarita
Sancellas
Binisalem
Sineu
Petra
Manacor
San Lorenzo
Son Servra
Morey 500
Artá
Cala Ratjada
Cala Millor
Porto Cristo
Cala D'Or
Porto Petro
San Salvador 509
Felanitx
Santany
Cabo de Salines
Cabo Blanco
Cabo Salines
Bahía de Alcudia
Alcudia
Estellencs
Bañalbufar
Valldemosa
Galilea
Puigpuñent
Andraitx
Calviá
Palma Nova
Magaluf
Santa Ponsa
Cabo Cala Figuera
Isla Dragonera
Calvo
Llebetx
PALMA DE MALLORCA
Bahía de Palma
Llucmayor
Campos
Porreras
Villafranca
Algaida
Montuiri
El Arenal
S'Estanyol
Colonia de S. Jordi

CABRERA
Isla Conejera
Isla de Cabrera
Punta Ensiola

## IBIZA
1° 30'
Punta Grosa
Isla de Tagomago
Cala San Vicente
S. Juan Bautista
Cabo Aubarca
Sta. Inés
San Miguel
San Mateo
S. Carlos
Sta. Eulalia
S. Lorenzo 409
S. Antonio
San Gertrudis
IBIZA
Ibiza
San Jorge 475
Salinas
Cabo Falcó
Isla Espartar
Punta del Pes
Cabo Llentrisca
Isla Vedra
Isla Conijera
1° 30'

## FORMENTERA
La Sabina
S. Francisco
S. Fernando
Isla Espalmador
Cabo de Berbería

## MADEIRA
1:800 000

NORTH ATLANTIC OCEAN

MADEIRA
Porto Moniz
Ponta do Pargo
Ponta do Sol
Ponta do Sol
Ribeira Brava
Câmara de Lobos
Funchal
Santa Cruz
Caniçal
Machico
Ponta de S. Lourenço
Pico Ruivo 1861
Ponta de São Jorge
Faial
São Vicente
Seixal
Santana

## CANARY ISLANDS
1:1 600 000

## LANZAROTE
Alegranza 259
Montaña Clara
Graciosa
Punta Fariones
Haría
Teguise
Arrecife
Mala
Puerto del Carmen
Playa Blanca Sur
Isla de Lobos

## FUERTEVENTURA
Corralejo
La Oliva
Puerto del Rosario
669
Pájara
Betancuria 724
Antigua
Tuineje
Punta de la Herradura
Esmeralda
Gran Tarajal
Morro Jable
Punta de Jandía

## GRAN CANARIA
Guia
Gáldar
Agaete
Teror
LAS PALMAS
Telde
Arucas 1949
Tejeda
San Nicolás
Punta de Maspalomas
Playa del Inglés
Maspalomas

## TENERIFE
Punta de Anaga
La Laguna
SANTA CRUZ DE TENERIFE
Tacoronte
Güímar
Puerto de la Cruz
Orotava
Teide 3718
Icod
Granadilla
El Médano
Guía de Isora
Adeje
Los Cristianos

## GOMERA
Agulo
Vallehermoso
San Sebastián de la Gomera
Garajonay 1487

## HIERRO
Valverde
Malpaso 1501 / 1477
Frontera
Sabinosa

## LA PALMA
Barlovento
Los Sauces
Santa Cruz de la Palma
Los Llanos de Aridane
Roque de los Muchachos 2423
Fuencaliente

CANARY ISLANDS
1:1 600 000

## MADEIRA

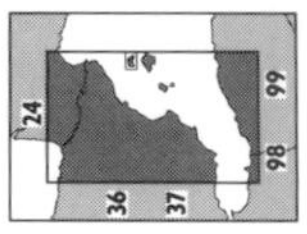

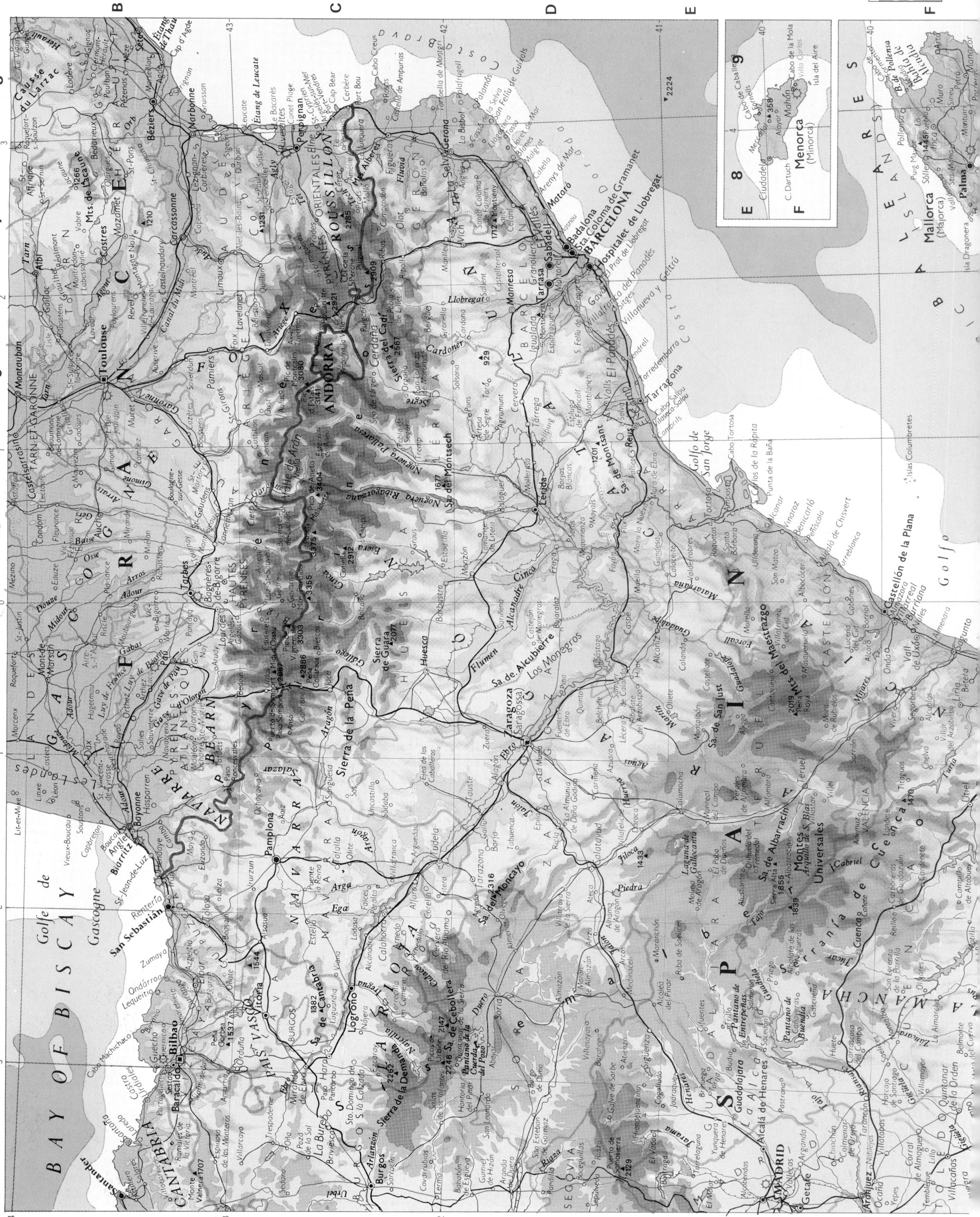
BAY OF BISCAY
Golfe de Gascogne
FRANCE
PYRÉNÉES
ANDORRA
ROUSSILLON
NAVARRA
ARAGÓN
CATALUÑA
SPAIN
Toulouse
Tarbes
Carcassonne
Perpignan
Narbonne
Béziers
Bayonne
Biarritz
San Sebastián
Bilbao
Vitoria
Pamplona
Logroño
Burgos
Zaragoza
Huesca
Lérida
Gerona
Barcelona
Badalona
Sabadell
Tarrasa
Manresa
Tarragona
Reus
Tortosa
Teruel
Castellón de la Plana
Sagunto
Cuenca
Guadalajara
Alcalá de Henares
MADRID
Getafe
Aranjuez
Soria
Menorca (Minorca)
Mahón
Ciudadela
Mallorca (Majorca)
Palma
BALEARES
Sierra de la Demanda
Sa. del Moncayo
Mts. del Maestrazgo
Montes Universales
Serranía de Cuenca
Sa. de Alcubierre
Los Monegros
Costa Brava
Golfo de San Jorge

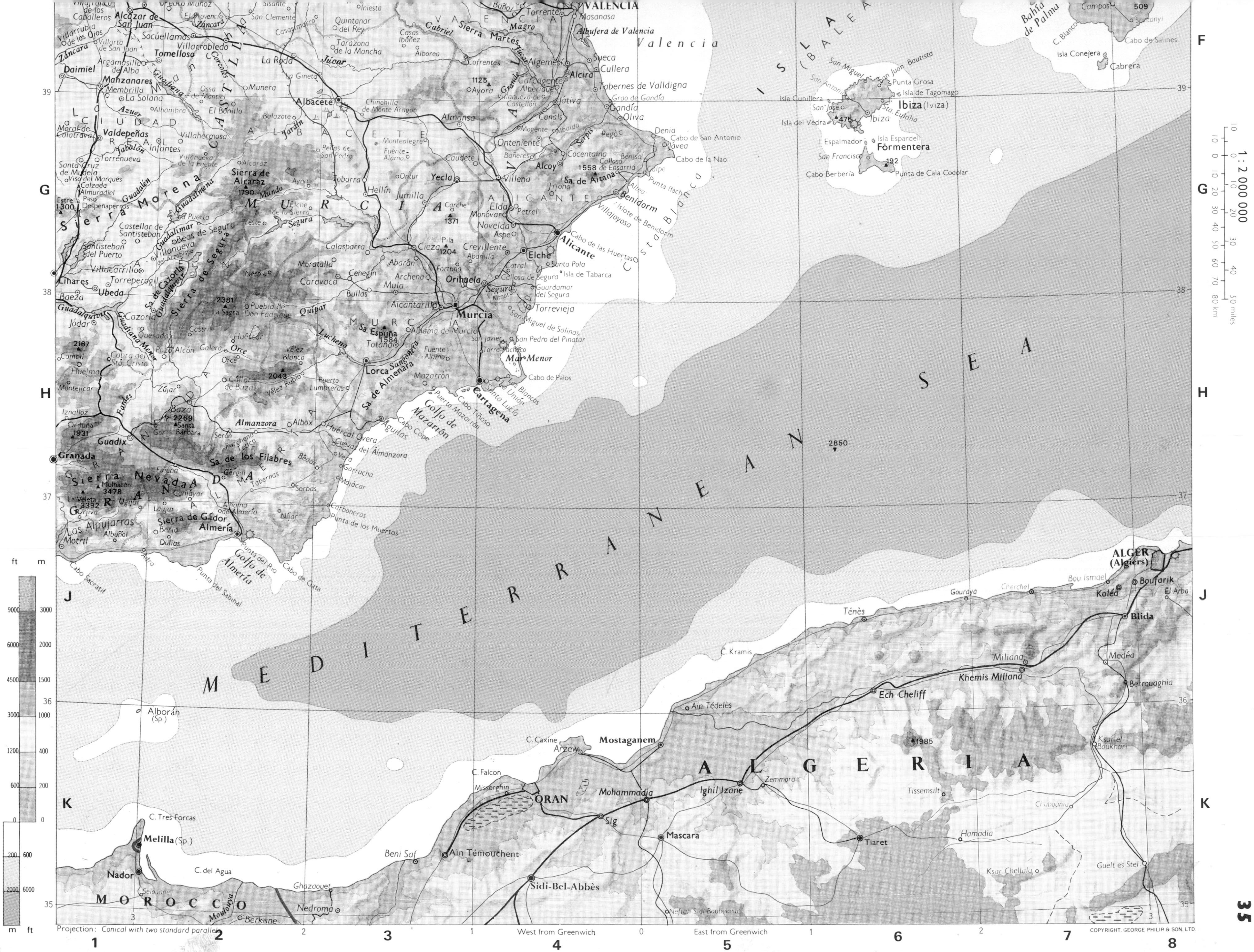

1 : 2 000 000

10    0    10    20    30    40    50 miles
10  0   10  20  30  40  50  60  70  80 km

F · G · H · J · K

MEDITERRANEAN SEA

BALEARIC ISLANDS

Bahía de Palma
Cabo Blanco
Isla Conejera
Cabrera
Cabo de Salines
509
Santanyi
Campos

San Antonio
San Miguel
Ibiza (Iviza)
Ibiza
Punta Grosa
Isla de Tagomago
Santa Eulalia
San José
475
Isla Cunillera
Isla del Vedra
San Francisco
Espalmador
Formentera
Punta de Cala Codolar
492
Cabo Berbería

2850

VALENCIA
Albufera de Valencia
Valencia
Torrente
Silla
Cullera
Sueca
Alcira
Algemesí
Carcagente
Játiva
Alberique
Tabernes de Valldigna
Gandía
Oliva
Denia
Cabo de San Antonio
Cabo de la Nao
Jávea
Villajoyosa
Benidorm
Islote de Benidorm
Altea
Calpe
Masanasa
Cocentaina
Alcoy
1558 Sa. de Aitana
1125
Sierra Martés
Cabriel
Sa. de Enguera
Ontiente
Onteniente
Villena
Sax
Elda
Petrel
Monóvar
Novelda
Aspe
Elche
Alicante
Cabo de las Huertas
Santa Pola
Isla de Tabarca
Guardamar del Segura
Torrevieja
Salinas de Torrevieja
San Miguel de Salinas
San Pedro del Pinatar
Cabo de Palos
Mar Menor
La Unión
Cartagena
Cabo Tiñoso

ALICANTE

Yecla
Jumilla
1371
Montealegre
Hellín
Tobarra
Almansa
Ayora
Alpera
Albacete
La Roda
La Gineta
Chinchilla de Monte Aragón
Pozo Cañada
Peñas de San Pedro
Montealegre del Castillo
Caudete
Pinoso
Monóvar

MURCIA
Murcia
Orihuela
Crevillente
Callosa de Segura
Molina de Segura
Alcantarilla
Mula
Archena
Cieza
Abarán
Blanca
Fortuna
Calasparra
Caravaca
Cehegín
Bullas
Totana
Sa. Espuña 1583
Lorca
Sa. de Almenara
Aguilas
Guazamara
Cuevas del Almanzora
Vera
Garrucha
Mojácar
Huércal Overa
Zurgena
Albox
Cantoria
Tíjola
Serón
Baza
Cúllar
La Sagra 2381
Huéscar
Puebla de Don Fadrique
Santiago de la Espada
2381
2045

Sierra de los Filabres
Almanzora
Tabernas
Gádor
Sierra de Gádor
Almería
Golfo de Almería
Punta del Río
Punta de los Muertos
Cabo de Gata
Punta del Sabinal
Punta de la Agua
Roquetas de Mar

Sierra Nevada
3392 Mulhacén
3478 Veleta
Granada
Guadix
Baza
Sierra de Baza
Las Alpujarras
Berja
Dalías
Adra
Motril
Órgiva
Ugíjar

Guadalquivir
Jaén
Úbeda
Baeza
Jódar
Quesada
Cazorla
Sierra de Cazorla
Sierra de Segura
2107

2269
Baza

Sierra Morena
Sierra de Alcaraz 1790
1798
Alcaraz
El Bonillo
Munera
Villarrobledo
Socuéllamos
Tomelloso
Alcázar de San Juan
Argamasilla de Alba
Manzanares
Membrilla
La Solana
Valdepeñas
Santa Cruz de Mudela
Viso del Marqués
Despeñaperros
1300
Infantes
Villanueva de los Infantes

Guadiana
Daimiel
Ciudad Real
Valdepeñas

CASTILLA
LA MANCHA

Júcar
Cabriel

MOROCCO
Melilla (Sp.)
Nador
C. Tres Forcas
C. del Agua
Berkane
Ghazaouet
Nedroma
Beni Saf

ALGERIA
ALGER (Algiers)
Boufarik
El Arba
Koléa
Blida
Bou Ismael
Medéa
Miliana
Khemis Miliana
Berrouaghia
Cherchel
Gouraya
Ténès
C. Kramis
Ech Cheliff
1985
Tiaret
Tissemsilt
Hamadia
Ksar Chellala
Guelt es Stel
Chullauma
Zemmora
Ain Tedelès
Mostaganem
Mohammadia
Sig
Mascara
ORAN
Arzew
Ayze(w
C. Caxine
C. Falcon
Misserghin
Sidi-Bel-Abbès
 Aïn Témouchent
Ain Tedelès
Ighil Izane
Ghar Rouban
Ksar el Boukhari
Ouled Si M'Bark
Ksar Chellala

West from Greenwich
East from Greenwich

Projection: Conical with two standard parallels

ft    m
9000
6000
4500
3000
1500
1000
400
200
0
3000
2000
1500
1000
400
200
0
m   ft
200  600
600 2000
2000 6000

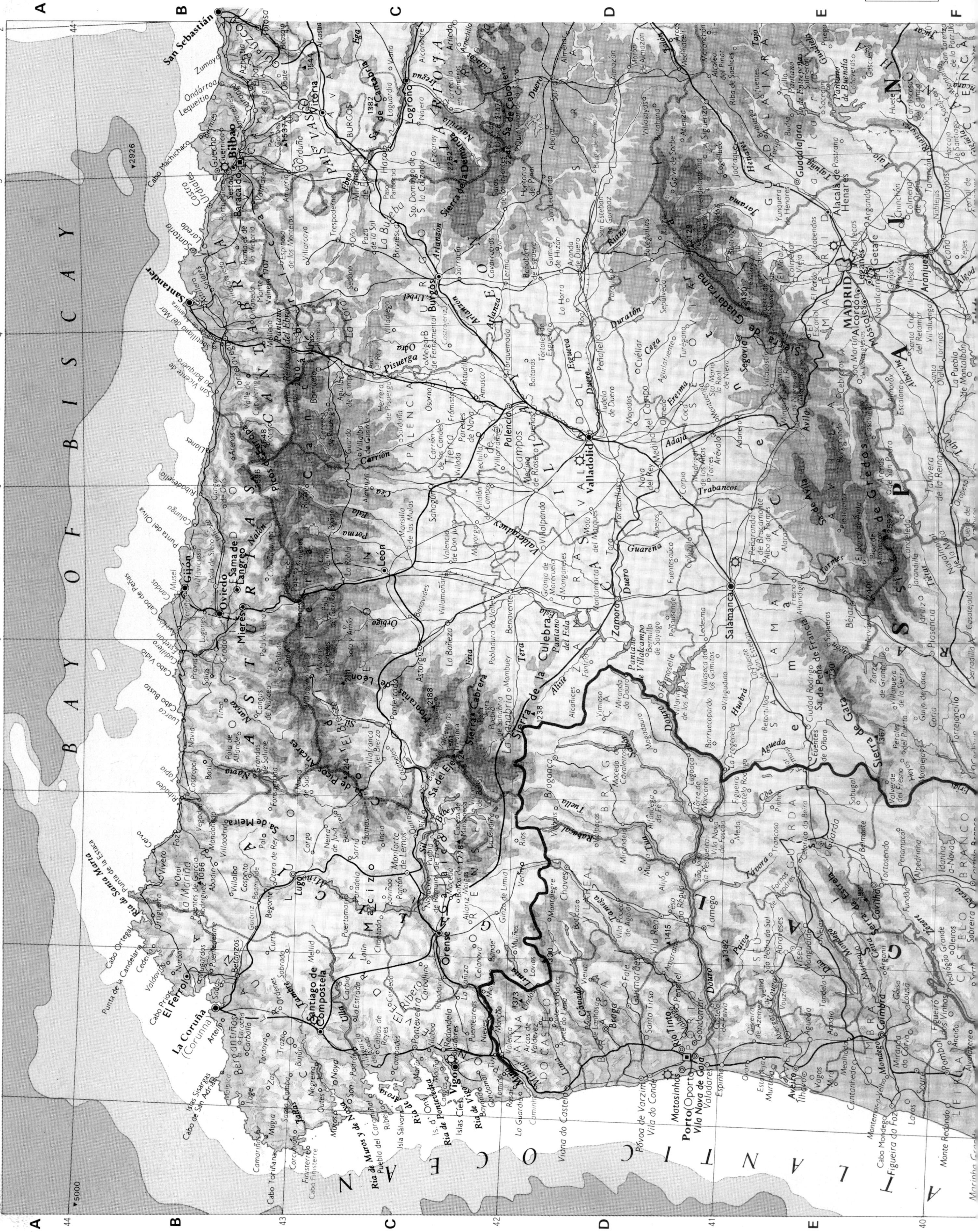

BAY OF BISCAY

ATLANTIC OCEAN

San Sebastián
Bilbao
Santander
Gijón
Oviedo
La Coruña (Corunna)
El Ferrol
Santiago de Compostela
Pontevedra
Vigo
Orense
Lugo
León
Palencia
Valladolid
Burgos
Vitoria
Logroño
Zamora
Salamanca
Ávila
Segovia
MADRID
Guadalajara
Alcalá de Henares
Aranjuez

PAÍS VASCO
LA RIOJA
CANTABRIA
ASTURIAS
GALICIA
CASTILLA
PORTUGAL

Porto (Oporto)
Vila Nova de Gaia
Matosinhos
Braga
Coimbra
Aveiro
Viana do Castelo
Chaves
Vila Real
Lamego
Bragança

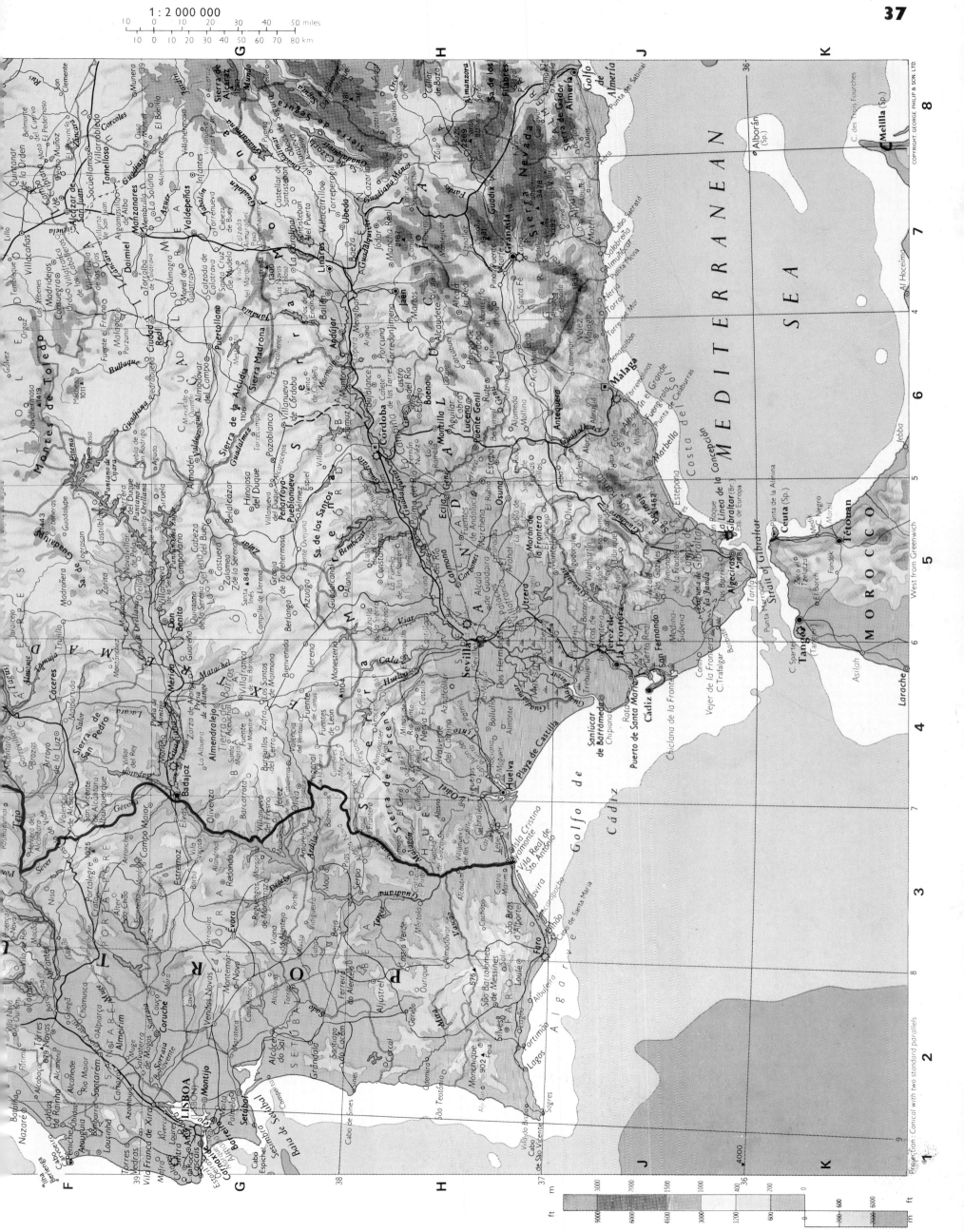

MEDITERRANEAN

SEA

MOROCCO

Melilla (Sp.)

Alborán (Sp.)

C. des Trois Fourches

Al Hoceima

Tétouan

Ceuta (Sp.)

Tánger

Larache

Asilah

Golfo de Almería

Almería

Golfo de Cádiz

Cabo de Santa María

Gibraltar (Br.)

La Línea de la Concepción

Algeciras

Strait of Gibraltar

Málaga

Sierra Nevada

GRANADA

Córdoba

Jaén

Sevilla

Cádiz

Huelva

LISBOA

Badajoz

Mérida

Cáceres

Évora

Setúbal

ALGARVE

Faro

Montes de Toledo

Valdepeñas

Daimil

Ciudad Real

Alcázar de San Juan

Linares

Puertollano

Projection: Conical with two standard parallels

1 : 2 000 000

10   0   10   20   30   40   50 miles

10   0   10   20   30   40   50   60   70   80 km

West from Greenwich

ft

m

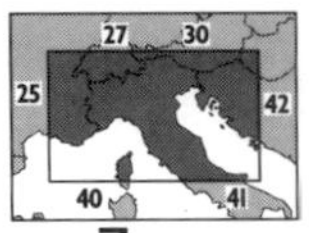

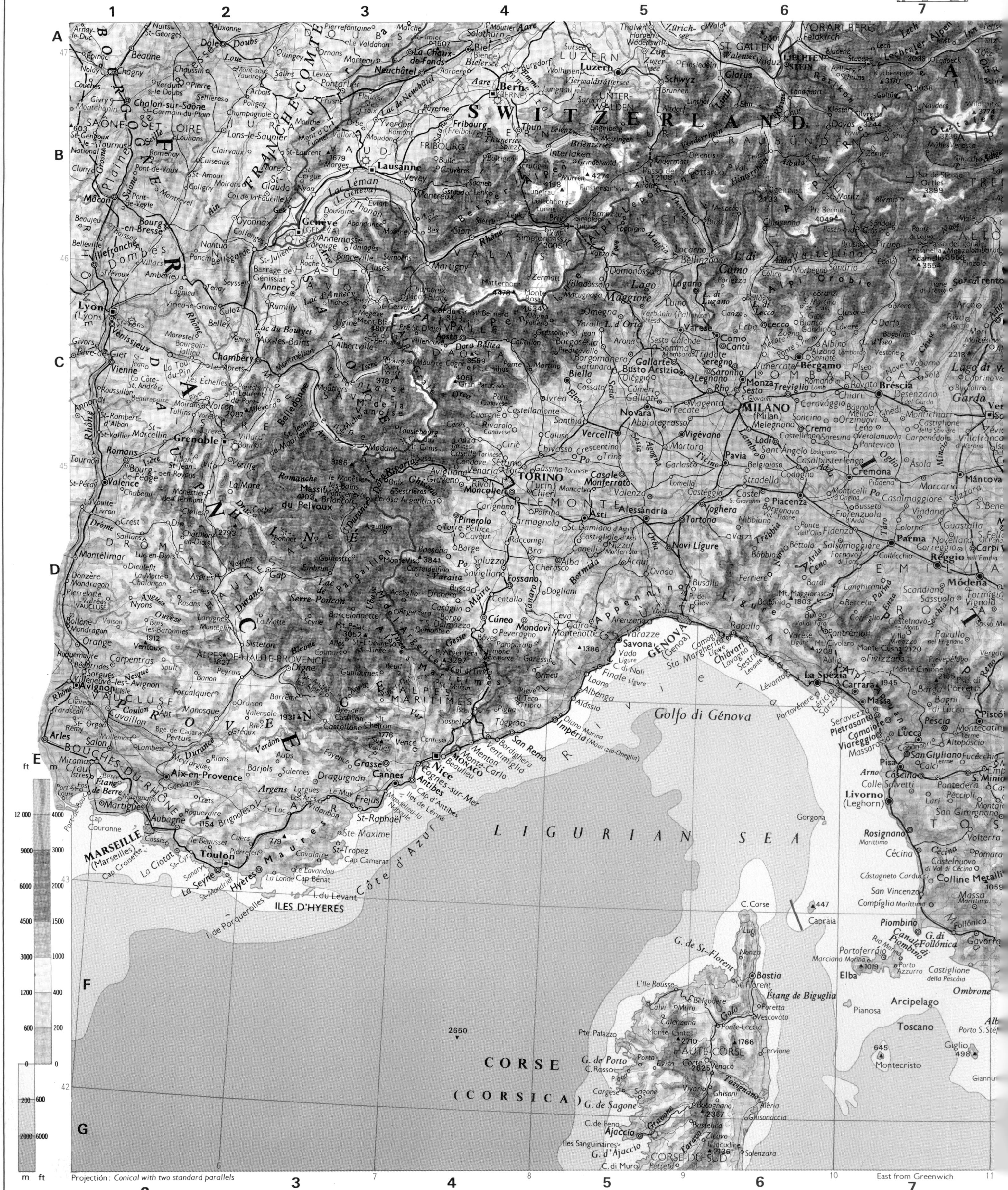

SWITZERLAND

FRANCE

ITALIA

BORGOGNA

FRANCHE-COMTÉ

SAVOIE

DAUPHINÉ

PROVENCE

PIEMONTE

LOMBARDIA

EMILIA

LIGURIAN SEA

Golfo di Génova

CORSE (CORSICA)

HAUTE CORSE

CORSE-DU-SUD

Lyon (Lyons)
Genève (GENEVA)
Lausanne
Bern
Luzern
ST GALLEN
VADUZ
LIECHTENSTEIN
VORARLBERG
MILANO (Milan)
TORINO (Turin)
GENOVA (Genoa)
Bréscia
Bérgamo
Párma
Módena
Réggio
Piacenza
Cremona
Mántova
Pavia
Novara
Vercelli
Cúneo
La Spézia
Livorno (Leghorn)
Lucca
Savona
MARSEILLE (Marseilles)
Toulon
Nice
MONACO
Monte-Carlo
Cannes
Antibes
Grenoble
Valence
Avignon
Arles
Aix-en-Provence
Bastia
Ajaccio

Projection: Conical with two standard parallels

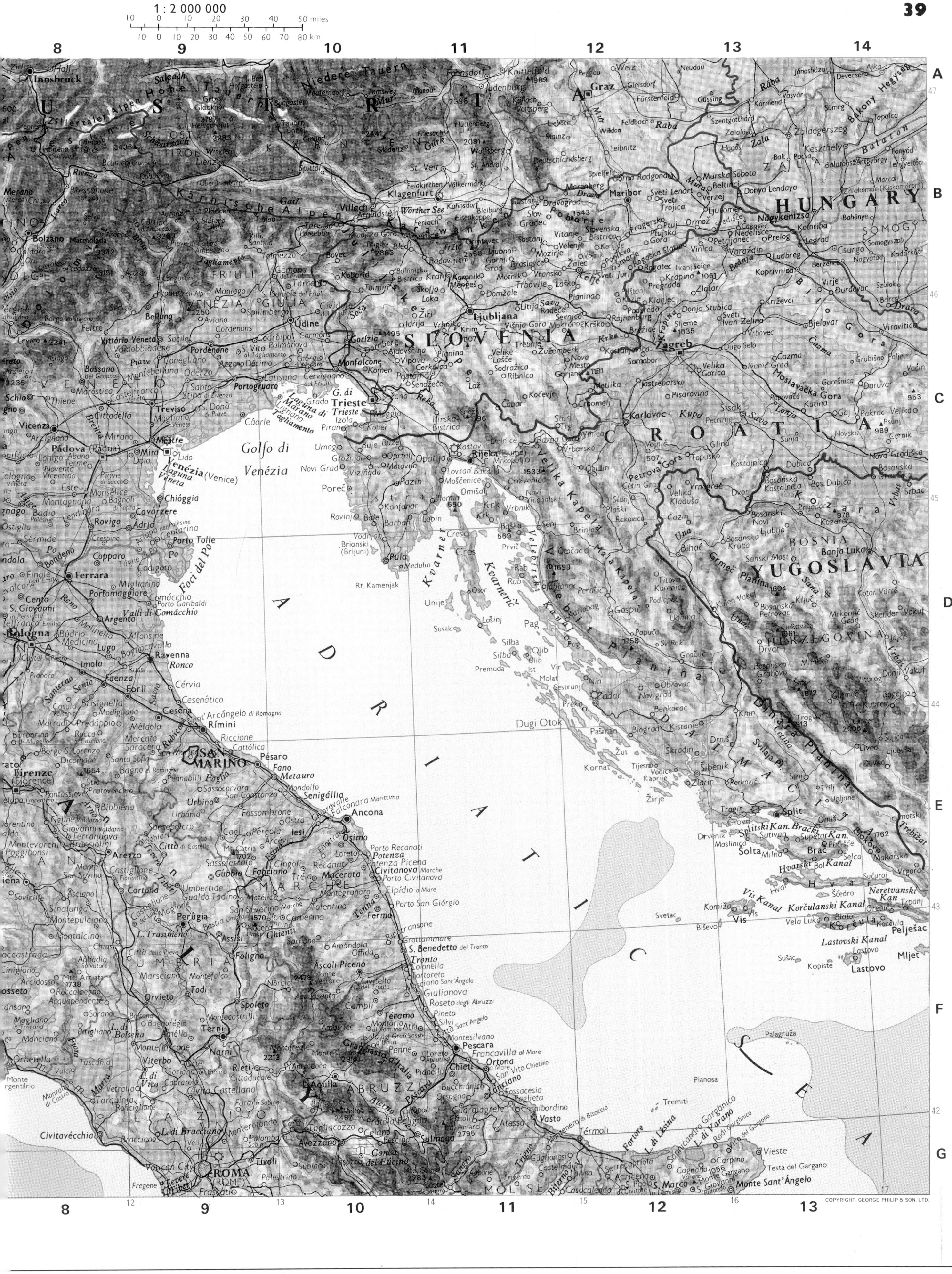

1 : 2 000 000

10  0  10  20  30  40  50 miles
10  0  10  20  30  40  50  60  70  80 km

 A U S T R I A

HUNGARY

SLOVENIA

CROATIA

YUGOSLAVIA

BOSNIA

HERZEGOVINA

VENETO

ADRIATIC   SEA

Golfo di Venézia

Innsbruck
Graz
Maribor
Ljubljana
Zagreb
Trieste
Venézia (Venice)
Pádova (Padua)
Vicenza
Ferrara
Bologna
Ravenna
Rímini
San Marino
Ancona
Perúgia
Firenze (Florence)
Arezzo
Terni
L'Aquila
Pescara
Roma (Rome)
Vatican City
Split
Zadar
Šibenik
Banja Luka

**Grid columns (top):** 1 2 3 4 5 6

**Grid rows (left):** A B C D E F

## Corsica / Corse

CORSE
CORSICA
CORSE-DU-SUD

Iles Sanguinaires
G. d'Ajaccio
C. di Muro
Petreto
Tarano
2136 Zonza
Levie
Favone
Solenzara
G. de Valinco
Sartène
Porto-Vecchio
Bonches de Bonifacio
Bonifacio
I. de Cavallo
Iles Cerbicales
Santa Teresa Gallura
Maddalena
Caprera
La Maddalena

## Sardegna / Sardinia

SARDEGNA
SARDINIA
Punta dello Scorno
Golfo dell' Asinara
Asinara
Coghinas
C. dell'Argentiera
Porto Tórres
Sássari
Sorso
Sennori
Osilo
Ferlitu
Alghero
Villanova Monteleone
Bosa
Tema
Macomer
Ghilarza
L. del Tirso
C. Mannu
Oristano
M. Arci 812
Golfo di Oristano
Arbatax
Abbasanta
Terralba
Uras
Guspini
Arbus
C. Pécora
Fluminimaggiore
1236 M. Linas
Iglesias
Gonnesa
Carbonia
Carloforte
Portoscuso
San Pietro
Sant'Antíoco
Sant' Antíoco
G. di Palmas
Porto Botte
Teulada
Pula
G. di Spartivento
C. Spartivento
Àggius
Témpia Pausania
1362 M. Limbara
Oschiri
Ozieri
Pattada
Buddusò
1259
Bonorva
Ittiri
Tissi
Nuoro
Orune
Bitti
Dorgali
Golfo di Orosei
Oliena
Mamoiada
Monti del Gennargentu 1834
Sorgono
Làconi
Bauni
C. di Monte Santu
Baunei
Tonara
Nurri
Flumendosa
Mandas
Serramanna
Senorbì
Sestu
Villacidro
Decimomannu
Dolianova
Siurgus
Sinnai 1069
Assèmini
Sìliqua
Quartu Sant'Elena
1116
Villaputzu
Muravera
S. Vito
C. Ferrato
Serpedro
Cágliari
Golfo di Cágliari
Serpentara
C. Carbonara
Santadi
Calangiànus
Golfo Aranci
G. di Ólbia
Ólbia
Tavolara
Posada
Siniscola
C. Comino
Tanaunella
Costa Smeralda
Arzachena
Pto. Cervo
Liscia

## Tyrrhenian Sea

TYRRHENIAN SEA
3719
3589
Ustica

## Italian mainland (Lazio / Campania)

ROMA (Rome)
Vatican City
Tívoli
Sabāudia
Fregene
Lido di Óstia (Lido di Roma)
Pràtica di Mare
Palestrina
Velletri
Albano
Anzio
Nettuno
Ponza
Ísole Ponziane
Palmarola
Zannone
283
Ventotene
Frosinone
Ferentino
Alatri
Véroli
Sora
Isola del Liri
Ceccano
Priverno
Pontecorvo
Cassino
Terracina
Monte Circeo 541
Gaeta
Golfo di Gaeta
Formia
Minturno
Garigliano
Mondragone
Volturno
Casal
Giugliano
788 Pro
Ísolo
Íschia (Naples)
Póz
Latina

## Sicily / Sicilia

SICILIA
PALERMO
Bagheria
C. San Vito
G. di Castellammare
Castellammare del Golfo
Favarotta
Mondello
Misilmeri
Partinico
Montelepre
1110
Levanzo
Trápani
Érice
Ísole Égadi
Maréttimo
Favignana
Stagnone
Alcamo
S. Giuseppe Iato
Piaceco
Calatafimi
Salemi
Sambuca
Marinco
Corleone
Camporeale
1613
Marsala
Gibellina
Partanna
Bisacquino
Prizzi
Belsit
Castelvetrano
Mazara del Vallo
Menfi
Sciacca
Santa Margherita
Belice
Campobello di Mazara
Burgio
Mussomeli
Castelfermi
Casteltérmini
San Cataldo
Caltan
Conica
Cattólica Eraclea
Ribera
Platani
Racalmuto
Siculiana
Lercara
Madd
Alia
SICI
Campobello di Licata
Porto Empédocle
Agrigento
Favara
Naro
Palma di Montechi
Licata

## Tunisia

TUNISIA
TUNIS
Halq el Oued
Bizerte (Binzert)
C. Blanc
Cani
C. Serrat
Plane
Menzel-Bourguiba
Mateur
Zembra
C. Bon
Golfe de Tunis
Iles de la Galite
El Kala
Tabarka
ALGERIA
Téborba
Béja
Bou Salem
Medjerda
Mejerda
Téboursouk
Zaghouan
Medjez
Soliman
Kelibia
Menzel-Temime
Nabeul
Hammamet
Mellègue
Pantelleria 836 (It.)
Sicilian Channel
Golfo di Gela

## Mediterranean

MEDITE
1319
Mali

Projection: Conical with two standard parallels

East from Greenwich

**Elevation scale (left):**
ft / m
9000 / 3000
6000 / 2000
4500 / 1500
3000 / 1000
1200 / 400
600 / 200
0 / 0
200 / 600
2000 / 6000
4000 / 12000
m / ft

1 : 2 000 000

10   0   10   20   30   40   50 miles
10   0   20   30   40   50   60   70   80 km

7     8     9     10     11     12

**ADRIATIC**

**SEA**

A B R U Z Z I

MOLISE

G. di Manfredónia

Monte Sant'Ángelo

Testa del Gargano

Vieste

Vico del Gargano

Manfredónia

Campobasso

Lucera

Fóggia

Cerignola

Cérvaro

Candela

Barletta

Trani

Biscéglie

Molfetta

Andria

Corato

Ruvo

Bitonto

**Bari**

Mola di Bari

Canosa

Ferlizzi

Giovinazzo

Monópoli

Altamura

Gravina

Gióia del Colle

Fasano

Ostuni

Martino Franca

Céglie Messápico

**Brindisi**

Francavilla Fontana

Mesagne

Mandúria

**Lecce**

Nardó Galatina

Máglie

Otranto

Galátone

Poggiardo

Gallípoli

Ugento

Tricase

C. Santa Maria di Leuca

Gáglianó del Capo

NÁPOLI

Salerno

G. di Salerno

Avellino

Benevento

Caserta

B A S I L I C A T A

Potenza

Matera

Grottáglie

Massafra

Táranto

Golfo di
Táranto

Ginosa

Pisticci

Senise

Lauria

G. di
Policastro

C. Palinuro

Morano
Cálabro

Castrovillari

Cassano Iónio

Trebisacce

Amendolara

**Crati**

Corigliano Cálabro

Rossano

Acri

C A L A B R I A

Cosenza

S. Giovanni in Fiore

Ciró

Paóla

La Sila

Crotone

C. delle Colonne

Catanzaro

Golfo di
Sant'Eufémia

Golfo di Squillace

I O N I A N

**SEA**

Pizzo

Vibo Valéntia

Mileto

Isole Eólie o Lípari (Æolian Is.)

Strómboli

Filicudi

Salina

Lípari

Vulcano

G. di Gióia

Palmi

Taurianova

Bagnara

Mílazzo

Barcellona

Mti Peloritani

**Messina**

**Réggio**

Str. di Messina

Palizzi

C. Spartivento

Mélito
di Porto Salvo

Bova Marina

Locri

Siderno Marina

Gioiosa Iónica

Roccella Iónica

Nébrodi

Monti

Etna
3340

Bronte

Adrano

Acireale

Paternò

**Catánia**

Golfo di
Catánia

Siracusa

Augusta

Lentini

Noto

Ávola

G. di
Noto

Caltagirone

Ráguso

Módica

Scicli

Ispica

Pachino

C. Passero

Cómiso

Vittória

**M E D I T E R R A N E A N   SEA**

Channel

Strait of Otranto

A L B A N I A

Durrësi
(Durazzo)

Tirana
(Tiranë)

Shkumbini

Vlorg (Valona)

B E R A T I

Kérkira
(Corfu)

Áyios Matthaíos

41

40

39

38

37

A

B

C

D

E

F

7     8     9     10     11     12

**HUNGARY**

**CROATIA**

**BOSNIA & HERZEGOVINA**

**SERBIA**

**MONTENEGRO**

**ALBANIA**

**MACEDONIA**

**CROATIA**

**ADRIATIC SEA**

Projection: Conical with two standard parallels

East from Greenwich

MONTENEGRO
Titograd (Podgorica)
Shkodër (Scutari)
Tiranë (Tirana)
Durrës (Durazzo)
Elbasan
Berat
Korçë
Vlorë (Valona)
Prizren
Priština
Niš
Skopje
Kumanovo
Bitola
Prilep
Sofiya
Pernik (Dimitrovo)
Kyustendil
Plovdiv
Stara Zagora
Pleven
Vratsa
Khaskovo
Edirne
Thessaloníki (Salonica)
Thermaikós Kólpos
Strimonikós Kólpos
Thásos
Samothráki
Límnos
Saros Körfezi
Çanakkale
Lárisa
Vólos
Ioánnina
Kérkira (Corfu)
Kateríni
Kastoriá
Komotiní
Xánthi
Kavála
Dráma
Sérrai

1 : 2 000 000

10   0   10   20   30   40   50 miles
10  0  10  20  30  40  50  60  70  80 km

AIYAÍON

Mitílni

Ayiásos

988

Plomárion

Kar Burun

Kara Agachu

1212

Onoúsa

Mólivos

1297

Khíos
(Chios)

1262

Foúrnoi

Ayios
Kírikos

Ikaría

957
822

Psará

Andípsara

Volissós

Khíos

Ákra Mástikho

Ákra Kastíon

Dhenoúsa

Khtapodhiá

Dhragónisi

Mélissa Óros

Kináros

Lévitha

Kínaros

Lídha

Astipálaia

Khamilónisi

Ákra Sídheros

Khondrí

Koufonísi

Gaídhouronísi

S E A

Mikonos

Tinos

Tinos

Náxos

Náxos

Koúfonísi

Káros

Amorgós

Amorgós

Anídhros

Andí

Anáfi

Makrá

Aygó

Ófidhoússa

Andros

Ákra Kafirévs

Yioúra

Síros

Síros

Ermoúpolis

Rinía

Dhílos

Páros

Páros

Andíparos

Dhespotikó

Íos

Íos

Síkinos

Folégandros

Thirasiá

Thíra
(Thíra)

Khristianá

Díai

Dia

K I K L Á D H E S
(C Y C L A D E S)

Kéa

Kíthnos

Sérifos

Sérifos

Sífnos

Sífnos

Kímolos

Mílos

Mílos

Andímilos

Ananes

Polyaigos

SÉRIPHOS

N O T I O S

A I Y A Í O N

S E A   O F   C R E T E
(Sea of Candia)

Khersónisos
Akrotíri
Soúdhas

Kólpos
Khaníon

Khaniá
(Canea)

K H A N I Á

Kólpos
Kisámou

Ákra Voúxa

Palaiokhóra

Kastélli

Kándanos

Elyros

Ayía
Rouméli

Loutró

RÉTHIMNON

Réthimnon

Khóra
Sfakíon

Tumbáki

Paximádha

Ákra Lithinon

Gávdhos

Gaídhopoúla

Ákra Spátha

Megalokástron

Iráklion
(Candia)

K R Í T I   (C R E T E)

2456

Ano Vianos

2153

Ídhi Óros

Mírtos

Melambes

Ierápetra

1231

Sitía

Ákra Sídheros

Kólpos Mirabéllou

Neápolis

Kólpos Mérabellou

Ákra Ayios Ioánnis

Yianisádhes

1476

Kritsá

STEREÁ

ELLAS

Skópelos

Skíathos

Skíros

792

Skíros

Vatiká

Skantzoúra

Ókhi Óros
1398

Káristos

Ayios
Kírikos

Psakho

1743

Khalkís
(Chalcis)

Kími

Dírfis

Vasilikí

Ílioupolis

Marathón

Pendélikon
Kifisiá

ATHÍNAI
(ATHENS)

Piraiévs

Ellevsís
(Eleusis)

Mégara

1413

Thívai
(Thebes)

Levádhia

Elikón

Korinthos

Corinth Canal

Argos

Náuplion
(Nauplia)

2376

Saronikós
Kólpos

Aíyina

Aíyina

Póros

Méthana

Póros

Ídhra
(Hydra)

Spétsai

Ermióni

Dhokós

Ídhra

Párnon Óros
1935

Leonídhion

Ástros

Trípolis

Spárti
(Sparta)

Taíyetos Óros
2407

L A K O N I A

Monemvasía

Taínaron Límera

Neápolis

Ákra Maléa

Elafónisos

Kíthira

Kíthira
(Cerigo)

Ákra Kapéllo

Andikíthira

P E L O P Ó N N I S O S

Gíthion

Areópolis

2404

Ákra Taínaron

5015

Kalamáta

M E S S I N I A

Messíni

Khóra

Pílos

Methóni

Ákra
Akrítas

Koróni

Petalídhion

Sikíza

Skíza

Ákra
Venétiko

Pírgos

Katákolon

Olimbía

Kiparissía

Kiparissiakós
Kólpos

Zákinthos
(Zante)

Zákinthos

Kéri

Marathiá

Strofádhes

1589

Messolóngion

Pátrai

Pátraïkós Kólpos

Aíyion

Vrakhóri

Agrínion

Amfilokhía

Árta

Préveza
(Santa Maura)

Levkás

Ayios
Nikólaos

Kefallínia
(Cephalonia)

Argostólion

Itháki
(Ithaca)

1628

Mesou Volímais

I O N I A N   S E A

I Ó N I O I   N Í S O I

Projection: Conical with two standard parallels

East from Greenwich

Continuation Eastwards
on same scale

Ródhos
(Rhodes)

Ródhos

Líndos

Ákra Líndos

Sími

Khálki

Tílos

Nísiros

Kos

Kálimnos

Léros

Pátmos

Sámos

Ikaría

846

D H O D E K Á N I S O S
(D O D E C A N E S E)

Stenón Kárpathos

Kárpathos

Kásos

Stenón Kasos

Astipálaia

Levítha

Ku̧sadasɪ

Kȗsadasi Körfezi

Samsun Daǧɪ
1229

Söke

Söke Ovasɪ

Bafa Gölü

D I D I M   D A Ǧ I
1357 Beşparmak Daǧɪ

M U Ǧ L A

Milâs

Bodrum
(Halicarnassus)

Mandalya Körfezi

1175

Marmaris

Kerme Körfezi

ft   m

9000   3000
6000   2000
4500   1500
3000   1000
1200   600
600    400
200    200
0      0

m   ft
200   600
0     0
2000  6000

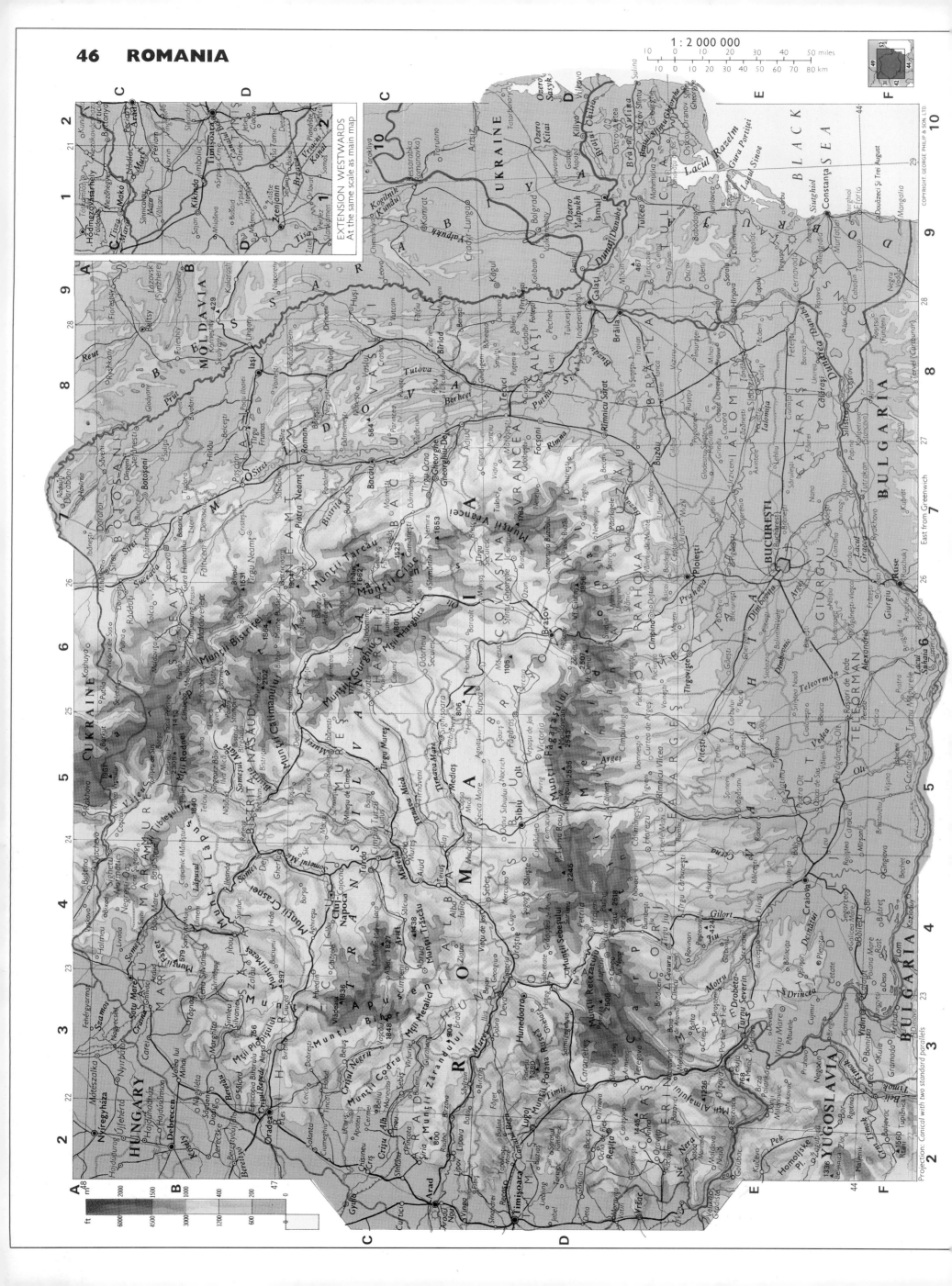

1 : 2 000 000

EXTENSION WESTWARDS
At the same scale as main map

1 : 2 000 000

10  0  10  20  30  40  50 miles
10  0  10  20  30  40  50  60  70  80 km

LITHUANIA

(RUSSIA)

BALTIC SEA

CZECHOSLOVAKIA

Zulew Szczecinski

Zatoka Gdańska

**Major places:**

Gdynia, Sopot, Gdańsk (Danzig), Gdynia, Szczecin (Stettin), Koszalin, Słupsk, Wejherowo, Kartuzy, Lębork, Bydgoszcz, Toruń, Włocławek, Grudziądz, Olsztyn, Elbląg, Malbork, Białystok, Grodno, Ełk, Łomża, Ostrołęka, Ciechanów, Płock, Warszawa (Warsaw), Siedlece, Łódź, Pabianice, Zgierz, Piotrków, Tomaszów Maz., Radom, Lublin, Chełm, Zamość, Kielce, Częstochowa, Katowice, Sosnowiec, Bytom, Zabrze, Gliwice, Ruda Śląska, Opole, Wrocław (Breslau), Legnica, Wałbrzych, Jelenia Góra, Zielona Góra, Gorzów Wielkopolski, Poznań, Gniezno, Kalisz, Leszno, Konin, Sieradz, Ostrów Wielkopolski

Projection: Conical with two standard parallels

East from Greenwich

COPYRIGHT GEORGE PHILIP & SON LTD.

ft  4500  3000  1500  1000  600  200  0  m

Odra (Oder)

Wisła

Bug

Narew

Warta

Noteć

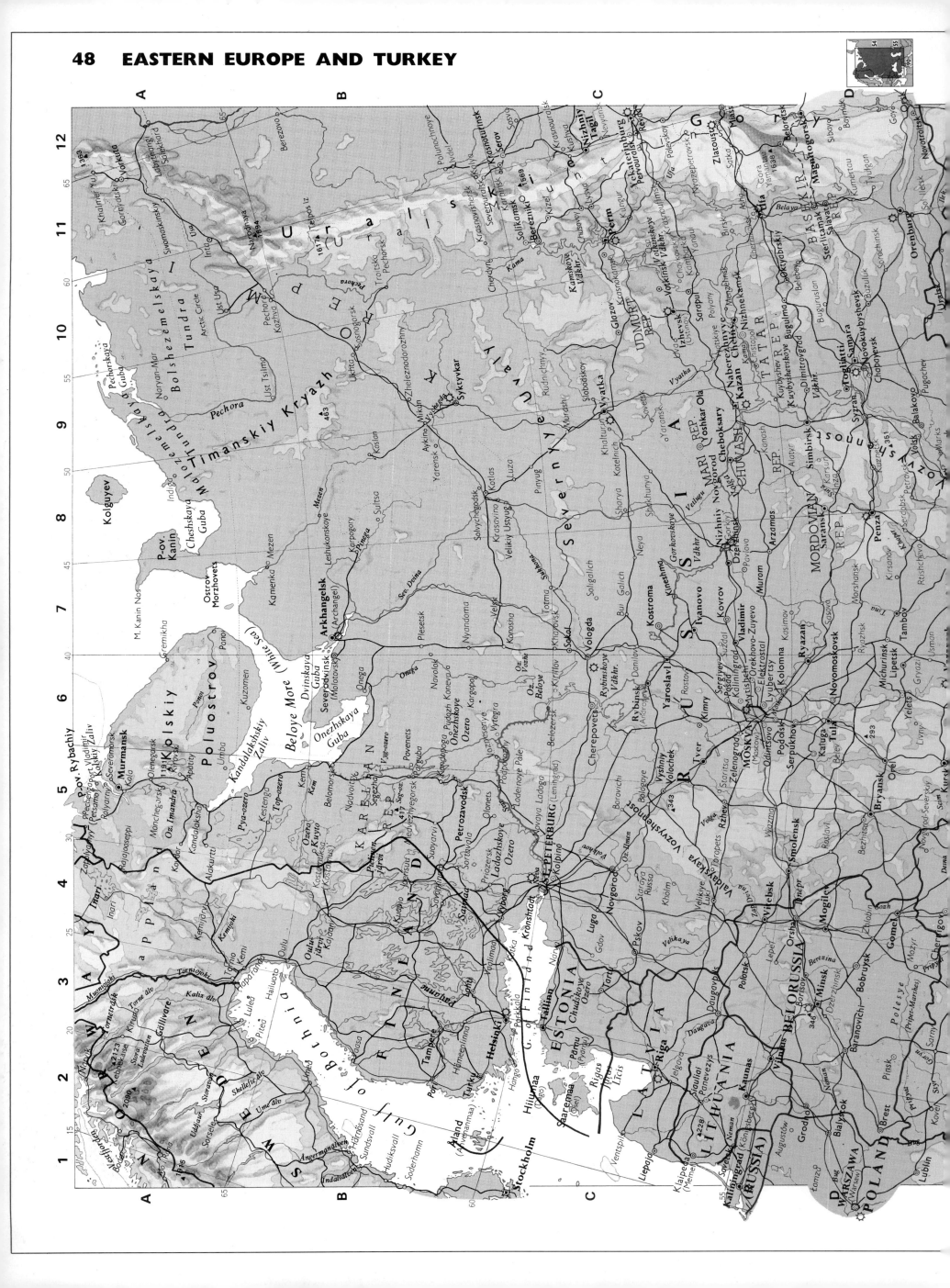

1 : 8 000 000

100   50   0   50   100   150   200 miles
100   0   100   200   300 km

E | F | G | H

9 | 8 | 7 | 6 | 5 | 4

Legend (inset box):
1  Kabardino-Balkar Rep.
2  North Ossetian Rep.
3  Nakhichevan Rep. (Azer.)
4  Checheno-Ingush Rep.
5  Karagiye Depression

**Seas and major water bodies**

CASPIAN SEA
BLACK SEA
Azovskoye More (Sea of Azov)
MEDITERRANEAN SEA
Levant
Zaliv Kara Bogaz Gol
Marmara Denizi
Krymskiy P-ov. (Crimea)
Karkinitskiy Zaliv

**Countries / Regions**

KAZAKHSTAN
Kirgiz Steppe
KALMYK A.S.S.R.
REP.
UKRAINE
MOLDAVIA
ROMANIA
BULGARIA
GEORGIA
ABKHAZ
DAGESTAN
AZERBAIJAN
ARMENIA
ADZHAR
TURKEY
SYRIA
IRAQ
IRAN
CYPRUS
Kuzey Anadolu Dağları
Toros Dağları
Anadolu
Elburz Mountains
Badiyat ash Sham

**Cities / Towns**

Aktyubinsk, Guryev, Astrakhan, Volgograd (Stalingrad), Volgodonsk, Rostov, Taganrog, Donetsk, Makeyevka, Zaporozhye, Dnepropetrovsk, Krivoy Rog, Kharkov, Belgorod, Poltava, Kremenchug, Cherkassy, Kiyev (Kiev), Zhitomir, Vinnitsa, Kishinev, Odessa, Nikolayev, Kherson, Simferopol, Sevastopol, Yalta, Feodosiya, Yevpatoriya, Krasnodar, Novorossiysk, Sochi, Sukhumi, Batumi, Trabzon, Samsun, Sinop, Zonguldak, Istanbul, Bursa, Izmir, Ankara, Eskişehir, Konya, Adana, Mersin, Antalya, Rodhos, Bucureşti (Bucharest), Braşov, Galaţi, Constanţa, Varna, Burgas, Baku, Sumgait, Makhachkala, Derbent, Groznyy, Vladikavkaz, Ordzhonikidze, Nalchik, Tbilisi, Kutaisi, Yerevan, Kirovakan, Kumayri, Erzurum, Kars, Van, Diyarbakir, Gaziantep, Malatya, Sivas, Kayseri, Halab, Hamāh, Hims, Dimashq (Damascus), Bayrūt (Beirut), BEIRUT, Al Mawşil, Kirkūk, Baghdad, Tehrān, Qom, Rasht, Qazvin, Zanjan, Tabriz, Hamadān, Urmiyeh

**Rivers / Physical features**

Don, Volga, Dnepr (Dnieper), Dnestr (Dniester), Kuban, Terek, Kura, Araks, Aras, Euphrates (Firat), Nahr Dijlah (Tigris), Prut, Siret, Tuz Gölü, Van Gölü, Sevan

Division between Greeks and Turks in Cyprus; Turks to the North.

Projection: Conical with two standard parallels

East from Greenwich

**Elevation scale (metres / feet)**
m: 4000 · 2000 · 1000 · 400 · 200 · 0
ft: 12 000 · 6000 · 3000 · 1200 · 600 · 0 · 200-600 · 2000-3000 · 6000-12 000

G. of Finland

**ESTONIA**

Tallinn

Paldiski · Kundo · Rakvere · Kohtla Järve

Bol'shoy Tyuters · Kronshtadt · **ST. PETERBURG** (Leningrad) · S_syastroy

Pushkin · Kolpino · Volkhov · Pasha

Gatchina · Tosno · Tikhvin · Pikalevo · Boksitogorsk

Ust Luga · Kingisepp · Narva · Slantsy · Lyuban · Kirishi

Hiiumaa (Khiuma) · Kärdla · Haapsalu · Rapla · Paide · Tapa · Tamsalu · Plyussa · Luga · Chudovo · Malaya Vishera · Lyubytino · Khvoynaya

Saaremaa (Sarema) · Virtsu · Viljandi · Tartu · Võru · Polna · Novgorod · Shimsk · Parakhino Padubye · Okulovka · Borovichi · Lesnoye

Kuressaare (Kingisepp) · Pärnu · Mõisaküla · Valga · Pechory · Pskov · Porkhov · Dno · Staraya Russa · Valday · Bologoye

Ruhnu · Ainaži · Valka · Munamäg 318▲ · Seredka · Oz. Ilmen · Demyansk · Vyshniy Volochek

**L A T V I A**

Rizhskiy Zaliv (Gulf of Riga) · Valmiera · Cēsis · Sigulda · Gulbene · Aluksne · Ostrov · Loknya · Kholm · Oz. Seliger · 343▲ · Torzhok · Likhoslavl

Ventspils · Kuldiga · Tukums · **Riga** · Gauja · Ergli · Madona · Oz. Lubana · Patalovo · Novorzhev · Velikaya · Opochka · 328▲ · R · Toropets · Peno · Selizharovo · Zapadnaya Dvina · Kuvshinovo

Liepāja · Saldus · Jelgava · Jaunjelgava · Plavinas · 311▲ · Rēzekne · Ludza · Pytalovo · Idritsa · Ostashkov · Andreapol · Zabadnaya Dvina · Staritsa

Priekule · Skuodas · Mažeikiai · Bauska · Jēkabpils · Ludza · Rezh · Novosokol'niki · Nelidovo · Olenino · Rzhev

Klaipeda · Kretinga · Telšiai · Joniškis · Biržai · Daugava · Velikiye Luki · Nevel · Zubtsov

**LITHUANIA**

Neringa · Šilutė · Plungė · Kuršėnai · Šiauliai · Seduva · Rokiškis · **Daugavpils** · Verkhnedvinsk (Drissa) · Demidov · Dukhovshchina · 320▲ · Vyazma

Taurage · Raseiniai · Panevežys · Zarasai · Disna · Novopolotsk · Gorodok · Velizh · Gzhatsk (Gagarin) · Borodino

Zelenogradsk · Polessk · Neman · Šakiai · Kėdainiai · Ukmerge · Braslav · **Polotsk** · Beshenkovichi · Senno · Rudnya · Smolensk · Yartsevo · Safonovo

**Kaliningrad (RUSSIA)** (Bagrationovsk) · Gusev · Jonava · Glubokoye · Lepel · Tolochin · Dorogobuzh · Yukhnov

Bartoszyce · Chernyakhovsk · Alytus · **Naujoji Vilnia** · Vilyka · Krulevshchina · **Vitebsk** · Liozno · Krasnyy (Krasnoye) · Pochinok · Yelnya · Spas-Demensk · Meshchovsk

Lidzbark Warmiński · Kętrzyn · 309▲ · Suwałki · **Vilnius** · Smorgon · Dolginovo · Osintorf · Dnepr · **Orsha** · Kopys · Shklov · Mstislavl · Gorki · Sukhinichi

Nidzica · Mrągowo · Pojezierze Mazurskie · Druskininkai · Varena · Smorgon · **Molodechno** · Vileyka · Viliya · Slavnoye · Kopys · Krasnyy · Roslavl · Kirov · Lyudinovo · Kozelsk

Chorzele · Szczytno · Pisz · Augustów · Lida · Yaratishky · Volozhin · Rakov 346▲ · Zhodino · Borisov · Mogilev · Petukhovka · Krichev · Klimovichi · Zhukovka · Dyatkovo · Fokino · Bezhitsa

Ostrołęka · Łomża · Grajewo · Grodno · Novogrudok · Stolbtsy · Dzerzhinsk · **Minsk** · Cherven · Berezina · Grodzyanka · Gorodok · Cherikov · Kostyukovichi · Kletnya · Bryansk · Karachev

**BELORUSSIA**

Ciechanów · Ostrów Mazowiecka · Knyszyn · 228▲ · Mosty · Dyatlovo · Novogrudok · Osipovichi · Sozh · Surazh · Unecha · Pochep · Mglin · Zhizdra

Wyszków · Ostrów · **Białystok** · Volkovysk · Slonim · Nesvizh · **Baranovichi** · Kletsk · Slutsk · Rogachev · **Bobruysk** · Zhlobin · Klintsy · Surazh · Starodub · Trubchevsk · Navlya · Sevsk

Różan · Łapy · Bielsk Podlaski · Białowieża · Hajnówka · Pruzhany · Byten · Lyakhovichi · Soligorsk · Glussk · Oktyabr'skiy · Svetlogorsk · Dobrush · Novozybkov · Semenovka · Dmitrovsk Orlovskiy

Rozmyn · Wołomin · Mińsk Mazowiecki · Ciechanowiec · Siemiatycze · Żeremcha · Drogichin · Yasel'da · Telekhany · Bereza · Lyuban · Rechitsa · **Gomel** · Novobelitsa · Dmitriev Lgovskiy · Zheleznogorsk

**WARSZAWA (Warsaw)** · Siedlce · Biała Podlaska · Drogichin · Ivanovo · **Pinsk** · Luninets · Pripyat (Pripet) · Ptich · Kalinkovichi · Vasilevichi · Starodub · Dmitrovsk

Otwock · **Brest** · Kobrin · Malorita · Stolin · Polesye · Mozyr · Loyev · Gorodnya · Novgorod-Severskiy · Shostka · Lgov

Radom · Łuków · Międzyrzec Podlaski · Włodawa · Łubartów · Ratno · Pripyat · David Gorodok · (Pripet Marshes) · Yelsk · Khoyniki · Gorodnya · Desna · Krolevets · Rylsk

Puławy · Chełm · Kamen Kashirskiy · Vysotsk · Dubrovitsa · Sarny · Ubort · Pripyat (Pripet) · Chernigov · Borzna · Glukhov · Putivl · Sudzha

Lublin · Kovel · Lyubomi · Olevsk · Belokorovichi · 316▲ · Ovruch · Chernobyl · Vorozhba · Bakhmach · Buryn · Belopolye · Sumy · Grayvoron

Sandomierz · Opole Lubelskie · Krasnik · Rejowiec · Fabryczny · Rozhishche · Styr · Starry Chartoriysk · Goryn · Korosten · Kievskoye Vdkhr. · Oster · Nezhin · Nosovka · Ichnya · Lebedin · Akhtyrka · Bogodukhov

Stalowa Wola · Nisko · Janów Lubelski · Novovolynsk · Vladimir Volynskiy · Kivertsy · Kostopol · Gorodnitsa · Malin · Radomyshl · Irpen · Brovary · Priluki · Lokhvitsa · Trostyanets · Krasnokutsk

Tarnobrzeg · Bilgoraj · **Lutsk** · Aleksandriya · Korets · Novograd-Volynskiy · Kozelets · Jagotin · Romny · Gadyach · Zolochev

Rzeszów · Łańcut · Leżajsk · Zamość · Rava Russkaya · 390▲ · Dubno · **Rovno** · Zdolbunov · Slavuta · Radomyshl · Vasilkov · **KIEV (Kiev)** · Pereyaslav Khmelnitskiy · Pyriatin · Sula · Lubny · Mirgorod · Krasnograd

Przemyśl · Mostiska · Gorodok · Krakovets · Lvov 471▲ · Zolochev · Brody · Kremenets · Izyaslav · Shepetovka · Polonnoye · Fastov · Dnepr · Belaya Tserkov · Lubny · Poltava

Sambor · Drogobych · Rogatin · Ternopol · Zbarazh · Starokonstantinov · Kazatin · Skvira · Berdichev · Pereyaslav · **U K R A I N E**

Krosno · Sanok · Lesko · Dnestr · Berezhany · Terebovlya · **Zhitomir** · Khmelnik · Tetiev · Boguslav · Korsun Shevchenkovskiy · Kremenchugskoye Vdkhr. · Kobelyaki

Stryj · Skole · Kalush · Monastyriska · Buchach · Kopychintsy · Proskurov · Vinnitsa · Karun · Gorodishche · **Cherkassy** · (Kremenchug) · Kremenchug

Uzhgorod · Ivano-Frankovsk (Stanislav) · 1345▲ · Nadvornaya · Kolomyya · Gorodenka · Edelshtein · 384▲ · **Khmelnitskiy** · Yuzhnyy Bug · Tulchin · Dashev · Bogslav · Zolotonosha · Smela · Svetlovodsk · Krasnograd

Mukachevo · **CZECHOSLOVAKIA** · 1881▲ · Kosiv · Chernovtsy · Kamenets-Podolskiy · Pechenizhin · Chortkov · Skala Podolskaya · Shargorod · Lipovets · Zhmerinka · Chigirin · Kremenchug

Projection: Conical with two standard parallels — East from Greenwich

ft m · 3000 · 1000 · 1200 · 400 · 600 · 200 · 0 · 0 · 200 · 600 · m ft

1 : 4 000 000

50 0 50 100 miles
50 0 50 100 150 km

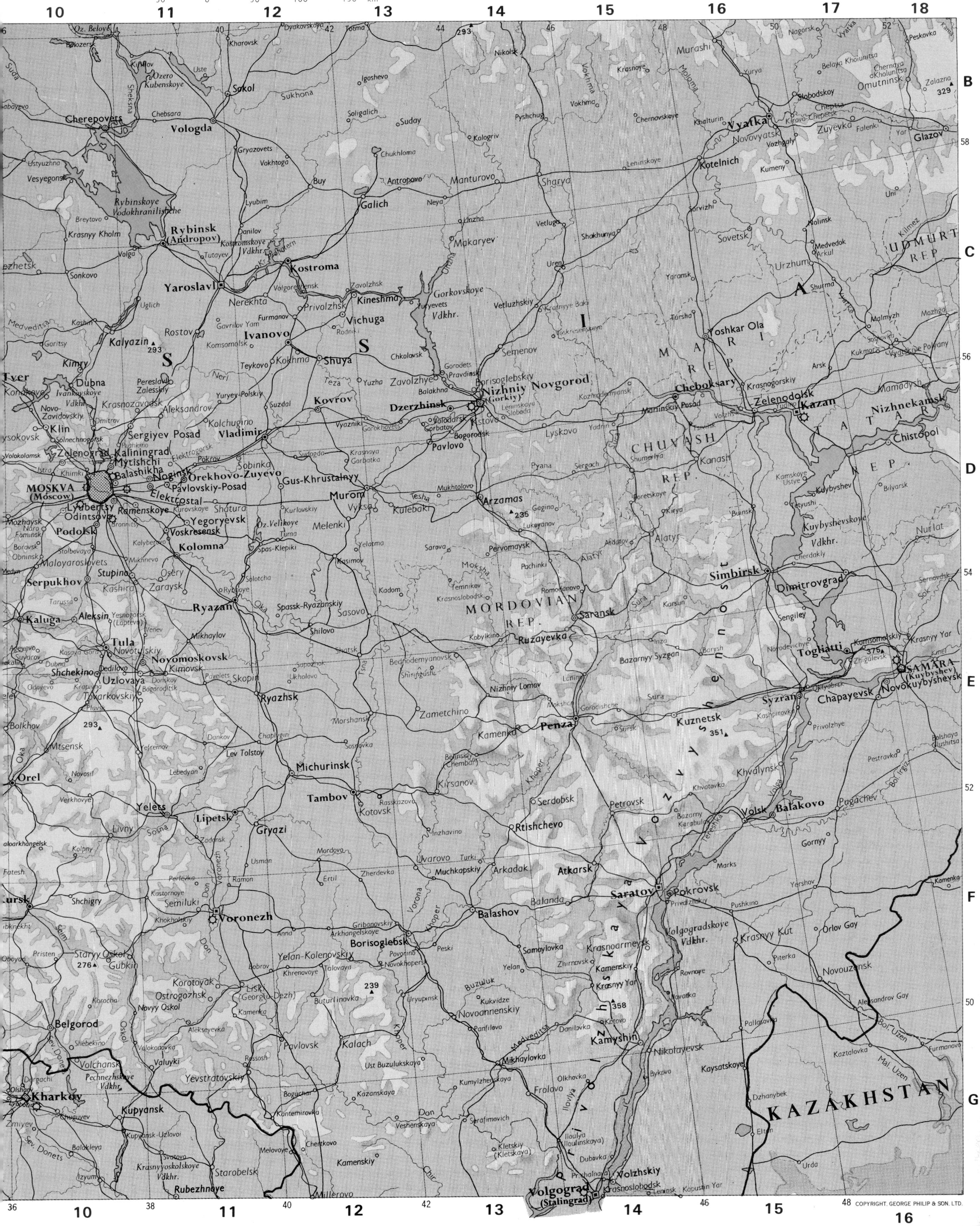

10 11 12 13 14 15 16 17 18

Oz. Beloye
Ozero Kubenskoye
Sheksna
Uste
Kirillov
Sokol
Sukhona
Soligalich
Suday
Igoshevo
Dyakovskaya
Totma
Kharovsk
Murashi
Nagorsk
Peskovka
Belozersk
Chebsara
Nikolsk
Vokhma
Krasnoye
Belaya Kholunitsa
Chernaya
Omutninsk
Zalazna 329
B

Cherepovets
Vologda
Gryazovets
Soligalich
Pyshchug
Chernavskoye
Khalturin
Kirovo
Zuyevka
Falenki
Yar
Glazov
58

Ustyuzhna
Vesyegonsk
Sheksna
Rybinskoye Vodokhranilishche
Buy
Lyubim
Antropovo
Manturovo
Sharya
Leninskoye
Novovyatsk
Vozhgaly
Kotelnich
Kumeny
Uni
UDMURT REP.

Breytovo
Krasnyy Kholm
Volga
Danilov
Kostromskoye Vdkhr.
Galich
Neya
Vetluga
Shabalino
Sovetsk
Yaransk
Urzhum
Arkul
Malmyzh
Mozhga
C

Kashin
Rybinsk (Andropov)
Tutayev
Nerekhta
Kostroma
Privolzhsk
Zavolzhsk
Kineshma
Gorkovskoye Vdkhr.
Vetluzhskiy
Krutyye Baki
Tonshayevo
Shurma
Yoshkar Ola
Kukmor
Vyatskiye Polyany
M A R I REP.
56

Medveditsa
Goritsy
Rostov
Gavrilov Yam
Komsomolsk
Furmanov
Rodniki
Vichuga
Chkalovsk
Gorodets
Semenov
Uren
Yaransk
Arsk
Mamadysh
Kazan
Nizhnekamsk

Tver
Dubna
Kalyazin 293
Kimry
Pereslavl Zalesskiy
Yuryev-Polskiy
Ivanovo
Teykovo
Kokhma
Shuya
Teza
Yuzha
Zavolzhye
Balakhna
Pravdinsk
Borisoglebsk
Nizhniy Novgorod (Gorkiy)
Kozhmodemyansk
Cheboksary
Krasnogorskiy
Zelenodolsk
T A T A R REP.
Chistopol
D

Klin
Novo-Zavidovskiy
Aleksandrov
Kolchugino
Suzdal
Vladimir
Kovrov
Vyazniki
Gorokhovets
Rostov
Dzerzhinsk
Volodarsk
Gorbatov
Bogorodsk
Lyskovo
Yadrin
CHUVASH REP.
Kanash
Shumerlya
Alatyr
Buinsk
Tetyushi
Bilyarsk
Kuybyshevskoye Vdkhr.
Nurlat

Zelenograd
Kaliningrad
Mytishchi
Balashikha
Noginsk
Orekhovo-Zuyevo
Pavlovskiy-Posad
Gus-Khrustalnyy
Murom
Pavlovo
Pyana
Sergach
Pervomaysk
Ardatov
Cherdakly
Dimitrovgrad

MOSKVA (Moscow)
Lyubertsy
Ramenskoye
Yegoryevsk
Shatura
Oz. Velikoye
Melenki
Vyksa
Kulebaki
Arzamas 235
Lukoyanov
Simbirsk
54

Odintsovo
Podolsk
Voskresensk
Kolomna
Spas-Klepiki
Tuma
Yelatma
Sarova
Moksha
Pachinki
Romodanovo
Saransk
Sura
Korsun
Sengiley
Syzran

Serpukhov
Stupino
Kashira
Zaraysk
Ryazan
Spassk-Ryazanskiy
Sasovo
Kadom
Temnikov
Krasnoslobodsk
MORDOVIAN REP.
Ruzayevka
Kobylkino
Bazarnyy Syzgan
Togliatti
SAMARA (Kuybyshev)
Novokuybyshevsk
E

Kaluga
Aleksin
Yesnogorsk (Laptevo)
Mikhaylov
Shilovo
Shatsk
Sapozhok
Zametchino
Nizhniy Lomov
Gorodishche
Kuznetsk 351
Kashpirovka
Chapayevsk

Tula
Novotulskiy
Novomoskovsk
Kimovsk
Skopin
Ryazhsk
Morshansk
Kamenka
Penza
Surok
Sura
Syzran
Privolzhye

Shchekino
Uzlovaya
Bogoroditsk
Dankov
Chaplygin
Sosnovka
Belinskiy (Chembar)
Lunino
Petrovsk
Khvalynsk
Balshaya Glushitsa

Orel
Mtsensk
Yefremov
Lebedyan
Lev Tolstoy
Michurinsk
Kirsanov
Serdobsk
Khvatovka
Volsk
Balakovo
Pugachev
52

Yelets
Lipetsk
Gryazi
Tambov
Kotovsk
Rasskazovo
Inzhavino
Rtishchevo
Petrovsk
Balkovo
Gornyy

Livny
Zadonsk
Mordovo
Usman
Uvarovo
Turki
Arkadak
Atkarsk
Marks
Pokrovsk
Saratov
F

Kursk
Shchigry
Semiluki
Khokhalskiy
Zherdevka
Ertil
Muchkapskiy
Balashov
Balanda
Privolzhye
Pushkino

Voronezh
Anna
Gribanovskiy
Arkhangelskoye
Peski
Samoylovka
Krasnoarmeysk
Volgogradskoye Vdkhr.
Krasnyy Kut
Orlov Gay

Staryy Oskol 276
Gubkin
Bobrov
Khrenovoye
Talovaya
Novokhopersk
Yelan
Zhirnovsk
Kamenskiy
Krasnyy Yar
Novouzensk

Belgorod
Ostrogozhsk
Novyy Oskol
Liski (Georgiu Dezh)
Buturlinovka
239
Buzuluk
Kukvidze
Novoannenskiy
Panfilovo
Medveditsa
Danilovka
358
Kamyshin
Pallasovka
Aleksandrov Gay
50

Shebekino
Alekseyevka
Korotoyak
Pavlovsk
Kalach
Kamenka
Ust Buzulukskaya
Uryupinsk
Mikhaylovka
Nikolayevsk
Kaysatskoye
Koztalovka

Volchansk
Pechenezhskoye Vdkhr.
Valuyki
Volokonovka
Rossosh
Boguchar
Kazanskaya
Kumylzhenskaya
Olkhovka
Bykovo
Dzhanybek
Mal. Uzen

Kharkov
Yevstratovskiy
Serafimovich
Ilovlya
Frolovo
KAZAKHSTAN
G

Kupyansk
Kantemirovka
Don
Veshenskaya
Kletskaya
Dubovka
Urda
Elton

Zmiyev
Balakleya
Millerovo
Chertkovo
Kamenskiy
Chir
Ilovlya (Iloulinskaya)
Volzhskiy
Krasnoslobodsk
Kapustin Yar

Izyum
Sev. Donets
Krasnyyoskolskoye Vdkhr.
Starobelsk
Rubezhnoye
Melovoye
Prishalnaya
Volgograd (Stalingrad)

36 10 38 11 40 12 42 13 14 46 15 48 16

COPYRIGHT. GEORGE PHILIP & SON. LTD.

1 2 3 4 5 6 7

A
Sokal Gorokhov Rovno Aleksandriya Korets Gorodnitsa Korosten Osto Kiyevskoye Vdkhr. Desna Bakhmach Belopolye Sudzha Pristen Starry Oskol
Chervonograd Dubno 29 Zdolbunov Novograd-Volynskiy Malin Irpen Nezhin Ichnya Sumy Rokitnoye 276
Kamenka-Bugskaya Radekhov Berestechko Ostrog Radomyshl Brovary KIYEV (Kiev) Priluki Romny Lebedin Grayvoron Belgorod
Lyov Kremenets Izyaslav Slavuta Shepetovka Zhitomir Fastov Vasilkov Baryshiv Jagotin Pereyaslav Khmelnitskiy Lokhvitsa Gadyach Akhtirka Bogodukhov Olshany Oskol Novvy Oskol
471 Zolochev Zbarazh Starokonstantinov Berdichev Belaya Tserkov Dnepr Sula Trostyanets Volchansk

B
Ternopol Skalat Khmelnitskiy Kazatin Bug Skvira Korsun Shevchenkovskiy Kharkov Kupyansk
Ivano-Frankovsk (Stanislav) Chortkov Gorodok 384 Vinnitsa U K R A I N E Tetiyev Gorodishche Cherkassy Poltava Krasnograd Kupyansk-Uzlo
Nadvornaya Zaleshchiki Skala Podolskaya Zhmerinka Baro Bogusi av Smela Vdkhr. Karlovka Sev. Donets Krasnyy Liman Barvenkovo
Kemenets-Podolskiy Khotin Mogilev-Podolskiy Uman Novomirgorod Znamenka Kremenchug Dneprodzerzhinskoye Vdkhr. Lozovaya Izyum Rubezhnoye

C
Chernovtsy Storozhinets Okintsa Tulchin Talnoye Yelizavetgrad Dneprodzerzhinsk Novomoskovsk Pavlograd Artemovsk Lisichans
Pervomaysk Bolshaya Vradiyevka Balta Dnepropetrovsk Konstantinovka Gorlovka
2102 Pietrosul Tirgu Neamt Beltsy Dubossary Vdkhr. 269 Zheltyye Vody Krivoy Rog Krasnoarmeisk Yenakiyevo Volchya Makeyevka
429 Rybnitsa Gayvoron Krivoy Rog Zaporozhye Donetsk (Stalino)
Iasi Orgeyev Kotovsk Voznesensk Nikopol Marganets Gulyaypole

D
ROMANIA Bacau Kishinev Bendery Tiraspol Nikolayev Melitopol Mariupol (Zhdanov)
Komrat Belgorod Dnestrovskiy Zhovtnevoye (Oktyabrskoye) Kherson Kakhovka Berdyansk Yeysk
Galati Ismail Odessa Ilyichevsk Karkinitskiy Zaliv AZOVSKOYE MORE (Sea of Azov)
Braila Buzau Ploiesti Dzhankoi Krymskiy P-ov. (Crimea) Kerch Slavyansk-na-Kubani
BUCURESTI (Bucharest) Yevpatoriya Simferopol Feodosiya Anapa Novorossiysk
Constanta Sevastopol Gora Roman-Kosh 1545 Yalta

E
Varna B L A C K S E A
BULGARIA Burgas 2135 2211 2137

F
Kirklareli Edirne Karadeniz Bogazi (Bosporus) Zonguldak Eregli Sinop Samsun
Corlu Tekirdag Istanbul Uskudar Izmit Adapazari Bolu Karabuk Bafra

G
Balikesir Bursa Ankara Corum Amasya Tokat

1 : 4 000 000

50    0    50    100 miles

50   0   50   100   150 km

8    9    10    11    12    13    14    15

**A**

40 Yelan-Kolenovskiy   Povorino   Peski   Krasnoarmeysk   Krasnyy Kut   Orlov Gay   50   Oz. Chalkar   52

Bobrov   Khrenovaya   Talovaya   Novokhoperskoye   Samoylovka   Zhirnovsk   Novouzensk   Chapayev

rotoyak   Ostrogozhsk   P.Liski (Georgiu-Dezh)   Uryupinsk   Yelan   Kamensk   Rovnoye   Mergenevo   Karsha   Dzhambeyty

Kamenka   Buturlinovka   239   Buzuluk   Krasnyy Yar   358   Vozyshennost   Volgogradskoye   Aleksandrov Gay

**50**

Alekseyevka   Kukvidze   Novoannenskiy   Panfilovo   Danilovka   Vdkh.   Piterka

Pavlovsk   Kalach   Ust Buzulukskaya   Mikhaylovka   Frolovo   Nikolayevsk   Novouzensk   Karsha   Bazartobe

Rossosh   Boguchar   Kazanskaya   Serafimovich   Iloulya   Kamyshin

**K A Z A K H S T A N**

**B**

Starobelsk   Melovoye   Chertkovo   Veshenskaya   Kletskiy (Kletskaya)   Ilovlya (Iloulinskaya)   Dzhanybek   Elton   IndErborskiy

everodonetsk   Kantemirovka   Kamenskiy   Don   Chir   Prichalinsk   Dubovka   Erda

irovsk   Kadiyevka   Millerovo   Volgograd (Stalingrad)   Volzhskiy   Leninsk   Bykovo

Bryanka   Lugansk (Voroshilovgrad)   Lenin   Morozovsk   Surovikino   Kalach na Donu   Krasnoslobodsk   Vladimirov   Kapustin Yar   Shungay

**48**

Kommunarsk   Krasnodon   Kamensk-Shakhtinskiy   Belaya Kalitva   Chernyshevsk   Volga   Akhtubinsk (Petropavlovsky)   Verkhniy Baskunchak

367   Krasnyy Luch   Sverdlovsk   Shakhov   Krasnodonetskaya   Tsimlyanskoye   Vdkhr.   Yerkhnii

Thorez   Rovenki   Gukovo   Krasny Sulin   Sinegorski

Snezhnoye   Novoshakhtinsk   Kamenolomni   Shakhty   Ust-Donetsky   Tsimlyansk   Kotelnikovo   Obilnoye   Kapornovka   Makhambet (Yamankhalinka)

**R U S S I A**

Novobogatinskoye

mvrosiyevka   Matveyev Kurgan   Tuzlov   Novocherkassk   Volgodonsk   Dubovskoye   Zavetnoye   Yenastayevka   Khyushkino   Guryev

aganrog   Rostov   Batysk   Azov   Bolshaya Martynovka   Zimovniki   Krasnyy Yar   -28

**C**

aliv   Port Katon   Zernograd   Veselovskoye Vdkhr.   Mechetinskaya   Manych   Kuberle   **K A L M Y K**   Astrakhan

rashchevskaya   Eya   Kushchevskaya   Proletarskaya   Remontnoye   **R E P.**   Kirovskiy

Stara-   Yegorlykskaya   Gigant   Oz. Manych-Gudilo   Krasnoye   Mamut

minskaya   Kanevskaya   Peschanokopskoye   Salsk   Yegorlyk   Elista (Stepnoi)   Limani   **46**

Pavlovskaya   Belaya Glina   Krasnogvardeyskoye   Priyutnoye   Beloye Ozero   -28   Kultay

Tikhoretsk   Novoaleksandrovskaya   Divnoye   Arzgir   Kaspiyskiy

Timashevsk   Izobil'nyy   Svetlograd (Petrovskoye)   Kalaus   Kuma   Kulaly   Mangyshlakskiy Zaliv

**D**

Korenovsk   Kropotkin   Blagodarnoye   M. Tyub Karagan

Krasnodar   Ust-Labinsk   Armavir   Kuban   Stavropol   Budennovsk   Neftekumsk   Staryy Biryuzyak   Fort Shevchenko   **P.-ov.**

  Kurganinsk (Kurgannaya)   831   Nevinnomyssk   Vladimirovka   Bryanskoye   Mangyshlak

Maykop   Labinsk   Kursavka   Zelenokumsk (Vorontsovo-Aleksandrovskoye)   Tyuleny   **44**

Khadyzhensk   Apsheronsk   Laba   Urup   Mineralnyye Vody   O. Chechen   Aktau

Jubga   Neftegorsk   Dakhovskaya   Cherkessk   Georgievsk   Aleksandriyskaya

Tuapse   **B**   Yessentuki   Pyatigorsk   Prokhladnyy   Mozdok   **CHECHENO-**   Lopatin

**E**

Kislovodsk   Karachayevsk   Mayskiy   Malgobek   **INGUSH**   Gudermes   Kizlyar

Sochi   Nalchik   Nartkala   Beslan   Groznyy   **REP.**   Khasavyurt   Kizil Yurt

Adler   Krasnaya Polyana   **KABARDINO-**   Tyrnyauz   Elkhotovo   Sulak   Makhachkala

Gagra   **BALKAR REP.**   Elbrus   5203   Vladikavkaz (Ordzhonikidze)   Kumtorkala   Kaspiysk

**ABKHAZ**   Gudauta   **C**   **NORTH OSSETIAN REP.**   Buynaksk   Novokayakent

Navy Afon   **REP.**   Tkvarcheli   Kazbek   5047   Tetnosi   Levberbash   Izberbash   **42**

Sukhumi   Goli   Dzhvari   Dagestanskiye Ogni   **C**

Ochamchire   Jedidi   Mtskheta   Tiyarda   Derbent   800   **A**

**GEORGIA**   Tkibuli   Tskhinvali   **a**   Akhvelis   **S**

Anaklia   Kutaisi   Chiatura   Dusheti   **u**   Kusunkent   **P**

Poti   Samtredia   Zestafoni   Khashuri   Telavi   Kvareli   **n**   Kakhmas   **I**

**F**

Kobuleti   Ozurgety   Senaki   Kaspi   Mtskheta   Logodekhi   Zakatayly   Kuba   Divichi   **A**

Batumi   **ADZHAR REP.**   Borzhomi   **Tbilisi**   Gori   Gurdzhaani   Sheki (Nukha)   Nazer Dyuzi   4466   Siazan   **N**

Hopa   Akhaltsikhe   Khrami   Marneuli   Signakhi   Alazan   Mingechaurskaya   Baba dag   3629   **Z**

Pazar   Achalkalaki   Shaumyani   Rustavi   Iori   Citel Ckaro   Mirzaani   Vdkhr.   Shemakha   **40**

Görele   Artvin   Ardahan   Alaverdi   Kura   Mingechaur   Agdash   Geokchay   Sumgait   Surokhany   Mashtaga

Tirebolu   Trabzon   Rize   3937   Borjka   3192   Karakalis   **Gyandzha (Kirovabad)**   **AZERBAIJAN**   Kozi Magomed   **BAKU**   Artem

Harsit   Akçaabat   Sürmene   Kaçkar   Kisir   Kars   **Kumayri**   Mir Bashir   Kürdamir   M. Byandovan

Çakirgol   3063   **D**   Artvin   Sarikamis   Aragats   4090   Kamo   **NAGORNO**   Sabirabad   **G**

Gümüshane   Bayburt   Oltu   Ispir   Narman   Sarikamis   Digor   **ARMENIA**   Ozm   Adzhibedi   Karachala

Ardanuç   Olur   Kôghizman   Echmiadzin   **Yerevan**   Masis   **KARABAKH**   Imishly   M. Byandovan

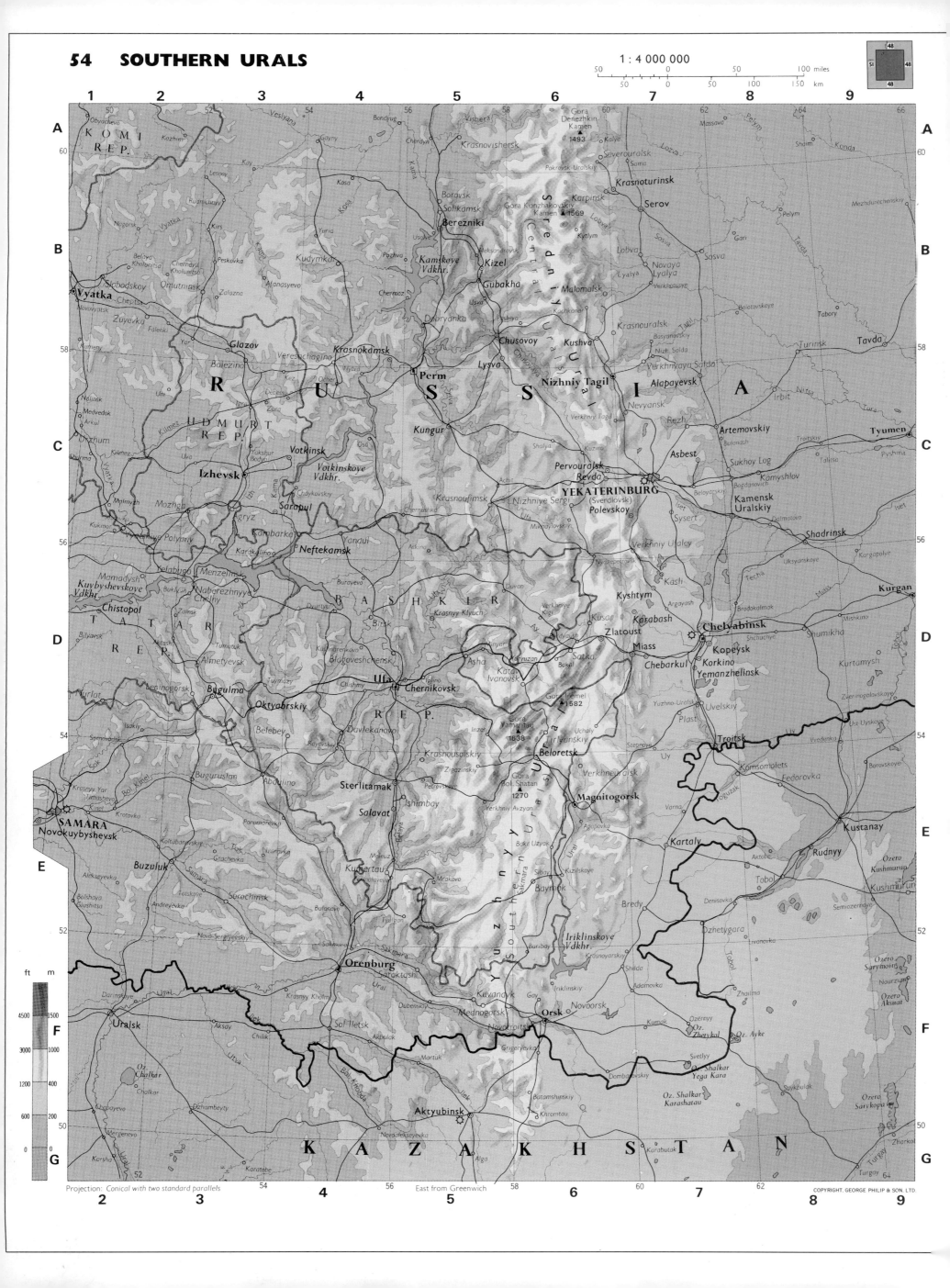

1 : 4 000 000

50    0    50    100 miles

50    0    50    100    150 km

48
51    48
48

**1** **2** **3** **4** **5** **6** **7** **8** **9**

50    52    54    56    58    60    62    64    66

**A**

KOMI
REP.

60

Gora
Denezhkin
Kamen
▲1493    Kalye    Massava    Polym    Shaim    Konda

Obyachevo    Kozhim    Vestyana    Bondyug    Vishera    Krasnovishersk    Saverouralsk    Soma    Gari    Mezhdurechensky

Krasnoturinsk

**B**

Vyatka    Slobodskoy    Peskovka    Chernaya    Kholunitsa    Kudymkar    Boravsk    Solikamsk    Gora Konzhakovsky    Karpinsk    Serov

58    Belaya    Kholunitsa    Pozhva    Kamskoye    Kizel    Vdkhr.    Gubakha    Malomalsk    Lobva    Novaya    Lyalya    Verkhoturye    Turinsk    Tavda

Glazov    Krasnokamsk    Dobryanka    Chusovoy    Kushva    Krasnouralsk    Basyanovsky

**R** Balezino    **U** Vereshchagino    **S** Perm    Lysva    **S** Nizhniy Tagil    **I** Alapayevsk    **A**

Kungur    Nevyansk    Rezh    Irbit

Votkinsk    Shalya    Kuzino    Artemovskiy    Tyumen

Izhevsk    Votkinskoye    Vdkhr.    Pervouralsk    Asbest    Sukhoy Log    Kamyshlov

Sarapul    Krasnoufimsk    Nizhniye Sergi    Revda    YEKATERINBURG    (Sverdlovsk)    Beloyarskiy    Bogdanovich    Kamensk    Uralskiy    Shadrinsk

Polevskoy

**D**

Chistopol    Naberezhnyye    Chelny    Verkhniy Ufaley    Kasli    Kurgan

**T**    **A**    **T**    **A**    **R**    Neftekamsk    **B**    **A**    **S**    **H**    **K**    **I**    **R**    Kyshtym    Kargapolye

Menzelinsk    Birsk    Karabash    Chelyabinsk

Almetyevsk    Blagoveshchensk    Zlatoust    Miass    Kopeysk    Shumikha

Bugulma    Ufa    Chernikovsk    Satka    Chebarkul    Korkino    Yemanzhelinsk

Oktyabrskiy    **R**    **E**    **P**.    Gora Iremel    ▲1582

Belebey    Davlekanovo    Gora Yamantau    1638    Beloretsk    Troitsk    Komsomolets

Sterlitamak    Ishimbay    Gora Bol. Shatan    ▲1270    Magnitogorsk    Kustanay

Salavat    Rudnyy

Buzuluk    Kumertau    Baymak

SAMARA    Novokuybyshevsk

Orenburg    Iriklinskoye    Vdkhr.    Orsk

Uralsk    Sol-Iletsk    Mednogorsk    Novotroitsk

Aktyubinsk

**K**    **A**    **Z**    **A**    **K**    **H**    **S**    **T**    **A**    **N**

Projection: Conical with two standard parallels    East from Greenwich    COPYRIGHT. GEORGE PHILIP & SON, LTD.

ft    m
4500    1500
3000    1000
1200    400
600    200
50    0
0    0

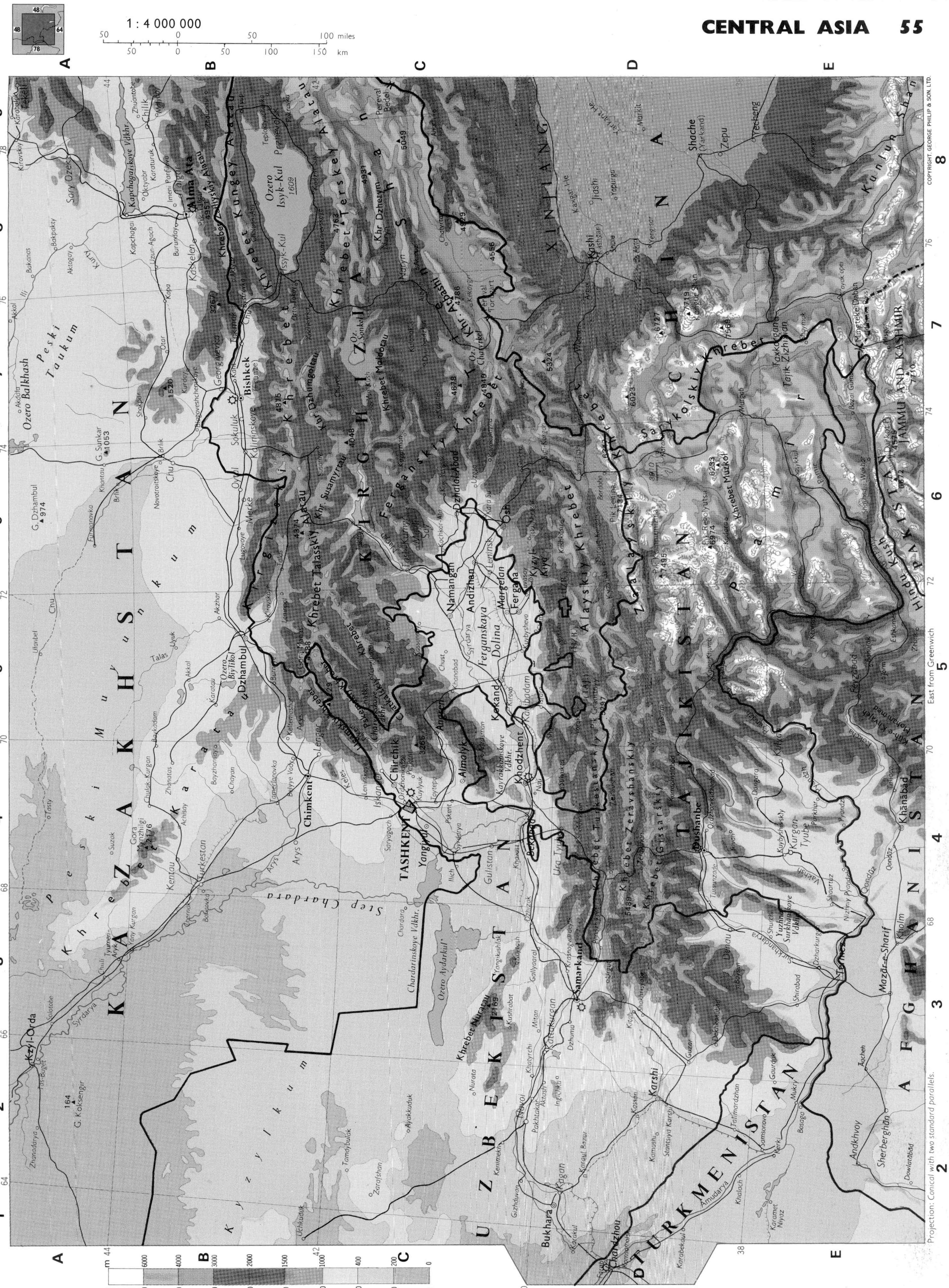

1 : 4 000 000

50 0 50 100 miles
50 0 100 150 km

KAZAKHSTAN

UZBEKISTAN

TURKMENISTAN

AFGHANISTAN

KIRGHIZIA

TAJIKISTAN

XINJIANG

CHINA

JAMMU AND KASHMIR

Pamir

Hindu Kush

Kun Lun Shan

Ozero Balkhash

Peski Taukum

Ozero Issyk-Kul

Khrebet Kungey Alatau

Khrebet Terskey Alatau

Khrebet Zailiyskiy Alatau

Alma Ata

Bishkek

Khrebet Talasskiy Alatau

Khrebet Moldotau

Ferganskiy Khrebet

Fergana Dolina

Ferganskaya Dolina

Alayskiy Khrebet

Zarafshanskiy Khrebet

Khrebet Zeravshanskiy

Khrebet (Gissarskiy)

Sarykol'skiy Khrebet

TASHKENT

Chirchik

Chimkent

Namangan

Andizhan

Margelan

Osh

Kokand

Almolyk

Khodzhent

Samarkand

Dushanbe

Kurgan-Tyube

Khanabad

Mazar-e-Sharif

Bukhara

Karshi

Kzyl-Orda

Syrdarya

Amudarya

Shache (Yarkand)

Zepu

Yecheng

Kashi

Kuqa

Peski
Taukum

Step Chardara

Kyzylkum

Kara-Kum

East from Greenwich

Projection: Conical with two standard parallels.

COPYRIGHT GEORGE PHILIP & SON. LTD.

ft m
18 000 6000
12 000 4000
9000 3000
6000 2000
4500 1500
3000 1000
1200 400
600 200
0 0

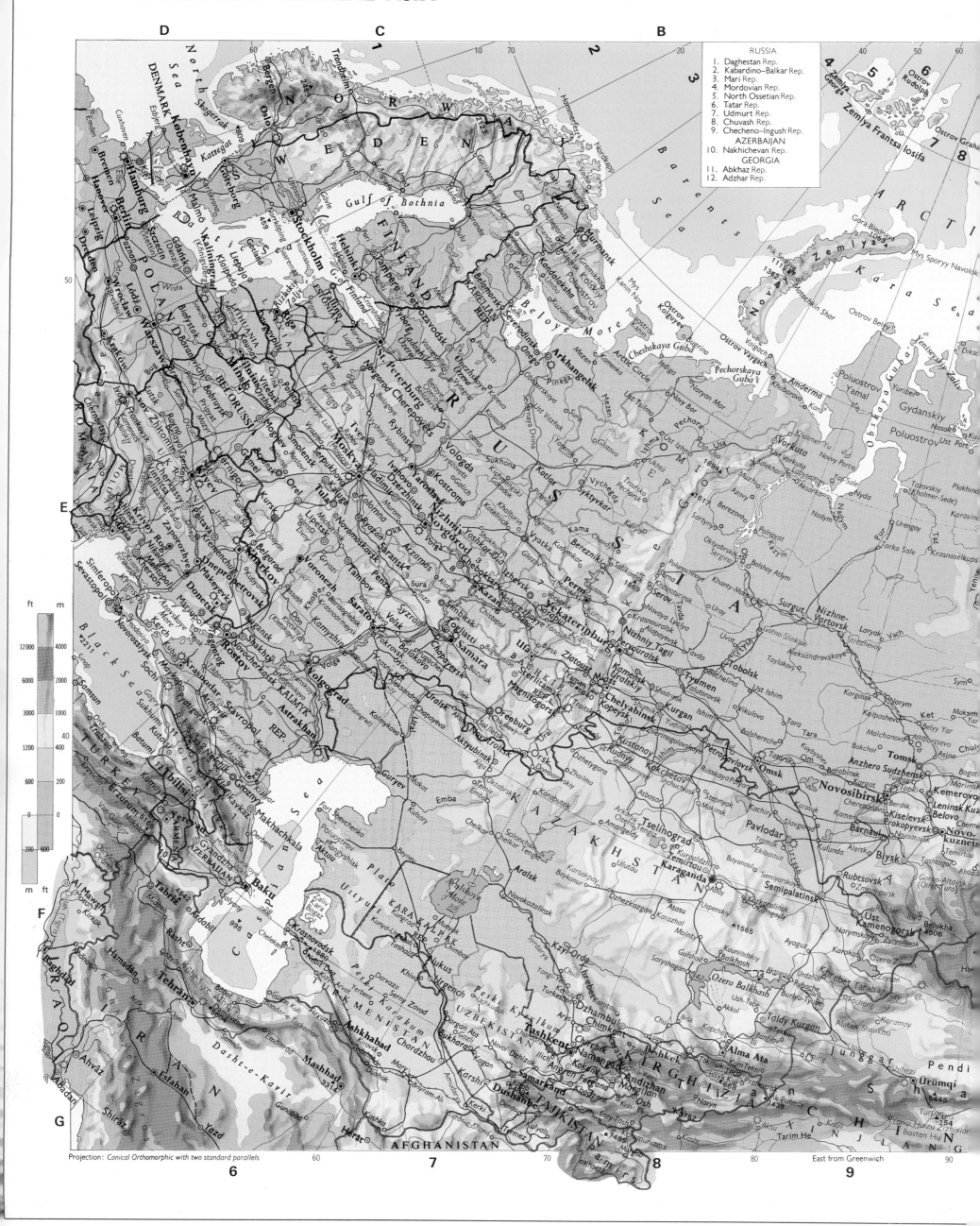

RUSSIA
1. Daghestan Rep.
2. Kabardino–Balkar Rep.
3. Mari Rep.
4. Mordovian Rep.
5. North Ossetian Rep.
6. Tatar Rep.
7. Udmurt Rep.
8. Chuvash Rep.
9. Checheno–Ingush Rep.
AZERBAIJAN
10. Nakhichevan Rep.
GEORGIA
11. Abkhaz Rep.
12. Adzhar Rep.

Projection: Conical Orthomorphic with two standard parallels

East from Greenwich

1 : 16 000 000

100   0   100   200   300   400 miles
100   0   100   200   300   400   500   600 km

A          B          C

9   10   11   12   13   14   15   16   17   18   19

ARCTIC OCEAN

Ostrov Shmidta
Mys Arkticheskiy
Ostrov Pioner
Ostrov Komsomolets
Ostrov Oktyabrskoy Revolyutsii
965
Ostrov Bolshevik
Severnaya Zemlya
Proliv Vilkitskogo

Ostrova Delong
Ostrov Henrietta
Ostrov Jeanette
Ostrov Bennett
Ostrov Zhokhova
Ostrova Novosibirskiye Ostrova
Ostrov Fadeyevskiy
Ostrov Novaya Sibir
Laptev Sea
3800
Ostrov Belkovskiy
Ostrov Molyy Lyakhovskiy
Ostrov Bolshoy Lyakhovskiy
Lyakhovskiye Ostrova
Proliv Dmitriya Lapteva
374
Ostrov Stolbovoy
Ostrov Kotelnyy

East Siberian Sea
Ostrova Medvezhi
Ostrov Vrangelya

Mys Dezhneva (East C.)
Chukotskoye More
St. Lawrence I. (U.S.A.)
1843
Providenya
Anadyrskiy Zaliv

Poluostrov Taymyr
Gory Byrranga
1146
Oz. Taymyr

Nordvik
Ust Olenek
Uryung-Khaya
Saskylakh
Olenek
Tiksi
Tit-Ary
Kyusyur
Bulun

Chukotskiy Khrebet
4562
Koryakskiy Khrebet
Bering Sea

Norilsk
Gory Putorana
1701
Zinka
apovo
Agapa
Volochanka
Kheta
Khatanga
Popigay
Novorybnoye
Dzhelinde

Verkhoyansk
2389
Verkhoyanskiy Khrebet
Yansky Khrebet
Khrebet Cherskogo
2958
Srednekolymsk
Kolyma
Indigirka
Zyryanka

Okhotsko Kolymskoye
Magadan
Gizhiginskaya Guba
Gizhiga
Penzhinskaya Guba
Sredinnyy Khrebet
Poluostrov Kamchatka
4750
Ust-Kamchatsk
Petropavlovsk-Kamchatskiy
3456

Norilsk
Arctic Circle
962
YAKUT REPUBLIC
Olenek
Vilyuy
Vilyuysk
Verkhnevilyuysk
Yakutsk
Lena
Aldan
Okhotsk
1780

Sea of Okhotsk

Ostrov Bolshoy Shantar
Sakhalinskiy Zaliv
Nikolayevsk-na-Am.
Sakhalin

Yeniseysk
Angara
Krasnoyarsk
Kansk
Achinsk
Bratsk
Nizhneudinsk
Ust-Ilimsk
Ust-Kut
Kirensk
Olekminsk
Vitim
Stanovoy Khrebet
2246
2482
Tynda
Skovorodino
Zeya
Komsomolsk
2078
Khrebet Sikhote-Alin
Sovetskaya Gavan
Khabarovsk
3669

Irkutsk
3491
Angarsk
1620
Ulan Ude
Chita
1054
Shilka
Blagoveshchensk
Amur
Birobidzhan
Ussuriysk
Vladivostok
Nakhodka
Hokkaido
Sapporo
Hakodate

TUVA REP.
Kyzyl
Hovsgol Nuur
Ulan Bator (Ulaanbaatar)
2800
Hentiyn Nuruu
Choybalsan
Qiqihar
Harbin
Jiamusi
Honshu

MONGOLIA
Hangayn Nuruu
Hyargas Nuur
Har Nuur
Uliastay (Javhlant)
Tsetserleg

1949
Changchun
Jilin
Chongjin
Sea of JAPAN

Edrengiyn Nuruu
3957
Saynshand
CHINESE REPUBLIC
Dongbei
Shenyang
Fushun
Anshan
Dandong
NORTH KOREA
Pyongyang
Wonsan
Niigata
To-yama

4266
Hami
Gaxun Nur
Baotou
Hohhot
Zhangjiakou
Beijing
Dalian
Inch'on
Soul
SOUTH KOREA
Taejon
Taegu
Pusan
Kanazawa

10   11   12   13   14

60
50
40
A B C D E F

Boundaries of Autonomous Republics

COPYRIGHT. GEORGE PHILIP & SON. LTD.

1 : 40 000 000

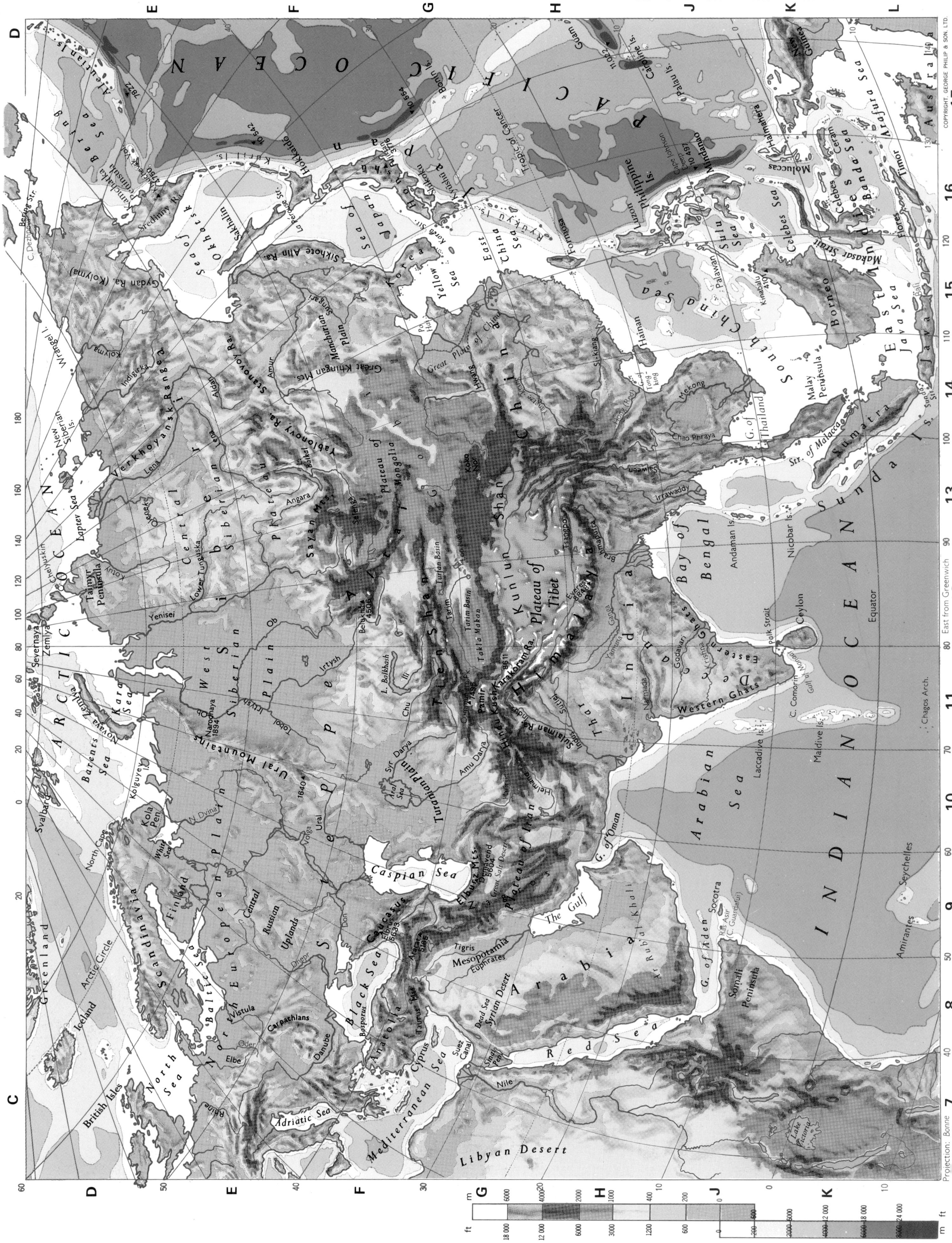

250    0    250    500    750    1000 miles

250    0    500    1000    1500 km

P A C I F I C    O C E A N

A R C T I C    O C E A N

ARCTIC OCEAN

I N D I A N    O C E A N

Caspian Sea

Black Sea

Red Sea

Arabian Sea

Bay of Bengal

South China Sea

Mediterranean Sea

Libyan Desert

Himalaya

Plateau of Tibet

Kunlun Shan

Tien Shan

Plateau of Mongolia

West Siberian Plain

Ural Mountains

Caucasus

Arabia

Rub' al Khali

Somali Peninsula

COPYRIGHT: GEORGE PHILIP & SON LTD.

Projection: Bonne

| m | ft |
| --- | --- |
| 6000 | 18 000 |
| 4000 | 12 000 |
| 2000 | 6000 |
| 1000 | 3000 |
| 400 | 1200 |
| 200 | 600 |
| 0 | 0 |

1 : 40 000 000

250   0   250   500   750   1000 miles
250   0   500   1000   1500 km

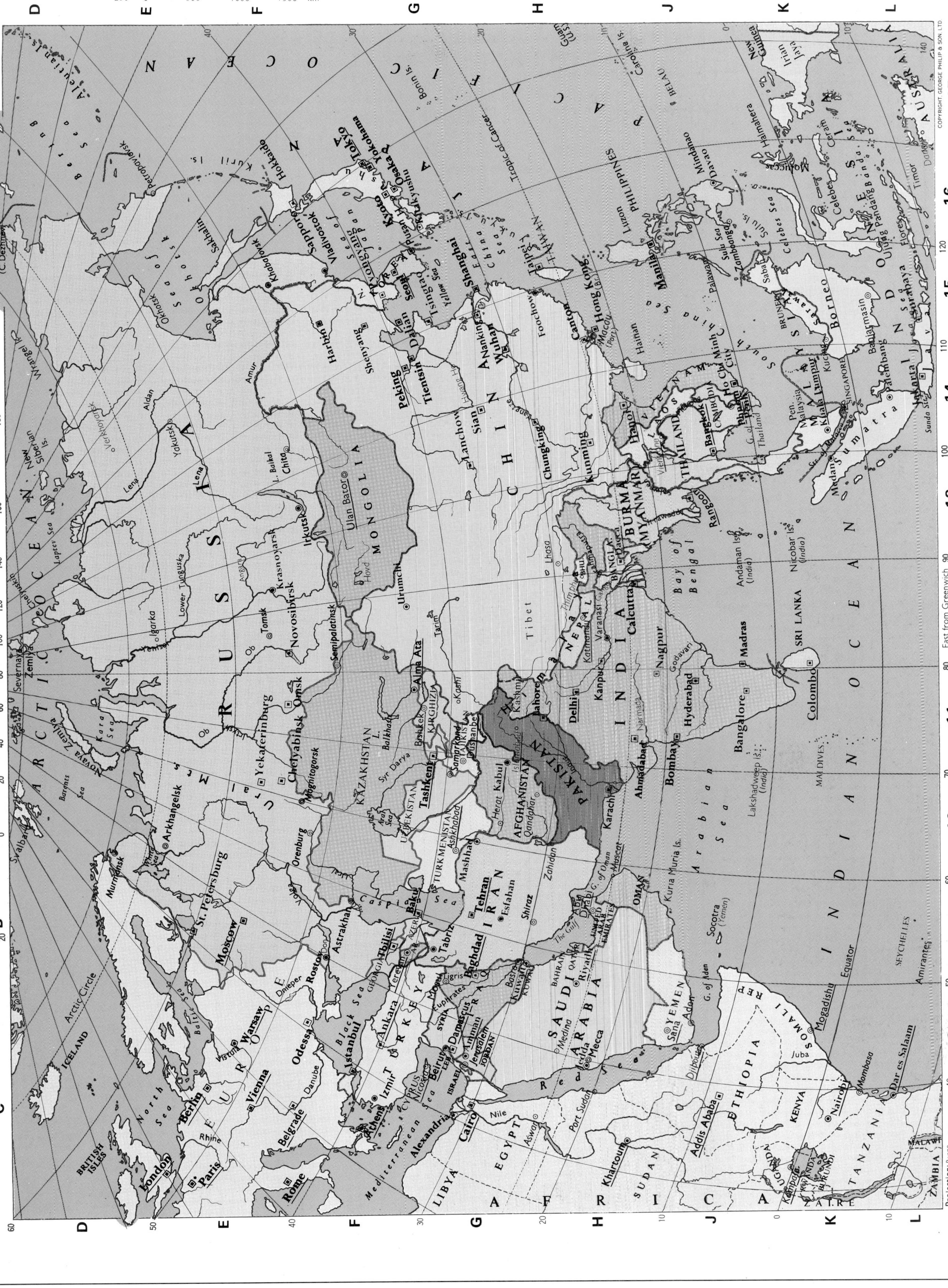

PACIFIC OCEAN

ARCTIC OCEAN

INDIAN OCEAN

R U S S I A

C H I N A

INDIA

MONGOLIA

KAZAKHSTAN

SAUDI ARABIA

IRAN

TURKEY

PAKISTAN

AFGHANISTAN

BURMA MYANMAR

THAILAND

MALAYSIA

PHILIPPINES

INDONESIA

AUSTRALIA

EGYPT

LIBYA

SUDAN

ETHIOPIA

SOMALI REP

KENYA

TANZANIA

ZAIRE

E U R O P E

A F R I C A

Peking  Tokyo  Moscow  Delhi  Tehran  Baghdad  Cairo  London  Paris  Rome

8 Peking  50 Capital Cities

East from Greenwich

Projection: Bonne

COPYRIGHT GEORGE PHILIP & SON LTD

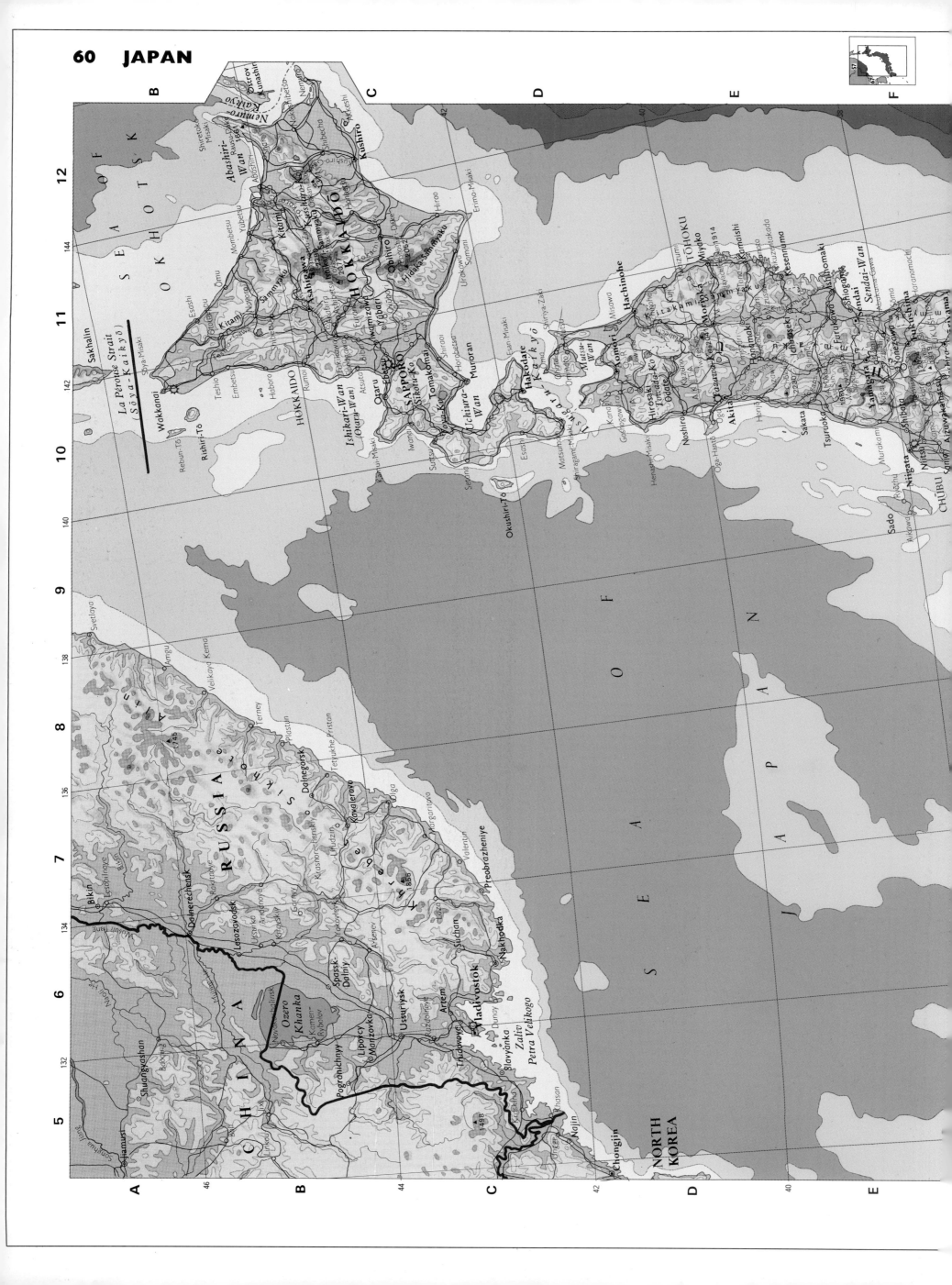

La Pérouse Strait
(Sōya-Kaikyō)

S E A   O F   O K H O T S K

HOKKAIDO

SAPPORO

TOHOKU

S E A   O F   J A P A N

RUSSIA

SIKHOTE-ALIN

CHINA

Ozero
Khanka

Vladivostok

Zaliv
Petra Velikogo

NORTH
KOREA

Chongjin

1 : 4 000 000

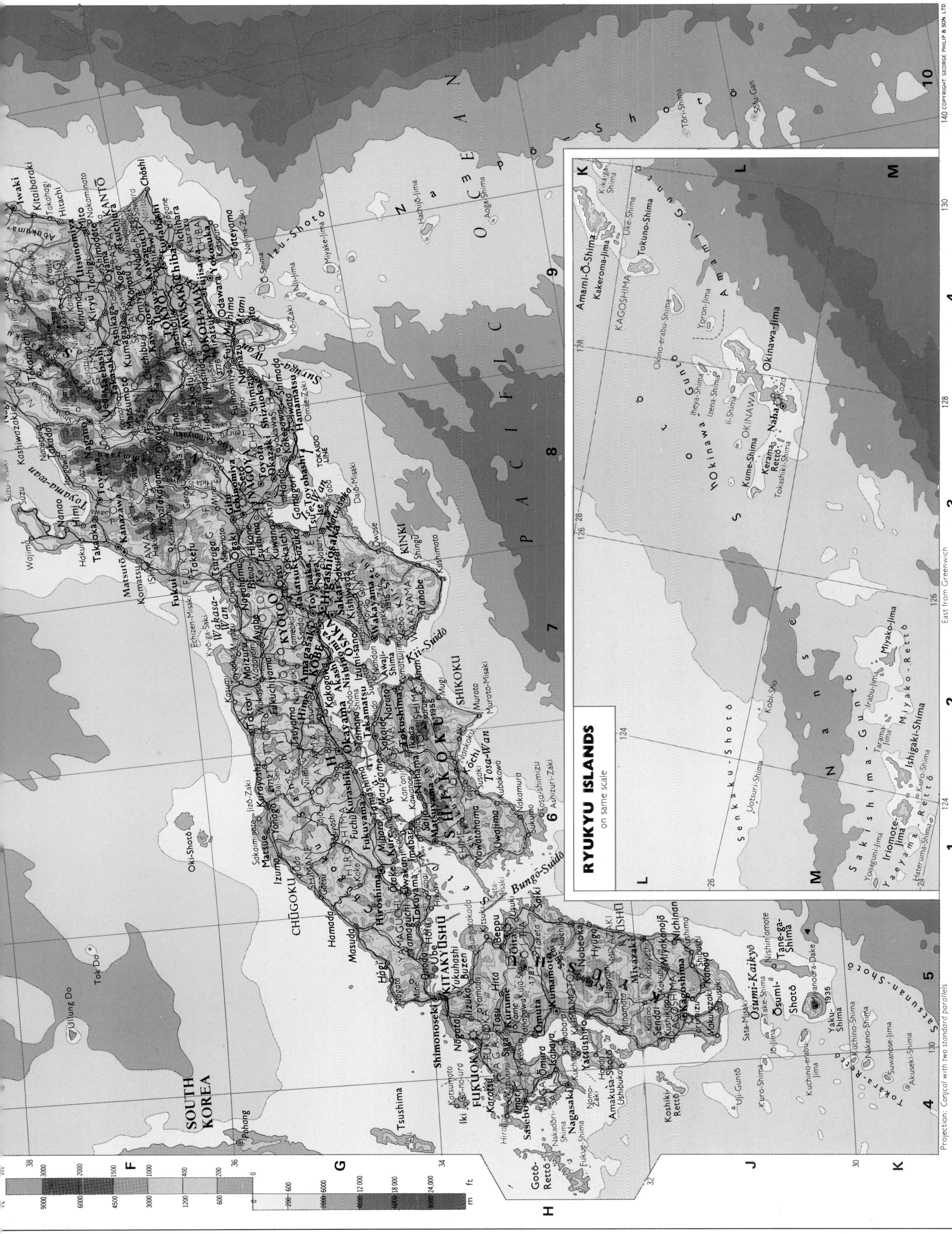

50   0   50   100 miles
50   0   50   100   150 km

**RYUKYU ISLANDS**
on same scale

SOUTH KOREA

PACIFIC OCEAN

KANTŌ
TŌKYŌ
YOKOHAMA
KAWASAKI
NAGOYA
KYŌTO
KOBE
OSAKA
KINKI
SHIKOKU
CHŪGOKU
KITAKYŪSHŪ
FUKUOKA
KYŪSHŪ
KAGOSHIMA
MIYAZAKI
KUMAMOTO
Shimonoseki
Nagasaki
Sasebo

AMAMI-Ō-SHIMA
KAGOSHIMA
OKINAWA
NAHA
RYUKYU
Miyako-Rettō
Sakishima-Guntō
Ishigaki-Shima

East from Greenwich

Projection: Conical with two standard parallels

140 COPYRIGHT GEORGE PHILIP & SON LTD.

ft
24,000
18,000
12,000
6000
3000
1500
600
0

m
6000
4000
2000
1000
500
200
0

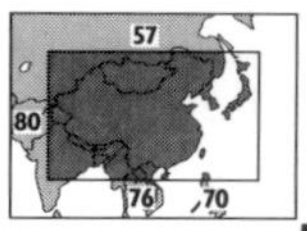

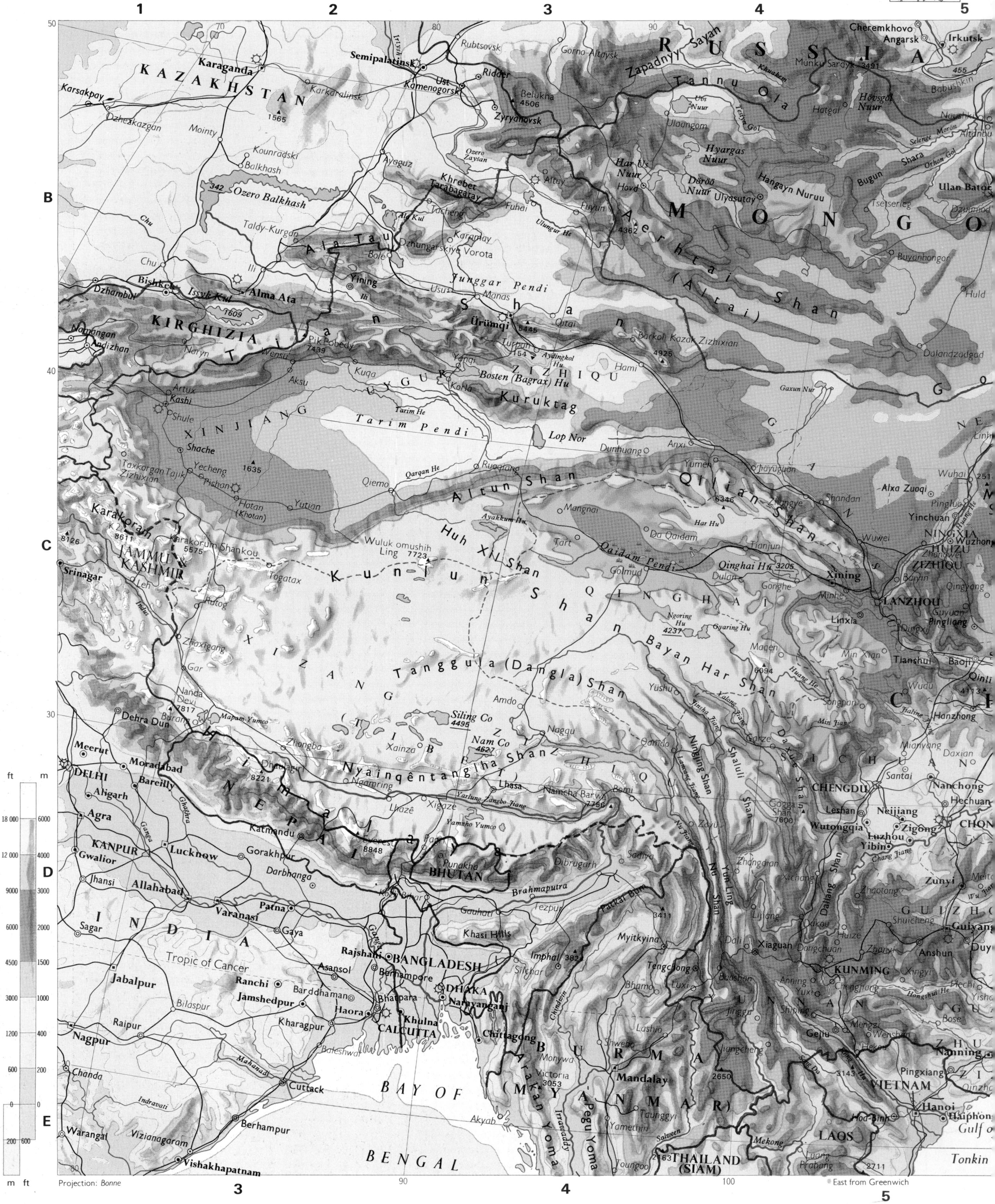

KAZAKHSTAN

Karaganda
Karsakpay
Dzheskazgan
Mointy
Kounradski
Balkhash
Ozero Balkhash
342
Taldy-Kurgan
Semipalatinsk
Ust Kamenogorsk
Ridder
Rubtsovsk
Karkaralinsk
Ayaguz
Ozero Zaysan
Zyryanovsk
Belukha 4506
Gorno-Altaysk
Zapadnyy Sayan
RUSSIA
Cheremkhovo
Angarsk
Irkutsk
Munku Sardyk 3491
Tannu Ola
Khovsgol Nuur
Babushkin
455

Chu
Bishkek
Dzhambul
Issyk-Kul
Alma Ata
Ili
1609
KIRGHIZIA
Namangan
Andizhan
Naryn
Pik Pobedy 7439
Wensu
Artux
Kashi
Shule
XINJIANG
Shache
Yecheng
Pishan
Hotan (Khotan)
Yutian
Taxkorgan Tajik Zizhixian
Ala Tau
Yining
Bole
Usu
Dzhungarskiye Vorota
Karamay
Manas
Shihezi
Ürümqi 5445
Turpan Aydingkol Hu -154
Yanqi
Korla
Bosten (Bagrax) Hu
Kuqa
Aksu
Tarim He
Tarim Pendi
Qiemo
Qarqan He
Ruoqiang
Lop Nor
Dunhuang
Anxi
Altun Shan
Junggar Pendi
Tian Shan
Fuhai
Ulungur He
Fuyun
4362
Altay
Qitai
Barkol Kazak Zizhixian
Hami
4925
Gaxun Nur
Yumen
Jiayuguan
Shandan
Qilian Shan 5346
Alxa Zuoqi
Wuhai
251
NINGXIA HUIZU ZIZHIQU
Yinchuan
Wuzhong
Lanzhou

ZIZHIQU
KURUKTAG
UYGUR
Togatax
Rutog
Zhaxigang
Gar
XIZANG
Karakorum Shankou 5575
JAMMU & KASHMIR
8126
8611
Srinagar
Leh
Nanda Devi 7817
Buram
Dehra Dun
Meerut
DELHI
Moradabad
Bareilly
Aligarh
Agra
KANPUR
Gwalior
Lucknow
Jhansi
Allahabad
Sagar
Jabalpur
INDIA
Nagpur
Raipur
Chanda
Warangal
Vizianagaram
Vishakhapatnam
Berhampur
Cuttack
Mahanadi
BAY OF BENGAL

Altun Shan
Huh Xil Shan
Wuluk omushih Ling 7723
Kun-lun Shan
Mapam Yumco
Tanggula (Dangla) Shan
Siling Co 4495
Nam Co 4627
Xainza
Amdo
Nagqu
Lhasa
Namcha Barwa 7756
Bomi
Nyainqêntanglha Shan
Ngamring
Lhazê
Xigaze
Yamzho Yumco
Zhongba
NEPAL
Dhaulagiri 8221
Katmandu
Gorakhpur
Darbhanga
Patna
Gaya
Everest 8848
BHUTAN
Thimphu
Punakha
Gauhati
Tezpur
Dibrugarh
Brahmaputra
Parkai Bum 3411
Sadiya
Imphal 3921
Silchar
Khasi Hills
Myitkyina
Bhamo
Lashio
Monywa
Shwebo
Mandalay
Chindwin
Akyab
Arakan Yoma
Pegu Yoma
Victoria 3053
Toungoo
Yamethin
Tuanggyi
THAILAND (SIAM) 2163
LAOS
Luang Prabang

Ngoring Hu 4237
Gyaring Hu
Qinghai Hu 3205
Golmud
Dulan
Magen
Yushu
Bayan Har Shan 6094
Qamdo
Garze
Qilian Shan
Xining
Linxia
Lanzhou
Tianshui
Baoji
Wudu
QINGHAI
SICHUAN
Songpan
Mianyang
Daxian
Hanzhong
Qinling
4113
Santai
Chengdu
Leshan
Neijiang
Nanchong
Hechuan
Gongga Shan 7600
Zigong
Yibin
Luzhou
Zunyi
GUIZHOU
Guiyang
Shuicheng
Anshun
KUNMING
Xiaguan
Dali
Dongchuan
Qujing
YUNNAN
Gejiu
Mengzi
Wenshan
VIETNAM
Hanoi
Haiphong
Gulf of Tonkin
Nanning
Pingxiang
2711

Projection: Bonne
East from Greenwich

ft m scale
18 000 6000
12 000 4000
9000 3000
6000 2000
4500 1500
3000 1000
1200 400
600 200
0 0
200 600
m ft

1 : 12 000 000

100    0    100    200    300    400 miles
100    0    100    200    300    400    500    600 km

7                    8                    9

**Map labels (west to east, north to south):**

Oz. Baykal
Ulan Ude
Chita
Sretensk
Nerchinsk
Yablonovy Khrebet
-baykalskiy
Olovyannaya
Borzya
Shilka
Bukaenacha
Yilehuli Shan
Svobodny
Shimanovsk
Aleksandrovsk
C. Terpeniya
Sakhalin
Poronaysk
Dolinsk
trovsk
'entiyn Nuruu
Dutulun Shan
Manzhouli
Hailar
Hulun Nur
Buir Nur
Choybalsan
Kerülen
Arxan
Butha Qi
Oroqen Zizhiqi
Nenjiang
Bei'an
Blagoveshchensk
Aihui
Bureya
Amur
Obluchye
Birobidzhan
Khabarovsk
Troitskoye
Komsomolsk
L. Bolon
Yuzhno-Sakhalinsk
Kholmsk
L I A
Saynshand
Abagnar Qi
Solon
Horqin Youyi Qianqi (Ulan Hot)
Baicheng
Yamusi
Shuangyashan
Bikin
Jixi
Mishan
Ozero Khanka
Ussuriysk
Sikhote Alin
Khrebet
Tatarskiy Proliv
La Perouse Str.
Wakkanai
Asahigawa
2290
Hokkaido
SAPPORO
Otaru
Kushiro
b i
Dzamin Üüd
Erenhot
Linxi
Chifeng
Duolun
Qiqihar
Anda
Suihua
Shuangcheng
HARBIN
Jilin
Mudanjiang
Dunhua
Yanji
Vladivostok
Nakhodka
Artem
Partizansk
Muroran
Hakodate
C. Erimo
Tsugaru-kaikyo
Aomori
Hachinohe
Morioka
MONGGOL
ZIZHIQU
Da Hinggan Ling
1949
Tongliao
Siping
Liaoyuan
Songhua Hu
Baektu
Chongjin
Akita
Sakata
Ishinomaki
SEA OF JAPAN
Sado
Niigata
Hohhot
Jining
Baotou
Datong
Zhangjiakou
Xuanhua
Fuxin
Chaoyang
CHANGCHUN
Shuangliao
FUSHUN
SHENYANG
Benxi
Liaoyang
ANSHAN
Dandong
Yalu Jiang
NORTH
Hungnam
Wonsan
JAPAN
Wajima
Toyama
Kanazawa
Utsunomiya
Koriyama
Sendai
Us
-mo
GREAT WALL
Yinchuan
BEIJING (Peking)
Baoding
TIANJIN SHI
2894
BEIJING SHI
TAIYUAN
Yangquan
Shijiazhuang
Dezhou
HEBEI
Cangzhou
Tangshan
Qinhuangdao
Jinzhou
Chengde
Yingkou
Liaodong Wan
Korea Bay
DALIAN
P'YONGYANG
Kaesong
SOUL
Inch'on
SOUTH
Taejon
Yantai
Weihai
Ye Xian
Weifang
Zibo
Jinan
HENAN
Yangcheng
QINGDAO
YELLOW SEA
KOBE
Okayama
OSAKA
NAGOYA
TOKYO
Kawasaki
YOKOHAMA
Yokosuka
Fuji-san 3776
Shizuoka
Hamamatsu
TAEGU
PUSAN
Masan
Kwangju
Kure
Hiroshima
Shimonoseki
KITAKYUSHU
FUKUOKA
Sasebo
Nagasaki
Kumamoto
Kyushu
Kagoshima
Tanega-shima
Wakayama
Sakai
Shikoku
Kochi
Matsuyama
Luoyang
Kaifeng
Zhengzhou
HENAN
Shangqiu
Huaibei
Xuzhou
Qingjiang
Nanyang
Pingdingshan
Shangshui
Fuyang
Bengbu
Huainan
Yangzhou
Taizhou
Nantong
XIAN
Shandi
Ankang
Han Shui
Zhumadian
Hefei
ANHUI
Ma'anshan
Changzhou
Wuxi
Suzhou
SHANGHAI SHI
SHANGHAI
Xiangfan
Dabie Shan
Zhongxiang
WUHAN
Anqing
Tongling
Wuhu
Wuxing
Jiaxing
HUBEI
EAST CHINA SEA
Amami-o-Shima
Vanxian
Yichang
Shashi
Huangshi
Hangzhou
Hangzhou Wan
Shaoxing
Ningbo
Changde
Yiyang
Dongting Hu
Nanchang
Jingdezhen
Jinhua
Qu Xian
Wenzhou
RYUKYU-retto
Naha
Okinawa
HUNAN
Changsha
Xiangtan
Pingxiang
JIANGXI
2120
Nanping
PACIFIC
Shaoyang
Ji'an
Sanming
Fuzhou
Hengyang
Ganzhou
Ruijin
Longyan
Quanzhou
FUJIAN
Jilong
TAIBEI
Taizhong
Sakishima Gunto
Tropic of Cancer
Guilin
Nan Ling
Shaoguan
Mei Xian
Zhangzhou
Xiamen
Jiayi
Yu Shan 3997
Taizhong
TAIWAN
GUANGXI
Wuzhou
GUANGDONG
GUANGZHOU
Huizhou
Shantou
Tainan
Gaoxiong
Pingdong
Foshan
Jiangmen
Macau (Port.)
HONG KONG (Br.)
Batan Is.
Maoming
Zhanjiang
Pratas
SOUTH CHINA SEA
Hainan Dao
1879
HAINAN
Haikou
Babuyan Is.
Qiongzhou Haixia
Formosa Strait

COPYRIGHT GEORGE PHILIP & SON LTD

6          120          7          130          8
110

B
Z
40
C
30
D
20
E

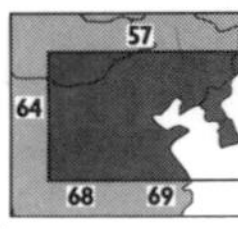

57
64 62
68 69

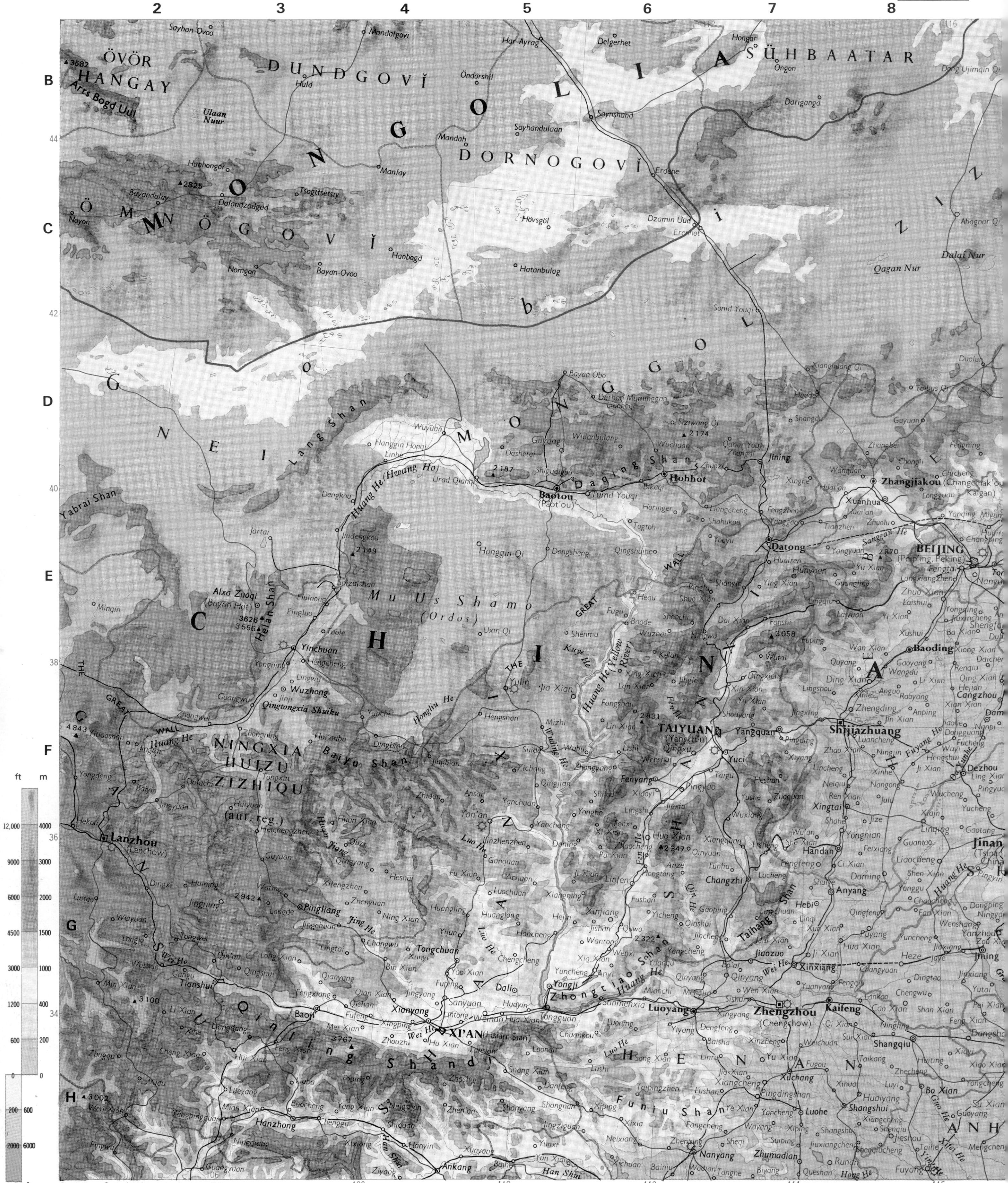

**2 3 4 5 6 7 8**

ÖVÖR
▲3582 HANGAY
Arts Bogd Uul

DUNDGOVĬ
Mandalgovi
Har-Ayrag
Delgerhet
Hongor
SÜHBAATAR
Öngon
Dariganga
Dong Ujimqin Qi

B
Sayhan-Ovoo
Öndörshil

O
N
G
O
L
I
A

Huld
Mandah
Sayhandulaan
Saynshand
Erdene
Darigang

44

Hanhongor
▲2825
Manlay
DORNOGOVĬ

Z
I
Z

Bayandalay
Dalandzadgad
Tsogttsetsiy

C
Noyon
Ö M
M N
Nomgon
Hanbogd
Hövsgöl
Hatanbulag
Dzamin Üüd
Ereenhot

Abagnar Qi
Dalai Nur

42
Bayan-Ovoo
b
Sonid Youqi
Qagan Nur
Duolun

G
O
V
Ĭ
G
o
b
i

M
O
N
G
G
O
L

Bayan Obo
Darhan Muminggan Lianhe
Xianghuang Qi
Huade
Zhangbei
Taibus Qi
Fengning

D
Langshan
Wuyuan
Hanggin Houqi
Linhe
Guyang
Wulanhua
Siziwang Qi
▲2174
Wuchuan
Qahar Youyi Zhongqi
Jining
Wanquan
Shangdu
Chongli
Guyuan

Yabrai Shan
▲2187
Dashetai
Shiguaigou
Daqing Shan
Hohhot
Baotou (Paot'ou)
Tumd Youqi
Bikeqi
Liangcheng
Fengzhen
Yanggao
Xinghe
Huai'an
Xuanhua
Zhangjiakou (Changchiak'ou) (Kalgan)
Huai'an
Chicheng

40
Huang He (Hwang Ho)
Urad Qianqi
Horinger
Shahukou
Youyu
Datong
Tianzhen
Zhuolu
Yanqing
Miyun
BEIJING (Peiping, Peking)
Fengtai

Dengkou
Jartai
Jinboshan
Hanggin Qi
Dongsheng
Qingshuihe
Togtoh
Huairen
Hunyuan
Ying Xian
Guangling
Yu Xian
Laishui
Langfang
Zhuo Xian

E
Alxa Zuoqi (Bayan Hot)
▲3626
3556
Huinong
Pingluo
Shizuishan
Mu Us Shamo (Ordos)
Uxin Qi
Shenmu
Hequ
Fugu
Baode
Wuzhai
Shuo Xian
Shanyin
Pinglu
GREAT
Shuo Xian
Baoding
Xiong Xian
Daicher
Gaoyang
Wangdu

Minqin
Helan Shan
Yinchuan
Tongxin
Yingchuan
Lingchuan
Kuye He
Yulin
Jia Xian
Huang He (Yellow River)
Kelan
Jingle
Dai Xian
▲3058
Wutai
Fanshi
Xin Xian
Ding Xian
Li Xian
Boye
Anguo
Renqiu

38
THE GREAT WALL
Yongning
Lingwu
Wuzhong
Qingtongxia Shuiku
Hongliu He
Hengshan
Mizhi
Lin Xian
Fen He
▲2831
TAIYUAN (Yangch'ü)
Yangquan
Pingding
SHIJIAZHUANG
Zhengding
Jin Xian
Cangzhou

▲4843
Yitiaoshan
Huang He
THE GREAT WALL
Zhongning
Hui'anbu
Baiyu Shan
Dingbian
Jingbian
Suide
Zichang
Zhongyang
Wenshui
Qingxu
Yuci
Shouyang
Taigu
Zhao Xian
Ningjin
Xinhe
Ji Xian
Dezhou

F
NINGXIA HUIZU ZIZHIQU (aut. reg.)
Zhongwei
Tongxin
Haiyuan
Huan Jiang
Huan Xian
Ansai
Yan'an
Yanchang
Xi Xian
Linfen
Fenxi
Xiaoyi
Pingyao
Heshun
Zuoquan
Xingtai
Julu
Pingxiang
Yucheng

36
Lanzhou (Lanchow)
Dingxi
Huining
Guyuan
Jingyuan
Quzi
Qingyang
Heichengzi
Luochuan
Yichuan
Ji Xian
Hongtong
Changzhi
Lucheng
Handan
Ci Xian
Daming
Shen Xian
Linqing
Guantao
Liaocheng
Jinan (Tsinan)

Weiyuan
Longxi
Tongwei
Qin'an
▲2942
Jingning
Pingliang
Jingchuan
Jing He
Changwu
Huangling
Hancheng
Jishan
Houma
Yicheng
Qinshui
Gaoping
Linfen
Tunliu
Anyang
Hebi
Qingfeng
Puyang
Fan Xian
Dongping

G
Swei Ho
Lintao
Weiyuan
Wushan
Longde
Qianyang
Ning Xian
Yijun
Luochuan
Wanrong
▲2347
Yangcheng
Qin He
Jiaozuo
Xinxiang
Changyuan
Heze
Jiye
Jining

▲3100
Tianshui
Li Xian
Min Xian
Qinyang
Qingshui
Fengxiang
Qishan
Baoji
Fufeng
Qianyang
Jingyang
Sanyuan
Dali
Zhongtiao Shan
Yongji
Yuncheng
Anyi
Mianchi
Meng Xian
Wen Xian
Xingyang
Qinyang
Xuanwu
Fengqiu
Dingtao
Jinxiang
Chengwu
Lankao

34
Zhouqu
Cheng Xian
Liangdang
Mei Xian
Feng He
▲3767
Xingping
Weinan
Hua Xian
Huayin
Tongguan
Sanmenxia
Luoyang (Chengchow)
Xingyang
Zhengzhou (Chengchow)
Kaifeng
Cao Xian
Shan Xian
Shangqiu

XI'AN (Hsian, Sian)
Zhouzhi
Hu Xian
Lantian
Chuankou
Luonan
Luoning
Yiyang
Dengfeng
Xinzheng
Yu Xian
Baisha
Weichuan
Xuchang
Huaiyang
Taikang
Zhecheng

H
▲3002
Wei Xian
Mian Xian
Liuba
Baocheng
Yang Xian
Fuping
Shang Xian
Danfeng
Lushi
Xichuan
Xixia
Neixiang
Funiu Shan
Ye Xian
Xihua
Luyi
Bo Xian

Qinling Shandi
Hanzhong
Chenggu
Zhenba
Xixiang
Shiquan
Zhen'an
Shangnan
Xiping
Yancheng
Wuyang
Fangcheng
Shangshui
Pingdingshan
ANHUI

Ningqiang
Lueyang
Han Shui
Hanyin
Xunyang
Yunxi
Yunxian
Xichuan
Zhenping
Xixia
Neixiang
Wayang
Sheqi
Biyang
Zhumadian
Xiping
Queshan

Bei
Zhiyang
Ankang
Ziyang
Han Shui
Nanyang
Zhumadian
Biyang
Hong He
Fuyang

ft m
12,000 4000
9000 3000
6000 2000
4500 1500
3000 1000
1200 400
600 200
0 0
200 600
2000 6000
m ft

1 : 4 800 000

50    0    50    100    150 miles

50    0    50    100    150    200    km

East from Greenwich

COPYRIGHT. GEORGE PHILIP & SON. LTD

**Map labels (west to east, north to south):**

HIQU

Horqin Youyi Qianqi
Zhenlai    Nen    HARBIN (Haerhpin)    Acheng    Jixi    Turiy Rog    Ozero Khanka
Hulin He    Baicheng    Songhua    Jiang    Shuangcheng    Linkou    RUSSIA
Tuquan    Tuowei He    Da'an    Maoxing    Zhaoyuan    Yimianpo    Shulan    Maqiaohe    Xiachengzi    Suyfenne
Tongyu    Tao'an    Songhua    Fuyu    Yushu    Wuchang    Mudanjiang    Hailin    Muling    Yangang    Dongning    Pokrovka
Jorud Qi    Qian Gorlos    Beitablaizhang    Sanchahe    Shangzhi    Shannetun    Ning'an    Dongjingcheng    Suiyang    luozigou    Ussuriysk (Voroshilov) Razdolnoye
Bairin Zuoqi    1949    Shenjingzi    Dehui    Gantang    Shulan    Chunyang    Artem
Changling    Fulongquan    Jiutai    Panshi    690 Zhangguangcailing (Manchuria)    Jingbo Hu    Vladivostok
Linxi    Fanjiatun    Wulajie    Jiaohe    Emu    Songjiangdian    Mingyuegue    Yanji    Tumen    Hunchun    Kraskino    Slavyanka
2029    Xinkai He    Changchun    Maolin    Huaidezhen    Huaide    Shuangyang    Hu    Xinzhan    Hua    Daxinggou    Wangqing    Tumen    Posyet    Paksikori
Bairin Youqi    Tongliao    Kailu    Shuangliao    Lishu    Yitong    Dunhua    Helong    Antu    Hoeryong    Musan    Unggi    Sosura
Xar Moron He    Xiligu-He    Siping    Liaoyuan    Dongfeng    Huinan    Lianjiang    1677    Puryong    Nanam    Kyongsong    Nojin
Ongniud Qi    Kangping    Zhangwu    Xifeng    Kaiyuan    Hailong    Fusong    Changbai Shan    Yupyongdong    Changbai    Chongjin    Onjoni    Ondejmi
2020    Lanha He    Hure Qi    Zhangwu    Shanchengzhen    Qingyuan    Huadian    Jingyu    2541    Hyhyangdong    Irhyangdong
Chifeng    Wutonghaolai    Xiawa    Faku    Tieling    Xinbin    Tonghua    Chungang-ni    Musan    Hochon    Kimchaek (Songjin)
Heishui    Beipiao    Qinghemen    Xinmin    FUSHUN    Huanren    Linjiang    Kanggye    1845    Pungsan    Kosong-ni    Tanchon
Weichang    Beizhen    SHENYANG (Mukden)    Heishan    Liaozhong    Hun    Jiang    Huaijianzi    Manpojin    Hapsu    Simpungdong
1885    Chaoyang    Liaoyang    Benxi    Qingheecheng    Supung Sk.    Kasan    Oro    Kapson
Chengde    Jinzhou    LIAONING    Anshan    Anpjng    Yalu    Jiang    Kuup-tong    2522    Kwongdeni    Pujon-chosuji    Changhungni    Kilju
Longhua    Jianchang    Daling He    Yi He    Niuzhuang    Haicheng    Lianshanguan    Xiuyan    Chosan    Changjin-chosuji    d'Changjin    Pukchong
Luangou    Pingquan    Panshan    Gai Xian    Kuandian    Chosan    Hyesan    Kosongni    Kimchaek
Luanping    Xingcheng    Jinxi    Yingkou    131    Fengcheng    Cao He    Pyoktong    Changjin    Hamhung    Hongwon    Tanchon
Shuangshanzi    Tianzhuangtai    Wantu    Dandong    Supung    Pukchin    Sinhung    Hongwon
Shangbaisheng    Jianchangying    Xiongyuecheng    Liaodong Bandao    Yongampo    Sinuiju    Taegwan    NORTH KOREA    Takchon    Hamhung    Hungnam    Tongwon
Zunhua    Fu Xian    Jin Xian    Gushao    Zhuanghe    Sonchon    Chongju    Anju    Songchon-ni    Wonsan    Kojo
TIANJIN (Tientsin) (Tienching)    Tangshan    Leting    Pikou    Dandong    Cho-do    Sukchon    Kangdong    P'YONGYANG    Sepo    Kosong    SEA OF
Tanggu    Luan Xian    Changli    Liaodong Wan    Chinnampo    Chunghwa    Suan    Pyonggang    Wonsan    Anbyon    Kojo    JAPAN
Dagu    Qinhuangdao    Lüshun    DALIAN (Lüda)    Korea Bay    Sariwon    Namch'on    Koksan    1638    Chango-ri    Kansong
Hangu    Oikou    Fuxin    Haeju    Kaesong    Panmunjom    Chorwon    Kumhwa    Hwachon-chosuji    1678    Yangyang
Bo Hai (Gulf of Chihli)    Changyon    Ongjin    Munsan    Uijongbu    Hongchon    Chunchon    Kangnung
Tangshan    Paengnyong-do    Yonan    Cease Fire Line    SEOUL    Ichon    Hongsong    Wonju    Yongwol    Samchok    Ullung-do
Luanxian    Huang He    Longkou    Huang Xian    Penglai    INCH'ON    Suwon    Pyongtaek    Yoju    Hoengsong    Yongwol    Ulchin
Zhanhua    Laizhou Wan    Duxinghai    Fushan    Yantai    Osan    Chechon    Chumunjin
Huimin    Kenli    Weihai    Chongju    Chungju    Tanyang
Shanghe    Guangrao    Qixia    923    Muping    SOUTH    Yongwol
Beizhen    Yidu    Ye Xian    Wendeng    Sosan    Chonan    KOREA    Chongju    Yechon    Andong    Yongdok
Qingcheng    Zibo    Shouguang    Laiyang    Shidao    Yesong    Yongju    Uisong    Chongha
Boshan    Weifang    Pingdu    Rushan    Hongsong    Taejon    Sangju    Pohang
Laiwu    1108    Linqu    Anqiu    Laixi    Nanhuang    Haiyang    Anmyon-do    Nonsan    Kimchon    Yongchon
Xintai    Mengyin    Jiao Xian    Gaomi    Lancun    Kumi    Andong    Ulsan
Sishui    Jinan    Changyang    Jiaozhou Wan    QINGDAO (Ch'ingtao)    Iri    Kunsan    Chonju    Koryong    Chongdo    Kyongju
Pingyi    Yishui    Wulian    HUANG HAI (Yellow Sea)    Namwon    Kochang    Hamyang    TAEGU    Miryang    Ulsan
Fei Xian    Rizhao    1915    Chinju    Tongnae
Teng Xian    Ganyu    Haizhou Wan    Sago-ri    Tamyang    Masan    PUSAN
Zaozhuang    Lianyungang    Sunchon    KWANGJU    Chinhae    Samchonpo    Chungmu    Tsushima    Iki
Hanzhuang    Haizhou    Lianyungang (Hsinhailien)    Mokpo    Suncheon    Pogil-ri    Yosu    Sasuna    Saka    Izuhara
Xuzhou    Guanyun    Xiangshui    Changhung    Korea Strait    Tsushima    Karatsu
Qingjiang    Qinjiangang    Chindo    JAPAN    Nagasaki    Inari
Bengbu    Guannan    Biaohi    Cheju    Cheju-do    Tsushima-Kaikyo    Sasebo    Kochinotsu
Fengyang    Da Yunhe    Hallim    1950    Onpyong-ni    Nakadori-jima    Ikinoura
Huaiyin    Suqian    Masipo    Sogwi-po    Fukue-jima    Kuchinotsu    Nagasaki
Qinglang    Funing    Yancheng    JIANGSU

Liaodong Bandao    Korea Bay    Shandong Bandao    Tsushima Strait

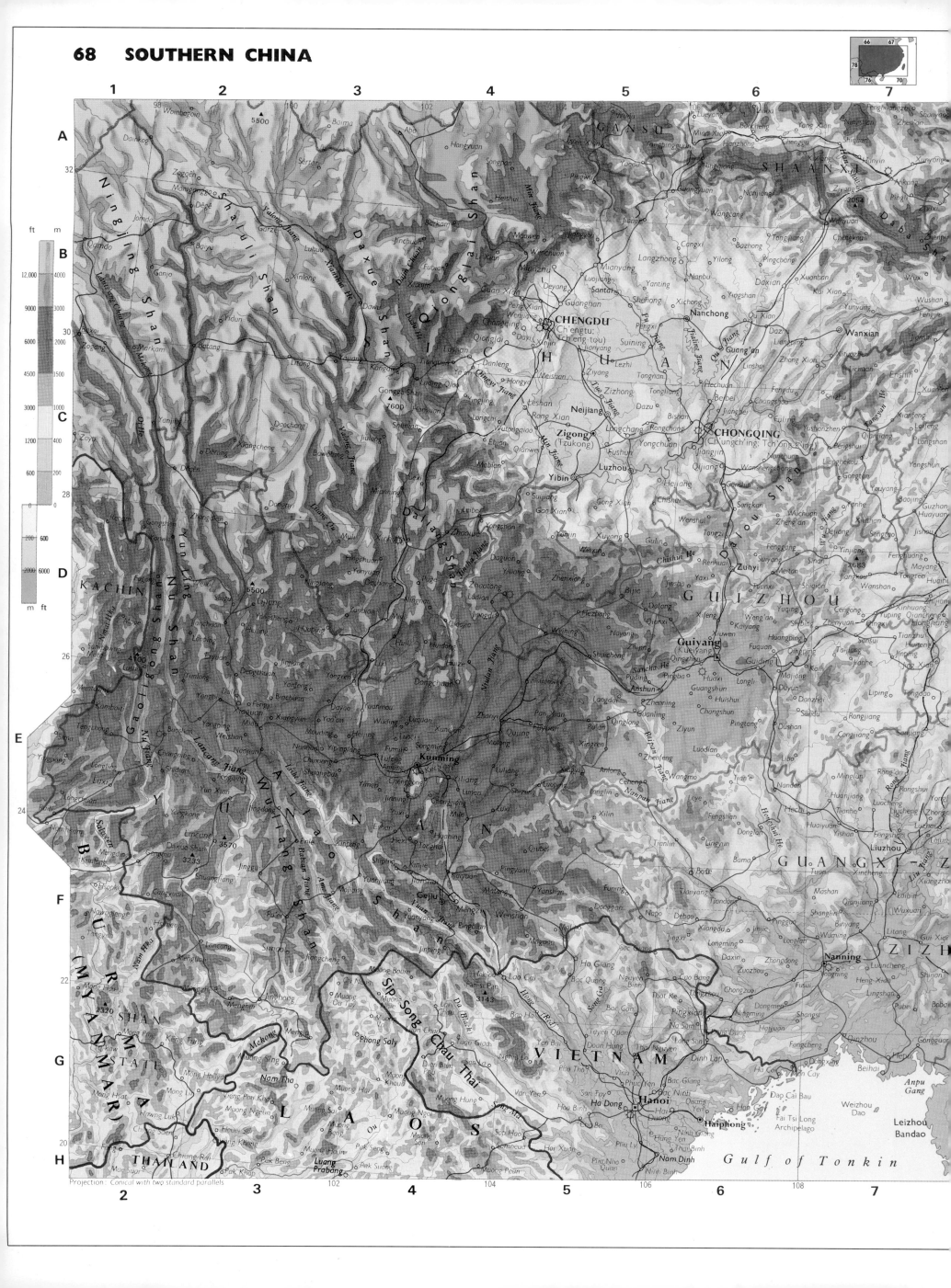

1 : 4 800 000

50 0 50 100 150 miles
50 0 50 100 150 200 km

HENAN
HUBEI
ANHUI
JIANGSU
ZHEJIANG
HUNAN
JIANGXI
FUJIAN
GUANGDONG
TAIWAN (FORMOSA)

Nanyang
Xinyang
Huainan
Bengbu
Hefei
NANJING (Nanking)
Changzhou
Wuxi
Suzhou (Soochow)
SHANGHAI (Changhai)
Songjiang
WUHAN (Wou-han)
Hankou
Hanyang
Huangshi
Yichang (Ichang)
Shashi
Hangzhou (Hangchow)
Ningbo (Ningpo)
Shaoxing
Tunxi
Zhoushan
Nanchang
Jingdezhen
Wenzhou (Wenchow)
Changsha
Xiangtan
Zhuzhou
Hengyang
Shaoyang
Ji'an
Ganzhou
Nanping
Fuzhou (Fuchow)
Sanming
Xiamen (Hsiamen; Amoy)
Zhangzhou
Quanzhou (Chuanchou)
Shantou (Swatow)
Guilin
Wuzhou
GUANGZHOU (Canton)
Foshan
HONG KONG (U.K.)
Kowloon
Macau (Macao) (Port.)
Zhanjiang
TAIBEI (Taipei)
Taizhong (Taichung)
Tainan
Gaoxiong (Kaohsiung)
Pingdong

Tropic of Cancer

SOUTH CHINA SEA
Luzon Strait
Hangzhou Wan

COPYRIGHT GEORGE PHILIP & SON LTD

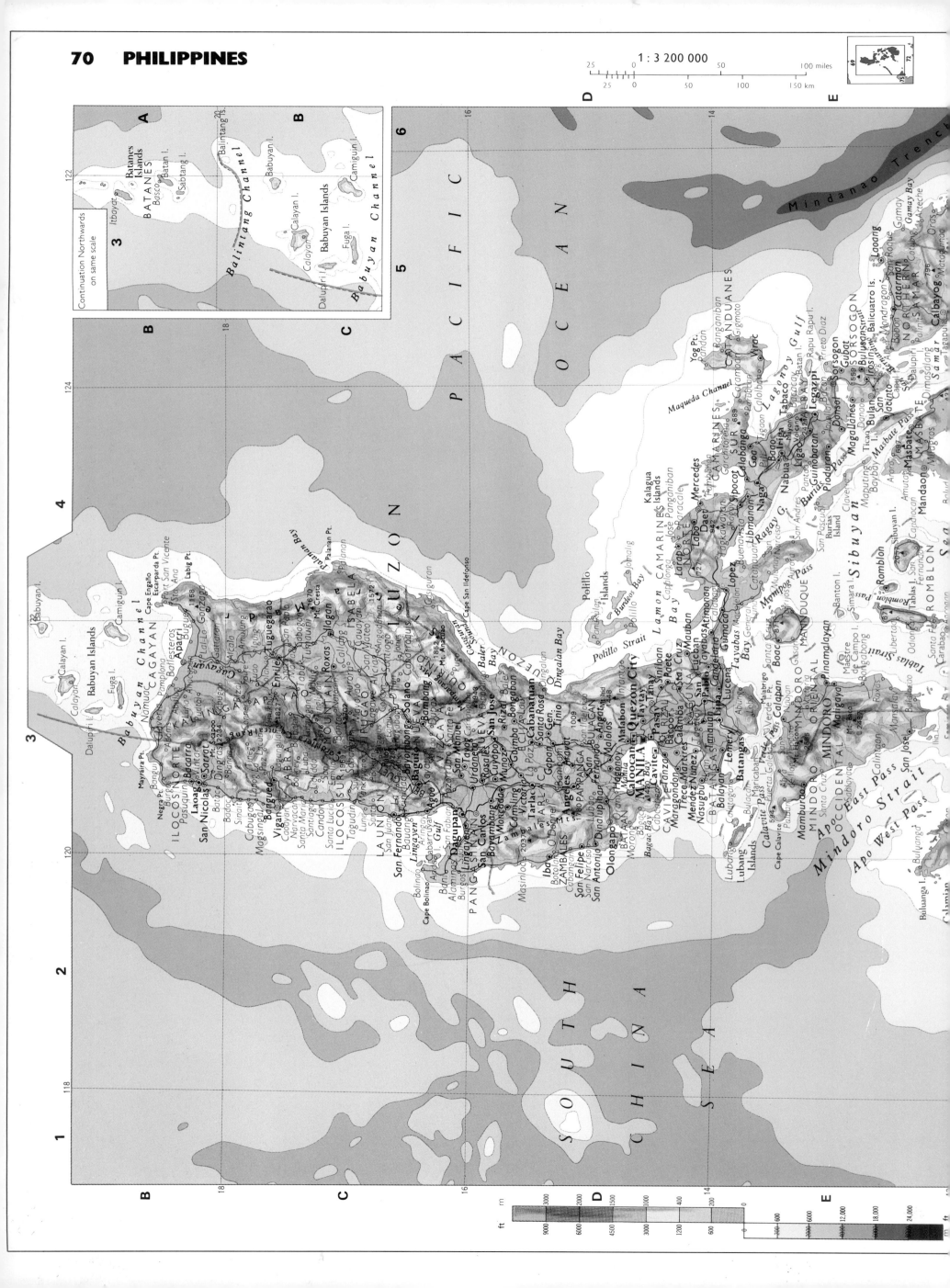

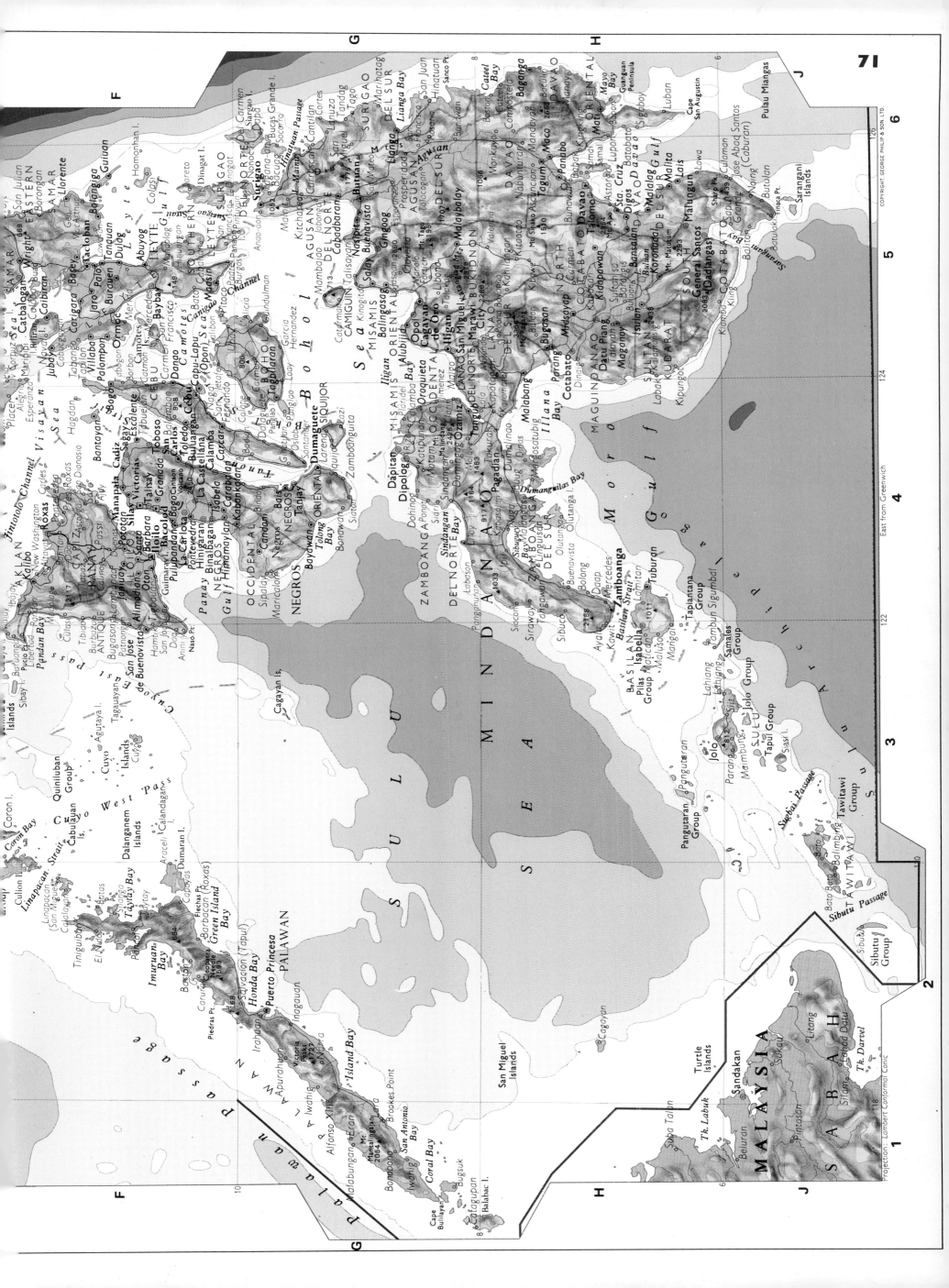

1  2  3

SULAWESI SEA

MALUKU SEA

A

BORNEO

Tawau
1346
Teluk
Sebuku
Lama
Malinau
Sesayap
Bunju
Tarakan
Nomeh
Berau
Tanjungselor
Tanjungbatu
Maratua
Tanjungredeb
Kongkemul
2053

Karakelong
Bulu
Beo
Kepulauan
Talaud
Kaburuang
Tahuna
Sangihe
Siau
Tohulandang
Biaro
Bangka

Morotai
Sopi
Rau Bereberu
Doi
Wayabulu
Tobelo
Akelamo

TIMUR
Equator
Telen
Muarakaman
Samarinda
Tenggarong
Sangasanga
Sungaitiram
Balikpapan
Tanahgrogot
Jangeru

Dumaring
Bontang
Balayan

Tolitoli
Dondo
Malino
Ogomas
2913
2707
Tomini

UTARA
2300
Tentolomatinan
Paleleh
Buol
Sumalata
Kuandang
Gambuta
Gorontolo
1954
Tilamuta
Muotong

Manado
2022
Kema
Tondano
Amurang
Kotamobagu
Tg. Flesko

Halmahera
Ternate
Ternate
Tidore
Soasiu
Mayu
Makian
Kayoa
Ibu
Jailolo
Weda
Teluk
Weda
Patani
Teluk
Buli
Wosi

0

Donggala
Toboli
Parigi
Palu
Lariang

Teluk
Tomini
Kepulauan
Toglan
Poh
Maliku
Luwuk

TENGAH
Poso
Tojo
Toili
Tokala
2630
Kolonodale

Peleng
Banggai

Kepulauan
Bacan
Obilatu
Obi
Loji
Sesepe
Mandioli
Bisa
Fluk
Loji
Fluk

B

Kepulauan
Balabalangan
(Paternoster)

Kotabaru
Sebuku
Kapambu
Pulau
Laut

SULAWESI
(CELEBES)
Balease
3016
Masamba
Mamuju
Onang
Makale
Palopo
Masamba
Polewali
SELATAN
3455
Rantekombola
Enrekang
Pinrang
Majene
Teluk
Mandar
Pangkajene

Tangkelebaoke
1782
Mekongga
2790
Kolaka
TENGGARA
Mondeodo
Kendari
Manui
Monse
Wowoni

Mangole
Taliabu
Auponhia
Sanana
Kepulauan Sula
Kepulauan Banggai
Teluk Tolo

SERAM

MOLUCCA

Kabalatmada
Namlea
Buru
2429
Womsasi
Tifu
Leksula
Namrole
Lima
Ambon
Ambon
Pidu
Kayeli

Parepare
Polewali
Watangsoppeng
Singkang
Rappang
Watampone
Sumpangbinangae
Pangkajene
Marek
Maros
Ujung
Pandang
Sinjai
Teluk Bone

Buapinang
Raha
Pising
Baubau
Muna
Butung
Lawele
Kabaena
Wangiwangi
Kepulauan
Tukangbesi
Binongko

INDO
NAT

5

Kepulauan
Masalima

Sungguminasa
Pattallassang
Lompobatang
2871
Bulukumba
Bontaeng
Bontosunggu

Batuata
(Watuata I.)

BANDA

Salayar

Benteng

Kepulauan
Bone Rate

Gunungapi

Tanahjampea
Kalao
Kalaotoa
Bone
Rate

C

FLORES SEA
Lesser Sunda Islands

Damar

Wetar
Westri
Romang
Iliwaki
Kepulauan

ft  m

12 000  4000

9000  3000

6000  2000

4500  1500

3000  1000

1200  400

600  200

0  0

m  ft

200  600

2000  6000

4000  12 000

6000  18 000

24 000

m  ft

Lombok
Rinjani
3726
Mataram
Kelong
Mojo
Sumbawa
Besar
Taliwang

Tambora
2821
Raba
Dompu
Parado

Sangeang
Komodo
Sape
Rinca

Labuhanbajo
Ruteng
Aimere
Ende

Flores
Maumere
Solor

Larantuka
Adonara
Lomblen

Pantar
Kalabahi
Alor

Atauro
Selat Wetar
Kisar
Bacon
Tutuala

Leti
Moa
Lakar
Kepulauan
Leti

Dili
Viqueque
TIMOR

Sumbawa
Selat Sumba
Memboro
Sumba
Waikabubak
Waingapu
Melolo
Boing

NUSA TENGGARA TIMUR

Narkliu
Ponte
Macassar
Atapupu
Atambua
Kefomenanu
Soe
Uato-Udo
Timor

SAWU SEA

TIMOR SEA

NUSA TENGGARA BARAT

Semau
Kupang
Pariti
Nikiniki

D

Raijua
Dana
Sawu
Baa
Roti

1 : 5 600 000

50    0    50    100    150    200 miles

50    0    50   100  150  200  250  300   km

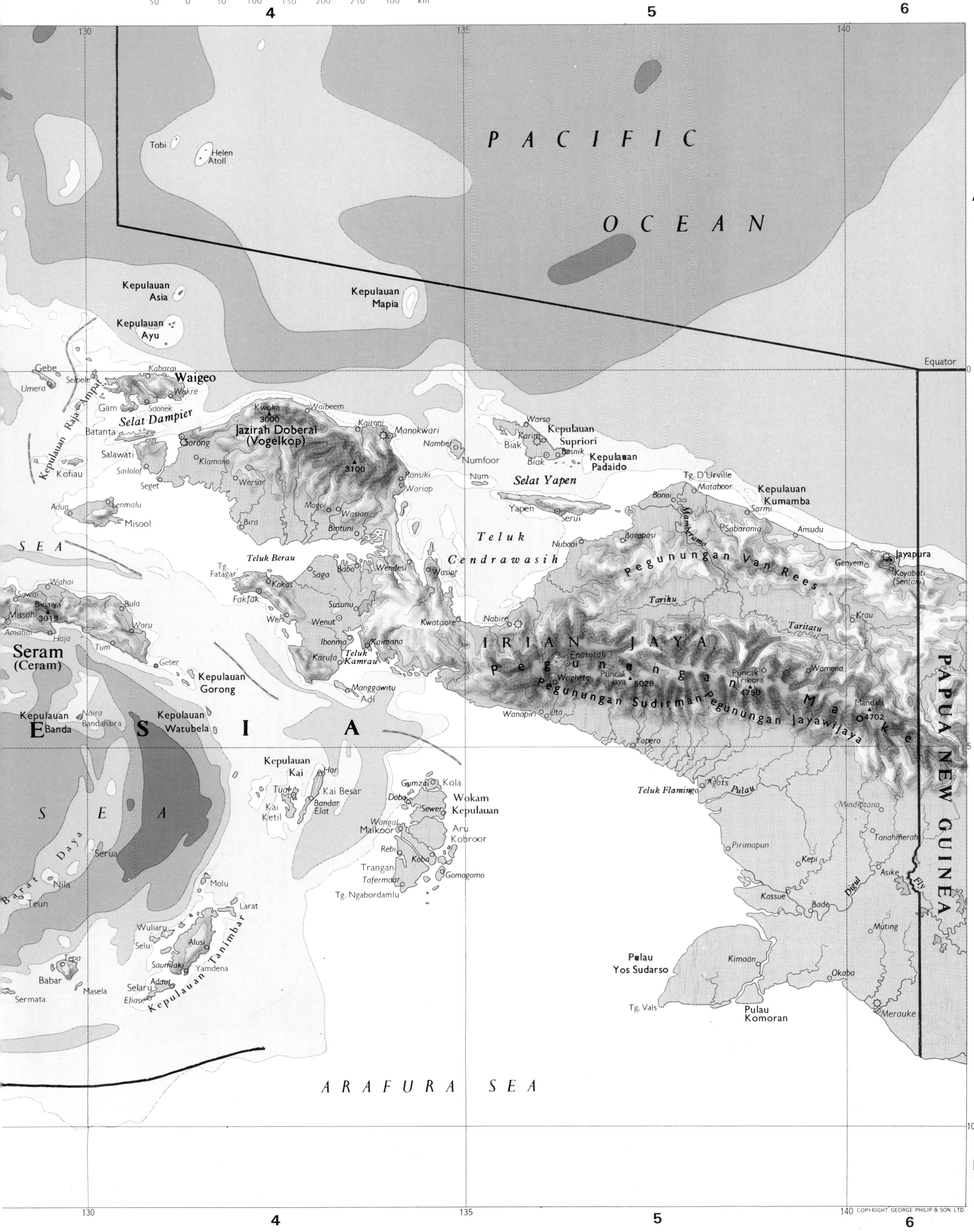

**4**                    **5**                    **6**

130                           135                          140

P A C I F I C

O C E A N

A

Tobi
Helen
Atoll

Kepulauan
Asia

Kepulauan
Mapia

Kepulauan
Ayu

Gebe
Umera
Selpele
Kabarai
Waigeo
Wokre
Gam    Saonek
Batanta    Selat Dampier
Salawati    Sorong
Sailolof    Klamano
Seget
Adua    Lenmalu
Misool
Kofiau
Kwoka
3000
Jazirah Doberai
(Vogelkop)
Waibeem
Kairani
Nambel
Manokwari
Numfoor
3100
Ransiki
Wariap

Worsa
Kepulauan
Karim    Supriori
Biak    Bosnik
Biak    Kepulauan
Padaido

Equator                0

Num
Numfoor
Selat Yapen
Yapen
Serui
Nuboai

Tg. D'Urville
Mataboor
Bonoi
Sarmi

Kepulauan
Kumamba
Sabarania    Ansudu

Jayapura
Genyem
Koyabati
(Sentani)

B

S E A

Wahai
Sawai
Masohi
3019
Amahai    Haja
Bina

Teluk Berau
Tg.
Fatagar    Saga
Fakfak    Kokas
Weri

Babo
Susunu
Wendesi

Teluk
Cendrawasih

Wasior
Kwatisore
Nabire

Barapasi
Tariku
Mamberamo

Pegunungan Van Rees

Taritatu
Taritatu

Krau

I R I A N     J A Y A

Wamena

Seram
(Ceram)

Woru
Tum
Geser

Wenut
Ibonma
Karufa    Teluk
Kamrau

Kaimana

Pegunungan    Maoke
Enarotali    Puncak    Puncak
Wagheto    Jaya    Trikora
5029    4750

Pegunungan Sudirman    Pegunungan Jayawijaya

Mandala
4702

Kepulauan
Gorong
Manggawitu
Adi

Wanapiri    Uta

Wapero

E    Kepulauan
Banda    Noira
Bandanaira    Kepulauan
Watubela

S    I    A

Yapero

Teluk Flaminga
Agats
Pulau

P A P U A     N E W     G U I N E A

Mindiptana

Kepulauan
Kai    Har
Tual
Kai Besar
Kai    Bandan
Ketil    Elat

Gymzai    Kola
Dobo
Sewer
Wokam
Kepulauan

Tanahmerah

Kepi

SEA

Barat Daya
Serua

Nila
Teun

Molu
Larat

Wuliaru
Selu    Alusi
Saumlaki    Yamdena
Tepa    Selaru    Adaut
Babar    Masela    Eliase
Sermata

Maikoor    Rebi
Wariga l
Trangan    Koba    Aru    Kobroor
Tafermaar    Gomogomo
Tg. Ngabordamlu

Pirimapun

Kassue
Bade

Muting

Asike
Digul    Fly

C

Pulau
Yos Sudarso

Kimaän

Okaba

Tg. Vals
Pulau
Komoran

Merauke

A R A F U R A     S E A

10

D

130                           135                          140   COPYRIGHT GEORGE PHILIP & SON LTD

**4**                    **5**                    **6**

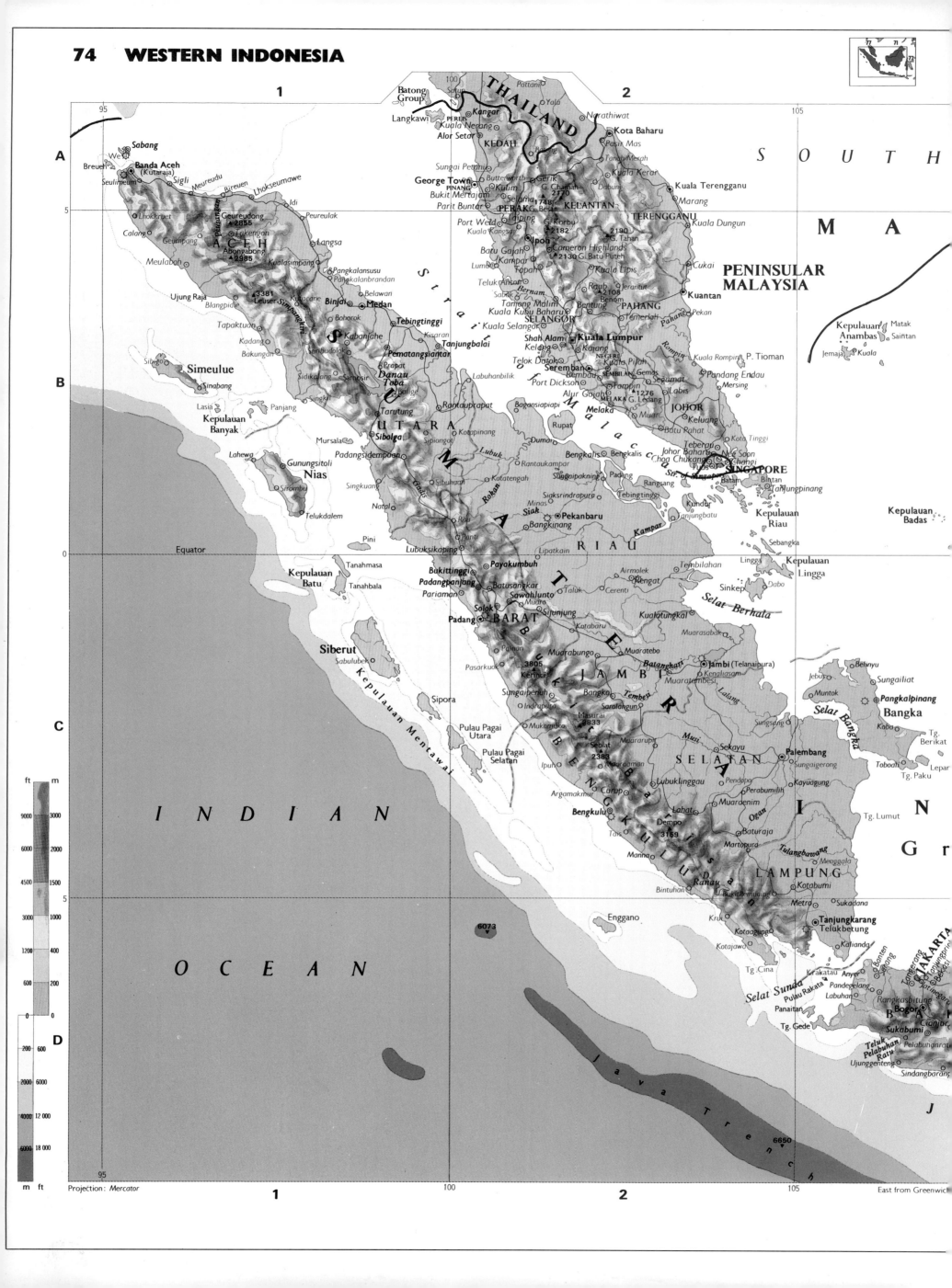

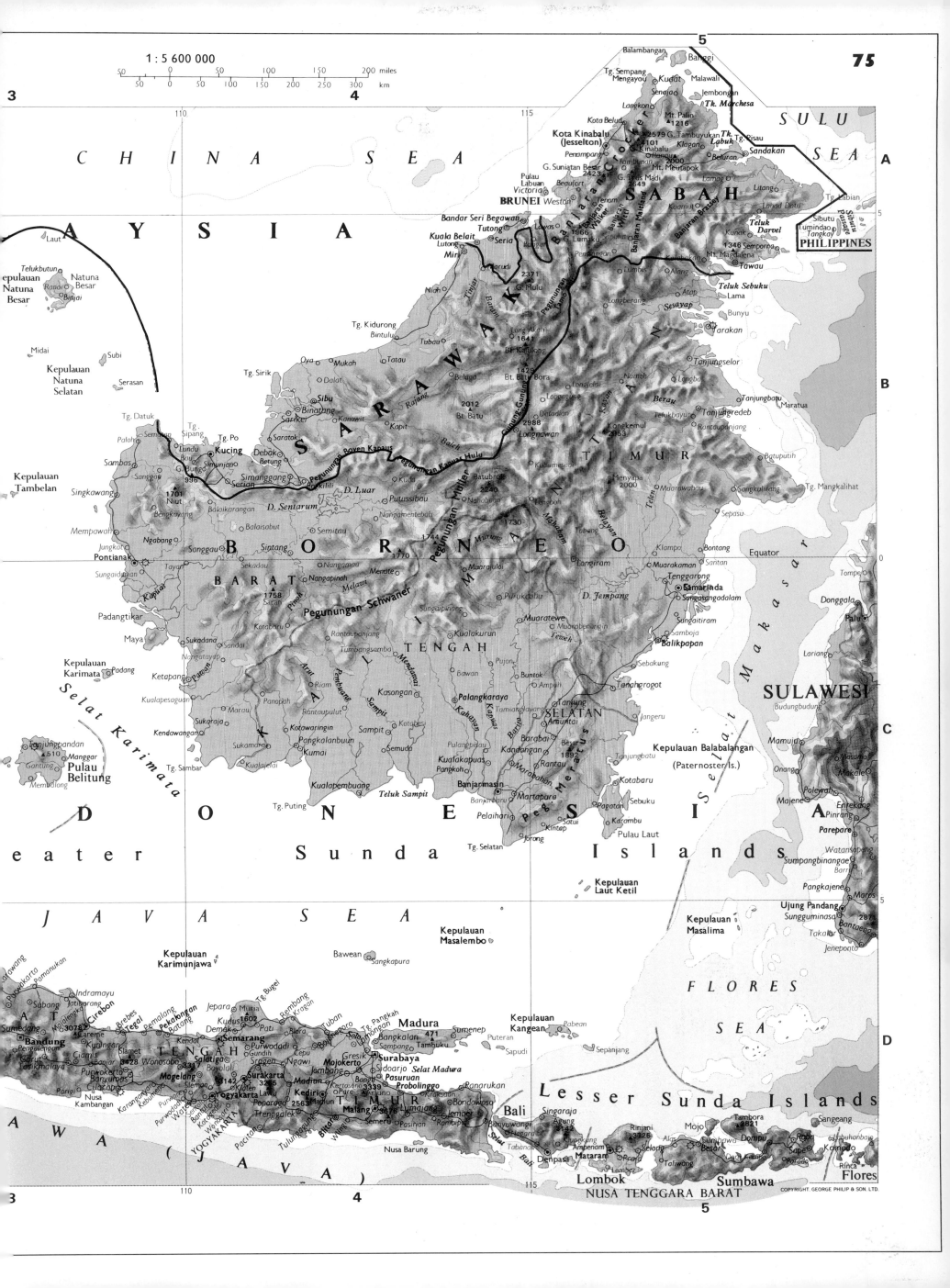

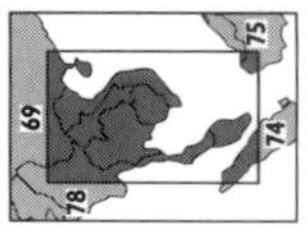

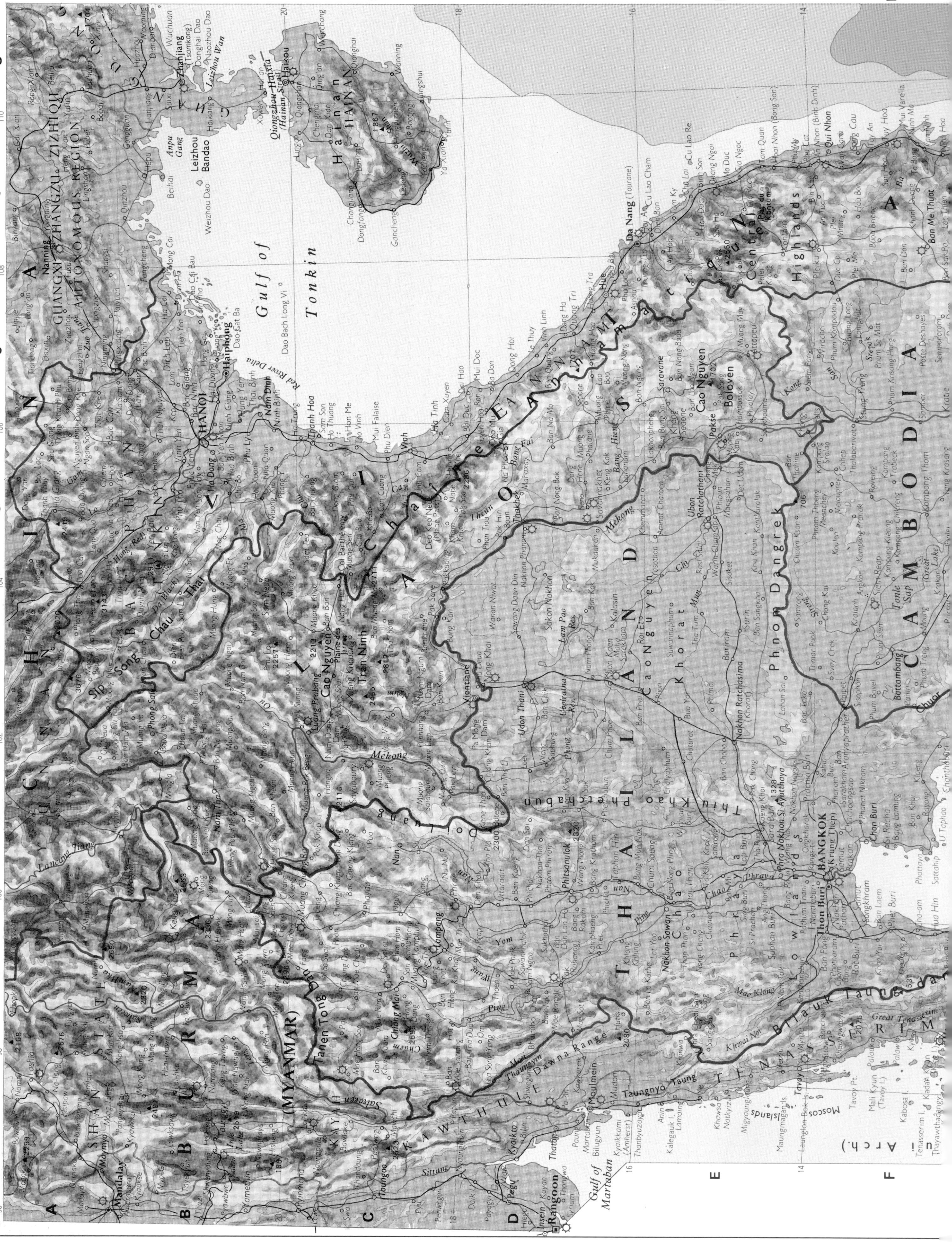

CHINA

GUANGXI ZHUANGZU ZIZHIQU AUTONOMOUS REGION

Nanning

GUANGDONG

Zhanjiang (Tsamkong)

HAINAN

Qiongzhou Haixia (Hainan Strait)

Haikou

Gulf of Tonkin

HANOI

Haiphong

Red River Delta

VIETNAM

Chaîne Annamitique

LAOS

Vientiane

THAILAND

Mekong

Khorat

Phnom Dangrek

CAMBODIA

BURMA (MYANMAR)

SHAN STATE

Mandalay

Chiang Mai

Bangkok (Krung Thep)

Chao Phraya Lowlands

TENASSERIM

Dawna Range

Salween

Gulf of Martaban

Rangoon

Pegu

Central Highlands

Da Nang (Tourane)

Mekong

Tonle Sap

Battambang

Mergui Arch.

Great Tenasserim

1 : 4 800 000

50   0   50   100   150 miles
50   0   50   100   150   200 km

SOUTH CHINA SEA

Gulf of Thailand

Strait of Malacca

PENINSULAR MALAYSIA

SINGAPORE

BORNEO

Kepulauan Natuna

Kepulauan Anambas

Mekong River

Con Son Islands

Isthmus of Kra (Kho Khot Kra)

Phnom Penh

Ho Chi Minh (Saigon)

Thanh Pho Ho Chi Minh

Phan Thiet

Nha Trang

Soc Trang

Rach Gia

George Town

Kuala Lumpur

Kuala Terengganu

Kota Baharu

Melaka

Johor Baharu

Seremban

Kelang

Butterworth

Alor Setar

Hat Yai

Songkhla (Singora)

Nakhon Si Thammarat

Medan

Binjai

Pematangsiantar

Sibolga

Tebingtinggi

Phuket

Kota Tinggi

Projection: Conical with two standard parallels

COPYRIGHT GEORGE PHILIP & SON LTD.

East from Greenwich

ft   m
9000   6000   4500   3000   1500   1200   600   200   0
m   ft   2000   4000   6000

1 : 4 800 000

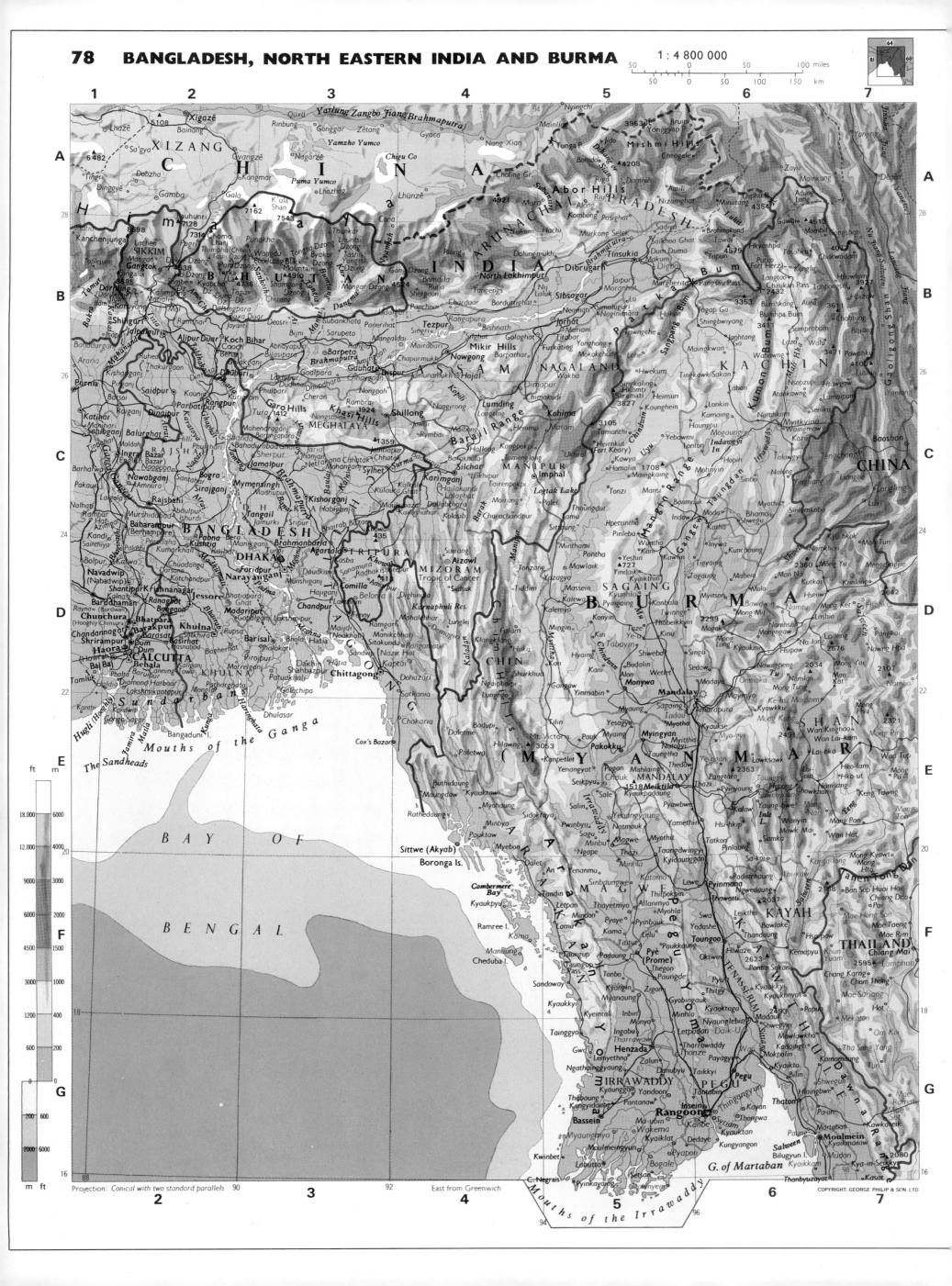

Projection: Conical with two standard parallels    East from Greenwich

1 : 5 600 000

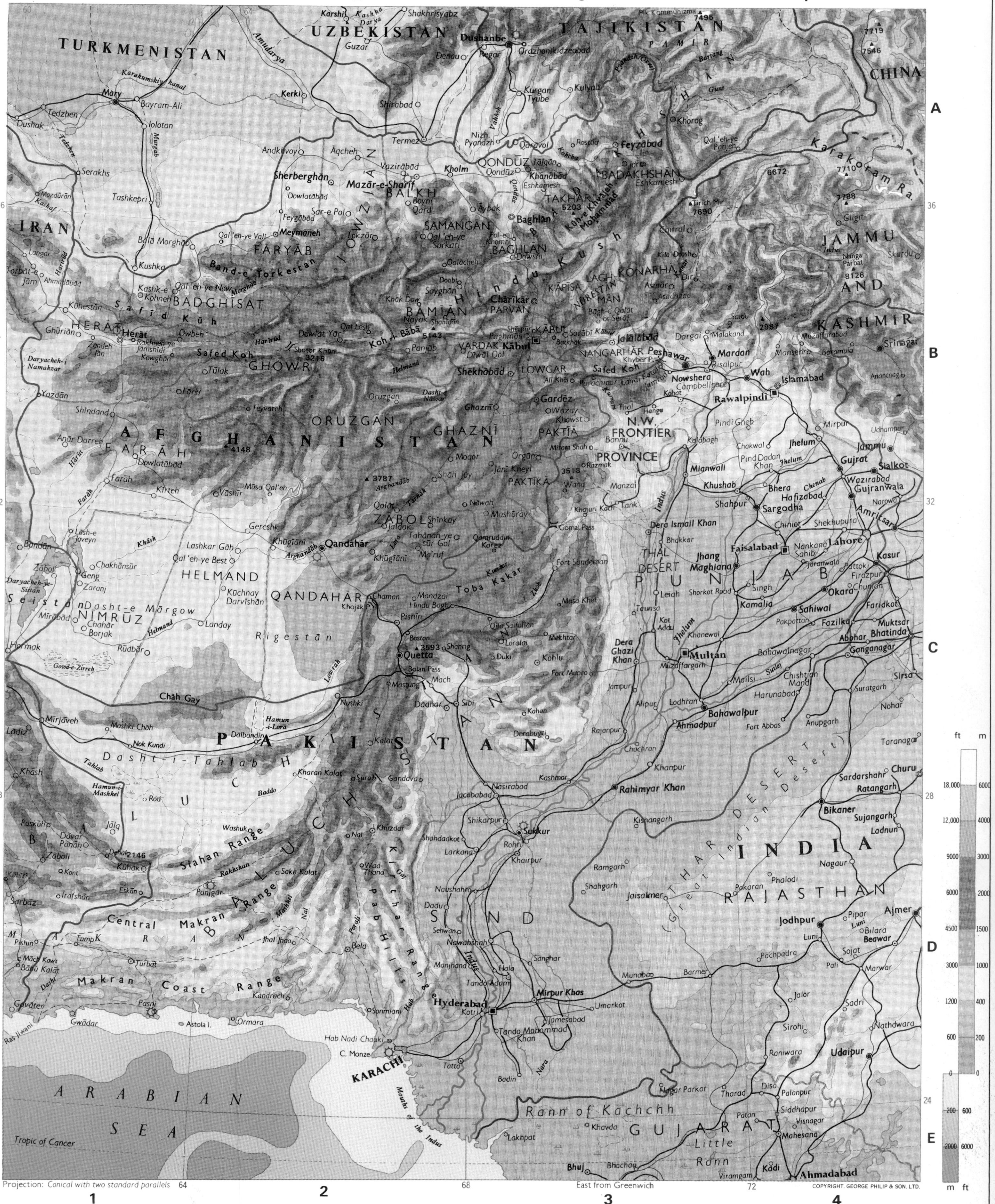

50    0    50    100    150    200 miles
50  0  50  100  150  200  250  300 km

**1**   **2**   **3**   **4**

## Countries and Regions

TURKMENISTAN
UZBEKISTAN
TAJIKISTAN
CHINA
IRAN
AFGHANISTAN
PAKISTAN
INDIA
JAMMU AND KASHMIR

### Afghanistan provinces / regions
FĀRYĀB
BĀDGHISĀT
HERĀT
GHOWR
FARĀH
ORUZGAN
GHAZNI
NIMRŪZ
HELMAND
QANDAHĀR
ZABOL
PAKTĪĀ
PAKTĪKĀ
LOWGAR
VARDAK
PARVAN
BĀMIĀN
SAMANGĀN
BALKH
JOWZJĀN
BAGHLĀN
TAKHĀR
BADAKHSHAN
KONARHA
NŪRESTĀN
KĀPISA
NANGARHĀR
LAGHMĀN

### Pakistan regions
N.W. FRONTIER PROVINCE
PUNJAB
BALUCHISTAN
SIND
THAL DESERT
THAR DESERT (Great Indian Desert)

### India regions
RAJASTHAN
GUJARAT

## Seas and physical features
ARABIAN SEA
Hindu Kush
Karakoram Ra.
Pamir
Safed Koh
Band-e Torkestan
Dasht-e Margow
Rigestan
Central Makran Range
Makran Coast Range
Siahan Range
Kirthar Range
Toba Kakar
Pab Hills
Seistan
Rann of Kachchh
Little Rann
Mouths of the Indus
Dasht-i-Tahlab
Tropic of Cancer

## Principal cities and towns
Maty, Tedzhen, Dushak, Bayram-Ali, Kerki, Iolotan, Serakhs, Tashkepri, Kushka, Andkhvoy, Āqcheh, Sherberghān, Mazar-e-Sharif, Meymaneh, Qal'eh-ye Vali, Dowlatabad, Sar-e Pol, Qondūz, Khānabād, Baghlān, Samangān, Feyzābād, Chitral, Gilgit, Skardu, Srinagar, Muzaffarabad, Herāt, Ghūriān, Shindand, Anār Darreh, Farāh, Qalāt, Ghazni, Gardēz, Kābul, Charikār, Jalālabād, Peshawar, Mardan, Nowshera, Rawalpindi, Islamabad, Jhelum, Gujrat, Sialkot, Jammu, Lashkar Gāh, Qandahār, Quetta, Chaman, Pishin, Loralai, Dera Ismail Khan, Mianwali, Khushab, Sargodha, Faisalabad, Lahore, Amritsar, Kasur, Multan, Bahawalpur, Sukkur, Shikarpur, Larkana, Khairpur, Rahimyar Khan, Bikaner, Churu, Jodhpur, Ajmer, Nawabshah, Hyderabad, Mirpur Khas, Karachi, Jaisalmer, Udaipur, Ahmadabad, Bhuj

## Elevation legend
ft    m
18,000  6000
12,000  4000
9000  3000
6000  2000
4500  1500
3000  1000
1200  400
600  200
0
200  600
2000  6000
m    ft

## Spot heights
7495, 7719, 7546, 7788, 7710, 6672, 8126, 7690 Tirich Mir, 2987, 5203, 5143, 3216, 4148, 3787, 3593, 3518, 2146, 2146

Projection: Conical with two standard parallels

East from Greenwich

AFGHANISTAN

PAKISTAN

BALUCHISTAN

N.W. FRONTIER PROVINCE

Kabul • Peshawar • Rawalpindi • Islamabad

Srinagar • KASHMIR • JAMMU

HIMACHAL PRADESH

Simla • Chandigarh • Dehra Dun

PUNJAB

Lahore • Amritsar • Jullundur • Ludhiana

Multan • Faisalabad • Gujranwala • Sialkot

Quetta

THAL DESERT

SIND

Karachi • Hyderabad • Sukkur • Larkana

HARYANA

DELHI • New Delhi

Meerut • Saharanpur • Panipat • Rohtak

THAR DESERT (Great Indian Desert)

RAJASTHAN

Bikaner • Jodhpur • Jaipur • Ajmer • Kota • Udaipur

Jaisalmer • Barmer • Bilara

Mouths of the Indus

Rann of Kachchh

Little Rann

ARABIAN SEA

Gulf of Kachchh

Tropic of Cancer

GUJARAT

AHMADABAD • Vadodara • Rajkot • Jamnagar • Bhavnagar • Bhuj • Porbandar • Junagadh

Gir Hills

MADHYA PRADESH

Indore • Bhopal • Ujjain • Gwalior

Agra • Mathura • Bharatpur

Vindhya Range

Satpura Range

Narmada

Tapi

Projection: Conical with two standard parallels

**1 : 4 800 000**

50  0  50  100 miles
50  0  50  100  150 km

East from Greenwich

**JAMMU AND KASHMIR**
On same scale as Main Map

CHINA

N.W. FRONTIER PROVINCE

PUNJAB

Rawalpindi
Islamabad

Srinagar
Nanga Parbat
Gilgit
Indus
Skardu
Leh

Mintaka Pass
Karakoram Pass

SODA PLAINS
Aksai Chin

KASHMIR
ZASKAR MOUNTAINS

Jammu
Sialkot
Wazirabad

HIMACHAL PRADESH

Ngangiong Kangri
Gangdisê Shan
Mapam Yumco

Nanda Devi
Badarinath

XIZANG (TIBET)

Mt. Everest 8848
Makalu
Kanchenjunga

SIKKIM
Gangtok

BHUTAN

Kathmandu
Lalitpur
Bhaktapur

N  E  P  A  L

Moradabad
Rampur
Bareilly
Budaun

Lucknow
Kanpur
Faizabad
Gorakhpur
Allahabad
Varanasi
Mirzapur

U  T  T  A  R   P  R  A  D  E  S  H

Jhansi

M  A  D  H  Y  A   P  R  A  D  E  S  H

Jabalpur
Bilaspur

Panna Hills
Kaimur Hills

Patna
Gaya
Bhagalpur
Munger

B  I  H  A  R

Ranchi
Jamshedpur
Raurkela
Hazaribag
Dhanbad
Asansol
Durgapur
Bardhaman

Kharagpur

W  E  S  T   B  E  N  G  A  L

BANGLADESH
DHAKA
Khulna
Jessore
Barisal

CALCUTTA
Haora
Medinipur

Mouths of the Ganga
The Sandheads

ASSAM

COPYRIGHT. GEORGE PHILIP & SON. LTD.

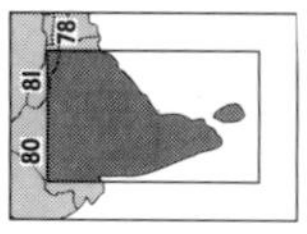

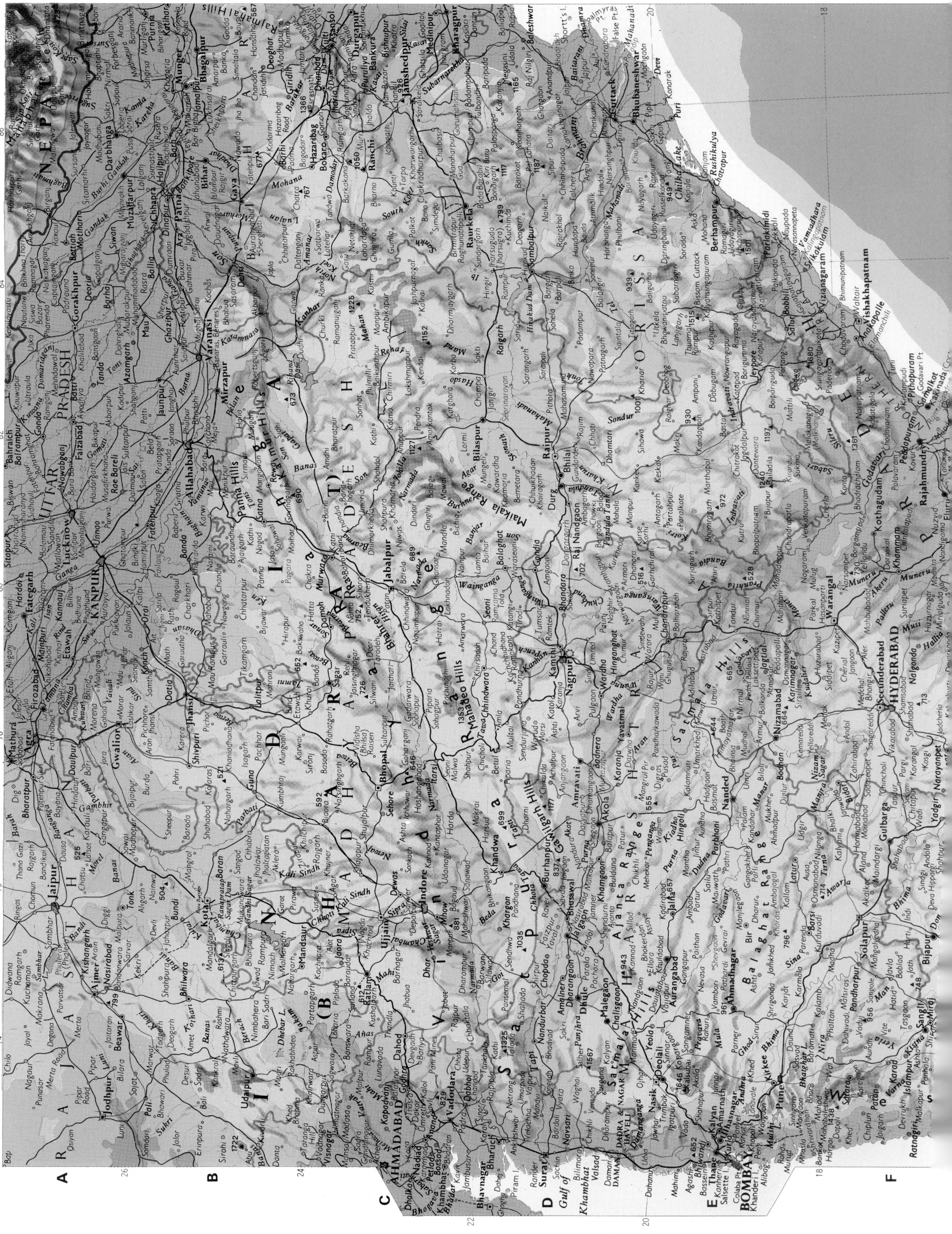

UTTAR PRADESH
MADHYA PRADESH
ORISSA
NEPAL
KANPUR
Lucknow
Allahabad
Varanasi
Jabalpur
Bhopal
Indore
Nagpur
Raipur
HYDERABAD
Secunderabad
AHMADABAD
Vadodara
BOMBAY
Pune
Solapur
Cuttack
Bhubaneshwar
Vishakhapatnam
Rajahmundry
Jaipur
Jodhpur
Udaipur
Gwalior
Jhansi
Gulf of Khambhat

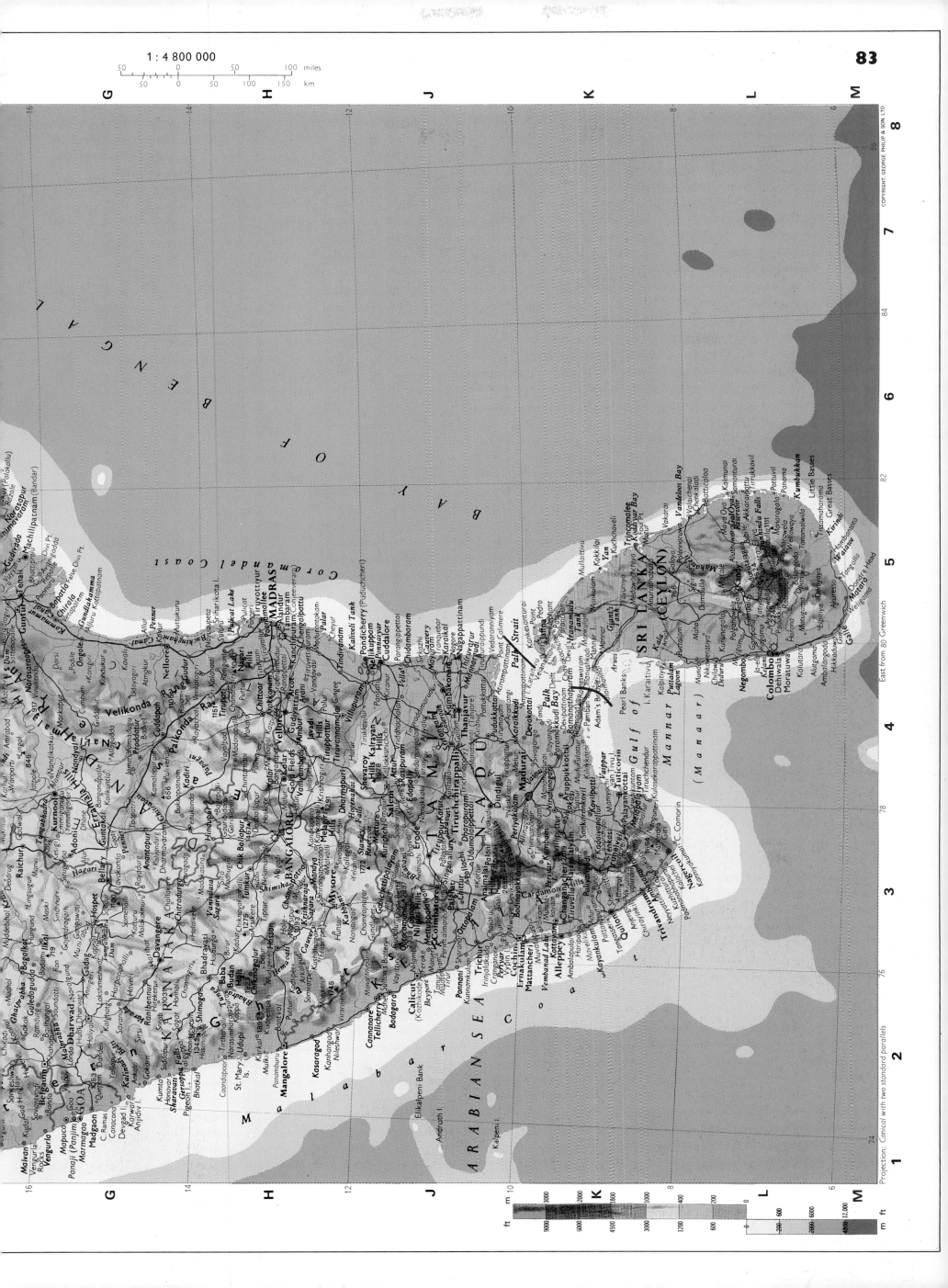

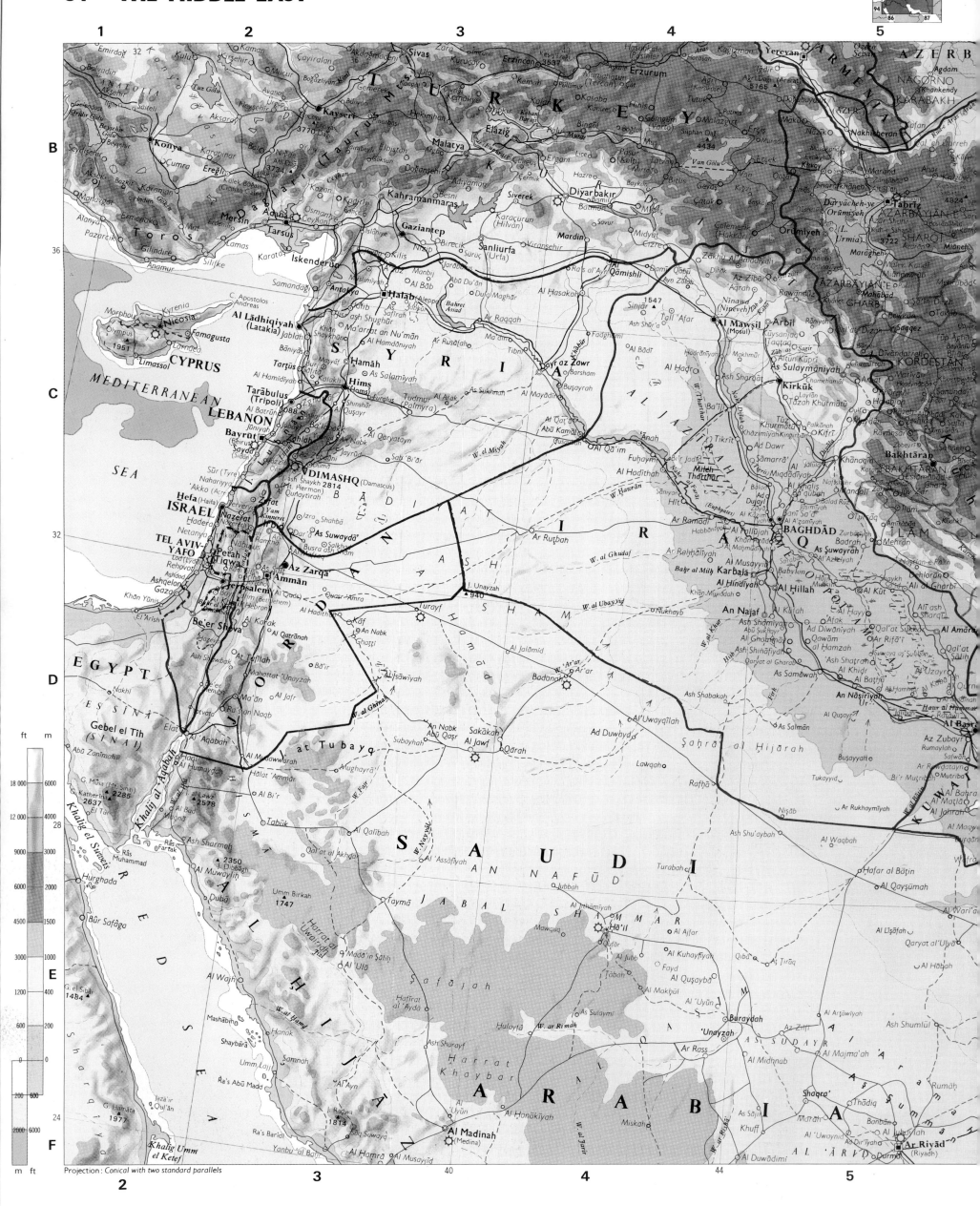

1 : 5 600 000

50 0 50 100 150 200 miles
50 0 50 100 150 200 250 300 km

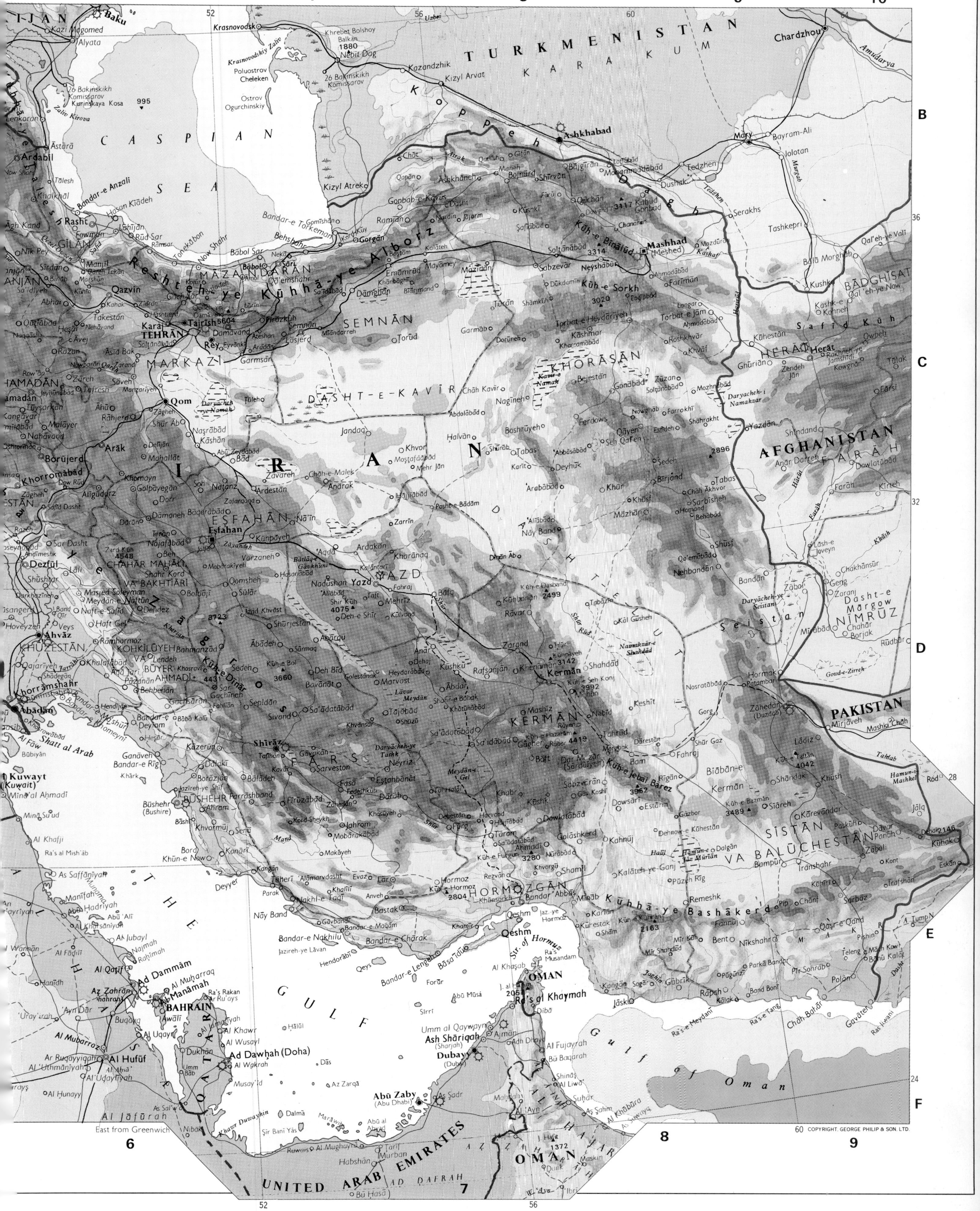

**TURKMENISTAN**

KARA KUM

**CASPIAN SEA**

Baku

Ashkhabad

Mary
Bayram-Ali

Chardzhou

Amudarya

Krasnovodsk

Nebit Dag

Kizyl Arvat

Mashhad (Meshed)

BADGHISAT

Gorgan

MAZANDARAN

Reshteh-ye Kūhhā-ye Alborz

SEMNĀN

KHORĀSĀN

HERĀT
Herāt

**AFGHANISTAN**

FARĀH

TEHRĀN

Karaj

Qom

Qazvin

MARKAZI

DASHT-E-KAVIR

HAMADĀN

Arāk

**IRAN**

ESFAHĀN
Esfahan

YAZD
Yazd

Ahvāz

KHŪZESTĀN

CHAHĀR MAHĀLL VA-BAKHTĪĀRĪ

KOHKILŪYEH VA BŪYER AHMADĪ

FĀRS

Shīrāz

KERMĀN
Kerman

SĪSTĀN VA BALŪCHESTĀN

**PAKISTAN**

Zāhedān (Duzdab)

Mirjāveh

Abādān

Khorramshahr

**Kuwayt (Kuwait)**

Būshehr (Bushire)

HORMOZGĀN

Kūhhā-ye Bashākerd

THE GULF

**BAHRAIN**
Al Manāmah

Ad Dammām

Az Zahrān

Al Hufūf

**QATAR**
Ad Dawḥah (Doha)

**OMAN**
Ra's al Khaymah

Dubay (Dubai)

Ash Shāriqah (Sharjah)

Abū Zaby (Abu Dhabi)

**UNITED ARAB EMIRATES**

Strait of Hormuz

Gulf of Oman

East from Greenwich

COPYRIGHT. GEORGE PHILIP & SON. LTD.

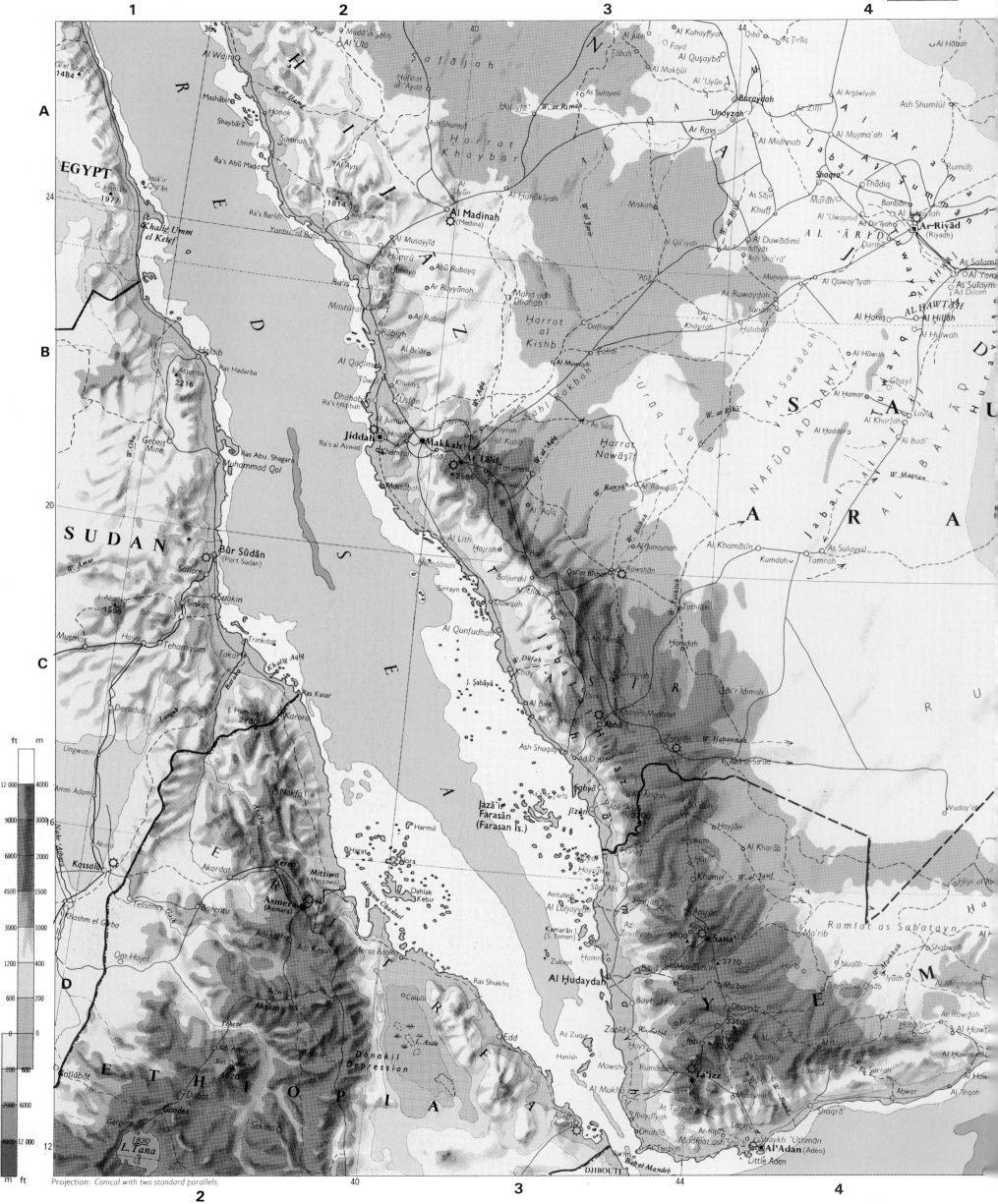

Projection: Conical with two standard parallels

1 : 5 600 000

50 0 50 100 150 200 miles
50 0 50 100 150 200 250 300 km

5  6  7  8

THE GULF

IRAN

Nāy Band · Gāvbandī · Bandar-e Maqām · Bastakū · Qeshm · Jaz-ye Hormoz · Kūhestak · Kūh-e Furgun 2163 · Mīr Kūh · Bent · Nīkshahr · Pannūr · Qasr-e Qand · Pīshīn

Bandar-e Nakhīlu · Jazīreh-ye Lāvan · Bandar-e Chārak · Khamīr · Shām · Mīr Shahdād · Parkā Bendar · Rāpch · Kūlak · Band Bonī · Sohrāb

Abū Hadrīyah · Abū 'Alī · Najmah · Rahīmah · Hendorābī · Qeys · Bandar-e Lengeh · Bāsa'īdū · Str. of Hormuz · Ra's-e Musandam · Jāskū · Ra's-e Meydanī · Chāh-Bahār · Ra's Jaddī

AL Khūsaniyah · Al Jubayl · Forūr · Abū Mūsā · Al Khaşab · Kangān · Sogār · Gabrīk · Ra's-e Tang · Gwātēr · Ras Jiwanī

Al Wannān · Al Fādilī · Ad Dammām · Al Muḩarraq · MANĀMAH · Ra's Rakan · Al Ru'ays · Sirrī · J. al Ḩarf 2057 · Ra's al Khaymah · Dibā · Gulf of Oman

Ḩanīdh · Az Zahrān (Dhahran) · BAHRAIN · Ḩalūl · Umm al Qaywayn · Ash Shāriqah (Sharjah) · Ajman · Adh Dhayd

'Uray'irah · 'Ayn Dār · Buqayq · Jawālī · Al Khawr · Al Wusayl · Das · Dubay (Dubai) · Al Fujayrah · Bū Baqarah

Al Mubarraz · Ar Ruqayyiqah · Al Hufūf · Dukhān · QATAR · Al Wakrah · Ad Dawḩah · Az Zarqā' · Abū Zaby (Abu Dhabi) · As Şadr · Shināş · Al Liwā · Şuḩār · 24

Al 'Uthmānīyah · Al Ihsā' · Al'Uḑayfiyah · Umm Bāb · Musay'id · Marāwiḩ · Abū al Abyad · Al Wāḩāt al Baraymī · 'Ayn · Saḩim · Al Khābūra · Barkā' · Masqaṭ (Muscat)

Khuray · Al Hunayy · As Salwā · Nibāk · Khawr Duwayhin · Dalmā · Şīr Banī Yās · Buwais · Al Mughoy · ḨAJAR · Ḩafīt 1372 · Dank · Miskin · Al Mufaddah · Sīmail · Al Qurayyāt · Tīwī

Harad · W. Sabāh · UNITED ARAB EMIRATES · Al Manā'if · Habshān · Murban · Tarif · AD ḐAFRAH · W. 'Ayn · Ibrī · 'Izkī · Ibrā 2151 · Sūr · Ra's al Ḩadd · Al Ḩadd

Al Khunn · Jirwān · Bū Ḩasa · Arādah · Istaihah · JIWA · Adam · W. Muqaybī · Sulaym · W. Baṭḩa · Al Kāmil · As Suwayḩ · B

'Azīz · Bunayyān · Al Quraynī · Al 'Urūq al Mutaridah · 'Uwayfī · OMAN · W. Ḩalfayn · W. Andam · Al Ashkharah

Al 'Ubaylah · At Tuwayrifah · R U B ' A L K H A L I · Ghalat

Hayy · Filīm · Dawwah · Maşīran · Hikmān · 20

Khalūl · Kalbūh · Duqm · Ra's Abū Raşāş · Khalīj Maşīrah

Jiddat al Ḩarāsī · Hayma · Ghubbat Sawqirah · C

W. Mughshin · W. Aṭnah · W. Quthī · W. Ghudun · Ra's al Madrakah

Ṣinaw · W. Rakhawt · Al Yahmadī · W. Shu'ayt · Na'mān · Shawqirah · Ra's ash Sharbatāt

Thamūd · Mukhaybub · Thāmit · W. Shihan · ẒUFĀR · Kuria Muria Bay · Ḩadbaram · Al Ḩallānīyah

Minwakh · Bi'r Fāmis · Fughmah · Qunfudhah · Ḩabarūt · J. al Qarā' · Jabal Samḩān 1678 · Ḩasik · Jazā'ir Khurīyā Murīyā (Kuria Muria Is.) (Oman)

2469 · Tarīm · Qabr Hūd · Al Qurḩ · Al Faydamī · J. al Qamar · Mirbāt · Ra's Nūws

Shibām · Aynāt · Sayḩūt · Rakhyūt · Ṣalālah · Damqawt · Al Fatk · 16

Al Qatn · Saywūn · W. Ḩaḑramawt · Al Ghayl · W. Jiz · Al Ghaydah · Ghubbat al Qamar · Khalūt

Al Hajarayn · Al Ghayl · 'Itāb · Qishn · A R A B I A N · S E A

Khuraybah · Ḩiṣn al Qarn · Al Ghaydah · Saybūt · Ra's Fartak · D

Ghayl Bā Wazīr · Shuḩayr · Al Mukallā · Ash Shiḩr

Burum · Al Ḩasy

Socotra (Yemen) · Qalansīyah · Ra's Kharwal · Tamareh

'Abd al Kūri · The Brothers · Ra's Qaṭanan · Qādib · Sīgīra · Ra's Mamī · 12

Ra's Layht · Ra's Shu'b · Fahr

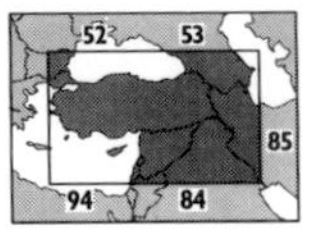

BLACK SEA

BULGARIA

GREECE

THRACE

İSTANBUL

Varna
Burgas
Dobrich
Kolarovgrad
Türnovo
Gabrovo
Stara Zagora
Sliven
Yambol
Elkhovo
Dimitrovgrad
Khaskovo
Kürdzhali
Edirne
Kırklareli
Çorlu
Tekirdağ
Gökçeada (İmroz)
Çanakkale

MYSIA
LYDIA
PHRYGIA
CARIA
LYCIA
PISIDIA
PAMPHYLIA
LYCAONIA
GALATIA
BITHYNIA
PAPHLAGONIA
CAPPADOCIA
CATAONIA
CILICIA

Zonguldak
Ereğli
Karabük
Bolu
Adapazarı (Sakarya)
İzmit (Kocaeli)
Gebze
Yalova
Bursa
İnegöl
Eskişehir
Kütahya
Ankara
Kırıkkale
Polatlı
Sincan
Çorum
Amasya
Samsun
Bafra
Sinop
Tokat
Turhal
Sivas
Kayseri
Nevşehir
Aksaray
Konya
Karaman
Ereğli
Niğde
Adana
Tarsus
Mersin (İçel)
Ceyhan
Osmaniye
Kahramanmaraş
Gaziantep
İskenderun
Kırıkhan
Antakya (Hatay)

Manisa
Turgutlu
İzmir (Smyrna)
Salihli
Uşak
Afyonkarahisar
Aydın
Nazilli
Denizli
Burdur
Isparta
Antalya
Balıkesir
Akhisar
Bandırma
Ayvacık

Anadolu (Anatolia)
Toros Dağları (Taurus Mountains)
Köroğlu Dağları
İlgaz Dağları
Küre Dağları
Aladağ Dağları
Sultan Dağı
Bey Dağları
Ak Dağ

CYPRUS
Nicosia
Famagusta
Larnaca
Limassol
Troodos
Paphos
Kyrenia

MEDITERRANEAN SEA

LEBANON
Bayrut (Beirut)
Sayda (Sidon)
Sür (Tyre)

SYRIA
Halab (Aleppo)
Idlib
Al Lādhiqiyah (Latakia)
Hamāh
Hims (Homs)
Tarābulus (Tripoli)
Dimashq (Damascus)

Rhodos (Rhodes)
Kárpathos
Kos
Sámos
Khíos (Chios)
Lésvos (Lesbos)
Dhodhekánisos (Dodecanese)

Provinces in Turkey are named after the chief towns which are underlined.

Division between Greeks and Turks in Cyprus; Turks to the North.

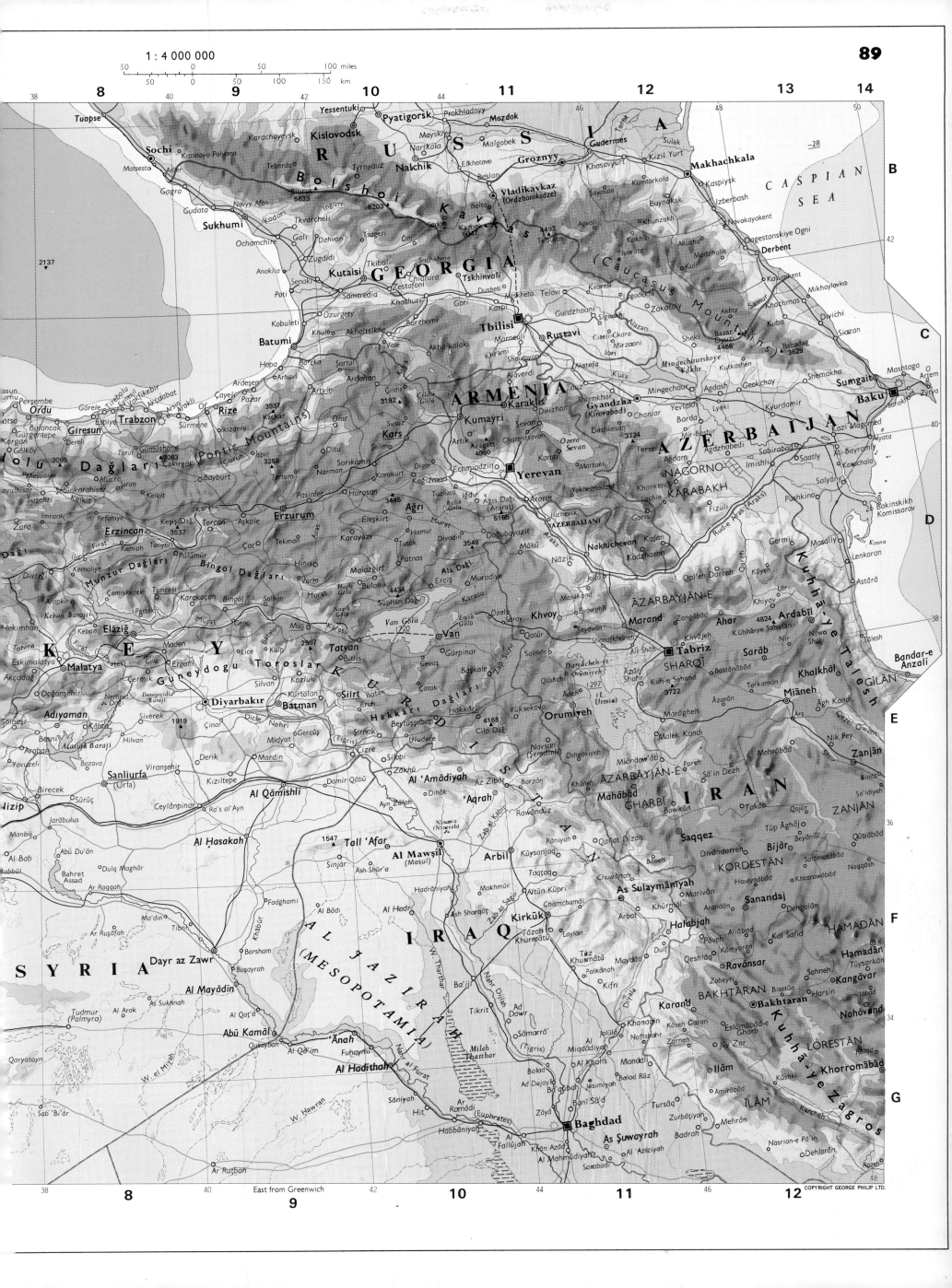

1 : 12 000 000

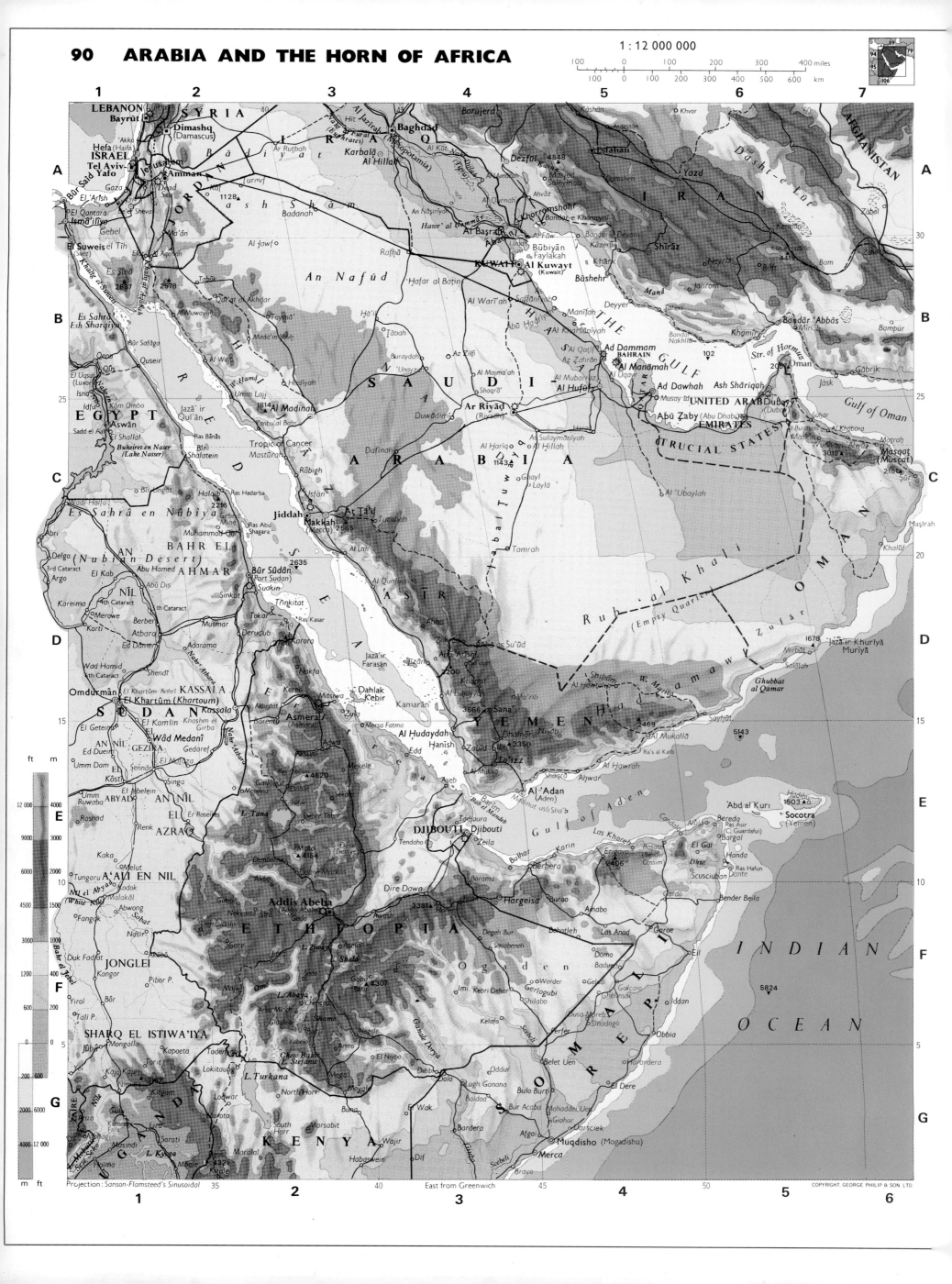

Projection: Sanson-Flamsteed's Sinusoidal    East from Greenwich    COPYRIGHT GEORGE PHILIP & SON LTD

1 : 2 000 000

10   0   10   20   30   40   50 miles
10   0  10 20 30 40 50 60 70 80 km

**CYPRUS**

Paphos
Limassol
Episkopi Bay
Akrotiri Bay
C. Gata

M E D I T E R R A N E A N

S E A

Al Hamidiyah
Tall Kalakh
Hims (Homs)
Shinshār
Furglus

Al Mīnā'
ASH SHAMĀL
Tarābulus (Tripoli)
Halba
Al Qaşay
Al Buray
Al Qaryatayn
Bi'r Ghadir

Al Batrūn
Jubayl
Ibrāhīmi
Jūniyah

**BAYRŪT (Beirut)**
Ash Shuwayfāt
Zahlah
DIMASHQ
**DIMASHQ (Damascus)**

**LEBANON**
**SYRIA**

Saydā (Sidon)
Jazzīn
An Nabatīyah at Tahtā
AL JANŪB
Şūr (Tyre)
Qiryat Shemo

Qatanā
A'jaj
Al Kiswah
Al Hijānah
Burqa
AS SAFĀ

Nahariyya
HAZOR
Golan His.
DARĀ
AS SUWAYDĀ'
'Akko (Acre)
Hagalil
W. al Harir
As Sanamayn
Shahba
Mifraz Hefa
Kinneret
 Izra'
As Suwaydā'
Hefa (Haifa)
Yarmūk
Dar'ā
Salkhad
Tirat Karmel
HAZAFON
Dāliyat el Karmel
Afula
Ailūn
Irbid
Isrā ash Shām
Umm al Qittayn

CAESAREA
SHOMRON
NABULUS
SAMARIA
Irbid
Az Zarqā'
Hadera
Ailūn
Jarash

**ISRAEL**
Netanya
Under Israeli Administration
AL BALQĀ'
**Az Zarqā'**
HAMERKAZ
Nabulus
Herzliyya
Benē Beraq
SHILO
West Bank
'AMMĀN
Petah Tiqwa
**Tel Aviv-Yafo**
Ramat Gan
Bat Yam
Rishon le Ziyyon
N. Soreq
AL QUDS
Ramla
Ram Allāh
Na'ūr
Ashdod
Madaba
Qiryat Mal'akhi
**Jerusalem (Yerushalayim) (Al Quds)**
Ashqelon
Bet Shemesh
Bethlehem
Qiryat Gat
TE LAKHISH
Gaza
N. Shiqma
AL KHALIL
W. al Haydān
Gaza Strip
Sederot
Az Zāhirīya
W. al Mawjib
Khān Yūnis
Rafah
Be'er Sheva
Arad
Al Qatrānah
Al Karak
AL 'ĀŞIMAH

**Būr Sa'īd (Port Said)**
Būr Fu'ād
Rās Burūn
Sabkhet el Bardawil
El 'Arīsh
Bīr el Garārāt
Bor Mashash
W. al Hasa
AL KARAK
Khalīg el Tīna
Romāni
Bīr el 'Abd
El Daheir
Dimona
Bīr Qatia
Bīr el Lahfān
W. al Ghadaf
El Qanţara
Bīr el Jafir
Bīr Kaseiba
HADAROM
W. Bāsīr
Wāhid
Bīr el Duweidar
Bīr Madkūr
Qezi'ot
**JORDAN**
Bīr Hasana
Birein
At Tafīlah
Ismâ'ilîya
Muweilih
W. Abu Saţar
Khamsa
El Buheirat el Murrat el Kubra (Gt. Bitter L.)
Muzbe Raman
Ma'ān
G. Yi'Allaq
Bīr Beiða
Qa'el Jafr
MA'ĀN
**Hanegev (Negev Desert)**
FETRA
Ma'ān
EL SUWEIS
**E G Y P T**
G. el Kabrīt
N. Paran
Mahattat 'Unayzah
El Suweis (Suez)
N. Hiyyon
Yotvata
Bīr Bad
Uyūn Mūsa
Nakhl
El Quntilla
Ras an Naqb
Mahattat ash Shidiyah
Ghubbet el Būs
Gebel el Tîh
Bīr el Biarāt
Al 'Aqabah
**SAUDI**
Bīr Abu Sundra
Rās Matarma
Sinai Peninsula
Bīr el Thamāda
El Thamod
**ARABIA**
Gebel el Tîh
Taba
'Ain Nuqayra
Naqb
J. as Tubayq

Projection: Polyconic        East from Greenwich        COPYRIGHT. GEORGE PHILIP & SON. LTD.

– – – 1949 Armistice Line, 1967 and 1974 Cease Fire Lines

ft   m
9000   3000
6000   2000
4500   1500
3000   1000
600    200
0      0
200    600
2000   6000
m   ft

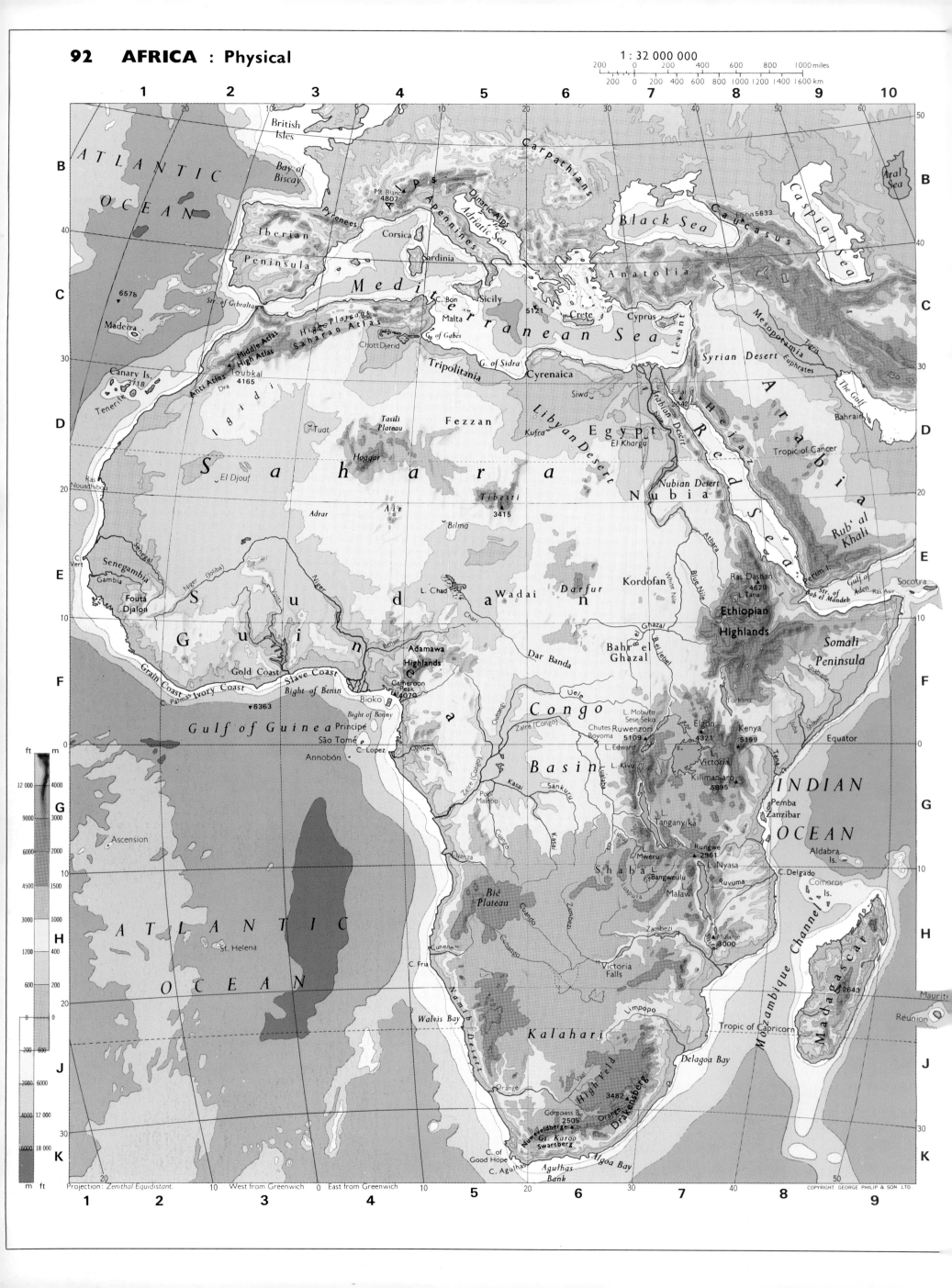

1 : 32 000 000

200  0  200  400  600  800  1000 miles
200  0  200 400 600 800 1000 1400 1600 km

**ATLANTIC OCEAN**

UNITED KINGDOM · London
GERMANY · POLAND · Warsaw
NETH. · BELG. · Paris · Prague · CZECHOSLOVAKIA · Kiev · RUSSIA · Volgograd
FRANCE · SWITZ. · AUSTRIA · Vienna · HUNGARY · ROMANIA · Odessa · UKRAINE · KAZAKHSTAN
Bay of Biscay · ITALY · YUGOSLAVIA · BULGARIA · Istanbul · Black Sea · Aral Sea
Corsica · Rome · Adriatic Sea · ALB. · GREECE · Athens · TURKEY · Ankara · Baku · Caspian Sea
Madrid · SPAIN · Sardinia · Sicily · MALTA · Crete · CYPRUS · Aleppo · Mosul · Tehran
Lisbon · PORTUGAL · Algiers · Annaba · Constantine · Tunis · SYRIA · Damascus · Baghdad · Esfahan
Madeira (Port.) · Casablanca · Rabat · Fès · Oran · Sfax · Tripoli · Tel Aviv-Jaffa · Jerusalem · ISRAEL · Syrian Desert · IRAN
MOROCCO · Marrakesh · Djerba · Misratah · Benghazi · Alexandria · Port Said · Suez · JORDAN · KUWAIT · Basra
Canary Is. (Sp.) · ALGERIA · Ghadames · CAIRO · El Faiyûm · Asyut · Nile · SAUDI · Riyadh · The Gulf · BAHRAIN I. · QATAR
Dakhla · WESTERN SAHARA · In Salah · LIBYA · Marzuq · Al Jawf · EGYPT · Aswan · Medina · ARABIA · Tropic of Cancer
El Aaiun · F'Dérik · Sahara · Wadi-Halfa · Pt. Sudan · Mecca · Jedda
MAURITANIA · Nouakchott · Tombouctou (Timbuktu) · Agades · NIGER · CHAD · Atbara · Omdurman · Kassala · Asmera · Mesewa · YEMEN · Socotra (Yemen)
St. Louis · SENEGAL · Dakar · MALI · Niamey · L. Chad · Abéché · El Fasher · SUDAN · KHARTOUM · Wad Medani · Ras Asir (C. Guardafui)
GAMBIA · Banjul · Bamako · BURKINA FASO · Ouagadougou · Kano · Maiduguri · Ndjamena (Ft. Lamy) · El Obeid · White Nile · Blue Nile · L. Tana · DJIBOUTI · G. of Aden
GUINEA BISSAU · Bissau · GUINEA · Bobo-Dioulasso · BENIN · NIGERIA · Kaduna · Benue · Chari · CENTRAL AFRICAN REPUBLIC · Malakal · Addis Ababa · Harer · Berbera
Conakry · SIERRA LEONE · Freetown · IVORY COAST · Bouaké · GHANA · Kumasi · TOGO · Ibadan · Abuja · Enugu · Wau · Bahr el Jebel · ETHIOPIA · SOMALI REP. · Mogadishu (Mogadiscio)
Monrovia · LIBERIA · Yamoussoukro · Accra · Lagos · Porto Novo · CAMEROON · Port Harcourt · Yaoundé · Bangui · Oubangui · L. Turkana · Equator
Abidjan · Sekondi-Takoradi · Bight of Benin · Bioko · Douala · EQUATORIAL GUINEA · Rio Muni · GABON · CONGO · Mbandaka · Kisangani · L. Mobutu Sese Seko · UGANDA · Kampala · KENYA · Kismayu · INDIAN OCEAN
**Gulf of Guinea** · SAO TOMÉ & PRINCIPE · C. Lopez · Libreville · Annobon · ZAIRE (Congo) · L. Edward · Kisumu · L. Victoria · Nairobi · Juba
Ascension (Br.) · Brazzaville · Kinshasa · Kasai · L. Kivu · RWANDA · Kigali · BURUNDI · Bujumbura · L. Tanganyika · TANZANIA · Mombasa · Zanzibar · Dodoma · Dar-es-Salaam · Aldabra Is.
Pointe Noire · CABINDA · Matadi · Kwango · Kananga · L. Mweru · Likasi · L. Nyasa (L. Malawi) · Ruvuma · C. Delgado · COMOROS · Antsiranana
Luanda · ANGOLA · Lobito · Huambo · Lubumbashi · Ndola · ZAMBIA · Lilongwe · MALAWI · Blantyre · Mozambique · Mahajanga · Antananarivo · MADAGASCAR · MAURITIUS
**ATLANTIC OCEAN** · St. Helena (Br.) · Namibe · Cunene · Cubango · Lusaka · Zambezi · Livingstone · MOZAMBIQUE · Beira · Mozambique Channel · Toamasina · Réunion (Fr.)
NAMIBIA · BOTSWANA · Harare · ZIMBABWE · Bulawayo · Limpopo · Tropic of Capricorn · Fianarantsoa
Walvis Bay (South Africa) · Windhoek · Gaborone · TRANSVAAL · Pretoria · Mbabane · SWAZILAND · Maputo
C. Fria · Orange · Johannesburg · ORANGE FREE STATE · Vaal · LESOTHO · NATAL · Durban
Kimberley · Bloemfontein · Maseru
**SOUTH AFRICA** · CAPE PROVINCE
Cape Town · C. of Good Hope · C. Agulhas · East London · Port Elizabeth

**INDIAN OCEAN**

Nairobi  Capital Cities

Projection: Zenithal Equidistant.
West from Greenwich  0  East from Greenwich
COPYRIGHT. GEORGE PHILIP & SON. LTD

1 : 6 400 000

50    0    100    150    200 miles

50    0    100    200    300 km

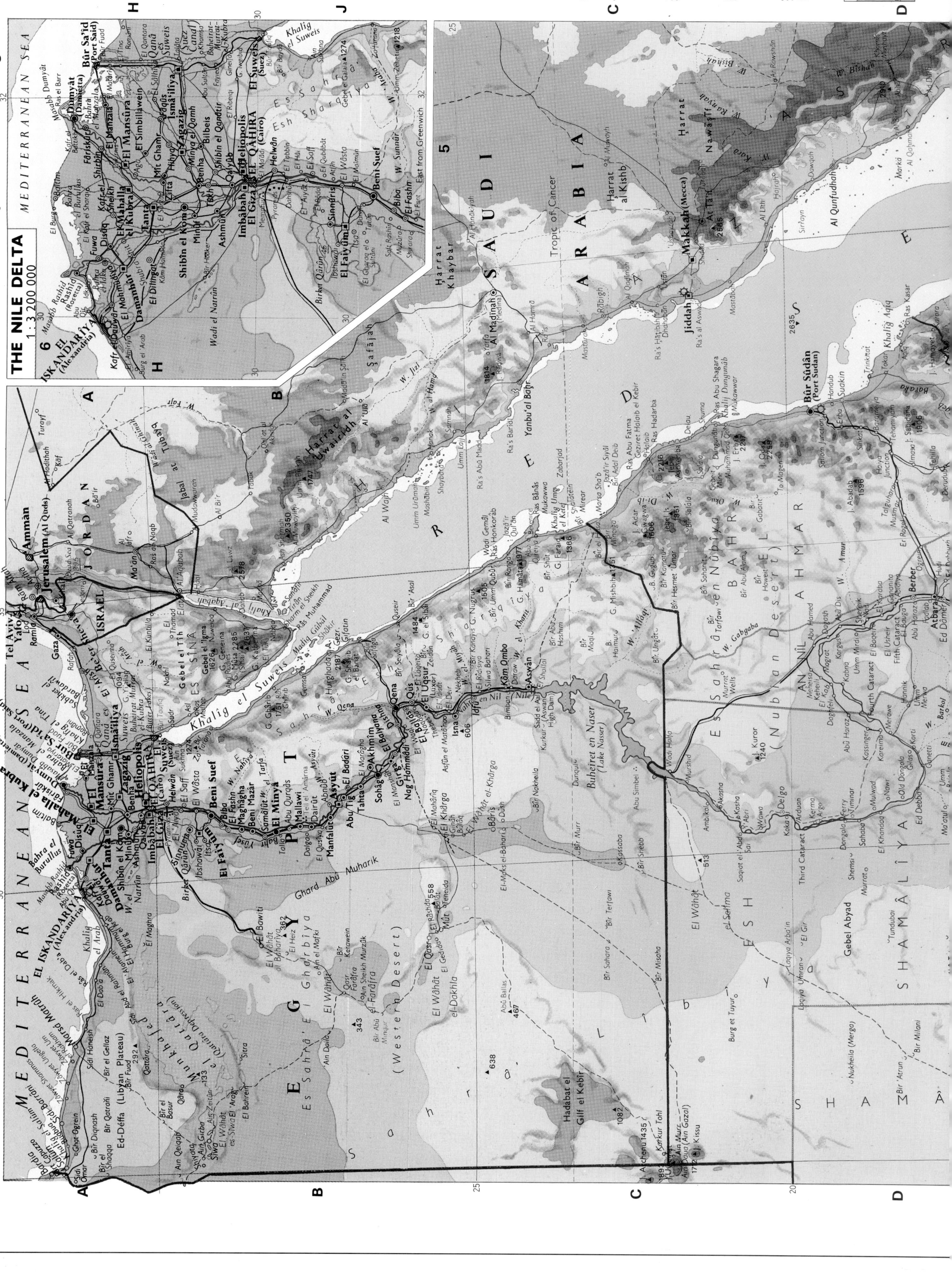

**THE NILE DELTA**
1 : 3 200 000

MEDITERRANEAN SEA

Bûr Sa'îd (Port Said)
Dimyât (Damietta)
El Mansûra
Ismâ'ilîya
El Suweis (Suez)
Tanta
El Mahalla el Kubra
EL QÂHIRA (Cairo)
Imbâbah
El Gîza
Heliopolis
Qalyûb
Zagazig
Benha
Helwân
Beni Suef
El Faiyûm
Shibîn el Kôm
EL ISKANDARÎYA (Alexandria)
Dumyât
Rashid (Rosetta)

SAUDI ARABIA

Al Madînah
Makkah (Mecca)
Jiddah
At Tâ'if
Al Qunfudhah

Tropic of Cancer

East from Greenwich

MEDITERRANEAN SEA

EL ISKANDARÎYA (Alexandria)
Bûr Sa'îd (Port Said)
Dimyât (Damietta)
El Mansûra
El Mahalla el Kubra
Tanta
Zagazig
Heliopolis
EL QÂHIRA (Cairo)
El Gîza
Imbâbah
Helwân
Beni Suef
El Faiyûm
El Minyâ
Mallawi
Asyût
El Bâdâri
Sohâg
Nag Hammâdi
Girga
Qena
El Uqsur (Luxor)
Isna
Idfu
Kôm Ombo
Aswân
El Wâhât el Khârga

EGYPT

ISRAEL
JORDAN
Jerusalem (Al Quds)
Ammân
Tel Aviv-Yafo
Gaza

SÎNÂ
ES SÎNÂ

Khalig el Suweis

RED SEA

Bûr Sûdân (Port Sudan)
Atbara
Berber

AN NÎL EL AHMAR
ESH SHAMÂLÎYA

Buhêret en Naser (Lake Nasser)
Abu Simbel
Wadi Halfa
Third Cataract
Fourth Cataract

Es Sahrâ el Gharbîya (Western Desert)

Gilf el Kebîr
Hadâbat el

Esh Sharqîya

YEMEN

DJIBOUTI

ETHIOPIA

ADDIS ABEBA
(Addis Abeba)

SUDAN

EL KHARTÛM
(Khartoum)

Omdurmân
El Khartûm Bahri
Wad Medani

KASSALA

Kassala
Gedaref

GONDER
Gonder
L. Tana
Chôke Mts.

ERITREA
Asmera
(Asmara)
Keren
Mitsiwa

Mekele
Aksum

Dese

Dire Dawa
Nazret
Debre Zeyit

GOJAM
BLUE NILE
(Blue Nile)

WELEGA
ILUBABOR
KEFA
SHEWA
WELO
 TIGRE
HARERGE
BALE
SIDAMO
GAMO-GOFA

Jima
Goba

EL OBEID
El Obeid
KORDOFÂN
SHAMÂL KORDOFÂN
JANÛB KORDOFÂN
 Jibâlan Nûbah (Nuba Mts.)

DÂRFÛR
SHAMÂL DÂRFÛR
JANÛB DÂRFÛR
El Fâsher

En Nahud
Ed Dueim
Kôsti
Ed Dein

Malakâl
UPPER NILE
A'ALI EN NIL

BAHR EL GHAZAL
Wâw

JUNGLEI
EL BUHAYRAT
Bôr

EQUATORIA
EL ISTIWÂ'IYA

CENTRAL AFRICAN REPUBLIC

ZAIRE

UGANDA

KENYA

SOMALI REP.

L. Turkana
(L. Rudolf)

Shendi

Jaza'ir Farasân al Kabîr
Farasân

DANAKIL
DESERT
Danakil Depression

AWASH

Red Sea

Projection: Lambert's Equivalent Azimuthal

East from Greenwich

| ft | m |
| --- | --- |
| 12,000 | 4000 |
| 9000 | 3000 |
| 6000 | 2000 |
| 4500 | 1500 |
| 3000 | 1000 |
| 1200 | 400 |
| 600 | 200 |
| 0 | 0 |

EGYPT

MEDITERRANEAN SEA

LIBYA

TUNISIA

ALGERIA

SICILIA

CATÁNIA

Siracusa

MALTA

Valletta

TUNIS

Banghāzī (Benghazi)

Tarābulus (Tripoli)

Khalīj Surt (Gulf of Sidra)

Sahra

Tropic of Cancer

1 : 6 400 000

50    0    50    100    150    200 miles
50  0   100   200   300 km

SHAMÂL  DÂRFÛR

JANUB DARFUR

SUDAN

ENNEDI

TIBESTI

Mortcha

TCHAD (CHAD)

BORKOU

DJOURAB

NIGER

Aïr (Azbine)

Ténéré

Erg du Ténéré

Manga

L. Tchad

L. Chad

Ndjamena

CENTRAL AFRICAN REPUBLIC

CAMEROUN

NIGERIA

KANO

BORNU

GONGOLA

Maiduguri

Garoua

Kano

Agadez

Abéché

Mongo

Moundou

Bongor

Massénya

Moussoro

Faya-Largeau

Emi Koussi 3415

Pic Toussidé 3265

COPYRIGHT. GEORGE PHILIP & SON, LTD.

Projection: Lambert's Equivalent Azimuthal

ft    m
9000  3000
6000  1800
4500  1500
3000  1000
1500  600
     400
     200
0    0
600
6000  2000
12,000  4000
m    ft

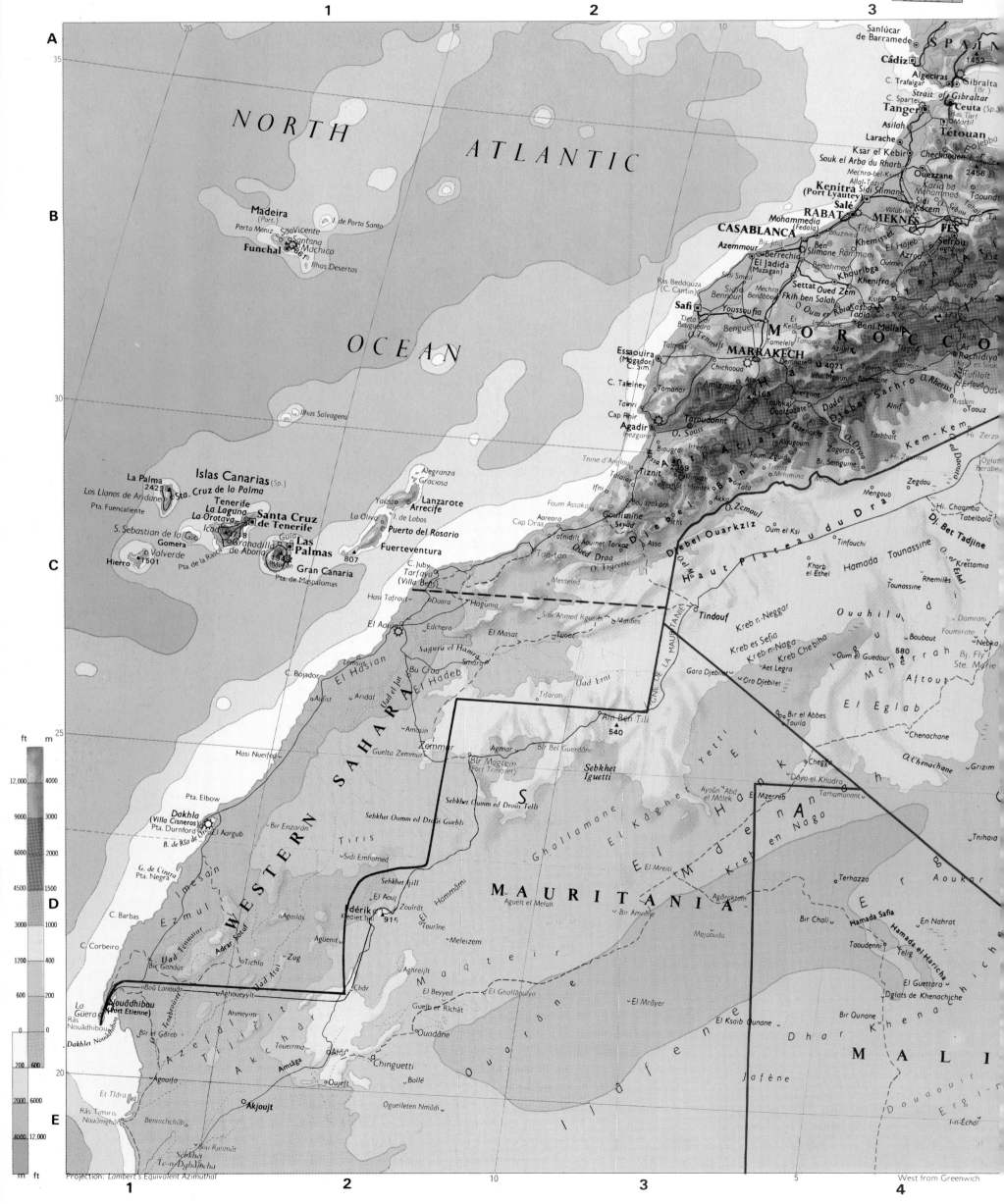

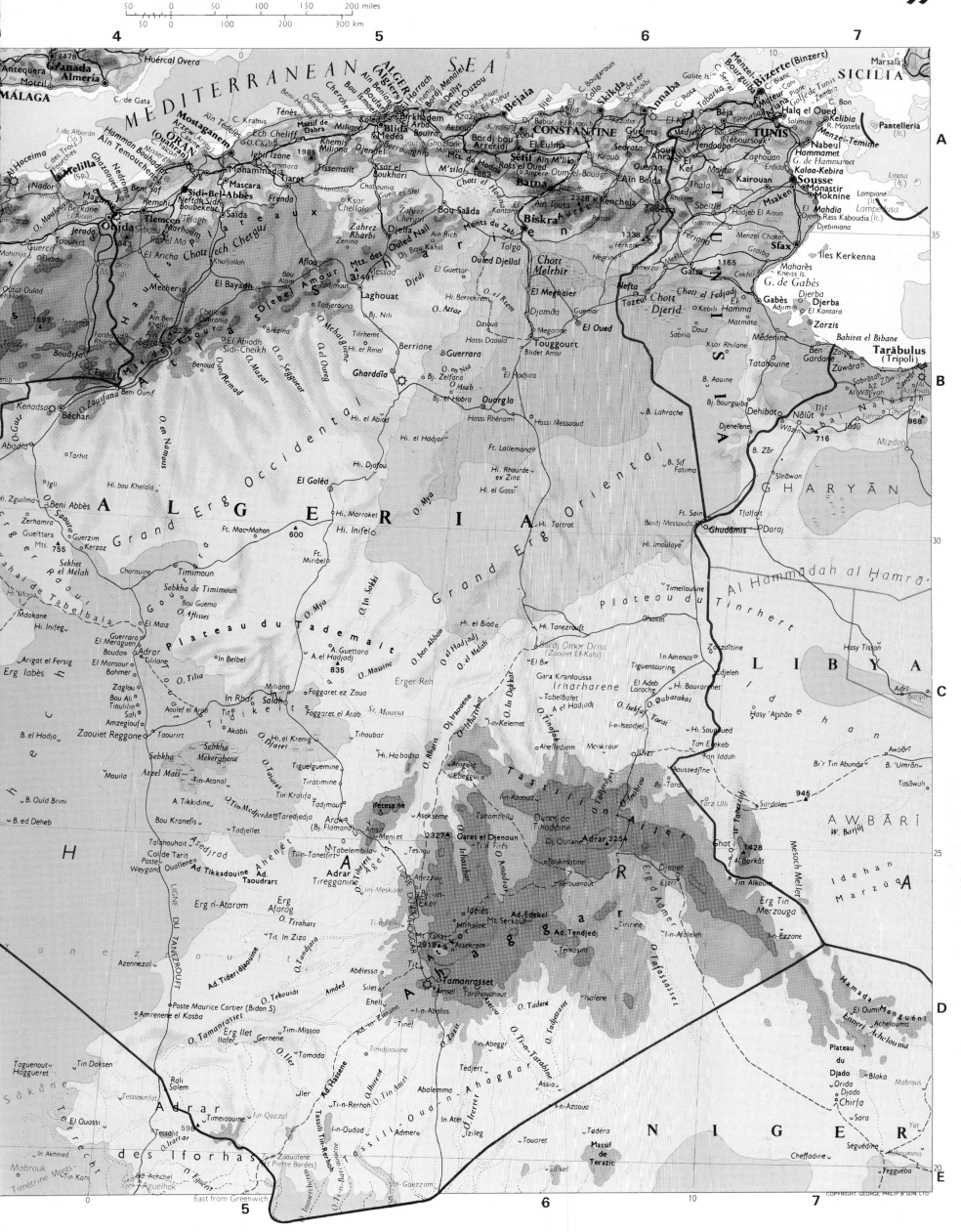

1 : 6 400 000

50    0    50    100    150    200 miles
50    0    100    200    300 km

**4**            **5**                 **6**            **7**

MEDITERRANEAN SEA

MÁLAGA

Granada
Almería
Antequera
Motril
Huércal Overa

C. de Gata

Melilla

I. de Alborán (Sp.)

El Hoceima
Nador

Oujda

Tlemcen

Oran (Ouahran)
Mostaganem
Arzew (Arzeu)

ALGER (Algiers)

Blida
Médéa

Bejaia

Skikda

Annaba

CONSTANTINE

Guelma

SICILIA

Pantelleria (It.)

Bizerte (Binzert)

TUNIS

Halq el Oued

Nabeul

Sousse
Monastir
Sfax

Kairouan

T  U  N  I  S  I  A

Béchar

Ghardaïa

Ouargla

Touggourt

El Oued

Gabès
Djerba

Tarābulus (Tripoli)

A L G E R I A

Grand Erg Occidental

Plateau du Tademaït

Grand Erg Oriental

Ghudāmis

Al Hammādah al Hamrā'

Plateau du Tinrhert

L  I  B  Y  A

AWBĀRĪ

Idehan Marzūq

Erg Tin Merzouga

Tamanrasset

A h a g g a r

Adrar des Iforhas

N  I  G  E  R

East from Greenwich

**5**                  **6**            **10**    **7**

COPYRIGHT. GEORGE PHILIP & SON LTD.

A

B

C

D

E

35

30

25

20

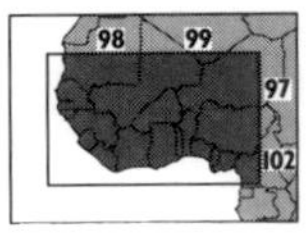

MAURITANIA

SENEGAL

GAMBIA

GUINEA-BISSAU
Arquipélago dos Bijagós

GUINEA

SIERRA LEONE

LIBERIA

IVORY COAST

MALI

BURKINA

DAKAR

Nouakchott

St. Louis

Banjul

Bissau

Conakry

Freetown

Monrovia

Bamako

Ségou

Mopti

Bobo Dioulasso

Bouaké

Abidjan

Grain Coast

Ivory Coast

GULF

Projection: Lambert's Equivalent Azimuthal

West from Greenwich

ft  m
12 000  4000
9000  3000
6000  2000
4500  1500
3000  1000
1200  400
600  200
0  0
200  600
2000  6000
4000  12 000
6000  18 000
m  ft

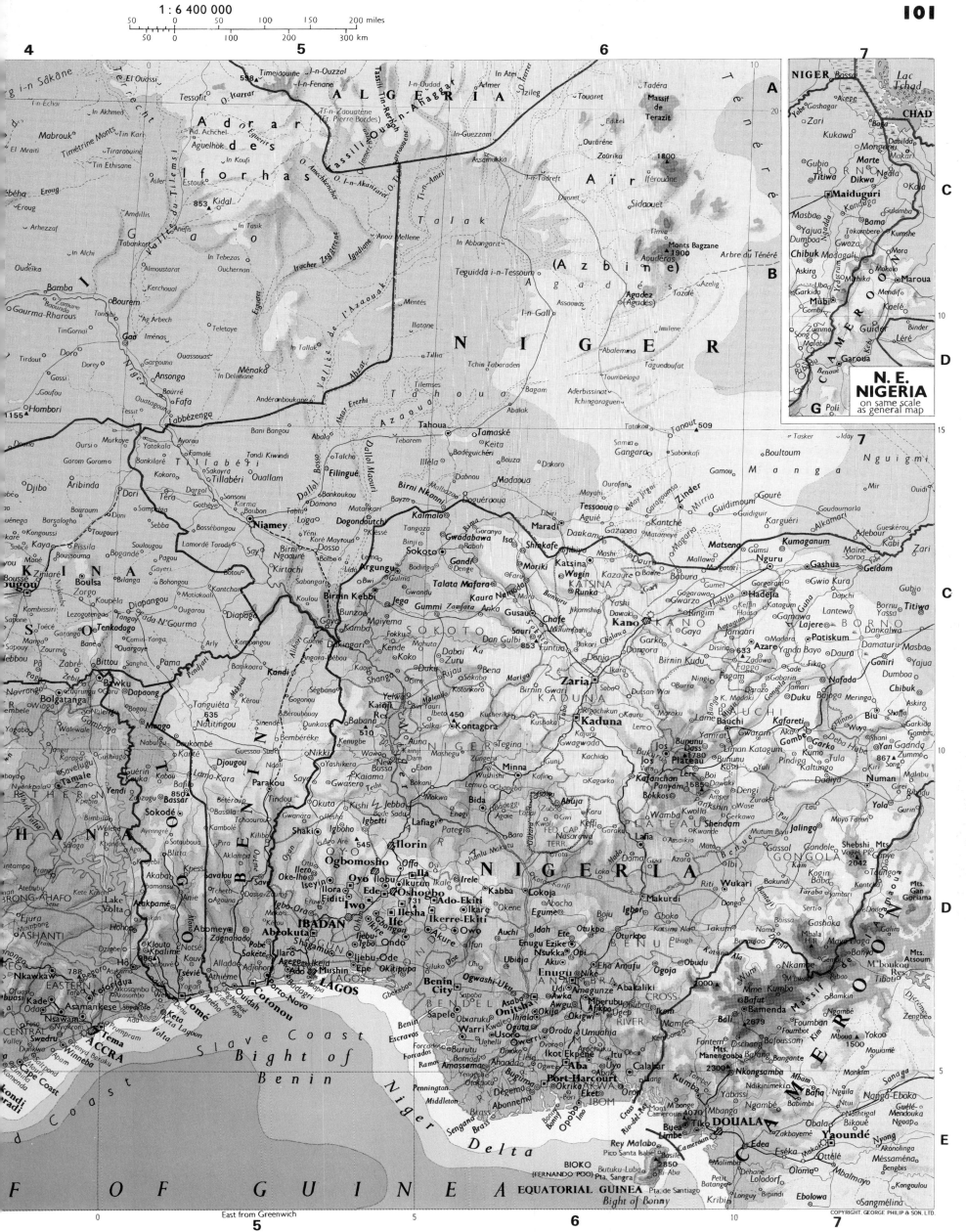

1 : 6 400 000

50    0    50    100    150    200 miles
50    0    100    200    300 km

NIGER
CHAD

N. E.
NIGERIA
on same scale
as general map

ALGERIA

NIGER

NIGERIA

BENIN

GHANA

CAMEROON

Bight of
Benin

Bight of Bonny

EQUATORIAL GUINEA

BIOKO
(FERNANDO POO)

Slave Coast

Niger
Delta

East from Greenwich

COPYRIGHT. GEORGE PHILIP & SON. LTD.

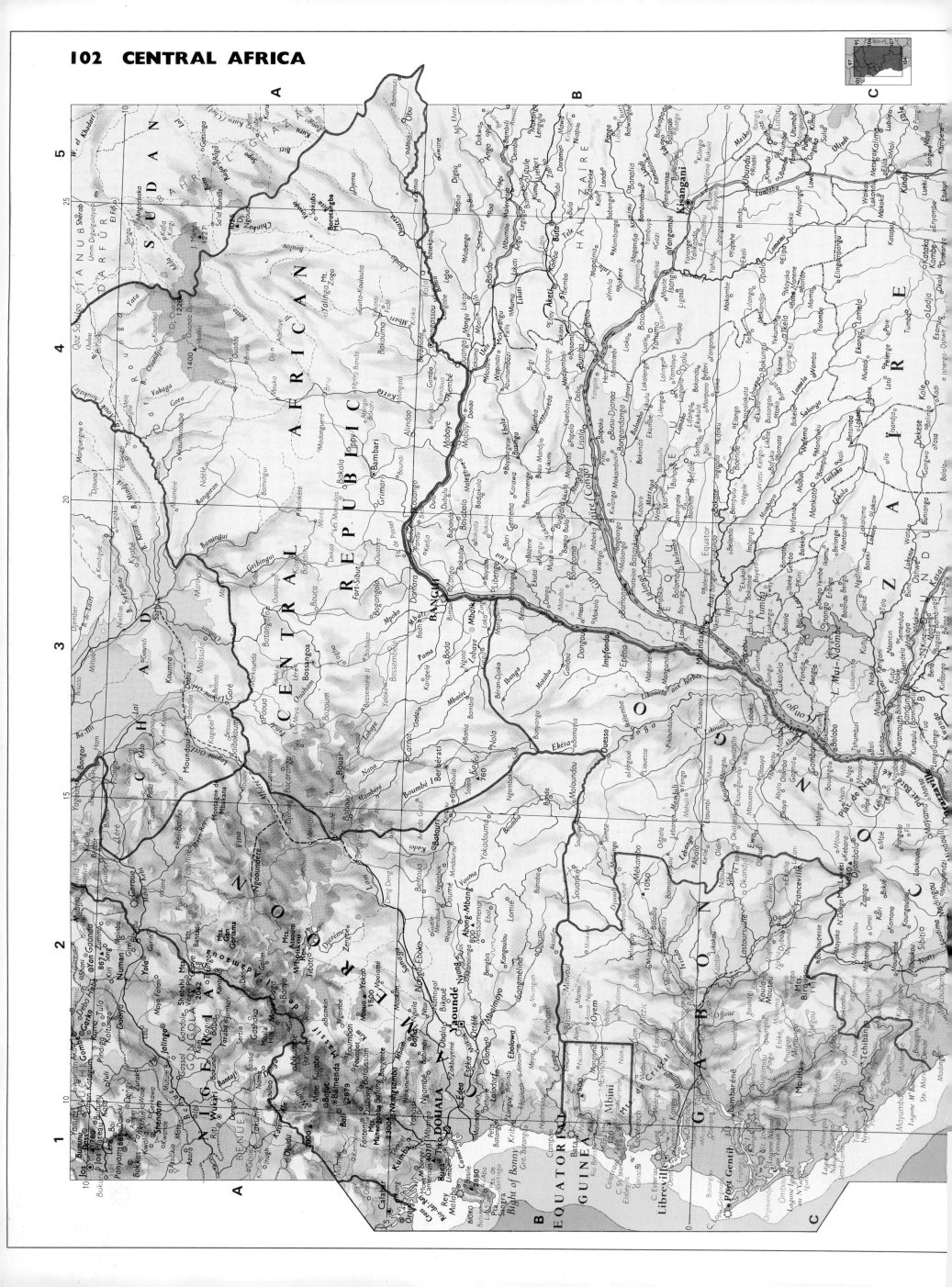

1 : 6 400 000

50  0  50  100  150  200 miles
50  0  50  100  200  300 km

Projection: Lambert's Equivalent Azimuthal

ZAIRE

KINSHASA

KASAI OCCIDENTAL

KASAI ORIENTAL

SHABA

ANGOLA

ZAMBIA

BOTSWANA

NAMIBIA

CABINDA (ANGOLA)

Pointe Noire

Matadi

Mbuji-Mayi

Kananga

Kamina

Kolwezi

Likasi

Lubumbashi (Elisabethville)

COPPERBELT

NORTH WESTERN

SOUTHERN

LUANDA

Lobito

Benguela

Namibe (Moçâmedes)

Huambo

Planalto de Bié

UIGE

CUANZA NORTE

CUANZA SUL

LUNDA NORTE

LUNDA SUL

MALANGE

HUAMBO

BENGUELA

CUNENE

HUÍLA

CUANDO CUBANGO

OKAVANGO

Hartmannberge

Baynes Mts.

ATLANTIC OCEAN

**SÃO TOMÉ AND PRÍNCIPE**
At the same scale as main map

Príncipe

São Tomé

Pico de S. Tomé 2024

Santo António

m
9000
6000
4500
3000
1500
600
0
ft
3000
2000
1500
1200
600
400
200
0
200
600
6000
12000
ft   m

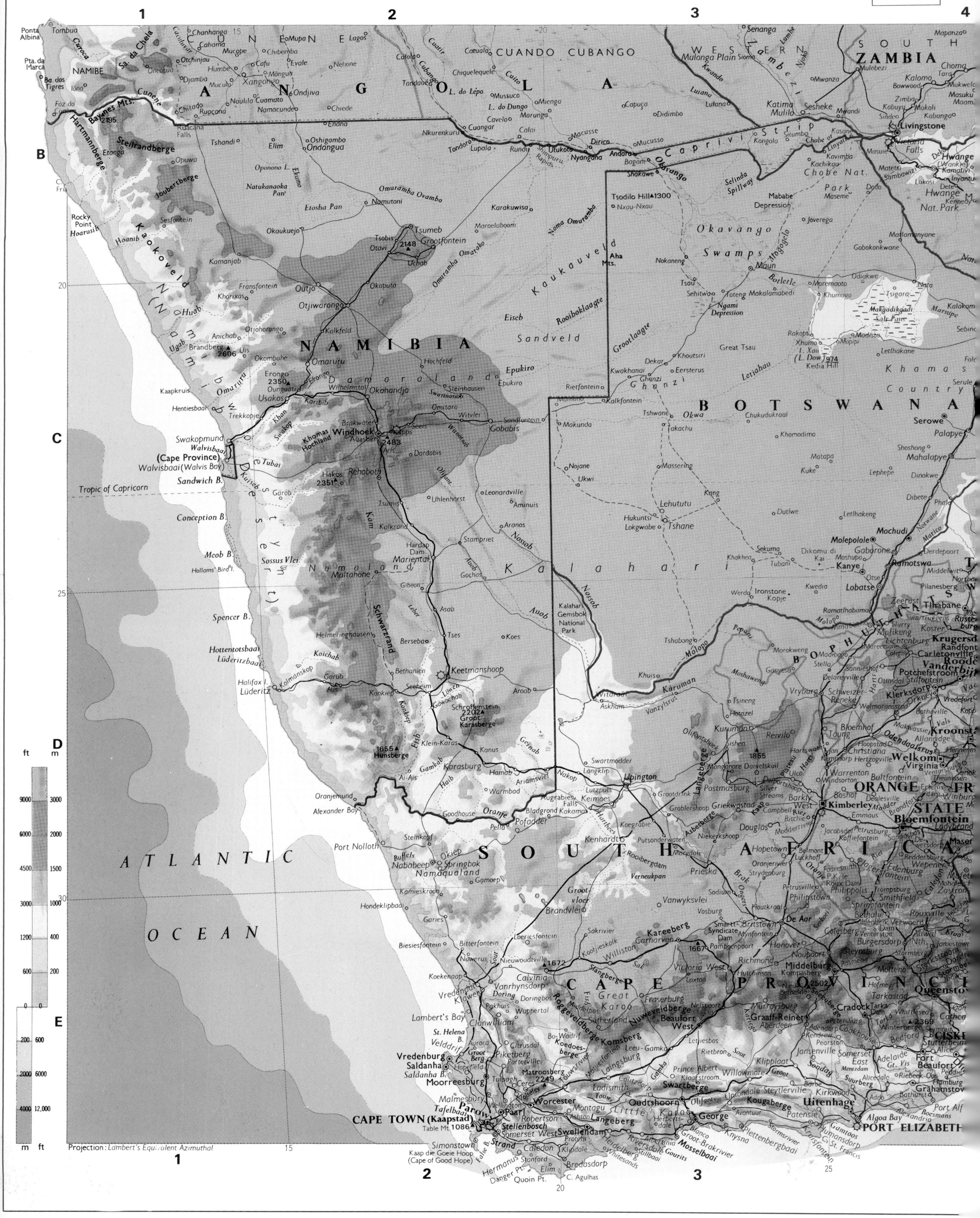

ANGOLA

CUANDO CUBANGO

SOUTH ZAMBIA

NAMIBIA

BOTSWANA

SOUTH AFRICA

CAPE PROVINCE

ORANGE FREE STATE

BOPHUTHATSWANA

ATLANTIC OCEAN

Kalahari

Namib (Desert)

Kaokoveld

Damaraland

Namaland

Namaqualand

Great Karoo

Little Karoo

Okavango Swamps

Etosha Pan

Tropic of Capricorn

Livingstone
Victoria Falls
Hwange
Chobe Nat. Park

Windhoek
Walvisbaai (Walvis Bay)
(Cape Province)
Swakopmund
Sandwich B.

Lüderitz
Lüderitzbaai

Keetmanshoop
Mariental
Rehoboth
Gobabis
Grootfontein
Tsumeb
Otjiwarongo
Otavi
Omaruru
Usakos
Karibib
Okahandja

Gaborone
Lobatse
Kanye
Molepolole
Mochudi
Serowe
Palapye
Mahalapye
Maun
Ghanzi

Upington
Kimberley
Bloemfontein
Welkom
Virginia
Kroonstad
Potchefstroom
Klerksdorp
Vryburg
Kuruman
Mafeking
Prieska
De Aar
Beaufort West
Oudtshoorn
George
Mosselbaai
Worcester
Paarl
Stellenbosch
CAPE TOWN (Kaapstad)
Table Mt 1086
Simonstown
Kaap die Goeie Hoop
(Cape of Good Hope)
C. Agulhas
PORT ELIZABETH
Algoa Bay
Uitenhage
Grahamstown
CISKEI
Port Nolloth
Springbok
Calvinia
Vredendal
Clanwilliam
Saldanha
Vredenburg
Malmesbury
Bredasdorp

Brandberg 2606
2350
Hunsberge 1655

Projection: Lambert's Equivalent Azimuthal

1 : 6 400 000

50    0    100    200    300 km

*MOZAMBIQUE CHANNEL*

**ZIMBABWE**

**MALAWI**

*TETE*

*MASHONALAND*

HARARE
Chitungwiza

Bulawayo
Gweru
Kwekwe
Kadoma

*MATABELELAND*

Masvingo

Beira

*MOZAMBIQUE*

Quelimane

Nova Sofala

I. do Bazaruto
I. Benguérua

Inhambane

Maputo
(Lourenço Marques)

**SWAZILAND**
Mbabane

Manzini

**PRETORIA**
**JOHANNESBURG**
Benoni
Springs
Soweto
Vereeniging

*TRANSVAAL*

*VENDA*

Messina
Beitbridge

*NATAL*

**DURBAN**
Pietermaritzburg
KwaMashu
Umlazi

**LESOTHO**

Umtata

East London

*INDIAN OCEAN*

**MADAGASCAR**

Antsiranana

Mahajanga

**ANTANANARIVO**
(Tananarive)

Antsirabe

Toamasina

Fianarantsoa

Morondava

Toliara

Tropic of Capricorn

Taolanaro

**MADAGASCAR**

On same scale as General Map

COPYRIGHT. GEORGE PHILIP & SON. LTD.

East from Greenwich

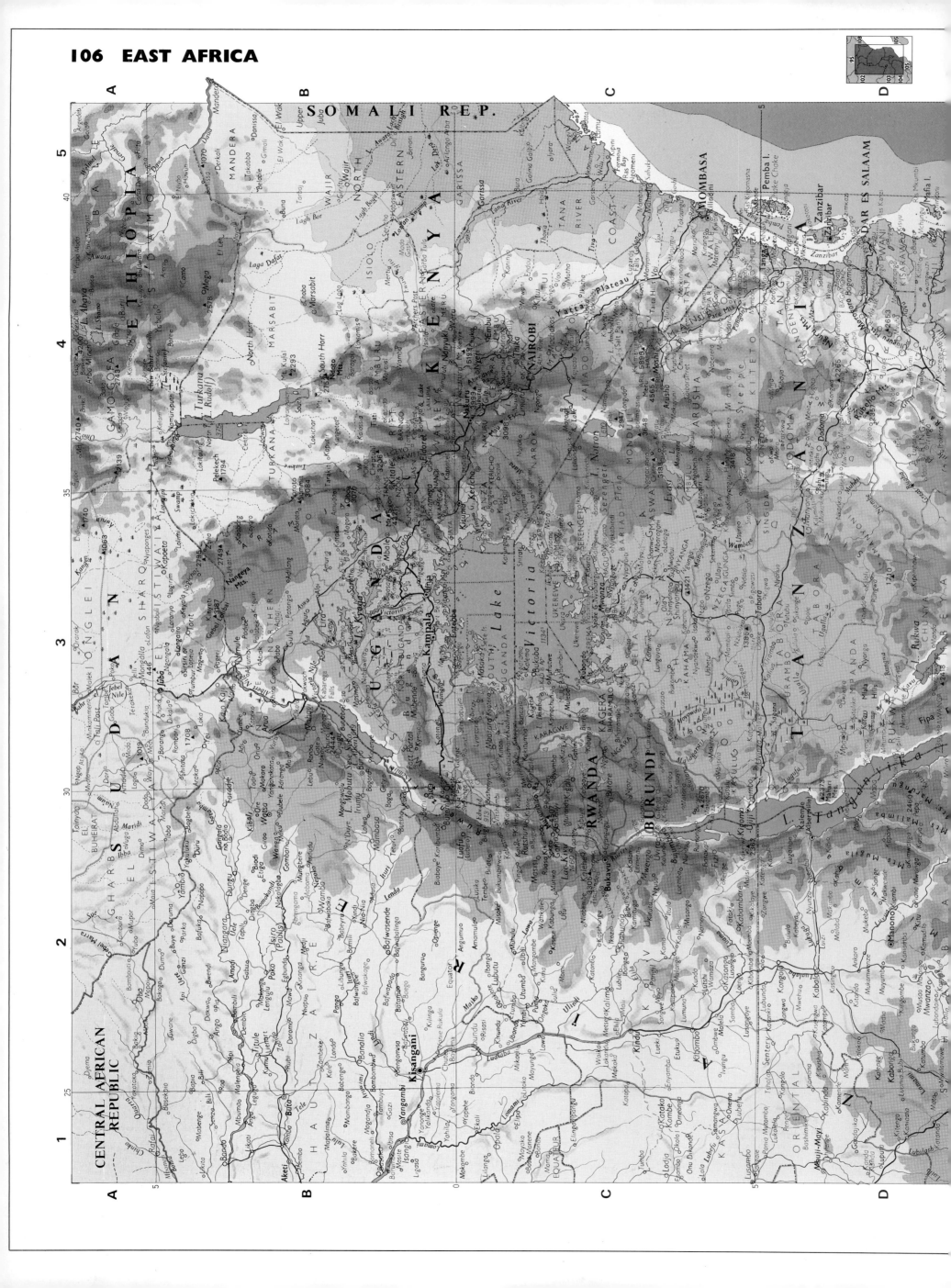

1 : 6 400 000

50   0   50   100   150   200 miles
50   0   100   200   300 km

COPYRIGHT GEORGE PHILIP & SON LTD

INDIAN

OCEAN

MALAWI

ZAMBIA

ZIMBABWE

MOZAMBIQUE

BOTSWANA

ANGOLA

SOUTH AFRICA

NORTHERN

SOUTHERN

WESTERN

Lusaka

HARARE

Bulawayo

Lilongwe

Blantyre

Beira

Lindi

Mtwara-Mikindani

Mufulira

Ndola

Kitwe

Luanshya

Kabwe

Likasi

Kolwezi

Kamina

Lubumbashi

Chingola

Livingstone

Gweru

L. Malawi

Lake Nyasa

ZAMBEZI

Projection : Lambert's Equivalent Azimuthal

East from Greenwich

m   ft
18 000
12 000
9000
6000
4500
3000
1200
600
0

ft   m
6000
4000
3000
2000
1500
1000
400
200
0
200-600
2000-6000

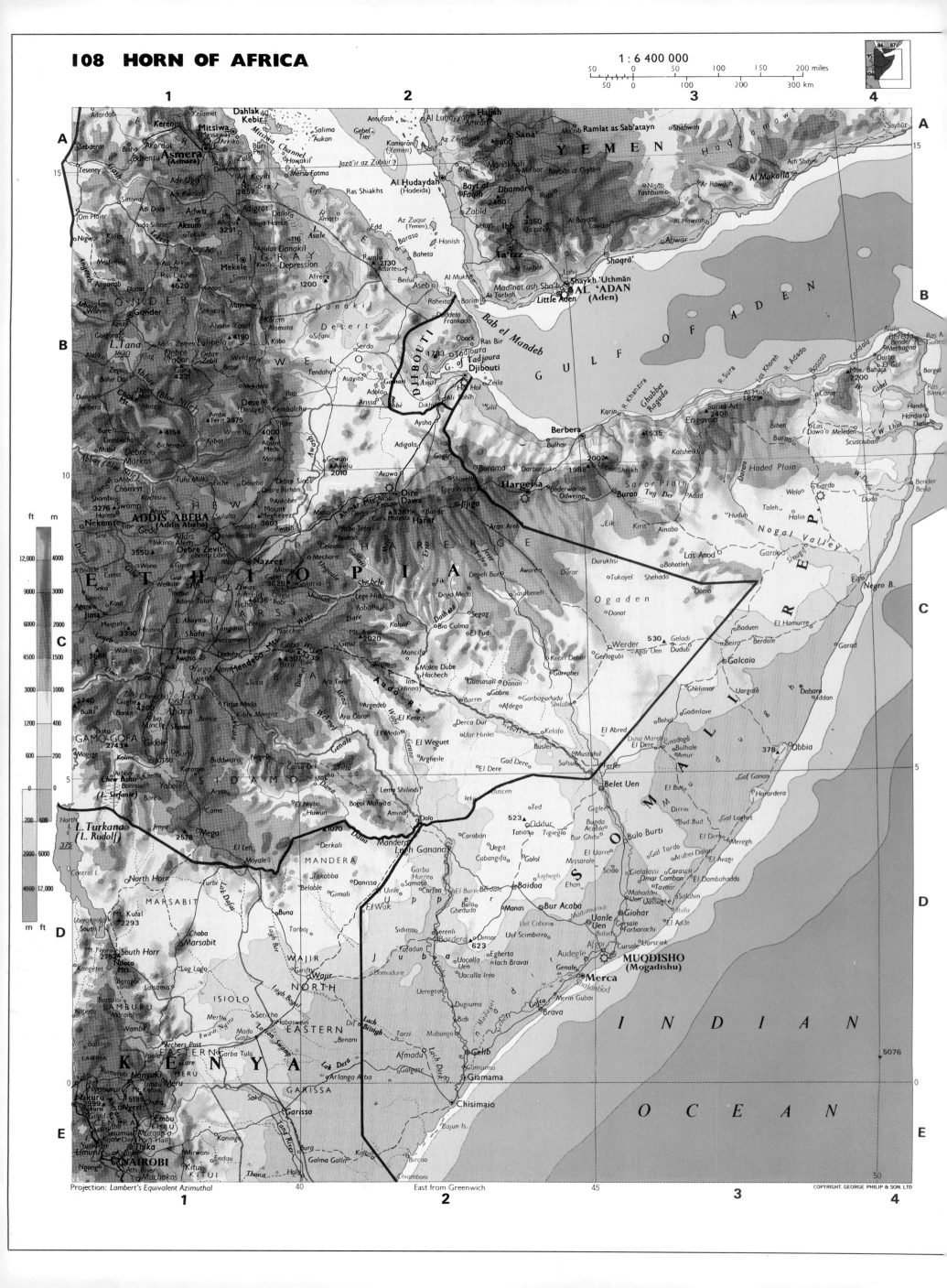

1 : 6 400 000

50    0    50    100    150    200 miles
50    0    100    200    300 km

86    87
95
104

**1**       **2**       **3**       **4**

Y E M E N

G U L F   O F   A D E N

D J I B O U T I

E T H I O P I A

S O M A L I   R E P.

Ogaden

K E N Y A

I N D I A N

O C E A N

Addis Abeba
(Addis Ababa)

Nazret

Hargeisa

Berbera

AL 'ADAN
(Aden)

Djibouti

Dire Dawa

Harer

Baidoa

MUQDISHO
(Mogadishu)

Merca

Chisimaio

NAIROBI

L. Turkana
(L. Rudolf)

L. Tana

Asmera
(Asmara)

Mitsiwa
Massawa

Galcaio

Obbia

Belet Uen

Brava

Projection: Lambert's Equivalent Azimuthal

East from Greenwich

COPYRIGHT. GEORGE PHILIP & SON, LTD

Equatorial Scale 1 : 40 000 000

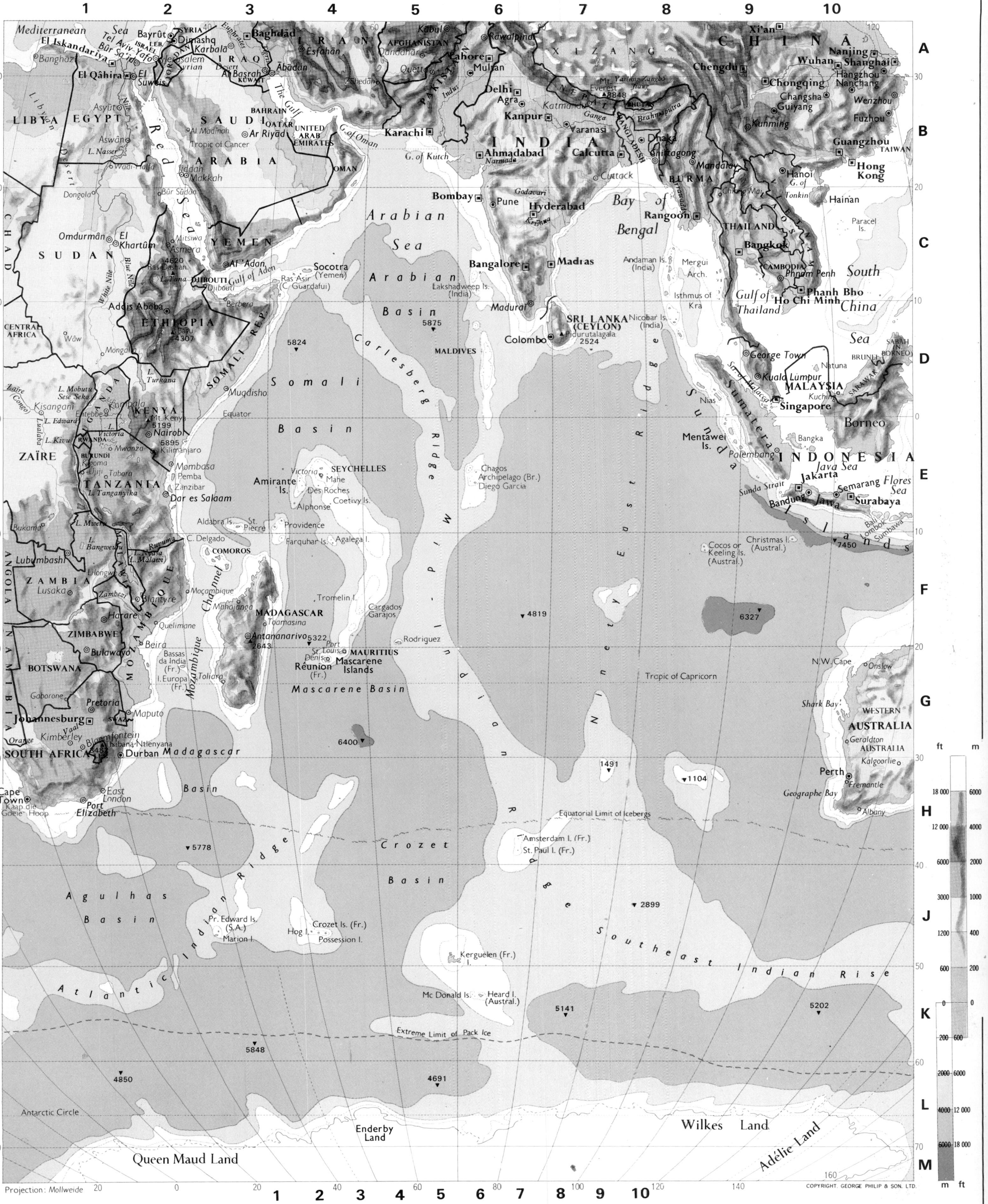

1 2 3 4 5 6 7 8 9 10

A B C D E F G H J K L M

Mediterranean Sea
El Iskandariya
Banghazi
El Qâhira
El Suweis
Bûr Saîd
LIBYA
EGYPT
Asyût
Aswân
L. Nasser
Wâdi Halfa
Dongola
CHAD
Omdurmân
El Khartûm
SUDAN
Wâw
Mongalla
CENTRAL AFRICA
Bûr Sûdân
Jiddah
Makkah
Al Madinah
SAUDI ARABIA
Tropic of Cancer
Red Sea
Mitsiwa
Asmera
Ras Dashan 4620
ETHIOPIA
Addis Abeba
Gimma 4307
YEMEN
Al Adan
DJIBOUTI
Djibouti
Gulf of Aden
Berbera
Socotra (Yemen)
Ras Asir (C. Guardafui)
SOMALI REP.
Muqdisho

Bayrût
Tel Aviv-Jaffa
Dimashq
Karbala
Baghdâd
IRAQ
Al Basrah
KUWAIT
BAHRAIN
QATAR
Ar Riyâd
UNITED ARAB EMIRATES
The Gulf
G. of Oman
OMAN
Esfahân
IRAN
Zâhedân
Qandahar
Quetta
Multan
Lahore
Rawalpindi
Kabul
AFGHANISTAN
PAKISTAN
Karachi
Delhi
Agra
Kanpur
Ahmadabad
Narmada
INDIA
Bombay
Pune
Hyderabad
Godavari
Krishna
Bangalore
Madras
Madurai

ARABIA
SYRIA
LEB.
ISRAEL
JORDAN

XIZANG
Mt. Yarlung Zangbo
Everest 8848
Katmandu
Ganga
Brahmaputra
Varanasi
Calcutta
Dhaka
BANGLADESH
Chittagong
Cuttack
Mandalay
BURMA
Rangoon

CHINA
Xi'an
Chengdu
Chongqing
Changsha
Guiyang
Kunming
Wuhan
Nanjing
Shanghai
Nanchang
Hangzhou
Wenzhou
Fuzhou
Guangzhou
TAIWAN
Hong Kong
Hainan
Hanoi
G. of Tonkin
Paracel Is.
South China Sea

Arabian Sea
Arabian Basin
5875
5824
Lakshadweep Is. (India)
MALDIVES
Carlesberg Ridge
Somali Basin
SRI LANKA (CEYLON)
Pidurutalagala 2524
Colombo
Andaman Is. (India)
Nicobar Is. (India)
Mergui Arch.
Isthmus of Kra
THAILAND
Bangkok
CAMBODIA
Phnom Penh
Phanh Bho
Ho Chi Minh
Gulf of Thailand

ZAÏRE
Kisangani
L. Mobutu Sese Seko
L. Edward
L. Kivu
RWANDA
BURUNDI
Kampala
Entebbe
UGANDA
L. Victoria
Mwanza
KENYA
Mt. Kenya 5199
Nairobi 5895
Kilimanjaro
TANZANIA
Mombasa
Pemba
Zanzibar
Dar es Salaam
L. Tanganyika
Tabora
Mongu
L. Turkana
Equator

SEYCHELLES
Victoria
Mahé
Amirante Is.
Des Roches
Coetivy Is.
Alphonse
Chagos Archipelago (Br.)
Diego Garcia
Mentawei Is.
Nias
Sumatera
George Town
Kuala Lumpur
MALAYSIA
Kuching
Singapore
SARAWAK
SABAH
BRUNEI
Natuna
Borneo
Bangka
Palembang
INDONESIA
Jakarta
Java Sea
Semarang
Surabaya
Flores Sea
Bandung
Java
Sunda Strait
Bali
Lombok
Sumbawa
Sunda Islands

ANGOLA
ZAMBIA
Lubumbashi
Lusaka
Zambezi
L. Mweru
L. Bangweulu
L. Nyasa (L. Malawi)
Lilongwe
Blantyre
MOZAMBIQUE
Beira
ZIMBABWE
Harare
Bulawayo
BOTSWANA
NAMIBIA
Gaborone
Pretoria
Johannesburg
Kimberley
Bloemfontein
SWAZ.
Maputo
Durban
SOUTH AFRICA
Cape Town
Kaap die Goeie Hoop
East London
Port Elizabeth

COMOROS
Aldabra Is.
St. Pierre
Providence
Farquhar Is.
Agalega I.
C. Delgado
Moçambique
Mozambique Channel
Mahajanga
Toamasina
MADAGASCAR
Antananarivo 2643
5322
Toliara
Bassas da India (Fr.)
I. Europa (Fr.)
Tromelin I.
Cargados Garajos
Rodriguez
St. Louis
Port
Denis
MAURITIUS
Réunion (Fr.)
Mascarene Islands
Mascarene Basin
Madagascar Basin

4819
6327
N.W. Cape
Onslow
Tropic of Capricorn
Shark Bay
Geraldton
WESTERN AUSTRALIA
AUSTRALIA
Kalgoorlie
Perth
Fremantle
Geographe Bay
Albany

Cocos or Keeling Is. (Austral.)
Christmas I. (Austral.)
7450

6400
1491
1104

Equatorial Limit of Icebergs
Amsterdam I. (Fr.)
St. Paul I. (Fr.)
5778
Crozet Basin
Agulhas Basin
Pr. Edward Is. (S.A.)
Marion I.
Hog I.
Crozet Is. (Fr.)
Possession I.
Atlantic Indian Ridge
Kerguelen (Fr.)
2899
Southeast Indian Rise
Mid-Indian Ridge
Ninety East Ridge
Indian Ridge

Mc Donald Is.
Heard I. (Austral.)
5141
5202
Extreme Limit of Pack Ice
5848
4850
4691
Antarctic Circle
Queen Maud Land
Enderby Land
Wilkes Land
Adélie Land

Projection: Mollweide
COPYRIGHT. GEORGE PHILIP & SON, LTD.

ft m
18 000  6000
12 000  4000
6000  2000
3000  1000
1200  400
600  200
0
200  600
2000  6000
4000  12 000
6000  18 000
m ft

Projection: Lambert's Equivalent Azimuthal
East from Greenwich

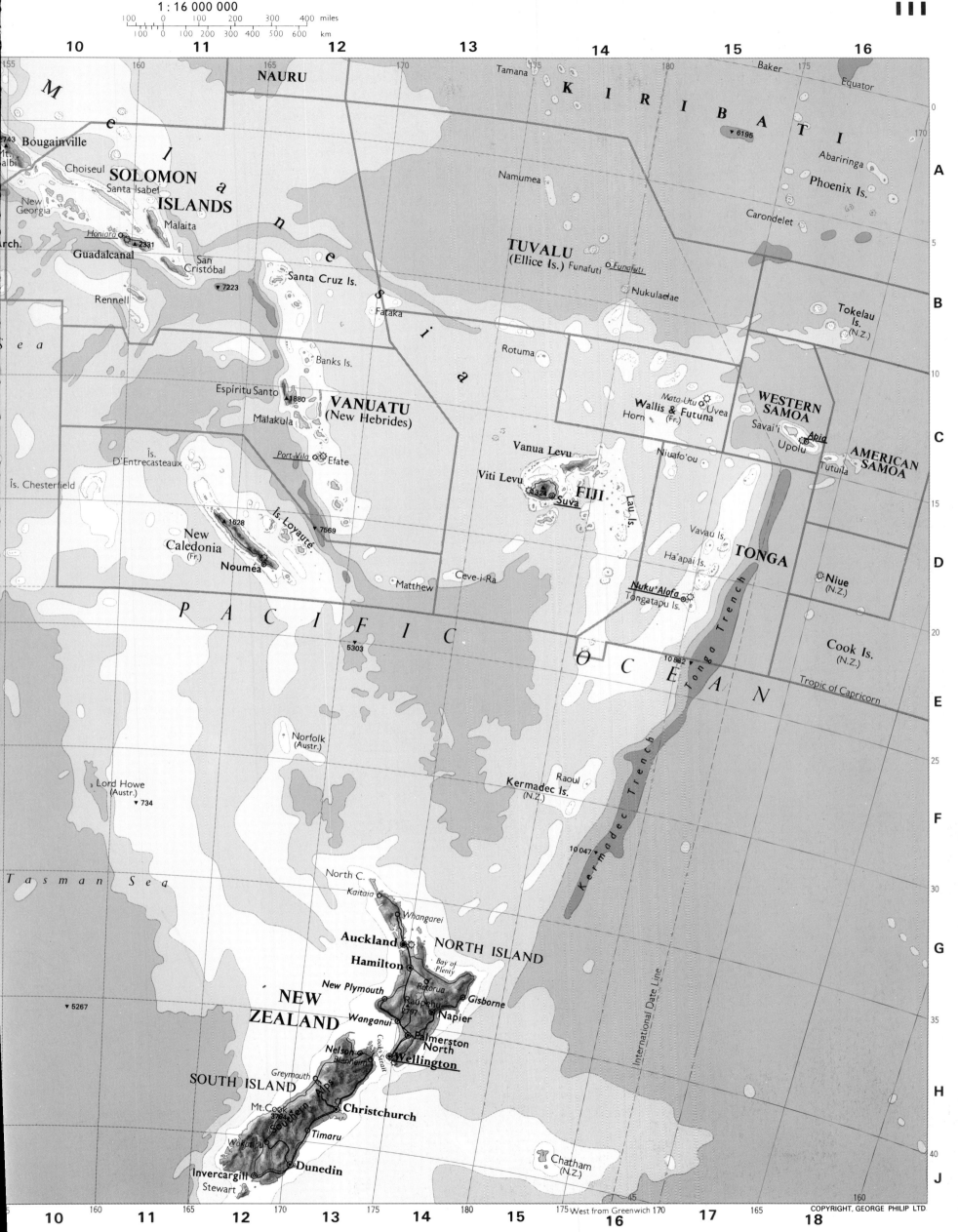

1 : 16 000 000

100   0   100   200   300   400 miles
100   0   100   200   300   400   500   600 km

**10**   **11**   **12**   **13**   **14**   **15**   **16**

155          160          165          170          175          180          175          170

NAURU          Tamana          Baker          Equator

M          KIRIBATI          170

2743 Bougainville          6195          Abariringa          **A**

Choiseul          Namumea          Phoenix Is.

SOLOMON          Carondelet

Santa Isabel          ISLANDS

New          Malaita          5

Georia          Honiara          2331          TUVALU          Tokelau          **B**

Guadalcanal          (Ellice Is.) Funafuti          Funafuti          Is.

San          Cristóbal          7223          Nukulaelae          (N.Z.)

Rennell          Fataka

Sea          Rotuma          10

Banks Is.          Mata-Utu  Uvea          WESTERN

Espíritu Santo          1880          VANUATU          Wallis & Futuna          SAMOA

(New Hebrides)          Horn   (Fr.)          Savai'i          Apia          **C**

Malakula          Vanua Levu          Niuafo'ou          Upolu          AMERICAN

Îs.          Port-Vila  Efate          Viti Levu          Tutuila          SAMOA

D'Entrecasteaux          FIJI

Îs. Chesterfield          1324          15

Suva          Lau Is.          Vavau Is.

1628          Is. Loyauté          7569          Ha'apai Is.          TONGA          **D**

New          Ceve-i-Ra          Nuku'Alofa          Niue

Caledonia          Matthew          Tongatapu Is.          (N.Z.)

(Fr.)          Nouméa          20

PACIFIC          10 882          Cook Is.

5303          (N.Z.)

Tropic of Capricorn          **E**

O          C          E          A          N          25

Norfolk          Raoul

(Austr.)          Kermadec Is.

Lord Howe          (N.Z.)          **F**

(Austr.)          734

10 047          30

Tasman Sea          North C.

Kaitaia          Whangarei          Auckland          **G**

5267          Bay of          Plenty

Hamilton          Rotorua          Gisborne          35

New Plymouth          Ruapehu          Napier

NEW          1797

ZEALAND          Wanganui          Palmerston          North

Nelson          North Island          Wellington          **H**

SOUTH ISLAND          Greymouth          Blenheim

Southern Alps          Mt.Cook          Christchurch          40

Wakatipu          Timaru          Chatham          **J**

Invercargill          Dunedin          (N.Z.)

Stewart          45   West from Greenwich 170          160

**10**   **11**   **12**   **13**   **14**   **15**   **16**   **17**   **18**

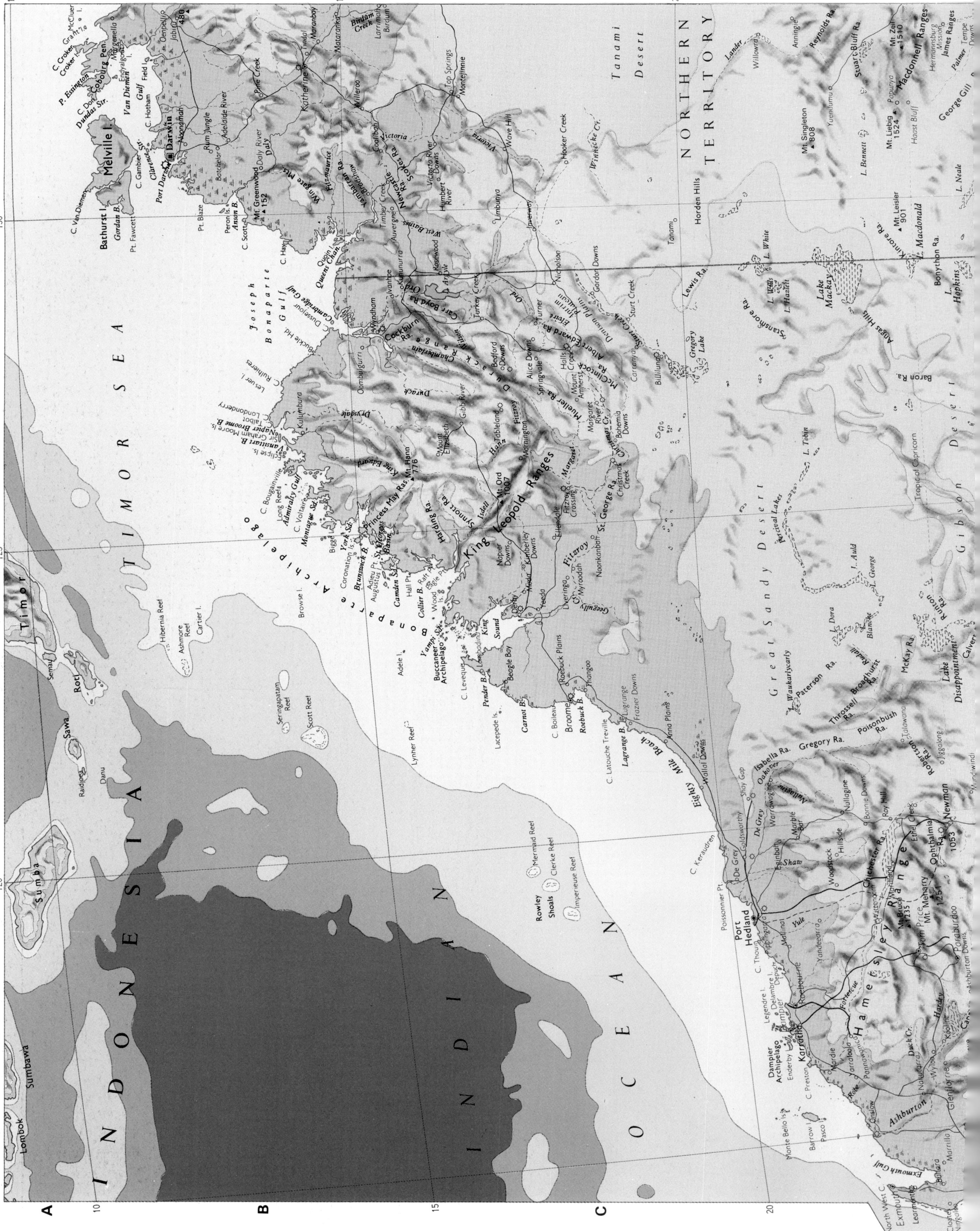
TIMOR SEA
INDONESIA
INDIAN OCEAN
NORTHERN TERRITORY
Tanami Desert
Great Sandy Desert
Gibson Desert
Melville I.
Bathurst I.
Darwin
Van Diemen Gulf
Cobourg Pen.
Joseph Bonaparte Gulf
Cambridge Gulf
Bonaparte Archipelago
King Leopold Ranges
King Sound
Derby
Broome
Roebuck B.
Eighty Mile Beach
Port Hedland
Dampier Archipelago
Karratha
Hamersley Range
Exmouth Gulf
Timor
Sumba
Sumbawa
Lombok
Sawa
Roti
Rowley Shoals
Scott Reef
Ashmore Reef
Cartier I.
Browse I.
Adele I.
Lacepede Is.
Katherine
Wyndham
Kununurra
Halls Creek
Fitzroy Crossing
Mt. Ord 1007
Mt. Hann 776
Lake Mackay
Lake Disappointment
Macdonnell Ranges
Tropic of Capricorn
Newman
Mt. Meharry 1251
Lagrange B.
Cockburn Ra.
Durack Range
Barrow I.
Monte Bello Is.
Onslow
North West C.
Exmouth

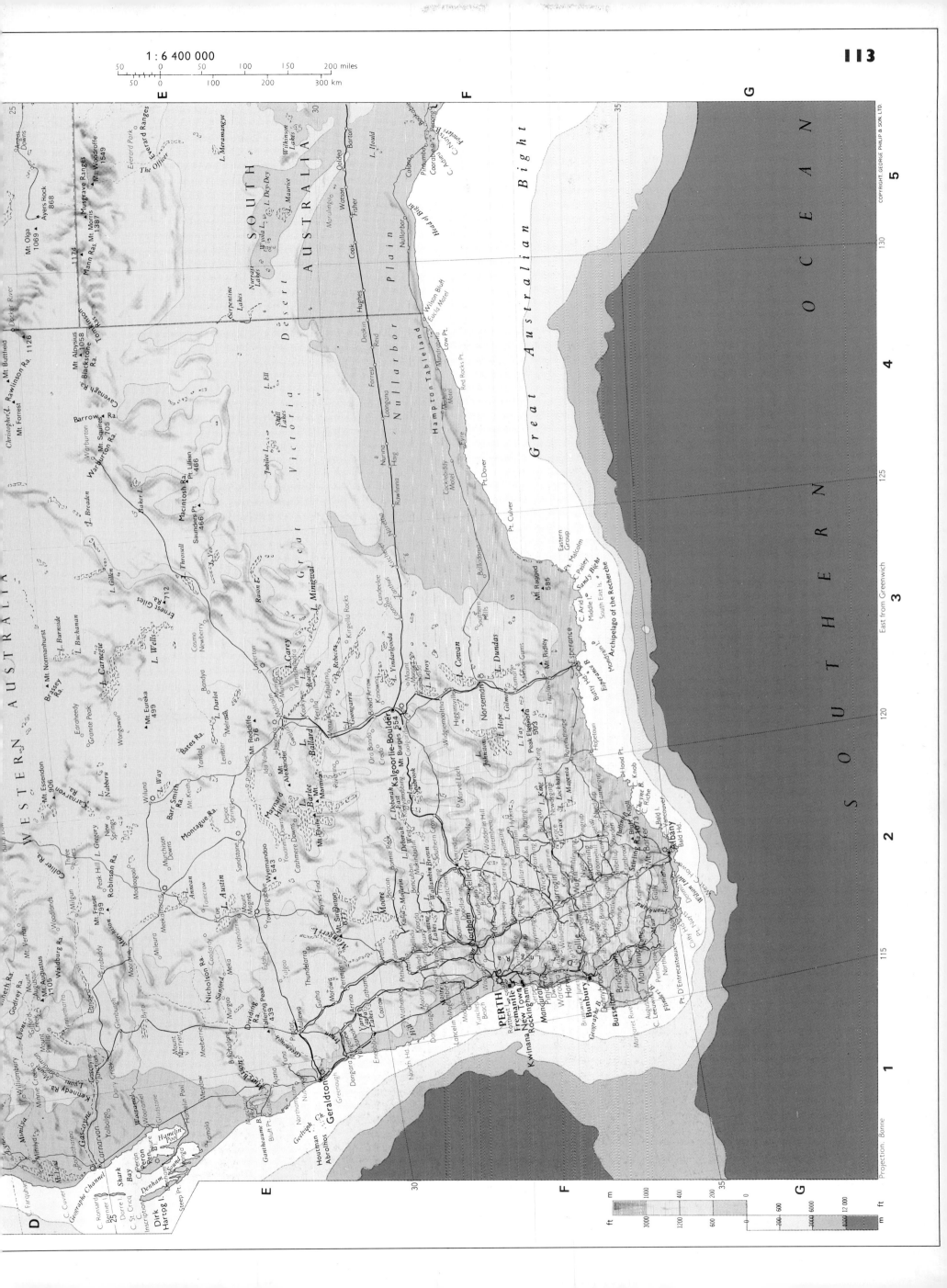

1 : 6 400 000

50    0    50    100   150   200 miles
50  0   100   200   300 km

WESTERN AUSTRALIA

SOUTH

AUSTRALIA

Great Victoria Desert

Nullarbor Plain

Hampton Tableland

Great Australian Bight

SOUTHERN OCEAN

PERTH
Fremantle
Rockingham
Kwinana
New

Geraldton

Bunbury
Busselton
Mandurah

Albany

Kalgoorlie-Boulder

Norseman

Esperance

Archipelago of the Recherche

East from Greenwich

Projection. Bonne

COPYRIGHT GEORGE PHILIP & SON LTD.

ft        m
3000    1000
         600
         400
         200
          0
        -200
        -600
       -2000
       -4000
m
12 000
6000
1200
600

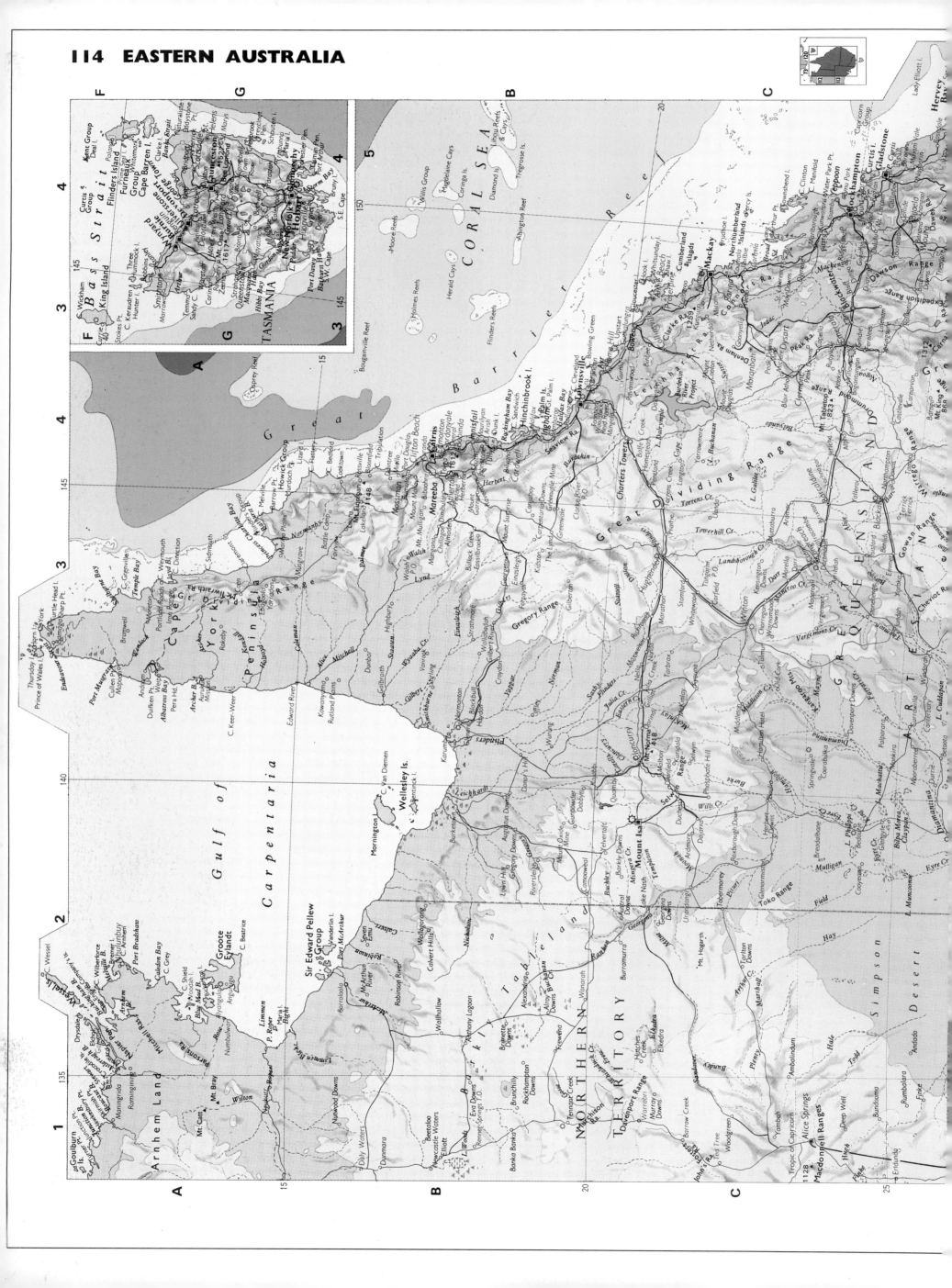

1 : 6 400 000

East from Greenwich

Projection: Bonne

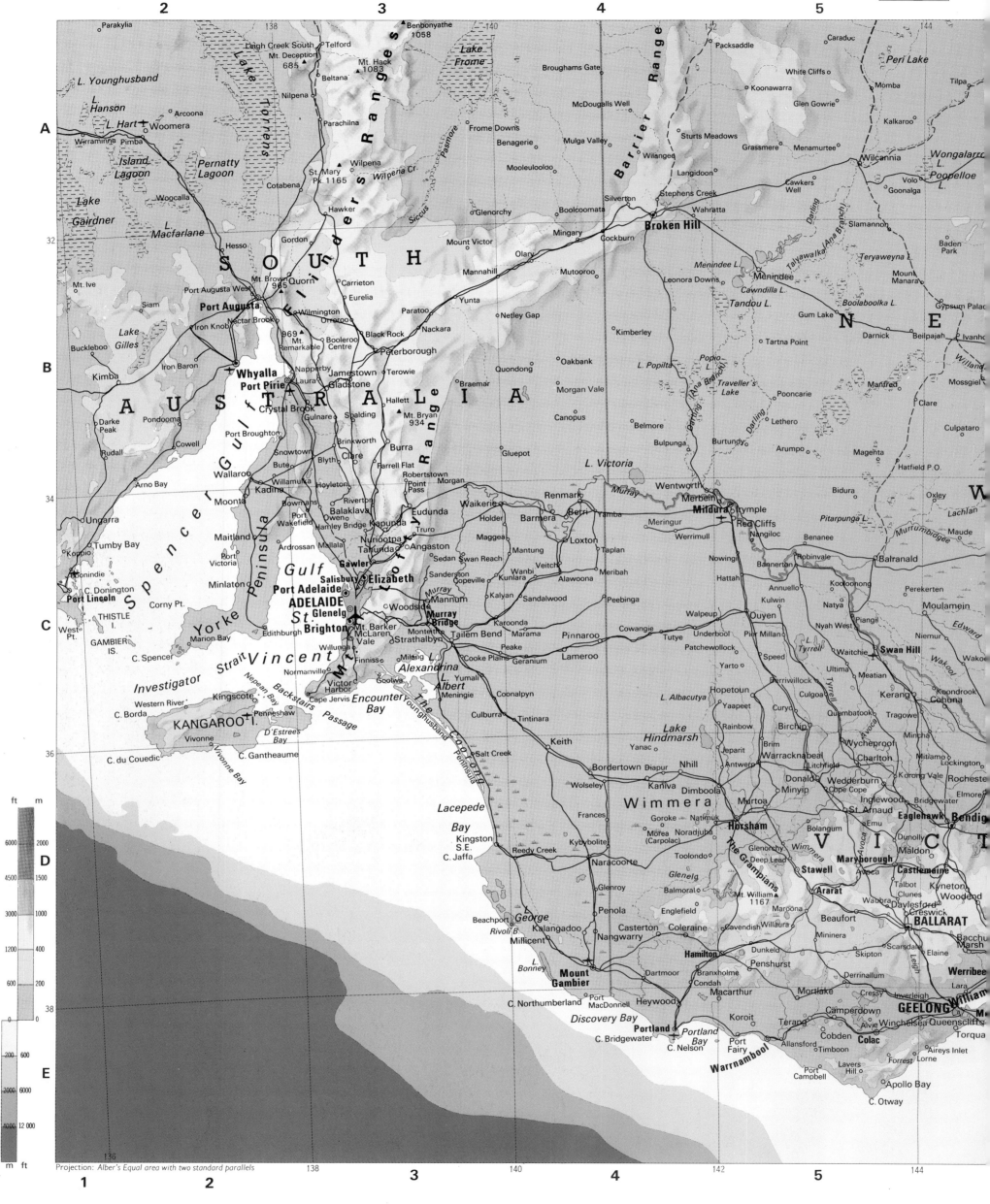

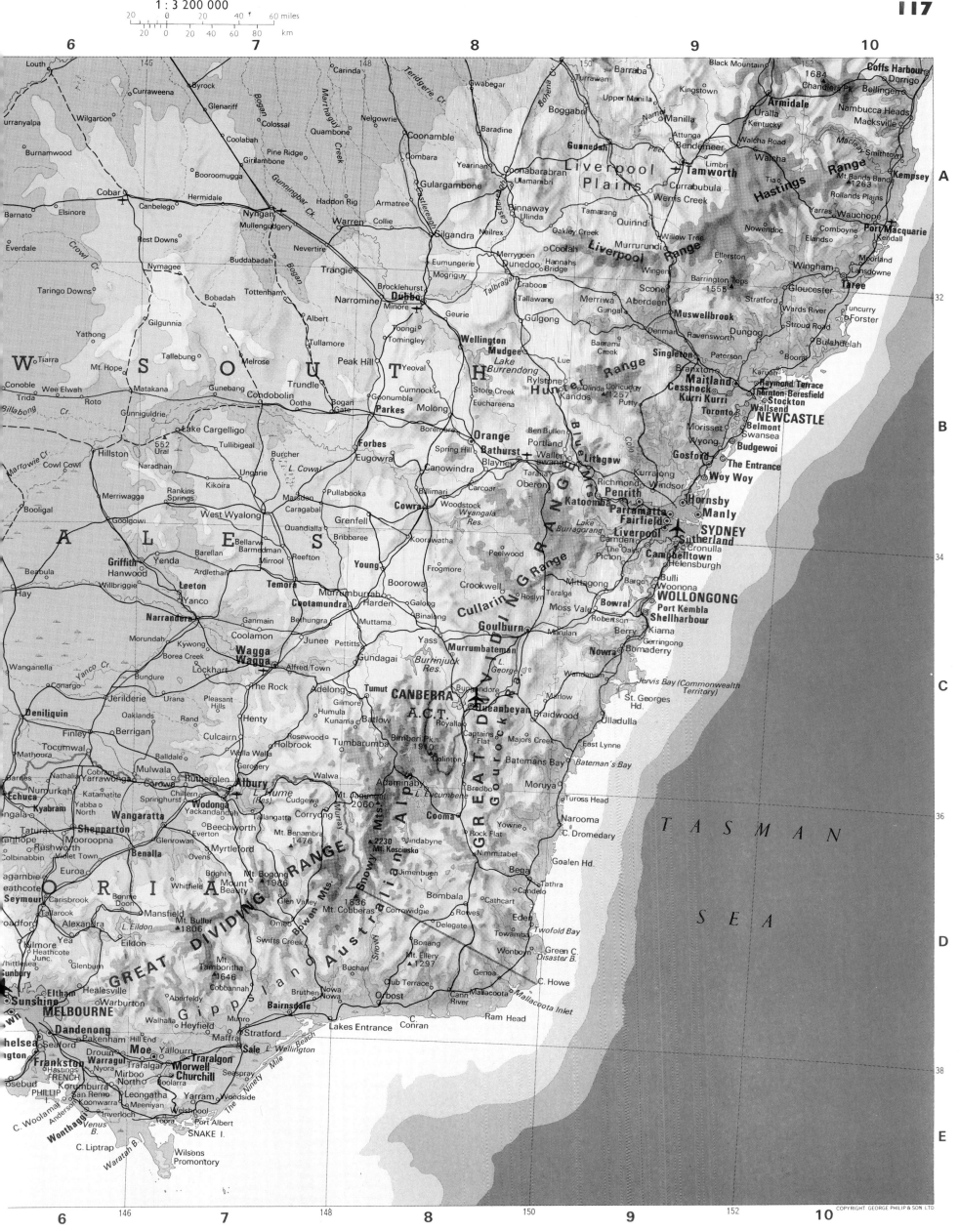

1 : 3 200 000

20    0    20    40    60 miles
20  0  20  40  60  80
km

**6** · 146 · **7** · 148 · **8** · 150 · **9** · 152 · **10**

A

B

C

D

E

Louth
Curraweena
Byrock
Carinda
Gwabegar
Barraba
Turrawan
Black Mountain
1684 Chandlers Pk
Coffs Harbour
Dorrigo
Bellingen

Wilgaroon
Glenariff
Bogan
Colossal
Nelgowrie
Coolabah
Pine Ridge
Quambone
Coonamble
Baradine
Teridgerie Cr.
Bokhara R.
Boggabri
Kingstown
Upper Manilla
Namoi
Manilla
Attunga
Bendemeer
Armidale
Uralla
Kentucky
Walcha Road
Nambucca Heads
Macksville
Maclay R. Smithtown

urranyalpa
Burnamwood
Booroomugga
Marthaguy Creek
Coonabarabran
Ulamambri
Binnaway
Ulinda
Gunnedah
Peel
Tamworth
Limbri
Currabubula
Walcha
Tia
Banda Banda
1263
Hastings
Range
Rollands Plains
Yarras Wauchope
Kempsey

Cobar
Hermidale
Haddon Rig
Warren
Collie
Gilgandra
Neilrex
Oakley Creek
Quirindi
Willow Tree
Murrurundi
Wingen
Ellerston
Nowendoc
Comboyne
Elands
Port Macquarie
Kendal

Canbelego
Nyngan
Mullengudgery
Nevertire
Merrygoen
Dunedoo
Eumungerie
Mogriguy
Tamarang
Scone
Barrington Tops
1555
Wingham
Lansdowne
Taree
Tuncurry
Forster

Everdale
Barnato
Elsinore
Rest Downs
Nymagee
Buddabadah
Trangie
Brocklehurst
Dubbo
Minore
Narromine
Talbragar
Craboon
Tallawang
Merriwa
Aberdeen
Gungal
Denman
Ravensworth
Dungog
Stroud Road
Stratford
Gloucester
Wards River
Bulahdelah
Booral

Crowl Cr.
Taringo Downs
Nymagee
Gilgunnia
Albert
Tottenham
Bobadah
Yoongi
Tominglen
Geurie
Gulgong
Baerami Creek
Muswellbrook
Paterson
Karuah

Yathong
Mt. Hope
Tallebung
Melrose
Trundle
Peak Hill
Yeoval
Wellington
Mudgee
Lake Burrendong
Rylstone
Olinda
Concudgy
1257
Kandos
Putty
Singleton
Branxton
Maitland
Cessnock
Kurri Kurri
Toronto
Raymond Terrace
Thornton-Beresfield
Stockton
Wallsend
NEWCASTLE

Conoble
Wee Elwah
Trida
Roto
Matakana
Gunebang
Condobolin
Ootha
Bogan Gate
Parkes
Goonumbla
Molong
Cumnock
Store Creek
Euchareena
Kandos
Hunter
Range
Belmont
Swansea
Budgewoi

W
Tiarra
S O U T H

Billabong Cr.
Marrowie Cr.
Cowl Cowl
Hillston
552
Ural
L. Cowal
Lake Cargelligo
Tullibigeal
Burcher
Forbes
Eugowra
Spring Hill
Orange
Bathurst
Portland
Lithgow
Wallerawang
Kurrajong
Richmond
Windsor
Gosford
Wyong
Morisset
The Entrance
Woy Woy

Booligal
Merriwagga
Rankins Springs
Kikoira
Maiden
Caragabal
Grenfell
Bribbaree
Billimari
Carcoar
Oberon
Taralga
Katoomba
Penrith
Parramatta
Hornsby
Manly

A L E S
Griffith
Hanwood
Yenda
Ardlethan
West Wyalong
Reefton
Young
Koorawatha
Woodstock
Wyangala Res.
Peelwood
Burragorang
Camden
Liverpool
Fairfield
SYDNEY
Sutherland
Cronulla

Beabula
Hay
Willbriggie
Leeton
Yanco
Barellan
Barmedman
Mirrool
Temora
Frogmore
Crookwell
Bargo
Helensburgh
Campbelltown
The Oaks
Picton
Bulli
Woonona

S
Wanganella
Narrandera
Coolamon
Junee
Pettitts
Galong
Binalong
Yass
Murrumbateman
Marulan
Mittagong
Bowral
Robertson
Berry
Gerringong
WOLLONGONG
Port Kembla
Shellharbour
Kiama

Morundah
Kywong
Borea Creek
Wagga
Wagga
Lockhart
Ganmain
Bethungra
Cootamundra
Harden
Muttama
Gundagai
Moss Vale
Nowra
Bomaderry

V I C T O R I A
Deniliquin
Finley
Berrigan
Jerilderie
Oaklands
Urana
Rand
Pleasant Hills
Henty
The Rock
Alfred Town
Adelong
Tumut
CANBERRA
A.C.T.
Queanbeyan
Bungendore
Braidwood
St. Georges Hd.
Jervis Bay (Commonwealth Territory)

Tocumwal
Mathoura
Barnes
Conargo
Yanco Cr.
Culcairn
Holbrook
Rosewood
Gilmore
Humula
Kunama
Batlow
Royalla
Captains Flat
Majors Creek
East Lynne
Ulladulla

Echuca
Kyabram
Yarrawonga
Cobram
Katamatite
Mulwala
Corowa
Rutherglen
Chiltern
Wodonga
Albury
Hume (Res.)
Wagra
Adaminaby
L. Eucumbene
Marlow
Batemans Bay
Bateman's Bay

Numurkah
Shepparton
Springhurst
Yabba North
Wangaratta
Beechworth
Yackandandah
Tallangatta
Corryong
Murray
L. Eucumbene
Cooma
Nimmitabel
Moruya
Tuross Head
C. Dromedary

Tatura
Stanhope
Rushworth
Violet Town
Everton
Myrtleford
Mt. Benambra
1476
Khancoban
Jindabyne
Yowrie
Narooma

Mooroopna
Benalla
Euroa
Ovens
Bright
Mount
Beauty
Mt. Bogong
1986
Mt. Kosciusko
2230
Rock Flat
Bega
Tathra
Goalen Hd.

Seymour
Carisbrook
Bonnie
Doon
Whitfield
Glen Valley
1836
Mt. Cobberas
Jimenbuen
Bombala
Cathcart
Candelo
Eden

Heathcote
Kilmore
Alexandra
Mansfield
Mt. Buller
1806
L. Eildon
Omeo
Swifts Creek
Bonang
1297
Mt. Ellery
Delegate
Bendoc
Rowes
Corrowidgie
Towamba
Twofold Bay

Whittlesea
Glenburn
Eildon
Mt. Tamboritha
1646
Cobbannah
Buchan
Genoa
Wonboyn
Green C.
Disaster B.

Sunbury
Healesville
Warburton
Abarfeldy
Walhalla
Nowa Nowa
Orbost
Cann River
Mallacoota
C. Howe
Mallacoota Inlet

Sunshine
MELBOURNE
Eltham
Hill End
Heyfield
Maffra
Stratford
Bruthen
Bairnsdale
Lakes Entrance
Ram Head
C. Conran

Dandenong
Pakenham
Yallourn
Sale
Wellington
Ninety Mile Beach

Frankston
Seaford
Chelsea
Drouin
Moe
Traralgon
Morwell
Churchill
Seaspray
Woodside

FRENCH
Hastings
Korumburra
Leongatha
Meeniyan
Yarram
Port Albert

PHILLIP
San Remo
Koonwarra
Woodside

C. Woolamai
Anderson
Wonthaggi
Venus B.
Inverloch
Toora
SNAKE I.

C. Liptrap
Waratah B.
Wilsons Promontory

GREAT
DIVIDING
RANGE
Gippsland
Australian
Alps
Snowy
Mts.
GREAT
DIVIDING
RANGE
Goulburn
Cullarin
Range
Blue
Mts.
Liverpool
Plains
Liverpool
Range
Hunter

T A S M A N

S E A

32

34

36

38

COPYRIGHT GEORGE PHILIP & SON LTD.

**6** · **7** · 148 · **8** · 150 · **9** · 152 · **10**

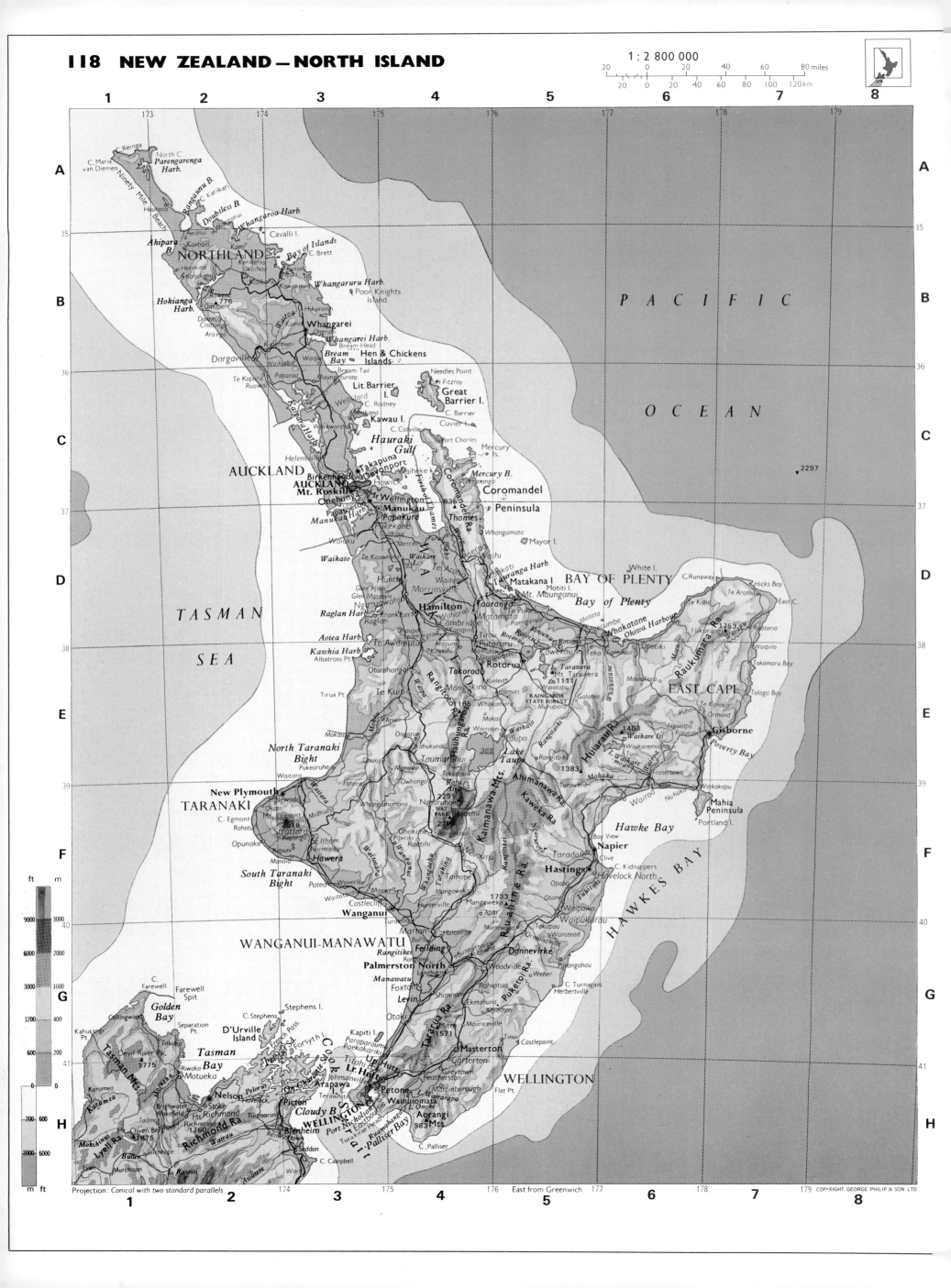

1 : 2 800 000

PACIFIC

OCEAN

NORTHLAND

Bay of Islands

Hokianga
Harb.

Ahipara
B.

Whangarei

Bream
Bay

Hen & Chickens
Islands

Dargaville

Lit. Barrier
I.

Great
Barrier I.

Kawau I.

Hauraki
Gulf

AUCKLAND

AUCKLAND
Mt. Roskill

Onehunga

Manukau

Papakura

Coromandel
Peninsula

Coromandel

2297

TASMAN

SEA

Waikato

Hamilton

Raglan Harb.

Raglan

Aotea Harb.

Kawhia Harb.
Albatross Pt.

Tauranga

BAY OF PLENTY

Bay of Plenty

Whakatane

Ohiwa Harbour
Opotiki

C. Runaway

Te Araroa

East C.

EAST CAPE

Hicks Bay

Raukumara Ra.

1753

Tokoroa

Rotorua

Te Kuiti

Mokau

Taumarunui

Lake
Taupo

369

Gisborne

Poverty Bay

North Taranaki
Bight

New Plymouth

TARANAKI

Mt. Egmont

Stratford

Opunake

Hawera

South Taranaki
Bight

Wanganui

Ahimanawa Ra.

Kaimanawa Mts.

Kaweka Ra.

1383

Hawke Bay

Napier

Hastings
Hovelock North

C. Kidnappers

WANGANUI-MANAWATU

Marton

Feilding

Palmerston North

Levin

Ruahine Ra.

1783

Dannevirke

Woodville

Puketoi Ra.

HAWKES BAY

C. Turnagain

Golden
Bay

Farewell
Spit

D'Urville
Island

Tasman
Bay

Stephens I.

Kapiti I.

Paraparaumu
Paekakariki

Tararua Ra.
1571

Masterton

Carterton

Castlepoint

WELLINGTON

Tasman Mts.

1775

Nelson

Richmond Ra.

1760

Picton

Cloudy B.

WELLINGTON

Blenheim

Cook
Strait

Lr. Hutt
Petone

Palliser Bay

C. Palliser

Flat Pt.

1 : 2 800 000

20  0  20  40  60  80 miles
20  0  20  40  80  100  120km

NELSON-MARLBOROUGH

**TASMAN SEA**

Golden Bay
Farewell Spit
C. Farewell
Collingwood
Kahurangi Pt.
D'Urville Island
C. Stephens
Stephens I.
French Pass
Pelorus Sd.
Forsyth I.
Jackson
Q'n Charlotte Sd.
Arapawa
Tasman Bay
Takaka
Riwaka
Motueka
Devil River Pt.
1775
Tasman Mts.
Karamea
Motupiko
Picton
Cloudy B.
Waikawa
Tuamarina
Karamea Bight
Waimarie
Granity
Millerton
Brightwater
Stoke
Nelson
Pelorus
Havelock
Renwicktown
Blenheim
Mt. Owen 1875
Richmond Ra.
Mt. Richmond 1760
Wairau
Seddon
C. Campbell
Ward
Wharanui
Westport
C. Foulwind
Wangamoa
Lyell Ra.
Dodville
Wakefield
Tadmor
Belgrove

Buller
Lyell
Buller Gorge
Mangahao Junction
Murchison
Rotoroa
L. Rotoiti
Spenser Mts.
St. Arnaud Ra.
Molesworth
Kaikoura Ra.
Tapuaenuku 2885
Mangamaunu
Reefton
Mt. Travers 2337
Mt. Franklin 2322
Seaward Kaikouras
2610
Kaikoura
Kaikoura Pen.

Runanga
Blackball
Inangahua
Grey
Ikamatua
Ahaura
Amuri Pass
Hanmer
Waiau
Kaikoura

Greymouth
Taramakau
Hokitika
Kumara
Kaimata
Harper Pass
Hope Pass
L. Sumner
L. Brunner
Jacksons
Otira
Arthur's Pass
Mt. Crossley 1772
Culverden
Waiau
Waiau
Parnassus
Ross
Kanieri
Browning Pass
Mt. Murchison 2400
Mt. Max 1832
Hurunui
Waikari
Waipara
Scargill
Domett

**WESTLAND BIGHT**

Wanganui
Abut Hd.
Whataroa
Okarito
Whataroa
L. Mapourika
Gillespie Pt.
Horihori
Otehake
Waimakariri
Lake Coleridge
Coleridge
Oxford
Ashley
Sefton
Rangiora
Kaiapoi
Pegasus Bay
New Brighton

Bruce B.
Tititira Hd.
Mt. Tasman 3498
Mt. Cook 3764
Whitcombe
White Cliffs
Springfield
Sheffield
Darfield
Rakaia
Belfast
Riccarton
Christchurch
Sumner
Lyttelton
919
Banks Peninsula

Open Bay Is.
Jackson
Jackson Hd. B.
Okuru
Cascade Pt.
Haast
3493
Heretaniwha
Two Thumb Ra.
Mt. Somers
Methven
L. Heron
Rakaia
Leeston
Lincoln
Little River
Akaroa
L. Ellesmere
Akaroa Harb.

Awarua Pt.
Awarua or Big B.
Yates Pt.
Milford Sd.
McKerrow
Olivine Ra.
Tutoko 2756
2819
Young Range
Barrier Ra.
3035
Wanaka
Mt. Earnslaw 2819
Bens Ohau
Aoraki Ra.
Tasman
Ben Ohau Ra.
L. Pukaki
Mackenzie Plains
Fairlie
Geraldine
Winchester
Temuka
Pleasant Point
Hinds
Ashburton
Tinwald
Canterbury Bight

Bligh Sd.
George Sd.
FIORDLAND
Caswell Sd.
Charles Sd.
NATIONAL
Franklin Mts.
Stuart Mts.
McKinnon Pass
Harris Mts.
L. Hawea
Mt. Bathans 2087
L. Ohau
Hakataramea
Karow
Kirkliston Ra.
The Hunter Hills
Timaru
St. Andrews
Hunter
Studholme Junction
Waihao
Waimate
Waihao Downs

Thompson Sd.
Secretary I.
Doubtful Sd.
Daggs Sd.
PARK
Murchison Mts.
Mt. Lyall 1858
L. Te Anau
Te Anau
Eyre Mts.
Garvie Mts.
Kawarau
Dunstan Mts.
Hawkdun Ra.
St. Bathans
Kakanui Mts.
Ngapara
Tokarahi
Waitaki
Glenavy
Marven
Oamaru

Breaksea Sd.
Resolution
Dusky Sd.
Cameron Mts.
Hauroko
Heath Mts.
Kaherekoau Mts.
Takitimu Mts.
SOUTHLAND
Manapouri
L. Manapouri
Monowai
OTAGO
Nokomai
Nevis
Alexandra
Roxburgh
Miller's Flat
Rough Ridge
Maniototo
1449
Waikouaiti Downs
Middlemarch
Sutton
Hyde
Naseby
Ranfurly
Windsor
Maheno
Hampden
Shag Pt.
Palmerston
Waikouaiti

Providence
Chalky Inlet
Preservation Inlet
Puysegur Pt.
1699
L. Hauroko
Tuatapere
Te Waewae B.
Pahia
Orepuki
Riverton
Wallacetown
Winton
Gore
Mataura
Waipahi
Clinton
Balclutha
Kaitangata
Milton
Stirling
Waihola
L. Waihola
Green Island
St. Kilda
Dunedin
Otago Harb.
Otago Pen.
C. Saunders
Port Chalmers
Waikaka
Warrington
Blanket B.
Mosgiel

**SOUTH PACIFIC OCEAN**

Solander I.
Mt. Anglem 980
Codfish I.
Halfmoon Bay
Oban
Mason B.
Daughboy B.
Stewart Island
Paterson Inlet
Port Pegasus
Southwest C.
Ruapuke I.
Waipapa Pt.
Bluff
Bluff Harb.
Toetoes
Toetoes B.
Foveaux Strait
Invercargill
South Invercargill
Fortrose
Waikawa
Tokanui
Chaslands Mistake
Long Pt.
Nugget Pt.
Owaka
Tahakopa

Projection: Conical with two standard parallels

East from Greenwich

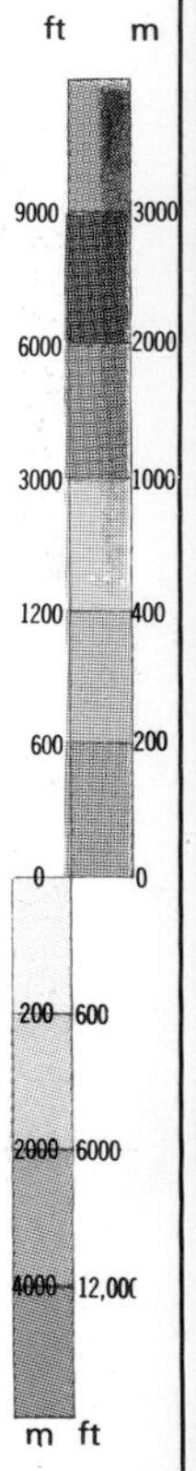

ft  m
9000  3000
6000  2000
3000  1000
1200  600
600  200
0  0
200  600
2000  6000
4000  12,000
m  ft

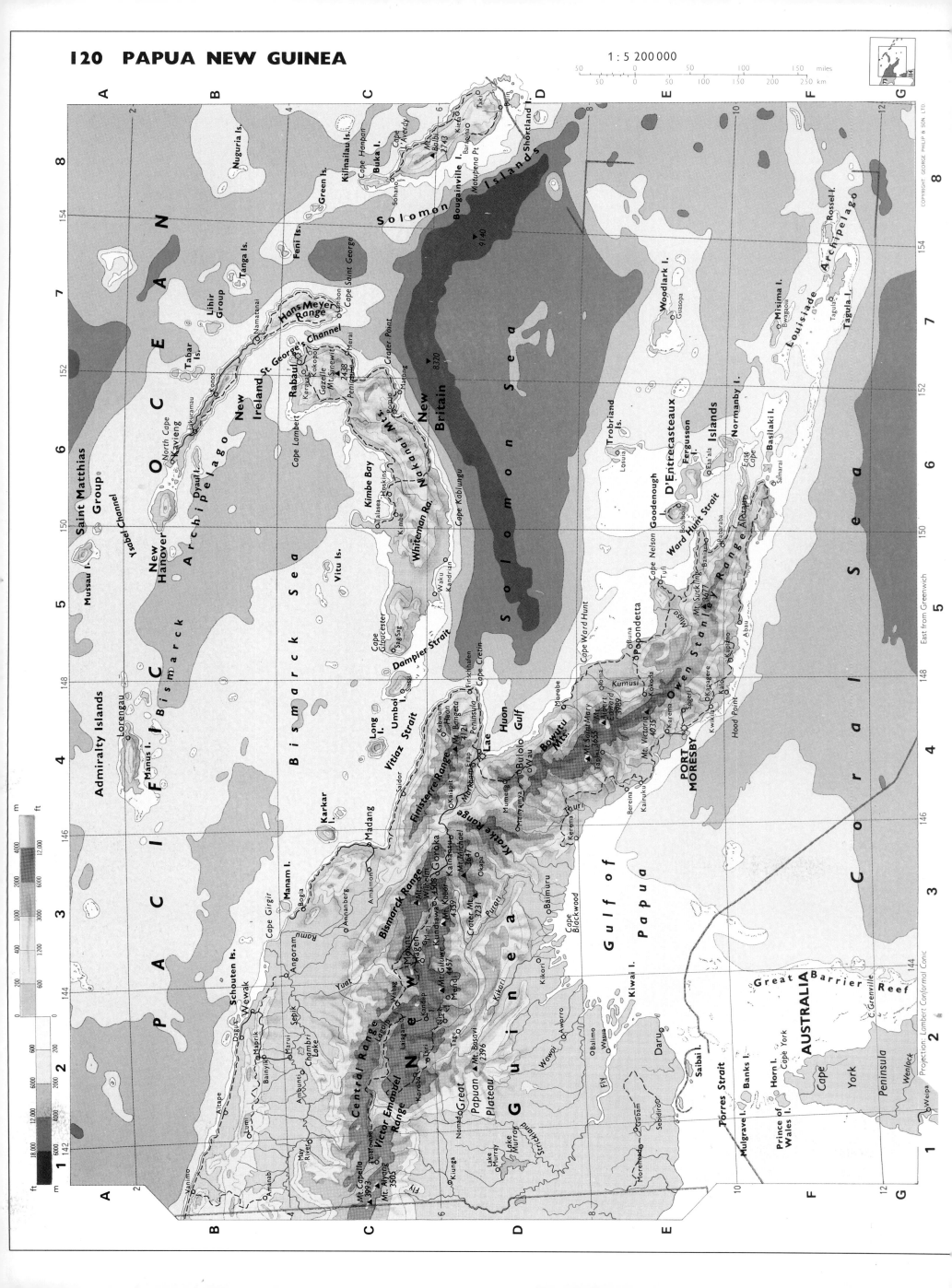

1 : 5 200 000

Projection: Lambert Conformal Conic

COPYRIGHT GEORGE PHILIP & SON, LTD.

East from Greenwich

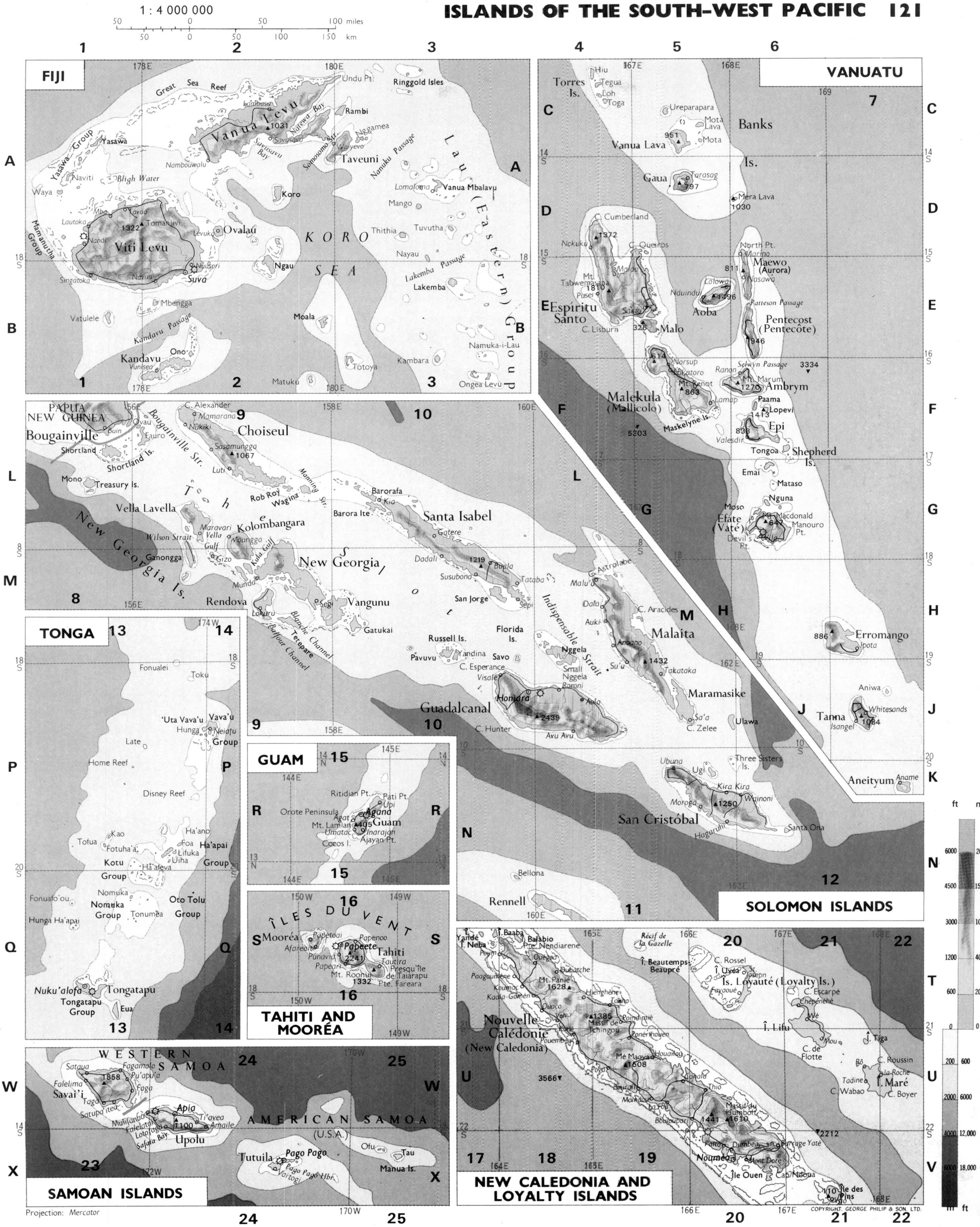

1 : 4 000 000

50 0 50 100 miles
50 0 50 100 150 km

**FIJI**

Great Sea Reef
Undu Pt.
Ringgold Isles
Vanua Levu
1031
Natewa Bay
Rambi
Nanuku Passage
Naggamea
Walyevu
Savusavu Bay
Somosomo Str.
Taveuni
Lomaloma
Vanua Mbalavu
Mango
Thithia
Tuvutha
Koro
Nayau
Lau (Eastern) Group
Yasawa Group
Naviti
Waya
Bligh Water
Nambouwalu
Mamanutha Group
Lautoka
Mba
Tavua
1322 Tomanivi
Nandi
Viti Levu
Nausori
Suva
Navua
Singatoka
Levuka
Ovalau
Ngau
KORO SEA
Lakemba Passage
Lakemba
Namuka-i-Lau
Kambara
Mbengga
Vatulele
Kandavu Passage
Kandavu
Ono
Vunisea
Moala
Totoya
Matuku
Ongea Levu

178E 180E

**VANUATU**

Hiu
Tegua
Loh
Toga
Torres Is.
Ureparapara
Mota Lava
951
Mota
Banks Is.
Vanua Lava
Gaua
797 Tarasag
Mera Lava
1030
C. Cumberland
1372 Nckulu
C. Queiros
North Pt.
C. Marina
811
Lolowa
Maewo (Aurora)
Mt. Tabwemasana
1810 Pusei
Malolo
Nduindui
1496
Aoba
Nasawa
Espiritu Santo
C. Lisburn
325 Malo
Pentecost (Pentecôte)
1946
Patteson Passage
674 Norsup
Pankatoro
3334
Mt. Renot
863 Lamap
Ranon
Mt. Marum
1270
Ambrym
Malekula (Mallicolo)
Paama
Lopevi
1413
Maskelyne Is.
5203
898
Epi
Valesdir
Tongoa
Shepherd Is.
Emai
Mataso
Nguna
Moso
Efate (Vate)
842 Mt. Macdonald
Manouro Pt.
Devil's Pt.
Erromango
886
Ipota
Aniwa
Tanna
1084 Whitesands
Isangel
Aneityum
Aname

167E 168E 169

**PAPUA NEW GUINEA**

Bougainville
C. Alexander
Mamareva
Buin
Nukiki
Bougainville Str.
9 10
Fauro Is.
Choiseul
Shortland Is.
Sasamungga
1067
Luti
Mono
Treasury Is.
Vella Lavella
Maravari
Vella Gulf
Rob Roy
Wagina
Manning Str.
Barorafa
Kia
Barora Ite
Kolombangara
Mounnga
Gatere
Santa Isabel
1219 Bugla
Dadali
Tataba
Sepi
New Georgia Is.
Ganongga
Gizo
Kula Gulf
Munda
New Georgia
San Jorge
Susubona
Rendova
Lokuru
Blanche Channel
Tetepare
Segi
Vangunu
Gatukai
Balfour Channel
Russell Is.
Yandina
Pavuvu
Savo
C. Esperance
Visale
Florida Is.
Nggela
Honiara
Guadalcanal
2439
C. Hunter
Avu Avu
Astrolabe
Malu'u
Dala
Auki
Aola
C. Aracides
Malaita
1432
Auala
Su'u
Takataka
Maramasike
Sa'a
C. Zelee
Ulawa
Indispensable Strait
Small Nggela
Baroni
Three Sisters Is.
Ubuna
Ugi
Kira Kira
Moroga
1250 Wainoni
San Cristóbal
Hogaruhi
Santa Ona
Bellona
Rennell
**SOLOMON ISLANDS** 12

156E 158E 160E 162E

**TONGA**

Fonualei
Toku
13 14
'Uta Vava'u
Vava'u Group
Hunga
Neiafu
Late
Home Reef
Disney Reef
Ha'ano
Tofua
Kao
Foa
Fotuha'a
Lifuka
Kotu Group
Uiha
Ha'apai Group
Ha'afeva
Fonuafo'ou
Nomuka Group
Tonumea
Oto Tolu Group
Hunga Ha'apai
Nuku'alofa
Tongatapu
Tongatapu Group
Eua

174W

**GUAM**

Ritidian Pt.
Pati Pt.
Upi
Orote Peninsula
Agat
Agana
Mt. Lamlam
405 Guam
Umatac
Inarajan
Cocos I.
Ajayan Pt.
15

144E 145E

**TAHITI AND MOORÉA**

ÎLES DU VENT
Mooréa
Papetoai
Papenoo
Afareaitu
Tahiti
Punavia
2241
Tautira
Papeari
Presqu'île de Taiarapu
Mt. Roohui
1332
Pte. Fareara
16

150W 149W

**NEW CALEDONIA AND LOYALTY ISLANDS**

Î. Baaba
Balabio
Yandé
Î. Neba
Poum
Nendiarene
Ouégoa
Récif de la Gazelle
20 21 22
C. Rossel
Î. Beautemps-Beaupré
Î. Uvéa
Îepn
Fayaoué
Is. Loyauté (Loyalty Is.)
Paagoumène
Koumac
Kaala-Gomén
Hienghène
Touho
Mt. Panié
1628
C. Escarpé
Chépénéhe
Î. Lifu
Voh
1385
Massif de Tchingou
Poindimié
Nouméa
Nouvelle Calédonie (New Caledonia)
Ponérihouen
Mé Maoya
1608
Houailou
Î. Mou
Î. Tiga
C. de Flotte
Poya
Bô
C. Roussin
3566
Kanala
Tadine
Î. Maré
Pouembout
Thio
C. Wabao
C. Boyer
Boulouparis
1441
Massif du Humboldt
1610
Païta
Dumbéa
2212
Nouméa
Passage Yate
Mont Dore
17 18 19
Île Ouen
Cap N'doua
Île des Pins
10

164E 165E 166E 167E 168E

**WESTERN SAMOA**

Satava
Falealima
1858
Pu'apu'a
Fagamalo
Faga
Savai'i
Taga
Satupa'itea
24 25
Apia
Mulifanua
Falelatai
Ti'avea
Amaile
1100
Lotofaga
Safata Bay
Upolu
AMERICAN SAMOA (U.S.A.)
Ofu
Tau
Manua Is.
Tutuila
Pago Pago
Pago Pago Hbr.
Vaitogi

172W 170W

**SAMOAN ISLANDS**

**NEW CALEDONIA AND LOYALTY ISLANDS**

Projection: Mercator

COPYRIGHT GEORGE PHILIP & SON LTD.

ft m
6000 2000
4500 1500
3000 1000
1200 400
600 200
0 0
200 600
2000 6000
4000 12,000
6000 18,000
m ft

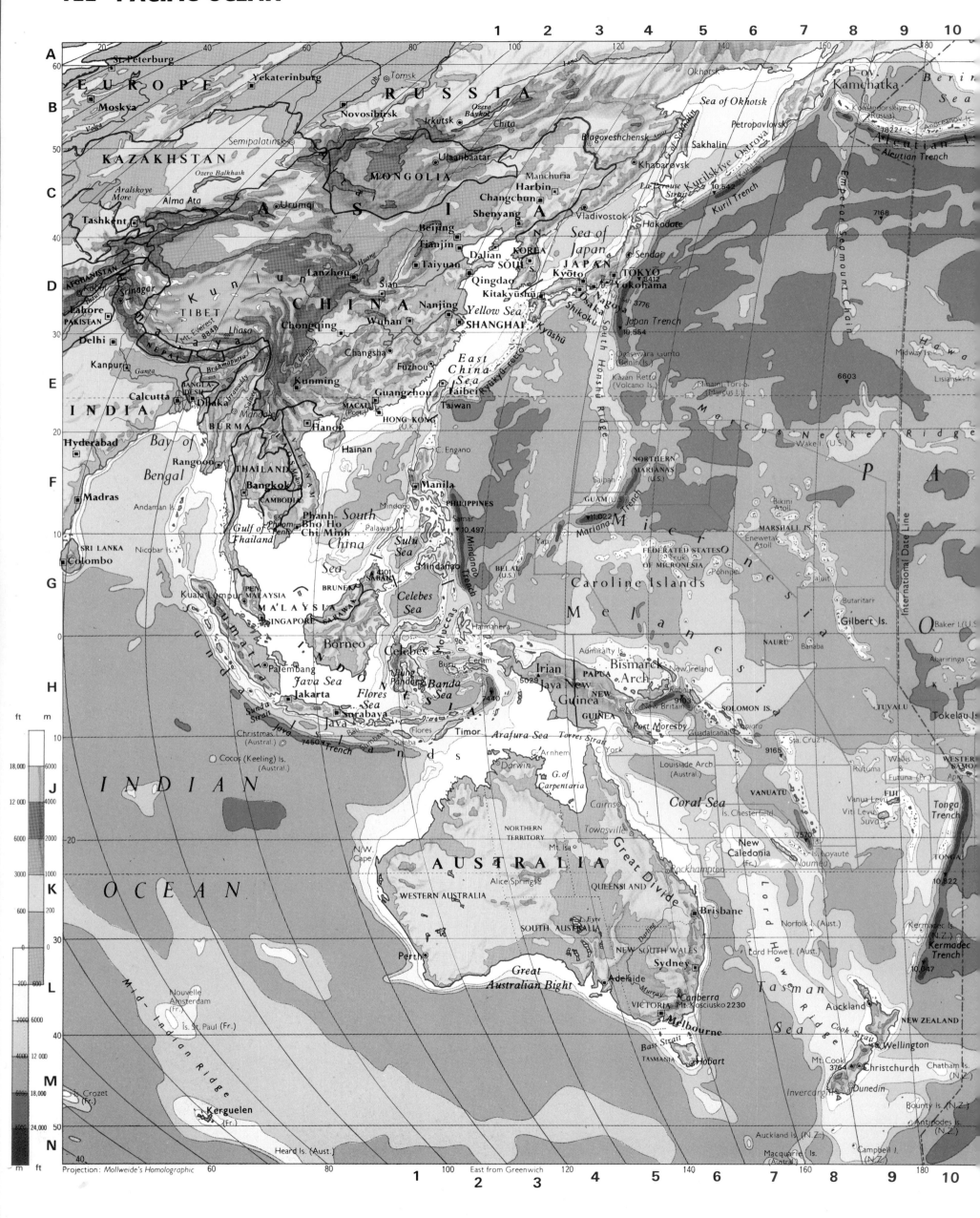

1 2 3 4 5 6 7 8 9 10

A
B
C
D
E
F
G
H
J
K
L
M
N

**St. Peterburg**
**EUROPE**
Yekaterinburg
**Moskva**
Volga
Novosibirsk
Semipalatinsk
**KAZAKHSTAN**
Ozero Balkhash
Aralskoye More
Alma Ata
Tashkent
**A**
Urumqi
Kunlun
**TIBET**
Mt. Everest 8848
Lhasa
**NEPAL**
Himalaya
Ganga
Brahmaputra
Delhi
**AFGHANISTAN**
Srinagar
**PAKISTAN**
Lahore
Kanpur
**INDIA**
Calcutta
**BANGLA-DESH**
Dhaka
Irrawaddy
**BURMA**
Hyderabad
Mandaly
**Madras**
Andaman Is.
Nicobar Is.
**SRI LANKA**
**Colombo**
Bay of Bengal
Rangoon
**THAILAND**
**Bangkok**
**CAMBODIA**
Gulf of Thailand
Phnom Penh
Phanh
Bho Ho Chi Minh
**VIETNAM**
Kuala Lumpur
**MALAYSIA**
**MALAYSIA**
SARAWAK
**SINGAPORE**
Sumatra
Borneo
Palembang
**INDONESIA**
Java Sea
**Jakarta**
Java
Surabaya
Flores Sea
Sunda Strait
Christmas I. (Austral.)
Cocos (Keeling) Is. (Austral.)

RUSSIA
Tomsk
Ob
Irkutsk
Ozero Baykal
Chita
MONGOLIA
Ulaanbaatar
Blagoveshchensk
Amur
Harbin
Changchun
Manchuria
Shenyang
Vladivostok
KOREA
Beijing
Tianjin
SOUL
S.
Dalian
Taiyuan
Qingdao
Kitakyushū
Sian
CHINA
Lanzhou
Huang
Nanjing
Yellow Sea
Chongqing
Wuhan
SHANGHAI
Changsha
East China Sea
Kunming
Fuzhou
Guangzhou
Taibei
MACAU (Port.)
HONG KONG (U.K.)
Taiwan
Hanoi
Hainan
C. Engano
South China Sea
Mindoro
Manila
PHILIPPINES
Palawan
Samar
Mindanao Trench
10.497
Sulu Sea
Mindanao
SABAH
4101
BRUNEI
Celebes Sea
BELAL (U.S.)
Celebes
Moluccas
Buru
Ceram
Halmahera
Banda Sea
Flores
Sumba
Timor
Arafura Sea
Java Trench 7460

Sea of Okhotsk
Okhotsk
P-ov. Kamchatka
Kamandorskiye O. (Russia)
Petropavlovsk
O. Sakhalin
Sakhalin
Khabarovsk
La Perouse Strait
Kurilskiye Ostrova
Kuril Trench
10.542
Hakodate
Sendai
Sea of Japan
JAPAN
TOKYO
Kyōto
Yokohama
8412
Nagoya
Shikoku
3776
Japan Trench
10.554
Kyūshū
Ryūkyū-rettō
South Honshū Ridge
Ogasawara Guntō (Benins)
Kazan Rettō (Volcano Is.)
Minami-Tori-s. (Marcus I.)
NORTHERN MARIANAS (U.S.)
Saipan
GUAM (U.S.)
10.022
Mariana Trench
Yap
FEDERATED STATES OF MICRONESIA
Pohnpei
Caroline Islands
Admiralty Is.
New Ireland
Bismarck Arch.
New Britain
Irian Jaya
PAPUA NEW GUINEA
5029
Port Moresby
9103
SOLOMON IS.
Guadalcanal
Torres Strait
C. York
G. of Carpentaria
C. Arnhem
Darwin
NORTHERN TERRITORY
N.W. Cape
WESTERN AUSTRALIA
Perth
Alice Springs
Mt. Isa
SOUTH AUSTRALIA
L. Eyre
AUSTRALIA
Cairns
Townsville
Great Divide
Rockhampton
QUEENSLAND
Brisbane
NEW SOUTH WALES
Darling
Murray
Sydney
Canberra
Mt. Kosciusko 2230
VICTORIA
Adelaide
Great Australian Bight
Melbourne
Bass Strait
TASMANIA
Hobart

Aleutian Trench
Emperor Seamount Chain
7168
Midway Is.
Hawaii
6603
Lisianski I.
Wake I. (U.S.)
Marcus Necker Ridge
PACIFIC
Bikini Atoll
MARSHALL IS.
Enewetak Atoll
Jaluit
NAURU
Banaba
Butaritarr
Gilbert Is.
Baker I. (U.S.)
Abariringa
Micronesia
Melanesia
TUVALU
Tokelau Is.
Santa Cruz Is.
9165
Rotuma
Walis & Futuna (Fr.)
WESTERN SAMOA
Louisiade Arch. (Austral.)
VANUATU
FIJI
Vanua Levu
Viti Levu
Suva
Coral Sea
Is. Chesterfield
New Caledonia (Fr.)
7570
Nouméa
Is. Loyauté
Norfolk I. (Aust.)
Lord Howe I. (Aust.)
Lord Howe Ridge
Tonga Trench
10.822
TONGA
Kermadec Is. (N.Z.)
Kermadec Trench
10.047
Tasman Sea
Norfolk Ridge
Auckland
Cook Strait
NEW ZEALAND
Wellington
Chatham Is. (N.Z.)
Mt. Cook 3764
Christchurch
Dunedin
Invercargill
Bounty Is. (N.Z.)
Antipodes Is. (N.Z.)
Auckland Is. (N.Z.)
Macquarie Is. (Austral.)
Campbell I. (N.Z.)

INDIAN
OCEAN
Mid-Indian Ridge
Nouvelle Amsterdam (Fr.)
Îs. St. Paul (Fr.)
Îs. Crozet (Fr.)
Kerguelen (Fr.)
Heard Is. (Aust.)

International Date Line

ft    m
18,000  6000
12 000  4000
6000   2000
3000   1000
600    200
0      0
200    600
2000   6000
4000   12 000
6000   18,000
m      ft

Projection: Mollweide's Homolographic

20 40 60 80 100 120 140 160 180

East from Greenwich

1 2 3 4 5 6 7 8 9 10

1 : 43 200 000

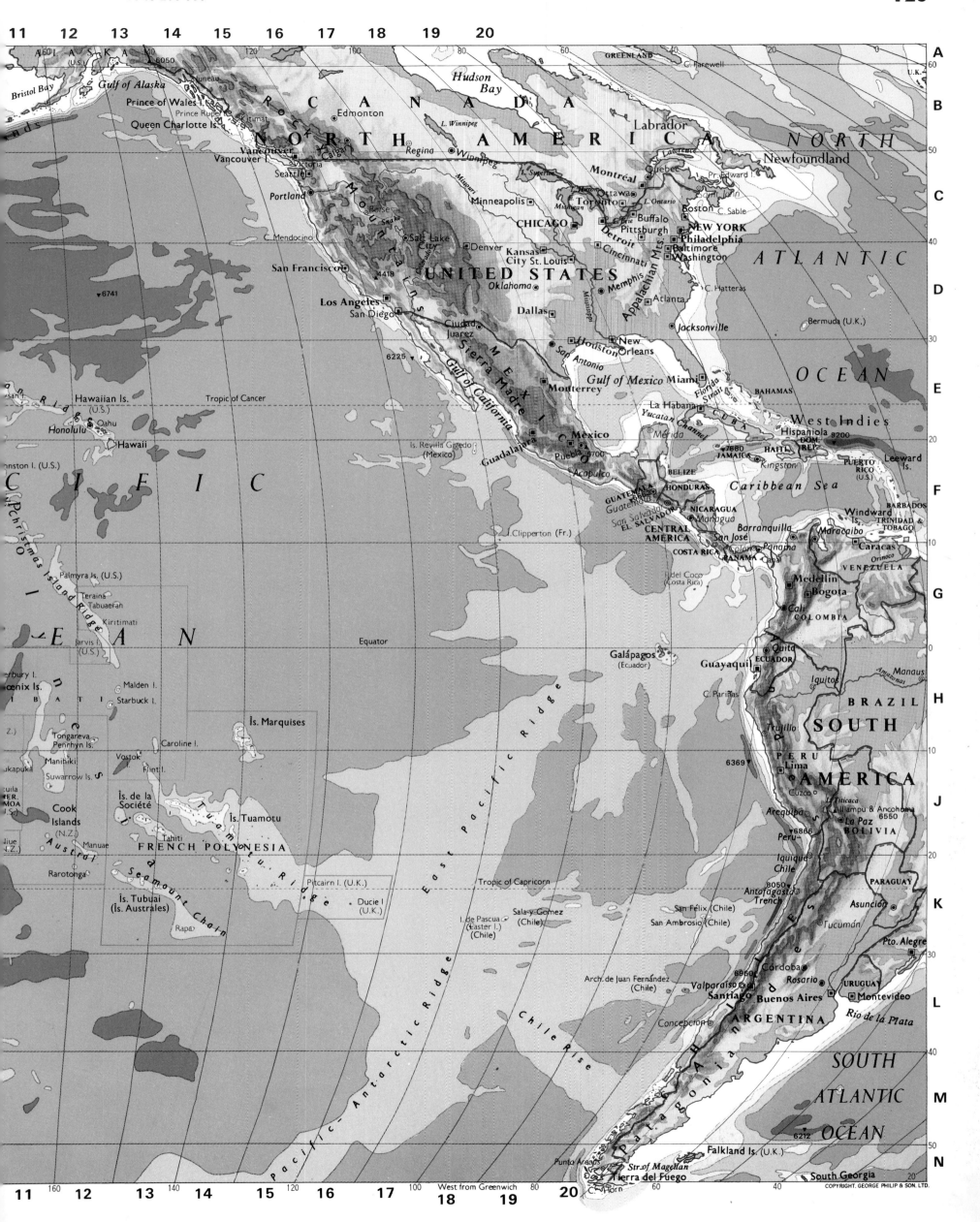

**11   12   13   14   15   16   17   18   19   20**

A L A S K A (U.S.)   6050   120   100   80   60   GREENLAND   40   C. Farewell   20   U.K.   A

Bristol Bay   Gulf of Alaska   Juneau   C A N A D A   NORTH   60   B

Prince of Wales I.   Edmonton   L. Winnipeg   Labrador   Newfoundland   50

Prince Rupert   Kitimat   NORTH AMERICA   Pr. Edward I.   C

Queen Charlotte Is.   Vancouver   Calgary   Regina   Winnipeg   L. Superior   Montréal   Québec

Vancouver I.   Seattle   Victoria   Boise   L. Michigan   Ottawa   Toronto   L. Ontario   Boston   St. John   C. Sable   ATLANTIC   40

Portland   Snake   Minneapolis   CHICAGO   Erie   Buffalo   NEW YORK

C. Mendocino   Salt Lake City   Denver   Kansas City   St. Louis   Detroit   Pittsburgh   Philadelphia   Baltimore   Washington   D

San Francisco   4418   UNITED STATES   Memphis   Cincinnati   Appalachian Mts.   C. Hatteras   Bermuda (U.K.)   30

Los Angeles   Oklahoma   Dallas   Atlanta   Jacksonville

San Diego   Ciudad Juárez   6225   San Antonio   Houston   New Orleans   OCEAN   E

Hawaiian Is. (U.S.)   Tropic of Cancer   Sierra Madre   Monterrey   Gulf of Mexico   Miami   Florida Strait   BAHAMAS

Oahu   Gulf of California   La Habana   CUBA   West Indies

Honolulu   Hawaii   México   Guadalajara   Mérida   Yucatán Channel   Hispaniola   DOM. REP.   9200   20

Is. Revilla Gigedo (Mexico)   Puebla   5700   HAITI   7680   JAMAICA   PUERTO RICO (U.S.)   Leeward Is.   F

P A C I F I C   Acapulco   BELIZE   Kingston   Caribbean Sea   BARBADOS

Christmas Island Ridge   GUATEMALA   Guatemala   HONDURAS   WINDWARD   TRINIDAD & TOBAGO

J. Clipperton (Fr.)   San Salvador   NICARAGUA   Managua   Barranquilla   Windward Is.

O C E A N   EL SALVADOR   CENTRAL   San José   Panamá   Maracaibo   Caracas   10

COSTA RICA   AMERICA   PANAMA   VENEZUELA   Orinoco   G

Palmyra Is. (U.S.)   I. del Coco (Costa Rica)   Medellín   Bogotá

Teraina   Tabuaeran   Kiritimati   Cali   COLOMBIA

Jarvis I. (U.S.)   Equator   Galápagos (Ecuador)   Quito   Ecuador   Manaus   0

Malden I.   Guayaquil   Iquitos   Amazonas

Phoenix Is.   Starbuck I.   C. Pariñas   BRAZIL   H

Îs. Marquises   Trujillo   SOUTH

Tongareva   Penrhyn Is.   Caroline I.   6369   PERU   Lima   AMERICA   10

Manihiki   Vostok   Flint I.   Cuzco   L. Titicaca

Pukapuka   Suwarrow Is.   Îs. de la Société   Îs. Tuamotu   Arequipa   Illampu & Ancohuma   6550   La Paz   BOLIVIA   J

SAMOA   Cook Islands (N.Z.)   Tahiti   6866   Perú

Niue (N.Z.)   Manuae   FRENCH POLYNESIA   Iquique   Chile   20

Rarotonga   Austral   Seamount Chain   Tropic of Capricorn   Antofagasta   8050   Trench   PARAGUAY

Pitcairn I. (U.K.)   San Félix (Chile)   Asunción   K

Îs. Tubuai (Îs. Australes)   Ducie I. (U.K.)   I. de Pascua (Easter I.) (Chile)   Sala-y-Gomez (Chile)   San Ambrosio (Chile)   Tucumán

Rapa   East Pacific Ridge   Pto. Alegre   30

Arch. de Juan Fernández (Chile)   Córdoba   Rosario   URUGUAY

Valparaíso   6960   L

Pacific - Antarctic Ridge   Santiago   Buenos Aires   Montevideo

Chile Rise   Concepción   ARGENTINA   Río de la Plata

Patagonia   Andes   SOUTH   40

ATLANTIC   M

6212   OCEAN

Punta Arenas   Str. of Magellan   Falkland Is. (U.K.)   50

West from Greenwich   C. Horn   Tierra del Fuego   South Georgia   20   N

**11   160   12   13   140   14   15   120   16   17   100   18   19   20   80   60   40**

COPYRIGHT. GEORGE PHILIP & SON LTD.

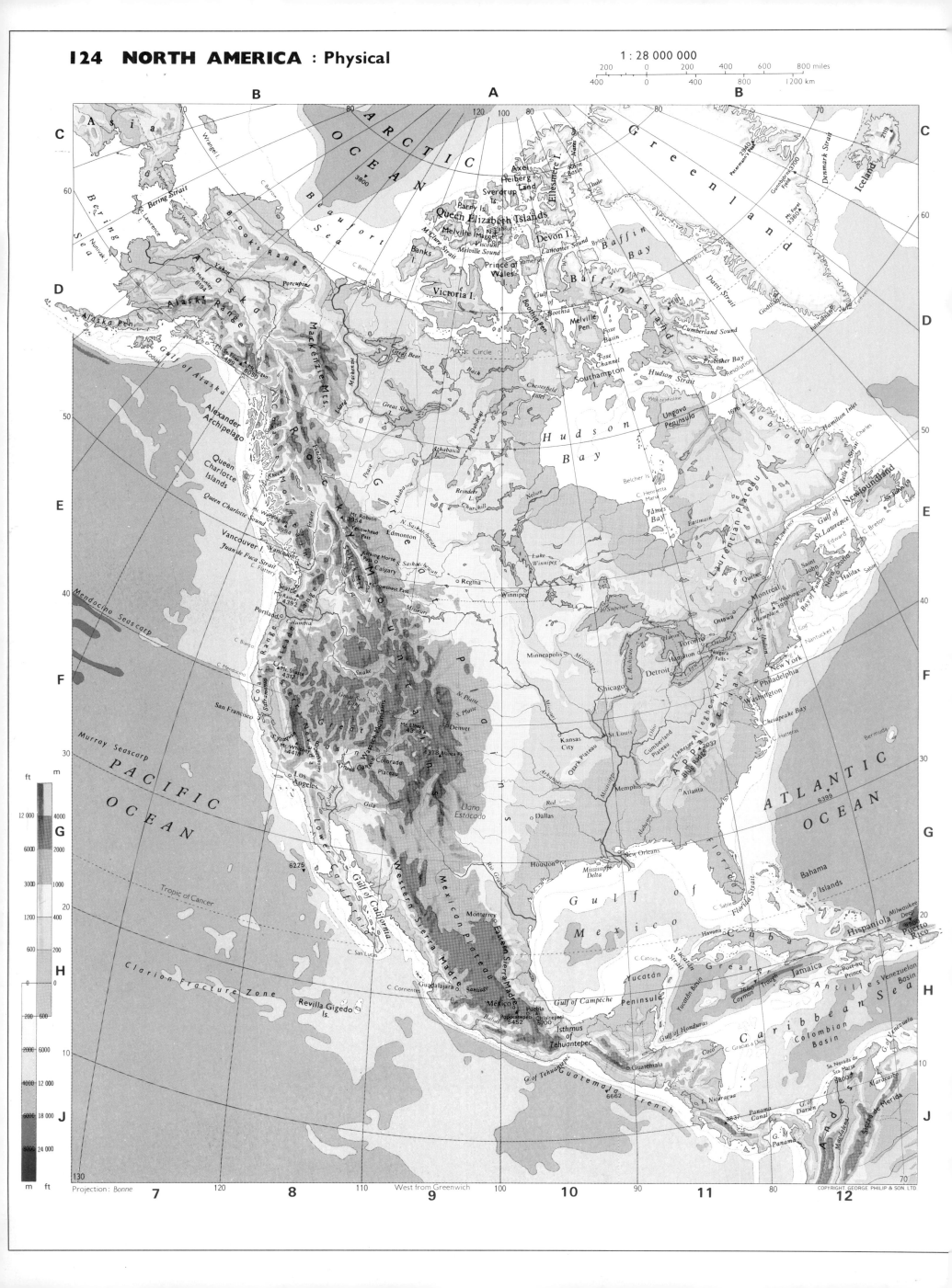

1 : 28 000 000

Projection: Bonne

West from Greenwich

COPYRIGHT. GEORGE PHILIP & SON. LTD

1 : 28 000 000

200 0 200 400 600 800 miles
400 0 400 800 1200 km

**ARCTIC OCEAN**

**GREENLAND (Denmark)**

RUSSIA

Bering Strait

Bering Sea

Beaufort Sea

Queen Elizabeth Is.

Ellesmere I.

Baffin Bay

Denmark Strait

ICELAND

Reykjavik

Arctic Circle

ALASKA

Yukon

Fairbanks

Anchorage

Gulf of Alaska

Porcupine

INUVIK

Victoria I.

KITIKMEOT

BAFFIN

Baffin I.

Goldhåb

C. Farvel

YUKON TERRITORY

Whitehorse

Mackenzie

Great Bear L.

Back

NORTHWEST TERRITORIES

Hudson Strait

NEWFOUNDLAND

FORT SMITH

Yellowknife

Great Slave L.

Liard

Finlay

Dubawnt

KEEWATIN

Hudson Bay

Labrador

Eastmain

BRITISH COLUMBIA

Skeena

Peace

L. Athabasca

Churchill

Nelson

Fraser

ALBERTA

Edmonton

N. Saskatchewan

SASKATCHEWAN

MANITOBA

QUÉBEC

St. Lawrence

SPM

Calgary

S. Saskatchewan

Regina

L. Winnipeg

ONTARIO

Québec

NEW BRUNSWICK

PR. EDWARD

Charlottetown

NOVA SCOTIA

Halifax

Victoria

Vancouver

WASHINGTON

Seattle

Olympia

Winnipeg

L. Superior

Montréal

MAINE

Fredericton

Montpelier

Augusta

Portland

Columbia

Salem

Missouri

NORTH DAKOTA

Bismarck

MINNESOTA

L. Huron

Toronto

L. Ontario

Buffalo

Ottawa

VER. N.H.

Concord

OREGON

MONTANA

Helena

Boise

IDAHO

Snake

Cheyenne

WYOMING

SOUTH DAKOTA

Pierre

Minneapolis

St. Paul

WISCONSIN

Madison

Milwaukee

MICHIGAN

Lansing

Detroit

Cleveland

L. Erie

PENNSYLVANIA

Pittsburgh

Harrisburg

Albany

NEW YORK

MASS.

Boston

Hartford

Providence R.I.

N.J.

Philadelphia

NEW YORK

Sacramento

Carson City

Salt Lake City

N. Platte

NEBRASKA

Lincoln

Des Moines

IOWA

Chicago

ILLINOIS

INDIANA

Columbus

OHIO

Cincinnati

Indianapolis

WEST VIRGINIA

Frankfort

Charleston

Washington D.C.

M. Dover

D.C.

VIRGINIA

Richmond

San Francisco

CALIFORNIA

San Jose

NEVADA

UTAH

Denver

COLORADO

Arkansas

KANSAS

Topeka

Kansas City

MISSOURI

St. Louis

Springfield

Jefferson City

KENTUCKY

Nashville

TENNESSEE

Tennessee

NORTH CAROLINA

Raleigh

Las Vegas

Columbia

Bermuda (Br.)

LOS ANGELES

Santa Fe

ARIZONA

Phoenix

NEW MEXICO

Albuquerque

Oklahoma City

OKLAHOMA

ARKANSAS

Little Rock

Memphis

Mississippi

Birmingham

Alabama

Atlanta

GEORGIA

SOUTH CAROLINA

San Diego

Colorado

Tucson

Gila

El Paso

Red River

Dallas

TEXAS

Austin

LOUISIANA

Baton Rouge

Jackson

MISSISSIPPI

Montgomery

ALABAMA

Tallahassee

FLORIDA

Jacksonville

ATLANTIC OCEAN

PACIFIC OCEAN

Rio Grande

Houston

New Orleans

Tampa

Miami

Nassau

BAHAMAS

Florida

Turks & Caicos (Br.)

Tropic of Cancer

MEXICO

Gulf of Mexico

Monterrey

Havana

CUBA

C. Sable

Cayman Is. (Br.)

DOMINICAN REP.

San Juan

PUERTO RICO

HAITI

Port-au-Prince

Santo Domingo

JAMAICA

Kingston

Guadalajara

Revilla Gigedo Is. (Mexico)

MEXICO

BELIZE

Belmopan

Caribbean Sea

GUATEMALA

HONDURAS

Guatemala

Tegucigalpa

Maracaibo

San Salvador

EL SALVADOR

NICARAGUA

L. Nicaragua

Barranquilla

VENEZUELA

Managua

Panama

PANAMA

COSTA RICA

San José

SOUTH AMERICA

Medellín

COLOMBIA

Bogotá

West from Greenwich

Projection: Bonne

**7** Washington Capital Cities

⊙ U.S. State Capitals and Canadian Provincial Capitals

| C | CONNECTICUT | N.H. | NEW HAMPSHIRE |
| D. | DELAWARE | N.J. | NEW JERSEY |
| D.C. | DISTRICT OF COLUMBIA | R.I. | RHODE ISLAND |
| M. | MARYLAND | VER. | VERMONT |
| MASS. | MASSACHUSETTS | SPM | ST. PIERRE ET MIQUELON |

ALASKA
1 : 24 000 000

Projection: Bonne

MANITOBA

HUDSON BAY

N.W. TERRITORIES

North Belcher Is.
Baker's Dozen Is.
Kugong
Belcher
Islands
Tukarak I.
Innetalling I.
Flaherty
Merry I.
C. Henrietta Maria

JAMES BAY

Akimiski I.
North Twin I.
South Twin I.
Weston I.
Charlton
Trodely I.

ONTARIO

QUÉBEC

Lake Nipigon
Thunder Bay

LAKE SUPERIOR

Duluth
Superior
Apostle Is.
Isle Royale

Timmins
Kirkland Lake
Kapuskasing
Cochrane

Sudbury
North Bay

LAKE HURON

Sault Ste. Marie

Manitoulin I.

Georgian Bay
Parry Sound

LAKE MICHIGAN

WISCONSIN

MILWAUKEE
Green Bay
CHICAGO
Grand Rapids
Flint
DETROIT
Windsor

MICHIGAN

OTTAWA
Trois-Rivières
Shawinigan
MONTRÉAL

TORONTO
HAMILTON
St. Catharines
Niagara Falls
BUFFALO
Rochester

LAKE ONTARIO

LAKE ERIE

CLEVELAND
Toledo

INDIANA   OHIO   PENNSYLVANIA

NEW YORK
Adirondack Mountains
Syracuse
Albany

Lambert's Equivalent Azimuthal

1 : 5 600 000

50  0  50  100  150  200 miles
50  0  50  100  150  200  250  300 km

**QUEBEC**
**LABRADOR**
**COAST OF** ... **NEWFOUNDLAND**
**NEW BRUNSWICK**
**NOVA SCOTIA**
**PRINCE EDWARD ISLAND**
**MAINE**
**NEWFOUNDLAND**

GULF OF ST. LAWRENCE
Cabot Strait
Cape Breton Island
Avalon Peninsula
SAINT-PIERRE ET MIQUELON (Fr.)
Str. of Belle Isle
Belle I.
Dét. de Jacques-Cartier
I. d'Anticosti
Jupiter
Heath Pt.
Î. Brion
Îs. de la Madeleine (Quebec)
Sable I. (Nova Scotia)

ATLANTIC OCEAN

Kaniapiskau Lake
Manicouagan
Labrador City
Happy Valley-Goose Bay
Churchill Falls
Smallwood Res.
Corner Brook
Gros Morne Nat. Park
St. John's
Gander
Grand Falls
Sept-Îles
Baie-Comeau
Gaspé
Pén. de Gaspé
Mts. Chic-Chocs
Rimouski
Rivière-du-Loup
Edmundston
Fredericton
Saint John
Moncton
Charlottetown
Summerside
Sydney
Glace Bay
New Waterford
Sydney Mines
Truro
Halifax
Dartmouth
New Glasgow
Yarmouth
Lunenburg
QUÉBEC
Chicoutimi
Jonquière
Sherbrooke
Thetford Mines
Asbestos
Bangor
Waterville
Augusta
Lewiston
Auburn
Portland
BOSTON
Brockton
Portsmouth
Manchester
Nashua
Lowell
Lynn
Rockland
Bath
Brunswick
Biddeford
Saco
Sanford
Dover
Concord

West from Greenwich

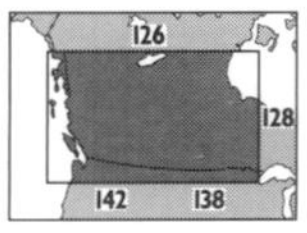

PACIFIC OCEAN

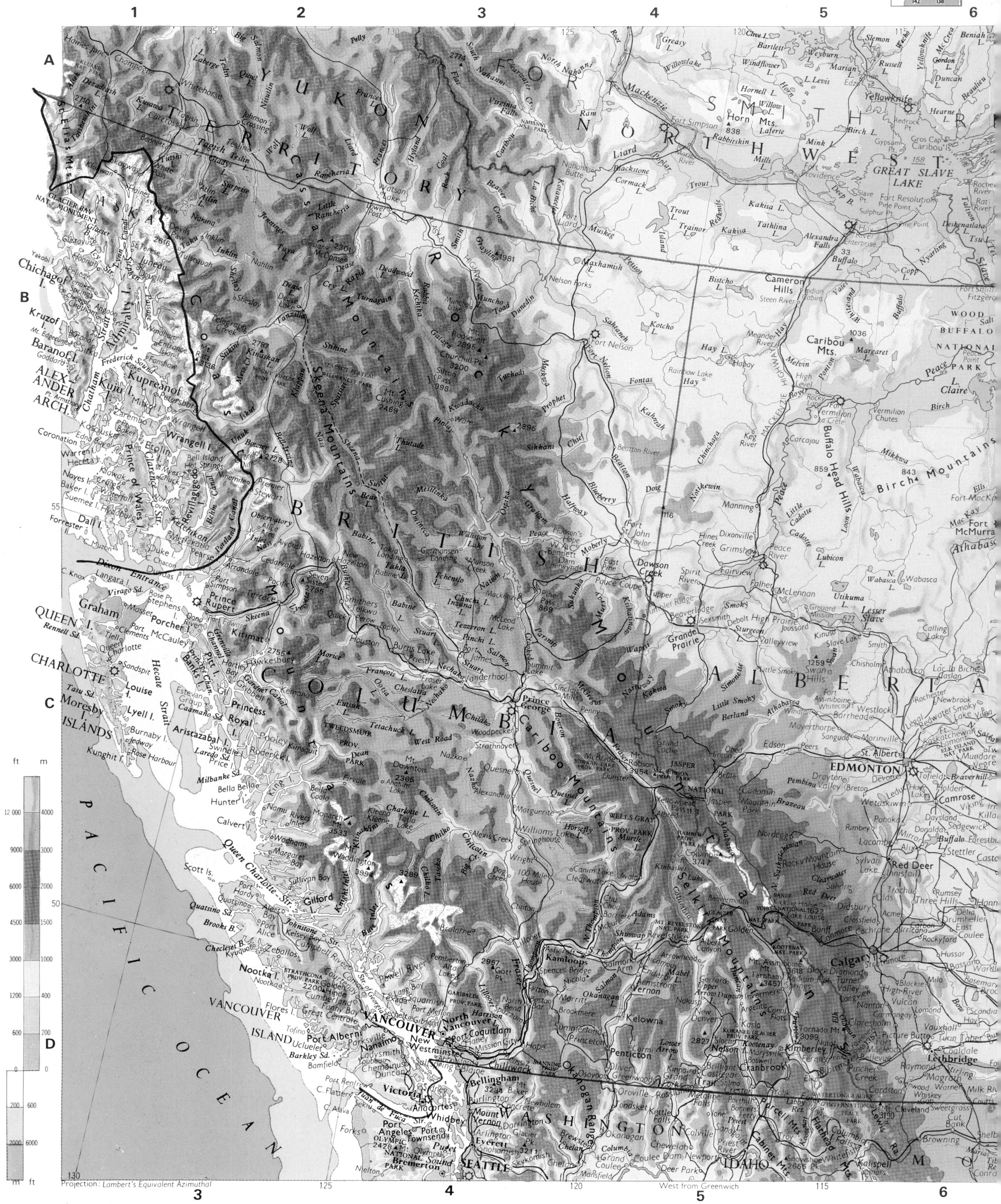

YUKON TERRITORY

NORTHWEST TERRITORIES

BRITISH COLUMBIA

ALBERTA

ALASKA

WASHINGTON

IDAHO

GREAT SLAVE LAKE

WOOD BUFFALO NATIONAL PARK

QUEEN CHARLOTTE ISLANDS

VANCOUVER ISLAND

ALEXANDER ARCH.

Birch Mountains

Cariboo Mountains

Selkirk Mountains

Rocky Mountains

Skeena Mountains

**Cities and towns:** Yellowknife, Fort Simpson, Fort Nelson, Fort St. John, Dawson Creek, Peace River, Grande Prairie, Edmonton, Red Deer, Calgary, Lethbridge, Camrose, Prince George, Prince Rupert, Kitimat, Kamloops, Kelowna, Penticton, Vernon, Nelson, Cranbrook, Kimberley, VANCOUVER, New Westminster, Victoria, Nanaimo, Port Alberni, Whitehorse, Juneau, SEATTLE, Bellingham, Everett, Bremerton

Juan de Fuca Strait

Hecate Strait

Dixon Entrance

ft   m
12 000  4000
9000   3000
6000   2000
4500   1500
3000   1000
1200   400
600    200
0      0
200    600
2000   6000
m   ft

Projection: Lambert's Equivalent Azimuthal

West from Greenwich

1 : 5 600 000

50  0  50  100  150  200 miles

50  0  50  100  150  200  250  300  km

7    8    9    10    11

A

B

C

D

TERRITORIES    KEEWATIN    REGION

HUDSON

BAY

SASKATCHEWAN

MANITOBA

ONTARIO

Lake Athabasca

Lake Winnipeg

LAKE WINNIPEG

Cree L.

Reindeer L.

Wollaston L.

Lac la Ronge

Saskatoon

Regina

Moose Jaw

Prince Albert

North Battleford

Swift Current

Medicine Hat

Yorkton

Brandon

WINNIPEG

Portage la Prairie

Selkirk

Dauphin

Flin Flon

Churchill

C. Churchill

NORTH DAKOTA

MINNESOTA

MONTANA

Duluth

Minot

Grand Forks

Williston

Bemidji

Hibbing

Grand Rapids

Virginia

International Falls

Fort Frances

Kenora

COPYRIGHT GEORGE PHILIP & SON LTD

110    105    100    95

7    8    9    10

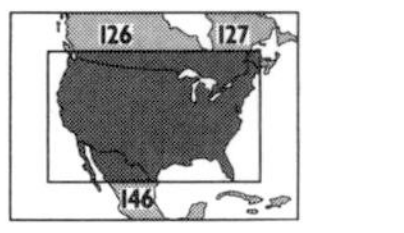

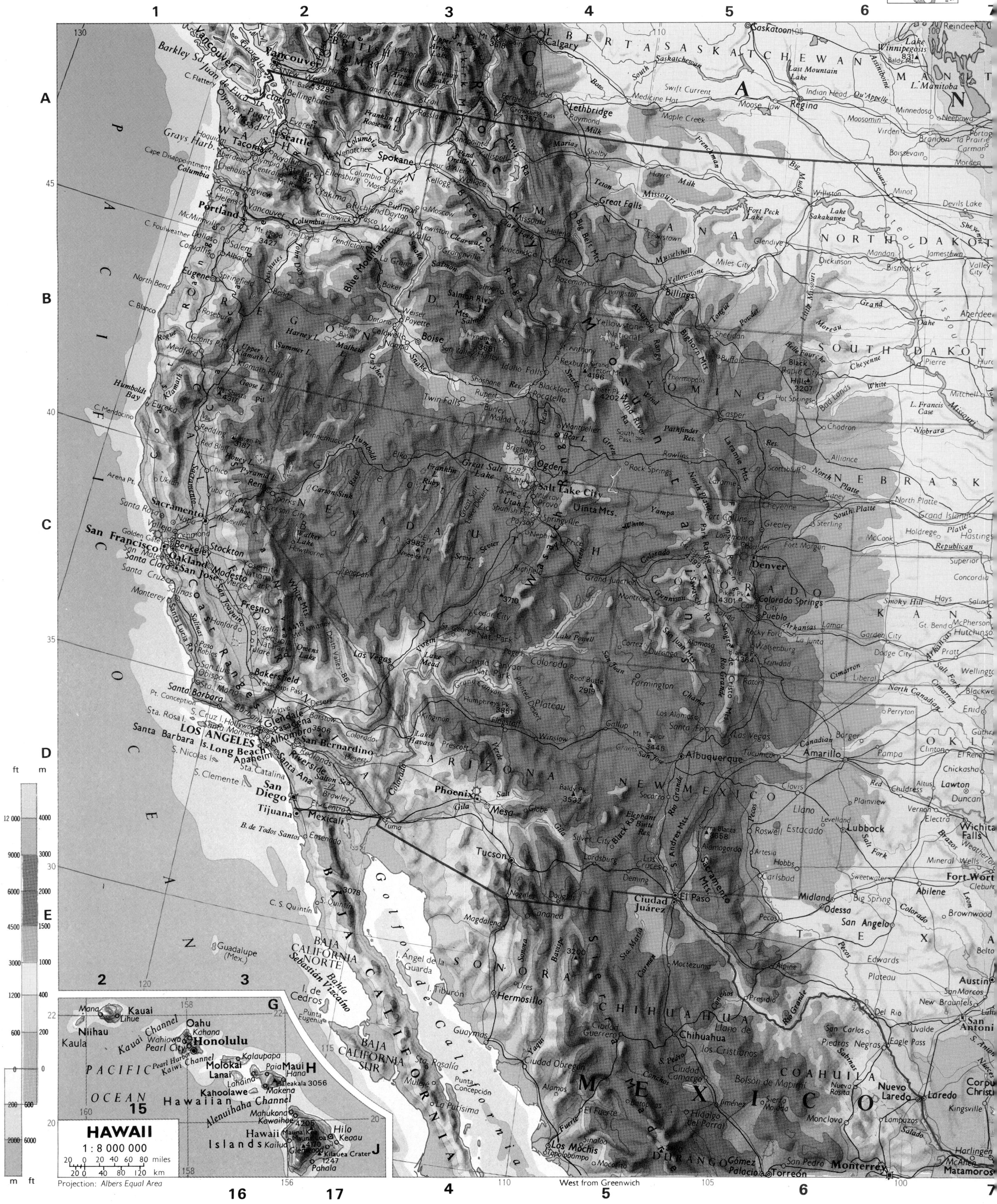

A B C D E F G H J

1 2 3 4 5 6 7

BRITISH COLUMBIA • ALBERTA • SASKATCHEWAN • MANITOBA

Vancouver I. • Vancouver • Victoria • Bellingham

WASHINGTON • Seattle • Tacoma • Olympia • Everett • Spokane

Calgary • Lethbridge • Regina • Moose Jaw • Saskatoon

Portland • Salem • Eugene • OREGON

Boise • IDAHO • MONTANA • Great Falls • Helena • Billings

NORTH DAKOTA • Bismarck • SOUTH DAKOTA • Pierre

Sacramento • San Francisco • Oakland • San Jose • Stockton • Modesto • Fresno • NEVADA • Reno • Carson Sink

UTAH • Salt Lake City • Ogden • Provo • WYOMING • Casper • Cheyenne

Denver • Colorado Springs • Pueblo • COLORADO • NEBRASKA • KANSAS

Las Vegas • Bakersfield • Santa Barbara • LOS ANGELES • Long Beach • Pasadena • San Bernardino • Riverside • Santa Ana • Anaheim

San Diego • Tijuana • Mexicali

ARIZONA • Phoenix • Mesa • Tucson • NEW MEXICO • Albuquerque • Santa Fe • Amarillo • Lubbock

BAJA CALIFORNIA NORTE • SONORA • Hermosillo • Guaymas

El Paso • Ciudad Juárez • Chihuahua • CHIHUAHUA • COAHUILA • TEXAS • Odessa • San Angelo • Abilene • Fort Worth • Austin • San Antonio

MEXICO • DURANGO • Torreón • Monterrey • Nuevo Laredo • Laredo • Corpus Christi • Matamoros

PACIFIC OCEAN • BAJA CALIFORNIA SUR • Golfo de California

West from Greenwich

ft m
12 000  4000
9000  3000
6000  2000
4500  1500
3000  1000
1500  400
600  200
0
600  200
2000  6000
m ft

2 3

HAWAII
1 : 8 000 000
Projection: Albers Equal Area

Kauai • Niihau • Oahu • Honolulu • Pearl City • Molokai • Lanai • Maui • Kahoolawe • Hawaii • Hilo • HAWAIIAN Islands • PACIFIC OCEAN

20 0 20 40 60 80 miles
20 0 20 40 60 80 120 km

16 17

1 : 9 600 000

50  0  50  100  150  200  250  300 miles
50  0  50  100 150 200 250 300 350 400 450 km

ATLANTIC OCEAN

GULF OF MEXICO

BAHAMAS

MINNESOTA · WISCONSIN · MICHIGAN · ILLINOIS · INDIANA · OHIO · KENTUCKY · TENNESSEE · MISSISSIPPI · ALABAMA · GEORGIA · LOUISIANA · FLORIDA · ARKANSAS · MISSOURI · MAINE · PENNSYLVANIA · WEST VIRGINIA · VIRGINIA · NORTH CAROLINA · SOUTH CAROLINA · NEW JERSEY · MARYLAND · NEW BRUNSWICK

Lake Winnipeg · Lake Superior · Lake Michigan · Lake Huron · Lake Erie · Lake Ontario

Winnipeg · Lake of the Woods · Duluth · Minneapolis · St. Paul · Thunder Bay · Sault Ste. Marie · Toronto · Montreal · Ottawa · Quebec · Buffalo · Rochester · Syracuse · Albany · Boston · New York · Philadelphia · Baltimore · Washington D.C. · Richmond · Norfolk · Pittsburgh · Cleveland · Detroit · Chicago · Milwaukee · Grand Rapids · Indianapolis · Cincinnati · Columbus · Dayton · St. Louis · Kansas City · Memphis · Nashville · Louisville · Knoxville · Chattanooga · Atlanta · Birmingham · Montgomery · Jackson · New Orleans · Baton Rouge · Houston · Dallas · Galveston · Shreveport · Little Rock · Tulsa · Oklahoma City · Wichita · Des Moines · Omaha · Sioux City · Topeka · Charlotte · Columbia · Savannah · Jacksonville · Orlando · Tampa · St. Petersburg · Miami · West Palm Beach

COPYRIGHT. GEORGE PHILIP & SON, LTD.

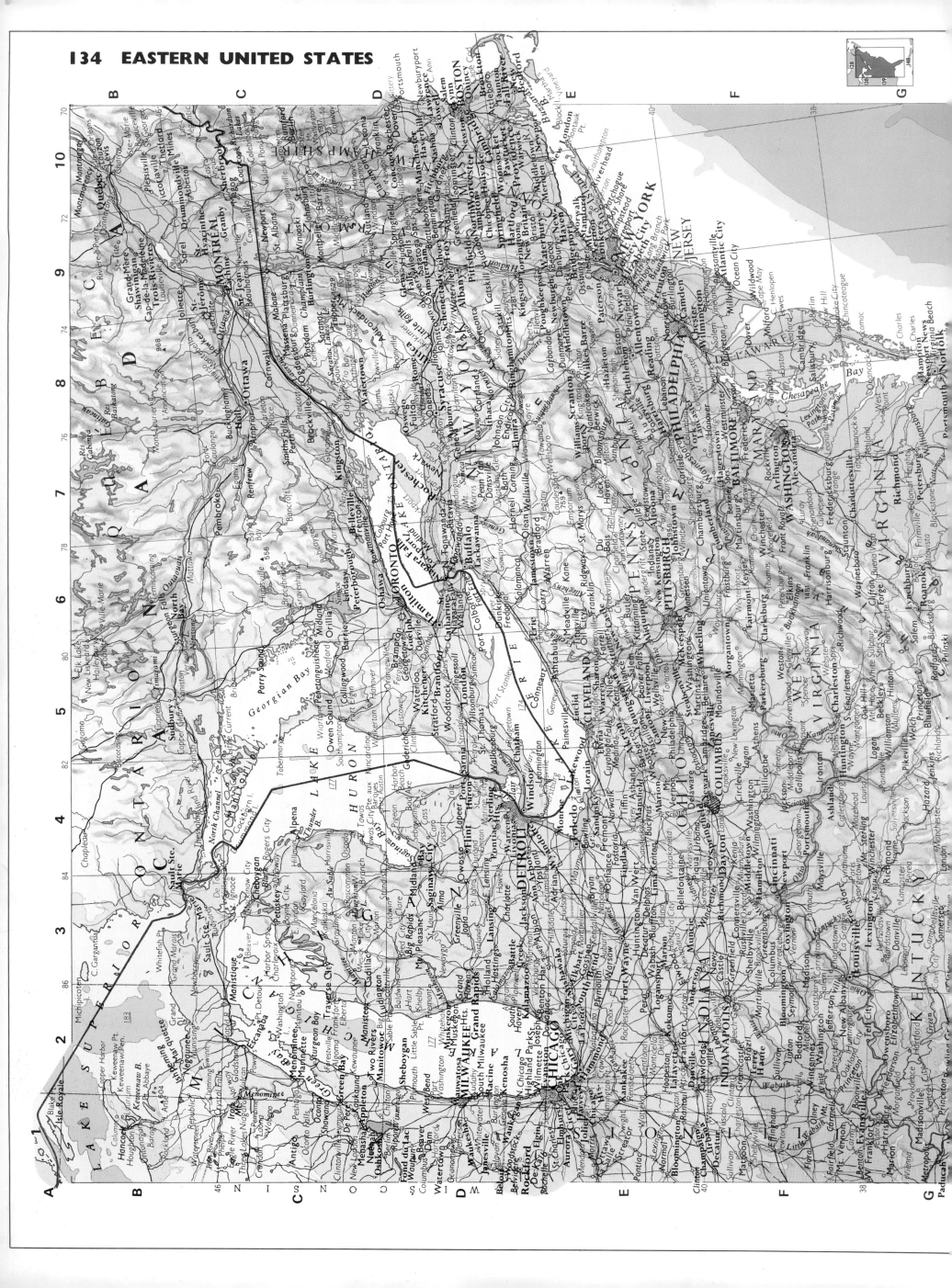

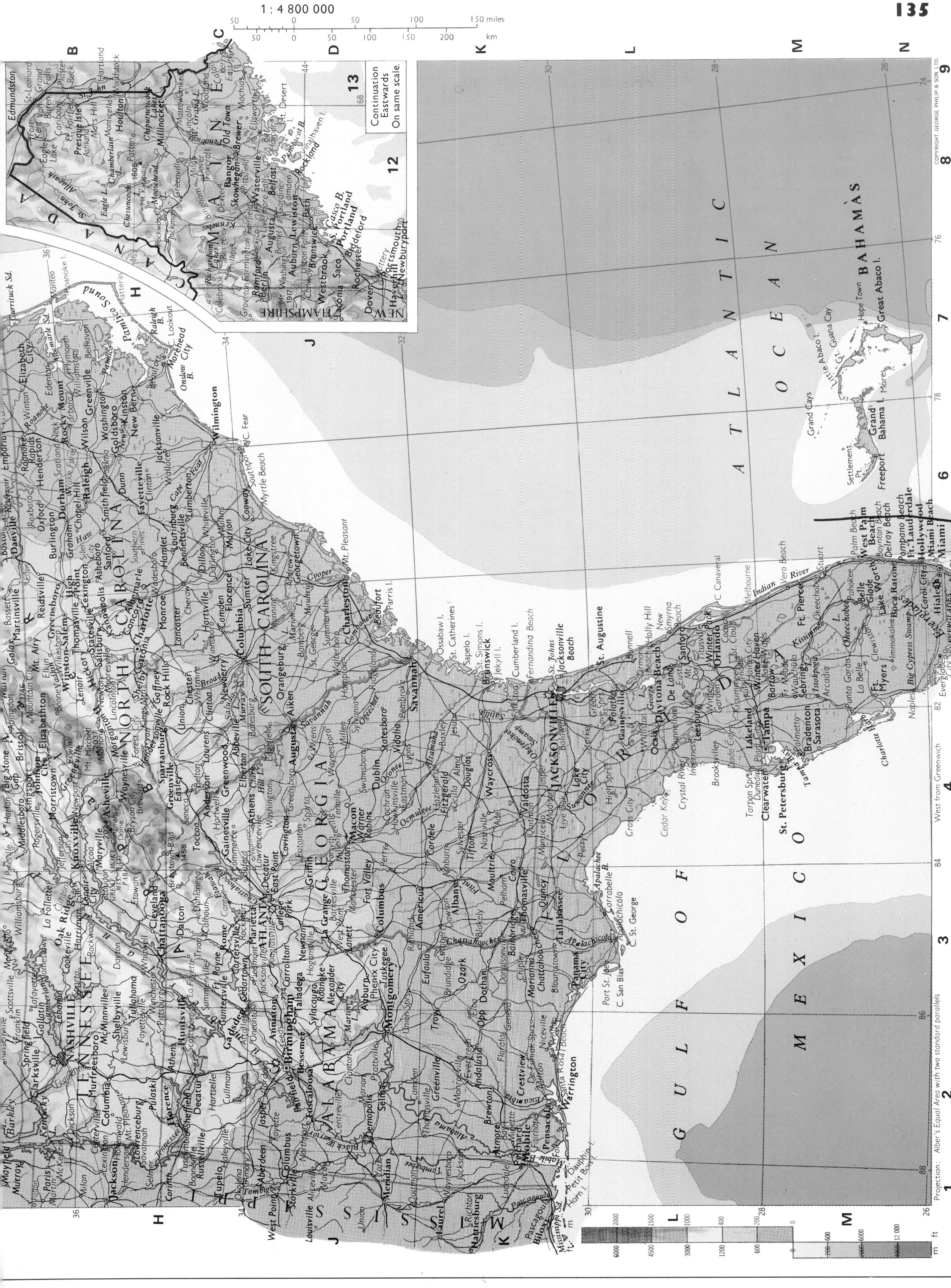

1 : 4 800 000
50 0 50 100 150 miles
50 0 50 100 150 200 km
Continuation Eastwards On same scale.
MAINE
NEW HAMPSHIRE
CANADA
TENNESSEE
NORTH CAROLINA
SOUTH CAROLINA
GEORGIA
ALABAMA
MISSISSIPPI
FLORIDA
ATLANTIC OCEAN
GULF OF MEXICO
BAHAMAS
Nashville
Atlanta
Birmingham
Montgomery
Jacksonville
Charleston
Savannah
Columbia
Raleigh
Charlotte
Tampa
Miami
Orlando
Tallahassee
Mobile
Chattanooga
Knoxville
Wilmington
Bangor
Portland
Augusta
Projection: Alber's Equal Area with two standard parallels
West from Greenwich
COPYRIGHT, GEORGE PHILIP & SON, LTD.
m ft

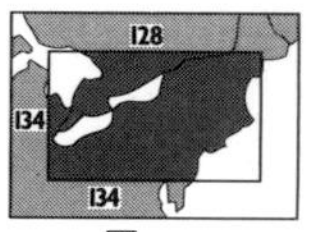

1  2  3  4  5  6  7

Georgian Bay

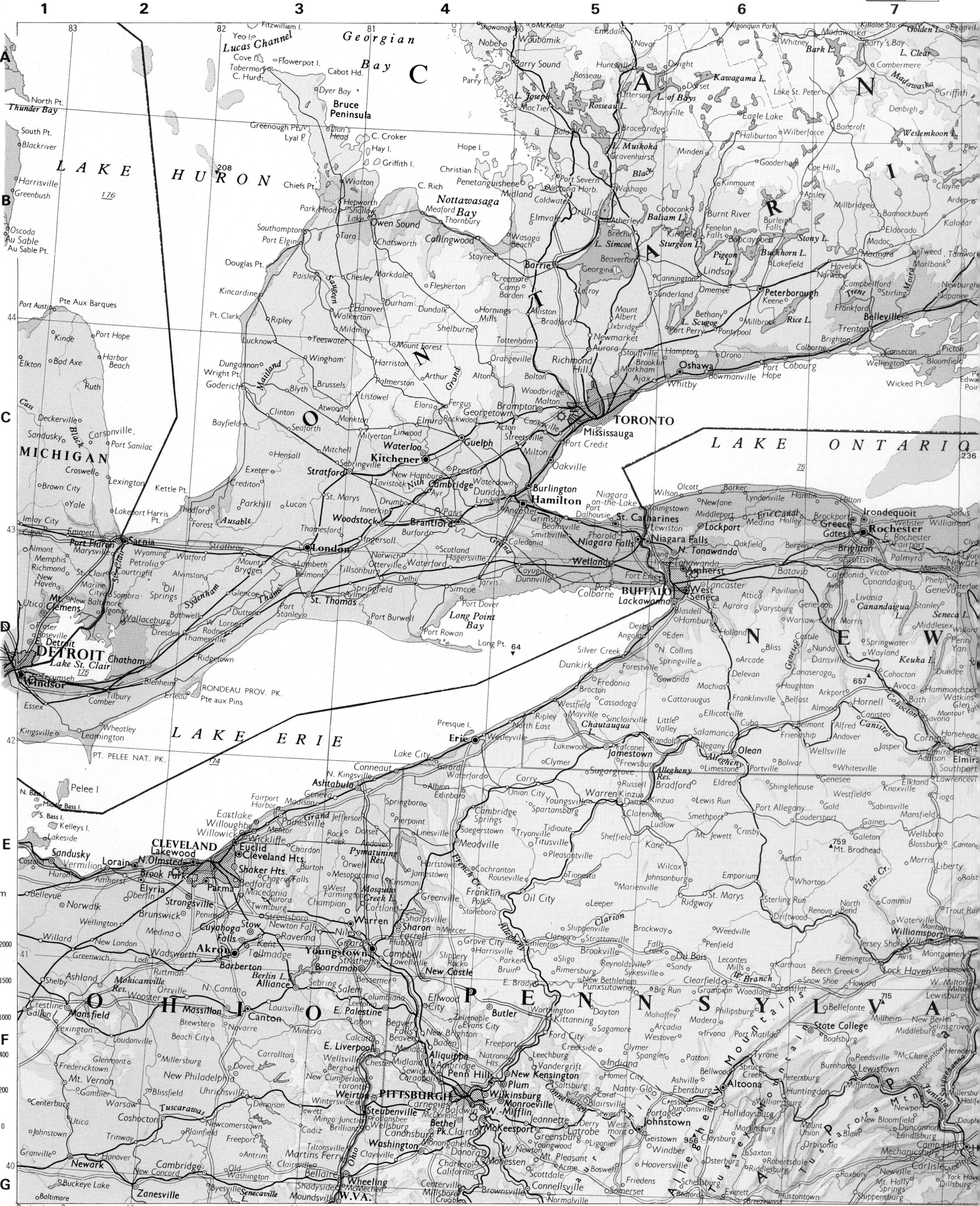

Lucas Channel
Cove
Tobermory
C. Hurd
Bruce Peninsula

Parry Sound
Rosseau
Huntsville
Dwight
Algonquin Park

LAKE HURON

Nottawasaga Bay

CANADA

ONTARIO

MICHIGAN

Owen Sound
Collingwood
Barrie
L. Simcoe
Orillia
Peterborough
Belleville

Kitchener
Waterloo
Guelph
TORONTO
Mississauga

LAKE ONTARIO

Hamilton
St. Catharines
Niagara Falls
BUFFALO
Rochester
Irondequoit
Greece

Sarnia
London
Woodstock
Brantford

DETROIT
Windsor
Lake St. Clair

Chatham

LAKE ERIE

Long Point Bay

PT. PELEE NAT. PK.

Erie

Dunkirk
Jamestown
Olean

NEW YORK

CLEVELAND
Lakewood
Euclid
Sandusky
Lorain
Elyria
Akron

Ashtabula

Warren
Youngstown
Boardman
New Castle

PENNSYLVANIA

OHIO

Canton
Massillon
Alliance

Butler

Mansfield

PITTSBURGH
Wilkinsburg
McKeesport
Monroeville

Altoona
State College

Wheeling
W. VA.

Newark
Zanesville

Projection: Bonne

2  3  4  5  6  7

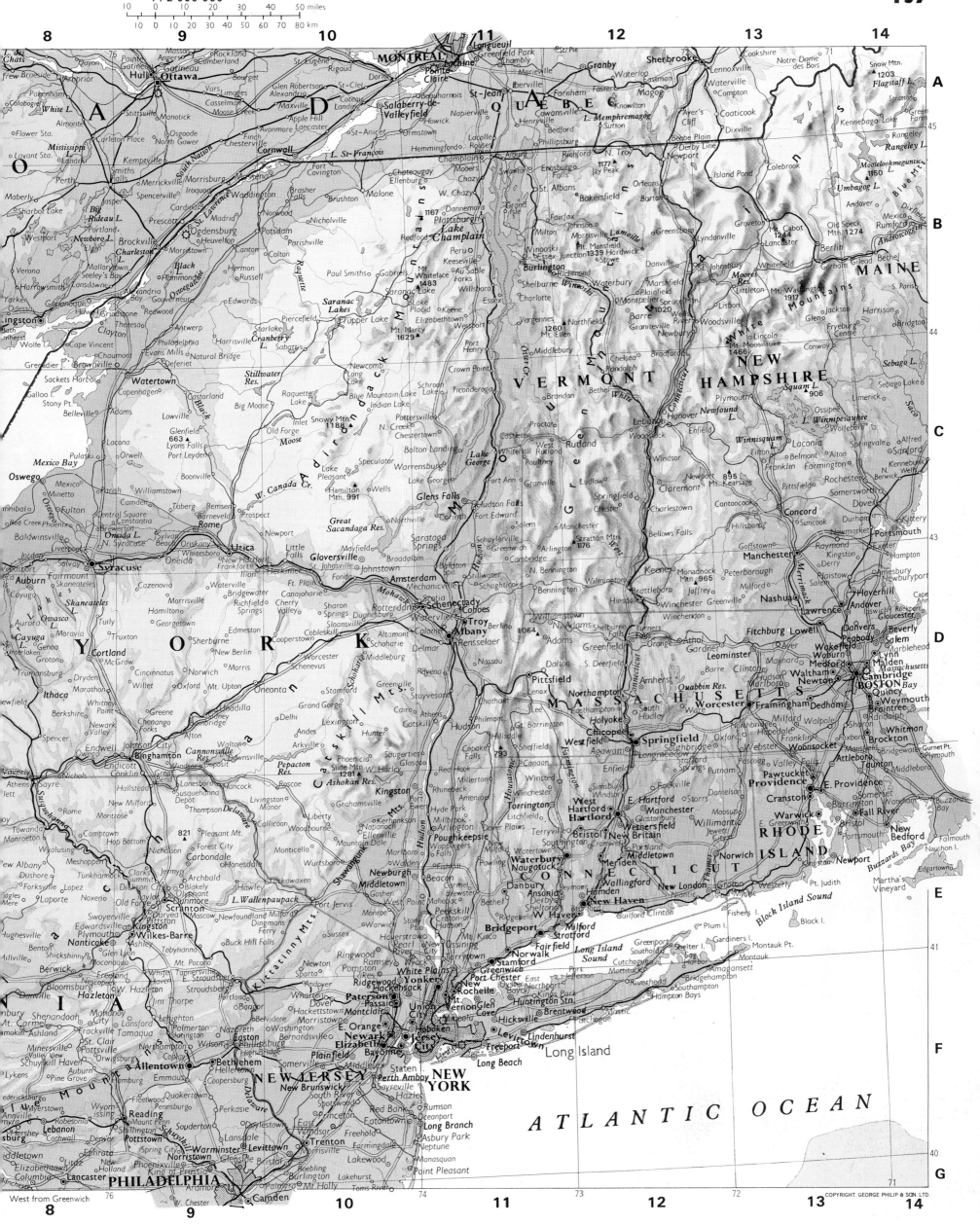

1 : 2 000 000

10   0   10   20   30   40   50 miles
10   0   10   20   30   40   50   60   70   80 km

8          9          10          11          12          13          14

CANADA

ONTARIO

QUEBEC

MONTREAL

Ottawa
Hull

Cornwall

Ogdensburg

Watertown

Oswego

Syracuse

Utica

NEW YORK

Binghamton

Scranton

Wilkes-Barre

Allentown

NEW JERSEY

NEW YORK

PHILADELPHIA

Camden

Trenton

Reading

Lancaster

Adirondack Mountains

Lake Champlain

Burlington

VERMONT

NEW HAMPSHIRE

MAINE

White Mountains

Montpelier

Lake George

Glens Falls

Saratoga Springs

Albany

Troy

Schenectady

Amsterdam

Gloversville

Catskill Mts.

Kingston

Poughkeepsie

Newburgh

Middletown

MASSACHUSETTS

Pittsfield

Springfield

Worcester

BOSTON

Cambridge

Concord

Manchester

Nashua

Lawrence

Lowell

Fitchburg

CONNECTICUT

Hartford

New Haven

Bridgeport

Stamford

Norwalk

Danbury

Waterbury

Meriden

New Britain

RHODE ISLAND

Providence

Pawtucket

Warwick

Fall River

New Bedford

Newport

Block Island Sound

Long Island Sound

Long Island

Montauk Pt.

Martha's Vineyard

Buzzards Bay

White Plains

Yonkers

New Rochelle

Paterson

Newark

Elizabeth

Jersey City

Long Beach

Freeport

Levittown

Hicksville

Huntington Stn.

Brentwood

ATLANTIC  OCEAN

A

B

C

D

E

F

G

45

44

43

41

40

West from Greenwich        76          10          74          11          73          12          72          13          14

COPYRIGHT. GEORGE PHILIP & SON. LTD.

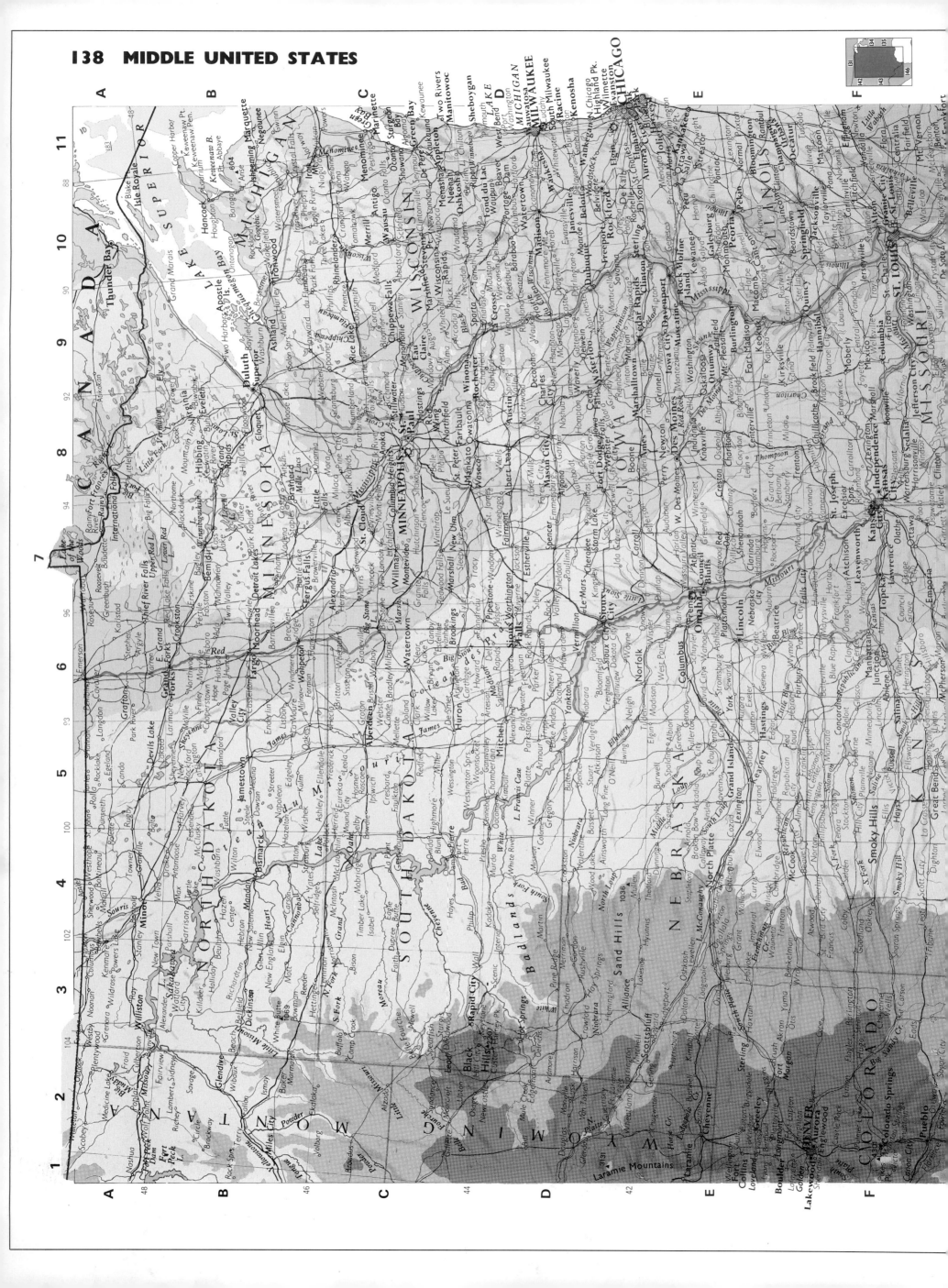

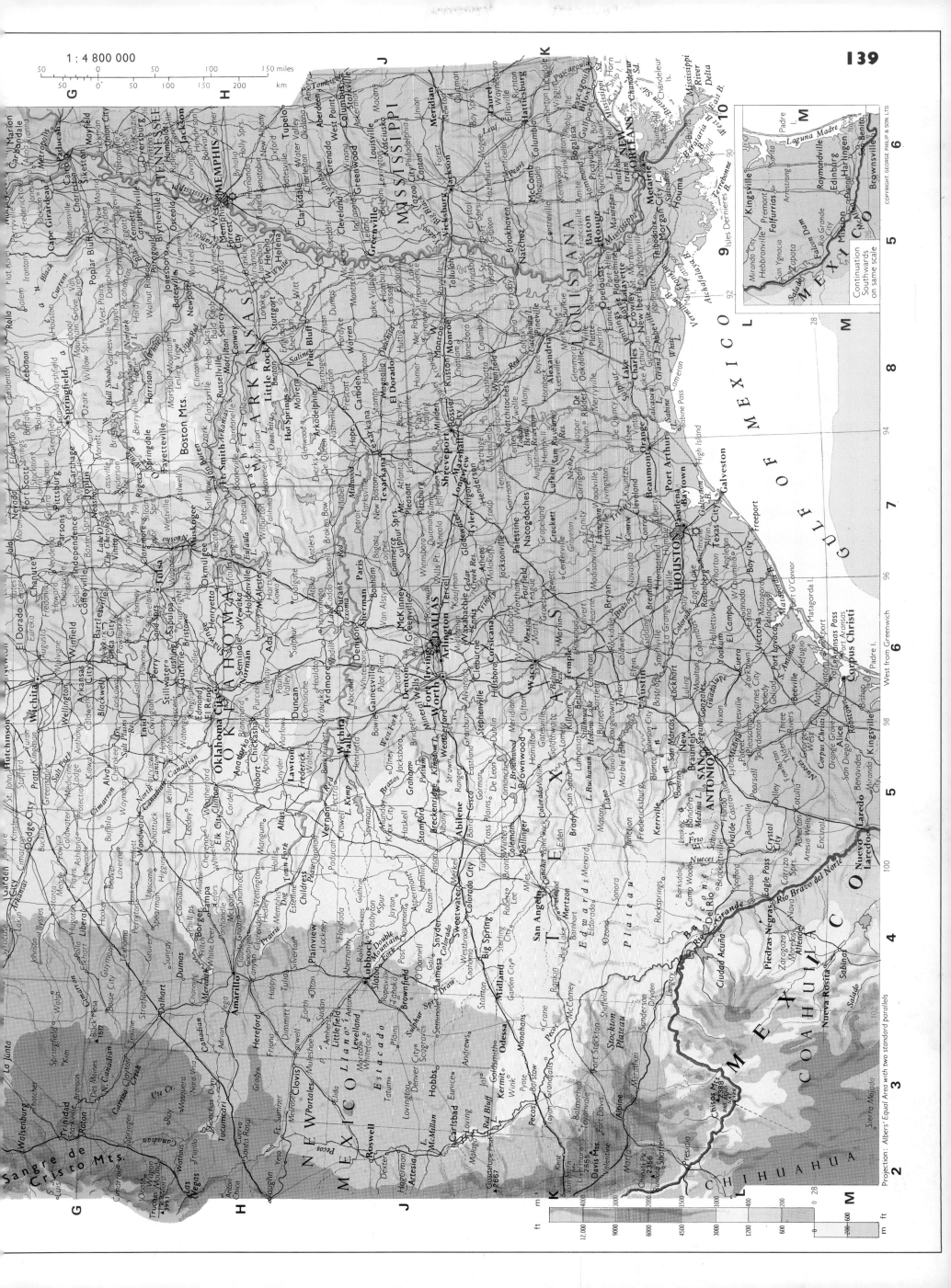

1 : 4 800 000

COPYRIGHT GEORGE PHILIP & SON LTD.

Projection: Albers' Equal Area with two standard parallels

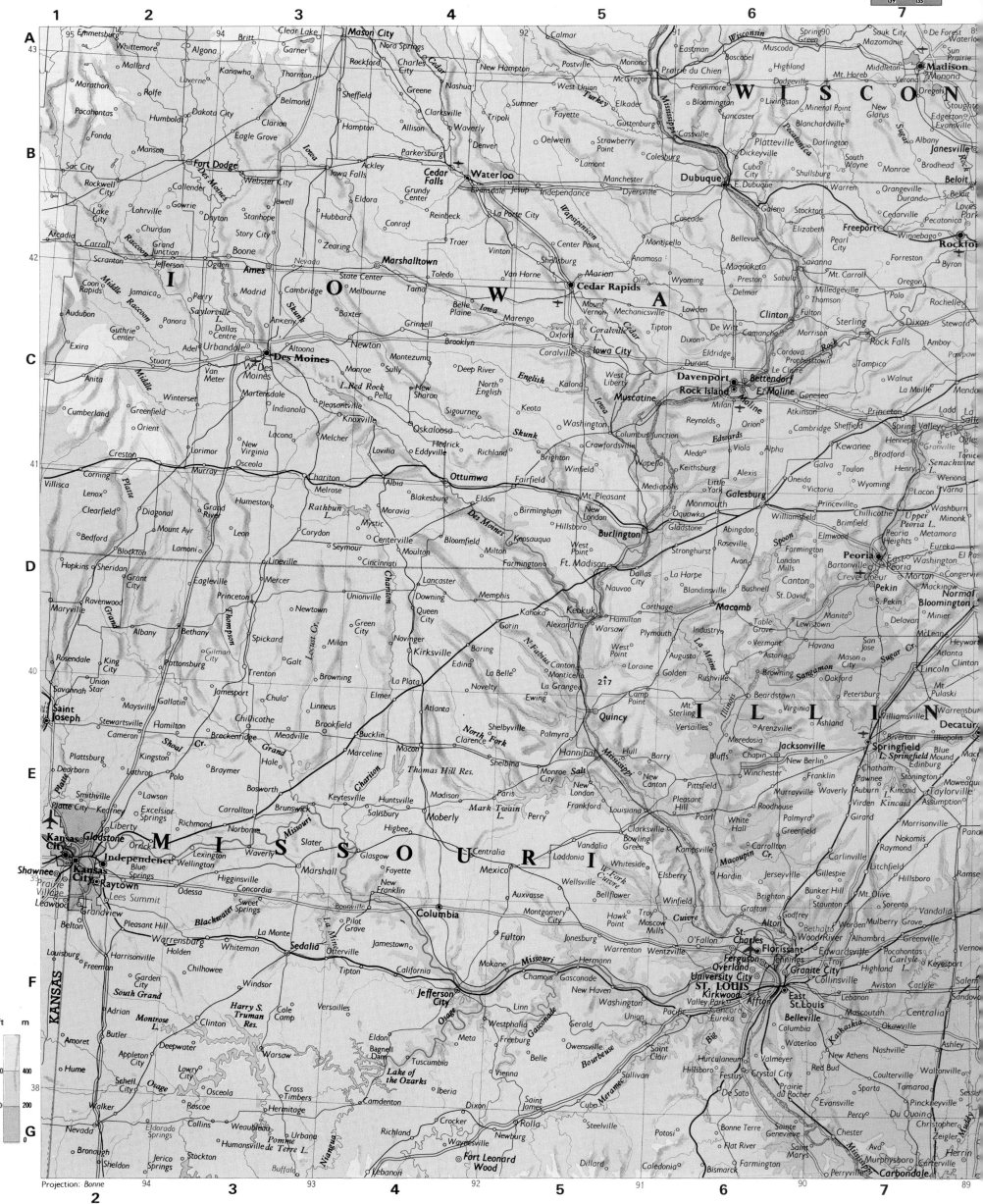

1 : 2 000 000

10  0  10  20  30  40  50 miles
10  0  10  20  30  40  50  60  70  80 km

8   9   10   11   12   13   14

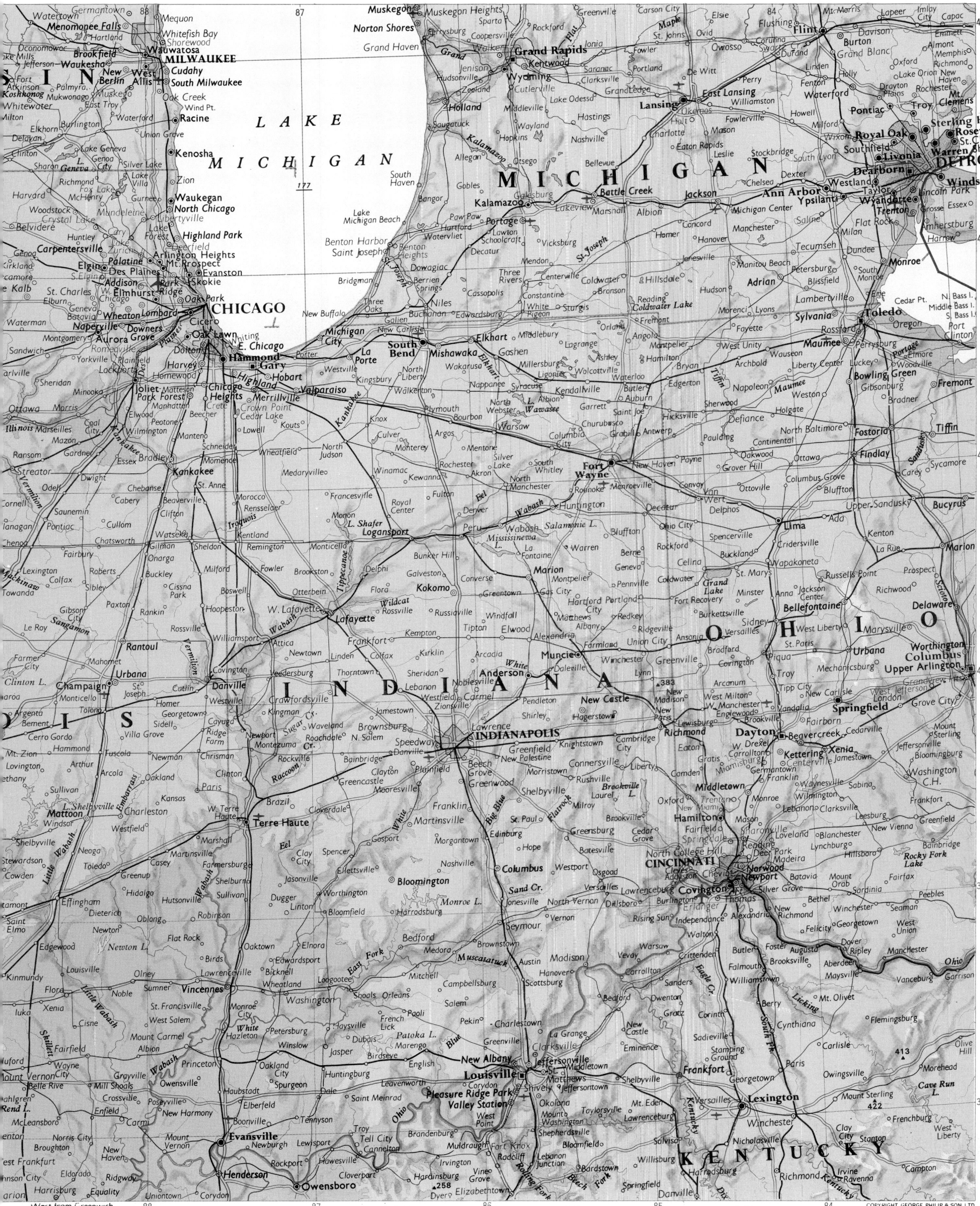

LAKE MICHIGAN

MILWAUKEE

WISCONSIN

MICHIGAN

Muskegon
Muskegon Heights
Norton Shores
Grand Haven
Grand Rapids
Wyoming
Kentwood
Holland
Lansing
East Lansing
Flint
Burton
Pontiac
Royal Oak
Southfield
Livonia
Warren
Dearborn
DETROIT
Windsor
Sterling Hts.
Roseville
St. Clair Shores

Kalamazoo
Battle Creek
Jackson
Ann Arbor
Ypsilanti
Westland
Taylor
Wyandotte
Monroe

Menomonee Falls
Brookfield
Wauwatosa
New Berlin
West Allis
Cudahy
South Milwaukee
Oak Creek
Racine
Kenosha
Waukegan
North Chicago
Highland Park
Arlington Heights
Des Plaines
Evanston
Skokie
Elmhurst
Oak Park
CHICAGO
Cicero
Oak Lawn
Harvey
Hammond
Gary
Hobart
Valparaiso
Merrillville
Joliet
Park Forest
Chicago Heights
Crown Point

Toledo
Maumee
Bowling Green
Fremont
Tiffin
Fostoria
Findlay
Lima

South Bend
Mishawaka
Elkhart
Goshen
Fort Wayne

INDIANA

OHIO

Kankakee

Lafayette
W. Lafayette
Kokomo
Logansport
Peru
Marion

Muncie
Anderson
New Castle
Richmond
Dayton
Kettering
Xenia
Springfield
Columbus
Upper Arlington
Worthington
Delaware
Bellefontaine

Champaign
Urbana
Danville
Crawfordsville

INDIANAPOLIS
Speedway
Greenwood
Beech Grove

Terre Haute
Brazil
Bloomington
Columbus

Hamilton
Middletown
CINCINNATI
Norwood
Newport
Covington

Vincennes

Bedford

New Albany
Louisville
Jeffersonville
Frankfort
Lexington

Evansville
Henderson
Owensboro

KENTUCKY

West from Greenwich

COPYRIGHT. GEORGE PHILIP & SON. LTD.

8   9   10   11   12   13

A  B  C  D  E  F  G

1 : 4 800 000

West from Greenwich

Projection : Albers' Equal Area with two standard parallels

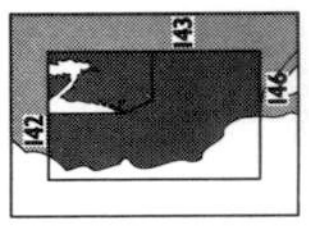

**SEATTLE-PORTLAND REGION**
On same scale

CANADA

Vancouver Island

Strait of Georgia

Strait of Juan de Fuca

Olympic Mountains
NATIONAL PARK

WASHINGTON

SEATTLE
Tacoma
Bellevue
Everett
Bellingham
Victoria
Vancouver

OREGON
PORTLAND

PACIFIC OCEAN

Pahute Mesa

White Mts.

Inyo Mts.

Owens

Sierra Nevada

CALIFORNIA

Reno
Sparks
Carson City

Sacramento
Stockton
Fresno
San Joaquin

SAN FRANCISCO
Oakland
Berkeley
San Jose
Santa Cruz
Monterey

Diablo Range

Santa Lucia Range

Napa
Santa Rosa

Palo Alto
Salinas

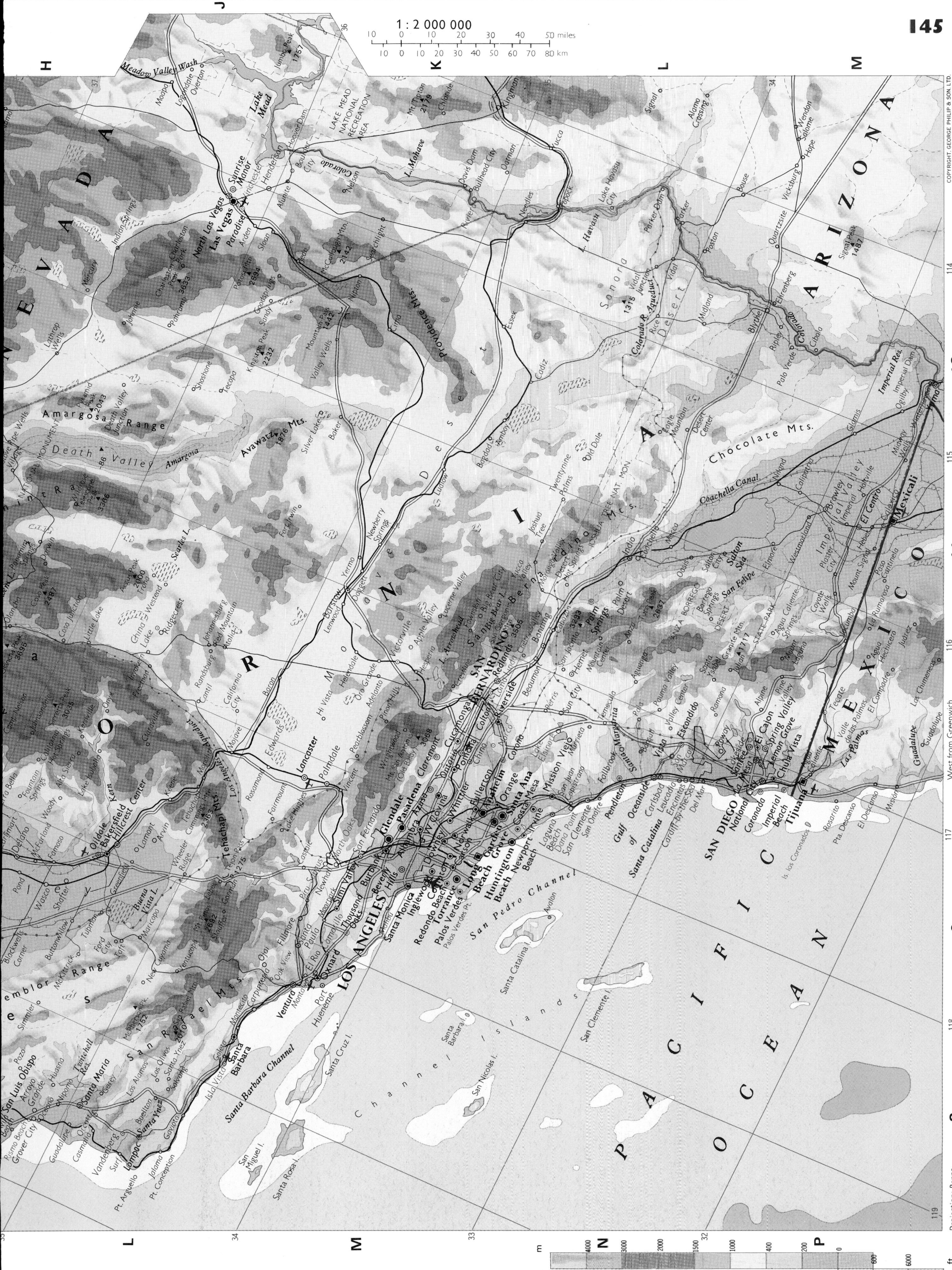

1 : 2 000 000

10  0  10  20  30  40  50 miles
10  0  10  20  30  40  50  60  70  80 km

NEVADA

ARIZONA

CALIFORNIA

MEXICO

PACIFIC OCEAN

Lake Mead

LAKE MEAD NATIONAL RECREATION AREA

Hoover Dam
Davis Dam
Parker Dam
Imperial Dam

Las Vegas
North Las Vegas
Paradise
Henderson
Boulder City
Kingman
Needles
Yuma
Mexicali
El Centro
Brawley
Calexico
Tijuana
San Diego
National City
Chula Vista
Coronado
Imperial Beach
Oceanside
Carlsbad
Encinitas
Del Mar
La Jolla
El Cajon
Escondido
Vista
San Clemente
Dana Point
Laguna Beach
Newport Beach
Huntington Beach
Costa Mesa
Santa Ana
Anaheim
Orange
Fullerton
Garden Grove
Long Beach
Torrance
Redondo Beach
Palos Verdes
Inglewood
Santa Monica
LOS ANGELES
Glendale
Pasadena
Burbank
Alhambra
Whittier
Pomona
Ontario
Claremont
Cucamonga
SAN BERNARDINO
Riverside
Colton
Redlands
San Fernando
Thousand Oaks
Simi Valley
Oxnard
Ventura
Santa Barbara
Santa Maria
San Luis Obispo
Lancaster
Palmdale
Edwards
Bakersfield
Victorville
Barstow
Palm Springs
Indio
Blythe
Twentynine Palms
Joshua Tree

Death Valley
Amargosa Range
Amargosa
Panamint Range
Searles L.
Mojave
Mojave Desert
Providence Mts.
Chocolate Mts.
Colorado Desert
San Bernardino Mts.
San Gabriel Mts.
San Jacinto Pk.
Santa Rosa Mts.
San Rafael Mts.
Tehachapi Mts.
Channel Islands
Santa Cruz I.
Santa Rosa I.
San Miguel I.
Santa Catalina
Santa Barbara I.
San Nicolas I.
San Clemente I.
Santa Catalina I.
San Pedro Channel
Santa Barbara Channel
Gulf of Santa Catalina

Colorado R.
Colorado R. Aqueduct
Coachella Canal
Lake Havasu
Lake Mohave
Imperial Valley
Imperial Res.
Tecate
ANZA BORREGO DESERT STATE PARK
JOSHUA TREE NAT. MON.

Projection: Bonne

West from Greenwich

m ft
4000  12 000
3000  9000
2000  6000
1500  4500
1000  3000
600  2000
400  1200
200  600
0  0
200  600
2000  6000
6000
m ft

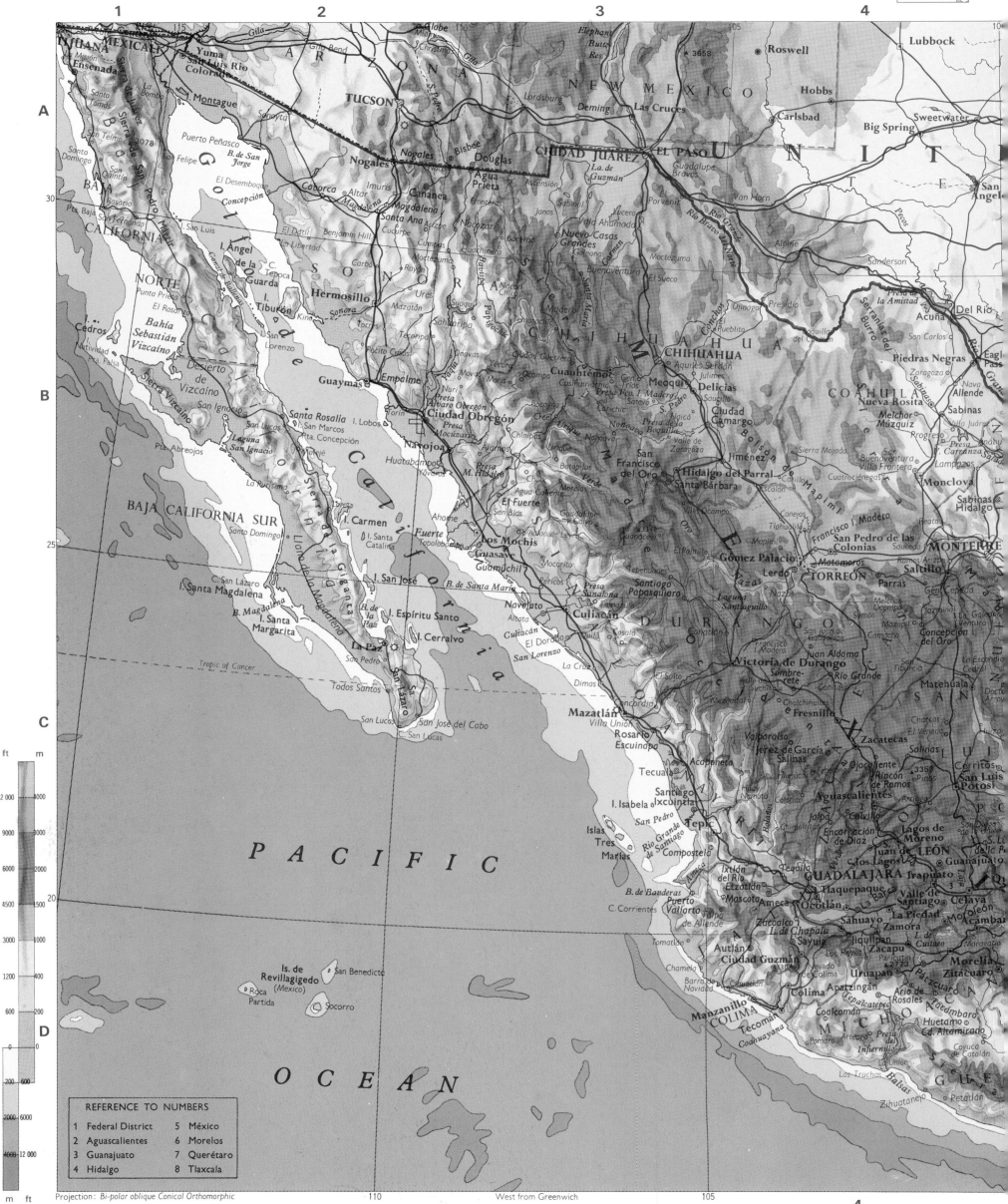

PACIFIC

OCEAN

REFERENCE TO NUMBERS
1 Federal District    5 México
2 Aguascalientes      6 Morelos
3 Guanajuato          7 Querétaro
4 Hidalgo             8 Tlaxcala

Projection: Bi-polar oblique Conical Orthomorphic    West from Greenwich

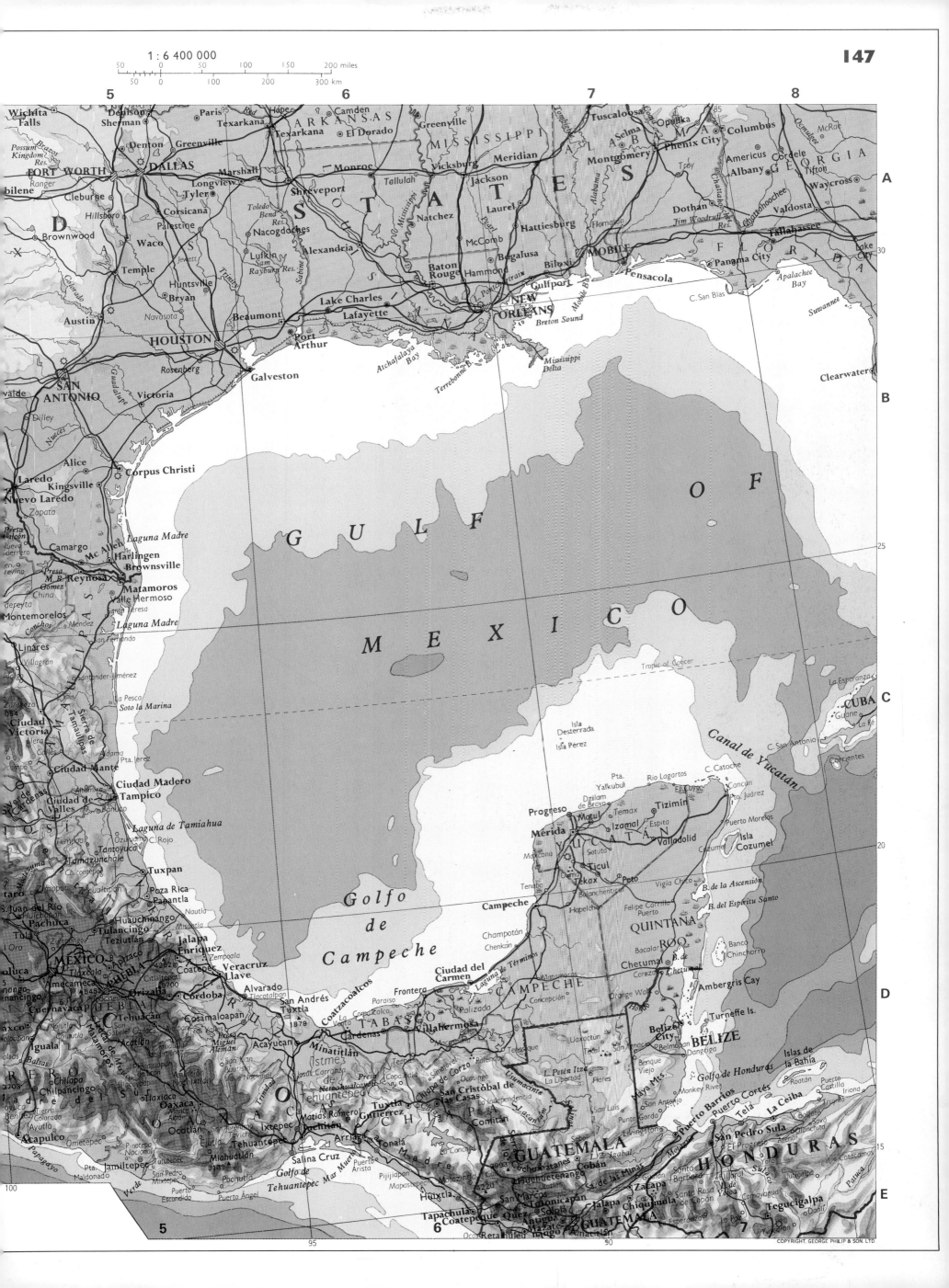

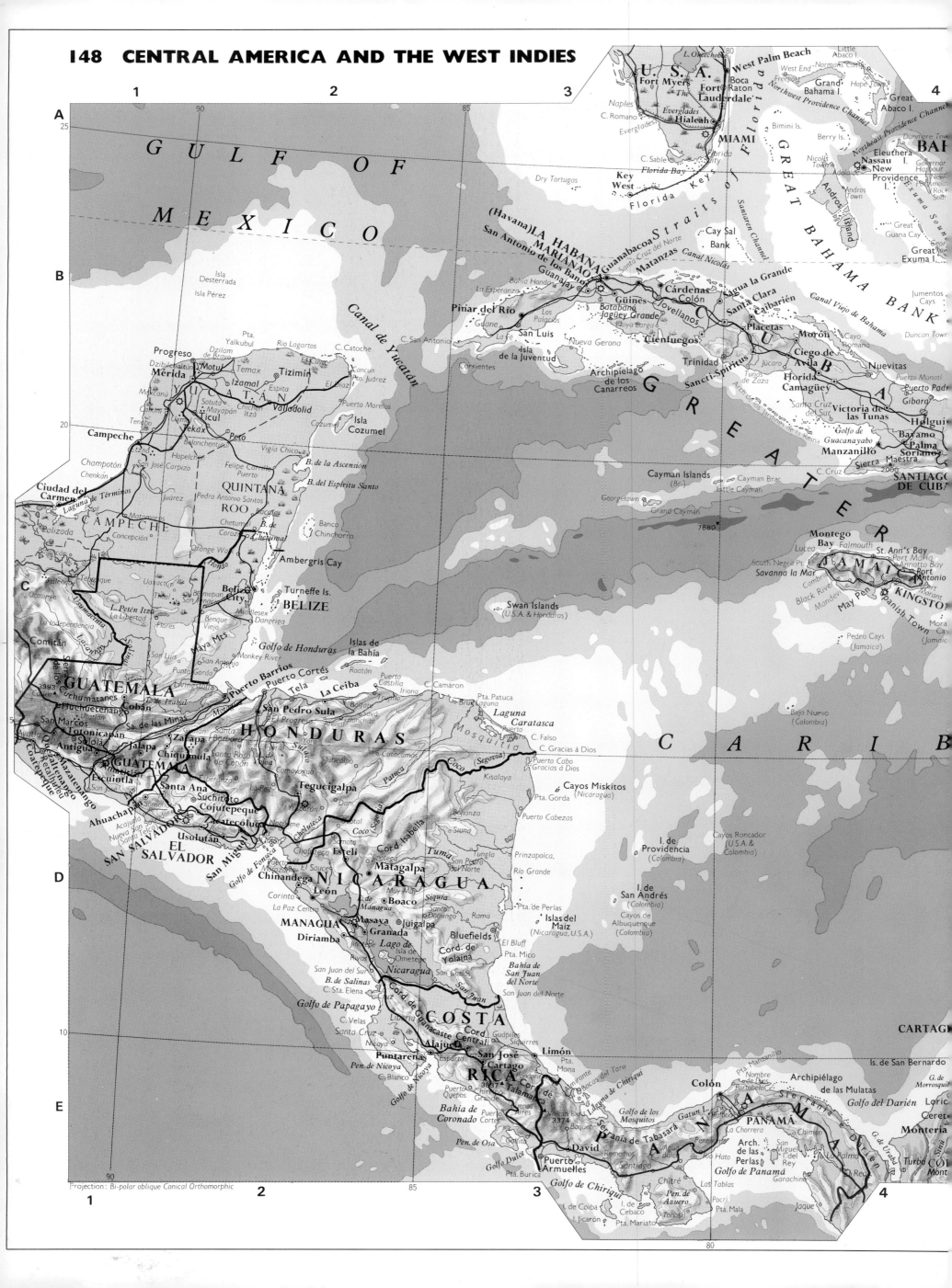

GULF OF MEXICO

U.S.A.
L. Okeechobee
Fort Myers
West Palm Beach
Naples
Boca Raton
Fort Lauderdale
C. Romano
Everglades
Hialeah
MIAMI
Everglades
C. Sable
Florida Bay
Key West
Dry Tortugas
Florida Keys

Little Abaco I.
Normans Cay
Freeport
Grand Bahama I.
Hope Town
Great Abaco I.
Bimini Is.
Berry Is.
Nicols Town
Adelaide
Nassau
New Providence
Andros Town
Andros Island

GREAT BAHAMA BANK

Eleuthera I.
Governor Harbour
Great Guana Cay
Great Exuma I.
Jumentos Cays

BAH

Straits of Florida

(Havana) LA HABANA
Guanabacoa
San Antonio de los Baños
MARIANAO
Guanajay
Bahia Honda
La Esperanza
Pinar del Rio
Guane
La Fé
Los Palacios
San Luis
Isla de la Juventud
Corrientes
C. San Antonio

Güines
Batabanó
Jagüey Grande
Playa Larga
Nueva Gerona
Archipiélago de los Canarreos

Matanzas
Cárdenas
Colón
Jovellanos
Santa Clara
Cienfuegos
Trinidad
Sancti Spíritus
Tunas de Zaza

Canal Nicolás
Sagua la Grande
Caibarién
Placetas
Morón
Ciego de Avila
Jucaro
Florida
Camagüey
Santa Cruz del Sur
Golfo de Guacanayabo

CUBA
GREATER

Canal Viejo de Bahama
Duncan Town
Cayo Romano
Nuevitas
Puerto Manati
Puerto Padr
Gibaro
Holgui
Bayamo
Palma Soriano
Manzanillo
Sierra Maestra
2000
C. Cruz
SANTIAGO DE CUBA

Cayman Islands (Br.)
Georgetown
Grand Cayman
Cayman Brac
Little Cayman
7680

Montego Bay
Lucea
Falmouth
St. Ann's Bay
Port Maria
South Negril Pt.
Savanna la Mar
Black River
Mandev
May Pen
Spanish Town
JAMAI
Port Antonio
KINGSTO

Pedro Cays (Jamaica)

CARIB

Progreso
Yalkubul
Pta.
Dzilam de Bravo
Rio Lagartos
C. Catoche
Motul
Temax
Izamal
Tizimín
Espita
Cancún
Pta. Juárez
Mérida
Macanú
Dzibalchaltun
Yucatán
Sotuta
Chichén Itzá
Valladolid
Puerto Morelos
Ticul
Mayapán
Peto
Isla Cozumel
Tekax
Balonchentick
Cozumel
Campeche
Champotón
Hopelchén
Chenkán
Vigia Chico
B. de la Ascensión

QUINTANA ROO
Felipe Carrillo Puerto
B. del Espíritu Santo
Banco Chinchorro

CAMPECHE
Ciudad del Carmen
Laguna de Términos
Palizada
Escárcega
Matamoros
Concepción
Juárez
Pedro Antonio Santos
Bacalar
Chetumal
B. de Corazal
Chetumal
Orange Wk
Ambergris Cay

BELIZE
Belize City
Belmopan
Turneffe Is.
Middlesex
Dangriga
Maya Mts.
Monkey River
Punta Gorda

Golfo de Honduras
Islas de la Bahía
Roatán

Swan Islands (U.S.A. & Honduras)

GUATEMALA
Cuchumatanes
Huehuetenango
Cobán
San Marcos
Totonicapán
Antigua
GUATEMALA
Escuintla
Mazatenango
Coatepeque

Puerto Barrios
Livingston
Puerto Cortés
Tela
San Pedro Sula
El Progreso
La Ceiba
Trujillo
C. Camarón

HONDURAS
Santa Rosa de Copán
Santa Bárbara
Comayagua
Tegucigalpa
Juticalpa
Catacamas
Danli

Pta. Patuca
Brus Laguna
C. Falso
Laguna Caratasca

Mosquitia

EL SALVADOR
Santa Ana
San Salvador
Cojutepeque
Zacatecoluca
Usulután
San Miguel
Golfo de Fonseca

Esteli
Matagalpa
Chinandega
León
Managua
Boaco

NICARAGUA
Cord. Isabella
Cord. de Yolaina
Bonanza
Siuna
Prinzapolca
Puerto Cabezas
Cayos Miskitos (Nicaragua)
Pta. Gorda
Puerto Cabo Gracias á Dios
C. Gracias á Dios
Coco (Segovia)
Kisalaya

MANAGUA
Masaya
Granada
Diriamba
Lago de Nicaragua
Rivas
B. de Salinas

COSTA RICA
Puntarenas
San José
Cartago
Alajuela
Limón
Golfo de Papagayo
Liberia
Santa Cruz
Nicoya
Pen. de Nicoya

Rio Grande
Bluefields
El Bluff
Bahia de San Juan del Norte
San Juan del Norte
Islas del Maiz (Nicaragua, U.S.A.)

I. de Providencia (Colombia)
Cayos Roncador (U.S.A. & Colombia)
I. de San Andrés (Colombia)
Cayos de Albuquenque (Colombia)

CARTAG

Puerto Armuelles
Golfo de Chiriqui
David
PANAMÁ
Colón
Gatun L.
La Chorrera
Arch. de las Perlas
Golfo de Panamá

Archipiélago de las Mulatas
Golfo del Darién
Turbo
COLON

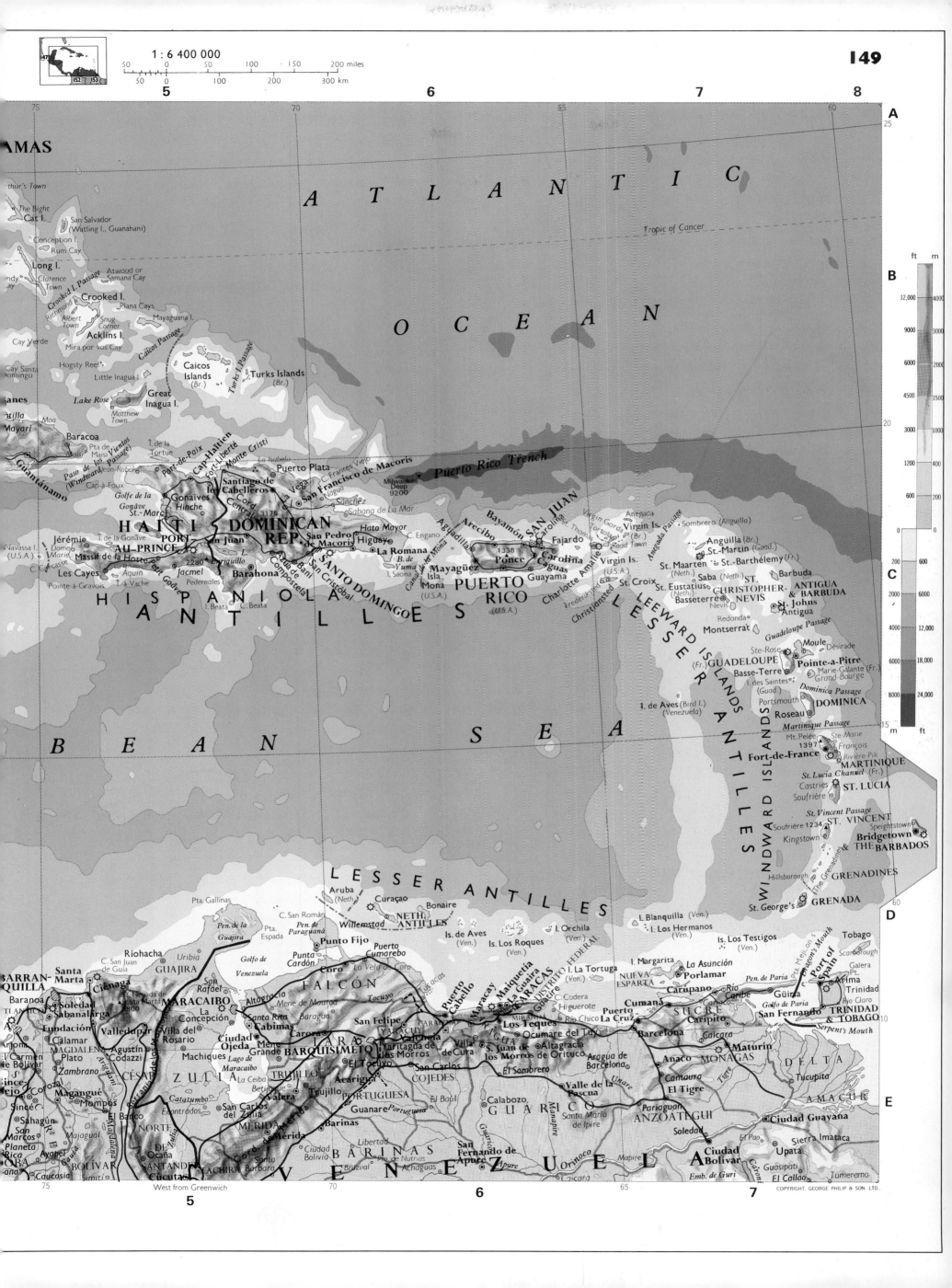

# 150 SOUTH AMERICA : Physical

1 : 24 000 000

Projection: Lambert's Equivalent Azimuthal

COPYRIGHT. GEORGE PHILIP & SON LTD.

West from Greenwich

1 : 24 000 000

100   0   100   200   300   400   500 miles
100   0   200   400   600   800 km

NORTH ATLANTIC OCEAN

SOUTH ATLANTIC OCEAN

PACIFIC OCEAN

COSTA RICA
San José
PANAMA
Golfo de Panamá
Golfo de Darién
Barranquilla
Cartagena
Maracaibo
Barquisimeto
Valencia
Caracas
Port of Spain
TRINIDAD AND TOBAGO
Medellín
Cúcuta
San Cristóbal
Bucaramanga
Bogotá
Cali
COLOMBIA
VENEZUELA
Orinoco
Ciudad Guayana
Georgetown
Paramaribo
Cayenne
GUYANA
SURINAM
FRENCH GUIANA
C. Orange
Meta
Orinoco
C. de San Francisco
Quito
ECUADOR
Guayaquil
G. de Guayaquil
Napo
Putumayo
Caquetá
Negro
Japurá
Iquitos
Marañón
Juruá
Purus
Madeira
Pôrto Velho
Tapajós
Xingu
Amazonas
Manaus
Santarém
Belém
Ilha de Marajó
Equator
São Luís
Teresina
Parnaíba
Fortaleza (Ceara)
C. de São Roque
Natal
João Pessoa
Recife (Pernambuco)
Maceió
Aracaju
Salvador
São Francisco
Pta. Aguja
Chiclayo
Trujillo
Chimbote
PERU
Callao
Lima
Cuzco
Madre de Dios
Ucayali
Guaporé
Mamoré
BRAZIL
Arequipa
Titicaca
La Paz
Cochabamba
BOLIVIA
Santa Cruz
Sucre
Cuiabá
Brasília
Goiânia
Belo Horizonte
Vitória
Campos
Iquique
Iberê Prêto
Campo Grande
Paraná
Campinas
Niterói
RIO DE JANEIRO
Santos
SÃO PAULO
Curitiba
Londrina
PARAGUAY
Pilcomayo
Asunción
Paraguay
Tropic of Capricorn
Antofagasta
Isla San Félix (Chile)
Isla San Ambrosio (Chile)
Salta
San Miguel de Tucumán
Resistencia
Corrientes
Uruguay
Pôrto Alegre
Lagoa dos Patos
Pelotas
CHILE
Viña del Mar
Valparaíso
Santiago
Córdoba
San Juan
Mendoza
ARGENTINA
Santa Fe
Paraná
Rosario
URUGUAY
Montevideo
BUENOS AIRES
La Plata
Río de la Plata
Talca
Concepción
Bahía Blanca
Mar del Plata
Salado
Valdivia
Negro
Colorado
Puerto Montt
Viedma
Chubut
Arch. de Juan Fernández (Chile)
Golfo Comodoro Rivadavia
San Jorge
G. de Penas
FALKLAND ISLANDS
West Falkland
Stanley
East Falkland
(U.K.)
Strait of Magellan
Tierra del Fuego
Cape Horn

West from Greenwich

Projection: Lambert's Equivalent Azimuthal

COPYRIGHT. GEORGE PHILIP & SON. LTD.

1 : 6 400 000

50    0    50    100    150    200 miles
50    0    100    200    300 km

**5**                    **6**                    **7**

*A T L A N T I C*

*O C E A N*

La Blanquilla (Ven.)
Los Hermanos (Ven.)
St. George's GRENADA
Is. Los Testigos (Ven.)
Tobago
NUEVA ESPARTA
Margarita
La Asunción
Pta. Arenas
Porlamar
Pta. Peñas
Scarborough
Pta. de Araya
I. Coche
Carúpano
Rio Caribe
Pen. de Paria
Guiria
**A**
Pto.
La Tortuga (Ven.)
Cariaco
Araya
Pen. de
Cumaná
**SUCRE**
S. Juan
Pilar
Irapa
Golfo de San
**TRINIDAD**
Pto.
La Cruz
Guanta
2596
Caripito
Fernando
**AND TOBAGO**
Barcelona
Paria
Arima
Serpent's Mouth
**Port of Spain**
Trinidad
Aragua de Barcelona
Anaco
**Maturín**
Amana
Boca de la Sierpe
Rio Claro
Galeota Point
**ANZOATEGUI**
Santa Maria de Ipire
**El Tigre**
Cantaura
**MONAGAS**
Guanipa
Tigre
Morichal Largo
Cano Macareo
**DELTA**
**10**
Zaraza
Pao
Pariaguán
Temblador
Barrancas
**AMACURO**
Boca Grande
I. Corocoro
Santa Cruz
Soledad
Pto. Ordaz
**Ciudad**
Tucupita
Grande
Morawhanna
Mapire
**Ciudad Guayana**
Orinoco
El Pao
Mabaruma
Maripa
**Ciudad Bolívar**
Guri Dam
Upata
Barima
Charity
**B**
Caicara
Caparo
Ciudad Piar
El Miamo
La Horqueta
Wani
Kokerite
Anna Regina
Nichas
**B**
**O**
Guri
El Palmar
La Paragua
El Callao
Tumeremo
Matthew's Ridge
Suddie
Serranía Turagua
Aro
**L**
El Dorado
Cuyuni
Parika
**Georgetown**
**I**
Supamo
Curatabaca
**I**
Peter's Mine
Bartisa
Buxton
**V**
**V**
Angel Falls
Luepa
**G U Y A N A**
Mazaruni
Hyde Park
Mahaicony
**A**
2560
La Gran
Imbaimadai
Issano
Rosignol
**New Amsterdam**
**R**
**Sabana**
Mt.
Apoteri
Wismar
**Linden**
Mara
Port Mourant
Nueva Esparta
Roraima 2772
**Nieuw Nickerie**
**Paramaribo**
Equelbo
Arabopó
Pakaraima
Kaieteur Falls
Ituni
Mahdia
**Nieuw Amsterdam**
Guaina
Sta. Teresa
Tumatumari
Kwakwani
**CORONIE**
**PARA**
Sierra del Zamuro
Icabaru
Orealla
Wageningen
Groningen
Moengo
Sinnamary
Icabarú
Orinduik
Kurupukari
Epira
Nickerie
**COMME-**
Albina
Iracoubo
Paragua
Majari
Surumu
**E**
Toka
Epira
**WIJNE**
St. Laurent
**Sa. Tepequem**
Irengo
**B**
Coppename
Brownsweg
Brokopondo
Gare Tigre
Arabela
Urariicaá
**Q**
**Prof. Dr. Ir. W. J.**
Langatabbetje
**5**
**5**
Motocurunya
Uraricuera
Lethem
Wichabai
Reva
**SARAMACCA**
**Van Blommestein**
Paul Isnard
Cacao
Catisirmiña
Boa Esperança
**I**
Rupununi
Pasoegroenoe
**Meer**
St. Elie
Regina
Parima
Boa Vista
Dadanawa
Shea
**SURINAM**
**Wilhelmina Geb.**
**BROKOPONDO**
Grand Santi
Cabo Orange
Matacuni
Mucajai
Isherton
New River
Julianatop
Benzdorp
**FRENCH**
Serra del
Apiaú
**BERBICE**
**1280**
**MAROWIJNE**
Eau
Maripasoula
St. Georges
**C**
Ocamo
Serra do Apiaú
Kamoa
Biloku
Alalaparu
Americankondre
Claire
Saül
Camopi
Oyapoque
Parima
Serra do Mucajaí
Mts.
Essequibo
**Serra Acara**
Tapanahoni
Alowike
**GUIANA**
Bienvenue
Clevelândia do Norte
Orinoco
Catrimani
734
Chiara
Litani
Camopi
Vila Velha
**R O R A I M A**
Caracaraí
**Serra Tumucumaque**
690
**C**
Tapirapecó
Serra Tabatinga
Anauá
Janaperi
Jarí
Paru
**A M A P Á**
Lourenço
Serra Curupira
Demini
San José do Anauá
Maracá
Calçoene
Padauari
Araçá
Catrimani
Maracá
Merirumá
Araguari
Amapá
**I. de**
**Maracá**
Preto
Branco
Bolaçu
Janaperi
Alalaú
Maraú
Serra do Navio
Teresinha
Aporema
Tapurucuará
Uatumã
Maecuru
Amapari
Porto Grande
Januacu
**50**
Negro
Jufari
Uatumã
Amapari
**Macapá**
Uaraxá
Maguru
Serra do Navio
Ilha Grande
Moreira
Nhamundá
Cuminá
Pôrto Santana
Cuiuni
Barcelos
Unini
Airão
Jacapu
São Tiago
Carapanatuba
Mazagão
Chaves
Caurés
Moura
Anajás
Caviana
**B**
**R**
Carvoeiro
Apuaú
Arquipélago das
Anavilhanas
Urubu
Uatumã
Faro
Óbidos
**Alenquer**
Prainha
Almeirim
I. Grande de Gurupá
Afuá
Agua Preta
Pauini
**A**
**Z**
**I**
**L**
Monte
Alegre
Gurupá
Ilha de
Marajó
Jaú
Uruará
Amazonas
Pôrto de Moz
Breves
L. Amaná
Mucura
Manacapuru
Santa Maria
Urucará
Urucurituba
**Santarém**
Aveiro
Juruti
Xingu
Carvalho
Arari
Piorini
Airão
Itapiranga
Silves
Belterra
Curuá
Jauari
Sousel
Portel
Alvarães
**MANAUS**
Itacoatiara
Barreirinha
**Parintins**
Anapu
Tefé
L. Badajós
Caapiranga
Manaquirú
Eva
Brasília Legal
João
**D**
Caapiranga
Careiro
Ilha Tupinambaranas
Maués
Nova Olinda
Itaituba
Altamira
Codajás
Anamá
Autazes
Itaituba
Tuaré
**Z**
**O**
**N**
**A**
L. de
Coari
Coari
Beruri
Axinim
Canumã
Brasília Legal
Iriri
Pôrto Alegre
Bacajá
Itanhauá
Purus
Paricatuba
Borba
Mundurucus
Abacaxis
**P A R Á**
Alvarães
Preto do Igapó-Açu
Aruma
Nova Aripuana
Abufari
Madeira
**Amazonas**
Itaboca
Tapajós

West from Greenwich

**5**                    **6**                    **7**

COPYRIGHT. GEORGE PHILIP & SON. LTD.

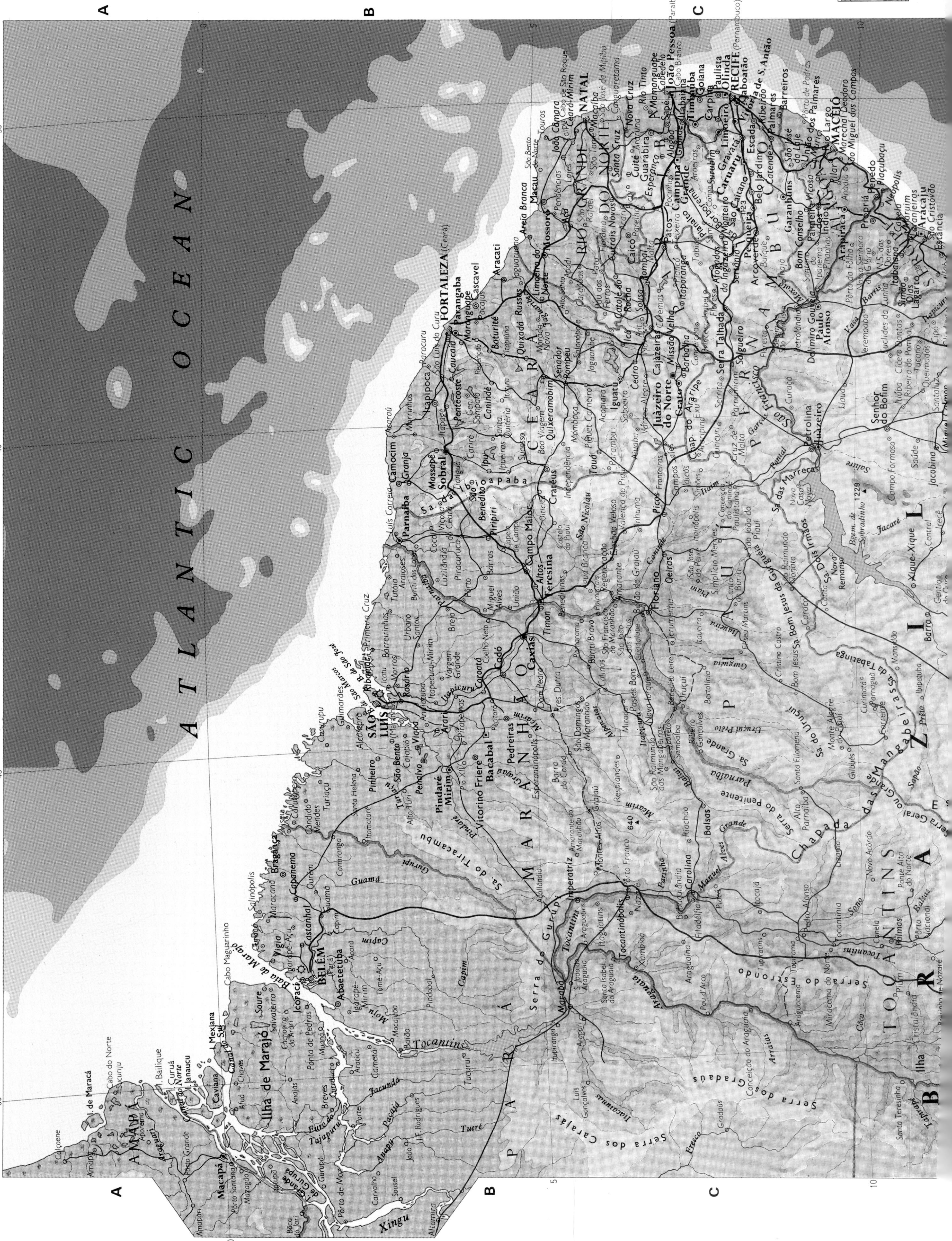

A T L A N T I C   O C E A N

## Major cities and features

FORTALEZA (Ceará)
NATAL
RIO GRANDE DO NORTE
João Pessoa (Paraíba)
RECIFE (Pernambuco)
Olinda
MACEIÓ
Aracaju
SÃO LUÍS
BELÉM (Pará)
Teresina
PIAUÍ
MARANHÃO
CEARÁ
PARAÍBA
PERNAMBUCO
ALAGOAS
SERGIPE
PARÁ
TOCANTINS
BAHIA

Ilha de Marajó
Baía de Marajó
Cabo do Norte
AMAPÁ
Macapá
Caviana
Mexiana
Ilha de S. Antão
Cabo de São Roque

Sobral
Parnaíba
Camocim
Granja
Caxias
Codó
Bacabal
Imperatriz
Tocantinópolis
Juazeiro do Norte
Mossoró
Campina Grande
Caruaru
Garanhuns
Crateús
Floriano
Oeiras
Picos
Piripiri

## Rivers

Tocantins
Xingu
Guamá
Parnaíba
São Francisco
Gurupi
Araguaia

Serra dos Carajás
Serra do Estrondo
Chapada das Mangabeiras
Chapada Diamantina

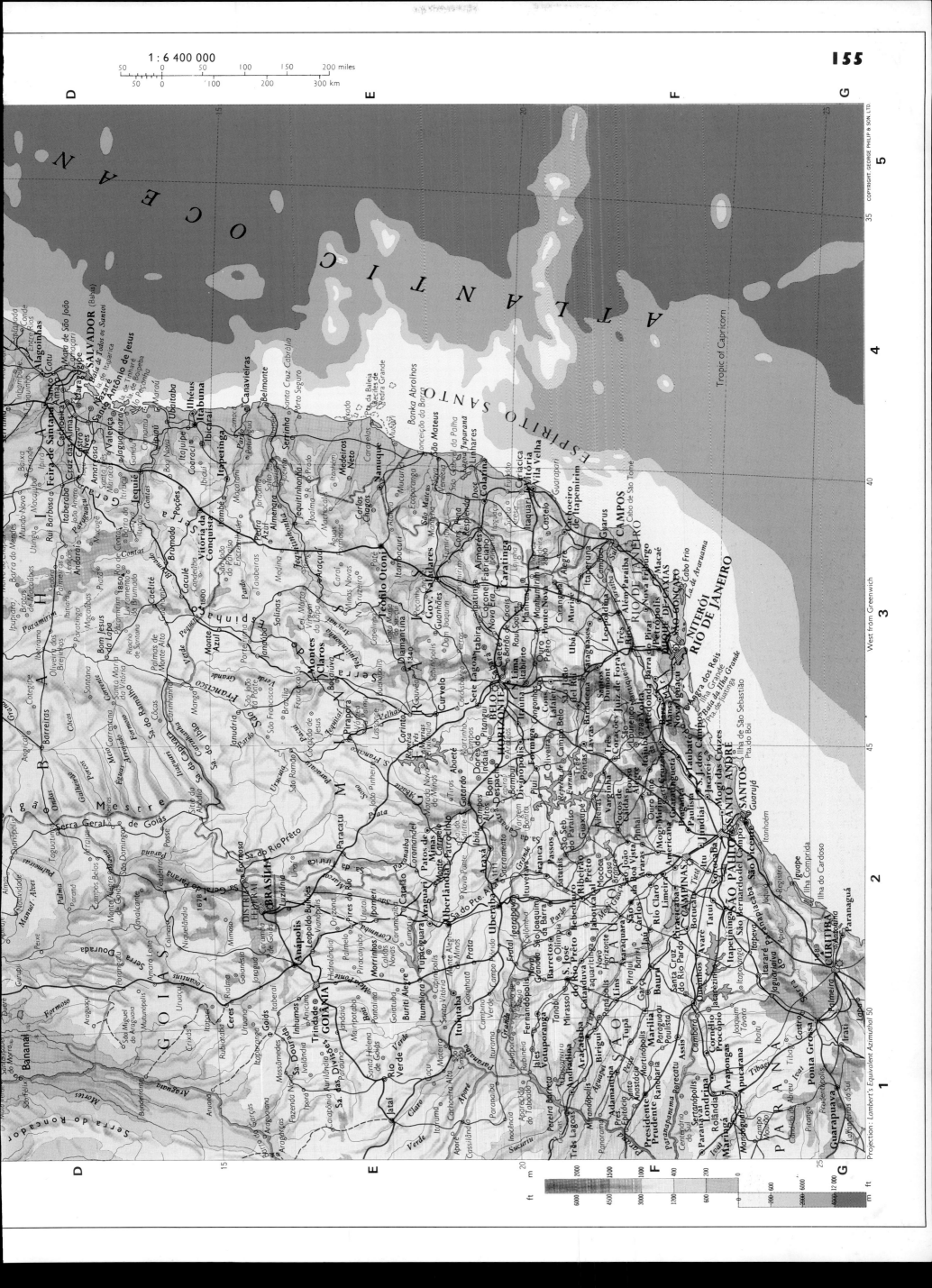

1 : 6 400 000

50   0   50   100   150   200 miles
50   0   100   200   300 km

ATLANTIC OCEAN

ESPÍRITO SANTO

Tropic of Capricorn

West from Greenwich

Projection: Lambert's Equivalent Azimuthal 50

SALVADOR (Bahia)

Feira de Santana

RIO DE JANEIRO
NITERÓI

BELO HORIZONTE

MINAS

GOIÁS

BRASÍLIA
DISTRITO FEDERAL

GOIÂNIA

SÃO PAULO
SANTO ANDRÉ
SÃO BERNARDO DO CAMPO
SANTOS
SÃO VICENTE

CAMPOS

PARANÁ

CURITIBA

Paranaguá
Ponta Grossa

Guarapuava

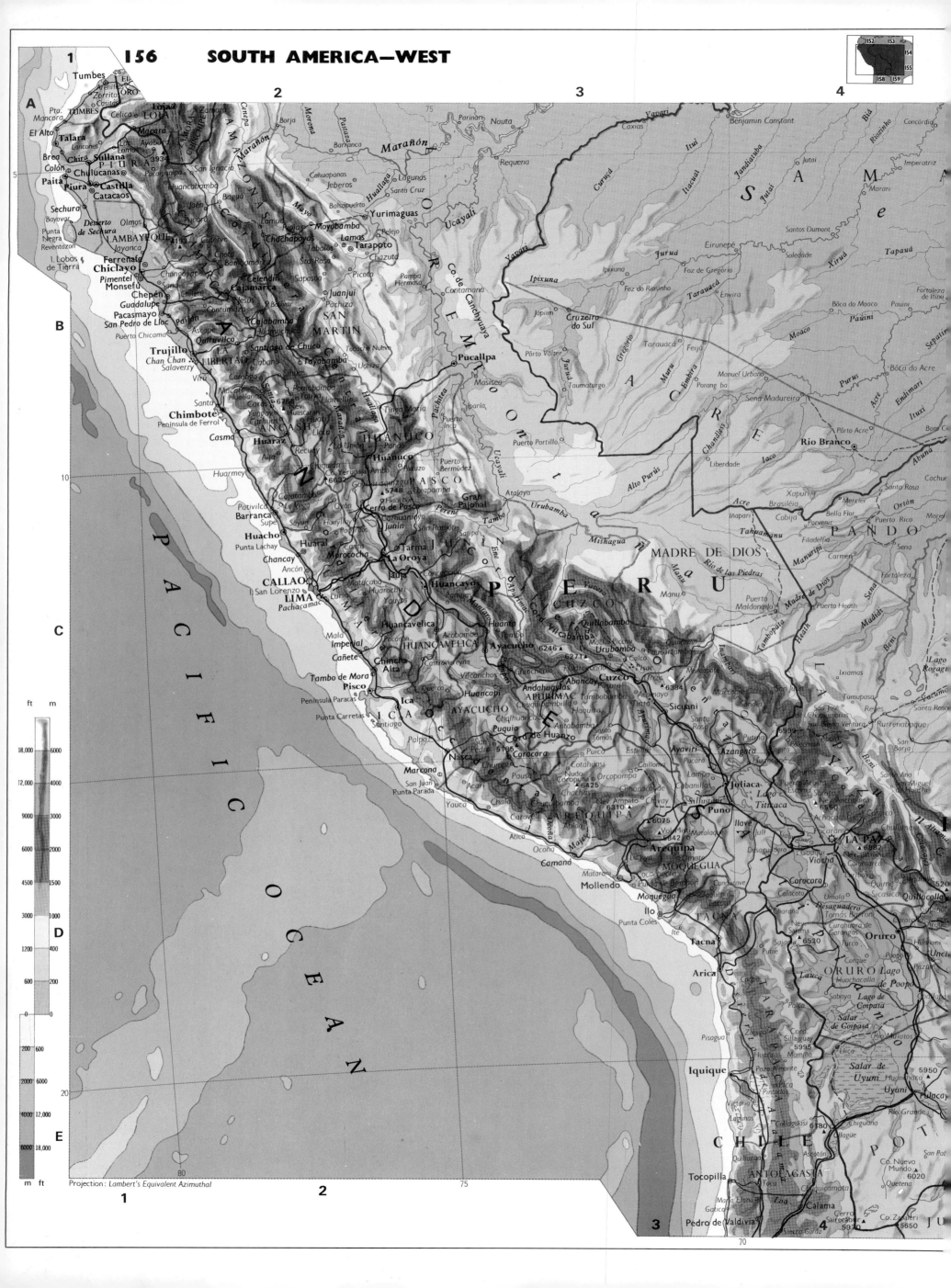

**PACIFIC OCEAN**

**PERU**

**AMAZONAS**

**PANDO**

**MADRE DE DIOS**

**CUZCO**

**AREQUIPA**

**CHILE**

**ANTOFAGASTA**

**ORURO**

Projection: Lambert's Equivalent Azimuthal

1 : 6 400 000

50   0   50   100   150   200 miles
50   0   100   200   300 km

5                           6                           7

A

**BRAZIL**

**ZONAS**

**PARÁ**

Itanhauá · Coari · Purus · Madeira · Preto do Igapó-Açu · Nova Aripuana · Abacaxis · Mundurucus · Tapajós · Iriri · Porto Alegre

Canutama · Abufari · Manicoré · Santa Maria dos Marmelos · Itapinima · Copoeira · Tucuraré · Entre Rios · Nazaré · São Fél.

Telj · Coari · Jaburu · Itatuba · Itapuá · Itaparaná · Manicoré · Prainha · Borba · Axinim · Canumã · Crepuri · Jamanxim · Curuá · Itaituba

B

Pinhua · Purus · Axioma · Tres Casas · Canumã · Miriti · Sai-Cinzo · Canudos · Recreio · Serra do Cachimbo · Cachimbo · Alto Iriri

Labrea · Humaitá · Aripuana · Barração do Barreto · S. Benedito · Curuá

Majuria · Calama · Marmelos · Jurvena · Cururu

C

Villa Bella · Guajará-Mirim · Sa. dos Pacaás Novos · Porto Velho · 404 · Bom Comércio · Abunã · Iciparaná · Nova Vida · Rondônia · Presidente Hermes · Peixoto de Azeredo · Serra Formosa · Manitsauá-Missu · Campo de Diauarum

Riberalta · Guayaramerín · Mamoré · Principe da Beira · Pimenta Bueno · Barão de Melgaço · Porto Cajueiro · Suiá Missu · Libertade

**RONDÔNIA** · Serra · 663 · Vilhena · Camararé · Nhambiquara · Juruena · Serra dos Caiabis · Romero · Porto dos Meinacos · Xingu

Puerto Siles · Lago Rogoaguado · San Joaquin · Versalles · Pedras Negras · Aripuã · Planalto · Culiseu · Serra do Roncador

Exaltación · Baures · Puerto Villazón · Serra de Huanchaca · Utiariti · Serra do Tombador · Arinos · Chavantina

**BENI** · Lago de San Luis · El Carmen · San Ramón · 995 · Mato Grosso · Guaporé · Nortelândia · Diamantino · Cuiabá · Planalto do · Aruanã

Trinidad · Loreto · San Javier · Perseverancia · 669 · Arenápolis · Alto Paraguai · Serra Azul · Mato 915 Grosso · Mortes

San Francisco · San Lorenzo · Añez · Santa Rosa de la Roca · Guaporé · Tapirapuã · Rosário Oeste · Barra do Bugres · Chapada dos Guimarães · Barro do Garças · Aragonças

D

Secure · San Ignacio · Negro · Santa Rosa del Palmar · Concepción · San Ignacio · Santa Ana · Porto Esperidão · Nossa Senhora do Livramento · Várzea Grande · Cuiabá · Coronel Ponce · Poxoreu · Tesouro · Rio das Garças · Araguáias

Cochabamba · Portachuelo · San Javier · San Miguel · San Matias · Cáceres · Poconé · Santo Antônio do Leverger · Barão de Melgaço · Jaciara · Rondonópolis · Guiratinga · Ponte Branca · Baliza · Sa. das Divisões

**BOLIVIA** · Montero · Warnes · El Cerro · Laguna Concepción · Chaco · Itiquira · São Lourenço · Alto Garças · Santa Rita do Araguaia · Caiapó · Rio Verde

**SANTA CRUZ** · Buena Vista · San José · Lagoa Uberaba · Pantanal do São Lourenço · Itiquira · Santa Rita do Araguaia · Mineiros · Jataí

Sucre · San Carlos · Cotoca · El Palmar · Llanos de Chiquitos · 1425 · Roboré · Serra Santiago de Santiago · La Cal · Lagoa Mandioré · Pantanal do Rio Negro · Rio Verde de Mato Grosso · Jaci · Baús · Verde · Itarumã · Açu · Cachoeira Alta

Villegrande · Abapó · Bañados de Izozog · Santa Ana · Puerto Suárez · Corumbá · **MATO GROSSO** · Apore · Cassilândia · Apore

**CHUQUISACA** · Gutiérrez · Lagunillas · Charagua · Fortin Ingavi · Fortin General Pando · Ladário · Nhecolândia · **DO SUL** · Aquidauana · Jaraguari · Ribas do Rio Pardo · Inocência · Aparecida do Taboado · Paranaíba

5614 · Camiri · Fortin Coronel Eugenio Garay · Bahia Negra · Aquidauana · Corumba · Aquidauana · Jardim · Rochedo · Agua Clara · Pereira Barreto

**NUEVA** · Carandaiti · Fortin Madrejón · **CHACO BOREAL** · Porto Esperança · Negro · Taquari · Campo Grande · Tres Lagoas · Andradina

**PARAGUAY** · Fortin Garrapatal · **ALTO PARAGUAY** · Fuerte Olimpo · Puerto Guaraní · Aquidauana · Miranda · Anhanduí · Mirandópolis · Aguapeí

E

**TARIJA** · Villa Montes · Camatindi · **PARAGUAY** · Porto Murtinho · Bonito · Nioaque · Maracaju · Xavantina · Panorama

**ASUNCIÓN** · La Esmeralda · Guia Lopes da Laguna · Garcias · Jardim

Tarija · Yacuiba · **BOQUERON** · Serra da Bodoquena · Aidrolândia

**SALTA** · Tartagal

5                           6                           7

West from Greenwich

65                    60                    55

Projection: Lambert's Equivalent Azimuthal

1 : 6 400 000

50   0   50   100   150   200 miles
50   0   100   200   300 km

BELO HORIZONTE

MATO GROSSO DO SUL

Três Lagoas · Andradina · Mirassol · S. Olímpia · Pardo · Batatais · Passos · Oliveira · Congonhas · Cons. Lafaiete · Ouro Prêto · Ponte Nova · Vitória · Itaquaí · Vila Velha

Xavantina · Araçatuba · Catanduva · Taquaritinga · S. do Rio Prêto · Bebedouro · Ribeirão Prêto · Guaxupé · São Seb. do Paraíso · Campo Belo · São João del Rei · Ubá · Muriaé · Itaperuna · Guarapari · Cachoeiro de Itapemirim

Mirandópolis · Birigui · Tietê · Penápolis · Novo Horizonte · Jaboticabal · Mococa · Três Pontas · Lavras · Barbacena · Cataguases · Leopoldina · Campos · Cabo de São Tomé

Pres. Epitácio · Adamantina · Tupã · Lins · Piraju · Araraquara · São Carlos · da Boa Vista · Poços de Caldas · Varginha · Três Corações · Juiz de Fora · Três Rios · Além Paraíba · Cambuci

Pôrto São José · Presidente Prudente · Martinópolis · Marília · Garça · Bauru · Ituá · Rio Claro · Limeira · Araras · Santos Dumont · Paraíba do Sul

Paranavaí · Centenário do Oeste · Rancharia · Paraguaçu Paulista · Assis · Cambará · Santa Cruz do Rio Pardo · Botucatu · Piracicaba · CAMPINAS · Americana · Mogi Mirim · Bragança · Pouso Alegre · Cruzeiro · Barra do Pirai · Nova Friburgo · Macaé

BRAZIL · Nova · Londrina · Rolândia · Avaré · Paulista · Volta Redonda · Angra dos Reis · RIO DE JANEIRO

Umuarama · Cianorte · Maringá · Arapongas · Cornélio Procópio · Jacarèzinho · Tatuí · Sorocaba · Jundiaí · SÃO PAULO · Mogi das Cruzes · Jacareí · Duque de Caxias · Petrópolis · NITERÓI

Guaíra · Apucarana · Mandaguari · Joaquim Távora · Ibaiti · Itapetininga · São Bernardo del Campo · SANTO ANDRÉ · S. dos Campos · Baía da Ilha Grande · L.ª de Araruama · Tropic of Capricorn

Cruzeiro do Oeste · Erê · PARANÁ · Itararé · Itapeva · São Vicente · Santos · Guarujá · Ilha de São Sebastião

CANINDEYÚ · Goio · Cândido de Abreu · Castro · Ponta Grossa · Itanhaém · Pta. do Boi

ITAGUAY · Cascavel · Guarapuava · Palmeira · CURITIBA · Antonina · Ilha do Cardoso · Iguape · Ilha Comprida · 25

Foz do Iguaçu · Iguaçu Falls · Irati · Lapa · Paranaguá · Guaratuba

PARANÁ · Bernardo de Irigoyen · União da Vitória · Rio Negro · Mafra · São Francisco do Sul · Joinvile

ITAPUÁ · MISIONES · Eldorado · Pto. União · Caçador · Itajaí · Blumenau · Brusque · SANTA CATARINA

Encarnación · Obera · Chapecó · Joaçaba · Campos Novos · Rio do Sul · Santa Cecília · Ilha de Santa Catarina · Florianópolis

N. Alem · Santa Rosa · Erechim · Lajes · 1808

Carázinho · Passo Fundo · Tubarão · Laguna

Santo Angelo · São Luís Gonzaga · Cruz Alta · Vacaria · Criciúma · Cabo Santa Marta Grande

RIO GRANDE · Guaporé · Bento Gonçalves · Araranguá

Santa Maria · Santa Cruz do Sul · Caxias do Sul · Montenegro · Nôvo Hamburgo · Taquara · 30

Alegrete · Cachoeira do Sul · Rio Pardo · São Leopoldo · Canoas · Viamão · Osório · PORTO ALEGRE

São Gabriel · Santana do Livramento · Rivera · Dom Pedrito · Caçapava do Sul · Camaquã · Lagoa dos Patos · Mostardas

Bagé · Sa. de Canguçu · Canguçu

URUGUAY · Tacuarembó · Melo · Pelotas · Rio Grande

San Gregorio · Jaguarão · Rio Branco · Lagoa Mirim

Sarandí del Yi · Lagoa Mangueira

Treinta y Tres · Santa Vitória do Palmar · ATLANTIC

José Batlle y Ordoñez · Lascano · Aigua · Castillos

Minas · Rocha · OCEAN

San Carlos · Maldonado

MONTEVIDEO

Rio de la Plata

West from Greenwich

COPYRIGHT. GEORGE PHILIP & SON. LTD

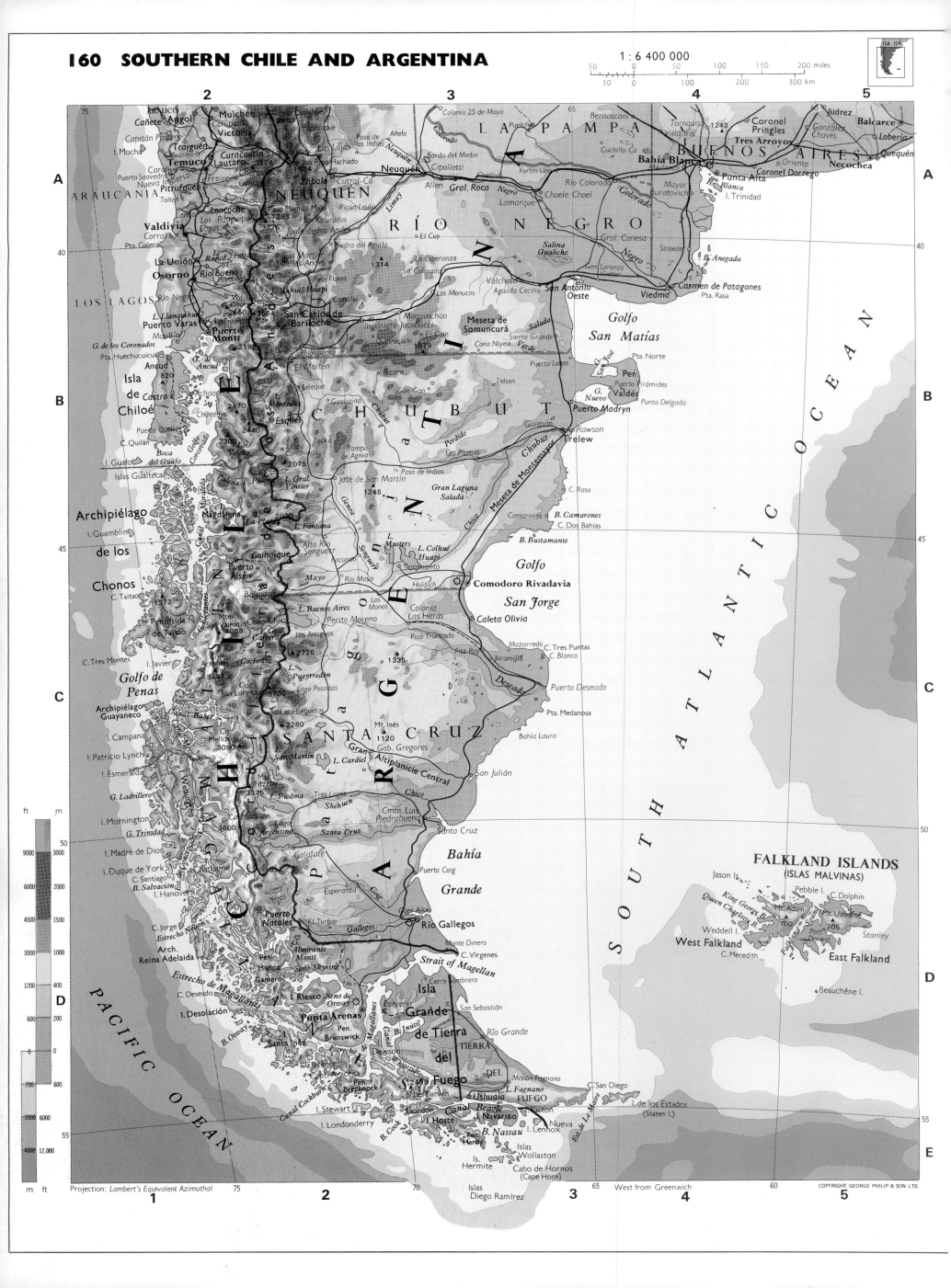

# INDEX

The index contains the names of all the principal places and features shown on the World Maps. Each name is followed by an additional entry in italics giving the country or region within which it is located. The alphabetical order of names composed of two or more words is governed primarily by the first word and then by the second. This is an example of the rule:

| | | | |
|---|---|---|---|
| Mīr Kūh, *Iran* | **85 E8** | 26 22 N | 58 55 E |
| Mīr Shahdād, *Iran* | **85 E8** | 26 15 N | 58 29 E |
| Miraj, *India* | **82 F2** | 16 50 N | 74 45 E |
| Miram Shah, *Pakistan* | **79 B3** | 33 0 N | 70 2 E |
| Miramar, *Mozam.* | **105 C6** | 23 50 S | 35 35 E |

Physical features composed of a proper name (Erie) and a description (Lake) are positioned alphabetically by the proper name. The description is positioned after the proper name and is usually abbreviated:

| | | | |
|---|---|---|---|
| Erie, L., *N. Amer.* | **136 D4** | 42 15 N | 81 0 W |

Where a description forms part of a settlement or administrative name however, it is always written in full and put in its true alphabetic position:

| | | | |
|---|---|---|---|
| Mount Morris, *U.S.A.* | **136 D7** | 42 43 N | 77 50 W |

Names beginning with M' and Mc are indexed as if they were spelt Mac. Names beginning St. are alphabetised under Saint, but Sankt, Sint, Sant', Santa and San are all spelt in full and are alphabetised accordingly. If the same place name occurs two or more times in the index and all are in the same country, each is followed by the name of the administrative subdivision in which it is located. The names are placed in the alphabetical order of the subdivisions. For example:

| | | | |
|---|---|---|---|
| Jackson, *Ky., U.S.A.* | **134 G4** | 37 35 N | 83 22 W |
| Jackson, *Mich., U.S.A.* | **141 B12** | 42 18 N | 84 25 W |
| Jackson, *Minn., U.S.A.* | **138 D7** | 43 35 N | 95 0 W |

The number in bold type which follows each name in the index refers to the number of the map page where that feature or place will be found. This is usually the largest scale at which the place or feature appears.

The letter and figure which are in bold type immediately after the page number give the grid square on the map page, within which the feature is situated. The letter represents the latitude and the figure the longitude.

In some cases the feature itself may fall within the specified square, while the name is outside. This is usually the case only with features which are larger than a grid square.

For a more precise location the geographical coordinates which follow the letter/figure references give the latitude and the longitude of each place. The first set of figures represent the latitude which is the distance north or south of the Equator measured as an angle at the centre of the earth. The Equator is latitude 0°, the North Pole is 90°N, and the South Pole 90°S.

The second set of figures represent the longitude, which is the distance East or West of the prime meridian, which runs through Greenwich, England. Longitude is also measured as an angle at the centre of the earth and is given East or West of the prime meridian, from 0° to 180° in either direction.

The unit of measurement for latitude and longitude is the degree, which is subdivided into 60 minutes. Each index entry states the position of a place in degrees and minutes, a space being left between the degrees and the minutes.

The latitude is followed by N(orth) or S(outh) and the longitude by E(ast) or W(est).

Rivers are indexed to their mouths or confluences, and carry the symbol → after their names. A solid square ■ follows the name of a country while, an open square □ refers to a first order administrative area.

## ABBREVIATIONS USED IN THE INDEX

*A.C.T.* — Australian Capital Territory
*Afghan.* — Afghanistan
*Ala.* — Alabama
*Alta.* — Alberta
*Amer.* — America(n)
*Arch.* — Archipelago
*Ariz.* — Arizona
*Ark.* — Arkansas
*Atl. Oc.* — Atlantic Ocean
*B.* — Baie, Bahía, Bay, Bucht, Bugt
*B.C.* — British Columbia
*Bangla.* — Bangladesh
*Barr.* — Barrage
*Bos.-H.* — Bosnia-Herzegovina
*C.* — Cabo, Cap, Cape, Coast
*C.A.R.* — Central African Republic
*C. Prov.* — Cape Province
*Calif.* — California
*Cent.* — Central
*Chan.* — Channel
*Colo.* — Colorado
*Conn.* — Connecticut
*Cord.* — Cordillera
*Cr.* — Creek
*Czech.* — Czechoslovakia
*D.C.* — District of Columbia
*Del.* — Delaware
*Dep.* — Dependency
*Des.* — Desert
*Dist.* — District
*Dj.* — Djebel
*Domin.* — Dominica
*Dom. Rep.* — Dominican Republic
*E.* — East
*El Salv.* — El Salvador

*Eq. Guin.* — Equatorial Guinea
*Fla.* — Florida
*Falk. Is.* — Falkland Is.
*G.* — Golfe, Golfo, Gulf, Guba, Gebel
*Ga.* — Georgia
*Gt.* — Great, Greater
*Guinea-Biss.* — Guinea-Bissau
*H.K.* — Hong Kong
*H.P.* — Himachal Pradesh
*Hants.* — Hampshire
*Harb.* — Harbor, Harbour
*Hd.* — Head
*Hts.* — Heights
*I.(s).* — Île, Ilha, Insel, Isla, Island, Isle
*Ill.* — Illinois
*Ind.* — Indiana
*Ind. Oc.* — Indian Ocean
*Ivory C.* — Ivory Coast
*J.* — Jabal, Jebel, Jazira
*Junc.* — Junction
*K.* — Kap, Kapp
*Kans.* — Kansas
*Kep.* — Kepulauan
*Ky.* — Kentucky
*L.* — Lac, Lacul, Lago, Lagoa, Lake, Limni, Loch, Lough
*La.* — Louisiana
*Liech.* — Liechtenstein
*Lux.* — Luxembourg
*Mad. P.* — Madhya Pradesh
*Madag.* — Madagascar
*Man.* — Manitoba
*Mass.* — Massachusetts
*Md.* — Maryland

*Me.* — Maine
*Medit. S.* — Mediterranean Sea
*Mich.* — Michigan
*Minn.* — Minnesota
*Miss.* — Mississippi
*Mo.* — Missouri
*Mont.* — Montana
*Mozam.* — Mozambique
*Mt.(e).* — Mont, Monte, Monti, Montaña, Mountain
*N.* — Nord, Norte, North, Northern, Nouveau
*N.B.* — New Brunswick
*N.C.* — North Carolina
*N. Cal.* — New Caledonia
*N. Dak.* — North Dakota
*N.H.* — New Hampshire
*N.I.* — North Island
*N.J.* — New Jersey
*N. Mex.* — New Mexico
*N.S.* — Nova Scotia
*N.S.W.* — New South Wales
*N.W.T.* — North West Territory
*N.Y.* — New York
*N.Z.* — New Zealand
*Nebr.* — Nebraska
*Neths.* — Netherlands
*Nev.* — Nevada
*Nfld.* — Newfoundland
*Nic.* — Nicaragua
*O.* — Oued, Ouadi
*Occ.* — Occidentale
*O.F.S.* — Orange Free State
*Okla.* — Oklahoma
*Ont.* — Ontario
*Or.* — Orientale

*Oreg.* — Oregon
*Os.* — Ostrov
*Oz.* — Ozero
*P.* — Pass, Passo, Pasul, Pulau
*P.E.I.* — Prince Edward Island
*Pa.* — Pennsylvania
*Pac. Oc.* — Pacific Ocean
*Papua N.G.* — Papua New Guinea
*Pass.* — Passage
*Pen.* — Peninsula, Péninsule
*Phil.* — Philippines
*Pk.* — Park, Peak
*Plat.* — Plateau
*P-ov.* — Poluostrov
*Prov.* — Province, Provincial
*Pt.* — Point
*Pta.* — Ponta, Punta
*Pte.* — Pointe
*Qué.* — Québec
*Queens.* — Queensland
*R.* — Rio, River
*R.I.* — Rhode Island
*Ra.(s).* — Range(s)
*Raj.* — Rajasthan
*Reg.* — Region
*Rep.* — Republic
*Res.* — Reserve, Reservoir
*S.* — San, South, Sea
*Si. Arabia* — Saudi Arabia
*S.C.* — South Carolina
*S. Dak.* — South Dakota
*S.I.* — South Island
*S. Leone* — Sierra Leone
*Sa.* — Serra, Sierra
*Sask.* — Saskatchewan
*Scot.* — Scotland

*Sd.* — Sound
*Sev.* — Severnaya
*Sib.* — Siberia
*Sprs.* — Springs
*St.* — Saint, Sankt, Sint
*Sta.* — Santa, Station
*Ste.* — Sainte
*Sto.* — Santo
*Str.* — Strait, Stretto
*Switz.* — Switzerland
*Tas.* — Tasmania
*Tenn.* — Tennessee
*Tex.* — Texas
*Tg.* — Tanjung
*Trin. & Tob.* — Trinidad & Tobago
*U.A.E.* — United Arab Emirates
*U.K.* — United Kingdom
*U.S.A.* — United States of America
*Ut. P.* — Uttar Pradesh
*Va.* — Virginia
*Vdkhr.* — Vodokhranilishche
*Vf.* — Vîrful
*Vic.* — Victoria
*Vol.* — Volcano
*Vt.* — Vermont
*W.* — Wadi, West
*W. Va.* — West Virginia
*Wash.* — Washington
*Wis.* — Wisconsin
*Wlkp.* — Wielkopolski
*Wyo.* — Wyoming
*Yorks.* — Yorkshire
*Yugo.* — Yugoslavia

162 Aachen

# A


Aachen, Germany 26 E2 50 47N 6 4 E
Aadorf, Switz. 29 B7 47 30N 8 55 E
Aalborg = Ålborg, Denmark 15 G3 57 2N 9 54 E
Aalen, Germany 27 G6 48 49N 10 6 E
A'âli en Nîl □, Sudan 95 F3 9 30N 31 30 E
Aalsmeer, Neths. 20 D5 52 17N 4 43 E
Aalst, Belgium 21 G4 50 56N 4 2 E
Aalst, Neths. 21 F6 51 23N 5 29 E
Aalten, Neths. 20 E9 51 56N 6 35 E
Aalter, Belgium 21 F2 51 5N 3 28 E
Aarau, Switz. 28 B6 47 23N 8 4 E
Aarberg, Switz. 28 B4 47 2N 7 16 E
Aardenburg, Belgium 21 F2 51 16N 3 28 E
Aare →, Switz. 28 A6 47 33N 8 14 E
Aargau □, Switz. 28 B6 47 26N 8 10 E
Aarhus = Århus, Denmark 15 H4 56 8N 10 11 E
Aarle, Neths. 21 E7 51 30N 5 38 E
Aarschot, Belgium 21 G5 50 59N 4 49 E
Aarsele, Belgium 21 G2 51 0N 3 26 E
Aartrijke, Belgium 21 F2 51 7N 3 6 E
Aarwangen, Switz. 28 B5 47 15N 7 46 E
Aba, China 68 A3 32 59N 101 42 E
Aba, Nigeria 101 D6 5 10N 7 19 E
Aba, Zaïre 106 B3 3 58N 30 17 E
Âbâ, Jazîrat, Sudan 95 E3 13 30N 32 31 E
Abacaxis →, Brazil 153 D6 3 54 S 58 47W
Ābādān, Iran 85 D6 30 22N 48 20 E
Abade, Ethiopia 95 F4 9 22N 38 3 E
Ābādeh, Iran 85 D7 31 8N 52 40 E
Abadin, Spain 36 B3 43 21N 7 29W
Abadla, Algeria 99 B4 31 2N 2 45W
Abaeté, Brazil 155 E2 19 9 S 45 27W
Abaeté →, Brazil 155 E2 18 2 S 45 12W
Abaetetuba, Brazil 154 B2 1 40 S 48 50W
Abagnar Qi, China 66 C9 43 52N 116 2 E
Abai, Paraguay 159 B4 25 58 S 55 54W
Abak, Nigeria 101 E6 4 58N 7 50 E
Abakaliki, Nigeria 101 D6 6 22N 8 2 E
Abakan, Russia 57 D10 53 40N 91 10 E
Abalemma, Niger 101 B6 16 12N 7 50 E
Abana, Turkey 88 C6 41 59N 34 1 E
Abancay, Peru 156 C3 13 35 S 72 55W
Abanilla, Spain 35 G3 38 12N 1 3W
Abano Terme, Italy 39 C8 45 22N 11 46 E
Abapó, Bolivia 157 D5 18 48 S 63 25W
Abarán, Spain 35 G3 38 12N 1 23W
Abariringa, Kiribati 122 H10 2 50 S 171 40W
Abarqū, Iran 85 D7 31 10N 53 20 E
Abashiri, Japan 60 B12 44 0N 144 15 E
Abashiri-Wan, Japan 60 B12 44 0N 144 30 E
Abau, Papua N. G. 120 F5 10 11 S 148 46 E
Abaújszántó, Hungary 31 C14 48 16N 21 12 E
Abay, Kazakhstan 56 E8 49 38N 72 53 E
Abaya, L., Ethiopia 95 F4 6 30N 37 50 E
Abaza, Russia 56 D10 52 39N 90 6 E
Abbadia San Salvatore, Italy 39 F8 42 53N 11 40 E
'Abbāsābād, Iran 85 C8 33 34N 58 23 E
Abbay = Nîl el Azraq →, Sudan 95 D3 15 38N 32 31 E
Abbaye, Pt., U.S.A. 134 B1 46 58N 88 4W
Abbé, L., Ethiopia 95 E5 11 8N 41 47 E
Abbeville, France 23 B8 50 6N 1 49 E
Abbeville, La., U.S.A. 139 K8 30 0N 92 7W
Abbeville, S.C., U.S.A. 135 H4 34 12N 82 21W
Abbiategrasso, Italy 38 C5 45 23N 8 55 E
Abbieglassie, Australia 115 D4 27 15 S 147 28 E
Abbot Ice Shelf, Antarctica 7 D16 73 0 S 92 0W
Abbotsford, Canada 130 D4 49 5N 122 20W
Abbotsford, U.S.A. 138 C9 44 55N 90 20W
Abbottabad, Pakistan 80 B5 34 10N 73 15 E
Abcoude, Neths. 20 D5 52 17N 4 59 E
Abd al Kūrī, Ind. Oc. 87 D6 12 5N 52 20 E
Ābdar, Iran 85 D7 30 16N 55 19 E
'Abdolābād, Iran 85 C8 34 12N 56 30 E
Abdulino, Russia 54 E3 53 42N 53 40 E
Abéché, Chad 97 F4 13 50N 20 35 E
Abejar, Spain 34 D2 41 48N 2 47W
Abekr, Sudan 95 E2 12 45N 28 50 E
Abêlessa, Algeria 99 D5 22 58N 4 47 E
Abengourou, Ivory C. 100 D4 6 42N 3 27W
Åbenrå, Denmark 15 J3 55 3N 9 25 E
Abensberg, Germany 27 G7 48 49N 11 51 E
Abeokuta, Nigeria 101 D5 7 3N 3 19 E
Aber, Uganda 106 B3 2 12N 32 25 E
Aberaeron, U.K. 17 E3 52 15N 4 16W
Aberayron = Aberaeron, U.K. 17 E3 52 15N 4 16W
Abercorn = Mbala, Zambia 107 D3 8 46 S 31 24 E
Abercorn, Australia 115 D5 25 12 S 151 5 E
Aberdare, U.K. 17 F4 51 43N 3 27W
Aberdare Ra., Kenya 106 C4 0 15 S 36 50 E
Aberdeen, Australia 117 B9 32 9 S 150 56 E
Aberdeen, Canada 131 C7 52 20N 106 8W
Aberdeen, S. Africa 104 E3 32 28 S 24 2 E
Aberdeen, U.K. 18 D6 57 9N 2 6W
Aberdeen, Ala., U.S.A. 135 J1 33 49N 88 33W
Aberdeen, Idaho, U.S.A. 142 E7 42 57N 112 50W
Aberdeen, Ohio, U.S.A. 141 F13 38 39N 83 46W
Aberdeen, S. Dak., U.S.A. 138 C5 45 30N 98 30W
Aberdeen, Wash., U.S.A. 144 D3 47 0N 123 50W
Aberdovey = Aberdyfi, U.K. 17 E3 52 33N 4 3W
Aberdyfi, U.K. 17 E3 52 33N 4 3W
Aberfeldy, Australia 117 D7 37 42 S 146 22 E
Aberfeldy, U.K. 18 E5 56 37N 3 50W
Abergaria-a-Velha, Portugal 36 E2 40 41N 8 32W
Abergavenny, U.K. 17 F4 51 49N 3 1W
Abernathy, U.S.A. 139 J4 33 49N 101 49W
Abert, L., U.S.A. 142 E3 42 40N 120 8W
Aberystwyth, U.K. 17 E3 52 25N 4 6W
Abha, Si. Arabia 94 D5 18 0N 42 34 E
Abhar, Iran 85 B6 36 9N 49 13 E
Abhayapuri, India 78 B3 26 24N 90 38 E
Abidiya, Sudan 94 D3 18 18N 34 3 E
Abidjan, Ivory C. 100 D4 5 26N 3 58W
Abilene, Kans., U.S.A. 138 F6 39 0N 97 16W
Abilene, Tex., U.S.A. 139 J5 32 22N 99 40W
Abingdon, U.K. 17 F6 51 40N 1 17W
Abingdon, Ill., U.S.A. 140 D6 40 53N 90 23W
Abingdon, Va., U.S.A. 135 G5 36 46N 81 56W
Abington Reef, Australia 114 B4 18 0 S 149 35 E
Abitau →, Canada 131 B7 59 53N 109 3W
Abitau L., Canada 131 A7 60 27N 107 15W
Abitibi L., Canada 128 C4 48 40N 79 40W
Abiy Adi, Ethiopia 95 E4 13 39N 39 3 E
Abkhaz Republic □, Georgia 53 E9 43 0N 41 0 E
Abkit, Russia 57 C16 64 10N 157 10 E
Abminga, Australia 115 D1 26 8 S 134 51 E
Abnûb, Egypt 94 B3 27 18N 31 4 E
Abo, Massif d', Chad 97 D3 21 41N 16 8 E
Abocho, Nigeria 101 D6 7 35N 6 56 E
Abohar, India 80 D6 30 10N 74 10 E
Aboisso, Ivory C. 100 D4 5 30N 3 5W
Abolo, Congo 102 B2 0 8N 14 16 E
Abomey, Benin 101 D5 7 10N 2 5 E
Abondance, France 25 B10 46 18N 6 43 E
Abong-Mbang, Cameroon 102 B2 4 0N 13 8 E
Abongabong, Indonesia 74 B1 4 15N 96 48 E
Abonnema, Nigeria 101 E6 4 41N 6 49 E
Abony, Hungary 31 D13 47 12N 20 3 E
Aboso, Ghana 100 D4 5 23N 1 57W
Abou-Deïa, Chad 97 F3 11 20N 19 20 E
Abou Goulem, Chad 97 F4 13 37N 21 38 E
Aboyne, U.K. 18 D6 57 4N 2 48W
Abra □, Phil. 70 C3 17 35N 120 45 E
Abra de Ilog, Phil. 70 E3 13 27N 120 44 E
Abra Pampa, Argentina 158 A2 22 43 S 65 42W
Abrantes, Portugal 37 F2 39 24N 8 7W
Abraveses, Portugal 36 E3 40 41N 7 55W
Abreojos, Pta., Mexico 146 B2 26 50N 113 40W
Abreschviller, France 23 D14 48 39N 7 6 E
Abri, Esh Shamâliya, Sudan 94 C3 20 50N 30 27 E
Abri, Janub Kordofân, Sudan 95 E3 11 40N 30 21 E
Abrolhos, Banka, Brazil 155 E4 18 0 S 38 0W
Abrud, Romania 46 C4 46 19N 23 5 E
Abruzzi □, Italy 39 F10 42 15N 14 0 E
Absaroka Ra., U.S.A. 142 D9 44 40N 110 0W
Abū al Khaṣīb, Iraq 85 D6 30 25N 48 0 E
Abū 'Alī, Si. Arabia 85 E6 27 20N 49 27 E
Abū 'Alī →, Lebanon 91 A4 34 25N 35 50 E
Abu 'Arīsh, Si. Arabia 86 C3 16 53N 42 48 E
Abû Ballas, Egypt 94 C2 24 26N 27 36 E
Abu Deleiq, Sudan 95 D3 15 57N 33 48 E
Abu Dhabi = Abū Ẓāby, U.A.E. 85 E7 24 28N 54 22 E
Abû Dis, Sudan 94 D3 19 12N 33 38 E
Abû Dom, Sudan 95 D3 16 18N 32 25 E
Abû Du'ān, Syria 84 B3 36 25N 38 15 E
Abu el Gairi, W. →, Egypt 91 F2 29 35N 33 30 E
Abû Gabra, Sudan 95 E2 11 2N 26 50 E
Abu Ga'da, W. →, Egypt 91 F1 29 15N 32 53 E
Abû Gubeiha, Sudan 95 E3 11 30N 31 15 E
Abu Habl, Khawr →, Sudan 95 E3 12 37N 31 0 E
Abū Ḥadrīyah, Si. Arabia 85 E6 27 20N 48 58 E
Abu Hamed, Sudan 94 D3 19 32N 33 13 E
Abu Haraz, An Nîl el Azraq, Sudan 95 E3 14 35N 33 30 E
Abu Haraz, Esh Shamâliya, Sudan 94 D3 19 8N 32 18 E
Abû Higar, Sudan 95 E3 12 50N 33 59 E
Abū Kamāl, Syria 84 C4 34 30N 41 0 E
Abū Madd, Ra's, Si. Arabia 84 E3 24 50N 37 7 E
Abu Matariq, Sudan 95 E2 10 59N 26 9 E
Abu Qir, Egypt 94 H7 31 18N 30 0 E
Abu Qireiya, Egypt 94 C4 24 5N 35 28 E
Abu Qurqâs, Egypt 94 J7 28 1N 30 44 E
Abū Raṣāṣ, Ra's, Oman 87 B7 20 10N 58 38 E
Abū Rubayq, Si. Arabia 86 B2 23 44N 39 42 E
Abu Ṣafāt, W. →, Jordan 91 E5 30 24N 36 7 E
Abû Simbel, Egypt 94 C3 22 18N 31 40 E
Abū Şukhayr, Iraq 84 D5 31 54N 44 30 E
Abu Tig, Egypt 94 B3 27 4N 31 15 E
Abu Tiga, Sudan 95 E3 12 47N 34 12 E
Abû Zabad, Sudan 95 E2 12 25N 29 10 E
Abū Ẓāby, U.A.E. 85 E7 24 28N 54 22 E
Abū Zeydābād, Iran 85 C6 33 54N 51 45 E
Abufari, Brazil 157 B5 5 25 S 62 59W
Abuja, Nigeria 101 D6 9 16N 7 2 E
Abukuma-Gawa →, Japan 60 E10 38 6N 140 52 E
Abukuma-Sammyaku, Japan 60 F10 37 30N 140 45 E
Abulug, Phil. 70 B3 18 27N 121 27 E
Abumombazi, Zaïre 102 B4 3 42N 22 10 E
Abunã, Brazil 157 B4 9 40 S 65 20W
Abunã →, Brazil 157 B4 9 41 S 65 20W
Abung, Phil. 70 E3 13 46N 121 26 E
Aburatsu, Japan 62 F3 31 34N 131 24 E
Aburo, Zaïre 106 B3 2 4N 30 53 E
Abut Hd., N.Z. 119 D5 43 7 S 170 15 E
Abwong, Sudan 95 F3 9 2N 32 14 E
Åby, Sweden 15 F10 58 40N 16 10 E
Aby, Lagune, Ivory C. 100 D4 5 15N 3 14W
Acacías, Colombia 152 C3 3 59N 73 46W
Acajutla, El Salv. 148 D2 13 36N 89 50W
Açailândia, Brazil 154 C2 5 0 S 47 30W
Acámbaro, Mexico 146 C4 20 0N 100 40W
Acanthus, Greece 44 D5 40 27N 23 47 E
Acaponeta, Mexico 146 C3 22 30N 105 20W
Acapulco, Mexico 147 D5 16 51N 99 56W
Acarai, Serra, Brazil 153 C6 1 50N 57 50W
Acaraú, Brazil 154 B3 2 53 S 40 7W
Acari, Brazil 154 C4 6 31 S 36 38W
Acarí, Peru 156 D3 15 25 S 74 36W
Acarigua, Venezuela 152 B4 9 33N 69 12W
Acatlán, Mexico 147 D5 18 10N 98 3W
Acayucan, Mexico 147 D6 17 59N 94 58W
Accéglio, Italy 38 D3 44 28N 6 59 E
Accomac, U.S.A. 134 G8 37 43N 75 40W
Accous, France 24 E3 43 0N 0 36W
Accra, Ghana 101 D4 5 35N 0 6W
Accrington, U.K. 16 D5 53 46N 2 22W
Acebal, Argentina 158 C3 33 20 S 60 50W
Acerenza, Italy 41 B8 40 50N 15 58 E
Acerra, Italy 41 B7 40 57N 14 22 E
Aceuchal, Spain 37 G4 38 39N 6 30W
Achacachi, Bolivia 156 D4 16 3 S 68 43W
Achaguas, Venezuela 152 B4 7 46N 68 14W
Achalpur, India 82 D3 21 22N 77 32 E
Achao, Chile 160 B2 42 28 S 73 30W
Achel, Belgium 21 F6 51 15N 5 29 E
Acheng, China 67 B14 45 30N 126 58 E
Achenkirch, Austria 30 D4 47 32N 11 45 E
Achensee, Austria 30 D4 47 26N 11 45 E
Acher, India 80 H5 23 10N 72 32 E
Achern, Germany 27 G4 48 37N 8 5 E
Acheron →, N.Z. 119 C8 42 16 S 173 4 E
Achill, Ireland 19 C2 53 56N 9 55W
Achill Hd., Ireland 19 C1 53 59N 10 15W
Achill I., Ireland 19 C1 53 58N 10 5W
Achill Sd., Ireland 19 C2 53 53N 9 55W
Achim, Germany 26 B5 53 1N 9 2 E
Achinsk, Russia 57 D10 56 20N 90 20 E
Achisay, Kazakhstan 55 B4 43 35N 68 53 E
Achit, Russia 54 C5 56 48N 57 54 E
Achol, Sudan 95 F3 6 35N 31 32 E
Acıgöl, Turkey 88 E3 37 50N 29 50 E
Acireale, Italy 41 E8 37 37N 15 9 E
Ackerman, U.S.A. 139 J10 33 20N 89 8W
Ackley, U.S.A. 140 B3 42 33N 93 3W
Acklins I., Bahamas 149 B5 22 30N 74 0W
Acme, Canada 130 C6 51 33N 113 30W
Acobamba, Peru 156 C3 12 52 S 74 35W
Acomayo, Peru 156 C3 13 55 S 71 38W
Aconcagua □, Chile 158 C1 32 15 S 70 30W
Aconcagua, Cerro, Argentina 158 C2 32 39 S 70 0W
Aconquija, Mt., Argentina 158 B2 27 0 S 66 0W
Acopiara, Brazil 154 C4 6 6 S 39 27W
Açores, Is. dos = Azores, Atl. Oc. 8 E6 38 44N 29 0W
Acorizal, Brazil 157 D6 15 12 S 56 22W
Acquapendente, Italy 39 F8 42 45N 11 50 E
Acquasanta, Italy 39 F10 42 46N 13 24 E
Acquaviva delle Fonti, Italy 41 B9 40 53N 16 50 E
Acqui, Italy 38 D5 44 40N 8 28 E
Acraman, L., Australia 115 E2 32 2 S 135 23 E
Acre = 'Akko, Israel 91 C4 32 55N 35 4 E
Acre □, Brazil 156 B3 9 1 S 71 0W
Acre →, Brazil 156 B4 8 45 S 67 22W
Acri, Italy 41 C9 39 29N 16 23 E
Acs, Hungary 31 D11 47 42N 18 2 E
Actium, Greece 45 F2 38 57N 20 45 E
Acton, Canada 136 C4 43 38N 80 3W
Açu, Brazil 154 C4 5 34 S 36 54W
Ad Dahnā, Si. Arabia 87 A5 24 30N 48 10 E
Ad Ḍāli', Yemen 86 D4 13 42N 44 44 E
Ad Dammām, Si. Arabia 85 E6 26 20N 50 5 E
Ad Darb, Si. Arabia 86 C3 18 2N 43 7 E
Ad Dawhah, Qatar 85 E6 25 15N 51 35 E
Ad Dawr, Iraq 84 C4 34 27N 43 47 E
Ad Ḍiffah, Libya 96 B4 30 30N 24 30 E
Ad Dilam, Si. Arabia 86 B4 23 55N 47 10 E
Ad Dir'īyah, Si. Arabia 84 E5 24 44N 46 35 E
Ad Dīwānīyah, Iraq 84 D5 32 0N 45 0 E
Ad Dujayl, Iraq 84 C5 33 51N 44 14 E
Ad Durūz, J., Jordan 91 C5 32 35N 36 40 E
Ada, Ghana 101 D5 5 44N 0 40 E
Ada, Serbia, Yug. 42 B5 45 49N 20 9 E
Ada, Minn., U.S.A. 138 B6 47 20N 96 30W
Ada, Ohio, U.S.A. 141 D13 40 46N 83 49W
Ada, Okla., U.S.A. 139 H6 34 50N 96 45W
Adad, Somali Rep. 108 C3 9 27N 46 49 E
Adaja →, Spain 36 D6 41 32N 4 52W
Ådalslinden, Sweden 14 A10 63 27N 16 55 E
Adam, Oman 87 B7 22 15N 57 28 E
Adam, Mt., Falk. Is. 160 D4 51 34 S 60 4W
Adamantina, Brazil 155 F1 21 42 S 51 4W
Adamaoua, Massif de l', Cameroon 101 D7 7 20N 12 20 E
Adamawa Highlands = Adamaoua, Massif de l', Cameroon 101 D7 7 20N 12 20 E
Adamello, Mt., Italy 38 B7 46 10N 10 34 E
Adami Tulu, Ethiopia 95 F4 7 53N 38 41 E
Adaminaby, Australia 117 D8 36 0 S 148 45 E
Adamovka, Russia 54 F6 51 32N 59 56 E
Adams, Phil. 70 B3 18 28N 120 54 E
Adams, Mass., U.S.A. 137 D11 42 38N 73 8W
Adams, N.Y., U.S.A. 137 C8 43 50N 76 3W
Adams, Wis., U.S.A. 138 D10 43 59N 89 50W
Adams, Mt., U.S.A. 144 D5 46 10N 121 28W
Adam's Bridge, Sri Lanka 83 K4 9 15N 79 40 E
Adams L., Canada 130 C5 51 10N 119 40W
Adam's Peak, Sri Lanka 83 L5 6 48N 80 30 E
Adamuz, Spain 37 G6 38 2N 4 32W
Adana, Turkey 88 E6 37 0N 35 16 E
Adana □, Turkey 88 E6 37 0N 35 30 E
Adanero, Spain 36 E6 40 56N 4 36W
Adapazarı, Turkey 88 C4 40 48N 30 25 E
Adarama, Sudan 95 D3 17 10N 34 52 E
Adare, C., Antarctica 7 D11 71 0 S 171 0 E
Adaut, Indonesia 73 C4 8 8 S 131 7 E
Adavale, Australia 115 D3 25 52 S 144 32 E
Adda →, Italy 38 C6 45 8N 9 53 E
Addis Ababa = Addis Abeba, Ethiopia 95 F4 9 2N 38 42 E
Addis Abeba, Ethiopia 95 F4 9 2N 38 42 E
Addis Alem, Ethiopia 95 F4 9 0N 38 17 E
Addison, Ill., U.S.A. 141 C8 41 56N 88 0W
Addison, N.Y., U.S.A. 136 D7 42 9N 77 15W
Addo, S. Africa 104 E4 33 32 S 25 45 E
Addyston, U.S.A. 141 E12 39 8N 84 43W
Adebour, Niger 97 F2 13 17N 11 50 E
Ādeh, Iran 84 B5 37 42N 45 11 E
Adel, Ga., U.S.A. 135 K4 31 10N 83 28W
Adel, Iowa, U.S.A. 140 C2 41 37N 94 1W
Adelaide, Australia 116 C3 34 52 S 138 30 E
Adelaide, Bahamas 148 A4 25 4N 77 31W
Adelaide, S. Africa 104 E4 32 42 S 26 20 E
Adelaide I., Antarctica 7 C17 67 15 S 68 30W
Adelaide Pen., Canada 126 B10 68 15N 97 30W
Adelaide River, Australia 112 B5 13 15 S 131 7 E
Adelanto, U.S.A. 145 L9 34 35N 117 22W
Adelboden, Switz. 28 D5 46 29N 7 33 E
Adele I., Australia 112 C3 15 32 S 123 9 E
Adélie, Terre, Antarctica 7 C10 68 0 S 140 0 E
Ademuz, Spain 34 E3 40 5N 1 13W
Aden = Al 'Adan, Yemen 86 D4 12 45N 45 0 E
Aden, G. of, Asia 90 E4 12 30N 47 30 E
Adendorp, S. Africa 104 E3 32 15 S 24 30 E
Adh Dhayd, U.A.E. 85 E7 25 17N 55 53 E
Adhoi, India 80 H4 23 26N 70 32 E
Adi, Indonesia 73 B4 4 15 S 133 30 E
Adi Daro, Ethiopia 95 E4 14 20N 38 14 E
Adi Keyih, Ethiopia 95 E4 14 51N 39 22 E
Adi Kwala, Ethiopia 95 E4 14 38N 38 48 E
Adi Ugri, Ethiopia 95 E4 14 58N 38 48 E
Adieu, C., Australia 113 F5 32 0 S 132 10 E
Adieu Pt., Australia 112 C3 15 14 S 124 35 E
Adigala, Ethiopia 95 E5 10 24N 42 15 E
Adige →, Italy 39 C9 45 9N 12 20 E
Adigrat, Ethiopia 95 E4 14 20N 39 26 E
Adilabad, India 82 E4 19 33N 78 20 E
Adin, U.S.A. 142 F3 41 10N 121 0W
Adinkerke, Belgium 21 F1 51 5N 2 36 E
Adirondack Mts., U.S.A. 137 C10 44 0N 74 15W
Adıyaman, Turkey 89 E8 37 45N 38 16 E
Adıyaman □, Turkey 89 E8 37 30N 38 10 E
Adjim, Tunisia 96 B2 33 47N 10 50 E
Adjohon, Benin 101 D5 6 41N 2 32 E
Adjud, Romania 46 C8 46 7N 27 10 E
Adjumani, Uganda 106 B3 3 20N 31 50 E
Adlavik Is., Canada 129 B8 55 2N 57 45W
Adler, Russia 53 E8 43 28N 39 52 E
Adliswil, Switz. 29 B7 47 19N 8 32 E
Admer, Algeria 99 D6 20 21N 5 27 E
Admer, Erg d', Algeria 99 D6 24 0N 9 5 E
Admiralty G., Australia 112 B4 14 20 S 125 55 E
Admiralty I., U.S.A. 126 C6 57 40N 134 35W
Admiralty Inlet, U.S.A. 142 C2 48 0N 122 40W
Admiralty Is., Papua N. G. 120 B4 2 0 S 147 0 E
Ado, Nigeria 101 D5 6 36N 2 56 E
Ado Ekiti, Nigeria 101 D6 7 38N 5 12 E
Adok, Sudan 95 F3 8 10N 30 20 E
Adola, Ethiopia 95 E5 11 14N 41 44 E
Adonara, Indonesia 72 C2 8 15 S 123 5 E
Adoni, India 83 G3 15 33N 77 18 E
Adony, Hungary 31 D11 47 6N 18 52 E
Adour →, France 24 E2 43 32N 1 32W
Adra, India 81 H12 23 30N 86 42 E
Adra, Spain 35 J1 36 43N 3 3W
Adrano, Italy 41 E7 37 40N 14 49 E
Adrar, Algeria 99 C4 27 51N 0 11W
Adrasman, Tajikistan 55 C4 40 38N 69 58 E
Adré, Chad 97 F4 13 40N 22 20 E
Adrī, Libya 96 C2 27 32N 13 2 E
Ádria, Italy 39 C9 45 4N 12 3 E
Adrian, Mich., U.S.A. 141 C12 41 55N 84 5W
Adrian, Mo., U.S.A. 140 F2 38 24N 94 21W
Adrian, Tex., U.S.A. 139 H3 35 19N 102 37W
Adriatic Sea, Europe 10 G8 43 0N 16 0 E
Adua, Indonesia 73 B3 1 45 S 129 50 E
Adula, Switz. 29 D8 46 30N 9 3 E
Adung Long, Burma 78 A6 28 7N 97 42 E
Adur, India 83 K3 9 8N 76 40 E
Adwa, Ethiopia 95 E4 14 15N 38 52 E
Adzhar Republic □, Georgia 53 F10 41 30N 42 0 E
Adzopé, Ivory C. 100 D4 6 7N 3 49W
Ægean Sea, Europe 45 F7 38 30N 25 0 E
Æolian Is. = Eólie, Is., Italy 41 D7 38 30N 14 50 E
Aerhtai Shan, Mongolia 64 B4 46 40N 92 45 E
Ærø, Denmark 15 K4 54 52N 10 25 E
Ærøskøbing, Denmark 15 K4 54 53N 10 24 E
Aesch, Switz. 28 B5 47 28N 7 36 E
Aëtós, Greece 45 G3 37 15N 21 50 E
Afafi, Massif d', Niger 97 D3 22 11N 15 10 E
'Afak, Iraq 84 C5 32 4N 45 15 E
Afanasyevo, Russia 54 B3 58 52N 53 15 E
Afándou, Greece 32 C10 36 18N 28 12 E
Afarag, Erg, Algeria 99 D5 23 50N 2 47 E
Afars & Issas, Terr. of = Djibouti ■, Africa 90 E3 12 0N 43 0 E
Afdega, Ethiopia 108 C2 6 4N 43 30 E
Affreville = Khemis Miliana, Algeria 99 A5 36 11N 2 14 E
Affton, U.S.A. 140 F6 38 33N 90 20W
Afghanistan ■, Asia 79 B2 33 0N 65 0 E
Afgoi, Somali Rep. 90 G3 2 7N 44 59 E
'Afif, Si. Arabia 86 B3 23 53N 42 56 E
Afikpo, Nigeria 101 D6 5 53N 7 54 E
Aflou, Algeria 99 B5 34 7N 2 3 E
Afmadu, Somali Rep. 108 D2 0 31N 42 4 E
Afogados da Ingàzeira, Brazil 154 C4 7 45 S 37 39W
Afognak I., U.S.A. 126 C4 58 10N 152 50W
Afragola, Italy 41 B7 40 54N 14 15 E
Afrera, Ethiopia 95 E5 13 16N 41 5 E
Africa 92 E6 10 0N 20 0 E
'Afrīn, Syria 84 B3 36 32N 36 50 E
Afşin, Turkey 88 D7 38 14N 36 55 E
Afton, U.S.A. 137 D9 42 14N 75 31W
Aftout, Algeria 98 C4 26 50N 3 45W
Afuá, Brazil 153 D7 0 15 S 50 20W
Afula, Israel 91 C4 32 37N 35 17 E
Afyonkarahisar, Turkey 88 D4 38 45N 30 33 E
Afyonkarahisar □, Turkey 88 D4 38 45N 30 30 E
Aga, Egypt 94 H7 30 55N 31 10 E
Agadès = Agadez, Niger 97 E1 16 58N 7 59 E
Agadez, Niger 97 E1 16 58N 7 59 E
Agadir, Morocco 98 B3 30 28N 9 55W
Agaete, Canary Is. 33 F4 28 6N 15 43W
Agailás, Mauritania 98 D2 22 37N 14 22W
Agana, Guam 121 R15 13 28N 144 45 E
Agapa, Russia 57 B9 71 27N 89 15 E
Agapovka, Russia 54 E6 53 18N 59 8 E
Agar, India 80 H7 23 40N 76 2 E
Agaro, Ethiopia 95 F4 7 50N 36 38 E
Agartala, India 78 D3 23 50N 91 23 E
Agăş, Romania 46 C7 46 28N 26 15 E
Agassiz, Canada 130 D4 49 14N 121 46W
Agats, Indonesia 73 C5 5 33 S 138 0 E
Agbélouvé, Togo 101 D5 6 35N 1 14 E
Agboville, Ivory C. 100 D4 5 55N 4 15W
Agcogan, Phil. 70 E3 12 4N 121 57 E
Agdam, Azerbaijan 53 G12 40 0N 46 58 E
Agdash, Azerbaijan 53 F12 40 44N 47 22 E
Agde, France 24 E7 43 19N 3 28 E
Agde, C. d', France 24 E7 43 16N 3 28 E
Agdz, Morocco 98 B3 30 47N 6 30W
Agdzhabedi, Azerbaijan 53 F12 40 5N 47 27 E
Agen, France 24 D4 44 12N 0 38 E
Ageo, Japan 63 B11 35 58N 139 36 E

Al Khawr 163

Ager Tay, Chad 97 E3 20 0N 17 41 E
Agersø, Denmark 15 J5 55 13N 11 12 E
Ageyevo, Russia 51 D10 54 10N 36 27 E
Agger, Denmark 15 H2 56 47N 8 13 E
Ággius, Italy 40 B2 40 56N 9 4 E
Āgh Kand, Iran 85 B6 37 15N 48 4 E
Aghoueyyît, Mauritania 98 D1 21 10N 15 6W
Aginskoye, Russia 57 D12 51 6N 114 32 E
Agira, Italy 41 E7 37 40N 14 30 E
Ağlasun, Turkey 88 E4 37 39N 30 31 E
Agly →, France 24 F7 42 46N 3 3 E
Agnibilékrou, Ivory C. 100 D4 7 10N 3 11W
Agnita, Romania 46 D5 45 59N 24 40 E
Agnone, Italy 41 A7 41 49N 14 20 E
Ago, Japan 63 C8 34 20N 136 51 E
Agofie, Ghana 101 D5 8 27N 0 15 E
Agogna →, Italy 38 C5 45 4N 8 52 E
Agogo, Sudan 95 F2 7 50N 28 45 E
Agon, France 22 C5 49 2N 1 34W
Agön, Sweden 14 C11 61 34N 17 23 E
Agoo, Phil. 70 C3 16 20N 120 22 E
Ágordo, Italy 39 B9 46 18N 12 2 E
Agout →, France 24 E5 43 47N 1 41 E
Agra, India 80 F7 27 17N 77 58 E
Agramunt, Spain 34 D6 41 48N 1 6 E
Agreda, Spain 34 D3 41 51N 1 55W
Ağri, Turkey 89 D10 39 44N 43 4 E
Ağri □, Turkey 89 D10 39 45N 43 5 E
Agri →, Italy 41 B9 40 13N 16 44 E
Ağrı Dağı, Turkey 89 D11 39 50N 44 15 E
Ağrı Karakose, Turkey 89 D10 39 44N 43 3 E
Agrigento, Italy 40 E6 37 19N 13 33 E
Agrinion, Greece 45 F3 38 37N 21 27 E
Agrópoli, Italy 41 B7 40 23N 14 59 E
Agryz, Russia 54 C3 56 33N 53 2 E
Água Branca, Brazil 154 C3 5 50 S 42 40W
Agua Caliente, Baja Calif. N., Mexico 145 N10 32 29N 116 59W
Agua Caliente, Sinaloa, Mexico 146 B3 26 30N 108 20W
Agua Caliente Springs, U.S.A. 145 N10 32 56N 116 19W
Água Clara, Brazil 157 E7 20 25 S 52 45W
Agua Hechicero, Mexico 145 N10 32 26N 116 14W
Agua Preta →, Brazil 153 D5 1 41 S 63 48W
Agua Prieta, Mexico 146 A3 31 20N 109 32W
Aguachica, Colombia 152 B3 8 19N 73 38W
Aguada Cecilio, Argentina 160 B3 40 51 S 65 51W
Aguadas, Colombia 152 B2 5 40N 75 38W
Aguadilla, Puerto Rico 149 C6 18 27N 67 10W
Aguadulce, Panama 148 E3 8 15N 80 32W
Aguanga, U.S.A. 145 M10 33 27N 116 51W
Aguanish, Canada 129 B7 50 14N 62 2W
Aguanus →, Canada 129 B7 50 13N 62 5W
Aguapeí, Brazil 157 D6 16 12 S 59 43W
Aguapeí →, Brazil 155 F1 21 0 S 51 0W
Aguapey →, Argentina 158 B4 29 7 S 56 36W
Aguaray Guazú →, Paraguay 158 A4 24 47 S 57 19W
Aguarico →, Ecuador 152 D2 0 59 S 75 11W
Aguas →, Spain 34 D4 41 20N 0 30W
Aguas Blancas, Chile 158 A2 24 15 S 69 55W
Aguas Calientes, Sierra de, Argentina 158 B2 25 26 S 66 40W
Águas Formosas, Brazil 155 E3 17 5 S 40 57W
Aguascalientes, Mexico 146 C4 21 53N 102 12W
Aguascalientes □, Mexico 146 C4 22 0N 102 20W
Agudo, Spain 37 G6 38 59N 4 52W
Águeda, Portugal 36 E2 40 34N 8 27W
Agueda →, Spain 36 D4 41 2N 6 56W
Aguié, Niger 101 C6 13 31N 7 46 E
Aguilafuente, Spain 36 D6 41 13N 4 7W
Aguilar, Spain 37 H6 37 31N 4 40W
Aguilar de Campóo, Spain 36 C6 42 47N 4 15W
Aguilares, Argentina 158 B2 27 26 S 65 35W
Aguilas, Spain 35 H3 37 23N 1 35W
Agüimes, Canary Is. 33 G4 27 58N 15 27W
Aguja, C. de la, Colombia 152 A3 11 18N 74 12W
Agulaa, Ethiopia 95 E4 13 40N 39 40 E
Agulhas, C., S. Africa 104 E3 34 52 S 20 0 E
Agulo, Canary Is. 33 F2 28 11N 17 12W
Agung, Indonesia 75 D5 8 20 S 115 28 E
Agur, Uganda 106 B3 2 28N 32 55 E
Agusan →, Phil. 71 G5 9 0N 125 30 E
Agusan del Norte □, Phil. 71 G5 9 20N 125 10 E
Agusan del Sur □, Phil. 71 G5 8 30N 125 30 E
Agustín Codazzi, Colombia 152 A3 10 2N 73 14W
Agutaya I., Phil. 71 F3 11 9N 120 58 E
Agvali, Russia 53 E12 42 36N 46 8 E
Aha Mts., Botswana 104 B3 19 45 S 21 0 E
Ahaggar, Algeria 99 D6 23 0N 6 30 E
Ahamansu, Ghana 101 D5 7 38N 0 35 E
Ahar, Iran 84 B5 38 35N 47 0 E
Ahaura →, N.Z. 119 C6 42 21 S 171 34 E
Ahaus, Germany 26 C3 52 4N 7 1 E
Ahelledjem, Algeria 99 C6 26 37N 6 58 E
Ahimanawa Ra., N.Z. 118 F5 39 3 S 176 30 E
Ahipara B., N.Z. 118 B2 35 5 S 173 5 E
Ahiri, India 82 E5 19 30N 80 0 E
Ahlen, Germany 26 D3 51 45N 7 52 E
Ahmad Wal, Pakistan 80 E1 29 18N 65 58 E
Ahmadabad, India 80 H5 23 0N 72 40 E
Aḩmadābād, Khorāsān, Iran 85 C9 35 3N 60 50 E
Aḩmadābād, Khorāsān, Iran 85 C8 35 49N 59 42 E
Aḩmadī, Iran 85 E8 27 56N 56 42 E
Ahmadnagar, India 82 E2 19 7N 74 46 E
Ahmadpur, Pakistan 80 E4 29 12N 71 10 E
Ahmar, Ethiopia 95 F5 9 20N 41 15 E
Ahmedabad = Ahmadabad, India 80 H5 23 0N 72 40 E
Ahmednagar = Ahmadnagar, India 82 E2 19 7N 74 46 E
Ahoada, Nigeria 101 D6 5 8N 6 36 E
Ahome, Mexico 146 B3 25 55N 109 11W
Ahr →, Germany 26 E3 50 33N 7 17 E
Ahram, Iran 85 D6 28 52N 51 16 E
Ahrax Pt., Malta 32 D1 35 59N 14 22 E
Ahrensbök, Germany 26 A6 54 2N 10 34 E
Ahrweiler, Germany 26 E3 50 31N 7 3 E
Āhū, Iran 85 C6 34 33N 50 2 E
Ahuachapán, El Salv. 148 D2 13 54N 89 52W
Ahuriri →, N.Z. 119 E5 44 31 S 170 12 E
Ahvāz, Iran 85 D6 31 20N 48 40 E
Ahvenanmaa = Åland, Finland 13 F16 60 15N 20 0 E
Aḩwar, Yemen 86 D4 13 30N 46 40 E
Ahzar, Mali 101 B5 15 30N 3 20 E
Aiari →, Brazil 152 C4 1 22N 68 36W
Aichach, Germany 27 G7 48 28N 11 9 E
Aichi □, Japan 63 B9 35 0N 137 15 E
Aidone, Italy 41 E7 37 26N 14 26 E
Aiello Cálabro, Italy 41 C9 39 6N 16 12 E
Aigle, Switz. 28 D3 46 18N 6 58 E
Aignay-le-Duc, France 23 E11 47 40N 4 43 E
Aigoual, Mt., France 24 D7 44 8N 3 35 E
Aigre, France 24 C4 45 54N 0 1 E
Aigua, Uruguay 159 C5 34 13 S 54 46W
Aigueperse, France 24 B7 46 3N 3 13 E
Aigues →, France 25 D8 44 7N 4 43 E
Aigues-Mortes, France 25 E8 43 35N 4 12 E
Aigues-Mortes, G. d', France 25 E8 43 31N 4 3 E
Aiguilles, France 25 D10 44 47N 6 51 E
Aiguillon, France 24 D4 44 18N 0 21 E
Aigurande, France 24 B5 46 27N 1 49 E
Aihui, China 65 A7 50 10N 127 30 E
Aija, Peru 156 B2 9 50 S 77 45W
Aikawa, Japan 60 E9 38 2N 138 15 E
Aiken, U.S.A. 135 J5 33 34N 81 50W
Ailao Shan, China 68 F3 24 0N 101 20 E
Aillant-sur-Tholon, France 23 E10 47 52N 3 20 E
Aillik, Canada 129 A8 55 11N 59 18W
Ailly-sur-Noye, France 23 C9 49 45N 2 20 E
Ailsa Craig, U.K. 18 F3 55 15N 5 7W
'Ailūn, Jordan 91 C4 32 18N 35 47 E
Aim, Russia 57 D14 59 0N 133 55 E
Aimere, Indonesia 72 C2 8 45 S 121 3 E
Aimogasta, Argentina 158 B2 28 33 S 66 50W
Aimorés, Brazil 155 E3 19 30 S 41 4W
Ain □, France 25 B9 46 5N 5 20 E
Ain →, France 25 C9 45 45N 5 11 E
Aïn Beïda, Algeria 99 A6 35 50N 7 29 E
Aïn Ben Khellil, Algeria 99 B4 33 15N 0 49W
Aïn Ben Tili, Mauritania 98 C3 25 59N 9 27W
Aïn Beni Mathar, Morocco 99 B4 34 1N 2 0W
Aïn Benian, Algeria 99 A5 36 48N 2 55 E
Ain Dalla, Egypt 94 B2 27 20N 27 23 E
Ain el Mafki, Egypt 94 B2 27 30N 28 15 E
Ain Girba, Egypt 94 B2 29 20N 25 14 E
Aïn M'lila, Algeria 99 A6 36 2N 6 35 E
Ain Qeiqab, Egypt 94 B1 29 42N 24 55 E
Aïn-Sefra, Algeria 99 B4 32 47N 0 37W
Ain Sheikh Murzûk, Egypt 94 B2 26 47N 27 45 E
'Ain Sudr, Egypt 91 F2 29 50N 33 6 E
Ain Sukhna, Egypt 94 J8 29 32N 32 20 E
Aïn Tédelès, Algeria 99 A5 36 0N 0 21 E
Aïn-Témouchent, Algeria 99 A4 35 16N 1 8W
Aïn Touta, Algeria 99 A6 35 26N 5 54 E
Ain Zeitûn, Egypt 94 B2 29 10N 25 48 E
Ain Zorah, Morocco 99 B4 34 37N 3 32W
Ainabo, Somali Rep. 90 F4 9 0N 46 25 E
Ainaži, Latvia 50 C4 57 50N 24 24 E
Aínos Óros, Greece 45 F2 38 10N 20 35 E
Ainsworth, U.S.A. 138 D5 42 33N 99 52W
Aioi, Japan 62 C6 34 48N 134 28 E
Aipe, Colombia 152 C2 3 13N 75 15W
Aiquile, Bolivia 157 D4 18 10 S 65 10W
Aïr, Niger 97 E1 18 30N 8 0 E
Air Hitam, Malaysia 77 M4 1 55N 103 11 E
Airaines, France 23 C8 49 58N 1 55 E
Airão, Brazil 153 D5 1 56 S 61 22W
Airdrie, U.K. 18 F5 55 53N 3 57W
Aire →, France 23 C11 49 18N 4 49 E
Aire →, U.K. 16 D7 53 42N 0 55W
Aire, I. del, Spain 33 B11 39 48N 4 16 E
Aire-sur-la-Lys, France 23 B9 50 37N 2 22 E
Aire-sur-l'Adour, France 24 E3 43 42N 0 15W
Aireys Inlet, Australia 116 E6 38 29 S 144 5 E
Airlie Beach, Australia 114 C4 20 16 S 148 43 E
Airolo, Switz. 29 C7 46 32N 8 37 E
Airvault, France 22 F6 46 50N 0 8W
Aisch →, Germany 27 F7 49 46N 11 1 E
Aisen □, Chile 160 C2 46 30 S 73 0W
Aisne □, France 23 C10 49 42N 3 40 E
Aisne →, France 23 C9 49 26N 2 50 E
Aitana, Sierra de, Spain 35 G4 38 35N 0 24W
Aitape, Papua N. G. 120 B2 3 11 S 142 22 E
Aitkin, U.S.A. 138 B8 46 32N 93 43W
Aitolía Kai Akarnanía □, Greece 45 F3 38 45N 21 18 E
Aitolikón, Greece 45 F3 38 26N 21 21 E
Aiuaba, Brazil 154 C3 6 38 S 40 7W
Aiud, Romania 46 C4 46 19N 23 44 E
Aix-en-Provence, France 25 E9 43 32N 5 27 E
Aix-la-Chapelle = Aachen, Germany 26 E2 50 47N 6 4 E
Aix-les-Bains, France 25 C9 45 41N 5 53 E
Aixe-sur-Vienne, France 24 C5 45 47N 1 9 E
Aiyang, Mt., Papua N. G. 120 C1 5 10 S 141 20 E
Aiyansh, Canada 130 B3 55 17N 129 2W
Aíyina, Greece 45 G5 37 45N 23 26 E
Aiyínion, Greece 44 D4 40 28N 22 28 E
Aiyion, Greece 45 F4 38 15N 22 5 E
Aizawl, India 78 D4 23 40N 92 44 E
Aizenay, France 22 F5 46 44N 1 38W
Aizpute, Latvia 50 C2 56 43N 21 40 E
Aizuwakamatsu, Japan 60 F9 37 30N 139 56 E
Ajaccio, France 25 G12 41 55N 8 40 E
Ajaccio, G. d', France 25 G12 41 52N 8 40 E
Ajaju →, Colombia 152 C3 0 59N 72 20W
Ajalpan, Mexico 147 D5 18 22N 97 15W
Ajanta Ra., India 82 D2 20 28N 75 50 E
Ajax, Canada 136 C5 43 50N 79 1W
Ajax, Mt., N.Z. 119 C7 42 35 S 172 5 E
Ajayan Pt., Guam 121 R15 13 15N 144 43 E
Ajdâbiyah, Libya 96 B4 30 54N 20 4 E
Ajdovščina, Slovenia 39 C10 45 54N 13 54 E
Ajibar, Ethiopia 95 E4 10 35N 38 36 E
Ajka, Hungary 31 D10 47 4N 17 31 E
'Ajmān, U.A.E. 85 E7 25 25N 55 30 E
Ajmer, India 80 F6 26 28N 74 37 E
Ajo, U.S.A. 143 K7 32 18N 112 54W
Ajoie, Switz. 28 B4 47 22N 7 0 E
Ajok, Sudan 95 F2 9 15N 28 28 E
Ajuy, Phil. 71 F4 11 11N 123 1 E
Ak Dağ, Antalya, Turkey 88 E3 36 30N 29 45 E
Ak Dağ, Sivas, Turkey 88 D7 39 40N 36 25 E
Akaba, Togo 101 D5 8 10N 1 2 E
Akabira, Japan 60 C11 43 33N 142 5 E
Akabli, Algeria 99 C5 26 49N 1 31 E
Akaishi-Dake, Japan 63 B10 35 27N 138 9 E
Akaishi-Sammyaku, Japan 63 B10 35 25N 138 10 E
Akaki Beseka, Ethiopia 95 F4 8 55N 38 45 E
Akala, Sudan 95 D4 15 39N 36 13 E
Akamas □, Cyprus 32 D11 35 3N 32 18 E
Akanthou, Cyprus 32 D12 35 22N 33 45 E
Akaroa, N.Z. 119 D7 43 49 S 172 59 E
Akaroa Harbour, N.Z. 119 D7 43 50 S 172 55 E
Akasha, Sudan 94 C3 21 10N 30 32 E
Akashi, Japan 62 C6 34 45N 134 58 E
Akbou, Algeria 99 A5 36 31N 4 31 E
Akbulak, Russia 54 F4 51 1N 55 37 E
Akçaabat, Turkey 89 C8 41 1N 39 34 E
Akçakoca, Turkey 88 C4 41 5N 31 8 E
Akchâr, Mauritania 98 D2 20 20N 14 28W
Akdağmadeni, Turkey 88 D6 39 39N 35 53 E
Akdala, Kazakhstan 55 A7 45 2N 74 35 E
Akechi, Japan 63 B9 35 18N 137 23 E
Akelamo, Indonesia 72 A3 1 35N 129 40 E
Akershus fylke □, Norway 14 E5 60 0N 11 10 E
Akeru →, India 82 F5 17 25N 80 5 E
Aketi, Zaïre 102 B4 2 38N 23 47 E
Akhaïa □, Greece 45 F3 38 5N 21 45 E
Akhalkalaki, Georgia 53 F10 41 27N 43 25 E
Akhaltsikhe, Georgia 53 F10 41 40N 43 0 E
Akharnaí, Greece 45 F5 38 5N 23 44 E
Akhelóös →, Greece 45 F3 38 36N 21 14 E
Akhendria, Greece 45 K7 34 58N 25 16 E
Akhéron →, Greece 44 E2 39 20N 20 29 E
Akhladhókambos, Greece 45 G4 37 31N 22 35 E
Akhmîm, Egypt 94 B3 26 31N 31 47 E
Akhnur, India 81 C6 32 52N 74 45 E
Akhtopol, Bulgaria 43 E12 42 6N 27 56 E
Akhtubinsk, Russia 53 B12 48 13N 46 7 E
Akhty, Russia 53 F12 41 30N 47 45 E
Akhtyrka, Ukraine 50 F9 50 25N 35 0 E
Aki, Japan 62 D5 33 30N 133 54 E
Aki-Nada, Japan 62 C4 34 5N 132 40 E
Akiéni, Gabon 102 C2 1 11 S 13 53 E
Akimiski I., Canada 128 B3 52 50N 81 30W
Akimovka, Ukraine 52 C6 46 44N 35 0 E
Akita, Japan 60 E10 39 45N 140 7 E
Akita □, Japan 60 E10 39 40N 140 30 E
Akjoujt, Mauritania 100 B2 19 45N 14 15W
Akka, Morocco 98 C3 29 22N 8 9W
Akkeshi, Japan 60 C12 43 2N 144 51 E
'Akko, Israel 91 C4 32 55N 35 4 E
Akkol, Kazakhstan 55 B5 43 36N 70 45 E
Akkol, Kazakhstan 56 E8 45 0N 75 39 E
Akköy, Turkey 45 G9 37 30N 27 18 E
Akkrum, Neths. 20 B7 53 3N 5 50 E
Aklampa, Benin 101 D5 8 15N 2 10 E
Aklan □, Phil. 71 F4 11 50N 122 30 E
Aklavik, Canada 126 B6 68 12N 135 0W
Akmolinsk = Tselinograd, Kazakhstan 56 D8 51 10N 71 30 E
Akmonte, Spain 37 H4 37 13N 6 38W
Akmuz, Kirghizia 55 C8 41 15N 76 10 E
Aknoul, Morocco 99 B4 34 40N 3 55W
Akō, Japan 62 C6 34 45N 134 24 E
Ako, Nigeria 101 C7 10 19N 10 48 E
Akobo →, Ethiopia 95 F3 7 48N 33 3 E
Akola, India 82 D3 20 42N 77 2 E
Akonolinga, Cameroon 101 E7 3 50N 12 18 E
Akordat, Ethiopia 95 D4 15 30N 37 40 E
Akosombo Dam, Ghana 101 D5 6 20N 0 5 E
Akot, India 82 D3 21 10N 77 10 E
Akot, Sudan 95 F3 6 31N 30 9 E
Akpatok I., Canada 127 B13 60 25N 68 8W
Akranes, Iceland 12 D3 64 19N 22 5W
Akreïjit, Mauritania 100 B3 18 19N 9 11W
Akrítas Venétiko, Ákra, Greece 45 H3 36 43N 21 54 E
Akron, Colo., U.S.A. 138 E3 40 13N 103 15W
Akron, Ind., U.S.A. 141 C10 41 2N 86 1W
Akron, Ohio, U.S.A. 136 E3 41 7N 81 31W
Akrotiri, Cyprus 32 E11 34 36N 32 57 E
Akrotíri, Ákra, Greece 44 D7 40 26N 25 27 E
Akrotiri Bay, Cyprus 32 E12 34 35N 33 10 E
Aksai Chih, India 81 B8 35 15N 79 55 E
Aksaray, Turkey 88 D6 38 25N 34 2 E
Aksarka, Russia 56 C7 66 31N 67 50 E
Aksay, Kazakhstan 54 F3 51 11N 53 0 E
Akşehir, Turkey 88 D4 38 18N 31 30 E
Akşehir Gölü, Turkey 88 D4 38 30N 31 25 E
Aksenovo Zilovskoye, Russia 57 D12 53 20N 117 40 E
Akstafa, Azerbaijan 53 F11 41 7N 45 27 E
Aksu, China 64 B3 41 5N 80 10 E
Aksu →, Turkey 88 E4 36 41N 30 54 E
Aksuat, Ozero, Kazakhstan 54 F9 51 32N 64 34 E
Aksum, Ethiopia 95 E4 14 5N 38 40 E
Aktash, Russia 54 D3 55 2N 52 0 E
Aktash, Uzbekistan 55 D2 39 55N 65 55 E
Aktogay, Kazakhstan 55 A8 44 25N 76 44 E
Aktogay, Kazakhstan 56 E8 46 57N 79 40 E
Aktyubinsk, Kazakhstan 49 D10 50 17N 57 10 E
Aktyuz, Kirghizia 55 B8 42 54N 76 7 E
Aku, Nigeria 101 D6 6 40N 7 18 E
Akula, Zaïre 102 B4 2 22N 20 12 E
Akune, Japan 62 E2 32 1N 130 12 E
Akure, Nigeria 101 D6 7 15N 5 5 E
Akureyri, Iceland 12 D4 65 40N 18 6W
Akuseki-Shima, Japan 61 K4 29 27N 129 37 E
Akusha, Russia 53 E12 42 18N 47 30 E
Akwa-Ibom □, Nigeria 101 E6 4 30N 7 30 E
Akyab = Sittwe, Burma 78 E4 20 18N 92 45 E
Akyazı, Turkey 88 C4 40 40N 30 38 E
Akzhar, Kazakhstan 55 B5 43 8N 71 37 E
Al Abyār, Libya 96 B4 32 9N 20 29 E
Al 'Adan, Yemen 86 D4 12 45N 45 0 E
Al Aḩsā, Si. Arabia 85 E6 25 50N 49 0 E
Al Ajfar, Si. Arabia 84 E4 27 26N 43 0 E
Al Amādīyah, Iraq 84 B4 37 5N 43 30 E
Al Amārah, Iraq 84 D5 31 55N 47 15 E
Al 'Aqabah, Jordan 91 F4 29 31N 35 0 E
Al' Aqīq, Si. Arabia 86 B3 20 39N 41 25 E
Al Arak, Syria 84 C3 34 38N 38 35 E
Al 'Aramah, Si. Arabia 84 E5 25 30N 46 0 E
Al 'Ariḑah, Si. Arabia 86 C3 17 3N 43 5 E
Al Arţāwīyah, Si. Arabia 84 E5 26 31N 45 20 E
Al Ashkhara, Oman 87 B7 21 50N 59 30 E
Al 'Āşimah □, Jordan 91 D5 31 40N 36 30 E
Al' Assāfīyah, Si. Arabia 84 D3 28 17N 38 59 E
Al 'Ayn, Oman 85 E7 24 15N 55 45 E
Al 'Ayn, Si. Arabia 84 E3 25 4N 38 6 E
Al A'zamīyah, Iraq 84 C5 33 22N 44 22 E
Al 'Azīzīyah, Iraq 84 C5 32 54N 45 4 E
Al 'Azīzīyah, Libya 96 B2 32 30N 13 1 E
Al Bāb, Syria 84 B3 36 23N 37 29 E
Al Bad', Si. Arabia 84 D2 28 28N 35 1 E
Al Bādī, Iraq 84 C4 35 56N 41 32 E
Al Badī', Si. Arabia 86 B4 22 0N 46 35 E
Al Baḩrah, Kuwait 84 D5 29 40N 47 52 E
Al Balqā' □, Jordan 91 C4 32 5N 35 45 E
Al Barkāt, Libya 96 D2 24 56N 10 14 E
Al Bārūk, J., Lebanon 91 B4 33 39N 35 40 E
Al Başrah, Iraq 84 D5 30 30N 47 50 E
Al Baţḩā, Iraq 84 D5 31 6N 45 53 E
Al Batrūn, Lebanon 91 A4 34 15N 35 40 E
Al Bayāḑ, Si. Arabia 86 B4 22 0N 47 0 E
Al Bayḑā', Yemen 86 D4 14 5N 45 42 E
Al Bayḑā □, Libya 96 B4 32 0N 21 30 E
Al Bi'ār, Si. Arabia 86 B2 22 39N 39 40 E
Al Bi'r, Si. Arabia 84 D3 28 51N 36 16 E
Al Birk, Si. Arabia 86 C3 18 13N 41 33 E
Al Bu'ayrāt, Libya 96 B3 31 24N 15 44 E
Al Burayj, Syria 91 A5 34 15N 36 46 E
Al Fallūjah, Iraq 84 C4 33 20N 43 55 E
Al Fatk, Yemen 87 C6 16 31N 52 41 E
Al Fāw, Iraq 85 D6 30 0N 48 30 E
Al Faydamī, Yemen 87 C6 16 25N 52 26 E
Al Fujayrah, U.A.E. 85 E8 25 7N 56 18 E
Al Ghadaf, W. →, Jordan 91 D5 31 26N 36 43 E
Al Ghammās, Iraq 84 D5 31 45N 44 37 E
Al Gharīb, Libya 96 B4 32 35N 21 11 E
Al Ghayḑah, Yemen 87 C6 16 13N 52 11 E
Al Ghayḑah, Yemen 87 D5 14 55N 50 0 E
Al Ghayl, Yemen 87 D5 15 30N 50 54 E
Al Hābah, Si. Arabia 84 E5 27 10N 47 0 E
Al Ḩadd, Oman 87 B7 22 35N 59 48 E
Al Ḩaddār, Si. Arabia 86 B4 21 58N 45 57 E
Al Ḩadīthah, Iraq 84 C4 34 0N 41 13 E
Al Ḩadīthah, Si. Arabia 84 D3 31 28N 37 8 E
Al Ḩājānah, Syria 91 B5 33 20N 36 33 E
Al Hajarayn, Yemen 87 D5 15 29N 48 20 E
Al Hallānīyah, Oman 87 C7 17 30N 56 1 E
Al Ḩāmad, Si. Arabia 84 D3 31 30N 39 30 E
Al Ḩamar, Si. Arabia 86 B4 22 26N 46 12 E
Al Hamdānīyah, Syria 84 C3 35 25N 36 50 E
Al Ḩamīdīyah, Syria 91 A4 34 42N 35 57 E
Al Ḩammādah al Ḩamrā', Libya 96 C2 29 30N 12 0 E
Al Ḩammār, Iraq 84 D5 30 57N 46 51 E
Al Ḩamrā', Si. Arabia 86 A2 24 2N 38 55 E
Al Ḩarīq, Si. Arabia 86 B4 23 29N 46 27 E
Al Harīr, W. →, Syria 91 C4 32 44N 35 59 E
Al Ḩarūj al Aswad, Libya 96 C3 27 0N 17 10 E
Al Ḩasā, W. →, Jordan 91 D4 31 4N 35 29 E
Al Ḩasakah, Syria 84 B4 36 35N 40 45 E
Al Ḩāsikīyah, Oman 87 C6 17 28N 55 36 E
Al Ḩasy, Yemen 86 D5 14 3N 48 40 E
Al Ḩawrah, Yemen 86 D4 13 50N 47 35 E
Al Ḩawţah, Yemen 86 D4 14 23N 47 24 E
Al Ḩawţah □, Si. Arabia 86 B4 23 30N 47 0 E
Al Ḩaydān, W. →, Jordan 91 D4 31 29N 35 34 E
Al Ḩayy, Iraq 84 C5 32 5N 46 5 E
Al Ḩijāz, Si. Arabia 86 A2 26 0N 37 30 E
Al Ḩillah, Iraq 84 C5 32 30N 44 25 E
Al Ḩillah, Si. Arabia 86 B4 23 35N 46 50 E
Al Hirmil, Lebanon 91 A5 34 26N 36 24 E
Al Hoceïma, Morocco 98 A4 35 8N 3 58W
Al Ḩudaydah, Yemen 86 D3 14 50N 43 0 E
Al Ḩufrah, Awbārī, Libya 96 C2 25 32N 14 1 E
Al Ḩufrah, Misrātah, Libya 96 C3 29 5N 18 3 E
Al Hufūf, Si. Arabia 85 E6 25 25N 49 45 E
Al Ḩulwah, Si. Arabia 86 B4 23 24N 46 48 E
Al Ḩumayḑah, Si. Arabia 84 D2 29 14N 34 56 E
Al Ḩunayy, Si. Arabia 85 E6 25 58N 48 45 E
Al Ḩurayḑah, Yemen 87 D5 15 36N 48 12 E
Al Husayyāt, Libya 96 B4 30 24N 20 37 E
Al Hūwah, Si. Arabia 86 B4 23 2N 45 48 E
Al Ḩuwaymī, Yemen 86 D4 13 23N 44 28 E
Al Irq, Libya 96 C4 29 5N 21 35 E
Al 'Irqah, Yemen 86 D4 13 39N 47 22 E
Al Işāwīyah, Si. Arabia 84 D3 30 43N 37 59 E
Al Ittihad = Madīnat ash Sha'b, Yemen 86 D4 12 50N 45 0 E
Al Jabal al Akhḑar, Libya 96 B4 32 0N 21 30 E
Al Jafr, Jordan 91 E5 30 18N 36 14 E
Al Jaghbūb, Libya 96 C4 29 42N 24 38 E
Al Jahrah, Kuwait 84 D5 29 25N 47 40 E
Al Jalāmīd, Si. Arabia 84 D3 31 20N 39 45 E
Al Jamalīyah, Qatar 85 E6 25 37N 51 5 E
Al Janūb □, Lebanon 91 B4 33 20N 35 20 E
Al Jawf, Libya 96 D4 24 10N 23 24 E
Al Jawf, Si. Arabia 84 D3 29 55N 39 40 E
Al Jazirah, Iraq 84 C5 33 30N 44 0 E
Al Jazirah, Libya 96 C4 26 10N 21 20 E
Al Jithāmīyah, Si. Arabia 84 E4 27 41N 41 43 E
Al Jubayl, Si. Arabia 85 E6 27 0N 49 50 E
Al Jubaylah, Si. Arabia 84 E5 24 55N 46 25 E
Al Jubb, Si. Arabia 84 E4 27 11N 42 17 E
Al Jumūm, Si. Arabia 86 B2 21 37N 39 42 E
Al Junaynah, Sudan 97 F4 13 27N 22 45 E
Al Kabā'ish, Iraq 84 D5 30 58N 47 0 E
Al Kāmil, Oman 87 B7 22 13N 59 12 E
Al Karak, Jordan 91 D4 31 11N 35 42 E
Al Karak □, Jordan 91 E5 31 0N 36 0 E
Al Kāzim Tyah, Iraq 84 C5 33 22N 44 12 E
Al Khābūra, Oman 87 B7 23 57N 57 5 E
Al Khalīl, Jordan 91 D4 31 32N 35 6 E
Al Khalīl □, Jordan 91 D4 31 35N 35 5 E
Al Khamāsīn, Si. Arabia 86 B4 20 29N 44 46 E
Al Kharāb, Yemen 86 C4 16 29N 44 18 E
Al Kharfah, Si. Arabia 86 B4 22 0N 46 35 E
Al Kharj, Si. Arabia 86 B4 24 0N 47 0 E
Al Khāşirah, Si. Arabia 86 B3 23 30N 43 47 E
Al Khawr, Qatar 85 E6 25 41N 51 30 E

164 Al Khiḍr


Al Khiḍr, *Iraq* **84** **D5** 31 12N 45 33 E
Al Khiyām, *Lebanon* **91** **B4** 33 20N 35 36 E
Al Khums, *Libya* **96** **B2** 32 40N 14 17 E
Al Khums □, *Libya* **96** **B2** 31 20N 14 10 E
Al Kiswah, *Syria* **91** **B5** 33 23N 36 14 E
Al Kufrah, *Libya* **96** **D4** 24 17N 23 15 E
Al Kuhayfīyah, *Si. Arabia* **84** **E4** 27 12N 43 3 E
Al Kūt, *Iraq* **84** **C5** 32 30N 46 0 E
Al Kuwayt, *Kuwait* **84** **D5** 29 30N 48 0 E
Al Labwah, *Lebanon* **91** **A5** 34 11N 36 20 E
Al Lādhiqīyah, *Syria* **84** **C2** 35 30N 35 45 E
Al Līth, *Si. Arabia* **86** **B3** 20 9N 40 15 E
Al Liwā', *Oman* **85** **E8** 24 31N 56 36 E
Al Luḥayyah, *Yemen* **86** **D3** 15 45N 42 40 E
Al Madīnah, *Iraq* **84** **D5** 30 57N 47 16 E
Al Madīnah, *Si. Arabia* **84** **E3** 24 35N 39 52 E
Al-Mafraq, *Jordan* **91** **C5** 32 17N 36 14 E
Al Maghārīm, *Yemen* **86** **D4** 15 1N 47 49 E
Al Maḥmūdīyah, *Iraq* **84** **C5** 33 3N 44 21 E
Al Majma'ah, *Si. Arabia* **84** **E5** 25 57N 45 22 E
Al Makhruq, W. →,
*Jordan* **91** **D6** 31 28N 37 0 E
Al Makḥūl, *Si. Arabia* **84** **E4** 26 37N 42 39 E
Al Makīlī, *Libya* **96** **B4** 32 10N 22 17 E
Al Manā'if, *Si. Arabia* **87** **B5** 23 49N 51 20 E
Al Manāmah, *Bahrain* **85** **E6** 26 10N 50 30 E
Al Manṣūrī, *Yemen* **86** **D4** 14 17N 45 16 E
Al Maqwa', *Kuwait* **84** **D5** 29 10N 47 59 E
Al Marj, *Libya* **96** **B4** 32 25N 20 30 E
Al Maṭlā, *Kuwait* **84** **D5** 29 24N 47 40 E
Al Mawjib, W. →,
*Jordan* **91** **D4** 31 28N 35 36 E
Al Mawṣil, *Iraq* **84** **B4** 36 15N 43 5 E
Al Mayādin, *Syria* **84** **C4** 35 1N 40 27 E
Al Mazār, *Jordan* **91** **D4** 31 4N 35 41 E
Al Midhnab, *Si. Arabia* **84** **E5** 25 50N 44 18 E
Al Mīfá, *Si. Arabia* **86** **C3** 18 54N 41 57 E
Al Mīnā', *Lebanon* **91** **A4** 34 24N 35 49 E
Al Miqdādīyah, *Iraq* **84** **C5** 34 0N 45 0 E
Al Mubarraz, *Si. Arabia* **85** **E6** 25 30N 49 40 E
Al Muḍaybī, *Oman* **87** **B7** 22 34N 58 7 E
Al Mughayrā', *U.A.E.* **85** **E7** 24 5N 53 32 E
Al Muḥarraq, *Bahrain* **85** **E6** 26 15N 50 40 E
Al Mukallā, *Yemen* **87** **D5** 14 33N 49 2 E
Al Mukhā, *Yemen* **86** **D3** 13 18N 43 15 E
Al Muladdah, *Oman* **87** **B7** 23 45N 57 34 E
Al Musayjīd, *Si. Arabia* **84** **E3** 24 5N 39 5 E
Al Musayyib, *Iraq* **84** **C5** 32 40N 44 25 E
Al Muwayliḥ, *Si. Arabia* **84** **E2** 27 40N 35 30 E
Al Owuho = Otukpa,
*Nigeria* **101** **D6** 7 9N 7 41 E
Al Qaddāhīyah, *Libya* **96** **B3** 31 15N 15 9 E
Al Qaḍīmah, *Si. Arabia* **86** **B2** 22 20N 39 13 E
Al Qaḥmah, *Si. Arabia* **86** **C3** 18 0N 41 41 E
Al Qā'im, *Iraq* **84** **C4** 34 21N 41 7 E
Al Qalībah, *Si. Arabia* **84** **D3** 28 24N 37 42 E
Al Qaryah ash Sharqīyah,
*Libya* **96** **B2** 30 28N 13 40 E
Al Qaryatayn, *Syria* **91** **A6** 34 12N 37 13 E
Al Qaṣabát, *Libya* **96** **B2** 32 39N 14 1 E
Al Qaṭ'ā, *Syria* **84** **C4** 34 40N 40 48 E
Al Qaṭīf, *Si. Arabia* **85** **E6** 26 35N 50 0 E
Al Qaṭn, *Yemen* **87** **D5** 15 51N 48 26 E
Al Qatrānah, *Jordan* **91** **D5** 31 14N 36 26 E
Al Qaṭrūn, *Libya* **96** **D3** 24 56N 15 3 E
Al Qayṣūmah, *Si. Arabia* **84** **D5** 28 20N 46 7 E
Al Qiblīyah, *Oman* **87** **C7** 17 30N 56 20 E
Al Quds = Jerusalem,
*Israel* **91** **D4** 31 47N 35 10 E
Al Quds □, *Jordan* **91** **D4** 31 50N 35 20 E
Al Qunaytirah, *Syria* **91** **C4** 32 55N 35 45 E
Al Qunfudhah, *Si. Arabia* **86** **C3** 19 3N 41 4 E
Al Qurḥ, *Yemen* **87** **C5** 16 44N 51 29 E
Al Qurnah, *Iraq* **84** **D5** 31 1N 47 25 E
Al Quṣayr, *Iraq* **84** **D5** 30 39N 45 50 E
Al Quṣayr, *Syria* **91** **A5** 34 31N 36 34 E
Al Quṭayfah, *Syria* **91** **B5** 33 44N 36 36 E
Al Quway'īyah,
*Si. Arabia* **86** **A4** 24 3N 45 15 E
Al 'Ubaylah, *Si. Arabia* **87** **B5** 21 59N 50 57 E
Al' Uḍaylīyah, *Si. Arabia* **85** **E6** 25 8N 49 18 E
Al 'Ulā, *Si. Arabia* **84** **E3** 26 35N 38 0 E
Al 'Ulayyah, *Si. Arabia* **86** **C3** 19 39N 41 54 E
Al Uqaylah ash
Sharqīgah, *Libya* **96** **B3** 30 12N 19 10 E
Al Uqayr, *Si. Arabia* **85** **E6** 25 40N 50 15 E
Al 'Uwaynid, *Si. Arabia* **84** **E5** 24 50N 46 0 E
Al' 'Uwayqīlah,
*Si. Arabia* **84** **D4** 30 30N 42 10 E
Al 'Uyūn, *Si. Arabia* **84** **E4** 26 30N 43 50 E
Al 'Uyūn, *Si. Arabia* **84** **E3** 24 33N 39 35 E
Al Wajh, *Si. Arabia* **84** **E3** 26 10N 36 30 E
Al Wakrah, *Qatar* **85** **E6** 25 10N 51 40 E
Al Wannān, *Si. Arabia* **85** **E6** 26 55N 48 24 E
Al Waqbah, *Si. Arabia* **84** **D5** 28 48N 45 33 E
Al Wari'āh, *Si. Arabia* **84** **E5** 27 51N 47 25 E
Al Wātīyah, *Libya* **96** **B2** 32 28N 11 57 E
Al Wusayl, *Qatar* **85** **E6** 25 29N 51 29 E
Ala, *Italy* **38** **C8** 45 46N 11 0 E
Ala Dağlari, *Turkey* **89** **D10** 39 15N 43 33 E
Ala Tau Shankou =
Dzhungarskiye Vorota,
*Kazakhstan* **64** **B3** 45 0N 82 0 E
Alabama □, *U.S.A.* **135** **J2** 33 0N 87 0W
Alabama →, *U.S.A.* **135** **K2** 31 8N 87 57W
Alaca, *Turkey* **88** **C6** 40 10N 34 51 E
Alaçam, *Turkey* **88** **C6** 41 36N 35 36 E
Alaçam Dağlari, *Turkey* **88** **D3** 39 15N 28 30 E
Alaçati, *Turkey* **45** **F8** 38 16N 26 23 E
Alaejos, *Spain* **36** **D5** 41 18N 5 13W
Alaérma, *Greece* **32** **C9** 36 9N 27 57 E
Alagna Valsésia, *Italy* **38** **C4** 45 51N 7 56 E
Alagoa Grande, *Brazil* **154** **C4** 7 3 S 35 35W
Alagoas □, *Brazil* **154** **C4** 9 0 S 36 0W
Alagoinhas, *Brazil* **155** **D4** 12 7 S 38 20W
Alagón, *Spain* **34** **D3** 41 46N 1 12W
Alagón →, *Spain* **37** **F4** 39 44N 6 53W
Alajero, *Canary Is.* **33** **F2** 28 3N 17 13W
Alajuela, *Costa Rica* **148** **D3** 10 2N 84 8W
Alakamisy, *Madag.* **105** **C8** 21 19 S 47 14 E
Alakurtti, *Russia* **48** **A5** 67 0N 30 30 E
Alalapura, *Surinam* **153** **C6** 2 20N 56 25W
Alalaú →, *Brazil* **153** **D5** 0 30 S 61 9W
Alameda, *Spain* **37** **H6** 37 12N 4 39W
Alameda, *Calif., U.S.A.* **144** **H4** 37 46N 122 15W
Alameda, *N. Mex.,*
*U.S.A.* **143** **J10** 35 10N 106 43W
Alaminos, *Phil.* **70** **C2** 16 10N 119 59 E
Alamo, *U.S.A.* **145** **J11** 36 21N 115 10W
Alamo Crossing, *U.S.A.* **145** **L13** 34 16N 113 33W
Alamogordo, *U.S.A.* **143** **K11** 32 59N 106 0W
Alamos, *Mexico* **146** **B3** 27 0N 109 0W
Alamosa, *U.S.A.* **143** **H11** 37 30N 106 0W
Åland, *Finland* **13** **F16** 60 15N 20 0 E
Aland, *India* **82** **F3** 17 36N 76 35 E
Alandroal, *Portugal* **37** **G3** 38 41N 7 24W
Ålands hav, *Sweden* **13** **G15** 60 0N 19 30 E
Alandur, *India* **83** **H5** 13 0N 80 15 E
Alange, Presa de, *Spain* **37** **G4** 38 45N 6 18W
Alanis, *Spain* **37** **G5** 38 3N 5 43W
Alanya, *Turkey* **88** **E4** 36 38N 32 0 E
Alaotra, Farihin', *Madag.* **105** **B8** 17 30 S 48 30 E
Alapayevsk, *Russia* **54** **C7** 57 52N 61 42 E
Alar del Rey, *Spain* **36** **C6** 42 38N 4 20W
Alaraz, *Spain* **36** **E5** 40 45N 5 17W
Alaşehir, *Turkey* **88** **D3** 38 23N 28 30 E
Alaska □, *U.S.A.* **126** **B5** 65 0N 150 0W
Alaska, G. of, *Pac. Oc.* **126** **C5** 58 0N 145 0W
Alaska Highway, *Canada* **130** **B3** 60 0N 130 0W
Alaska Pen., *U.S.A.* **126** **C4** 56 0N 160 0W
Alaska Range, *U.S.A.* **126** **B4** 62 50N 151 0W
Alássio, *Italy* **38** **D5** 44 1N 8 10 E
Alatri, *Italy* **40** **A6** 41 44N 13 21 E
Alatyr, *Russia* **51** **D15** 54 45N 46 35 E
Alatyr →, *Russia* **51** **D15** 54 52N 46 36 E
Alausi, *Ecuador* **152** **D2** 2 0 S 78 50W
Álava □, *Spain* **34** **C2** 42 48N 2 28W
Alava, C., *U.S.A.* **142** **B1** 48 10N 124 40W
Alaverdi, *Armenia* **53** **F11** 41 15N 44 37 E
Alawoona, *Australia* **116** **C4** 34 45 S 140 30 E
'Alayh, *Lebanon* **91** **B4** 33 46N 35 33 E
Alaykel, *Kirghizia* **55** **C7** 40 15N 74 25 E
Alayor, *Spain* **33** **B11** 39 57N 4 8 E
Alayskiy Khrebet,
*Kirghizia* **55** **D6** 39 45N 72 0 E
Alazan →, *Azerbaijan* **53** **F12** 41 5N 46 40 E
Alba, *Italy* **38** **D5** 44 41N 8 1 E
Alba □, *Romania* **46** **C4** 46 10N 23 30 E
Alba de Tormes, *Spain* **36** **E5** 40 50N 5 30W
Alba Iulia, *Romania* **46** **C4** 46 8N 23 39 E
Albac, *Romania* **46** **C4** 46 28N 23 1 E
Albacete, *Spain* **35** **G3** 39 0N 1 50W
Albacete □, *Spain* **35** **G3** 38 50N 2 0W
Albacutya, L., *Australia* **116** **C4** 35 45 S 141 58 E
Ålbæk, *Denmark* **15** **G4** 57 36N 10 25 E
Ålbæk Bugt, *Denmark* **15** **G4** 57 35N 10 40 E
Albaida, *Spain* **35** **G4** 38 51N 0 31W
Albalate de las Nogueras,
*Spain* **34** **E2** 40 22N 2 18W
Albalate del Arzobispo,
*Spain* **34** **D4** 41 6N 0 31W
Albania ■, *Europe* **44** **C2** 41 0N 20 0 E
Albano Laziale, *Italy* **40** **A5** 41 44N 12 40 E
Albany, *Australia* **113** **G2** 35 1 S 117 58 E
Albany, *Ga., U.S.A.* **135** **K3** 31 40N 84 10W
Albany, *Ind., U.S.A.* **141** **D11** 40 18N 85 13W
Albany, *Minn., U.S.A.* **138** **C7** 45 37N 94 38W
Albany, *Mo., U.S.A.* **140** **D2** 40 15N 94 20W
Albany, *N.Y., U.S.A.* **137** **D11** 42 35N 73 47W
Albany, *Oreg., U.S.A.* **142** **D2** 44 41N 123 0W
Albany, *Tex., U.S.A.* **139** **J5** 32 45N 99 20W
Albany, *Wis., U.S.A.* **140** **B7** 42 43N 89 26W
Albany →, *Canada* **128** **B3** 52 17N 81 31W
Albardón, *Argentina* **158** **C2** 31 20 S 68 30W
Albarracín, *Spain* **34** **E3** 40 25N 1 26W
Albarracín, Sierra de,
*Spain* **34** **E3** 40 30N 1 30W
Albatross B., *Australia* **114** **A3** 12 45 S 141 30 E
Albatross Pt., *N.Z.* **118** **E3** 38 7 S 174 44 E
Albay □, *Phil.* **70** **E4** 13 13N 123 33 E
Albegna →, *Italy* **39** **F8** 42 30N 11 11 E
Albemarle, *U.S.A.* **135** **H5** 35 27N 80 15W
Albemarle Sd., *U.S.A.* **135** **H7** 36 0N 76 30W
Albenga, *Italy* **38** **D5** 44 3N 8 12 E
Alberche →, *Spain* **36** **F6** 39 58N 4 46W
Alberdi, *Paraguay* **158** **B4** 26 14 S 58 20W
Alberes, Mts., *Spain* **34** **C7** 42 28N 2 56 E
Alberique, *Spain* **35** **F4** 39 7N 0 31W
Albersdorf, *Germany* **26** **A5** 54 8N 9 19 E
Albert, *Australia* **117** **B7** 32 22 S 147 30 E
Albert, *France* **23** **B9** 50 0N 2 38 E
Albert, L. = Mobutu
Sese Seko, L., *Africa* **106** **B3** 1 30N 31 0 E
Albert, L., *Australia* **116** **C3** 35 30 S 139 10 E
Albert Canyon, *Canada* **130** **C5** 51 8N 117 41W
Albert Edward, Mt.,
*Papua N. G.* **120** **E4** 8 20 S 147 24 E
Albert Edward Ra.,
*Australia* **112** **C4** 18 17 S 127 57 E
Albert Lea, *U.S.A.* **138** **D8** 43 32N 93 20W
Albert Nile →, *Uganda* **106** **B3** 3 36N 32 2 E
Albert Town, *Bahamas* **149** **B5** 22 37N 74 33W
Alberta □, *Canada* **130** **C6** 54 40N 115 0W
Alberti, *Argentina* **158** **D3** 35 1 S 60 16W
Albertinia, *S. Africa* **104** **E3** 34 11 S 21 34 E
Albertirsa, *Hungary* **31** **D12** 47 14N 19 37 E
Albertkanaal →,
*Belgium* **21** **F4** 51 14N 4 26 E
Alberton, *Canada* **129** **C7** 46 50N 64 0W
Albertville = Kalemie,
*Zaïre* **106** **D2** 5 55 S 29 9 E
Albertville, *France* **25** **C10** 45 40N 6 22 E
Albi, *France* **24** **E6** 43 56N 2 9 E
Albia, *U.S.A.* **140** **C4** 41 2N 92 50W
Albina, *Surinam* **153** **B7** 5 37N 54 15W
Albina, Ponta, *Angola* **103** **F2** 15 52 S 11 44 E
Albino, *Italy* **38** **C6** 45 47N 9 48 E
Albion, *Idaho, U.S.A.* **142** **E7** 42 21N 113 37W
Albion, *Ill., U.S.A.* **141** **F8** 38 23N 88 4W
Albion, *Ind., U.S.A.* **141** **C11** 41 24N 85 25W
Albion, *Mich., U.S.A.* **141** **B12** 42 15N 84 45W
Albion, *Nebr., U.S.A.* **138** **E5** 41 47N 98 0W
Albion, *Pa., U.S.A.* **136** **E4** 41 53N 80 21W
Alblasserdam, *Neths.* **20** **E5** 51 52N 4 40 E
Albocácer, *Spain* **34** **E5** 40 21N 0 1 E
Alborán, *Medit. S.* **37** **K7** 35 57N 3 0W
Alborea, *Spain* **35** **F3** 39 17N 1 24W
Ålborg, *Denmark* **15** **G3** 57 2N 9 54 E
Ålborg Bugt, *Denmark* **15** **H4** 56 50N 10 35 E
Alborz, Reshteh-ye
Kūhhā-ye, *Iran* **85** **C7** 36 0N 52 0 E
Albox, *Spain* **35** **H2** 37 23N 2 8W
Albreda, *Canada* **130** **C5** 52 35N 119 10W
Albufeira, *Portugal* **37** **H2** 37 5N 8 15W
Albula →, *Switz.* **29** **C8** 46 38N 9 28 E
Albuñol, *Spain* **35** **J1** 36 48N 3 11W
Albuquerque, *Brazil* **157** **D6** 19 23 S 57 26W
Albuquerque, *U.S.A.* **143** **J10** 35 5N 106 47W
Albuquerque, Cayos de,
*Caribbean* **148** **D3** 12 10N 81 50W
Alburg, *U.S.A.* **137** **B11** 44 58N 73 19W
Alburno, Mte., *Italy* **41** **B8** 40 32N 15 15 E
Alburquerque, *Spain* **37** **F4** 39 15N 6 59W
Albury, *Australia* **117** **D7** 36 3 S 146 56 E
Alby, *Sweden* **14** **B9** 62 30N 15 28 E
Alcácer do Sal, *Portugal* **37** **G2** 38 22N 8 33W
Alcaçovas, *Portugal* **37** **G2** 38 23N 8 9W
Alcala, *Phil.* **70** **C3** 17 54N 121 39 E
Alcalá de Chisvert, *Spain* **34** **E5** 40 19N 0 13 E
Alcalá de Guadaira,
*Spain* **37** **H5** 37 20N 5 50W
Alcalá de Henares, *Spain* **34** **E1** 40 28N 3 22W
Alcalá de los Gazules,
*Spain* **37** **J5** 36 29N 5 43W
Alcalá la Real, *Spain* **37** **H7** 37 27N 3 57W
Alcamo, *Italy* **40** **E5** 37 59N 12 55 E
Alcanadre, *Spain* **34** **C2** 42 24N 2 7W
Alcanadre →, *Spain* **34** **D4** 41 43N 0 12W
Alcanar, *Spain* **34** **E5** 40 33N 0 28 E
Alcanede, *Portugal* **37** **F2** 39 25N 8 49W
Alcanena, *Portugal* **37** **F2** 39 27N 8 40W
Alcañices, *Spain* **36** **D4** 41 41N 6 21W
Alcaníz, *Spain* **34** **D4** 41 2N 0 8W
Alcântara, *Brazil* **154** **B3** 2 20 S 44 30W
Alcántara, *Spain* **37** **F4** 39 41N 6 57W
Alcantara L., *Canada* **131** **A7** 60 57N 108 9W
Alcantarilla, *Spain* **35** **H3** 37 59N 1 12W
Alcaracejos, *Spain* **37** **G6** 38 24N 4 58W
Alcaraz, *Spain* **35** **G2** 38 40N 2 29W
Alcaraz, Sierra de, *Spain* **35** **G2** 38 40N 2 20W
Alcaudete, *Spain* **37** **H6** 37 35N 4 5W
Alcázar de San Juan,
*Spain* **35** **F1** 39 24N 3 12W
Alcira, *Spain* **35** **F4** 39 9N 0 30W
Alcoa, *U.S.A.* **135** **H4** 35 50N 84 0W
Alcobaça, *Portugal* **37** **F2** 39 32N 8 58W
Alcobendas, *Spain* **34** **E1** 40 32N 3 38W
Alcolea del Pinar, *Spain* **34** **D2** 41 2N 2 28W
Alcora, *Spain* **34** **E4** 40 5N 0 14W
Alcorcón, *Spain* **36** **E7** 40 20N 3 50W
Alcoutim, *Portugal* **37** **H3** 37 25N 7 28W
Alcova, *U.S.A.* **142** **E10** 42 37N 106 52W
Alcoy, *Spain* **35** **G4** 38 43N 0 30W
Alcubierre, Sierra de,
*Spain* **34** **D4** 41 45N 0 22W
Alcublas, *Spain* **34** **F4** 39 48N 0 43W
Alcudia, *Spain* **33** **B10** 39 51N 3 7 E
Alcudia, B. de, *Spain* **33** **B10** 39 47N 3 15 E
Alcudia, Sierra de la,
*Spain* **37** **G6** 38 34N 4 30W
Aldabra Is., *Seychelles* **109** **E3** 9 22 S 46 28 E
Aldama, *Mexico* **147** **C5** 23 0N 98 4W
Aldan, *Russia* **57** **D13** 58 40N 125 30 E
Aldan →, *Russia* **57** **C13** 63 28N 129 35 E
Aldea, Pta. de la,
*Canary Is.* **33** **G4** 28 0N 15 50W
Aldeburgh, *U.K.* **17** **E9** 52 9N 1 35 E
Aldeia Nova, *Portugal* **37** **H3** 37 55N 7 24W
Alder, *U.S.A.* **142** **D7** 45 27N 112 3W
Alder Pk., *U.S.A.* **144** **K5** 35 53N 121 22W
Alderney, *Chan. Is.* **17** **H5** 49 42N 2 12W
Aldershot, *U.K.* **17** **F7** 51 15N 0 43W
Aledo, *U.S.A.* **140** **C6** 41 10N 90 50W
Alefa, *Ethiopia* **95** **E4** 11 55N 36 55 E
Aleg, *Mauritania* **100** **B2** 17 3N 13 55W
Alegranza, *Canary Is.* **33** **E6** 29 23N 13 32W
Alegranza, I., *Canary Is.* **33** **E6** 29 23N 13 32W
Alegre, *Brazil* **155** **F3** 20 50 S 41 30W
Alegrete, *Brazil* **159** **B4** 29 40 S 56 0W
Alegria, *Phil.* **71** **F5** 11 47N 124 3 E
Aleisk, *Russia* **56** **D9** 52 40N 83 0 E
Aleksandriya, *Ukraine* **50** **F5** 50 37N 26 19 E
Aleksandriya, *Ukraine* **52** **B5** 48 42N 33 3 E
Aleksandriyskaya, *Russia* **53** **E12** 43 59N 47 0 E
Aleksandrov, *Russia* **51** **C11** 56 23N 38 44 E
Aleksandrovac,
*Serbia, Yug.* **42** **D6** 43 28N 21 3 E
Aleksandrovac,
*Serbia, Yug.* **42** **C6** 44 28N 21 13 E
Aleksandrovka, *Ukraine* **52** **B5** 48 55N 32 20 E
Aleksandrovo, *Bulgaria* **43** **D9** 43 14N 24 51 E
Aleksandrovsk, *Russia* **54** **B5** 59 9N 57 33 E
Aleksandrovsk-
Sakhalinskiy, *Russia* **57** **D15** 50 50N 142 20 E
Aleksandrovskiy Zavod,
*Russia* **57** **D12** 50 40N 117 50 E
Aleksandrovskoye, *Russia* **56** **C8** 60 35N 77 50 E
Aleksandrów Kujawski,
*Poland* **47** **C5** 52 53N 18 43 E
Aleksandrów Łódźki,
*Poland* **47** **D6** 51 49N 19 17 E
Alekseyevka, *Russia* **51** **F11** 50 43N 38 40 E
Alekseyevka, *Russia* **54** **E2** 52 35N 51 17 E
Aleksin, *Russia* **51** **D10** 54 31N 37 9 E
Aleksinac, *Serbia, Yug.* **42** **D6** 43 31N 21 42 E
Além Paraíba, *Brazil* **155** **F3** 21 52 S 42 41W
Alemania, *Argentina* **158** **B2** 25 40 S 65 30W
Alemania, *Chile* **158** **B2** 25 10 S 69 55W
Ålen, *Norway* **14** **B5** 62 51N 11 17 E
Alençon, *France* **22** **D7** 48 27N 0 4 E
Alenuihaha Chan.,
*U.S.A.* **132** **H17** 20 25N 156 0W
Aleppo = Ḥalab, *Syria* **84** **B3** 36 10N 37 15 E
Aléria, *France* **25** **F13** 42 5N 9 26 E
Alert Bay, *Canada* **130** **C3** 50 30N 126 55W
Alès, *France* **25** **D8** 44 9N 4 5 E
Aleşd, *Romania* **46** **B3** 47 3N 22 22 E
Alessándria, *Italy* **38** **D5** 44 54N 8 37 E
Ålestrup, *Denmark* **15** **H3** 56 42N 9 29 E
Ålesund, *Norway* **12** **E9** 62 28N 6 12 E
Alet-les-Bains, *France* **24** **F6** 42 59N 2 14 E
Aletschhorn, *Switz.* **28** **D6** 46 28N 8 0 E
Aleutian Is., *Pac. Oc.* **126** **C2** 52 0N 175 0W
Aleutian Trench,
*Pac. Oc.* **122** **B10** 48 0N 180 0 E
Alexander, *U.S.A.* **138** **B3** 47 51N 103 40W
Alexander, Mt., *Australia* **113** **E3** 28 58 S 120 16 E
Alexander Arch., *U.S.A.* **130** **B2** 57 0N 135 0W
Alexander B., *S. Africa* **104** **D2** 28 36 S 16 33 E
Alexander Bay, *S. Africa* **104** **D2** 28 40 S 16 30 E
Alexander City, *U.S.A.* **135** **J3** 32 58N 85 57W
Alexander I., *Antarctica* **7** **C17** 69 0 S 70 0W
Alexandra, *Australia* **117** **D6** 37 8 S 145 40 E
Alexandra, *N.Z.* **119** **F4** 45 14 S 169 25 E
Alexandra Falls, *Canada* **130** **A5** 60 29N 116 18W
Alexandretta =
İskenderun, *Turkey* **88** **E7** 36 32N 36 10 E
Alexandria = El
Iskandarîya, *Egypt* **94** **H6** 31 0N 30 0 E
Alexandria, *Australia* **114** **B2** 19 5 S 136 40 E
Alexandria, *B.C., Canada* **130** **C4** 52 35N 122 27W
Alexandria, *Ont., Canada* **128** **C5** 45 19N 74 38W
Alexandria, *Romania* **46** **F6** 43 57N 25 24 E
Alexandria, *S. Africa* **104** **E4** 33 38 S 26 28 E
Alexandria, *Ind., U.S.A.* **141** **D11** 40 18N 85 40W
Alexandria, *Ky., U.S.A.* **141** **F12** 38 58N 84 23W
Alexandria, *La., U.S.A.* **139** **K8** 31 20N 92 30W
Alexandria, *Minn.,*
*U.S.A.* **138** **C7** 45 50N 95 20W
Alexandria, *Mo., U.S.A.* **140** **D5** 40 27N 91 28W
Alexandria, *S. Dak.,*
*U.S.A.* **138** **D6** 43 40N 97 45W
Alexandria, *Va., U.S.A.* **134** **F7** 38 47N 77 1W
Alexandria Bay, *U.S.A.* **137** **B9** 44 20N 75 52W
Alexandrina, L., *Australia* **116** **C3** 35 25 S 139 10 E
Alexandroúpolis, *Greece* **44** **D7** 40 50N 25 54 E
Alexis, *U.S.A.* **140** **C6** 41 4N 90 33W
Alexis →, *Canada* **129** **B8** 52 33N 56 8W
Alexis Creek, *Canada* **130** **C4** 52 10N 123 20W
Alfabia, *Spain* **33** **B9** 39 44N 2 44 E
Alfambra, *Spain* **34** **E3** 40 33N 1 5W
Alfândega da Fé,
*Portugal* **36** **D4** 41 20N 6 59W
Alfaro, *Spain* **34** **C3** 42 10N 1 50W
Alfatar, *Bulgaria* **43** **D12** 43 59N 27 13 E
Alfeld, *Germany* **26** **D5** 52 0N 9 49 E
Alfenas, *Brazil* **159** **A6** 21 20 S 46 10W
Alfiós →, *Greece* **45** **G3** 37 40N 21 33 E
Alfonsine, *Italy* **39** **D9** 44 30N 12 1 E
Alfonso XIII, *Phil.* **71** **G1** 9 15N 117 59 E
Alford, *U.K.* **18** **D6** 57 13N 2 42W
Alfred, *Maine, U.S.A.* **137** **C14** 43 28N 70 40W
Alfred, *N.Y., U.S.A.* **136** **D7** 42 15N 77 45W
Alfred Town, *Australia* **117** **C7** 35 8 S 147 30 E
Alfredton, *N.Z.* **118** **G4** 40 41 S 175 54 E
Alfreton, *U.K.* **16** **D6** 53 6N 1 22W
Alga, *Kazakhstan* **49** **E10** 49 53N 57 20 E
Algaida, *Spain* **33** **B9** 39 33N 2 53 E
Algar, *Spain* **37** **J5** 36 40N 5 39W
Algarinejo, *Spain* **37** **H6** 37 19N 4 9W
Algarve, *Portugal* **37** **J2** 36 58N 8 20W
Algeciras, *Spain* **37** **J5** 36 9N 5 28W
Algemesí, *Spain* **35** **F4** 39 11N 0 27W
Alger, *Algeria* **99** **A5** 36 42N 3 8 E
Algeria ■, *Africa* **99** **C5** 28 30N 2 0 E
Alghero, *Italy* **40** **B1** 40 34N 8 20 E
Algiers = Alger, *Algeria* **99** **A5** 36 42N 3 8 E
Algoa B., *S. Africa* **104** **E4** 33 50 S 25 45 E
Algodonales, *Spain* **37** **J5** 36 54N 5 24W
Algodor →, *Spain* **36** **F7** 39 55N 3 53W
Algoma, *U.S.A.* **134** **C2** 44 35N 87 27W
Algona, *U.S.A.* **140** **A2** 43 4N 94 14W
Algonac, *U.S.A.* **136** **D2** 42 37N 82 32W
Alhama de Almería,
*Spain* **35** **J2** 36 57N 2 34W
Alhama de Aragón, *Spain* **34** **D3** 41 18N 1 54W
Alhama de Granada,
*Spain* **37** **J7** 37 0N 3 59W
Alhama de Murcia, *Spain* **35** **H3** 37 51N 1 25W
Alhambra, *Spain* **35** **G1** 38 54N 3 4W
Alhambra, *Calif., U.S.A.* **145** **L8** 34 2N 118 10W
Alhambra, *Ill., U.S.A.* **140** **F7** 38 52N 89 45W
Alhaurín el Grande,
*Spain* **37** **J6** 36 39N 4 41W
Alhucemas = Al
Hoceïma, *Morocco* **98** **A4** 35 8N 3 58W
'Alī al Gharbī, *Iraq* **84** **C5** 32 30N 46 45 E
Alī ash Sharqī, *Iraq* **84** **C5** 32 7N 46 44 E
Ali Bayramly, *Azerbaijan* **53** **G13** 39 59N 48 52 E
'Alī Khēl, *Afghan.* **79** **B3** 33 57N 69 43 E
Ali Sahîh, *Djibouti* **95** **E5** 11 10N 42 44 E
Alī Shāh, *Iran* **84** **B5** 38 9N 45 50 E
Ália, *Italy* **40** **E6** 37 47N 13 42 E
'Alīābād, *Khorāsān, Iran* **85** **C8** 32 30N 57 30 E
Alīābād, *Kordestān, Iran* **84** **C5** 35 4N 46 58 E
'Alīābād, *Yazd, Iran* **85** **D7** 31 41N 53 49 E
Aliaga, *Spain* **34** **E4** 40 40N 0 42W
Aliağa, *Turkey* **88** **D2** 38 47N 26 59 E
Aliákmon →, *Greece* **44** **D4** 40 30N 22 36 E
Alibag, *India* **82** **E1** 18 38N 72 56 E
Alibo, *Ethiopia* **95** **F4** 9 52N 37 5 E
Alibunar, *Serbia, Yug.* **42** **B5** 45 5N 20 57 E
Alicante, *Spain* **35** **G4** 38 23N 0 30W
Alicante □, *Spain* **35** **G4** 38 30N 0 37W
Alice, *S. Africa* **104** **E4** 32 48 S 26 55 E
Alice, *U.S.A.* **139** **M5** 27 47N 98 1W
Alice →, *Queens.,*
*Australia* **114** **C3** 24 2 S 144 50 E
Alice →, *Queens.,*
*Australia* **114** **B3** 15 35 S 142 20 E
Alice, Punta dell', *Italy* **41** **C10** 39 23N 17 10 E
Alice Arm, *Canada* **130** **B3** 55 29N 129 31W
Alice Downs, *Australia* **112** **C4** 17 45 S 127 56 E
Alice Springs, *Australia* **114** **C1** 23 40 S 133 50 E
Alicedale, *S. Africa* **104** **E4** 33 15 S 26 4 E
Aliceville, *U.S.A.* **135** **J1** 33 9N 88 10W
Alicia, *Phil.* **71** **G5** 9 54N 124 26 E
Alick Cr. →, *Australia* **114** **C3** 20 55 S 142 20 E
Alicudi, I., *Italy* **41** **D7** 38 33N 14 20 E
Alida, *Canada* **131** **D8** 49 25N 101 55W
Aligarh, *Raj., India* **80** **G7** 25 55N 76 15 E
Aligarh, *Ut. P., India* **80** **F8** 27 55N 78 10 E
Alīgūdarz, *Iran* **85** **C6** 33 25N 49 45 E
Alijó, *Portugal* **36** **D3** 41 16N 7 27W
Alimena, *Italy* **41** **E7** 37 42N 14 4 E
Alimnía, *Greece* **32** **C9** 36 16N 27 43 E
Alimodian, *Phil.* **71** **F4** 10 49N 122 26 E
Alindao, *C.A.R.* **102** **A4** 5 2N 21 13 E
Alingsås, *Sweden* **15** **G6** 57 56N 12 31 E
Alipur, *Pakistan* **80** **E4** 29 25N 70 55 E
Alipur Duar, *India* **78** **B2** 26 30N 89 35 E
Aliquippa, *U.S.A.* **136** **F4** 40 38N 80 18W
Aliste →, *Spain* **36** **D5** 41 34N 5 58W
Alitus, *Lithuania* **50** **D4** 54 24N 24 3 E
Alivérion, *Greece* **45** **F6** 38 24N 24 2 E
Aliwal North, *S. Africa* **104** **E4** 30 45 S 26 45 E
Alix, *Canada* **130** **C6** 52 24N 113 11W
Aljezur, *Portugal* **37** **H2** 37 18N 8 49W

'Amrān 165


Aljustrel, *Portugal* 37 H2 37 55N 8 10W
Alkamari, *Niger* 97 F2 13 27N 11 10 E
Alken, *Belgium* 21 G6 50 53N 5 18 E
Alkmaar, *Neths.* 20 C5 52 37N 4 45 E
All American Canal, *U.S.A.* 143 K6 32 45N 115 0W
Allacapan, *Phil.* 70 B3 18 15N 121 35 E
Allada, *Benin* 101 D5 6 41N 2 9 E
Allah Dad, *Pakistan* 80 G2 25 38N 67 34 E
Allahabad, *India* 81 G9 25 25N 81 58 E
Allakh-Yun, *Russia* 57 C14 60 50N 137 5 E
Allal Tazi, *Morocco* 98 B3 34 30N 6 20W
Allan, *Canada* 131 C7 51 53N 106 4W
Allanche, *France* 24 C6 45 14N 2 57 E
Allanmyo, *Burma* 78 F5 19 30N 95 17 E
Allanridge, *S. Africa* 104 D4 27 45 S 26 40 E
Allansford, *Australia* 116 E5 38 26 S 142 39 E
Allanton, *N.Z.* 119 F5 45 55 S 170 15 E
Allanwater, *Canada* 128 B1 50 14N 90 10W
Allaqi, Wadi →, *Egypt* 94 C3 23 7N 32 47 E
Allariz, *Spain* 36 C3 42 11N 7 50W
Allassac, *France* 24 C5 45 15N 1 29 E
Alle, *Belgium* 21 J5 49 51N 4 58 E
Allegan, *U.S.A.* 141 B11 42 32N 85 52W
Allegany, *U.S.A.* 136 D6 42 6N 78 30W
Allegheny →, *U.S.A.* 136 F5 40 27N 80 0W
Allegheny Plateau, *U.S.A.* 134 G6 38 0N 80 0W
Allegheny Res., *U.S.A.* 136 E6 42 0N 78 55W
Allègre, *France* 24 C7 45 12N 3 41 E
Allen, *Argentina* 160 A3 38 58 S 67 50W
Allen, *Phil.* 70 E5 12 30N 124 17 E
Allen, Bog of, *Ireland* 19 C4 53 15N 7 0W
Allen, L., *Ireland* 19 B3 54 12N 8 5W
Allende, *Mexico* 146 B4 28 20N 100 50W
Allentown, *U.S.A.* 137 F9 40 36N 75 30W
Allentsteig, *Austria* 30 C8 48 41N 15 20 E
Alleppey, *India* 83 K3 9 30N 76 28 E
Aller →, *Germany* 26 C5 52 57N 9 10 E
Alleur, *Belgium* 21 G7 50 39N 5 31 E
Allevard, *France* 25 C10 45 24N 6 5 E
Alliance, *Surinam* 153 B7 5 50N 54 50W
Alliance, *Nebr., U.S.A.* 138 D3 42 10N 102 50W
Alliance, *Ohio, U.S.A.* 136 F3 40 53N 81 7W
Allier □, *France* 24 B6 46 25N 2 40 E
Allier →, *France* 23 F10 46 57N 3 4 E
Allingåbro, *Denmark* 15 H4 56 28N 10 20 E
Allison, *U.S.A.* 140 B4 42 45N 92 48W
Alliston, *Canada* 128 D4 44 9N 79 52W
Alloa, *U.K.* 18 E5 56 7N 3 49W
Allora, *Australia* 115 D5 28 2 S 152 0 E
Allos, *France* 25 D10 44 15N 6 38 E
Alluitsup Paa = Sydprøven, *Greenland* 6 C5 60 30N 45 35W
Alma, *Canada* 129 C5 48 35N 71 40W
Alma, *Ga., U.S.A.* 135 K4 31 33N 82 28W
Alma, *Kans., U.S.A.* 138 F6 39 1N 96 22W
Alma, *Mich., U.S.A.* 134 D3 43 25N 84 40W
Alma, *Nebr., U.S.A.* 138 E5 40 10N 99 25W
Alma, *Wis., U.S.A.* 138 C9 44 19N 91 54W
Alma Ata, *Kazakhstan* 55 B8 43 15N 76 57 E
Almada, *Portugal* 37 G1 38 40N 9 9W
Almaden, *Australia* 114 B3 17 22 S 144 40 E
Almadén, *Spain* 37 G6 38 49N 4 52W
Almagro, *Spain* 35 G7 38 50N 3 45W
Almagro I., *Phil.* 71 F5 11 56N 124 18 E
Almalyk, *Uzbekistan* 55 C4 40 50N 69 35 E
Almanor, L., *U.S.A.* 142 F3 40 15N 121 11W
Almansa, *Spain* 35 G3 38 51N 1 5W
Almanza, *Spain* 36 C5 42 39N 5 3W
Almanzor, Pico de, *Spain* 36 E5 40 15N 5 18W
Almanzora →, *Spain* 35 H3 37 14N 1 46W
Almas, *Brazil* 155 D2 11 33 S 47 9W
Almaş, Mţii., *Romania* 46 E3 44 49N 22 12 E
Almazán, *Spain* 34 D2 41 30N 2 30W
Almazora, *Spain* 34 F4 39 57N 0 3W
Almeirim, *Brazil* 153 D7 1 30 S 52 34W
Almeirim, *Portugal* 37 F2 39 12N 8 37W
Almelo, *Neths.* 20 D9 52 22N 6 42 E
Almenar, *Spain* 34 D2 41 43N 2 12W
Almenara, *Brazil* 155 E3 16 11 S 40 42W
Almenara, *Spain* 34 F4 39 46N 0 14W
Almenara, Sierra de, *Spain* 35 H3 37 34N 1 32W
Almendralejo, *Spain* 37 G4 38 41N 6 26W
Almería, *Spain* 35 J2 36 52N 2 27W
Almería □, *Spain* 35 H2 37 20N 2 20W
Almería, G. de, *Spain* 35 J2 36 41N 2 28W
Almetyevsk, *Russia* 54 D3 54 53N 52 20 E
Almirante, *Panama* 148 E3 9 10N 82 30W
Almirante Montt, G., *Chile* 160 D2 51 52 S 72 50W
Almiropótamos, *Greece* 45 F6 38 16N 24 11 E
Almirós, *Greece* 45 E4 39 11N 22 45 E
Almiroú, Kólpos, *Greece* 32 D6 35 23N 24 20 E
Almodôvar, *Portugal* 37 H2 37 31N 8 2W
Almodóvar del Campo, *Spain* 37 G6 38 43N 4 10W
Almogia, *Spain* 37 J6 36 50N 4 32W
Almonaster la Real, *Spain* 37 H4 37 52N 6 48W
Almont, *U.S.A.* 136 D1 42 53N 83 2W
Almonte, *Canada* 137 A8 45 14N 76 12W
Almonte →, *Spain* 37 F4 39 41N 6 28W
Almora, *India* 81 E8 29 38N 79 40 E
Almoradi, *Spain* 35 G4 38 7N 0 46W
Almorox, *Spain* 36 E6 40 14N 4 24W
Almoustarat, *Mali* 101 B5 17 35N 0 8 E
Almuñécar, *Spain* 37 J7 36 43N 3 41W
Alnif, *Morocco* 98 B3 31 10N 5 8W
Alnwick, *U.K.* 16 B6 55 25N 1 42W
Aloi, *Uganda* 106 B3 2 16N 33 10 E
Alon, *Burma* 78 D5 22 12N 95 5 E
Alor, *Indonesia* 72 C2 8 15 S 124 30 E
Alor Setar, *Malaysia* 77 J3 6 7N 100 22 E
Alora, *Spain* 37 J6 36 49N 4 46W
Alosno, *Spain* 37 H3 37 33N 7 7W
Alotau, *Papua N. G.* 120 F6 10 16 S 150 30 E
Alougoum, *Morocco* 98 B3 30 17N 6 56W
Aloysius, Mt., *Australia* 113 E4 26 0 S 128 38 E
Alpaugh, *U.S.A.* 144 K7 35 53N 119 29W
Alpedrinha, *Portugal* 36 E3 40 6N 7 27W
Alpena, *U.S.A.* 134 C4 45 4N 83 27W
Alpercatas →, *Brazil* 154 C3 6 2 S 44 19W
Alpes-de-Haute-Provence □, *France* 25 D10 44 8N 6 10 E
Alpes-Maritimes □, *France* 25 E11 43 55N 7 10 E
Alpha, *Australia* 114 C4 23 39 S 146 37 E
Alpha, *U.S.A.* 140 C6 41 11N 90 23W
Alphen, *Neths.* 21 F5 51 29N 4 58 E
Alphen aan den Rijn, *Neths.* 20 D5 52 7N 4 40 E
Alphonse, *Seychelles* 109 E4 7 0 S 52 45 E
Alpiarça, *Portugal* 37 F2 39 15N 8 35W
Alpine, *Ariz., U.S.A.* 143 K9 33 57N 109 4W
Alpine, *Calif., U.S.A.* 145 N10 32 50N 116 46W
Alpine, *Tex., U.S.A.* 139 K3 30 25N 103 35W
Alpnach, *Switz.* 29 C6 46 57N 8 17 E
Alps, *Europe* 10 F7 46 30N 9 30 E
Alpu, *Turkey* 88 D4 39 46N 30 58 E
Alrø, *Denmark* 15 J4 55 52N 10 5 E
Alroy Downs, *Australia* 114 B2 19 20 S 136 5 E
Alsace, *France* 23 D14 48 15N 7 25 E
Alsask, *Canada* 131 C7 51 21N 109 59W
Alsásua, *Spain* 34 C2 42 54N 2 10W
Alsen, *Sweden* 14 A7 63 23N 13 56 E
Alsfeld, *Germany* 26 E5 50 44N 9 19 E
Alsónémedi, *Hungary* 31 D12 47 20N 19 15 E
Alsten, *Norway* 12 D12 65 58N 12 40 E
Alta, *Norway* 12 B17 69 57N 23 10 E
Alta, Sierra, *Spain* 34 E3 40 31N 1 30W
Alta Gracia, *Argentina* 158 C3 31 40 S 64 30W
Alta Lake, *Canada* 130 C4 50 10N 123 0W
Alta Sierra, *U.S.A.* 145 K8 35 42N 118 33W
Altaelva →, *Norway* 12 B17 69 46N 23 45 E
Altafjorden, *Norway* 12 A17 70 5N 23 5 E
Altagracia, *Venezuela* 152 A3 10 45N 71 30W
Altagracia de Orituco, *Venezuela* 152 B4 9 52N 66 23W
Altai = Aerhtai Shan, *Mongolia* 64 B4 46 40N 92 45 E
Altamachi →, *Bolivia* 156 D4 16 8 S 66 50W
Altamaha →, *U.S.A.* 135 K5 31 19N 81 17W
Altamira, *Brazil* 153 D7 3 12 S 52 10W
Altamira, *Chile* 158 B2 25 47 S 69 51W
Altamira, *Colombia* 152 C2 2 3N 75 47W
Altamira, *Mexico* 147 C5 22 24N 97 55W
Altamira, Cuevas de, *Spain* 36 B6 43 20N 4 5W
Altamont, *Ill., U.S.A.* 141 E8 39 4N 88 45W
Altamont, *N.Y., U.S.A.* 137 D10 42 43N 74 3W
Altamura, *Italy* 41 B9 40 50N 16 33 E
Altanbulag, *Mongolia* 64 A5 50 16N 106 30 E
Altar, *Mexico* 146 A2 30 40N 111 50W
Altata, *Mexico* 146 C3 24 30N 108 0W
Altavas, *Phil.* 71 F4 11 32N 122 29 E
Altavista, *U.S.A.* 134 G6 37 9N 79 22W
Altay, *China* 64 B3 47 48N 88 10 E
Altdorf, *Switz.* 29 C7 46 52N 8 36 E
Alte Mellum, *Germany* 26 B4 53 45N 8 6 E
Altea, *Spain* 35 G4 38 38N 0 2W
Altenberg, *Germany* 26 E9 50 46N 13 47 E
Altenbruch, *Germany* 26 B4 53 48N 8 44 E
Altenburg, *Germany* 26 E8 50 59N 12 28 E
Altenkirchen, *Mecklenburg-Vorpommern, Germany* 26 A9 54 38N 13 20 E
Altenkirchen, *Rhld-Pfz., Germany* 26 E3 50 41N 7 38 E
Altenmarkt, *Austria* 30 D7 47 43N 14 39 E
Altenteptow, *Germany* 26 B9 53 42N 13 15 E
Alter do Chão, *Portugal* 37 F3 39 12N 7 40W
Altıntaş, *Turkey* 88 D4 39 4N 30 10 E
Altiplano, *Bolivia* 156 D4 17 0 S 68 0W
Altkirch, *France* 23 E14 47 37N 7 15 E
Altmühl →, *Germany* 27 G7 48 54N 11 54 E
Alto Adige = Trentino-Alto Adige □, *Italy* 38 B8 46 30N 11 0 E
Alto Araguaia, *Brazil* 157 D7 17 15 S 53 20W
Alto Cuchumatanes = Cuchumatanes, Sierra de los, *Guatemala* 148 C1 15 35N 91 25W
Alto Cuito, *Angola* 103 E3 13 27 S 18 49 E
Alto del Inca, *Chile* 158 A2 24 10 S 68 10W
Alto Garças, *Brazil* 157 D7 16 56 S 53 32W
Alto Iriri →, *Brazil* 157 B7 8 50 S 53 25W
Alto Ligonha, *Mozam.* 107 F4 15 30 S 38 11 E
Alto Molocue, *Mozam.* 107 F4 15 50 S 37 35 E
Alto Paraguai, *Brazil* 157 C6 14 30 S 56 31W
Alto Paraguay □, *Paraguay* 158 A4 21 0 S 58 30W
Alto Paraná □, *Paraguay* 159 B5 25 30 S 54 50W
Alto Parnaíba, *Brazil* 154 C2 9 6 S 45 57W
Alto Purús →, *Peru* 156 B3 9 12 S 70 28W
Alto Río Senguerr, *Argentina* 160 C2 45 2 S 70 50W
Alto Santo, *Brazil* 154 C4 5 31 S 38 15W
Alto Sucuriú, *Brazil* 157 D7 19 19 S 52 47W
Alto Turi, *Brazil* 154 B2 2 54 S 45 38W
Alton, *Canada* 136 C4 43 54N 80 5W
Alton, *U.S.A.* 140 F6 38 55N 90 5W
Alton Downs, *Australia* 115 D2 26 7 S 138 57 E
Altoona, *Iowa, U.S.A.* 140 C3 41 39N 93 28W
Altoona, *Pa., U.S.A.* 136 F6 40 32N 78 24W
Altopáscio, *Italy* 38 E7 43 50N 10 40 E
Altos, *Brazil* 154 C3 5 3 S 42 28W
Altötting, *Germany* 27 G8 48 14N 12 41 E
Altstätten, *Switz.* 29 B9 47 22N 9 33 E
Altūn Kūprī, *Iraq* 84 C5 35 45N 44 9 E
Altun Shan, *China* 64 C3 38 30N 88 0 E
Alturas, *U.S.A.* 142 F3 41 36N 120 37W
Altus, *U.S.A.* 139 H5 34 30N 99 25W
Alubijid, *Phil.* 71 G5 8 35N 124 29 E
Alucra, *Turkey* 53 F8 40 22N 38 47 E
Aluksne, *Latvia* 50 C5 57 24N 27 3 E
Alùla, *Somali Rep.* 90 E5 11 50N 50 45 E
Alunite, *U.S.A.* 145 K12 35 59N 114 55W
Alupka, *Ukraine* 52 D6 44 23N 34 2 E
Alur Gajah, *Malaysia* 74 B2 2 23N 102 13 E
Alushta, *Ukraine* 52 D6 44 40N 34 25 E
Alusi, *Indonesia* 73 C4 7 35 S 131 40 E
Alustante, *Spain* 34 E3 40 36N 1 40W
Al'Uzayr, *Iraq* 84 D5 31 19N 47 25 E
Alva, *U.S.A.* 139 G5 36 50N 98 50W
Alvaiázere, *Portugal* 36 F2 39 49N 8 23W
Älvängen, *Sweden* 15 G6 57 58N 12 8 E
Alvarado, *Mexico* 147 D5 18 40N 95 50W
Alvarado, *U.S.A.* 139 J6 32 25N 97 15W
Alvarães, *Brazil* 153 D5 3 12 S 64 50W
Alvaro Obregón, Presa, *Mexico* 146 B3 27 55N 109 52W
Alvdal, *Norway* 14 B4 62 6N 10 37 E
Alvear, *Argentina* 158 B4 29 5 S 56 30W
Alverca, *Portugal* 37 G1 38 56N 9 1W
Alveringen, *Belgium* 21 F1 51 1N 2 43 E
Alvesta, *Sweden* 13 H13 56 54N 14 35 E
Alvie, *Australia* 116 E5 38 14 S 143 30 E
Alvin, *U.S.A.* 139 L7 29 23N 95 12W
Alvinston, *Canada* 136 D3 42 49N 81 52W
Alvito, *Portugal* 37 G3 38 15N 8 0W
Älvkarleby, *Sweden* 13 F14 60 34N 17 26 E
Älvros, *Sweden* 14 B8 62 3N 14 38 E
Älvsborgs län □, *Sweden* 15 F6 58 30N 12 30 E
Älvsbyn, *Sweden* 12 D16 65 40N 21 0 E
Älvsered, *Sweden* 15 G6 57 14N 12 51 E
Alwar, *India* 80 F7 27 38N 76 34 E
Alwaye, *India* 83 J3 10 8N 76 24 E
Alxa Zuoqi, *China* 66 E3 38 50N 105 40 E
Alyaskitovyy, *Russia* 57 C15 64 45N 141 30 E
Alyata, *Azerbaijan* 53 G13 39 58N 49 25 E
Alyth, *U.K.* 18 E5 56 38N 3 15W
Alzada, *U.S.A.* 138 C2 45 3N 104 22W
Alzano Lombardo, *Italy* 38 C6 45 44N 9 43 E
Alzette →, *Lux.* 21 J8 49 45N 6 6 E
Alzey, *Germany* 27 F4 49 48N 8 4 E
Am Dam, *Chad* 97 F4 12 40N 20 35 E
Am Géréda, *Chad* 97 F4 12 53N 21 14 E
Am-Timan, *Chad* 97 F4 11 0N 20 10 E
Amacuro □, *Venezuela* 153 B5 8 50N 61 5W
Amadeus, L., *Australia* 113 D5 24 54 S 131 0 E
Amâdi, *Sudan* 95 F3 5 29N 30 25 E
Amadi, *Zaïre* 106 B2 3 40N 26 40 E
Amadjuak, *Canada* 127 B12 64 0N 72 39W
Amadjuak L., *Canada* 127 B12 65 0N 71 8W
Amadora, *Portugal* 37 G1 38 45N 9 13W
Amagasaki, *Japan* 63 C7 34 42N 135 20 E
Amager, *Denmark* 15 J6 55 37N 12 35 E
Amagi, *Japan* 62 D2 33 25N 130 39 E
Amahai, *Indonesia* 73 B3 3 20 S 128 55 E
Amaimon, *Papua N. G.* 120 C3 5 12 S 145 30 E
Amakusa-Nada, *Japan* 62 E2 32 35N 130 5 E
Amakusa-Shotō, *Japan* 62 E2 32 15N 130 10 E
Amalapuram, *India* 83 F5 16 35N 81 55 E
Amalfi, *Colombia* 152 B2 6 55N 75 4W
Amalfi, *Italy* 41 B7 40 39N 14 34 E
Amaliás, *Greece* 45 G3 37 47N 21 22 E
Amalner, *India* 82 D2 21 5N 75 5 E
Amambaí, *Brazil* 159 A4 23 5 S 55 13W
Amambaí →, *Brazil* 159 A5 23 22 S 53 56W
Amambay □, *Paraguay* 159 A4 23 0 S 56 0W
Amambay, Cordillera de, *S. Amer.* 159 A4 23 0 S 55 45W
Amami-Guntō, *Japan* 61 L4 27 16N 129 21 E
Amami-Ō-Shima, *Japan* 61 L4 28 0N 129 0 E
Amana →, *Venezuela* 153 B5 9 45N 62 39W
Amaná, L., *Brazil* 153 D5 2 35 S 64 40W
Amanab, *Papua N. G.* 120 B1 3 40 S 141 14 E
Amanda Park, *U.S.A.* 144 C3 47 28N 123 55W
Amándola, *Italy* 39 F10 42 59N 13 21 E
Amangeldy, *Kazakhstan* 56 D7 50 10N 65 10 E
Amantea, *Italy* 41 C9 39 8N 16 3 E
Amapá, *Brazil* 153 C7 2 5N 50 50W
Amapá □, *Brazil* 153 C7 1 40N 52 0W
Amapari, *Brazil* 153 C7 0 37N 51 39W
Amara, *Sudan* 95 E3 10 25N 34 10 E
Amarante, *Brazil* 154 C3 6 14 S 42 50W
Amarante, *Portugal* 36 D2 41 16N 8 5W
Amarante do Maranhão, *Brazil* 154 C2 5 36 S 46 45W
Amaranth, *Canada* 131 C9 50 36N 98 43W
Amarapura, *Burma* 78 E6 21 54N 96 3 E
Amaravati →, *India* 83 J4 11 0N 78 15 E
Amareleja, *Portugal* 37 G3 38 12N 7 13W
Amargosa, *Brazil* 155 D4 13 2 S 39 36W
Amargosa →, *U.S.A.* 145 J10 36 14N 116 51W
Amargosa Ra., *U.S.A.* 145 J10 36 25N 116 40W
Amári, *Greece* 32 D6 35 13N 24 40 E
Amarillo, *U.S.A.* 139 H4 35 14N 101 46W
Amarnath, *India* 82 E1 19 12N 73 22 E
Amaro, Mt., *Italy* 39 F11 42 5N 14 6 E
Amaro Leite, *Brazil* 155 D2 13 58 S 49 9W
Amarpur, *India* 81 G12 25 5N 87 0 E
Amasra, *Turkey* 88 C5 41 45N 32 23 E
Amassama, *Nigeria* 101 D6 5 1N 6 2 E
Amasya, *Turkey* 88 C6 40 40N 35 50 E
Amasya □, *Turkey* 88 C6 40 40N 35 50 E
Amataurá, *Brazil* 152 D4 3 29 S 68 6W
Amatikulu, *S. Africa* 105 D5 29 3 S 31 33 E
Amatitlán, *Guatemala* 148 D1 14 29N 90 38W
Amatrice, *Italy* 39 F10 42 38N 13 16 E
Amay, *Belgium* 21 G6 50 33N 5 19 E
Amazon = Amazonas →, *S. Amer.* 153 D7 0 5 S 50 0W
Amazonas □, *Brazil* 157 B5 5 0 S 65 0W
Amazonas □, *Peru* 156 B2 5 0 S 78 0W
Amazonas □, *Venezuela* 152 C4 3 30N 66 0W
Amazonas →, *S. Amer.* 153 D7 0 5 S 50 0W
Ambad, *India* 82 E2 19 38N 75 50 E
Ambahakily, *Madag.* 105 C7 21 36 S 43 41 E
Ambala, *India* 80 D7 30 23N 76 56 E
Ambalangoda, *Sri Lanka* 83 L5 6 15N 80 5 E
Ambalapulai, *India* 83 K3 9 25N 76 25 E
Ambalavao, *Madag.* 105 C8 21 50 S 46 56 E
Ambalindum, *Australia* 114 C2 23 23 S 135 0 E
Ambam, *Cameroon* 102 B2 2 20N 11 15 E
Ambanja, *Madag.* 105 A8 13 40 S 48 27 E
Ambarchik, *Russia* 57 C17 69 40N 162 20 E
Ambarijeby, *Madag.* 105 A8 14 56 S 47 41 E
Ambaro, Helodranon', *Madag.* 105 A8 13 23 S 48 38 E
Ambartsevo, *Russia* 56 D9 57 30N 83 52 E
Ambasamudram, *India* 83 K3 8 43N 77 25 E
Ambato, *Ecuador* 152 D2 1 5 S 78 42W
Ambato, Sierra de, *Argentina* 158 B2 28 25 S 66 10W
Ambato Boeny, *Madag.* 105 B8 16 28 S 46 43 E
Ambatofinandrahana, *Madag.* 105 C8 20 33 S 46 48 E
Ambatolampy, *Madag.* 105 B8 19 20 S 47 35 E
Ambatondrazaka, *Madag.* 105 B8 17 55 S 48 28 E
Ambatosoratra, *Madag.* 105 B8 17 37 S 48 31 E
Ambenja, *Madag.* 105 B8 15 17 S 46 58 E
Amberg, *Germany* 27 F7 49 25N 11 52 E
Ambergris Cay, *Belize* 147 D7 18 0N 88 0W
Ambérieu-en-Bugey, *France* 25 C9 45 57N 5 20 E
Amberley, *N.Z.* 119 D7 43 9 S 172 44 E
Ambert, *France* 24 C7 45 33N 3 44 E
Ambidédi, *Mali* 100 C2 14 35N 11 47W
Ambikapur, *India* 81 H10 23 15N 83 15 E
Ambikol, *Sudan* 94 C3 21 20N 30 50 E
Ambilobé, *Madag.* 105 A8 13 10 S 49 3 E
Ambinanindrano, *Madag.* 105 C8 20 5 S 48 23 E
Ambjörnarp, *Sweden* 15 G7 57 25N 13 17 E
Ambleside, *U.K.* 16 C5 54 26N 2 58W
Amblève, *Belgium* 21 H8 50 21N 6 10 E
Amblève →, *Belgium* 21 H7 50 25N 5 45 E
Ambo, *Ethiopia* 95 E4 12 20N 37 30 E
Ambo, *Peru* 156 C2 10 5 S 76 10W
Ambodifototra, *Madag.* 105 B8 16 59 S 49 52 E
Ambodilazana, *Madag.* 105 B8 18 6 S 49 10 E
Ambohimahasoa, *Madag.* 105 C8 21 7 S 47 13 E
Ambohimanga, *Madag.* 105 C8 20 52 S 47 36 E
Ambohitra, *Madag.* 105 A8 12 30 S 49 10 E
Ambon, *Indonesia* 72 B3 3 43 S 128 12 E
Ambon, *Indonesia* 72 B3 3 35 S 128 20 E
Amboseli L., *Kenya* 106 C4 2 40 S 37 10 E
Ambositra, *Madag.* 105 C8 20 31 S 47 25 E
Ambovombé, *Madag.* 105 D8 25 11 S 46 5 E
Amboy, *Calif., U.S.A.* 145 L11 34 33N 115 51W
Amboy, *Ill., U.S.A.* 140 C7 41 44N 89 20W
Ambridge, *U.S.A.* 136 F4 40 36N 80 15W
Ambriz, *Angola* 103 D2 7 48 S 13 8 E
Ambrym, *Vanuatu* 121 F6 16 15 S 168 10 E
Ambunti, *Papua N. G.* 120 C2 4 13 S 142 52 E
Ambur, *India* 83 H4 12 48N 78 43 E
Amby, *Australia* 115 D4 26 30 S 148 11 E
Amchitka I., *U.S.A.* 126 C1 51 30N 179 0 E
Amderma, *Russia* 56 C7 69 45N 61 30 E
Ameca, *Mexico* 146 C4 20 30N 104 0W
Ameca →, *Mexico* 146 C3 20 40N 105 15W
Amecameca, *Mexico* 147 D5 19 7N 98 46W
Ameland, *Neths.* 20 B7 53 27N 5 45 E
Amélia, *Italy* 39 F9 42 34N 12 25 E
Amélie-les-Bains-Palalda, *France* 24 F6 42 29N 2 41 E
Amen, *Russia* 57 C18 68 45N 180 0 E
Amendolaro, *Italy* 41 C9 39 58N 16 34 E
America, *Neths.* 21 F7 51 27N 5 59 E
American Falls, *U.S.A.* 142 E7 42 46N 112 56W
American Falls Res., *U.S.A.* 142 E7 43 0N 112 50W
American Highland, *Antarctica* 7 D6 73 0 S 75 0 E
American Samoa ■, *Pac. Oc.* 121 X24 14 20 S 170 40W
Americana, *Brazil* 159 A6 22 45 S 47 20W
Americus, *U.S.A.* 135 J3 32 0N 84 10W
Amersfoort, *Neths.* 20 D6 52 9N 5 23 E
Amersfoort, *S. Africa* 105 D4 26 59 S 29 53 E
Amery, *Australia* 113 F2 31 9 S 117 5 E
Amery, *Canada* 131 B10 56 34N 94 3W
Amery Ice Shelf, *Antarctica* 7 C6 69 30 S 72 0 E
Ames, *U.S.A.* 140 B3 42 0N 93 40W
Amesbury, *U.S.A.* 137 D14 42 50N 70 52W
Amfíklia, *Greece* 45 F4 38 38N 22 35 E
Amfilokhía, *Greece* 45 F3 38 52N 21 9 E
Amfípolis, *Greece* 44 D5 40 48N 23 52 E
Ámfissa, *Greece* 45 F4 38 32N 22 22 E
Amga, *Russia* 57 C14 60 50N 132 0 E
Amga →, *Russia* 57 C14 62 38N 134 32 E
Amgu, *Russia* 57 E14 45 45N 137 15 E
Amgun →, *Russia* 57 D14 52 56N 139 38 E
Amherst, *Canada* 129 C7 45 48N 64 8W
Amherst, *Mass., U.S.A.* 137 D12 42 21N 72 30W
Amherst, *N.Y., U.S.A.* 136 D6 42 59N 78 48W
Amherst, *Ohio, U.S.A.* 136 E2 41 23N 82 15W
Amherst, *Tex., U.S.A.* 139 H3 34 0N 102 24W
Amherst I., *Canada* 137 B8 44 8N 76 43W
Amherstburg, *Canada* 128 D3 42 6N 83 6W
Amiata, Mte., *Italy* 39 F8 42 54N 11 40 E
Amiens, *France* 23 C9 49 54N 2 16 E
Amigdhalokefáli, *Greece* 45 J5 35 23N 23 30 E
Amili, *India* 78 A5 28 25N 95 52 E
Amindaion, *Greece* 44 D3 40 42N 21 42 E
Amīrābād, *Iran* 84 C5 33 20N 46 16 E
Amirante Is., *Seychelles* 109 E4 6 0 S 53 0 E
Amisk L., *Canada* 131 C8 54 35N 102 15W
Amistad, Presa de la, *Mexico* 146 B4 29 24N 101 0W
Amite, *U.S.A.* 139 K9 30 47N 90 31W
Amizmiz, *Morocco* 98 B3 31 12N 8 15W
Åmli, *Norway* 15 F2 58 45N 8 32 E
Amlwch, *U.K.* 16 D3 53 24N 4 21W
Amm Adam, *Sudan* 95 D4 16 20N 36 1 E
'Ammān, *Jordan* 91 D4 31 57N 35 52 E
Ammanford, *U.K.* 17 F3 51 48N 4 4W
Ammassalik = Angmagssalik, *Greenland* 6 C6 65 40N 37 20W
Ammerån, *Sweden* 14 A10 63 9N 16 13 E
Ammerån →, *Sweden* 14 A10 63 9N 16 13 E
Ammersee, *Germany* 27 G7 48 0N 11 7 E
Ammerzoden, *Neths.* 20 E6 51 45N 5 13 E
Amnat Charoen, *Thailand* 76 E5 15 51N 104 38 E
Amo Jiang →, *China* 68 F3 23 0N 101 50 E
Āmol, *Iran* 85 B7 36 23N 52 20 E
Amorebieta, *Spain* 34 B2 43 13N 2 44W
Amoret, *U.S.A.* 140 F2 38 15N 94 35W
Amorgós, *Greece* 45 H7 36 50N 25 57 E
Amory, *U.S.A.* 135 J1 33 59N 88 29W
Amos, *Canada* 128 C4 48 35N 78 5W
Åmot, *Buskerud, Norway* 14 E3 59 54N 9 54 E
Åmot, *Telemark, Norway* 14 E2 59 34N 8 0 E
Åmotsdal, *Norway* 14 E2 59 37N 8 26 E
Amour, Djebel, *Algeria* 99 B5 33 42N 1 37 E
Amoy = Xiamen, *China* 69 E12 24 25N 118 4 E
Ampang, *Malaysia* 77 L3 3 8N 101 45 E
Ampanihy, *Madag.* 105 C7 24 40 S 44 45 E
Ampasindava, Helodranon', *Madag.* 105 A8 13 40 S 48 15 E
Ampasindava, Saikanosy, *Madag.* 105 A8 13 42 S 47 55 E
Ampato, Nevado, *Peru* 156 D3 15 40 S 71 56W
Ampenan, *Indonesia* 75 D5 8 35 S 116 13 E
Amper, *Nigeria* 101 D6 9 25N 9 40 E
Amper →, *Germany* 27 G7 48 30N 11 57 E
Ampère, *Algeria* 99 A6 35 44N 5 27 E
Ampezzo, *Italy* 39 B9 46 25N 12 48 E
Amposta, *Spain* 34 E5 40 43N 0 34 E
Ampotaka, *Madag.* 105 D7 25 3 S 44 41 E
Ampoza, *Madag.* 105 C7 22 20 S 44 44 E
Amqui, *Canada* 129 C6 48 28N 67 27W
'Amrān, *Yemen* 86 D3 15 41N 43 55 E

168 Arizaro, Salar de


Arizaro, Salar de, Argentina 158 A2 24 40 S 67 50W
Arizona, Argentina 158 D2 35 45 S 65 25W
Arizona □, U.S.A. 143 J8 34 20N 111 30W
Arizpe, Mexico 146 A2 30 20N 110 11W
Arjeplog, Sweden 12 C15 66 3N 18 2 E
Arjona, Colombia 152 A2 10 14N 75 22W
Arjona, Spain 37 H6 37 56N 4 4W
Arjuno, Indonesia 75 D4 7 49 S 112 34 E
Arka, Russia 57 C15 60 15N 142 0 E
Arkadak, Russia 51 F13 51 58N 43 19 E
Arkadelphia, U.S.A. 139 H8 34 5N 93 0W
Arkadhía □, Greece 45 G4 37 30N 22 20 E
Arkaig, L., U.K. 18 E3 56 58N 5 10W
Arkalyk, Kazakhstan 56 D7 50 13N 66 50 E
Arkansas □, U.S.A. 139 H8 35 0N 92 30W
Arkansas →, U.S.A. 139 J9 33 48N 91 4W
Arkansas City, U.S.A. 139 G6 37 4N 97 3W
Árkathos →, Greece 44 E3 39 20N 21 4 E
Arkhángelos, Greece 32 C10 36 13N 28 7 E
Arkhangelsk, Russia 48 B7 64 40N 41 0 E
Arkhangelskoye, Russia 51 F12 51 32N 40 58 E
Arkiko, Ethiopia 95 D4 15 33N 39 30 E
Arklow, Ireland 19 D5 52 48N 6 10W
Árkoi, Greece 45 G8 37 24N 26 44 E
Arkona, Kap, Germany 26 A9 54 41N 13 26 E
Arkösund, Sweden 15 F10 58 29N 16 56 E
Arkoúdhi, Greece 45 F2 38 33N 20 43 E
Arkticheskiy, Mys, Russia 57 A10 81 10N 95 0 E
Arkul, Russia 54 C2 57 17N 50 3 E
Arlanc, France 24 C7 45 25N 3 42 E
Arlanza →, Spain 36 C6 42 6N 4 9W
Arlanzón →, Spain 36 C6 42 3N 4 17W
Arlberg Pass, Austria 27 H6 47 9N 10 12 E
Arlee, U.S.A. 142 C6 47 10N 114 4W
Arles, France 25 E8 43 41N 4 40 E
Arlesheim, Switz. 28 B5 47 30N 7 37 E
Arlington, S. Africa 105 D4 28 1 S 27 53 E
Arlington, Oreg., U.S.A. 142 D3 45 48N 120 6W
Arlington, S. Dak., U.S.A. 138 C6 44 25N 97 4W
Arlington, Va., U.S.A. 134 F7 38 52N 77 5W
Arlington, Wash., U.S.A. 144 B4 48 11N 122 4W
Arlington Heights, U.S.A. 141 B9 42 5N 87 59W
Arlon, Belgium 21 J7 49 42N 5 49 E
Arlöv, Sweden 15 J7 55 38N 13 5 E
Arly, Burkina Faso 101 C5 11 35N 1 28 E
Armagh, U.K. 19 B5 54 22N 6 40W
Armagh □, U.K. 19 B5 54 18N 6 37W
Armagnac, France 24 E4 43 50N 0 10 E
Armançon →, France 23 E10 47 59N 3 30 E
Armavir, Russia 53 D9 45 2N 41 7 E
Armenia, Colombia 152 C2 4 35N 75 45W
Armenia ■, Asia 53 F11 40 20N 45 0 E
Armeniş, Romania 46 D3 45 13N 22 17 E
Armenistís, Ákra, Greece 32 C9 36 8N 27 42 E
Armentières, France 23 B9 50 40N 2 50 E
Armidale, Australia 117 A9 30 30 S 151 40 E
Armour, U.S.A. 138 D5 43 20N 98 25W
Armstrong, B.C., Canada 130 C5 50 25N 119 10W
Armstrong, Ont., Canada 128 B2 50 18N 89 4W
Armstrong, U.S.A. 139 M6 26 59N 97 48W
Armstrong →, Australia 112 C5 16 35 S 131 40 E
Armur, India 82 E4 18 48N 78 16 E
Arnaía, Greece 44 D5 40 30N 23 40 E
Arnarfjörður, Iceland 12 D2 65 48N 23 40W
Arnaud →, Canada 127 B12 60 0N 70 0W
Arnauti, C., Cyprus 32 D11 35 6N 32 17 E
Arnay-le-Duc, France 23 E11 47 10N 4 27 E
Arnedillo, Spain 34 C2 42 13N 2 14W
Arnedo, Spain 34 C2 42 12N 2 5W
Arnemuiden, Neths. 21 F3 51 30N 3 40 E
Árnes, Iceland 12 C3 66 1N 21 31W
Årnes, Norway 14 D5 60 7N 11 28 E
Arnett, U.S.A. 139 G5 36 9N 99 44W
Arnhem, Neths. 20 E7 51 58N 5 55 E
Arnhem, C., Australia 114 A2 12 20 S 137 30 E
Arnhem B., Australia 114 A2 12 20 S 136 10 E
Arnhem Land, Australia 114 A1 13 10 S 134 30 E
Árnissa, Greece 44 D3 40 47N 21 49 E
Arno →, Italy 38 E7 43 41N 10 17 E
Arno Bay, Australia 116 B2 33 54 S 136 34 E
Arnold, Calif., U.S.A. 144 G6 38 15N 120 20W
Arnold, Nebr., U.S.A. 138 E4 41 29N 100 10W
Arnoldstein, Austria 30 E6 46 33N 13 43 E
Arnon →, France 23 E9 47 13N 2 1 E
Arnot, Canada 131 B9 55 56N 96 41W
Arnøy, Norway 12 A16 70 9N 20 40 E
Arnprior, Canada 128 C4 45 26N 76 21W
Arnsberg, Germany 26 D4 51 25N 8 2 E
Arnstadt, Germany 26 E6 50 50N 10 56 E
Aro →, Venezuela 153 B5 8 1N 64 11W
Aroab, Namibia 104 D2 26 41 S 19 39 E
Aroánia Óri, Greece 45 G4 37 56N 22 12 E
Aroche, Spain 37 H4 37 56N 6 57W
Aroeiras, Brazil 154 C4 7 31 S 35 41W
Arolla, Switz. 28 D4 46 2N 7 29 E
Arolsen, Germany 26 D5 51 23N 9 1 E
Aron →, France 24 B7 46 50N 3 28 E
Arona, Italy 38 C5 45 45N 8 32 E
Aroroy, Phil. 70 E4 12 31N 123 24 E
Arosa, Switz. 29 C9 46 47N 9 41 E
Arosa, Ria de, Spain 36 C2 42 28N 8 57W
Arpajon, France 23 D9 48 36N 2 15 E
Arpajon-sur-Cère, France 24 D6 44 53N 2 28 E
Arpino, Italy 40 A6 41 40N 13 35 E
Arque, Bolivia 156 D4 17 48 S 66 23W
Arrabury, Australia 115 D3 26 45 S 141 0 E
Arraias, Brazil 155 D2 12 56 S 46 57W
Arraias →, Mato Grosso, Brazil 157 C7 11 10 S 53 35W
Arraias →, Pará, Brazil 154 C2 7 30 S 49 20W
Arraiolos, Portugal 37 G3 38 44N 7 59W
Arran, U.K. 18 F3 55 34N 5 12W
Arrandale, Canada 130 C3 54 57N 130 0W
Arras, France 23 B9 50 17N 2 46 E
Arrats →, France 24 D4 44 6N 0 52 E
Arreau, France 24 F4 42 54N 0 22 E
Arrecife, Canary Is. 33 F6 28 57N 13 37W
Arrecifes, Argentina 158 C3 34 6 S 60 9W
Arrée, Mts. d', France 22 D3 48 26N 3 55W
Arriaga, Chiapas, Mexico 147 D6 16 15N 93 52W
Arriaga, San Luis Potosí, Mexico 146 C4 21 55N 101 23W
Arrilalah P.O., Australia 114 C3 23 43 S 143 54 E
Arrino, Australia 113 E2 29 30 S 115 40 E
Arrojado →, Brazil 155 D3 13 24 S 44 20W
Arromanches-les-Bains, France 22 C6 49 20N 0 38W
Arronches, Portugal 37 F3 39 8N 7 16W
Arros →, France 24 E3 43 40N 0 2W
Arrou, France 22 D8 48 6N 1 8 E
Arrow, L., Ireland 19 B3 54 3N 8 20W
Arrow Rock Res., U.S.A. 142 E6 43 45N 115 50W
Arrowhead, Canada 130 C5 50 40N 117 55W
Arrowhead, L., U.S.A. 145 L9 34 16N 117 10W
Arrowsmith, Mt., N.Z. 119 D5 43 20 S 170 55 E
Arrowtown, N.Z. 119 E3 44 57 S 168 50 E
Arroyo de la Luz, Spain 37 F4 39 30N 6 38W
Arroyo Grande, U.S.A. 145 K6 35 9N 120 32W
Års, Denmark 15 H3 56 48N 9 30 E
Ars, Iran 84 B5 37 9N 47 46 E
Ars-en-Ré, France 24 B2 46 12N 1 31W
Ars-sur-Moselle, France 23 C13 49 5N 6 4 E
Arsenault L., Canada 131 B7 55 6N 108 32W
Arsenev, Russia 60 B6 44 10N 133 15 E
Arsi □, Ethiopia 95 F4 7 45N 39 0 E
Arsiero, Italy 39 C8 45 49N 11 22 E
Arsikere, India 83 H3 13 15N 76 15 E
Arsin, Turkey 89 C8 41 8N 39 55 E
Arsk, Russia 51 C16 56 10N 49 50 E
Árta, Greece 44 E3 39 8N 21 2 E
Artá, Spain 33 B10 39 41N 3 21 E
Árta □, Greece 44 E3 39 15N 21 5 E
Arteaga, Mexico 146 D4 18 50N 102 20W
Arteche, Phil. 70 E5 12 17N 125 22 E
Arteijo, Spain 36 B2 43 19N 8 29W
Artem, Russia 60 C6 43 22N 132 13 E
Artem, Ostrov, Azerbaijan 53 F14 40 28N 50 20 E
Artemovsk, Russia 57 D10 54 45N 93 35 E
Artemovsk, Ukraine 52 B8 48 35N 38 0 E
Artemovskiy, Russia 53 C9 47 45N 40 16 E
Artemovskiy, Russia 54 C7 57 21N 61 54 E
Artenay, France 23 D8 48 5N 1 50 E
Artern, Germany 26 D7 51 22N 11 18 E
Artesa de Segre, Spain 34 D6 41 54N 1 3 E
Artesia = Mosomane, Botswana 104 C4 24 2 S 26 19 E
Artesia, U.S.A. 139 J2 32 55N 104 25W
Artesia Wells, U.S.A. 139 L5 28 17N 99 18W
Artesian, U.S.A. 138 C6 44 2N 97 54W
Arth, Switz. 29 B7 47 4N 8 31 E
Arthez-de-Béarn, France 24 E3 43 29N 0 38W
Arthington, Liberia 100 D2 6 35N 10 45W
Arthur, U.S.A. 141 E8 39 43N 88 28W
Arthur →, Australia 114 G3 41 2 S 144 40 E
Arthur Cr. →, Australia 114 C2 22 30 S 136 25 E
Arthur Pt., Australia 114 C5 22 7 S 150 3 E
Arthur's Pass, N.Z. 119 C6 42 54 S 171 35 E
Arthur's Town, Bahamas 149 B4 24 38N 75 42W
Artigas, Uruguay 158 C4 30 20 S 56 30W
Artik, Armenia 53 F10 40 38N 43 58 E
Artillery L., Canada 131 A7 63 9N 107 52W
Artois, France 23 B9 50 20N 2 30 E
Artotína, Greece 45 F4 38 42N 22 2 E
Artsiz, Ukraine 52 C3 46 4N 29 26 E
Artvin, Turkey 53 F9 41 14N 41 44 E
Artvin □, Turkey 89 C9 41 10N 41 50 E
Aru, Kepulauan, Indonesia 73 C4 6 0 S 134 30 E
Aru Is. = Aru, Kepulauan, Indonesia 73 C4 6 0 S 134 30 E
Aru Meru □, Tanzania 106 C4 3 20 S 36 50 E
Arua, Uganda 106 B3 3 1N 30 58 E
Aruanã, Brazil 155 D1 14 54 S 51 10W
Aruba, Neth. Ant. 149 D6 12 30N 70 0W
Arucas, Canary Is. 33 F4 28 7N 15 32W
Arudy, France 24 E3 43 7N 0 28W
Arumã, Brazil 153 D5 4 44 S 62 8W
Arumpo, Australia 116 B5 33 48 S 142 55 E
Arun →, Nepal 81 F12 26 55N 87 10 E
Arunachal Pradesh □, India 78 A5 28 0N 95 0 E
Aruppukottai, India 83 K4 9 31N 78 8 E
Arusha, Tanzania 106 C4 3 20 S 36 40 E
Arusha □, Tanzania 106 C4 4 0 S 36 30 E
Arusha Chini, Tanzania 106 C4 3 32 S 37 20 E
Arut →, Indonesia 75 C4 2 42 S 111 34 E
Aruvi →, Sri Lanka 83 K4 8 48N 79 53 E
Aruwimi →, Zaïre 106 B1 1 13N 23 36 E
Arvada, U.S.A. 142 D10 44 43N 106 6W
Arvakalu, Sri Lanka 83 K4 8 20N 79 58 E
Arve →, France 25 B10 46 11N 6 8 E
Árvi, Greece 32 E7 34 59N 25 28 E
Arvi, India 82 D4 20 59N 78 16 E
Arvida, Canada 129 C5 48 25N 71 14W
Arvidsjaur, Sweden 12 D15 65 35N 19 10 E
Arvika, Sweden 13 G12 59 40N 12 36 E
Arvin, U.S.A. 145 K8 35 12N 118 50W
Arxan, China 65 B6 47 11N 119 57 E
Aryirádhes, Greece 32 B3 39 27N 19 58 E
Aryiroúpolis, Greece 32 D6 35 17N 24 20 E
Arys, Kazakhstan 55 B4 42 26N 68 48 E
Arys →, Kazakhstan 55 B4 42 45N 68 15 E
Arzachena, Italy 40 A2 41 5N 9 27 E
Arzamas, Russia 51 D13 55 27N 43 55 E
Arzew, Algeria 99 A4 35 50N 0 23W
Arzgir, Russia 53 D11 45 18N 44 23 E
Arzignano, Italy 39 C8 45 30N 11 20 E
As, Belgium 21 F7 51 1N 5 35 E
Aš, Czech. 30 A5 50 13N 12 12 E
Aş Şadr, U.A.E. 85 E7 24 40N 54 41 E
Aş Şafā, Syria 91 B6 33 10N 37 0 E
'As Saffānīyah, Si. Arabia 86 D6 28 5N 48 50 E
As Safīrah, Syria 84 B3 36 5N 37 21 E
Aş Şahm, Oman 85 E8 24 10N 56 53 E
As Sājir, Si. Arabia 84 E5 25 11N 44 36 E
As Salamīyah, Si. Arabia 86 A4 24 12N 47 18 E
As Salamīyah, Syria 84 C3 35 1N 37 2 E
As Salt, Jordan 91 C4 32 2N 35 43 E
As Sal'w'a, Qatar 85 E6 24 23N 50 50 E
As Samāwah, Iraq 84 D5 31 15N 45 15 E
As Sanamayn, Syria 91 B5 33 3N 36 10 E
As Sawādah, Si. Arabia 86 B4 22 24N 44 28 E
As Sayl al Kabīr, Si. Arabia 86 B3 21 38N 40 25 E
As Sukhnah, Syria 84 C3 34 52N 38 52 E
As Sulaymānīyah, Iraq 84 C5 35 35N 45 29 E
As Sulaymānīyah, Si. Arabia 86 A4 24 9N 47 18 E
As Sulaymī, Si. Arabia 84 E4 26 17N 41 21 E
As Sulayyil, Si. Arabia 86 B4 20 27N 45 34 E
As Sulṭan, Libya 96 B3 31 4N 17 8 E
As Summān, Si. Arabia 84 E5 25 0N 47 0 E
As Sūq, Si. Arabia 86 B3 21 54N 42 3 E
Aş Şurrah, Yemen 86 D4 13 57N 46 14 E
As Suwaydā', Syria 91 C5 32 40N 36 30 E
As Suwaydā' □, Syria 91 C5 32 45N 36 45 E
As Suwayh, Oman 87 B7 22 10N 59 33 E
As Suwayq, Oman 87 B7 23 51N 57 26 E
Aş Şuwayrah, Iraq 84 C5 32 55N 45 0 E
Asab, Namibia 104 D2 25 30 S 18 0 E
Asaba, Nigeria 101 D6 6 12N 6 38 E
Asafo, Ghana 100 D4 6 20N 2 40W
Asahi, Japan 63 B12 35 43N 140 39 E
Asahi-Gawa →, Japan 62 C5 34 36N 133 58 E
Asahigawa, Japan 60 C11 43 46N 142 22 E
Asale, L., Ethiopia 95 E5 14 0N 40 20 E
Asama-Yama, Japan 63 A10 36 24N 138 31 E
Asamankese, Ghana 101 D4 5 50N 0 40W
Asansol, India 81 H12 23 40N 87 1 E
Åsarna, Sweden 14 B8 62 39N 14 22 E
Asbe Teferi, Ethiopia 95 F5 9 4N 40 49 E
Asbesberge, S. Africa 104 D3 29 0 S 23 0 E
Asbest, Russia 54 C7 57 0N 61 30 E
Asbestos, Canada 129 C5 45 47N 71 58W
Asbury Park, U.S.A. 137 F10 40 15N 74 1W
Ascensión, Mexico 146 A3 31 6N 107 59W
Ascensión, B. de la, Mexico 147 D7 19 50N 87 20W
Ascension I., Atl. Oc. 9 J7 8 0 S 14 15W
Aschach, Austria 30 C7 48 22N 14 2 E
Aschaffenburg, Germany 27 F5 49 58N 9 8 E
Aschendorf, Germany 26 B3 53 2N 7 22 E
Aschersleben, Germany 26 D7 51 45N 11 28 E
Asciano, Italy 39 E8 43 14N 11 32 E
Áscoli Piceno, Italy 39 F10 42 51N 13 34 E
Áscoli Satriano, Italy 41 A8 41 11N 15 32 E
Ascona, Switz. 29 D7 46 9N 8 46 E
Ascope, Peru 156 B2 7 46 S 79 8W
Ascotán, Chile 158 A2 21 45 S 68 17W
Ascuncion, Phil. 71 H5 7 35N 125 45 E
Aseb, Ethiopia 90 E3 13 0N 42 40 E
Asedjrad, Algeria 99 D5 24 51N 1 29 E
Asela, Ethiopia 95 F4 8 0N 39 0 E
Asenovgrad, Bulgaria 43 E9 42 1N 24 51 E
Asfeld, France 23 C11 49 27N 4 5 E
Asfûn el Matâ'na, Egypt 94 B3 25 26N 32 30 E
Åsgårdstrand, Norway 14 E4 59 22N 10 27 E
Asgata, Cyprus 32 E12 34 46N 33 15 E
Ash Fork, U.S.A. 143 J7 35 14N 112 32W
Ash Grove, U.S.A. 139 G8 37 21N 93 36W
Ash Shamāl □, Lebanon 91 A5 34 25N 36 0 E
Ash Shāmīyah, Iraq 84 D5 31 55N 44 35 E
Ash Sha'rā', Si. Arabia 86 A4 24 16N 44 11 E
Ash Shāriqah, U.A.E. 85 E7 25 23N 55 26 E
Ash Sharmah, Si. Arabia 84 D2 28 1N 35 16 E
Ash Sharqāt, Iraq 84 C4 35 27N 43 16 E
Ash Sharqi, Al Jabal, Lebanon 91 B5 33 40N 36 10 E
Ash Shaṭrah, Iraq 84 D5 31 30N 46 10 E
Ash Shawbak, Jordan 84 D2 30 32N 35 34 E
Ash Shawmari, J., Jordan 91 E5 30 35N 36 35 E
Ash Shaykh, J., Lebanon 91 B4 33 25N 35 50 E
Ash Shiḥr, Yemen 87 D5 14 45N 49 36 E
Ash Shināfīyah, Iraq 84 D5 31 35N 44 39 E
Ash Shu'aybah, Si. Arabia 84 E5 27 53N 44 43 E
Ash Shumlūl, Si. Arabia 84 E5 26 31N 47 20 E
Ash Shuqayq, Si. Arabia 86 C3 17 44N 42 1 E
Ash Shūr'a, Iraq 84 C4 35 58N 43 13 E
Ash Shurayf, Si. Arabia 84 E3 25 43N 39 14 E
Ash Shuwayfāt, Lebanon 91 B4 33 45N 35 30 E
Asha, Russia 54 D5 55 0N 57 16 E
Ashanti □, Ghana 101 D4 7 30N 1 30W
Ashau, Vietnam 76 D6 16 6N 107 22 E
Ashburn, U.S.A. 135 K4 31 42N 83 40W
Ashburton, N.Z. 119 D6 43 53 S 171 48 E
Ashburton →, Australia 112 D1 21 40 S 114 56 E
Ashburton, North Branch →, N.Z. 119 D6 43 54 S 171 44 E
Ashburton, South Branch →, N.Z. 119 D6 43 54 S 171 44 E
Ashburton Downs, Australia 112 D2 23 25 S 117 4 E
Ashby de la Zouch, U.K. 16 E6 52 45N 1 29W
Ashcroft, Canada 130 C4 50 40N 121 20W
Ashdod, Israel 91 D3 31 49N 34 35 E
Asheboro, U.S.A. 135 H6 35 43N 79 46W
Asherton, U.S.A. 139 L5 28 25N 99 43W
Asheville, U.S.A. 135 H4 35 39N 82 30W
Asheweig →, Canada 128 B2 54 17N 87 12W
Ashford, Australia 115 D5 29 15 S 151 3 E
Ashford, U.K. 17 F8 51 8N 0 53 E
Ashford, U.S.A. 142 C2 46 45N 122 2W
Ashibetsu, Japan 60 C11 43 31N 142 11 E
Ashikaga, Japan 63 A11 36 28N 139 29 E
Ashio, Japan 63 A11 36 38N 139 27 E
Ashizuri-Zaki, Japan 62 E5 32 44N 133 0 E
Ashkarkot, Afghan. 80 C2 33 3N 67 58 E
Ashkhabad, Turkmenistan 56 F6 38 0N 57 50 E
Ashland, Ill., U.S.A. 140 E6 39 53N 90 0W
Ashland, Kans., U.S.A. 139 G5 37 13N 99 43W
Ashland, Ky., U.S.A. 134 F4 38 25N 82 40W
Ashland, Maine, U.S.A. 129 C6 46 34N 68 26W
Ashland, Mont., U.S.A. 142 D10 45 41N 106 12W
Ashland, Nebr., U.S.A. 138 E6 41 5N 96 27W
Ashland, Ohio, U.S.A. 136 F2 40 52N 82 19W
Ashland, Oreg., U.S.A. 142 E2 42 10N 122 38W
Ashland, Pa., U.S.A. 137 F8 40 45N 76 22W
Ashland, Va., U.S.A. 134 G7 37 46N 77 30W
Ashland, Wis., U.S.A. 138 B9 46 40N 90 52W
Ashley, Ill., U.S.A. 140 F7 38 20N 89 11W
Ashley, Ind., U.S.A. 141 C11 41 32N 85 4W
Ashley, N. Dak., U.S.A. 138 B5 46 3N 99 23W
Ashley, Pa., U.S.A. 137 E9 41 12N 75 55W
Ashley →, N.Z. 119 D7 43 17 S 172 44 E
Ashmont, Canada 130 C6 54 7N 111 35W
Ashmore Reef, Australia 112 B3 12 14 S 123 5 E
Ashmûn, Egypt 94 H7 30 18N 30 55 E
Ashq'elon, Israel 91 D3 31 42N 34 35 E
Ashtabula, U.S.A. 136 E4 41 52N 80 50W
Ashti, India 82 E2 18 50N 75 15 E
Ashton, S. Africa 104 E3 33 50 S 20 5 E
Ashton, U.S.A. 142 D8 44 6N 111 30W
Ashton under Lyne, U.K. 16 D5 53 30N 2 8W
Ashuanipi, L., Canada 129 B6 52 45N 66 15W
Ashurst, N.Z. 118 G4 40 16 S 175 55 E
Asia 58 E11 45 0N 75 0 E
Asia, Kepulauan, Indonesia 73 A4 1 0N 131 13 E
Āsīā Bak, Iran 85 C6 35 19N 50 30 E
Asiago, Italy 39 C8 45 52N 11 30 E
Asidonhoppo, Surinam 153 C6 3 50N 55 30W
Asifabad, India 82 E4 19 20N 79 24 E
Asike, Indonesia 73 C6 6 39 S 140 24 E
Asilah, Morocco 98 A3 35 29N 6 0W
Asinara, Italy 40 A1 41 5N 8 15 E
Asinara, G. dell', Italy 40 B1 41 0N 8 30 E
Asino, Russia 56 D9 57 0N 86 0 E
'Asīr □, Si. Arabia 86 C3 18 40N 42 30 E
Asir, Ras, Somali Rep. 90 E5 11 55N 51 10 E
Aska, India 82 E7 19 2N 84 42 E
Aşkale, Turkey 89 D9 39 55N 40 41 E
Asker, Norway 14 E4 59 50N 10 26 E
Askersund, Sweden 15 F8 58 53N 14 55 E
Askham, S. Africa 104 D3 26 59 S 20 47 E
Askim, Norway 14 E5 59 35N 11 10 E
Askino, Russia 54 C5 56 5N 56 34 E
Askja, Iceland 12 D5 65 3N 16 48W
Asl, Egypt 94 J8 29 33N 32 44 E
Asmār, Afghan. 79 B3 35 10N 71 27 E
Asmara = Asmera, Ethiopia 95 D4 15 19N 38 55 E
Asmera, Ethiopia 95 D4 15 19N 38 55 E
Asnæs, Denmark 15 J5 55 40N 11 0 E
Asni, Morocco 98 B3 31 17N 7 58W
Aso, Japan 62 E3 32 55N 131 5 E
Aso-Zan, Japan 62 E3 32 53N 131 6 E
Ásola, Italy 38 C7 45 12N 10 25 E
Asoteriba, Jebel, Sudan 94 C4 21 51N 36 30 E
Asotin, U.S.A. 142 C5 46 20N 117 3W
Aspe, Spain 35 G4 38 20N 0 40W
Aspen, U.S.A. 143 G10 39 12N 106 56W
Aspendos, Turkey 88 E4 36 54N 31 7 E
Aspermont, U.S.A. 139 J4 33 11N 100 15W
Aspiring, Mt., N.Z. 119 E3 44 23 S 168 46 E
Aspres-sur-Buëch, France 25 D9 44 32N 5 44 E
Asprókavos, Ákra, Greece 32 B4 39 21N 20 6 E
Aspromonte, Italy 41 D8 38 10N 15 55 E
Aspur, India 80 H6 23 58N 74 7 E
Asquith, Canada 131 C7 52 8N 107 13W
Assa, Morocco 98 C3 28 35N 9 6W
Assâba, Mauritania 100 B2 16 10N 11 45W
Assam □, India 78 B4 26 0N 93 0 E
Assamakka, Niger 101 B6 19 21N 5 38 E
Asse, Belgium 21 H4 50 24N 4 10 E
Assebroek, Belgium 21 F2 51 11N 3 17 E
Assekrem, Algeria 99 D6 23 16N 5 49 E
Assémini, Italy 40 C2 39 18N 9 0 E
Assen, Neths. 20 C9 53 0N 6 35 E
Assendelft, Neths. 20 D5 52 29N 4 45 E
Assenede, Belgium 21 F3 51 14N 3 46 E
Assens, Århus, Denmark 15 H4 56 41N 10 3 E
Assens, Fyn, Denmark 15 J3 55 16N 9 55 E
Assesse, Belgium 21 H6 50 22N 5 2 E
Assini, Ivory C. 100 D4 5 9N 3 17W
Assiniboia, Canada 131 D7 49 40N 105 59W
Assiniboine →, Canada 131 D9 49 53N 97 8W
Assis, Brazil 159 A5 22 40 S 50 20W
Assisi, Italy 39 E9 43 4N 12 36 E
Ássos, Greece 45 F2 38 22N 20 33 E
Assumption, U.S.A. 140 E7 39 31N 89 3W
Assus, Turkey 44 E8 39 32N 26 22 E
Assynt, L., U.K. 18 C3 58 25N 5 15W
Astaffort, France 24 D4 44 4N 0 40 E
Astakidha, Greece 45 J8 35 53N 26 50 E
Astara, Azerbaijan 89 D13 38 30N 48 50 E
Asten, Neths. 21 F7 51 24N 5 45 E
Asteroúsia, Greece 32 E7 34 59N 25 3 E
Asti, Italy 38 D5 44 54N 8 11 E
Astipálaia, Greece 45 H8 36 32N 26 22 E
Astorga, Mindanao, Phil. 71 H5 6 54N 125 27 E
Astorga, Panay, Phil. 71 F4 11 15N 122 48 E
Astorga, Spain 36 C4 42 29N 6 8W
Astoria, Ill., U.S.A. 140 D6 40 14N 90 21W
Astoria, Oreg., U.S.A. 144 D3 46 16N 123 50W
Åstorp, Sweden 15 H6 56 6N 12 55 E
Astrakhan, Russia 53 C13 46 25N 48 5 E
Astrakhan-Bazàr, Azerbaijan 49 G8 39 14N 48 30 E
Astudillo, Spain 36 C6 42 12N 4 22W
Asturias, Spain 36 B5 43 15N 6 0W
Asunción, Paraguay 158 B4 25 10 S 57 30W
Asunción Nochixtlán, Mexico 147 D5 17 28N 97 14W
Asutri, Sudan 95 D4 15 25N 35 45 E
Aswa →, Uganda 106 B3 3 43N 31 55 E
Aswad, Ras al, Si. Arabia 86 B2 21 20N 39 0 E
Aswân, Egypt 94 C3 24 4N 32 57 E
Aswân High Dam = Sadd el Aali, Egypt 94 C3 23 54N 32 54 E
Asyût, Egypt 94 B3 27 11N 31 4 E
Asyûti, Wadi →, Egypt 94 B3 27 11N 31 16 E
Aszód, Hungary 31 D12 47 39N 19 28 E
At Ṭafīlah, Jordan 91 E4 30 45N 35 30 E
At Tā'if, Si. Arabia 86 B3 21 5N 40 27 E
At Tāj, Libya 96 D4 24 13N 23 18 E
At Tamīmī, Libya 96 B4 32 20N 23 4 E
Aţ Ţirāq, Si. Arabia 84 E5 27 19N 44 33 E
At Turbah, Yemen 86 D4 13 13N 44 7 E
At Turbah, Yemen 86 D3 12 40N 43 30 E
Aţ Ţuwayrifah, Si. Arabia 87 B5 21 30N 49 35 E
Atacama □, Chile 158 B2 27 30 S 70 0W
Atacama, Desierto de, Chile 158 A2 24 0 S 69 20W
Atacama, Salar de, Chile 158 A2 23 30 S 68 20W
Atacoo, Colombia 152 C2 3 35N 75 23W
Atakor, Algeria 99 D6 23 27N 5 31 E
Atakpamé, Togo 101 D5 7 31N 1 13 E
Atalándi, Greece 45 F4 38 39N 22 58 E
Atalaya, Peru 156 C3 10 45 S 73 50W
Atalaya de Femes, Canary Is. 33 F6 28 56N 13 47W
Ataléia, Brazil 155 E3 18 3 S 41 6W
Atambua, Indonesia 72 C2 9 7 S 124 54 E
Atami, Japan 63 B11 35 5N 139 4 E
Atankawng, Burma 78 C6 25 50N 97 47 E
Atapupu, Indonesia 72 C2 9 0 S 124 51 E
Atâr, Mauritania 98 D2 20 30N 13 5W
Atara, Russia 57 C13 63 10N 129 10 E
Ataram, Erg n-, Algeria 99 D5 23 57N 2 0 E
Atarfe, Spain 37 H7 37 13N 3 40W
Atascadero, U.S.A. 143 J3 35 32N 120 44W

Azuero, Pen. de 169


Atascadero, Calif., U.S.A. 144 K6 35 29N 120 40W
Atasu, Kazakhstan 56 E8 48 30N 71 0 E
Atauro, Indonesia 72 C3 8 10 S 125 30 E
Atbara, Sudan 94 D3 17 42N 33 59 E
'Atbara →, Sudan 94 D3 17 40N 33 56 E
Atbasar, Kazakhstan 56 D7 51 48N 68 20 E
Atbashi, Kirghizia 55 C7 41 10N 75 48 E
Atbashi, Khrebet, Kirghizia 55 C7 40 50N 75 30 E
Atchafalaya B., U.S.A. 139 L9 29 30N 91 20W
Atchison, U.S.A. 138 F7 39 40N 95 10W
Atebubu, Ghana 101 D4 7 47N 1 0W
Ateca, Spain 34 D3 41 20N 1 49W
Aterno →, Italy 39 F10 42 11N 13 51 E
Atesine, Alpi, Italy 38 B8 46 55N 11 30 E
Atessa, Italy 39 F11 42 5N 14 27 E
Ath, Belgium 21 G3 50 38N 3 47 E
Athabasca, Canada 130 C6 54 45N 113 20W
Athabasca →, Canada 131 B6 58 40N 110 50W
Athabasca, L., Canada 131 B7 59 15N 109 15W
Athboy, Ireland 19 C5 53 37N 6 55W
Athenry, Ireland 19 C3 53 18N 8 45W
Athens = Athínai, Greece 45 G5 37 58N 23 46 E
Athens, Ala., U.S.A. 135 H2 34 49N 86 58W
Athens, Ga., U.S.A. 135 J4 33 56N 83 24W
Athens, N.Y., U.S.A. 137 D11 42 15N 73 48W
Athens, Ohio, U.S.A. 134 F4 39 25N 82 6W
Athens, Pa., U.S.A. 137 E8 41 57N 76 36W
Athens, Tenn., U.S.A. 135 H3 35 45N 84 38W
Athens, Tex., U.S.A. 139 J7 32 11N 95 48W
Atherley, Canada 136 B5 44 37N 79 20W
Atherton, Australia 114 B4 17 17 S 145 30 E
Athiéme, Benin 101 D5 6 37N 1 40 E
Athienou, Cyprus 32 D12 35 3N 33 32 E
Athínai, Greece 45 G5 37 58N 23 46 E
Athlone, Ireland 19 C4 53 26N 7 57W
Athna, Cyprus 32 D12 35 3N 33 47 E
Athni, India 82 F2 16 44N 75 6 E
Athol, N.Z. 119 F3 45 30 S 168 35 E
Atholl, Forest of, U.K. 18 E5 56 51N 3 50W
Atholville, Canada 129 C6 47 59N 66 43W
Áthos, Greece 44 D6 40 9N 24 22 E
Athus, Belgium 21 J7 49 34N 5 50 E
Athy, Ireland 19 D5 53 0N 7 0W
Ati, Chad 97 F3 13 13N 18 20 E
Ati, Sudan 95 E2 13 5N 29 2 E
Atiak, Uganda 106 B3 3 12N 32 2 E
Atiamuri, N.Z. 118 E5 38 24 S 176 5 E
Atico, Peru 156 D3 16 14 S 73 40W
Atienza, Spain 34 D2 41 12N 2 52W
Atikokan, Canada 128 C1 48 45N 91 37W
Atikonak L., Canada 129 B7 52 40N 64 32W
Atimonan, Phil. 70 D3 14 0N 121 55 E
'Ātinah, W. →, Oman 87 C6 18 23N 53 28 E
Atirampattinam, India 83 J4 10 28N 79 20 E
Atka, Russia 57 C16 60 50N 151 48 E
Atkarsk, Russia 51 F14 51 55N 45 2 E
Atkinson, Ill., U.S.A. 140 C6 41 25N 90 1W
Atkinson, Nebr., U.S.A. 138 D5 42 35N 98 59W
Atlanta, Ga., U.S.A. 135 J3 33 50N 84 24W
Atlanta, Ill., U.S.A. 140 D7 40 16N 89 14W
Atlanta, Mo., U.S.A. 140 E4 39 54N 92 29W
Atlanta, Tex., U.S.A. 139 J7 33 7N 94 8W
Atlantic, U.S.A. 138 E7 41 25N 95 0W
Atlantic City, U.S.A. 134 F8 39 25N 74 25W
Atlantic Ocean 8 H7 0 0 20 0W
Atlántico □, Colombia 152 A2 10 45N 75 0W
Atlas Mts. = Haut Atlas, Morocco 98 B3 32 30N 5 0W
Atlin, Canada 130 B2 59 31N 133 41W
Atlin, L., Canada 130 B2 59 26N 133 45W
Atmakur, India 83 G4 14 37N 79 40 E
Atmore, U.S.A. 135 K2 31 2N 87 30W
Atō, Japan 62 C3 34 25N 131 40 E
Atok, Phil. 70 C3 16 35N 120 41 E
Atoka, U.S.A. 139 H6 34 22N 96 10W
Átokos, Greece 45 F2 38 28N 20 49 E
Atolia, U.S.A. 145 K9 35 19N 117 37W
Atouguia, Portugal 37 F1 39 20N 9 20W
Atoyac →, Mexico 147 D5 16 30N 97 31W
Atrak →, Iran 85 B8 37 50N 57 0 E
Åtran, Sweden 15 G6 57 7N 12 57 E
Atrato →, Colombia 152 B2 8 17N 76 58W
Atrauli, India 80 E8 28 2N 78 20 E
Atri, Italy 39 F10 42 35N 14 0 E
Atsbi, Ethiopia 95 E4 13 52N 39 50 E
Atsoum, Mts., Cameroon 101 D7 6 41N 12 57 E
Atsugi, Japan 63 B11 35 25N 139 21 E
Atsumi, Japan 63 C9 34 35N 137 4 E
Atsumi-Wan, Japan 63 C9 34 44N 137 13 E
Atsuta, Japan 60 C10 43 24N 141 26 E
Attalla, U.S.A. 135 H2 34 2N 86 5W
Attáviros, Greece 32 C9 36 12N 27 50 E
Attawapiskat, Canada 128 B3 52 56N 82 24W
Attawapiskat →, Canada 128 B3 52 57N 82 18W
Attawapiskat, L., Canada 128 B2 52 18N 87 54W
Attendorn, Germany 26 D3 51 8N 7 54 E
Attersee, Austria 30 D6 47 55N 13 32 E
Attert, Belgium 21 J7 49 45N 5 47 E
Attica, U.S.A. 141 D9 40 20N 87 15W
Attichy, France 23 C10 49 25N 3 3 E
Attigny, France 23 C11 49 28N 4 35 E
Attikamagen L., Canada 129 A6 55 0N 66 30W
Attikí □, Greece 45 F5 38 10N 23 40 E
Attleboro, U.S.A. 137 E13 41 56N 71 18W
Attock, Pakistan 80 C5 33 52N 72 20 E
Attopeu, Laos 76 E6 14 48N 106 50 E
Attunga, Australia 117 A9 30 55 S 150 50 E
Attur, India 83 J4 11 35N 78 30 E
'Atūd, Yemen 87 D5 14 53N 48 10 E
Atuel →, Argentina 158 D2 36 17 S 66 50W
Atvacik, Turkey 88 D2 39 36N 26 24 E
Åtvidaberg, Sweden 15 F10 58 12N 16 0 E
Atwater, U.S.A. 144 H6 37 21N 120 37W
Atwood, Canada 136 C3 43 40N 81 1W
Atwood, U.S.A. 138 F4 39 52N 101 3W
Au Sable →, U.S.A. 134 C4 44 25N 83 20W
Au Sable Pt., U.S.A. 128 C2 46 40N 86 10W
Aubagne, France 25 E9 43 17N 5 37 E
Aubange, Belgium 21 J7 49 34N 5 48 E
Aubarca, C., Spain 33 B7 39 4N 1 22 E
Aube □, France 23 D11 48 15N 4 10 E
Aube →, France 23 D10 48 34N 3 43 E
Aubel, Belgium 21 G7 50 42N 5 51 E
Aubenas, France 25 D8 44 37N 4 24 E
Aubenton, France 23 C11 49 50N 4 12 E
Auberry, U.S.A. 144 H7 37 7N 119 29W
Aubigny-sur-Nère, France 23 E9 47 30N 2 24 E
Aubin, France 24 D6 44 33N 2 15 E
Aubrac, Mts. d', France 24 D7 44 40N 3 2 E
Auburn, Ala., U.S.A. 135 J3 32 37N 85 30W
Auburn, Calif., U.S.A. 144 G5 38 53N 121 4W
Auburn, Ill., U.S.A. 140 E7 39 36N 89 45W
Auburn, Ind., U.S.A. 141 C11 41 20N 85 5W
Auburn, N.Y., U.S.A. 137 D8 42 57N 76 39W
Auburn, Nebr., U.S.A. 138 E7 40 25N 95 50W
Auburn, Wash., U.S.A. 144 C4 47 18N 122 13W
Auburn Ra., Australia 115 D5 25 15 S 150 30 E
Auburndale, U.S.A. 135 L5 28 5N 81 45W
Aubusson, France 24 C6 45 57N 2 11 E
Auch, France 24 E4 43 39N 0 36 E
Auchel, France 23 B9 50 30N 2 29 E
Auchi, Nigeria 101 D6 7 6N 6 13 E
Auckland, N.Z. 118 C3 36 52 S 174 46 E
Auckland □, N.Z. 118 E6 36 50 S 175 0 E
Auckland Is., Pac. Oc. 122 N8 50 40 S 166 5 E
Aude □, France 24 E6 43 8N 2 28 E
Aude →, France 24 E7 43 13N 3 14 E
Audegle, Somali Rep. 108 D2 1 59N 44 50 E
Auden, Canada 128 B2 50 14N 87 53W
Auderghem, Belgium 21 G4 50 49N 4 26 E
Auderville, France 22 C5 49 43N 1 57W
Audierne, France 22 D2 48 1N 4 34W
Audincourt, France 23 E13 47 30N 6 50 E
Audo, Ethiopia 95 F5 6 20N 41 50 E
Audubon, U.S.A. 140 C2 41 43N 94 56W
Aue, Germany 26 E8 50 34N 12 43 E
Auerbach, Germany 26 E8 50 30N 12 25 E
Aueti Paraná →, Brazil 152 D4 1 51 S 65 37W
Aufist, W. Sahara 98 C2 25 44N 14 39W
Augathella, Australia 115 D4 25 48 S 146 35 E
Augrabies Falls, S. Africa 104 D3 28 35 S 20 20 E
Augsburg, Germany 27 G6 48 22N 10 54 E
Augusta, Italy 41 E8 37 14N 15 12 E
Augusta, Ark., U.S.A. 139 H9 35 17N 91 25W
Augusta, Ga., U.S.A. 135 J5 33 29N 81 59W
Augusta, Ill., U.S.A. 140 D6 40 14N 90 57W
Augusta, Kans., U.S.A. 139 G6 37 40N 97 0W
Augusta, Ky., U.S.A. 141 F12 38 47N 84 0W
Augusta, Maine, U.S.A. 129 D6 44 20N 69 46W
Augusta, Mont., U.S.A. 142 C7 47 30N 112 29W
Augusta, Wis., U.S.A. 138 C9 44 41N 91 8W
Augustenborg, Denmark 15 K3 54 57N 9 53 E
Augustów, Poland 47 B9 53 51N 23 0 E
Augustus, Mt., Australia 112 D2 24 20 S 116 50 E
Augustus Downs, Australia 114 B2 18 35 S 139 55 E
Augustus I., Australia 112 C3 15 20 S 124 30 E
Aukan, Ethiopia 95 D5 15 29N 40 50 E
Auki, Solomon Is. 121 M11 8 45 S 160 42 E
Aukum, U.S.A. 144 G6 38 34N 120 43W
Auld, L., Australia 112 D3 22 25 S 123 50 E
Aulla, Italy 38 D6 44 12N 10 0 E
Aulnay, France 24 B3 46 2N 0 22W
Aulne →, France 22 D2 48 17N 4 16W
Aulnoye-Aymeries, France 23 B10 50 12N 3 50 E
Ault, France 22 B8 50 8N 1 26 E
Ault, U.S.A. 138 E2 40 40N 104 42W
Aulus-les-Bains, France 24 F5 42 49N 1 19 E
Aumale, France 23 C8 49 46N 1 46 E
Aumont-Aubrac, France 24 D7 44 43N 3 17 E
Auna, Nigeria 101 C5 10 9N 4 42 E
Aundh, India 82 F2 17 33N 74 23 E
Aunis, France 24 B3 46 5N 0 50W
Auponhia, Indonesia 72 B3 1 58 S 125 27 E
Aups, France 25 E10 43 37N 6 15 E
Aur, P., Malaysia 77 L5 2 35N 104 10 E
Aura, Burma 78 B6 26 59N 97 57 E
Auraiya, India 81 F8 26 28N 79 33 E
Aurangabad, Bihar, India 81 G11 24 45N 84 18 E
Aurangabad, Maharashtra, India 82 E2 19 50N 75 23 E
Auray, France 22 E4 47 40N 2 59W
Aurès, Algeria 99 A6 35 8N 6 30 E
Aurich, Germany 26 B3 53 28N 7 30 E
Aurilândia, Brazil 155 E1 16 44 S 50 28W
Aurillac, France 24 D6 44 55N 2 26 E
Auronza, Italy 39 B9 46 33N 12 27 E
Aurora = Maewo, Vanuatu 121 E6 15 10 S 168 10 E
Aurora, Canada 136 C5 44 0N 79 28W
Aurora, Isabela, Phil. 70 C3 16 59N 121 38 E
Aurora, Quezon, Phil. 70 E4 13 21N 122 31 E
Aurora, S. Africa 104 E2 32 40 S 18 29 E
Aurora, Colo., U.S.A. 138 F2 39 44N 104 55W
Aurora, Ill., U.S.A. 141 C8 41 42N 88 12W
Aurora, Mo., U.S.A. 139 G8 36 58N 93 42W
Aurora, Nebr., U.S.A. 138 E6 40 55N 98 0W
Aurora, Ohio, U.S.A. 136 E3 41 21N 81 20W
Aursmoen, Norway 14 E5 59 55N 11 26 E
Aurukun Mission, Australia 114 A3 13 20 S 141 45 E
Aus, Namibia 104 D2 26 35 S 16 12 E
Auschwitz = Oświecim, Poland 31 A12 50 2N 19 11 E
Aust-Agder fylke □, Norway 13 G9 58 55N 7 40 E
Austerlitz = Slavkov, Czech. 31 B9 49 10N 16 52 E
Austin, Ind., U.S.A. 141 F11 38 45N 85 49W
Austin, Minn., U.S.A. 138 D8 43 37N 92 59W
Austin, Nev., U.S.A. 142 G5 39 30N 117 1W
Austin, Pa., U.S.A. 136 E6 41 40N 78 7W
Austin, Tex., U.S.A. 139 K6 30 20N 97 45W
Austin, L., Australia 113 E2 27 40 S 118 0 E
Austral Downs, Australia 114 C2 20 30 S 137 45 E
Austral Is. = Tubuai Is., Pac. Oc. 123 K12 25 0 S 150 0W
Austral Seamount Chain, Pac. Oc. 123 K13 24 0 S 150 0W
Australia ■, Oceania 122 K5 23 0 S 135 0 E
Australian Alps, Australia 117 D8 36 30 S 148 30 E
Australian Capital Territory □, Australia 115 F4 35 30 S 149 0 E
Austria ■, Europe 30 E7 47 0N 14 0 E
Austvågøy, Norway 12 B13 68 20N 14 40 E
Autazes, Brazil 153 D6 3 35 S 59 8W
Autelbas, Belgium 21 J7 49 39N 5 52 E
Auterive, France 24 E5 43 21N 1 29 E
Authie →, France 23 B8 50 22N 1 38 E
Authon-du-Perche, France 22 D7 48 12N 0 54 E
Autlán, Mexico 146 D4 19 40N 104 30W
Autun, France 23 F11 46 58N 4 17 E
Auvelais, Belgium 21 H5 50 27N 4 38 E
Auvergne, Australia 112 C5 15 39 S 130 1 E
Auvergne, France 24 C7 45 20N 3 15 E
Auvergne, Mts. d', France 24 C6 45 20N 2 55 E
Auvézère →, France 24 C4 45 12N 0 50 E
Auxerre, France 23 E10 47 48N 3 32 E
Auxi-le-Château, France 23 B9 50 15N 2 8 E
Auxonne, France 23 E12 47 10N 5 20 E
Auxvasse, U.S.A. 140 E5 39 1N 91 54W
Auzances, France 24 B6 46 2N 2 30 E
Auzat-sur-Allier, France 24 C7 45 27N 3 19 E
Ava, U.S.A. 140 G7 37 53N 89 30W
Avallon, France 23 E10 47 30N 3 53 E
Avalon, U.S.A. 145 M8 33 21N 118 20W
Avalon Pen., Canada 129 C9 47 30N 53 20W
Avanigadda, India 83 G5 16 0N 80 56 E
Avaré, Brazil 159 A6 23 4 S 48 58W
Ávas, Greece 44 D7 40 57N 25 56 E
Avawatz Mts., U.S.A. 145 K10 35 30N 116 20W
Aveiro, Brazil 153 D6 3 10 S 55 5W
Aveiro, Portugal 36 E2 40 37N 8 38W
Aveiro □, Portugal 36 E2 40 40N 8 35W
Āvej, Iran 85 C6 35 40N 49 15 E
Avelgem, Belgium 21 G2 50 47N 3 27 E
Avellaneda, Argentina 158 C4 34 50 S 58 10W
Avellino, Italy 41 B7 40 54N 14 46 E
Avenal, U.S.A. 144 K6 36 0N 120 8W
Avenches, Switz. 28 C4 46 53N 7 2 E
Averøya, Norway 14 A1 63 5N 7 35 E
Aversa, Italy 41 B7 40 58N 14 11 E
Avery, U.S.A. 142 C6 47 22N 115 56W
Aves, I. de, W. Indies 149 C7 15 45N 63 55W
Aves, Is. de, Venezuela 149 D6 12 0N 67 30W
Avesnes-sur-Helpe, France 23 B10 50 8N 3 55 E
Avesta, Sweden 13 F14 60 9N 16 10 E
Aveyron □, France 24 D6 44 22N 2 45 E
Aveyron →, France 24 D5 44 5N 1 16 E
Avezzano, Italy 39 F10 42 2N 13 24 E
Avgó, Greece 45 J7 35 33N 25 37 E
Aviá Terai, Argentina 158 B3 26 45 S 60 50W
Aviano, Italy 39 B9 46 3N 12 35 E
Avigliana, Italy 38 C4 45 7N 7 13 E
Avigliano, Italy 41 B8 40 44N 15 41 E
Avignon, France 25 E8 43 57N 4 50 E
Ávila, Spain 36 E6 40 39N 4 43W
Ávila □, Spain 36 E6 40 30N 5 0W
Ávila, Sierra de, Spain 36 E5 40 40N 5 15W
Avila Beach, U.S.A. 145 K6 35 11N 120 44W
Avilés, Spain 36 B5 43 35N 5 57W
Avionárion, Greece 45 F6 38 31N 24 8 E
Avisio →, Italy 39 B8 46 7N 11 5 E
Aviston, U.S.A. 140 F7 38 36N 89 36W
Aviz, Portugal 37 F3 39 4N 7 53W
Avize, France 23 D11 48 59N 4 1 E
Avoca, Ireland 19 D5 52 52N 6 13W
Avoca, U.S.A. 136 D7 42 24N 77 25W
Avoca →, Australia 116 C5 35 40 S 143 43 E
Avola, Canada 130 C5 51 45N 119 19W
Avola, Italy 41 F8 36 56N 15 7 E
Avon, Ill., U.S.A. 140 D6 40 40N 90 26W
Avon, N.Y., U.S.A. 136 D7 42 55N 77 42W
Avon, S. Dak., U.S.A. 138 D5 43 0N 98 3W
Avon □, U.K. 17 F5 51 30N 2 40W
Avon →, Australia 113 F2 31 40 S 116 7 E
Avon →, Avon, U.K. 17 F5 51 30N 2 43W
Avon →, Hants., U.K. 17 G6 50 44N 1 45W
Avon →, Warks., U.K. 17 F5 51 57N 2 9W
Avondale, Zimbabwe 107 F3 17 43 S 30 58 E
Avonlea, Canada 131 D7 50 0N 105 0W
Avonmore, Canada 137 A10 45 10N 74 58W
Avonmouth, U.K. 17 F5 51 30N 2 42W
Avramov, Bulgaria 43 E11 42 45N 26 38 E
Avranches, France 22 D5 48 40N 1 20W
Avre →, France 22 D8 48 47N 1 22 E
Avrig, Romania 46 D5 45 43N 24 21 E
Avtovac, Bos.-H., Yug. 42 D3 43 9N 18 35 E
Avu Avu, Solomon Is. 121 M11 9 50 S 160 22 E
Awag el Baqar, Sudan 95 E3 10 10N 33 10 E
A'waj →, Syria 91 B5 33 23N 36 20 E
Awaji, Japan 63 C7 34 32N 135 1 E
Awaji-Shima, Japan 62 C6 34 30N 134 50 E
'Awālī, Bahrain 85 E6 26 0N 50 30 E
Awantipur, India 81 C6 33 55N 75 3 E
Awanui, N.Z. 118 B2 35 4 S 173 17 E
Awarja →, India 82 F3 17 5N 76 15 E
Awarua B., N.Z. 119 E3 44 28 S 168 4 E
Awarua Pt., N.Z. 119 E3 44 15 S 168 5 E
Awasa, L., Ethiopia 95 F4 7 0N 38 30 E
Awash, Ethiopia 90 F3 9 1N 40 10 E
Awash →, Ethiopia 95 E5 11 45N 41 5 E
Awaso, Ghana 100 D4 6 15N 2 22W
Awatere →, N.Z. 119 B9 41 37 S 174 10 E
Awbārī, Libya 96 C2 26 46N 12 57 E
Awbārī □, Libya 96 C2 26 35N 12 46 E
Awe, L., U.K. 18 E3 56 15N 5 15W
Aweil, Sudan 95 F2 8 42N 27 20 E
Awgu, Nigeria 101 D6 6 4N 7 24 E
Awjilah, Libya 96 C4 29 8N 21 7 E
Aworro, Papua N. G. 120 D2 7 43 S 143 11 E
Ax-les-Thermes, France 24 F5 42 44N 1 50 E
Axarfjörður, Iceland 12 C5 66 15N 16 45W
Axel, Neths. 21 F3 51 16N 3 55 E
Axel Heiberg I., Canada 6 B3 80 0N 90 0W
Axim, Ghana 100 E4 4 51N 2 15W
Axinim, Brazil 153 D6 4 2 S 59 22W
Axintele, Romania 46 E7 44 37N 26 47 E
Axioma, Brazil 157 B5 6 45 S 64 31W
Axiós →, Greece 44 D4 40 57N 22 35 E
Axminster, U.K. 17 G4 50 47N 3 1W
Axvall, Sweden 15 F7 58 23N 13 34 E
Ay, France 23 C11 49 3N 4 1 E
Ay →, Russia 54 C5 56 8N 57 40 E
Ayaantang, Eq. Guin. 102 B2 1 58N 10 24 E
Ayabaca, Peru 156 A2 4 40 S 79 53W
Ayabe, Japan 63 B7 35 20N 135 20 E
Ayacucho, Argentina 158 D4 37 5 S 58 20W
Ayacucho, Peru 156 C3 13 0 S 74 0W
Ayaguz, Kazakhstan 56 E9 48 10N 80 10 E
Ayakkuduk, Uzbekistan 55 C2 41 12N 65 12 E
Ayakudi, India 83 J3 10 28N 77 56 E
Ayala, Phil. 71 H3 6 57N 121 57 E
Ayamonte, Spain 37 H3 37 12N 7 24W
Ayan, Russia 57 D14 56 30N 138 16 E
Ayancık, Turkey 52 F6 41 57N 34 35 E
Ayapel, Colombia 152 B2 8 19N 75 9W
Ayas, Turkey 52 F5 40 2N 32 21 E
Ayaviri, Peru 156 C3 14 50 S 70 35W
Āybak, Afghan. 79 A3 36 15N 68 5 E
Aybastı, Turkey 88 C7 40 41N 37 23 E
Aydim, W. →, Oman 87 C6 18 8N 53 8 E
Aydın, Turkey 88 E2 37 51N 27 51 E
Aydin □, Turkey 88 E2 37 50N 28 0 E
Aye, Belgium 21 H6 50 14N 5 18 E
Ayenngré, Togo 101 D5 8 40N 1 1 E
Ayer's Cliff, Canada 137 A12 45 10N 72 3W
Ayers Rock, Australia 113 E5 25 23 S 131 5 E
Ayiá, Greece 44 E4 39 43N 22 45 E
Ayía Aikateríni, Ákra, Greece 32 A3 39 50N 19 50 E
Ayía Ánna, Greece 45 F5 38 52N 23 24 E
Ayia Dhéka, Greece 32 D6 35 3N 24 58 E
Ayia Gálini, Greece 32 D6 35 6N 24 41 E
Ayía Marína, Kásos, Greece 45 J8 35 27N 26 53 E
Ayía Marína, Leros, Greece 45 G8 37 11N 26 48 E
Ayia Napa, Cyprus 32 E13 34 59N 34 0 E
Ayía Paraskeví, Greece 44 E8 39 14N 26 16 E
Áyia Phyla, Cyprus 32 E12 34 43N 33 1 E
Ayía Rouméli, Greece 45 J5 35 14N 23 58 E
Ayia Varvára, Greece 32 D7 35 8N 25 1 E
Ayiássos, Greece 45 E8 39 5N 26 23 E
Áyion Óros, Greece 44 D6 40 25N 24 6 E
Áyios Amvrósios, Cyprus 32 D12 35 20N 33 35 E
Áyios Andréas, Greece 45 G4 37 21N 22 45 E
Áyios Evstrátios, Greece 44 E6 39 34N 24 58 E
Áyios Ioánnis, Ákra, Greece 32 D7 35 20N 25 40 E
Áyios Isidhoros, Greece 32 C9 36 9N 27 51 E
Áyios Kiríkos, Greece 45 G8 37 34N 26 17 E
Áyios Matthaíos, Greece 32 B3 39 30N 19 47 E
Áyios Míroni, Greece 45 J7 35 15N 25 1 E
Áyios Nikólaos, Greece 32 D7 35 11N 25 41 E
Áyios Pétros, Greece 45 F2 38 38N 20 33 E
Áyios Seryíos, Cyprus 32 D12 35 12N 33 53 E
Ayios Theodhoros, Cyprus 32 D13 35 22N 34 1 E
Áyios Yeóryios, Greece 45 G5 37 28N 23 57 E
Aykathonisi, Greece 45 G8 37 28N 27 0 E
Ayke, Ozero, Kazakhstan 54 F7 50 57N 61 36 E
Aykin, Russia 48 B8 62 15N 49 56 E
Aylesbury, U.K. 17 F7 51 48N 0 49W
Aylmer, Canada 136 D4 42 46N 80 59W
Aylmer, L., Canada 126 B8 64 0N 110 8W
'Ayn al Ghazālah, Libya 96 B4 32 10N 23 20 E
'Ayn Zaqqūt, Libya 96 C3 29 0N 19 30 E
Ayna, Spain 35 G2 38 34N 2 3W
Aynāt, Yemen 87 C5 16 4N 49 9 E
Ayni, Tajikistan 55 D4 39 23N 68 32 E
Ayolas, Paraguay 158 B4 27 10 S 56 59W
Ayom, Sudan 95 F2 7 49N 28 23 E
Ayon, Ostrov, Russia 57 C17 69 50N 169 0 E
Ayora, Spain 35 F3 39 3N 1 3W
Ayr, Australia 114 B4 19 35 S 147 25 E
Ayr, U.K. 18 F4 55 28N 4 37W
Ayr →, U.K. 18 F4 55 29N 4 40W
Ayrancı, Turkey 88 E5 37 21N 33 41 E
Ayre, Pt. of, U.K. 16 C3 54 27N 4 21W
Aysha, Ethiopia 95 E5 10 50N 42 23 E
Aytos, Bulgaria 43 E12 42 42N 27 16 E
Aytoska Planina, Bulgaria 43 E12 42 45N 27 30 E
Ayu, Kepulauan, Indonesia 73 A4 0 35N 131 5 E
Ayutla, Guatemala 148 D1 14 40N 92 10W
Ayutla, Mexico 147 D5 16 58N 99 17W
Ayvacık, Turkey 88 C7 40 59N 36 38 E
Ayvalık, Turkey 88 D2 39 20N 26 46 E
Aywaille, Belgium 21 H7 50 28N 5 40 E
Az Zabdānī, Syria 91 B5 33 43N 36 5 E
Az Ẓāhirīyah, Jordan 91 D3 31 25N 34 58 E
Az Ẓahrān, Si. Arabia 85 E6 26 10N 50 7 E
Az Zarqā, Jordan 91 C5 32 5N 36 4 E
Az Zāwiyah, Libya 96 B2 32 52N 12 56 E
Az Zaydīyah, Yemen 86 D3 15 20N 43 1 E
Az Zībār, Iraq 84 B5 36 52N 44 4 E
Az-Zilfī, Si. Arabia 84 E5 26 12N 44 52 E
Az Zubayr, Iraq 84 D5 30 20N 47 50 E
Az Zuqur, Yemen 86 D3 14 0N 42 45 E
Azambuja, Portugal 37 F2 39 4N 8 51W
Azamgarh, India 81 F10 26 5N 83 13 E
Azangaro, Peru 156 C3 14 55 S 70 13W
Azaouak, Vallée de l', Mali 101 B5 15 50N 3 20 E
Āzār Shahr, Iran 84 B5 37 45N 45 59 E
Āzarbāyjān-e Gharbī □, Iran 84 B5 37 0N 44 30 E
Āzarbāyjān-e Sharqī □, Iran 84 B5 37 20N 47 0 E
Azare, Nigeria 101 C7 11 55N 10 10 E
Azay-le-Rideau, France 22 E7 47 16N 0 30 E
A'zāz, Syria 84 B3 36 36N 37 4 E
Azazga, Algeria 99 A5 36 48N 4 22 E
Azbine = Aïr, Niger 97 E1 18 30N 8 0 E
Azefal, Mauritania 98 D2 21 0N 14 45W
Azeffoun, Algeria 99 A5 36 51N 4 26 E
Azemmour, Morocco 98 B3 33 20N 9 20W
Azerbaijan ■, Asia 53 F12 40 20N 48 0 E
Azezo, Ethiopia 95 E4 12 28N 37 15 E
Azimganj, India 81 G13 24 14N 88 16 E
Aznalcóllar, Spain 37 H4 37 32N 6 17W
Azogues, Ecuador 152 D2 2 35 S 78 0W
Azores, Atl. Oc. 8 C8 38 44N 29 0W
Azov, Russia 53 C8 47 3N 39 25 E
Azov Sea = Azovskoye More, Europe 52 C7 46 0N 36 30 E
Azovskoye More, Europe 52 C7 46 0N 36 30 E
Azovy, Russia 56 C7 64 55N 64 35 E
Azpeitia, Spain 34 B2 43 12N 2 19W
Azrou, Morocco 98 B3 33 28N 5 19W
Aztec, U.S.A. 143 H10 36 54N 108 0W
Azúa, Dom. Rep. 149 C5 18 25N 70 44W
Azuaga, Spain 37 G5 38 16N 5 39W
Azuara, Spain 34 D4 41 15N 0 53W
Azuay □, Ecuador 152 D2 2 55 S 79 0W
Azuer →, Spain 37 F7 39 8N 3 36W
Azuero, Pen. de, Panama 148 E3 7 30N 80 30W

# 172 Barcellona Pozzo di Gotto



Barcellona Pozzo di Gotto, *Italy* 41 **D8** 38 8N 15 15 E
Barcelona, *Spain* 34 **D7** 41 21N 2 10 E
Barcelona, *Venezuela* 153 **A5** 10 10N 64 40W
Barcelona □, *Spain* 34 **D7** 41 30N 2 0 E
Barcelonette, *France* 25 **D10** 44 23N 6 40 E
Barcelos, *Brazil* 153 **D5** 1 0 S 63 0W
Barcin, *Poland* 47 **C4** 52 52N 17 55 E
Barcoo →, *Australia* 114 **D3** 25 30 S 142 50 E
Barcs, *Hungary* 31 **F10** 45 58N 17 28 E
Barczewo, *Poland* 47 **B7** 53 50N 20 42 E
Barda, *Azerbaijan* 53 **F12** 40 25N 47 10 E
Barda del Medio, *Argentina* 160 **A3** 38 45 S 68 11W
Bardai, *Chad* 97 **D3** 21 25N 17 0 E
Bardas Blancas, *Argentina* 158 **D2** 35 49 S 69 45W
Barddhaman, *India* 81 **H12** 23 14N 87 39 E
Bardejov, *Czech.* 31 **B14** 49 18N 21 15 E
Bardera, *Somali Rep.* 90 **G3** 2 20N 42 27 E
Bardi, *Italy* 38 **D6** 44 38N 9 43 E
Bardia, *Libya* 96 **B5** 31 45N 25 5 E
Bardo, *Poland* 47 **E3** 50 31N 16 42 E
Bardoli, *India* 82 **D1** 21 12N 73 5 E
Bardolino, *Italy* 38 **C7** 45 33N 10 43 E
Bardsey I., *U.K.* 16 **E3** 52 46N 4 47W
Bardstown, *U.S.A.* 141 **G11** 37 50N 85 29W
Bareilly, *India* 81 **E8** 28 22N 79 27 E
Barellan, *Australia* 117 **C7** 34 16 S 146 24 E
Barentin, *France* 22 **C7** 49 33N 0 58 E
Barenton, *France* 22 **D6** 48 38N 0 50W
Barents Sea, *Arctic* 6 **B9** 73 0N 39 0 E
Barentu, *Ethiopia* 95 **D4** 15 2N 37 35 E
Barfleur, *France* 22 **C5** 49 40N 1 17W
Barfleur, Pte. de, *France* 22 **C5** 49 42N 1 16W
Barga, *Italy* 38 **D7** 44 5N 10 30 E
Bargal, *Somali Rep.* 90 **E5** 11 25N 51 0 E
Bargara, *Australia* 114 **C5** 24 50 S 152 25 E
Barge, *Italy* 38 **D4** 44 43N 7 19 E
Bargnop, *Sudan* 95 **F2** 9 32N 28 25 E
Bargo, *Australia* 117 **C9** 34 18 S 150 35 E
Bargteheide, *Germany* 26 **B6** 53 42N 10 13 E
Barguzin, *Russia* 57 **D11** 53 37N 109 37 E
Barh, *India* 81 **G11** 25 29N 85 46 E
Barhaj, *India* 81 **F10** 26 18N 83 44 E
Barhi, *India* 81 **G11** 24 15N 85 25 E
Bari, *India* 80 **F7** 26 39N 77 39 E
Bari, *Italy* 41 **A9** 41 6N 16 52 E
Bari Doab, *Pakistan* 80 **D5** 30 20N 73 0 E
Bariadi □, *Tanzania* 106 **C3** 2 45 S 34 40 E
Barīm, *Yemen* 86 **D3** 12 39N 43 25 E
Barima →, *Guyana* 153 **B5** 8 33N 60 25W
Barinas, *Venezuela* 152 **B3** 8 36N 70 15W
Barinas □, *Venezuela* 152 **B4** 8 10N 69 50W
Baring, *U.S.A.* 140 **D4** 40 15N 92 12W
Baring, C., *Canada* 126 **B8** 70 0N 117 30W
Baringa, *Zaïre* 102 **B4** 0 45N 20 52 E
Baringo, *Kenya* 106 **B4** 0 47N 36 16 E
Baringo □, *Kenya* 106 **B4** 0 55N 36 0 E
Baringo, L., *Kenya* 106 **B4** 0 47N 36 16 E
Barinitas, *Venezuela* 152 **B3** 8 45N 70 25W
Baripada, *India* 82 **D8** 21 57N 86 45 E
Bariri, *Brazil* 155 **F2** 22 4 S 48 44W
Bârîs, *Egypt* 94 **C3** 24 42N 30 31 E
Barisal, *Bangla.* 78 **D3** 22 45N 90 20 E
Barito →, *Indonesia* 75 **C4** 4 0 S 114 50 E
Barjac, *France* 25 **D8** 44 20N 4 22 E
Barjols, *France* 25 **E10** 43 34N 6 2 E
Barjūj, Wadi →, *Libya* 96 **C2** 25 26N 12 12 E
Bark L., *Canada* 136 **A7** 45 27N 77 51W
Barka = Baraka →, *Sudan* 94 **D4** 18 13N 37 35 E
Barkam, *China* 68 **B4** 31 51N 102 28 E
Barker, *U.S.A.* 136 **C6** 43 20N 78 35W
Barkley Sound, *Canada* 130 **D3** 48 50N 125 10W
Barkly Downs, *Australia* 114 **C2** 20 30 S 138 30 E
Barkly East, *S. Africa* 104 **E4** 30 58 S 27 33 E
Barkly Tableland, *Australia* 114 **B2** 17 50 S 136 40 E
Barkly West, *S. Africa* 104 **D3** 28 5 S 24 31 E
Barkol, *China* 64 **B4** 43 37N 93 2 E
Barkol, Wadi →, *Sudan* 94 **D3** 17 40N 32 0 E
Barksdale, *U.S.A.* 139 **L4** 29 47N 100 2W
Barlee, L., *Australia* 113 **E2** 29 15 S 119 30 E
Barlee, Mt., *Australia* 113 **D4** 24 38 S 128 13 E
Barletta, *Italy* 41 **A9** 41 20N 16 17 E
Barlinek, *Poland* 47 **C2** 53 0N 15 15 E
Barlovento, *Canary Is.* 33 **F2** 28 48N 17 48W
Barlow L., *Canada* 131 **A8** 62 0N 103 0W
Barmedman, *Australia* 117 **C7** 34 9 S 147 21 E
Barmer, *India* 80 **G4** 25 45N 71 20 E
Barmera, *Australia* 116 **C4** 34 15 S 140 28 E
Barmouth, *U.K.* 16 **E3** 52 44N 4 3W
Barmstedt, *Germany* 26 **B5** 53 47N 9 46 E
Barnagar, *India* 80 **H6** 23 7N 75 19 E
Barnard Castle, *U.K.* 16 **C6** 54 33N 1 55W
Barnato, *Australia* 117 **A6** 31 38 S 145 0 E
Barnaul, *Russia* 56 **D9** 53 20N 83 40 E
Barnesville, *U.S.A.* 135 **J3** 33 6N 84 9W
Barnet, *U.K.* 17 **F7** 51 37N 0 15W
Barneveld, *Neths.* 20 **D7** 52 7N 5 36 E
Barneveld, *U.S.A.* 137 **C9** 43 16N 75 14W
Barneville-Cartevert, *France* 22 **C5** 49 23N 1 46W
Barngo, *Australia* 114 **D4** 25 3 S 147 20 E
Barnhart, *U.S.A.* 139 **K4** 31 10N 101 8W
Barnsley, *U.K.* 16 **D6** 53 33N 1 29W
Barnstaple, *U.K.* 17 **F3** 51 5N 4 3W
Barnsville, *U.S.A.* 138 **B6** 46 43N 96 28W
Baro, *Nigeria* 101 **D6** 8 35N 6 18 E
Baro →, *Ethiopia* 95 **F3** 8 26N 33 13 E
Baroda = Vadodara, *India* 80 **H5** 22 20N 73 10 E
Baroda, *India* 80 **G7** 25 29N 76 35 E
Baroe, *S. Africa* 104 **E3** 33 13 S 24 33 E
Baron Ra., *Australia* 112 **D4** 23 30 S 127 45 E
Barora Ite, *Solomon Is.* 121 **L10** 7 36 S 158 24 E
Barorafa, *Solomon Is.* 121 **L10** 7 30 S 158 20 E
Barpali, *India* 82 **D6** 21 11N 83 35 E
Barpathar, *India* 78 **B4** 26 17N 93 53 E
Barpeta, *India* 78 **B3** 26 20N 91 10 E
Barqin, *Libya* 96 **C2** 27 33N 13 34 E
Barques, Pte. aux, *U.S.A.* 134 **C4** 44 5N 82 55W
Barquinha, *Portugal* 37 **F2** 39 28N 8 25W
Barquísimeto, *Venezuela* 152 **A4** 10 4N 69 19W
Barr, *France* 23 **D14** 48 25N 7 28 E
Barra, *Brazil* 154 **D3** 11 5 S 43 10W
Barra, *U.K.* 18 **E1** 57 0N 7 30W
Barra, Sd. of, *U.K.* 18 **D1** 57 4N 7 25W
Barra da Estiva, *Brazil* 155 **D3** 13 38 S 41 19W
Barra de Navidad, *Mexico* 146 **D4** 19 12N 104 41W
Barra do Corda, *Brazil* 154 **C2** 5 30 S 45 10W
Barra do Dande, *Angola* 103 **D2** 8 28 S 13 22 E
Barra do Mendes, *Brazil* 155 **D3** 11 43 S 42 4W
Barra do Piraí, *Brazil* 155 **F3** 22 30 S 43 50W
Barra Falsa, Pta. da, *Mozam.* 105 **C6** 22 58 S 35 37 E
Barra Hd., *U.K.* 18 **E1** 56 47N 7 40W
Barra Mansa, *Brazil* 155 **F3** 22 35 S 44 12W
Barraba, *Australia* 117 **A9** 30 21 S 150 35 E
Barracão do Barreto, *Brazil* 157 **B6** 8 48 S 58 24W
Barrackpur = Barakpur, *India* 81 **H13** 22 44N 88 30 E
Barrafranca, *Italy* 41 **E7** 37 22N 14 10 E
Barranca, *Lima, Peru* 156 **C2** 10 45 S 77 50W
Barranca, *Loreto, Peru* 152 **D2** 4 50 S 76 50W
Barrancabermeja, *Colombia* 152 **B3** 7 0N 73 50W
Barrancas, *Colombia* 152 **A3** 10 57N 72 50W
Barrancas, *Venezuela* 153 **B5** 8 55N 62 5W
Barrancos, *Portugal* 37 **G4** 38 10N 6 58W
Barranqueras, *Argentina* 158 **B4** 27 30 S 59 0W
Barranquilla, *Colombia* 152 **A3** 11 0N 74 50W
Barras, *Brazil* 154 **B3** 4 15 S 42 18W
Barras, *Colombia* 152 **D3** 1 45 S 73 13W
Barraute, *Canada* 128 **C4** 48 26N 77 38W
Barre, *Mass., U.S.A.* 137 **D12** 42 26N 72 6W
Barre, *Vt., U.S.A.* 137 **B12** 44 15N 72 30W
Barre do Bugres, *Brazil* 157 **C6** 15 0 S 57 11W
Barreal, *Argentina* 158 **C2** 31 33 S 69 28W
Barrei, *Ethiopia* 108 **C2** 6 10N 42 49 E
Barreiras, *Brazil* 155 **D3** 12 8 S 45 0W
Barreirinha, *Brazil* 153 **D6** 2 47 S 57 3W
Barreirinhas, *Brazil* 154 **B3** 2 30 S 42 50W
Barreiro, *Portugal* 37 **G1** 38 40N 9 6W
Barreiros, *Brazil* 154 **C4** 8 49 S 35 12W
Barrême, *France* 25 **E10** 43 57N 6 23 E
Barren, Nosy, *Madag.* 105 **B7** 18 25 S 43 40 E
Barretos, *Brazil* 155 **F2** 20 30 S 48 35W
Barrhead, *Canada* 130 **C6** 54 10N 114 24W
Barrie, *Canada* 128 **D4** 44 24N 79 40W
Barrier, C., *N.Z.* 118 **C4** 36 25 S 175 32 E
Barrier Ra., *Australia* 116 **A4** 31 0 S 141 30 E
Barrier Ra., *Otago, N.Z.* 119 **E4** 44 15 S 169 32 E
Barrier Ra., *W. Coast, N.Z.* 119 **E3** 44 30 S 168 30 E
Barrière, *Canada* 130 **C4** 51 12N 120 7W
Barrington, *U.S.A.* 137 **E13** 41 43N 71 20W
Barrington L., *Canada* 131 **B8** 56 55N 100 15W
Barrington Tops, *Australia* 117 **B9** 32 6 S 151 28 E
Barringun, *Australia* 115 **D4** 29 1 S 145 41 E
Barro do Garças, *Brazil* 157 **D7** 15 54 S 52 16W
Barrow, *U.S.A.* 126 **A4** 71 16N 156 50W
Barrow →, *Ireland* 19 **D4** 52 10N 6 57W
Barrow, C., *U.S.A.* 124 **B4** 71 10N 156 20W
Barrow Creek, *Australia* 114 **C1** 21 30 S 133 55 E
Barrow I., *Australia* 112 **D2** 20 45 S 115 20 E
Barrow-in-Furness, *U.K.* 16 **C4** 54 8N 3 15W
Barrow Pt., *Australia* 114 **A3** 14 20 S 144 40 E
Barrow Ra., *Australia* 113 **E4** 26 0 S 127 40 E
Barrow Str., *Canada* 6 **B3** 74 20N 95 0W
Barruecopardo, *Spain* 36 **D4** 41 4N 6 40W
Barruelo, *Spain* 36 **C6** 42 54N 4 17W
Barry, *U.K.* 17 **F4** 51 23N 3 19W
Barry, *U.S.A.* 140 **E5** 39 42N 91 2W
Barry's Bay, *Canada* 128 **C4** 45 29N 77 41W
Barsalogho, *Burkina Faso* 101 **C4** 13 25N 1 3W
Barsat, *Pakistan* 81 **A5** 36 10N 72 45 E
Barsham, *Syria* 84 **C4** 35 21N 40 33 E
Barsi, *India* 82 **E2** 18 10N 75 50 E
Barsø, *Denmark* 15 **J3** 55 7N 9 33 E
Barstow, *Calif., U.S.A.* 145 **L9** 34 58N 117 2W
Barstow, *Tex., U.S.A.* 139 **K3** 31 28N 103 24W
Barth, *Germany* 26 **A8** 54 20N 12 36 E
Barthélemy, Col, *Vietnam* 76 **C5** 19 26N 104 6 E
Bartica, *Guyana* 153 **B6** 6 25N 58 40W
Bartin, *Turkey* 88 **C5** 41 38N 32 21 E
Bartle Frere, *Australia* 110 **D8** 17 27 S 145 50 E
Bartlesville, *U.S.A.* 139 **G7** 36 50N 95 58W
Bartlett, *Calif., U.S.A.* 144 **J8** 36 29N 118 2W
Bartlett, *Tex., U.S.A.* 139 **K6** 30 46N 97 30W
Bartlett, L., *Canada* 130 **A5** 63 5N 118 20W
Bartolomeu Dias, *Mozam.* 107 **G4** 21 10 S 35 8 E
Barton, *Australia* 113 **F5** 30 31 S 132 39 E
Barton, *Phil.* 71 **F2** 10 24N 119 8 E
Barton upon Humber, *U.K.* 16 **D7** 53 41N 0 27W
Bartonville, *U.S.A.* 140 **D7** 40 39N 89 39W
Bartoszyce, *Poland* 47 **A7** 54 15N 20 55 E
Bartow, *U.S.A.* 135 **M5** 27 53N 81 49W
Barú, I. de, *Colombia* 152 **A2** 10 15N 75 35W
Barú, Volcan, *Panama* 148 **E3** 8 55N 82 35W
Barumba, *Zaïre* 106 **B1** 1 3N 23 37 E
Baruth, *Germany* 26 **C9** 52 3N 13 31 E
Barvaux, *Belgium* 21 **H6** 50 21N 5 29 E
Barvenkovo, *Ukraine* 52 **B7** 48 57N 37 0 E
Barwani, *India* 80 **H6** 22 2N 74 57 E
Barycz →, *Poland* 47 **D3** 51 42N 16 15 E
Barysh, *Russia* 51 **E15** 53 39N 47 8 E
Barzān, *Iraq* 84 **B5** 36 55N 44 3 E
Bas-Rhin □, *France* 23 **D14** 48 40N 7 30 E
Bašaid, *Serbia, Yug.* 42 **B5** 45 38N 20 25 E
Bāsa'idū, *Iran* 85 **E7** 26 35N 55 20 E
Basal, *Pakistan* 80 **C5** 33 33N 72 13 E
Basankusa, *Zaïre* 102 **B3** 1 5N 19 50 E
Basawa, *Afghan.* 80 **B4** 34 15N 70 50 E
Bascharage, *Lux.* 21 **J7** 49 34N 5 55 E
Basco, *Phil.* 70 **A3** 20 27N 121 58 E
Bascuñán, C., *Chile* 158 **B1** 28 52 S 71 35W
Basècles, *Belgium* 21 **G3** 50 32N 3 39 E
Basel, *Switz.* 28 **A5** 47 35N 7 35 E
Basel-Stadt □, *Switz.* 28 **A5** 47 35N 7 35 E
Baselland □, *Switz.* 28 **B5** 47 26N 7 45 E
Basento →, *Italy* 41 **B9** 40 21N 16 50 E
Basey, *Phil.* 71 **F5** 11 17N 125 4 E
Bāshī, *Iran* 85 **D6** 28 41N 51 4 E
Bashkir Republic □, *Russia* 54 **D5** 54 0N 57 0 E
Basilaki I., *Papua N. G.* 120 **F6** 10 35 S 151 0 E
Basilan, *Phil.* 71 **H4** 6 35N 122 0 E
Basilan □, *Phil.* 71 **H4** 6 33N 122 4 E
Basilan Str., *Phil.* 71 **H4** 6 50N 122 0 E
Basildon, *U.K.* 17 **F8** 51 34N 0 29 E
Basilicata □, *Italy* 41 **B9** 40 30N 16 0 E
Basim = Washim, *India* 82 **D3** 20 3N 77 0 E
Basin, *U.S.A.* 142 **D9** 44 22N 108 2W
Basingstoke, *U.K.* 17 **F6** 51 15N 1 5W
Basirhat, *Bangla.* 78 **D2** 22 40N 88 54 E
Baška, *Croatia* 39 **D11** 44 58N 14 45 E
Başkale, *Turkey* 89 **D10** 38 2N 43 59 E
Baskatong, Rés., *Canada* 128 **C4** 46 46N 75 50W
Basle = Basel, *Switz.* 28 **A5** 47 35N 7 35 E
Basmat, *India* 82 **E3** 19 15N 77 12 E
Basoda, *India* 80 **H7** 23 52N 77 54 E
Basodino, *Switz.* 29 **D6** 46 25N 8 28 E
Basoka, *Zaïre* 106 **B1** 1 16N 23 40 E
Basongo, *Zaïre* 103 **C4** 4 15 S 20 20 E
Basque, Pays, *France* 24 **E2** 43 15N 1 20W
Basque Provinces = País Vasco □, *Spain* 34 **C2** 42 50N 2 45W
Basra = Al Başrah, *Iraq* 84 **D5** 30 30N 47 50 E
Bass Rock, *U.K.* 18 **E6** 56 5N 2 40W
Bass Str., *Australia* 114 **F4** 39 15 S 146 30 E
Bassano, *Canada* 130 **C6** 50 48N 112 20W
Bassano del Grappa, *Italy* 39 **C8** 45 45N 11 45 E
Bassar, *Togo* 101 **D5** 9 19N 0 57 E
Basse Santa-Su, *Gambia* 100 **C2** 13 13N 14 15W
Basse-Terre, *Guadeloupe* 149 **C7** 16 0N 61 44W
Bassecourt, *Switz.* 28 **B4** 47 20N 7 15 E
Bassein, *Burma* 78 **G5** 16 45N 94 30 E
Bassein, *India* 82 **E1** 19 26N 72 48 E
Basseterre, *St. Christopher-Nevis* 149 **C7** 17 17N 62 43W
Bassett, *Nebr., U.S.A.* 138 **D5** 42 37N 99 30W
Bassett, *Va., U.S.A.* 135 **G6** 36 48N 79 59W
Bassevelde, *Belgium* 21 **F3** 51 15N 3 41 E
Bassi, *India* 80 **D7** 30 44N 76 21 E
Bassigny, *France* 23 **E12** 48 0N 5 30 E
Bassikounou, *Mauritania* 100 **B3** 15 55N 6 1W
Bassilly, *Belgium* 21 **G3** 50 40N 3 56 E
Bassum, *Germany* 26 **C4** 52 50N 8 42 E
Båstad, *Sweden* 15 **H6** 56 25N 12 51 E
Bastak, *Iran* 85 **E7** 27 15N 54 25 E
Baştām, *Iran* 85 **B7** 36 29N 55 4 E
Bastar, *India* 82 **E5** 19 15N 81 40 E
Bastelica, *France* 25 **F13** 42 1N 9 3 E
Basti, *India* 81 **F10** 26 52N 82 55 E
Bastia, *France* 25 **F13** 42 40N 9 30 E
Bastia Umbra, *Italy* 39 **E9** 43 4N 12 34 E
Bastogne, *Belgium* 21 **H7** 50 1N 5 43 E
Bastrop, *U.S.A.* 139 **K6** 30 5N 97 22W
Basyanovskiy, *Russia* 54 **B7** 58 19N 60 44 E
Bat Yam, *Israel* 91 **C3** 32 2N 34 44 E
Bata, *Eq. Guin.* 102 **B1** 1 57N 9 50 E
Bata, *Romania* 46 **C3** 46 1N 22 4 E
Bataan, *Phil.* 70 **D3** 14 40N 120 25 E
Batabanó, *Cuba* 148 **B3** 22 40N 82 20W
Batabanó, G. de, *Cuba* 148 **B3** 22 30N 82 30W
Batac, *Phil.* 70 **B3** 18 3N 120 34 E
Batagoy, *Russia* 57 **C14** 67 38N 134 38 E
Batak, *Bulgaria* 43 **F9** 41 57N 24 12 E
Batalha, *Portugal* 37 **F2** 39 40N 8 50W
Batam, *Indonesia* 74 **B2** 1 5N 104 3 E
Batama, *Zaïre* 106 **B2** 0 58N 26 33 E
Batamay, *Russia* 57 **C13** 63 30N 129 15 E
Batamshinskiy, *Kazakhstan* 54 **F6** 50 36N 58 16 E
Batan I., *Phil.* 70 **A3** 20 30N 121 50 E
Batanes □, *Phil.* 70 **A3** 20 40N 121 55 E
Batanes Is., *Phil.* 70 **A3** 20 30N 121 50 E
Batang, *China* 68 **B2** 30 1N 99 0 E
Batang, *Indonesia* 75 **D3** 6 55 S 109 45 E
Batangafo, *C.A.R.* 102 **A3** 7 25N 18 20 E
Batangas, *Phil.* 70 **E3** 13 35N 121 10 E
Batangas □, *Phil.* 70 **E3** 13 15N 121 5 E
Batanghari, *Indonesia* 74 **C2** 1 36 S 103 37 E
Batanta, *Indonesia* 73 **B4** 0 55 S 130 40 E
Batas, *Phil.* 71 **F2** 11 10N 119 37 E
Batas I., *Phil.* 71 **F2** 11 10N 119 36 E
Batatais, *Brazil* 159 **A6** 20 54 S 47 37W
Batavia, *Ind., U.S.A.* 141 **C8** 41 55N 88 17W
Batavia, *N.Y., U.S.A.* 136 **D6** 43 0N 78 10W
Batavia, *Ohio, U.S.A.* 141 **E12** 39 5N 84 11W
Bataysk, *Russia* 53 **C8** 47 3N 39 45 E
Batchelor, *Australia* 112 **B5** 13 4 S 131 1 E
Batéké, Plateau, *Congo* 102 **C3** 3 30 S 15 45 E
Bateman's B., *Australia* 117 **C9** 35 40 S 150 12 E
Batemans Bay, *Australia* 117 **C9** 35 44 S 150 11 E
Bates Ra., *Australia* 113 **E3** 27 27 S 121 5 E
Batesburg, *U.S.A.* 135 **J5** 33 54N 81 32W
Batesville, *Ark., U.S.A.* 139 **H9** 35 48N 91 40W
Batesville, *Ind., U.S.A.* 141 **E11** 39 18N 85 13W
Batesville, *Miss., U.S.A.* 139 **H10** 34 17N 89 58W
Batesville, *Tex., U.S.A.* 139 **L5** 28 59N 99 38W
Bath, *U.K.* 17 **F5** 51 22N 2 22W
Bath, *Maine, U.S.A.* 129 **D6** 43 50N 69 49W
Bath, *N.Y., U.S.A.* 136 **D7** 42 20N 77 17W
Batheay, *Cambodia* 77 **G5** 11 59N 104 57 E
Bathgate, *U.K.* 18 **F5** 55 54N 3 38W
Bathmen, *Neths.* 20 **D8** 52 15N 6 29 E
Bathurst = Banjul, *Gambia* 100 **C1** 13 28N 16 40W
Bathurst, *Australia* 117 **B8** 33 25 S 149 31 E
Bathurst, *Canada* 129 **C6** 47 37N 65 43W
Bathurst, *S. Africa* 104 **E4** 33 30 S 26 50 E
Bathurst, C., *Canada* 126 **A7** 70 34N 128 0W
Bathurst B., *Australia* 114 **A3** 14 16 S 144 25 E
Bathurst Harb., *Australia* 114 **G4** 43 15 S 146 10 E
Bathurst I., *Australia* 112 **B5** 11 30 S 130 10 E
Bathurst I., *Canada* 6 **B2** 76 0N 100 30W
Bathurst Inlet, *Canada* 126 **B9** 66 50N 108 1W
Batie, *Burkina Faso* 100 **D4** 9 53N 2 53W
Batlow, *Australia* 117 **C8** 35 31 S 148 9 E
Batman, *Turkey* 89 **E9** 37 55N 41 5 E
Batna, *Algeria* 99 **A6** 35 34N 6 15 E
Bato, *Leyte, Phil.* 71 **F5** 10 13N 124 48 E
Bato, *Sulu, Phil.* 71 **J3** 5 15N 120 3 E
Bato Bato, *Phil.* 71 **J3** 5 6N 119 49 E
Batoala, *Gabon* 102 **B2** 0 48N 13 27 E
Batobato, *Phil.* 71 **H6** 6 50N 126 5 E
Batočina, *Serbia, Yug.* 42 **C6** 44 7N 21 5 E
Batoka, *Zambia* 107 **F2** 16 45 S 27 15 E
Baton Rouge, *U.S.A.* 139 **K9** 30 30N 91 5W
Batong, Ko, *Thailand* 77 **J2** 6 32N 99 12 E
Bátonyterenye, *Hungary* 31 **C12** 48 3N 19 50 E
Batopilas, *Mexico* 146 **B3** 27 0N 107 45W
Batouri, *Cameroon* 102 **B2** 4 30N 14 25 E
Battambang, *Cambodia* 76 **F4** 13 7N 103 12 E
Batticaloa, *Sri Lanka* 83 **L5** 7 43N 81 45 E
Battice, *Belgium* 21 **G7** 50 39N 5 50 E
Battipáglia, *Italy* 41 **B7** 40 38N 15 0 E
Battle, *U.K.* 17 **G8** 50 55N 0 30 E
Battle →, *Canada* 131 **C7** 52 43N 108 15W
Battle Camp, *Australia* 114 **B3** 15 20 S 144 40 E
Battle Creek, *U.S.A.* 141 **B11** 42 20N 85 6W
Battle Ground, *U.S.A.* 144 **E4** 45 47N 122 32W
Battle Harbour, *Canada* 129 **B8** 52 16N 55 35W
Battle Lake, *U.S.A.* 138 **B7** 46 20N 95 43W
Battle Mountain, *U.S.A.* 142 **F5** 40 45N 117 0W
Battlefields, *Zimbabwe* 107 **F2** 18 37 S 29 47 E
Battleford, *Canada* 131 **C7** 52 45N 108 15W
Battonya, *Hungary* 31 **E14** 46 16N 21 3 E
Batu, *Ethiopia* 90 **F2** 6 55N 39 45 E
Batu, Bukit, *Malaysia* 75 **B4** 2 16N 113 43 E
Batu, Kepulauan, *Indonesia* 74 **C1** 0 30 S 98 25 E
Batu Bora, Bukit, *Malaysia* 75 **B4** 2 43N 114 43 E
Batu Caves, *Malaysia* 77 **L3** 3 15N 101 40 E
Batu Gajah, *Malaysia* 77 **K3** 4 28N 101 3 E
Batu Is. = Batu, Kepulauan, *Indonesia* 74 **C1** 0 30 S 98 25 E
Batu Pahat, *Malaysia* 77 **M4** 1 50N 102 56 E
Batu Puteh, Gunong, *Malaysia* 74 **B2** 4 15N 101 31 E
Batuata, *Indonesia* 72 **C2** 6 12 S 122 42 E
Batulaki, *Phil.* 71 **J5** 5 34N 125 19 E
Batumi, *Georgia* 53 **F9** 41 30N 41 30 E
Baturaja, *Indonesia* 74 **C2** 4 11 S 104 15 E
Baturité, *Brazil* 154 **B4** 4 28 S 38 45W
Batusangkar, *Indonesia* 74 **C2** 0 27 S 100 35 E
Bau, *Malaysia* 75 **B4** 1 25N 110 9 E
Bauang, *Phil.* 70 **C3** 16 31N 120 20 E
Baubau, *Indonesia* 72 **C2** 5 25 S 122 38 E
Bauchi, *Nigeria* 101 **C6** 10 22N 9 48 E
Bauchi □, *Nigeria* 101 **C6** 10 30N 10 0 E
Baud, *France* 22 **E3** 47 52N 3 1W
Baudette, *U.S.A.* 138 **A7** 48 46N 94 35W
Baudour, *Belgium* 21 **H3** 50 29N 3 50 E
Bauer, C., *Australia* 115 **E1** 32 44 S 134 4 E
Baugé, *France* 22 **E6** 47 31N 0 8W
Bauhinia Downs, *Australia* 114 **C4** 24 35 S 149 18 E
Bauma, *Switz.* 29 **B7** 47 23N 8 53 E
Baume-les-Dames, *France* 23 **E13** 47 22N 6 22 E
Baunatal, *Germany* 26 **D5** 51 13N 9 25 E
Baunei, *Italy* 40 **B2** 40 2N 9 41 E
Baures, *Bolivia* 157 **C5** 13 35 S 63 35W
Bauru, *Brazil* 159 **A6** 22 10 S 49 0W
Baús, *Brazil* 157 **D7** 18 22 S 52 47W
Bauska, *Latvia* 50 **C4** 56 24N 24 15 E
Bautzen, *Germany* 26 **D10** 51 11N 14 25 E
Bavānāt, *Iran* 85 **D7** 30 28N 53 27 E
Bavanište, *Serbia, Yug.* 42 **C5** 44 49N 20 53 E
Bavaria = Bayern □, *Germany* 27 **F7** 49 7N 11 30 E
Båven, *Sweden* 14 **F10** 59 0N 16 56 E
Bavi Sadri, *India* 80 **G6** 24 28N 74 30 E
Bavispe →, *Mexico* 146 **B3** 29 30N 109 11W
Bawdwin, *Burma* 78 **D6** 23 5N 97 20 E
Bawean, *Indonesia* 75 **D4** 5 46 S 112 35 E
Bawku, *Ghana* 101 **C4** 11 3N 0 19W
Bawlake, *Burma* 78 **F6** 19 11N 97 21 E
Bawolung, *China* 68 **C3** 28 50N 101 16 E
Baxley, *U.S.A.* 135 **K4** 31 43N 82 23W
Baxoi, *China* 68 **B1** 30 1N 96 50 E
Baxter, *U.S.A.* 140 **C3** 41 49N 93 9W
Baxter Springs, *U.S.A.* 139 **G7** 37 3N 94 45W
Bay Bulls, *Canada* 129 **C9** 47 19N 52 50W
Bay City, *Mich., U.S.A.* 134 **D4** 43 35N 83 51W
Bay City, *Oreg., U.S.A.* 142 **D2** 45 45N 123 58W
Bay City, *Tex., U.S.A.* 139 **L7** 28 59N 95 55W
Bay de Verde, *Canada* 129 **C9** 48 5N 52 54W
Bay Minette, *U.S.A.* 135 **K2** 30 54N 87 43W
Bay St. Louis, *U.S.A.* 139 **K10** 30 18N 89 22W
Bay Springs, *U.S.A.* 139 **K10** 31 58N 89 18W
Bay View, *N.Z.* 118 **F5** 39 25 S 176 50 E
Baya, *Zaïre* 107 **E2** 11 53 S 27 25 E
Bayambang, *Phil.* 70 **D3** 15 49N 120 27 E
Bayamo, *Cuba* 148 **B4** 20 20N 76 40W
Bayamón, *Puerto Rico* 149 **C6** 18 24N 66 10W
Bayan Har Shan, *China* 64 **C4** 34 0N 98 0 E
Bayan Hot = Alxa Zuoqi, *China* 66 **E3** 38 50N 105 40 E
Bayan Obo, *China* 66 **D5** 41 52N 109 59 E
Bayan-Ovoo, *Mongolia* 66 **C4** 42 55N 106 5 E
Bayana, *India* 80 **F7** 26 55N 77 18 E
Bayanaul, *Kazakhstan* 56 **D8** 50 45N 75 45 E
Bayandalay, *Mongolia* 66 **C2** 43 30N 103 29 E
Bayanhongor, *Mongolia* 64 **B5** 46 8N 102 43 E
Bayard, *U.S.A.* 138 **E3** 41 48N 103 17W
Bayawan, *Phil.* 71 **G4** 9 46N 122 45 E
Baybay, *Phil.* 71 **F5** 10 40N 124 55 E
Bayburt, *Turkey* 89 **C9** 40 15N 40 20 E
Bayerischer Wald, *Germany* 27 **F8** 49 0N 12 50 E
Bayern □, *Germany* 27 **F7** 49 7N 11 30 E
Bayeux, *France* 22 **C6** 49 17N 0 42W
Bayfield, *Canada* 136 **C3** 43 34N 81 42W
Bayfield, *U.S.A.* 138 **B9** 46 50N 90 48W
Bayḩān al Qiṣāb, *Yemen* 86 **D4** 15 48N 45 44 E
Bayındır, *Turkey* 88 **D2** 38 13N 27 39 E
Baykadam, *Kazakhstan* 55 **B4** 43 48N 69 58 E
Baykal, Oz., *Russia* 57 **D11** 53 0N 108 0 E
Baykit, *Russia* 57 **C10** 61 50N 95 50 E
Baykonur, *Kazakhstan* 56 **E7** 47 48N 65 50 E
Baymak, *Russia* 54 **E6** 52 36N 58 19 E
Baynes Mts., *Namibia* 104 **B1** 17 15 S 13 0 E
Bayombong, *Phil.* 70 **C3** 16 30N 121 10 E
Bayon, *France* 23 **D13** 48 30N 6 20 E
Bayona, *Spain* 36 **C2** 42 6N 8 52W
Bayonne, *France* 24 **E2** 43 30N 1 28W
Bayonne, *U.S.A.* 137 **F10** 40 41N 74 7W
Bayovar, *Peru* 156 **B1** 5 50 S 81 0W
Bayram-Ali, *Turkmenistan* 56 **F7** 37 37N 62 10 E
Bayramiç, *Turkey* 88 **D2** 39 48N 26 36 E
Bayreuth, *Germany* 27 **F7** 49 56N 11 35 E
Bayrischzell, *Germany* 27 **H8** 47 39N 12 1 E
Bayrūt, *Lebanon* 91 **B4** 33 53N 35 31 E
Baysun, *Uzbekistan* 55 **D3** 38 12N 67 12 E
Bayt al Faqīh, *Yemen* 86 **D3** 14 31N 43 19 E
Bayt Lahm, *Jordan* 91 **D4** 31 43N 35 12 E
Baytown, *U.S.A.* 139 **L7** 29 42N 94 57W
Bayzhansay, *Kazakhstan* 55 **B4** 43 14N 69 54 E
Bayzo, *Niger* 101 **C5** 13 52N 4 35 E

Benagerie 173


Baza, Spain 35 H2 37 30N 2 47W
Bazar Dyuzi, Russia 53 F12 41 12N 47 50 E
Bazarny Karabulak, Russia 51 E15 52 15N 46 20 E
Bazarnyy Syzgan, Russia 51 E15 53 45N 46 40 E
Bazartobe, Kazakhstan 53 B14 49 26N 51 45 E
Bazaruto, I. do, Mozam. 105 C6 21 40 S 35 28 E
Bazas, France 24 D3 44 27N 0 13W
Bazhong, China 68 B6 31 52N 106 46 E
Bazmān, Kūh-e, Iran 85 D9 28 4N 60 1 E
Beabula, Australia 117 C6 34 26 S 145 9 E
Beach, U.S.A. 138 B3 46 57N 103 58W
Beach City, U.S.A. 136 F3 40 38N 81 35W
Beachport, Australia 116 D3 37 29 S 140 0 E
Beachy Hd., U.K. 17 G8 50 44N 0 16 E
Beacon, Australia 113 F2 30 26 S 117 52 E
Beacon, U.S.A. 137 E11 41 32N 73 58W
Beaconia, Canada 131 C9 50 25N 96 31W
Beagle, Canal, S. Amer. 160 E3 55 0 S 68 30W
Beagle Bay, Australia 112 C3 16 58 S 122 40 E
Bealanana, Madag. 105 A8 14 33 S 48 44 E
Beamsville, Canada 136 C5 43 12N 79 28W
Bear →, U.S.A. 144 G5 38 56N 121 36W
Béar, C., France 24 F7 42 31N 3 8 E
Bear I., Ireland 19 E2 51 38N 9 50W
Bear L., B.C., Canada 130 B3 56 10N 126 52W
Bear L., Man., Canada 131 B9 55 8N 96 0W
Bear L., U.S.A. 142 E8 42 0N 111 20W
Bearcreek, U.S.A. 142 D9 45 11N 109 6W
Beardmore, Canada 128 C2 49 36N 87 57W
Beardmore Glacier, Antarctica 7 E11 84 30 S 170 0 E
Beardstown, U.S.A. 140 D6 40 0N 90 25W
Béarn, France 24 E3 43 20N 0 30W
Bearpaw Mts., U.S.A. 142 B9 48 15N 109 30W
Bearskin Lake, Canada 128 B1 53 58N 91 2W
Beas de Segura, Spain 35 G2 38 15N 2 53W
Beasain, Spain 34 B2 43 3N 2 11W
Beata, C., Dom. Rep. 149 C5 17 40N 71 30W
Beata, I., Dom. Rep. 149 C5 17 34N 71 31W
Beatrice, U.S.A. 138 E6 40 20N 96 40W
Beatrice, Zimbabwe 107 F3 18 15 S 30 55 E
Beatrice, C., Australia 114 A2 14 20 S 136 55 E
Beatton →, Canada 130 B4 56 15N 120 45W
Beatton River, Canada 130 B4 57 26N 121 20W
Beatty, U.S.A. 144 J10 36 58N 116 46W
Beaucaire, France 25 E8 43 48N 4 39 E
Beauce, Plaine de la, France 23 D8 48 10N 1 45 E
Beauceville, Canada 129 C5 46 13N 70 46W
Beauchêne, I., Falk. Is. 160 D5 52 55 S 59 15W
Beaudesert, Australia 115 D5 27 59 S 153 0 E
Beaufort, Australia 116 D5 37 25 S 143 25 E
Beaufort, Malaysia 75 A5 5 30N 115 40 E
Beaufort, N.C., U.S.A. 135 H7 34 45N 76 40W
Beaufort, S.C., U.S.A. 135 J5 32 25N 80 40W
Beaufort Sea, Arctic 124 B6 72 0N 140 0W
Beaufort West, S. Africa 104 E3 32 18 S 22 36 E
Beaugency, France 23 E8 47 47N 1 38 E
Beauharnois, Canada 128 C5 45 20N 73 52W
Beaujeu, France 25 B8 46 10N 4 35 E
Beaulieu →, Canada 130 A6 62 3N 113 11W
Beaulieu-sur-Dordogne, France 24 D5 44 58N 1 50 E
Beaulieu-sur-Mer, France 25 E11 43 42N 7 20 E
Beauly, U.K. 18 D4 57 29N 4 27W
Beauly →, U.K. 18 D4 57 26N 4 28W
Beaumaris, U.K. 16 D3 53 16N 4 7W
Beaumetz-lès-Loges, France 23 B9 50 15N 2 38 E
Beaumont, Belgium 21 H4 50 15N 4 14 E
Beaumont, France 24 D4 44 45N 0 46 E
Beaumont, N.Z. 119 F4 45 50 S 169 33 E
Beaumont, Calif., U.S.A. 145 M10 33 56N 116 58W
Beaumont, Tex., U.S.A. 139 K7 30 5N 94 8W
Beaumont-de-Lomagne, France 24 E4 43 53N 1 0 E
Beaumont-le-Roger, France 22 C7 49 4N 0 47 E
Beaumont-sur-Oise, France 23 C9 49 9N 2 17 E
Beaumont-sur-Sarthe, France 22 D7 48 13N 0 8 E
Beaune, France 23 E11 47 2N 4 50 E
Beaune-la-Rolande, France 23 D9 48 4N 2 25 E
Beaupréau, France 22 E6 47 12N 0 59W
Beauraing, Belgium 21 H5 50 7N 4 57 E
Beauséjour, Canada 131 C9 50 5N 96 35W
Beautemps-Beaupré, I., N. Cal. 121 K4 20 24 S 166 9 E
Beauvais, France 23 C9 49 25N 2 8 E
Beauval, Canada 131 B7 55 9N 107 37W
Beauvoir-sur-Mer, France 22 F4 46 55N 2 2W
Beauvoir-sur-Niort, France 24 B3 46 12N 0 30W
Beaver, Alaska, U.S.A. 126 B5 66 20N 147 30W
Beaver, Okla., U.S.A. 139 G4 36 52N 100 31W
Beaver, Pa., U.S.A. 136 F4 40 40N 80 18W
Beaver, Utah, U.S.A. 143 G7 38 20N 112 45W
Beaver →, B.C., Canada 130 B4 59 52N 124 20W
Beaver →, Ont., Canada 128 A2 55 55N 87 48W
Beaver →, Sask., Canada 131 B7 55 26N 107 45W
Beaver City, U.S.A. 138 E5 40 13N 99 50W
Beaver Dam, U.S.A. 138 D10 43 28N 88 50W
Beaver Falls, U.S.A. 136 F4 40 44N 80 20W
Beaver Hill L., Canada 131 C10 54 5N 94 50W
Beaver I., U.S.A. 134 C3 45 40N 85 31W
Beavercreek, U.S.A. 141 E12 39 43N 84 11W
Beaverhill L., Alta., Canada 130 C6 53 27N 112 32W
Beaverhill L., N.W.T., Canada 131 A8 63 2N 104 22W
Beaverlodge, Canada 130 B5 55 11N 119 29W
Beavermouth, Canada 130 C5 51 32N 117 23W
Beaverstone →, Canada 128 B2 54 59N 89 25W
Beaverton, Canada 136 B5 44 26N 79 9W
Beaverton, U.S.A. 144 E4 45 29N 122 48W
Beaverville, U.S.A. 141 D9 40 57N 87 39W
Beawar, India 80 F6 26 3N 74 18 E
Bebedouro, Brazil 159 A6 21 0 S 48 25W
Beboa, Madag. 105 B7 17 22 S 44 33 E
Bebra, Germany 26 E5 50 59N 9 48 E
Beccles, U.K. 17 E9 52 27N 1 33 E
Bečej, Serbia, Yug. 42 B5 45 36N 20 3 E
Beceni, Romania 46 D7 45 23N 26 48 E
Becerreá, Spain 36 C3 42 51N 7 10W
Béchar, Algeria 99 B4 31 38N 2 18W
Bechyně, Czech. 30 B7 49 17N 14 29 E
Beckley, U.S.A. 134 G5 37 50N 81 8W
Beckum, Germany 26 D4 51 46N 8 3 E
Bečva →, Czech. 31 B10 49 31N 17 40 E
Bédar, Spain 35 H3 37 11N 1 59W
Bédarieux, France 24 E7 43 37N 3 10 E
Bédarrides, France 25 D8 44 2N 4 54 E
Beddouza, Ras, Morocco 98 B3 32 33N 9 9W
Bedel, Pereval, Kirghizia 55 C9 41 26N 78 26 E
Bedele, Ethiopia 95 F4 8 31N 36 23 E
Bederkesa, Germany 26 B4 53 37N 8 50 E
Bederwanak, Somali Rep. 108 C2 9 34N 44 23 E
Bedeso, Ethiopia 95 F5 9 58N 40 52 E
Bedford, Canada 128 C5 45 7N 72 59W
Bedford, S. Africa 104 E4 32 40 S 26 10 E
Bedford, U.K. 17 E7 52 8N 0 29W
Bedford, Ind., U.S.A. 141 F10 38 50N 86 30W
Bedford, Iowa, U.S.A. 140 D2 40 40N 94 41W
Bedford, Ky., U.S.A. 141 F11 38 36N 85 19W
Bedford, Ohio, U.S.A. 136 E3 41 23N 81 32W
Bedford, Pa., U.S.A. 136 F6 40 1N 78 30W
Bedford, Va., U.S.A. 134 G6 37 25N 79 30W
Bedford, C., Australia 114 B4 15 14 S 145 21 E
Bedford Downs, Australia 112 C4 17 19 S 127 20 E
Bedfordshire □, U.K. 17 E7 52 4N 0 28W
Bedi, Chad 97 F3 11 6N 18 33 E
Będków, Poland 47 D6 51 36N 19 44 E
Bednja →, Croatia 39 B13 46 20N 16 52 E
Bednodemyanovsk, Russia 51 E13 53 55N 43 15 E
Bedónia, Italy 38 D6 44 28N 9 36 E
Bedourie, Australia 114 C2 24 30 S 139 30 E
Bedretto, Switz. 29 C7 46 31N 8 31 E
Bedum, Neths. 20 B9 53 18N 6 36 E
Będzin, Poland 47 E6 50 19N 19 7 E
Beech Fork →, U.S.A. 141 G11 37 55N 85 50W
Beech Grove, U.S.A. 141 E10 39 40N 86 2W
Beecher, U.S.A. 141 C9 41 21N 87 38W
Beechworth, Australia 117 D7 36 22 S 146 43 E
Beechy, Canada 131 C7 50 53N 107 24W
Beek, Gelderland, Neths. 20 E8 51 55N 6 11 E
Beek, Limburg, Neths. 21 G7 50 57N 5 48 E
Beek, Noord-Brabant, Neths. 21 E7 51 32N 5 38 E
Beekbergen, Neths. 20 D7 52 10N 5 58 E
Beelitz, Germany 26 C8 52 14N 12 58 E
Beenleigh, Australia 115 D5 27 43 S 153 10 E
Be'er Menuha, Israel 84 D2 30 19N 35 8 E
Be'er Sheva', Israel 91 D3 31 15N 34 48 E
Beersheba = Be'er Sheva', Israel 91 D3 31 15N 34 48 E
Beerta, Neths. 20 B10 53 11N 7 6 E
Beerze →, Neths. 20 E6 51 39N 5 20 E
Beesd, Neths. 20 E6 51 53N 5 11 E
Beeskow, Germany 26 C10 52 9N 14 14 E
Beeston, U.K. 16 E6 52 55N 1 11W
Beetaloo, Australia 114 B1 17 15 S 133 50 E
Beetsterzwaag, Neths. 20 B8 53 4N 6 5 E
Beetzendorf, Germany 26 C7 52 42N 11 6 E
Beeville, U.S.A. 139 L6 28 27N 97 44W
Befale, Zaïre 102 B4 0 25N 20 45 E
Befandriana, Madag. 105 C7 21 55 S 44 0 E
Befotaka, Madag. 105 C8 23 49 S 47 0 E
Bega, Australia 117 D8 36 41 S 149 51 E
Bega, Canalul, Romania 42 B5 45 37N 20 46 E
Bégard, France 22 D3 48 38N 3 18W
Bègles, France 24 D3 44 45N 0 35W
Begna →, Norway 14 D4 60 35N 10 0 E
Begonte, Spain 36 B3 43 10N 7 40W
Begusarai, India 81 G12 25 24N 86 9 E
Behābād, Iran 85 C8 32 24N 59 47 E
Behara, Madag. 105 C8 24 55 S 46 20 E
Behbehān, Iran 85 D6 30 30N 50 15 E
Behshahr, Iran 85 B7 36 45N 53 35 E
Bei Jiang →, China 69 F9 23 2N 112 58 E
Bei'an, China 65 B7 48 10N 126 20 E
Beigang, Taiwan 69 F13 23 38N 120 16 E
Beihai, China 68 G7 21 28N 109 6 E
Beijing, China 66 E9 39 55N 116 20 E
Beijing □, China 66 E9 39 55N 116 20 E
Beilen, Neths. 20 C8 52 52N 6 27 E
Beiliu, China 69 F8 22 41N 110 21 E
Beilngries, Germany 27 F7 49 1N 11 27 E
Beilpajah, Australia 116 B5 32 54 S 143 52 E
Beilul, Ethiopia 95 E5 13 2N 42 20 E
Beipiao, China 67 D11 41 52N 120 32 E
Beira, Mozam. 107 F3 19 50 S 34 52 E
Beira, Somali Rep. 108 C3 6 57N 47 19 E
Beirut = Bayrūt, Lebanon 91 B4 33 53N 35 31 E
Beitaolaizhao, China 67 B13 44 58N 125 58 E
Beitbridge, Zimbabwe 107 G3 22 12 S 30 0 E
Beiuş, Romania 46 C3 46 40N 22 21 E
Beizhen, Liaoning, China 67 D11 41 38N 121 54 E
Beizhen, Shandong, China 67 F10 37 20N 118 2 E
Beizhengzhen, China 67 B12 44 31N 123 30 E
Beja, Portugal 37 G3 38 2N 7 53W
Béja, Tunisia 96 A1 36 43N 9 12 E
Beja □, Portugal 37 H3 37 55N 7 55W
Bejaia, Algeria 99 A6 36 42N 5 2 E
Béjar, Spain 36 E5 40 23N 5 46W
Bejestān, Iran 85 C8 34 30N 58 5 E
Bekabad, Uzbekistan 55 C4 40 13N 69 14 E
Bekasi, Indonesia 74 D3 6 14 S 106 59 E
Békés, Hungary 31 E14 46 47N 21 9 E
Békés □, Hungary 31 E13 46 45N 21 0 E
Békéscsaba, Hungary 31 E14 46 40N 21 5 E
Bekily, Madag. 105 C8 24 13 S 45 19 E
Bekkevoort, Belgium 21 G5 50 57N 4 58 E
Bekoji, Ethiopia 95 F4 7 40N 39 17 E
Bekok, Malaysia 77 L4 2 20N 103 7 E
Bekwai, Ghana 101 D4 6 30N 1 34W
Bela, India 81 G9 25 50N 82 0 E
Bela, Pakistan 79 D2 26 12N 66 20 E
Bela Crkva, Serbia, Yug. 42 C6 44 55N 21 27 E
Bela Palanka, Serbia, Yug. 42 D7 43 13N 22 17 E
Bela Vista, Brazil 158 A4 22 12 S 56 20W
Bela Vista, Mozam. 105 D5 26 10 S 32 44 E
Bélâbre, France 24 B5 46 34N 1 8 E
Belaga, Malaysia 75 B4 2 42N 113 47 E
Belalcázar, Spain 37 G5 38 35N 5 10W
Belanovica, Serbia, Yug. 42 C5 44 15N 20 23 E
Belarus = Belorussia ■, Europe 50 E5 53 30N 27 0 E
Belas, Angola 103 D2 8 55 S 13 9 E
Belau I., Pac. Oc. 122 G5 7 30N 134 30 E
Belavenona, Madag. 105 C8 24 50 S 47 4 E
Belawan, Indonesia 74 B1 3 33N 98 32 E
Belaya, Ethiopia 95 E4 11 25N 36 8 E
Belaya →, Russia 54 D4 54 40N 56 0 E
Belaya Glina, Russia 53 C9 46 5N 40 48 E
Belaya Kalitva, Russia 53 B9 48 13N 40 50 E
Belaya Kholunitsa, Russia 54 B2 58 41N 50 13 E
Belaya Tserkov, Ukraine 50 G7 49 45N 30 10 E
Belayan →, Indonesia 75 C5 0 14 S 116 36 E
Belceşti, Romania 46 B8 47 19N 27 7 E
Bełchatów, Poland 47 D6 51 21N 19 22 E
Belcher Is., Canada 127 C12 56 15N 78 45W
Belchite, Spain 34 D4 41 18N 0 43W
Belden, U.S.A. 144 E5 40 2N 121 17W
Belebey, Russia 54 D4 54 7N 54 7 E
Belém, Brazil 154 B2 1 20 S 48 30W
Belém de São Francisco, Brazil 154 C4 8 46 S 38 58W
Belén, Argentina 158 B2 27 40 S 67 5W
Belén, Colombia 152 C2 1 26N 75 56W
Belén, Paraguay 158 A4 23 30 S 57 6W
Belen, U.S.A. 143 J10 34 40N 106 50W
Belene, Bulgaria 43 D10 43 39N 25 10 E
Bélesta, France 24 F5 42 55N 1 56 E
Belet Uen, Somali Rep. 90 G4 4 30N 45 5 E
Belev, Russia 51 E10 53 50N 36 5 E
Belfair, U.S.A. 144 C4 47 27N 122 50W
Belfast, N.Z. 119 D7 43 27 S 172 39 E
Belfast, S. Africa 105 D5 25 42 S 30 2 E
Belfast, U.K. 19 B6 54 35N 5 56W
Belfast, Maine, U.S.A. 129 D6 44 30N 69 0W
Belfast, N.Y., U.S.A. 136 D6 42 21N 78 9W
Belfast □, U.K. 19 B6 54 35N 5 56W
Belfast L., U.K. 19 B6 54 40N 5 50W
Belfeld, Neths. 21 F8 51 18N 6 6 E
Belfield, U.S.A. 138 B3 46 54N 103 11W
Belfort, France 23 E13 47 38N 6 50 E
Belfort, Territoire de □, France 23 E13 47 40N 6 55 E
Belfry, U.S.A. 142 D9 45 10N 109 2W
Belgaum, India 83 G2 15 55N 74 35 E
Belgioioso, Italy 38 C6 45 9N 9 21 E
Belgium ■, Europe 21 G5 50 30N 5 0 E
Belgorod, Russia 51 F10 50 35N 36 35 E
Belgorod-Dnestrovskiy, Ukraine 52 C4 46 11N 30 23 E
Belgrade = Beograd, Serbia, Yug. 42 C5 44 50N 20 37 E
Belgrade, U.S.A. 142 D8 45 50N 111 10W
Belgrove, N.Z. 119 B7 41 27 S 172 59 E
Belhaven, U.S.A. 135 H7 35 34N 76 35W
Beli Drim →, Europe 42 E5 42 6N 20 25 E
Beli Manastir, Croatia 42 B3 45 45N 18 36 E
Beli Timok →, Serbia, Yug. 42 D7 43 53N 22 14 E
Belice →, Italy 40 E5 37 35N 12 55 E
Belin-Béliet, France 24 D3 44 29N 0 47W
Belinga, Gabon 102 B2 1 10N 13 2 E
Belinskiy, Russia 51 E13 53 0N 43 25 E
Belinţ, Romania 42 B6 45 48N 21 54 E
Belinyu, Indonesia 74 C3 1 35 S 105 50 E
Belitung, Indonesia 75 C3 3 10 S 107 50 E
Beliu, Romania 46 C3 46 30N 22 0 E
Belize ■, Cent. Amer. 147 D7 17 0N 88 30W
Belize City, Belize 147 D7 17 25N 88 0W
Beljanica, Serbia, Yug. 42 C6 44 8N 21 43 E
Belkovskiy, Ostrov, Russia 57 B14 75 32N 135 44 E
Bell →, Canada 128 C4 49 48N 77 38W
Bell Bay, Australia 114 G4 41 6 S 146 53 E
Bell I., Canada 129 B8 50 46N 55 35W
Bell-Irving →, Canada 130 B3 56 12N 129 5W
Bell Peninsula, Canada 127 B11 63 50N 82 0W
Bell Ville, Argentina 158 C3 32 40 S 62 40W
Bella Bella, Canada 130 C3 52 10N 128 10W
Bella Coola, Canada 130 C3 52 25N 126 40W
Bella Flor, Bolivia 156 C4 11 9 S 67 49W
Bella Unión, Uruguay 158 C4 30 15 S 57 40W
Bella Vista, Corrientes, Argentina 158 B4 28 33 S 59 0W
Bella Vista, Tucuman, Argentina 158 B2 27 10 S 65 25W
Bellac, France 24 B5 46 7N 1 3 E
Bellágio, Italy 38 C6 45 59N 9 15 E
Bellaire, U.S.A. 136 F4 40 1N 80 46W
Bellary, India 83 G3 15 10N 76 56 E
Bellata, Australia 115 D4 29 53 S 149 46 E
Belle, U.S.A. 140 F5 38 17N 91 43W
Belle Fourche, U.S.A. 138 C3 44 43N 103 52W
Belle Fourche →, U.S.A. 138 C3 44 25N 102 19W
Belle Glade, U.S.A. 135 M5 26 43N 80 38W
Belle-Ile, France 22 E3 47 20N 3 10W
Belle Isle, Canada 129 B8 51 57N 55 25W
Belle Isle, Str. of, Canada 129 B8 51 30N 56 30W
Belle-Isle-en-Terre, France 22 D3 48 33N 3 23W
Belle Plaine, Iowa, U.S.A. 140 C4 41 51N 92 18W
Belle Plaine, Minn., U.S.A. 138 C8 44 35N 93 48W
Belle Rive, U.S.A. 141 F8 38 14N 88 45W
Belle Yella, Liberia 100 D3 7 24N 10 0W
Belledonne, Chaîne de, France 25 C10 45 20N 6 10 E
Belledune, Canada 129 C6 47 55N 65 50W
Bellefontaine, U.S.A. 141 D13 40 20N 83 45W
Bellefonte, U.S.A. 136 F7 40 56N 77 45W
Bellegarde, France 23 E9 47 59N 2 26 E
Bellegarde-en-Marche, France 24 C6 45 59N 2 18 E
Bellegarde-sur-Valserine, France 25 B9 46 4N 5 50 E
Bellême, France 22 D7 48 22N 0 34 E
Belleoram, Canada 129 C8 47 31N 55 25W
Belleville, Canada 128 D4 44 10N 77 23W
Belleville, France 25 B8 46 7N 4 45 E
Belleville, Ill., U.S.A. 140 F7 38 30N 90 0W
Belleville, Kans., U.S.A. 138 F6 39 51N 97 38W
Belleville, N.Y., U.S.A. 137 C8 43 46N 76 10W
Belleville-sur-Vie, France 22 F5 46 46N 1 25W
Bellevue, Canada 130 D6 49 35N 114 22W
Bellevue, Idaho, U.S.A. 142 E6 43 25N 114 23W
Bellevue, Iowa, U.S.A. 140 B6 42 16N 90 26W
Bellevue, Mich., U.S.A. 141 B11 42 27N 85 1W
Bellevue, Ohio, U.S.A. 136 E2 41 20N 82 48W
Bellevue, Wash., U.S.A. 144 C4 47 37N 122 12W
Belley, France 25 C9 45 45N 5 41 E
Bellflower, U.S.A. 140 E5 39 0N 91 21W
Bellin, Canada 127 B13 60 0N 70 0W
Bellingen, Australia 117 A10 30 25 S 152 50 E
Bellingham, U.S.A. 144 B4 48 45N 122 27W
Bellingshausen Sea, Antarctica 7 C17 66 0 S 80 0W
Bellinzona, Switz. 29 D8 46 11N 9 1 E
Bello, Colombia 152 B2 6 20N 75 33W
Bellona, Solomon Is. 121 N10 11 17 S 159 47 E
Bellows Falls, U.S.A. 137 C12 43 10N 72 30W
Bellpat, Pakistan 80 E3 29 0N 68 5 E
Bellpuig, Spain 34 D6 41 37N 1 1 E
Belluno, Italy 39 B9 46 8N 12 13 E
Bellville, U.S.A. 139 L6 29 58N 96 18W
Bellwood, U.S.A. 136 F6 40 36N 78 21W
Bélmez, Spain 37 G5 38 17N 5 17W
Belmond, U.S.A. 140 B3 42 51N 93 37W
Belmont, Australia 117 B9 33 4 S 151 42 E
Belmont, Canada 136 D3 42 53N 81 5W
Belmont, S. Africa 104 D3 29 28 S 24 22 E
Belmont, U.S.A. 136 D6 42 14N 78 3W
Belmonte, Brazil 155 E4 16 0 S 39 0W
Belmonte, Portugal 36 E3 40 21N 7 20W
Belmonte, Spain 34 F2 39 34N 2 43W
Belmopan, Belize 147 D7 17 18N 88 30W
Belmore, Australia 116 B4 33 34 S 141 13 E
Belmullet, Ireland 19 B2 54 13N 9 58W
Belo Horizonte, Brazil 155 E3 19 55 S 43 56W
Belo Jardim, Brazil 154 C4 8 20 S 36 26W
Belo-sur-Mer, Madag. 105 C7 20 42 S 44 0 E
Belo-Tsiribihina, Madag. 105 B7 19 40 S 44 30 E
Belogorsk, Russia 57 D13 51 0N 128 20 E
Belogorsk, Ukraine 52 D6 45 3N 34 35 E
Belogradchik, Bulgaria 42 D7 43 53N 22 15 E
Belogradets, Bulgaria 43 D12 43 22N 27 18 E
Beloha, Madag. 105 D8 25 10 S 45 3 E
Beloit, Kans., U.S.A. 138 F5 39 32N 98 9W
Beloit, Wis., U.S.A. 140 B7 42 35N 89 3W
Belokorovichi, Ukraine 50 F6 51 7N 28 2 E
Belomorsk, Russia 48 B5 64 35N 34 30 E
Belonia, India 78 D3 23 15N 91 30 E
Belopolye, Ukraine 50 F9 51 14N 34 20 E
Beloretsk, Russia 54 E6 53 58N 58 24 E
Belorussia ■, Europe 50 E5 53 30N 27 0 E
Belovo, Russia 56 D9 54 30N 86 0 E
Beloyarskiy, Russia 54 C7 56 45N 61 24 E
Beloye, Oz., Russia 48 B6 60 10N 37 35 E
Beloye More, Russia 48 A6 66 30N 38 0 E
Beloye Ozero, Russia 53 D12 45 15N 46 50 E
Belozem, Bulgaria 43 E10 42 12N 25 2 E
Belozersk, Russia 51 A10 60 4N 37 30 E
Belpasso, Italy 41 E7 37 37N 15 0 E
Belsele, Belgium 21 F4 51 9N 4 6 E
Belsito, Italy 40 E6 37 50N 13 47 E
Beltana, Australia 116 A3 30 48 S 138 25 E
Belterra, Brazil 153 D7 2 45 S 55 0W
Beltinci, Slovenia 39 B13 46 37N 16 20 E
Belton, S.C., U.S.A. 135 H4 34 31N 82 39W
Belton, Tex., U.S.A. 139 K6 31 4N 97 30W
Belton Res., U.S.A. 139 K6 31 8N 97 32W
Beltsy, Moldavia 52 C3 47 48N 28 0 E
Belturbet, Ireland 19 B4 54 6N 7 28W
Belukha, Russia 56 E9 49 50N 86 50 E
Beluša, Czech. 31 B11 49 5N 18 27 E
Belušić, Serbia, Yug. 42 D6 43 50N 21 10 E
Belvedere Maríttimo, Italy 41 C8 39 37N 15 52 E
Belvès, France 24 D5 44 46N 1 0 E
Belvidere, Ill., U.S.A. 138 D10 42 15N 88 55W
Belvidere, N.J., U.S.A. 137 F9 40 48N 75 5W
Belvis de la Jara, Spain 37 F6 39 45N 4 57W
Belyando →, Australia 114 C4 21 38 S 146 50 E
Belyy, Russia 50 D8 55 48N 32 51 E
Belyy, Ostrov, Russia 56 B8 73 30N 71 0 E
Belyy Yar, Russia 56 D9 58 26N 84 39 E
Belyye Vody, Kazakhstan 55 B4 42 25N 69 50 E
Belzig, Germany 26 C8 52 8N 12 36 E
Belzoni, U.S.A. 139 J9 33 12N 90 30W
Bełżyce, Poland 47 D9 51 11N 22 17 E
Bemaraha, Lembalemban' i, Madag. 105 B7 18 40 S 44 45 E
Bemarivo, Madag. 105 C7 21 45 S 44 45 E
Bemarivo →, Madag. 105 B8 15 27 S 47 40 E
Bemavo, Madag. 105 C8 21 33 S 45 25 E
Bembéréke, Benin 101 C5 10 11N 2 43 E
Bembesi, Zimbabwe 107 F2 20 0 S 28 58 E
Bembesi →, Zimbabwe 107 F2 18 57 S 27 47 E
Bembézar →, Spain 37 H5 37 45N 5 13W
Bement, U.S.A. 141 E8 39 55N 88 34W
Bemidji, U.S.A. 138 B7 47 30N 94 50W
Bemmel, Neths. 20 E7 51 54N 5 54 E
Ben, Iran 85 C6 32 32N 50 45 E
Ben Bullen, Australia 117 B9 33 12 S 150 2 E
Ben Cruachan, U.K. 18 E3 56 26N 5 8W
Ben Dearg, U.K. 18 D4 57 47N 4 58W
Ben Gardane, Tunisia 96 B2 33 11N 11 11 E
Ben Hope, U.K. 18 C4 58 24N 4 36W
Ben Lawers, U.K. 18 E4 56 33N 4 13W
Ben Lomond, N.S.W., Australia 115 E5 30 1 S 151 43 E
Ben Lomond, Tas., Australia 114 G4 41 38 S 147 42 E
Ben Lomond, U.K. 18 E4 56 12N 4 39W
Ben Luc, Vietnam 77 G6 10 39N 106 29 E
Ben Macdhui, U.K. 18 D5 57 4N 3 40W
Ben Mhor, U.K. 18 D1 57 16N 7 21W
Ben More, Central, U.K. 18 E4 56 23N 4 31W
Ben More, Strath., U.K. 18 E2 56 26N 6 2W
Ben More Assynt, U.K. 18 C4 58 7N 4 51W
Ben Nevis, U.K. 18 E4 56 48N 4 58W
Ben Ohau Ra., N.Z. 119 E5 44 1 S 170 4 E
Ben Quang, Vietnam 76 D6 17 3N 106 55 E
Ben Slimane, Morocco 98 B3 33 38N 7 7W
Ben Tre, Vietnam 77 G6 10 3N 106 36 E
Ben Vorlich, U.K. 18 E4 56 22N 4 15W
Ben Wyvis, U.K. 18 D4 57 40N 4 35W
Bena, Nigeria 101 C6 11 20N 5 50 E
Bena Dibele, Zaïre 103 C4 4 4 S 22 50 E
Bena-Leka, Zaïre 103 D4 5 8 S 22 10 E
Bena-Tshadi, Zaïre 103 C4 4 40 S 22 50 E
Benadir, Somali Rep. 108 D2 1 30N 44 30 E
Benagalbón, Spain 37 J6 36 45N 4 15W
Benagerie, Australia 116 A4 31 25 S 140 22 E

174 Benahmed


Benahmed, *Morocco* 98 B3 33 4N 7 9W
Benalla, *Australia* 117 D7 36 30 S 146 0 E
Benambra, Mt., *Australia* 117 D7 36 31 S 147 34 E
Benamejí, *Spain* 37 H6 37 16N 4 33W
Benares = Varanasi, *India* 81 G10 25 22N 83 0 E
Bénat, C., *France* 25 E10 43 5N 6 22 E
Benavente, *Portugal* 37 G2 38 59N 8 49W
Benavente, *Spain* 36 C5 42 2N 5 43W
Benavides, *Spain* 36 C5 42 30N 5 54W
Benavides, *U.S.A.* 139 M5 27 35N 98 28W
Benbecula, *U.K.* 18 D1 57 26N 7 21W
Benbonyathe, *Australia* 116 A3 30 25 S 139 11 E
Bencubbin, *Australia* 113 F2 30 48 S 117 52 E
Bend, *U.S.A.* 142 D3 44 2N 121 15W
Bendel □, *Nigeria* 101 D6 6 0N 6 0 E
Bendela, *Zaïre* 102 C3 3 18 S 17 36 E
Bender Beila, *Somali Rep.* 90 F5 9 30N 50 48 E
Bender Merchagno, *Somali Rep.* 108 B4 11 41N 50 34 E
Bendering, *Australia* 113 F2 32 23 S 118 18 E
Bendery, *Moldavia* 52 C3 46 50N 29 30 E
Bendigo, *Australia* 116 D6 36 40 S 144 15 E
Bendorf, *Germany* 26 E3 50 26N 7 34 E
Benē Beraq, *Israel* 91 C3 32 6N 34 51 E
Beneden Knijpe, *Neths.* 20 C7 52 58N 5 59 E
Beneditinos, *Brazil* 154 C3 5 27 S 42 22W
Benedito Leite, *Brazil* 154 C3 7 13 S 44 34W
Bénéna, *Mali* 100 C4 13 9N 4 17W
Benenitra, *Madag.* 105 C8 23 27 S 45 5 E
Benešŏv, *Czech.* 30 B7 49 46N 14 41 E
Bénestroff, *France* 23 D13 48 54N 6 45 E
Benet, *France* 24 B3 46 22N 0 35W
Benevento, *Italy* 41 A7 41 7N 14 45 E
Benfeld, *France* 23 D14 48 22N 7 34 E
Benga, *Mozam.* 107 F3 16 11 S 33 40 E
Bengal, Bay of, *Ind. Oc.* 58 H13 15 0N 90 0 E
Bengbu, *China* 67 H9 32 58N 117 20 E
Benghazi = Banghāzī, *Libya* 96 B4 32 11N 20 3 E
Bengkalis, *Indonesia* 74 B2 1 30N 102 10 E
Bengkulu, *Indonesia* 74 C2 3 50 S 102 12 E
Bengough, *Canada* 131 D7 49 25N 105 10W
Benguela, *Angola* 103 E2 12 37 S 13 25 E
Benguela □, *Angola* 103 E2 13 0S 13 30 E
Benguerir, *Morocco* 98 B3 32 16N 7 56W
Benguérua, I., *Mozam.* 105 C6 21 58 S 35 28 E
Benguet □, *Phil.* 70 C3 16 30N 120 40 E
Benha, *Egypt* 94 H7 30 26N 31 8 E
Beni, *Zaïre* 106 B2 0 30N 29 27 E
Beni □, *Bolivia* 157 C4 14 0S 65 0W
Beni →, *Bolivia* 157 C4 10 23 S 65 24W
Beni Abbès, *Algeria* 99 B4 30 5N 2 5W
Beni-Haoua, *Algeria* 99 A5 36 30N 1 30 E
Beni Mazâr, *Egypt* 94 J7 28 32N 30 44 E
Beni Mellal, *Morocco* 98 B3 32 21N 6 21W
Beni Ounif, *Algeria* 99 B4 32 0N 1 10W
Beni Saf, *Algeria* 99 A4 35 17N 1 15W
Beni Suef, *Egypt* 94 J7 29 5N 31 6 E
Beniah L., *Canada* 130 A6 63 23N 112 17W
Benicarló, *Spain* 34 E5 40 23N 0 23 E
Benicia, *U.S.A.* 144 G4 38 3N 122 9W
Benidorm, *Spain* 35 G4 38 33N 0 9W
Benidorm, Islote de, *Spain* 35 G4 38 31N 0 9W
Benin ■, *Africa* 101 D5 10 0N 2 0 E
Benin, Bight of, *W. Afr.* 101 D5 5 0N 3 0 E
Benin City, *Nigeria* 101 D6 6 20N 5 31 E
Benisa, *Spain* 35 G5 38 43N 0 3 E
Benitses, *Greece* 32 A3 39 32N 19 55 E
Benjamin Aceval, *Paraguay* 158 A4 24 58 S 57 34W
Benjamin Constant, *Brazil* 152 D3 4 40 S 70 15W
Benjamin Hill, *Mexico* 146 A2 30 10N 111 10W
Benkelman, *U.S.A.* 138 E4 40 7N 101 32W
Benkovac, *Croatia* 39 D12 44 2N 15 37 E
Benlidi, *Australia* 114 C3 24 35 S 144 50 E
Benmore Pk., *N.Z.* 119 E5 44 25 S 170 8 E
Bennebroek, *Neths.* 20 D5 52 19N 4 36 E
Bennekom, *Neths.* 20 D7 52 0N 5 41 E
Bennett, *Canada* 130 B2 59 56N 134 53W
Bennett, L., *Australia* 112 D5 22 50 S 131 2 E
Bennett, Ostrov, *Russia* 57 B15 76 21N 148 56 E
Bennettsville, *U.S.A.* 135 H6 34 38N 79 39W
Bennington, *U.S.A.* 137 D11 42 52N 73 12W
Bénodet, *France* 22 E2 47 53N 4 7W
Benoni, *S. Africa* 105 D4 26 11 S 28 18 E
Benoud, *Algeria* 99 B5 32 20N 0 16 E
Benoy, *Chad* 97 G3 8 59N 16 19 E
Benque Viejo, *Belize* 147 D7 17 5N 89 8W
Bensheim, *Germany* 27 F4 49 40N 8 38 E
Benson, *U.S.A.* 143 L8 31 59N 110 19W
Bent, *Iran* 85 E8 26 20N 59 31 E
Benteng, *Indonesia* 72 C2 6 10 S 120 30 E
Bentinck I., *Australia* 114 B2 17 3 S 139 35 E
Bentiu, *Sudan* 95 F2 9 10N 29 55 E
Bento Gonçalves, *Brazil* 159 B5 29 10 S 51 31W
Benton, *Ark., U.S.A.* 139 H8 34 30N 92 35W
Benton, *Calif., U.S.A.* 144 H8 37 48N 118 32W
Benton, *Ill., U.S.A.* 140 G8 38 0N 88 55W
Benton Harbor, *U.S.A.* 141 B10 42 10N 86 28W
Bentu Liben, *Ethiopia* 95 F4 8 32N 38 21 E
Bentung, *Malaysia* 77 L3 3 31N 101 55 E
Benue □, *Nigeria* 101 D6 7 30N 7 30 E
Benue →, *Nigeria* 101 D6 7 48N 6 46 E
Benxi, *China* 67 D12 41 20N 123 48 E
Benzdorp, *Surinam* 153 C7 3 44N 54 5W
Beo, *Indonesia* 72 A3 4 25N 126 50 E
Beograd, *Serbia, Yug.* 42 C5 44 50N 20 37 E
Beowawe, *U.S.A.* 142 F5 40 35N 116 30W
Bepan Jiang →, *China* 68 E6 24 55N 106 5 E
Beppu, *Japan* 62 D3 33 15N 131 30 E
Beppu-Wan, *Japan* 62 D3 33 18N 131 34 E
Bera, *Bangla.* 78 C2 24 5N 89 37 E
Berati, *Albania* 44 D1 40 43N 19 59 E
Berau →, *Indonesia* 75 B5 2 10N 117 42 E
Berau, Teluk, *Indonesia* 73 B4 2 30 S 132 30 E
Berber, *Sudan* 94 D3 18 0N 34 0 E
Berbera, *Somali Rep.* 90 E4 10 30N 45 2 E
Berbérati, *C.A.R.* 102 B3 4 15N 15 40 E
Berberia, C. del, *Spain* 33 C7 38 39N 1 24 E
Berbice □, *Guyana* 153 C6 4 0N 58 0W
Berbice →, *Guyana* 153 B6 6 20N 57 32W
Berceto, *Italy* 38 D7 44 30N 10 0 E
Berchtesgaden, *Germany* 27 H8 47 37N 12 58 E
Berdale, *Somali Rep.* 108 C3 7 4N 47 51 E
Berdichev, *Ukraine* 52 B3 49 57N 28 30 E
Berdsk, *Russia* 56 D9 54 47N 83 2 E
Berdyansk, *Ukraine* 52 C7 46 45N 36 50 E
Berdyaush, *Russia* 54 D6 55 9N 59 9 E
Berea, *U.S.A.* 134 G3 37 35N 84 18W
Berebere, *Indonesia* 72 A3 2 25N 128 45 E
Bereda, *Somali Rep.* 90 E5 11 45N 51 0 E
Bereina, *Papua N. G.* 120 E4 8 39 S 146 30 E
Berekum, *Ghana* 100 D4 7 29N 2 34W
Berenice, *Egypt* 94 C4 24 2N 35 25 E
Berens →, *Canada* 131 C9 52 25N 97 2W
Berens I., *Canada* 131 C9 52 18N 97 18W
Berens River, *Canada* 131 C9 52 25N 97 0W
Berestechko, *Ukraine* 50 F4 50 22N 25 5 E
Bereşti, *Romania* 46 C8 46 6N 27 50 E
Beretău →, *Romania* 46 B2 47 10N 21 50 E
Berettyo →, *Hungary* 31 E14 46 59N 21 7 E
Berettyóújfalu, *Hungary* 31 D14 47 13N 21 33 E
Berevo, *Mahajanga, Madag.* 105 B7 17 14 S 44 17 E
Berevo, *Toliara, Madag.* 105 B7 19 44 S 44 58 E
Bereza, *Belorussia* 50 E4 52 31N 24 51 E
Berezhany, *Ukraine* 50 G4 49 26N 24 58 E
Berezina →, *Belorussia* 50 E7 52 33N 30 14 E
Berezna, *Ukraine* 50 F7 51 35N 31 46 E
Berezniki, *Russia* 54 B5 59 24N 56 46 E
Berezovka, *Ukraine* 52 C4 47 14N 30 55 E
Berezovo, *Russia* 48 B11 64 0N 65 0 E
Berga, *Spain* 34 C6 42 6N 1 48 E
Bergama, *Turkey* 88 D2 39 8N 27 15 E
Bergambacht, *Neths.* 20 E5 51 56N 4 48 E
Bérgamo, *Italy* 38 C6 45 42N 9 40 E
Bergantiños, *Spain* 36 B2 43 20N 8 40W
Bergara, *Spain* 34 B2 43 9N 2 28W
Bergedorf, *Germany* 26 B6 53 28N 10 12 E
Bergeijk, *Neths.* 21 F6 51 19N 5 21 E
Bergen, *Germany* 26 A9 54 24N 13 26 E
Bergen, *Neths.* 20 C5 52 40N 4 43 E
Bergen, *Norway* 13 F8 60 23N 5 20 E
Bergen, *U.S.A.* 136 C7 43 5N 77 56W
Bergen-op-Zoom, *Neths.* 21 F4 51 28N 4 18 E
Bergerac, *France* 24 D4 44 51N 0 30 E
Bergheim, *Germany* 26 E2 50 57N 6 38 E
Berghem, *Neths.* 20 E7 51 46N 5 33 E
Bergisch-Gladbach, *Germany* 26 E3 50 59N 7 9 E
Bergschenhoek, *Neths.* 20 E5 51 59N 4 30 E
Bergsjö, *Sweden* 14 C11 61 59N 17 3 E
Bergues, *France* 23 B9 50 58N 2 24 E
Bergum, *Neths.* 20 B7 53 13N 5 59 E
Bergville, *S. Africa* 105 D4 28 52 S 29 18 E
Berhala, Selat, *Indonesia* 74 C2 1 0 S 104 15 E
Berhampore = Baharampur, *India* 81 G13 24 2N 88 27 E
Berhampur, *India* 82 E7 19 15N 84 54 E
Berheci →, *Romania* 46 C8 46 7N 27 19 E
Bering Sea, *Pac. Oc.* 126 C1 58 0N 171 0 E
Bering Str., *U.S.A.* 126 B3 66 0N 170 0W
Beringen, *Belgium* 21 F6 51 3N 5 14 E
Beringen, *Switz.* 29 A7 47 38N 8 34 E
Beringovskiy, *Russia* 57 C18 63 3N 179 19 E
Berislav, *Ukraine* 52 C5 46 50N 33 30 E
Berisso, *Argentina* 158 C4 34 56 S 57 50W
Berja, *Spain* 35 J2 36 50N 2 56W
Berkane, *Morocco* 99 B4 34 52N 2 20W
Berkel →, *Neths.* 20 D8 52 8N 6 12 E
Berkeley, *U.K.* 17 F5 51 41N 2 28W
Berkeley, *U.S.A.* 144 H4 37 52N 122 20W
Berkeley Springs, *U.S.A.* 134 F6 39 38N 78 12W
Berkhout, *Neths.* 20 C5 52 38N 4 59 E
Berkner I., *Antarctica* 7 D18 79 30 S 50 0W
Berkovitsa, *Bulgaria* 43 D8 43 16N 23 8 E
Berkshire □, *U.K.* 17 F6 51 30N 1 20W
Berlaar, *Belgium* 21 F5 51 7N 4 39 E
Berland →, *Canada* 130 C5 54 0N 116 50W
Berlanga, *Spain* 37 G5 38 17N 5 50W
Berlare, *Belgium* 21 F4 51 2N 4 2 E
Berlenga, I., *Portugal* 37 F1 39 25N 9 30W
Berlin, *Germany* 26 C9 52 32N 13 24 E
Berlin, *Md., U.S.A.* 134 F8 38 19N 75 12W
Berlin, *N.H., U.S.A.* 137 B13 44 29N 71 10W
Berlin, *Wis., U.S.A.* 134 D1 43 58N 88 55W
Bermeja, Sierra, *Spain* 37 J5 36 30N 5 11W
Bermejo →, *Formosa, Argentina* 158 B4 26 51 S 58 23W
Bermejo →, *San Juan, Argentina* 158 C2 32 30 S 67 30W
Bermeo, *Spain* 34 B2 43 25N 2 47W
Bermillo de Sayago, *Spain* 36 D4 41 22N 6 8W
Bermuda ■, *Atl. Oc.* 8 E2 32 45N 65 0W
Bern, *Switz.* 28 C4 46 57N 7 28 E
Bern □, *Switz.* 28 C5 46 45N 7 40 E
Bernado, *U.S.A.* 143 J10 34 30N 106 53W
Bernalda, *Italy* 41 B9 40 24N 16 44 E
Bernalillo, *U.S.A.* 143 J10 35 17N 106 37W
Bernam →, *Malaysia* 74 B2 3 45N 101 5 E
Bernardo de Irigoyen, *Argentina* 159 B5 26 15 S 53 40W
Bernardo O'Higgins □, *Chile* 158 C1 34 15 S 70 45W
Bernasconi, *Argentina* 158 D3 37 55 S 63 44W
Bernau, *Bayern, Germany* 27 H8 47 45N 12 20 E
Bernau, *Brandenburg, Germany* 26 C9 52 40N 13 35 E
Bernay, *France* 22 C7 49 5N 0 35 E
Bernburg, *Germany* 26 D7 51 40N 11 42 E
Berndorf, *Austria* 30 D9 47 59N 16 1 E
Berne = Bern, *Switz.* 28 C4 46 57N 7 28 E
Berne = Bern □, *Switz.* 28 C5 46 45N 7 40 E
Berne, *U.S.A.* 141 D12 40 39N 84 57W
Berner Alpen, *Switz.* 28 D5 46 27N 7 35 E
Bernese Oberland = Oberland, *Switz.* 28 C5 46 35N 7 38 E
Bernier I., *Australia* 113 D1 24 50 S 113 12 E
Bernina, Piz, *Switz.* 29 D9 46 20N 9 54 E
Bernina, Pizzo, *Switz.* 29 D9 46 22N 9 54 E
Bernissart, *Belgium* 21 H3 50 28N 3 39 E
Bernkastel-Kues, *Germany* 27 F3 49 55N 7 4 E
Beroroha, *Madag.* 105 C8 21 40 S 45 10 E
Béroubouay, *Benin* 101 C5 10 34N 2 46 E
Beroun, *Czech.* 30 B7 49 57N 14 5 E
Berounka →, *Czech.* 30 B7 50 0N 14 22 E
Berovo, *Macedonia, Yug.* 42 F7 41 38N 22 51 E
Berrahal, *Algeria* 99 A6 36 54N 7 33 E
Berre, Étang de, *France* 25 E9 43 27N 5 5 E
Berrechid, *Morocco* 98 B3 33 18N 7 36W
Berri, *Australia* 116 C4 34 14 S 140 35 E
Berriane, *Algeria* 99 B5 32 50N 3 46 E
Berrien Springs, *U.S.A.* 141 C10 41 57N 86 20W
Berrigan, *Australia* 117 C6 35 38 S 145 49 E
Berriwillock, *Australia* 116 C5 35 36 S 142 59 E
Berrouaghia, *Algeria* 99 A5 36 10N 2 53 E
Berry, *Australia* 117 C9 34 46 S 150 43 E
Berry, *France* 23 F8 46 50N 2 0 E
Berry, *U.S.A.* 141 F12 38 31N 84 23W
Berry Is., *Bahamas* 148 A4 25 40N 77 50W
Berryessa, L., *U.S.A.* 144 G4 38 31N 122 6W
Berryville, *U.S.A.* 139 G8 36 23N 93 35W
Bersenbrück, *Germany* 26 C3 52 33N 7 56 E
Berthold, *U.S.A.* 138 A4 48 19N 101 45W
Berthoud, *U.S.A.* 138 E2 40 21N 105 5W
Bertincourt, *France* 23 B9 50 5N 2 58 E
Bertoua, *Cameroon* 102 B2 4 30N 13 45 E
Bertrand, *U.S.A.* 138 E5 40 35N 99 38W
Bertrange, *Lux.* 21 J8 49 37N 6 3 E
Bertrix, *Belgium* 21 J6 49 51N 5 15 E
Berufjörður, *Iceland* 12 D6 64 48N 14 29W
Beruri, *Brazil* 153 D5 3 54 S 61 22W
Berwick, *U.S.A.* 137 E8 41 4N 76 17W
Berwick-upon-Tweed, *U.K.* 16 B5 55 47N 2 0W
Berwyn Mts., *U.K.* 16 E4 52 54N 3 26W
Berzasca, *Romania* 42 C6 44 39N 21 58 E
Berzence, *Hungary* 31 E10 46 12N 17 11 E
Besal, *Pakistan* 81 B5 35 4N 73 56 E
Besalampy, *Madag.* 105 B7 16 43 S 44 29 E
Besançon, *France* 23 E13 47 15N 6 2 E
Besar, *Indonesia* 75 C5 2 40 S 116 0 E
Besar, Gunong, *Malaysia* 74 A2 5 10N 101 18 E
Beshenkovichi, *Belorussia* 50 D6 55 2N 29 29 E
Beška, *Serbia, Yug.* 42 B5 45 8N 20 6 E
Beskids = Beskydy, *Europe* 31 B11 49 35N 18 40 E
Beskydy, *Europe* 31 B11 49 35N 18 40 E
Beslan, *Russia* 53 E11 43 15N 44 28 E
Besna Kobila, *Serbia, Yug.* 42 E7 42 31N 22 10 E
Besnard L., *Canada* 131 B7 55 25N 106 0W
Besni, *Turkey* 89 E7 37 41N 37 52 E
Besor, N. →, *Egypt* 91 D3 31 28N 34 22 E
Beşparmak Dağı, *Turkey* 45 G9 37 32N 27 30 E
Bessa Monteiro, *Angola* 103 D2 7 7 S 13 44 E
Bessarabiya, *Moldavia* 46 C9 47 0N 28 10 E
Bessarabka, *Moldavia* 52 C3 46 21N 28 58 E
Besseges, *France* 25 D8 44 18N 4 8 E
Bessemer, *Ala., U.S.A.* 135 J2 33 25N 86 57W
Bessemer, *Mich., U.S.A.* 138 B9 46 27N 90 5W
Bessin, *France* 22 C5 49 18N 1 0W
Bessines-sur-Gartempe, *France* 24 B5 46 6N 1 22 E
Best, *Neths.* 21 E6 51 31N 5 23 E
Bet She'an, *Israel* 91 C4 32 30N 35 30 E
Bet Shemesh, *Israel* 91 D3 31 44N 35 0 E
Bet Tadjine, Djebel, *Algeria* 98 C4 29 0N 3 30W
Betafo, *Madag.* 105 B8 19 50 S 46 51 E
Betancuria, *Canary Is.* 33 F5 28 25N 14 3W
Betanzos, *Bolivia* 157 D4 19 34 S 65 27W
Betanzos, *Spain* 36 B2 43 15N 8 12W
Bétaré Oya, *Cameroon* 102 A2 5 40N 14 5 E
Bétera, *Spain* 34 F4 39 35N 0 28W
Bethal, *S. Africa* 105 D4 26 27 S 29 28 E
Bethanien, *Namibia* 104 D2 26 31 S 17 8 E
Bethany, *S. Africa* 104 D4 29 34 S 25 59 E
Bethany, *Ill., U.S.A.* 141 E8 39 39N 88 45W
Bethany, *Mo., U.S.A.* 140 D2 40 18N 94 3W
Bethel, *Alaska, U.S.A.* 126 B3 60 50N 161 50W
Bethel, *Ohio, U.S.A.* 141 F12 38 58N 84 5W
Bethel, *Vt., U.S.A.* 137 C12 43 50N 72 38W
Bethel Park, *U.S.A.* 136 F4 40 20N 80 2W
Bethlehem = Bayt Lahm, *Jordan* 91 D4 31 43N 35 12 E
Bethlehem, *S. Africa* 105 D4 28 14 S 28 18 E
Bethlehem, *U.S.A.* 137 F9 40 39N 75 24W
Bethulie, *S. Africa* 104 E4 30 30 S 25 59 E
Béthune, *France* 23 B9 50 30N 2 38 E
Béthune →, *France* 22 C8 49 53N 1 9 E
Bethungra, *Australia* 117 C7 34 45 S 147 51 E
Betijoque, *Venezuela* 152 B3 9 23N 70 44W
Betim, *Brazil* 155 E3 19 58 S 44 7W
Betioky, *Madag.* 105 C7 23 48 S 44 20 E
Beton-Bazoches, *France* 23 D10 48 42N 3 15 E
Betong, *Thailand* 77 K3 5 45N 101 5 E
Betoota, *Australia* 114 D3 25 45 S 140 42 E
Betroka, *Madag.* 105 C8 23 16 S 46 0 E
Betsiamites, *Canada* 129 C6 48 56N 68 40W
Betsiamites →, *Canada* 129 C6 48 56N 68 38W
Betsiboka →, *Madag.* 105 B8 16 3 S 46 36 E
Betsjoeanaland, *S. Africa* 104 D3 26 30 S 22 30 E
Bettembourg, *Lux.* 21 J8 49 31N 6 6 E
Bettendorf, *U.S.A.* 140 C6 41 32N 90 30W
Bettiah, *India* 81 F11 26 48N 84 33 E
Bèttola, *Italy* 38 D6 44 44N 9 32 E
Betul, *India* 82 D3 21 58N 77 59 E
Betung, *Malaysia* 75 B4 1 24N 111 31 E
Betzdorf, *Germany* 26 E3 50 47N 7 53 E
Beuca, *Romania* 46 E5 44 14N 24 56 E
Beuil, *France* 25 D10 44 6N 6 59 E
Beulah, *U.S.A.* 138 B4 47 18N 101 47W
Beuvron →, *France* 22 E8 47 29N 1 15 E
Beveren, *Belgium* 21 F4 51 12N 4 16 E
Beverley, *Australia* 113 F2 32 9 S 116 56 E
Beverley, *U.K.* 16 D7 53 52N 0 26W
Beverlo, *Belgium* 21 F6 51 7N 5 13 E
Beverly, *Mass., U.S.A.* 137 D14 42 32N 70 50W
Beverly, *Wash., U.S.A.* 142 C4 46 55N 119 59W
Beverly Hills, *U.S.A.* 145 L8 34 4N 118 29W
Beverwijk, *Neths.* 20 D5 52 28N 4 38 E
Bex, *Switz.* 28 D4 46 15N 7 0 E
Bey Dağları, *Turkey* 88 E4 36 45N 30 15 E
Beyānlū, *Iran* 84 C5 36 0N 47 51 E
Beyin, *Ghana* 100 D4 5 1N 2 41W
Beykoz, *Turkey* 43 F14 41 8N 29 7 E
Beyla, *Guinea* 100 D3 8 30N 8 38W
Beynat, *France* 24 C5 45 8N 1 44 E
Beyneu, *Kazakhstan* 49 E10 45 10N 55 3 E
Beypazarı, *Turkey* 88 C4 40 10N 31 56 E
Beypore →, *India* 83 J2 11 10N 75 47 E
Beyşehir Gölü, *Turkey* 88 E4 37 40N 31 45 E
Beytüşşebap, *Turkey* 89 E10 37 35N 43 10 E
Bezdan, *Serbia, Yug.* 42 B3 45 50N 18 57 E
Bezhetsk, *Russia* 51 C10 57 47N 36 39 E
Bezhitsa, *Russia* 50 E9 53 19N 34 17 E
Béziers, *France* 24 E7 43 20N 3 12 E
Bezwada = Vijayawada, *India* 83 F5 16 31N 80 39 E
Bhadarwah, *India* 81 C6 32 58N 75 46 E
Bhadra →, *India* 83 H2 14 0N 75 20 E
Bhadrakh, *India* 82 D8 21 10N 86 30 E
Bhadravati, *India* 83 H2 13 49N 75 40 E
Bhagalpur, *India* 81 G12 25 10N 87 0 E
Bhainsa, *India* 82 E3 19 10N 77 58 E
Bhairab →, *Bangla.* 78 D2 22 51N 89 34 E
Bhairab Bazar, *Bangla.* 78 C3 24 4N 90 58 E
Bhakkar, *Pakistan* 79 C3 31 40N 71 5 E
Bhakra Dam, *India* 80 D7 31 30N 76 45 E
Bhamo, *Burma* 78 C6 24 15N 97 15 E
Bhamragarh, *India* 82 E5 19 30N 80 40 E
Bhandara, *India* 82 D4 21 5N 79 42 E
Bhanrer Ra., *India* 80 H8 23 40N 79 45 E
Bharat = India ■, *Asia* 59 H11 20 0N 78 0 E
Bharatpur, *India* 80 F7 27 15N 77 30 E
Bharuch, *India* 82 D1 21 47N 73 0 E
Bhatghar L., *India* 82 E1 18 10N 73 48 E
Bhatiapara Ghat, *Bangla.* 78 D2 23 13N 89 42 E
Bhatinda, *India* 80 D6 30 15N 74 57 E
Bhatkal, *India* 83 H2 13 58N 74 35 E
Bhatpara, *India* 81 H13 22 50N 88 25 E
Bhattiprolu, *India* 83 F5 16 7N 80 45 E
Bhaun, *Pakistan* 80 C5 32 55N 72 40 E
Bhaunagar = Bhavnagar, *India* 80 J5 21 45N 72 10 E
Bhavani, *India* 83 J3 11 27N 77 43 E
Bhavani →, *India* 83 J4 11 0N 78 15 E
Bhavnagar, *India* 80 J5 21 45N 72 10 E
Bhawanipatna, *India* 82 E5 19 55N 80 10 E
Bhera, *Pakistan* 80 C5 32 29N 72 57 E
Bhilsa = Vidisha, *India* 80 H7 23 28N 77 53 E
Bhilwara, *India* 80 G6 25 25N 74 38 E
Bhima →, *India* 82 F3 16 25N 77 17 E
Bhimavaram, *India* 83 F5 16 30N 81 30 E
Bhimbar, *Pakistan* 81 C6 32 59N 74 3 E
Bhind, *India* 81 F8 26 30N 78 46 E
Bhiwandi, *India* 82 E1 19 20N 73 0 E
Bhiwani, *India* 80 E7 28 50N 76 9 E
Bhola, *Bangla.* 78 D3 22 45N 90 35 E
Bhongir, *India* 82 F4 17 30N 78 56 E
Bhopal, *India* 80 H7 23 20N 77 30 E
Bhor, *India* 82 E1 18 12N 73 53 E
Bhubaneshwar, *India* 82 D7 20 15N 85 50 E
Bhuj, *India* 80 H3 23 15N 69 49 E
Bhumiphol Dam = Phumiphon, Khuan, *Thailand* 76 D2 17 15N 98 58 E
Bhusaval, *India* 82 D2 21 3N 75 46 E
Bhutan ■, *Asia* 78 B3 27 25N 90 30 E
Biá →, *Brazil* 152 D4 3 28 S 67 23W
Biafra, B. of = Bonny, Bight of, *Africa* 101 E6 3 30N 9 20 E
Biak, *Indonesia* 73 B5 1 10 S 136 6 E
Biała, *Poland* 47 E4 50 24N 17 40 E
Biała →, *Białystok, Poland* 47 B10 53 11N 23 4 E
Biała →, *Tarnów, Poland* 31 A13 50 3N 20 55 E
Biała Piska, *Poland* 47 B9 53 37N 22 5 E
Biała Podlaska, *Poland* 47 C10 52 4N 23 6 E
Biała Podlaska □, *Poland* 47 D10 52 0N 23 0 E
Biała Rawska, *Poland* 47 D7 51 48N 20 29 E
Białobrzegi, *Poland* 47 C8 52 27N 21 3 E
Białogard, *Poland* 47 A2 54 2N 15 58 E
Białowieza, *Poland* 47 C10 52 41N 23 49 E
Biały Bór, *Poland* 47 B3 53 53N 16 51 E
Białystok, *Poland* 47 B10 53 10N 23 10 E
Białystok □, *Poland* 47 B10 53 9N 23 10 E
Biancavilla, *Italy* 41 E7 37 39N 14 50 E
Bīārjmand, *Iran* 85 B7 36 6N 55 53 E
Biaro, *Indonesia* 72 A3 2 5N 125 26 E
Biarritz, *France* 24 E2 43 29N 1 33W
Biasca, *Switz.* 29 D7 46 22N 8 58 E
Biba, *Egypt* 94 J7 28 55N 31 0 E
Bibai, *Japan* 60 C10 43 19N 141 52 E
Bibala, *Angola* 103 E2 14 44 S 13 24 E
Bibane, Bahiret el, *Tunisia* 96 B2 33 16N 11 13 E
Bibassé, *Gabon* 102 B2 1 27N 11 37 E
Bibbiena, *Italy* 39 E8 43 43N 11 50 E
Bibby I., *Canada* 131 A10 61 55N 93 0W
Biberach, *Germany* 27 G5 48 5N 9 49 E
Biberist, *Switz.* 28 B5 47 11N 7 34 E
Bibey →, *Spain* 36 C3 42 24N 7 13W
Bibiani, *Ghana* 100 D4 6 30N 2 8W
Bibile, *Sri Lanka* 83 L5 7 10N 81 25 E
Biboohra, *Australia* 114 B4 16 56 S 145 25 E
Bibungwa, *Zaïre* 106 C2 2 40 S 28 15 E
Bic, *Canada* 129 C6 48 20N 68 41W
Bicaj, *Albania* 44 C2 41 58N 20 25 E
Bicaz, *Romania* 46 C7 46 53N 26 5 E
Biccari, *Italy* 41 A8 41 23N 15 12 E
Bichena, *Ethiopia* 95 E4 10 28N 38 10 E
Bickerton I., *Australia* 114 A2 13 45 S 136 10 E
Bicknell, *Ind., U.S.A.* 141 F9 38 50N 87 20W
Bicknell, *Utah, U.S.A.* 143 G8 38 16N 111 35W
Bida, *Nigeria* 101 D6 9 3N 5 58 E
Bida, *Zaïre* 102 B3 4 55N 19 56 E
Bidar, *India* 82 F3 17 55N 77 35 E
Biddeford, *U.S.A.* 129 D5 43 30N 70 28W
Biddwara, *Ethiopia* 95 F4 5 11N 38 34 E
Bideford, *U.K.* 17 F3 51 1N 4 13W
Bidon 5 = Poste Maurice Cortier, *Algeria* 99 D5 22 14N 1 2 E
Bidor, *Malaysia* 77 K3 4 6N 101 15 E
Bidura, *Australia* 116 C5 34 10 S 143 21 E
Bié □, *Angola* 103 E3 12 30 S 17 0 E
Bié, Planalto de, *Angola* 103 E3 12 0 S 16 0 E
Bieber, *U.S.A.* 142 F3 41 4N 121 6W
Biebrza →, *Poland* 47 B9 53 13N 22 25 E
Biecz, *Poland* 31 B14 49 44N 21 15 E
Biel, *Switz.* 28 B4 47 8N 7 14 E
Bielawa, *Poland* 47 E3 50 43N 16 37 E
Bielé Karpaty, *Czech.* 31 B10 49 5N 18 0 E
Bielefeld, *Germany* 26 C4 52 2N 8 31 E
Bielersee, *Switz.* 28 B4 47 6N 7 5 E
Biella, *Italy* 38 C5 45 33N 8 3 E
Bielsk Podlaski, *Poland* 47 C10 52 47N 23 12 E
Bielsko-Biała, *Poland* 31 B12 49 50N 19 2 E
Bielsko-Biała □, *Poland* 31 B12 49 45N 19 15 E
Bien Hoa, *Vietnam* 77 G6 10 57N 106 49 E

Blaenau Ffestiniog 175

Bienfait, *Canada* 131 **D8** 49 10N 102 50W
Bienne = Biel, *Switz.* 28 **B4** 47 8N 7 14 E
Bienvenida, *Spain* 37 **G4** 38 18N 6 12W
Bienvenue, *Fr. Guiana* 153 **C7** 3 0N 52 30W
Bienville, L., *Canada* 128 **A5** 55 5N 72 40W
Biescas, *Spain* 34 **C4** 42 37N 0 20W
Biese →, *Germany* 26 **C7** 52 53N 11 46 E
Biesiesfontein, *S. Africa* 104 **E2** 30 57 S 17 58 E
Bietigheim, *Germany* 27 **G5** 48 57N 9 8 E
Bievre, *Belgium* 21 **J6** 49 57N 5 1 E
Biferno →, *Italy* 41 **A8** 41 59N 15 2 E
Bifoum, *Gabon* 102 **C2** 0 20 S 10 23 E
Big →, *Canada* 129 **B8** 54 50N 58 55W
Big →, *U.S.A.* 140 **F6** 38 27N 90 37W
Big B., *Canada* 129 **A7** 55 43N 60 35W
Big B., *N.Z.* 119 **E3** 44 28 S 168 4 E
Big Bear City, *U.S.A.* 145 **L10** 34 16N 116 51W
Big Bear L., *U.S.A.* 145 **L10** 34 15N 116 56W
Big Beaver, *Canada* 131 **D7** 49 10N 105 10W
Big Belt Mts., *U.S.A.* 142 **C8** 46 50N 111 30W
Big Bend, *Swaziland* 105 **D5** 26 50 S 31 58 E
Big Bend Nat. Park, *U.S.A.* 139 **L3** 29 15N 103 15W
Big Black →, *U.S.A.* 139 **J9** 32 0N 91 5W
Big Blue →, *Ind., U.S.A.* 141 **E11** 39 12N 85 56W
Big Blue →, *Kans., U.S.A.* 138 **F6** 39 11N 96 40W
Big Cr. →, *Canada* 130 **C4** 51 42N 122 41W
Big Creek, *U.S.A.* 144 **H7** 37 11N 119 14W
Big Cypress Swamp, *U.S.A.* 135 **M5** 26 12N 81 10W
Big Falls, *U.S.A.* 138 **A8** 48 11N 93 48W
Big Fork →, *U.S.A.* 138 **A8** 48 31N 93 43W
Big Horn Mts. = Bighorn Mts., *U.S.A.* 142 **D10** 44 30N 107 30W
Big Lake, *U.S.A.* 139 **K4** 31 12N 101 25W
Big Moose, *U.S.A.* 137 **C10** 43 49N 74 58W
Big Muddy →, *Ill., U.S.A.* 140 **G8** 38 0N 89 0W
Big Muddy →, *Mont., U.S.A.* 138 **A2** 48 8N 104 36W
Big Pine, *U.S.A.* 144 **H8** 37 12N 118 17W
Big Piney, *U.S.A.* 142 **E8** 42 32N 110 3W
Big Quill L., *Canada* 131 **C8** 51 55N 104 50W
Big Rapids, *U.S.A.* 134 **D3** 43 42N 85 27W
Big River, *Canada* 131 **C7** 53 50N 107 0W
Big Run, *U.S.A.* 136 **F6** 40 57N 78 55W
Big Sable Pt., *U.S.A.* 134 **C2** 44 5N 86 30W
Big Sand L., *Canada* 131 **B9** 57 45N 99 45W
Big Sandy, *U.S.A.* 142 **B8** 48 12N 110 9W
Big Sandy Cr. →, *U.S.A.* 138 **F3** 38 6N 102 29W
Big Sioux →, *U.S.A.* 138 **D6** 42 30N 96 25W
Big Spring, *U.S.A.* 139 **J4** 32 10N 101 25W
Big Springs, *U.S.A.* 138 **E3** 41 4N 102 3W
Big Stone City, *U.S.A.* 138 **C6** 45 20N 96 30W
Big Stone Gap, *U.S.A.* 135 **G4** 36 52N 82 45W
Big Stone L., *U.S.A.* 138 **C6** 45 30N 96 35W
Big Sur, *U.S.A.* 144 **J5** 36 15N 121 48W
Big Timber, *U.S.A.* 142 **D9** 45 53N 110 0W
Big Trout L., *Canada* 128 **B1** 53 40N 90 0W
Biğa, *Turkey* 88 **C2** 40 13N 27 14 E
Bigadiç, *Turkey* 88 **D3** 39 22N 28 7 E
Biganos, *France* 24 **D3** 44 39N 0 59W
Bigfork, *U.S.A.* 142 **B6** 48 3N 114 2W
Biggar, *Canada* 131 **C7** 52 4N 108 0W
Biggar, *U.K.* 18 **F5** 55 38N 3 31W
Bigge I., *Australia* 112 **B4** 14 35 S 125 10 E
Biggenden, *Australia* 115 **D5** 25 31 S 152 4 E
Biggs, *U.S.A.* 144 **F5** 39 24N 121 43W
Bighorn, *U.S.A.* 142 **C10** 46 11N 107 25W
Bighorn →, *U.S.A.* 142 **C10** 46 9N 107 28W
Bighorn Mts., *U.S.A.* 142 **D10** 44 30N 107 30W
Bignona, *Senegal* 100 **C1** 12 52N 16 14W
Bigorre, *France* 24 **E4** 43 10N 0 5 E
Bigstone L., *Canada* 131 **C9** 53 42N 95 44W
Bigwa, *Tanzania* 106 **D4** 7 10 S 39 10 E
Bihać, *Bos.-H., Yug.* 39 **D12** 44 49N 15 57 E
Bihar, *India* 81 **G11** 25 5N 85 40 E
Bihar □, *India* 81 **G11** 25 0N 86 0 E
Biharamulo, *Tanzania* 106 **C3** 2 25 S 31 25 E
Biharamulo □, *Tanzania* 106 **C3** 2 30 S 31 20 E
Biharkeresztes, *Hungary* 31 **D14** 47 8N 21 44 E
Bihor □, *Romania* 46 **C3** 47 0N 22 10 E
Bihor, Munţii, *Romania* 46 **C3** 46 29N 22 47 E
Bijagós, Arquipélago dos, *Guinea-Biss.* 100 **C1** 11 15N 16 10W
Bijaipur, *India* 80 **F7** 26 2N 77 20 E
Bijapur, *Karnataka, India* 82 **F2** 16 50N 75 55 E
Bijapur, *Mad. P., India* 82 **E5** 18 50N 80 50 E
Bījār, *Iran* 84 **C5** 35 52N 47 35 E
Bijeljina, *Bos.-H., Yug.* 42 **C4** 44 46N 19 17 E
Bijelo Polje, *Montenegro, Yug.* 42 **D4** 43 1N 19 45 E
Bijie, *China* 68 **D5** 27 20N 105 16 E
Bijni, *India* 78 **B3** 26 30N 90 40 E
Bijnor, *India* 80 **E8** 29 27N 78 11 E
Bikaner, *India* 80 **E5** 28 2N 73 18 E
Bikapur, *India* 81 **F10** 26 30N 82 7 E
Bikeqi, *China* 66 **D6** 40 43N 111 20 E
Bikfayyā, *Lebanon* 91 **B4** 33 55N 35 41 E
Bikin, *Russia* 57 **E14** 46 50N 134 20 E
Bikin →, *Russia* 60 **A7** 46 51N 134 2 E
Bikini Atoll, *Pac. Oc.* 122 **F8** 12 0N 167 30 E
Bikoro, *Zaïre* 102 **C3** 0 48 S 18 15 E
Bikoué, *Cameroon* 101 **E7** 3 55N 11 50 E
Bilara, *India* 80 **F5** 26 14N 73 53 E
Bilaspara, *India* 78 **B3** 26 13N 90 14 E
Bilaspur, *Mad. P., India* 81 **H10** 22 2N 82 15 E
Bilaspur, *Punjab, India* 80 **D7** 31 19N 76 50 E
Bilauk Taungdan, *Thailand* 76 **F2** 13 0N 99 0 E
Bilbao, *Spain* 34 **B2** 43 16N 2 56W
Bilbeis, *Egypt* 94 **H7** 30 25N 31 34 E
Bilbor, *Romania* 46 **B6** 47 6N 25 30 E
Bíldudalur, *Iceland* 12 **D2** 65 41N 23 36W
Bileća, *Bos.-H., Yug.* 42 **E3** 42 53N 18 27 E
Bilecik, *Turkey* 88 **C4** 40 5N 30 5 E
Bilecik □, *Turkey* 88 **C4** 40 0N 30 0 E
Bilgoraj, *Poland* 47 **E9** 50 33N 22 42 E
Bilibino, *Russia* 57 **C17** 68 3N 166 20 E
Bilibiza, *Mozam.* 107 **E5** 12 30 S 40 20 E
Bilin, *Burma* 78 **G6** 17 14N 97 15 E
Bilir, *Russia* 57 **C14** 65 40N 131 20 E
Biliran I., *Phil.* 71 **F5** 11 35N 124 28 E
Bilishti, *Albania* 44 **D3** 40 37N 21 2 E
Bill, *U.S.A.* 138 **D2** 43 18N 105 18W
Billabalong, *Australia* 113 **E2** 27 25 S 115 49 E
Billiluna, *Australia* 112 **C4** 19 37 S 127 41 E
Billingham, *U.K.* 16 **C6** 54 36N 1 18W
Billings, *U.S.A.* 142 **D9** 45 43N 108 29W
Billiton Is. = Belitung, *Indonesia* 75 **C3** 3 10 S 107 50 E
Billom, *France* 24 **C7** 45 43N 3 20 E
Bilma, *Niger* 97 **E2** 18 50N 13 30 E
Bilo Gora, *Croatia* 42 **B2** 45 53N 17 15 E
Biloela, *Australia* 114 **C5** 24 24 S 150 31 E
Biloku, *Guyana* 153 **C6** 1 50N 58 25W
Biloxi, *U.S.A.* 139 **K10** 30 24N 88 53W
Bilpa Morea Claypan, *Australia* 114 **D2** 25 0 S 140 0 E
Bilthoven, *Neths.* 20 **D6** 52 8N 5 12 E
Biltine, *Chad* 97 **F4** 14 40N 20 50 E
Bilugyun, *Burma* 78 **G6** 16 24N 97 32 E
Bilyana, *Australia* 114 **B4** 18 5 S 145 50 E
Bilyarsk, *Russia* 54 **D2** 54 58N 50 22 E
Bilzen, *Belgium* 21 **G7** 50 52N 5 31 E
Bima, *Indonesia* 75 **D5** 8 22 S 118 49 E
Bimban, *Egypt* 94 [illegible] 24 24N 32 54 E
Bimberi Pk., *Australia* 117 [illegible] 35 44 S 148 51 E
Bimbila, *Ghana* 101 **D5** 8 54N 0 [illegible] E
Bimbo, *C.A.R.* 102 **B3** 4 15N 18 33 E
Bimini Is., *Bahamas* 148 **A4** 25 42N 79 25W
Bin Xian, *Heilongjiang, China* 67 **B14** 45 42N 127 32 E
Bin Xian, *Shaanxi, China* 66 **G5** 35 2N 108 4 E
Bina-Etawah, *India* 80 **G8** 24 13N 78 14 E
Bināb, *Iran* 85 **B6** 36 35N 48 41 E
Binaiya, *Indonesia* 73 **B3** 3 11 S 129 26 E
Binalbagan, *Phil.* 71 **F4** 10 12N 122 50 E
Binalong, *Australia* 117 **C8** 34 40 S 148 39 E
Bīnālūd, Kūh-e, *Iran* 85 **B8** 36 30N 58 30 E
Binatang, *Malaysia* 75 **B4** 2 10N 111 40 E
Binbee, *Australia* 114 **C4** 20 19 S 147 56 E
Binche, *Belgium* 21 **H4** 50 26N 4 10 E
Binchuan, *China* 68 **E3** 25 42N 100 38 E
Binda, *Australia* 115 **D4** 27 52 S 147 21 E
Binda, *Zaïre* 103 **D2** 5 52 S 13 14 E
Bindle, *Australia* 115 **D4** 27 40 S 148 45 E
Bindoy, *Phil.* 71 **G4** 9 48N 123 5 E
Bindura, *Zimbabwe* 107 **F3** 17 18 S 31 18 E
Bingara, *N.S.W., Australia* 115 **D5** 29 52 S 150 36 E
Bingara, *Queens., Australia* 115 **D3** 28 10 S 144 37 E
Bingen, *Germany* 27 **F3** 49 57N 7 53 E
Bingerville, *Ivory C.* 100 **D4** 5 18N 3 49W
Bingham, *U.S.A.* 129 **C6** 45 5N 69 50W
Bingham Canyon, *U.S.A.* 142 **F7** 40 31N 112 10W
Binghamton, *U.S.A.* 137 **D9** 42 9N 75 54W
Bingöl, *Turkey* 89 **D9** 38 53N 40 29 E
Bingöl □, *Turkey* 89 **D9** 38 55N 40 30 E
Bingöl Dağları, *Turkey* 89 **D9** 39 20N 40 40 E
Binh Dinh = An Nhon, *Vietnam* 76 **F7** 13 55N 109 7 E
Binh Khe, *Vietnam* 76 **F7** 13 57N 108 51 E
Binh Son, *Vietnam* 76 **E7** 15 20N 108 40 E
Binhai, *China* 67 **G10** 34 2N 119 49 E
Binisatua, *Spain* 33 **B11** 39 50N 4 11 E
Binjai, *Indonesia* 74 **B1** 3 20N 98 30 E
Binnaway, *Australia* 117 **A8** 31 28 S 149 24 E
Binongko, *Indonesia* 72 **C2** 5 55 S 123 55 E
Binscarth, *Canada* 131 **C8** 50 37N 101 17W
Bintan, *Indonesia* 74 **B2** 1 0N 104 0 E
Bintuni, *Indonesia* 73 **B4** 2 7 S 133 32 E
Binyang, *China* 68 **F7** 23 12N 108 47 E
Binz, *Germany* 26 **A9** 54 23N 13 37 E
Binza, *Zaïre* 103 **C3** 4 21 S 15 14 E
Binzert = Bizerte, *Tunisia* 96 **A1** 37 15N 9 50 E
Bío Bío □, *Chile* 158 **D1** 37 35 S 72 0W
Biograd, *Croatia* 39 **E12** 43 56N 15 29 E
Bioko, *Eq. Guin.* 101 **E6** 3 30N 8 40 E
Biokovo, *Croatia* 42 **D2** 43 23N 17 0 E
Biougra, *Morocco* 98 **B3** 30 15N 9 14W
Bir, *India* 82 **E2** 19 4N 75 46 E
Bir, Ras, *Djibouti* 95 **E5** 12 0N 43 20 E
Bîr Abu Hashim, *Egypt* 94 **C3** 23 42N 34 6 E
Bîr Abu M'nqar, *Egypt* 94 **B2** 26 33N 27 33 E
Bîr Abu Muḥammad, *Egypt* 91 **F3** 29 44N 34 14 E
Bi'r ad Dabbāghāt, *Jordan* 91 **E4** 30 26N 35 32 E
Bîr Adal Deib, *Sudan* 94 **C4** 22 35N 36 10 E
Bi'r al Butayyihāt, *Jordan* 91 **F4** 29 47N 35 20 E
Bi'r al Malfa, *Libya* 96 **B3** 31 58N 15 18 E
Bi'r al Mārī, *Jordan* 91 **E4** 30 4N 35 33 E
Bi'r al Qattār, *Jordan* 91 **F4** 29 47N 35 32 E
Bir 'Ali, *Yemen* 87 **D5** 14 1N 48 20 E
Bir Aouine, *Tunisia* 96 **B1** 32 25N 9 18 E
Bîr 'Asal, *Egypt* 94 **B3** 25 55N 34 20 E
Bir Autrun, *Sudan* 95 **D2** 18 15N 26 40 E
Bîr Beiḍa, *Egypt* 91 **E3** 30 25N 34 29 E
Bi'r Dhu'fān, *Libya* 96 **B2** 31 59N 14 32 E
Bîr Diqnash, *Egypt* 94 **A2** 31 3N 25 23 E
Bir el Abbes, *Algeria* 98 **C3** 26 7N 6 9W
Bîr el 'Abd, *Egypt* 91 **D2** 31 2N 33 0 E
Bir el Ater, *Algeria* 99 **B6** 34 46N 8 3 E
Bîr el Basur, *Egypt* 94 **B2** 29 51N 25 49 E
Bîr el Biarât, *Egypt* 91 **F3** 29 30N 34 43 E
Bîr el Duweidar, *Egypt* 91 **E1** 30 56N 32 32 E
Bîr el Garârât, *Egypt* 91 **D2** 31 3N 33 34 E
Bîr el Gellaz, *Egypt* 94 **A2** 30 50N 26 40 E
Bîr el Heisi, *Egypt* 91 **F3** 29 22N 34 36 E
Bîr el Jafir, *Egypt* 91 **E1** 30 50N 32 41 E
Bîr el Mâlḥi, *Egypt* 91 **E2** 30 38N 33 19 E
Bîr el Shaqqa, *Egypt* 94 **A2** 30 54N 25 1 E
Bîr el Thamâda, *Egypt* 91 **E2** 30 12N 33 27 E
Bîr Fuad, *Egypt* 94 **A2** 30 35N 26 28 E
Bir Gara, *Chad* 97 **F3** 13 11N 15 58 E
Bîr Gebeil Ḥiṣn, *Egypt* 91 **E2** 30 2N 33 18 E
Bi'r Ghadīr, *Syria* 91 **A6** 34 6N 37 3 E
Bîr Haimur, *Egypt* 94 **C3** 22 45N 33 40 E
Bîr Ḥasana, *Egypt* 91 **E2** 30 29N 33 46 E
Bir Ìdimah, *Si. Arabia* 86 **C4** 18 31N 44 12 E
Bi'r Jadīd, *Iraq* 84 **C4** 34 1N 42 54 E
Bir Jdid, *Morocco* 98 **B3** 33 26N 8 0W
Bîr Kanayis, *Egypt* 94 **C3** 24 59N 33 15 E
Bîr Kaseiba, *Egypt* 91 **E2** 31 0N 33 17 E
Bîr Kerawein, *Egypt* 94 **B2** 27 10N 28 25 E
Bîr Lahfân, *Egypt* 91 **D2** 31 0N 33 51 E
Bir Lahrache, *Algeria* 99 **B6** 32 1N 8 12 E
Bîr Madkûr, *Egypt* 91 **E1** 30 44N 32 33 E
Bîr Maql, *Egypt* 94 **C3** 23 7N 33 40 E
Bîr Misaha, *Egypt* 94 **C2** 22 13N 27 59 E
Bir Mogrein, *Mauritania* 98 **C2** 25 10N 11 25W
Bi'r Muṭribah, *Kuwait* 84 **D5** 29 54N 47 17 E
Bîr Murr, *Egypt* 94 **C3** 23 28N 30 10 E
Bîr Nakheila, *Egypt* 94 **C3** 24 1N 30 50 E
Bîr Qaṭia, *Egypt* 91 **E1** 30 58N 32 45 E
Bîr Qatrani, *Egypt* 94 **A2** 30 55N 26 10 E
Bîr Ranga, *Egypt* 94 **C4** 24 25N 35 15 E
Bîr Sahara, *Egypt* 94 **C2** 22 54N 28 40 E
Bîr Seiyâla, *Egypt* 94 **B3** 26 10N 33 50 E
Bir Semguine, *Morocco* 98 **B3** 30 1N 5 39W
Bîr Shalatein, *Egypt* 94 **C4** 23 5N 35 25 E
Bîr Shebb, *Egypt* 94 **C2** 22 25N 29 40 E
Bîr Shût, *Egypt* 94 **C4** 23 50N 35 15 E
Bi'r Tamis, *Yemen* 87 **C5** 16 45N 48 48 E
Bîr Terfawi, *Egypt* 94 **C2** 22 57N 28 55 E
Bîr Umm Qubûr, *Egypt* 94 **C3** 24 35N 34 2 E
Bîr Ungât, *Egypt* 94 **C3** 22 8N 33 48 E
Bîr Za'farâna, *Egypt* 94 **J8** 29 10N 32 40 E
Bîr Zāmūs, *Libya* 96 **D3** 24 16N 15 6 E
Bîr Zeidûn, *Egypt* 94 **B3** 25 45N 33 40 E
Bira, *Indonesia* 73 **B4** 2 3 S 132 2 E
Bîra, *Romania* 46 **B8** 47 2N 27 3 E
Biramféro, *Guinea* 100 **C3** 11 40N 9 10W
Birao, *C.A.R.* 102 **A4** 10 20N 22 47 E
Bir[illegible], *Zaïre* 106 **C2** 2 20 S 28 48 E
Bîrca, *Romania* 46 **F4** 43 59N 23 36 E
Birch Hills, *Canada* 131 **C7** 52 59N 105 25W
Birch I., *Canada* 131 **C9** 52 26N 99 54W
Birch L., *N.W.T., Canada* 130 **A5** 62 4N 116 33W
Birch L., *Ont., Canada* 128 **B1** 51 23N 92 18W
Birch L., *U.S.A.* 128 **C1** 47 48N 91 43W
Birch Mts., *Canada* 130 **B6** 57 30N 113 10W
Birch River, *Canada* 131 **C8** 52 24N 101 6W
Birchip, *Australia* 116 **C5** 35 56 S 142 55 E
Birchiş, *Romania* 46 **D3** 45 58N 22 9 E
Birchwood, *N.Z.* 119 **F2** 45 55 S 167 53 E
Bird, *Canada* 131 **B10** 56 30N 94 13W
Bird City, *U.S.A.* 138 **F4** 39 48N 101 33W
Bird I. = Aves, I. de, *W. Indies* 149 **C7** 15 45N 63 55W
Bird I., *S. Africa* 104 **E2** 32 3 S 18 17 E
Birdaard, *Neths.* 20 **B7** 53 18N 5 53 E
Birdlip, *U.K.* 17 **F5** 51 50N 2 7W
Birds, *U.S.A.* 141 **F9** 38 50N 87 40W
Birdseye, *U.S.A.* 141 **F10** 38 19N 86 42W
Birdsville, *Australia* 114 **D2** 25 51 S 139 20 E
Birdum, *Australia* 112 **C5** 15 39 S 133 13 E
Birein, *Israel* 91 **E3** 30 50N 34 28 E
Bireuen, *Indonesia* 74 **A1** 5 14N 96 39 E
Birifo, *Gambia* 100 **C2** 13 30N 14 0W
Birigui, *Brazil* 159 **A5** 21 18 S 50 16W
Birini, *C.A.R.* 102 **A4** 7 51N 22 24 E
Birkenfeld, *Germany* 27 **F3** 49 39N 7 11 E
Birkenhead, *N.Z.* 118 **C3** 36 49 S 174 46 E
Birkenhead, *U.K.* 16 **D4** 53 24N 3 1W
Birket Qârûn, *Egypt* 94 **J7** 29 30N 30 40 E
Birkfeld, *Austria* 30 **D8** 47 21N 15 45 E
Birkhadem, *Algeria* 99 **A5** 36 43N 3 3 E
Bîrlad, *Romania* 46 **C8** 46 15N 27 38 E
Birmingham, *U.K.* 17 **E6** 52 30N 1 55W
Birmingham, *Ala., U.S.A.* 135 **J2** 33 31N 86 50W
Birmingham, *Iowa, U.S.A.* 140 **D5** 40 53N 91 57W
Birmitrapur, *India* 82 **C7** 22 24N 84 46 E
Birni Ngaouré, *Niger* 101 **C5** 13 5N 2 51 E
Birni Nkonni, *Niger* 101 **C6** 13 55N 5 15 E
Birnin Gwari, *Nigeria* 101 **C6** 11 0N 6 45 E
Birnin Kebbi, *Nigeria* 101 **C5** 12 32N 4 12 E
Birnin Kudu, *Nigeria* 101 **C6** 11 30N 9 29 E
Birobidzhan, *Russia* 57 **E14** 48 50N 132 50 E
Birougou, Mts., *Gabon* 102 **C2** 1 51 S 12 20 E
Birr, *Ireland* 19 **C4** 53 7N 7 55W
Birrie →, *Australia* 115 **D4** 29 43 S 146 37 E
Birs →, *Switz.* 28 **B5** 47 24N 7 32 E
Birsilpur, *India* 80 **E5** 28 11N 72 15 E
Birsk, *Russia* 54 **D4** 55 25N 55 30 E
Birtin, *Romania* 46 **C3** 46 59N 22 31 E
Birtle, *Canada* 131 **C8** 50 30N 101 5W
Biryuchiy, *Ukraine* 52 **C6** 46 10N 35 0 E
Birzai, *Lithuania* 50 **C4** 56 11N 24 45 E
Bîrzava, *Romania* 46 **C2** 46 7N 21 59 E
Birzebugga, *Malta* 32 **D2** 35 49N 14 32 E
Bisa, *Indonesia* 72 **B3** 1 15 S 127 28 E
Bisáccia, *Italy* 41 **A8** 41 0N 15 20 E
Bisacquino, *Italy* 40 **E6** 37 42N 13 13 E
Bisai, *Japan* 63 **B8** 35 16N 136 44 E
Bisalpur, *India* 81 **E8** 28 14N 79 48 E
Bisbee, *U.S.A.* 143 **L9** 31 30N 110 0W
Biscarrosse et de Parentis, Étang de, *France* 24 **D2** 44 21N 1 10W
Biscay, B. of, *Atl. Oc.* 8 **D8** 45 0N 2 0W
Biscayne B., *U.S.A.* 135 **N5** 25 40N 80 12W
Bisceglie, *Italy* 41 **A9** 41 14N 16 30 E
Bischofshofen, *Austria* 30 **D6** 47 26N 13 14 E
Bischofswerda, *Germany* 26 **D10** 51 8N 14 11 E
Bischofszell, *Switz.* 29 **B8** 47 29N 9 15 E
Bischwiller, *France* 23 **D14** 48 46N 7 50 E
Biscoe Bay, *Antarctica* 7 **D13** 77 0 S 152 0W
Biscoe Is., *Antarctica* 7 **C17** 66 0 S 67 0W
Biscostasing, *Canada* 128 **C3** 47 18N 82 9W
Biscucuy, *Venezuela* 152 **B4** 9 22N 69 59W
Biševo, *Croatia* 39 **F13** 42 57N 16 3 E
Bisha, *Ethiopia* 95 **D4** 15 30N 37 31 E
Bishah, W. →, *Si. Arabia* 86 **B3** 21 24N 43 26 E
Bishan, *China* 68 **C6** 29 33N 106 12 E
Bishkek, *Kirghizia* 55 **B7** 42 54N 74 46 E
Bishnupur, *India* 81 **H12** 23 8N 87 20 E
Bisho, *S. Africa* 105 **E4** 32 50 S 27 23 E
Bishop, *Calif., U.S.A.* 144 **H8** 37 20N 118 26W
Bishop, *Tex., U.S.A.* 139 **M6** 27 35N 97 49W
Bishop Auckland, *U.K.* 16 **C6** 54 40N 1 40W
Bishop's Falls, *Canada* 129 **C8** 49 2N 55 30W
Bishop's Stortford, *U.K.* 17 **F8** 51 52N 0 11 E
Bisignano, *Italy* 41 **C9** 39 30N 16 17 E
Bisina, L., *Uganda* 106 **B3** 1 38N 33 56 E
Biskra, *Algeria* 99 **B6** 34 50N 5 44 E
Biskupiec, *Poland* 47 **B7** 53 53N 20 58 E
Bismarck, *Mo., U.S.A.* 140 **G6** 37 46N 90 38W
Bismarck, *N. Dak., U.S.A.* 138 **B4** 46 49N 100 49W
Bismarck Arch., *Papua N. G.* 120 **B5** 2 30 S 150 0 E
Bismarck Ra., *Papua N. G.* 120 **C3** 5 35 S 145 0 E
Bismarck Sea, *Papua N. G.* 120 **C4** 4 10 S 146 50 E
Bismark, *Germany* 26 **C7** 52 39N 11 31 E
Biso, *Uganda* 106 **B3** 1 44N 31 26 E
Bison, *U.S.A.* 138 **C3** 45 34N 102 28W
Bīsotūn, *Iran* 84 **C5** 34 23N 47 26 E
Bispfors, *Sweden* 12 **E14** 63 1N 16 37 E
Bispgården, *Sweden* 14 **A10** 63 2N 16 40 E
Bissagos = Bijagós, Arquipélago dos, *Guinea-Biss.* 100 **C1** 11 15N 16 10W
Bissau, *Guinea-Biss.* 100 **C1** 11 45N 15 45W
Bissett, *Canada* 131 **C9** 51 2N 95 41W
Bissikrima, *Guinea* 100 **C2** 10 50N 10 58W
Bistcho L., *Canada* 130 **B5** 59 45N 118 50W
Bistreţu, *Romania* 46 **E4** 43 54N 23 23 E
Bistrica = Ilirska-Bistrica, *Slovenia* 39 **C11** 45 34N 14 14 E
Bistriţa, *Romania* 46 **B5** 47 9N 24 35 E
Bistriţa →, *Romania* 46 **C7** 46 30N 26 57 E
Bistriţa Năsăud □, *Romania* 46 **B5** 47 15N 24 30 E
Bistriţei, Munţii, *Romania* 46 **B6** 47 15N 25 40 E
Biswan, *India* 81 **F9** 27 29N 81 2 E
Bisztynek, *Poland* 47 **A7** 54 8N 20 53 E
Bitam, *Gabon* 102 **B2** 2 5N 11 25 E
Bitburg, *Germany* 27 **F2** 49 58N 6 32 E
Bitche, *France* 23 **C14** 49 2N 7 25 E
Bithynia, *Turkey* 88 **C4** 40 40N 31 0 E
Bitkine, *Chad* 97 **F3** 11 59N 18 13 E
Bitlis, *Turkey* 89 **D10** 38 20N 42 3 E
Bitlis □, *Turkey* 89 **D10** 38 20N 42 5 E
Bitola, *Macedonia, Yug.* 42 **F6** 41 5N 21 10 E
Bitolj = Bitola, *Macedonia, Yug.* 42 **F6** 41 5N 21 10 E
Bitonto, *Italy* 41 **A9** 41 7N 16 40 E
Bitter Creek, *U.S.A.* 142 **F9** 41 39N 108 36W
Bitter L. = Buheirat-Murrat-el-Kubra, *Egypt* 94 **H8** 30 15N 32 40 E
Bitterfeld, *Germany* 26 **D8** 51 36N 12 20 E
Bitterfontein, *S. Africa* 104 **E2** 31 1 S 18 32 E
Bitterroot →, *U.S.A.* 142 **C6** 46 52N 114 6W
Bitterroot Range, *U.S.A.* 142 **D6** 46 0N 114 20W
Bitterwater, *U.S.A.* 144 **J6** 36 23N 121 0W
Bitti, *Italy* 40 **B2** 40 29N 9 20 E
Bittou, *Burkina Faso* 101 **C4** 11 17N 0 18W
Biu, *Nigeria* 101 **C7** 10 40N 12 3 E
Bivolari, *Romania* 46 **B8** 47 31N 27 27 E
Bivolu, *Romania* 46 **B6** 47 16N 25 58 E
Biwa-Ko, *Japan* 63 **B8** 35 15N 136 10 E
Biwabik, *U.S.A.* 138 **B8** 47 33N 92 19W
Bixad, *Romania* 46 **B4** 47 56N 23 28 E
Biyang, *China* 66 **H7** 32 38N 113 21 E
Biylikol, Ozero, *Kazakhstan* 55 **B5** 43 5N 70 45 E
Biysk, *Russia* 56 **D9** 52 40N 85 0 E
Bizana, *S. Africa* 105 **E4** 30 50 S 29 52 E
Bizen, *Japan* 62 **C6** 34 43N 134 8 E
Bizerte, *Tunisia* 96 **A1** 37 15N 9 50 E
Bjargtangar, *Iceland* 12 **D1** 65 30N 24 30W
Bjelasica, *Montenegro, Yug.* 42 **E4** 42 50N 19 40 E
Bjelašnica, *Bos.-H., Yug.* 42 **D3** 43 43N 18 9 E
Bjelovar, *Croatia* 42 **B1** 45 56N 16 49 E
Bjerringbro, *Denmark* 15 **H3** 56 23N 9 39 E
Bjørnøya, *Arctic* 6 **B8** 74 30N 19 0 E
Bjuv, *Sweden* 15 **H6** 56 5N 12 55 E
Blace, *Serbia, Yug.* 42 **D6** 43 18N 21 17 E
Blachownia, *Poland* 47 **E5** 50 49N 18 56 E
Black = Da →, *Vietnam* 76 **B5** 21 15N 105 20 E
Black →, *Canada* 136 **B5** 44 42N 79 19W
Black →, *Ark., U.S.A.* 139 **H9** 35 38N 91 19W
Black →, *N.Y., U.S.A.* 137 **C8** 43 59N 76 4W
Black →, *Wis., U.S.A.* 138 **D9** 43 52N 91 22W
Black Diamond, *Canada* 130 **C6** 50 45N 114 14W
Black Forest = Schwarzwald, *Germany* 27 **H4** 48 0N 8 0 E
Black Hills, *U.S.A.* 138 **C3** 44 0N 103 50W
Black I., *Canada* 131 **C9** 51 12N 96 30W
Black L., *Canada* 131 **B7** 59 12N 105 15W
Black L., *U.S.A.* 134 **C3** 45 28N 84 15W
Black Mesa, *U.S.A.* 139 **G3** 36 57N 102 55W
Black Mt. = Mynydd Du, *U.K.* 17 **F4** 51 45N 3 45W
Black Mountain, *Australia* 117 **A9** 30 18 S 151 39 E
Black Mts., *U.K.* 17 **F4** 51 52N 3 5W
Black Range, *U.S.A.* 143 **K10** 33 30N 107 55W
Black River, *Jamaica* 148 **C4** 18 0N 77 50W
Black River Falls, *U.S.A.* 138 **C9** 44 23N 90 52W
Black Rock, *Australia* 116 **B3** 32 50 S 138 44 E
Black Sea, *Europe* 52 **E6** 43 30N 35 0 E
Black Volta →, *Africa* 100 **D4** 8 41N 1 33W
Black Warrior →, *U.S.A.* 135 **J2** 32 32N 87 51W
Blackall, *Australia* 114 **C4** 24 25 S 145 45 E
Blackball, *N.Z.* 119 **C6** 42 22 S 171 26 E
Blackbull, *Australia* 114 **B3** 17 55 S 141 45 E
Blackburn, *U.K.* 16 **D5** 53 44N 2 30W
Blackduck, *U.S.A.* 138 **B7** 47 43N 94 32W
Blackfoot, *U.S.A.* 142 **E7** 43 13N 112 12W
Blackfoot →, *U.S.A.* 142 **C7** 46 52N 113 53W
Blackfoot Res., *U.S.A.* 142 **E8** 43 0N 111 35W
Blackie, *Canada* 130 **C6** 50 36N 113 37W
Blackpool, *U.K.* 16 **D4** 53 48N 3 3W
Blackriver, *U.S.A.* 136 **B1** 44 46N 83 17W
Blacks Harbour, *Canada* 129 **C6** 45 3N 66 49W
Blacksburg, *U.S.A.* 134 **G5** 37 17N 80 23W
Blacksod B., *Ireland* 19 **B2** 54 6N 10 0W
Blackstone, *U.S.A.* 134 **G6** 37 6N 78 0W
Blackstone →, *Canada* 130 **A4** 61 5N 122 55W
Blackstone Ra., *Australia* 113 **E4** 26 0 S 128 30 E
Blackville, *Canada* 129 **C6** 46 44N 65 50W
Blackwater, *Australia* 114 **C4** 23 35 S 148 53 E
Blackwater →, *Ireland* 19 **E4** 51 55N 7 50W
Blackwater →, *U.K.* 19 **B5** 54 31N 6 35W
Blackwater →, *U.S.A.* 140 **F4** 38 59N 92 59W
Blackwater Cr. →, *Australia* 115 **D3** 25 56 S 144 30 E
Blackwell, *U.S.A.* 139 **G6** 36 55N 97 20W
Blackwells Corner, *U.S.A.* 145 **K7** 35 37N 119 47W
Blackwood, C., *Papua N. G.* 120 **D3** 7 49 S 144 31 E
Bladel, *Neths.* 21 **F6** 51 22N 5 13 E
Blaenau Ffestiniog, *U.K.* 16 **E4** 52 59N 3 57W

176 Blagaj


Blagaj, Bos.-H., Yug. 42 D2 43 16N 17 55 E
Blagodarnoye, Russia 53 D10 45 7N 43 37 E
Blagoevgrad, Bulgaria 42 E8 42 2N 23 5 E
Blagoveshchensk, Russia 54 D4 55 1N 55 59 E
Blagoveshchensk, Amur, Russia 57 D13 50 20N 127 30 E
Blagoveshchenskoye, Kazakhstan 55 B7 43 18N 74 12 E
Blain, France 22 E5 47 29N 1 45W
Blaine, U.S.A. 144 B4 48 59N 122 43W
Blaine Lake, Canada 131 C7 52 51N 106 52W
Blainville-sur-l'Eau, France 23 D13 48 33N 6 23 E
Blair, U.S.A. 138 E6 41 38N 96 10W
Blair Athol, Australia 114 C4 22 42 S 147 31 E
Blair Atholl, U.K. 18 E5 56 46N 3 50W
Blairgowrie, U.K. 18 E5 56 36N 3 20W
Blairmore, Canada 130 D6 49 40N 114 25W
Blairsden, U.S.A. 144 F6 39 47N 120 37W
Blairsville, U.S.A. 136 F5 40 27N 79 15W
Blaj, Romania 46 C4 46 10N 23 57 E
Blake Pt., U.S.A. 138 A10 48 12N 88 27W
Blakely, U.S.A. 135 K3 31 22N 85 0W
Blakesburg, U.S.A. 140 D4 40 58N 92 38W
Blâmont, France 23 D13 48 35N 6 50 E
Blanc, C., Tunisia 96 A1 37 15N 9 56 E
Blanc, Mont, Alps 25 C10 45 48N 6 50 E
Blanca, B., Argentina 160 A4 39 10 S 61 30W
Blanca Peak, U.S.A. 143 H11 37 35N 105 29W
Blanchard, U.S.A. 139 H6 35 8N 97 40W
Blanchardville, U.S.A. 140 B7 42 48N 89 52W
Blanche, C., Australia 115 E1 33 1 S 134 9 E
Blanche, L., S. Austral., Australia 115 D2 29 15 S 139 40 E
Blanche, L., W. Austral., Australia 112 D3 22 25 S 123 17 E
Blanche Channel, Solomon Is. 121 M9 8 30 S 157 30 E
Blanchester, U.S.A. 141 E13 39 17N 83 59W
Blanco, S. Africa 104 E3 33 55 S 22 23 E
Blanco, U.S.A. 139 K5 30 7N 98 30W
Blanco →, Argentina 158 C2 30 20 S 68 42W
Blanco, C., Costa Rica 148 E2 9 34N 85 8W
Blanco, C., Spain 33 B9 39 21N 2 51 E
Blanco, C., U.S.A. 142 E1 42 50N 124 40W
Blanda →, Iceland 12 D4 65 20N 19 40W
Blandford Forum, U.K. 17 G5 50 52N 2 10W
Blanding, U.S.A. 143 H9 37 35N 109 30W
Blandinsville, U.S.A. 140 D6 40 33N 90 52W
Blanes, Spain 34 D7 41 40N 2 48 E
Blangy-sur-Bresle, France 23 C8 49 55N 1 37 E
Blanice →, Czech. 30 B7 49 10N 14 5 E
Blankenberge, Belgium 21 F2 51 20N 3 9 E
Blankenburg, Germany 26 D6 51 46N 10 56 E
Blanquefort, France 24 D3 44 55N 0 38W
Blanquillo, Uruguay 159 C4 32 53 S 55 37W
Blansko, Czech. 31 B9 49 22N 16 40 E
Blantyre, Malawi 107 F4 15 45 S 35 0 E
Blaricum, Neths. 20 D6 52 16N 5 14 E
Blarney, Ireland 19 E3 51 57N 8 35W
Błaski, Poland 47 D5 51 38N 18 30 E
Blatná, Czech. 30 B6 49 25N 13 52 E
Blatnitsa, Bulgaria 43 D13 43 41N 28 32 E
Blato, Croatia 39 F13 42 56N 16 48 E
Blatten, Switz. 28 D5 46 20N 7 50 E
Blaubeuren, Germany 27 G5 48 24N 9 47 E
Blåvands Huk, Denmark 13 J10 55 33N 8 4 E
Blaydon, U.K. 16 C6 54 56N 1 47W
Blaye, France 24 C3 45 8N 0 40W
Blaye-les-Mines, France 24 D6 44 1N 2 8 E
Blayney, Australia 117 B8 33 32 S 149 14 E
Blaze, Pt., Australia 112 B5 12 56 S 130 11 E
Błazowa, Poland 31 B15 49 53N 22 7 E
Bleckede, Germany 26 B6 53 18N 10 43 E
Bled, Slovenia 39 B11 46 27N 14 7 E
Blednaya, Gora, Russia 56 B7 76 20N 65 0 E
Bléharis, Belgium 21 G2 50 31N 3 25 E
Bleiburg, Austria 30 E7 46 35N 14 49 E
Blejeşti, Romania 46 E6 44 19N 25 27 E
Blekinge län □, Sweden 13 H13 56 20N 15 20 E
Blenheim, Canada 136 D2 42 20N 82 0W
Blenheim, N.Z. 119 B8 41 38 S 173 57 E
Bléone →, France 25 D10 44 5N 6 0 E
Blerick, Neths. 21 F8 51 22N 6 9 E
Bletchley, U.K. 17 F7 51 59N 0 44W
Blida, Algeria 99 A5 36 30N 2 49 E
Blidet Amor, Algeria 99 B6 32 59N 5 58 E
Blidö, Sweden 14 E12 59 37N 18 53 E
Bligh Sound, N.Z. 119 E2 44 47 S 167 32 E
Bligh Water, Fiji 121 A2 17 0 S 178 0 E
Blind River, Canada 128 C3 46 10N 82 58W
Blinishti, Albania 44 C1 41 52N 19 58 E
Blinnenhorn, Switz. 29 D6 46 26N 8 19 E
Blissfield, U.S.A. 141 C13 41 50N 83 52W
Blitar, Indonesia 75 D4 8 5 S 112 11 E
Blitta, Togo 101 D5 8 23N 1 6 E
Block I., U.S.A. 137 E13 41 11N 71 35W
Block Island Sd., U.S.A. 137 E13 41 17N 71 35W
Blockton, U.S.A. 140 D2 40 37N 94 29W
Blodgett Iceberg Tongue, Antarctica 7 C9 66 8 S 130 35 E
Bloemendaal, Neths. 20 D5 52 24N 4 39 E
Bloemfontein, S. Africa 104 D4 29 6 S 26 7 E
Bloemhof, S. Africa 104 D4 27 38 S 25 32 E
Blois, France 22 E8 47 35N 1 20 E
Blokziji, Neths. 20 C7 52 43N 5 58 E
Blönduós, Iceland 12 D3 65 40N 20 12W
Blonie, Poland 47 C7 52 12N 20 37 E
Bloodvein →, Canada 131 C9 51 47N 96 43W
Bloody Foreland, Ireland 19 A3 55 10N 8 18W
Bloomer, U.S.A. 138 C9 45 8N 91 30W
Bloomfield, Australia 114 B4 15 56 S 145 22 E
Bloomfield, Canada 136 C7 43 59N 77 14W
Bloomfield, Ind., U.S.A. 141 E10 39 1N 86 57W
Bloomfield, Iowa, U.S.A. 140 D4 40 44N 92 26W
Bloomfield, Ky., U.S.A. 141 G11 37 55N 85 19W
Bloomfield, N. Mex., U.S.A. 143 H10 36 46N 107 59W
Bloomfield, Nebr., U.S.A. 138 D6 42 38N 97 40W
Bloomingburg, U.S.A. 141 E13 39 36N 83 24W
Bloomington, Ill., U.S.A. 140 D7 40 27N 89 0W
Bloomington, Ind., U.S.A. 141 E10 39 10N 86 30W
Bloomington, Wis., U.S.A. 140 B6 42 53N 90 55W
Bloomsburg, U.S.A. 137 F8 41 0N 76 30W
Blora, Indonesia 75 D4 6 57 S 111 25 E
Blossburg, U.S.A. 136 E7 41 40N 77 4W
Blouberg, S. Africa 105 C4 23 8 S 28 59 E
Blountstown, U.S.A. 135 K3 30 28N 85 5W
Bludenz, Austria 30 D2 47 10N 9 50 E
Blue →, U.S.A. 141 F10 38 11N 86 18W
Blue Island, U.S.A. 134 E2 41 40N 87 40W
Blue Lake, U.S.A. 142 F2 40 53N 124 0W
Blue Mesa Res., U.S.A. 143 G10 38 30N 107 15W
Blue Mound, U.S.A. 140 E7 39 42N 89 7W
Blue Mts., Australia 117 B9 33 40 S 150 0 E
Blue Mts., Oreg., U.S.A. 142 D4 45 15N 119 0W
Blue Mts., Pa., U.S.A. 137 F8 40 30N 76 30W
Blue Mud B., Australia 114 A2 13 30 S 136 0 E
Blue Nile = An Nîl el Azraq □, Sudan 95 E3 12 30N 34 30 E
Blue Nile = Nîl el Azraq →, Sudan 95 D3 15 38N 32 31 E
Blue Rapids, U.S.A. 138 F6 39 41N 96 39W
Blue Ridge Mts., U.S.A. 135 G5 36 30N 80 15W
Blue Springs, U.S.A. 140 E2 39 1N 94 17W
Blue Stack Mts., Ireland 19 B3 54 46N 8 5W
Blueberry →, Canada 130 B4 56 45N 120 49W
Bluefield, U.S.A. 134 G5 37 18N 81 14W
Bluefields, Nic. 148 D3 12 20N 83 50W
Blueskin B., N.Z. 119 F5 45 44 S 170 38 E
Bluff, Australia 114 C4 23 35 S 149 4 E
Bluff, N.Z. 119 G3 46 37 S 168 20 E
Bluff, U.S.A. 143 H9 37 17N 109 33W
Bluff Harbour, N.Z. 119 G3 46 36 S 168 21 E
Bluff Knoll, Australia 113 F2 34 24 S 118 15 E
Bluff Pt., Australia 113 E1 27 50 S 114 5 E
Bluffs, U.S.A. 140 E6 39 45N 90 32W
Bluffton, Ind., U.S.A. 141 D11 40 43N 85 9W
Bluffton, Ohio, U.S.A. 141 D13 40 54N 83 54W
Bluford, U.S.A. 141 F8 38 20N 88 45W
Blumenau, Brazil 159 B6 27 0 S 49 0W
Blümisalphorn, Switz. 28 D5 46 28N 7 47 E
Blunt, U.S.A. 138 C4 44 32N 100 0W
Bly, U.S.A. 142 E3 42 23N 121 0W
Blyth, Canada 136 C3 43 44N 81 26W
Blyth, U.K. 16 B6 55 8N 1 32W
Blyth Bridge, U.K. 16 E5 52 58N 2 4W
Blythe, U.S.A. 145 M12 33 40N 114 33W
Bø, Norway 14 E3 59 25N 9 3 E
Bo, S. Leone 100 D2 7 55N 11 50W
Bo Duc, Vietnam 77 G6 11 58N 106 50 E
Bo Hai, China 67 E10 39 0N 119 0 E
Bō-no-Misaki, Japan 62 F2 31 15N 130 13 E
Bo Xian, China 66 H8 33 55N 115 41 E
Boa Esperança, Brazil 153 C5 3 21N 61 23W
Boa Nova, Brazil 155 D3 14 22 S 40 10W
Boa Viagem, Brazil 154 C4 5 7 S 39 44W
Boa Vista, Brazil 153 C5 2 48N 60 30W
Boac, Phil. 70 E3 13 27N 121 50 E
Boaco, Nic. 148 D2 12 29N 85 35W
Bo'ai, China 66 G7 35 10N 113 3 E
Boal, Spain 36 B4 43 25N 6 49W
Boali, C.A.R. 102 B3 4 48N 18 7 E
Boardman, U.S.A. 136 E4 41 2N 80 40W
Boatman, Australia 115 D4 27 16 S 146 55 E
Bobadah, Australia 117 B7 32 19 S 146 41 E
Bobai, China 68 F7 22 17N 109 59 E
Bobbili, India 82 E6 18 35N 83 30 E
Bóbbio, Italy 38 D6 44 47N 9 22 E
Bobcaygeon, Canada 128 D4 44 33N 78 33W
Böblingen, Germany 27 G5 48 41N 9 1 E
Bobo-Dioulasso, Burkina Faso 100 C4 11 8N 4 13W
Boboc, Romania 46 D7 45 13N 26 59 E
Bobolice, Poland 47 B3 53 58N 16 37 E
Bobon, Davao, Phil. 71 H6 6 53N 126 19 E
Bobon, Samar, Phil. 70 E5 12 32N 124 34 E
Bobonaza →, Ecuador 152 D2 2 36 S 76 38W
Boboshevo, Bulgaria 42 E7 42 9N 23 0 E
Bobov Dol, Bulgaria 42 E7 42 20N 23 0 E
Bóbr →, Poland 47 C2 52 4N 15 4 E
Bobraomby, Tanjon' i, Madag. 105 A8 12 40 S 49 10 E
Bobrinets, Ukraine 52 B5 48 4N 32 5 E
Bobrov, Russia 51 F12 51 5N 40 2 E
Bobruysk, Belorussia 50 E6 53 10N 29 15 E
Bobures, Venezuela 152 B3 9 15N 71 11W
Boca de Drago, Venezuela 153 A5 11 0N 61 50W
Bôca do Acre, Brazil 156 B4 8 50 S 67 27W
Bôca do Jari, Brazil 153 D7 1 7 S 51 58W
Bôca do Moaco, Brazil 156 B4 7 41 S 68 17W
Boca Grande, Venezuela 153 B5 8 40N 60 40W
Boca Raton, U.S.A. 135 M5 26 21N 80 5W
Bocaiúva, Brazil 155 E3 17 7 S 43 49W
Bocanda, Ivory C. 100 D4 7 5N 4 31W
Bocaranga, C.A.R. 102 A3 7 0N 15 35 E
Bocas del Toro, Panama 148 E3 9 15N 82 20W
Boceguillas, Spain 34 D1 41 20N 3 39W
Bochnia, Poland 31 B13 49 58N 20 27 E
Bocholt, Belgium 21 F7 51 10N 5 35 E
Bocholt, Germany 26 D2 51 50N 6 35 E
Bochov, Czech. 30 A6 50 9N 13 3 E
Bochum, Germany 26 D3 51 28N 7 12 E
Bockenem, Germany 26 C6 52 1N 10 8 E
Boćki, Poland 47 C10 52 39N 23 3 E
Bocognano, France 25 F13 42 5N 9 4 E
Boconó, Venezuela 152 B3 9 15N 70 16W
Boconó →, Venezuela 152 B4 8 43N 69 34W
Bocoyna, Mexico 146 B3 27 52N 107 35W
Bocq →, Belgium 21 H5 50 20N 4 55 E
Bocşa, Romania 42 B6 45 21N 21 47 E
Boda, C.A.R. 102 B3 4 19N 17 26 E
Bodaybo, Russia 57 D12 57 50N 114 0 E
Boddington, Australia 113 F2 32 50 S 116 30 E
Bodega Bay, U.S.A. 144 G3 38 20N 123 3W
Bodegraven, Neths. 20 D5 52 5N 4 46 E
Boden, Sweden 12 D16 65 50N 21 42 E
Bodensee, Europe 29 A8 47 35N 9 25 E
Bodenteich, Germany 26 C6 52 49N 10 41 E
Bodhan, India 82 E3 18 40N 77 44 E
Bodinayakkanur, India 83 J3 10 2N 77 10 E
Bodinga, Nigeria 101 C6 12 58N 5 10 E
Bodio, Switz. 29 D7 46 23N 8 55 E
Bodmin, U.K. 17 G3 50 28N 4 44W
Bodmin Moor, U.K. 17 G3 50 33N 4 36W
Bodoquena, Serra da, Brazil 157 E6 21 0 S 56 50W
Bodoupa, C.A.R. 102 A3 5 43N 17 36 E
Bodrog →, Hungary 31 C14 48 15N 21 35 E
Bodrum, Turkey 88 E2 37 5N 27 30 E
Bódva →, Hungary 31 C13 48 19N 20 45 E
Boechout, Belgium 21 F5 51 10N 4 30 E
Boegoebergdam, S. Africa 104 D3 29 7 S 22 9 E
Boekelo, Neths. 20 D9 52 12N 6 49 E
Boelenslaan, Neths. 20 B8 53 10N 6 10 E
Boembé, Congo 102 C3 2 54 S 15 39 E
Boën, France 25 C8 45 44N 4 0 E
Boende, Zaïre 102 C4 0 24 S 21 12 E
Boerne, U.S.A. 139 L5 29 48N 98 41W
Boertange, Neths. 20 B10 53 1N 7 12 E
Boezinge, Belgium 21 G1 50 54N 2 52 E
Boffa, Guinea 100 C2 10 16N 14 3W
Bogale, Burma 78 G5 16 17N 95 24 E
Bogalusa, U.S.A. 139 K10 30 50N 89 55W
Bogan →, Australia 117 A7 29 59 S 146 17 E
Bogan Gate, Australia 117 B7 33 7 S 147 49 E
Bogangolo, C.A.R. 102 A3 5 34N 18 15 E
Bogantungan, Australia 114 C4 23 41 S 147 17 E
Bogata, U.S.A. 139 J7 33 26N 95 10W
Bogatić, Serbia, Yug. 42 C4 44 51N 19 30 E
Boğazlıyan, Turkey 88 D6 39 11N 35 14 E
Bogdanovitch, Russia 54 C8 56 47N 62 1 E
Bogense, Denmark 15 J4 55 34N 10 5 E
Boggabilla, Australia 115 D5 28 36 S 150 24 E
Boggabri, Australia 117 A9 30 45 S 150 5 E
Boggeragh Mts., Ireland 19 D3 52 2N 8 55W
Bogia, Papua N. G. 120 C3 4 9 S 145 0 E
Bognor Regis, U.K. 17 G7 50 47N 0 40W
Bogø, Denmark 15 K6 54 55N 12 2 E
Bogo, Phil. 71 F4 11 3N 124 0 E
Bogodukhov, Ukraine 52 A6 50 9N 35 33 E
Bogong, Mt., Australia 117 D7 36 47 S 147 17 E
Bogor, Indonesia 74 D3 6 36 S 106 48 E
Bogoroditsk, Russia 51 E11 53 47N 38 8 E
Bogorodsk, Russia 51 C13 56 4N 43 30 E
Bogorodskoye, Russia 57 D15 52 22N 140 30 E
Bogoso, Ghana 100 D4 5 38N 2 3W
Bogotá, Colombia 152 C3 4 34N 74 0W
Bogotol, Russia 56 D9 56 15N 89 50 E
Bogra, Bangla. 78 C2 24 51N 89 22 E
Boguchany, Russia 57 D10 58 40N 97 30 E
Boguchar, Russia 53 B9 49 55N 40 32 E
Bogué, Mauritania 100 B2 16 45N 14 10W
Boguslav, Ukraine 52 B4 49 47N 30 53 E
Boguszów, Poland 47 E3 50 45N 16 12 E
Bohain-en-Vermandois, France 23 C10 49 59N 3 28 E
Bohemia, Czech. 30 B7 50 0N 14 0 E
Bohemia Downs, Australia 112 C4 18 53 S 126 14 E
Bohemian Forest = Böhmerwald, Germany 27 F8 49 30N 12 40 E
Bohena Cr. →, Australia 115 E4 30 17 S 149 42 E
Bohinjska Bistrica, Slovenia 39 B11 46 17N 14 1 E
Böhmerwald, Germany 27 F8 49 30N 12 40 E
Bohmte, Germany 26 C4 52 24N 8 20 E
Bohol, Phil. 71 G5 9 50N 124 10 E
Bohol, Somali Rep. 108 C3 5 45N 46 9 E
Bohol Str., Phil. 71 G4 9 45N 123 40 E
Bohotleh, Somali Rep. 90 F4 8 20N 46 25 E
Boi, Nigeria 101 D6 9 35N 9 27 E
Boi, Pta. de, Brazil 159 A6 23 55 S 45 15W
Boiaçu, Brazil 153 D5 0 27 S 61 46W
Boiano, Italy 41 A7 41 28N 14 29 E
Boileau, C., Australia 112 C3 17 40 S 122 7 E
Boinitsa, Bulgaria 42 D7 43 58N 22 32 E
Boipeba, I. de, Brazil 155 D4 13 39 S 38 55W
Bois →, Brazil 155 E1 18 35 S 50 2W
Boischot, Belgium 21 F5 51 3N 4 47 E
Boise, U.S.A. 142 E5 43 43N 116 9W
Boise City, U.S.A. 139 G3 36 45N 102 30W
Boissevain, Canada 131 D8 49 15N 100 5W
Boite →, Italy 39 B9 46 5N 12 5 E
Boitzenburg, Germany 26 B9 53 16N 13 36 E
Boizenburg, Germany 26 B6 53 22N 10 42 E
Bojador C., W. Sahara 98 C2 26 0N 14 30W
Bojana →, Albania 44 F4 41 52N 19 22 E
Bojanowo, Poland 47 D3 51 43N 16 42 E
Bojnūrd, Iran 85 B8 37 30N 57 20 E
Bojonegoro, Indonesia 75 D4 7 11 S 111 54 E
Boju, Nigeria 101 D6 7 22N 7 55 E
Boka, Serbia, Yug. 42 B5 45 22N 20 52 E
Boka Kotorska, Montenegro, Yug. 42 E3 42 23N 18 32 E
Bokada, Zaïre 102 B3 4 8N 19 23 E
Bokala, Ivory C. 100 D4 8 31N 4 33W
Bokatola, Zaïre 102 C3 0 38 S 18 46 E
Boké, Guinea 100 C2 10 56N 14 17W
Bokhara →, Australia 115 D4 29 55 S 146 42 E
Bokkos, Nigeria 101 D6 9 17N 9 1 E
Boknafjorden, Norway 13 G8 59 14N 5 40 E
Bokombayevskoye, Kirghizia 55 B8 42 10N 76 55 E
Bokoro, Chad 97 F3 12 25N 17 14 E
Bokote, Zaïre 102 C4 0 12 S 21 8 E
Boksitogorsk, Russia 50 B8 59 32N 33 56 E
Bokungu, Zaïre 102 C4 0 35 S 22 50 E
Bol, Chad 97 F2 13 30N 14 40 E
Bol, Croatia 39 E13 43 18N 16 38 E
Bolama, Guinea-Biss. 100 C1 11 30N 15 30W
Bolan Pass, Pakistan 79 C2 29 50N 67 20 E
Bolangum, Australia 116 D5 36 42 S 142 54 E
Bolaños →, Mexico 146 C4 21 14N 104 8W
Bolbec, France 22 C7 49 30N 0 30 E
Boldājī, Iran 85 D6 31 56N 51 3 E
Boldeşti, Romania 46 D7 45 3N 26 2 E
Bole, China 64 B3 45 11N 81 37 E
Bole, Ethiopia 95 F4 6 36N 37 20 E
Bolekhov, Ukraine 50 G3 49 0N 23 57 E
Bolesławiec, Poland 47 D2 51 17N 15 37 E
Bolgatanga, Ghana 101 C4 10 44N 0 53W
Bolgrad, Ukraine 52 D3 45 40N 28 32 E
Boli, Sudan 95 F2 6 2N 28 48 E
Bolinao, Phil. 70 C2 16 23N 119 54 E
Bolinao C., Phil. 70 C2 16 23N 119 55 E
Boliney, Phil. 70 C3 17 24N 120 48 E
Bolívar, Argentina 158 D3 36 15 S 60 53W
Bolívar, Antioquía, Colombia 152 B2 5 50N 76 1W
Bolívar, Cauca, Colombia 152 C2 2 0N 77 0W
Bolívar, Peru 156 B2 7 18 S 77 48W
Bolivar, Mo., U.S.A. 139 G8 37 38N 93 22W
Bolivar, Tenn., U.S.A. 139 H10 35 14N 89 0W
Bolívar □, Colombia 152 B3 9 0N 74 40W
Bolívar □, Ecuador 152 D2 1 15 S 79 5W
Bolívar □, Venezuela 153 B5 6 20N 63 30W
Bolivia ■, S. Amer. 157 D5 17 6 S 64 0W
Bolivian Plateau, S. Amer. 150 D3 20 0 S 67 30W
Boljevac, Serbia, Yug. 42 D6 43 51N 21 58 E
Bolkhov, Russia 51 E10 53 25N 36 0 E
Bollène, France 25 D8 44 18N 4 45 E
Bollnäs, Sweden 14 C10 61 21N 16 24 E
Bollon, Australia 115 D4 28 2 S 147 29 E
Bollstabruk, Sweden 14 A11 63 1N 17 40 E
Bollullos, Spain 37 H4 37 19N 6 32W
Bolobo, Zaïre 102 C3 2 6 S 16 20 E
Bologna, Italy 39 D8 44 30N 11 20 E
Bologne, France 23 D12 48 10N 5 8 E
Bologoye, Russia 50 C9 57 55N 34 5 E
Bolomba, Zaïre 102 B3 0 35N 19 0 E
Bolonchenticul, Mexico 147 D7 20 0N 89 49W
Bolong, Phil. 71 H4 7 6N 122 14 E
Bolotovskoye, Russia 54 B8 58 31N 62 28 E
Boloven, Cao Nguyen, Laos 76 E6 15 10N 106 30 E
Bolpur, India 81 H12 23 40N 87 45 E
Bolsena, Italy 39 F8 42 40N 11 58 E
Bolsena, L. di, Italy 39 F8 42 35N 11 55 E
Bolshaya Glushitsa, Russia 54 E2 52 28N 50 30 E
Bolshaya Khobda →, Kazakhstan 54 F4 50 56N 54 34 E
Bolshaya Kinel →, Russia 54 E2 53 14N 50 30 E
Bolshaya Martynovka, Russia 53 C9 47 12N 41 46 E
Bolshaya Shatan, Gora, Russia 54 E6 53 37N 58 3 E
Bolshaya Vradiyevka, Ukraine 52 C4 47 50N 30 40 E
Bolshereche, Russia 56 D8 56 4N 74 45 E
Bolshevik, Ostrov, Russia 57 B11 78 30N 102 0 E
Bolshezemelskaya Tundra, Russia 48 A10 67 0N 56 0 E
Bolshoi Kavkas, Asia 53 E11 42 50N 44 0 E
Bolshoy Anyuy →, Russia 57 C17 68 30N 160 49 E
Bolshoy Atlym, Russia 56 C7 62 25N 66 50 E
Bolshoy Begichev, Ostrov, Russia 57 B12 74 20N 112 30 E
Bolshoy Lyakhovskiy, Ostrov, Russia 57 B15 73 35N 142 0 E
Bolshoy Tokmak, Ukraine 52 C6 47 16N 35 42 E
Bol'shoy Tyuters, Estonia 50 B5 59 51N 27 13 E
Bolsward, Neths. 20 B7 53 3N 5 32 E
Boltaña, Spain 34 C5 42 28N 0 4 E
Boltigen, Switz. 28 C4 46 38N 7 24 E
Bolton, Canada 136 C5 43 54N 79 45W
Bolton, U.K. 16 D5 53 35N 2 26W
Bolu, Turkey 88 C4 40 45N 31 35 E
Bolu □, Turkey 88 C4 40 40N 31 30 E
Bolubolu, Papua N. G. 120 E6 9 21 S 150 20 E
Boluo, China 69 F10 23 3N 114 21 E
Bolvadin, Turkey 88 D4 38 45N 31 4 E
Bolzano, Italy 39 B8 46 30N 11 20 E
Bom Comércio, Brazil 157 B4 9 45 S 65 54W
Bom Conselho, Brazil 154 C4 9 10 S 36 41W
Bom Despacho, Brazil 155 E2 19 43 S 45 15W
Bom Jesus, Brazil 154 C3 9 4 S 44 22W
Bom Jesus da Gurguéia, Serra, Brazil 154 C3 9 0 S 43 0W
Bom Jesus da Lapa, Brazil 155 D3 13 15 S 43 25W
Boma, Zaïre 103 D2 5 50 S 13 4 E
Bomaderry, Australia 117 C9 34 52 S 150 37 E
Bomandjokou, Congo 102 B2 0 34N 14 23 E
Bomassa, Congo 102 B3 2 12N 16 12 E
Bombala, Australia 117 D8 36 56 S 149 15 E
Bombarral, Portugal 37 F1 39 15N 9 9W
Bombay, India 82 E1 18 55N 72 50 E
Bomboma, Zaïre 102 B3 2 25N 18 55 E
Bombombwa, Zaïre 106 B2 1 40N 25 40 E
Bomi Hills, Liberia 100 D2 7 1N 10 38W
Bomili, Zaïre 106 B2 1 45N 27 5 E
Bommel, Neths. 20 E4 51 43N 4 26 E
Bomokandi →, Zaïre 106 B2 3 39N 26 8 E
Bomongo, Zaïre 102 B3 1 27N 18 21 E
Bomu →, C.A.R. 102 B4 4 40N 22 30 E
Bon, C., Tunisia 96 A2 37 1N 11 2 E
Bon Sar Pa, Vietnam 76 F6 12 24N 107 35 E
Bonaduz, Switz. 29 C8 46 49N 9 25 E
Bonaire, Neth. Ant. 149 D6 12 10N 68 15W
Bonang, Australia 117 D8 37 11 S 148 41 E
Bonanza, Nic. 148 D3 13 54N 84 35W
Bonaparte Arch., Australia 112 B3 14 0 S 124 30 E
Boñar, Spain 36 C5 42 52N 5 19W
Bonaventure, Canada 129 C6 48 5N 65 32W
Bonavista, Canada 129 C9 48 40N 53 5W
Bonavista, C., Canada 129 C9 48 42N 53 5W
Bonawan, Phil. 71 G4 9 8N 122 55 E
Bondeno, Italy 39 D8 44 53N 11 22 E
Bondo, Zaïre 102 B4 3 55N 23 53 E
Bondoukou, Ivory C. 100 D4 8 2N 2 47W
Bondowoso, Indonesia 75 D4 7 55 S 113 49 E
Bondyug, Russia 54 A6 60 29N 55 56 E
Bone, Teluk, Indonesia 72 B2 4 10 S 120 50 E
Bone Rate, Indonesia 72 C2 7 25 S 121 5 E
Bone Rate, Kepulauan, Indonesia 72 C2 6 30 S 121 10 E
Bonefro, Italy 41 A7 41 42N 14 55 E
Bo'ness, U.K. 18 E5 56 0N 3 38W
Bong Son = Hoai Nhon, Vietnam 76 E7 14 28N 109 1 E
Bongabon, Phil. 70 D3 15 38N 121 8 E
Bongabong, Phil. 70 E3 12 45N 121 29 E
Bongandanga, Zaïre 102 B4 1 24N 21 3 E
Bongo, Zaïre 102 C3 1 47 S 17 41 E
Bongor, Chad 97 F3 10 35N 15 20 E
Bongouanou, Ivory C. 100 D4 6 42N 4 15W
Bonham, U.S.A. 139 J6 33 30N 96 10W
Bonheiden, Belgium 21 F5 51 1N 4 32 E
Bonifacio, France 25 G13 41 24N 9 10 E
Bonifacio, Bouches de, Medit. S. 40 A2 41 12N 9 15 E
Bonin Is. = Ogasawara Gunto, Pac. Oc. 122 E6 27 0N 142 0 E
Bonke, Ethiopia 95 F4 6 5N 37 16 E
Bonn, Germany 26 E3 50 43N 7 6 E
Bonnat, France 24 B5 46 20N 1 54 E
Bonne Terre, U.S.A. 139 G9 37 57N 90 33W

**Brake 177**


Bonners Ferry, *U.S.A.* 142 B5 48 38N 116 21W
Bonnétable, *France* 22 D7 48 11N 0 25 E
Bonneuil-Matours, *France* 22 F7 46 41N 0 34 E
Bonneval, *France* 22 D8 48 11N 1 24 E
Bonneville, *France* 25 B10 46 4N 6 24 E
Bonney, L., *Australia* 116 D4 37 50 S 140 20 E
Bonnie Doon, *Australia* 117 D6 37 2 S 145 53 E
Bonnie Downs, *Australia* 114 C3 22 7 S 143 50 E
Bonnie Rock, *Australia* 113 F2 30 29 S 118 22 E
Bonny, *Nigeria* 101 E6 4 25N 7 13 E
Bonny →, *Nigeria* 101 E6 4 20N 7 10 E
Bonny, Bight of, *Africa* 101 E6 3 30N 9 20 E
Bonny-sur-Loire, *France* 23 E9 47 33N 2 50 E
Bonnyville, *Canada* 131 C6 54 20N 110 45W
Bonobono, *Phil.* 71 G1 8 40N 117 36 E
Bonoi, *Indonesia* 73 B5 1 45 S 137 41 E
Bonorva, *Italy* 40 B1 40 25N 8 47 E
Bonsall, *U.S.A.* 145 M9 33 16N 117 14W
Bontang, *Indonesia* 75 B5 0 10N 117 30 E
Bonthain, *Indonesia* 72 C1 5 34 S 119 56 E
Bonthe, *S. Leone* 100 D2 7 30N 12 33W
Bontoc, *Phil.* 70 C3 17 7N 120 58 E
Bonyeri, *Ghana* 100 D4 5 1N 2 46W
Bonyhád, *Hungary* 31 E11 46 18N 18 32 E
Bonython Ra., *Australia* 112 D4 23 40 S 128 45 E
Bookabie, *Australia* 113 F5 31 50 S 132 41 E
Booker, *U.S.A.* 139 G4 36 29N 100 30W
Boolaboolka L., *Australia* 116 B5 32 38 S 143 10 E
Boolarra, *Australia* 117 E7 38 20 S 146 20 E
Boolcoomata, *Australia* 116 A4 31 57 S 140 33 E
Booleroo Centre,
*Australia* 116 B3 32 53 S 138 21 E
Booligal, *Australia* 117 B6 33 58 S 144 53 E
Boom, *Belgium* 21 F4 51 6N 4 20 E
Boonah, *Australia* 115 D5 27 58 S 152 41 E
Boone, *Iowa, U.S.A.* 140 B3 42 5N 93 53W
Boone, *N.C., U.S.A.* 135 G5 36 14N 81 43W
Booneville, *Ark., U.S.A.* 139 H8 35 10N 93 54W
Booneville, *Miss., U.S.A.* 135 H1 34 39N 88 34W
Boonville, *Calif., U.S.A.* 144 F3 39 1N 123 22W
Boonville, *Ind., U.S.A.* 141 F9 38 3N 87 13W
Boonville, *Mo., U.S.A.* 140 F4 38 57N 92 45W
Boonville, *N.Y., U.S.A.* 137 C9 43 31N 75 20W
Booral, *Australia* 117 B9 32 30 S 151 56 E
Boorindal, *Australia* 115 E4 30 22 S 146 11 E
Booroomugga, *Australia* 117 A7 31 17 S 146 27 E
Boorowa, *Australia* 117 C8 34 28 S 148 44 E
Boothia, Gulf of, *Canada* 127 A11 71 0N 90 0W
Boothia Pen., *Canada* 126 A10 71 0N 94 0W
Bootle, *Cumb., U.K.* 16 C4 54 17N 3 24W
Bootle, *Mersey., U.K.* 16 D4 53 28N 3 1W
Booué, *Gabon* 102 C2 0 5 S 11 55 E
Bophuthatswana □,
*S. Africa* 104 D4 25 49 S 25 30 E
Boppard, *Germany* 27 E3 50 13N 7 36 E
Boquerón □, *Paraguay* 157 E5 23 0 S 60 0W
Boquete, *Panama* 148 E3 8 46N 82 27W
Boquilla, Presa de la,
*Mexico* 146 B3 27 40N 105 30W
Boquillas del Carmen,
*Mexico* 146 B4 29 17N 102 53W
Bor, *Czech.* 30 B5 49 41N 12 45 E
Bor, *Serbia, Yug.* 42 C7 44 5N 22 7 E
Bôr, *Sudan* 95 F3 6 10N 31 40 E
Bor, *Turkey* 88 E6 37 54N 34 32 E
Bor Mashash, *Israel* 91 D3 31 7N 34 50 E
Boradā →, *Syria* 91 B5 33 33N 36 34 E
Borah Pk., *U.S.A.* 142 D7 44 19N 113 46W
Borama, *Somali Rep.* 90 F3 9 55N 43 7 E
Borang, *Sudan* 95 G3 4 50N 30 59 E
Borangapara, *India* 78 C3 25 14N 90 14 E
Borås, *Sweden* 15 G6 57 43N 12 56 E
Borāzjān, *Iran* 85 D6 29 22N 51 10 E
Borba, *Brazil* 153 D6 4 12 S 59 34W
Borba, *Portugal* 37 G3 38 50N 7 26W
Borbon, *Phil.* 71 F5 10 50N 124 2 E
Borborema, Planalto da,
*Brazil* 154 C4 7 0 S 37 0W
Borçka, *Turkey* 53 F9 41 25N 41 41 E
Borculo, *Neths.* 20 D9 52 7N 6 31 E
Bord Khūn-e Now, *Iran* 85 D6 28 3N 51 28 E
Borda, C., *Australia* 116 C2 35 45 S 136 34 E
Bordeaux, *France* 24 D3 44 50N 0 36W
Borden, *Australia* 113 F2 34 3 S 118 12 E
Borden, *Canada* 129 C7 46 18N 63 47W
Borden I., *Canada* 6 B2 78 30N 111 30W
Borders □, *U.K.* 18 F6 55 35N 2 50W
Bordertown, *Australia* 116 D4 36 19 S 140 45 E
Borðeyri, *Iceland* 12 D3 65 12N 21 6W
Bordighera, *Italy* 38 E4 43 47N 7 40 E
Bordj bou Arreridj,
*Algeria* 99 A5 36 4N 4 45 E
Bordj Bourguiba, *Tunisia* 96 B2 32 12N 10 2 E
Bordj el Hobra, *Algeria* 99 B5 32 9N 4 51 E
Bordj Fly Ste. Marie,
*Algeria* 98 C4 27 19N 2 32W
Bordj-in-Eker, *Algeria* 99 D6 24 9N 5 3 E
Bordj Menaiel, *Algeria* 99 A5 36 46N 3 43 E
Bordj Messouda, *Algeria* 99 B6 30 12N 9 25 E
Bordj Nili, *Algeria* 99 B5 33 28N 3 2 E
Bordj Omar Driss,
*Algeria* 99 C6 28 10N 6 40 E
Bordj-Tarat, *Algeria* 99 C6 25 55N 9 3 E
Bordj Zelfana, *Algeria* 99 B5 32 27N 4 15 E
Bordoba, *Kirghizia* 55 D6 39 31N 73 16 E
Borea Creek, *Australia* 117 C7 35 5 S 146 35 E
Borek Wielkopolski,
*Poland* 47 D4 51 54N 17 11 E
Boremore, *Australia* 117 B8 33 15 S 149 0 E
Boren Kapuas,
Pegunungan, *Malaysia* 75 B4 1 25N 113 15 E
Borensberg, *Sweden* 15 F9 58 34N 15 17 E
Borgå, *Finland* 13 F18 60 24N 25 40 E
Borgarnes, *Iceland* 12 D3 64 32N 21 55W
Børgefjellet, *Norway* 12 D12 65 20N 13 45 E
Borger, *Neths.* 20 C9 52 54N 6 44 E
Borger, *U.S.A.* 139 H4 35 40N 101 20W
Borgerhout, *Belgium* 21 F4 51 12N 4 28 E
Borghamn, *Sweden* 15 F8 58 23N 14 41 E
Borgholm, *Sweden* 13 H14 56 52N 16 39 E
Bórgia, *Italy* 41 D9 38 50N 16 30 E
Borgloon, *Belgium* 21 G6 50 48N 5 21 E
Borgo San Dalmazzo,
*Italy* 38 D4 44 19N 7 29 E
Borgo San Lorenzo, *Italy* 39 E8 43 57N 11 21 E
Borgo Valsugano, *Italy* 39 B8 46 3N 11 27 E
Borgomanero, *Italy* 38 C5 45 41N 8 28 E
Borgonovo Val Tidone,
*Italy* 38 C6 45 1N 9 28 E
Borgorose, *Italy* 39 F10 42 12N 13 14 E
Borgosésia, *Italy* 38 C5 45 43N 8 17 E
Borgvattnet, *Sweden* 14 A9 63 26N 15 48 E
Borikhane, *Laos* 76 C4 18 33N 103 43 E
Borislav, *Ukraine* 50 G3 49 18N 23 28 E
Borisoglebsk, *Russia* 51 F13 51 27N 42 5 E
Borisoglebskiy, *Russia* 51 C13 56 28N 43 59 E
Borisov, *Belorussia* 50 D6 54 17N 28 28 E
Borisovka, *Kazakhstan* 55 B4 43 15N 68 10 E
Borispol, *Ukraine* 50 F7 50 21N 30 59 E
Borja, *Peru* 152 D2 4 20 S 77 40W
Borja, *Spain* 34 D3 41 48N 1 34W
Borjas Blancas, *Spain* 34 D5 41 31N 0 52 E
Borken, *Germany* 26 D2 51 51N 6 52 E
Borkou, *Chad* 97 E3 18 15N 18 50 E
Borkum, *Germany* 26 B2 53 36N 6 42 E
Borlänge, *Sweden* 13 F13 60 29N 15 26 E
Borley, C., *Antarctica* 7 C5 66 15 S 52 30 E
Bormida →, *Italy* 38 D5 44 23N 8 13 E
Bórmio, *Italy* 38 B7 46 28N 10 22 E
Born, *Neths.* 21 F7 51 2N 5 49 E
Borna, *Germany* 26 D8 51 8N 12 31 E
Borndiep, *Neths.* 20 B7 53 27N 5 35 E
Borne, *Neths.* 20 D9 52 18N 6 46 E
Bornem, *Belgium* 21 F4 51 6N 4 14 E
Borneo, *E. Indies* 75 B4 1 0N 115 0 E
Bornholm, *Denmark* 13 J13 55 10N 15 0 E
Borno □, *Nigeria* 101 C7 12 30N 12 30 E
Bornos, *Spain* 37 J5 36 48N 5 42W
Bornu Yassa, *Nigeria* 101 C7 12 14N 12 25 E
Borobudur, *Indonesia* 75 D4 7 36 S 110 13 E
Borodino, *Russia* 50 D9 55 31N 35 40 E
Borogontsy, *Russia* 57 C14 62 42N 131 8 E
Boromo, *Burkina Faso* 100 C4 11 45N 2 58W
Boron, *U.S.A.* 145 L9 35 0N 117 39W
Borongа Is., *Burma* 78 F4 19 58N 93 6 E
Borongan, *Phil.* 71 F5 11 37N 125 26 E
Bororen, *Australia* 114 C5 24 13 S 151 33 E
Borotangba Mts., *C.A.R.* 95 F1 6 30N 25 0 E
Borovan, *Bulgaria* 43 D8 43 27N 23 45 E
Borovichi, *Russia* 50 B8 58 25N 33 55 E
Borovsk, *Russia* 51 D10 55 12N 36 24 E
Borovsk, *Russia* 54 B5 59 43N 56 40 E
Borovskoye, *Kazakhstan* 54 E9 53 48N 64 12 E
Borrego Springs, *U.S.A.* 145 M10 33 15N 116 23W
Borriol, *Spain* 34 E4 40 4N 0 4W
Borroloola, *Australia* 114 B2 16 4 S 136 17 E
Borşa, *Romania* 46 B5 47 41N 24 50 E
Borsod-Abaúj-
Zemplén □, *Hungary* 31 C13 48 20N 21 0 E
Borssele, *Neths.* 21 F3 51 26N 3 45 E
Bort-les-Orgues, *France* 24 C6 45 24N 2 29 E
Borth, *U.K.* 17 E3 52 29N 4 3W
Borujerd, *Iran* 85 C6 33 55N 48 50 E
Borzhomi, *Georgia* 53 F10 41 48N 43 28 E
Borzna, *Ukraine* 50 F8 51 18N 32 26 E
Borzya, *Russia* 57 D12 50 24N 116 31 E
Bosa, *Italy* 40 B1 40 17N 8 32 E
Bosaga, *Turkmenistan* 55 E2 37 33N 65 41 E
Bosanska Brod,
*Bos.-H., Yug.* 42 B3 45 10N 18 0 E
Bosanska Dubica,
*Bos.-H., Yug.* 39 C13 45 10N 16 50 E
Bosanska Gradiška,
*Bos.-H., Yug.* 42 B2 45 10N 17 15 E
Bosanska Kostajnica,
*Bos.-H., Yug.* 39 C13 45 11N 16 33 E
Bosanska Krupa,
*Bos.-H., Yug.* 39 D13 44 53N 16 10 E
Bosanski Novi,
*Bos.-H., Yug.* 39 C13 45 2N 16 22 E
Bosanski Šamac,
*Bos.-H., Yug.* 42 B3 45 3N 18 29 E
Bosansko Grahovo,
*Bos.-H., Yug.* 39 D13 44 12N 16 26 E
Bosansko Petrovac,
*Bos.-H., Yug.* 39 D13 44 35N 16 21 E
Bosaso, *Somali Rep.* 90 E4 11 12N 49 18 E
Bosavi, Mt., *Papua N. G.* 120 D2 6 30 S 142 49 E
Boscastle, *U.K.* 17 G3 50 42N 4 42W
Boscobel, *U.S.A.* 140 A6 43 8N 90 42W
Boscotrecase, *Italy* 41 B7 40 46N 14 28 E
Bose, *China* 68 F6 23 53N 106 35 E
Boshan, *China* 67 F9 36 28N 117 49 E
Boshoek, *S. Africa* 104 D4 25 30 S 27 9 E
Boshof, *S. Africa* 104 D4 28 31 S 25 13 E
Boshrūyeh, *Iran* 85 C8 33 50N 57 30 E
Bosilegrad, *Serbia, Yug.* 42 E7 42 30N 22 27 E
Boskoop, *Neths.* 20 D5 52 4N 4 40 E
Boskovice, *Czech.* 31 B9 49 29N 16 40 E
Bosna →, *Bos.-H., Yug.* 42 B3 45 4N 18 29 E
Bosna i Hercegovina =
Bosnia-Herzegovina □,
*Bos.-H., Yug.* 42 D2 44 0N 17 0 E
Bosnia-Herzegovina □,
*Bos.-H., Yug.* 42 D2 44 0N 17 0 E
Bosnik, *Indonesia* 73 B5 1 5 S 136 10 E
Bōsō-Hantō, *Japan* 63 B12 35 20N 140 20 E
Bosobolo, *Zaïre* 102 B3 4 15N 19 50 E
Bosporus = Karadeniz
Boğazı, *Turkey* 88 C3 41 10N 29 10 E
Bossangoa, *C.A.R.* 102 A3 6 35N 17 30 E
Bossekop, *Norway* 12 B17 69 57N 23 15 E
Bossembélé, *C.A.R.* 102 A3 5 25N 17 40 E
Bossembélé II, *C.A.R.* 102 A3 5 41N 16 38 E
Bossier City, *U.S.A.* 139 J8 32 28N 93 48W
Bosso, *Niger* 97 F2 13 43N 13 19 E
Bostānābād, *Iran* 84 B5 37 50N 46 50 E
Bosten Hu, *China* 64 B3 41 55N 87 40 E
Boston, *Phil.* 71 H6 7 52N 126 22 E
Boston, *U.K.* 16 E7 52 59N 0 2W
Boston, *U.S.A.* 137 D13 42 20N 71 5W
Boston Bar, *Canada* 130 D4 49 52N 121 30W
Bosusulu, *Zaïre* 102 B4 0 50N 20 45 E
Bosut →, *Croatia* 42 B3 45 20N 18 45 E
Boswell, *Canada* 130 D5 49 28N 116 45W
Boswell, *Ind., U.S.A.* 141 D9 40 30N 87 23W
Boswell, *Okla., U.S.A.* 139 H7 34 1N 95 50W
Boswell, *Pa., U.S.A.* 136 F5 40 9N 79 2W
Bosworth, *U.S.A.* 140 E3 39 28N 93 20W
Botad, *India* 80 H4 22 15N 71 40 E
Botan →, *Turkey* 89 E9 37 44N 41 47 E
Botany B., *Australia* 115 E5 34 0 S 151 14 E
Botene, *Laos* 76 D3 17 35N 101 12 E
Botevgrad, *Bulgaria* 43 E8 42 55N 23 47 E
Bothaville, *S. Africa* 104 D4 27 23 S 26 34 E
Bothnia, G. of, *Europe* 12 E16 63 0N 20 15 E
Bothwell, *Australia* 114 G4 42 20 S 147 1 E
Bothwell, *Canada* 136 D3 42 38N 81 52W
Boticas, *Portugal* 36 D3 41 41N 7 40W
Botletle →, *Botswana* 104 C3 20 10 S 23 15 E
Botolan, *Phil.* 70 D3 15 17N 120 1 E
Botoroaga, *Romania* 46 E6 44 8N 25 32 E
Botoşani, *Romania* 46 B7 47 42N 26 41 E
Botoşani □, *Romania* 46 B7 47 50N 26 50 E
Botro, *Ivory C.* 100 D3 7 51N 5 19W
Botswana ■, *Africa* 104 C3 22 0 S 24 0 E
Bottineau, *U.S.A.* 138 A4 48 49N 100 25W
Bottrop, *Germany* 21 E9 51 34N 6 59 E
Botucatu, *Brazil* 159 A6 22 55 S 48 30W
Botwood, *Canada* 129 C8 49 6N 55 23W
Bou Alam, *Algeria* 99 B5 33 50N 1 26 E
Bou Ali, *Algeria* 99 C4 27 11N 0 4W
Bou Djébéha, *Mali* 100 B4 18 25N 2 45W
Bou Guema, *Algeria* 99 C5 28 49N 0 19 E
Bou Ismael, *Algeria* 99 A5 36 38N 2 42 E
Bou Izakarn, *Morocco* 98 C3 29 12N 9 46W
Boû Lanouâr, *Mauritania* 98 D1 21 12N 16 34W
Bou Saâda, *Algeria* 99 A5 35 11N 4 9 E
Bou Salem, *Tunisia* 96 A1 36 45N 9 2 E
Bouaké, *Ivory C.* 100 D3 7 40N 5 2W
Bouanga, *Congo* 102 C3 2 7 S 16 8 E
Bouar, *C.A.R.* 102 A3 6 0N 15 40 E
Bouârfa, *Morocco* 99 B4 32 32N 1 58W
Bouca, *C.A.R.* 102 A3 6 45N 18 25 E
Boucau, *France* 24 E2 43 32N 1 29W
Boucaut B., *Australia* 114 A1 12 0 S 134 25 E
Bouches-du-Rhône □,
*France* 25 E9 43 37N 5 2 E
Bouda, *Algeria* 99 C4 27 50N 0 27W
Boudenib, *Morocco* 98 B4 31 59N 3 31W
Boudry, *Switz.* 28 C3 46 57N 6 50 E
Boufarik, *Algeria* 99 A5 36 34N 2 58 E
Bougainville, C.,
*Australia* 112 B4 13 57 S 126 4 E
Bougainville I.,
*Solomon Is.* 121 L8 6 0 S 155 0 E
Bougainville Reef,
*Australia* 114 B4 15 30 S 147 5 E
Bougainville Str.,
*Solomon Is.* 121 L9 6 40 S 156 10 E
Bougaroun, C., *Algeria* 99 A6 37 6N 6 30 E
Bougie = Bejaia, *Algeria* 99 A6 36 42N 5 2 E
Bougouni, *Mali* 100 C3 11 30N 7 20W
Bouillon, *Belgium* 21 J6 49 44N 5 3 E
Bouïra, *Algeria* 99 A5 36 20N 3 59 E
Boulder, *Colo., U.S.A.* 138 E2 40 3N 105 10W
Boulder, *Mont., U.S.A.* 142 C7 46 14N 112 4W
Boulder City, *U.S.A.* 145 K12 35 58N 114 50W
Boulder Creek, *U.S.A.* 144 H4 37 7N 122 7W
Boulder Dam = Hoover
Dam, *U.S.A.* 145 K12 36 0N 114 45W
Boulembo, *Gabon* 102 C2 1 26 S 12 0 E
Bouli, *Mauritania* 100 B2 15 17N 12 18W
Boulia, *Australia* 114 C2 22 52 S 139 51 E
Bouligny, *France* 23 C12 49 17N 5 45 E
Boulogne →, *France* 22 E5 47 12N 1 47W
Boulogne-sur-Gesse,
*France* 24 E4 43 18N 0 38 E
Boulogne-sur-Mer, *France* 23 B8 50 42N 1 36 E
Bouloire, *France* 22 E7 47 59N 0 45 E
Bouloupari, *N. Cal.* 121 U20 21 52 S 166 4 E
Boulsa, *Burkina Faso* 101 C4 12 39N 0 34W
Boultoum, *Niger* 97 F2 14 45N 10 25 E
Boumalne, *Morocco* 98 B3 31 25N 6 0W
Boun Neua, *Laos* 76 B3 21 38N 101 54 E
Boun Tai, *Laos* 76 B3 21 23N 101 58 E
Bouna, *Ivory C.* 100 D4 9 10N 3 0W
Boundary Pk., *U.S.A.* 144 H8 37 51N 118 21W
Boundiali, *Ivory C.* 100 D3 9 30N 6 20W
Bountiful, *U.S.A.* 142 F8 40 57N 111 58W
Bounty Is., *Pac. Oc.* 122 M9 48 0 S 178 30 E
Bourail, *N. Cal.* 121 U19 21 34 S 165 30 E
Bourbeuse →, *U.S.A.* 140 F6 38 24N 90 54W
Bourbon, *U.S.A.* 141 C10 41 18N 86 7W
Bourbon-Lancy, *France* 24 B7 46 37N 3 45 E
Bourbon-l'Archambault,
*France* 24 B7 46 36N 3 4 E
Bourbonnais, *France* 24 B7 46 28N 3 0 E
Bourbonne-les-Bains,
*France* 23 E12 47 54N 5 45 E
Bourem, *Mali* 101 B4 17 0N 0 24W
Bourg, *France* 24 C3 45 3N 0 34W
Bourg-Argental, *France* 25 C8 45 18N 4 32 E
Bourg-de-Péage, *France* 25 C9 45 2N 5 3 E
Bourg-en-Bresse, *France* 25 B9 46 13N 5 12 E
Bourg-St.-Andéol, *France* 25 D8 44 23N 4 39 E
Bourg-St.-Maurice,
*France* 25 C10 45 35N 6 46 E
Bourg-St.-Pierre, *Switz.* 28 E4 45 57N 7 12 E
Bourganeuf, *France* 24 C5 45 57N 1 45 E
Bourges, *France* 23 E9 47 9N 2 25 E
Bourget, *Canada* 137 A9 45 26N 75 9W
Bourget, L. du, *France* 25 C9 45 44N 5 52 E
Bourgneuf, B. de, *France* 22 E4 47 3N 2 10W
Bourgneuf-en-Retz,
*France* 22 E5 47 2N 1 58W
Bourgogne, *France* 23 F11 47 0N 4 50 E
Bourgoin-Jallieu, *France* 25 C9 45 36N 5 17 E
Bourgueil, *France* 22 E7 47 17N 0 10 E
Bourke, *Australia* 115 E4 30 8 S 145 55 E
Bournemouth, *U.K.* 17 G6 50 43N 1 53W
Bourriot-Bergonce,
*France* 24 D3 44 7N 0 14W
Bouse, *U.S.A.* 145 M13 33 55N 114 0W
Boussac, *France* 24 B6 46 22N 2 13 E
Boussens, *France* 24 E4 43 12N 0 58 E
Bousso, *Chad* 97 F3 10 34N 16 52 E
Boussu, *Belgium* 21 H3 50 26N 3 48 E
Boutilimit, *Mauritania* 100 B2 17 45N 14 40W
Bouvet I. = Bouvetøya,
*Antarctica* 9 P9 54 26 S 3 24 E
Bouvetøya, *Antarctica* 9 P9 54 26 S 3 24 E
Bouznika, *Morocco* 98 B3 33 46N 7 6W
Bouzonville, *France* 23 C13 49 17N 6 32 E
Bova Marina, *Italy* 41 E8 37 59N 15 56 E
Bovalino Marina, *Italy* 41 D9 38 9N 16 10 E
Bovec, *Slovenia* 39 B10 46 20N 13 33 E
Bovenkarspel, *Neths.* 20 C6 52 41N 5 14 E
Bovigny, *Belgium* 21 H7 50 12N 5 55 E
Bovill, *U.S.A.* 142 C5 46 58N 116 27W
Bovino, *Italy* 41 A8 41 15N 15 20 E
Bow Island, *Canada* 130 D6 49 50N 111 23W
Bowbells, *U.S.A.* 138 A3 48 47N 102 19W
Bowdle, *U.S.A.* 138 C5 45 30N 99 40W
Bowelling, *Australia* 113 F2 33 25 S 116 30 E
Bowen, *Australia* 114 C4 20 0 S 148 16 E
Bowen Mts., *Australia* 117 D7 37 0 S 147 50 E
Bowie, *Ariz., U.S.A.* 143 K9 32 15N 109 30W
Bowie, *Tex., U.S.A.* 139 J6 33 33N 97 50W
Bowkān, *Iran* 84 B5 36 31N 46 12 E
Bowland, Forest of, *U.K.* 16 D5 54 0N 2 30W
Bowling Green, *Ky.*,
*U.S.A.* 134 G2 37 0N 86 25W
Bowling Green, *Mo.*,
*U.S.A.* 140 E5 39 21N 91 12W
Bowling Green, *Ohio*,
*U.S.A.* 141 C13 41 22N 83 40W
Bowling Green, C.,
*Australia* 114 B4 19 19 S 147 25 E
Bowman, *U.S.A.* 138 B3 46 12N 103 21W
Bowman I., *Antarctica* 7 C8 65 0 S 104 0 E
Bowmans, *Australia* 116 C3 34 10 S 138 17 E
Bowmanville, *Canada* 128 D4 43 55N 78 41W
Bowmore, *U.K.* 18 F2 55 45N 6 18W
Bowral, *Australia* 117 C9 34 26 S 150 27 E
Bowraville, *Australia* 115 E5 30 37 S 152 52 E
Bowron →, *Canada* 130 C4 54 3N 121 50W
Bowser L., *Canada* 130 B3 56 30N 129 30W
Bowsman, *Canada* 131 C8 52 14N 101 12W
Bowutu Mts.,
*Papua N. G.* 120 D4 7 45 S 147 10 E
Bowwood, *Zambia* 107 F2 17 5 S 26 20 E
Boxholm, *Sweden* 15 F9 58 12N 15 3 E
Boxmeer, *Neths.* 21 E7 51 38N 5 56 E
Boxtel, *Neths.* 21 E6 51 36N 5 20 E
Boyabat, *Turkey* 52 F6 41 28N 34 42 E
Boyabo, *Zaïre* 102 B3 3 43N 18 46 E
Boyaca = Casanare □,
*Colombia* 152 B3 6 0N 73 0W
Boyce, *U.S.A.* 139 K8 31 25N 92 39W
Boyer →, *Canada* 130 B5 58 27N 115 57W
Boyer, C., *N. Cal.* 121 U22 21 37 S 168 6 E
Boyle, *Ireland* 19 C3 53 58N 8 19W
Boyne →, *Ireland* 19 C5 53 43N 6 15W
Boyne City, *U.S.A.* 134 C3 45 13N 85 1W
Boyni Qara, *Afghan.* 79 A2 36 20N 67 0 E
Boynton Beach, *U.S.A.* 135 M5 26 31N 80 3W
Boyolali, *Indonesia* 75 D4 7 32 S 110 35 E
Boyoma, Chutes, *Zaïre* 102 B5 0 35N 25 23 E
Boyup Brook, *Australia* 113 F2 33 50 S 116 23 E
Boz Dağ, *Turkey* 88 E3 37 18N 29 11 E
Boz Dağları, *Turkey* 88 D3 38 20N 28 0 E
Bozburun, *Turkey* 45 H10 36 43N 28 8 E
Bozcaada, *Turkey* 44 E8 39 49N 26 3 E
Bozdoğan, *Turkey* 88 E3 37 40N 28 17 E
Bozeman, *U.S.A.* 142 D8 45 40N 111 0W
Bozen = Bolzano, *Italy* 39 B8 46 30N 11 20 E
Bozene, *Zaïre* 102 B3 2 56N 19 12 E
Bożepole Wielkopolskie,
*Poland* 47 A4 54 33N 17 56 E
Boževac, *Serbia, Yug.* 42 C6 44 32N 21 24 E
Bozkır, *Turkey* 88 E5 37 11N 32 14 E
Bozouls, *France* 24 D6 44 28N 2 43 E
Bozoum, *C.A.R.* 102 A3 6 25N 16 35 E
Bozova, *Turkey* 89 E8 37 21N 38 32 E
Bozovici, *Romania* 46 E3 44 56N 22 1 E
Bozüyük, *Turkey* 88 D4 39 54N 30 3 E
Bra, *Italy* 38 D4 44 41N 7 50 E
Brabant □, *Belgium* 21 G5 50 46N 4 30 E
Brabant L., *Canada* 131 B8 55 58N 103 43W
Brabrand, *Denmark* 15 H4 56 9N 10 7 E
Brač, *Croatia* 39 E13 43 20N 16 40 E
Bracadale, L., *U.K.* 18 D2 57 20N 6 30W
Bracciano, *Italy* 39 F9 42 6N 12 10 E
Bracciano, L. di, *Italy* 39 F9 42 8N 12 11 E
Bracebridge, *Canada* 128 C4 45 2N 79 19W
Brach, *Libya* 96 C2 27 31N 14 20 E
Bracieux, *France* 23 E8 47 30N 1 30 E
Bräcke, *Sweden* 14 B9 62 45N 15 26 E
Brackettville, *U.S.A.* 139 L4 29 21N 100 20W
Bracki Kanal, *Croatia* 39 E13 43 24N 16 40 E
Brad, *Romania* 46 C3 46 10N 22 50 E
Brádano →, *Italy* 41 B9 40 23N 16 51 E
Bradenton, *U.S.A.* 135 M4 27 25N 82 35W
Bradford, *Canada* 136 B5 44 7N 79 34W
Bradford, *U.K.* 16 D6 53 47N 1 45W
Bradford, *Ill., U.S.A.* 140 C7 41 11N 89 39W
Bradford, *Ohio, U.S.A.* 141 D12 40 8N 84 27W
Bradford, *Pa., U.S.A.* 136 E6 41 58N 78 41W
Bradford, *Vt., U.S.A.* 137 C12 43 59N 72 9W
Brădiceni, *Romania* 46 D4 45 3N 23 4 E
Bradley, *Ark., U.S.A.* 139 J8 33 7N 93 39W
Bradley, *Calif., U.S.A.* 144 K6 35 52N 120 48W
Bradley, *Ill., U.S.A.* 141 C9 41 9N 87 52W
Bradley, *S. Dak., U.S.A.* 138 C6 45 10N 97 40W
Bradley Institute,
*Zimbabwe* 107 F3 17 7 S 31 25 E
Bradore Bay, *Canada* 129 B8 51 27N 57 18W
Bradshaw, *Australia* 112 C5 15 21 S 130 16 E
Brady, *U.S.A.* 139 K5 31 9N 99 20W
Brædstrup, *Denmark* 15 J3 55 58N 9 37 E
Braemar, *Australia* 116 B3 33 12 S 139 35 E
Braeside, *Canada* 137 A8 45 28N 76 24W
Braga, *Portugal* 36 D2 41 35N 8 25W
Braga □, *Portugal* 36 D2 41 30N 8 30W
Bragado, *Argentina* 158 D3 35 2 S 60 27W
Bragança, *Brazil* 154 B2 1 0 S 47 2W
Bragança, *Portugal* 36 D4 41 48N 6 50W
Bragança □, *Portugal* 36 D4 41 30N 6 45W
Bragança Paulista, *Brazil* 159 A6 22 55 S 46 32W
Brahmanbaria, *Bangla.* 78 D3 23 58N 91 15 E
Brahmani →, *India* 82 D8 20 39N 86 46 E
Brahmaputra →, *India* 78 D2 23 58N 89 50 E
Braich-y-pwll, *U.K.* 16 E3 52 47N 4 46W
Braidwood, *Australia* 117 C8 35 27 S 149 49 E
Brăila, *Romania* 46 D8 45 19N 27 59 E
Brăila □, *Romania* 46 D8 45 5N 27 30 E
Braine-l'Alleud, *Belgium* 21 G4 50 42N 4 23 E
Braine-le-Comte, *Belgium* 21 G4 50 37N 4 8 E
Brainerd, *U.S.A.* 138 B7 46 20N 94 10W
Braintree, *U.K.* 17 F8 51 53N 0 34 E
Braintree, *U.S.A.* 137 D14 42 11N 71 0W
Brak →, *S. Africa* 104 D3 29 35 S 22 55 E
Brake, *Niedersachsen*,
*Germany* 26 B4 53 19N 8 30 E
Brake,
*Nordrhein-Westfalen*,
*Germany* 26 D5 51 43N 9 12 E

Bustamante, B. 179


Bryansk, *Russia* 50 E9 53 13N 34 25 E
Bryanskoye, *Russia* 53 D12 44 20N 47 10 E
Bryant, *U.S.A.* 138 C6 44 35N 97 28W
Bryne, *Norway* 13 G8 58 44N 5 38 E
Bryson City, *U.S.A.* 135 H4 35 28N 83 25W
Brza Palanka, *Serbia, Yug.* 42 C7 44 28N 22 27 E
Brzava →, *Serbia, Yug.* 42 B5 45 21N 20 45 E
Brzeg, *Poland* 47 E4 50 52N 17 30 E
Brzeg Din, *Poland* 47 D3 51 16N 16 41 E
Brześć Kujawski, *Poland* 47 C5 52 36N 18 55 E
Brzesko, *Poland* 31 B13 49 59N 20 34 E
Brzeszcze, *Poland* 31 B12 49 59N 19 10 E
Brzeziny, *Poland* 47 D6 51 49N 19 42 E
Brzozów, *Poland* 31 B15 49 41N 22 3 E
Bsharri, *Lebanon* 91 A5 34 15N 36 0 E
Bū Athlah, *Libya* 96 B3 30 9N 15 39 E
Bū Baqarah, *U.A.E.* 85 E8 25 35N 56 25 E
Bu Craa, *W. Sahara* 98 C2 26 45N 12 50W
Bū Ḥasā, *U.A.E.* 85 F7 23 30N 53 20 E
Bua Yai, *Thailand* 76 E4 15 33N 102 26 E
Buad I., *Phil.* 71 F5 11 40N 124 51 E
Buala, *Solomon Is.* 121 M10 8 10 S 159 35 E
Buapinang, *Indonesia* 72 B2 4 40 S 121 30 E
Buba, *Guinea-Biss.* 100 C2 11 40N 14 59W
Bubanda, *Zaïre* 102 B3 4 14N 19 38 E
Bubanza, *Burundi* 106 C2 3 6 S 29 23 E
Būbiyān, *Kuwait* 85 D6 29 45N 48 15 E
Bucak, *Turkey* 88 E4 37 28N 30 36 E
Bucaramanga, *Colombia* 152 B3 7 0N 73 0W
Bucas Grande I., *Phil.* 71 G5 9 40N 125 57 E
Buccaneer Arch., *Australia* 112 C3 16 7 S 123 20 E
Bucchiánico, *Italy* 39 F11 42 20N 14 10 E
Bucecea, *Romania* 46 B7 47 47N 26 28 E
Buchach, *Ukraine* 50 G4 49 5N 25 25 E
Buchan, *Australia* 117 D8 37 30 S 148 12 E
Buchan, *U.K.* 18 D6 57 32N 2 8W
Buchan Ness, *U.K.* 18 D7 57 29N 1 48W
Buchanan, *Canada* 131 C8 51 40N 102 45W
Buchanan, *Liberia* 100 D2 5 57N 10 2W
Buchanan, *U.S.A.* 141 C10 41 50N 86 22W
Buchanan, L., *Queens., Australia* 114 C4 21 35 S 145 52 E
Buchanan, L., *W. Austral., Australia* 113 E3 25 33 S 123 2 E
Buchanan, L., *U.S.A.* 139 K5 30 50N 98 25W
Buchanan Cr. →, *Australia* 114 B2 19 13 S 136 33 E
Buchans, *Canada* 129 C8 48 50N 56 52W
Bucharest = Bucureşti, *Romania* 46 E7 44 27N 26 10 E
Buchholz, *Germany* 26 B5 53 19N 9 51 E
Buchloe, *Germany* 27 G6 48 3N 10 45 E
Buchon, Pt., *U.S.A.* 144 K6 35 15N 120 54W
Buchs, *Switz.* 29 B8 47 10N 9 28 E
Bückeburg, *Germany* 26 C5 52 16N 9 2 E
Buckeye, *U.S.A.* 143 K7 33 28N 112 40W
Buckhannon, *U.S.A.* 134 F5 39 2N 80 10W
Buckhaven, *U.K.* 18 E5 56 10N 3 2W
Buckie, *U.K.* 18 D6 57 40N 2 58W
Buckingham, *Canada* 128 C4 45 37N 75 24W
Buckingham, *U.K.* 17 F7 52 0N 0 59W
Buckingham B., *Australia* 114 A2 12 10 S 135 40 E
Buckingham Canal, *India* 83 G5 14 0N 80 5 E
Buckinghamshire □, *U.K.* 17 F7 51 50N 0 55W
Buckland, *U.S.A.* 141 D12 40 37N 84 16W
Buckle Hd., *Australia* 112 B4 14 26 S 127 52 E
Buckleboo, *Australia* 116 B2 32 54 S 136 12 E
Buckley, *Ill., U.S.A.* 141 D8 40 35N 88 2W
Buckley, *Wash., U.S.A.* 142 C2 47 10N 122 2W
Buckley →, *Australia* 114 C2 20 10 S 138 49 E
Bucklin, *Kans., U.S.A.* 139 G5 37 37N 99 40W
Bucklin, *Mo., U.S.A.* 140 E4 39 47N 92 53W
Bucks L., *U.S.A.* 144 F5 39 54N 121 12W
Buco Zau, *Angola* 103 C2 4 46 S 12 33 E
Bucquoy, *France* 23 B9 50 9N 2 43 E
Buctouche, *Canada* 129 C7 46 30N 64 45W
Bucureşti, *Romania* 46 E7 44 27N 26 10 E
Bucyrus, *U.S.A.* 141 D14 40 48N 82 58W
Budafok, *Hungary* 31 D12 47 26N 19 2 E
Budalin, *Burma* 78 D5 22 20N 95 10 E
Budapest, *Hungary* 31 D12 47 29N 19 5 E
Budaun, *India* 81 E8 28 5N 79 10 E
Budd Coast, *Antarctica* 7 C8 68 0 S 112 0 E
Buddabadah, *Australia* 117 A7 31 56 S 147 14 E
Buddusò, *Italy* 40 B2 40 35N 9 18 E
Bude, *U.K.* 17 G3 50 49N 4 33W
Budel, *Neths.* 21 F7 51 17N 5 34 E
Budennovsk, *Russia* 53 D11 44 50N 44 10 E
Budeşti, *Romania* 46 E7 44 13N 26 30 E
Budge Budge = Baj Baj, *India* 81 H13 22 30N 88 5 E
Budgewoi, *Australia* 117 B9 33 13 S 151 34 E
Búðareyri, *Iceland* 12 D6 65 2N 14 13W
Búðir, *Iceland* 12 D2 64 49N 23 23W
Budia, *Spain* 34 E2 40 38N 2 46W
Budjala, *Zaïre* 102 B3 2 50N 19 40 E
Búdrio, *Italy* 39 D8 44 31N 11 31 E
Budva, *Montenegro, Yug.* 42 E3 42 17N 18 50 E
Budzyń, *Poland* 47 C3 52 54N 16 59 E
Buea, *Cameroon* 101 E6 4 10N 9 9 E
Buellton, *U.S.A.* 145 L6 34 37N 120 12W
Buena Vista, *Bolivia* 157 D5 17 27 S 63 40W
Buena Vista, *Colo., U.S.A.* 143 G10 38 56N 106 6W
Buena Vista, *Va., U.S.A.* 134 G6 37 47N 79 23W
Buena Vista L., *U.S.A.* 145 K7 35 15N 119 21W
Buenaventura, *Colombia* 152 C2 3 53N 77 4W
Buenaventura, *Mexico* 146 B3 29 50N 107 30W
Buenaventura, B. de, *Colombia* 152 C2 3 48N 77 17W
Buenavista, *Luzon, Phil.* 70 E4 13 35N 122 34 E
Buenavista, *Mindanao, Phil.* 71 G5 8 59N 125 24 E
Buenavista, *Zamboanga del S., Phil.* 71 H4 7 15N 122 16 E
Buendía, Pantano de, *Spain* 34 E2 40 25N 2 43W
Buenópolis, *Brazil* 155 E3 17 54 S 44 11W
Buenos Aires, *Argentina* 158 C4 34 30 S 58 20W
Buenos Aires, *Colombia* 152 C3 1 36N 73 18W
Buenos Aires, *Costa Rica* 148 E3 9 10N 83 20W
Buenos Aires □, *Argentina* 158 D4 36 30 S 60 0W
Buenos Aires, L., *Chile* 160 C2 46 35 S 72 30W
Buesaco, *Colombia* 152 C2 1 23N 77 9W
Buffalo, *Mo., U.S.A.* 139 G8 37 40N 93 5W
Buffalo, *N.Y., U.S.A.* 136 D6 42 55N 78 50W
Buffalo, *Okla., U.S.A.* 139 G5 36 55N 99 42W
Buffalo, *S. Dak., U.S.A.* 138 C3 45 39N 103 31W
Buffalo, *Wyo., U.S.A.* 142 D10 44 25N 106 50W
Buffalo →, *Canada* 130 A5 60 5N 115 5W
Buffalo Head Hills, *Canada* 130 B5 57 25N 115 55W
Buffalo L., *Canada* 130 C6 52 27N 112 54W
Buffalo Narrows, *Canada* 131 B7 55 51N 108 29W
Buffels →, *S. Africa* 104 D2 29 36 S 17 3 E
Buford, *U.S.A.* 135 H4 34 5N 84 0W
Bug →, *Poland* 47 C8 52 31N 21 5 E
Bug →, *Ukraine* 52 C4 46 59N 31 58 E
Buga, *Colombia* 152 C2 4 0N 76 15W
Buganda, *Uganda* 106 C3 0 0 31 30 E
Buganga, *Uganda* 106 C3 0 3 S 32 0 E
Bugasan, *Phil.* 71 H5 7 27N 124 14 E
Bugasong, *Phil.* 71 F4 11 3N 122 4 E
Bugeat, *France* 24 C5 45 36N 1 55 E
Bugel, Tanjung, *Indonesia* 75 D4 6 26 S 111 3 E
Buggenhout, *Belgium* 21 F4 51 1N 4 12 E
Bugibba, *Malta* 32 D1 35 57N 14 25 E
Bugojno, *Bos.-H., Yug.* 42 C2 44 2N 17 25 E
Bugsuk, *Phil.* 71 G1 8 15N 117 15 E
Buguey, *Phil.* 70 B3 18 17N 121 50 E
Bugulma, *Russia* 54 D3 54 33N 52 48 E
Buguma, *Nigeria* 101 E6 4 42N 6 55 E
Bugun Shara, *Mongolia* 64 B5 49 0N 104 0 E
Bugun Shara, *Mongolia* 64 B5 49 0N 104 0 E
Buguruslan, *Russia* 54 E3 53 39N 52 26 E
Buhăeşti, *Romania* 46 C8 46 47N 27 32 E
Buheirat-Murrat-el-Kubra, *Egypt* 94 H8 30 15N 32 40 E
Buhl, *Idaho, U.S.A.* 142 E6 42 35N 114 54W
Buhl, *Minn., U.S.A.* 138 B8 47 30N 92 46W
Buhuşi, *Romania* 46 C7 46 41N 26 45 E
Buick, *U.S.A.* 139 G9 37 38N 91 2W
Builth Wells, *U.K.* 17 E4 52 10N 3 26W
Buin, *Papua N. G.* 121 L8 6 48 S 155 42 E
Buinsk, *Russia* 51 D16 55 0N 48 18 E
Buíque, *Brazil* 154 C4 8 37 S 37 9W
Buir Nur, *Mongolia* 65 B6 47 50N 117 42 E
Buis-les-Baronnies, *France* 25 D9 44 17N 5 16 E
Buitenpost, *Neths.* 20 B8 53 15N 6 9 E
Buitrago, *Spain* 36 E7 40 58N 3 38W
Bujalance, *Spain* 37 H6 37 54N 4 23W
Buján, *Spain* 36 C2 42 59N 8 36W
Bujanovac, *Serbia, Yug.* 42 E6 42 28N 21 44 E
Bujaraloz, *Spain* 34 D4 41 29N 0 10W
Buje, *Croatia* 39 C10 45 24N 13 39 E
Bujumbura, *Burundi* 106 C2 3 16 S 29 18 E
Bük, *Hungary* 31 D9 47 22N 16 45 E
Buk, *Poland* 47 C3 52 21N 16 30 E
Buka I., *Papua N. G.* 120 C8 5 10 S 154 35 E
Bukachacha, *Russia* 57 D12 52 55N 116 50 E
Bukama, *Zaïre* 107 D2 9 10 S 25 50 E
Bukavu, *Zaïre* 106 C2 2 20 S 28 52 E
Bukene, *Tanzania* 106 C3 4 15 S 32 48 E
Bukhara, *Uzbekistan* 55 D2 39 48N 64 25 E
Bukidnon □, *Phil.* 71 G5 8 0N 125 0 E
Bukima, *Tanzania* 106 C3 1 50 S 33 25 E
Bukit Mertajam, *Malaysia* 77 K3 5 22N 100 28 E
Bukittinggi, *Indonesia* 74 C2 0 20 S 100 20 E
Bukkapatnam, *India* 83 G3 14 14N 77 46 E
Buklyan, *Russia* 54 D3 55 42N 52 10 E
Bukoba, *Tanzania* 106 C3 1 20 S 31 49 E
Bukoba □, *Tanzania* 106 C3 1 30 S 32 0 E
Bukowno, *Poland* 31 A12 50 17N 19 35 E
Bukuru, *Nigeria* 101 D6 9 42N 8 48 E
Bukuya, *Uganda* 106 B3 0 40N 31 52 E
Bula, *Guinea-Biss.* 100 C1 12 7N 15 43W
Bula, *Indonesia* 73 B4 3 6 S 130 30 E
Bulacan, *Phil.* 70 E3 13 40N 120 21 E
Bulacan □, *Phil.* 70 D3 15 0N 121 5 E
Bülach, *Switz.* 29 A7 47 31N 8 32 E
Bulahdelah, *Australia* 117 B10 32 23 S 152 13 E
Bulalacao, *Phil.* 70 E3 12 31N 121 26 E
Bulan, *Phil.* 70 E4 12 40N 123 52 E
Bulanash, *Russia* 54 C8 57 16N 62 0 E
Bulancak, *Turkey* 89 C8 40 56N 38 14 E
Bulandshahr, *India* 80 E7 28 28N 77 51 E
Bulanık, *Turkey* 89 D10 39 4N 42 14 E
Bulanovo, *Russia* 54 E4 52 27N 55 10 E
Bûlâq, *Egypt* 94 B3 25 10N 30 38 E
Bulawayo, *Zimbabwe* 107 G2 20 7 S 28 32 E
Buldan, *Turkey* 88 D3 38 2N 28 50 E
Buldana, *India* 82 D3 20 30N 76 18 E
Buldon, *Phil.* 71 H5 7 33N 124 25 E
Bulgaria ■, *Europe* 43 E10 42 35N 25 30 E
Bulgroo, *Australia* 115 D3 25 47 S 143 58 E
Bulgunnia, *Australia* 115 E1 30 10 S 134 53 E
Bulhale, *Somali Rep.* 108 C3 5 20N 46 29 E
Bulhar, *Somali Rep.* 108 E3 10 25N 44 30 E
Buli, Teluk, *Indonesia* 72 A3 1 5N 128 25 E
Buliluyan, C., *Phil.* 71 G1 8 20N 117 15 E
Bulki, *Ethiopia* 95 F4 6 11N 36 31 E
Bulkley →, *Canada* 130 B3 55 15N 127 40W
Bull Shoals L., *U.S.A.* 139 G8 36 40N 93 5W
Bullange, *Belgium* 21 H8 50 24N 6 15 E
Bullaque →, *Spain* 37 G6 38 59N 4 17W
Bullara, *Australia* 112 D1 22 40 S 114 3 E
Bullaring, *Australia* 113 F2 32 30 S 117 45 E
Bullas, *Spain* 35 G3 38 2N 1 40W
Bulle, *Switz.* 28 C4 46 37N 7 3 E
Buller →, *N.Z.* 119 B6 41 44 S 171 36 E
Buller, Mt., *Australia* 117 D7 37 10 S 146 28 E
Buller Gorge, *N.Z.* 119 B7 41 40 S 172 10 E
Bulli, *Australia* 117 C9 34 15 S 150 57 E
Bullock Creek, *Australia* 114 B3 17 43 S 144 31 E
Bulloo →, *Australia* 115 D3 28 43 S 142 30 E
Bulloo Downs, *Queens., Australia* 115 D3 28 31 S 142 57 E
Bulloo Downs, *W. Austral., Australia* 112 D2 24 0 S 119 32 E
Bulloo L., *Australia* 115 D3 28 43 S 142 25 E
Bulls, *N.Z.* 118 G4 40 10 S 175 24 E
Bully-les-Mines, *France* 23 B9 50 27N 2 44 E
Bulnes, *Chile* 158 D1 36 42 S 72 19W
Bulo Burti, *Somali Rep.* 90 G4 3 50N 45 33 E
Bulo Ghedudo, *Somali Rep.* 108 D2 2 52N 43 1 E
Bulolo, *Papua N. G.* 120 D4 7 10 S 146 40 E
Bulongo, *Zaïre* 103 C4 4 45 S 21 30 E
Bulpunga, *Australia* 116 B4 33 47 S 141 45 E
Bulqiza, *Albania* 44 C2 41 30N 20 21 E
Bulsar = Valsad, *India* 82 D1 20 40N 72 58 E
Bultfontein, *S. Africa* 104 D4 28 18 S 26 10 E
Buluan, L., *Phil.* 71 H5 6 40N 124 49 E
Buluangan, *Phil.* 71 F4 10 24N 123 20 E
Bulukumba, *Indonesia* 72 C2 5 33 S 120 11 E
Bulun, *Russia* 57 B13 70 37N 127 30 E
Bulungu, *Zaïre* 103 D4 6 4 S 21 54 E
Bulusan, *Phil.* 70 E5 12 45N 124 8 E
Bumba, *Zaïre* 102 B4 2 13N 22 30 E
Bumbiri I., *Tanzania* 106 C3 1 40 S 31 55 E
Bumhkang, *Burma* 78 B6 26 51N 97 40 E
Bumhpa Bum, *Burma* 78 B6 26 51N 97 14 E
Bumi →, *Zimbabwe* 107 F2 17 0 S 28 20 E
Bumtang →, *Bhutan* 78 B3 26 56N 90 53 E
Buna, *Kenya* 106 B4 2 58N 39 30 E
Buna, *Papua N. G.* 120 E5 8 42 S 148 27 E
Bunawan, *Agusan del S., Phil.* 71 G5 8 12N 125 57 E
Bunawan, *Davao del S., Phil.* 71 H5 7 14N 125 38 E
Bunazi, *Tanzania* 106 C3 1 3 S 31 23 E
Bunbah, Khalīj, *Libya* 96 B4 32 20N 23 15 E
Bunbury, *Australia* 113 F2 33 20 S 115 35 E
Buncrana, *Ireland* 19 A4 55 8N 7 28W
Bundaberg, *Australia* 115 C5 24 54 S 152 22 E
Bünde, *Germany* 26 C4 52 11N 8 33 E
Bundey →, *Australia* 114 C2 21 46 S 135 37 E
Bundi, *India* 80 G6 25 30N 75 35 E
Bundooma, *Australia* 114 C1 24 54 S 134 16 E
Bundoran, *Ireland* 19 B3 54 24N 8 17W
Bundukia, *Sudan* 95 F3 5 14N 30 55 E
Bundure, *Australia* 117 C7 35 10 S 146 1 E
Bung Kan, *Thailand* 76 C4 18 23N 103 37 E
Bungatakada, *Japan* 62 D3 33 35N 131 25 E
Bungendore, *Australia* 117 C8 35 14 S 149 30 E
Bungil Cr. →, *Australia* 114 D4 27 5 S 149 5 E
Bungo, Gunong, *Malaysia* 75 B4 1 16N 110 9 E
Bungo-Suidō, *Japan* 62 E4 33 0N 132 15 E
Bungoma, *Kenya* 106 B3 0 34N 34 34 E
Bungu, *Tanzania* 106 D4 7 35 S 39 0 E
Bunia, *Zaïre* 106 B3 1 35N 30 20 E
Bunji, *Pakistan* 81 B6 35 45N 74 40 E
Bunker Hill, *Ill., U.S.A.* 140 E7 39 3N 89 57W
Bunker Hill, *Ind., U.S.A.* 141 D10 40 40N 86 6W
Bunkie, *U.S.A.* 139 K8 31 1N 92 12W
Bunnell, *U.S.A.* 135 L5 29 28N 81 12W
Bunnik, *Neths.* 20 D6 52 4N 5 12 E
Bunnythorpe, *N.Z.* 118 G4 40 16 S 175 39 E
Buñol, *Spain* 35 F4 39 25N 0 47W
Bunsbeek, *Belgium* 21 G5 50 50N 4 56 E
Bunschoten, *Neths.* 20 D6 52 14N 5 22 E
Buntok, *Indonesia* 75 C4 1 40 S 114 58 E
Bununu, *Nigeria* 101 D6 9 51N 9 32 E
Bununu Dass, *Nigeria* 101 C6 10 0N 9 31 E
Bünyan, *Turkey* 88 D6 38 51N 35 51 E
Bunyu, *Indonesia* 75 B5 3 35N 117 50 E
Bunza, *Nigeria* 101 C5 12 8N 4 0 E
Buol, *Indonesia* 72 A2 1 15N 121 32 E
Buon Brieng, *Vietnam* 76 F7 13 9N 108 12 E
Buon Me Thuot, *Vietnam* 76 F7 12 40N 108 3 E
Buong Long, *Cambodia* 76 F6 13 44N 106 59 E
Buorkhaya, Mys, *Russia* 57 B14 71 50N 132 40 E
Buqayq, *Si. Arabia* 85 E6 26 0N 49 45 E
Buqbua, *Egypt* 94 A2 31 29N 25 29 E
Bur Acaba, *Somali Rep.* 90 G3 3 12N 44 20 E
Bûr Fuad, *Egypt* 94 H8 31 15N 32 20 E
Bur Ghibi, *Somali Rep.* 108 D3 3 56N 45 7 E
Bûr Safâga, *Egypt* 94 B3 26 43N 33 57 E
Bûr Sa'îd, *Egypt* 94 H8 31 16N 32 18 E
Bûr Sûdân, *Sudan* 94 D4 19 32N 37 9 E
Bûr Taufiq, *Egypt* 94 J8 29 54N 32 32 E
Bura, *Kenya* 106 C4 1 4 S 39 58 E
Buran, *Somali Rep.* 108 B3 10 14N 48 44 E
Burao, *Somali Rep.* 90 F4 9 32N 45 32 E
Burāq, *Syria* 91 B5 33 11N 36 29 E
Buras, *U.S.A.* 139 L10 29 20N 89 33W
Burauen, *Phil.* 71 F5 10 58N 124 53 E
Buraydah, *Si. Arabia* 84 E5 26 20N 44 8 E
Burayevo, *Russia* 54 D4 55 50N 55 24 E
Burbank, *U.S.A.* 145 L8 34 9N 118 23W
Burcher, *Australia* 117 B7 33 30 S 147 16 E
Burdekin →, *Australia* 114 B4 19 38 S 147 25 E
Burdeos Bay, *Phil.* 70 D4 14 44N 122 6 E
Burdett, *Canada* 130 D6 49 50N 111 32W
Burdur, *Turkey* 88 E4 37 45N 30 17 E
Burdur □, *Turkey* 88 E4 37 45N 30 15 E
Burdur Gölü, *Turkey* 88 E4 37 44N 30 10 E
Burdwan = Barddhaman, *India* 81 H12 23 14N 87 39 E
Bure, *Ethiopia* 95 E4 10 40N 37 4 E
Bure →, *U.K.* 16 E9 52 38N 1 45 E
Büren, *Germany* 26 D4 51 33N 8 34 E
Buren, *Neths.* 20 E6 51 55N 5 20 E
Bureya →, *Russia* 57 E13 49 27N 129 30 E
Burford, *Canada* 136 C4 43 7N 80 27W
Burg, *Sachsen-Anhalt, Germany* 26 C7 52 16N 11 50 E
Burg, *Schleswig-Holstein, Germany* 26 A7 54 25N 11 10 E
Burg el Arab, *Egypt* 94 H6 30 54N 29 32 E
Burg et Tuyur, *Sudan* 94 C2 20 55N 27 56 E
Burg Stargard, *Germany* 26 B9 53 29N 13 19 E
Burgas, *Bulgaria* 43 E12 42 33N 27 29 E
Burgaski Zaliv, *Bulgaria* 43 E12 42 30N 27 39 E
Burgdorf, *Germany* 26 C5 52 27N 10 0 E
Burgdorf, *Switz.* 28 B5 47 3N 7 37 E
Burgenland □, *Austria* 31 D9 47 20N 16 20 E
Burgeo, *Canada* 129 C8 47 37N 57 38W
Burgersdorp, *S. Africa* 104 E4 31 0 S 26 20 E
Burges, Mt., *Australia* 113 F3 30 50 S 121 5 E
Burghausen, *Germany* 27 G8 48 10N 12 50 E
Búrgio, *Italy* 40 E6 37 35N 13 18 E
Bürglen, *Switz.* 29 C7 46 53N 8 40 E
Burglengenfeld, *Germany* 27 F8 49 11N 12 2 E
Burgo de Osma, *Spain* 34 D1 41 35N 3 4W
Burgohondo, *Spain* 36 E6 40 26N 4 47W
Burgos, *Ilocos N., Phil.* 70 B3 18 31N 120 39 E
Burgos, *Pangasinan, Phil.* 70 C3 16 4N 119 52 E
Burgos, *Spain* 34 C1 42 21N 3 41W
Burgos □, *Spain* 34 C1 42 21N 3 42W
Burgstädt, *Germany* 26 E8 50 55N 12 49 E
Burgsvik, *Sweden* 13 H15 57 3N 18 19 E
Burguillos del Cerro, *Spain* 37 G4 38 23N 6 35W
Burgundy = Bourgogne, *France* 23 F11 47 0N 4 50 E
Burhanpur, *India* 82 D3 21 18N 76 14 E
Burhou, *U.K.* 22 C4 49 45N 2 15W
Buri Pen., *Ethiopia* 95 D4 15 25N 39 55 E
Burias, *Phil.* 70 E4 12 55N 123 5 E
Burias Pass, *Phil.* 70 E4 13 0N 123 15 E
Buribay, *Russia* 54 F6 51 57N 58 10 E
Burica, Pta., *Costa Rica* 148 E3 8 3N 82 51W
Burigi, L., *Tanzania* 106 C3 2 2 S 31 22 E
Burin, *Canada* 129 C8 47 1N 55 14W
Buriram, *Thailand* 76 E4 15 0N 103 0 E
Buriti Alegre, *Brazil* 155 E2 18 9 S 49 3W
Buriti Bravo, *Brazil* 154 C3 5 50 S 43 50W
Buriti dos Lopes, *Brazil* 154 B3 3 10 S 41 52W
Burj Sāfitā, *Syria* 84 C3 34 48N 36 7 E
Burji, *Ethiopia* 95 F4 5 29N 37 51 E
Burkburnett, *U.S.A.* 139 H5 34 7N 98 35W
Burke, *U.S.A.* 142 C6 47 31N 115 56W
Burke →, *Australia* 114 C2 23 12 S 139 33 E
Burketown, *Australia* 114 B2 17 45 S 139 33 E
Burkettsville, *U.S.A.* 141 D12 40 21N 84 39W
Burkina Faso ■, *Africa* 100 C4 12 0N 1 0W
Burk's Falls, *Canada* 128 C4 45 37N 79 24W
Burley, *U.S.A.* 142 E7 42 37N 113 55W
Burlingame, *U.S.A.* 144 H4 37 35N 122 21W
Burlington, *Canada* 136 C5 43 18N 79 45W
Burlington, *Colo., U.S.A.* 138 F3 39 21N 102 18W
Burlington, *Ill., U.S.A.* 141 B8 42 3N 88 33W
Burlington, *Iowa, U.S.A.* 140 D5 40 50N 91 5W
Burlington, *Kans., U.S.A.* 138 F7 38 15N 95 47W
Burlington, *Ky., U.S.A.* 141 E12 39 2N 84 43W
Burlington, *N.C., U.S.A.* 135 G6 36 7N 79 27W
Burlington, *N.J., U.S.A.* 137 F10 40 5N 74 50W
Burlington, *Vt., U.S.A.* 137 B11 44 27N 73 14W
Burlington, *Wash., U.S.A.* 144 B4 48 29N 122 19W
Burlington, *Wis., U.S.A.* 134 D1 42 41N 88 18W
Burlyu-Tyube, *Kazakhstan* 56 E8 46 30N 79 10 E
Burma ■, *Asia* 78 E6 21 0N 96 30 E
Burnaby I., *Canada* 130 C2 52 25N 131 19W
Burnamwood, *Australia* 117 A6 31 7 S 144 53 E
Burnet, *U.S.A.* 139 K5 30 45N 98 11W
Burney, *U.S.A.* 142 F3 40 56N 121 41W
Burngup, *Australia* 113 F2 33 2 S 118 42 E
Burnham, *U.S.A.* 136 F7 40 37N 77 34W
Burnie, *Australia* 114 G4 41 4 S 145 56 E
Burnley, *U.K.* 16 D5 53 47N 2 15W
Burnoye, *Kazakhstan* 55 B5 42 36N 70 47 E
Burns, *Oreg., U.S.A.* 142 E4 43 40N 119 4W
Burns, *Wyo., U.S.A.* 138 E2 41 13N 104 18W
Burns Lake, *Canada* 130 C3 54 20N 125 45W
Burnside →, *Canada* 126 B9 66 51N 108 4W
Burnside, L., *Australia* 113 E3 25 22 S 123 0 E
Burnt River, *Canada* 136 B6 44 41N 78 42W
Burntwood →, *Canada* 131 B9 56 8N 96 34W
Burntwood L., *Canada* 131 B8 55 22N 100 26W
Burqān, *Kuwait* 84 D5 29 0N 47 57 E
Burra, *Australia* 116 B3 33 40 S 138 55 E
Burragorang, L., *Australia* 117 B9 33 52 S 150 37 E
Burramurra, *Australia* 114 C2 20 25 S 137 15 E
Burreli, *Albania* 44 C2 41 36N 20 1 E
Burren Junction, *Australia* 115 E4 30 7 S 148 59 E
Burrendong, L., *Australia* 117 B8 32 45 S 149 10 E
Burrendong Dam, *Australia* 115 E4 32 39 S 149 6 E
Burriana, *Spain* 34 F4 39 50N 0 4W
Burrinjuck Res., *Australia* 117 C8 35 0 S 148 34 E
Burro, Serranías del, *Mexico* 146 B4 29 0N 102 0W
Burruyacú, *Argentina* 158 B3 26 30 S 64 40W
Burry Port, *U.K.* 17 F3 51 41N 4 17W
Bursa, *Turkey* 88 C3 40 15N 29 5 E
Bursa □, *Turkey* 88 C3 40 10N 30 0 E
Burseryd, *Sweden* 15 G7 57 12N 13 17 E
Burstall, *Canada* 131 C7 50 39N 109 54W
Burton, *U.S.A.* 141 B13 43 0N 83 40W
Burton L., *Canada* 128 B4 54 45N 78 20W
Burton upon Trent, *U.K.* 16 E6 52 48N 1 39W
Burtundy, *Australia* 116 B5 33 45 S 142 15 E
Buru, *Indonesia* 72 B3 3 30 S 126 30 E
Buruanga, *Phil.* 71 F3 11 51N 121 53 E
Burullus, Bahra el, *Egypt* 94 H7 31 25N 31 0 E
Burūm, *Yemen* 87 D5 14 22N 48 59 E
Burûn, Râs, *Egypt* 91 D2 31 14N 33 7 E
Burunday, *Kazakhstan* 55 B8 43 20N 76 51 E
Burundi ■, *Africa* 106 C3 3 15 S 30 0 E
Bururi, *Burundi* 106 C2 3 57 S 29 37 E
Burutu, *Nigeria* 101 D6 5 20N 5 29 E
Burwell, *U.S.A.* 138 E5 41 49N 99 8W
Bury, *U.K.* 16 D5 53 36N 2 19W
Bury St. Edmunds, *U.K.* 17 E8 52 15N 0 42 E
Buryat Republic □, *Russia* 57 D11 53 0N 110 0 E
Buryn, *Ukraine* 50 F8 51 13N 33 50 E
Burzenin, *Poland* 47 D5 51 28N 18 47 E
Busalla, *Italy* 38 D5 44 34N 8 58 E
Busango Swamp, *Zambia* 107 E2 14 15 S 25 45 E
Buşayrah, *Syria* 84 C4 35 9N 40 26 E
Buşayyah, *Iraq* 84 D5 30 0N 46 10 E
Busca, *Italy* 38 D4 44 31N 7 29 E
Bushati, *Albania* 44 C1 41 58N 19 34 E
Būshehr, *Iran* 85 D6 28 55N 50 55 E
Būshehr □, *Iran* 85 D6 28 20N 51 45 E
Bushell, *Canada* 131 B7 59 31N 108 45W
Bushenyi, *Uganda* 106 C3 0 35 S 30 10 E
Bushire = Būshehr, *Iran* 85 D6 28 55N 50 55 E
Bushnell, *Ill., U.S.A.* 138 E9 40 32N 90 30W
Bushnell, *Nebr., U.S.A.* 138 E3 41 18N 103 50W
Busia □, *Kenya* 106 B3 0 25N 34 6 E
Busie, *Ghana* 100 C4 10 29N 2 22W
Businga, *Zaïre* 102 B4 3 16N 20 59 E
Buskerud fylke □, *Norway* 14 D3 60 13N 9 0 E
Busko Zdrój, *Poland* 47 E7 50 28N 20 42 E
Buslei, *Ethiopia* 108 C2 5 28N 44 25 E
Busoga □, *Uganda* 106 B3 0 5N 33 30 E
Busovača, *Bos.-H., Yug.* 42 C2 44 6N 17 53 E
Busra ash Shām, *Syria* 91 C5 32 30N 36 25 E
Bussang, *France* 23 E13 47 50N 6 50 E
Busselton, *Australia* 113 F2 33 42 S 115 15 E
Busseto, *Italy* 38 D7 44 59N 10 2 E
Bussigny, *Switz.* 28 C3 46 33N 6 33 E
Bussum, *Neths.* 20 D6 52 16N 5 10 E
Bustamante, B., *Argentina* 160 C3 45 5 S 66 18W

Carberry 181


Camanche, *U.S.A.* ..... **140** **C6** 41 47N 90 15W
Camanche Res., *U.S.A.* . **144** **G6** 38 16N 120 51W
Camanongue, *Angola* ... **103** **E4** 11 24 S 20 17 E
Camaquã ⟶, *Brazil* .... **159** **C5** 31 17 S 51 47W
Câmara de Lobos, *Madeira* ............ **33** **D3** 32 39N 16 59W
Camararé ⟶, *Brazil* ... **157** **C6** 12 15 S 58 55W
Camarat, C., *France* .... **25** **E10** 43 12N 6 41 E
Camaret, *France* ....... **22** **D2** 48 16N 4 37W
Camargo, *Bolivia* ...... **157** **E4** 20 38 S 65 15W
Camargue, *France* ...... **25** **E8** 43 34N 4 34 E
Camarillo, *U.S.A.* ...... **145** **L7** 34 13N 119 2W
Camariñas, *Spain* ...... **36** **B1** 43 8N 9 12W
Camarines Norte □, *Phil.* **70** **D4** 14 10N 122 45 E
Camarines Sur □, *Phil.* . **70** **E4** 13 40N 123 20 E
Camarón, C., *Honduras* **148** **C2** 16 0N 85 5W
Camarones, *Argentina* .. **160** **B3** 44 50 S 65 40W
Camarones, B., *Argentina* **160** **B3** 44 45 S 65 35W
Camas, *U.S.A.* ......... **144** **E4** 45 35N 122 24W
Camas Valley, *U.S.A.* .. **142** **E2** 43 0N 123 46W
Camaxilo, *Angola* ...... **103** **D3** 8 21 S 18 56 E
Cambados, *Spain* ....... **36** **C2** 42 31N 8 49W
Cambamba, *Angola* .... **103** **D2** 8 53 S 14 44 E
Cambará, *Brazil* ....... **159** **A5** 23 2 S 50 5W
Cambay = Khambhat, *India* .............. **80** **H5** 22 23N 72 33 E
Cambil, *Spain* ......... **35** **H1** 37 40N 3 33W
Cambo-les-Bains, *France* **24** **E2** 43 22N 1 23W
Cambodia ■, *Asia* ..... **76** **F5** 12 15N 105 0 E
Camborne, *U.K.* ....... **17** **G2** 50 13N 5 18W
Cambrai, *France* ....... **23** **B10** 50 11N 3 14 E
Cambria, *U.S.A.* ....... **144** **K5** 35 39N 121 6W
Cambrian Mts., *U.K.* ... **17** **E4** 52 25N 3 52W
Cambridge, *Canada* .... **128** **D3** 43 23N 80 15W
Cambridge, *Jamaica* .... **148** **C4** 18 18N 77 54W
Cambridge, *N.Z.* ....... **118** **D4** 37 54 S 175 29 E
Cambridge, *U.K.* ....... **17** **E8** 52 13N 0 8 E
Cambridge, *Idaho, U.S.A.* ............. **142** **D5** 44 36N 116 40W
Cambridge, *Ill., U.S.A.* . **140** **C6** 41 18N 90 12W
Cambridge, *Iowa, U.S.A.* **140** **C3** 41 54N 93 32W
Cambridge, *Mass., U.S.A.* ............ **137** **D13** 42 20N 71 8W
Cambridge, *Md., U.S.A.* **134** **F7** 38 33N 76 2W
Cambridge, *Minn., U.S.A.* ............ **138** **C8** 45 34N 93 15W
Cambridge, *N.Y., U.S.A.* **137** **C11** 43 2N 73 22W
Cambridge, *Nebr., U.S.A.* ............ **138** **E4** 40 20N 100 12W
Cambridge, *Ohio, U.S.A.* **136** **F3** 40 1N 81 35W
Cambridge Bay, *Canada* **126** **B9** 69 10N 105 0W
Cambridge City, *U.S.A.* **141** **E11** 39 49N 85 10W
Cambridge G., *Australia* **112** **B4** 14 55 S 128 15 E
Cambridge Springs, *U.S.A.* ............ **136** **E4** 41 47N 80 4W
Cambridgeshire □, *U.K.* **17** **E8** 52 12N 0 7 E
Cambrils, *Spain* ........ **34** **D6** 41 8N 1 3 E
Cambuci, *Brazil* ....... **155** **F3** 21 35 S 41 55W
Cambundi-Catembo, *Angola* ............. **103** **E3** 10 10 S 17 35 E
Camden, *Australia* ..... **117** **C9** 34 1 S 150 43 E
Camden, *Ala., U.S.A.* .. **135** **K2** 31 59N 87 15W
Camden, *Ark., U.S.A.* .. **139** **J8** 33 40N 92 50W
Camden, *Maine, U.S.A.* **129** **D6** 44 14N 69 6W
Camden, *N.J., U.S.A.* .. **137** **G9** 39 57N 75 7W
Camden, *Ohio, U.S.A.* . **141** **E12** 39 38N 84 39W
Camden, *S.C., U.S.A.* .. **135** **H5** 34 17N 80 34W
Camden Sd., *Australia* . **112** **C3** 15 27 S 124 25 E
Camdenton, *U.S.A.* .... **139** **F8** 38 1N 92 45W
Çameli, *Turkey* ........ **88** **E3** 37 5N 29 24 E
Camembert, *France* .... **22** **D7** 48 53N 0 10 E
Cámeri, *Italy* .......... **38** **C5** 45 30N 8 40 E
Camerino, *Italy* ........ **39** **E10** 43 10N 13 4 E
Cameron, *Ariz., U.S.A.* **143** **J8** 35 55N 111 31W
Cameron, *La., U.S.A.* .. **139** **L8** 29 50N 93 18W
Cameron, *Mo., U.S.A.* . **140** **E2** 39 42N 94 14W
Cameron, *Tex., U.S.A.* . **139** **K6** 30 53N 97 0W
Cameron Falls, *Canada* . **128** **C2** 49 8N 88 19W
Cameron Highlands, *Malaysia* ........... **77** **K3** 4 27N 101 22 E
Cameron Hills, *Canada* . **130** **B5** 59 48N 118 0W
Cameron Mts., *N.Z.* .... **119** **G1** 46 1 S 167 0 E
Cameroon ■, *Africa* .... **102** **A2** 6 0N 12 30 E
Camerota, *Italy* ........ **41** **B8** 40 2N 15 21 E
Cameroun ⟶, *Cameroon* **101** **E6** 4 0N 9 35 E
Cameroun, Mt., *Cameroon* .......... **101** **E6** 4 13N 9 10 E
Cametá, *Brazil* ......... **154** **B2** 2 12 S 49 30W
Camiguin □, *Phil.* ...... **71** **G5** 9 11N 124 42 E
Camiguin I., *Phil.* ...... **70** **B3** 18 56N 121 55 E
Camiling, *Phil.* ......... **70** **D3** 15 42N 120 24 E
Caminha, *Portugal* ..... **36** **D2** 41 50N 8 50W
Camino, *U.S.A.* ........ **144** **G6** 38 47N 120 40W
Camira Creek, *Australia* **115** **D5** 29 15 S 152 58 E
Camiranga, *Brazil* ..... **154** **B2** 1 48 S 46 17W
Camiri, *Bolivia* ........ **157** **E5** 20 3 S 63 31W
Camissombo, *Angola* ... **103** **D4** 8 7 S 20 38 E
Cammal, *U.S.A.* ....... **136** **E7** 41 24N 77 28W
Camocim, *Brazil* ....... **154** **B3** 2 55 S 40 50W
Camogli, *Italy* ......... **38** **D6** 44 21N 9 9 E
Camooweal, *Australia* .. **114** **B2** 19 56 S 138 7 E
Camopi, *Fr. Guiana* .... **153** **C7** 3 12N 52 17W
Camopi ⟶, *Fr. Guiana* . **153** **C7** 3 10N 52 20W
Camotes Is., *Phil.* ...... **71** **F5** 10 40N 124 24 E
Camotes Sea, *Phil.* ..... **71** **F5** 10 30N 124 15 E
Camp Crook, *U.S.A.* ... **138** **C3** 45 36N 103 59W
Camp Nelson, *U.S.A.* .. **145** **J8** 36 8N 118 39W
Camp Point, *U.S.A.* .... **140** **D5** 40 3N 91 4W
Camp Wood, *U.S.A.* ... **139** **L4** 29 41N 100 0W
Campagna, *Italy* ....... **41** **B8** 40 40N 15 5 E
Campana, *Argentina* ... **158** **C4** 34 10 S 58 55W
Campana, I., *Chile* ..... **160** **C1** 48 20 S 75 20W
Campanário, *Madeira* ... **33** **D2** 32 39N 17 2W
Campanario, *Spain* ..... **37** **G5** 38 52N 5 36W
Campania □, *Italy* ...... **41** **B7** 40 50N 14 45 E
Campbell, *S. Africa* .... **104** **D3** 28 48 S 23 44 E
Campbell, *Calif., U.S.A.* **144** **H5** 37 17N 121 57W
Campbell, *Ohio, U.S.A.* **136** **E4** 41 5N 80 36W
Campbell, C., *N.Z.* .... **119** **B9** 41 47 S 174 18 E
Campbell I., *Pac. Oc.* .. **122** **N8** 52 30 S 169 0 E
Campbell L., *Canada* ... **131** **A7** 63 14N 106 55W
Campbell River, *Canada* **130** **C3** 50 5N 125 20W
Campbell Town, *Australia* **114** **G4** 41 52 S 147 30 E
Campbellford, *Canada* .. **136** **B7** 44 18N 77 48W
Campbellpur, *Pakistan* .. **80** **C5** 33 46N 72 26 E
Campbellsburg, *U.S.A.* . **141** **F10** 38 39N 86 16W
Campbellsville, *U.S.A.* .. **134** **G3** 37 23N 85 21W
Campbellton, *Canada* ... **129** **C6** 47 57N 66 43W
Campbelltown, *Australia* **117** **C9** 34 4 S 150 49 E
Campbeltown, *U.K.* .... **18** **F3** 55 25N 5 36W
Campeche, *Mexico* ..... **147** **D6** 19 50N 90 32W
Campeche □, *Mexico* ... **147** **D6** 19 50N 90 32W
Campeche, B. de, *Mexico* **147** **D6** 19 30N 93 0W
Camperdown, *Australia* . **116** **E5** 38 14 S 143 9 E
Camperville, *Canada* ... **131** **C8** 51 59N 100 9W
Campi Salentina, *Italy* .. **41** **B11** 40 22N 18 2 E
Campidano, *Italy* ....... **40** **C1** 39 30N 8 40 E
Campíglia Maríttima, *Italy* .............. **38** **E7** 43 4N 10 37 E
Campillo de Altobuey, *Spain* .............. **34** **F3** 39 36N 1 49W
Campillo de Llerena, *Spain* .............. **37** **G5** 38 30N 5 50W
Campillos, *Spain* ....... **37** **H6** 37 4N 4 51W
Campina Grande, *Brazil* **154** **C4** 7 20 S 35 47W
Campina Verde, *Brazil* . **155** **E2** 19 31 S 49 28W
Campinas, *Brazil* ....... **159** **A6** 22 50 S 47 0W
Campine, *Belgium* ..... **21** **F6** 51 8N 5 20 E
Campli, *Italy* .......... **39** **F10** 42 44N 13 40 E
Campo, *Cameroon* ..... **102** **B1** 2 22N 9 50 E
Campo, *Spain* ......... **34** **C5** 42 25N 0 24 E
Campo Belo, *Brazil* .... **155** **F2** 20 52 S 45 16W
Campo de Criptana, *Spain* .............. **35** **F1** 39 24N 3 7W
Campo de Diauarum, *Brazil* .............. **157** **C7** 11 12 S 53 14W
Campo de Gibraltar, *Spain* .............. **37** **J5** 36 15N 5 25W
Campo Flórido, *Brazil* .. **155** **E2** 19 47 S 48 35W
Campo Formoso, *Brazil* . **154** **D3** 10 30 S 40 20W
Campo Grande, *Brazil* .. **157** **E7** 20 25 S 54 40W
Campo Maíor, *Brazil* ... **154** **B3** 4 50 S 42 12W
Campo Maior, *Portugal* . **37** **G3** 38 59N 7 7W
Campo Mourão, *Brazil* . **159** **A5** 24 3 S 52 22W
Campo Tencia, *Switz.* .. **29** **D7** 46 26N 8 43 E
Campo Túres, *Italy* ..... **39** **B8** 46 53N 11 55 E
Campoalegre, *Colombia* **152** **C2** 2 41N 75 20W
Campobasso, *Italy* ...... **41** **A7** 41 34N 14 40 E
Campobello di Licata, *Italy* .............. **40** **E6** 37 16N 13 55 E
Campobello di Mazara, *Italy* .............. **40** **E5** 37 38N 12 45 E
Campofelice, *Italy* ...... **40** **E6** 37 54N 13 53 E
Camporeale, *Italy* ...... **40** **E6** 37 53N 13 3 E
Campos, *Brazil* ......... **155** **F3** 21 50 S 41 20W
Campos Altos, *Brazil* ... **155** **E2** 19 47 S 46 10W
Campos Belos, *Brazil* ... **155** **D2** 13 10 S 47 3W
Campos del Puerto, *Spain* **33** **B10** 39 26N 3 1 E
Campos Novos, *Brazil* .. **159** **B5** 27 21 S 51 50W
Campos Sales, *Brazil* ... **154** **C3** 7 4 S 40 23W
Camprodón, *Spain* ..... **34** **C7** 42 19N 2 23 E
Campton, *U.S.A.* ...... **141** **G13** 37 44N 83 33W
Camptonville, *U.S.A.* ... **144** **F5** 39 27N 121 3W
Campuya ⟶, *Peru* ..... **152** **D3** 1 40 S 73 30W
Camrose, *Canada* ...... **130** **C6** 53 0N 112 50W
Camsell Portage, *Canada* **131** **B7** 59 37N 109 15W
Çan, *Turkey* ........... **88** **C2** 40 2N 27 3 E
Can Clavo, *Spain* ...... **33** **C7** 38 57N 1 27 E
Can Creu, *Spain* ....... **33** **C7** 38 58N 1 28 E
Can Gio, *Vietnam* ...... **77** **G6** 10 25N 106 58 E
Can Tho, *Vietnam* ..... **77** **G5** 10 2N 105 46 E
Canaan, *U.S.A.* ....... **137** **D11** 42 1N 73 20W
Canada ■, *N. Amer.* ... **126** **C10** 60 0N 100 0W
Cañada de Gómez, *Argentina* ........... **158** **C3** 32 40 S 61 30W
Canadian, *U.S.A.* ...... **139** **H4** 35 56N 100 25W
Canadian ⟶, *U.S.A.* ... **139** **H7** 35 27N 95 3W
Çanakkale, *Turkey* ..... **44** **D8** 40 8N 26 24 E
Çanakkale □, *Turkey* ... **88** **C2** 40 10N 26 25 E
Çanakkale Boğazı, *Turkey* ............. **44** **D8** 40 17N 26 32 E
Canal Flats, *Canada* ... **130** **C5** 50 10N 115 48W
Canala, *N. Cal.* ........ **121** **U19** 21 32 S 165 57 E
Canalejas, *Argentina* ... **158** **D2** 35 15 S 66 34W
Canals, *Argentina* ..... **158** **C3** 33 35 S 62 53W
Canals, *Spain* ......... **35** **G4** 38 58N 0 35W
Canandaigua, *U.S.A.* ... **136** **D7** 42 55N 77 18W
Cananea, *Mexico* ...... **146** **A2** 31 0N 110 20W
Cañar, *Ecuador* ........ **152** **D2** 2 33 S 78 56W
Cañar □, *Ecuador* ...... **152** **D2** 2 30 S 79 0W
Canarias, Is., *Atl. Oc.* .. **33** **F4** 28 30N 16 0W
Canarreos, Arch. de los, *Cuba* .............. **148** **B3** 21 35N 81 40W
Canary Is. = Canarias, Is., *Atl. Oc.* ........ **33** **F4** 28 30N 16 0W
Canastra, Serra da, *Brazil* **155** **F2** 20 0 S 46 20W
Canatlán, *Mexico* ...... **146** **C4** 24 31N 104 47W
Canaveral, C., *U.S.A.* .. **135** **L5** 28 28N 80 31W
Cañaveras, *Spain* ...... **34** **E2** 40 27N 2 24W
Canavieiras, *Brazil* .... **155** **E4** 15 39 S 39 0W
Canbelego, *Australia* ... **117** **A7** 31 32 S 146 18 E
Canberra, *Australia* .... **117** **C8** 35 15 S 149 8 E
Canby, *Calif., U.S.A.* .. **142** **F3** 41 26N 120 58W
Canby, *Minn., U.S.A.* . **138** **C6** 44 44N 96 15W
Canby, *Oreg., U.S.A.* .. **144** **E4** 45 16N 122 42W
Cancale, *France* ....... **22** **D5** 48 40N 1 50W
Canche ⟶, *France* ..... **23** **B8** 50 31N 1 39 E
Canchyuaya, Cordillera de, *Peru* ........... **156** **B3** 7 30 S 74 0W
Cancún, *Mexico* ....... **147** **C7** 21 8N 86 44W
Candala, *Somali Rep.* ... **90** **E4** 11 30N 49 58 E
Candarave, *Peru* ....... **156** **D3** 17 15 S 70 13W
Candas, *Spain* ......... **36** **B5** 43 35N 5 45W
Candé, *France* ........ **22** **E5** 47 34N 1 2W
Candeias ⟶, *Brazil* .... **157** **B5** 8 39 S 63 31W
Candela, *Italy* ......... **41** **A8** 41 8N 15 31 E
Candelaria, *Argentina* .. **159** **B4** 27 29 S 55 44W
Candelaria, *Canary Is.* .. **33** **F3** 28 22N 16 22W
Candelaria, *Phil.* ....... **70** **E3** 13 56N 121 25 E
Candelaria, Pta. de la, *Spain* .............. **36** **B2** 43 45N 8 0W
Candeleda, *Spain* ...... **36** **E5** 40 10N 5 14W
Candelo, *Australia* ..... **117** **D8** 36 47 S 149 43 E
Candia = Iráklion, *Greece* .............. **32** **D7** 35 20N 25 12 E
Candia, Sea of = Crete, Sea of, *Greece* ....... **45** **H6** 36 0N 25 0 E
Cândido de Abreu, *Brazil* **155** **F1** 24 35 S 51 20W
Cândido Mendes, *Brazil* **154** **B2** 1 27 S 45 43W
Candle L., *Canada* ..... **131** **C7** 53 50N 105 18W
Candlemas I., *Antarctica* **7** **B1** 57 3 S 26 40W
Cando, *U.S.A.* ......... **138** **A5** 48 30N 99 14W
Candon, *Phil.* .......... **70** **C3** 17 12N 120 27 E
Candoni, *Phil.* ......... **71** **G4** 9 48N 122 30 E
Canea = Khaniá, *Greece* **32** **D6** 35 30N 24 4 E
Canela, *Brazil* ......... **154** **D2** 10 15 S 48 25W
Canelli, *Italy* .......... **38** **D5** 44 44N 8 18 E
Canelones, *Uruguay* .... **159** **C4** 34 32 S 56 17W
Canet-Plage, *France* .... **24** **F7** 42 41N 3 2 E
Cañete, *Chile* .......... **158** **D1** 37 50 S 73 30W
Cañete, *Peru* .......... **156** **C2** 13 8 S 76 30W
Cañete, *Spain* ......... **34** **E3** 40 3N 1 54W
Cañete de las Torres, *Spain* .............. **37** **H6** 37 53N 4 19W
Canfranc, *Spain* ....... **34** **C4** 42 42N 0 31W
Cangamba, *Angola* ..... **103** **E3** 13 40 S 19 54 E
Cangandala, *Angola* .... **103** **D3** 9 45 S 16 33 E
Cangas, *Spain* ......... **36** **C2** 42 16N 8 47W
Cangas de Narcea, *Spain* **36** **B4** 43 10N 6 32W
Cangas de Onís, *Spain* .. **36** **B5** 43 21N 5 8W
Cangoa, *Angola* ........ **103** **E3** 13 8 S 18 30 E
Cangombo, *Angola* ..... **103** **E3** 14 24 S 19 59 E
Cangongo, *Angola* ..... **103** **D3** 9 24 S 17 30 E
Canguaretama, *Brazil* .. **154** **C4** 6 20 S 35 5W
Canguçu, *Brazil* ....... **159** **C5** 31 22 S 52 43W
Cangxi, *China* ......... **68** **B5** 31 47N 105 59 E
Cangyuan, *China* ...... **68** **F2** 23 12N 99 14 E
Cangzhou, *China* ...... **66** **E9** 38 19N 116 52 E
Canhoca, *Angola* ...... **103** **D2** 9 15 S 14 41 E
Cani, I., *Tunisia* ...... **96** **A2** 36 21N 10 5 E
Canicattì, *Italy* ........ **40** **E6** 37 21N 13 50 E
Canicattini, *Italy* ...... **41** **E8** 37 1N 15 3 E
Canigao Channel, *Phil.* . **71** **F5** 10 15N 124 42 E
Canim Lake, *Canada* ... **130** **C4** 51 47N 120 54W
Canindé, *Brazil* ........ **154** **B4** 4 22 S 39 19W
Canindé ⟶, *Brazil* ..... **154** **C3** 6 15 S 42 52W
Canindeyu □, *Paraguay* . **159** **A4** 24 10 S 55 0W
Canisteo, *U.S.A.* ....... **136** **D7** 42 17N 77 37W
Canisteo ⟶, *U.S.A.* .... **136** **D7** 42 5N 77 8W
Cañitas, *Mexico* ....... **146** **C4** 23 36N 102 43W
Cañizal, *Spain* ......... **36** **D5** 41 12N 5 22W
Canjáyar, *Spain* ....... **35** **H2** 37 1N 2 44W
Canjinge, *Angola* ...... **103** **E4** 10 12 S 21 17 E
Çankırı, *Turkey* ........ **88** **C5** 40 40N 33 37 E
Çankırı □, *Turkey* ...... **88** **C5** 40 40N 33 30 E
Cankuzo, *Burundi* ...... **106** **C3** 3 10 S 30 31 E
Canmore, *Canada* ...... **130** **C5** 51 7N 115 18W
Cann River, *Australia* ... **117** **D8** 37 35 S 149 7 E
Canna, *U.K.* ........... **18** **D2** 57 3N 6 33W
Cannanore, *India* ...... **83** **J2** 11 53N 75 27 E
Cannelton, *U.S.A.* ..... **141** **G10** 37 55N 86 45W
Cannes, *France* ........ **25** **E11** 43 32N 7 1 E
Canning Town = Port Canning, *India* ....... **81** **H13** 22 23N 88 40 E
Cannington, *Canada* .... **136** **B5** 44 20N 79 2W
Cannock, *U.K.* ........ **16** **E5** 52 42N 2 2W
Cannon Ball ⟶, *U.S.A.* . **138** **B4** 46 20N 100 38W
Cannondale Mt., *Australia* ............ **114** **D4** 25 13 S 148 57 E
Caño Colorado, *Colombia* **152** **C4** 2 18N 68 22W
Canoas, *Brazil* ......... **159** **B5** 29 56 S 51 11W
Canoe L., *Canada* ...... **131** **B7** 55 10N 108 15W
Canon City, *U.S.A.* .... **138** **F2** 38 27N 105 14W
Canopus, *Australia* ..... **116** **B4** 33 29 S 140 42 E
Canora, *Canada* ........ **131** **C8** 51 40N 102 30W
Canosa di Púglia, *Italy* .. **41** **A9** 41 13N 16 4 E
Canowindra, *Australia* .. **117** **B8** 33 35 S 148 38 E
Canso, *Canada* ......... **129** **C7** 45 20N 61 0W
Canta, *Peru* ........... **156** **C2** 11 29 S 76 37W
Cantabria □, *Spain* ..... **36** **B6** 43 10N 4 0W
Cantabria, Sierra de, *Spain* .............. **34** **C2** 42 40N 2 30W
Cantabrian Mts. = Cantábrica, Cordillera, *Spain* .............. **36** **C5** 43 0N 5 10W
Cantábrica, Cordillera, *Spain* .............. **36** **C5** 43 0N 5 10W
Cantal □, *France* ....... **24** **C6** 45 5N 2 45 E
Cantal, Plomb du, *France* **24** **C6** 45 3N 2 45 E
Cantanhede, *Portugal* ... **36** **E2** 40 20N 8 36W
Cantaura, *Venezuela* ... **153** **B5** 9 19N 64 21W
Cantavieja, *Spain* ...... **34** **E4** 40 31N 0 25W
Čantavir, *Serbia, Yug.* .. **42** **B4** 45 55N 19 46 E
Canterbury, *Australia* ... **114** **D3** 25 23 S 141 53 E
Canterbury, *U.K.* ...... **17** **F9** 51 17N 1 5 E
Canterbury □, *N.Z.* .... **119** **D6** 43 45 S 171 19 E
Canterbury Bight, *N.Z.* . **119** **E6** 44 16 S 171 55 E
Canterbury Plains, *N.Z.* . **119** **D6** 43 55 S 171 22 E
Cantil, *U.S.A.* ......... **145** **K9** 35 18N 117 58W
Cantilan, *Phil.* ......... **71** **G5** 9 20N 125 58 E
Cantillana, *Spain* ...... **37** **H5** 37 36N 5 50W
Canto do Buriti, *Brazil* . **154** **C3** 8 7 S 42 58W
Canton = Guangzhou, *China* .............. **69** **F9** 23 5N 113 10 E
Canton, *Ga., U.S.A.* .... **135** **H3** 34 13N 84 29W
Canton, *Ill., U.S.A.* .... **140** **D6** 40 32N 90 5W
Canton, *Miss., U.S.A.* .. **139** **J9** 32 40N 90 1W
Canton, *Mo., U.S.A.* ... **140** **D5** 40 10N 91 33W
Canton, *N.Y., U.S.A.* ... **137** **B9** 44 32N 75 3W
Canton, *Ohio, U.S.A.* .. **136** **F3** 40 47N 81 22W
Canton, *Okla., U.S.A.* .. **139** **G5** 36 5N 98 36W
Canton, *S. Dak., U.S.A.* **138** **D6** 43 20N 96 35W
Canton L., *U.S.A.* ..... **139** **G5** 36 12N 98 40W
Cantù, *Italy* ........... **38** **C6** 45 44N 9 8 E
Canudos, *Brazil* ........ **157** **B6** 7 13 S 58 5W
Canumã, *Amazonas, Brazil* .............. **153** **D6** 4 2 S 59 4W
Canumã, *Amazonas, Brazil* .............. **157** **B5** 6 8 S 60 10W
Canumã ⟶, *Brazil* ..... **153** **A6** 3 55 S 59 10W
Canutama, *Brazil* ...... **157** **B5** 6 30 S 64 20W
Canutillo, *U.S.A.* ...... **143** **L10** 31 58N 106 36W
Canyon, *Tex., U.S.A.* .. **139** **H4** 35 0N 101 57W
Canyon, *Wyo., U.S.A.* .. **142** **D8** 44 43N 110 36W
Canyonlands Nat. Park, *U.S.A.* ............ **143** **G9** 38 25N 109 30W
Canyonville, *U.S.A.* .... **142** **E2** 42 55N 123 14W
Canzo, *Italy* ........... **38** **C6** 45 54N 9 18 E
Cao Bang, *Vietnam* .... **76** **A6** 22 40N 106 15 E
Cao He ⟶, *China* ...... **67** **D13** 40 10N 124 32 E
Cao Lanh, *Vietnam* .... **77** **G5** 10 27N 105 38 E
Cao Xian, *China* ....... **66** **G8** 34 50N 115 35 E
Caoayan, *Phil.* ......... **70** **C3** 17 37N 120 23 E
Cáorle, *Italy* .......... **39** **C9** 45 36N 12 51 E
Cap-aux-Meules, *Canada* **129** **C7** 47 23N 61 52W
Cap-Chat, *Canada* ..... **129** **C6** 49 6N 66 40W
Cap-de-la-Madeleine, *Canada* ............ **128** **C5** 46 22N 72 31W
Cap-Haïtien, *Haiti* ..... **149** **C5** 19 40N 72 20W
Cap St.-Jacques = Vung Tau, *Vietnam* ........ **77** **G6** 10 21N 107 4 E
Capa, *Vietnam* ........ **76** **A4** 22 21N 103 50 E
Capa Stilo, *Italy* ........ **41** **D9** 38 25N 16 35 E
Capáccio, *Italy* ........ **41** **B8** 40 26N 15 4 E
Capaia, *Angola* ........ **103** **D4** 8 27 S 20 13 E
Capalonga, *Phil.* ....... **70** **D4** 14 20N 122 30 E
Capanaparo ⟶, *Venezuela* ............ **152** **B4** 7 1N 67 7W
Capanema, *Brazil* ...... **154** **B2** 1 12 S 47 11W
Caparo ⟶, *Barinas, Venezuela* ............ **152** **B3** 7 46N 70 23W
Caparo ⟶, *Bolívar, Venezuela* ............ **153** **B5** 7 30N 64 0W
Capatárida, *Venezuela* .. **152** **A3** 11 11N 70 37W
Capayas, *Phil.* ......... **71** **F2** 10 28N 119 39 E
Capbreton, *France* ..... **24** **E2** 43 39N 1 26W
Capdenac, *France* ...... **24** **D6** 44 34N 2 5 E
Cape ⟶, *Australia* ..... **114** **C4** 20 59 S 146 51 E
Cape Barren I., *Australia* **114** **G4** 40 25 S 148 15 E
Cape Breton Highlands Nat. Park, *Canada* ... **129** **C7** 46 50N 60 40W
Cape Breton I., *Canada* . **129** **C7** 46 0N 60 30W
Cape Charles, *U.S.A.* ... **134** **G8** 37 15N 75 59W
Cape Coast, *Ghana* ..... **101** **D4** 5 5N 1 15W
Cape Dorset, *Canada* ... **127** **B12** 64 14N 76 32W
Cape Dyer, *Canada* .... **127** **B13** 66 30N 61 22W
Cape Fear ⟶, *U.S.A.* .. **135** **H6** 34 30N 78 25W
Cape Girardeau, *U.S.A.* **139** **G10** 37 20N 89 30W
Cape Jervis, *Australia* .. **116** **C3** 35 40 S 138 5 E
Cape May, *U.S.A.* ..... **134** **F8** 39 1N 74 53W
Cape May Pt., *U.S.A.* .. **133** **C12** 38 56N 74 56W
Cape Palmas, *Liberia* ... **100** **E3** 4 25N 7 49W
Cape Province □, *S. Africa* ............ **104** **E3** 32 0 S 23 0 E
Cape Tormentine, *Canada* ............ **129** **C7** 46 8N 63 47W
Cape Town, *S. Africa* ... **104** **E2** 33 55 S 18 22 E
Cape Verde Is. ■, *Atl. Oc.* ............. **8** **G6** 17 10N 25 20W
Cape Vincent, *U.S.A.* .. **137** **B8** 44 9N 76 21W
Cape York Peninsula, *Australia* ........... **114** **A3** 12 0 S 142 30 E
Capela, *Brazil* ......... **154** **D4** 10 30 S 37 0W
Capela de Campo, *Brazil* **154** **B3** 4 40 S 41 55W
Capele, *Angola* ........ **103** **E2** 13 39 S 14 53 E
Capelinha, *Brazil* ...... **155** **E3** 17 42 S 42 31W
Capella, *Australia* ..... **114** **C4** 23 2 S 148 1 E
Capella, Mt., *Papua N. G.* .......... **120** **C1** 5 4 S 141 8 E
Capenda Camulemba, *Angola* ............. **103** **D3** 9 24 S 18 27 E
Capendu, *France* ....... **24** **E6** 43 11N 2 31 E
Capestang, *France* ..... **24** **E7** 43 20N 3 2 E
Capim, *Brazil* .......... **154** **B2** 1 41 S 47 47W
Capim ⟶, *Brazil* ....... **154** **B2** 1 40 S 47 47W
Capinópolis, *Brazil* ..... **155** **E2** 18 41 S 49 35W
Capinota, *Bolivia* ...... **156** **D4** 17 43 S 66 14W
Capitan, *U.S.A.* ........ **143** **K11** 33 33N 105 41W
Capitán Aracena, I., *Chile* .............. **160** **D2** 54 10 S 71 20W
Capitán Pastene, *Chile* .. **160** **A2** 38 13 S 73 1W
Capitola, *U.S.A.* ....... **144** **J5** 36 59N 121 57W
Capivara, Serra da, *Brazil* **155** **D4** 14 35 S 45 0W
Capiz □, *Phil.* ......... **71** **F4** 11 35N 122 30 E
Capizzi, *Italy* .......... **41** **E7** 37 50N 14 26 E
Čapljina, *Bos.-H., Yug.* . **42** **D2** 43 10N 17 43 E
Capoche ⟶, *Mozam.* ... **107** **F3** 15 35 S 33 0 E
Capoeira, *Brazil* ....... **157** **B6** 5 37 S 59 33W
Capolo, *Angola* ........ **103** **E2** 10 22 S 14 7 E
Cappadocia, *Turkey* .... **88** **D6** 39 0N 35 0 E
Capraia, *Italy* ......... **38** **E6** 43 2N 9 50 E
Caprarola, *Italy* ....... **39** **F9** 42 21N 12 11 E
Capreol, *Canada* ....... **128** **C3** 46 43N 80 56W
Caprera, *Italy* ......... **40** **A2** 41 12N 9 28 E
Capri, *Italy* ........... **41** **B7** 40 34N 14 15 E
Capricorn Group, *Australia* ........... **114** **C5** 23 30 S 151 55 E
Capricorn Ra., *Australia* **112** **D2** 23 20 S 116 50 E
Caprino Veronese, *Italy* . **38** **C7** 45 37N 10 47 E
Caprivi Strip, *Namibia* .. **104** **B3** 18 0 S 23 0 E
Captainganj, *India* ..... **81** **F10** 26 55N 83 45 E
Captain's Flat, *Australia* **117** **C8** 35 35 S 149 27 E
Captieux, *France* ....... **24** **D3** 44 18N 0 16W
Capu-Lapu, *Phil.* ....... **71** **F4** 10 20N 123 55 E
Cápua, *Italy* ........... **41** **A7** 41 7N 14 15 E
Capul I., *Phil.* ......... **70** **E5** 12 26N 124 10 E
Caquetá □, *Colombia* .. **152** **C3** 1 0N 74 0W
Caquetá ⟶, *Colombia* . **152** **D4** 1 15 S 69 15W
Carabalan, *Phil.* ....... **71** **F4** 10 6N 122 57 E
Carabao I., *Phil.* ....... **70** **E3** 12 4N 121 56 E
Carabobo, *Venezuela* ... **152** **A4** 10 2N 68 5W
Carabobo □, *Venezuela* . **152** **A4** 10 10N 68 5W
Caracal, *Romania* ...... **46** **E5** 44 8N 24 22 E
Caracaraí, *Brazil* ...... **153** **C5** 1 50N 61 8W
Caracas, *Venezuela* .... **152** **A4** 10 30N 66 55W
Caracol, *Brazil* ........ **154** **C3** 9 15 S 43 22W
Caracollo, *Bolivia* ..... **156** **D4** 17 39 S 67 10W
Caradoc, *Australia* ..... **116** **A5** 30 35 S 143 5 E
Caragabal, *Australia* ... **117** **B7** 33 49 S 147 45 E
Caráglio, *Italy* ......... **38** **D4** 44 25N 7 25 E
Carahue, *Chile* ........ **160** **A2** 38 43 S 73 12W
Caraí, *Brazil* .......... **155** **E3** 17 12 S 41 42W
Carajás, Serra dos, *Brazil* **154** **C1** 6 0 S 51 30W
Caramoan, *Phil.* ....... **70** **E4** 13 46N 123 52 E
Caranapatuba, *Brazil* ... **157** **B5** 6 38 S 62 34W
Carandaiti, *Bolivia* ..... **157** **E5** 20 45 S 63 4W
Carangola, *Brazil* ...... **155** **F3** 20 44 S 42 5W
Carani, *Australia* ...... **113** **F2** 30 57 S 116 28 E
Caransebeş, *Romania* ... **46** **D3** 45 28N 22 18 E
Carantec, *France* ...... **22** **D3** 48 40N 3 55W
Caraparaná ⟶, *Colombia* .......... **152** **D3** 1 45 S 73 13W
Carapelle ⟶, *Italy* ..... **41** **A8** 41 3N 15 55 E
Caras, *Peru* ........... **156** **B2** 9 3 S 77 47W
Caraş Severin □, *Romania* ........... **42** **B7** 45 10N 22 10 E
Caraşova, *Romania* .... **42** **B6** 45 11N 21 51 E
Caratasca, L., *Honduras* **148** **C3** 15 20N 83 40W
Caratinga, *Brazil* ...... **155** **E3** 19 50 S 42 10W
Caraúbas, *Brazil* ...... **154** **C4** 5 43 S 37 33W
Caravaca, *Spain* ....... **35** **G3** 38 8N 1 52W
Caravággio, *Italy* ...... **38** **C6** 45 30N 9 39 E
Caravelas, *Brazil* ...... **155** **E4** 17 45 S 39 15W
Caraveli, *Peru* ........ **156** **D3** 15 45 S 73 25W
Caràzinho, *Brazil* ...... **159** **B5** 28 16 S 52 46W
Carballino, *Spain* ...... **36** **C2** 42 26N 8 5W
Carballo, *Spain* ....... **36** **B2** 43 13N 8 41W
Carberry, *Canada* ...... **131** **D9** 49 50N 99 25W

Cíes, Is. 185


Chiamussu = Jiamusi, China 65 B8 46 40N 130 26 E
Chiang Dao, Thailand 76 C2 19 22N 98 58 E
Chiang Kham, Thailand 76 C3 19 32N 100 18 E
Chiang Khan, Thailand 76 D3 17 52N 101 36 E
Chiang Khong, Thailand 76 B3 20 17N 100 24 E
Chiang Mai, Thailand 76 C2 18 47N 98 59 E
Chiang Saen, Thailand 76 B3 20 16N 100 5 E
Chiange, Angola 103 F2 15 35 S 13 40 E
Chiapa →, Mexico 147 D6 16 42N 93 0W
Chiapa de Corzo, Mexico 147 D6 16 42N 93 0W
Chiapas □, Mexico 147 D6 17 0N 92 45W
Chiaramonte Gulfi, Italy 41 E7 37 1N 14 41 E
Chiaravalle, Italy 39 E10 43 38N 13 17 E
Chiaravalle Centrale, Italy 41 D9 38 41N 16 25 E
Chiari, Italy 38 C6 45 31N 9 55 E
Chiasso, Switz. 29 E8 45 50N 9 2 E
Chiatura, Georgia 53 E10 42 15N 43 17 E
Chiautla, Mexico 147 D5 18 18N 98 34W
Chiávari, Italy 38 D6 44 20N 9 20 E
Chiavenna, Italy 38 B6 46 18N 9 23 E
Chiba, Japan 63 B12 35 30N 140 7 E
Chiba □, Japan 63 B12 35 30N 140 20 E
Chibabava, Mozam. 105 C5 20 17 S 33 35 E
Chibemba, Cunene, Angola 103 F2 15 48 S 14 8 E
Chibemba, Huila, Angola 103 F3 16 20 S 15 20 E
Chibia, Angola 103 F2 15 10 S 13 42 E
Chibougamau, Canada 128 C5 49 56N 74 24W
Chibougamau L., Canada 128 C5 49 50N 74 20W
Chibuk, Nigeria 101 C7 10 52N 12 50 E
Chic-Chocs, Mts., Canada 129 C6 48 55N 66 0W
Chicacole = Srikakulam, India 82 E6 18 14N 83 58 E
Chicago, U.S.A. 141 C9 41 53N 87 40W
Chicago Heights, U.S.A. 141 C9 41 29N 87 37W
Chichagof I., U.S.A. 130 B1 58 0N 136 0W
Chichaoua, Morocco 98 B3 31 32N 8 44W
Chicheng, China 66 D8 40 55N 115 55 E
Chichester, U.K. 17 G7 50 50N 0 47W
Chichibu, Japan 63 A11 36 5N 139 10 E
Ch'ich'ihaerh = Qiqihar, China 65 B7 47 26N 124 0 E
Chickasha, U.S.A. 139 H5 35 0N 98 0W
Chiclana de la Frontera, Spain 37 J4 36 26N 6 9W
Chiclayo, Peru 156 B2 6 42 S 79 50W
Chico, U.S.A. 144 F5 39 45N 121 54W
Chico →, Chubut, Argentina 160 B3 44 0 S 67 0W
Chico →, Santa Cruz, Argentina 160 C3 50 0 S 68 30W
Chicomo, Mozam. 105 C5 24 31 S 34 6 E
Chicontepec, Mexico 147 C5 20 58N 98 10W
Chicopee, U.S.A. 137 D12 42 6N 72 37W
Chicoutimi, Canada 129 C5 48 28N 71 5W
Chicualacuala, Mozam. 105 C5 22 6 S 31 42 E
Chidambaram, India 83 J4 11 20N 79 45 E
Chidenguele, Mozam. 105 C5 24 55 S 34 11 E
Chidley, C., Canada 127 B13 60 23N 64 26W
Chiede, Angola 103 F3 17 15 S 16 22 E
Chiefs Pt., Canada 136 B3 44 41N 81 18W
Chiem Hoa, Vietnam 76 A5 22 12N 105 17 E
Chiemsee, Germany 27 H8 47 53N 12 27 E
Chiengi, Zambia 107 D2 8 45 S 29 10 E
Chiengmai = Chiang Mai, Thailand 76 C2 18 47N 98 59 E
Chiengo, Angola 103 E4 13 20 S 21 55 E
Chienti →, Italy 39 E10 43 18N 13 45 E
Chieri, Italy 38 D4 45 0N 7 50 E
Chiers →, France 23 C11 49 39N 4 59 E
Chiese →, Italy 38 C7 45 8N 10 25 E
Chieti, Italy 39 F11 42 22N 14 10 E
Chièvres, Belgium 21 G3 50 35N 3 48 E
Chifeng, China 67 C10 42 18N 118 58 E
Chigasaki, Japan 63 B11 35 19N 139 24 E
Chigirin, Ukraine 52 B5 49 4N 32 38 E
Chignecto B., Canada 129 C7 45 30N 64 40W
Chigorodó, Colombia 152 B2 7 41N 76 42W
Chiguana, Bolivia 158 A2 21 0 S 67 58W
Chiha-ri, N. Korea 67 E14 38 40N 126 30 E
Chihli, G. of = Bo Hai, China 67 E10 39 0N 119 0 E
Chihuahua, Mexico 146 B3 28 40N 106 3W
Chihuahua □, Mexico 146 B3 28 40N 106 3W
Chiili, Kazakhstan 55 A3 44 20N 66 15 E
Chik Bollapur, India 83 H3 13 25N 77 45 E
Chikhli, India 82 D3 20 20N 76 18 E
Chikmagalur, India 83 H2 13 15N 75 45 E
Chikodi, India 83 F2 16 26N 74 38 E
Chikugo, Japan 62 D2 33 14N 130 28 E
Chikuma-Gawa →, Japan 63 A10 36 59N 138 35 E
Chikwawa, Malawi 107 F3 16 2 S 34 50 E
Chilac, Mexico 147 D5 18 20N 97 24W
Chilako →, Canada 130 C4 53 53N 122 57W
Chilam Chavki, Pakistan 81 B6 35 5N 75 5 E
Chilanga, Zambia 107 F2 15 33 S 28 16 E
Chilapa, Mexico 147 D5 17 40N 99 11W
Chilas, Pakistan 81 B6 35 25N 74 5 E
Chilcotin →, Canada 130 C4 51 44N 122 23W
Childers, Australia 115 D5 25 15 S 152 17 E
Childress, U.S.A. 139 H4 34 30N 100 15W
Chile ■, S. Amer. 160 B2 35 0 S 72 0W
Chile Chico, Chile 160 C2 46 33 S 71 44W
Chile Rise, Pac. Oc. 123 L18 38 0 S 92 0W
Chilecito, Argentina 158 B2 29 10 S 67 30W
Chilete, Peru 156 B2 7 10 S 78 50W
Chilhowee, U.S.A. 140 F3 38 36N 93 51W
Chilia, Braţul →, Romania 46 D10 45 25N 29 20 E
Chilik, Kazakhstan 54 F3 51 7N 53 55 E
Chilik, Kazakhstan 55 B9 43 33N 78 17 E
Chililabombwe, Zambia 107 E2 12 18 S 27 43 E
Chilin = Jilin, China 67 C14 43 44N 126 30 E
Chilka L., India 82 E7 19 40N 85 25 E
Chilko →, Canada 130 C4 52 0N 123 40W
Chilko, L., Canada 130 C4 51 20N 124 10W
Chillagoe, Australia 114 B3 17 7 S 144 33 E
Chillán, Chile 158 D1 36 40 S 72 10W
Chillicothe, Ill., U.S.A. 140 D7 40 55N 89 32W
Chillicothe, Mo., U.S.A. 140 E3 39 45N 93 30W
Chillicothe, Ohio, U.S.A. 134 F4 39 20N 82 58W
Chilliwack, Canada 130 D4 49 10N 121 54W
Chilo, India 80 F5 27 25N 73 32 E
Chiloane, I., Mozam. 105 C5 20 40 S 34 55 E
Chiloé □, Chile 160 B2 43 0 S 73 0W
Chiloé, I. de, Chile 160 B2 42 30 S 73 50W
Chilonda, Angola 103 E3 11 19 S 16 12 E
Chilpancingo, Mexico 147 D5 17 30N 99 30W
Chiltern, Australia 117 D7 36 10 S 146 36 E
Chiltern Hills, U.K. 17 F7 51 44N 0 42W
Chilton, U.S.A. 134 C1 44 1N 88 12W
Chiluage, Angola 103 D4 9 30 S 21 50 E
Chilubi, Zambia 107 E2 11 5 S 29 58 E
Chilubula, Zambia 107 E3 10 14 S 30 51 E
Chilumba, Malawi 107 E3 10 28 S 34 12 E
Chilwa, L., Malawi 107 F4 15 15 S 35 40 E
Chimaltitán, Mexico 146 C4 21 46N 103 50W
Chimán, Panama 148 E4 8 45N 78 40W
Chimay, Belgium 21 H4 50 3N 4 20 E
Chimbay, Uzbekistan 56 E6 42 57N 59 47 E
Chimborazo, Ecuador 152 D2 1 29 S 78 55W
Chimborazo □, Ecuador 152 D2 1 0 S 78 40W
Chimbote, Peru 156 B2 9 0 S 78 35W
Chimion, Uzbekistan 55 C5 40 15N 71 32 E
Chimishliya, Moldavia 46 C9 46 34N 28 44 E
Chimkent, Kazakhstan 55 B4 42 18N 69 36 E
Chimoio, Mozam. 107 F3 19 4 S 33 30 E
Chimpembe, Zambia 107 D2 9 31 S 29 33 E
Chin □, Burma 78 D4 22 0N 93 0 E
Chin Hills, Burma 78 D4 22 30N 93 30 E
Chin Ling Shan = Qinling Shandi, China 66 H5 33 50N 108 10 E
China, Mexico 147 B5 25 40N 99 20W
China ■, Asia 65 D6 30 0N 110 0 E
China Lake, U.S.A. 145 K9 35 44N 117 37W
Chinacota, Colombia 152 B3 7 37N 72 36W
Chinan = Jinan, China 66 F9 36 38N 117 1 E
Chinandega, Nic. 148 D2 12 35N 87 12W
Chinati Pk., U.S.A. 139 K2 30 0N 104 25W
Chincha Alta, Peru 156 C2 13 25 S 76 7W
Chinchilla, Australia 115 D5 26 45 S 150 38 E
Chinchilla de Monte Aragón, Spain 35 G3 38 53N 1 40W
Chinchón, Spain 34 E1 40 9N 3 26W
Chinchorro, Banco, Mexico 147 D7 18 35N 87 20W
Chinchou = Jinzhou, China 67 D11 41 5N 121 3 E
Chinchoua, Gabon 102 B1 0 1N 9 48 E
Chincoteague, U.S.A. 134 G8 37 58N 75 21W
Chinde, Mozam. 107 F4 18 35 S 36 30 E
Chindo, S. Korea 67 G14 34 28N 126 15 E
Chindwin →, Burma 78 E5 21 26N 95 15 E
Chineni, India 81 C6 33 2N 75 15 E
Chinga, Mozam. 107 F4 15 13 S 38 35 E
Chingola, Zambia 107 E2 12 31 S 27 53 E
Chingole, Malawi 107 E3 13 4 S 34 17 E
Chingoroi, Angola 103 E2 13 37 S 14 1 E
Ch'ingtao = Qingdao, China 67 F11 36 5N 120 20 E
Chinguar, Angola 103 E3 12 25 S 16 45 E
Chinguetti, Mauritania 98 D2 20 25N 12 24W
Chingune, Mozam. 105 C5 20 33 S 34 58 E
Chinhae, S. Korea 67 G15 35 9N 128 47 E
Chinhanguanine, Mozam. 105 D5 25 21 S 32 30 E
Chinhoyi, Zimbabwe 107 F3 17 20 S 30 8 E
Chiniot, Pakistan 79 C4 31 45N 73 0 E
Chínipas, Mexico 146 B3 27 22N 108 32W
Chinju, S. Korea 67 G15 35 12N 128 2 E
Chinle, U.S.A. 143 H9 36 14N 109 38W
Chinnamanur, India 83 K3 9 50N 77 24 E
Chinnampo, N. Korea 67 E13 38 52N 125 10 E
Chinnur, India 82 E4 18 57N 79 49 E
Chino, Japan 63 B10 35 59N 138 9 E
Chino, U.S.A. 145 L9 34 1N 117 41W
Chino Valley, U.S.A. 143 J7 34 54N 112 28W
Chinon, France 22 E7 47 10N 0 15 E
Chinook, Canada 131 C6 51 28N 110 59W
Chinook, U.S.A. 142 B9 48 35N 109 19W
Chinsali, Zambia 107 E3 10 30 S 32 2 E
Chintamani, India 83 H4 13 26N 78 3 E
Chióggia, Italy 39 C9 45 13N 12 15 E
Chíos = Khíos, Greece 45 F8 38 27N 26 9 E
Chipata, Zambia 107 E3 13 38 S 32 28 E
Chipewyan L., Canada 131 B9 58 0N 98 27W
Chipinge, Zimbabwe 107 G3 20 13 S 32 28 E
Chipiona, Spain 37 J4 36 44N 6 26W
Chipley, U.S.A. 135 K3 30 45N 85 32W
Chiplun, India 82 F1 17 31N 73 34 E
Chipman, Canada 129 C6 46 6N 65 53W
Chipoka, Malawi 107 E3 13 57 S 34 28 E
Chippenham, U.K. 17 F5 51 27N 2 7W
Chippewa →, U.S.A. 138 C8 44 25N 92 10W
Chippewa Falls, U.S.A. 138 C9 44 55N 91 22W
Chiprovtsi, Bulgaria 42 D7 43 24N 22 52 E
Chiquián, Peru 156 C2 10 10 S 77 0W
Chiquimula, Guatemala 148 D2 14 51N 89 37W
Chiquinquira, Colombia 152 B3 5 37N 73 50W
Chiquitos, Llanos de, Bolivia 157 D5 18 0 S 61 30W
Chir →, Russia 53 B10 48 30N 43 0 E
Chirala, India 83 G5 15 50N 80 26 E
Chiramba, Mozam. 107 F3 16 55 S 34 39 E
Chiran, Japan 62 F2 31 22N 130 27 E
Chirawa, India 80 E6 28 14N 75 42 E
Chirayinkil, India 83 K3 8 41N 76 49 E
Chirchik, Uzbekistan 55 C4 41 29N 69 35 E
Chirfa, Niger 97 D2 20 55N 12 22 E
Chirgua →, Venezuela 152 B4 8 54N 67 58W
Chiricahua Pk., U.S.A. 143 L9 31 53N 109 14W
Chiriquí, G. de, Panama 148 E3 8 0N 82 10W
Chiriquí, L. de, Panama 148 E3 9 10N 82 0W
Chirivira Falls, Zimbabwe 107 G3 21 10 S 32 12 E
Chirnogi, Romania 46 E7 44 7N 26 32 E
Chirpan, Bulgaria 43 E10 42 10N 25 19 E
Chirripó Grande, Cerro, Costa Rica 148 E3 9 29N 83 29W
Chisamba, Zambia 107 E2 14 55 S 28 20 E
Chishmy, Russia 54 D4 54 35N 55 23 E
Chisholm, Canada 130 C6 54 55N 114 10W
Chishtian Mandi, Pakistan 80 E5 29 50N 72 55 E
Chishui, China 68 C5 28 30N 105 42 E
Chishui He →, China 68 C5 28 49N 105 50 E
Chisimaio, Somali Rep. 108 E2 0 22 S 42 32 E
Chisimba Falls, Zambia 107 E3 10 12 S 30 56 E
Chisineu Criş, Romania 46 C2 46 32N 21 37 E
Chisone →, Italy 38 D4 44 49N 7 25 E
Chisos Mts., U.S.A. 139 L3 29 20N 103 15W
Chistopol, Russia 51 D17 55 25N 50 38 E
Chita, Colombia 152 B3 6 11N 72 28W
Chita, Russia 57 D12 52 0N 113 35 E
Chitado, Angola 103 F2 17 10 S 14 8 E
Chitapur, India 82 F3 17 10N 77 5 E
Chitembo, Angola 103 E3 13 30 S 16 50 E
Chitipa, Malawi 107 D3 9 41 S 33 19 E
Chitose, Japan 60 C10 42 49N 141 39 E
Chitrakot, India 82 E5 19 10N 81 40 E
Chitral, Pakistan 79 B3 35 50N 71 56 E
Chitravati →, India 83 G4 14 45N 78 15 E
Chitré, Panama 148 E3 7 59N 80 27W
Chittagong, Bangla. 78 D3 22 19N 91 48 E
Chittagong □, Bangla. 78 C3 24 5N 91 0 E
Chittaurgarh, India 80 G6 24 52N 74 38 E
Chittoor, India 83 H4 13 15N 79 5 E
Chittur, India 83 J3 10 40N 76 45 E
Chitungwiza, Zimbabwe 107 F3 18 0 S 31 6 E
Chiumba, Angola 103 E3 12 29 S 16 8 E
Chiume, Angola 103 F4 15 3 S 21 14 E
Chiusa, Italy 39 B8 46 38N 11 34 E
Chiusi, Italy 39 E8 43 1N 11 58 E
Chiva, Spain 35 F4 39 27N 0 41W
Chivacoa, Venezuela 152 A4 10 10N 68 54W
Chivasso, Italy 38 C4 45 10N 7 52 E
Chivay, Peru 156 D3 15 40 S 71 35W
Chivhu, Zimbabwe 107 F3 19 2 S 30 52 E
Chivilcoy, Argentina 158 C4 34 55 S 60 0W
Chiwanda, Tanzania 107 E3 11 23 S 34 55 E
Chixi, China 69 G9 22 0N 112 58 E
Chizera, Zambia 107 E1 13 10 S 25 0 E
Chkalov = Orenburg, Russia 54 F4 51 45N 55 6 E
Chkolovsk, Russia 51 C13 56 50N 43 10 E
Chloride, U.S.A. 145 K12 35 25N 114 12W
Chlumec, Czech. 30 A8 50 9N 15 29 E
Chmielnik, Poland 47 E7 50 37N 20 43 E
Cho Bo, Vietnam 76 B5 20 46N 105 10 E
Cho-do, N. Korea 67 E13 38 30N 124 40 E
Cho Phuoc Hai, Vietnam 77 G6 10 26N 107 18 E
Choa Chukang, Malaysia 74 B2 1 22N 103 41 E
Choba, Kenya 106 B4 2 30N 38 5 E
Chobe National Park, Botswana 104 B3 18 0 S 25 0 E
Chochiwŏn, S. Korea 67 F14 36 37N 127 18 E
Chocianów, Poland 47 D2 51 27N 15 55 E
Chociwel, Poland 47 B2 53 29N 15 21 E
Chocó □, Colombia 152 B2 6 0N 77 0W
Chocontá, Colombia 152 B3 5 9N 73 41W
Choctawhatchee B., U.S.A. 133 D9 30 15N 86 30W
Chodaków, Poland 47 C7 52 16N 20 18 E
Chodavaram, India 82 F6 17 50N 82 57 E
Chodecz, Poland 47 C6 52 24N 19 2 E
Chodziez, Poland 47 C3 52 58N 16 58 E
Choele Choel, Argentina 160 A3 39 11 S 65 40W
Chōfu, Japan 63 B11 35 39N 139 33 E
Choiseul, Solomon Is. 121 L9 7 0 S 156 40 E
Choisy-le-Roi, France 23 D9 48 45N 2 24 E
Choix, Mexico 146 B3 26 40N 108 23W
Chojna, Poland 47 C1 52 58N 14 25 E
Chojnice, Poland 47 B4 53 42N 17 32 E
Chojnów, Poland 47 D2 51 18N 15 58 E
Chōkai-San, Japan 60 E10 39 6N 140 3 E
Choke, Ethiopia 95 E4 11 18N 37 15 E
Chokurdakh, Russia 57 B15 70 38N 147 55 E
Cholame, U.S.A. 144 K6 35 44N 120 18W
Cholet, France 22 E6 47 4N 0 52W
Cholpon-Ata, Kirghizia 55 B8 42 40N 77 6 E
Choluteca, Honduras 148 D2 13 20N 87 14W
Choluteca →, Honduras 148 D2 13 0N 87 20W
Chom Bung, Thailand 76 F2 13 37N 99 36 E
Chom Thong, Thailand 76 C2 18 25N 98 41 E
Choma, Zambia 107 F2 16 48 S 26 59 E
Chomen Swamp, Ethiopia 95 F4 9 20N 37 10 E
Chomun, India 80 F6 27 15N 75 40 E
Chomutov, Czech. 30 A6 50 28N 13 23 E
Chon Buri, Thailand 76 F3 13 21N 101 1 E
Chon Thanh, Vietnam 77 G6 11 24N 106 36 E
Chonan, S. Korea 67 F14 36 48N 127 9 E
Chone, Ecuador 152 D2 0 40 S 80 0W
Chong Kai, Cambodia 76 F4 13 57N 103 35 E
Chong Mek, Thailand 76 E5 15 10N 105 27 E
Chong'an, China 69 D12 27 45N 118 0 E
Chongde, China 69 B13 30 32N 120 26 E
Chŏngdo, S. Korea 67 G15 35 38N 128 42 E
Chŏngha, S. Korea 67 F15 36 12N 129 21 E
Chŏngjin, N. Korea 67 D15 41 47N 129 50 E
Chŏngju, N. Korea 67 E13 39 40N 125 5 E
Chŏngju, S. Korea 67 F14 36 39N 127 27 E
Chongli, China 66 D8 40 58N 115 15 E
Chongming, China 69 B13 31 38N 121 23 E
Chongming Dao, China 69 B13 31 40N 121 30 E
Chongoyape, Peru 156 B2 6 35 S 79 25W
Chongqing, Sichuan, China 68 C6 29 35N 106 25 E
Chongqing, Sichuan, China 68 B4 30 38N 103 40 E
Chongren, China 69 D11 27 46N 116 3 E
Chŏngŭp, S. Korea 67 G14 35 35N 126 50 E
Chongzuo, China 68 F6 22 23N 107 20 E
Chŏnju, S. Korea 67 G14 35 50N 127 4 E
Chonos, Arch. de los, Chile 160 C2 45 0 S 75 0W
Chopda, India 82 D2 21 20N 75 15 E
Chopim →, Brazil 159 B5 25 35 S 53 5W
Chorbat La, India 81 B7 34 42N 76 37 E
Chorley, U.K. 16 D5 53 39N 2 39W
Chorolque, Cerro, Bolivia 158 A2 20 59 S 66 5W
Choroszcz, Poland 47 B9 53 10N 22 59 E
Chorregon, Australia 114 C3 22 40 S 143 32 E
Chortkov, Ukraine 50 G4 49 2N 25 46 E
Chŏrwŏn, S. Korea 67 E14 38 15N 127 10 E
Chorzele, Poland 47 B7 53 15N 20 55 E
Chorzów, Poland 47 E5 50 18N 18 57 E
Chos-Malal, Argentina 158 D1 37 20 S 70 15W
Chosan, N. Korea 67 D13 40 50N 125 47 E
Chōshi, Japan 63 B12 35 45N 140 51 E
Choszczno, Poland 47 B2 53 7N 15 25 E
Chota, Peru 156 B2 6 33 S 78 39W
Choteau, U.S.A. 142 C7 47 50N 112 10W
Chotila, India 80 H4 22 23N 71 15 E
Chowchilla, U.S.A. 144 H6 37 11N 120 12W
Chowkham, Burma 78 E6 20 52N 97 28 E
Choybalsan, Mongolia 65 B6 48 4N 114 30 E
Chrisman, U.S.A. 141 E9 39 48N 87 41W
Christchurch, N.Z. 119 D7 43 33 S 172 47 E
Christchurch, U.K. 17 G6 50 44N 1 45W
Christian I., Canada 136 B4 44 50N 80 12W
Christiana, S. Africa 104 D4 27 52 S 25 8 E
Christiansfeld, Denmark 15 J3 55 21N 9 29 E
Christiansted, Virgin Is. 149 C7 17 45N 64 42W
Christie B., Canada 131 A6 62 32N 111 10W
Christina →, Canada 131 B6 56 40N 111 3W
Christmas Cr. →, Australia 112 C4 18 29 S 125 23 E
Christmas Creek, Australia 112 C4 18 29 S 125 23 E
Christmas I. = Kiritimati, Kiribati 123 G12 1 58N 157 27W
Christmas I., Ind. Oc. 109 F9 10 30 S 105 40 E
Christopher L., Australia 113 D4 24 49 S 127 42 E
Chrudim, Czech. 30 B8 49 58N 15 43 E
Chrzanów, Poland 31 A12 50 10N 19 21 E
Chtimba, Malawi 107 E3 10 35 S 34 13 E
Chu, Kazakhstan 55 B6 43 36N 73 42 E
Chu →, Kazakhstan 55 A3 45 0N 67 44 E
Chu →, Vietnam 76 C5 19 53N 105 45 E
Chu Chua, Canada 130 C4 51 22N 120 10W
Chu Lai, Vietnam 76 E7 15 28N 108 45 E
Chu Xian, China 69 A12 32 19N 118 20 E
Chuadanga, Bangla. 78 D2 23 38N 88 51 E
Ch'uanchou = Quanzhou, China 69 E12 24 55N 118 34 E
Chuankou, China 66 G6 34 20N 110 59 E
Chūbu □, Japan 63 A9 36 45N 137 30 E
Chubut □, Argentina 160 B3 43 30 S 69 0W
Chubut →, Argentina 160 B3 43 20 S 65 5W
Chuchi L., Canada 130 B4 55 12N 124 30W
Chudovo, Russia 50 B7 59 10N 31 41 E
Chudskoye, Oz., Estonia 50 B5 58 13N 27 30 E
Chūgoku □, Japan 62 C4 35 0N 133 0 E
Chūgoku-Sanchi, Japan 62 C4 35 0N 133 0 E
Chuguyev, Ukraine 52 B7 49 55N 36 45 E
Chugwater, U.S.A. 138 E2 41 48N 104 47W
Chukhloma, Russia 51 B13 58 45N 42 40 E
Chukotskiy Khrebet, Russia 57 C18 68 0N 175 0 E
Chukotskoye More, Russia 57 C19 68 0N 175 0W
Chula, U.S.A. 140 E3 39 55N 93 29W
Chula Vista, U.S.A. 145 N9 32 39N 117 8W
Chulak-Kurgan, Kazakhstan 55 B4 43 46N 69 9 E
Chulman, Russia 57 D13 56 52N 124 52 E
Chulucanas, Peru 156 B1 5 8 S 80 10W
Chulumani, Bolivia 156 D4 16 24 S 67 31W
Chulym →, Russia 56 D9 57 43N 83 51 E
Chum Phae, Thailand 76 D4 16 40N 102 6 E
Chum Saeng, Thailand 76 E3 15 55N 100 15 E
Chuma, Bolivia 156 D4 15 24 S 68 56W
Chumar, India 81 C8 32 40N 78 35 E
Chumbicha, Argentina 158 B2 29 0 S 66 10W
Chumerna, Bulgaria 43 E10 42 45N 25 55 E
Chumikan, Russia 57 D14 54 40N 135 10 E
Chumphon, Thailand 77 G2 10 35N 99 14 E
Chumpi, Peru 156 D3 15 4 S 73 46W
Chumuare, Mozam. 107 E3 14 31 S 31 50 E
Chumunjin, S. Korea 67 F15 37 55N 128 54 E
Chuna →, Russia 57 D10 57 47N 94 37 E
Chun'an, China 69 C12 29 35N 119 3 E
Chunchŏn, S. Korea 67 F14 37 58N 127 44 E
Chunchura, India 81 H13 22 53N 88 27 E
Chunga, Zambia 107 F2 15 0 S 26 2 E
Chunggang-ŭp, N. Korea 67 D14 41 48N 126 48 E
Chunghwa, N. Korea 67 E13 38 52N 125 47 E
Chungju, S. Korea 67 F14 36 58N 127 58 E
Chungking = Chongqing, China 68 C6 29 35N 106 25 E
Chungmu, S. Korea 67 G15 34 50N 128 20 E
Chungt'iaoshan = Zhongtiao Shan, China 66 G6 35 0N 111 10 E
Chunian, Pakistan 80 D6 30 57N 74 0 E
Chunya, Tanzania 107 D3 8 30 S 33 27 E
Chunya □, Tanzania 106 D3 7 48 S 33 0 E
Chunyang, China 67 C15 43 38N 129 23 E
Chuquibamba, Peru 156 D3 15 47 S 72 44W
Chuquibambilla, Peru 156 C3 14 7 S 72 41W
Chuquicamata, Chile 158 A2 22 15 S 69 0W
Chuquisaca □, Bolivia 157 E5 20 30 S 63 30W
Chur, Switz. 29 C9 46 52N 9 32 E
Churachandpur, India 78 C4 24 20N 93 40 E
Churchill, Canada 131 B10 58 47N 94 11W
Churchill →, Man., Canada 131 B10 58 47N 94 12W
Churchill →, Nfld., Canada 129 B7 53 19N 60 10W
Churchill, C., Canada 131 B10 58 46N 93 12W
Churchill Falls, Canada 129 B7 53 36N 64 19W
Churchill L., Canada 131 B7 55 55N 108 20W
Churchill Pk., Canada 130 B3 58 10N 125 10W
Churdan, U.S.A. 140 B2 42 9N 94 29W
Churfisten, Switz. 29 B8 47 8N 9 17 E
Churu, India 80 E6 28 20N 74 50 E
Churubusco, U.S.A. 141 C11 41 14N 85 19W
Churwalden, Switz. 29 C9 46 47N 9 33 E
Chushal, India 81 C8 33 40N 78 40 E
Chusovaya →, Russia 54 B5 58 18N 56 22 E
Chusovoy, Russia 54 B5 58 15N 57 40 E
Chust, Uzbekistan 55 C5 41 0N 71 13 E
Chuuronjang, N. Korea 67 D15 41 35N 129 40 E
Chuvash Republic□, Russia 51 D15 55 30N 47 0 E
Chuwārtah, Iraq 84 C5 35 43N 45 34 E
Chuxiong, China 68 E3 25 2N 101 28 E
Ci Xian, China 66 F8 36 20N 114 25 E
Ciacova, Romania 46 D2 45 35N 21 10 E
Ciamis, Indonesia 75 D3 7 20 S 108 21 E
Cianjur, Indonesia 74 D3 6 49 S 107 8 E
Cibola, U.S.A. 145 M12 33 17N 114 42W
Cicero, U.S.A. 134 E2 41 48N 87 48W
Cicero, Ill., U.S.A. 141 C9 41 51N 87 45W
Cícero Dantas, Brazil 154 D4 10 36 S 38 23W
Cidacos →, Spain 34 C3 42 21N 1 38W
Cide, Turkey 52 F5 41 53N 33 1 E
Ciechanów, Poland 47 C7 52 52N 20 38 E
Ciechanów □, Poland 47 B7 53 0N 20 30 E
Ciechanowiec, Poland 47 C9 52 40N 22 31 E
Ciechocinek, Poland 47 C5 52 53N 18 45 E
Ciego de Avila, Cuba 148 B4 21 50N 78 50W
Ciénaga, Colombia 152 A3 11 1N 74 15W
Ciénaga de Oro, Colombia 152 B2 8 53N 75 37W
Cienfuegos, Cuba 148 B3 22 10N 80 30W
Cieplice Slaskie Zdrój, Poland 47 E2 50 50N 15 40 E
Cierp, France 24 F4 42 55N 0 40 E
Cíes, Is., Spain 36 C2 42 12N 8 55W

186 Cieszanów


Cieszanów, *Poland* 47 **E10** 50 14N 23 8 E
Cieszyn, *Poland* 31 **B11** 49 45N 18 35 E
Cieza, *Spain* 35 **G3** 38 17N 1 23W
Çifteler, *Turkey* 88 **D4** 39 22N 31 2 E
Cifuentes, *Spain* 34 **E2** 40 47N 2 37W
Cihanbeyli, *Turkey* 88 **D5** 38 40N 32 55 E
Cihuatlán, *Mexico* 146 **D4** 19 14N 104 35W
Cijara, Pantano de, *Spain* 37 **F6** 39 18N 4 52W
Cilacap, *Indonesia* 75 **D3** 7 43 S 109 0 E
Çıldır, *Turkey* 53 **F10** 41 7N 43 8 E
Çıldır Gölü, *Turkey* 89 **C10** 41 5N 43 15 E
Cili, *China* 69 **C8** 29 30N 111 8 E
Cilicia, *Turkey* 88 **E5** 36 30N 33 40 E
Cîlnicu, *Romania* 46 **E4** 44 54N 23 4 E
Cilo Dağı, *Turkey* 89 **E10** 37 28N 43 55 E
Cima, *U.S.A.* 145 **K11** 35 14N 115 30W
Cimarron, *Kans., U.S.A.* 139 **G4** 37 50N 100 20W
Cimarron, *N. Mex., U.S.A.* 139 **G2** 36 30N 104 52W
Cimarron →, *U.S.A.* 139 **G6** 36 10N 96 17W
Cimone, Mte., *Italy* 38 **D7** 44 10N 10 40 E
Cîmpic Turzii, *Romania* 46 **C4** 46 34N 23 53 E
Cîmpina, *Romania* 46 **D6** 45 10N 25 45 E
Cîmpulung, *Argeş, Romania* 46 **D6** 45 17N 25 3 E
Cîmpulung, *Suceava, Romania* 46 **B6** 47 32N 25 30 E
Cîmpuri, *Romania* 46 **C7** 46 0N 26 50 E
Çinar, *Turkey* 89 **E9** 37 46N 40 19 E
Cinca →, *Spain* 34 **D5** 41 26N 0 21 E
Cincer, *Bos.-H., Yug.* 42 **D2** 43 55N 17 5 E
Cincinnati, *Iowa, U.S.A.* 140 **D4** 40 38N 92 56W
Cincinnati, *Ohio, U.S.A.* 141 **E12** 39 10N 84 26W
Cîndeşti, *Romania* 46 **D7** 45 15N 26 42 E
Çine, *Turkey* 88 **E3** 37 37N 28 2 E
Ciney, *Belgium* 21 **H6** 50 18N 5 5 E
Cíngoli, *Italy* 39 **E10** 43 23N 13 10 E
Cinigiano, *Italy* 39 **F8** 42 53N 11 23 E
Cinto, Mte., *France* 25 **F12** 42 24N 8 54 E
Ciorani, *Romania* 46 **E7** 44 45N 26 25 E
Čiovo, *Croatia* 39 **E13** 43 30N 16 17 E
Cipó, *Brazil* 154 **D4** 11 6 S 38 31W
Circeo, Monte, *Italy* 40 **A6** 41 14N 13 3 E
Çirçir, *Turkey* 88 **C7** 40 5N 36 47 E
Circle, *Alaska, U.S.A.* 126 **B5** 65 50N 144 10W
Circle, *Mont., U.S.A.* 138 **B2** 47 26N 105 35W
Circleville, *Ohio, U.S.A.* 134 **F4** 39 35N 82 57W
Circleville, *Utah, U.S.A.* 143 **G7** 38 12N 112 24W
Cirebon, *Indonesia* 75 **D3** 6 45 S 108 32 E
Cirencester, *U.K.* 17 **F6** 51 43N 1 59W
Cireşu, *Romania* 46 **E3** 44 47N 22 31 E
Cirey-sur-Vezouze, *France* 23 **D13** 48 35N 6 57 E
Ciriè, *Italy* 38 **C4** 45 14N 7 35 E
Cirium, *Cyprus* 32 **E11** 34 40N 32 53 E
Cirò, *Italy* 41 **C10** 39 23N 17 3 E
Ciron →, *France* 24 **D3** 44 36N 0 18W
Cisco, *U.S.A.* 139 **J5** 32 25N 99 0W
Ciskei □, *S. Africa* 105 **E4** 33 0 S 27 0 E
Cislău, *Romania* 46 **D7** 45 14N 26 20 E
Cisna, *Poland* 31 **B15** 49 12N 22 20 E
Cisnădie, *Romania* 46 **D5** 45 42N 24 9 E
Cisne, *U.S.A.* 141 **F8** 38 31N 88 26W
Cisneros, *Colombia* 152 **B2** 6 33N 75 4W
Cissna Park, *U.S.A.* 141 **D9** 40 34N 87 54W
Cisterna di Latina, *Italy* 40 **A5** 41 35N 12 50 E
Cisternino, *Italy* 41 **B10** 40 45N 17 26 E
Citaré →, *Brazil* 153 **C7** 1 11N 54 41W
Citeli-Ckaro, *Georgia* 53 **F12** 41 33N 46 0 E
Citlaltépetl, *Mexico* 147 **D5** 19 0N 97 20W
Citrus Heights, *U.S.A.* 144 **G5** 38 42N 121 17W
Citrusdal, *S. Africa* 104 **E2** 32 35 S 19 0 E
Città della Pieve, *Italy* 39 **F9** 42 57N 12 0 E
Città di Castello, *Italy* 39 **E9** 43 27N 12 14 E
Città Sant' Angelo, *Italy* 39 **F11** 42 32N 14 5 E
Cittadella, *Italy* 39 **C8** 45 39N 11 48 E
Cittaducale, *Italy* 39 **F9** 42 24N 12 58 E
Cittanova, *Italy* 41 **D9** 38 22N 16 5 E
Ciuc, Munţii, *Romania* 46 **C7** 46 25N 26 5 E
Ciucaş, *Romania* 46 **D6** 45 31N 25 56 E
Ciudad Altamirano, *Mexico* 146 **D4** 18 20N 100 40W
Ciudad Bolívar, *Venezuela* 153 **B5** 8 5N 63 36W
Ciudad Camargo, *Mexico* 146 **B3** 27 41N 105 10W
Ciudad Chetumal, *Mexico* 147 **D7** 18 30N 88 20W
Ciudad de Valles, *Mexico* 147 **C5** 22 0N 99 0W
Ciudad del Carmen, *Mexico* 147 **D6** 18 38N 91 50W
Ciudad Delicias = Delicias, *Mexico* 146 **B3** 28 10N 105 30W
Ciudad Guayana, *Venezuela* 153 **B5** 8 0N 62 30W
Ciudad Guerrero, *Mexico* 146 **B3** 28 33N 107 28W
Ciudad Guzmán, *Mexico* 146 **D4** 19 40N 103 30W
Ciudad Juárez, *Mexico* 146 **A3** 31 40N 106 28W
Ciudad Madero, *Mexico* 147 **C5** 22 19N 97 50W
Ciudad Mante, *Mexico* 147 **C5** 22 50N 99 0W
Ciudad Obregón, *Mexico* 146 **B3** 27 28N 109 59W
Ciudad Ojeda, *Venezuela* 152 **A3** 10 12N 71 19W
Ciudad Real, *Spain* 37 **G7** 38 59N 3 55W
Ciudad Real □, *Spain* 37 **G7** 38 50N 4 0W
Ciudad Rodrigo, *Spain* 36 **E4** 40 35N 6 32W
Ciudad Trujillo = Santo Domingo, *Dom. Rep.* 149 **C6** 18 30N 69 59W
Ciudad Victoria, *Mexico* 147 **C5** 23 41N 99 9W
Ciudadela, *Spain* 33 **B10** 40 0N 3 50 E
Ciulnița, *Romania* 46 **E8** 44 26N 27 22 E
Civa Burnu, *Turkey* 88 **C7** 41 21N 36 38 E
Cividale del Friuli, *Italy* 39 **B10** 46 6N 13 25 E
Cívita Castellana, *Italy* 39 **F9** 42 18N 12 24 E
Civitanova Marche, *Italy* 39 **E10** 43 18N 13 41 E
Civitavécchia, *Italy* 39 **F8** 42 6N 11 46 E
Civitella del Tronto, *Italy* 39 **F10** 42 48N 13 40 E
Civray, *France* 24 **B4** 46 10N 0 17 E
Çivril, *Turkey* 88 **D3** 38 20N 29 43 E
Cixerri →, *Italy* 40 **C1** 39 20N 8 40 E
Cizre, *Turkey* 89 **E10** 37 19N 42 10 E
Clacton-on-Sea, *U.K.* 17 **F9** 51 47N 1 10 E
Clain →, *France* 22 **F7** 46 47N 0 33 E
Claire, L., *Canada* 130 **B6** 58 35N 112 5W
Clairemont, *U.S.A.* 139 **J4** 33 9N 100 44W
Clairton, *U.S.A.* 136 **F5** 40 18N 79 54W
Clairvaux-les-Lacs, *France* 25 **B9** 46 35N 5 45 E
Clallam Bay, *U.S.A.* 144 **B2** 48 15N 124 16W
Clamecy, *France* 23 **E10** 47 28N 3 30 E
Clanton, *U.S.A.* 135 **J2** 32 48N 86 36W
Clanwilliam, *S. Africa* 104 **E2** 32 11 S 18 52 E
Clara, *Ireland* 19 **C4** 53 20N 7 38W
Clara →, *Australia* 114 **B3** 19 8 S 142 30 E
Claraville, *U.S.A.* 145 **K8** 35 24N 118 20W
Clare, *Australia* 116 **B3** 33 50 S 138 37 E
Clare, *U.S.A.* 134 **D3** 43 47N 84 45W
Clare □, *Ireland* 19 **D3** 52 45N 9 0W
Clare →, *Ireland* 19 **C2** 53 22N 9 5W
Clare I., *Ireland* 19 **C2** 53 48N 10 0W
Claremont, *Calif., U.S.A.* 145 **L9** 34 6N 117 43W
Claremont, *N.H., U.S.A.* 137 **C12** 43 23N 72 20W
Claremont Pt., *Australia* 114 **A3** 14 1 S 143 41 E
Claremore, *U.S.A.* 139 **G7** 36 40N 95 37W
Claremorris, *Ireland* 19 **C3** 53 45N 9 0W
Clarence, *U.S.A.* 140 **E4** 39 45N 92 16W
Clarence →, *Australia* 115 **D5** 29 25 S 153 22 E
Clarence →, *N.Z.* 119 **C8** 42 10 S 173 56 E
Clarence, I., *Chile* 160 **D2** 54 0 S 72 0W
Clarence I., *Antarctica* 7 **C18** 61 10 S 54 0W
Clarence Str., *Australia* 112 **B5** 12 0 S 131 0 E
Clarence Str., *U.S.A.* 130 **B2** 55 40N 132 10W
Clarence Town, *Bahamas* 149 **B5** 23 6N 74 59W
Clarendon, *Ark., U.S.A.* 139 **H9** 34 41N 91 20W
Clarendon, *Tex., U.S.A.* 139 **H4** 34 58N 100 54W
Clarenville, *Canada* 129 **C9** 48 10N 54 1W
Claresholm, *Canada* 130 **C6** 50 0N 113 33W
Clarie Coast, *Antarctica* 7 **C9** 68 0 S 135 0 E
Clarin, *Phil.* 71 **G4** 8 12N 123 52 E
Clarinda, *U.S.A.* 138 **E7** 40 45N 95 0W
Clarion, *Iowa, U.S.A.* 140 **B3** 42 41N 93 46W
Clarion, *Pa., U.S.A.* 136 **E5** 41 12N 79 22W
Clarion →, *U.S.A.* 136 **E5** 41 9N 79 41W
Clark, *U.S.A.* 138 **C6** 44 55N 97 45W
Clark, Pt., *Canada* 136 **B3** 44 4N 81 45W
Clark Fork, *U.S.A.* 142 **B5** 48 9N 116 9W
Clark Fork →, *U.S.A.* 142 **B5** 48 9N 116 15W
Clark Hill Res., *U.S.A.* 135 **J4** 33 45N 82 20W
Clarkdale, *U.S.A.* 143 **J7** 34 53N 112 3W
Clarke City, *Canada* 129 **B6** 50 12N 66 38W
Clarke I., *Australia* 114 **G4** 40 32 S 148 10 E
Clarke L., *Canada* 131 **C7** 54 24N 106 54W
Clarke Ra., *Australia* 114 **C4** 20 40 S 148 30 E
Clark's Fork →, *U.S.A.* 142 **D9** 45 39N 108 43W
Clark's Harbour, *Canada* 129 **D6** 43 25N 65 38W
Clarks Summit, *U.S.A.* 137 **E9** 41 31N 75 44W
Clarksburg, *U.S.A.* 134 **F5** 39 18N 80 21W
Clarksdale, *U.S.A.* 139 **H9** 34 12N 90 33W
Clarkston, *U.S.A.* 142 **C5** 46 28N 117 2W
Clarksville, *Ark., U.S.A.* 139 **H8** 35 29N 93 27W
Clarksville, *Iowa, U.S.A.* 140 **B4** 42 47N 92 40W
Clarksville, *Mich., U.S.A.* 141 **B11** 42 50N 85 15W
Clarksville, *Ohio, U.S.A.* 141 **E13** 39 24N 83 59W
Clarksville, *Tenn., U.S.A.* 135 **G2** 36 32N 87 20W
Clarksville, *Tex., U.S.A.* 139 **J7** 33 37N 94 59W
Claro →, *Brazil* 155 **E1** 19 8 S 50 40W
Clatskanie, *U.S.A.* 144 **D3** 46 9N 123 12W
Claude, *U.S.A.* 139 **H4** 35 8N 101 22W
Claveria, *Cagayan, Phil.* 70 **E4** 12 54N 123 15 E
Claveria, *Masbate, Phil.* 71 **G5** 8 38N 124 55 E
Claveria, *Mindanao, Phil.* 70 **B3** 18 37N 121 4 E
Clay, *U.S.A.* 144 **G5** 38 17N 121 10W
Clay Center, *U.S.A.* 138 **F6** 39 27N 97 9W
Clay City, *Ind., U.S.A.* 141 **E9** 39 17N 87 7W
Clay City, *Ky., U.S.A.* 141 **G13** 37 52N 83 55W
Claypool, *U.S.A.* 143 **K8** 33 27N 110 55W
Claysville, *U.S.A.* 136 **F4** 40 5N 80 25W
Clayton, *Idaho, U.S.A.* 142 **D6** 44 12N 114 31W
Clayton, *Ind., U.S.A.* 141 **E10** 39 41N 86 31W
Clayton, *N. Mex., U.S.A.* 139 **G3** 36 30N 103 10W
Cle Elum, *U.S.A.* 142 **C3** 47 15N 120 57W
Clear, C., *Ireland* 19 **E2** 51 26N 9 30W
Clear I., *Ireland* 19 **E2** 51 26N 9 30W
Clear L., *U.S.A.* 144 **F4** 39 5N 122 47W
Clear Lake, *Iowa, U.S.A.* 140 **A3** 43 8N 93 23W
Clear Lake, *S. Dak., U.S.A.* 138 **C6** 44 48N 96 41W
Clear Lake, *Wash., U.S.A.* 142 **B2** 48 27N 122 15W
Clear Lake Res., *U.S.A.* 142 **F3** 41 55N 121 10W
Clearfield, *Iowa, U.S.A.* 140 **D2** 40 48N 94 29W
Clearfield, *Pa., U.S.A.* 134 **E6** 41 0N 78 27W
Clearfield, *Utah, U.S.A.* 142 **F7** 41 10N 112 0W
Clearlake Highlands, *U.S.A.* 144 **G4** 38 57N 122 38W
Clearmont, *U.S.A.* 142 **D10** 44 43N 106 29W
Clearwater, *Canada* 130 **C4** 51 38N 120 2W
Clearwater, *U.S.A.* 135 **M4** 27 58N 82 45W
Clearwater →, *Alta., Canada* 130 **C6** 52 22N 114 57W
Clearwater →, *Alta., Canada* 131 **B6** 56 44N 111 23W
Clearwater Cr. →, *Canada* 130 **A3** 61 36N 125 30W
Clearwater Mts., *U.S.A.* 142 **C6** 46 20N 115 30W
Clearwater Prov. Park, *Canada* 131 **C8** 54 0N 101 0W
Cleburne, *U.S.A.* 139 **J6** 32 18N 97 25W
Cleethorpes, *U.K.* 16 **D7** 53 33N 0 2W
Cleeve Hill, *U.K.* 17 **F6** 51 54N 2 0W
Clelles, *France* 25 **D9** 44 50N 5 38 E
Clemency, *Lux.* 21 **J7** 49 35N 5 53 E
Cleopatra Needle, *Phil.* 71 **F2** 10 7N 118 58 E
Clerke Reef, *Australia* 112 **C2** 17 22 S 119 20 E
Clermont, *Australia* 114 **C4** 22 49 S 147 39 E
Clermont, *France* 23 **C9** 49 23N 2 24 E
Clermont-en-Argonne, *France* 23 **C12** 49 5N 5 4 E
Clermont-Ferrand, *France* 24 **C7** 45 46N 3 4 E
Clermont-l'Hérault, *France* 24 **E7** 43 38N 3 26 E
Clerval, *France* 23 **E13** 47 25N 6 30 E
Clervaux, *Lux.* 21 **H8** 50 4N 6 2 E
Cléry-St.-André, *France* 23 **E8** 47 50N 1 46 E
Cles, *Italy* 38 **B8** 46 21N 11 4 E
Cleveland, *Australia* 115 **D5** 27 30 S 153 15 E
Cleveland, *Miss., U.S.A.* 139 **J9** 33 43N 90 43W
Cleveland, *Ohio, U.S.A.* 136 **E3** 41 28N 81 43W
Cleveland, *Okla., U.S.A.* 139 **G6** 36 21N 96 33W
Cleveland, *Tenn., U.S.A.* 135 **H3** 35 9N 84 52W
Cleveland, *Tex., U.S.A.* 139 **K7** 30 18N 95 0W
Cleveland □, *U.K.* 16 **C6** 54 35N 1 8 E
Cleveland, C., *Australia* 114 **B4** 19 11 S 147 1 E
Cleveland Heights, *U.S.A.* 136 **E3** 41 32N 81 30W
Clevelândia, *Brazil* 159 **B5** 26 24 S 52 23W
Clevelândia do Norte, *Brazil* 153 **C7** 3 49N 51 52W
Cleves, *U.S.A.* 141 **E12** 39 10N 84 45W
Clew B., *Ireland* 19 **C2** 53 54N 9 50W
Clewiston, *U.S.A.* 135 **M5** 26 44N 80 50W
Clifden, *Ireland* 19 **C1** 53 30N 10 2W
Clifden, *N.Z.* 119 **G2** 46 1 S 167 42 E
Cliffdell, *U.S.A.* 144 **D5** 46 56N 121 5W
Clifton, *Australia* 115 **D5** 27 59 S 151 53 E
Clifton, *Ariz., U.S.A.* 143 **K9** 33 8N 109 23W
Clifton, *Ill., U.S.A.* 141 **D9** 40 56N 87 56W
Clifton, *Tex., U.S.A.* 139 **K6** 31 46N 97 35W
Clifton Beach, *Australia* 114 **B4** 16 46 S 145 39 E
Clifton Forge, *U.S.A.* 134 **G6** 37 49N 79 51W
Clifton Hills, *Australia* 115 **D2** 27 1 S 138 54 E
Climax, *Canada* 131 **D7** 49 10N 108 20W
Clinch →, *U.S.A.* 135 **H3** 36 0N 84 29W
Clingmans Dome, *U.S.A.* 135 **H4** 35 35N 83 30W
Clint, *U.S.A.* 143 **L10** 31 37N 106 11W
Clinton, *B.C., Canada* 130 **C4** 51 6N 121 35W
Clinton, *Ont., Canada* 128 **D3** 43 37N 81 32W
Clinton, *N.Z.* 119 **G4** 46 12 S 169 23 E
Clinton, *Ark., U.S.A.* 139 **H8** 35 37N 92 30W
Clinton, *Ill., U.S.A.* 138 **E10** 40 8N 89 0W
Clinton, *Ind., U.S.A.* 141 **E9** 39 40N 87 22W
Clinton, *Iowa, U.S.A.* 140 **C6** 41 50N 90 12W
Clinton, *Mass., U.S.A.* 137 **D13** 42 26N 71 40W
Clinton, *Mo., U.S.A.* 140 **F3** 38 20N 93 46W
Clinton, *N.C., U.S.A.* 135 **H6** 35 5N 78 15W
Clinton, *Okla., U.S.A.* 139 **H5** 35 30N 99 0W
Clinton, *S.C., U.S.A.* 135 **H5** 34 30N 81 54W
Clinton, *Tenn., U.S.A.* 135 **G3** 36 6N 84 10W
Clinton, *Wash., U.S.A.* 144 **C4** 47 59N 122 22W
Clinton, *Wis., U.S.A.* 141 **B8** 42 34N 88 52W
Clinton C., *Australia* 114 **C5** 22 30 S 150 45 E
Clinton Colden L., *Canada* 126 **B9** 63 58N 107 27W
Clintonville, *U.S.A.* 138 **C10** 44 35N 88 46W
Clipperton, I., *Pac. Oc.* 123 **F17** 10 18N 109 13W
Clisson, *France* 22 **E5** 47 5N 1 16W
Clive, *N.Z.* 118 **F5** 39 36 S 176 58 E
Clive L., *Canada* 130 **A5** 63 13N 118 54W
Cliza, *Bolivia* 157 **D4** 17 36 S 65 56W
Cloates, Pt., *Australia* 112 **D1** 22 43 S 113 40 E
Clocolan, *S. Africa* 105 **D4** 28 55 S 27 34 E
Clodomira, *Argentina* 158 **B3** 27 35 S 64 14W
Clonakilty, *Ireland* 19 **E3** 51 37N 8 53W
Clonakilty B., *Ireland* 19 **E3** 51 33N 8 50W
Cloncurry, *Australia* 114 **C3** 20 40 S 140 28 E
Cloncurry →, *Australia* 114 **B3** 18 37 S 140 40 E
Clones, *Ireland* 19 **B4** 54 10N 7 13W
Clonmel, *Ireland* 19 **D4** 52 22N 7 42W
Cloppenburg, *Germany* 26 **C4** 52 50N 8 3 E
Cloquet, *U.S.A.* 138 **B8** 46 40N 92 30W
Clorinda, *Argentina* 158 **B4** 25 16 S 57 45W
Cloud Peak, *U.S.A.* 142 **D10** 44 23N 107 10W
Cloudcroft, *U.S.A.* 143 **K11** 33 0N 105 48W
Cloudy B., *N.Z.* 119 **B9** 41 25 S 174 10 E
Cloverdale, *Calif., U.S.A.* 144 **G4** 38 49N 123 0W
Cloverdale, *Ind., U.S.A.* 141 **E10** 39 31N 86 47W
Cloverport, *U.S.A.* 141 **G10** 37 50N 86 38W
Clovis, *Calif., U.S.A.* 144 **J7** 36 47N 119 45W
Clovis, *N. Mex., U.S.A.* 139 **H3** 34 20N 103 10W
Cloyes-sur-le-Loir, *France* 22 **E8** 48 0N 1 14 E
Club Terrace, *Australia* 117 **D8** 37 35 S 148 58 E
Cluj □, *Romania* 46 **C4** 46 45N 23 30 E
Cluj-Napoca, *Romania* 46 **C4** 46 47N 23 38 E
Clunes, *Australia* 116 **D5** 37 20 S 143 45 E
Cluny, *France* 25 **B8** 46 26N 4 38 E
Cluses, *France* 25 **B10** 46 5N 6 35 E
Clusone, *Italy* 38 **C6** 45 54N 9 58 E
Clutha →, *N.Z.* 119 **G4** 46 20 S 169 49 E
Clwyd □, *U.K.* 16 **D4** 53 5N 3 20W
Clwyd →, *U.K.* 16 **D4** 53 20N 3 30W
Clyde, *N.Z.* 119 **F4** 45 12 S 169 20 E
Clyde, *U.S.A.* 136 **C8** 43 8N 76 52W
Clyde →, *U.K.* 18 **F4** 55 56N 4 29W
Clyde, Firth of, *U.K.* 18 **F4** 55 20N 5 0W
Clyde River, *Canada* 127 **A13** 70 30N 68 30W
Clydebank, *U.K.* 18 **F4** 55 54N 4 25W
Clymer, *U.S.A.* 136 **D5** 40 42N 79 3W
Côa →, *Portugal* 36 **D3** 41 5N 7 6W
Coachella, *U.S.A.* 145 **M10** 33 44N 116 13W
Coachella Canal, *U.S.A.* 145 **N12** 32 43N 114 57W
Coahoma, *U.S.A.* 139 **J4** 32 17N 101 20W
Coahuayana →, *Mexico* 146 **D4** 18 41N 103 45W
Coahuayutla, *Mexico* 146 **D4** 18 19N 101 42W
Coahuila □, *Mexico* 146 **B4** 27 0N 103 0W
Coal →, *Canada* 130 **B3** 59 39N 126 57W
Coal City, *U.S.A.* 141 **C8** 41 17N 88 17W
Coal I., *N.Z.* 119 **G1** 46 8 S 166 40 E
Coalane, *Mozam.* 107 **F4** 17 48 S 37 2 E
Coalcomán, *Mexico* 146 **D4** 18 40N 103 10W
Coaldale, *Canada* 130 **D6** 49 45N 112 35W
Coalgate, *U.S.A.* 139 **H6** 34 35N 96 13W
Coalinga, *U.S.A.* 144 **J6** 36 10N 120 21W
Coalville, *U.K.* 16 **E6** 52 43N 1 21W
Coalville, *U.S.A.* 142 **F8** 40 58N 111 24W
Coaraci, *Brazil* 155 **D4** 14 38 S 39 32W
Coari, *Brazil* 153 **D5** 4 8 S 63 7W
Coari →, *Brazil* 153 **D5** 4 30 S 63 33W
Coari, L. de, *Brazil* 153 **D5** 4 15 S 63 22W
Coast □, *Kenya* 106 **C4** 2 40 S 39 45 E
Coast Mts., *Canada* 130 **C3** 55 0N 129 20W
Coast Ranges, *U.S.A.* 124 **E7** 41 0N 123 0W
Coatbridge, *U.K.* 18 **F4** 55 52N 4 2W
Coatepec, *Mexico* 147 **D5** 19 27N 96 58W
Coatepeque, *Guatemala* 148 **D1** 14 46N 91 55W
Coatesville, *U.S.A.* 134 **F8** 39 59N 75 55W
Coaticook, *Canada* 129 **C5** 45 10N 71 46W
Coats I., *Canada* 127 **B11** 62 30N 83 0W
Coats Land, *Antarctica* 7 **D1** 77 0 S 25 0W
Coatzacoalcos, *Mexico* 147 **D6** 18 7N 94 25W
Cobadin, *Romania* 46 **E9** 44 5N 28 13 E
Cobalt, *Canada* 128 **C4** 47 25N 79 42W
Cobán, *Guatemala* 148 **C1** 15 30N 90 21W
Cobar, *Australia* 117 **A6** 31 27 S 145 48 E
Cobberas, Mt., *Australia* 117 **D8** 36 53 S 148 12 E
Cobden, *Australia* 116 **E5** 38 20 S 143 3 E
Cóbh, *Ireland* 19 **E3** 51 50N 8 18W
Cobham, *Australia* 115 **E3** 30 18 S 142 7 E
Cobija, *Bolivia* 156 **C4** 11 0 S 68 50W
Cobleskill, *U.S.A.* 137 **D10** 42 40N 74 30W
Coboconk, *Canada* 136 **B6** 44 39N 78 48W
Cobourg, *Canada* 128 **D4** 43 58N 78 10W
Cobourg Pen., *Australia* 112 **B5** 11 20 S 132 15 E
Cobram, *Australia* 117 **C6** 35 54 S 145 40 E
Cobre, *U.S.A.* 142 **F6** 41 6N 114 25W
Cóbué, *Mozam.* 107 **E3** 12 0 S 34 58 E
Coburg, *Germany* 27 **E6** 50 15N 10 58 E
Coca, *Spain* 36 **D6** 41 13N 4 32W
Coca →, *Ecuador* 152 **D2** 0 29 S 76 58W
Cocachacra, *Peru* 156 **D3** 17 5 S 71 45W
Cocal, *Brazil* 154 **B3** 3 28 S 41 34W
Cocanada = Kakinada, *India* 82 **F6** 16 57N 82 11 E
Cocentaina, *Spain* 35 **G4** 38 45N 0 27W
Cochabamba, *Bolivia* 157 **D4** 17 26 S 66 10W
Coche, I., *Venezuela* 153 **A5** 10 47N 63 56W
Cochem, *Germany* 27 **E3** 50 8N 7 7 E
Cochemane, *Mozam.* 107 **F3** 17 0 S 32 54 E
Cochin, *India* 83 **K3** 9 59N 76 22 E
Cochin China = Nam-Phan, *Vietnam* 77 **G6** 10 30N 106 0 E
Cochise, *U.S.A.* 143 **K9** 32 6N 109 58W
Cochran, *U.S.A.* 135 **J4** 32 25N 83 23W
Cochrane, *Alta., Canada* 130 **C6** 51 11N 114 30W
Cochrane, *Ont., Canada* 128 **C3** 49 0N 81 0W
Cochrane →, *Canada* 131 **B8** 59 0N 103 40W
Cochrane, L., *Chile* 160 **C2** 47 10 S 72 0W
Cockburn, *Australia* 116 **B4** 32 5 S 141 0 E
Cockburn, Canal, *Chile* 160 **D2** 54 30 S 72 0W
Cockburn I., *Canada* 128 **C3** 45 55N 83 22W
Cockburn Ra., *Australia* 112 **C4** 15 46 S 128 0 E
Cocklebiddy Motel, *Australia* 113 **F4** 32 0 S 126 3 E
Coco →, *Cent. Amer.* 148 **D3** 15 0N 83 8W
Coco, Pta., *Colombia* 152 **C2** 2 58N 77 43W
Cocoa, *U.S.A.* 135 **L5** 28 22N 80 40W
Cocobeach, *Gabon* 102 **B1** 0 59N 9 34 E
Cocora, *Romania* 46 **E8** 44 45N 27 3 E
Côcos, *Brazil* 155 **D3** 14 10 S 44 33W
Côcos →, *Brazil* 155 **D3** 12 44 S 44 48W
Cocos, I. del, *Pac. Oc.* 123 **G19** 5 25N 87 55W
Cocos I., *Guam* 121 **R15** 13 14N 144 39 E
Cocos Is., *Ind. Oc.* 109 **F8** 12 10 S 96 55 E
Cod, C., *U.S.A.* 133 **B13** 42 8N 70 10W
Codajás, *Brazil* 153 **D5** 3 55 S 62 0W
Codera, C., *Venezuela* 152 **A4** 10 35N 66 4W
Coderre, *Canada* 131 **C7** 50 11N 106 31W
Codfish I., *N.Z.* 119 **G2** 46 47 S 167 38 E
Codigoro, *Italy* 39 **D9** 44 50N 12 5 E
Codó, *Brazil* 154 **B3** 4 30 S 43 55W
Codogno, *Italy* 38 **C6** 45 10N 9 42 E
Codpa, *Chile* 156 **D4** 18 50 S 69 44W
Codróipo, *Italy* 39 **C10** 45 57N 13 0 E
Codru, Munţii, *Romania* 46 **C3** 46 30N 22 15 E
Cody, *U.S.A.* 142 **D9** 44 35N 109 0W
Coe Hill, *Canada* 128 **D4** 44 52N 77 50W
Coelemu, *Chile* 158 **D1** 36 30 S 72 48W
Coelho Neto, *Brazil* 154 **B3** 4 15 S 43 0W
Coen, *Australia* 114 **A3** 13 52 S 143 12 E
Coeroeni →, *Surinam* 153 **C6** 3 21N 57 31W
Coesfeld, *Germany* 26 **D3** 51 56N 7 10 E
Coetivy Is., *Seychelles* 109 **E4** 7 8 S 56 16 E
Cœur d'Alene, *U.S.A.* 142 **C5** 47 45N 116 51W
Cœur d'Alene L., *U.S.A.* 142 **C5** 47 32N 116 48W
Coevorden, *Neths.* 20 **C9** 52 40N 6 44 E
Cofete, *Canary Is.* 33 **F5** 28 6N 14 23W
Coffeyville, *U.S.A.* 139 **G7** 37 0N 95 40W
Coffin B., *Australia* 115 **E2** 34 38 S 135 28 E
Coffin Bay Peninsula, *Australia* 115 **E2** 34 32 S 135 15 E
Coffs Harbour, *Australia* 117 **A10** 30 16 S 153 5 E
Cofrentes, *Spain* 35 **F3** 39 13N 1 5W
Cogealac, *Romania* 46 **E9** 44 36N 28 36 E
Coghinas →, *Italy* 40 **B1** 40 55N 8 48 E
Coghinas, L. di, *Italy* 40 **B2** 40 46N 9 3 E
Cognac, *France* 24 **C3** 45 41N 0 20W
Cogne, *Italy* 38 **C4** 45 37N 7 21 E
Cogolludo, *Spain* 34 **E1** 40 59N 3 10W
Cohagen, *U.S.A.* 142 **C10** 47 2N 106 36W
Cohoes, *U.S.A.* 137 **D11** 42 47N 73 42W
Cohuna, *Australia* 116 **C6** 35 45 S 144 15 E
Coiba, I., *Panama* 148 **E3** 7 30N 81 40W
Coig →, *Argentina* 160 **D3** 51 0 S 69 10W
Coihaique, *Chile* 160 **C2** 45 30 S 71 45W
Coimbatore, *India* 83 **J3** 11 2N 76 59 E
Coimbra, *Brazil* 157 **D6** 19 55 S 57 48W
Coimbra, *Portugal* 36 **E2** 40 15N 8 27W
Coimbra □, *Portugal* 36 **E2** 40 12N 8 25W
Coín, *Spain* 37 **J6** 36 40N 4 48W
Coipasa, L. de, *Bolivia* 156 **D4** 19 12 S 68 7W
Coipasa, Salar de, *Bolivia* 156 **D4** 19 26 S 68 9W
Cojata, *Peru* 156 **D4** 15 2 S 69 25W
Cojedes □, *Venezuela* 152 **B4** 9 20N 68 20W
Cojedes →, *Venezuela* 152 **B4** 8 34N 68 5W
Cojimies, *Ecuador* 156 **A2** 0 20N 80 0W
Cojocna, *Romania* 46 **C4** 46 45N 23 50 E
Cojutepequé, *El Salv.* 148 **D2** 13 41N 88 54W
Čoka, *Serbia, Yug.* 42 **B5** 45 57N 20 12 E
Cokeville, *U.S.A.* 142 **E8** 42 4N 111 0W
Colaba Pt., *India* 82 **E1** 18 54N 72 47 E
Colac, *Australia* 116 **E5** 38 21 S 143 35 E
Colachel = Kolachel, *India* 83 **K3** 8 10N 77 15 E
Colares, *Portugal* 37 **G1** 38 48N 9 30W
Colasi, *Phil.* 71 **F5** 10 43N 125 44 E
Colatina, *Brazil* 155 **E3** 19 32 S 40 37W
Colbeck, C., *Antarctica* 7 **D13** 77 6 S 157 48W
Colbinabbin, *Australia* 117 **D6** 36 38 S 144 48 E
Colborne, *Canada* 136 **B7** 44 0N 77 53W
Colby, *U.S.A.* 138 **F4** 39 27N 101 2W
Colchagua □, *Chile* 158 **C1** 34 30 S 71 0W
Colchester, *U.K.* 17 **F8** 51 54N 0 55 E
Coldstream, *U.K.* 18 **F6** 55 39N 2 14W
Coldwater, *Canada* 136 **B5** 44 42N 79 40W
Coldwater, *Kans., U.S.A.* 139 **G5** 37 18N 99 24W
Coldwater, *Mich., U.S.A.* 141 **C11** 41 57N 85 0W
Coldwater, *Ohio, U.S.A.* 141 **D12** 40 29N 84 38W
Coldwater, L., *U.S.A.* 141 **C12** 41 48N 84 59W
Cole Camp, *U.S.A.* 140 **F3** 38 28N 93 12W
Colebrook, *Australia* 114 **G4** 42 31 S 147 21 E
Colebrook, *U.S.A.* 137 **B13** 44 54N 71 29W
Coleman, *Canada* 130 **D6** 49 40N 114 30W
Coleman, *U.S.A.* 139 **K5** 31 52N 99 28W
Coleman →, *Australia* 114 **B3** 15 6 S 141 38 E
Colenso, *S. Africa* 105 **D4** 28 44 S 29 50 E
Coleraine, *Australia* 116 **D4** 37 36 S 141 40 E
Coleraine, *U.K.* 19 **A5** 55 8N 6 40W
Coleraine □, *U.K.* 19 **A5** 55 8N 6 40W
Coleridge, L., *N.Z.* 119 **D6** 43 17 S 171 30 E
Coleroon →, *India* 83 **J4** 11 25N 79 50 E
Colesberg, *S. Africa* 104 **E4** 30 45 S 25 5 E
Colesburg, *U.S.A.* 140 **B5** 42 38N 91 12W
Coleville, *U.S.A.* 144 **G7** 38 34N 119 30W

Colfax, Calif., U.S.A. 144 F6 39 6N 120 57W
Colfax, Ill., U.S.A. 141 D8 40 34N 88 37W
Colfax, Ind., U.S.A. 141 D10 40 12N 86 40W
Colfax, La., U.S.A. 139 K8 31 35N 92 39W
Colfax, Wash., U.S.A. 142 C5 46 57N 117 28W
Colhué Huapi, L., Argentina 160 C3 45 30 S 69 0W
Cólico, Italy 38 B6 46 8N 9 22 E
Coligny, France 25 B9 46 23N 5 21 E
Coligny, S. Africa 105 D4 26 17 S 26 15 E
Colima, Mexico 146 D4 19 10N 103 40W
Colima □, Mexico 146 D4 19 10N 103 40W
Colima, Nevado de, Mexico 146 D4 19 35N 103 45W
Colina, Chile 158 C1 33 13 S 70 45W
Colina do Norte, Guinea-Biss. 100 C2 12 28N 15 0W
Colinas, Goiás, Brazil 155 D2 14 15 S 48 2W
Colinas, Maranhão, Brazil 154 C3 6 0 S 44 10W
Colinton, Australia 117 C8 35 50 S 149 10 E
Coll, U.K. 18 E2 56 40N 6 35W
Collaguasi, Chile 158 A2 21 5 S 68 45W
Collarada, Peña, Spain 34 C4 42 43N 0 29W
Collarenebri, Australia 115 D4 29 33 S 148 34 E
Collbran, U.S.A. 143 G10 39 16N 107 58W
Colle di Val d'Elsa, Italy 39 E8 43 25N 11 7 E
Colle Salvetti, Italy 38 E7 43 34N 10 27 E
Colle Sannita, Italy 41 A7 41 22N 14 48 E
Collécchio, Italy 38 D7 44 45N 10 10 E
Colleen Bawn, Zimbabwe 107 G2 21 0 S 29 12 E
College Park, U.S.A. 135 J3 33 42N 84 27W
Collette, Canada 129 C6 46 40N 65 30W
Collie, N.S.W., Australia 117 A8 31 41 S 148 18 E
Collie, W. Austral., Australia 113 F2 33 22 S 116 8 E
Collier B., Australia 112 C3 16 10 S 124 15 E
Collier Ra., Australia 112 D2 24 45 S 119 10 E
Colline Metallifere, Italy 38 E7 43 10N 11 0 E
Collingwood, Canada 128 D3 44 29N 80 13W
Collingwood, N.Z. 119 A7 40 41 S 172 40 E
Collins, Canada 128 B2 50 17N 89 27W
Collins, U.S.A. 140 G3 37 54N 93 37W
Collinsville, Australia 114 C4 20 30 S 147 56 E
Collinsville, U.S.A. 140 F7 38 40N 89 59W
Collipulli, Chile 158 D1 37 55 S 72 30W
Collo, Algeria 99 A6 36 58N 6 37 E
Collonges, France 25 B9 46 9N 5 52 E
Collooney, Ireland 19 B3 54 11N 8 28W
Colmar, France 23 D14 48 5N 7 20 E
Colmars, France 25 D10 44 11N 6 39 E
Colmenar, Spain 37 J6 36 54N 4 20W
Colmenar de Oreja, Spain 34 E1 40 6N 3 25W
Colmenar Viejo, Spain 36 E7 40 39N 3 47W
Colne, U.K. 16 D5 53 51N 2 11W
Colo →, Australia 117 B9 33 25 S 150 52 E
Cologna Véneta, Italy 39 C8 45 19N 11 21 E
Cologne = Köln, Germany 26 E2 50 56N 6 58 E
Colom, I., Spain 33 B11 39 58N 4 16 E
Coloma, U.S.A. 144 G6 38 49N 120 53W
Colomb-Béchar = Béchar, Algeria 99 B4 31 38N 2 18W
Colombey-les-Belles, France 23 D12 48 32N 5 54 E
Colombey-les-Deux-Églises, France 23 D11 48 13N 4 50 E
Colômbia, Brazil 155 F2 20 10 S 48 40W
Colombia ■, S. Amer. 152 C3 3 45N 73 0W
Colombier, Switz. 28 C3 46 58N 6 53 E
Colombo, Sri Lanka 83 L4 6 56N 79 58 E
Colome, U.S.A. 138 D5 43 20N 99 44W
Colón, Argentina 158 C4 32 12 S 58 10W
Colón, Cuba 148 B3 22 42N 80 54W
Colón, Panama 148 E4 9 20N 79 54W
Colón, Peru 156 A1 5 0 S 81 0W
Colona, Australia 113 F5 31 38 S 132 4 E
Colonella, Italy 39 F10 42 52N 13 50 E
Colonia, Uruguay 158 C4 34 25 S 57 50W
Colonia de San Jordi, Spain 33 B9 39 19N 2 59 E
Colonia Dora, Argentina 158 B3 28 34 S 62 59W
Colonial Heights, U.S.A. 134 G7 37 19N 77 25W
Colonne, C. delle, Italy 41 C10 39 2N 17 11 E
Colonsay, Canada 131 C7 51 59N 105 52W
Colonsay, U.K. 18 E2 56 4N 6 12W
Colorado □, U.S.A. 132 C5 37 40N 106 0W
Colorado →, Argentina 160 A4 39 50 S 62 8W
Colorado →, N. Amer. 143 L6 31 45N 114 40W
Colorado →, U.S.A. 139 L7 28 36N 95 58W
Colorado City, U.S.A. 139 J4 32 25N 100 50W
Colorado Desert, U.S.A. 132 D3 34 20N 116 0W
Colorado Plateau, U.S.A. 143 H8 36 40N 110 30W
Colorado River Aqueduct, U.S.A. 145 L12 34 17N 114 10W
Colorado Springs, U.S.A. 138 F2 38 55N 104 50W
Colorno, Italy 38 D7 44 55N 10 21 E
Colotlán, Mexico 146 C4 22 6N 103 16W
Colquechaca, Bolivia 157 D4 18 40 S 66 1W
Colton, Calif., U.S.A. 145 L9 34 4N 117 20W
Colton, N.Y., U.S.A. 137 B10 44 34N 74 58W
Colton, Wash., U.S.A. 142 C5 46 41N 117 6W
Columbia, Ill., U.S.A. 140 F6 38 26N 90 12W
Columbia, La., U.S.A. 139 J8 32 7N 92 5W
Columbia, Miss., U.S.A. 139 K10 31 16N 89 50W
Columbia, Mo., U.S.A. 140 F4 38 58N 92 20W
Columbia, Pa., U.S.A. 137 F8 40 2N 76 30W
Columbia, S.C., U.S.A. 135 H5 34 0N 81 0W
Columbia, Tenn., U.S.A. 135 H2 35 40N 87 0W
Columbia →, N. Amer. 142 C1 46 15N 124 5W
Columbia, C., Canada 6 A4 83 0N 70 0W
Columbia, District of □, U.S.A. 134 F7 38 55N 77 0W
Columbia, Mt., Canada 130 C5 52 8N 117 20W
Columbia Basin, U.S.A. 142 C4 47 30N 118 30W
Columbia Falls, U.S.A. 142 B6 48 25N 114 16W
Columbia Heights, U.S.A. 138 C8 45 5N 93 10W
Columbiana, U.S.A. 136 F4 40 53N 80 40W
Columbretes, Is., Spain 34 F5 39 50N 0 50 E
Columbus, Ga., U.S.A. 135 J3 32 30N 84 58W
Columbus, Ind., U.S.A. 141 E11 39 14N 85 55W
Columbus, Kans., U.S.A. 139 G7 37 15N 94 30W
Columbus, Miss., U.S.A. 135 J1 33 30N 88 26W
Columbus, Mont., U.S.A. 142 D9 45 38N 109 14W
Columbus, N. Dak., U.S.A. 138 A3 48 52N 102 48W
Columbus, N. Mex., U.S.A. 143 L10 31 54N 107 43W
Columbus, Nebr., U.S.A. 138 E6 41 30N 97 25W
Columbus, Ohio, U.S.A. 141 E13 39 57N 83 1W
Columbus, Tex., U.S.A. 139 L6 29 42N 96 33W
Columbus, Wis., U.S.A. 138 D10 43 20N 89 2W
Columbus Grove, U.S.A. 141 D12 40 55N 84 4W
Columbus Junction, U.S.A. 140 C5 41 17N 91 22W
Colunga, Spain 36 B5 43 29N 5 16W
Colusa, U.S.A. 144 F4 39 15N 122 1W
Colville, U.S.A. 142 B5 48 33N 117 54W
Colville →, U.S.A. 126 A4 70 25N 151 0W
Colville, C., N.Z. 118 C4 36 29 S 175 21 E
Colwyn Bay, U.K. 16 D4 53 17N 3 44W
Coma, Ethiopia 95 F4 8 29N 36 53 E
Comácchio, Italy 39 D9 44 41N 12 10 E
Comalcalco, Mexico 147 D6 18 16N 93 13W
Comallo, Argentina 160 B2 41 0 S 70 5W
Comana, Romania 46 E7 44 10N 26 10 E
Comanche, Okla., U.S.A. 139 H6 34 27N 97 58W
Comanche, Tex., U.S.A. 139 K5 31 55N 98 35W
Comandante Luis Piedrabuena, Argentina 160 C3 49 59 S 68 54W
Comăneşti, Romania 46 C7 46 25N 26 26 E
Comarapa, Bolivia 157 D5 17 54 S 64 29W
Comayagua, Honduras 148 D2 14 25N 87 37W
Combahee →, U.S.A. 135 J5 32 30N 80 31W
Combara, Australia 117 A8 31 10 S 148 22 E
Combeaufontaine, France 23 E12 47 38N 5 54 E
Comber, Canada 136 D2 42 14N 82 33W
Combermere Bay, Burma 78 F4 19 37N 93 34 E
Comblain-au-Pont, Belgium 21 H7 50 29N 5 35 E
Combles, France 23 B9 50 2N 2 50 E
Combourg, France 22 D5 48 25N 1 46W
Comboyne, Australia 117 A10 31 34 S 152 27 E
Combronde, France 24 C7 45 58N 3 5 E
Comeragh Mts., Ireland 19 D4 52 17N 7 35W
Comet, Australia 114 C4 23 36 S 148 38 E
Comilla, Bangla. 78 D3 23 28N 91 10 E
Comines, Belgium 21 G1 50 46N 3 0 E
Comino, Malta 32 C1 36 2N 14 20 E
Comino, C., Italy 40 B2 40 28N 9 47 E
Cómiso, Italy 41 F7 36 57N 14 35 E
Comitán, Mexico 147 D6 16 18N 92 9W
Commentry, France 24 B6 46 20N 2 46 E
Commerce, Ga., U.S.A. 135 H4 34 10N 83 25W
Commerce, Tex., U.S.A. 139 J7 33 15N 95 50W
Commercy, France 23 D12 48 43N 5 34 E
Commewijne □, Surinam 153 B7 5 25N 54 45W
Committee B., Canada 127 B11 68 30N 86 30W
Commonwealth B., Antarctica 7 C10 67 0 S 144 0 E
Commonwealth of Independent States ■, Eurasia 57 D11 60 0N 100 0 E
Commoron Cr. →, Australia 115 D5 28 22 S 150 8 E
Communism Pk. = Kommunizma, Pik, Tajikistan 55 D6 39 0N 72 2 E
Como, Italy 38 C6 45 48N 9 5 E
Como, L. di, Italy 38 B6 46 5N 9 17 E
Comodoro Rivadavia, Argentina 160 C3 45 50 S 67 40W
Comorin, C., India 83 K3 8 3N 77 40 E
Comorişte, Romania 46 D2 45 10N 21 35 E
Comoro Is. ■, Ind. Oc. 93 H8 12 10 S 44 15 E
Comox, Canada 130 D4 49 42N 124 55W
Compiègne, France 23 C9 49 24N 2 50 E
Comporta, Portugal 37 G2 38 22N 8 46W
Compostela, Mexico 146 C4 21 15N 104 53W
Compostela, Phil. 71 H6 7 40N 126 2 E
Comprida, I., Brazil 159 A6 24 50 S 47 42W
Compton, U.S.A. 145 M8 33 54N 118 13W
Compton Downs, Australia 115 E4 30 28 S 146 30 E
Con Cuong, Vietnam 76 C5 19 2N 104 54 E
Con Son, Is., Vietnam 77 H6 8 41N 106 37 E
Cona Niyeu, Argentina 160 B3 41 58 S 67 0W
Conakry, Guinea 100 D2 9 29N 13 49W
Conara Junction, Australia 114 G4 41 50 S 147 26 E
Conargo, Australia 117 C6 35 16 S 145 10 E
Concarneau, France 22 E3 47 52N 3 56W
Conceição, Brazil 154 C4 7 33 S 38 31W
Conceição, Mozam. 107 F4 18 47 S 36 7 E
Conceição da Barra, Brazil 155 E4 18 35 S 39 45W
Conceição do Araguaia, Brazil 154 C2 8 0 S 49 2W
Conceição do Canindé, Brazil 154 C3 7 54 S 41 34W
Concepción, Argentina 158 B2 27 20 S 65 35W
Concepción, Bolivia 157 D5 16 15 S 62 8W
Concepción, Chile 158 D1 36 50 S 73 0W
Concepción, Mexico 147 D6 18 15N 90 5W
Concepción, Paraguay 158 A4 23 22 S 57 26W
Concepción, Peru 156 C2 11 54 S 75 19W
Concepción □, Chile 158 D1 37 0 S 72 30W
Concepción →, Mexico 146 A2 30 32N 113 2W
Concepción, Est. de, Chile 160 D2 50 30 S 74 55W
Concepción, L., Bolivia 157 D5 17 20 S 61 20W
Concepción, Punta, Mexico 146 B2 26 55N 111 59W
Concepción del Oro, Mexico 146 C4 24 40N 101 30W
Concepción del Uruguay, Argentina 158 C4 32 35 S 58 20W
Conception, Pt., U.S.A. 145 L6 34 30N 120 34W
Conception B., Namibia 104 C1 23 55 S 14 22 E
Conception I., Bahamas 149 B4 23 52N 75 9W
Concession, Zimbabwe 107 F3 17 27 S 30 56 E
Conchas Dam, U.S.A. 139 H2 35 25N 104 10W
Conche, Canada 129 B8 50 55N 55 58W
Concho, U.S.A. 143 J9 34 32N 109 43W
Concho →, U.S.A. 139 K5 31 30N 99 45W
Conchos →, Chihuahua, Mexico 146 B4 29 32N 105 0W
Conchos →, Tamaulipas, Mexico 147 B5 25 9N 98 35W
Concord, Calif., U.S.A. 144 H4 37 59N 122 2W
Concord, Mich., U.S.A. 141 B12 42 11N 84 38W
Concord, N.C., U.S.A. 135 H5 35 28N 80 35W
Concord, N.H., U.S.A. 137 C13 43 12N 71 30W
Concordia, Argentina 158 C4 31 20 S 58 2W
Concórdia, Brazil 152 D4 4 36 S 66 36W
Concordia, Mexico 146 C3 23 18N 106 2W
Concordia, Kans., U.S.A. 138 F6 39 35N 97 40W
Concordia, Mo., U.S.A. 140 F3 38 59N 93 34W
Concots, France 24 D5 44 26N 1 40 E
Concrete, U.S.A. 142 B3 48 35N 121 49W
Condah, Australia 116 D4 37 57 S 141 44 E
Condamine, Australia 115 D5 26 56 S 150 9 E
Condat, France 24 C6 45 21N 2 46 E
Condé, Angola 103 E2 10 50 S 14 37 E
Conde, Brazil 155 D4 11 49 S 37 37W
Conde, U.S.A. 138 C5 45 13N 98 5W
Condé-sur-l'Escaut, France 23 B10 50 26N 3 34 E
Condé-sur-Noireau, France 22 D6 48 51N 0 33W
Condeúba, Brazil 155 D3 14 52 S 42 0W
Condobolin, Australia 115 E4 33 4 S 147 6 E
Condom, France 24 E4 43 57N 0 22 E
Condon, U.S.A. 142 D3 45 15N 120 8W
Condove, Italy 38 C4 45 8N 7 19 E
Conegliano, Italy 39 C9 45 53N 12 18 E
Conejera, I., Spain 33 B9 39 11N 2 58 E
Conejos, Mexico 146 B4 26 14N 103 53W
Conflans-en-Jarnisy, France 23 C12 49 10N 5 52 E
Confolens, France 24 B4 46 2N 0 40 E
Confuso →, Paraguay 158 B4 25 9 S 57 34W
Congjiang, China 68 E7 25 43N 108 52 E
Congleton, U.K. 16 D5 53 10N 2 12W
Congo = Zaïre →, Africa 103 D2 6 4 S 12 24 E
Congo, Brazil 154 C4 7 48 S 36 40W
Congo (Kinshasa) = Zaïre ■, Africa 103 C4 3 0 S 23 0 E
Congo ■, Africa 102 C3 1 0 S 16 0 E
Congo Basin, Africa 92 G6 0 10 S 24 30 E
Congonhas, Brazil 155 F3 20 30 S 43 52W
Congress, U.S.A. 143 J7 34 11N 112 56W
Conil, Spain 37 J4 36 17N 6 10W
Coniston, Canada 128 C3 46 29N 80 51W
Conjeeveram = Kanchipuram, India 83 H4 12 52N 79 45 E
Conjuboy, Australia 114 B3 18 35 S 144 35 E
Conklin, Canada 131 B6 55 38N 111 5W
Conlea, Australia 115 E3 30 7 S 144 35 E
Conn, L., Ireland 19 B2 54 3N 9 15W
Connacht, Ireland 19 C3 53 23N 8 40W
Conneaut, U.S.A. 136 E4 41 55N 80 32W
Connecticut □, U.S.A. 137 E12 41 40N 72 40W
Connecticut →, U.S.A. 137 E12 41 17N 72 21W
Connell, U.S.A. 142 C4 46 36N 118 51W
Connellsville, U.S.A. 136 F5 40 3N 79 32W
Connemara, Ireland 19 C2 53 29N 9 45W
Connemaugh →, U.S.A. 136 F5 40 38N 79 42W
Conner, Phil. 70 C3 17 48N 121 19 E
Connerré, France 22 D7 48 3N 0 30 E
Connersville, U.S.A. 141 E11 39 40N 85 10W
Connors Ra., Australia 114 C4 21 40 S 149 10 E
Conoble, Australia 117 B6 32 55 S 144 33 E
Cononaco →, Ecuador 152 D2 1 32 S 75 35W
Cononbridge, U.K. 18 D4 57 32N 4 30W
Conquest, Canada 131 C7 51 32N 107 14W
Conrad, Iowa, U.S.A. 140 B4 42 14N 92 52W
Conrad, Mont., U.S.A. 142 B8 48 11N 111 58W
Conran, C., Australia 117 D8 37 49 S 148 44 E
Conroe, U.S.A. 139 K7 30 15N 95 28W
Conselheiro Lafaiete, Brazil 155 F3 20 40 S 43 48W
Conselheiro Pena, Brazil 155 E3 19 10 S 41 30W
Consort, Canada 131 C6 52 1N 110 46W
Constance = Konstanz, Germany 27 H5 47 39N 9 10 E
Constance, L. = Bodensee, Europe 29 A8 47 35N 9 25 E
Constanţa, Romania 46 E9 44 14N 28 38 E
Constanţa □, Romania 46 E9 44 15N 28 15 E
Constantina, Spain 37 H5 37 51N 5 40W
Constantine, Algeria 99 A6 36 25N 6 42 E
Constantine, U.S.A. 141 C11 41 50N 85 40W
Constitución, Chile 158 D1 35 20 S 72 30W
Constitución, Uruguay 158 C4 31 0 S 57 50W
Consuegra, Spain 37 F7 39 28N 3 36W
Consul, Canada 131 D7 49 20N 109 30W
Contact, U.S.A. 142 F6 41 50N 114 56W
Contai, India 81 J12 21 54N 87 46 E
Contamana, Peru 156 B3 7 19 S 74 55W
Contarina, Italy 39 C9 45 2N 12 13 E
Contas →, Brazil 155 D4 14 17 S 39 1W
Contes, France 25 E11 43 49N 7 19 E
Conthey, Switz. 28 D4 46 14N 7 18 E
Continental, U.S.A. 141 C12 41 6N 84 16W
Contoocook, U.S.A. 137 C13 43 13N 71 45W
Contra Costa, Mozam. 105 D5 25 9 S 33 30 E
Contres, France 22 E8 47 24N 1 26 E
Contrexéville, France 23 D12 48 10N 5 53 E
Contumaza, Peru 156 B2 7 23 S 78 57W
Convención, Colombia 152 B3 8 28N 73 21W
Conversano, Italy 41 B10 40 57N 17 8 E
Converse, U.S.A. 141 D11 40 34N 85 52W
Convoy, U.S.A. 141 D12 40 55N 84 43W
Conway = Conwy, U.K. 16 D4 53 17N 3 50W
Conway = Conwy →, U.K. 16 D4 53 18N 3 50W
Conway, Ark., U.S.A. 139 H8 35 5N 92 30W
Conway, N.H., U.S.A. 137 C13 43 58N 71 8W
Conway, S.C., U.S.A. 135 J6 33 49N 79 2W
Conway, L., Australia 115 D2 28 17 S 135 35 E
Conwy, U.K. 16 D4 53 17N 3 50W
Conwy →, U.K. 16 D4 53 18N 3 50W
Coober Pedy, Australia 115 D1 29 1 S 134 43 E
Cooch Behar = Koch Bihar, India 78 B2 26 22N 89 29 E
Coodardy, Australia 113 E2 27 15 S 117 39 E
Cook, Australia 113 F5 30 37 S 130 25 E
Cook, U.S.A. 138 B8 47 49N 92 39W
Cook, B., Chile 160 E2 55 10 S 70 0W
Cook, Mt., N.Z. 119 D5 43 36 S 170 9 E
Cook Inlet, U.S.A. 126 C4 59 0N 151 0W
Cook Is., Pac. Oc. 123 J11 17 0 S 160 0W
Cook Strait, N.Z. 118 H3 41 15 S 174 29 E
Cooke Plains, Australia 116 C3 35 23 S 139 34 E
Cookeville, U.S.A. 135 G3 36 12N 85 30W
Cookhouse, S. Africa 104 E4 32 44 S 25 47 E
Cookshire, Canada 137 A13 45 25N 71 38W
Cookstown, U.K. 19 B5 54 40N 6 43W
Cookstown □, U.K. 19 B5 54 40N 6 43W
Cooksville, Canada 136 C5 43 36N 79 35W
Cooktown, Australia 114 B4 15 30 S 145 16 E
Coolabah, Australia 117 A7 31 1 S 146 43 E
Cooladdi, Australia 115 D4 26 37 S 145 23 E
Coolah, Australia 117 A8 31 48 S 149 41 E
Coolamon, Australia 117 C7 34 46 S 147 8 E
Coolangatta, Australia 115 D5 28 11 S 153 29 E
Coolgardie, Australia 113 F3 30 55 S 121 8 E
Coolibah, Australia 112 C5 15 33 S 130 56 E
Coolidge, U.S.A. 143 K8 33 1N 111 35W
Coolidge Dam, U.S.A. 143 K8 33 10N 110 30W
Cooma, Australia 117 D8 36 12 S 149 8 E
Coon Rapids, U.S.A. 140 C2 41 53N 94 41W
Coonabarabran, Australia 117 A8 31 14 S 149 18 E
Coonalpyn, Australia 116 C3 35 43 S 139 52 E
Coonamble, Australia 117 A8 30 56 S 148 27 E
Coonana, Australia 113 F3 31 0 S 123 0 E
Coondapoor, India 83 H2 13 42N 74 40 E
Coongie, Australia 115 D3 27 9 S 140 8 E
Coongoola, Australia 115 D4 27 43 S 145 51 E
Cooninie, L., Australia 115 D2 26 4 S 139 59 E
Coonoor, India 83 J3 11 21N 76 45 E
Cooper, U.S.A. 139 J7 33 20N 95 40W
Cooper →, U.S.A. 135 J6 33 0N 79 55W
Cooper Cr. →, N. Terr., Australia 110 C5 12 7 S 132 41 E
Cooper Cr. →, S. Austral., Australia 115 D2 28 29 S 137 46 E
Cooperstown, N. Dak., U.S.A. 138 B5 47 30N 98 6W
Cooperstown, N.Y., U.S.A. 137 D10 42 42N 74 57W
Coopersville, U.S.A. 141 A11 43 4N 85 57W
Coorabie, Australia 113 F5 31 54 S 132 18 E
Coorabulka, Australia 114 C3 23 41 S 140 20 E
Coorow, Australia 113 E2 29 53 S 116 2 E
Cooroy, Australia 115 D5 26 22 S 152 54 E
Coos Bay, U.S.A. 142 E1 43 26N 124 7W
Cootamundra, Australia 117 C8 34 36 S 148 1 E
Cootehill, Ireland 19 B4 54 5N 7 5W
Cooyar, Australia 115 D5 26 59 S 151 51 E
Cooyeana, Australia 114 C2 24 29 S 138 45 E
Copahue Paso, Argentina 158 D1 37 49 S 71 8W
Copainalá, Mexico 147 D6 17 8N 93 11W
Copán, Honduras 148 D2 14 50N 89 9W
Copatana, Brazil 152 D4 2 48 S 67 4W
Cope, U.S.A. 138 F3 39 44N 102 50W
Cope, C., Spain 35 H3 37 26N 1 28W
Cope Cope, Australia 116 D5 36 27 S 143 5 E
Copenhagen = København, Denmark 15 J6 55 41N 12 34 E
Copertino, Italy 41 B11 40 17N 18 2 E
Copeville, Australia 116 C3 34 47 S 139 51 E
Copiapó, Chile 158 B1 27 30 S 70 20W
Copiapó →, Chile 158 B1 27 19 S 70 56W
Copley, Australia 116 A3 30 36 S 138 26 E
Copp L., Canada 130 A6 60 14N 114 40W
Copparo, Italy 39 D8 44 52N 11 49 E
Coppename →, Surinam 153 B6 5 48N 55 55W
Copper Center, U.S.A. 126 B5 62 10N 145 25W
Copper Cliff, Canada 128 C3 46 28N 81 4W
Copper Harbor, U.S.A. 134 B2 47 31N 87 55W
Copper Queen, Zimbabwe 107 F2 17 29 S 29 18 E
Copperbelt □, Zambia 107 E2 13 15 S 27 30 E
Coppermine, Canada 126 B8 67 50N 115 5W
Coppermine →, Canada 126 B8 67 49N 116 4W
Copperopolis, U.S.A. 144 H6 37 58N 120 38W
Coquet →, U.K. 16 B6 55 18N 1 45W
Coquilhatville = Mbandaka, Zaïre 102 B3 0 1N 18 18 E
Coquille, U.S.A. 142 E1 43 15N 124 12W
Coquimbo, Chile 158 B1 30 0 S 71 20W
Coquimbo □, Chile 158 C1 31 0 S 71 0W
Corabia, Romania 46 F5 43 48N 24 30 E
Coração de Jesus, Brazil 155 E3 16 43 S 44 22W
Coracora, Peru 156 D3 15 5 S 73 45W
Coradi, Is., Italy 41 B10 40 27N 17 10 E
Coral Bay, Phil. 71 G1 8 25N 117 20 E
Coral Gables, U.S.A. 135 N5 25 45N 80 16W
Coral Harbour, Canada 127 B11 64 8N 83 10W
Coral Sea, Pac. Oc. 122 J7 15 0 S 150 0 E
Coralville, U.S.A. 140 C5 41 42N 91 34W
Coralville Res., U.S.A. 140 C5 41 50N 91 40W
Corantijn →, Surinam 153 B6 5 50N 57 8W
Coraopolis, U.S.A. 136 F4 40 30N 80 10W
Corato, Italy 41 A9 41 12N 16 22 E
Corbeil-Essonnes, France 23 D9 48 36N 2 26 E
Corbie, France 23 C9 49 54N 2 30 E
Corbières, France 24 F6 42 55N 2 35 E
Corbigny, France 23 E10 47 16N 3 40 E
Corbin, U.S.A. 134 G3 37 0N 84 3W
Corbion, Belgium 21 J6 49 48N 5 0 E
Corbones →, Spain 37 H5 37 36N 5 39W
Corby, U.K. 17 E7 52 29N 0 41W
Corby Glen, U.K. 17 E7 52 49N 0 31W
Corcoles →, Spain 35 F1 39 40N 3 18W
Corcoran, U.S.A. 144 J7 36 6N 119 35W
Corcubión, Spain 36 C1 42 56N 9 12W
Cordele, U.S.A. 135 K4 31 55N 83 49W
Cordell, U.S.A. 139 H5 35 18N 99 0W
Cordenons, Italy 39 C9 45 59N 12 42 E
Cordes, France 24 D5 44 5N 1 57 E
Cordisburgo, Brazil 155 E3 19 7 S 44 21W
Córdoba, Argentina 158 C3 31 20 S 64 10W
Córdoba, Mexico 147 D5 18 50N 97 0W
Córdoba, Spain 37 H6 37 50N 4 50W
Córdoba □, Argentina 158 C3 31 22 S 64 15W
Córdoba □, Colombia 152 B2 8 20N 75 40W
Córdoba □, Spain 37 G6 38 5N 5 0W
Córdoba, Sierra de, Argentina 158 C3 31 10 S 64 25W
Cordon, Phil. 70 C3 16 42N 121 32 E
Cordova, Ala., U.S.A. 135 J2 33 45N 87 12W
Cordova, Alaska, U.S.A. 126 B5 60 36N 145 45W
Cordova, Ill., U.S.A. 140 C6 41 41N 90 19W
Corella, Spain 34 C3 42 7N 1 48W
Corella →, Australia 114 B3 19 34 S 140 47 E
Coremas, Brazil 154 C4 7 1 S 37 58W
Corentyne →, Guyana 153 B6 5 50N 57 8W
Corfield, Australia 114 C3 21 40 S 143 21 E
Corfu = Kérkira, Greece 32 A3 39 38N 19 50 E
Corfu, Str of, Greece 32 A4 39 34N 20 0 E
Corgo, Spain 36 C3 42 56N 7 25W
Corguinho, Brazil 157 D7 19 53 S 54 52W
Cori, Italy 40 A5 41 39N 12 53 E

190 Dam Doi


Dam Doi, Vietnam 77 H5 8 50N 105 12 E
Dam Ha, Vietnam 76 B6 21 21N 107 36 E
Daman, India 82 D1 20 25N 72 57 E
Daman □, India 82 D1 20 25N 72 58 E
Dāmaneh, Iran 85 C6 33 1N 50 29 E
Damanhûr, Egypt 94 H7 31 0N 30 30 E
Damanzhuang, China 66 E9 38 5N 116 35 E
Damar, Indonesia 72 C3 7 7 S 128 40 E
Damara, C.A.R. 102 B3 4 58N 18 42 E
Damaraland, Namibia 104 C2 21 0 S 17 0 E
Damascus = Dimashq, Syria 91 B5 33 30N 36 18 E
Damaturu, Nigeria 101 C7 11 45N 11 55 E
Damāvand, Iran 85 C7 35 47N 52 0 E
Damāvand, Qolleh-ye, Iran 85 C7 35 56N 52 10 E
Damba, Angola 103 D3 6 44 S 15 20 E
Dame Marie, Haiti 149 C5 18 36N 74 26W
Dāmghān, Iran 85 B7 36 10N 54 17 E
Dămienesti, Romania 46 C8 46 44N 27 1 E
Damietta = Dumyât, Egypt 94 H7 31 24N 31 48 E
Daming, China 66 F8 36 15N 115 6 E
Damīr Qābū, Syria 84 B4 36 58N 41 51 E
Dammarie, France 22 D8 48 20N 1 30 E
Dammartin-en-Goële, France 23 C9 49 3N 2 41 E
Dammastock, Switz. 29 C6 46 38N 8 24 E
Damme, Germany 26 C4 52 32N 8 12 E
Damodar →, India 81 H12 23 17N 87 35 E
Damoh, India 81 H8 23 50N 79 28 E
Damous, Algeria 99 A5 36 31N 1 42 E
Dampier, Australia 112 D2 20 41 S 116 42 E
Dampier, Selat, Indonesia 73 B4 0 40 S 131 0 E
Dampier Arch., Australia 112 D2 20 38 S 116 32 E
Dampier Str., Papua N. G. 120 C5 5 50 S 148 0 E
Damqawt, Yemen 87 C6 16 34N 52 50 E
Damrei, Chuor Phnum, Cambodia 77 G4 11 30N 103 0 E
Damville, France 22 D8 48 51N 1 5 E
Damvillers, France 23 C12 49 20N 5 21 E
Dan-Gulbi, Nigeria 101 C6 11 40N 6 15 E
Dana, Indonesia 72 D2 11 0 S 122 52 E
Dana, L., Canada 128 B4 50 53N 77 20W
Dana, Mt., U.S.A. 144 H7 37 54N 119 12W
Danakil Depression, Ethiopia 95 E5 12 45N 41 0 E
Danao, Cebu, Phil. 71 F5 10 31N 124 1 E
Danao, Sorsogon, Phil. 70 E4 12 44N 123 51 E
Danbury, U.S.A. 137 E11 41 23N 73 29W
Danby L., U.S.A. 143 J6 34 17N 115 0W
Dand, Afghan. 80 D1 31 28N 65 32 E
Dandaragan, Australia 113 F2 30 40 S 115 40 E
Dandeldhura, Nepal 81 E9 29 20N 80 35 E
Dandenong, Australia 117 E6 38 0 S 145 15 E
Dandong, China 67 D13 40 10N 124 20 E
Danfeng, China 66 H6 33 45N 110 25 E
Danforth, U.S.A. 129 C6 45 39N 67 57W
Dangan Liedao, China 69 F10 22 2N 114 8 E
Dangara, Tajikistan 55 D4 38 6N 69 22 E
Danger Is. = Pukapuka, Cook Is. 123 J11 10 53 S 165 49W
Danger Pt., S. Africa 104 E2 34 40 S 19 17 E
Dangla, Ethiopia 95 E4 11 18N 36 56 E
Dangora, Nigeria 101 C6 11 30N 8 7 E
Dangrek, Phnom, Thailand 76 E5 14 15N 105 0 E
Dangriga, Belize 147 D7 17 0N 88 13W
Dangshan, China 66 G9 34 27N 116 22 E
Dangtu, China 69 B12 31 32N 118 25 E
Dangyang, China 69 B8 30 52N 111 44 E
Daniel, U.S.A. 142 E8 42 56N 110 2W
Daniel's Harbour, Canada 129 B8 50 13N 57 35W
Danielskuil, S. Africa 104 D3 28 11 S 23 33 E
Danielson, U.S.A. 137 E13 41 50N 71 52W
Danilov, Russia 51 B12 58 16N 40 13 E
Danilovgrad, Montenegro, Yug. 42 E4 42 38N 19 9 E
Danilovka, Russia 51 F14 50 25N 44 12 E
Daning, China 66 F6 36 28N 110 45 E
Danissa, Kenya 106 B5 3 15N 40 58 E
Danja, Nigeria 101 C6 11 21N 7 30 E
Danje-ia-Menha, Angola 103 D2 9 32 S 14 39 E
Ḍank, Oman 87 B7 23 33N 56 16 E
Dankalwa, Nigeria 101 C7 11 52N 12 12 E
Dankama, Nigeria 101 C6 13 20N 7 44 E
Dankov, Russia 51 E11 53 20N 39 5 E
Danleng, China 68 B4 30 1N 103 31 E
Danlí, Honduras 148 D2 14 4N 86 35W
Dannemora, Sweden 13 F14 60 12N 17 51 E
Dannemora, U.S.A. 137 B11 44 41N 73 44W
Dannenberg, Germany 26 B7 53 7N 11 4 E
Dannevirke, N.Z. 118 G5 40 12 S 176 8 E
Dannhauser, S. Africa 105 D5 28 0 S 30 3 E
Danot, Ethiopia 108 C3 7 33N 45 17 E
Danshui, Taiwan 69 E13 25 12N 121 25 E
Dansville, U.S.A. 136 D7 42 32N 77 41W
Dantan, India 81 J12 21 57N 87 20 E
Dante, Somali Rep. 90 E5 10 25N 51 16 E
Danube →, Europe 46 D10 45 20N 29 40 E
Danubyu, Burma 78 G5 17 15N 95 35 E
Danukandi, Bangla. 78 D3 23 32N 90 43 E
Danvers, U.S.A. 137 D14 42 34N 70 55W
Danville, Ill., U.S.A. 141 D9 40 10N 87 40W
Danville, Ind., U.S.A. 141 E10 39 46N 86 32W
Danville, Ky., U.S.A. 141 G12 37 40N 84 45W
Danville, Va., U.S.A. 135 G6 36 40N 79 20W
Danyang, China 69 B12 32 0N 119 31 E
Danzhai, China 68 D6 26 11N 107 48 E
Danzig = Gdańsk, Poland 47 A5 54 22N 18 40 E
Dao, Antique, Phil. 71 F3 10 30N 121 57 E
Dao, Capiz, Phil. 71 F4 11 24N 122 41 E
Dão →, Portugal 36 E2 40 20N 8 11W
Dao Xian, China 69 E8 25 36N 111 31 E
Daocheng, China 68 C3 29 0N 100 10 E
Daora, W. Sahara 98 C2 27 5N 12 59W
Daoud = Aïn Beïda, Algeria 99 A6 35 50N 7 29 E
Daoulas, France 22 D2 48 22N 4 17W
Dapa, Phil. 71 G6 9 46N 126 3 E
Dapitan, Phil. 71 G4 8 39N 123 25 E
Dapong, Togo 101 C5 10 55N 0 16 E
Daqing Shan, China 66 D6 40 40N 111 0 E
Daqu Shan, China 69 B14 30 25N 122 20 E
Dar es Salaam, Tanzania 106 D4 6 50 S 39 12 E
Dar Mazār, Iran 85 D8 29 14N 57 20 E
Dar'ā, Syria 91 C5 32 36N 36 7 E
Dar'ā □, Syria 91 C5 32 55N 36 10 E
Dārāb, Iran 85 D7 28 50N 54 30 E
Darabani, Romania 46 A7 48 10N 26 39 E
Daraj, Libya 96 B2 30 10N 10 28 E
Dārān, Iran 85 C6 32 59N 50 24 E
Daraut Kurgan, Kirghizia 55 D6 39 33N 72 11 E
Daravica, Serbia, Yug. 42 E5 42 32N 20 8 E
Daraw, Egypt 94 C3 24 22N 32 51 E
Dārayyā, Syria 91 B5 33 28N 36 15 E
Darazo, Nigeria 101 C7 11 1N 10 24 E
Darband, Pakistan 80 B5 34 20N 72 50 E
Darband, Kūh-e, Iran 85 D8 31 34N 57 8 E
Darbhanga, India 81 F11 26 15N 85 55 E
Darburruk, Somali Rep. 108 C2 9 44N 44 31 E
Darby, U.S.A. 142 C6 46 2N 114 7W
Darda, Croatia 42 B3 45 40N 18 41 E
Dardanelle, Ark., U.S.A. 139 H8 35 12N 93 9W
Dardanelle, Calif., U.S.A. 144 G7 38 15N 119 50W
Dardanelles = Çanakkale Boğazı, Turkey 44 D8 40 17N 26 32 E
Darende, Turkey 88 D7 38 31N 37 30 E
Dārestān, Iran 85 D8 29 9N 58 42 E
Darfield, N.Z. 119 D7 43 29 S 172 7 E
Darfo, Italy 38 C7 45 52N 10 11 E
Dârfûr, Sudan 92 E6 13 40N 24 0 E
Dargai, Pakistan 79 B3 34 25N 71 55 E
Dargan Ata, Uzbekistan 56 E7 40 29N 62 10 E
Dargaville, N.Z. 118 B2 35 57 S 173 52 E
Darhan Muminggan Lianheqi, China 66 D6 41 40N 110 28 E
Dari, Sudan 95 F3 5 48N 30 26 E
Darién, G. del, Colombia 152 B2 9 0N 77 0W
Darién, Serranía del, Colombia 152 B2 8 30N 77 30W
Dariganga, Mongolia 66 B7 45 21N 113 45 E
Darinskoye, Kazakhstan 54 F2 51 20N 51 44 E
Darjeeling = Darjiling, India 81 F13 27 3N 88 18 E
Darjiling, India 81 F13 27 3N 88 18 E
Dark Cove, Canada 129 C9 48 47N 54 13W
Darkan, Australia 113 F2 33 20 S 116 43 E
Darke Peak, Australia 116 B2 33 27 S 136 12 E
Darkhazīneh, Iran 85 D6 31 54N 48 39 E
Darkot Pass, Pakistan 81 A5 36 45N 73 26 E
Darling →, Australia 116 C4 34 4 S 141 54 E
Darling Downs, Australia 115 D5 27 30 S 150 30 E
Darling Ra., Australia 113 F2 32 30 S 116 0 E
Darlington, U.K. 16 C6 54 33N 1 33W
Darlington, S.C., U.S.A. 135 H6 34 18N 79 50W
Darlington, Wis., U.S.A. 140 B6 42 43N 90 7W
Darlot, L., Australia 113 E3 27 48 S 121 35 E
Darłowo, Poland 47 A3 54 25N 16 25 E
Dărmăneşti, Romania 46 C7 46 21N 26 33 E
Darmstadt, Germany 27 F4 49 51N 8 40 E
Darnah, Libya 96 B4 32 40N 22 35 E
Darnah □, Libya 96 B4 31 0N 23 40 E
Darnall, S. Africa 105 D5 29 23 S 31 18 E
Darnétal, France 22 C8 49 25N 1 10 E
Darney, France 23 D13 48 5N 6 2 E
Darnick, Australia 116 B5 32 48 S 143 38 E
Darnley, C., Antarctica 7 C6 68 0 S 69 0 E
Darnley B., Canada 126 B7 69 30N 123 30W
Daroca, Spain 34 D3 41 9N 1 25W
Darr, Australia 114 C3 23 13 S 144 7 E
Darr →, Australia 114 C3 23 39 S 143 50 E
Darran Mts., N.Z. 119 E2 44 37 S 167 59 E
Darrington, U.S.A. 142 B3 48 14N 121 37W
Darsana, Bangla. 78 D2 23 35N 88 48 E
Darsi, India 83 G4 15 46N 79 44 E
Darsser Ort, Germany 26 A8 54 29N 12 31 E
Dart →, U.K. 17 G4 50 24N 3 36W
Dart, C., Antarctica 7 D14 73 6 S 126 20W
Dartmoor, Australia 116 D4 37 56 S 141 19 E
Dartmoor, U.K. 17 G4 50 36N 4 0W
Dartmouth, Australia 114 C3 23 31 S 144 44 E
Dartmouth, Canada 129 D7 44 40N 63 30W
Dartmouth, U.K. 17 G4 50 21N 3 35W
Dartmouth, L., Australia 115 D4 26 4 S 145 18 E
Dartuch, C., Spain 33 B10 39 55N 3 49 E
Daru, Papua N. G. 120 E2 9 3 S 143 13 E
Daruvar, Croatia 42 B2 45 35N 17 14 E
Darvaza, Turkmenistan 56 E6 40 11N 58 24 E
Darvel, Teluk, Malaysia 75 B5 4 50N 118 20 E
Darwha, India 82 D3 20 15N 77 45 E
Darwin, Australia 112 B5 12 25 S 130 51 E
Darwin, U.S.A. 145 J9 36 15N 117 35W
Darwin, Mt., Chile 160 D3 54 47 S 69 55W
Darwin River, Australia 112 B5 12 50 S 130 58 E
Daryapur, India 82 D3 20 55N 77 20 E
Dās, U.A.E. 85 E7 25 20N 53 30 E
Dashetai, China 66 D5 41 0N 109 5 E
Dashkesan, Azerbaijan 53 F12 40 25N 46 0 E
Dasht, Iran 85 B8 37 17N 56 7 E
Dasht →, Pakistan 79 D1 25 10N 61 40 E
Dasht-i-Nawar, Afghan. 80 C3 33 52N 68 0 E
Daska, Pakistan 80 C6 32 20N 74 20 E
Dassa-Zoume, Benin 101 D5 7 46N 2 14 E
Dasseneiland, S. Africa 104 E2 33 25 S 18 3 E
Datça, Turkey 45 H9 36 46N 27 40 E
Datia, India 81 G8 25 39N 78 27 E
Datian, China 69 E11 25 40N 117 50 E
Datong, Anhui, China 69 B11 30 48N 117 44 E
Datong, Shanxi, China 66 D7 40 6N 113 18 E
Dattapur = Dhamangaon, India 82 D4 20 45N 78 15 E
Datu, Tanjung, Indonesia 75 B3 2 5N 109 39 E
Datu Piang, Phil. 71 H5 7 2N 124 30 E
Datuk, Tanjong, Malaysia 75 B3 2 5N 109 39 E
Daugava →, Latvia 50 C4 57 4N 24 3 E
Daugavpils, Latvia 50 D5 55 53N 26 32 E
Daulatabad, India 82 E2 19 57N 75 15 E
Daule, Ecuador 152 D1 2 56 S 79 56W
Daule →, Ecuador 152 D2 2 10 S 79 52W
Daulpur, India 80 F7 26 45N 77 59 E
Daun, Germany 27 E2 50 10N 6 53 E
Daund, India 82 E2 18 26N 74 40 E
Dauphin, Canada 131 C8 51 9N 100 5W
Dauphin I., U.S.A. 135 K1 30 16N 88 10W
Dauphin L., Canada 131 C9 51 20N 99 45W
Dauphiné, France 25 C9 45 15N 5 25 E
Daura, Borno, Nigeria 101 C7 11 31N 11 24 E
Daura, Kaduna, Nigeria 101 C6 13 2N 8 21 E
Dausa, India 80 F7 26 52N 76 20 E
Davangere, India 83 G2 14 25N 75 55 E
Davao, Phil. 71 H5 7 0N 125 40 E
Davao □, Phil. 71 H5 7 0N 125 55 E
Davao, G. of, Phil. 71 H5 6 30N 125 48 E
Davao del Sur □, Phil. 71 H5 6 30N 125 25 E
Davao Oriental □, Phil. 71 H6 7 10N 126 30 E
Dāvar Panāh, Iran 85 E9 27 25N 62 15 E
Davenport, Calif., U.S.A. 144 H4 37 1N 122 12W
Davenport, Iowa, U.S.A. 140 C6 41 30N 90 40W
Davenport, Wash., U.S.A. 142 C4 47 40N 118 5W
Davenport Downs, Australia 114 C3 24 8 S 141 7 E
Davenport Ra., Australia 114 C1 20 28 S 134 0 E
David, Panama 148 E3 8 30N 82 30W
David City, U.S.A. 138 E6 41 18N 97 10W
David Gorodok, Belorussia 50 E5 52 4N 27 8 E
Davidson, Canada 131 C7 51 16N 105 59W
Davis, U.S.A. 144 G5 38 33N 121 44W
Davis Dam, U.S.A. 145 K12 35 11N 114 35W
Davis Inlet, Canada 129 A7 55 50N 60 59W
Davis Mts., U.S.A. 139 K2 30 42N 104 15W
Davis Sea, Antarctica 7 C7 66 0 S 92 0 E
Davis Str., N. Amer. 127 B14 65 0N 58 0W
Davlekanovo, Russia 54 D4 54 13N 55 3 E
Davos, Switz. 29 C9 46 48N 9 49 E
Davy L., Canada 131 B7 58 53N 108 18W
Dawa →, Ethiopia 95 G5 4 11N 42 6 E
Dawaki, Bauchi, Nigeria 101 D6 9 25N 9 33 E
Dawaki, Kano, Nigeria 101 C6 12 5N 8 23 E
Dawes Ra., Australia 114 C5 24 40 S 150 40 E
Dawna Range, Burma 78 G7 16 30N 98 30 E
Dawnyein, Burma 78 G5 15 54N 95 36 E
Dawqah, Si. Arabia 86 C3 19 36N 40 54 E
Dawson, Canada 126 B6 64 10N 139 30W
Dawson, Ga., U.S.A. 135 K3 31 45N 84 28W
Dawson, N. Dak., U.S.A. 138 B5 46 56N 99 45W
Dawson, I., Chile 160 D2 53 50 S 70 50W
Dawson Creek, Canada 130 B4 55 45N 120 15W
Dawson Inlet, Canada 131 A10 61 50N 93 25W
Dawson Ra., Australia 114 C4 24 30 S 149 48 E
Dawu, China 68 B3 30 55N 101 10 E
Dawwah, Oman 87 B7 20 33N 58 48 E
Dax, France 24 E2 43 44N 1 3W
Daxi, Taiwan 69 E13 24 52N 121 20 E
Daxian, China 68 B6 31 15N 107 23 E
Daxin, China 68 F6 22 50N 107 11 E
Daxindian, China 67 F11 37 30N 120 50 E
Daxinggou, China 67 C15 43 25N 129 40 E
Daxue Shan, Sichuan, China 68 B3 30 30N 101 30 E
Daxue Shan, Yunnan, China 68 F2 23 42N 99 48 E
Dayao, China 68 E3 25 43N 101 20 E
Daye, China 69 B10 30 6N 114 58 E
Dayi, China 68 B4 30 41N 103 29 E
Daylesford, Australia 116 D6 37 21 S 144 9 E
Dayong, China 69 C8 29 11N 110 30 E
Dayr az Zawr, Syria 84 C4 35 20N 40 5 E
Daysland, Canada 130 C6 52 50N 112 20W
Dayton, Iowa, U.S.A. 140 B2 42 14N 94 6W
Dayton, Ky., U.S.A. 141 E12 39 47N 84 28W
Dayton, Nev., U.S.A. 144 F7 39 15N 119 34W
Dayton, Ohio, U.S.A. 134 F3 39 45N 84 10W
Dayton, Pa., U.S.A. 136 F5 40 54N 79 18W
Dayton, Tenn., U.S.A. 135 H3 35 30N 85 1W
Dayton, Wash., U.S.A. 142 C4 46 20N 118 10W
Daytona Beach, U.S.A. 135 L5 29 14N 81 0W
Dayu, China 69 E10 25 24N 114 22 E
Dayville, U.S.A. 142 D4 44 33N 119 37W
Dazhu, China 68 B6 30 41N 107 15 E
Dazu, China 68 C5 29 40N 105 42 E
De Aar, S. Africa 104 E3 30 39 S 24 0 E
De Bilt, Neths. 20 D6 52 6N 5 11 E
De Forest, U.S.A. 140 A7 43 15N 89 20W
De Funiak Springs, U.S.A. 135 K2 30 42N 86 10W
De Grey, Australia 112 D2 20 12 S 119 12 E
De Grey →, Australia 112 D2 20 12 S 119 13 E
De Kalb, U.S.A. 138 E10 41 55N 88 45W
De Koog, Neths. 20 B5 53 6N 4 46 E
De Land, U.S.A. 135 L5 29 1N 81 19W
De Leon, U.S.A. 139 J5 32 9N 98 35W
De Panne, Belgium 21 F1 51 6N 2 34 E
De Pere, U.S.A. 134 C1 44 28N 88 1W
De Queen, U.S.A. 139 H7 34 3N 94 24W
De Quincy, U.S.A. 139 K8 30 30N 93 27W
De Ridder, U.S.A. 139 K8 30 48N 93 15W
De Rijp, Neths. 20 C5 52 33N 4 51 E
De Smet, U.S.A. 138 C6 44 25N 97 35W
De Soto, U.S.A. 140 F6 38 7N 90 33W
De Tour, U.S.A. 134 C4 45 59N 83 56W
De Witt, Ark., U.S.A. 139 H9 34 19N 91 20W
De Witt, Iowa, U.S.A. 140 C6 41 49N 90 33W
De Witt, Mich., U.S.A. 141 B12 42 50N 84 33W
Dead Sea, Asia 86 A1 31 30N 35 30 E
Deadwood, U.S.A. 138 C3 44 23N 103 44W
Deadwood L., Canada 130 B3 59 10N 128 30W
Deakin, Australia 113 F4 30 46 S 128 58 E
Deal, U.K. 17 F9 51 13N 1 25 E
Deal I., Australia 114 F4 39 30 S 147 20 E
Dealesville, S. Africa 104 D4 28 41 S 25 44 E
De'an, China 69 C10 29 21N 115 46 E
Dean, Forest of, U.K. 17 F5 51 50N 2 35W
Deán Funes, Argentina 158 C3 30 20 S 64 20W
Dearborn, Mich., U.S.A. 128 D3 42 18N 83 15W
Dearborn, Mo., U.S.A. 140 E2 39 32N 94 46W
Dease →, Canada 130 B3 59 56N 128 32W
Dease L., Canada 130 B2 58 40N 130 5W
Dease Lake, Canada 130 B2 58 25N 130 6W
Death Valley, U.S.A. 145 J10 36 19N 116 52W
Death Valley Junction, U.S.A. 145 J10 36 21N 116 30W
Death Valley Nat. Monument, U.S.A. 145 J10 36 30N 117 0W
Deauville, France 22 C7 49 23N 0 2 E
Deba Habe, Nigeria 101 C7 10 14N 11 20 E
Debak, Malaysia 75 B4 1 34N 111 25 E
Debaltsevo, Ukraine 52 B8 48 22N 38 26 E
Debao, China 68 F6 23 21N 106 46 E
Debar, Macedonia, Yug. 42 F5 41 31N 20 30 E
Debden, Canada 131 C7 53 30N 106 50W
Debdou, Morocco 99 B4 33 59N 3 0W
Debessy, Russia 54 C3 57 39N 53 49 E
Dębica, Poland 31 A14 50 2N 21 25 E
Dęblin, Poland 47 D8 51 34N 21 50 E
Debno, Poland 47 C1 52 44N 14 41 E
Débo, L., Mali 100 B4 15 14N 4 15W
Debolt, Canada 130 B5 55 12N 118 1W
Deborah East, L., Australia 113 F2 30 45 S 119 0 E
Deborah West, L., Australia 113 F2 30 45 S 118 50 E
Debrc, Serbia, Yug. 42 C4 44 38N 19 53 E
Debre Birhan, Ethiopia 95 F4 9 41N 39 31 E
Debre Markos, Ethiopia 95 E4 10 20N 37 40 E
Debre May, Ethiopia 95 E4 11 20N 37 25 E
Debre Sina, Ethiopia 95 F4 9 51N 39 50 E
Debre Tabor, Ethiopia 95 E4 11 50N 38 26 E
Debre Zebit, Ethiopia 95 E4 11 48N 38 30 E
Debrecen, Hungary 31 D14 47 33N 21 42 E
Dečani, Serbia, Yug. 42 E5 42 30N 20 10 E
Decatur, Ala., U.S.A. 135 H2 34 35N 87 0W
Decatur, Ga., U.S.A. 135 J3 33 47N 84 17W
Decatur, Ill., U.S.A. 140 E8 39 50N 88 55W
Decatur, Ind., U.S.A. 141 D12 40 50N 84 56W
Decatur, Mich., U.S.A. 141 B11 42 7N 85 58W
Decatur, Tex., U.S.A. 139 J6 33 15N 97 35W
Decazeville, France 24 D6 44 34N 2 15 E
Deccan, India 82 F4 18 0N 79 0 E
Deception, Mt., Australia 116 A3 30 42 S 138 16 E
Deception L., Canada 131 B8 56 33N 104 13W
Dechang, China 68 D4 27 25N 102 11 E
Děčín, Czech. 30 A7 50 47N 14 12 E
Decize, France 23 F10 46 50N 3 28 E
Deckerville, U.S.A. 136 C2 43 33N 82 46W
Decollatura, Italy 41 C9 39 2N 16 21 E
Decorah, U.S.A. 138 D9 43 20N 91 50W
Deda, Romania 46 C5 46 56N 24 50 E
Dedaye, Burma 78 G5 16 24N 95 53 E
Dedéagach = Alexandroúpolis, Greece 44 D7 40 50N 25 54 E
Dedegöl Dağları, Turkey 88 E4 37 15N 31 18 E
Dedemsvaart, Neths. 20 C8 52 36N 6 28 E
Dedham, U.S.A. 137 D13 42 14N 71 10W
Dedilovo, Russia 51 E10 53 59N 37 50 E
Dédougou, Burkina Faso 100 C4 12 30N 3 25W
Deduru Oya, Sri Lanka 83 L4 7 32N 79 50 E
Dedza, Malawi 107 E3 14 20 S 34 20 E
Dee →, Clwyd, U.K. 16 D4 53 15N 3 7W
Dee →, Gramp., U.K. 18 D6 57 4N 2 7W
Deep B., Canada 130 A5 61 15N 116 35W
Deep Lead, Australia 116 D5 37 0 S 142 43 E
Deep River, U.S.A. 140 C4 41 35N 92 22W
Deep Well, Australia 114 C1 24 20 S 134 0 E
Deepwater, Australia 115 D5 29 25 S 151 51 E
Deepwater, U.S.A. 140 F3 38 18N 93 46W
Deer →, Canada 131 B10 58 23N 94 13W
Deer Lake, Nfld., Canada 129 C8 49 11N 57 27W
Deer Lake, Ont., Canada 131 C10 52 36N 94 20W
Deer Lodge, U.S.A. 142 C7 46 25N 112 40W
Deer Park, Ohio, U.S.A. 141 E12 39 13N 84 23W
Deer Park, Wash., U.S.A. 142 C5 47 55N 117 21W
Deer River, U.S.A. 138 B8 47 21N 93 44W
Deeral, Australia 114 B4 17 14 S 145 55 E
Deerdepoort, S. Africa 104 C4 24 37 S 26 27 E
Deerlijk, Belgium 21 G2 50 51N 3 22 E
Deferiet, U.S.A. 137 B9 44 2N 75 41W
Defiance, U.S.A. 141 C12 41 20N 84 20W
Dêgê, China 68 B2 31 44N 98 39 E
Degebe →, Portugal 37 G3 38 13N 7 29W
Degeh Bur, Ethiopia 90 F3 8 11N 43 31 E
Degema, Nigeria 101 E6 4 50N 6 48 E
Degersheim, Switz. 29 B8 47 23N 9 12 E
Deggendorf, Germany 27 G8 48 49N 12 59 E
Deh Bīd, Iran 85 D7 30 39N 53 11 E
Deh-e Shīr, Iran 85 D7 31 29N 53 45 E
Dehaj, Iran 85 D7 30 42N 54 53 E
Dehak, Iran 79 D1 27 11N 62 37 E
Dehdez, Iran 85 D6 31 43N 50 17 E
Dehestān, Iran 85 D7 28 30N 55 35 E
Dehgolān, Iran 84 C5 35 17N 47 25 E
Dehibat, Tunisia 96 B2 32 0N 10 47 E
Dehiwala, Sri Lanka 83 L4 6 50N 79 51 E
Dehlorān, Iran 84 C5 32 41N 47 16 E
Dehnow-e Kūhestān, Iran 85 E8 27 58N 58 32 E
Dehra Dun, India 80 D8 30 20N 78 4 E
Dehri, India 81 G11 24 50N 84 15 E
Dehua, China 69 E12 25 26N 118 14 E
Dehui, China 67 B13 44 30N 125 40 E
Deinze, Belgium 21 G3 50 59N 3 32 E
Dej, Romania 46 B4 47 10N 23 52 E
Dejiang, China 68 C7 28 18N 108 7 E
Dekemhare, Ethiopia 95 D4 15 6N 39 0 E
Dekese, Zaïre 102 C4 3 24 S 21 24 E
Dekhkanabad, Uzbekistan 55 D3 38 21N 66 30 E
Dekoa, C.A.R. 102 A3 6 19N 19 4 E
Del Carmen, Phil. 71 G6 9 50N 126 0 E
Del Mar, U.S.A. 145 N9 32 58N 117 16W
Del Norte, U.S.A. 143 H10 37 40N 106 27W
Del Rio, U.S.A. 139 L4 29 23N 100 50W
Delai, Sudan 94 D4 17 21N 36 6 E
Delano, U.S.A. 145 K7 35 48N 119 13W
Delareyville, S. Africa 104 D4 26 41 S 25 26 E
Delavan, Ill., U.S.A. 140 D7 40 22N 89 33W
Delavan, Wis., U.S.A. 138 D10 42 40N 88 39W
Delaware, U.S.A. 141 D13 40 20N 83 5W
Delaware □, U.S.A. 134 F8 39 0N 75 40W
Delaware →, U.S.A. 134 F8 39 20N 75 25W
Delaware B., U.S.A. 133 C12 38 50N 75 0W
Delčevo, Macedonia, Yug. 42 F7 41 58N 22 46 E
Delegate, Australia 117 D8 37 4 S 148 56 E
Delémont, Switz. 28 B4 47 22N 7 20 E
Delft, Neths. 20 D4 52 1N 4 22 E
Delft I., Sri Lanka 83 K4 9 30N 79 40 E
Delfzijl, Neths. 20 B9 53 20N 6 55 E
Delgado, C., Mozam. 107 E5 10 45 S 40 40 E
Delgerhet, Mongolia 66 B6 45 50N 110 30 E
Delgo, Sudan 94 C3 20 6N 30 40 E
Delhi, Canada 136 D4 42 51N 80 30W
Delhi, India 80 E7 28 38N 77 17 E
Delhi, U.S.A. 137 D10 42 17N 74 56W
Deli Jovan, Serbia, Yug. 42 C7 44 13N 22 9 E
Delia, Canada 130 C6 51 38N 112 23W
Delice, Turkey 88 D6 39 54N 34 2 E
Delice →, Turkey 88 D6 39 45N 34 15 E
Delicias, Mexico 146 B3 28 10N 105 30W
Delījān, Iran 85 C6 33 59N 50 40 E
Delitzsch, Germany 26 D8 51 32N 12 22 E

Dinh Lap 191


Dell City, *U.S.A.* 143 L11 31 58N 105 19W
Dell Rapids, *U.S.A.* 138 D6 43 53N 96 44W
Delle, *France* 23 E14 47 30N 7 2 E
Dellys, *Algeria* 99 A5 36 57N 3 57 E
Delmar, *Iowa, U.S.A.* 140 C6 42 0N 90 37W
Delmar, *N.Y., U.S.A.* 137 D11 42 37N 73 47W
Delmenhorst, *Germany* 26 B4 53 3N 8 37 E
Delmiro Gouveia, *Brazil* 154 C4 9 24 S 38 6W
Delnice, *Croatia* 39 C11 45 23N 14 50 E
Delong, Ostrova, *Russia* 57 B15 76 40N 149 20 E
Deloraine, *Australia* 114 G4 41 30 S 146 40 E
Deloraine, *Canada* 131 D8 49 15N 100 29W
Delphi, *Greece* 45 F4 38 28N 22 30 E
Delphi, *U.S.A.* 141 D10 40 37N 86 40W
Delphos, *U.S.A.* 141 D12 40 51N 84 17W
Delportshoop, *S. Africa* 104 D3 28 22 S 24 20 E
Delray Beach, *U.S.A.* 135 M5 26 27N 80 4W
Delsbo, *Sweden* 14 C10 61 48N 16 32 E
Delta, *Colo., U.S.A.* 143 G9 38 44N 108 5W
Delta, *Utah, U.S.A.* 142 G7 39 21N 112 35W
Delta Amacuro □, *Venezuela* 153 B5 8 30N 61 30W
Delungra, *Australia* 115 D5 29 39 S 150 51 E
Delvina, *Albania* 44 E2 39 59N 20 4 E
Delvinákion, *Greece* 44 E2 39 57N 20 32 E
Demak, *Indonesia* 75 D4 6 53 S 110 38 E
Demanda, Sierra de la, *Spain* 34 C1 42 15N 3 0W
Demba, *Zaïre* 103 D4 5 28 S 22 15 E
Demba Chio, *Angola* 103 D2 9 41 S 13 41 E
Dembecha, *Ethiopia* 95 E4 10 32N 37 30 E
Dembi, *Ethiopia* 95 F4 8 5N 36 25 E
Dembia, *Zaïre* 106 B2 3 33N 25 48 E
Dembidolo, *Ethiopia* 95 F3 8 34N 34 50 E
Demer →, *Belgium* 21 G5 50 57N 4 42 E
Demerara □, *Guyana* 153 B6 6 0N 58 30W
Demetrias, *Greece* 44 E5 39 22N 23 1 E
Demidov, *Russia* 50 D7 55 16N 31 30 E
Deming, *N. Mex., U.S.A.* 143 K10 32 10N 107 50W
Deming, *Wash., U.S.A.* 144 B4 48 49N 122 13W
Demini →, *Brazil* 153 D5 0 46 S 62 56W
Demirci, *Turkey* 88 D3 39 2N 28 38 E
Demirköy, *Turkey* 88 C2 41 49N 27 45 E
Demmin, *Germany* 26 B9 53 54N 13 2 E
Demnate, *Morocco* 98 B3 31 44N 6 59W
Demonte, *Italy* 38 D4 44 18N 7 18 E
Demopolis, *U.S.A.* 135 J2 32 30N 87 48W
Dempo, *Indonesia* 74 C2 4 2 S 103 15 E
Demyansk, *Russia* 50 C8 57 40N 32 27 E
Den Burg, *Neths.* 20 B5 53 3N 4 47 E
Den Chai, *Thailand* 76 D3 17 59N 100 4 E
Den Dungen, *Neths.* 21 E6 51 41N 5 22 E
Den Haag = 's-Gravenhage, *Neths.* 20 D4 52 7N 4 17 E
Den Ham, *Neths.* 20 D8 52 28N 6 30 E
Den Helder, *Neths.* 20 C5 52 57N 4 45 E
Den Hulst, *Neths.* 20 C8 52 36N 6 16 E
Den Oever, *Neths.* 20 C6 52 56N 5 2 E
Denain, *France* 23 B10 50 20N 3 22 E
Denair, *U.S.A.* 144 H6 37 32N 120 48W
Denau, *Uzbekistan* 55 D3 38 16N 67 54 E
Denbigh, *U.K.* 16 D4 53 12N 3 26W
Dendang, *Indonesia* 75 C3 3 7 S 107 56 E
Dender →, *Belgium* 21 F4 51 2N 4 6 E
Denderhoutem, *Belgium* 21 G4 50 53N 4 2 E
Denderleeuw, *Belgium* 21 G4 50 54N 4 5 E
Dendermonde, *Belgium* 21 F4 51 2N 4 5 E
Deneba, *Ethiopia* 95 F4 9 47N 39 10 E
Denekamp, *Neths.* 20 D10 52 22N 7 1 E
Denezhkin Kamen, Gora, *Russia* 54 A6 60 25N 59 32 E
Deng Deng, *Cameroon* 102 A2 5 12N 13 31 E
Deng Xian, *China* 69 A9 32 34N 112 4 E
Dengchuan, *China* 68 E3 25 59N 100 3 E
Denge, *Nigeria* 101 C6 12 52N 5 21 E
Dengfeng, *China* 66 G7 34 25N 113 2 E
Dengi, *Nigeria* 101 D6 9 25N 9 55 E
Dengkou, *China* 66 D4 40 18N 106 55 E
Denham, *Australia* 113 E1 25 56 S 113 31 E
Denham Ra., *Australia* 114 C4 21 55 S 147 46 E
Denham Sd., *Australia* 113 E1 25 45 S 113 15 E
Denia, *Spain* 35 G5 38 49N 0 8 E
Denial B., *Australia* 115 E1 32 14 S 133 32 E
Deniliquin, *Australia* 117 C6 35 30 S 144 58 E
Denison, *Iowa, U.S.A.* 138 D7 42 0N 95 18W
Denison, *Tex., U.S.A.* 139 J6 33 50N 96 40W
Denison Plains, *Australia* 112 C4 18 35 S 128 0 E
Denisovka, *Kazakhstan* 54 E7 52 28N 61 46 E
Denizli, *Turkey* 88 E3 37 42N 29 2 E
Denizli □, *Turkey* 88 E3 37 45N 29 5 E
Denman, *Australia* 117 B9 32 24 S 150 42 E
Denman Glacier, *Antarctica* 7 C7 66 45 S 99 25 E
Denmark, *Australia* 113 F2 34 59 S 117 25 E
Denmark ■, *Europe* 15 J3 55 30N 9 0 E
Denmark Str., *Atl. Oc.* 124 C17 66 0N 30 0W
Dennison, *U.S.A.* 136 F3 40 21N 81 21W
Denton, *Mont., U.S.A.* 142 C9 47 25N 109 56W
Denton, *Tex., U.S.A.* 139 J6 33 12N 97 10W
D'Entrecasteaux, Pt., *Australia* 113 F2 34 50 S 115 57 E
D'Entrecasteaux Is., *Papua N. G.* 120 E6 9 0 S 151 0 E
Dents du Midi, *Switz.* 28 D3 46 10N 6 56 E
Denu, *Ghana* 101 D5 6 4N 1 8 E
Denver, *Colo., U.S.A.* 138 F2 39 45N 105 0W
Denver, *Ind., U.S.A.* 141 D10 40 52N 86 5W
Denver, *Iowa, U.S.A.* 140 B4 42 40N 92 20W
Denver City, *U.S.A.* 139 J3 32 58N 102 48W
Deoband, *India* 80 E7 29 42N 77 43 E
Deobhog, *India* 82 E6 19 53N 82 44 E
Deogarh, *India* 82 D7 21 32N 84 45 E
Deoghar, *India* 81 G12 24 30N 86 42 E
Deolali, *India* 82 E1 19 58N 73 50 E
Deoli = Devli, *India* 80 G6 25 50N 75 20 E
Deoria, *India* 81 F10 26 31N 83 48 E
Deosai Mts., *Pakistan* 81 B6 35 40N 75 0 E
Deping, *China* 67 F9 37 25N 116 58 E
Deposit, *U.S.A.* 137 D9 42 5N 75 23W
Depot Springs, *Australia* 113 E3 27 55 S 120 3 E
Deputatskiy, *Russia* 57 C14 69 18N 139 54 E
Dêqên, *China* 68 C2 28 34N 98 51 E
Deqing, *China* 69 F8 23 8N 111 42 E
Dera Ghazi Khan, *Pakistan* 79 C3 30 5N 70 43 E
Dera Ismail Khan, *Pakistan* 79 C3 31 50N 70 50 E
Derbent, *Russia* 53 E13 42 5N 48 15 E
Derby, *Australia* 112 C3 17 18 S 123 38 E
Derby, *U.K.* 16 E6 52 55N 1 28W
Derby, *Conn., U.S.A.* 137 E11 41 20N 73 5W
Derby, *N.Y., U.S.A.* 136 D6 42 40N 78 59W
Derbyshire □, *U.K.* 16 E6 52 55N 1 28W
Derecske, *Hungary* 31 D14 47 20N 21 33 E
Dereli, *Turkey* 89 C8 40 44N 38 26 E
Derg →, *U.K.* 19 B4 54 42N 7 26W
Derg, L., *Ireland* 19 D3 53 0N 8 20W
Dergachi, *Ukraine* 52 A7 50 9N 36 11 E
Derik, *Turkey* 89 E9 37 21N 40 18 E
Derinkuyu, *Turkey* 88 D6 38 22N 34 45 E
Dermantsi, *Bulgaria* 43 D9 43 8N 24 17 E
Dernieres Isles, *U.S.A.* 139 L9 29 0N 90 45W
Dêrong, *China* 68 C2 28 44N 99 9 E
Derrinallum, *Australia* 116 D5 37 57 S 143 15 E
Derry = Londonderry, *U.K.* 19 B4 55 0N 7 23W
Derryveagh Mts., *Ireland* 19 B3 55 0N 8 4W
Derudub, *Sudan* 94 D4 17 31N 36 7 E
Derval, *France* 22 E5 47 40N 1 41W
Dervéni, *Greece* 45 F4 38 8N 22 25 E
Derventa, *Bos.-H., Yug.* 42 C2 44 59N 17 55 E
Derwent, *Canada* 131 C6 53 41N 110 58W
Derwent →, *Derby, U.K.* 16 E6 52 53N 1 17W
Derwent →, *N. Yorks., U.K.* 16 D7 53 45N 0 57W
Derwent Water, *U.K.* 16 C4 54 35N 3 9W
Des Moines, *Iowa, U.S.A.* 140 C3 41 35N 93 37W
Des Moines, *N. Mex., U.S.A.* 139 G3 36 50N 103 51W
Des Moines →, *U.S.A.* 138 E9 40 23N 91 25W
Des Plaines, *U.S.A.* 141 B9 42 3N 87 52W
Des Plaines →, *U.S.A.* 141 C8 41 23N 88 15W
Desaguadero →, *Argentina* 158 C2 34 30 S 66 46W
Desaguadero →, *Bolivia* 156 D4 16 35 S 69 5W
Descanso, Pta., *Mexico* 145 N9 32 21N 117 3W
Descartes, *France* 24 B4 46 59N 0 42 E
Deschaillons, *Canada* 129 C5 46 32N 72 7W
Descharme →, *Canada* 131 B7 56 51N 109 13W
Deschutes →, *U.S.A.* 142 D3 45 30N 121 0W
Dese, *Ethiopia* 90 E2 11 5N 39 40 E
Deseado, C., *Chile* 160 D2 52 45 S 74 42W
Desenzano del Gardo, *Italy* 38 C7 45 28N 10 32 E
Desert Center, *U.S.A.* 145 M11 33 45N 115 27W
Desert Hot Springs, *U.S.A.* 145 M10 33 58N 116 30W
Désirade, I., *Guadeloupe* 149 C7 16 18N 61 3W
Deskenatlata L., *Canada* 130 A6 60 55N 112 3W
Desna →, *Ukraine* 50 F7 50 33N 30 32 E
Desnătui →, *Romania* 46 E4 44 15N 23 27 E
Desolación, I., *Chile* 160 D2 53 0 S 74 0W
Despeñaperros, Paso, *Spain* 35 G1 38 24N 3 30W
Despotovac, *Serbia, Yug.* 42 C6 44 6N 21 30 E
Dessau, *Germany* 26 D8 51 49N 12 15 E
Dessel, *Belgium* 21 F6 51 15N 5 7 E
Dessye = Dese, *Ethiopia* 90 E2 11 5N 39 40 E
D'Estrees B., *Australia* 116 C2 35 55 S 137 45 E
Desuri, *India* 80 G5 25 18N 73 35 E
Desvres, *France* 23 B8 50 40N 1 48 E
Det Udom, *Thailand* 76 E5 14 54N 105 5 E
Deta, *Romania* 42 B6 45 24N 21 13 E
Dete, *Zimbabwe* 107 F2 18 38 S 26 50 E
Detinja →, *Serbia, Yug.* 42 D4 43 51N 20 5 E
Detmold, *Germany* 26 D4 51 55N 8 50 E
Detour Pt., *U.S.A.* 134 C2 45 37N 86 35W
Detroit, *Mich., U.S.A.* 128 D3 42 23N 83 5W
Detroit, *Tex., U.S.A.* 139 J7 33 40N 95 10W
Detroit Lakes, *U.S.A.* 138 B7 46 50N 95 50W
Deurne, *Belgium* 21 F4 51 12N 4 24 E
Deurne, *Neths.* 21 F7 51 27N 5 49 E
Deutsche Bucht, *Germany* 26 A4 54 15N 8 0 E
Deutschlandsberg, *Austria* 30 E8 46 49N 15 14 E
Deux-Sèvres □, *France* 22 F6 46 35N 0 20W
Deva, *Romania* 46 D3 45 53N 22 55 E
Devakottai, *India* 83 K4 9 55N 78 45 E
Devaprayag, *India* 81 D8 30 13N 78 35 E
Dévaványa, *Hungary* 31 D13 47 2N 20 59 E
Deveci Dağı, *Turkey* 52 F7 40 10N 36 0 E
Deveci Dağları, *Turkey* 88 C6 40 10N 35 50 E
Devecser, *Hungary* 31 D10 47 6N 17 26 E
Develi, *Turkey* 88 D6 38 23N 35 29 E
Deventer, *Neths.* 20 D8 52 15N 6 10 E
Deveron →, *U.K.* 18 D6 57 40N 2 31W
Devesel, *Romania* 46 E3 44 28N 22 41 E
Devgad I., *India* 83 G2 14 48N 74 5 E
Devgadh Bariya, *India* 80 H5 22 40N 73 55 E
Devil River Pk., *N.Z.* 119 A7 40 56 S 172 37 E
Devils Den, *U.S.A.* 144 K7 35 46N 119 58W
Devils Lake, *U.S.A.* 138 A5 48 5N 98 50W
Devils Paw, *Canada* 130 B2 58 47N 134 0W
Devil's Pt., *Sri Lanka* 83 K5 9 26N 80 6 E
Devil's Pt., *Vanuatu* 121 G6 17 44 S 168 11 E
Devin, *Bulgaria* 43 F9 41 44N 24 24 E
Devizes, *U.K.* 17 F6 51 21N 2 0W
Devli, *India* 80 G6 25 50N 75 20 E
Devnya, *Bulgaria* 43 D12 43 13N 27 33 E
Devolii →, *Albania* 44 D2 40 57N 20 15 E
Devon, *Canada* 130 C6 53 24N 113 44W
Devon □, *U.K.* 17 G4 50 50N 3 40W
Devon I., *Canada* 6 B3 75 10N 85 0W
Devonport, *Australia* 114 G4 41 10 S 146 22 E
Devonport, *N.Z.* 118 C3 36 49 S 174 49 E
Devonport, *U.K.* 17 G3 50 23N 4 11W
Devrek, *Turkey* 88 C4 41 13N 31 57 E
Devrekâni, *Turkey* 88 C5 41 36N 33 50 E
Devrez →, *Turkey* 88 C6 41 6N 34 25 E
Dewas, *India* 80 H7 22 59N 76 3 E
Dewetsdorp, *S. Africa* 104 D4 29 33 S 26 39 E
Dewsbury, *U.K.* 16 D6 53 42N 1 38W
Dexing, *China* 69 C11 28 46N 117 30 E
Dexter, *Mich., U.S.A.* 141 B13 42 20N 83 53W
Dexter, *Mo., U.S.A.* 139 G9 36 50N 90 0W
Dexter, *N. Mex., U.S.A.* 139 J2 33 15N 104 25W
Dey-Dey, L., *Australia* 113 E5 29 12 S 131 4 E
Deyang, *China* 68 B5 31 3N 104 27 E
Deyhūk, *Iran* 85 C8 33 15N 57 30 E
Deyyer, *Iran* 85 E6 27 55N 51 55 E
Dezadeash L., *Canada* 130 A1 60 28N 136 58W
Dezfūl, *Iran* 85 C6 32 20N 48 30 E
Dezhneva, Mys, *Russia* 57 C19 66 5N 169 40W
Dezhou, *China* 66 F9 37 26N 116 18 E
Dháfni, *Greece* 45 G4 37 48N 22 1 E
Dháfni, *Kríti, Greece* 32 D7 35 13N 25 3 E
Dhahaban, *Si. Arabia* 86 B2 21 58N 39 3 E
Dhahiriya = Az Zāhirīyah, *Jordan* 91 D3 31 25N 34 58 E
Dhahran = Az Zahrān, *Si. Arabia* 85 E6 26 10N 50 7 E
Dhaka, *Bangla.* 78 D3 23 43N 90 26 E
Dhaka □, *Bangla.* 78 C3 24 25N 90 25 E
Dhali, *Cyprus* 32 D12 35 1N 33 25 E
Dhamangaon, *India* 82 D4 20 45N 78 15 E
Dhamar, *Yemen* 86 D4 14 30N 44 20 E
Dhamási, *Greece* 44 E4 39 43N 22 11 E
Dhampur, *India* 81 E8 29 19N 78 33 E
Dhamtari, *India* 82 D5 20 42N 81 35 E
Dhanbad, *India* 81 H12 23 50N 86 30 E
Dhankuta, *Nepal* 81 F12 26 55N 87 40 E
Dhanora, *India* 82 D5 20 20N 80 22 E
Dhar, *India* 80 H6 22 35N 75 26 E
Dharampur, *Gujarat, India* 82 D1 20 32N 73 17 E
Dharampur, *Mad. P., India* 80 H6 22 13N 75 18 E
Dharamsala = Dharmsala, *India* 80 C7 32 16N 76 23 E
Dharapuram, *India* 83 J3 10 45N 77 34 E
Dharmapuri, *India* 83 H4 12 10N 78 10 E
Dharmavaram, *India* 83 G3 14 29N 77 44 E
Dharmsala, *India* 80 C7 32 16N 76 23 E
Dharwad, *India* 83 G2 15 22N 75 15 E
Dhaulagiri, *Nepal* 81 E10 28 39N 83 28 E
Dhebar, L., *India* 80 G6 24 10N 74 0 E
Dheftera, *Cyprus* 32 D12 35 5N 33 16 E
Dhenkanal, *India* 82 D7 20 45N 85 35 E
Dhenoúsa, *Greece* 45 G7 37 8N 25 48 E
Dherinia, *Cyprus* 32 D12 35 3N 33 57 E
Dheskáti, *Greece* 44 E3 39 55N 21 49 E
Dhespotikó, *Greece* 45 H6 36 57N 24 58 E
Dhestina, *Greece* 45 F4 38 25N 22 31 E
Dhiarrizos →, *Cyprus* 32 E11 34 41N 32 34 E
Dhībān, *Jordan* 91 D4 31 30N 35 46 E
Dhidhimótikhon, *Greece* 44 C8 41 22N 26 29 E
Dhíkti Óros, *Greece* 32 D7 35 8N 25 22 E
Dhilianáta, *Greece* 45 F2 38 15N 20 34 E
Dhílos, *Greece* 45 G7 37 23N 25 15 E
Dhimitsána, *Greece* 45 G4 37 36N 22 3 E
Dhírfis, *Greece* 45 F5 38 40N 23 54 E
Dhodhekánisos, *Greece* 45 H8 36 35N 27 0 E
Dhokós, *Greece* 45 G5 37 20N 23 20 E
Dholiana, *Greece* 44 E2 39 54N 20 32 E
Dholka, *India* 80 H5 22 44N 72 29 E
Dhomokós, *Greece* 45 E4 39 10N 22 18 E
Dhoraji, *India* 80 J4 21 45N 70 37 E
Dhoxáton, *Greece* 44 C6 41 9N 24 16 E
Dhragonísi, *Greece* 45 G7 37 27N 25 29 E
Dhráhstis, Ákra, *Greece* 32 A3 39 48N 19 40 E
Dhrangadhra, *India* 80 H4 22 59N 71 31 E
Dhrápanon, Ákra, *Greece* 32 D6 35 28N 24 14 E
Dhriopís, *Greece* 45 G6 37 25N 24 35 E
Dhrol, *India* 80 H4 22 33N 70 25 E
Dhubāb, *Yemen* 86 D3 12 56N 43 25 E
Dhuburi, *India* 78 B2 26 2N 89 59 E
Dhulasar, *Bangla.* 78 E3 21 52N 90 14 E
Dhule, *India* 82 D2 20 58N 74 50 E
Dhupdhara, *India* 78 B3 26 10N 91 4 E
Dhut →, *Somali Rep.* 90 E5 10 30N 50 0 E
Di Linh, *Vietnam* 77 G7 11 35N 108 4 E
Di Linh, Cao Nguyen, *Vietnam* 77 G7 11 30N 108 0 E
Día, *Greece* 32 D7 35 28N 25 14 E
Diablo, Mt., *U.S.A.* 144 H5 37 53N 121 56W
Diablo Range, *U.S.A.* 144 J5 37 0N 121 5W
Diafarabé, *Mali* 100 C4 14 9N 4 57W
Diagonal, *U.S.A.* 140 D2 40 49N 94 20W
Diala, *Mali* 100 C3 14 10N 9 58W
Dialakoro, *Mali* 100 C3 12 18N 7 54W
Diallassagou, *Mali* 100 C4 13 47N 3 41W
Diamante, *Argentina* 158 C3 32 5 S 60 40W
Diamante →, *Argentina* 158 C2 34 30 S 66 46W
Diamantina, *Brazil* 155 E3 18 17 S 43 40W
Diamantina →, *Australia* 115 D2 26 45 S 139 10 E
Diamantino, *Brazil* 157 C6 14 30 S 56 30W
Diamond Harbour, *India* 81 H13 22 11N 88 14 E
Diamond Is., *Australia* 114 B5 17 25 S 151 5 E
Diamond Mts., *U.S.A.* 142 G6 40 0N 115 58W
Diamond Springs, *U.S.A.* 144 G6 38 42N 120 49W
Diamondville, *U.S.A.* 142 F8 41 51N 110 30W
Dianbai, *China* 69 G8 21 33N 111 0 E
Diancheng, *China* 69 G8 21 30N 111 4 E
Diano Marina, *Italy* 38 E5 43 55N 8 3 E
Dianópolis, *Brazil* 155 D2 11 38 S 46 50W
Dianra, *Ivory C.* 100 D3 8 45N 6 14W
Diapaga, *Burkina Faso* 101 C5 12 5N 1 46 E
Diapangou, *Burkina Faso* 101 C5 12 5N 0 10 E
Diapur, *Australia* 116 D4 36 19 S 141 29 E
Diariguila, *Guinea* 100 C2 10 35N 10 2W
Dībā, *Oman* 85 E8 25 45N 56 16 E
Dibaya, *Zaïre* 103 D4 6 30 S 22 57 E
Dibaya-Lubue, *Zaïre* 103 C3 4 12 S 19 54 E
Dibbi, *Ethiopia* 90 G3 4 10N 41 52 E
Dibete, *Botswana* 104 C4 23 45 S 26 32 E
Dibrugarh, *India* 78 B5 27 29N 94 55 E
Dickeyville, *U.S.A.* 140 B6 42 38N 90 36W
Dickinson, *U.S.A.* 138 B3 46 50N 102 48W
Dickson, *U.S.A.* 135 G2 36 5N 87 22W
Dickson City, *U.S.A.* 137 E9 41 29N 75 40W
Dicomano, *Italy* 39 E8 43 53N 11 30 E
Didam, *Neths.* 20 E8 51 57N 6 8 E
Didesa, W. →, *Ethiopia* 95 E4 10 2N 35 32 E
Didiéni, *Mali* 100 C3 13 53N 8 6W
Didsbury, *Canada* 130 C6 51 35N 114 10W
Didwana, *India* 80 F6 27 23N 74 36 E
Die, *France* 25 D9 44 47N 5 22 E
Diébougou, *Burkina Faso* 100 C4 11 0N 3 15W
Diefenbaker L., *Canada* 131 C7 51 0N 106 55W
Diego Garcia, *Ind. Oc.* 109 E6 7 50 S 72 50 E
Diekirch, *Lux.* 21 J8 49 52N 6 10 E
Diélette, *France* 22 C5 49 33N 1 52W
Diéma, *Mali* 100 C3 14 32N 9 12W
Diembéring, *Senegal* 100 C1 12 29N 16 47W
Diemen, *Neths.* 20 D5 52 21N 4 58 E
Dien Ban, *Vietnam* 76 E7 15 53N 108 16 E
Dien Bien, *Vietnam* 76 B4 21 20N 103 0 E
Dien Khanh, *Vietnam* 77 F7 12 15N 109 6 E
Diepenbeek, *Belgium* 21 G6 50 54N 5 25 E
Diepenheim, *Neths.* 20 D9 52 12N 6 33 E
Diepenveen, *Neths.* 20 D8 52 18N 6 9 E
Diepholz, *Germany* 26 C4 52 37N 8 22 E
Diepoldsau, *Switz.* 29 B9 47 23N 9 40 E
Dieppe, *France* 22 C8 49 54N 1 4 E
Dieren, *Neths.* 20 D8 52 3N 6 6 E
Dierks, *U.S.A.* 139 H7 34 9N 94 0W
Diessen, *Neths.* 21 F6 51 29N 5 10 E
Diessenhofen, *Switz.* 29 A7 47 42N 8 46 E
Diest, *Belgium* 21 G6 50 58N 5 4 E
Dieterich, *U.S.A.* 141 E8 39 4N 88 23W
Dietikon, *Switz.* 29 B6 47 24N 8 24 E
Dieulefit, *France* 25 D9 44 32N 5 4 E
Dieuze, *France* 23 D13 48 49N 6 43 E
Diever, *Neths.* 20 C8 52 51N 6 19 E
Differdange, *Lux.* 21 J7 49 31N 5 54 E
Diffun, *Phil.* 70 C3 16 36N 121 33 E
Dig, *India* 80 F7 27 28N 77 20 E
Digba, *Zaïre* 106 B2 4 25N 25 48 E
Digboi, *India* 78 B5 27 23N 95 38 E
Digby, *Canada* 129 D6 44 38N 65 50W
Digges, *Canada* 131 B10 58 40N 94 0W
Digges Is., *Canada* 127 B12 62 40N 77 50W
Dighinala, *Bangla.* 78 D4 23 15N 92 5 E
Dighton, *U.S.A.* 138 F4 38 30N 100 26W
Diglur, *India* 82 E3 18 34N 77 33 E
Digne, *France* 25 D10 44 5N 6 12 E
Digoin, *France* 24 B7 46 29N 3 58 E
Digor, *Turkey* 89 C10 40 22N 43 25 E
Digos, *Phil.* 71 H5 6 45N 125 20 E
Digranes, *Iceland* 12 C6 66 4N 14 44W
Digras, *India* 82 D3 20 6N 77 45 E
Digul →, *Indonesia* 73 C5 7 7 S 138 42 E
Dīhōk, *Iraq* 84 B3 36 55N 38 57 E
Dijlah, Nahr →, *Asia* 84 D5 31 0N 47 25 E
Dijle →, *Belgium* 21 G5 50 58N 4 41 E
Dijon, *France* 23 E12 47 20N 5 3 E
Dikala, *Sudan* 95 G3 4 45N 31 28 E
Dikkil, *Djibouti* 95 E5 11 8N 42 20 E
Dikomu di Kai, *Botswana* 104 C3 24 58 S 24 36 E
Diksmuide, *Belgium* 21 F1 51 2N 2 52 E
Dikson, *Russia* 56 B9 73 40N 80 5 E
Dikwa, *Nigeria* 101 C7 12 4N 13 30 E
Dila, *Ethiopia* 95 F4 6 21N 38 22 E
Dilbeek, *Belgium* 21 G4 50 51N 4 17 E
Dili, *Indonesia* 72 C3 8 39 S 125 34 E
Dilizhan, *Armenia* 53 F11 40 46N 44 57 E
Dilj, *Croatia* 42 B3 45 29N 18 1 E
Dillard, *U.S.A.* 140 G5 37 44N 91 13W
Dillenburg, *Germany* 26 E4 50 44N 8 17 E
Dilley, *U.S.A.* 139 L5 28 40N 99 12W
Dilling, *Sudan* 95 E2 12 3N 29 35 E
Dillingen, *Germany* 27 G6 48 32N 10 29 E
Dillingham, *U.S.A.* 126 C4 59 5N 158 30W
Dillon, *Canada* 131 B7 55 56N 108 35W
Dillon, *Mont., U.S.A.* 142 D7 45 9N 112 36W
Dillon, *S.C., U.S.A.* 135 H6 34 26N 79 20W
Dillon →, *Canada* 131 B7 55 56N 108 56W
Dillsboro, *U.S.A.* 141 E11 39 1N 85 4W
Dilolo, *Zaïre* 103 E4 10 28 S 22 18 E
Dilsen, *Belgium* 21 F7 51 2N 5 44 E
Dilston, *Australia* 114 G4 41 22 S 147 10 E
Dimapur, *India* 78 C4 25 54N 93 45 E
Dimas, *Mexico* 146 C3 23 43N 106 47W
Dimasalang, *Phil.* 70 E4 12 12N 123 51 E
Dimashq, *Syria* 91 B5 33 30N 36 18 E
Dimashq □, *Syria* 91 B5 33 30N 36 30 E
Dimbaza, *S. Africa* 105 E4 32 50 S 27 14 E
Dimbelenge, *Zaïre* 103 D4 5 33 S 23 7 E
Dimbokro, *Ivory C.* 100 D4 6 45N 4 46W
Dimboola, *Australia* 116 D5 36 28 S 142 7 E
Dîmboviţa □, *Romania* 46 E6 45 0N 25 30 E
Dîmboviţa →, *Romania* 46 E7 44 5N 26 35 E
Dîmbovnic →, *Romania* 46 E6 44 28N 25 18 E
Dimbulah, *Australia* 114 B4 17 8 S 145 4 E
Dimitrovgrad, *Bulgaria* 43 E10 42 5N 25 35 E
Dimitrovgrad, *Russia* 51 D16 54 14N 49 39 E
Dimitrovgrad, *Serbia, Yug.* 42 D7 43 2N 22 48 E
Dimitrovo = Pernik, *Bulgaria* 42 E8 42 35N 23 2 E
Dimmitt, *U.S.A.* 139 H3 34 36N 102 16W
Dimo, *Sudan* 95 F2 5 19N 29 10 E
Dimona, *Israel* 91 D4 31 2N 35 1 E
Dimovo, *Bulgaria* 42 D7 43 43N 22 50 E
Dinagat, *Phil.* 71 F5 10 10N 125 40 E
Dinaig, *Phil.* 71 H5 7 11N 124 10 E
Dinajpur, *Bangla.* 78 C2 25 33N 88 43 E
Dinalupihan, *Phil.* 70 D3 14 52N 120 28 E
Dinan, *France* 22 D4 48 28N 2 2W
Dīnān Āb, *Iran* 85 C8 32 4N 56 49 E
Dinant, *Belgium* 21 H5 50 16N 4 55 E
Dinapur, *India* 81 G11 25 38N 85 5 E
Dinar, *Turkey* 88 D4 38 5N 30 10 E
Dinara Planina, *Croatia* 39 E13 44 0N 16 30 E
Dinard, *France* 22 D4 48 38N 2 6W
Dinaric Alps = Dinara Planina, *Croatia* 39 E13 44 0N 16 30 E
Dinas, *Phil.* 71 H4 7 38N 123 20 E
Dinder, Nahr ed →, *Sudan* 95 E3 14 6N 33 40 E
Dindi →, *India* 83 F4 16 24N 78 15 E
Dindigul, *India* 83 J3 10 25N 78 0 E
Ding Xian, *China* 66 E8 38 30N 114 59 E
Dingalan, *Phil.* 70 D3 15 18N 121 25 E
Dingalan Bay, *Phil.* 70 D3 15 18N 121 25 E
Dingbian, *China* 66 F4 37 35N 107 32 E
Dingelstädt, *Germany* 26 D6 51 19N 10 19 E
Dinghai, *China* 69 B14 30 1N 122 6 E
Dingle, *Ireland* 19 D1 52 9N 10 17W
Dingle B., *Ireland* 19 D1 52 3N 10 20W
Dingmans Ferry, *U.S.A.* 137 E10 41 13N 74 55W
Dingnan, *China* 69 E10 24 45N 115 0 E
Dingo, *Australia* 114 C4 23 38 S 149 19 E
Dingolfing, *Germany* 27 G8 48 38N 12 30 E
Dingras, *Phil.* 70 B3 18 6N 120 42 E
Dingtao, *China* 66 G8 35 5N 115 35 E
Dinguiraye, *Guinea* 100 C2 11 18N 10 49W
Dingwall, *U.K.* 18 D4 57 36N 4 26W
Dingxi, *China* 66 G3 35 30N 104 33 E
Dingxiang, *China* 66 E7 38 30N 112 58 E
Dingyuan, *China* 69 A11 32 32N 117 41 E
Dinh, Mui, *Vietnam* 77 G7 11 22N 109 1 E
Dinh Lap, *Vietnam* 76 B6 21 33N 107 6 E

192 Dinhata


Dinhata, *India* **78 B2** 26 8N 89 27 E
Dinkel →, *Neths.* **20 D9** 52 30N 6 58 E
Dinokwe, *Botswana* **104 C4** 23 29 S 26 37 E
Dinosaur National Monument, *U.S.A.* **142 F9** 40 30N 108 58W
Dinslaken, *Germany* **21 E9** 51 34N 6 41 E
Dinsor, *Somali Rep.* **108 D2** 2 24N 42 59 E
Dintel →, *Neths.* **21 E4** 51 39N 4 22 E
Dinteloord, *Neths.* **21 E4** 51 38N 4 22 E
Dinuba, *U.S.A.* **144 J7** 36 31N 119 22W
Dinxperlo, *Neths.* **20 E9** 51 52N 6 30 E
Diósgyör, *Hungary* **31 C13** 48 7N 20 43 E
Diosig, *Romania* **46 B3** 47 18N 22 2 E
Diourbel, *Senegal* **100 C1** 14 39N 16 12W
Dipaculao, *Phil.* **70 D3** 15 51N 121 32 E
Diphu Pass, *India* **78 A6** 28 9N 97 20 E
Diplo, *Pakistan* **80 G3** 24 35N 69 35 E
Dipolog, *Phil.* **71 G4** 8 36N 123 20 E
Dipşa, *Romania* **46 C5** 46 58N 24 27 E
Dipton, *N.Z.* **119 F3** 45 54 S 168 22 E
Dir, *Pakistan* **79 B3** 35 8N 71 59 E
Diré, *Mali* **100 B4** 16 20N 3 25W
Dire Dawa, *Ethiopia* **90 F3** 9 35N 41 45 E
Diriamba, *Nic.* **148 D2** 11 51N 86 19W
Dirico, *Angola* **103 F4** 17 50 S 20 42 E
Dirk Hartog I., *Australia* **113 E1** 25 50 S 113 5 E
Dirkou, *Niger* **97 E2** 19 1N 12 53 E
Dirranbandi, *Australia* **115 D4** 28 33 S 148 17 E
Dirs, *Si. Arabia* **86 C3** 18 32N 42 5 E
Disa, *India* **80 G5** 24 18N 72 10 E
Disa, *Sudan* **95 E3** 12 5N 34 15 E
Disappointment, C., *U.S.A.* **142 C1** 46 20N 124 0W
Disappointment, L., *Australia* **112 D3** 23 20 S 122 40 E
Disaster B., *Australia* **117 D8** 37 15 S 149 58 E
Discovery B., *Australia* **116 E4** 38 10 S 140 40 E
Disentis, *Switz.* **29 C7** 46 42N 8 50 E
Dishna, *Egypt* **94 B3** 26 9N 32 32 E
Disina, *Nigeria* **101 C6** 11 35N 9 50 E
Disko, *Greenland* **6 C5** 69 45N 53 30W
Disko Bugt, *Greenland* **6 C5** 69 10N 52 0W
Disna →, *Belorussia* **50 D6** 55 34N 28 12 E
Disney Reef, *Tonga* **121 P13** 19 17 S 174 7W
Dison, *Belgium* **21 G7** 50 37N 5 51 E
Disteghil Sar, *Pakistan* **81 A6** 36 20N 75 12 E
Distrito Federal □, *Brazil* **155 E2** 15 45 S 47 45W
Distrito Federal □, *Venezuela* **152 A4** 10 30N 66 55W
Disûq, *Egypt* **94 H7** 31 8N 30 35 E
Ditu, *Zaïre* **103 D4** 5 23 S 21 27 E
Diu, *India* **80 J4** 20 45N 70 58 E
Diuata Mts., *Phil.* **71 G5** 9 0N 125 50 E
Dīvāndarreh, *Iran* **84 C5** 35 55N 47 2 E
Dives →, *France* **22 C6** 49 18N 0 7W
Dives-sur-Mer, *France* **22 C6** 49 18N 0 8W
Divi Pt., *India* **83 G5** 15 59N 81 9 E
Divichi, *Azerbaijan* **53 F13** 41 15N 48 57 E
Divide, *U.S.A.* **142 D7** 45 48N 112 47W
Dividing Ra., *Australia* **113 E2** 27 45 S 116 0 E
Divinópolis, *Brazil* **155 F3** 20 10 S 44 54W
Divisões, Serra dos, *Brazil* **155 E1** 17 0 S 51 0W
Divnoye, *Russia* **53 D10** 45 55N 43 21 E
Divo, *Ivory C.* **100 D3** 5 48N 5 15W
Divriği, *Turkey* **89 D8** 39 22N 38 7 E
Dīwāl Kol, *Afghan.* **79 B2** 34 23N 67 52 E
Dix →, *U.S.A.* **141 G12** 37 49N 84 44W
Dixie Mt., *U.S.A.* **144 F6** 39 55N 120 16W
Dixon, *Calif., U.S.A.* **144 G5** 38 27N 121 49W
Dixon, *Ill., U.S.A.* **140 C7** 41 50N 89 30W
Dixon, *Iowa, U.S.A.* **140 C6** 41 45N 90 47W
Dixon, *Mo., U.S.A.* **140 G4** 37 59N 92 6W
Dixon, *Mont., U.S.A.* **142 C6** 47 19N 114 25W
Dixon, *N. Mex., U.S.A.* **143 H11** 36 15N 105 57W
Dixon Entrance, *U.S.A.* **130 C2** 54 30N 132 0W
Dixonville, *Canada* **130 B5** 56 32N 117 40W
Diyadin, *Turkey* **89 D10** 39 33N 43 40 E
Diyarbakır, *Turkey* **89 E9** 37 55N 40 18 E
Diyarbakir □, *Turkey* **89 E9** 38 0N 40 10 E
Djado, *Niger* **97 D2** 21 4N 12 14 E
Djado, Plateau du, *Niger* **97 D2** 21 29N 12 21 E
Djakarta = Jakarta, *Indonesia* **74 D3** 6 9 S 106 49 E
Djamâa, *Algeria* **99 B6** 33 32N 5 59 E
Djamba, *Angola* **103 F2** 16 45 S 13 58 E
Djambala, *Congo* **102 C2** 2 32 S 14 30 E
Djanet, *Algeria* **99 D6** 24 35N 9 32 E
Djaul I., *Papua N. G.* **120 B6** 2 58 S 150 57 E
Djawa = Jawa, *Indonesia* **75 D4** 7 0 S 110 0 E
Djebiniana, *Tunisia* **96 A2** 35 1N 11 0 E
Djédaa, *Chad* **97 F3** 13 31N 18 34 E
Djelfa, *Algeria* **99 B5** 34 40N 3 15 E
Djema, *C.A.R.* **102 A5** 6 3N 25 15 E
Djember, *Chad* **97 F3** 10 25N 17 50 E
Djendel, *Algeria* **99 A5** 36 15N 2 25 E
Djeneïene, *Tunisia* **96 B2** 31 45N 10 9 E
Djenné, *Mali* **100 C4** 14 0N 4 30W
Djenoun, Garet el, *Algeria* **99 C6** 25 4N 5 31 E
Djerba, *Tunisia* **96 B2** 33 52N 10 51 E
Djerba, I. de, *Tunisia* **96 B2** 33 50N 10 48 E
Djerid, Chott, *Tunisia* **96 B1** 33 42N 8 30 E
Djiba, *Gabon* **102 C2** 1 20 S 13 9 E
Djibo, *Burkina Faso* **101 C4** 14 9N 1 35W
Djibouti, *Djibouti* **90 E3** 11 30N 43 5 E
Djibouti ■, *Africa* **90 E3** 12 0N 43 0 E
Djolu, *Zaïre* **102 B4** 0 35N 22 5 E
Djougou, *Benin* **101 D5** 9 40N 1 45 E
Djoum, *Cameroon* **102 B2** 2 41N 12 35 E
Djourab, *Chad* **97 E3** 16 40N 18 50 E
Djugu, *Zaïre* **106 B3** 1 55N 30 35 E
Djúpivogur, *Iceland* **12 D6** 64 39N 14 17W
Djursholm, *Sweden* **14 E12** 59 25N 18 6 E
Djursland, *Denmark* **15 H4** 56 27N 10 45 E
Dmitriev-Lgovskiy, *Russia* **50 E9** 52 10N 35 0 E
Dmitriya Lapteva, Proliv, *Russia* **57 B15** 73 0N 140 0 E
Dmitrov, *Russia* **51 C10** 56 25N 37 32 E
Dmitrovsk-Orlovskiy, *Russia* **50 E9** 52 29N 35 10 E
Dnepr →, *Ukraine* **52 C5** 46 30N 32 18 E
Dneprodzerzhinsk, *Ukraine* **52 B6** 48 32N 34 37 E
Dneprodzerzhinskoye Vdkhr., *Ukraine* **52 B6** 49 0N 34 0 E
Dnepropetrovsk, *Ukraine* **52 B6** 48 30N 35 0 E
Dneprorudnoye, *Ukraine* **52 C6** 47 21N 34 58 E
Dnestr →, *Europe* **52 C4** 46 18N 30 17 E
Dnestrovski = Belgorod, *Russia* **51 F10** 50 35N 36 35 E
Dnieper = Dnepr →, *Ukraine* **52 C5** 46 30N 32 18 E
Dniester = Dnestr →, *Europe* **52 C4** 46 18N 30 17 E
Dno, *Russia* **50 C6** 57 50N 29 58 E
Doabi, *Afghan.* **79 A3** 36 1N 69 32 E
Doan Hung, *Vietnam* **76 B5** 21 30N 105 10 E
Doba, *Chad* **97 G3** 8 40N 16 50 E
Dobbiaco, *Italy* **39 B9** 46 44N 12 13 E
Dobbyn, *Australia* **114 B3** 19 44 S 140 2 E
Dobczyce, *Poland* **31 B13** 49 52N 20 25 E
Döbeln, *Germany* **26 D9** 51 7N 13 10 E
Doberai, Jazirah, *Indonesia* **73 B4** 1 25 S 133 0 E
Dobiegniew, *Poland* **47 C2** 52 59N 15 45 E
Doblas, *Argentina* **158 D3** 37 5 S 64 0W
Dobo, *Indonesia* **73 C4** 5 45 S 134 15 E
Doboj, *Bos.-H., Yug.* **42 C3** 44 46N 18 6 E
Dobra, *Konin, Poland* **47 D5** 51 55N 18 37 E
Dobra, *Szczecin, Poland* **47 B2** 53 34N 15 20 E
Dobra, *Dîmbovita, Romania* **46 E6** 44 52N 25 40 E
Dobra, *Hunedoara, Romania* **46 D3** 45 54N 22 36 E
Dobre Miasto, *Poland* **47 B7** 53 58N 20 26 E
Dobreta-Turnu-Severin, *Romania* **46 E3** 44 39N 22 41 E
Dobrinishta, *Bulgaria* **43 F8** 41 49N 23 34 E
Dobříš, *Czech.* **30 B7** 49 46N 14 10 E
Dobrodzień, *Poland* **47 E5** 50 45N 18 25 E
Dobropole, *Ukraine* **52 B7** 48 25N 37 2 E
Dobruja, *Romania* **46 E9** 44 30N 28 15 E
Dobrush, *Belorussia* **50 E7** 52 28N 30 19 E
Dobryanka, *Russia* **54 B5** 58 27N 56 25 E
Dobrzyń nad Wisłą, *Poland* **47 C6** 52 39N 19 22 E
Dobtong, *Sudan* **95 F3** 6 25N 31 40 E
Doc, Mui, *Vietnam* **76 D6** 17 58N 106 30 E
Doce →, *Brazil* **155 E4** 19 37 S 39 49W
Doda, *India* **81 C6** 33 10N 75 34 E
Dodecanese = Dhodhekánisos, *Greece* **45 H8** 36 35N 27 0 E
Dodewaard, *Neths.* **20 E7** 51 55N 5 39 E
Dodge Center, *U.S.A.* **138 C8** 44 1N 92 50W
Dodge City, *U.S.A.* **139 G5** 37 42N 100 0W
Dodge L., *Canada* **131 B7** 59 50N 105 36W
Dodgeville, *U.S.A.* **140 B6** 42 55N 90 8W
Dodo, *Sudan* **95 F2** 5 10N 29 57 E
Dodola, *Ethiopia* **95 F4** 6 59N 39 11 E
Dodoma, *Tanzania* **106 D4** 6 8 S 35 45 E
Dodoma □, *Tanzania* **106 D4** 6 0 S 36 0 E
Dodona, *Greece* **44 E2** 39 40N 20 46 E
Dodsland, *Canada* **131 C7** 51 50N 108 45W
Dodson, *U.S.A.* **142 B9** 48 23N 108 16W
Doesburg, *Neths.* **20 D8** 52 1N 6 9 E
Doetinchem, *Neths.* **20 E8** 51 59N 6 18 E
Doftana, *Romania* **46 D6** 45 11N 25 45 E
Dog Creek, *Canada* **130 C4** 51 35N 122 14W
Dog L., *Man., Canada* **131 C9** 51 2N 98 31W
Dog L., *Ont., Canada* **128 C2** 48 48N 89 30W
Doğanbey, *Turkey* **45 G9** 37 40N 27 10 E
Doğanşehir, *Turkey* **89 D7** 38 5N 37 53 E
Dogger Bank, *N. Sea* **10 E6** 54 50N 2 0 E
Dogliani, *Italy* **38 D4** 44 35N 7 55 E
Dōgo, *Japan* **62 A5** 36 15N 133 16 E
Dōgo-San, *Japan* **62 B5** 35 2N 133 13 E
Dogondoutchi, *Niger* **101 C5** 13 38N 4 2 E
Dogran, *Pakistan* **80 D5** 31 48N 73 35 E
Doğubayazıt, *Turkey* **89 D11** 39 31N 44 5 E
Doguéraoua, *Niger* **101 C6** 14 0N 5 31 E
Dohinog, *Phil.* **71 G4** 8 32N 123 12 E
Doi, *Indonesia* **72 A3** 2 14N 127 49 E
Doi Luang, *Thailand* **76 C3** 18 30N 101 0 E
Doi Saket, *Thailand* **76 C2** 18 52N 99 9 E
Doig →, *Canada* **130 B4** 56 25N 120 40W
Dois Irmãos, Sa., *Brazil* **154 C3** 9 0 S 42 30W
Dojransko Jezero, *Macedonia, Yug.* **42 F7** 41 13N 22 44 E
Dokka, *Norway* **13 F11** 60 49N 10 7 E
Dokka →, *Norway* **14 D4** 60 50N 10 6 E
Dokkum, *Neths.* **20 B7** 53 20N 5 59 E
Dokkumer Ee →, *Neths.* **20 B7** 53 18N 5 52 E
Dokri, *Pakistan* **80 F3** 27 25N 68 7 E
Dol-de-Bretagne, *France* **22 D5** 48 34N 1 47W
Doland, *U.S.A.* **138 C5** 44 55N 98 5W
Dolbeau, *Canada* **129 C5** 48 53N 72 18W
Dole, *France* **23 E12** 47 7N 5 31 E
Doleib, Wadi →, *Sudan* **95 E3** 12 10N 33 15 E
Dolgellau, *U.K.* **16 E4** 52 44N 3 53W
Dolgelley = Dolgellau, *U.K.* **16 E4** 52 44N 3 53W
Dolginovo, *Belorussia* **50 D5** 54 39N 27 29 E
Dolianova, *Italy* **40 C2** 39 23N 9 11 E
Dolinskaya, *Ukraine* **52 B5** 48 6N 32 46 E
Dolj □, *Romania* **46 E4** 44 10N 23 30 E
Dollart, *Neths.* **20 B10** 53 20N 7 10 E
Dolna Banya, *Bulgaria* **43 E8** 42 18N 23 44 E
Dolni Dŭbnik, *Bulgaria* **43 D9** 43 24N 24 26 E
Dolo, *Ethiopia* **95 G5** 4 11N 42 3 E
Dolo, *Italy* **39 C9** 45 25N 12 4 E
Dolomites = Dolomiti, *Italy* **39 B8** 46 30N 11 40 E
Dolomiti, *Italy* **39 B8** 46 30N 11 40 E
Dolores, *Argentina* **158 D4** 36 20 S 57 40W
Dolores, *Phil.* **70 E5** 12 2N 125 29 E
Dolores, *Uruguay* **158 C4** 33 34 S 58 15W
Dolores, *U.S.A.* **143 H9** 37 30N 108 30W
Dolores →, *U.S.A.* **143 G9** 38 49N 108 17W
Đolovo, *Serbia, Yug.* **42 C5** 44 55N 20 52 E
Dolphin, C., *Falk. Is.* **160 D5** 51 10 S 59 0W
Dolphin and Union Str., *Canada* **126 B8** 69 5N 114 45W
Dolsk, *Poland* **47 D4** 51 59N 17 3 E
Dolton, *U.S.A.* **141 C9** 41 38N 87 36W
Dom, *Switz.* **28 D5** 46 6N 7 50 E
Dom Joaquim, *Brazil* **155 E3** 18 57 S 43 16W
Dom Pedrito, *Brazil* **159 C5** 31 0 S 54 40W
Dom Pedro, *Brazil* **154 B3** 4 59 S 44 27W
Doma, *Nigeria* **101 D6** 8 25N 8 18 E
Domaniç, *Turkey* **88 D3** 39 48N 29 36 E
Domasi, *Malawi* **107 F4** 15 15 S 35 22 E
Domat Ems, *Switz.* **29 C8** 46 50N 9 27 E
Domažlice, *Czech.* **30 B5** 49 28N 12 58 E
Dombarovskiy, *Russia* **54 F6** 50 46N 59 32 E
Dombås, *Norway* **13 E10** 62 4N 9 8 E
Dombasle-sur-Meurthe, *France* **23 D13** 48 38N 6 21 E
Dombes, *France* **25 B8** 45 58N 5 0 E
Dombóvár, *Hungary* **31 E11** 46 21N 18 9 E
Dombrád, *Hungary* **31 C14** 48 13N 21 54 E
Domburg, *Neths.* **21 E3** 51 34N 3 30 E
Domérat, *France* **24 B6** 46 21N 2 32 E
Domett, *N.Z.* **119 C8** 42 53 S 173 12 E
Domeyko, *Chile* **158 B1** 29 0 S 71 0W
Domeyko, Cordillera, *Chile* **158 A2** 24 30 S 69 0W
Domfront, *France* **22 D6** 48 37N 0 40W
Dominador, *Chile* **158 A2** 24 21 S 69 20W
Dominica ■, *W. Indies* **149 C7** 15 20N 61 20W
Dominica Passage, *W. Indies* **149 C7** 15 10N 61 20W
Dominican Rep. ■, *W. Indies* **149 C5** 19 0N 70 30W
Domiongo, *Zaïre* **103 C4** 4 37 S 21 15 E
Dömitz, *Germany* **26 B7** 53 9N 11 13 E
Domme, *France* **24 D5** 44 48N 1 12 E
Dommel →, *Neths.* **21 E6** 51 38N 5 20 E
Domo, *Ethiopia* **90 F4** 7 50N 47 10 E
Domodóssola, *Italy* **38 B5** 46 6N 8 19 E
Dompaire, *France* **23 D13** 48 14N 6 14 E
Dompierre-sur-Besbre, *France* **24 B7** 46 31N 3 41 E
Dompim, *Ghana* **100 D4** 5 10N 2 5W
Dompu, *Indonesia* **72 C1** 8 32 S 118 28 E
Domrémy-la-Pucelle, *France* **23 D12** 48 26N 5 40 E
Domsjö, *Sweden* **14 A12** 63 16N 18 41 E
Domville, Mt., *Australia* **115 D5** 28 1 S 151 15 E
Domvraína, *Greece* **45 F4** 38 15N 22 59 E
Domžale, *Slovenia* **39 B11** 46 9N 14 35 E
Don →, *India* **83 F3** 16 20N 76 15 E
Don →, *Russia* **53 C8** 47 4N 39 18 E
Don →, *Gramp., U.K.* **18 D6** 57 14N 2 5W
Don →, *S. Yorks., U.K.* **16 D7** 53 41N 0 51W
Don, C., *Australia* **112 B5** 11 18 S 131 46 E
Don Benito, *Spain* **37 G5** 38 53N 5 51W
Don Duong, *Vietnam* **77 G7** 11 51N 108 35 E
Don Martín, Presa de, *Mexico* **146 B4** 27 30N 100 50W
Dona Ana = Nhamaabué, *Mozam.* **107 F4** 17 25 S 35 5 E
Donaghadee, *U.K.* **19 B6** 54 38N 5 32W
Donald, *Australia* **116 D5** 36 23 S 143 0 E
Donalda, *Canada* **130 C6** 52 35N 112 34W
Donaldsonville, *U.S.A.* **139 K9** 30 2N 91 0W
Donalsonville, *U.S.A.* **135 K3** 31 3N 84 52W
Donau →, *Austria* **31 C10** 48 10N 17 0 E
Donaueschingen, *Germany* **27 H4** 47 57N 8 30 E
Donauwörth, *Germany* **27 G6** 48 42N 10 47 E
Donawitz, *Austria* **30 D8** 47 22N 15 4 E
Doncaster, *U.K.* **16 D6** 53 31N 1 9W
Dondo, *Angola* **103 D2** 9 45 S 14 25 E
Dondo, *Mozam.* **107 F3** 19 33 S 34 46 E
Dondo, *Zaïre* **102 B4** 4 11N 21 39 E
Dondo, Teluk, *Indonesia* **72 A2** 0 29N 120 30 E
Dondra Head, *Sri Lanka* **83 M5** 5 55N 80 40 E
Donegal, *Ireland* **19 B3** 54 39N 8 8W
Donegal □, *Ireland* **19 B4** 54 53N 8 0W
Donegal B., *Ireland* **19 B3** 54 30N 8 35W
Donets →, *Russia* **53 C9** 47 33N 40 55 E
Donetsk, *Ukraine* **52 C7** 48 0N 37 45 E
Dong Ba Thin, *Vietnam* **77 F7** 12 8N 109 13 E
Dong Dang, *Vietnam* **76 B6** 21 54N 106 42 E
Dong Giam, *Vietnam* **76 C5** 19 25N 105 31 E
Dong Ha, *Vietnam* **76 D6** 16 55N 107 8 E
Dong Hene, *Laos* **76 D5** 16 40N 105 18 E
Dong Hoi, *Vietnam* **76 D6** 17 29N 106 36 E
Dong Jiang →, *China* **69 F10** 23 6N 114 0 E
Dong Khe, *Vietnam* **76 A6** 22 26N 106 27 E
Dong Ujimqin Qi, *China* **66 B9** 45 32N 116 55 E
Dong Van, *Vietnam* **76 A5** 23 16N 105 22 E
Dong Xoai, *Vietnam* **77 G6** 11 32N 106 55 E
Donga, *Nigeria* **101 D7** 7 45N 10 2 E
Dong'an, *China* **69 D8** 26 23N 111 12 E
Dongara, *Australia* **113 E1** 29 14 S 114 57 E
Dongargarh, *India* **82 D5** 21 10N 80 40 E
Dongbei, *China* **67 D13** 42 0N 125 0 E
Dongchuan, *China* **68 D4** 26 8N 103 1 E
Dongen, *Neths.* **21 E5** 51 38N 4 56 E
Donges, *France* **22 E4** 47 18N 2 4W
Dongfang, *China* **76 C7** 18 50N 108 33 E
Dongfeng, *China* **67 C13** 42 40N 125 34 E
Donggala, *Indonesia* **72 B1** 0 30 S 119 40 E
Donggan, *China* **68 F5** 23 22N 105 9 E
Donggou, *China* **67 E13** 39 52N 124 10 E
Dongguan, *China* **69 F9** 22 58N 113 44 E
Dongguang, *China* **66 F9** 37 50N 116 30 E
Donghai Dao, *China* **69 G8** 21 0N 110 15 E
Dongjingcheng, *China* **67 B15** 44 5N 129 10 E
Donglan, *China* **68 E6** 24 30N 107 21 E
Dongliu, *China* **69 B11** 30 13N 116 55 E
Dongmen, *China* **68 F6** 22 20N 107 48 E
Dongning, *China* **67 B16** 44 2N 131 5 E
Dongnyi, *China* **68 C3** 28 3N 100 15 E
Dongo, *Angola* **103 E3** 14 36 S 15 48 E
Dongola, *Sudan* **94 D3** 19 9N 30 22 E
Dongou, *Congo* **102 B3** 2 0N 18 5 E
Dongping, *China* **66 G9** 35 55N 116 20 E
Dongshan, *China* **69 F11** 23 43N 117 30 E
Dongsheng, *China* **66 E6** 39 50N 110 0 E
Dongshi, *Taiwan* **69 E13** 24 18N 120 49 E
Dongtai, *China* **67 H11** 32 51N 120 21 E
Dongting Hu, *China* **69 C9** 29 18N 112 45 E
Dongxiang, *China* **69 C11** 28 11N 116 34 E
Dongxing, *China* **68 G7** 21 34N 108 0 E
Dongyang, *China* **69 C13** 29 13N 120 15 E
Dongzhi, *China* **69 B11** 30 9N 117 0 E
Donington, C., *Australia* **116 C2** 34 45 S 136 0 E
Doniphan, *U.S.A.* **139 G9** 36 40N 90 50W
Donja Stubica, *Croatia* **39 C13** 45 59N 16 0 E
Donji Dušnik, *Serbia, Yug.* **42 D7** 43 12N 22 5 E
Donji Miholjac, *Croatia* **42 B3** 45 45N 18 10 E
Donji Milanovac, *Serbia, Yug.* **42 C7** 44 28N 22 6 E
Donji Vakuf, *Bos.-H., Yug.* **42 C2** 44 8N 17 24 E
Dønna, *Norway* **12 C12** 66 6N 12 30 E
Donna, *U.S.A.* **139 M5** 26 12N 98 2W
Donnaconna, *Canada* **129 C5** 46 41N 71 41W
Donnelly's Crossing, *N.Z.* **118 B2** 35 42 S 173 38 E
Donnybrook, *Australia* **113 F2** 33 34 S 115 48 E
Donnybrook, *S. Africa* **105 D4** 29 59 S 29 48 E
Donora, *U.S.A.* **136 F5** 40 11N 79 50W
Donor's Hill, *Australia* **114 B3** 18 42 S 140 33 E
Donostia = San Sebastián, *Spain* **34 B3** 43 17N 1 58W
Donque, *Angola* **103 F2** 15 28 S 14 6 E
Donskoy, *Russia* **51 E11** 53 55N 38 15 E
Donsol, *Phil.* **70 E4** 12 54N 123 36 E
Donya Lendava, *Slovenia* **39 B13** 46 35N 16 25 E
Donzère, *France* **25 D8** 44 28N 4 43 E
Donzère-Mondragon, Barr. de, *France* **25 D8** 44 13N 4 42 E
Donzy, *France* **23 E10** 47 20N 3 6 E
Doon →, *U.K.* **18 F4** 55 26N 4 41W
Doorn, *Neths.* **20 D6** 52 2N 5 20 E
Dora, L., *Australia* **112 D3** 22 0 S 123 0 E
Dora Báltea →, *Italy* **38 C5** 45 11N 8 5 E
Dora Riparia →, *Italy* **38 C4** 45 5N 7 44 E
Doran L., *Canada* **131 A7** 61 13N 108 6W
Dorchester, *U.K.* **17 G5** 50 42N 2 28W
Dorchester, C., *Canada* **127 B12** 65 27N 77 27W
Dordogne □, *France* **24 C4** 45 5N 0 40 E
Dordogne →, *France* **24 C3** 45 2N 0 36W
Dordrecht, *Neths.* **20 E5** 51 48N 4 39 E
Dordrecht, *S. Africa* **104 E4** 31 20 S 27 3 E
Dore →, *France* **24 C7** 45 50N 3 35 E
Dore, Mts., *France* **24 C6** 45 32N 2 50 E
Doré L., *Canada* **131 C7** 54 46N 107 17W
Doré Lake, *Canada* **131 C7** 54 38N 107 36W
Dores do Indaiá, *Brazil* **155 E2** 19 27 S 45 36W
Dorfen, *Germany* **27 G8** 48 16N 12 10 E
Dorgali, *Italy* **40 B2** 40 18N 9 35 E
Dori, *Burkina Faso* **101 C4** 14 3N 0 2W
Doring →, *S. Africa* **104 E2** 31 54 S 18 39 E
Doringbos, *S. Africa* **104 E2** 31 59 S 19 16 E
Dorion, *Canada* **128 C5** 45 23N 74 3W
Dormaa-Ahenkro, *Ghana* **100 D4** 7 15N 2 52W
Dormo, Ras, *Ethiopia* **95 E5** 13 14N 42 35 E
Dornach, *Switz.* **28 B5** 47 29N 7 37 E
Dornberg, *Slovenia* **39 C10** 45 45N 13 50 E
Dornbirn, *Austria* **30 D2** 47 25N 9 45 E
Dornes, *France* **23 F10** 46 48N 3 18 E
Dornoch, *U.K.* **18 D4** 57 52N 4 5W
Dornoch Firth, *U.K.* **18 D4** 57 52N 4 0W
Dornogovĭ □, *Mongolia* **66 B6** 44 0N 110 0 E
Doro, *Mali* **101 B4** 16 9N 0 51W
Dorog, *Hungary* **31 D11** 47 42N 18 45 E
Dorogobuzh, *Russia* **50 D8** 54 50N 33 18 E
Dorohoi, *Romania* **46 B7** 47 56N 26 30 E
Döröö Nuur, *Mongolia* **64 B4** 48 0N 93 0 E
Dorr, *Iran* **85 C6** 33 17N 50 38 E
Dorre I., *Australia* **113 E1** 25 13 S 113 12 E
Dorrigo, *Australia* **117 A10** 30 20 S 152 44 E
Dorris, *U.S.A.* **142 F3** 41 59N 121 58W
Dorset, *Canada* **136 A6** 45 14N 78 54W
Dorset, *U.S.A.* **136 E4** 41 4N 80 40W
Dorset □, *U.K.* **17 G5** 50 48N 2 25W
Dorsten, *Germany* **26 D2** 51 40N 6 55 E
Dortmund, *Germany* **26 D3** 51 32N 7 28 E
Dörtyol, *Turkey* **88 E7** 36 50N 36 13 E
Dorum, *Germany* **26 B4** 53 40N 8 33 E
Doruma, *Zaïre* **106 B2** 4 42N 27 33 E
Dorūneh, *Iran* **85 C8** 35 10N 57 18 E
Dos Bahías, C., *Argentina* **160 B3** 44 58 S 65 32W
Dos Hermanas, *Spain* **37 H5** 37 16N 5 55W
Dos Palos, *U.S.A.* **144 J6** 36 59N 120 37W
Dosso, *Niger* **101 C5** 13 0N 3 13 E
Dothan, *U.S.A.* **135 K3** 31 10N 85 25W
Dottignies, *Belgium* **21 G2** 50 44N 3 19 E
Doty, *U.S.A.* **144 D3** 46 38N 123 17W
Douai, *France* **23 B10** 50 21N 3 4 E
Douala, *Cameroon* **101 E6** 4 0N 9 45 E
Douarnenez, *France* **22 D2** 48 6N 4 21W
Douăzeci Şi Trei August, *Romania* **46 F9** 43 55N 28 40 E
Double Island Pt., *Australia* **115 D5** 25 56 S 153 11 E
Doubrava →, *Czech.* **30 B8** 49 40N 15 30 E
Doubs □, *France* **23 E13** 47 10N 6 20 E
Doubs →, *France* **23 F12** 46 53N 5 1 E
Doubtful Sd., *N.Z.* **119 F1** 45 20 S 166 49 E
Doubtless B., *N.Z.* **118 A2** 34 55 S 173 26 E
Doudeville, *France* **22 C7** 49 43N 0 47 E
Doué-la-Fontaine, *France* **22 E6** 47 11N 0 16W
Douentza, *Mali* **100 C4** 14 58N 2 48W
Doughboy B., *N.Z.* **119 H2** 47 2 S 167 40 E
Douglas, *S. Africa* **104 D3** 29 4 S 23 46 E
Douglas, *U.K.* **16 C3** 54 9N 4 29W
Douglas, *Alaska, U.S.A.* **130 B2** 58 23N 134 24W
Douglas, *Ariz., U.S.A.* **143 L9** 31 21N 109 30W
Douglas, *Ga., U.S.A.* **135 K4** 31 32N 82 52W
Douglas, *Wyo., U.S.A.* **138 D2** 42 45N 105 20W
Douglastown, *Canada* **129 C7** 48 46N 64 24W
Douglasville, *U.S.A.* **135 J3** 33 46N 84 43W
Douirat, *Morocco* **98 B4** 33 2N 4 11W
Doukáton, Ákra, *Greece* **45 F2** 38 34N 20 30 E
Doulevant-le-Château, *France* **23 D11** 48 23N 4 55 E
Doullens, *France* **23 B9** 50 10N 2 20 E
Doumé, *Cameroon* **102 B2** 4 15N 13 25 E
Douna, *Mali* **100 C3** 13 13N 6 0W
Dounan, *Taiwan* **69 F13** 23 41N 120 26 E
Dounguila, *Congo* **102 C2** 2 53 S 11 58 E
Dounreay, *U.K.* **18 C5** 58 34N 3 44W
Dour, *Belgium* **21 H3** 50 24N 3 46 E
Dourada, Serra, *Brazil* **155 D2** 13 10 S 48 45W
Dourados, *Brazil* **159 A5** 22 9 S 54 50W
Dourados →, *Brazil* **159 A5** 21 58 S 54 18W
Dourdan, *France* **23 D9** 48 30N 2 1 E
Douro →, *Europe* **36 D2** 41 8N 8 40W
Douvaine, *France* **25 B10** 46 19N 6 16 E
Douz, *Tunisia* **96 B1** 33 25N 9 0 E
Douze →, *France* **24 E3** 43 54N 0 30W
Dove →, *U.K.* **16 E6** 52 51N 1 36W
Dove Creek, *U.S.A.* **143 H9** 37 46N 108 59W
Dover, *Australia* **114 G4** 43 18 S 147 2 E
Dover, *U.K.* **17 F9** 51 7N 1 19 E
Dover, *Del., U.S.A.* **134 F8** 39 10N 75 31W
Dover, *Ky., U.S.A.* **141 F13** 38 43N 83 52W
Dover, *N.H., U.S.A.* **137 C14** 43 12N 70 51W
Dover, *N.J., U.S.A.* **137 F10** 40 53N 74 34W

Dzuumod 193


Dover, Ohio, U.S.A. 136 F3 40 32N 81 30W
Dover, Pt., Australia 113 F4 32 32 S 125 32 E
Dover, Str. of, Europe 22 B8 51 0N 1 30 E
Dover-Foxcroft, U.S.A. 129 C6 45 14N 69 14W
Dover Plains, U.S.A. 137 E11 41 43N 73 35W
Dovey = Dyfi →, U.K. 17 E4 52 32N 4 0W
Dovrefjell, Norway 14 B3 62 15N 9 33 E
Dow Rūd, Iran 85 C6 33 28N 49 4 E
Dowa, Malawi 107 E3 13 38 S 33 58 E
Dowagiac, U.S.A. 141 C10 41 58N 86 8W
Dowgha'i, Iran 85 B8 36 54N 58 32 E
Dowlat Yār, Afghan. 79 B2 34 30N 65 45 E
Dowlatābād, Farāh, Afghan. 79 B1 32 47N 62 40 E
Dowlatābād, Fāryāb, Afghan. 79 A2 36 26N 64 55 E
Dowlatābād, Iran 85 D8 28 20N 56 40 E
Down □, U.K. 19 B6 54 20N 5 47W
Downers Grove, U.S.A. 141 C8 41 49N 88 1W
Downey, Calif., U.S.A. 145 M8 33 56N 118 7W
Downey, Utah, U.S.A. 142 E7 42 29N 112 3W
Downham Market, U.K. 17 E8 52 36N 0 22 E
Downieville, U.S.A. 144 F6 39 34N 120 50W
Downing, U.S.A. 140 D4 40 29N 92 22W
Downpatrick, U.K. 19 B6 54 20N 5 43W
Downpatrick Hd., Ireland 19 B2 54 20N 9 21W
Dowsārī, Iran 85 D8 28 25N 57 59 E
Dowshī, Afghan. 79 B3 35 35N 68 43 E
Doyle, U.S.A. 144 E6 40 2N 120 6W
Doylestown, U.S.A. 137 F9 40 21N 75 10W
Draa, C., Morocco 98 C2 28 47N 11 0W
Draa, Oued →, Morocco 98 C2 28 40N 11 10W
Drac →, France 25 C9 45 12N 5 42 E
Drachten, Neths. 20 B8 53 7N 6 5 E
Drăgănești, Romania 46 E5 44 9N 24 32 E
Drăgănești-Vlașca, Romania 46 E6 44 5N 25 33 E
Dragaš, Serbia, Yug. 42 E5 42 5N 20 35 E
Drăgășani, Romania 46 E5 44 39N 24 17 E
Dragina, Serbia, Yug. 42 C4 44 30N 19 25 E
Dragocvet, Serbia, Yug. 42 D6 43 58N 21 15 E
Dragoman, Prokhod, Bulgaria 42 E7 42 58N 22 53 E
Dragonera, I., Spain 33 B9 39 35N 2 19 E
Dragovishtitsa, Bulgaria 42 E7 42 22N 22 39 E
Draguignan, France 25 E10 43 32N 6 27 E
Drain, U.S.A. 142 E2 43 45N 123 17W
Drake, Australia 115 D5 28 55 S 152 25 E
Drake, U.S.A. 138 B4 47 56N 100 21W
Drake Passage, S. Ocean 7 B17 58 0 S 68 0W
Drakensberg, S. Africa 105 E4 31 0 S 28 0 E
Dráma, Greece 44 C6 41 9N 24 10 E
Dráma □, Greece 44 C6 41 20N 24 0 E
Drammen, Norway 14 E4 59 42N 10 12 E
Drangajökull, Iceland 12 C2 66 9N 22 15W
Drangedal, Norway 14 E3 59 6N 9 3 E
Dranov, Ostrov, Romania 46 E10 44 55N 29 30 E
Dras, India 81 B6 34 25N 75 48 E
Drau = Drava →, Croatia 31 F11 45 33N 18 55 E
Drava →, Croatia 31 F11 45 33N 18 55 E
Draveil, France 23 D9 48 41N 2 25 E
Dravograd, Slovenia 39 B12 46 36N 15 5 E
Drawa →, Poland 47 C2 52 52N 15 59 E
Drawno, Poland 47 B2 53 13N 15 46 E
Drawsko Pomorskie, Poland 47 B2 53 35N 15 50 E
Drayton Plains, U.S.A. 141 B13 42 42N 83 23W
Drayton Valley, Canada 130 C6 53 12N 114 58W
Dreibergen, Neths. 20 D6 52 3N 5 17 E
Dren, Serbia, Yug. 42 D5 43 8N 20 44 E
Drenthe □, Neths. 20 C9 52 52N 6 40 E
Drentsche Hoofdvaart, Neths. 20 C8 52 39N 6 4 E
Drepanum, C., Cyprus 32 E11 34 54N 32 19 E
Dresden, Canada 136 D2 42 35N 82 11W
Dresden, Germany 26 D9 51 2N 13 45 E
Dreux, France 22 D8 48 44N 1 23 E
Drexel, U.S.A. 141 E12 39 45N 84 18W
Drezdenko, Poland 47 C2 52 50N 15 49 E
Driel, Neths. 20 E7 51 57N 5 49 E
Driffield = Great Driffield, U.K. 16 C7 54 0N 0 25W
Driftwood, U.S.A. 136 E6 41 22N 78 9W
Driggs, U.S.A. 142 E8 43 50N 111 8W
Drin i zi →, Albania 44 C2 41 37N 20 28 E
Drina →, Bos.-H., Yug. 42 C4 44 53N 19 21 E
Drincea →, Romania 46 E3 44 20N 22 55 E
Drînceni, Romania 46 C9 46 49N 28 10 E
Drini →, Albania 42 B2 42 20N 20 0 E
Drinjača →, Bos.-H., Yug. 42 C4 44 15N 19 8 E
Drivstua, Norway 14 B3 62 26N 9 47 E
Drniš, Croatia 39 E13 43 51N 16 10 E
Drøbak, Norway 14 E4 59 39N 10 39 E
Drobin, Poland 47 C6 52 42N 19 58 E
Drogheda, Ireland 19 C5 53 45N 6 20W
Drogichin, Belorussia 50 E4 52 15N 25 8 E
Drogobych, Ukraine 50 G3 49 20N 23 30 E
Drohiczyn, Poland 47 C9 52 24N 22 39 E
Droichead Nua, Ireland 19 C5 53 11N 6 50W
Droitwich, U.K. 17 E5 52 16N 2 10W
Drôme □, France 25 D9 44 38N 5 15 E
Drôme →, France 25 D8 44 46N 4 46 E
Dromedary, C., Australia 117 D9 36 17 S 150 10 E
Dronero, Italy 38 D4 44 29N 7 22 E
Dronfield, Australia 114 C3 21 12 S 140 3 E
Dronne →, France 24 C3 45 2N 0 9W
Dronninglund, Denmark 15 G4 57 10N 10 19 E
Dronrijp, Neths. 20 B7 53 11N 5 39 E
Dropt →, France 24 D3 44 35N 0 6W
Drosendorf, Austria 30 C8 48 52N 15 37 E
Drouin, Australia 117 E6 38 10 S 145 53 E
Drouzhba, Bulgaria 43 D13 43 15N 28 0 E
Drumbo, Canada 136 C4 43 16N 80 35W
Drumheller, Canada 130 C6 51 25N 112 40W
Drummond, U.S.A. 142 C7 46 40N 113 4W
Drummond I., U.S.A. 128 C3 46 0N 83 40W
Drummond Pt., Australia 115 E2 34 9 S 135 16 E
Drummond Ra., Australia 114 C4 23 45 S 147 10 E
Drummondville, Canada 128 C5 45 55N 72 25W
Drumright, U.S.A. 139 H6 35 59N 96 38W
Drunen, Neths. 21 E6 51 41N 5 8 E
Druskininkai, Lithuania 50 D3 54 3N 23 58 E
Drut →, Belorussia 50 E7 53 8N 30 5 E
Druten, Neths. 20 E7 51 53N 5 36 E
Druya, Latvia 50 D5 55 45N 27 28 E
Druzhina, Russia 57 C15 68 14N 145 18 E
Drvar, Bos.-H., Yug. 39 D13 44 21N 16 23 E
Drvenik, Croatia 39 E13 43 27N 16 3 E
Drwęca →, Poland 47 C5 53 0N 18 42 E
Dry Tortugas, U.S.A. 148 B3 24 38N 82 55W
Dryanovo, Bulgaria 43 E10 42 59N 25 28 E
Dryden, Canada 131 D10 49 47N 92 50W
Dryden, U.S.A. 139 K3 30 3N 102 3W
Drygalski I., Antarctica 7 C7 66 0 S 92 0 E
Drysdale →, Australia 112 B4 13 59 S 126 51 E
Drysdale I., Australia 114 A2 11 41 S 136 0 E
Drzewiczka →, Poland 47 D7 51 36N 20 36 E
Dschang, Cameroon 101 D7 5 32N 10 3 E
Du Bois, U.S.A. 136 E6 41 8N 78 46W
Du Quoin, U.S.A. 140 F7 38 0N 89 10W
Duanesburg, U.S.A. 137 D10 42 45N 74 11W
Duaringa, Australia 114 C4 23 42 S 149 42 E
Ḍubā, Si. Arabia 84 E2 27 10N 35 40 E
Dubai = Dubayy, U.A.E. 85 E7 25 18N 55 20 E
Dubawnt →, Canada 131 A8 64 33N 100 6W
Dubawnt, L., Canada 131 A8 63 4N 101 42W
Dubayy, U.A.E. 85 E7 25 18N 55 20 E
Dubbeldam, Neths. 20 E5 51 47N 4 43 E
Dubbo, Australia 117 B8 32 11 S 148 35 E
Dubele, Zaïre 106 B2 2 56N 29 35 E
Dübendorf, Switz. 29 B7 47 24N 8 37 E
Dubenskiy, Russia 54 F5 51 27N 56 38 E
Dubica, Croatia 39 C13 45 11N 16 48 E
Dublin, Ireland 19 C5 53 20N 6 18W
Dublin, Ga., U.S.A. 135 J4 32 30N 82 34W
Dublin, Tex., U.S.A. 139 J5 32 5N 98 20W
Dublin □, Ireland 19 C5 53 24N 6 20W
Dublin B., Ireland 19 C5 53 18N 6 5W
Dubna, Russia 51 C10 56 44N 37 10 E
Dubna, Russia 51 D10 54 8N 36 59 E
Dubno, Ukraine 50 F4 50 25N 25 45 E
Dubois, Idaho, U.S.A. 142 D7 44 7N 112 9W
Dubois, Ind., U.S.A. 141 F10 38 26N 86 48W
Dubossary, Moldavia 52 C3 47 15N 29 10 E
Dubossary Vdkhr., Moldavia 52 C3 47 30N 29 0 E
Dubovka, Russia 53 B11 49 5N 44 50 E
Dubovskoye, Russia 53 C10 47 28N 42 46 E
Dubrajpur, India 81 H12 23 48N 87 25 E
Dubréka, Guinea 100 D2 9 46N 13 31W
Dubrovitsa, Ukraine 50 F5 51 31N 26 35 E
Dubrovnik, Croatia 42 E3 42 39N 18 6 E
Dubrovskoye, Russia 57 D12 58 55N 111 10 E
Dubulu, Zaïre 102 B4 4 18N 20 16 E
Dubuque, U.S.A. 140 B6 42 30N 90 41W
Duchang, China 69 C11 29 18N 116 12 E
Duchesne, U.S.A. 142 F8 40 14N 110 22W
Duchess, Australia 114 C2 21 20 S 139 50 E
Ducie I., Pac. Oc. 123 K15 24 40 S 124 48W
Duck Cr. →, Australia 112 D2 22 37 S 116 53 E
Duck Lake, Canada 131 C7 52 50N 106 16W
Duck Mountain Prov. Park, Canada 131 C8 51 45N 101 0W
Duckwall, Mt., U.S.A. 144 H6 37 58N 120 7W
Düdelange, Lux. 21 K8 49 29N 6 5 E
Duderstadt, Germany 26 D6 51 30N 10 15 E
Dudhnai, India 78 C3 25 59N 90 47 E
Düdingen, Switz. 28 C4 46 52N 7 12 E
Dudinka, Russia 57 C9 69 30N 86 13 E
Dudley, U.K. 17 E5 52 30N 2 5W
Dudna →, India 82 E3 19 17N 76 54 E
Dudo, Somali Rep. 108 C4 9 20N 50 12 E
Dudub, Ethiopia 108 C3 6 55N 46 43 E
Duenas, Phil. 71 F4 11 4N 122 37 E
Dueñas, Spain 36 D6 41 52N 4 33W
Dueré, Brazil 155 D2 11 20 S 49 17W
Duero = Douro →, Europe 36 D2 41 8N 8 40W
Dūfah, W. →, Si. Arabia 86 C3 18 45N 41 49 E
Duffel, Belgium 21 F5 51 6N 4 30 E
Dufftown, U.K. 18 D5 57 26N 3 9W
Dufourspitz, Switz. 28 E5 45 56N 7 52 E
Dugger, U.S.A. 141 E9 39 4N 87 16W
Dugi Otok, Croatia 39 E12 44 0N 15 3 E
Dugiuma, Somali Rep. 108 D2 1 15N 42 34 E
Dugo Selo, Croatia 39 C13 45 51N 16 18 E
Duifken Pt., Australia 114 A3 12 33 S 141 38 E
Duisburg, Germany 26 D2 51 27N 6 42 E
Duitama, Colombia 152 B3 5 50N 73 2W
Duiveland, Neths. 21 E4 51 38N 4 0 E
Duiwelskloof, S. Africa 105 C5 23 42 S 30 10 E
Dukati, Albania 44 D1 40 16N 19 32 E
Dūkdamīn, Iran 85 C8 35 59N 57 43 E
Duke I., U.S.A. 130 C2 54 50N 131 20W
Dukelský průsmyk, Czech. 31 B14 49 25N 21 42 E
Dukhān, Qatar 85 E6 25 25N 50 50 E
Dukhovshchina, Russia 50 D8 55 15N 32 27 E
Duki, Pakistan 79 C3 30 14N 68 25 E
Dukla, Poland 31 B14 49 30N 21 35 E
Duku, Bauchi, Nigeria 101 C7 10 43N 10 43 E
Duku, Sokoto, Nigeria 101 C5 11 11N 4 55 E
Dulag, Phil. 71 F5 10 57N 125 2 E
Dulce →, Argentina 158 C3 30 32 S 62 33W
Dulce, G., Costa Rica 148 E3 8 40N 83 20W
Dulf, Iraq 84 C5 35 7N 45 51 E
Dŭlgopol, Bulgaria 43 D12 43 3N 27 22 E
Duliu, China 66 E9 39 2N 116 55 E
Dullewala, Pakistan 80 D4 31 50N 71 25 E
Dülmen, Germany 26 D3 51 49N 7 18 E
Dulovo, Bulgaria 43 D12 43 48N 27 9 E
Dulq Maghār, Syria 84 B3 36 22N 38 39 E
Dululu, Australia 114 C5 23 48 S 150 15 E
Duluth, U.S.A. 138 B8 46 48N 92 10W
Dum Dum, India 81 H13 22 39N 88 33 E
Dum Hadjer, Chad 97 F3 13 18N 19 41 E
Dūmā, Lebanon 91 A4 34 12N 35 50 E
Dūmā, Syria 91 B5 33 34N 36 24 E
Dumaguete, Phil. 71 G4 9 17N 123 15 E
Dumai, Indonesia 74 B2 1 35N 101 28 E
Dumalinao, Phil. 71 H4 7 49N 123 23 E
Dumanguilas Bay, Phil. 71 H4 7 34N 123 4 E
Dumaran, Phil. 71 F2 10 33N 119 50 E
Dumas, Ark., U.S.A. 139 J9 33 52N 91 30W
Dumas, Tex., U.S.A. 139 H4 35 50N 101 58W
Dumbarton, U.K. 18 F4 55 58N 4 35W
Dumbea, N. Cal. 121 V20 22 10 S 166 27 E
Dumbleyung, Australia 113 F2 33 17 S 117 42 E
Dumbo, Angola 103 E3 14 6 S 17 24 E
Dumbrăveni, Romania 46 C5 46 14N 24 34 E
Dumfries, U.K. 18 F5 55 4N 3 37W
Dumfries & Galloway □, U.K. 18 F5 55 5N 4 0W
Dumingag, Phil. 71 G4 8 20N 123 20 E
Dumka, India 81 G12 24 12N 87 15 E
Dümmersee, Germany 26 C4 52 30N 8 21 E
Dumoine →, Canada 128 C4 46 13N 77 51W
Dumoine L., Canada 128 C4 46 55N 77 55W
Dumraon, India 81 G11 25 33N 84 8 E
Dumyât, Egypt 94 H7 31 24N 31 48 E
Dumyât, Masabb, Egypt 94 H7 31 28N 31 51 E
Dun Laoghaire, Ireland 19 C5 53 17N 6 9W
Dun-le-Palestel, France 24 B5 46 18N 1 39 E
Dun-sur-Auron, France 23 F9 46 53N 2 33 E
Duna →, Hungary 31 F11 45 51N 18 48 E
Dunaföldvár, Hungary 31 E11 46 50N 18 57 E
Dunaj →, Czech. 31 D11 47 50N 18 50 E
Dunajec →, Poland 31 A13 50 15N 20 44 E
Dunajska Streda, Czech. 31 D10 48 0N 17 37 E
Dunapatai, Hungary 31 E12 46 39N 19 4 E
Dunărea →, Romania 46 D10 45 20N 29 40 E
Dunaszekcsö, Hungary 31 E11 46 6N 18 45 E
Dunaújváros, Hungary 31 E11 47 0N 18 57 E
Dunav →, Serbia, Yug. 42 C6 44 47N 20 20 E
Dunavtsi, Bulgaria 42 D7 43 57N 22 53 E
Dunay, Russia 60 C6 42 52N 132 22 E
Dunback, N.Z. 119 F5 45 23 S 170 36 E
Dunbar, Australia 114 B3 16 0 S 142 22 E
Dunbar, U.K. 18 E6 56 0N 2 32W
Dunblane, U.K. 18 E5 56 10N 3 58W
Duncan, Canada 130 D4 48 45N 123 40W
Duncan, Ariz., U.S.A. 143 K9 32 46N 109 6W
Duncan, Okla., U.S.A. 139 H6 34 25N 98 0W
Duncan, L., Canada 128 B4 53 29N 77 58W
Duncan L., Canada 130 A6 62 51N 113 58W
Duncan Town, Bahamas 148 B4 22 15N 75 45W
Duncannon, U.S.A. 136 F7 40 23N 77 2W
Dundalk, Canada 136 B4 44 10N 80 24W
Dundalk, Ireland 19 B5 54 1N 6 25W
Dundalk Bay, Ireland 19 C5 53 55N 6 15W
Dundas, Canada 128 D4 43 17N 79 59W
Dundas, L., Australia 113 F3 32 35 S 121 50 E
Dundas I., Canada 130 C2 54 30N 130 50W
Dundas Str., Australia 112 B5 11 15 S 131 35 E
Dundee, S. Africa 105 D5 28 11 S 30 15 E
Dundee, U.K. 18 E6 56 29N 3 0W
Dundee, U.S.A. 141 C13 41 57N 83 40W
Dundgovĭ □, Mongolia 66 B4 45 10N 106 0 E
Dundoo, Australia 115 D3 27 40 S 144 37 E
Dundrum, U.K. 19 B6 54 17N 5 50W
Dundrum B., U.K. 19 B6 54 12N 5 40W
Dundwara, India 81 F8 27 48N 79 9 E
Dunedin, N.Z. 119 F5 45 50 S 170 33 E
Dunedin, U.S.A. 135 L4 28 1N 82 45W
Dunedin →, Canada 130 B4 59 30N 124 5W
Dunfermline, U.K. 18 E5 56 5N 3 28W
Dungannon, Canada 136 C3 43 51N 81 36W
Dungannon, U.K. 19 B5 54 30N 6 47W
Dungannon □, U.K. 19 B5 54 30N 6 55W
Dungarpur, India 80 H5 23 52N 73 45 E
Dungarvan, Ireland 19 D4 52 6N 7 40W
Dungarvan Bay, Ireland 19 D4 52 5N 7 35W
Dungeness, U.K. 17 G8 50 54N 0 59 E
Dungo, L. do, Angola 103 F3 17 15 S 19 0 E
Dungog, Australia 117 B9 32 22 S 151 46 E
Dungu, Zaïre 106 B2 3 40N 28 32 E
Dungunâb, Sudan 94 C4 21 10N 37 9 E
Dungunâb, Khalij, Sudan 94 C4 21 5N 37 12 E
Dunhinda Falls, Sri Lanka 83 L5 7 5N 81 6 E
Dunhua, China 67 C15 43 20N 128 14 E
Dunhuang, China 64 B4 40 8N 94 36 E
Dunières, France 25 C8 45 13N 4 20 E
Dunk I., Australia 114 B4 17 59 S 146 29 E
Dunkeld, Australia 116 D5 37 40 S 142 22 E
Dunkeld, U.K. 18 E5 56 34N 3 36W
Dunkerque, France 23 A9 51 2N 2 20 E
Dunkery Beacon, U.K. 17 F4 51 15N 3 37W
Dunkirk = Dunkerque, France 23 A9 51 2N 2 20 E
Dunkirk, U.S.A. 136 D5 42 30N 79 18W
Dunkuj, Sudan 95 E3 12 50N 32 49 E
Dunkwa, Central, Ghana 100 D4 6 0N 1 47W
Dunkwa, Central, Ghana 101 D4 5 30N 1 0W
Dunlap, U.S.A. 138 E7 41 50N 95 36W
Dúnleary = Dun Laoghaire, Ireland 19 C5 53 17N 6 9W
Dunmanus B., Ireland 19 E2 51 31N 9 50W
Dunmara, Australia 114 B1 16 42 S 133 25 E
Dunmore, U.S.A. 137 E9 41 27N 75 38W
Dunmore Hd., Ireland 19 D1 52 10N 10 35W
Dunmore Town, Bahamas 148 A4 25 30N 76 39W
Dunn, U.S.A. 135 H6 35 18N 78 36W
Dunnellon, U.S.A. 135 L4 29 4N 82 28W
Dunnet Hd., U.K. 18 C5 58 38N 3 22W
Dunning, U.S.A. 138 E4 41 52N 100 4W
Dunnville, Canada 136 D5 42 54N 79 36W
Dunolly, Australia 116 D5 36 51 S 143 44 E
Dunoon, U.K. 18 F4 55 57N 4 56W
Dunqul, Egypt 94 C3 23 26N 31 37 E
Duns, U.K. 18 F6 55 47N 2 20W
Dunseith, U.S.A. 138 A4 48 49N 100 2W
Dunsmuir, U.S.A. 142 F2 41 10N 122 18W
Dunstable, U.K. 17 F7 51 53N 0 31W
Dunstan Mts., N.Z. 119 E4 44 53 S 169 35 E
Dunster, Canada 130 C5 53 8N 119 50W
Duntroon, N.Z. 119 E5 44 51 S 170 40 E
Dunvegan L., Canada 131 A7 60 8N 107 10W
Duolun, China 66 C9 42 12N 116 28 E
Duong Dong, Vietnam 77 G4 10 13N 103 58 E
Dupax, Phil. 70 C3 16 17N 121 5 E
Dupree, U.S.A. 138 C4 45 4N 101 35W
Dupuyer, U.S.A. 142 B7 48 11N 112 31W
Duqm, Oman 87 C7 19 39N 57 42 E
Duque de Caxias, Brazil 155 F3 22 45 S 43 19W
Duque de York, I., Chile 160 D1 50 37 S 75 25W
Durack →, Australia 112 C4 15 33 S 127 52 E
Durack Ra., Australia 112 C4 16 50 S 127 40 E
Durağan, Turkey 88 C6 41 25N 35 3 E
Durance →, France 25 E8 43 55N 4 45 E
Durand, Ill., U.S.A. 140 B7 42 26N 89 20W
Durand, Mich., U.S.A. 141 B13 42 54N 83 58W
Durango = Victoria de Durango, Mexico 146 C4 24 3N 104 39W
Durango, Spain 34 B2 43 13N 2 40W
Durango, U.S.A. 143 H10 37 16N 107 50W
Durango □, Mexico 146 C4 25 0N 105 0W
Duranillin, Australia 113 F2 33 30 S 116 45 E
Durant, Iowa, U.S.A. 140 C6 41 36N 90 54W
Durant, Okla., U.S.A. 139 J6 34 0N 96 25W
Duratón →, Spain 36 D6 41 37N 4 7W
Durazno, Uruguay 158 C4 33 25 S 56 31W
Durazzo = Durrësi, Albania 44 C1 41 19N 19 28 E
Durban, France 24 F6 42 59N 2 49 E
Durban, S. Africa 105 D5 29 49 S 31 1 E
Durbo, Somali Rep. 108 B4 11 37N 50 20 E
Dúrcal, Spain 37 J7 37 0N 3 34W
Đurđevac, Croatia 42 A2 46 2N 17 3 E
Düren, Germany 26 E2 50 48N 6 30 E
Durg, India 82 D5 21 15N 81 22 E
Durgapur, India 81 H12 23 30N 87 20 E
Durham, Canada 128 D3 44 10N 80 49W
Durham, U.K. 16 C6 54 47N 1 34W
Durham, Calif., U.S.A. 144 F5 39 39N 121 48W
Durham, N.C., U.S.A. 135 G6 36 0N 78 55W
Durham □, U.K. 16 C6 54 42N 1 45W
Durham Downs, Australia 115 D4 26 6 S 149 5 E
Ḍurmā, Si. Arabia 86 A4 24 37N 46 8 E
Durness, U.K. 18 C4 58 34N 4 45W
Durrësi, Albania 44 C1 41 19N 19 28 E
Durrie, Australia 114 D3 25 40 S 140 15 E
Dursunbey, Turkey 88 D3 39 35N 28 37 E
Durtal, France 22 E6 47 40N 0 18W
Duru, Zaïre 106 B2 4 14N 28 50 E
D'Urville, Tanjung, Indonesia 73 B5 1 28 S 137 54 E
D'Urville I., N.Z. 119 A8 40 50 S 173 55 E
Duryea, U.S.A. 137 E9 41 20N 75 45W
Dusa Mareb, Somali Rep. 90 F4 5 30N 46 15 E
Dûsh, Egypt 94 C3 24 35N 30 41 E
Dushak, Turkmenistan 56 F7 37 13N 60 1 E
Dushan, China 68 E6 25 48N 107 30 E
Dushanbe, Tajikistan 55 D4 38 33N 68 48 E
Dusheti, Georgia 53 E11 42 10N 44 42 E
Dusky Sd., N.Z. 119 F1 45 47 S 166 30 E
Dussejour, C., Australia 112 B4 14 45 S 128 13 E
Düsseldorf, Germany 26 D2 51 15N 6 46 E
Dussen, Neths. 20 E5 51 44N 4 59 E
Duszniki-Zdrój, Poland 47 E3 50 24N 16 24 E
Dutch Harbor, U.S.A. 126 C3 53 54N 166 35W
Dutlwe, Botswana 104 C3 23 58 S 23 46 E
Dutsan Wai, Nigeria 101 C6 10 50N 8 10 E
Dutton, Canada 136 D3 42 39N 81 30W
Dutton →, Australia 114 C3 20 44 S 143 10 E
Duvan, Russia 54 D5 55 42N 57 54 E
Duved, Sweden 14 A6 63 24N 12 55 E
Duvno, Bos.-H., Yug. 42 D2 43 42N 17 13 E
Duyun, China 68 D6 26 18N 107 29 E
Düzce, Turkey 88 C4 40 50N 31 10 E
Duzdab = Zāhedān, Iran 85 D9 29 30N 60 50 E
Dve Mogili, Bulgaria 43 D10 43 35N 25 55 E
Dvina, Sev. →, Russia 48 B7 64 32N 40 30 E
Dvinsk = Daugavpils, Latvia 50 D5 55 53N 26 32 E
Dvinskaya Guba, Russia 48 B6 65 0N 39 0 E
Dvor, Croatia 39 C13 45 4N 16 22 E
Dvorce, Czech. 31 B10 49 50N 17 34 E
Dvur Králové, Czech. 30 A8 50 27N 15 50 E
Dwarka, India 80 H3 22 18N 69 8 E
Dwellingup, Australia 113 F2 32 43 S 116 4 E
Dwight, Canada 136 A5 45 20N 79 1W
Dwight, U.S.A. 141 C8 41 5N 88 25W
Dyakovskoya, Russia 51 A12 60 5N 41 12 E
Dyatkovo, Russia 50 E9 53 40N 34 27 E
Dyatlovo, Belorussia 50 E4 53 28N 25 28 E
Dyer, U.S.A. 141 G10 37 24N 86 13W
Dyer, C., Canada 127 B13 66 40N 61 0W
Dyer Plateau, Antarctica 7 D17 70 45 S 65 30W
Dyerbeldzhin, Kirghizia 55 C7 41 13N 74 54 E
Dyersburg, U.S.A. 139 G10 36 2N 89 20W
Dyersville, U.S.A. 140 B5 42 29N 91 8W
Dyfed □, U.K. 17 E3 52 0N 4 30W
Dyfi →, U.K. 17 E4 52 32N 4 0W
Dyje →, Czech. 31 C9 48 37N 16 56 E
Dyle →, Belgium 21 G5 50 58N 4 41 E
Dynevor Downs, Australia 115 D3 28 10 S 144 20 E
Dynów, Poland 31 B15 49 50N 22 11 E
Dysart, Canada 131 C8 50 57N 104 2W
Dyurtyuli, Russia 54 D4 55 9N 54 40 E
Dzamin Üüd, Mongolia 66 C6 43 50N 111 58 E
Dzerzhinsk, Belorussia 50 E5 53 40N 27 1 E
Dzerzhinsk, Russia 51 C13 56 14N 43 30 E
Dzhalal-Abad, Kirghizia 55 C6 40 56N 73 0 E
Dzhalinda, Russia 57 D13 53 26N 124 0 E
Dzhambeyty, Kazakhstan 53 A15 50 16N 52 35 E
Dzhambul, Kazakhstan 55 B5 42 54N 71 22 E
Dzhambul, Gora, Kazakhstan 55 A6 44 54N 73 0 E
Dzhankoi, Ukraine 52 D6 45 40N 34 20 E
Dzhanybek, Kazakhstan 53 B12 49 25N 46 50 E
Dzhardzhan, Russia 57 C13 68 10N 124 10 E
Dzharkurgan, Uzbekistan 55 E3 37 31N 67 25 E
Dzhelinde, Russia 57 C12 70 0N 114 20 E
Dzhetygara, Kazakhstan 54 E7 52 11N 61 12 E
Dzhetym, Khrebet, Kirghizia 55 C8 41 30N 77 0 E
Dzhezkazgan, Kazakhstan 56 E7 47 44N 67 40 E
Dzhikimde, Russia 57 D13 59 1N 121 47 E
Dzhizak, Uzbekistan 55 C3 40 6N 67 50 E
Dzhugdzur, Khrebet, Russia 57 D14 57 30N 138 0 E
Dzhuma, Uzbekistan 55 D3 39 42N 66 40 E
Dzhumgoltau, Khrebet, Kirghizia 55 B7 42 15N 74 30 E
Dzhungarskiye Vorota, Kazakhstan 64 B3 45 0N 82 0 E
Dzhvari, Georgia 53 E10 42 42N 42 4 E
Działdowo, Poland 47 B7 53 15N 20 15 E
Działoszyce, Poland 47 E7 50 22N 20 20 E
Działoszyn, Poland 47 D5 51 6N 18 50 E
Dzierzgoń, Poland 47 B6 53 58N 19 20 E
Dzierżoniów, Poland 47 E3 50 45N 16 39 E
Dzilam de Bravo, Mexico 147 C7 21 24N 88 53W
Dzioua, Algeria 99 B6 33 14N 5 14 E
Dziwnów, Poland 47 A1 54 2N 14 45 E
Dzungaria = Junggar Pendi, China 64 B3 44 30N 86 0 E
Dzungarian Gates = Dzhungarskiye Vorota, Kazakhstan 64 B3 45 0N 82 0 E
Dzuumod, Mongolia 64 B5 47 45N 106 58 E

194 Eabamet, L.

# E


Eabamet, L., Canada 128 B2 51 30N 87 46W
Eads, U.S.A. 138 F3 38 30N 102 46W
Eagle, U.S.A. 142 G10 39 39N 106 55W
Eagle →, Canada 129 B8 53 36N 57 26W
Eagle Butt, U.S.A. 138 C4 45 1N 101 12W
Eagle Cr. →, U.S.A. 141 F11 38 36N 85 4W
Eagle Grove, U.S.A. 140 B3 42 37N 93 53W
Eagle L., Calif., U.S.A. 142 F3 40 35N 120 50W
Eagle L., Maine, U.S.A. 129 C6 46 23N 69 22W
Eagle Lake, U.S.A. 139 L6 29 35N 96 21W
Eagle Mountain, U.S.A. 145 M11 33 52N 115 26W
Eagle Nest, U.S.A. 143 H11 36 33N 105 13W
Eagle Pass, U.S.A. 139 L4 28 45N 100 35W
Eagle Pk., U.S.A. 144 G7 38 10N 119 25W
Eagle Pt., Australia 112 C3 16 11 S 124 23 E
Eagle River, U.S.A. 138 C10 45 55N 89 17W
Eagleville, U.S.A. 140 D3 40 28N 93 59W
Ealing, U.K. 17 F7 51 30N 0 19W
Earaheedy, Australia 113 E3 25 34 S 121 29 E
Earl Grey, Canada 131 C8 50 57N 104 43W
Earle, U.S.A. 139 H9 35 18N 90 26W
Earlimart, U.S.A. 145 K7 35 53N 119 16W
Earlville, U.S.A. 141 C8 41 35N 88 55W
Earn →, U.K. 18 E5 56 20N 3 19W
Earn, L., U.K. 18 E4 56 23N 4 14W
Earnslaw, Mt., N.Z. 119 E3 44 32 S 168 27 E
Earth, U.S.A. 139 H3 34 18N 102 30W
Easley, U.S.A. 135 H4 34 52N 82 35W
East Angus, Canada 129 C5 45 30N 71 40W
East Aurora, U.S.A. 136 D6 42 46N 78 38W
East B., U.S.A. 139 L10 29 2N 89 16W
East Beskids = Vychodné Beskydy, Europe 31 B15 49 20N 22 0 E
East Brady, U.S.A. 136 F5 40 59N 79 36W
East C., N.Z. 118 D7 37 42 S 178 35 E
East C., Papua N. G. 120 F6 10 13 S 150 53 E
East Chicago, U.S.A. 141 C9 41 40N 87 30W
East China Sea, Asia 65 C7 30 5N 126 0 E
East Coast Bays, N.Z. 118 C3 36 46 S 174 46 E
East Coulee, Canada 130 C6 51 23N 112 27W
East Dubuque, U.S.A. 140 B6 42 29N 90 39W
East Falkland, Falk. Is. 160 D5 51 30 S 58 30W
East Grand Forks, U.S.A. 138 B6 47 55N 97 5W
East Greenwich, U.S.A. 137 E13 41 39N 71 27W
East Hartford, U.S.A. 137 E12 41 45N 72 39W
East Helena, U.S.A. 142 C8 46 37N 111 58W
East Indies, Asia 58 K15 0 0 120 0 E
East Jordan, U.S.A. 134 C3 45 10N 85 7W
East Lansing, U.S.A. 141 B12 42 44N 84 29W
East Liverpool, U.S.A. 136 F4 40 39N 80 35W
East London, S. Africa 105 E4 33 0 S 27 55 E
East Lynne, Australia 117 C9 35 35 S 150 16 E
East Main = Eastmain, Canada 128 B4 52 10N 78 30W
East Moline, U.S.A. 140 C6 41 31N 90 25W
East Orange, U.S.A. 137 F10 40 46N 74 13W
East Pacific Ridge, Pac. Oc. 123 J17 15 0 S 110 0W
East Pakistan = Bangladesh ■, Asia 78 C3 24 0N 90 0 E
East Palestine, U.S.A. 136 F4 40 50N 80 32W
East Peoria, U.S.A. 140 D7 40 40N 89 34W
East Pine, Canada 130 B4 55 48N 120 12W
East Pt., Canada 129 C7 46 27N 61 58W
East Point, U.S.A. 135 J3 33 40N 84 28W
East Providence, U.S.A. 137 E13 41 48N 71 22W
East Retford, U.K. 16 D7 53 19N 0 55W
East St. Louis, U.S.A. 140 F6 38 37N 90 4W
East Schelde → = Oosterschelde, Neths. 21 E4 51 33N 4 0 E
East Siberian Sea, Russia 57 B17 73 0N 160 0 E
East Stroudsburg, U.S.A. 137 E9 41 1N 75 11W
East Sussex □, U.K. 17 G8 51 0N 0 20 E
East Tawas, U.S.A. 134 C4 44 17N 83 31W
East Toorale, Australia 115 E4 30 27 S 145 28 E
East Troy, U.S.A. 141 B8 42 47N 88 24W
East Walker →, U.S.A. 144 G7 38 52N 119 10W
Eastbourne, N.Z. 118 H3 41 19 S 174 55 E
Eastbourne, U.K. 17 G8 50 46N 0 18 E
Eastend, Canada 131 D7 49 32N 108 50W
Easter Islands = Pascua, I. de, Pac. Oc. 123 K17 27 0 S 109 0W
Eastern □, Kenya 106 B4 0 0 38 30 E
Eastern □, Uganda 106 B3 1 50N 33 45 E
Eastern Cr. →, Australia 114 C3 20 40 S 141 35 E
Eastern Ghats, India 83 J4 14 0N 78 50 E
Eastern Group = Lau Group, Fiji 121 A3 17 0 S 178 30W
Eastern Group, Australia 113 F3 33 30 S 124 30 E
Eastern Province □, S. Leone 100 D2 8 15N 11 0W
Eastern Samar □, Phil. 71 F5 11 40N 125 40 E
Easterville, Canada 131 C9 53 8N 99 49W
Easthampton, U.S.A. 137 D12 42 15N 72 41W
Eastland, U.S.A. 139 J5 32 26N 98 45W
Eastleigh, U.K. 17 G6 50 58N 1 21W
Eastmain, Canada 128 B4 52 10N 78 30W
Eastmain →, Canada 128 B4 52 27N 78 26W
Eastman, Canada 137 A12 45 18N 72 19W
Eastman, Ga., U.S.A. 135 J4 32 13N 83 20W
Eastman, Wis., U.S.A. 140 A5 43 10N 91 1W
Easton, Md., U.S.A. 134 F7 38 47N 76 7W
Easton, Pa., U.S.A. 137 F9 40 41N 75 15W
Easton, Wash., U.S.A. 144 C5 47 14N 121 8W
Eastport, U.S.A. 129 D6 44 57N 67 0W
Eastsound, U.S.A. 144 B4 48 42N 122 55W
Eaton, Colo., U.S.A. 138 E2 40 35N 104 42W
Eaton, Ohio, U.S.A. 141 E12 39 45N 84 38W
Eaton Rapids, U.S.A. 141 B12 42 31N 84 39W
Eatonia, Canada 131 C7 51 13N 109 25W
Eatonton, U.S.A. 135 J4 33 22N 83 24W
Eatontown, U.S.A. 137 F10 40 18N 74 7W
Eatonville, U.S.A. 144 D4 46 52N 122 16W
Eau Claire, Fr. Guiana 153 C7 3 30N 53 40W
Eau Claire, U.S.A. 138 C9 44 46N 91 30W
Eauze, France 24 E4 43 53N 0 7 E
Ebagoola, Australia 114 A3 14 15 S 143 12 E
Eban, Nigeria 101 D5 9 40N 4 50 E
Ebangalakata, Zaïre 102 C4 0 29 S 21 29 E
Ebbw Vale, U.K. 17 F4 51 47N 3 12W
Ebebiyín, Eq. Guin. 102 B2 2 9N 11 20 E
Ebeggui, Algeria 99 C6 26 2N 6 0 E
Ebel, Gabon 102 B2 0 7N 11 5 E
Ebeltoft, Denmark 13 H11 56 12N 10 41 E
Ebensburg, U.S.A. 136 F6 40 29N 78 43W
Ebensee, Austria 30 D6 47 48N 13 46 E
Eber Gölü, Turkey 88 D4 38 38N 31 11 E
Eberbach, Germany 27 F4 49 27N 8 59 E
Eberswalde, Germany 26 C9 52 49N 13 50 E
Ebetsu, Japan 60 C10 43 7N 141 34 E
Ebian, China 68 C4 29 11N 103 13 E
Ebikon, Switz. 29 B6 47 5N 8 21 E
Ebingen, Germany 27 G5 48 13N 9 1 E
Ebino, Japan 62 E2 32 2N 130 48 E
Ebnat-Kappel, Switz. 29 B8 47 16N 9 7 E
Eboli, Italy 41 B8 40 39N 15 2 E
Ebolowa, Cameroon 101 E7 2 55N 11 10 E
Ebrach, Germany 27 F6 49 50N 10 30 E
Ébrié, Lagune, Ivory C. 100 D4 5 12N 4 26W
Ebro →, Spain 34 E5 40 43N 0 54 E
Ebro, Pantano del, Spain 36 B7 43 0N 3 58W
Ebstorf, Germany 26 B6 53 2N 10 23 E
Ecaussines-d' Enghien, Belgium 21 G4 50 35N 4 11 E
Eceabat, Turkey 44 D8 40 11N 26 21 E
Ech Cheliff, Algeria 99 A5 36 10N 1 20 E
Echallens, Switz. 28 C3 46 38N 6 38 E
Echeng, China 69 B10 30 23N 114 50 E
Echigo-Sammyaku, Japan 61 F9 36 50N 139 50 E
Echizen-Misaki, Japan 63 B7 35 59N 135 57 E
Echmiadzin, Armenia 53 F11 40 12N 44 19 E
Echo Bay, N.W.T., Canada 126 B8 66 5N 117 55W
Echo Bay, Ont., Canada 128 C3 46 29N 84 4W
Echoing →, Canada 131 B10 55 51N 92 5W
Echt, Neths. 21 F7 51 7N 5 52 E
Echternach, Lux. 21 J8 49 49N 6 25 E
Echuca, Australia 117 D6 36 10 S 144 20 E
Ecija, Spain 37 H5 37 30N 5 10W
Eckernförde, Germany 26 A5 54 26N 9 50 E
Eclipse Is., Australia 112 B4 13 54 S 126 19 E
Écommoy, France 22 E7 47 50N 0 17 E
Ecoporanga, Brazil 155 E3 18 23 S 40 50W
Écos, France 23 C8 49 9N 1 35 E
Écouché, France 22 D6 48 42N 0 10W
Ecuador ■, S. Amer. 152 D2 2 0 S 78 0W
Écueillé, France 22 E8 47 5N 1 21 E
Ed, Sweden 15 F5 58 55N 11 55 E
Ed Dabbura, Sudan 94 D3 17 40N 34 15 E
Ed Dâmer, Sudan 94 D3 17 27N 34 0 E
Ed Debba, Sudan 94 D3 18 0N 30 51 E
Ed-Déffa, Egypt 94 A2 30 40N 26 30 E
Ed Deim, Sudan 95 E2 10 10N 28 20 E
Ed Dueim, Sudan 95 E3 14 0N 32 10 E
Edah, Australia 113 E2 28 16 S 117 10 E
Edam, Canada 131 C7 53 11N 108 46W
Edam, Neths. 20 C6 52 31N 5 3 E
Edapally, India 83 J4 11 19N 78 3 E
Eday, U.K. 18 B6 59 11N 2 47W
Edd, Ethiopia 90 E3 14 0N 41 38 E
Eddrachillis B., U.K. 18 C3 58 16N 5 10W
Eddystone, U.K. 17 G3 50 11N 4 16W
Eddystone Pt., Australia 114 G4 40 59 S 148 20 E
Eddyville, U.S.A. 140 C4 41 9N 92 38W
Ede, Neths. 20 D7 52 4N 5 40 E
Ede, Nigeria 101 D5 7 45N 4 29 E
Édea, Cameroon 101 E7 3 51N 10 9 E
Edegem, Belgium 21 F4 51 10N 4 27 E
Edehon L., Canada 131 A9 60 25N 97 15W
Edekel, Adrar, Algeria 99 D6 23 56N 6 47 E
Eden, Australia 117 D8 37 3 S 149 55 E
Eden, N.C., U.S.A. 135 G6 36 29N 79 53W
Eden, N.Y., U.S.A. 136 D6 42 39N 78 55W
Eden, Tex., U.S.A. 139 K5 31 16N 99 50W
Eden, Wyo., U.S.A. 142 E9 42 2N 109 27W
Eden →, U.K. 16 C4 54 57N 3 2W
Eden L., Canada 131 B8 56 38N 100 15W
Edenburg, S. Africa 104 D4 29 43 S 25 58 E
Edendale, N.Z. 119 G3 46 19 S 168 48 E
Edendale, S. Africa 105 D5 29 39 S 30 18 E
Edenderry, Ireland 19 C4 53 21N 7 3W
Edenton, U.S.A. 135 G7 36 5N 76 36W
Edenville, S. Africa 105 D4 27 37 S 27 34 E
Eder →, Germany 26 D5 51 15N 9 25 E
Ederstausee, Germany 26 D4 51 11N 9 0 E
Edgar, U.S.A. 138 E5 40 25N 98 0W
Edgartown, U.S.A. 137 E14 41 22N 70 28W
Edge Hill, U.K. 17 E6 52 7N 1 28W
Edgecumbe, N.Z. 118 D5 37 59 S 176 47 E
Edgefield, U.S.A. 135 J5 33 50N 81 59W
Edgeley, U.S.A. 138 B5 46 27N 98 41W
Edgemont, U.S.A. 138 D3 43 15N 103 53W
Edgeøya, Svalbard 6 B9 77 45N 22 30 E
Edgerton, Ohio, U.S.A. 141 C12 41 27N 84 45W
Edgerton, Wis., U.S.A. 140 B7 42 50N 89 4W
Edgewood, U.S.A. 141 F8 38 55N 88 40W
Édhessa, Greece 44 D4 40 48N 22 5 E
Edievale, N.Z. 119 F4 45 49 S 169 22 E
Edina, Liberia 100 D2 6 0N 10 10W
Edina, U.S.A. 140 D4 40 6N 92 10W
Edinburg, Ill., U.S.A. 140 E7 39 39N 89 23W
Edinburg, Ind., U.S.A. 141 E11 39 21N 85 58W
Edinburg, Tex., U.S.A. 139 M5 26 22N 98 10W
Edinburgh, U.K. 18 F5 55 57N 3 12W
Edirne, Turkey 43 F11 41 40N 26 34 E
Edirne □, Turkey 88 C2 41 40N 26 30 E
Edison, U.S.A. 144 B4 48 33N 122 27W
Edithburgh, Australia 116 C2 35 5 S 137 43 E
Edjeleh, Algeria 99 C6 28 38N 9 50 E
Edjudina, Australia 113 E3 29 48 S 122 23 E
Edmeston, U.S.A. 137 D9 42 42N 75 15W
Edmond, U.S.A. 139 H6 35 37N 97 30W
Edmonds, U.S.A. 144 C4 47 47N 122 22W
Edmonton, Australia 114 B4 17 2 S 145 46 E
Edmonton, Canada 130 C6 53 30N 113 30W
Edmund L., Canada 131 C10 54 45N 93 17W
Edmundston, Canada 129 C6 47 23N 68 20W
Edna, U.S.A. 139 L6 29 0N 96 40W
Edna Bay, U.S.A. 130 B2 55 55N 133 40W
Edolo, Italy 38 B7 46 10N 10 21 E
Edremit, Turkey 88 D2 39 34N 27 0 E
Edremit Körfezi, Turkey 88 D2 39 30N 26 45 E
Edsbyn, Sweden 14 C9 61 23N 15 49 E
Edsele, Sweden 14 A10 63 25N 16 32 E
Edson, Canada 130 C5 53 35N 116 28W
Eduardo Castex, Argentina 158 D3 35 50 S 64 18W
Edward →, Australia 116 C5 35 5 S 143 30 E
Edward, L., Africa 106 C2 0 25 S 29 40 E
Edward I., Canada 128 C2 48 22N 88 37W
Edward River, Australia 114 A3 14 59 S 141 26 E
Edward VII Land, Antarctica 7 E13 80 0 S 150 0W
Edwards, U.S.A. 145 L9 34 55N 117 51W
Edwards →, U.S.A. 140 C6 41 10N 90 59W
Edwards Plateau, U.S.A. 139 K4 30 30N 101 5W
Edwardsburg, U.S.A. 141 C10 41 48N 86 6W
Edwardsport, U.S.A. 141 F9 38 49N 87 15W
Edwardsville, Ill., U.S.A. 140 F7 38 49N 89 57W
Edwardsville, Pa., U.S.A. 137 E9 41 15N 75 56W
Edzo, Canada 130 A5 62 49N 116 4W
Eefde, Neths. 20 D8 52 10N 6 13 E
Eekloo, Belgium 21 F3 51 11N 3 33 E
Eel →, Ind., U.S.A. 141 E10 39 7N 86 58W
Eel →, Ind., U.S.A. 141 D10 40 45N 86 22W
Eelde, Neths. 20 B9 53 8N 6 34 E
Eem →, Neths. 20 D6 52 16N 5 20 E
Eems →, Neths. 20 B9 53 26N 6 57 E
Eems Kanaal, Neths. 20 B9 53 18N 6 46 E
Eenrum, Neths. 20 B8 53 22N 6 28 E
Eernegem, Belgium 21 F2 51 8N 3 2 E
Eerste Valthermond, Neths. 20 C9 52 53N 6 58 E
Efate, I., Vanuatu 121 G6 17 40 S 168 25 E
Eferding, Austria 30 C7 48 18N 14 1 E
Eferi, Algeria 99 D6 24 30N 9 28 E
Effingham, U.S.A. 141 E8 39 8N 88 30W
Effretikon, Switz. 29 B7 47 25N 8 42 E
Eforie Sud, Romania 46 E9 44 1N 28 37 E
Ega →, Spain 34 C3 42 19N 1 55W
Égadi, Ísole, Italy 40 E5 37 55N 12 16 E
Eganville, Canada 128 C4 45 32N 77 5W
Egeland, U.S.A. 138 A5 48 42N 99 6W
Egenolf L., Canada 131 B9 59 3N 100 0W
Eger = Cheb, Czech. 30 A5 50 9N 12 28 E
Eger, Hungary 31 D13 47 53N 20 27 E
Eger →, Hungary 31 D13 47 38N 20 50 E
Egersund, Norway 13 G9 58 26N 6 1 E
Egg L., Canada 131 B7 55 5N 105 30W
Eggenburg, Austria 30 C8 48 38N 15 50 E
Eggenfelden, Germany 27 G8 48 24N 12 46 E
Eggiwil, Switz. 28 C5 46 52N 7 47 E
Egherta, Somali Rep. 108 D2 2 4N 43 11 E
Éghezée, Belgium 21 G5 50 35N 4 55 E
Eginbah, Australia 112 D2 20 53 S 119 47 E
Egito, Angola 103 E2 12 4 S 13 58 E
Égletons, France 24 C6 45 24N 2 3 E
Eglisau, Switz. 29 A7 47 35N 8 31 E
Egmond-aan-Zee, Neths. 20 C5 52 37N 4 38 E
Egmont, C., N.Z. 118 F2 39 16 S 173 45 E
Egmont, Mt., N.Z. 118 F3 39 17 S 174 5 E
Eğridir, Turkey 88 E4 37 52N 30 51 E
Eğridir Gölü, Turkey 88 E4 37 53N 30 50 E
Egtved, Denmark 15 J3 55 38N 9 18 E
Éguas →, Brazil 155 D3 13 26 S 44 14W
Egume, Nigeria 101 D6 7 30N 7 14 E
Éguzon, France 24 B5 46 27N 1 33 E
Egvekinot, Russia 57 C19 66 19N 179 50W
Egyek, Hungary 31 D13 47 39N 20 52 E
Egypt ■, Africa 94 J7 28 0N 31 0 E
Eha Amufu, Nigeria 101 D6 6 30N 7 46 E
Ehime □, Japan 62 D4 33 30N 132 40 E
Ehingen, Germany 27 G5 48 16N 9 43 E
Ehrenberg, U.S.A. 145 M12 33 36N 114 31W
Ehrwald, Austria 30 D3 47 24N 10 56 E
Eibar, Spain 34 B2 43 11N 2 28W
Eibergen, Neths. 20 D9 52 6N 6 39 E
Eichstätt, Germany 27 G7 48 53N 11 12 E
Eider →, Germany 26 A4 54 19N 8 58 E
Eidsvold, Australia 115 D5 25 25 S 151 12 E
Eidsvoll, Norway 13 F11 60 19N 11 14 E
Eifel, Germany 27 E2 50 10N 6 45 E
Eiffel Flats, Zimbabwe 107 F3 18 20 S 30 0 E
Eigg, U.K. 18 E2 56 54N 6 10W
Eighty Mile Beach, Australia 112 C3 19 30 S 120 40 E
Eil, Somali Rep. 90 F4 8 0N 49 50 E
Eil, L., U.K. 18 E3 56 50N 5 15W
Eildon, Australia 117 D6 37 14 S 145 55 E
Eildon, L., Australia 115 F4 37 10 S 146 0 E
Eileen L., Canada 131 A7 62 16N 107 37W
Eilenburg, Germany 26 D8 51 28N 12 38 E
Ein el Luweiqa, Sudan 95 E3 14 5N 33 50 E
Einasleigh, Australia 114 B3 18 32 S 144 5 E
Einasleigh →, Australia 114 B3 17 30 S 142 17 E
Einbeck, Germany 26 D5 51 48N 9 50 E
Eindhoven, Neths. 21 F6 51 26N 5 28 E
Einsiedeln, Switz. 29 B7 47 7N 8 46 E
Eire ■, Europe 19 D4 53 0N 8 0W
Eiríksjökull, Iceland 12 D3 64 46N 20 24W
Eirlandsche Gat, Neths. 20 B5 53 12N 4 54 E
Eirunepé, Brazil 156 B4 6 35 S 69 53W
Eisden, Belgium 21 G7 50 59N 5 42 E
Eisenach, Germany 26 E6 50 58N 10 18 E
Eisenberg, Germany 26 E7 50 59N 11 50 E
Eisenerz, Austria 30 D7 47 32N 14 54 E
Eisenhüttenstadt, Germany 26 C10 52 9N 14 41 E
Eisenkappel, Austria 30 E7 46 29N 14 36 E
Eisenstadt, Austria 31 D9 47 51N 16 31 E
Eiserfeld, Germany 26 E3 50 50N 7 59 E
Eisfeld, Germany 26 E6 50 25N 10 54 E
Eisleben, Germany 26 D7 51 31N 11 31 E
Ejby, Denmark 15 J3 55 25N 9 56 E
Eje, Sierra del, Spain 36 C4 42 24N 6 54W
Ejea de los Caballeros, Spain 34 C3 42 7N 1 9W
Ejutla, Mexico 147 D5 16 34N 96 44W
Ekalaka, U.S.A. 138 C2 45 55N 104 30W
Ekalla, Gabon 102 C2 1 27 S 14 0 E
Ekanga, Zaïre 102 C4 2 23 S 23 14 E
Ekawasaki, Japan 62 D4 33 13N 132 46 E
Ekeren, Belgium 21 F4 51 17N 4 25 E
Eket, Nigeria 101 E6 4 38N 7 56 E
Eketahuna, N.Z. 118 G4 40 38 S 175 43 E
Ekhínos, Greece 44 C7 41 16N 25 1 E
Ekibastuz, Kazakhstan 56 D8 51 50N 75 10 E
Ekimchan, Russia 57 D14 53 0N 133 0 E
Ekoli, Zaïre 102 C4 0 23 S 24 13 E
Eksel, Belgium 21 F6 51 9N 5 24 E
Ekwan →, Canada 128 B3 53 12N 82 15W
Ekwan Pt., Canada 128 B3 53 16N 82 7W
El Aaiún, W. Sahara 98 C2 27 9N 13 12W
El Aargub, Mauritania 98 D1 23 37N 15 52W
El Abiodh-Sidi-Cheikh, Algeria 99 B5 32 53N 0 31 E
El Adde, Somali Rep. 108 D3 2 35N 46 9 E
El 'Agrûd, Egypt 91 E3 30 14N 34 24 E
El Aïoun, Morocco 99 B4 34 33N 2 30W
El 'Aiyat, Egypt 94 J7 29 36N 31 15 E
El Alamein, Egypt 94 H6 30 48N 28 58 E
El Alto, Peru 156 A1 4 15 S 81 14W
El 'Aqaba, W. →, Egypt 91 E2 30 7N 33 54 E
El 'Arag, Egypt 94 B2 28 40N 26 20 E
El Arahal, Spain 37 H5 37 15N 5 33W
El Arenal, Spain 33 B9 39 30N 2 45 E
El Aricha, Algeria 99 B4 34 13N 1 10W
El Arīhā, Jordan 91 D4 31 52N 35 27 E
El Arish, Australia 114 B4 17 35 S 146 1 E
El 'Arîsh, Egypt 91 D2 31 8N 33 50 E
El 'Arîsh, W. →, Egypt 91 D2 31 8N 33 47 E
El Arrouch, Algeria 99 A6 36 37N 6 53 E
El Asnam = Ech Cheliff, Algeria 99 A5 36 10N 1 20 E
El Astillero, Spain 36 B7 43 24N 3 49W
El Badâri, Egypt 94 B3 27 4N 31 25 E
El Bahrein, Egypt 94 B2 28 30N 26 25 E
El Ballâs, Egypt 94 B3 26 2N 32 43 E
El Balyana, Egypt 94 B3 26 10N 32 3 E
El Banco, Colombia 152 B3 9 0N 73 58W
El Baqeir, Sudan 94 D3 18 40N 33 40 E
El Barco de Ávila, Spain 36 E5 40 21N 5 31W
El Barco de Valdeorras, Spain 36 C4 42 23N 6 58W
El Bauga, Sudan 94 D3 18 18N 33 52 E
El Baúl, Venezuela 152 B4 8 57N 68 17W
El Bawiti, Egypt 94 J6 28 25N 28 45 E
El Bayadh, Algeria 99 B5 33 40N 1 1 E
El Bierzo, Spain 36 C4 42 45N 6 30W
El Bluff, Nic. 148 D3 11 59N 83 40W
El Bolsón, Argentina 160 B2 41 55 S 71 30W
El Bonillo, Spain 35 G2 38 57N 2 35W
El Brûk, W. →, Egypt 91 E2 30 15N 33 50 E
El Buheirat □, Sudan 95 F2 7 0N 30 0 E
El Bur, Somali Rep. 108 D3 4 40N 46 37 E
El Caín, Argentina 160 B3 41 38 S 68 19W
El Cajon, U.S.A. 145 N10 32 49N 117 0W
El Callao, Venezuela 153 B5 7 18N 61 50W
El Camp, Spain 34 D6 41 5N 1 10 E
El Campo, U.S.A. 139 L6 29 10N 96 20W
El Carmen, Bolivia 157 C5 13 40 S 63 55W
El Carmen, Venezuela 152 C4 1 16N 66 52W
El Castillo, Spain 37 H4 37 41N 6 19W
El Centro, U.S.A. 145 N11 32 50N 115 40W
El Cerro, Bolivia 157 D5 17 30 S 61 40W
El Cerro, Spain 37 H4 37 45N 6 57W
El Cocuy, Colombia 152 B3 6 25N 72 27W
El Compadre, Mexico 145 N10 32 20N 116 14W
El Corcovado, Argentina 160 B2 43 25 S 71 35W
El Coronil, Spain 37 H5 37 5N 5 38W
El Cuy, Argentina 160 A3 39 55 S 68 25W
El Cuyo, Mexico 147 C7 21 30N 87 40W
El Dab'a, Egypt 94 H6 31 0N 28 27 E
El Daheir, Egypt 91 D3 31 13N 34 10 E
El Dambahaddo, Somali Rep. 108 D3 3 17N 46 40 E
El Deir, Egypt 94 B3 25 25N 32 20 E
El Dere, Ethiopia 108 C2 5 6N 43 5 E
El Dere, Somali Rep. 108 C3 5 22N 46 11 E
El Dere, Somali Rep. 90 G4 3 50N 47 8 E
El Descanso, Mexico 145 N10 32 12N 116 58W
El Desemboque, Mexico 146 A2 30 30N 112 57W
El Dilingat, Egypt 94 H7 30 50N 30 31 E
El Diviso, Colombia 152 C2 1 22N 78 14W
El Djem, Tunisia 96 A2 35 18N 10 42 E
El Djouf, Mauritania 92 D3 20 0N 9 0W
El Dorado, Ark., U.S.A. 139 J8 33 10N 92 40W
El Dorado, Kans., U.S.A. 139 G6 37 55N 96 56W
El Dorado, Venezuela 153 B5 6 55N 61 37W
El Eglab, Algeria 98 C4 26 20N 4 30W
El Escorial, Spain 36 E6 40 35N 4 7W
El Eulma, Algeria 99 A6 36 9N 5 42 E
El Faiyûm, Egypt 94 J7 29 19N 30 50 E
El Fâsher, Sudan 95 E2 13 33N 25 26 E
El Fashn, Egypt 94 J7 28 50N 30 54 E
El Ferrol, Spain 36 B2 43 29N 8 15W
El Fifi, Sudan 95 E1 10 4N 25 0 E
El Fud, Ethiopia 108 C2 7 15N 42 52 E
El Fuerte, Mexico 146 B3 26 30N 108 40W
El Gal, Somali Rep. 90 E5 10 58N 50 20 E
El Gebir, Sudan 95 E2 13 40N 29 40 E
El Gedida, Egypt 94 B2 25 40N 28 30 E
El Geteina, Sudan 95 E3 14 50N 32 27 E
El Gezira □, Sudan 95 E3 15 0N 33 0 E
El Gîza, Egypt 94 H7 30 0N 31 10 E
El Goléa, Algeria 99 B5 30 30N 2 50 E
El Guettar, Algeria 99 B5 34 5N 4 38 E
El Hadeb, W. Sahara 98 C2 25 51N 13 0W
El Hadjira, Algeria 99 B6 32 36N 5 30 E
El Hagiz, Sudan 95 D4 15 15N 35 50 E
El Hajeb, Morocco 98 B3 33 43N 5 13W
El Hammam, Egypt 94 H6 30 52N 29 25 E
El Hammâmi, Mauritania 98 D2 23 3N 11 30W
El Hamurre, Somali Rep. 108 C3 7 13N 48 54 E
El Hank, Mauritania 98 D3 24 30N 7 0W
El Harrach, Algeria 99 A5 36 45N 3 5 E
El Hasian, W. Sahara 98 C2 26 20N 14 0W
El Hawata, Sudan 95 E3 13 25N 34 42 E
El Heiz, Egypt 94 B2 27 50N 28 40 E
El 'Idisât, Egypt 94 B3 25 30N 32 35 E
El Iskandarîya, Egypt 94 H6 31 0N 30 0 E
El Jadida, Morocco 98 B3 33 11N 8 17W
El Jebelein, Sudan 95 E3 12 40N 32 55 E
El Kab, Sudan 94 D3 19 27N 32 46 E
El Kabrît, G., Egypt 91 F2 29 42N 33 16 E
El Kala, Algeria 99 A6 36 50N 8 30 E
El Kalâa, Morocco 98 B3 32 4N 7 27W
El Kamlin, Sudan 95 D3 15 3N 33 11 E
El Kantara, Algeria 99 A6 35 14N 5 45 E
El Kantara, Tunisia 96 B2 33 45N 10 58 E
El Karaba, Sudan 94 D3 18 32N 33 41 E
El Kef, Tunisia 96 A1 36 12N 8 47 E
El Khandaq, Sudan 94 D3 18 30N 30 30 E
El Khârga, Egypt 94 B3 25 30N 30 33 E
El Khartûm, Sudan 95 D3 15 31N 32 35 E
El Khartûm □, Sudan 95 D3 16 0N 33 0 E
El Khartûm Bahrî, Sudan 95 D3 15 40N 32 31 E
El Khroub, Algeria 99 A6 36 10N 6 55 E
El Kseur, Algeria 99 A5 36 46N 4 49 E
El Ksiba, Morocco 98 B3 32 45N 6 1W
El Kuntilla, Egypt 91 E3 30 1N 34 45 E
El Laqâwa, Sudan 95 E2 11 25N 29 1 E

Entrepeñas, Pantano de 195


El Laqeita, *Egypt* 94 B3 25 50N 33 15 E
El Leiya, *Sudan* 95 D4 16 15N 35 28 E
El Mafâza, *Sudan* 95 E3 13 38N 34 30 E
El Mahalla el Kubra, *Egypt* 94 H7 31 0N 31 0 E
El Mahârîq, *Egypt* 94 B3 25 35N 30 35 E
El Mahmûdîya, *Egypt* 94 H7 31 10N 30 32 E
El Maitén, *Argentina* 160 B2 42 3 S 71 10W
El Maiz, *Algeria* 99 C4 28 19N 0 9W
El-Maks el-Bahari, *Egypt* 94 C3 24 30N 30 40 E
El Manshâh, *Egypt* 94 B3 26 26N 31 50 E
El Mansour, *Algeria* 99 C4 27 47N 0 14W
El Mansûra, *Egypt* 94 H7 31 0N 31 19 E
El Mantico, *Venezuela* 153 B5 7 38N 62 45W
El Manzala, *Egypt* 94 H7 31 10N 31 50 E
El Marâgha, *Egypt* 94 B3 26 35N 31 10 E
El Masid, *Sudan* 95 D3 15 15N 33 0 E
El Matariya, *Egypt* 94 H8 31 15N 32 0 E
El Medano, *Canary Is.* 33 F3 28 3N 16 32W
El Meghaier, *Algeria* 99 B6 33 55N 5 58 E
El Meraguen, *Algeria* 99 C4 28 0N 0 7W
El Metemma, *Sudan* 95 D3 16 50N 33 10 E
El Miamo, *Venezuela* 153 B5 7 39N 61 46W
El Milagro, *Argentina* 158 C2 30 59 S 65 59W
El Milia, *Algeria* 99 A6 36 51N 6 13 E
El Minyâ, *Egypt* 94 J7 28 7N 30 33 E
El Molar, *Spain* 34 E1 40 42N 3 45W
El Mreyye, *Mauritania* 100 B3 18 0N 6 0W
El Nido, *Phil.* 71 F2 11 10N 119 25 E
El Obeid, *Sudan* 95 E3 13 8N 30 10 E
El Odaiya, *Sudan* 95 E2 12 8N 28 12 E
El Oro, *Mexico* 147 D4 19 48N 100 8W
El Oro □, *Ecuador* 152 D2 3 30 S 79 50W
El Oued, *Algeria* 99 B6 33 20N 6 58 E
El Palmar, *Bolivia* 157 D5 17 50 S 63 9W
El Palmar, *Venezuela* 153 B5 7 58N 61 53W
El Palmito, Presa, *Mexico* 146 B3 25 40N 105 30W
El Panadés, *Spain* 34 D6 41 10N 1 30 E
El Pardo, *Spain* 36 E7 40 31N 3 47W
El Paso, *Ill., U.S.A.* 140 D7 40 44N 89 1W
El Paso, *Tex., U.S.A.* 143 L10 31 50N 106 30W
El Paso Robles, *U.S.A.* 144 K6 35 38N 120 41W
El Pedernoso, *Spain* 35 F2 39 29N 2 45W
El Pedroso, *Spain* 37 H5 37 51N 5 45W
El Pobo de Dueñas, *Spain* 34 E3 40 46N 1 39W
El Portal, *U.S.A.* 144 H7 37 44N 119 49W
El Porvenir, *Mexico* 146 A3 31 15N 105 51W
El Prat de Llobregat, *Spain* 34 D7 41 18N 2 3 E
El Progreso, *Honduras* 148 C2 15 26N 87 51W
El Provencío, *Spain* 35 F2 39 23N 2 35W
El Pueblito, *Mexico* 146 B3 29 3N 105 4W
El Pueblo, *Canary Is.* 33 F2 28 36N 17 47W
El Qâhira, *Egypt* 94 H7 30 1N 31 14 E
El Qantara, *Egypt* 91 E1 30 51N 32 20 E
El Qasr, *Egypt* 94 B2 25 44N 28 42 E
El Quseima, *Egypt* 91 E3 30 40N 34 15 E
El Qusîya, *Egypt* 94 B3 27 29N 30 44 E
El Râshda, *Egypt* 94 B2 25 36N 28 57 E
El Reno, *U.S.A.* 139 H6 35 30N 98 0W
El Ribero, *Spain* 36 C2 42 30N 8 30W
El Rîdisiya, *Egypt* 94 C3 24 56N 32 51 E
El Rio, *U.S.A.* 145 L7 34 14N 119 10W
El Ronquillo, *Spain* 37 H4 37 44N 6 10W
El Roque, Pta., *Canary Is.* 33 F4 28 10N 15 25W
El Rosarito, *Mexico* 146 B2 28 38N 114 4W
El Rubio, *Spain* 37 H5 37 22N 5 0W
El Saff, *Egypt* 94 J7 29 34N 31 16 E
El Saheira, W. →, *Egypt* 91 E2 30 5N 33 25 E
El Salto, *Mexico* 146 C3 23 47N 105 22W
El Salvador ■, *Cent. Amer.* 148 D2 13 50N 89 0W
El Sancejo, *Spain* 37 H5 37 4N 5 6W
El Sauce, *Nic.* 148 D2 13 0N 86 40W
El Shallal, *Egypt* 94 C3 24 0N 32 53 E
El Simbillawein, *Egypt* 94 H7 30 48N 31 13 E
El Sombrero, *Venezuela* 152 B4 9 23N 67 3W
El Suweis, *Egypt* 94 J8 29 58N 32 31 E
El Tamarâni, W. →, *Egypt* 91 E3 30 7N 34 43 E
El Thamad, *Egypt* 91 F3 29 40N 34 28 E
El Tigre, *Venezuela* 153 B5 8 44N 64 15W
El Tîh, G., *Egypt* 91 F2 29 40N 33 50 E
El Tîna, Khalîg, *Egypt* 91 D1 31 10N 32 40 E
El Tocuyo, *Venezuela* 152 B4 9 47N 69 48W
El Tofo, *Chile* 158 B1 29 22 S 71 18W
El Tránsito, *Chile* 158 B1 28 52 S 70 17W
El Tûr, *Egypt* 94 J8 28 14N 33 36 E
El Turbio, *Argentina* 160 D2 51 45 S 72 5W
El Uinle, *Somali Rep.* 108 D2 3 4N 41 42 E
El Uqsur, *Egypt* 94 B3 25 41N 32 38 E
El Vado, *Spain* 34 D1 41 2N 3 18W
El Vallés, *Spain* 34 D7 41 35N 2 20 E
El Venado, *Mexico* 146 C4 22 56N 101 10W
El Vigía, *Venezuela* 152 B3 8 38N 71 39W
El Wabeira, *Egypt* 91 F2 29 34N 33 6 E
El Wak, *Kenya* 106 B5 2 49N 40 56 E
El Wak, *Somali Rep.* 108 D2 2 44N 41 1 E
El Waqf, *Egypt* 94 B3 25 45N 32 15 E
El Wâsta, *Egypt* 94 J7 29 19N 31 12 E
El Weguet, *Ethiopia* 95 F5 5 28N 42 17 E
El Wuz, *Sudan* 95 D3 15 5N 30 7 E
Elafónisos, *Greece* 45 H4 36 29N 22 56 E
Elaine, *Australia* 116 D6 37 44 S 144 2 E
Elamanchili, *India* 82 F6 17 33N 82 50 E
Elands, *Australia* 117 A10 31 37 S 152 20 E
Elandsvlei, *S. Africa* 104 E2 32 19 S 19 31 E
Élassa, *Greece* 45 J8 35 18N 26 21 E
Elassón, *Greece* 44 E4 39 53N 22 12 E
Elat, *Israel* 91 F3 29 30N 34 56 E
Eláthia, *Greece* 45 F4 38 37N 22 46 E
Elâzığ, *Turkey* 89 D8 38 37N 39 14 E
Elâzığ □, *Turkey* 89 D8 38 40N 39 15 E
Elba, *Italy* 38 F7 42 48N 10 15 E
Elba, *U.S.A.* 135 K2 31 27N 86 4W
Elbasani, *Albania* 44 C2 41 9N 20 9 E
Elbasani-Berati □, *Albania* 44 D2 40 58N 20 0 E
Elbe, *U.S.A.* 144 D4 46 45N 122 10W
Elbe →, *Europe* 26 B4 53 50N 9 0 E
Elbe-Seiten Kanal, *Germany* 26 C6 52 45N 10 32 E
Elberfeld, *U.S.A.* 141 F9 38 10N 87 27W
Elbert, Mt., *U.S.A.* 143 G10 39 5N 106 27W
Elberta, *U.S.A.* 134 C2 44 35N 86 14W
Elberton, *U.S.A.* 135 H4 34 7N 82 51W
Elbeuf, *France* 22 C8 49 17N 1 2 E
Elbing = Elbląg, *Poland* 47 A6 54 10N 19 25 E
Elbistan, *Turkey* 88 D7 38 12N 36 11 E
Elbląg, *Poland* 47 A6 54 10N 19 25 E
Elbląg □, *Poland* 47 A6 54 15N 19 30 E
Elbow, *Canada* 131 C7 51 7N 106 35W
Elbrus, *Asia* 53 E10 43 21N 42 30 E
Elburg, *Neths.* 20 D7 52 26N 5 50 E
Elburn, *U.S.A.* 141 C8 41 54N 88 28W
Elburz Mts. = Alborz, Reshteh-ye Kūhhā-ye, *Iran* 85 C7 36 0N 52 0 E
Elche, *Spain* 35 G4 38 15N 0 42W
Elche de la Sierra, *Spain* 35 G2 38 27N 2 3W
Elcho I., *Australia* 114 A2 11 55 S 135 45 E
Elda, *Spain* 35 G4 38 29N 0 47W
Eldon, *Mo., U.S.A.* 140 F4 38 20N 92 38W
Eldon, *Wash., U.S.A.* 144 C3 47 32N 123 4W
Eldora, *U.S.A.* 140 B3 42 20N 93 5W
Eldorado, *Argentina* 159 B5 26 28 S 54 43W
Eldorado, *Canada* 131 B7 59 35N 108 30W
Eldorado, *Mexico* 146 C3 24 20N 107 22W
Eldorado, *Ill., U.S.A.* 141 G8 37 50N 88 25W
Eldorado, *Tex., U.S.A.* 139 K4 30 52N 100 35W
Eldorado Springs, *U.S.A.* 139 G8 37 54N 93 59W
Eldoret, *Kenya* 106 B4 0 30N 35 17 E
Eldred, *U.S.A.* 136 E6 41 57N 78 24W
Eldridge, *U.S.A.* 140 C6 41 39N 90 35W
Elea, C., *Cyprus* 32 D13 35 19N 34 4 E
Electra, *U.S.A.* 139 H5 34 5N 99 0W
Elefantes →, *Mozam.* 105 C5 24 10 S 32 40 E
Elefantes, G., *Chile* 160 C2 46 28 S 73 49W
Elektrogorsk, *Russia* 51 D11 55 56N 38 50 E
Elektrostal, *Russia* 51 D11 55 41N 38 32 E
Elele, *Nigeria* 101 D6 5 5N 6 50 E
Elena, *Bulgaria* 43 E10 42 55N 25 53 E
Elephant Butte Res., *U.S.A.* 143 K10 33 45N 107 30W
Elephant I., *Antarctica* 7 C18 61 0 S 55 0W
Elephant Pass, *Sri Lanka* 83 K5 9 35N 80 25 E
Elesbão Veloso, *Brazil* 154 C3 6 13 S 42 8W
Eleshnitsa, *Bulgaria* 43 F8 41 52N 23 36 E
Eleşkirt, *Turkey* 89 D10 39 50N 42 50 E
Eleuthera, *Bahamas* 148 A4 25 0N 76 20W
Elevsís, *Greece* 45 F5 38 4N 23 26 E
Elevtheroúpolis, *Greece* 44 D6 40 52N 24 20 E
Elgepiggen, *Norway* 14 B5 62 10N 11 21 E
Elgeyo-Marakwet □, *Kenya* 106 B4 0 45N 35 30 E
Elgg, *Switz.* 29 B7 47 29N 8 52 E
Elgin, *N.B., Canada* 129 C6 45 48N 65 10W
Elgin, *Ont., Canada* 137 B8 44 36N 76 13W
Elgin, *U.K.* 18 D5 57 39N 3 20W
Elgin, *Ill., U.S.A.* 141 B8 42 5N 88 20W
Elgin, *N. Dak., U.S.A.* 138 B4 46 24N 101 46W
Elgin, *Nebr., U.S.A.* 138 E5 41 58N 98 3W
Elgin, *Nev., U.S.A.* 143 H6 37 21N 114 20W
Elgin, *Oreg., U.S.A.* 142 D5 45 37N 118 0W
Elgin, *Tex., U.S.A.* 139 K6 30 21N 97 22W
Elgon, Mt., *Africa* 106 B3 1 10N 34 30 E
Eliase, *Indonesia* 73 C4 8 21 S 130 48 E
Elida, *U.S.A.* 139 J3 33 56N 103 41W
Elikón, *Greece* 45 F4 38 18N 22 45 E
Elim, *S. Africa* 104 E2 34 35 S 19 45 E
Elin Pelin, *Bulgaria* 43 E8 42 40N 23 36 E
Elisabethville = Lubumbashi, *Zaïre* 107 E2 11 40 S 27 28 E
Eliseu Martins, *Brazil* 154 C3 8 13 S 43 42W
Elista, *Russia* 53 C11 46 16N 44 14 E
Elizabeth, *Australia* 116 C3 34 42 S 138 41 E
Elizabeth, *Ill., U.S.A.* 140 B6 42 19N 90 13W
Elizabeth, *N.J., U.S.A.* 137 F10 40 37N 74 12W
Elizabeth City, *U.S.A.* 135 G7 36 18N 76 16W
Elizabethton, *U.S.A.* 135 G4 36 20N 82 13W
Elizabethtown, *Ky., U.S.A.* 134 G3 37 40N 85 54W
Elizabethtown, *N.Y., U.S.A.* 137 B11 44 13N 73 36W
Elizabethtown, *Pa., U.S.A.* 137 F8 40 8N 76 36W
Elizondo, *Spain* 34 B3 43 12N 1 30W
Ełk, *Poland* 47 B9 53 50N 22 21 E
Ełk →, *Poland* 47 B9 53 41N 22 28 E
Elk City, *U.S.A.* 139 H5 35 25N 99 25W
Elk Creek, *U.S.A.* 144 F4 39 36N 122 32W
Elk Grove, *U.S.A.* 144 G5 38 25N 121 22W
Elk Island Nat. Park, *Canada* 130 C6 53 35N 112 59W
Elk Lake, *Canada* 128 C3 47 40N 80 25W
Elk Point, *Canada* 131 C6 53 54N 110 55W
Elk River, *Idaho, U.S.A.* 142 C5 46 50N 116 8W
Elk River, *Minn., U.S.A.* 138 C8 45 17N 93 34W
Elkader, *U.S.A.* 140 B5 42 51N 91 24W
Elkedra, *Australia* 114 C2 21 9 S 135 33 E
Elkedra →, *Australia* 114 C2 21 8 S 136 22 E
Elkhart, *Ind., U.S.A.* 141 C11 41 42N 85 55W
Elkhart, *Kans., U.S.A.* 139 G4 37 3N 101 54W
Elkhart →, *U.S.A.* 141 C11 41 41N 85 58W
Elkhorn, *Canada* 131 D8 49 59N 101 14W
Elkhorn, *U.S.A.* 141 B8 42 40N 88 33W
Elkhorn →, *U.S.A.* 138 E6 41 7N 96 15W
Elkhotovo, *Russia* 53 E11 43 19N 44 15 E
Elkhovo, *Bulgaria* 43 E11 42 10N 26 40 E
Elkin, *U.S.A.* 135 G5 36 17N 80 50W
Elkins, *U.S.A.* 134 F6 38 53N 79 53W
Elko, *Canada* 130 D5 49 20N 115 10W
Elko, *U.S.A.* 142 F6 40 50N 115 50W
Ell, L., *Australia* 113 E4 29 13 S 127 46 E
Ellecom, *Neths.* 20 D8 52 2N 6 6 E
Ellef Ringnes I., *Canada* 6 B2 78 30N 102 2W
Ellendale, *Australia* 112 C3 17 56 S 124 48 E
Ellendale, *U.S.A.* 138 B5 46 3N 98 30W
Ellensburg, *U.S.A.* 142 C3 47 0N 120 30W
Ellenville, *U.S.A.* 137 E10 41 42N 74 23W
Ellerston, *Australia* 117 A9 31 49 S 151 20 E
Ellery, Mt., *Australia* 117 D8 37 28 S 148 47 E
Ellesmere, L., *N.Z.* 119 H7 47 47 S 172 28 E
Ellesmere I., *Canada* 6 B4 79 30N 80 0W
Ellesmere Port, *U.K.* 16 D5 53 17N 2 55W
Ellettsville, *U.S.A.* 141 E10 39 14N 86 38W
Ellezelles, *Belgium* 21 G3 50 44N 3 42 E
Ellice Is. = Tuvalu ■, *Pac. Oc.* 122 H9 8 0 S 178 0 E
Ellinwood, *U.S.A.* 138 F5 38 27N 98 37W
Elliot, *Australia* 114 B1 17 33 S 133 32 E
Elliot, *S. Africa* 105 E4 31 22 S 27 48 E
Elliot Lake, *Canada* 128 C3 46 25N 82 35W
Elliotdale = Xhora, *S. Africa* 105 E4 31 55 S 28 38 E
Ellis, *U.S.A.* 138 F5 39 0N 99 39W
Elliston, *Australia* 115 E1 33 39 S 134 53 E
Ellisville, *U.S.A.* 139 K10 31 38N 89 12W
Ellon, *U.K.* 18 D6 57 21N 2 5W
Ellore = Eluru, *India* 82 F5 16 48N 81 8 E
Ells →, *Canada* 130 B6 57 18N 111 40W
Ellsworth, *U.S.A.* 138 F5 38 47N 98 15W
Ellsworth Land, *Antarctica* 7 D16 76 0 S 89 0W
Ellsworth Mts., *Antarctica* 7 D16 78 30 S 85 0W
Ellwangen, *Germany* 27 G6 48 57N 10 9 E
Ellwood City, *U.S.A.* 136 F4 40 52N 80 19W
Elm, *Switz.* 29 C8 46 54N 9 10 E
Elma, *Canada* 131 D9 49 52N 95 55W
Elma, *U.S.A.* 144 D3 47 0N 123 30W
Elmadağ, *Turkey* 88 D5 39 55N 33 14 E
Elmalı, *Turkey* 88 E3 36 44N 29 56 E
Elmer, *U.S.A.* 140 E4 39 57N 92 39W
Elmhurst, *U.S.A.* 141 C9 41 52N 87 58W
Elmina, *Ghana* 101 D4 5 5N 1 21W
Elmira, *Canada* 136 C4 43 36N 80 33W
Elmira, *U.S.A.* 136 D8 42 8N 76 49W
Elmore, *Australia* 116 D6 36 30 S 144 37 E
Elmore, *Calif., U.S.A.* 145 M11 33 7N 115 49W
Elmore, *Minn., U.S.A.* 141 C13 41 29N 83 18W
Elmshorn, *Germany* 26 B5 53 44N 9 40 E
Elmvale, *Canada* 136 B5 44 35N 79 52W
Elmwood, *U.S.A.* 140 D6 40 47N 90 0W
Elne, *France* 24 F6 42 36N 2 58 E
Elnora, *U.S.A.* 141 F9 38 53N 87 5W
Elora, *Canada* 136 C4 43 41N 80 26W
Elorza, *Venezuela* 152 B4 7 3N 69 31W
Elos, *Greece* 45 H4 36 46N 22 43 E
Eloúnda, *Greece* 32 D7 35 16N 25 42 E
Eloy, *U.S.A.* 143 K8 32 46N 111 33W
Éloyes, *France* 23 D13 48 6N 6 36 E
Elrose, *Canada* 131 C7 51 12N 108 0W
Elsas, *Canada* 128 C3 48 32N 82 55W
Elsie, *U.S.A.* 144 E3 45 52N 123 35W
Elsinore = Helsingør, *Denmark* 15 H6 56 2N 12 35 E
Elsinore, *Australia* 117 A6 31 35 S 145 11 E
Elsinore, *U.S.A.* 143 G7 38 40N 112 2W
Elspe, *Germany* 26 D4 51 10N 8 1 E
Elspeet, *Neths.* 20 D7 52 17N 5 48 E
Elst, *Neths.* 20 E7 51 55N 5 51 E
Elster →, *Germany* 26 D7 51 25N 11 57 E
Elsterwerda, *Germany* 26 D9 51 27N 13 32 E
Elten, *Neths.* 20 E8 51 52N 6 9 E
Eltham, *Australia* 117 D6 37 43 S 145 12 E
Eltham, *N.Z.* 118 F3 39 26 S 174 19 E
Elton, *Russia* 53 B12 49 5N 46 52 E
Eluanbi, *Taiwan* 69 G13 21 51N 120 50 E
Eluru, *India* 82 F5 16 48N 81 8 E
Elvas, *Portugal* 37 G3 38 50N 7 10W
Elven, *France* 22 E4 47 44N 2 36W
Elverum, *Norway* 14 D5 60 53N 11 34 E
Elvire →, *Australia* 112 C4 17 51 S 128 11 E
Elvo →, *Italy* 38 C5 45 23N 8 21 E
Elvran, *Norway* 14 A5 63 24N 11 3 E
Elwood, *Ill., U.S.A.* 141 C8 41 24N 88 7W
Elwood, *Ind., U.S.A.* 141 D11 40 20N 85 50W
Elwood, *Nebr., U.S.A.* 138 E5 40 38N 99 51W
Ely, *U.K.* 17 E8 52 24N 0 16 E
Ely, *Minn., U.S.A.* 138 B9 47 54N 91 52W
Ely, *Nev., U.S.A.* 142 G6 39 10N 114 50W
Elyria, *U.S.A.* 136 E2 41 22N 82 8W
Elyrus, *Greece* 45 J5 35 15N 23 45 E
Elz →, *Germany* 27 G3 48 21N 7 45 E
Emai, *Vanuatu* 121 G6 17 4 S 168 24 E
Emāmrūd, *Iran* 85 B7 36 30N 55 0 E
Emba, *Kazakhstan* 56 E6 48 50N 58 8 E
Emba →, *Kazakhstan* 49 E9 46 38N 53 14 E
Embarcación, *Argentina* 158 A3 23 10 S 64 0W
Embarras Portage, *Canada* 131 B6 58 27N 111 28W
Embarrass →, *U.S.A.* 141 F9 38 39N 87 37W
Embetsu, *Japan* 60 B10 44 44N 141 47 E
Embira →, *Brazil* 156 B3 7 19 S 70 15W
Embóna, *Greece* 32 C9 36 13N 27 51 E
Embrach, *Switz.* 29 A7 47 30N 8 36 E
Embrun, *France* 25 D10 44 34N 6 30 E
Embu, *Kenya* 106 C4 0 32 S 37 38 E
Embu □, *Kenya* 106 C4 0 30 S 37 35 E
Emden, *Germany* 26 B3 53 22N 7 12 E
Emerald, *Australia* 114 C4 23 32 S 148 10 E
Emerson, *Canada* 131 D9 49 0N 97 10W
Emery, *U.S.A.* 143 G8 38 59N 111 17W
Emet, *Turkey* 88 D3 39 20N 29 15 E
Emi Koussi, *Chad* 97 E3 19 45N 18 55 E
Emilia-Romagna □, *Italy* 38 D7 44 33N 10 40 E
Emilius, Mte., *Italy* 38 C4 45 41N 7 23 E
Eminabad, *Pakistan* 80 C6 32 2N 74 8 E
Emine, Nos, *Bulgaria* 43 E12 42 40N 27 56 E
Eminence, *U.S.A.* 141 F11 38 22N 85 11W
Emirdağ, *Turkey* 88 D4 39 2N 31 8 E
Emlenton, *U.S.A.* 136 E5 41 11N 79 41W
Emlichheim, *Germany* 26 C2 52 37N 6 51 E
Emme →, *Switz.* 28 B5 47 14N 7 32 E
Emmeloord, *Neths.* 20 C7 52 44N 5 46 E
Emmen, *Neths.* 20 C9 52 48N 6 57 E
Emmendingen, *Germany* 27 G3 48 7N 7 51 E
Emmental, *Switz.* 28 C4 46 55N 7 20 E
Emmer-Compascuum, *Neths.* 20 C10 52 49N 7 2 E
Emmerich, *Germany* 26 D2 51 50N 6 12 E
Emmet, *Australia* 114 C3 24 45 S 144 30 E
Emmetsburg, *U.S.A.* 140 A2 43 3N 94 40W
Emmett, *U.S.A.* 142 E5 43 51N 116 33W
Emöd, *Hungary* 31 D13 47 57N 20 47 E
Emona, *Bulgaria* 43 E12 42 43N 27 53 E
Empalme, *Mexico* 146 B2 28 1N 110 49W
Empangeni, *S. Africa* 105 D5 28 50 S 31 52 E
Empedrado, *Argentina* 158 B4 28 0 S 58 46W
Emperor Seamount Chain, *Pac. Oc.* 122 D9 40 0N 170 0 E
Empoli, *Italy* 38 E7 43 43N 10 57 E
Emporia, *Kans., U.S.A.* 138 F6 38 25N 96 10W
Emporia, *Va., U.S.A.* 135 G7 36 41N 77 32W
Emporium, *U.S.A.* 136 E6 41 30N 78 17W
Empress, *Canada* 131 C6 50 57N 110 0W
Emptinne, *Belgium* 21 H6 50 19N 5 8 E
Empty Quarter = Rub' al Khali, *Si. Arabia* 87 C5 18 0N 48 0 E
Ems →, *Germany* 26 B3 53 22N 7 15 E
Emsdale, *Canada* 136 A5 45 32N 79 19W
Emsdetten, *Germany* 26 C3 52 11N 7 31 E
Emu, *Australia* 116 D5 36 44 S 143 26 E
Emu, *China* 67 C15 43 40N 128 6 E
Emu Park, *Australia* 114 C5 23 13 S 150 50 E
'En 'Avrona, *Israel* 91 F3 29 43N 35 0 E
En Nahud, *Sudan* 95 E2 12 45N 28 25 E
Ena, *Japan* 63 B9 35 25N 137 25 E
Ena-San, *Japan* 63 B9 35 26N 137 36 E
Enafors, *Sweden* 14 A6 63 17N 12 20 E
Enambú, *Colombia* 152 C3 1 1N 70 17W
Enana, *Namibia* 104 B2 17 30 S 16 23 E
Enånger, *Sweden* 14 C11 61 30N 17 9 E
Enaratoli, *Indonesia* 73 B5 3 55 S 136 21 E
Enard B., *U.K.* 18 C3 58 5N 5 20W
Enare = Inarijärvi, *Finland* 12 B19 69 0N 28 0 E
Encantadas, Serra, *Brazil* 159 C5 30 40 S 53 0W
Encarnación, *Paraguay* 159 B4 27 15 S 55 50W
Encarnación de Diaz, *Mexico* 146 C4 21 30N 102 13W
Enchi, *Ghana* 100 D4 5 53N 2 48W
Encinal, *U.S.A.* 139 L5 28 3N 99 25W
Encinitas, *U.S.A.* 145 M9 33 3N 117 17W
Encino, *U.S.A.* 143 J11 34 38N 105 40W
Encontrados, *Venezuela* 152 B3 9 3N 72 14W
Encounter B., *Australia* 116 C3 35 45 S 138 45 E
Encruzilhada, *Brazil* 155 E3 15 31 S 40 54W
Ende, *Indonesia* 72 C2 8 45 S 121 40 E
Endeavour, *Canada* 131 C8 52 10N 102 39W
Endeavour Str., *Australia* 114 A3 10 45 S 142 0 E
Endelave, *Denmark* 15 J4 55 46N 10 18 E
Enderbury I., *Kiribati* 122 H10 3 8 S 171 5W
Enderby, *Canada* 130 C5 50 35N 119 10W
Enderby I., *Australia* 112 D2 20 35 S 116 30 E
Enderby Land, *Antarctica* 7 C5 66 0 S 53 0 E
Enderlin, *U.S.A.* 138 B6 46 37N 97 41W
Endicott, *N.Y., U.S.A.* 137 D8 42 6N 76 2W
Endicott, *Wash., U.S.A.* 142 C5 47 0N 117 45W
Endimari →, *Brazil* 156 B4 8 46 S 66 7W
Endröd, *Hungary* 31 E13 46 55N 20 47 E
Endyalgout I., *Australia* 112 B5 11 40 S 132 35 E
Ene →, *Peru* 156 C3 11 10 S 74 18W
Enewetak Atoll, *Pac. Oc.* 122 F8 11 30N 162 15 E
Enez, *Turkey* 44 D8 40 45N 26 5 E
Enfida, *Tunisia* 96 A2 36 6N 10 28 E
Enfield, *U.K.* 17 F7 51 39N 0 4W
Enfield, *U.S.A.* 141 F8 38 6N 88 20W
Engadin, *Switz.* 27 J6 46 45N 10 10 E
Engaño, C., *Dom. Rep.* 149 C6 18 30N 68 20W
Engaño, C., *Phil.* 70 B4 18 35N 122 23 E
Engcobo, *S. Africa* 105 E4 31 37 S 28 0 E
Engelberg, *Switz.* 29 C6 46 48N 8 26 E
Engels = Pokrovsk, *Russia* 51 F15 51 28N 46 6 E
Engemann L., *Canada* 131 B7 58 0N 106 55W
Enger, *Norway* 14 D4 60 35N 10 20 E
Enggano, *Indonesia* 74 D2 5 20 S 102 40 E
Enghien, *Belgium* 21 G4 50 37N 4 2 E
Engil, *Morocco* 98 B4 33 12N 4 32W
Engkilili, *Malaysia* 75 B4 1 3N 111 42 E
England, *U.S.A.* 139 H9 34 30N 91 58W
England □, *U.K.* 11 E5 53 0N 2 0W
Englee, *Canada* 129 B8 50 45N 56 5W
Englefield, *Australia* 116 D4 37 21 S 141 48 E
Englehart, *Canada* 128 C4 47 49N 79 52W
Engler L., *Canada* 131 B7 59 8N 106 52W
Englewood, *Colo., U.S.A.* 138 F2 39 40N 105 0W
Englewood, *Kans., U.S.A.* 139 G5 37 7N 99 59W
Englewood, *Ohio, U.S.A.* 141 E12 39 53N 84 18W
English, *U.S.A.* 141 F10 38 20N 86 28W
English →, *Canada* 131 C10 50 35N 93 30W
English →, *U.S.A.* 140 C5 41 29N 91 32W
English Bazar = Ingraj Bazar, *India* 81 G13 24 58N 88 10 E
English Channel, *Europe* 17 G6 50 0N 2 0W
English River, *Canada* 128 C1 49 14N 91 0W
Enid, *U.S.A.* 139 G6 36 26N 97 52W
Enipévs →, *Greece* 44 E4 39 22N 22 17 E
Enkhuizen, *Neths.* 20 C6 52 42N 5 17 E
Enköping, *Sweden* 14 E11 59 37N 17 4 E
Enle, *China* 68 E3 24 0N 101 9 E
Enna, *Italy* 41 E7 37 34N 14 15 E
Ennadai, *Canada* 131 A8 61 8N 100 53W
Ennadai L., *Canada* 131 A8 61 0N 101 0W
Ennedi, *Chad* 97 E4 17 15N 22 0 E
Enngonia, *Australia* 115 D4 29 21 S 145 50 E
Ennis, *Ireland* 19 D3 52 51N 8 59W
Ennis, *Mont., U.S.A.* 142 D8 45 20N 111 42W
Ennis, *Tex., U.S.A.* 139 J6 32 15N 96 40W
Enniscorthy, *Ireland* 19 D5 52 30N 6 35W
Enniskillen, *U.K.* 19 B4 54 20N 7 40W
Ennistimon, *Ireland* 19 D2 52 56N 9 18W
Enns, *Austria* 30 C7 48 12N 14 28 E
Enns →, *Austria* 30 C7 48 14N 14 32 E
Enontekiö, *Finland* 12 B17 68 23N 23 37 E
Enping, *China* 69 F9 22 16N 112 21 E
Enrekang, *Indonesia* 72 B1 3 34 S 119 47 E
Enrile, *Phil.* 70 C3 17 34N 121 42 E
Enriquillo, L., *Dom. Rep.* 149 C5 18 20N 72 5W
Ens, *Neths.* 20 C7 52 38N 5 50 E
Enschede, *Neths.* 20 D9 52 13N 6 53 E
Ensenada, *Argentina* 158 C4 34 55 S 57 55W
Ensenada, *Mexico* 146 A1 31 50N 116 50W
Enshi, *China* 68 B7 30 18N 109 29 E
Enshū-Nada, *Japan* 63 C9 34 27N 137 38 E
Ensiola, Pta., *Spain* 33 B9 39 7N 2 55 E
Ensisheim, *France* 23 E14 47 50N 7 20 E
Entebbe, *Uganda* 106 B3 0 4N 32 28 E
Enter, *Neths.* 20 D9 52 17N 6 35 E
Enterprise, *Canada* 130 A5 60 47N 115 45W
Enterprise, *Oreg., U.S.A.* 142 D5 45 30N 117 18W
Enterprise, *Utah, U.S.A.* 143 H7 37 37N 113 36W
Entlebuch, *Switz.* 28 C6 46 59N 8 4 E
Entre Ríos, *Bolivia* 158 A3 21 30 S 64 25W
Entre Rios, *Bahia, Brazil* 155 D4 11 56 S 38 5W
Entre Rios, *Pará, Brazil* 157 B7 5 24 S 54 21W
Entre Ríos □, *Argentina* 158 C4 30 30 S 58 30W
Entrepeñas, Pantano de, *Spain* 34 E2 40 34N 2 42W

Fiditi 197

# F


Fabens, U.S.A. 143 L10 31 30N 106 8W
Fåborg, Denmark 15 J4 55 6N 10 15 E
Fabriano, Italy 39 E9 43 20N 12 52 E
Făcăeni, Romania 46 E8 44 32N 27 53 E
Facatativá, Colombia 152 C3 4 49N 74 22W
Fachi, Niger 97 E2 18 6N 11 34 E
Facture, France 24 D3 44 39N 0 58W
Fada, Chad 97 E4 17 13N 21 34 E
Fada-n-Gourma, Burkina Faso 101 C5 12 10N 0 30 E
Fadd, Hungary 31 E11 46 28N 18 49 E
Faddeyevskiy, Ostrov, Russia 57 B15 76 0N 144 0 E
Fadghāmī, Syria 84 C4 35 53N 40 52 E
Fadlab, Sudan 94 D3 17 42N 34 2 E
Faenza, Italy 39 D8 44 17N 11 53 E
Fafa, Mali 101 B5 15 22N 0 48 E
Fafe, Portugal 36 D2 41 27N 8 11W
Faga, W. Samoa 121 W23 13 39 S 172 8W
Fagam, Nigeria 101 C7 11 1N 10 1 E
Fagamalo, W. Samoa 121 W23 13 25 S 172 21W
Făgăras, Romania 46 D5 45 48N 24 58 E
Făgăras, Munţii, Romania 46 D5 45 40N 24 40 E
Fågelsjö, Sweden 14 C8 61 50N 14 35 E
Fagernes, Norway 13 F10 60 59N 9 14 E
Fagersta, Sweden 13 F13 60 1N 15 46 E
Făget, Romania 46 D3 45 52N 22 10 E
Făget, Munţii, Romania 46 B4 47 40N 23 10 E
Fagnano, L., Argentina 160 D3 54 30 S 68 0W
Fagnano Castello, Italy 41 C9 39 31N 16 4 E
Fagnières, France 23 D11 48 58N 4 20 E
Fahlīān, Iran 85 D6 30 11N 51 28 E
Fahr, Yemen 87 D6 12 26N 54 8 E
Fahraj, Kermān, Iran 85 D8 29 0N 59 0 E
Fahraj, Yazd, Iran 85 D7 31 46N 54 36 E
Faial, Madeira 33 D3 32 47N 16 53W
Faido, Switz. 29 D7 46 29N 8 48 E
Fair Hd., U.K. 19 A5 55 14N 6 10W
Fair Oaks, U.S.A. 144 G5 38 39N 121 16W
Fairbank, U.S.A. 143 L8 31 44N 110 12W
Fairbanks, U.S.A. 126 B5 64 50N 147 50W
Fairborn, U.S.A. 141 E12 39 52N 84 2W
Fairbury, Ill., U.S.A. 141 D8 40 45N 88 31W
Fairbury, Nebr., U.S.A. 138 E6 40 5N 97 5W
Faire, Phil. 70 C3 17 53N 121 34 E
Fairfax, Ohio, U.S.A. 141 E13 39 5N 83 37W
Fairfax, Okla., U.S.A. 139 G6 36 37N 96 45W
Fairfield, Australia 117 B9 33 53 S 150 57 E
Fairfield, Ala., U.S.A. 135 J2 33 30N 87 0W
Fairfield, Calif., U.S.A. 144 G4 38 14N 122 1W
Fairfield, Conn., U.S.A. 137 E11 41 8N 73 16W
Fairfield, Idaho, U.S.A. 142 E6 43 21N 114 46W
Fairfield, Ill., U.S.A. 141 F8 38 20N 88 20W
Fairfield, Iowa, U.S.A. 140 C5 41 0N 91 58W
Fairfield, Mont., U.S.A. 142 C8 47 40N 112 0W
Fairfield, Ohio, U.S.A. 141 E12 39 21N 84 34W
Fairfield, Tex., U.S.A. 139 K7 31 40N 96 0W
Fairford, Canada 131 C9 51 37N 98 38W
Fairhope, U.S.A. 135 K2 30 35N 87 50W
Fairlie, N.Z. 119 E5 44 5 S 170 49 E
Fairmead, U.S.A. 144 H6 37 5N 120 10W
Fairmont, Minn., U.S.A. 138 D7 43 37N 94 30W
Fairmont, W. Va., U.S.A. 134 F5 39 29N 80 10W
Fairmount, U.S.A. 145 L8 34 45N 118 26W
Fairplay, U.S.A. 143 G11 39 9N 105 40W
Fairport, N.Y., U.S.A. 136 C7 43 8N 77 29W
Fairport, Ohio, U.S.A. 136 E3 41 45N 81 17W
Fairview, Australia 114 B3 15 31 S 144 17 E
Fairview, Canada 130 B5 56 5N 118 25W
Fairview, N. Dak., U.S.A. 138 B2 47 49N 104 7W
Fairview, Okla., U.S.A. 139 G5 36 19N 98 30W
Fairview, Utah, U.S.A. 142 G8 39 50N 111 0W
Fairweather, Mt., U.S.A. 126 C6 58 55N 137 45W
Faisalabad, Pakistan 79 C4 31 30N 73 5 E
Faith, U.S.A. 138 C3 45 2N 102 4W
Faizabad, India 81 F10 26 45N 82 10 E
Faizpur, India 82 D2 21 14N 75 49 E
Fajardo, Puerto Rico 149 C6 18 20N 65 39W
Fakam, Yemen 86 C3 16 38N 43 49 E
Fakfak, Indonesia 73 B4 3 0 S 132 15 E
Fakiya, Bulgaria 43 E12 42 10N 27 6 E
Fakobli, Ivory C. 100 D3 7 23N 7 23W
Fakse, Denmark 15 J6 55 15N 12 8 E
Fakse B., Denmark 15 J6 55 11N 12 15 E
Fakse Ladeplads, Denmark 15 J6 55 11N 12 9 E
Faku, China 67 C12 42 32N 123 21 E
Falaise, France 22 D6 48 54N 0 12W
Falaise, Mui, Vietnam 76 C5 19 6N 105 45 E
Falakrón Óros, Greece 44 C5 41 15N 23 58 E
Falam, Burma 78 D4 23 0N 93 45 E
Falces, Spain 34 C3 42 24N 1 48W
Fălciu, Romania 46 C9 46 17N 28 7 E
Falcón □, Venezuela 152 A4 11 0N 69 50W
Falcón, C., Spain 33 C7 38 50N 1 23 E
Falcon, C., Algeria 99 A4 35 50N 0 50W
Falcon Dam, U.S.A. 139 M5 26 50N 99 20W
Falconara Marittima, Italy 39 E10 43 37N 13 23 E
Falconer, U.S.A. 136 D5 42 7N 79 13W
Faléa, Mali 100 C2 12 16N 11 17W
Falelatai, W. Samoa 121 W24 13 55 S 171 59W
Falelima, W. Samoa 121 W23 13 32 S 172 41W
Falenki, Russia 54 B2 58 22N 51 35 E
Faleshty, Moldavia 52 C2 47 32N 27 44 E
Falfurrias, U.S.A. 139 M5 27 14N 98 8W
Falher, Canada 130 B5 55 44N 117 15W
Falirakí, Greece 32 C10 36 22N 28 12 E
Falkenberg, Germany 26 D9 51 34N 13 13 E
Falkenberg, Sweden 15 H6 56 54N 12 30 E
Falkensee, Germany 26 C9 52 35N 13 6 E
Falkenstein, Germany 26 E8 50 27N 12 24 E
Falkirk, U.K. 18 F5 56 0N 3 47W
Falkland, East, I., Falk. Is. 160 D5 51 40 S 58 30W
Falkland, West, I., Falk. Is. 160 D4 51 40 S 60 0W
Falkland Is., Atl. Oc. 160 D5 51 30 S 59 0W
Falkland Is. Dependency □, Atl. Oc. 7 B1 57 0 S 40 0W
Falkland Sd., Falk. Is. 160 D5 52 0 S 60 0W
Falkonéra, Greece 45 H5 36 50N 23 52 E
Falköping, Sweden 15 F7 58 12N 13 33 E
Fall River, U.S.A. 137 E13 41 45N 71 5W
Fall River Mills, U.S.A. 142 F3 41 1N 121 30W
Fallbrook, U.S.A. 143 K5 33 25N 117 12W
Fallbrook, U.S.A. 145 M9 33 23N 117 15W
Fallon, Mont., U.S.A. 138 B2 46 52N 105 8W
Fallon, Nev., U.S.A. 142 G4 39 31N 118 51W
Falls City, Nebr., U.S.A. 138 E7 40 5N 95 40W
Falls City, Oreg., U.S.A. 142 D2 44 54N 123 29W
Falls Creek, U.S.A. 136 E6 41 8N 78 49W
Falmouth, Jamaica 148 C4 18 30N 77 40W
Falmouth, U.K. 17 G2 50 9N 5 5W
Falmouth, U.S.A. 141 F12 38 40N 84 20W
False B., S. Africa 104 E2 34 15 S 18 40 E
False Divi Pt., India 83 G5 15 43N 80 50 E
Falset, Spain 34 D5 41 7N 0 50 E
Falso, C., Honduras 148 C3 15 12N 83 21W
Falster, Denmark 15 K5 54 45N 11 55 E
Falsterbo, Sweden 15 J6 55 23N 12 50 E
Fălticeni, Romania 46 B7 47 21N 26 20 E
Falun, Sweden 13 F13 60 37N 15 37 E
Famagusta, Cyprus 32 D12 35 8N 33 55 E
Famagusta Bay, Cyprus 32 D13 35 15N 34 0 E
Famatina, Sierra de, Argentina 158 B2 27 30 S 68 0W
Family L., Canada 131 C9 51 54N 95 27W
Famoso, U.S.A. 145 K7 35 37N 119 12W
Fan Xian, China 66 G8 35 55N 115 38 E
Fana, Mali 100 C3 13 0N 6 56W
Fanárion, Greece 44 E3 39 24N 21 47 E
Fandriana, Madag. 105 C8 20 14 S 47 21 E
Fang, Thailand 76 C2 19 55N 99 13 E
Fang Xian, China 69 A8 32 3N 110 40 E
Fangchang, China 69 B12 31 5N 118 4 E
Fangcheng, Guangxi Zhuangzu, China 68 G7 21 42N 108 21 E
Fangcheng, Henan, China 66 H7 33 18N 112 59 E
Fangliao, Taiwan 69 F13 22 22N 120 38 E
Fangshan, China 66 E6 38 3N 111 25 E
Fangzi, China 67 F10 36 33N 119 10 E
Fani i Madh →, Albania 44 C2 41 56N 20 16 E
Fanjiatun, China 67 C13 43 40N 125 15 E
Fannich, L., U.K. 18 D4 57 40N 5 0W
Fannūj, Iran 85 E8 26 35N 59 38 E
Fanny Bay, Canada 130 D4 49 37N 124 48W
Fanø, Denmark 15 J2 55 25N 8 25 E
Fano, Italy 39 E10 43 50N 13 0 E
Fanshaw, U.S.A. 130 B2 57 11N 133 30W
Fanshi, China 66 E7 39 12N 113 20 E
Fao = Al Fāw, Iraq 85 D6 30 0N 48 30 E
Faqirwali, Pakistan 80 E5 29 27N 73 0 E
Fara in Sabina, Italy 39 F9 42 13N 12 44 E
Farab, Turkmenistan 55 D1 39 9N 63 36 E
Faradje, Zaïre 106 B2 3 50N 29 45 E
Farafangana, Madag. 105 C8 22 49 S 47 50 E
Farâfra, El Wâhât el-, Egypt 94 B2 27 15N 28 20 E
Farāh, Afghan. 79 B1 32 20N 62 7 E
Farāh □, Afghan. 79 B1 32 25N 62 10 E
Farahalana, Madag. 105 A9 14 26 S 50 10 E
Faraid, Gebel, Egypt 94 C4 23 33N 35 19 E
Faramana, Burkina Faso 100 C4 11 56N 4 45W
Faranah, Guinea 100 C2 10 3N 10 45W
Farasān, Jazā'ir, Si. Arabia 86 C3 16 45N 41 55 E
Farasan Is. = Farasān, Jazā'ir, Si. Arabia 86 C3 16 45N 41 55 E
Faratsiho, Madag. 105 B8 19 24 S 46 57 E
Farbarachi, Somali Rep. 108 D3 2 30N 45 30 E
Fardes →, Spain 35 H1 37 35N 3 0W
Fareham, U.K. 17 G6 50 52N 1 11W
Farewell, C., N.Z. 119 A7 40 29 S 172 43 E
Farewell C. = Farvel, Kap, Greenland 124 D15 59 48N 43 55W
Farewell Spit, N.Z. 119 A8 40 35 S 173 0 E
Fargo, U.S.A. 138 B6 46 52N 96 40W
Fari'a →, Jordan 91 C4 32 12N 35 27 E
Faribault, U.S.A. 138 C8 44 15N 93 19W
Faridkot, India 80 D6 30 44N 74 45 E
Faridpur, Bangla. 78 D2 23 15N 89 55 E
Färila, Sweden 14 C9 61 48N 15 50 E
Farim, Guinea-Biss. 100 C1 12 27N 15 9W
Farīmān, Iran 85 C8 35 40N 59 49 E
Farina, Australia 115 E2 30 3 S 138 15 E
Farinha →, Brazil 154 C2 6 51 S 47 30W
Fariones, Pta., Canary Is. 33 E6 29 13N 13 28W
Fâriskûr, Egypt 94 H7 31 20N 31 43 E
Farmakonisi, Greece 45 G9 37 17N 27 8 E
Farmer City, U.S.A. 141 D8 40 15N 88 39W
Farmersburg, U.S.A. 141 E9 39 15N 87 23W
Farmerville, U.S.A. 139 J8 32 48N 92 23W
Farmington, Calif., U.S.A. 144 H6 37 56N 121 0W
Farmington, Ill., U.S.A. 140 D6 40 42N 90 0W
Farmington, Iowa, U.S.A. 140 D5 40 38N 91 44W
Farmington, Mo., U.S.A. 140 G6 37 47N 90 25W
Farmington, N.H., U.S.A. 137 C13 43 25N 71 7W
Farmington, N. Mex., U.S.A. 143 H9 36 45N 108 28W
Farmington, Utah, U.S.A. 142 F8 41 0N 111 12W
Farmington →, U.S.A. 137 E12 41 51N 72 38W
Farmland, U.S.A. 141 D11 40 15N 85 5W
Farmville, U.S.A. 134 G6 37 19N 78 22W
Farnborough, U.K. 17 F7 51 17N 0 46W
Farne Is., U.K. 16 B6 55 38N 1 37W
Farnham, Canada 137 A12 45 17N 72 59W
Faro, Brazil 153 D6 2 10 S 56 39W
Faro, Portugal 37 H3 37 2N 7 55W
Fårö, Sweden 13 H15 57 55N 19 5 E
Faro □, Portugal 37 H2 37 12N 8 10W
Faroe Is. = Føroyar, Atl. Oc. 8 B8 62 0N 7 0W
Farquhar, C., Australia 113 D1 23 50 S 113 36 E
Farquhar Is., Seychelles 109 F4 11 0 S 52 0 E
Farrars Cr. →, Australia 114 D3 25 35 S 140 43 E
Farrāshband, Iran 85 D7 28 57N 52 5 E
Farrell, U.S.A. 136 E4 41 13N 80 29W
Farrell Flat, Australia 116 B3 33 48 S 138 48 E
Farrokhī, Iran 85 C8 33 50N 59 31 E
Farruch, C., Spain 33 B10 39 47N 3 21 E
Farrukhabad-cum-Fatehgarh, India 81 F8 27 30N 79 32 E
Fārs □, Iran 85 D7 29 30N 55 0 E
Fársala, Greece 44 E4 39 17N 22 23 E
Fārsī, Afghan. 79 B1 33 47N 63 15 E
Farsø, Denmark 15 H3 56 46N 9 19 E
Farsund, Norway 13 G9 58 5N 6 55 E
Fartak, Râs, Si. Arabia 84 D2 28 5N 34 34 E
Fartak, Ra's, Yemen 87 D6 15 38N 52 15 E
Fartura, Serra da, Brazil 159 B5 26 21 S 52 52W
Faru, Nigeria 101 C6 12 48N 6 12 E
Fārūj, Iran 85 B8 37 14N 58 14 E
Farum, Denmark 15 J6 55 49N 12 21 E
Farvel, Kap, Greenland 124 D15 59 48N 43 55W
Farwell, U.S.A. 139 H3 34 25N 103 0W
Fāryāb □, Afghan. 79 B2 36 0N 65 0 E
Fasā, Iran 85 D7 29 0N 53 39 E
Fasano, Italy 41 B10 40 50N 17 20 E
Fashoda, Sudan 95 F3 9 50N 32 2 E
Fastnet Rock, Ireland 19 E2 51 22N 9 37W
Fastov, Ukraine 50 F6 50 7N 29 57 E
Fatagar, Tanjung, Indonesia 73 B4 2 46 S 131 57 E
Fatehgarh, India 81 F8 27 25N 79 35 E
Fatehpur, Raj., India 80 F6 28 0N 74 40 E
Fatehpur, Ut. P., India 81 G9 25 56N 81 13 E
Fatesh, Russia 51 E9 52 8N 35 57 E
Fatick, Senegal 100 C1 14 19N 16 27W
Fatima, Canada 129 C7 47 24N 61 53W
Fátima, Portugal 37 F2 39 37N 8 39W
Fatoya, Guinea 100 C3 11 37N 9 10W
Faucille, Col de la, France 25 B10 46 22N 6 2 E
Faulkton, U.S.A. 138 C5 45 4N 99 8W
Faulquemont, France 23 C13 49 3N 6 36 E
Fauquembergues, France 23 B9 50 36N 2 5 E
Faure I., Australia 113 E1 25 52 S 113 50 E
Făurei, Romania 46 D8 45 6N 27 19 E
Fauresmith, S. Africa 104 D4 29 44 S 25 17 E
Fauro, Solomon Is. 121 L9 6 55 S 156 7 E
Fauske, Norway 12 C13 67 17N 15 25 E
Fauvillers, Belgium 21 J7 49 51N 5 40 E
Favara, Italy 40 E6 37 19N 13 39 E
Favaritx, C., Spain 33 A11 40 0N 4 15 E
Favignana, Italy 40 E5 37 56N 12 18 E
Favignana, I., Italy 40 E5 37 56N 12 18 E
Favourable Lake, Canada 128 B1 52 50N 93 39W
Fawn →, Canada 128 A2 55 20N 87 35W
Fawnskin, U.S.A. 145 L10 34 16N 116 56W
Faxaflói, Iceland 12 D2 64 29N 23 0W
Faya-Largeau, Chad 97 E3 17 58N 19 6 E
Fayaoué, Vanuatu 121 K4 20 38 S 166 33 E
Fayd, Si. Arabia 84 E4 27 1N 42 52 E
Fayence, France 25 E10 43 38N 6 42 E
Fayette, Ala., U.S.A. 135 J2 33 40N 87 50W
Fayette, Iowa, U.S.A. 140 B5 42 51N 91 48W
Fayette, Mo., U.S.A. 140 E4 39 10N 92 40W
Fayette, Ohio, U.S.A. 141 C12 41 40N 84 20W
Fayetteville, Ark., U.S.A. 139 G7 36 5N 94 5W
Fayetteville, N.C., U.S.A. 135 H6 35 0N 78 58W
Fayetteville, Tenn., U.S.A. 135 H2 35 8N 86 30W
Fayón, Spain 34 D5 41 15N 0 20 E
Fazenda Libongo, Angola 103 D2 8 24 S 13 24 E
Fazenda Nova, Brazil 155 E1 16 11 S 50 48W
Fazilka, India 80 D6 30 27N 74 2 E
Fazilpur, Pakistan 80 E4 29 18N 70 29 E
Fdérik, Mauritania 98 D2 22 40N 12 45W
Feale →, Ireland 19 D2 52 26N 9 40W
Fear, C., U.S.A. 135 J7 33 51N 78 0W
Feather →, U.S.A. 142 G3 38 47N 121 36W
Feather Falls, U.S.A. 144 F5 39 36N 121 16W
Featherston, N.Z. 118 H4 41 6 S 175 20 E
Featherstone, Zimbabwe 107 F3 18 42 S 30 55 E
Fécamp, France 22 C7 49 45N 0 22 E
Fedala = Mohammedia, Morocco 98 B3 33 44N 7 21W
Federación, Argentina 158 C4 31 0 S 57 55W
Fedeshkūh, Iran 85 D7 28 49N 53 50 E
Fedjadj, Chott el, Tunisia 96 B1 33 52N 9 14 E
Fedorovka, Kazakhstan 54 E8 53 38N 62 42 E
Fehérgyarmat, Hungary 31 D15 48 0N 22 30 E
Fehmarn, Germany 26 A7 54 26N 11 10 E
Fehmarn Bælt, Denmark 26 A7 54 35N 11 20 E
Fei Xian, China 67 G9 35 18N 117 59 E
Feijó, Brazil 156 B3 8 9S 70 21W
Feilding, N.Z. 118 G4 40 13 S 175 35 E
Feira de Santana, Brazil 155 D4 12 15 S 38 57W
Feixiang, China 66 F8 36 30N 114 45 E
Fejér □, Hungary 31 D11 47 9N 18 30 E
Fejø, Denmark 15 K5 54 55N 11 30 E
Feke, Turkey 88 E6 37 48N 35 56 E
Fekete →, Hungary 31 F11 45 47N 18 15 E
Felanitx, Spain 33 B10 39 28N 3 9 E
Feldbach, Austria 30 E8 46 57N 15 52 E
Feldberg, Baden-W., Germany 27 H3 47 51N 7 58 E
Feldberg, Mecklenburg-Vorpommern, Germany 26 B9 53 20N 13 26 E
Feldkirch, Austria 30 D2 47 15N 9 37 E
Feldkirchen, Austria 30 E7 46 44N 14 6 E
Felicity, U.S.A. 141 F12 38 51N 84 6W
Felipe Carrillo Puerto, Mexico 147 D7 19 38N 88 3W
Felixlândia, Brazil 155 E3 18 47 S 44 55W
Felixstowe, U.K. 17 F9 51 58N 1 22 E
Felletin, France 24 C6 45 53N 2 11 E
Felton, U.K. 16 B6 55 18N 1 42W
Felton, U.S.A. 144 H4 37 3N 122 4W
Feltre, Italy 39 B8 46 1N 11 55 E
Femø, Denmark 15 K5 54 58N 11 53 E
Femunden, Norway 14 B5 62 10N 11 53 E
Fen He →, China 66 G6 35 36N 110 42 E
Fenelon Falls, Canada 136 B6 44 32N 78 45W
Feneroa, Ethiopia 95 E4 13 5N 39 3 E
Feng Xian, Jiangsu, China 66 G9 34 43N 116 35 E
Feng Xian, Shaanxi, China 66 H4 33 54N 106 40 E
Fengári, Greece 44 D7 40 25N 25 32 E
Fengcheng, Jiangxi, China 69 C10 28 12N 115 48 E
Fengcheng, Liaoning, China 67 D13 40 28N 124 5 E
Fengdu, China 68 C6 29 55N 107 41 E
Fengfeng, China 66 F8 36 28N 114 8 E
Fenggang, China 68 D6 27 57N 107 47 E
Fenghua, China 69 C13 29 40N 121 25 E
Fenghuang, China 68 D7 27 57N 109 29 E
Fenghuangzui, China 68 A7 33 30N 109 23 E
Fengjie, China 68 B7 31 5N 109 36 E
Fengkai, China 69 F8 23 24N 111 30 E
Fengle, China 69 B9 31 29N 112 29 E
Fengning, China 66 D9 41 10N 116 33 E
Fengqing, China 68 E2 24 38N 99 55 E
Fengqiu, China 66 G8 35 2N 114 25 E
Fengrun, China 67 E10 39 48N 118 8 E
Fengshan, Guangxi Zhuangzu, China 68 E7 24 39N 109 15 E
Fengshan, Guangxi Zhuangzu, China 68 E6 24 31N 107 3 E
Fengtai, Anhui, China 69 A11 32 50N 116 40 E
Fengtai, Beijing, China 66 E9 39 50N 116 18 E
Fengxian, China 69 B13 30 55N 121 26 E
Fengxiang, China 66 G4 34 29N 107 25 E
Fengxin, China 69 C10 28 41N 115 18 E
Fengyang, China 67 H9 32 51N 117 29 E
Fengyi, China 68 E3 25 37N 100 20 E
Fengzhen, China 66 D7 40 25N 113 2 E
Feni Is., Papua N. G. 120 C7 4 0 S 153 40 E
Fenit, Ireland 19 D2 52 17N 9 51W
Fennimore, U.S.A. 140 B6 42 58N 90 41W
Fenny, Bangla. 78 D3 22 55N 91 32 E
Feno, C. de, France 25 G12 41 58N 8 33 E
Fenoarivo Afovoany, Madag. 105 B8 18 26 S 46 34 E
Fenoarivo Atsinanana, Madag. 105 B8 17 22 S 49 25 E
Fens, The, U.K. 16 E8 52 45N 0 2 E
Fenton, U.S.A. 141 B13 42 47N 83 44W
Fenxi, China 66 F6 36 40N 111 31 E
Fenyang, China 65 C6 37 19N 111 48 E
Fenyang, Shanxi, China 66 F6 37 18N 111 48 E
Fenyi, China 69 D10 27 45N 114 47 E
Feodosiya, Ukraine 52 D6 45 2N 35 16 E
Fer, C. de, Algeria 99 A6 37 3N 7 10 E
Ferdows, Iran 85 C8 33 58N 58 2 E
Fère-Champenoise, France 23 D10 48 45N 3 59 E
Fère-en-Tardenois, France 23 C10 49 10N 3 30 E
Ferentino, Italy 40 A6 41 42N 13 14 E
Ferfer, Somali Rep. 90 F4 5 4N 45 9 E
Fergana, Uzbekistan 55 C5 40 23N 71 19 E
Ferganskaya Dolina, Uzbekistan 55 C5 40 50N 71 30 E
Ferganskiy Khrebet, Kirghizia 55 C6 41 0N 73 50 E
Fergus, Canada 128 D3 43 43N 80 24W
Fergus Falls, U.S.A. 138 B6 46 18N 96 7W
Ferguson, U.S.A. 140 F6 38 45N 90 18W
Fergusson I., Papua N. G. 120 E6 9 30 S 150 45 E
Fériana, Tunisia 96 B1 34 59N 8 33 E
Feričanci, Croatia 42 B3 45 32N 18 0 E
Ferkane, Algeria 99 B6 34 37N 7 26 E
Ferkéssédougou, Ivory C. 100 D3 9 35N 5 6W
Ferlach, Austria 30 E7 46 32N 14 18 E
Ferland, Canada 128 B2 50 19N 88 27W
Ferlo, Vallée du, Senegal 100 B2 15 15N 14 15W
Fermanagh □, U.K. 19 B4 54 21N 7 40W
Fermo, Italy 39 E10 43 10N 13 42 E
Fermoselle, Spain 36 D4 41 19N 6 27W
Fermoy, Ireland 19 D3 52 4N 8 18W
Fernán Nuñéz, Spain 37 H6 37 40N 4 44W
Fernández, Argentina 158 B3 27 55 S 63 50W
Fernandina Beach, U.S.A. 135 K5 30 40N 81 30W
Fernando de Noronha, Brazil 154 B5 4 0 S 33 10W
Fernando Póo = Bioko, Eq. Guin. 101 E6 3 30N 8 40 E
Fernandópolis, Brazil 155 F1 20 16 S 50 14W
Ferndale, Calif., U.S.A. 142 F1 40 37N 124 12W
Ferndale, Wash., U.S.A. 144 B4 48 51N 122 41W
Fernie, Canada 130 D5 49 30N 115 5W
Fernlees, Australia 114 C4 23 51 S 148 7 E
Fernley, U.S.A. 142 G4 39 36N 119 14W
Feroke, India 83 J2 11 9N 75 46 E
Ferozepore = Firozpur, India 80 D6 30 55N 74 40 E
Férrai, Greece 44 D8 40 53N 26 10 E
Ferrandina, Italy 41 B9 40 30N 16 28 E
Ferrara, Italy 39 D8 44 50N 11 36 E
Ferrato, C., Italy 40 C2 39 18N 9 39 E
Ferreira do Alentejo, Portugal 37 G2 38 4N 8 6W
Ferreñafe, Peru 156 B2 6 42 S 79 50W
Ferrerías, Spain 33 B11 39 59N 4 1 E
Ferret, C., France 24 D2 44 38N 1 15W
Ferrette, France 23 E14 47 30N 7 20 E
Ferriday, U.S.A. 139 K9 31 35N 91 33W
Ferrières, France 23 D9 48 5N 2 48 E
Ferriete, Italy 38 D6 44 40N 9 30 E
Ferrol, Pen. de, Peru 156 B2 9 10 S 78 35W
Ferron, U.S.A. 143 G8 39 3N 111 3W
Ferros, Brazil 155 E3 19 14 S 43 2W
Ferryland, Canada 129 C9 47 2N 52 53W
Ferrysburg, U.S.A. 141 A10 43 5N 86 13W
Fertile, U.S.A. 138 B6 47 31N 96 18W
Fertília, Italy 40 B1 40 37N 8 13 E
Fertöszentmiklós, Hungary 31 D9 47 35N 16 53 E
Fès, Morocco 98 B4 34 0N 5 0W
Feschaux, Belgium 21 H5 50 9N 4 54 E
Feshi, Zaïre 103 D3 6 8 S 18 10 E
Fessenden, U.S.A. 138 B5 47 42N 99 38W
Festus, U.S.A. 140 F6 38 13N 90 24W
Feteşti, Romania 46 E8 44 22N 27 51 E
Fethiye, Turkey 88 E3 36 36N 29 10 E
Fetlar, U.K. 18 A8 60 36N 0 52W
Feuerthalen, Switz. 29 A7 47 37N 8 38 E
Feuilles →, Canada 127 C12 58 47N 70 4W
Feurs, France 25 C8 45 45N 4 13 E
Feyzābād, Badākhshān, Afghan. 79 A3 37 7N 70 33 E
Feyzābād, Fāryāb, Afghan. 79 A2 36 17N 64 52 E
Fezzan, Libya 92 D5 27 0N 15 0 E
Ffestiniog, U.K. 16 E4 52 58N 3 56W
Fiambalá, Argentina 158 B2 27 45 S 67 37W
Fianarantsoa, Madag. 105 C8 21 26 S 47 5 E
Fianarantsoa □, Madag. 105 B8 19 30 S 47 0 E
Fianga, Cameroon 97 G3 9 55N 15 9 E
Fibiş, Romania 46 D2 45 57N 21 26 E
Fichtelgebirge, Germany 27 E7 50 10N 12 0 E
Ficksburg, S. Africa 105 D4 28 51 S 27 53 E
Fidenza, Italy 38 D7 44 51N 10 3 E
Fiditi, Nigeria 101 D5 7 45N 3 53 E

Giraltovce 201


Gazli, *Uzbekistan* 56 E7 40 14N 63 24 E
Gbarnga, *Liberia* 100 D3 7 19N 9 13W
Gbekebo, *Nigeria* 101 D5 6 20N 4 56 E
Gboko, *Nigeria* 101 D6 7 17N 9 4 E
Gbongan, *Nigeria* 101 D5 7 28N 4 20 E
Gcuwa, *S. Africa* 105 E4 32 20 S 28 11 E
Gdańsk, *Poland* 47 A5 54 22N 18 40 E
Gdańsk □, *Poland* 47 A5 54 10N 18 30 E
Gdańska, Zatoka, *Poland* 47 A6 54 30N 19 20 E
Gdov, *Russia* 50 B5 58 48N 27 55 E
Gdynia, *Poland* 47 A5 54 35N 18 33 E
Gebe, *Indonesia* 73 A3 0 5N 129 25 E
Gebeit Mine, *Sudan* 94 C4 21 3N 36 29 E
Gebel Mûsa, *Egypt* 94 J8 28 32N 33 59 E
Gebze, *Turkey* 88 C3 40 47N 29 25 E
Gecha, *Ethiopia* 95 F4 7 30N 35 18 E
Gedaref, *Sudan* 95 E4 14 2N 35 28 E
Gede, Tanjung, *Indonesia* 74 D3 6 46 S 105 12 E
Gedinne, *Belgium* 21 J5 49 59N 4 56 E
Gediz, *Turkey* 88 D3 39 1N 29 24 E
Gediz →, *Turkey* 88 D2 38 35N 26 48 E
Gedo, *Ethiopia* 95 F4 9 2N 37 25 E
Gèdre, *France* 24 F4 42 47N 0 2 E
Gedser, *Denmark* 15 K5 54 35N 11 55 E
Gedser Odde, *Denmark* 15 K5 54 30N 11 58 E
Geegully Cr. →,
*Australia* 112 C3 18 32 S 123 41 E
Geel, *Belgium* 21 F5 51 10N 4 59 E
Geelong, *Australia* 116 E6 38 10 S 144 22 E
Geelvink Chan., *Australia* 113 E1 28 30 S 114 0 E
Geer →, *Belgium* 21 G7 50 51N 5 42 E
Geesthacht, *Germany* 26 B6 53 25N 10 20 E
Geffen, *Neths.* 20 E6 51 44N 5 28 E
Geidam, *Nigeria* 101 C7 12 57N 11 57 E
Geikie →, *Canada* 131 B8 57 45N 103 52W
Geili, *Sudan* 95 D3 16 1N 32 37 E
Geilo, *Norway* 14 D2 60 32N 8 14 E
Geinica, *Czech.* 31 C13 48 51N 20 55 E
Geisingen, *Germany* 27 H4 47 55N 8 37 E
Geislingen, *Germany* 27 G5 48 37N 9 51 E
Geita, *Tanzania* 106 C3 2 48 S 32 12 E
Geita □, *Tanzania* 106 C3 2 50 S 32 10 E
Gejiu, *China* 68 F4 23 20N 103 10 E
Gel →, *Sudan* 95 F2 7 5N 29 10 E
Gel River, *Sudan* 95 F2 7 5N 29 10 E
Gela, *Italy* 41 E7 37 6N 14 18 E
Gela, G. di, *Italy* 41 F7 37 0N 14 8 E
Geladi, *Ethiopia* 90 F4 6 59N 46 30 E
Gelderland □, *Neths.* 20 D8 52 5N 6 10 E
Geldermalsen, *Neths.* 20 E6 51 53N 5 17 E
Geldern, *Germany* 26 D2 51 32N 6 18 E
Geldrop, *Neths.* 21 F7 51 25N 5 32 E
Geleen, *Neths.* 21 G7 50 57N 5 49 E
Gelehun, *S. Leone* 100 D2 8 20N 11 40W
Gelendost, *Turkey* 88 D4 38 7N 31 1 E
Gelendzhik, *Russia* 52 D8 44 33N 38 10 E
Gelib, *Somali Rep.* 108 D2 0 29N 42 46 E
Gelibolu, *Turkey* 44 D8 40 28N 26 43 E
Gelidonya Burnu, *Turkey* 88 E4 36 12N 30 24 E
Gelnhausen, *Germany* 27 E5 50 12N 9 12 E
Gelsenkirchen, *Germany* 26 D3 51 30N 7 5 E
Gelting, *Germany* 26 A5 54 43N 9 53 E
Gemas, *Malaysia* 77 L4 2 37N 102 36 E
Gembloux, *Belgium* 21 G5 50 34N 4 43 E
Gemena, *Zaïre* 102 B3 3 13N 19 48 E
Gemerek, *Turkey* 88 D7 39 15N 36 10 E
Gemert, *Neths.* 21 E7 51 33N 5 41 E
Gemlik, *Turkey* 88 C3 40 26N 29 9 E
Gemona del Friuli, *Italy* 39 B10 46 16N 13 7 E
Gemsa, *Egypt* 94 B3 27 39N 33 35 E
Gemünden, *Germany* 27 E5 50 3N 9 43 E
Genale, *Ethiopia* 95 F4 6 0N 39 30 E
Genale, *Somali Rep.* 108 D2 1 48N 44 42 E
Genappe, *Belgium* 21 G4 50 37N 4 30 E
Genç, *Turkey* 89 D9 38 44N 40 34 E
Gençay, *France* 24 B4 46 23N 0 23 E
Gendringen, *Neths.* 20 E8 51 52N 6 21 E
Gendt, *Neths.* 20 E7 51 53N 5 59 E
Geneina, Gebel, *Egypt* 94 J8 29 2N 33 55 E
Genemuiden, *Neths.* 20 C8 52 38N 6 2 E
General Acha, *Argentina* 158 D3 37 20 S 64 38W
General Alvear,
*Buenos Aires,*
*Argentina* 158 D3 36 0 S 60 0W
General Alvear,
*Mendoza, Argentina* 158 D2 35 0 S 67 40W
General Artigas,
*Paraguay* 158 B4 26 52 S 56 16W
General Belgrano,
*Argentina* 158 D4 36 35 S 58 47W
General Cabrera,
*Argentina* 158 C3 32 53 S 63 52W
General Carrera, L.,
*Chile* 160 C2 46 35 S 72 0W
General Cepeda, *Mexico* 146 B4 25 23N 101 27W
General Conesa,
*Argentina* 160 B4 40 6 S 64 25W
General Guido, *Argentina* 158 D4 36 40 S 57 50W
General Juan Madariaga,
*Argentina* 158 D4 37 0 S 57 0W
General La Madrid,
*Argentina* 158 D3 37 17 S 61 20W
General Lorenzo Vintter,
*Argentina* 160 B4 40 45 S 64 26W
General Luna, *Phil.* 70 E4 13 41N 122 10 E
General MacArthur, *Phil.* 71 F5 11 18N 125 28 E
General Martin Miguel de
Güemes, *Argentina* 158 A3 24 50 S 65 0W
General Paz, *Argentina* 158 B4 27 45 S 57 36W
General Pico, *Argentina* 158 D3 35 45 S 63 50W
General Pinedo,
*Argentina* 158 B3 27 15 S 61 20W
General Pinto, *Argentina* 158 C3 34 45 S 61 50W
General Sampaio, *Brazil* 154 B4 4 2 S 39 29W
General Santos, *Phil.* 71 H5 6 5N 125 14 E
General Tinio, *Phil.* 70 D3 15 39N 121 10 E
General Toshevo,
*Bulgaria* 43 D13 43 42N 28 6 E
General Trevino, *Mexico* 147 B5 26 14N 99 29W
General Trías, *Mexico* 146 B3 28 21N 106 22W
General Viamonte,
*Argentina* 158 D3 35 1 S 61 3W
General Villegas,
*Argentina* 158 D3 35 5 S 63 0W
General Vintter, L.,
*Argentina* 160 B2 43 55 S 71 40W
Generoso, Mte., *Switz.* 29 E8 45 56N 9 2 E
Genesee, *Idaho, U.S.A.* 142 C5 46 31N 116 59W
Genesee, *Pa., U.S.A.* 136 E7 41 59N 77 54W
Genesee →, *U.S.A.* 136 C7 43 16N 77 36W
Geneseo, *Ill., U.S.A.* 140 C6 41 25N 90 10W
Geneseo, *Kans., U.S.A.* 138 F5 38 32N 98 8W
Geneseo, *N.Y., U.S.A.* 136 D7 42 49N 77 49W
Geneva = Genève, *Switz.* 28 D2 46 12N 6 9 E
Geneva, *Ala., U.S.A.* 135 K3 31 2N 85 52W
Geneva, *Ill., U.S.A.* 141 C8 41 53N 88 18W
Geneva, *Ind., U.S.A.* 141 D12 40 36N 84 57W
Geneva, *N.Y., U.S.A.* 136 D7 42 53N 77 0W
Geneva, *Nebr., U.S.A.* 138 E6 40 35N 97 35W
Geneva, *Ohio, U.S.A.* 136 E4 41 49N 80 58W
Geneva, L. = Léman,
Lac, *Switz.* 28 D3 46 26N 6 30 E
Geneva, L., *U.S.A.* 141 B8 42 38N 88 30W
Genève, *Switz.* 28 D2 46 12N 6 9 E
Genève □, *Switz.* 28 D2 46 10N 6 10 E
Geng, *Afghan.* 79 C1 31 22N 61 28 E
Gengenbach, *Germany* 27 G4 48 25N 8 2 E
Gengma, *China* 68 F2 23 32N 99 20 E
Genichesk, *Ukraine* 52 C6 46 12N 34 50 E
Genil →, *Spain* 37 H5 37 42N 5 19W
Génissiat, Barr. de,
*France* 25 B9 46 1N 5 48 E
Genk, *Belgium* 21 G7 50 58N 5 32 E
Genkai-Nada, *Japan* 62 D2 34 0N 130 0 E
Genlis, *France* 23 E12 47 11N 5 12 E
Gennargentu, Mti. del,
*Italy* 40 C2 40 0N 9 10 E
Gennep, *Neths.* 21 E7 51 41N 5 59 E
Gennes, *France* 22 E6 47 20N 0 17W
Genoa = Génova, *Italy* 38 D5 44 24N 8 56 E
Genoa, *Australia* 117 D8 37 29 S 149 35 E
Genoa, *Ill., U.S.A.* 141 B8 42 6N 88 42W
Genoa, *N.Y., U.S.A.* 137 D8 42 40N 76 32W
Genoa, *Nebr., U.S.A.* 138 E6 41 31N 97 44W
Genoa, *Nev., U.S.A.* 144 F7 39 2N 119 50W
Genoa →, *Argentina* 160 B2 44 55 S 70 5W
Genoa City, *U.S.A.* 141 B8 42 30N 88 20W
Génova, *Italy* 38 D5 44 24N 8 56 E
Génova, G. di, *Italy* 38 E6 44 0N 9 0 E
Gent, *Belgium* 21 F3 51 2N 3 42 E
Gentbrugge, *Belgium* 21 F3 51 3N 3 47 E
Genthin, *Germany* 26 C8 52 24N 12 10 E
Gentio do Ouro, *Brazil* 154 D3 11 25 S 42 30W
Geographe B., *Australia* 113 F2 33 30 S 115 15 E
Geographe Chan.,
*Australia* 113 D1 24 30 S 113 0 E
Geokchay, *Azerbaijan* 53 F12 40 42N 47 43 E
Georga, Zemlya, *Russia* 56 A5 80 30N 49 0 E
George, *S. Africa* 104 E3 33 58 S 22 29 E
George →, *Canada* 129 A6 58 49N 66 10W
George, L., *N.S.W.,*
*Australia* 117 C8 35 10 S 149 25 E
George, L., *S. Austral.,*
*Australia* 116 D4 37 25 S 140 0 E
George, L., *W. Austral.,*
*Australia* 112 D3 22 45 S 123 40 E
George, L., *Uganda* 106 B3 0 5N 30 10 E
George, L., *Fla., U.S.A.* 135 L5 29 15N 81 35W
George, L., *N.Y., U.S.A.* 137 C11 43 30N 73 30W
George Gill Ra.,
*Australia* 112 D5 24 22 S 131 45 E
George River = Port
Nouveau-Québec,
*Canada* 127 C13 58 30N 65 59W
George Sound, *N.Z.* 119 E2 44 52 S 167 25 E
George Town, *Bahamas* 148 B4 23 33N 75 47W
George Town, *Malaysia* 77 K3 5 25N 100 15 E
George V Land,
*Antarctica* 7 C10 69 0 S 148 0 E
George VI Sound,
*Antarctica* 7 D17 71 0 S 68 0W
George West, *U.S.A.* 139 L5 28 18N 98 5W
Georgetown, *Australia* 114 B3 18 17 S 143 33 E
Georgetown, *Ont.,*
*Canada* 128 D4 43 40N 79 56W
Georgetown, *P.E.I.,*
*Canada* 129 C7 46 13N 62 24W
Georgetown, *Cayman Is.* 148 C3 19 20N 81 24W
Georgetown, *Gambia* 100 C2 13 30N 14 47W
Georgetown, *Guyana* 153 B6 6 50N 58 12W
Georgetown, *Calif.,*
*U.S.A.* 144 G6 38 54N 120 50W
Georgetown, *Colo.,*
*U.S.A.* 142 G11 39 46N 105 49W
Georgetown, *Ill., U.S.A.* 141 E9 39 59N 87 38W
Georgetown, *Ky., U.S.A.* 134 F3 38 13N 84 33W
Georgetown, *Ohio,*
*U.S.A.* 141 F13 38 50N 83 50W
Georgetown, *S.C.,*
*U.S.A.* 135 J6 33 22N 79 15W
Georgetown, *Tex.,*
*U.S.A.* 139 K6 30 40N 97 45W
Georgi Dimitrov,
*Bulgaria* 43 E8 42 15N 23 54 E
Georgi Dimitrov,
Yazovir, *Bulgaria* 43 E10 42 37N 25 18 E
Georgia □, *U.S.A.* 135 J4 32 0N 82 0W
Georgia ■, *Asia* 53 E10 42 0N 43 0 E
Georgia, Str. of, *Canada* 130 D4 49 25N 124 0W
Georgian B., *Canada* 128 C3 45 15N 81 0W
Georgievsk, *Russia* 53 D10 44 12N 43 28 E
Georgina →, *Australia* 114 C2 23 30 S 139 47 E
Georgina Downs,
*Australia* 114 C2 21 10 S 137 40 E
Georgiu-Dezh = Liski,
*Russia* 51 F11 51 3N 39 30 E
Georgiyevka, *Kazakhstan* 55 B7 43 3N 74 43 E
Gera, *Germany* 26 E8 50 53N 12 11 E
Geraardsbergen, *Belgium* 21 G3 50 45N 3 53 E
Geral, Serra, *Bahia,*
*Brazil* 155 D3 14 0 S 41 0W
Geral, Serra, *Goiás,*
*Brazil* 154 D2 11 15 S 46 30W
Geral, Serra,
*Sta. Catarina, Brazil* 159 B6 26 25 S 50 0W
Geral de Goiás, Serra,
*Brazil* 155 D2 12 0 S 46 0W
Geral do Paraná Serra,
*Brazil* 155 E2 15 0 S 47 30W
Gerald, *U.S.A.* 140 F5 38 24N 91 21W
Geraldine, *N.Z.* 119 E6 44 5 S 171 15 E
Geraldine, *U.S.A.* 142 C8 47 36N 110 18W
Geraldton, *Australia* 113 E1 28 48 S 114 32 E
Geraldton, *Canada* 128 C2 49 44N 86 59W
Geranium, *Australia* 116 C4 35 23 S 140 11 E
Gérardmer, *France* 23 D13 48 3N 6 50 E
Gercüş, *Turkey* 89 E9 37 34N 41 23 E
Gerede, *Turkey* 52 F5 40 45N 32 10 E
Gereshk, *Afghan.* 79 C2 31 47N 64 35 E
Gérgal, *Spain* 35 H2 37 7N 2 31W
Gerik, *Malaysia* 77 K3 5 50N 101 15 E
Gering, *U.S.A.* 138 E3 41 51N 103 30W
Gerlach, *U.S.A.* 142 F4 40 43N 119 27W
Gerlachovka, *Czech.* 31 B13 49 11N 20 7 E
Gerlogubi, *Ethiopia* 90 F4 6 53N 45 3 E
German Planina,
*Macedonia, Yug.* 42 E7 42 20N 22 0 E
Germansen Landing,
*Canada* 130 B4 55 43N 124 40W
Germantown, *U.S.A.* 141 E12 39 38N 84 22W
Germany ■, *Europe* 26 E6 51 0N 10 0 E
Germersheim, *Germany* 27 F4 49 13N 8 20 E
Germiston, *S. Africa* 105 D4 26 15 S 28 10 E
Gernsheim, *Germany* 27 F4 49 44N 8 29 E
Gero, *Japan* 63 B9 35 48N 137 14 E
Gerolstein, *Germany* 27 E2 50 12N 6 40 E
Gerolzhofen, *Germany* 27 F6 49 54N 10 21 E
Gerona, *Spain* 34 D7 41 58N 2 46 E
Gerona □, *Spain* 34 C7 42 11N 2 30 E
Gérouville, *Belgium* 21 J6 49 37N 5 26 E
Gerrard, *Canada* 130 C5 50 30N 117 17W
Gerringong, *Australia* 117 C9 34 46 S 150 47 E
Gers □, *France* 24 E4 43 35N 0 30 E
Gers →, *France* 24 D4 44 9N 0 39 E
Gersfeld, *Germany* 26 E5 50 27N 9 57 E
Gersoppa Falls, *India* 83 G2 14 12N 74 46 E
Gerze, *Turkey* 88 C6 41 48N 35 12 E
Geseke, *Germany* 26 D4 51 38N 8 29 E
Geser, *Indonesia* 73 B4 3 50 S 130 54 E
Gesso →, *Italy* 38 D4 44 24N 7 33 E
Gestro, Wabi →,
*Ethiopia* 95 G5 4 12N 42 2 E
Gesves, *Belgium* 21 H6 50 24N 5 4 E
Getafe, *Spain* 36 E7 40 18N 3 44W
Gethsémani, *Canada* 129 B7 50 13N 60 40W
Gettysburg, *Pa., U.S.A.* 134 F7 39 47N 77 18W
Gettysburg, *S. Dak.,*
*U.S.A.* 138 C5 45 3N 99 56W
Getz Ice Shelf, *Antarctica* 7 D14 75 0 S 130 0W
Geul →, *Neths.* 21 G7 50 53N 5 43 E
Geureudong, Mt.,
*Indonesia* 74 B1 4 13N 96 42 E
Geurie, *Australia* 117 B8 32 22 S 148 50 E
Gevaş, *Turkey* 89 D10 38 15N 43 6 E
Gévaudan, *France* 24 D7 44 40N 3 40 E
Gevgelija,
*Macedonia, Yug.* 42 F7 41 9N 22 30 E
Gévora →, *Spain* 37 G4 38 53N 6 57W
Gex, *France* 25 B10 46 21N 6 3 E
Geyikli, *Turkey* 44 E8 39 50N 26 12 E
Geyser, *U.S.A.* 142 C8 47 17N 110 30W
Geyserville, *U.S.A.* 144 G4 38 42N 122 54W
Geysir, *Iceland* 12 D3 64 19N 20 18W
Geyve, *Turkey* 88 C4 40 30N 30 18 E
Ghâbat el Arab = Wang
Kai, *Sudan* 95 F2 9 3N 29 23 E
Ghaghara →, *India* 81 G11 25 45N 84 40 E
Ghalat, *Oman* 87 B7 21 6N 58 53 E
Ghalla, Wadi el →,
*Sudan* 95 E2 10 25N 27 32 E
Ghallamane, *Mauritania* 98 D3 23 15N 10 0W
Ghana ■, *W. Afr.* 101 D4 8 0N 1 0W
Ghansor, *India* 81 H9 22 39N 80 1 E
Ghanzi, *Botswana* 104 C3 21 50 S 21 34 E
Ghanzi □, *Botswana* 104 C3 21 50 S 21 45 E
Gharb el Istiwa'iya □,
*Sudan* 95 F2 5 0N 30 0 E
Gharbîya, Es Sahrâ el,
*Egypt* 94 B2 27 40N 26 30 E
Ghard Abû Muharik,
*Egypt* 94 B2 26 50N 30 0 E
Ghardaïa, *Algeria* 99 B5 32 20N 3 37 E
Ghârib, G., *Egypt* 94 J8 28 6N 32 54 E
Ghârib, Râs, *Egypt* 94 J8 28 6N 33 18 E
Gharm, W. →, *Oman* 87 C7 19 57N 57 38 E
Gharyān, *Libya* 96 B2 32 10N 13 0 E
Gharyān □, *Libya* 96 B2 30 35N 12 0 E
Ghat, *Libya* 96 D2 24 59N 10 11 E
Ghatal, *India* 81 H12 22 40N 87 46 E
Ghatampur, *India* 81 F9 26 8N 80 13 E
Ghatere, *Solomon Is.* 121 L10 7 55 S 159 0 E
Ghatprabha →, *India* 83 F2 16 15N 75 20 E
Ghaţţi, *Si. Arabia* 84 D3 31 16N 37 31 E
Ghawdex = Gozo, *Malta* 32 C1 36 3N 14 13 E
Ghayl, *Si. Arabia* 86 B4 21 40N 46 20 E
Ghayl Bā Wazīr, *Yemen* 87 D5 14 47N 49 22 E
Ghazal, Bahr el →,
*Chad* 97 F3 13 0N 15 47 E
Ghazâl, Bahr el →,
*Sudan* 95 F3 9 31N 30 25 E
Ghazaouet, *Algeria* 99 A4 35 8N 1 50W
Ghaziabad, *India* 80 E7 28 42N 77 26 E
Ghazipur, *India* 81 G10 25 38N 83 35 E
Ghaznī, *Afghan.* 79 B3 33 30N 68 28 E
Ghaznī □, *Afghan.* 79 B3 32 10N 68 20 E
Ghedi, *Italy* 38 C7 45 24N 10 16 E
Ghelari, *Romania* 46 D3 45 38N 22 45 E
Ghèlinsor, *Somali Rep.* 90 F4 6 28N 46 39 E
Ghent = Gent, *Belgium* 21 F3 51 2N 3 42 E
Gheorghe Gheorghiu-Dej,
*Romania* 46 C7 46 17N 26 47 E
Gheorgheni, *Romania* 46 C6 46 43N 25 41 E
Ghergani, *Romania* 46 E6 44 37N 25 37 E
Gherla, *Romania* 46 B4 47 2N 23 57 E
Ghilarza, *Italy* 40 B1 40 8N 8 50 E
Ghisonaccia, *France* 25 F13 42 1N 9 26 E
Ghisoni, *France* 25 F13 42 7N 9 12 E
Ghizao, *Afghan.* 80 C1 33 20N 65 44 E
Ghizar →, *Pakistan* 81 A5 36 15N 73 43 E
Ghod →, *India* 82 E2 18 30N 74 35 E
Ghogha, *India* 80 J5 21 40N 72 20 E
Ghot Ogrein, *Egypt* 94 A2 31 10N 25 20 E
Ghotaru, *India* 80 F4 27 20N 70 1 E
Ghotki, *Pakistan* 80 E3 28 5N 69 21 E
Ghowr □, *Afghan.* 79 B2 34 0N 64 20 E
Ghudaf, W. al →, *Iraq* 84 C4 32 56N 43 30 E
Ghudāmis, *Libya* 96 B1 30 11N 9 29 E
Ghughri, *India* 81 H9 22 39N 80 41 E
Ghugus, *India* 82 E4 19 58N 79 12 E
Ghulam Mohammad
Barrage, *Pakistan* 80 G3 25 30N 68 20 E
Ghurayrah, *Si. Arabia* 86 C3 18 37N 42 41 E
Ghūrīān, *Afghan.* 79 B1 34 17N 61 25 E
Gia Dinh, *Vietnam* 77 G6 10 49N 106 42 E
Gia Lai = Pleiku,
*Vietnam* 76 F7 13 57N 108 0 E
Gia Nghia, *Vietnam* 77 G6 11 58N 107 42 E
Gia Ngoc, *Vietnam* 76 E7 14 50N 108 58 E
Gia Vuc, *Vietnam* 76 E7 14 42N 108 34 E
Giamama, *Somali Rep.* 108 D2 0 4N 42 44 E
Giannutri, *Italy* 38 F8 42 16N 11 5 E
Giant Forest, *U.S.A.* 144 J8 36 36N 118 43W
Giant Mts. = Krkonoše,
*Czech.* 30 A8 50 50N 15 35 E
Giants Causeway, *U.K.* 19 A5 55 15N 6 30W
Giarabub = Al Jaghbūb,
*Libya* 96 C4 29 42N 24 38 E
Giarre, *Italy* 41 E8 37 44N 15 10 E
Giaveno, *Italy* 38 C4 45 3N 7 20 E
Gibara, *Cuba* 148 B4 21 9N 76 11W
Gibb River, *Australia* 112 C4 16 26 S 126 26 E
Gibbon, *U.S.A.* 138 E5 40 49N 98 45W
Gibe →, *Ethiopia* 95 F4 7 20N 37 36 E
Gibellina, *Italy* 40 E6 37 48N 13 0 E
Gibraléon, *Spain* 37 H4 37 23N 6 58W
Gibraltar, *Europe* 37 J5 36 7N 5 22W
Gibraltar, Str. of,
*Medit. S.* 37 K5 35 55N 5 40W
Gibson City, *U.S.A.* 141 D8 40 28N 88 22W
Gibson Desert, *Australia* 112 D4 24 0 S 126 0 E
Gibsonburg, *U.S.A.* 141 C13 41 23N 83 19W
Gibsons, *Canada* 130 D4 49 24N 123 32W
Gibsonville, *U.S.A.* 144 F6 39 46N 120 54W
Giddalur, *India* 83 G4 15 20N 78 57 E
Giddings, *U.S.A.* 139 K6 30 11N 96 58W
Gidole, *Ethiopia* 95 F4 5 40N 37 25 E
Gien, *France* 23 E9 47 40N 2 36 E
Giessen, *Germany* 26 E4 50 34N 8 40 E
Gieten, *Neths.* 20 B9 53 1N 6 46 E
Gīfān, *Iran* 85 B8 37 54N 57 28 E
Gifatin, Geziret, *Egypt* 94 B3 27 10N 33 50 E
Gifford Creek, *Australia* 112 D2 24 3 S 116 16 E
Gifhorn, *Germany* 26 C6 52 29N 10 32 E
Gifu, *Japan* 63 B8 35 30N 136 45 E
Gifu □, *Japan* 63 B8 35 40N 137 0 E
Gigant, *Russia* 53 C9 46 28N 41 20 E
Giganta, Sa. de la,
*Mexico* 146 B2 25 30N 111 30W
Gigen, *Bulgaria* 43 D9 43 40N 24 28 E
Gigha, *U.K.* 18 F3 55 42N 5 45W
Giglei, *Somali Rep.* 108 C3 5 25N 45 20 E
Giglio, *Italy* 38 F7 42 20N 10 52 E
Gigmoto, *Phil.* 70 E5 13 47N 124 23 E
Gignac, *France* 24 E7 43 39N 3 32 E
Gigüela →, *Spain* 35 F1 39 8N 3 44W
Gijón, *Spain* 36 B5 43 32N 5 42W
Gil I., *Canada* 130 C3 53 12N 129 15W
Gila →, *U.S.A.* 143 K6 32 43N 114 33W
Gila Bend, *U.S.A.* 143 K7 33 0N 112 46W
Gila Bend Mts., *U.S.A.* 143 K7 33 15N 113 0W
Gīlān □, *Iran* 85 B6 37 0N 50 0 E
Gilău, *Romania* 46 C4 46 45N 23 23 E
Gilbert →, *Australia* 114 B3 16 35 S 141 15 E
Gilbert Is., *Kiribati* 122 G9 1 0N 176 0 E
Gilbert Plains, *Canada* 131 C8 51 9N 100 28W
Gilbert River, *Australia* 114 B3 18 9 S 142 52 E
Gilberton, *Australia* 114 B3 19 16 S 143 35 E
Gilbués, *Brazil* 154 C2 9 50 S 45 21W
Gilf el Kebîr, Hadabat el,
*Egypt* 94 C2 23 50N 25 50 E
Gilford I., *Canada* 130 C3 50 40N 126 30W
Gilgandra, *Australia* 117 A8 31 43 S 148 39 E
Gilgil, *Kenya* 106 C4 0 30 S 36 20 E
Gilgit, *India* 81 B6 35 50N 74 15 E
Gilgit →, *Pakistan* 81 B6 35 44N 74 37 E
Gilgunnia, *Australia* 117 B7 32 26 S 146 2 E
Giljeva Planina,
*Serbia, Yug.* 42 D4 43 9N 20 0 E
Gillam, *Canada* 131 B10 56 20N 94 40W
Gilleleje, *Denmark* 15 H6 56 8N 12 19 E
Gillen, L., *Australia* 113 E3 26 11 S 124 38 E
Gilles, L., *Australia* 116 B2 32 50 S 136 45 E
Gillespie, *U.S.A.* 140 E7 39 7N 89 49W
Gillespies Pt., *N.Z.* 119 D4 43 24 S 169 49 E
Gillette, *U.S.A.* 138 C2 44 20N 105 30W
Gilliat, *Australia* 114 C3 20 40 S 141 28 E
Gillingham, *U.K.* 17 F8 51 23N 0 34 E
Gilly, *Belgium* 21 H4 50 25N 4 29 E
Gilman, *U.S.A.* 141 D9 40 46N 88 0W
Gilman City, *U.S.A.* 140 D3 40 8N 93 53W
Gilmer, *U.S.A.* 139 J7 32 44N 94 55W
Gilmore, *Australia* 117 C8 35 20 S 148 12 E
Gilmore, L., *Australia* 113 F3 32 29 S 121 37 E
Gilmour, *Canada* 128 D4 44 48N 77 37W
Gilo →, *Ethiopia* 95 F3 8 10N 33 15 E
Gilort →, *Romania* 46 E4 44 38N 23 32 E
Gilroy, *U.S.A.* 144 H5 37 1N 121 37W
Giluwe, Mt.,
*Papua N. G.* 120 D2 6 8 S 143 52 E
Gilze, *Neths.* 21 E5 51 32N 4 57 E
Gimbi, *Ethiopia* 95 F4 9 3N 35 42 E
Gimigliano, *Italy* 41 D9 38 58N 16 32 E
Gimli, *Canada* 131 C9 50 40N 97 0W
Gimone →, *France* 24 E5 44 0N 1 6 E
Gimont, *France* 24 E4 43 38N 0 52 E
Gin →, *Sri Lanka* 83 L5 6 5N 80 7 E
Gin Gin, *Australia* 115 D5 25 0 S 151 58 E
Ginâh, *Egypt* 94 B3 25 21N 30 30 E
Ginatilan, *Phil.* 71 G4 9 34N 123 19 E
Gindie, *Australia* 114 C4 23 44 S 148 8 E
Gingin, *Australia* 113 F2 31 22 S 115 54 E
Gîngiova, *Romania* 46 F4 43 54N 23 50 E
Gingoog, *Phil.* 71 G5 8 50N 125 7 E
Ginir, *Ethiopia* 90 F3 7 6N 40 40 E
Ginosa, *Italy* 41 B9 40 35N 16 45 E
Ginzo de Limia, *Spain* 36 C3 42 3N 7 47W
Giohar, *Somali Rep.* 90 G4 2 48N 45 30 E
Gióia, G. di, *Italy* 41 D8 38 30N 15 50 E
Gióia del Colle, *Italy* 41 B9 40 49N 16 55 E
Gióia Táuro, *Italy* 41 D8 38 26N 15 53 E
Gioiosa Iónica, *Italy* 41 D9 38 20N 16 19 E
Gióna, Óros, *Greece* 45 F4 38 38N 22 14 E
Giovi, Passo dei, *Italy* 38 D5 44 33N 8 57 E
Giovinazzo, *Italy* 41 A9 41 10N 16 40 E
Gir Hills, *India* 80 J4 21 0N 71 0 E
Girab, *India* 80 F4 26 2N 70 38 E
Girâfi, W. →, *Egypt* 91 F3 29 58N 34 39 E
Giraltovce, *Czech.* 31 B14 49 7N 21 32 E

204 Green Cove Springs


Green Cove Springs, U.S.A. 135 L5 29 59N 81 40W
Green Is., Papua N. G. 120 C8 4 35 S 154 10 E
Green Island Bay, Phil. 71 F2 10 12N 119 22 E
Green River, U.S.A. 143 G8 38 59N 110 10W
Greenbank, U.S.A. 144 B4 48 6N 122 34W
Greenbush, Mich., U.S.A. 136 B1 44 35N 83 19W
Greenbush, Minn., U.S.A. 138 A6 48 46N 96 10W
Greencastle, U.S.A. 141 E10 39 40N 86 48W
Greene, Iowa, U.S.A. 140 B4 42 54N 92 48W
Greene, N.Y., U.S.A. 137 D9 42 20N 75 45W
Greenfield, Calif., U.S.A. 144 J5 36 19N 121 15W
Greenfield, Calif., U.S.A. 145 K8 35 15N 119 0W
Greenfield, Ill., U.S.A. 140 E6 39 21N 90 12W
Greenfield, Ind., U.S.A. 141 E11 39 47N 85 51W
Greenfield, Iowa, U.S.A. 140 C2 41 18N 94 28W
Greenfield, Mass., U.S.A. 137 D12 42 38N 72 38W
Greenfield, Miss., U.S.A. 139 G8 37 28N 93 50W
Greenfield, Ohio, U.S.A. 141 E13 39 21N 83 23W
Greenfield Park, Canada 137 A11 45 29N 73 29W
Greenland ■, N. Amer. 6 C5 66 0N 45 0W
Greenland Sea, Arctic 6 B7 73 0N 10 0W
Greenock, U.K. 18 F4 55 57N 4 46W
Greenore, Ireland 19 B5 54 2N 6 8W
Greenore Pt., Ireland 19 D5 52 15N 6 20W
Greenough →, Australia 113 E1 28 51 S 114 38 E
Greenport, U.S.A. 137 E12 41 5N 72 23W
Greensboro, Ga., U.S.A. 135 J4 33 34N 83 12W
Greensboro, N.C., U.S.A. 135 G6 36 7N 79 46W
Greensburg, Ind., U.S.A. 141 E11 39 20N 85 30W
Greensburg, Kans., U.S.A. 139 G5 37 38N 99 20W
Greensburg, Pa., U.S.A. 136 F5 40 18N 79 31W
Greentown, U.S.A. 141 D11 40 29N 85 58W
Greenup, U.S.A. 141 E8 39 15N 88 10W
Greenville, Liberia 100 D3 5 1N 9 6W
Greenville, Ala., U.S.A. 135 K2 31 50N 86 37W
Greenville, Calif., U.S.A. 144 E6 40 8N 120 57W
Greenville, Ill., U.S.A. 140 F7 38 53N 89 22W
Greenville, Ind., U.S.A. 141 F11 38 22N 85 59W
Greenville, Maine, U.S.A. 129 C6 45 30N 69 32W
Greenville, Mich., U.S.A. 141 A11 43 12N 85 14W
Greenville, Miss., U.S.A. 139 J9 33 25N 91 0W
Greenville, N.C., U.S.A. 135 H7 35 37N 77 26W
Greenville, Ohio, U.S.A. 141 D12 40 5N 84 38W
Greenville, Pa., U.S.A. 136 E4 41 23N 80 22W
Greenville, S.C., U.S.A. 135 H4 34 54N 82 24W
Greenville, Tenn., U.S.A. 135 G4 36 13N 82 51W
Greenville, Tex., U.S.A. 139 J6 33 5N 96 5W
Greenwater Lake Prov. Park, Canada 131 C8 52 32N 103 30W
Greenwich, U.K. 17 F8 51 28N 0 0 E
Greenwich, Conn., U.S.A. 137 E11 41 1N 73 38W
Greenwich, N.Y., U.S.A. 137 C11 43 2N 73 36W
Greenwich, Ohio, U.S.A. 136 E2 41 1N 82 32W
Greenwood, Canada 130 D5 49 10N 118 40W
Greenwood, Ind., U.S.A. 141 E10 39 37N 86 7W
Greenwood, Miss., U.S.A. 139 J9 33 30N 90 4W
Greenwood, S.C., U.S.A. 135 H4 34 13N 82 13W
Greenwood, Mt., Australia 112 B5 13 48 S 130 4 E
Gregório →, Brazil 156 B3 6 50 S 70 46W
Gregory, U.S.A. 138 D5 43 14N 99 20W
Gregory →, Australia 114 B2 17 53 S 139 17 E
Gregory, L., S. Austral., Australia 115 D2 28 55 S 139 0 E
Gregory, L., W. Austral., Australia 113 E2 25 38 S 119 58 E
Gregory Downs, Australia 114 B2 18 35 S 138 45 E
Gregory L., Australia 112 D4 20 0 S 127 40 E
Gregory Ra., Queens., Australia 114 B3 19 30 S 143 40 E
Gregory Ra., W. Austral., Australia 112 D3 21 20 S 121 12 E
Greiffenberg, Germany 26 B9 53 6N 13 57 E
Greifswald, Germany 26 A9 54 6N 13 23 E
Greifswalder Bodden, Germany 26 A9 54 12N 13 35 E
Grein, Austria 30 C7 48 14N 14 51 E
Greiner Wald, Austria 30 C7 48 30N 15 0 E
Greiz, Germany 26 E8 50 39N 12 12 E
Gremikha, Russia 48 A6 67 50N 39 40 E
Grenå, Denmark 15 H4 56 25N 10 53 E
Grenada, U.S.A. 139 J10 33 45N 89 50W
Grenada ■, W. Indies 149 D7 12 10N 61 40W
Grenade, France 24 E5 43 47N 1 17 E
Grenadines, W. Indies 149 D7 12 40N 61 20W
Grenchen, Switz. 28 B4 47 12N 7 24 E
Grenen, Denmark 15 G4 57 44N 10 40 E
Grenfell, Australia 117 B8 33 52 S 148 8 E
Grenfell, Canada 131 C8 50 30N 102 56W
Grenoble, France 25 C9 45 12N 5 42 E
Grenora, U.S.A. 138 A3 48 38N 103 54W
Grenville, C., Australia 114 A3 12 0 S 143 13 E
Grenville Chan., Canada 130 C3 53 40N 129 46W
Gréoux-les-Bains, France 25 E9 43 45N 5 52 E
Gresham, U.S.A. 144 E4 45 30N 122 25W
Gresik, Indonesia 75 D4 7 13 S 112 38 E
Grëssoney St. Jean, Italy 38 C4 45 49N 7 47 E
Gretna Green, U.K. 18 F5 55 0N 3 3W
Grevelingen Krammer, Neths. 20 E4 51 44N 4 0 E
Greven, Germany 26 C3 52 7N 7 36 E
Grevená, Greece 44 D3 40 4N 21 25 E
Grevená □, Greece 44 D3 40 2N 21 25 E
Grevenbroich, Germany 26 D2 51 6N 6 32 E
Grevenmacher, Lux. 21 J8 49 41N 6 26 E
Grevesmühlen, Germany 26 B7 53 51N 11 10 E
Grevie, Sweden 15 H6 56 22N 12 46 E
Grey →, N.Z. 119 C6 42 27 S 171 12 E
Grey, C., Australia 114 A2 13 0 S 136 35 E
Grey Ra., Australia 115 D3 27 0 S 143 30 E
Grey Res., Canada 129 C8 48 20N 56 30W
Greybull, U.S.A. 142 D9 44 30N 108 3W
Greymouth, N.Z. 119 C6 42 29 S 171 13 E
Greytown, N.Z. 118 H4 41 5 S 175 29 E
Greytown, S. Africa 105 D5 29 1 S 30 36 E
Gribanovskiy, Russia 51 F12 51 28N 41 50 E
Gribbell I., Canada 130 C3 53 23N 129 0W
Gridley, U.S.A. 144 F5 39 27N 121 47W
Griekwastad, S. Africa 104 D3 28 49 S 23 15 E
Griffin, U.S.A. 135 J3 33 17N 84 14W
Griffith, Australia 117 C7 34 18 S 146 2 E
Grigoryevka, Kazakhstan 54 F6 50 48N 58 18 E
Grijpskerk, Neths. 20 B8 53 16N 6 18 E
Grillby, Sweden 14 E11 59 38N 17 15 E
Grimari, C.A.R. 102 A4 5 43N 20 6 E
Grimaylov, Ukraine 50 G5 49 20N 26 5 E
Grimbergen, Belgium 21 G4 50 56N 4 22 E
Grimes, U.S.A. 144 F5 39 4N 121 54W
Grimma, Germany 26 D8 51 14N 12 44 E
Grimmen, Germany 26 A9 54 6N 13 2 E
Grimsby, Canada 136 C5 43 12N 79 34W
Grimsby, U.K. 16 D7 53 35N 0 5W
Grimselpass, Switz. 29 C6 46 34N 8 23 E
Grímsey, Iceland 12 C5 66 33N 17 58W
Grimshaw, Canada 130 B5 56 10N 117 40W
Grimstad, Norway 15 F2 58 22N 8 35 E
Grindelwald, Switz. 28 C6 46 38N 8 2 E
Grindsted, Denmark 15 J2 55 46N 8 55 E
Grindu, Romania 46 E7 44 44N 26 50 E
Grinnell, U.S.A. 140 C4 41 45N 92 43W
Griñón, Spain 36 E7 40 13N 3 51W
Grintavec, Slovenia 39 B11 46 22N 14 32 E
Grip, Norway 14 A1 63 16N 7 37 E
Gris-Nez, C., France 23 B8 50 52N 1 35 E
Grisolles, France 24 E5 43 49N 1 19 E
Grisons = Graubünden □, Switz. 29 C9 46 45N 9 30 E
Grivegnée, Belgium 21 G7 50 37N 5 36 E
Grmeč Planina, Bos.-H., Yug. 39 D13 44 43N 16 16 E
Groais I., Canada 129 B8 50 55N 55 35W
Groblersdal, S. Africa 105 D4 25 15 S 29 25 E
Grobming, Austria 30 D6 47 27N 13 54 E
Grocka, Serbia, Yug. 42 C5 44 40N 20 42 E
Gródek, Poland 47 B10 53 6N 23 40 E
Grodkow, Poland 47 E4 50 43N 17 21 E
Grodno, Belorussia 50 E3 53 42N 23 52 E
Grodzisk Mázowiecki, Poland 47 C7 52 7N 20 37 E
Grodzisk Wielkopolski, Poland 47 C3 52 15N 16 22 E
Grodzyanka, Belorussia 50 E6 53 31N 28 42 E
Groenlo, Neths. 20 D9 52 2N 6 37 E
Groesbeck, U.S.A. 139 K6 31 32N 96 34W
Groesbeek, Neths. 20 E7 51 47N 5 58 E
Groix, France 22 E3 47 38N 3 29W
Groix, I. de, France 22 E3 47 38N 3 28W
Grójec, Poland 47 D7 51 50N 20 58 E
Grolloo, Neths. 20 C9 52 56N 6 41 E
Gronau, Niedersachsen, Germany 26 C5 52 5N 9 47 E
Gronau, Nordrhein-Westfalen, Germany 26 C3 52 13N 7 2 E
Grong, Norway 12 D12 64 25N 12 8 E
Groningen, Neths. 20 B9 53 15N 6 35 E
Groningen, Surinam 153 B6 5 48N 55 28W
Groningen □, Neths. 20 B9 53 16N 6 40 E
Groninger Wad, Neths. 20 B9 53 27N 6 30 E
Gronsveld, Neths. 21 G7 50 49N 5 44 E
Groom, U.S.A. 139 H4 35 12N 100 59W
Groot →, S. Africa 104 E3 33 45 S 24 36 E
Groot Berg →, S. Africa 104 E2 32 47 S 18 8 E
Groot-Brakrivier, S. Africa 104 E3 34 2 S 22 18 E
Groot-Kei →, S. Africa 105 E4 32 41 S 28 22 E
Groot Vis →, S. Africa 104 E4 33 28 S 27 5 E
Groote Eylandt, Australia 114 A2 14 0 S 136 40 E
Grootebroek, Neths. 20 C6 52 41N 5 13 E
Grootfontein, Namibia 104 B2 19 31 S 18 6 E
Grootlaagte →, Africa 104 C3 20 55 S 21 27 E
Grootvloer, S. Africa 104 E3 30 0 S 20 40 E
Gros C., Canada 130 A6 61 59N 113 32W
Grosa, Pta., Spain 33 B8 39 6N 1 36 E
Grósio, Italy 38 B7 46 18N 10 17 E
Grosne →, France 25 B8 46 42N 4 56 E
Gross Glockner, Austria 30 D5 47 5N 12 40 E
Grossenbrode, Germany 26 A7 54 21N 11 4 E
Grossenhain, Germany 26 D9 51 17N 13 32 E
Grosseto, Italy 38 F8 42 45N 11 7 E
Grossgerungs, Austria 30 C7 48 34N 14 57 E
Groswater B., Canada 129 B8 54 20N 57 40W
Grote Gette →, Neths. 21 G6 50 51N 5 6 E
Grote Nete →, Belgium 21 F5 51 8N 4 34 E
Groton, Conn., U.S.A. 137 E12 41 22N 72 12W
Groton, S. Dak., U.S.A. 138 C5 45 27N 98 6W
Grottáglie, Italy 41 B10 40 32N 17 25 E
Grottaminarda, Italy 41 A8 41 5N 15 4 E
Grottammare, Italy 39 F10 42 59N 13 52 E
Grouard Mission, Canada 130 B5 55 33N 116 9W
Grouin, Pte. du, France 22 D5 48 43N 1 51W
Groundhog →, Canada 128 C3 48 45N 82 58W
Grouse Creek, U.S.A. 142 F7 41 44N 113 57W
Grouw, Neths. 20 B7 53 5N 5 51 E
Grove City, Ohio, U.S.A. 141 E13 39 53N 83 6W
Grove City, Pa., U.S.A. 136 E4 41 10N 80 5W
Groveland, U.S.A. 144 H6 37 50N 120 14W
Grover City, U.S.A. 145 K6 35 7N 120 37W
Grover Hill, U.S.A. 141 C12 41 1N 84 29W
Groveton, N.H., U.S.A. 137 B13 44 34N 71 30W
Groveton, Tex., U.S.A. 139 K7 31 5N 95 4W
Grožnjan, Croatia 39 C10 45 22N 13 43 E
Groznyy, Russia 53 E11 43 20N 45 45 E
Grubbenvorst, Neths. 21 F8 51 25N 6 9 E
Grubišno Polje, Croatia 42 B2 45 44N 17 12 E
Grudovo, Bulgaria 43 E12 42 21N 27 10 E
Grudusk, Poland 47 B7 53 3N 20 38 E
Grudziądz, Poland 47 B5 53 30N 18 47 E
Gruissan, France 24 E7 43 8N 3 7 E
Grumo Áppula, Italy 41 A9 41 2N 16 43 E
Grünberg, Germany 26 E4 50 37N 8 55 E
Grundy Center, U.S.A. 140 B4 42 22N 92 45W
Gruver, U.S.A. 139 G4 36 19N 101 20W
Gruyères, Switz. 28 C4 46 35N 7 4 E
Gruža, Serbia, Yug. 42 D5 43 54N 20 46 E
Gryazi, Russia 51 E11 52 30N 39 58 E
Gryazovets, Russia 51 B12 58 50N 40 10 E
Grybów, Poland 31 B13 49 36N 20 55 E
Gryfice, Poland 47 B2 53 55N 15 13 E
Gryfino, Poland 47 B1 53 16N 14 29 E
Gryfow Sl., Poland 47 D2 51 2N 15 24 E
Gstaad, Switz. 28 D4 46 28N 7 18 E
Gua Musang, Malaysia 77 K3 4 53N 101 58 E
Guacanayabo, G. de, Cuba 148 B4 20 40N 77 20W
Guacara, Venezuela 152 A4 10 14N 67 53W
Guachípas →, Argentina 158 B2 25 40 S 65 30W
Guachiría →, Colombia 152 B3 5 27N 70 36W
Guadajoz →, Spain 37 H6 37 50N 4 51W
Guadalajara, Mexico 146 C4 20 40N 103 20W
Guadalajara, Spain 34 E1 40 37N 3 12W
Guadalajara □, Spain 34 E2 40 47N 2 30W
Guadalcanal, Solomon Is. 121 M11 9 32 S 160 12 E
Guadalcanal, Spain 37 G5 38 5N 5 52W
Guadalén →, Spain 37 G7 38 5N 3 32W
Guadales, Argentina 158 C2 34 30 S 67 55W
Guadalete →, Spain 37 J4 36 35N 6 13W
Guadalhorce →, Spain 37 J6 36 41N 4 27W
Guadalimar →, Spain 35 G1 38 5N 3 28W
Guadalmena →, Spain 35 G2 38 19N 2 56W
Guadalmez →, Spain 37 G5 38 46N 5 4W
Guadalope →, Spain 34 D4 41 15N 0 3W
Guadalquivir →, Spain 37 J4 36 47N 6 22W
Guadalupe = Guadeloupe ■, W. Indies 149 C7 16 20N 61 40W
Guadalupe, Brazil 154 C3 6 44 S 43 47W
Guadalupe, Mexico 145 N10 32 4N 116 32W
Guadalupe, Spain 37 F5 39 27N 5 17W
Guadalupe, U.S.A. 145 L6 34 59N 120 33W
Guadalupe →, Mexico 145 N10 32 6N 116 51W
Guadalupe →, U.S.A. 139 L6 28 30N 96 53W
Guadalupe, Sierra de, Spain 37 F5 39 28N 5 30W
Guadalupe Bravos, Mexico 146 A3 31 20N 106 10W
Guadalupe Pk., U.S.A. 143 L11 31 50N 105 30W
Guadalupe y Calvo, Mexico 146 B3 26 6N 106 58W
Guadarrama, Sierra de, Spain 36 E7 41 0N 4 0W
Guadeloupe ■, W. Indies 149 C7 16 20N 61 40W
Guadeloupe Passage, W. Indies 149 C7 16 50N 62 15W
Guadiamar →, Spain 37 J4 36 55N 6 24W
Guadiana →, Portugal 37 H3 37 14N 7 22W
Guadiana Menor →, Spain 35 H1 37 56N 3 15W
Guadiaro →, Spain 37 J5 36 17N 5 17W
Guadiato →, Spain 37 H5 37 48N 5 5W
Guadiela →, Spain 34 E2 40 22N 2 49W
Guadix, Spain 35 H1 37 18N 3 11W
Guafo, Boca del, Chile 160 B2 43 35 S 74 0W
Guafo, I., Chile 160 B2 43 35 S 74 50W
Guainía □, Colombia 152 C4 2 30N 69 0W
Guainía →, Colombia 152 C4 2 1N 67 7W
Guaíra, Brazil 159 A5 24 5 S 54 10W
Guaitecas, Is., Chile 160 B2 44 0 S 74 30W
Guajará-Mirim, Brazil 157 C4 10 50 S 65 20W
Guajira □, Colombia 152 A3 11 30N 72 30W
Guajira, Pen. de la, Colombia 152 A3 12 0N 72 0W
Gualaceo, Ecuador 152 D2 2 54 S 78 47W
Gualán, Guatemala 148 C2 15 8N 89 22W
Gualdo Tadino, Italy 39 E9 43 14N 12 46 E
Gualeguay, Argentina 158 C4 33 10 S 59 14W
Gualeguaychú, Argentina 158 C4 33 3 S 59 31W
Gualicho, Salina, Argentina 160 B3 40 25 S 65 20W
Gualjaina, Argentina 160 B2 42 45 S 70 30W
Guam, Pac. Oc. 121 R15 13 27N 144 45 E
Guamá, Brazil 154 B2 1 37 S 47 29W
Guamá →, Brazil 154 B2 1 29 S 48 30W
Guamblin, I., Chile 160 B1 44 50 S 75 0W
Guaminí, Argentina 158 D3 37 1 S 62 28W
Guamote, Ecuador 152 D2 1 56 S 78 43W
Guampí, Sierra de, Venezuela 153 B4 6 0N 65 35W
Guamúchil, Mexico 146 B3 25 25N 108 3W
Guan Xian, China 68 B4 31 2N 103 38 E
Guanabacoa, Cuba 148 B3 23 8N 82 18W
Guanacaste, Cordillera del, Costa Rica 148 D2 10 40N 85 4W
Guanaceví, Mexico 146 B3 25 40N 106 0W
Guanahani = San Salvador, Bahamas 149 B5 24 0N 74 40W
Guanajay, Cuba 148 B3 22 56N 82 42W
Guanajuato, Mexico 146 C4 21 0N 101 20W
Guanajuato □, Mexico 146 C4 20 40N 101 20W
Guanambi, Brazil 155 D3 14 13 S 42 47W
Guanare, Venezuela 152 B4 8 42N 69 12W
Guanare →, Venezuela 152 B4 8 13N 67 46W
Guandacol, Argentina 158 B2 29 30 S 68 40W
Guane, Cuba 148 B3 22 10N 84 7W
Guang'an, China 68 B6 30 28N 106 35 E
Guangchang, China 69 D11 26 50N 116 21 E
Guangde, China 69 B12 30 54N 119 25 E
Guangdong □, China 69 F9 23 0N 113 0 E
Guangfeng, China 69 C12 28 20N 118 15 E
Guanghan, China 68 B5 30 58N 104 17 E
Guanghua, China 69 A8 32 22N 111 38 E
Guangji, China 69 C10 29 52N 115 30 E
Guangling, China 66 E8 39 47N 114 22 E
Guangning, China 69 F9 23 40N 112 22 E
Guangrao, China 67 F10 37 5N 118 25 E
Guangshun, China 68 D6 26 8N 106 21 E
Guanguan Peninsula, Phil. 71 H6 6 50N 126 19 E
Guangwu, China 66 F3 37 48N 105 57 E
Guangxi Zhuangzu Zizhiqu □, China 68 E7 24 0N 109 0 E
Guangyuan, China 68 A5 32 26N 105 51 E
Guangze, China 69 D11 27 30N 117 12 E
Guangzhou, China 69 F9 23 5N 113 10 E
Guanhães, Brazil 155 E3 18 47 S 42 57W
Guanipa →, Venezuela 153 B5 9 56N 62 26W
Guanling, China 68 E5 25 56N 105 35 E
Guannan, China 67 G10 34 8N 119 21 E
Guanta, Venezuela 153 A5 10 14N 64 36W
Guantánamo, Cuba 149 B4 20 10N 75 14W
Guantao, China 66 F8 36 42N 115 25 E
Guanyang, China 69 E8 25 30N 111 8 E
Guanyun, China 67 G10 34 20N 119 18 E
Guapí, Colombia 152 C2 2 36N 77 54W
Guápiles, Costa Rica 148 D3 10 10N 83 46W
Guaporé →, Brazil 157 C4 11 55 S 65 4W
Guaqui, Bolivia 156 D4 16 41 S 68 54W
Guara, Sierra de, Spain 34 C4 42 19N 0 15W
Guarabira, Brazil 154 C4 6 51 S 35 29W
Guaranda, Ecuador 152 D2 1 36 S 79 0W
Guarapari, Brazil 155 F3 20 40 S 40 30W
Guarapuava, Brazil 159 B5 25 20 S 51 30W
Guaratinguetá, Brazil 159 A6 22 49 S 45 9W
Guaratuba, Brazil 159 B6 25 53 S 48 38W
Guarda, Portugal 36 E3 40 32N 7 20W
Guarda □, Portugal 36 E3 40 40N 7 20W
Guardafui, C. = Asir, Ras, Somali Rep. 90 E5 11 55N 51 10 E
Guardamar del Segura, Spain 35 G4 38 5N 0 39W
Guardavalle, Italy 41 D9 38 31N 16 30 E
Guardiagrele, Italy 39 F11 42 11N 14 11 E
Guardo, Spain 36 C6 42 47N 4 50W
Guareña, Spain 37 G4 38 51N 6 6W
Guareña →, Spain 36 D5 41 29N 5 23W
Guaria □, Paraguay 158 B4 25 45 S 56 30W
Guárico □, Venezuela 152 B4 8 40N 66 35W
Guarrojo →, Colombia 152 C3 4 6N 70 42W
Guarujá, Brazil 159 A6 24 2 S 46 25W
Guarus, Brazil 155 F3 21 44 S 41 20W
Guasave, Mexico 146 B3 25 34N 108 27W
Guascama, Pta., Colombia 152 C2 2 32N 78 24W
Guasdualito, Venezuela 152 B3 7 15N 70 44W
Guasipati, Venezuela 153 B5 7 28N 61 54W
Guasopa, Papua N. G. 120 E7 9 12 S 152 56 E
Guastalla, Italy 38 D7 44 55N 10 40 E
Guatemala, Guatemala 148 D1 14 40N 90 22W
Guatemala ■, Cent. Amer. 148 C1 15 40N 90 30W
Guatire, Venezuela 152 A4 10 28N 66 32W
Guaviare □, Colombia 152 C3 2 0N 72 30W
Guaviare →, Colombia 152 C4 4 3N 67 44W
Guaxupé, Brazil 159 A6 21 10 S 47 5W
Guayabero →, Colombia 152 C3 2 36N 72 47W
Guayama, Puerto Rico 149 C6 17 59N 66 7W
Guayaneco, Arch., Chile 160 C1 47 45 S 75 10W
Guayaquil, Ecuador 152 D2 2 15 S 79 52W
Guayaquil, G. de, Ecuador 152 D1 3 10 S 81 0W
Guayaramerín, Bolivia 157 C4 10 48 S 65 23W
Guayas →, Ecuador 152 D2 2 36 S 79 52W
Guaymas, Mexico 146 B2 27 59N 110 54W
Guazhou, China 69 A12 32 17N 119 21 E
Guba, Zaïre 107 E2 10 38 S 26 27 E
Gubakha, Russia 54 B5 58 52N 57 36 E
Gûbâl, Madîq, Egypt 94 B3 27 30N 34 0 E
Gubam, Papua N. G. 120 E1 8 39 S 141 53 E
Gubat, Phil. 70 E5 12 55N 124 7 E
Gúbbio, Italy 39 E9 43 20N 12 34 E
Gubin, Poland 47 D1 51 57N 14 43 E
Gubio, Nigeria 101 C7 12 30N 12 42 E
Gubkin, Russia 51 F10 51 17N 37 32 E
Guča, Serbia, Yug. 42 D5 43 46N 20 15 E
Gudalur, India 83 J3 11 30N 76 29 E
Gudata, Georgia 53 E9 43 7N 40 32 E
Gudbrandsdalen, Norway 13 F10 61 33N 9 55 E
Gudenå, Denmark 15 H3 56 27N 9 40 E
Gudermes, Russia 53 E12 43 24N 46 5 E
Gudivada, India 83 F5 16 30N 81 3 E
Gudiyattam, India 83 H4 12 57N 78 55 E
Gudur, India 83 G4 14 12N 79 55 E
Guebwiller, France 23 E14 47 55N 7 12 E
Guecho, Spain 34 B2 43 21N 2 59W
Guékédou, Guinea 100 D2 8 40N 10 5W
Guelma, Algeria 99 A6 36 25N 7 29 E
Guelph, Canada 128 D3 43 35N 80 20W
Guelt es Stel, Algeria 99 A5 35 12N 3 1 E
Gueltara, Algeria 99 C4 29 23N 2 10W
Guemar, Algeria 99 B6 33 30N 6 49 E
Guéméné-Penfao, France 22 E5 47 38N 1 50W
Guéméné-sur-Scorff, France 22 D3 48 4N 3 13W
Guéné, Benin 101 C5 11 44N 3 16 E
Güepi, Peru 152 D2 0 9 S 75 10W
Guer, France 22 E4 47 54N 2 8W
Güer Aike, Argentina 160 D3 51 39 S 69 35W
Guera Pk., Chad 97 F3 11 55N 18 12 E
Guérande, France 22 E4 47 20N 2 26W
Guercif, Morocco 99 B4 34 14N 3 21W
Guéréda, Chad 97 F4 14 31N 22 5 E
Guéret, France 24 B5 46 11N 1 51 E
Guérigny, France 23 E10 47 6N 3 10 E
Guerneville, U.S.A. 144 G4 38 30N 123 0W
Guernica, Spain 34 B2 43 19N 2 40W
Guernsey, U.K. 17 H5 49 30N 2 35W
Guernsey, U.S.A. 138 D2 42 19N 104 45W
Guerrara, Oasis, Algeria 99 B5 32 51N 4 22 E
Guerrara, Saoura, Algeria 99 C4 28 5N 0 8W
Guerrero □, Mexico 147 D5 17 30N 100 0W
Guerzim, Algeria 99 C4 29 39N 1 40W
Gueugnon, France 25 B8 46 36N 4 4 E
Gueydan, U.S.A. 139 K8 30 3N 92 30W
Gūgher, Iran 85 D8 29 28N 56 27 E
Guglionesi, Italy 41 A7 41 55N 14 54 E
Gui Jiang →, China 69 F8 23 30N 111 15 E
Gui Xian, China 68 F7 23 8N 109 35 E
Guia, Canary Is. 33 F4 28 8N 15 38W
Guia de Isora, Canary Is. 33 F3 28 12N 16 46W
Guia Lopes da Laguna, Brazil 159 A4 21 26 S 56 7W
Guichi, China 69 B11 30 39N 117 27 E
Guider, Cameroon 101 D7 9 56N 13 57 E
Guidimouni, Niger 97 F1 13 42N 9 31 E
Guiding, China 68 D6 26 34N 107 11 E
Guidong, China 69 D9 26 7N 113 57 E
Guiglo, Ivory C. 100 D3 6 45N 7 30W
Guijá, Mozam. 105 C5 24 27 S 33 0 E
Guijo de Coria, Spain 36 E4 40 6N 6 28W
Guildford, U.K. 17 F7 51 14N 0 34W
Guilford, U.S.A. 129 C6 45 12N 69 25W
Guilin, China 69 E8 25 18N 110 15 E
Guillaumes, France 25 D10 44 5N 6 52 E
Guillestre, France 25 D10 44 39N 6 40 E
Guilvinec, France 22 E2 47 48N 4 17W
Güímar, Canary Is. 33 F3 28 18N 16 24W
Guimarães, Brazil 154 B3 2 9 S 44 42W
Guimarães, Portugal 36 D2 41 28N 8 24W
Guimaras, Phil. 71 F4 10 35N 122 37 E
Guimba, Phil. 70 D3 15 40N 120 46 E
Guinda, U.S.A. 144 G4 38 50N 122 12W
Guindulman, Phil. 71 G5 9 46N 124 29 E
Guinea ■, W. Afr. 100 C2 10 20N 11 30W
Guinea, Gulf of, Atl. Oc. 101 E5 3 0N 2 30 E
Guinea-Bissau ■, Africa 100 C2 12 0N 15 0W
Güines, Cuba 148 B3 22 50N 82 0W
Guingamp, France 22 D3 48 34N 3 10W
Guinobatan, Phil. 70 E4 13 11N 123 36 E
Guiom, Phil. 71 F4 11 59N 123 44 E
Guipavas, France 22 D2 48 26N 4 29W

Hamersley Ra. 205


Guiping, *China* 69 **F8** 23 21N 110 2 E
Guipúzcoa □, *Spain* 34 **B2** 43 12N 2 15W
Guir, O. →, *Algeria* 99 **B4** 31 29N 2 17W
Guiratinga, *Brazil* 157 **D7** 16 21 S 53 45W
Güiria, *Venezuela* 153 **A5** 10 32N 62 18W
Guiscard, *France* 23 **C10** 49 40N 3 1 E
Guise, *France* 23 **C10** 49 52N 3 35 E
Guitiriz, *Spain* 36 **B3** 43 11N 7 50W
Guiuan, *Phil.* 71 **F5** 11 5N 125 55 E
Guixi, *China* 69 **C11** 28 16N 117 15 E
Guiyang, *Guizhou, China* 68 **D6** 26 32N 106 40 E
Guiyang, *Hunan, China* 69 **E9** 25 46N 112 42 E
Guizhou □, *China* 68 **D6** 27 0N 107 0 E
Gujan-Mestras, *France* 24 **D2** 44 38N 1 4W
Gujarat □, *India* 80 **H4** 23 20N 71 0 E
Gujiang, *China* 69 **D10** 27 11N 114 47 E
Gujranwala, *Pakistan* 79 **B4** 32 10N 74 12 E
Gujrat, *Pakistan* 79 **B4** 32 40N 74 2 E
Gukovo, *Russia* 53 **B8** 48 1N 39 58 E
Gulargambone, *Australia* 117 **A8** 31 20 S 148 30 E
Gulbarga, *India* 82 **F3** 17 20N 76 50 E
Gulbene, *Latvia* 50 **C5** 57 8N 26 52 E
Gulcha, *Kirghizia* 55 **C6** 40 19N 73 26 E
Guledagudda, *India* 83 **F2** 16 3N 75 48 E
Gulf, The, *Asia* 85 **E6** 27 0N 50 0 E
Gulfport, *U.S.A.* 139 **K10** 30 21N 89 3W
Gulgong, *Australia* 117 **B8** 32 20 S 149 49 E
Gulin, *China* 68 **C5** 28 1N 105 50 E
Gulistan, *Pakistan* 80 **D2** 30 30N 66 35 E
Gulistan, *Uzbekistan* 55 **C4** 40 29N 68 46 E
Gull Lake, *Canada* 131 **C7** 50 10N 108 29W
Gullegem, *Belgium* 21 **G2** 50 51N 3 13 E
Güllük, *Turkey* 88 **E2** 37 14N 27 35 E
Gulma, *Nigeria* 101 **C5** 12 40N 4 23 E
Gulmarg, *India* 81 **B6** 34 3N 74 25 E
Gülnar, *Turkey* 88 **E5** 36 19N 33 24 E
Gulnare, *Australia* 116 **B3** 33 27 S 138 27 E
Gulpen, *Neths.* 21 **G7** 50 49N 5 53 E
Gülpinar, *Turkey* 44 **E8** 39 32N 26 10 E
Gülşehir, *Turkey* 88 **D6** 38 44N 34 37 E
Gulshad, *Kazakhstan* 56 **E8** 46 45N 74 25 E
Gulsvik, *Norway* 14 **D3** 60 24N 9 38 E
Gulu, *Uganda* 106 **B3** 2 48N 32 17 E
Gulwe, *Tanzania* 106 **D4** 6 30 S 36 25 E
Gulyaypole, *Ukraine* 52 **C7** 47 45N 36 21 E
Gum Lake, *Australia* 116 **B5** 32 42 S 143 9 E
Gumaca, *Phil.* 70 **E4** 13 55N 122 6 E
Gumal →, *Pakistan* 80 **D4** 31 40N 71 50 E
Gumbaz, *Pakistan* 80 **D3** 30 2N 69 0 E
Gumel, *Nigeria* 101 **C6** 12 39N 9 22 E
Gumiel de Hizán, *Spain* 34 **D1** 41 46N 3 41W
Gumlu, *Australia* 114 **B4** 19 53 S 147 41 E
Gumma □, *Japan* 63 **A10** 36 30N 138 20 E
Gummersbach, *Germany* 26 **D3** 51 2N 7 32 E
Gummi, *Nigeria* 101 **C6** 12 4N 5 9 E
Gümüşhaciköy, *Turkey* 52 **F6** 40 50N 35 18 E
Gümüşhane, *Turkey* 89 **C8** 40 30N 39 30 E
Gümüşhane □, *Turkey* 89 **C8** 40 35N 39 25 E
Gumzai, *Indonesia* 73 **C4** 5 28 S 134 42 E
Guna, *Ethiopia* 95 **E4** 11 50N 37 40 E
Guna, *India* 80 **G7** 24 40N 77 19 E
Gundagai, *Australia* 117 **C8** 35 3 S 148 6 E
Gundelfingen, *Germany* 27 **G6** 48 33N 10 22 E
Gundih, *Indonesia* 75 **D4** 7 10 S 110 56 E
Gundlakamma →, *India* 83 **G5** 15 30N 80 15 E
Gunebang, *Australia* 117 **B7** 33 1 S 146 38 E
Guneydogu Toroslar,
*Turkey* 89 **D9** 38 40N 40 30 E
Gungal, *Australia* 117 **B9** 32 17 S 150 32 E
Gungu, *Zaïre* 103 **D3** 5 43 S 19 20 E
Gunisao →, *Canada* 131 **C9** 53 56N 97 53W
Gunisao L., *Canada* 131 **C9** 53 33N 96 15W
Gunnbjørn Fjeld,
*Greenland* 6 **C6** 68 55N 29 47W
Gunnedah, *Australia* 117 **A9** 30 59 S 150 15 E
Gunniguldrie, *Australia* 117 **B7** 33 12 S 146 8 E
Gunningbar Cr. →,
*Australia* 117 **A7** 31 14 S 147 6 E
Gunnison, *Colo., U.S.A.* 143 **G10** 38 32N 106 56W
Gunnison, *Utah, U.S.A.* 142 **G8** 39 11N 111 48W
Gunnison →, *U.S.A.* 143 **G9** 39 3N 108 30W
Gunpowder, *Australia* 114 **B2** 19 42 S 139 22 E
Guntakal, *India* 83 **G3** 15 11N 77 27 E
Guntersville, *U.S.A.* 135 **H2** 34 18N 86 16W
Guntong, *Malaysia* 77 **K3** 4 36N 101 3 E
Guntur, *India* 83 **F5** 16 23N 80 30 E
Gunungapi, *Indonesia* 72 **C3** 6 45 S 126 30 E
Gunungsitoli, *Indonesia* 74 **B1** 1 15N 97 30 E
Gunupur, *India* 82 **E6** 19 5N 83 50 E
Günz →, *Germany* 27 **G6** 48 27N 10 16 E
Gunza, *Angola* 103 **E2** 10 50 S 13 50 E
Günzburg, *Germany* 27 **G6** 48 27N 10 16 E
Gunzenhausen, *Germany* 27 **F6** 49 6N 10 45 E
Guo He →, *China* 67 **H9** 32 59N 117 10 E
Guoyang, *China* 66 **H9** 33 32N 116 12 E
Gupis, *Pakistan* 81 **A5** 36 15N 73 20 E
Gura Humorului,
*Romania* 46 **B6** 47 35N 25 53 E
Gura-Teghii, *Romania* 46 **D7** 45 30N 26 25 E
Gurag, *Ethiopia* 95 **F4** 8 20N 38 20 E
Gurdaspur, *India* 80 **C6** 32 5N 75 31 E
Gurdon, *U.S.A.* 139 **J8** 33 55N 93 10W
Gurdzhaani, *Georgia* 53 **F11** 41 43N 45 52 E
Gurgaon, *India* 80 **E7** 28 27N 77 1 E
Gürgentepe, *Turkey* 89 **C8** 40 45N 38 18 E
Gurghiu, Munţii,
*Romania* 46 **C6** 46 41N 25 15 E
Gurguéia →, *Brazil* 154 **C3** 6 50 S 43 24W
Gurha, *India* 80 **G4** 25 12N 71 39 E
Guri, Embalse de,
*Venezuela* 153 **B5** 7 50N 62 52W
Gurk →, *Austria* 30 **E7** 46 35N 14 31 E
Gurkha, *Nepal* 81 **E11** 28 5N 84 40 E
Gurley, *Australia* 115 **D4** 29 45 S 149 48 E
Gurnee, *U.S.A.* 141 **B9** 42 22N 87 55W
Gurué, *Mozam.* 107 **F4** 15 25 S 36 58 E
Gurun, *Malaysia* 77 **K3** 5 49N 100 27 E
Gürün, *Turkey* 88 **D7** 38 43N 37 15 E
Gurupá, *Brazil* 153 **D7** 1 25 S 51 35W
Gurupá, I. Grande de,
*Brazil* 153 **D7** 1 25 S 51 45W
Gurupi, *Brazil* 155 **D2** 11 43 S 49 4W
Gurupi →, *Brazil* 154 **B2** 1 13 S 46 6W
Gurupi, Serra do, *Brazil* 154 **C2** 5 0 S 47 50W
Guryev, *Kazakhstan* 53 **C14** 47 5N 52 0 E
Gus-Khrustalnyy, *Russia* 51 **D12** 55 42N 40 44 E
Gusau, *Nigeria* 101 **C6** 12 12N 6 40 E
Gusev, *Russia* 50 **D3** 54 35N 22 10 E
Gushan, *China* 67 **E12** 39 50N 123 35 E
Gushi, *China* 69 **A10** 32 11N 115 41 E
Gushiago, *Ghana* 101 **D4** 9 55N 0 15W
Gusinje,
*Montenegro, Yug.* 42 **E4** 42 35N 19 50 E
Gusinoozersk, *Russia* 57 **D11** 51 16N 106 27 E
Gúspini, *Italy* 40 **C1** 39 32N 8 38 E
Güssing, *Austria* 31 **D9** 47 3N 16 20 E
Gustanj, *Slovenia* 39 **B11** 46 36N 14 59 E
Gustine, *U.S.A.* 144 **H6** 37 14N 121 0W
Güstrow, *Germany* 26 **B8** 53 47N 12 12 E
Gusum, *Sweden* 15 **F10** 58 16N 16 30 E
Guta = Kalárovo, *Czech.* 31 **D11** 47 54N 18 0 E
Gütersloh, *Germany* 26 **D4** 51 54N 8 25 E
Gutha, *Australia* 113 **E2** 28 58 S 115 55 E
Guthalongra, *Australia* 114 **B4** 19 52 S 147 50 E
Guthrie, *U.S.A.* 139 **H6** 35 55N 97 30W
Guthrie Center, *U.S.A.* 140 **C2** 41 41N 94 30W
Gutian, *China* 69 **D12** 26 32N 118 43 E
Gutiérrez, *Bolivia* 157 **D5** 19 25 S 63 34W
Guttannen, *Switz.* 29 **C6** 46 38N 8 18 E
Guttenberg, *U.S.A.* 140 **B5** 42 46N 91 10W
Guyana ■, *S. Amer.* 153 **B6** 5 0N 59 0W
Guyang, *China* 66 **D6** 41 0N 110 5 E
Guyenne, *France* 24 **D4** 44 30N 0 40 E
Guymon, *U.S.A.* 139 **G4** 36 45N 101 30W
Guyra, *Australia* 115 **E5** 30 15 S 151 40 E
Guyuan, *Hebei, China* 66 **D8** 41 37N 115 40 E
Guyuan, *Ningxia Huizu,*
*China* 66 **F4** 36 0N 106 20 E
Guzar, *Uzbekistan* 55 **D3** 38 36N 66 15 E
Guzhang, *China* 68 **C7** 28 42N 109 58 E
Guzhen, *China* 67 **H9** 33 22N 117 18 E
Guzmán, L. de, *Mexico* 146 **A3** 31 25N 107 25W
Gwa, *Burma* 78 **G5** 17 36N 94 34 E
Gwaai, *Zimbabwe* 107 **F2** 19 15 S 27 45 E
Gwabegar, *Australia* 117 **A8** 30 31 S 149 0 E
Gwadabawa, *Nigeria* 101 **C6** 13 28N 5 15 E
Gwādar, *Pakistan* 79 **D1** 25 10N 62 18 E
Gwagwada, *Nigeria* 101 **C6** 10 15N 7 15 E
Gwalia, *Australia* 113 **E3** 28 54 S 121 20 E
Gwalior, *India* 80 **F8** 26 12N 78 10 E
Gwanda, *Zimbabwe* 107 **G2** 20 55 S 29 0 E
Gwandu, *Nigeria* 101 **C5** 12 30N 4 41 E
Gwane, *Zaïre* 106 **B2** 4 45N 25 48 E
Gwaram, *Nigeria* 101 **C7** 10 15N 10 25 E
Gwarzo, *Nigeria* 101 **C6** 12 20N 8 55 E
Gwda →, *Poland* 47 **B3** 53 3N 16 44 E
Gweebarra B., *Ireland* 19 **B3** 54 52N 8 21W
Gweedore, *Ireland* 19 **A3** 55 4N 8 15W
Gwent □, *U.K.* 17 **F5** 51 45N 2 55W
Gweru, *Zimbabwe* 107 **F2** 19 28 S 29 45 E
Gwi, *Nigeria* 101 **D6** 9 0N 7 10 E
Gwinn, *U.S.A.* 134 **B2** 46 15N 87 29W
Gwio Kura, *Nigeria* 101 **C7** 12 40N 11 2 E
Gwol, *Ghana* 100 **C4** 10 58N 1 59W
Gwoza, *Nigeria* 101 **C7** 11 5N 13 40 E
Gwydir →, *Australia* 115 **D4** 29 27 S 149 48 E
Gwynedd □, *U.K.* 16 **E4** 53 0N 4 0W
Gyandzha, *Azerbaijan* 53 **F12** 40 45N 46 20 E
Gyaring Hu, *China* 64 **C4** 34 50N 97 40 E
Gydanskiy P-ov., *Russia* 56 **C8** 70 0N 78 0 E
Gympie, *Australia* 115 **D5** 26 11 S 152 38 E
Gyobingauk, *Burma* 78 **F5** 18 13N 95 39 E
Gyoda, *Japan* 63 **A11** 36 10N 139 30 E
Gyoma, *Hungary* 31 **E13** 46 56N 20 50 E
Gyöngyös, *Hungary* 31 **D12** 47 48N 19 56 E
Györ, *Hungary* 31 **D10** 47 41N 17 40 E
Györ-Sopron □, *Hungary* 31 **D10** 47 40N 17 20 E
Gypsum Palace, *Australia* 116 **B6** 32 37 S 144 9 E
Gypsum Pt., *Canada* 130 **A6** 61 53N 114 35W
Gypsumville, *Canada* 131 **C9** 51 45N 98 40W
Gyula, *Hungary* 31 **E14** 46 38N 21 17 E
Gzhatsk, *Russia* 50 **D9** 55 38N 35 0 E


# H


Ha 'Arava →, *Israel* 91 **E4** 30 50N 35 20 E
Ha Coi, *Vietnam* 76 **B6** 21 26N 107 46 E
Ha Dong, *Vietnam* 76 **B5** 20 58N 105 46 E
Ha Giang, *Vietnam* 76 **A5** 22 50N 104 59 E
Ha Tien, *Vietnam* 77 **G5** 10 23N 104 29 E
Ha Tinh, *Vietnam* 76 **C5** 18 20N 105 54 E
Ha Trung, *Vietnam* 76 **C5** 19 58N 105 50 E
Haacht, *Belgium* 21 **G5** 50 59N 4 37 E
Ha'afeva, *Tonga* 121 **P13** 19 57 S 174 43W
Haag, *Germany* 27 **G8** 48 11N 12 12 E
Haaksbergen, *Neths.* 20 **D9** 52 9N 6 45 E
Haaltert, *Belgium* 21 **G4** 50 55N 4 1 E
Haamstede, *Neths.* 21 **E3** 51 42N 3 45 E
Ha'ano, *Tonga* 121 **P13** 19 41 S 174 18W
Ha'apai Group, *Tonga* 121 **P13** 19 47 S 174 27W
Haapamäki, *Finland* 12 **E18** 62 18N 24 28 E
Haapsalu, *Estonia* 50 **B3** 58 56N 23 30 E
Haarlem, *Neths.* 20 **D5** 52 23N 4 39 E
Haast, *N.Z.* 119 **D4** 43 51 S 169 1 E
Haast →, *N.Z.* 119 **D4** 43 50 S 169 2 E
Haast Bluff, *Australia* 112 **D5** 23 22 S 132 0 E
Haast Pass, *N.Z.* 119 **E4** 44 6 S 169 21 E
Haastrecht, *Neths.* 20 **E5** 52 0N 4 47 E
Hab Nadi Chauki,
*Pakistan* 80 **G2** 25 0N 66 50 E
Ḩabarūt, *Yemen* 87 **C6** 17 18N 52 44 E
Habaswein, *Kenya* 106 **B4** 1 2N 39 30 E
Ḩabawnah, W. →,
*Si. Arabia* 86 **C4** 17 57N 44 58 E
Habay, *Canada* 130 **B5** 58 50N 118 44W
Habay-la-Neuve, *Belgium* 21 **J7** 49 44N 5 38 E
Ḩabbān, *Yemen* 86 **D4** 14 21N 47 5 E
Ḩabbānīyah, *Iraq* 84 **C4** 33 17N 43 29 E
Habiganj, *Bangla.* 78 **C3** 24 24N 91 30 E
Haboro, *Japan* 60 **B10** 44 22N 141 42 E
Haccourt, *Belgium* 21 **G7** 50 44N 5 40 E
Hachenburg, *Germany* 26 **E3** 50 40N 7 49 E
Hachijō-Jima, *Japan* 63 **D11** 33 5N 139 45 E
Hachinohe, *Japan* 60 **D10** 40 30N 141 29 E
Hachiōji, *Japan* 63 **B11** 35 40N 139 20 E
Hachŏn, *N. Korea* 67 **D15** 41 29N 129 2 E
Hachy, *Belgium* 21 **J7** 49 42N 5 41 E
Hacıbektaş, *Turkey* 88 **D6** 38 56N 34 33 E
Hacılar, *Turkey* 88 **D6** 38 38N 35 26 E
Hackensack, *U.S.A.* 137 **F10** 40 53N 74 3W
Haçli Gölü, *Turkey* 89 **D10** 39 0N 42 17 E
Hadali, *Pakistan* 80 **C5** 32 16N 72 11 E
Hadarba, Ras, *Sudan* 94 **C4** 22 4N 36 51 E
Hadarom □, *Israel* 91 **E3** 31 0N 35 0 E
Ḩadbaram, *Oman* 87 **C6** 17 27N 55 15 E
Hadd, Ras al, *Oman* 87 **B7** 22 35N 59 50 E
Ḩaddā, *Si. Arabia* 86 **B2** 21 27N 39 34 E
Haddington, *U.K.* 18 **F6** 55 57N 2 48W
Haddon Rig, *Australia* 117 **A7** 31 27 S 147 52 E
Haded Plain, *Somali Rep.* 108 **C3** 9 46N 48 2 E
Hadejia, *Nigeria* 101 **C7** 12 30N 10 5 E
Hadejia →, *Nigeria* 101 **C7** 12 50N 10 51 E
Haden, *Australia* 115 **D5** 27 13 S 151 54 E
Hadera, *Israel* 91 **C3** 32 27N 34 55 E
Hadera, N. →, *Israel* 91 **C3** 32 28N 34 52 E
Haderslev, *Denmark* 15 **J3** 55 15N 9 30 E
Hadházteglás, *Hungary* 31 **D14** 47 40N 21 40 E
Hadhramaut =
Ḩaḑramawt, *Yemen* 87 **D5** 15 30N 49 30 E
Hadım, *Turkey* 88 **E5** 36 58N 32 26 E
Hadjeb El Aïoun, *Tunisia* 96 **A1** 35 21N 9 32 E
Hadong, *S. Korea* 67 **G14** 35 5N 127 44 E
Ḩaḑramawt, *Yemen* 87 **D5** 15 30N 49 30 E
Ḩaḑramawt, W. →,
*Yemen* 87 **D5** 16 0N 48 53 E
Ḩadrānīyah, *Iraq* 84 **C4** 35 38N 43 14 E
Hadrian's Wall, *U.K.* 16 **C5** 55 0N 2 30W
Hadsten, *Denmark* 15 **H4** 56 19N 10 3 E
Hadsund, *Denmark* 15 **H4** 56 44N 10 8 E
Haeju, *N. Korea* 67 **E13** 38 3N 125 45 E
Haenam, *S. Korea* 67 **G14** 34 34N 126 35 E
Haerhpin = Harbin,
*China* 67 **B14** 45 48N 126 40 E
Hafar al Bāţin, *Si. Arabia* 84 **D5** 28 25N 46 0 E
Hafik, *Turkey* 88 **D7** 39 51N 37 23 E
Ḩafīrat al 'Aydā,
*Si. Arabia* 84 **E3** 26 26N 39 12 E
Ḩafit, *Oman* 87 **B6** 23 59N 55 49 E
Hafizabad, *Pakistan* 80 **C5** 32 5N 73 40 E
Haflong, *India* 78 **C4** 25 10N 93 5 E
Hafnarfjörður, *Iceland* 12 **D3** 64 4N 21 57W
Hafun, Ras, *Somali Rep.* 90 **E5** 10 29N 51 30 E
Hagalil, *Israel* 91 **C4** 32 53N 35 18 E
Hagari →, *India* 83 **G3** 15 40N 77 0 E
Hagdan, *Phil.* 71 **F4** 11 20N 123 54 E
Hagen, *Germany* 26 **D3** 51 21N 7 29 E
Hagenow, *Germany* 26 **B7** 53 25N 11 10 E
Hagerman, *U.S.A.* 139 **J2** 33 5N 104 22W
Hagerstown, *Ind., U.S.A.* 141 **E11** 39 55N 85 10W
Hagerstown, *Md., U.S.A.* 134 **F7** 39 39N 77 46W
Hagetmau, *France* 24 **E3** 43 39N 0 37W
Hagfors, *Sweden* 13 **F12** 60 3N 13 45 E
Häggenås, *Sweden* 14 **A8** 63 24N 14 55 E
Hagi, *Iceland* 12 **D2** 65 28N 23 25W
Hagi, *Japan* 62 **C3** 34 30N 131 22 E
Hagolan, *Syria* 91 **B4** 33 0N 35 45 E
Hagondange-Briey,
*France* 23 **C13** 49 16N 6 11 E
Hagonoy, *Phil.* 70 **D3** 14 50N 120 44 E
Hags Hd., *Ireland* 19 **D2** 52 57N 9 30W
Hague, C. de la, *France* 22 **C5** 49 44N 1 56W
Hague, The = 's-
Gravenhage, *Neths.* 20 **D4** 52 7N 4 17 E
Haguenau, *France* 23 **D14** 48 49N 7 47 E
Hai □, *Tanzania* 106 **C4** 3 10 S 37 10 E
Hai Duong, *Vietnam* 76 **B6** 20 56N 106 19 E
Hai'an, *Guangdong,*
*China* 69 **G8** 20 18N 110 11 E
Hai'an, *Jiangsu, China* 69 **A13** 32 37N 120 27 E
Haicheng, *Fujian, China* 69 **E11** 24 23N 117 48 E
Haicheng, *Liaoning,*
*China* 67 **D12** 40 50N 122 45 E
Haidar Khel, *Afghan.* 80 **C3** 33 58N 68 38 E
Haifa = Hefa, *Israel* 91 **C3** 32 46N 35 0 E
Haifeng, *China* 69 **F10** 22 58N 115 10 E
Haig, *Australia* 113 **F4** 30 55 S 126 10 E
Haiger, *Germany* 26 **E4** 50 44N 8 12 E
Haikang, *China* 69 **G8** 20 52N 110 8 E
Haikou, *China* 65 **D6** 20 1N 110 16 E
Ḩā'il, *Si. Arabia* 84 **E4** 27 28N 41 45 E
Hailakandi, *India* 78 **C4** 24 42N 92 34 E
Hailar, *China* 65 **B6** 49 10N 119 38 E
Hailey, *U.S.A.* 142 **E6** 43 30N 114 15W
Haileybury, *Canada* 128 **C4** 47 30N 79 38W
Hailin, *China* 67 **B15** 44 37N 129 30 E
Hailing Dao, *China* 69 **G8** 21 35N 111 47 E
Hailong, *China* 67 **C13** 42 32N 125 40 E
Hailuoto, *Finland* 12 **D18** 65 3N 24 45 E
Haimen, *Guangdong,*
*China* 69 **F11** 23 15N 116 38 E
Haimen, *Jiangsu, China* 69 **B13** 31 52N 121 10 E
Haimen, *Zhejiang, China* 69 **C13** 28 40N 121 24 E
Hainan □, *China* 65 **E5** 19 0N 109 30 E
Hainaut □, *Belgium* 21 **H4** 50 30N 4 0 E
Hainburg, *Austria* 31 **C9** 48 9N 16 56 E
Haines, *U.S.A.* 142 **D5** 44 51N 117 59W
Haines City, *U.S.A.* 135 **L5** 28 6N 81 35W
Haines Junction, *Canada* 130 **A1** 60 45N 137 30W
Hainfeld, *Austria* 30 **C8** 48 3N 15 48 E
Haining, *China* 69 **B13** 30 28N 120 40 E
Haiphong, *Vietnam* 64 **D5** 20 47N 106 41 E
Haiti ■, *W. Indies* 149 **C5** 19 0N 72 30W
Haiya Junction, *Sudan* 94 **D4** 18 20N 36 21 E
Haiyan, *China* 69 **B13** 30 28N 120 58 E
Haiyang, *China* 67 **F11** 36 47N 121 9 E
Haiyuan,
*Guangxi Zhuangzu,*
*China* 68 **F6** 22 8N 107 35 E
Haiyuan, *Ningxia Huizu,*
*China* 66 **F3** 36 35N 105 52 E
Haizhou, *China* 67 **G10** 34 37N 119 7 E
Haizhou Wan, *China* 67 **G10** 34 50N 119 20 E
Haja, *Indonesia* 73 **B3** 3 19 S 129 37 E
Hajar Bangar, *Sudan* 97 **F4** 10 40N 22 45 E
Hajdú-Bihar □, *Hungary* 31 **D14** 47 30N 21 30 E
Hajdúböszörmény,
*Hungary* 31 **D14** 47 40N 21 30 E
Hajdúdurog, *Hungary* 31 **D14** 47 48N 21 30 E
Hajdúnánás, *Hungary* 31 **D14** 47 50N 21 26 E
Hajdúsámson, *Hungary* 31 **D14** 47 37N 21 42 E
Hajdúszobaszló, *Hungary* 31 **D14** 47 27N 21 22 E
Hajiganj, *Bangla.* 78 **D3** 23 15N 90 50 E
Hajipur, *India* 81 **G11** 25 45N 85 13 E
Ḩajjah, *Yemen* 86 **D3** 15 42N 43 36 E
Ḩājjī Muḩsin, *Iraq* 84 **C5** 32 35N 45 29 E
Ḩājjīābād, *Eşfahan, Iran* 85 **C7** 33 41N 54 50 E
Ḩājjīābād, *Hormozgān,*
*Iran* 85 **D7** 28 19N 55 55 E
Hajnówka, *Poland* 47 **C10** 52 47N 23 35 E
Ḩajrah, *Si. Arabia* 86 **B3** 20 14N 41 3 E
Haka, *Burma* 78 **D4** 22 39N 93 37 E
Hakansson, Mts., *Zaïre* 103 **D5** 8 40 S 25 45 E
Håkantorp, *Sweden* 15 **F6** 58 18N 12 55 E
Hakataramea, *N.Z.* 119 **E5** 44 43 S 170 30 E
Ḩakkan, *Oman* 87 **B7** 20 22N 58 47 E
Hakkâri, *Turkey* 89 **E10** 37 34N 43 44 E
Hakkâri □, *Turkey* 89 **E10** 37 30N 44 0 E
Hakkâri Dağları, *Turkey* 89 **E10** 37 45N 42 35 E
Hakken-Zan, *Japan* 63 **C7** 34 10N 135 54 E
Hakodate, *Japan* 60 **D10** 41 45N 140 44 E
Hakota, *Japan* 63 **A12** 36 5N 140 30 E
Haku-San, *Japan* 63 **A8** 36 9N 136 46 E
Hakui, *Japan* 61 **F8** 36 53N 136 47 E
Hakun, *Burma* 78 **B5** 26 46N 95 42 E
Hala, *Pakistan* 79 **D3** 25 43N 68 20 E
Ḩalab, *Syria* 84 **B3** 36 10N 37 15 E
Ḩalaban, *Si. Arabia* 86 **B4** 23 29N 44 23 E
Ḩalabjah, *Iraq* 84 **C5** 35 10N 45 58 E
Halaib, *Sudan* 94 **C4** 22 12N 36 30 E
Halanzy, *Belgium* 21 **J7** 49 33N 5 44 E
Hālat 'Ammār, *Si. Arabia* 84 **D3** 29 10N 36 4 E
Halbā, *Lebanon* 91 **A5** 34 34N 36 6 E
Halberstadt, *Germany* 26 **D7** 51 53N 11 2 E
Halcombe, *N.Z.* 118 **G4** 40 8 S 175 30 E
Halcon, Mt., *Phil.* 70 **E3** 13 0N 121 30 E
Halden, *Norway* 14 **E5** 59 9N 11 23 E
Haldensleben, *Germany* 26 **C7** 52 17N 11 30 E
Haldwani, *India* 81 **E8** 29 31N 79 30 E
Hale, *U.S.A.* 140 **E3** 39 36N 93 20W
Hale →, *Australia* 114 **C2** 24 56 S 135 53 E
Haleakala Crater, *U.S.A.* 132 **H16** 20 43N 156 12W
Halen, *Belgium* 21 **G6** 50 57N 5 6 E
Haleyville, *U.S.A.* 135 **H2** 34 15N 87 40W
Half Assini, *Ghana* 100 **D4** 5 1N 2 50W
Halfmoon Bay, *N.Z.* 119 **G3** 46 50 S 168 5 E
Halfway →, *Canada* 130 **B4** 56 12N 121 32W
Haliburton, *Canada* 128 **C4** 45 3N 78 30W
Halicarnassus, *Turkey* 45 **G9** 37 3N 27 30 E
Halifax, *Australia* 114 **B4** 18 32 S 146 22 E
Halifax, *Canada* 129 **D7** 44 38N 63 35W
Halifax, *U.K.* 16 **D6** 53 43N 1 51W
Halifax B., *Australia* 114 **B4** 18 50 S 147 0 E
Halifax I., *Namibia* 104 **D2** 26 38 S 15 4 E
Halīl →, *Iran* 85 **E8** 27 40N 58 30 E
Halin, *Somali Rep.* 108 **C3** 9 6N 48 37 E
Hall, *Austria* 30 **D4** 47 17N 11 30 E
Hall Beach, *Canada* 127 **B11** 68 46N 81 12W
Hall Pt., *Australia* 112 **C3** 15 40 S 124 23 E
Hallands län □, *Sweden* 15 **H6** 56 50N 12 50 E
Hallands Väderö, *Sweden* 15 **H6** 56 27N 12 34 E
Hallandsås, *Sweden* 15 **H7** 56 22N 13 0 E
Halle, *Belgium* 21 **G4** 50 44N 4 13 E
Halle,
*Nordrhein-Westfalen,*
*Germany* 26 **C4** 52 4N 8 20 E
Halle, *Sachsen-Anhalt,*
*Germany* 26 **D7** 51 29N 12 0 E
Hällefors, *Sweden* 13 **G13** 59 47N 14 31 E
Hallein, *Austria* 30 **D6** 47 40N 13 5 E
Hällekis, *Sweden* 15 **F7** 58 38N 13 27 E
Hallett, *Australia* 116 **B3** 33 25 S 138 55 E
Hallettsville, *U.S.A.* 139 **L6** 29 28N 96 57W
Hällevadsholm, *Sweden* 15 **F5** 58 35N 11 33 E
Hallia →, *India* 82 **F4** 16 55N 79 20 E
Halliday, *U.S.A.* 138 **B3** 47 20N 102 25W
Halliday L., *Canada* 131 **A7** 61 21N 108 56W
Hallim, *S. Korea* 67 **H14** 33 24N 126 15 E
Hallingdal →, *Norway* 13 **F10** 60 34N 9 12 E
Hällnäs, *Sweden* 12 **D15** 64 19N 19 36 E
Hallock, *U.S.A.* 131 **D9** 48 47N 97 0W
Halls Creek, *Australia* 112 **C4** 18 16 S 127 38 E
Hallstahammar, *Sweden* 14 **E10** 59 38N 16 15 E
Hallstatt, *Austria* 30 **D6** 47 33N 13 38 E
Hallstead, *U.S.A.* 137 **E9** 41 56N 75 45W
Halmahera, *Indonesia* 72 **A3** 0 40N 128 0 E
Halmeu, *Romania* 46 **B4** 47 57N 23 2 E
Halmstad, *Sweden* 15 **H6** 56 41N 12 52 E
Halq el Oued, *Tunisia* 96 **A2** 36 53N 10 18 E
Hals, *Denmark* 15 **H4** 56 59N 10 18 E
Halsafjorden, *Norway* 14 **A2** 63 5N 8 10 E
Hälsingborg =
Helsingborg, *Sweden* 15 **H6** 56 3N 12 42 E
Halstad, *U.S.A.* 138 **B6** 47 21N 96 50W
Haltdalen, *Norway* 14 **B5** 62 56N 11 8 E
Haltern, *Germany* 26 **D3** 51 44N 7 10 E
Halul, *Qatar* 85 **E7** 25 40N 52 40 E
Ḩalvān, *Iran* 85 **C8** 33 57N 56 15 E
Ham, *France* 23 **C10** 49 45N 3 4 E
Ham Tan, *Vietnam* 77 **G6** 10 40N 107 45 E
Ham Yen, *Vietnam* 76 **A5** 22 4N 105 3 E
Hamab, *Namibia* 104 **D2** 28 7 S 19 16 E
Hamad, *Sudan* 95 **D3** 15 20N 33 32 E
Hamada, *Japan* 62 **C4** 34 56N 132 4 E
Hamadān, *Iran* 85 **C6** 34 52N 48 32 E
Hamadān □, *Iran* 85 **C6** 35 0N 49 0 E
Hamadia, *Algeria* 99 **A5** 35 28N 1 57 E
Hamāh, *Syria* 84 **C3** 35 5N 36 40 E
Hamakita, *Japan* 63 **C9** 34 45N 137 47 E
Hamamatsu, *Japan* 63 **C9** 34 45N 137 45 E
Hamar, *Norway* 14 **D5** 60 48N 11 7 E
Hamarøy, *Norway* 12 **B13** 68 5N 15 38 E
Hamâta, Gebel, *Egypt* 94 **C3** 24 17N 35 0 E
Hamber Prov. Park,
*Canada* 130 **C5** 52 20N 118 0W
Hamburg, *Germany* 26 **B5** 53 32N 9 59 E
Hamburg, *Ark., U.S.A.* 139 **J9** 33 15N 91 47W
Hamburg, *Iowa, U.S.A.* 138 **E7** 40 37N 95 38W
Hamburg, *N.Y., U.S.A.* 136 **D6** 42 44N 78 50W
Hamburg, *Pa., U.S.A.* 137 **F9** 40 33N 76 0W
Hamburg □, *Germany* 26 **B6** 53 30N 10 0 E
Ḩamḑ, W. al →,
*Si. Arabia* 84 **E3** 24 55N 36 20 E
Ḩamḑah, *Si. Arabia* 86 **C3** 19 2N 43 36 E
Ḩamdānah, *Si. Arabia* 86 **C3** 19 59N 40 34 E
Hamden, *U.S.A.* 137 **E12** 41 21N 72 56W
Hame □ = Hämeen
lääni □, *Finland* 13 **F18** 61 30N 24 0 E
Hämeen lääni □, *Finland* 13 **F18** 61 30N 24 0 E
Hämeenlinna, *Finland* 13 **F18** 61 0N 24 28 E
Hamélé, *Ghana* 100 **C4** 10 56N 2 45W
Hamelin Pool, *Australia* 113 **E1** 26 22 S 114 20 E
Hameln, *Germany* 26 **C5** 52 7N 9 24 E
Hamer Koke, *Ethiopia* 95 **F4** 5 15N 36 45 E
Hamerkaz □, *Israel* 91 **C3** 32 15N 34 55 E
Hamersley Ra., *Australia* 112 **D2** 22 0 S 117 45 E

Icha, *Russia* 57 D16 55 30N 156 0 E
Ich'ang = Yichang, *China* 69 B8 30 40N 111 20 E
Ichchapuram, *India* 82 E7 19 10N 84 40 E
Ichihara, *Japan* 63 B12 35 28N 140 5 E
Ichikawa, *Japan* 63 B11 35 44N 139 55 E
Ichilo →, *Bolivia* 157 D5 15 57 S 64 50W
Ichinohe, *Japan* 60 D10 40 13N 141 17 E
Ichinomiya, *Gifu, Japan* 63 B8 35 18N 136 48 E
Ichinomiya, *Kumamoto, Japan* 62 E3 32 58N 131 5 E
Ichinoseki, *Japan* 60 E10 38 55N 141 8 E
Ichnya, *Ukraine* 50 F8 50 52N 32 24 E
Ichŏn, *S. Korea* 67 F14 37 17N 127 27 E
Icht, *Morocco* 98 C3 29 6N 8 54W
Ichtegem, *Belgium* 21 F2 51 5N 3 1 E
Icó, *Brazil* 154 C4 6 24 S 38 51W
Icod, *Canary Is.* 33 F3 28 22N 16 43W
Icoraci, *Brazil* 154 B2 1 18 S 48 28W
Icy Str., *U.S.A.* 130 B1 58 20N 135 30W
Ida Grove, *U.S.A.* 138 D7 42 20N 95 25W
Ida Valley, *Australia* 113 E3 28 42 S 120 29 E
Idabel, *U.S.A.* 139 J7 33 53N 94 50W
Idaga Hamus, *Ethiopia* 95 E4 14 13N 39 48 E
Idah, *Nigeria* 101 D6 7 5N 6 40 E
Idaho □, *U.S.A.* 142 D6 44 10N 114 0W
Idaho City, *U.S.A.* 142 E6 43 50N 115 52W
Idaho Falls, *U.S.A.* 142 E7 43 30N 112 1W
Idaho Springs, *U.S.A.* 142 G11 39 49N 105 30W
Idanha-a-Nova, *Portugal* 36 F3 39 50N 7 15W
Idar-Oberstein, *Germany* 27 F3 49 43N 7 19 E
Idd el Ghanam, *Sudan* 97 F4 11 30N 24 19 E
Iddan, *Somali Rep.* 90 F4 6 10N 48 55 E
Idehan, *Libya* 96 C2 27 10N 11 30 E
Idehan Marzūq, *Libya* 96 D2 24 50N 13 51 E
Idelès, *Algeria* 99 D6 23 50N 5 53 E
Idfû, *Egypt* 94 C3 24 55N 32 49 E
Ídhi Óros, *Greece* 32 D6 35 15N 24 45 E
Ídhra, *Greece* 45 G5 37 20N 23 28 E
Idi, *Indonesia* 74 A1 5 2N 97 37 E
Idiofa, *Zaïre* 103 C3 4 55 S 19 42 E
Idku, Bahra el, *Egypt* 94 H7 31 18N 30 18 E
Idlib, *Syria* 84 C3 35 55N 36 36 E
Idria, *U.S.A.* 144 J6 36 25N 120 41W
Idrija, *Slovenia* 39 B11 46 0N 14 5 E
Idritsa, *Russia* 50 C6 56 25N 28 30 E
Idstein, *Germany* 27 E4 50 13N 8 17 E
Idutywa, *S. Africa* 105 E4 32 8 S 28 18 E
Ieper, *Belgium* 21 G1 50 51N 2 53 E
Ierápetra, *Greece* 32 E7 35 0N 25 44 E
Ierissós, *Greece* 44 D5 40 22N 23 52 E
Ierissóu Kólpos, *Greece* 44 D5 40 27N 23 57 E
Ierzu, *Italy* 40 C2 39 48N 9 32 E
Ieshima-Shotō, *Japan* 62 C6 34 40N 134 32 E
Iesi, *Italy* 39 E10 43 32N 13 12 E
Ifach, Punta, *Spain* 35 G5 38 38N 0 5 E
'Ifāl, W. al →, *Si. Arabia* 84 D2 28 7N 35 3 E
Ifanadiana, *Madag.* 105 C8 21 19 S 47 39 E
Ife, *Nigeria* 101 D5 7 30N 4 31 E
Iférouâne, *Niger* 97 E1 19 5N 8 24 E
Iffley, *Australia* 114 B3 18 53 S 141 12 E
Ifni, *Morocco* 98 C2 29 29N 10 12W
Ifon, *Nigeria* 101 D6 6 58N 5 40 E
Iforas, Adrar des, *Mali* 101 B5 19 40N 1 40 E
Ifould, L., *Australia* 113 F5 30 52 S 132 6 E
Ifrane, *Morocco* 98 B3 33 33N 5 7W
Ifugao □, *Phil.* 70 C3 16 40N 121 10 E
Iga, *Japan* 63 C8 34 45N 136 10 E
Iganga, *Uganda* 106 B3 0 37N 33 28 E
Igara Paraná →, *Colombia* 152 D3 2 9 S 71 47W
Igarapava, *Brazil* 155 F2 20 3 S 47 47W
Igarapé Açu, *Brazil* 154 B2 1 4 S 47 33W
Igarapé-Mirim, *Brazil* 154 B2 1 59 S 48 58W
Igarka, *Russia* 56 C9 67 30N 86 33 E
Igatimi, *Paraguay* 159 A4 24 5 S 55 40W
Igatpuri, *India* 82 E1 19 40N 73 35 E
Igbetti, *Nigeria* 101 D5 8 44N 4 8 E
Igbo-Ora, *Nigeria* 101 D5 7 29N 3 15 E
Igboho, *Nigeria* 101 D5 8 53N 3 50 E
Iğdır, *Turkey* 89 D11 39 55N 44 2 E
Iggesund, *Sweden* 14 C11 61 39N 17 10 E
Ighil Izane, *Algeria* 99 A5 35 44N 0 31 E
Iglésias, *Italy* 40 C1 39 19N 8 27 E
Igli, *Algeria* 99 B4 30 25N 2 19W
Iglino, *Russia* 54 D5 54 50N 56 26 E
Igloolik, *Canada* 127 B11 69 20N 81 49W
Igma, Gebel el, *Egypt* 94 J8 28 55N 34 0 E
Ignace, *Canada* 128 C1 49 30N 91 40W
İğneada Burnu, *Turkey* 88 C3 41 53N 28 2 E
Igoshevo, *Russia* 51 B13 59 25N 42 35 E
Igoumenítsa, *Greece* 44 E2 39 32N 20 18 E
Igra, *Russia* 54 C3 57 33N 53 7 E
Iguaçu →, *Brazil* 159 B5 25 36 S 54 36W
Iguaçu, Cat. del, *Brazil* 159 B5 25 41 S 54 26W
Iguaçu Falls = Iguaçu, Cat. del, *Brazil* 159 B5 25 41 S 54 26W
Iguala, *Mexico* 147 D5 18 20N 99 40W
Igualada, *Spain* 34 D6 41 37N 1 37 E
Iguape, *Brazil* 155 F2 24 43 S 47 33W
Iguassu = Iguaçu →, *Brazil* 159 B5 25 36 S 54 36W
Iguatu, *Brazil* 154 C4 6 20 S 39 18W
Iguéla, *Gabon* 102 C1 2 0 S 9 16 E
Iguig, *Phil.* 70 C3 17 45N 121 44 E
Igunga □, *Tanzania* 106 C3 4 20 S 33 45 E
Iheya-Shima, *Japan* 61 L3 27 4N 127 58 E
Ihiala, *Nigeria* 101 D6 5 51N 6 55 E
Ihosy, *Madag.* 105 C8 22 24 S 46 8 E
Ihotry, L., *Madag.* 105 C7 21 56 S 43 41 E
Ii, *Finland* 12 D18 65 19N 25 22 E
Ii-Shima, *Japan* 61 L3 26 43N 127 47 E
Iida, *Japan* 63 B9 35 35N 137 50 E
Iijoki →, *Finland* 12 D18 65 20N 25 20 E
Iisalmi, *Finland* 12 E19 63 32N 27 10 E
Iiyama, *Japan* 61 F9 36 51N 138 22 E
Iizuka, *Japan* 62 D2 33 38N 130 42 E
Ijâfene, *Mauritania* 98 D3 20 40N 8 0W
Ijebu-Igbo, *Nigeria* 101 D5 6 56N 4 1 E
Ijebu-Ode, *Nigeria* 101 D5 6 47N 3 58 E
IJmuiden, *Neths.* 20 D5 52 28N 4 35 E
IJssel →, *Neths.* 20 C7 52 35N 5 50 E
IJsselmeer, *Neths.* 20 C6 52 45N 5 20 E
IJsselmuiden, *Neths.* 20 C7 52 34N 5 57 E
IJsselstein, *Neths.* 20 D6 52 1N 5 2 E
Ijuí →, *Brazil* 159 B4 27 58 S 55 20W
Ijūin, *Japan* 62 F2 31 37N 130 24 E
IJzendijke, *Neths.* 21 F3 51 19N 3 37 E
IJzer →, *Belgium* 21 F1 51 9N 2 44 E
Ik →, *Russia* 54 D3 55 55N 52 36 E
Ikale, *Nigeria* 101 D6 7 40N 5 37 E
Ikare, *Nigeria* 101 D6 7 32N 5 40 E
Ikaría, *Greece* 45 G8 37 35N 26 10 E
Ikast, *Denmark* 15 H3 56 8N 9 10 E
Ikawa, *Japan* 63 B10 35 13N 138 15 E
Ikeda, *Japan* 62 C5 34 1N 133 48 E
Ikeja, *Nigeria* 101 D5 6 36N 3 23 E
Ikela, *Zaïre* 102 C4 1 6 S 23 6 E
Ikenge, *Zaïre* 102 C3 0 8 S 18 8 E
Ikerre-Ekiti, *Nigeria* 101 D6 7 25N 5 19 E
Ikhtiman, *Bulgaria* 43 E8 42 27N 23 48 E
Iki, *Japan* 62 D1 33 45N 129 42 E
Iki-Kaikyō, *Japan* 62 D1 33 40N 129 45 E
Ikimba L., *Tanzania* 106 C3 1 30 S 31 20 E
Ikire, *Nigeria* 101 D5 7 23N 4 15 E
Ikitsuki-Shima, *Japan* 62 D1 33 23N 129 26 E
İkizdere, *Turkey* 89 C9 40 46N 40 32 E
Ikom, *Nigeria* 101 D6 6 0N 8 42 E
Ikopa →, *Madag.* 105 B8 16 45 S 46 40 E
Ikot Ekpene, *Nigeria* 101 D6 5 12N 7 40 E
'Ikrimah, *Libya* 96 B4 32 2N 23 41 E
Ikungu, *Tanzania* 106 C3 1 33 S 33 42 E
Ikuno, *Japan* 62 B6 35 10N 134 48 E
Ikurun, *Nigeria* 101 D5 7 54N 4 40 E
Ila, *Nigeria* 101 D5 8 0N 4 39 E
Ilagan, *Phil.* 70 C3 17 7N 121 53 E
Īlām, *Iran* 84 C5 33 0N 46 0 E
Ilam, *Nepal* 81 F12 26 58N 87 58 E
Ilanskiy, *Russia* 57 D10 56 14N 96 3 E
Ilanz, *Switz.* 29 C8 46 46N 9 12 E
Ilaro, *Nigeria* 101 D5 6 53N 3 3 E
Iława, *Poland* 47 B6 53 36N 19 34 E
Ilayangudi, *India* 83 K4 9 34N 78 37 E
Ilbilbie, *Australia* 114 C4 21 45 S 149 20 E
Ile-à-la-Crosse, *Canada* 131 B7 55 27N 107 53W
Ile-à-la-Crosse, Lac, *Canada* 131 B7 55 40N 107 45W
Île-de-France, *France* 23 D9 49 0N 2 20 E
Ilebo, *Zaïre* 103 C4 4 17 S 20 55 E
Ileje □, *Tanzania* 107 D3 9 30 S 33 25 E
Ilek, *Russia* 54 F3 51 32N 53 21 E
Ilek →, *Russia* 54 F3 51 30N 53 22 E
Ilero, *Nigeria* 101 D5 8 0N 3 20 E
Ilesha, *Kwara, Nigeria* 101 D5 8 57N 3 28 E
Ilesha, *Oyo, Nigeria* 101 D5 7 37N 4 40 E
Ilford, *Canada* 131 B9 56 4N 95 35W
Ilfracombe, *Australia* 114 C3 23 30 S 144 30 E
Ilfracombe, *U.K.* 17 F3 51 13N 4 8W
Ilgaz, *Turkey* 88 C5 40 55N 33 37 E
Ilgaz Dağları, *Turkey* 88 C5 41 10N 33 50 E
Ilgın, *Turkey* 88 D4 38 16N 31 55 E
Ilha Grande, *Brazil* 153 D4 0 27 S 65 2W
Ilha Grande, B. da, *Brazil* 155 F3 23 9 S 44 30W
Ílhavo, *Portugal* 36 E2 40 33N 8 43W
Ilhéus, *Brazil* 155 D4 14 49 S 39 2W
Ili →, *Kazakhstan* 55 A8 45 53N 77 10 E
Ilia, *Romania* 46 D3 45 57N 22 40 E
Ilia □, *Greece* 45 G3 37 45N 21 35 E
Iliç, *Turkey* 89 D8 39 27N 38 33 E
Ilich, *Kazakhstan* 55 C4 40 50N 68 27 E
Iliff, *U.S.A.* 138 E3 40 50N 103 3W
Iligan, *Phil.* 71 G5 8 12N 124 13 E
Iligan Bay, *Phil.* 71 G5 8 25N 124 5 E
Ilíki, L., *Greece* 45 F5 38 24N 23 15 E
Ilin I., *Phil.* 70 E3 12 14N 121 5 E
Iliodhrómia, *Greece* 44 E5 39 12N 23 50 E
Ilion, *U.S.A.* 137 D9 43 0N 75 3W
Ilirska-Bistrica, *Slovenia* 39 C11 45 34N 14 14 E
Ilkal, *India* 83 G3 15 57N 76 8 E
Ilkeston, *U.K.* 16 E6 52 59N 1 19W
Illampu = Ancohuma, Nevada, *Bolivia* 156 D4 16 0 S 68 50W
Illana B., *Phil.* 71 H4 7 35N 123 45 E
Illapel, *Chile* 158 C1 32 0 S 71 10W
Ille-et-Vilaine □, *France* 22 D5 48 10N 1 30W
Ille-sur-Têt, *France* 24 F6 42 40N 2 38 E
Iller →, *Germany* 27 G5 48 23N 9 58 E
Illescas, *Spain* 36 E7 40 8N 3 51W
Illetas, *Spain* 33 B9 39 32N 2 35 E
Illiers-Combray, *France* 22 D8 48 18N 1 15 E
Illimani, *Bolivia* 156 D4 16 30 S 67 50W
Illinois □, *U.S.A.* 140 D7 40 15N 89 30W
Illinois →, *U.S.A.* 140 F6 38 55N 90 28W
Illiopolis, *U.S.A.* 140 E7 39 51N 89 15W
Illium = Troy, *Turkey* 44 E8 39 57N 26 12 E
Illizi, *Algeria* 99 C6 26 31N 8 32 E
Illora, *Spain* 37 H7 37 17N 3 53W
Ilm →, *Germany* 26 D7 51 7N 11 45 E
Ilmen, Oz., *Russia* 50 B7 58 15N 31 10 E
Ilmenau, *Germany* 26 E6 50 41N 10 55 E
Ilo, *Peru* 156 D3 17 40 S 71 20W
Ilobu, *Nigeria* 101 D5 7 45N 4 25 E
Ilocos Norte □, *Phil.* 70 B3 18 10N 120 45 E
Ilocos Sur □, *Phil.* 70 C3 17 20N 120 35 E
Iloilo, *Phil.* 71 F4 10 45N 122 33 E
Iloilo □, *Phil.* 71 F4 11 0N 122 40 E
Ilok, *Croatia* 42 B4 45 15N 19 20 E
Ilora, *Nigeria* 101 D5 7 45N 3 50 E
Ilorin, *Nigeria* 101 D5 8 30N 4 35 E
Iloulya, *Russia* 53 B11 49 15N 44 2 E
Ilovatka, *Russia* 51 F14 50 30N 45 50 E
Ilovlya →, *Russia* 53 B10 49 14N 43 54 E
Iłowa, *Poland* 47 D2 51 30N 15 10 E
Ilubabor □, *Ethiopia* 95 F3 7 25N 35 0 E
Ilukste, *Latvia* 50 D5 55 55N 26 20 E
Ilva Mică, *Romania* 46 B5 47 17N 24 40 E
Ilwaco, *U.S.A.* 144 D2 46 19N 124 3W
Ilwaki, *Indonesia* 72 C3 7 55 S 126 30 E
Ilyichevsk, *Ukraine* 52 C4 46 20N 30 35 E
Iłża, *Poland* 47 D8 51 10N 21 15 E
Iłżanka →, *Poland* 47 D8 51 14N 21 48 E
Imabari, *Japan* 62 C5 34 4N 133 0 E
Imaichi, *Japan* 63 A11 36 43N 139 46 E
Imaloto →, *Madag.* 105 C8 23 27 S 45 13 E
İmamoğlu, *Turkey* 88 E6 37 15N 35 38 E
Imandra, Oz., *Russia* 48 A5 67 30N 33 0 E
Imari, *Japan* 62 D1 33 15N 129 52 E
Imasa, *Sudan* 94 D4 18 0N 36 12 E
Imathía □, *Greece* 44 D4 40 30N 22 15 E
Imbâbah, *Egypt* 94 H7 30 5N 31 12 E
Imbabura □, *Ecuador* 152 C2 0 30N 78 45W
Imbaimadai, *Guyana* 153 B5 5 44N 60 17W
Imbler, *U.S.A.* 142 D5 45 31N 118 0W
Imdahane, *Morocco* 98 B3 32 8N 7 0W
imeni 26 Bakinskikh Komissarov, *Azerbaijan* 89 D13 39 19N 49 12 E
imeni 26 Bakinskikh Komissarov, *Turkmenistan* 49 G9 39 22N 54 10 E
Imeni Panfilova, *Kazakhstan* 55 B8 43 23N 77 7 E
Imeni Poliny Osipenko, *Russia* 57 D14 52 30N 136 29 E
Imeri, Serra, *Brazil* 152 C4 0 50N 65 25W
Imerimandroso, *Madag.* 105 B8 17 26 S 48 35 E
Imesan, *Mauritania* 98 D1 22 54N 15 30W
Imi, *Ethiopia* 90 F3 6 28N 42 10 E
Imishly, *Azerbaijan* 53 G13 39 55N 48 4 E
Imitek, *Morocco* 98 C3 29 43N 8 10W
Imlay, *U.S.A.* 142 F4 40 45N 118 9W
Imlay City, *U.S.A.* 136 C1 43 0N 83 2W
Immenstadt, *Germany* 27 H6 47 34N 10 13 E
Immingham, *U.K.* 16 D7 53 37N 0 12W
Immokalee, *U.S.A.* 135 M5 26 25N 81 26W
Imo □, *Nigeria* 101 D6 5 15N 7 20 E
Imola, *Italy* 39 D8 44 20N 11 42 E
Imotski, *Croatia* 42 D2 43 27N 17 12 E
Imperatriz, *Amazonas, Brazil* 156 B4 5 18 S 67 11W
Imperatriz, *Maranhão, Brazil* 154 C2 5 30 S 47 29W
Impéria, *Italy* 38 E5 43 52N 8 3 E
Imperial, *Canada* 131 C7 51 21N 105 28W
Imperial, *Peru* 156 C2 13 4 S 76 21W
Imperial, *Calif., U.S.A.* 145 N11 32 52N 115 34W
Imperial, *Nebr., U.S.A.* 138 E4 40 38N 101 39W
Imperial Beach, *U.S.A.* 145 N9 32 35N 117 8W
Imperial Dam, *U.S.A.* 145 N12 32 50N 114 30W
Imperial Res., *U.S.A.* 145 N12 32 53N 114 28W
Imperial Valley, *U.S.A.* 145 N11 32 55N 115 30W
Imperieuse Reef, *Australia* 112 C2 17 36 S 118 50 E
Impfondo, *Congo* 102 B3 1 40N 18 0 E
Imphal, *India* 78 C4 24 48N 93 56 E
Imphy, *France* 24 B7 46 55N 3 16 E
İmralı, *Turkey* 88 C3 40 32N 28 31 E
İmranlı, *Turkey* 89 D8 39 54N 38 7 E
İmroz = Gökçeada, *Turkey* 44 D7 40 10N 25 50 E
Imst, *Austria* 30 D3 47 15N 10 44 E
Imuruan B., *Phil.* 71 F2 10 40N 119 10 E
In Belbel, *Algeria* 99 C5 27 55N 1 12 E
In Delimane, *Mali* 101 B5 15 52N 1 31 E
In Rhar, *Algeria* 99 C5 27 10N 1 59 E
In Salah, *Algeria* 99 C5 27 10N 2 32 E
In Tallak, *Mali* 101 B5 16 19N 3 15 E
Ina, *Japan* 63 B9 35 50N 137 55 E
Ina-Bonchi, *Japan* 63 B9 35 45N 137 58 E
Inagauan, *Phil.* 71 G2 9 33N 118 39 E
Inajá, *Brazil* 154 C4 8 54 S 37 49W
Inangahua Junction, *N.Z.* 119 B6 41 52 S 171 59 E
Inanwatan, *Indonesia* 73 B4 2 10 S 132 14 E
Iñapari, *Peru* 156 C4 11 0 S 69 40W
Inarajan, *Guam* 121 R15 13 16N 144 45 E
Inari, *Finland* 12 B19 68 54N 27 5 E
Inarijärvi, *Finland* 12 B19 69 0N 28 0 E
Inawashiro-Ko, *Japan* 60 F10 37 29N 140 6 E
Inazawa, *Japan* 63 B8 35 15N 136 47 E
Inca, *Spain* 33 B9 39 43N 2 54 E
Incaguasi, *Chile* 158 B1 29 12 S 71 5W
İnce-Burnu, *Turkey* 52 E6 42 7N 34 56 E
İncekum Burnu, *Turkey* 88 E5 36 13N 33 57 E
Inchon, *S. Korea* 67 F14 37 27N 126 40 E
Incio, *Spain* 36 C3 42 39N 7 21W
İncirliova, *Turkey* 88 E2 37 50N 27 41 E
Incomáti →, *Mozam.* 105 D5 25 46 S 32 43 E
Inda Silase, *Ethiopia* 95 E4 14 10N 38 15 E
Indalsälven →, *Sweden* 14 B11 62 36N 17 30 E
Indaw, *Burma* 78 C6 24 15N 96 5 E
Indbir, *Ethiopia* 95 F4 8 7N 37 52 E
Independence, *Calif., U.S.A.* 144 J8 36 51N 118 14W
Independence, *Iowa, U.S.A.* 140 B5 42 27N 91 52W
Independence, *Kans., U.S.A.* 139 G7 37 10N 95 43W
Independence, *Ky., U.S.A.* 141 F12 38 57N 84 33W
Independence, *Mo., U.S.A.* 140 E2 39 3N 94 25W
Independence, *Oreg., U.S.A.* 142 D2 44 53N 123 12W
Independence Fjord, *Greenland* 6 A6 82 10N 29 0W
Independence Mts., *U.S.A.* 142 F5 41 30N 116 2W
Independência, *Brazil* 154 C3 5 23 S 40 19W
Independenţa, *Romania* 46 D8 45 25N 27 42 E
Inderborskiy, *Kazakhstan* 53 B14 48 30N 51 42 E
Index, *U.S.A.* 144 C5 47 50N 121 33W
India ■, *Asia* 59 H11 20 0N 78 0 E
Indian →, *U.S.A.* 135 M5 27 59N 80 34W
Indian Cabins, *Canada* 130 B5 59 52N 117 40W
Indian Harbour, *Canada* 129 B8 54 27N 57 13W
Indian Head, *Canada* 131 C8 50 30N 103 41W
Indian Ocean 58 K11 5 0 S 75 0 E
Indian Springs, *U.S.A.* 145 J11 36 35N 115 40W
Indiana, *U.S.A.* 136 F5 40 38N 79 9W
Indiana □, *U.S.A.* 141 D11 40 0N 86 0W
Indianapolis, *U.S.A.* 141 E10 39 42N 86 10W
Indianola, *Iowa, U.S.A.* 140 C3 41 20N 93 32W
Indianola, *Miss., U.S.A.* 139 J9 33 27N 90 40W
Indiapora, *Brazil* 155 E1 19 57 S 50 17W
Indiga, *Russia* 48 A8 67 50N 48 50 E
Indigirka →, *Russia* 57 B15 70 48N 148 54 E
Inđija, *Serbia, Yug.* 42 B5 45 6N 20 7 E
Indio, *U.S.A.* 145 M10 33 46N 116 15W
Indispensable Strait, *Solomon Is.* 121 M11 9 0 S 160 30 E
Indonesia ■, *Asia* 75 C4 5 0 S 115 0 E
Indore, *India* 80 H6 22 42N 75 53 E
Indramayu, *Indonesia* 75 D3 6 20 S 108 19 E
Indravati →, *India* 82 E5 19 20N 80 20 E
Indre □, *France* 23 F8 46 50N 1 39 E
Indre →, *France* 22 E7 47 16N 0 11 E
Indre-et-Loire □, *France* 22 E7 47 20N 0 40 E
Indungo, *Angola* 103 E3 14 48 S 16 17 E
Indus →, *Pakistan* 79 D2 24 20N 67 47 E
Indus, Mouth of the, *Pakistan* 79 E3 24 0N 68 0 E
Industry, *U.S.A.* 140 D6 40 20N 90 36W
İnebolu, *Turkey* 88 C5 41 55N 33 40 E
İnegöl, *Turkey* 88 C3 40 5N 29 31 E
Inés, Mt., *Argentina* 160 C3 48 30 S 69 40W
Ineu, *Romania* 46 C2 46 26N 21 51 E
Inezgane, *Morocco* 98 B3 30 25N 9 29W
Infanta, *Phil.* 70 D3 14 45N 121 39 E
Infantes, *Spain* 35 G1 38 43N 3 1W
Infiernillo, Presa del, *Mexico* 146 D4 18 9N 102 0W
Infiesto, *Spain* 36 B5 43 21N 5 21W
Inganda, *Zaïre* 102 C4 0 5 S 20 57 E
Ingapirca, *Ecuador* 152 D2 2 38 S 78 56W
Ingelmunster, *Belgium* 21 G2 50 56N 3 16 E
Ingende, *Zaïre* 102 C3 0 12 S 18 57 E
Ingeniero Jacobacci, *Argentina* 160 B3 41 20 S 69 36W
Ingenio, *Canary Is.* 33 G4 27 55N 15 26W
Ingenio Santa Ana, *Argentina* 158 B2 27 25 S 65 40W
Ingersoll, *Canada* 136 C4 43 4N 80 55W
Ingham, *Australia* 114 B4 18 43 S 146 10 E
Ingichka, *Uzbekistan* 55 D2 39 47N 65 58 E
Ingleborough, *U.K.* 16 C5 54 11N 2 23W
Inglewood, *Queens., Australia* 115 D5 28 25 S 151 2 E
Inglewood, *Vic., Australia* 116 D5 36 29 S 143 53 E
Inglewood, *N.Z.* 118 F3 39 9 S 174 14 E
Inglewood, *U.S.A.* 145 M8 33 58N 118 21W
Ingólfshöfði, *Iceland* 12 E5 63 48N 16 39W
Ingolstadt, *Germany* 27 G7 48 45N 11 26 E
Ingomar, *U.S.A.* 142 C10 46 35N 107 21W
Ingonish, *Canada* 129 C7 46 42N 60 18W
Ingore, *Guinea-Biss.* 100 C1 12 24N 15 48W
Ingraj Bazar, *India* 81 G13 24 58N 88 10 E
Ingrid Christensen Coast, *Antarctica* 7 C6 69 30 S 76 0 E
Ingul →, *Ukraine* 52 C5 46 50N 32 0 E
Ingulec, *Ukraine* 52 C5 47 42N 33 14 E
Ingulets →, *Ukraine* 52 C5 46 35N 32 48 E
Inguri →, *Georgia* 53 E9 42 38N 41 35 E
Ingwavuma, *S. Africa* 105 D5 27 9 S 31 59 E
Inhaca, I., *Mozam.* 105 D5 26 1 S 32 57 E
Inhafenga, *Mozam.* 105 C5 20 36 S 33 53 E
Inhambane, *Mozam.* 105 C6 23 54 S 35 30 E
Inhambane □, *Mozam.* 105 C5 22 30 S 34 20 E
Inhambupe, *Brazil* 155 D4 11 47 S 38 21W
Inhaminga, *Mozam.* 107 F4 18 26 S 35 0 E
Inharrime, *Mozam.* 105 C6 24 30 S 35 0 E
Inharrime →, *Mozam.* 105 C6 24 30 S 35 0 E
Inhuma, *Brazil* 154 C3 6 40 S 41 42W
Inhumas, *Brazil* 155 E2 16 22 S 49 30W
Iniesta, *Spain* 35 F3 39 27N 1 45W
Ining = Yining, *China* 64 B3 43 58N 81 10 E
Inini □, *Fr. Guiana* 153 C7 4 0N 53 0W
Inírida →, *Colombia* 152 C4 3 55N 67 52W
Inishbofin, *Ireland* 19 C1 53 35N 10 12W
Inishmore, *Ireland* 19 C2 53 8N 9 45W
Inishowen, *Ireland* 19 A4 55 14N 7 15W
Injune, *Australia* 115 D4 25 53 S 148 32 E
Inklin, *Canada* 130 B2 58 56N 133 5W
Inklin →, *Canada* 130 B2 58 50N 133 10W
Inkom, *U.S.A.* 142 E7 42 51N 112 15W
Inle L., *Burma* 78 E6 20 30N 96 58 E
Inn →, *Austria* 27 G9 48 35N 13 28 E
Innamincka, *Australia* 115 D3 27 44 S 140 46 E
Inner Hebrides, *U.K.* 18 D2 57 0N 6 30W
Inner Mongolia = Nei Monggol Zizhiqu □, *China* 66 C6 42 0N 112 0 E
Inner Sound, *U.K.* 18 D3 57 30N 5 55W
Innerkip, *Canada* 136 C4 43 13N 80 42W
Innerkirchen, *Switz.* 28 C6 46 43N 8 14 E
Innerste →, *Germany* 26 C5 52 45N 9 40 E
Innetalling I., *Canada* 128 A4 56 0N 79 0W
Innisfail, *Australia* 114 B4 17 33 S 146 5 E
Innisfail, *Canada* 130 C6 52 0N 113 57W
In'no-shima, *Japan* 62 C5 34 19N 133 10 E
Innsbruck, *Austria* 30 D4 47 16N 11 23 E
Inny →, *Ireland* 19 C4 53 30N 7 50W
Ino, *Japan* 62 D5 33 33N 133 26 E
Inocência, *Brazil* 155 E1 19 47 S 51 48W
Inongo, *Zaïre* 102 C3 1 55 S 18 30 E
Inoni, *Congo* 102 C3 3 4 S 15 39 E
Inoucdjouac, *Canada* 127 C12 58 25N 78 15W
Inowrocław, *Poland* 47 C5 52 50N 18 12 E
Inpundong, *N. Korea* 67 D14 41 25N 126 34 E
Inquisivi, *Bolivia* 156 D4 16 50 S 67 10W
Ins, *Switz.* 28 B4 47 1N 7 7 E
Inscription, C., *Australia* 113 E1 25 29 S 112 59 E
Insein, *Burma* 78 G6 16 50N 96 5 E
Însurăţei, *Romania* 46 E8 44 50N 27 40 E
Inta, *Russia* 48 A11 66 5N 60 8 E
Intendente Alvear, *Argentina* 158 D3 35 12 S 63 32W
Interior, *U.S.A.* 138 D4 43 46N 101 59W
Interlaken, *Switz.* 23 F14 46 41N 7 50 E
International Falls, *U.S.A.* 138 A8 48 36N 93 25W
Intiyaco, *Argentina* 158 B3 28 43 S 60 5W
Intragna, *Switz.* 29 D7 46 11N 8 42 E
Intutu, *Peru* 152 D3 3 32 S 74 48W
Inubō-Zaki, *Japan* 63 B12 35 42N 140 52 E
Inútil, B., *Chile* 160 D2 53 30 S 70 15W
Inuvik, *Canada* 126 B6 68 16N 133 40W
Inuyama, *Japan* 63 B8 35 23N 136 56 E
Inveraray, *U.K.* 18 E3 56 13N 5 5W
Inverbervie, *U.K.* 18 E6 56 50N 2 17W
Invercargill, *N.Z.* 119 G3 46 24 S 168 24 E
Inverell, *Australia* 115 D5 29 45 S 151 8 E
Invergordon, *U.K.* 18 D4 57 41N 4 10W
Inverleigh, *Australia* 116 E6 38 6 S 144 3 E
Invermere, *Canada* 130 C5 50 30N 116 2W
Inverness, *Canada* 129 C7 46 15N 61 19W
Inverness, *U.K.* 18 D4 57 29N 4 12W
Inverness, *U.S.A.* 135 L4 28 50N 82 20W
Inverurie, *U.K.* 18 D6 57 15N 2 21W
Inverway, *Australia* 112 C4 17 50 S 129 38 E
Investigator Group, *Australia* 115 E1 34 45 S 134 20 E
Investigator Str., *Australia* 116 C2 35 30 S 137 0 E
Inya, *Russia* 56 D9 50 28N 86 37 E

Izyum 211


Inyanga, *Zimbabwe* .... 107 F3 18 12 S 32 40 E
Inyangani, *Zimbabwe* ... 107 F3 18 5 S 32 50 E
Inyantue, *Zimbabwe* .... 107 F2 18 30 S 26 40 E
Inyo Mts., *U.S.A.* ...... 143 H5 37 0N 118 0W
Inyokern, *U.S.A.* ...... 145 K9 35 38N 117 48W
Inywa, *Burma* ........ 78 D6 23 56N 96 17 E
Inza, *Russia* .......... 51 E15 53 55N 46 25 E
Inzer, *Russia* .......... 54 D5 54 14N 57 34 E
Inzhavino, *Russia* ...... 51 E13 52 22N 42 30 E
Iō-Jima, *Japan* ........ 61 J5 30 48N 130 18 E
Ioánnina, *Greece* ....... 44 E2 39 42N 20 47 E
Ioánnina □, *Greece* ..... 44 E2 39 39N 20 57 E
Iola, *U.S.A.* .......... 139 G7 38 0N 95 20W
Ioma, *Papua N. G.* ..... 120 E4 8 19 S 147 52 E
Ion Corvin, *Romania* ... 46 E8 44 7N 27 50 E
Iona, *U.K.* ............ 18 E2 56 20N 6 25W
Ione, *Calif., U.S.A.* .... 144 G6 38 20N 120 56W
Ione, *Wash., U.S.A.* .... 142 B5 48 44N 117 29W
Ionia, *U.S.A.* .......... 141 B11 42 59N 85 7W
Ionian Is. = Iónioi Nísoi, *Greece* ............. 45 F2 38 40N 20 0 E
Ionian Sea, *Europe* ..... 10 H9 37 30N 17 30 E
Iónioi Nísoi, *Greece* ... 45 F2 38 40N 20 0 E
Iori →, *Azerbaijan* ..... 53 F12 41 3N 46 17 E
Íos, *Greece* ........... 45 H7 36 41N 25 20 E
Iowa □, *U.S.A.* ........ 138 D8 42 18N 93 30W
Iowa →, *U.S.A.* ....... 140 C5 41 10N 91 1W
Iowa City, *U.S.A.* ...... 140 C5 41 40N 91 35W
Iowa Falls, *U.S.A.* ..... 140 B3 42 30N 93 15W
Ipala, *Tanzania* ........ 106 C3 4 30 S 32 52 E
Ipameri, *Brazil* ........ 155 E2 17 44 S 48 9W
Iparía, *Peru* .......... 156 B3 9 17 S 74 29W
Ipáti, *Greece* .......... 45 F4 38 52N 22 14 E
Ipatinga, *Brazil* ....... 155 E3 19 32 S 42 30W
Ipatovo, *Russia* ....... 53 D10 45 45N 42 50 E
Ipel →, *Europe* ....... 31 C12 48 10N 19 35 E
Ipiales, *Colombia* ...... 152 C2 0 50N 77 37W
Ipiaú, *Brazil* .......... 155 D4 14 8 S 39 44W
Ipil, *Phil.* ............ 71 H4 7 47N 122 35 E
Ipin = Yibin, *China* .... 68 C5 28 45N 104 32 E
Ipirá, *Brazil* .......... 155 D4 12 10 S 39 44W
Ipiranga, *Brazil* ....... 152 D4 3 13 S 65 57W
Ípiros □, *Greece* ...... 44 E2 39 30N 20 30 E
Ipixuna, *Brazil* ......... 156 B3 7 0 S 71 40W
Ipixuna →, *Amazonas, Brazil* .............. 156 B3 7 11 S 71 51W
Ipixuna →, *Amazonas, Brazil* .............. 157 B5 5 45 S 63 2W
Ipoh, *Malaysia* ........ 77 K3 4 35N 101 5 E
Iporá, *Brazil* .......... 155 D1 11 23 S 50 40W
Ippy, *C.A.R.* .......... 102 A4 6 5N 21 7 E
Ipsala, *Turkey* ........ 44 D8 40 55N 26 23 E
Ipsárion Óros, *Greece* .. 44 D6 40 40N 24 40 E
Ipswich, *Australia* ..... 115 D5 27 35 S 152 40 E
Ipswich, *U.K.* ......... 17 E9 52 4N 1 9 E
Ipswich, *Mass., U.S.A.* . 137 D14 42 40N 70 50W
Ipswich, *S. Dak., U.S.A.* 138 C5 45 28N 99 1W
Ipu, *Brazil* ........... 154 B3 4 23 S 40 44W
Ipueiras, *Brazil* ....... 154 B3 4 33 S 40 43W
Ipupiara, *Brazil* ....... 155 D3 11 49 S 42 37W
Iput →, *Belorussia* ..... 50 E7 52 26N 31 2 E
Iqaluit, *Canada* ........ 127 B13 63 44N 68 31W
Iquique, *Chile* ........ 156 E3 20 19 S 70 5W
Iquitos, *Peru* ......... 152 D3 3 45 S 73 10W
Irabu-Jima, *Japan* ...... 61 M2 24 50N 125 10 E
Iracoubo, *Fr. Guiana* ... 153 B7 5 30N 53 10W
Īrafshān, *Iran* ......... 85 E9 26 42N 61 56 E
Irahuan, *Phil.* ......... 71 G2 9 48N 118 41 E
Iráklia, *Greece* ........ 45 H7 36 50N 25 28 E
Iráklion, *Greece* ....... 32 D7 35 20N 25 12 E
Iráklion □, *Greece* ..... 32 D7 35 10N 25 10 E
Irako-Zaki, *Japan* ...... 63 C9 34 35N 137 1 E
Irala, *Paraguay* ....... 159 B5 25 55 S 54 35W
Iramba □, *Tanzania* .... 106 C3 4 30 S 34 30 E
Iran ■, *Asia* .......... 85 C7 33 0N 53 0 E
Iran, Gunung-Gunung, *Malaysia* ........... 75 B4 2 20N 114 50 E
Iran Ra. = Iran, Gunung-Gunung, *Malaysia* .... 75 B4 2 20N 114 50 E
Iranamadu Tank, *Sri Lanka* ........... 83 K5 9 23N 80 29 E
Īrānshahr, *Iran* ........ 85 E9 27 15N 60 40 E
Irapa, *Venezuela* ....... 153 A5 10 34N 62 35W
Irapuato, *Mexico* ...... 146 C4 20 40N 101 30W
Iraq ■, *Asia* .......... 84 C5 33 0N 44 0 E
Irarrar, O. →, *Mali* .... 99 D5 20 0N 1 30 E
Irati, *Brazil* ........... 159 B5 25 25 S 50 38W
Irbid, *Jordan* ......... 91 C4 32 35N 35 48 E
Irbid □, *Jordan* ....... 91 C5 32 15N 36 35 E
Irbit, *Russia* ......... 54 C8 57 41N 63 3 E
Irebu, *Zaïre* .......... 102 C3 0 40 S 17 46 E
Irecê, *Brazil* .......... 154 D3 11 18 S 41 52W
Iregua →, *Spain* ....... 34 C7 42 27N 2 24 E
Ireland ■, *Europe* ...... 19 D4 53 0N 8 0W
Ireland's Eye, *Ireland* ... 19 C5 53 25N 6 4W
Irele, *Nigeria* ......... 101 D6 7 40N 5 40 E
Iremel, Gora, *Russia* ... 54 D6 54 33N 58 50 E
Ireng →, *Brazil* ....... 153 C6 3 33N 59 51W
Iret, *Russia* ........... 57 C16 60 3N 154 20 E
Irgiz, Bolshaya →, *Russia* .............. 51 E16 52 10N 49 10 E
Irhârharene, *Algeria* .... 99 C6 27 37N 7 30 E
Irharrhar, O. →, *Algeria* 99 C6 28 3N 6 15 E
Irherm, *Morocco* ....... 98 B3 30 7N 8 18W
Irhil Mgoun, *Morocco* .. 98 B3 31 30N 6 28W
Irhyangdong, *N. Korea* . 67 D15 41 15N 129 30 E
Iri, *S. Korea* .......... 67 G14 35 59N 127 0 E
Irian Jaya □, *Indonesia* . 73 B5 4 0 S 137 0 E
Iriba, *Chad* ........... 97 E4 15 7N 22 15 E
Irid, Mt., *Phil.* ........ 70 D3 14 47N 121 19 E
Irié, *Guinea* .......... 100 D3 8 15N 9 10W
Iriga, *Phil.* ........... 70 E4 13 25N 123 25 E
Iriklinskiy, *Russia* ..... 54 F6 51 39N 58 38 E
Iriklinskoye Vdkhr., *Russia* .............. 54 E6 52 0N 59 0 E
Iringa, *Tanzania* ...... 106 D4 7 48 S 35 43 E
Iringa □, *Tanzania* .... 106 D4 7 48 S 35 43 E
Irinjalakuda, *India* ..... 83 J3 10 21N 76 14 E
Iriomote-Jima, *Japan* ... 61 M1 24 19N 123 48 E
Iriona, *Honduras* ....... 148 C2 15 57N 85 11W
Iriri →, *Brazil* ........ 153 D7 3 52 S 52 37W
Iriri Novo →, *Brazil* ... 157 B7 8 46 S 53 22W
Irish Republic ■, *Europe* 19 D4 53 0N 8 0W
Irish Sea, *Europe* ...... 16 D3 54 0N 5 0W
Irkeshtam, *Kirghizia* .... 55 D6 39 41N 73 55 E
Irkineyeva, *Russia* ..... 57 D10 58 30N 96 49 E
Irkutsk, *Russia* ........ 57 D11 52 18N 104 20 E
Irma, *Canada* .......... 131 C6 52 55N 111 14W
Irō-Zaki, *Japan* ........ 63 C10 34 36N 138 51 E
Iroise, Mer d', *France* .. 22 D2 48 15N 4 45W
Iron Baron, *Australia* ... 116 B2 32 58 S 137 11 E
Iron Gate = Portile de Fier, *Europe* ......... 46 E3 44 42N 22 30 E
Iron Knob, *Australia* ... 116 B2 32 46 S 137 8 E
Iron Mountain, *U.S.A.* . 134 C1 45 49N 88 4W
Iron Ra., *Australia* ..... 114 A3 12 46 S 143 16 E
Iron River, *U.S.A.* ..... 138 B10 46 6N 88 40W
Ironbridge, *U.K.* ....... 17 E5 52 38N 2 29W
Irondequoit, *U.S.A.* .... 136 C7 43 13N 77 35W
Ironstone Kopje, *Botswana* ........... 104 D3 25 17 S 24 5 E
Ironton, *Mo., U.S.A.* ... 139 G9 37 40N 90 40W
Ironton, *Ohio, U.S.A.* .. 134 F4 38 35N 82 40W
Ironwood, *U.S.A.* ...... 138 B9 46 30N 90 10W
Iroquois →, *U.S.A.* .... 141 C9 41 5N 87 49W
Iroquois Falls, *Canada* .. 128 C3 48 46N 80 41W
Irosin, *Phil.* ........... 70 E5 12 42N 124 2 E
Irpen, *Ukraine* ......... 50 F7 50 30N 30 15 E
Irrara Cr. →, *Australia* . 115 D4 29 35 S 145 31 E
Irrawaddy □, *Burma* .... 78 G5 17 0N 95 0 E
Irrawaddy →, *Burma* ... 78 G5 15 50N 95 6 E
Irsina, *Italy* ........... 41 B9 40 45N 16 15 E
Irtysh →, *Russia* ...... 56 C7 61 4N 68 52 E
Irumu, *Zaïre* .......... 106 B2 1 32N 29 53 E
Irún, *Spain* ........... 34 B3 43 20N 1 52W
Irurzun, *Spain* ........ 34 C3 42 55N 1 50W
Irvine, *Canada* ........ 131 D6 49 57N 110 16W
Irvine, *U.K.* ........... 18 F4 55 37N 4 40W
Irvine, *U.S.A.* ......... 141 G13 37 42N 83 58W
Irvine, *Calif., U.S.A.* ... 145 M9 33 41N 117 46W
Irvinestown, *U.K.* ...... 19 B4 54 28N 7 38W
Irvington, *U.S.A.* ...... 141 G10 37 53N 86 17W
Irvona, *U.S.A.* ......... 136 F6 40 46N 78 35W
Irwin →, *Australia* .... 113 E1 29 15 S 114 54 E
Irymple, *Australia* ..... 116 C5 34 14 S 142 8 E
Is-sur-Tille, *France* ..... 23 E12 47 30N 5 8 E
Isa, *Nigeria* ........... 101 C6 13 14N 6 24 E
Isaac →, *Australia* .... 114 C4 22 55 S 149 20 E
Isabel, *U.S.A.* ......... 138 C4 45 27N 101 22W
Isabela, *Phil.* ......... 71 F4 10 12N 122 59 E
Isabela □, *Phil.* ....... 70 C4 17 0N 122 0 E
Isabela, I., *Mexico* .... 146 C3 21 51N 105 55W
Isabella, *Phil.* ......... 71 H4 6 40N 122 10 E
Isabella, Cord., *Nic.* .... 148 D2 13 30N 85 25W
Isabella Ra., *Australia* .. 112 D3 21 0 S 121 4 E
Ísafjarðardjúp, *Iceland* .. 12 C2 66 10N 23 0W
Ísafjörður, *Iceland* ..... 12 C2 66 5N 23 9W
Isagarh, *India* ......... 80 G7 24 48N 77 51 E
Isahaya, *Japan* ........ 62 E2 32 52N 130 2 E
Isaka, *Tanzania* ....... 106 C3 3 56 S 32 59 E
Isakly, *Russia* ......... 54 D2 54 8N 51 32 E
Isana = Içana →, *Brazil* 152 C4 0 26N 67 19W
Isangi, *Zaïre* .......... 102 B4 0 52N 24 10 E
Isar →, *Germany* ...... 27 G8 48 49N 12 58 E
Isarco →, *Italy* ....... 39 B8 46 57N 11 18 E
Ísari, *Greece* .......... 45 G3 37 22N 22 0 E
Isbergues, *France* ...... 23 B9 50 36N 2 28 E
Isbiceni, *Romania* ...... 46 F5 43 45N 24 40 E
Iscayachi, *Bolivia* ...... 157 E4 21 31 S 65 3W
Íschia, *Italy* ........... 40 B6 40 45N 13 51 E
Iscuandé, *Colombia* .... 152 C2 2 28N 77 59W
Isdell →, *Australia* .... 112 C3 16 27 S 124 51 E
Ise, *Japan* ............ 63 C8 34 25N 136 45 E
Ise-Heiya, *Japan* ....... 63 C8 34 40N 136 30 E
Ise-Wan, *Japan* ........ 63 C8 34 43N 136 43 E
Isefjord, *Denmark* ...... 15 J5 55 53N 11 50 E
Iseltwald, *Switz.* ....... 28 C5 46 43N 7 58 E
Isenthal, *Switz.* ........ 29 C7 46 55N 8 34 E
Iseo, *Italy* ............ 38 C7 45 40N 10 3 E
Iseo, L. d', *Italy* ...... 38 C7 45 45N 10 3 E
Iseramagazi, *Tanzania* .. 106 C3 4 37 S 32 10 E
Isère □, *France* ........ 25 C9 45 15N 5 40 E
Isère →, *France* ....... 25 D8 44 59N 4 51 E
Iserlohn, *Germany* ..... 26 D3 51 22N 7 40 E
Isérnia, *Italy* .......... 41 A7 41 35N 14 12 E
Isesaki, *Japan* ......... 63 A11 36 19N 139 12 E
Iseyin, *Nigeria* ........ 101 D5 8 0N 3 36 E
Isfara, *Tajikistan* ...... 55 C5 40 7N 70 38 E
Isherton, *Guyana* ...... 153 C6 2 20N 59 25W
Ishigaki-Shima, *Japan* ... 61 M2 24 20N 124 10 E
Ishikari-Gawa →, *Japan* 60 C10 43 15N 141 23 E
Ishikari-Sammyaku, *Japan* 60 C11 43 30N 143 0 E
Ishikari-Wan, *Japan* .... 60 C10 43 25N 141 1 E
Ishikawa □, *Japan* ..... 63 A8 36 30N 136 30 E
Ishim, *Russia* ......... 56 D7 56 10N 69 30 E
Ishim →, *Russia* ...... 56 D8 57 45N 71 10 E
Ishimbay, *Russia* ....... 54 E5 53 28N 56 2 E
Ishinomaki, *Japan* ...... 60 E10 38 32N 141 20 E
Ishioka, *Japan* ......... 63 A12 36 11N 140 16 E
Ishizuchi-Yama, *Japan* .. 62 D5 33 45N 133 6 E
Ishkashim = Eshkamish, *Tajikistan* ............ 55 E5 36 44N 71 37 E
Ishkuman, *Pakistan* .... 81 A5 36 30N 73 50 E
Ishmi, *Albania* ......... 44 C1 41 33N 19 34 E
Ishpeming, *U.S.A.* ..... 134 B2 46 30N 87 40W
Ishurdi, *Bangla.* ....... 78 C2 24 9N 89 3 E
Isigny-sur-Mer, *France* .. 22 C5 49 19N 1 6W
Isil Kul, *Russia* ........ 56 D8 54 55N 71 16 E
Isiolo, *Kenya* ......... 106 B4 0 24N 37 33 E
Isiolo □, *Kenya* ....... 106 B4 2 30N 37 30 E
Isipingo Beach, *S. Africa* 105 E5 30 0 S 30 57 E
Isiro, *Zaïre* ........... 106 B2 2 53N 27 40 E
Isisford, *Australia* ..... 114 C3 24 15 S 144 21 E
Iskander, *Uzbekistan* ... 55 C4 41 36N 69 41 E
İskederun, *Turkey* ...... 88 E7 36 9N 36 35 E
İskenderun, *Turkey* ..... 88 E7 36 32N 36 10 E
İskenderun Körfezi, *Turkey* .............. 88 E6 36 40N 35 50 E
Iski-Naukat, *Kirghizia* .. 55 C6 40 16N 72 36 E
İskilip, *Turkey* ......... 52 F6 40 45N 34 29 E
Iskūr →, *Bulgaria* ..... 43 D9 43 45N 24 25 E
Iskūr, Yazovir, *Bulgaria* 43 E8 42 23N 23 30 E
Iskut →, *Canada* ...... 130 B2 56 45N 131 49W
Isla →, *U.K.* ......... 18 E5 56 32N 3 20W
Isla Cristina, *Spain* .... 37 H3 37 13N 7 17W
Isla Vista, *U.S.A.* ..... 145 L7 34 27N 119 52W
İslâhiye, *Turkey* ....... 88 E7 37 0N 36 35 E
Islamabad, *Pakistan* .... 79 B4 33 40N 73 10 E
Islamkot, *Pakistan* ..... 80 G4 24 42N 70 13 E
Islampur, *India* ........ 82 F2 17 2N 74 20 E
Island →, *Canada* ..... 130 A4 60 25N 121 12W
Island Bay, *Phil.* ....... 71 G2 9 6N 118 10 E
Island Falls, *Canada* .... 128 C3 49 35N 81 20W
Island Falls, *U.S.A.* .... 129 C6 46 0N 68 16W
Island L., *Canada* ...... 131 C10 53 47N 94 25W
Island Lagoon, *Australia* 116 A2 31 30 S 136 40 E
Island Pond, *U.S.A.* .... 137 B13 44 50N 71 50W
Islands, B. of, *Canada* .. 129 C8 49 11N 58 15W
Islands, B. of, *N.Z.* .... 118 B3 35 15 S 174 6 E
Islay, *U.K.* ............ 18 F2 55 46N 6 10W
Isle →, *France* ........ 24 D3 44 55N 0 15W
Isle aux Morts, *Canada* . 129 C8 47 35N 59 0W
Isle of Wight □, *U.K.* .. 17 G6 50 40N 1 20W
Isle Royale, *U.S.A.* .... 138 A10 48 0N 88 50W
Isleta, *U.S.A.* ......... 143 J10 34 58N 106 46W
Isleton, *U.S.A.* ........ 144 G5 38 10N 121 37W
Ismail, *Ukraine* ........ 52 D3 45 22N 28 46 E
Ismâ'ilîya, *Egypt* ...... 94 H8 30 37N 32 18 E
Ismaning, *Germany* ..... 27 G7 48 14N 11 41 E
Ismay, *U.S.A.* ......... 138 B2 46 33N 104 44W
Isna, *Egypt* ............ 94 B3 25 17N 32 30 E
Isogstalo, *India* ........ 81 B8 34 15N 78 46 E
Isola del Gran Sasso d'Italia, *Italy* ......... 39 F10 42 30N 13 40 E
Ísola del Liri, *Italy* ..... 40 A6 41 39N 13 32 E
Ísola della Scala, *Italy* .. 38 C8 45 16N 11 0 E
Ísola di Capo Rizzuto, *Italy* ............... 41 D10 38 56N 17 5 E
Isparta, *Turkey* ........ 88 E4 37 47N 30 30 E
Isparta □, *Turkey* ...... 88 E4 38 0N 31 0 E
Isperikh, *Bulgaria* ...... 43 D11 43 43N 26 50 E
Íspica, *Italy* ........... 41 F7 36 47N 14 53 E
Ispir, *Turkey* .......... 53 F9 40 28N 41 1 E
Israel ■, *Asia* ......... 91 D3 32 0N 34 50 E
Issano, *Guyana* ........ 153 B6 5 49N 59 26W
Issia, *Ivory C.* ......... 100 D3 6 33N 6 33W
Issoire, *France* ........ 24 C7 45 32N 3 15 E
Issoudun, *France* ...... 23 F8 46 57N 2 0 E
Issyk-Kul, *Kirghizia* .... 55 B8 42 26N 76 12 E
Issyk-Kul, Ozero, *Kirghizia* ............ 55 B8 42 25N 77 15 E
Ist, *Croatia* ........... 39 D11 44 17N 14 47 E
Istaihah, *U.A.E.* ....... 85 F7 23 19N 54 4 E
İstanbul, *Turkey* ....... 88 C3 41 0N 29 0 E
İstanbul □, *Turkey* ..... 88 C3 41 0N 29 0 E
Istiaía, *Greece* ......... 45 F5 38 57N 23 9 E
Istmina, *Colombia* ...... 152 B2 5 10N 76 39W
Istok, *Serbia, Yug.* ..... 42 E5 42 45N 20 24 E
Istokpoga, L., *U.S.A.* .. 135 M5 27 22N 81 14W
Istra, *Croatia* .......... 39 C11 45 10N 14 0 E
Istra, *Russia* .......... 51 D10 55 55N 36 50 E
İstranca Dağları, *Turkey* 43 F12 41 48N 27 36 E
Istres, *France* ......... 25 E8 43 31N 4 59 E
Istria = Istra, *Croatia* .. 39 C11 45 10N 14 0 E
Isulan, *Phil.* .......... 71 H5 6 30N 124 29 E
Itá, *Paraguay* ......... 158 B4 25 29 S 57 21W
'Itāb, *Yemen* .......... 87 D5 15 20N 51 29 E
Itabaiana, *Paraíba, Brazil* 154 C4 7 18 S 35 19W
Itabaiana, *Sergipe, Brazil* 154 D4 10 41 S 37 37W
Itabaianinha, *Brazil* .... 154 D4 11 16 S 37 47W
Itaberaba, *Brazil* ...... 155 D3 12 32 S 40 18W
Itaberaí, *Brazil* ........ 155 E2 16 2 S 49 48W
Itabira, *Brazil* ......... 155 E3 19 37 S 43 13W
Itabirito, *Brazil* ........ 155 F3 20 15 S 43 48W
Itaboca, *Brazil* ........ 153 D5 4 50 S 62 40W
Itabuna, *Brazil* ........ 155 D4 14 48 S 39 16W
Itacajá, *Brazil* ........ 154 C2 8 19 S 47 46W
Itacaunas →, *Brazil* .... 154 C2 5 21 S 49 8W
Itacoatiara, *Brazil* ...... 153 D6 3 8 S 58 25W
Itacuaí →, *Brazil* ...... 156 A3 4 20 S 70 12W
Itaguaçu, *Brazil* ....... 155 E3 19 48 S 40 51W
Itaguari →, *Brazil* ..... 155 D3 14 11 S 44 40W
Itaguatins, *Brazil* ...... 154 C2 5 47 S 47 29W
Itaim →, *Brazil* ....... 154 C3 7 2 S 42 2W
Itainópolis, *Brazil* ..... 154 C3 7 24 S 41 31W
Itaipu Dam, *Brazil* ..... 159 B5 25 30 S 54 30W
Itaituba, *Brazil* ........ 153 D6 4 10 S 55 50W
Itajaí, *Brazil* .......... 159 B6 27 50 S 48 39W
Itajubá, *Brazil* ......... 155 F2 22 24 S 45 30W
Itajuípe, *Brazil* ........ 155 D4 14 41 S 39 22W
Itaka, *Tanzania* ........ 107 D3 8 50 S 32 49 E
Itako, *Japan* ........... 63 B12 35 56N 140 33 E
Italy ■, *Europe* ........ 11 G8 42 0N 13 0 E
Itamataré, *Brazil* ...... 154 B2 2 16 S 46 24W
Itambacuri, *Brazil* ...... 155 E3 18 1 S 41 42W
Itambé, *Brazil* ......... 155 E3 15 15 S 40 37W
Itampolo, *Madag.* ...... 105 C7 24 41 S 43 57 E
Itanhauã →, *Brazil* .... 153 D5 4 45 S 63 48W
Itanhém, *Brazil* ........ 155 E3 17 9 S 40 20W
Itano, *Japan* .......... 62 C6 34 7N 134 28 E
Itapaci, *Brazil* ......... 155 D2 14 57 S 49 34W
Itapagé, *Brazil* ........ 154 B4 3 41 S 39 34W
Itaparica, I. de, *Brazil* .. 155 D4 12 54 S 38 42W
Itapebi, *Brazil* ......... 155 E4 15 56 S 39 32W
Itapecuru-Mirim, *Brazil* . 154 B3 3 24 S 44 20W
Itaperuna, *Brazil* ...... 155 F3 21 10 S 41 54W
Itapetinga, *Brazil* ...... 155 E3 15 15 S 40 15W
Itapetininga, *Brazil* ..... 159 A6 23 36 S 48 7W
Itapeva, *Brazil* ......... 159 A6 23 59 S 48 59W
Itapicuru →, *Bahia, Brazil* ............... 154 D4 11 47 S 37 32W
Itapicuru →, *Maranhão, Brazil* ............... 154 B3 2 52 S 44 12W
Itapinima, *Brazil* ....... 157 B5 5 25 S 60 44W
Itapipoca, *Brazil* ....... 154 B4 3 30 S 39 35W
Itapiranga, *Brazil* ...... 153 D6 2 45 S 58 1W
Itapiúna, *Brazil* ........ 154 B4 4 33 S 38 57W
Itaporanga, *Brazil* ...... 154 C4 7 18 S 38 0W
Itapuá □, *Paraguay* .... 159 B4 26 40 S 55 40W
Itapuranga, *Brazil* ...... 155 E2 15 40 S 49 59W
Itaquari, *Brazil* ........ 155 F3 20 20 S 40 25W
Itaquatiara, *Brazil* ...... 153 D6 2 58 S 58 30W
Itaquí, *Brazil* .......... 158 B4 29 8 S 56 30W
Itararé, *Brazil* ......... 159 A6 24 6 S 49 23W
Itarsi, *India* ........... 80 H7 22 36N 77 51 E
Itarumã, *Brazil* ........ 155 E1 18 42 S 51 25W
Itatí, *Argentina* ........ 158 B4 27 16 S 58 15W
Itatira, *Brazil* ......... 154 B4 4 30 S 39 37W
Itatuba, *Brazil* ......... 157 B5 5 46 S 63 20W
Itatupa, *Brazil* ......... 153 D7 0 37 S 51 12W
Itaueira, *Brazil* ........ 154 C3 7 36 S 43 2W
Itaueira →, *Brazil* ..... 154 C3 6 41 S 42 55W
Itaúna, *Brazil* .......... 155 F3 20 4 S 44 34W
Itbayat, *Phil.* .......... 70 A3 20 47N 121 51 E
Itbayat I., *Phil.* ........ 70 A3 20 46N 121 50 E
Itchen →, *U.K.* ....... 17 G6 50 57N 1 20W
Ite, *Peru* .............. 156 D3 17 55 S 70 57W
Itéa, *Greece* ........... 45 F4 38 25N 22 25 E
Itezhi Tezhi, L., *Zambia* 107 F2 15 30 S 25 30 E
Ithaca = Itháki, *Greece* . 45 F2 38 25N 20 40 E
Ithaca, *U.S.A.* ......... 137 D8 42 25N 76 30W
Itháki, *Greece* ......... 45 F2 38 25N 20 40 E
Itinga, *Brazil* .......... 155 E3 16 36 S 41 47W
Itiquira, *Brazil* ........ 157 D7 17 12 S 54 7W
Itiquira →, *Brazil* ..... 157 D6 17 18 S 56 44W
Itiruçu, *Brazil* ......... 155 D3 13 31 S 40 9W
Itiúba, *Brazil* .......... 154 D4 10 43 S 39 51W
Ito, *Japan* ............. 63 C11 34 58N 139 5 E
Itoigawa, *Japan* ........ 61 F8 37 2N 137 51 E
Iton →, *France* ........ 22 C8 49 9N 1 12 E
Itonamas →, *Bolivia* ... 157 C5 12 28 S 64 24W
Itsa, *Egypt* ............ 94 J7 29 15N 30 47 E
Itsukaichi, *Japan* ....... 62 C4 34 22N 132 22 E
Itsuki, *Japan* .......... 62 E2 32 24N 130 50 E
Íttiri, *Italy* ............ 40 B1 40 38N 8 32 E
Ittoqqortoormiit = Scoresbysund, *Greenland* .......... 6 B6 70 20N 23 0W
Itu, *Brazil* ............ 159 A6 23 17 S 47 15W
Itu, *Nigeria* ........... 101 D6 5 10N 7 58 E
Ituaçu, *Brazil* ......... 155 D3 13 50 S 41 18W
Ituango, *Colombia* ..... 152 B2 7 4N 75 45W
Ituiutaba, *Brazil* ....... 155 E2 19 0 S 49 25W
Itumbiara, *Brazil* ....... 155 E2 18 20 S 49 10W
Ituna, *Canada* ......... 131 C8 51 10N 103 24W
Itunge Port, *Tanzania* .. 107 D3 9 40 S 33 55 E
Ituni, *Guyana* ......... 153 B6 5 28N 58 15W
Itupiranga, *Brazil* ...... 154 C2 5 9 S 49 20W
Iturama, *Brazil* ........ 155 E1 19 44 S 50 11W
Iturbe, *Argentina* ...... 158 A2 23 0 S 65 25W
Ituri →, *Zaïre* ......... 106 B2 1 40N 27 1 E
Iturup, Ostrov, *Russia* .. 57 E15 45 0N 148 0 E
Ituverava, *Brazil* ....... 155 F2 20 20 S 47 47W
Ituxi →, *Brazil* ........ 157 B5 7 18 S 64 51W
Ituyuro →, *Argentina* .. 158 A3 22 40 S 63 50W
Itzehoe, *Germany* ...... 26 B5 53 56N 9 31 E
Iuka, *U.S.A.* .......... 141 F8 38 37N 88 47W
Ivaí →, *Brazil* ........ 159 A5 23 18 S 53 42W
Ivalo, *Finland* ......... 12 B19 68 38N 27 35 E
Ivalojoki →, *Finland* ... 12 B19 68 40N 27 40 E
Ivangorod, *Russia* ...... 50 B6 59 37N 28 40 E
Ivangrad, *Montenegro, Yug.* .... 42 E4 42 51N 19 52 E
Ivanhoe, *N.S.W., Australia* .............. 116 B6 32 56 S 144 20 E
Ivanhoe, *W. Austral., Australia* ............ 112 C4 15 41 S 128 41 E
Ivanhoe, *U.S.A.* ....... 144 J7 36 25N 119 13W
Ivanhoe L., *Canada* .... 131 A7 60 25N 106 30W
Ivanić Grad, *Croatia* .... 39 C13 45 41N 16 25 E
Ivanjica, *Serbia, Yug.* ... 42 D5 43 35N 20 12 E
Ivanjšcice, *Croatia* ..... 39 B13 46 12N 16 13 E
Ivankoyskoye Vdkhr., *Russia* .............. 51 C10 56 37N 36 32 E
Ivano-Frankovsk, *Ukraine* 50 G4 48 40N 24 40 E
Ivanovka, *Russia* ....... 54 E3 52 44N 53 45 E
Ivanovo, *Belorussia* .... 50 E4 52 7N 25 29 E
Ivanovo, *Russia* ....... 51 C12 57 5N 41 0 E
Ivato, *Madag.* ......... 105 C8 20 37 S 47 10 E
Ivaylovgrad, *Bulgaria* ... 43 F11 41 32N 26 8 E
Ivdel, *Russia* .......... 48 B11 60 42N 60 24 E
Ive, Mt., *Australia* ..... 116 B2 32 25 S 136 5 E
Ivindo →, *Gabon* ...... 102 C2 0 9 S 12 9 E
Ivinheima →, *Brazil* ... 159 A5 23 14 S 53 42W
Iviza = Ibiza, *Spain* .... 33 C7 38 54N 1 26 E
Ivohibe, *Madag.* ....... 105 C8 22 31 S 46 57 E
Ivolândia, *Brazil* ....... 155 E1 16 34 S 50 51W
Ivory Coast ■, *Africa* ... 100 D3 7 30N 5 0W
Ivrea, *Italy* ........... 38 C4 45 30N 7 52 E
Ivugivik, *Canada* ....... 127 B12 62 24N 77 55W
Iwahig, *Palawan, Phil.* .. 71 G2 9 19N 118 5 E
Iwahig, *Palawan, Phil.* .. 71 G1 8 36N 117 32 E
Iwai-Jima, *Japan* ....... 62 D3 33 47N 131 58 E
Iwaizumi, *Japan* ........ 60 E10 39 50N 141 45 E
Iwaki, *Japan* .......... 61 F10 37 3N 140 55 E
Iwakuni, *Japan* ........ 62 C4 34 15N 132 8 E
Iwami, *Japan* .......... 62 B6 35 32N 134 15 E
Iwamizawa, *Japan* ...... 60 C10 43 12N 141 46 E
Iwanai, *Japan* ......... 60 C10 42 58N 140 30 E
Iwase, *Japan* .......... 63 A12 36 21N 140 6 E
Iwata, *Japan* .......... 63 C9 34 42N 137 51 E
Iwate □, *Japan* ........ 60 E10 39 30N 141 30 E
Iwate-San, *Japan* ...... 60 E10 39 51N 141 0 E
Iwo, *Nigeria* .......... 101 D5 7 39N 4 9 E
Iwonicz-Zdrój, *Poland* .. 31 B14 49 37N 21 47 E
Iwungu, *Zaïre* ......... 103 D3 5 16 S 19 17 E
Ixiamas, *Bolivia* ....... 156 C4 13 50 S 68 5W
Ixopo, *S. Africa* ........ 105 E5 30 11 S 30 5 E
Ixtepec, *Mexico* ........ 147 D5 16 32N 95 10W
Ixtlán del Río, *Mexico* .. 146 C4 21 5N 104 21W
'Iyādh, *Yemen* ......... 86 D4 14 59N 46 51 E
Iyo, *Japan* ............ 62 D4 33 45N 132 45 E
Iyo-mishima, *Japan* ..... 62 D5 33 58N 133 30 E
Iyo-Nada, *Japan* ....... 62 D3 33 40N 132 20 E
Izabal, L. de, *Guatemala* 148 C2 15 30N 89 10W
Izamal, *Mexico* ........ 147 C7 20 56N 89 1W
Izberbash, *Russia* ...... 53 E12 42 35N 47 52 E
Izbica, *Poland* ......... 47 E10 50 53N 23 10 E
Izbica Kujawska, *Poland* 47 C5 52 25N 18 30 E
Izegem, *Belgium* ....... 21 G2 50 55N 3 12 E
Izena-Shima, *Japan* .... 61 L3 26 56N 127 56 E
Izgrev, *Bulgaria* ....... 43 D11 43 36N 26 58 E
Izh →, *Russia* ........ 54 D3 56 36N 52 38 E
Izhevsk, *Russia* ....... 54 C3 56 51N 53 14 E
Izkī, *Oman* ........... 87 B7 22 56N 57 46 E
İzmir, *Turkey* ......... 88 D2 38 25N 27 8 E
İzmir □, *Turkey* ....... 88 D2 38 25N 27 10 E
İzmit, *Turkey* ......... 88 C3 40 45N 29 50 E
Iznajar, *Spain* ......... 37 H6 37 15N 4 19W
Iznalloz, *Spain* ........ 35 H1 37 24N 3 30W
İznik Gölü, *Turkey* ..... 88 C3 40 27N 29 30 E
Izobil'nyy, *Russia* ...... 53 D9 45 25N 41 44 E
Izola, *Slovenia* ......... 39 C10 45 32N 13 39 E
Izozog, Bañados de, *Bolivia* ............. 157 D5 18 48 S 62 10W
Izra, *Syria* ............ 91 C5 32 51N 36 15 E
Iztochni Rodopi, *Bulgaria* 43 F10 41 45N 25 30 E
Izu-Hantō, *Japan* ...... 63 C10 34 45N 139 0 E
Izu-Shotō, *Japan* ....... 61 G10 34 30N 140 0 E
Izuhara, *Japan* ........ 62 C1 34 12N 129 17 E
Izumi, *Japan* .......... 62 E2 32 5N 130 22 E
Izumi-sano, *Japan* ..... 63 C7 34 23N 135 18 E
Izumiotsu, *Japan* ...... 63 C7 34 30N 135 24 E
Izumo, *Japan* .......... 62 B4 35 20N 132 46 E
Izyaslav, *Ukraine* ...... 50 F5 50 5N 26 50 E
Izyum, *Ukraine* ........ 52 B7 49 12N 37 19 E

212 J.F. Rodrigues

# J


J.F. Rodrigues, Brazil 154 B1 2 55 S 50 20W
Jaba, Ethiopia 95 F4 6 20N 35 7 E
Jabal el Awlîya, Sudan 95 D3 15 10N 32 31 E
Jabal Lubnān, Lebanon 91 B4 33 45N 35 40 E
Jabalón →, Spain 37 G6 38 53N 4 5W
Jabalpur, India 81 H8 23 9N 79 58 E
Jabbūl, Syria 84 B3 36 4N 37 30 E
Jablah, Syria 84 C3 35 20N 36 0 E
Jablanac, Croatia 39 D11 44 42N 14 56 E
Jablonec, Czech. 30 A8 50 43N 15 10 E
Jablonica, Czech. 31 C10 48 37N 17 26 E
Jabłonowo, Poland 47 B6 53 23N 19 10 E
Jaboatão, Brazil 154 C4 8 7 S 35 1W
Jabonga, Phil. 71 G5 9 20N 125 32 E
Jaboticabal, Brazil 159 A6 21 15 S 48 17W
Jabukovac, Serbia, Yug. 42 C7 44 22N 22 21 E
Jaburu, Brazil 157 B5 5 30 S 64 0W
Jaca, Spain 34 C4 42 35N 0 33W
Jacaré →, Brazil 154 D3 10 3 S 42 13W
Jacareí, Brazil 159 A6 23 20 S 46 0W
Jacarèzinho, Brazil 159 A6 23 5 S 49 58W
Jáchymov, Czech. 30 A5 50 22N 12 55 E
Jaciara, Brazil 157 D7 15 59 S 54 57W
Jacinto, Brazil 155 E3 16 10 S 40 17W
Jaciparaná, Brazil 157 B5 9 15 S 64 23W
Jackman, U.S.A. 129 C5 45 35N 70 17W
Jacksboro, U.S.A. 139 J5 33 14N 98 15W
Jackson, Australia 115 D4 26 39 S 149 39 E
Jackson, Ala., U.S.A. 135 K2 31 32N 87 53W
Jackson, Calif., U.S.A. 144 G6 38 19N 120 47W
Jackson, Ky., U.S.A. 134 G4 37 35N 83 22W
Jackson, Mich., U.S.A. 141 B12 42 18N 84 25W
Jackson, Minn., U.S.A. 138 D7 43 35N 95 0W
Jackson, Miss., U.S.A. 139 J9 32 20N 90 10W
Jackson, Mo., U.S.A. 139 G10 37 25N 89 42W
Jackson, Ohio, U.S.A. 134 F4 39 0N 82 40W
Jackson, Tenn., U.S.A. 135 H1 35 40N 88 50W
Jackson, Wyo., U.S.A. 142 E8 43 30N 110 49W
Jackson, C., N.Z. 119 A9 40 59 S 174 20 E
Jackson, L., U.S.A. 142 E8 43 55N 110 40W
Jackson B., N.Z. 119 D3 43 58 S 168 42 E
Jackson Center, U.S.A. 141 D12 40 27N 84 4W
Jackson Hd., N.Z. 119 D3 43 58 S 168 37 E
Jacksons, N.Z. 119 C6 42 46 S 171 32 E
Jacksonville, Ala., U.S.A. 135 J3 33 49N 85 45W
Jacksonville, Calif., U.S.A. 144 H6 37 52N 120 24W
Jacksonville, Fla., U.S.A. 135 K5 30 15N 81 38W
Jacksonville, Ill., U.S.A. 140 E6 39 42N 90 15W
Jacksonville, N.C., U.S.A. 135 H7 34 50N 77 29W
Jacksonville, Oreg., U.S.A. 142 E2 42 19N 122 56W
Jacksonville, Tex., U.S.A. 139 K7 31 58N 95 19W
Jacksonville Beach, U.S.A. 135 K5 30 19N 81 26W
Jacmel, Haiti 149 C5 18 14N 72 32W
Jacob Lake, U.S.A. 143 H7 36 45N 112 12W
Jacobabad, Pakistan 79 C3 28 20N 68 29 E
Jacobina, Brazil 154 D3 11 11 S 40 30W
Jacques-Cartier, Mt., Canada 129 C6 48 57N 66 0W
Jacqueville, Ivory C. 100 D4 5 12N 4 25W
Jacuí →, Brazil 159 C5 30 2 S 51 15W
Jacumba, U.S.A. 145 N10 32 37N 116 11W
Jacundá →, Brazil 154 B1 1 57 S 50 26W
Jade, Germany 26 B4 53 22N 8 14 E
Jadebusen, Germany 26 B4 53 30N 8 15 E
Jadoigne, Belgium 21 G5 50 43N 4 52 E
Jadotville = Likasi, Zaïre 107 E2 10 55 S 26 48 E
Jadovnik, Serbia, Yug. 42 D4 43 20N 19 45 E
Jadów, Poland 47 C8 52 28N 21 38 E
Jadraque, Spain 34 E2 40 55N 2 55W
Jādū, Libya 96 B2 32 0N 12 0 E
Jaén, Peru 156 B2 5 25 S 78 40W
Jaén, Spain 37 H7 37 44N 3 43W
Jaén □, Spain 37 H7 37 50N 3 30W
Jafène, Africa 98 D3 20 35N 5 30W
Jaffa = Tel Aviv-Yafo, Israel 91 C3 32 4N 34 48 E
Jaffa, C., Australia 116 D3 36 58 S 139 40 E
Jaffna, Sri Lanka 83 K5 9 45N 80 2 E
Jagadhri, India 80 D7 30 10N 77 20 E
Jagadishpur, India 81 G11 25 30N 84 21 E
Jagdalpur, India 82 E5 19 3N 82 0 E
Jagersfontein, S. Africa 104 D4 29 44 S 25 27 E
Jagst →, Germany 27 F5 49 14N 9 11 E
Jagtial, India 82 E4 18 50N 79 0 E
Jaguaquara, Brazil 155 D4 13 32 S 39 58W
Jaguariaíva, Brazil 159 A6 24 10 S 49 50W
Jaguaribe, Brazil 154 C4 5 53 S 38 37W
Jaguaribe →, Brazil 154 B4 4 25 S 37 45W
Jaguaruana, Brazil 154 B4 4 50 S 37 47W
Jagüey Grande, Cuba 148 B3 22 35N 81 7W
Jagungal, Mt., Australia 117 D8 36 8 S 148 22 E
Jahangirabad, India 80 E8 28 19N 78 4 E
Jahrom, Iran 85 D7 28 30N 53 31 E
Jaicós, Brazil 154 C3 7 21 S 41 8W
Jailolo, Indonesia 72 A3 1 5N 127 30 E
Jailolo, Selat, Indonesia 73 A3 0 5N 129 5 E
Jaintiapur, Bangla. 78 C4 25 8N 92 7 E
Jaipur, India 80 F6 27 0N 75 50 E
Jājarm, Iran 85 B8 36 58N 56 27 E
Jajce, Bos.-H., Yug. 42 C2 44 19N 17 17 E
Jajpur, India 82 D8 20 53N 86 22 E
Jakarta, Indonesia 74 D3 6 9 S 106 49 E
Jakobstad, Finland 12 E17 63 40N 22 43 E
Jakupica, Macedonia, Yug. 42 F6 41 45N 21 22 E
Jal, U.S.A. 139 J3 32 8N 103 8W
Jalalabad, Afghan. 79 B3 34 30N 70 29 E
Jalalabad, India 81 F8 27 41N 79 42 E
Jalalpur Jattan, Pakistan 80 C6 32 38N 74 11 E
Jalama, U.S.A. 145 L6 34 29N 120 29W
Jalapa, Guatemala 148 D2 14 39N 89 59W
Jalapa Enríquez, Mexico 147 D5 19 32N 96 55W
Jalaun, India 81 F8 26 8N 79 25 E
Jaldak, Afghan. 79 C2 31 58N 66 43 E
Jales, Brazil 155 F1 20 10 S 50 33W
Jaleswar, Nepal 81 F11 26 38N 85 48 E
Jalgaon, Maharashtra, India 82 D3 21 2N 76 31 E
Jalgaon, Maharashtra, India 82 D2 21 0N 75 42 E
Jalhay, Belgium 21 G7 50 33N 5 58 E
Jalībah, Iraq 84 D5 30 35N 46 32 E
Jalingo, Nigeria 101 D7 8 55N 11 25 E
Jalisco □, Mexico 146 C4 20 0N 104 0W
Jalkot, Pakistan 81 B5 35 14N 73 24 E
Jallas →, Spain 36 C1 42 54N 9 8W
Jalna, India 82 E2 19 48N 75 38 E
Jalón →, Spain 34 D3 41 47N 1 4W
Jalpa, Mexico 146 C4 21 38N 102 58W
Jalpaiguri, India 78 B2 26 32N 88 46 E
Jalq, Iran 79 D1 27 35N 62 46 E
Jaluit I., Pac. Oc. 122 G8 6 0N 169 30 E
Jalūlā, Iraq 84 C5 34 16N 45 10 E
Jamaari, Nigeria 101 C6 11 44N 9 53 E
Jamaica, U.S.A. 140 C2 41 51N 94 18W
Jamaica ■, W. Indies 148 C4 18 10N 77 30W
Jamalpur, Bangla. 78 C2 24 52N 89 56 E
Jamalpur, India 81 G12 25 18N 86 28 E
Jamalpurganj, India 81 H13 23 2N 88 1 E
Jamanxim →, Brazil 157 A6 4 43 S 56 18W
Jamari, Brazil 157 B5 8 45 S 63 27W
Jamari →, Brazil 157 B5 8 27 S 63 30W
Jambe, Indonesia 73 B4 1 15 S 132 10 E
Jambes, Belgium 21 H5 50 27N 4 52 E
Jambi, Indonesia 74 C2 1 38 S 103 30 E
Jambi □, Indonesia 74 C2 1 30 S 102 30 E
Jambusar, India 80 H5 22 3N 72 51 E
James →, U.S.A. 138 D6 42 52N 97 18W
James B., Canada 127 C11 51 30N 80 0W
James Ras., Australia 112 D5 24 10 S 132 30 E
James Ross I., Antarctica 7 C18 63 58 S 57 50W
Jamesport, U.S.A. 140 E3 39 58N 93 48W
Jamestown, Australia 116 B3 33 10 S 138 32 E
Jamestown, S. Africa 104 E4 31 6 S 26 45 E
Jamestown, Ind., U.S.A. 141 E10 39 56N 86 38W
Jamestown, Ky., U.S.A. 134 G3 37 0N 85 5W
Jamestown, Mo., U.S.A. 140 F4 38 48N 92 30W
Jamestown, N. Dak., U.S.A. 138 B5 46 54N 98 42W
Jamestown, N.Y., U.S.A. 136 D5 42 5N 79 18W
Jamestown, Ohio, U.S.A. 141 E13 39 39N 83 44W
Jamestown, Pa., U.S.A. 136 E4 41 32N 80 27W
Jamestown, Tenn., U.S.A. 135 G3 36 25N 85 0W
Jamīlābād, Iran 85 C6 34 24N 48 28 E
Jamiltepec, Mexico 147 D5 16 17N 97 49W
Jamkhandi, India 82 F2 16 30N 75 15 E
Jammalamadugu, India 83 G4 14 51N 78 25 E
Jammerbugt, Denmark 15 G3 57 15N 9 20 E
Jammu, India 80 C6 32 43N 74 54 E
Jammu & Kashmir □, India 81 B7 34 25N 77 0 E
Jamnagar, India 80 H4 22 30N 70 6 E
Jamner, India 82 D2 20 45N 75 52 E
Jamoigne, Belgium 21 J6 49 41N 5 24 E
Jampur, Pakistan 79 C3 29 39N 70 40 E
Jamrud, Pakistan 79 B3 33 59N 71 24 E
Jamshedpur, India 81 H12 22 44N 86 12 E
Jamtara, India 81 H12 23 59N 86 49 E
Jämtlands län □, Sweden 14 B7 62 40N 13 50 E
Jamuna →, Bangla. 78 D2 23 51N 89 45 E
Jamurki, Bangla. 78 C3 24 9N 90 2 E
Jan Kempdorp, S. Africa 104 D3 27 55 S 24 51 E
Jan L., Canada 131 C8 54 56N 102 55W
Jan Mayen, Arctic 6 B7 71 0N 9 0W
Janaúba, Brazil 155 E3 15 48 S 43 19W
Janaucu, I., Brazil 154 A1 0 30N 50 10W
Jand, Pakistan 80 C5 33 30N 72 6 E
Janda, L. de la, Spain 37 J5 36 15N 5 45W
Jandaia, Brazil 155 E1 17 6 S 50 7W
Jandaq, Iran 85 C7 34 3N 54 22 E
Jandia, Canary Is. 33 F5 28 6N 14 21W
Jandia, Pta. de, Canary Is. 33 F5 28 3N 14 31W
Jandiatuba →, Brazil 152 D4 3 28 S 68 42W
Jandola, Pakistan 80 C4 32 20N 70 9 E
Jandowae, Australia 115 D5 26 45 S 151 7 E
Jandrain-Jandrenouilles, Belgium 21 G5 50 40N 4 58 E
Jándula →, Spain 37 G6 38 3N 4 6W
Jane Pk., N.Z. 119 F3 45 15 S 168 20 E
Janesville, U.S.A. 140 B7 42 39N 89 1W
Janga, Ghana 101 C4 10 5N 1 0W
Jango, Brazil 157 E6 20 27 S 55 29W
Jangoon, India 82 F4 17 44N 79 5 E
Janhtang Ga, Burma 78 B6 26 32N 96 38 E
Jānī Kheyl, Afghan. 79 B3 32 46N 68 24 E
Janikowo, Poland 47 C5 52 45N 18 7 E
Janīn, Jordan 91 C4 32 28N 35 18 E
Janinà = Ioánnina □, Greece 44 E2 39 39N 20 57 E
Janiuay, Phil. 71 F4 10 58N 122 30 E
Janja, Bos.-H., Yug. 42 C4 44 40N 19 17 E
Janjevo, Serbia, Yug. 42 E6 42 35N 21 19 E
Janjina, Croatia 42 E2 42 58N 17 25 E
Janos, Mexico 146 A3 30 45N 108 10W
Jánoshalma, Hungary 31 E12 46 18N 19 21 E
Jánosháza, Hungary 31 D10 47 8N 17 12 E
Jánossomorja, Hungary 31 D10 47 47N 17 11 E
Janów, Poland 47 E6 50 44N 19 27 E
Janów Lubelski, Poland 47 E9 50 48N 22 23 E
Janów Podlaski, Poland 47 C10 52 11N 23 11 E
Janowiec Wielkopolski, Poland 47 C4 52 45N 17 30 E
Januária, Brazil 155 E3 15 25 S 44 25W
Janub Dârfûr □, Sudan 95 E2 11 0N 25 0 E
Janub Kordofân □, Sudan 95 E3 12 0N 30 0 E
Janubio, Canary Is. 33 F6 28 56N 13 50W
Janville, France 23 D8 48 10N 1 50 E
Janzé, France 22 E5 47 55N 1 28W
Jaora, India 80 H6 23 40N 75 10 E
Japan ■, Asia 61 G8 36 0N 136 0 E
Japan, Sea of, Asia 60 E7 40 0N 135 0 E
Japan Trench, Pac. Oc. 122 D6 32 0N 142 0 E
Japen = Yapen, Indonesia 73 B5 1 50 S 136 0 E
Japurá →, Brazil 152 D4 3 8 S 65 46W
Jaque, Panama 152 B2 7 27N 78 8W
Jarābulus, Syria 84 B3 36 49N 38 1 E
Jaraguá, Brazil 155 E2 15 45 S 49 20W
Jaraguari, Brazil 157 E7 20 9 S 54 35W
Jaraicejo, Spain 37 F5 39 40N 5 49W
Jaraiz, Spain 36 E5 40 4N 5 45W
Jarama →, Spain 34 E1 40 2N 3 39W
Jaramillo, Argentina 160 C3 47 10 S 67 7W
Jarandilla, Spain 36 E5 40 8N 5 39W
Jaranwala, Pakistan 79 C4 31 15N 73 26 E
Jarash, Jordan 91 C4 32 17N 35 54 E
Jarauçu →, Brazil 153 D7 1 48 S 52 22W
Jardas al 'Abīd, Libya 96 B4 32 18N 20 59 E
Jardim, Brazil 158 A4 21 28 S 56 2W
Jardín →, Spain 35 G2 38 50N 2 10W
Jardines de la Reina, Is., Cuba 148 B4 20 50N 78 50W
Jargalang, China 67 C12 43 5N 122 55 E
Jargalant = Hovd, Mongolia 64 B4 48 2N 91 37 E
Jargeau, France 23 E9 47 50N 2 1 E
Jari →, Brazil 153 D7 1 9 S 51 54W
Jarīr, W. al →, Si. Arabia 84 E4 25 38N 42 30 E
Jarmen, Germany 26 B9 53 56N 13 20 E
Jarnac, France 24 C3 45 40N 0 11W
Jarny, France 23 C12 49 9N 5 53 E
Jaro, Phil. 71 F5 11 11N 124 47 E
Jarocin, Poland 47 D4 51 59N 17 29 E
Jaroměr, Czech. 30 A8 50 22N 15 52 E
Jarosław, Poland 31 A15 50 2N 22 42 E
Järpås, Sweden 15 F6 58 23N 12 57 E
Järpen, Sweden 14 A7 63 21N 13 26 E
Jarrahdale, Australia 113 F2 32 24 S 116 5 E
Jarres, Plaine des, Laos 76 C4 19 27N 103 10 E
Jarso, Ethiopia 95 F4 5 15N 37 30 E
Jartai, China 66 E3 39 45N 105 48 E
Jaru, Brazil 157 C5 10 26 S 62 27W
Jaru →, Brazil 157 C5 10 5 S 61 59W
Jarud Qi, China 67 B11 44 28N 120 50 E
Jarvis, Canada 136 D4 42 53N 80 6W
Jarvis I., Pac. Oc. 123 H12 0 15 S 159 55W
Jarvornik, Czech. 31 A10 50 23N 17 2 E
Jarwa, India 81 F10 27 38N 82 30 E
Jaša Tomić, Serbia, Yug. 42 B5 45 26N 20 50 E
Jasaan, Phil. 71 G5 8 39N 124 45 E
Jasien, Poland 47 D2 51 46N 15 0 E
Jāsimīyah, Iraq 84 C5 33 45N 44 41 E
Jasin, Malaysia 77 L4 2 20N 102 26 E
Jāsk, Iran 85 E8 25 38N 57 45 E
Jasło, Poland 31 B14 49 45N 21 30 E
Jason, Is., Falk. Is. 160 D4 51 0 S 61 0W
Jasonville, U.S.A. 141 E9 39 10N 87 13W
Jasper, Alta., Canada 130 C5 52 55N 118 5W
Jasper, Ont., Canada 137 B9 44 52N 75 57W
Jasper, Ala., U.S.A. 135 J2 33 48N 87 16W
Jasper, Fla., U.S.A. 135 K4 30 31N 82 58W
Jasper, Ind., U.S.A. 141 F10 38 24N 86 56W
Jasper, Minn., U.S.A. 138 D6 43 52N 96 22W
Jasper, Tex., U.S.A. 139 K8 30 59N 93 58W
Jasper Nat. Park, Canada 130 C5 52 50N 118 8W
Jassy = Iaşi, Romania 46 B8 47 10N 27 40 E
Jastrebarsko, Croatia 39 C12 45 41N 15 39 E
Jastrowie, Poland 47 B3 53 26N 16 49 E
Jastrzębie Zdrój, Poland 31 B11 49 57N 18 35 E
Jászapáti, Hungary 31 D13 47 32N 20 10 E
Jászárokszállás, Hungary 31 D13 47 39N 20 1 E
Jászberény, Hungary 31 D12 47 30N 19 55 E
Jászkiser, Hungary 31 D13 47 27N 20 20 E
Jászladány, Hungary 31 D13 47 23N 20 10 E
Jataí, Brazil 155 E1 17 58 S 51 48W
Jatapu →, Brazil 153 D6 2 13 S 58 17W
Jati, Pakistan 80 G3 24 20N 68 19 E
Jatibarang, Indonesia 75 D3 6 28 S 108 18 E
Jatinegara, Indonesia 74 D3 6 13 S 106 52 E
Játiva, Spain 35 G4 39 0N 0 32W
Jatobal, Brazil 154 B2 4 35 S 49 33W
Jáu, Angola 103 F2 15 12 S 13 31 E
Jaú, Brazil 159 A6 22 10 S 48 30W
Jaú →, Brazil 153 D5 1 54 S 61 26W
Jauaperí →, Brazil 153 D5 1 26 S 61 35W
Jauche, Belgium 21 G5 50 41N 4 57 E
Jauja, Peru 156 C2 11 45 S 75 15W
Jaunjelgava, Latvia 50 C4 56 35N 25 0 E
Jaunpur, India 81 G10 25 46N 82 44 E
Jauru →, Brazil 157 D6 16 22 S 57 46W
Java = Jawa, Indonesia 75 D4 7 0 S 110 0 E
Java Sea, Indonesia 75 C3 4 35 S 107 15 E
Java Trench, Ind. Oc. 74 D2 9 0 S 105 0 E
Javadi Hills, India 83 H4 12 40N 78 40 E
Jávea, Spain 35 G5 38 48N 0 10 E
Javhlant = Ulyasutay, Mongolia 64 B4 47 56N 97 28 E
Javier, I., Chile 160 C2 47 5 S 74 25W
Javla, India 82 F2 17 18N 75 9 E
Javron, France 22 D6 48 25N 0 25W
Jawa, Indonesia 75 D4 7 0 S 110 0 E
Jawf, W. al →, Yemen 86 D4 15 50N 45 30 E
Jawor, Poland 47 D3 51 4N 16 11 E
Jaworzno, Poland 31 A12 50 13N 19 11 E
Jay, U.S.A. 139 G7 36 25N 94 46W
Jaya, Puncak, Indonesia 73 B5 3 57 S 137 17 E
Jayanca, Peru 156 B2 6 24 S 79 50W
Jayanti, India 78 B2 26 45N 89 40 E
Jayapura, Indonesia 73 B6 2 28 S 140 38 E
Jayawijaya, Pegunungan, Indonesia 73 B5 5 0 S 139 0 E
Jayrūd, Syria 84 C3 33 49N 36 44 E
Jayton, U.S.A. 139 J4 33 17N 100 35W
Jazīreh-ye Shīf, Iran 85 D6 29 4N 50 54 E
Jazminal, Mexico 146 C4 24 56N 101 25W
Jazzīn, Lebanon 91 B4 33 31N 35 35 E
Jean, U.S.A. 145 K11 35 47N 115 20W
Jean Marie River, Canada 130 A4 61 32N 120 38W
Jean Rabel, Haiti 149 C5 19 50N 73 5W
Jeanerette, U.S.A. 139 L9 29 52N 91 38W
Jeanette, Ostrov, Russia 57 B16 76 43N 158 0 E
Jeannette, U.S.A. 136 F5 40 20N 79 36W
Jebba, Morocco 98 A4 35 11N 4 43W
Jebba, Nigeria 101 D5 9 9N 4 48 E
Jebel, Bahr el →, Sudan 95 F3 9 30N 30 25 E
Jebel Qerri, Sudan 95 D3 16 16N 32 50 E
Jeberos, Peru 156 B2 5 15 S 76 10W
Jedburgh, U.K. 18 F6 55 28N 2 33W
Jedda = Jiddah, Si. Arabia 86 B2 21 29N 39 10 E
Jedlicze, Poland 31 B14 49 43N 21 40 E
Jedlnia-Letnisko, Poland 47 D8 51 25N 21 19 E
Jędrzejów, Poland 47 E7 50 35N 20 15 E
Jedwabne, Poland 47 B9 53 17N 22 18 E
Jedway, Canada 130 C2 52 17N 131 14W
Jeetzel →, Germany 26 B7 53 9N 11 6 E
Jefferson, Iowa, U.S.A. 140 B2 42 3N 94 23W
Jefferson, Ohio, U.S.A. 136 E4 41 40N 80 46W
Jefferson, Tex., U.S.A. 139 J7 32 45N 94 23W
Jefferson, Wis., U.S.A. 138 D10 43 0N 88 49W
Jefferson, Mt., Nev., U.S.A. 142 G5 38 51N 117 0W
Jefferson, Mt., Oreg., U.S.A. 142 D3 44 45N 121 50W
Jefferson City, Mo., U.S.A. 140 F4 38 34N 92 10W
Jefferson City, Tenn., U.S.A. 135 G4 36 8N 83 30W
Jeffersontown, U.S.A. 141 F11 38 17N 85 44W
Jeffersonville, Ind., U.S.A. 141 F11 38 20N 85 42W
Jeffersonville, Ohio, U.S.A. 141 E13 39 38N 83 34W
Jega, Nigeria 101 C5 12 15N 4 23 E
Jekabpils, Latvia 50 C4 56 29N 25 57 E
Jelenia Góra, Poland 47 E2 50 50N 15 45 E
Jelenia Góra □, Poland 47 D2 51 0N 15 30 E
Jelgava, Latvia 13 H17 56 41N 23 49 E
Jelica, Serbia, Yug. 42 D5 43 50N 20 17 E
Jelli, Sudan 95 F3 5 25N 31 45 E
Jellicoe, Canada 128 C2 49 40N 87 30W
Jelšava, Czech. 31 C13 48 37N 20 15 E
Jemaja, Indonesia 74 B3 3 5N 105 45 E
Jemaluang, Malaysia 77 L4 2 16N 103 52 E
Jemappes, Belgium 21 H3 50 27N 3 54 E
Jember, Indonesia 75 D4 8 11 S 113 41 E
Jemeppe, Belgium 21 G7 50 37N 5 30 E
Jemnice, Czech. 30 B8 49 1N 15 34 E
Jena, Germany 26 E7 50 56N 11 33 E
Jena, U.S.A. 139 K8 31 41N 92 7W
Jenbach, Austria 30 D4 47 24N 11 47 E
Jendouba, Tunisia 96 A1 36 29N 8 47 E
Jeneponto, Indonesia 72 C1 5 41 S 119 42 E
Jenkins, U.S.A. 134 G4 37 13N 82 41W
Jenner, U.S.A. 144 G3 38 27N 123 7W
Jennings, La., U.S.A. 139 K8 30 10N 92 45W
Jennings, Mo., U.S.A. 140 F6 38 43N 90 16W
Jennings →, Canada 130 B2 59 38N 132 5W
Jepara, Indonesia 75 D3 7 40 S 109 14 E
Jeparit, Australia 116 D5 36 8 S 142 1 E
Jequié, Brazil 155 D3 13 51 S 40 5W
Jequitaí →, Brazil 155 E3 17 4 S 44 50W
Jequitinhonha, Brazil 155 E3 16 30 S 41 0W
Jequitinhonha →, Brazil 155 E4 15 51 S 38 53W
Jerada, Morocco 99 B4 34 17N 2 10W
Jerantut, Malaysia 77 L4 3 56N 102 22 E
Jérémie, Haiti 149 C5 18 40N 74 10W
Jeremoabo, Brazil 154 D4 10 4 S 38 21W
Jerez, Punta, Mexico 147 C5 22 58N 97 40W
Jerez de García Salinas, Mexico 146 C4 22 39N 103 0W
Jerez de la Frontera, Spain 37 J4 36 41N 6 7W
Jerez de los Caballeros, Spain 37 G4 38 20N 6 45W
Jericho = Arīḩā, Syria 84 C3 35 49N 36 35 E
Jericho = El Arīḩā, Jordan 91 D4 31 52N 35 27 E
Jericho, Australia 114 C4 23 38 S 146 6 E
Jerichow, Germany 26 C8 52 30N 12 2 E
Jerico Springs, U.S.A. 140 G2 37 37N 94 1W
Jerilderie, Australia 117 C6 35 20 S 145 41 E
Jermyn, U.S.A. 137 E9 41 31N 75 31W
Jerome, U.S.A. 143 J8 34 50N 112 0W
Jersey, Chan. Is. 17 H5 49 13N 2 7W
Jersey City, U.S.A. 137 F10 40 41N 74 8W
Jersey Shore, U.S.A. 136 E7 41 17N 77 18W
Jerseyville, U.S.A. 140 E6 39 5N 90 20W
Jerusalem, Israel 91 D4 31 47N 35 10 E
Jervis B., Australia 117 C9 35 8 S 150 46 E
Jesenice, Slovenia 39 B11 46 28N 14 3 E
Jeseník, Czech. 31 B10 50 0N 17 8 E
Jesenké, Czech. 31 C13 48 20N 20 10 E
Jesselton = Kota Kinabalu, Malaysia 75 A5 6 0N 116 4 E
Jessnitz, Germany 26 D8 51 42N 12 19 E
Jessore, Bangla. 78 D2 23 10N 89 10 E
Jesup, U.S.A. 135 K5 31 36N 81 54W
Jesup, U.S.A. 140 B4 42 29N 92 4W
Jesús, Peru 156 B2 7 15 S 78 25W
Jesús Carranza, Mexico 147 D5 17 28N 95 1W
Jesús María, Argentina 158 C3 30 59 S 64 5W
Jetafe, Phil. 71 F5 10 9N 124 9 E
Jetmore, U.S.A. 139 F5 38 10N 99 57W
Jetpur, India 80 J4 21 45N 70 10 E
Jette, Belgium 21 G4 50 53N 4 20 E
Jevnaker, Norway 14 D4 60 15N 10 26 E
Jewell, U.S.A. 140 B3 42 20N 93 39W
Jewett, Ohio, U.S.A. 136 F3 40 22N 81 2W
Jewett, Tex., U.S.A. 139 K6 31 20N 96 8W
Jewett City, U.S.A. 137 E13 41 36N 71 58W
Jeyhūnābād, Iran 85 C6 34 58N 48 59 E
Jeypore, India 82 E6 18 50N 82 38 E
Jeziorak, Jezioro, Poland 47 B6 53 40N 19 35 E
Jeziorany, Poland 47 B7 53 58N 20 46 E
Jeziorka →, Poland 47 D7 51 59N 20 57 E
Jhajjar, India 80 E7 28 37N 76 42 E
Jhal Jhao, Pakistan 79 D2 26 20N 65 35 E
Jhalakati, Bangla. 78 D3 22 39N 90 12 E
Jhalawar, India 80 G7 24 40N 76 10 E
Jhang Maghiana, Pakistan 79 C4 31 15N 72 22 E
Jhansi, India 81 G8 25 30N 78 36 E
Jharia, India 81 H12 23 45N 86 26 E
Jharsuguda, India 82 D7 21 56N 84 5 E
Jhelum, Pakistan 79 B4 33 0N 73 45 E
Jhelum →, Pakistan 80 D5 31 20N 72 10 E
Jhunjhunu, India 80 E6 28 10N 75 30 E
Ji Xian, Hebei, China 66 F8 37 35N 115 30 E
Ji Xian, Henan, China 66 G8 35 22N 114 5 E
Ji Xian, Shanxi, China 66 F6 36 7N 110 40 E
Jia Xian, Henan, China 66 H7 33 59N 113 12 E
Jia Xian, Shaanxi, China 66 E6 38 12N 110 28 E
Jiading, China 69 B13 31 22N 121 15 E
Jiahe, China 69 E9 25 38N 112 19 E
Jiali, Taiwan 69 F13 23 10N 120 10 E
Jialing Jiang →, China 68 C6 29 30N 106 20 E
Jiamusi, China 65 B8 46 40N 130 26 E
Ji'an, Jiangxi, China 69 D10 27 6N 114 59 E
Ji'an, Jilin, China 67 D14 41 5N 126 10 E
Jianchang, China 67 D11 40 55N 120 35 E
Jianchangying, China 67 D10 40 10N 118 50 E
Jianchuan, China 68 D2 26 38N 99 55 E
Jiande, China 69 C12 29 23N 119 15 E
Jiangbei, China 68 C6 29 40N 106 34 E
Jiangcheng, China 68 F3 22 36N 101 52 E
Jiangdi, China 68 D4 26 57N 103 37 E
Jiange, China 68 A5 32 4N 105 32 E

Kadina 213


Jiangjin, *China* ........ 68 C6 29 14N 106 14 E
Jiangkou, *China* ........ 68 D7 27 40N 108 49 E
Jiangle, *China* ........ 69 D11 26 42N 117 23 E
Jiangling, *China* ........ 69 B9 30 25N 112 12 E
Jiangmen, *China* ...... 69 F9 22 32N 113 0 E
Jiangshan, *China* ...... 69 C12 28 40N 118 37 E
Jiangsu □, *China* ...... 67 H10 33 0N 120 0 E
Jiangxi □, *China* ...... 69 D10 27 30N 116 0 E
Jiangyin, *China* ...... 69 B13 31 54N 120 17 E
Jiangyong, *China* ...... 69 E8 25 20N 111 22 E
Jiangyou, *China* ........ 68 B5 31 44N 104 43 E
Jianhe, *China* .......... 68 D7 26 37N 108 31 E
Jianli, *China* .......... 69 C9 29 46N 112 56 E
Jianning, *China* ........ 69 D11 26 50N 116 50 E
Jian'ou, *China* ........ 69 D12 27 3N 118 17 E
Jianshi, *China* ........ 68 B7 30 37N 109 38 E
Jianshui, *China* ........ 68 F4 23 36N 102 43 E
Jianyang, *Fujian, China* . 69 D12 27 20N 118 5 E
Jianyang, *Sichuan, China* 68 B5 30 24N 104 33 E
Jiao Xian, *China* ...... 67 F11 36 18N 120 1 E
Jiaohe, *Hebei, China* ... 66 E9 38 2N 116 20 E
Jiaohe, *Jilin, China* .... 67 C14 43 40N 127 22 E
Jiaoling, *China* ........ 69 E11 24 41N 116 12 E
Jiaozhou Wan, *China* ... 67 F11 36 5N 120 10 E
Jiaozuo, *China* ........ 66 G7 35 16N 113 12 E
Jiashan, *China* ........ 69 A11 32 46N 117 59 E
Jiawang, *China* ........ 67 G9 34 28N 117 26 E
Jiaxiang, *China* ........ 66 G9 35 25N 116 20 E
Jiaxing, *China* ........ 69 B13 30 49N 120 45 E
Jiayi, *Taiwan* .......... 69 F13 23 30N 120 24 E
Jiayu, *China* .......... 69 C9 29 55N 113 55 E
Jibão, Serra do, *Brazil* .. 155 D3 14 48 S 45 0W
Jibiya, *Nigeria* ........ 101 C6 13 5N 7 12 E
Jibou, *Romania* ........ 46 B4 47 15N 23 17 E
Jibuti = Djibouti ■,
*Africa* .............. 90 E3 12 0N 43 0 E
Jicarón, I., *Panama* .... 148 E3 7 10N 81 50W
Jičín, *Czech.* .......... 30 A8 50 25N 15 28 E
Jiddah, *Si. Arabia* ...... 86 B2 21 29N 39 10 E
Jieshou, *China* ........ 66 H8 33 18N 115 22 E
Jiexiu, *China* .......... 66 F6 37 2N 111 55 E
Jieyang, *China* ........ 69 F11 23 35N 116 21 E
Jiggalong, *Australia* .... 112 D3 23 21 S 120 47 E
Jihlava, *Czech.* ........ 30 B8 49 28N 15 35 E
Jihlava →, *Czech.* ...... 30 C9 48 55N 16 36 E
Jihočeský □, *Czech.* .... 30 B7 49 8N 14 35 E
Jihomoravský □, *Czech.* 31 B9 49 5N 16 30 E
Jijel, *Algeria* .......... 99 A6 36 52N 5 50 E
Jijiga, *Ethiopia* ........ 90 F3 9 20N 42 50 E
Jijona, *Spain* .......... 35 G4 38 34N 0 30W
Jikamshi, *Nigeria* ...... 101 C6 12 12N 7 45 E
Jilin, *China* .......... 67 C14 43 44N 126 30 E
Jilin □, *China* ........ 67 C13 44 0N 127 0 E
Jiloca →, *Spain* ...... 34 D3 41 21N 1 39W
Jilong, *Taiwan* ........ 69 E13 25 8N 121 42 E
Jílové, *Czech.* .......... 30 B7 49 52N 14 29 E
Jima, *Ethiopia* ........ 95 F4 7 40N 36 47 E
Jimbolia, *Romania* ...... 46 D1 45 47N 20 43 E
Jimena de la Frontera,
*Spain* .............. 37 J5 36 27N 5 24W
Jimenbuen, *Australia* ... 117 D8 36 42 S 148 53 E
Jiménez, *Mexico* ...... 146 B4 27 10N 104 54W
Jimenez, *Phil.* ........ 71 G4 8 20N 123 50 E
Jimo, *China* .......... 67 F11 36 23N 120 30 E
Jin Jiang →, *China* .... 69 C10 28 24N 115 48 E
Jin Xian, *Hebei, China* .. 66 E8 38 2N 115 2 E
Jin Xian, *Liaoning, China* 67 E11 38 55N 121 42 E
Jinan, *China* .......... 66 F9 36 38N 117 1 E
Jincheng, *China* ........ 66 G7 35 29N 112 50 E
Jinchuan, *China* ........ 68 B4 31 30N 102 3 E
Jind, *India* ............ 80 E7 29 19N 76 22 E
Jindabyne, *Australia* .... 117 D8 36 25 S 148 35 E
Jindrichuv Hradeç,
*Czech.* .............. 30 B8 49 10N 15 2 E
Jing He →, *China* .... 66 G5 34 27N 109 4 E
Jing Shan, *China* ...... 69 B8 31 20N 111 35 E
Jing Xian, *Anhui, China* 69 B12 30 38N 118 25 E
Jing Xian, *Hunan, China* 68 D7 26 33N 109 40 E
Jing'an, *China* ........ 69 C10 28 50N 115 17 E
Jingbian, *China* ........ 66 F5 37 20N 108 30 E
Jingchuan, *China* ...... 66 G4 35 20N 107 20 E
Jingde, *China* .......... 69 B12 30 15N 118 27 E
Jingdezhen, *China* ...... 69 C11 29 20N 117 11 E
Jingdong, *China* ........ 68 E3 24 23N 100 47 E
Jinggu, *China* .......... 68 F3 23 35N 100 41 E
Jinghai, *China* ........ 66 E9 38 55N 116 55 E
Jinghong, *China* ........ 68 F3 22 0N 100 45 E
Jingjiang, *China* ........ 69 A13 32 2N 120 16 E
Jingle, *China* .......... 66 E6 38 20N 111 55 E
Jingmen, *China* ........ 69 B9 31 0N 112 10 E
Jingning, *China* ........ 66 G3 35 30N 105 43 E
Jingpo Hu, *China* ...... 67 C15 43 55N 128 55 E
Jingshan, *China* ........ 69 B9 31 1N 113 7 E
Jingtai, *China* .......... 66 F3 37 10N 104 6 E
Jingxi, *China* .......... 68 F6 23 8N 106 27 E
Jingxing, *China* ........ 66 E8 38 2N 114 8 E
Jingyang, *China* ........ 66 G5 34 30N 108 50 E
Jingyu, *China* .......... 67 C14 42 25N 126 45 E
Jingyuan, *China* ........ 66 F3 36 30N 104 40 E
Jingziguan, *China* ...... 66 H6 33 15N 111 0 E
Jinhua, *China* .......... 69 C12 29 8N 119 38 E
Jining,
*Nei Mongol Zizhiqu,*
*China* .............. 66 D7 41 5N 113 0 E
Jining, *Shandong, China* 66 G9 35 22N 116 34 E
Jinja, *Uganda* .......... 106 B3 0 25N 33 12 E
Jinjang, *Malaysia* ...... 77 L3 3 13N 101 39 E
Jinji, *China* .......... 66 F4 37 58N 106 8 E
Jinjiang, *Fujian, China* .. 69 E12 24 43N 118 33 E
Jinjiang, *Yunnan, China* 68 D3 26 14N 100 34 E
Jinjie, *China* .......... 68 F6 23 15N 107 18 E
Jinjini, *Ghana* ........ 100 D4 7 26N 3 42W
Jinkou, *China* .......... 69 B10 30 20N 114 8 E
Jinmen Dao, *China* ...... 69 E12 24 25N 118 25 E
Jinning, *China* ........ 68 E4 24 38N 102 38 E
Jinotega, *Nic.* .......... 148 D2 13 6N 85 59W
Jinotepe, *Nic.* .......... 148 D2 11 50N 86 10W
Jinping, *Guizhou, China* 68 D7 26 41N 109 10 E
Jinping, *Yunnan, China* . 68 F4 22 45N 103 18 E
Jinsha, *China* .......... 68 D6 27 29N 106 12 E
Jinsha Jiang →, *China* . 68 C5 28 50N 104 36 E
Jinshan, *China* ........ 69 B13 30 54N 121 10 E
Jinshi, *China* .......... 69 C8 29 40N 111 50 E
Jintan, *China* .......... 69 B12 31 42N 119 36 E
Jintotolo Channel, *Phil.* . 71 F4 11 48N 123 5 E
Jinxi, *Jiangxi, China* .... 69 D11 27 56N 116 45 E
Jinxi, *Liaoning, China* .. 67 D11 40 52N 120 50 E
Jinxian, *China* ........ 69 C11 28 26N 116 17 E
Jinxiang, *China* ........ 66 G9 35 5N 116 22 E
Jinyun, *China* .......... 69 C13 28 35N 120 5 E
Jinzhai, *China* ........ 69 B10 31 40N 115 53 E
Jinzhou, *China* ........ 67 D11 41 5N 121 3 E
Jiparaná →, *Brazil* .... 157 B5 8 3 S 62 52W
Jipijapa, *Ecuador* ...... 152 D1 1 0 S 80 40W
Jiquilpan, *Mexico* ...... 146 D4 19 57N 102 42W
Jirwān, *Si. Arabia* ...... 87 B5 23 27N 50 53 E
Jishan, *China* .......... 66 G6 35 34N 110 58 E
Jishou, *China* .......... 68 C7 28 21N 109 43 E
Jishui, *China* .......... 69 D10 27 12N 115 8 E
Jisr ash Shughūr, *Syria* .. 84 C3 35 49N 36 18 E
Jitarning, *Australia* .... 113 F2 32 48 S 117 57 E
Jitra, *Malaysia* ........ 77 J3 6 16N 100 25 E
Jiu →, *Romania* ...... 46 F4 43 47N 23 48 E
Jiudengkou, *China* ...... 66 E4 39 56N 106 40 E
Jiujiang, *Guangdong,*
*China* .............. 69 F9 22 50N 113 0 E
Jiujiang, *Jiangxi, China* . 69 C10 29 42N 115 58 E
Jiuling Shan, *China* .... 69 C10 28 40N 114 40 E
Jiulong, *China* ........ 68 C3 28 57N 101 31 E
Jiutai, *China* .......... 67 B13 44 10N 125 50 E
Jiuxiangcheng, *China* .... 66 H8 33 12N 114 50 E
Jiuxincheng, *China* ...... 66 E8 39 17N 115 59 E
Jiuyuhang, *China* ...... 69 B12 30 18N 119 56 E
Jixi, *Anhui, China* ...... 69 B12 30 5N 118 34 E
Jixi, *Heilongjiang, China* 67 B16 45 20N 130 50 E
Jiyang, *China* .......... 67 F9 37 0N 117 12 E
Jiz', W. →, *Yemen* .... 87 C6 16 12N 52 14 E
Jīzān, *Si. Arabia* ...... 86 C3 17 0N 42 20 E
Jize, *China* .......... 66 F8 36 54N 114 56 E
Jizera →, *Czech.* ...... 30 A7 50 10N 14 43 E
Jizō-Zaki, *Japan* ...... 62 B5 35 34N 133 20 E
Joaçaba, *Brazil* ........ 159 B5 27 5 S 51 31W
Joaíma, *Brazil* ........ 155 E3 16 39 S 41 2W
João, *Brazil* .......... 154 B1 2 46 S 50 59W
João Amaro, *Brazil* .... 155 D3 12 46 S 40 22W
João Câmara, *Brazil* .... 154 C4 5 32 S 35 48W
João Pessoa, *Brazil* .... 154 C5 7 10 S 34 52W
João Pinheiro, *Brazil* ... 155 E2 17 45 S 46 10W
Joaquim Távora, *Brazil* . 155 F2 23 30 S 49 58W
Joaquín V. González,
*Argentina* .......... 158 B3 25 10 S 64 0W
Jobourg, Nez de, *France* 22 C5 49 41N 1 57W
Jódar, *Spain* .......... 35 H1 37 50N 3 21W
Jodhpur, *India* ........ 80 F5 26 23N 73 8 E
Joensuu, *Finland* ...... 48 B4 62 37N 29 49 E
Jœuf, *France* .......... 23 C13 49 12N 6 0 E
Jofane, *Mozam.* ........ 105 C5 21 15 S 34 18 E
Joggins, *Canada* ........ 129 C7 45 42N 64 27W
Jogjakarta = Yogyakarta,
*Indonesia* .......... 75 D4 7 49 S 110 22 E
Jōhana, *Japan* ........ 63 A8 36 30N 136 57 E
Johannesburg, *S. Africa* . 105 D4 26 10 S 28 2 E
Johannesburg, *U.S.A.* .. 145 K9 35 26N 117 38W
Jōhen, *Japan* .......... 62 E4 32 58N 132 32 E
John Day, *U.S.A.* ...... 142 D4 44 25N 118 57W
John Day →, *U.S.A.* .. 142 D3 45 44N 120 39W
John H. Kerr Res.,
*U.S.A.* .............. 135 G6 36 20N 78 30W
John o' Groats, *U.K.* ... 18 C5 58 39N 3 3W
Johnnie, *U.S.A.* ........ 145 J10 36 25N 116 5W
John's Ra., *Australia* ... 114 C1 21 55 S 133 23 E
Johnson, *U.S.A.* ........ 139 G4 37 35N 101 48W
Johnson City, *Ill., U.S.A.* 140 G8 37 49N 88 56W
Johnson City, *N.Y.,*
*U.S.A.* .............. 137 D9 42 7N 75 57W
Johnson City, *Tenn.,*
*U.S.A.* .............. 135 G4 36 18N 82 21W
Johnson City, *Tex.,*
*U.S.A.* .............. 139 K5 30 15N 98 24W
Johnsonburg, *U.S.A.* .... 136 E6 41 30N 78 40W
Johnsondale, *U.S.A.* .... 145 K8 35 58N 118 32W
Johnson's Crossing,
*Canada* .............. 130 A2 60 29N 133 18W
Johnsonville, *N.Z.* ...... 118 H3 41 13 S 174 48 E
Johnston, L., *Australia* .. 113 F3 32 25 S 120 30 E
Johnston Falls =
Mambilima Falls,
*Zambia* .............. 107 E2 10 31 S 28 45 E
Johnston I., *Pac. Oc.* .... 123 F11 17 10N 169 8W
Johnstone Str., *Canada* . 130 C3 50 28N 126 0W
Johnstown, *N.Y., U.S.A.* 137 C10 43 1N 74 20W
Johnstown, *Pa., U.S.A.* . 136 F6 40 19N 78 53W
Johor □, *Malaysia* ...... 74 B2 2 0N 103 30 E
Johor Baharu, *Malaysia* . 77 M4 1 28N 103 46 E
Joigny, *France* .......... 23 E10 47 58N 3 20 E
Joinvile, *Brazil* ........ 159 B6 26 15 S 48 55W
Joinville, *France* ........ 23 D12 48 27N 5 10 E
Joinville I., *Antarctica* .. 7 C18 65 0 S 55 30W
Jojutla, *Mexico* ........ 147 D5 18 37N 99 11W
Jokkmokk, *Sweden* ...... 12 C15 66 35N 19 50 E
Jökulsá á Bru →, *Iceland* 12 D6 65 40N 14 16W
Jökulsá á Fjöllum →,
*Iceland* .............. 12 C5 66 10N 16 30W
Jolfā, *Āzarbājān-e Sharqī,*
*Iran* .............. 84 B5 38 57N 45 38 E
Jolfā, *Eşfahan, Iran* .... 85 C6 32 58N 51 37 E
Joliet, *U.S.A.* .......... 141 C8 41 30N 88 5W
Joliette, *Canada* ........ 128 C5 46 3N 73 24W
Jolo, *Phil.* ............ 71 H3 6 0N 121 0 E
Jolo Group, *Phil.* ...... 71 J3 6 0N 121 9 E
Jolon, *U.S.A.* .......... 144 K5 35 58N 121 9W
Jomalig, *Phil.* .......... 70 D4 14 42N 122 22 E
Jombang, *Indonesia* .... 75 D4 7 33 S 112 14 E
Jomda, *China* .......... 68 B2 31 28N 98 12 E
Jome, *Indonesia* ........ 72 B3 1 16 S 127 30 E
Jomfruland, *Norway* .... 15 F3 58 52N 9 36 E
Jönåker, *Sweden* ........ 15 F10 58 44N 16 40 E
Jonava, *Lithuania* ...... 50 D4 55 8N 24 12 E
Jones, *Phil.* .......... 70 C3 16 33N 121 42 E
Jones Sound, *Canada* .... 6 B3 76 0N 85 0W
Jonesboro, *Ark., U.S.A.* 139 H9 35 50N 90 45W
Jonesboro, *Ill., U.S.A.* .. 139 G10 37 26N 89 18W
Jonesboro, *La., U.S.A.* . 139 J8 32 15N 92 41W
Jonesburg, *U.S.A.* ...... 140 F5 38 51N 91 18W
Jonesport, *U.S.A.* ...... 129 D6 44 32N 67 38W
Jonesville, *Ind., U.S.A.* . 141 E11 39 5N 85 54W
Jonesville, *Mich., U.S.A.* 141 C12 41 59N 84 40W
Jonglei, *Sudan* .......... 95 F3 6 25N 30 50 E
Jonglei □, *Sudan* ...... 95 F3 7 30N 32 30 E
Joniskis, *Lithuania* .... 50 C3 56 13N 23 35 E
Jönköping, *Sweden* ...... 13 H13 57 45N 14 10 E
Jönköpings län □, *Sweden* 13 H13 57 30N 14 30 E
Jonquière, *Canada* ...... 129 C5 48 27N 71 14W
Jonsberg, *Sweden* ...... 15 F10 58 30N 16 48 E
Jonsered, *Sweden* ...... 15 G6 57 45N 12 10 E
Jonzac, *France* ........ 24 C3 45 27N 0 28W
Joplin, *U.S.A.* ........ 139 G7 37 0N 94 31W
Jordan, *U.S.A.* ........ 142 C10 47 25N 106 58W
Jordan ■, *Asia* ........ 91 E5 31 0N 36 0 E
Jordan →, *Asia* ........ 91 D4 31 48N 35 32 E
Jordan Valley, *U.S.A.* .. 142 E5 43 0N 117 2W
Jordânia, *Brazil* ........ 155 E3 15 55 S 40 11W
Jordanów, *Poland* ...... 31 B12 49 41N 19 49 E
Jorge, C., *Chile* ........ 160 D1 51 40 S 75 35W
Jorhat, *India* .......... 78 B5 26 45N 94 12 E
Jorm, *Afghan.* .......... 79 A3 36 50N 70 52 E
Jörn, *Sweden* .......... 12 D16 65 4N 20 1 E
Jorong, *Indonesia* ...... 75 C4 3 58 S 114 56 E
Jorquera →, *Chile* .... 158 B2 28 3 S 69 58W
Jos, *Nigeria* .......... 101 D6 9 53N 8 51 E
Jošanička Banja,
*Serbia, Yug.* .......... 42 D5 43 24N 20 47 E
Jose Abad Santos, *Phil.* . 71 J5 5 55N 125 39 E
José Batlle y Ordóñez,
*Uruguay* .............. 159 C4 33 20 S 55 10W
José de San Martín,
*Argentina* .......... 160 B2 44 4 S 70 26W
Jose Panganiban, *Phil.* .. 70 D4 14 17N 122 41 E
Joseni, *Romania* ........ 46 C6 46 42N 25 29 E
Joseph, *U.S.A.* ........ 142 D5 45 27N 117 13W
Joseph, L., *Nfld., Canada* 129 B6 52 45N 65 18W
Joseph, L., *Ont., Canada* 136 A5 45 10N 79 44W
Joseph Bonaparte G.,
*Australia* ............ 112 B4 14 35 S 128 50 E
Joseph City, *U.S.A.* .... 143 J8 35 0N 110 16W
Joshua Tree, *U.S.A.* .... 145 L10 34 8N 116 19W
Joshua Tree Nat. Mon.,
*U.S.A.* .............. 145 M10 33 56N 116 5W
Josselin, *France* ........ 22 E4 47 57N 2 33W
Jostedal, *Norway* ...... 14 C2 61 35N 7 15 E
Jotunheimen, *Norway* .. 14 C2 61 35N 8 25 E
Jourdanton, *U.S.A.* .... 139 L5 28 54N 98 32W
Joure, *Neths.* .......... 20 C7 52 58N 5 48 E
Joussard, *Canada* ...... 130 B5 55 22N 115 50W
Jovellanos, *Cuba* ...... 148 B3 22 40N 81 10W
Jovellar, *Phil.* .......... 70 E4 13 4N 123 36 E
Jowai, *India* .......... 78 C4 25 26N 92 12 E
Jowzjān □, *Afghan.* .... 79 A2 36 10N 66 0 E
Joyeuse, *France* ........ 25 D8 44 29N 4 16 E
Józefów, *Poland* ........ 47 C8 52 10N 21 11 E
Ju Xian, *China* ........ 67 F10 36 35N 118 20 E
Juan Aldama, *Mexico* .... 146 C4 24 20N 103 23W
Juan Bautista Alberdi,
*Argentina* .......... 158 C3 34 26 S 61 48W
Juan de Fuca Str.,
*Canada* .............. 144 B2 48 15N 124 0W
Juan de Nova, *Ind. Oc.* . 105 B7 17 3 S 43 45 E
Juan Fernández, Arch.
de, *Pac. Oc.* .......... 123 L20 33 50 S 80 0W
Juan José Castelli,
*Argentina* .......... 158 B3 25 27 S 60 57W
Juan L. Lacaze, *Uruguay* 158 C4 34 26 S 57 25W
Juanjuí, *Peru* .......... 156 B2 7 10 S 76 45W
Juárez, *Argentina* ...... 158 D4 37 40 S 59 43W
Juárez, *Mexico* ........ 145 N11 32 20N 115 57W
Juárez, Sierra de, *Mexico* 146 A1 32 0N 116 0W
Juatinga, Ponta de, *Brazil* 155 F3 23 17 S 44 30W
Juàzeiro, *Brazil* ........ 154 C3 9 30 S 40 30W
Juàzeiro do Norte, *Brazil* 154 C4 7 10 S 39 18W
Jubay, *Phil.* .......... 71 F5 11 33N 124 18 E
Jubayl, *Lebanon* ........ 91 A4 34 5N 35 39 E
Jubbah, *Si. Arabia* ...... 84 D4 28 2N 40 56 E
Jubbulpore = Jabalpur,
*India* .............. 81 H8 23 9N 79 58 E
Jübek, *Germany* ........ 26 A5 54 31N 9 24 E
Jubga, *Russia* .......... 53 D8 44 19N 38 48 E
Jubilee L., *Australia* .... 113 E4 29 0 S 126 50 E
Júcar →, *Spain* ........ 35 F4 39 5N 0 10W
Júcaro, *Cuba* .......... 148 B4 21 37N 78 51W
Juchitán, *Mexico* ...... 147 D5 16 27N 95 5W
Judaea = Har Yehuda,
*Israel* .............. 91 D3 31 35N 34 57 E
Judenburg, *Austria* .... 30 D7 47 12N 14 38 E
Judith →, *U.S.A.* .... 142 C9 47 44N 109 38W
Judith Gap, *U.S.A.* .... 142 C9 46 40N 109 46W
Judith Pt., *U.S.A.* ...... 137 E13 41 20N 71 30W
Jufari →, *Brazil* ...... 153 D5 1 13 S 62 0W
Jugoslavia =
Yugoslavia ■, *Europe* 42 D5 44 0N 20 0 E
Juigalpa, *Nic.* .......... 148 D2 12 6N 85 26W
Juillac, *France* .......... 24 C5 45 20N 1 19 E
Juist, *Germany* .......... 26 B2 53 40N 7 0 E
Juiz de Fora, *Brazil* .... 155 F3 21 43 S 43 19W
Jujuy □, *Argentina* .... 158 A2 23 20 S 65 40W
Julesburg, *U.S.A.* ...... 138 E3 41 0N 102 20W
Juli, *Peru* .............. 156 D4 16 10 S 69 25W
Julia Cr. →, *Australia* .. 114 C3 20 0 S 141 11 E
Julia Creek, *Australia* .. 114 C3 20 39 S 141 44 E
Juliaca, *Peru* .......... 156 D3 15 25 S 70 10W
Julian, *U.S.A.* .......... 145 M10 33 4N 116 38W
Julian Alps = Julijske
Alpe, *Slovenia* ...... 39 B11 46 15N 14 1 E
Julianakanaal, *Neths.* ... 21 F7 51 6N 5 52 E
Julianatop, *Surinam* .... 153 C6 3 40N 56 30W
Julianehåb, *Greenland* .. 6 C5 60 43N 46 0W
Jülich, *Germany* ........ 26 E2 50 55N 6 20 E
Julierpass, *Switz.* ...... 29 D9 46 28N 9 32 E
Julijske Alpe, *Slovenia* .. 39 B11 46 15N 14 1 E
Julimes, *Mexico* ........ 146 B3 28 25N 105 27W
Jullundur, *India* ........ 80 D6 31 20N 75 40 E
Julu, *China* ............ 66 F8 37 15N 115 2 E
Jumbo, *Zimbabwe* ...... 107 F3 17 30 S 30 58 E
Jumbo Pk., *U.S.A.* .... 145 J12 36 12N 114 11W
Jumentos Cays, *Bahamas* 149 B4 23 0N 75 40W
Jumet, *Belgium* ........ 21 H4 50 27N 4 25 E
Jumilla, *Spain* .......... 35 G3 38 28N 1 19W
Jumla, *Nepal* .......... 81 E10 29 15N 82 13 E
Jumna = Yamuna →,
*India* .............. 81 G9 25 30N 81 53 E
Junagadh, *India* ........ 80 J4 21 30N 70 30 E
Junaynah, *Si. Arabia* .... 86 B4 22 33N 46 18 E
Junction, *Tex., U.S.A.* .. 139 K5 30 29N 99 48W
Junction, *Utah, U.S.A.* . 143 G7 38 10N 112 15W
Junction B., *Australia* .. 114 A1 11 52 S 133 55 E
Junction City, *Kans.,*
*U.S.A.* .............. 138 F6 39 4N 96 55W
Junction City, *Oreg.,*
*U.S.A.* .............. 142 D2 44 14N 123 12W
Junction Pt., *Australia* . 114 A1 11 45 S 133 50 E
Jundah, *Australia* ...... 114 C3 24 46 S 143 2 E
Jundiaí, *Brazil* .......... 159 A6 24 30 S 47 0W
Juneau, *U.S.A.* ........ 126 C6 58 20N 134 20W
Junee, *Australia* ........ 117 C7 34 53 S 147 35 E
Jungfrau, *Switz.* ........ 28 C5 46 32N 7 58 E
Junggar Pendi, *China* ... 64 B3 44 30N 86 0 E
Junglinster, *Lux.* ........ 21 J8 49 43N 6 15 E
Jungshahi, *Pakistan* .... 80 G2 24 52N 67 44 E
Juniata →, *U.S.A.* .... 136 F7 40 30N 77 40W
Junín, *Argentina* ...... 158 C3 34 33 S 60 57W
Junín, *Peru* ............ 156 C2 11 12 S 76 0W
Junín □, *Peru* .......... 156 C3 11 30 S 75 0W
Junín de los Andes,
*Argentina* .......... 160 A2 39 45 S 71 0W
Jūniyah, *Lebanon* ...... 91 B4 33 59N 35 38 E
Junnar, *India* .......... 82 E1 19 12N 73 58 E
Juntura, *U.S.A.* ........ 142 E4 43 44N 118 4W
Juparanã, L., *Brazil* .... 155 E3 19 16 S 40 8W
Jupiter →, *Canada* .... 129 C7 49 29N 63 37W
Juquiá, *Brazil* .......... 155 F2 24 19 S 47 38W
Jur, Nahr el →, *Sudan* . 95 F2 8 45N 29 15 E
Jura, *Europe* .......... 23 F13 46 35N 6 5 E
Jura, *U.K.* ............ 18 F3 56 0N 5 50W
Jura □, *France* ........ 23 F12 46 47N 5 45 E
Jura, Mts. du, *Europe* .. 25 B10 46 40N 6 5 E
Jura, Sd. of, *U.K.* ...... 18 F3 55 57N 5 45W
Jura Suisse, *Switz.* ...... 28 B3 47 10N 7 0 E
Jurado, *Colombia* ...... 152 B2 7 7N 77 46W
Jurilovca, *Romania* .... 46 E9 44 46N 28 52 E
Jurong, *China* .......... 69 B12 31 57N 119 9 E
Juruá →, *Brazil* ...... 152 D4 2 37 S 65 44W
Juruena, *Brazil* ........ 157 C6 13 0 S 58 10W
Juruena →, *Brazil* .... 157 B6 7 20 S 58 3W
Juruti, *Brazil* .......... 153 D6 2 9 S 56 4W
Jussey, *France* ........ 23 E12 47 50N 5 55 E
Justo Daract, *Argentina* . 158 C2 33 52 S 65 12W
Jutaí, *Brazil* .......... 156 B4 5 11 S 68 54W
Jutaí →, *Brazil* ........ 152 D4 2 43 S 66 57W
Jüterbog, *Germany* .... 26 D9 52 0N 13 6 E
Juticalpa, *Honduras* .... 148 D2 14 40N 86 12W
Jutland = Jylland,
*Denmark* ............ 15 H3 56 25N 9 30 E
Jutphaas, *Neths.* ...... 20 D6 52 2N 5 6 E
Juventud, I. de la, *Cuba* 148 B3 21 40N 82 40W
Juvigny-sous-Andaine,
*France* .............. 22 D6 48 32N 0 30W
Juvisy-sur-Orge, *France* . 23 D9 48 42N 2 22 E
Jūy Zar, *Iran* .......... 84 C5 33 50N 46 18 E
Juye, *China* .......... 66 G9 35 22N 116 5 E
Juzennecourt, *France* ... 23 D11 48 10N 4 58 E
Jylland, *Denmark* ...... 15 H3 56 25N 9 30 E
Jyväskylä, *Finland* ...... 12 E18 62 14N 25 50 E


# K


K2, Mt., *Pakistan* ...... 81 B7 35 58N 76 32 E
Kaala-Gomén, *N. Cal.* .. 121 T18 20 40 S 164 25 E
Kaap die Goeie Hoop,
*S. Africa* .......... 104 E2 34 24 S 18 30 E
Kaap Plateau, *S. Africa* . 104 D3 28 30 S 24 0 E
Kaapkruis, *Namibia* .... 104 C1 21 55 S 13 57 E
Kaapstad = Cape Town,
*S. Africa* .......... 104 E2 33 55 S 18 22 E
Kaatsheuvel, *Neths.* .... 21 E6 51 39N 5 2 E
Kabacan, *Phil.* .......... 71 H5 7 8N 124 49 E
Kabaena, *Indonesia* .... 72 C2 5 15 S 122 0 E
Kabala, *S. Leone* ...... 100 D2 9 38N 11 37W
Kabale, *Uganda* ........ 106 C3 1 15 S 30 0 E
Kabalo, *Zaïre* .......... 103 D5 6 0 S 27 0 E
Kabambare, *Zaïre* ...... 106 C2 4 41 S 27 39 E
Kabango, *Zaïre* ........ 107 D2 8 35 S 28 30 E
Kabanjahe, *Indonesia* ... 74 B1 3 6N 98 30 E
Kabankalan, *Phil.* ...... 71 G4 9 59N 122 49 E
Kabara, *Mali* .......... 100 B4 16 40N 2 50W
Kabardinka, *Russia* .... 52 D7 44 40N 37 57 E
Kabardino-Balkar
Republic □, *Russia* ... 53 E10 43 30N 43 30 E
Kabare, *Indonesia* ...... 73 B4 0 4 S 130 58 E
Kabarega Falls, *Uganda* . 106 B3 2 15N 31 30 E
Kabasalan, *Phil.* ........ 71 H4 7 47N 122 44 E
Kabba, *Nigeria* ........ 101 D6 7 50N 6 3 E
Kabe, *Japan* .......... 62 C4 34 31N 132 31 E
Kabi, *Niger* .......... 97 F2 13 30N 12 35 E
Kabin Buri, *Thailand* ... 76 F3 13 57N 101 43 E
Kabinakagami L., *Canada* 128 C3 48 54N 84 25W
Kabīr, Zab al →, *Iraq* . 84 C4 36 0N 43 0 E
Kabkabīyah, *Sudan* .... 97 F4 13 50N 24 0 E
Kablungu, C.,
*Papua N. G.* ........ 120 D6 6 20 S 150 1 E
Kabna, *Sudan* .......... 94 D3 19 6N 32 40 E
Kabo, *C.A.R.* .......... 102 A3 7 35N 18 38 E
Kabompo, *Zambia* ...... 107 E1 13 36 S 24 14 E
Kabondo, *Zaïre* ........ 103 D5 8 58 S 25 40 E
Kabongo, *Zaïre* ........ 103 D5 7 22 S 25 33 E
Kabou, *Togo* .......... 101 D5 9 28N 0 55 E
Kaboudia, Rass, *Tunisia* 96 A2 35 13N 11 10 E
Kabra, *Australia* ...... 114 C5 23 25 S 150 25 E
Kabūd Gonbad, *Iran* .... 85 B8 37 5N 59 45 E
Kabugao, *Phil.* .......... 70 B3 18 2N 121 11 E
Kābul, *Afghan.* .......... 79 B3 34 28N 69 11 E
Kābul □, *Afghan.* ...... 79 B3 34 30N 69 0 E
Kabul →, *Pakistan* .... 79 B4 33 55N 72 14 E
Kabunga, *Zaïre* ........ 106 C2 1 38 S 28 3 E
Kaburuang, *Indonesia* .. 72 A3 3 50N 126 30 E
Kabushiya, *Sudan* ...... 95 D3 16 54N 33 41 E
Kabwe, *Zambia* ........ 107 E2 14 30 S 28 29 E
Kabwum, *Papua N. G.* . 120 D4 6 11 S 147 15 E
Kačanik, *Serbia, Yug.* .. 42 E6 42 13N 21 12 E
Kachanovo, *Russia* .... 50 C5 57 25N 27 38 E
Kachchh, Gulf of, *India* . 80 H3 22 50N 69 15 E
Kachchh, Rann of, *India* 80 G4 24 0N 70 0 E
Kachebera, *Zambia* .... 107 E3 13 50 S 32 50 E
Kachin □, *Burma* ...... 78 B6 26 0N 97 30 E
Kachira, L., *Uganda* .... 106 C3 0 40 S 31 7 E
Kachiry, *Kazakhstan* .... 56 D8 53 10N 75 50 E
Kachisi, *Ethiopia* ...... 95 F4 9 40N 37 50 E
Kachkanar, *Russia* .... 54 B6 58 42N 59 33 E
Kachot, *Cambodia* ...... 77 G4 11 30N 103 3 E
Kackar, *Turkey* ........ 53 F9 40 45N 41 10 E
Kadaingti, *Burma* ...... 78 G6 17 37N 97 32 E
Kadaiyanallur, *India* .... 83 K3 9 3N 77 22 E
Kadanai →, *Afghan.* .... 80 D1 31 22N 65 45 E
Kadarkút, *Hungary* .... 31 E10 46 13N 17 39 E
Kade, *Ghana* .......... 101 D4 6 7N 0 56W
Kadi, *India* .......... 80 H5 23 18N 72 23 E
Kadina, *Australia* ...... 116 B2 33 55 S 137 43 E

214 Kadınhanı


Kadınhanı, *Turkey* 88 **D5** 38 14N 32 13 E
Kadiri, *India* 83 **G4** 14 12N 78 13 E
Kadirli, *Turkey* 88 **E7** 37 23N 36 5 E
Kadiyevka, *Ukraine* 53 **B8** 48 35N 38 40 E
Kadoka, *U.S.A.* 138 **D4** 43 50N 101 31W
Kadom, *Russia* 51 **D13** 54 37N 42 30 E
Kadoma, *Zimbabwe* 107 **F2** 18 20 S 29 52 E
Kâdugli, *Sudan* 95 **E2** 11 0N 29 45 E
Kaduna, *Nigeria* 101 **C6** 10 30N 7 21 E
Kaduna □, *Nigeria* 101 **C6** 11 0N 7 30 E
Kadzhi-Say, *Kirghizia* 55 **B8** 42 8N 77 10 E
Kaédi, *Mauritania* 100 **B2** 16 9N 13 28W
Kaelé, *Cameroon* 101 **C7** 10 7N 14 27 E
Kaeng Khoï, *Thailand* 76 **E3** 14 35N 101 0 E
Kaeo, *N.Z.* 118 **B2** 35 6 S 173 49 E
Kaesŏng, *N. Korea* 67 **F14** 37 58N 126 35 E
Kāf, *Si. Arabia* 84 **D3** 31 25N 37 29 E
Kafakumba, *Zaïre* 103 **D4** 9 38 S 23 46 E
Kafan, *Armenia* 89 **D12** 39 18N 46 15 E
Kafanchan, *Nigeria* 101 **D6** 9 40N 8 20 E
Kafareti, *Nigeria* 101 **C7** 10 25N 11 12 E
Kaffrine, *Senegal* 100 **C1** 14 8N 15 36W
Kafia Kingi, *Sudan* 102 **A4** 9 20N 24 25 E
Kafinda, *Zambia* 107 **E3** 12 32 S 30 20 E
Kafirévs, Ákra, *Greece* 45 **F6** 38 9N 24 38 E
Kafr el Dauwâr, *Egypt* 94 **H7** 31 8N 30 8 E
Kafr el Sheikh, *Egypt* 94 **H7** 31 15N 30 50 E
Kafue, *Zambia* 107 **F2** 15 46 S 28 9 E
Kafue Flats, *Zambia* 107 **F2** 15 40 S 27 25 E
Kafue Nat. Park, *Zambia* 107 **F2** 15 0 S 25 30 E
Kafulwe, *Zambia* 107 **D2** 9 0 S 29 1 E
Kaga, *Afghan.* 80 **B4** 34 14N 70 10 E
Kaga, *Japan* 63 **A8** 36 16N 136 15 E
Kaga Bandoro, *C.A.R.* 102 **A3** 7 0N 19 10 E
Kagan, *Uzbekistan* 55 **D2** 39 43N 64 33 E
Kagawa □, *Japan* 62 **C6** 34 15N 134 0 E
Kagera □, *Tanzania* 106 **C3** 2 0 S 31 30 E
Kagera →, *Uganda* 106 **C3** 0 57 S 31 47 E
Kağizman, *Turkey* 89 **C10** 40 5N 43 10 E
Kagoshima, *Japan* 62 **F2** 31 35N 130 33 E
Kagoshima □, *Japan* 62 **F2** 31 30N 130 30 E
Kagoshima-Wan, *Japan* 62 **F2** 31 25N 130 40 E
Kagul, *Moldavia* 52 **D3** 45 50N 28 15 E
Kahak, *Iran* 85 **B6** 36 6N 49 46 E
Kahama, *Tanzania* 106 **C3** 4 8 S 32 30 E
Kahama □, *Tanzania* 106 **C3** 3 50 S 32 0 E
Kahang, *Malaysia* 77 **L4** 2 12N 103 32 E
Kahayan →, *Indonesia* 75 **C4** 3 40 S 114 0 E
Kahe, *Tanzania* 106 **C4** 3 30 S 37 25 E
Kahemba, *Zaïre* 103 **D3** 7 18 S 18 55 E
Kaherekoau Mts., *N.Z.* 119 **F2** 45 45 S 167 15 E
Kahil, Djebel bou, *Algeria* 99 **B5** 34 26N 4 0 E
Kahilangan, *Phil.* 71 **H5** 7 48N 124 48 E
Kahniah →, *Canada* 130 **B4** 58 15N 120 55W
Kahnūj, *Iran* 85 **E8** 27 55N 57 40 E
Kahoka, *U.S.A.* 140 **D5** 40 25N 91 42W
Kahoolawe, *U.S.A.* 132 **H16** 20 33N 156 35W
Kahramanmaraş, *Turkey* 88 **E7** 37 37N 36 53 E
Kahramanmaraş □, *Turkey* 88 **E7** 37 35N 36 33 E
Kâhta, *Turkey* 89 **E8** 37 46N 38 36 E
Kahurangi, Pt., *N.Z.* 119 **A7** 40 50 S 172 10 E
Kahuta, *Pakistan* 80 **C5** 33 35N 73 24 E
Kai, Kepulauan, *Indonesia* 73 **C4** 5 55 S 132 45 E
Kai Besar, *Indonesia* 73 **C4** 5 35 S 133 0 E
Kai Is. = Kai, Kepulauan, *Indonesia* 73 **C4** 5 55 S 132 45 E
Kai-Ketil, *Indonesia* 73 **C4** 5 45 S 132 40 E
Kai Xian, *China* 68 **B7** 31 11N 108 21 E
Kaiama, *Nigeria* 101 **D5** 9 36N 4 1 E
Kaiapit, *Papua N. G.* 120 **D4** 6 18 S 146 18 E
Kaiapoi, *N.Z.* 119 **D7** 43 24 S 172 40 E
Kaibara, *Japan* 63 **B7** 35 8N 135 5 E
Kaieteur Falls, *Guyana* 153 **B6** 5 1N 59 10W
Kaifeng, *China* 66 **G8** 34 48N 114 21 E
Kaihua, *China* 69 **C12** 29 12N 118 20 E
Kaikohe, *N.Z.* 118 **B2** 35 25 S 173 49 E
Kaikoura, *N.Z.* 119 **C8** 42 25 S 173 43 E
Kaikoura Pen., *N.Z.* 119 **C8** 42 25 S 173 43 E
Kaikoura Ra., *N.Z.* 119 **B8** 41 59 S 173 41 E
Kailahun, *S. Leone* 100 **D2** 8 18N 10 39W
Kailashahar, *India* 78 **C4** 24 19N 92 0 E
Kaili, *China* 68 **D6** 26 33N 107 59 E
Kailu, *China* 67 **C11** 43 38N 121 18 E
Kailua, *U.S.A.* 132 **J17** 19 39N 156 0W
Kaimana, *Indonesia* 73 **B4** 3 39 S 133 45 E
Kaimanawa Mts., *N.Z.* 118 **F4** 39 15 S 175 56 E
Kaimata, *N.Z.* 119 **C6** 42 34 S 171 28 E
Kaimganj, *India* 81 **F8** 27 33N 79 24 E
Kaimon-Dake, *Japan* 62 **F2** 31 11N 130 32 E
Kaimur Hills, *India* 81 **G9** 24 30N 82 0 E
Kainan, *Japan* 63 **C7** 34 9N 135 12 E
Kainantu, *Papua N. G.* 120 **D3** 6 18 S 145 52 E
Kaingaroa Forest, *N.Z.* 118 **E5** 38 24 S 176 30 E
Kainji Res., *Nigeria* 101 **C5** 10 1N 4 40 E
Kaipara Harbour, *N.Z.* 118 **C3** 36 25 S 174 14 E
Kaiping, *China* 69 **F9** 22 23N 112 42 E
Kaipokok B., *Canada* 129 **B8** 54 54N 59 47W
Kairana, *India* 80 **E7** 29 24N 77 15 E
Kaironi, *Indonesia* 73 **B4** 0 47 S 133 40 E
Kairouan, *Tunisia* 96 **A2** 35 45N 10 5 E
Kairuku, *Papua N. G.* 120 **E4** 8 51 S 146 35 E
Kaiserslautern, *Germany* 27 **F3** 49 30N 7 43 E
Kaitaia, *N.Z.* 118 **B2** 35 8 S 173 17 E
Kaitangata, *N.Z.* 119 **G4** 46 17 S 169 51 E
Kaithal, *India* 80 **E7** 29 48N 76 26 E
Kaitu →, *Pakistan* 80 **C4** 33 10N 70 30 E
Kaiwi Channel, *U.S.A.* 132 **H16** 21 13N 157 30W
Kaiyang, *China* 68 **D6** 27 4N 106 59 E
Kaiyuan, *Liaoning, China* 67 **C13** 42 28N 124 1 E
Kaiyuan, *Yunnan, China* 68 **F4** 23 40N 103 12 E
Kajaani, *Finland* 12 **D19** 64 17N 27 46 E
Kajabbi, *Australia* 114 **B3** 20 0 S 140 1 E
Kajana = Kajaani, *Finland* 12 **D19** 64 17N 27 46 E
Kajang, *Malaysia* 77 **L3** 2 59N 101 48 E
Kajiado, *Kenya* 106 **C4** 1 53 S 36 48 E
Kajiado □, *Kenya* 106 **C4** 2 0 S 36 30 E
Kajiki, *Japan* 62 **F2** 31 44N 130 40 E
Kajo Kaji, *Sudan* 95 **G3** 3 58N 31 40 E
Kaka, *Sudan* 95 **E3** 10 38N 32 10 E
Kakabeka Falls, *Canada* 128 **C2** 48 24N 89 37W
Kakamas, *S. Africa* 104 **D3** 28 45 S 20 33 E
Kakamega, *Kenya* 106 **B3** 0 20N 34 46 E
Kakamega □, *Kenya* 106 **B3** 0 20N 34 46 E
Kakamigahara, *Japan* 63 **B8** 35 28N 136 48 E
Kakanj, *Bos.-H., Yug.* 42 **C3** 44 9N 18 7 E
Kakanui Mts., *N.Z.* 119 **F5** 45 10 S 170 30 E
Kake, *Japan* 62 **C4** 34 36N 132 19 E
Kakegawa, *Japan* 63 **C10** 34 45N 138 1 E
Kakeroma-Jima, *Japan* 61 **K4** 28 8N 129 14 E
Kakhib, *Russia* 53 **E12** 42 28N 46 34 E
Kakhovka, *Ukraine* 52 **C5** 46 40N 33 15 E
Kakhovskoye Vdkhr., *Ukraine* 52 **C6** 47 5N 34 0 E
Kakinada, *India* 82 **F6** 16 57N 82 11 E
Kakisa →, *Canada* 130 **A5** 61 3N 118 10W
Kakisa L., *Canada* 130 **A5** 60 56N 117 43W
Kakogawa, *Japan* 62 **C6** 34 46N 134 51 E
Kakwa →, *Canada* 130 **C5** 54 37N 118 28W
Kāl Gūsheh, *Iran* 85 **D8** 30 59N 58 12 E
Kal Safīd, *Iran* 84 **C5** 34 52N 47 23 E
Kala, *Nigeria* 101 **C7** 12 2N 14 40 E
Kala Oya →, *Sri Lanka* 83 **K4** 8 20N 79 45 E
Kalaa-Kebira, *Tunisia* 96 **A2** 35 59N 10 32 E
Kalabagh, *Pakistan* 79 **B3** 33 0N 71 28 E
Kalabahi, *Indonesia* 72 **C2** 8 13 S 124 31 E
Kalabáka, *Greece* 44 **E3** 39 42N 21 39 E
Kalabakan, *Malaysia* 75 **B5** 4 25N 117 29 E
Kalabo, *Zambia* 103 **E4** 14 58 S 22 40 E
Kalach, *Russia* 51 **F12** 50 22N 41 0 E
Kalach na Donu, *Russia* 53 **B10** 48 43N 43 32 E
Kaladar, *Canada* 136 **B7** 44 37N 77 5W
Kalagua Is., *Phil.* 70 **D4** 14 30N 122 55 E
Kalahari, *Africa* 104 **C3** 24 0 S 21 30 E
Kalahari Gemsbok Nat. Park, *S. Africa* 104 **D3** 25 30 S 20 30 E
Kalai-Khumb, *Tajikistan* 55 **D5** 38 28N 70 46 E
Kālak, *Iran* 85 **E8** 25 29N 59 22 E
Kalakamati, *Botswana* 105 **C4** 20 40 S 27 25 E
Kalakan, *Russia* 57 **D12** 55 15N 116 45 E
Kalakh, *Syria* 84 **C3** 34 55N 36 10 E
K'alak'unlun Shank'ou, *Pakistan* 81 **B7** 35 33N 77 46 E
Kalam, *Pakistan* 81 **B5** 35 34N 72 30 E
Kalama, *U.S.A.* 144 **E4** 46 0N 122 55W
Kalama, *Zaïre* 106 **C2** 2 52 S 28 35 E
Kalamansig, *Phil.* 71 **H5** 6 33N 124 3 E
Kalamariá, *Greece* 44 **D4** 40 33N 22 55 E
Kalamata, *Greece* 45 **G4** 37 3N 22 10 E
Kalamazoo, *U.S.A.* 141 **B11** 42 20N 85 35W
Kalamazoo →, *U.S.A.* 141 **B10** 42 40N 86 12W
Kalamb, *India* 82 **E2** 18 3N 74 48 E
Kalambo Falls, *Tanzania* 107 **D3** 8 37 S 31 35 E
Kálamos, *Attiki, Greece* 45 **F5** 38 17N 23 52 E
Kálamos, *Ionioi Nísoi, Greece* 45 **F2** 38 37N 20 55 E
Kalamoti, *Greece* 45 **F8** 38 15N 26 4 E
Kalangadoo, *Australia* 116 **D4** 37 34 S 140 41 E
Kalannie, *Australia* 113 **F2** 30 22 S 117 5 E
Kalāntarī, *Iran* 85 **C7** 32 10N 54 8 E
Kalao, *Indonesia* 72 **C2** 7 21 S 121 0 E
Kalaotoa, *Indonesia* 72 **C2** 7 20 S 121 50 E
Kälarne, *Sweden* 14 **B10** 62 59N 16 8 E
Kalárovo, *Czech.* 31 **D11** 47 54N 18 0 E
Kalasin, *Thailand* 76 **D4** 16 26N 103 30 E
Kalat, *Pakistan* 79 **C2** 29 8N 66 31 E
Kalāteh, *Iran* 85 **B7** 36 33N 55 41 E
Kalāteh-ye-Ganj, *Iran* 85 **E8** 27 31N 57 55 E
Kálathos, *Greece* 45 **H10** 36 9N 28 8 E
Kalaus →, *Russia* 53 **D11** 45 40N 44 7 E
Kalávrita, *Greece* 45 **F4** 38 3N 22 8 E
Kalaw, *Burma* 78 **E6** 20 38N 96 34 E
Kalbān, *Oman* 87 **B7** 20 18N 58 38 E
Kalbarri, *Australia* 113 **E1** 27 40 S 114 10 E
Kale, *Turkey* 88 **E3** 37 27N 28 49 E
Kalecik, *Turkey* 52 **F5** 40 4N 33 26 E
Kalehe, *Zaïre* 106 **C2** 2 6 S 28 50 E
Kalema, *Tanzania* 106 **C3** 1 12 S 31 55 E
Kalemie, *Zaïre* 106 **D2** 5 55 S 29 9 E
Kalemyo, *Burma* 78 **D5** 23 11N 94 4 E
Kalety, *Poland* 47 **E5** 50 35N 18 52 E
Kalewa, *Burma* 78 **D5** 23 10N 94 15 E
Kálfafellsstaður, *Iceland* 12 **D6** 64 11N 15 53W
Kalgan = Zhangjiakou, *China* 66 **D8** 40 48N 114 55 E
Kalgoorlie-Boulder, *Australia* 113 **F3** 30 40 S 121 22 E
Kaliakra, Nos, *Bulgaria* 43 **D13** 43 21N 28 30 E
Kalianda, *Indonesia* 74 **D3** 5 50 S 105 45 E
Kalibo, *Phil.* 71 **F4** 11 43N 122 22 E
Kaliganj, *Bangla.* 81 **H13** 22 25N 89 8 E
Kalima, *Zaïre* 106 **C2** 2 33 S 26 32 E
Kalimantan, *Indonesia* 75 **C4** 0 0 114 0 E
Kalimantan Barat □, *Indonesia* 75 **C4** 0 0 110 30 E
Kalimantan Selatan □, *Indonesia* 75 **C5** 2 30 S 115 30 E
Kalimantan Tengah □, *Indonesia* 75 **C4** 2 0 S 113 30 E
Kalimantan Timur □, *Indonesia* 75 **B5** 1 30N 116 30 E
Kálimnos, *Greece* 45 **H8** 37 0N 27 0 E
Kalimpong, *India* 81 **F13** 27 4N 88 35 E
Kalinadi →, *India* 83 **G2** 14 50N 74 7 E
Kalinga □, *Phil.* 70 **C3** 17 30N 121 20 E
Kalinin = Tver, *Russia* 51 **C9** 56 55N 35 55 E
Kaliningrad, *Russia* 50 **D2** 54 42N 20 32 E
Kaliningrad, *Russia* 51 **D10** 55 58N 37 54 E
Kalininskoye, *Kirghizia* 55 **B6** 42 50N 73 49 E
Kalinkovichi, *Belorussia* 50 **E6** 52 12N 29 20 E
Kalinovik, *Bos.-H., Yug.* 42 **D3** 43 31N 18 29 E
Kalipetrovo, *Bulgaria* 43 **C12** 44 5N 27 14 E
Kaliro, *Uganda* 106 **B3** 0 56N 33 30 E
Kalirrákhi, *Greece* 44 **D6** 40 40N 24 35 E
Kalispell, *U.S.A.* 142 **B6** 48 10N 114 22W
Kalisz, *Poland* 47 **D5** 51 45N 18 8 E
Kalisz □, *Poland* 47 **D4** 51 30N 18 0 E
Kalisz Pomorski, *Poland* 47 **B2** 53 17N 15 55 E
Kaliua, *Tanzania* 106 **D3** 5 5 S 31 48 E
Kaliveli Tank, *India* 83 **H4** 12 5N 79 50 E
Kalix →, *Sweden* 12 **D17** 65 50N 23 11 E
Kalka, *India* 80 **D7** 30 46N 76 57 E
Kalkan, *Turkey* 88 **E3** 36 15N 29 23 E
Kalkaroo, *Australia* 116 **A5** 31 12 S 143 54 E
Kalkaska, *U.S.A.* 134 **C3** 44 44N 85 11W
Kalkfeld, *Namibia* 104 **C2** 20 57 S 16 14 E
Kalkfontein, *Botswana* 104 **C3** 22 4 S 20 57 E
Kalkrand, *Namibia* 104 **C2** 24 1 S 17 35 E
Kallakkurichchi, *India* 83 **J4** 11 44N 79 1 E
Kållandsö, *Sweden* 15 **F7** 58 40N 13 5 E
Kallidaikurichi, *India* 83 **K3** 8 38N 77 31 E
Kallithéa, *Greece* 45 **G5** 37 55N 23 41 E
Kallmeti, *Albania* 44 **C1** 41 51N 19 41 E
Kallonís, Kólpos, *Greece* 45 **E8** 39 10N 26 10 E
Kallsjön, *Sweden* 12 **E12** 63 38N 13 0 E
Kalmalo, *Nigeria* 101 **C6** 13 40N 5 20 E
Kalmar, *Sweden* 13 **H14** 56 40N 16 20 E
Kalmthout, *Belgium* 21 **F4** 51 23N 4 29 E
Kalmyk Republic □, *Russia* 53 **C12** 46 5N 46 1 E
Kalmykovo, *Kazakhstan* 53 **B14** 49 0N 51 47 E
Kalna, *India* 81 **H13** 23 13N 88 25 E
Kalo, *Papua N. G.* 120 **F4** 10 1 S 147 48 E
Kalocsa, *Hungary* 31 **E12** 46 32N 19 0 E
Kalofer, *Bulgaria* 43 **E9** 42 37N 24 59 E
Kalokhorio, *Cyprus* 32 **E12** 34 51N 33 2 E
Kaloko, *Zaïre* 103 **D5** 6 47 S 25 48 E
Kalol, *Gujarat, India* 80 **H5** 22 37N 73 31 E
Kalol, *Gujarat, India* 80 **H5** 23 15N 72 33 E
Kalolímnos, *Greece* 45 **G9** 37 4N 27 8 E
Kalomo, *Zambia* 107 **F2** 17 0 S 26 30 E
Kalona, *U.S.A.* 140 **C5** 41 29N 91 43W
Kalonerón, *Greece* 45 **G3** 37 20N 21 38 E
Kalpi, *India* 81 **F8** 26 8N 79 47 E
Kalrayan Hills, *India* 83 **J4** 11 45N 78 40 E
Kalsubai, *India* 82 **E1** 19 35N 73 45 E
Kaltbrunn, *Switz.* 29 **B8** 47 13N 9 2 E
Kaltungo, *Nigeria* 101 **D7** 9 48N 11 19 E
Kalu, *Pakistan* 80 **G2** 25 5N 67 39 E
Kaluga, *Russia* 51 **D10** 54 35N 36 10 E
Kalulong, Bukit, *Malaysia* 75 **B4** 3 14N 114 39 E
Kalulushi, *Zambia* 107 **E2** 12 50 S 28 3 E
Kalundborg, *Denmark* 15 **J5** 55 41N 11 5 E
Kalush, *Ukraine* 50 **G4** 49 3N 24 23 E
Kałuszyn, *Poland* 47 **C8** 52 13N 21 52 E
Kalutara, *Sri Lanka* 83 **L4** 6 35N 80 0 E
Kalwaria, *Poland* 31 **B12** 49 53N 19 41 E
Kalya, *Russia* 54 **A6** 60 15N 59 59 E
Kalyan, *Australia* 116 **C3** 34 55 S 139 49 E
Kalyan, *India* 82 **D2** 20 30N 74 3 E
Kalyazin, *Russia* 51 **C10** 57 15N 37 55 E
Kama, *Burma* 78 **F5** 19 1N 95 4 E
Kama, *Zaïre* 106 **C2** 3 30 S 27 5 E
Kama →, *Russia* 54 **D3** 55 45N 52 0 E
Kamachumu, *Tanzania* 106 **C3** 1 37 S 31 37 E
Kamae, *Japan* 62 **E3** 32 48N 131 56 E
Kamaing, *Burma* 78 **C6** 25 26N 96 35 E
Kamaishi, *Japan* 60 **E10** 39 16N 141 53 E
Kamakura, *Japan* 63 **B11** 35 19N 139 33 E
Kamalia, *Pakistan* 80 **D5** 30 44N 72 42 E
Kamamaung, *Burma* 78 **G6** 17 21N 97 40 E
Kamapanda, *Zambia* 107 **E1** 12 5 S 24 0 E
Kamaran, *Yemen* 86 **D3** 15 21N 42 35 E
Kamashi, *Uzbekistan* 55 **D2** 38 51N 65 23 E
Kamativi, *Zimbabwe* 107 **F2** 18 15 S 27 27 E
Kamba, *Nigeria* 101 **C5** 11 50N 3 45 E
Kambalda, *Australia* 113 **F3** 31 10 S 121 37 E
Kambam, *India* 83 **K3** 9 45N 77 16 E
Kambar, *Pakistan* 80 **F3** 27 37N 68 1 E
Kambarka, *Russia* 54 **C4** 56 15N 54 11 E
Kambia, *S. Leone* 100 **D2** 9 3N 12 53W
Kambolé, *Zambia* 107 **D3** 8 47 S 30 48 E
Kambos, *Cyprus* 32 **D11** 35 2N 32 44 E
Kambove, *Zaïre* 107 **E2** 10 51 S 26 33 E
Kambuie, *Zaïre* 103 **D4** 6 59 S 22 19 E
Kamchatka, P-ov., *Russia* 57 **D16** 57 0N 160 0 E
Kamen, *Russia* 56 **D9** 53 50N 81 30 E
Kamen Kashirskiy, *Ukraine* 50 **F4** 51 39N 24 56 E
Kamen-Rybolov, *Russia* 60 **B6** 44 46N 132 2 E
Kamenets-Podolskiy, *Ukraine* 52 **B2** 48 45N 26 40 E
Kamenica, *Serbia, Yug.* 42 **D7** 43 27N 22 27 E
Kamenica, *Serbia, Yug.* 42 **C4** 44 25N 19 40 E
Kamenice, *Czech.* 30 **B8** 49 18N 15 2 E
Kamenjak, Rt., *Croatia* 39 **D10** 44 47N 13 55 E
Kamenka, *Russia* 48 **A7** 65 58N 44 0 E
Kamenka, *Russia* 51 **E14** 53 10N 44 5 E
Kamenka, *Russia* 51 **F11** 50 47N 39 20 E
Kamenka, *Ukraine* 52 **B5** 49 3N 32 6 E
Kamenka Bugskaya, *Ukraine* 50 **F4** 50 8N 24 16 E
Kamenka Dneprovskaya, *Ukraine* 52 **C6** 47 29N 34 14 E
Kameno, *Bulgaria* 43 **E12** 42 34N 27 18 E
Kamenolomini, *Russia* 53 **C9** 47 40N 40 14 E
Kamensk-Shakhtinskiy, *Russia* 53 **B9** 48 23N 40 20 E
Kamensk Uralskiy, *Russia* 54 **C8** 56 25N 62 2 E
Kamenskiy, *Russia* 51 **F14** 50 48N 45 25 E
Kamenskiy, *Russia* 53 **B9** 49 20N 41 15 E
Kamenskoye, *Russia* 57 **C17** 62 45N 165 30 E
Kamenyak, *Bulgaria* 43 **D11** 43 24N 26 57 E
Kamenz, *Germany* 26 **D10** 51 17N 14 7 E
Kameoka, *Japan* 63 **B7** 35 0N 135 35 E
Kameyama, *Japan* 63 **C8** 34 51N 136 27 E
Kami, *Albania* 44 **B2** 42 17N 20 18 E
Kami-Jima, *Japan* 62 **E2** 32 27N 130 20 E
Kami-koshiki-Jima, *Japan* 62 **F1** 31 50N 129 52 E
Kamiah, *U.S.A.* 142 **C5** 46 12N 116 2W
Kamień Krajeński, *Poland* 47 **B4** 53 32N 17 32 E
Kamień Pomorski, *Poland* 47 **B1** 53 57N 14 43 E
Kamienna →, *Poland* 47 **D8** 51 6N 21 47 E
Kamienna Góra, *Poland* 47 **E3** 50 47N 16 2 E
Kamiensk, *Poland* 47 **D6** 51 12N 19 29 E
Kamieskroon, *S. Africa* 104 **E2** 30 9 S 17 56 E
Kamiita, *Japan* 62 **C6** 34 6N 134 22 E
Kamilukuak, L., *Canada* 131 **A8** 62 22N 101 40W
Kamina, *Zaïre* 103 **D5** 8 45 S 25 0 E
Kaminak L., *Canada* 131 **A9** 62 10N 95 0W
Kaminoyama, *Japan* 60 **E10** 38 9N 140 17 E
Kamioka, *Japan* 63 **A9** 36 25N 137 15 E
Kamiros, *Greece* 32 **C9** 36 20N 27 56 E
Kamituga, *Zaïre* 106 **C2** 3 2 S 28 10 E
Kamloops, *Canada* 130 **C4** 50 40N 120 20W
Kamnik, *Slovenia* 39 **B11** 46 14N 14 37 E
Kamo, *Armenia* 53 **F11** 40 21N 45 7 E
Kamo, *Japan* 60 **F9** 37 39N 139 3 E
Kamo, *N.Z.* 118 **B3** 35 42 S 174 20 E
Kamoa Mts., *Guyana* 153 **C6** 1 30N 59 0W
Kamogawa, *Japan* 63 **B12** 35 5N 140 5 E
Kamoke, *Pakistan* 80 **C6** 32 4N 74 4 E
Kamp →, *Austria* 30 **C8** 48 23N 15 42 E
Kampala, *Uganda* 106 **B3** 0 20N 32 30 E
Kampar, *Malaysia* 77 **K3** 4 18N 101 9 E
Kampar →, *Indonesia* 74 **B2** 0 30N 103 8 E
Kampen, *Neths.* 20 **C7** 52 33N 5 53 E
Kamperland, *Neths.* 21 **E3** 51 34N 3 43 E
Kamphaeng Phet, *Thailand* 76 **D2** 16 28N 99 30 E
Kampolombo, L., *Zambia* 107 **E2** 11 37 S 29 42 E
Kampong To, *Thailand* 77 **J3** 6 3N 101 13 E
Kampot, *Cambodia* 77 **G5** 10 36N 104 10 E
Kampsville, *U.S.A.* 140 **E6** 39 18N 90 37W
Kamptee, *India* 82 **D4** 21 9N 79 19 E
Kampti, *Burkina Faso* 100 **C4** 10 7N 3 25W
Kampuchea = Cambodia ■, *Asia* 76 **F5** 12 15N 105 0 E
Kampung →, *Indonesia* 73 **C5** 5 44 S 138 24 E
Kampung Air Putih, *Malaysia* 77 **K4** 4 15N 103 10 E
Kampung Jerangau, *Malaysia* 77 **K4** 4 50N 103 10 E
Kampung Raja, *Malaysia* 77 **K4** 5 45N 102 35 E
Kampungbaru = Tolitoli, *Indonesia* 72 **A2** 1 5N 120 50 E
Kamrau, Teluk, *Indonesia* 73 **B4** 3 30 S 133 36 E
Kamsack, *Canada* 131 **C8** 51 34N 101 54W
Kamskoye Ustye, *Russia* 51 **D16** 55 10N 49 20 E
Kamskoye Vdkhr., *Russia* 54 **B5** 58 0N 56 0 E
Kamuchawie L., *Canada* 131 **B8** 56 18N 101 59W
Kamui-Misaki, *Japan* 60 **C10** 43 20N 140 21 E
Kāmyārān, *Iran* 84 **C5** 34 47N 46 56 E
Kamyshin, *Russia* 51 **F14** 50 10N 45 24 E
Kamyshlov, *Russia* 54 **C8** 56 50N 62 43 E
Kamyzyak, *Russia* 53 **C13** 46 4N 48 10 E
Kan, *Burma* 78 **D5** 22 25N 94 5 E
Kanaaupscow, *Canada* 128 **B4** 54 2N 76 30W
Kanab, *U.S.A.* 143 **H7** 37 3N 112 29W
Kanab Creek, *U.S.A.* 143 **H7** 37 0N 112 40W
Kanagawa □, *Japan* 63 **B11** 35 20N 139 20 E
Kanagi, *Japan* 60 **D10** 40 54N 140 27 E
Kanairiktok →, *Canada* 129 **A7** 55 2N 60 18W
Kanakapura, *India* 83 **H3** 12 33N 77 28 E
Kanália, *Greece* 44 **E4** 39 30N 22 53 E
Kananga, *Zaïre* 103 **D4** 5 55 S 22 18 E
Kanarraville, *U.S.A.* 143 **H7** 37 34N 113 12W
Kanash, *Russia* 51 **D15** 55 30N 47 32 E
Kanaskat, *U.S.A.* 144 **C5** 47 19N 121 54W
Kanastraíon, Ákra, *Greece* 44 **E5** 39 57N 23 45 E
Kanawha →, *U.S.A.* 134 **F4** 38 50N 82 8W
Kanazawa, *Japan* 63 **A8** 36 30N 136 38 E
Kanbalu, *Burma* 78 **D5** 23 12N 95 31 E
Kanchanaburi, *Thailand* 76 **E2** 14 2N 99 31 E
Kanchenjunga, *Nepal* 81 **F13** 27 50N 88 10 E
Kanchipuram, *India* 83 **H4** 12 52N 79 45 E
Kańczuga, *Poland* 31 **B15** 49 59N 22 25 E
Kanda Kanda, *Zaïre* 103 **D4** 6 52 S 23 48 E
Kandahar = Qandahār, *Afghan.* 79 **C2** 31 32N 65 30 E
Kandalaksha, *Russia* 48 **A5** 67 9N 32 30 E
Kandalakshkiy Zaliv, *Russia* 48 **A5** 66 0N 35 0 E
Kandangan, *Indonesia* 75 **C5** 2 50 S 115 20 E
Kandanos, *Greece* 45 **J5** 35 19N 23 44 E
Kandanos, *Kríti, Greece* 32 **D5** 35 20N 23 45 E
Kandavu, *Fiji* 121 **B2** 19 0 S 178 15 E
Kandavu Passage, *Fiji* 121 **B2** 18 45 S 178 0 E
Kandep, *Papua N. G.* 120 **C2** 5 54 S 143 32 E
Kander →, *Switz.* 28 **C5** 46 33N 7 38 E
Kandersteg, *Switz.* 28 **D5** 46 28N 7 40 E
Kandhíla, *Greece* 45 **G4** 37 46N 22 22 E
Kandhkot, *Pakistan* 80 **E3** 28 16N 69 8 E
Kandhla, *India* 80 **E7** 29 18N 77 19 E
Kandi, *Benin* 101 **C5** 11 7N 2 55 E
Kandi, *India* 81 **H13** 23 58N 88 5 E
Kandıra, *Turkey* 88 **C4** 41 4N 30 9 E
Kandla, *India* 80 **H4** 23 0N 70 10 E
Kandos, *Australia* 117 **B8** 32 45 S 149 58 E
Kandrian, *Papua N. G.* 120 **D5** 6 14 S 149 37 E
Kandy, *Sri Lanka* 83 **L5** 7 18N 80 43 E
Kane, *U.S.A.* 136 **E6** 41 39N 78 53W
Kane Basin, *Greenland* 6 **B4** 79 1N 70 0W
Kanevskaya, *Russia* 53 **C8** 46 3N 39 3 E
Kanfanar, *Croatia* 39 **C10** 45 7N 13 50 E
Kangaba, *Mali* 100 **C3** 11 56N 8 25W
Kangal, *Turkey* 88 **D7** 39 14N 37 23 E
Kangān, *Fārs, Iran* 85 **E7** 27 50N 52 3 E
Kangān, *Hormozgān, Iran* 85 **E8** 25 48N 57 28 E
Kangar, *Malaysia* 77 **J3** 6 27N 100 12 E
Kangaroo I., *Australia* 116 **C2** 35 45 S 137 0 E
Kangavar, *Iran* 85 **C6** 34 40N 48 0 E
Kangding, *China* 68 **B3** 30 2N 101 57 E
Kăngdong, *N. Korea* 67 **E14** 39 9N 126 5 E
Kangean, Kepulauan, *Indonesia* 75 **D5** 6 55 S 115 23 E
Kangean Is. = Kangean, Kepulauan, *Indonesia* 75 **D5** 6 55 S 115 23 E
Kanggye, *N. Korea* 67 **D14** 41 0N 126 35 E
Kanggyŏng, *S. Korea* 67 **F14** 36 10N 127 0 E
Kanghwa, *S. Korea* 67 **F14** 37 45N 126 30 E
Kangnŭng, *S. Korea* 67 **F15** 37 45N 128 54 E
Kango, *Gabon* 102 **B2** 0 11N 10 5 E
Kangoya, *Zaïre* 103 **D4** 9 55 S 22 48 E
Kangping, *China* 67 **C12** 42 43N 123 18 E
Kangpokpi, *India* 78 **C4** 25 8N 93 58 E
Kangyidaung, *Burma* 78 **G5** 16 56N 94 54 E
Kanhangad, *India* 83 **H2** 12 21N 74 58 E
Kanheri, *India* 82 **E1** 19 13N 72 50 E
Kani, *Ivory C.* 100 **D3** 8 29N 6 36W
Kaniama, *Zaïre* 103 **D4** 7 30 S 24 12 E
Kaniapiskau →, *Canada* 129 **A6** 56 40N 69 30W
Kaniapiskau L., *Canada* 129 **B6** 54 10N 69 55W
Kanibadam, *Tajikistan* 55 **C5** 40 17N 70 25 E
Kaniere, L., *N.Z.* 119 **C6** 42 50 S 171 10 E
Kanin, P-ov., *Russia* 48 **A8** 68 0N 45 0 E
Kanin Nos, Mys, *Russia* 48 **A7** 68 45N 43 20 E
Kanina, *Albania* 44 **D1** 40 23N 19 30 E
Kaniva, *Australia* 116 **D4** 36 22 S 141 18 E
Kanjiža, *Serbia, Yug.* 42 **A5** 46 3N 20 4 E
Kanjut Sar, *Pakistan* 81 **A6** 36 7N 75 25 E
Kankakee, *U.S.A.* 141 **C9** 41 6N 87 50W
Kankakee →, *U.S.A.* 141 **C8** 41 23N 88 16W
Kankan, *Guinea* 100 **C3** 10 23N 9 15W
Kanker, *India* 82 **D5** 20 10N 81 40 E
Kankunskiy, *Russia* 57 **D13** 57 37N 126 8 E
Kanmuri-Yama, *Japan* 62 **C4** 34 30N 132 4 E
Kannabe, *Japan* 62 **C5** 34 32N 133 23 E
Kannapolis, *U.S.A.* 135 **H5** 35 32N 80 37W
Kannauj, *India* 81 **F8** 27 3N 79 56 E
Kano, *Nigeria* 101 **C6** 12 2N 8 30 E
Kano □, *Nigeria* 101 **C6** 11 45N 9 0 E

Kawachi-Nagano 215


Kan'onji, *Japan* 62 C5 34 7N 133 39 E
Kanoroba, *Ivory C.* 100 D3 9 7N 6 8W
Kanowha, *U.S.A.* 140 B3 42 57N 93 47W
Kanowit, *Malaysia* 75 B4 2 14N 112 20 E
Kanowna, *Australia* 113 F3 30 32 S 121 31 E
Kanoya, *Japan* 62 F2 31 25N 130 50 E
Kanpetlet, *Burma* 78 E4 21 10N 93 59 E
Kanpur, *India* 81 F9 26 28N 80 20 E
Kansas, *U.S.A.* 141 E9 39 33N 87 56W
Kansas □, *U.S.A.* 138 F6 38 40N 98 0W
Kansas →, *U.S.A.* 138 F7 39 7N 94 36W
Kansas City, *Kans., U.S.A.* 140 E2 39 5N 94 40W
Kansas City, *Mo., U.S.A.* 140 E2 39 3N 94 30W
Kansenia, *Zaïre* 107 E2 10 20 S 26 0 E
Kansk, *Russia* 57 D10 56 20N 95 37 E
Kansŏng, *S. Korea* 67 E15 38 24N 128 30 E
Kansu = Gansu □, *China* 66 G3 36 0N 104 0 E
Kant, *Kirghizia* 55 B7 42 53N 74 51 E
Kantang, *Thailand* 77 J2 7 25N 99 31 E
Kantché, *Niger* 97 F1 13 31N 8 30 E
Kanté, *Togo* 101 D5 9 57N 1 3 E
Kantemirovka, *Russia* 53 B8 49 43N 39 55 E
Kantharalak, *Thailand* 76 E5 14 39N 104 39 E
Kantō □, *Japan* 63 A11 36 15N 139 30 E
Kantō-Heiya, *Japan* 63 A11 36 0N 139 30 E
Kantō-Sanchi, *Japan* 63 B10 35 59N 138 50 E
Kantu-long, *Burma* 78 F6 19 57N 97 36 E
Kanturk, *Ireland* 19 D3 52 10N 8 55W
Kanuma, *Japan* 63 A11 36 34N 139 42 E
Kanus, *Namibia* 104 D2 27 50 S 18 39 E
Kanye, *Botswana* 104 C4 24 55 S 25 28 E
Kanzenze, *Zaïre* 103 E5 10 30 S 25 12 E
Kanzi, Ras, *Tanzania* 106 D4 7 1 S 39 33 E
Kao, *Fiji* 121 P13 19 40 S 175 1W
Kaohsiung = Gaoxiong, *Taiwan* 69 F13 22 38N 120 18 E
Kaokoveld, *Namibia* 104 B1 19 15 S 14 30 E
Kaolack, *Senegal* 100 C1 14 5N 16 8W
Kaoshan, *China* 67 B13 44 38N 124 50 E
Kaouar, *Niger* 97 E2 19 5N 12 52 E
Kapadvanj, *India* 80 H5 23 5N 73 0 E
Kapagere, *Papua N. G.* 120 E4 9 46 S 147 42 E
Kapanga, *Zaïre* 103 D4 8 30 S 22 40 E
Kapatagan, *Phil.* 71 H4 7 52N 123 44 E
Kapchagai, *Kazakhstan* 55 B8 43 51N 77 14 E
Kapchagaiskoye Vdkhr., *Kazakhstan* 55 B8 43 45N 77 50 E
Kapellen, *Belgium* 21 F4 51 19N 4 25 E
Kapéllo, Ákra, *Greece* 45 H5 36 9N 23 3 E
Kapema, *Zaïre* 107 E2 10 45 S 28 22 E
Kapfenberg, *Austria* 30 D8 47 26N 15 18 E
Kapia, *Zaïre* 103 C3 4 17 S 19 46 E
Kapiri Mposhi, *Zambia* 107 E2 13 59 S 28 43 E
Kāpīsā □, *Afghan.* 79 B3 35 0N 69 20 E
Kapiskau →, *Canada* 128 B3 52 47N 81 55W
Kapit, *Malaysia* 75 B4 2 0N 112 55 E
Kapiti I., *N.Z.* 118 G3 40 50 S 174 56 E
Kapka, Massif du, *Chad* 97 E4 15 7N 21 45 E
Kaplice, *Czech.* 30 C7 48 42N 14 30 E
Kapoe, *Thailand* 77 H2 9 34N 98 32 E
Kapoeta, *Sudan* 95 G3 4 50N 33 35 E
Kápolnásnyék, *Hungary* 31 D11 47 16N 18 41 E
Kaponga, *N.Z.* 118 F3 39 29 S 174 9 E
Kapos →, *Hungary* 31 E11 46 44N 18 30 E
Kaposvár, *Hungary* 31 E10 46 25N 17 47 E
Kapowsin, *U.S.A.* 144 D4 46 59N 122 13W
Kappeln, *Germany* 26 A5 54 37N 9 56 E
Kapps, *Namibia* 104 C2 22 32 S 17 18 E
Kaprije, *Croatia* 39 E12 43 42N 15 43 E
Kaprijke, *Belgium* 21 F3 51 13N 3 38 E
Kapsan, *N. Korea* 67 D15 41 4N 128 19 E
Kapsukas = Mariyampol, *Lithuania* 50 D3 54 33N 23 19 E
Kapuas, *Indonesia* 75 C4 3 10 S 114 5 E
Kapuas →, *Indonesia* 75 C3 0 25 S 109 20 E
Kapuas Hulu, Pegunungan, *Malaysia* 75 B4 1 30N 113 30 E
Kapuas Hulu Ra. = Kapuas Hulu, Pegunungan, *Malaysia* 75 B4 1 30N 113 30 E
Kapulo, *Zaïre* 107 D2 8 18 S 29 15 E
Kapunda, *Australia* 116 C3 34 20 S 138 56 E
Kapuni, *N.Z.* 118 F3 39 29 S 174 8 E
Kapurthala, *India* 80 D6 31 23N 75 25 E
Kapuskasing, *Canada* 128 C3 49 25N 82 30W
Kapuskasing →, *Canada* 128 C3 49 49N 82 0W
Kapustin Yar, *Russia* 53 B11 48 37N 45 40 E
Kaputar, *Australia* 115 E5 30 15 S 150 10 E
Kaputir, *Kenya* 106 B4 2 5N 35 28 E
Kapuvár, *Hungary* 31 D10 47 36N 17 1 E
Kara, *Russia* 56 C7 69 10N 65 0 E
Kara, *Turkey* 45 H9 36 58N 27 30 E
Kara Bogaz Gol, Zaliv, *Turkmenistan* 49 F9 41 0N 53 30 E
Kara Kalpak Republic □, *Uzbekistan* 56 E6 43 0N 58 0 E
Kara Kum = Karakum, Peski, *Turkmenistan* 56 F6 39 30N 60 0 E
Kara-Saki, *Japan* 62 C1 34 41N 129 30 E
Kara Sea, *Russia* 56 B7 75 0N 70 0 E
Kara Su, *Kirghizia* 55 C6 40 44N 72 53 E
Karabash, *Russia* 54 D7 55 29N 60 14 E
Karabekaul, *Turkmenistan* 55 D2 38 30N 64 8 E
Karabük, *Turkey* 52 F5 41 12N 32 37 E
Karabulak, *Kazakhstan* 55 A9 44 54N 78 30 E
Karaburun, *Turkey* 45 F8 38 41N 26 28 E
Karaburuni, *Albania* 44 D1 40 25N 19 20 E
Karabutak, *Kazakhstan* 54 G7 49 59N 60 14 E
Karacabey, *Turkey* 88 C3 40 12N 28 21 E
Karacasu, *Turkey* 88 E3 37 43N 28 35 E
Karachala, *Azerbaijan* 53 G13 39 45N 48 53 E
Karachayevsk, *Russia* 53 E9 43 50N 41 55 E
Karachev, *Russia* 50 E9 53 10N 35 5 E
Karachi, *Pakistan* 79 D2 24 53N 67 0 E
Karád, *Hungary* 31 E10 46 41N 17 51 E
Karad, *India* 82 F2 17 15N 74 10 E
Karadeniz Boğazı, *Turkey* 88 C3 41 10N 29 10 E
Karaga, *Ghana* 101 D4 9 58N 0 28W
Karaganda, *Kazakhstan* 56 E8 49 50N 73 10 E
Karagayly, *Kazakhstan* 56 E8 49 26N 76 0 E
Karaginskiy, Ostrov, *Russia* 57 D17 58 45N 164 0 E
Karagiye Depression, *Kazakhstan* 49 F9 43 27N 51 45 E
Karagüney Dağları, *Turkey* 88 C6 40 30N 34 40 E
Karagwe □, *Tanzania* 106 C3 2 0 S 31 0 E
Karaikal, *India* 83 J4 10 59N 79 50 E
Karaikkudi, *India* 83 J4 10 5N 78 45 E
Karaisali, *Turkey* 88 E6 37 16N 35 2 E
Karaitivu I., *Sri Lanka* 83 K4 9 45N 79 52 E
Karaj, *Iran* 85 C6 35 48N 51 0 E
Karak, *Malaysia* 77 L4 3 25N 102 2 E
Karakas, *Kazakhstan* 56 E9 48 20N 83 30 E
Karakitang, *Indonesia* 72 A3 3 14N 125 28 E
Karaklis, *Armenia* 53 F11 40 48N 44 30 E
Karakoçan, *Turkey* 89 D9 38 57N 40 2 E
Karakoram Pass, *Pakistan* 81 B7 35 33N 77 50 E
Karakoram Ra., *Pakistan* 81 B7 35 30N 77 0 E
Karakul, *Tajikistan* 55 D6 39 2N 73 33 E
Karakul, *Uzbekistan* 55 D1 39 22N 63 50 E
Karakuldzha, *Kirghizia* 55 C6 40 39N 73 26 E
Karakulino, *Russia* 54 C3 56 1N 53 43 E
Karakum, Peski, *Turkmenistan* 56 F6 39 30N 60 0 E
Karakurt, *Turkey* 89 C10 40 10N 42 37 E
Karal, *Chad* 97 F2 12 50N 14 46 E
Karalon, *Russia* 57 D12 57 5N 115 50 E
Karaman, *Turkey* 88 E5 37 14N 33 13 E
Karamay, *China* 64 B3 45 30N 84 58 E
Karambu, *Indonesia* 75 C5 3 53 S 116 6 E
Karamea, *N.Z.* 119 B7 41 14 S 172 6 E
Karamea →, *N.Z.* 119 B7 41 13 S 172 26 E
Karamea Bight, *N.Z.* 119 B6 41 22 S 171 40 E
Karamet Niyaz, *Turkmenistan* 55 E2 37 45N 64 34 E
Karamoja □, *Uganda* 106 B3 3 0N 34 15 E
Karamsad, *India* 80 H5 22 35N 72 50 E
Karand, *Iran* 84 C5 34 16N 46 15 E
Karanganyar, *Indonesia* 75 D3 7 38 S 109 37 E
Karanja, *India* 82 D3 20 29N 77 31 E
Karapınar, *Turkey* 88 E5 37 13N 33 32 E
Karapiro, *N.Z.* 118 D4 37 53 S 175 32 E
Karasburg, *Namibia* 104 D2 28 0 S 18 44 E
Karasino, *Russia* 56 C9 66 50N 86 50 E
Karasjok, *Norway* 12 B18 69 27N 25 30 E
Karasu, *Turkey* 88 C4 41 4N 30 46 E
Karasu →, *Turkey* 89 D8 39 42N 39 25 E
Karasuk, *Russia* 56 D8 53 44N 78 2 E
Karasuyama, *Japan* 63 A12 36 39N 140 9 E
Karataş Burnu, *Turkey* 88 E6 36 32N 35 1 E
Karatau, *Kazakhstan* 55 B5 43 10N 70 28 E
Karatau, Khrebet, *Kazakhstan* 55 B4 43 30N 69 30 E
Karatepe, *Turkey* 88 E7 37 22N 36 16 E
Karativu, *Sri Lanka* 83 K4 8 22N 79 47 E
Karatobe, *Kazakhstan* 54 G3 49 44N 53 30 E
Karatoya →, *India* 78 C2 24 7N 89 36 E
Karaturuk, *Kazakhstan* 55 B8 43 35N 77 50 E
Karaul-Bazar, *Uzbekistan* 55 D2 39 30N 64 48 E
Karauli, *India* 80 F7 26 30N 77 4 E
Karávi, *Greece* 45 H5 36 49N 23 37 E
Karavostasi, *Cyprus* 32 D11 35 8N 32 50 E
Karawa, *Zaïre* 102 B4 3 18N 20 17 E
Karawang, *Indonesia* 75 D3 6 30 S 107 15 E
Karawanken, *Europe* 30 E7 46 30N 14 40 E
Karayazı, *Turkey* 89 D10 39 41N 42 9 E
Karazhal, *Kazakhstan* 56 E8 48 2N 70 49 E
Karbalā, *Iraq* 84 C5 32 36N 44 3 E
Kårböle, *Sweden* 14 C9 61 59N 15 22 E
Karcag, *Hungary* 31 D13 47 19N 20 57 E
Karcha →, *Pakistan* 81 B7 34 45N 76 10 E
Karda, *Russia* 57 D11 55 0N 103 16 E
Kardhámila, *Greece* 45 F8 38 35N 26 5 E
Kardhítsa, *Greece* 44 E3 39 23N 21 54 E
Kardhítsa □, *Greece* 44 E3 39 15N 21 50 E
Kärdla, *Estonia* 50 B3 58 50N 22 40 E
Kareeberge, *S. Africa* 104 E3 30 59 S 21 50 E
Kareima, *Sudan* 94 D3 18 30N 31 49 E
Karelian Republic □, *Russia* 48 A5 65 30N 32 30 E
Karema, *Papua N. G.* 120 E4 9 12 S 147 18 E
Karevāndar, *Iran* 85 E9 27 53N 60 44 E
Kargapolye, *Russia* 54 D9 55 57N 64 24 E
Kargasok, *Russia* 56 D9 59 3N 80 53 E
Kargat, *Russia* 56 D9 55 10N 80 15 E
Kargı, *Turkey* 52 F6 41 11N 34 30 E
Kargil, *India* 81 B7 34 32N 76 12 E
Kargopol, *Russia* 48 B6 61 30N 38 58 E
Kargowa, *Poland* 47 C2 52 5N 15 51 E
Karguéri, *Niger* 97 F2 13 27N 10 30 E
Karia ba Mohammed, *Morocco* 98 B3 34 22N 5 12W
Kariaí, *Greece* 44 D6 40 14N 24 19 E
Karīān, *Iran* 85 E8 26 57N 57 14 E
Kariba, *Zimbabwe* 107 F2 16 28 S 28 50 E
Kariba, L., *Zimbabwe* 107 F2 16 40 S 28 25 E
Kariba Dam, *Zimbabwe* 107 F2 16 30 S 28 35 E
Kariba Gorge, *Zambia* 107 F2 16 30 S 28 50 E
Karibib, *Namibia* 104 C2 22 0 S 15 56 E
Karikari, C., *N.Z.* 118 A2 34 46 S 173 24 E
Karimata, Kepulauan, *Indonesia* 75 C3 1 25 S 109 0 E
Karimata, Selat, *Indonesia* 75 C3 2 0 S 108 40 E
Karimata I. = Karimata, Kepulauan, *Indonesia* 75 C3 1 25 S 109 0 E
Karimnagar, *India* 82 E4 18 26N 79 10 E
Karimunjawa, Kepulauan, *Indonesia* 75 D4 5 50 S 110 30 E
Karin, *Somali Rep.* 90 E4 10 50N 45 52 E
Karístos, *Greece* 45 F6 38 1N 24 29 E
Karīt, *Iran* 85 C8 33 29N 56 55 E
Kariya, *Japan* 63 C9 34 58N 137 1 E
Karkal, *India* 83 H2 13 15N 74 56 E
Karkar I., *Papua N. G.* 120 C4 4 40 S 146 0 E
Karkaralinsk, *Kazakhstan* 56 E8 49 26N 75 30 E
Karkinitskiy Zaliv, *Ukraine* 52 D5 45 56N 33 0 E
Karkur Tohl, *Egypt* 94 C2 22 5N 25 5 E
Karl Libknekht, *Russia* 50 F9 51 40N 35 35 E
Karl-Marx-Stadt = Chemnitz, *Germany* 26 E8 50 50N 12 55 E
Karla, L. = Voiviïs Límni, *Greece* 44 E4 39 30N 22 45 E
Karlino, *Poland* 47 A2 54 3N 15 53 E
Karlobag, *Croatia* 39 D12 44 32N 15 5 E
Karlovac, *Croatia* 39 C12 45 31N 15 36 E
Karlovka, *Ukraine* 52 B6 49 29N 35 8 E
Karlovy Vary, *Czech.* 30 A5 50 13N 12 51 E
Karlsbad = Karlovy Vary, *Czech.* 30 A5 50 13N 12 51 E
Karlsborg, *Sweden* 15 F8 58 33N 14 33 E
Karlshamn, *Sweden* 13 H13 56 10N 14 51 E
Karlskoga, *Sweden* 13 G13 59 22N 14 33 E
Karlskrona, *Sweden* 13 H13 56 10N 15 35 E
Karlsruhe, *Germany* 27 F4 49 3N 8 23 E
Karlstad, *Sweden* 13 G12 59 23N 13 30 E
Karlstad, *U.S.A.* 138 A6 48 38N 96 30W
Karlstadt, *Germany* 27 F5 49 57N 9 46 E
Karnal, *India* 80 E7 29 42N 77 2 E
Karnali →, *Nepal* 81 E9 28 45N 81 16 E
Karnaphuli Res., *Bangla.* 78 D4 22 40N 92 20 E
Karnataka □, *India* 83 H3 13 15N 77 0 E
Karnes City, *U.S.A.* 139 L6 28 53N 97 53W
Karnische Alpen, *Europe* 30 E6 46 36N 13 0 E
Kärnten □, *Austria* 30 E6 46 52N 13 30 E
Karo, *Mali* 100 C4 12 16N 3 18W
Karoi, *Zimbabwe* 107 F2 16 48 S 29 45 E
Karomatan, *Phil.* 71 H4 7 55N 123 44 E
Karonga, *Malawi* 107 D3 9 57 S 33 55 E
Karoonda, *Australia* 116 C3 35 1 S 139 59 E
Karora, *Sudan* 94 D4 17 44N 38 15 E
Káros, *Greece* 45 H7 36 54N 25 40 E
Karousádhes, *Greece* 44 E1 39 47N 19 45 E
Karpasia □, *Cyprus* 32 D13 35 32N 34 15 E
Kárpathos, *Greece* 45 J9 35 37N 27 10 E
Kárpathos, Stenón, *Greece* 45 J9 36 0N 27 30 E
Karpinsk, *Russia* 54 B7 59 45N 60 1 E
Karpogory, *Russia* 48 B7 63 59N 44 27 E
Karrebæk, *Denmark* 15 J5 55 12N 11 39 E
Kars, *Turkey* 53 F10 40 40N 43 5 E
Kars □, *Turkey* 89 C10 40 40N 43 0 E
Karsakpay, *Kazakhstan* 56 E7 47 55N 66 40 E
Karsha, *Kazakhstan* 53 B14 49 45N 51 35 E
Karshi, *Uzbekistan* 55 D2 38 53N 65 48 E
Karsiyang, *India* 81 F13 26 56N 88 18 E
Karst, *Croatia* 39 C11 45 35N 14 0 E
Karsun, *Russia* 51 D15 54 14N 46 57 E
Kartál Óros, *Greece* 44 C7 41 15N 25 13 E
Kartaly, *Russia* 54 E7 53 3N 60 40 E
Kartapur, *India* 80 D6 31 27N 75 32 E
Karthaus, *U.S.A.* 136 E6 41 8N 78 9W
Kartuzy, *Poland* 47 A5 54 22N 18 10 E
Karuah, *Australia* 117 B9 32 37 S 151 56 E
Karufa, *Indonesia* 73 B4 3 50 S 133 20 E
Karumba, *Australia* 114 B3 17 31 S 140 50 E
Karumo, *Tanzania* 106 C3 2 25 S 32 50 E
Karumwa, *Tanzania* 106 C3 3 12 S 32 38 E
Karungu, *Kenya* 106 C3 0 50 S 34 10 E
Karup, *Denmark* 15 H3 56 19N 9 10 E
Karur, *India* 83 J4 10 59N 78 2 E
Karviná, *Czech.* 31 B11 49 53N 18 25 E
Karwi, *India* 81 G9 25 12N 80 57 E
Kaş, *Turkey* 88 E3 36 11N 29 37 E
Kasache, *Malawi* 107 E3 13 25 S 34 20 E
Kasai, *Japan* 62 C6 34 55N 134 52 E
Kasai →, *Zaïre* 103 C3 3 30 S 16 10 E
Kasai Occidental □, *Zaïre* 103 D4 6 0 S 22 0 E
Kasai Oriental □, *Zaïre* 103 D4 5 0 S 24 30 E
Kasaji, *Zaïre* 103 E4 10 25 S 23 27 E
Kasama, *Japan* 63 A12 36 23N 140 16 E
Kasama, *Zambia* 107 E3 10 16 S 31 9 E
Kasan-dong, *N. Korea* 67 D14 41 18N 126 55 E
Kasane, *Namibia* 104 B3 17 34 S 24 50 E
Kasanga, *Tanzania* 107 D3 8 30 S 31 10 E
Kasangulu, *Zaïre* 103 C3 4 33 S 15 15 E
Kasaoka, *Japan* 62 C5 34 30N 133 30 E
Kasaragod, *India* 83 H2 12 30N 74 58 E
Kasat, *Burma* 78 G7 15 56N 98 13 E
Kasba, *Bangla.* 78 D3 23 45N 91 2 E
Kasba L., *Canada* 131 A8 60 20N 102 10W
Kasba Tadla, *Morocco* 98 B3 32 36N 6 17W
Kaseda, *Japan* 62 F2 31 25N 130 19 E
Kāseh Garān, *Iran* 84 C5 34 5N 46 2 E
Kasempa, *Zambia* 107 E2 13 30 S 25 44 E
Kasenga, *Zaïre* 107 E2 10 20 S 28 45 E
Kasese, *Uganda* 106 B3 0 13N 30 3 E
Kasewa, *Zambia* 107 E2 14 28 S 28 53 E
Kasganj, *India* 81 F8 27 48N 78 42 E
Kashabowie, *Canada* 128 C1 48 40N 90 26W
Kāshān, *Iran* 85 C6 34 5N 51 30 E
Kashi, *China* 64 C2 39 30N 76 2 E
Kashihara, *Japan* 63 C7 34 27N 135 46 E
Kashima, *Ibaraki, Japan* 63 B12 35 58N 140 38 E
Kashima, *Saga, Japan* 62 D2 33 7N 130 6 E
Kashima-Nada, *Japan* 63 B12 36 0N 140 45 E
Kashimbo, *Zaïre* 107 E2 11 12 S 26 19 E
Kashin, *Russia* 51 C10 57 20N 37 36 E
Kashipur, *Orissa, India* 82 E6 19 16N 83 3 E
Kashipur, *Ut. P., India* 81 E8 29 15N 79 0 E
Kashira, *Russia* 51 D11 54 45N 38 10 E
Kashiwa, *Japan* 63 B11 35 52N 139 59 E
Kashiwazaki, *Japan* 61 F9 37 22N 138 33 E
Kashk-e Kohneh, *Afghan.* 79 B1 34 55N 62 30 E
Kashkasu, *Kirghizia* 55 D6 39 54N 72 44 E
Kāshmar, *Iran* 85 C8 35 16N 58 26 E
Kashmir, *Asia* 81 C7 34 0N 76 0 E
Kashmor, *Pakistan* 79 C3 28 28N 69 32 E
Kashpirovka, *Russia* 51 E16 53 0N 48 30 E
Kashun Noerh = Gaxun Nur, *China* 64 B5 42 22N 100 30 E
Kasimov, *Russia* 51 D12 54 55N 41 20 E
Kasinge, *Zaïre* 106 D2 6 15 S 26 58 E
Kasiruta, *Indonesia* 72 B3 0 25 S 127 12 E
Kaskaskia →, *U.S.A.* 140 G7 37 58N 89 57W
Kaskattama →, *Canada* 131 B10 57 3N 90 4W
Kaskelen, *Kazakhstan* 55 B8 43 20N 76 35 E
Kaskinen, *Finland* 12 E16 62 22N 21 15 E
Kaskö, *Finland* 12 E16 62 22N 21 15 E
Kasli, *Russia* 54 D7 55 53N 60 46 E
Kaslo, *Canada* 130 D5 49 55N 116 55W
Kasmere L., *Canada* 131 B8 59 34N 101 10W
Kasongan, *Indonesia* 75 C4 2 0 S 113 23 E
Kasongo, *Zaïre* 106 C2 4 30 S 26 33 E
Kasongo Lunda, *Zaïre* 103 D3 6 35 S 16 49 E
Kásos, *Greece* 45 J8 35 20N 26 55 E
Kásos, Stenón, *Greece* 45 J8 35 30N 26 30 E
Kaspi, *Georgia* 53 F11 41 54N 44 17 E
Kaspichan, *Bulgaria* 43 D12 43 18N 27 11 E
Kaspiysk, *Russia* 53 E12 42 52N 47 40 E
Kaspiyskiy, *Russia* 53 D12 45 22N 47 23 E
Kassab ed Doleib, *Sudan* 95 E3 13 30N 33 35 E
Kassaba, *Egypt* 94 C2 22 40N 29 55 E
Kassala, *Sudan* 95 D4 15 30N 36 0 E
Kassalâ □, *Sudan* 95 D4 15 20N 36 26 E
Kassan, *Uzbekistan* 55 D2 39 2N 65 35 E
Kassándra, *Greece* 44 D5 40 0N 23 30 E
Kassansay, *Uzbekistan* 55 C5 41 15N 71 31 E
Kassel, *Germany* 26 D5 51 19N 9 32 E
Kassinger, *Sudan* 94 D3 18 46N 31 51 E
Kassiópi, *Greece* 32 A3 39 48N 19 53 E
Kassue, *Indonesia* 73 C5 6 58 S 139 21 E
Kastamonu, *Turkey* 88 C5 41 25N 33 43 E
Kastamonu □, *Turkey* 88 C5 41 20N 34 0 E
Kastav, *Croatia* 39 C11 45 22N 14 20 E
Kastélli, *Greece* 32 D5 35 29N 23 38 E
Kastéllion, *Greece* 32 D7 35 12N 25 20 E
Kastellou, Ákra, *Greece* 45 J9 35 30N 27 15 E
Kasterlee, *Belgium* 21 F5 51 15N 4 59 E
Kastóri, *Greece* 45 G4 37 10N 22 17 E
Kastoría, *Greece* 44 D3 40 30N 21 19 E
Kastoría □, *Greece* 44 D3 40 30N 21 15 E
Kastorías, L., *Greece* 44 D3 40 30N 21 20 E
Kastornoye, *Russia* 51 F11 51 55N 38 2 E
Kastós, *Greece* 45 F2 38 35N 20 55 E
Kástron, *Greece* 44 E7 39 50N 25 2 E
Kastrosikiá, *Greece* 45 E2 39 6N 20 36 E
Kasugai, *Japan* 63 B8 35 12N 136 59 E
Kasukabe, *Japan* 63 B11 35 58N 139 49 E
Kasulu, *Tanzania* 106 C3 4 37 S 30 5 E
Kasulu □, *Tanzania* 106 C3 4 37 S 30 5 E
Kasumi, *Japan* 62 B6 35 38N 134 38 E
Kasumiga-Ura, *Japan* 63 B12 36 0N 140 25 E
Kasumkent, *Azerbaijan* 53 F13 41 47N 48 15 E
Kasungu, *Malawi* 107 E3 13 0 S 33 29 E
Kasur, *Pakistan* 79 C4 31 5N 74 25 E
Kata, *Russia* 57 D11 58 46N 102 40 E
Kataba, *Zambia* 107 F2 16 5 S 25 10 E
Katako Kombe, *Zaïre* 102 C4 3 25 S 24 20 E
Katákolon, *Greece* 45 G3 37 38N 21 19 E
Katale, *Tanzania* 106 C3 4 52 S 31 7 E
Katamatite, *Australia* 117 D6 36 6 S 145 41 E
Katanda, *Kivu, Zaïre* 106 C2 0 55 S 29 21 E
Katanda, *Shaba, Zaïre* 103 D4 7 52 S 24 13 E
Katangi, *India* 82 D4 21 56N 79 50 E
Katanglad Mts., *Phil.* 71 G5 8 6N 124 54 E
Katangli, *Russia* 57 D15 51 42N 143 14 E
Katapakishi, *Zaïre* 103 D4 8 15 S 22 49 E
Katastári, *Greece* 45 G2 37 50N 20 45 E
Katav Ivanovsk, *Russia* 54 D6 54 45N 58 12 E
Katavi Swamp, *Tanzania* 106 D3 6 50 S 31 10 E
Katchiungo, *Angola* 103 E3 12 35 S 16 13 E
Kateríni, *Greece* 44 D4 40 18N 22 37 E
Katherîna, Gebel, *Egypt* 94 J8 28 30N 33 57 E
Katherine, *Australia* 112 B5 14 27 S 132 20 E
Kathiawar, *India* 80 H4 22 20N 71 0 E
Kathikas, *Cyprus* 32 E11 34 55N 32 25 E
Kati, *Mali* 100 C3 12 41N 8 4W
Katihar, *India* 81 G12 25 34N 87 36 E
Katikati, *N.Z.* 118 D4 37 32 S 175 57 E
Katima Mulilo, *Zambia* 104 B3 17 28 S 24 13 E
Katimbira, *Malawi* 107 E3 12 40 S 34 0 E
Katingan = Mendawai →, *Indonesia* 75 C4 3 30 S 113 0 E
Katiola, *Ivory C.* 100 D3 8 10N 5 10W
Katipunan, *Phil.* 71 G4 8 31N 123 17 E
Katlanovo, *Macedonia, Yug.* 42 F6 41 52N 21 40 E
Katmandu, *Nepal* 81 F11 27 45N 85 20 E
Kato Akhaïa, *Greece* 45 F3 38 8N 21 33 E
Káto Arkhánai, *Greece* 32 D7 35 15N 25 10 E
Káto Khorió, *Greece* 32 D7 35 3N 25 47 E
Kato Pyrgos, *Cyprus* 32 D11 35 11N 32 41 E
Káto Stavros, *Greece* 44 D5 40 39N 23 43 E
Katol, *India* 82 D4 21 17N 78 38 E
Katompe, *Zaïre* 103 D5 6 2 S 26 23 E
Katonga →, *Uganda* 106 B3 0 34N 31 50 E
Katoomba, *Australia* 117 B9 33 41 S 150 19 E
Katowice, *Poland* 47 E6 50 17N 19 5 E
Katowice □, *Poland* 47 E6 50 10N 19 0 E
Katrine, L., *U.K.* 18 E4 56 15N 4 30W
Katrineholm, *Sweden* 14 E10 59 9N 16 12 E
Katsepe, *Madag.* 105 B8 15 45 S 46 15 E
Katsina, *Nigeria* 101 C6 13 0N 7 32 E
Katsina □, *Nigeria* 101 C6 12 30N 7 30 E
Katsina Ala →, *Nigeria* 101 D6 7 10N 9 20 E
Katsumoto, *Japan* 62 D1 33 51N 129 42 E
Katsuta, *Japan* 63 A12 36 25N 140 31 E
Katsuura, *Japan* 63 B12 35 10N 140 20 E
Katsuyama, *Japan* 63 A8 36 3N 136 30 E
Kattakurgan, *Uzbekistan* 55 D3 39 55N 66 15 E
Kattaviá, *Greece* 32 D9 35 57N 27 46 E
Kattegatt, *Denmark* 15 H5 57 0N 11 20 E
Katumba, *Zaïre* 103 D5 7 40 S 25 17 E
Katungu, *Kenya* 106 C5 2 55 S 40 3 E
Katwa, *India* 81 H13 23 30N 88 5 E
Katwijk-aan-Zee, *Neths.* 20 D4 52 12N 4 24 E
Katy, *Poland* 47 D3 51 2N 16 45 E
Kauai, *U.S.A.* 132 H15 22 0N 159 30W
Kauai Chan., *U.S.A.* 132 H15 21 45N 158 50W
Kaub, *Germany* 27 E3 50 5N 7 46 E
Kaufbeuren, *Germany* 27 H6 47 50N 10 37 E
Kaufman, *U.S.A.* 139 J6 32 35N 96 20W
Kaukauna, *U.S.A.* 134 C1 44 20N 88 13W
Kaukauveld, *Namibia* 104 C3 20 0 S 20 15 E
Kaukonen, *Finland* 12 C18 67 31N 24 53 E
Kauliranta, *Finland* 12 C17 66 27N 23 41 E
Kaunas, *Lithuania* 50 D3 54 54N 23 54 E
Kaunghein, *Burma* 78 C5 25 41N 95 26 E
Kaupalatmada, Mt., *Indonesia* 72 B3 3 30 S 126 10 E
Kaura Namoda, *Nigeria* 101 C6 12 37N 6 33 E
Kautokeino, *Norway* 12 B17 69 0N 23 4 E
Kavacha, *Russia* 57 C17 60 16N 169 51 E
Kavadarci, *Macedonia, Yug.* 42 F7 41 26N 22 3 E
Kavaja, *Albania* 44 C1 41 11N 19 33 E
Kavak, *Turkey* 88 C7 41 4N 36 3 E
Kavalerovo, *Russia* 60 B7 44 15N 135 4 E
Kavali, *India* 83 G5 14 55N 80 1 E
Kavála, *Greece* 44 D6 40 57N 24 28 E
Kavála □, *Greece* 44 C6 41 5N 24 30 E
Kavála Kólpos, *Greece* 44 D6 40 50N 24 25 E
Kavār, *Iran* 85 D7 29 11N 52 44 E
Kavarna, *Bulgaria* 43 D13 43 26N 28 22 E
Kavieng, *Papua N. G.* 120 B6 2 36 S 150 51 E
Kavos, *Greece* 32 B4 39 23N 20 3 E
Kavoúsi, *Greece* 45 J7 35 7N 25 51 E
Kaw, *Fr. Guiana* 153 C7 4 30N 52 15W
Kawa, *Sudan* 95 E3 13 42N 32 34 E
Kawachi-Nagano, *Japan* 63 C7 34 28N 135 31 E

Kisar 217


Khemissèt, Morocco 98 B3 33 50N 6 1W
Khemmarat, Thailand 76 D5 16 10N 105 15 E
Khenāmān, Iran 85 D8 30 27N 56 29 E
Khenchela, Algeria 99 A6 35 28N 7 11 E
Khenifra, Morocco 98 B3 32 58N 5 46W
Kherrata, Algeria 99 A6 36 27N 5 13 E
Khérson, Greece 44 C4 41 5N 22 47 E
Kherson, Ukraine 52 C5 46 35N 32 35 E
Khersónisos Akrotíri, Greece 32 D6 35 30N 24 10 E
Kheta →, Russia 57 B11 71 54N 102 6 E
Khiliomódhion, Greece 45 G4 37 48N 22 51 E
Khilok, Russia 57 D12 51 30N 110 45 E
Khimki, Russia 51 D10 55 50N 37 20 E
Khíos, Greece 45 F8 38 27N 26 9 E
Khirbat Qanāfār, Lebanon 91 B4 33 39N 35 43 E
Khisar-Momina Banya, Bulgaria 43 E9 42 30N 24 44 E
Khiuma = Hiiumaa, Estonia 50 B3 58 50N 22 45 E
Khiva, Uzbekistan 56 E7 41 30N 60 18 E
Khīyāv, Iran 84 B5 38 30N 47 45 E
Khlebarovo, Bulgaria 43 D11 43 37N 26 15 E
Khlong Khlung, Thailand 76 D2 16 12N 99 43 E
Khmelnitskiy, Ukraine 50 G5 49 23N 27 0 E
Khmer Rep. = Cambodia ■, Asia 76 F5 12 15N 105 0 E
Khoai, Hon, Vietnam 77 H5 8 26N 104 50 E
Khodzent, Tajikistan 55 C4 40 17N 69 37 E
Khojak P., Afghan. 79 C2 30 55N 66 30 E
Khok Kloi, Thailand 77 H2 8 17N 98 19 E
Khok Pho, Thailand 77 J3 6 43N 101 6 E
Khokholskiy, Russia 51 F11 51 35N 38 40 E
Kholm, Afghan. 79 A2 36 45N 67 40 E
Kholm, Russia 50 C7 57 10N 31 15 E
Kholmsk, Russia 57 E15 47 40N 142 5 E
Khomas Hochland, Namibia 104 C2 22 40 S 16 0 E
Khomayn, Iran 85 C6 33 40N 50 7 E
Khon Kaen, Thailand 76 D4 16 30N 102 47 E
Khong, Laos 76 E5 14 7N 105 51 E
Khong Sedone, Laos 76 E5 15 34N 105 49 E
Khonu, Russia 57 C15 66 30N 143 12 E
Khoper →, Russia 51 G13 49 30N 42 20 E
Khor el 'Atash, Sudan 95 E3 13 20N 34 15 E
Khóra, Greece 45 G3 37 3N 21 42 E
Khóra Sfakíon, Greece 32 D6 35 15N 24 9 E
Khorāsān □, Iran 85 C8 34 0N 58 0 E
Khorat = Nakhon Ratchasima, Thailand 76 E4 14 59N 102 12 E
Khorat, Cao Nguyen, Thailand 76 E4 15 30N 102 50 E
Khorb el Ethel, Algeria 98 C3 28 30N 6 17W
Khorixas, Namibia 104 C1 20 16 S 14 59 E
Khorog, Tajikistan 55 E5 37 30N 71 36 E
Khorol, Ukraine 52 B5 49 48N 33 15 E
Khorramābād, Khorāsān, Iran 85 C8 35 6N 57 57 E
Khorramābād, Lorestān, Iran 85 C6 33 30N 48 25 E
Khorrāmshahr, Iran 85 D6 30 29N 48 15 E
Khosravī, Iran 85 D6 30 48N 51 28 E
Khosrowābād, Khuzestān, Iran 85 D6 30 10N 48 25 E
Khosrowābād, Kordestān, Iran 84 C5 35 31N 47 38 E
Khosūyeh, Iran 85 D7 28 32N 54 26 E
Khotin, Ukraine 52 B2 48 31N 26 27 E
Khouribga, Morocco 98 B3 32 58N 6 57W
Khowai, Bangla. 78 C3 24 5N 91 40 E
Khoyniki, Belorussia 50 F6 51 54N 29 55 E
Khrami →, Azerbaijan 53 F11 41 25N 45 0 E
Khrenovoye, Russia 51 F12 51 4N 40 16 E
Khristianá, Greece 45 H7 36 14N 25 13 E
Khromtau, Kazakhstan 54 F6 50 17N 58 27 E
Khrysokhou B., Cyprus 32 D11 35 6N 32 25 E
Khtapodhiá, Greece 45 G7 37 24N 25 34 E
Khu Khan, Thailand 76 E5 14 42N 104 12 E
Khudrah, W. →, Yemen 87 C5 18 10N 50 20 E
Khuff, Si. Arabia 84 E5 24 55N 44 53 E
Khūgīānī, Qandahar, Afghan. 79 C2 31 34N 66 32 E
Khūgīānī, Qandahar, Afghan. 79 C2 31 28N 65 14 E
Khulayṣ, Si. Arabia 86 B2 22 9N 39 19 E
Khulna, Bangla. 78 D2 22 45N 89 34 E
Khulna □, Bangla. 78 D2 22 25N 89 35 E
Khulo, Georgia 53 F10 41 33N 42 19 E
Khumago, Botswana 104 C3 20 26 S 24 32 E
Khumrah, Si. Arabia 86 B2 21 22N 39 13 E
Khūnsorkh, Iran 85 E8 27 9N 56 7 E
Khunzakh, Russia 53 E12 42 35N 46 42 E
Khūr, Iran 85 C8 32 55N 58 18 E
Khurai, India 80 G8 24 3N 78 23 E
Khuraydah, Yemen 87 D5 15 33N 48 18 E
Khurayṣ, Si. Arabia 85 E6 25 6N 48 2 E
Khūrīyā Mūrīyā, Jazā 'ir, Oman 87 C6 17 30N 55 58 E
Khurja, India 80 E7 28 15N 77 58 E
Khūsf, Iran 85 C8 32 46N 58 53 E
Khushab, Pakistan 79 B4 32 20N 72 20 E
Khuzdar, Pakistan 79 D2 27 52N 66 30 E
Khūzestān □, Iran 85 D6 31 0N 49 0 E
Khvājeh, Iran 84 B5 38 9N 46 35 E
Khvājeh Moḥammad, Kūh-e, Afghan. 79 A3 36 22N 70 17 E
Khvalynsk, Russia 51 E16 52 30N 48 2 E
Khvānsār, Iran 85 D7 29 56N 54 8 E
Khvatovka, Russia 51 E15 52 24N 46 32 E
Khvor, Iran 85 C7 33 45N 55 0 E
Khvorgū, Iran 85 E8 27 34N 56 27 E
Khvormūj, Iran 85 D6 28 40N 51 30 E
Khvoy, Iran 84 B5 38 35N 45 0 E
Khvoynaya, Russia 50 B9 58 58N 34 28 E
Khyber Pass, Afghan. 79 B3 34 10N 71 8 E
Kia, Solomon Is. 121 L10 7 32 S 158 26 E
Kiabukwa, Zaïre 103 D4 8 40 S 24 48 E
Kiadho →, India 82 E3 19 37N 77 40 E
Kiama, Australia 117 C9 34 40 S 150 50 E
Kiamba, Phil. 71 H5 6 2N 124 46 E
Kiambi, Zaïre 106 D2 7 15 S 28 0 E
Kiambu, Kenya 106 C4 1 8 S 36 50 E
Kiangsi = Jiangxi □, China 69 D10 27 30N 116 0 E
Kiangsu = Jiangsu □, China 67 H10 33 0N 120 0 E
Kiáton, Greece 45 F4 38 2N 22 43 E
Kibæk, Denmark 15 H2 56 2N 8 51 E
Kibanga Port, Uganda 106 B3 0 10N 32 58 E
Kibangou, Congo 102 C2 3 26 S 12 22 E
Kibara, Tanzania 106 C3 2 8 S 33 30 E
Kibare, Mts., Zaïre 106 D2 8 25 S 27 10 E
Kibawe, Phil. 71 H5 7 34N 125 0 E
Kibombo, Zaïre 103 C5 3 57 S 25 53 E
Kibondo, Tanzania 106 C3 3 35 S 30 45 E
Kibondo □, Tanzania 106 C3 4 0 S 30 55 E
Kibumbu, Burundi 106 C2 3 32 S 29 45 E
Kibungu, Rwanda 106 C3 2 10 S 30 32 E
Kibuye, Burundi 106 C2 3 39 S 29 59 E
Kibuye, Rwanda 106 C2 2 3 S 29 21 E
Kibwesa, Tanzania 106 D2 6 30 S 29 58 E
Kibwezi, Kenya 106 C4 2 27 S 37 57 E
Kičevo, Macedonia, Yug. 42 F5 41 34N 20 59 E
Kichiga, Russia 57 D17 59 50N 163 5 E
Kicking Horse Pass, Canada 130 C5 51 28N 116 16W
Kidal, Mali 101 B5 18 26N 1 22 E
Kidapawan, Phil. 71 H5 7 1N 125 3 E
Kidderminster, U.K. 17 E5 52 24N 2 13W
Kidete, Tanzania 106 D4 6 25 S 37 17 E
Kidira, Senegal 100 C2 14 28N 12 13W
Kidnappers, C., N.Z. 118 F6 39 38 S 177 5 E
Kidston, Australia 114 B3 18 52 S 144 8 E
Kidugallo, Tanzania 106 D4 6 49 S 38 15 E
Kidurong, Tanjong, Malaysia 75 B4 3 16N 113 3 E
Kiel, Germany 26 A6 54 16N 10 8 E
Kiel Kanal = Nord-Ostsee Kanal, Germany 26 A5 54 15N 9 40 E
Kielce, Poland 47 E7 50 52N 20 42 E
Kielce □, Poland 47 E7 50 40N 20 40 E
Kieldrecht, Belgium 21 F4 51 17N 4 11 E
Kieler Bucht, Germany 26 A6 54 30N 10 30 E
Kien Binh, Vietnam 77 H5 9 55N 105 19 E
Kien Tan, Vietnam 77 G5 10 7N 105 17 E
Kienge, Zaïre 107 E2 10 30 S 27 30 E
Kiessé, Niger 101 C5 13 29N 4 1 E
Kieta, Papua N. G. 120 D8 6 12 S 155 36 E
Kiev = Kiyev, Ukraine 50 F7 50 30N 30 28 E
Kiffa, Mauritania 100 B2 16 37N 11 24W
Kifisiá, Greece 45 F5 38 4N 23 49 E
Kifissós →, Greece 45 F5 38 35N 23 20 E
Kifrī, Iraq 84 C5 34 45N 45 0 E
Kigali, Rwanda 106 C3 1 59 S 30 4 E
Kigarama, Tanzania 106 C3 1 1 S 31 50 E
Kigoma □, Tanzania 106 D2 5 0 S 30 0 E
Kigoma-Ujiji, Tanzania 106 C2 4 55 S 29 36 E
Kigomasha, Ras, Tanzania 106 C4 4 58 S 38 58 E
Kihee, Australia 115 D3 27 23 S 142 37 E
Kihikihi, N.Z. 118 E4 38 2 S 175 22 E
Kii-Hantō, Japan 63 D7 34 0N 135 45 E
Kii-Sanchi, Japan 63 C8 34 20N 136 0 E
Kii-Suidō, Japan 62 D6 33 40N 134 45 E
Kikaiga-Shima, Japan 61 K4 28 19N 129 59 E
Kikinda, Serbia, Yug. 42 B5 45 50N 20 30 E
Kikládhes, Greece 45 G6 37 20N 24 30 E
Kikládhes □, Greece 45 G6 37 0N 25 0 E
Kikoira, Australia 117 B7 33 39 S 146 40 E
Kikori, Papua N. G. 120 D3 7 25 S 144 15 E
Kikori →, Papua N. G. 120 D3 7 38 S 144 20 E
Kikuchi, Japan 62 E2 32 59N 130 47 E
Kikwit, Zaïre 103 D3 5 0 S 18 45 E
Kila' Drosh, Pakistan 79 B3 35 33N 71 52 E
Kilakkarai, India 83 K4 9 12N 78 47 E
Kílalki, Greece 45 H9 36 15N 27 35 E
Kilauea Crater, U.S.A. 132 J17 19 24N 155 17W
Kilchberg, Switz. 29 B7 47 18N 8 33 E
Kilcoy, Australia 115 D5 26 59 S 152 30 E
Kildare, Ireland 19 C5 53 10N 6 50W
Kildare □, Ireland 19 C5 53 10N 6 50W
Kilembe, Zaïre 103 D3 5 42 S 19 55 E
Kilgore, U.S.A. 139 J7 32 22N 94 55W
Kilifi, Kenya 106 C4 3 40 S 39 48 E
Kilifi □, Kenya 106 C4 3 30 S 39 40 E
Kilimanjaro, Tanzania 106 C4 3 7 S 37 20 E
Kilimanjaro □, Tanzania 106 C4 4 0 S 38 0 E
Kilinailau Is., Papua N. G. 120 C8 4 45 S 155 20 E
Kilindini, Kenya 106 C4 4 4 S 39 40 E
Kilis, Turkey 88 E7 36 42N 37 6 E
Kiliya, Ukraine 52 D3 45 28N 29 16 E
Kilju, N. Korea 67 D15 40 57N 129 25 E
Kilkee, Ireland 19 D2 52 41N 9 40W
Kilkenny, Ireland 19 D4 52 40N 7 17W
Kilkenny □, Ireland 19 D4 52 35N 7 15W
Kilkieran B., Ireland 19 C2 53 18N 9 45W
Kilkís, Greece 44 D4 40 58N 22 57 E
Kilkís □, Greece 44 C4 41 5N 22 50 E
Killala, Ireland 19 B2 54 13N 9 12W
Killala B., Ireland 19 B2 54 20N 9 12W
Killaloe, Ireland 19 D3 52 48N 8 28W
Killaloe Sta., Canada 136 A7 45 33N 77 25W
Killam, Canada 130 C6 52 47N 111 51W
Killarney, Australia 115 D5 28 20 S 152 18 E
Killarney, Canada 128 C3 45 55N 81 30W
Killarney, Ireland 19 D2 52 2N 9 30W
Killarney, Lakes of, Ireland 19 E2 52 0N 9 30W
Killary Harbour, Ireland 19 C2 53 38N 9 52W
Killdeer, Canada 131 D7 49 6N 106 22W
Killdeer, U.S.A. 138 B3 47 26N 102 48W
Killeen, U.S.A. 139 K6 31 7N 97 45W
Killiecrankie, Pass of, U.K. 18 E5 56 44N 3 46W
Killin, U.K. 18 E4 56 28N 4 20W
Killíni, Ilía, Greece 45 G3 37 55N 21 8 E
Killíni, Korinthía, Greece 45 G4 37 54N 22 25 E
Killybegs, Ireland 19 B3 54 38N 8 26W
Kilmarnock, U.K. 18 F4 55 36N 4 30W
Kilmez, Russia 54 C2 56 58N 50 55 E
Kilmez →, Russia 54 C2 56 58N 50 28 E
Kilmore, Australia 117 D6 37 25 S 144 53 E
Kilondo, Tanzania 107 D3 9 45 S 34 20 E
Kilosa, Tanzania 106 D4 6 48 S 37 0 E
Kilosa □, Tanzania 106 D4 6 48 S 37 0 E
Kilrush, Ireland 19 D2 52 39N 9 30W
Kilwa □, Tanzania 107 D4 9 0 S 39 0 E
Kilwa Kisiwani, Tanzania 107 D4 8 58 S 39 32 E
Kilwa Kivinje, Tanzania 107 D4 8 45 S 39 25 E
Kilwa Masoko, Tanzania 107 D4 8 55 S 39 30 E
Kim, U.S.A. 139 G3 37 18N 103 20W
Kimaam, Indonesia 73 C5 7 58 S 138 53 E
Kimamba, Tanzania 106 D4 6 45 S 37 10 E
Kimba, Australia 116 B2 33 8 S 136 23 E
Kimball, Nebr., U.S.A. 138 E3 41 17N 103 40W
Kimball, S. Dak., U.S.A. 138 D5 43 47N 98 57W
Kimbe, Papua N. G. 120 C6 5 33 S 150 11 E
Kimbe B., Papua N. G. 120 C6 5 15 S 150 30 E
Kimberley, Australia 116 B4 32 50 S 141 4 E
Kimberley, Canada 130 D5 49 40N 115 59W
Kimberley, S. Africa 104 D3 28 43 S 24 46 E
Kimberley Downs, Australia 112 C3 17 24 S 124 22 E
Kimberley Plateau, Australia 110 D4 16 20 S 127 0 E
Kimberly, U.S.A. 142 E6 42 33N 114 25W
Kimchaek, N. Korea 67 D15 40 40N 129 10 E
Kimchŏn, S. Korea 67 F15 36 11N 128 4 E
Kími, Greece 45 F6 38 38N 24 6 E
Kimje, S. Korea 67 G14 35 48N 126 45 E
Kímolos, Greece 45 H6 36 48N 24 37 E
Kimovsk, Russia 51 D11 54 0N 38 29 E
Kimparana, Mali 100 C4 12 48N 5 0W
Kimry, Russia 51 C10 56 55N 37 15 E
Kimsquit, Canada 130 C3 52 45N 126 57W
Kimstad, Sweden 15 F9 58 35N 15 58 E
Kimvula, Zaïre 103 D3 5 44 S 15 58 E
Kinabalu, Gunong, Malaysia 75 A5 6 3N 116 14 E
Kínaros, Greece 45 H8 36 59N 26 15 E
Kinaskan L., Canada 130 B2 57 38N 130 8W
Kinbasket L., Canada 130 C5 52 0N 118 10W
Kincaid, Canada 131 D7 49 40N 107 0W
Kincaid, U.S.A. 140 E7 39 35N 89 25W
Kincardine, Canada 128 D3 44 10N 81 40W
Kinda, Kasai Or., Zaïre 103 D5 9 18 S 25 4 E
Kinda, Shaba, Zaïre 103 C4 4 47 S 21 48 E
Kinder Scout, U.K. 16 D6 53 24N 1 53W
Kindersley, Canada 131 C7 51 30N 109 10W
Kindia, Guinea 100 C2 10 0N 12 52W
Kindu, Zaïre 102 C5 2 55 S 25 50 E
Kinel, Russia 54 E2 53 15N 50 40 E
Kineshma, Russia 51 C13 57 30N 42 5 E
Kinesi, Tanzania 106 C3 1 25 S 33 50 E
King, L., Australia 113 F2 33 10 S 119 35 E
King, Mt., Australia 114 D4 25 10 S 147 30 E
King City, Calif., U.S.A. 144 J5 36 11N 121 8W
King City, Mo., U.S.A. 140 D2 40 3N 94 31W
King Cr. →, Australia 114 C2 24 35 S 139 30 E
King Edward →, Australia 112 B4 14 14 S 126 35 E
King Frederick VI Land = Kong Frederik VI.s Kyst, Greenland 6 C5 63 0N 43 0W
King George B., Falk. Is. 160 D4 51 30 S 60 30W
King George I., Antarctica 7 C18 60 0 S 60 0W
King George Is., Canada 127 C11 57 20N 80 30W
King I., Australia 114 F3 39 50 S 144 0 E
King I., Canada 130 C3 52 10N 127 40W
King Leopold Ras., Australia 112 C4 17 30 S 125 45 E
King Sd., Australia 112 C3 16 50 S 123 20 E
King William I., Canada 126 B10 69 10N 97 25W
King William's Town, S. Africa 104 E4 32 51 S 27 22 E
Kingaroy, Australia 115 D5 26 32 S 151 51 E
Kingfisher, U.S.A. 139 H6 35 50N 97 55W
Kingirbān, Iraq 84 C5 34 40N 44 54 E
Kingisepp = Kuressaare, Estonia 50 B3 58 15N 22 30 E
Kingisepp, Russia 50 B6 59 25N 28 40 E
Kingking, Phil. 71 H5 7 9N 125 54 E
Kingman, Ariz., U.S.A. 145 K12 35 12N 114 2W
Kingman, Ind., U.S.A. 141 E9 39 58N 87 18W
Kingman, Kans., U.S.A. 139 G5 37 41N 98 9W
Kingoonya, Australia 115 E2 30 55 S 135 19 E
Kings →, U.S.A. 144 J7 36 10N 119 50W
Kings Canyon National Park, U.S.A. 144 J8 37 0N 118 35W
King's Lynn, U.K. 16 E8 52 45N 0 25 E
Kings Mountain, U.S.A. 135 H5 35 13N 81 20W
King's Peak, U.S.A. 142 F8 40 46N 110 27W
Kingsbridge, U.K. 17 G4 50 17N 3 46W
Kingsburg, U.S.A. 144 J7 36 35N 119 36W
Kingsbury, U.S.A. 141 C10 41 31N 86 42W
Kingscote, Australia 116 C2 35 40 S 137 38 E
Kingscourt, Ireland 19 C5 53 55N 6 48W
Kingsley, U.S.A. 138 D7 42 37N 95 58W
Kingsport, U.S.A. 135 G4 36 33N 82 36W
Kingston, Canada 128 D4 44 14N 76 30W
Kingston, Jamaica 148 C4 18 0N 76 50W
Kingston, N.Z. 119 F3 45 20 S 168 43 E
Kingston, Mo., U.S.A. 140 E2 39 38N 94 2W
Kingston, N.Y., U.S.A. 137 E10 41 55N 74 0W
Kingston, Pa., U.S.A. 137 E9 41 19N 75 58W
Kingston, R.I., U.S.A. 137 E13 41 29N 71 30W
Kingston Pk., U.S.A. 145 K11 35 45N 115 54W
Kingston South East, Australia 116 D3 36 51 S 139 55 E
Kingston upon Hull, U.K. 16 D7 53 45N 0 20W
Kingston-upon-Thames, U.K. 17 F7 51 23N 0 20W
Kingstown, Australia 117 A9 30 29 S 151 6 E
Kingstown, St. Vincent 149 D7 13 10N 61 10W
Kingstree, U.S.A. 135 J6 33 40N 79 48W
Kingsville, Canada 128 D3 42 2N 82 45W
Kingsville, U.S.A. 139 M6 27 30N 97 53W
Kingussie, U.K. 18 D4 57 5N 4 2W
Kinistino, Canada 131 C7 52 57N 105 2W
Kinkala, Congo 103 C2 4 18 S 14 49 E
Kinki □, Japan 63 D8 33 45N 136 0 E
Kinleith, N.Z. 118 E4 38 20 S 175 56 E
Kinmount, Canada 136 B6 44 48N 78 45W
Kinmundy, U.S.A. 141 F8 38 46N 88 51W
Kinna, Sweden 15 G6 57 32N 12 42 E
Kinnaird, Canada 130 D5 49 17N 117 39W
Kinnairds Hd., U.K. 18 D7 57 40N 2 0W
Kinnared, Sweden 15 G7 57 2N 13 7 E
Kinnarodden, Norway 11 A11 71 8N 27 40 E
Kino, Mexico 146 B2 28 45N 111 59W
Kinogitan, Phil. 71 G5 9 0N 124 48 E
Kinoje →, Canada 128 B3 52 8N 81 25W
Kinomoto, Japan 63 B8 35 30N 136 13 E
Kinoni, Uganda 106 C3 0 41 S 30 28 E
Kinrooi, Belgium 21 F7 51 9N 5 45 E
Kinross, U.K. 18 E5 56 13N 3 25W
Kinsale, Ireland 19 E3 51 42N 8 31W
Kinsale, Old Hd. of, Ireland 19 E3 51 37N 8 32W
Kinshasa, Zaïre 103 C3 4 20 S 15 15 E
Kinsley, U.S.A. 139 G5 37 57N 99 30W
Kinston, U.S.A. 135 H7 35 18N 77 35W
Kintampo, Ghana 101 D4 8 5N 1 41W
Kintap, Indonesia 75 C5 3 51 S 115 13 E
Kintore Ra., Australia 112 D4 23 15 S 128 47 E
Kintyre, U.K. 18 F3 55 30N 5 35W
Kintyre, Mull of, U.K. 18 F3 55 17N 5 55W
Kinu, Burma 78 D5 22 46N 95 37 E
Kinu-Gawa →, Japan 63 B11 35 36N 139 57 E
Kinushseo →, Canada 128 A3 55 15N 83 45W
Kinuso, Canada 130 B5 55 20N 115 25W
Kinyangiri, Tanzania 106 C3 4 25 S 34 37 E
Kinzig →, Germany 27 G3 48 37N 7 49 E
Kinzua, U.S.A. 136 E6 41 52N 78 58W
Kinzua Dam, U.S.A. 136 E5 41 53N 79 0W
Kióni, Greece 45 F2 38 27N 20 41 E
Kiosk, Canada 128 C4 46 6N 78 53W
Kiowa, Kans., U.S.A. 139 G5 37 3N 98 30W
Kiowa, Okla., U.S.A. 139 H7 34 45N 95 50W
Kipahigan L., Canada 131 B8 55 20N 101 55W
Kipanga, Tanzania 106 D4 6 15 S 35 20 E
Kiparissía, Greece 45 G3 37 15N 21 40 E
Kiparissiakós Kólpos, Greece 45 G3 37 25N 21 25 E
Kipembawe, Tanzania 106 D3 7 38 S 33 27 E
Kipengere Ra., Tanzania 107 D3 9 12 S 34 15 E
Kipili, Tanzania 106 D3 7 28 S 30 32 E
Kipini, Kenya 106 C5 2 30 S 40 32 E
Kipling, Canada 131 C8 50 6N 102 38W
Kippure, Ireland 19 C5 53 11N 6 23W
Kipungot, Phil. 71 H5 6 24N 124 4 E
Kipushi, Zaïre 107 E2 11 48 S 27 12 E
Kira Kira, Solomon Is. 121 N11 10 27 S 161 56 E
Kirandul, India 82 E5 18 33N 81 10 E
Kiratpur, India 80 E8 29 32N 78 12 E
Kirchberg, Switz. 28 B5 47 5N 7 35 E
Kirchhain, Germany 26 E4 50 49N 8 54 E
Kirchheim, Germany 27 G5 48 38N 9 20 E
Kirchheim-Bolanden, Germany 27 F4 49 40N 8 0 E
Kirchschlag, Austria 31 D9 47 30N 16 19 E
Kirensk, Russia 57 D11 57 50N 107 55 E
Kirgella Rocks, Australia 113 F3 30 5 S 122 50 E
Kirghizia ■, Asia 55 C7 42 0N 75 0 E
Kirgizia = Kirghizia ■, Asia 55 C7 42 0N 75 0 E
Kirgiziya Steppe, Kazakhstan 49 D10 50 0N 55 0 E
Kiri, Zaïre 102 C3 1 29 S 19 0 E
Kiri Buru, India 82 D7 22 0N 85 0 E
Kiribati ■, Pac. Oc. 122 H9 5 0 S 176 0 E
Kırıkhan, Turkey 88 E7 36 31N 36 21 E
Kırıkkale, Turkey 88 D5 39 51N 33 32 E
Kirikopuni, N.Z. 118 B3 35 50 S 174 1 E
Kirillov, Russia 51 B11 59 51N 38 14 E
Kirin = Jilin, China 67 C14 43 44N 126 30 E
Kirin = Jilin □, China 67 C13 44 0N 127 0 E
Kirindi →, Sri Lanka 83 L5 6 15N 81 20 E
Kirishi, Russia 50 B7 59 28N 31 59 E
Kirishima-Yama, Japan 62 F2 31 58N 130 55 E
Kiritimati, Kiribati 123 G12 1 58N 157 27W
Kırka, Turkey 88 D4 39 16N 30 31 E
Kirkcaldy, U.K. 18 E5 56 7N 3 10W
Kirkcudbright, U.K. 18 G4 54 50N 4 3W
Kirkee, India 82 E1 18 34N 73 56 E
Kirkenær, Norway 14 D6 60 27N 12 3 E
Kirkenes, Norway 12 B21 69 40N 30 5 E
Kirkintilloch, U.K. 18 F4 55 57N 4 10W
Kirkjubæjarklaustur, Iceland 12 E4 63 47N 18 4W
Kirkland, Ariz., U.S.A. 143 J7 34 29N 112 46W
Kirkland, Ill., U.S.A. 141 B8 42 5N 88 51W
Kirkland Lake, Canada 128 C3 48 9N 80 2W
Kırklareli, Turkey 43 F12 41 44N 27 15 E
Kırklareli □, Turkey 88 C2 41 45N 27 15 E
Kirklin, U.S.A. 141 D10 40 12N 86 22W
Kirkliston Ra., N.Z. 119 E5 44 25 S 170 34 E
Kirksville, U.S.A. 140 D4 40 8N 92 35W
Kirkūk, Iraq 84 C5 35 30N 44 21 E
Kirkwall, U.K. 18 C6 58 59N 2 59W
Kirkwood, S. Africa 104 E4 33 22 S 25 15 E
Kirkwood, U.S.A. 140 F6 38 35N 90 24W
Kirlampudi, India 82 F6 17 12N 82 12 E
Kirn, Germany 27 F3 49 46N 7 29 E
Kirov = Vyatka, Russia 54 B1 58 35N 49 40 E
Kirov, Russia 50 D9 54 3N 34 20 E
Kirovabad = Gyandzha, Azerbaijan 53 F12 40 45N 46 20 E
Kirovakan = Karaklis, Armenia 53 F11 40 48N 44 30 E
Kirovo, Uzbekistan 55 C5 40 26N 70 36 E
Kirovo-Chepetsk, Russia 51 B17 58 28N 50 0 E
Kirovograd = Yelizavetgrad, Ukraine 52 B5 48 35N 32 20 E
Kirovsk, Russia 48 A5 67 48N 33 50 E
Kirovsk, Turkmenistan 56 F7 37 42N 60 23 E
Kirovsk, Ukraine 53 B8 48 35N 38 30 E
Kirovski, Russia 53 D13 45 51N 48 11 E
Kirovskiy, Kazakhstan 55 A9 44 52N 78 12 E
Kirovskiy, Russia 57 D16 54 27N 155 42 E
Kirovskiy, Russia 60 B6 45 7N 133 30 E
Kirovskoye, Kirghizia 55 B5 42 39N 71 35 E
Kirriemuir, U.K. 18 E6 56 41N 2 58W
Kirs, Russia 54 B3 59 21N 52 14 E
Kirsanov, Russia 51 E13 52 35N 42 40 E
Kırşehir, Turkey 88 D6 39 14N 34 5 E
Kırşehir □, Turkey 88 D6 39 10N 34 10 E
Kirstonia, S. Africa 104 D3 25 30 S 23 45 E
Kirtachi, Niger 101 C5 12 52N 2 30 E
Kīrteh, Afghan. 79 B1 32 15N 63 0 E
Kirthar Range, Pakistan 79 D2 27 0N 67 0 E
Kiruna, Sweden 12 C16 67 52N 20 15 E
Kirundu, Zaïre 102 C5 0 50 S 25 35 E
Kirup, Australia 113 F2 33 40 S 115 50 E
Kirya, Russia 51 D15 55 5N 46 45 E
Kiryū, Japan 63 A11 36 24N 139 20 E
Kisaga, Tanzania 106 C3 4 30 S 34 23 E
Kisalaya, Nic. 148 D3 14 40N 84 3W
Kisambo, Zaïre 103 D3 6 25 S 18 14 E
Kisámou, Kólpos, Greece 32 D5 35 30N 23 38 E
Kisanga, Zaïre 106 B2 2 30N 26 35 E
Kisangani, Zaïre 106 B2 0 35N 25 15 E
Kisantu, Zaïre 103 D3 5 7 S 15 5 E
Kisar, Indonesia 72 C3 8 5 S 127 10 E

Krichev 219


Kong Frederik VIII.s Land, Greenland 6 B6 78 30N 26 0W
Kong Oscar Fjord, Greenland 6 B6 72 20N 24 0W
Kongbo, C.A.R. 102 B4 4 44N 21 23 E
Kongeå →, Denmark 15 J3 55 23N 8 39 E
Kongju, S. Korea 67 F14 36 30N 127 0 E
Kongkemul, Indonesia 75 B4 1 52N 112 11 E
Konglu, Burma 78 B6 27 13N 97 57 E
Kongolo, Kasai Or., Zaïre 103 D4 5 26 S 24 49 E
Kongolo, Shaba, Zaïre 106 D2 5 22 S 27 0 E
Kongor, Sudan 95 F3 7 1N 31 27 E
Kongoussi, Burkina Faso 101 C4 13 19N 1 32W
Kongsberg, Norway 14 E3 59 39N 9 39 E
Kongsvinger, Norway 14 D6 60 12N 12 2 E
Kongwa, Tanzania 106 D4 6 11 S 36 26 E
Koni, Zaïre 107 E2 10 40 S 27 11 E
Koni, Mts., Zaïre 107 E2 10 36 S 27 10 E
Koniecpol, Poland 47 E6 50 46N 19 40 E
Königsberg = Kaliningrad, Russia 50 D2 54 42N 20 32 E
Königslutter, Germany 26 C6 52 14N 10 50 E
Königswusterhausen, Germany 26 C9 52 19N 13 38 E
Konin, Poland 47 C5 52 12N 18 15 E
Konin □, Poland 47 C5 52 15N 18 30 E
Konispoli, Albania 44 E2 39 42N 20 10 E
Kónitsa, Greece 44 D2 40 5N 20 48 E
Köniz, Switz. 28 C4 46 56N 7 25 E
Konjic, Bos.-H., Yug. 42 D2 43 42N 17 58 E
Konjice, Slovenia 39 B12 46 20N 15 28 E
Konkiep, Namibia 104 D2 26 49 S 17 15 E
Konkouré →, Guinea 100 D2 9 50N 13 42W
Könnern, Germany 26 D7 51 40N 11 45 E
Konnur, India 83 F2 16 14N 74 49 E
Kono, S. Leone 100 D2 8 30N 11 5W
Konolfingen, Switz. 28 C5 46 54N 7 38 E
Konongo, Ghana 101 D4 6 40N 1 15W
Konos, Papua N. G. 120 B6 3 10 S 151 44 E
Konosha, Russia 48 B11 61 0N 40 5 E
Kōnosu, Japan 63 A11 36 3N 139 31 E
Konotop, Ukraine 50 F8 51 12N 33 7 E
Końskie, Poland 47 D7 51 15N 20 23 E
Konstantinovka, Ukraine 52 B7 48 32N 37 39 E
Konstantinovski, Russia 53 C9 47 33N 41 10 E
Konstantynów Łódźki, Poland 47 D6 51 45N 19 20 E
Konstanz, Germany 27 H5 47 39N 9 10 E
Kont, Iran 85 E9 26 55N 61 50 E
Kontagora, Nigeria 101 C6 10 23N 5 27 E
Kontich, Belgium 21 F4 51 8N 4 26 E
Kontum, Vietnam 76 E7 14 24N 108 0 E
Kontum, Plateau du, Vietnam 76 E7 14 30N 108 30 E
Konya, Turkey 88 E5 37 52N 32 35 E
Konya □, Turkey 88 E5 37 46N 32 20 E
Konya Ovasi, Turkey 88 D5 38 30N 33 0 E
Konyin, Burma 78 D5 22 58N 94 42 E
Konz, Germany 27 F2 49 41N 6 36 E
Konza, Kenya 106 C4 1 45 S 37 7 E
Konzhakovskiy Kamen, Gora, Russia 54 B6 59 38N 59 8 E
Kookynie, Australia 113 E3 29 17 S 121 22 E
Kooline, Australia 112 D2 22 57 S 116 20 E
Kooloonong, Australia 116 C5 34 48 S 143 10 E
Koolyanobbing, Australia 113 F2 30 48 S 119 36 E
Koondrook, Australia 116 C6 35 33 S 144 8 E
Koonibba, Australia 115 E1 31 54 S 133 25 E
Koorawatha, Australia 117 C8 34 2 S 148 33 E
Koorda, Australia 113 F2 30 48 S 117 35 E
Kooskia, U.S.A. 142 C6 46 9N 115 59W
Kootenai →, Canada 142 B5 49 15N 117 39W
Kootenay L., Canada 130 D5 49 45N 116 50W
Kootenay Nat. Park, Canada 130 C5 51 0N 116 0W
Kootjieskolk, S. Africa 104 E3 31 15 S 20 21 E
Kopa, Kazakhstan 55 B7 43 31N 75 50 E
Kopanovka, Russia 53 C12 47 28N 46 50 E
Kopaonik, Serbia, Yug. 42 D6 43 10N 20 50 E
Kopargaon, India 82 E2 19 51N 74 28 E
Kópavogur, Iceland 12 D3 64 6N 21 55W
Koper, Slovenia 39 C10 45 31N 13 44 E
Kopervik, Norway 13 G8 59 17N 5 17 E
Kopeysk, Russia 54 D7 55 7N 61 37 E
Kopi, Australia 115 E2 33 24 S 135 40 E
Köping, Sweden 14 E10 59 31N 16 3 E
Kopiste, Croatia 39 F13 42 48N 16 42 E
Kopliku, Albania 44 B1 42 15N 19 25 E
Köpmanholmen, Sweden 14 A12 63 10N 18 35 E
Koppal, India 83 G3 15 23N 76 5 E
Koppang, Norway 14 C5 61 34N 11 3 E
Kopparberg, Sweden 13 G13 59 52N 15 0 E
Kopparbergs län □, Sweden 13 F13 61 20N 14 15 E
Kopperå, Norway 14 A5 63 24N 11 50 E
Koppies, S. Africa 105 D4 27 20 S 27 30 E
Koppio, Australia 116 C1 34 26 S 135 51 E
Koprivlen, Bulgaria 43 F8 41 36N 23 53 E
Koprivnica, Croatia 39 B13 46 12N 16 45 E
Koprivshtitsa, Bulgaria 43 E9 42 40N 24 19 E
Kopychintsy, Ukraine 50 G4 49 7N 25 58 E
Kopys, Belorussia 50 D7 54 20N 30 17 E
Korab, Macedonia, Yug. 42 F5 41 44N 20 40 E
Korakiána, Greece 32 A3 39 42N 19 45 E
Koraput, India 82 E6 18 50N 82 40 E
Korba, India 81 H10 22 20N 82 45 E
Korbach, Germany 26 D4 51 17N 8 50 E
Korbu, G., Malaysia 77 K3 4 41N 101 18 E
Korça, Albania 44 D2 40 37N 20 50 E
Korça □, Albania 44 D2 40 40N 20 50 E
Korce = Korça, Albania 44 D2 40 37N 20 50 E
Korčula, Croatia 39 F14 42 57N 17 8 E
Korčulanski Kanal, Croatia 39 E13 43 3N 16 40 E
Kord Kūy, Iran 85 B7 36 48N 54 7 E
Kord Sheykh, Iran 85 D7 28 31N 52 53 E
Kordestān □, Iran 84 C5 36 0N 47 0 E
Korea, North ■, Asia 67 E14 40 0N 127 0 E
Korea, South ■, Asia 67 F15 36 0N 128 0 E
Korea Bay, Korea 67 E13 39 0N 124 0 E
Korea Strait, Asia 67 G15 34 0N 129 30 E
Koregaon, India 82 F2 17 40N 74 10 E
Korenevo, Russia 50 F9 51 27N 34 55 E
Korenovsk, Russia 53 D8 45 30N 39 22 E
Korets, Ukraine 50 F5 50 40N 27 5 E
Korgan, Turkey 89 C7 40 44N 37 13 E
Korgus, Sudan 94 D3 19 16N 33 29 E
Korhogo, Ivory C. 100 D3 9 29N 5 28W
Koribundu, S. Leone 100 D2 7 41N 11 46W
Korim, Indonesia 73 B5 0 58 S 136 10 E
Korinthía □, Greece 45 G4 37 50N 22 35 E
Korinthiakós Kólpos, Greece 45 F4 38 16N 22 30 E
Kórinthos, Greece 45 G4 37 56N 22 55 E
Korioumé, Mali 100 B4 16 35N 3 0W
Korissa, Límni, Greece 32 B3 39 27N 19 53 E
Kōriyama, Japan 60 F10 37 24N 140 23 E
Korkino, Russia 54 D7 54 54N 61 23 E
Korkuteli, Turkey 88 E4 37 2N 30 11 E
Korla, China 64 B3 41 45N 86 4 E
Kormakiti, C., Cyprus 32 D11 35 23N 32 56 E
Körmend, Hungary 31 D9 47 5N 16 35 E
Kornat, Croatia 39 E12 43 50N 15 20 E
Korneshty, Moldavia 52 C3 47 21N 28 1 E
Korneuburg, Austria 31 C9 48 20N 16 20 E
Kornsjø, Norway 14 F5 58 57N 11 39 E
Kornstad, Norway 14 B1 62 59N 7 27 E
Koro, Fiji 121 A2 17 19 S 179 23 E
Koro, Ivory C. 100 D3 8 32N 7 30W
Koro, Mali 100 C4 14 1N 2 58W
Koro Sea, Fiji 121 A3 17 30 S 179 45W
Koro Toro, Chad 97 E3 16 5N 18 30 E
Koroba, Papua N. G. 120 C2 5 44 S 142 47 E
Korocha, Russia 51 F10 50 55N 37 30 E
Köroğlu Dağları, Turkey 88 C4 40 30N 31 50 E
Korogwe, Tanzania 106 D4 5 5S 38 25 E
Korogwe □, Tanzania 106 D4 5 0S 38 20 E
Koroit, Australia 116 E5 38 18 S 142 24 E
Koronadal, Phil. 71 H5 6 12N 125 1 E
Korong Vale, Australia 116 D5 36 22 S 143 45 E
Koróni, Greece 45 H3 36 48N 21 57 E
Korónia, Limni, Greece 44 D5 40 47N 23 37 E
Koronís, Greece 45 G7 37 12N 25 35 E
Koronowo, Poland 47 B4 53 19N 17 55 E
Körös →, Hungary 31 E13 46 43N 20 12 E
Köröstarcsa, Hungary 31 E14 46 53N 21 3 E
Korosten, Ukraine 50 F6 50 57N 28 25 E
Korotoyak, Russia 51 F11 51 1N 39 2 E
Korraraika, Helodranon' i, Madag. 105 B7 17 45 S 43 57 E
Korsakov, Russia 57 E15 46 36N 142 42 E
Korshunovo, Russia 57 D12 58 37N 110 10 E
Korsør, Denmark 13 J11 55 20N 11 9 E
Korsun Shevchenkovskiy, Ukraine 52 B4 49 26N 31 16 E
Korsze, Poland 47 A8 54 11N 21 9 E
Kortemark, Belgium 21 F2 51 2N 3 3 E
Kortessem, Belgium 21 G6 50 52N 5 23 E
Korti, Sudan 94 D3 18 6N 31 33 E
Kortrijk, Belgium 21 G2 50 50N 3 17 E
Korumburra, Australia 117 E6 38 26 S 145 50 E
Korwai, India 80 G8 24 7N 78 5 E
Koryakskiy Khrebet, Russia 57 C18 61 0N 171 0 E
Koryŏng, S. Korea 67 G15 35 44N 128 15 E
Kos, Greece 45 H9 36 50N 27 15 E
Kosa, Ethiopia 95 F4 7 50N 36 50 E
Kosa, Russia 54 B4 59 56N 55 0 E
Kosa →, Russia 54 B4 60 11N 55 10 E
Kosaya Gora, Russia 51 D10 54 10N 37 30 E
Koschagyl, Kazakhstan 49 E9 46 40N 54 0 E
Kościan, Poland 47 C3 52 5N 16 40 E
Kościerzyna, Poland 47 A4 54 8N 17 59 E
Kosciusko, U.S.A. 139 J10 33 3N 89 34W
Kosciusko, Mt., Australia 117 D8 36 27 S 148 16 E
Kosciusko I., U.S.A. 130 B2 56 0N 133 40W
Kösély →, Hungary 31 D14 47 25N 21 5 E
Kosgi, India 82 F3 16 58N 77 43 E
Kosha, Sudan 94 C3 20 50N 30 30 E
Koshigaya, Japan 63 B11 35 54N 139 48 E
K'oshih = Kashi, China 64 C2 39 30N 76 2 E
Koshiki-Rettō, Japan 62 F1 31 45N 129 49 E
Koshkonong, L., U.S.A. 141 B8 42 53N 88 58W
Kōshoku, Japan 63 A10 36 38N 138 6 E
Koshtëbë, Kirghizia 55 C7 41 5N 74 15 E
Kosi, India 80 F7 27 48N 77 29 E
Kosi-meer, S. Africa 105 D5 27 0S 32 50 E
Košice, Czech. 31 C14 48 42N 21 15 E
Kosjerić, Serbia, Yug. 42 D4 44 0N 19 55 E
Koskhinoú, Greece 32 C10 36 23N 28 13 E
Koslan, Russia 48 B8 63 28N 48 52 E
Kosŏng, N. Korea 67 E15 38 40N 128 22 E
Kosovo, Soc. Aut. Pokrajina □, Serbia, Yug. 42 E5 42 30N 21 0 E
Kosovska-Mitrovica, Serbia, Yug. 42 E5 42 54N 20 52 E
Kostajnica, Croatia 39 C13 45 17N 16 30 E
Kostamuksa, Russia 48 B5 62 34N 32 44 E
Kostanjevica, Slovenia 39 C12 45 51N 15 27 E
Kostelec, Czech. 31 A9 50 14N 16 35 E
Kostenets, Bulgaria 43 E8 42 15N 23 52 E
Koster, S. Africa 104 D4 25 52 S 26 54 E
Kôstî, Sudan 95 E3 13 8N 32 43 E
Kostolac, Serbia, Yug. 42 C6 44 37N 21 15 E
Kostopol, Ukraine 50 F5 50 51N 26 22 E
Kostroma, Russia 51 C12 57 50N 40 58 E
Kostromskoye Vdkhr., Russia 51 C12 57 52N 40 49 E
Kostrzyn, Gorzow Wlkp., Poland 47 C1 52 35N 14 39 E
Kostrzyn, Poznań, Poland 47 C4 52 24N 17 14 E
Kostyukovichi, Belorussia 50 E8 53 20N 32 4 E
Koszalin, Poland 47 A3 54 11N 16 8 E
Koszalin □, Poland 47 B3 53 40N 16 10 E
Kőszeg, Hungary 31 D9 47 23N 16 33 E
Kot Addu, Pakistan 79 C3 30 30N 71 0 E
Kot Moman, Pakistan 80 C5 32 13N 73 0 E
Kota, India 80 G6 25 14N 75 49 E
Kota Baharu, Malaysia 77 J4 6 7N 102 14 E
Kota Belud, Malaysia 75 A5 6 21N 116 26 E
Kota Kinabalu, Malaysia 75 A5 6 0N 116 4 E
Kota Tinggi, Malaysia 77 M4 1 44N 103 53 E
Kotaagung, Indonesia 74 D2 5 38 S 104 29 E
Kotabaru, Indonesia 75 C5 3 20 S 116 20 E
Kotabumi, Indonesia 74 C2 4 49 S 104 54 E
Kotagede, Indonesia 75 D4 7 54 S 110 26 E
Kotamobagu, Indonesia 72 A2 0 57N 124 31 E
Kotaneelee →, Canada 130 A4 60 11N 123 42W
Kotawaringin, Indonesia 75 C4 2 28 S 111 27 E
Kotchandpur, Bangla. 78 D2 23 24N 89 1 E
Kotcho L., Canada 130 B4 59 7N 121 12W
Kotel, Bulgaria 43 E11 42 52N 26 26 E
Kotelnich, Russia 51 B16 58 20N 48 10 E
Kotelnikovo, Russia 53 C10 47 38N 43 8 E
Kotelnyy, Ostrov, Russia 57 B14 75 10N 139 0 E
Kothagudam, India 82 F5 17 30N 80 40 E
Kothapet, India 82 E4 19 21N 79 28 E
Köthen, Germany 26 D7 51 44N 11 59 E
Kothi, India 81 G9 24 45N 80 40 E
Kotiro, Pakistan 80 F2 26 17N 67 13 E
Kotka, Finland 13 F19 60 28N 26 58 E
Kotlas, Russia 48 B8 61 15N 47 0 E
Kotlenska Planina, Bulgaria 43 E11 42 56N 26 30 E
Kotli, Pakistan 80 C5 33 30N 73 55 E
Kotmul, Pakistan 81 B6 35 32N 75 10 E
Kotohira, Japan 62 C5 34 11N 133 49 E
Kotonkoro, Nigeria 101 C6 11 3N 5 58 E
Kotor, Montenegro, Yug. 42 E3 42 25N 18 47 E
Kotor Varoš, Bos.-H., Yug. 42 C2 44 38N 17 22 E
Kotoriba, Croatia 39 B13 46 23N 16 48 E
Kotovo, Russia 51 F14 50 22N 44 45 E
Kotovsk, Ukraine 52 C3 47 45N 29 35 E
Kotputli, India 80 F7 27 43N 76 12 E
Kotri, Pakistan 79 D3 25 22N 68 22 E
Kotri →, India 82 E5 19 15N 80 35 E
Kótronas, Greece 45 H4 36 38N 22 29 E
Kötschach-Mauthen, Austria 30 E6 46 41N 13 1 E
Kottayam, India 83 K3 9 35N 76 33 E
Kottur, India 83 J3 10 34N 76 56 E
Kotuy →, Russia 57 B11 71 54N 102 6 E
Kotzebue, U.S.A. 126 B3 66 50N 162 40W
Kouango, C.A.R. 102 B4 5 0N 20 10 E
Koudekerke, Neths. 21 F3 51 29N 3 33 E
Koudougou, Burkina Faso 100 C4 12 10N 2 20W
Koufonísi, Greece 32 E8 34 56N 26 8 E
Koufonísia, Greece 45 H7 36 57N 25 35 E
Kougaberge, S. Africa 104 E3 33 48 S 23 50 E
Kouibli, Ivory C. 100 D3 7 15N 7 14W
Kouilou →, Congo 103 C2 4 10 S 12 5 E
Kouki, C.A.R. 102 A3 7 22N 17 3 E
Koula Moutou, Gabon 102 C2 1 15 S 12 25 E
Koulen, Cambodia 76 F5 13 50N 104 40 E
Koulikoro, Mali 100 C3 12 40N 7 50W
Kouloúra, Greece 32 A3 39 42N 19 54 E
Koúm-bournoú, Ákra, Greece 32 C10 36 15N 28 11 E
Koumac, N. Cal. 121 T18 20 33 S 164 17 E
Koumala, Australia 114 C4 21 38 S 149 15 E
Koumankou, Mali 100 C3 11 58N 6 6W
Koumbia, Burkina Faso 100 C4 11 10N 3 50W
Koumbia, Guinea 100 C2 11 48N 13 29W
Koumboum, Guinea 100 C2 10 25N 13 0W
Koumpenntoum, Senegal 100 C2 13 59N 14 34W
Koumra, Chad 97 G3 8 50N 17 35 E
Koundara, Guinea 100 C2 12 29N 13 18W
Koundé, C.A.R. 102 A2 6 7N 14 38 E
Kounradskiy, Kazakhstan 56 E8 46 59N 75 0 E
Kountze, U.S.A. 139 K7 30 20N 94 22W
Koupéla, Burkina Faso 101 C4 12 11N 0 21W
Kouris →, Cyprus 32 E11 34 38N 32 54 E
Kourizo, Passe de, Chad 96 D3 22 28N 15 27 E
Kourou, Fr. Guiana 153 B7 5 9N 52 39W
Kouroussa, Guinea 100 C3 10 45N 9 45W
Koussané, Mali 100 C2 14 53N 11 14W
Kousseri, Cameroon 97 F2 12 0N 14 55 E
Koutiala, Mali 100 C3 12 25N 5 23W
Kouto, Ivory C. 100 D3 9 53N 6 25W
Kouts, U.S.A. 141 C9 41 18N 87 2W
Kouvé, Togo 101 D5 6 25N 1 25 E
Kovačica, Serbia, Yug. 42 B5 45 5N 20 38 E
Kovdor, Russia 48 A5 67 34N 30 24 E
Kovel, Ukraine 50 F4 51 10N 24 20 E
Kovilpatti, India 83 K3 9 10N 77 50 E
Kovin, Serbia, Yug. 42 C5 44 44N 20 59 E
Kovrov, Russia 51 C12 56 25N 41 25 E
Kovur, Andhra Pradesh, India 82 F5 17 3N 81 39 E
Kovur, Andhra Pradesh, India 83 G5 14 30N 80 1 E
Kowal, Poland 47 C6 52 32N 19 7 E
Kowalewo Pomorskie, Poland 47 B5 53 10N 18 52 E
Kowanyama, Australia 114 B3 15 29 S 141 44 E
Kowghān, Afghan. 79 B1 34 12N 63 2 E
Kowkash, Canada 128 B2 50 20N 87 12W
Kowloon, H.K. 69 F10 22 20N 114 15 E
Kowŏn, N. Korea 67 E14 39 26N 127 14 E
Koyabuti, Indonesia 73 B6 2 36 S 140 37 E
Kōyama, Japan 62 F2 31 20N 130 56 E
Köyceğiz, Turkey 88 E3 36 57N 28 40 E
Koytash, Uzbekistan 55 C3 40 11N 67 19 E
Koyuk, U.S.A. 126 B3 64 55N 161 20W
Koyukuk →, U.S.A. 126 B4 64 56N 157 30W
Koyulhisar, Turkey 52 F7 40 20N 37 52 E
Koza, Japan 61 L3 26 19N 127 46 E
Kozan, Turkey 88 E6 37 26N 35 50 E
Kozáni, Greece 44 D3 40 19N 21 47 E
Kozáni □, Greece 44 D3 40 18N 21 45 E
Kozara, Bos.-H., Yug. 39 D14 45 0N 17 0 E
Kozarac, Bos.-H., Yug. 39 D13 44 58N 16 48 E
Kozelsk, Russia 50 D9 54 2N 35 48 E
Kozhikode = Calicut, India 83 J2 11 15N 75 43 E
Kozhva, Russia 48 A10 65 10N 57 0 E
Koziegłowy, Poland 47 E6 50 37N 19 8 E
Kozienice, Poland 47 D8 51 35N 21 34 E
Kozje, Slovenia 39 B12 46 5N 15 35 E
Kozle, Poland 47 E5 50 20N 18 8 E
Kozloduy, Bulgaria 43 D8 43 45N 23 42 E
Kozlovets, Bulgaria 43 D10 43 30N 25 20 E
Kozlu, Turkey 88 C4 41 26N 31 45 E
Kozluk, Turkey 89 D9 38 11N 41 31 E
Koźmin, Poland 47 D4 51 48N 17 27 E
Kozmodemyansk, Russia 51 C15 56 20N 46 36 E
Kōzu-Shima, Japan 63 C11 34 13N 139 10 E
Kozuchów, Poland 47 D2 51 45N 15 31 E
Kpabia, Ghana 101 D4 9 10N 0 20W
Kpalimé, Togo 101 D5 6 57N 0 44 E
Kpandae, Ghana 101 D4 8 30N 0 2W
Kpessi, Togo 101 D5 8 4N 1 16 E
Kra, Isthmus of = Kra, Kho Khot, Thailand 77 G2 10 15N 99 30 E
Kra, Kho Khot, Thailand 77 G2 10 15N 99 30 E
Kra Buri, Thailand 77 G2 10 22N 98 46 E
Krabbendijke, Neths. 21 F4 51 26N 4 7 E
Krabi, Thailand 77 H2 8 4N 98 55 E
Kragan, Indonesia 75 D4 6 43 S 111 38 E
Kragerø, Norway 14 F3 58 52N 9 25 E
Kragujevac, Serbia, Yug. 42 C5 44 2N 20 56 E
Krajenka, Poland 47 B3 53 18N 16 59 E
Krakatau = Rakata, Pulau, Indonesia 74 D3 6 10 S 105 20 E
Krakor, Cambodia 76 F5 12 32N 104 12 E
Kraków, Poland 31 A12 50 4N 19 57 E
Kraków □, Poland 31 A13 50 0N 20 0 E
Kraksaan, Indonesia 75 D4 7 43 S 113 23 E
Kråkstad, Norway 14 E4 59 39N 10 55 E
Kralanh, Cambodia 76 F4 13 35N 103 25 E
Králiky, Czech. 31 A9 50 6N 16 45 E
Kraljevo, Serbia, Yug. 42 D5 43 44N 20 41 E
Kralovice, Czech. 30 B6 49 59N 13 29 E
Královský Chlmec, Czech. 31 C14 48 27N 22 0 E
Kralupy, Czech. 30 A7 50 13N 14 20 E
Kramatorsk, Ukraine 52 B7 48 50N 37 30 E
Kramfors, Sweden 14 B11 62 55N 17 48 E
Kramis, C., Algeria 99 A5 36 26N 0 45 E
Krångede, Sweden 14 A10 63 9N 16 10 E
Kraniá, Greece 44 E3 39 53N 21 18 E
Kranídhion, Greece 45 G5 37 20N 23 10 E
Kranj, Slovenia 39 B11 46 16N 14 22 E
Kranjska Gora, Slovenia 39 B10 46 29N 13 48 E
Krankskop, S. Africa 105 D5 28 0 S 30 47 E
Krapina, Croatia 39 B12 46 10N 15 52 E
Krapina →, Croatia 39 C12 45 50N 15 50 E
Krapivna, Russia 51 D10 53 58N 37 10 E
Krapkowice, Poland 47 E4 50 29N 17 56 E
Krasavino, Russia 48 B8 60 58N 46 29 E
Krashyy Klyuch, Russia 54 D5 55 23N 56 39 E
Kraskino, Russia 57 E14 42 44N 130 48 E
Kraslice, Czech. 30 A5 50 19N 12 31 E
Krasnaya Gorbatka, Russia 51 D12 55 52N 41 45 E
Krasnaya Polyana, Russia 53 E9 43 40N 40 13 E
Kraśnik, Poland 47 E9 50 55N 22 5 E
Kraśnik Fabryczny, Poland 47 E9 50 58N 22 11 E
Krasnoarmeisk, Ukraine 52 B7 48 18N 37 11 E
Krasnoarmeysk, Russia 51 F14 51 0N 45 42 E
Krasnoarmeysk, Russia 53 B11 48 30N 44 25 E
Krasnodar, Russia 53 D8 45 5N 39 0 E
Krasnodon, Ukraine 53 B8 48 17N 39 44 E
Krasnodonetskaya, Russia 53 B9 48 5N 40 50 E
Krasnogorskiy, Russia 51 C16 56 10N 48 28 E
Krasnograd, Ukraine 52 B6 49 27N 35 27 E
Krasnogvardeysk, Uzbekistan 55 D3 39 46N 67 16 E
Krasnogvardeyskoye, Russia 53 D9 45 52N 41 33 E
Krasnogvardyesk, Ukraine 52 D6 45 32N 34 16 E
Krasnokamsk, Russia 54 B4 58 4N 55 48 E
Krasnokutsk, Ukraine 50 F9 50 10N 34 50 E
Krasnoperekopsk, Ukraine 52 D5 46 0N 33 54 E
Krasnorechenskiy, Russia 60 B7 44 41N 135 14 E
Krasnoselkupsk, Russia 56 C9 65 20N 82 10 E
Krasnoslobodsk, Russia 51 D13 54 25N 43 45 E
Krasnoslobodsk, Russia 53 B11 48 42N 44 33 E
Krasnoturinsk, Russia 54 B7 59 46N 60 12 E
Krasnoufimsk, Russia 54 C5 56 57N 57 46 E
Krasnouralsk, Russia 54 B7 58 21N 60 3 E
Krasnousolskiy, Russia 54 E5 53 54N 56 27 E
Krasnovishersk, Russia 54 A5 60 23N 57 3 E
Krasnovodsk, Turkmenistan 49 F9 40 0N 52 52 E
Krasnoyarsk, Russia 57 D10 56 8N 93 0 E
Krasnoyarskiy, Russia 54 F6 51 58N 59 55 E
Krasnoye = Krasnyy, Russia 50 D7 54 25N 31 30 E
Krasnoye, Russia 51 B15 59 15N 47 40 E
Krasnoye, Russia 53 C11 46 16N 45 0 E
Krasnozavodsk, Russia 51 C11 56 27N 38 25 E
Krasny Liman, Ukraine 52 B7 48 58N 37 50 E
Krasny Sulin, Russia 53 C9 47 52N 40 8 E
Krasnystaw, Poland 47 E10 50 57N 23 5 E
Krasnyy, Russia 50 D7 54 25N 31 30 E
Krasnyy Kholm, Russia 51 B10 58 10N 37 10 E
Krasnyy Kholm, Russia 54 F4 51 35N 54 9 E
Krasnyy Kut, Russia 51 F15 50 50N 47 0 E
Krasnyy Luch, Ukraine 53 B8 48 13N 39 0 E
Krasnyy Profintern, Russia 51 C12 57 45N 40 27 E
Krasnyy Yar, Russia 51 F14 50 42N 44 45 E
Krasnyy Yar, Russia 53 C13 46 43N 48 23 E
Krasnyy Yar, Russia 54 E2 53 30N 50 22 E
Krasnyye Baki, Russia 51 C14 57 8N 45 10 E
Krasnyyoskolskoye Vdkhr., Ukraine 52 B7 49 30N 37 30 E
Kraszna →, Hungary 31 C15 48 4N 22 20 E
Kratie, Cambodia 76 F6 12 32N 106 10 E
Kratke Ra., Papua N. G. 120 D3 6 45 S 146 0 E
Kratovo, Macedonia, Yug. 42 E7 42 6N 22 10 E
Krau, Indonesia 73 B6 3 19 S 140 5 E
Kravanh, Chuor Phnum, Cambodia 77 G4 12 0N 103 32 E
Krefeld, Germany 26 D2 51 20N 6 32 E
Krémaston, Límni, Greece 45 F3 38 52N 21 30 E
Kremenchug, Ukraine 52 B5 49 5N 33 25 E
Kremenchugskoye Vdkhr., Ukraine 52 B5 49 20N 32 30 E
Kremenets, Ukraine 52 A1 50 8N 25 43 E
Kremenica, Macedonia, Yug. 44 D3 40 55N 21 25 E
Kremennaya, Ukraine 52 B8 49 1N 38 10 E
Kremges = Svetlovodsk, Ukraine 50 G8 49 2N 33 13 E
Kremikovtsi, Bulgaria 43 E8 42 46N 23 28 E
Kremmen, Germany 26 C9 52 45N 13 1 E
Kremmling, U.S.A. 142 F10 40 10N 106 30W
Kremnica, Czech. 31 C11 48 45N 18 50 E
Krems, Austria 30 C8 48 25N 15 36 E
Kremsmünster, Austria 30 C7 48 3N 14 8 E
Kretinga, Lithuania 50 D2 55 53N 21 15 E
Krettamia, Algeria 98 C4 28 47N 3 27W
Krettsy, Russia 50 B8 58 15N 32 30 E
Kreuzberg, Germany 27 E5 50 22N 9 58 E
Kreuzlingen, Switz. 29 A8 47 38N 9 10 E
Kribi, Cameroon 101 E6 2 57N 9 56 E
Krichem, Bulgaria 43 E9 42 8N 24 28 E
Krichev, Belorussia 50 E7 53 45N 31 50 E

Laghmān 221


Kwangju, *S. Korea* 67 **G14** 35 9N 126 54 E
Kwango →, *Zaïre* 102 **C3** 3 14 S 17 22 E
Kwangsi-Chuang = Guangxi Zhuangzu Zizhiqu □, *China* 68 **E7** 24 0N 109 0 E
Kwangtung = Guangdong □, *China* 69 **F9** 23 0N 113 0 E
Kwara □, *Nigeria* 101 **D5** 8 0N 5 0 E
Kwataboahegan →, *Canada* 128 **B3** 51 9N 80 50W
Kwatisore, *Indonesia* 73 **B4** 3 18 S 134 50 E
Kweichow = Guizhou □, *China* 68 **D6** 27 0N 107 0 E
Kwekwe, *Zimbabwe* 107 **F2** 18 58 S 29 48 E
Kwidzyn, *Poland* 47 **B5** 53 44N 18 55 E
Kwikila, *Papua N. G.* 120 **E4** 9 49 S 147 38 E
Kwimba □, *Tanzania* 106 **C3** 3 0 S 33 0 E
Kwinana New Town, *Australia* 113 **F2** 32 15 S 115 47 E
Kwisa →, *Poland* 47 **D2** 51 34N 15 24 E
Kwoka, *Indonesia* 73 **B4** 0 31 S 132 27 E
Kya-in-Seikkyi, *Burma* 78 **G7** 16 2N 98 8 E
Kyabé, *Chad* 97 **G3** 9 30N 19 0 E
Kyabra Cr. →, *Australia* 115 **D3** 25 36 S 142 55 E
Kyabram, *Australia* 115 **F4** 36 19 S 145 4 E
Kyaiklat, *Burma* 78 **G5** 16 25N 95 40 E
Kyaikmaraw, *Burma* 78 **G6** 16 23N 97 44 E
Kyaikthin, *Burma* 78 **D5** 23 32N 95 40 E
Kyaikto, *Burma* 76 **D1** 17 20N 97 3 E
Kyakhta, *Russia* 57 **D11** 50 30N 106 25 E
Kyancutta, *Australia* 115 **E2** 33 8 S 135 33 E
Kyangin, *Burma* 78 **F5** 18 20N 95 20 E
Kyaukhnyat, *Burma* 78 **F6** 18 15N 97 31 E
Kyaukse, *Burma* 78 **E6** 21 36N 96 10 E
Kyauktaw, *Burma* 78 **E4** 20 51N 92 59 E
Kyawkku, *Burma* 78 **E6** 21 48N 96 56 E
Kyburz, *U.S.A.* 144 **G6** 38 47N 120 18W
Kybybolite, *Australia* 116 **D4** 36 53 S 140 55 E
Kycen, *Russia* 57 **D11** 51 45N 101 45 E
Kyeintali, *Burma* 78 **G5** 18 0N 94 29 E
Kyenjojo, *Uganda* 106 **B3** 0 40N 30 37 E
Kyidaunggan, *Burma* 78 **F6** 19 53N 96 12 E
Kyle Dam, *Zimbabwe* 107 **G3** 20 15 S 31 0 E
Kyle of Lochalsh, *U.K.* 18 **D3** 57 17N 5 43W
Kyll →, *Germany* 27 **F2** 49 48N 6 42 E
Kyllburg, *Germany* 27 **E2** 50 2N 6 35 E
Kyneton, *Australia* 116 **D6** 37 10 S 144 29 E
Kynuna, *Australia* 114 **C3** 21 37 S 141 55 E
Kyō-ga-Saki, *Japan* 63 **B7** 35 45N 135 15 E
Kyoga, L., *Uganda* 106 **B3** 1 35N 33 0 E
Kyogle, *Australia* 115 **D5** 28 40 S 153 0 E
Kyongju, *S. Korea* 67 **G15** 35 51N 129 14 E
Kyŏngsŏng, *N. Korea* 67 **D15** 41 35N 129 36 E
Kyōto, *Japan* 63 **B7** 35 0N 135 45 E
Kyōto □, *Japan* 63 **B7** 35 15N 135 45 E
Kyparissovouno, *Cyprus* 32 **D12** 35 19N 33 10 E
Kyperounda, *Cyprus* 32 **E11** 34 56N 32 58 E
Kyrenia, *Cyprus* 32 **D12** 35 20N 33 20 E
Kyritz, *Germany* 26 **C8** 52 57N 12 25 E
Kyshtym, *Russia* 54 **D7** 55 42N 60 34 E
Kystatyam, *Russia* 57 **C13** 67 20N 123 10 E
Kytal Ktakh, *Russia* 57 **C13** 65 30N 123 40 E
Kythréa, *Cyprus* 32 **D12** 35 15N 33 29 E
Kytlym, *Russia* 54 **B6** 59 30N 59 12 E
Kyu-hkok, *Burma* 78 **C7** 24 4N 98 4 E
Kyulyunken, *Russia* 57 **C14** 64 10N 137 5 E
Kyunhla, *Burma* 78 **D5** 23 25N 95 15 E
Kyuquot, *Canada* 130 **C3** 50 3N 127 25W
Kyurdamir, *Azerbaijan* 53 **F13** 40 25N 48 3 E
Kyūshū, *Japan* 62 **E3** 33 0N 131 0 E
Kyūshū □, *Japan* 62 **E3** 33 0N 131 0 E
Kyūshū-Sanchi, *Japan* 62 **E3** 32 35N 131 17 E
Kyustendil, *Bulgaria* 42 **E7** 42 16N 22 41 E
Kyusyur, *Russia* 57 **B13** 70 19N 127 30 E
Kywong, *Australia* 117 **C7** 34 58 S 146 44 E
Kyzyl, *Russia* 57 **D10** 51 50N 94 30 E
Kyzyl-Kiya, *Kirghizia* 55 **C6** 40 16N 72 8 E
Kyzylkum, Peski, *Uzbekistan* 55 **B2** 42 30N 65 0 E
Kyzylsu →, *Kirghizia* 55 **D6** 38 50N 70 0 E
Kzyl-Orda, *Kazakhstan* 55 **A2** 44 48N 65 28 E


# L


La Albuera, *Spain* 37 **G4** 38 45N 6 49W
La Alcarria, *Spain* 34 **E2** 40 31N 2 45W
La Algaba, *Spain* 37 **H4** 37 27N 6 1W
La Almarcha, *Spain* 34 **F2** 39 41N 2 24W
La Almunia de Doña Godina, *Spain* 34 **D3** 41 29N 1 23W
La Asunción, *Venezuela* 153 **A5** 11 2N 63 53W
La Banda, *Argentina* 158 **B3** 27 45 S 64 10W
La Bañeza, *Spain* 36 **C5** 42 17N 5 54W
La Barca, *Mexico* 146 **C4** 20 20N 102 40W
La Barge, *U.S.A.* 142 **E8** 42 12N 110 4W
La Bassée, *France* 23 **B9** 50 31N 2 49 E
La Bastide-Puylaurent, *France* 24 **D7** 44 35N 3 55 E
La Baule, *France* 22 **E4** 47 17N 2 24W
La Belle, *Fla., U.S.A.* 135 **M5** 26 45N 81 22W
La Belle, *Mo., U.S.A.* 140 **D5** 40 7N 91 55W
La Biche →, *Canada* 130 **B4** 59 57N 123 50W
La Bisbal, *Spain* 34 **D8** 41 58N 3 2 E
La Blanquilla, *Venezuela* 153 **A5** 11 51N 64 37W
La Bomba, *Mexico* 146 **A1** 31 53N 115 2W
La Bresse, *France* 23 **D13** 48 2N 6 53 E
La Bureba, *Spain* 34 **C1** 42 36N 3 24W
La Cal →, *Bolivia* 157 **D6** 17 27 S 58 15W
La Calera, *Chile* 158 **C1** 32 50 S 71 10W
La Campiña, *Spain* 37 **H6** 37 45N 4 45W
La Canal, *Spain* 33 **C7** 38 51N 1 23 E
La Cañiza, *Spain* 36 **C2** 42 13N 8 16W
La Capelle, *France* 23 **C10** 49 59N 3 50 E
La Carlota, *Argentina* 158 **C3** 33 30 S 63 20W
La Carlota, *Phil.* 71 **F4** 10 25N 122 55 E
La Carolina, *Spain* 37 **G7** 38 17N 3 38W
La Castellana, *Phil.* 71 **F4** 10 20N 123 3 E
La Cavalerie, *France* 24 **D7** 44 1N 3 10 E
La Ceiba, *Honduras* 148 **C2** 15 40N 86 50W
La Chaise-Dieu, *France* 24 **C7** 45 18N 3 42 E
La Chaize-le-Vicomte, *France* 22 **F5** 46 40N 1 18W
La Chapelle d'Angillon, *France* 23 **E9** 47 21N 2 25 E
La Chapelle-Glain, *France* 22 **E5** 47 38N 1 11W
La Charité-sur-Loire, *France* 23 **E10** 47 10N 3 1 E
La Chartre-sur-le-Loir, *France* 22 **E7** 47 44N 0 34 E
La Châtaigneraie, *France* 24 **B3** 46 39N 0 44W
La Châtre, *France* 24 **B5** 46 35N 2 0 E
La Chaux de Fonds, *Switz.* 28 **B3** 47 7N 6 50 E
La Chorrera, *Colombia* 152 **D3** 0 44 S 73 1W
La Ciotat, *France* 25 **E9** 43 10N 5 37 E
La Clayette, *France* 25 **B8** 46 17N 4 19 E
La Cocha, *Argentina* 158 **B2** 27 50 S 65 40W
La Concepción = Ri-Aba, *Eq. Guin.* 101 **E6** 3 28N 8 40 E
La Concepción, *Venezuela* 152 **A3** 10 30N 71 50W
La Concordia, *Mexico* 147 **D6** 16 8N 92 38W
La Conner, *U.S.A.* 142 **B2** 48 22N 122 27W
La Coruña, *Spain* 36 **B2** 43 20N 8 25W
La Coruña □, *Spain* 36 **B2** 43 10N 8 30W
La Côte, *Switz.* 28 **D2** 46 25N 6 15 E
La Côte-St.-André, *France* 25 **C9** 45 24N 5 15 E
La Courtine-le-Trucq, *France* 24 **C6** 45 41N 2 15 E
La Crau, *France* 25 **E8** 43 32N 4 40 E
La Crete, *Canada* 130 **B5** 58 11N 116 24W
La Crosse, *Kans., U.S.A.* 138 **F5** 38 33N 99 20W
La Crosse, *Wis., U.S.A.* 138 **D9** 43 48N 91 13W
La Cruz, *Costa Rica* 148 **D2** 11 4N 85 39W
La Cruz, *Mexico* 146 **C3** 23 55N 106 54W
La Dorada, *Colombia* 152 **B3** 5 30N 74 40W
La Ensenada, *Chile* 160 **B2** 41 12 S 72 33W
La Escondida, *Mexico* 146 **C5** 24 6N 99 55W
La Esmeralda, *Paraguay* 158 **A3** 22 16 S 62 33W
La Esperanza, *Argentina* 160 **B3** 40 26 S 68 32W
La Esperanza, *Cuba* 148 **B3** 22 46N 83 44W
La Esperanza, *Honduras* 148 **D2** 14 15N 88 10W
La Estrada, *Spain* 36 **C2** 42 43N 8 27W
La Fayette, *U.S.A.* 135 **H3** 34 44N 85 15W
La Fé, *Cuba* 148 **B3** 22 2N 84 15W
La Fère, *France* 23 **C10** 49 39N 3 21 E
La Ferté-Bernard, *France* 22 **D7** 48 10N 0 40 E
La Ferté-Macé, *France* 22 **D6** 48 35N 0 22W
La Ferté-St.-Aubin, *France* 23 **E8** 47 42N 1 57 E
La Ferté-sous-Jouarre, *France* 23 **D10** 48 56N 3 8 E
La Ferté-Vidame, *France* 22 **D7** 48 37N 0 53 E
La Flèche, *France* 22 **E6** 47 42N 0 4W
La Foa, *N. Cal.* 121 **U19** 21 43 S 165 50 E
La Follette, *U.S.A.* 135 **G3** 36 23N 84 9W
La Fontaine, *U.S.A.* 141 **D11** 40 40N 85 43W
La Fregeneda, *Spain* 36 **E4** 40 58N 6 54W
La Fría, *Venezuela* 152 **B3** 8 13N 72 15W
La Fuente de San Esteban, *Spain* 36 **E4** 40 49N 6 15W
La Gineta, *Spain* 35 **F2** 39 8N 2 1W
La Gloria, *Colombia* 152 **B3** 8 37N 73 48W
La Gran Sabana, *Venezuela* 153 **B5** 5 30N 61 30W
La Grand-Combe, *France* 25 **D8** 44 13N 4 2 E
La Grande, *U.S.A.* 142 **D4** 45 15N 118 10W
La Grande-Motte, *France* 25 **E8** 43 23N 4 5 E
La Grange, *U.S.A.* 144 **H6** 37 42N 120 27W
La Grange, *Ga., U.S.A.* 135 **J3** 33 4N 85 0W
La Grange, *Ky., U.S.A.* 134 **F3** 38 20N 85 20W
La Grange, *Mo., U.S.A.* 140 **D5** 40 3N 91 35W
La Grange, *Tex., U.S.A.* 139 **L6** 29 54N 96 52W
La Grita, *Venezuela* 152 **B3** 8 8N 71 59W
La Guaira, *Venezuela* 152 **A4** 10 36N 66 56W
La Guardia, *Spain* 36 **D2** 41 56N 8 52W
La Gudiña, *Spain* 36 **C3** 42 4N 7 8W
La Güera, *Mauritania* 98 **D1** 20 51N 17 0W
La Guerche-de-Bretagne, *France* 22 **E5** 47 57N 1 16W
La Guerche-sur-l'Aubois, *France* 23 **F9** 46 58N 2 56 E
La Habana, *Cuba* 148 **B3** 23 8N 82 22W
La Harpe, *U.S.A.* 140 **D6** 40 30N 91 0W
La Haye-du-Puits, *France* 22 **C5** 49 17N 1 33W
La Horqueta, *Venezuela* 153 **B5** 7 55N 60 20W
La Horra, *Spain* 36 **D7** 41 44N 3 53W
La Independencia, *Mexico* 147 **D6** 16 31N 91 47W
La Isabela, *Dom. Rep.* 149 **C5** 19 58N 71 2W
La Jara, *U.S.A.* 143 **H11** 37 16N 106 0W
La Joya, *Peru* 156 **D3** 16 43 S 71 52W
La Junquera, *Spain* 34 **C7** 42 25N 2 53 E
La Junta, *U.S.A.* 139 **F3** 38 5N 103 30W
La Laguna, *Canary Is.* 33 **F3** 28 28N 16 18W
La Libertad, *Guatemala* 148 **C1** 16 47N 90 7W
La Libertad, *Mexico* 146 **B2** 29 55N 112 41W
La Libertad □, *Peru* 156 **B2** 8 0 S 78 30W
La Ligua, *Chile* 158 **C1** 32 30 S 71 16W
La Línea de la Concepción, *Spain* 37 **J5** 36 15N 5 23W
La Loche, *Canada* 131 **B7** 56 29N 109 26W
La Londe-les-Maures, *France* 25 **E10** 43 8N 6 14 E
La Lora, *Spain* 36 **C7** 42 45N 4 0W
La Loupe, *France* 22 **D8** 48 29N 1 1 E
La Louvière, *Belgium* 21 **H4** 50 27N 4 10 E
La Machine, *France* 23 **F10** 46 54N 3 27 E
La Maddalena, *Italy* 40 **A2** 41 13N 9 25 E
La Malbaie, *Canada* 129 **C5** 47 40N 70 10W
La Mancha, *Spain* 35 **F2** 39 10N 2 54W
La Mariña, *Spain* 36 **B3** 43 30N 7 40W
La Mesa, *Calif., U.S.A.* 145 **N9** 32 48N 117 5W
La Mesa, *N. Mex., U.S.A.* 143 **K10** 32 6N 106 48W
La Misión, *Mexico* 146 **A1** 32 5N 116 50W
La Moille, *U.S.A.* 140 **C7** 41 32N 89 17W
La Moine →, *U.S.A.* 140 **E6** 39 58N 90 32W
La Monte, *U.S.A.* 140 **F3** 38 47N 93 27W
La Mothe-Achard, *France* 22 **F5** 46 37N 1 40W
La Motte, *France* 25 **D10** 44 20N 6 3 E
La Motte-Chalançon, *France* 25 **D9** 44 30N 5 21 E
La Moure, *U.S.A.* 138 **B5** 46 27N 98 17W
La Muela, *Spain* 34 **D3** 41 36N 1 7W
La Mure, *France* 25 **D9** 44 55N 5 48 E
La Negra, *Chile* 158 **A1** 23 46 S 70 18W
La Neuveville, *Switz.* 28 **B4** 47 4N 7 6 E
La Oliva, *Canary Is.* 33 **F6** 28 36N 13 57W
La Oraya, *Peru* 156 **C2** 11 32 S 75 54W
La Orotava, *Canary Is.* 33 **F3** 28 22N 16 31W
La Pacaudière, *France* 24 **B7** 46 11N 3 52 E
La Palma, *Canary Is.* 33 **F2** 28 40N 17 50W
La Palma, *Panama* 148 **E4** 8 15N 78 0W
La Palma, *Spain* 37 **H4** 37 21N 6 38W
La Paloma, *Chile* 158 **C1** 30 35 S 71 0W
La Pampa □, *Argentina* 158 **D2** 36 50 S 66 0W
La Paragua, *Venezuela* 153 **B5** 6 50N 63 20W
La Paz, *Entre Ríos, Argentina* 158 **C4** 30 50 S 59 45W
La Paz, *San Luis, Argentina* 158 **C2** 33 30 S 67 20W
La Paz, *Bolivia* 156 **D4** 16 20 S 68 10W
La Paz, *Honduras* 148 **D2** 14 20N 87 47W
La Paz, *Mexico* 146 **C2** 24 10N 110 20W
La Paz, *Phil.* 70 **D3** 15 26N 120 45 E
La Paz □, *Bolivia* 156 **D4** 15 30 S 68 0W
La Paz Centro, *Nic.* 148 **D2** 12 20N 86 41W
La Pedrera, *Colombia* 152 **D4** 1 18 S 69 43W
La Perouse Str., *Asia* 60 **B11** 45 40N 142 0 E
La Pesca, *Mexico* 147 **C5** 23 46N 97 47W
La Piedad, *Mexico* 146 **C4** 20 20N 102 1W
La Pine, *U.S.A.* 142 **E3** 43 40N 121 30W
La Plant, *U.S.A.* 138 **C4** 45 11N 100 40W
La Plata, *Argentina* 158 **D4** 35 0 S 57 55W
La Plata, *Colombia* 152 **C2** 2 23N 75 53W
La Plata, *U.S.A.* 140 **D4** 40 2N 92 29W
La Plata, L., *Argentina* 160 **B2** 44 55 S 71 50W
La Pobla de Lillet, *Spain* 34 **C6** 42 16N 1 59 E
La Pola de Gordón, *Spain* 36 **C5** 42 51N 5 41W
La Porte, *U.S.A.* 141 **C10** 41 36N 86 43W
La Porte City, *U.S.A.* 140 **B4** 42 19N 92 12W
La Puebla, *Spain* 34 **F8** 39 46N 3 1 E
La Puebla de Cazalla, *Spain* 37 **H5** 37 10N 5 20W
La Puebla de los Infantes, *Spain* 37 **H5** 37 47N 5 24W
La Puebla de Montalbán, *Spain* 36 **F6** 39 52N 4 22W
La Puerta, *Spain* 35 **G2** 38 22N 2 45W
La Punt, *Switz.* 29 **C9** 46 35N 9 56 E
La Purísima, *Mexico* 146 **B2** 26 10N 112 4W
La Push, *U.S.A.* 144 **C2** 47 55N 124 38W
La Quiaca, *Argentina* 158 **A2** 22 5 S 65 35W
La Rambla, *Spain* 37 **H6** 37 37N 4 45W
La Reine, *Canada* 128 **C4** 48 50N 79 30W
La Réole, *France* 24 **D3** 44 35N 0 1W
La Restinga, *Canary Is.* 33 **G2** 27 38N 17 59W
La Rioja, *Argentina* 158 **B2** 29 20 S 67 0W
La Rioja □, *Argentina* 158 **B2** 29 30 S 67 0W
La Rioja □, *Spain* 34 **C2** 42 20N 2 20W
La Robla, *Spain* 36 **C5** 42 50N 5 41W
La Roche, *Switz.* 28 **C4** 46 42N 7 7 E
La Roche-Bernard, *France* 22 **E4** 47 31N 2 19W
La Roche-Canillac, *France* 24 **C5** 45 12N 1 57 E
La Roche-en-Ardenne, *Belgium* 21 **H7** 50 11N 5 35 E
La Roche-sur-Yon, *France* 22 **F5** 46 40N 1 25W
La Rochefoucauld, *France* 24 **C4** 45 44N 0 24 E
La Rochelle, *France* 24 **B2** 46 10N 1 9W
La Roda, *Albacete, Spain* 35 **F2** 39 13N 2 15W
La Roda, *Sevilla, Spain* 37 **H6** 37 12N 4 46W
La Romana, *Dom. Rep.* 149 **C6** 18 27N 68 57W
La Ronge, *Canada* 131 **B7** 55 5N 105 20W
La Rue, *U.S.A.* 141 **D13** 40 35N 83 23W
La Rumorosa, *Mexico* 145 **N10** 32 33N 116 4W
La Sabina, *Spain* 33 **C7** 38 44N 1 25 E
La Sagra, *Spain* 35 **H2** 37 57N 2 35W
La Salle, *U.S.A.* 140 **C7** 41 20N 89 6W
La Sanabria, *Spain* 36 **C4** 42 0N 6 30W
La Santa, *Canary Is.* 33 **E6** 29 5N 13 40W
La Sarraz, *Switz.* 28 **C3** 46 38N 6 32 E
La Sarre, *Canada* 128 **C4** 48 45N 79 15W
La Scie, *Canada* 129 **C8** 49 57N 55 36W
La Selva, *Spain* 34 **D7** 42 0N 2 45 E
La Selva Beach, *U.S.A.* 144 **J5** 36 56N 121 51W
La Serena, *Chile* 158 **B1** 29 55 S 71 10W
La Serena, *Spain* 37 **G5** 38 45N 5 40W
La Seyne, *France* 25 **E9** 43 7N 5 52 E
La Sila, *Italy* 41 **C9** 39 15N 16 35 E
La Solana, *Spain* 35 **G1** 38 59N 3 14W
La Souterraine, *France* 24 **B5** 46 15N 1 30 E
La Spézia, *Italy* 38 **D6** 44 8N 9 50 E
La Suze-sur-Sarthe, *France* 22 **E7** 47 53N 0 2 E
La Tagua, *Colombia* 152 **C3** 0 3N 74 40W
La Teste, *France* 24 **D2** 44 37N 1 8W
La Tortuga, *Venezuela* 149 **D6** 11 0N 65 22W
La Tour-du-Pin, *France* 25 **C9** 45 33N 5 27 E
La Tranche-sur-Mer, *France* 22 **F5** 46 20N 1 27W
La Tremblade, *France* 24 **C2** 45 46N 1 8W
La Trinidad, *Phil.* 70 **C3** 16 28N 120 35 E
La Tuque, *Canada* 128 **C5** 47 30N 72 50W
La Unión, *Chile* 160 **B2** 40 10 S 73 0W
La Unión, *Colombia* 152 **C2** 1 35N 77 5W
La Unión, *El Salv.* 148 **D2** 13 20N 87 50W
La Unión, *Mexico* 146 **D4** 17 58N 101 49W
La Unión, *Peru* 156 **B2** 9 43 S 76 45W
La Unión, *Spain* 35 **H4** 37 38N 0 53W
La Union □, *Phil.* 70 **C3** 16 30N 120 25 E
La Urbana, *Venezuela* 152 **B4** 7 8N 66 56W
La Vecilla, *Spain* 36 **C5** 42 51N 5 27W
La Vega, *Dom. Rep.* 149 **C5** 19 20N 70 30W
La Vega, *Peru* 156 **C2** 10 41 S 77 44W
La Vela, *Venezuela* 152 **A4** 11 27N 69 34W
La Veleta, *Spain* 37 **H7** 37 1N 3 22W
La Venta, *Mexico* 147 **D6** 18 8N 94 3W
La Ventura, *Mexico* 146 **C4** 24 38N 100 54W
La Venturosa, *Colombia* 152 **B4** 6 8N 68 48W
La Victoria, *Venezuela* 152 **A4** 10 14N 67 20W
La Voulte-sur-Rhône, *France* 25 **D8** 44 48N 4 46 E
La Zarza, *Spain* 37 **H4** 37 42N 6 51W
Laa, *Austria* 31 **C9** 48 43N 16 23 E
Laaber →, *Germany* 27 **G8** 48 55N 12 30 E
Laage, *Germany* 26 **B8** 53 55N 12 21 E
Laba →, *Russia* 53 **D8** 45 11N 39 42 E
Laban, *Burma* 78 **C6** 25 52N 96 40 E
Labason, *Phil.* 71 **G4** 8 4N 122 31 E
Labastide-Murat, *France* 24 **D5** 44 39N 1 33 E
Labastide-Rouairoux, *France* 24 **E6** 43 28N 2 39 E
Labbézenga, *Mali* 101 **B5** 15 2N 0 48 E
Labdah = Leptis Magna, *Libya* 96 **B2** 32 40N 14 12 E
Labe = Elbe →, *Europe* 26 **B4** 53 50N 9 0 E
Labé, *Guinea* 100 **C2** 11 24N 12 16W
Laberec →, *Czech.* 31 **C14** 48 37N 21 58 E
Laberge, L., *Canada* 130 **A1** 61 11N 135 12W
Labian, Tanjong, *Malaysia* 75 **A5** 5 9N 119 13 E
Labig Pt., *Phil.* 70 **B4** 18 25N 122 25 E
Labin, *Croatia* 39 **C11** 45 5N 14 8 E
Labinsk, *Russia* 53 **D9** 44 40N 40 48 E
Labis, *Malaysia* 77 **L4** 2 22N 103 2 E
Labiszyn, *Poland* 47 **C4** 52 57N 17 54 E
Labo, *Phil.* 70 **D4** 14 9N 122 51 E
Laboe, *Germany* 26 **A6** 54 25N 10 13 E
Laboka, *Gabon* 102 **B2** 0 19N 11 32 E
Labouheyre, *France* 24 **D3** 44 13N 0 55W
Laboulaye, *Argentina* 158 **C3** 34 10 S 63 30W
Labra, Peña, *Spain* 36 **B6** 43 3N 4 26W
Labrador, Coast of □, *Canada* 129 **B7** 53 20N 61 0W
Labrador City, *Canada* 129 **B6** 52 57N 66 55W
Lábrea, *Brazil* 157 **B5** 7 15 S 64 51W
Labrède, *France* 24 **D3** 44 41N 0 32W
Labuan, Pulau, *Malaysia* 75 **A5** 5 21N 115 13 E
Labuha, *Indonesia* 72 **B3** 0 30 S 127 30 E
Labuhan, *Indonesia* 74 **D3** 6 22 S 105 50 E
Labuhanbajo, *Indonesia* 72 **C2** 8 28 S 120 1 E
Labuissière, *Belgium* 21 **H4** 50 19N 4 11 E
Labuk, Telok, *Malaysia* 75 **A5** 6 10N 117 50 E
Labutta, *Burma* 78 **G5** 16 9N 94 46 E
Labyrinth, L., *Australia* 115 **E2** 30 40 S 135 11 E
Labytnangi, *Russia* 48 **A12** 66 39N 66 21 E
Łabżenica, *Poland* 47 **B4** 53 18N 17 15 E
Lac Allard, *Canada* 129 **B7** 50 33N 63 24W
Lac Bouchette, *Canada* 129 **C5** 48 16N 72 11W
Lac du Flambeau, *U.S.A.* 138 **B10** 46 1N 89 51W
Lac Édouard, *Canada* 128 **C5** 47 40N 72 16W
Lac La Biche, *Canada* 130 **C6** 54 45N 111 58W
Lac la Martre, *Canada* 126 **B8** 63 8N 117 16W
Lac-Mégantic, *Canada* 129 **C5** 45 35N 70 53W
Lac Seul, Res., *Canada* 128 **B1** 50 25N 92 30W
Lac Thien, *Vietnam* 76 **F7** 12 25N 108 11 E
Lacanau, *France* 24 **D2** 44 58N 1 5W
Lacanau, Étang de, *France* 24 **D2** 44 58N 1 7W
Lacantúm →, *Mexico* 147 **D6** 16 36N 90 40W
Lacara →, *Spain* 37 **G4** 38 55N 6 25W
Lacaune, *France* 24 **E6** 43 43N 2 40 E
Lacaune, Mts. de, *France* 24 **E6** 43 43N 2 50 E
Laccadive Is. = Lakshadweep Is., *Ind. Oc.* 58 **J11** 10 0N 72 30 E
Lacepede B., *Australia* 116 **D3** 36 40 S 139 40 E
Lacepede Is., *Australia* 112 **C3** 16 55 S 122 0 E
Lacerdónia, *Mozam.* 107 **F4** 18 3 S 35 35 E
Lacey, *U.S.A.* 144 **C4** 47 7N 122 49W
Lachay, Pta., *Peru* 156 **C2** 11 17 S 77 44W
Lachen, *India* 78 **B2** 27 46N 88 36 E
Lachen, *Switz.* 29 **B7** 47 12N 8 51 E
Lachhmangarh, *India* 80 **F6** 27 50N 75 4 E
Lachi, *Pakistan* 80 **C4** 33 25N 71 20 E
Lachine, *Canada* 128 **C5** 45 30N 73 40W
Lachlan →, *Australia* 116 **C5** 34 22 S 143 55 E
Lachute, *Canada* 128 **C5** 45 39N 74 21W
Lackawanna, *U.S.A.* 136 **D6** 42 49N 78 50W
Lacolle, *Canada* 137 **A11** 45 5N 73 22W
Lacombe, *Canada* 130 **C6** 52 30N 113 44W
Lacon, *U.S.A.* 140 **C7** 41 2N 89 24W
Lacona, *Iowa, U.S.A.* 140 **C3** 41 11N 93 23W
Lacona, *N.Y., U.S.A.* 137 **C8** 43 37N 76 5W
Láconi, *Italy* 40 **C2** 39 54N 9 4 E
Laconia, *U.S.A.* 137 **C13** 43 32N 71 30W
Lacq, *France* 24 **E3** 43 25N 0 35W
Lacrosse, *U.S.A.* 142 **C5** 46 51N 117 58W
Lacub, *Phil.* 70 **C3** 17 40N 120 53 E
Ladakh Ra., *India* 81 **B8** 34 0N 78 0 E
Ladário, *Brazil* 157 **D6** 19 1 S 57 35W
Ladd, *U.S.A.* 140 **C7** 41 23N 89 13W
Laddonia, *U.S.A.* 140 **E5** 39 15N 91 39W
Lądekzdrój, *Poland* 47 **E3** 50 21N 16 53 E
Ládhon →, *Greece* 45 **G3** 37 40N 21 50 E
Lâdik, *Turkey* 52 **F6** 40 57N 35 58 E
Ladismith, *S. Africa* 104 **E3** 33 28 S 21 15 E
Lādīz, *Iran* 85 **D9** 28 55N 61 15 E
Ladnun, *India* 80 **F6** 27 38N 74 25 E
Ladoga, L. = Ladozhskoye Ozero, *Russia* 48 **B5** 61 15N 30 30 E
Ladon, *France* 23 **D9** 48 0N 2 30 E
Ladozhskoye Ozero, *Russia* 48 **B5** 61 15N 30 30 E
Ladrillero, G., *Chile* 160 **C1** 49 20 S 75 35W
Lady Grey, *S. Africa* 104 **E4** 30 43 S 27 13 E
Ladybrand, *S. Africa* 104 **D4** 29 9 S 27 29 E
Ladysmith, *Canada* 130 **D4** 49 0N 123 49W
Ladysmith, *S. Africa* 105 **D4** 28 32 S 29 46 E
Ladysmith, *U.S.A.* 138 **C9** 45 27N 91 4W
Lae, *Papua N. G.* 120 **D4** 6 40 S 147 2 E
Laem Ngop, *Thailand* 77 **F4** 12 10N 102 26 E
Laem Pho, *Thailand* 77 **J3** 6 55N 101 19 E
Læsø, *Denmark* 15 **G4** 57 15N 10 53 E
Læsø Rende, *Denmark* 15 **G4** 57 20N 10 45 E
Lafayette, *Colo., U.S.A.* 138 **F2** 40 0N 105 2W
Lafayette, *Ind., U.S.A.* 141 **D10** 40 25N 86 54W
Lafayette, *La., U.S.A.* 139 **K9** 30 18N 92 0W
Lafayette, *Tenn., U.S.A.* 135 **G3** 36 35N 86 0W
Laferte →, *Canada* 130 **A5** 61 53N 117 44W
Lafia, *Nigeria* 101 **D6** 8 30N 8 34 E
Lafiagi, *Nigeria* 101 **D6** 8 52N 5 20 E
Lafleche, *Canada* 131 **D7** 49 45N 106 40W
Lafon, *Sudan* 95 **F3** 5 5N 32 29 E
Laforsen, *Sweden* 14 **C9** 61 56N 15 3 E
Lagaip →, *Papua N. G.* 120 **C2** 5 4 S 142 52 E
Lagan →, *Sweden* 15 **H7** 56 56N 13 58 E
Lagan →, *U.K.* 19 **B6** 54 35N 5 55W
Lagangilang, *Phil.* 70 **C3** 17 37N 120 44 E
Lagarfljót →, *Iceland* 12 **D6** 65 40N 14 18W
Lagarto, *Brazil* 154 **D4** 10 54 S 37 41W
Lagawe, *Phil.* 70 **C3** 16 49N 121 6 E
Lage, *Germany* 26 **D4** 51 58N 8 47 E
Lage, *Spain* 36 **B2** 43 13N 9 0W
Lage-Mierde, *Neths.* 21 **F6** 51 25N 5 9 E
Lågen →, *Norway* 13 **F11** 61 8N 10 25 E
Lägerdorf, *Germany* 26 **B5** 53 53N 9 35 E
Laghmān □, *Afghan.* 79 **B3** 34 20N 70 0 E

**Leopoldina 223**


Las Tablas, *Panama* 148 E3 7 49N 80 14W
Las Termas, *Argentina* 158 B3 27 29 S 64 52W
Las Truchas, *Mexico* 146 D4 17 57N 102 13W
Las Varillas, *Argentina* 158 C3 31 50 S 62 50W
Las Vegas, *N. Mex.*, *U.S.A.* 143 J11 35 35N 105 10W
Las Vegas, *Nev.*, *U.S.A.* 145 J11 36 10N 115 5W
Lascano, *Uruguay* 159 C5 33 35 S 54 12W
Lashburn, *Canada* 131 C7 53 10N 109 40W
Lashio, *Burma* 78 D6 22 56N 97 45 E
Lashkar, *India* 80 F8 26 10N 78 10 E
Lashkar Gāh, *Afghan.* 79 C2 31 35N 64 21 E
Łasin, *Poland* 47 B6 53 30N 19 2 E
Lasíthi, *Greece* 32 D7 35 11N 25 31 E
Lasíthi □, *Greece* 32 D7 35 5N 25 50 E
Lask, *Poland* 47 D6 51 34N 19 8 E
Łaskarzew, *Poland* 47 D8 51 48N 21 36 E
Laško, *Slovenia* 39 B12 46 10N 15 16 E
Lassance, *Brazil* 155 E3 17 54 S 44 34W
Lassay, *France* 22 D6 48 27N 0 30W
Lassen Pk., *U.S.A.* 142 F3 40 29N 121 31W
Last Mountain L., *Canada* 131 C7 51 5N 105 14W
Lastchance Cr. →, *U.S.A.* 144 E5 40 2N 121 15W
Lastoursville, *Gabon* 102 C2 0 55 S 12 38 E
Lastovo, *Croatia* 39 F13 42 46N 16 55 E
Lastovski Kanal, *Croatia* 39 F13 42 50N 17 0 E
Lat Yao, *Thailand* 76 E2 15 45N 99 48 E
Latacunga, *Ecuador* 152 D2 0 50 S 78 35W
Latakia = Al Lādhiqīyah, *Syria* 84 C2 35 30N 35 45 E
Latchford, *Canada* 128 C4 47 20N 79 50W
Late, *Tonga* 121 P13 18 48 S 174 39W
Laterza, *Italy* 41 B9 40 38N 16 47 E
Latham, *Australia* 113 E2 29 44 S 116 20 E
Lathen, *Germany* 26 C3 52 51N 7 21 E
Lathrop, *U.S.A.* 140 E2 39 33N 94 20W
Lathrop Wells, *U.S.A.* 145 J10 36 39N 116 24W
Latiano, *Italy* 41 B10 40 33N 17 43 E
Latina, *Italy* 40 A5 41 26N 12 53 E
Latisana, *Italy* 39 C10 45 47N 13 1 E
Latium = Lazio □, *Italy* 39 F9 42 10N 12 30 E
Laton, *U.S.A.* 144 J7 36 26N 119 41W
Latorica →, *Czech.* 31 C14 48 28N 21 50 E
Latouche Treville, C., *Australia* 112 C3 18 27 S 121 49 E
Latrobe, *Australia* 114 G4 41 14 S 146 30 E
Latrobe, *U.S.A.* 136 F5 40 19N 79 21W
Latrónico, *Italy* 41 B9 40 5N 16 0 E
Latur, *India* 82 E3 18 25N 76 40 E
Latvia ■, *Europe* 50 C3 56 50N 24 0 E
Lau Group, *Fiji* 121 A3 17 0 S 178 30W
Lauca →, *Bolivia* 156 D4 19 9 S 68 10W
Lauchhammer, *Germany* 26 D9 51 35N 13 48 E
Lauenburg, *Germany* 26 B6 53 23N 10 33 E
Läufelfingen, *Switz.* 28 B5 47 24N 7 52 E
Laufen, *Switz.* 28 B5 47 25N 7 30 E
Lauffen, *Germany* 27 F5 49 4N 9 9 E
Laugarbakki, *Iceland* 12 D3 65 20N 20 55W
Laujar, *Spain* 35 J2 37 0N 2 54W
Launceston, *Australia* 114 G4 41 24 S 147 8 E
Launceston, *U.K.* 17 G3 50 38N 4 21W
Laune →, *Ireland* 19 D2 52 5N 9 40W
Laupheim, *Germany* 27 G5 48 13N 9 53 E
Laur, *Phil.* 70 D3 15 35N 121 11 E
Laura, *Queens.*, *Australia* 114 B3 15 32 S 144 32 E
Laura, *S. Austral.*, *Australia* 116 B3 33 10 S 138 18 E
Laureana di Borrello, *Italy* 41 D9 38 28N 16 5 E
Laurel, *Ind.*, *U.S.A.* 141 E11 39 31N 85 11W
Laurel, *Miss.*, *U.S.A.* 139 K10 31 41N 89 9W
Laurel, *Mont.*, *U.S.A.* 142 D9 45 46N 108 49W
Laurencekirk, *U.K.* 18 E6 56 50N 2 30W
Laurens, *U.S.A.* 135 H4 34 32N 82 2W
Laurentian Plateau, *Canada* 129 B6 52 0N 70 0W
Laurentides, Parc Prov. des, *Canada* 129 C5 47 45N 71 15W
Lauria, *Italy* 41 B8 40 3N 15 50 E
Laurie L., *Canada* 131 B8 56 35N 101 57W
Laurinburg, *U.S.A.* 135 H6 34 50N 79 25W
Laurium, *U.S.A.* 134 B1 47 14N 88 26W
Lausanne, *Switz.* 28 C3 46 32N 6 38 E
Laut, *Indonesia* 75 B3 4 45N 108 0 E
Laut, Pulau, *Indonesia* 75 C5 3 40 S 116 10 E
Laut Ketil, Kepulauan, *Indonesia* 75 C5 4 45 S 115 40 E
Lautaro, *Chile* 160 A2 38 31 S 72 27W
Lauterbach, *Germany* 26 E5 50 39N 9 23 E
Lauterbrunnen, *Switz.* 28 C5 46 36N 7 55 E
Lauterecken, *Germany* 27 F3 49 38N 7 35 E
Lautoka, *Fiji* 121 A1 17 37 S 177 27 E
Lauwe, *Belgium* 21 G2 50 47N 3 12 E
Lauwers, *Neths.* 20 A8 53 32N 6 23 E
Lauwers Zee, *Neths.* 20 B8 53 21N 6 13 E
Lauzon, *Canada* 129 C5 46 48N 71 10W
Lava Hot Springs, *U.S.A.* 142 E7 42 38N 112 1W
Lavadores, *Spain* 36 C2 42 14N 8 41W
Lavagna, *Italy* 38 D6 44 18N 9 22 E
Laval, *France* 22 D6 48 4N 0 48W
Lavalle, *Argentina* 158 B2 28 15 S 65 15W
Lávara, *Greece* 44 C8 41 19N 26 22 E
Lavardac, *France* 24 D4 44 12N 0 20 E
Lavaur, *France* 24 E5 43 40N 1 49 E
Lavaux, *Switz.* 28 D3 46 30N 6 45 E
Lavelanet, *France* 24 F5 42 57N 1 51 E
Lavello, *Italy* 41 A8 41 4N 15 47 E
Laverne, *U.S.A.* 139 G5 36 43N 99 58W
Lavers Hill, *Australia* 116 E5 38 40 S 143 25 E
Laverton, *Australia* 113 E3 28 44 S 122 29 E
Lávkos, *Greece* 45 E5 39 9N 23 14 E
Lavos, *Portugal* 36 E2 40 6N 8 49W
Lavras, *Brazil* 155 F3 21 20 S 45 0W
Lavre, *Portugal* 37 G2 38 46N 8 22W
Lavrentiya, *Russia* 57 C19 65 35N 171 0W
Lávrion, *Greece* 45 G6 37 40N 24 4 E
Lávris, *Greece* 32 D6 35 25N 24 40 E
Lavumisa, *Swaziland* 105 D5 27 20 S 31 55 E
Lawa, *Phil.* 71 H5 6 12N 125 41 E
Lawa-an, *Phil.* 71 F5 11 51N 125 5 E
Lawas, *Malaysia* 75 B5 4 55N 115 25 E
Lawdar, *Yemen* 86 D4 13 53N 45 52 E
Lawele, *Indonesia* 72 C2 5 16 S 123 3 E
Lawksawk, *Burma* 78 E6 21 15N 96 52 E
Lawn Hill, *Australia* 114 B2 18 36 S 138 33 E
Lawqar, *Si. Arabia* 84 D4 29 49N 42 45 E
Lawra, *Ghana* 100 C4 10 39N 2 51W
Lawrence, *N.Z.* 119 F4 45 55 S 169 41 E
Lawrence, *Ind.*, *U.S.A.* 141 E10 39 50N 86 2W
Lawrence, *Kans.*, *U.S.A.* 138 F7 39 0N 95 10W
Lawrence, *Mass.*, *U.S.A.* 137 D13 42 40N 71 9W
Lawrenceburg, *Ind.*, *U.S.A.* 141 E12 39 5N 84 50W
Lawrenceburg, *Ky.*, *U.S.A.* 141 F12 38 2N 84 54W
Lawrenceburg, *Tenn.*, *U.S.A.* 135 H2 35 12N 87 19W
Lawrenceville, *Ga.*, *U.S.A.* 135 J4 33 55N 83 59W
Lawrenceville, *Ill.*, *U.S.A.* 141 F9 38 44N 87 41W
Laws, *U.S.A.* 144 H8 37 24N 118 20W
Lawson, *U.S.A.* 140 E2 39 26N 94 12W
Lawton, *Mich.*, *U.S.A.* 141 B11 42 10N 85 50W
Lawton, *Okla.*, *U.S.A.* 139 H5 34 33N 98 25W
Lawu, *Indonesia* 75 D4 7 40 S 111 13 E
Laxford, L., *U.K.* 18 C3 58 25N 5 10W
Layht, Ra's, *Yemen* 87 D6 12 38N 53 25 E
Laylá, *Si. Arabia* 86 B4 22 10N 46 40 E
Laylān, *Iraq* 84 C5 35 18N 44 31 E
Layon →, *France* 22 E6 47 20N 0 45W
Laysan I., *Pac. Oc.* 123 E11 25 30N 167 0W
Laytonville, *U.S.A.* 142 G2 39 44N 123 29W
Laza, *Burma* 78 B6 26 30N 97 38 E
Lazarevac, *Serbia, Yug.* 42 C5 44 23N 20 17 E
Lazi, *Phil.* 71 G4 9 8N 123 38 E
Lazio □, *Italy* 39 F9 42 10N 12 30 E
Lazo, *Russia* 60 C6 43 25N 133 55 E
Łazy, *Poland* 47 E6 50 27N 19 24 E
Le Barcarès, *France* 24 F7 42 47N 3 2 E
Le Beausset, *France* 25 E9 43 12N 5 48 E
Le Blanc, *France* 24 B5 46 37N 1 3 E
Le Bleymard, *France* 24 D7 44 30N 3 42 E
Le Bourgneuf-la-Fôret, *France* 22 D6 48 10N 0 59W
Le Bouscat, *France* 24 D3 44 53N 0 37W
Le Brassus, *Switz.* 28 C2 46 35N 6 13 E
Le Bugue, *France* 24 D4 44 55N 0 56 E
Le Canourgue, *France* 24 D7 44 26N 3 13 E
Le Cateau, *France* 23 B10 50 7N 3 32 E
Le Chambon-Feugerolles, *France* 25 C8 45 24N 4 19 E
Le Château-d'Oléron, *France* 24 C2 45 54N 1 12W
Le Châtelard, *Switz.* 28 D3 46 4N 6 57 E
Le Châtelet, *France* 24 B6 46 38N 2 16 E
Le Châtelet-en-Brie, *France* 23 D9 48 31N 2 48 E
Le Chesne, *France* 23 C11 49 30N 4 45 E
Le Cheylard, *France* 25 D8 44 55N 4 25 E
Le Claire, *U.S.A.* 140 C6 41 36N 90 21W
Le Conquet, *France* 22 D2 48 21N 4 46W
Le Creusot, *France* 23 F11 46 48N 4 24 E
Le Croisic, *France* 22 E4 47 18N 2 30W
Le Donjon, *France* 24 B7 46 22N 3 48 E
Le Dorat, *France* 24 B5 46 14N 1 5 E
Le François, *Martinique* 149 D7 14 38N 60 57W
Le Grand-Lucé, *France* 22 E7 47 52N 0 28 E
Le Grand-Pressigny, *France* 22 F7 46 55N 0 48 E
Le Havre, *France* 22 C7 49 30N 0 5 E
Le Lavandou, *France* 25 E10 43 8N 6 22 E
Le Lion-d'Angers, *France* 22 E6 47 37N 0 43W
Le Locle, *Switz.* 28 B3 47 3N 6 44 E
Le Louroux-Béconnais, *France* 22 E6 47 30N 0 55W
Le Luc, *France* 25 E10 43 23N 6 21 E
Le Madonie, *Italy* 40 E6 37 50N 13 50 E
Le Maire, Est. de, *Argentina* 160 D4 54 50 S 65 0W
Le Mans, *France* 22 E7 48 0N 0 10 E
Le Marinel, *Zaïre* 103 E5 10 25 S 25 17 E
Le Mars, *U.S.A.* 138 D6 43 0N 96 5W
Le Mêle-sur-Sarthe, *France* 22 D7 48 31N 0 22 E
Le Merlerault, *France* 22 D7 48 41N 0 16 E
Le Monastier-sur-Gazeille, *France* 24 D7 44 57N 3 59 E
Le Monêtier-les-Bains, *France* 25 D10 44 58N 6 30 E
Le Mont d'Or, *France* 23 F13 46 45N 6 18 E
Le Mont-Dore, *France* 24 C6 45 35N 2 49 E
Le Mont-St.-Michel, *France* 22 D5 48 40N 1 30W
Le Moule, *Guadeloupe* 149 C7 16 20N 61 22W
Le Muy, *France* 25 E10 43 28N 6 34 E
Le Palais, *France* 22 E3 47 20N 3 10W
Le Perthus, *France* 24 F6 42 30N 2 53 E
Le Pont, *Switz.* 28 C2 46 41N 6 20 E
Le Pouldu, *France* 22 E3 47 41N 3 36W
Le Puy, *France* 24 C7 45 3N 3 52 E
Le Quesnoy, *France* 23 B10 50 15N 3 38 E
Le Roy, *Ill.*, *U.S.A.* 141 D8 40 21N 88 46W
Le Roy, *Kans.*, *U.S.A.* 139 F7 38 8N 95 35W
Le Sentier, *Switz.* 28 C2 46 37N 6 15 E
Le Sueur, *U.S.A.* 138 C8 44 25N 93 52W
Le Teil, *France* 25 D8 44 33N 4 40 E
Le Teilleul, *France* 22 D6 48 32N 0 53W
Le Theil, *France* 22 D7 48 16N 0 42 E
Le Thillot, *France* 23 E13 47 53N 6 46 E
Le Thuy, *Vietnam* 76 D6 17 14N 106 49 E
Le Touquet-Paris-Plage, *France* 23 B8 50 30N 1 36 E
Le Tréport, *France* 22 B8 50 3N 1 20 E
Le Val-d'Ajol, *France* 23 E13 47 55N 6 30 E
Le Verdon-sur-Mer, *France* 24 C2 45 33N 1 4W
Le Vigan, *France* 24 E7 43 59N 3 36 E
Lea →, *U.K.* 17 F7 51 30N 0 10W
Leach, *Cambodia* 77 F4 12 21N 103 46 E
Lead, *U.S.A.* 138 C3 44 20N 103 40W
Leader, *Canada* 131 C7 50 50N 109 30W
Leadhills, *U.K.* 18 F5 55 25N 3 47W
Leadville, *U.S.A.* 143 G10 39 17N 106 23W
Leaf →, *U.S.A.* 139 K10 31 0N 88 45W
Leakey, *U.S.A.* 139 L5 29 45N 99 45W
Lealui, *Zambia* 103 F4 15 10 S 23 2 E
Leamington, *Canada* 128 D3 42 3N 82 36W
Leamington, *N.Z.* 118 D4 37 55 S 175 30 E
Leamington, *U.S.A.* 142 G7 39 37N 112 17W
Leamington Spa = Royal Leamington Spa, *U.K.* 17 E6 52 18N 1 32W
Le'an, *China* 69 D10 27 22N 115 48 E
Leandro Norte Alem, *Argentina* 159 B4 27 34 S 55 15W
Learmonth, *Australia* 112 D1 22 13 S 114 10 E
Leask, *Canada* 131 C7 53 5N 106 45W
Leavenworth, *Ind.*, *U.S.A.* 141 F10 38 12N 86 21W
Leavenworth, *Kans.*, *U.S.A.* 138 F7 39 25N 95 0W
Leavenworth, *Wash.*, *U.S.A.* 142 C3 47 44N 120 37W
Leawood, *U.S.A.* 140 F2 38 57N 94 37W
Łeba, *Poland* 47 A4 54 45N 17 32 E
Łeba →, *Poland* 47 A4 54 46N 17 33 E
Lebak, *Phil.* 71 H5 6 32N 124 5 E
Lebam, *U.S.A.* 144 D3 46 34N 123 33W
Lebane, *Serbia, Yug.* 42 E6 42 56N 21 44 E
Lebango, *Congo* 102 B2 0 39N 14 21 E
Lebanon, *Ill.*, *U.S.A.* 140 F7 38 38N 89 49W
Lebanon, *Ind.*, *U.S.A.* 141 D10 40 3N 86 28W
Lebanon, *Kans.*, *U.S.A.* 138 F5 39 50N 98 35W
Lebanon, *Ky.*, *U.S.A.* 134 G3 37 35N 85 15W
Lebanon, *Mo.*, *U.S.A.* 139 G8 37 40N 92 40W
Lebanon, *Ohio*, *U.S.A.* 141 E12 39 26N 84 13W
Lebanon, *Oreg.*, *U.S.A.* 142 D2 44 31N 122 57W
Lebanon, *Pa.*, *U.S.A.* 137 F8 40 20N 76 28W
Lebanon, *Tenn.*, *U.S.A.* 135 G2 36 15N 86 20W
Lebanon ■, *Asia* 91 B4 34 0N 36 0 E
Lebanon Junction, *U.S.A.* 141 G11 37 50N 85 44W
Lebbeke, *Belgium* 21 G4 50 58N 4 8 E
Lebec, *U.S.A.* 145 L8 34 50N 118 59W
Lebedin, *Ukraine* 50 F9 50 35N 34 30 E
Lebedyan, *Russia* 51 E11 53 0N 39 10 E
Lebomboberge, *S. Africa* 105 C5 24 30 S 32 0 E
Lębork, *Poland* 47 A4 54 33N 17 46 E
Lebrija, *Spain* 37 J4 36 53N 6 5W
Łebsko, Jezioro, *Poland* 47 A4 54 40N 17 25 E
Lebu, *Chile* 158 D1 37 40 S 73 47W
Lecce, *Italy* 41 B11 40 20N 18 10 E
Lecco, *Italy* 38 C6 45 50N 9 27 E
Lecco, L. di, *Italy* 38 C6 45 51N 9 22 E
Lécera, *Spain* 34 D4 41 13N 0 43W
Lech, *Austria* 30 D3 47 13N 10 9 E
Lech →, *Germany* 27 G6 48 44N 10 56 E
Lechang, *China* 69 E9 25 10N 113 20 E
Lechtaler Alpen, *Austria* 30 D3 47 15N 10 30 E
Lectoure, *France* 24 E4 43 56N 0 38 E
Łeczna, *Poland* 47 D9 51 18N 22 53 E
Łęczyca, *Poland* 47 C6 52 5N 19 15 E
Ledang, Gunong, *Malaysia* 74 B2 2 22N 102 37 E
Ledbury, *U.K.* 17 E5 52 3N 2 25W
Lede, *Belgium* 21 G3 50 58N 3 59 E
Ledeberg, *Belgium* 21 F3 51 2N 3 45 E
Ledeč, *Czech.* 30 B8 49 41N 15 18 E
Ledesma, *Spain* 36 D5 41 6N 5 59W
Ledong, *China* 76 C7 18 41N 109 5 E
Leduc, *Canada* 130 C6 53 15N 113 30W
Ledyczek, *Poland* 47 B3 53 33N 16 59 E
Lee, *U.S.A.* 137 D11 42 17N 73 18W
Lee →, *Ireland* 19 E3 51 50N 8 30W
Lee Vining, *U.S.A.* 144 H7 37 58N 119 7W
Leech L., *U.S.A.* 138 B7 47 9N 94 23W
Leedey, *U.S.A.* 139 H5 35 53N 99 24W
Leeds, *U.K.* 16 D6 53 48N 1 34W
Leeds, *U.S.A.* 135 J2 33 32N 86 30W
Leek, *Neths.* 20 B8 53 10N 6 24 E
Leek, *U.K.* 16 D5 53 7N 2 2W
Leende, *Neths.* 21 F7 51 21N 5 33 E
Leer, *Germany* 26 B3 53 13N 7 29 E
Leerdam, *Neths.* 20 E6 51 54N 5 6 E
Leersum, *Neths.* 20 E6 52 0N 5 26 E
Lee's Summit, *U.S.A.* 140 F2 38 55N 94 23W
Leesburg, *Fla.*, *U.S.A.* 135 L5 28 47N 81 52W
Leesburg, *Ohio*, *U.S.A.* 141 E13 39 21N 83 33W
Leeston, *N.Z.* 119 D7 43 45 S 172 19 E
Leesville, *U.S.A.* 139 K8 31 12N 93 15W
Leeton, *Australia* 117 C7 34 33 S 146 23 E
Leetonia, *U.S.A.* 136 F4 40 53N 80 45W
Leeu Gamka, *S. Africa* 104 E3 32 47 S 21 59 E
Leeuwarden, *Neths.* 20 B7 53 15N 5 48 E
Leeuwin, C., *Australia* 113 F2 34 20 S 115 9 E
Leeward Is., *Atl. Oc.* 149 C7 16 30N 63 30W
Léfini, *Congo* 102 C3 2 55 S 15 39 E
Lefka, *Cyprus* 32 D11 35 6N 32 51 E
Lefkoniko, *Cyprus* 32 D12 35 18N 33 44 E
Lefors, *U.S.A.* 139 H4 35 30N 100 50W
Lefroy, L., *Australia* 113 F3 31 21 S 121 40 E
Łeg →, *Poland* 47 E8 50 42N 21 50 E
Legal, *Canada* 130 C6 53 55N 113 35W
Leganés, *Spain* 36 E7 40 19N 3 45W
Legazpi, *Phil.* 70 E4 13 10N 123 45 E
Legendre I., *Australia* 112 D2 20 22 S 116 55 E
Leghorn = Livorno, *Italy* 38 E7 43 32N 10 18 E
Legionowo, *Poland* 47 C7 52 25N 20 50 E
Léglise, *Belgium* 21 J7 49 48N 5 32 E
Legnago, *Italy* 39 C8 45 10N 11 19 E
Legnano, *Italy* 38 C5 45 35N 8 55 E
Legnica, *Poland* 47 D3 51 12N 16 10 E
Legnica □, *Poland* 47 D3 51 30N 16 0 E
Legrad, *Croatia* 39 B13 46 17N 16 51 E
Legume, *Australia* 115 D5 28 20 S 152 19 E
Leh, *India* 81 B7 34 9N 77 35 E
Lehi, *U.S.A.* 142 F8 40 20N 111 51W
Lehighton, *U.S.A.* 137 F9 40 50N 75 44W
Lehliu, *Romania* 46 E7 44 29N 26 20 E
Lehrte, *Germany* 26 C5 52 22N 9 58 E
Lehututu, *Botswana* 104 C3 23 54 S 21 55 E
Lei Shui →, *China* 69 D9 26 55N 112 35 E
Leiah, *Pakistan* 79 C3 30 58N 70 58 E
Leibnitz, *Austria* 30 E8 46 47N 15 34 E
Leibo, *China* 68 C4 28 11N 103 34 E
Leicester, *U.K.* 17 E6 52 39N 1 9W
Leicestershire □, *U.K.* 17 E6 52 40N 1 10W
Leichhardt →, *Australia* 114 B2 17 35 S 139 48 E
Leichhardt Ra., *Australia* 114 C4 20 46 S 147 40 E
Leiden, *Neths.* 20 D5 52 9N 4 30 E
Leiderdorp, *Neths.* 20 D5 52 9N 4 32 E
Leidschendam, *Neths.* 20 D4 52 5N 4 24 E
Leie →, *Belgium* 23 A10 51 2N 3 45 E
Leigh →, *Australia* 116 E6 38 18 S 144 30 E
Leignon, *Belgium* 21 H6 50 16N 5 7 E
Leikhto, *Burma* 78 F6 19 13N 96 35 E
Leine →, *Germany* 26 C5 52 20N 9 50 E
Leinster, *Australia* 113 E3 27 51 S 120 36 E
Leinster □, *Ireland* 19 C4 53 0N 7 10W
Leinster, Mt., *Ireland* 19 D5 52 38N 6 47W
Leipzig, *Germany* 26 D8 51 20N 12 23 E
Leiria, *Portugal* 37 F2 39 46N 8 53W
Leiria □, *Portugal* 37 F2 39 46N 8 53W
Leisler, Mt., *Australia* 112 D4 23 23 S 129 20 E
Leith, *U.K.* 18 F5 55 59N 3 10W
Leith Hill, *U.K.* 17 F7 51 10N 0 23W
Leitha →, *Europe* 31 D10 47 41N 17 40 E
Leitrim, *Ireland* 19 B3 54 0N 8 5W
Leitrim □, *Ireland* 19 B3 54 8N 8 0W
Leiyang, *China* 69 D9 26 27N 112 45 E
Leiza, *Spain* 34 B3 43 5N 1 55W
Leizhou Bandao, *China* 65 D6 21 0N 110 0 E
Leizhou Wan, *China* 69 G8 20 50N 110 20 E
Lek →, *Neths.* 20 E5 51 54N 4 35 E
Lekáni, *Greece* 44 C6 41 10N 24 35 E
Leke, *Belgium* 21 F1 51 6N 2 54 E
Lekhainá, *Greece* 45 G3 37 57N 21 16 E
Lekkerkerk, *Neths.* 20 E5 51 54N 4 41 E
Leksula, *Indonesia* 72 B3 3 46 S 126 31 E
Leland, *U.S.A.* 139 J9 33 25N 90 52W
Leland Lakes, *Canada* 131 A6 60 0N 110 59W
Leleque, *Argentina* 160 B2 42 28 S 71 0W
Lelu, *Burma* 78 F5 19 4N 95 30 E
Lelystad, *Neths.* 20 D6 52 30N 5 25 E
Lema, *Nigeria* 101 C5 12 58N 4 13 E
Léman, Lac, *Switz.* 28 D3 46 26N 6 30 E
Lemelerveld, *Neths.* 20 D8 52 26N 6 20 E
Lemera, *Zaïre* 106 C2 3 0 S 28 55 E
Lemery, *Phil.* 70 E3 13 51N 120 56 E
Lemfu, *Zaïre* 103 D3 5 18 S 15 13 E
Lemgo, *Germany* 26 C4 52 2N 8 52 E
Lemhi Ra., *U.S.A.* 142 D7 44 30N 113 30W
Lemmer, *Neths.* 20 C7 52 51N 5 43 E
Lemmon, *U.S.A.* 138 C3 45 59N 102 10W
Lemon Grove, *U.S.A.* 145 N9 32 45N 117 2W
Lemoore, *U.S.A.* 144 J7 36 23N 119 46W
Lempdes, *France* 24 C7 45 22N 3 17 E
Lemsid, *W. Sahara* 98 C2 26 33N 13 51W
Lemvig, *Denmark* 15 H2 56 33N 8 20 E
Lemyethna, *Burma* 78 G5 17 36N 95 9 E
Lena →, *Russia* 57 B13 72 52N 126 40 E
Lenartovce, *Czech.* 31 C13 48 18N 20 19 E
Lencloître, *France* 22 F7 46 50N 0 20 E
Lençóis, *Brazil* 155 D3 12 35 S 41 24W
Léndas, *Greece* 32 E6 34 56N 24 56 E
Lendeh, *Iran* 85 D6 30 58N 50 25 E
Lendelede, *Belgium* 21 G2 50 53N 3 16 E
Lendinara, *Italy* 39 C8 45 4N 11 37 E
Lenger, *Kazakhstan* 55 B4 42 12N 69 54 E
Lengerich, *Germany* 26 C3 52 12N 7 50 E
Lenggong, *Malaysia* 77 K3 5 6N 100 58 E
Lenggries, *Germany* 27 H7 47 41N 11 34 E
Lengua de Vaca, Pta., *Chile* 158 C1 30 14 S 71 38W
Lengyeltóti, *Hungary* 31 E10 46 40N 17 40 E
Lenin, *Russia* 53 B9 48 20N 40 56 E
Lenina, Pik, *Kirghizia* 55 D6 39 20N 72 55 E
Leninabad = Khodzent, *Tajikistan* 55 C4 40 17N 69 37 E
Leninakan = Kumayri, *Armenia* 53 F10 40 47N 43 50 E
Leningrad = Sankt-Peterburg, *Russia* 50 B7 59 55N 30 20 E
Lenino, *Ukraine* 52 D6 45 17N 35 46 E
Leninogorsk = Ridder, *Kazakhstan* 56 D9 50 20N 83 30 E
Leninogorsk, *Russia* 54 D3 54 36N 52 30 E
Leninpol, *Kirghizia* 55 B5 42 29N 71 55 E
Leninsk, *Russia* 53 B11 48 40N 45 15 E
Leninsk, *Russia* 53 C10 46 10N 43 46 E
Leninsk, *Uzbekistan* 55 C6 40 38N 72 15 E
Leninsk-Kuznetskiy, *Russia* 56 D9 54 44N 86 10 E
Leninskaya Sloboda, *Russia* 51 C14 56 7N 44 29 E
Leninskoye, *Kazakhstan* 55 C4 41 45N 69 23 E
Leninskoye, *Russia* 51 B15 58 23N 47 3 E
Leninskoye, *Russia* 57 E14 47 56N 132 38 E
Lenk, *Switz.* 28 D4 46 27N 7 28 E
Lenkoran, *Azerbaijan* 89 D13 39 45N 48 50 E
Lenmalu, *Indonesia* 73 B4 1 45 S 130 15 E
Lenne →, *Germany* 26 D3 51 25N 7 30 E
Lennox, I., *Chile* 160 E3 55 18 S 66 50W
Lennoxville, *Canada* 137 A13 45 22N 71 51W
Leno, *Italy* 38 C7 45 24N 10 14 E
Lenoir, *U.S.A.* 135 H5 35 55N 81 36W
Lenoir City, *U.S.A.* 135 H3 35 40N 84 20W
Lenora, *U.S.A.* 138 F4 39 39N 100 1W
Lenore L., *Canada* 131 C8 52 30N 104 59W
Lenox, *Iowa*, *U.S.A.* 140 D2 40 53N 94 34W
Lenox, *Mass.*, *U.S.A.* 137 D11 42 20N 73 18W
Lens, *Belgium* 21 G3 50 33N 3 54 E
Lens, *France* 23 B9 50 26N 2 50 E
Lens St. Remy, *Belgium* 21 G6 50 39N 5 7 E
Lensk, *Russia* 57 C12 60 48N 114 55 E
Lenskoye, *Ukraine* 52 D6 45 3N 34 1 E
Lent, *Neths.* 20 E7 51 52N 5 52 E
Lenti, *Hungary* 31 E9 46 37N 16 33 E
Lentini, *Italy* 41 E8 37 18N 15 0 E
Lentvaric, *Lithuania* 50 D4 54 39N 25 3 E
Lenwood, *U.S.A.* 145 L9 34 53N 117 7W
Lenzburg, *Switz.* 28 B6 47 23N 8 11 E
Lenzen, *Germany* 26 B7 53 6N 11 26 E
Lenzerheide, *Switz.* 29 C9 46 44N 9 34 E
Léo, *Burkina Faso* 100 C4 11 3N 2 2W
Leoben, *Austria* 30 D8 47 22N 15 5 E
Leola, *U.S.A.* 138 C5 45 47N 98 58W
Leominster, *U.K.* 17 E5 52 15N 2 43W
Leominster, *U.S.A.* 137 D13 42 32N 71 45W
Léon, *France* 24 E2 43 53N 1 18W
León, *Mexico* 146 C4 21 7N 101 30W
León, *Nic.* 148 D2 12 20N 86 51W
León, *Spain* 36 C5 42 38N 5 34W
Leon, *U.S.A.* 140 D3 40 40N 93 40W
León □, *Spain* 36 C5 42 40N 5 55W
León, Montañas de, *Spain* 36 C4 42 30N 6 18W
Leonardtown, *U.S.A.* 134 F7 38 19N 76 39W
Leone, Mte., *Switz.* 28 D6 46 15N 8 5 E
Leonforte, *Italy* 41 E7 37 39N 14 22 E
Leongatha, *Australia* 117 E6 38 30 S 145 58 E
Leonídhion, *Greece* 45 G4 37 9N 22 52 E
Leonora, *Australia* 113 E3 28 49 S 121 19 E
Leonora Downs, *Australia* 116 B5 32 29 S 142 5 E
Léopold II, Lac = Mai-Ndombe, L., *Zaïre* 102 C3 2 0 S 18 20 E
Leopoldina, *Brazil* 155 F3 21 28 S 42 40W

# M

228 Madagali


Madagali, *Nigeria* **101** **C7** 10 56N 13 33 E
Madagascar ■, *Africa* **105** **C8** 20 0 S 47 0 E
Madā'in Sālih, *Si. Arabia* **84** **E3** 26 46N 37 57 E
Madalag, *Phil.* **71** **F4** 11 32N 122 18 E
Madama, *Niger* **97** **D2** 22 0N 13 40 E
Madame I., *Canada* **129** **C7** 45 30N 60 58W
Madan, *Bulgaria* **43** **F9** 41 30N 24 57 E
Madanapalle, *India* **83** **H4** 13 33N 78 28 E
Madang, *Papua N. G.* **120** **C3** 5 12 S 145 49 E
Madaoua, *Niger* **101** **C6** 14 5N 6 27 E
Madara, *Nigeria* **101** **C7** 11 45N 10 35 E
Madaripur, *Bangla.* **78** **D3** 23 19N 90 15 E
Madauk, *Burma* **78** **G6** 17 56N 96 52 E
Madawaska, *Canada* **136** **A7** 45 30N 78 0W
Madawaska →, *Canada* **128** **C4** 45 27N 76 21W
Madaya, *Burma* **78** **D6** 22 12N 96 10 E
Madbar, *Sudan* **95** **F3** 6 17N 30 45 E
Maddaloni, *Italy* **41** **A7** 41 4N 14 23 E
Made, *Neths.* **21** **E5** 51 41N 4 49 E
Madeira, *Atl. Oc.* **33** **D3** 32 50N 17 0W
Madeira, *U.S.A.* **141** **E12** 39 11N 84 22W
Madeira →, *Brazil* **153** **D6** 3 22 S 58 45W
Madeleine, Is. de la, *Canada* **129** **C7** 47 30N 61 40W
Maden, *Turkey* **89** **D8** 38 23N 39 40 E
Madera, *U.S.A.* **144** **J6** 36 58N 120 1W
Madgaon, *India* **83** **G1** 15 12N 73 58 E
Madha, *India* **82** **F2** 18 0N 75 30 E
Madhubani, *India* **81** **F12** 26 21N 86 7 E
Madhumati →, *Bangla.* **78** **D2** 22 53N 89 52 E
Madhya Pradesh □, *India* **80** **J7** 21 50N 78 0 E
Madian, *China* **69** **A11** 33 0N 116 6 E
Madidi →, *Bolivia* **156** **C4** 12 32 S 66 52W
Madikeri, *India* **83** **H2** 12 30N 75 45 E
Madill, *U.S.A.* **139** **H6** 34 5N 96 49W
Madimba, *Angola* **103** **D2** 6 36 S 14 23 E
Madimba, *Zaïre* **103** **C3** 4 58 S 15 5 E
Ma'din, *Syria* **84** **C3** 35 45N 39 36 E
Madīnat ash Sha'b, *Yemen* **86** **D4** 12 50N 45 0 E
Madingou, *Congo* **102** **C2** 4 10 S 13 33 E
Madirovalo, *Madag.* **105** **B8** 16 26 S 46 32 E
Madison, *Calif., U.S.A.* **144** **G5** 38 41N 121 59W
Madison, *Fla., U.S.A.* **135** **K4** 30 29N 83 39W
Madison, *Ind., U.S.A.* **141** **F11** 38 42N 85 20W
Madison, *Mo., U.S.A.* **140** **E4** 39 28N 92 13W
Madison, *Nebr., U.S.A.* **138** **E6** 41 53N 97 25W
Madison, *Ohio, U.S.A.* **136** **E3** 41 45N 81 4W
Madison, *S. Dak., U.S.A.* **138** **D6** 44 0N 97 8W
Madison, *Wis., U.S.A.* **140** **A7** 43 5N 89 25W
Madison →, *U.S.A.* **142** **D8** 45 56N 111 30W
Madisonville, *Ky., U.S.A.* **134** **G2** 37 20N 87 30W
Madisonville, *Tex., U.S.A.* **139** **K7** 30 57N 95 55W
Madista, *Botswana* **104** **C4** 21 15 S 25 6 E
Madiun, *Indonesia* **75** **D4** 7 38 S 111 32 E
Madley, *U.K.* **17** **E5** 52 3N 2 51W
Madol, *Sudan* **95** **F2** 9 3N 27 45 E
Madon →, *France* **23** **D13** 48 36N 6 6 E
Madona, *Latvia* **50** **C5** 56 53N 26 5 E
Madrakah, Ra's al, *Oman* **87** **C7** 19 0N 57 50 E
Madras = Tamil Nadu □, *India* **83** **J3** 11 0N 77 0 E
Madras, *India* **83** **H5** 13 8N 80 19 E
Madras, *U.S.A.* **142** **D3** 44 40N 121 10W
Madre, L., *Mexico* **147** **B5** 25 0N 97 30W
Madre, L., *U.S.A.* **139** **M6** 26 15N 97 40W
Madre, Sierra, *Phil.* **70** **C4** 17 0N 122 0 E
Madre de Dios □, *Peru* **156** **C3** 12 0 S 70 15W
Madre de Dios →, *Bolivia* **156** **C4** 10 59 S 66 8W
Madre de Dios, I., *Chile* **160** **D1** 50 20 S 75 10W
Madre del Sur, Sierra, *Mexico* **147** **D5** 17 30N 100 0W
Madre Occidental, Sierra, *Mexico* **146** **B3** 27 0N 107 0W
Madre Oriental, Sierra, *Mexico* **146** **C4** 25 0N 100 0W
Madri, *India* **80** **G5** 24 16N 73 32 E
Madrid, *Spain* **36** **E7** 40 25N 3 45W
Madrid, *U.S.A.* **140** **C3** 41 53N 93 49W
Madrid □, *Spain* **36** **E7** 40 30N 3 45W
Madridejos, *Spain* **37** **F7** 39 28N 3 33W
Madrigal de las Altas Torres, *Spain* **36** **D6** 41 5N 5 0W
Madrona, Sierra, *Spain* **37** **G6** 38 27N 4 16W
Madroñera, *Spain* **37** **F5** 39 26N 5 42W
Madu, *Sudan* **95** **E2** 14 37N 26 4 E
Madura, Selat, *Indonesia* **75** **D4** 7 30 S 113 20 E
Madura Motel, *Australia* **113** **F4** 31 55 S 127 0 E
Madurai, *India* **83** **K4** 9 55N 78 10 E
Madurantakam, *India* **83** **H4** 12 30N 79 50 E
Madzhalis, *Russia* **53** **E12** 42 9N 47 47 E
Mae Chan, *Thailand* **76** **B2** 20 9N 99 52 E
Mae Hong Son, *Thailand* **76** **C2** 19 16N 98 1 E
Mae Khlong →, *Thailand* **76** **F3** 13 24N 100 0 E
Mae Phrik, *Thailand* **76** **D2** 17 27N 99 7 E
Mae Ramat, *Thailand* **76** **D2** 16 58N 98 31 E
Mae Rim, *Thailand* **76** **C2** 18 54N 98 57 E
Mae Sot, *Thailand* **76** **D2** 16 43N 98 34 E
Mae Suai, *Thailand* **76** **C2** 19 39N 99 33 E
Mae Tha, *Thailand* **76** **C2** 18 28N 99 8 E
Maebaru, *Japan* **62** **D2** 33 33N 130 12 E
Maebashi, *Japan* **63** **A11** 36 24N 139 4 E
Maella, *Spain* **34** **D5** 41 8N 0 7 E
Măeruş, *Romania* **46** **D6** 45 53N 25 31 E
Maesteg, *U.K.* **17** **F4** 51 36N 3 40W
Maestra, Sierra, *Cuba* **148** **B4** 20 15N 77 0W
Maestrazgo, Mts. del, *Spain* **34** **E4** 40 30N 0 25W
Maestre de Campo I., *Phil.* **70** **E3** 12 56N 121 42 E
Maevatanana, *Madag.* **105** **B8** 16 56 S 46 49 E
Maewo, *Vanuatu* **121** **E6** 15 10 S 168 10 E
Ma'fan, *Libya* **96** **C2** 25 56N 14 29 E
Mafeking = Mafikeng, *S. Africa* **104** **D4** 25 50 S 25 38 E
Mafeking, *Canada* **131** **C8** 52 40N 101 10W
Maféré, *Ivory C.* **100** **D4** 5 30N 3 2W
Mafeteng, *Lesotho* **104** **D4** 29 51 S 27 15 E
Maffe, *Belgium* **21** **H6** 50 21N 5 19 E
Maffra, *Australia* **117** **D7** 37 53 S 146 58 E
Mafia I., *Tanzania* **106** **D4** 7 45 S 39 50 E
Mafikeng, *S. Africa* **104** **D4** 25 50 S 25 38 E
Mafra, *Brazil* **159** **B6** 26 10 S 49 55W
Mafra, *Portugal* **37** **G1** 38 55N 9 20W
Mafungabusi Plateau, *Zimbabwe* **107** **F2** 18 30 S 29 8 E
Magadan, *Russia* **57** **D16** 59 38N 150 50 E
Magadi, *Kenya* **106** **C4** 1 54 S 36 19 E
Magadi, L., *Kenya* **106** **C4** 1 54 S 36 19 E
Magaliesburg, *S. Africa* **105** **D4** 26 0 S 27 32 E
Magallanes, *Phil.* **70** **E4** 12 50N 123 50 E
Magallanes □, *Chile* **160** **D2** 52 0 S 72 0W
Magallanes, Estrecho de, *Chile* **160** **D2** 52 30 S 75 0W
Magangué, *Colombia* **152** **B3** 9 14N 74 45W
Maganoy, *Phil.* **71** **H5** 6 51N 124 31 E
Magaria, *Niger* **97** **F1** 13 4N 9 5 E
Magburaka, *S. Leone* **100** **D2** 8 47N 12 0W
Magdalena, *Argentina* **158** **D4** 35 5 S 57 30W
Magdalena, *Bolivia* **157** **C5** 13 13 S 63 57W
Magdalena, *Mexico* **146** **A2** 30 50N 112 0W
Magdalena, *U.S.A.* **143** **J10** 34 10N 107 20W
Magdalena □, *Colombia* **152** **A3** 10 0N 74 0W
Magdalena →, *Colombia* **152** **A3** 11 6N 74 51W
Magdalena →, *Mexico* **146** **A2** 30 40N 112 25W
Magdalena, B., *Mexico* **146** **C2** 24 30N 112 10W
Magdalena, I., *Chile* **160** **B2** 44 40 S 73 0W
Magdalena, Llano de la, *Mexico* **146** **C2** 25 0N 111 30W
Magdeburg, *Germany* **26** **C7** 52 8N 11 36 E
Magdelaine Cays, *Australia* **114** **B5** 16 33 S 150 18 E
Magdub, *Sudan* **95** **E2** 13 42N 25 5 E
Magee, *U.S.A.* **139** **K10** 31 53N 89 45W
Magee, I., *U.K.* **19** **B6** 54 48N 5 44W
Magelang, *Indonesia* **75** **D4** 7 29 S 110 13 E
Magellan's Str. = Magallanes, Estrecho de, *Chile* **160** **D2** 52 30 S 75 0W
Magenta, *Australia* **116** **B5** 33 51 S 143 34 E
Magenta, *Italy* **38** **C5** 45 28N 8 53 E
Magenta, L., *Australia* **113** **F2** 33 30 S 119 2 E
Maggea, *Australia* **116** **C4** 34 28 S 140 2 E
Maggia, *Switz.* **29** **D7** 46 15N 8 42 E
Maggia →, *Switz.* **29** **D7** 46 18N 8 36 E
Maggiorasca, Mte., *Italy* **38** **D6** 44 33N 9 29 E
Maggiore, L., *Italy* **38** **C5** 46 0N 8 35 E
Maghama, *Mauritania* **100** **B2** 15 32N 12 57W
Magherafelt, *U.K.* **19** **B5** 54 44N 6 37W
Maghnia, *Algeria* **99** **B4** 34 50N 1 43W
Magione, *Italy* **39** **E9** 43 10N 12 12 E
Maglaj, *Bos.-H., Yug.* **42** **C3** 44 33N 18 7 E
Magliano in Toscana, *Italy* **39** **F8** 42 36N 11 18 E
Máglie, *Italy* **41** **B11** 40 8N 18 17 E
Magnac-Laval, *France* **24** **B5** 46 13N 1 11 E
Magnetic Pole (North) = North Magnetic Pole, *Canada* **6** **B2** 77 58N 102 8 E
Magnetic Pole (South) = South Magnetic Pole, *Antarctica* **7** **C9** 64 8 S 138 8 E
Magnisía □, *Greece* **44** **E4** 39 15N 22 45 E
Magnitogorsk, *Russia* **54** **E6** 53 27N 59 4 E
Magnolia, *Ark., U.S.A.* **139** **J8** 33 18N 93 12W
Magnolia, *Miss., U.S.A.* **139** **K9** 31 8N 90 28W
Magnor, *Norway* **14** **E6** 59 56N 12 15 E
Magny-en-Vexin, *France* **23** **C8** 49 9N 1 47 E
Magog, *Canada* **129** **C5** 45 18N 72 9W
Magoro, *Uganda* **106** **B3** 1 45N 34 12 E
Magosa = Famagusta, *Cyprus* **32** **D12** 35 8N 33 55 E
Magouládhes, *Greece* **32** **A3** 39 45N 19 42 E
Magoye, *Zambia* **107** **F2** 16 1 S 27 30 E
Magpie L., *Canada* **129** **B7** 51 0N 64 41W
Magrath, *Canada* **130** **D6** 49 25N 112 50W
Magro →, *Spain* **35** **F4** 39 11N 0 25W
Magrur, Wadi →, *Sudan* **95** **D2** 16 5N 26 30 E
Magsingal, *Phil.* **70** **C3** 17 41N 120 25 E
Magu □, *Tanzania* **106** **C3** 2 31 S 33 28 E
Maguan, *China* **68** **F5** 23 0N 104 21 E
Maguarinho, C., *Brazil* **154** **B2** 0 15 S 48 30W
Maguindanao □, *Phil.* **71** **H5** 7 5N 124 0 E
Maguse L., *Canada* **131** **A9** 61 40N 95 10W
Maguse Pt., *Canada* **131** **A10** 61 20N 93 50W
Magwe, *Burma* **78** **E5** 20 10N 95 0 E
Maha Sarakham, *Thailand* **76** **D4** 16 12N 103 16 E
Mahābād, *Iran* **84** **B5** 36 50N 45 45 E
Mahabaleshwar, *India* **82** **F1** 17 58N 73 43 E
Mahabharat Lekh, *Nepal* **81** **E9** 28 30N 82 0 E
Mahabo, *Madag.* **105** **C7** 20 23 S 44 40 E
Mahad, *India* **82** **E1** 18 6N 73 29 E
Mahaddei Uen, *Somali Rep.* **108** **D3** 2 58N 45 32 E
Mahadeo Hills, *India* **80** **H8** 22 20N 78 30 E
Mahadeopur, *India* **82** **E5** 18 48N 80 0 E
Mahagi, *Zaïre* **106** **B3** 2 20N 31 0 E
Mahaicony, *Guyana* **153** **B6** 6 36N 57 48W
Mahajamba →, *Madag.* **105** **B8** 15 33 S 47 8 E
Mahajamba, Helodranon' i, *Madag.* **105** **B8** 15 24 S 47 5 E
Mahajan, *India* **80** **E5** 28 48N 73 56 E
Mahajanga, *Madag.* **105** **B8** 15 40 S 46 25 E
Mahajanga □, *Madag.* **105** **B8** 17 0 S 47 0 E
Mahajilo →, *Madag.* **105** **B8** 19 42 S 45 22 E
Mahakam →, *Indonesia* **75** **C5** 0 35 S 117 17 E
Mahalapye, *Botswana* **104** **C4** 23 1 S 26 51 E
Maḩallāt, *Iran* **85** **C6** 33 55N 50 30 E
Māhān, *Iran* **85** **D8** 30 5N 57 18 E
Mahanadi →, *India* **82** **D8** 20 20N 86 25 E
Mahanoro, *Madag.* **105** **B8** 19 54 S 48 48 E
Mahanoy City, *U.S.A.* **137** **F8** 40 48N 76 10W
Mahaplag, *Phil.* **71** **F5** 10 35N 124 57 E
Maharashtra □, *India* **82** **D2** 20 30N 75 30 E
Maharès, *Tunisia* **96** **B2** 34 32N 10 29 E
Mahari Mts., *Tanzania* **106** **D2** 6 20 S 30 0 E
Mahasham, W. →, *Egypt* **91** **E3** 30 15N 34 10 E
Mahasolo, *Madag.* **105** **B8** 19 7 S 46 22 E
Mahattat ash Shīdīyah, *Jordan* **91** **F4** 29 55N 35 55 E
Mahattat 'Unayzah, *Jordan* **91** **E4** 30 30N 35 47 E
Mahaweli →, *Sri Lanka* **83** **K5** 8 30N 81 15 E
Mahaxay, *Laos* **76** **D5** 17 22N 105 12 E
Mahbes, *W. Sahara* **98** **C3** 27 10N 9 50W
Mahbubabad, *India* **82** **F5** 17 42N 80 2 E
Mahbubnagar, *India* **82** **F3** 16 45N 77 59 E
Maḩḑah, *Oman* **85** **E7** 24 24N 55 59 E
Mahdia, *Guyana* **153** **B6** 5 13N 59 8W
Mahdia, *Tunisia* **96** **A2** 35 28N 11 0 E
Mahe, *Jammu & Kashmir, India* **81** **C8** 33 10N 78 32 E
Mahé, *Pondicherry, India* **83** **J2** 11 42N 75 34 E
Mahé, *Seychelles* **109** **E4** 5 0 S 55 30 E
Mahendra Giri, *India* **83** **K3** 8 20N 77 30 E
Mahendraganj, *India* **78** **C2** 25 20N 89 45 E
Mahenge, *Tanzania* **107** **D4** 8 45 S 36 41 E
Maheno, *N.Z.* **119** **F5** 45 10 S 170 50 E
Mahesana, *India* **80** **H5** 23 39N 72 26 E
Mahia Pen., *N.Z.* **118** **F6** 39 9 S 177 55 E
Mahirija, *Morocco* **99** **B4** 34 0N 3 16W
Mahlaing, *Burma* **78** **E5** 21 6N 95 39 E
Mahmiya, *Sudan* **95** **D3** 17 12N 33 43 E
Mahmud Kot, *Pakistan* **80** **D4** 30 16N 71 0 E
Mahmudia, *Romania* **46** **D10** 45 5N 29 5 E
Mahnomen, *U.S.A.* **138** **B7** 47 22N 95 57W
Mahoba, *India* **81** **G8** 25 15N 79 55 E
Mahomet, *U.S.A.* **141** **D8** 40 12N 88 24W
Mahón, *Spain* **33** **B11** 39 53N 4 16 E
Mahone Bay, *Canada* **129** **D7** 44 30N 64 20W
Mahuta, *Nigeria* **101** **C5** 11 32N 4 58 E
Mai-Ndombe, L., *Zaïre* **102** **C3** 2 0 S 18 20 E
Mai-Sai, *Thailand* **76** **B2** 20 20N 99 55 E
Maibara, *Japan* **63** **B8** 35 19N 136 17 E
Maicao, *Colombia* **152** **A3** 11 23N 72 13W
Maîche, *France* **23** **E13** 47 16N 6 48 E
Maici →, *Brazil* **157** **B5** 6 30 S 61 43W
Maicurú →, *Brazil* **153** **D7** 2 14 S 54 17W
Máida, *Italy* **41** **D9** 38 51N 16 21 E
Maidan Khula, *Afghan.* **80** **C3** 33 36N 69 50 E
Maidenhead, *U.K.* **17** **F7** 51 31N 0 42W
Maidi, *Yemen* **95** **D5** 16 20N 42 45 E
Maidstone, *Canada* **131** **C7** 53 5N 109 20W
Maidstone, *U.K.* **17** **F8** 51 16N 0 31 E
Maiduguri, *Nigeria* **101** **C7** 12 0N 13 20 E
Maignelay, *France* **23** **C9** 49 32N 2 30 E
Maigo, *Phil.* **71** **G4** 8 10N 123 57 E
Maigualida, Sierra, *Venezuela* **153** **B4** 5 30N 65 10W
Maigudo, *Ethiopia* **95** **F4** 7 30N 37 8 E
Maijdi, *Bangla.* **78** **D3** 22 48N 91 10 E
Maikala Ra., *India* **82** **D5** 22 0N 81 0 E
Maikoor, *Indonesia* **73** **C4** 6 8 S 134 6 E
Mailly-le-Camp, *France* **23** **D11** 48 41N 4 12 E
Mailsi, *Pakistan* **80** **E5** 29 48N 72 15 E
Maimbung, *Phil.* **71** **J3** 5 56N 121 2 E
Main →, *Germany* **27** **F4** 50 0N 8 18 E
Main →, *U.K.* **19** **B5** 54 49N 6 20W
Main Centre, *Canada* **131** **C7** 50 35N 107 21W
Mainburg, *Germany* **27** **G7** 48 37N 11 49 E
Maine, *France* **22** **E6** 47 55N 0 25W
Maine □, *U.S.A.* **129** **C6** 45 20N 69 0W
Maine →, *Ireland* **19** **D2** 52 10N 9 40W
Maine-et-Loire □, *France* **22** **E6** 47 31N 0 30W
Maïne-Soroa, *Niger* **101** **C7** 13 13N 12 2 E
Maingkwan, *Burma* **78** **B6** 26 15N 96 37 E
Mainit, *Phil.* **71** **G5** 9 32N 125 32 E
Mainit, L., *Phil.* **71** **G5** 9 31N 125 30 E
Mainkaing, *Burma* **78** **C5** 24 48N 95 16 E
Mainland, *Orkney, U.K.* **18** **C5** 59 0N 3 10W
Mainland, *Shet., U.K.* **18** **A7** 60 15N 1 22W
Mainpuri, *India* **81** **F8** 27 18N 79 4 E
Maintenon, *France* **23** **D8** 48 35N 1 35 E
Maintirano, *Madag.* **105** **B7** 18 3 S 44 1 E
Mainvault, *Belgium* **21** **G3** 50 39N 3 43 E
Mainz, *Germany* **27** **F4** 50 0N 8 17 E
Maipú, *Argentina* **158** **D4** 36 52 S 57 50W
Maiquetía, *Venezuela* **152** **A4** 10 36N 66 57W
Maira →, *Italy* **38** **D4** 44 49N 7 38 E
Mairabari, *India* **78** **B4** 26 30N 92 22 E
Mairipotaba, *Brazil* **155** **E2** 17 18 S 49 28W
Maisí, *Cuba* **149** **B5** 20 17N 74 9W
Maisi, Pta. de, *Cuba* **149** **B5** 20 10N 74 10W
Maisse, *France* **23** **D9** 48 24N 2 21 E
Maissin, *Belgium* **21** **J6** 49 58N 5 10 E
Maitland, *N.S.W., Australia* **117** **B9** 32 33 S 151 36 E
Maitland, *S. Austral., Australia* **116** **C2** 34 23 S 137 40 E
Maitland →, *Canada* **136** **C3** 43 45N 81 43W
Maitland, Banjaran, *Malaysia* **75** **B5** 4 55N 116 37 E
Maiyema, *Nigeria* **101** **C5** 12 5N 4 25 E
Maiyuan, *China* **69** **E11** 25 34N 117 28 E
Maiz, Is. del, *Nic.* **148** **D3** 12 15N 83 4W
Maizuru, *Japan* **63** **B7** 35 25N 135 22 E
Majagual, *Colombia* **152** **B3** 8 33N 74 38W
Majalengka, *Indonesia* **75** **D3** 6 50 S 108 13 E
Majari →, *Brazil* **153** **C5** 3 29N 60 58W
Majene, *Indonesia* **72** **B1** 3 38 S 118 57 E
Majes →, *Peru* **156** **D3** 16 40 S 72 44W
Majevica, *Bos.-H., Yug.* **42** **C3** 44 45N 18 50 E
Maji, *Ethiopia* **95** **F4** 6 12N 35 30 E
Majiang, *China* **68** **D6** 26 28N 107 32 E
Major, *Canada* **131** **C7** 51 52N 109 37W
Majorca = Mallorca, *Spain* **33** **B10** 39 30N 3 0 E
Majors Creek, *Australia* **117** **C8** 35 33 S 149 45 E
Majuriã, *Brazil* **157** **B5** 7 30 S 64 55W
Maka, *Senegal* **100** **C2** 13 40N 14 10W
Makak, *Cameroon* **101** **E7** 3 36N 11 0 E
Makakou, *Gabon* **102** **C2** 0 11 S 12 12 E
Makale, *Indonesia* **72** **B1** 3 6 S 119 51 E
Makamba, *Burundi* **106** **C2** 4 8 S 29 49 E
Makarewa, *N.Z.* **119** **G3** 46 20 S 168 21 E
Makarikari = Makgadikgadi Salt Pans, *Botswana* **104** **C4** 20 40 S 25 45 E
Makarovo, *Russia* **57** **D11** 57 40N 107 45 E
Makarska, *Croatia* **42** **D2** 43 20N 17 2 E
Makaryev, *Russia* **51** **C13** 57 52N 43 50 E
Makasar = Ujung Pandang, *Indonesia* **72** **C1** 5 10 S 119 20 E
Makasar, Selat, *Indonesia* **72** **B1** 1 0 S 118 20 E
Makasar, Str. of = Makasar, Selat, *Indonesia* **72** **B1** 1 0 S 118 20 E
Makat, *Kazakhstan* **49** **E9** 47 39N 53 19 E
Makedhonía □, *Greece* **44** **D3** 40 39N 22 0 E
Makedonija = Macedonia □, *Macedonia, Yug.* **42** **F6** 41 53N 21 40 E
Makena, *U.S.A.* **132** **H16** 20 39N 156 27W
Makeni, *S. Leone* **100** **D2** 8 55N 12 5W
Makeyevka, *Ukraine* **52** **B7** 48 0N 38 0 E
Makgadikgadi Salt Pans, *Botswana* **104** **C4** 20 40 S 25 45 E
Makhachkala, *Russia* **53** **E12** 43 0N 47 30 E
Makhambet, *Kazakhstan* **53** **C14** 47 43N 51 40 E
Makharadze = Ozurgety, *Georgia* **53** **F10** 41 55N 42 2 E
Makhmūr, *Iraq* **84** **C4** 35 46N 43 35 E
Makhyah, W. →, *Yemen* **87** **C5** 17 40N 49 1 E
Makian, *Indonesia* **72** **A3** 0 20N 127 20 E
Makindu, *Kenya* **106** **C4** 2 18 S 37 50 E
Makinsk, *Kazakhstan* **56** **D8** 52 37N 70 26 E
Makkah, *Si. Arabia* **86** **B2** 21 30N 39 54 E
Makkovik, *Canada* **129** **A8** 55 10N 59 10W
Makkum, *Neths.* **20** **B6** 53 3N 5 25 E
Makó, *Hungary* **31** **E13** 46 14N 20 33 E
Makok, *Gabon* **102** **C1** 0 1 S 9 35 E
Makokou, *Gabon* **102** **B2** 0 40N 12 50 E
Makongo, *Zaïre* **106** **B2** 3 25N 26 17 E
Makoro, *Zaïre* **106** **B2** 3 10N 29 59 E
Makoua, *Congo* **102** **C3** 0 5 S 15 50 E
Maków Mazowiecki, *Poland* **47** **C8** 52 52N 21 6 E
Maków Podhal, *Poland* **31** **B12** 49 43N 19 45 E
Makrá, *Greece* **45** **H7** 36 15N 25 54 E
Makran, *Asia* **79** **D1** 26 13N 61 30 E
Makran Coast Range, *Pakistan* **79** **D2** 25 40N 64 0 E
Makrana, *India* **80** **F6** 27 2N 74 46 E
Mákri, *Greece* **44** **D7** 40 52N 25 40 E
Makriyialos, *Greece* **32** **D7** 35 2N 25 59 E
Maksimkin Yar, *Russia* **56** **D9** 58 42N 86 50 E
Maktar, *Tunisia* **96** **A1** 35 48N 9 12 E
Mākū, *Iran* **84** **B5** 39 15N 44 31 E
Makum, *India* **78** **B5** 27 30N 95 23 E
Makumbi, *Zaïre* **103** **D4** 5 50 S 20 43 E
Makunda, *Botswana* **104** **C3** 22 30 S 20 7 E
Makurazaki, *Japan* **62** **F2** 31 15N 130 20 E
Makurdi, *Nigeria* **101** **D6** 7 43N 8 35 E
Makūyeh, *Iran* **85** **D7** 28 7N 53 9 E
Makwassie, *S. Africa* **104** **D4** 27 17 S 26 0 E
Mal, *India* **78** **B2** 26 51N 88 45 E
Mal B., *Ireland* **19** **D2** 52 50N 9 30W
Mal i Gjalicës së Lumës, *Albania* **44** **B2** 42 2N 20 25 E
Mal i Gribës, *Albania* **44** **D1** 40 17N 19 45 E
Mal i Nemërçkës, *Albania* **44** **D2** 40 15N 20 15 E
Mal i Tomorit, *Albania* **44** **D2** 40 42N 20 11 E
Mala, *Peru* **156** **C2** 12 40 S 76 38W
Mala, Pta., *Panama* **148** **E3** 7 28N 80 2W
Mala Kapela, *Croatia* **39** **D12** 44 45N 15 30 E
Malabang, *Phil.* **71** **H5** 7 36N 124 3 E
Malabar Coast, *India* **83** **J2** 11 0N 75 0 E
Malabo = Rey Malabo, *Eq. Guin.* **101** **E6** 3 45N 8 50 E
Malabon, *Phil.* **70** **D3** 14 21N 121 0 E
Malabrigo Pt., *Phil.* **70** **E3** 13 36N 121 15 E
Malabungan, *Phil.* **71** **G1** 9 3N 117 38 E
Malacca, Str. of, *Indonesia* **77** **L3** 3 0N 101 0 E
Malacky, *Czech.* **31** **C10** 48 27N 17 0 E
Malad City, *U.S.A.* **142** **E7** 42 10N 112 20W
Málaga, *Colombia* **152** **B3** 6 42N 72 44W
Málaga, *Spain* **37** **J6** 36 43N 4 23W
Malaga, *U.S.A.* **139** **J2** 32 12N 104 2W
Málaga □, *Spain* **37** **J6** 36 38N 4 58W
Malagarasi, *Tanzania* **106** **D3** 5 5 S 30 50 E
Malagarasi →, *Tanzania* **106** **D2** 5 12 S 29 47 E
Malagón, *Spain* **37** **F7** 39 11N 3 52W
Malagón →, *Spain* **37** **H3** 37 35N 7 29W
Malaimbandy, *Madag.* **105** **C8** 20 20 S 45 36 E
Malaita, *Pac. Oc.* **121** **M11** 9 0 S 161 0 E
Malakâl, *Sudan* **95** **F3** 9 33N 31 40 E
Malakand, *Pakistan* **79** **B3** 34 40N 71 55 E
Malakoff, *U.S.A.* **139** **J7** 32 10N 95 55W
Malalag, *Phil.* **71** **H5** 6 36N 125 24 E
Malam, *Chad* **97** **F4** 11 27N 20 59 E
Malamyzh, *Russia* **57** **E14** 49 50N 136 50 E
Malang, *Indonesia* **75** **D4** 7 59 S 112 45 E
Malangas, *Phil.* **71** **H4** 7 37N 123 1 E
Malange, *Angola* **103** **D3** 9 36 S 16 17 E
Malange □, *Angola* **103** **D3** 9 30 S 16 0 E
Mälaren, *Sweden* **14** **E11** 59 30N 17 10 E
Malargüe, *Argentina* **158** **D2** 35 32 S 69 30W
Malartic, *Canada* **128** **C4** 48 9N 78 9W
Malatya, *Turkey* **89** **D8** 38 25N 38 20 E
Malatya □, *Turkey* **89** **D8** 38 15N 38 0 E
Malawali, *Malaysia* **75** **A5** 7 3N 117 18 E
Malawi ■, *Africa* **107** **E3** 11 55 S 34 0 E
Malawi, L., *Africa* **107** **E3** 12 30 S 34 30 E
Malay, *Phil.* **71** **F3** 11 54N 121 55 E
Malay Pen., *Asia* **77** **J3** 7 25N 100 0 E
Malaya Belozërka, *Ukraine* **52** **C6** 47 12N 34 56 E
Malaya Vishera, *Russia* **50** **B8** 58 55N 32 25 E
Malaya Viska, *Ukraine* **52** **B4** 48 39N 31 36 E
Malaybalay, *Phil.* **71** **G5** 8 5N 125 7 E
Malāyer, *Iran* **85** **C6** 34 19N 48 51 E
Malaysia ■, *Asia* **74** **B4** 5 0N 110 0 E
Malazgirt, *Turkey* **89** **D10** 39 10N 42 33 E
Malbon, *Australia* **114** **C3** 21 5 S 140 17 E
Malbooma, *Australia* **115** **E1** 30 41 S 134 11 E
Malbork, *Poland* **47** **A6** 54 3N 19 1 E
Malca Dube, *Ethiopia* **108** **C2** 6 47N 42 4 E
Malcésine, *Italy* **38** **C7** 45 46N 10 48 E
Malchin, *Germany* **26** **B8** 53 43N 12 44 E
Malchow, *Germany* **26** **B8** 53 29N 12 25 E
Malcolm, *Australia* **113** **E3** 28 51 S 121 25 E
Malcolm, Pt., *Australia* **113** **F3** 33 48 S 123 45 E
Malczyce, *Poland* **47** **D3** 51 14N 16 29 E
Maldegem, *Belgium* **21** **F2** 51 14N 3 26 E
Malden, *Mass., U.S.A.* **137** **D13** 42 26N 71 5W
Malden, *Mo., U.S.A.* **139** **G10** 36 35N 90 0W
Malden I., *Kiribati* **123** **H12** 4 3 S 155 1W
Maldives ■, *Ind. Oc.* **58** **J11** 5 0N 73 0 E
Maldon, *Australia* **116** **D6** 37 0 S 144 6 E
Maldonado, *Uruguay* **159** **C5** 34 59 S 55 0W
Maldonado, Punta, *Mexico* **147** **D5** 16 19N 98 35W
Malé, *Italy* **38** **B7** 46 20N 10 55 E
Malé Karpaty, *Czech.* **31** **C10** 48 30N 17 20 E
Maléa, Ákra, *Greece* **45** **H5** 36 28N 23 7 E
Malebo, Pool, *Africa* **103** **C3** 4 17 S 15 20 E
Malegaon, *India* **82** **D2** 20 30N 74 38 E
Malei, *Mozam.* **107** **F4** 17 12 S 36 58 E
Malek Kandī, *Iran* **84** **B5** 37 9N 46 6 E
Malekula, *Vanuatu* **121** **F5** 16 15 S 167 30 E
Malela, *Bas Zaïre, Zaïre* **103** **D2** 5 59 S 12 37 E

Manzai 229


Malela, Kivu, Zaïre 103 C5 4 22 S 26 8 E
Malema, Mozam. 107 E4 14 57 S 37 20 E
Máleme, Greece 32 D5 35 31N 23 49 E
Malerkotla, India 80 D6 30 32N 75 58 E
Máles, Greece 32 D7 35 6N 25 35 E
Malesherbes, France 23 D9 48 15N 2 24 E
Maleshevska Planina, Europe 42 F8 41 38N 23 7 E
Malestroit, France 22 E4 47 49N 2 25W
Malfa, Italy 41 D7 38 35N 14 50 E
Malgobek, Russia 53 E11 43 30N 44 34 E
Malgomaj, Sweden 12 D14 64 40N 16 30 E
Malgrat, Spain 34 D7 41 39N 2 46 E
Malha, Sudan 95 D2 15 8N 25 10 E
Malheur →, U.S.A. 142 D5 44 3N 116 59W
Malheur L., U.S.A. 142 E4 43 19N 118 42W
Mali, Guinea 100 C2 12 10N 12 20W
Mali ■, Africa 100 B4 17 0N 3 0W
Mali Hka →, Burma 78 C6 25 42N 97 30 E
Mali Kanal, Serbia, Yug. 42 B4 45 36N 19 24 E
Malibu, U.S.A. 145 L8 34 2N 118 41W
Maligaya, Phil. 70 E3 12 59N 121 30 E
Malik, Indonesia 72 B2 0 39 S 123 16 E
Malili, Indonesia 72 B2 2 42 S 121 6 E
Malimba, Mts., Zaïre 106 D2 7 30 S 29 30 E
Malin, Ukraine 50 F6 50 46N 29 3 E
Malin Hd., Ireland 19 A4 55 18N 7 24W
Malindang, Mt., Phil. 71 G4 8 13N 123 38 E
Malindi, Kenya 106 C5 3 12 S 40 5 E
Malines = Mechelen, Belgium 21 F4 51 2N 4 29 E
Maling, Indonesia 72 A2 1 0N 121 0 E
Malinyi, Tanzania 107 D4 8 56 S 36 0 E
Malipo, China 68 F5 23 7N 104 42 E
Maliqi, Albania 44 D2 40 45N 20 48 E
Malita, Phil. 71 H5 6 19N 125 39 E
Maljenik, Serbia, Yug. 42 D6 43 59N 21 55 E
Malkapur, Maharashtra, India 82 F3 16 57N 76 17 E
Malkapur, Maharashtra, India 82 D1 20 53N 73 58 E
Malkara, Turkey 88 C2 40 53N 26 53 E
Małkinia Górna, Poland 47 C9 52 42N 22 5 E
Malko Tŭrnovo, Bulgaria 43 F12 41 59N 27 31 E
Mallacoota, Australia 117 D8 37 40 S 149 40 E
Mallacoota Inlet, Australia 117 D8 37 34 S 149 40 E
Mallaig, U.K. 18 E3 57 0N 5 50W
Mallala, Australia 116 C3 34 26 S 138 30 E
Mallard, U.S.A. 140 B2 42 56N 94 41W
Mallawan, India 81 F9 27 4N 80 12 E
Mallawi, Egypt 94 B3 27 44N 30 44 E
Malleco □, Chile 160 A2 38 10 S 72 20W
Mallemort, France 25 E9 43 43N 5 11 E
Málles Venosta, Italy 38 B7 46 42N 10 32 E
Mállia, Greece 32 D7 35 17N 25 27 E
Mallicolo = Malekula, Vanuatu 121 F5 16 15 S 167 30 E
Mallig, Phil. 70 C3 17 8N 121 42 E
Mallión, Kólpos, Greece 32 D7 35 19N 25 27 E
Mallorca, Spain 33 B10 39 30N 3 0 E
Mallorytown, Canada 137 B9 44 29N 75 53W
Mallow, Ireland 19 D3 52 8N 8 40W
Malmberget, Sweden 12 C16 67 11N 20 40 E
Malmédy, Belgium 21 H8 50 25N 6 2 E
Malmesbury, S. Africa 104 E2 33 28 S 18 41 E
Malmö, Sweden 15 J6 55 36N 12 59 E
Malmöhus län □, Sweden 15 J7 55 45N 13 30 E
Malmslätt, Sweden 15 F9 58 27N 15 33 E
Malmyzh, Russia 54 C2 56 31N 50 41 E
Malnaş, Romania 46 C6 46 2N 25 49 E
Malo, Vanuatu 121 E5 15 40 S 167 11 E
Malo Konare, Bulgaria 43 E9 42 12N 24 24 E
Maloarkhangelsk, Russia 51 E10 52 28N 36 30 E
Maloca, Brazil 153 C6 0 43 S 55 57W
Maloja, Switz. 29 D9 46 25N 9 35 E
Maloja, P., Switz. 29 D9 46 23N 9 42 E
Malolos, Phil. 70 D3 14 50N 120 49 E
Malomalsk, Russia 54 B6 58 45N 59 53 E
Malombe L., Malawi 107 E4 14 40 S 35 15 E
Malomir, Bulgaria 43 E11 42 16N 26 30 E
Malone, U.S.A. 137 B10 44 50N 74 19W
Malong, China 68 E4 25 24N 103 34 E
Malonga, Zaïre 103 E4 10 24 S 23 10 E
Malorad, Bulgaria 43 D8 43 28N 23 41 E
Malorita, Belorussia 50 F4 51 50N 24 3 E
Maloyaroslovets, Russia 51 D10 55 2N 36 20 E
Malozemelskaya Tundra, Russia 48 A9 67 0N 50 0 E
Malpartida, Spain 37 F4 39 26N 6 30W
Malpaso, Canary Is. 33 G1 27 43N 18 3W
Malpelo, Colombia 156 A1 4 3N 81 35W
Malpica, Spain 36 B2 43 19N 8 50W
Malprabha →, India 83 F3 16 20N 76 5 E
Malta, Brazil 154 C4 6 54 S 37 31W
Malta, Idaho, U.S.A. 142 E7 42 15N 113 30W
Malta, Mont., U.S.A. 142 B10 48 20N 107 55W
Malta ■, Europe 32 D1 35 50N 14 30 E
Malta Channel, Medit. S. 40 F6 36 40N 14 0 E
Maltahöhe, Namibia 104 C2 24 55 S 17 0 E
Malters, Switz. 28 B6 47 3N 8 11 E
Malton, Canada 136 C5 43 42N 79 38W
Malton, U.K. 16 C7 54 9N 0 48W
Malu'a, Solomon Is. 121 M11 8 0 S 160 0 E
Maluku, Indonesia 72 B3 1 0 S 127 0 E
Maluku □, Indonesia 72 B3 3 0 S 128 0 E
Maluku Sea, Indonesia 72 A3 4 0 S 124 0 E
Malumfashi, Nigeria 101 C6 11 48N 7 39 E
Malungun, Phil. 71 H5 6 16N 125 14 E
Maluso, Phil. 71 H3 6 33N 121 53 E
Malvalli, India 83 H3 12 28N 77 8 E
Malvan, India 83 F1 16 2N 73 30 E
Malvern, U.S.A. 139 H8 34 22N 92 50W
Malvern Hills, U.K. 17 E5 52 0N 2 19W
Malvik, Norway 14 A4 63 25N 10 40 E
Malvinas, Is. = Falkland Is., Atl. Oc. 160 D5 51 30 S 59 0W
Malya, Tanzania 106 C3 3 5 S 33 38 E
Malybay, Kazakhstan 55 B9 43 30N 78 25 E
Malyy Lyakhovskiy, Ostrov, Russia 57 B15 74 7N 140 36 E
Mama, Russia 57 D12 58 18N 112 54 E
Mamadysh, Russia 54 D2 55 44N 51 23 E
Mamaia, Romania 46 E9 44 18N 28 37 E
Mamaku, N.Z. 118 E5 38 5 S 176 8 E
Mamanguape, Brazil 154 C4 6 50 S 35 4W
Mamasa, Indonesia 72 B1 2 55 S 119 20 E
Mambajao, Phil. 71 G5 9 15N 124 43 E
Mambasa, Zaïre 106 B2 1 22N 29 3 E
Mamberamo →, Indonesia 73 B5 2 0 S 137 50 E
Mambilima Falls, Zambia 107 E2 10 31 S 28 45 E
Mambirima, Zaïre 107 E2 11 25 S 27 33 E
Mambo, Tanzania 106 C4 4 52 S 38 22 E
Mambrui, Kenya 106 C5 3 5 S 40 5 E
Mamburao, Phil. 70 E3 13 13N 120 39 E
Mameigwess L., Canada 128 B2 52 35N 87 50W
Mamer, Lux. 21 J8 49 38N 6 2 E
Mamers, France 22 D7 48 21N 0 22 E
Mamfe, Cameroon 101 D6 5 50N 9 15 E
Māmī, Ra's, Yemen 87 D6 12 32N 54 30 E
Mamiña, Chile 156 E4 20 5 S 69 14W
Mámmola, Italy 41 D9 38 23N 16 13 E
Mammoth, U.S.A. 143 K8 32 46N 110 43W
Mamoré →, Bolivia 157 C4 10 23 S 65 53W
Mamou, Guinea 100 C2 10 15N 12 0W
Mamparang Mts., Phil. 70 C3 16 21N 121 28 E
Mampatá, Guinea-Biss. 100 C2 11 54N 14 53W
Mampong, Ghana 101 D4 7 6N 1 26W
Mamry, Jezioro, Poland 47 A8 54 5N 21 50 E
Mamuil Malal, Paso, S. Amer. 160 A2 39 35 S 71 28W
Mamuju, Indonesia 72 B1 2 41 S 118 50 E
Ma'mūl, Oman 87 C6 18 8N 55 16 E
Man, Ivory C. 100 D3 7 30N 7 40W
Man →, India 82 F2 17 31N 75 32 E
Man, I. of, U.K. 16 C3 54 15N 4 30W
Man Na, Burma 78 D6 23 27N 97 19 E
Man Tun, Burma 78 D7 23 52N 98 38 E
Mana, Fr. Guiana 153 B7 5 45N 53 55W
Mana →, Fr. Guiana 153 B7 5 45N 53 55W
Måna →, Norway 14 E2 59 55N 8 50 E
Manaar, G. of = Mannar, G. of, Asia 83 K4 8 30N 79 0 E
Manabí □, Ecuador 152 D1 0 40 S 80 5W
Manacacías →, Colombia 152 C3 4 23N 72 4W
Manacapuru, Brazil 153 D5 3 16 S 60 37W
Manacapuru →, Brazil 153 D5 3 18 S 60 37W
Manacor, Spain 33 B10 39 34N 3 13 E
Manado, Indonesia 72 A2 1 29N 124 51 E
Manage, Belgium 21 G4 50 31N 4 15 E
Managua, Nic. 148 D2 12 6N 86 20W
Managua, L., Nic. 148 D2 12 20N 86 30W
Manaia, N.Z. 118 F3 39 33 S 174 8 E
Manakara, Madag. 105 C8 22 8 S 48 1 E
Manakau Mt., N.Z. 119 C8 42 15 S 173 42 E
Manākhah, Yemen 86 D3 15 5N 43 44 E
Manakino, N.Z. 118 E4 38 22 S 175 47 E
Manam I., Papua N. G. 120 C3 4 5 S 145 0 E
Manambao →, Madag. 105 B7 17 35 S 44 0 E
Manambato, Madag. 105 A8 13 43 S 49 7 E
Manambolo →, Madag. 105 B7 19 18 S 44 22 E
Manambolosy, Madag. 105 B8 16 2 S 49 40 E
Mananara, Madag. 105 B8 16 10 S 49 46 E
Mananara →, Madag. 105 C8 23 21 S 47 42 E
Mananjary, Madag. 105 C8 21 13 S 48 20 E
Manantenina, Madag. 105 C8 24 17 S 47 19 E
Manaos = Manaus, Brazil 153 D6 3 0 S 60 0W
Manapala, Phil. 71 F4 10 58N 123 5 E
Manapire →, Venezuela 152 B4 7 42N 66 7W
Manapouri, N.Z. 119 F2 45 34 S 167 39 E
Manapouri, L., N.Z. 119 F2 45 32 S 167 32 E
Manar →, India 82 E3 18 50N 77 20 E
Manār, Jabal, Yemen 86 D4 14 2N 44 17 E
Manas, China 64 B3 44 17N 85 56 E
Manas, Somali Rep. 108 D2 2 57N 43 28 E
Manas, Gora, Kirghizia 55 B5 42 22N 71 2 E
Manaslu, Nepal 81 E11 28 33N 84 33 E
Manasquan, U.S.A. 137 F10 40 7N 74 3W
Manassa, U.S.A. 143 H11 37 12N 105 58W
Manaung, Burma 78 F4 18 45N 93 40 E
Manaus, Brazil 153 D6 3 0 S 60 0W
Manavgat, Turkey 88 E4 36 47N 31 26 E
Manawan L., Canada 131 B8 55 24N 103 14W
Manawatu →, N.Z. 118 G4 40 28 S 175 12 E
Manay, Phil. 71 H6 7 17N 126 33 E
Manbij, Syria 84 B3 36 31N 37 57 E
Mancelona, U.S.A. 134 C3 44 54N 85 5W
Mancha Real, Spain 37 H7 37 48N 3 39W
Manche □, France 22 C5 49 10N 1 20W
Manchegorsk, Russia 48 A5 67 40N 32 40 E
Manchester, U.K. 16 D5 53 30N 2 15W
Manchester, Calif., U.S.A. 144 G3 38 58N 123 41W
Manchester, Conn., U.S.A. 137 E12 41 47N 72 30W
Manchester, Ga., U.S.A. 135 J3 32 53N 84 32W
Manchester, Iowa, U.S.A. 140 B5 42 28N 91 27W
Manchester, Ky., U.S.A. 134 G4 37 9N 83 45W
Manchester, Mich., U.S.A. 141 B12 42 9N 84 2W
Manchester, N.H., U.S.A. 137 D13 42 58N 71 29W
Manchester, N.Y., U.S.A. 136 D7 42 56N 77 16W
Manchester, Vt., U.S.A. 137 C11 43 10N 73 5W
Manchester L., Canada 131 A7 61 28N 107 29W
Manchuria = Dongbei, China 67 D13 42 0N 125 0 E
Manciano, Italy 39 F8 42 35N 11 30 E
Mancifa, Ethiopia 95 F5 6 53N 41 50 E
Mancora, Pta., Peru 156 A1 4 9 S 81 1W
Mand →, Iran 85 D7 28 20N 52 30 E
Manda, Chunya, Tanzania 106 D3 6 51 S 32 29 E
Manda, Ludewe, Tanzania 107 E3 10 30 S 34 40 E
Mandabé, Madag. 105 C7 21 0 S 44 55 E
Mandaguari, Brazil 159 A5 23 32 S 51 42W
Mandah, Mongolia 66 B5 44 27N 108 2 E
Mandal, Norway 13 G9 58 2N 7 25 E
Mandalay, Burma 78 D6 22 0N 96 4 E
Mandale = Mandalay, Burma 78 D6 22 0N 96 4 E
Mandalgovi, Mongolia 66 B4 45 45N 106 10 E
Mandalī, Iraq 84 C5 33 43N 45 28 E
Mandalya Körfezi, Turkey 45 G9 37 15N 27 20 E
Mandan, U.S.A. 138 B4 46 50N 101 0W
Mandaon, Phil. 70 E4 12 13N 123 17 E
Mandapeta, India 82 F5 16 47N 81 56 E
Mandar, Teluk, Indonesia 72 B1 3 35 S 119 15 E
Mandas, Italy 40 C2 39 40N 9 8 E
Mandasor = Mandsaur, India 80 G6 24 3N 75 8 E
Mandaue, Phil. 71 F4 10 20N 123 56 E
Mandayar, Phil. 71 H6 7 34N 126 14 E
Mandelieu-la-Napoule, France 25 E10 43 34N 6 57 E
Mandera, Kenya 106 B5 3 55N 41 53 E
Mandera □, Kenya 106 B5 3 30N 41 0 E
Manderfeld, Belgium 21 H8 50 20N 6 20 E
Mandi, India 80 D7 31 39N 76 58 E
Mandimba, Mozam. 107 E4 14 20 S 35 40 E
Mandioli, Indonesia 72 B3 0 40 S 127 20 E
Mandioré, L., S. Amer. 157 D6 18 8 S 57 33W
Mandji I. = Lopez I., Gabon 102 C1 0 50 S 8 47 E
Mandla, India 81 H9 22 39N 80 30 E
Mandø, Denmark 15 J2 55 18N 8 33 E
Mandoto, Madag. 105 B8 19 34 S 46 17 E
Mandoúdhion, Greece 45 F5 38 48N 23 29 E
Mandra, Pakistan 80 C5 33 23N 73 12 E
Mandráki, Greece 45 H9 36 36N 27 11 E
Mandrare →, Madag. 105 D8 25 10 S 46 30 E
Mandritsara, Madag. 105 B8 15 50 S 48 49 E
Mandsaur, India 80 G6 24 3N 75 8 E
Mandurah, Australia 113 F2 32 36 S 115 48 E
Mandúria, Italy 41 B10 40 25N 17 38 E
Mandvi, India 80 H3 22 51N 69 22 E
Mandya, India 83 H3 12 30N 77 0 E
Mandzai, Pakistan 80 D2 30 55N 67 6 E
Mané, Burkina Faso 101 C4 12 59N 1 21W
Maneh, Iran 85 B8 37 39N 57 7 E
Manenguba, Mts., Cameroon 101 D6 5 0N 9 50 E
Maner →, India 82 E4 18 30N 79 40 E
Maneroo, Australia 114 C3 23 22 S 143 53 E
Maneroo Cr. →, Australia 114 C3 23 21 S 143 53 E
Manfalût, Egypt 94 B3 27 20N 30 52 E
Manfred, Australia 116 B5 33 19 S 143 45 E
Manfredónia, Italy 41 A8 41 40N 15 55 E
Manfredónia, G. di, Italy 41 A9 41 30N 16 10 E
Manga, Brazil 155 D3 14 46 S 43 56W
Manga, Burkina Faso 101 C4 11 40N 1 4W
Manga, Niger 97 F2 15 0N 14 0 E
Mangabeiras, Chapada das, Brazil 154 D2 10 0 S 46 30W
Mangal, Phil. 71 H3 6 25N 121 58 E
Mangalagiri, India 83 F5 16 26N 80 36 E
Mangaldai, India 78 B4 26 26N 92 2 E
Mangalia, Romania 46 F9 43 50N 28 35 E
Mangalore, Australia 117 D6 36 56 S 145 10 E
Mangalore, India 83 H2 12 55N 74 47 E
Manganeses, Spain 36 D5 41 45N 5 43W
Mangaon, India 82 E1 18 15N 73 20 E
Mangaweka, N.Z. 118 F4 39 48 S 175 47 E
Mangaweka, Mt., N.Z. 118 F5 39 49 S 176 5 E
Mange, Zaïre 102 B4 0 54N 20 30 E
Manggar, Indonesia 75 C3 2 50 S 108 10 E
Manggawitu, Indonesia 73 B4 4 8 S 133 32 E
Mangin Range, Burma 78 C5 24 15N 95 45 E
Mangkalihat, Tanjung, Indonesia 75 B5 1 2N 118 59 E
Mangla Dam, Pakistan 81 C5 33 9N 73 44 E
Manglares, C., Colombia 152 C2 1 36N 79 2W
Manglaur, India 80 E7 29 44N 77 49 E
Mangnai, China 64 C4 37 52N 91 43 E
Mango, Togo 101 C5 10 20N 0 30 E
Mangoche, Malawi 107 E4 14 25 S 35 16 E
Mangoky →, Madag. 105 C7 21 29 S 43 41 E
Mangole, Indonesia 72 B3 1 50 S 125 55 E
Mangombe, Zaïre 106 C2 1 20 S 26 48 E
Mangonui, N.Z. 118 B2 35 1 S 173 32 E
Mangualde, Portugal 36 E3 40 38N 7 48W
Mangueigne, Chad 97 F4 10 30N 21 15 E
Mangueira, L. da, Brazil 159 C5 33 0 S 52 50W
Manguéni, Hamada, Niger 96 D2 22 35N 12 40 E
Mangum, U.S.A. 139 H5 34 50N 99 30W
Mangyshlak Poluostrov, Kazakhstan 53 D15 44 30N 52 30 E
Mangyshlakskiy Zaliv, Kazakhstan 53 D14 44 40N 50 50 E
Manhattan, U.S.A. 138 F6 39 10N 96 40W
Manhatten, U.S.A. 141 C9 41 26N 87 59W
Manhiça, Mozam. 105 D5 25 23 S 32 49 E
Manhuaçu, Brazil 155 F3 20 15 S 42 2W
Manhumirim, Brazil 155 F3 20 22 S 41 57W
Maní, Colombia 152 C3 4 49N 72 17W
Mania →, Madag. 105 B8 19 42 S 45 22 E
Maniago, Italy 39 B9 46 11N 12 40 E
Manica, Mozam. 105 B5 18 58 S 32 59 E
Manica e Sofala □, Mozam. 105 B5 19 10 S 33 45 E
Manicaland □, Zimbabwe 107 F3 19 0 S 32 30 E
Manicoré, Brazil 157 B5 5 48 S 61 16W
Manicoré →, Brazil 157 B5 5 51 S 61 19W
Manicouagan →, Canada 129 C6 49 30N 68 30W
Manīfah, Si. Arabia 85 E6 27 44N 49 0 E
Manifold, Australia 114 C5 22 41 S 150 40 E
Manifold, C., Australia 114 C5 22 41 S 150 50 E
Manigganggo, China 68 B2 31 56N 99 10 E
Manigotagan, Canada 131 C9 51 6N 96 18W
Manihiki, Cook Is. 123 J11 10 24 S 161 1W
Manika, Plateau de la, Zaïre 107 E2 10 0 S 25 5 E
Manikganj, Bangla. 78 D3 23 52N 90 0 E
Manila, Phil. 70 D3 14 40N 121 3 E
Manila, U.S.A. 142 F9 41 0N 109 44W
Manila B., Phil. 70 D3 14 40N 120 35 E
Manilla, Australia 117 A9 30 45 S 150 43 E
Manimpé, Mali 100 C3 14 11N 5 28W
Maningrida, Australia 114 A1 12 3 S 134 13 E
Manipur □, India 78 C4 25 0N 94 0 E
Manipur →, Burma 78 D5 23 45N 94 20 E
Manisa, Turkey 88 D2 38 38N 27 30 E
Manisa □, Turkey 88 D2 38 40N 27 30 E
Manistee, U.S.A. 134 C2 44 15N 86 20W
Manistee →, U.S.A. 134 C2 44 15N 86 21W
Manistique, U.S.A. 134 C2 45 59N 86 18W
Manito, U.S.A. 140 D7 40 25N 89 47W
Manito L., Canada 131 C7 52 43N 109 43W
Manitoba □, Canada 131 B9 55 30N 97 0W
Manitoba, L., Canada 131 C9 51 0N 98 45W
Manitou, Canada 131 D9 49 15N 98 32W
Manitou Beach, U.S.A. 141 C12 41 58N 84 19W
Manitou I., U.S.A. 128 C2 47 22N 87 30W
Manitou Is., U.S.A. 134 C2 45 8N 86 0W
Manitou L., Canada 129 B6 50 55N 65 17W
Manitou Springs, U.S.A. 138 F2 38 52N 104 55W
Manitoulin I., Canada 128 C3 45 40N 82 30W
Manitowaning, Canada 128 C3 45 46N 81 49W
Manitowoc, U.S.A. 134 C2 44 8N 87 40W
Manitsauá-Missu →, Brazil 157 C7 10 58 S 53 20W
Manizales, Colombia 152 B2 5 5N 75 32W
Manja, Madag. 105 C7 21 26 S 44 20 E
Manjacaze, Mozam. 105 C5 24 45 S 34 0 E
Manjakandriana, Madag. 105 B8 18 55 S 47 47 E
Manjeri, India 83 J3 11 7N 76 11 E
Manjhand, Pakistan 79 D3 25 50N 68 10 E
Manjil, Iran 85 B6 36 46N 49 30 E
Manjimup, Australia 113 F2 34 15 S 116 6 E
Manjra →, India 82 E3 18 49N 77 52 E
Mankato, Kans., U.S.A. 138 F5 39 49N 98 11W
Mankato, Minn., U.S.A. 138 C8 44 8N 93 59W
Mankayan, Phil. 70 C3 16 52N 120 47 E
Mankayane, Swaziland 105 D5 26 40 S 31 4 E
Mankono, Ivory C. 100 D3 8 1N 6 10W
Mankota, Canada 131 D7 49 25N 107 5W
Manlay, Mongolia 66 B4 44 9N 107 0 E
Manlleu, Spain 34 C7 42 2N 2 17 E
Manly, Australia 117 B9 33 48 S 151 17 E
Manmad, India 82 D2 20 18N 74 28 E
Mann Ras., Australia 113 E5 26 6 S 130 5 E
Manna, Indonesia 74 C2 4 25 S 102 55 E
Mannahill, Australia 116 B3 32 25 S 140 0 E
Mannar, Sri Lanka 83 K4 9 1N 79 54 E
Mannar, G. of, Asia 83 K4 8 30N 79 0 E
Mannar I., Sri Lanka 83 K4 9 5N 79 45 E
Mannargudi, India 83 J4 10 45N 79 51 E
Mannduque □, Phil. 70 E4 13 18N 122 0 E
Männedorf, Switz. 29 B7 47 15N 8 43 E
Mannheim, Germany 27 F4 49 28N 8 29 E
Manning, Canada 130 B5 56 53N 117 39W
Manning, Oreg., U.S.A. 144 E3 45 45N 123 13W
Manning, S.C., U.S.A. 135 J5 33 40N 80 9W
Manning Prov. Park, Canada 130 D4 49 5N 120 45W
Manning Str., Solomon Is. 121 L10 7 30 S 158 0 E
Mannington, U.S.A. 134 F5 39 35N 80 25W
Mannu →, Italy 40 C2 39 15N 9 32 E
Mannu, C., Italy 40 B1 40 2N 8 24 E
Mannum, Australia 116 C3 34 50 S 139 20 E
Mano, S. Leone 100 D2 8 3N 12 2W
Manoa, Bolivia 157 B4 9 40 S 65 27W
Manokwari, Indonesia 73 B4 0 54 S 134 0 E
Manolás, Greece 45 F3 38 4N 21 21 E
Manolo Fortich, Phil. 71 G5 8 28N 124 50 E
Manombo, Madag. 105 C7 22 57 S 43 28 E
Manono, Zaïre 106 D2 7 15 S 27 25 E
Manosque, France 25 E9 43 49N 5 47 E
Manouane, L., Canada 129 B5 50 45N 70 45W
Manouro, Pt., Vanuatu 121 G6 17 41 S 168 36 E
Manpojin, N. Korea 67 D14 41 6N 126 24 E
Manresa, Spain 34 D6 41 48N 1 50 E
Mansa, Gujarat, India 80 H5 23 27N 72 45 E
Mansa, Punjab, India 80 E6 30 0N 75 27 E
Mansa, Zambia 107 E2 11 13 S 28 55 E
Mansalay, Phil. 70 E3 12 31N 121 26 E
Mansehra, Pakistan 80 B5 34 20N 73 15 E
Mansel I., Canada 127 B11 62 0N 80 0W
Mansfield, Australia 117 D7 37 4 S 146 6 E
Mansfield, U.K. 16 D6 53 8N 1 12W
Mansfield, La., U.S.A. 139 J8 32 2N 93 40W
Mansfield, Mass., U.S.A. 137 D13 42 2N 71 12W
Mansfield, Ohio, U.S.A. 136 F2 40 45N 82 30W
Mansfield, Pa., U.S.A. 136 E7 41 48N 77 4W
Mansfield, Wash., U.S.A. 142 C4 47 51N 119 44W
Mansi, Burma 78 C5 24 48N 95 52 E
Mansidão, Brazil 154 D3 10 43 S 44 2W
Mansilla de las Mulas, Spain 36 C5 42 30N 5 25W
Mansle, France 24 C4 45 52N 0 12 E
Manso →, Brazil 155 D2 13 50 S 47 0W
Mansoa, Guinea-Biss. 100 C1 12 0N 15 20W
Manson, U.S.A. 140 B2 42 32N 94 32W
Manson Creek, Canada 130 B4 55 37N 124 32W
Mansoura, Algeria 99 A5 36 1N 4 31 E
Manta, Ecuador 152 D1 1 0 S 80 40W
Manta, B. de, Ecuador 152 D1 0 54 S 80 44W
Mantalingajan, Mt., Phil. 71 G1 8 55N 117 45 E
Mantare, Tanzania 106 C3 2 42 S 33 13 E
Manteca, U.S.A. 144 H5 37 50N 121 12W
Mantecal, Venezuela 152 B4 7 34N 69 17W
Mantena, Brazil 155 E3 18 47 S 40 59W
Manteno, U.S.A. 141 C9 41 15N 87 50W
Manteo, U.S.A. 135 H8 35 55N 75 41W
Mantes-la-Jolie, France 23 D8 48 58N 1 41 E
Manthani, India 82 E4 18 40N 79 35 E
Manthelan, France 22 E7 47 9N 0 47 E
Manti, U.S.A. 142 G8 39 23N 111 32W
Mantiqueira, Serra da, Brazil 155 F3 22 0 S 44 0W
Manton, U.S.A. 134 C3 44 23N 85 25W
Mantorp, Sweden 15 F9 58 21N 15 20 E
Mántova, Italy 38 C7 45 20N 10 42 E
Mänttä, Finland 12 E18 62 0N 24 40 E
Mantua = Mántova, Italy 38 C7 45 20N 10 42 E
Mantung, Australia 116 C4 34 35 S 140 3 E
Manturovo, Russia 51 B14 58 30N 44 30 E
Manu, Peru 156 C3 12 10 S 70 51W
Manu →, Peru 156 C3 12 16 S 70 55W
Manua Is., Amer. Samoa 121 X25 14 13 S 169 35W
Manuae, Cook Is. 123 J12 19 30 S 159 0W
Manuel Alves →, Brazil 155 D2 11 19 S 48 28W
Manuel Alves Grande →, Brazil 154 C2 7 27 S 47 35W
Manuel Urbano, Brazil 156 B4 8 53 S 69 18W
Manui, Indonesia 72 B2 3 35 S 123 5 E
Manukau Harbour, N.Z. 118 D3 37 3 S 174 45 E
Manunui, N.Z. 118 E4 38 54 S 175 21 E
Manurewa, N.Z. 118 D3 37 1 S 174 54 E
Manuripi →, Bolivia 156 C4 11 6 S 67 36W
Manus I., Papua N. G. 120 B4 2 0 S 147 0 E
Manvi, India 83 G3 15 57N 76 59 E
Manville, U.S.A. 138 D2 42 48N 104 36W
Manwath, India 82 E3 19 19N 76 32 E
Many, U.S.A. 139 K8 31 36N 93 28W
Manyara, L., Tanzania 106 C4 3 40 S 35 50 E
Manych →, Russia 53 C8 47 15N 39 45 E
Manych-Gudilo, Oz., Russia 53 C10 46 24N 42 38 E
Manyonga →, Tanzania 106 C3 4 10 S 34 15 E
Manyoni, Tanzania 106 D3 5 45 S 34 55 E
Manyoni □, Tanzania 106 D3 6 30 S 34 30 E
Manzai, Pakistan 79 B3 32 12N 70 15 E

230 Manzala, Bahra el


Manzala, Bahra el, *Egypt* **94 H7** 31 10N 31 56 E
Manzanares, *Spain* **35 F1** 39 2N 3 22W
Manzaneda, Cabeza de, *Spain* **36 C3** 42 12N 7 15W
Manzanillo, *Cuba* **148 B4** 20 20N 77 31W
Manzanillo, *Mexico* **146 D4** 19 0N 104 20W
Manzanillo, Pta., *Panama* **148 E4** 9 30N 79 40W
Manzano Mts., *U.S.A.* **143 J10** 34 30N 106 45W
Manzarīyeh, *Iran* **85 C6** 34 53N 50 50 E
Manzhouli, *China* **65 B6** 49 35N 117 25 E
Manzini, *Swaziland* **105 D5** 26 30 S 31 25 E
Mao, *Chad* **97 F3** 14 4N 15 19 E
Maoke, Pegunungan, *Indonesia* **73 B5** 3 40 S 137 30 E
Maolin, *China* **67 C12** 43 58N 123 30 E
Maoming, *China* **69 G8** 21 50N 110 54 E
Maowen, *China* **68 B4** 31 41N 103 49 E
Maoxing, *China* **67 B13** 45 28N 124 40 E
Mapam Yumco, *China* **64 C3** 30 45N 81 28 E
Mapastepec, *Mexico* **147 D6** 15 26N 92 54W
Mapia, Kepulauan, *Indonesia* **73 A4** 0 50N 134 20 E
Mapimí, *Mexico* **146 B4** 25 50N 103 50W
Mapimí, Bolsón de, *Mexico* **146 B4** 27 30N 104 15W
Maping, *China* **69 B9** 31 34N 113 32 E
Mapinga, *Tanzania* **106 D4** 6 40 S 39 12 E
Mapinhane, *Mozam.* **105 C6** 22 20 S 35 0 E
Mapire, *Venezuela* **153 B5** 7 45N 64 42W
Maple →, *U.S.A.* **141 B12** 42 58N 84 56W
Maple Creek, *Canada* **131 D7** 49 55N 109 29W
Maple Valley, *U.S.A.* **144 C4** 47 25N 122 3W
Mapleton, *U.S.A.* **142 D2** 44 4N 123 58W
Mapourika, L., *N.Z.* **119 D5** 43 16 S 170 12 E
Maprik, *Papua N. G.* **120 B2** 3 44 S 143 3 E
Mapuca, *India* **83 G1** 15 36N 73 46 E
Mapuera →, *Brazil* **153 D6** 1 5 S 57 2W
Maputing Baybay, *Phil.* **70 E4** 12 45N 123 20 E
Maputo, *Mozam.* **105 D5** 25 58 S 32 32 E
Maputo, B. de, *Mozam.* **105 D5** 25 50 S 32 45 E
Maqiaohe, *China* **67 B16** 44 40N 130 30 E
Maqnā, *Si. Arabia* **84 D2** 28 25N 34 50 E
Maqran, W. →, *Si. Arabia* **86 B4** 20 55N 47 12 E
Maqteïr, *Mauritania* **98 D2** 21 50N 11 40W
Maqueda Channel, *Phil.* **70 E5** 13 42N 124 1 E
Maquela do Zombo, *Angola* **103 D3** 6 0 S 15 15 E
Maquinchao, *Argentina* **160 B3** 41 15 S 68 50W
Maquoketa, *U.S.A.* **140 B6** 42 4N 90 40W
Mar, Serra do, *Brazil* **159 B6** 25 30 S 49 0W
Mar Chiquita, L., *Argentina* **158 C3** 30 40 S 62 50W
Mar del Plata, *Argentina* **158 D4** 38 0 S 57 30W
Mar Menor, L., *Spain* **35 H4** 37 40N 0 45W
Mara, *Guyana* **153 B6** 6 0N 57 36W
Mara, *India* **78 A5** 28 11N 94 14 E
Mara, *Tanzania* **106 C3** 1 30 S 34 32 E
Mara □, *Tanzania* **106 C3** 1 45 S 34 20 E
Maraã, *Brazil* **152 D4** 1 52 S 65 25W
Marabá, *Brazil* **154 C2** 5 20 S 49 5W
Maracá, I. de, *Brazil* **153 C7** 2 10N 50 30W
Maracaibo, *Venezuela* **152 A3** 10 40N 71 37W
Maracaibo, L. de, *Venezuela* **152 B3** 9 40N 71 30W
Maracaju, *Brazil* **159 A4** 21 38 S 55 9W
Maracajú, Serra de, *Brazil* **157 E6** 23 57 S 55 1W
Maracanã, *Brazil* **154 B2** 0 46 S 47 27W
Maracás, *Brazil* **155 D3** 13 26 S 40 18W
Maracay, *Venezuela* **152 A4** 10 15N 67 28W
Marādah, *Libya* **96 C3** 29 15N 19 15 E
Maradi, *Niger* **101 C6** 13 29N 7 20 E
Maradun, *Nigeria* **101 C6** 12 35N 6 18 E
Marāgheh, *Iran* **84 B5** 37 30N 46 12 E
Maragogipe, *Brazil* **155 D4** 12 46 S 38 55W
Maragondon, *Phil.* **70 D3** 14 16N 120 44 E
Marāh, *Si. Arabia* **84 E5** 25 0N 45 35 E
Marajó, B. de, *Brazil* **154 B2** 1 0 S 48 30W
Marajó, I. de, *Brazil* **154 B2** 1 0S 49 30W
Marākand, *Iran* **84 B5** 38 51N 45 16 E
Maralal, *Kenya* **106 B4** 1 0N 36 38 E
Maralinga, *Australia* **113 F5** 30 13 S 131 32 E
Marama, *Australia* **116 C4** 35 10 S 140 10 E
Maramasike, *Solomon Is.* **121 M11** 9 30 S 161 25 E
Marampa, *S. Leone* **100 D2** 8 45N 12 28W
Maramureș □, *Romania* **46 B4** 47 45N 24 0 E
Maran, *Malaysia* **77 L4** 3 35N 102 45 E
Marana, *U.S.A.* **143 K8** 32 30N 111 9W
Maranboy, *Australia* **112 B5** 14 40 S 132 39 E
Maranchón, *Spain* **34 D2** 41 6N 2 15W
Marand, *Iran* **84 B5** 38 30N 45 45 E
Marang, *Malaysia* **77 K4** 5 12N 103 13 E
Maranguape, *Brazil* **154 B4** 3 55 S 38 50W
Maranhão = São Luís, *Brazil* **154 B3** 2 39 S 44 15W
Maranhão □, *Brazil* **154 B2** 5 0 S 46 0W
Marano, L. di, *Italy* **39 C10** 45 42N 13 13 E
Maranoa →, *Australia* **115 D4** 27 50 S 148 37 E
Marañón →, *Peru* **156 A3** 4 30 S 73 35W
Marão, *Mozam.* **105 C5** 24 18 S 34 2 E
Marapi →, *Brazil* **153 C6** 0 37N 55 58W
Marari, *Brazil* **156 B4** 5 43 S 67 47W
Maraș = Kahramanmaraș, *Turkey* **88 E7** 37 37N 36 53 E
Mărășești, *Romania* **46 D8** 45 52N 27 14 E
Maratea, *Italy* **41 C8** 39 59N 15 43 E
Marateca, *Portugal* **37 G2** 38 34N 8 40W
Marathasa □, *Cyprus* **32 E11** 34 59N 32 51 E
Marathókambos, *Greece* **45 G8** 37 43N 26 42 E
Marathon, *Australia* **114 C3** 20 51 S 143 32 E
Marathon, *Canada* **128 C2** 48 44N 86 23W
Marathón, *Greece* **45 F5** 38 11N 23 58 E
Marathon, *Iowa, U.S.A.* **140 B2** 42 52N 94 59W
Marathon, *N.Y., U.S.A.* **137 D8** 42 25N 76 3W
Marathon, *Tex., U.S.A.* **139 K3** 30 15N 103 15W
Marathóvouno, *Cyprus* **32 D12** 35 13N 33 37 E
Maratua, *Indonesia* **75 B5** 2 10N 118 35 E
Maraú, *Brazil* **155 D4** 14 6 S 39 0W
Maravatío, *Mexico* **146 D4** 19 51N 100 25W
Marawi City, *Phil.* **71 G5** 8 0N 124 21 E
Marāwih, *U.A.E.* **85 E7** 24 18N 53 18 E
Marbella, *Spain* **37 J6** 36 30N 4 57W
Marble Bar, *Australia* **112 D2** 21 9 S 119 44 E
Marble Falls, *U.S.A.* **139 K5** 30 30N 98 15W
Marblehead, *U.S.A.* **137 D14** 42 29N 70 51W
Marburg, *Germany* **26 E4** 50 49N 8 36 E
Marby, *Sweden* **14 A8** 63 7N 14 18 E
Marcal →, *Hungary* **31 D10** 47 41N 17 32 E
Marcali, *Hungary* **31 E10** 46 35N 17 25 E
Marcapata, *Peru* **156 C3** 13 31 S 70 52W
Marcaria, *Italy* **38 C7** 45 7N 10 34 E
Marceline, *U.S.A.* **140 E4** 39 43N 92 57W
March, *U.K.* **17 E8** 52 33N 0 5 E
Marchal, *Zaïre* **103 D2** 5 16 S 14 58 E
Marchand = Rommani, *Morocco* **98 B3** 33 31N 6 40W
Marche, *France* **24 B5** 46 5N 1 20 E
Marche □, *Italy* **39 E10** 43 22N 13 10 E
Marche-en-Famenne, *Belgium* **21 H6** 50 14N 5 19 E
Marchena, *Spain* **37 H5** 37 18N 5 23W
Marches = Marche □, *Italy* **39 E10** 43 22N 13 10 E
Marciana Marina, *Italy* **38 F7** 42 44N 10 12 E
Marcianise, *Italy* **41 A7** 41 3N 14 16 E
Marcigny, *France* **25 B8** 46 17N 4 2 E
Marcillat-en-Combraille, *France* **24 B6** 46 12N 2 38 E
Marcinelle, *Belgium* **21 H4** 50 24N 4 26 E
Marck, *France* **23 B8** 50 57N 1 57 E
Marckolsheim, *France* **23 D14** 48 10N 7 30 E
Marcona, *Peru* **156 D2** 15 10 S 75 0W
Marcos Juárez, *Argentina* **158 C3** 32 42 S 62 5W
Marcus I. = Minami-Tori-Shima, *Pac. Oc.* **122 E7** 24 0N 153 45 E
Marcus Necker Ridge, *Pac. Oc.* **122 F9** 20 0N 175 0 E
Marcy Mt., *U.S.A.* **137 B11** 44 7N 73 55W
Mardan, *Pakistan* **79 B4** 34 20N 72 0 E
Mardie, *Australia* **112 D2** 21 12 S 115 59 E
Mardin, *Turkey* **89 E9** 37 20N 40 43 E
Maré, I., *N. Cal.* **121 U22** 21 30 S 168 0 E
Marechal Deodoro, *Brazil* **154 C4** 9 43 S 35 54W
Maree L., *U.K.* **18 D3** 57 40N 5 30W
Mareeba, *Australia* **114 B4** 16 59 S 145 28 E
Marek = Stanke Dimitrov, *Bulgaria* **42 E8** 42 17N 23 9 E
Marek, *Indonesia* **72 B2** 4 41 S 120 24 E
Maremma, *Italy* **38 F8** 42 45N 11 15 E
Maréna, *Mali* **100 C3** 14 0N 7 20W
Marenberg, *Slovenia* **39 B12** 46 38N 15 13 E
Marengo, *U.S.A.* **140 C4** 41 42N 92 5W
Marennes, *France* **24 C2** 45 49N 1 7W
Marenyi, *Kenya* **106 C4** 4 22 S 39 8 E
Marerano, *Madag.* **105 C7** 21 23 S 44 52 E
Maréttimo, *Italy* **40 E5** 37 58N 12 5 E
Mareuil-sur-Lay, *France* **24 B2** 46 32N 1 14W
Marfa, *U.S.A.* **139 K2** 30 15N 104 5W
Marfa Pt., *Malta* **32 D1** 35 59N 14 19 E
Marganets, *Ukraine* **52 C6** 47 40N 34 40 E
Margaret →, *Australia* **112 C4** 18 9 S 125 41 E
Margaret Bay, *Canada* **130 C3** 51 20N 127 35W
Margaret L., *Canada* **130 B5** 58 56N 115 25W
Margaret River, *Australia* **112 C4** 18 38 S 126 52 E
Margarita, I. de, *Venezuela* **153 A5** 11 0N 64 0W
Margarítion, *Greece* **44 E2** 39 22N 20 26 E
Margaritovo, *Russia* **60 C7** 43 25N 134 45 E
Margate, *S. Africa* **105 E5** 30 50 S 30 20 E
Margate, *U.K.* **17 F9** 51 23N 1 24 E
Margelan, *Uzbekistan* **55 C5** 40 27N 71 42 E
Margeride, Mts. de la, *France* **24 D7** 44 43N 3 38 E
Margherita, *India* **78 B5** 27 16N 95 40 E
Margherita di Savola, *Italy* **41 A9** 41 25N 16 5 E
Marghita, *Romania* **46 B3** 47 22N 22 22 E
Margonin, *Poland* **47 C4** 52 58N 17 5 E
Margosatubig, *Phil.* **71 H4** 7 34N 123 10 E
Marguerite, *Canada* **130 C4** 52 30N 122 25W
Marhoum, *Algeria* **99 B4** 34 27N 0 11W
Mari Republic □, *Russia* **51 C16** 56 30N 48 0 E
María Elena, *Chile* **158 A2** 22 18 S 69 40W
María Grande, *Argentina* **158 C4** 31 45 S 59 55W
Maria I., *N. Terr., Australia* **114 A2** 14 52 S 135 45 E
Maria I., *Tas., Australia* **114 G4** 42 35 S 148 0 E
Maria van Diemen, C., *N.Z.* **118 A1** 34 29 S 172 40 E
Mariager, *Denmark* **15 H4** 56 40N 10 0 E
Mariager Fjord, *Denmark* **15 H4** 56 42N 10 19 E
Mariakani, *Kenya* **106 C4** 3 50 S 39 27 E
Marian L., *Canada* **130 A5** 63 0N 116 15W
Mariana Trench, *Pac. Oc.* **122 F6** 13 0N 145 0 E
Marianao, *Cuba* **148 B3** 23 8N 82 24W
Mariani, *India* **78 B5** 26 39N 94 19 E
Marianna, *Ark., U.S.A.* **139 H9** 34 48N 90 48W
Marianna, *Fla., U.S.A.* **135 K3** 30 45N 85 15W
Mariánske Lázně, *Czech.* **30 B5** 49 48N 12 41 E
Marias →, *U.S.A.* **142 C8** 47 56N 110 30W
Mariato, Punta, *Panama* **148 E3** 7 12N 80 52W
Mariazell, *Austria* **30 D8** 47 47N 15 19 E
Ma'rib, *Yemen* **86 D4** 15 25N 45 21 E
Maribo, *Denmark* **15 K5** 54 48N 11 30 E
Maribor, *Slovenia* **39 B12** 46 36N 15 40 E
Maricaban I., *Phil.* **70 E3** 13 39N 120 53 E
Maricalom, *Phil.* **71 G4** 9 42N 122 25 E
Marico →, *Africa* **104 C4** 23 35 S 26 57 E
Maricopa, *Ariz., U.S.A.* **143 K7** 33 5N 112 2W
Maricopa, *Calif., U.S.A.* **145 K7** 35 7N 119 27W
Marîdî, *Sudan* **95 G2** 4 55N 29 25 E
Maridi, Wadi →, *Sudan* **95 F2** 6 15N 29 21 E
Marié →, *Brazil* **152 D4** 0 27 S 66 26W
Marie Byrd Land, *Antarctica* **7 D14** 79 30 S 125 0W
Marie-Galante, *Guadeloupe* **149 C7** 15 56N 61 16W
Mariecourt, *Canada* **127 B12** 61 30N 72 0W
Mariefred, *Sweden* **14 E11** 59 15N 17 12 E
Mariehamn, *Finland* **13 F15** 60 5N 19 55 E
Marienbad = Mariánské Lázně, *Czech.* **30 B5** 49 48N 12 41 E
Marienberg, *Germany* **26 E9** 50 40N 13 10 E
Marienberg, *Neths.* **20 D9** 52 2N 6 35 E
Marienbourg, *Belgium* **21 H5** 50 6N 4 31 E
Mariental, *Namibia* **104 C2** 24 36 S 18 0 E
Marienville, *U.S.A.* **136 E5** 41 27N 79 8W
Mariestad, *Sweden* **15 F7** 58 43N 13 50 E
Marietta, *Ga., U.S.A.* **135 J3** 33 55N 84 30W
Marietta, *Ohio, U.S.A.* **134 F5** 39 27N 81 27W
Marieville, *Canada* **137 A11** 45 26N 73 10W
Marignane, *France* **25 E9** 43 25N 5 13 E
Marihatag, *Phil.* **71 G6** 8 48N 126 18 E
Mariinsk, *Russia* **56 D9** 56 10N 87 20 E
Mariinskiy Posad, *Russia* **51 C15** 56 10N 47 45 E
Marília, *Brazil* **159 A5** 22 13 S 50 0W
Marillana, *Australia* **112 D2** 22 37 S 119 16 E
Marimba, *Angola* **103 D3** 8 28 S 17 8 E
Marín, *Spain* **36 C2** 42 23N 8 42W
Marina, *U.S.A.* **144 J5** 36 41N 121 48W
Marina di Cirò, *Italy* **41 C10** 39 22N 17 8 E
Marina Plains, *Australia* **114 A3** 14 37 S 143 57 E
Marinduque, *Phil.* **70 E3** 13 25N 122 0 E
Marine City, *U.S.A.* **134 D4** 42 45N 82 29W
Marineo, *Italy* **40 E6** 37 57N 13 23 E
Marinette, *U.S.A.* **134 C2** 45 4N 87 40W
Maringá, *Brazil* **159 A5** 23 26 S 52 2W
Marinha Grande, *Portugal* **37 F2** 39 45N 8 56W
Marion, *Ala., U.S.A.* **135 J2** 32 33N 87 20W
Marion, *Ill., U.S.A.* **139 G10** 37 45N 88 55W
Marion, *Ind., U.S.A.* **141 D11** 40 35N 85 40W
Marion, *Iowa, U.S.A.* **140 B5** 42 2N 91 36W
Marion, *Kans., U.S.A.* **138 F6** 38 25N 97 2W
Marion, *Mich., U.S.A.* **134 C3** 44 7N 85 8W
Marion, *N.C., U.S.A.* **135 H5** 35 42N 82 0W
Marion, *Ohio, U.S.A.* **141 D13** 40 38N 83 8W
Marion, *S.C., U.S.A.* **135 H6** 34 11N 79 22W
Marion, *Va., U.S.A.* **135 G5** 36 51N 81 29W
Marion, L., *U.S.A.* **135 J5** 33 30N 80 15W
Marion Bay, *Australia* **116 C2** 35 12 S 136 59 E
Marion I., *Ind. Oc.* **109 J2** 47 0 S 38 0 E
Maripa, *Venezuela* **153 B4** 7 26N 65 9W
Maripasoula, *Fr. Guiana* **153 C7** 3 40N 54 4W
Maripipi I., *Phil.* **71 F5** 11 47N 124 19 E
Mariposa, *U.S.A.* **144 H7** 37 31N 119 59W
Mariscal Estigarribia, *Paraguay* **158 A3** 22 3 S 60 40W
Maritime Alps = Maritimes, Alpes, *Europe* **25 D11** 44 10N 7 10 E
Maritimes, Alpes, *Europe* **25 D11** 44 10N 7 10 E
Maritsa, *Bulgaria* **43 E10** 42 1N 25 50 E
Maritsa, *Greece* **32 C10** 36 22N 28 10 E
Maritsa →, *Bulgaria* **43 F11** 41 40N 26 34 E
Mariupol, *Ukraine* **52 C7** 47 5N 37 31 E
Marīvān, *Iran* **84 C5** 35 30N 46 25 E
Mariyampol, *Lithuania* **50 D3** 54 33N 23 19 E
Markah, W. →, *Yemen* **86 D4** 14 59N 46 36 E
Markam, *China* **68 C2** 29 42N 98 38 E
Markapur, *India* **83 G4** 15 44N 79 19 E
Markazī □, *Iran* **85 C6** 35 0N 49 30 E
Markdale, *Canada* **136 B4** 44 19N 80 39W
Marke, *Belgium* **21 G2** 50 48N 3 14 E
Marked Tree, *U.S.A.* **139 H9** 35 35N 90 24W
Markelsdorfer Huk, *Germany* **26 A6** 54 33N 11 0 E
Marken, *Neths.* **20 D6** 52 26N 5 12 E
Markermeer, *Neths.* **20 C6** 52 33N 5 15 E
Market Drayton, *U.K.* **16 E5** 52 55N 2 30W
Market Harborough, *U.K.* **17 E7** 52 29N 0 55W
Markham, *Canada* **136 C5** 43 52N 79 16W
Markham →, *Papua N. G.* **120 D4** 6 41 S 147 2 E
Markham, Mt., *Antarctica* **7 E11** 83 0 S 164 0 E
Markham L., *Canada* **131 A8** 62 30N 102 35W
Marki, *Poland* **47 C8** 52 20N 21 2 E
Markleeville, *U.S.A.* **144 G7** 38 44N 119 47W
Markoupoulon, *Greece* **45 G5** 37 53N 23 57 E
Markovac, *Serbia, Yug.* **42 C6** 44 14N 21 7 E
Markovo, *Russia* **57 C17** 64 40N 169 40 E
Markoye, *Burkina Faso* **101 C5** 14 39N 0 2 E
Marks, *Russia* **51 F15** 51 45N 46 50 E
Marksville, *U.S.A.* **139 K8** 31 10N 92 2W
Markt Schwaben, *Germany* **27 G7** 48 14N 11 49 E
Marktredwitz, *Germany* **27 E8** 50 1N 12 2 E
Marla, *Australia* **115 D1** 27 19 S 133 33 E
Marlboro, *U.S.A.* **137 D13** 42 19N 71 33W
Marlborough, *Australia* **114 C4** 22 46 S 149 52 E
Marlborough Downs, *U.K.* **17 F6** 51 25N 1 55W
Marle, *France* **23 C10** 49 43N 3 47 E
Marlin, *U.S.A.* **139 K6** 31 25N 96 50W
Marlow, *Germany* **26 A8** 54 8N 12 34 E
Marlow, *U.S.A.* **139 H6** 34 40N 97 58W
Marly-le-Grand, *Switz.* **28 C4** 46 47N 7 10 E
Marmagao, *India* **83 G1** 15 25N 73 56 E
Marmande, *France* **24 D4** 44 30N 0 10 E
Marmara, *Turkey* **52 F2** 40 35N 27 38 E
Marmara, Sea of = Marmara Denizi, *Turkey* **88 C3** 40 45N 28 15 E
Marmara Denizi, *Turkey* **88 C3** 40 45N 28 15 E
Marmara Gölü, *Turkey* **88 D3** 38 37N 28 0 E
Marmaris, *Turkey* **88 E3** 36 50N 28 14 E
Marmarth, *U.S.A.* **138 B3** 46 21N 103 52W
Marmelos →, *Brazil* **157 B5** 6 6 S 61 46W
Marmion, Mt., *Australia* **113 E2** 29 16 S 119 50 E
Marmion L., *Canada* **128 C1** 48 55N 91 20W
Marmolada, Mte., *Italy* **39 B8** 46 25N 11 55 E
Marmolejo, *Spain* **37 G6** 38 3N 4 13W
Marmora, *Canada* **128 D4** 44 28N 77 41W
Marnay, *France* **23 E12** 47 16N 5 48 E
Marne, *Germany* **26 B5** 53 57N 9 1 E
Marne □, *France* **23 D11** 48 50N 4 10 E
Marne →, *France* **23 D9** 48 48N 2 24 E
Marneuli, *Georgia* **53 F11** 41 30N 44 48 E
Maro, *Chad* **97 G3** 8 30N 19 0 E
Maroa, *Venezuela* **152 C4** 2 43N 67 33W
Maroala, *Madag.* **105 B8** 15 23 S 47 59 E
Maroantsetra, *Madag.* **105 B8** 15 26 S 49 44 E
Maromandia, *Madag.* **105 A8** 14 13 S 48 5 E
Marondera, *Zimbabwe* **107 F3** 18 5 S 31 42 E
Maroni →, *Fr. Guiana* **153 B7** 5 30N 54 0W
Marónia, *Greece* **44 D7** 40 53N 25 24 E
Maronne →, *France* **24 C5** 45 5N 1 56 E
Maroochydore, *Australia* **115 D5** 26 29 S 153 5 E
Maroona, *Australia* **116 D5** 37 27 S 142 54 E
Maros, *Indonesia* **72 C1** 5 0 S 119 34 E
Maros →, *Hungary* **31 E13** 46 15N 20 13 E
Marosakoa, *Madag.* **105 B8** 15 26 S 46 38 E
Marostica, *Italy* **39 C8** 45 44N 11 40 E
Maroua, *Cameroon* **101 C7** 10 40N 14 20 E
Marovoay, *Madag.* **105 B8** 16 6 S 46 39 E
Marowijne □, *Surinam* **153 C7** 4 0N 55 0W
Marowijne →, *Surinam* **153 B7** 5 45N 53 58W
Marquard, *S. Africa* **104 D4** 28 40 S 27 28 E
Marqueira, *Portugal* **37 G1** 38 41N 9 9W
Marquesas Is. = Marquises, Is., *Pac. Oc.* **123 H14** 9 30 S 140 0W
Marquette, *U.S.A.* **134 B2** 46 30N 87 21W
Marquise, *France* **23 B8** 50 50N 1 40 E
Marquises, Is., *Pac. Oc.* **123 H14** 9 30 S 140 0W
Marra, Gebel, *Sudan* **95 F2** 7 20N 27 35 E
Marracuene, *Mozam.* **105 D5** 25 45 S 32 35 E
Marradi, *Italy* **39 D8** 44 5N 11 37 E
Marrakech, *Morocco* **98 B3** 31 9N 8 0W
Marrawah, *Australia* **114 G3** 40 55 S 144 42 E
Marrecas, Serra das, *Brazil* **154 C3** 9 0 S 41 0W
Marree, *Australia* **115 D2** 29 39 S 138 1 E
Marrilla, *Australia* **112 D1** 22 31 S 114 25 E
Marrimane, *Mozam.* **105 C5** 22 58 S 33 34 E
Marromeu, *Mozam.* **105 B6** 18 15 S 36 25 E
Marroquí, Punta, *Spain* **37 K5** 36 0N 5 37W
Marrowie Cr. →, *Australia* **117 B6** 33 23 S 145 40 E
Marrubane, *Mozam.* **107 F4** 18 0 S 37 0 E
Marrum, *Neths.* **20 B7** 53 19N 5 48 E
Marrupa, *Mozam.* **107 E4** 13 8 S 37 30 E
Marsa Brega, *Libya* **96 B3** 30 24N 19 37 E
Marsá Matrûh, *Egypt* **94 A2** 31 19N 27 9 E
Marsá Susah, *Libya* **96 B4** 32 52N 21 59 E
Marsabit, *Kenya* **106 B4** 2 18N 38 0 E
Marsabit □, *Kenya* **106 B4** 2 45N 37 45 E
Marsala, *Italy* **40 E5** 37 48N 12 25 E
Marsalforn, *Malta* **32 C1** 36 4N 14 15 E
Marsberg, *Germany* **26 D4** 51 28N 8 52 E
Marsciano, *Italy* **39 F9** 42 54N 12 20 E
Marsden, *Australia* **117 B7** 33 47 S 147 32 E
Marsdiep, *Neths.* **20 C5** 52 58N 4 46 E
Marseillan, *France* **24 E7** 43 23N 3 31 E
Marseille, *France* **25 E9** 43 18N 5 23 E
Marseilles = Marseille, *France* **25 E9** 43 18N 5 23 E
Marseilles, *U.S.A.* **141 C8** 41 20N 88 43W
Marsh I., *U.S.A.* **139 L9** 29 35N 91 50W
Marsh L., *U.S.A.* **138 C6** 45 5N 96 0W
Marshall, *Liberia* **100 D2** 6 8N 10 22W
Marshall, *Ark., U.S.A.* **139 H8** 35 58N 92 40W
Marshall, *Ill., U.S.A.* **141 E9** 39 23N 87 42W
Marshall, *Mich., U.S.A.* **141 B12** 42 17N 84 59W
Marshall, *Minn., U.S.A.* **138 C7** 44 25N 95 45W
Marshall, *Mo., U.S.A.* **140 E3** 39 8N 93 15W
Marshall, *Tex., U.S.A.* **139 J7** 32 29N 94 20W
Marshall →, *Australia* **114 C2** 22 59 S 136 59 E
Marshall Is., *Pac. Oc.* **122 G9** 9 0N 171 0 E
Marshalltown, *U.S.A.* **140 B4** 42 5N 92 56W
Marshfield, *Mo., U.S.A.* **139 G8** 37 20N 92 58W
Marshfield, *Wis., U.S.A.* **138 C9** 44 42N 90 10W
Marshūn, *Iran* **85 B6** 36 19N 49 23 E
Mársico Nuovo, *Italy* **41 B8** 40 26N 15 43 E
Märsta, *Sweden* **14 E11** 59 37N 17 52 E
Marstal, *Denmark* **15 K4** 54 51N 10 30 E
Marstrand, *Sweden* **15 G5** 57 53N 11 35 E
Mart, *U.S.A.* **139 K6** 31 34N 96 51W
Marta →, *Italy* **39 F8** 42 14N 11 42 E
Martaban, *Burma* **78 G6** 16 30N 97 35 E
Martaban, G. of, *Burma* **78 G6** 16 5N 96 30 E
Martano, *Italy* **41 B11** 40 14N 18 18 E
Martapura, *Kalimantan, Indonesia* **75 C4** 3 22 S 114 47 E
Martapura, *Sumatera, Indonesia* **74 C2** 4 19 S 104 22 E
Marte, *Nigeria* **101 C7** 12 23N 13 46 E
Martel, *France* **24 D5** 44 57N 1 37 E
Martelange, *Belgium* **21 J7** 49 49N 5 43 E
Martensdale, *U.S.A.* **140 C3** 41 23N 93 45W
Martés, Sierra, *Spain* **35 F4** 39 20N 1 0W
Martha's Vineyard, *U.S.A.* **137 E14** 41 25N 70 35W
Martigné-Ferchaud, *France* **22 E5** 47 50N 1 20W
Martigny, *Switz.* **28 D4** 46 6N 7 3 E
Martigues, *France* **25 E9** 43 24N 5 4 E
Martil, *Morocco* **98 A3** 35 36N 5 15W
Martin, *Czech.* **31 B11** 49 6N 18 48 E
Martin, *S. Dak., U.S.A.* **138 D4** 43 11N 101 45W
Martin, *Tenn., U.S.A.* **139 G10** 36 23N 88 51W
Martín →, *Spain* **34 D4** 41 18N 0 19W
Martin, L., *U.S.A.* **135 J3** 32 45N 85 50W
Martina, *Switz.* **29 C10** 46 53N 10 28 E
Martina Franca, *Italy* **41 B10** 40 42N 17 20 E
Martinborough, *N.Z.* **118 H4** 41 14 S 175 29 E
Martinez, *U.S.A.* **144 G4** 38 1N 122 8W
Martinho Campos, *Brazil* **155 E2** 19 20 S 45 13W
Martinique ■, *W. Indies* **149 D7** 14 40N 61 0W
Martinique Passage, *W. Indies* **149 C7** 15 15N 61 0W
Martínon, *Greece* **45 F5** 38 35N 23 15 E
Martinópolis, *Brazil* **159 A5** 22 11 S 51 12W
Martins Ferry, *U.S.A.* **136 F4** 40 5N 80 46W
Martinsberg, *Austria* **30 C8** 48 22N 15 9 E
Martinsburg, *Pa., U.S.A.* **136 F6** 40 18N 78 21W
Martinsburg, *W. Va., U.S.A.* **134 F7** 39 30N 77 57W
Martinsville, *Ill., U.S.A.* **141 E9** 39 20N 87 53W
Martinsville, *Ind., U.S.A.* **141 E10** 39 29N 86 23W
Martinsville, *Va., U.S.A.* **135 G6** 36 41N 79 52W
Marton, *N.Z.* **118 G4** 40 4 S 175 23 E
Martorell, *Spain* **34 D6** 41 28N 1 56 E
Martos, *Spain* **37 H7** 37 44N 3 58W
Martūbah, *Libya* **96 B4** 32 35N 22 46 E
Martuk, *Kazakhstan* **54 F5** 50 46N 56 31 E
Martuni, *Armenia* **53 F11** 40 9N 45 10 E
Maru, *Nigeria* **101 C6** 12 22N 6 22 E
Marudi, *Malaysia* **75 B4** 4 11N 114 19 E
Ma'ruf, *Afghan.* **79 C2** 31 30N 67 6 E
Marugame, *Japan* **62 C5** 34 15N 133 40 E
Marúggio, *Italy* **41 B10** 40 20N 17 33 E
Marui, *Papua N. G.* **120 C2** 4 4 S 143 2 E
Maruia →, *N.Z.* **119 B7** 41 47 S 172 13 E
Maruim, *Brazil* **154 D4** 10 45 S 37 5W
Marulan, *Australia* **117 C9** 34 43 S 150 3 E
Marum, *Neths.* **20 B8** 53 9N 6 16 E
Marum, Mt., *Vanuatu* **121 F6** 16 15 S 168 7 E
Marunga, *Angola* **103 F4** 17 28 S 20 2 E
Marungu, Mts., *Zaïre* **106 D2** 7 30 S 30 0 E
Maruoka, *Japan* **63 A8** 36 9N 136 16 E
Marvast, *Iran* **85 D7** 30 30N 54 15 E
Marvejols, *France* **24 D7** 44 33N 3 19 E
Marwar, *India* **80 G5** 25 43N 73 45 E
Mary, *Turkmenistan* **56 F7** 37 40N 61 50 E

Minobu-Sanchi 233


Městys Zelezná Ruda, Czech. 30 B6 49 8N 13 15 E
Meta, U.S.A. 140 F4 38 19N 92 10W
Meta □, Colombia 152 C3 3 30N 73 0W
Meta →, S. Amer. 152 B4 6 12N 67 28W
Metairie, U.S.A. 139 L9 29 59N 90 9W
Metalici, Munţii, Romania 46 C3 46 15N 22 50 E
Metaline Falls, U.S.A. 142 B5 48 52N 117 22W
Metamora, U.S.A. 140 D7 40 47N 89 22W
Metán, Argentina 158 B3 25 30 S 65 0W
Metangula, Mozam. 107 E3 12 40 S 34 50 E
Metauro →, Italy 39 E10 43 50N 13 3 E
Metema, Ethiopia 95 E4 12 56N 36 13 E
Metengobalame, Mozam. 107 E3 14 49 S 34 30 E
Méthana, Greece 45 G5 37 35N 23 23 E
Methóni, Greece 45 H3 36 49N 21 42 E
Methven, N.Z. 119 D6 43 38 S 171 40 E
Methy L., Canada 131 B7 56 28N 109 30W
Metil, Mozam. 107 F4 16 24 S 39 0 E
Metkovets, Bulgaria 43 D8 43 37N 23 10 E
Metković, Croatia 42 D2 43 6N 17 39 E
Metlakatla, U.S.A. 130 B2 55 10N 131 33W
Metlaoui, Tunisia 96 B1 34 24N 8 24 E
Metlika, Slovenia 39 C12 45 40N 15 20 E
Metro, Indonesia 74 D3 5 5 S 105 20 E
Metropolis, U.S.A. 139 G10 37 10N 88 47W
Métsovon, Greece 44 E3 39 48N 21 12 E
Mettet, Belgium 21 H5 50 19N 4 41 E
Mettuppalaiyam, India 83 J3 11 18N 76 59 E
Mettur, India 83 J3 11 48N 77 47 E
Metz, France 23 C13 49 8N 6 10 E
Meulaboh, Indonesia 74 B1 4 11N 96 3 E
Meulan, France 23 C8 49 3N 1 55 E
Meung-sur-Loire, France 23 E8 47 50N 1 40 E
Meureudu, Indonesia 74 A1 5 19N 96 10 E
Meurthe →, France 23 D13 48 47N 6 9 E
Meurthe-et-Moselle □, France 23 D13 48 52N 6 0 E
Meuse □, France 23 C12 49 8N 5 25 E
Meuse →, Europe 21 G7 50 45N 5 41 E
Meuselwitz, Germany 26 D8 51 3N 12 18 E
Meutapok, Mt., Malaysia 75 A5 5 40N 117 0 E
Mexborough, U.K. 16 D6 53 29N 1 18W
Mexia, U.S.A. 139 K6 31 38N 96 32W
Mexiana, I., Brazil 154 A2 0 0 49 30W
Mexicali, Mexico 146 A1 32 40N 115 30W
México, Mexico 147 D5 19 20N 99 10W
Mexico, Maine, U.S.A. 137 B14 44 35N 70 30W
Mexico, Mo., U.S.A. 140 E5 39 10N 91 55W
México □, Mexico 146 D5 19 20N 99 10W
Mexico ■, Cent. Amer. 146 C4 25 0N 105 0W
Mexico, G. of, Cent. Amer. 147 C7 25 0N 90 0W
Meyenburg, Germany 26 B8 53 19N 12 15 E
Meymac, France 24 C6 45 32N 2 10 E
Meymaneh, Afghan. 79 B2 35 53N 64 38 E
Meyrargues, France 25 E9 43 38N 5 32 E
Meyrueis, France 24 D7 44 12N 3 27 E
Meyssac, France 24 C5 45 3N 1 40 E
Mezdra, Bulgaria 43 D8 43 12N 23 42 E
Mèze, France 24 E7 43 27N 3 36 E
Mezen, Russia 48 A7 65 50N 44 20 E
Mezen →, Russia 48 A7 66 11N 43 59 E
Mézenc, Mt., France 25 D8 44 54N 4 11 E
Mezeş, Munţii, Romania 46 B4 47 5N 23 5 E
Mezha →, Russia 50 D7 55 50N 31 45 E
Mezhdurechenskiy, Russia 54 B9 59 36N 65 56 E
Mézidon, France 22 C6 49 5N 0 1W
Mézilhac, France 25 D8 44 49N 4 21 E
Mézin, France 24 D4 44 4N 0 16 E
Mezöberény, Hungary 31 E14 46 49N 21 3 E
Mezöfalva, Hungary 31 E11 46 55N 18 49 E
Mezöhegyes, Hungary 31 E13 46 19N 20 49 E
Mezökövácsháza, Hungary 31 E13 46 25N 20 57 E
Mezökövesd, Hungary 31 D13 47 49N 20 35 E
Mézos, France 24 D2 44 5N 1 10W
Mezötúr, Hungary 31 E13 46 58N 20 41 E
Mezquital, Mexico 146 C4 23 29N 104 23W
Mezzolombardo, Italy 38 B8 46 13N 11 5 E
Mgeta, Tanzania 107 D4 8 22 S 36 6 E
Mglin, Russia 50 E8 53 2N 32 50 E
Mhlaba Hills, Zimbabwe 107 F3 18 30 S 30 30 E
Mhow, India 80 H6 22 33N 75 50 E
Mi-Shima, Japan 62 C3 34 46N 131 9 E
Miahuatlán, Mexico 147 D5 16 21N 96 36W
Miajadas, Spain 37 F5 39 9N 5 54W
Miallo, Australia 114 B4 16 28 S 145 22 E
Miami, Ariz., U.S.A. 143 K8 33 25N 110 54W
Miami, Fla., U.S.A. 135 N5 25 45N 80 15W
Miami, Tex., U.S.A. 139 H4 35 44N 100 38W
Miami →, U.S.A. 134 F3 39 20N 84 40W
Miami Beach, U.S.A. 135 N5 25 49N 80 6W
Miamisburg, U.S.A. 141 E12 39 40N 84 11W
Mian Xian, China 66 H4 33 10N 106 32 E
Mianchi, China 66 G6 34 48N 111 48 E
Mīāndowāb, Iran 84 B5 37 0N 46 5 E
Miandrivazo, Madag. 105 B8 19 31 S 45 29 E
Mīāneh, Iran 84 B5 37 30N 47 40 E
Mianning, China 68 C4 28 32N 102 9 E
Mianwali, Pakistan 79 B3 32 38N 71 28 E
Mianyang, Hubei, China 69 B9 30 25N 113 25 E
Mianyang, Sichuan, China 68 B5 31 22N 104 47 E
Mianzhu, China 68 B5 31 22N 104 7 E
Miaoli, Taiwan 69 E13 24 37N 120 49 E
Miarinarivo, Madag. 105 B8 18 57 S 46 55 E
Miass, Russia 54 D7 54 59N 60 6 E
Miass →, Russia 54 C9 56 6N 64 30 E
Miasteczko Kraj, Poland 47 B4 53 7N 17 1 E
Miastko, Poland 47 A3 54 0N 16 58 E
Micăsasa, Romania 46 C5 46 7N 24 7 E
Michael, Mt., Papua N. G. 120 D3 6 27 S 145 22 E
Michalovce, Czech. 31 C14 48 47N 21 58 E
Michelstadt, Germany 27 F5 49 40N 9 0 E
Michigan □, U.S.A. 133 B9 44 40N 85 40W
Michigan, L., U.S.A. 134 C2 44 0N 87 0W
Michigan Center, U.S.A. 141 B12 42 14N 84 20W
Michigan City, U.S.A. 141 C10 41 42N 86 56W
Michikamau L., Canada 129 B7 54 20N 63 10W
Michipicoten, Canada 128 C3 47 55N 84 55W
Michipicoten I., Canada 128 C2 47 40N 85 40W
Michoacan □, Mexico 146 D4 19 0N 102 0W
Michurin, Bulgaria 43 E12 42 9N 27 51 E
Michurinsk, Russia 51 E12 52 58N 40 27 E
Miclere, Australia 114 C4 22 34 S 147 32 E
Mico, Pta., Nic. 148 D3 12 0N 83 30W
Micronesia, Federated States of ■, Pac. Oc. 122 G7 9 0N 150 0 E
Mid Glamorgan □, U.K. 17 F4 51 40N 3 25W
Mid-Indian Ridge, Ind. Oc. 109 H6 30 0 S 75 0 E
Midai, P., Indonesia 75 B3 3 0N 107 47 E
Midale, Canada 131 D8 49 25N 103 20W
Middagsfjället, Sweden 14 A6 63 27N 12 19 E
Middelbeers, Neths. 21 F6 51 28N 5 15 E
Middelburg, Neths. 21 F3 51 30N 3 36 E
Middelburg, C. Prov., S. Africa 104 E3 31 30 S 25 0 E
Middelburg, Trans., S. Africa 105 D4 25 49 S 29 28 E
Middelfart, Denmark 15 J3 55 30N 9 43 E
Middelharnis, Neths. 20 E4 51 46N 4 10 E
Middelkerke, Belgium 21 F1 51 11N 2 49 E
Middelrode, Neths. 21 E6 51 41N 5 26 E
Middelwit, S. Africa 104 C4 24 51 S 27 3 E
Middle →, U.S.A. 140 C3 41 26N 93 30W
Middle Alkali L., U.S.A. 142 F3 41 30N 120 3W
Middle Fork Feather →, U.S.A. 144 F5 39 35N 121 25W
Middle I., Australia 113 F3 34 6 S 123 11 E
Middle Loup →, U.S.A. 138 E5 41 17N 98 23W
Middle Raccoon →, U.S.A. 140 C3 41 35N 93 35W
Middleboro, U.S.A. 137 E14 41 56N 70 52W
Middleburg, N.Y., U.S.A. 137 D10 42 36N 74 19W
Middleburg, Pa., U.S.A. 136 F7 40 46N 77 5W
Middlebury, Ind., U.S.A. 141 C11 41 41N 85 42W
Middlebury, Vt., U.S.A. 137 B11 44 2N 73 9W
Middlemarch, N.Z. 119 F5 45 30 S 170 9 E
Middleport, U.S.A. 134 F4 39 0N 82 5W
Middlesboro, U.S.A. 133 C10 36 40N 83 40W
Middlesboro, U.S.A. 135 G4 36 36N 83 43W
Middlesbrough, U.K. 16 C6 54 35N 1 14W
Middlesex, Belize 148 C2 17 2N 88 31W
Middlesex, U.S.A. 137 F10 40 36N 74 30W
Middleton, Australia 114 C3 22 22 S 141 32 E
Middleton, Canada 129 D6 44 57N 65 4W
Middleton, U.S.A. 140 A7 43 6N 89 30W
Middletown, Calif., U.S.A. 144 G4 38 45N 122 37W
Middletown, Conn., U.S.A. 137 E12 41 37N 72 40W
Middletown, N.Y., U.S.A. 137 E10 41 28N 74 28W
Middletown, Ohio, U.S.A. 141 E12 39 29N 84 25W
Middletown, Pa., U.S.A. 137 F8 40 12N 76 44W
Middleville, U.S.A. 141 B11 42 43N 85 28W
Midelt, Morocco 98 B4 32 46N 4 44W
Midhirst, N.Z. 118 F3 39 17 S 174 18 E
Midi, Canal du →, France 24 E5 43 45N 1 21 E
Midi d'Ossau, Pic du, France 24 F3 42 50N 0 26W
Midland, Canada 128 D4 44 45N 79 50W
Midland, Calif., U.S.A. 145 M12 33 52N 114 48W
Midland, Mich., U.S.A. 134 D3 43 37N 84 17W
Midland, Pa., U.S.A. 136 F4 40 39N 80 27W
Midland, Tex., U.S.A. 139 K3 32 0N 102 3W
Midlands □, Zimbabwe 107 F2 19 40 S 29 0 E
Midleton, Ireland 19 E3 51 52N 8 12W
Midlothian, U.S.A. 139 J6 32 30N 97 0W
Midongy, Tangorombohitr' i, Madag. 105 C8 23 30 S 47 0 E
Midongy Atsimo, Madag. 105 C8 23 35 S 47 1 E
Midou →, France 24 E3 43 54N 0 30W
Midouze →, France 24 E3 43 48N 0 51W
Midsayap, Phil. 71 H5 7 12N 124 32 E
Midu, China 68 E3 25 18N 100 30 E
Midway Is., Pac. Oc. 122 E10 28 13N 177 22W
Midway Wells, U.S.A. 145 N11 32 41N 115 7W
Midwest, U.S.A. 142 E10 43 27N 106 19W
Midwolda, Neths. 20 B9 53 12N 6 52 E
Midyat, Turkey 89 E9 37 25N 41 23 E
Midzur, Bulgaria 42 D7 43 24N 22 40 E
Mie □, Japan 63 C8 34 30N 136 10 E
Miechów, Poland 47 E7 50 21N 20 5 E
Miedwie, Jezioro, Poland 47 B1 53 17N 14 54 E
Międzybód, Poland 47 D4 51 25N 17 34 E
Międzychód, Poland 47 C2 52 35N 15 53 E
Międzylesie, Poland 47 E3 50 8N 16 40 E
Międzyrzec Podlaski, Poland 47 D9 51 58N 22 45 E
Międzyrzecz, Poland 47 C2 52 26N 15 35 E
Międzyzdroje, Poland 47 B1 53 56N 14 26 E
Miejska, Poland 47 D3 51 39N 16 58 E
Miélan, France 24 E4 43 27N 0 19 E
Mielec, Poland 47 E8 50 15N 21 25 E
Mienga, Angola 103 F3 17 12 S 19 48 E
Miercurea Ciuc, Romania 46 C6 46 21N 25 48 E
Mieres, Spain 36 B5 43 18N 5 48W
Mierlo, Neths. 21 F7 51 27N 5 37 E
Mieroszów, Poland 47 E3 50 40N 16 11 E
Mieso, Ethiopia 95 F5 9 15N 40 43 E
Mieszkowice, Poland 47 C1 52 47N 14 30 E
Mifflintown, U.S.A. 136 F7 40 34N 77 24W
Mifraz Hefa, Israel 91 C4 32 52N 35 0 E
Migdāl, Israel 91 C4 32 51N 35 30 E
Migennes, France 23 E10 47 58N 3 31 E
Migliarino, Italy 39 D8 44 45N 11 56 E
Miguel Alemán, Presa, Mexico 147 D5 18 15N 96 40W
Miguel Alves, Brazil 154 B3 4 11 S 42 55W
Miguel Calmon, Brazil 154 D3 11 26 S 40 36W
Mihaliççık, Turkey 88 D4 39 53N 31 30 E
Mihara, Japan 62 C5 34 24N 133 5 E
Mihara-Yama, Japan 63 C11 34 43N 139 23 E
Mijares →, Spain 34 F4 39 55N 0 1W
Mijas, Spain 37 J6 36 36N 4 40W
Mikese, Tanzania 106 D4 6 48 S 37 55 E
Mikha-Tskhakaya = Senaki, Georgia 53 E10 42 15N 42 7 E
Mikhailovka, Ukraine 52 C6 47 36N 35 16 E
Mikhaylovgrad, Bulgaria 43 D8 43 27N 23 16 E
Mikhaylovka, Azerbaijan 53 F13 41 31N 48 52 E
Mikhaylovka, Russia 51 D11 54 14N 39 0 E
Mikhaylovka, Russia 51 F13 50 3N 43 5 E
Mikhaylovski, Russia 54 C6 56 27N 59 7 E
Mikhnevo, Russia 51 D10 55 4N 37 59 E
Miki, Hyōgo, Japan 62 C6 34 48N 134 59 E
Miki, Kagawa, Japan 62 C6 34 12N 134 7 E
Mikínai, Greece 45 G4 37 43N 22 46 E
Mikkeli, Finland 13 F19 61 43N 27 15 E
Mikkeli □ = Mikkelin lääni □, Finland 12 E19 61 56N 28 0 E
Mikkelin lääni □, Finland 12 E19 61 56N 28 0 E
Mikkwa →, Canada 130 B6 58 25N 114 46W
Mikniya, Sudan 95 D3 17 0N 33 45 E
Mikołajki, Poland 47 B8 53 49N 21 37 E
Mikołów, Poland 31 A11 50 10N 18 50 E
Míkonos, Greece 45 G7 37 30N 25 25 E
Mikrí Préspa, Límni, Greece 44 D3 40 47N 21 3 E
Mikrón Dhérion, Greece 44 C8 41 19N 26 6 E
Mikstat, Poland 47 D4 51 32N 17 59 E
Mikulov, Czech. 31 C9 48 48N 16 39 E
Mikumi, Tanzania 106 D4 7 26 S 37 0 E
Mikun, Russia 48 B9 62 20N 50 0 E
Mikuni, Japan 63 A8 36 13N 136 9 E
Mikuni-Tōge, Japan 63 A10 36 50N 138 50 E
Mikura-Jima, Japan 63 D11 33 52N 139 36 E
Milaca, U.S.A. 138 C8 45 45N 93 40W
Milagro, Ecuador 152 D2 2 11 S 79 36W
Milagros, Phil. 70 E4 12 13N 123 30 E
Milan = Milano, Italy 38 C6 45 28N 9 10 E
Milan, Ill., U.S.A. 140 C6 41 27N 90 34W
Milan, Mich., U.S.A. 141 B13 42 5N 83 40W
Milan, Mo., U.S.A. 140 D4 40 10N 93 5W
Milan, Tenn., U.S.A. 135 H1 35 55N 88 45W
Milang, S. Austral., Australia 115 E2 32 2 S 139 10 E
Milang, S. Austral., Australia 116 C3 35 24 S 138 58 E
Milange, Mozam. 107 F4 16 3 S 35 45 E
Milano, Italy 38 C6 45 28N 9 10 E
Milâs, Turkey 88 E2 37 20N 27 50 E
Milatos, Greece 32 D7 35 18N 25 34 E
Milazzo, Italy 41 D8 38 13N 15 13 E
Milbank, U.S.A. 138 C6 45 17N 96 38W
Milden, Canada 131 C7 51 29N 107 32W
Mildmay, Canada 136 B3 44 3N 81 7W
Mildura, Australia 116 C5 34 13 S 142 9 E
Mile, China 68 E4 24 28N 103 20 E
Miléai, Greece 44 E5 39 20N 23 9 E
Mileh Tharthār, Iraq 84 C4 34 0N 43 15 E
Miles, Australia 115 D5 26 40 S 150 9 E
Miles, U.S.A. 139 K4 31 39N 100 11W
Miles City, U.S.A. 138 B2 46 24N 105 50W
Milestone, Canada 131 D8 49 59N 104 31W
Mileto, Italy 41 D9 38 37N 16 3 E
Miletto, Mte., Italy 41 A7 41 26N 14 23 E
Miletus, Turkey 45 G9 37 30N 27 18 E
Mileura, Australia 113 E2 26 22 S 117 20 E
Milevsko, Czech. 30 B7 49 27N 14 21 E
Milford, Calif., U.S.A. 144 E6 40 10N 120 22W
Milford, Conn., U.S.A. 137 E11 41 13N 73 4W
Milford, Del., U.S.A. 134 F8 38 52N 75 27W
Milford, Ill., U.S.A. 141 D9 40 40N 87 43W
Milford, Mass., U.S.A. 137 D13 42 8N 71 30W
Milford, Mich., U.S.A. 141 B13 42 35N 83 36W
Milford, Pa., U.S.A. 137 E10 41 20N 74 47W
Milford, Utah, U.S.A. 143 G7 38 20N 113 0W
Milford Haven, U.K. 17 F2 51 43N 5 2W
Milford Sd., N.Z. 119 E2 44 41 S 167 47 E
Milgun, Australia 113 D2 24 56 S 118 18 E
Milh, Bahr al, Iraq 84 C4 32 40N 43 35 E
Miliana, Aïn Salah, Algeria 99 C5 27 20N 2 32 E
Miliana, Médéa, Algeria 99 A5 36 20N 2 15 E
Milicz, Poland 47 D4 51 31N 17 19 E
Miling, Australia 113 F2 30 30 S 116 17 E
Militello in Val di Catánia, Italy 41 E7 37 16N 14 46 E
Milk →, N. Amer. 142 B10 48 5N 106 15W
Milk, Wadi el →, Sudan 94 D3 17 55N 30 20 E
Milk River, Canada 130 D6 49 10N 112 5W
Mill, Neths. 21 E7 51 41N 5 48 E
Mill City, U.S.A. 142 D2 44 45N 122 28W
Mill I., Antarctica 7 C8 66 0 S 101 30 E
Mill Shoals, U.S.A. 141 F8 38 15N 88 21W
Mill Valley, U.S.A. 144 H4 37 54N 122 32W
Millau, France 24 D7 44 8N 3 4 E
Millbridge, Canada 136 B7 44 41N 77 36W
Millbrook, Canada 136 B6 44 10N 78 29W
Mille Lacs, L., U.S.A. 138 B8 46 10N 93 30W
Mille Lacs, L. des, Canada 128 C1 48 45N 90 35W
Milledgeville, Ga., U.S.A. 135 J4 33 7N 83 15W
Milledgeville, Ill., U.S.A. 140 C7 41 58N 89 46W
Millen, U.S.A. 135 J5 32 50N 81 57W
Miller, U.S.A. 138 C5 44 35N 98 59W
Millerovo, Russia 53 B9 48 57N 40 28 E
Miller's Flat, N.Z. 119 F4 45 39 S 169 23 E
Millersburg, Ind., U.S.A. 141 C11 41 32N 85 42W
Millersburg, Ohio, U.S.A. 136 F3 40 32N 81 52W
Millersburg, Pa., U.S.A. 136 F8 40 32N 76 58W
Millerton, N.Z. 119 B6 41 39 S 171 54 E
Millerton, U.S.A. 137 E11 41 57N 73 32W
Millerton L., U.S.A. 144 J7 37 0N 119 42W
Millevaches, Plateau de, France 24 C6 45 45N 2 0 E
Millicent, Australia 116 D4 37 34 S 140 21 E
Millingen, Neths. 20 E8 51 52N 6 2 E
Millinocket, U.S.A. 129 C6 45 45N 68 45W
Millmerran, Australia 115 D5 27 53 S 151 16 E
Mills L., Canada 130 A5 61 30N 118 20W
Millsboro, U.S.A. 136 G4 40 0N 80 0W
Milltown Malbay, Ireland 19 D2 52 51N 9 25W
Millville, U.S.A. 134 F8 39 22N 75 0W
Millwood Res., U.S.A. 139 J8 33 45N 94 0W
Milly-la-Forêt, France 23 D9 48 24N 2 28 E
Milna, Croatia 39 E13 43 20N 16 28 E
Milne →, Australia 114 C2 21 10 S 137 33 E
Milne Inlet, Canada 127 A11 72 30N 80 0W
Milnor, U.S.A. 138 B6 46 19N 97 29W
Milo, Canada 130 C6 50 34N 112 53W
Mílos, Greece 45 H6 36 44N 24 25 E
Miloševo, Serbia, Yug. 42 B5 45 42N 20 20 E
Miłosław, Poland 47 C4 52 12N 17 32 E
Milparinka P.O., Australia 115 D3 29 46 S 141 57 E
Milroy, U.S.A. 141 E11 39 30N 85 28W
Miltenberg, Germany 27 F5 49 41N 9 13 E
Milton, Canada 136 C5 43 31N 79 53W
Milton, N.Z. 119 G4 46 7 S 169 59 E
Milton, U.K. 18 D4 57 18N 4 32W
Milton, Calif., U.S.A. 144 G6 38 3N 120 51W
Milton, Fla., U.S.A. 135 K2 30 38N 87 0W
Milton, Iowa, U.S.A. 140 D4 40 41N 92 10W
Milton, Pa., U.S.A. 136 F8 41 0N 76 53W
Milton, Wis., U.S.A. 141 B8 42 47N 88 56W
Milton-Freewater, U.S.A. 142 D4 45 57N 118 24W
Milton Keynes, U.K. 17 E7 52 3N 0 42W
Miltou, Chad 97 F3 10 14N 17 26 E
Milverton, Canada 136 C4 43 34N 80 55W
Milwaukee, U.S.A. 141 A9 43 9N 87 58W
Milwaukee Deep, Atl. Oc. 8 G2 19 50N 68 0W
Milwaukie, U.S.A. 144 E4 45 27N 122 39W
Mim, Ghana 100 D4 6 57N 2 33W
Mimizan, France 24 D2 44 12N 1 13W
Mimon, Czech. 30 A7 50 38N 14 43 E
Mimongo, Gabon 102 C2 1 11 S 11 36 E
Mimoso, Brazil 155 E2 15 10 S 48 5W
Min Chiang →, China 69 E12 26 0N 119 35 E
Min Jiang →, China 68 C5 28 45N 104 40 E
Min-Kush, Kirghizia 55 C7 41 40N 74 28 E
Min Xian, China 66 G3 34 25N 104 5 E
Mina, U.S.A. 143 G4 38 21N 118 9W
Mina Pirquitas, Argentina 158 A2 22 40 S 66 30W
Mīnā Su'ud, Si. Arabia 85 D6 28 45N 48 28 E
Mīnā'al Aḩmadī, Kuwait 85 D6 29 5N 48 10 E
Mīnāb, Iran 85 E8 27 10N 57 1 E
Minago →, Canada 131 C9 54 33N 98 59W
Minakami, Japan 63 A10 36 49N 138 59 E
Minaki, Canada 131 D10 49 59N 94 40W
Minakuchi, Japan 63 C8 34 58N 136 10 E
Minamata, Japan 62 E2 32 10N 130 30 E
Minami-Tori-Shima, Pac. Oc. 122 E7 24 0N 153 45 E
Minas, Uruguay 159 C4 34 20 S 55 10W
Minas, Sierra de las, Guatemala 148 C2 15 9N 89 31W
Minas Basin, Canada 129 C7 45 20N 64 12W
Minas de Rio Tinto, Spain 37 H4 37 42N 6 35W
Minas de San Quintín, Spain 37 G6 38 49N 4 23W
Minas Gerais □, Brazil 155 E2 18 50 S 46 0W
Minas Novas, Brazil 155 E3 17 15 S 42 36W
Minatitlán, Mexico 147 D6 17 58N 94 35W
Minbu, Burma 78 E5 20 10N 94 52 E
Minbya, Burma 78 E4 20 22N 93 16 E
Mincio →, Italy 38 C7 45 4N 10 59 E
Mindanao, Phil. 71 H5 8 0N 125 0 E
Mindanao Trench, Pac. Oc. 70 E5 12 0N 126 6 E
Mindel →, Germany 27 G6 48 31N 10 23 E
Mindelheim, Germany 27 G6 48 4N 10 30 E
Minden, Canada 136 B6 44 55N 78 43W
Minden, Germany 26 C4 52 18N 8 45 E
Minden, La., U.S.A. 139 J8 32 40N 93 20W
Minden, Nev., U.S.A. 144 G7 38 57N 119 48W
Mindiptana, Indonesia 73 C6 5 55 S 140 22 E
Mindon, Burma 78 F5 19 21N 94 44 E
Mindoro, Phil. 70 E3 13 0N 121 0 E
Mindoro Occidental □, Phil. 70 E3 13 0N 120 55 E
Mindoro Oriental □, Phil. 70 E3 13 0N 121 5 E
Mindoro Str., Phil. 70 E3 12 30N 120 30 E
Mindouli, Congo 103 C2 4 12 S 14 28 E
Mine, Japan 62 C3 34 12N 131 7 E
Minehead, U.K. 17 F4 51 12N 3 29W
Mineiros, Brazil 157 D7 17 34 S 52 34W
Mineola, U.S.A. 139 J7 32 40N 95 30W
Mineral King, U.S.A. 144 J8 36 27N 118 36W
Mineral Point, U.S.A. 140 B6 42 52N 90 11W
Mineral Wells, U.S.A. 139 J5 32 50N 98 5W
Mineralnyye Vody, Russia 53 D10 44 15N 43 8 E
Minersville, Pa., U.S.A. 137 F8 40 11N 76 17W
Minersville, Utah, U.S.A. 143 G7 38 14N 112 58W
Minerva, U.S.A. 136 F3 40 43N 81 8W
Minervino Murge, Italy 41 A9 41 6N 16 4 E
Minetto, U.S.A. 137 C8 43 24N 76 28W
Mingan, Canada 129 B7 50 20N 64 0W
Mingary, Australia 116 B4 32 8 S 140 45 E
Mingechaur, Azerbaijan 53 F12 40 45N 47 0 E
Mingechaurskoye Vdkhr., Azerbaijan 53 F12 40 56N 47 20 E
Mingela, Australia 114 B4 19 52 S 146 38 E
Mingenew, Australia 113 E2 29 12 S 115 21 E
Mingera Cr. →, Australia 114 C2 20 38 S 137 45 E
Minggang, China 69 A10 32 24N 114 3 E
Mingin, Burma 78 D5 22 50N 94 30 E
Minglanilla, Spain 34 F3 39 34N 1 38W
Minglun, China 68 E7 25 10N 108 21 E
Mingorria, Spain 36 E6 40 45N 4 40W
Mingt'iehkaitafan = Mintaka Pass, Pakistan 81 A6 37 0N 74 58 E
Mingxi, China 69 D11 26 18N 117 12 E
Mingyuegue, China 67 C15 43 2N 128 50 E
Minhou, China 69 E12 26 0N 119 15 E
Minićevo, Serbia, Yug. 42 D7 43 42N 22 18 E
Minidoka, U.S.A. 142 E7 42 47N 113 34W
Minier, U.S.A. 140 D7 40 26N 89 19W
Minigwal, L., Australia 113 E3 29 31 S 123 14 E
Minilya, Australia 113 D1 23 55 S 114 0 E
Minilya →, Australia 113 D1 23 45 S 114 0 E
Mininera, Australia 116 D5 37 37 S 142 58 E
Minipi, L., Canada 129 B7 52 25N 60 45W
Minj, Papua N. G. 120 C3 5 54 S 144 37 E
Mink L., Canada 130 A5 61 54N 117 40W
Minlaton, Australia 116 C2 34 45 S 137 35 E
Minna, Nigeria 101 D6 9 37N 6 30 E
Minneapolis, Kans., U.S.A. 138 F6 39 11N 97 40W
Minneapolis, Minn., U.S.A. 138 C8 44 58N 93 20W
Minnedosa, Canada 131 C9 50 14N 99 50W
Minnesota □, U.S.A. 138 B7 46 40N 94 0W
Minnesund, Norway 14 D5 60 23N 11 14 E
Minnie Creek, Australia 113 D2 24 3 S 115 42 E
Minnipa, Australia 115 E2 32 51 S 135 9 E
Minnitaki L., Canada 128 C1 49 57N 92 10W
Mino, Japan 63 B8 35 32N 136 55 E
Miño →, Spain 36 D2 41 52N 8 40W
Mino-Kamo, Japan 63 B9 35 23N 137 2 E
Mino-Mikawa-Kōgen, Japan 63 B9 35 10N 137 23 E
Minoa, Greece 45 J7 35 6N 25 45 E
Minobu, Japan 63 B10 35 22N 138 26 E
Minobu-Sanchi, Japan 63 E10 35 14N 138 20 E

234 Minonk


Minonk, U.S.A. 140 D7 40 54N 89 2W
Minooka, U.S.A. 141 C8 41 27N 88 16W
Minorca = Menorca, Spain 33 B11 40 0N 4 0 E
Minore, Australia 117 B8 32 14 S 148 27 E
Minot, U.S.A. 138 A4 48 10N 101 15W
Minqin, China 66 E2 38 38N 103 20 E
Minqing, China 69 D12 26 15N 118 50 E
Minsen, Germany 26 B3 53 43N 7 58 E
Minsk, Belorussia 50 E5 53 52N 27 30 E
Mińsk Mazowiecki, Poland 47 C8 52 10N 21 33 E
Minster, U.S.A. 141 D12 40 24N 84 23W
Mintaka Pass, Pakistan 81 A6 37 0N 74 58 E
Minthami, Burma 78 D5 23 55N 94 16 E
Minto, U.S.A. 126 B5 64 55N 149 20W
Minton, Canada 131 D8 49 10N 104 35W
Mintoum, Gabon 102 B2 0 27N 12 16 E
Minturn, U.S.A. 142 G10 39 35N 106 25W
Minturno, Italy 40 A6 41 15N 13 43 E
Minûf, Egypt 94 H7 30 26N 30 52 E
Minusinsk, Russia 57 D10 53 50N 91 20 E
Minutang, India 78 A6 28 15N 96 30 E
Minvoul, Gabon 102 B2 2 9N 12 8 E
Minwakh, Yemen 87 C5 16 48N 48 6 E
Minya el Qamh, Egypt 94 H7 30 31N 31 21 E
Minyar, Russia 54 D5 55 4N 57 33 E
Minyip, Australia 116 D5 36 29 S 142 36 E
Mionica, Serbia, Yug. 42 C5 44 14N 20 6 E
Mir, Niger 97 F2 14 5N 11 59 E
Mir-Bashir, Azerbaijan 53 F12 40 20N 46 58 E
Mīr Kūh, Iran 85 E8 26 22N 58 55 E
Mīr Shahdād, Iran 85 E8 26 15N 58 29 E
Mira, Italy 39 C9 45 26N 12 9 E
Mira, Portugal 36 E2 40 26N 8 44W
Mira →, Colombia 152 C2 1 36N 79 1W
Mira →, Portugal 37 H2 37 43N 8 47W
Mira por vos Cay, Bahamas 149 B5 22 9N 74 30W
Mīrābād, Afghan. 79 C1 30 25N 61 50 E
Mirabella Eclano, Italy 41 A7 41 3N 14 59 E
Miracema do Norte, Brazil 154 C2 9 33 S 48 24W
Mirador, Brazil 154 C3 6 22 S 44 22W
Miraflores, Colombia 152 C3 1 25N 72 13W
Miraj, India 82 F2 16 50N 74 45 E
Miram Shah, Pakistan 79 B3 33 0N 70 2 E
Miramar, Argentina 158 D4 38 15 S 57 50W
Miramar, Mozam. 105 C6 23 50 S 35 35 E
Miramas, France 25 E8 43 33N 4 59 E
Mirambeau, France 24 C3 45 23N 0 35W
Miramichi B., Canada 129 C7 47 15N 65 0W
Miramont-de-Guyenne, France 24 D4 44 37N 0 21 E
Miranda, Brazil 157 E6 20 10 S 56 15W
Miranda □, Venezuela 152 A4 10 15N 66 25W
Miranda →, Brazil 157 D6 19 25 S 57 20W
Miranda de Ebro, Spain 34 C2 42 41N 2 57W
Miranda do Corvo, Spain 36 E2 40 6N 8 20W
Miranda do Douro, Portugal 36 D4 41 30N 6 16W
Mirande, France 24 E4 43 31N 0 25 E
Mirandela, Portugal 36 D3 41 32N 7 10W
Mirando City, U.S.A. 139 M5 27 28N 98 59W
Mirandola, Italy 38 D8 44 53N 11 2 E
Mirandópolis, Brazil 159 A5 21 9 S 51 6W
Mirango, Malawi 107 E3 13 32 S 34 58 E
Mirani, Australia 114 C4 21 9 S 148 53 E
Mirano, Italy 39 C9 45 29N 12 6 E
Mirassol, Brazil 159 A6 20 46 S 49 28W
Mirbāţ, Oman 87 C6 17 0N 54 45 E
Mirboo North, Australia 117 E7 38 24 S 146 10 E
Mirear, Egypt 94 C4 23 15N 35 41 E
Mirebeau, Côte-d'Or, France 23 E12 47 25N 5 20 E
Mirebeau, Vienne, France 22 F7 46 49N 0 10 E
Mirecourt, France 23 D13 48 20N 6 10 E
Mirgorod, Ukraine 50 G8 49 58N 33 37 E
Miri, Malaysia 75 B4 4 23N 113 59 E
Miriam Vale, Australia 114 C5 24 20 S 151 33 E
Mirim, L., S. Amer. 159 C5 32 45 S 52 50W
Mirimire, Venezuela 152 A4 11 10N 68 43W
Miriti, Brazil 157 B6 6 15 S 59 0W
Mirnyy, Russia 57 C12 62 33N 113 53 E
Miroč, Serbia, Yug. 42 C7 44 32N 22 16 E
Mirond L., Canada 131 B8 55 6N 102 47W
Mirosławiec, Poland 47 B3 53 20N 16 5 E
Mirpur, Pakistan 79 B4 33 32N 73 56 E
Mirpur Bibiwari, Pakistan 80 E2 28 33N 67 44 E
Mirpur Khas, Pakistan 79 D3 25 30N 69 0 E
Mirpur Sakro, Pakistan 80 G2 24 33N 67 41 E
Mirria, Niger 97 F1 13 43N 9 7 E
Mirror, Canada 130 C6 52 30N 113 7W
Mîrşani, Romania 46 E4 44 1N 23 59 E
Mirsk, Poland 47 E2 50 58N 15 23 E
Miryang, S. Korea 67 G15 35 31N 128 44 E
Mirzaani, Georgia 53 F12 41 24N 46 5 E
Mirzapur, India 81 G10 25 10N 82 34 E
Mirzapur-cum-Vindhyachal = Mirzapur, India 81 G10 25 10N 82 34 E
Misamis Occidental □, Phil. 71 G4 8 20N 123 42 E
Misamis Oriental □, Phil. 71 G5 8 45N 125 0 E
Misantla, Mexico 147 D5 19 56N 96 50W
Misawa, Japan 60 D10 40 41N 141 24 E
Miscou I., Canada 129 C7 47 57N 64 31W
Mish'āb, Ra'as al, Si. Arabia 85 D6 28 15N 48 43 E
Mishagua →, Peru 156 C3 11 12 S 72 58W
Mishan, China 65 B8 45 37N 131 48 E
Mishawaka, U.S.A. 141 C10 41 40N 86 8W
Mishbih, Gebel, Egypt 94 C3 22 38N 34 44 E
Mishima, Japan 63 B10 35 10N 138 52 E
Mishkino, Russia 54 D8 55 20N 63 55 E
Mishmi Hills, India 78 A5 29 0N 96 0 E
Misilmeri, Italy 40 D6 38 2N 13 25 E
Misima I., Papua N. G. 120 F7 10 40 S 152 45 E
Misión, Mexico 145 N10 32 6N 116 53W
Misión Fagnano, Argentina 160 D3 54 32 S 67 17W
Misiones □, Argentina 159 B5 27 0 S 55 0W
Misiones □, Paraguay 158 B4 27 0 S 56 0W
Miskah, Si. Arabia 84 E4 24 49N 42 56 E
Miskitos, Cayos, Nic. 148 D3 14 26N 82 50W
Miskolc, Hungary 31 C13 48 7N 20 50 E
Misoke, Zaïre 106 C2 0 42 S 28 2 E
Misool, Indonesia 73 B4 1 52 S 130 10 E
Misrātah, Libya 96 B3 32 24N 15 3 E
Misrātah □, Libya 96 C3 29 0N 16 0 E
Missanabie, Canada 128 C3 48 20N 84 6W
Missão Velha, Brazil 154 C4 7 15 S 39 10W
Missinaibi →, Canada 128 B3 50 43N 81 29W
Missinaibi L., Canada 128 C3 48 23N 83 40W
Mission, S. Dak., U.S.A. 138 D4 43 21N 100 36W
Mission, Tex., U.S.A. 139 M5 26 15N 98 20W
Mission City, Canada 130 D4 49 10N 122 15W
Mission Viejo, U.S.A. 145 M9 33 41N 117 46W
Missisa L., Canada 128 B2 52 20N 85 7W
Missisagi →, Canada 128 C3 46 15N 83 9W
Mississinewa Res., U.S.A. 141 D10 40 46N 86 3W
Mississippi □, U.S.A. 133 D9 33 0N 90 0W
Mississippi →, U.S.A. 139 L10 29 0N 89 15W
Mississippi, Delta of the, U.S.A. 139 L9 29 15N 90 30W
Mississippi L., Canada 137 A8 45 5N 76 10W
Mississippi Sd., U.S.A. 139 K10 30 25N 89 0W
Missoula, U.S.A. 142 C6 46 52N 114 0W
Missour, Morocco 98 B4 33 3N 4 0W
Missouri □, U.S.A. 138 F8 38 25N 92 30W
Missouri →, U.S.A. 138 F9 38 50N 90 8W
Missouri Valley, U.S.A. 138 E7 41 33N 95 53W
Mist, U.S.A. 144 E3 45 59N 123 15W
Mistake B., Canada 131 A10 62 8N 93 0W
Mistassini →, Canada 129 C5 48 42N 72 20W
Mistassini L., Canada 128 B5 51 0N 73 30W
Mistastin L., Canada 129 A7 55 57N 63 20W
Mistatim, Canada 131 C8 52 52N 103 22W
Mistelbach, Austria 31 C9 48 34N 16 34 E
Misterbianco, Italy 41 E8 37 32N 15 2 E
Mistretta, Italy 41 E7 37 56N 14 20 E
Misty L., Canada 131 B8 58 53N 101 40W
Misugi, Japan 63 C8 34 31N 136 16 E
Misumi, Japan 62 E2 32 37N 130 27 E
Mît Ghamr, Egypt 94 H7 30 42N 31 12 E
Mitaka, Japan 63 B11 35 40N 139 33 E
Mitan, Uzbekistan 55 C3 40 5N 66 35 E
Mitatib, Sudan 95 D4 15 59N 36 12 E
Mitchell, Australia 115 D4 26 29 S 147 58 E
Mitchell, Canada 136 C3 43 28N 81 12W
Mitchell, Ind., U.S.A. 141 F10 38 42N 86 25W
Mitchell, Nebr., U.S.A. 138 E3 41 58N 103 45W
Mitchell, Oreg., U.S.A. 142 D3 44 31N 120 8W
Mitchell, S. Dak., U.S.A. 138 D5 43 40N 98 0W
Mitchell →, Australia 114 B3 15 12 S 141 35 E
Mitchell, Mt., U.S.A. 135 H4 35 40N 82 20W
Mitchell Ras., Australia 114 A2 12 49 S 135 36 E
Mitchelstown, Ireland 19 D3 52 16N 8 18W
Mitha Tiwana, Pakistan 80 C5 32 13N 72 6 E
Míthimna, Greece 44 E8 39 20N 26 12 E
Mitiamo, Australia 116 D6 36 12 S 144 15 E
Mitilíni, Greece 45 E8 39 6N 26 35 E
Mitilinoí, Greece 45 G8 37 42N 26 56 E
Mito, Japan 63 A12 36 20N 140 30 E
Mitre, Mt., N.Z. 118 G4 40 50 S 175 30 E
Mitsinjo, Madag. 105 B8 16 1 S 45 52 E
Mitsiwa, Ethiopia 95 D4 15 35N 39 25 E
Mitsiwa Channel, Ethiopia 95 D5 15 30N 40 0 E
Mitsukaidō, Japan 63 A11 36 1N 139 59 E
Mittagong, Australia 117 C9 34 28 S 150 29 E
Mittelland, Switz. 28 C4 46 50N 7 23 E
Mittelland Kanal, Germany 26 C3 52 23N 7 45 E
Mittenwalde, Germany 26 C9 52 16N 13 33 E
Mitterteich, Germany 27 F8 49 57N 12 15 E
Mittweida, Germany 26 E8 50 59N 13 0 E
Mitú, Colombia 152 C3 1 8N 70 3W
Mituas, Colombia 152 C4 3 52N 68 49W
Mitumba, Tanzania 106 D3 7 8 S 31 2 E
Mitumba, Chaîne des, Zaïre 106 D2 7 0 S 27 30 E
Mitwaba, Zaïre 107 D2 8 2 S 27 17 E
Mityana, Uganda 106 B3 0 23N 32 2 E
Mitzic, Gabon 102 B2 0 45N 11 40 E
Miura, Japan 63 B11 35 12N 139 40 E
Mixteco →, Mexico 147 D5 18 11N 98 30W
Miyagi □, Japan 60 E10 38 15N 140 45 E
Miyāh, W. el →, Egypt 94 B3 25 0N 33 23 E
Miyāh, W. el →, Syria 84 C3 34 44N 39 57 E
Miyake-Jima, Japan 63 C11 34 5N 139 30 E
Miyako, Japan 60 E10 39 40N 141 59 E
Miyako-Jima, Japan 61 M2 24 45N 125 20 E
Miyako-Rettō, Japan 61 M2 24 24N 125 0 E
Miyakonojō, Japan 62 F3 31 40N 131 5 E
Miyanojō, Japan 62 F2 31 54N 130 27 E
Miyanoura-Dake, Japan 61 J5 30 20N 130 31 E
Miyata, Japan 62 D2 33 49N 130 42 E
Miyazaki, Japan 62 F3 31 56N 131 30 E
Miyazaki □, Japan 62 E3 32 30N 131 30 E
Miyazu, Japan 63 B7 35 35N 135 10 E
Miyet, Bahr el = Dead Sea, Asia 86 A1 31 30N 35 30 E
Miyi, China 68 D4 26 47N 102 9 E
Miyoshi, Japan 62 C4 34 48N 132 51 E
Miyun, China 66 D9 40 28N 116 50 E
Miyun Shuiku, China 67 D9 40 30N 117 0 E
Mizamis = Ozamis, Phil. 71 G4 8 15N 123 50 E
Mizdah, Libya 96 B2 31 30N 13 0 E
Mizen Hd., Cork, Ireland 19 E2 51 27N 9 50W
Mizen Hd., Wick., Ireland 19 D5 52 52N 6 4W
Mizhi, China 66 F6 37 47N 110 12 E
Mizil, Romania 46 E7 44 59N 26 29 E
Mizoram □, India 78 D4 23 30N 92 40 E
Mizpe Ramon, Israel 91 E3 30 34N 34 49 E
Mizuho, Japan 63 B7 35 6N 135 17 E
Mizunami, Japan 63 B9 35 22N 137 15 E
Mizusawa, Japan 60 E10 39 8N 141 8 E
Mjöbäck, Sweden 15 G6 57 28N 12 53 E
Mjölby, Sweden 15 F9 58 20N 15 10 E
Mjörn, Sweden 15 G6 57 55N 12 25 E
Mjøsa, Norway 14 D5 60 48N 11 0 E
Mkata, Tanzania 106 D4 5 45 S 38 20 E
Mkokotoni, Tanzania 106 D4 5 55 S 39 15 E
Mkomazi, Tanzania 106 C4 4 40 S 38 7 E
Mkomazi →, S. Africa 105 E5 30 12 S 30 50 E
Mkulwe, Tanzania 107 D3 8 37 S 32 20 E
Mkumbi, Ras, Tanzania 106 D4 7 38 S 39 55 E
Mkushi, Zambia 107 E2 14 25 S 29 15 E
Mkushi River, Zambia 107 E2 13 32 S 29 45 E
Mkuze, S. Africa 105 D5 27 10 S 32 0 E
Mkuze →, S. Africa 105 D5 27 45 S 32 30 E
Mladá Boleslav, Czech. 30 A7 50 27N 14 53 E
Mladenovac, Serbia, Yug. 42 C5 44 28N 20 44 E
Mlala Hills, Tanzania 106 D3 6 50 S 31 40 E
Mlange, Malawi 107 F4 16 2 S 35 33 E
Mlava →, Serbia, Yug. 42 C6 44 45N 21 13 E
Mława, Poland 47 B7 53 9N 20 25 E
Mlinište, Bos.-H., Yug. 39 D13 44 15N 16 50 E
Mljet, Croatia 42 E2 42 43N 17 30 E
Mljetski Kanal, Croatia 42 E2 42 48N 17 35 E
Młynary, Poland 47 A6 54 12N 19 46 E
Mmabatho, S. Africa 104 D4 25 49 S 25 30 E
Mme, Cameroon 101 D7 6 18N 10 14 E
Mo i Rana, Norway 12 C13 66 15N 14 7 E
Moa, Indonesia 72 C3 8 0 S 128 0 E
Moa →, S. Leone 100 D2 6 59N 11 36W
Moab, U.S.A. 143 G9 38 40N 109 35W
Moabi, Gabon 102 C2 2 24 S 10 59 E
Moaco →, Brazil 156 B4 7 41 S 68 18W
Moala, Fiji 121 B2 18 36 S 179 53 E
Moalie Park, Australia 115 D3 29 42 S 143 3 E
Moaña, Spain 36 C2 42 18N 8 43W
Moba, Zaïre 106 D2 7 0 S 29 48 E
Mobara, Japan 63 B12 35 25N 140 18 E
Mobārakābād, Iran 85 D7 28 24N 53 20 E
Mobārakīyeh, Iran 85 C6 35 5N 51 47 E
Mobaye, C.A.R. 102 B4 4 25N 21 5 E
Mobayi, Zaïre 102 B4 4 15N 21 8 E
Moberly, U.S.A. 140 E4 39 25N 92 25W
Moberly →, Canada 130 B4 56 12N 120 55W
Mobile, U.S.A. 135 K1 30 41N 88 3W
Mobile B., U.S.A. 135 K2 30 30N 88 0W
Mobridge, U.S.A. 138 C4 45 31N 100 28W
Mobutu Sese Seko, L., Africa 106 B3 1 30N 31 0 E
Moc Chau, Vietnam 76 B5 20 50N 104 38 E
Moc Hoa, Vietnam 77 G5 10 46N 105 56 E
Mocaba, Sa. de, Angola 103 D3 7 12 S 15 0 E
Mocabe Kasari, Zaïre 107 D2 9 58 S 26 12 E
Mocajuba, Brazil 154 B2 2 35 S 49 30W
Moçambique, Mozam. 107 F5 15 3 S 40 42 E
Moçâmedes = Namibe, Angola 103 F2 15 7 S 12 11 E
Mocapra →, Venezuela 152 B4 7 56N 66 46W
Mocha, I., Chile 160 A2 38 22 S 73 56W
Mochudi, Botswana 104 C4 24 27 S 26 7 E
Mocimboa da Praia, Mozam. 107 E5 11 25 S 40 20 E
Mociu, Romania 46 C5 46 46N 24 3 E
Moclips, U.S.A. 144 C2 47 14N 124 10W
Mocoa, Colombia 152 C2 1 7N 76 35W
Mococa, Brazil 159 A6 21 28 S 47 0W
Mocorito, Mexico 146 B3 25 30N 107 53W
Moctezuma, Mexico 146 B3 29 50N 109 0W
Moctezuma →, Mexico 147 C5 21 59N 98 34W
Mocuba, Mozam. 107 F4 16 54 S 36 57 E
Mocúzari, Presa, Mexico 146 B3 27 10N 109 10W
Moda, Burma 78 C6 24 22N 96 29 E
Modane, France 25 C10 45 12N 6 40 E
Modasa, India 80 H5 23 30N 73 21 E
Modave, Belgium 21 H6 50 27N 5 18 E
Modder →, S. Africa 104 D3 29 2 S 24 37 E
Modderrivier, S. Africa 104 D3 29 2 S 24 38 E
Módena, Italy 38 D7 44 39N 10 55 E
Modena, U.S.A. 143 H7 37 55N 113 56W
Modesto, U.S.A. 144 H6 37 43N 121 0W
Módica, Italy 41 F7 36 52N 14 45 E
Modigliana, Italy 39 D8 44 9N 11 48 E
Modjamboli, Zaïre 102 B4 2 28N 22 6 E
Modlin, Poland 47 C7 52 24N 20 41 E
Mödling, Austria 31 C9 48 5N 16 17 E
Modo, Sudan 95 F3 5 31N 30 33 E
Modra, Czech. 31 C10 48 19N 17 20 E
Modriča, Bos.-H., Yug. 42 C3 44 57N 18 17 E
Moe, Australia 117 E7 38 12 S 146 19 E
Moebase, Mozam. 107 F4 17 3 S 38 41 E
Moëlan-sur-Mer, France 22 E3 47 49N 3 38W
Moengo, Surinam 153 B7 5 45N 54 20W
Moergestel, Neths. 21 E6 51 33N 5 11 E
Moers, Germany 21 F9 51 27N 6 38 E
Moësa →, Switz. 29 D8 46 12N 9 10 E
Moffat, U.K. 18 F5 55 20N 3 27W
Moga, India 80 D6 30 48N 75 8 E
Mogadishu = Muqdisho, Somali Rep. 90 G4 2 2N 45 25 E
Mogador = Essaouira, Morocco 98 B3 31 32N 9 42W
Mogadouro, Portugal 36 D4 41 22N 6 47W
Mogalakwena →, S. Africa 105 C4 22 38 S 28 40 E
Mogami →, Japan 60 E10 38 45N 140 0 E
Mogán, Canary Is. 33 G4 27 53N 15 43W
Mogaung, Burma 78 C6 25 20N 97 0 E
Møgeltønder, Denmark 15 K2 54 57N 8 48 E
Mogente, Spain 35 G4 38 52N 0 45W
Mogho, Ethiopia 95 G5 4 54N 40 16 E
Mogi das Cruzes, Brazil 159 A6 23 31 S 46 11W
Mogi-Guaçu →, Brazil 159 A6 20 53 S 48 10W
Mogi-Mirim, Brazil 159 A6 22 29 S 47 0W
Mogielnica, Poland 47 D7 51 42N 20 41 E
Mogilev, Belorussia 50 E7 53 55N 30 18 E
Mogilev-Podolskiy, Moldavia 52 B2 48 20N 27 40 E
Mogilno, Poland 47 C4 52 39N 17 55 E
Mogincual, Mozam. 107 F5 15 35 S 40 25 E
Mogliano Véneto, Italy 39 C9 45 33N 12 15 E
Mogocha, Russia 57 D12 53 40N 119 50 E
Mogoi, Indonesia 73 B4 1 55 S 133 10 E
Mogok, Burma 78 D6 23 0N 96 40 E
Mogriguy, Australia 117 B8 32 3 S 148 40 E
Moguer, Spain 37 H4 37 15N 6 52W
Mogumber, Australia 113 F2 31 2 S 116 3 E
Mohács, Hungary 31 F11 45 58N 18 41 E
Mohaka →, N.Z. 118 F6 39 7 S 177 12 E
Mohales Hoek, Lesotho 104 E4 30 7 S 27 26 E
Mohall, U.S.A. 138 A4 48 46N 101 30W
Moḩammadābād, Iran 85 B8 37 52N 59 5 E
Mohammadia, Algeria 99 A5 35 33N 0 3 E
Mohammedia, Morocco 98 B3 33 44N 7 21W
Mohave, L., U.S.A. 145 K12 35 25N 114 36W
Mohawk →, U.S.A. 137 D11 42 47N 73 42W
Möhne →, Germany 26 D3 51 29N 7 57 E
Mohnyin, Burma 78 C6 24 47N 96 22 E
Moholm, Sweden 15 F8 58 37N 14 5 E
Mohoro, Tanzania 106 D4 8 6 S 39 8 E
Moia, Sudan 95 F2 5 3N 28 2 E
Moidart, L., U.K. 18 E3 56 47N 5 40W
Moinabad, India 82 F3 17 44N 77 16 E
Moindou, N. Cal. 121 U19 21 42 S 165 41 E
Moineşti, Romania 46 C7 46 28N 26 31 E
Mointy, Kazakhstan 56 E8 47 10N 73 18 E
Moirans, France 25 C9 45 20N 5 33 E
Moirans-en-Montagne, France 25 B9 46 26N 5 43 E
Moíres, Greece 32 D6 35 4N 24 56 E
Moisakula, Estonia 50 B4 58 3N 25 12 E
Moisie, Canada 129 B6 50 12N 66 1W
Moisie →, Canada 129 B6 50 14N 66 5W
Moissac, France 24 D5 44 7N 1 5 E
Moïssala, Chad 97 G3 8 21N 17 46 E
Moita, Portugal 37 G2 38 38N 8 58W
Mojácar, Spain 35 H3 37 6N 1 55W
Mojados, Spain 36 D6 41 26N 4 40W
Mojave, U.S.A. 145 K8 35 8N 118 8W
Mojave Desert, U.S.A. 145 L10 35 0N 116 30W
Mojiang, China 68 F3 23 37N 101 35 E
Mojo, Bolivia 158 A2 21 48 S 65 33W
Mojo, Ethiopia 95 F4 8 35N 39 5 E
Mojokerto, Indonesia 75 D4 7 28 S 112 26 E
Mojos, Llanos de, Bolivia 157 D5 15 10 S 65 0W
Moju →, Brazil 154 B2 1 40 S 48 25W
Mokai, N.Z. 118 E4 38 32 S 175 56 E
Mokambo, Zaïre 107 E2 12 25 S 28 20 E
Mokameh, India 81 G11 25 24N 85 55 E
Mokane, U.S.A. 140 F5 38 41N 91 53W
Mokau, N.Z. 118 E3 38 42 S 174 39 E
Mokau →, N.Z. 118 E3 38 35 S 174 35 E
Mokelumne →, U.S.A. 144 G5 38 23N 121 25W
Mokelumne Hill, U.S.A. 144 G6 38 18N 120 43W
Mokhós, Greece 32 D7 35 16N 25 27 E
Mokhotlong, Lesotho 105 D4 29 22 S 29 2 E
Mokihinui →, N.Z. 119 B6 41 33 S 171 58 E
Moknine, Tunisia 96 A2 35 35N 10 58 E
Mokpalin, Burma 78 G6 17 26N 96 53 E
Mokra Gora, Serbia, Yug. 42 E5 42 50N 20 30 E
Mokronog, Slovenia 39 C12 45 57N 15 9 E
Moksha →, Russia 51 D12 54 45N 41 53 E
Mokshan, Russia 51 E14 53 25N 44 35 E
Mol, Belgium 21 F6 51 11N 5 5 E
Mola, C. de la, Spain 34 F9 39 40N 4 20 E
Mola di Bari, Italy 41 A10 41 3N 17 5 E
Moláoi, Greece 45 H4 36 49N 22 56 E
Molat, Croatia 39 D11 44 15N 14 50 E
Molave, Phil. 71 G4 8 5N 123 30 E
Molchanovo, Russia 56 D9 57 40N 83 50 E
Mold, U.K. 16 D4 53 10N 3 10W
Moldava nad Bodvou, Czech. 31 C14 48 38N 21 0 E
Moldavia = Moldova, Romania 46 C8 46 30N 27 0 E
Moldavia ■, Europe 52 C3 47 0N 28 0 E
Molde, Norway 12 E9 62 45N 7 9 E
Moldotau, Khrebet, Kirghizia 55 C7 41 35N 75 0 E
Moldova, Romania 46 C8 46 30N 27 0 E
Moldova Nouă, Romania 46 E2 44 45N 21 41 E
Moldoveanu, Romania 46 D5 45 36N 24 45 E
Molepolole, Botswana 104 C4 24 28 S 25 28 E
Moléson, Switz. 28 C4 46 33N 7 1 E
Molesworth, N.Z. 119 C8 42 5 S 173 16 E
Molfetta, Italy 41 A9 41 12N 16 35 E
Molina de Aragón, Spain 34 E3 40 46N 1 52W
Moline, U.S.A. 140 C6 41 30N 90 30W
Molinella, Italy 39 D8 44 38N 11 40 E
Molinos, Argentina 158 B2 25 28 S 66 15W
Moliro, Zaïre 106 D3 8 12 S 30 30 E
Molise □, Italy 39 G11 41 45N 14 30 E
Moliterno, Italy 41 B8 40 14N 15 50 E
Mollahat, Bangla. 81 H13 22 56N 89 48 E
Mölle, Sweden 15 H6 56 17N 12 31 E
Molledo, Spain 36 B6 43 8N 4 6W
Mollendo, Peru 156 D3 17 0 S 72 0W
Mollerin, L., Australia 113 F2 30 30 S 117 35 E
Mollerusa, Spain 34 D5 41 37N 0 54 E
Mollina, Spain 37 H6 37 8N 4 38W
Mölln, Germany 26 B6 53 37N 10 41 E
Mölltorp, Sweden 15 F8 58 30N 14 26 E
Mölndal, Sweden 15 G6 57 40N 12 3 E
Molo, Burma 78 D6 23 22N 96 53 E
Molochansk, Ukraine 52 C6 47 15N 35 35 E
Molochnaya →, Ukraine 52 C6 46 44N 35 15 E
Molodechno, Belorussia 50 D5 54 20N 26 50 E
Molokai, U.S.A. 132 H16 21 8N 157 0W
Moloma →, Russia 51 B16 58 20N 48 15 E
Molong, Australia 117 B8 33 5 S 148 54 E
Molopo →, Africa 104 D3 27 30 S 20 13 E
Mólos, Greece 45 F4 38 47N 22 37 E
Molotov = Perm, Russia 54 C5 58 0N 56 10 E
Moloundou, Cameroon 102 B3 2 8N 15 15 E
Molsheim, France 23 D14 48 33N 7 29 E
Molson L., Canada 131 C9 54 22N 96 40W
Molteno, S. Africa 104 E4 31 22 S 26 22 E
Molu, Indonesia 73 C4 6 45 S 131 40 E
Molucca Sea = Maluku Sea, Indonesia 72 A3 4 0 S 124 0 E
Moluccas = Maluku, Indonesia 72 B3 1 0 S 127 0 E
Molundo, Phil. 71 H5 7 57N 124 23 E
Moma, Mozam. 107 F4 16 47 S 39 4 E
Moma, Zaïre 102 C4 1 35 S 23 52 E
Momba, Australia 116 A5 30 58 S 143 30 E
Mombaça, Brazil 154 C4 5 43 S 39 45W
Mombasa, Kenya 106 C4 4 2 S 39 43 E
Mombetsu, Japan 60 B11 44 21N 143 22 E
Mombil, Burma 78 B7 27 46N 98 6 E
Mombuey, Spain 36 C4 42 3N 6 20W
Momchilgrad, Bulgaria 43 F10 41 33N 25 23 E
Momence, U.S.A. 141 C9 41 10N 87 40W
Momi, Zaïre 106 C2 1 42 S 27 0 E
Momignies, Belgium 21 H4 50 2N 4 10 E
Mompog Pass, Phil. 70 E4 13 34N 122 13 E
Mompós, Colombia 152 B3 9 14N 74 26W
Møn, Denmark 15 K6 54 57N 12 15 E
Mona, Canal de la, W. Indies 149 C6 18 30N 67 45W
Mona, I., Puerto Rico 149 C6 18 5N 67 54W
Mona, Pta., Costa Rica 148 E3 9 37N 82 36W
Mona, Pta., Spain 37 J7 36 43N 3 45W
Mona Quimbundo, Angola 103 D3 9 55 S 19 58 E
Monach Is., U.K. 18 D1 57 32N 7 40W
Monaco ■, Europe 25 E11 43 46N 7 23 E
Monadhliath Mts., U.K. 18 D4 57 10N 4 4W
Monagas □, Venezuela 153 B5 9 20N 63 0W
Monaghan, Ireland 19 B5 54 15N 6 58W
Monaghan □, Ireland 19 B5 54 15N 7 0W

Moree 235


Monahans, *U.S.A.* ..... 139 **K3** 31 35N 102 50W
Monapo, *Mozam.* ...... 107 **E5** 14 56 S 40 19 E
Monarch Mt., *Canada* .. 130 **C3** 51 55N 125 57W
Monastir = Bitola, *Macedonia, Yug.* ..... 42 **F6** 41 5N 21 10 E
Monastir, *Tunisia* ..... 96 **A2** 35 50N 10 49 E
Monastyriska, *Ukraine* .. 50 **G4** 49 8N 25 14 E
Moncada, *Phil.* ........ 70 **D3** 15 44N 120 34 E
Moncada, *Spain* ....... 34 **F4** 39 30N 0 24W
Moncalieri, *Italy* ...... 38 **D4** 45 0N 7 40 E
Moncalvo, *Italy* ....... 38 **C5** 45 3N 8 15 E
Moncão, *Portugal* ..... 36 **C2** 42 4N 8 27W
Moncarapacho, *Portugal* 37 **H3** 37 5N 7 46W
Moncayo, Sierra del, *Spain* .............. 34 **D3** 41 48N 1 50W
Mönchengladbach, *Germany* ........... 26 **D2** 51 12N 6 23 E
Monchique, *Portugal* ... 37 **H2** 37 19N 8 38W
Monclova, *Mexico* ...... 146 **B4** 26 50N 101 30W
Moncontour, *France* .... 22 **D4** 48 22N 2 38W
Moncoutant, *France* .... 24 **B3** 46 43N 0 35W
Moncton, *Canada* ...... 129 **C7** 46 7N 64 51W
Mondego →, *Portugal* . 36 **E2** 40 9N 8 52W
Mondego, C., *Portugal* . 36 **E2** 40 11N 8 54W
Mondeodo, *Indonesia* ... 72 **B2** 3 34 S 122 9 E
Mondo, *Chad* ......... 97 **F3** 13 47N 15 32 E
Mondolfo, *Italy* ....... 39 **E10** 43 45N 13 8 E
Mondoñedo, *Spain* ..... 36 **B3** 43 25N 7 23W
Mondovi, *Italy* ........ 38 **D4** 44 23N 7 49 E
Mondovi, *U.S.A.* ...... 138 **C9** 44 37N 91 40W
Mondragon, *France* .... 25 **D8** 44 13N 4 44 E
Mondragon, *Phil.* ...... 70 **E5** 12 31N 124 45 E
Mondragone, *Italy* ..... 40 **A6** 41 8N 13 52 E
Mondrain I., *Australia* .. 113 **F3** 34 9 S 122 14 E
Monduli □, *Tanzania* ... 106 **C4** 3 0 S 36 0 E
Monemvasía, *Greece* .... 45 **H5** 36 41N 23 3 E
Monessen, *U.S.A.* ..... 136 **F5** 40 9N 79 50W
Monesterio, *Spain* ...... 37 **G4** 38 6N 6 15W
Monestier-de-Clermont, *France* ............. 25 **D9** 44 55N 5 38 E
Monett, *U.S.A.* ....... 139 **G8** 36 55N 93 56W
Monfalcone, *Italy* ...... 39 **C10** 45 49N 13 32 E
Monflanquin, *France* ... 24 **D4** 44 32N 0 47 E
Monforte, *Portugal* .... 37 **F3** 39 6N 7 25W
Monforte de Lemos, *Spain* .............. 36 **C3** 42 31N 7 33W
Mong Hta, *Burma* ...... 78 **F7** 19 50N 98 35 E
Mong Ket, *Burma* ...... 78 **D7** 23 8N 98 22 E
Mong Kung, *Burma* ..... 78 **E6** 21 35N 97 35 E
Mong Kyawt, *Burma* ... 78 **F7** 19 56N 98 45 E
Mong Nai, *Burma* ...... 78 **E6** 20 32N 97 46 E
Mong Ping, *Burma* ..... 78 **E7** 21 22N 99 2 E
Mong Pu, *Burma* ...... 78 **E7** 20 55N 98 44 E
Mong Ton, *Burma* ..... 78 **E7** 20 17N 98 45 E
Mong Tung, *Burma* .... 78 **D6** 22 2N 97 41 E
Mong Yai, *Burma* ...... 78 **D7** 22 21N 98 3 E
Monga, *Zaïre* ......... 102 **B4** 4 12N 22 49 E
Mongalla, *Sudan* ...... 95 **F3** 5 8N 31 42 E
Mongers, L., *Australia* .. 113 **E2** 29 25 S 117 5 E
Monghyr = Munger, *India* .............. 81 **G12** 25 23N 86 30 E
Mongla, *Bangla.* ....... 78 **D2** 22 8N 89 35 E
Mongngaw, *Burma* ..... 78 **D6** 22 47N 96 59 E
Mongo, *Chad* ......... 97 **F3** 12 14N 18 43 E
Mongó, *Eq. Guin.* ..... 102 **B2** 1 52N 10 10 E
Mongolia ■, *Asia* ..... 64 **B5** 47 0N 103 0 E
Mongomo, *Eq. Guin.* ... 102 **B2** 1 38N 11 19 E
Mongonu, *Nigeria* ..... 101 **C7** 12 40N 13 32 E
Mongororo, *Chad* ...... 97 **F4** 12 3N 22 26 E
Mongu, *Zambia* ........ 103 **F4** 15 16 S 23 12 E
Môngua, *Angola* ....... 103 **F3** 16 43 S 15 20 E
Monistrol-d'Allier, *France* 24 **D7** 44 58N 3 38 E
Monistrol-sur-Loire, *France* ............. 25 **C8** 45 17N 4 11 E
Monkayo, *Phil.* ........ 71 **H6** 7 50N 126 5 E
Monkey Bay, *Malawi* ... 107 **E4** 14 7 S 35 1 E
Monkey River, *Belize* ... 147 **D7** 16 22N 88 29W
Mońki, *Poland* ......... 47 **B9** 53 23N 22 48 E
Monkira, *Australia* ..... 114 **C3** 24 46 S 140 30 E
Monkoto, *Zaïre* ........ 102 **C4** 1 38 S 20 35 E
Monmouth, *U.K.* ....... 17 **F5** 51 48N 2 43W
Monmouth, *U.S.A.* ..... 140 **D6** 40 50N 90 40W
Mono, *Solomon Is.* ..... 121 **L8** 7 20 S 155 35 E
Mono, L., *U.S.A.* ...... 144 **H7** 38 0N 119 9W
Monolith, *U.S.A.* ...... 145 **K8** 35 7N 118 22W
Monólithos, *Greece* ..... 32 **C9** 36 7N 27 45 E
Monon, *U.S.A.* ........ 141 **D10** 40 52N 86 53W
Monona, *Iowa, U.S.A.* .. 140 **A5** 43 3N 91 24W
Monona, *Wis., U.S.A.* .. 140 **A7** 43 4N 89 20W
Monongahela, *U.S.A.* ... 136 **F5** 40 12N 79 56W
Monópoli, *Italy* ........ 41 **B10** 40 57N 17 18 E
Monor, *Hungary* ....... 31 **D12** 47 21N 19 27 E
Monóvar, *Spain* ....... 35 **G4** 38 28N 0 53W
Monowai, *N.Z.* ........ 119 **F2** 45 53 S 167 31 E
Monowai, L., *N.Z.* ..... 119 **F2** 45 53 S 167 25 E
Monqoumba, *C.A.R.* .... 102 **B3** 3 33N 18 40 E
Monreal del Campo, *Spain* .............. 34 **E3** 40 47N 1 20W
Monreale, *Italy* ........ 40 **D6** 38 6N 13 16 E
Monroe, *Ga., U.S.A.* ... 135 **J4** 33 47N 83 43W
Monroe, *Iowa, U.S.A.* .. 140 **C3** 41 31N 93 6W
Monroe, *La., U.S.A.* ... 139 **J8** 32 32N 92 4W
Monroe, *Mich., U.S.A.* .. 141 **C13** 41 55N 83 26W
Monroe, *N.C., U.S.A.* .. 135 **H5** 35 2N 80 37W
Monroe, *N.Y., U.S.A.* .. 137 **E10** 41 19N 74 11W
Monroe, *Ohio, U.S.A.* .. 141 **E12** 39 27N 84 22W
Monroe, *Utah, U.S.A.* .. 143 **G7** 38 45N 112 5W
Monroe, *Wash., U.S.A.* . 144 **C5** 47 51N 121 58W
Monroe, *Wis., U.S.A.* .. 140 **B7** 42 38N 89 40W
Monroe City, *U.S.A.* ... 140 **E5** 39 40N 91 40W
Monroe Res., *U.S.A.* ... 141 **E10** 39 1N 86 31W
Monroeville, *Ala., U.S.A.* 135 **K2** 31 33N 87 15W
Monroeville, *Ind., U.S.A.* 141 **D12** 40 59N 84 52W
Monroeville, *Pa., U.S.A.* 136 **F5** 40 26N 79 45W
Monrovia, *Liberia* ...... 100 **D2** 6 18N 10 47W
Monrovia, *U.S.A.* ...... 143 **J4** 34 7N 118 1W
Mons, *Belgium* ......... 21 **H3** 50 27N 3 58 E
Monsaraz, *Portugal* ..... 37 **G3** 38 28N 7 22W
Monse, *Indonesia* ...... 72 **B2** 4 0 S 123 10 E
Monsefú, *Peru* ......... 156 **B2** 6 52 S 79 52W
Monségur, *France* ...... 24 **D4** 44 38N 0 4 E
Monsélice, *Italy* ........ 39 **C8** 45 16N 11 46 E
Monster, *Neths.* ........ 20 **D4** 52 1N 4 10 E
Mont Cenis, Col du, *France* ............. 25 **C10** 45 15N 6 55 E
Mont-de-Marsan, *France* 24 **E3** 43 54N 0 31W
Mont-Joli, *Canada* ..... 129 **C6** 48 37N 68 10W
Mont-Laurier, *Canada* .. 128 **C4** 46 35N 75 30W
Mont-St.-Michel, Le = Le Mont-St.-Michel, *France* ............. 22 **D5** 48 40N 1 30W
Mont-sous-Vaudrey, *France* ............. 23 **F12** 46 58N 5 36 E
Mont-sur-Marchienne, *Belgium* ............ 21 **H4** 50 23N 4 24 E
Mont Tremblant Prov. Park, *Canada* ....... 128 **C5** 46 30N 74 30W
Montabaur, *Germany* ... 26 **E3** 50 26N 7 49 E
Montagnac, *France* ..... 24 **E7** 43 29N 3 28 E
Montagnana, *Italy* ...... 39 **C8** 45 13N 11 29 E
Montagu, *S. Africa* ..... 104 **E3** 33 45 S 20 8 E
Montagu I., *Antarctica* .. 7 **B1** 58 25 S 26 20W
Montague, *Canada* ..... 129 **C7** 46 10N 62 39W
Montague, *U.S.A.* ...... 142 **F2** 41 47N 122 30W
Montague, I., *Mexico* ... 146 **A2** 31 40N 114 56W
Montague Ra., *Australia* 113 **E2** 27 15 S 119 30 E
Montague Sd., *Australia* 112 **B4** 14 28 S 125 20 E
Montaigu, *France* ...... 22 **F5** 46 59N 1 18W
Montalbán, *Spain* ...... 34 **E4** 40 50N 0 45W
Montalbano di Elicona, *Italy* ............... 41 **D8** 38 1N 15 0 E
Montalbano Iónico, *Italy* 41 **B9** 40 17N 16 33 E
Montalbo, *Spain* ....... 34 **F2** 39 53N 2 42W
Montalcino, *Italy* ....... 39 **E8** 43 4N 11 30 E
Montalegre, *Portugal* ... 36 **D3** 41 49N 7 47W
Montalto di Castro, *Italy* 39 **F8** 42 20N 11 36 E
Montalto Uffugo, *Italy* .. 41 **C9** 39 25N 16 9 E
Montalvo, *U.S.A.* ...... 145 **L7** 34 15N 119 12W
Montamarta, *Spain* ..... 36 **D5** 41 39N 5 49W
Montaña, *Peru* ........ 156 **B3** 6 0 S 73 0W
Montana, *Switz.* ........ 28 **D4** 46 19N 7 29 E
Montana □, *U.S.A.* .... 132 **A5** 47 0N 110 0W
Montaña Clara, I., *Canary Is.* ........... 33 **E6** 29 17N 13 33W
Montánchez, *Spain* ..... 37 **F4** 39 15N 6 8W
Montañita, *Colombia* ... 152 **C2** 1 22N 75 28W
Montargis, *France* ...... 23 **E9** 47 59N 2 43 E
Montauban, *France* ..... 24 **D5** 44 2N 1 21 E
Montauk, *U.S.A.* ...... 137 **E13** 41 3N 71 57W
Montauk Pt., *U.S.A.* .... 137 **E13** 41 4N 71 52W
Montbard, *France* ...... 23 **E11** 47 38N 4 20 E
Montbéliard, *France* .... 23 **E13** 47 31N 6 48 E
Montblanch, *Spain* ..... 34 **D6** 41 23N 1 4 E
Montbrison, *France* ..... 25 **C8** 45 36N 4 3 E
Montcalm, Pic de, *France* 24 **F5** 42 40N 1 25 E
Montceau-les-Mines, *France* ............. 23 **F11** 46 40N 4 23 E
Montchanin, *France* .... 25 **B8** 46 47N 4 30 E
Montclair, *U.S.A.* ..... 137 **F10** 40 53N 74 13W
Montcornet, *France* .... 23 **C11** 49 40N 4 1 E
Montcuq, *France* ...... 24 **D5** 44 21N 1 13 E
Montdidier, *France* ..... 23 **C9** 49 38N 2 35 E
Monte Albán, *Mexico* .. 147 **D5** 17 2N 96 45W
Monte Alegre, *Brazil* ... 153 **D7** 2 0 S 54 0W
Monte Alegre de Goiás, *Brazil* .............. 155 **D2** 13 14 S 47 10W
Monte Alegre de Minas, *Brazil* .............. 155 **E2** 18 52 S 48 52W
Monte Azul, *Brazil* ..... 155 **E3** 15 9 S 42 53W
Monte Bello Is., *Australia* 112 **D2** 20 30 S 115 45 E
Monte-Carlo, *Monaco* .. 25 **E11** 43 46N 7 23 E
Monte Carmelo, *Brazil* . 155 **E2** 18 43 S 47 29W
Monte Caseros, *Argentina* 158 **C4** 30 10 S 57 50W
Monte Comán, *Argentina* 158 **C2** 34 40 S 67 53W
Monte Cristi, *Dom. Rep.* 149 **C5** 19 52N 71 39W
Monte Dinero, *Argentina* 160 **D3** 52 18 S 68 33W
Monte Lindo →, *Paraguay* ............ 158 **A4** 23 56 S 57 12W
Monte Quemado, *Argentina* ........... 158 **B3** 25 53 S 62 41W
Monte Redondo, *Portugal* 36 **F2** 39 53N 8 50W
Monte Rio, *U.S.A.* ..... 144 **G4** 38 28N 123 0W
Monte San Giovanni, *Italy* ............... 40 **A6** 41 39N 13 33 E
Monte San Savino, *Italy* . 39 **E8** 43 20N 11 42 E
Monte Sant' Ángelo, *Italy* 41 **A8** 41 42N 15 59 E
Monte Santu, C. di, *Italy* 40 **B2** 40 5N 9 42 E
Monte Vista, *U.S.A.* ... 143 **H10** 37 40N 106 8W
Monteagudo, *Argentina* . 159 **B5** 27 14 S 54 8W
Monteagudo, *Bolivia* ... 157 **D5** 19 49 S 63 59W
Montealegre, *Spain* ..... 35 **G3** 38 48N 1 17W
Montebello, *Canada* .... 128 **C5** 45 40N 74 55W
Montebelluna, *Italy* ..... 39 **C9** 45 47N 12 3 E
Montebourg, *France* .... 22 **C5** 49 30N 1 20W
Montecastrilli, *Italy* .... 39 **F9** 42 40N 12 30 E
Montecatini Terme, *Italy* 38 **E7** 43 55N 10 48 E
Montecito, *U.S.A.* ..... 145 **L7** 34 26N 119 40W
Montecristi, *Ecuador* ... 152 **D1** 1 0 S 80 40W
Montecristo, *Italy* ...... 38 **F7** 42 20N 10 20 E
Montefalco, *Italy* ...... 39 **F9** 42 53N 12 38 E
Montefiascone, *Italy* .... 39 **F9** 42 31N 12 2 E
Montefrío, *Spain* ....... 37 **H6** 37 20N 4 0W
Montegnée, *Belgium* .... 21 **G7** 50 38N 5 31 E
Montego Bay, *Jamaica* .. 148 **C4** 18 30N 78 0W
Montegranaro, *Italy* .... 39 **E10** 43 13N 13 38 E
Monteiro, *Brazil* ....... 154 **C4** 7 48 S 37 2W
Monteith, *Australia* .... 116 **C3** 35 11 S 139 23 E
Montejicar, *Spain* ...... 35 **H1** 37 33N 3 30W
Montejinnie, *Australia* .. 112 **C5** 16 40 S 131 38 E
Montelíbano, *Colombia* . 152 **B2** 8 5N 75 29W
Montélimar, *France* .... 25 **D8** 44 33N 4 45 E
Montella, *Italy* ......... 41 **B8** 40 50N 15 2 E
Montellano, *Spain* ...... 37 **J5** 36 59N 5 36W
Montello, *U.S.A.* ...... 138 **D10** 43 49N 89 21W
Montelupo Fiorentino, *Italy* ............... 38 **E8** 43 44N 11 2 E
Montemor-o-Novo, *Portugal* ............ 37 **G2** 38 40N 8 12W
Montemor-o-Velho, *Portugal* ............ 36 **E2** 40 11N 8 40W
Montemorelos, *Mexico* .. 147 **B5** 25 11N 99 42W
Montendre, *France* ..... 24 **C3** 45 16N 0 26W
Montenegro, *Brazil* ..... 159 **B5** 29 39 S 51 29W
Montenegro □, *Montenegro, Yug.* ..... 42 **E4** 42 40N 19 20 E
Montenero di Bisaccia, *Italy* ............... 39 **G11** 41 58N 14 47 E
Montepuez, *Mozam.* .... 107 **E4** 13 8 S 38 59 E
Montepuez →, *Mozam.* 107 **E5** 12 32 S 40 27 E
Montepulciano, *Italy* .... 39 **E8** 43 5N 11 46 E
Montereale, *Italy* ...... 39 **F10** 42 31N 13 13 E
Montereau-Fault-Yonne, *France* ............. 23 **D9** 48 22N 2 57 E
Monterey, *Calif., U.S.A.* 144 **J5** 36 35N 121 57W
Monterey, *Ind., U.S.A.* . 141 **C10** 41 11N 86 30W
Monterey B., *U.S.A.* ... 144 **J5** 36 50N 121 55W
Montería, *Colombia* .... 152 **B2** 8 46N 75 53W
Montero, *Bolivia* ....... 157 **D5** 17 20 S 63 15W
Monteros, *Argentina* .... 158 **B2** 27 11 S 65 30W
Monterotondo, *Italy* .... 39 **F9** 42 3N 12 36 E
Monterrey, *Mexico* ..... 146 **B4** 25 40N 100 30W
Montes Altos, *Brazil* ... 154 **C2** 5 50 S 47 4W
Montes Claros, *Brazil* .. 155 **E3** 16 30 S 43 50W
Montesano, *U.S.A.* .... 144 **D3** 46 58N 123 39W
Montesárchio, *Italy* ..... 41 **A7** 41 5N 14 37 E
Montescaglioso, *Italy* ... 41 **B9** 40 34N 16 40 E
Montesilvano, *Italy* ..... 39 **F11** 42 30N 14 8 E
Montevarchi, *Italy* ..... 39 **E8** 43 30N 11 32 E
Montevideo, *Uruguay* ... 159 **C4** 34 50 S 56 11W
Montevideo, *U.S.A.* .... 138 **C7** 44 55N 95 40W
Montezuma, *Ind., U.S.A.* 141 **E9** 39 47N 87 22W
Montezuma, *Iowa, U.S.A.* .............. 140 **C4** 41 32N 92 35W
Montfaucon, *France* .... 23 **C12** 49 16N 5 8 E
Montfaucon-en-Velay, *France* ............. 25 **C8** 45 11N 4 20 E
Montfort, *France* ....... 22 **D5** 48 9N 1 58W
Montfort, *Neths.* ....... 21 **F7** 51 7N 5 58 E
Montfort-l'Amaury, *France* ............. 23 **D8** 48 47N 1 49 E
Montgenèvre, *France* ... 25 **D10** 44 56N 6 43 E
Montgomery = Sahiwal, *Pakistan* ........... 79 **C4** 30 45N 73 8 E
Montgomery, *U.K.* ..... 17 **E4** 52 34N 3 9W
Montgomery, *Ala., U.S.A.* .............. 135 **J2** 32 20N 86 20W
Montgomery, *Ill., U.S.A.* 141 **C8** 41 44N 88 21W
Montgomery, *W. Va., U.S.A.* .............. 134 **F5** 38 9N 81 21W
Montgomery City, *U.S.A.* 140 **F5** 38 59N 91 30W
Montguyon, *France* ..... 24 **C3** 45 12N 0 12W
Monthey, *Switz.* ........ 28 **D3** 46 15N 6 56 E
Monticelli d'Ongina, *Italy* 38 **C6** 45 3N 9 56 E
Monticello, *Ark., U.S.A.* 139 **J9** 33 40N 91 48W
Monticello, *Fla., U.S.A.* 135 **K4** 30 35N 83 50W
Monticello, *Ill., U.S.A.* . 141 **D8** 40 1N 88 34W
Monticello, *Ind., U.S.A.* 141 **D10** 40 40N 86 45W
Monticello, *Iowa, U.S.A.* 140 **B5** 42 18N 91 12W
Monticello, *Ky., U.S.A.* 135 **G3** 36 52N 84 50W
Monticello, *Minn., U.S.A.* .............. 138 **C8** 45 17N 93 52W
Monticello, *Miss., U.S.A.* 139 **K9** 31 35N 90 8W
Monticello, *Mo., U.S.A.* 140 **D5** 40 7N 91 43W
Monticello, *N.Y., U.S.A.* 137 **E10** 41 37N 74 42W
Monticello, *Utah, U.S.A.* 143 **H9** 37 55N 109 27W
Montichiari, *Italy* ...... 38 **C7** 45 28N 10 29 E
Montier-en-Der, *France* . 23 **D11** 48 30N 4 45 E
Montignac, *France* ..... 24 **C5** 45 4N 1 10 E
Montignies-sur-Sambre, *Belgium* ............ 21 **H4** 50 24N 4 29 E
Montigny, *France* ...... 23 **C13** 49 7N 6 10 E
Montigny-sur-Aube, *France* ............. 23 **E11** 47 57N 4 45 E
Montijo, *Spain* ........ 37 **G4** 38 52N 6 39W
Montijo, Presa de, *Spain* 37 **G4** 38 55N 6 26W
Montilla, *Spain* ........ 37 **H6** 37 36N 4 40W
Montlhéry, *France* ..... 23 **D9** 48 39N 2 15 E
Montluçon, *France* ..... 24 **B6** 46 22N 2 36 E
Montmagny, *Canada* ... 129 **C5** 46 58N 70 34W
Montmarault, *France* ... 24 **B6** 46 19N 2 57 E
Montmartre, *Canada* ... 131 **C8** 50 14N 103 27W
Montmédy, *France* ..... 23 **C12** 49 30N 5 20 E
Montmélian, *France* .... 25 **C10** 45 30N 6 4 E
Montmirail, *France* ..... 23 **D10** 48 51N 3 30 E
Montmoreau-St.-Cybard, *France* ............. 24 **C4** 45 23N 0 8 E
Montmorency, *Canada* .. 129 **C5** 46 53N 71 11W
Montmorillon, *France* ... 24 **B4** 46 26N 0 50 E
Montmort, *France* ...... 23 **D10** 48 55N 3 49 E
Monto, *Australia* ...... 114 **C5** 24 52 S 151 6 E
Montoir-sur-le-Loir, *France* ............. 22 **E7** 47 45N 0 52 E
Montório al Vomano, *Italy* ............... 39 **F10** 42 35N 13 38 E
Montoro, *Spain* ........ 37 **G6** 38 1N 4 27W
Montour Falls, *U.S.A.* .. 136 **D8** 42 20N 76 51W
Montpelier, *Idaho, U.S.A.* .............. 142 **E8** 42 15N 111 20W
Montpelier, *Ind., U.S.A.* 141 **D11** 40 33N 85 17W
Montpelier, *Ohio, U.S.A.* 141 **C12** 41 34N 84 40W
Montpelier, *Vt., U.S.A.* . 137 **B12** 44 15N 72 38W
Montpellier, *France* .... 24 **E7** 43 37N 3 52 E
Montpezat-de-Quercy, *France* ............. 24 **D5** 44 15N 1 30 E
Montpon-Ménestérol, *France* ............. 24 **D4** 45 0N 0 11 E
Montréal, *Canada* ..... 128 **C5** 45 31N 73 34W
Montréal, *France* ...... 24 **E6** 43 13N 2 8 E
Montreal L., *Canada* ... 131 **C7** 54 20N 105 45W
Montreal Lake, *Canada* . 131 **C7** 54 3N 105 46W
Montredon-Labessonnié, *France* ............. 24 **E6** 43 45N 2 18 E
Montréjeau, *France* ..... 24 **E4** 43 6N 0 35 E
Montrésor, *France* ..... 22 **E8** 47 10N 1 10 E
Montreuil, *France* ...... 23 **B8** 50 27N 1 45 E
Montreuil-Bellay, *France* 22 **E6** 47 8N 0 9W
Montreux, *Switz.* ....... 28 **D3** 46 26N 6 55 E
Montrevault, *France* .... 22 **E5** 47 17N 1 2W
Montrevel-en-Bresse, *France* ............. 25 **B9** 46 21N 5 8 E
Montrichard, *France* .... 22 **E8** 47 20N 1 10 E
Montrose, *U.K.* ........ 18 **E6** 56 43N 2 28W
Montrose, *Colo., U.S.A.* 143 **G10** 38 30N 107 52W
Montrose, *Pa., U.S.A.* .. 137 **E9** 41 50N 75 55W
Montrose, L., *U.S.A.* ... 140 **F3** 38 18N 93 50W
Monts, Pte. des, *Canada* 129 **C6** 49 20N 67 12W
Monts-sur-Guesnes, *France* ............. 22 **F7** 46 55N 0 13 E
Montsalvy, *France* ..... 24 **D6** 44 41N 2 30 E
Montsant, Sierra de, *Spain* .............. 34 **D5** 41 17N 1 0 E
Montsauche, *France* .... 23 **E11** 47 13N 4 2 E
Montsech, Sierra del, *Spain* .............. 34 **C5** 42 0N 0 45 E
Montseny, *Spain* ....... 34 **D2** 41 55N 2 25W
Montserrat, *Spain* ...... 34 **D6** 41 36N 1 49 E
Montserrat, *W. Indies* .. 149 **C7** 16 40N 62 10W
Montuenga, *Spain* ...... 36 **D6** 41 3N 4 38W
Montuiri, *Spain* ........ 33 **B9** 39 34N 2 59 E
Monveda, *Zaïre* ........ 102 **B4** 2 52N 21 30 E
Monyo, *Burma* ........ 78 **G5** 17 59N 95 30 E
Monywa, *Burma* ....... 78 **D5** 22 7N 95 11 E
Monza, *Italy* .......... 38 **C6** 45 35N 9 15 E
Monze, *Zambia* ........ 107 **F2** 16 17 S 27 29 E
Monze, C., *Pakistan* .... 79 **D2** 24 47N 66 37 E
Monzón, *Spain* ........ 34 **D5** 41 52N 0 10 E
Mooi River, *S. Africa* ... 105 **D4** 29 13 S 29 50 E
Mook, *Neths.* .......... 20 **E7** 51 46N 5 54 E
Mo'oka, *Japan* ......... 63 **A12** 36 26N 140 1 E
Moolawatana, *Australia* . 115 **D2** 29 55 S 139 45 E
Mooleulooloo, *Australia* 116 **A4** 31 36 S 140 32 E
Mooliabeenee, *Australia* 113 **F2** 31 20 S 116 2 E
Mooloogool, *Australia* .. 113 **E2** 26 2 S 119 5 E
Moomin Cr. →, *Australia* ........... 115 **D4** 29 44 S 149 20 E
Moonah →, *Australia* .. 114 **C2** 22 3 S 138 33 E
Moonbeam, *Canada* .... 128 **C3** 49 20N 82 10W
Moonda, L., *Australia* .. 114 **D3** 25 52 S 140 25 E
Moonie, *Australia* ..... 115 **D5** 27 46 S 150 20 E
Moonie →, *Australia* .. 115 **D4** 29 19 S 148 43 E
Moonta, *Australia* ..... 116 **C2** 34 6 S 137 32 E
Moora, *Australia* ...... 113 **F2** 30 37 S 115 58 E
Mooraberree, *Australia* . 114 **D3** 25 13 S 140 54 E
Moorarie, *Australia* .... 113 **E2** 25 56 S 117 35 E
Moorcroft, *U.S.A.* ..... 138 **C2** 44 17N 104 58W
Moore →, *Australia* ... 113 **F2** 31 22 S 115 30 E
Moore, L., *Australia* ... 113 **E2** 29 50 S 117 35 E
Moore Reefs, *Australia* . 114 **B4** 16 0 S 149 5 E
Moorefield, *U.S.A.* ..... 134 **F6** 39 5N 78 59W
Moores Res., *U.S.A.* ... 137 **B13** 44 45N 71 50W
Mooresville, *Ind., U.S.A.* 141 **E10** 39 37N 86 22W
Mooresville, *N.C., U.S.A.* .............. 135 **H5** 35 36N 80 45W
Moorfoot Hills, *U.K.* ... 18 **F5** 55 44N 3 8W
Moorhead, *U.S.A.* ..... 138 **B6** 46 51N 96 44W
Moorland, *Australia* .... 117 **A10** 31 46 S 152 38 E
Mooroopna, *Australia* .. 117 **D6** 36 25 S 145 22 E
Moorpark, *U.S.A.* ...... 145 **L8** 34 17N 118 53W
Moorreesburg, *S. Africa* 104 **E2** 33 6 S 18 38 E
Moorslede, *Belgium* .... 21 **G2** 50 54N 3 4 E
Moosburg, *Germany* .... 27 **G7** 48 28N 11 57 E
Moose →, *Canada* ..... 128 **B3** 51 20N 80 25W
Moose Factory, *Canada* . 128 **B3** 51 16N 80 32W
Moose I., *Canada* ...... 131 **C9** 51 42N 97 10W
Moose Jaw, *Canada* .... 131 **C7** 50 24N 105 30W
Moose Jaw →, *Canada* . 131 **C7** 50 34N 105 18W
Moose Lake, *Canada* ... 131 **C8** 53 43N 100 20W
Moose Lake, *U.S.A.* ... 138 **B8** 46 27N 92 48W
Moose Mountain Cr. →, *Canada* ............. 131 **D8** 49 13N 102 12W
Moose Mountain Prov. Park, *Canada* ....... 131 **D8** 49 48N 102 25W
Moose River, *Canada* ... 128 **B3** 50 48N 81 17W
Moosehead L., *U.S.A.* .. 129 **C6** 45 34N 69 40W
Moosomin, *Canada* ..... 131 **C8** 50 9N 101 40W
Moosonee, *Canada* ..... 128 **B3** 51 17N 80 39W
Moosup, *U.S.A.* ....... 137 **E13** 41 44N 71 52W
Mopeia Velha, *Mozam.* . 107 **F4** 17 30 S 35 40 E
Mopipi, *Botswana* ...... 104 **C3** 21 6 S 24 55 E
Mopoi, *C.A.R.* ......... 102 **A5** 5 6N 26 54 E
Mopti, *Mali* ........... 100 **C4** 14 30N 4 0W
Moqatta, *Sudan* ....... 95 **E4** 14 38N 35 50 E
Moquegua, *Peru* ....... 156 **D3** 17 15 S 70 46W
Moquegua □, *Peru* ..... 156 **D3** 16 50 S 70 55W
Mór, *Hungary* ......... 31 **D11** 47 25N 18 12 E
Móra, *Portugal* ........ 37 **G2** 38 55N 8 10W
Mora, *Sweden* ......... 13 **F13** 61 2N 14 38 E
Mora, *Minn., U.S.A.* ... 138 **C8** 45 52N 93 19W
Mora, *N. Mex., U.S.A.* . 143 **J11** 35 58N 105 21W
Mora de Ebro, *Spain* ... 34 **D5** 41 6N 0 38 E
Mora de Rubielos, *Spain* 34 **E4** 40 15N 0 45W
Mora la Nueva, *Spain* .. 34 **D5** 41 7N 0 39 E
Morača →, *Montenegro, Yug.* .... 42 **E4** 42 20N 19 9 E
Morada Nova, *Brazil* ... 154 **C4** 5 7 S 38 23W
Morada Nova de Minas, *Brazil* .............. 155 **E2** 18 37 S 45 22W
Moradabad, *India* ...... 81 **E8** 28 50N 78 50 E
Morafenobe, *Madag.* .... 105 **B7** 17 50 S 44 53 E
Morąg, *Poland* ......... 47 **B6** 53 55N 19 56 E
Moral de Calatrava, *Spain* 35 **G1** 38 51N 3 33W
Moraleja, *Spain* ........ 36 **E4** 40 6N 6 43W
Morales, *Colombia* ..... 152 **C2** 2 45N 76 38W
Moramanga, *Madag.* .... 105 **B8** 18 56 S 48 12 E
Moran, *Kans., U.S.A.* .. 139 **G7** 37 53N 94 35W
Moran, *Wyo., U.S.A.* .. 142 **E8** 43 53N 110 37W
Moranbah, *Australia* .... 114 **C4** 22 1 S 148 6 E
Morano Cálabro, *Italy* .. 41 **C9** 39 51N 16 8 E
Morant Cays, *Jamaica* .. 148 **C4** 17 22N 76 0W
Morant Pt., *Jamaica* .... 148 **C4** 17 55N 76 12W
Morar, L., *U.K.* ....... 18 **E3** 56 57N 5 40W
Moratalla, *Spain* ....... 35 **G3** 38 14N 1 49W
Moratuwa, *Sri Lanka* ... 83 **L4** 6 45N 79 55 E
Morava →, *Czech.* ..... 31 **C9** 48 10N 16 59 E
Moravia, *U.S.A.* ....... 140 **D4** 40 50N 92 50W
Moravian Hts. = Ceskomoravská Vrchovina, *Czech.* .... 30 **B8** 49 30N 15 40 E
Moravica →, *Serbia, Yug.* ........ 42 **D5** 43 52N 20 8 E
Moravice →, *Czech.* ... 31 **B10** 49 50N 17 43 E
Moravița, *Romania* ..... 42 **B6** 45 17N 21 14 E
Moravská Třebová, *Czech.* ............. 31 **B9** 49 45N 16 40 E
Moravské Budějovice, *Czech.* ............. 30 **B8** 49 4N 15 49 E
Morawa, *Australia* ...... 113 **E2** 29 13 S 116 0 E
Morawhanna, *Guyana* ... 153 **B6** 8 30N 59 40W
Moray Firth, *U.K.* ..... 18 **D5** 57 50N 3 30W
Morbach, *Germany* ..... 27 **F3** 49 48N 7 7 E
Morbegno, *Italy* ........ 38 **B6** 46 8N 9 34 E
Morbi, *India* .......... 80 **H4** 22 50N 70 42 E
Morbihan □, *France* ... 22 **E4** 47 55N 2 50W
Morcenx, *France* ....... 24 **D3** 44 3N 0 55W
Mordelles, *France* ...... 22 **D5** 48 5N 1 52W
Morden, *Canada* ....... 131 **D9** 49 15N 98 10W
Mordovian Republic □, *Russia* ............. 51 **D14** 54 20N 44 30 E
Mordovo, *Russia* ....... 51 **E12** 52 6N 40 50 E
Mordy, *Poland* ........ 47 **C9** 52 13N 22 31 E
Møre og Romsdal fylke □, *Norway* .... 14 **B2** 62 30N 8 0 E
Morea, *Australia* ....... 116 **D4** 36 45 S 141 18 E
Morea, *Greece* ......... 10 **H10** 37 45N 22 10 E
Moreau →, *U.S.A.* .... 138 **C4** 45 15N 100 43W
Morecambe, *U.K.* ...... 16 **C5** 54 5N 2 52W
Morecambe B., *U.K.* .... 16 **C5** 54 7N 3 0W
Moree, *Australia* ....... 115 **D4** 29 28 S 149 54 E

Mu Gia, Deo, *Vietnam* 76 **D5** 17 40N 105 47 E
Mu Us Shamo, *China* 66 **E5** 39 0N 109 0 E
Muacandalo, *Angola* 103 **E3** 10 2S 19 40 E
Muaná, *Brazil* 154 **B2** 1 25S 49 15W
Muanda, *Zaïre* 103 **D2** 6 0S 12 20 E
Muang Chiang Rai, *Thailand* 76 **C2** 19 52N 99 50 E
Muang Lamphun, *Thailand* 76 **C2** 18 40N 99 2 E
Muang Pak Beng, *Laos* 76 **C3** 19 54N 101 8 E
Muar, *Malaysia* 77 **L4** 2 3N 102 34 E
Muarabungo, *Indonesia* 74 **C2** 1 28S 102 52 E
Muaraenim, *Indonesia* 74 **C2** 3 40S 103 50 E
Muarajuloi, *Indonesia* 75 **C4** 0 12S 114 3 E
Muarakaman, *Indonesia* 75 **C5** 0 2S 116 45 E
Muaratebo, *Indonesia* 74 **C2** 1 30S 102 26 E
Muaratembesi, *Indonesia* 74 **C2** 1 42S 103 8 E
Muaratewe, *Indonesia* 75 **C4** 0 58S 114 52 E
Mubarakpur, *India* 81 **F10** 26 6N 83 18 E
Mubarraz = Al Mubarraz, *Si. Arabia* 85 **E6** 25 30N 49 40 E
Mubende, *Uganda* 106 **B3** 0 33N 31 22 E
Mubi, *Nigeria* 101 **C7** 10 18N 13 16 E
Mubur, P., *Indonesia* 77 **L6** 3 20N 106 12 E
Mucajaí →, *Brazil* 153 **C5** 2 25N 60 52W
Mucajaí, Serra do, *Brazil* 153 **C5** 2 23N 61 10W
Mucari, *Angola* 103 **D3** 9 30S 16 54 E
Muchachos, Roque de los, *Canary Is.* 33 **F2** 28 44N 17 52W
Mücheln, *Germany* 26 **D7** 51 18N 11 49 E
Muchinga Mts., *Zambia* 107 **E3** 11 30S 31 30 E
Muchkapskiy, *Russia* 51 **F13** 51 52N 42 28 E
Muck, *U.K.* 18 **E2** 56 50N 6 15W
Muckadilla, *Australia* 115 **D4** 26 35S 148 23 E
Muco →, *Colombia* 152 **C3** 4 15N 70 21W
Mucoma, *Angola* 103 **F2** 15 18S 13 39 E
Muconda, *Angola* 103 **E4** 10 31S 21 15 E
Mucuim →, *Brazil* 157 **B5** 6 33S 64 18W
Mucur, *Turkey* 88 **D6** 39 3N 34 22 E
Mucura, *Brazil* 153 **D5** 2 31S 62 43W
Mucuri, *Brazil* 155 **E4** 18 0S 39 36W
Mucurici, *Brazil* 155 **E3** 18 6S 40 31W
Mucusso, *Angola* 103 **F4** 18 1S 21 25 E
Muda, *Canary Is.* 33 **F6** 28 34N 13 57W
Mudan Jiang →, *China* 67 **A15** 46 20N 129 30 E
Mudanjiang, *China* 67 **B15** 44 38N 129 30 E
Mudanya, *Turkey* 52 **F3** 40 25N 28 50 E
Muddy →, *U.S.A.* 143 **H8** 38 0N 110 22W
Mudgee, *Australia* 117 **B8** 32 32S 149 31 E
Mudjatik →, *Canada* 131 **B7** 56 1N 107 36W
Mudon, *Burma* 78 **G6** 16 15N 97 44 E
Mudugh, *Somali Rep.* 108 **C3** 7 0N 47 30 E
Mudurnu, *Turkey* 88 **C4** 40 27N 31 12 E
Muecate, *Mozam.* 107 **E4** 14 55S 39 40 E
Muêda, *Mozam.* 107 **E4** 11 36S 39 28 E
Mueller Ra., *Australia* 112 **C4** 18 18S 126 46 E
Muende, *Mozam.* 107 **E3** 14 28S 33 0 E
Muerto, Mar, *Mexico* 147 **D6** 16 10N 94 10W
Muertos, Punta de los, *Spain* 35 **J3** 36 57N 1 54W
Mufindi □, *Tanzania* 107 **D4** 8 30S 35 20 E
Mufu Shan, *China* 69 **C10** 29 20N 114 30 E
Mufulira, *Zambia* 107 **E2** 12 32S 28 15 E
Mufumbiro Range, *Africa* 106 **C2** 1 25S 29 30 E
Mugardos, *Spain* 36 **B2** 43 27N 8 15W
Muge, *Portugal* 37 **F2** 39 3N 8 40W
Muge →, *Portugal* 37 **F2** 39 8N 8 44W
Múggia, *Italy* 39 **C10** 45 36N 13 47 E
Mughayrā', *Si. Arabia* 84 **D3** 29 17N 37 41 E
Mugi, *Japan* 62 **D6** 33 40N 134 25 E
Mugia, *Spain* 36 **B1** 43 3N 9 10W
Mugila, Mts., *Zaïre* 106 **D2** 7 0S 28 50 E
Muğla, *Turkey* 88 **E3** 37 15N 28 22 E
Muğla □, *Turkey* 88 **E3** 37 0N 28 0 E
Müglizh, *Bulgaria* 43 **E10** 42 37N 25 32 E
Mugu, *Nepal* 81 **E10** 29 45N 82 30 E
Muhammad, Râs, *Egypt* 94 **B3** 27 44N 34 16 E
Muhammad Qol, *Sudan* 94 **C4** 20 53N 37 9 E
Muhammadabad, *India* 81 **F10** 26 4N 83 25 E
Muḩayriqah, *Si. Arabia* 86 **B4** 23 59N 45 4 E
Muhesi →, *Tanzania* 106 **D4** 7 0S 35 20 E
Muheza □, *Tanzania* 106 **C4** 5 0S 39 0 E
Mühldorf, *Germany* 27 **G8** 48 14N 12 33 E
Mühlhausen, *Germany* 26 **D6** 51 12N 10 29 E
Mühlig Hofmann fjella, *Antarctica* 7 **D3** 72 30S 5 0 E
Muhutwe, *Tanzania* 106 **C3** 1 35S 31 45 E
Muiden, *Neths.* 20 **D6** 52 20N 5 4 E
Muikamachi, *Japan* 61 **F9** 37 15N 138 50 E
Muine Bheag, *Ireland* 19 **D5** 52 42N 6 57W
Muiños, *Spain* 36 **D3** 41 58N 7 59W
Muir, L., *Australia* 113 **F2** 34 30S 116 40 E
Mukachevo, *Ukraine* 50 **G3** 48 27N 22 45 E
Mukah, *Malaysia* 75 **B4** 2 55N 112 5 E
Mukawwa, Geziret, *Egypt* 94 **C4** 23 55N 35 53 E
Mukdahan, *Thailand* 76 **D5** 16 32N 104 43 E
Mukden = Shenyang, *China* 67 **D12** 41 48N 123 27 E
Mukhtolovo, *Russia* 51 **D13** 55 29N 43 15 E
Mukhtuya = Lensk, *Russia* 57 **C12** 60 48N 114 55 E
Mukinbudin, *Australia* 113 **F2** 30 55S 118 5 E
Mukishi, *Zaïre* 103 **D4** 8 30S 24 44 E
Mukomuko, *Indonesia* 74 **C2** 2 30S 101 10 E
Mukomwenze, *Zaïre* 106 **D2** 6 49S 27 15 E
Mukry, *Turkmenistan* 55 **E2** 37 54N 65 12 E
Muktsar, *India* 80 **D6** 30 30N 74 30 E
Mukur, *Afghan.* 80 **C2** 32 50N 67 42 E
Mukutawa →, *Canada* 131 **C9** 53 10N 97 24W
Mukwela, *Zambia* 107 **F2** 17 0S 26 40 E
Mukwonago, *U.S.A.* 141 **B8** 42 52N 88 20W
Mula, *Spain* 35 **G3** 38 3N 1 33W
Mula →, *India* 82 **E2** 18 34N 74 21 E
Mulanay, *Phil.* 70 **E4** 13 31N 122 24 E
Mulange, *Zaïre* 106 **C2** 3 40S 27 10 E
Mulberry Grove, *U.S.A.* 140 **F7** 38 55N 89 16W
Mulchén, *Chile* 158 **D1** 37 45S 72 20W
Mulde →, *Germany* 26 **D8** 51 50N 12 15 E
Muldraugh, *U.S.A.* 141 **G11** 37 56N 85 59W
Mule Creek, *U.S.A.* 138 **D2** 43 19N 104 8W
Muleba, *Tanzania* 106 **C3** 1 50S 31 37 E
Muleba □, *Tanzania* 106 **C3** 2 0S 31 30 E
Mulegns, *Switz.* 29 **C9** 46 32N 9 38 E
Muleshoe, *U.S.A.* 139 **H3** 34 17N 102 42W
Mulga Valley, *Australia* 116 **A4** 31 8S 141 3 E
Mulgathing, *Australia* 115 **E1** 30 15S 134 8 E
Mulgrave, *Canada* 129 **C7** 45 38N 61 31W
Mulgrave I., *Papua N. G.* 120 **F2** 10 5S 142 10 E
Mulhacén, *Spain* 35 **H1** 37 4N 3 20W
Mülheim, *Germany* 26 **D2** 51 26N 6 53 E
Mulhouse, *France* 23 **E14** 47 40N 7 20 E
Muli, *China* 68 **D3** 27 52N 101 8 E
Mulifanua, *W. Samoa* 121 **W24** 13 50S 171 59W
Muling, *China* 67 **B16** 44 35N 130 10 E
Mull, *U.K.* 18 **E3** 56 27N 6 0W
Mullaittvu, *Sri Lanka* 83 **K5** 9 15N 80 49 E
Mullen, *U.S.A.* 138 **D4** 42 5N 101 0W
Mullengudgery, *Australia* 117 **A7** 31 43S 147 23 E
Mullens, *U.S.A.* 134 **G5** 37 34N 81 22W
Muller, Pegunungan, *Indonesia* 75 **B4** 0 30N 113 30 E
Mullet Pen., *Ireland* 19 **B1** 54 10N 10 2W
Mullewa, *Australia* 113 **E2** 28 29S 115 30 E
Müllheim, *Germany* 27 **H3** 47 48N 7 37 E
Mulligan →, *Australia* 114 **C2** 25 0S 139 0 E
Mullin, *U.S.A.* 139 **K5** 31 33N 98 38W
Mullingar, *Ireland* 19 **C4** 53 31N 7 20W
Mullins, *U.S.A.* 135 **H6** 34 12N 79 15W
Mullumbimby, *Australia* 115 **D5** 28 30S 153 30 E
Mulobezi, *Zambia* 107 **F2** 16 45S 25 7 E
Mulshi L., *India* 82 **E1** 18 30N 73 48 E
Multai, *India* 82 **D4** 21 50N 78 21 E
Multan, *Pakistan* 79 **C3** 30 15N 71 36 E
Multrå, *Sweden* 14 **A11** 63 10N 17 24 E
Mulu, Gunong, *Malaysia* 75 **B4** 4 3N 114 56 E
Mulumbe, Mts., *Zaïre* 107 **D2** 8 40S 27 30 E
Mulungushi Dam, *Zambia* 107 **E2** 14 48S 28 48 E
Mulvane, *U.S.A.* 139 **G6** 37 30N 97 15W
Mulwad, *Sudan* 94 **D3** 18 45N 30 39 E
Mulwala, *Australia* 117 **C7** 35 59S 146 0 E
Mumbondo, *Angola* 103 **E2** 10 9S 14 15 E
Mumbwa, *Zambia* 107 **E2** 15 0S 27 0 E
Mumeng, *Papua N. G.* 120 **D4** 7 1S 146 37 E
Mumra, *Russia* 53 **D12** 45 45N 47 41 E
Mun →, *Thailand* 76 **E5** 15 19N 105 30 E
Muna, *Indonesia* 72 **B2** 5 0S 122 30 E
Munamagi, *Estonia* 50 **C5** 57 43N 27 4 E
Münchberg, *Germany* 27 **E7** 50 11N 11 48 E
Müncheberg, *Germany* 26 **C10** 52 30N 14 9 E
München, *Germany* 27 **G7** 48 8N 11 33 E
Munchen-Gladbach = Mönchengladbach, *Germany* 26 **D2** 51 12N 6 23 E
Muncho Lake, *Canada* 130 **B3** 59 0N 125 50W
Munchŏn, *N. Korea* 67 **E14** 39 14N 127 19 E
Münchwilen, *Switz.* 29 **B7** 47 28N 8 59 E
Muncie, *U.S.A.* 141 **D11** 40 10N 85 20W
Muncoonie, L., *Australia* 114 **D2** 25 12S 138 40 E
Munda, *Solomon Is.* 121 **M9** 8 20S 157 16 E
Mundakayam, *India* 83 **K3** 9 30N 76 50 E
Mundala, *Indonesia* 73 **B6** 4 30S 141 0 E
Mundare, *Canada* 130 **C6** 53 35N 112 20W
Munday, *U.S.A.* 139 **J5** 33 26N 99 39W
Münden, *Germany* 26 **D5** 51 25N 9 42 E
Mundiwindi, *Australia* 112 **D3** 23 47S 120 9 E
Mundo →, *Spain* 35 **G2** 38 30N 2 15W
Mundo Novo, *Brazil* 155 **D3** 11 50S 40 29W
Mundra, *India* 80 **H3** 22 54N 69 48 E
Mundrabilla, *Australia* 113 **F4** 31 52S 127 51 E
Munducurus, *Brazil* 153 **D6** 4 47S 58 16W
Munenga, *Angola* 103 **E2** 10 2S 14 41 E
Munera, *Spain* 35 **F2** 39 2N 2 29W
Muneru →, *India* 83 **F5** 16 45N 80 3 E
Mungallala, *Australia* 115 **D4** 26 28S 147 34 E
Mungallala Cr. →, *Australia* 115 **D4** 28 53S 147 5 E
Mungana, *Australia* 114 **B3** 17 8S 144 27 E
Mungaoli, *India* 80 **G8** 24 24N 78 7 E
Mungari, *Mozam.* 107 **F3** 17 12S 33 30 E
Mungbere, *Zaïre* 106 **B2** 2 36N 28 28 E
Munger, *India* 81 **G12** 25 23N 86 30 E
Mungindi, *Australia* 115 **D4** 28 58S 149 1 E
Munhango, *Angola* 103 **E3** 12 10S 18 38 E
Munich = München, *Germany* 27 **G7** 48 8N 11 33 E
Munising, *U.S.A.* 134 **B2** 46 25N 86 39W
Munka-Ljungby, *Sweden* 15 **H6** 56 16N 12 58 E
Munkedal, *Sweden* 15 **F5** 58 28N 11 40 E
Munku-Sardyk, *Russia* 57 **D11** 51 45N 100 20 E
Münnerstadt, *Germany* 27 **E6** 50 15N 10 11 E
Munoz, *Phil.* 70 **D3** 15 43N 120 54 E
Muñoz Gamero, Pen., *Chile* 160 **D2** 52 30S 73 5W
Munro, *Australia* 117 **D7** 37 56S 147 11 E
Munroe L., *Canada* 131 **B9** 59 13N 98 35W
Munsan, *S. Korea* 67 **F14** 37 51N 126 48 E
Munshiganj, *Bangla.* 78 **D3** 23 33N 90 32 E
Münsingen, *Switz.* 28 **C5** 46 52N 7 32 E
Munster, *France* 23 **D14** 48 2N 7 8 E
Munster, *Niedersachsen, Germany* 26 **C6** 52 59N 10 5 E
Münster, *Nordrhein-Westfalen, Germany* 26 **D3** 51 58N 7 37 E
Münster, *Switz.* 29 **D6** 46 29N 8 17 E
Munster □, *Ireland* 19 **D3** 52 20N 8 40W
Muntadgin, *Australia* 113 **F2** 31 45S 118 33 E
Muntele Mare, *Romania* 46 **C4** 46 30N 23 12 E
Muntok, *Indonesia* 74 **C3** 2 5S 105 10 E
Munyak, *Uzbekistan* 56 **E6** 43 30N 59 15 E
Munyama, *Zambia* 107 **F2** 16 5S 28 31 E
Muong Beng, *Laos* 76 **B3** 20 23N 101 46 E
Muong Boum, *Vietnam* 76 **A4** 22 24N 102 49 E
Muong Et, *Laos* 76 **B5** 20 49N 104 1 E
Muong Hai, *Laos* 76 **B3** 21 3N 101 49 E
Muong Hiem, *Laos* 76 **B4** 20 5N 103 22 E
Muong Houn, *Laos* 76 **B3** 20 8N 101 23 E
Muong Hung, *Vietnam* 76 **B4** 20 56N 103 53 E
Muong Kau, *Laos* 76 **E5** 15 6N 105 47 E
Muong Khao, *Laos* 76 **C4** 19 38N 103 32 E
Muong Khoua, *Laos* 76 **B4** 21 5N 102 31 E
Muong Liep, *Laos* 76 **C3** 18 29N 101 40 E
Muong May, *Laos* 76 **E6** 14 49N 106 56 E
Muong Ngeun, *Laos* 76 **B3** 20 36N 101 3 E
Muong Ngoi, *Laos* 76 **B4** 20 43N 102 41 E
Muong Nhie, *Vietnam* 76 **A4** 22 12N 102 28 E
Muong Nong, *Laos* 76 **D6** 16 22N 106 30 E
Muong Ou Tay, *Laos* 76 **A3** 22 7N 101 48 E
Muong Oua, *Laos* 76 **C3** 18 18N 101 20 E
Muong Peun, *Laos* 76 **B4** 20 13N 103 52 E
Muong Phalane, *Laos* 76 **D5** 16 39N 105 34 E
Muong Phieng, *Laos* 76 **C3** 19 6N 101 32 E
Muong Phine, *Laos* 76 **D6** 16 32N 106 2 E
Muong Sai, *Laos* 76 **B3** 20 42N 101 59 E
Muong Saiapoun, *Laos* 76 **C3** 18 24N 101 31 E
Muong Sen, *Vietnam* 76 **C5** 19 24N 104 8 E
Muong Sing, *Laos* 76 **B3** 21 11N 101 9 E
Muong Son, *Laos* 76 **B4** 20 27N 103 19 E
Muong Soui, *Laos* 76 **C4** 19 33N 102 52 E
Muong Va, *Laos* 76 **B4** 21 53N 102 19 E
Muong Xia, *Vietnam* 76 **B5** 20 19N 104 50 E
Muonio, *Finland* 12 **C17** 67 57N 23 40 E
Muotathal, *Switz.* 29 **C7** 46 58N 8 46 E
Mupa, *Angola* 103 **F3** 16 5S 15 50 E
Muping, *China* 67 **F11** 37 22N 121 36 E
Muqaddam, Wadi →, *Sudan* 94 **D3** 18 4N 31 30 E
Muqdisho, *Somali Rep.* 90 **G4** 2 2N 45 25 E
Muqshin, W. →, *Oman* 87 **C6** 19 44N 55 14 E
Muquequete, *Angola* 103 **E2** 14 50S 14 16 E
Mur →, *Austria* 30 **E9** 46 35N 16 3 E
Mur-de-Bretagne, *France* 22 **D4** 48 12N 3 0W
Mura →, *Slovenia* 39 **B13** 46 30N 16 33 E
Muradiye, *Turkey* 89 **D10** 39 0N 43 44 E
Murakami, *Japan* 60 **E9** 38 14N 139 29 E
Murallón, Cuerro, *Chile* 160 **C2** 49 48S 73 30W
Muralto, *Switz.* 29 **D7** 46 11N 8 49 E
Muranda, *Rwanda* 106 **C2** 1 52S 29 20 E
Murang'a, *Kenya* 106 **C4** 0 45S 37 9 E
Murashi, *Russia* 51 **B16** 59 30N 49 0 E
Murat, *France* 24 **C6** 45 7N 2 53 E
Murat →, *Turkey* 89 **D8** 38 39N 39 50 E
Muratlı, *Turkey* 88 **C2** 41 10N 27 29 E
Murau, *Austria* 30 **D7** 47 6N 14 10 E
Muravera, *Italy* 40 **C2** 39 25N 9 35 E
Murayama, *Japan* 60 **E10** 38 30N 140 25 E
Murban, *U.A.E.* 85 **F7** 23 50N 53 45 E
Murça, *Portugal* 36 **D3** 41 24N 7 28W
Murchison, *N.Z.* 119 **B7** 41 49S 172 21 E
Murchison →, *Australia* 113 **E1** 27 45S 114 0 E
Murchison, Mt., *Antarctica* 7 **D11** 73 0S 168 0 E
Murchison Falls = Kabarega Falls, *Uganda* 106 **B3** 2 15N 31 30 E
Murchison House, *Australia* 113 **E1** 27 39S 114 14 E
Murchison Mt., *N.Z.* 119 **D6** 43 0S 171 22 E
Murchison Mts., *N.Z.* 119 **F2** 45 13S 167 23 E
Murchison Ra., *Australia* 114 **C1** 20 0S 134 10 E
Murchison Rapids, *Malawi* 107 **F3** 15 55S 34 35 E
Murcia, *Spain* 35 **G3** 38 5N 1 10W
Murcia □, *Spain* 35 **H3** 37 50N 1 30W
Murdo, *U.S.A.* 138 **D4** 43 56N 100 43W
Murdoch Pt., *Australia* 114 **A3** 14 37S 144 55 E
Mureş □, *Romania* 46 **C5** 46 45N 24 40 E
Mureş →, *Romania* 46 **C1** 46 15N 20 13 E
Mureşul = Mureş →, *Romania* 46 **C1** 46 15N 20 13 E
Muret, *France* 24 **E5** 43 30N 1 20 E
Murfatlar, *Romania* 46 **E9** 44 10N 28 26 E
Murfreesboro, *U.S.A.* 135 **H2** 35 50N 86 21W
Murg, *Switz.* 29 **B8** 47 6N 9 13 E
Murg →, *Germany* 27 **G4** 48 55N 8 10 E
Murgab, *Tajikistan* 55 **D7** 38 10N 74 2 E
Murgeni, *Romania* 46 **C9** 46 12N 28 1 E
Murgenthal, *Switz.* 28 **B5** 47 16N 7 50 E
Murgon, *Australia* 115 **D5** 26 15S 151 54 E
Murgoo, *Australia* 113 **E2** 27 24S 116 28 E
Muri, *Switz.* 29 **B6** 47 17N 8 21 E
Muria, *Indonesia* 75 **D4** 6 36S 110 53 E
Muriaé, *Brazil* 155 **F3** 21 8S 42 23W
Murias de Paredes, *Spain* 36 **C4** 42 52N 6 11W
Murici, *Brazil* 154 **C4** 9 19S 35 56W
Muriége, *Angola* 103 **D4** 9 58S 21 11 E
Muriel Mine, *Zimbabwe* 107 **F3** 17 14S 30 40 E
Murila, *Angola* 103 **E4** 10 44S 20 20 E
Müritz See, *Germany* 26 **B8** 53 25N 12 40 E
Murka, *Kenya* 106 **C4** 3 27S 38 0 E
Murmansk, *Russia* 48 **A5** 68 57N 33 10 E
Murmerwoude, *Neths.* 20 **B8** 53 18N 6 0 E
Murnau, *Germany* 27 **H7** 47 40N 11 11 E
Muro, *France* 25 **F12** 42 34N 8 54 E
Muro, *Spain* 33 **B10** 39 44N 3 3 E
Muro, C. de, *France* 25 **G12** 41 44N 8 37 E
Muro Lucano, *Italy* 41 **B8** 40 45N 15 30 E
Murom, *Russia* 51 **D13** 55 35N 42 3 E
Muroran, *Japan* 60 **C10** 42 25N 141 0 E
Muros, *Spain* 36 **C1** 42 45N 9 5W
Muros y de Noya, Ría de, *Spain* 36 **C2** 42 45N 9 0W
Muroto, *Japan* 62 **D6** 33 18N 134 9 E
Muroto-Misaki, *Japan* 62 **D6** 33 15N 134 10 E
Murowana Goślina, *Poland* 47 **C4** 52 35N 17 0 E
Murphy, *U.S.A.* 142 **E5** 43 11N 116 33W
Murphys, *U.S.A.* 144 **G6** 38 8N 120 28W
Murphysboro, *U.S.A.* 139 **G10** 37 50N 89 20W
Murrat, *Sudan* 94 **D2** 18 51N 29 33 E
Murray, *Iowa, U.S.A.* 140 **C3** 41 3N 93 57W
Murray, *Ky., U.S.A.* 135 **G1** 36 40N 88 20W
Murray, *Utah, U.S.A.* 142 **F8** 40 41N 111 58W
Murray →, *Australia* 116 **C3** 35 20S 139 22 E
Murray →, *Canada* 130 **B4** 56 11N 120 45W
Murray, L., *Papua N. G.* 120 **D1** 7 0S 141 35 E
Murray, L., *U.S.A.* 135 **H5** 34 8N 81 30W
Murray Bridge, *Australia* 116 **C3** 35 6S 139 14 E
Murray Downs, *Australia* 114 **C1** 21 4S 134 40 E
Murray Harbour, *Canada* 129 **C7** 46 0N 62 28W
Murraysburg, *S. Africa* 104 **E3** 31 58S 23 47 E
Murrayville, *U.S.A.* 140 **E6** 39 35N 90 15W
Murree, *Pakistan* 80 **C5** 33 56N 73 28 E
Murrieta, *U.S.A.* 145 **M9** 33 33N 117 13W
Murrin Murrin, *Australia* 113 **E3** 28 58S 121 33 E
Murrumbidgee →, *Australia* 116 **C5** 34 43S 143 12 E
Murrumburrah, *Australia* 117 **C8** 34 32S 148 22 E
Murrurundi, *Australia* 117 **A9** 31 42S 150 51 E
Mursala, *Indonesia* 74 **B1** 1 41N 98 28 E
Murshid, *Sudan* 94 **C3** 21 40N 31 10 E
Murshidabad, *India* 81 **G13** 24 11N 88 19 E
Murska Sobota, *Slovenia* 39 **B13** 46 39N 16 12 E
Murtazapur, *India* 82 **D3** 20 40N 77 25 E
Murten, *Switz.* 28 **C4** 46 56N 7 4 E
Murtensee, *Switz.* 28 **C4** 46 56N 7 7 E
Murtle L., *Canada* 130 **C5** 52 8N 119 38W
Murtoa, *Australia* 116 **D5** 36 35S 142 28 E
Murtosa, *Portugal* 36 **E2** 40 44N 8 40W
Muru →, *Brazil* 156 **B3** 8 9S 70 45W
Murungu, *Tanzania* 106 **C3** 4 12S 31 10 E
Murupara, *N.Z.* 118 **E5** 38 28S 176 42 E
Murwara, *India* 81 **H9** 23 46N 80 28 E
Murwillumbah, *Australia* 115 **D5** 28 18S 153 27 E
Mürz →, *Austria* 30 **D8** 47 30N 15 25 E
Mürzzuschlag, *Austria* 30 **D8** 47 36N 15 41 E
Muş, *Turkey* 89 **D9** 38 45N 41 30 E
Muş □, *Turkey* 89 **D9** 38 45N 41 30 E
Musa, *Zaïre* 102 **B3** 2 40N 19 18 E
Musa →, *Papua N. G.* 120 **E5** 9 3S 148 55 E
Mûsa, G., *Egypt* 94 **J8** 28 33N 33 59 E
Musa Khel, *Pakistan* 79 **C3** 30 59N 69 52 E
Mūsá Qal'eh, *Afghan.* 79 **B2** 32 20N 64 50 E
Musala, *Bulgaria* 43 **E8** 42 13N 23 37 E
Musan, *N. Korea* 67 **C15** 42 12N 129 12 E
Musangu, *Zaïre* 103 **E4** 10 28S 23 55 E
Musasa, *Tanzania* 106 **C3** 3 25S 31 30 E
Musashino, *Japan* 63 **B11** 35 42N 139 34 E
Musay'īd, *Qatar* 85 **E6** 25 0N 51 33 E
Musaymīr, *Yemen* 86 **D4** 13 27N 44 37 E
Muscat = Masqat, *Oman* 87 **B7** 23 37N 58 36 E
Muscat & Oman = Oman ■, *Asia* 87 **B7** 23 0N 58 0 E
Muscatine, *U.S.A.* 140 **C5** 41 25N 91 5W
Muscoda, *U.S.A.* 140 **A6** 43 11N 90 27W
Musel, *Spain* 36 **B5** 43 34N 5 42W
Musgrave, *Australia* 114 **A3** 14 47S 143 30 E
Musgrave Ras., *Australia* 113 **E5** 26 0S 132 0 E
Mushie, *Zaïre* 102 **C3** 2 56S 16 55 E
Mushin, *Nigeria* 101 **D5** 6 32N 3 21 E
Musi →, *India* 82 **F4** 16 41N 79 40 E
Musi →, *Indonesia* 74 **C2** 2 20S 104 56 E
Muskeg →, *Canada* 130 **A4** 60 20N 123 20W
Muskegon, *U.S.A.* 141 **A10** 43 15N 86 17W
Muskegon →, *U.S.A.* 134 **D2** 43 25N 86 25W
Muskegon Heights, *U.S.A.* 141 **A10** 43 12N 86 17W
Muskogee, *U.S.A.* 139 **H7** 35 50N 95 25W
Muskwa →, *Canada* 130 **B4** 58 47N 122 48W
Muslīmiyah, *Syria* 84 **B3** 36 19N 37 12 E
Musmar, *Sudan* 94 **D4** 18 13N 35 40 E
Musofu, *Zambia* 107 **E2** 13 30S 29 0 E
Musoma, *Tanzania* 106 **C3** 1 30S 33 48 E
Musoma □, *Tanzania* 106 **C3** 1 50S 34 30 E
Musquaro, L., *Canada* 129 **B7** 50 38N 61 5W
Musquodoboit Harbour, *Canada* 129 **D7** 44 50N 63 9W
Mussau I., *Papua N. G.* 120 **A5** 1 30S 149 40 E
Musselburgh, *U.K.* 18 **F5** 55 57N 3 3W
Musselkanaal, *Neths.* 20 **C10** 52 57N 7 0 E
Musselshell →, *U.S.A.* 142 **C10** 47 21N 107 58W
Mussende, *Angola* 103 **E3** 10 32S 16 5 E
Mussidan, *France* 24 **C4** 45 2N 0 22 E
Mussolo, *Angola* 103 **D3** 9 59S 17 19 E
Mussomeli, *Italy* 40 **E6** 37 35N 13 43 E
Musson, *Belgium* 21 **J7** 49 33N 5 42 E
Mussoorie, *India* 80 **D8** 30 27N 78 6 E
Mussuco, *Angola* 103 **F3** 17 2S 19 3 E
Mustafakemalpaşa, *Turkey* 88 **C3** 40 2N 28 24 E
Mustahil, *Ethiopia* 108 **C2** 5 16N 44 45 E
Mustang, *Nepal* 81 **E10** 29 10N 83 55 E
Musters, L., *Argentina* 160 **C3** 45 20S 69 25W
Musudan, *N. Korea* 67 **D15** 40 50N 129 43 E
Muswellbrook, *Australia* 117 **B9** 32 16S 150 56 E
Muszyna, *Poland* 31 **B13** 49 22N 20 55 E
Mût, *Egypt* 94 **B2** 25 28N 28 58 E
Mut, *Turkey* 88 **E5** 36 40N 33 28 E
Mutanda, *Mozam.* 105 **C5** 21 0S 33 34 E
Mutanda, *Zambia* 107 **E2** 12 24S 26 13 E
Mutaray, *Russia* 57 **C11** 60 56N 101 0 E
Mutare, *Zimbabwe* 107 **F3** 18 58S 32 38 E
Mu'tariḑah, Al 'Urūq al, *Si. Arabia* 87 **B6** 21 15N 54 0 E
Muting, *Indonesia* 73 **C6** 7 23S 140 20 E
Mutooroo, *Australia* 116 **B4** 32 26S 140 55 E
Mutoto, *Zaïre* 103 **D4** 5 42S 22 42 E
Mutshatsha, *Zaïre* 103 **E4** 10 35S 24 20 E
Mutsu, *Japan* 60 **D10** 41 5N 140 55 E
Mutsu-Wan, *Japan* 60 **D10** 41 5N 140 55 E
Muttaburra, *Australia* 114 **C3** 22 38S 144 29 E
Muttama, *Australia* 117 **C8** 34 46S 148 8 E
Mutuáli, *Mozam.* 107 **E4** 14 55S 37 0 E
Mutunópolis, *Brazil* 155 **D2** 13 40S 49 15W
Muvatupusha, *India* 83 **K3** 9 53N 76 35 E
Muweilih, *Egypt* 91 **E3** 30 42N 34 19 E
Muxima, *Angola* 103 **D2** 9 33S 13 58 E
Muy Muy, *Nic.* 148 **D2** 12 39N 85 36W
Muya, *Russia* 57 **D12** 56 27N 115 50 E
Muyinga, *Burundi* 106 **C3** 3 14S 30 33 E
Muyunkum, Peski, *Kazakhstan* 55 **A5** 44 12N 71 0 E
Muzaffarabad, *Pakistan* 81 **B5** 34 25N 73 30 E
Muzaffargarh, *Pakistan* 79 **C3** 30 5N 71 14 E
Muzaffarnagar, *India* 80 **E7** 29 26N 77 40 E
Muzaffarpur, *India* 81 **F11** 26 7N 85 23 E
Muzeze, *Angola* 103 **F3** 15 3S 17 43 E
Muzhi, *Russia* 56 **C7** 65 25N 64 40 E
Muzillac, *France* 22 **E4** 47 35N 2 30W
Muzkol, Khrebet, *Tajikistan* 55 **D6** 38 22N 73 20 E
Muzon C., *U.S.A.* 130 **C2** 54 40N 132 40W
Mvadhi-Ousyé, *Gabon* 102 **B2** 1 13N 13 12 E
Mvam, *Gabon* 102 **C1** 0 13S 9 39 E
Mvôlô, *Sudan* 95 **F2** 6 2N 29 53 E
Mvuma, *Zimbabwe* 107 **F3** 19 16S 30 30 E
Mvurwi, *Zimbabwe* 107 **F3** 17 0S 30 57 E
Mwadui, *Tanzania* 106 **C3** 3 26S 33 32 E
Mwambo, *Tanzania* 107 **E5** 10 30S 40 22 E
Mwandi, *Zambia* 107 **F1** 17 30S 24 51 E
Mwanza, *Tanzania* 106 **C3** 2 30S 32 58 E
Mwanza, *Zaïre* 103 **D5** 7 55S 26 43 E
Mwanza, *Zambia* 107 **F1** 16 58S 24 28 E
Mwanza □, *Tanzania* 106 **C3** 2 0S 33 0 E
Mwaya, *Tanzania* 107 **D3** 9 32S 33 55 E
Mweelrea, *Ireland* 19 **C2** 53 37N 9 48W
Mweka, *Zaïre* 103 **C4** 4 50S 21 34 E
Mwendjila, *Zaïre* 103 **D3** 7 12S 18 51 E
Mwene, *Zaïre* 103 **D4** 6 35S 22 27 E
Mwenezi, *Zimbabwe* 107 **G3** 21 15S 30 48 E
Mwenezi →, *Mozam.* 107 **G3** 22 40S 31 50 E
Mwenga, *Zaïre* 106 **C2** 3 1S 28 28 E
Mweru, L., *Zambia* 107 **D2** 9 0S 28 40 E
Mweza Range, *Zimbabwe* 107 **G3** 21 0S 30 0 E
Mwilambwe, *Zaïre* 103 **D5** 8 7S 25 5 E
Mwimbi, *Tanzania* 107 **D3** 8 38S 31 39 E
Mwinilunga, *Zambia* 107 **E1** 11 43S 24 25 E
My Tho, *Vietnam* 77 **G6** 10 29N 106 23 E
Mya, O. →, *Algeria* 99 **B5** 30 46N 4 54 E

238 Myajlar


Myajlar, *India* 80 F4 26 15N 70 20 E
Myanaung, *Burma* 78 F5 18 18N 95 22 E
Myanmar = Burma ■, *Asia* 78 E6 21 0N 96 30 E
Myaungmya, *Burma* 78 G5 16 30N 94 40 E
Mycenae = Mikínai, *Greece* 45 G4 37 43N 22 46 E
Myeik Kyunzu, *Burma* 77 G1 11 30N 97 30 E
Myerstown, *U.S.A.* 137 F8 40 22N 76 18W
Myingyan, *Burma* 78 E5 21 30N 95 20 E
Myitkyina, *Burma* 78 C6 25 24N 97 26 E
Myittha →, *Burma* 78 D5 23 12N 94 17 E
Myjava, *Czech.* 31 C10 48 41N 17 37 E
Mymensingh, *Bangla.* 78 C3 24 45N 90 24 E
Myndus, *Turkey* 45 G9 37 3N 27 14 E
Mynydd Du, *U.K.* 17 F4 51 45N 3 45W
Mynzhilgi, Gora, *Kazakhstan* 55 B4 43 48N 68 51 E
Mýrdalsjökull, *Iceland* 12 E4 63 40N 19 6W
Myroodah, *Australia* 112 C3 18 7 S 124 16 E
Myrtle Beach, *U.S.A.* 135 J6 33 43N 78 50W
Myrtle Creek, *U.S.A.* 142 E2 43 0N 123 9W
Myrtle Point, *U.S.A.* 142 E1 43 0N 124 4W
Myrtleford, *Australia* 117 D7 36 34 S 146 44 E
Myrtou, *Cyprus* 32 D12 35 18N 33 4 E
Mysen, *Norway* 14 E5 59 33N 11 20 E
Mysia, *Turkey* 88 D2 39 50N 27 0 E
Myslenice, *Poland* 31 B12 49 51N 19 57 E
Myślibórz, *Poland* 47 C1 52 55N 14 50 E
Mysłowice, *Poland* 31 A12 50 15N 19 12 E
Mysore = Karnataka □, *India* 83 H3 13 15N 77 0 E
Mysore, *India* 83 H3 12 17N 76 41 E
Mystic, *Conn., U.S.A.* 137 E13 41 21N 71 58W
Mystic, *Iowa, U.S.A.* 140 D4 40 47N 92 57W
Myszków, *Poland* 47 E6 50 45N 19 22 E
Myszyniec, *Poland* 47 B8 53 23N 21 21 E
Mythen, *Switz.* 29 B7 47 2N 8 42 E
Mytishchi, *Russia* 51 D10 55 50N 37 50 E
Myton, *U.S.A.* 142 F8 40 10N 110 2W
Mývatn, *Iceland* 12 D5 65 36N 17 0W
Mze →, *Czech.* 30 B6 49 46N 13 24 E
Mzimba, *Malawi* 107 E3 11 55 S 33 39 E
Mzimkulu →, *S. Africa* 105 E5 30 44 S 30 28 E
Mzimvubu →, *S. Africa* 105 E4 31 38 S 29 33 E
Mzuzu, *Malawi* 107 E3 11 30 S 33 55 E


## N


N' Dioum, *Senegal* 100 B2 16 31N 14 39W
Na-lang, *Burma* 78 D6 22 42N 97 33 E
Na Noi, *Thailand* 76 C3 18 19N 100 43 E
Na Phao, *Laos* 76 D5 17 35N 105 44 E
Na Sam, *Vietnam* 76 A6 22 3N 106 37 E
Na San, *Vietnam* 76 B5 21 12N 104 2 E
Naab →, *Germany* 27 F8 49 1N 12 2 E
Naaldwijk, *Neths.* 20 E4 51 59N 4 13 E
Na'am, *Sudan* 95 F2 9 42N 28 27 E
Naantali, *Finland* 13 F17 60 29N 22 2 E
Naarden, *Neths.* 20 D6 52 18N 5 9 E
Naas, *Ireland* 19 C5 53 12N 6 40W
Nababiep, *S. Africa* 104 D2 29 36 S 17 46 E
Nabadwip = Navadwip, *India* 81 H13 23 34N 88 20 E
Nabari, *Japan* 63 C8 34 37N 136 5 E
Nabawa, *Australia* 113 E1 28 30 S 114 48 E
Nabberu, L., *Australia* 113 E3 25 50 S 120 30 E
Nabburg, *Germany* 27 F8 49 27N 12 11 E
Naberezhnyye Chelny, *Russia* 54 D3 55 42N 52 19 E
Nabeul, *Tunisia* 96 A2 36 30N 10 44 E
Nabha, *India* 80 D7 30 26N 76 14 E
Nabīd, *Iran* 85 D8 29 40N 57 38 E
Nabire, *Indonesia* 73 B5 3 15 S 135 26 E
Nabisar, *Pakistan* 80 G3 25 8N 69 40 E
Nabisipi →, *Canada* 129 B7 50 14N 62 13W
Nabiswera, *Uganda* 106 B3 1 27N 32 15 E
Nablus = Nābulus, *Jordan* 91 C4 32 14N 35 15 E
Naboomspruit, *S. Africa* 105 C4 24 32 S 28 40 E
Nabua, *Phil.* 70 E4 13 24N 123 22 E
Nābulus, *Jordan* 91 C4 32 14N 35 15 E
Nābulus □, *Jordan* 91 C4 32 20N 35 20 E
Nabunturan, *Phil.* 71 H5 7 35N 125 58 E
Nacala, *Mozam.* 107 E5 14 31 S 40 34 E
Nacala-Velha, *Mozam.* 107 E5 14 32 S 40 34 E
Nacaome, *Honduras* 148 D2 13 31N 87 30W
Nacaroa, *Mozam.* 107 E4 14 22 S 39 56 E
Naches, *U.S.A.* 142 C3 46 48N 120 42W
Naches →, *U.S.A.* 144 D6 46 38N 120 31W
Nachikatsuura, *Japan* 63 D7 33 33N 135 58 E
Nachingwea, *Tanzania* 107 E4 10 23 S 38 49 E
Nachingwea □, *Tanzania* 107 E4 10 30 S 38 30 E
Nachna, *India* 80 F4 27 34N 71 41 E
Náchod, *Czech.* 31 A9 50 25N 16 8 E
Nacimiento Res., *U.S.A.* 144 K6 35 46N 121 0W
Nacka, *Sweden* 14 E12 59 17N 18 12 E
Nackara, *Australia* 116 B3 32 48 S 139 12 E
Naco, *Mexico* 146 A3 31 20N 109 56W
Naco, *U.S.A.* 143 L9 31 24N 109 58W
Nacogdoches, *U.S.A.* 139 K7 31 33N 94 39W
Nácori Chico, *Mexico* 146 B3 29 39N 109 1W
Nacozari, *Mexico* 146 A3 30 24N 109 39W
Nadi, *Sudan* 94 D3 18 40N 33 41 E
Nadiad, *India* 80 H5 22 41N 72 56 E
Nădlac, *Romania* 46 C1 46 10N 20 50 E
Nador, *Morocco* 99 A4 35 14N 2 58W
Nadur, *Malta* 32 C1 36 2N 14 17 E
Nadūshan, *Iran* 85 C7 32 2N 53 35 E
Nadvoitsy, *Russia* 48 B5 63 52N 34 14 E
Nadvornaya, *Ukraine* 52 B1 48 37N 24 30 E
Nadym, *Russia* 56 C8 65 35N 72 42 E
Nadym →, *Russia* 56 C8 66 12N 72 0 E
Næstved, *Denmark* 15 J5 55 13N 11 44 E
Nafada, *Nigeria* 101 C7 11 8N 11 20 E
Näfels, *Switz.* 29 B8 47 6N 9 4 E
Naftshahr, *Iran* 84 C5 34 0N 45 30 E
Nafūsah, Jabal, *Libya* 96 B2 32 12N 12 30 E
Nag Hammâdi, *Egypt* 94 B3 26 2N 32 18 E
Naga, *Cebu, Phil.* 71 F4 10 13N 123 45 E
Naga, *Luzon, Phil.* 70 E4 13 38N 123 15 E
Naga, *Zamboanga del S., Phil.* 71 H4 7 46N 122 45 E
Naga, Kreb en, *Africa* 98 D3 24 12N 6 0W
Naga-Shima, *Kagoshima, Japan* 62 E2 32 10N 130 9 E
Naga-Shima, *Yamaguchi, Japan* 62 D4 33 49N 132 5 E
Nagagami →, *Canada* 128 C3 49 40N 84 40W
Nagahama, *Ehime, Japan* 62 D4 33 36N 132 29 E
Nagahama, *Shiga, Japan* 63 B8 35 23N 136 16 E
Nagai, *Japan* 60 E10 38 6N 140 2 E
Nagaland □, *India* 78 B5 26 0N 94 30 E
Nagambie, *Australia* 117 D6 36 47 S 145 10 E
Nagano, *Japan* 63 A10 36 40N 138 10 E
Nagano □, *Japan* 63 A10 36 15N 138 0 E
Nagaoka, *Japan* 61 F9 37 27N 138 51 E
Nagappattinam, *India* 83 J4 10 46N 79 51 E
Nagar Parkar, *Pakistan* 80 G4 24 28N 70 46 E
Nagara →, *Japan* 63 B8 35 40N 136 43 E
Nagari Hills, *India* 83 H4 13 3N 79 45 E
Nagarjuna Sagar, *India* 83 F4 16 35N 79 17 E
Nagasaki, *Japan* 62 E1 32 47N 129 50 E
Nagasaki □, *Japan* 62 E1 32 50N 129 40 E
Nagato, *Japan* 62 C3 34 19N 131 5 E
Nagaur, *India* 80 F5 27 15N 73 45 E
Nagbhir, *India* 82 D4 20 34N 79 55 E
Nagercoil, *India* 83 K3 8 12N 77 26 E
Nagina, *India* 81 E8 29 30N 78 30 E
Nagīneh, *Iran* 85 C8 34 20N 57 15 E
Nagir, *Pakistan* 81 A6 36 12N 74 42 E
Nagold, *Germany* 27 G4 48 33N 8 43 E
Nagold →, *Germany* 27 G4 48 52N 8 42 E
Nagoorin, *Australia* 114 C5 24 17 S 151 15 E
Nagornyy, *Russia* 57 D13 55 58N 124 57 E
Nagorsk, *Russia* 54 B2 59 18N 50 48 E
Nagoya, *Japan* 63 B8 35 10N 136 50 E
Nagpur, *India* 82 D4 21 8N 79 10 E
Nagua, *Dom. Rep.* 149 C6 19 23N 69 50W
Nagyatád, *Hungary* 31 E10 46 14N 17 22 E
Nagyecsed, *Hungary* 31 D15 47 53N 22 24 E
Nagykanizsa, *Hungary* 31 E10 46 28N 17 0 E
Nagykörös, *Hungary* 31 D12 47 5N 19 48 E
Nagyléta, *Hungary* 31 D14 47 23N 21 55 E
Naha, *Japan* 61 L3 26 13N 127 42 E
Nahanni Butte, *Canada* 130 A4 61 2N 123 31W
Nahanni Nat. Park, *Canada* 130 A3 61 15N 125 0W
Nahariyya, *Israel* 84 C2 33 1N 35 5 E
Nahāvand, *Iran* 85 C6 34 10N 48 22 E
Nahe →, *Germany* 27 F3 49 58N 7 57 E
Nahīya, Wadi →, *Egypt* 94 J7 28 55N 31 0 E
Nahlin, *Canada* 130 B2 58 55N 131 38W
Nahuel Huapi, L., *Argentina* 160 B2 41 0 S 71 32W
Naicá, *Mexico* 146 B3 27 53N 105 31W
Naicam, *Canada* 131 C8 52 30N 104 30W
Nā'ifah, *Si. Arabia* 90 D5 19 59N 50 46 E
Naila, *Germany* 27 E7 50 19N 11 43 E
Nain, *Canada* 129 A7 56 34N 61 40W
Nā'īn, *Iran* 85 C7 32 54N 53 0 E
Naini Tal, *India* 81 E8 29 30N 79 30 E
Naintré, *France* 22 F7 46 46N 0 29 E
Naipu, *Romania* 46 E6 44 12N 25 47 E
Naira, *Indonesia* 73 B3 4 28 S 130 0 E
Nairn, *U.K.* 18 D5 57 35N 3 54W
Nairobi, *Kenya* 106 C4 1 17 S 36 48 E
Naivasha, *Kenya* 106 C4 0 40 S 36 30 E
Naivasha, L., *Kenya* 106 C4 0 48 S 36 20 E
Najac, *France* 24 D5 44 14N 1 58 E
Najafābād, *Iran* 85 C6 32 40N 51 15 E
Nájera, *Spain* 34 C2 42 26N 2 48W
Najerilla →, *Spain* 34 C2 42 32N 2 48W
Najibabad, *India* 80 E8 29 40N 78 20 E
Najin, *N. Korea* 67 C16 42 12N 130 15 E
Najmah, *Si. Arabia* 85 E6 26 42N 50 6 E
Naju, *S. Korea* 67 G14 35 3N 126 43 E
Naka →, *Japan* 63 A12 36 20N 140 36 E
Nakadōri-Shima, *Japan* 61 H4 32 57N 129 4 E
Nakalagba, *Zaïre* 106 B2 2 50N 27 58 E
Nakama, *Japan* 62 D2 33 56N 130 43 E
Nakaminato, *Japan* 63 A12 36 21N 140 36 E
Nakamura, *Japan* 62 E4 32 59N 132 56 E
Nakanai Mts., *Papua N. G.* 120 C6 5 40 S 151 0 E
Nakano, *Japan* 63 A10 36 45N 138 22 E
Nakano-Shima, *Japan* 61 K4 29 51N 129 52 E
Nakanojō, *Japan* 63 A10 36 35N 138 51 E
Nakashibetsu, *Japan* 60 C12 43 33N 144 59 E
Nakatsu, *Japan* 62 D3 33 34N 131 15 E
Nakatsugawa, *Japan* 63 B9 35 29N 137 30 E
Nakfa, *Ethiopia* 95 D4 16 40N 38 32 E
Nakhichevan, *Azerbaijan* 89 D11 39 12N 45 15 E
Nakhichevan Republic □, *Azerbaijan* 49 G8 39 14N 45 30 E
Nakhl, *Egypt* 91 F2 29 55N 33 43 E
Nakhl-e Taqī, *Iran* 85 E7 27 28N 52 36 E
Nakhodka, *Russia* 57 E14 42 53N 132 54 E
Nakhon Nayok, *Thailand* 76 E3 14 12N 101 13 E
Nakhon Pathom, *Thailand* 76 F3 13 49N 100 3 E
Nakhon Phanom, *Thailand* 76 D5 17 23N 104 43 E
Nakhon Ratchasima, *Thailand* 76 E4 14 59N 102 12 E
Nakhon Sawan, *Thailand* 76 E3 15 35N 100 10 E
Nakhon Si Thammarat, *Thailand* 77 H3 8 29N 100 0 E
Nakhon Thai, *Thailand* 76 D3 17 5N 100 44 E
Nakina, *B.C., Canada* 130 B2 59 12N 132 52W
Nakina, *Ont., Canada* 128 B2 50 10N 86 40W
Nakło nad Notecią, *Poland* 47 B4 53 9N 17 38 E
Nakodar, *India* 80 D6 31 8N 75 31 E
Nakskov, *Denmark* 15 K5 54 50N 11 8 E
Näkten, *Sweden* 14 B8 62 48N 14 38 E
Naktong →, *S. Korea* 67 G15 35 7N 128 57 E
Nakuru, *Kenya* 106 C4 0 15 S 36 4 E
Nakuru □, *Kenya* 106 C4 0 15 S 35 5 E
Nakuru, L., *Kenya* 106 C4 0 23 S 36 5 E
Nakusp, *Canada* 130 C5 50 20N 117 45W
Nal →, *Pakistan* 79 D2 25 20N 65 30 E
Nalchik, *Russia* 53 E10 43 30N 43 33 E
Nälden, *Sweden* 14 A8 63 21N 14 14 E
Näldsjön, *Sweden* 14 A8 63 25N 14 15 E
Nalerigu, *Ghana* 101 C4 10 35N 0 25W
Nalgonda, *India* 82 F4 17 6N 79 15 E
Nalhati, *India* 81 G12 24 17N 87 52 E
Nalinnes, *Belgium* 21 H4 50 19N 4 27 E
Nallamalai Hills, *India* 83 G4 15 30N 78 50 E
Nallıhan, *Turkey* 88 C4 40 11N 31 20 E
Nalón →, *Spain* 36 B4 43 32N 6 4W
Nālūt, *Libya* 96 B2 31 54N 11 0 E
Nam Can, *Vietnam* 77 H5 8 46N 104 59 E
Nam Co, *China* 64 C4 30 30N 90 45 E
Nam Dinh, *Vietnam* 76 B6 20 25N 106 5 E
Nam Du, Hon, *Vietnam* 77 H5 9 41N 104 21 E
Nam Ngum Dam, *Laos* 76 C4 18 35N 102 34 E
Nam-Phan, *Vietnam* 77 G6 10 30N 106 0 E
Nam Phong, *Thailand* 76 D4 16 42N 102 52 E
Nam Tha, *Laos* 76 B3 20 58N 101 30 E
Nam Tok, *Thailand* 76 E2 14 21N 99 4 E
Namachire, *Angola* 103 E4 11 26 S 22 43 E
Namacunde, *Angola* 103 F3 17 18 S 15 50 E
Namacurra, *Mozam.* 105 B6 17 30 S 36 50 E
Namak, Daryācheh-ye, *Iran* 85 C7 34 30N 52 0 E
Namak, Kavir-e, *Iran* 85 C8 34 30N 57 30 E
Namakkal, *India* 83 J4 11 13N 78 13 E
Namaland, *Namibia* 104 C2 24 30 S 17 0 E
Namangan, *Uzbekistan* 55 C5 41 0N 71 40 E
Namapa, *Mozam.* 107 E4 13 43 S 39 50 E
Namaqualand, *S. Africa* 104 D2 30 0 S 17 25 E
Namasagali, *Uganda* 106 B3 1 2N 33 0 E
Namatanai, *Papua N. G.* 120 B7 3 40 S 152 29 E
Namber, *Indonesia* 73 B4 1 2 S 134 49 E
Nambour, *Australia* 115 D5 26 32 S 152 58 E
Nambouwalu, *Fiji* 121 A2 17 0 S 178 45 E
Nambucca Heads, *Australia* 117 A10 30 37 S 153 0 E
Namcha Barwa, *China* 64 D4 29 40N 95 10 E
Namche Bazar, *Nepal* 81 F12 27 51N 86 47 E
Namchonjŏm, *N. Korea* 67 E14 38 15N 126 26 E
Namêche, *Belgium* 21 H6 50 28N 5 0 E
Namecunda, *Mozam.* 107 E4 14 54 S 37 37 E
Nameh, *Indonesia* 75 B5 2 34N 116 21 E
Nameponda, *Mozam.* 107 F4 15 50 S 39 50 E
Namerikawa, *Japan* 63 A9 36 46N 137 20 E
Náměšť' nad Oslavou, *Czech.* 31 B9 49 12N 16 10 E
Námestovo, *Czech.* 31 B12 49 24N 19 25 E
Nametil, *Mozam.* 107 F4 15 40 S 39 21 E
Namew L., *Canada* 131 C8 54 14N 101 56W
Namhsan, *Burma* 78 D6 22 48N 97 2 E
Namib Desert = Namibwoestyn, *Namibia* 104 C2 22 30 S 15 0 E
Namibe, *Angola* 103 F2 15 7 S 12 11 E
Namibe □, *Angola* 103 F2 16 35 S 12 30 E
Namibia ■, *Africa* 104 C2 22 0 S 18 9 E
Namibwoestyn, *Namibia* 104 C2 22 30 S 15 0 E
Namkhan, *Burma* 78 D6 23 50N 97 41 E
Namlea, *Indonesia* 72 B3 3 18 S 127 5 E
Namoi →, *Australia* 117 A8 30 12 S 149 30 E
Namous, O. en →, *Algeria* 99 B4 31 0N 0 15W
Nampa, *U.S.A.* 142 E5 43 34N 116 34W
Nampō-Shotō, *Japan* 61 J10 32 0N 140 0 E
Nampula, *Mozam.* 107 F4 15 6 S 39 15 E
Namrole, *Indonesia* 72 B3 3 46 S 126 46 E
Namsen →, *Norway* 12 D11 64 27N 11 42 E
Namsos, *Norway* 12 D11 64 29N 11 30 E
Namtay, *Russia* 57 C13 62 43N 129 37 E
Namtu, *Burma* 78 D6 23 5N 97 28 E
Namtumbo, *Tanzania* 107 E4 10 30 S 36 4 E
Namu, *Canada* 130 C3 51 52N 127 50W
Namuac, *Phil.* 70 B3 18 37N 121 10 E
Namur, *Belgium* 21 H5 50 27N 4 52 E
Namur □, *Belgium* 21 H6 50 17N 5 0 E
Namutoni, *Namibia* 104 B2 18 49 S 16 55 E
Namwala, *Zambia* 107 F2 15 44 S 26 30 E
Namwŏn, *S. Korea* 67 G14 35 23N 127 23 E
Namysłów, *Poland* 47 D4 51 6N 17 42 E
Nan, *Thailand* 76 C3 18 48N 100 46 E
Nan →, *Thailand* 76 E3 15 42N 100 9 E
Nan Xian, *China* 69 C9 29 20N 112 22 E
Nana, *Romania* 46 E7 44 17N 26 34 E
Nanaimo, *Canada* 130 D4 49 10N 124 0W
Nanam, *N. Korea* 67 D15 41 44N 129 40 E
Nanan, *China* 69 E12 24 59N 118 21 E
Nanango, *Australia* 115 D5 26 40 S 152 0 E
Nan'ao, *China* 69 F11 23 28N 117 5 E
Nanao, *Japan* 61 F8 37 0N 137 0 E
Nanbu, *China* 68 B6 31 18N 106 3 E
Nanchang, *China* 69 C10 28 42N 115 55 E
Nancheng, *China* 69 D11 27 33N 116 35 E
Nanching = Nanjing, *China* 65 C6 32 2N 118 47 E
Nanchong, *China* 68 B6 30 43N 106 2 E
Nanchuan, *China* 68 C6 29 9N 107 6 E
Nancy, *France* 23 D13 48 42N 6 12 E
Nanda Devi, *India* 81 D8 30 23N 79 59 E
Nandan, *China* 68 E6 24 58N 107 29 E
Nandan, *Japan* 62 C6 34 10N 134 42 E
Nanded, *India* 82 E3 19 10N 77 20 E
Nandewar Ra., *Australia* 115 E5 30 15 S 150 35 E
Nandi □, *Kenya* 106 B4 0 15N 35 0 E
Nandikotkur, *India* 83 G4 15 52N 78 18 E
Nandura, *India* 82 D3 20 52N 76 25 E
Nandurbar, *India* 82 D2 21 20N 74 15 E
Nandyal, *India* 83 G4 15 30N 78 30 E
Nanfeng, *Guangdong, China* 69 F8 23 45N 111 47 E
Nanfeng, *Jiangxi, China* 69 D11 27 12N 116 28 E
Nanga, *Australia* 113 E1 26 7 S 113 45 E
Nanga-Eboko, *Cameroon* 101 E7 4 41N 12 22 E
Nanga Parbat, *Pakistan* 81 B6 35 10N 74 35 E
Nangade, *Mozam.* 107 E4 11 5 S 39 36 E
Nangapinoh, *Indonesia* 75 C4 0 20 S 111 44 E
Nangarhár □, *Afghan.* 79 B3 34 20N 70 0 E
Nangatayap, *Indonesia* 75 C4 1 32 S 110 34 E
Nangeya Mts., *Uganda* 106 B3 3 30N 33 30 E
Nangis, *France* 23 D10 48 33N 3 1 E
Nangong, *China* 66 F8 37 23N 115 22 E
Nangwarry, *Australia* 116 D4 37 33 S 140 48 E
Nanhua, *China* 68 E3 25 13N 101 21 E
Nanhuang, *China* 67 F11 36 58N 121 48 E
Nanhui, *China* 69 B13 31 5N 121 44 E
Nanjangud, *India* 83 H3 12 6N 76 43 E
Nanjeko, *Zambia* 107 F1 15 31 S 23 30 E
Nanji Shan, *China* 69 D13 27 27N 121 4 E
Nanjian, *China* 68 E3 25 2N 100 25 E
Nanjiang, *China* 68 A6 32 28N 106 51 E
Nanjing, *Fujian, China* 69 E11 24 25N 117 20 E
Nanjing, *Jiangsu, China* 65 C6 32 2N 118 47 E
Nanjirinji, *Tanzania* 107 D4 9 41 S 39 5 E
Nankana Sahib, *Pakistan* 80 D5 31 27N 73 38 E
Nankang, *China* 69 E10 25 40N 114 45 E
Nanking = Nanjing, *China* 65 C6 32 2N 118 47 E
Nankoku, *Japan* 62 D5 33 39N 133 44 E
Nanling, *China* 69 B12 30 55N 118 20 E
Nanning, *China* 68 F7 22 48N 108 20 E
Nannup, *Australia* 113 F2 33 59 S 115 48 E
Nanpan Jiang →, *China* 68 E6 25 10N 106 5 E
Nanpara, *India* 81 F9 27 52N 81 33 E
Nanpi, *China* 66 E9 38 2N 116 45 E
Nanping, *Fujian, China* 69 D12 26 38N 118 10 E
Nanping, *Henan, China* 69 C9 29 55N 112 3 E
Nanri Dao, *China* 69 E12 25 15N 119 25 E
Nanripe, *Mozam.* 107 E4 13 52 S 38 52 E
Nansei-Shotō = Ryūkyū-rettō, *Japan* 61 M2 26 0N 126 0 E
Nansen Sd., *Canada* 6 A3 81 0N 91 0W
Nansio, *Tanzania* 106 C3 2 3 S 33 4 E
Nant, *France* 24 D7 44 1N 3 18 E
Nantes, *France* 22 E5 47 12N 1 33W
Nanteuil-le-Haudouin, *France* 23 C9 49 9N 2 48 E
Nantiat, *France* 24 B5 46 1N 1 11 E
Nanticoke, *U.S.A.* 137 E8 41 12N 76 1W
Nanton, *Canada* 130 C6 50 21N 113 46W
Nantong, *China* 69 A13 32 1N 120 52 E
Nantua, *France* 25 B9 46 10N 5 35 E
Nantucket I., *U.S.A.* 124 E12 41 16N 70 3W
Nanuku Passage, *Fiji* 121 A3 16 45 S 179 15W
Nanuque, *Brazil* 155 E3 17 50 S 40 21W
Nanutarra, *Australia* 112 D2 22 32 S 115 30 E
Nanxiong, *China* 69 E10 25 6N 114 15 E
Nanyang, *China* 66 H7 33 11N 112 30 E
Nanyi Hu, *China* 69 B12 31 5N 119 0 E
Nan'yō, *Japan* 62 C3 34 3N 131 49 E
Nanyuan, *China* 66 E9 39 44N 116 22 E
Nanyuki, *Kenya* 106 B4 0 2N 37 4 E
Nanzhang, *China* 69 B8 31 45N 111 50 E
Náo, C. de la, *Spain* 35 G5 38 44N 0 14 E
Naococane L., *Canada* 129 B5 52 50N 70 45W
Naoetsu, *Japan* 61 F9 37 12N 138 10 E
Naogaon, *Bangla.* 78 C2 24 52N 88 52 E
Náousa, *Greece* 44 D4 40 42N 22 9 E
Naozhou Dao, *China* 69 G8 20 55N 110 20 E
Napa, *U.S.A.* 144 G4 38 18N 122 17W
Napa →, *U.S.A.* 144 G4 38 10N 122 19W
Napanee, *Canada* 128 D4 44 15N 77 0W
Napanoch, *U.S.A.* 137 E10 41 44N 74 22W
Nape, *Laos* 76 C5 18 18N 105 6 E
Nape Pass = Keo Neua, Deo, *Vietnam* 76 C5 18 23N 105 10 E
Naperville, *U.S.A.* 141 C8 41 46N 88 9W
Napf, *Switz.* 28 B5 47 1N 7 56 E
Napier, *N.Z.* 118 F5 39 30 S 176 56 E
Napier Broome B., *Australia* 112 B4 14 2 S 126 37 E
Napier Downs, *Australia* 112 C3 17 11 S 124 36 E
Napier Pen., *Australia* 114 A2 12 4 S 135 43 E
Naples = Nápoli, *Italy* 41 B7 40 50N 14 17 E
Naples, *U.S.A.* 135 M5 26 10N 81 45W
Napo, *China* 68 F5 23 22N 105 50 E
Napo □, *Ecuador* 152 D2 0 30 S 77 0W
Napo →, *Peru* 152 D3 3 20 S 72 40W
Napoleon, *N. Dak., U.S.A.* 138 B5 46 32N 99 49W
Napoleon, *Ohio, U.S.A.* 141 C12 41 24N 84 7W
Nápoli, *Italy* 41 B7 40 50N 14 17 E
Nápoli, G. di, *Italy* 41 B7 40 40N 14 10 E
Napopo, *Zaïre* 106 B2 4 15N 28 0 E
Nappa Merrie, *Australia* 115 D3 27 36 S 141 7 E
Nappanee, *U.S.A.* 141 C11 41 27N 86 0W
Naqāda, *Egypt* 94 B3 25 53N 32 42 E
Naqqāsh, *Iran* 85 C6 35 40N 49 6 E
Nara, *Japan* 63 C7 34 40N 135 49 E
Nara, *Mali* 100 B3 15 10N 7 20W
Nara □, *Japan* 63 C7 34 30N 136 0 E
Nara Canal, *Pakistan* 80 G3 24 30N 69 20 E
Nara Visa, *U.S.A.* 139 H3 35 39N 103 10W
Naracoorte, *Australia* 116 D4 36 58 S 140 45 E
Naradhan, *Australia* 117 B7 33 34 S 146 17 E
Narasapur, *India* 83 F5 16 26N 81 40 E
Narasaropet, *India* 83 F5 16 14N 80 4 E
Narathiwat, *Thailand* 77 J3 6 30N 101 48 E
Narayanganj, *Bangla.* 78 D3 23 40N 90 33 E
Narayanpet, *India* 82 F3 16 45N 77 30 E
Narbonne, *France* 24 E7 43 11N 3 0 E
Narcea →, *Spain* 36 B4 43 33N 6 44W
Nardīn, *Iran* 85 B7 37 3N 55 59 E
Nardò, *Italy* 41 B11 40 10N 18 0 E
Narembeen, *Australia* 113 F2 32 7 S 118 24 E
Nares Str., *Arctic* 124 B13 80 0N 70 0W
Naretha, *Australia* 113 F3 31 0 S 124 45 E
Narew, *Poland* 47 C10 52 55N 23 31 E
Narew →, *Poland* 47 C7 52 26N 20 41 E
Nari →, *Pakistan* 80 E2 28 0N 67 40 E
Narindra, Helodranon' i, *Madag.* 105 A8 14 55 S 47 30 E
Narino □, *Colombia* 152 C2 1 30N 78 0W
Narita, *Japan* 63 B12 35 47N 140 19 E
Narmada →, *India* 80 J5 21 38N 72 36 E
Narman, *Turkey* 89 C9 40 26N 41 57 E
Narnaul, *India* 80 E7 28 5N 76 11 E
Narni, *Italy* 39 F9 42 30N 12 30 E
Naro, *Ghana* 100 C4 10 22N 2 27W
Naro, *Italy* 40 E6 37 18N 13 48 E
Naro Fominsk, *Russia* 51 D10 55 23N 36 43 E
Narodnaya, *Russia* 48 A10 65 5N 59 58 E
Narok, *Kenya* 106 C4 1 55 S 35 52 E
Narok □, *Kenya* 106 C4 1 20 S 36 30 E
Narón, *Spain* 36 B2 43 32N 8 9W
Narooma, *Australia* 117 D9 36 14 S 150 4 E
Narowal, *Pakistan* 79 B4 32 6N 74 52 E
Narrabri, *Australia* 115 E4 30 19 S 149 46 E
Narran →, *Australia* 115 D4 28 37 S 148 12 E
Narrandera, *Australia* 117 C7 34 42 S 146 31 E
Narraway →, *Canada* 130 B5 55 44N 119 55W
Narrogin, *Australia* 113 F2 32 58 S 117 14 E
Narromine, *Australia* 117 B8 32 12 S 148 12 E
Narsampet, *India* 82 F4 17 57N 79 58 E
Narsimhapur, *India* 81 H8 22 54N 79 14 E
Nartkala, *Russia* 53 E10 43 33N 43 51 E
Naruto, *Kantō, Japan* 62 C6 34 11N 134 37 E
Narutō, *Shikoku, Japan* 63 B12 35 36N 140 25 E
Naruto-Kaikyō, *Japan* 62 C6 34 14N 134 39 E
Narva, *Estonia* 50 B6 59 23N 28 12 E
Narva →, *Russia* 50 B6 59 27N 28 2 E
Narvacan, *Phil.* 70 C3 17 25N 120 28 E
Narvik, *Norway* 12 B14 68 28N 17 26 E

Nevinnomyssk 239


Narvskoye Vdkhr., Russia 50 B6 59 18N 28 14 E
Narwana, India 80 E7 29 39N 76 6 E
Naryan-Mar, Russia 48 A9 68 0N 53 0 E
Naryilco, Australia 115 D3 28 37 S 141 53 E
Narym, Russia 56 D9 59 0N 81 30 E
Narymskoye, Kazakhstan 56 E9 49 10N 84 15 E
Naryn, Kirghizia 55 C7 41 26N 75 58 E
Naryn →, Uzbekistan 55 C5 40 52N 71 36 E
Nasa, Norway 12 C13 66 29N 15 23 E
Nasarawa, Nigeria 101 D6 8 32N 7 41 E
Năsăud, Romania 46 B5 47 19N 24 29 E
Nasawa, Vanuatu 121 E6 15 0 S 168 0 E
Naseby, N.Z. 119 F5 45 1 S 170 10 E
Naselle, U.S.A. 144 D3 46 22N 123 49W
Naser, Buheirat en, Egypt 94 C3 23 0N 32 30 E
Nashua, Iowa, U.S.A. 140 B4 42 55N 92 34W
Nashua, Mont., U.S.A. 142 B10 48 10N 106 25W
Nashua, N.H., U.S.A. 137 D13 42 50N 71 25W
Nashville, Ark., U.S.A. 139 J8 33 56N 93 50W
Nashville, Ga., U.S.A. 135 K4 31 3N 83 15W
Nashville, Ill., U.S.A. 140 F7 38 21N 89 23W
Nashville, Ind., U.S.A. 141 E10 39 12N 86 14W
Nashville, Mich., U.S.A. 141 B11 42 36N 85 5W
Nashville, Tenn., U.S.A. 135 G2 36 12N 86 46W
Našice, Croatia 42 B3 45 32N 18 4 E
Nasielsk, Poland 47 C7 52 35N 20 50 E
Nasik, India 82 E1 19 58N 73 50 E
Nasipit, Phil. 71 G5 8 57N 125 19 E
Nasirabad, India 80 F6 26 15N 74 45 E
Naskaupi →, Canada 129 B7 53 47N 60 51W
Naso, Italy 41 D7 38 8N 14 46 E
Naso Pt., Phil. 71 F3 10 25N 121 57 E
Naṣriān-e Pā'īn, Iran 84 C5 32 52N 46 52 E
Nass →, Canada 130 B3 55 0N 129 40W
Nassau, Bahamas 148 A4 25 5N 77 20W
Nassau, U.S.A. 137 D11 42 30N 73 34W
Nassau, B., Chile 160 E3 55 20 S 68 0W
Nasser, L. = Naser, Buheirat en, Egypt 94 C3 23 0N 32 30 E
Nasser City = Kôm Ombo, Egypt 94 C3 24 25N 32 52 E
Nassian, Ivory C. 100 D4 8 28N 3 28W
Nässjö, Sweden 13 H13 57 39N 14 42 E
Nasugbu, Phil. 70 D3 14 5N 120 38 E
Näsviken, Sweden 14 C10 61 46N 16 52 E
Nata, Botswana 104 C4 20 12 S 26 12 E
Natagaima, Colombia 152 C2 3 37N 75 6W
Natal, Brazil 154 C4 5 47 S 35 13W
Natal, Canada 130 D6 49 43N 114 51W
Natal, Indonesia 74 B1 0 35N 99 7 E
Natal □, S. Africa 105 D5 28 30 S 30 30 E
Natalinci, Serbia, Yug. 42 C5 44 15N 20 49 E
Naṭanz, Iran 85 C6 33 30N 51 55 E
Natashquan, Canada 129 B7 50 14N 61 46W
Natashquan →, Canada 129 B7 50 7N 61 50W
Natchez, U.S.A. 139 K9 31 35N 91 25W
Natchitoches, U.S.A. 139 K8 31 47N 93 4W
Naters, Switz. 28 D5 46 19N 7 58 E
Natewa B., Fiji 121 A2 16 35 S 179 40 E
Nathalia, Australia 117 D6 36 1 S 145 13 E
Nathdwara, India 80 G5 24 55N 73 50 E
Nati, Pta., Spain 33 A10 40 3N 3 50 E
Natimuk, Australia 116 D4 36 42 S 142 0 E
Nation →, Canada 130 B4 55 30N 123 32W
National City, U.S.A. 145 N9 32 39N 117 7W
Natitingou, Benin 101 C5 10 20N 1 26 E
Natividad, I., Mexico 146 B1 27 50N 115 10W
Natogyi, Burma 78 E5 21 25N 95 39 E
Natoma, U.S.A. 138 F5 39 14N 99 0W
Natonin, Phil. 70 C3 17 6N 121 18 E
Natron, L., Tanzania 106 C4 2 20 S 36 0 E
Natrona Heights, U.S.A. 136 F5 40 39N 79 43W
Natrûn, W. el →, Egypt 94 H7 30 25N 30 13 E
Natuna Besar, Kepulauan, Indonesia 77 L7 4 0N 108 15 E
Natuna Is. = Natuna Besar, Kepulauan, Indonesia 77 L7 4 0N 108 15 E
Natuna Selatan, Kepulauan, Indonesia 75 B3 2 45N 109 0 E
Natural Bridge, U.S.A. 137 B9 44 5N 75 30W
Naturaliste, C., Australia 114 G4 40 50 S 148 15 E
Natya, Australia 116 C5 34 57 S 143 13 E
Nau, Tajikistan 55 C4 40 9N 69 22 E
Nau Qala, Afghan. 80 B3 34 5N 68 5 E
Naubinway, U.S.A. 128 C2 46 7N 85 27W
Naucelle, France 24 D6 44 13N 2 20 E
Nauders, Austria 30 E3 46 54N 10 30 E
Nauen, Germany 26 C8 52 36N 12 52 E
Naugatuck, U.S.A. 137 E11 41 28N 73 4W
Naujan, Phil. 70 E3 13 20N 121 18 E
Naujoji Vilnia, Lithuania 50 D4 54 48N 25 27 E
Naumburg, Germany 26 D7 51 10N 11 48 E
Nā'ūr at Tunayb, Jordan 91 D4 31 48N 35 57 E
Nauru ■, Pac. Oc. 122 H8 1 0 S 166 0 E
Naurzum, Kazakhstan 54 F9 51 32N 64 34 E
Naushahra = Nowshera, Pakistan 79 B3 34 0N 72 0 E
Nausori, Fiji 121 B2 18 2 S 178 32 E
Nauta, Peru 152 D3 4 31 S 73 35W
Nautla, Mexico 147 C5 20 20N 96 50W
Nauvoo, U.S.A. 140 D5 40 33N 91 23W
Nava, Mexico 146 B4 28 25N 100 46W
Nava del Rey, Spain 36 D5 41 22N 5 6W
Navacerrada, Puerto de, Spain 36 E7 40 47N 4 0W
Navadwip, India 81 H13 23 34N 88 20 E
Navahermosa, Spain 37 F6 39 41N 4 28W
Navajo Res., U.S.A. 143 H10 36 55N 107 30W
Naval, Phil. 71 F5 11 34N 124 23 E
Navalcarnero, Spain 36 E6 40 17N 4 5W
Navalmoral de la Mata, Spain 36 F5 39 52N 5 33W
Navalvillar de Pela, Spain 37 F5 39 9N 5 24W
Navan = An Uaimh, Ireland 19 C5 53 39N 6 40W
Navarino, I., Chile 160 E3 55 0 S 67 40W
Navarra □, Spain 34 C3 42 40N 1 40W
Navarre, U.S.A. 136 F3 40 43N 81 31W
Navarrenx, France 24 E3 43 20N 0 45W
Navarro, U.S.A. 144 F3 39 10N 123 32W
Navasota, U.S.A. 139 K6 30 20N 96 5W
Navassa, W. Indies 149 C4 18 30N 75 0W
Nave, Italy 38 C7 45 35N 10 17 E
Naver →, U.K. 18 C4 58 34N 4 15W
Navia, Spain 36 B4 43 35N 6 42W
Navia →, Spain 36 B4 43 15N 6 50W
Navia de Suarna, Spain 36 C4 42 58N 6 59W
Navidad, Chile 158 C1 33 57 S 71 50W
Navlya, Russia 50 E9 52 53N 34 30 E
Navoi, Uzbekistan 55 C2 40 9N 65 22 E
Navojoa, Mexico 146 B3 27 0N 109 30W
Navolato, Mexico 146 C3 24 47N 107 42W
Navolok, Russia 48 B6 62 33N 39 57 E
Návpaktos, Greece 45 F3 38 23N 21 50 E
Návplion, Greece 45 G4 37 33N 22 50 E
Navrongo, Ghana 101 C4 10 51N 1 3W
Navsari, India 82 D1 20 57N 72 59 E
Nawa Kot, Pakistan 80 E4 28 21N 71 24 E
Nawabganj, Bangla. 78 C2 24 35N 88 14 E
Nawabganj, Ut. P., India 81 F9 26 56N 81 14 E
Nawabganj, Ut. P., India 81 E8 28 32N 79 40 E
Nawabshah, Pakistan 79 D3 26 15N 68 25 E
Nawada, India 81 G11 24 50N 85 33 E
Nāwah, Afghan. 79 B2 32 19N 67 53 E
Nawakot, Nepal 81 F11 27 55N 85 10 E
Nawalgarh, India 80 F6 27 50N 75 15 E
Nawanshahr, India 81 C6 32 33N 74 48 E
Nawapara, India 82 D6 20 46N 82 33 E
Nawāsīf, Harrat, Si. Arabia 86 B3 21 20N 42 10 E
Nawi, Sudan 94 D3 18 32N 30 50 E
Nawng Hpa, Burma 78 D7 22 30N 98 30 E
Nawṣ, Ra's, Oman 87 C6 17 15N 55 16 E
Náxos, Greece 45 G7 37 8N 25 25 E
Nay, France 24 E3 43 10N 0 18W
Nāy Band, Iran 85 E7 27 20N 52 40 E
Naya →, Colombia 152 C2 3 13N 77 22W
Nayakhan, Russia 57 C16 61 56N 159 0 E
Nayarit □, Mexico 146 C4 22 0N 105 0W
Nayé, Senegal 100 C2 14 28N 12 12W
Nayong, China 68 D5 26 50N 105 20 E
Nayoro, Japan 60 B11 44 21N 142 28 E
Nayyāl, W. →, Si. Arabia 84 D3 28 35N 39 4 E
Nazaré, Bahia, Brazil 155 D4 13 2 S 39 0W
Nazaré, Goiás, Brazil 154 C2 6 23 S 47 40W
Nazaré, Pará, Brazil 157 B7 6 25 S 52 29W
Nazaré, Portugal 37 F1 39 36N 9 4W
Nazareth = Nazerat, Israel 91 C4 32 42N 35 17 E
Nazas, Mexico 146 B4 25 10N 104 6W
Nazas →, Mexico 146 B4 25 35N 103 25W
Naze, The, U.K. 17 F9 51 53N 1 19 E
Nazerat, Israel 91 C4 32 42N 35 17 E
Nāzīk, Iran 84 B5 39 1N 45 4 E
Nazik Gölü, Turkey 89 D10 38 50N 42 16 E
Nazilli, Turkey 88 E3 37 55N 28 15 E
Nazir Hat, Bangla. 78 D3 22 35N 91 49 E
Nazko, Canada 130 C4 53 1N 123 37W
Nazko →, Canada 130 C4 53 7N 123 34W
Nazret, Ethiopia 95 F4 8 32N 39 22 E
Nazwá, Oman 87 B7 22 56N 57 32 E
Nchanga, Zambia 107 E2 12 30 S 27 49 E
Ncheu, Malawi 107 E3 14 50 S 34 47 E
Ndala, Tanzania 106 C3 4 45 S 33 15 E
Ndalatando, Angola 103 D2 9 12 S 14 48 E
Ndali, Benin 101 D5 9 50N 2 46 E
Ndareda, Tanzania 106 C4 4 12 S 35 30 E
Ndélé, C.A.R. 102 A4 8 25N 20 36 E
Ndendé, Gabon 102 C2 2 22 S 11 23 E
Ndjamena, Chad 97 F2 12 10N 14 59 E
Ndjolé, Gabon 102 C2 0 10 S 10 45 E
Ndola, Zambia 107 E2 13 0 S 28 34 E
Ndoto Mts., Kenya 106 B4 2 0N 37 0 E
Ndoua, C., N. Cal. 121 V20 22 24 S 166 56 E
Nduguti, Tanzania 106 C3 4 18 S 34 41 E
Nduindui, Vanuatu 121 E5 15 24 S 167 46 E
Nea →, Norway 14 A5 63 15N 11 0 E
Néa Epídhavros, Greece 45 G5 37 40N 23 7 E
Néa Flippiás, Greece 44 E2 39 12N 20 53 E
Néa Kallikrátia, Greece 44 D5 40 21N 23 1 E
Néa Víssi, Greece 44 C8 41 34N 26 33 E
Neagari, Japan 63 A8 36 26N 136 25 E
Neagh, Lough, U.K. 19 B5 54 35N 6 25W
Neah Bay, U.S.A. 144 B2 48 25N 124 40W
Neale, L., Australia 112 D5 24 15 S 130 0 E
Neamţ □, Romania 46 C7 47 0N 26 20 E
Neápolis, Kozan, Greece 44 D3 40 20N 21 24 E
Neápolis, Kríti, Greece 32 D7 35 15N 25 37 E
Neápolis, Lakonía, Greece 45 H5 36 27N 23 8 E
Near Is., U.S.A. 126 C1 53 0N 172 0 E
Neath, U.K. 17 F4 51 39N 3 49W
Nebbou, Burkina Faso 101 C4 11 9N 1 51W
Nebine Cr. →, Australia 115 D4 29 27 S 146 56 E
Nebit Dag, Turkmenistan 49 G9 39 30N 54 22 E
Nebolchy, Russia 50 B8 59 8N 33 18 E
Nebraska □, U.S.A. 138 E5 41 30N 100 0W
Nebraska City, U.S.A. 138 E7 40 40N 95 52W
Nébrodi, Monti, Italy 41 E7 37 55N 14 50 E
Necedah, U.S.A. 138 C9 44 2N 90 7W
Nechako →, Canada 130 C4 53 30N 122 44W
Neches →, U.S.A. 139 L8 29 55N 93 52W
Neckar →, Germany 27 F4 49 31N 8 26 E
Necochea, Argentina 158 D4 38 30 S 58 50W
Nectar Brook, Australia 116 B2 32 43 S 137 57 E
Nedelišće, Croatia 39 B13 46 23N 16 22 E
Neder Rijn →, Neths. 20 E8 51 57N 6 2 E
Nederbrakel, Belgium 21 G3 50 48N 3 46 E
Nederweert, Neths. 21 F7 51 17N 5 45 E
Nédha →, Greece 45 G3 37 25N 21 45 E
Nedroma, Algeria 99 A4 35 1N 1 45W
Nee Soon, Singapore 74 B2 1 24N 103 49 E
Neede, Neths. 20 D9 52 8N 6 37 E
Needles, U.S.A. 145 L12 34 50N 114 35W
Needles, The, U.K. 17 G6 50 39N 1 35W
Needles Pt., N.Z. 118 C4 36 3 S 175 25 E
Ñeembucú □, Paraguay 158 B4 27 0 S 58 0W
Neemuch = Nimach, India 80 G6 24 30N 74 56 E
Neenah, U.S.A. 134 C1 44 10N 88 30W
Neepawa, Canada 131 C9 50 15N 99 30W
Neer, Neths. 21 F7 51 16N 5 59 E
Neerpelt, Belgium 21 F6 51 13N 5 26 E
Neft-chala = imeni 26 Bakinskikh Komissarov, Azerbaijan 89 D13 39 19N 49 12 E
Nefta, Tunisia 96 B1 33 53N 7 50 E
Neftah Sidi Boubekeur, Algeria 99 A5 35 1N 0 4 E
Neftegorsk, Russia 53 D8 44 25N 39 45 E
Neftekumsk, Russia 53 D11 44 46N 44 50 E
Neftenbach, Switz. 29 A7 47 32N 8 41 E
Neftyannyye Kamni, Azerbaijan 49 F9 40 20N 50 55 E
Negapatam = Nagappattinam, India 83 J4 10 46N 79 51 E
Negaunee, U.S.A. 134 B2 46 30N 87 36W
Negele, Ethiopia 90 F2 5 20N 39 36 E
Negeri Sembilan □, Malaysia 74 B2 2 45N 102 10 E
Negev Desert = Hanegev, Israel 91 E3 30 50N 35 0 E
Negoiul, Vf., Romania 46 D5 45 38N 24 35 E
Negombo, Sri Lanka 83 L4 7 12N 79 50 E
Negotin, Serbia, Yug. 42 C7 44 16N 22 37 E
Negotino, Macedonia, Yug. 42 F7 41 29N 22 9 E
Negra, Peña, Spain 36 C4 42 11N 6 30W
Negra, Pta., Mauritania 98 D1 22 54N 16 18W
Negra, Pta., Peru 156 B1 6 6 S 81 10W
Negra Pt., Phil. 70 B3 18 40N 120 50 E
Negrais C., Burma 78 G5 16 0N 94 12 E
Negreira, Spain 36 C2 42 54N 8 45W
Negreşti, Romania 46 C8 46 50N 27 30 E
Négrine, Algeria 99 B6 34 30N 7 30 E
Negro →, Argentina 160 B4 41 2 S 62 47W
Negro →, Bolivia 157 C5 14 11 S 63 7W
Negro →, Brazil 153 D6 3 0 S 60 0W
Negro →, Uruguay 159 C4 33 24 S 58 22W
Negros, Phil. 71 G4 9 30N 122 40 E
Negru Vodă, Romania 46 F9 43 47N 28 21 E
Nehalem →, U.S.A. 144 E3 45 40N 123 56W
Nehāvand, Iran 85 C6 35 56N 49 31 E
Nehbandān, Iran 85 D9 31 35N 60 5 E
Neheim, Germany 26 D3 51 27N 7 58 E
Nehoiaşu, Romania 46 D7 45 24N 26 20 E
Nei Monggol Zizhiqu □, China 66 C6 42 0N 112 0 E
Neiafu, Tonga 121 P14 18 39 S 173 59W
Neidpath, Canada 131 C7 50 12N 107 20W
Neihart, U.S.A. 142 C8 47 0N 110 44W
Neijiang, China 68 C5 29 35N 104 55 E
Neilrex, Australia 117 A8 31 44 S 149 20 E
Neilton, U.S.A. 142 C2 47 24N 123 52W
Neiqiu, China 66 F8 37 15N 114 30 E
Neira de Jusá, Spain 36 C3 42 53N 7 14W
Neisse →, Europe 26 C10 52 4N 14 46 E
Neiva, Colombia 152 C2 2 56N 75 18W
Neixiang, China 66 H6 33 10N 111 52 E
Nejanilini L., Canada 131 B9 59 33N 97 48W
Nejo, Ethiopia 95 F4 9 30N 35 28 E
Nekā, Iran 85 B7 36 39N 53 19 E
Nekemte, Ethiopia 95 F4 9 4N 36 30 E
Nêkheb, Egypt 94 B3 25 10N 32 48 E
Neksø, Denmark 13 J13 55 4N 15 8 E
Nelas, Portugal 36 E3 40 32N 7 52W
Nelia, Australia 114 C3 20 39 S 142 12 E
Nelidovo, Russia 50 C8 56 13N 32 49 E
Neligh, U.S.A. 138 D5 42 11N 98 2W
Nelkan, Russia 57 D14 57 40N 136 4 E
Nellikuppam, India 83 J4 11 46N 79 43 E
Nellore, India 83 G4 14 27N 79 59 E
Nelma, Russia 57 E14 47 39N 139 0 E
Nelson, Canada 130 D5 49 30N 117 20W
Nelson, N.Z. 119 B8 41 18 S 173 16 E
Nelson, U.K. 16 D5 53 50N 2 14W
Nelson, U.S.A. 143 J7 35 35N 113 16W
Nelson →, Canada 131 C9 54 33N 98 2W
Nelson, C., Australia 116 E4 38 26 S 141 32 E
Nelson, C., Papua N. G. 120 E5 9 0 S 149 20 E
Nelson, Estrecho, Chile 160 D2 51 30 S 75 0W
Nelson Forks, Canada 130 B4 59 30N 124 0W
Nelson House, Canada 131 B9 55 47N 98 51W
Nelson L., Canada 131 B8 55 48N 100 7W
Nelspoort, S. Africa 104 E3 32 7 S 23 0 E
Nelspruit, S. Africa 105 D5 25 29 S 30 59 E
Néma, Mauritania 100 B3 16 40N 7 15W
Neman →, Lithuania 50 D2 55 25N 21 10 E
Neméa, Greece 45 G4 37 49N 22 40 E
Nemeiben L., Canada 131 B7 55 20N 105 20W
Nemira, Romania 46 C7 46 17N 26 19 E
Nemours, France 23 D9 48 16N 2 40 E
Nemunas = Neman →, Lithuania 50 D2 55 25N 21 10 E
Nemuro, Japan 60 C12 43 20N 145 35 E
Nemuro-Kaikyō, Japan 60 C12 43 30N 145 30 E
Nemuy, Russia 57 D14 55 40N 136 9 E
Nen Jiang →, China 67 B13 45 28N 124 30 E
Nenagh, Ireland 19 D3 52 52N 8 11W
Nenana, U.S.A. 126 B5 64 30N 149 20W
Nenasi, Malaysia 77 L4 3 9N 103 23 E
Nendiarene, Pte., N. Cal. 121 T18 20 14 S 164 19 E
Nene →, U.K. 16 E8 52 38N 0 13 E
Nenjiang, China 65 B7 49 10N 125 10 E
Neno, Malawi 107 F3 15 25 S 34 40 E
Neodesha, U.S.A. 139 G7 37 30N 95 37W
Neoga, U.S.A. 141 E8 39 19N 88 27W
Néon Petrítsi, Greece 44 C5 41 16N 23 15 E
Neópolis, Brazil 154 D4 10 18 S 36 35W
Neosho, U.S.A. 139 G7 36 56N 94 28W
Neosho →, U.S.A. 139 H7 35 59N 95 10W
Nepal ■, Asia 81 F11 28 0N 84 30 E
Nepalganj, Nepal 81 E9 28 5N 81 40 E
Nephi, U.S.A. 142 G8 39 43N 111 52W
Nephin, Ireland 19 B2 54 1N 9 21W
Nepomuk, Czech. 30 B6 49 29N 13 35 E
Neptune City, U.S.A. 137 F10 40 13N 74 4W
Néra →, Romania 42 C6 44 48N 21 25 E
Nérac, France 24 D4 44 8N 0 21 E
Nerastro, Sarīr, Libya 96 D4 24 20N 20 37 E
Nerchinsk, Russia 57 D12 52 0N 116 39 E
Nerchinskiy Zavod, Russia 57 D12 51 20N 119 40 E
Nereju, Romania 46 D7 45 43N 26 43 E
Nerekhta, Russia 51 C12 57 26N 40 38 E
Néret L., Canada 129 B5 54 45N 70 44W
Neretva →, Croatia 42 D2 43 1N 17 27 E
Neretvanski Kanal, Croatia 42 D2 43 7N 17 10 E
Neringa, Lithuania 50 D2 55 30N 21 5 E
Nerja, Spain 37 J7 36 43N 3 55W
Nerl →, Russia 51 C12 56 11N 40 34 E
Nerokoúrou, Greece 45 J6 35 29N 24 3 E
Nerpio, Spain 35 G2 38 11N 2 16W
Nerva, Spain 37 H4 37 42N 6 30W
Nes, Iceland 12 D5 65 53N 17 24W
Nes, Neths. 20 B7 53 26N 5 47 E
Nesbyen, Norway 14 D3 60 34N 9 35 E
Nesebŭr, Bulgaria 43 E12 42 41N 27 46 E
Neskaupstaður, Iceland 12 D7 65 9N 13 42W
Nesland, Norway 14 E1 59 31N 7 59 E
Neslandsvatn, Norway 14 F3 58 57N 9 10 E
Nesle, France 23 C9 49 45N 2 53 E
Nesodden, Norway 14 E4 59 48N 10 40 E
Nesque →, France 25 E8 43 59N 4 59 E
Ness, L., U.K. 18 D4 57 15N 4 30W
Nesslau, Switz. 29 B8 47 14N 9 13 E
Nestórion, Greece 44 D3 40 24N 21 5 E
Néstos →, Greece 44 C6 41 20N 24 35 E
Nesttun, Norway 13 F8 60 19N 5 21 E
Nesvizh, Belorussia 50 E5 53 14N 26 38 E
Netanya, Israel 91 C3 32 20N 34 51 E
Nète →, Belgium 21 F4 51 7N 4 14 E
Netherdale, Australia 114 C4 21 10 S 148 33 E
Netherlands ■, Europe 20 E6 52 0N 5 30 E
Netherlands Antilles ■, S. Amer. 152 A4 12 15N 69 0W
Netherlands Guiana = Surinam ■, S. Amer. 153 C6 4 0N 56 0W
Netley Gap, Australia 116 B3 32 43 S 139 59 E
Neto →, Italy 41 C10 39 13N 17 8 E
Netrakona, Bangla. 78 C3 24 53N 90 47 E
Nettancourt, France 23 D11 48 51N 4 57 E
Nettilling L., Canada 127 B12 66 30N 71 0W
Nettuno, Italy 40 A5 41 29N 12 40 E
Netzahualcoyotl, Presa, Mexico 147 D6 17 10N 93 30W
Neu-Isenburg, Germany 27 E4 50 3N 8 42 E
Neu-Ulm, Germany 27 G6 48 23N 10 2 E
Neubrandenburg, Germany 26 B9 53 33N 13 17 E
Neubukow, Germany 26 A7 54 1N 11 40 E
Neuburg, Germany 27 G7 48 43N 11 11 E
Neuchâtel, Switz. 28 C3 47 0N 6 55 E
Neuchâtel □, Switz. 28 C3 47 0N 6 55 E
Neuchâtel, Lac de, Switz. 28 C3 46 53N 6 50 E
Neudau, Austria 30 D9 47 11N 16 6 E
Neuenegg, Switz. 28 C4 46 54N 7 18 E
Neuenhaus, Germany 26 C2 52 30N 6 55 E
Neuf-Brisach, France 23 D14 48 1N 7 30 E
Neufahrn, Germany 27 G8 48 44N 12 11 E
Neufchâteau, Belgium 21 J6 49 50N 5 25 E
Neufchâteau, France 23 D12 48 21N 5 40 E
Neufchâtel-en-Bray, France 22 C8 49 44N 1 26 E
Neufchâtel-sur-Aisne, France 23 C11 49 26N 4 1 E
Neuhaus, Germany 26 B6 53 16N 10 54 E
Neuhausen, Switz. 29 A7 47 41N 8 37 E
Neuillé-Pont-Pierre, France 22 E7 47 33N 0 33 E
Neuilly-St.-Front, France 23 C10 49 10N 3 15 E
Neukalen, Germany 26 B8 53 49N 12 48 E
Neumarkt, Germany 27 F7 49 16N 11 28 E
Neumarkt-Sankt Veit, Germany 27 G8 48 22N 12 30 E
Neumünster, Germany 26 A5 54 4N 9 58 E
Neung-sur-Beuvron, France 23 E8 47 30N 1 50 E
Neunkirchen, Austria 30 D9 47 43N 16 4 E
Neunkirchen, Germany 27 F3 49 23N 7 12 E
Neuquén, Argentina 160 A3 38 55 S 68 0W
Neuquén □, Argentina 158 D2 38 0 S 69 50W
Neuquén →, Argentina 160 A3 38 59 S 68 0W
Neuruppin, Germany 26 C8 52 56N 12 48 E
Neuse →, U.S.A. 135 H7 35 5N 76 30W
Neusiedl, Austria 31 D9 47 57N 16 50 E
Neusiedler See, Austria 31 D9 47 50N 16 47 E
Neuss, Germany 21 F9 51 12N 6 39 E
Neussargues-Moissac, France 24 C7 45 9N 3 0 E
Neustadt, Baden-W., Germany 27 H4 47 54N 8 13 E
Neustadt, Bayern, Germany 27 F8 49 42N 12 10 E
Neustadt, Bayern, Germany 27 G7 48 48N 11 47 E
Neustadt, Bayern, Germany 27 F6 49 34N 10 37 E
Neustadt, Bayern, Germany 27 E7 50 23N 11 7 E
Neustadt, Brandenburg, Germany 26 C8 52 50N 12 27 E
Neustadt, Hessen, Germany 26 E5 50 51N 9 9 E
Neustadt, Niedersachsen, Germany 26 C5 52 30N 9 30 E
Neustadt, Rhld-Pfz., Germany 27 F4 49 21N 8 10 E
Neustadt, Schleswig-Holstein, Germany 26 A6 54 6N 10 49 E
Neustadt, Thüringen, Germany 26 E7 50 45N 11 43 E
Neustrelitz, Germany 26 B9 53 22N 13 4 E
Neuvic, France 24 C6 45 23N 2 16 E
Neuville, Belgium 21 H5 50 11N 4 32 E
Neuville-aux-Bois, France 23 D9 48 4N 2 3 E
Neuville-de-Poitou, France 24 B4 46 41N 0 15 E
Neuville-sur-Saône, France 25 C8 45 52N 4 51 E
Neuvy-le-Roi, France 22 E7 47 36N 0 36 E
Neuvy-St.-Sépulchre, France 24 B5 46 35N 1 48 E
Neuvy-sur-Barangeon, France 23 E9 47 20N 2 15 E
Neuwerk, Germany 26 B4 53 55N 8 30 E
Neuwied, Germany 26 E3 50 26N 7 29 E
Neva →, Russia 48 C5 59 50N 30 30 E
Nevada, Iowa, U.S.A. 140 B3 42 1N 93 27W
Nevada, Mo., U.S.A. 139 G7 37 51N 94 22W
Nevada □, U.S.A. 142 G5 39 20N 117 0W
Nevada, Sierra, Spain 35 H1 37 3N 3 15W
Nevada, Sierra, U.S.A. 142 G3 39 0N 120 30W
Nevada City, U.S.A. 144 F6 39 20N 121 0W
Nevado, Cerro, Argentina 158 D2 35 30 S 68 32W
Nevanka, Russia 57 D10 56 31N 98 55 E
Nevasa, India 82 E2 19 34N 75 0 E
Nevel, Russia 50 D6 56 0N 29 55 E
Nevele, Belgium 21 F3 51 3N 3 33 E
Nevers, France 23 F10 47 0N 3 9 E
Nevertire, Australia 117 A7 31 50 S 147 44 E
Nevesinje, Bos.-H., Yug. 42 D3 43 14N 18 6 E
Neville, Canada 131 D7 49 58N 107 39W
Nevinnomyssk, Russia 53 D9 44 40N 42 0 E

Norwich 241


Nioaque, *Brazil* **159 A4** 21 5 S 55 50W
Niobrara, *U.S.A.* **138 D6** 42 48N 97 59W
Niobrara →, *U.S.A.* **138 D6** 42 45N 98 0W
Nioki, *Zaïre* **102 C3** 2 47 S 17 40 E
Niono, *Mali* **100 C3** 14 15N 6 0W
Nioro du Rip, *Senegal* **100 C1** 13 40N 15 50W
Nioro du Sahel, *Mali* **100 B3** 15 15N 9 30W
Niort, *France* **24 B3** 46 19N 0 29W
Nipa, *Papua N. G.* **120 D2** 6 9 S 143 29 E
Nipani, *India* **83 F2** 16 20N 74 25 E
Nipawin, *Canada* **131 C8** 53 20N 104 0W
Nipawin Prov. Park, *Canada* **131 C8** 54 0N 104 37W
Nipigon, *Canada* **128 C2** 49 0N 88 17W
Nipigon, L., *Canada* **128 C2** 49 50N 88 30W
Nipin →, *Canada* **131 B7** 55 46N 108 35W
Nipishish L., *Canada* **129 B7** 54 12N 60 45W
Nipissing L., *Canada* **128 C4** 46 20N 80 0W
Nipomo, *U.S.A.* **145 K6** 35 4N 120 29W
Nipton, *U.S.A.* **145 K11** 35 28N 115 16W
Niquelândia, *Brazil* **155 D2** 14 33 S 48 23W
Nīr, *Iran* **84 B5** 38 2N 47 59 E
Nira →, *India* **82 F2** 17 58N 75 8 E
Nirasaki, *Japan* **63 B10** 35 42N 138 27 E
Nirmal, *India* **82 E4** 19 3N 78 20 E
Nirmali, *India* **81 F12** 26 20N 86 35 E
Niš, *Serbia, Yug.* **42 D6** 43 19N 21 58 E
Nisa, *Portugal* **37 F3** 39 30N 7 41W
Nişāb, *Yemen* **86 D4** 14 25N 46 29 E
Nišava →, *Serbia, Yug.* **42 D6** 43 20N 21 46 E
Niscemi, *Italy* **41 E7** 37 8N 14 21 E
Nishi-Sonogi-Hantō, *Japan* **62 E1** 32 55N 129 45 E
Nishinomiya, *Japan* **63 C7** 34 45N 135 20 E
Nishin'omote, *Japan* **61 J5** 30 43N 130 59 E
Nishio, *Japan* **63 C9** 34 52N 137 3 E
Nishiwaki, *Japan* **62 C6** 34 59N 134 58 E
Nísíros, *Greece* **45 H9** 36 35N 27 12 E
Niskibi →, *Canada* **128 A2** 56 29N 88 9W
Nisko, *Poland* **47 E9** 50 35N 22 7 E
Nispen, *Neths.* **21 F4** 51 29N 4 28 E
Nisporeny, *Moldavia* **46 B9** 47 4N 28 10 E
Nisqually →, *U.S.A.* **144 C4** 47 6N 122 42W
Nissáki, *Greece* **32 A3** 39 43N 19 52 E
Nissan →, *Sweden* **15 H6** 56 40N 12 51 E
Nissedal, *Norway* **14 E2** 59 10N 8 30 E
Nisser, *Norway* **14 E2** 59 7N 8 28 E
Nissum Fjord, *Denmark* **15 H2** 56 20N 8 11 E
Nistelrode, *Neths.* **21 E7** 51 42N 5 34 E
Nisutlin →, *Canada* **130 A2** 60 14N 132 34W
Nitchequon, *Canada* **129 B5** 53 10N 70 58W
Niterói, *Brazil* **155 F3** 22 52 S 43 0W
Nith →, *U.K.* **18 F5** 55 20N 3 5W
Nitra, *Czech.* **31 C11** 48 19N 18 4 E
Nitra →, *Czech.* **31 D11** 47 46N 18 10 E
Nitsa →, *Russia* **54 C9** 57 29N 64 33 E
Nittedal, *Norway* **14 D4** 60 1N 10 57 E
Nittendau, *Germany* **27 F8** 49 12N 12 16 E
Niuafo'ou, *Tonga* **111 D15** 15 30 S 175 58W
Niue, *Cook Is.* **123 J11** 19 2 S 169 54W
Niulan Jiang →, *China* **68 D4** 27 30N 103 5 E
Niut, *Indonesia* **75 B4** 0 55N 110 6 E
Niutou Shan, *China* **69 C13** 29 5N 121 59 E
Niuzhuang, *China* **67 D12** 40 58N 122 28 E
Nivelles, *Belgium* **21 G4** 50 35N 4 20 E
Nivernais, *France* **23 E10** 47 15N 3 30 E
Nixon, *U.S.A.* **139 L6** 29 17N 97 45W
Nizam Sagar, *India* **82 E3** 18 10N 77 58 E
Nizamabad, *India* **82 E4** 18 45N 78 7 E
Nizamghat, *India* **78 A5** 28 20N 95 45 E
Nizhiye Sergi, *Russia* **54 C6** 56 40N 59 18 E
Nizhne Kolymsk, *Russia* **57 C17** 68 34N 160 55 E
Nizhne-Vartovsk, *Russia* **56 C8** 60 56N 76 38 E
Nizhneangarsk, *Russia* **57 D11** 55 47N 109 30 E
Nizhnegorskiy, *Ukraine* **52 D6** 45 27N 34 38 E
Nizhnekamsk, *Russia* **54 D2** 55 38N 51 49 E
Nizhneudinsk, *Russia* **57 D10** 54 54N 99 3 E
Nizhneyansk, *Russia* **57 B14** 71 26N 136 4 E
Nizhniy Lomov, *Russia* **51 E13** 53 34N 43 38 E
Nizhniy Novgorod, *Russia* **51 C14** 56 20N 44 0 E
Nizhniy Pyandzh, *Tajikistan* **55 E4** 37 12N 68 35 E
Nizhniy Tagil, *Russia* **54 C6** 57 55N 59 57 E
Nizhny Salda, *Russia* **54 B7** 58 8N 60 42 E
Nizip, *Turkey* **89 E7** 37 5N 37 50 E
Nizké Tatry, *Czech.* **31 C12** 48 55N 19 30 E
Nizza Monferrato, *Italy* **38 D5** 44 46N 8 22 E
Njakwa, *Malawi* **107 E3** 11 1 S 33 56 E
Njanji, *Zambia* **107 E3** 14 25 S 31 46 E
Njinjo, *Tanzania* **107 D4** 8 48 S 38 54 E
Njombe, *Tanzania* **107 D3** 9 20 S 34 50 E
Njombe □, *Tanzania* **107 D3** 9 20 S 34 49 E
Njombe →, *Tanzania* **106 D4** 6 56 S 35 6 E
Nkambe, *Cameroon* **101 D7** 6 35N 10 40 E
Nkana, *Zambia* **107 E2** 12 50 S 28 8 E
Nkawkaw, *Ghana* **101 D4** 6 36N 0 49W
Nkayi, *Zimbabwe* **107 F2** 19 41 S 29 20 E
Nkhota Kota, *Malawi* **107 E3** 12 56 S 34 15 E
Nkolabona, *Gabon* **102 B2** 1 14N 11 43 E
Nkone, *Zaïre* **102 C4** 1 2 S 22 20 E
Nkongsamba, *Cameroon* **101 E6** 4 55N 9 55 E
Nkunga, *Zaïre* **103 C3** 4 41 S 18 34 E
Nkurenkuru, *Namibia* **104 B2** 17 42 S 18 32 E
Nkwanta, *Ghana* **100 D4** 6 10N 2 10W
Noakhali = Maijdi, *Bangla.* **78 D3** 22 48N 91 10 E
Noatak, *U.S.A.* **126 B3** 67 32N 162 59W
Nobel, *Canada* **136 A4** 45 25N 80 6W
Nobeoka, *Japan* **62 E3** 32 36N 131 41 E
Nōbi-Heiya, *Japan* **63 B8** 35 15N 136 45 E
Noble, *U.S.A.* **141 F8** 38 42N 88 14W
Noblejas, *Spain* **34 F1** 39 58N 3 26W
Noblesville, *U.S.A.* **141 D11** 40 1N 85 59W
Noce →, *Italy* **38 B8** 46 9N 11 4 E
Nocera Inferiore, *Italy* **41 B7** 40 45N 14 37 E
Nocera Terinese, *Italy* **41 C9** 39 2N 16 9 E
Nocera Umbra, *Italy* **39 E9** 43 8N 12 47 E
Noci, *Italy* **41 B10** 40 47N 17 7 E
Nockatunga, *Australia* **115 D3** 27 42 S 142 42 E
Nocona, *U.S.A.* **139 J6** 33 48N 97 45W
Nocrich, *Romania* **46 D5** 45 55N 24 26 E
Noda, *Japan* **63 B11** 35 56N 139 52 E
Noel, *U.S.A.* **139 G7** 36 36N 94 29W
Nogal Valley, *Somali Rep.* **108 C3** 8 35N 48 35 E
Nogales, *Mexico* **146 A2** 31 20N 110 56W
Nogales, *U.S.A.* **143 L8** 31 33N 110 56W
Nogat →, *Poland* **47 A6** 54 17N 19 17 E
Nōgata, *Japan* **62 D2** 33 48N 130 44 E
Nogent-en-Bassigny, *France* **23 D12** 48 1N 5 20 E
Nogent-le-Rotrou, *France* **22 D7** 48 20N 0 50 E
Nogent-sur-Seine, *France* **23 D10** 48 30N 3 30 E
Noggerup, *Australia* **113 F2** 33 32 S 116 5 E
Noginsk, *Russia* **51 D11** 55 50N 38 25 E
Noginsk, *Sib., Russia* **57 C10** 64 30N 90 50 E
Nogoa →, *Australia* **114 C4** 23 40 S 147 55 E
Nogoyá, *Argentina* **158 C4** 32 24 S 59 48W
Nógrád □, *Hungary* **31 D12** 48 0N 19 30 E
Nogueira de Ramuin, *Spain* **36 C3** 42 21N 7 43W
Noguera Pallaresa →, *Spain* **34 D5** 41 55N 0 55 E
Noguera Ribagorzana →, *Spain* **34 D5** 41 40N 0 43 E
Nohar, *India* **80 E6** 29 11N 74 49 E
Noing, *Phil.* **71 J5** 5 40N 125 28 E
Noire, Mt., *France* **22 D3** 48 11N 3 40W
Noirétable, *France* **24 C7** 45 48N 3 46 E
Noirmoutier, I. de, *France* **22 F4** 46 58N 2 10W
Noirmoutier-en-l'Ile, *France* **22 F4** 47 0N 2 14W
Nojane, *Botswana* **104 C3** 23 15 S 20 14 E
Nojima-Zaki, *Japan* **63 C11** 34 54N 139 53 E
Nok Kundi, *Pakistan* **79 C1** 28 50N 62 45 E
Nokaneng, *Botswana* **104 B3** 19 40 S 22 17 E
Nokhtuysk, *Russia* **57 C12** 60 0N 117 45 E
Nokomis, *Canada* **131 C8** 51 35N 105 0W
Nokomis, *U.S.A.* **140 E7** 39 18N 89 18W
Nokomis L., *Canada* **131 B8** 57 0N 103 0W
Nokou, *Chad* **97 F2** 14 35N 14 47 E
Nol, *Sweden* **15 G6** 57 56N 12 5 E
Nola, *C.A.R.* **102 B3** 3 35N 16 4 E
Nola, *Italy* **41 B7** 40 54N 14 29 E
Nolay, *France* **23 F11** 46 58N 4 35 E
Noli, C. di, *Italy* **38 D5** 44 12N 8 26 E
Nolinsk, *Russia* **54 C1** 57 28N 49 57 E
Noma Omuramba →, *Namibia* **104 B3** 18 52 S 20 53 E
Noma-Saki, *Japan* **62 F2** 31 25N 130 7 E
Nomad, *Papua N. G.* **120 D2** 6 19 S 142 13 E
Noman L., *Canada* **131 A7** 62 15N 108 55W
Nombre de Dios, *Panama* **148 E4** 9 34N 79 28W
Nome, *U.S.A.* **126 B3** 64 30N 165 24W
Nomo-Zaki, *Japan* **62 E1** 32 35N 129 44 E
Nomuka, *Tonga* **121 Q13** 20 17 S 174 48W
Nomuka Group, *Tonga* **121 Q13** 20 20 S 174 48W
Nonacho L., *Canada* **131 A7** 61 42N 109 40W
Nonancourt, *France* **22 D8** 48 47N 1 11 E
Nonant-le-Pin, *France* **22 D7** 48 42N 0 12 E
Nonda, *Australia* **114 C3** 20 40 S 142 28 E
Nong Chang, *Thailand* **76 E2** 15 23N 99 51 E
Nong Het, *Laos* **76 C4** 19 29N 103 59 E
Nong Khai, *Thailand* **76 D4** 17 50N 102 46 E
Nong'an, *China* **67 B13** 44 25N 125 5 E
Nongoma, *S. Africa* **105 D5** 27 58 S 31 35 E
Nonoava, *Mexico* **146 B3** 27 28N 106 44W
Nonoc I., *Phil.* **71 G5** 9 51N 125 37 E
Nonthaburi, *Thailand* **76 F3** 13 51N 100 34 E
Nontron, *France* **24 C4** 45 31N 0 40 E
Nonza, *France* **25 F13** 42 47N 9 21 E
Noonamah, *Australia* **112 B5** 12 40 S 131 4 E
Noonan, *U.S.A.* **138 A3** 48 51N 102 59W
Noondoo, *Australia* **115 D4** 28 35 S 148 30 E
Noonkanbah, *Australia* **112 C3** 18 30 S 124 50 E
Noord-Bergum, *Neths.* **20 B8** 53 14N 6 1 E
Noord Brabant □, *Neths.* **21 E6** 51 40N 5 0 E
Noord Holland □, *Neths.* **20 D5** 52 30N 4 45 E
Noordbeveland, *Neths.* **21 E3** 51 35N 3 50 E
Noordeloos, *Neths.* **20 E5** 51 55N 4 56 E
Noordhollandsch Kanaal, *Neths.* **20 C5** 52 55N 4 48 E
Noordhorn, *Neths.* **20 B8** 53 16N 6 24 E
Noordoostpolder, *Neths.* **20 C7** 52 45N 5 45 E
Noordwijk aan Zee, *Neths.* **20 D4** 52 14N 4 26 E
Noordwijk-Binnen, *Neths.* **20 D4** 52 14N 4 27 E
Noordwijkerhout, *Neths.* **20 D5** 52 16N 4 30 E
Noordzee Kanaal, *Neths.* **20 D5** 52 28N 4 35 E
Noorwolde, *Neths.* **20 C8** 52 54N 6 8 E
Nootka, *Canada* **130 D3** 49 38N 126 38W
Nootka I., *Canada* **130 D3** 49 32N 126 42W
Nóqui, *Angola* **103 D2** 5 55 S 13 30 E
Nora, *Ethiopia* **95 D5** 16 6N 40 4 E
Nora Springs, *U.S.A.* **140 A4** 43 9N 93 0W
Noranda, *Canada* **128 C4** 48 20N 79 0W
Norborne, *U.S.A.* **140 E3** 39 18N 93 40W
Nórcia, *Italy* **39 F10** 42 50N 13 5 E
Norco, *U.S.A.* **145 M9** 33 56N 117 33W
Nord □, *France* **23 B10** 50 15N 3 30 E
Nord-Ostsee Kanal, *Germany* **26 A5** 54 15N 9 40 E
Nord-Trøndelag fylke □, *Norway* **12 D12** 64 20N 12 10 E
Nordagutu, *Norway* **14 E3** 59 25N 9 20 E
Nordaustlandet, *Svalbard* **6 B9** 79 14N 23 0 E
Nordborg, *Denmark* **15 J3** 55 5N 9 50 E
Nordby, *Århus, Denmark* **15 J4** 55 58N 10 32 E
Nordby, *Ribe, Denmark* **15 J2** 55 27N 8 24 E
Norddeich, *Germany* **26 B3** 53 37N 7 10 E
Nordegg, *Canada* **130 C5** 52 29N 116 5W
Norden, *Germany* **26 B3** 53 35N 7 12 E
Nordenham, *Germany* **26 B4** 53 29N 8 28 E
Norderhov, *Norway* **14 D4** 60 7N 10 17 E
Norderney, *Germany* **26 B3** 53 42N 7 15 E
Nordfriesische Inseln, *Germany* **26 A4** 54 40N 8 20 E
Nordhausen, *Germany* **26 D6** 51 29N 10 47 E
Nordhorn, *Germany* **26 C3** 52 27N 7 4 E
Nordjyllands Amtskommune □, *Denmark* **15 H4** 57 0N 10 0 E
Nordkapp, *Norway* **12 A18** 71 10N 25 44 E
Nordkapp, *Svalbard* **6 A9** 80 31N 20 0 E
Nordkinn = Kinnarodden, *Norway* **10 A11** 71 8N 27 40 E
Nordland fylke □, *Norway* **12 D12** 65 40N 13 0 E
Nördlingen, *Germany* **27 G6** 48 50N 10 30 E
Nordrhein-Westfalen □, *Germany* **26 D3** 51 45N 7 30 E
Nordstrand, *Germany* **26 A4** 54 27N 8 50 E
Nordvik, *Russia* **57 B12** 74 2N 111 32 E
Nore, *Norway* **14 D3** 60 10N 9 0 E
Norefjell, *Norway* **14 D3** 60 16N 9 29 E
Norembega, *Canada* **128 C3** 48 59N 80 43W
Noresund, *Norway* **14 D3** 60 11N 9 37 E
Norfolk, *Nebr., U.S.A.* **138 D6** 42 3N 97 25W
Norfolk, *Va., U.S.A.* **134 G7** 36 40N 76 15W
Norfolk □, *U.K.* **16 E9** 52 39N 1 0 E
Norfolk Broads, *U.K.* **16 E9** 52 30N 1 15 E
Norfolk I., *Pac. Oc.* **122 K8** 28 58 S 168 3 E
Norfork Res., *U.S.A.* **139 G8** 36 13N 92 15W
Norg, *Neths.* **20 B8** 53 4N 6 28 E
Norilsk, *Russia* **57 C9** 69 20N 88 6 E
Norley, *Australia* **115 D3** 27 45 S 143 48 E
Norma, Mt., *Australia* **114 C3** 20 55 S 140 42 E
Normal, *U.S.A.* **140 D8** 40 30N 88 55W
Norman, *U.S.A.* **139 H6** 35 12N 97 30W
Norman →, *Australia* **114 B3** 19 18 S 141 51 E
Norman Wells, *Canada* **126 B7** 65 17N 126 51W
Normanby, *N.Z.* **118 F3** 39 32 S 174 18 E
Normanby →, *Australia* **114 A3** 14 23 S 144 10 E
Normanby I., *Papua N. G.* **120 F6** 10 5 S 151 5 E
Normandie, *France* **22 D7** 48 45N 0 10 E
Normandie, Collines de, *France* **22 D6** 48 45N 0 45W
Normandin, *Canada* **128 C5** 48 49N 72 31W
Normandy = Normandie, *France* **22 D7** 48 45N 0 10 E
Normanhurst, Mt., *Australia* **113 E3** 25 4 S 122 30 E
Normanton, *Australia* **114 B3** 17 40 S 141 10 E
Normanville, *Australia* **116 C3** 35 27 S 138 18 E
Norquay, *Canada* **131 C8** 51 53N 102 5W
Norquinco, *Argentina* **160 B2** 41 51 S 70 55W
Norrbotten □, *Sweden* **12 C17** 66 30N 22 30 E
Norrby, *Sweden* **12 D15** 64 55N 18 15 E
Nørre Åby, *Denmark* **15 J3** 55 27N 9 52 E
Nørre Nebel, *Denmark* **15 J2** 55 47N 8 17 E
Nørresundby, *Denmark* **15 G3** 57 5N 9 52 E
Norris, *U.S.A.* **142 D8** 45 40N 111 40W
Norris City, *U.S.A.* **141 G8** 37 59N 88 20W
Norristown, *U.S.A.* **137 F9** 40 9N 75 21W
Norrköping, *Sweden* **15 F10** 58 37N 16 11 E
Norrland, *Sweden* **12 E13** 62 15N 15 45 E
Norrtälje, *Sweden* **14 E12** 59 46N 18 42 E
Norseman, *Australia* **113 F3** 32 8 S 121 43 E
Norsewood, *N.Z.* **118 G5** 40 3 S 176 13 E
Norsholm, *Sweden* **15 F9** 58 31N 15 59 E
Norsk, *Russia* **57 D14** 52 30N 130 5 E
Norsup, *Vanuatu* **121 F5** 16 3 S 167 24 E
Norte, Pta., *Argentina* **160 B4** 42 5 S 63 46W
Norte, Pta. del, *Canary Is.* **33 G2** 27 51N 17 57W
Norte de Santander □, *Colombia* **152 B3** 8 0N 73 0W
Nortelândia, *Brazil* **157 C6** 14 25 S 56 48W
North Adams, *U.S.A.* **137 D11** 42 42N 73 6W
North America **124 F10** 40 0N 100 0W
North Atlantic Ocean, *Atl. Oc.* **8 F4** 30 0N 50 0W
North Baltimore, *U.S.A.* **141 C13** 41 11N 83 41W
North Battleford, *Canada* **131 C7** 52 50N 108 17W
North Bay, *Canada* **128 C4** 46 20N 79 30W
North Belcher Is., *Canada* **128 A4** 56 50N 79 50W
North Bend, *Canada* **130 D4** 49 50N 121 27W
North Bend, *Oreg., U.S.A.* **142 E1** 43 28N 124 14W
North Bend, *Pa., U.S.A.* **136 E7** 41 20N 77 42W
North Bend, *Wash., U.S.A.* **144 C5** 47 30N 121 47W
North Berwick, *U.K.* **18 E6** 56 4N 2 44W
North Berwick, *U.S.A.* **137 C14** 43 18N 70 43W
North Buganda □, *Uganda* **106 B3** 1 0N 32 0 E
North Canadian →, *U.S.A.* **139 H7** 35 17N 95 31W
North C., *Canada* **129 C7** 47 2N 60 20W
North C., *N.Z.* **118 A2** 34 23 S 173 4 E
North C., *Papua N. G.* **120 B6** 2 32 S 150 50 E
North Caribou L., *Canada* **128 B1** 52 50N 90 40W
North Carolina □, *U.S.A.* **135 H5** 35 30N 80 0W
North Channel, *Canada* **128 C3** 46 0N 83 0W
North Channel, *U.K.* **18 G3** 55 0N 5 30W
North Chicago, *U.S.A.* **141 B9** 42 19N 87 50W
North College Hill, *U.S.A.* **141 E12** 39 13N 84 33W
North Cotabato □, *Phil.* **71 H5** 7 10N 125 0 E
North Dakota □, *U.S.A.* **138 B5** 47 30N 100 0W
North Dandalup, *Australia* **113 F2** 32 30 S 115 57 E
North Down □, *U.K.* **19 B6** 54 40N 5 45W
North Downs, *U.K.* **17 F8** 51 17N 0 30 E
North East, *U.S.A.* **136 D5** 42 17N 79 50W
North East Frontier Agency = Arunachal Pradesh □, *India* **78 A5** 28 0N 95 0 E
North East Providence Chan., *W. Indies* **148 A4** 26 0N 76 0W
North Eastern □, *Kenya* **106 B5** 1 30N 40 0 E
North English, *U.S.A.* **140 C4** 41 31N 92 5W
North Esk →, *U.K.* **18 E6** 56 44N 2 25W
North European Plain, *Europe* **10 D11** 55 0N 25 0 E
North Fabius →, *U.S.A.* **140 E5** 39 54N 91 28W
North Foreland, *U.K.* **17 F9** 51 22N 1 28 E
North Fork, *U.S.A.* **144 H7** 37 14N 119 21W
North Fork, Salt →, *U.S.A.* **140 E5** 39 26N 91 53W
North Fork American →, *U.S.A.* **144 G5** 38 45N 121 8W
North Fork Feather →, *U.S.A.* **144 F5** 39 17N 121 38W
North Frisian Is. = Nordfriesische Inseln, *Germany* **26 A4** 54 40N 8 20 E
North Henik L., *Canada* **131 A9** 61 45N 97 40W
North Highlands, *U.S.A.* **144 G5** 38 40N 121 25W
North Horr, *Kenya* **106 B4** 3 20N 37 8 E
North I., *Kenya* **106 B4** 4 5N 36 5 E
North I., *N.Z.* **118 E4** 38 0 S 175 0 E
North Judson, *U.S.A.* **141 C10** 41 13N 86 46W
North Kingsville, *U.S.A.* **136 E4** 41 53N 80 42W
North Knife →, *Canada* **131 B10** 58 53N 94 45W
North Koel →, *India* **81 G10** 24 45N 83 50 E
North Korea ■, *Asia* **67 E14** 40 0N 127 0 E
North Lakhimpur, *India* **78 B5** 27 14N 94 7 E
North Las Vegas, *U.S.A.* **145 J11** 36 15N 115 6W
North Liberty, *U.S.A.* **141 C10** 41 32N 86 26W
North Loup →, *U.S.A.* **138 E5** 41 17N 98 23W
North Magnetic Pole, *Canada* **6 B2** 77 58N 102 8 E
North Manchester, *U.S.A.* **141 D11** 41 0N 85 46W
North Minch, *U.K.* **18 C3** 58 5N 5 55W
North Nahanni →, *Canada* **130 A4** 62 15N 123 20W
North Olmsted, *U.S.A.* **136 E3** 41 25N 81 56W
North Ossetian Republic □, *Russia* **53 E11** 43 30N 44 30 E
North Pagai, I. = Pagai Utara, *Indonesia* **74 C2** 2 35 S 100 0 E
North Palisade, *U.S.A.* **144 H8** 37 6N 118 32W
North Platte, *U.S.A.* **138 E4** 41 10N 100 50W
North Platte →, *U.S.A.* **138 E4** 41 15N 100 45W
North Pt., *Canada* **129 C7** 47 5N 64 0W
North Pt., *Vanuatu* **121 D6** 14 56 S 168 6 E
North Pole, *Arctic* **6 A** 90 0N 0 0 E
North Portal, *Canada* **131 D8** 49 0N 102 33W
North Powder, *U.S.A.* **142 D5** 45 2N 117 59W
North Ronaldsay, *U.K.* **18 B6** 59 20N 2 30W
North Saskatchewan →, *Canada* **131 C7** 53 15N 105 5W
North Sea, *Europe* **10 D6** 56 0N 4 0 E
North Sporades = Voríai Sporádhes, *Greece* **45 E5** 39 15N 23 30 E
North Sydney, *Canada* **129 C7** 46 12N 60 15W
North Taranaki Bight, *N.Z.* **118 E3** 38 50 S 174 15 E
North Thompson →, *Canada* **130 C4** 50 40N 120 20W
North Tonawanda, *U.S.A.* **136 C6** 43 5N 78 50W
North Troy, *U.S.A.* **137 B12** 44 59N 72 24W
North Truchas Pk., *U.S.A.* **143 J11** 36 0N 105 30W
North Twin I., *Canada* **128 B3** 53 20N 80 0W
North Tyne →, *U.K.* **16 C5** 54 59N 2 7W
North Uist, *U.K.* **18 D1** 57 40N 7 15W
North Vancouver, *Canada* **130 D4** 49 25N 123 3W
North Vernon, *U.S.A.* **141 E11** 39 0N 85 35W
North Wabasca L., *Canada* **130 B6** 56 0N 113 55W
North Walsham, *U.K.* **16 E9** 52 49N 1 22 E
North Webster, *U.S.A.* **141 C11** 41 25N 85 48W
North West C., *Australia* **112 D1** 21 45 S 114 9 E
North West Christmas I. Ridge, *Pac. Oc.* **123 G11** 6 30N 165 0W
North West Frontier □, *Pakistan* **79 B3** 34 0N 71 0 E
North West Highlands, *U.K.* **18 D3** 57 35N 5 2W
North West Providence Channel, *W. Indies* **148 A4** 26 0N 78 0W
North West River, *Canada* **129 B7** 53 30N 60 10W
North West Territories □, *Canada* **126 B9** 67 0N 110 0W
North Western □, *Zambia* **107 E2** 13 30 S 25 30 E
North York Moors, *U.K.* **16 C7** 54 25N 0 50W
North Yorkshire □, *U.K.* **16 C6** 54 15N 1 25W
Northallerton, *U.K.* **16 C6** 54 20N 1 26W
Northam, *S. Africa* **104 C4** 24 56 S 27 18 E
Northampton, *Australia* **113 E1** 28 27 S 114 33 E
Northampton, *U.K.* **17 E7** 52 14N 0 54W
Northampton, *Mass., U.S.A.* **137 D12** 42 22N 72 31W
Northampton, *Pa., U.S.A.* **137 F9** 40 38N 75 24W
Northampton Downs, *Australia* **114 C4** 24 35 S 145 48 E
Northamptonshire □, *U.K.* **17 E7** 52 16N 0 55W
Northbridge, *U.S.A.* **137 D13** 42 12N 71 40W
Northcliffe, *Australia* **113 F2** 34 39 S 116 7 E
Northeim, *Germany* **26 D6** 51 42N 10 0 E
Northern □, *Malawi* **107 E3** 11 0 S 34 0 E
Northern □, *Uganda* **106 B3** 3 5N 32 30 E
Northern □, *Zambia* **107 E3** 10 30 S 31 0 E
Northern Circars, *India* **82 F6** 17 30N 82 30 E
Northern Indian L., *Canada* **131 B9** 57 20N 97 20W
Northern Ireland □, *U.K.* **19 B5** 54 45N 7 0W
Northern Light, L., *Canada* **128 C1** 48 15N 90 39W
Northern Marianas □, *Pac. Oc.* **122 F6** 17 0N 145 0 E
Northern Province □, *S. Leone* **100 D2** 9 15N 11 30W
Northern Samar □, *Phil.* **70 E5** 12 30N 124 40 E
Northern Territory □, *Australia* **112 D5** 20 0 S 133 0 E
Northfield, *U.S.A.* **138 C8** 44 30N 93 10W
Northland □, *N.Z.* **118 B2** 35 30 S 173 30 E
Northome, *U.S.A.* **138 B7** 47 53N 94 15W
Northport, *Ala., U.S.A.* **135 J2** 33 15N 87 35W
Northport, *Mich., U.S.A.* **134 C3** 45 8N 85 39W
Northport, *Wash., U.S.A.* **142 B5** 48 55N 117 48W
Northumberland □, *U.K.* **16 B5** 55 12N 2 0W
Northumberland, C., *Australia* **116 E4** 38 5 S 140 40 E
Northumberland Is., *Australia* **114 C4** 21 30 S 149 50 E
Northumberland Str., *Canada* **129 C7** 46 20N 64 0W
Northwich, *U.K.* **16 D5** 53 16N 2 30W
Northwood, *Iowa, U.S.A.* **138 D8** 43 27N 93 0W
Northwood, *N. Dak., U.S.A.* **138 B6** 47 44N 97 30W
Norton, *U.S.A.* **138 F5** 39 50N 99 53W
Norton, *Zimbabwe* **107 F3** 17 52 S 30 40 E
Norton Sd., *U.S.A.* **126 B3** 64 0N 164 0W
Norton Shores, *U.S.A.* **141 A10** 43 8N 86 15W
Nortorf, *Germany* **26 A5** 54 14N 9 47 E
Norwalk, *Calif., U.S.A.* **145 M8** 33 54N 118 5W
Norwalk, *Conn., U.S.A.* **137 E11** 41 9N 73 25W
Norwalk, *Ohio, U.S.A.* **136 E2** 41 13N 82 38W
Norway, *U.S.A.* **134 C2** 45 46N 87 57W
Norway ■, *Europe* **12 E11** 63 0N 11 0 E
Norway House, *Canada* **131 C9** 53 59N 97 50W
Norwegian Sea, *Atl. Oc.* **8 B9** 66 0N 1 0 E
Norwich, *Canada* **136 D4** 42 59N 80 36W

Norwich, U.K. 16 E9 52 38N 1 17 E
Norwich, Conn., U.S.A. 137 E12 41 33N 72 5W
Norwich, N.Y., U.S.A. 137 D9 42 32N 75 30W
Norwood, Canada 136 B7 44 23N 77 59W
Norwood, U.S.A. 141 E12 39 10N 84 27W
Noshiro, Japan 60 D10 40 12N 140 0 E
Nosok, Russia 56 B9 70 10N 82 20 E
Nosovka, Ukraine 50 F7 50 50N 31 37 E
Noss Hd., U.K. 18 C5 58 29N 3 4W
Nossa Senhora da Glória, Brazil 154 D4 10 14 S 37 25W
Nossa Senhora das Dores, Brazil 154 D4 10 29 S 37 13W
Nossa Senhora do Livramento, Brazil 157 D6 15 48 S 56 22W
Nossebro, Sweden 15 F6 58 12N 12 43 E
Nossob →, S. Africa 104 D3 26 55 S 20 45 E
Nosy Boraha, Madag. 105 B8 16 50 S 49 55 E
Nosy Varika, Madag. 105 C8 20 35 S 48 32 E
Noteć →, Poland 47 C2 52 44N 15 26 E
Notigi Dam, Canada 131 B9 56 40N 99 10W
Notikewin →, Canada 130 B5 57 2N 117 38W
Notios Evvoïkos Kólpos, Greece 45 F5 38 20N 24 0 E
Noto, Italy 41 F8 36 52N 15 4 E
Noto, G. di, Italy 41 F8 36 50N 15 10 E
Notodden, Norway 14 E3 59 35N 9 17 E
Notre-Dame, Canada 129 C7 46 18N 64 46W
Notre Dame B., Canada 129 C8 49 45N 55 30W
Notre Dame de Koartac = Koartac, Canada 127 B13 60 55N 69 40W
Notre Dame d'Ivugivic = Ivugivik, Canada 127 B12 62 24N 77 55W
Notsé, Togo 101 D5 7 0N 1 17 E
Nottaway →, Canada 128 B4 51 22N 78 55W
Nøtterøy, Norway 14 E4 59 14N 10 24 E
Nottingham, U.K. 16 E6 52 57N 1 10W
Nottinghamshire □, U.K. 16 D7 53 10N 1 0W
Nottoway →, U.S.A. 134 G7 36 33N 76 55W
Notwane →, Botswana 104 C4 23 35 S 26 58 E
Nouâdhibou, Mauritania 98 D1 20 54N 17 0W
Nouâdhibou, Ras, Mauritania 98 D1 20 50N 17 0W
Nouakchott, Mauritania 100 B1 18 9N 15 58W
Nouméa, N. Cal. 122 K8 22 17 S 166 30 E
Noupoort, S. Africa 104 E3 31 10 S 24 57 E
Nouveau Comptoir, Canada 128 B4 53 0N 78 49W
Nouvelle-Calédonie = New Caledonia, Pac. Oc. 121 U19 21 0 S 165 0 E
Nouzonville, France 23 C11 49 48N 4 44 E
Nová Baňa, Czech. 31 C11 48 28N 18 39 E
Nová Bystřice, Czech. 30 B8 49 2N 15 8 E
Nova Casa Nova, Brazil 154 C3 9 25 S 41 5W
Nova Cruz, Brazil 154 C4 6 28 S 35 25W
Nova Era, Brazil 155 E3 19 45 S 43 3W
Nova Esperança, Brazil 159 A5 23 8 S 52 24W
Nova Friburgo, Brazil 155 F3 22 16 S 42 30W
Nova Gaia = Cambundi-Catembo, Angola 103 E3 10 10 S 17 35 E
Nova Gradiška, Croatia 42 B2 45 17N 17 28 E
Nova Granada, Brazil 155 F2 20 30 S 49 20W
Nova Iguaçu, Brazil 155 F3 22 45 S 43 28W
Nova Iorque, Brazil 154 C3 7 0 S 44 5W
Nova Lamego, Guinea-Biss. 100 C2 12 19N 14 11W
Nova Lima, Brazil 159 A7 19 59 S 43 51W
Nova Lisboa = Huambo, Angola 103 E3 12 42 S 15 54 E
Nova Lusitânia, Mozam. 107 F3 19 50 S 34 34 E
Nova Mambone, Mozam. 105 C6 21 0 S 35 3 E
Nova Mesto, Slovenia 39 C12 45 47N 15 12 E
Nova Paka, Czech. 30 A8 50 29N 15 30 E
Nova Ponte, Brazil 155 E2 19 8 S 47 41W
Nova Scotia □, Canada 129 C7 45 10N 63 0W
Nova Sofala, Mozam. 105 C5 20 7 S 34 42 E
Nova Varoš, Serbia, Yug. 42 D4 43 29N 19 48 E
Nova Venécia, Brazil 155 E3 18 45 S 40 24W
Nova Vida, Brazil 157 C5 10 11 S 62 47W
Nova Zagora, Bulgaria 43 E10 42 32N 25 59 E
Novaci, Macedonia, Yug. 42 F6 41 5N 21 29 E
Novaci, Romania 46 D4 45 10N 23 42 E
Novaleksandrovskaya, Russia 53 D9 45 29N 41 17 E
Novannenskiy, Russia 51 F13 50 32N 42 39 E
Novara, Italy 38 C5 45 27N 8 36 E
Novata, U.S.A. 144 G4 38 6N 122 35W
Novaya Kakhovka, Ukraine 52 C5 46 42N 33 27 E
Novaya Ladoga, Russia 48 B5 60 7N 32 16 E
Novaya Lyalya, Russia 54 B7 59 10N 60 35 E
Novaya Sibir, Ostrov, Russia 57 B16 75 10N 150 0 E
Novaya Zemlya, Russia 56 B6 75 0N 56 0 E
Nové Město, Czech. 31 C10 48 45N 17 50 E
Nové Zámky, Czech. 31 C11 48 2N 18 8 E
Novelda, Spain 35 G4 38 24N 0 45W
Novellara, Italy 38 D7 44 50N 10 43 E
Novelty, U.S.A. 140 D4 40 1N 92 12W
Noventa Vicentina, Italy 39 C8 45 18N 11 30 E
Novgorod, Russia 50 B7 58 30N 31 25 E
Novgorod-Severskiy, Ukraine 50 E8 52 2N 33 10 E
Novi Bečej, Serbia, Yug. 42 B5 45 36N 20 10 E
Novi Grad, Croatia 39 C10 45 19N 13 33 E
Novi Kneževa, Serbia, Yug. 42 A5 46 4N 20 8 E
Novi Krichim, Bulgaria 43 E9 42 8N 24 31 E
Novi Lígure, Italy 38 D5 44 45N 8 47 E
Novi Pazar, Bulgaria 43 D12 43 25N 27 15 E
Novi Pazar, Serbia, Yug. 42 D5 43 12N 20 28 E
Novi Sad, Serbia, Yug. 42 B4 45 18N 19 52 E
Novi Vinodolski, Croatia 39 C11 45 10N 14 48 E
Novigrad, Croatia 39 D12 44 10N 15 32 E
Noville, Belgium 21 H7 50 4N 5 46 E
Novinger, U.S.A. 140 D4 40 14N 92 43W
Novo Acôrdo, Brazil 154 D2 10 10 S 46 48W
Novo Aripuanã, Brazil 153 E5 5 8 S 60 22W
Nôvo Cruzeiro, Brazil 155 E3 17 29 S 41 53W
Nôvo Hamburgo, Brazil 159 B5 29 37 S 51 7W
Novo Horizonte, Brazil 155 F2 21 25 S 49 10W
Novo Remanso, Brazil 154 C3 9 41 S 42 4W
Novo-Sergiyevskiy, Russia 54 E3 52 5N 53 38 E
Novo-Zavidovskiy, Russia 51 C10 56 32N 36 29 E
Novoakrainka, Ukraine 52 B4 48 25N 31 30 E
Novoalekseyevka, Kazakhstan 54 F4 50 8N 55 39 E
Novoataysk, Russia 56 D9 53 30N 84 0 E
Novoazovsk, Ukraine 52 C8 47 15N 38 4 E
Novobelitsa, Belorussia 50 E7 52 27N 31 2 E
Novobogatinskoye, Kazakhstan 53 C14 47 20N 51 11 E
Novocherkassk, Russia 53 C9 47 27N 40 15 E
Novodevichye, Russia 51 E16 53 37N 48 50 E
Novograd-Volynskiy, Ukraine 50 F5 50 34N 27 35 E
Novogrudok, Belorussia 50 E4 53 40N 25 50 E
Novokachalinsk, Russia 60 B6 45 5N 132 0 E
Novokayakent, Russia 53 E12 42 30N 47 52 E
Novokazalinsk, Kazakhstan 56 E7 45 48N 62 6 E
Novokhopersk, Russia 51 F12 51 5N 41 39 E
Novokuybyshevsk, Russia 54 E1 53 7N 49 58 E
Novokuznetsk, Russia 56 D9 53 45N 87 10 E
Novomirgorod, Ukraine 52 B4 48 45N 31 33 E
Novomoskovsk, Russia 51 D11 54 5N 38 15 E
Novomoskovsk, Ukraine 52 B6 48 33N 35 17 E
Novoorsk, Russia 54 F6 51 21N 59 2 E
Novopolotsk, Belorussia 50 D6 55 32N 28 37 E
Novorossiysk, Russia 52 D7 44 43N 37 46 E
Novorybnoye, Russia 57 B11 72 50N 105 50 E
Novorzhev, Russia 50 C6 57 3N 29 25 E
Novoselitsa, Ukraine 52 B2 48 14N 26 15 E
Novoshakhtinsk, Russia 53 C8 47 46N 39 58 E
Novosibirsk, Russia 56 D9 55 0N 83 5 E
Novosibirskiye Ostrova, Russia 57 B15 75 0N 142 0 E
Novosil, Russia 51 E10 52 59N 37 2 E
Novosokolniki, Russia 50 C7 56 33N 30 5 E
Novotroitsk, Russia 54 F6 51 10N 58 15 E
Novotroitskoye, Kazakhstan 55 B6 43 42N 73 46 E
Novotulskiy, Russia 51 D10 54 10N 37 43 E
Novouzensk, Russia 51 F16 50 32N 48 17 E
Novovolynsk, Ukraine 50 F4 50 45N 24 4 E
Novovyatsk, Russia 54 B1 58 24N 49 45 E
Novozybkov, Russia 50 E8 52 30N 32 0 E
Novska, Croatia 42 B2 45 19N 17 0 E
Novvy Port, Russia 56 C8 67 40N 72 30 E
Novy Bug, Ukraine 52 C5 47 34N 32 29 E
Nový Bydzov, Czech. 30 A8 50 14N 15 29 E
Novy Dwór Mazowiecki, Poland 47 C7 52 26N 20 44 E
Nový Jičín, Czech. 31 B11 49 30N 18 2 E
Novyy Afon, Georgia 53 E9 43 7N 40 50 E
Novyy Oskol, Russia 51 F10 50 44N 37 55 E
Now Shahr, Iran 85 B6 36 40N 51 30 E
Nowa Deba, Poland 47 E8 50 26N 21 41 E
Nowa Huta, Poland 31 A13 50 5N 20 30 E
Nowa Nowa, Australia 117 D8 37 44 S 148 3 E
Nowa Ruda, Poland 47 E3 50 35N 16 30 E
Nowa Skalmierzyce, Poland 47 D5 51 43N 18 0 E
Nowa Sól, Poland 47 D2 51 48N 15 44 E
Nowbarān, Iran 85 C6 35 8N 49 42 E
Nowe, Poland 47 B5 53 41N 18 44 E
Nowe Miasteczko, Poland 47 D2 51 42N 15 42 E
Nowe Miasto, Poland 47 D7 51 38N 20 34 E
Nowe Miasto Lubawskie, Poland 47 B6 53 27N 19 33 E
Nowe Warpno, Poland 47 B1 53 42N 14 18 E
Nowendoc, Australia 117 A9 31 32 S 151 44 E
Nowghāb, Iran 85 C8 33 53N 59 4 E
Nowgong, India 78 B4 26 20N 92 50 E
Nowingi, Australia 116 C5 34 33 S 142 15 E
Nowogard, Poland 47 B2 53 41N 15 10 E
Nowogród, Poland 47 B8 53 14N 21 53 E
Nowra, Australia 117 C9 34 53 S 150 35 E
Nowshera, Pakistan 79 B3 34 0N 72 0 E
Nowy Dwór, Białystok, Poland 47 B10 53 40N 23 30 E
Nowy Dwór, Gdańsk, Poland 47 A6 54 13N 19 7 E
Nowy Korczyn, Poland 47 E7 50 19N 20 48 E
Nowy Sącz, Poland 31 B13 49 40N 20 41 E
Nowy Sącz □, Poland 31 B13 49 30N 20 30 E
Nowy Staw, Poland 47 A6 54 13N 19 2 E
Nowy Tomyśl, Poland 47 C3 52 19N 16 10 E
Noxen, U.S.A. 137 E8 41 25N 76 4W
Noxon, U.S.A. 142 C6 48 0N 115 43W
Noya, Spain 36 C2 42 48N 8 53W
Noyant, France 22 E7 47 30N 0 6 E
Noyers, France 23 E10 47 40N 4 0 E
Noyes I., U.S.A. 130 B2 55 30N 133 40W
Noyon, France 23 C9 49 34N 2 59 E
Noyon, Mongolia 66 C2 43 2N 102 4 E
Nozay, France 22 E5 47 34N 1 38W
Nsa, O. en →, Algeria 99 B6 32 28N 5 24 E
Nsa, Plateau de, Congo 102 C3 2 26 S 15 20 E
Nsah, Congo 102 C3 2 22 S 15 19 E
Nsanje, Malawi 107 F4 16 55 S 35 12 E
Nsawam, Ghana 101 D4 5 50N 0 24W
Nsomba, Zambia 107 E2 10 45 S 29 51 E
Nsopzup, Burma 78 C6 25 51N 97 30 E
Nsukka, Nigeria 101 D6 6 51N 7 29 E
Ntoum, Gabon 102 B1 0 22N 9 47 E
Nu Jiang →, China 68 C1 29 58N 97 25 E
Nu Shan, China 68 D2 26 0N 99 20 E
Nuba Mts. = Nubah, Jibalan, Sudan 95 E3 12 0N 31 0 E
Nubah, Jibalan, Sudan 95 E3 12 0N 31 0 E
Nubian Desert = Nûbîya, Es Sahrâ En, Sudan 94 C3 21 30N 33 30 E
Nûbîya, Es Sahrâ En, Sudan 94 C3 21 30N 33 30 E
Ñuble □, Chile 158 D1 37 0 S 72 0W
Nuboai, Indonesia 73 B5 2 10 S 136 30 E
Nubra →, India 81 B7 34 35N 77 35 E
Nueces →, U.S.A. 139 M6 27 50N 97 30W
Nueltin L., Canada 131 A9 60 30N 99 30W
Nuenen, Neths. 21 F7 51 29N 5 33 E
Nueva, I., Chile 160 E3 55 13 S 66 30W
Nueva Antioquia, Colombia 152 B4 6 5N 69 26W
Nueva Asunción □, Paraguay 158 A3 21 0 S 61 0W
Nueva Ecija □, Phil. 70 D3 15 35N 121 0 E
Nueva Esparta □, Venezuela 153 A5 11 0N 64 0W
Nueva Gerona, Cuba 148 B3 21 53N 82 49W
Nueva Imperial, Chile 160 A2 38 45 S 72 58W
Nueva Palmira, Uruguay 158 C4 33 52 S 58 20W
Nueva Rosita, Mexico 146 B4 28 0N 101 11W
Nueva San Salvador, El Salv. 148 D2 13 40N 89 18W
Nueva Vizcaya □, Phil. 70 C3 16 20N 121 20 E
Nuéve de Julio, Argentina 158 D3 35 30 S 61 0W
Nuevitas, Cuba 148 B4 21 30N 77 20W
Nuevo, G., Argentina 160 B4 43 0 S 64 30W
Nuevo Guerrero, Mexico 147 B5 26 34N 99 15W
Nuevo Laredo, Mexico 147 B5 27 30N 99 30W
Nuevo León □, Mexico 146 C4 25 0N 100 0W
Nuevo Mundo, Cerro, Bolivia 156 E4 21 55 S 66 53W
Nuevo Rocafuerte, Ecuador 152 D2 0 55 S 75 27W
Nugget Pt., N.Z. 119 G4 46 27 S 169 50 E
Nugrus, Gebel, Egypt 94 C3 24 47N 34 35 E
Nuhaka, N.Z. 118 F6 39 3 S 177 45 E
Nuits-St.-Georges, France 23 E11 47 10N 4 56 E
Nukey Bluff, Australia 115 E2 32 26 S 135 29 E
Nukheila, Sudan 94 D2 19 1N 26 21 E
Nuku'alofa, Tonga 121 Q14 21 10 S 174 0W
Nukus, Uzbekistan 56 E6 42 20N 59 7 E
Nuland, Neths. 20 E6 51 44N 5 26 E
Nulato, U.S.A. 126 B4 64 40N 158 10W
Nules, Spain 34 F4 39 51N 0 9W
Nullagine →, Australia 112 D3 21 20 S 120 20 E
Nullarbor, Australia 113 F5 31 28 S 130 55 E
Nullarbor Plain, Australia 113 F4 31 10 S 129 0 E
Numalla, L., Australia 115 D3 28 43 S 144 20 E
Numan, Nigeria 101 D7 9 29N 12 3 E
Numansdorp, Neths. 20 E4 51 43N 4 26 E
Numata, Japan 63 A11 36 45N 139 4 E
Numatinna →, Sudan 95 F2 7 38N 27 20 E
Numazu, Japan 63 B10 35 7N 138 51 E
Numbulwar, Australia 114 A2 14 15 S 135 45 E
Numfoor, Indonesia 73 B4 1 0 S 134 50 E
Numurkah, Australia 117 D6 36 5 S 145 26 E
Nunaksaluk I., Canada 129 A7 55 49N 60 20W
Nuneaton, U.K. 17 E6 52 32N 1 29W
Nungo, Mozam. 107 E4 13 23 S 37 43 E
Nungwe, Tanzania 106 C3 2 48 S 32 2 E
Nunivak, U.S.A. 126 B3 60 10N 166 0W
Nunkun, India 81 C7 33 57N 76 2 E
Nunspeet, Neths. 20 D7 52 21N 5 45 E
Nuoro, Italy 40 B2 40 20N 9 20 E
Nuqayy, Jabal, Libya 96 D3 23 11N 19 30 E
Nuqūb, Yemen 86 D4 14 59N 45 48 E
Nuquí, Colombia 152 B2 5 42N 77 17W
Nūrābād, Iran 85 E8 27 47N 57 12 E
Nurata, Uzbekistan 55 C2 40 33N 65 41 E
Nuratau, Khrebet, Uzbekistan 55 C3 40 40N 66 30 E
Nure →, Italy 38 C6 45 3N 9 49 E
Nuremburg = Nürnberg, Germany 27 F7 49 26N 11 5 E
Nūrestān, Afghan. 79 B3 35 30N 70 45 E
Nuri, Mexico 146 B3 28 2N 109 22W
Nurina, Australia 113 F4 30 56 S 126 33 E
Nuriootpa, Australia 116 C3 34 27 S 139 0 E
Nurlat, Russia 54 D2 54 29N 50 45 E
Nürnberg, Germany 27 F7 49 26N 11 5 E
Nurran, L. = Terewah, L., Australia 115 D4 29 52 S 147 35 E
Nurrari Lakes, Australia 113 E5 29 1 S 130 5 E
Nurri, Italy 40 C2 39 43N 9 13 E
Nurzec →, Poland 47 C9 52 37N 22 25 E
Nusa Barung, Indonesia 75 D4 8 10 S 113 30 E
Nusa Kambangan, Indonesia 75 D3 7 40 S 108 10 E
Nusa Tenggara Barat □, Indonesia 75 D5 8 50 S 117 30 E
Nusa Tenggara Timur □, Indonesia 72 C2 9 30 S 122 0 E
Nusaybin, Turkey 49 G7 37 3N 41 10 E
Nushki, Pakistan 79 C2 29 35N 66 0 E
Nutak, Canada 127 C13 57 28N 61 59W
Nuth, Neths. 21 G7 50 55N 5 53 E
Nutwood Downs, Australia 114 B1 15 49 S 134 10 E
Nuuk = Godthåb, Greenland 127 B14 64 10N 51 35W
Nuwakot, Nepal 81 E10 28 10N 83 55 E
Nuwara Eliya, Sri Lanka 83 L5 6 58N 80 48 E
Nuweiba', Egypt 94 B3 28 59N 34 39 E
Nuweveldberge, S. Africa 104 E3 32 10 S 21 45 E
Nuyts, C., Australia 113 F5 32 2 S 132 21 E
Nuyts Arch., Australia 115 E1 32 35 S 133 20 E
Nuzvid, India 82 F5 16 47N 80 53 E
Nxau-Nxau, Botswana 104 B3 18 57 S 21 4 E
Nyaake, Liberia 100 E3 4 52N 7 37W
Nyack, U.S.A. 137 E11 41 5N 73 57W
Nyadal, Sweden 14 B11 62 48N 17 59 E
Nyah West, Australia 116 C5 35 16 S 143 21 E
Nyahanga, Tanzania 106 C3 2 20 S 33 37 E
Nyahua, Tanzania 106 D3 5 25 S 33 23 E
Nyahururu, Kenya 106 B4 0 2N 36 27 E
Nyainqentanglha Shan, China 64 D3 30 0N 90 0 E
Nyakanazi, Tanzania 106 C3 3 2 S 31 10 E
Nyakrom, Ghana 101 D4 5 40N 0 50W
Nyâlâ, Sudan 95 E1 12 2N 24 58 E
Nyamandhlovu, Zimbabwe 107 F2 19 55 S 28 16 E
Nyambiti, Tanzania 106 C3 2 48 S 33 27 E
Nyamwaga, Tanzania 106 C3 1 27 S 34 33 E
Nyandekwa, Tanzania 106 C3 3 57 S 32 32 E
Nyanding →, Sudan 95 F3 8 40N 32 41 E
Nyandoma, Russia 48 B7 61 40N 40 12 E
Nyanga →, Gabon 102 C2 2 58 S 10 15 E
Nyangana, Namibia 104 B3 18 0 S 20 40 E
Nyanguge, Tanzania 106 C3 2 30 S 33 12 E
Nyankpala, Ghana 101 D4 9 21N 0 58W
Nyanza, Burundi 106 C2 4 21 S 29 36 E
Nyanza, Rwanda 106 C2 2 20 S 29 42 E
Nyanza □, Kenya 106 C3 0 10 S 34 15 E
Nyarling →, Canada 130 A6 60 41N 113 23W
Nyasa, L. = Malawi, L., Africa 107 E3 12 30 S 34 30 E
Nyaunglebin, Burma 78 G6 17 52N 96 42 E
Nyazepetrovsk, Russia 54 C6 56 3N 59 36 E
Nyazura, Zimbabwe 107 F3 18 40 S 32 16 E
Nyazwidzi →, Zimbabwe 107 F3 20 0 S 31 17 E
Nyborg, Denmark 15 J4 55 18N 10 47 E
Nybro, Sweden 13 H13 56 44N 15 55 E
Nyda, Russia 56 C8 66 40N 72 58 E
Nyeri, Kenya 106 C4 0 23 S 36 56 E
Nyerol, Sudan 95 F3 8 41N 32 1 E
Nyhem, Sweden 14 B9 62 54N 15 37 E
Nyiel, Sudan 95 F3 6 9N 31 13 E
Nyinahin, Ghana 100 D4 6 43N 2 3W
Nyirbátor, Hungary 31 D15 47 49N 22 9 E
Nyíregyháza, Hungary 31 D14 47 58N 21 47 E
Nykarleby, Finland 12 E17 63 22N 22 31 E
Nykøbing, Sjælland, Denmark 15 J5 55 55N 11 40 E
Nykøbing, Storstrøm, Denmark 15 K5 54 56N 11 52 E
Nykøbing, Viborg, Denmark 15 H2 56 48N 8 51 E
Nyköping, Sweden 15 F11 58 45N 17 0 E
Nykvarn, Sweden 14 E11 59 11N 17 25 E
Nyland, Sweden 14 A11 63 1N 17 45 E
Nylstroom, S. Africa 105 C4 24 42 S 28 22 E
Nymagee, Australia 117 B7 32 7 S 146 20 E
Nymburk, Czech. 30 A8 50 10N 15 1 E
Nynäshamn, Sweden 14 F11 58 54N 17 57 E
Nyngan, Australia 115 E4 31 30 S 147 8 E
Nyon, Switz. 28 D2 46 23N 6 14 E
Nyong →, Cameroon 101 E6 3 17N 9 54 E
Nyons, France 25 D9 44 22N 5 10 E
Nyora, Australia 117 E6 38 20 S 145 41 E
Nyord, Denmark 15 J6 55 4N 12 13 E
Nyou, Burkina Faso 101 C4 12 42N 2 1W
Nysa, Poland 47 E4 50 30N 17 22 E
Nysa →, Europe 47 C1 52 4N 14 46 E
Nyssa, U.S.A. 142 E5 43 56N 117 2W
Nysted, Denmark 15 K5 54 40N 11 44 E
Nytva, Russia 54 C4 57 56N 55 20 E
Nyūgawa, Japan 62 D5 33 56N 133 5 E
Nyunzu, Zaïre 106 D2 5 57 S 27 58 E
Nyurba, Russia 57 C12 63 17N 118 28 E
Nzega, Tanzania 106 C3 4 10 S 33 12 E
Nzega □, Tanzania 106 C3 4 10 S 33 10 E
N'Zérékoré, Guinea 100 D3 7 49N 8 48W
Nzeto, Angola 103 D2 7 10 S 12 52 E
Nzilo, Chutes de, Zaïre 103 E5 10 18 S 25 27 E
Nzubuka, Tanzania 106 C3 4 45 S 32 50 E

## O

Ō-Shima, Fukuoka, Japan 62 D2 33 54N 130 25 E
Ō-Shima, Nagasaki, Japan 62 C1 34 29N 129 33 E
Ō-Shima, Shizuoka, Japan 63 C11 34 44N 139 24 E
Oacoma, U.S.A. 138 D5 43 50N 99 26W
Oahe Dam, U.S.A. 138 C4 44 28N 100 25W
Oahe L., U.S.A. 138 C4 45 30N 100 25W
Oahu, U.S.A. 132 H16 21 30N 158 0W
Oak Creek, Colo., U.S.A. 142 F10 40 15N 106 59W
Oak Creek, Wis., U.S.A. 141 B9 42 52N 87 55W
Oak Harbour, U.S.A. 144 B4 48 20N 122 38W
Oak Hill, U.S.A. 134 G5 38 0N 81 7W
Oak Lawn, U.S.A. 141 C9 41 43N 87 44W
Oak Park, U.S.A. 141 C9 41 53N 87 47W
Oak Ridge, U.S.A. 135 G3 36 1N 84 12W
Oak View, U.S.A. 145 L7 34 24N 119 18W
Oakan-Dake, Japan 60 C12 43 27N 144 10 E
Oakbank, Australia 116 B4 33 4 S 140 33 E
Oakdale, Calif., U.S.A. 144 H6 37 45N 120 55W
Oakdale, La., U.S.A. 139 K8 30 50N 92 38W
Oakengates, U.K. 16 E5 52 42N 2 29W
Oakes, U.S.A. 138 B5 46 14N 98 4W
Oakesdale, U.S.A. 142 C5 47 11N 117 15W
Oakey, Australia 115 D5 27 25 S 151 43 E
Oakford, U.S.A. 140 D7 40 6N 89 58W
Oakham, U.K. 16 E7 52 40N 0 43W
Oakhurst, U.S.A. 144 H7 37 19N 119 40W
Oakland, Calif., U.S.A. 144 H4 37 50N 122 18W
Oakland, Ill., U.S.A. 141 E8 39 39N 88 2W
Oakland, Oreg., U.S.A. 142 E2 43 23N 123 18W
Oakland City, U.S.A. 141 F9 38 20N 87 20W
Oaklands, Australia 117 C7 35 34 S 146 10 E
Oakley, Idaho, U.S.A. 142 E7 42 14N 113 55W
Oakley, Kans., U.S.A. 138 F4 39 8N 100 51W
Oakley Creek, Australia 117 A8 31 37 S 149 46 E
Oakover →, Australia 112 D3 21 0 S 120 40 E
Oakridge, U.S.A. 142 E2 43 47N 122 31W
Oaktown, U.S.A. 141 F9 38 52N 87 27W
Oakville, U.S.A. 144 D3 46 50N 123 14W
Oakwood, U.S.A. 141 C12 41 6N 84 23W
Oamaru, N.Z. 119 F5 45 5 S 170 59 E
Ōamishirasato, Japan 63 B12 35 31N 140 18 E
Oarai, Japan 63 A12 36 21N 140 34 E
Oasis, Calif., U.S.A. 145 M10 33 28N 116 6W
Oasis, Nev., U.S.A. 144 H9 37 29N 117 55W
Oates Land, Antarctica 7 C11 69 0 S 160 0 E
Oatman, U.S.A. 145 K12 35 1N 114 19W
Oaxaca, Mexico 147 D5 17 2N 96 40W
Oaxaca □, Mexico 147 D5 17 0N 97 0W
Ob →, Russia 56 C7 66 45N 69 30 E
Oba, Canada 128 C3 49 4N 84 7W
Obala, Cameroon 101 E7 4 9N 11 32 E
Obama, Fukui, Japan 63 B7 35 30N 135 45 E
Obama, Nagasaki, Japan 62 E2 32 43N 130 13 E
Oban, U.K. 18 E3 56 25N 5 30W
Obbia, Somali Rep. 90 F4 5 25N 48 30 E
Obdam, Neths. 20 C5 52 41N 4 55 E
Obed, Canada 130 C5 53 30N 117 10W
Ober-Aagau, Switz. 28 B5 47 10N 7 45 E
Obera, Argentina 159 B4 27 21 S 55 2W
Oberalppass, Switz. 29 C7 46 39N 8 35 E
Oberalpstock, Switz. 29 C7 46 45N 8 47 E
Oberammergau, Germany 27 H7 47 35N 11 3 E
Oberdrauburg, Austria 30 E5 46 44N 12 58 E
Oberengadin, Switz. 29 C9 46 35N 9 55 E
Oberentfelden, Switz. 28 B6 47 21N 8 2 E
Oberhausen, Germany 26 D2 51 28N 6 50 E
Oberkirch, Germany 27 G4 48 31N 8 5 E
Oberland, Switz. 28 C5 46 35N 7 38 E
Oberlin, Kans., U.S.A. 138 F4 39 52N 100 31W
Oberlin, La., U.S.A. 139 K8 30 42N 92 42W
Oberlin, Ohio, U.S.A. 136 E2 41 15N 82 10W
Obernai, France 23 D14 48 28N 7 30 E
Oberndorf, Germany 27 G4 48 17N 8 35 E
Oberon, Australia 117 B8 33 45 S 149 52 E
Oberösterreich □, Austria 30 C6 48 10N 14 0 E
Oberpfälzer Wald, Germany 27 F8 49 30N 12 25 E
Obersiggenthal, Switz. 29 B6 47 29N 8 18 E

Oberstdorf, *Germany* 27 **H6** 47 25N 10 16 E
Oberting, *Gabon* 102 **C1** 0 22 S 9 46 E
Oberwil, *Switz.* 28 **A5** 47 32N 7 33 E
Obi, Kepulauan, *Indonesia* 72 **B3** 1 23 S 127 45 E
Obi Is. = Obi, Kepulauan, *Indonesia* 72 **B3** 1 23 S 127 45 E
Obiaruku, *Nigeria* 101 **D6** 5 51N 6 9 E
Óbidos, *Brazil* 153 **D6** 1 50 S 55 30W
Óbidos, *Portugal* 37 **F1** 39 19N 9 10W
Obihiro, *Japan* 60 **C11** 42 56N 143 12 E
Obilatu, *Indonesia* 72 **B3** 1 25 S 127 20 E
Obilnoye, *Russia* 53 **C11** 47 32N 44 30 E
Obing, *Germany* 27 **H8** 48 0N 12 25 E
Öbisfelde, *Germany* 26 **C6** 52 27N 10 57 E
Objat, *France* 24 **C5** 45 16N 1 24 E
Oblong, *U.S.A.* 141 **E9** 39 0N 87 55W
Obluchye, *Russia* 57 **E14** 49 1N 131 4 E
Obninsk, *Russia* 51 **D10** 55 8N 36 37 E
Obo, *C.A.R.* 102 **A5** 5 20N 26 32 E
Obo, *Ethiopia* 95 **G4** 3 46N 38 52 E
Oboa, Mt., *Uganda* 106 **B3** 1 45N 34 45 E
Obock, *Djibouti* 95 **E5** 12 0N 43 20 E
Oborniki, *Poland* 47 **C3** 52 39N 16 50 E
Oborniki Śląskie, *Poland* 47 **D3** 51 17N 16 53 E
Obouya, *Congo* 102 **C3** 0 56 S 15 43 E
Oboyan, *Russia* 51 **F10** 51 13N 36 37 E
Obozerskaya, *Russia* 56 **C5** 63 20N 40 15 E
Obrenovac, *Serbia, Yug.* 42 **C5** 44 40N 20 11 E
Obrovac, *Croatia* 39 **D12** 44 11N 15 41 E
Obruk, *Turkey* 88 **D5** 38 18N 33 12 E
Observatory Inlet, *Canada* 130 **B3** 55 10N 129 54W
Obshchi Syrt, *Kazakhstan* 10 **E16** 52 0N 53 0 E
Obskaya Guba, *Russia* 56 **C8** 69 0N 73 0 E
Obuasi, *Ghana* 101 **D4** 6 17N 1 40W
Obubra, *Nigeria* 101 **D6** 6 8N 8 20 E
Obwalden □, *Switz.* 28 **C6** 46 55N 8 15 E
Obyachevo, *Russia* 54 **A1** 60 20N 49 37 E
Obzor, *Bulgaria* 43 **E12** 42 50N 27 52 E
Ocala, *U.S.A.* 135 **L4** 29 11N 82 5W
Ocamo →, *Venezuela* 153 **C4** 2 48N 65 14W
Ocampo, *Mexico* 146 **B3** 28 9N 108 24W
Ocaña, *Colombia* 152 **B3** 8 15N 73 20W
Ocaña, *Spain* 34 **F1** 39 55N 3 30W
Ocanomowoc, *U.S.A.* 138 **D10** 43 7N 88 30W
Ocate, *U.S.A.* 139 **G2** 36 12N 104 59W
Occidental, Cordillera, *Colombia* 152 **C3** 5 0N 76 0W
Occidental, Cordillera, *Peru* 156 **C3** 14 0 S 74 0W
Ocean City, *N.J., U.S.A.* 134 **F8** 39 18N 74 34W
Ocean City, *Wash., U.S.A.* 144 **C2** 47 4N 124 10W
Ocean I. = Banaba, *Kiribati* 122 **H8** 0 45 S 169 50 E
Ocean Park, *U.S.A.* 144 **D2** 46 30N 124 2W
Oceano, *U.S.A.* 145 **K6** 35 6N 120 37W
Oceanport, *U.S.A.* 137 **F10** 40 20N 74 3W
Oceanside, *U.S.A.* 145 **M9** 33 13N 117 26W
Ochagavia, *Spain* 34 **C3** 42 55N 1 5W
Ochamchire, *Georgia* 53 **E9** 42 46N 41 32 E
Ochamps, *Belgium* 21 **J6** 49 56N 5 16 E
Ocher, *Russia* 54 **C4** 57 53N 54 42 E
Ochiai, *Japan* 62 **B5** 35 1N 133 45 E
Ochil Hills, *U.K.* 18 **E5** 56 14N 3 40W
Ochre River, *Canada* 131 **C9** 51 4N 99 47W
Ochsenfurt, *Germany* 27 **F6** 49 38N 10 3 E
Ochsenhausen, *Germany* 27 **G5** 48 4N 9 57 E
Ocilla, *U.S.A.* 135 **K4** 31 35N 83 12W
Ocmulgee →, *U.S.A.* 135 **K4** 31 58N 82 33W
Ocna Mureş, *Romania* 46 **C4** 46 23N 23 55 E
Ocna Sibiului, *Romania* 46 **D5** 45 52N 24 2 E
Ocnele Mari, *Romania* 46 **D5** 45 8N 24 18 E
Ocoña, *Peru* 156 **D3** 16 26 S 73 8W
Ocoña →, *Peru* 156 **D3** 16 28 S 73 8W
Oconee →, *U.S.A.* 135 **K4** 31 58N 82 32W
Oconomowoc, *U.S.A.* 141 **A8** 43 6N 88 30W
Oconto, *U.S.A.* 134 **C2** 44 52N 87 53W
Oconto Falls, *U.S.A.* 134 **C1** 44 52N 88 10W
Ocosingo, *Mexico* 147 **D6** 17 10N 92 15W
Ocotal, *Nic.* 148 **D2** 13 41N 86 31W
Ocotlán, *Mexico* 146 **C4** 20 21N 102 42W
Ocquier, *Belgium* 21 **H6** 50 24N 5 24 E
Ocreza →, *Portugal* 37 **F3** 39 32N 7 50W
Ócsa, *Hungary* 31 **D12** 47 17N 19 15 E
Octave, *U.S.A.* 143 **J7** 34 10N 112 43W
Octeville, *France* 22 **C5** 49 38N 1 40W
Ocumare del Tuy, *Venezuela* 152 **A4** 10 7N 66 46W
Ocuri, *Bolivia* 157 **D4** 18 45 S 65 50W
Oda, *Ghana* 101 **D4** 5 50N 0 51W
Oda, *Ehime, Japan* 62 **D4** 33 36N 132 53 E
Ōda, *Shimane, Japan* 62 **B4** 35 11N 132 30 E
Oda, J., *Sudan* 94 **C4** 20 21N 36 39 E
Ódáðahraun, *Iceland* 12 **D5** 65 5N 17 0W
Ödåkra, *Sweden* 15 **H6** 56 7N 12 45 E
Odate, *Japan* 60 **D10** 40 16N 140 34 E
Odawara, *Japan* 63 **B11** 35 20N 139 6 E
Odda, *Norway* 13 **F9** 60 3N 6 35 E
Odder, *Denmark* 15 **J4** 55 58N 10 10 E
Oddur, *Somali Rep.* 90 **G3** 4 11N 43 52 E
Ödeborg, *Sweden* 15 **F5** 58 32N 11 58 E
Odei →, *Canada* 131 **B9** 56 6N 96 54W
Odell, *U.S.A.* 141 **D8** 41 0N 88 31W
Odemira, *Portugal* 37 **H2** 37 35N 8 40W
Ödemiş, *Turkey* 88 **D3** 38 15N 28 0 E
Odendaalsrus, *S. Africa* 104 **D4** 27 48 S 26 45 E
Odense, *Denmark* 15 **J4** 55 22N 10 23 E
Odenwald, *Germany* 27 **F5** 49 30N 9 0 E
Oder →, *Germany* 26 **B10** 53 33N 14 38 E
Oderzo, *Italy* 39 **C9** 45 47N 12 29 E
Odessa, *Canada* 137 **B8** 44 17N 76 43W
Odessa, *Ukraine* 52 **C4** 46 30N 30 45 E
Odessa, *Mo., U.S.A.* 140 **F3** 39 0N 93 57W
Odessa, *Tex., U.S.A.* 139 **K3** 31 51N 102 23W
Odessa, *Wash., U.S.A.* 142 **C4** 47 19N 118 35W
Odiakwe, *Botswana* 104 **C4** 20 12 S 25 17 E
Odiel →, *Spain* 37 **H4** 37 10N 6 55W
Odienné, *Ivory C.* 100 **D3** 9 30N 7 34W
Odintsovo, *Russia* 51 **D10** 55 39N 37 15 E
Odiongan, *Phil.* 70 **E3** 12 24N 121 59 E
Odobeşti, *Romania* 46 **D8** 45 43N 27 4 E
Odolanów, *Poland* 47 **D4** 51 34N 17 40 E
O'Donnell, *Phil.* 70 **D3** 15 21N 120 27 E
O'Donnell, *U.S.A.* 139 **J4** 33 0N 101 48W
Odoorn, *Neths.* 20 **C9** 52 51N 6 51 E
Odorheiu Secuiesc, *Romania* 46 **C6** 46 21N 25 21 E
Odoyevo, *Russia* 51 **E10** 53 56N 36 42 E
Odra →, *Poland* 47 **B1** 53 33N 14 38 E
Odra →, *Spain* 36 **C6** 42 14N 4 17W
Odweina, *Somali Rep.* 108 **C3** 9 25N 45 4 E
Odžaci, *Serbia, Yug.* 42 **B4** 45 30N 19 17 E
Odžak, *Bos.-H., Yug.* 42 **B3** 45 3N 18 18 E
Odzi, *Zimbabwe* 105 **B5** 19 0 S 32 20 E
Oedelem, *Belgium* 21 **F2** 51 10N 3 21 E
Oegstgeest, *Neths.* 20 **D4** 52 11N 4 29 E
Oeiras, *Brazil* 154 **C3** 7 0 S 42 8W
Oeiras, *Portugal* 37 **G1** 38 41N 9 18W
Oelrichs, *U.S.A.* 138 **D3** 43 11N 103 14W
Oelsnitz, *Germany* 26 **E8** 50 24N 12 11 E
Oelwein, *U.S.A.* 138 **D9** 42 41N 91 55W
Oenpelli, *Australia* 112 **B5** 12 20 S 133 4 E
Of, *Turkey* 89 **C9** 40 59N 40 23 E
O'Fallon, *U.S.A.* 140 **F6** 38 50N 90 43W
Ofanto →, *Italy* 41 **A9** 41 22N 16 13 E
Offa, *Nigeria* 101 **D5** 8 13N 4 42 E
Offaly □, *Ireland* 19 **C4** 53 15N 7 30W
Offenbach, *Germany* 27 **E4** 50 6N 8 46 E
Offenburg, *Germany* 27 **G3** 48 29N 7 56 E
Offerdal, *Sweden* 14 **A8** 63 28N 14 0 E
Offida, *Italy* 39 **F10** 42 56N 13 40 E
Offranville, *France* 22 **C8** 49 52N 1 1 E
Ofidhousa, *Greece* 45 **H8** 36 33N 26 8 E
Ofotfjorden, *Norway* 12 **B14** 68 27N 16 40 E
Ofu, *Amer. Samoa* 121 **X25** 14 11 S 169 41W
Ōfunato, *Japan* 60 **E10** 39 4N 141 43 E
Oga, *Japan* 60 **E9** 39 55N 139 50 E
Oga-Hantō, *Japan* 60 **E9** 39 58N 139 47 E
Ogaden, *Ethiopia* 108 **C3** 7 30N 45 30 E
Ogahalla, *Canada* 128 **B2** 50 6N 85 51W
Ōgaki, *Japan* 63 **B8** 35 21N 136 37 E
Ogallala, *U.S.A.* 138 **E4** 41 12N 101 40W
Ogan →, *Indonesia* 74 **C2** 3 1 S 104 44 E
Ogasawara Gunto, *Pac. Oc.* 122 **E6** 27 0N 142 0 E
Ogbomosho, *Nigeria* 101 **D5** 8 1N 4 11 E
Ogden, *Iowa, U.S.A.* 140 **B2** 42 3N 94 0W
Ogden, *Utah, U.S.A.* 142 **F7** 41 13N 112 1W
Ogdensburg, *U.S.A.* 137 **B9** 44 40N 75 27W
Ogeechee →, *U.S.A.* 135 **K5** 31 51N 81 6W
Ogilby, *U.S.A.* 145 **N12** 32 49N 114 50W
Oglesby, *U.S.A.* 140 **C7** 41 21N 89 3W
Oglio →, *Italy* 38 **C7** 45 2N 10 39 E
Ogmore, *Australia* 114 **C4** 22 37 S 149 35 E
Ognon →, *France* 23 **E12** 47 16N 5 28 E
Ogo Mas, *Indonesia* 72 **A2** 0 50N 120 5 E
Ogoja, *Nigeria* 101 **D6** 6 38N 8 39 E
Ogoki →, *Canada* 128 **B2** 51 38N 85 57W
Ogoki L., *Canada* 128 **B2** 50 50N 87 10W
Ogoki Res., *Canada* 128 **B2** 50 45N 88 15W
Ogooué →, *Gabon* 102 **C1** 1 0 S 9 0 E
Ōgori, *Japan* 62 **C3** 34 6N 131 24 E
Ogosta →, *Bulgaria* 43 **D8** 43 48N 23 55 E
Ogowe = Ogooué →, *Gabon* 102 **C1** 1 0 S 9 0 E
Ogr = Sharafa, *Sudan* 95 **E2** 11 59N 27 7 E
Ograźden, *Macedonia, Yug.* 42 **F7** 41 30N 22 50 E
Ogrein, *Sudan* 94 **D3** 17 55N 34 50 E
Ogulin, *Croatia* 39 **C12** 45 16N 15 16 E
Ogun □, *Nigeria* 101 **D5** 7 0N 3 0 E
Oguni, *Japan* 62 **D3** 33 11N 131 8 E
Oguta, *Nigeria* 101 **D6** 5 44N 6 44 E
Ogwashi-Uku, *Nigeria* 101 **D6** 6 15N 6 30 E
Ogwe, *Nigeria* 101 **E6** 5 0N 7 14 E
Ohai, *N.Z.* 119 **F3** 45 55 S 168 0 E
Ohakune, *N.Z.* 118 **F4** 39 24 S 175 24 E
Ohanet, *Algeria* 99 **C6** 28 44N 8 46 E
Ōhara, *Japan* 63 **B12** 35 15N 140 23 E
Ohata, *Japan* 60 **D10** 41 24N 141 10 E
Ohau, L., *N.Z.* 119 **E4** 44 15 S 169 53 E
Ohaupo, *N.Z.* 118 **D4** 37 56 S 175 20 E
Ohey, *Belgium* 21 **H6** 50 26N 5 8 E
Ohio □, *U.S.A.* 134 **E3** 40 20N 84 10W
Ohio →, *U.S.A.* 134 **G1** 36 59N 89 8W
Ohio City, *U.S.A.* 141 **D12** 40 46N 84 37W
Ohiwa Harbour, *N.Z.* 118 **D6** 37 59 S 177 10 E
Ohre →, *Czech.* 30 **A7** 50 30N 14 10 E
Ohre →, *Germany* 26 **C7** 52 18N 11 47 E
Ohrid, *Macedonia, Yug.* 42 **F5** 41 8N 20 52 E
Ohridsko, Jezero, *Macedonia, Yug.* 42 **F5** 41 8N 20 52 E
Ohrigstad, *S. Africa* 105 **C5** 24 39 S 30 36 E
Öhringen, *Germany* 27 **F5** 49 11N 9 31 E
Ohura, *N.Z.* 118 **E3** 38 51 S 174 59 E
Oiapoque →, *Brazil* 153 **C7** 4 8N 51 40W
Oikou, *China* 67 **E9** 38 35N 117 42 E
Oil City, *U.S.A.* 136 **E5** 41 26N 79 40W
Oildale, *U.S.A.* 145 **K7** 35 25N 119 1W
Oinousa, *Greece* 45 **F8** 38 33N 26 14 E
Oirschot, *Neths.* 21 **E6** 51 30N 5 18 E
Oise □, *France* 23 **C9** 49 28N 2 30 E
Oise →, *France* 23 **D9** 49 0N 2 4 E
Oisterwijk, *Neths.* 21 **E6** 51 35N 5 12 E
Ōita, *Japan* 62 **D3** 33 14N 131 36 E
Ōita □, *Japan* 62 **D3** 33 15N 131 30 E
Oiticica, *Brazil* 154 **C3** 5 3 S 41 5W
Ojai, *U.S.A.* 145 **L7** 34 28N 119 16W
Ojinaga, *Mexico* 146 **B4** 29 34N 104 25W
Ojiya, *Japan* 61 **F9** 37 18N 138 48 E
Ojos del Salado, Cerro, *Argentina* 158 **B2** 27 0 S 68 40W
Oka →, *Russia* 51 **C13** 56 20N 43 59 E
Okaba, *Indonesia* 73 **C5** 8 6 S 139 42 E
Okahandja, *Namibia* 104 **C2** 22 0 S 16 59 E
Okahukura, *N.Z.* 118 **E4** 38 48 S 175 14 E
Okaihau, *N.Z.* 118 **B2** 35 19 S 173 47 E
Okanagan L., *Canada* 130 **C5** 50 0N 119 30W
Okandja, *Gabon* 102 **C2** 0 35 S 13 45 E
Okanogan, *U.S.A.* 142 **B4** 48 6N 119 43W
Okanogan →, *U.S.A.* 142 **B4** 48 6N 119 43W
Okány, *Hungary* 31 **E14** 46 52N 21 21 E
Okapa, *Papua N. G.* 120 **D3** 6 38 S 145 39 E
Okaputa, *Namibia* 104 **C2** 20 5 S 17 0 E
Okara, *Pakistan* 79 **C4** 30 50N 73 31 E
Okarito, *N.Z.* 119 **D5** 43 15 S 170 9 E
Okato, *N.Z.* 118 **F2** 39 12 S 173 53 E
Okaukuejo, *Namibia* 104 **B2** 19 10 S 16 0 E
Okavango Swamps, *Botswana* 104 **B3** 18 45 S 22 45 E
Okawa, *Japan* 62 **D2** 33 9N 130 21 E
Okawville, *U.S.A.* 140 **F7** 38 26N 89 33W
Okaya, *Japan* 63 **A10** 36 5N 138 10 E
Okayama, *Japan* 62 **C5** 34 40N 133 54 E
Okayama □, *Japan* 62 **C5** 35 0N 133 50 E
Okazaki, *Japan* 63 **C9** 34 57N 137 10 E
Oke-Iho, *Nigeria* 101 **D5** 8 1N 3 18 E
Okeechobee, *U.S.A.* 135 **M5** 27 16N 80 46W
Okeechobee, L., *U.S.A.* 135 **M5** 27 0N 80 50W
Okefenokee Swamp, *U.S.A.* 135 **K4** 30 50N 82 15W
Okehampton, *U.K.* 17 **G3** 50 44N 4 1W
Okene, *Nigeria* 101 **D6** 7 32N 6 11 E
Oker →, *Germany* 26 **C6** 52 30N 10 22 E
Okha, *Russia* 57 **D15** 53 40N 143 0 E
Ókhi Óros, *Greece* 45 **F6** 38 5N 24 25 E
Okhotsk, *Russia* 57 **D15** 59 20N 143 10 E
Okhotsk, Sea of, *Asia* 57 **D15** 55 0N 145 0 E
Okhotskiy Perevoz, *Russia* 57 **C14** 61 52N 135 35 E
Okhotsko Kolymskoye, *Russia* 57 **C16** 63 0N 157 0 E
Oki-no-Shima, *Japan* 62 **E4** 32 44N 132 33 E
Oki-Shotō, *Japan* 62 **A5** 36 5N 133 15 E
Okiep, *S. Africa* 104 **D2** 29 39 S 17 53 E
Okigwi, *Nigeria* 101 **D6** 5 52N 7 20 E
Okija, *Nigeria* 101 **D6** 5 54N 6 55 E
Okinawa □, *Japan* 61 **L3** 26 40N 128 0 E
Okinawa-Guntō, *Japan* 61 **L3** 26 40N 128 0 E
Okinawa-Jima, *Japan* 61 **L4** 26 32N 128 0 E
Okino-erabu-Shima, *Japan* 61 **L4** 27 21N 128 33 E
Okitipupa, *Nigeria* 101 **D5** 6 31N 4 50 E
Oklahoma □, *U.S.A.* 139 **H6** 35 20N 97 30W
Oklahoma City, *U.S.A.* 139 **H6** 35 25N 97 30W
Okmulgee, *U.S.A.* 139 **H7** 35 38N 96 0W
Oknitsa, *Ukraine* 52 **B2** 48 25N 27 30 E
Okolo, *Uganda* 106 **B3** 2 37N 31 8 E
Okolona, *Ky., U.S.A.* 141 **F11** 38 8N 85 41W
Okolona, *Miss., U.S.A.* 139 **H10** 34 0N 88 45W
Okonek, *Poland* 47 **B3** 53 32N 16 51 E
Okrika, *Nigeria* 101 **E6** 4 40N 7 10 E
Oktabrsk, *Kazakhstan* 49 **E10** 49 28N 57 25 E
Oktyabr, *Kazakhstan* 55 **B8** 43 41N 77 12 E
Oktyabrsk, *Russia* 51 **E16** 53 11N 48 40 E
Oktyabrskiy, *Belorussia* 50 **E6** 52 38N 28 53 E
Oktyabrskiy, *Russia* 54 **D3** 54 28N 53 28 E
Oktyabrskoy Revolyutsii, Os., *Russia* 57 **B10** 79 30N 97 0 E
Oktyabrskoye = Zhovtnevoye, *Ukraine* 52 **C5** 46 54N 32 3 E
Oktyabrskoye, *Russia* 56 **C7** 62 28N 66 3 E
Ōkuchi, *Japan* 62 **E2** 32 4N 130 37 E
Okulovka, *Russia* 50 **B8** 58 25N 33 19 E
Okuru, *N.Z.* 119 **D3** 43 55 S 168 55 E
Okushiri-Tō, *Japan* 60 **C9** 42 15N 139 30 E
Okuta, *Nigeria* 101 **D5** 9 14N 3 12 E
Okwa →, *Botswana* 104 **C3** 22 30 S 23 0 E
Ola, *U.S.A.* 139 **H8** 35 2N 93 10W
Ólafsfjörður, *Iceland* 12 **C4** 66 4N 18 39W
Ólafsvík, *Iceland* 12 **D2** 64 53N 23 43W
Olancha, *U.S.A.* 145 **J8** 36 15N 118 1W
Olancha Pk., *U.S.A.* 145 **J8** 36 15N 118 7W
Olanchito, *Honduras* 148 **C2** 15 30N 86 30W
Öland, *Sweden* 13 **H14** 56 45N 16 38 E
Olargues, *France* 24 **E6** 43 34N 2 53 E
Olary, *Australia* 116 **B4** 32 18 S 140 19 E
Olascoaga, *Argentina* 158 **D3** 35 15 S 60 39W
Olathe, *U.S.A.* 138 **F7** 38 50N 94 50W
Olavarría, *Argentina* 158 **D3** 36 55 S 60 20W
Oława, *Poland* 47 **E4** 50 57N 17 20 E
Ólbia, *Italy* 40 **B2** 40 55N 9 30 E
Ólbia, G. di, *Italy* 40 **B2** 40 55N 9 35 E
Old Bahama Chan. = Bahama, Canal Viejo de, *W. Indies* 148 **B4** 22 10N 77 30W
Old Baldy Pk. = San Antonio, Mt., *U.S.A.* 145 **L9** 34 17N 117 38W
Old Castile = Castilla y Leon □, *Spain* 36 **D6** 42 0N 5 0W
Old Castle, *Ireland* 19 **C4** 53 46N 7 10W
Old Cork, *Australia* 114 **C3** 22 57 S 141 52 E
Old Crow, *Canada* 126 **B6** 67 30N 139 55W
Old Dale, *U.S.A.* 145 **L11** 34 8N 115 47W
Old Dongola, *Sudan* 94 **D3** 18 11N 30 44 E
Old Fletton, *U.K.* 17 **E7** 52 34N 0 13W
Old Forge, *N.Y., U.S.A.* 137 **C10** 43 43N 74 58W
Old Forge, *Pa., U.S.A.* 137 **E9** 41 20N 75 46W
Old Fort →, *Canada* 131 **B6** 58 36N 110 24W
Old Shinyanga, *Tanzania* 106 **C3** 3 33 S 33 27 E
Old Speck, Mt., *U.S.A.* 137 **B14** 44 35N 70 57W
Old Town, *U.S.A.* 129 **D6** 45 0N 68 41W
Old Wives L., *Canada* 131 **C7** 50 5N 106 0W
Oldbury, *U.K.* 17 **F5** 51 38N 2 30W
Oldeani, *Tanzania* 106 **C4** 3 22 S 35 35 E
Oldenburg, *Niedersachsen, Germany* 26 **B4** 53 10N 8 10 E
Oldenburg, *Schleswig-Holstein, Germany* 26 **A6** 54 16N 10 53 E
Oldenzaal, *Neths.* 20 **D9** 52 19N 6 53 E
Oldham, *U.K.* 16 **D5** 53 33N 2 8W
Oldman →, *Canada* 130 **D6** 49 57N 111 42W
Olds, *Canada* 130 **C6** 51 50N 114 10W
Olean, *U.S.A.* 136 **D6** 42 8N 78 25W
Olecko, *Poland* 47 **A9** 54 2N 22 31 E
Oléggio, *Italy* 38 **C5** 45 36N 8 38 E
Oleiros, *Portugal* 36 **F3** 39 56N 7 56W
Olekma →, *Russia* 57 **C13** 60 22N 120 42 E
Olekminsk, *Russia* 57 **C13** 60 25N 120 30 E
Olema, *U.S.A.* 144 **G4** 38 3N 122 47W
Olen, *Belgium* 21 **F5** 51 9N 4 52 E
Olenegorsk, *Russia* 48 **A5** 68 9N 33 18 E
Olenek, *Russia* 57 **C12** 68 28N 112 18 E
Olenek →, *Russia* 57 **B13** 73 0N 120 10 E
Olenino, *Russia* 50 **C8** 56 15N 33 30 E
Oléron, I. d', *France* 24 **C2** 45 55N 1 15W
Oleśnica, *Poland* 47 **D4** 51 13N 17 22 E
Olesno, *Poland* 47 **E5** 50 51N 18 26 E
Olevsk, *Ukraine* 50 **F5** 51 12N 27 39 E
Olga, *Russia* 57 **E14** 43 50N 135 14 E
Olga, L., *Canada* 128 **C4** 49 47N 77 15W
Olga, Mt., *Australia* 113 **E5** 25 20 S 130 50 E
Ølgod, *Denmark* 15 **J2** 55 49N 8 36 E
Olhão, *Portugal* 37 **H3** 37 3N 7 48W
Olib, *Croatia* 39 **D11** 44 23N 14 44 E
Oliena, *Italy* 40 **B2** 40 18N 9 22 E
Oliete, *Spain* 34 **D4** 41 1N 0 41W
Olifants →, *Africa* 105 **C5** 23 57 S 31 58 E
Olifantshoek, *S. Africa* 104 **D3** 27 57 S 22 42 E
Ólimbos, *Greece* 45 **J9** 35 44N 27 11 E
Ólimbos, Óros, *Greece* 44 **D4** 40 6N 22 23 E
Olímpia, *Brazil* 159 **A6** 20 44 S 48 54W
Olin, *U.S.A.* 140 **B5** 42 0N 91 9W
Olinda, *Brazil* 154 **C5** 8 1 S 34 51W
Olindiná, *Brazil* 154 **D4** 11 22 S 38 21W
Olite, *Spain* 34 **C3** 42 29N 1 40W
Oliva, *Argentina* 158 **C3** 32 0 S 63 38W
Oliva, *Spain* 35 **G4** 38 58N 0 9W
Oliva, Punta del, *Spain* 36 **B5** 43 37N 5 28W
Oliva de la Frontera, *Spain* 37 **G4** 38 17N 6 54W
Olivares, *Spain* 34 **F2** 39 46N 2 20W
Olive Hill, *U.S.A.* 141 **F13** 38 18N 83 13W
Olivehurst, *U.S.A.* 144 **F5** 39 6N 121 34W
Oliveira, *Brazil* 155 **F3** 20 39 S 44 50W
Oliveira de Azemeis, *Portugal* 36 **E2** 40 49N 8 29W
Oliveira dos Brejinhos, *Brazil* 155 **D3** 12 19 S 42 54W
Olivenza, *Spain* 37 **G3** 38 41N 7 9W
Oliver, *Canada* 130 **D5** 49 13N 119 37W
Oliver L., *Canada* 131 **B8** 56 56N 103 22W
Olivine Ra., *N.Z.* 119 **E3** 44 15 S 168 30 E
Olivone, *Switz.* 29 **C7** 46 32N 8 57 E
Olkhovka, *Russia* 53 **B11** 49 48N 44 32 E
Olkusz, *Poland* 47 **E6** 50 18N 19 33 E
Ollagüe, *Chile* 158 **A2** 21 15 S 68 10W
Olloy, *Belgium* 21 **H5** 50 5N 4 36 E
Olmedo, *Spain* 36 **D6** 41 20N 4 43W
Olmos, *Peru* 156 **B2** 5 59 S 79 46W
Olney, *Ill., U.S.A.* 141 **F8** 38 40N 88 5W
Olney, *Tex., U.S.A.* 139 **J5** 33 25N 98 45W
Oloma, *Cameroon* 101 **E7** 3 29N 11 19 E
Olomane →, *Canada* 129 **B7** 50 14N 60 37W
Olombo, *Congo* 102 **C3** 1 18 S 15 53 E
Olomouc, *Czech.* 31 **B10** 49 38N 17 12 E
Olonets, *Russia* 48 **B5** 61 10N 33 0 E
Olongapo, *Phil.* 70 **D3** 14 50N 120 18 E
Oloron, Gave d' →, *France* 24 **E2** 43 33N 1 5W
Oloron-Ste.-Marie, *France* 24 **E3** 43 11N 0 38W
Olot, *Spain* 34 **C7** 42 11N 2 30 E
Olovo, *Bos.-H., Yug.* 42 **C3** 44 8N 18 35 E
Olovo, *Yugoslavia* 42 **C3** 44 10N 19 0 E
Olovyannaya, *Russia* 57 **D12** 50 58N 115 35 E
Oloy →, *Russia* 57 **C16** 66 29N 159 29 E
Olpe, *Germany* 26 **D3** 51 2N 7 50 E
Olshanka, *Ukraine* 52 **B4** 48 16N 30 58 E
Olshany, *Ukraine* 52 **A6** 50 3N 35 53 E
Olst, *Neths.* 20 **D8** 52 20N 6 7 E
Olsztyn, *Poland* 47 **B7** 53 48N 20 29 E
Olsztyn □, *Poland* 47 **B7** 54 0N 21 0 E
Olsztynek, *Poland* 47 **B7** 53 34N 20 19 E
Olt □, *Romania* 46 **E5** 44 20N 24 30 E
Olt →, *Romania* 46 **F5** 43 43N 24 51 E
Olten, *Switz.* 28 **B5** 47 21N 7 53 E
Olteniţa, *Romania* 46 **E7** 44 7N 26 42 E
Olton, *U.S.A.* 139 **H3** 34 16N 102 7W
Oltu, *Turkey* 89 **C9** 40 35N 41 58 E
Olur, *Turkey* 89 **C10** 40 49N 42 8 E
Olutanga, *Phil.* 71 **H4** 7 26N 122 54 E
Olutanga I., *Phil.* 71 **H4** 7 22N 122 52 E
Olvega, *Spain* 34 **D3** 41 47N 2 0W
Olvera, *Spain* 37 **J5** 36 55N 5 18W
Olymbos, *Cyprus* 32 **D12** 35 21N 33 45 E
Olympia, *Greece* 45 **G3** 37 39N 21 39 E
Olympia, *U.S.A.* 144 **D4** 47 0N 122 58W
Olympic Mts., *U.S.A.* 144 **C3** 47 50N 123 45W
Olympic Nat. Park, *U.S.A.* 144 **C3** 47 48N 123 30W
Olympus, *Cyprus* 32 **E11** 34 56N 32 52 E
Olympus, Mt. = Ólimbos, Óros, *Greece* 44 **D4** 40 6N 22 23 E
Olympus, Mt., *U.S.A.* 144 **C3** 47 52N 123 40W
Olyphant, *U.S.A.* 137 **E9** 41 27N 75 36W
Om →, *Russia* 56 **D8** 54 59N 73 22 E
Om Hajer, *Ethiopia* 95 **E4** 14 20N 36 41 E
Om Koi, *Thailand* 76 **D2** 17 48N 98 22 E
Ōma, *Japan* 60 **D10** 41 45N 141 5 E
Ōmachi, *Japan* 63 **A9** 36 30N 137 50 E
Omae-Zaki, *Japan* 63 **C10** 34 36N 138 14 E
Ōmagari, *Japan* 60 **E10** 39 27N 140 29 E
Omagh, *U.K.* 19 **B4** 54 36N 7 20W
Omagh □, *U.K.* 19 **B4** 54 35N 7 15W
Omaha, *U.S.A.* 138 **E7** 41 15N 95 55W
Omak, *U.S.A.* 142 **B4** 48 24N 119 31W
Omalos, *Greece* 32 **D5** 35 19N 23 55 E
Oman ■, *Asia* 87 **B7** 23 0N 58 0 E
Oman, G. of, *Asia* 85 **E8** 24 30N 58 30 E
Omapere, *N.Z.* 118 **B2** 35 37 S 173 25 E
Omar Combon, *Somali Rep.* 108 **D3** 3 10N 45 47 E
Omaruru, *Namibia* 104 **C2** 21 26 S 16 0 E
Omaruru →, *Namibia* 104 **C1** 22 7 S 14 15 E
Omate, *Peru* 156 **D3** 16 45 S 71 0W
Ombai, Selat, *Indonesia* 72 **C2** 8 30 S 124 50 E
Omboué, *Gabon* 102 **C1** 1 35 S 9 15 E
Ombrone →, *Italy* 38 **F8** 42 39N 11 0 E
Omchi, *Chad* 97 **D3** 21 22N 17 53 E
Omdurmân, *Sudan* 95 **D3** 15 40N 32 28 E
Ōme, *Japan* 63 **B11** 35 47N 139 15 E
Omegna, *Italy* 38 **C5** 45 52N 8 23 E
Omeonga, *Zaïre* 102 **C4** 3 40 S 24 22 E
Ometepe, I. de, *Nic.* 148 **D2** 11 32N 85 35W
Ometepec, *Mexico* 147 **D5** 16 39N 98 23W
Ōmi-Shima, *Ehime, Japan* 62 **C5** 34 15N 133 0 E
Ōmi-Shima, *Yamaguchi, Japan* 62 **C3** 34 25N 131 9 E
Omihachiman, *Japan* 63 **B8** 35 7N 136 3 E
Ominato, *Japan* 60 **D10** 41 17N 141 10 E
Omineca →, *Canada* 130 **B4** 56 3N 124 16W
Omiš, *Croatia* 39 **E13** 43 28N 16 40 E
Omišalj, *Croatia* 39 **C11** 45 13N 14 32 E
Omitara, *Namibia* 104 **C2** 22 16 S 18 2 E
Ōmiya, *Japan* 63 **B11** 35 54N 139 38 E
Omme Å →, *Denmark* 15 **J2** 55 56N 8 32 E
Ommen, *Neths.* 20 **C8** 52 31N 6 26 E
Ömnögovĭ □, *Mongolia* 66 **C3** 43 15N 104 0 E
Omo →, *Ethiopia* 95 **F4** 6 25N 36 10 E

244 Omodhos


Omodhos, *Cyprus* 32 **E11** 34 51N 32 48 E
Omolon →, *Russia* 57 **C16** 68 42N 158 36 E
Omono-Gawa →, *Japan* 60 **E10** 39 46N 140 3 E
Omsk, *Russia* 56 **D8** 55 0N 73 12 E
Omsukchan, *Russia* 57 **C16** 62 32N 155 48 E
Ōmu, *Japan* 60 **B11** 44 34N 142 58 E
Omul, Vf., *Romania* 46 **D6** 45 27N 25 29 E
Omulew →, *Poland* 47 **B8** 53 5N 21 33 E
Ōmura, *Japan* 62 **E1** 32 56N 129 57 E
Omura-Wan, *Japan* 62 **E1** 32 57N 129 52 E
Omurtag, *Bulgaria* 43 **D11** 43 8N 26 26 E
Ōmuta, *Japan* 62 **D2** 33 5N 130 26 E
Omutninsk, *Russia* 54 **B3** 58 45N 52 4 E
On, *Belgium* 21 **H6** 50 11N 5 18 E
On-Take, *Japan* 62 **F2** 31 35N 130 39 E
Oña, *Spain* 34 **C1** 42 43N 3 25W
Onaga, *U.S.A.* 138 **F6** 39 32N 96 12W
Onalaska, *U.S.A.* 138 **D9** 43 53N 91 14W
Onamia, *U.S.A.* 138 **B8** 46 4N 93 38W
Onancock, *U.S.A.* 134 **G8** 37 42N 75 49W
Onang, *Indonesia* 72 **B1** 3 2 S 118 49 E
Onaping L., *Canada* 128 **C3** 47 3N 81 30W
Onarga, *U.S.A.* 141 **D8** 40 43N 88 1W
Onarhā, *Afghan.* 79 **B3** 35 30N 71 0 E
Oñate, *Spain* 34 **B2** 43 3N 2 25W
Onavas, *Mexico* 146 **B3** 28 28N 109 30W
Onawa, *U.S.A.* 138 **D6** 42 2N 96 2W
Onaway, *U.S.A.* 134 **C3** 45 21N 84 11W
Oncesti, *Romania* 46 **F6** 43 56N 25 52 E
Oncócua, *Angola* 103 **F2** 16 30 S 13 25 E
Onda, *Spain* 34 **F4** 39 55N 0 17W
Ondaejin, *N. Korea* 67 **D15** 41 34N 129 40 E
Ondangua, *Namibia* 104 **B2** 17 57 S 16 4 E
Ondárroa, *Spain* 34 **B2** 43 19N 2 25W
Ondas →, *Brazil* 155 **D3** 12 8 S 44 55W
Ondava →, *Czech.* 31 **C14** 48 27N 21 48 E
Onderdijk, *Neths.* 20 **C6** 52 45N 5 8 E
Ondjiva, *Angola* 103 **F3** 16 48 S 15 50 E
Ondo, *Japan* 62 **C4** 34 11N 132 32 E
Ondo, *Nigeria* 101 **D5** 7 4N 4 47 E
Ondo □, *Nigeria* 101 **D6** 7 0N 5 0 E
Öndörshil, *Mongolia* 66 **B5** 45 13N 108 5 E
Öndverðarnes, *Iceland* 12 **D1** 64 52N 24 0W
Onega, *Russia* 48 **B6** 64 0N 38 10 E
Onega →, *Russia* 48 **B6** 63 58N 37 55 E
Onega, G. of = Onezhskaya Guba, *Russia* 48 **B6** 64 30N 37 0 E
Onega, L. = Onezhskoye Ozero, *Russia* 48 **B6** 62 0N 35 30 E
Onehunga, *N.Z.* 118 **C3** 36 55 S 174 48 E
Oneida, *Ill., U.S.A.* 140 **C6** 41 4N 90 13W
Oneida, *N.Y., U.S.A.* 137 **C9** 43 5N 75 40W
Oneida L., *U.S.A.* 137 **C9** 43 12N 76 0W
O'Neill, *U.S.A.* 138 **D5** 42 30N 98 38W
Onekotan, Ostrov, *Russia* 57 **E16** 49 25N 154 45 E
Onema, *Zaïre* 103 **C4** 4 35 S 24 30 E
Oneonta, *Ala., U.S.A.* 135 **J2** 33 58N 86 29W
Oneonta, *N.Y., U.S.A.* 137 **D9** 42 26N 75 5W
Onerahi, *N.Z.* 118 **B3** 35 45 S 174 22 E
Onezhskaya Guba, *Russia* 48 **B6** 64 30N 37 0 E
Onezhskoye Ozero, *Russia* 48 **B6** 62 0N 35 30 E
Ongarue, *N.Z.* 118 **E4** 38 42 S 175 19 E
Ongea Levu, *Fiji* 121 **B3** 19 8 S 178 24W
Ongerup, *Australia* 113 **F2** 33 58 S 118 28 E
Ongjin, *N. Korea* 67 **F13** 37 56N 125 21 E
Ongkharak, *Thailand* 76 **E3** 14 8N 101 1 E
Ongniud Qi, *China* 67 **C10** 43 0N 118 38 E
Ongoka, *Zaïre* 106 **C2** 1 20 S 26 0 E
Ongole, *India* 83 **G5** 15 33N 80 2 E
Ongon, *Mongolia* 66 **B7** 45 41N 113 5 E
Onguren, *Russia* 57 **D11** 53 38N 107 36 E
Onhaye, *Belgium* 21 **H5** 50 15N 4 50 E
Oni, *Georgia* 53 **E10** 42 33N 43 26 E
Onida, *U.S.A.* 138 **C4** 44 42N 100 5W
Onilahy →, *Madag.* 105 **C7** 23 34 S 43 45 E
Onitsha, *Nigeria* 101 **D6** 6 6N 6 42 E
Onmaka, *Burma* 78 **D6** 22 17N 96 41 E
Ono, *Fiji* 121 **B2** 18 55 S 178 29 E
Ono, *Fukui, Japan* 63 **B8** 35 59N 136 29 E
Ono, *Hyōgo, Japan* 62 **C6** 34 51N 134 56 E
Onoda, *Japan* 62 **C3** 34 2N 131 25 E
Onoke, L., *N.Z.* 118 **H4** 41 22 S 175 8 E
Onomichi, *Japan* 62 **C5** 34 25N 133 12 E
Onpyŏng-ni, *S. Korea* 67 **H14** 33 25N 126 55 E
Ons, Is. d', *Spain* 36 **C2** 42 23N 8 55W
Onsala, *Sweden* 15 **G6** 57 26N 12 0 E
Onslow, *Australia* 112 **D2** 21 40 S 115 12 E
Onslow B., *U.S.A.* 135 **H7** 34 20N 77 20W
Onstwedde, *Neths.* 20 **B10** 53 2N 7 4 E
Ontake-San, *Japan* 63 **B9** 35 53N 137 29 E
Ontaneda, *Spain* 36 **B7** 43 12N 3 57W
Ontario, *Calif., U.S.A.* 145 **L9** 34 2N 117 40W
Ontario, *Oreg., U.S.A.* 142 **D5** 44 1N 117 1W
Ontario □, *Canada* 128 **B2** 52 0N 88 10W
Ontario, L., *N. Amer.* 128 **D4** 43 40N 78 0W
Onteniente, *Spain* 35 **G4** 38 50N 0 35W
Ontonagon, *U.S.A.* 138 **B10** 46 52N 89 19W
Ontur, *Spain* 35 **G3** 38 38N 1 29W
Onyx, *U.S.A.* 145 **K8** 35 41N 118 14W
Oodnadatta, *Australia* 115 **D2** 27 33 S 135 30 E
Ooldea, *Australia* 113 **F5** 30 27 S 131 50 E
Ooltgensplaat, *Neths.* 21 **E4** 51 41N 4 21 E
Oombulgurri, *Australia* 112 **C4** 15 15 S 127 45 E
Oona River, *Canada* 130 **C2** 53 57N 130 16W
Oordegem, *Belgium* 21 **G3** 50 58N 3 54 E
Oorindi, *Australia* 114 **C3** 20 40 S 141 1 E
Oost-Vlaanderen □, *Belgium* 21 **F3** 51 5N 3 50 E
Oost-Vlieland, *Neths.* 20 **B6** 53 18N 5 4 E
Oostakker, *Belgium* 21 **F3** 51 6N 3 46 E
Oostburg, *Neths.* 21 **F3** 51 19N 3 30 E
Oostduinkerke, *Belgium* 21 **F1** 51 7N 2 41 E
Oostelijk-Flevoland, *Neths.* 20 **C7** 52 31N 5 38 E
Oostende, *Belgium* 21 **F1** 51 15N 2 54 E
Oosterbeek, *Neths.* 20 **E7** 51 59N 5 51 E
Oosterdijk, *Neths.* 20 **C6** 52 44N 5 14 E
Oosterend, *Friesland, Neths.* 20 **B6** 53 24N 5 23 E
Oosterend, *Noord-Holland, Neths.* 20 **B5** 53 5N 4 52 E
Oosterhout, *Noord-Brabant, Neths.* 21 **E7** 51 53N 5 50 E
Oosterhout, *Noord-Brabant, Neths.* 21 **E5** 51 39N 4 47 E
Oosterschelde, *Neths.* 21 **E4** 51 33N 4 0 E
Oosterwolde, *Neths.* 20 **B8** 53 0N 6 17 E
Oosterzele, *Belgium* 21 **G3** 50 57N 3 48 E
Oostkamp, *Belgium* 21 **F2** 51 9N 3 14 E
Oostmalle, *Belgium* 21 **F5** 51 18N 4 44 E
Oostrozebekke, *Belgium* 21 **G2** 50 55N 3 21 E
Oostvleteven, *Belgium* 21 **G1** 50 56N 2 45 E
Oostvoorne, *Neths.* 20 **E4** 51 55N 4 5 E
Oostzaan, *Neths.* 20 **D5** 52 26N 4 52 E
Ootacamund, *India* 83 **J3** 11 30N 76 44 E
Ootha, *Australia* 117 **B7** 33 6 S 147 29 E
Ootmarsum, *Neths.* 20 **D9** 52 24N 6 54 E
Ootsa L., *Canada* 130 **C3** 53 50N 126 2W
Opaka, *Bulgaria* 43 **D11** 43 28N 26 10 E
Opala, *Russia* 57 **D16** 51 58N 156 30 E
Opala, *Zaïre* 102 **C4** 0 40 S 24 20 E
Opalenica, *Poland* 47 **C3** 52 18N 16 24 E
Opan, *Bulgaria* 43 **E10** 42 13N 25 41 E
Opanake, *Sri Lanka* 83 **L5** 6 35N 80 40 E
Opapa, *N.Z.* 118 **F5** 39 47 S 176 42 E
Opasatika, *Canada* 128 **C3** 49 30N 82 50W
Opasquia, *Canada* 131 **C10** 53 16N 93 34W
Opatija, *Croatia* 39 **C11** 45 21N 14 17 E
Opatów, *Poland* 47 **E8** 50 50N 21 27 E
Opava, *Czech.* 31 **B10** 49 57N 17 58 E
Opeinde, *Neths.* 20 **B8** 53 8N 6 4 E
Opelousas, *U.S.A.* 139 **K8** 30 35N 92 7W
Opémisca, L., *Canada* 128 **C5** 49 56N 74 52W
Open Bay Is., *N.Z.* 119 **D3** 43 51 S 168 51 E
Opglabbeek, *Belgium* 21 **F7** 51 3N 5 35 E
Opheim, *U.S.A.* 142 **B10** 48 52N 106 30W
Ophthalmia Ra., *Australia* 112 **D2** 23 15 S 119 30 E
Opi, *Nigeria* 101 **D6** 6 36N 7 28 E
Opinaca →, *Canada* 128 **B4** 52 15N 78 2W
Opinaca L., *Canada* 128 **B4** 52 39N 76 20W
Opiskotish, L., *Canada* 129 **B6** 53 10N 67 50W
Oploo, *Neths.* 21 **E7** 51 37N 5 52 E
Opmeer, *Neths.* 20 **C5** 52 42N 4 57 E
Opobo, *Nigeria* 101 **E6** 4 35N 7 34 E
Opochka, *Russia* 50 **C6** 56 42N 28 45 E
Opoczno, *Poland* 47 **D7** 51 22N 20 18 E
Opol, *Phil.* 71 **G5** 8 31N 124 34 E
Opole, *Poland* 47 **E4** 50 42N 17 58 E
Opole □, *Poland* 47 **E4** 50 40N 17 56 E
Opon = Capu-Lapu, *Phil.* 71 **F4** 10 20N 123 55 E
Oporto = Porto, *Portugal* 36 **D2** 41 8N 8 40W
Opotiki, *N.Z.* 118 **E6** 38 1 S 177 19 E
Opp, *U.S.A.* 135 **K2** 31 19N 86 13W
Oppenheim, *Germany* 27 **F4** 49 50N 8 22 E
Opperdoes, *Neths.* 20 **C6** 52 45N 5 4 E
Óppido Mamertina, *Italy* 41 **D8** 38 16N 15 59 E
Oppland fylke □, *Norway* 14 **C3** 61 15N 9 40 E
Oppstad, *Norway* 14 **D5** 60 17N 11 40 E
Oprtalj, *Croatia* 39 **C10** 45 23N 13 50 E
Opua, *N.Z.* 118 **B3** 35 19 S 174 9 E
Opunake, *N.Z.* 118 **F2** 39 26 S 173 52 E
Opuzen, *Croatia* 42 **D2** 43 1N 17 34 E
Oquawka, *U.S.A.* 140 **D6** 40 56N 90 57W
Ora, *Cyprus* 32 **E12** 34 51N 33 12 E
Ora, *Italy* 39 **B8** 46 20N 11 19 E
Ora Banda, *Australia* 113 **F3** 30 20 S 121 0 E
Oracle, *U.S.A.* 143 **K8** 32 36N 110 46W
Oradea, *Romania* 46 **B2** 47 2N 21 58 E
Öræfajökull, *Iceland* 12 **D5** 64 2N 16 39W
Orahovac, *Serbia, Yug.* 42 **E5** 42 24N 20 40 E
Orahovica, *Croatia* 42 **B2** 45 35N 17 52 E
Orai, *India* 81 **G8** 25 58N 79 30 E
Oraison, *France* 25 **E9** 43 55N 5 55 E
Oran, *Algeria* 99 **A4** 35 45N 0 39W
Oran, *Argentina* 158 **A3** 23 10 S 64 20W
Orange = Oranje →, *S. Africa* 104 **D2** 28 41 S 16 28 E
Orange, *Australia* 117 **B8** 33 15 S 149 7 E
Orange, *France* 25 **D8** 44 8N 4 47 E
Orange, *Calif., U.S.A.* 145 **M9** 33 47N 117 51W
Orange, *Mass., U.S.A.* 137 **D12** 42 35N 72 15W
Orange, *Tex., U.S.A.* 139 **K8** 30 10N 93 50W
Orange, *Va., U.S.A.* 134 **F6** 38 17N 78 5W
Orange, C., *Brazil* 153 **C7** 4 20N 51 30W
Orange Cove, *U.S.A.* 144 **J7** 36 38N 119 19W
Orange Free State □, *S. Africa* 104 **D4** 28 30 S 27 0 E
Orange Grove, *U.S.A.* 139 **M6** 27 57N 97 57W
Orange Walk, *Belize* 147 **D7** 18 6N 88 33W
Orangeburg, *U.S.A.* 135 **J5** 33 35N 80 53W
Orangeville, *Canada* 128 **D3** 43 55N 80 5W
Orangeville, *U.S.A.* 140 **B7** 42 28N 89 39W
Orani, *Phil.* 70 **D3** 14 49N 120 32 E
Oranienburg, *Germany* 26 **C9** 52 45N 13 15 E
Oranje →, *S. Africa* 104 **D2** 28 41 S 16 28 E
Oranje Vrystaat = Orange Free State □, *S. Africa* 104 **D4** 28 30 S 27 0 E
Oranjemund, *Namibia* 104 **D2** 28 38 S 16 29 E
Oranjerivier, *S. Africa* 104 **D3** 29 40 S 24 12 E
Oras, *Phil.* 70 **E5** 12 9N 125 28 E
Orašje, *Bos.-H., Yug.* 42 **B3** 45 1N 18 42 E
Orăştie, *Romania* 46 **D4** 45 50N 23 10 E
Oraşul Stalin = Braşov, *Romania* 46 **D6** 45 38N 25 35 E
Orava →, *Czech.* 31 **B12** 49 24N 19 20 E
Oravita, *Romania* 46 **B6** 45 2N 21 43 E
Orawia, *N.Z.* 119 **G2** 46 1 S 167 50 E
Orb →, *France* 24 **E7** 43 15N 3 18 E
Orba →, *Italy* 38 **D5** 44 53N 8 37 E
Ørbæk, *Denmark* 15 **J4** 55 17N 10 39 E
Orbe, *Switz.* 28 **C3** 46 43N 6 32 E
Orbec, *France* 22 **C7** 49 1N 0 23 E
Orbetello, *Italy* 39 **F8** 42 26N 11 11 E
Órbigo →, *Spain* 36 **C5** 42 5N 5 42W
Orbost, *Australia* 117 **D8** 37 40 S 148 29 E
Orce, *Spain* 35 **H2** 37 44N 2 28W
Orce →, *Spain* 35 **H2** 37 44N 2 28W
Orchies, *France* 23 **B10** 50 28N 3 14 E
Orchila, I., *Venezuela* 152 **A4** 11 48N 66 10W
Orco →, *Italy* 38 **C4** 45 10N 7 52 E
Orcopampa, *Peru* 156 **D3** 15 20 S 72 23W
Orcutt, *U.S.A.* 145 **L6** 34 52N 120 27W
Ord →, *Australia* 112 **C4** 15 33 S 128 15 E
Ord, Mt., *Australia* 112 **C4** 17 20 S 125 34 E
Ordenes, *Spain* 36 **B2** 43 5N 8 29W
Orderville, *U.S.A.* 143 **H7** 37 18N 112 43W
Ording, *Germany* 26 **A4** 54 23N 8 32 E
Ordos = Mu Us Shamo, *China* 66 **E5** 39 0N 109 0 E
Ordu, *Turkey* 89 **C7** 40 55N 37 53 E
Ordu □, *Turkey* 89 **C7** 41 0N 37 50 E
Orduña, *Álava, Spain* 34 **C7** 42 58N 2 58 E
Orduña, *Granada, Spain* 35 **H1** 37 20N 3 30W
Ordway, *U.S.A.* 138 **F3** 38 15N 103 42W
Ordzhonikidze = Vladikavkaz, *Russia* 53 **E11** 43 0N 44 35 E
Ordzhonikidze, *Ukraine* 52 **C6** 47 39N 34 3 E
Ordzhonikidze, *Uzbekistan* 55 **C4** 41 21N 69 22 E
Ordzhonikidzeabad, *Tajikistan* 55 **D4** 38 34N 69 1 E
Ore, *Zaïre* 106 **B2** 3 17N 29 30 E
Ore Mts. = Erzgebirge, *Germany* 26 **E9** 50 25N 13 0 E
Orealla, *Guyana* 153 **B6** 5 15N 57 23W
Orebić, *Croatia* 42 **D2** 43 0N 17 11 E
Örebro, *Sweden* 13 **G13** 59 20N 15 18 E
Örebro län □, *Sweden* 13 **G13** 59 27N 15 0 E
Oregon, *Ill., U.S.A.* 140 **B7** 42 1N 89 20W
Oregon, *Ohio, U.S.A.* 141 **C13** 41 38N 83 25W
Oregon, *Wis., U.S.A.* 140 **B7** 42 56N 89 23W
Oregon □, *U.S.A.* 142 **E3** 44 0N 121 0W
Oregon City, *U.S.A.* 144 **E4** 45 21N 122 35W
Orekhov, *Ukraine* 52 **C6** 47 30N 35 48 E
Orekhovo-Zuyevo, *Russia* 51 **D11** 55 50N 38 55 E
Orel, *Russia* 51 **E10** 52 57N 36 3 E
Orel →, *Ukraine* 52 **B6** 48 45N 34 20 E
Orellana, Canal de, *Spain* 37 **F5** 39 2N 6 0W
Orellana, Pantano de, *Spain* 37 **F5** 39 5N 5 10W
Orellana la Vieja, *Spain* 37 **F5** 39 1N 5 32W
Orem, *U.S.A.* 142 **F8** 40 20N 111 45W
Ören, *Turkey* 45 **G9** 37 3N 27 57 E
Orenburg, *Russia* 54 **F4** 51 45N 55 6 E
Orense, *Spain* 36 **C3** 42 19N 7 55W
Orense □, *Spain* 36 **C3** 42 15N 7 51W
Orepuki, *N.Z.* 119 **G2** 46 19 S 167 46 E
Orestiás, *Greece* 44 **C8** 41 30N 26 33 E
Øresund, *Europe* 15 **J6** 55 45N 12 45 E
Oreti →, *N.Z.* 119 **G3** 46 28 S 168 14 E
Orford Ness, *U.K.* 17 **E9** 52 6N 1 31 E
Organà, *Spain* 34 **C6** 42 13N 1 20 E
Organos, Pta. de los, *Canary Is.* 33 **F2** 28 12N 17 17W
Orgaz, *Spain* 37 **F7** 39 39N 3 53W
Orgeyev, *Moldavia* 52 **C3** 47 24N 28 50 E
Orgon, *France* 25 **E9** 43 47N 5 3 E
Orgūn, *Afghan.* 79 **B3** 32 55N 69 12 E
Orhaneli, *Turkey* 88 **D3** 39 54N 28 59 E
Orhangazi, *Turkey* 88 **C3** 40 29N 29 18 E
Orhon Gol →, *Mongolia* 64 **A5** 50 21N 106 0 E
Ória, *Italy* 41 **B10** 40 30N 17 38 E
Orient, *Australia* 115 **D3** 28 7 S 142 50 E
Orient, *U.S.A.* 140 **C2** 41 12N 94 25W
Oriental, Cordillera, *Bolivia* 157 **D4** 17 0 S 66 0W
Oriental, Cordillera, *Colombia* 152 **B3** 6 0N 73 0W
Oriente, *Argentina* 158 **D3** 38 44 S 60 37W
Origny-Ste.-Benoîte, *France* 23 **C10** 49 50N 3 30 E
Orihuela, *Spain* 35 **G4** 38 7N 0 55W
Orihuela del Tremedal, *Spain* 34 **E3** 40 33N 1 39W
Oriku, *Albania* 44 **D1** 40 20N 19 30 E
Orinduik, *Guyana* 153 **C5** 4 40N 60 3W
Orinoco →, *Venezuela* 153 **B5** 9 15N 61 30W
Orion, *U.S.A.* 140 **C6** 41 21N 90 23W
Orissa □, *India* 82 **D6** 20 0N 84 0 E
Oristano, *Italy* 40 **C1** 39 54N 8 35 E
Oristano, G. di, *Italy* 40 **C1** 39 50N 8 22 E
Orituco →, *Venezuela* 152 **B4** 8 45N 67 27W
Orizaba, *Mexico* 147 **D5** 18 50N 97 10W
Orizare, *Bulgaria* 43 **E12** 42 44N 27 39 E
Orizona, *Brazil* 155 **E2** 17 3 S 48 18W
Orjen, *Bos.-H., Yug.* 42 **E3** 42 35N 18 34 E
Orjiva, *Spain* 35 **J1** 36 53N 3 24W
Orkanger, *Norway* 14 **A3** 63 18N 9 52 E
Örkelljunga, *Sweden* 15 **H7** 56 17N 13 17 E
Örkény, *Hungary* 31 **D12** 47 9N 19 26 E
Orkla →, *Norway* 14 **A3** 63 18N 9 51 E
Orkney, *S. Africa* 104 **D4** 26 58 S 26 40 E
Orkney □, *U.K.* 18 **C6** 59 0N 3 0W
Orkney Is., *U.K.* 18 **C6** 59 0N 3 0W
Orla, *Poland* 47 **C10** 52 42N 23 20 E
Orland, *Calif., U.S.A.* 144 **F4** 39 46N 122 12W
Orland, *Ind., U.S.A.* 141 **C11** 41 47N 85 12W
Orlando, *U.S.A.* 135 **L5** 28 30N 81 25W
Orlando, C. d', *Italy* 41 **D7** 38 10N 14 43 E
Orléanais, *France* 23 **E9** 48 0N 2 0 E
Orléans, *France* 23 **E8** 47 54N 1 52 E
Orleans, *U.S.A.* 137 **B12** 44 49N 72 10W
Orléans, I. d', *Canada* 129 **C5** 46 54N 70 58W
Orlice →, *Czech.* 30 **A9** 50 5N 16 10 E
Orlické Hory, *Czech.* 31 **A9** 50 15N 16 30 E
Orlov, *Czech.* 31 **B13** 49 17N 20 51 E
Orlov Gay, *Russia* 51 **F16** 50 56N 48 19 E
Orlovat, *Serbia, Yug.* 42 **B5** 45 14N 20 33 E
Ormara, *Pakistan* 79 **D2** 25 16N 64 33 E
Ormea, *Italy* 38 **D4** 44 9N 7 54 E
Ormília, *Greece* 44 **D5** 40 16N 23 39 E
Ormoc, *Phil.* 71 **F5** 11 0N 124 37 E
Ormond, *N.Z.* 118 **E6** 38 33 S 177 56 E
Ormond Beach, *U.S.A.* 135 **L5** 29 13N 81 5W
Ormondville, *N.Z.* 118 **G5** 40 5 S 176 19 E
Ormož, *Slovenia* 39 **B13** 46 25N 16 10 E
Ormstown, *Canada* 137 **A11** 45 8N 74 0W
Ornans, *France* 23 **E13** 47 7N 6 10 E
Orne □, *France* 22 **D7** 48 40N 0 5 E
Orne →, *France* 22 **C6** 49 18N 0 15W
Orneta, *Poland* 47 **A7** 54 8N 20 9 E
Ørnhøj, *Denmark* 15 **H2** 56 13N 8 34 E
Ornö, *Sweden* 14 **E12** 59 4N 18 24 E
Örnsköldsvik, *Sweden* 14 **A12** 63 17N 18 40 E
Oro, *N. Korea* 67 **D14** 40 1N 127 27 E
Oro →, *Mexico* 146 **B3** 25 35N 105 2W
Oro Grande, *U.S.A.* 145 **L9** 34 36N 117 20W
Orobie, Alpi, *Italy* 38 **B6** 46 7N 10 0 E
Orocué, *Colombia* 152 **C3** 4 48N 71 20W
Orodo, *Nigeria* 101 **D6** 5 34N 7 4 E
Orogrande, *U.S.A.* 143 **K10** 32 20N 106 4W
Orol, *Spain* 36 **B3** 43 34N 7 39W
Oromocto, *Canada* 129 **C6** 45 54N 66 29W
Oron, *Nigeria* 101 **E6** 4 48N 8 14 E
Oron, *Switz.* 28 **C3** 46 34N 6 50 E
Orono, *Canada* 136 **C6** 43 59N 78 37W
Oropesa, *Spain* 36 **F5** 39 57N 5 10W
Oroqen Zizhiqi, *China* 65 **A7** 50 34N 123 43 E
Oroquieta, *Phil.* 71 **G4** 8 32N 123 44 E
Orós, *Brazil* 154 **C4** 6 15 S 38 55W
Orosei, G. di, *Italy* 40 **B2** 40 15N 9 40 E
Orosháza, *Hungary* 31 **E13** 46 32N 20 42 E
Orote Pen., *Guam* 121 **R15** 13 26N 144 38 E
Orotukan, *Russia* 57 **C16** 62 16N 151 42 E
Oroville, *Calif., U.S.A.* 144 **F5** 39 31N 121 30W
Oroville, *Wash., U.S.A.* 142 **B4** 48 58N 119 30W
Oroville Res., *U.S.A.* 144 **F5** 39 33N 121 29W
Orrick, *U.S.A.* 140 **E2** 39 13N 94 7W
Orroroo, *Australia* 116 **B3** 32 43 S 138 38 E
Orrville, *U.S.A.* 136 **F3** 40 50N 81 46W
Orsara di Púglia, *Italy* 41 **A8** 41 17N 15 16 E
Orsha, *Belorussia* 50 **D7** 54 30N 30 25 E
Orsières, *Switz.* 28 **D4** 46 2N 7 9 E
Orsk, *Russia* 54 **F6** 51 12N 58 34 E
Ørslev, *Denmark* 15 **J5** 55 3N 11 56 E
Orsogna, *Italy* 39 **F11** 42 13N 14 17 E
Orşova, *Romania* 46 **E3** 44 41N 22 25 E
Ørsted, *Denmark* 15 **H4** 56 30N 10 20 E
Orta, L. d', *Italy* 38 **C5** 45 48N 8 21 E
Orta Nova, *Italy* 41 **A8** 41 20N 15 40 E
Ortaca, *Turkey* 88 **E3** 36 49N 28 45 E
Ortaköy, *Çorum, Turkey* 88 **C6** 40 16N 35 15 E
Ortaköy, *Niğde, Turkey* 88 **D6** 38 44N 34 3 E
Orte, *Italy* 39 **F9** 42 28N 12 23 E
Ortegal, C., *Spain* 36 **B3** 43 43N 7 52W
Orteguaza →, *Colombia* 152 **C2** 0 43N 75 16W
Orthez, *France* 24 **E3** 43 29N 0 48W
Ortho, *Belgium* 21 **H7** 50 8N 5 37 E
Ortigueira, *Spain* 36 **B3** 43 40N 7 50W
Orting, *U.S.A.* 144 **C4** 47 6N 122 12W
Ortles, *Italy* 38 **B7** 46 31N 10 33 E
Orto, Tokay, *Kirghizia* 55 **B8** 42 20N 76 1 E
Ortón →, *Bolivia* 156 **C4** 10 50 S 67 0W
Ortona, *Italy* 39 **F11** 42 21N 14 24 E
Orūmīyeh, *Iran* 84 **B5** 37 40N 45 0 E
Orūmīyeh, Daryācheh-ye, *Iran* 84 **B5** 37 50N 45 30 E
Orune, *Italy* 40 **B2** 40 25N 9 20 E
Oruro, *Bolivia* 156 **D4** 18 0 S 67 9W
Oruro□, *Bolivia* 156 **D4** 18 40 S 67 30W
Orust, *Sweden* 15 **F5** 58 10N 11 40 E
Oruzgān □, *Afghan.* 79 **B2** 33 30N 66 0 E
Orvault, *France* 22 **E5** 47 17N 1 38W
Orvieto, *Italy* 39 **F9** 42 43N 12 8 E
Orwell, *U.S.A.* 136 **E4** 41 32N 80 52W
Orwell →, *U.K.* 17 **E9** 52 2N 1 12 E
Oryakhovo, *Bulgaria* 43 **D8** 43 40N 23 57 E
Orzinuovi, *Italy* 38 **C6** 45 24N 9 55 E
Orzyc →, *Poland* 47 **C8** 52 46N 21 14 E
Orzysz, *Poland* 47 **B8** 53 50N 21 58 E
Osa, *Russia* 54 **C4** 57 17N 55 26 E
Osa →, *Poland* 47 **B5** 53 33N 18 46 E
Osa, Pen. de, *Costa Rica* 148 **E3** 8 0N 84 0W
Osage, *Iowa, U.S.A.* 138 **D8** 43 15N 92 50W
Osage, *Wyo., U.S.A.* 138 **D2** 43 59N 104 25W
Osage →, *U.S.A.* 140 **F5** 38 35N 91 57W
Osage City, *U.S.A.* 138 **F7** 38 43N 95 51W
Ōsaka, *Japan* 63 **C7** 34 40N 135 30 E
Ōsaka □, *Japan* 63 **C7** 34 30N 135 30 E
Ōsaka-Wan, *Japan* 63 **C7** 34 30N 135 18 E
Osan, *S. Korea* 67 **F14** 37 11N 127 4 E
Osawatomie, *U.S.A.* 138 **F7** 38 30N 94 55W
Osborne, *U.S.A.* 138 **F5** 39 30N 98 45W
Osceola, *Ark., U.S.A.* 139 **H10** 35 40N 90 0W
Osceola, *Iowa, U.S.A.* 140 **C3** 41 3N 93 20W
Osceola, *Mo., U.S.A.* 140 **F3** 38 3N 93 42W
Oschatz, *Germany* 26 **D9** 51 17N 13 8 E
Oschersleben, *Germany* 26 **C7** 52 2N 11 13 E
Ōschiri, *Italy* 40 **B2** 40 43N 9 7 E
Oscoda, *U.S.A.* 136 **B1** 44 26N 83 20W
Osečina, *Serbia, Yug.* 42 **C4** 44 23N 19 34 E
Ösel = Saaremaa, *Estonia* 50 **B3** 58 30N 22 30 E
Osëry, *Russia* 51 **D11** 54 52N 38 28 E
Osgood, *U.S.A.* 141 **E11** 39 8N 85 18W
Osh, *Kirghizia* 55 **C6** 40 37N 72 49 E
Oshawa, *Canada* 128 **D4** 43 50N 78 50W
Oshima, *Japan* 62 **D4** 33 55N 132 14 E
Oshkosh, *Nebr., U.S.A.* 138 **E3** 41 27N 102 20W
Oshkosh, *Wis., U.S.A.* 138 **C10** 44 3N 88 35W
Oshmyany, *Belorussia* 50 **D4** 54 26N 25 52 E
Oshnovīyeh, *Iran* 84 **B5** 37 2N 45 6 E
Oshogbo, *Nigeria* 101 **D5** 7 48N 4 37 E
Oshtorīnān, *Iran* 85 **C6** 34 1N 48 38 E
Oshwe, *Zaïre* 102 **C3** 3 25 S 19 28 E
Osica de Jos, *Romania* 46 **E5** 44 14N 24 20 E
Osieczna, *Poland* 47 **D3** 51 55N 16 40 E
Osijek, *Croatia* 42 **B3** 45 34N 18 41 E
Ōsilo, *Italy* 40 **B1** 40 45N 8 41 E
Osimo, *Italy* 39 **E10** 43 28N 13 30 E
Osintorf, *Belorussia* 50 **D7** 54 40N 30 39 E
Osipenko = Berdyansk, *Ukraine* 52 **C7** 46 45N 36 50 E
Osipovichi, *Belorussia* 50 **E6** 53 19N 28 33 E
Osizweni, *S. Africa* 105 **D5** 27 49 S 30 7 E
Oskaloosa, *U.S.A.* 140 **C4** 41 18N 92 40W
Oskarshamn, *Sweden* 13 **H14** 57 15N 16 27 E
Oskélanéo, *Canada* 128 **C4** 48 5N 75 15W
Oskol →, *Ukraine* 51 **G10** 49 6N 37 25 E
Oslo, *Norway* 14 **E4** 59 55N 10 45 E
Oslob, *Phil.* 71 **G4** 9 31N 123 26 E
Oslofjorden, *Norway* 14 **E4** 59 20N 10 35 E
Osmanabad, *India* 82 **E3** 18 5N 76 10 E
Osmancık, *Turkey* 52 **F6** 40 58N 34 47 E
Osmaniye, *Turkey* 88 **E7** 37 5N 36 10 E
Ösmo, *Sweden* 14 **F11** 58 58N 17 55 E
Osnabrück, *Germany* 26 **C4** 52 16N 8 2 E
Ośno Lubuskie, *Poland* 47 **C1** 52 28N 14 51 E
Osobláha, *Czech.* 31 **A10** 50 17N 17 44 E
Osogovska Planina, *Macedonia, Yug.* 42 **E7** 42 10N 22 30 E
Osor, *Italy* 39 **D11** 44 42N 14 24 E
Osorio, *Brazil* 159 **B5** 29 53 S 50 17W
Osorno, *Chile* 160 **B2** 40 25 S 73 0W
Osorno, *Spain* 36 **C6** 42 24N 4 22W
Osorno □, *Chile* 160 **B2** 40 34 S 73 9W
Osorno, Vol., *Chile* 160 **B2** 41 0 S 72 30W
Osoyoos, *Canada* 130 **D5** 49 0N 119 30W
Ospika →, *Canada* 130 **B4** 56 20N 124 0W
Osprey Reef, *Australia* 114 **A4** 13 52 S 146 36 E
Oss, *Neths.* 20 **E7** 51 46N 5 32 E
Ossa, Mt., *Australia* 114 **G4** 41 52 S 146 3 E

Päijänne 245


Óssa, Oros, Greece 44 E4 39 47N 22 42 E
Ossa de Montiel, Spain 35 G2 38 58N 2 45W
Ossabaw I., U.S.A. 135 K5 31 45N 81 8W
Osse →, France 24 D4 44 7N 0 17 E
Ossendrecht, Neths. 21 F4 51 24N 4 20 E
Ossining, U.S.A. 137 E11 41 9N 73 50W
Ossipee, U.S.A. 137 C13 43 41N 71 9W
Ossokmanuan L., Canada 129 B7 53 25N 65 0W
Ossora, Russia 57 D17 59 20N 163 13 E
Ostashkov, Russia 50 C8 57 4N 33 2 E
Oste →, Germany 26 B5 53 30N 9 12 E
Ostend = Oostende, Belgium 21 F1 51 15N 2 54 E
Oster, Ukraine 50 F7 50 57N 30 53 E
Osterburg, Germany 26 C7 52 47N 11 44 E
Osterburken, Germany 27 F5 49 26N 9 25 E
Österdalälven →, Sweden 13 F12 61 30N 13 45 E
Östergötlands län □, Sweden 15 F9 58 35N 15 45 E
Osterholz-Scharmbeck, Germany 26 B4 53 14N 8 48 E
Østerild, Denmark 15 G2 57 2N 8 51 E
Ostermundigen, Switz. 28 C4 46 58N 7 27 E
Östersund, Sweden 14 A8 63 10N 14 38 E
Østfold fylke □, Norway 14 E5 59 25N 11 25 E
Ostfriesische Inseln, Germany 26 B3 53 45N 7 15 E
Ostfriesland, Germany 26 B3 53 20N 7 30 E
Óstia, Lido di, Italy 40 A5 41 43N 12 17 E
Ostiglía, Italy 39 C8 45 4N 11 9 E
Ostra, Italy 39 E10 43 40N 13 5 E
Ostrava, Czech. 31 B11 49 51N 18 18 E
Ostróda, Poland 47 B6 53 42N 19 58 E
Ostrog, Ukraine 50 F5 50 20N 26 30 E
Ostrogozhsk, Russia 51 F11 50 55N 39 7 E
Ostrogróg Sźamotuły, Poland 47 C3 52 37N 16 33 E
Ostrołęka, Poland 47 B8 53 4N 21 32 E
Ostrołeka □, Poland 47 C8 53 0N 21 30 E
Ostrov, Bulgaria 43 D9 43 40N 24 9 E
Ostrov, Romania 46 E8 44 6N 27 24 E
Ostrov, Russia 50 C6 57 25N 28 20 E
Ostrów Lubelski, Poland 47 D9 51 29N 22 51 E
Ostrów Mazowiecka, Poland 47 C8 52 50N 21 51 E
Ostrów Wielkopolski, Poland 47 D4 51 36N 17 44 E
Ostrowiec-Świętokrzyski, Poland 47 E8 50 55N 21 22 E
Ostrozac, Bos.-H., Yug. 42 D2 43 43N 17 49 E
Ostrzeszów, Poland 47 D4 51 25N 17 52 E
Ostseebad-Külungsborn, Germany 26 A7 54 10N 11 40 E
Osttirol □, Austria 27 J8 46 50N 12 30 E
Ostuni, Italy 41 B10 40 44N 17 34 E
Osum →, Bulgaria 43 D9 43 40N 24 50 E
Osumi →, Albania 44 D2 40 40N 20 10 E
Ōsumi-Hantō, Japan 62 F2 31 20N 130 55 E
Ōsumi-Kaikyō, Japan 61 J5 30 55N 131 0 E
Ōsumi-Shotō, Japan 61 J5 30 30N 130 0 E
Osuna, Spain 37 H5 37 14N 5 8W
Oswego, U.S.A. 137 C8 43 29N 76 30W
Oswestry, U.K. 16 E4 52 52N 3 3W
Oświecim, Poland 31 A12 50 2N 19 11 E
Ōta, Japan 63 A11 36 18N 139 22 E
Ota-Gawa →, Japan 62 C4 34 21N 132 18 E
Otago □, N.Z. 119 E4 45 15 S 170 0 E
Otago Harbour, N.Z. 119 F5 45 47 S 170 42 E
Otago Pen., N.Z. 119 F5 45 48 S 170 39 E
Otahuhu, N.Z. 118 C3 36 56 S 174 51 E
Ōtake, Japan 62 C4 34 12N 132 13 E
Ōtaki, Japan 63 B12 35 17N 140 15 E
Otaki, N.Z. 118 G4 40 45 S 175 10 E
Otane, N.Z. 118 F5 39 54 S 176 39 E
Otar, Kazakhstan 55 B7 43 32N 75 12 E
Otaru, Japan 60 C10 43 10N 141 0 E
Otaru-Wan = Ishikari-Wan, Japan 60 C10 43 25N 141 1 E
Otautau, N.Z. 119 G3 46 9 S 168 1 E
Otava →, Czech. 30 B7 49 26N 14 12 E
Otavalo, Ecuador 152 C2 0 13N 78 20W
Otavi, Namibia 104 B2 19 40 S 17 24 E
Otchinjau, Angola 103 F2 16 30 S 13 56 E
Otelec, Romania 46 D1 45 36N 20 50 E
Otero de Rey, Spain 36 B3 43 6N 7 36W
Othello, U.S.A. 142 C4 46 53N 119 8W
Othonoí, Greece 44 E1 39 52N 19 22 E
Óthris, Óros, Greece 45 E4 39 4N 22 42 E
Otira, N.Z. 119 C6 42 49 S 171 35 E
Otira Gorge, N.Z. 119 C6 42 53 S 171 33 E
Otis, U.S.A. 138 E3 40 12N 102 58W
Otjiwarongo, Namibia 104 C2 20 30 S 16 33 E
Otmuchów, Poland 47 E4 50 28N 17 10 E
Oto Tolu Group, Tonga 121 Q13 20 21 S 174 32W
Otočac, Croatia 39 D12 44 53N 15 12 E
Otoineppu, Japan 60 B11 44 44N 142 16 E
Oton, Phil. 71 F4 10 42N 122 29 E
Otorohanga, N.Z. 118 E4 38 12 S 175 14 E
Otoskwin →, Canada 128 B2 52 13N 88 6W
Otosquen, Canada 131 C8 53 17N 102 1W
Ōtoyo, Japan 62 D5 33 43N 133 45 E
Otranto, Italy 41 B11 40 9N 18 28 E
Otranto, C. d', Italy 41 B11 40 7N 18 30 E
Otranto, Str. of, Italy 41 B11 40 15N 18 40 E
Otse, S. Africa 104 D4 25 2 S 25 45 E
Otsego, U.S.A. 141 B11 42 27N 85 42W
Ōtsu, Japan 63 B7 35 0N 135 50 E
Ōtsuki, Japan 63 B10 35 36N 138 57 E
Otta, Norway 14 C3 61 46N 9 32 E
Ottapalam, India 83 J3 10 46N 76 23 E
Ottawa = Outaouais →, Canada 128 C5 45 27N 74 8W
Ottawa, Canada 128 C4 45 27N 75 42W
Ottawa, Ill., U.S.A. 138 E10 41 20N 88 55W
Ottawa, Kans., U.S.A. 138 F7 38 40N 95 6W
Ottawa, Ohio, U.S.A. 141 C12 41 1N 84 3W
Ottawa Is., Canada 127 C11 59 35N 80 10W
Ottélé, Cameroon 101 E7 3 38N 11 19 E
Ottensheim, Austria 30 C7 48 21N 14 12 E
Otter L., Canada 131 B8 55 35N 104 39W
Otter Rapids, Ont., Canada 128 B3 50 11N 81 39W
Otter Rapids, Sask., Canada 131 B8 55 38N 104 44W
Otterbein, U.S.A. 141 D9 40 29N 87 6W
Otterndorf, Germany 26 B4 53 47N 8 52 E
Otterup, Denmark 15 J4 55 30N 10 22 E
Otterville, Canada 136 D4 42 55N 80 36W
Otterville, U.S.A. 140 F4 38 42N 93 0W
Ottignies, Belgium 21 G5 50 40N 4 33 E
Otto Beit Bridge, Zimbabwe 107 F2 15 59 S 28 56 E
Ottosdal, S. Africa 104 D4 26 46 S 25 59 E
Ottoshoop, S. Africa 104 D4 25 45 S 25 58 E
Ottoville, U.S.A. 141 D12 40 57N 84 22W
Ottsjön, Sweden 14 A7 63 13N 13 2 E
Ottumwa, U.S.A. 140 C4 41 0N 92 25W
Otu, Nigeria 101 D5 8 14N 3 22 E
Otukpa, Nigeria 101 D6 7 9N 7 41 E
Oturkpo, Nigeria 101 D6 7 16N 8 8 E
Otway, B., Chile 160 D2 53 30 S 74 0W
Otway, C., Australia 116 E5 38 52 S 143 30 E
Otwock, Poland 47 C8 52 5N 21 20 E
Ötz, Austria 30 D3 47 13N 10 53 E
Ötz →, Austria 30 D3 47 14N 10 50 E
Ötztaler Alpen, Austria 30 E4 46 56N 11 0 E
Ou →, Laos 76 B4 20 4N 102 13 E
Ou Neua, Laos 76 A3 22 18N 101 48 E
Ou-Sammyaku, Japan 60 E10 39 20N 140 35 E
Ouachita →, U.S.A. 139 K9 31 38N 91 49W
Ouachita, L., U.S.A. 139 H8 34 40N 93 25W
Ouachita Mts., U.S.A. 139 H7 34 50N 94 30W
Ouaco, N. Cal. 121 T18 20 50 S 164 29 E
Ouadâne, Mauritania 98 D2 20 50N 11 40W
Ouadda, C.A.R. 102 A4 8 15N 22 20 E
Ouagadougou, Burkina Faso 101 C4 12 25N 1 30W
Ouagam, Chad 97 F2 14 22N 14 42 E
Ouahigouya, Burkina Faso 100 C4 13 31N 2 25W
Ouahila, Algeria 98 C3 27 50N 5 0W
Ouahran = Oran, Algeria 99 A4 35 45N 0 39W
Oualâta, Mauritania 100 B3 17 20N 6 55W
Ouallene, Algeria 99 D5 24 41N 1 11 E
Ouanda Djallé, C.A.R. 102 A4 8 55N 22 53 E
Ouandago, C.A.R. 102 A3 7 13N 18 50 E
Ouango, C.A.R. 102 B4 4 19N 22 30 E
Ouarâne, Mauritania 98 D2 21 0N 10 30W
Ouargla, Algeria 99 B6 31 59N 5 16 E
Ouarkziz, Djebel, Algeria 98 C3 28 50N 8 0W
Ouarzazate, Morocco 98 B3 30 55N 6 50W
Ouatagouna, Mali 101 B5 15 11N 0 43 E
Ouatere, C.A.R. 102 A3 5 30N 19 8 E
Oubangi →, Zaïre 102 C3 0 30 S 17 50 E
Oubarakai, O. →, Algeria 99 C6 27 20N 9 0 E
Oubatche, N. Cal. 121 T18 20 26 S 164 39 E
Ouche →, France 23 E12 47 6N 5 16 E
Oud-Beijerland, Neths. 20 E4 51 50N 4 25 E
Oud-Gastel, Neths. 21 E4 51 35N 4 28 E
Oud Turnhout, Belgium 21 F6 51 19N 5 0 E
Ouddorp, Neths. 20 E3 51 50N 3 57 E
Oude-Pekela, Neths. 20 B10 53 6N 7 0 E
Oude Rijn →, Neths. 20 D4 52 12N 4 24 E
Oudega, Neths. 20 B8 53 8N 6 0 E
Oudenaarde, Belgium 21 G3 50 50N 3 37 E
Oudenbosch, Neths. 21 E5 51 35N 4 32 E
Oudenburg, Belgium 21 F2 51 11N 3 1 E
Ouderkerk, Utrecht, Neths. 20 D5 52 18N 4 55 E
Ouderkerk, Zuid-Holland, Neths. 20 E5 51 56N 4 38 E
Oudeschild, Neths. 20 B5 53 2N 4 50 E
Oudewater, Neths. 20 D5 52 2N 4 52 E
Oudkarspel, Neths. 20 C5 52 43N 4 49 E
Oudon, France 22 E5 47 22N 1 19W
Oudtshoorn, S. Africa 104 E3 33 35 S 22 14 E
Oued Zem, Morocco 98 B3 32 52N 6 34W
Ouégoa, N. Cal. 121 T18 20 20 S 164 26 E
Ouellé, Ivory C. 100 D4 7 26N 4 1W
Ouen, I., N. Cal. 121 V20 22 26 S 166 49 E
Ouenza, Algeria 99 A6 35 57N 8 4 E
Ouessa, Burkina Faso 100 C4 11 4N 2 47W
Ouessant, I. d', France 22 D1 48 28N 5 6W
Ouesso, Congo 102 B3 1 37N 16 5 E
Ouest, Pte., Canada 129 C7 49 52N 64 40W
Ouezzane, Morocco 98 B3 34 51N 5 35W
Ouffet, Belgium 21 H6 50 26N 5 28 E
Ouidah, Benin 101 D5 6 25N 2 0 E
Ouistreham, France 22 C6 49 17N 0 18W
Oujda, Morocco 99 B4 34 41N 1 55W
Oujeft, Mauritania 98 D2 20 2N 13 0W
Ould Yenjé, Mauritania 100 B2 15 38N 12 16W
Ouled Djellal, Algeria 99 B6 34 28N 5 2 E
Ouled Naïl, Mts. des, Algeria 99 B5 34 30N 3 30 E
Oulmès, Morocco 98 B3 33 17N 6 0W
Oulu, Finland 12 D18 65 1N 25 29 E
Oulu □ = Oulun lääni □, Finland 12 D19 64 36N 27 20 E
Oulujärvi, Finland 12 D19 64 25N 27 15 E
Oulujoki →, Finland 12 D18 65 1N 25 30 E
Oulun lääni □, Finland 12 D19 64 36N 27 20 E
Oulx, Italy 38 C3 45 2N 6 49 E
Oum Chalouba, Chad 97 E4 15 48N 20 46 E
Oum-el-Bouaghi, Algeria 99 A6 35 55N 7 6 E
Oum el Ksi, Algeria 98 C3 29 4N 6 59W
Oum-er-Rbia, O. →, Morocco 98 B3 33 19N 8 21W
Oumè, Ivory C. 100 D3 6 21N 5 27W
Ounane, Dj., Algeria 99 C6 25 4N 7 19 E
Ounguati, Namibia 104 C2 22 0 S 15 46 E
Ounianga-Kébir, Chad 97 E4 19 4N 20 29 E
Ounianga Sérir, Chad 97 E4 18 54N 20 51 E
Our →, Lux. 21 J8 49 55N 6 5 E
Ouray, U.S.A. 143 G10 38 3N 107 40W
Ourcq →, France 23 C10 49 1N 3 1 E
Oureg, Oued el →, Algeria 99 B5 32 34N 2 10 E
Ourém, Brazil 154 B2 1 33 S 47 6W
Ouricuri, Brazil 154 C3 7 53 S 40 5W
Ourinhos, Brazil 159 A6 23 0 S 49 54W
Ourique, Portugal 37 H2 37 38N 8 16W
Ouro Fino, Brazil 159 A6 22 16 S 46 25W
Ouro Prêto, Brazil 155 F3 20 20 S 43 30W
Ouro Sogui, Senegal 100 B2 15 36N 13 19W
Oursi, Burkina Faso 101 C4 14 41N 0 27W
Ourthe →, Belgium 21 H7 50 29N 5 35 E
Ouse, Australia 114 G4 42 38 S 146 42 E
Ouse →, E. Susx., U.K. 17 G8 50 43N 0 3 E
Ouse →, N. Yorks., U.K. 16 C8 54 3N 0 7 E
Oust, France 24 F5 42 52N 1 13 E
Oust →, France 22 E4 47 35N 2 6W
Outaouais →, Canada 128 C5 45 27N 74 8W
Outardes →, Canada 129 C6 49 24N 69 30W
Outat Oulad el Haj, Morocco 99 B4 33 22N 3 42W
Outer Hebrides, U.K. 18 D1 57 30N 7 40W
Outer I., Canada 129 B8 51 10N 58 35W
Outes, Spain 36 C2 42 52N 8 55W
Outjo, Namibia 104 C2 20 5 S 16 7 E
Outlook, Canada 131 C7 51 30N 107 0W
Outlook, U.S.A. 138 A2 48 53N 104 46W
Outreau, France 23 B8 50 40N 1 36 E
Ouvèze →, France 25 E8 43 59N 4 51 E
Ouyen, Australia 116 C5 35 1 S 142 22 E
Ouzouer-le-Marché, France 23 E8 47 54N 1 32 E
Ovada, Italy 38 D5 44 39N 8 40 E
Ovalau, Fiji 121 A2 17 40 S 178 48 E
Ovalle, Chile 158 C1 30 33 S 71 18W
Ovar, Portugal 36 E2 40 51N 8 40W
Ovejas, Colombia 152 B2 9 32N 75 14W
Ovens, Australia 117 D7 36 35 S 146 46 E
Overdinkel, Neths. 20 D10 52 14N 7 2 E
Overflakkee, Neths. 20 E4 51 44N 4 10 E
Overijse, Belgium 21 G5 50 47N 4 32 E
Overijssel □, Neths. 20 D9 52 25N 6 35 E
Overijsselsch Kanaal →, Neths. 20 C8 52 31N 6 6 E
Overland, U.S.A. 140 F6 38 41N 90 23W
Overpelt, Belgium 21 F6 51 12N 5 20 E
Overton, U.S.A. 145 J12 36 32N 114 31W
Övertorneå, Sweden 12 C17 66 23N 23 38 E
Ovid, Colo., U.S.A. 138 E3 41 0N 102 17W
Ovid, Mich., U.S.A. 141 A12 43 1N 84 22W
Ovidiopol, Ukraine 52 C4 46 15N 30 30 E
Oviedo, Spain 36 B5 43 25N 5 50W
Oviedo □, Spain 36 B5 43 20N 6 0W
Oviken, Sweden 14 A8 63 0N 14 23 E
Oviksfjällen, Sweden 14 B7 63 0N 13 49 E
Övör Hangay □, Mongolia 66 B2 45 0N 102 30 E
Ovoro, Nigeria 101 D6 5 26N 7 16 E
Ovruch, Ukraine 50 F6 51 25N 28 45 E
Owaka, N.Z. 119 G4 46 27 S 169 40 E
Owando, Congo 102 C3 0 29 S 15 55 E
Owase, Japan 63 C8 34 7N 136 12 E
Owatonna, U.S.A. 138 C8 44 3N 93 10W
Owbeh, Afghan. 79 B1 34 28N 63 10 E
Owego, U.S.A. 137 D8 42 6N 76 17W
Owen, Australia 116 C3 34 15 S 138 32 E
Owen Falls, Uganda 106 B3 0 30N 33 5 E
Owen Mt., N.Z. 119 B7 41 35 S 172 33 E
Owen Sound, Canada 128 D3 44 35N 80 55W
Owen Stanley Ra., Papua N. G. 120 E4 8 30 S 147 0 E
Owendo, Gabon 102 B1 0 17N 9 30 E
Owens →, U.S.A. 144 J9 36 32N 117 59W
Owens L., U.S.A. 145 J9 36 20N 118 0W
Owensboro, U.S.A. 141 G9 37 40N 87 5W
Owensville, Ind., U.S.A. 141 F9 38 16N 87 41W
Owensville, Mo., U.S.A. 140 F5 38 20N 91 30W
Owenton, U.S.A. 141 F12 38 32N 84 50W
Owerri, Nigeria 101 D6 5 29N 7 0 E
Owhango, N.Z. 118 F4 39 0 S 175 23 E
Owingsville, U.S.A. 141 F13 38 9N 83 46W
Owl →, Canada 131 B10 57 51N 92 44W
Owo, Nigeria 101 D6 7 10N 5 39 E
Owosso, U.S.A. 141 B12 43 0N 84 10W
Owyhee, U.S.A. 142 F5 42 0N 116 3W
Owyhee →, U.S.A. 142 E5 43 46N 117 2W
Owyhee, L., U.S.A. 142 E5 43 40N 117 16W
Ox Mts., Ireland 19 B3 54 6N 9 0W
Oxapampa, Peru 156 C2 10 33 S 75 26W
Oxelösund, Sweden 15 F11 58 43N 17 15 E
Oxford, N.Z. 119 D7 43 18 S 172 11 E
Oxford, U.K. 17 F6 51 45N 1 15W
Oxford, Iowa, U.S.A. 140 C5 41 43N 91 47W
Oxford, Mich., U.S.A. 141 B13 42 49N 83 16W
Oxford, Miss., U.S.A. 139 H10 34 22N 89 30W
Oxford, N.C., U.S.A. 135 G6 36 19N 78 36W
Oxford, Ohio, U.S.A. 141 E12 39 30N 84 40W
Oxford L., Canada 131 C9 54 51N 95 37W
Oxfordshire □, U.K. 17 F6 51 45N 1 15W
Oxía, Greece 45 F3 38 16N 21 5 E
Oxílithos, Greece 45 F6 38 35N 24 7 E
Oxley, Australia 116 C6 34 11 S 144 6 E
Oxnard, U.S.A. 145 L7 34 10N 119 14W
Oxus = Amudarya →, Uzbekistan 56 E6 43 40N 59 0 E
Oya, Malaysia 75 B4 2 55N 111 55 E
Oyabe, Japan 63 A8 36 47N 136 56 E
Oyama, Japan 63 A11 36 18N 139 48 E
Oyana, Japan 62 E2 32 32N 130 30 E
Oyapock →, Fr. Guiana 153 C7 4 8N 51 40W
Oyem, Gabon 102 B2 1 34N 11 31 E
Oyen, Canada 131 C6 51 22N 110 28W
Øyeren, Norway 14 E5 59 50N 11 15 E
Oykel →, U.K. 18 D4 57 55N 4 26W
Oymyakon, Russia 57 C15 63 25N 142 44 E
Oyo, Nigeria 101 D5 7 46N 3 56 E
Oyo □, Nigeria 101 D5 8 0N 3 30 E
Oyón, Peru 156 C2 10 37 S 76 47W
Oyonnax, France 25 B9 46 16N 5 40 E
Oyster Bay, U.S.A. 137 F11 40 52N 73 32W
Oytal, Kazakhstan 55 B6 42 54N 73 17 E
Ōyūbari, Japan 60 C11 43 1N 142 5 E
Özalp, Turkey 89 D10 38 39N 43 59 E
Ozamis, Phil. 71 G4 8 15N 123 50 E
Ozark, Ala., U.S.A. 135 K3 31 29N 85 39W
Ozark, Ark., U.S.A. 139 H8 35 30N 93 50W
Ozark, Mo., U.S.A. 139 G8 37 0N 93 15W
Ozark Plateau, U.S.A. 139 G9 37 20N 91 40W
Ozarks, L. of the, U.S.A. 140 F4 38 10N 92 40W
Ózd, Hungary 31 C13 48 14N 20 15 E
Ozërnyy, Russia 54 F7 51 8N 60 50 E
Ozette, L., U.S.A. 144 B2 48 6N 124 38W
Ozieri, Italy 40 B2 40 35N 9 0 E
Ozimek, Poland 47 E5 50 41N 18 11 E
Ozona, U.S.A. 139 K4 30 43N 101 11W
Ozorków, Poland 47 D6 51 57N 19 16 E
Ozren, Bos.-H., Yug. 42 D3 43 55N 18 29 E
Ozu, Ehime, Japan 62 D4 33 30N 132 33 E
Ozu, Kumamoto, Japan 62 E2 32 52N 130 52 E
Ozuluama, Mexico 147 C5 21 40N 97 50W
Ozun, Romania 46 D6 45 47N 25 50 E
Ozurgety, Georgia 53 F10 41 55N 42 2 E


# P


P.K. le Roux Dam, S. Africa 104 E3 30 4 S 24 40 E
Pa, Burkina Faso 100 C4 11 33N 3 19W
Pa-an, Burma 78 G6 16 51N 97 40 E
Pa Mong Dam, Thailand 76 D4 18 0N 102 22 E
Paagoumène, N. Cal. 121 T18 20 29 S 164 11 E
Paal, Belgium 21 F6 51 2N 5 10 E
Paama, Vanuatu 121 F6 16 28 S 168 14 E
Paamiut = Frederikshåb, Greenland 6 C5 62 0N 49 43W
Paar →, Germany 27 G6 48 13N 10 59 E
Paarl, S. Africa 104 E2 33 45 S 18 56 E
Paatsi →, Russia 12 B20 68 55N 29 0 E
Paauilo, U.S.A. 132 H17 20 3N 155 22W
Pab Hills, Pakistan 79 D2 26 30N 66 45 E
Pabianice, Poland 47 D6 51 40N 19 20 E
Pabna, Bangla. 78 C2 24 1N 89 18 E
Pabo, Uganda 106 B3 3 1N 32 10 E
Pacaás Novos, Serra dos, Brazil 157 C5 10 45 S 64 15W
Pacaipampa, Peru 156 B2 5 35 S 79 39W
Pacaja →, Brazil 154 B1 1 56 S 50 50W
Pacajus, Brazil 154 B4 4 10 S 38 31W
Pacaraima, Sierra, Venezuela 153 C5 4 0N 62 30W
Pacarán, Peru 156 C2 12 50 S 76 3W
Pacaraos, Peru 156 C2 11 12 S 76 42W
Pacasmayo, Peru 156 B2 7 20 S 79 35W
Paceco, Italy 40 E5 37 59N 12 32 E
Pachacamac, Peru 156 C2 12 14 S 77 53W
Pachhar, India 80 G7 24 40N 77 42 E
Pachino, Italy 41 F8 36 43N 15 4 E
Pachitea →, Peru 156 B3 8 46 S 74 33W
Pachiza, Peru 156 B2 7 16 S 76 46W
Pacho, Colombia 152 B3 5 8N 74 10W
Pachora, India 82 D2 20 38N 75 29 E
Pachuca, Mexico 147 C5 20 10N 98 40W
Pacific, Canada 130 C3 54 48N 128 28W
Pacific, U.S.A. 140 F6 38 29N 90 45W
Pacific-Antarctic Ridge, Pac. Oc. 123 M16 43 0 S 115 0W
Pacific Grove, U.S.A. 144 J5 36 38N 121 58W
Pacific Ocean, Pac. Oc. 123 G14 10 0N 140 0W
Pacifica, U.S.A. 144 H4 37 36N 122 30W
Pacitan, Indonesia 75 D4 8 12 S 111 7 E
Packsaddle, Australia 116 A4 30 36 S 141 58 E
Packwood, U.S.A. 144 D5 46 36N 121 40W
Pacov, Czech. 30 B8 49 27N 15 0 E
Pacsa, Hungary 31 E10 46 44N 17 2 E
Pacuí →, Brazil 155 E2 16 46 S 45 1W
Paczków, Poland 47 E4 50 28N 17 0 E
Padaido, Kepulauan, Indonesia 73 B5 1 5 S 138 0 E
Padang, Indonesia 74 C2 1 0 S 100 20 E
Padang Endau, Malaysia 74 B2 2 40N 103 38 E
Padangpanjang, Indonesia 74 C2 0 40 S 100 20 E
Padangsidempuan, Indonesia 74 B1 1 30N 99 15 E
Padangtikar, Indonesia 75 C3 0 44 S 109 15 E
Padatchuang, Burma 78 F5 19 46N 94 48 E
Padauari →, Brazil 153 D5 0 15 S 64 5W
Padborg, Denmark 15 K3 54 49N 9 21 E
Padcaya, Bolivia 157 E5 21 52 S 64 48W
Paddockwood, Canada 131 C7 53 30N 105 30W
Paderborn, Germany 26 D4 51 42N 8 44 E
Padeşul, Romania 46 D3 45 40N 22 22 E
Padilla, Bolivia 157 D5 19 19 S 64 20W
Padina, Romania 46 E8 44 50N 27 8 E
Padloping Island, Canada 127 B13 67 0N 62 50W
Padma →, Bangla. 78 D3 23 22N 90 32 E
Padmanabhapuram, India 83 K3 8 16N 77 17 E
Pádova, Italy 39 C8 45 24N 11 52 E
Padra, India 80 H5 22 15N 73 7 E
Padrauna, India 81 F10 26 54N 83 59 E
Padre Burgos, Phil. 71 F5 10 1N 125 0 E
Padre I., U.S.A. 139 M6 27 0N 97 20W
Padro, Mte., France 25 F12 42 28N 8 59 E
Padrón, Spain 36 C2 42 41N 8 39W
Padstow, U.K. 17 G3 50 33N 4 57W
Padua = Pádova, Italy 39 C8 45 24N 11 52 E
Paducah, Ky., U.S.A. 134 G1 37 0N 88 40W
Paducah, Tex., U.S.A. 139 H4 34 3N 100 16W
Padul, Spain 37 H7 37 1N 3 38W
Padula, Italy 41 B8 40 20N 15 40 E
Padwa, India 82 E6 18 27N 82 47 E
Paekakariki, N.Z. 118 G3 40 59 S 174 58 E
Paengaroa, N.Z. 118 D5 37 49 S 176 29 E
Paengnyong-do, S. Korea 67 F13 37 57N 124 40 E
Paeroa, N.Z. 118 D4 37 23 S 175 41 E
Paesana, Italy 38 D4 44 40N 7 18 E
Paete, Phil. 70 D3 14 23N 121 29 E
Pafúri, Mozam. 105 C5 22 28 S 31 17 E
Pag, Croatia 39 D11 44 30N 14 50 E
Paga, Ghana 101 C4 11 1N 1 8W
Pagadian, Phil. 71 H4 7 55N 123 30 E
Pagai Selatan, P., Indonesia 74 C2 3 0 S 100 15 E
Pagai Utara, Indonesia 74 C2 2 35 S 100 0 E
Pagalu = Annobón, Atl. Oc. 93 G4 1 25 S 5 36 E
Pagastikós Kólpos, Greece 44 E5 39 15N 23 0 E
Pagatan, Indonesia 75 C5 3 33 S 115 59 E
Page, Ariz., U.S.A. 143 H8 36 57N 111 27W
Page, N. Dak., U.S.A. 138 B6 47 11N 97 37W
Paglieta, Italy 39 F11 42 10N 14 30 E
Pagny-sur-Moselle, France 23 D13 48 59N 6 2 E
Pago Pago, Amer. Samoa 121 X24 14 16 S 170 43W
Pagosa Springs, U.S.A. 143 H10 37 16N 107 4W
Pagwa River, Canada 128 B2 50 2N 85 14W
Pahala, U.S.A. 132 J17 19 12N 155 25W
Pahang □, Malaysia 74 B2 3 30N 102 45 E
Pahang →, Malaysia 77 L4 3 30N 103 9 E
Pahia Pt., N.Z. 119 G2 46 20 S 167 41 E
Pahiatua, N.Z. 118 G4 40 27 S 175 50 E
Pahokee, U.S.A. 135 M5 26 50N 80 40W
Pahrump, U.S.A. 145 J11 36 15N 116 0W
Pahute Mesa, U.S.A. 144 H10 37 25N 116 50W
Pai, Thailand 76 C2 19 19N 98 27 E
Paia, U.S.A. 132 H16 20 54N 156 22W
Paicines, U.S.A. 144 J5 36 44N 121 17W
Paide, Estonia 50 B4 58 57N 25 31 E
Paignton, U.K. 17 G4 50 26N 3 33W
Paiján, Peru 156 B2 7 42 S 79 20W
Päijänne, Finland 13 F18 61 30N 25 30 E

**246 Paimbœuf**


Paimbœuf, *France* 22 **E4** 47 17N 2 3W
Paimpol, *France* 22 **D3** 48 48N 3 4W
Painan, *Indonesia* 74 **C2** 1 21 S 100 34 E
Painesville, *U.S.A.* 136 **E3** 41 42N 81 18W
Paint Hills = Nouveau Comptoir, *Canada* 128 **B4** 53 0N 78 49W
Paint L., *Canada* 131 **B9** 55 28N 97 57W
Paint Rock, *U.S.A.* 139 **K5** 31 30N 99 56W
Painted Desert, *U.S.A.* 143 **J8** 36 0N 111 30W
Paintsville, *U.S.A.* 134 **G4** 37 50N 82 50W
País Vasco □, *Spain* 34 **C2** 42 50N 2 45W
Paisley, *Canada* 136 **B3** 44 18N 81 16W
Paisley, *U.K.* 18 **F4** 55 51N 4 27W
Paisley, *U.S.A.* 142 **E3** 42 43N 120 40W
Paita, *N. Cal.* 121 **V20** 22 8 S 166 22 E
Paita, *Peru* 156 **B1** 5 11 S 81 9W
Paiva →, *Portugal* 36 **D2** 41 4N 8 16W
Paizhou, *China* 69 **B9** 30 12N 113 55 E
Pajares, *Spain* 36 **B5** 43 1N 5 46W
Pajares, Puerto de, *Spain* 36 **C5** 42 58N 5 46W
Pajeczno, *Poland* 47 **D6** 51 10N 19 0 E
Pak Lay, *Laos* 76 **C3** 18 15N 101 27 E
Pak Phanang, *Thailand* 77 **H3** 8 21N 100 12 E
Pak Sane, *Laos* 76 **C4** 18 22N 103 39 E
Pak Song, *Laos* 76 **E6** 15 11N 106 14 E
Pak Suong, *Laos* 76 **C4** 19 58N 102 15 E
Pakala, *India* 83 **H4** 13 29N 79 8 E
Pakaraima Mts., *Guyana* 153 **B5** 6 0N 60 0W
Pakenham, *Australia* 117 **E6** 38 6 S 145 30 E
Pákhnes, *Greece* 32 **D6** 35 16N 24 4 E
Pakhtakor, *Uzbekistan* 55 **C2** 40 2N 65 46 E
Pakistan ■, *Asia* 79 **C3** 30 0N 70 0 E
Pakistan, East = Bangladesh ■, *Asia* 78 **C3** 24 0N 90 0 E
Pakkading, *Laos* 76 **C4** 18 19N 103 59 E
Pakokku, *Burma* 78 **E5** 21 20N 95 0 E
Pakosc, *Poland* 47 **C5** 52 48N 18 6 E
Pakpattan, *Pakistan* 79 **C4** 30 25N 73 27 E
Pakrac, *Croatia* 42 **B2** 45 27N 17 12 E
Paks, *Hungary* 31 **E11** 46 38N 18 55 E
Pakse, *Laos* 76 **E5** 15 5N 105 52 E
Paktīā □, *Afghan.* 79 **B3** 33 0N 69 15 E
Paktīkā □, *Afghan.* 79 **B3** 32 30N 69 0 E
Pakwach, *Uganda* 106 **B3** 2 28N 31 27 E
Pala, *Chad* 97 **G3** 9 25N 15 5 E
Pala, *U.S.A.* 145 **M9** 33 22N 117 5W
Pala, *Zaïre* 106 **D2** 6 45 S 29 30 E
Palabek, *Uganda* 106 **B3** 3 22N 32 33 E
Palacios, *U.S.A.* 139 **L6** 28 44N 96 12W
Palafrugell, *Spain* 34 **D8** 41 55N 3 10 E
Palagiano, *Italy* 41 **B10** 40 35N 17 2 E
Palagonía, *Italy* 41 **E7** 37 20N 14 43 E
Palagruža, *Croatia* 39 **F13** 42 24N 16 15 E
Palaiokastron, *Greece* 45 **J8** 35 12N 26 18 E
Palaiókastron, *Kríti, Greece* 32 **D8** 35 12N 26 15 E
Palaiokhóra, *Greece* 32 **D5** 35 16N 23 39 E
Pálairos, *Greece* 45 **F2** 38 45N 20 51 E
Palakol, *India* 83 **F5** 16 31N 81 46 E
Palam, *India* 82 **E3** 19 0N 77 0 E
Palamás, *Greece* 44 **E4** 39 26N 22 4 E
Palamós, *Spain* 34 **D8** 41 50N 3 10 E
Palampur, *India* 80 **C7** 32 10N 76 30 E
Palana, *Australia* 114 **F4** 39 45 S 147 55 E
Palana, *Russia* 57 **D16** 59 10N 159 59 E
Palanan, *Phil.* 70 **C4** 17 8N 122 29 E
Palanan Bay, *Phil.* 70 **C4** 17 9N 122 27 E
Palanan Pt., *Phil.* 70 **C4** 17 17N 122 30 E
Palandri, *Pakistan* 81 **C5** 33 42N 73 40 E
Palangkaraya, *Indonesia* 75 **C4** 2 16 S 113 56 E
Palani, *India* 83 **J3** 10 30N 77 30 E
Palani Hills, *India* 83 **J3** 10 14N 77 33 E
Palanpur, *India* 80 **G5** 24 10N 72 25 E
Palapye, *Botswana* 104 **C4** 22 30 S 27 7 E
Palar →, *India* 83 **H5** 12 27N 80 13 E
Palas, *Pakistan* 81 **B5** 35 4N 73 14 E
Palatine, *U.S.A.* 141 **B8** 42 7N 88 3W
Palatka, *Russia* 57 **C16** 60 6N 150 54 E
Palatka, *U.S.A.* 135 **L5** 29 40N 81 40W
Palawan, *Phil.* 71 **G2** 9 30N 118 30 E
Palawan □, *Phil.* 71 **G2** 10 0N 119 0 E
Palawan Passage, *Phil.* 71 **G1** 10 0N 118 0 E
Palayankottai, *India* 83 **K3** 8 45N 77 45 E
Palazzo, Pte., *France* 25 **F12** 42 28N 8 30 E
Palazzo San Gervásio, *Italy* 41 **B8** 40 53N 15 58 E
Palazzolo Acreide, *Italy* 41 **E7** 37 4N 14 54 E
Palca, *Chile* 156 **D4** 19 7 S 69 9W
Paldiski, *Estonia* 50 **B4** 59 23N 24 9 E
Pale, *Bos.-H., Yug.* 42 **D3** 43 50N 18 38 E
Palel, *India* 78 **C5** 24 27N 94 2 E
Paleleh, *Indonesia* 72 **A2** 1 10N 121 50 E
Palembang, *Indonesia* 74 **C2** 3 0 S 104 50 E
Palena →, *Chile* 160 **B2** 43 50 S 73 50W
Palena, L., *Chile* 160 **B2** 43 55 S 71 40W
Palencia, *Spain* 36 **C6** 42 1N 4 34W
Palencia □, *Spain* 36 **C6** 42 31N 4 33W
Paleokastrítsa, *Greece* 32 **A3** 39 40N 19 41 E
Paleometokho, *Cyprus* 32 **D12** 35 7N 33 11 E
Palermo, *Colombia* 152 **C2** 2 54N 75 26W
Palermo, *Italy* 40 **D6** 38 8N 13 20 E
Palermo, *U.S.A.* 142 **G3** 39 30N 121 37W
Palestine, *Asia* 91 **D4** 32 0N 35 0 E
Palestine, *U.S.A.* 139 **K7** 31 42N 95 35W
Palestrina, *Italy* 40 **A5** 41 50N 12 52 E
Paletwa, *Burma* 78 **E4** 21 10N 92 50 E
Palghat, *India* 83 **J3** 10 46N 76 42 E
Palgrave, Mt., *Australia* 112 **D2** 23 22 S 115 58 E
Pali, *India* 80 **G5** 25 50N 73 20 E
Palin, Mt., *Malaysia* 75 **A5** 6 10N 117 10 E
Palinit, *Phil.* 70 **E5** 12 15N 124 20 E
Palinuro, C., *Italy* 41 **B8** 40 1N 15 14 E
Palisade, *U.S.A.* 138 **E4** 40 21N 101 10W
Paliseul, *Belgium* 21 **J6** 49 54N 5 8 E
Palitana, *India* 80 **J4** 21 32N 71 49 E
Palizada, *Mexico* 147 **D6** 18 18N 92 8W
Palizzi, *Italy* 41 **E8** 37 58N 15 59 E
Palk Bay, *Asia* 83 **K4** 9 30N 79 15 E
Palk Strait, *Asia* 83 **K4** 10 0N 79 45 E
Palkānah, *Iraq* 84 **C5** 35 49N 44 26 E
Palkonda, *India* 82 **E6** 18 36N 83 48 E
Palkonda Ra., *India* 83 **H4** 13 50N 79 20 E
Palla Road = Dinokwe, *Botswana* 104 **C4** 23 29 S 26 37 E
Pallanza = Verbánia, *Italy* 38 **C5** 45 56N 8 43 E
Pallasovka, *Russia* 51 **F15** 50 4N 47 0 E
Palleru →, *India* 82 **F5** 16 45N 80 2 E
Pallisa, *Uganda* 106 **B3** 1 12N 33 43 E
Palliser, C., *N.Z.* 118 **H4** 41 37 S 175 14 E
Palliser B., *N.Z.* 118 **H4** 41 26 S 175 5 E
Pallu, *India* 80 **E6** 28 59N 74 14 E
Palm Beach, *U.S.A.* 135 **M6** 26 46N 80 0W
Palm Desert, *U.S.A.* 145 **M10** 33 43N 116 22W
Palm Is., *Australia* 114 **B4** 18 40 S 146 35 E
Palm Springs, *U.S.A.* 145 **M10** 33 51N 116 35W
Palma, *Mozam.* 107 **E5** 10 46 S 40 29 E
Palma →, *Brazil* 155 **D2** 12 33 S 47 52W
Palma, B. de, *Spain* 33 **B9** 39 30N 2 39 E
Palma de Mallorca, *Spain* 33 **B9** 39 35N 2 39 E
Palma del Río, *Spain* 37 **H5** 37 43N 5 17W
Palma di Montechiaro, *Italy* 40 **E6** 37 12N 13 46 E
Palma Soriano, *Cuba* 148 **B4** 20 15N 76 0W
Palmanova, *Italy* 39 **C10** 45 54N 13 18 E
Palmares, *Brazil* 154 **C4** 8 41 S 35 28W
Palmarito, *Venezuela* 152 **B3** 7 37N 70 10W
Palmarola, *Italy* 40 **B5** 40 57N 12 50 E
Palmas, *Brazil* 159 **B5** 26 29 S 52 0W
Palmas, C., *Liberia* 100 **E3** 4 27N 7 46W
Pálmas, G. di, *Italy* 40 **C1** 39 0N 8 30 E
Palmas de Monte Alto, *Brazil* 155 **D3** 14 16 S 43 10W
Palmdale, *U.S.A.* 145 **L8** 34 36N 118 7W
Palmeira, *Brazil* 155 **G2** 25 25 S 50 0W
Palmeira dos Índios, *Brazil* 154 **C4** 9 25 S 36 37W
Palmeirais, *Brazil* 154 **C3** 6 0 S 43 0W
Palmeiras →, *Brazil* 155 **D2** 12 22 S 47 8W
Palmeirinhas, Pta. das, *Angola* 103 **D2** 9 2 S 12 57 E
Palmela, *Portugal* 37 **G2** 38 32N 8 57W
Palmelo, *Brazil* 155 **E2** 17 20 S 48 27W
Palmer, *U.S.A.* 126 **B5** 61 35N 149 10W
Palmer →, *Australia* 114 **B3** 16 0 S 142 26 E
Palmer Arch., *Antarctica* 7 **C17** 64 15 S 65 0W
Palmer Lake, *U.S.A.* 138 **F2** 39 10N 104 52W
Palmer Land, *Antarctica* 7 **D18** 73 0 S 60 0W
Palmerston, *Canada* 136 **C4** 43 50N 80 51W
Palmerston, *N.Z.* 119 **F5** 45 29 S 170 43 E
Palmerston North, *N.Z.* 118 **G4** 40 21 S 175 39 E
Palmerton, *U.S.A.* 137 **F9** 40 47N 75 36W
Palmetto, *U.S.A.* 135 **M4** 27 33N 82 33W
Palmi, *Italy* 41 **D8** 38 21N 15 51 E
Palmira, *Argentina* 158 **C2** 32 59 S 68 34W
Palmira, *Colombia* 152 **C2** 3 32N 76 16W
Palmyra = Tudmur, *Syria* 84 **C3** 34 36N 38 15 E
Palmyra, *Ill., U.S.A.* 140 **E6** 39 26N 90 0W
Palmyra, *Mo., U.S.A.* 140 **E5** 39 45N 91 30W
Palmyra, *N.Y., U.S.A.* 136 **C7** 43 5N 77 18W
Palmyra, *Wis., U.S.A.* 141 **B8** 42 52N 88 36W
Palmyra Is., *Pac. Oc.* 123 **G11** 5 52N 162 5W
Palo, *Phil.* 71 **F5** 11 10N 124 59 E
Palo Alto, *U.S.A.* 144 **H4** 37 25N 122 8W
Palo del Colle, *Italy* 41 **A9** 41 4N 16 43 E
Palo Verde, *U.S.A.* 145 **M12** 33 26N 114 45W
Palombara Sabina, *Italy* 39 **F9** 42 4N 12 45 E
Palompon, *Phil.* 71 **F5** 11 3N 124 23 E
Palopo, *Indonesia* 72 **B2** 3 0 S 120 16 E
Palos, C. de, *Spain* 35 **H4** 37 38N 0 40W
Palos Verdes, *U.S.A.* 145 **M8** 33 48N 118 23W
Palos Verdes, Pt., *U.S.A.* 145 **M8** 33 43N 118 26W
Palouse, *U.S.A.* 142 **C5** 46 59N 117 5W
Palpa, *Peru* 156 **C2** 14 30 S 75 15W
Palparara, *Australia* 114 **C3** 24 47 S 141 28 E
Pålsboda, *Sweden* 14 **E9** 59 3N 15 22 E
Palu, *Indonesia* 72 **B1** 1 0 S 119 52 E
Palu, *Turkey* 49 **G7** 38 45N 40 0 E
Paluan, *Phil.* 70 **E3** 13 26N 120 29 E
Palwal, *India* 80 **E7** 28 8N 77 19 E
Pama, *Burkina Faso* 101 **C5** 11 19N 0 44 E
Pamanukan, *Indonesia* 75 **D3** 6 16 S 107 49 E
Pamban I., *India* 83 **K4** 9 15N 79 20 E
Pambuhan, *Phil.* 70 **E4** 13 59N 123 5 E
Pamekasan, *Indonesia* 75 **D4** 7 10 S 113 28 E
Pamiers, *France* 24 **E5** 43 7N 1 39 E
Pamir →, *Tajikistan* 55 **E6** 37 1N 72 41 E
Pamirs, *Tajikistan* 55 **E6** 37 40N 73 0 E
Pamlico →, *U.S.A.* 135 **H7** 35 25N 76 30W
Pamlico Sd., *U.S.A.* 135 **H8** 35 20N 76 0W
Pampa, *U.S.A.* 139 **H4** 35 35N 100 58W
Pampa de Agma, *Argentina* 160 **B3** 43 45 S 69 40W
Pampa de las Salinas, *Argentina* 158 **C2** 32 1 S 66 58W
Pampa Grande, *Bolivia* 157 **D5** 18 5 S 64 6W
Pampa Hermosa, *Peru* 156 **B2** 7 7 S 75 4W
Pampanga □, *Phil.* 70 **D3** 15 4N 120 40 E
Pampanua, *Indonesia* 72 **B2** 4 16 S 120 8 E
Pamparato, *Italy* 38 **D4** 44 16N 7 54 E
Pampas, *Argentina* 158 **D3** 35 0 S 63 0W
Pampas, *Peru* 156 **C3** 12 20 S 74 50W
Pampas →, *Peru* 156 **C3** 13 24 S 73 12W
Pamphylia, *Turkey* 88 **E4** 37 0N 31 20 E
Pamplona, *Colombia* 152 **B3** 7 23N 72 39W
Pamplona, *Phil.* 70 **B3** 18 31N 121 20 E
Pamplona, *Spain* 34 **C3** 42 48N 1 38W
Pampoenpoort, *S. Africa* 104 **E3** 31 3 S 22 40 E
Pamukkale, *Turkey* 88 **E3** 37 57N 28 50 E
Pan Xian, *China* 68 **E5** 25 46N 104 38 E
Pana, *U.S.A.* 140 **E7** 39 25N 89 10W
Panabo, *Phil.* 71 **H5** 7 19N 125 42 E
Panaca, *U.S.A.* 143 **H6** 37 51N 114 23W
Panagyurishte, *Bulgaria* 43 **E9** 42 30N 24 15 E
Panaitan, *Indonesia* 74 **D3** 6 36 S 105 12 E
Panaji, *India* 83 **G1** 15 25N 73 50 E
Panamá, *Panama* 148 **E4** 9 0N 79 25W
Panama ■, *Cent. Amer.* 148 **E4** 8 48N 79 55W
Panamá, G. de, *Panama* 148 **E4** 8 4N 79 20W
Panama Canal, *Panama* 148 **E4** 9 10N 79 37W
Panama City, *U.S.A.* 135 **K3** 30 10N 85 41W
Panamint Ra., *U.S.A.* 145 **J9** 36 20N 117 20W
Panamint Springs, *U.S.A.* 145 **J9** 36 20N 117 28W
Panão, *Peru* 156 **B2** 9 55 S 75 55W
Panaon I., *Phil.* 71 **F5** 10 3N 125 13 E
Panare, *Thailand* 77 **J3** 6 51N 101 30 E
Panarea, *Italy* 41 **D8** 38 38N 15 3 E
Panaro →, *Italy* 38 **D8** 44 55N 11 25 E
Panarukan, *Indonesia* 75 **D4** 7 42 S 113 56 E
Panay, *Phil.* 71 **F4** 11 10N 122 30 E
Panay, G., *Phil.* 71 **F4** 11 0N 122 30 E
Pancake Ra., *U.S.A.* 143 **G6** 38 30N 116 0W
Pančevo, *Serbia, Yug.* 42 **C5** 44 52N 20 41 E
Panciu, *Romania* 46 **D8** 45 54N 27 8 E
Pancol, *Phil.* 71 **F2** 10 52N 119 25 E
Pancorbo, Paso, *Spain* 34 **C1** 42 32N 3 5W
Pandan, *Antique, Phil.* 71 **F4** 11 45N 122 10 E
Pandan, *Catanduanes, Phil.* 70 **D5** 14 3N 124 10 E
Pandan Bay, *Phil.* 71 **F4** 11 43N 122 0 E
Pandegelang, *Indonesia* 74 **D3** 6 25 S 106 5 E
Pandharpur, *India* 82 **F2** 17 41N 75 20 E
Pandhurna, *India* 82 **D4** 21 36N 78 35 E
Pandilla, *Spain* 34 **D1** 41 32N 3 43W
Pando, *Uruguay* 159 **C4** 34 44 S 56 0W
Pando □, *Bolivia* 156 **C4** 11 20 S 67 40W
Pando, L. = Hope, L., *Australia* 115 **D2** 28 24 S 139 18 E
Pandokrátor, *Greece* 32 **A3** 39 45N 19 50 E
Pandora, *Costa Rica* 148 **E3** 9 43N 83 3W
Pandu, *Zaïre* 102 **B3** 4 59N 19 16 E
Panevezys, *Lithuania* 50 **D4** 55 42N 24 25 E
Panfilov, *Kazakhstan* 56 **E8** 44 10N 80 0 E
Panfilovo, *Russia* 51 **F13** 50 25N 42 46 E
Panga, *Zaïre* 106 **B2** 1 52N 26 18 E
Pangaíon Óros, *Greece* 44 **D6** 40 50N 24 0 E
Pangala, *Congo* 102 **C2** 4 1 S 13 52 E
Pangalanes, Canal des, *Madag.* 105 **C8** 22 48 S 47 50 E
Pangani, *Tanzania* 106 **D4** 5 25 S 38 58 E
Pangani □, *Tanzania* 106 **D4** 5 25 S 39 0 E
Pangani →, *Tanzania* 106 **D4** 5 26 S 38 58 E
Panganiban, *Phil.* 70 **E5** 13 55N 124 18 E
Panganuran, *Phil.* 71 **G4** 8 2N 122 22 E
Pangasinan □, *Phil.* 70 **D3** 15 55N 120 20 E
Pangfou = Bengbu, *China* 67 **H9** 32 58N 117 20 E
Pangil, *Zaïre* 106 **C2** 3 10 S 26 35 E
Pangkah, Tanjung, *Indonesia* 75 **D4** 6 51 S 112 33 E
Pangkai, *Burma* 78 **D7** 22 40N 98 40 E
Pangkajene, *Indonesia* 72 **B1** 4 46 S 119 34 E
Pangkalanbrandan, *Indonesia* 74 **B1** 4 1N 98 20 E
Pangkalanbuun, *Indonesia* 75 **C4** 2 41 S 111 37 E
Pangkalansusu, *Indonesia* 74 **B1** 4 2N 98 13 E
Pangkalpinang, *Indonesia* 74 **C3** 2 0 S 106 0 E
Pangkoh, *Indonesia* 75 **C4** 3 5 S 114 8 E
Panglao, *Phil.* 71 **G4** 9 35N 123 45 E
Panglao I., *Phil.* 71 **G4** 9 35N 123 48 E
Pangnirtung, *Canada* 127 **B13** 66 8N 65 54W
Pangrango, *Indonesia* 74 **D3** 6 46 S 107 1 E
Pangsau Pass, *Burma* 78 **B6** 27 15N 96 10 E
Pangtara, *Burma* 78 **E6** 20 57N 96 40 E
Panguipulli, *Chile* 160 **A2** 39 38 S 72 20W
Panguitch, *U.S.A.* 143 **H7** 37 52N 112 30W
Pangutaran, *Phil.* 71 **H3** 6 18N 120 34 E
Pangutaran Group, *Phil.* 71 **H3** 6 18N 120 34 E
Panhandle, *U.S.A.* 139 **H4** 35 23N 101 23W
Pani Mines, *India* 80 **H5** 22 29N 73 50 E
Pania-Mutombo, *Zaïre* 103 **D4** 5 11 S 23 51 E
Panié, Mt., *N. Cal.* 121 **T18** 20 36 S 164 46 E
Panipat, *India* 80 **E7** 29 25N 77 2 E
Panitan, *Phil.* 71 **F4** 11 28N 122 46 E
Panjal Range, *India* 80 **C7** 32 30N 76 50 E
Panjgur, *Pakistan* 79 **D2** 27 0N 64 5 E
Panjim = Panaji, *India* 83 **G1** 15 25N 73 50 E
Panjwai, *Afghan.* 80 **D1** 31 26N 65 27 E
Pankshin, *Nigeria* 101 **D6** 9 16N 9 25 E
Panmunjŏm, *N. Korea* 67 **F14** 37 59N 126 38 E
Panna, *India* 81 **G9** 24 40N 80 15 E
Panna Hills, *India* 81 **G9** 24 40N 81 15 E
Pano Lefkara, *Cyprus* 32 **E12** 34 53N 33 20 E
Pano Panayia, *Cyprus* 32 **E11** 34 55N 32 38 E
Panora, *U.S.A.* 140 **C2** 41 41N 94 22W
Panorama, *Brazil* 159 **A5** 21 21 S 51 51W
Pánormon, *Greece* 32 **D6** 35 25N 24 41 E
Panruti, *India* 83 **J4** 11 46N 79 35 E
Panshan, *China* 67 **D12** 41 3N 122 2 E
Panshi, *China* 67 **C14** 42 58N 126 5 E
Pantao, *Phil.* 70 **E4** 13 12N 123 20 E
Pantar, *Indonesia* 72 **C2** 8 28 S 124 10 E
Pantelleria, *Italy* 40 **F5** 36 52N 12 0 E
Pantha, *Burma* 78 **D5** 23 55N 94 35 E
Pantin Sakan, *Burma* 78 **F6** 18 38N 97 33 E
Pantón, *Spain* 36 **C3** 42 31N 7 37W
Pánuco, *Mexico* 147 **C5** 22 0N 98 15W
Panukulan, *Phil.* 70 **D3** 14 56N 121 49 E
Panyam, *Nigeria* 101 **D6** 9 27N 9 8 E
Panyu, *China* 69 **F9** 22 51N 113 20 E
Pao →, *Anzoátegui, Venezuela* 153 **B5** 8 6N 64 17W
Pao →, *Apure, Venezuela* 152 **B4** 8 33N 68 1W
Páola, *Italy* 41 **C9** 39 21N 16 2 E
Paola, *Malta* 32 **D2** 35 52N 14 30 E
Paola, *U.S.A.* 138 **F7** 38 36N 94 50W
Paoli, *U.S.A.* 141 **F10** 38 33N 86 28W
Paonia, *U.S.A.* 143 **G10** 38 56N 107 37W
Paoting = Baoding, *China* 66 **E8** 38 50N 115 28 E
Paot'ou = Baotou, *China* 66 **D6** 40 32N 110 2 E
Paoua, *C.A.R.* 102 **A3** 7 9N 16 20 E
Pápa, *Hungary* 31 **D10** 47 22N 17 30 E
Papagayo →, *Mexico* 147 **D5** 16 36N 99 43W
Papagayo, G. de, *Costa Rica* 148 **D2** 10 30N 85 50W
Papagni →, *India* 83 **G3** 15 35N 77 45 E
Papakura, *N.Z.* 118 **D3** 37 4 S 174 59 E
Papantla, *Mexico* 147 **C5** 20 30N 97 30W
Paparoa, *N.Z.* 118 **C3** 36 6 S 174 16 E
Paparoa Nat. Park, *N.Z.* 119 **C6** 42 7 S 171 26 E
Paparoa Ra., *N.Z.* 119 **C6** 42 5 S 171 35 E
Pápas, Ákra, *Greece* 45 **F3** 38 13N 21 20 E
Papatoetoe, *N.Z.* 118 **C3** 36 59 S 174 51 E
Papenburg, *Germany* 26 **B3** 53 7N 7 25 E
Paphlagonia, *Turkey* 88 **C5** 41 30N 33 0 E
Paphos, *Cyprus* 32 **E11** 34 46N 32 25 E
Papien Chiang = Da →, *Vietnam* 76 **B5** 21 15N 105 20 E
Papigochic →, *Mexico* 146 **B3** 29 9N 109 40W
Paposo, *Chile* 158 **B1** 25 0 S 70 30W
Papoutsa, *Cyprus* 32 **E12** 34 54N 33 4 E
Papua, G. of, *Papua N. G.* 120 **E3** 9 0 S 144 50 E
Papua New Guinea ■, *Oceania* 120 **D3** 8 0 S 145 0 E
Papuča, *Croatia* 39 **D12** 44 22N 15 30 E
Papudo, *Chile* 158 **C1** 32 29 S 71 27W
Papuk, *Croatia* 42 **B2** 45 30N 17 30 E
Papun, *Burma* 78 **F6** 18 2N 97 30 E
Papunya, *Australia* 112 **D5** 23 15 S 131 54 E
Pará = Belém, *Brazil* 154 **B2** 1 20 S 48 30W
Pará □, *Brazil* 157 **A7** 3 20 S 52 0W
Pará □, *Surinam* 153 **B6** 5 20N 55 5W
Parábita, *Italy* 41 **B11** 40 3N 18 8 E
Paraburdoo, *Australia* 112 **D2** 23 14 S 117 32 E
Paracale, *Phil.* 70 **D4** 14 17N 122 48 E
Paracas, Pen., *Peru* 156 **C2** 13 53 S 76 20W
Paracatu, *Brazil* 155 **E2** 17 10 S 46 50W
Paracatu →, *Brazil* 155 **E2** 16 30 S 45 4W
Parachilna, *Australia* 116 **A3** 31 10 S 138 21 E
Parachinar, *Pakistan* 79 **B3** 33 55N 70 5 E
Paraćin, *Serbia, Yug.* 42 **D6** 43 54N 21 27 E
Paracuru, *Brazil* 154 **B4** 3 24 S 39 4W
Parada, Punta, *Peru* 156 **D2** 15 22 S 75 11W
Paradas, *Spain* 37 **H5** 37 18N 5 29W
Paradela, *Spain* 36 **C3** 42 44N 7 37W
Paradhísi, *Greece* 32 **C10** 36 18N 28 7 E
Paradip, *India* 82 **D8** 20 15N 86 35 E
Paradise, *Calif., U.S.A.* 144 **F5** 39 46N 121 37W
Paradise, *Mont., U.S.A.* 142 **C6** 47 27N 114 17W
Paradise, *Nev., U.S.A.* 145 **J11** 36 4N 115 7W
Paradise →, *Canada* 129 **B8** 53 27N 57 19W
Paradise Valley, *U.S.A.* 142 **F5** 41 30N 117 28W
Parado, *Indonesia* 75 **D5** 8 42 S 118 30 E
Paradyz, *Poland* 47 **D7** 51 19N 20 2 E
Paragould, *U.S.A.* 139 **G9** 36 5N 90 30W
Paraguá →, *Bolivia* 157 **C5** 13 34 S 61 53W
Paragua →, *Venezuela* 153 **B5** 6 55N 62 55W
Paraguaçu →, *Brazil* 155 **D4** 12 45 S 38 54W
Paraguaçu Paulista, *Brazil* 159 **A5** 22 22 S 50 35W
Paraguaipoa, *Venezuela* 152 **A3** 11 21N 71 57W
Paraguaná, Pen. de, *Venezuela* 152 **A3** 12 0N 70 0W
Paraguarí, *Paraguay* 158 **B4** 25 36 S 57 0W
Paraguarí □, *Paraguay* 158 **B4** 26 0 S 57 10W
Paraguay ■, *S. Amer.* 158 **A4** 23 0 S 57 0W
Paraguay →, *Paraguay* 158 **B4** 27 18 S 58 38W
Paraíba = João Pessoa, *Brazil* 154 **C5** 7 10 S 34 52W
Paraíba □, *Brazil* 154 **C4** 7 0 S 36 0W
Paraíba do Sul →, *Brazil* 155 **F3** 21 37 S 41 3W
Parainen, *Finland* 13 **F17** 60 18N 22 18 E
Paraiso, *Mexico* 147 **D6** 18 24N 93 14W
Parak, *Iran* 85 **E7** 27 38N 52 25 E
Parakhino Paddubye, *Russia* 50 **B8** 58 26N 33 10 E
Parakou, *Benin* 101 **D5** 9 25N 2 40 E
Parakylia, *Australia* 116 **A2** 30 24 S 136 25 E
Paralimni, *Cyprus* 32 **D12** 35 2N 33 58 E
Parálion-Astrous, *Greece* 45 **G4** 37 25N 22 45 E
Paramakkudi, *India* 83 **K4** 9 31N 78 39 E
Paramaribo, *Surinam* 153 **B6** 5 50N 55 10W
Parambu, *Brazil* 154 **C3** 6 13 S 40 43W
Paramillo, Nudo del, *Colombia* 152 **B2** 7 4N 75 55W
Paramirim, *Brazil* 155 **D3** 13 26 S 42 15W
Paramirim →, *Brazil* 155 **D3** 11 34 S 43 18W
Paramithiá, *Greece* 44 **E2** 39 30N 20 35 E
Paramushir, Ostrov, *Russia* 57 **D16** 50 24N 156 0 E
Paran →, *Israel* 91 **E4** 30 20N 35 10 E
Paraná, *Argentina* 158 **C3** 31 45 S 60 30W
Paranã, *Brazil* 155 **D2** 12 30 S 47 48W
Paraná □, *Brazil* 159 **A5** 24 30 S 51 0W
Paraná →, *Argentina* 158 **C4** 33 43 S 59 15W
Paranaguá, *Brazil* 159 **B6** 25 30 S 48 30W
Paranaíba →, *Brazil* 155 **F1** 20 6 S 51 4W
Paranapanema →, *Brazil* 159 **A5** 22 40 S 53 9W
Paranapiacaba, Serra do, *Brazil* 159 **A6** 24 31 S 48 35W
Paranavaí, *Brazil* 159 **A5** 23 4 S 52 56W
Parang, *Jolo, Phil.* 71 **J3** 5 55N 120 54 E
Parang, *Mindanao, Phil.* 71 **H5** 7 23N 124 16 E
Parangaba, *Brazil* 154 **B4** 3 45 S 38 33W
Parangippettai, *India* 83 **J4** 11 30N 79 38 E
Paraparaumu, *N.Z.* 118 **G4** 40 57 S 175 3 E
Parapóla, *Greece* 45 **H5** 36 55N 23 27 E
Paraspóri, Ákra, *Greece* 45 **J9** 35 55N 27 15 E
Paratinga, *Brazil* 155 **D3** 12 40 S 43 10W
Paratoo, *Australia* 116 **B3** 32 42 S 139 20 E
Parattah, *Australia* 114 **G4** 42 22 S 147 23 E
Paraúna, *Brazil* 155 **E1** 16 55 S 50 26W
Paray-le-Monial, *France* 25 **B8** 46 27N 4 7 E
Parbati →, *India* 80 **G7** 25 50N 76 30 E
Parbatipur, *Bangla.* 78 **C2** 25 39N 88 55 E
Parbhani, *India* 82 **E3** 19 8N 76 52 E
Parchim, *Germany* 26 **B7** 53 25N 11 50 E
Parczew, *Poland* 47 **D9** 51 40N 22 52 E
Pardes Hanna, *Israel* 91 **C3** 32 28N 34 57 E
Pardilla, *Spain* 36 **D7** 41 33N 3 43W
Pardo →, *Bahia, Brazil* 155 **E4** 15 40 S 39 0W
Pardo →, *Mato Grosso, Brazil* 159 **A5** 21 46 S 52 9W
Pardo →, *Minas Gerais, Brazil* 155 **E3** 15 48 S 44 48W
Pardo →, *São Paulo, Brazil* 155 **F2** 20 10 S 48 38W
Pardubice, *Czech.* 30 **A8** 50 3N 15 45 E
Pare, *Indonesia* 75 **D4** 7 43 S 112 12 E
Pare □, *Tanzania* 106 **C4** 4 10 S 38 0 E
Pare Mts., *Tanzania* 106 **C4** 4 0 S 37 45 E
Parecis, Serra dos, *Brazil* 157 **C6** 13 0 S 60 0W
Paredes de Nava, *Spain* 36 **C6** 42 9N 4 42W
Pareh, *Iran* 84 **B5** 38 52N 45 42 E
Parelhas, *Brazil* 154 **C4** 6 41 S 36 39W
Paren, *Russia* 57 **C17** 62 30N 163 15 E
Parengarenga Harbour, *N.Z.* 118 **A1** 34 31 S 173 0 E
Parent, *Canada* 128 **C5** 47 55N 74 35W
Parent, L., *Canada* 128 **C4** 48 31N 77 1W
Parentis-en-Born, *France* 24 **D2** 44 21N 1 4W
Parepare, *Indonesia* 72 **B1** 4 0 S 119 40 E
Parfino, *Russia* 50 **C7** 57 59N 31 34 E
Pargo, Pta. do, *Madeira* 33 **D2** 32 49N 17 17W
Parguba, *Russia* 48 **B5** 62 20N 34 27 E
Paria, G. de, *Venezuela* 153 **A5** 10 20N 62 0W
Paria, Pen. de, *Venezuela* 153 **A5** 10 50N 62 30W
Pariaguán, *Venezuela* 153 **B5** 8 51N 64 34W
Pariaman, *Indonesia* 74 **C2** 0 47 S 100 11 E
Paricatuba, *Brazil* 153 **D5** 4 26 S 61 53W
Paricutín, Cerro, *Mexico* 146 **D4** 19 28N 102 15W
Parigi, *Java, Indonesia* 75 **D3** 7 42 S 108 29 E
Parigi, *Sulawesi, Indonesia* 72 **B2** 0 50 S 120 5 E
Parika, *Guyana* 153 **B6** 6 50N 58 20W
Parima, Serra, *Brazil* 153 **C5** 2 30N 64 0W

Pendelikón 247


Parinari, Peru 156 A3 4 35 S 74 25W
Parincea, Romania 46 C8 46 27N 27 9 E
Parîng, Romania 46 D4 45 20N 23 37 E
Parintins, Brazil 153 D6 2 40 S 56 50W
Paris, Canada 128 D3 43 12N 80 25W
Paris, France 23 D9 48 50N 2 20 E
Paris, Idaho, U.S.A. 142 E8 42 13N 111 30W
Paris, Ill., U.S.A. 141 E9 39 36N 87 42W
Paris, Ky., U.S.A. 141 F12 38 12N 84 12W
Paris, Mo., U.S.A. 140 E5 39 29N 92 0W
Paris, Tenn., U.S.A. 135 G1 36 20N 88 20W
Paris, Tex., U.S.A. 139 J7 33 40N 95 30W
Paris, Ville de □, France 23 D9 48 50N 2 20 E
Parish, U.S.A. 137 C8 43 24N 76 9W
Pariti, Indonesia 72 D2 10 15 S 123 45 E
Park, U.S.A. 144 B4 48 45N 122 18W
Park City, U.S.A. 142 F8 40 42N 111 35W
Park Falls, U.S.A. 138 C9 45 58N 90 27W
Park Forest, U.S.A. 141 C9 41 29N 87 40W
Park Range, U.S.A. 142 G10 40 0N 106 30W
Park Rapids, U.S.A. 138 B7 46 56N 95 0W
Park Ridge, U.S.A. 141 B9 42 2N 87 51W
Park River, U.S.A. 138 A6 48 25N 97 43W
Park Rynie, S. Africa 105 E5 30 25 S 30 45 E
Parkā Bandar, Iran 85 E8 25 55N 59 35 E
Parkent, Uzbekistan 55 C4 41 18N 69 40 E
Parker, Ariz., U.S.A. 145 L12 34 8N 114 16W
Parker, S. Dak., U.S.A. 138 D6 43 25N 97 7W
Parker Dam, U.S.A. 145 L12 34 13N 114 5W
Parkersburg, Iowa, U.S.A. 140 B4 42 35N 92 47W
Parkersburg, W. Va., U.S.A. 134 F5 39 18N 81 31W
Parkerview, Canada 131 C8 51 21N 103 18W
Parkes, Australia 117 B8 33 9 S 148 11 E
Parkfield, U.S.A. 144 K6 35 54N 120 26W
Parkhar, Tajikistan 55 E4 37 30N 69 34 E
Parkland, U.S.A. 144 C4 47 9N 122 26W
Parkside, Canada 131 C7 53 10N 106 33W
Parkston, U.S.A. 138 D5 43 25N 98 0W
Parksville, Canada 130 D4 49 20N 124 21W
Parlakimidi, India 82 E7 18 45N 84 5 E
Parli, India 82 E3 18 50N 76 35 E
Parma, Italy 38 D7 44 50N 10 20 E
Parma, Idaho, U.S.A. 142 E5 43 49N 116 59W
Parma, Ohio, U.S.A. 136 E3 41 25N 81 42W
Parma →, Italy 38 D7 44 56N 10 26 E
Parnaguá, Brazil 154 D3 10 10 S 44 38W
Parnaíba, Piauí, Brazil 154 B3 2 54 S 41 47W
Parnaíba, São Paulo, Brazil 157 D7 19 34 S 51 14W
Parnaíba →, Brazil 154 B3 3 0 S 41 50W
Parnamirim, Brazil 154 C4 8 5 S 39 34W
Parnarama, Brazil 154 C3 5 31 S 43 6W
Parnassós, Greece 45 F4 38 35N 22 30 E
Parnassus, N.Z. 119 C8 42 42 S 173 23 E
Párnis, Greece 45 F5 38 14N 23 45 E
Párnon Óros, Greece 45 G4 37 15N 22 45 E
Pärnu, Estonia 50 B4 58 28N 24 33 E
Parola, India 82 D2 20 47N 75 7 E
Paroo →, Australia 115 E3 31 28 S 143 32 E
Páros, Greece 45 G7 37 5N 25 12 E
Parowan, U.S.A. 143 H7 37 54N 112 56W
Parpaillon, France 25 D10 44 30N 6 40 E
Parral, Chile 158 D1 36 10 S 71 52W
Parramatta, Australia 117 B9 33 48 S 151 1 E
Parras, Mexico 146 B4 25 30N 102 20W
Parrett →, U.K. 17 F5 51 7N 2 58W
Parris I., U.S.A. 135 J5 32 20N 80 30W
Parrsboro, Canada 129 C7 45 30N 64 25W
Parry Is., Canada 6 B2 77 0N 110 0W
Parry Sound, Canada 128 C3 45 20N 80 0W
Parsberg, Germany 27 F7 49 10N 11 43 E
Parseta →, Poland 47 A2 54 11N 15 34 E
Parshall, U.S.A. 138 B3 47 56N 102 11W
Parsnip →, Canada 130 B4 55 10N 123 2W
Parsons, U.S.A. 139 G7 37 20N 95 17W
Parsons Ra., Australia 114 A2 13 30 S 135 15 E
Partabpur, India 82 E5 20 0N 80 42 E
Partanna, Italy 40 E5 37 43N 12 51 E
Parthenay, France 22 F6 46 38N 0 16W
Partinico, Italy 40 D6 38 3N 13 6 E
Partur, India 82 E3 19 40N 76 14 E
Paru →, Brazil 153 D7 1 33 S 52 38W
Parú →, Venezuela 152 C4 4 20N 66 27W
Paru de Oeste →, Brazil 153 C6 1 30N 56 0W
Parubcan, Phil. 70 E4 13 43N 123 45 E
Parucito →, Venezuela 152 B4 5 18N 65 59W
Parur, India 83 J3 10 13N 76 14 E
Paruro, Peru 156 C3 13 45 S 71 50W
Parvān □, Afghan. 79 B3 35 0N 69 0 E
Parvatipuram, India 82 E6 18 50N 83 25 E
Parys, S. Africa 104 D4 26 52 S 27 29 E
Pas-de-Calais □, France 23 B9 50 30N 2 10 E
Pasadena, Calif., U.S.A. 145 L8 34 5N 118 9W
Pasadena, Tex., U.S.A. 139 L7 29 45N 95 14W
Pasaje, Ecuador 152 D2 3 23 S 79 50W
Pasaje →, Argentina 158 B3 25 39 S 63 56W
Pasay, Phil. 70 D3 14 33N 121 0 E
Pascagoula, U.S.A. 139 K10 30 21N 88 30W
Pascagoula →, U.S.A. 139 K10 30 21N 88 35W
Paşcani, Romania 46 B7 47 14N 26 45 E
Pasco, U.S.A. 142 C4 46 10N 119 0W
Pasco □, Peru 156 C2 10 40 S 75 0W
Pasco, Cerro de, Peru 156 C2 10 45 S 76 10W
Pascua, I. de, Pac. Oc. 123 K17 27 0 S 109 0W
Pasewalk, Germany 26 B10 53 30N 14 0 E
Pasfield L., Canada 131 B7 58 24N 105 20W
Pasha →, Russia 50 B8 60 29N 32 55 E
Pashiwari, Pakistan 81 B6 34 40N 75 10 E
Pashiya, Russia 54 B6 58 33N 58 26 E
Pashmakli = Smolyan, Bulgaria 43 F9 41 36N 24 38 E
Pasighat, India 78 A5 28 4N 95 21 E
Pasinler, Turkey 89 D9 39 59N 41 41 E
Pasir Mas, Malaysia 74 A2 6 2N 102 8 E
Pasirian, Indonesia 75 D4 8 13 S 113 8 E
Paskūh, Iran 85 E9 27 34N 61 39 E
Pasłeka →, Poland 47 A6 54 26N 19 46 E
Pasley, C., Australia 113 F3 33 52 S 123 35 E
Pašman, Croatia 39 E12 43 58N 15 20 E
Pasmore →, Australia 116 A3 31 5 S 139 49 E
Pasni, Pakistan 79 D1 25 15N 63 27 E
Paso Cantinela, Mexico 145 N11 32 33N 115 47W
Paso de Indios, Argentina 160 B3 43 55 S 69 0W
Paso de los Libres, Argentina 158 B4 29 44 S 57 10W
Paso de los Toros, Uruguay 158 C4 32 45 S 56 30W
Paso Flores, Argentina 160 B2 40 35 S 70 38W
Paso Robles, U.S.A. 143 J3 35 40N 120 45W
Pasorapa, Bolivia 157 D5 18 16 S 64 37W
Paspébiac, Canada 129 C6 48 3N 65 17W
Pasrur, Pakistan 80 C6 32 16N 74 43 E
Passage West, Ireland 19 E3 51 52N 8 20W
Passaic, U.S.A. 137 F10 40 50N 74 8W
Passau, Germany 27 G9 48 34N 13 27 E
Passendale, Belgium 21 G2 50 54N 3 2 E
Passero, C., Italy 41 F8 36 42N 15 8 E
Passi, Phil. 71 F4 11 6N 122 38 E
Passo Fundo, Brazil 159 B5 28 10 S 52 20W
Passos, Brazil 155 F2 20 45 S 46 37W
Passow, Germany 26 B10 53 13N 14 10 E
Passwang, Switz. 28 B5 47 22N 7 41 E
Passy, France 25 C10 45 55N 6 41 E
Pastaza □, Ecuador 152 D2 2 0 S 77 0W
Pastaza →, Peru 152 D2 4 50 S 76 52W
Pastęk, Poland 47 A6 54 3N 19 41 E
Pasto, Colombia 152 C2 1 13N 77 17W
Pastos Bons, Brazil 154 C3 6 36 S 44 5W
Pastrana, Spain 34 E2 40 27N 2 53W
Pasuquin, Phil. 70 B3 18 20N 120 37 E
Pasuruan, Indonesia 75 D4 7 40 S 112 44 E
Pasym, Poland 47 B7 53 48N 20 49 E
Pásztó, Hungary 31 D12 47 52N 19 43 E
Patagonia, Argentina 160 C2 45 0 S 69 0W
Patagonia, U.S.A. 143 L8 31 35N 110 45W
Patambar, Iran 85 D9 29 45N 60 17 E
Patan, Gujarat, India 82 F1 17 22N 73 57 E
Patan, Maharashtra, India 80 H5 23 54N 72 14 E
Patani, Indonesia 72 A3 0 20N 128 50 E
Pataudi, India 80 E7 28 18N 76 48 E
Patay, France 23 D8 48 2N 1 40 E
Patchewollock, Australia 116 C5 35 22 S 142 12 E
Patchogue, U.S.A. 137 F11 40 46N 73 1W
Patea, N.Z. 118 F3 39 45 S 174 30 E
Pategi, Nigeria 101 D6 8 50N 5 45 E
Patensie, S. Africa 104 E3 33 46 S 24 49 E
Paternò, Italy 41 E7 37 34N 14 53 E
Pateros, U.S.A. 142 B4 48 4N 119 58W
Paterson, Australia 117 B9 32 35 S 151 36 E
Paterson, U.S.A. 137 F10 40 55N 74 10W
Paterson Inlet, N.Z. 119 G3 46 56 S 168 12 E
Paterson Ra., Australia 112 D3 21 45 S 122 10 E
Paterswolde, Neths. 20 B9 53 9N 6 34 E
Pathankot, India 80 C6 32 18N 75 45 E
Patharghata, Bangla. 78 D2 22 2N 89 58 E
Pathfinder Res., U.S.A. 142 E10 42 30N 107 0W
Pathiu, Thailand 77 G2 10 42N 99 19 E
Pathum Thani, Thailand 76 E3 14 1N 100 32 E
Pati, Indonesia 75 D4 6 45 S 111 1 E
Pati Pt., Guam 121 R15 13 40N 144 50 E
Patía, Colombia 152 C2 2 4N 77 4W
Patía →, Colombia 152 C2 2 13N 78 40W
Patiala, India 80 D7 30 23N 76 26 E
Patine Kouka, Senegal 100 C2 12 45N 13 45W
Pativilca, Peru 156 C2 10 42 S 77 48W
Patkai Bum, India 78 B5 27 0N 95 30 E
Pátmos, Greece 45 G8 37 21N 26 36 E
Patna, India 81 G11 25 35N 85 12 E
Patnongon, Phil. 71 F3 10 55N 122 0 E
Patnos, Turkey 89 D10 39 13N 42 51 E
Patonga, Uganda 106 B3 2 45N 33 15 E
Patos, Brazil 154 C4 6 55 S 37 16W
Patos, L. dos, Brazil 159 C5 31 20 S 51 0W
Patos de Minas, Brazil 155 E2 18 35 S 46 32W
Patosi, Albania 44 D1 40 42N 19 38 E
Patquía, Argentina 158 C2 30 2 S 66 55W
Pátrai, Greece 45 F3 38 14N 21 47 E
Pátraikós Kólpos, Greece 45 F3 38 17N 21 30 E
Patricio Lynch, I., Chile 160 C1 48 35 S 75 30W
Patrocínio, Brazil 155 E2 18 57 S 47 0W
Patta, Kenya 106 C5 2 10 S 41 0 E
Pattada, Italy 40 B2 40 35N 9 7 E
Pattanapuram, India 83 K3 9 6N 76 50 E
Pattani, Thailand 77 J3 6 48N 101 15 E
Patten, U.S.A. 129 C6 45 59N 68 28W
Patterson, Calif., U.S.A. 144 H5 37 30N 121 9W
Patterson, La., U.S.A. 139 L9 29 44N 91 20W
Patterson, Mt., U.S.A. 144 G7 38 29N 119 20W
Patteson, Passage, Vanuatu 121 E6 15 26 S 168 12 E
Patti, India 80 D6 31 17N 74 54 E
Patti, Italy 41 D7 38 8N 14 57 E
Pattoki, Pakistan 80 D5 31 5N 73 52 E
Patton, U.S.A. 136 F6 40 38N 78 40W
Pattonsburg, U.S.A. 140 D2 40 3N 94 8W
Pattukkattai, India 83 J4 10 25N 79 20 E
Patu, Brazil 154 C4 6 6 S 37 38W
Patuakhali, Bangla. 78 D3 22 20N 90 25 E
Patuca →, Honduras 148 C3 15 50N 84 18W
Patuca, Punta, Honduras 148 C3 15 49N 84 14W
Pâturages, Belgium 21 H3 50 25N 3 52 E
Pátzcuaro, Mexico 146 D4 19 30N 101 40W
Pau, France 24 E3 43 19N 0 25W
Pau, Gave de →, France 24 E2 43 33N 1 12W
Pau d' Arco, Brazil 154 C2 7 30 S 49 22W
Pau dos Ferros, Brazil 154 C4 6 7 S 38 10W
Paucartambo, Peru 156 C3 13 19 S 71 35W
Pauillac, France 24 C3 45 11N 0 46W
Pauini, Brazil 156 B4 7 40 S 66 58W
Pauini →, Brazil 153 D5 1 42 S 62 50W
Pauk, Burma 78 E5 21 27N 94 30 E
Paul I., Canada 129 A7 56 30N 61 20W
Paul Isnard, Fr. Guiana 153 C7 4 47N 54 1W
Paulding, U.S.A. 141 C12 41 8N 84 35W
Paulhan, France 24 E7 43 33N 3 28 E
Paulis = Isiro, Zaïre 106 B2 2 53N 27 40 E
Paulista, Brazil 154 C5 7 57 S 34 53W
Paulistana, Brazil 154 C3 8 9 S 41 9W
Paullina, U.S.A. 138 D7 42 55N 95 40W
Paulo Afonso, Brazil 154 C4 9 21 S 38 15W
Paulo de Faria, Brazil 155 F2 20 2 S 49 24W
Paulpietersburg, S. Africa 105 D5 27 23 S 30 50 E
Pauls Valley, U.S.A. 139 H6 34 40N 97 17W
Pauma Valley, U.S.A. 145 M10 33 16N 116 58W
Paungde, Burma 78 F5 18 29N 95 30 E
Pauni, India 82 D4 20 48N 79 40 E
Pausa, Peru 156 D3 15 16 S 73 22W
Pauto →, Colombia 152 B3 5 9N 70 55W
Pāveh, Iran 84 C5 35 3N 46 22 E
Pavelets, Russia 51 E11 53 49N 39 14 E
Pavia, Italy 38 C6 45 10N 9 10 E
Pavlikeni, Bulgaria 43 D10 43 14N 25 20 E
Pavlodar, Kazakhstan 56 D8 52 33N 77 0 E
Pavlograd, Ukraine 52 B6 48 30N 35 52 E
Pavlovo, Russia 51 D13 55 58N 43 5 E
Pavlovo, Russia 57 C12 63 5N 115 25 E
Pavlovsk, Russia 51 F12 50 26N 40 5 E
Pavlovskaya, Russia 53 C8 46 17N 39 47 E
Pavlovskiy-Posad, Russia 51 D11 55 47N 38 42 E
Pavullo nel Frignano, Italy 38 D7 44 20N 10 50 E
Pavuvu, Solomon Is. 121 M10 9 4 S 159 8 E
Paw Paw, U.S.A. 141 B11 42 13N 85 53W
Pawahku, Burma 78 B7 26 11N 98 40 E
Pawan →, Indonesia 75 C4 1 55 S 110 0 E
Pawhuska, U.S.A. 139 G6 36 40N 96 25W
Pawling, U.S.A. 137 E11 41 35N 73 37W
Pawnee, Ill., U.S.A. 140 E7 39 35N 89 35W
Pawnee, Okla., U.S.A. 139 G6 36 24N 96 50W
Pawnee City, U.S.A. 138 E6 40 8N 96 10W
Pawpaw, U.S.A. 140 C8 41 41N 88 59W
Pawtucket, U.S.A. 137 E13 41 51N 71 22W
Paximádhia, Greece 32 D6 35 0N 24 35 E
Paxoí, Greece 44 E2 39 14N 20 12 E
Paxton, Ill., U.S.A. 141 D8 40 25N 88 7W
Paxton, Nebr., U.S.A. 138 E4 41 12N 101 27W
Payakumbuh, Indonesia 74 C2 0 20 S 100 35 E
Payerne, Switz. 28 C3 46 49N 6 56 E
Payette, U.S.A. 142 D5 44 5N 117 0W
Paymogo, Spain 37 H3 37 44N 7 21W
Payne, U.S.A. 141 C12 41 5N 84 44W
Payne Bay = Bellin, Canada 127 B13 60 0N 70 0W
Payne L., Canada 127 C12 59 30N 74 30W
Paynes Find, Australia 113 E2 29 15 S 117 42 E
Paynesville, Liberia 100 D2 6 20N 10 45W
Paynesville, U.S.A. 138 C7 45 21N 94 44W
Paysandú, Uruguay 158 C4 32 19 S 58 8W
Payson, Ariz., U.S.A. 143 J8 34 17N 111 15W
Payson, Utah, U.S.A. 142 F8 40 8N 111 41W
Paz →, Guatemala 148 D1 13 44N 90 10W
Paz, B. la, Mexico 146 C2 24 15N 110 25W
Pāzanān, Iran 85 D6 30 35N 49 59 E
Pazar, Turkey 89 C9 41 10N 40 50 E
Pazarcık, Turkey 88 E7 37 30N 37 17 E
Pazardzhik, Bulgaria 43 E9 42 12N 24 20 E
Pazin, Croatia 39 C10 45 14N 13 56 E
Pazña, Bolivia 156 D4 18 36 S 66 55W
Pčinja →, Macedonia, Yug. 42 F6 41 50N 21 45 E
Pe Ell, U.S.A. 144 D3 46 30N 123 18W
Peabody, U.S.A. 137 D14 42 31N 70 56W
Peace →, Canada 130 B6 59 0N 111 25W
Peace Point, Canada 130 B6 59 7N 112 27W
Peace River, Canada 130 B5 56 15N 117 18W
Peach Springs, U.S.A. 143 J7 35 36N 113 30W
Peak Downs, Australia 114 C4 22 55 S 148 5 E
Peak Downs Mine, Australia 114 C4 22 17 S 148 11 E
Peak Hill, N.S.W., Australia 117 B8 32 47 S 148 11 E
Peak Hill, W. Austral., Australia 113 E2 25 35 S 118 43 E
Peak Ra., Australia 114 C4 22 50 S 148 20 E
Peake, Australia 116 C3 35 25 S 139 55 E
Peake Cr. →, Australia 115 D2 28 2 S 136 7 E
Peale Mt., U.S.A. 143 G9 38 25N 109 12W
Pearblossom, U.S.A. 145 L9 34 30N 117 55W
Pearl, U.S.A. 140 E6 39 28N 90 38W
Pearl →, U.S.A. 139 K10 30 23N 89 45W
Pearl Banks, Sri Lanka 83 K4 8 45N 79 45 E
Pearl City, Hawaii, U.S.A. 132 H16 21 24N 158 0W
Pearl City, Ill., U.S.A. 140 B7 42 16N 89 50W
Pearsall, U.S.A. 139 L5 28 55N 99 8W
Pearse I., Canada 130 C2 54 52N 130 14W
Peary Land, Greenland 6 A6 82 40N 33 0W
Pease →, U.S.A. 139 H5 34 12N 99 7W
Pebane, Mozam. 107 F4 17 10 S 38 8 E
Pebas, Peru 152 D3 3 10 S 71 46W
Pebble, I., Falk. Is. 160 D5 51 20 S 59 40W
Pebble Beach, U.S.A. 144 J5 36 34N 121 57W
Peč, Serbia, Yug. 42 E5 42 40N 20 17 E
Peçanha, Brazil 155 E3 18 33 S 42 34W
Pecatonica, U.S.A. 140 B7 42 19N 89 22W
Pecatonica →, U.S.A. 140 B7 42 26N 89 17W
Péccioli, Italy 38 E7 43 32N 10 43 E
Pechea, Romania 46 D8 45 36N 27 49 E
Pechenezhin, Ukraine 52 B1 48 30N 24 48 E
Pechenga, Russia 48 A5 69 30N 31 25 E
Pechiguera, Pta., Canary Is. 33 F6 28 51N 13 53W
Pechnezhskoye Vdkhr., Ukraine 52 A7 50 0N 37 10 E
Pechora →, Russia 48 A9 68 13N 54 15 E
Pechorskaya Guba, Russia 48 A9 68 40N 54 0 E
Pechory, Russia 50 C5 57 48N 27 40 E
Pecica, Romania 46 C2 46 10N 21 3 E
Pečka, Serbia, Yug. 42 C4 44 18N 19 33 E
Pécora, C., Italy 40 C1 39 28N 8 23 E
Pecos, U.S.A. 139 K3 31 25N 103 30W
Pecos →, U.S.A. 139 L3 29 42N 102 30W
Pécs, Hungary 31 E11 46 5N 18 15 E
Peddapalli, India 82 E4 18 40N 79 24 E
Peddapuram, India 82 F6 17 6N 82 8 E
Pedder, L., Australia 114 G4 42 55 S 146 10 E
Peddie, S. Africa 105 E4 33 14 S 27 7 E
Pédernales, Dom. Rep. 149 C5 18 2N 71 44W
Pedieos →, Cyprus 32 D12 35 10N 33 54 E
Pedirka, Australia 115 D2 26 40 S 135 14 E
Pedra Azul, Brazil 155 E3 16 2 S 41 17W
Pedra Grande, Recifes de, Brazil 155 E4 17 45 S 38 58W
Pedras Negras, Brazil 157 C5 12 51 S 62 54W
Pedreiras, Brazil 154 B3 4 32 S 44 40W
Pedro Afonso, Brazil 154 C2 9 0 S 48 10W
Pedro Cays, Jamaica 148 C4 17 5N 77 48W
Pedro Chico, Colombia 152 C3 1 4N 70 25W
Pedro de Valdivia, Chile 158 A2 22 55 S 69 38W
Pedro Juan Caballero, Paraguay 159 A4 22 30 S 55 40W
Pedro Muñoz, Spain 35 F2 39 25N 2 56W
Pedrógão Grande, Portugal 36 F2 39 55N 8 9W
Peebinga, Australia 116 C4 34 52 S 140 57 E
Peebles, U.K. 18 F5 55 40N 3 12W
Peebles, U.S.A. 141 F13 38 57N 83 23W
Peekskill, U.S.A. 137 E11 41 18N 73 57W
Peel, U.K. 16 C3 54 13N 4 41W
Peel →, Australia 117 A9 30 50 S 150 29 E
Peel →, Canada 126 B6 67 0N 135 0W
Peelwood, Australia 117 C8 34 7 S 149 27 E
Peene →, Germany 26 A9 54 9N 13 46 E
Peera Peera Poolanna L., Australia 115 D2 26 30 S 138 0 E
Peers, Canada 130 C5 53 40N 116 0W
Pegasus Bay, N.Z. 119 D8 43 20 S 173 10 E
Peggau, Austria 30 D8 47 12N 15 21 E
Pegnitz, Germany 27 F7 49 45N 11 33 E
Pegnitz →, Germany 27 F6 49 29N 10 59 E
Pego, Spain 35 G4 38 51N 0 8W
Pegu, Burma 78 G6 17 20N 96 29 E
Pegu Yoma, Burma 78 F5 19 0N 96 0 E
Pehčevo, Macedonia, Yug. 42 F7 41 41N 22 55 E
Pehuajó, Argentina 158 D3 35 45 S 62 0W
Pei Xian, China 66 G9 34 44N 116 55 E
Peine, Chile 158 A2 23 45 S 68 8W
Peine, Germany 26 C6 52 19N 10 12 E
Peip'ing = Beijing, China 66 E9 39 55N 116 20 E
Peissenberg, Germany 27 H7 47 48N 11 4 E
Peitz, Germany 26 D10 51 50N 14 23 E
Peixe, Brazil 155 D2 12 0 S 48 40W
Peixe →, Brazil 155 F1 21 31 S 51 58W
Peixoto de Azeredo →, Brazil 157 C6 10 6 S 55 31W
Peize, Neths. 20 B8 53 9N 6 30 E
Pek →, Serbia, Yug. 42 C6 44 45N 21 29 E
Pekalongan, Indonesia 75 D3 6 53 S 109 40 E
Pekan, Malaysia 77 L4 3 30N 103 25 E
Pekanbaru, Indonesia 74 B2 0 30N 101 15 E
Pekin, U.S.A. 140 D7 40 35N 89 40W
Peking = Beijing, China 66 E9 39 55N 116 20 E
Pelabuhan Kelang, Malaysia 77 L3 3 0N 101 23 E
Pelabuhan Ratu, Teluk, Indonesia 74 D3 7 5 S 106 30 E
Pelabuhanratu, Indonesia 74 D3 7 0 S 106 32 E
Pélagos, Greece 44 E6 39 17N 24 4 E
Pelaihari, Indonesia 75 C4 3 55 S 114 45 E
Pelat, Mt., France 25 D10 44 16N 6 42 E
Pełczyce, Poland 47 B2 53 3N 15 16 E
Peleaga, Romania 46 D3 45 22N 22 55 E
Pelechuco, Bolivia 156 C4 14 48 S 69 4W
Pelée, Mt., Martinique 149 D7 14 48N 61 10W
Pelee, Pt., Canada 128 D3 41 54N 82 31W
Pelee I., Canada 128 D3 41 47N 82 40W
Pelejo, Peru 156 B2 6 10 S 75 49W
Pelekech, Kenya 106 B4 3 52N 35 8 E
Peleng, Indonesia 72 B2 1 20 S 123 30 E
Pelham, U.S.A. 135 K3 31 5N 84 6W
Pelhřimov, Czech. 30 B8 49 24N 15 12 E
Pelican L., Canada 131 C8 52 28N 100 20W
Pelican Narrows, Canada 131 B8 55 10N 102 56W
Pelican Rapids, Canada 131 C8 52 45N 100 42W
Peljesac, Croatia 42 E2 42 55N 17 25 E
Pelkosenniemi, Finland 12 C19 67 6N 27 28 E
Pella, Greece 44 D4 40 46N 22 23 E
Pella, S. Africa 104 D2 29 1 S 19 6 E
Pella, U.S.A. 140 C4 41 30N 92 54W
Pélla □, Greece 44 D4 40 52N 22 0 E
Péllaro, Italy 41 D8 38 1N 15 40 E
Pellworm, Germany 26 A4 54 30N 8 40 E
Pelly →, Canada 126 B6 62 47N 137 19W
Pelly Bay, Canada 127 B11 68 38N 89 50W
Pelly L., Canada 126 B9 66 0N 102 0W
Peloponnese = Pelopónnisos □, Greece 45 G4 37 10N 22 0 E
Pelopónnisos □, Greece 45 G4 37 10N 22 0 E
Peloritani, Monti, Italy 41 D8 38 2N 15 25 E
Peloro, C., Italy 41 D8 38 15N 15 40 E
Pelorus →, N.Z. 119 B8 41 16 S 173 45 E
Pelorus Sd., N.Z. 119 A8 40 59 S 173 59 E
Pelotas, Brazil 159 C5 31 42 S 52 23W
Pelòvo, Bulgaria 43 D9 43 26N 24 17 E
Pelvoux, Massif de, France 25 D10 44 52N 6 20 E
Pelym →, Russia 54 B8 59 39N 63 26 E
Pemalang, Indonesia 75 D3 6 53 S 109 23 E
Pematangsiantar, Indonesia 74 B1 2 57N 99 5 E
Pemba, Mozam. 107 E5 12 58 S 40 30 E
Pemba, Zambia 107 F2 16 30 S 27 28 E
Pemba Channel, Tanzania 106 D4 5 0 S 39 37 E
Pemba I., Tanzania 106 D4 5 0 S 39 45 E
Pemberton, Australia 113 F2 34 30 S 116 0 E
Pemberton, Canada 130 C4 50 25N 122 50W
Pembina, U.S.A. 131 D9 48 58N 97 15W
Pembina →, U.S.A. 131 D9 49 0N 98 12W
Pembine, U.S.A. 134 C2 45 38N 87 59W
Pembino, U.S.A. 138 A6 48 58N 97 15W
Pembroke, Canada 128 C4 45 50N 77 7W
Pembroke, U.K. 17 F3 51 41N 4 57W
Pembroke, U.S.A. 135 J5 32 5N 81 32W
Pembuang →, Indonesia 75 C4 3 24 S 112 33 E
Pen-y-Ghent, U.K. 16 C5 54 10N 2 15W
Peña, Sierra de la, Spain 34 C4 42 32N 0 45W
Peña de Francia, Sierra de, Spain 36 E4 40 32N 6 10W
Peñafiel, Portugal 36 D2 41 12N 8 17W
Peñafiel, Spain 36 D6 41 35N 4 7W
Peñaflor, Spain 37 H5 37 43N 5 21W
Peñalara, Pico, Spain 36 E7 40 51N 3 57W
Penalva, Brazil 154 B2 3 18 S 45 10W
Penamacôr, Portugal 36 E3 40 10N 7 10W
Penang = Pinang, Malaysia 77 K3 5 25N 100 15 E
Penápolis, Brazil 159 A6 21 30 S 50 0W
Peñaranda de Bracamonte, Spain 36 E5 40 53N 5 13W
Peñarroya-Pueblonuevo, Spain 37 G5 38 19N 5 16W
Peñas, C. de, Spain 36 B5 43 42N 5 52W
Penas, G. de, Chile 160 C2 47 0 S 75 0W
Peñas, Pta., Venezuela 153 A5 11 17N 62 0W
Peñas de San Pedro, Spain 35 G2 38 44N 2 0W
Peñas del Chache, Canary Is. 33 E6 29 6N 13 33W
Peñausende, Spain 36 D5 41 17N 5 52W
Pench'i = Benxi, China 67 D12 41 20N 123 48 E
Pend Oreille →, U.S.A. 142 B5 49 4N 117 37W
Pend Oreille, L., U.S.A. 142 C5 48 0N 116 30W
Pendálofon, Greece 44 D3 40 14N 21 12 E
Pendelikón, Greece 45 F5 38 10N 23 53 E

248 Pendembu

Pendembu, *S. Leone* **100** **D2** 9 7N 12 14W
Pendências, *Brazil* **154** **C4** 5 15 S 36 43W
Pender B., *Australia* **112** **C3** 16 45 S 122 42 E
Pendleton, *Calif., U.S.A.* **145** **M9** 33 16N 117 23W
Pendleton, *Ind., U.S.A.* **141** **E11** 40 0N 85 45W
Pendleton, *Oreg., U.S.A.* **142** **D4** 45 35N 118 50W
Pendzhikent, *Tajikistan* **55** **D3** 39 29N 67 37 E
Penedo, *Brazil* **154** **D4** 10 15 S 36 36W
Penetanguishene, *Canada* **128** **D4** 44 50N 79 55W
Peng Xian, *China* **68** **B4** 31 4N 103 32 E
Pengalengan, *Indonesia* **75** **D3** 7 9 S 107 30 E
Penge, *Kasai Or., Zaïre* **103** **D4** 5 30 S 24 33 E
Penge, *Kivu, Zaïre* **106** **C2** 4 27 S 28 25 E
Penglai, *China* **67** **F11** 37 48N 120 42 E
Pengshui, *China* **68** **C7** 29 17N 108 12 E
Penguin, *Australia* **114** **G4** 41 8 S 146 6 E
Pengxi, *China* **68** **B5** 30 44N 105 45 E
Pengze, *China* **69** **C11** 29 52N 116 32 E
Penhalonga, *Zimbabwe* **107** **F3** 18 52 S 32 40 E
Peniche, *Portugal* **37** **F1** 39 19N 9 22W
Penicuik, *U.K.* **18** **F5** 55 50N 3 14W
Penida, *Indonesia* **75** **D5** 8 45 S 115 30 E
Peninsular Malaysia □, *Malaysia* **77** **L4** 4 0N 102 0 E
Peñíscola, *Spain* **34** **E5** 40 22N 0 24 E
Penitente, Serra dos, *Brazil* **154** **C2** 8 45 S 46 20W
Penmarch, *France* **22** **E2** 47 49N 4 21W
Penmarch, Pte. de, *France* **22** **E2** 47 48N 4 22W
Penn Hills, *U.S.A.* **136** **F5** 40 28N 79 52W
Penn Yan, *U.S.A.* **136** **D7** 42 39N 77 7W
Pennabilli, *Italy* **39** **E9** 43 50N 12 17 E
Pennant, *Canada* **131** **C7** 50 32N 108 14W
Penne, *Italy* **39** **F10** 42 28N 13 56 E
Penner →, *India* **83** **G5** 14 35N 80 10 E
Penneshaw, *Australia* **116** **C2** 35 44 S 137 56 E
Pennine, Alpi, *Alps* **38** **B4** 46 4N 7 30 E
Pennines, *U.K.* **16** **C5** 54 50N 2 20W
Pennington, *U.S.A.* **144** **F5** 39 15N 121 47W
Pennino, Mte., *Italy* **39** **E9** 43 6N 12 54 E
Pennsylvania □, *U.S.A.* **134** **E6** 40 50N 78 0W
Pennville, *U.S.A.* **141** **D11** 40 30N 85 9W
Penny, *Canada* **130** **C4** 53 51N 121 20W
Peno, *Russia* **50** **C8** 57 2N 32 49 E
Penola, *Australia* **116** **D4** 37 25 S 140 48 E
Penong, *Australia* **110** **G5** 31 59 S 133 5 E
Penong, *S. Austral., Australia* **113** **F5** 31 56 S 133 1 E
Penonomé, *Panama* **148** **E3** 8 31N 80 21W
Penot, Mt., *Vanuatu* **121** **F5** 16 20 S 167 31 E
Penrith, *Australia* **117** **B9** 33 43 S 150 38 E
Penrith, *U.K.* **16** **C5** 54 40N 2 45W
Pensacola, *U.S.A.* **135** **K2** 30 30N 87 10W
Pensacola Mts., *Antarctica* **7** **E1** 84 0 S 40 0W
Pense, *Canada* **131** **C8** 50 25N 104 59W
Penshurst, *Australia* **116** **D5** 37 49 S 142 20 E
Pensiangan, *Malaysia* **75** **B5** 4 33N 116 19 E
Pentecost = Pentecôte, *Vanuatu* **121** **E6** 15 42 S 168 10 E
Pentecoste, *Brazil* **154** **B4** 3 48 S 39 17W
Pentecôte, *Vanuatu* **121** **E6** 15 42 S 168 10 E
Penticton, *Canada* **130** **D5** 49 30N 119 38W
Pentland, *Australia* **114** **C4** 20 32 S 145 25 E
Pentland Firth, *U.K.* **18** **C5** 58 43N 3 10W
Pentland Hills, *U.K.* **18** **F5** 55 48N 3 25W
Penukonda, *India* **83** **G3** 14 5N 77 38 E
Penylan L., *Canada* **131** **A7** 61 50N 106 20W
Penza, *Russia* **51** **E14** 53 15N 45 5 E
Penzance, *U.K.* **17** **G2** 50 7N 5 32W
Penzberg, *Germany* **27** **H7** 47 46N 11 23 E
Penzhino, *Russia* **57** **C17** 63 30N 167 55 E
Penzhinskaya Guba, *Russia* **57** **C17** 61 30N 163 0 E
Penzlin, *Germany* **26** **B9** 53 32N 13 6 E
Peoria, *Ariz., U.S.A.* **143** **K7** 33 40N 112 15W
Peoria, *Ill., U.S.A.* **140** **D7** 40 40N 89 40W
Peoria Heights, *U.S.A.* **140** **D7** 40 45N 89 35W
Peotone, *U.S.A.* **141** **C9** 41 20N 87 48W
Pepingen, *Belgium* **21** **G4** 50 46N 4 10 E
Pepinster, *Belgium* **21** **G7** 50 34N 5 47 E
Peqini, *Albania* **44** **C1** 41 4N 19 44 E
Pera Hd., *Australia* **114** **A3** 12 55 S 141 37 E
Perabumilih, *Indonesia* **74** **C2** 3 27 S 104 15 E
Perak □, *Malaysia* **74** **A2** 5 0N 101 0 E
Perakhóra, *Greece* **45** **F4** 38 2N 22 56 E
Perales de Alfambra, *Spain* **34** **E3** 40 38N 1 0W
Perales del Puerto, *Spain* **36** **E4** 40 10N 6 40W
Peralta, *Spain* **34** **C3** 42 21N 1 49W
Pérama, *Kérkira, Greece* **32** **A3** 39 34N 19 54 E
Pérama, *Kríti, Greece* **32** **D6** 35 20N 24 40 E
Perast, *Montenegro, Yug.* **42** **E3** 42 31N 18 47 E
Percé, *Canada* **129** **C7** 48 31N 64 13W
Perche, *France* **22** **D8** 48 31N 1 1 E
Perche, Collines du, *France* **22** **D7** 48 30N 0 40 E
Percival Lakes, *Australia* **112** **D4** 21 25 S 125 0 E
Percy, *France* **22** **D5** 48 55N 1 11W
Percy, *U.S.A.* **140** **F7** 38 5N 89 41W
Percy Is., *Australia* **114** **C5** 21 39 S 150 16 E
Perdido →, *Argentina* **160** **B3** 42 55 S 67 0W
Perdido, Mte., *Spain* **24** **F4** 42 40N 0 5 E
Perdu, Mt. = Perdido, Mte., *Spain* **24** **F4** 42 40N 0 5 E
Pereira, *Colombia* **152** **C2** 4 49N 75 43W
Pereira Barreto, *Brazil* **155** **F1** 20 38 S 51 7W
Perekerten, *Australia* **116** **C5** 34 55 S 143 40 E
Perené →, *Peru* **156** **C3** 11 9 S 74 14W
Perenjori, *Australia* **113** **E2** 29 26 S 116 16 E
Pereslavi-Zalesskiy, *Russia* **51** **C11** 56 45N 38 50 E
Pereyaslav Khmelnitskiy, *Ukraine* **50** **F7** 50 3N 31 28 E
Pérez, I., *Mexico* **147** **C7** 22 24N 89 42W
Perg, *Austria* **30** **C7** 48 15N 14 38 E
Pergamino, *Argentina* **158** **C3** 33 52 S 60 30W
Pérgine Valsugano, *Italy* **39** **B8** 46 4N 11 15 E
Pérgola, *Italy* **39** **E9** 43 35N 12 50 E
Perham, *U.S.A.* **138** **B7** 46 36N 95 36W
Perhentian, Kepulauan, *Malaysia* **77** **K4** 5 54N 102 42 E
Peri L., *Australia* **116** **A5** 30 45 S 143 35 E
Periam, *Romania* **46** **C1** 46 2N 20 59 E
Péribonca →, *Canada* **129** **C5** 48 45N 72 5W
Péribonca, L., *Canada* **129** **B5** 50 1N 71 10W
Perico, *Argentina* **158** **A2** 24 20 S 65 5W
Pericos, *Mexico* **146** **B3** 25 3N 107 42W
Périers, *France* **22** **C5** 49 11N 1 25W
Périgord, *France* **24** **D4** 45 0N 0 40 E
Périgueux, *France* **24** **C4** 45 10N 0 42 E
Perijá, Sierra de, *Colombia* **152** **B3** 9 30N 73 3W
Peristéra, *Greece* **45** **E5** 39 15N 23 58 E
Peristerona →, *Cyprus* **32** **D12** 35 8N 33 5 E
Perito Moreno, *Argentina* **160** **C2** 46 36 S 70 56W
Peritoró, *Brazil* **154** **B3** 4 20 S 44 18W
Perivol = Dragovishtitsa, *Bulgaria* **42** **E7** 42 22N 22 39 E
Periyakulam, *India* **83** **J3** 10 5N 77 30 E
Periyar →, *India* **83** **J3** 10 15N 76 10 E
Periyar, L., *India* **83** **K3** 9 25N 77 10 E
Perković, *Croatia* **39** **E13** 43 41N 16 10 E
Perlas, Arch. de las, *Panama* **148** **E4** 8 41N 79 7W
Perlas, Punta de, *Nic.* **148** **D3** 12 30N 83 30W
Perleberg, *Germany* **26** **B7** 53 5N 11 50 E
Perlevka, *Russia* **51** **F11** 51 58N 38 57 E
Perlez, *Serbia, Yug.* **42** **B5** 45 11N 20 22 E
Perlis □, *Malaysia* **74** **A2** 6 30N 100 15 E
Perm, *Russia* **54** **C5** 58 0N 56 10 E
Përmeti, *Albania* **44** **D2** 40 15N 20 21 E
Pernambuco = Recife, *Brazil* **154** **C5** 8 0 S 35 0W
Pernambuco □, *Brazil* **154** **C4** 8 0 S 37 0W
Pernatty Lagoon, *Australia* **116** **A2** 31 30 S 137 12 E
Pernik, *Bulgaria* **42** **E8** 42 35N 23 2 E
Peron, C., *Australia* **113** **E1** 25 30 S 113 30 E
Peron Is., *Australia* **112** **B5** 13 9 S 130 4 E
Peron Pen., *Australia* **113** **E1** 26 0 S 113 10 E
Péronne, *France* **23** **C9** 49 55N 2 57 E
Péronnes, *Belgium* **21** **H4** 50 27N 4 9 E
Perosa Argentina, *Italy* **38** **D4** 44 57N 7 11 E
Perow, *Canada* **130** **C3** 54 35N 126 10W
Perpendicular Pt., *Australia* **115** **E5** 31 37 S 152 52 E
Perpignan, *France* **24** **F6** 42 42N 2 53 E
Perris, *U.S.A.* **145** **M9** 33 47N 117 14W
Perros-Guirec, *France* **22** **D3** 48 49N 3 28W
Perry, *Fla., U.S.A.* **135** **K4** 30 9N 83 40W
Perry, *Ga., U.S.A.* **135** **J4** 32 25N 83 41W
Perry, *Iowa, U.S.A.* **140** **C2** 41 48N 94 5W
Perry, *Maine, U.S.A.* **135** **C12** 44 59N 67 20W
Perry, *Mich., U.S.A.* **141** **B12** 42 50N 84 13W
Perry, *Mo., U.S.A.* **140** **E5** 39 26N 91 40W
Perry, *Okla., U.S.A.* **139** **G6** 36 20N 97 20W
Perrysburg, *U.S.A.* **141** **C13** 41 34N 83 38W
Perryton, *U.S.A.* **139** **G4** 36 28N 100 48W
Perryville, *U.S.A.* **139** **G10** 37 42N 89 50W
Perşembe, *Turkey* **89** **C7** 41 5N 37 46 E
Perseverancia, *Bolivia* **157** **C5** 14 44 S 62 48W
Persia = Iran ■, *Asia* **85** **C7** 33 0N 53 0 E
Persian Gulf = Gulf, The, *Asia* **85** **E6** 27 0N 50 0 E
Perstorp, *Sweden* **15** **H7** 56 10N 13 25 E
Pertek, *Turkey* **89** **D8** 38 51N 39 19 E
Perth, *Australia* **113** **F2** 31 57 S 115 52 E
Perth, *Canada* **128** **D4** 44 55N 76 15W
Perth, *U.K.* **18** **E5** 56 24N 3 27W
Perth Amboy, *U.S.A.* **137** **F10** 40 31N 74 16W
Pertuis, *France* **25** **E9** 43 42N 5 30 E
Peru, *Ill., U.S.A.* **140** **C7** 41 18N 89 12W
Peru, *Ind., U.S.A.* **141** **D10** 40 42N 86 5W
Peru ■, *S. Amer.* **152** **D2** 4 0 S 75 0W
Peru-Chile Trench, *Pac. Oc.* **123** **K20** 20 0 S 72 0W
Perúgia, *Italy* **39** **E9** 43 6N 12 24 E
Perušić, *Croatia* **39** **D12** 44 40N 15 22 E
Péruwelz, *Belgium* **21** **G3** 50 31N 3 36 E
Pervomaysk, *Russia* **51** **D13** 54 56N 43 58 E
Pervomaysk, *Ukraine* **52** **B4** 48 10N 30 46 E
Pervouralsk, *Russia* **54** **C6** 56 55N 59 45 E
Perwez, *Belgium* **21** **G5** 50 38N 4 48 E
Pes, Pta. del, *Spain* **33** **C7** 38 46N 1 26 E
Pésaro, *Italy* **39** **E9** 43 55N 12 53 E
Pescara, *Italy* **39** **F11** 42 28N 14 13 E
Pescara →, *Italy* **39** **F11** 42 28N 14 13 E
Peschanokopskoye, *Russia* **53** **C9** 46 14N 41 4 E
Péscia, *Italy* **38** **E7** 43 54N 10 40 E
Pescina, *Italy* **39** **G10** 42 0N 13 39 E
Peseux, *Switz.* **28** **C3** 46 59N 6 53 E
Peshawar, *Pakistan* **79** **B3** 34 2N 71 37 E
Peshkopia, *Albania* **44** **C2** 41 41N 20 25 E
Peshtera, *Bulgaria* **43** **E9** 42 2N 24 18 E
Peshtigo, *U.S.A.* **134** **C2** 45 4N 87 46W
Peski, *Russia* **51** **F13** 51 14N 42 29 E
Peskovka, *Russia* **51** **B18** 59 23N 52 20 E
Peskovka, *Russia* **54** **B3** 59 4N 52 22 E
Pêso da Régua, *Portugal* **36** **D3** 41 10N 7 47W
Pesqueira, *Brazil* **154** **C4** 8 20 S 36 42W
Pessac, *France* **24** **D3** 44 48N 0 37W
Pessoux, *Belgium* **21** **H6** 50 17N 5 11 E
Pest □, *Hungary* **31** **D12** 47 29N 19 5 E
Pestovo, *Russia* **50** **B9** 58 33N 35 42 E
Pestravka, *Russia* **51** **E16** 52 28N 49 57 E
Péta, *Greece* **45** **E3** 39 10N 21 2 E
Petah Tiqwa, *Israel* **91** **C3** 32 6N 34 53 E
Petalídhion, *Greece* **45** **H3** 36 57N 21 55 E
Petaling Jaya, *Malaysia* **77** **L3** 3 4N 101 42 E
Petaloudhes, *Greece* **32** **C10** 36 18N 28 5 E
Petaluma, *U.S.A.* **144** **G4** 38 13N 122 39W
Petange, *Lux.* **21** **J7** 49 33N 5 55 E
Petatlán, *Mexico* **146** **D4** 17 31N 101 16W
Petauke, *Zambia* **107** **E3** 14 14 S 31 20 E
Petawawa, *Canada* **128** **C4** 45 54N 77 17W
Petegem, *Belgium* **21** **G3** 50 59N 3 32 E
Petén Itzá, L., *Guatemala* **148** **C2** 16 58N 89 50W
Peter I.s Øy, *Antarctica* **7** **C16** 69 0 S 91 0W
Peter Pond L., *Canada* **131** **B7** 55 55N 108 44W
Peterbell, *Canada* **128** **C3** 48 36N 83 21W
Peterborough, *Australia* **116** **B3** 32 58 S 138 51 E
Peterborough, *Canada* **136** **B6** 44 20N 78 20W
Peterborough, *U.K.* **17** **E7** 52 35N 0 14W
Peterborough, *U.S.A.* **137** **D13** 42 55N 71 59W
Peterhead, *U.K.* **18** **D7** 57 30N 1 49W
Petermann Bjerg, *Greenland* **124** **B17** 73 7N 28 25W
Peter's Mine, *Guyana* **153** **B6** 6 14N 59 20W
Petersburg, *Alaska, U.S.A.* **130** **B2** 56 50N 133 0W
Petersburg, *Ill., U.S.A.* **140** **D7** 40 1N 89 51W
Petersburg, *Ind., U.S.A.* **141** **F9** 38 30N 87 15W
Petersburg, *Va., U.S.A.* **134** **G7** 37 17N 77 26W
Petersburg, *W. Va., U.S.A.* **134** **F6** 38 59N 79 10W
Petford, *Australia* **114** **B3** 17 20 S 144 58 E
Petília Policastro, *Italy* **41** **C9** 39 7N 16 48 E
Petit Bois I., *U.S.A.* **135** **K1** 30 16N 88 25W
Petit-Cap, *Canada* **129** **C7** 49 3N 64 30W
Petit Goâve, *Haiti* **149** **C5** 18 27N 72 51W
Petit Lac Manicouagan, *Canada* **129** **B6** 51 25N 67 40W
Petit Saint Bernard, Col du, *Italy* **38** **C3** 45 40N 6 52 E
Petitcodiac, *Canada* **129** **C6** 45 57N 65 11W
Petite Baleine →, *Canada* **128** **A4** 56 0N 76 45W
Petite Saguenay, *Canada* **129** **C5** 48 15N 70 4W
Petitsikapau, L., *Canada* **129** **B6** 54 37N 66 25W
Petlad, *India* **80** **H5** 22 30N 72 45 E
Peto, *Mexico* **147** **C7** 20 10N 88 53W
Petone, *N.Z.* **118** **H3** 41 13 S 174 53 E
Petoskey, *U.S.A.* **134** **C3** 45 22N 84 57W
Petra, *Jordan* **91** **E4** 30 20N 35 22 E
Petra, *Spain* **33** **B10** 39 37N 3 6 E
Petra, Ostrova, *Russia* **6** **B13** 76 15N 118 30 E
Petra Velikogo, Zaliv, *Russia* **60** **C5** 42 40N 132 0 E
Petralia, *Italy* **41** **E7** 37 49N 14 4 E
Petrel, *Spain* **35** **G4** 38 30N 0 46W
Petreto-Bicchisano, *France* **25** **G12** 41 47N 8 58 E
Petrich, *Bulgaria* **43** **F8** 41 24N 23 13 E
Petrijanec, *Croatia* **39** **B13** 46 23N 16 17 E
Petrikov, *Belorussia* **50** **E6** 52 11N 28 29 E
Petrila, *Romania* **46** **D4** 45 29N 23 29 E
Petrinja, *Croatia* **39** **C13** 45 28N 16 18 E
Petrograd = Sankt-Peterburg, *Russia* **50** **B7** 59 55N 30 20 E
Petrolândia, *Brazil* **154** **C4** 9 5 S 38 20W
Petrolia, *Canada* **128** **D3** 42 54N 82 9W
Petrolina, *Brazil* **154** **C3** 9 24 S 40 30W
Petromagoúla, *Greece* **45** **F5** 38 31N 23 0 E
Petropavlovsk, *Kazakhstan* **56** **D7** 54 53N 69 13 E
Petropavlovsk-Kamchatskiy, *Russia* **57** **D16** 53 3N 158 43 E
Petropavlovskiy = Akhtubinsk, *Russia* **53** **B12** 48 13N 46 7 E
Petrópolis, *Brazil* **155** **F3** 22 33 S 43 9W
Petroşeni, *Romania* **46** **D4** 45 28N 23 20 E
Petrova Gora, *Croatia* **39** **C12** 45 15N 15 45 E
Petrovac, *Montenegro, Yug.* **42** **E3** 42 13N 18 57 E
Petrovac, *Serbia, Yug.* **42** **C6** 44 22N 21 26 E
Petrovaradin, *Serbia, Yug.* **42** **B4** 45 16N 19 55 E
Petrovsk, *Russia* **51** **E14** 52 22N 45 19 E
Petrovsk-Zabaykalskiy, *Russia* **57** **D11** 51 20N 108 55 E
Petrovskoye = Svetlograd, *Russia* **53** **D10** 45 25N 42 58 E
Petrovskoye, *Russia* **54** **E5** 53 37N 56 23 E
Petrozavodsk, *Russia* **48** **B5** 61 41N 34 20 E
Petrus Steyn, *S. Africa* **105** **D4** 27 38 S 28 8 E
Petrusburg, *S. Africa* **104** **D4** 29 4 S 25 26 E
Pettitts, *Australia* **117** **C8** 34 56 S 148 10 E
Petukhovka, *Belorussia* **50** **E7** 53 42N 30 54 E
Peumo, *Chile* **158** **C1** 34 21 S 71 12W
Peureulak, *Indonesia* **74** **B1** 4 48N 97 45 E
Peusangan →, *Indonesia* **74** **A1** 5 16N 96 51 E
Pevek, *Russia* **57** **C18** 69 41N 171 19 E
Peveragno, *Italy* **38** **D4** 44 20N 7 37 E
Peyrehorade, *France* **24** **E2** 43 34N 1 7W
Peyruis, *France* **25** **D9** 44 1N 5 56 E
Pézenas, *France* **24** **E7** 43 28N 3 24 E
Pezinok, *Czech.* **31** **C10** 48 17N 17 17 E
Pfaffenhofen, *Germany* **27** **G7** 48 31N 11 31 E
Pfäffikon, *Switz.* **29** **B7** 47 13N 8 46 E
Pfarrkirchen, *Germany* **27** **G8** 48 25N 12 57 E
Pfeffenhausen, *Germany* **27** **G7** 48 40N 11 58 E
Pforzheim, *Germany* **27** **G4** 48 53N 8 43 E
Pfullendorf, *Germany* **27** **H5** 47 55N 9 15 E
Pfungstadt, *Germany* **27** **F4** 49 47N 8 36 E
Phaistós, *Greece* **32** **D6** 35 2N 24 50 E
Phala, *Botswana* **104** **C4** 23 45 S 26 50 E
Phalera = Phulera, *India* **80** **F6** 26 52N 75 16 E
Phalodi, *India* **80** **F5** 27 12N 72 24 E
Phalsbourg, *France* **23** **D14** 48 46N 7 15 E
Phan, *Thailand* **76** **C2** 19 28N 99 43 E
Phan Rang, *Vietnam* **77** **G7** 11 34N 109 0 E
Phan Ri = Hoa Da, *Vietnam* **77** **G7** 11 16N 108 40 E
Phan Thiet, *Vietnam* **77** **G7** 11 1N 108 9 E
Phanae, *Greece* **45** **F7** 38 8N 25 57 E
Phanat Nikhom, *Thailand* **76** **F3** 13 27N 101 11 E
Phangan, Ko, *Thailand* **77** **H3** 9 45N 100 0 E
Phangnga, *Thailand* **77** **H2** 8 28N 98 30 E
Phanh Bho Ho Chi Minh, *Vietnam* **77** **G6** 10 58N 106 40 E
Phanom Sarakham, *Thailand* **76** **F3** 13 45N 101 21 E
Pharenda, *India* **81** **F10** 27 5N 83 17 E
Phatthalung, *Thailand* **77** **J3** 7 39N 100 6 E
Phayao, *Thailand* **76** **C2** 19 11N 99 55 E
Phelps, *N.Y., U.S.A.* **136** **D7** 42 57N 77 5W
Phelps, *Wis., U.S.A.* **138** **B10** 46 2N 89 2W
Phelps L., *Canada* **131** **B8** 59 15N 103 15W
Phenix City, *U.S.A.* **135** **J3** 32 30N 84 55W
Phet Buri, *Thailand* **76** **F2** 13 1N 99 55 E
Phetchabun, *Thailand* **76** **D3** 16 25N 101 8 E
Phetchabun, Thiu Khao, *Thailand* **76** **E3** 16 0N 101 20 E
Phetchaburi = Phet Buri, *Thailand* **76** **F2** 13 1N 99 55 E
Phi Phi, Ko, *Thailand* **77** **J2** 7 45N 98 46 E
Phiafay, *Laos* **76** **E6** 14 48N 106 0 E
Phibun Mangsahan, *Thailand* **76** **E5** 15 14N 105 14 E
Phichai, *Thailand* **76** **D3** 17 22N 100 10 E
Phichit, *Thailand* **76** **D3** 16 26N 100 22 E
Philadelphia, *Miss., U.S.A.* **139** **J10** 32 47N 89 5W
Philadelphia, *N.Y., U.S.A.* **137** **B9** 44 9N 75 40W
Philadelphia, *Pa., U.S.A.* **137** **F9** 40 0N 75 10W
Philip, *U.S.A.* **138** **C4** 44 4N 101 42W
Philippeville, *Belgium* **21** **H5** 50 12N 4 33 E
Philippi, *Greece* **44** **C6** 41 1N 24 16 E
Philippi L., *Australia* **114** **C2** 24 20 S 138 55 E
Philippines ■, *Asia* **70** **E4** 12 0N 123 0 E
Philippolis, *S. Africa* **104** **E4** 30 15 S 25 16 E
Philippopolis = Plovdiv, *Bulgaria* **43** **E9** 42 8N 24 44 E
Philipsburg, *Mont., U.S.A.* **142** **C7** 46 20N 113 21W
Philipsburg, *Pa., U.S.A.* **136** **F6** 40 53N 78 10W
Philipstown, *S. Africa* **104** **E3** 30 28 S 24 30 E
Phillip I., *Australia* **117** **E6** 38 30 S 145 12 E
Phillips, *Tex., U.S.A.* **139** **H4** 35 48N 101 17W
Phillips, *Wis., U.S.A.* **138** **C9** 45 41N 90 22W
Phillipsburg, *Kans., U.S.A.* **138** **F5** 39 48N 99 20W
Phillipsburg, *Pa., U.S.A.* **137** **F9** 40 43N 75 12W
Phillott, *Australia* **115** **D4** 27 53 S 145 50 E
Philmont, *U.S.A.* **137** **D11** 42 14N 73 37W
Philomath, *U.S.A.* **142** **D2** 44 28N 123 21W
Phimai, *Thailand* **76** **E4** 15 13N 102 30 E
Phitsanulok, *Thailand* **76** **D3** 16 50N 100 12 E
Phnom Dangrek, *Thailand* **76** **E5** 14 20N 104 0 E
Phnom Penh, *Cambodia* **77** **G5** 11 33N 104 55 E
Phoenix, *Ariz., U.S.A.* **143** **K7** 33 30N 112 10W
Phoenix, *N.Y., U.S.A.* **137** **C8** 43 13N 76 18W
Phoenix Is., *Kiribati* **122** **H10** 3 30 S 172 0W
Phoenixville, *U.S.A.* **137** **F9** 40 12N 75 29W
Phon, *Thailand* **76** **E4** 15 49N 102 36 E
Phon Tiou, *Laos* **76** **D5** 17 53N 104 37 E
Phong →, *Thailand* **76** **D4** 16 23N 102 56 E
Phong Saly, *Laos* **76** **B4** 21 42N 102 9 E
Phong Tho, *Vietnam* **76** **A4** 22 32N 103 21 E
Phonhong, *Laos* **76** **C4** 18 30N 102 25 E
Phonum, *Thailand* **77** **H2** 8 49N 98 48 E
Phosphate Hill, *Australia* **114** **C2** 21 53 S 139 58 E
Photharam, *Thailand* **76** **F2** 13 41N 99 51 E
Phra Chedi Sam Ong, *Thailand* **76** **E2** 15 16N 98 23 E
Phra Nakhon Si Ayutthaya, *Thailand* **76** **E3** 14 25N 100 30 E
Phra Thong, Ko, *Thailand* **77** **H2** 9 5N 98 17 E
Phrae, *Thailand* **76** **C3** 18 7N 100 9 E
Phrom Phiram, *Thailand* **76** **D3** 17 2N 100 12 E
Phrygia, *Turkey* **88** **D3** 38 40N 30 0 E
Phu Dien, *Vietnam* **76** **C5** 18 58N 105 31 E
Phu Loi, *Laos* **76** **B4** 20 14N 103 14 E
Phu Ly, *Vietnam* **76** **B5** 20 35N 105 50 E
Phu Tho, *Vietnam* **76** **B5** 21 24N 105 13 E
Phuc Yen, *Vietnam* **76** **B5** 21 16N 105 45 E
Phuket, *Thailand* **77** **J2** 7 52N 98 22 E
Phuket, Ko, *Thailand* **77** **J2** 8 0N 98 22 E
Phulbari, *India* **78** **C3** 25 55N 90 2 E
Phulera, *India* **80** **F6** 26 52N 75 16 E
Phumiphon, Khuan, *Thailand* **76** **D2** 17 15N 98 58 E
Phun Phin, *Thailand* **77** **H2** 9 7N 99 12 E
Piacá, *Brazil* **154** **C2** 7 42 S 47 18W
Piacenza, *Italy* **38** **C6** 45 2N 9 42 E
Piaçubaçu, *Brazil* **154** **D4** 10 24 S 36 25W
Piádena, *Italy* **38** **C7** 45 8N 10 22 E
Piako →, *N.Z.* **118** **D4** 37 12 S 175 30 E
Pialba, *Australia* **115** **D5** 25 20 S 152 45 E
Pian Cr. →, *Australia* **115** **E4** 30 2 S 148 12 E
Piana, *France* **25** **F12** 42 15N 8 34 E
Pianella, *Italy* **39** **F11** 42 24N 14 5 E
Piangil, *Australia* **116** **C5** 35 5 S 143 20 E
Pianoro, *Italy* **39** **D8** 44 20N 11 20 E
Pianosa, *Puglia, Italy* **39** **F12** 42 12N 15 44 E
Pianosa, *Toscana, Italy* **38** **F7** 42 36N 10 4 E
Piapot, *Canada* **131** **D7** 49 59N 109 8W
Piare →, *Italy* **39** **C9** 45 32N 12 44 E
Pias, *Portugal* **37** **G3** 38 1N 7 29W
Piaseczno, *Poland* **47** **C8** 52 5N 21 2 E
Piaski, *Poland* **47** **D9** 51 8N 22 52 E
Piastów, *Poland* **47** **C7** 52 12N 20 48 E
Piatã, *Brazil* **155** **D3** 13 9 S 41 48W
Piatra, *Romania* **46** **F6** 43 51N 25 9 E
Piatra Neamţ, *Romania* **46** **C7** 46 56N 26 21 E
Piatra Olt, *Romania* **46** **E5** 44 22N 24 16 E
Piauí □, *Brazil* **154** **C3** 7 0 S 43 0W
Piaui →, *Brazil* **154** **C3** 6 38 S 42 42W
Piave →, *Italy* **39** **C9** 45 32N 12 44 E
Piazza Ármerina, *Italy* **41** **E7** 37 21N 14 20 E
Pibor →, *Sudan* **95** **F3** 7 35N 33 0 E
Pibor Post, *Sudan* **95** **F3** 6 47N 33 3 E
Pica, *Chile* **156** **E4** 20 35 S 69 25W
Picardie, *France* **23** **C9** 49 50N 3 0 E
Picardie, Plaine de, *France* **23** **C9** 50 0N 2 0 E
Picardy = Picardie, *France* **23** **C9** 49 50N 3 0 E
Picayune, *U.S.A.* **139** **K10** 30 31N 89 40W
Picerno, *Italy* **41** **B8** 40 40N 15 37 E
Pichilemu, *Chile* **158** **C1** 34 22 S 72 0W
Pichincha, □, *Ecuador* **152** **D2** 0 10 S 78 40W
Pickerel L., *Canada* **128** **C1** 48 40N 91 25W
Pickle Lake, *Canada* **128** **B1** 51 30N 90 12W
Pico Truncado, *Argentina* **160** **C3** 46 40 S 68 0W
Picos, *Brazil* **154** **C3** 7 5 S 41 28W
Picos Ancares, Sierra de, *Spain* **36** **C4** 42 51N 6 52W
Picota, *Peru* **156** **B2** 6 54 S 76 24W
Picquigny, *France* **23** **C9** 49 56N 2 10 E
Picton, *Australia* **117** **C9** 34 12 S 150 34 E
Picton, *Canada* **128** **D4** 44 1N 77 9W
Picton, *N.Z.* **119** **B9** 41 18 S 174 3 E
Picton, I., *Chile* **160** **E3** 55 2 S 66 57W
Pictou, *Canada* **129** **C7** 45 41N 62 42W
Picture Butte, *Canada* **130** **D6** 49 55N 112 45W
Picuí, *Brazil* **154** **C4** 6 31 S 36 21W
Picún Leufú, *Argentina* **160** **A3** 39 30 S 69 5W
Pidurutalagala, *Sri Lanka* **83** **L5** 7 10N 80 50 E
Piedecuesta, *Colombia* **152** **B3** 6 59N 73 3W
Piedicavallo, *Italy* **38** **C4** 45 41N 7 57 E
Piedmont = Piemonte □, *Italy* **38** **D4** 45 0N 7 30 E
Piedmont, *U.S.A.* **135** **J3** 33 55N 85 39W
Piedmont Plateau, *U.S.A.* **135** **J5** 34 0N 81 30W
Piedmonte d'Alife, *Italy* **41** **A7** 41 22N 14 22 E
Piedra →, *Spain* **34** **D3** 41 18N 1 47W
Piedra del Anguila, *Argentina* **160** **B2** 40 2 S 70 4W
Piedra Lais, *Venezuela* **152** **C4** 3 10N 65 50W
Piedrabuena, *Spain* **37** **F6** 39 0N 4 10W
Piedrahita, *Spain* **36** **E5** 40 28N 5 23W

Rakkestad 253


Qaryat al Gharab, *Iraq* . 84 **D5** 31 27N 44 48 E
Qaryat al 'Ulyā,
*Si. Arabia* .......... 84 **E5** 27 33N 47 42 E
Qasr 'Amra, *Jordan* .... 84 **D3** 31 48N 36 35 E
Qaşr Bū Hadi, *Libya* ... 96 **B3** 31 1N 16 45 E
Qaşr-e Qand, *Iran* ...... 85 **E9** 26 15N 60 45 E
Qasr Farâfra, *Egypt* .... 94 **B2** 27 0N 28 1 E
Qat Lesh, *Afghan.* ..... 79 **B2** 34 40N 66 18 E
Qa'ṭabah, *Yemen* ...... 86 **D4** 13 51N 44 42 E
Qatanā, *Syria* ......... 91 **B5** 33 26N 36 4 E
Qaṭānan, Ra's, *Yemen* .. 87 **D6** 12 21N 53 33 E
Qatar ■, *Asia* ........ 85 **E6** 25 30N 51 15 E
Qatlīsh, *Iran* .......... 85 **B8** 37 50N 57 19 E
Qattâra, *Egypt* ........ 94 **A2** 30 12N 27 3 E
Qattâra, Munkhafed el,
*Egypt* .............. 94 **B2** 29 30N 27 30 E
Qattâra Depression =
Qattâra, Munkhafed el,
*Egypt* .............. 94 **B2** 29 30N 27 30 E
Qawām al Ḩamzah, *Iraq* 84 **D5** 31 43N 44 58 E
Qāyen, *Iran* .......... 85 **C8** 33 40N 59 10 E
Qazvin, *Iran* .......... 85 **B6** 36 15N 50 0 E
Qena, *Egypt* .......... 94 **B3** 26 10N 32 43 E
Qena, Wadi →, *Egypt* . 94 **B3** 26 12N 32 44 E
Qeqertarsuag = Disko,
*Greenland* .......... 6 **C5** 69 45N 53 30W
Qeqertarsuaq =
Godhavn, *Greenland* . 6 **C5** 69 15N 53 38W
Qeshlāq, *Iran* ......... 84 **C5** 34 55N 46 28 E
Qeshm, *Iran* .......... 85 **E8** 26 55N 56 10 E
Qezi'ot, *Israel* ........ 91 **E3** 30 52N 34 26 E
Qi Xian, *China* ........ 66 **G8** 34 40N 114 48 E
Qian Gorlos, *China* .... 67 **B13** 45 5N 124 42 E
Qian Xian, *China* ...... 66 **G5** 34 31N 108 15 E
Qiancheng, *China* ...... 68 **D7** 27 12N 109 50 E
Qianjiang,
*Guangxi Zhuangzu,*
*China* .............. 68 **F7** 23 38N 108 58 E
Qianjiang, *Hubei, China* 69 **B9** 30 24N 112 55 E
Qianjiang, *Sichuan, China* 68 **C7** 29 33N 108 47 E
Qianshan, *China* ...... 69 **B11** 30 37N 116 35 E
Qianwei, *China* ....... 68 **C4** 29 13N 103 56 E
Qianxi, *China* ......... 68 **D6** 27 3N 106 3 E
Qianyang, *Hunan, China* 69 **D8** 27 18N 110 10 E
Qianyang, *Shaanxi, China* 66 **G4** 34 40N 107 8 E
Qianyang, *Zhejiang,*
*China* .............. 69 **B12** 30 11N 119 25 E
Qiaojia, *China* ........ 68 **D4** 26 56N 102 58 E
Qibā', *Si. Arabia* ...... 84 **E5** 27 24N 44 20 E
Qichun, *China* ........ 69 **B10** 30 18N 115 25 E
Qidong, *Hunan, China* .. 69 **D9** 26 49N 112 7 E
Qidong, *Jiangsu, China* . 69 **B13** 31 48N 121 38 E
Qijiang, *China* ........ 68 **C6** 28 57N 106 35 E
Qila Saifullāh, *Pakistan* . 79 **C3** 30 45N 68 17 E
Qilian Shan, *China* ..... 64 **C4** 38 30N 96 0 E
Qimen, *China* ......... 69 **C11** 29 50N 117 42 E
Qin He →, *China* ...... 66 **G7** 35 1N 113 22 E
Qin Jiang →, *China* ... 69 **D10** 26 15N 115 55 E
Qin Ling = Qinling
Shandi, *China* ...... 66 **H5** 33 50N 108 10 E
Qināb, W. →, *Yemen* .. 87 **C5** 17 55N 49 59 E
Qin'an, *China* ........ 66 **G3** 34 48N 105 40 E
Qing Xian, *China* ...... 66 **E9** 38 35N 116 45 E
Qingcheng, *China* ..... 67 **F9** 37 15N 117 40 E
Qingdao, *China* ....... 67 **F11** 36 5N 120 20 E
Qingfeng, *China* ....... 66 **G8** 35 52N 115 8 E
Qinghai □, *China* ..... 64 **C4** 36 0N 98 0 E
Qinghai Hu, *China* ..... 64 **C5** 36 40N 100 10 E
Qinghecheng, *China* .... 67 **D13** 41 15N 124 30 E
Qinghemen, *China* ..... 67 **D11** 41 48N 121 25 E
Qingjian, *China* ....... 66 **F6** 37 8N 110 8 E
Qingjiang, *Jiangsu, China* 67 **H10** 33 30N 119 2 E
Qingjiang, *Jiangxi, China* 69 **C10** 28 4N 115 29 E
Qingliu, *China* ........ 69 **D11** 26 11N 116 48 E
Qinglong, *China* ....... 68 **E5** 25 49N 105 12 E
Qingping, *China* ....... 68 **D6** 26 39N 107 47 E
Qingpu, *China* ........ 69 **B13** 31 10N 121 6 E
Qingshui, *China* ....... 66 **G4** 34 48N 106 8 E
Qingshuihe, *China* ..... 66 **E6** 39 55N 111 35 E
Qingtian, *China* ....... 69 **C13** 28 12N 120 15 E
Qingtongxia Shuiku,
*China* .............. 66 **F3** 37 50N 105 58 E
Qingxi, *China* ........ 68 **D7** 27 8N 108 43 E
Qingxu, *China* ........ 66 **F7** 37 34N 112 22 E
Qingyang, *Anhui, China* 69 **B11** 30 38N 117 50 E
Qingyang, *Gansu, China* 66 **F4** 36 2N 107 55 E
Qingyi Jiang →, *China* . 68 **C4** 29 32N 103 44 E
Qingyuan, *Guangdong,*
*China* .............. 69 **F9** 23 40N 112 59 E
Qingyuan, *Liaoning,*
*China* .............. 67 **C13** 42 10N 124 55 E
Qingyuan, *Zhejiang,*
*China* .............. 69 **D12** 27 36N 119 3 E
Qingyun, *China* ....... 67 **F9** 37 45N 117 20 E
Qingzhen, *China* ...... 68 **D6** 26 31N 106 25 E
Qinhuangdao, *China* ... 67 **E10** 39 56N 119 30 E
Qinling Shandi, *China* .. 66 **H5** 33 50N 108 10 E
Qinshui, *China* ........ 66 **G7** 35 40N 112 8 E
Qinyang, *China* ....... 66 **G7** 35 7N 112 57 E
Qinyuan, *China* ....... 66 **F7** 36 29N 112 20 E
Qinzhou, *China* ....... 68 **G7** 21 58N 108 38 E
Qionghai, *China* ...... 76 **C8** 19 15N 110 26 E
Qionglai, *China* ....... 68 **B4** 30 25N 103 31 E
Qionglai Shan, *China* .. 68 **B4** 31 0N 102 30 E
Qiongshan, *China* ..... 76 **C8** 19 51N 110 26 E
Qiongzhou Haixia, *China* 76 **B8** 20 10N 110 15 E
Qiqihar, *China* ........ 65 **B7** 47 26N 124 0 E
Qiraîya, W. →, *Egypt* .. 91 **E3** 30 27N 34 0 E
Qiryat Ata, *Israel* ...... 91 **C4** 32 47N 35 6 E
Qiryat Gat, *Israel* ...... 91 **D3** 31 32N 34 46 E
Qiryat Mal'akhi, *Israel* .. 91 **D3** 31 44N 34 44 E
Qiryat Shemona, *Israel* . 91 **B4** 33 13N 35 35 E
Qiryat Yam, *Israel* ..... 91 **C4** 32 51N 35 4 E
Qishan, *China* ........ 66 **G4** 34 25N 107 38 E
Qishan, *Taiwan* ....... 69 **F13** 22 52N 120 25 E
Qishn, *Yemen* ........ 87 **D5** 15 26N 51 40 E
Qitai, *China* .......... 64 **B3** 44 2N 89 35 E
Qitbīt, W. →, *Oman* ... 87 **C6** 19 15N 54 23 E
Qiubei, *China* ........ 68 **E5** 24 2N 104 12 E
Qixia, *China* ......... 67 **F11** 37 17N 120 52 E
Qiyang, *China* ........ 69 **D8** 26 35N 111 50 E
Qojūr, *Iran* .......... 84 **B5** 36 12N 47 55 E
Qom, *Iran* ............ 85 **C6** 34 40N 51 0 E
Qomsheh, *Iran* ........ 85 **D6** 32 0N 51 55 E
Qondūz, *Afghan.* ...... 79 **A3** 36 50N 68 50 E
Qondūz □, *Afghan.* .... 79 **A3** 36 50N 68 50 E
Qu Jiang →, *China* .... 68 **B6** 30 1N 106 24 E
Qu Xian, *Sichuan, China* 68 **B6** 30 48N 106 58 E
Qu Xian, *Zhejiang, China* 69 **C12** 28 57N 118 54 E
Quackenbrück, *Germany* 26 **C3** 52 40N 7 59 E
Quairading, *Australia* ... 113 **F2** 32 0 S 117 21 E
Quakertown, *U.S.A.* ... 137 **F9** 40 27N 75 20W
Qualeup, *Australia* ..... 113 **F2** 33 48 S 116 48 E
Quambatook, *Australia* . 116 **C5** 35 49 S 143 34 E
Quambone, *Australia* ... 117 **A7** 30 57 S 147 53 E
Quamby, *Australia* ..... 114 **C3** 20 22 S 140 17 E
Quan Long, *Vietnam* ... 77 **H5** 9 7N 105 8 E
Quanah, *U.S.A.* ....... 139 **H5** 34 20N 99 45W
Quandialla, *Australia* ... 117 **C7** 34 1 S 147 47 E
Quang Ngai, *Vietnam* ... 76 **E7** 15 13N 108 58 E
Quang Yen, *Vietnam* ... 76 **B6** 20 56N 106 52 E
Quannan, *China* ....... 69 **E10** 24 45N 114 33 E
Quantock Hills, *U.K.* ... 17 **F4** 51 8N 3 10W
Quanzhou, *Fujian, China* 69 **E12** 24 55N 118 34 E
Quanzhou,
*Guangxi Zhuangzu,*
*China* .............. 69 **E8** 25 57N 111 5 E
Quaraí, *Brazil* ........ 158 **C4** 30 15 S 56 20W
Quarré-les-Tombes,
*France* ............. 23 **E10** 47 21N 4 0 E
Quartu Sant' Elena, *Italy* 40 **C2** 39 15N 9 10 E
Quartzsite, *U.S.A.* ..... 145 **M12** 33 44N 114 16W
Quatsino, *Canada* ..... 130 **C3** 50 30N 127 40W
Quatsino Sd., *Canada* .. 130 **C3** 50 25N 127 58W
Qūchān, *Iran* ......... 85 **B8** 37 10N 58 27 E
Queanbeyan, *Australia* .. 117 **C8** 35 17 S 149 14 E
Québec, *Canada* ....... 129 **C5** 46 52N 71 13W
Québec □, *Canada* .... 129 **B6** 50 0N 70 0W
Quedlinburg, *Germany* . 26 **D7** 51 47N 11 9 E
Queen Alexandra Ra.,
*Antarctica* .......... 7 **E11** 85 0 S 170 0 E
Queen Charlotte, *Canada* 130 **C2** 53 15N 132 2W
Queen Charlotte Bay,
*Falk. Is.* ............ 160 **D4** 51 50 S 60 40W
Queen Charlotte Is.,
*Canada* ............ 130 **C2** 53 20N 132 10W
Queen Charlotte Sd.,
*N.Z.* ............... 119 **B9** 41 10 S 174 15 E
Queen Charlotte Str.,
*Canada* ............ 130 **C3** 51 0N 128 0W
Queen City, *U.S.A.* .... 140 **D4** 40 25N 92 34W
Queen Elizabeth Is.,
*Canada* ............ 124 **B10** 76 0N 95 0W
Queen Elizabeth Nat.
Park, *Uganda* ....... 106 **C3** 0 0 30 0 E
Queen Mary Land,
*Antarctica* .......... 7 **D7** 70 0 S 95 0 E
Queen Maud G., *Canada* 126 **B9** 68 15N 102 30W
Queen Maud Land,
*Antarctica* .......... 7 **D3** 72 30 S 12 0 E
Queen Maud Mts.,
*Antarctica* .......... 7 **E13** 86 0 S 160 0W
Queens Chan., *Australia* 112 **C4** 15 0 S 129 30 E
Queenscliff, *Australia* ... 115 **F3** 38 16 S 144 39 E
Queensland □, *Australia* 114 **C3** 22 0 S 142 0 E
Queenstown, *Australia* .. 114 **G4** 42 4 S 145 35 E
Queenstown, *N.Z.* ..... 119 **F3** 45 1 S 168 40 E
Queenstown, *S. Africa* .. 104 **E4** 31 52 S 26 52 E
Queets, *U.S.A.* ....... 144 **C2** 47 32N 124 20W
Queguay Grande →,
*Uruguay* ........... 158 **C4** 32 9 S 58 9W
Queimadas, *Brazil* ..... 154 **D4** 11 0 S 39 38W
Queiros, C., *Vanuatu* ... 121 **D5** 14 55 S 167 1 E
Quela, *Angola* ........ 103 **D3** 9 10 S 16 56 E
Quelimane, *Mozam.* .... 107 **F4** 17 53 S 36 58 E
Quelpart = Cheju Do,
*S. Korea* ........... 67 **H14** 33 29N 126 34 E
Quemado, *N. Mex.,*
*U.S.A.* ............. 143 **J9** 34 17N 108 28W
Quemado, *Tex., U.S.A.* . 139 **L4** 28 58N 100 35W
Quemú-Quemú,
*Argentina* .......... 158 **D3** 36 3 S 63 36W
Quequén, *Argentina* .... 158 **D4** 38 30 S 58 30W
Querco, *Peru* ......... 156 **C3** 13 50 S 74 52W
Querétaro, *Mexico* ..... 146 **C4** 20 40N 100 23W
Querétaro □, *Mexico* ... 146 **C5** 20 30N 100 0W
Querfurt, *Germany* ..... 26 **D7** 51 22N 11 33 E
Quesada, *Spain* ....... 35 **H1** 37 51N 3 4W
Queshan, *China* ....... 66 **H8** 32 55N 114 2 E
Quesnel, *Canada* ...... 130 **C4** 53 0N 122 30W
Quesnel →, *Canada* ... 130 **C4** 52 58N 122 29W
Quesnel L., *Canada* .... 130 **C4** 52 30N 121 20W
Questa, *U.S.A.* ....... 143 **H11** 36 45N 105 35W
Questembert, *France* ... 22 **E4** 47 40N 2 28W
Quetena, *Bolivia* ...... 156 **E4** 22 10 S 67 25W
Quetico Prov. Park,
*Canada* ............ 128 **C1** 48 30N 91 45W
Quetrequile, *Argentina* .. 160 **B3** 41 33 S 69 22W
Quetta, *Pakistan* ...... 79 **C2** 30 15N 66 55 E
Quevedo, *Ecuador* ..... 152 **D2** 1 2 S 79 29W
Quezaltenango,
*Guatemala* .......... 148 **D1** 14 50N 91 30W
Quezon □, *Phil.* ...... 70 **D3** 14 40N 121 30 E
Quezon City, *Phil.* ..... 70 **D3** 14 38N 121 0 E
Qufār, *Si. Arabia* ...... 84 **E4** 27 26N 41 37 E
Qui Nhon, *Vietnam* .... 76 **F7** 13 40N 109 13 E
Quibala, *Angola* ....... 103 **E2** 10 46 S 14 59 E
Quibaxe, *Angola* ...... 103 **D2** 8 24 S 14 27 E
Quibdo, *Colombia* ..... 152 **B2** 5 42N 76 40W
Quiberon, *France* ...... 22 **E3** 47 29N 3 9W
Quíbor, *Venezuela* ..... 152 **B4** 9 56N 69 37W
Quick, *Canada* ........ 130 **C3** 54 36N 126 54W
Quickborn, *Germany* ... 26 **B5** 53 42N 9 52 E
Quiet L., *Canada* ..... 130 **A2** 61 5N 133 5W
Quiévrain, *Belgium* .... 21 **H3** 50 24N 3 41 E
Quiindy, *Paraguay* ..... 158 **B4** 25 58 S 57 14W
Quila, *Mexico* ........ 146 **C3** 24 23N 107 13W
Quilán, C., *Chile* ..... 160 **B2** 43 15 S 74 30W
Quilcene, *U.S.A.* ..... 144 **C4** 47 49N 122 53W
Quilengues, *Angola* .... 103 **E2** 14 12 S 14 12 E
Quilimarí, *Chile* ...... 158 **C1** 32 5 S 71 30W
Quilino, *Argentina* ..... 158 **C3** 30 14 S 64 29W
Quillabamba, *Peru* ..... 156 **C3** 12 50 S 72 50W
Quillacollo, *Bolivia* .... 156 **D4** 17 26 S 66 17W
Quillagua, *Chile* ...... 158 **A2** 21 40 S 69 40W
Quillaicillo, *Chile* ..... 158 **C1** 31 17 S 71 40W
Quillan, *France* ....... 24 **F6** 42 53N 2 10 E
Quillebeuf-sur-Seine,
*France* ............. 22 **C7** 49 28N 0 30 E
Quillota, *Chile* ....... 158 **C1** 32 54 S 71 16W
Quilmes, *Argentina* .... 158 **C4** 34 43 S 58 15W
Quilon, *India* ........ 83 **K3** 8 50N 76 38 E
Quilpie, *Australia* ..... 115 **D3** 26 35 S 144 11 E
Quilpué, *Chile* ....... 158 **C1** 33 5 S 71 33W
Quilua, *Mozam.* ....... 107 **F4** 16 17 S 39 54 E
Quimbele, *Angola* ..... 103 **D3** 6 17 S 16 41 E
Quimbonge, *Angola* .... 103 **D3** 8 36 S 18 30 E
Quime, *Bolivia* ....... 156 **D4** 17 2 S 67 15W
Quimilí, *Argentina* .... 158 **B3** 27 40 S 62 30W
Quimper, *France* ...... 22 **D2** 48 0N 4 9W
Quimperlé, *France* ..... 22 **E3** 47 53N 3 33W
Quinault →, *U.S.A.* ... 144 **C2** 47 23N 124 18W
Quincemil, *Peru* ...... 156 **C3** 13 15 S 70 40W
Quincy, *Calif., U.S.A.* .. 144 **F6** 39 56N 120 56W
Quincy, *Fla., U.S.A.* ... 135 **K3** 30 34N 84 34W
Quincy, *Ill., U.S.A.* .... 138 **F9** 39 55N 91 20W
Quincy, *Mass., U.S.A.* .. 137 **D14** 42 14N 71 0W
Quincy, *Wash., U.S.A.* . 142 **C4** 47 22N 119 56W
Quines, *Argentina* ..... 158 **C2** 32 13 S 65 48W
Quinga, *Mozam.* ...... 107 **F5** 15 49 S 40 15 E
Quingey, *France* ...... 23 **E12** 47 7N 5 52 E
Quiniluban Group, *Phil.* 71 **F3** 11 27N 120 48 E
Quintana de la Serena,
*Spain* .............. 37 **G5** 38 45N 5 40W
Quintana Roo □, *Mexico* 147 **D7** 19 0N 88 0W
Quintanar de la Orden,
*Spain* .............. 34 **F1** 39 36N 3 5W
Quintanar de la Sierra,
*Spain* .............. 34 **D2** 41 57N 2 55W
Quintanar del Rey, *Spain* 35 **F3** 39 21N 1 56W
Quintero, *Chile* ....... 158 **C1** 32 45 S 71 30W
Quintin, *France* ....... 22 **D4** 48 26N 2 56W
Quinto, *Spain* ........ 34 **D4** 41 25N 0 32W
Quinyambie, *Australia* .. 115 **E3** 30 15 S 141 0 E
Quípar →, *Spain* ..... 35 **G3** 38 15N 1 40W
Quipungo, *Angola* ..... 103 **E2** 14 37 S 14 40 E
Quirihue, *Chile* ....... 158 **D1** 36 15 S 72 35W
Quirimbo, *Angola* ..... 103 **E2** 10 36 S 14 12 E
Quirindi, *Australia* .... 117 **A9** 31 28 S 150 40 E
Quirino □, *Phil.* ...... 70 **C3** 16 15N 121 40 E
Quiroga, *Spain* ....... 36 **C3** 42 28N 7 18W
Quiruvilca, *Peru* ...... 156 **B2** 8 1 S 78 19W
Quissac, *France* ...... 25 **E8** 43 55N 4 0 E
Quissanga, *Mozam.* .... 107 **E5** 12 24 S 40 28 E
Quitapa, *Angola* ...... 103 **E3** 10 20 S 18 19 E
Quitilipi, *Argentina* .... 158 **B3** 26 50 S 60 13W
Quitman, *Ga., U.S.A.* .. 135 **K4** 30 49N 83 35W
Quitman, *Miss., U.S.A.* . 135 **J1** 32 2N 88 42W
Quitman, *Tex., U.S.A.* .. 139 **J7** 32 48N 95 25W
Quito, *Ecuador* ....... 152 **D2** 0 15 S 78 35W
Quixadá, *Brazil* ...... 154 **B4** 4 55 S 39 0W
Quixaxe, *Mozam.* ..... 107 **F5** 15 17 S 40 4 E
Quixeramobim, *Brazil* .. 154 **C4** 5 12 S 39 17W
Quixinge, *Angola* ..... 103 **D2** 9 52 S 14 23 E
Quizenga, *Angola* ..... 103 **D3** 9 21 S 15 28 E
Qujing, *China* ........ 68 **E4** 25 32N 103 41 E
Qul'ân, Jazâ'ir, *Egypt* .. 94 **C4** 24 22N 35 31 E
Qumbu, *S. Africa* ..... 105 **E4** 31 10 S 28 48 E
Quneitra, *Syria* ....... 91 **B4** 33 7N 35 48 E
Qunfudh, *Yemen* ...... 87 **C5** 16 39N 49 33 E
Quoin I., *Australia* .... 112 **B4** 14 54 S 129 32 E
Quoin Pt., *S. Africa* ... 104 **E2** 34 46 S 19 37 E
Quondong, *Australia* ... 116 **B4** 33 6 S 140 18 E
Quorn, *Australia* ..... 116 **B3** 32 25 S 138 5 E
Qurein, *Sudan* ....... 95 **E3** 13 30N 34 50 E
Qurnat as Sawdā',
*Lebanon* ........... 91 **A5** 34 18N 36 6 E
Qûs, *Egypt* .......... 94 **B3** 25 55N 32 50 E
Qusaybah, *Iraq* ....... 84 **C4** 34 24N 40 59 E
Quşay'ir, *Yemen* ..... 87 **D5** 14 55N 50 20 E
Quseir, *Egypt* ........ 94 **B3** 26 7N 34 16 E
Qūshchī, *Iran* ........ 84 **B5** 37 59N 45 3 E
Quthing, *Lesotho* ..... 105 **E4** 30 25 S 27 36 E
Qūṭīābād, *Iran* ....... 85 **C6** 35 47N 48 30 E
Quwo, *China* ......... 66 **G6** 35 38N 111 25 E
Quyang, *China* ....... 66 **E8** 38 35N 114 40 E
Quynh Nhai, *Vietnam* .. 76 **B4** 21 49N 103 33 E
Quzi, *China* ......... 66 **F4** 36 20N 107 20 E
Qytet Stalin, *Albania* .. 44 **D1** 40 47N 19 57 E

# R

Ra, Ko, *Thailand* ...... 77 **H2** 9 13N 98 16 E
Råå, *Sweden* ........ 15 **J6** 56 0N 12 45 E
Raab, *Austria* ........ 30 **C6** 48 21N 13 39 E
Raahe, *Finland* ...... 12 **D18** 64 40N 24 28 E
Raalte, *Neths.* ....... 20 **D8** 52 23N 6 16 E
Raamsdonksveer, *Neths.* 21 **E5** 51 43N 4 52 E
Raasay, *U.K.* ........ 18 **D2** 57 25N 6 4W
Raasay, Sd. of, *U.K.* ... 18 **D2** 57 30N 6 8W
Rab, *Croatia* ........ 39 **D11** 44 45N 14 45 E
Raba, *Indonesia* ...... 72 **C1** 8 36 S 118 55 E
Rába →, *Hungary* .... 31 **D10** 47 38N 17 38 E
Raba →, *Poland* ..... 31 **A13** 50 8N 20 30 E
Rabaçal →, *Portugal* .. 36 **D3** 41 30N 7 12W
Rabah, *Nigeria* ....... 101 **C6** 13 5N 5 30 E
Rabai, *Kenya* ........ 106 **C4** 3 50 S 39 31 E
Rabaraba, *Papua N. G.* . 120 **E5** 9 58 S 149 49 E
Rabastens, *France* .... 24 **E5** 43 50N 1 43 E
Rabastens-de-Bigorre,
*France* ............. 24 **E4** 43 23N 0 9 E
Rabat, *Malta* ........ 32 **D1** 35 53N 14 25 E
Rabat, *Morocco* ...... 98 **B3** 34 2N 6 48W
Rabaul, *Papua N. G.* ... 120 **C7** 4 24 S 152 18 E
Rabbit →, *Canada* .... 130 **B3** 59 41N 127 12W
Rabbit Lake, *Canada* ... 131 **C7** 53 8N 107 46W
Rabbitskin →, *Canada* . 130 **A4** 61 47N 120 42W
Rābigh, *Si. Arabia* .... 86 **B2** 22 50N 39 5 E
Rabka, *Poland* ....... 31 **B12** 49 37N 19 59 E
Rābor, *Iran* ......... 85 **D8** 29 17N 56 55 E
Rača, *Serbia, Yug.* .... 42 **C5** 44 14N 21 0 E
Răcale, *Italy* ........ 41 **C11** 39 57N 18 6 E
Racalmuto, *Italy* ..... 40 **E6** 37 25N 13 41 E
Răcăşdia, *Romania* ... 42 **C6** 44 59N 21 36 E
Racconigi, *Italy* ...... 38 **D4** 44 47N 7 41 E
Raccoon →, *U.S.A.* ... 140 **C3** 41 35N 93 37W
Raccoon Cr. →, *U.S.A.* 141 **E9** 39 47N 87 23W
Race, C., *Canada* ..... 129 **C9** 46 40N 53 5W
Rach Gia, *Vietnam* .... 77 **G5** 10 5N 105 5 E
Raciąż, *Poland* ...... 47 **C7** 52 46N 20 10 E
Racibórz, *Poland* ..... 31 **A11** 50 7N 18 18 E
Racine, *U.S.A.* ...... 141 **B9** 42 41N 87 51W
Rackerby, *U.S.A.* .... 144 **F5** 39 26N 121 22W
Radama, Nosy, *Madag.* . 105 **A8** 14 0 S 47 47 E
Radama, Saikanosy,
*Madag.* ............ 105 **A8** 14 16 S 47 53 E
Radan, *Serbia, Yug.* ... 42 **E6** 42 59N 21 29 E
Rădăuţi, *Romania* .... 46 **B6** 47 50N 25 59 E
Radbuza →, *Czech.* ... 30 **B6** 49 35N 13 5 E
Radcliff, *U.S.A.* ..... 141 **G11** 37 51N 85 57W
Radeburg, *Germany* ... 26 **D9** 51 6N 13 55 E
Radeče, *Slovenia* ..... 39 **B12** 46 5N 15 14 E
Radekhov, *Ukraine* .... 50 **F4** 50 25N 24 32 E
Radew →, *Poland* .... 47 **A2** 54 2N 15 52 E
Radford, *U.S.A.* ..... 134 **G5** 37 8N 80 32W
Radhanpur, *India* ..... 80 **H4** 23 50N 71 38 E
Radiska →,
*Macedonia, Yug.* ..... 42 **F5** 41 38N 20 37 E
Radisson, *Canada* .... 131 **C7** 52 30N 107 20W
Radium Hot Springs,
*Canada* ............ 130 **C5** 50 35N 116 2W
Radków, *Poland* ..... 47 **E3** 50 30N 16 24 E
Radlin, *Poland* ...... 31 **A11** 50 3N 18 29 E
Radna, *Romania* ..... 42 **A6** 46 7N 21 41 E
Radnevo, *Bulgaria* .... 43 **E10** 42 17N 25 58 E
Radnice, *Czech.* ..... 30 **B6** 49 51N 13 35 E
Radnor Forest, *U.K.* ... 17 **E4** 52 17N 3 10W
Radolfzell, *Germany* ... 27 **H4** 47 44N 8 58 E
Radom, *Poland* ...... 47 **D8** 51 23N 21 12 E
Radom □, *Poland* .... 47 **D8** 51 30N 21 0 E
Radomir, *Bulgaria* .... 42 **E8** 42 37N 23 4 E
Radomka →, *Poland* .. 47 **D8** 51 31N 21 11 E
Radomsko, *Poland* .... 47 **D6** 51 5N 19 28 E
Radomyshl, *Ukraine* ... 50 **F6** 50 30N 29 12 E
Radomysl Wielki, *Poland* 31 **A14** 50 14N 21 15 E
Radoszyce, *Poland* .... 47 **D7** 51 4N 20 15 E
Radoviš,
*Macedonia, Yug.* ..... 42 **F7** 41 38N 22 28 E
Radovljica, *Slovenia* ... 39 **B11** 46 22N 14 12 E
Radstadt, *Austria* .... 30 **D6** 47 24N 13 28 E
Radstock, *U.K.* ...... 17 **F5** 51 17N 2 25W
Radstock, C., *Australia* . 115 **E1** 33 12 S 134 20 E
Răducăneni, *Romania* .. 46 **C8** 46 58N 27 54 E
Raduša, *Serbia, Yug.* .. 42 **E6** 42 7N 21 15 E
Radviliškis, *Lithuania* .. 50 **D3** 55 49N 23 33 E
Radville, *Canada* ..... 131 **D8** 49 30N 104 15W
Radymno, *Poland* .... 31 **B15** 49 59N 22 52 E
Radzanów, *Poland* .... 47 **C7** 52 56N 20 8 E
Radziejów, *Poland* .... 47 **C5** 52 40N 18 30 E
Radzymin, *Poland* .... 47 **C8** 52 25N 21 11 E
Radzyń Chełmiński,
*Poland* ............ 47 **B5** 53 23N 18 55 E
Radzyń Podlaski, *Poland* 47 **D9** 51 47N 22 37 E
Rae, *Canada* ........ 130 **A5** 62 50N 116 3W
Rae Bareli, *India* ..... 81 **F9** 26 18N 81 20 E
Rae Isthmus, *Canada* .. 127 **B11** 66 40N 87 30W
Raeren, *Belgium* ..... 21 **G8** 50 41N 6 7 E
Raeside, L., *Australia* .. 113 **E3** 29 20 S 122 0 E
Raetihi, *N.Z.* ....... 118 **F4** 39 25 S 175 17 E
Rafaela, *Argentina* ... 158 **C3** 31 10 S 61 30W
Rafah, *Egypt* ....... 91 **D3** 31 18N 34 14 E
Rafai, *C.A.R.* ...... 102 **B4** 4 59N 23 58 E
Raffadali, *Italy* ..... 40 **E6** 37 23N 13 29 E
Rafḩā, *Si. Arabia* .... 84 **D4** 29 35N 43 35 E
Rafsanjān, *Iran* ..... 85 **D8** 30 30N 56 5 E
Raft Pt., *Australia* ... 112 **C3** 16 4 S 124 26 E
Ragag, *Sudan* ....... 95 **E1** 10 59N 24 40 E
Ragang, Mt., *Phil.* ... 71 **H5** 7 43N 124 32 E
Ragay, *Phil.* ........ 70 **E4** 13 49N 122 47 E
Ragay G., *Phil.* ..... 70 **E4** 13 30N 122 45 E
Ragged, Mt., *Australia* . 113 **F3** 33 27 S 123 25 E
Raglan, *Australia* .... 114 **C5** 23 42 S 150 49 E
Raglan, *N.Z.* ....... 118 **D3** 37 55 S 174 55 E
Raglan Harbour, *N.Z.* .. 118 **D3** 37 47 S 174 50 E
Ragunda, *Sweden* .... 14 **A10** 63 6N 16 23 E
Ragusa, *Italy* ....... 41 **F7** 36 56N 14 42 E
Raha, *Indonesia* ..... 72 **B2** 4 55 S 123 0 E
Rahad, Nahr ed →,
*Sudan* ............ 95 **E3** 14 28N 33 31 E
Rahad al Bardī, *Sudan* .. 97 **F4** 11 20N 23 40 E
Rahaeng = Tak, *Thailand* 76 **D2** 16 52N 99 8 E
Rahden, *Germany* .... 26 **C4** 52 26N 8 36 E
Raheita, *Ethiopia* .... 95 **E5** 12 46N 43 4 E
Raḩīmah, *Si. Arabia* .. 85 **E6** 26 42N 50 4 E
Rahimyar Khan, *Pakistan* 79 **C3** 28 30N 70 25 E
Rāhjerd, *Iran* ....... 85 **C6** 34 22N 50 22 E
Rahotu, *N.Z.* ....... 118 **F2** 39 20 S 173 49 E
Raichur, *India* ...... 83 **F3** 16 10N 77 20 E
Raiganj, *India* ...... 81 **G13** 25 37N 88 10 E
Raigarh, *India* ...... 82 **D6** 21 56N 83 25 E
Raighar, *India* ...... 82 **E6** 19 51N 82 6 E
Raijua, *Indonesia* .... 72 **D2** 10 37 S 121 36 E
Railton, *Australia* ... 114 **G4** 41 25 S 146 28 E
Rainbow, *Australia* ... 116 **C5** 35 55 S 142 0 E
Rainbow Lake, *Canada* . 130 **B5** 58 30N 119 23W
Rainier, *U.S.A.* ..... 144 **D4** 46 4N 122 58W
Rainier, Mt., *U.S.A.* .. 144 **D5** 46 50N 121 50W
Rainy L., *Canada* .... 131 **D10** 48 42N 93 10W
Rainy River, *Canada* .. 131 **D10** 48 43N 94 29W
Raipur, *India* ....... 82 **D5** 21 17N 81 45 E
Raj Nandgaon, *India* .. 82 **D5** 21 5N 81 5 E
Raja, Ujung, *Indonesia* . 74 **B1** 3 40N 96 25 E
Raja Ampat, Kepulauan,
*Indonesia* .......... 73 **B4** 0 30 S 130 0 E
Rajahmundry, *India* ... 82 **F5** 17 1N 81 48 E
Rajajooseppi, *Finland* .. 12 **B20** 68 28N 28 29 E
Rajang →, *Malaysia* .. 75 **B4** 2 30N 112 0 E
Rajapalaiyam, *India* ... 83 **K3** 9 25N 77 35 E
Rajasthan □, *India* ... 80 **F5** 26 45N 73 30 E
Rajasthan Canal, *India* . 80 **E5** 28 0N 72 0 E
Rajauri, *India* ...... 81 **C6** 33 25N 74 21 E
Rajbari, *Bangla.* ..... 78 **D2** 23 47N 89 41 E
Rajgarh, *Mad. P., India* 80 **G7** 24 2N 76 45 E
Rajgarh, *Raj., India* ... 80 **E6** 28 40N 75 25 E
Rajgród, *Poland* ..... 47 **B9** 53 42N 22 42 E
Rajhenburg, *Slovenia* .. 39 **B12** 46 1N 15 29 E
Rajkot, *India* ....... 80 **H4** 22 15N 70 56 E
Rajmahal Hills, *India* .. 81 **G12** 24 30N 87 30 E
Rajpipla, *India* ...... 82 **D1** 21 50N 73 30 E
Rajpura, *India* ...... 80 **D7** 30 25N 76 32 E
Rajshahi, *Bangla.* .... 78 **C2** 24 22N 88 39 E
Rajshahi □, *Bangla.* .. 81 **G13** 25 0N 89 0 E
Rakaia, *N.Z.* ....... 119 **D7** 43 45 S 172 1 E
Rakaia →, *N.Z.* ..... 119 **D7** 43 36 S 172 15 E
Rakan, Ra's, *Qatar* ... 85 **E6** 26 10N 51 20 E
Rakaposhi, *Pakistan* .. 81 **A6** 36 10N 74 25 E
Rakata, Pulau, *Indonesia* 74 **D3** 6 10 S 105 20 E
Rakhawt, W. →, *Yemen* 87 **C5** 18 16N 51 50 E
Rakhneh-ye Jamshīdī,
*Afghan.* ........... 79 **B1** 34 22N 62 19 E
Rakhni, *Pakistan* .... 80 **D3** 30 4N 69 56 E
Rakhyūt, *Oman* ..... 87 **C6** 16 44N 53 20 E
Rakitnoye, *Russia* ... 60 **B7** 45 36N 134 17 E
Rakitovo, *Bulgaria* ... 43 **F9** 41 59N 24 5 E
Rakkestad, *Norway* ... 14 **E5** 59 25N 11 21 E

254 Rakoniewice


Rakoniewice, *Poland* **47** **C3** 52 10N 16 16 E
Rakops, *Botswana* **104** **C3** 21 1 S 24 28 E
Rákospalota, *Hungary* **31** **D12** 47 30N 19 5 E
Rakov, *Belorussia* **50** **E5** 53 58N 26 59 E
Rakovica, *Croatia* **39** **D12** 44 59N 15 38 E
Rakovník, *Czech.* **30** **A6** 50 6N 13 42 E
Rakovski, *Bulgaria* **43** **E9** 42 21N 24 57 E
Rakvere, *Estonia* **50** **B5** 59 20N 26 25 E
Raleigh, *U.S.A.* **135** **H6** 35 47N 78 39W
Raleigh B., *U.S.A.* **135** **H7** 34 50N 76 15W
Ralja, *Serbia, Yug.* **42** **C5** 44 33N 20 34 E
Ralls, *U.S.A.* **139** **J4** 33 40N 101 20W
Ram →, *Canada* **130** **A4** 62 1N 123 41W
Râm Allâh, *Jordan* **91** **D4** 31 55N 35 10 E
Ram Hd., *Australia* **117** **D8** 37 47 S 149 30 E
Rama, *Nic.* **148** **D3** 12 9N 84 15W
Ramacca, *Italy* **41** **E7** 37 24N 14 40 E
Ramachandrapuram, *India* **82** **F6** 16 50N 82 4 E
Ramales de la Victoria, *Spain* **34** **B1** 43 15N 3 28W
Ramalho, Serra do, *Brazil* **155** **D3** 13 45 S 44 0W
Raman, *Thailand* **77** **J3** 6 29N 101 18 E
Ramanathapuram, *India* **83** **K4** 9 25N 78 55 E
Ramanetaka, B. de, *Madag.* **105** **A8** 14 13 S 47 52 E
Ramas C., *India* **83** **G1** 15 5N 73 55 E
Ramat Gan, *Israel* **91** **C3** 32 4N 34 48 E
Ramatlhabama, *S. Africa* **104** **D4** 25 37 S 25 33 E
Ramban, *India* **81** **C6** 33 14N 75 12 E
Rambervillers, *France* **23** **D13** 48 20N 6 38 E
Rambi, *Fiji* **121** **A3** 16 30 S 179 59W
Rambipuji, *Indonesia* **75** **D4** 8 12 S 113 37 E
Rambouillet, *France* **23** **D8** 48 39N 1 50 E
Ramdurg, *India* **83** **G2** 15 58N 75 22 E
Ramea, *Canada* **129** **C8** 47 31N 57 23W
Ramechhap, *Nepal* **81** **F12** 27 25N 86 10 E
Ramelau, *Indonesia* **72** **C3** 8 55 S 126 22 E
Ramenskoye, *Russia* **51** **D11** 55 32N 38 15 E
Ramgarh, *Bihar, India* **81** **H11** 23 40N 85 35 E
Ramgarh, *Raj., India* **80** **F6** 27 16N 75 14 E
Ramgarh, *Raj., India* **80** **F4** 27 30N 70 36 E
Râmhormoz, *Iran* **85** **D6** 31 15N 49 35 E
Ramīān, *Iran* **85** **B7** 37 3N 55 16 E
Ramingining, *Australia* **114** **A2** 12 19 S 135 3 E
Ramla, *Israel* **91** **D3** 31 55N 34 52 E
Ramlat Zalṭan, *Libya* **96** **C3** 28 30N 19 30 E
Ramlu, *Ethiopia* **95** **E5** 13 32N 41 40 E
Ramme, *Denmark* **15** **H2** 56 30N 8 11 E
Ramnad = Ramanathapuram, *India* **83** **K4** 9 25N 78 55 E
Ramnagar, *India* **81** **C6** 32 47N 75 18 E
Ramnäs, *Sweden* **14** **E10** 59 46N 16 12 E
Ramon, *Russia* **51** **F11** 51 55N 39 21 E
Ramona, *U.S.A.* **145** **M10** 33 1N 116 56W
Ramore, *Canada* **128** **C3** 48 30N 80 25W
Ramotswa, *Botswana* **104** **C4** 24 50 S 25 52 E
Rampur, *H.P., India* **80** **D7** 31 26N 77 43 E
Rampur, *Mad. P., India* **80** **H5** 23 25N 73 53 E
Rampur, *Orissa, India* **82** **D6** 21 48N 83 58 E
Rampur, *Ut. P., India* **81** **E8** 28 50N 79 5 E
Rampur Hat, *India* **81** **G12** 24 10N 87 50 E
Rampura, *India* **80** **G6** 24 30N 75 27 E
Râmsar, *Iran* **85** **B6** 36 53N 50 41 E
Ramsel, *Belgium* **21** **F5** 51 2N 4 50 E
Ramsey, *Canada* **128** **C3** 47 25N 82 20W
Ramsey, *U.K.* **16** **C3** 54 20N 4 21W
Ramsey, *U.S.A.* **140** **E7** 39 8N 89 7W
Ramsgate, *U.K.* **17** **F9** 51 20N 1 25 E
Ramshai, *India* **78** **B2** 26 44N 88 51 E
Ramsjö, *Sweden* **14** **B9** 62 11N 15 37 E
Ramtek, *India* **82** **D4** 21 20N 79 15 E
Ramu →, *Papua N. G.* **120** **C3** 4 0 S 144 41 E
Ramvik, *Sweden* **14** **B11** 62 49N 17 51 E
Ranaghat, *India* **81** **H13** 23 15N 88 35 E
Ranahu, *Pakistan* **80** **G3** 25 55N 69 45 E
Rancagua, *Chile* **158** **C1** 34 10 S 70 50W
Rance, *Belgium* **21** **H4** 50 9N 4 16 E
Rance →, *France* **22** **D5** 48 34N 1 59W
Rance, Barrage de la, *France* **22** **D4** 48 30N 2 3W
Rancharia, *Brazil* **155** **F1** 22 15 S 50 55W
Rancheria →, *Canada* **130** **A3** 60 13N 129 7W
Ranchester, *U.S.A.* **142** **D10** 44 57N 107 12W
Ranchi, *India* **81** **H11** 23 19N 85 27 E
Ranco, L., *Chile* **160** **B2** 40 15 S 72 25W
Rancu, *Romania* **46** **E5** 44 32N 24 15 E
Rand, *Australia* **117** **C7** 35 33 S 146 32 E
Randan, *France* **24** **B7** 46 2N 3 21 E
Randazzo, *Italy* **41** **E7** 37 53N 14 56 E
Randers, *Denmark* **15** **H4** 56 29N 10 1 E
Randers Fjord, *Denmark* **15** **H4** 56 37N 10 20 E
Randfontein, *S. Africa* **105** **D4** 26 8 S 27 45 E
Randle, *U.S.A.* **144** **D5** 46 32N 121 57W
Randolph, *Mass., U.S.A.* **137** **D13** 42 10N 71 3W
Randolph, *N.Y., U.S.A.* **136** **D6** 42 10N 78 59W
Randolph, *Utah, U.S.A.* **142** **F8** 41 43N 111 10W
Randolph, *Vt., U.S.A.* **137** **C12** 43 55N 72 39W
Randsfjord, *Norway* **14** **D4** 60 15N 10 25 E
Råne älv →, *Sweden* **12** **D17** 65 50N 22 20 E
Ranfurly, *N.Z.* **119** **F5** 45 7 S 170 6 E
Rangae, *Thailand* **77** **J3** 6 19N 101 44 E
Rangamati, *Bangla.* **78** **D4** 22 38N 92 12 E
Rangataua, *N.Z.* **118** **F4** 39 26 S 175 28 E
Rangaunu B., *N.Z.* **118** **A2** 34 51 S 173 15 E
Rångedala, *Sweden* **15** **G7** 57 47N 13 9 E
Rangeley, *U.S.A.* **137** **B14** 44 58N 70 33W
Rangely, *U.S.A.* **142** **F9** 40 3N 108 53W
Ranger, *U.S.A.* **139** **J5** 32 30N 98 42W
Rangia, *India* **78** **B3** 26 28N 91 38 E
Rangiora, *N.Z.* **119** **D7** 43 19 S 172 36 E
Rangitaiki, *N.Z.* **118** **E5** 38 52 S 176 24 E
Rangitaiki →, *N.Z.* **118** **D5** 37 54 S 176 49 E
Rangitata →, *N.Z.* **119** **D6** 43 45 S 171 15 E
Rangitikei →, *N.Z.* **118** **G4** 40 17 S 175 15 E
Rangitoto Ra., *N.Z.* **118** **E4** 38 25 S 175 35 E
Rangkasbitung, *Indonesia* **74** **D3** 6 21 S 106 15 E
Rangoon, *Burma* **78** **G6** 16 45N 96 20 E
Rangpur, *Bangla.* **78** **C2** 25 42N 89 22 E
Rangsang, *Indonesia* **74** **B2** 1 20N 103 30 E
Rangsit, *Thailand* **76** **F3** 13 59N 100 37 E
Ranibennur, *India* **83** **G2** 14 35N 75 30 E
Raniganj, *India* **81** **H12** 23 40N 87 5 E
Ranippettai, *India* **83** **H4** 12 56N 79 23 E
Rāniyah, *Iraq* **84** **B5** 36 15N 44 53 E
Ranken →, *Australia* **114** **C2** 20 31 S 137 36 E
Rankin, *Ill., U.S.A.* **141** **D9** 40 28N 87 54W
Rankin, *Tex., U.S.A.* **139** **K4** 31 16N 101 56W
Rankin Inlet, *Canada* **126** **B10** 62 30N 93 0W
Rankins Springs, *Australia* **117** **B7** 33 49 S 146 14 E
Rannoch, L., *U.K.* **18** **E4** 56 41N 4 20W
Rannoch Moor, *U.K.* **18** **E4** 56 38N 4 48W
Ranobe, Helodranon' i, *Madag.* **105** **C7** 23 3 S 43 33 E
Ranohira, *Madag.* **105** **C8** 22 29 S 45 24 E
Ranomafana, *Toamasina, Madag.* **105** **B8** 18 57 S 48 50 E
Ranomafana, *Toliara, Madag.* **105** **C8** 24 34 S 47 0 E
Ranong, *Thailand* **77** **H2** 9 56N 98 40 E
Rānsa, *Iran* **85** **C6** 33 39N 48 18 E
Ransiki, *Indonesia* **73** **B4** 1 30 S 134 10 E
Ransom, *U.S.A.* **141** **C8** 41 9N 88 39W
Rantau, *Indonesia* **75** **C5** 2 56 S 115 9 E
Rantauprapat, *Indonesia* **74** **B1** 2 15N 99 50 E
Rantekombola, *Indonesia* **72** **B1** 3 15 S 119 57 E
Rantoul, *U.S.A.* **141** **D8** 40 18N 88 10W
Ranum, *Denmark* **15** **H3** 56 54N 9 14 E
Ranyah, W. →, *Si. Arabia* **86** **B3** 21 18N 43 20 E
Raon l'Étape, *France* **23** **D13** 48 24N 6 50 E
Raoui, Erg er, *Algeria* **99** **C4** 29 0N 2 0W
Raoyang, *China* **66** **E8** 38 15N 115 45 E
Rapa, *Pac. Oc.* **123** **K13** 27 35 S 144 20W
Rapallo, *Italy* **38** **D6** 44 21N 9 12 E
Rāpch, *Iran* **85** **E8** 25 40N 59 15 E
Rapid →, *Canada* **130** **B3** 59 15N 129 5W
Rapid City, *U.S.A.* **138** **D3** 44 0N 103 0W
Rapid River, *U.S.A.* **134** **C2** 45 55N 87 0W
Rapides des Joachims, *Canada* **128** **C4** 46 13N 77 43W
Rapla, *Estonia* **50** **B4** 59 1N 24 52 E
Rapperswil, *Switz.* **29** **B7** 47 14N 8 45 E
Rapu Rapu I., *Phil.* **70** **E5** 13 12N 124 9 E
Rarotonga, *Cook Is.* **123** **K12** 21 30 S 160 0W
Ra's al' Ayn, *Syria* **84** **B4** 36 51N 40 4 E
Ra's al Khaymah, *U.A.E.* **85** **E8** 25 50N 56 5 E
Ra's al-Unuf, *Libya* **96** **B3** 30 25N 18 15 E
Ra's an Naqb, *Jordan* **91** **F4** 30 0N 35 29 E
Ras Bânâs, *Egypt* **94** **C4** 23 57N 35 59 E
Ras Dashen, *Ethiopia* **95** **E4** 13 8N 38 26 E
Ras el Ma, *Algeria* **99** **B4** 34 26N 0 50W
Ras Mallap, *Egypt* **94** **J8** 29 18N 32 50 E
Râs Timirist, *Mauritania* **100** **B1** 19 21N 16 30W
Rasa, Punta, *Argentina* **160** **B4** 40 50 S 62 15W
Rasca, Pta. de la, *Canary Is.* **33** **G3** 27 59N 16 41W
Raseiniai, *Lithuania* **50** **D3** 55 25N 23 5 E
Rashad, *Sudan* **95** **E3** 11 55N 31 0 E
Rashîd, *Egypt* **94** **H7** 31 21N 30 22 E
Rashîd, Masabb, *Egypt* **94** **H7** 31 22N 30 17 E
Rasht, *Iran* **85** **B6** 37 20N 49 40 E
Rasi Salai, *Thailand* **76** **E5** 15 20N 104 9 E
Rasipuram, *India* **83** **J4** 11 30N 78 15 E
Raška, *Serbia, Yug.* **42** **D5** 43 19N 20 39 E
Rason L., *Australia* **113** **E3** 28 45 S 124 25 E
Raşova, *Romania* **46** **E8** 44 15N 27 55 E
Rasovo, *Bulgaria* **43** **D8** 43 42N 23 17 E
Rasra, *India* **81** **G10** 25 50N 83 50 E
Rass el Oued, *Algeria* **99** **A6** 35 57N 5 2 E
Rasskazovo, *Russia* **51** **E12** 52 35N 41 50 E
Rastatt, *Germany* **27** **G4** 48 50N 8 12 E
Rastu, *Romania* **46** **F4** 43 53N 23 16 E
Raszków, *Poland* **47** **D4** 51 43N 17 40 E
Rat Buri, *Thailand* **76** **F2** 13 30N 99 54 E
Rat Is., *U.S.A.* **126** **C1** 51 50N 178 15 E
Rat River, *Canada* **130** **A6** 61 7N 112 36W
Ratangarh, *India* **80** **E6** 28 5N 74 35 E
Raṭāwī, *Iraq* **84** **D5** 30 38N 47 13 E
Rath, *India* **81** **G8** 25 36N 79 37 E
Rath Luirc, *Ireland* **19** **D3** 52 21N 8 40W
Rathbun Res., *U.S.A.* **140** **D4** 40 49N 92 53W
Rathdrum, *Ireland* **19** **D5** 52 57N 6 13W
Rathedaung, *Burma* **78** **E4** 20 29N 92 45 E
Rathenow, *Germany* **26** **C8** 52 38N 12 23 E
Rathkeale, *Ireland* **19** **D3** 52 32N 8 57W
Rathlin, *U.K.* **19** **A5** 55 18N 6 14W
Rathlin O'Birne I., *Ireland* **19** **B3** 54 40N 8 50W
Ratibor = Racibórz, *Poland* **31** **A11** 50 7N 18 18 E
Rätikon, *Austria* **30** **D2** 47 0N 9 55 E
Ratlam, *India* **80** **H6** 23 20N 75 0 E
Ratnagiri, *India* **82** **F1** 16 57N 73 18 E
Ratnapura, *Sri Lanka* **83** **L5** 6 40N 80 20 E
Raton, *U.S.A.* **139** **G2** 37 0N 104 30W
Rattaphum, *Thailand* **77** **J3** 7 8N 100 16 E
Ratten, *Austria* **30** **D8** 47 28N 15 44 E
Rattray Hd., *U.K.* **18** **D7** 57 38N 1 50W
Ratz, Mt., *Canada* **130** **B2** 57 23N 132 12W
Ratzeburg, *Germany* **26** **B6** 53 41N 10 46 E
Raub, *Malaysia* **77** **L3** 3 47N 101 52 E
Rauch, *Argentina* **158** **D4** 36 45 S 59 5W
Raufarhöfn, *Iceland* **12** **C6** 66 27N 15 57W
Raufoss, *Norway* **14** **D4** 60 44N 10 37 E
Raukumara Ra., *N.Z.* **118** **E6** 38 5 S 177 55 E
Raul Soares, *Brazil* **155** **F3** 20 5 S 42 22W
Rauland, *Norway* **14** **E2** 59 43N 8 0 E
Rauma, *Finland* **13** **F16** 61 10N 21 30 E
Rauma →, *Norway* **14** **B1** 62 34N 7 43 E
Raurkela, *India* **81** **H11** 22 14N 84 50 E
Rausu-Dake, *Japan* **60** **B12** 44 4N 145 7 E
Rava Russkaya, *Ukraine* **50** **F3** 50 15N 23 42 E
Ravānsar, *Iran* **84** **C5** 34 43N 46 40 E
Ravanusa, *Italy* **40** **E6** 37 16N 13 58 E
Rāvar, *Iran* **85** **D8** 31 20N 56 51 E
Ravels, *Belgium* **21** **F6** 51 22N 5 0 E
Ravena, *U.S.A.* **137** **D11** 42 28N 73 49W
Ravenna, *Italy* **39** **D9** 44 28N 12 15 E
Ravenna, *Ky., U.S.A.* **141** **G13** 37 42N 83 55W
Ravenna, *Nebr., U.S.A.* **138** **E5** 41 3N 98 58W
Ravenna, *Ohio, U.S.A.* **136** **E3** 41 11N 81 15W
Ravensburg, *Germany* **27** **H5** 47 48N 9 38 E
Ravenshoe, *Australia* **114** **B4** 17 37 S 145 29 E
Ravenstein, *Neths.* **20** **E7** 51 47N 5 39 E
Ravensthorpe, *Australia* **113** **F3** 33 35 S 120 2 E
Ravenswood, *Australia* **114** **C4** 20 6 S 146 54 E
Ravenswood, *U.S.A.* **134** **F5** 38 58N 81 47W
Ravensworth, *Australia* **117** **B9** 32 26 S 151 4 E
Ravenwood, *U.S.A.* **140** **D2** 40 23N 94 41W
Ravi →, *Pakistan* **80** **D4** 30 35N 71 49 E
Ravna Gora, *Croatia* **39** **C11** 45 24N 14 50 E
Ravna Reka, *Serbia, Yug.* **42** **D6** 43 59N 21 35 E
Rawa Mazowiecka, *Poland* **47** **D7** 51 46N 20 12 E
Rawalpindi, *Pakistan* **79** **B4** 33 38N 73 8 E
Rawāndūz, *Iraq* **84** **B5** 36 40N 44 30 E
Rawang, *Malaysia* **77** **L3** 3 20N 101 35 E
Rawdon, *Canada* **128** **C5** 46 3N 73 40W
Rawene, *N.Z.* **118** **B2** 35 25 S 173 32 E
Rawicz, *Poland* **47** **D3** 51 36N 16 52 E
Rawka →, *Poland* **47** **C7** 52 9N 20 8 E
Rawlinna, *Australia* **113** **F4** 30 58 S 125 28 E
Rawlins, *U.S.A.* **142** **F10** 41 50N 107 20W
Rawlinson Ra., *Australia* **113** **D4** 24 40 S 128 30 E
Rawson, *Argentina* **160** **B3** 43 15 S 65 5W
Ray, *U.S.A.* **138** **A3** 48 21N 103 6W
Ray, C., *Canada* **129** **C8** 47 33N 59 15W
Rayachoti, *India* **83** **G4** 14 4N 78 50 E
Rayadurg, *India* **83** **G3** 14 40N 76 50 E
Rayagada, *India* **82** **E6** 19 15N 83 20 E
Raychikhinsk, *Russia* **57** **E13** 49 46N 129 25 E
Rāyen, *Iran* **85** **D8** 29 34N 57 26 E
Rayevskiy, *Russia* **54** **D4** 54 4N 54 56 E
Raymond, *Canada* **130** **D6** 49 30N 112 35W
Raymond, *Calif., U.S.A.* **144** **H7** 37 13N 119 54W
Raymond, *Ill., U.S.A.* **140** **E7** 39 19N 89 34W
Raymond, *Wash., U.S.A.* **144** **D3** 46 45N 123 48W
Raymond Terrace, *Australia* **117** **B9** 32 45 S 151 44 E
Raymondville, *U.S.A.* **139** **M6** 26 30N 97 50W
Raymore, *Canada* **131** **C8** 51 25N 104 31W
Rayne, *U.S.A.* **139** **K8** 30 16N 92 16W
Rayón, *Mexico* **146** **B2** 29 43N 110 35W
Rayong, *Thailand* **76** **F3** 12 40N 101 20 E
Raytown, *U.S.A.* **140** **E2** 39 1N 94 28W
Rayville, *U.S.A.* **139** **J9** 32 30N 91 45W
Raz, Pte. du, *France* **22** **D2** 48 2N 4 47W
Razan, *Iran* **85** **C6** 35 23N 49 2 E
Ražana, *Serbia, Yug.* **42** **C4** 44 6N 19 55 E
Ražanj, *Serbia, Yug.* **42** **D6** 43 40N 21 31 E
Razdelna, *Bulgaria* **43** **D12** 43 13N 27 41 E
Razdel'naya, *Ukraine* **52** **C4** 46 50N 30 2 E
Razdolnoye, *Russia* **60** **C5** 43 30N 131 52 E
Razdolnoye, *Ukraine* **52** **D5** 45 46N 33 29 E
Razeh, *Iran* **85** **C6** 32 47N 48 9 E
Razelm, Lacul, *Romania* **46** **E10** 44 50N 29 0 E
Razgrad, *Bulgaria* **43** **D11** 43 33N 26 34 E
Razlog, *Bulgaria* **43** **F8** 41 53N 23 28 E
Razmak, *Pakistan* **79** **B3** 32 45N 69 50 E
Razole, *India* **83** **F5** 16 36N 81 48 E
Ré, I. de, *France* **24** **B2** 46 12N 1 30W
Reading, *U.K.* **17** **F7** 51 27N 0 57W
Reading, *Mich., U.S.A.* **141** **C12** 41 50N 84 45W
Reading, *Ohio, U.S.A.* **141** **E12** 39 13N 84 26W
Reading, *Pa., U.S.A.* **137** **F9** 40 20N 75 53W
Real, Cordillera, *Bolivia* **156** **D4** 17 0 S 67 10W
Realicó, *Argentina* **158** **D3** 35 0 S 64 15W
Réalmont, *France* **24** **E6** 43 48N 2 10 E
Reata, *Mexico* **146** **B4** 26 8N 101 5W
Rebais, *France* **23** **D10** 48 50N 3 10 E
Rebecca, L., *Australia* **113** **F3** 30 0 S 122 15 E
Rebi, *Indonesia* **73** **C4** 6 23 S 134 7 E
Rebiana, *Libya* **96** **D4** 24 12N 22 10 E
Rebun-Tō, *Japan* **60** **B10** 45 23N 141 2 E
Recanati, *Italy* **39** **E10** 43 24N 13 32 E
Recaş, *Romania* **46** **D2** 45 46N 21 30 E
Recherche, Arch. of the, *Australia* **113** **F3** 34 15 S 122 50 E
Rechitsa, *Belorussia* **50** **E7** 52 13N 30 15 E
Recht, *Belgium* **21** **H8** 50 20N 6 3 E
Recife, *Brazil* **154** **C5** 8 0 S 35 0W
Recklinghausen, *Germany* **21** **E10** 51 36N 7 10 E
Reconquista, *Argentina* **158** **B4** 29 10 S 59 45W
Recreio, *Brazil* **157** **B6** 8 0 S 58 25W
Recreo, *Argentina* **158** **B2** 29 25 S 65 10W
Recuay, *Peru* **156** **B2** 9 43 S 77 28W
Recz, *Poland* **47** **B2** 53 16N 15 31 E
Red →, *N. Amer.* **138** **A6** 50 24N 96 48W
Red →, *U.S.A.* **139** **K9** 31 0N 91 40W
Red Bank, *U.S.A.* **137** **F10** 40 21N 74 4W
Red Bay, *Canada* **129** **B8** 51 44N 56 25W
Red Bluff, *U.S.A.* **142** **F2** 40 11N 122 11W
Red Bluff L., *U.S.A.* **139** **K3** 31 59N 103 58W
Red Bud, *U.S.A.* **140** **F7** 38 13N 90 0W
Red Cliffs, *Australia* **116** **C5** 34 19 S 142 11 E
Red Cloud, *U.S.A.* **138** **E5** 40 5N 98 33W
Red Deer, *Canada* **130** **C6** 52 20N 113 50W
Red Deer →, *Alta., Canada* **131** **C6** 50 58N 110 0W
Red Deer →, *Man., Canada* **131** **C8** 52 53N 101 1W
Red Deer L., *Canada* **131** **C8** 52 55N 101 20W
Red Indian L., *Canada* **129** **C8** 48 35N 57 0W
Red Lake, *Canada* **131** **C10** 51 3N 93 49W
Red Lake Falls, *U.S.A.* **138** **B6** 47 54N 96 15W
Red Lodge, *U.S.A.* **142** **D9** 45 10N 109 10W
Red Mountain, *U.S.A.* **145** **K9** 35 22N 117 38W
Red Oak, *U.S.A.* **138** **E7** 41 0N 95 10W
Red Rock, *Canada* **128** **C2** 48 55N 88 15W
Red Rock, L., *U.S.A.* **140** **C3** 41 30N 93 15W
Red Rocks Pt., *Australia* **113** **F4** 32 13 S 127 32 E
Red Sea, *Asia* **90** **C2** 25 0N 36 0 E
Red Slate Mt., *U.S.A.* **144** **H8** 37 31N 118 52W
Red Sucker L., *Canada* **131** **C10** 54 9N 93 40W
Red Tower Pass = Turnu Rosu Pasul, *Romania* **46** **D5** 45 33N 24 17 E
Red Wing, *U.S.A.* **138** **C8** 44 32N 92 35W
Reda, *Poland* **47** **A5** 54 40N 18 19 E
Rédange, *Lux.* **21** **J7** 49 46N 5 52 E
Redbridge, *U.K.* **17** **F8** 51 35N 0 7 E
Redcar, *U.K.* **16** **C6** 54 37N 1 4W
Redcliff, *Canada* **131** **C6** 50 10N 110 50W
Redcliffe, *Australia* **115** **D5** 27 12 S 153 0 E
Redcliffe, Mt., *Australia* **113** **E3** 28 30 S 121 30 E
Reddersburg, *S. Africa* **104** **D4** 29 41 S 26 10 E
Redding, *U.S.A.* **142** **F2** 40 30N 122 25W
Redditch, *U.K.* **17** **E6** 52 18N 1 57W
Redenção, *Brazil* **154** **B4** 4 13 S 38 43W
Redfield, *U.S.A.* **138** **C5** 45 0N 98 30W
Redkey, *U.S.A.* **141** **D11** 40 21N 85 9W
Redknife →, *Canada* **130** **A5** 61 14N 119 22W
Redlands, *U.S.A.* **145** **M9** 34 0N 117 11W
Redmond, *Australia* **113** **F2** 34 55 S 117 40 E
Redmond, *Oreg., U.S.A.* **142** **D3** 44 19N 121 11W
Redmond, *Wash., U.S.A.* **144** **C4** 47 40N 122 7W
Redon, *France* **22** **E4** 47 40N 2 6W
Redonda, *Antigua* **149** **C7** 16 58N 62 19W
Redondela, *Spain* **36** **C2** 42 15N 8 38W
Redondo, *Portugal* **37** **G3** 38 39N 7 37W
Redondo Beach, *U.S.A.* **145** **M8** 33 50N 118 23W
Redrock Pt., *Canada* **130** **A5** 62 11N 115 2W
Redruth, *U.K.* **17** **G2** 50 14N 5 14W
Redvers, *Canada* **131** **D8** 49 35N 101 40W
Redwater, *Canada* **130** **C6** 53 55N 113 6W
Redwood, *U.S.A.* **137** **B9** 44 18N 75 48W
Redwood City, *U.S.A.* **144** **H4** 37 30N 122 15W
Redwood Falls, *U.S.A.* **138** **C7** 44 30N 95 2W
Ree, L., *Ireland* **19** **C4** 53 35N 8 0W
Reed, L., *Canada* **131** **C8** 54 38N 100 30W
Reed City, *U.S.A.* **134** **D3** 43 52N 85 30W
Reeder, *U.S.A.* **138** **B3** 46 7N 102 52W
Reedley, *U.S.A.* **144** **J7** 36 36N 119 27W
Reedsburg, *U.S.A.* **138** **D9** 43 34N 90 5W
Reedsport, *U.S.A.* **142** **E1** 43 45N 124 4W
Reedy Creek, *Australia* **116** **D4** 36 58 S 140 2 E
Reefton, *Australia* **117** **C7** 34 15 S 147 27 E
Reefton, *N.Z.* **119** **C6** 42 6 S 171 51 E
Refahiye, *Turkey* **89** **D8** 39 54N 38 47 E
Refugio, *U.S.A.* **139** **L6** 28 18N 97 17W
Rega →, *Poland* **47** **A2** 54 10N 15 18 E
Regalbuto, *Italy* **41** **E7** 37 40N 14 38 E
Regen, *Germany* **27** **G9** 48 58N 13 9 E
Regen →, *Germany* **27** **F8** 49 2N 12 6 E
Regeneração, *Brazil* **154** **C3** 6 15 S 42 41W
Regensburg, *Germany* **27** **F8** 49 1N 12 7 E
Regensdorf, *Switz* **29** **B6** 47 26N 8 28 E
Réggio di Calábria, *Italy* **41** **D8** 38 7N 15 38 E
Réggio nell' Emilia, *Italy* **38** **D7** 44 42N 10 38 E
Regina, *Canada* **131** **C8** 50 27N 104 35W
Régina, *Fr. Guiana* **153** **C7** 4 19N 52 8W
Registro, *Brazil* **159** **A6** 24 29 S 47 49W
Reguengos de Monsaraz, *Portugal* **37** **G3** 38 25N 7 32W
Rehar →, *India* **81** **H10** 23 55N 82 40 E
Rehoboth, *Namibia* **104** **C2** 23 15 S 17 4 E
Rehovot, *Israel* **91** **D3** 31 54N 34 48 E
Rei-Bouba, *Cameroon* **102** **A2** 8 40N 14 15 E
Reichenbach, *Germany* **26** **E8** 50 36N 12 19 E
Reichenbach, *Switz.* **28** **C5** 46 38N 7 42 E
Reid, *Australia* **113** **F4** 30 49 S 128 26 E
Reid River, *Australia* **114** **B4** 19 40 S 146 48 E
Reiden, *Switz.* **28** **B5** 47 14N 7 59 E
Reidsville, *U.S.A.* **135** **G6** 36 21N 79 40W
Reigate, *U.K.* **17** **F7** 51 14N 0 11W
Reillo, *Spain* **34** **F3** 39 54N 1 53W
Reims, *France* **23** **C11** 49 15N 4 1 E
Reina Adelaida, Arch., *Chile* **160** **D2** 52 20 S 74 0W
Reinach, *Aargau, Switz.* **28** **B6** 47 14N 8 11 E
Reinach, *Basel, Switz.* **28** **B5** 47 29N 7 35 E
Reinbeck, *U.S.A.* **140** **B4** 42 18N 92 40W
Reindeer →, *Canada* **131** **B8** 55 36N 103 11W
Reindeer I., *Canada* **131** **C9** 52 30N 98 0W
Reindeer L., *Canada* **131** **B8** 57 15N 102 15W
Reinga, C., *N.Z.* **118** **A1** 34 25 S 172 43 E
Reinosa, *Spain* **36** **B6** 43 2N 4 15W
Reinosa, Paso, *Spain* **36** **C6** 42 56N 4 10W
Reitdiep, *Neths.* **20** **B8** 53 20N 6 20 E
Reitz, *S. Africa* **105** **D4** 27 48 S 28 29 E
Reivilo, *S. Africa* **104** **D3** 27 36 S 24 8 E
Rejmyre, *Sweden* **15** **F9** 58 50N 15 55 E
Rejowiec Fabryczny, *Poland* **47** **D10** 51 5N 23 17 E
Reka →, *Slovenia* **39** **C11** 45 40N 14 0 E
Rekinniki, *Russia* **57** **C17** 60 51N 163 40 E
Rekovac, *Serbia, Yug.* **42** **D6** 43 51N 21 3 E
Reliance, *Canada* **131** **A7** 63 0N 109 20W
Remad, Oued →, *Algeria* **99** **B4** 33 28N 1 20W
Rémalard, *France* **22** **D7** 48 26N 0 47 E
Remarkable, Mt., *Australia* **116** **B3** 32 48 S 138 10 E
Rembang, *Indonesia* **75** **D4** 6 42 S 111 21 E
Rembau, *Malaysia* **74** **B2** 2 35N 102 6 E
Remchi, *Algeria* **99** **A4** 35 2N 1 26W
Remedios, *Colombia* **152** **B3** 7 2N 74 41W
Remedios, *Panama* **148** **E3** 8 15N 81 50W
Remeshk, *Iran* **85** **E8** 26 55N 58 50 E
Remetea, *Romania* **46** **C6** 46 45N 25 29 E
Remich, *Lux.* **21** **J8** 49 32N 6 22 E
Remington, *U.S.A.* **141** **D9** 40 45N 87 8W
Rémire, *Fr. Guiana* **153** **C7** 4 53N 52 17W
Remiremont, *France* **23** **D13** 48 2N 6 36 E
Remo, *Ethiopia* **95** **F5** 6 48N 41 20 E
Remontnoye, *Russia* **53** **C10** 46 34N 43 37 E
Remoulins, *France* **25** **E8** 43 55N 4 35 E
Remscheid, *Germany* **26** **D3** 51 11N 7 12 E
Ren Xian, *China* **66** **F8** 37 8N 114 40 E
Renascença, *Brazil* **152** **D4** 3 50 S 66 21W
Rend L., *U.S.A.* **140** **F8** 38 2N 88 58W
Rende, *Italy* **41** **C9** 39 19N 16 11 E
Rendeux, *Belgium* **21** **H7** 50 14N 5 30 E
Rendína, *Greece* **45** **E3** 39 4N 21 58 E
Rendova, *Solomon Is.* **121** **M9** 8 33 S 157 17 E
Rendsburg, *Germany* **26** **A5** 54 18N 9 41 E
Rene, *Russia* **57** **C19** 66 2N 179 25W
Renfrew, *Canada* **128** **C4** 45 30N 76 40W
Renfrew, *U.K.* **18** **F4** 55 52N 4 24W
Rengat, *Indonesia* **74** **C2** 0 30 S 102 45 E
Rengo, *Chile* **158** **C1** 34 24 S 70 50W
Renhua, *China* **69** **E9** 25 5N 113 40 E
Renhuai, *China* **68** **D6** 27 48N 106 24 E
Reni, *Moldavia* **52** **D3** 45 28N 28 15 E
Renigunta, *India* **83** **H4** 13 38N 79 30 E
Renk, *Sudan* **95** **E3** 11 50N 32 50 E
Renkum, *Neths.* **20** **E7** 51 58N 5 43 E
Renmark, *Australia* **116** **C4** 34 11 S 140 43 E
Rennell, *Solomon Is.* **121** **N11** 11 40 S 160 10 E
Rennell Sd., *Canada* **130** **C2** 53 23N 132 35W
Renner Springs T.O., *Australia* **114** **B1** 18 20 S 133 47 E
Rennes, *France* **22** **D5** 48 7N 1 41W
Rennes, Bassin de, *France* **22** **E5** 48 0N 1 30W
Reno, *U.S.A.* **144** **F7** 39 30N 119 50W
Reno →, *Italy* **39** **D9** 44 37N 12 17 E
Renovo, *U.S.A.* **136** **E7** 41 20N 77 47W
Renqiu, *China* **66** **E9** 38 43N 116 5 E
Rensselaer, *Ind., U.S.A.* **141** **D9** 40 57N 87 10W

**Roag, L. 255**


Rensselaer, *N.Y., U.S.A.* 137 **D11** 42 38N 73 41W
Rentería, *Spain* 34 **B3** 43 19N 1 54W
Renton, *U.S.A.* 144 **C4** 47 30N 122 9W
Renwick, *N.Z.* 119 **B8** 41 30 S 173 51 E
Réo, *Burkina Faso* 100 **C4** 12 28N 2 35W
Reotipur, *India* 81 **G10** 25 33N 83 45 E
Repalle, *India* 83 **F5** 16 2N 80 45 E
Répcelak, *Hungary* 31 **D10** 47 24N 17 1 E
Republic, *Mich., U.S.A.* 134 **B2** 46 25N 87 59W
Republic, *Wash., U.S.A.* 142 **B4** 48 38N 118 42W
Republican →, *U.S.A.* 138 **F6** 39 3N 96 48W
Republican City, *U.S.A.* 138 **E5** 40 9N 99 20W
Republiek, *Surinam* 153 **B6** 5 30N 55 13W
Repulse Bay, *Canada* 127 **B11** 66 30N 86 30W
Requena, *Peru* 156 **B3** 5 5 S 73 52W
Requena, *Spain* 35 **F3** 39 30N 1 4W
Resadiye = Datça, *Turkey* 45 **H9** 36 46N 27 40 E
Reşadiye, *Turkey* 88 **C7** 40 23N 37 20 E
Resele, *Sweden* 14 **A11** 63 20N 17 5 E
Resen, *Macedonia, Yug.* 42 **F6** 41 5N 21 0 E
Reserve, *Canada* 131 **C8** 52 28N 102 39W
Reserve, *U.S.A.* 143 **K9** 33 50N 108 54W
Resht = Rasht, *Iran* 85 **B6** 37 20N 49 40 E
Resistencia, *Argentina* 158 **B4** 27 30 S 59 0W
Reşiţa, *Romania* 42 **B6** 45 18N 21 53 E
Resko, *Poland* 47 **B2** 53 47N 15 25 E
Resolution I., *Canada* 127 **B13** 61 30N 65 0W
Resolution I., *N.Z.* 119 **F1** 45 40 S 166 40 E
Resplandes, *Brazil* 154 **C2** 6 17 S 45 13W
Resplendor, *Brazil* 155 **E3** 19 20 S 41 15W
Ressano Garcia, *Mozam.* 105 **D5** 25 25 S 32 0 E
Reston, *Canada* 131 **D8** 49 33N 101 6W
Reszel, *Poland* 47 **A8** 54 4N 21 10 E
Retalhuleu, *Guatemala* 148 **D1** 14 33N 91 46W
Reteag, *Romania* 46 **B5** 47 10N 24 0 E
Retenue, L. de, *Zaïre* 107 **E2** 11 0 S 27 0 E
Rethel, *France* 23 **C11** 49 30N 4 20 E
Rethem, *Germany* 26 **C5** 52 47N 9 25 E
Réthímnon, *Greece* 32 **D6** 35 18N 24 30 E
Réthímnon □, *Greece* 32 **D6** 35 23N 24 28 E
Retiche, Alpi, *Switz.* 29 **D10** 46 30N 10 0 E
Retie, *Belgium* 21 **F6** 51 16N 5 5 E
Retiers, *France* 22 **E5** 47 55N 1 23W
Retortillo, *Spain* 36 **E4** 40 48N 6 21W
Rétság, *Hungary* 31 **D12** 47 58N 19 10 E
Reuland, *Belgium* 21 **H8** 50 12N 6 8 E
Réunion ■, *Ind. Oc.* 109 **G4** 21 0 S 56 0 E
Reus, *Spain* 34 **D6** 41 10N 1 5 E
Reusel, *Neths.* 21 **F6** 51 21N 5 9 E
Reuss →, *Switz.* 29 **B6** 47 16N 8 24 E
Reutlingen, *Germany* 27 **G5** 48 28N 9 13 E
Reutte, *Austria* 30 **D3** 47 29N 10 42 E
Reuver, *Neths.* 21 **F8** 51 17N 6 5 E
Reval = Tallinn, *Estonia* 50 **B4** 59 22N 24 48 E
Revda, *Russia* 54 **C6** 56 48N 59 57 E
Revel, *France* 24 **E6** 43 28N 2 0 E
Revelganj, *India* 81 **G11** 25 50N 84 40 E
Revelstoke, *Canada* 130 **C5** 51 0N 118 10W
Reventazón, *Peru* 156 **B1** 6 10 S 80 58W
Revigny-sur-Ornain, *France* 23 **D11** 48 49N 4 59 E
Revilla Gigedo, Is., *Pac. Oc.* 123 **F16** 18 40N 112 0W
Revillagigedo I., *U.S.A.* 130 **B2** 55 50N 131 20W
Revin, *France* 23 **C11** 49 55N 4 39 E
Revolyutsii, Pik, *Tajikistan* 55 **D6** 38 31N 72 21 E
Revuè →, *Mozam.* 107 **F3** 19 50 S 34 0 E
Rewa, *India* 81 **G9** 24 33N 81 25 E
Rewa →, *Guyana* 153 **C6** 3 19N 58 42W
Rewari, *India* 80 **E7** 28 15N 76 40 E
Rexburg, *U.S.A.* 142 **E8** 43 55N 111 50W
Rey, *Iran* 85 **C6** 35 35N 51 25 E
Rey, Rio del →, *Nigeria* 101 **E6** 4 30N 8 48 E
Rey Malabo, *Eq. Guin.* 101 **E6** 3 45N 8 50 E
Reyes, *Bolivia* 156 **C4** 14 19 S 67 23W
Reyes, Pt., *U.S.A.* 144 **H3** 37 59N 123 2W
Reykjahlið, *Iceland* 12 **D5** 65 40N 16 55W
Reykjanes, *Iceland* 12 **E2** 63 48N 22 40W
Reykjavík, *Iceland* 12 **D3** 64 10N 21 57W
Reynolds, *Canada* 131 **D9** 49 40N 95 55W
Reynolds, *U.S.A.* 140 **C6** 41 20N 90 40W
Reynolds Ra., *Australia* 112 **D5** 22 30 S 133 0 E
Reynoldsville, *U.S.A.* 136 **E6** 41 5N 78 58W
Reynosa, *Mexico* 147 **B5** 26 5N 98 18W
Rezekne, *Latvia* 50 **C5** 56 30N 27 17 E
Rezh, *Russia* 54 **C7** 57 23N 61 24 E
Rezovo, *Bulgaria* 43 **E13** 42 0N 28 0 E
Rezvān, *Iran* 85 **E8** 27 34N 56 6 E
Rgotina, *Serbia, Yug.* 42 **C7** 44 1N 22 17 E
Rhamnus, *Greece* 45 **F6** 38 12N 24 3 E
Rharis, O. →, *Algeria* 99 **C6** 26 0N 5 4 E
Rhayader, *U.K.* 17 **E4** 52 19N 3 30W
Rheden, *Neths.* 20 **D8** 52 3N 6 3 E
Rhein, *Canada* 131 **C8** 51 25N 102 15W
Rhein →, *Europe* 20 **E8** 51 52N 6 2 E
Rhein-Main-Donau-Kanal, *Germany* 27 **F7** 49 1N 11 27 E
Rheinbach, *Germany* 26 **E2** 50 38N 6 54 E
Rheine, *Germany* 26 **C3** 52 17N 7 25 E
Rheineck, *Switz.* 29 **B9** 47 28N 9 31 E
Rheinfelden, *Switz.* 28 **A5** 47 32N 7 47 E
Rheinland-Pfalz □, *Germany* 27 **E2** 50 0N 7 0 E
Rheinsberg, *Germany* 26 **B8** 53 6N 12 52 E
Rheinwaldhorn, *Switz.* 29 **D8** 46 30N 9 3 E
Rhenen, *Neths.* 20 **E7** 51 58N 5 33 E
Rheriss, Oued →, *Morocco* 98 **B4** 30 50N 4 34W
Rheydt, *Germany* 26 **D2** 51 10N 6 24 E
Rhin = Rhein →, *Europe* 20 **E8** 51 52N 6 2 E
Rhinau, *France* 23 **D14** 48 19N 7 43 E
Rhine = Rhein →, *Europe* 20 **E8** 51 52N 6 2 E
Rhineland-Palatinate □ = Rheinland-Pfalz □, *Germany* 27 **E2** 50 0N 7 0 E
Rhinelander, *U.S.A.* 138 **C10** 45 38N 89 29W
Rhino Camp, *Uganda* 106 **B3** 3 0N 31 22 E
Rhir, Cap, *Morocco* 98 **B3** 30 38N 9 54W
Rhisnes, *Belgium* 21 **G5** 50 31N 4 48 E
Rho, *Italy* 38 **C6** 45 31N 9 2 E
Rhode Island □, *U.S.A.* 137 **E13** 41 38N 71 37W
Rhodes = Ródhos, *Greece* 32 **C10** 36 15N 28 10 E
Rhodesia = Zimbabwe ■, *Africa* 107 **F2** 19 0 S 30 0 E
Rhodope Mts. = Rhodopi Planina, *Bulgaria* 43 **F9** 41 40N 24 20 E
Rhodopi Planina, *Bulgaria* 43 **F9** 41 40N 24 20 E
Rhondda, *U.K.* 17 **F4** 51 39N 3 30W
Rhône □, *France* 25 **C8** 45 54N 4 35 E
Rhône →, *France* 25 **E8** 43 28N 4 42 E
Rhum, *U.K.* 18 **E2** 57 0N 6 20W
Rhyl, *U.K.* 16 **D4** 53 19N 3 29W
Rhymney, *U.K.* 17 **F4** 51 45N 3 17W
Ri-Aba, *Eq. Guin.* 101 **E6** 3 28N 8 40 E
Riachão, *Brazil* 154 **C2** 7 20 S 46 37W
Riacho de Santana, *Brazil* 155 **D3** 13 37 S 42 57W
Rialma, *Brazil* 155 **E2** 15 18 S 49 34W
Riang, *India* 78 **B4** 27 31N 92 56 E
Riaño, *Spain* 36 **C5** 42 59N 5 0W
Rians, *France* 25 **E9** 43 37N 5 44 E
Riansares →, *Spain* 34 **F1** 39 32N 3 18W
Riasi, *India* 81 **C6** 33 10N 74 50 E
Riau, Kepulauan, *Indonesia* 74 **B2** 0 30N 104 20 E
Riau Arch. = Riau, Kepulauan, *Indonesia* 74 **B2** 0 30N 104 20 E
Riaza, *Spain* 34 **D1** 41 18N 3 30W
Riaza →, *Spain* 34 **D1** 41 42N 3 55W
Riba de Saelices, *Spain* 34 **E2** 40 55N 2 17W
Ribadavia, *Spain* 36 **C2** 42 17N 8 8W
Ribadeo, *Spain* 36 **B3** 43 35N 7 5W
Ribadesella, *Spain* 36 **B5** 43 30N 5 7W
Ribamar, *Brazil* 154 **B3** 2 33 S 44 3W
Ribas, *Spain* 34 **C7** 42 19N 2 15 E
Ribas do Rio Pardo, *Brazil* 157 **E7** 20 27 S 53 46W
Ribāţ, *Yemen* 86 **D4** 14 18N 44 15 E
Ribble →, *U.K.* 16 **C5** 54 13N 2 20W
Ribe, *Denmark* 15 **J2** 55 19N 8 44 E
Ribeauvillé, *France* 23 **D14** 48 10N 7 20 E
Ribécourt, *France* 23 **C9** 49 30N 2 55 E
Ribeira, *Spain* 36 **C2** 42 36N 8 58W
Ribeira Brava, *Madeira* 33 **D2** 32 41N 17 4W
Ribeira do Pombal, *Brazil* 154 **D4** 10 50 S 38 32W
Ribeirão Prêto, *Brazil* 159 **A6** 21 10 S 47 50W
Ribeiro Gonçalves, *Brazil* 154 **C2** 7 32 S 45 14W
Ribemont, *France* 23 **C10** 49 47N 3 27 E
Ribera, *Italy* 40 **E6** 37 30N 13 13 E
Ribérac, *France* 24 **C4** 45 15N 0 20 E
Riberalta, *Bolivia* 157 **C4** 11 0 S 66 0W
Ribnica, *Slovenia* 39 **C11** 45 45N 14 45 E
Ribnitz-Damgarten, *Germany* 26 **A8** 54 14N 12 24 E
Ričany, *Czech.* 30 **B7** 50 0N 14 40 E
Riccarton, *N.Z.* 119 **D7** 43 32 S 172 37 E
Riccia, *Italy* 41 **A7** 41 30N 14 50 E
Riccione, *Italy* 39 **D9** 44 0N 12 39 E
Rice, *U.S.A.* 145 **L12** 34 5N 114 51W
Rice L., *Canada* 136 **B6** 44 12N 78 10W
Rice Lake, *U.S.A.* 138 **C9** 45 30N 91 42W
Rich, *Morocco* 98 **B4** 32 16N 4 30W
Rich Hill, *U.S.A.* 139 **F7** 38 5N 94 22W
Richards Bay, *S. Africa* 105 **D5** 28 48 S 32 6 E
Richards L., *Canada* 131 **B7** 59 10N 107 10W
Richardson →, *Canada* 131 **B6** 58 25N 111 14W
Richardson Mts., *N.Z.* 119 **E3** 44 49 S 168 34 E
Richardson Springs, *U.S.A.* 144 **F5** 39 51N 121 46W
Richardton, *U.S.A.* 138 **B3** 46 56N 102 22W
Riche, C., *Australia* 113 **F2** 34 36 S 118 47 E
Richelieu, *France* 22 **E7** 47 0N 0 20 E
Richey, *U.S.A.* 138 **B2** 47 42N 105 5W
Richfield, *Idaho, U.S.A.* 142 **E6** 43 2N 114 5W
Richfield, *Utah, U.S.A.* 143 **G8** 38 50N 112 0W
Richford, *U.S.A.* 137 **B12** 45 0N 72 40W
Richibucto, *Canada* 129 **C7** 46 42N 64 54W
Richland, *Ga., U.S.A.* 135 **J3** 32 7N 84 40W
Richland, *Iowa, U.S.A.* 140 **C4** 41 13N 92 0W
Richland, *Mo., U.S.A.* 140 **G4** 37 51N 92 26W
Richland, *Oreg., U.S.A.* 142 **D5** 44 49N 117 9W
Richland, *Wash., U.S.A.* 142 **C4** 46 15N 119 15W
Richland Center, *U.S.A.* 138 **D9** 43 21N 90 22W
Richlands, *U.S.A.* 134 **G5** 37 7N 81 49W
Richmond, *N.S.W., Australia* 117 **B9** 33 35 S 150 42 E
Richmond, *Queens., Australia* 114 **C3** 20 43 S 143 8 E
Richmond, *N.Z.* 119 **B8** 41 20 S 173 12 E
Richmond, *S. Africa* 105 **D5** 29 51 S 30 18 E
Richmond, *U.K.* 16 **C6** 54 24N 1 43W
Richmond, *Calif., U.S.A.* 144 **H4** 37 58N 122 21W
Richmond, *Ind., U.S.A.* 141 **E12** 39 50N 84 50W
Richmond, *Ky., U.S.A.* 141 **G12** 37 40N 84 20W
Richmond, *Mich., U.S.A.* 136 **D2** 42 47N 82 45W
Richmond, *Mo., U.S.A.* 138 **F8** 39 15N 93 58W
Richmond, *Tex., U.S.A.* 139 **L7** 29 32N 95 42W
Richmond, *Utah, U.S.A.* 142 **F8** 41 55N 111 48W
Richmond, *Va., U.S.A.* 134 **G7** 37 33N 77 27W
Richmond, Mt., *N.Z.* 119 **B8** 41 32 S 173 22 E
Richmond Ra., *Australia* 115 **D5** 29 0 S 152 45 E
Richmond Ra., *N.Z.* 119 **B8** 41 32 S 173 22 E
Richmond-upon-Thames, *U.K.* 17 **F7** 51 28N 0 18W
Richterswil, *Switz.* 29 **B7** 47 13N 8 43 E
Richton, *U.S.A.* 135 **K1** 31 23N 88 58W
Richwood, *Ohio, U.S.A.* 141 **D13** 40 26N 83 18W
Richwood, *W. Va., U.S.A.* 134 **F5** 38 17N 80 32W
Ricla, *Spain* 34 **D3** 41 31N 1 24W
Ricupe, *Angola* 103 **E4** 14 37 S 21 25 E
Ridā', *Yemen* 86 **D4** 14 25N 44 50 E
Ridder, *Kazakhstan* 56 **D9** 50 20N 83 30 E
Ridderkerk, *Neths.* 20 **E5** 51 52N 4 35 E
Riddes, *Switz.* 28 **D4** 46 11N 7 14 E
Ridge Farm, *U.S.A.* 141 **E9** 39 54N 87 39W
Ridgecrest, *U.S.A.* 145 **K9** 35 37N 117 40W
Ridgedale, *Canada* 131 **C8** 53 0N 104 10W
Ridgefield, *U.S.A.* 144 **E4** 45 49N 122 45W
Ridgeland, *U.S.A.* 135 **J5** 32 30N 80 58W
Ridgelands, *Australia* 114 **C5** 23 16 S 150 17 E
Ridgetown, *Canada* 128 **D3** 42 26N 81 52W
Ridgeville, *U.S.A.* 141 **D11** 40 18N 85 2W
Ridgewood, *U.S.A.* 137 **F10** 40 59N 74 7W
Ridgway, *Ill., U.S.A.* 141 **G8** 37 48N 88 16W
Ridgway, *Pa., U.S.A.* 136 **E6** 41 25N 78 43W
Riding Mountain Nat. Park, *Canada* 131 **C8** 50 50N 100 0W
Ridley, Mt., *Australia* 113 **F3** 33 12 S 122 7 E
Ried, *Austria* 30 **C6** 48 14N 13 30 E
Riedlingen, *Germany* 27 **G5** 48 9N 9 28 E
Riel, *Neths.* 21 **E6** 51 31N 5 1 E
Rienza →, *Italy* 39 **B8** 46 49N 11 47 E
Riesa, *Germany* 26 **D9** 51 19N 13 19 E
Riesco, I., *Chile* 160 **D2** 52 55 S 72 40W
Riesi, *Italy* 41 **E7** 37 16N 14 4 E
Riet →, *S. Africa* 104 **D3** 29 0 S 23 54 E
Rieti, *Italy* 39 **F9** 42 23N 12 50 E
Rieupeyroux, *France* 24 **D6** 44 19N 2 12 E
Riez, *France* 25 **E10** 43 49N 6 6 E
Riffe, L., *U.S.A.* 144 **D4** 46 30N 122 20W
Rifle, *U.S.A.* 142 **G10** 39 40N 107 50W
Rifstangi, *Iceland* 12 **C5** 66 32N 16 12W
Rift Valley □, *Kenya* 106 **B4** 0 20N 36 0 E
Rig Rig, *Chad* 97 **F2** 14 13N 14 25 E
Riga, *Latvia* 50 **C4** 56 53N 24 8 E
Riga, G. of = Rīgas Jūras Līcis, *Latvia* 50 **C3** 57 40N 23 45 E
Rīgān, *Iran* 85 **D8** 28 37N 58 58 E
Rīgas Jūras Līcis, *Latvia* 50 **C3** 57 40N 23 45 E
Rigaud, *Canada* 137 **A10** 45 29N 74 18W
Rigby, *U.S.A.* 142 **E8** 43 41N 111 58W
Rīgestān □, *Afghan.* 79 **C2** 30 15N 65 0 E
Riggins, *U.S.A.* 142 **D5** 45 29N 116 26W
Rignac, *France* 24 **D6** 44 25N 2 16 E
Rigolet, *Canada* 129 **B8** 54 10N 58 23W
Riihimäki, *Finland* 13 **F18** 60 45N 24 48 E
Riiser-Larsen-halvøya, *Antarctica* 7 **C4** 68 0 S 35 0 E
Rijau, *Nigeria* 101 **C6** 11 8N 5 17 E
Rijeka, *Croatia* 39 **C11** 45 20N 14 21 E
Rijeka Crnojevica, *Montenegro, Yug.* 42 **E4** 42 24N 19 1 E
Rijen, *Neths.* 21 **E5** 51 35N 4 55 E
Rijkevorsel, *Belgium* 21 **F5** 51 21N 4 46 E
Rijn →, *Neths.* 20 **D4** 52 12N 4 21 E
Rijnsberg, *Neths.* 20 **D4** 52 11N 4 27 E
Rijsbergen, *Neths.* 21 **E5** 51 31N 4 41 E
Rijssen, *Neths.* 20 **D9** 52 19N 6 31 E
Rijswijk, *Neths.* 20 **D4** 52 4N 4 22 E
Rikā', W. ar →, *Si. Arabia* 86 **B4** 22 25N 44 50 E
Rike, *Ethiopia* 95 **E4** 10 50N 39 53 E
Rikuzentakada, *Japan* 60 **E10** 39 0N 141 40 E
Rila, *Bulgaria* 43 **E8** 42 7N 23 7 E
Rila Planina, *Bulgaria* 42 **E8** 42 10N 23 0 E
Riley, *U.S.A.* 142 **E4** 43 35N 119 33W
Rima →, *Nigeria* 101 **C6** 13 4N 5 10 E
Rimah, Wadi ar →, *Si. Arabia* 84 **E4** 26 5N 41 30 E
Rimavská Sobota, *Czech.* 31 **C13** 48 22N 20 2 E
Rimbey, *Canada* 130 **C6** 52 35N 114 15W
Rimbo, *Sweden* 14 **E12** 59 44N 18 21 E
Rimi, *Nigeria* 101 **C6** 12 58N 7 43 E
Rímini, *Italy* 39 **D9** 44 3N 12 33 E
Rîmna →, *Romania* 46 **D8** 45 36N 27 3 E
Rîmnicu Sărat, *Romania* 46 **D8** 45 26N 27 3 E
Rîmnicu Vîlcea, *Romania* 46 **D5** 45 9N 24 21 E
Rimouski, *Canada* 129 **C6** 48 27N 68 30W
Rimrock, *U.S.A.* 144 **D5** 46 38N 121 10W
Rinca, *Indonesia* 72 **C1** 8 45 S 119 35 E
Rincón de Romos, *Mexico* 146 **C4** 22 14N 102 18W
Rinconada, *Argentina* 158 **A2** 22 26 S 66 10W
Ringarum, *Sweden* 15 **F10** 58 21N 16 26 E
Ringe, *Denmark* 15 **J4** 55 13N 10 28 E
Ringgold Is., *Fiji* 121 **A3** 16 15 S 179 25W
Ringim, *Nigeria* 101 **C6** 12 13N 9 10 E
Ringkøbing, *Denmark* 15 **H2** 56 5N 8 15 E
Ringling, *U.S.A.* 142 **C8** 46 16N 110 56W
Ringsaker, *Norway* 14 **D4** 60 54N 10 45 E
Ringsted, *Denmark* 15 **J5** 55 25N 11 46 E
Ringvassøy, *Norway* 12 **B15** 69 56N 19 15 E
Rinía, *Greece* 45 **G7** 37 23N 25 13 E
Rinjani, *Indonesia* 75 **D5** 8 24 S 116 28 E
Rinteln, *Germany* 26 **C5** 52 11N 9 3 E
Río, Punta del, *Spain* 35 **J2** 36 49N 2 24W
Rio Branco, *Brazil* 156 **B4** 9 58 S 67 49W
Río Branco, *Uruguay* 159 **C5** 32 40 S 53 40W
Rio Brilhante, *Brazil* 159 **A5** 21 48 S 54 33W
Río Bueno, *Chile* 160 **B2** 40 19 S 72 58W
Río Chico, *Venezuela* 152 **A4** 10 19N 65 59W
Rio Claro, *Brazil* 159 **A6** 22 19 S 47 35W
Rio Claro, *Trin. & Tob.* 149 **D7** 10 20N 61 25W
Río Colorado, *Argentina* 160 **A4** 39 0 S 64 0W
Río Cuarto, *Argentina* 158 **C3** 33 10 S 64 25W
Rio das Pedras, *Mozam.* 105 **C6** 23 8 S 35 28 E
Rio de Contas, *Brazil* 155 **D3** 13 36 S 41 48W
Rio de Janeiro, *Brazil* 155 **F3** 23 0 S 43 12W
Rio de Janeiro □, *Brazil* 155 **F3** 22 50 S 43 0W
Rio do Prado, *Brazil* 155 **E3** 16 35 S 40 34W
Rio do Sul, *Brazil* 159 **B6** 27 13 S 49 37W
Río Gallegos, *Argentina* 160 **D3** 51 35 S 69 15W
Río Grande, *Argentina* 160 **D3** 53 50 S 67 45W
Río Grande, *Bolivia* 156 **E4** 20 51 S 67 17W
Rio Grande, *Brazil* 159 **C5** 32 0 S 52 20W
Río Grande, *Mexico* 146 **C4** 23 50N 103 2W
Río Grande, *Nic.* 148 **D3** 12 54N 83 33W
Rio Grande →, *U.S.A.* 139 **N6** 25 57N 97 9W
Rio Grande City, *U.S.A.* 139 **M5** 26 23N 98 49W
Río Grande del Norte →, *N. Amer.* 133 **E7** 26 0N 97 0W
Rio Grande do Norte □, *Brazil* 154 **C4** 5 40 S 36 0W
Rio Grande do Sul □, *Brazil* 159 **C5** 30 0 S 53 0W
Río Hato, *Panama* 148 **E3** 8 22N 80 10W
Río Lagartos, *Mexico* 147 **C7** 21 36N 88 10W
Rio Largo, *Brazil* 154 **C4** 9 28 S 35 50W
Rio Maior, *Portugal* 37 **F2** 39 19N 8 57W
Rio Marina, *Italy* 38 **F7** 42 48N 10 25 E
Río Mayo, *Argentina* 160 **C2** 45 40 S 70 15W
Río Mulatos, *Bolivia* 156 **D4** 19 40 S 66 50W
Río Muni = Mbini □, *Eq. Guin.* 102 **B2** 1 30N 10 0 E
Rio Negro, *Brazil* 159 **B6** 26 0 S 49 55W
Río Negro, *Chile* 160 **B2** 40 47 S 73 14W
Rio Negro, Pantanal do, *Brazil* 157 **D6** 19 0 S 56 0W
Rio Pardo, *Brazil* 159 **C5** 30 0 S 52 30W
Río Pico, *Argentina* 160 **B2** 44 0 S 70 22W
Rio Real, *Brazil* 155 **D4** 11 28 S 37 56W
Río Segundo, *Argentina* 158 **C3** 31 40 S 63 59W
Río Tercero, *Argentina* 158 **C3** 32 15 S 64 8W
Rio Tinto, *Brazil* 154 **C4** 6 48 S 35 5W
Rio Tinto, *Portugal* 36 **D2** 41 11N 8 34W
Rio Verde, *Brazil* 155 **E1** 17 50 S 51 0W
Río Verde, *Mexico* 147 **C5** 21 56N 99 59W
Rio Verde de Mato Grosso, *Brazil* 157 **D7** 18 56 S 54 52W
Rio Vista, *U.S.A.* 144 **G5** 38 11N 121 44W
Ríobamba, *Ecuador* 152 **D2** 1 50 S 78 45W
Ríohacha, *Colombia* 152 **A3** 11 33N 72 55W
Rioja, *Peru* 156 **B2** 6 11 S 77 5W
Riom, *France* 24 **C7** 45 54N 3 7 E
Riom-ès-Montagnes, *France* 24 **C6** 45 17N 2 39 E
Rion-des-Landes, *France* 24 **E3** 43 55N 0 56W
Rionegro, *Colombia* 152 **B2** 6 9N 75 22W
Rionero in Vúlture, *Italy* 41 **B8** 40 55N 15 40 E
Rioni →, *Georgia* 53 **E9** 42 5N 41 50 E
Rios, *Spain* 36 **D3** 41 58N 7 16W
Riosucio, *Caldas, Colombia* 152 **B2** 5 30N 75 40W
Ríosucio, *Choco, Colombia* 152 **B2** 7 27N 77 7W
Riou L., *Canada* 131 **B7** 59 7N 106 25W
Rioz, *France* 23 **E13** 47 26N 6 5 E
Riozinho →, *Brazil* 152 **D4** 2 55 S 67 7W
Riparia, Dora →, *Italy* 38 **C4** 45 7N 7 24 E
Ripatransone, *Italy* 39 **F10** 43 0N 13 45 E
Ripley, *Canada* 136 **B3** 44 4N 81 35W
Ripley, *Calif., U.S.A.* 145 **M12** 33 32N 114 39W
Ripley, *N.Y., U.S.A.* 136 **D5** 42 16N 79 44W
Ripley, *Ohio, U.S.A.* 141 **F13** 38 45N 83 51W
Ripley, *Tenn., U.S.A.* 139 **H10** 35 43N 89 34W
Ripoll, *Spain* 34 **C7** 42 15N 2 13 E
Ripon, *U.K.* 16 **C6** 54 8N 1 31W
Ripon, *Calif., U.S.A.* 144 **H5** 37 44N 121 7W
Ripon, *Wis., U.S.A.* 134 **D1** 43 51N 88 50W
Riposto, *Italy* 41 **E8** 37 44N 15 12 E
Risalpur, *Pakistan* 80 **B4** 34 3N 71 59 E
Risan, *Montenegro, Yug.* 42 **E3** 42 32N 18 42 E
Risaralda □, *Colombia* 152 **B2** 5 0N 76 10W
Riscle, *France* 24 **E3** 43 39N 0 5W
Rishā', W. ar →, *Si. Arabia* 84 **E5** 25 33N 44 5 E
Rishiri-Tō, *Japan* 60 **B10** 45 11N 141 15 E
Rishon le Ziyyon, *Israel* 91 **D3** 31 58N 34 48 E
Rising Sun, *U.S.A.* 141 **F12** 38 57N 84 51W
Risle →, *France* 22 **C7** 49 26N 0 23 E
Rîşnov, *Romania* 46 **D6** 45 35N 25 27 E
Rison, *U.S.A.* 139 **J8** 33 57N 92 11W
Risør, *Norway* 15 **F3** 58 43N 9 13 E
Rissani, *Morocco* 98 **B4** 31 18N 4 12W
Riti, *Nigeria* 101 **D6** 7 57N 9 41 E
Ritidian Pt., *Guam* 121 **R15** 13 39N 144 51 E
Rittman, *U.S.A.* 136 **F3** 40 57N 81 48W
Ritzville, *U.S.A.* 142 **C4** 47 10N 118 21W
Riu, *India* 78 **A5** 28 19N 95 3 E
Riva Bella, *France* 22 **C6** 49 17N 0 18W
Riva del Garda, *Italy* 38 **C7** 45 53N 10 50 E
Rivadavia, *Buenos Aires, Argentina* 158 **D3** 35 29 S 62 59W
Rivadavia, *Mendoza, Argentina* 158 **C2** 33 13 S 68 30W
Rivadavia, *Salta, Argentina* 158 **A3** 24 5 S 62 54W
Rivadavia, *Chile* 158 **B1** 29 57 S 70 35W
Rivarolo Canavese, *Italy* 38 **C4** 45 20N 7 42 E
Rivas, *Nic.* 148 **D2** 11 30N 85 50W
Rive-de-Gier, *France* 25 **C8** 45 32N 4 37 E
River Cess, *Liberia* 100 **D3** 5 30N 9 32W
Rivera, *Uruguay* 159 **C4** 31 0 S 55 50W
Riverdale, *U.S.A.* 144 **J7** 36 26N 119 52W
Riverdsale, *S. Africa* 104 **E3** 34 7 S 21 15 E
Riverhead, *U.S.A.* 137 **F12** 40 53N 72 40W
Riverhurst, *Canada* 131 **C7** 50 55N 106 50W
Riverina, *Australia* 113 **E3** 29 45 S 120 40 E
Rivers, *Canada* 131 **C8** 50 2N 100 14W
Rivers □, *Nigeria* 101 **E6** 5 0N 6 30 E
Rivers, L. of the, *Canada* 131 **D7** 49 49N 105 44W
Rivers Inlet, *Canada* 130 **C3** 51 42N 127 15W
Riversdale, *N.Z.* 119 **F3** 45 54 S 168 44 E
Riverside, *Calif., U.S.A.* 145 **M9** 33 58N 117 22W
Riverside, *Wyo., U.S.A.* 142 **F10** 41 12N 106 57W
Riversleigh, *Australia* 114 **B2** 19 5 S 138 40 E
Riverton, *Australia* 116 **C3** 34 10 S 138 46 E
Riverton, *Canada* 131 **C9** 51 1N 97 0W
Riverton, *N.Z.* 119 **G2** 46 21 S 168 0 E
Riverton, *Ill., U.S.A.* 140 **E7** 39 51N 89 33W
Riverton, *Wyo., U.S.A.* 142 **E9** 43 1N 108 27W
Riverton Heights, *U.S.A.* 144 **C4** 47 28N 122 17W
Rives, *France* 25 **C9** 45 21N 5 31 E
Rivesaltes, *France* 24 **F6** 42 47N 2 50 E
Riviera, *Europe* 38 **E5** 44 0N 8 30 E
Rivière-à-Pierre, *Canada* 129 **C5** 46 59N 72 11W
Rivière-au-Renard, *Canada* 129 **C7** 48 59N 64 23W
Rivière-du-Loup, *Canada* 129 **C6** 47 50N 69 30W
Rivière-Pentecôte, *Canada* 129 **C6** 49 57N 67 1W
Rivière-Pilot, *Martinique* 149 **D7** 14 26N 60 53W
Rívoli, *Italy* 38 **C4** 45 3N 7 31 E
Rivoli B., *Australia* 116 **D4** 37 32 S 140 3 E
Riwaka, *N.Z.* 119 **B7** 41 5 S 172 59 E
Rixensart, *Belgium* 21 **G5** 50 43N 4 32 E
Riyadh = Ar Riyāḍ, *Si. Arabia* 84 **E5** 24 41N 46 42 E
Rizal, *Cagayan, Phil.* 70 **C3** 17 51N 121 21 E
Rizal, *Nueva Ecija, Phil.* 70 **D3** 15 43N 121 6 E
Rizal, *Zamboanga del N., Phil.* 71 **G4** 8 35N 123 26 E
Rize, *Turkey* 89 **C9** 41 0N 40 30 E
Rize □, *Turkey* 89 **C9** 41 0N 40 30 E
Rizhao, *China* 67 **G10** 35 25N 119 30 E
Rizokarpaso, *Cyprus* 32 **D13** 35 36N 34 23 E
Rizzuto, C., *Italy* 41 **D10** 38 54N 17 5 E
Rjukan, *Norway* 14 **E2** 59 54N 8 33 E
Rô, *N. Cal.* 121 **U21** 21 22 S 167 50 E
Roa, *Norway* 14 **D4** 60 17N 10 37 E
Roa, *Spain* 36 **D7** 41 41N 3 56W
Roachdale, *U.S.A.* 141 **E10** 39 51N 86 48W
Road Town, *Virgin Is.* 149 **C7** 18 27N 64 37W
Roag, L., *U.K.* 18 **C2** 58 10N 6 55W

Şa'in Dezh 257


Rovigo, *Italy* 39 C8 45 4N 11 48 E
Rovinari, *Romania* 46 E4 44 56N 23 10 E
Rovinj, *Croatia* 39 C10 45 5N 13 40 E
Rovira, *Colombia* 152 C2 4 15N 75 20W
Rovno, *Ukraine* 50 F5 50 40N 26 10 E
Rovnoye, *Russia* 51 F15 50 52N 46 3 E
Rovuma →, *Tanzania* 107 E5 10 29 S 40 28 E
Row'ān, *Iran* 85 C6 35 8N 48 51 E
Rowena, *Australia* 115 D4 29 48 S 148 55 E
Rowes, *Australia* 117 D8 37 0 S 149 6 E
Rowley Shoals, *Australia* 112 C2 17 30 S 119 0 E
Roxa, *Guinea-Biss.* 100 C1 11 15N 15 45W
Roxas = Barbacan, *Phil.* 71 F2 10 20N 119 21 E
Roxas, *Capiz, Phil.* 71 F4 11 36N 122 49 E
Roxas, *Isabela, Phil.* 70 C3 17 8N 121 36 E
Roxas, *Mindoro, Phil.* 70 E3 12 35N 121 31 E
Roxboro, *U.S.A.* 135 G6 36 24N 78 59W
Roxborough Downs, *Australia* 114 C2 22 30 S 138 45 E
Roxburgh, *N.Z.* 119 F4 45 33 S 169 19 E
Roxen, *Sweden* 15 F9 58 30N 15 40 E
Roy, *Mont., U.S.A.* 142 C9 47 17N 109 0W
Roy, *N. Mex., U.S.A.* 139 H2 35 57N 104 8W
Roy Hill, *Australia* 112 D2 22 37 S 119 58 E
Roya, Peña, *Spain* 34 E4 40 25N 0 40W
Royal Center, *U.S.A.* 141 D10 40 52N 86 30W
Royal Leamington Spa, *U.K.* 17 E6 52 18N 1 32W
Royalla, *Australia* 117 C8 35 30 S 149 9 E
Royan, *France* 24 C2 45 37N 1 2W
Roye, *France* 23 C9 49 42N 2 48 E
Røyken, *Norway* 14 E4 59 45N 10 23 E
Rožaj, *Montenegro, Yug.* 42 E5 42 50N 20 15 E
Rózan, *Poland* 47 C8 52 52N 21 25 E
Rozay-en-Brie, *France* 23 D9 48 41N 2 58 E
Rozhishche, *Ukraine* 50 F4 50 54N 25 15 E
Rožňava, *Czech.* 31 C13 48 37N 20 35 E
Rozogi, *Poland* 47 B8 53 48N 21 9 E
Rozoy-sur-Serre, *France* 23 C11 49 40N 4 8 E
Rozwadów, *Poland* 47 E9 50 37N 22 2 E
Rrësheni, *Albania* 44 C1 41 47N 19 49 E
Rrogozhino, *Albania* 44 C1 41 2N 19 50 E
Rtanj, *Serbia, Yug.* 42 D6 43 45N 21 50 E
Rtishchevo, *Russia* 51 D13 55 16N 43 50 E
Rúa, *Spain* 36 C3 42 24N 7 6W
Ruacaná, *Angola* 103 F2 17 20 S 14 12 E
Ruahine Ra., *N.Z.* 118 F5 39 55 S 176 2 E
Ruamahanga →, *N.Z.* 118 H4 41 24 S 175 8 E
Ruapehu, *N.Z.* 118 F4 39 17 S 175 35 E
Ruapuke I., *N.Z.* 119 G3 46 46 S 168 31 E
Ruâq, W. →, *Egypt* 91 F2 30 0N 33 49 E
Ruatoria, *N.Z.* 118 D7 37 55 S 178 20 E
Ruaus, Wadi →, *Libya* 96 B3 30 26N 15 24 E
Ruawai, *N.Z.* 118 C2 36 8 S 173 59 E
Rub' al Khali, *Si. Arabia* 87 C5 18 0N 48 0 E
Rubeho Mts., *Tanzania* 106 D4 6 50 S 36 25 E
Rubezhnoye, *Ukraine* 52 B8 49 6N 38 25 E
Rubh a' Mhail, *U.K.* 18 F2 55 55N 6 10W
Rubha Hunish, *U.K.* 18 D2 57 42N 6 20W
Rubiataba, *Brazil* 155 E2 15 8 S 49 48W
Rubicon →, *U.S.A.* 144 G5 38 53N 121 4W
Rubicone →, *Italy* 39 D9 44 8N 12 28 E
Rubinéia, *Brazil* 155 F1 20 13 S 51 2W
Rubino, *Ivory C.* 100 D4 6 4N 4 18W
Rubio, *Venezuela* 152 B3 7 43N 72 22W
Rubtsovsk, *Russia* 56 D9 51 30N 81 10 E
Ruby L., *U.S.A.* 142 F6 40 10N 115 28W
Ruby Mts., *U.S.A.* 142 F6 40 30N 115 30W
Rucava, *Latvia* 50 C2 56 9N 21 12 E
Rucheng, *China* 69 E9 25 33N 113 38 E
Ruciane-Nida, *Poland* 47 B8 53 40N 21 32 E
Rud, *Norway* 14 D4 60 1N 10 1 E
Rūd Sar, *Iran* 85 B6 37 8N 50 18 E
Ruda Śląska, *Poland* 47 E5 50 16N 18 50 E
Rudall, *Australia* 116 B2 33 43 S 136 17 E
Rudall →, *Australia* 112 D3 22 34 S 122 13 E
Rūdbār, *Afghan.* 79 C1 30 9N 62 36 E
Ruden, *Germany* 26 A9 54 13N 13 47 E
Rüdersdorf, *Germany* 26 C9 52 28N 13 48 E
Rudewa, *Tanzania* 107 E3 10 7 S 34 40 E
Rudkøbing, *Denmark* 15 K4 54 56N 10 41 E
Rudna, *Poland* 47 D3 51 30N 16 17 E
Rudnichnyy, *Russia* 54 B3 59 38N 52 26 E
Rudnik, *Bulgaria* 43 E12 42 36N 27 30 E
Rudnik, *Poland* 47 E9 50 26N 22 15 E
Rudnik, *Serbia, Yug.* 42 C5 44 7N 20 35 E
Rudnogorsk, *Russia* 57 D11 57 15N 103 42 E
Rudnya, *Russia* 50 D7 54 55N 31 7 E
Rudnyy, *Kazakhstan* 54 E8 52 57N 63 7 E
Rudo, *Bos.-H., Yug.* 42 D4 43 41N 19 23 E
Rudolf, Ostrov, *Russia* 56 A6 81 45N 58 30 E
Rudolstadt, *Germany* 26 E7 50 44N 11 20 E
Rudong, *China* 69 A13 32 20N 121 12 E
Rudozem, *Bulgaria* 43 F9 41 29N 24 51 E
Rudyard, *U.S.A.* 134 B3 46 14N 84 35W
Rue, *France* 23 B8 50 15N 1 40 E
Ruelle, *France* 24 C4 45 41N 0 14 E
Rufa'a, *Sudan* 95 E3 14 44N 33 22 E
Ruffec, *France* 24 B4 46 2N 0 12 E
Rufiji □, *Tanzania* 106 D4 8 0 S 38 30 E
Rufiji →, *Tanzania* 106 D4 7 50 S 39 15 E
Rufino, *Argentina* 158 C3 34 20 S 62 50W
Rufisque, *Senegal* 100 C1 14 40N 17 15W
Rufunsa, *Zambia* 107 F2 15 4 S 29 34 E
Rugao, *China* 69 A13 32 23N 120 31 E
Rugby, *U.K.* 17 E6 52 23N 1 16W
Rugby, *U.S.A.* 138 A5 48 21N 100 0W
Rügen, *Germany* 26 A9 54 22N 13 25 E
Rugles, *France* 22 D7 48 50N 0 40 E
Ruhea, *Bangla.* 78 B2 26 10N 88 25 E
Ruhengeri, *Rwanda* 106 C2 1 30 S 29 36 E
Ruhla, *Germany* 26 E6 50 53N 10 21 E
Ruhland, *Germany* 26 D9 51 27N 13 52 E
Ruhr →, *Germany* 26 D2 51 25N 6 44 E
Ruhuhu →, *Tanzania* 107 E3 10 31 S 34 34 E
Rui Barbosa, *Brazil* 155 D3 12 18 S 40 27W
Rui'an, *China* 69 D13 27 47N 120 40 E
Ruichang, *China* 69 C10 29 40N 115 39 E
Ruidosa, *U.S.A.* 139 L2 29 59N 104 39W
Ruidoso, *U.S.A.* 143 K11 33 19N 105 39W
Ruili, *China* 68 E1 24 1N 97 43 E
Ruinen, *Neths.* 20 C8 52 46N 6 21 E
Ruinerwold, *Neths.* 20 C8 52 44N 6 15 E
Ruiten A Kanaal →, *Neths.* 20 C10 52 54N 7 8 E
Ruivo, Pico, *Madeira* 33 D3 32 45N 16 56W
Ruj, *Bulgaria* 42 E7 42 52N 22 42 E
Rujen, *Macedonia, Yug.* 42 E7 42 9N 22 30 E
Rujm Tal'at al Jamā'ah, *Jordan* 91 E4 30 24N 35 30 E
Ruk, *Pakistan* 80 F3 27 50N 68 42 E
Rukwa □, *Tanzania* 106 D3 7 0 S 31 30 E
Rukwa L., *Tanzania* 106 D3 8 0 S 32 20 E
Rulhieres, C., *Australia* 112 B4 13 56 S 127 22 E
Rulles, *Belgium* 21 J7 49 43N 5 32 E
Rum Cay, *Bahamas* 149 B5 23 40N 74 58W
Rum Jungle, *Australia* 112 B5 13 0 S 130 59 E
Ruma, *Serbia, Yug.* 42 B4 45 0N 19 50 E
Rumādah, *Yemen* 86 D3 13 34N 43 52 E
Rumāḥ, *Si. Arabia* 84 E5 25 29N 47 10 E
Rumania = Romania ■, *Europe* 46 C5 46 0N 25 0 E
Rumaylah, *Iraq* 84 D5 30 47N 47 37 E
Rumaylah, 'Urūq ar, *Si. Arabia* 86 B4 21 0N 47 30 E
Rumbalara, *Australia* 114 D1 25 20 S 134 29 E
Rumbêk, *Sudan* 95 F2 6 54N 29 37 E
Rumbeke, *Belgium* 21 G2 50 56N 3 10 E
Rumburk, *Czech.* 30 A7 50 57N 14 32 E
Rumelange, *Lux.* 21 K8 49 27N 6 2 E
Rumford, *U.S.A.* 137 B14 44 30N 70 30W
Rumia, *Poland* 47 A5 54 37N 18 25 E
Rumilly, *France* 25 C9 45 53N 5 56 E
Rumoi, *Japan* 60 C10 43 56N 141 39 E
Rumonge, *Burundi* 106 C2 3 59 S 29 26 E
Rumsey, *Canada* 130 C6 51 51N 112 48W
Rumula, *Australia* 114 B4 16 35 S 145 20 E
Rumuruti, *Kenya* 106 B4 0 17N 36 32 E
Runan, *China* 66 H8 33 0N 114 30 E
Runanga, *N.Z.* 119 C6 42 25 S 171 15 E
Runaway, C., *N.Z.* 118 D6 37 32 S 177 59 E
Runcorn, *U.K.* 16 D5 53 20N 2 44W
Rungwa, *Tanzania* 106 D3 6 55 S 33 32 E
Rungwa →, *Tanzania* 106 D3 7 36 S 31 50 E
Rungwe, *Tanzania* 107 D3 9 11 S 33 32 E
Rungwe □, *Tanzania* 107 D3 9 25 S 33 32 E
Runka, *Nigeria* 101 C6 12 28N 7 20 E
Runton Ra., *Australia* 112 D3 23 31 S 123 6 E
Ruoqiang, *China* 64 C3 38 55N 88 10 E
Rupa, *India* 78 B4 27 15N 92 21 E
Rupar, *India* 80 D7 31 2N 76 38 E
Rupat, *Indonesia* 74 B2 1 45N 101 40 E
Rupea, *Romania* 46 C6 46 2N 25 13 E
Rupert →, *Canada* 128 B4 51 29N 78 45W
Rupert House = Fort Rupert, *Canada* 128 B4 51 30N 78 40W
Rupsa, *Bangla.* 78 E2 21 44N 89 30 E
Rupununi →, *Guyana* 153 C6 4 3N 58 35W
Rur →, *Germany* 26 E2 50 54N 6 24 E
Rurrenabaque, *Bolivia* 156 C4 14 30 S 67 32W
Rus →, *Spain* 35 F2 39 30N 2 30W
Rusambo, *Zimbabwe* 107 F3 16 30 S 32 4 E
Rusape, *Zimbabwe* 107 F3 18 35 S 32 8 E
Ruschuk = Ruse, *Bulgaria* 43 D10 43 48N 25 59 E
Ruse, *Bulgaria* 43 D10 43 48N 25 59 E
Ruşeţu, *Romania* 46 E8 44 57N 27 14 E
Rushan, *China* 67 F11 36 56N 121 30 E
Rushden, *U.K.* 17 E7 52 17N 0 37W
Rushford, *U.S.A.* 138 D9 43 48N 91 46W
Rushville, *Ill., U.S.A.* 140 D6 40 6N 90 35W
Rushville, *Ind., U.S.A.* 141 E11 39 38N 85 22W
Rushville, *Nebr., U.S.A.* 138 D3 42 43N 102 28W
Rushworth, *Australia* 117 D6 36 32 S 145 1 E
Russas, *Brazil* 154 B4 4 55 S 37 50W
Russell, *Canada* 131 C8 50 50N 101 20W
Russell, *N.Z.* 118 B3 35 16 S 174 10 E
Russell, *U.S.A.* 138 F5 38 56N 98 55W
Russell Is., *Solomon Is.* 121 M10 9 4 S 159 12 E
Russell L., *Man., Canada* 131 B8 56 15N 101 30W
Russell L., *N.W.T., Canada* 130 A5 63 5N 115 44W
Russellkonda, *India* 82 E7 19 57N 84 42 E
Russellville, *Ala., U.S.A.* 135 H2 34 30N 87 44W
Russellville, *Ark., U.S.A.* 139 H8 35 15N 93 8W
Russellville, *Ky., U.S.A.* 135 G2 36 50N 86 50W
Russi, *Italy* 39 D9 44 21N 12 1 E
Russian →, *U.S.A.* 144 G3 38 27N 123 8W
Russian Federation ■, *Eurasia* 57 C11 62 0N 105 0 E
Russiaville, *U.S.A.* 141 D10 40 25N 86 16W
Russkaya Polyana, *Kazakhstan* 56 D8 53 47N 73 53 E
Russkoye Ustie, *Russia* 6 B15 71 0N 149 0 E
Rust, *Austria* 31 D9 47 49N 16 42 E
Rustam, *Pakistan* 80 B5 34 25N 72 13 E
Rustam Shahr, *Pakistan* 80 F2 26 58N 66 6 E
Rustavi, *Georgia* 53 F11 41 30N 45 0 E
Rustenburg, *S. Africa* 104 D4 25 41 S 27 14 E
Ruston, *U.S.A.* 139 J8 32 30N 92 58W
Ruswil, *Switz.* 28 B6 47 5N 8 8 E
Rutana, *Burundi* 106 C2 3 55 S 30 0 E
Rute, *Spain* 37 H6 37 19N 4 23W
Ruteng, *Indonesia* 72 C2 8 35 S 120 30 E
Ruth, *Mich., U.S.A.* 136 C2 43 42N 82 45W
Ruth, *Nev., U.S.A.* 142 G6 39 15N 115 1W
Rutherford, *U.S.A.* 144 G4 38 26N 122 24W
Rutherglen, *Australia* 117 D7 36 5 S 146 29 E
Rutherglen, *U.K.* 18 F4 55 50N 4 11W
Rüti, *Switz.* 29 B7 47 16N 8 51 E
Rutigliano, *Italy* 41 A10 41 1N 17 0 E
Rutland Plains, *Australia* 114 B3 15 38 S 141 43 E
Rutledge →, *Canada* 131 A6 61 4N 112 0W
Rutledge L., *Canada* 131 A6 61 33N 110 47W
Rutshuru, *Zaïre* 106 C2 1 13 S 29 25 E
Ruurlo, *Neths.* 20 D8 52 5N 6 24 E
Ruvo di Púglia, *Italy* 41 A9 41 7N 16 27 E
Ruvu, *Tanzania* 106 D4 6 49 S 38 43 E
Ruvu →, *Tanzania* 106 D4 6 23 S 38 52 E
Ruvuma □, *Tanzania* 107 E4 10 20 S 36 0 E
Ruwais, *U.A.E.* 85 E7 24 5N 52 50 E
Ruwenzori, *Africa* 106 B2 0 30N 29 55 E
Ruyigi, *Burundi* 106 C3 3 29 S 30 15 E
Ruyuan, *China* 69 E9 24 46N 113 16 E
Ruzayevka, *Russia* 51 D14 54 4N 45 0 E
Růzhevo Konare, *Bulgaria* 43 E9 42 23N 24 46 E
Ružomberok, *Czech.* 31 B12 49 3N 19 17 E
Rwanda ■, *Africa* 106 C3 2 0 S 30 0 E
Ry, *Denmark* 15 H3 56 5N 9 45 E
Ryakhovo, *Bulgaria* 43 D11 43 58N 26 18 E
Ryan, L., *U.K.* 18 G3 55 0N 5 2W
Ryazan, *Russia* 51 D11 54 40N 39 40 E
Ryazhsk, *Russia* 51 E12 53 45N 40 3 E
Rybache, *Kazakhstan* 56 E9 46 40N 81 20 E
Rybachiy Poluostrov, *Russia* 48 A5 69 43N 32 0 E
Rybachye = Issyk-Kul, *Kirghizia* 55 B8 42 26N 76 12 E
Rybinsk, *Russia* 51 B11 58 5N 38 50 E
Rybinskoye Vdkhr., *Russia* 51 B11 58 30N 38 25 E
Rybnik, *Poland* 31 A11 50 6N 18 32 E
Rybnitsa, *Moldavia* 52 C3 47 45N 29 0 E
Rybnoye, *Russia* 51 D11 54 45N 39 30 E
Rychwał, *Poland* 47 C5 52 4N 18 10 E
Ryde, *U.K.* 17 G6 50 44N 1 9W
Ryderwood, *U.S.A.* 144 D3 46 23N 123 3W
Rydöbruk, *Sweden* 15 H7 56 58N 13 7 E
Rydultowy, *Poland* 31 A11 50 4N 18 23 E
Rydzyna, *Poland* 47 D3 51 47N 16 39 E
Rye, *U.K.* 17 G8 50 57N 0 46 E
Rye →, *U.K.* 16 C7 54 12N 0 53W
Rye Patch Res., *U.S.A.* 142 F4 40 38N 118 20W
Ryegate, *U.S.A.* 142 C9 46 21N 109 15W
Ryki, *Poland* 47 D8 51 38N 21 56 E
Rylsk, *Russia* 50 F9 51 36N 34 43 E
Rylstone, *Australia* 117 B8 32 46 S 149 58 E
Rymanów, *Poland* 31 B14 49 35N 21 51 E
Ryn, *Poland* 47 B8 53 57N 21 34 E
Ryōhaku-Sanchi, *Japan* 63 A8 36 9N 136 49 E
Ryōthu, *Japan* 60 E9 38 5N 138 26 E
Rypin, *Poland* 47 B6 53 3N 19 25 E
Ryūgasaki, *Japan* 63 B12 35 54N 140 11 E
Ryūkyū Is. = Ryūkyū-rettō, *Japan* 61 M2 26 0N 126 0 E
Ryūkyū-rettō, *Japan* 61 M2 26 0N 126 0 E
Rzepin, *Poland* 47 C1 52 20N 14 49 E
Rzeszów, *Poland* 31 A14 50 5N 21 58 E
Rzeszów □, *Poland* 31 B15 50 0N 22 0 E
Rzhev, *Russia* 50 C9 56 20N 34 20 E


## S


Sa, *Thailand* 76 C3 18 34N 100 45 E
Sa Dec, *Vietnam* 77 G5 10 20N 105 46 E
Sa-koi, *Burma* 78 F6 19 54N 97 3 E
Sa'ādatābād, *Fārs, Iran* 85 D7 30 10N 53 5 E
Sa'ādatābād, *Kermān, Iran* 85 D7 28 3N 55 53 E
Saale →, *Germany* 26 D7 51 57N 11 56 E
Saaler Bodden, *Germany* 26 A8 54 20N 12 25 E
Saalfeld, *Germany* 26 E7 50 39N 11 21 E
Saalfelden, *Austria* 30 D5 47 25N 12 51 E
Saane →, *Switz.* 28 B4 47 8N 7 10 E
Saar →, *Europe* 23 C13 49 41N 6 32 E
Saarbrücken, *Germany* 27 F2 49 15N 6 58 E
Saarburg, *Germany* 27 F2 49 36N 6 32 E
Saaremaa, *Estonia* 50 B3 58 30N 22 30 E
Saariselkä, *Finland* 12 B20 68 16N 28 15 E
Saarland □, *Germany* 27 C13 49 15N 7 0 E
Saarlouis, *Germany* 27 F2 49 19N 6 45 E
Saas Fee, *Switz.* 28 D5 46 7N 7 56 E
Sab 'Bi'ār, *Syria* 84 C3 33 46N 37 41 E
Saba, *W. Indies* 149 C7 17 42N 63 26W
Šabac, *Serbia, Yug.* 42 C4 44 48N 19 42 E
Sabadell, *Spain* 34 D7 41 28N 2 7 E
Sabae, *Japan* 63 B8 35 57N 136 11 E
Sabah □, *Malaysia* 75 A5 6 0N 117 0 E
Sabak Bernam, *Malaysia* 77 L3 3 46N 100 58 E
Sábana de la Mar, *Dom. Rep.* 149 C6 19 7N 69 24W
Sábanalarga, *Colombia* 152 A3 10 38N 74 55W
Sabang, *Indonesia* 74 A1 5 50N 95 15 E
Sabangan, *Phil.* 70 C3 17 0N 120 55 E
Sabará, *Brazil* 155 E3 19 55 S 43 46W
Sabarania, *Indonesia* 73 B5 2 5 S 138 18 E
Sabari →, *India* 82 F5 17 35N 81 16 E
Sab'atayn, Ramlat as, *Yemen* 86 D4 15 30N 46 10 E
Sabattis, *U.S.A.* 137 B10 44 6N 74 40W
Sabáudia, *Italy* 40 A6 41 17N 13 2 E
Sabaya, *Bolivia* 156 D4 19 1 S 68 23W
Sabāyā, Jaz., *Si. Arabia* 86 C3 18 35N 41 3 E
Sabhah, *Libya* 96 C2 27 9N 14 29 E
Sabhah □, *Libya* 96 C2 26 0N 14 0 E
Sabie, *S. Africa* 105 D5 25 10 S 30 48 E
Sabina, *U.S.A.* 141 E13 39 29N 83 38W
Sabinal, *Mexico* 146 A3 30 58N 107 25W
Sabinal, *U.S.A.* 139 L5 29 20N 99 27W
Sabinal, Punta del, *Spain* 35 J2 36 43N 2 44W
Sabinas, *Mexico* 146 B4 27 50N 101 10W
Sabinas →, *Mexico* 146 B4 27 37N 100 42W
Sabinas Hidalgo, *Mexico* 146 B4 26 33N 100 10W
Sabine →, *U.S.A.* 139 L8 30 0N 93 35W
Sabine L., *U.S.A.* 139 L8 29 50N 93 50W
Sabine Pass, *U.S.A.* 139 L8 29 42N 93 54W
Sabinópolis, *Brazil* 155 E3 18 40 S 43 6W
Sabinov, *Czech.* 31 B14 49 6N 21 5 E
Sabirabad, *Azerbaijan* 53 F13 40 5N 48 30 E
Sabkhat Tāwurghā', *Libya* 96 B3 31 48N 15 30 E
Sabkhet el Bardawîl, *Egypt* 91 D2 31 10N 33 15 E
Sablayan, *Phil.* 70 E3 12 50N 120 50 E
Sable, C., *Canada* 129 D6 43 29N 65 38W
Sable, C., *U.S.A.* 133 E10 25 13N 81 0W
Sable I., *Canada* 129 D8 44 0N 60 0W
Sablé-sur-Sarthe, *France* 22 E6 47 50N 0 20W
Saboeiro, *Brazil* 154 C4 6 32 S 39 54W
Sabolev, *Russia* 57 D16 54 20N 155 30 E
Sabor →, *Portugal* 36 D3 41 10N 7 7W
Sabou, *Burkina Faso* 100 C4 12 1N 2 15W
Sabrātah, *Libya* 96 B2 32 47N 12 29 E
Sabria, *Tunisia* 96 B1 33 22N 8 45 E
Sabrina Coast, *Antarctica* 7 C9 68 0 S 120 0 E
Sabtang I., *Phil.* 70 A3 20 19N 121 52 E
Sabugal, *Portugal* 36 E3 40 20N 7 5W
Sabula, *U.S.A.* 140 B6 42 5N 90 23W
Sabulubek, *Indonesia* 74 C1 1 36 S 98 40 E
Şabyā, *Si. Arabia* 86 C3 17 9N 42 37 E
Sabzevār, *Iran* 85 B8 36 15N 57 40 E
Sabzvārān, *Iran* 85 D8 28 45N 57 50 E
Sac City, *U.S.A.* 140 B2 42 26N 95 0W
Sacedón, *Spain* 34 E2 40 29N 2 41W
Sachigo →, *Canada* 128 A2 55 6N 88 58W
Sachigo, L., *Canada* 128 B1 53 50N 92 12W
Sachkhere, *Georgia* 53 E10 42 25N 43 28 E
Sachseln, *Switz.* 29 C6 46 52N 8 15 E
Sachsen □, *Germany* 26 E9 51 0N 13 0 E
Sachsen-Anhalt □, *Germany* 26 D8 52 0N 12 0 E
Sacile, *Italy* 39 C9 45 58N 12 30 E
Sackets Harbor, *U.S.A.* 137 C8 43 56N 76 7W
Saco, *Maine, U.S.A.* 135 D10 43 30N 70 27W
Saco, *Mont., U.S.A.* 142 B10 48 28N 107 19W
Sacramento, *Brazil* 155 E2 19 53 S 47 27W
Sacramento, *U.S.A.* 144 G5 38 33N 121 30W
Sacramento →, *U.S.A.* 144 G5 38 3N 121 56W
Sacramento Mts., *U.S.A.* 143 K11 32 30N 105 30W
Sacramento Valley, *U.S.A.* 144 G5 39 0N 122 0W
Sacratif, C., *Spain* 35 J1 36 42N 3 28W
Săcueni, *Romania* 46 B3 47 20N 22 5 E
Sada, *Spain* 36 B2 43 22N 8 15W
Sada-Misaki-Hantō, *Japan* 62 D4 33 22N 132 1 E
Sádaba, *Spain* 34 C3 42 19N 1 12W
Sadani, *Tanzania* 106 D4 5 58 S 38 35 E
Sadao, *Thailand* 77 J3 6 38N 100 26 E
Sadaseopet, *India* 82 F3 17 38N 77 59 E
Sadd el Aali, *Egypt* 94 C3 23 54N 32 54 E
Saddle Mt., *U.S.A.* 144 E3 45 58N 123 41W
Sade, *Nigeria* 101 C7 11 22N 10 45 E
Şadḩ, *Oman* 87 C6 17 3N 55 4 E
Sadieville, *U.S.A.* 141 F12 38 23N 84 32W
Sadimi, *Zaïre* 103 D4 9 25 S 23 32 E
Sadiya, *India* 78 B5 27 50N 95 40 E
Sado, *Japan* 60 E9 38 0N 138 25 E
Sado →, *Portugal* 37 G2 38 29N 8 55W
Sadon, *Russia* 53 E10 42 52N 43 58 E
Sæby, *Denmark* 15 G4 57 21N 10 30 E
Saegerstown, *U.S.A.* 136 E4 41 42N 80 10W
Saelices, *Spain* 34 F2 39 55N 2 49W
Safaga, *Egypt* 94 B3 26 42N 34 0 E
Şafājah, *Si. Arabia* 84 E3 26 25N 39 0 E
Šafárikovo, *Czech.* 31 C13 48 25N 20 20 E
Safata B., *W. Samoa* 121 X24 14 0 S 171 50W
Safed Koh, *Afghan.* 79 B3 34 0N 70 0 E
Säffle, *Sweden* 13 G12 59 8N 12 55 E
Safford, *U.S.A.* 143 K9 32 50N 109 43W
Saffron Walden, *U.K.* 17 E8 52 2N 0 15 E
Safi, *Morocco* 98 B3 32 18N 9 20W
Şafīābād, *Iran* 85 B8 36 45N 57 58 E
Safīd Dasht, *Iran* 85 C6 33 27N 48 11 E
Safīd Kūh, *Afghan.* 79 B1 34 45N 63 0 E
Safonovo, *Russia* 50 D8 55 4N 33 16 E
Safranbolu, *Turkey* 52 F5 41 15N 32 41 E
Safwān, *Iraq* 84 D5 30 7N 47 43 E
Sag Harbor, *U.S.A.* 137 F12 40 59N 72 17W
Sag Sag, *Papua N. G.* 120 C5 5 32 S 148 23 E
Saga, *Indonesia* 73 B4 2 40 S 132 55 E
Saga, *Kōchi, Japan* 62 D5 33 5N 133 6 E
Saga, *Saga, Japan* 62 D2 33 15N 130 16 E
Saga □, *Japan* 62 D2 33 15N 130 20 E
Sagae, *Japan* 60 E10 38 22N 140 17 E
Sagaing □, *Burma* 78 D5 23 55N 95 56 E
Sagala, *Mali* 100 C3 14 9N 6 38W
Sagami-Nada, *Japan* 63 C11 34 58N 139 30 E
Sagami-Wan, *Japan* 63 B11 35 15N 139 25 E
Sagamihara, *Japan* 63 B11 35 33N 139 25 E
Saganoseki, *Japan* 62 D3 33 15N 131 53 E
Sagar, *India* 83 G2 14 14N 75 6 E
Sagara, *Japan* 63 C10 34 41N 138 12 E
Sagara, L., *Tanzania* 106 D3 5 20 S 31 0 E
Sagawa, *Japan* 62 D5 33 28N 133 11 E
Sagay, *Phil.* 71 F4 10 57N 123 25 E
Saginaw, *U.S.A.* 134 D4 43 26N 83 55W
Saginaw B., *U.S.A.* 134 D4 43 50N 83 40W
Sagīr, Zab as →, *Iraq* 84 C4 35 10N 43 20 E
Sagleipie, *Liberia* 100 D3 7 0N 8 52W
Saglouc, *Canada* 127 B12 62 14N 75 38W
Sagŏ-ri, *S. Korea* 67 G14 35 25N 126 49 E
Sagone, *France* 25 F12 42 7N 8 42 E
Sagone, G. de, *France* 25 F12 42 4N 8 40 E
Sagres, *Portugal* 37 J2 37 0N 8 58W
Sagu, *Burma* 78 E5 20 13N 94 46 E
Sagua la Grande, *Cuba* 148 B3 22 50N 80 10W
Saguache, *U.S.A.* 143 G10 38 10N 106 10W
Saguenay →, *Canada* 129 C5 48 22N 71 0W
Sagunto, *Spain* 34 F4 39 42N 0 18W
Sahaba, *Sudan* 94 D3 18 57N 30 25 E
Sahagún, *Colombia* 152 B2 8 57N 75 27W
Sahagún, *Spain* 36 C5 42 18N 5 2W
Saḩam al Jawlān, *Syria* 91 C4 32 45N 35 55 E
Sahand, Kūh-e, *Iran* 84 B5 37 44N 46 27 E
Sahara, *Africa* 92 D4 23 0N 5 0 E
Saharan Atlas = Saharien, Atlas, *Algeria* 99 B5 33 30N 1 0 E
Saharanpur, *India* 80 E7 29 58N 77 33 E
Saharien, Atlas, *Algeria* 99 B5 33 30N 1 0 E
Sahasinaka, *Madag.* 105 C8 21 49 S 47 49 E
Sahaswan, *India* 81 E8 28 5N 78 45 E
Sahel, Canal du, *Mali* 100 C3 14 20N 6 0W
Sahibganj, *India* 81 G12 25 12N 87 40 E
Sahiwal, *Pakistan* 79 C4 30 45N 73 8 E
Şahneh, *Iran* 84 C5 34 29N 47 41 E
Sahtaneh →, *Canada* 130 B4 59 2N 122 28W
Sahuaripa, *Mexico* 146 B3 29 0N 109 13W
Sahuarita, *U.S.A.* 143 L8 31 58N 110 59W
Sahuayo, *Mexico* 146 C4 20 4N 102 43W
Sahy, *Czech.* 31 C11 48 4N 18 55 E
Sai Buri, *Thailand* 77 J3 6 43N 101 45 E
Sai-Cinza, *Brazil* 157 B6 6 17 S 57 42W
Saibai I., *Australia* 120 E2 9 25 S 142 40 E
Sa'id Bundas, *Sudan* 97 G4 8 24N 24 48 E
Saïda, *Algeria* 99 B5 34 50N 0 11 E
Saīdābād, *Kermān, Iran* 85 D7 29 30N 55 45 E
Sa'īdābād, *Semnān, Iran* 85 B7 36 8N 54 11 E
Saïdia, *Morocco* 99 A4 35 5N 2 14W
Sa'īdiyeh, *Iran* 85 B6 36 20N 48 55 E
Saidor, *Papua N. G.* 120 C4 5 40 S 146 29 E
Saidpur, *Bangla.* 78 C2 25 48N 89 0 E
Saidu, *Pakistan* 79 B4 34 43N 72 24 E
Saignelégier, *Switz.* 28 B3 47 15N 7 0 E
Saignes, *France* 24 C6 45 20N 2 31 E
Saigō, *Japan* 62 A5 36 12N 133 20 E
Saigon = Phanh Bho Ho Chi Minh, *Vietnam* 77 G6 10 58N 106 40 E
Saijō, *Ehime, Japan* 62 D5 33 55N 133 11 E
Saijō, *Hiroshima, Japan* 62 C4 34 25N 132 45 E
Saiki, *Japan* 62 E3 32 58N 131 51 E
Saillans, *France* 25 D9 44 42N 5 12 E
Sailolof, *Indonesia* 73 B4 1 7 S 130 46 E
Saimbeyli, *Turkey* 88 E7 37 59N 36 6 E
Şa'in Dezh, *Iran* 84 B5 36 40N 46 25 E

San Daniele del Friuli 259


Ste.-Foy-la-Grande, *France* 24 **D4** 44 50N 0 13 E
Ste. Genevieve, *U.S.A.* 140 **G6** 37 59N 90 2W
Ste.-Hermine, *France* 24 **B2** 46 32N 1 4W
Ste.-Livrade-sur-Lot, *France* 24 **D4** 44 24N 0 36 E
Ste-Marguerite →, *Canada* 129 **B6** 50 9N 66 36W
Ste.-Marie, *Martinique* 149 **D7** 14 48N 61 1W
Ste.-Marie-aux-Mines, *France* 23 **D14** 48 15N 7 12 E
Ste-Marie de la Madeleine, *Canada* 129 **C5** 46 26N 71 0W
Ste.-Maure-de-Touraine, *France* 22 **E7** 47 7N 0 37 E
Ste.-Maxime, *France* 25 **E10** 43 19N 6 39 E
Ste.-Menehould, *France* 23 **C11** 49 5N 4 54 E
Ste.-Mère-Église, *France* 22 **C5** 49 24N 1 19W
Ste.-Rose, *Guadeloupe* 149 **C7** 16 20N 61 45W
Ste. Rose du Lac, *Canada* 131 **C9** 51 4N 99 30W
Saintes, *France* 24 **C3** 45 45N 0 37W
Saintes, I. des, *Guadeloupe* 149 **C7** 15 50N 61 35W
Stes.-Maries-de-la-Mer, *France* 25 **E8** 43 26N 4 26 E
Saintonge, *France* 24 **C3** 45 40N 0 50W
Saipan, *Pac. Oc.* 122 **F6** 15 12N 145 45 E
Sairecábur, Cerro, *Bolivia* 158 **A2** 22 43 S 67 54W
Saitama □, *Japan* 63 **A11** 36 25N 139 30 E
Saito, *Japan* 62 **E3** 32 3N 131 24 E
Sajama, *Bolivia* 156 **D4** 18 7 S 69 0W
Sajan, *Serbia, Yug.* 42 **B5** 45 50N 20 20 E
Sajószentpéter, *Hungary* 31 **C13** 48 12N 20 44 E
Sajum, *India* 81 **C8** 33 20N 79 0 E
Sak →, *S. Africa* 104 **E3** 30 52 S 20 25 E
Sakai, *Japan* 63 **C7** 34 30N 135 30 E
Sakaide, *Japan* 62 **C5** 34 15N 133 50 E
Sakaiminato, *Japan* 62 **B5** 35 38N 133 11 E
Sakākah, *Si. Arabia* 84 **D4** 30 0N 40 8 E
Sakakawea, L., *U.S.A.* 138 **B3** 47 30N 102 0W
Sakami, L., *Canada* 128 **B4** 53 15N 77 0W
Sâkâne, 'Erg i-n, *Mali* 98 **D4** 20 30N 1 30W
Sakania, *Zaïre* 107 **E2** 12 43 S 28 30 E
Sakarya = Adapazarı, *Turkey* 88 **C4** 40 48N 30 25 E
Sakarya □, *Turkey* 88 **C4** 40 45N 30 25 E
Sakarya →, *Turkey* 52 **F4** 41 7N 30 39 E
Sakashima-Guntō, *Japan* 61 **M2** 24 46N 124 0 E
Sakata, *Japan* 60 **E9** 38 55N 139 50 E
Sakchu, *N. Korea* 67 **D13** 40 23N 125 2 E
Sakeny →, *Madag.* 105 **C8** 20 0 S 45 25 E
Sakété, *Benin* 101 **D5** 6 40N 2 45 E
Sakhalin, *Russia* 57 **D15** 51 0N 143 0 E
Sakhalinskiy Zaliv, *Russia* 57 **D15** 54 0N 141 0 E
Sakhi Gopal, *India* 82 **E7** 19 58N 85 50 E
Saki, *Ukraine* 52 **D5** 45 9N 33 34 E
Sakiai, *Lithuania* 50 **D3** 54 59N 23 0 E
Sakmara, *Russia* 54 **E4** 52 0N 55 20 E
Sakmara →, *Russia* 54 **F4** 51 46N 55 1 E
Sakon Nakhon, *Thailand* 76 **D5** 17 10N 104 9 E
Sakrand, *Pakistan* 80 **F3** 26 10N 68 15 E
Sakri, *India* 82 **D2** 21 2N 74 20 E
Sakrivier, *S. Africa* 104 **E3** 30 54 S 20 28 E
Sakskøbing, *Denmark* 15 **K5** 54 49N 11 39 E
Saku, *Japan* 63 **A10** 36 17N 138 31 E
Sakuma, *Japan* 63 **B9** 35 3N 137 49 E
Sakura, *Japan* 63 **B12** 35 43N 140 14 E
Sakurai, *Japan* 63 **C7** 34 30N 135 51 E
Sal →, *Russia* 53 **C9** 47 31N 40 45 E
Šal'a, *Czech.* 31 **C10** 48 10N 17 50 E
Sala, *Sweden* 13 **G14** 59 58N 16 35 E
Sala Consilina, *Italy* 41 **B8** 40 23N 15 35 E
Sala-y-Gómez, *Pac. Oc.* 123 **K17** 26 28 S 105 28W
Salaberry-de-Valleyfield, *Canada* 128 **C5** 45 15N 74 8W
Saladas, *Argentina* 158 **B4** 28 15 S 58 40W
Saladillo, *Argentina* 158 **D4** 35 40 S 59 55W
Salado →, *Buenos Aires, Argentina* 158 **D4** 35 44 S 57 22W
Salado →, *La Pampa, Argentina* 160 **A3** 37 30 S 67 0W
Salado →, *Río Negro, Argentina* 160 **B3** 41 34 S 65 3W
Salado →, *Santa Fe, Argentina* 158 **C3** 31 40 S 60 41W
Salado →, *Mexico* 146 **B5** 26 52N 99 19W
Salaga, *Ghana* 101 **D4** 8 31N 0 31W
Salāh, *Syria* 91 **C5** 32 40N 36 45 E
Sălaj □, *Romania* 46 **B4** 47 15N 23 0 E
Sálakhos, *Greece* 32 **C9** 36 17N 27 57 E
Salala, *Liberia* 100 **D2** 6 42N 10 7W
Salala, *Sudan* 94 **C4** 21 17N 36 16 E
Salālah, *Oman* 87 **C6** 16 56N 53 59 E
Salamanca, *Chile* 158 **C1** 31 46 S 70 59W
Salamanca, *Spain* 36 **E5** 40 58N 5 39W
Salamanca, *U.S.A.* 136 **D6** 42 10N 78 42W
Salamanca □, *Spain* 36 **E5** 40 57N 5 40W
Salāmatābād, *Iran* 84 **C5** 35 39N 47 50 E
Salamina, *Colombia* 152 **B2** 5 25N 75 29W
Salamis, *Cyprus* 32 **D12** 35 11N 33 54 E
Salamis, *Greece* 45 **G5** 37 56N 23 30 E
Salamonie, Res., *U.S.A.* 141 **D11** 40 45N 85 35W
Salar de Atacama, *Chile* 158 **A2** 23 30 S 68 25W
Salar de Uyuni, *Bolivia* 156 **E4** 20 30 S 67 45W
Sălard, *Romania* 46 **B3** 47 12N 22 3 E
Salas, *Spain* 36 **B4** 43 25N 6 15W
Salas de los Infantes, *Spain* 34 **C1** 42 2N 3 17W
Salatiga, *Indonesia* 75 **D4** 7 19 S 110 30 E
Salavat, *Russia* 54 **E4** 53 21N 55 55 E
Salaverry, *Peru* 156 **B2** 8 15 S 79 0W
Salawati, *Indonesia* 73 **B4** 1 7 S 130 52 E
Salay, *Phil.* 71 **G5** 8 52N 124 47 E
Salayar, *Indonesia* 72 **C2** 6 7 S 120 30 E
Salazar →, *Spain* 34 **C3** 42 40N 1 20W
Salbris, *France* 23 **E9** 47 25N 2 3 E
Salcia, *Romania* 46 **F5** 43 56N 24 55 E
Salcombe, *U.K.* 17 **G4** 50 14N 3 47W
Salda Gölü, *Turkey* 88 **E3** 37 22N 29 41 E
Saldaña, *Spain* 36 **C6** 42 32N 4 48W
Saldanha, *S. Africa* 104 **E2** 33 0 S 17 58 E
Saldanha B., *S. Africa* 104 **E2** 33 6 S 18 0 E
Saldus, *Latvia* 50 **C3** 56 38N 22 30 E
Sale, *Australia* 117 **E7** 38 6 S 147 6 E
Salé, *Morocco* 98 **B3** 34 3N 6 48W
Sale, *U.K.* 16 **D5** 53 26N 2 19W
Salekhard, *Russia* 48 **A12** 66 30N 66 35 E
Salem, *India* 83 **J4** 11 40N 78 11 E
Salem, *Ill., U.S.A.* 140 **F8** 38 38N 88 57W
Salem, *Ind., U.S.A.* 141 **F10** 38 38N 86 6W
Salem, *Mass., U.S.A.* 137 **D14** 42 29N 70 53W
Salem, *Mo., U.S.A.* 139 **G9** 37 40N 91 30W
Salem, *N.J., U.S.A.* 134 **F8** 39 34N 75 29W
Salem, *Ohio, U.S.A.* 136 **F4** 40 52N 80 50W
Salem, *Oreg., U.S.A.* 142 **D2** 45 0N 123 0W
Salem, *S. Dak., U.S.A.* 138 **D6** 43 44N 97 23W
Salem, *Va., U.S.A.* 134 **G5** 37 19N 80 8W
Salemi, *Italy* 40 **E5** 37 49N 12 47 E
Salernes, *France* 25 **E10** 43 34N 6 15 E
Salerno, *Italy* 41 **B7** 40 40N 14 44 E
Salerno, G. di, *Italy* 41 **B7** 40 35N 14 45 E
Salford, *U.K.* 16 **D5** 53 30N 2 17W
Salgir →, *Ukraine* 52 **D6** 45 38N 35 1 E
Salgótarján, *Hungary* 31 **C12** 48 5N 19 47 E
Salgueiro, *Brazil* 154 **C4** 8 4 S 39 6W
Salida, *U.S.A.* 132 **C5** 38 35N 106 0W
Salies-de-Béarn, *France* 24 **E3** 43 28N 0 56W
Şalif, *Yemen* 86 **D3** 15 18N 42 41 E
Salihli, *Turkey* 88 **D3** 38 28N 28 8 E
Salin, *Burma* 78 **E5** 20 35N 94 40 E
Salina, *Italy* 41 **D7** 38 35N 14 50 E
Salina, *U.S.A.* 138 **F6** 38 50N 97 40W
Salina Cruz, *Mexico* 147 **D5** 16 10N 95 10W
Salinas, *Brazil* 155 **E3** 16 10 S 42 10W
Salinas, *Chile* 158 **A2** 23 31 S 69 29W
Salinas, *Ecuador* 152 **D1** 2 10 S 80 58W
Salinas, *U.S.A.* 144 **J5** 36 40N 121 41W
Salinas →, *Guatemala* 147 **D6** 16 28N 90 31W
Salinas →, *U.S.A.* 144 **J5** 36 45N 121 48W
Salinas, B. de, *Nic.* 148 **D2** 11 4N 85 45W
Salinas, C. de, *Spain* 33 **B10** 39 16N 3 4 E
Salinas, Pampa de las, *Argentina* 158 **C2** 31 58 S 66 42W
Salinas Ambargasta, *Argentina* 158 **B3** 29 0 S 65 0W
Salinas de Hidalgo, *Mexico* 146 **C4** 22 30N 101 40W
Salinas Grandes, *Argentina* 158 **B2** 30 0 S 65 0W
Saline →, *Ark., U.S.A.* 139 **J8** 33 10N 92 8W
Saline →, *Kans., U.S.A.* 138 **F6** 38 51N 97 30W
Salines, *Spain* 33 **B10** 39 21N 3 3 E
Salinópolis, *Brazil* 154 **B2** 0 40 S 47 20W
Salins-les-Bains, *France* 23 **F12** 46 58N 5 52 E
Salir, *Portugal* 37 **H2** 37 14N 8 2W
Salisbury = Harare, *Zimbabwe* 107 **F3** 17 43 S 31 2 E
Salisbury, *Australia* 116 **C3** 34 46 S 138 40 E
Salisbury, *U.K.* 17 **F6** 51 4N 1 48W
Salisbury, *Md., U.S.A.* 134 **F8** 38 20N 75 38W
Salisbury, *Mo., U.S.A.* 140 **E4** 39 25N 92 48W
Salisbury, *N.C., U.S.A.* 135 **H5** 35 20N 80 29W
Salisbury Plain, *U.K.* 17 **F6** 51 13N 1 50W
Săliște, *Romania* 46 **D4** 45 45N 23 56 E
Salitre →, *Brazil* 154 **C3** 9 29 S 40 39W
Salka, *Nigeria* 101 **C5** 10 20N 4 58 E
Salkhad, *Jordan* 91 **C5** 32 30N 36 43 E
Sallent, *Spain* 34 **D6** 41 49N 1 54 E
Salles-Curan, *France* 24 **D6** 44 11N 2 48 E
Salling, *Denmark* 15 **H2** 56 40N 8 55 E
Sallisaw, *U.S.A.* 139 **H7** 35 26N 94 45W
Sallom Junction, *Sudan* 94 **D4** 19 17N 37 6 E
Salmās, *Iran* 84 **B5** 38 11N 44 47 E
Salmerón, *Spain* 34 **E2** 40 33N 2 29W
Salmo, *Canada* 130 **D5** 49 10N 117 20W
Salmon, *U.S.A.* 142 **D7** 45 12N 113 56W
Salmon →, *Canada* 130 **C4** 54 3N 122 40W
Salmon →, *U.S.A.* 142 **D5** 45 51N 116 46W
Salmon Arm, *Canada* 130 **C5** 50 40N 119 15W
Salmon Falls, *U.S.A.* 142 **E6** 42 48N 114 59W
Salmon Gums, *Australia* 113 **F3** 32 59 S 121 38 E
Salmon Res., *Canada* 129 **C8** 48 5N 56 0W
Salmon River Mts., *U.S.A.* 142 **D6** 45 0N 114 30W
Salo, *Finland* 13 **F17** 60 22N 23 10 E
Salò, *Italy* 38 **C7** 45 37N 10 32 E
Salobreña, *Spain* 37 **J7** 36 44N 3 35W
Salome, *U.S.A.* 145 **M13** 33 51N 113 37W
Salon-de-Provence, *France* 25 **E9** 43 39N 5 6 E
Salonica = Thessaloníki, *Greece* 44 **D4** 40 38N 22 58 E
Salonta, *Romania* 46 **C2** 46 49N 21 42 E
Salor →, *Spain* 37 **F3** 39 39N 7 3W
Salou, C., *Spain* 34 **D6** 41 3N 1 10 E
Salsacate, *Argentina* 158 **C2** 31 20 S 65 5W
Salses, *France* 24 **F6** 42 50N 2 55 E
Salsette I., *India* 82 **E1** 19 5N 72 50 E
Salsk, *Russia* 53 **C9** 46 28N 41 30 E
Salso →, *Italy* 40 **E6** 37 6N 13 55 E
Salsomaggiore, *Italy* 38 **D6** 44 48N 9 59 E
Salt →, *Canada* 130 **B6** 60 0N 112 25W
Salt →, *Ariz., U.S.A.* 143 **K7** 33 23N 112 18W
Salt →, *Mo., U.S.A.* 140 **E5** 39 29N 91 5W
Salt Creek, *Australia* 116 **D3** 36 8 S 139 38 E
Salt Fork →, *U.S.A.* 139 **G6** 36 37N 97 7W
Salt Lake City, *U.S.A.* 142 **F8** 40 45N 111 58W
Salt Range, *Pakistan* 80 **C5** 32 30N 72 25 E
Salta, *Argentina* 158 **A2** 24 57 S 65 25W
Salta □, *Argentina* 158 **A2** 24 48 S 65 30W
Saltcoats, *U.K.* 18 **F4** 55 38N 4 47W
Saltee Is., *Ireland* 19 **D5** 52 7N 6 37W
Saltfjorden, *Norway* 12 **C13** 67 15N 14 10 E
Saltholm, *Denmark* 15 **J6** 55 38N 12 43 E
Salthólmavík, *Iceland* 12 **D3** 65 24N 21 57W
Saltillo, *Mexico* 146 **B4** 25 30N 100 57W
Salto, *Argentina* 158 **C3** 34 20 S 60 15W
Salto, *Uruguay* 158 **C4** 31 27 S 57 50W
Salto da Divisa, *Brazil* 155 **E4** 16 0 S 39 57W
Salton City, *U.S.A.* 145 **M11** 33 29N 115 51W
Salton Sea, *U.S.A.* 145 **M11** 33 15N 115 50W
Saltpond, *Ghana* 101 **D4** 5 15N 1 3W
Saltsjöbaden, *Sweden* 14 **E12** 59 15N 18 20 E
Saltville, *U.S.A.* 134 **G5** 36 53N 81 46W
Saluda →, *U.S.A.* 135 **H5** 34 0N 81 4W
Salûm, *Egypt* 94 **A2** 31 31N 25 7 E
Salûm, Khâlig el, *Egypt* 94 **A2** 31 30N 25 9 E
Salur, *India* 82 **E6** 18 27N 83 18 E
Salut, Is. du, *Fr. Guiana* 153 **B7** 5 15N 52 35W
Saluzzo, *Italy* 38 **D4** 44 39N 7 29 E
Salvacion, *Phil.* 71 **G2** 9 56N 118 47 E
Salvación, B., *Chile* 160 **D1** 50 50 S 75 10W
Salvador, *Brazil* 155 **D4** 13 0 S 38 30W
Salvador, *Canada* 131 **C7** 52 10N 109 32W
Salvador, L., *U.S.A.* 139 **L9** 29 46N 90 16W
Salvaterra, *Brazil* 154 **B2** 0 46 S 48 31W
Salvaterra de Magos, *Portugal* 37 **F2** 39 1N 8 47W
Salvisa, *U.S.A.* 141 **G12** 37 54N 84 51W
Sálvora, I., *Spain* 36 **C2** 42 30N 8 58W
Salween →, *Burma* 78 **G6** 16 31N 97 37 E
Salyany, *Azerbaijan* 89 **D13** 39 10N 48 50 E
Salyersville, *U.S.A.* 134 **G4** 37 45N 83 4W
Salza →, *Austria* 30 **D7** 47 40N 14 43 E
Salzach →, *Austria* 30 **C5** 48 12N 12 56 E
Salzburg, *Austria* 30 **D6** 47 48N 13 2 E
Salzburg □, *Austria* 30 **D6** 47 15N 13 0 E
Salzgitter, *Germany* 26 **C6** 52 13N 10 22 E
Salzwedel, *Germany* 26 **C7** 52 50N 11 11 E
Sam, *Gabon* 102 **B2** 0 58N 11 16 E
Sam Neua, *Laos* 76 **B5** 20 29N 104 5 E
Sam Ngao, *Thailand* 76 **D2** 17 18N 99 0 E
Sam Rayburn Res., *U.S.A.* 139 **K7** 31 15N 94 20W
Sam Son, *Vietnam* 76 **C5** 19 44N 105 54 E
Sam Teu, *Laos* 76 **C5** 19 59N 104 38 E
Sama, *Russia* 54 **A7** 60 12N 60 22 E
Sama de Langreo, *Spain* 36 **B5** 43 18N 5 40W
Samacimbo, *Angola* 103 **E3** 13 33 S 16 59 E
Samagaltai, *Russia* 57 **D10** 50 36N 95 3 E
Samā'il, *Oman* 87 **B7** 23 40N 57 50 E
Samaipata, *Bolivia* 157 **D5** 18 9 S 63 52W
Samal, *Phil.* 71 **H5** 7 5N 125 42 E
Samal I., *Phil.* 71 **H5** 7 3N 125 44 E
Samales Group, *Phil.* 71 **J3** 6 0N 122 0 E
Samalkot, *India* 82 **F6** 17 3N 82 13 E
Samâlût, *Egypt* 94 **J7** 28 20N 30 42 E
Samana, *India* 80 **D7** 30 10N 76 13 E
Samana Cay, *Bahamas* 149 **B5** 23 3N 73 45W
Samandağı, *Turkey* 88 **E6** 36 5N 35 59 E
Samanga, *Tanzania* 107 **D4** 8 20 S 39 13 E
Samangān □, *Afghan.* 79 **A3** 36 15N 68 3 E
Samangwa, *Zaïre* 103 **C4** 4 23 S 24 10 E
Samani, *Japan* 60 **C11** 42 7N 142 56 E
Samar, *Phil.* 71 **E5** 12 0N 125 0 E
Samar □, *Phil.* 71 **F5** 11 50N 125 0 E
Samar Sea, *Phil.* 70 **E5** 12 0N 124 15 E
Samara, *Russia* 51 **E17** 53 8N 50 6 E
Samara →, *Russia* 54 **E2** 53 10N 50 4 E
Samarai, *Papua N. G.* 120 **F6** 10 39 S 150 41 E
Samaria = Shōmrōn, *Jordan* 91 **C4** 32 15N 35 13 E
Samariá, *Greece* 32 **D5** 35 17N 23 58 E
Samarinda, *Indonesia* 75 **C5** 0 30 S 117 9 E
Samarkand, *Uzbekistan* 55 **D3** 39 40N 66 55 E
Sāmarrā, *Iraq* 84 **C4** 34 12N 43 52 E
Samastipur, *India* 81 **G11** 25 50N 85 50 E
Samatan, *France* 24 **E4** 43 29N 0 55 E
Samaúma, *Brazil* 157 **B5** 7 50 S 60 2W
Samba, *India* 81 **C6** 32 32N 75 10 E
Samba, *Zaïre* 103 **C5** 4 38 S 26 22 E
Samba Caju, *Angola* 103 **D3** 8 46 S 15 24 E
Sambaíba, *Brazil* 154 **C2** 7 8 S 45 21W
Sambalpur, *India* 82 **D7** 21 28N 84 4 E
Sambar, Tanjung, *Indonesia* 75 **C4** 2 59 S 110 19 E
Sambas, *Indonesia* 75 **B3** 1 20N 109 20 E
Sambava, *Madag.* 105 **A9** 14 16 S 50 10 E
Sambawizi, *Zimbabwe* 107 **F2** 18 24 S 26 13 E
Sambhal, *India* 81 **E8** 28 35N 78 37 E
Sambhar, *India* 80 **F6** 26 52N 75 6 E
Sambiase, *Italy* 41 **D9** 38 58N 16 16 E
Sambonifacio, *Italy* 38 **C8** 45 24N 11 16 E
Sambor, *Cambodia* 76 **F6** 12 46N 106 0 E
Sambor, *Ukraine* 50 **G3** 49 30N 23 10 E
Sambre →, *Europe* 21 **H5** 50 27N 4 52 E
Sambuca di Sicilia, *Italy* 40 **E6** 37 39N 13 6 E
Samburu □, *Kenya* 106 **B4** 1 10N 37 0 E
Samchŏk, *S. Korea* 67 **F15** 37 30N 129 10 E
Samchonpo, *S. Korea* 67 **G15** 35 0N 128 6 E
Same, *Tanzania* 106 **C4** 4 2 S 37 38 E
Samedan, *Switz.* 29 **C9** 46 32N 9 52 E
Samer, *France* 23 **B8** 50 38N 1 44 E
Samfya, *Zambia* 107 **E2** 11 22 S 29 31 E
Samhān, Jabal, *Oman* 87 **C6** 17 12N 54 55 E
Sámi, *Greece* 45 **F2** 38 15N 20 39 E
Samnah, *Si. Arabia* 84 **E3** 25 10N 37 15 E
Samnaun, *Switz.* 29 **C10** 46 57N 10 22 E
Samnū, *Libya* 96 **C2** 27 15N 14 55 E
Samo Alto, *Chile* 158 **C1** 30 22 S 71 0W
Samoan Is., *Pac. Oc.* 121 **X24** 14 0 S 171 0W
Samobor, *Croatia* 39 **C12** 45 47N 15 44 E
Samoëns, *France* 25 **B10** 46 5N 6 45 E
Samokov, *Bulgaria* 43 **E8** 42 18N 23 35 E
Samoorombón, B., *Argentina* 158 **D4** 36 5 S 57 20W
Samorogouan, *Burkina Faso* 100 **C4** 11 21N 4 57W
Sámos, *Greece* 45 **G8** 37 45N 26 50 E
Samoš, *Serbia, Yug.* 42 **B5** 45 13N 20 49 E
Samos, *Spain* 36 **C3** 42 44N 7 20W
Samosir, *Indonesia* 74 **B1** 2 55N 98 50 E
Samothráki, *Évros, Greece* 44 **D7** 40 28N 25 28 E
Samothráki, *Ionioi Nisoi, Greece* 44 **E1** 39 48N 19 31 E
Samothráki, *Kérkira, Greece* 32 **A3** 39 48N 19 31 E
Samoylovka, *Russia* 51 **F13** 51 12N 43 43 E
Sampa, *Ghana* 100 **D4** 8 0N 2 36W
Sampacho, *Argentina* 158 **C3** 33 20 S 64 50W
Sampang, *Indonesia* 75 **D4** 7 11 S 113 13 E
Samper de Calanda, *Spain* 34 **D4** 41 11N 0 28W
Sampit, *Indonesia* 75 **C4** 2 34 S 113 0 E
Sampit →, *Indonesia* 75 **C4** 2 44 S 112 54 E
Sampit, Teluk, *Indonesia* 75 **C4** 3 5 S 113 3 E
Samrée, *Belgium* 21 **H7** 50 13N 5 39 E
Samrong, *Cambodia* 76 **E4** 14 15N 103 30 E
Samrong, *Thailand* 76 **E3** 15 10N 100 40 E
Samsø, *Denmark* 15 **J4** 55 50N 10 35 E
Samsø Bælt, *Denmark* 15 **J4** 55 45N 10 45 E
Samsonovo, *Turkmenistan* 55 **E2** 37 53N 65 15 E
Samsun, *Turkey* 88 **C7** 41 15N 36 22 E
Samsun Dağı, *Turkey* 45 **G9** 37 45N 27 10 E
Samtredia, *Georgia* 53 **E10** 42 7N 42 24 E
Samui, Ko, *Thailand* 77 **H3** 9 30N 100 0 E
Samun □, *Turkey* 88 **C7** 41 10N 36 10 E
Samur →, *Azerbaijan* 53 **F13** 41 53N 48 32 E
Samusole, *Zaïre* 103 **E4** 10 2 S 24 0 E
Samut Prakan, *Thailand* 76 **F3** 13 32N 100 40 E
Samut Sakhon, *Thailand* 76 **F3** 13 31N 100 13 E
Samut Songkhram →, *Thailand* 76 **F3** 13 24N 100 1 E
Samwari, *Pakistan* 80 **E2** 28 30N 66 46 E
San, *Mali* 100 **C4** 13 15N 4 57W
San →, *Cambodia* 76 **F5** 13 32N 105 57 E
San →, *Poland* 31 **A14** 50 45N 21 51 E
San Adrián, C. de, *Spain* 36 **B2** 43 21N 8 50W
San Agustín, *Colombia* 152 **C2** 1 53N 76 16W
San Agustin, C., *Phil.* 71 **H6** 6 20N 126 13 E
San Agustín de Valle Fértil, *Argentina* 158 **C2** 30 35 S 67 30W
San Ambrosio, *Pac. Oc.* 123 **K20** 26 28 S 79 53W
San Andreas, *U.S.A.* 144 **G6** 38 15N 120 39W
San Andres, *Phil.* 70 **E4** 13 19N 122 41 E
San Andrés, I. de, *Caribbean* 148 **D3** 12 42N 81 46W
San Andres Mts., *U.S.A.* 143 **K10** 33 0N 106 45W
San Andrés Tuxtla, *Mexico* 147 **D5** 18 30N 95 20W
San Angelo, *U.S.A.* 139 **K4** 31 30N 100 30W
San Anselmo, *U.S.A.* 144 **H4** 37 59N 122 34W
San Antonio, *Belize* 147 **D7** 16 15N 89 2W
San Antonio, *Chile* 158 **C1** 33 40 S 71 40W
San Antonio, *Phil.* 70 **D3** 14 57N 120 5 E
San Antonio, *N. Mex., U.S.A.* 143 **K10** 33 58N 106 57W
San Antonio, *Tex., U.S.A.* 139 **L5** 29 30N 98 30W
San Antonio, *Venezuela* 152 **C4** 3 30N 66 44W
San Antonio →, *U.S.A.* 139 **L6** 28 30N 96 50W
San Antonio, C., *Argentina* 158 **D4** 36 15 S 56 40W
San Antonio, C., *Cuba* 148 **B3** 21 50N 84 57W
San Antonio, C. de, *Spain* 35 **G5** 38 48N 0 12 E
San Antonio, Mt., *U.S.A.* 145 **L9** 34 17N 117 38W
San Antonio Abad, *Spain* 33 **C7** 38 59N 1 19 E
San Antonio Bay, *Phil.* 71 **G1** 8 38N 117 35 E
San Antonio de los Baños, *Cuba* 148 **B3** 22 54N 82 31W
San Antonio de los Cobres, *Argentina* 158 **A2** 24 10 S 66 17W
San Antonio Oeste, *Argentina* 160 **B4** 40 40 S 65 0W
San Arcángelo, *Italy* 41 **B9** 40 14N 16 14 E
San Ardo, *U.S.A.* 144 **J6** 36 1N 120 54W
San Augustín, *Canary Is.* 33 **G4** 27 47N 15 32W
San Augustine, *U.S.A.* 139 **K7** 31 30N 94 7W
San Bartolomé, *Canary Is.* 33 **F6** 28 59N 13 37W
San Bartolomé de Tirajana, *Canary Is.* 33 **G4** 27 54N 15 34W
San Bartolomeo in Galdo, *Italy* 41 **A8** 41 23N 15 2 E
San Benedetto, *Italy* 38 **C7** 45 2N 10 57 E
San Benedetto del Tronto, *Italy* 39 **F10** 42 57N 13 52 E
San Benedicto, I., *Mexico* 146 **D2** 19 18N 110 49W
San Benito, *U.S.A.* 139 **M6** 26 5N 97 39W
San Benito →, *U.S.A.* 144 **J5** 36 53N 121 50W
San Benito Mt., *U.S.A.* 144 **J6** 36 22N 120 37W
San Bernardino, *U.S.A.* 145 **L9** 34 7N 117 19W
San Bernardino, Paso del, *Switz.* 29 **D8** 46 28N 9 11 E
San Bernardino Mts., *U.S.A.* 145 **L10** 34 10N 116 45W
San Bernardino Str., *Phil.* 70 **E5** 13 0N 125 0 E
San Bernardo, *Chile* 158 **C1** 33 40 S 70 50W
San Bernardo, I. de, *Colombia* 152 **B2** 9 45N 75 50W
San Blas, *Mexico* 146 **B3** 26 4N 108 46W
San Blas, Arch. de, *Panama* 148 **E4** 9 50N 78 31W
San Blas, C., *U.S.A.* 135 **L3** 29 40N 85 12W
San Borja, *Bolivia* 156 **C4** 14 50 S 66 52W
San Buenaventura, *Bolivia* 156 **C4** 14 28 S 67 35W
San Buenaventura, *Mexico* 146 **B4** 27 5N 101 32W
San Carlos = Butuku-Luba, *Eq. Guin.* 101 **E6** 3 29N 8 33 E
San Carlos, *Argentina* 158 **C2** 33 50 S 69 0W
San Carlos, *Bolivia* 157 **D5** 17 24 S 63 45W
San Carlos, *Chile* 158 **D1** 36 10 S 72 0W
San Carlos, *Mexico* 146 **B4** 29 0N 100 54W
San Carlos, *Nic.* 148 **D3** 11 12N 84 50W
San Carlos, *Negros, Phil.* 71 **F4** 10 29N 123 25 E
San Carlos, *Pangasinan, Phil.* 70 **D3** 15 55N 120 20 E
San Carlos, *Spain* 33 **B8** 39 3N 1 34 E
San Carlos, *Uruguay* 159 **C5** 34 46 S 54 58W
San Carlos, *U.S.A.* 143 **K8** 33 24N 110 27W
San Carlos, *Amazonas, Venezuela* 152 **C4** 1 55N 67 4W
San Carlos, *Cojedes, Venezuela* 152 **B4** 9 40N 68 36W
San Carlos de Bariloche, *Argentina* 160 **B2** 41 10 S 71 25W
San Carlos de la Rápita, *Spain* 34 **E5** 40 37N 0 35 E
San Carlos del Zulia, *Venezuela* 152 **B3** 9 1N 71 55W
San Carlos L., *U.S.A.* 143 **K8** 33 15N 110 25W
San Cataldo, *Italy* 40 **E6** 37 30N 13 58 E
San Celoni, *Spain* 34 **D7** 41 42N 2 30 E
San Clemente, *Chile* 158 **D1** 35 30 S 71 29W
San Clemente, *Spain* 35 **F2** 39 24N 2 25W
San Clemente, *U.S.A.* 145 **M9** 33 29N 117 36W
San Clemente I., *U.S.A.* 145 **N8** 32 53N 118 30W
San Constanzo, *Italy* 39 **E10** 43 46N 13 5 E
San Cristóbal, *Argentina* 158 **C3** 30 20 S 61 10W
San Cristóbal, *Colombia* 152 **D3** 2 18 S 73 2W
San Cristóbal, *Dom. Rep.* 149 **C5** 18 25N 70 6W
San Cristóbal, *Mexico* 147 **D6** 16 50N 92 33W
San Cristóbal, *Solomon Is.* 121 **N11** 10 30 S 161 0 E
San Cristóbal, *Spain* 33 **B11** 39 57N 4 3 E
San Cristóbal, *Venezuela* 152 **B3** 7 46N 72 14W
San Damiano d'Asti, *Italy* 38 **D5** 44 51N 8 4 E
San Daniele del Friuli, *Italy* 39 **B10** 46 10N 13 0 E

São Bento do Norte 261


Sandover →, *Australia* 114 **C2** 21 43 S 136 32 E
Sandpoint, *U.S.A.* 142 **B5** 48 20N 116 34W
Sandringham, *U.K.* 16 **E8** 52 50N 0 30 E
Sandslån, *Sweden* 14 **A11** 63 2N 17 49 E
Sandspit, *Canada* 130 **C2** 53 14N 131 49W
Sandstone, *Australia* 113 **E2** 27 59 S 119 16 E
Sandu, *China* 68 **E6** 26 0N 107 52 E
Sandusky, *Mich., U.S.A.* 128 **D3** 43 26N 82 50W
Sandusky, *Ohio, U.S.A.* 136 **E2** 41 25N 82 40W
Sandusky →, *U.S.A.* 141 **C14** 41 27N 83 0W
Sandvig, *Sweden* 15 **J8** 55 18N 14 47 E
Sandviken, *Sweden* 13 **F14** 60 38N 16 46 E
Sandwich, *U.S.A.* 141 **C8** 41 39N 88 37W
Sandwich, C., *Australia* 114 **B4** 18 14 S 146 18 E
Sandwich B., *Canada* 129 **B8** 53 40N 57 15W
Sandwich B., *Namibia* 104 **C1** 23 25 S 14 20 E
Sandy, *Nev., U.S.A.* 145 **K11** 35 49N 115 36W
Sandy, *Oreg., U.S.A.* 144 **E4** 45 24N 122 16W
Sandy Bight, *Australia* 113 **F3** 33 50 S 123 20 E
Sandy C., *Queens., Australia* 114 **C5** 24 42 S 153 15 E
Sandy C., *Tas., Australia* 114 **G3** 41 25 S 144 45 E
Sandy Cay, *Bahamas* 149 **B4** 23 13N 75 18W
Sandy Cr. →, *U.S.A.* 142 **F9** 41 15N 109 47W
Sandy L., *Canada* 128 **B1** 53 2N 93 0W
Sandy Lake, *Canada* 128 **B1** 53 0N 93 15W
Sandy Narrows, *Canada* 131 **B8** 55 5N 103 4W
Sanford, *Fla., U.S.A.* 135 **L5** 28 45N 81 20W
Sanford, *Maine, U.S.A.* 137 **C14** 43 28N 70 47W
Sanford, *N.C., U.S.A.* 135 **H6** 35 30N 79 10W
Sanford →, *Australia* 113 **E2** 27 22 S 115 53 E
Sanford Mt., *U.S.A.* 126 **B5** 62 30N 143 0W
Sang-i-Masha, *Afghan.* 80 **C2** 33 8N 67 27 E
Sanga, *Mozam.* 107 **E4** 12 22 S 35 21 E
Sanga →, *Congo* 102 **C3** 1 5 S 17 0 E
Sanga-Tolon, *Russia* 57 **C15** 61 50N 149 40 E
Sangamner, *India* 82 **E2** 19 37N 74 15 E
Sangamon →, *U.S.A.* 140 **D6** 40 2N 90 21W
Sangar, *Afghan.* 80 **C1** 32 56N 65 30 E
Sangar, *Russia* 57 **C13** 64 2N 127 31 E
Sangar Sarai, *Afghan.* 80 **B4** 34 27N 70 35 E
Sangasangadalam, *Indonesia* 75 **C5** 0 36 S 117 13 E
Sangay, *Ecuador* 152 **D2** 2 0 S 78 20W
Sange, *Zaïre* 106 **D2** 6 58 S 28 21 E
Sangeang, *Indonesia* 72 **C1** 8 12 S 119 6 E
Sanger, *U.S.A.* 144 **J7** 36 41N 119 35W
Sangerhausen, *Germany* 26 **D7** 51 28N 11 18 E
Sanggan He →, *China* 66 **E9** 38 12N 117 15 E
Sanggau, *Indonesia* 75 **B4** 0 5N 110 30 E
Sangihe, Kepulauan, *Indonesia* 72 **A3** 3 0N 126 0 E
Sangihe, P., *Indonesia* 72 **A3** 3 45N 125 30 E
Sangju, *S. Korea* 67 **F15** 36 25N 128 10 E
Sangkapura, *Indonesia* 75 **D4** 5 52 S 112 40 E
Sangkhla, *Thailand* 76 **E2** 14 57N 98 28 E
Sangli, *India* 82 **F2** 16 55N 74 33 E
Sangmélina, *Cameroon* 101 **E7** 2 57N 12 1 E
Sangonera →, *Spain* 35 **H3** 37 59N 1 4W
Sangpang Bum, *Burma* 78 **B5** 26 30N 95 50 E
Sangre de Cristo Mts., *U.S.A.* 139 **G2** 37 0N 105 0W
Sangro →, *Italy* 39 **F11** 42 14N 14 32 E
Sangudo, *Canada* 130 **C6** 53 50N 114 54W
Sangue →, *Brazil* 157 **C6** 11 1 S 58 39W
Sangüesa, *Spain* 34 **C3** 42 37N 1 17W
Sanguinaires, Is., *France* 25 **G12** 41 51N 8 36 E
Sangzhi, *China* 69 **C8** 29 25N 110 12 E
Sanhala, *Ivory C.* 100 **C3** 10 3N 6 51W
Sāniyah, *Iraq* 84 **C4** 33 49N 42 43 E
Sanje, *Uganda* 106 **C3** 0 49 S 31 30 E
Sanjiang, *China* 68 **E7** 25 48N 109 37 E
Sanjo, *Japan* 60 **F9** 37 37N 138 57 E
Sankarankovil, *India* 83 **K3** 9 10N 77 35 E
Sankeshwar, *India* 83 **F2** 16 23N 74 32 E
Sankosh →, *India* 78 **B2** 26 24N 89 47 E
Sankt Andrä, *Austria* 30 **E7** 46 46N 14 50 E
Sankt Antönien, *Switz.* 29 **C9** 46 58N 9 48 E
Sankt Blasien, *Germany* 27 **H4** 47 47N 8 7 E
Sankt Gallen, *Switz.* 29 **B8** 47 26N 9 22 E
Sankt Gallen □, *Switz.* 29 **B8** 47 25N 9 22 E
Sankt Goar, *Germany* 27 **E3** 50 12N 7 43 E
Sankt Ingbert, *Germany* 27 **F3** 49 16N 7 6 E
Sankt Johann, *Salzburg, Austria* 30 **D6** 47 22N 13 12 E
Sankt Johann, *Tirol, Austria* 30 **D5** 47 30N 12 25 E
Sankt Margrethen, *Switz.* 29 **B9** 47 28N 9 37 E
Sankt Moritz, *Switz.* 29 **D9** 46 30N 9 50 E
Sankt-Peterburg, *Russia* 50 **B7** 59 55N 30 20 E
Sankt Pölten, *Austria* 30 **C8** 48 12N 15 38 E
Sankt Valentin, *Austria* 30 **C7** 48 11N 14 33 E
Sankt Veit, *Austria* 30 **E7** 46 54N 14 22 E
Sankt Wendel, *Germany* 27 **F3** 49 27N 7 9 E
Sankt Wolfgang, *Austria* 30 **D6** 47 43N 13 27 E
Sankuru →, *Zaïre* 103 **C4** 4 17 S 20 25 E
Sanlúcar de Barrameda, *Spain* 37 **J4** 36 46N 6 21W
Sanlúcar la Mayor, *Spain* 37 **H4** 37 26N 6 18W
Sanluri, *Italy* 40 **C1** 39 35N 8 55 E
Sanmenxia, *China* 66 **G6** 34 47N 111 12 E
Sanming, *China* 65 **D6** 26 13N 117 35 E
Sanming, *Fujian, China* 69 **D11** 26 15N 117 40 E
Sannan, *Japan* 63 **B7** 35 2N 135 1 E
Sannaspos, *S. Africa* 104 **D4** 29 6 S 26 34 E
Sannicandro Gargánico, *Italy* 41 **A8** 41 50N 15 34 E
Sannidal, *Norway* 14 **F3** 58 55N 9 15 E
Sannieshof, *S. Africa* 104 **D4** 26 30 S 25 47 E
Sannīn, J., *Lebanon* 91 **B4** 33 57N 35 52 E
Sano, *Japan* 63 **A11** 36 19N 139 35 E
Sanok, *Poland* 31 **B15** 49 35N 22 10 E
Sanquhar, *U.K.* 18 **F5** 55 21N 3 56W
Sansanding Dam, *Mali* 100 **C3** 13 48N 6 0W
Sansepolcro, *Italy* 39 **E9** 43 34N 12 8 E
Sansha, *China* 69 **D13** 26 58N 120 12 E
Sanshui, *China* 69 **F9** 23 10N 112 56 E
Sanski Most, *Bos.-H., Yug.* 39 **D13** 44 46N 16 40 E
Sansui, *China* 68 **D7** 26 58N 108 39 E
Santa, *Peru* 156 **B2** 8 59 S 78 40W
Sant' Ágata de Goti, *Italy* 41 **A7** 41 6N 14 30 E
Sant' Ágata di Militello, *Italy* 41 **D7** 38 2N 14 8 E
Santa Ana, *Beni, Bolivia* 157 **C4** 13 50 S 65 40W
Santa Ana, *Santa Cruz, Bolivia* 157 **D6** 18 43 S 58 44W
Santa Ana, *Santa Cruz, Bolivia* 157 **D5** 16 37 S 60 43W
Santa Ana, *Ecuador* 152 **D1** 1 16 S 80 20W
Santa Ana, *El Salv.* 148 **D2** 14 0N 89 31W
Santa Ana, *Mexico* 146 **A2** 30 31N 111 8W
Santa Ana, *Phil.* 70 **B4** 18 28N 122 20 E
Santa Ana, *U.S.A.* 145 **M9** 33 48N 117 55W
Santa Ana →, *Venezuela* 152 **B3** 9 30N 71 57W
Sant' Ángelo Lodigiano, *Italy* 38 **C6** 45 14N 9 25 E
Sant' Antíoco, *Italy* 40 **C1** 39 2N 8 30 E
Sant' Arcángelo di Romagna, *Italy* 39 **D9** 44 4N 12 26 E
Santa Bárbara, *Colombia* 152 **B2** 5 53N 75 35W
Santa Barbara, *Honduras* 148 **D2** 14 53N 88 14W
Santa Bárbara, *Mexico* 146 **B3** 26 48N 105 50W
Santa Barbara, *Phil.* 71 **F4** 10 50N 122 32 E
Santa Bárbara, *Spain* 34 **E5** 40 42N 0 29 E
Santa Barbara, *U.S.A.* 145 **L7** 34 25N 119 40W
Santa Bárbara, *Venezuela* 152 **B3** 7 47N 71 10W
Santa Bárbara, Mt., *Spain* 35 **H2** 37 23N 2 50W
Santa Barbara Channel, *U.S.A.* 145 **L7** 34 20N 120 0W
Santa Barbara I., *U.S.A.* 145 **M7** 33 29N 119 2W
Santa Catalina, *Colombia* 152 **A2** 10 36N 75 17W
Santa Catalina, *Mexico* 146 **B2** 25 40N 110 50W
Santa Catalina, G. of, *U.S.A.* 145 **N9** 33 0N 118 0W
Santa Catalina I., *U.S.A.* 145 **M8** 33 20N 118 30W
Santa Catarina □, *Brazil* 159 **B6** 27 25 S 48 30W
Santa Catarina, I. de, *Brazil* 159 **B6** 27 30 S 48 40W
Santa Caterina Villarmosa, *Italy* 41 **E7** 37 37N 14 1 E
Santa Cecília, *Brazil* 159 **B5** 26 56 S 50 18W
Santa Clara, *Cuba* 148 **B4** 22 20N 80 0W
Santa Clara, *Calif., U.S.A.* 144 **H5** 37 21N 122 0W
Santa Clara, *Utah, U.S.A.* 143 **H7** 37 10N 113 38W
Santa Clara de Olimar, *Uruguay* 159 **C5** 32 50 S 54 54W
Santa Clotilde, *Peru* 152 **D3** 2 33 S 73 45W
Santa Coloma de Farners, *Spain* 34 **D7** 41 50N 2 39 E
Santa Coloma de Gramanet, *Spain* 34 **D7** 41 27N 2 13 E
Santa Comba, *Spain* 36 **B2** 43 2N 8 49W
Santa Croce Camerina, *Italy* 41 **F7** 36 50N 14 30 E
Santa Croce di Magliano, *Italy* 41 **A7** 41 43N 14 59 E
Santa Cruz, *Argentina* 160 **D3** 50 0 S 68 32W
Santa Cruz, *Bolivia* 157 **D5** 17 43 S 63 10W
Santa Cruz, *Brazil* 154 **C4** 6 13 S 36 1W
Santa Cruz, *Chile* 158 **C1** 34 38 S 71 27W
Santa Cruz, *Costa Rica* 148 **D2** 10 15N 85 35W
Santa Cruz, *Madeira* 33 **D3** 32 42N 16 46W
Santa Cruz, *Peru* 156 **B2** 5 40 S 75 56W
Santa Cruz, *Davao del S., Phil.* 71 **H5** 6 50N 125 25 E
Santa Cruz, *Laguna, Phil.* 70 **D3** 14 20N 121 24 E
Santa Cruz, *Marinduque, Phil.* 70 **E4** 13 28N 122 2 E
Santa Cruz, *U.S.A.* 144 **J4** 36 55N 122 1W
Santa Cruz, *Venezuela* 153 **B5** 8 3N 64 27W
Santa Cruz □, *Argentina* 160 **C3** 49 0 S 70 0W
Santa Cruz □, *Bolivia* 157 **D5** 17 43 S 63 10W
Santa Cruz →, *Argentina* 160 **D3** 50 10 S 68 20W
Santa Cruz Cabrália, *Brazil* 155 **E4** 16 17 S 39 2W
Santa Cruz de la Palma, *Canary Is.* 33 **F2** 28 41N 17 46W
Santa Cruz de Mudela, *Spain* 35 **G1** 38 39N 3 28W
Santa Cruz de Tenerife, *Canary Is.* 33 **F3** 28 28N 16 15W
Santa Cruz del Norte, *Cuba* 148 **B3** 23 9N 81 55W
Santa Cruz del Retamar, *Spain* 36 **E6** 40 8N 4 14W
Santa Cruz del Sur, *Cuba* 148 **B4** 20 44N 78 0W
Santa Cruz do Rio Pardo, *Brazil* 159 **A6** 22 54 S 49 37W
Santa Cruz do Sul, *Brazil* 159 **B5** 29 42 S 52 25W
Santa Cruz I., *Solomon Is.* 122 **J8** 10 30 S 166 0 E
Santa Cruz I., *U.S.A.* 145 **M7** 34 0N 119 45W
Santa Domingo, Cay, *Bahamas* 148 **B4** 21 25N 75 15W
Santa Elena, *Argentina* 158 **C4** 30 58 S 59 47W
Santa Elena, *Ecuador* 152 **D1** 2 16 S 80 52W
Santa Elena, C., *Costa Rica* 148 **D2** 10 54N 85 56W
Sant' Eufémia, G. di, *Italy* 41 **D9** 38 50N 16 10 E
Santa Eugenia, Pta., *Mexico* 146 **B1** 27 50N 115 5W
Santa Eulalia, *Spain* 33 **C8** 38 59N 1 32 E
Santa Fe, *Argentina* 158 **C3** 31 35 S 60 41W
Santa Fe, *Nueva Viscaya, Phil.* 70 **C3** 16 10N 120 57 E
Santa Fe, *Tablas, Phil.* 70 **E4** 12 10N 122 0 E
Santa Fe, *Spain* 37 **H7** 37 11N 3 43W
Santa Fe, *U.S.A.* 143 **J11** 35 40N 106 0W
Santa Fé □, *Argentina* 158 **C3** 31 50 S 60 55W
Santa Filomena, *Brazil* 154 **C2** 9 6 S 45 50W
Santa Galdana, *Spain* 33 **B10** 39 56N 3 58 E
Santa Gertrudis, *Spain* 33 **B7** 39 0N 1 26 E
Santa Helena, *Brazil* 154 **B2** 2 14 S 45 18W
Santa Helena de Goiás, *Brazil* 155 **E1** 17 53 S 50 35W
Santa Inês, *Brazil* 155 **D4** 13 17 S 39 48W
Santa Inés, *Baleares, Spain* 33 **B7** 39 3N 1 21 E
Santa Inés, *Extremadura, Spain* 37 **G5** 38 32N 5 37W
Santa Inés, I., *Chile* 160 **D2** 54 0 S 73 0W
Santa Isabel = Rey Malabo, *Eq. Guin.* 101 **E6** 3 45N 8 50 E
Santa Isabel, *Argentina* 158 **D2** 36 10 S 66 54W
Santa Isabel, *Brazil* 155 **D1** 11 45 S 51 30W
Santa Isabel, *Solomon Is.* 121 **M10** 8 0 S 159 0 E
Santa Isabel, Pico, *Eq. Guin.* 101 **E6** 3 36N 8 49 E
Santa Isabel do Araguaia, *Brazil* 154 **C2** 6 7 S 48 19W
Santa Isabel do Morro, *Brazil* 155 **D1** 11 34 S 50 40W
Santa Lucía, *Corrientes, Argentina* 158 **B4** 28 58 S 59 5W
Santa Lucía, *San Juan, Argentina* 158 **C2** 31 30 S 68 30W
Santa Lucia, *Phil.* 70 **C3** 17 7N 120 27 E
Santa Lucía, *Spain* 35 **H4** 37 35N 0 58W
Santa Lucía, *Uruguay* 158 **C4** 34 27 S 56 24W
Santa Lucia Range, *U.S.A.* 144 **K5** 36 0N 121 20W
Santa Magdalena, I., *Mexico* 146 **C2** 24 40N 112 15W
Santa Margarita, *Argentina* 158 **D3** 38 28 S 61 35W
Santa Margarita, *Mexico* 146 **C2** 24 30N 111 50W
Santa Margarita, *Spain* 33 **B10** 39 42N 3 6 E
Santa Margarita, *U.S.A.* 144 **K6** 35 23N 120 37W
Santa Margarita →, *U.S.A.* 145 **M9** 33 13N 117 23W
Santa Margherita, *Italy* 38 **D6** 44 20N 9 11 E
Santa María, *Argentina* 158 **B2** 26 40 S 66 0W
Santa Maria, *Brazil* 159 **B5** 29 40 S 53 48W
Santa Maria, *Ilocos S., Phil.* 70 **C3** 17 22N 120 29 E
Santa Maria, *Isabela, Phil.* 70 **C3** 17 28N 121 45 E
Santa Maria, *Spain* 33 **B9** 39 38N 2 47 E
Santa Maria, *Switz.* 29 **C10** 46 36N 10 25 E
Santa Maria, *U.S.A.* 145 **L6** 34 58N 120 29W
Santa María →, *Mexico* 146 **A3** 31 0N 107 14W
Santa María, B. de, *Mexico* 146 **B3** 25 10N 108 40W
Santa Maria, C. de, *Portugal* 37 **J3** 36 58N 7 53W
Santa Maria Capua Vetere, *Italy* 41 **A7** 41 3N 14 15 E
Santa Maria da Vitória, *Brazil* 155 **D3** 13 24 S 44 12W
Santa María de Ipire, *Venezuela* 153 **B4** 8 49N 65 19W
Santa Maria di Leuca, C., *Italy* 41 **C11** 39 48N 18 20 E
Santa Maria do Suaçuí, *Brazil* 155 **E3** 18 12 S 42 25W
Santa Maria dos Marmelos, *Brazil* 157 **B5** 6 7 S 61 51W
Santa María la Real de Nieva, *Spain* 36 **D6** 41 4N 4 24W
Santa Marta, *Colombia* 152 **A3** 11 15N 74 13W
Santa Marta, *Spain* 37 **G4** 38 37N 6 39W
Santa Marta, Ría de, *Spain* 36 **B3** 43 44N 7 45W
Santa Marta, Sierra Nevada de, *Colombia* 152 **A3** 10 55N 73 50W
Santa Marta Grande, C., *Brazil* 159 **B6** 28 43 S 48 50W
Santa Maura = Levkás, *Greece* 45 **F2** 38 40N 20 43 E
Santa Monica, *U.S.A.* 145 **M8** 34 0N 118 30W
Santa Olalla, *Huelva, Spain* 37 **H4** 37 54N 6 14W
Santa Olalla, *Toledo, Spain* 36 **E6** 40 2N 4 25W
Sant' Onofrio, *Italy* 41 **D9** 38 42N 16 10 E
Santa Pola, *Spain* 35 **G4** 38 13N 0 35W
Santa Ponsa, *Spain* 33 **B9** 39 30N 2 28 E
Santa Quitéria, *Brazil* 154 **B3** 4 20 S 40 10W
Santa Rita, *U.S.A.* 143 **K10** 32 50N 108 0W
Santa Rita, *Guarico, Venezuela* 152 **B4** 8 8N 66 16W
Santa Rita, *Zulia, Venezuela* 152 **A3** 10 32N 71 32W
Santa Rita do Araquaia, *Brazil* 157 **D7** 17 20 S 53 12W
Santa Rosa, *La Pampa, Argentina* 158 **D3** 36 40 S 64 17W
Santa Rosa, *San Luis, Argentina* 158 **C2** 32 21 S 65 10W
Santa Rosa, *Bolivia* 156 **C4** 10 36 S 67 20W
Santa Rosa, *Brazil* 159 **B5** 27 52 S 54 29W
Santa Rosa, *Colombia* 152 **C4** 3 32N 69 48W
Santa Rosa, *Ecuador* 152 **D2** 3 27 S 79 58W
Santa Rosa, *Peru* 156 **C3** 14 30 S 70 50W
Santa Rosa, *Phil.* 70 **D3** 15 25N 120 57 E
Santa Rosa, *Calif., U.S.A.* 144 **G4** 38 26N 122 43W
Santa Rosa, *N. Mex., U.S.A.* 139 **H2** 34 58N 104 40W
Santa Rosa, *Venezuela* 152 **C4** 1 29N 66 55W
Santa Rosa de Cabal, *Colombia* 152 **C2** 4 52N 75 38W
Santa Rosa de Copán, *Honduras* 148 **D2** 14 47N 88 46W
Santa Rosa de Osos, *Colombia* 152 **B2** 6 39N 75 28W
Santa Rosa de Río Primero, *Argentina* 158 **C3** 31 8 S 63 20W
Santa Rosa de Viterbo, *Colombia* 152 **B3** 5 53N 72 59W
Santa Rosa del Palmar, *Bolivia* 157 **D5** 16 54 S 62 24W
Santa Rosa I., *Calif., U.S.A.* 145 **M6** 34 0N 120 6W
Santa Rosa I., *Fla., U.S.A.* 135 **K2** 30 23N 87 0W
Santa Rosa Ra., *U.S.A.* 142 **F5** 41 45N 117 30W
Santa Rosalía, *Mexico* 146 **B2** 27 20N 112 20W
Santa Sofia, *Italy* 39 **E8** 43 57N 11 55 E
Santa Sylvina, *Argentina* 158 **B3** 27 50 S 61 10W
Santa Tecla = Nueva San Salvador, *El Salv.* 148 **D2** 13 40N 89 18W
Santa Teresa, *Argentina* 158 **C3** 33 25 S 60 47W
Santa Teresa, *Brazil* 155 **E3** 19 55 S 40 36W
Santa Teresa, *Mexico* 147 **B5** 25 17N 97 51W
Santa Teresa, *Venezuela* 153 **C5** 4 43N 61 4W
Santa Teresa di Riva, *Italy* 41 **E8** 37 58N 15 21 E
Santa Teresa Gallura, *Italy* 40 **A2** 41 14N 9 12 E
Santa Vitória, *Brazil* 155 **E1** 18 50 S 50 8W
Santa Vitória do Palmar, *Brazil* 159 **C5** 33 32 S 53 25W
Santa Ynez, *U.S.A.* 145 **L6** 34 37N 120 5W
Santa Ynez →, *U.S.A.* 145 **L6** 34 37N 120 41W
Santa Ysabel, *U.S.A.* 145 **M10** 33 7N 116 40W
Santadi, *Italy* 40 **C1** 39 5N 8 42 E
Santahar, *Bangla.* 78 **C2** 24 48N 88 59 E
Santai, *China* 68 **B5** 31 5N 104 58 E
Santaluz, *Brazil* 154 **D4** 11 15 S 39 22W
Santana, *Brazil* 155 **D3** 13 2 S 44 5W
Santana, *Madeira* 33 **D3** 32 48N 16 52W
Santana, Coxilha de, *Brazil* 159 **C4** 30 50 S 55 35W
Santana do Ipanema, *Brazil* 154 **C4** 9 22 S 37 14W
Santana do Livramento, *Brazil* 159 **C4** 30 55 S 55 30W
Santanayi, *Spain* 33 **B10** 39 20N 3 5 E
Santander, *Colombia* 152 **C2** 3 1N 76 28W
Santander, *Phil.* 71 **G4** 9 25N 123 20 E
Santander, *Spain* 36 **B7** 43 27N 3 51W
Santander Jiménez, *Mexico* 147 **C5** 24 11N 98 29W
Santaquin, *U.S.A.* 142 **G8** 40 0N 111 51W
Santarém, *Brazil* 153 **D7** 2 25 S 54 42W
Santarém, *Portugal* 37 **F2** 39 12N 8 42W
Santarém □, *Portugal* 37 **F2** 39 10N 8 40W
Santaren Channel, *W. Indies* 148 **B4** 24 0N 79 30W
Santee, *U.S.A.* 145 **N10** 32 50N 116 58W
Santéramo in Colle, *Italy* 41 **B9** 40 48N 16 45 E
Santerno →, *Italy* 39 **D8** 44 10N 11 38 E
Santhia, *Italy* 38 **C5** 45 20N 8 10 E
Santiago, *Bolivia* 157 **D6** 18 19 S 59 34W
Santiago, *Brazil* 159 **B5** 29 11 S 54 52W
Santiago, *Chile* 158 **C1** 33 24 S 70 40W
Santiago, *Panama* 148 **E3** 8 0N 81 0W
Santiago, *Peru* 156 **C2** 14 11 S 75 43W
Santiago, *Ilocos S., Phil.* 70 **C3** 17 18N 120 27 E
Santiago, *Isabela, Phil.* 70 **C3** 16 41N 121 33 E
Santiago □, *Chile* 158 **C1** 33 30 S 70 50W
Santiago →, *Peru* 152 **D2** 4 27 S 77 38W
Santiago, C., *Chile* 160 **D1** 50 46 S 75 27W
Santiago, Punta de, *Eq. Guin.* 101 **E6** 3 12N 8 40 E
Santiago, Serranía de, *Bolivia* 157 **D6** 18 25 S 59 25W
Santiago de Chuco, *Peru* 156 **B2** 8 9 S 78 11W
Santiago de Compostela, *Spain* 36 **C2** 42 52N 8 37W
Santiago de Cuba, *Cuba* 148 **C4** 20 0N 75 49W
Santiago de los Cabelleros, *Dom. Rep.* 149 **C5** 19 30N 70 40W
Santiago del Estero, *Argentina* 158 **B3** 27 50 S 64 15W
Santiago del Estero □, *Argentina* 158 **B3** 27 40 S 63 15W
Santiago del Teide, *Canary Is.* 33 **F3** 28 17N 16 48W
Santiago do Cacém, *Portugal* 37 **G2** 38 1N 8 42W
Santiago Ixcuintla, *Mexico* 146 **C3** 21 50N 105 11W
Santiago Papasquiaro, *Mexico* 146 **B3** 25 0N 105 20W
Santiaguillo, L. de, *Mexico* 146 **C4** 24 50N 104 50W
Santillana del Mar, *Spain* 36 **B6** 43 24N 4 6W
Säntis, *Switz.* 29 **B8** 47 15N 9 22 E
Santisteban del Puerto, *Spain* 35 **G1** 38 17N 3 15W
Santo, *Vanuatu* 121 **E5** 15 27 S 167 10 E
Santo →, *Peru* 156 **B2** 8 56 S 78 37W
Santo Amaro, *Brazil* 155 **D4** 12 30 S 38 43W
Santo Anastácio, *Brazil* 159 **A5** 21 58 S 51 39W
Santo André, *Brazil* 159 **A6** 23 39 S 46 29W
Santo Ângelo, *Brazil* 159 **B5** 28 15 S 54 15W
Santo Antonio, *Brazil* 157 **D6** 15 50 S 56 0W
Santo Antônio de Jesus, *Brazil* 155 **D4** 12 58 S 39 16W
Santo Antônio do Içá, *Brazil* 152 **D4** 3 5 S 67 57W
Santo Antônio do Leverger, *Brazil* 157 **D6** 15 52 S 56 5W
Santo Corazón, *Bolivia* 157 **D6** 18 0 S 58 45W
Santo Domingo, *Dom. Rep.* 149 **C6** 18 30N 69 59W
Santo Domingo, *Baja Calif. N., Mexico* 146 **A1** 30 43N 116 2W
Santo Domingo, *Baja Calif. S., Mexico* 146 **B2** 25 32N 112 2W
Santo Domingo, *Nic.* 148 **D3** 12 14N 84 59W
Santo Domingo de la Calzada, *Spain* 34 **C2** 42 26N 2 57W
Santo Domingo de los Colorados, *Ecuador* 152 **D2** 0 15 S 79 9W
Santo Nino I., *Phil.* 71 **F5** 11 55N 124 27 E
Santo Stéfano di Camastro, *Italy* 41 **D7** 38 1N 14 22 E
Santo Stino di Livenza, *Italy* 39 **C9** 45 45N 12 40 E
Santo Tirso, *Portugal* 36 **D2** 41 21N 8 28W
Santo Tomás, *Mexico* 146 **A1** 31 33N 116 24W
Santo Tomás, *Peru* 156 **C3** 14 26 S 72 8W
Santo Tomé, *Argentina* 159 **B4** 28 40 S 56 5W
Santo Tomé de Guayana = Ciudad Guayana, *Venezuela* 153 **B5** 8 0N 62 30W
Santol, *Phil.* 70 **C3** 16 47N 120 27 E
Santoña, *Spain* 36 **B7** 43 29N 3 27W
Santos, *Brazil* 159 **A6** 24 0 S 46 20W
Santos, Sierra de los, *Spain* 37 **G5** 38 7N 5 12W
Santos Dumont, *Brazil* 155 **F3** 22 55 S 43 10W
Santpoort, *Neths.* 20 **D5** 52 26N 4 39 E
Sanvignes-les-Mines, *France* 23 **F11** 46 40N 4 18 E
San'yō, *Japan* 62 **C3** 34 2N 131 5 E
Sanyuan, *China* 66 **G5** 34 35N 108 58 E
Sanyuki-Sammyaku, *Japan* 62 **C6** 34 5N 134 0 E
Sanza Pombo, *Angola* 103 **D3** 7 18 S 15 56 E
São Anastácio, *Brazil* 159 **A5** 22 0 S 51 40W
São Bartolomeu de Messines, *Portugal* 37 **H2** 37 15N 8 17W
São Benedito, *Brazil* 154 **B3** 4 3 S 40 53W
São Bento, *Brazil* 154 **B3** 2 42 S 44 50W
São Bento do Norte, *Brazil* 154 **C4** 5 4 S 36 2W

**Serdobsk 263**


Schiers, *Switz.* 29 **C9** 46 58N 9 41 E
Schifferstadt, *Germany* 27 **F4** 49 22N 8 23 E
Schifflange, *Lux.* 21 **K8** 49 30N 6 1 E
Schijndel, *Neths.* 21 **E6** 51 37N 5 27 E
Schiltigheim, *France* 23 **D14** 48 35N 7 45 E
Schio, *Italy* 39 **C8** 45 42N 11 21 E
Schipbeek, *Neths.* 20 **D8** 52 14N 6 10 E
Schipluiden, *Neths.* 20 **E4** 51 59N 4 19 E
Schirmeck, *France* 23 **D14** 48 29N 7 12 E
Schladming, *Austria* 30 **D6** 47 23N 13 41 E
Schlei →, *Germany* 26 **A5** 54 45N 9 52 E
Schleiden, *Germany* 26 **E2** 50 32N 6 26 E
Schleiz, *Germany* 26 **E7** 50 35N 11 49 E
Schleswig, *Germany* 26 **A5** 54 32N 9 34 E
Schleswig-Holstein □, *Germany* 26 **A5** 54 10N 9 40 E
Schlieren, *Switz.* 29 **B6** 47 26N 8 27 E
Schlüchtern, *Germany* 27 **E5** 50 20N 9 32 E
Schmalkalden, *Germany* 26 **E6** 50 43N 10 28 E
Schmölln, *Brandenburg, Germany* 26 **B10** 53 15N 14 6 E
Schmölln, *Thüringen, Germany* 26 **E8** 50 54N 12 22 E
Schneeberg, *Austria* 30 **D8** 47 47N 15 48 E
Schneeberg, *Germany* 26 **E8** 50 35N 12 39 E
Schneider, *U.S.A.* 141 **C9** 41 13N 87 28W
Schoenberg, *Belgium* 21 **H8** 50 17N 6 16 E
Schofield, *U.S.A.* 138 **C10** 44 54N 89 39W
Scholls, *U.S.A.* 144 **E4** 45 24N 122 56W
Schönberg, *Mecklenburg-Vorpommern, Germany* 26 **B6** 53 50N 10 55 E
Schönberg, *Schleswig-Holstein, Germany* 26 **A6** 54 23N 10 20 E
Schönebeck, *Germany* 26 **C7** 52 2N 11 42 E
Schönenwerd, *Switz.* 28 **B5** 47 23N 8 0 E
Schongau, *Germany* 27 **H6** 47 49N 10 54 E
Schöningen, *Germany* 26 **C6** 52 8N 10 57 E
Schoolcraft, *U.S.A.* 141 **B11** 42 7N 85 38W
Schoondijke, *Neths.* 21 **F3** 51 21N 3 33 E
Schoonebeek, *Neths.* 20 **C9** 52 39N 6 52 E
Schoonhoven, *Neths.* 20 **E5** 51 57N 4 51 E
Schoorl, *Neths.* 20 **C5** 52 42N 4 42 E
Schortens, *Germany* 26 **B3** 53 37N 7 51 E
Schoten, *Belgium* 21 **F5** 51 16N 4 30 E
Schouten I., *Australia* 114 **G4** 42 20 S 148 20 E
Schouten Is. = Supriori, Kepulauan, *Indonesia* 73 **B5** 1 0 S 136 0 E
Schouwen, *Neths.* 21 **E3** 51 43N 3 45 E
Schramberg, *Germany* 27 **G4** 48 12N 8 24 E
Schrankogl, *Austria* 30 **D4** 47 3N 11 7 E
Schreckhorn, *Switz.* 28 **C6** 46 36N 8 7 E
Schreiber, *Canada* 128 **C2** 48 45N 87 20W
Schrobenhausen, *Germany* 27 **G7** 48 33N 11 16 E
Schruns, *Austria* 30 **D2** 47 5N 9 56 E
Schuler, *Canada* 131 **C6** 50 20N 110 6W
Schuls, *Switz.* 29 **C10** 46 48N 10 18 E
Schumacher, *Canada* 128 **C3** 48 30N 81 16W
Schüpfen, *Switz.* 28 **B4** 47 2N 7 24 E
Schüpfheim, *Switz.* 28 **C6** 46 57N 8 2 E
Schurz, *U.S.A.* 142 **G4** 38 57N 118 48W
Schuyler, *U.S.A.* 138 **E6** 41 30N 97 3W
Schuylkill Haven, *U.S.A.* 137 **F8** 40 37N 76 11W
Schwabach, *Germany* 27 **F7** 49 19N 11 3 E
Schwäbisch Gmünd, *Germany* 27 **G5** 48 49N 9 48 E
Schwäbisch Hall, *Germany* 27 **F5** 49 7N 9 45 E
Schwäbische Alb, *Germany* 27 **G5** 48 30N 9 30 E
Schwabmünchen, *Germany* 27 **G6** 48 11N 10 45 E
Schwanden, *Switz.* 29 **C8** 46 58N 9 5 E
Schwandorf, *Germany* 27 **F8** 49 20N 12 7 E
Schwaner, Pegunungan, *Indonesia* 75 **C4** 1 0 S 112 30 E
Schwarmstedt, *Germany* 26 **C5** 52 41N 9 37 E
Schwarzach →, *Austria* 30 **E5** 46 56N 12 35 E
Schwärze, *Germany* 26 **C9** 52 50N 13 49 E
Schwarze Elster →, *Germany* 26 **D8** 51 49N 12 51 E
Schwarzenberg, *Germany* 26 **E8** 50 31N 12 49 E
Schwarzenburg, *Switz.* 28 **C4** 46 49N 7 20 E
Schwarzwald, *Germany* 27 **H4** 48 0N 8 0 E
Schwaz, *Austria* 30 **D4** 47 20N 11 44 E
Schwedt, *Germany* 26 **B10** 53 4N 14 18 E
Schweinfurt, *Germany* 27 **E6** 50 3N 10 12 E
Schweizer Mittelland, *Switz.* 28 **C4** 47 0N 7 15 E
Schweizer-Reneke, *S. Africa* 104 **D4** 27 11 S 25 18 E
Schwenningen, *Germany* 27 **G4** 48 3N 8 29 E
Schwerin, *Germany* 26 **B7** 53 37N 11 22 E
Schweriner See, *Germany* 26 **B7** 53 45N 11 26 E
Schwetzingen, *Germany* 27 **F4** 49 22N 8 35 E
Schwyz, *Switz.* 29 **B7** 47 2N 8 39 E
Schwyz □, *Switz.* 29 **B7** 47 2N 8 39 E
Sciacca, *Italy* 40 **E6** 37 30N 13 3 E
Sciao, *Somali Rep.* 108 **D3** 3 26N 45 21 E
Scicli, *Italy* 41 **F7** 36 48N 14 41 E
Scilla, *Italy* 41 **D8** 38 18N 15 44 E
Scilly, Isles of, *U.K.* 17 **H1** 49 55N 6 15W
Ścinawa, *Poland* 47 **D3** 51 25N 16 26 E
Scione, *Greece* 44 **E5** 39 57N 23 36 E
Scioto →, *U.S.A.* 134 **F4** 38 44N 83 0W
Scobey, *U.S.A.* 138 **A2** 48 47N 105 30W
Scone, *Australia* 117 **B9** 32 5 S 150 52 E
Scordia, *Italy* 41 **E7** 37 19N 14 50 E
Scoresbysund, *Greenland* 6 **B6** 70 20N 23 0W
Scorno, Punta dello, *Italy* 40 **A1** 41 7N 8 23 E
Scotia, *Calif., U.S.A.* 142 **F1** 40 36N 124 4W
Scotia, *N.Y., U.S.A.* 137 **D11** 42 50N 73 58W
Scotia Sea, *Antarctica* 7 **B18** 56 5 S 56 0W
Scotland, *U.S.A.* 138 **D6** 43 10N 97 45W
Scotland □, *U.K.* 18 **E5** 57 0N 4 0W
Scotland Neck, *U.S.A.* 135 **G7** 36 6N 77 32W
Scott, C., *Australia* 112 **B4** 13 30 S 129 49 E
Scott City, *U.S.A.* 138 **F4** 38 30N 100 52W
Scott Glacier, *Antarctica* 7 **C8** 66 15 S 100 5 E
Scott I., *Antarctica* 7 **C11** 67 0 S 179 0 E
Scott Inlet, *Canada* 127 **A12** 71 0N 71 0W
Scott Is., *Canada* 130 **C3** 50 48N 128 40W
Scott L., *Canada* 131 **B7** 59 55N 106 18W
Scott Reef, *Australia* 112 **B3** 14 0 S 121 50 E
Scottburgh, *S. Africa* 105 **E5** 30 15 S 30 47 E
Scottdale, *U.S.A.* 136 **F5** 40 8N 79 35W
Scottsbluff, *U.S.A.* 138 **E3** 41 55N 103 35W
Scottsboro, *U.S.A.* 135 **H2** 34 40N 86 0W
Scottsburg, *U.S.A.* 141 **F11** 38 40N 85 46W
Scottsdale, *Australia* 114 **G4** 41 9 S 147 31 E
Scottsville, *Ky., U.S.A.* 135 **G2** 36 48N 86 10W
Scottsville, *N.Y., U.S.A.* 136 **C7** 43 2N 77 47W
Scottville, *U.S.A.* 134 **D2** 43 57N 86 18W
Scranton, *Iowa, U.S.A.* 140 **B2** 42 1N 94 33W
Scranton, *Pa., U.S.A.* 137 **E9** 41 22N 75 41W
Scugog, L., *Canada* 136 **B6** 44 10N 78 55W
Scunthorpe, *U.K.* 16 **D7** 53 35N 0 38W
Scuol, *Switz.* 29 **C10** 46 48N 10 17 E
Scusciuban, *Somali Rep.* 90 **E5** 10 18N 50 12 E
Scutari = Üsküdar, *Turkey* 49 **F4** 41 0N 29 5 E
Seabra, *Brazil* 155 **D3** 12 25 S 41 46W
Seabrook, L., *Australia* 113 **F2** 30 55 S 119 40 E
Seaford, *U.S.A.* 134 **F8** 38 37N 75 36W
Seaforth, *Canada* 128 **D3** 43 35N 81 25W
Seagraves, *U.S.A.* 139 **J3** 32 56N 102 30W
Seal →, *Canada* 131 **B10** 59 4N 94 48W
Seal Cove, *Canada* 129 **C8** 49 57N 56 22W
Seal L., *Canada* 129 **B7** 54 20N 61 30W
Sealy, *U.S.A.* 139 **L6** 29 46N 96 9W
Seaman, *U.S.A.* 141 **F13** 38 57N 83 34W
Searchlight, *U.S.A.* 145 **K12** 35 31N 114 55W
Searcy, *U.S.A.* 139 **H9** 35 15N 91 45W
Searles L., *U.S.A.* 145 **K9** 35 47N 117 17W
Seaside, *Calif., U.S.A.* 144 **J5** 36 37N 121 50W
Seaside, *Oreg., U.S.A.* 144 **E3** 45 59N 123 55W
Seaspray, *Australia* 117 **E7** 38 25 S 147 15 E
Seattle, *U.S.A.* 144 **C4** 47 41N 122 15W
Seaview Ra., *Australia* 114 **B4** 18 40 S 145 45 E
Seaward Kaikouras, Mts., *N.Z.* 119 **C8** 42 10 S 173 44 E
Sebangka, *Indonesia* 74 **B2** 0 7N 104 36 E
Sebastián Vizcaíno, B., *Mexico* 146 **B2** 28 0N 114 30W
Sebastopol = Sevastopol, *Ukraine* 52 **D5** 44 35N 33 30 E
Sebastopol, *U.S.A.* 144 **G4** 38 24N 122 49W
Sebderat, *Ethiopia* 95 **D4** 15 26N 36 42 E
Sebdou, *Algeria* 99 **B4** 34 38N 1 19W
Seben, *Turkey* 88 **C4** 40 24N 31 34 E
Sebeş, *Romania* 46 **D4** 45 58N 23 34 E
Sebeşului, Munţii, *Romania* 46 **D4** 45 36N 23 40 E
Sebewaing, *U.S.A.* 134 **D4** 43 45N 83 27W
Sebezh, *Russia* 50 **C6** 56 14N 28 22 E
Sébi, *Mali* 100 **B4** 15 50N 4 12W
Şebinkarahisar, *Turkey* 52 **F8** 40 22N 38 28 E
Sebiş, *Romania* 46 **C3** 46 23N 22 13 E
Sebkhet Te-n-Dghâmcha, *Mauritania* 100 **B1** 18 30N 15 55W
Sebkra Azzel Mati, *Algeria* 99 **C5** 26 10N 0 43 E
Sebkra Mekerghene, *Algeria* 99 **C5** 26 21N 1 30 E
Seblat, *Indonesia* 74 **C2** 3 14 S 101 38 E
Sebnitz, *Germany* 26 **E10** 50 58N 14 17 E
Sebou, Oued →, *Morocco* 98 **B3** 34 16N 6 40W
Sebring, *Fla., U.S.A.* 135 **M5** 27 30N 81 26W
Sebring, *Ohio, U.S.A.* 136 **F3** 40 55N 81 2W
Sebringville, *Canada* 136 **C3** 43 24N 81 4W
Sebta = Ceuta, *Morocco* 98 **A3** 35 52N 5 18W
Sebuku, *Indonesia* 75 **C5** 3 30 S 116 25 E
Sebuku, Teluk, *Malaysia* 75 **B5** 4 0N 118 10 E
Sečanj, *Serbia, Yug.* 42 **B5** 45 25N 20 47 E
Secchia →, *Italy* 38 **C8** 45 4N 11 0 E
Sechelt, *Canada* 130 **D4** 49 25N 123 42W
Sechura, *Peru* 156 **B1** 5 39 S 80 50W
Sechura, Desierto de, *Peru* 156 **B1** 6 0 S 80 30W
Seclin, *France* 23 **B10** 50 33N 3 2 E
Secondigny, *France* 22 **F6** 46 37N 0 26W
Sečovce, *Czech.* 31 **C14** 48 42N 21 40 E
Secretary I., *N.Z.* 119 **F1** 45 15 S 166 56 E
Secunderabad, *India* 82 **F4** 17 28N 78 30 E
Sécure →, *Bolivia* 157 **D5** 15 10 S 64 52W
Sedalia, *U.S.A.* 140 **F3** 38 40N 93 18W
Sedan, *Australia* 116 **C3** 34 34 S 139 19 E
Sedan, *France* 23 **C11** 49 43N 4 57 E
Sedan, *U.S.A.* 139 **G6** 37 10N 96 11W
Sedano, *Spain* 34 **C1** 42 43N 3 49W
Seddon, *N.Z.* 119 **B9** 41 40 S 174 7 E
Seddonville, *N.Z.* 119 **B7** 41 33 S 172 1 E
Sedeh, *Fārs, Iran* 85 **D7** 30 45N 52 11 E
Sedeh, *Khorāsān, Iran* 85 **C8** 33 20N 59 14 E
Sederot, *Israel* 91 **D3** 31 32N 34 37 E
Sedgewick, *Canada* 130 **C6** 52 48N 111 41W
Sedhiou, *Senegal* 100 **C1** 12 44N 15 30W
Sedičany, *Czech.* 30 **B7** 49 40N 14 25 E
Sedico, *Italy* 39 **B9** 46 8N 12 6 E
Sedienie, *Bulgaria* 43 **E9** 42 16N 24 33 E
Sedley, *Canada* 131 **C8** 50 10N 104 0W
Sedova, Pik, *Russia* 56 **B6** 73 29N 54 58 E
Sedrata, *Algeria* 99 **A6** 36 7N 7 31 E
Sedro Woolley, *U.S.A.* 144 **B4** 48 30N 122 15W
Sedrun, *Switz.* 29 **C7** 46 36N 8 47 E
Seduva, *Lithuania* 50 **D3** 55 45N 23 45 E
Sedziszów Małapolski, *Poland* 31 **A14** 50 5N 21 45 E
Seebad Ahlbeck, *Germany* 26 **B10** 53 56N 14 10 E
Seefeld, *Austria* 30 **D4** 47 19N 11 13 E
Seehausen, *Germany* 26 **C7** 52 52N 11 43 E
Seeheim, *Namibia* 104 **D2** 26 50 S 17 45 E
Seekoei →, *S. Africa* 104 **E4** 30 18 S 25 1 E
Seelaw, *Germany* 26 **C10** 52 32N 14 22 E
Sées, *France* 22 **D7** 48 38N 0 10 E
Seesen, *Germany* 26 **D6** 51 53N 10 10 E
Sefadu, *S. Leone* 100 **D2** 8 35N 10 58W
Seferihisar, *Turkey* 88 **D2** 38 10N 26 50 E
Séfeto, *Mali* 100 **C3** 14 8N 9 49W
Sefrou, *Morocco* 98 **B4** 33 52N 4 52W
Sefton, *N.Z.* 119 **D7** 43 15 S 172 41 E
Sefuri-San, *Japan* 62 **D2** 33 28N 130 18 E
Sefwi Bekwai, *Ghana* 100 **D4** 6 10N 2 25W
Seg-ozero, *Russia* 50 **A8** 63 0N 33 10 E
Segag, *Ethiopia* 108 **C2** 7 39N 42 50 E
Segamat, *Malaysia* 77 **L4** 2 30N 102 50 E
Segarcea, *Romania* 46 **E4** 44 6N 23 43 E
Segbwema, *S. Leone* 100 **D2** 8 0N 11 0W
Seget, *Indonesia* 73 **B4** 1 24 S 130 58 E
Segezha, *Russia* 48 **B5** 63 44N 34 19 E
Seggueur, O. →, *Algeria* 99 **B5** 32 4N 2 4 E
Segonzac, *France* 24 **C3** 45 36N 0 14W
Segorbe, *Spain* 34 **F4** 39 50N 0 30W
Ségou, *Mali* 100 **C3** 13 30N 6 16W
Segovia = Coco →, *Cent. Amer.* 148 **D3** 15 0N 83 8W
Segovia, *Colombia* 152 **B3** 7 7N 74 42W
Segovia, *Spain* 36 **E6** 40 57N 4 10W
Segovia □, *Spain* 36 **E6** 40 55N 4 10W
Segré, *France* 22 **E6** 47 40N 0 52W
Segre →, *Spain* 34 **D5** 41 40N 0 43 E
Séguéla, *Ivory C.* 100 **D3** 7 55N 6 40W
Seguin, *U.S.A.* 139 **L6** 29 34N 97 58W
Segundo →, *Argentina* 158 **C3** 30 53 S 62 44W
Segura →, *Spain* 35 **G4** 38 6N 0 54W
Segura, Sierra de, *Spain* 35 **G2** 38 5N 2 45W
Seh Qal'eh, *Iran* 85 **C8** 33 40N 58 24 E
Sehitwa, *Botswana* 104 **C3** 20 30 S 22 30 E
Sehore, *India* 80 **H7** 23 10N 77 5 E
Sehwan, *Pakistan* 79 **D2** 26 28N 67 53 E
Şeica Mare, *Romania* 46 **C5** 46 1N 24 7 E
Seikpyu, *Burma* 78 **E5** 20 54N 94 48 E
Seiland, *Norway* 12 **A17** 70 25N 23 15 E
Seiling, *U.S.A.* 139 **G5** 36 10N 98 56W
Seille →, *France* 25 **B8** 46 31N 4 57 E
Seilles, *Belgium* 21 **G6** 50 30N 5 6 E
Sein, I. de, *France* 22 **D2** 48 2N 4 52W
Seinäjoki →, *Finland* 12 **E17** 62 40N 22 45 E
Seine →, *France* 22 **C7** 49 26N 0 26 E
Seine, B. de la, *France* 22 **C6** 49 40N 0 40W
Seine-et-Marne □, *France* 23 **D9** 48 45N 3 0 E
Seine-Maritime □, *France* 22 **C7** 49 40N 1 0 E
Seine-St.-Denis □, *France* 23 **D9** 48 58N 2 24 E
Seini, *Romania* 46 **B4** 47 44N 23 21 E
Seistan, *Iran* 85 **D9** 30 50N 61 0 E
Sejerø, *Denmark* 15 **J5** 55 54N 11 9 E
Sejerø Bugt, *Denmark* 15 **J5** 55 53N 11 15 E
Sejny, *Poland* 47 **A10** 54 6N 23 21 E
Seka, *Ethiopia* 95 **F4** 8 10N 36 52 E
Sekayu, *Indonesia* 74 **C2** 2 51 S 103 51 E
Seke, *Tanzania* 106 **C3** 3 20 S 33 31 E
Seke-Banza, *Zaïre* 103 **D2** 5 20 S 13 16 E
Sekenke, *Tanzania* 106 **C3** 4 18 S 34 11 E
Seki, *Japan* 63 **B8** 35 29N 136 55 E
Sekigahara, *Japan* 63 **B8** 35 22N 136 28 E
Sekken Veøy, *Norway* 14 **B1** 62 45N 7 30 E
Sekondi-Takoradi, *Ghana* 100 **E4** 4 58N 1 45W
Sekuma, *Botswana* 104 **C3** 24 36 S 23 50 E
Selah, *U.S.A.* 142 **C3** 46 44N 120 30W
Selama, *Malaysia* 77 **K3** 5 12N 100 42 E
Selangor □, *Malaysia* 74 **B2** 3 10N 101 30 E
Selárgius, *Italy* 40 **C2** 39 14N 9 14 E
Selaru, *Indonesia* 73 **C4** 8 9 S 131 0 E
Selb, *Germany* 27 **E8** 50 9N 12 9 E
Selby, *U.K.* 16 **D6** 53 47N 1 5W
Selby, *U.S.A.* 138 **C4** 45 34N 100 2W
Selca, *Croatia* 39 **E13** 43 20N 16 50 E
Selçuk, *Turkey* 88 **E2** 37 56N 27 22 E
Selden, *U.S.A.* 138 **F4** 39 30N 100 39W
Sele →, *Italy* 41 **B7** 40 27N 14 58 E
Selemdzha →, *Russia* 57 **D13** 51 42N 128 53 E
Selenga = Selenge Mörön →, *Asia* 64 **A5** 52 16N 106 16 E
Selenge, *Zaïre* 102 **C3** 1 58 S 18 11 E
Selenge Mörön →, *Asia* 64 **A5** 52 16N 106 16 E
Selenica, *Albania* 44 **D1** 40 33N 19 39 E
Selenter See, *Germany* 26 **A6** 54 19N 10 26 E
Sélestat, *France* 23 **D14** 48 16N 7 26 E
Seletan, Tg., *Indonesia* 75 **C4** 4 10 S 114 40 E
Seletin, *Romania* 46 **B6** 47 50N 25 12 E
Selevac, *Serbia, Yug.* 42 **C5** 44 28N 20 52 E
Selfridge, *U.S.A.* 138 **B4** 46 3N 100 57W
Sélibabi, *Mauritania* 100 **B2** 15 10N 12 15W
Seliger, Oz., *Russia* 50 **C8** 57 15N 33 0 E
Seligman, *U.S.A.* 143 **J7** 35 17N 112 56W
Şelim, *Turkey* 53 **F10** 40 30N 42 46 E
Selîma, El Wâhât el, *Sudan* 94 **C2** 21 22N 29 19 E
Selinda Spillway, *Botswana* 104 **B3** 18 35 S 23 10 E
Selinoús, *Greece* 45 **G3** 37 35N 21 37 E
Selizharovo, *Russia* 50 **C8** 56 51N 33 27 E
Seljord, *Norway* 14 **E2** 59 30N 8 40 E
Selkirk, *Canada* 131 **C9** 50 10N 96 55W
Selkirk, *U.K.* 18 **F6** 55 33N 2 50W
Selkirk I., *Canada* 131 **C9** 53 20N 99 6W
Selkirk Mts., *Canada* 130 **C5** 51 15N 117 40W
Selles-sur-Cher, *France* 23 **E8** 47 16N 1 33 E
Sellía, *Greece* 32 **D6** 35 12N 24 23 E
Sellières, *France* 23 **F12** 46 50N 5 32 E
Sells, *U.S.A.* 143 **L8** 31 57N 111 57W
Sellye, *Hungary* 31 **F10** 45 52N 17 51 E
Selma, *Ala., U.S.A.* 135 **J2** 32 30N 87 0W
Selma, *Calif., U.S.A.* 144 **J7** 36 39N 119 39W
Selma, *N.C., U.S.A.* 135 **H6** 35 32N 78 15W
Selmer, *U.S.A.* 135 **H1** 35 9N 88 36W
Selo, *Greece* 44 **C7** 41 10N 25 53 E
Selong, *Indonesia* 75 **D5** 8 39 S 116 32 E
Selongey, *France* 23 **E12** 47 36N 5 11 E
Selowandoma Falls, *Zimbabwe* 107 **G3** 21 15 S 31 50 E
Selpele, *Indonesia* 73 **B4** 0 1 S 130 5 E
Selsey Bill, *U.K.* 17 **G7** 50 44N 0 47W
Seltz, *France* 23 **D15** 48 54N 8 4 E
Selu, *Indonesia* 73 **C4** 7 32 S 130 55 E
Sélune →, *France* 22 **D5** 48 38N 1 22W
Selva, *Argentina* 158 **B3** 29 50 S 62 0W
Selva, *Italy* 39 **B8** 46 33N 11 46 E
Selva, *Spain* 34 **D6** 41 13N 1 8 E
Selvas, *Brazil* 156 **B4** 6 30 S 67 0W
Selwyn, *Australia* 114 **C3** 21 32 S 140 30 E
Selwyn L., *Canada* 131 **A8** 60 0N 104 30W
Selwyn Passage, *Vanuatu* 121 **F6** 16 3 S 168 12 E
Selwyn Ra., *Australia* 114 **C3** 21 10 S 140 0 E
Seman →, *Albania* 44 **D1** 40 45N 19 50 E
Semara, *W. Sahara* 98 **C2** 26 48N 11 41W
Semarang, *Indonesia* 75 **D4** 7 0 S 110 26 E
Sematan, *Malaysia* 75 **B3** 1 48N 109 46 E
Semau, *Indonesia* 72 **D2** 10 13 S 123 22 E
Sembabule, *Uganda* 106 **C3** 0 4 S 31 25 E
Sembé, *Congo* 102 **B2** 1 39N 14 36 E
Sémé, *Senegal* 100 **B2** 15 4N 13 41W
Semeih, *Sudan* 95 **E3** 12 43N 30 53 E
Semenov, *Russia* 51 **C14** 56 43N 44 30 E
Semenovka, *Ukraine* 50 **E8** 52 8N 32 36 E
Semenovka, *Ukraine* 52 **B5** 49 37N 33 10 E
Semeru, *Indonesia* 75 **D4** 8 4 S 112 55 E
Semiluki, *Russia* 51 **F11** 51 41N 39 2 E
Seminoe Res., *U.S.A.* 142 **E10** 42 0N 107 0W
Seminole, *Okla., U.S.A.* 139 **H6** 35 15N 96 45W
Seminole, *Tex., U.S.A.* 139 **J3** 32 41N 102 38W
Semiozernoye, *Kazakhstan* 54 **E9** 52 22N 64 8 E
Semipalatinsk, *Kazakhstan* 56 **D9** 50 30N 80 10 E
Semirara I., *Phil.* 70 **E3** 12 4N 121 23 E
Semirara Is., *Phil.* 71 **F3** 12 0N 121 20 E
Semisopochnoi, *U.S.A.* 126 **C2** 52 0N 179 40W
Semitau, *Indonesia* 75 **B4** 0 29N 111 57 E
Semiyarskoye, *Kazakhstan* 56 **D8** 50 55N 78 23 E
Semmering Pass, *Austria* 30 **D8** 47 41N 15 45 E
Semnān, *Iran* 85 **C7** 35 55N 53 25 E
Semnān □, *Iran* 85 **C7** 36 0N 54 0 E
Semois →, *Europe* 21 **J5** 49 53N 4 44 E
Sempang Mengayou, Tanjong, *Malaysia* 75 **A5** 7 0N 116 40 E
Semporna, *Malaysia* 75 **B5** 4 30N 118 33 E
Semuda, *Indonesia* 75 **C4** 2 51 S 112 58 E
Semur-en-Auxois, *France* 23 **E11** 47 30N 4 20 E
Sena, *Bolivia* 156 **C4** 11 32 S 67 11W
Senā, *Iran* 85 **D6** 28 27N 51 36 E
Sena, *Mozam.* 107 **F3** 17 25 S 35 0 E
Sena →, *Bolivia* 156 **C4** 11 31 S 67 11W
Sena Madureira, *Brazil* 156 **B4** 9 5 S 68 45W
Senador Pompeu, *Brazil* 154 **C4** 5 40 S 39 20W
Senaja, *Malaysia* 75 **A5** 6 45N 117 3 E
Senaki, *Georgia* 53 **E10** 42 15N 42 7 E
Senanga, *Zambia* 104 **B3** 16 2 S 23 14 E
Senatobia, *U.S.A.* 139 **H10** 34 38N 89 57W
Sendafa, *Ethiopia* 95 **F4** 9 11N 39 3 E
Sendai, *Kagoshima, Japan* 62 **F2** 31 50N 130 20 E
Sendai, *Miyagi, Japan* 60 **E10** 38 15N 140 53 E
Sendai-Wan, *Japan* 60 **E10** 38 15N 141 0 E
Sendamangalam, *India* 83 **J4** 11 17N 78 17 E
Sendenhorst, *Germany* 26 **D3** 51 50N 7 49 E
Sendurjana, *India* 82 **D4** 21 32N 78 17 E
Senec, *Czech.* 31 **C10** 48 12N 17 23 E
Seneca, *Oreg., U.S.A.* 142 **D4** 44 10N 119 2W
Seneca, *S.C., U.S.A.* 135 **H4** 34 43N 82 59W
Seneca Falls, *U.S.A.* 137 **D8** 42 55N 76 50W
Seneca L., *U.S.A.* 136 **D8** 42 40N 76 58W
Seneffe, *Belgium* 21 **G4** 50 32N 4 16 E
Senegal ■, *W. Afr.* 100 **C2** 14 30N 14 30W
Senegal →, *W. Afr.* 100 **B1** 15 48N 16 32W
Senegambia, *Africa* 92 **E2** 12 45N 12 0W
Senekal, *S. Africa* 105 **D4** 28 20 S 27 36 E
Senftenberg, *Germany* 26 **D10** 51 30N 14 1 E
Senga Hill, *Zambia* 107 **D3** 9 19 S 31 11 E
Senge Khambab = Indus →, *Pakistan* 79 **D2** 24 20N 67 47 E
Sengerema □, *Tanzania* 106 **C3** 2 10 S 32 20 E
Sengiley, *Russia* 51 **E16** 53 58N 48 46 E
Sengkang, *Indonesia* 72 **B2** 4 8 S 120 1 E
Sengua →, *Zimbabwe* 107 **F2** 17 7 S 28 5 E
Senguerr →, *Argentina* 160 **C3** 45 35 S 68 50W
Senhor-do-Bonfim, *Brazil* 154 **D3** 10 30 S 40 10W
Senica, *Czech.* 31 **C10** 48 41N 17 25 E
Senigállia, *Italy* 39 **E10** 43 42N 13 12 E
Seniku, *Burma* 78 **C6** 25 32N 97 48 E
Senio →, *Italy* 39 **D9** 44 35N 12 15 E
Senirkent, *Turkey* 88 **D4** 38 6N 30 33 E
Senise, *Italy* 41 **B9** 40 6N 16 15 E
Senj, *Croatia* 39 **D11** 45 0N 14 58 E
Senja, *Norway* 12 **B14** 69 25N 17 30 E
Senlis, *France* 23 **C9** 49 13N 2 35 E
Senmonorom, *Cambodia* 76 **F6** 12 27N 107 12 E
Sennâr, *Sudan* 95 **E3** 13 30N 33 35 E
Senne →, *Belgium* 21 **G4** 50 42N 4 13 E
Senneterre, *Canada* 128 **C4** 48 25N 77 15W
Senniquelle, *Liberia* 100 **D3** 7 19N 8 38W
Senno, *Belorussia* 50 **D6** 54 45N 29 43 E
Sennori, *Italy* 40 **B1** 40 49N 8 36 E
Seno, *Laos* 76 **D5** 16 35N 104 50 E
Senonches, *France* 22 **D8** 48 34N 1 2 E
Senorbì, *Italy* 40 **C2** 39 33N 9 8 E
Senožeče, *Slovenia* 39 **C11** 45 43N 14 3 E
Sens, *France* 23 **D10** 48 11N 3 15 E
Senta, *Serbia, Yug.* 42 **B5** 45 55N 20 3 E
Sentery, *Zaïre* 103 **D5** 5 17 S 25 42 E
Sentinel, *U.S.A.* 143 **K7** 32 45N 113 13W
Sentolo, *Indonesia* 75 **D4** 7 55 S 110 13 E
Senya Beraku, *Ghana* 101 **D4** 5 28N 0 31W
Senye, *Eq. Guin.* 102 **B1** 1 34N 9 50 E
Seo de Urgel, *Spain* 34 **C6** 42 22N 1 23 E
Seohara, *India* 81 **E8** 29 15N 78 33 E
Seoni, *India* 81 **H8** 22 5N 79 30 E
Seoriuarayan, *India* 82 **D6** 21 45N 82 34 E
Seoul = Sŏul, *S. Korea* 67 **F14** 37 31N 126 58 E
Separation Point, *Canada* 129 **B8** 53 37N 57 25W
Separation Pt., *N.Z.* 119 **A7** 40 47 S 172 59 E
Sepīdān, *Iran* 85 **D7** 30 20N 52 5 E
Sepik →, *Papua N. G.* 120 **B3** 3 49 S 144 30 E
Sepo-ri, *N. Korea* 67 **E14** 38 57N 127 25 E
Sępólno Krajeńskie, *Poland* 47 **B4** 53 26N 17 30 E
Sepone, *Laos* 76 **D6** 16 45N 106 13 E
Sepopol, *Poland* 47 **A8** 54 16N 21 2 E
Sept-Îles, *Canada* 129 **B6** 50 13N 66 22W
Septemvri, *Bulgaria* 43 **E9** 42 13N 24 6 E
Sepúlveda, *Spain* 36 **D7** 41 18N 3 45W
Sequeros, *Spain* 36 **E4** 40 31N 6 2W
Sequim, *U.S.A.* 144 **B3** 48 3N 123 9W
Sequoia Nat. Park, *U.S.A.* 144 **J8** 36 30N 118 30W
Serafimovich, *Russia* 53 **B10** 49 36N 42 43 E
Seraing, *Belgium* 21 **G7** 50 35N 5 32 E
Seraja, *Indonesia* 77 **L7** 2 41N 108 35 E
Serakhis →, *Cyprus* 32 **D11** 35 13N 32 55 E
Seram, *Indonesia* 73 **B3** 3 10 S 129 0 E
Seram Laut, Kepulauan, *Indonesia* 73 **B4** 4 5 S 131 25 E
Seram Sea, *Indonesia* 72 **B3** 2 30 S 128 30 E
Serang, *Indonesia* 74 **D3** 6 8 S 106 10 E
Serasan, *Indonesia* 75 **B3** 2 29N 109 4 E
Seravezza, *Italy* 38 **E7** 43 59N 10 13 E
Serbia □, *Serbia, Yug.* 42 **D5** 43 30N 21 0 E
Sercaia, *Romania* 46 **D6** 45 49N 25 9 E
Serdo, *Ethiopia* 95 **E5** 11 56N 41 14 E
Serdobsk, *Russia* 51 **E14** 52 28N 44 10 E

Şimleu-Silvaniei 265

Shibām, Yemen 87 D5 16 0N 48 36 E
Shibata, Japan 60 F9 37 57N 139 20 E
Shibecha, Japan 60 C12 43 17N 144 36 E
Shibetsu, Japan 60 B11 44 10N 142 23 E
Shibîn el Kôm, Egypt 94 H7 30 31N 30 55 E
Shibîn el Qanâtir, Egypt 94 H7 30 19N 31 19 E
Shibing, China 68 D7 27 2N 108 7 E
Shibogama L., Canada 128 B2 53 35N 88 15W
Shibukawa, Japan 63 A10 36 29N 139 0 E
Shibushi, Japan 62 F3 31 25N 131 8 E
Shibushi-Wan, Japan 62 F3 31 24N 131 8 E
Shicheng, China 69 D11 26 22N 116 20 E
Shidād, Si. Arabia 86 B3 21 19N 40 3 E
Shidao, China 67 F12 36 50N 122 25 E
Shidian, China 68 E2 24 40N 99 5 E
Shido, Japan 62 C6 34 19N 134 10 E
Shiel, L., U.K. 18 E3 56 48N 5 32W
Shield, C., Australia 114 A2 13 20 S 136 20 E
Shiga □, Japan 63 B8 35 20N 136 0 E
Shigaib, Sudan 97 E4 15 5N 23 35 E
Shigaraki, Japan 63 C8 34 57N 136 2 E
Shigu, China 68 D2 26 51N 99 56 E
Shiguaigou, China 66 D6 40 52N 110 15 E
Shihan, W. →, Yemen 87 C5 17 24N 51 26 E
Shihchiachuangi = Shijiazhuang, China 66 E8 38 2N 114 28 E
Shiiba, Japan 62 E3 32 29N 131 4 E
Shijaku, Albania 44 C1 41 21N 19 33 E
Shijiazhuang, China 66 E8 38 2N 114 28 E
Shijiu Hu, China 69 B12 31 25N 118 50 E
Shikarpur, India 80 E8 28 17N 78 7 E
Shikarpur, Pakistan 79 D3 27 57N 68 39 E
Shikine-Jima, Japan 63 C11 34 19N 139 13 E
Shikoku, Japan 62 D5 33 30N 133 30 E
Shikoku □, Japan 62 D5 33 30N 133 30 E
Shikoku-Sanchi, Japan 62 D5 33 30N 133 30 E
Shilabo, Ethiopia 90 F3 6 22N 44 32 E
Shilda, Russia 54 F6 51 49N 59 47 E
Shiliguri, India 78 B2 26 45N 88 25 E
Shilka, Russia 57 D12 52 0N 115 55 E
Shilka →, Russia 57 D13 53 20N 121 26 E
Shillelagh, Ireland 19 D5 52 46N 6 32W
Shillong, India 78 C3 25 35N 91 53 E
Shilo, Jordan 91 C4 32 4N 35 18 E
Shilong, China 69 F9 23 5N 113 52 E
Shilou, China 66 F6 37 0N 110 48 E
Shilovo, Russia 51 D12 54 25N 40 57 E
Shima-Hantō, Japan 63 C8 34 22N 136 45 E
Shimabara, Japan 62 E2 32 48N 130 20 E
Shimada, Japan 63 C10 34 49N 138 10 E
Shimane □, Japan 62 C4 35 0N 132 30 E
Shimane-Hantō, Japan 62 B5 35 30N 133 0 E
Shimanovsk, Russia 57 D13 52 15N 127 30 E
Shimen, China 69 C8 29 35N 111 20 E
Shimenjie, China 69 C11 29 29N 116 48 E
Shimian, China 68 C4 29 17N 102 23 E
Shimizu, Japan 63 C10 35 0N 138 30 E
Shimo-Jima, Japan 62 E2 32 15N 130 7 E
Shimo-Koshiki-Jima, Japan 62 F1 31 40N 129 43 E
Shimoda, Japan 63 C10 34 40N 138 57 E
Shimodate, Japan 63 A11 36 20N 139 55 E
Shimoga, India 83 H2 13 57N 75 32 E
Shimoni, Kenya 106 C4 4 38 S 39 20 E
Shimonita, Japan 63 A10 36 13N 138 47 E
Shimonoseki, Japan 62 D2 33 58N 130 55 E
Shimotsuma, Japan 63 A11 36 11N 139 58 E
Shimpuru Rapids, Angola 103 F3 17 45 S 19 55 E
Shimsha →, India 83 H3 13 15N 77 10 E
Shimsk, Russia 50 B7 58 15N 30 50 E
Shin, L., U.K. 18 C4 58 7N 4 30W
Shin-Tone →, Japan 63 B12 35 44N 140 51 E
Shinan, China 68 F7 22 44N 109 53 E
Shinano →, Japan 61 F9 36 50N 138 30 E
Shīndand, Afghan. 79 B1 33 12N 62 8 E
Shingbwiyang, Burma 78 B6 26 41N 96 13 E
Shingleton, U.S.A. 128 C2 46 25N 86 33W
Shingū, Japan 63 D7 33 40N 135 55 E
Shinji, Japan 62 B4 35 24N 132 54 E
Shinji Ko, Japan 62 B4 35 26N 132 57 E
Shinjō, Japan 60 E10 38 46N 140 18 E
Shinkafe, Nigeria 101 C6 13 8N 6 29 E
Shīnkay, Afghan. 79 C2 31 57N 67 26 E
Shinminato, Japan 63 A9 36 47N 137 4 E
Shinonoi, Japan 63 A10 36 35N 138 9 E
Shinshār, Syria 91 A5 34 36N 36 43 E
Shinshiro, Japan 63 C9 34 54N 137 30 E
Shinyanga, Tanzania 106 C3 3 45 S 33 27 E
Shinyanga □, Tanzania 106 C3 3 50 S 34 0 E
Shio-no-Misaki, Japan 63 D7 33 25N 135 45 E
Shiogama, Japan 60 E10 38 19N 141 1 E
Shiojiri, Japan 63 A9 36 6N 137 58 E
Ship I., U.S.A. 139 K10 30 16N 88 55W
Shipehenski Prokhod, Bulgaria 43 E10 42 45N 25 15 E
Shiping, China 68 F4 23 45N 102 23 E
Shippegan, Canada 129 C7 47 45N 64 45W
Shippensburg, U.S.A. 136 F7 40 4N 77 32W
Shiprock, U.S.A. 143 H9 36 51N 108 45W
Shiqian, China 68 D7 27 32N 108 13 E
Shiqma, N. →, Israel 91 D3 31 37N 34 30 E
Shiquan, China 66 H5 33 5N 108 15 E
Shīr Kūh, Iran 85 D7 31 39N 54 3 E
Shirabad, Uzbekistan 55 E3 37 40N 67 1 E
Shiragami-Misaki, Japan 60 D10 41 24N 140 12 E
Shirahama, Japan 63 D7 33 41N 135 20 E
Shirakawa, Fukushima, Japan 61 F10 37 7N 140 13 E
Shirakawa, Gifu, Japan 63 A8 36 17N 136 56 E
Shirane-San, Gumma, Japan 63 A11 36 48N 139 22 E
Shirane-San, Yamanashi, Japan 63 B10 35 42N 138 9 E
Shiraoi, Japan 60 C10 42 33N 141 21 E
Shīrāz, Iran 85 D7 29 42N 52 30 E
Shirbin, Egypt 94 H7 31 11N 31 32 E
Shire →, Africa 107 F4 17 42 S 35 19 E
Shiretoko-Misaki, Japan 60 B12 44 21N 145 20 E
Shirinab →, Pakistan 80 D2 30 15N 66 28 E
Shiringushi, Russia 51 E13 53 51N 42 46 E
Shiriya-Zaki, Japan 60 D10 41 25N 141 30 E
Shirley, U.S.A. 141 E11 39 53N 85 35W
Shiroishi, Japan 60 E10 38 0N 140 37 E
Shirol, India 82 F2 16 47N 74 41 E
Shirpur, India 82 D2 21 21N 74 57 E
Shīrvān, Iran 85 B8 37 30N 57 50 E
Shirwa, L. = Chilwa, L., Malawi 107 F4 15 15 S 35 40 E
Shishmanova, Bulgaria 43 E8 42 58N 23 12 E
Shishou, China 69 C9 29 38N 112 22 E
Shitai, China 69 B11 30 12N 117 25 E
Shively, U.S.A. 141 F11 38 12N 85 49W
Shivpuri, India 80 G7 25 26N 77 42 E
Shixian, China 67 C15 43 5N 129 50 E
Shixing, China 69 E10 24 46N 114 5 E
Shiyan, China 69 A8 32 35N 110 45 E
Shiyata, Egypt 94 B2 29 25N 25 7 E
Shizhu, China 68 C7 29 58N 108 7 E
Shizong, China 68 E5 24 50N 104 0 E
Shizuishan, China 66 E4 39 15N 106 50 E
Shizuoka, Japan 63 C10 34 57N 138 24 E
Shizuoka □, Japan 63 B10 35 15N 138 40 E
Shklov, Belorussia 50 D7 54 16N 30 15 E
Shkoder = Shkodra, Albania 44 B1 42 6N 19 20 E
Shkodra, Albania 44 B1 42 6N 19 20 E
Shkodra □, Albania 44 B1 42 25N 19 20 E
Shkumbini →, Albania 44 C1 41 5N 19 50 E
Shmidta, O., Russia 57 A10 81 0N 91 0 E
Shō-Gawa →, Japan 63 A9 36 47N 137 4 E
Shoal Cr. →, U.S.A. 140 E3 39 39N 93 35W
Shoal Lake, Canada 131 C8 50 30N 100 35W
Shoals, U.S.A. 141 F10 38 40N 86 47W
Shōbara, Japan 62 C5 34 51N 133 1 E
Shōdo-Shima, Japan 62 C6 34 30N 134 15 E
Shoeburyness, U.K. 17 F8 51 31N 0 49 E
Shokpar, Kazakhstan 55 B7 43 49N 74 21 E
Sholapur = Solapur, India 82 F2 17 43N 75 56 E
Shologontsy, Russia 57 C12 66 13N 114 0 E
Shōmrōn, Jordan 91 C4 32 15N 35 13 E
Shoranur, India 83 J3 10 46N 76 19 E
Shorapur, India 83 F3 16 31N 76 48 E
Shortland I., Solomon Is. 121 L8 7 0 S 155 45 E
Shoshone, Calif., U.S.A. 145 K10 35 58N 116 16W
Shoshone, Idaho, U.S.A. 142 E6 43 0N 114 27W
Shoshone L., U.S.A. 142 D8 44 30N 110 40W
Shoshone Mts., U.S.A. 142 G5 39 30N 117 30W
Shoshong, Botswana 104 C4 22 56 S 26 31 E
Shoshoni, U.S.A. 142 E9 43 13N 108 5W
Shostka, Ukraine 50 F8 51 57N 33 32 E
Shou Xian, China 69 A11 32 37N 116 42 E
Shouchang, China 69 C12 29 18N 119 12 E
Shouguang, China 67 F10 37 52N 118 45 E
Shouning, China 69 D12 27 27N 119 31 E
Shouyang, China 66 F7 37 54N 113 8 E
Show Low, U.S.A. 143 J9 34 16N 110 0W
Shpola, Ukraine 52 B4 49 1N 31 30 E
Shreveport, U.S.A. 139 J8 32 30N 93 50W
Shrewsbury, U.K. 16 E5 52 42N 2 45W
Shrirampur, India 81 H13 22 44N 88 21 E
Shrirangapattana, India 83 H3 12 26N 76 43 E
Shropshire □, U.K. 17 E5 52 36N 2 45W
Shuangbai, China 68 E3 24 42N 101 38 E
Shuangcheng, China 67 B14 45 20N 126 15 E
Shuangfeng, China 69 D9 27 29N 112 11 E
Shuanggou, China 67 G9 34 2N 117 30 E
Shuangjiang, China 68 F2 23 26N 99 58 E
Shuangliao, China 67 C12 43 29N 123 30 E
Shuangshanzi, China 67 D10 40 20N 119 8 E
Shuangyang, China 67 C13 43 28N 125 40 E
Shuangyashan, China 65 B8 46 28N 131 5 E
Shu'b, Ra's, Yemen 87 D6 12 30N 53 25 E
Shucheng, China 69 B11 31 28N 116 57 E
Shuguri Falls, Tanzania 107 D4 8 33 S 37 22 E
Shuḥayr, Yemen 87 D5 14 41N 49 23 E
Shuicheng, China 68 D5 26 38N 104 48 E
Shuiji, China 69 D12 27 13N 118 20 E
Shuiye, China 66 F8 36 7N 114 8 E
Shujalpur, India 80 H7 23 18N 76 46 E
Shukpa Kunzang, India 81 B8 34 22N 78 22 E
Shulan, China 67 B14 44 28N 127 0 E
Shule, China 64 C2 39 25N 76 3 E
Shullsburg, U.S.A. 140 B6 42 35N 90 15W
Shumagin Is., U.S.A. 126 C4 55 0N 159 0W
Shumerlya, Russia 51 D15 55 30N 46 25 E
Shumikha, Russia 54 D8 55 10N 63 15 E
Shunchang, China 69 D11 26 54N 117 48 E
Shunde, China 69 F9 22 42N 113 14 E
Shungay, Kazakhstan 53 B12 48 30N 46 45 E
Shungnak, U.S.A. 126 B4 66 55N 157 10W
Shuo Xian, China 66 E7 39 20N 112 33 E
Shūr →, Iran 85 D7 28 30N 55 0 E
Shūr Āb, Iran 85 C6 34 23N 51 11 E
Shūr Gaz, Iran 85 D8 29 10N 59 20 E
Shūrāb, Iran 85 C8 33 43N 56 29 E
Shurab, Tajikistan 55 C5 40 3N 70 33 E
Shurchi, Uzbekistan 55 E3 37 59N 67 47 E
Shūrjestān, Iran 85 D7 31 24N 52 25 E
Shurkhua, Burma 78 D4 22 15N 93 38 E
Shurma, Russia 54 C2 56 58N 50 21 E
Shurugwi, Zimbabwe 107 F3 19 40 S 30 0 E
Shūsf, Iran 85 D9 31 50N 60 5 E
Shūshtar, Iran 85 D6 32 0N 48 50 E
Shuswap L., Canada 130 C5 50 55N 119 3W
Shuya, Russia 51 C12 56 50N 41 28 E
Shuyang, China 67 G10 34 10N 118 42 E
Shuzenji, Japan 63 C10 34 58N 138 56 E
Shūzū, Iran 85 D7 29 52N 54 30 E
Shwebo, Burma 78 D5 22 30N 95 45 E
Shwegu, Burma 78 C6 24 15N 96 26 E
Shwegun, Burma 78 G6 17 9N 97 39 E
Shwenyaung, Burma 78 E6 20 46N 96 57 E
Shyok, India 81 B8 34 15N 78 12 E
Shyok →, Pakistan 81 B6 35 13N 75 53 E
Si Chon, Thailand 77 H2 9 0N 99 54 E
Si Kiang = Xi Jiang →, China 69 F9 22 5N 113 20 E
Si Prachan, Thailand 76 E3 14 37N 100 9 E
Si Racha, Thailand 76 F3 13 10N 100 48 E
Si Xian, China 67 H9 33 30N 117 50 E
Siahan Range, Pakistan 79 D2 27 30N 64 40 E
Siak →, Indonesia 74 B2 1 13N 102 9 E
Siaksrindrapura, Indonesia 74 B2 0 51N 102 0 E
Sialkot, Pakistan 79 B4 32 32N 74 30 E
Sialsuk, India 78 D4 23 24N 92 45 E
Siam = Thailand ■, Asia 76 E4 16 0N 102 0 E
Siam, Australia 116 B2 32 35 S 136 41 E
Sian = Xi'an, China 66 G5 34 15N 109 0 E
Siantan, P., Indonesia 77 L6 3 10N 106 15 E
Siàpo →, Venezuela 152 C4 2 7N 66 28W
Sīāreh, Iran 85 D9 28 5N 60 14 E
Siargao, Phil. 71 G6 9 52N 126 3 E
Siari, Pakistan 81 B7 34 55N 76 40 E
Siari, Phil. 71 G4 8 19N 122 58 E
Siasi I., Phil. 71 J3 5 33N 120 51 E
Siassi, Papua N. G. 120 C4 5 40 S 147 51 E
Siátista, Greece 44 D3 40 15N 21 33 E
Siaton, Phil. 71 G4 9 4N 123 2 E
Siau, Indonesia 72 A3 2 50N 125 25 E
Šiauliai, Lithuania 50 D3 55 56N 23 15 E
Siaya □, Kenya 106 B3 0 0 34 20 E
Siazan, Azerbaijan 53 F13 41 3N 49 10 E
Sibâi, Gebel el, Egypt 94 B3 25 45N 34 10 E
Sibang, Gabon 102 B1 0 25N 9 31 E
Sibari, Italy 41 C9 39 47N 16 27 E
Sibasa, S. Africa 105 C5 22 53 S 30 33 E
Sibay, Russia 54 E6 52 42N 58 39 E
Sibay I., Phil. 71 F3 11 51N 121 29 E
Sibayi, L., S. Africa 105 D5 27 20 S 32 45 E
Šibenik, Croatia 39 E12 43 48N 15 54 E
Siberia, Russia 58 D14 60 0N 100 0 E
Siberut, Indonesia 74 C1 1 30 S 99 0 E
Sibi, Pakistan 79 C2 29 30N 67 54 E
Sibil, Indonesia 73 B6 4 59 S 140 35 E
Sibiti, Congo 102 C2 3 38 S 13 19 E
Sibiu, Romania 46 D5 45 45N 24 9 E
Sibiu □, Romania 46 D5 45 50N 24 15 E
Sibley, Ill., U.S.A. 141 D8 40 35N 88 23W
Sibley, Iowa, U.S.A. 138 D7 43 21N 95 43W
Sibley, La., U.S.A. 139 J8 32 34N 93 16W
Sibolga, Indonesia 74 B1 1 42N 98 45 E
Sibret, Belgium 21 J7 49 58N 5 38 E
Sibsagar, India 78 B5 27 0N 94 36 E
Sibu, Malaysia 75 B4 2 18N 111 49 E
Sibuco, Phil. 71 H4 7 20N 122 10 E
Sibuguey B., Phil. 71 H4 7 50N 122 45 E
Sibutu, Phil. 71 J2 4 45N 119 30 E
Sibutu Group, Phil. 71 J2 4 45N 119 20 E
Sibutu Passage, E. Indies 71 J2 4 50N 120 0 E
Sibuyan, Phil. 70 E4 12 25N 122 40 E
Sibuyan Sea, Phil. 70 E4 12 30N 122 20 E
Sicamous, Canada 130 C5 50 49N 119 0W
Sicapoo, Mt., Phil. 70 B3 18 1N 120 56 E
Sichuan □, China 68 B5 31 0N 104 0 E
Sicilia, Italy 41 E7 37 30N 14 30 E
Sicilia □, Italy 41 E7 37 30N 14 30 E
Sicilia, Canale di, Italy 40 E5 37 25N 12 30 E
Sicilian Channel = Sicilia, Canale di, Italy 40 E5 37 25N 12 30 E
Sicily = Sicilia, Italy 41 E7 37 30N 14 30 E
Sicuani, Peru 156 C3 14 21 S 71 10W
Siculiana, Italy 40 E6 37 20N 13 23 E
Šid, Serbia, Yug. 42 B4 45 8N 19 14 E
Sidamo □, Ethiopia 95 G4 5 0N 37 50 E
Sidaouet, Niger 97 E1 18 34N 8 3 E
Sidári, Greece 32 A3 39 47N 19 41 E
Siddeburen, Neths. 20 B9 53 15N 6 52 E
Siddhapur, India 80 H5 23 56N 72 25 E
Siddipet, India 82 E4 18 5N 78 51 E
Side, Turkey 88 E4 36 45N 31 23 E
Sidell, U.S.A. 141 E9 39 55N 87 49W
Sidéradougou, Burkina Faso 100 C4 10 42N 4 12W
Siderno Marina, Italy 41 D9 38 16N 16 17 E
Sídheros, Ákra, Greece 32 D8 35 19N 26 19 E
Sidhirókastron, Greece 44 C5 41 13N 23 24 E
Sîdi Abd el Rahmân, Egypt 94 H6 30 55N 29 44 E
Sîdi Barrâni, Egypt 94 A2 31 38N 25 58 E
Sidi-bel-Abbès, Algeria 99 A4 35 13N 0 39W
Sidi Bennour, Morocco 98 B3 32 40N 8 25W
Sidi Haneish, Egypt 94 A2 31 10N 27 35 E
Sidi Kacem, Morocco 98 B3 34 11N 5 49W
Sidi Omar, Egypt 94 A1 31 24N 24 57 E
Sidi Slimane, Morocco 98 B3 34 16N 5 56W
Sidi Smaïl, Morocco 98 B3 32 50N 8 31W
Sidi 'Uzayz, Libya 96 B4 31 41N 24 55 E
Sidlaw Hills, U.K. 18 E5 56 32N 3 10W
Sidley, Mt., Antarctica 7 D14 77 2 S 126 2W
Sidmouth, U.K. 17 G4 50 40N 3 13W
Sidmouth, C., Australia 114 A3 13 25 S 143 36 E
Sidney, Canada 130 D4 48 39N 123 24W
Sidney, Mont., U.S.A. 138 B2 47 42N 104 7W
Sidney, N.Y., U.S.A. 137 D9 42 18N 75 20W
Sidney, Nebr., U.S.A. 138 E3 41 12N 103 0W
Sidney, Ohio, U.S.A. 141 D12 40 18N 84 6W
Sidoarjo, Indonesia 75 D4 7 27 S 112 43 E
Sidoktaya, Burma 78 E5 20 27N 94 15 E
Sidon = Saydā, Lebanon 91 B4 33 35N 35 25 E
Sidra, G. of = Surt, Khalīj, Libya 96 B3 31 40N 18 30 E
Siedlce, Poland 47 C9 52 10N 22 20 E
Siedlce □, Poland 47 C9 52 0N 22 0 E
Sieg →, Germany 26 E3 50 46N 7 7 E
Siegburg, Germany 26 E3 50 48N 7 12 E
Siegen, Germany 26 E4 50 52N 8 2 E
Siem Pang, Cambodia 76 E6 14 7N 106 23 E
Siem Reap, Cambodia 76 F4 13 20N 103 52 E
Siena, Italy 39 E8 43 20N 11 20 E
Sieniawa, Poland 31 A15 50 11N 22 38 E
Sieradź, Poland 47 D5 51 37N 18 41 E
Sieraków, Poland 47 C3 52 39N 16 2 E
Sierck-les-Bains, France 23 C13 49 26N 6 20 E
Sierpc, Poland 47 C6 52 55N 19 43 E
Sierpe, Bocas de la, Venezuela 153 B5 10 0N 61 30W
Sierra Blanca, U.S.A. 143 L11 31 11N 105 17W
Sierra Blanca Pk., U.S.A. 143 K11 33 20N 105 54W
Sierra City, U.S.A. 144 F6 39 34N 120 42W
Sierra Colorada, Argentina 160 B3 40 35 S 67 50W
Sierra de Yeguas, Spain 37 H6 37 7N 4 52W
Sierra Gorda, Chile 158 A2 22 50 S 69 15W
Sierra Grande, Argentina 160 B3 41 36 S 65 22W
Sierra Leone ■, W. Afr. 100 D2 9 0N 12 0W
Sierra Madre, Mexico 147 D6 16 0N 93 0W
Sierra Mojada, Mexico 146 B4 27 19N 103 42W
Sierraville, U.S.A. 144 F6 39 36N 120 22W
Sierre, Switz. 28 D5 46 17N 7 31 E
Sif Fatima, Algeria 99 B6 31 6N 8 41 E
Sífnos, Greece 45 H6 37 0N 24 45 E
Sifton, Canada 131 C8 51 21N 100 8W
Sifton Pass, Canada 130 B3 57 52N 126 15W
Sig, Algeria 99 A4 35 32N 0 12W
Sigaboy, Phil. 71 H6 6 39N 126 5 E
Sigdal, Norway 14 D3 60 4N 9 38 E
Sigean, France 24 E6 43 2N 2 58 E
Sighetu-Marmatiei, Romania 46 B4 47 57N 23 52 E
Sighişoara, Romania 46 C5 46 12N 24 50 E
Sigira, Yemen 87 D6 12 37N 54 20 E
Sigli, Indonesia 74 A1 5 25N 96 0 E
Siglufjörður, Iceland 12 C4 66 12N 18 55W
Sigmaringen, Germany 27 G5 48 5N 9 13 E
Signakhi, Georgia 53 F11 41 40N 45 57 E
Signal, U.S.A. 145 L13 34 30N 113 38W
Signal Pk., U.S.A. 145 M12 33 25N 114 4W
Signau, Switz. 28 C5 46 56N 7 45 E
Signy-l'Abbaye, France 23 C11 49 40N 4 25 E
Sigourney, U.S.A. 140 C4 41 20N 92 12W
Sigsig, Ecuador 152 D2 3 0 S 78 50W
Sigtuna, Sweden 14 E11 59 36N 17 44 E
Sigüenza, Spain 34 D2 41 3N 2 40W
Siguiri, Guinea 100 C3 11 31N 9 10W
Sigulda, Latvia 50 C4 57 10N 24 55 E
Sigurd, U.S.A. 143 G8 38 49N 112 0W
Sihanoukville = Kompong Som, Cambodia 77 G4 10 38N 103 30 E
Sihaus, Peru 156 B2 8 40 S 77 40W
Sihui, China 69 F9 23 20N 112 40 E
Siirt, Turkey 89 E9 37 57N 41 55 E
Siirt □, Turkey 89 E9 37 55N 41 55 E
Siit, Phil. 71 J5 5 59N 124 13 E
Sijarira Ra., Zimbabwe 107 F2 17 36 S 27 45 E
Sijungjung, Indonesia 74 C2 0 42 S 100 58 E
Sikao, Thailand 77 J2 7 34N 99 21 E
Sikar, India 80 F6 27 33N 75 10 E
Sikasso, Mali 100 C3 11 18N 5 35W
Sikeston, U.S.A. 139 G10 36 52N 89 35W
Sikhote Alin, Khrebet, Russia 57 E14 45 0N 136 0 E
Sikiá., Greece 44 D5 40 2N 23 56 E
Síkinos, Greece 45 H7 36 40N 25 8 E
Sikkani Chief →, Canada 130 B4 57 47N 122 15W
Sikkim □, India 78 B2 27 50N 88 30 E
Siklós, Hungary 31 F11 45 50N 18 19 E
Sikotu-Ko, Japan 60 C10 42 45N 141 25 E
Sil →, Spain 36 C3 42 27N 7 43W
Silacayoapan, Mexico 147 D5 17 30N 98 9W
Silandro, Italy 38 B7 46 38N 10 48 E
Silanga, Phil. 71 F2 11 1N 119 34 E
Silay, Phil. 71 F4 10 47N 123 14 E
Silba, Croatia 39 D11 44 24N 14 41 E
Silchar, India 78 C4 24 49N 92 48 E
Silcox, Canada 131 B10 57 12N 94 10W
Şile, Turkey 88 C3 41 10N 29 37 E
Silenrieux, Belgium 21 H4 50 14N 4 27 E
Siler City, U.S.A. 135 H6 35 44N 79 30W
Sileru →, India 82 F5 17 49N 81 24 E
Silet, Algeria 99 D5 22 44N 4 37 E
Silgarhi Doti, Nepal 81 E9 29 15N 81 0 E
Silghat, India 78 B4 26 35N 93 0 E
Silifke, Turkey 88 E5 36 22N 33 58 E
Siling Co, China 64 C3 31 50N 89 20 E
Silíqua, Italy 40 C1 39 20N 8 49 E
Silistra, Bulgaria 43 C12 44 6N 27 19 E
Silivri, Turkey 88 C3 41 4N 28 14 E
Siljan, Sweden 13 F13 60 55N 14 45 E
Silkeborg, Denmark 15 H3 56 10N 9 32 E
Sillajhuay, Cordillera, Chile 156 D4 19 46 S 68 40W
Sillé-le-Guillaume, France 22 D6 48 10N 0 8W
Sillustani, Peru 156 D3 15 50 S 70 7W
Siloam Springs, U.S.A. 139 G7 36 15N 94 31W
Silopi, Turkey 89 E10 37 15N 42 27 E
Silsbee, U.S.A. 139 K7 30 20N 94 8W
Silute, Lithuania 50 D2 55 21N 21 33 E
Silva Porto = Kuito, Angola 103 E3 12 22 S 16 55 E
Silvan, Turkey 89 D9 38 7N 41 2 E
Silvaplana, Switz. 29 D9 46 28N 9 48 E
Silver City, N. Mex., U.S.A. 143 K9 32 50N 108 18W
Silver City, Nev., U.S.A. 142 G4 39 15N 119 48W
Silver Cr. →, U.S.A. 142 E4 43 16N 119 13W
Silver Creek, U.S.A. 136 D5 42 33N 79 9W
Silver Grove, U.S.A. 141 E12 39 2N 84 24W
Silver L., U.S.A. 144 G6 38 39N 120 6W
Silver Lake, Calif., U.S.A. 145 K10 35 21N 116 7W
Silver Lake, Ind., U.S.A. 141 C11 41 4N 85 53W
Silver Lake, Oreg., U.S.A. 142 E3 43 9N 121 4W
Silver Lake, Wis., U.S.A. 141 B8 42 33N 88 13W
Silver Streams, S. Africa 104 D3 28 20 S 23 33 E
Silverton, Australia 116 A4 31 52 S 141 10 E
Silverton, Colo., U.S.A. 143 H10 37 51N 107 45W
Silverton, Tex., U.S.A. 139 H4 34 30N 101 16W
Silves, Portugal 37 H2 37 11N 8 26W
Silvi, Italy 39 F11 42 32N 14 5 E
Silvia, Colombia 152 C2 2 37N 76 21W
Silvies →, U.S.A. 142 E4 43 22N 118 48W
Silvolde, Neths. 20 E8 51 55N 6 23 E
Silvretta-Gruppe, Switz. 29 C10 46 50N 10 6 E
Silwa Bahari, Egypt 94 C3 24 45N 32 55 E
Silz, Austria 30 D3 47 16N 10 56 E
Sim, C., Morocco 98 B3 31 26N 9 51W
Simanggang, Malaysia 75 B4 1 15N 111 32 E
Simao, China 68 F3 22 47N 101 5 E
Simão Dias, Brazil 154 D4 10 44 S 37 49W
Simara I., Phil. 70 E4 12 48N 122 3 E
Simard, L., Canada 128 C4 47 40N 78 40W
Simărtin, Romania 46 C6 46 19N 25 58 E
Simav, Turkey 88 D3 39 4N 28 58 E
Simba, Tanzania 106 C4 2 10 S 37 36 E
Simbach, Germany 27 G9 48 16N 13 3 E
Simbirsk, Russia 51 D16 54 20N 48 25 E
Simbo, Tanzania 106 C2 4 51 S 29 41 E
Simcoe, Canada 128 D3 42 50N 80 20W
Simcoe, L., Canada 128 D4 44 25N 79 20W
Simenga, Russia 57 C11 62 42N 108 25 E
Simeto →, Italy 41 E8 37 25N 15 10 E
Simeulue, Indonesia 74 B1 2 45N 95 45 E
Simferopol, Ukraine 52 D6 44 55N 34 3 E
Sími, Greece 45 H9 36 35N 27 50 E
Simi Valley, U.S.A. 145 L8 34 16N 118 47W
Simikot, Nepal 81 E9 30 0N 81 50 E
Simití, Colombia 152 B3 7 58N 73 57W
Simitli, Bulgaria 42 F8 41 52N 23 7 E
Simla, India 80 D7 31 2N 77 9 E
Şimleu-Silvaniei, Romania 46 B3 47 17N 22 50 E

266 Simme


Simme →, Switz. 28 C4 46 38N 7 25 E
Simmern, Germany 27 F3 49 59N 7 32 E
Simmie, Canada 131 D7 49 56N 108 6W
Simmler, U.S.A. 145 K7 35 21N 119 59W
Simões, Brazil 154 C3 7 36 S 40 49W
Simojärvi, Finland 12 C19 66 5N 27 3 E
Simojoki →, Finland 12 D18 65 35N 25 1 E
Simojovel, Mexico 147 D6 17 12N 92 38W
Simonette →, Canada 130 B5 55 9N 118 15W
Simonstown, S. Africa 104 E2 34 14 S 18 26 E
Simontornya, Hungary 31 E11 46 45N 18 33 E
Simpangkiri →, Indonesia 74 B1 2 50N 97 40 E
Simplício Mendes, Brazil 154 C3 7 51 S 41 54W
Simplon, Switz. 28 D6 46 12N 8 4 E
Simplon Pass = Simplonpass, Switz. 28 D6 46 15N 8 3 E
Simplon Tunnel, Switz. 28 D6 46 15N 8 7 E
Simplonpass, Switz. 28 D6 46 15N 8 3 E
Simpson Desert, Australia 114 D2 25 0 S 137 0 E
Simpungdong, N. Korea 67 D15 40 56N 129 29 E
Simunjan, Malaysia 75 B4 1 25N 110 45 E
Simushir, Ostrov, Russia 57 E16 46 50N 152 30 E
Sina →, India 82 F2 17 30N 75 55 E
Sinabang, Indonesia 74 B1 2 30N 96 24 E
Sinadogo, Somali Rep. 90 F4 5 50N 47 0 E
Sinai = Es Sînâ', Egypt 94 J8 29 0N 34 0 E
Sinai, Mt. = Mûsa, G., Egypt 94 J8 28 33N 33 59 E
Sinai Peninsula, Egypt 91 F2 29 30N 34 0 E
Sinaia, Romania 46 D6 45 21N 25 38 E
Sinait, Phil. 70 C3 17 52N 120 27 E
Sinako, Mt., Phil. 71 H5 7 30N 125 17 E
Sinaloa □, Mexico 146 C3 25 0N 107 30W
Sinaloa de Levya, Mexico 146 B3 25 50N 108 20W
Sinalunga, Italy 39 E8 43 12N 11 43 E
Sinan, China 68 D7 27 56N 108 13 E
Sînandrei, Romania 46 D2 45 52N 21 13 E
Sinarádhes, Greece 32 A3 39 34N 19 51 E
Sīnāwan, Libya 96 B2 31 0N 10 37 E
Sinbaungwe, Burma 78 F5 19 43N 95 10 E
Sinbo, Burma 78 C6 24 46N 97 3 E
Sincé, Colombia 152 B2 9 15N 75 9W
Sincelejo, Colombia 152 B2 9 18N 75 24W
Sinchang, N. Korea 67 D15 40 7N 128 28 E
Sinchang-ni, N. Korea 67 E14 39 24N 126 8 E
Sinclair, U.S.A. 142 F10 41 47N 107 10W
Sinclair Mills, Canada 130 C4 54 5N 121 40W
Sincorá, Serra do, Brazil 155 D3 13 30 S 41 0W
Sind, Pakistan 80 G3 26 0N 68 30 E
Sind □, Pakistan 79 D3 26 0N 69 0 E
Sind →, India 81 B6 34 18N 74 45 E
Sind Sagar Doab, Pakistan 80 D4 32 0N 71 30 E
Sindal, Denmark 15 G4 57 28N 10 10 E
Sindangan, Phil. 71 G4 8 10N 123 5 E
Sindangan Bay, Phil. 71 G4 8 11N 122 50 E
Sindangbarang, Indonesia 75 D3 7 27 S 107 1 E
Sinde, Zambia 107 F2 17 28 S 25 51 E
Sinegorski, Russia 53 C9 47 55N 40 52 E
Sinelnikovo, Ukraine 52 B6 48 25N 35 30 E
Sines, Portugal 37 H2 37 56N 8 51W
Sines, C. de, Portugal 37 H2 37 58N 8 53W
Sineu, Spain 33 B10 39 38N 3 1 E
Sinewit, Mt., Papua N. G. 120 C7 4 44 S 152 2 E
Sinfra, Ivory C. 100 D3 6 35N 5 56W
Sing Buri, Thailand 76 E3 14 53N 100 25 E
Singa, Sudan 95 E3 13 10N 33 57 E
Singanallur, India 83 J3 11 2N 77 1 E
Singapore ■, Asia 77 M4 1 17N 103 51 E
Singapore, Straits of, Asia 77 M5 1 15N 104 0 E
Singaraja, Indonesia 75 D5 8 6 S 115 10 E
Singen, Germany 27 H4 47 45N 8 50 E
Singida, Tanzania 106 C3 4 49 S 34 48 E
Singida □, Tanzania 106 D3 6 0 S 34 30 E
Singitikós Kólpos, Greece 44 D5 40 6N 24 0 E
Singkaling Hkamti, Burma 78 C5 26 0N 95 39 E
Singkawang, Indonesia 75 B3 1 0N 108 57 E
Singleton, Australia 117 B9 32 33 S 151 0 E
Singleton, Mt., N. Terr., Australia 112 D5 22 0 S 130 46 E
Singleton, Mt., W. Austral., Australia 113 E2 29 27 S 117 15 E
Singoli, India 80 G6 25 0N 75 22 E
Singora = Songkhla, Thailand 77 J3 7 13N 100 37 E
Singosan, N. Korea 67 E14 38 52N 127 25 E
Sinhung, N. Korea 67 D14 40 11N 127 34 E
Sînî □, Egypt 91 F2 30 0N 34 0 E
Siniátsikon, Óros, Greece 44 D3 40 25N 21 35 E
Siniloan, Phil. 70 D3 14 25N 121 27 E
Siniscóla, Italy 40 B2 40 35N 9 40 E
Sinj, Croatia 39 E13 43 42N 16 39 E
Sinjai, Indonesia 72 C2 5 7 S 120 20 E
Sinjajevina, Montenegro, Yug. 42 E4 42 57N 19 22 E
Sinjār, Iraq 84 B4 36 19N 41 52 E
Sinkat, Sudan 94 D4 18 55N 36 49 E
Sinkiang Uighur = Xinjiang Uygur Zizhiqu □, China 64 B3 42 0N 86 0 E
Sinmak, N. Korea 67 E14 38 25N 126 14 E
Sinnai, Italy 40 C2 39 18N 9 13 E
Sinnar, India 82 E2 19 48N 74 0 E
Sinni →, Italy 41 B9 40 9N 16 42 E
Sînnicolau Maré, Romania 42 A5 46 5N 20 39 E
Sinnuris, Egypt 94 J7 29 26N 30 31 E
Sinoe, L., Romania 46 E9 44 35N 28 50 E
Sinop, Turkey 52 E6 42 1N 35 11 E
Sinop □, Turkey 88 C6 42 0N 35 0 E
Sinpo, N. Korea 67 E15 40 0N 128 13 E
Sins, Switz. 29 B6 47 12N 8 24 E
Sinskoye, Russia 57 C13 61 8N 126 48 E
Sint-Amandsberg, Belgium 21 F3 51 4N 3 45 E
Sint Annaland, Neths. 21 E4 51 36N 4 6 E
Sint Annaparoch, Neths. 20 B7 53 16N 5 40 E
Sint-Denijs, Belgium 21 G2 50 45N 3 23 E
Sint Eustatius, I., Neth. Ant. 149 C7 17 30N 62 59W
Sint-Genesius-Rode, Belgium 21 G4 50 45N 4 22 E
Sint-Gillis-Waas, Belgium 21 F4 51 13N 4 6 E
Sint-Huibrechts-Lille, Belgium 21 F6 51 13N 5 29 E
Sint-Katelinje-Waver, Belgium 21 F5 51 5N 4 32 E
Sint-Kruis, Belgium 21 F2 51 13N 3 15 E
Sint-Laureins, Belgium 21 F3 51 14N 3 32 E
Sint Maarten, I., W. Indies 149 C7 18 4N 63 4W
Sint-Michiels, Belgium 21 F2 51 11N 3 15 E
Sint Nicolaasga, Neths. 20 C7 52 55N 5 45 E
Sint Niklaas, Belgium 21 F4 51 10N 4 9 E
Sint Oedenrode, Neths. 21 E6 51 35N 5 29 E
Sint Pancras, Neths. 20 C5 52 40N 4 48 E
Sint Philipsland, Neths. 21 E4 51 37N 4 10 E
Sint Truiden, Belgium 21 G6 50 48N 5 10 E
Sint Willebrord, Neths. 21 E5 51 33N 4 33 E
Sîntana, Romania 46 C2 46 20N 21 30 E
Sintang, Indonesia 75 B4 0 5N 111 35 E
Sintjohannesga, Neths. 20 C7 52 55N 5 52 E
Sinton, U.S.A. 139 L6 28 1N 97 30W
Sintra, Portugal 37 G1 38 47N 9 25W
Sinugif, Somali Rep. 108 C3 8 33N 48 59 E
Sinŭiju, N. Korea 67 D13 40 5N 124 24 E
Sinyukha →, Ukraine 52 B4 48 3N 30 51 E
Siocon, Phil. 71 H4 7 40N 122 10 E
Siófok, Hungary 31 E11 46 54N 18 3 E
Sioma, Zambia 104 B3 16 25 S 23 28 E
Sion, Switz. 28 D4 46 14N 7 20 E
Sioux City, U.S.A. 138 D6 42 32N 96 25W
Sioux Falls, U.S.A. 138 D6 43 35N 96 40W
Sioux Lookout, Canada 128 B1 50 10N 91 50W
Sip Song Chau Thai, Vietnam 76 B4 21 30N 103 30 E
Sipalay, Phil. 71 G4 9 45N 122 24 E
Šipan, Croatia 42 E2 42 45N 17 52 E
Sipang, Tanjong, Malaysia 75 B4 1 48N 110 20 E
Siping, China 67 C13 43 8N 124 21 E
Sipiwesk L., Canada 131 B9 55 5N 97 35W
Sipocot, Phil. 70 E4 13 46N 122 58 E
Sipora, Indonesia 74 C1 2 18 S 99 40 E
Siquia →, Nic. 148 D3 12 10N 84 20W
Siquijor, Phil. 71 G4 9 12N 123 35 E
Siquijor □, Phil. 71 G4 9 11N 123 35 E
Siquirres, Costa Rica 148 D3 10 6N 83 30W
Siquisique, Venezuela 152 A4 10 34N 69 42W
Sir Edward Pellew Group, Australia 114 B2 15 40 S 137 10 E
Sir Graham Moore Is., Australia 112 B4 13 53 S 126 34 E
Sira, India 83 H3 13 41N 76 49 E
Siracusa, Italy 41 E8 37 4N 15 17 E
Sirajganj, Bangla. 81 G13 24 25N 89 47 E
Sirakoro, Mali 100 C3 12 41N 9 14W
Şiran, Turkey 89 C8 40 11N 39 7 E
Sirasso, Ivory C. 100 D3 9 16N 6 6W
Siraway, Phil. 71 H4 7 34N 122 8 E
Sīrdān, Iran 85 B6 36 39N 49 12 E
Sirer, Spain 33 C7 38 56N 1 22 E
Siret, Romania 46 B7 47 55N 26 5 E
Siret →, Romania 46 D9 45 24N 28 1 E
Şiria, Romania 46 C2 46 16N 21 38 E
Sirik, Tanjong, Malaysia 75 B4 2 47N 111 15 E
Sirino, Monte, Italy 41 B8 40 7N 15 50 E
Sirkali = Sirkazhi, India 83 J4 11 15N 79 41 E
Sirkazhi, India 83 J4 11 15N 79 41 E
Sírna, Greece 45 H8 36 22N 26 42 E
Sirnach, Switz. 29 B7 47 28N 8 59 E
Şirnak, Turkey 89 E10 37 32N 42 28 E
Sirohi, India 80 G5 24 52N 72 53 E
Široki Brijeg, Bos.-H., Yug. 42 D2 43 21N 17 36 E
Sironj, India 80 G7 24 5N 77 39 E
Síros, Greece 45 G6 37 28N 24 57 E
Sirrayn, Si. Arabia 86 C3 19 38N 40 36 E
Sirretta Pk., U.S.A. 145 K8 35 56N 118 19W
Sirsa, India 80 E6 29 33N 75 4 E
Sirsi, India 83 G2 14 40N 74 49 E
Siruela, Spain 37 G5 38 58N 5 3W
Sisak, Croatia 39 C13 45 30N 16 21 E
Sisaket, Thailand 76 E5 15 8N 104 23 E
Sisante, Spain 35 F2 39 25N 2 12W
Sisargas, Is., Spain 36 B2 43 21N 8 50W
Sishen, S. Africa 104 D3 27 47 S 22 59 E
Sishui, Henan, China 66 G7 34 48N 113 15 E
Sishui, Shandong, China 67 G9 35 42N 117 18 E
Sisipuk L., Canada 131 B8 55 45N 101 50W
Sisophon, Cambodia 76 F4 13 38N 102 59 E
Sissach, Switz. 28 B5 47 27N 7 48 E
Sisseton, U.S.A. 138 C6 45 43N 97 3W
Sissonne, France 23 C10 49 34N 3 51 E
Sīstān va Balūchestān □, Iran 85 E9 27 0N 62 0 E
Sisteron, France 25 D9 44 12N 5 57 E
Sisters, U.S.A. 142 D3 44 21N 121 32W
Sitamarhi, India 81 F11 26 37N 85 30 E
Sitapur, India 81 F9 27 38N 80 45 E
Siteki, Swaziland 105 D5 26 32 S 31 58 E
Sitges, Spain 34 D6 41 17N 1 47 E
Sithoniá, Greece 44 D5 40 0N 23 45 E
Sitía, Greece 32 D8 35 13N 26 6 E
Sítio da Abadia, Brazil 155 D2 14 48 S 46 16W
Sitka, U.S.A. 126 C6 57 9N 135 20W
Sitoti, Botswana 104 C3 23 15 S 23 40 E
Sitra, Egypt 94 B2 28 40N 26 53 E
Sittang Myit →, Burma 78 G6 17 20N 96 45 E
Sittard, Neths. 21 G7 51 0N 5 52 E
Sittaung, Burma 78 C5 24 10N 94 35 E
Sittensen, Germany 26 B5 53 17N 9 32 E
Sittona, Ethiopia 95 E4 14 25N 37 23 E
Sittwe, Burma 78 E4 20 18N 92 45 E
Siuna, Nic. 148 D3 13 37N 84 45W
Siuri, India 81 H12 23 50N 87 34 E
Sivaganga, India 83 K4 9 50N 78 28 E
Sivagiri, India 83 K3 9 16N 77 26 E
Sivakasi, India 83 K3 9 24N 77 47 E
Sivana, India 80 E8 28 37N 78 6 E
Sīvand, Iran 85 D7 30 5N 52 55 E
Sivas, Turkey 88 D7 39 43N 36 58 E
Sivas □, Turkey 88 D7 39 45N 37 0 E
Siverek, Turkey 89 E8 37 50N 39 19 E
Sivomaskinskiy, Russia 48 A11 66 40N 62 35 E
Sivrihisar, Turkey 88 D4 39 30N 31 35 E
Sivry, Belgium 21 H4 50 10N 4 12 E
Sīwa, Egypt 94 B2 29 11N 25 31 E
Sīwa, El Wâhât es, Egypt 94 B2 29 10N 25 30 E
Siwalik Range, Nepal 81 F10 28 0N 83 0 E
Siwan, India 81 F11 26 13N 84 21 E
Siyâl, Jazâ'ir, Egypt 94 C4 22 49N 36 12 E
Sizewell, U.K. 17 E9 52 13N 1 38 E
Siziwang Qi, China 66 D6 41 25N 111 40 E
Sjælland, Denmark 15 J5 55 30N 11 30 E
Sjællands Odde, Denmark 15 J5 56 0N 11 15 E
Själevad, Sweden 14 A12 63 18N 18 36 E
Sjarinska Banja, Yugoslavia 42 E6 42 45N 21 38 E
Sjenica, Serbia, Yug. 42 D4 43 16N 20 0 E
Sjoa, Norway 14 C3 61 41N 9 33 E
Sjöbo, Sweden 15 J7 55 37N 13 45 E
Sjösa, Sweden 15 F11 58 47N 17 4 E
Sjumen = Šumen, Bulgaria 43 D11 43 18N 26 55 E
Skadarsko Jezero, Montenegro, Yug. 42 E4 42 10N 19 20 E
Skadovsk, Ukraine 52 C5 46 17N 32 52 E
Skagafjörður, Iceland 12 D4 65 54N 19 35W
Skagastølstindane, Norway 13 F9 61 28N 7 52 E
Skagen, Denmark 15 G4 57 43N 10 35 E
Skagerrak, Denmark 15 G3 57 30N 9 0 E
Skagit →, U.S.A. 144 B4 48 20N 122 25W
Skagway, U.S.A. 130 B1 59 23N 135 20W
Skaidi, Norway 12 A18 70 26N 24 30 E
Skala Podolskaya, Ukraine 52 B2 48 50N 26 15 E
Skalat, Ukraine 50 G4 49 23N 25 55 E
Skalbmierz, Poland 47 E7 50 20N 20 25 E
Skalica, Czech. 31 C10 48 50N 17 15 E
Skalni Dol = Kamenyak, Bulgaria 43 D11 43 24N 26 57 E
Skals, Denmark 15 H3 56 34N 9 24 E
Skanderborg, Denmark 15 H3 56 2N 9 55 E
Skanör, Sweden 15 J6 55 24N 12 50 E
Skantzoúra, Greece 45 E6 39 5N 24 6 E
Skara, Sweden 13 G12 58 25N 13 30 E
Skaraborgs län □, Sweden 13 G12 58 20N 13 30 E
Skardu, Pakistan 81 B6 35 20N 75 44 E
Skarrild, Denmark 15 J2 55 58N 8 53 E
Skarszewy, Poland 47 A5 54 4N 18 25 E
Skaryszew, Poland 47 D8 51 19N 21 15 E
Skarzysko Kamienna, Poland 47 D7 51 7N 20 52 E
Skebokvarn, Sweden 14 E10 59 7N 16 45 E
Skeena →, Canada 130 C2 54 9N 130 5W
Skeena Mts., Canada 130 B3 56 40N 128 30W
Skegness, U.K. 16 D8 53 9N 0 20 E
Skeldon, Guyana 153 B6 5 55N 57 20W
Skellefte älv →, Sweden 12 D16 64 45N 21 10 E
Skellefteå, Sweden 12 D16 64 45N 20 50 E
Skelleftehamn, Sweden 12 D16 64 40N 20 59 E
Skender Vakuf, Bos.-H., Yug. 42 C2 44 29N 17 22 E
Skene, Sweden 15 G6 57 30N 12 37 E
Skerries, The, U.K. 16 D3 53 27N 4 40W
Skhíza, Greece 45 H3 36 41N 21 40 E
Skhoinoúsa, Greece 45 H7 36 53N 25 31 E
Ski, Norway 14 E4 59 43N 10 52 E
Skíathos, Greece 45 E5 39 12N 23 30 E
Skibbereen, Ireland 19 E2 51 33N 9 16W
Skiddaw, U.K. 16 C4 54 39N 3 9W
Skien, Norway 14 E3 59 12N 9 35 E
Skierniewice, Poland 47 D7 51 58N 20 10 E
Skierniewice □, Poland 47 D7 52 0N 20 10 E
Skikda, Algeria 99 A6 36 50N 6 58 E
Skillett Fork, Little Wabash →, U.S.A. 141 F8 38 6N 88 9W
Skilloura, Cyprus 32 D12 35 14N 33 10 E
Skinári, Ákra, Greece 45 G2 37 56N 20 40 E
Skipton, Australia 116 D5 37 39 S 143 40 E
Skipton, U.K. 16 D5 53 57N 2 1W
Skirmish Pt., Australia 114 A1 11 59 S 134 17 E
Skiropoúla, Greece 45 F6 38 50N 24 21 E
Skíros, Greece 45 F6 38 55N 24 34 E
Skivarp, Sweden 15 J7 55 26N 13 34 E
Skive, Denmark 15 H3 56 33N 9 2 E
Skjálfandafljót →, Iceland 12 D5 65 59N 17 25W
Skjálfandi, Iceland 12 C5 66 5N 17 30W
Skjeberg, Norway 14 E5 59 12N 11 12 E
Skjern, Denmark 15 J2 55 57N 8 30 E
Skoczów, Poland 31 B11 49 49N 18 45 E
Škofja Loka, Slovenia 39 B11 46 9N 14 19 E
Skoghall, Sweden 13 G12 59 20N 13 30 E
Skoki, Poland 47 C4 52 40N 17 11 E
Skokie, U.S.A. 141 B9 42 3N 87 45W
Skole, Ukraine 50 G3 49 3N 23 30 E
Skópelos, Greece 45 E5 39 9N 23 47 E
Skopí, Greece 32 D8 35 11N 26 2 E
Skopin, Russia 51 E11 53 55N 39 32 E
Skopje, Macedonia, Yug. 42 E6 42 1N 21 32 E
Skórcz, Poland 47 B5 53 47N 18 30 E
Skövde, Sweden 13 G12 58 24N 13 50 E
Skovorodino, Russia 57 D13 54 0N 124 0 E
Skowhegan, U.S.A. 129 D6 44 49N 69 40W
Skownan, Canada 131 C9 51 58N 99 35W
Skradin, Croatia 39 E12 43 52N 15 53 E
Skreanäs, Sweden 15 H6 56 52N 12 35 E
Skrwa →, Poland 47 C6 52 35N 19 32 E
Skudeneshavn, Norway 13 G8 59 10N 5 10 E
Skull, Ireland 19 E2 51 32N 9 40W
Skultorp, Sweden 15 F7 58 24N 13 51 E
Skunk →, U.S.A. 140 D5 40 42N 91 7W
Skuodas, Lithuania 50 C2 56 21N 21 45 E
Skurup, Sweden 15 J7 55 28N 13 30 E
Skutskär, Sweden 14 D11 60 37N 17 25 E
Skvira, Ukraine 52 B3 49 44N 29 40 E
Skwierzyna, Poland 47 C2 52 33N 15 30 E
Skye, U.K. 18 D2 57 15N 6 10W
Skykomish, U.S.A. 142 C3 47 43N 121 16W
Skyros = Skíros, Greece 45 F6 38 55N 24 34 E
Slagelse, Denmark 15 J5 55 23N 11 19 E
Slagharen, Neths. 20 C9 52 37N 6 34 E
Slamannon, Australia 116 B5 32 1 S 143 41 E
Slamet, Indonesia 75 D3 7 16 S 109 8 E
Slaney →, Ireland 19 D5 52 52N 6 45W
Slangerup, Denmark 15 J6 55 50N 12 11 E
Slănic, Romania 46 D6 45 14N 25 58 E
Slankamen, Serbia, Yug. 42 B5 45 8N 20 15 E
Slano, Croatia 42 E2 42 48N 17 53 E
Slantsy, Russia 50 B6 59 7N 28 5 E
Slany, Czech. 30 A7 50 13N 14 6 E
Slate Is., Canada 128 C2 48 40N 87 0W
Slater, U.S.A. 140 E3 39 13N 93 4W
Slatina, Romania 46 E5 44 28N 24 22 E
Slaton, U.S.A. 139 J4 33 27N 101 38W
Slave →, Canada 130 A6 61 18N 113 39W
Slave Coast, W. Afr. 101 D5 6 0N 2 30 E
Slave Lake, Canada 130 B6 55 17N 114 43W
Slave Pt., Canada 130 A5 61 11N 115 56W
Slavgorod, Russia 56 D8 53 1N 78 37 E
Slavinja, Serbia, Yug. 42 D7 43 9N 22 50 E
Slavkov, Czech. 31 B9 49 10N 16 52 E
Slavnoye, Belorussia 50 D6 54 24N 29 15 E
Slavonska Požega, Croatia 42 B2 45 20N 17 40 E
Slavonski Brod, Croatia 42 B3 45 11N 18 0 E
Slavuta, Ukraine 50 F5 50 15N 27 2 E
Slavyanka, Russia 60 C5 42 53N 131 21 E
Slavyansk, Ukraine 52 B7 48 55N 37 36 E
Slavyansk-na-Kubani, Russia 52 D8 45 15N 38 11 E
Sława, Poland 47 D3 51 52N 16 2 E
Sławno, Poland 47 A3 54 20N 16 41 E
Sławoborze, Poland 47 B2 53 55N 15 42 E
Sleaford, U.K. 16 E7 53 0N 0 22W
Sleaford B., Australia 115 E2 34 55 S 135 45 E
Sleat, Sd. of, U.K. 18 D3 57 5N 5 47W
Sleeper Is., Canada 127 C11 58 30N 81 0W
Sleepy Eye, U.S.A. 138 C7 44 15N 94 45W
Sleidinge, Belgium 21 F3 51 8N 3 41 E
Sleman, Indonesia 75 D4 7 40 S 110 20 E
Slemon L., Canada 130 A5 63 13N 116 4W
Ślesin, Poland 47 C5 52 22N 18 14 E
Slidell, U.S.A. 139 K10 30 20N 89 48W
Sliedrecht, Neths. 20 E5 51 50N 4 45 E
Sliema, Malta 32 D2 35 54N 14 30 E
Slieve Aughty, Ireland 19 C3 53 4N 8 30W
Slieve Bloom, Ireland 19 C4 53 4N 7 40W
Slieve Donard, U.K. 19 B6 54 10N 5 57W
Slieve Gullion, U.K. 19 B5 54 8N 6 26W
Slieve Mish, Ireland 19 D2 52 12N 9 50W
Slievenamon, Ireland 19 D4 52 25N 7 37W
Sligo, Ireland 19 B3 54 17N 8 28W
Sligo □, Ireland 19 B3 54 10N 8 35W
Sligo B., Ireland 19 B3 54 20N 8 40W
Slijpe, Belgium 21 F1 51 9N 2 51 E
Slikkerveer, Neths. 20 E5 51 53N 4 36 E
Slite, Sweden 13 H15 57 42N 18 48 E
Sliven, Bulgaria 43 E11 42 42N 26 19 E
Slivnitsa, Bulgaria 42 E8 42 50N 23 0 E
Sljeme, Croatia 39 C12 45 57N 15 58 E
Sloan, U.S.A. 145 K11 35 57N 115 13W
Sloansville, U.S.A. 137 D10 42 45N 74 22W
Slobodskoy, Russia 54 B2 58 40N 50 6 E
Slobozia, Argeş, Romania 46 E6 44 30N 25 14 E
Slobozia, Ialomiţa, Romania 46 E8 44 34N 27 23 E
Slocan, Canada 130 D5 49 48N 117 28W
Slochteren, Neths. 20 B9 53 12N 6 48 E
Slöinge, Sweden 15 H6 56 51N 12 42 E
Słomniki, Poland 47 E7 50 16N 20 4 E
Slonim, Belorussia 50 E4 53 4N 25 19 E
Slotermeer, Neths. 20 C7 52 55N 5 38 E
Slough, U.K. 17 F7 51 30N 0 35W
Sloughhouse, U.S.A. 144 G5 38 26N 121 12W
Slovakian Ore Mts. = Slovenské Rudohorie, Czech. 31 C12 48 45N 20 0 E
Slovenia ■, Europe 39 C11 45 58N 14 30 E
Slovenija = Slovenia ■, Europe 39 C11 45 58N 14 30 E
Slovenj Gradec, Slovenia 39 B12 46 31N 15 5 E
Slovenska Bistrica, Slovenia 39 B12 46 24N 15 35 E
Slovenská Republika □, Czech. 31 C13 48 30N 20 0 E
Slovenské Rudohorie, Czech. 31 C12 48 45N 20 0 E
Słubice, Poland 47 C1 52 22N 14 35 E
Sluch →, Ukraine 50 F5 51 37N 26 38 E
Sluis, Neths. 21 F2 51 18N 3 23 E
Slunchev Bryag, Bulgaria 43 E12 42 40N 27 41 E
Slunj, Croatia 39 C12 45 6N 15 33 E
Słupca, Poland 47 C4 52 15N 17 52 E
Słupia →, Poland 47 A3 54 35N 16 51 E
Słupsk, Poland 47 A4 54 30N 17 3 E
Słupsk □, Poland 47 A4 54 15N 17 30 E
Slurry, S. Africa 104 D4 25 49 S 25 42 E
Slutsk, Belorussia 50 E5 53 2N 27 31 E
Slyne Hd., Ireland 19 C1 53 25N 10 10W
Slyudyanka, Russia 57 D11 51 40N 103 40 E
Smålandsfarvandet, Denmark 15 J5 55 10N 11 20 E
Smålandsstenar, Sweden 15 G7 57 10N 13 25 E
Small Nggela, Solomon Is. 121 M11 9 0 S 160 0 E
Smalltree L., Canada 131 A7 61 0N 105 0W
Smarje, Slovenia 39 B12 46 15N 15 34 E
Smartt Syndicate Dam, S. Africa 104 E3 30 45 S 23 10 E
Smartville, U.S.A. 144 F5 39 13N 121 18W
Smeaton, Canada 131 C8 53 30N 104 49W
Smederevo, Serbia, Yug. 42 C5 44 40N 20 57 E
Smederevska Palanka, Serbia, Yug. 42 C5 44 22N 20 58 E
Smela, Ukraine 52 B4 49 15N 31 58 E
Smethport, U.S.A. 136 E6 41 50N 78 28W
Smidovich, Russia 57 E14 48 36N 133 49 E
Smigiel, Poland 47 C3 52 1N 16 32 E
Smilde, Neths. 20 C8 52 58N 6 28 E
Smiley, Canada 131 C7 51 38N 109 29W
Smilyan, Bulgaria 43 F9 41 29N 24 46 E
Smith, Canada 130 B6 55 10N 114 0W
Smith →, Canada 130 B3 59 34N 126 30W
Smith Arm, Canada 126 B7 66 15N 123 0W
Smith Center, U.S.A. 138 F5 39 50N 98 50W
Smith Sund, Greenland 6 B4 78 30N 74 0W
Smithburne →, Australia 114 B3 17 3 S 140 57 E
Smithers, Canada 130 C3 54 45N 127 10W
Smithfield, S. Africa 105 E4 30 9 S 26 30 E
Smithfield, N.C., U.S.A. 135 H6 35 31N 78 16W
Smithfield, Utah, U.S.A. 142 F8 41 50N 111 50W
Smiths Falls, Canada 128 D4 44 55N 76 0W
Smithton, Australia 114 G4 40 53 S 145 6 E
Smithtown, Australia 117 A10 30 58 S 152 48 E
Smithville, Canada 136 C5 43 6N 79 33W
Smithville, Mo., U.S.A. 140 E2 39 23N 94 35W
Smithville, Tex., U.S.A. 139 K6 30 2N 97 12W

South Henik, L. 267


Smoky →, Canada 130 B5 56 10N 117 21W
Smoky Bay, Australia 115 E1 32 22 S 134 13 E
Smoky Falls, Canada 128 B3 50 4N 82 10W
Smoky Hill →, U.S.A. 138 F6 39 3N 96 48W
Smoky Lake, Canada 130 C6 54 10N 112 30W
Smøla, Norway 14 A2 63 23N 8 3 E
Smolensk, Russia 50 D8 54 45N 32 5 E
Smolikas, Óros, Greece 44 D2 40 9N 20 58 E
Smolník, Czech. 31 C13 48 43N 20 44 E
Smolyan, Bulgaria 43 F9 41 36N 24 38 E
Smooth Rock Falls, Canada 128 C3 49 17N 81 37W
Smoothstone L., Canada 131 C7 54 40N 106 50W
Smorgon, Belorussia 50 D5 54 20N 26 24 E
Smulţi, Romania 46 D8 45 57N 27 44 E
Smyadovo, Bulgaria 43 D12 43 2N 27 1 E
Smyrna = İzmir, Turkey 88 D2 38 25N 27 8 E
Snaefell, U.K. 16 C3 54 18N 4 26W
Snæfellsjökull, Iceland 12 D2 64 49N 23 46W
Snake →, U.S.A. 142 C4 46 12N 119 2W
Snake I., Australia 117 E7 38 47 S 146 33 E
Snake L., Canada 131 B7 55 32N 106 35W
Snake Ra., U.S.A. 142 G6 39 0N 114 30W
Snake River Plain, U.S.A. 142 E7 43 13N 113 0W
Snarum, Norway 14 D3 60 1N 9 54 E
Snedsted, Denmark 15 H2 56 55N 8 32 E
Sneek, Neths. 20 B7 53 2N 5 40 E
Sneeker-meer, Neths. 20 B7 53 2N 5 45 E
Sneeuberge, S. Africa 104 E3 31 46 S 24 20 E
Snejbjerg, Denmark 15 H2 56 8N 8 54 E
Snelling, U.S.A. 144 H6 37 31N 120 26W
Snezhnoye, Ukraine 53 C8 48 0N 38 58 E
Sněžka, Europe 30 A8 50 41N 15 50 E
Snežnik, Slovenia 39 C11 45 36N 14 35 E
Sniadowo, Poland 47 B8 53 2N 22 0 E
Sniardwy, Jezioro, Poland 47 B8 53 48N 21 50 E
Snigirevka, Ukraine 52 C5 47 2N 32 49 E
Snina, Czech. 31 C15 48 58N 22 9 E
Snizort, L., U.K. 18 D2 57 33N 6 28W
Snøhetta, Norway 14 B3 62 19N 9 16 E
Snohomish, U.S.A. 144 C4 47 53N 122 6W
Snoul, Cambodia 77 F6 12 4N 106 26 E
Snow Hill, U.S.A. 134 F8 38 10N 75 21W
Snow Lake, Canada 131 C8 54 52N 100 3W
Snow Mt., U.S.A. 144 F4 39 22N 122 44W
Snowbird L., Canada 131 A8 60 45N 103 0W
Snowdon, U.K. 16 D3 53 4N 4 8W
Snowdrift, Canada 131 A6 62 24N 110 44W
Snowdrift →, Canada 131 A6 62 24N 110 44W
Snowflake, U.S.A. 143 J8 34 30N 110 4W
Snowshoe Pk., U.S.A. 142 B6 48 13N 115 41W
Snowtown, Australia 116 B3 33 46 S 138 14 E
Snowville, U.S.A. 142 F7 41 59N 112 47W
Snowy →, Australia 117 D8 37 46 S 148 30 E
Snowy Mts., Australia 117 D8 36 30 S 148 20 E
Snug Corner, Bahamas 149 B5 22 33N 73 52W
Snyatyn, Ukraine 52 B1 48 30N 25 50 E
Snyder, Okla., U.S.A. 139 H5 34 40N 99 0W
Snyder, Tex., U.S.A. 139 J4 32 45N 100 57W
Soacha, Colombia 152 C3 4 35N 74 13W
Soahanina, Madag. 105 B7 18 42 S 44 13 E
Soalala, Madag. 105 B8 16 6 S 45 20 E
Soan →, Pakistan 80 C4 33 1N 71 44 E
Soanierana-Ivongo, Madag. 105 B8 16 55 S 49 35 E
Soap Lake, U.S.A. 142 C4 47 23N 119 31W
Sobat, Nahr →, Sudan 95 F3 9 22N 31 33 E
Soběslav, Czech. 30 B7 49 16N 14 45 E
Sobhapur, India 80 H8 22 47N 78 17 E
Sobinka, Russia 51 D12 56 0N 40 0 E
Sobo-Yama, Japan 62 E3 32 51N 131 22 E
Sobótka, Poland 47 E3 50 54N 16 44 E
Sobrado, Spain 36 B2 43 2N 8 2W
Sobral, Brazil 154 B3 3 50 S 40 20W
Sobreira Formosa, Portugal 37 F3 39 46N 7 51W
Soc Giang, Vietnam 76 A6 22 54N 106 1 E
Soc Trang, Vietnam 77 H5 9 37N 105 50 E
Soča →, Europe 39 B10 46 20N 13 40 E
Sochaczew, Poland 47 C7 52 15N 20 13 E
Soch'e = Shache, China 64 C2 38 20N 77 10 E
Sochi, Russia 53 E8 43 35N 39 40 E
Société, Is. de la, Pac. Oc. 123 J12 17 0 S 151 0W
Society Is. = Société, Is. de la, Pac. Oc. 123 J12 17 0 S 151 0W
Socompa, Portezuelo de, Chile 158 A2 24 27 S 68 18W
Socorro, Colombia 152 B3 6 29N 73 16W
Socorro, Phil. 71 G5 9 37N 125 58 E
Socorro, U.S.A. 143 J10 34 4N 106 54W
Socorro, I., Mexico 146 D2 18 45N 110 58W
Socotra, Ind. Oc. 87 D6 12 30N 54 0 E
Socuéllamos, Spain 35 F2 39 16N 2 47W
Soda L., U.S.A. 143 J5 35 7N 116 2W
Soda Plains, India 81 B8 35 30N 79 0 E
Soda Springs, U.S.A. 142 E8 42 40N 111 40W
Söderhamn, Sweden 13 F14 61 18N 17 10 E
Söderköping, Sweden 13 G14 58 31N 16 20 E
Södermanlands län □, Sweden 14 E10 59 10N 16 30 E
Södertälje, Sweden 14 E11 59 12N 17 39 E
Sodiri, Sudan 95 E2 14 27N 29 0 E
Sodo, Ethiopia 95 F4 7 0N 37 41 E
Sodražica, Slovenia 39 C11 45 45N 14 39 E
Sodus, U.S.A. 136 C7 43 13N 77 5W
Soe, Indonesia 72 C2 9 52 S 124 17 E
Soekmekaar, S. Africa 105 C4 23 30 S 29 55 E
Soest, Germany 26 D4 51 34N 8 7 E
Soest, Neths. 20 D6 52 9N 5 19 E
Soestdijk, Neths. 20 D6 52 11N 5 17 E
Sofádhes, Greece 44 E4 39 20N 22 4 E
Sofara, Mali 100 C4 13 59N 4 9W
Sofia = Sofiya, Bulgaria 43 E8 42 45N 23 20 E
Sofia →, Madag. 105 B8 15 27 S 47 23 E
Sofievka, Ukraine 52 B5 48 6N 33 55 E
Sofiiski, Russia 57 D14 52 15N 133 59 E
Sofikón, Greece 45 G5 37 47N 23 3 E
Sofiya, Bulgaria 43 E8 42 45N 23 20 E
Sōfu-Gan, Japan 61 K10 29 49N 140 21 E
Sogakofe, Ghana 101 D5 6 2N 0 39 E
Sogamoso, Colombia 152 B3 5 43N 72 56W
Sogār, Iran 85 E8 25 53N 58 6 E
Sögel, Germany 26 C3 52 50N 7 32 E
Sogeri, Papua N. G. 120 E4 9 26 S 147 35 E
Sogn og Fjordane fylke □, Norway 13 F9 61 40N 6 0 E
Sogndalsfjøra, Norway 13 F9 61 14N 7 5 E
Sognefjorden, Norway 13 F8 61 10N 5 50 E
Söğüt, Turkey 88 C4 40 2N 30 11 E
Söğüt Gölü, Turkey 88 E3 37 3N 29 51 E
Sŏgwi-po, S. Korea 67 H14 33 13N 126 34 E
Soh, Iran 85 C6 33 26N 51 27 E
Sohâg, Egypt 94 B3 26 33N 31 43 E
Sohano, Papua N. G. 120 C8 5 22 S 154 37 E
Sŏhori, N. Korea 67 D15 40 7N 128 23 E
Soignies, Belgium 21 G4 50 35N 4 5 E
Soira, Ethiopia 95 E4 14 45N 39 30 E
Soissons, France 23 C10 49 25N 3 19 E
Sōja, Japan 62 C5 34 40N 133 45 E
Sojat, India 80 G5 25 55N 73 45 E
Sok →, Russia 54 E2 53 24N 50 8 E
Sokal, Ukraine 50 F4 50 31N 24 15 E
Söke, Turkey 45 G9 37 48N 27 28 E
Sokelo, Zaïre 103 D4 9 55 S 24 36 E
Sokhós, Greece 44 D5 40 48N 23 22 E
Sokki, Oued In →, Algeria 99 C5 29 30N 3 42 E
Sokna, Norway 14 D3 60 16N 9 50 E
Soknedal, Norway 14 B4 62 57N 10 13 E
Soko Banja, Serbia, Yug. 42 D6 43 40N 21 51 E
Sokodé, Togo 101 D5 9 0N 1 11 E
Sokol, Russia 51 B12 59 30N 40 5 E
Sokolac, Bos.-H., Yug. 42 D3 43 56N 18 48 E
Sokółka, Poland 47 B10 53 25N 23 30 E
Sokolo, Mali 100 C3 14 53N 6 8W
Sokolov, Czech. 30 A5 50 12N 12 40 E
Sokołów Małpolski, Poland 31 A15 50 12N 22 7 E
Sokołów Podlaski, Poland 47 C9 52 25N 22 15 E
Sokoły, Poland 47 C9 52 59N 22 42 E
Sokoto, Nigeria 101 C6 13 2N 5 16 E
Sokoto □, Nigeria 101 C6 12 30N 5 0 E
Sokoto →, Nigeria 101 C5 11 20N 4 10 E
Sokuluk, Kirghizia 55 B7 42 52N 74 18 E
Sol Iletsk, Russia 54 F4 51 10N 55 0 E
Sola →, Poland 31 A12 50 4N 19 15 E
Solai, Kenya 106 B4 0 2N 36 12 E
Solana, Phil. 70 C3 17 39N 121 41 E
Solander I., N.Z. 119 G1 46 34 S 166 54 E
Solano, Phil. 70 C3 16 31N 121 15 E
Solapur, India 82 F2 17 43N 75 56 E
Solares, Spain 36 B7 43 23N 3 43W
Solca, Romania 46 B6 47 40N 25 50 E
Soléa □, Cyprus 32 D12 35 5N 33 4 E
Solec Kujawski, Poland 47 B5 53 5N 18 14 E
Soledad, Colombia 152 A3 10 55N 74 46W
Soledad, U.S.A. 144 J5 36 27N 121 16W
Soledad, Venezuela 153 B5 8 10N 63 34W
Solent, The, U.K. 17 G6 50 45N 1 25W
Solenzara, France 25 G13 41 53N 9 23 E
Solesmes, France 23 B10 50 10N 3 30 E
Solfonn, Norway 13 F9 60 2N 6 57 E
Solhan, Turkey 89 D9 38 57N 41 3 E
Soligalich, Russia 51 B13 59 5N 42 10 E
Soligorsk, Belorussia 50 E5 52 51N 27 27 E
Solikamsk, Russia 54 B5 59 38N 56 50 E
Solila, Madag. 105 C8 21 25 S 46 37 E
Solimões = Amazonas →, S. Amer. 153 D7 0 5 S 50 0W
Solingen, Germany 21 F10 51 10N 7 4 E
Sollebrunn, Sweden 15 F6 58 8N 12 32 E
Sollefteå, Sweden 14 A11 63 12N 17 20 E
Sollentuna, Sweden 14 E11 59 26N 17 56 E
Sóller, Spain 33 B9 39 46N 2 43 E
Solling, Germany 26 D5 51 44N 9 36 E
Solna, Sweden 14 E12 59 22N 18 1 E
Solnechnogorsk, Russia 51 C10 56 10N 36 57 E
Sologne, France 23 E8 47 40N 1 45 E
Solok, Indonesia 74 C2 0 45 S 100 40 E
Sololá, Guatemala 148 D1 14 49N 91 10W
Solomon, N. Fork →, U.S.A. 138 F5 39 29N 98 26W
Solomon, S. Fork →, U.S.A. 138 F5 39 25N 99 12W
Solomon Is. ■, Pac. Oc. 121 L8 6 0 S 155 0 E
Solomon Sea, Papua N. G. 120 D6 7 0 S 150 0 E
Solon, China 65 B7 46 32N 121 10 E
Solon Springs, U.S.A. 138 B9 46 19N 91 47W
Solonópole, Brazil 154 C4 5 44 S 39 1W
Solor, Indonesia 72 C2 8 27 S 123 0 E
Solotcha, Russia 51 D11 54 48N 39 53 E
Solothurn, Switz. 28 B5 47 13N 7 32 E
Solothurn □, Switz. 28 B5 47 18N 7 40 E
Solotobe, Kazakhstan 55 A3 44 37N 66 3 E
Solsona, Spain 34 D6 42 0N 1 31 E
Solt, Hungary 31 E12 46 45N 19 1 E
Solta, Croatia 39 E13 43 24N 16 15 E
Solţānābād, Khorāsān, Iran 85 C8 34 13N 59 58 E
Solţānābād, Khorāsān, Iran 85 B8 36 29N 58 5 E
Solţānābād, Markazī, Iran 85 C6 35 31N 51 10 E
Soltau, Germany 26 C5 52 59N 9 50 E
Soltsy, Russia 50 B7 58 10N 30 30 E
Solunska Glava, Macedonia, Yug. 42 F6 41 44N 21 31 E
Solvang, U.S.A. 145 L6 34 36N 120 8W
Solvay, U.S.A. 137 C8 43 5N 76 17W
Solvychegodsk, Russia 48 B8 61 21N 46 56 E
Solway Firth, U.K. 16 C4 54 45N 3 38W
Solwezi, Zambia 107 E2 12 11 S 26 21 E
Sōma, Japan 60 F10 37 40N 140 50 E
Soma, Turkey 88 D2 39 10N 27 35 E
Somali Rep. ■, Africa 90 F4 7 0N 47 0 E
Sombe Dzong, Bhutan 78 B2 27 13N 89 8 E
Sombernon, France 23 E11 47 20N 4 40 E
Sombor, Serbia, Yug. 42 B4 45 46N 19 9 E
Sombra, Canada 136 D2 42 43N 82 29W
Sombrerete, Mexico 146 C4 23 40N 103 40W
Sombrero, Anguilla 149 C7 18 37N 63 30W
Someren, Neths. 21 F7 51 23N 5 42 E
Somers, U.S.A. 142 B6 48 4N 114 18W
Somerset, Canada 131 D9 49 25N 98 39W
Somerset, Colo., U.S.A. 143 G10 38 55N 107 30W
Somerset, Ky., U.S.A. 134 G3 37 5N 84 40W
Somerset, Mass., U.S.A. 137 E13 41 45N 71 10W
Somerset, Pa., U.S.A. 136 F5 40 1N 79 4W
Somerset □, U.K. 17 F5 51 9N 3 0W
Somerset East, S. Africa 104 E4 32 42 S 25 35 E
Somerset I., Canada 126 A10 73 30N 93 0W
Somerset West, S. Africa 104 E2 34 8 S 18 50 E
Somerton, U.S.A. 143 K6 32 35N 114 47W
Somerville, U.S.A. 137 F10 40 34N 74 36W
Someş →, Romania 46 B3 47 49N 22 43 E
Someşul Mare →, Romania 46 B5 47 18N 24 30 E
Somma Lombardo, Italy 38 C5 45 41N 8 42 E
Somma Vesuviana, Italy 41 B7 40 52N 14 23 E
Sommariva, Australia 115 D4 26 24 S 146 36 E
Sommatino, Italy 40 E6 37 20N 14 0 E
Somme □, France 23 C9 49 57N 2 20 E
Somme →, France 23 B8 50 11N 1 38 E
Somme, B. de la, France 22 B8 50 14N 1 33 E
Sommelsdijk, Neths. 20 E4 51 46N 4 9 E
Sommepy-Tahure, France 23 C11 49 15N 4 31 E
Sömmerda, Germany 26 D7 51 10N 11 8 E
Sommesous, France 23 D11 48 44N 4 12 E
Sommières, France 25 E8 43 47N 4 6 E
Somogy □, Hungary 31 E10 46 19N 17 30 E
Somogyszob, Hungary 31 E10 46 18N 17 20 E
Somosomo Str., Fiji 121 A3 16 0 S 180 0 E
Somoto, Nic. 148 D2 13 28N 86 37W
Sompolno, Poland 47 C5 52 26N 18 30 E
Somport, Paso, Spain 34 C4 42 48N 0 31W
Somport, Puerto de, Spain 34 C4 42 48N 0 31W
Somuncurá, Meseta de, Argentina 160 B3 41 30 S 67 0W
Son, Neths. 21 E6 51 31N 5 30 E
Son, Norway 14 E4 59 32N 10 42 E
Son, Spain 36 C2 42 43N 8 58W
Son Ha, Vietnam 76 E7 15 3N 108 34 E
Son Hoa, Vietnam 76 F7 13 2N 108 58 E
Son La, Vietnam 76 B4 21 20N 103 50 E
Son Tay, Vietnam 76 B5 21 8N 105 30 E
Soná, Panama 148 E3 8 0N 81 20W
Sonamarg, India 81 B6 34 18N 75 21 E
Sonamukhi, India 81 H12 23 18N 87 27 E
Sonamura, India 78 D3 23 29N 91 15 E
Sŏnchŏn, N. Korea 67 E13 39 48N 124 55 E
Soncino, Italy 38 C6 45 24N 9 52 E
Sondags →, S. Africa 104 E4 33 44 S 25 51 E
Sóndalo, Italy 38 B7 46 20N 10 20 E
Sondar, India 81 C6 33 28N 75 56 E
Sønder Omme, Denmark 15 J2 55 50N 8 54 E
Sønder Tornby, Denmark 15 G3 57 31N 9 58 E
Sønderborg, Denmark 15 K3 54 55N 9 49 E
Sønderjyllands Amtskommune □, Denmark 15 J3 55 10N 9 10 E
Sondershausen, Germany 26 D6 51 22N 10 50 E
Sóndrio, Italy 38 B6 46 10N 9 53 E
Sone, Mozam. 107 F3 17 23 S 34 55 E
Sonepur, India 82 D6 20 55N 83 50 E
Song, Thailand 76 C3 18 28N 100 11 E
Song Cau, Vietnam 76 F7 13 27N 109 18 E
Song Xian, China 66 G7 34 12N 112 8 E
Songchŏn, N. Korea 67 E14 39 12N 126 15 E
Songea, Tanzania 107 E4 10 40 S 35 40 E
Songea □, Tanzania 107 E4 10 30 S 36 0 E
Songeons, France 23 C8 49 32N 1 50 E
Songhua Hu, China 67 C14 43 35N 126 50 E
Songhua Jiang →, China 65 B8 47 45N 132 30 E
Songjiang, China 69 B13 31 1N 121 12 E
Songjin, N. Korea 67 D15 40 40N 129 10 E
Songjŏng-ni, S. Korea 67 G14 35 8N 126 47 E
Songkan, China 68 C6 28 35N 106 52 E
Songkhla, Thailand 77 J3 7 13N 100 37 E
Songming, China 68 E4 25 12N 103 2 E
Songnim, N. Korea 67 E13 38 45N 125 39 E
Songo, Angola 103 D2 7 22 S 14 51 E
Songololo, Zaïre 103 D2 5 42 S 14 2 E
Songpan, China 68 A4 32 40N 103 30 E
Songtao, China 68 C7 28 11N 109 10 E
Songwe, Zaïre 106 C2 3 20 S 26 16 E
Songwe →, Africa 107 D3 9 44 S 33 58 E
Songxi, China 69 D12 27 31N 118 44 E
Songzi, China 69 B8 30 12N 111 45 E
Sonid Youqi, China 66 C7 42 45N 112 48 E
Sonipat, India 80 E7 29 0N 77 5 E
Sonkel, Ozero, Kirghizia 55 C7 41 50N 75 12 E
Sonkovo, Russia 51 C10 57 50N 37 5 E
Sonmiani, Pakistan 79 D2 25 25N 66 40 E
Sonnino, Italy 40 A6 41 25N 13 13 E
Sono →, Goiás, Brazil 154 C2 9 58 S 48 11W
Sono →, Minas Gerais, Brazil 155 E2 17 2 S 45 32W
Sonobe, Japan 63 B7 35 6N 135 28 E
Sonogno, Switz. 29 D7 46 22N 8 47 E
Sonora, Calif., U.S.A. 144 H6 37 59N 120 27W
Sonora, Tex., U.S.A. 139 K4 30 33N 100 37W
Sonora □, Mexico 146 B2 29 0N 111 0W
Sonora →, Mexico 146 B2 28 50N 111 33W
Sonora Desert, U.S.A. 145 M12 33 40N 114 15W
Sonoyta, Mexico 146 A2 31 51N 112 50W
Sŏnsan, S. Korea 67 F15 36 14N 128 17 E
Sonsonate, El Salv. 148 D2 13 43N 89 44W
Sonthofen, Germany 27 H6 47 31N 10 16 E
Soochow = Suzhou, China 69 B13 31 19N 120 38 E
Sop Hao, Laos 76 B5 20 33N 104 27 E
Sop Prap, Thailand 76 D2 17 53N 99 20 E
Sopachuy, Bolivia 157 D5 19 29 S 64 31W
Sopi, Indonesia 72 A3 2 34N 128 28 E
Sopo, Nahr →, Sudan 95 F2 8 40N 26 30 E
Sopot, Poland 47 A5 54 27N 18 31 E
Sopot, Serbia, Yug. 42 C5 44 29N 20 30 E
Sopotnica, Macedonia, Yug. 42 F6 41 23N 21 13 E
Sopron, Hungary 31 D9 47 45N 16 32 E
Sop's Arm, Canada 129 C8 49 46N 56 56W
Sopur, India 81 B6 34 18N 74 27 E
Sør-Rondane, Antarctica 7 D4 72 0 S 25 0 E
Sør-Trøndelag fylke □, Norway 14 B3 63 0N 9 30 E
Sora, Italy 40 A6 41 45N 13 36 E
Sorada, India 82 E7 19 45N 84 26 E
Sorah, Pakistan 80 F3 27 13N 68 56 E
Söråker, Sweden 14 B11 62 30N 17 32 E
Sorano, Italy 39 F8 42 40N 11 42 E
Sorata, Bolivia 156 D4 15 50 S 68 40W
Sorbas, Spain 35 H2 37 6N 2 7W
Sorel, Canada 128 C5 46 0N 73 10W
Sörenberg, Switz. 28 C6 46 50N 8 2 E
Sorento, U.S.A. 140 E7 39 0N 89 34W
Soreq, N. →, Israel 91 D3 31 57N 34 43 E
Soresina, Italy 38 C6 45 17N 9 51 E
Sorgono, Italy 40 B2 40 1N 9 6 E
Sorgues, France 25 D8 44 1N 4 53 E
Sorgun, Turkey 88 D6 39 29N 35 22 E
Soria, Spain 34 D2 41 43N 2 32W
Soria □, Spain 34 D2 41 46N 2 28W
Soriano, Uruguay 158 C4 33 24 S 58 19W
Soriano nel Cimino, Italy 39 F9 42 25N 12 14 E
Sorkh, Kuh-e, Iran 85 C8 35 40N 58 30 E
Sorø, Denmark 15 J5 55 26N 11 32 E
Soro, Guinea 100 C3 10 9N 9 48W
Sorocaba, Brazil 159 A6 23 31 S 47 27W
Sorochinsk, Russia 54 E3 52 26N 53 10 E
Soroki, Moldavia 52 B3 48 8N 28 12 E
Soroksár, Hungary 31 D12 47 24N 19 9 E
Soron, India 81 F8 27 55N 78 45 E
Sorong, Indonesia 73 B4 0 55 S 131 15 E
Soroní, Greece 32 C10 36 21N 28 1 E
Soroti, Uganda 106 B3 1 43N 33 35 E
Sørøya, Norway 12 A17 70 40N 22 30 E
Sørøysundet, Norway 12 A17 70 25N 23 0 E
Sorraia →, Portugal 37 G2 38 55N 8 53W
Sorrento, Australia 115 F3 38 22 S 144 47 E
Sorrento, Italy 41 B7 40 38N 14 23 E
Sorsele, Sweden 12 D14 65 31N 17 30 E
Sorso, Italy 40 B1 40 50N 8 34 E
Sorsogon, Phil. 70 E5 13 0N 124 0 E
Sorsogon □, Phil. 70 E4 12 50N 123 55 E
Sortavala, Russia 48 B5 61 42N 30 41 E
Sortino, Italy 41 E8 37 9N 15 1 E
Sorūbī, Afghan. 79 B3 34 36N 69 43 E
Sorvizhi, Russia 51 C16 57 52N 48 32 E
Sos, Spain 34 C3 42 30N 1 13W
Sŏsan, S. Korea 67 F14 36 47N 126 27 E
Soscumica, L., Canada 128 B4 50 15N 77 27W
Sosna →, Russia 51 E11 52 42N 38 55 E
Sosnogorsk, Russia 48 B9 63 37N 53 51 E
Sosnovka, Russia 51 E12 53 13N 41 24 E
Sosnovka, Russia 57 D11 54 9N 109 35 E
Sosnowiec, Poland 47 E6 50 20N 19 10 E
Sospel, France 25 E11 43 52N 7 27 E
Šoštanj, Slovenia 39 B12 46 23N 15 4 E
Sŏsura, N. Korea 67 C16 42 16N 130 36 E
Sosva, Russia 54 B7 59 10N 61 50 E
Sosva →, Russia 54 B8 59 32N 62 20 E
Soto la Marina →, Mexico 147 C5 23 40N 97 40W
Soto y Amío, Spain 36 C5 42 46N 5 53W
Sotteville-lès-Rouen, France 22 C8 49 24N 1 5 E
Sotuta, Mexico 147 C7 20 29N 89 43W
Souanké, Congo 102 B2 2 10N 14 3 E
Soúdha, Greece 32 D6 35 29N 24 4 E
Soúdhas, Kólpos, Greece 32 D6 35 25N 24 10 E
Soufflay, Congo 102 B2 2 1N 14 54 E
Souflíon, Greece 44 C8 41 12N 26 18 E
Sougne-Remouchamps, Belgium 21 H7 50 29N 5 42 E
Souillac, France 24 D5 44 53N 1 29 E
Souk-Ahras, Algeria 99 A6 36 23N 7 57 E
Souk el Arba du Rharb, Morocco 98 B3 34 43N 5 59W
Soukhouma, Laos 76 E5 14 38N 105 48 E
Sŏul, S. Korea 67 F14 37 31N 126 58 E
Soulac-sur-Mer, France 24 C2 45 30N 1 7W
Soultz-sous-Forêts, France 23 D14 48 57N 7 52 E
Soumagne, Belgium 21 G7 50 37N 5 44 E
Sound, The = Øresund, Europe 15 J6 55 45N 12 45 E
Sound, The, U.K. 17 G3 50 20N 4 10W
Soúnion, Ákra, Greece 45 G6 37 37N 24 1 E
Sour el Ghozlane, Algeria 99 A5 36 10N 3 45 E
Sources, Mt. aux, Lesotho 105 D4 28 45 S 28 50 E
Sourdeval, France 22 D6 48 43N 0 55W
Soure, Brazil 154 B2 0 35 S 48 30W
Soure, Portugal 36 E2 40 4N 8 38W
Souris, Man., Canada 131 D8 49 40N 100 20W
Souris, P.E.I., Canada 129 C7 46 21N 62 15W
Souris →, Canada 138 A5 49 40N 99 34W
Soúrpi, Greece 45 E4 39 6N 22 54 E
Sousa, Brazil 154 C4 6 45 S 38 10W
Sousel, Brazil 154 B1 2 38 S 52 29W
Sousel, Portugal 37 G3 38 57N 7 40W
Souss, O. →, Morocco 98 B3 30 27N 9 31W
Sousse, Tunisia 96 A2 35 50N 10 38 E
Soustons, France 24 E2 43 45N 1 19W
South Africa ■, Africa 104 E3 32 0 S 23 0 E
South Atlantic Ocean 9 L8 20 0 S 10 0W
South Aulatsivik I., Canada 129 A7 56 45N 61 30W
South Australia □, Australia 115 E2 32 0 S 139 0 E
South Baldy, U.S.A. 143 J10 33 6N 107 27W
South Beloit, U.S.A. 140 B7 42 29N 89 2W
South Bend, Ind., U.S.A. 141 C10 41 38N 86 20W
South Bend, Wash., U.S.A. 144 D3 46 44N 123 52W
South Boston, U.S.A. 135 G6 36 42N 78 58W
South Branch, Canada 129 C8 47 55N 59 2W
South Brook, Canada 129 C8 49 26N 56 5W
South Buganda □, Uganda 106 C3 0 15 S 31 30 E
South Carolina □, U.S.A. 135 J5 33 45N 81 0W
South Charleston, U.S.A. 134 F5 38 20N 81 40W
South China Sea, Asia 122 G3 10 0N 113 0 E
South Cotabato □, Phil. 71 H5 6 0N 125 0 E
South Dakota □, U.S.A. 138 C5 45 0N 100 0W
South Downs, U.K. 17 G7 50 53N 0 10W
South East C., Australia 114 G4 43 40 S 146 50 E
South East Is., Australia 113 F3 34 17 S 123 30 E
South Esk →, U.K. 18 E5 56 44N 3 3W
South Foreland, U.K. 17 F9 51 7N 1 23 E
South Fork →, U.S.A. 142 C7 47 54N 113 15W
South Fork, American →, U.S.A. 144 G5 38 45N 121 5W
South Fork, Feather →, U.S.A. 144 F5 39 17N 121 36W
South Georgia, Antarctica 7 B1 54 30 S 37 0W
South Glamorgan □, U.K. 17 F4 51 30N 3 20W
South Grand →, U.S.A. 140 F3 38 17N 93 55W
South Haven, U.S.A. 141 B10 42 22N 86 20W
South Henik, L., Canada 131 A9 61 30N 97 30W

Sultsa 269


Stellarton, *Canada* ..... 129 **C7** 45 32N 62 30W
Stellenbosch, *S. Africa* .. 104 **E2** 33 58 S 18 50 E
Stellendam, *Neths.* ..... 20 **E4** 51 49N 4 1 E
Stelvio, Paso dello, *Italy* 29 **C10** 46 32N 10 27 E
Stemshaug, *Norway* .... 14 **A2** 63 19N 8 44 E
Stendal, *Germany* ...... 26 **C7** 52 36N 11 50 E
Stene, *Belgium* ......... 21 **F1** 51 12N 2 56 E
Stensele, *Sweden* ....... 12 **D14** 65 3N 17 8 E
Stenstorp, *Sweden* ...... 15 **F7** 58 17N 13 45 E
Stepanakert =
Khankendy, *Azerbaijan* 89 **D12** 39 40N 46 25 E
Stephan, *U.S.A.* ....... 138 **A6** 48 30N 96 53W
Stephens, C., *N.Z.* ..... 119 **A8** 40 42 S 173 58 E
Stephens Creek, *Australia* 116 **A4** 31 50 S 141 30 E
Stephens I., *Canada* .... 130 **C2** 54 10N 130 45W
Stephens I., *N.Z.* ...... 119 **A9** 40 40 S 174 1 E
Stephenville, *Canada* ... 129 **C8** 48 31N 58 35W
Stephenville, *U.S.A.* .... 139 **J5** 32 12N 98 12W
Stepnica, *Poland* ....... 47 **B1** 53 38N 14 36 E
Stepnoi = Elista, *Russia* 53 **C11** 46 16N 44 14 E
Stepnoye, *Russia* ....... 54 **D7** 54 4N 60 26 E
Stepnyak, *Kazakhstan* .. 56 **D8** 52 50N 70 50 E
Steppe, *Asia* .......... 58 **E9** 50 0N 50 0 E
Stereá Ellas □, *Greece* .. 45 **F4** 38 50N 22 0 E
Sterkstroom, *S. Africa* .. 104 **E4** 31 32 S 26 32 E
Sterling, *Colo., U.S.A.* . 138 **E3** 40 40N 103 15W
Sterling, *Ill., U.S.A.* .... 140 **C7** 41 45N 89 45W
Sterling, *Kans., U.S.A.* . 138 **F5** 38 17N 98 13W
Sterling City, *U.S.A.* ... 139 **K4** 31 50N 100 59W
Sterling Heights, *U.S.A.* 141 **B13** 42 35N 83 5W
Sterling Run, *U.S.A.* ... 136 **E6** 41 25N 78 12W
Sterlitamak, *Russia* ..... 54 **E4** 53 40N 56 0 E
Sternberg, *Germany* .... 26 **B7** 53 42N 11 48 E
Šternberk, *Czech.* ...... 31 **B10** 49 45N 17 15 E
Stérnes, *Greece* ........ 32 **D6** 35 30N 24 9 E
Stettin = Szczecin,
*Poland* ............. 47 **B1** 53 27N 14 27 E
Stettiner Haff, *Germany* 26 **B10** 53 50N 14 25 E
Stettler, *Canada* ........ 130 **C6** 52 19N 112 40W
Steubenville, *U.S.A.* .... 136 **F4** 40 21N 80 39W
Stevens Point, *U.S.A.* .. 138 **C10** 44 32N 89 34W
Stevenson, *U.S.A.* ...... 144 **E5** 45 42N 121 53W
Stevenson L., *Canada* .. 131 **C9** 53 55N 96 0W
Stevns Klint, *Denmark* .. 15 **J6** 55 17N 12 28 E
Steward, *U.S.A.* ....... 140 **C7** 41 51N 89 1W
Stewardson, *U.S.A.* .... 141 **E8** 39 16N 88 38W
Stewart, *B.C., Canada* .. 130 **B3** 55 56N 129 57W
Stewart, *N.W.T., Canada* 126 **B6** 63 19N 139 26W
Stewart, *U.S.A.* ........ 144 **F7** 39 5N 119 46W
Stewart, C., *Australia* ... 114 **A1** 11 57 S 134 56 E
Stewart, I., *Chile* ....... 160 **D2** 54 50 S 71 15W
Stewart I., *N.Z.* ........ 119 **G2** 46 58 S 167 54 E
Stewarts Point, *U.S.A.* .. 144 **G3** 38 39N 123 20W
Stewartsville, *U.S.A.* ... 140 **E2** 39 45N 94 30W
Stewiacke, *Canada* ..... 129 **C7** 45 9N 63 22W
Steynsburg, *S. Africa* ... 104 **E4** 31 15 S 25 49 E
Steyr, *Austria* .......... 30 **C7** 48 3N 14 25 E
Steyr →, *Austria* ...... 30 **C7** 48 17N 14 15 E
Steytlerville, *S. Africa* .. 104 **E3** 33 17 S 24 19 E
Stia, *Italy* ............. 39 **E8** 43 48N 11 41 E
Stiens, *Neths.* .......... 20 **B7** 53 16N 5 46 E
Stigler, *U.S.A.* ......... 139 **H7** 35 19N 95 6W
Stigliano, *Italy* ......... 41 **B9** 40 24N 16 13 E
Stigsnæs, *Denmark* ..... 15 **J5** 55 13N 11 18 E
Stigtomta, *Sweden* ...... 15 **F10** 58 47N 16 48 E
Stikine →, *Canada* .... 130 **B2** 56 40N 132 30W
Stilfontein, *S. Africa* ... 104 **D4** 26 51 S 26 50 E
Stílis, *Greece* .......... 45 **F4** 38 55N 22 47 E
Stillwater, *N.Z.* ........ 119 **C6** 42 27 S 171 20 E
Stillwater, *Minn., U.S.A.* 138 **C8** 45 3N 92 47W
Stillwater, *N.Y., U.S.A.* 137 **D11** 42 55N 73 41W
Stillwater, *Okla., U.S.A.* 139 **G6** 36 5N 97 3W
Stillwater Ra., *U.S.A.* .. 142 **G4** 39 45N 118 6W
Stilwell, *U.S.A.* ........ 139 **H7** 35 52N 94 36W
Stimfalías, L., *Greece* ... 45 **G4** 37 51N 22 27 E
Štip, *Macedonia, Yug.* .. 42 **F7** 41 42N 22 10 E
Stíra, *Greece* .......... 45 **F6** 38 9N 24 14 E
Stirling, *Australia* ..... 114 **B3** 17 12 S 141 35 E
Stirling, *Canada* ....... 130 **D6** 49 30N 112 30W
Stirling, *N.Z.* .......... 119 **G4** 46 14 S 169 49 E
Stirling, *U.K.* .......... 18 **E5** 56 7N 3 57W
Stirling Ra., *Australia* ... 113 **F2** 34 23 S 118 0 E
Stittsville, *Canada* ..... 137 **A9** 45 15N 75 55W
Stockach, *Germany* ..... 27 **H5** 47 51N 9 1 E
Stockbridge, *U.S.A.* .... 141 **B12** 42 27N 84 11W
Stockerau, *Austria* ..... 31 **C9** 48 24N 16 12 E
Stockett, *U.S.A.* ....... 142 **C8** 47 23N 111 7W
Stockholm, *Sweden* ..... 14 **E12** 59 20N 18 3 E
Stockholms län □,
*Sweden* ............ 14 **E12** 59 30N 18 20 E
Stockhorn, *Switz.* ...... 28 **C5** 46 42N 7 33 E
Stockport, *U.K.* ........ 16 **D5** 53 25N 2 11W
Stockton, *Australia* ..... 117 **B9** 32 50 S 151 47 E
Stockton, *Calif., U.S.A.* 144 **H5** 37 58N 121 20W
Stockton, *Ill., U.S.A.* ... 140 **B6** 42 21N 90 1W
Stockton, *Kans., U.S.A.* 138 **F5** 39 30N 99 20W
Stockton, *Mo., U.S.A.* .. 139 **G8** 37 40N 93 48W
Stockton-on-Tees, *U.K.* . 16 **C6** 54 34N 1 20W
Stockvik, *Sweden* ...... 14 **B11** 62 17N 17 23 E
Stoczek Łukowski,
*Poland* ............. 47 **D8** 51 58N 21 58 E
Stöde, *Sweden* ......... 14 **B10** 62 28N 16 35 E
Stogovo,
*Macedonia, Yug.* ..... 42 **F5** 41 31N 20 38 E
Stoke, *N.Z.* ........... 119 **B8** 41 19 S 173 14 E
Stoke on Trent, *U.K.* ... 16 **D5** 53 1N 2 11W
Stokes Bay, *Canada* .... 128 **C3** 45 0N 81 28W
Stokes Pt., *Australia* ... 114 **G3** 40 10 S 143 56 E
Stokes Ra., *Australia* ... 112 **C5** 15 50 S 130 50 E
Stokkseyri, *Iceland* ..... 12 **E3** 63 50N 21 2W
Stokksnes, *Iceland* ...... 12 **D6** 64 14N 14 58W
Stolac, *Bos.-H., Yug.* ... 42 **D2** 43 8N 17 59 E
Stolberg, *Germany* ..... 26 **E2** 50 48N 6 13 E
Stolbovaya, *Russia* ..... 51 **D10** 55 10N 37 32 E
Stolbovaya, *Russia* ..... 57 **C16** 64 50N 153 50 E
Stolbovoy, Ostrov, *Russia* 57 **D17** 74 44N 135 14 E
Stolbtsy, *Belorussia* ..... 50 **E5** 53 30N 26 43 E
Stolin, *Belorussia* ....... 50 **F5** 51 53N 26 50 E
Stolnici, *Romania* ...... 46 **E5** 44 31N 24 48 E
Stolwijk, *Neths.* ........ 20 **E5** 51 59N 4 47 E
Stomíon, *Greece* ....... 32 **D5** 35 21N 23 32 E
Ston, *Croatia* .......... 42 **E2** 42 51N 17 43 E
Stonehaven, *U.K.* ...... 18 **E6** 56 58N 2 11W
Stonehenge, *Australia* ... 114 **C3** 24 22 S 143 17 E
Stonewall, *Canada* ..... 131 **C9** 50 10N 97 19W
Stonington, *U.S.A.* ..... 140 **E7** 39 44N 89 12W
Stony L., *Man., Canada* 131 **B9** 58 51N 98 40W
Stony L., *Ont., Canada* . 136 **B6** 44 30N 78 5W
Stony Rapids, *Canada* .. 131 **B7** 59 16N 105 50W
Stony Tunguska =
Podkamennaya
Tunguska →, *Russia* . 57 **C10** 61 50N 90 13 E
Stonyford, *U.S.A.* ...... 144 **F4** 39 23N 122 33W
Stopnica, *Poland* ....... 47 **E7** 50 27N 20 57 E
Stora Lulevatten, *Sweden* 12 **C15** 67 10N 19 30 E
Stora Sjöfallet, *Sweden* .. 12 **C15** 67 29N 18 40 E
Storavan, *Sweden* ...... 12 **D15** 65 45N 18 10 E
Store Bælt, *Denmark* ... 15 **J5** 55 20N 11 0 E
Store Creek, *Australia* .. 117 **B8** 32 54 S 149 6 E
Store Heddinge, *Denmark* 15 **J6** 55 18N 12 23 E
Støren, *Norway* ........ 14 **A4** 63 3N 10 18 E
Storm B., *Australia* ..... 114 **G4** 43 10 S 147 30 E
Storm Lake, *U.S.A.* .... 138 **D7** 42 35N 95 11W
Stormberge, *S. Africa* ... 104 **E4** 31 16 S 26 17 E
Stormsrivier, *S. Africa* .. 104 **E3** 33 59 S 23 52 E
Stornoway, *U.K.* ....... 18 **C2** 58 12N 6 23W
Storozhinets, *Ukraine* ... 52 **B1** 48 14N 25 45 E
Storsjö, *Sweden* ........ 14 **B7** 62 49N 13 5 E
Storsjøen, *Hedmark,*
*Norway* ............. 14 **D5** 60 20N 11 40 E
Storsjøen, *Hedmark,*
*Norway* ............. 14 **C5** 61 30N 11 14 E
Storsjön, *Sweden* ...... 14 **B7** 62 50N 13 8 E
Storstrøms Amt. □,
*Denmark* ............ 15 **K5** 54 50N 11 45 E
Storuman, *Sweden* ..... 12 **D14** 65 5N 17 10 E
Story City, *U.S.A.* ..... 140 **B3** 42 11N 93 36W
Stoughton, *Canada* ..... 131 **D8** 49 40N 103 0W
Stoughton, *U.S.A.* ..... 140 **B8** 42 55N 88 59W
Stour →, *Dorset, U.K.* . 17 **G5** 50 48N 2 7W
Stour →,
*Here. & Worcs., U.K.* 17 **E5** 52 25N 2 13W
Stour →, *Kent, U.K.* ... 17 **F9** 51 15N 1 20 E
Stour →, *Suffolk, U.K.* 17 **F9** 51 55N 1 5 E
Stourbridge, *U.K.* ...... 17 **E5** 52 28N 2 8W
Stout, L., *Canada* ...... 131 **C10** 52 0N 94 40W
Stove Pipe Wells Village,
*U.S.A.* .............. 145 **J9** 36 35N 117 11W
Stowmarket, *U.K.* ...... 17 **E9** 52 11N 1 0 E
Strabane, *U.K.* ........ 19 **B4** 54 50N 7 28W
Strabane □, *U.K.* ...... 19 **B4** 54 45N 7 25W
Stracin, *Macedonia, Yug.* 42 **E7** 42 13N 22 2 E
Stradella, *Italy* ......... 38 **C6** 45 4N 9 20 E
Strahan, *Australia* ..... 114 **G4** 42 9 S 145 20 E
Strakonice, *Czech.* ..... 30 **B6** 49 15N 13 53 E
Straldzha, *Bulgaria* ..... 43 **E11** 42 35N 26 40 E
Stralsund, *Germany* .... 26 **A9** 54 17N 13 5 E
Strand, *S. Africa* ...... 104 **E2** 34 9 S 18 48 E
Strangford L., *U.K.* .... 19 **B6** 54 30N 5 37W
Strängnäs, *Sweden* ..... 14 **E11** 59 23N 17 2 E
Strangsville, *U.S.A.* .... 136 **E3** 41 19N 81 50W
Stranraer, *U.K.* ........ 18 **G3** 54 54N 5 0W
Strasbourg, *Canada* .... 131 **C8** 51 4N 104 55W
Strasbourg, *France* ..... 23 **D14** 48 35N 7 42 E
Strasburg, *Germany* .... 26 **B9** 53 30N 13 44 E
Strasburg, *U.S.A.* ...... 138 **B4** 46 12N 100 9W
Strassen, *Lux.* ......... 21 **J8** 49 37N 6 4 E
Stratford, *N.S.W.,*
*Australia* ............ 117 **B9** 32 7 S 151 55 E
Stratford, *Vic., Australia* 117 **D7** 37 59 S 147 7 E
Stratford, *Canada* ...... 128 **D3** 43 23N 81 0W
Stratford, *N.Z.* ........ 118 **F3** 39 20 S 174 19 E
Stratford, *Calif., U.S.A.* 144 **J7** 36 10N 119 49W
Stratford, *Conn., U.S.A.* 137 **E11** 41 13N 73 8W
Stratford, *Tex., U.S.A.* . 139 **G3** 36 20N 102 3W
Stratford-upon-Avon,
*U.K.* ................ 17 **E6** 52 12N 1 42W
Strath Spey, *U.K.* ...... 18 **D5** 57 15N 3 40W
Strathalbyn, *Australia* ... 116 **C3** 35 13 S 138 53 E
Strathclyde □, *U.K.* .... 18 **F4** 56 0N 4 50W
Strathcona Prov. Park,
*Canada* ............. 130 **D3** 49 38N 125 40W
Strathmore, *Australia* ... 114 **B3** 17 50 S 142 35 E
Strathmore, *Canada* .... 130 **C6** 51 5N 113 18W
Strathmore, *U.K.* ...... 18 **E5** 56 40N 3 4W
Strathmore, *U.S.A.* .... 144 **J7** 36 9N 119 4W
Strathnaver, *Canada* .... 130 **C4** 53 20N 122 33W
Strathpeffer, *U.K.* ...... 18 **D4** 57 35N 4 32W
Strathroy, *Canada* ..... 128 **D3** 42 58N 81 38W
Strathy Pt., *U.K.* ....... 18 **C4** 58 35N 4 3W
Stratton, *U.S.A.* ....... 138 **F3** 39 20N 102 36W
Straubing, *Germany* .... 27 **G8** 48 53N 12 35 E
Straumnes, *Iceland* ..... 12 **C2** 66 26N 23 8W
Strausberg, *Germany* ... 26 **C9** 52 40N 13 52 E
Strawberry Point, *U.S.A.* 140 **B5** 42 41N 91 32W
Strawberry Res., *U.S.A.* 142 **F8** 40 10N 111 7W
Strawn, *U.S.A.* ........ 139 **J5** 32 36N 98 30W
Strážnice, *Czech.* ...... 31 **C10** 48 54N 17 19 E
Streaky B., *Australia* ... 115 **E1** 32 48 S 134 13 E
Streaky Bay, *Australia* .. 115 **E1** 32 51 S 134 18 E
Streator, *U.S.A.* ....... 138 **E10** 41 9N 88 52W
Středočeský □, *Czech.* .. 30 **B7** 49 55N 14 30 E
Středoslovenský □,
*Czech.* .............. 31 **C12** 48 30N 19 15 E
Streé, *Belgium* ......... 21 **H4** 50 17N 4 18 E
Streeter, *U.S.A.* ........ 138 **B5** 46 39N 99 21W
Streetsville, *Canada* .... 136 **C5** 43 35N 79 42W
Strehaia, *Romania* ..... 46 **E4** 44 37N 23 10 E
Strelcha, *Bulgaria* ..... 43 **E9** 42 25N 24 19 E
Strelka, *Russia* ........ 57 **D10** 58 5N 93 3 E
Streng →, *Cambodia* ... 76 **F4** 13 12N 103 37 E
Strésa, *Italy* ........... 38 **C5** 45 52N 8 28 E
Strezhevoy, *Russia* ..... 56 **C8** 60 42N 77 34 E
Střibro, *Czech.* ........ 30 **B6** 49 44N 13 0 E
Strickland →,
*Papua N. G.* ......... 120 **D1** 7 35 S 141 36 E
Strijen, *Neths.* ......... 20 **E5** 51 45N 4 33 E
Strimón →, *Greece* .... 44 **D5** 40 46N 23 51 E
Strimonikós Kólpos,
*Greece* .............. 44 **D5** 40 33N 24 0 E
Stroeder, *Argentina* ..... 160 **B4** 40 12 S 62 37W
Strofádhes, *Greece* ..... 45 **G3** 37 15N 21 0 E
Strömbacka, *Sweden* .... 14 **C10** 61 58N 16 44 E
Strómboli, *Italy* ......... 41 **D8** 38 48N 15 12 E
Stromeferry, *U.K.* ...... 18 **D3** 57 20N 5 33W
Stromness, *U.K.* ....... 18 **C5** 58 58N 3 18W
Ströms vattudal, *Sweden* 12 **D13** 64 15N 14 55 E
Strömstad, *Sweden* ..... 13 **G11** 58 55N 11 15 E
Strömsund, *Sweden* ..... 12 **E13** 63 51N 15 33 E
Stronghurst, *U.S.A.* .... 140 **D6** 40 45N 90 55W
Stróngoli, *Italy* ........ 41 **C10** 39 16N 17 2 E
Stronsay, *U.K.* ........ 18 **B6** 59 8N 2 38W
Stronsburg, *U.S.A.* ..... 138 **E6** 41 7N 97 36W
Stropkov, *Czech.* ....... 31 **B14** 49 13N 21 39 E
Stroud, *U.K.* ........... 17 **F5** 51 44N 2 12W
Stroud Road, *Australia* . 117 **B9** 32 18 S 151 57 E
Stroudsberg, *U.S.A.* .... 137 **F9** 40 59N 75 15W
Stroumbi, *Cyprus* ...... 32 **E11** 34 53N 32 29 E
Struer, *Denmark* ....... 15 **H2** 56 30N 8 35 E
Struga, *Macedonia, Yug.* 42 **F5** 41 13N 20 44 E
Strugi Krasnyye, *Russia* . 50 **B6** 58 21N 29 1 E
Strumica,
*Macedonia, Yug.* ..... 42 **F7** 41 28N 22 41 E
Strumica →, *Europe* ... 42 **F8** 41 20N 23 22 E
Struthers, *Canada* ...... 128 **C2** 48 41N 85 51W
Struthers, *U.S.A.* ...... 136 **E4** 41 6N 80 38W
Stryama, *Bulgaria* ...... 43 **E9** 42 16N 24 54 E
Stryi, *Ukraine* ......... 50 **G3** 49 16N 23 48 E
Stryker, *U.S.A.* ........ 142 **B6** 48 40N 114 44W
Stryków, *Poland* ....... 47 **D6** 51 55N 19 33 E
Strzegom, *Poland* ...... 47 **E3** 50 58N 16 20 E
Strzelce Krajeńskie,
*Poland* ............. 47 **C2** 52 52N 15 33 E
Strzelce Opolskie, *Poland* 47 **E5** 50 31N 18 18 E
Strzelecki Cr. →,
*Australia* ............ 115 **D2** 29 37 S 139 59 E
Strzelin, *Poland* ....... 47 **E4** 50 46N 17 2 E
Strzelno, *Poland* ....... 47 **C5** 52 35N 18 9 E
Strzybnica, *Poland* ..... 47 **E5** 50 28N 18 48 E
Strzyżów, *Poland* ...... 31 **B14** 49 52N 21 47 E
Stuart, *Fla., U.S.A.* .... 135 **M5** 27 11N 80 12W
Stuart, *Iowa, U.S.A.* ... 140 **C2** 41 30N 94 19W
Stuart, *Nebr., U.S.A.* ... 138 **D5** 42 39N 99 8W
Stuart →, *Canada* ..... 130 **C4** 54 0N 123 35W
Stuart Bluff Ra.,
*Australia* ............ 112 **D5** 22 50 S 131 52 E
Stuart L., *Canada* ..... 130 **C4** 54 30N 124 30W
Stuart Mts., *N.Z.* ...... 119 **F2** 45 2 S 167 39 E
Stuart Ra., *Australia* ... 115 **D1** 29 10 S 134 56 E
Stubbekøbing, *Denmark* 15 **K6** 54 53N 12 9 E
Stuben, *Austria* ........ 30 **D3** 47 10N 10 8 E
Studen Kladenets,
Yazovir, *Bulgaria* .... 43 **F10** 41 37N 25 30 E
Studholme, *N.Z.* ....... 119 **E6** 44 42 S 171 9 E
Stugun, *Sweden* ....... 14 **A9** 63 10N 15 40 E
Stull, L., *Canada* ...... 128 **B1** 54 24N 92 34W
Stung Treng, *Cambodia* . 76 **F5** 13 31N 105 58 E
Stupart →, *Canada* .... 131 **B10** 56 0N 93 25W
Stupino, *Russia* ........ 51 **D11** 54 57N 38 2 E
Sturgeon B., *Canada* ... 131 **C9** 52 0N 97 50W
Sturgeon Bay, *U.S.A.* .. 134 **C2** 44 52N 87 20W
Sturgeon Falls, *Canada* . 128 **C4** 46 25N 79 57W
Sturgeon L., *Alta.,*
*Canada* ............. 130 **B5** 55 6N 117 32W
Sturgeon L., *Ont.,*
*Canada* ............. 128 **B1** 50 0N 90 45W
Sturgeon L., *Ont.,*
*Canada* ............. 136 **B6** 44 28N 78 43W
Sturgis, *Mich., U.S.A.* .. 141 **C11** 41 50N 85 25W
Sturgis, *S. Dak., U.S.A.* 138 **C3** 44 25N 103 30W
Štúrovo, *Czech.* ........ 31 **D11** 47 48N 18 41 E
Sturt Cr. →, *Australia* . 112 **C4** 19 8 S 127 50 E
Sturt Creek, *Australia* .. 112 **C4** 19 12 S 128 8 E
Sturts Meadows, *Australia* 116 **A4** 31 18 S 141 42 E
Stutterheim, *S. Africa* .. 104 **E4** 32 33 S 27 28 E
Stuttgart, *Germany* .... 27 **G5** 48 46N 9 10 E
Stuttgart, *U.S.A.* ...... 139 **H9** 34 30N 91 33W
Stuyvesant, *U.S.A.* ..... 137 **D11** 42 23N 73 45W
Stykkishólmur, *Iceland* .. 12 **D2** 65 2N 22 40W
Styr →, *Belorussia* ..... 50 **E5** 52 7N 26 35 E
Styria = Steiermark □,
*Austria* ............. 30 **D8** 47 26N 15 0 E
Su-no-Saki, *Japan* ..... 63 **C11** 34 58N 139 45 E
Su Xian, *China* ........ 66 **H9** 33 41N 116 59 E
Suakin, *Sudan* ......... 94 **D4** 19 8N 37 20 E
Sual, *Phil.* ............. 70 **C3** 16 4N 120 5 E
Suan, *N. Korea* ........ 67 **E14** 38 42N 126 22 E
Suapure →, *Venezuela* . 152 **B4** 6 48N 67 1W
Suaqui, *Mexico* ........ 146 **B3** 29 12N 109 41W
Suatá →, *Venezuela* ... 153 **B4** 7 52N 65 22W
Subang, *Indonesia* ..... 75 **D3** 6 34 S 107 45 E
Subansiri →, *India* .... 78 **B4** 26 48N 93 50 E
Subayhah, *Si. Arabia* ... 84 **D3** 30 2N 38 50 E
Subi, *Indonesia* ........ 75 **B3** 2 58N 108 50 E
Subiaco, *Italy* ......... 39 **G10** 41 56N 13 5 E
Subotica, *Serbia, Yug.* .. 42 **A4** 46 6N 19 39 E
Success, *Canada* ....... 131 **C7** 50 28N 108 6W
Suceava, *Romania* ..... 46 **B7** 47 38N 26 16 E
Suceava □, *Romania* ... 46 **B6** 47 37N 25 40 E
Suceava →, *Romania* .. 46 **B7** 47 38N 26 16 E
Sucha-Beskidzka, *Poland* 31 **B12** 49 44N 19 35 E
Suchan, *Poland* ........ 47 **B2** 53 18N 15 18 E
Suchan, *Russia* ........ 60 **C6** 43 8N 133 9 E
Suchedniów, *Poland* .... 47 **D7** 51 3N 20 49 E
Suchitoto, *El Salv.* ..... 148 **D2** 13 56N 89 0W
Suchou = Suzhou, *China* 69 **B13** 31 19N 120 38 E
Süchow = Xuzhou, *China* 67 **G9** 34 18N 117 10 E
Suchowola, *Poland* ..... 47 **B10** 53 33N 23 3 E
Sucio →, *Colombia* .... 152 **B2** 7 27N 77 7W
Suck →, *Ireland* ....... 19 **C3** 53 17N 8 18W
Suckling, Mt.,
*Papua N. G.* ......... 120 **E5** 9 49 S 148 53 E
Sucre, *Bolivia* .......... 157 **D4** 19 0 S 65 15W
Sucre, *Colombia* ....... 152 **B3** 8 49N 74 44W
Sucre □, *Colombia* ..... 152 **B2** 8 50N 75 40W
Sucre □, *Venezuela* .... 153 **A5** 10 25N 63 30W
Sucuaro, *Colombia* ..... 152 **C4** 4 34N 68 50W
Sućuraj, *Croatia* ....... 39 **E14** 43 10N 17 8 E
Sucuriju, *Brazil* ........ 154 **A2** 1 39N 49 57W
Sucuriú →, *Brazil* ..... 157 **E7** 20 47 S 51 38W
Sud, Pte., *Canada* ..... 129 **C7** 49 3N 62 14W
Sud-Ouest, Pte. du,
*Canada* ............. 129 **C7** 49 23N 63 36W
Suda →, *Russia* ....... 51 **B10** 59 0N 37 40 E
Sudak, *Ukraine* ........ 52 **D6** 44 51N 34 57 E
Sudan, *U.S.A.* ......... 139 **H3** 34 4N 102 32W
Sudan ■, *Africa* ....... 95 **E3** 15 0N 30 0 E
Suday, *Russia* ......... 51 **B13** 59 0N 43 0 E
Sudbury, *Canada* ...... 128 **C3** 46 30N 81 0W
Sudbury, *U.K.* ......... 17 **E8** 52 2N 0 44 E
Sûdd, *Sudan* .......... 95 **F2** 8 20N 30 0 E
Suddie, *Guyana* ....... 153 **B6** 7 8N 58 29W
Süderbrarup, *Germany* .. 26 **A5** 54 38N 9 47 E
Süderlügum, *Germany* .. 26 **A4** 54 50N 8 55 E
Süderoog-Sand, *Germany* 26 **A4** 54 27N 8 30 E
Sudeten Mts. = Sudety,
*Europe* ............. 31 **A9** 50 20N 16 45 E
Sudety, *Europe* ........ 31 **A9** 50 20N 16 45 E
Sudi, *Tanzania* ........ 107 **E4** 10 11 S 39 57 E
Sudirman, Pegunungan,
*Indonesia* ............ 73 **B5** 4 30 S 137 0 E
Sudiți, *Romania* ........ 46 **E8** 44 35N 27 38 E
Sudogda, *Russia* ....... 51 **D12** 55 55N 40 50 E
Sudr, *Egypt* ........... 94 **J8** 29 40N 32 42 E
Sudzha, *Russia* ........ 50 **F9** 51 14N 35 17 E
Sueca, *Spain* .......... 35 **F4** 39 12N 0 21W
Suedala, *Sweden* ....... 15 **J7** 55 30N 13 15 E
Suez = El Suweis, *Egypt* 94 **J8** 29 58N 32 31 E
Suez, G. of = Suweis,
Khalîg el, *Egypt* ...... 94 **J8** 28 40N 33 0 E
Suez Canal = Suweis,
Qanâl es, *Egypt* ..... 94 **H8** 31 0N 32 20 E
Suffield, *Canada* ....... 131 **C6** 50 12N 111 10W
Suffolk, *U.S.A.* ........ 134 **G7** 36 47N 76 33W
Suffolk □, *U.K.* ........ 17 **E9** 52 16N 1 0 E
Sufi-Kurgan, *Kirghizia* .. 55 **C6** 40 2N 73 30 E
Suga no-Sen, *Japan* .... 62 **B6** 35 25N 134 25 E
Sugag, *Romania* ....... 46 **D4** 45 47N 23 37 E
Sugar →, *Ill., U.S.A.* .. 140 **B7** 42 25N 89 15W
Sugar →, *Ind., U.S.A.* . 141 **E9** 39 50N 87 23W
Sugar City, *U.S.A.* ..... 138 **F3** 38 18N 103 38W
Sugar Cr. →, *U.S.A.* ... 140 **D7** 40 12N 89 41W
Sugbai Passage, *Phil.* ... 71 **J3** 5 22N 120 33 E
Suğla Gölü, *Turkey* .... 88 **E5** 37 20N 32 0 E
Sugluk = Saglouc,
*Canada* ............. 127 **B12** 62 14N 75 38W
Sugny, *Belgium* ........ 21 **J5** 49 49N 4 54 E
Suhaia, L., *Romania* .... 46 **F6** 43 45N 25 15 E
Suhār, *Oman* .......... 85 **E8** 24 20N 56 40 E
Sühbaatar □, *Mongolia* . 66 **B8** 45 30N 114 0 E
Suhl, *Germany* ........ 26 **E6** 50 35N 10 40 E
Suhr, *Switz.* ........... 28 **B6** 47 22N 8 5 E
Şuhut, *Turkey* ......... 88 **D4** 38 31N 30 32 E
Sui Xian, *Henan, China* . 66 **G8** 34 25N 115 2 E
Sui Xian, *Henan, China* . 69 **B9** 31 42N 113 24 E
Suiá Missu →, *Brazil* .. 157 **C7** 11 13 S 53 15W
Suichang, *China* ....... 69 **C12** 28 29N 119 15 E
Suichuan, *China* ....... 69 **D10** 26 20N 114 32 E
Suide, *China* .......... 66 **F6** 37 30N 110 12 E
Suifenhe, *China* ....... 67 **B16** 44 25N 131 10 E
Suihua, *China* ......... 65 **B7** 46 32N 126 55 E
Suijiang, *China* ........ 68 **C4** 28 40N 103 59 E
Suining, *Hunan, China* .. 69 **D8** 26 35N 110 10 E
Suining, *Jiangsu, China* . 67 **H9** 33 56N 117 58 E
Suining, *Sichuan, China* . 68 **B5** 30 26N 105 35 E
Suiping, *China* ........ 66 **H7** 33 10N 113 59 E
Suippes, *France* ....... 23 **C11** 49 8N 4 30 E
Suir →, *Ireland* ....... 19 **D4** 52 15N 7 10W
Suita, *Japan* ........... 63 **C7** 34 45N 135 32 E
Suixi, *China* ........... 69 **G8** 21 19N 110 18 E
Suiyang, *Guizhou, China* 68 **D6** 27 58N 107 18 E
Suiyang, *Heilongjiang,*
*China* ............... 67 **B16** 44 30N 130 56 E
Suizhong, *China* ....... 67 **D11** 40 21N 120 20 E
Sujangarh, *India* ....... 80 **F6** 27 42N 74 31 E
Sujica, *Bos.-H., Yug.* ... 42 **D2** 43 52N 17 11 E
Sukabumi, *Indonesia* ... 74 **D3** 6 56 S 106 50 E
Sukadana, *Kalimantan,*
*Indonesia* ............ 75 **C4** 1 10 S 110 0 E
Sukadana, *Sumatera,*
*Indonesia* ............ 74 **D3** 5 5 S 105 33 E
Sukagawa, *Japan* ....... 61 **F10** 37 17N 140 23 E
Sukaraja, *Indonesia* ..... 75 **C4** 2 28 S 110 25 E
Sukarnapura = Jayapura,
*Indonesia* ............ 73 **B6** 2 28 S 140 38 E
Sukchŏn, *N. Korea* ..... 67 **E13** 39 22N 125 35 E
Sukhindol, *Bulgaria* .... 43 **D10** 43 11N 25 10 E
Sukhinichi, *Russia* ..... 50 **D9** 54 8N 35 10 E
Sukhona →, *Russia* .... 48 **C6** 59 40N 39 45 E
Sukhothai, *Thailand* .... 76 **D2** 17 1N 99 49 E
Sukhoy Log, *Russia* .... 54 **C8** 56 55N 62 1 E
Sukhumi, *Georgia* ..... 53 **E9** 43 0N 41 0 E
Sukkur, *Pakistan* ...... 79 **D3** 27 42N 68 54 E
Sukkur Barrage, *Pakistan* 80 **F3** 27 40N 68 50 E
Sukma, *India* .......... 82 **E5** 18 24N 81 45 E
Sukovo, *Serbia, Yug.* ... 42 **D7** 43 4N 22 37 E
Sukumo, *Japan* ........ 62 **E4** 32 56N 132 44 E
Sukunka →, *Canada* ... 130 **B4** 55 45N 121 15W
Sul, Canal do, *Brazil* ... 154 **B2** 0 10 S 48 30W
Sula →, *Ukraine* ...... 50 **G8** 49 40N 32 41 E
Sula, Kepulauan,
*Indonesia* ............ 72 **B3** 1 45 S 125 0 E
Sulaco →, *Honduras* ... 148 **C2** 15 2N 87 44W
Sulaiman Range, *Pakistan* 80 **D3** 30 30N 69 50 E
Sulak →, *Russia* ...... 53 **E12** 43 20N 47 34 E
Sūlār, *Iran* ............ 85 **D6** 31 53N 51 54 E
Sulawesi □, *Indonesia* .. 72 **B2** 2 0 S 120 0 E
Sulawesi Sea, *Indonesia* . 72 **A2** 3 0N 123 0 E
Sulechów, *Poland* ...... 47 **C2** 52 5N 15 40 E
Sulęcin, *Poland* ........ 47 **C2** 52 26N 15 10 E
Sulejów, *Poland* ....... 47 **D6** 51 26N 19 53 E
Sulejówek, *Poland* ..... 47 **C8** 52 13N 21 17 E
Sulgen, *Switz.* ......... 29 **A8** 47 33N 9 7 E
Sulima, *S. Leone* ...... 100 **D2** 6 58N 11 32W
Sulina, *Romania* ....... 46 **D10** 45 10N 29 40 E
Sulina, Braţul →,
*Romania* ............ 46 **D10** 45 10N 29 20 E
Sulingen, *Germany* ..... 26 **C4** 52 41N 8 47 E
Sulița, *Romania* ........ 46 **B7** 47 39N 26 59 E
Sulitälma, *Sweden* ..... 12 **C14** 67 17N 17 28 E
Sulitjelma, *Norway* ..... 12 **C14** 67 9N 16 3 E
Sułkowice, *Poland* ..... 31 **B12** 49 50N 19 49 E
Sullana, *Peru* .......... 156 **A1** 4 52 S 80 39W
Sullivan, *Ill., U.S.A.* ... 138 **F10** 39 40N 88 40W
Sullivan, *Ind., U.S.A.* .. 141 **E9** 39 5N 87 26W
Sullivan, *Mo., U.S.A.* .. 140 **F5** 38 10N 91 10W
Sullivan Bay, *Canada* ... 130 **C3** 50 55N 126 50W
Sully, *U.S.A.* .......... 140 **C4** 41 34N 92 50W
Sully-sur-Loire, *France* .. 23 **E9** 47 45N 2 20 E
Sulmierzyce, *Poland* .... 47 **D4** 51 37N 17 32 E
Sulmona, *Italy* ......... 39 **F10** 42 3N 13 55 E
Sulphur, *La., U.S.A.* ... 139 **K8** 30 13N 93 22W
Sulphur, *Okla., U.S.A.* . 139 **H6** 34 35N 97 0W
Sulphur Pt., *Canada* ... 130 **A6** 60 56N 114 48W
Sulphur Springs, *U.S.A.* 139 **J7** 33 5N 95 36W
Sulphur Springs
Draw →, *U.S.A.* ..... 139 **J4** 32 12N 101 36W
Sulsul, *Ethiopia* ........ 108 **C2** 5 5N 44 50 E
Sultan, *Canada* ........ 128 **C3** 47 36N 82 47W
Sultan, *U.S.A.* ........ 144 **C5** 47 51N 121 49W
Sultan Kudarat □, *Phil.* . 71 **H5** 6 30N 124 10 E
Sultan sa Barongis, *Phil.* 71 **H5** 6 45N 124 35 E
Sultanpur, *India* ....... 81 **F10** 26 18N 82 4 E
Sultsa, *Russia* ......... 48 **B8** 63 27N 46 2 E

Thonze 273


Telén, Argentina 158 D2 36 15 S 65 31W
Telen →, Indonesia 75 C5 0 10 S 117 20 E
Teleng, Iran 85 E9 25 47N 61 3 E
Teleño, Spain 36 C4 42 23N 6 22W
Teleorman □, Romania 46 E6 44 0N 25 0 E
Teleorman →, Romania 46 E6 44 15N 25 20 E
Teles Pires →, Brazil 157 B6 7 21 S 58 3W
Telescope Peak, U.S.A. 145 J9 36 6N 117 7W
Teletaye, Mali 101 B5 16 31N 1 30 E
Telford, U.K. 16 E5 52 42N 2 31W
Telfs, Austria 30 D4 47 19N 11 4 E
Télimélé, Guinea 100 C2 10 54N 13 2W
Telkwa, Canada 130 C3 54 41N 127 5W
Tell City, U.S.A. 141 G10 37 55N 86 44W
Tellicherry, India 83 J2 11 45N 75 30 E
Tellin, Belgium 21 H6 50 5N 5 13 E
Telluride, U.S.A. 143 H10 37 58N 107 48W
Telok Datok, Malaysia 74 B2 2 49N 101 31 E
Teloloapán, Mexico 147 D5 18 21N 99 51W
Telpos Iz, Russia 48 B10 63 35N 57 30 E
Telsen, Argentina 160 B3 42 30 S 66 50W
Telšiai, Lithuania 50 D3 55 59N 22 14 E
Teltow, Germany 26 C9 52 24N 13 15 E
Teluk Anson, Malaysia 77 K3 4 3N 101 0 E
Teluk Betung = Tanjungkarang Telukbetung, Indonesia 74 D3 5 20 S 105 10 E
Teluk Intan = Teluk Anson, Malaysia 77 K3 4 3N 101 0 E
Telukbutun, Indonesia 75 B3 4 13N 108 12 E
Telukdalem, Indonesia 74 B1 0 33N 97 50 E
Tema, Ghana 101 D5 5 41N 0 0 E
Temanggung, Indonesia 75 D4 7 18 S 110 10 E
Temapache, Mexico 147 C5 21 4N 97 38W
Temax, Mexico 147 C7 21 10N 88 50W
Temba, S. Africa 105 D4 25 20 S 28 17 E
Tembe, Zaïre 106 C2 0 16 S 28 14 E
Tembesi, Indonesia 74 C2 1 43 S 103 6 E
Tembilahan, Indonesia 74 C2 0 19 S 103 9 E
Temblador, Venezuela 153 B5 8 59N 62 44W
Tembleque, Spain 34 F1 39 41N 3 30W
Temblor Ra., U.S.A. 145 K7 35 30N 120 0W
Teme →, U.K. 17 E5 52 23N 2 15W
Temecula, U.S.A. 145 M9 33 26N 117 6W
Temerloh, Malaysia 77 L4 3 27N 102 25 E
Temir, Kazakhstan 56 E6 49 21N 57 3 E
Temirtau, Kazakhstan 56 D8 50 5N 72 56 E
Temirtau, Russia 56 D9 53 10N 87 30 E
Témiscaming, Canada 128 C4 46 44N 79 5W
Temma, Australia 114 G3 41 12 S 144 48 E
Temnikov, Russia 51 D13 54 40N 43 11 E
Temo →, Italy 40 B1 40 20N 8 30 E
Temora, Australia 117 C7 34 30 S 147 30 E
Temosachic, Mexico 146 B3 28 58N 107 50W
Tempe, U.S.A. 143 K8 33 26N 111 59W
Tempe Downs, Australia 112 D5 24 22 S 132 24 E
Témpio Pausania, Italy 40 B2 40 53N 9 6 E
Tempiute, U.S.A. 144 H11 37 39N 115 38W
Temple, U.S.A. 139 K6 31 5N 97 22W
Temple B., Australia 114 A3 12 15 S 143 3 E
Templemore, Ireland 19 D4 52 48N 7 50W
Templeton, U.S.A. 144 K6 35 33N 120 42W
Templeton →, Australia 114 C2 21 0 S 138 40 E
Templeuve, Belgium 21 G2 50 39N 3 17 E
Templin, Germany 26 B9 53 8N 13 31 E
Tempoal, Mexico 147 C5 21 31N 98 23W
Temryuk, Russia 52 D7 45 15N 37 24 E
Temse, Belgium 21 F4 51 7N 4 13 E
Temska →, Serbia, Yug. 42 D7 43 17N 22 33 E
Temuco, Chile 160 A2 38 45 S 72 40W
Temuka, N.Z. 119 E6 44 14 S 171 17 E
Ten Boer, Neths. 20 B9 53 16N 6 42 E
Tena, Ecuador 152 D2 0 59 S 77 49W
Tenabo, Mexico 147 C6 20 2N 90 12W
Tenaha, U.S.A. 139 K7 31 57N 94 25W
Tenali, India 83 F5 16 15N 80 35 E
Tenancingo, Mexico 147 D5 19 0N 99 33W
Tenango, Mexico 147 D5 19 7N 99 33W
Tenasserim, Burma 77 F2 12 6N 99 3 E
Tenasserim □, Burma 76 F2 14 0N 98 30 E
Tenay, France 25 C9 45 55N 5 31 E
Tenby, U.K. 17 F3 51 40N 4 42W
Tenda, Col di, France 25 D11 44 7N 7 36 E
Tendaho, Ethiopia 90 E3 11 48N 40 54 E
Tende, France 25 D11 44 5N 7 35 E
Tendelti, Sudan 95 E3 13 1N 31 55 E
Tendjedi, Adrar, Algeria 99 D6 23 41N 7 32 E
Tendrara, Morocco 99 B4 33 3N 1 58W
Tendre, Mt., Switz. 28 C2 46 35N 6 18 E
Teneida, Egypt 94 B2 25 30N 29 19 E
Tenente Marques →, Brazil 157 C6 11 10 S 59 56W
Ténéré, Niger 97 E2 19 0N 10 30 E
Ténéré, Erg du, Niger 97 E2 17 35N 10 55 E
Tenerife, Canary Is. 33 F3 28 15N 16 35W
Tenerife, Pico, Canary Is. 33 G1 27 43N 18 1W
Ténès, Algeria 99 A5 36 31N 1 14 E
Teng Xian, Guangxi Zhuangzu, China 69 F8 23 21N 110 56 E
Teng Xian, Shandong, China 67 G9 35 5N 117 10 E
Tengah □, Indonesia 72 B2 2 0 S 122 0 E
Tengah Kepulauan, Indonesia 75 D5 7 5 S 118 15 E
Tengchong, China 68 E2 25 0N 98 28 E
Tengchowfu = Penglai, China 67 F11 37 48N 120 42 E
Tenggara □, Indonesia 72 B2 3 0 S 122 0 E
Tenggarong, Indonesia 75 C5 0 24 S 116 58 E
Tenggol, P., Malaysia 77 K4 4 48N 103 41 E
Tengiz, Ozero, Kazakhstan 56 D7 50 30N 69 0 E
Tenigerbad, Switz. 29 C7 46 42N 8 57 E
Tenino, U.S.A. 144 D4 46 51N 122 51W
Tenkasi, India 83 K3 8 55N 77 20 E
Tenke, Shaba, Zaïre 107 E2 11 22 S 26 40 E
Tenke, Shaba, Zaïre 107 E2 10 32 S 26 7 E
Tenkodogo, Burkina Faso 101 C4 11 54N 0 19W
Tenna →, Italy 39 E10 43 12N 13 47 E
Tennant Creek, Australia 114 B1 19 30 S 134 15 E
Tennessee □, U.S.A. 133 C9 36 0N 86 30W
Tennessee →, U.S.A. 134 G1 37 4N 88 34W
Tenneville, Belgium 21 H7 50 6N 5 32 E
Tennille, U.S.A. 135 J4 32 58N 82 50W
Tennsift, Oued →, Morocco 98 B3 32 3N 9 28W
Tennyson, U.S.A. 141 F9 38 5N 87 7W
Teno, Pta. de, Canary Is. 33 F3 28 21N 16 55W
Tenom, Malaysia 75 A5 5 4N 115 57 E
Tenosique, Mexico 147 D6 17 30N 91 24W
Tenri, Japan 63 C7 34 39N 135 49 E
Tenryū, Japan 63 C9 34 52N 137 49 E
Tenryū-Gawa →, Japan 63 B9 35 39N 137 48 E
Tent L., Canada 131 A7 62 25N 107 54W
Tentelomatinan, Indonesia 72 A2 0 56N 121 48 E
Tenterfield, Australia 115 D5 29 0 S 152 0 E
Teófilo Otoni, Brazil 155 E3 17 50 S 41 30W
Teotihuacán, Mexico 147 D5 19 44N 98 50W
Tepa, Indonesia 73 C3 7 52 S 129 31 E
Tepalcatepec →, Mexico 146 D4 18 35N 101 59W
Tepehuanes, Mexico 146 B3 25 21N 105 44W
Tepelena, Albania 44 D2 40 17N 20 2 E
Tepequem, Serra, Brazil 153 C5 3 45N 61 45W
Tepetongo, Mexico 146 C4 22 28N 103 9W
Tepic, Mexico 146 C4 21 30N 104 54W
Teplice, Czech. 30 A6 50 40N 13 48 E
Teploklyuchenka, Kirghizia 55 B9 42 30N 78 30 E
Tepoca, C., Mexico 146 A2 30 20N 112 25W
Tequila, Mexico 146 C4 20 54N 103 47W
Ter →, Spain 34 C8 42 2N 3 12 E
Ter Apel, Neths. 20 C10 52 53N 7 5 E
Téra, Niger 101 C5 14 0N 0 45 E
Tera →, Spain 36 D5 41 54N 5 44W
Teraina, Kiribati 123 G11 4 43N 160 25W
Téramo, Italy 39 F10 42 40N 13 40 E
Terang, Australia 116 E5 38 15 S 142 55 E
Terawhiti, C., N.Z. 118 H3 41 16 S 174 38 E
Terazit, Massif de, Niger 97 D1 20 2N 8 30 E
Terborg, Neths. 20 E8 51 56N 6 22 E
Tercan, Turkey 89 D9 39 47N 40 23 E
Tercero →, Argentina 158 C3 32 58 S 61 47W
Terdal, India 82 F2 16 33N 75 3 E
Terebovlya, Ukraine 50 G4 49 18N 25 44 E
Teregova, Romania 46 D3 45 10N 22 16 E
Terek →, Russia 53 E12 44 0N 47 30 E
Terek-Say, Kirghizia 55 C5 41 30N 71 11 E
Terengganu □, Malaysia 74 B2 4 55N 103 0 E
Terenos, Brazil 157 E7 20 26 S 54 50W
Tereshka →, Russia 51 F15 51 48N 46 26 E
Teresina, Brazil 154 C3 5 9 S 42 45W
Teresinha, Brazil 153 C7 0 58N 52 2W
Terespol, Poland 47 C10 52 5N 23 37 E
Terewah, L., Australia 115 D4 29 52 S 147 35 E
Terges →, Portugal 37 H3 37 49N 7 41W
Tergnier, France 23 C10 49 40N 3 17 E
Terhazza, Mali 98 D3 23 38N 5 22W
Terheijden, Neths. 21 E5 51 38N 4 45 E
Teridgerie Cr. →, Australia 115 E4 30 25 S 148 50 E
Terifa, Yemen 86 D3 14 24N 43 48 E
Terlizzi, Italy 41 A9 41 8N 16 32 E
Terme, Turkey 52 F7 41 11N 37 0 E
Termez, Uzbekistan 55 E3 37 15N 67 15 E
Términi Imerese, Italy 40 E6 37 58N 13 42 E
Términos, L. de, Mexico 147 D6 18 35N 91 30W
Térmoli, Italy 39 F12 42 0N 15 0 E
Ternate, Indonesia 72 A3 0 45N 127 25 E
Terneuzen, Neths. 21 F3 51 20N 3 50 E
Terney, Russia 57 E14 45 3N 136 37 E
Terni, Italy 39 F9 42 34N 12 38 E
Ternitz, Austria 30 D9 47 43N 16 2 E
Ternopol, Ukraine 52 B1 49 30N 25 40 E
Terowie, N.S.W., Australia 115 E4 32 27 S 147 52 E
Terowie, S. Austral., Australia 115 E2 33 8 S 138 55 E
Terra Bella, U.S.A. 145 K7 35 58N 119 3W
Terrace, Canada 130 C3 54 30N 128 35W
Terrace Bay, Canada 128 C2 48 47N 87 5W
Terracina, Italy 40 A6 41 17N 13 12 E
Terralba, Italy 40 C1 39 42N 8 38 E
Terranova = Ólbia, Italy 40 B2 40 55N 9 30 E
Terranuova Bracciolini, Italy 39 E8 43 31N 11 35 E
Terrasini Favarotta, Italy 40 D6 38 10N 13 4 E
Terrasson-la-Villedieu, France 24 C5 45 8N 1 18 E
Terre Haute, U.S.A. 141 E9 39 28N 87 24W
Terrebonne B., U.S.A. 139 L9 29 15N 90 28W
Terrecht, Mali 99 D4 20 10N 0 10W
Terrell, U.S.A. 139 J6 32 44N 96 19W
Terrenceville, Canada 129 C9 47 40N 54 44W
Terrick Terrick, Australia 114 C4 24 44 S 145 5 E
Terry, U.S.A. 138 B2 46 47N 105 20W
Terschelling, Neths. 20 B6 53 25N 5 20 E
Terskey Alatau, Khrebet, Kirghizia 55 C8 41 50N 77 0 E
Terter →, Azerbaijan 53 F12 40 25N 47 10 E
Teruel, Spain 34 E3 40 22N 1 8W
Teruel □, Spain 34 E4 40 48N 1 0W
Tervel, Bulgaria 43 D12 43 45N 27 28 E
Tervola, Finland 12 C18 66 6N 24 49 E
Teryaweyna L., Australia 116 B5 32 18 S 143 22 E
Tešanj, Bos.-H., Yug. 42 C2 44 38N 18 1 E
Teseney, Ethiopia 95 D4 15 5N 36 42 E
Tesha →, Russia 51 D13 55 38N 42 9 E
Teshio, Japan 60 B10 44 53N 141 44 E
Teshio-Gawa →, Japan 60 B10 44 53N 141 45 E
Tešica, Serbia, Yug. 42 D6 43 27N 21 45 E
Tesiyn Gol →, Mongolia 64 A4 50 40N 93 20 E
Teslić, Bos.-H., Yug. 42 C2 44 37N 17 54 E
Teslin, Canada 130 A2 60 10N 132 43W
Teslin →, Canada 130 A2 61 34N 134 35W
Teslin L., Canada 130 A2 60 15N 132 57W
Tesouro, Brazil 157 D7 16 4 S 53 34W
Tessalit, Mali 101 A5 20 12N 1 0 E
Tessaoua, Niger 97 F1 13 47N 7 56 E
Tessenderlo, Belgium 21 F6 51 4N 5 5 E
Tessin, Germany 26 A8 54 2N 12 28 E
Tessit, Mali 101 B5 15 13N 0 18 E
Test →, U.K. 17 F6 51 7N 1 30W
Testa del Gargano, Italy 41 A9 41 50N 16 10 E
Tét, Hungary 31 D10 47 30N 17 33 E
Têt →, France 24 F7 42 44N 3 2 E
Tetachuck L., Canada 130 C3 53 18N 125 55W
Tetas, Pta., Chile 158 A1 23 31 S 70 38W
Tete, Mozam. 107 F3 16 13 S 33 33 E
Tete □, Mozam. 107 F3 15 15 S 32 40 E
Teterev →, Ukraine 50 F7 51 1N 30 5 E
Teteringen, Neths. 21 E5 51 37N 4 49 E
Teterow, Germany 26 B8 53 45N 12 34 E
Teteven, Bulgaria 43 E9 42 58N 24 17 E
Tethul →, Canada 130 A6 60 35N 112 12W
Tetiyev, Ukraine 52 B3 49 22N 29 38 E
Teton →, U.S.A. 142 C8 47 58N 111 0W
Tétouan, Morocco 98 A3 35 35N 5 21W
Tetovo, Macedonia, Yug. 42 E6 42 1N 21 2 E
Tetuán = Tétouan, Morocco 98 A3 35 35N 5 21W
Tetyukhe Pristan, Russia 60 B7 44 22N 135 48 E
Tetyushi, Russia 51 D16 54 55N 48 49 E
Teuco →, Argentina 158 B3 25 35 S 60 11W
Teufen, Switz. 29 B8 47 24N 9 23 E
Teulada, Italy 40 D1 38 59N 8 47 E
Teulon, Canada 131 C9 50 23N 97 16W
Teun, Indonesia 73 C3 6 59 S 129 8 E
Teutoburger Wald, Germany 26 C4 52 5N 8 20 E
Tevere →, Italy 39 G9 41 44N 12 14 E
Teverya, Israel 91 C4 32 47N 35 32 E
Teviot →, U.K. 18 F6 55 21N 2 51W
Tewantin, Australia 115 D5 26 27 S 153 3 E
Tewkesbury, U.K. 17 F5 51 59N 2 8W
Texada I., Canada 130 D4 49 40N 124 25W
Texarkana, Ark., U.S.A. 139 J8 33 25N 94 0W
Texarkana, Tex., U.S.A. 139 J7 33 25N 94 3W
Texas, Australia 115 D5 28 49 S 151 9 E
Texas □, U.S.A. 139 K5 31 40N 98 30W
Texas City, U.S.A. 139 L7 29 20N 94 55W
Texel, Neths. 20 B5 53 5N 4 50 E
Texhoma, U.S.A. 139 G4 36 32N 101 47W
Texline, U.S.A. 139 G3 36 26N 103 0W
Texoma L., U.S.A. 139 J6 34 0N 96 38W
Teykovo, Russia 51 C12 56 55N 40 30 E
Teyvareh, Afghan. 79 B2 33 30N 64 24 E
Teza →, Russia 51 C12 56 32N 41 53 E
Tezin, Afghan. 80 B3 34 24N 69 30 E
Teziutlán, Mexico 147 D5 19 50N 97 22W
Tezpur, India 78 B4 26 40N 92 45 E
Tezzeron L., Canada 130 C4 54 43N 124 30W
Tha-anne →, Canada 131 A10 60 31N 94 37W
Tha Deua, Laos 76 D4 17 57N 102 53 E
Tha Deua, Laos 76 C3 19 26N 101 50 E
Tha Pla, Thailand 76 D3 17 48N 100 32 E
Tha Rua, Thailand 76 E3 14 34N 100 44 E
Tha Sala, Thailand 77 H2 8 40N 99 56 E
Tha Song Yang, Thailand 76 D1 17 34N 97 55 E
Thaba Nchu, S. Africa 104 D4 29 17 S 26 52 E
Thaba Putsoa, Lesotho 105 D4 29 45 S 28 0 E
Thabana Ntlenyana, Lesotho 105 D4 29 30 S 29 16 E
Thabazimbi, S. Africa 105 C4 24 40 S 27 21 E
Thabeikkyin, Burma 78 D5 22 53N 95 59 E
Thai Binh, Vietnam 76 B6 20 35N 106 1 E
Thai Hoa, Vietnam 76 C5 19 20N 105 20 E
Thai Muang, Thailand 77 H2 8 24N 98 16 E
Thai Nguyen, Vietnam 76 B5 21 35N 105 55 E
Thailand ■, Asia 76 E4 16 0N 102 0 E
Thailand, G. of, Asia 77 G3 11 30N 101 0 E
Thakhek, Laos 76 D5 17 25N 104 45 E
Thakurgaon, Bangla. 78 B2 26 2N 88 34 E
Thal, Pakistan 79 B3 33 28N 70 33 E
Thal Desert, Pakistan 80 D4 31 10N 71 30 E
Thala, Tunisia 96 A1 35 35N 8 40 E
Thalabarivat, Cambodia 76 F5 13 33N 105 57 E
Thalkirch, Switz. 29 C8 46 39N 9 17 E
Thallon, Australia 115 D4 28 39 S 148 49 E
Thalwil, Switz. 29 B7 47 17N 8 35 E
Thamarit, Oman 87 C6 17 39N 54 2 E
Thame →, U.K. 17 F6 51 35N 1 8W
Thames, N.Z. 118 D4 37 7 S 175 34 E
Thames →, Canada 128 D3 42 20N 82 25W
Thames →, U.K. 17 F8 51 30N 0 35 E
Thames →, U.S.A. 137 E12 41 18N 72 9W
Thames, Firth of, N.Z. 118 D4 37 0 S 175 25 E
Thamesford, Canada 136 C3 43 4N 81 0W
Thamesville, Canada 136 D3 42 33N 81 59W
Thāmit, W. →, Libya 96 B3 30 51N 16 14 E
Thamūd, Yemen 87 C5 17 18N 49 55 E
Than Uyen, Vietnam 76 B4 22 0N 103 54 E
Thanbyuzayat, Burma 78 G6 15 58N 97 44 E
Thane, India 82 E1 19 12N 72 59 E
Thanesar, India 80 D7 30 1N 76 52 E
Thanet, I. of, U.K. 17 F9 51 21N 1 20 E
Thangoo, Australia 112 C3 18 10 S 122 22 E
Thangool, Australia 114 C5 24 38 S 150 42 E
Thanh Hoa, Vietnam 76 C5 19 48N 105 46 E
Thanh Hung, Vietnam 77 H5 9 55N 105 43 E
Thanh Pho Ho Chi Minh = Phanh Bho Ho Chi Minh, Vietnam 77 G6 10 58N 106 40 E
Thanh Thuy, Vietnam 76 A5 22 55N 104 51 E
Thanjavur, India 83 J4 10 48N 79 12 E
Thann, France 23 E14 47 48N 7 5 E
Thaon-les-Vosges, France 23 D13 48 15N 6 24 E
Thap Sakae, Thailand 77 G2 11 30N 99 37 E
Thap Than, Thailand 76 E2 15 27N 99 54 E
Thar Desert, India 80 F4 28 0N 72 0 E
Tharad, India 80 G4 24 30N 71 44 E
Thargomindah, Australia 115 D3 27 58 S 143 46 E
Tharrawaddy, Burma 78 G5 17 38N 95 48 E
Tharrawaw, Burma 78 G5 17 41N 95 28 E
Tharthar, W. →, Iraq 84 C4 33 59N 43 12 E
Thasopoúla, Greece 44 D6 40 49N 24 45 E
Thásos, Greece 44 D6 40 40N 24 40 E
That Khe, Vietnam 76 A6 22 16N 106 28 E
Thatcher, Ariz., U.S.A. 143 K9 32 54N 109 46W
Thatcher, Colo., U.S.A. 139 G2 37 38N 104 6W
Thaton, Burma 78 G6 16 55N 97 22 E
Thau, Bassin de, France 24 E7 43 23N 3 36 E
Thaungdut, Burma 78 C5 24 30N 94 40 E
Thayer, U.S.A. 139 G9 36 34N 91 34W
Thayetmyo, Burma 78 F5 19 20N 95 10 E
Thayngen, Switz. 29 A7 47 49N 8 43 E
The Alberga →, Australia 115 D2 27 6 S 135 33 E
The Bight, Bahamas 149 B4 24 19N 75 24W
The Brothers, Yemen 87 D6 12 8N 53 10 E
The Coorong, Australia 116 C3 35 50 S 139 20 E
The Dalles, U.S.A. 142 D3 45 40N 121 11W
The English Company's Is., Australia 114 A2 11 50 S 136 32 E
The Entrance, Australia 117 B9 33 21 S 151 30 E
The Frome →, Australia 115 D2 29 8 S 137 54 E
The Grampians, Australia 116 D5 37 0 S 142 20 E
The Great Divide = Great Dividing Ra., Australia 114 C4 23 0 S 146 0 E
The Hague = 's-Gravenhage, Neths. 20 D4 52 7N 4 17 E
The Hamilton →, Australia 115 D2 26 40 S 135 19 E
The Hunter Hills, N.Z. 119 E5 44 26 S 170 46 E
The Macumba →, Australia 115 D2 27 52 S 137 12 E
The Neales →, Australia 115 D2 28 8 S 136 47 E
The Oaks, Australia 117 C9 34 3 S 150 34 E
The Officer →, Australia 113 E5 27 46 S 132 30 E
The Pas, Canada 131 C8 53 45N 101 15W
The Range, Zimbabwe 107 F3 19 2 S 31 2 E
The Remarkables, N.Z. 119 F3 45 10 S 168 50 E
The Rock, Australia 117 F4 35 15 S 147 2 E
The Salt L., Australia 115 E3 30 6 S 142 8 E
The Stevenson →, Australia 115 D2 27 6 S 135 33 E
The Warburton →, Australia 115 D2 28 4 S 137 28 E
Thebes = Thívai, Greece 45 F5 38 19N 23 19 E
Thebes, Egypt 94 B3 25 40N 32 35 E
Thedford, Canada 136 C3 43 9N 81 51W
Thedford, U.S.A. 138 E4 41 59N 100 31W
Theebine, Australia 115 D5 25 57 S 152 34 E
Thekulthili L., Canada 131 A7 61 3N 110 0W
Thelon →, Canada 131 A8 62 35N 104 3W
Thénezay, France 22 F6 46 44N 0 2W
Thenia, Algeria 99 A5 36 44N 3 33 E
Thenon, France 24 C5 45 9N 1 4 E
Theodore, Australia 114 C5 24 55 S 150 3 E
Thepha, Thailand 77 J3 6 52N 100 58 E
Thérain →, France 23 C9 49 15N 2 27 E
Theresa, U.S.A. 137 B9 44 13N 75 50W
Thermaïkos Kólpos, Greece 44 D4 40 15N 22 45 E
Thermopolis, U.S.A. 142 E9 43 35N 108 10W
Thermopylae P., Greece 45 F4 38 48N 22 35 E
Thesprotía □, Greece 44 E2 39 27N 20 22 E
Thessalía □, Greece 44 E4 38 25N 21 50 E
Thessalon, Canada 128 C3 46 20N 83 30W
Thessaloníki, Greece 44 D4 40 38N 22 58 E
Thessaloníki □, Greece 44 D5 40 45N 23 0 E
Thessaloniki, Gulf of = Thermaïkos Kólpos, Greece 44 D4 40 15N 22 45 E
Thessaly = Thessalía □, Greece 44 E4 38 25N 21 50 E
Thetford, U.K. 17 E8 52 25N 0 44 E
Thetford Mines, Canada 129 C5 46 8N 71 18W
Theun →, Laos 76 C5 18 19N 104 0 E
Theunissen, S. Africa 104 D4 28 26 S 26 43 E
Theux, Belgium 21 G7 50 32N 5 49 E
Thevenard, Australia 115 E1 32 9 S 133 38 E
Thiámis →, Greece 44 E2 39 15N 20 6 E
Thiberville, France 22 C7 49 8N 0 27 E
Thibodaux, U.S.A. 139 L9 29 48N 90 49W
Thicket Portage, Canada 131 B9 55 19N 97 42W
Thief River Falls, U.S.A. 138 A6 48 15N 96 48W
Thiel Mts., Antarctica 7 E16 85 15 S 91 0W
Thiene, Italy 39 C8 45 42N 11 29 E
Thiérache, France 23 C10 49 51N 3 45 E
Thiers, France 24 C7 45 52N 3 33 E
Thies, Senegal 100 C1 14 50N 16 51W
Thiet, Sudan 95 F2 7 37N 28 49 E
Thika, Kenya 106 C4 1 1 S 37 5 E
Thille-Boubacar, Senegal 100 B1 16 31N 15 5W
Thimphu, Bhutan 78 B2 27 31N 89 45 E
þingvallavatn, Iceland 12 D3 64 11N 21 9W
Thio, N. Cal. 121 U20 21 37 S 166 14 E
Thionville, France 23 C13 49 20N 6 10 E
Thíra, Greece 45 H7 36 23N 25 27 E
Thirasía, Greece 45 H7 36 26N 25 21 E
Thirsk, U.K. 16 C6 54 15N 1 20W
Thiruvarur, India 83 J4 10 46N 79 38 E
Thisted, Denmark 13 H10 56 58N 8 40 E
Thistle I., Australia 116 C2 35 0 S 136 8 E
Thitgy, Burma 78 F6 18 15N 96 13 E
Thithia, Fiji 121 A3 17 45 S 179 18W
Thitpokpin, Burma 78 F5 19 24N 95 58 E
Thívai, Greece 45 F5 38 19N 23 19 E
Thiviers, France 24 C4 45 25N 0 54 E
Thizy, France 25 B8 46 2N 4 18 E
þjórsá →, Iceland 12 E3 63 47N 20 48W
Thlewiaza →, Man., Canada 131 B8 59 43N 100 5W
Thlewiaza →, N.W.T., Canada 131 A10 60 29N 94 40W
Thmar Puok, Cambodia 76 F4 13 57N 103 4 E
Tho Vinh, Vietnam 76 C5 19 16N 105 42 E
Thoa →, Canada 131 A7 60 31N 109 47W
Thoen, Thailand 76 D2 17 43N 99 12 E
Thoeng, Thailand 76 C3 19 41N 100 12 E
Thoissey, France 25 B8 46 12N 4 48 E
Tholdi, Pakistan 81 B7 35 5N 76 6 E
Tholen, Neths. 21 E4 51 32N 4 13 E
Thomas, Okla., U.S.A. 139 H5 35 48N 98 48W
Thomas, W. Va., U.S.A. 134 F6 39 10N 79 30W
Thomas, L., Australia 115 D2 26 4 S 137 58 E
Thomas Hill Res., U.S.A. 140 E4 39 34N 92 39W
Thomaston, U.S.A. 135 J3 32 54N 84 20W
Thomasville, Ala., U.S.A. 135 K2 31 55N 87 42W
Thomasville, Ga., U.S.A. 135 K3 30 50N 84 0W
Thomasville, N.C., U.S.A. 135 H5 35 55N 80 4W
Thommen, Belgium 21 H8 50 14N 6 5 E
Thompson, Canada 131 B9 55 45N 97 52W
Thompson, U.S.A. 143 G9 39 0N 109 50W
Thompson →, Canada 130 C4 50 15N 121 24W
Thompson →, U.S.A. 138 F8 39 46N 93 37W
Thompson Falls, U.S.A. 142 C6 47 37N 115 20W
Thompson Landing, Canada 131 A6 62 56N 110 40W
Thompson Pk., U.S.A. 142 F2 41 0N 123 3W
Thompson Sd., N.Z. 119 F1 45 8 S 166 46 E
Thomson, U.S.A. 140 C6 41 58N 90 6W
Thomson's Falls = Nyahururu, Kenya 106 B4 0 2N 36 27 E
Thon Buri, Thailand 77 F3 13 43N 100 29 E
Thônes, France 25 C10 45 54N 6 18 E
Thongwa, Burma 78 G6 16 45N 96 33 E
Thonon-les-Bains, France 25 B10 46 22N 6 29 E
Thonze, Burma 78 G5 17 38N 95 47 E

Trabzon 275


Tochigi, *Japan* .......... 63 **A11** 36 25N 139 45 E
Tochigi □, *Japan* ....... 63 **A11** 36 45N 139 45 E
Tocina, *Spain* .......... 37 **H5** 37 37N 5 44W
Tocopilla, *Chile* ........ 158 **A1** 22 5 S 70 10W
Tocumwal, *Australia* .... 117 **C6** 35 51 S 145 31 E
Tocuyo →, *Venezuela* .. 152 **A4** 11 3N 68 23W
Tocuyo de la Costa, *Venezuela* .......... 152 **A4** 11 2N 68 23W
Todd →, *Australia* ..... 114 **C2** 24 52 S 135 48 E
Todeli, *Indonesia* ....... 72 **B2** 1 38 S 124 34 E
Todenyang, *Kenya* ..... 106 **B4** 4 35N 35 56 E
Todi, *Italy* ............. 39 **F9** 42 47N 12 24 E
Tödi, *Switz.* ........... 29 **C7** 46 48N 8 55 E
Todos os Santos, B. de, *Brazil* .............. 155 **D4** 12 48 S 38 38W
Todos Santos, *Mexico* .. 146 **C2** 23 27N 110 13W
Todtnau, *Germany* ..... 27 **H3** 47 50N 7 56 E
Toecé, *Burkina Faso* ... 101 **C4** 11 50N 1 16W
Toetoes B., *N.Z.* ....... 119 **G3** 46 42 S 168 41 E
Tofield, *Canada* ........ 130 **C6** 53 25N 112 40W
Tofino, *Canada* ........ 130 **D3** 49 11N 125 55W
Töfsingdalens nationalpark, *Sweden* . 14 **B6** 62 15N 12 44 E
Toftlund, *Denmark* ..... 15 **J3** 55 11N 9 2 E
Tofua, *Tonga* .......... 121 **P13** 19 45 S 175 5W
Toga, *Vanuatu* ......... 121 **C4** 13 26 S 166 42 E
Tōgane, *Japan* ......... 63 **B12** 35 33N 140 22 E
Togba, *Mauritania* ...... 100 **B2** 17 26N 10 12W
Togbo, *C.A.R.* ......... 102 **A3** 6 0N 17 27 E
Toggenburg, *Switz.* ..... 29 **B8** 47 16N 9 9 E
Togian, Kepulauan, *Indonesia* ........... 72 **B2** 0 20 S 121 50 E
Togliatti, *Russia* ........ 51 **E16** 53 32N 49 24 E
Togo ■, *W. Afr.* ....... 101 **D5** 8 30N 1 35 E
Togtoh, *China* .......... 66 **D6** 40 15N 111 10 E
Toguzak →, *Kazakhstan* 54 **D8** 54 3N 62 44 E
Tohma →, *Turkey* ...... 89 **D8** 38 29N 38 23 E
Tōhoku □, *Japan* ...... 60 **E10** 39 50N 141 45 E
Toi, *Japan* ............ 63 **C10** 34 54N 138 47 E
Toinya, *Sudan* ......... 95 **F2** 6 17N 29 46 E
Tojo, *Indonesia* ........ 72 **B2** 1 20 S 121 15 E
Tōjō, *Japan* ........... 62 **C5** 34 53N 133 16 E
Tok →, *Russia* ......... 54 **E3** 52 46N 52 22 E
Toka, *Guyana* ......... 153 **C6** 3 58N 59 17W
Tokaanu, *N.Z.* ......... 118 **E4** 38 58 S 175 46 E
Tokachi-Dake, *Japan* ... 60 **C11** 43 17N 142 5 E
Tokachi-Gawa →, *Japan* 60 **C11** 42 44N 143 42 E
Tokai, *Japan* .......... 63 **B8** 35 2N 136 55 E
Tokaj, *Hungary* ........ 31 **C14** 48 8N 21 27 E
Tokala, *Indonesia* ...... 72 **B2** 1 30 S 121 40 E
Tōkamachi, *Japan* ..... 61 **F9** 37 8N 138 43 E
Tokanui, *N.Z.* ......... 119 **G3** 46 34 S 168 56 E
Tokar, *Sudan* .......... 94 **D4** 18 27N 37 56 E
Tokara-Rettō, *Japan* ... 61 **K4** 29 37N 129 43 E
Tokarahi, *N.Z.* ......... 119 **E5** 44 56 S 170 39 E
Tokashiki-Shima, *Japan* . 61 **L3** 26 11N 127 21 E
Tokat, *Turkey* ......... 88 **C7** 40 22N 36 35 E
Tokat □, *Turkey* ....... 88 **C7** 40 15N 36 30 E
Tŏkchŏn, *N. Korea* ..... 67 **E14** 39 45N 126 18 E
Tokeland, *U.S.A.* ...... 144 **D3** 46 42N 123 59W
Tokelau Is., *Pac. Oc.* ... 122 **H10** 9 0 S 171 45W
Toki, *Japan* ........... 63 **B9** 35 18N 137 8 E
Tokmak, *Kirghizia* ..... 55 **B7** 42 49N 75 15 E
Toko Ra., *Australia* .... 114 **C2** 23 5 S 138 20 E
Tokomaru Bay, *N.Z.* ... 118 **E7** 38 8 S 178 22 E
Tokoname, *Japan* ...... 63 **C8** 34 53N 136 51 E
Tokoro-Gawa →, *Japan* 60 **B12** 44 7N 144 5 E
Tokoroa, *N.Z.* ......... 118 **E4** 38 13 S 175 50 E
Tokorozawa, *Japan* ..... 63 **B11** 35 47N 139 28 E
Toktogul, *Kirghizia* ..... 55 **C6** 41 50N 72 50 E
Toku, *Tonga* .......... 121 **P13** 18 10 S 174 11W
Tokuji, *Japan* ......... 62 **C3** 34 11N 131 42 E
Tokuno-Shima, *Japan* ... 61 **L4** 27 56N 128 55 E
Tokushima, *Japan* ...... 62 **C6** 34 4N 134 34 E
Tokushima □, *Japan* .... 62 **D6** 33 55N 134 0 E
Tokuyama, *Japan* ...... 62 **C3** 34 3N 131 50 E
Tōkyō, *Japan* .......... 63 **B11** 35 45N 139 45 E
Tōkyō □, *Japan* ....... 63 **B11** 35 40N 139 30 E
Tōkyō-Wan, *Japan* ..... 63 **B11** 35 25N 139 47 E
Tokzār, *Afghan.* ....... 79 **B2** 35 52N 66 26 E
Tolaga Bay, *N.Z.* ...... 118 **E7** 38 21 S 178 20 E
Tolbukhin, *Bulgaria* .... 43 **D12** 43 37N 27 49 E
Toledo, *Phil.* .......... 71 **F4** 10 23N 123 38 E
Toledo, *Spain* ......... 36 **F6** 39 50N 4 2W
Toledo, *Ill., U.S.A.* ..... 141 **E8** 39 16N 88 15W
Toledo, *Iowa, U.S.A.* ... 140 **B4** 42 0N 92 35W
Toledo, *Ohio, U.S.A.* .. 141 **C13** 41 37N 83 33W
Toledo, *Oreg., U.S.A.* .. 142 **D2** 44 40N 123 59W
Toledo, *Wash., U.S.A.* . 142 **C2** 46 29N 122 51W
Toledo, Montes de, *Spain* 37 **F6** 39 33N 4 20W
Tolentino, *Italy* ........ 39 **E10** 43 12N 13 17 E
Tolga, *Algeria* ......... 99 **B6** 34 40N 5 22 E
Tolga, *Norway* ......... 14 **B5** 62 26N 11 1 E
Toliara, *Madag.* ........ 105 **C7** 23 21 S 43 40 E
Toliara □, *Madag.* ..... 105 **C8** 21 0 S 45 0 E
Tolima, *Colombia* ...... 152 **C2** 4 40N 75 19W
Tolima □, *Colombia* .... 152 **C2** 3 45N 75 15W
Tolitoli, *Indonesia* ...... 72 **A2** 1 5N 120 50 E
Tolkamer, *Neths.* ....... 20 **E8** 51 52N 6 6 E
Tolkmicko, *Poland* ...... 47 **A6** 54 19N 19 31 E
Tolleson, *U.S.A.* ....... 143 **K7** 33 29N 112 10W
Tollhouse, *U.S.A.* ...... 144 **H7** 37 1N 119 24W
Tolmachevo, *Russia* .... 50 **B6** 58 56N 29 51 E
Tolmezzo, *Italy* ........ 39 **B10** 46 23N 13 2 E
Tolmin, *Slovenia* ....... 39 **B10** 46 11N 13 45 E
Tolna, *Hungary* ........ 31 **E11** 46 25N 18 48 E
Tolna □, *Hungary* ..... 31 **E11** 46 30N 18 30 E
Tolo, *Zaïre* ........... 102 **C3** 2 55 S 18 34 E
Tolo, Teluk, *Indonesia* .. 72 **B2** 2 20 S 122 10 E
Tolochin, *Belorussia* .... 50 **D6** 54 25N 29 42 E
Tolong Bay, *Phil.* ...... 71 **G4** 9 20N 122 49 E
Tolono, *U.S.A.* ........ 141 **E8** 39 59N 88 16W
Tolosa, *Spain* .......... 34 **B2** 43 8N 2 5W
Tolox, *Spain* .......... 37 **J6** 36 41N 4 54W
Toltén, *Chile* .......... 160 **A2** 39 13 S 74 14W
Toluca, *Mexico* ........ 147 **D5** 19 20N 99 40W
Tom Burke, *S. Africa* ... 105 **C4** 23 5 S 28 0 E
Tom Price, *Australia* .... 112 **D2** 22 40 S 117 48 E
Tomah, *U.S.A.* ........ 138 **D9** 43 59N 90 30W
Tomahawk, *U.S.A.* ..... 138 **C10** 45 28N 89 40W
Tomakomai, *Japan* ..... 60 **C10** 42 38N 141 36 E
Tomales, *U.S.A.* ....... 144 **G4** 38 15N 122 53W
Tomales B., *U.S.A.* .... 144 **G3** 38 15N 123 58W
Tomanivi, *Fiji* ......... 121 **A2** 17 37 S 178 1 E
Tomar, *Portugal* ....... 37 **F2** 39 36N 8 25W
Tómaros Óros, *Greece* .. 44 **E2** 39 29N 20 48 E
Tomarza, *Turkey* ....... 88 **D6** 38 27N 35 48 E
Tomás Barrón, *Bolivia* .. 156 **D4** 17 35 S 67 31W
Tomaszów Mazowiecki, *Poland* .............. 47 **D6** 51 30N 19 57 E
Tomatlán, *Mexico* ...... 146 **D3** 19 56N 105 15W
Tombador, Serra do, *Brazil* .............. 157 **C6** 12 0 S 58 0W
Tombé, *Sudan* ......... 95 **F3** 5 53N 31 40 E
Tombigbee →, *U.S.A.* . 135 **K2** 31 4N 87 58W
Tombôco, *Angola* ...... 103 **D2** 6 48 S 13 18 E
Tombouctou, *Mali* ..... 100 **B4** 16 50N 3 0W
Tombstone, *U.S.A.* ..... 143 **L8** 31 40N 110 4W
Tombua, *Angola* ....... 103 **F2** 15 55 S 11 55 E
Tomé, *Chile* ........... 158 **D1** 36 36 S 72 57W
Tomé-Açu, *Brazil* ...... 154 **B2** 2 25 S 48 9W
Tomelilla, *Sweden* ...... 15 **J7** 55 33N 13 58 E
Tomelloso, *Spain* ...... 35 **F1** 39 10N 3 2W
Tomingley, *Australia* .... 117 **B8** 32 26 S 148 16 E
Tomini, *Indonesia* ...... 72 **A2** 0 30N 120 30 E
Tomini, Teluk, *Indonesia* 72 **B2** 0 10 S 122 0 E
Tominian, *Mali* ......... 100 **C4** 13 17N 4 35W
Tomiño, *Spain* ......... 36 **D2** 41 59N 8 46W
Tomkinson Ras., *Australia* ............ 113 **E4** 26 11 S 129 5 E
Tommot, *Russia* ....... 57 **D13** 59 4N 126 20 E
Tomnavoulin, *U.K.* ..... 18 **D5** 57 19N 3 18W
Tomnop Ta Suos, *Cambodia* ........... 77 **G5** 11 20N 104 15 E
Tomo, *Colombia.* ....... 152 **C4** 2 38N 67 32W
Tomo, *Japan* .......... 62 **C5** 34 23N 133 23 E
Tomo →, *Colombia* .... 152 **B4** 5 20N 67 48W
Tomobe, *Japan* ........ 63 **A12** 36 20N 140 20 E
Toms Place, *U.S.A.* .... 144 **H8** 37 34N 118 41W
Toms River, *U.S.A.* .... 137 **G10** 39 59N 74 12W
Tomsk, *Russia* ......... 56 **D9** 56 30N 85 5 E
Tonalá, *Mexico* ........ 147 **D6** 16 8N 93 41W
Tonale, Passo del, *Italy* . 38 **B7** 46 15N 10 34 E
Tonalea, *U.S.A.* ....... 143 **H8** 36 17N 110 58W
Tonami, *Japan* ......... 63 **A8** 36 40N 136 58 E
Tonantins, *Brazil* ...... 152 **D4** 2 45 S 67 45W
Tonasket, *U.S.A.* ...... 142 **B4** 48 45N 119 30W
Tonate, *Fr. Guiana* .... 153 **C7** 5 0N 52 28W
Tonawanda, *U.S.A.* .... 136 **D6** 43 0N 78 54W
Tonbridge, *U.K.* ....... 17 **F8** 51 12N 0 18 E
Tondano, *Indonesia* .... 72 **A2** 1 35N 124 54 E
Tondela, *Portugal* ...... 36 **E2** 40 31N 8 5W
Tønder, *Denmark* ...... 15 **K2** 54 58N 8 50 E
Tondi, *India* .......... 83 **K4** 9 45N 79 4 E
Tondi Kiwindi, *Niger* ... 101 **C5** 14 28N 2 2 E
Tondibi, *Mali* ......... 101 **B4** 16 39N 0 14W
Tonekābon, *Iran* ....... 85 **B6** 36 45N 51 12 E
Tong Xian, *China* ...... 66 **E9** 39 55N 116 35 E
Tonga ■, *Pac. Oc.* ..... 121 **P13** 19 50 S 174 30W
Tonga Trench, *Pac. Oc.* 122 **J10** 18 0 S 175 0W
Tongaat, *S. Africa* ..... 105 **D5** 29 33 S 31 9 E
Tongala, *Australia* ..... 117 **D6** 36 14 S 144 56 E
Tong'an, *China* ........ 69 **E12** 24 37N 118 8 E
Tongareva, *Cook Is.* .... 123 **H12** 9 0 S 158 0W
Tongatapu, *Tonga* ...... 121 **Q14** 21 10 S 174 0W
Tongatapu Group, *Tonga* 121 **Q13** 21 0 S 175 0W
Tongbai, *China* ......... 69 **A9** 32 20N 113 23 E
Tongcheng, *Anhui, China* 69 **B11** 31 4N 116 56 E
Tongcheng, *Hubei, China* 69 **C9** 29 15N 113 50 E
Tongchŏn-ni, *N. Korea* . 67 **E14** 39 50N 127 25 E
Tongchuan, *China* ...... 66 **G5** 35 6N 109 3 E
Tongdao, *China* ........ 68 **D7** 26 10N 109 42 E
Tongeren, *Belgium* ..... 21 **G6** 50 47N 5 28 E
Tonggu, *China* ......... 69 **C10** 28 31N 114 20 E
Tongguan, *China* ...... 66 **G6** 34 40N 110 25 E
Tonghai, *China* ........ 68 **E4** 24 10N 102 53 E
Tonghua, *China* ........ 67 **D13** 41 42N 125 58 E
Tongjiang, *China* ...... 68 **B6** 31 58N 107 11 E
Tongjosŏn Man, *N. Korea* 67 **E14** 39 30N 128 0 E
Tongking, G. of = Tonkin, G. of, *Asia* ... 76 **B7** 20 0N 108 0 E
Tongliang, *China* ...... 68 **C6** 29 50N 106 3 E
Tongliao, *China* ........ 67 **C12** 43 38N 122 18 E
Tongling, *China* ........ 69 **B11** 30 55N 117 48 E
Tonglu, *China* ......... 69 **C12** 29 45N 119 37 E
Tongnae, *S. Korea* ..... 67 **G15** 35 12N 129 5 E
Tongnan, *China* ....... 68 **B5** 30 9N 105 50 E
Tongoa, *Vanuatu* ...... 121 **F6** 16 54 S 168 34 E
Tongobory, *Madag.* .... 105 **C7** 23 32 S 44 20 E
Tongoy, *Chile* ......... 158 **C1** 30 16 S 71 31W
Tongren, *China* ........ 68 **D7** 27 43N 109 11 E
Tongres = Tongeren, *Belgium* ............. 21 **G6** 50 47N 5 28 E
Tongsa Dzong, *Bhutan* .. 78 **B3** 27 31N 90 31 E
Tongue, *U.K.* ......... 18 **C4** 58 29N 4 25W
Tongue →, *U.S.A.* ..... 138 **B2** 46 24N 105 52W
Tongwei, *China* ........ 66 **G3** 35 0N 105 5 E
Tongxin, *China* ........ 66 **F3** 36 59N 105 58 E
Tongyang, *N. Korea* .... 67 **E14** 39 9N 126 53 E
Tongyu, *China* ......... 67 **B12** 44 45N 123 4 E
Tongzi, *China* ......... 68 **C6** 28 9N 106 49 E
Tonica, *U.S.A.* ........ 140 **C7** 41 13N 89 4W
Tonj, *Sudan* .......... 95 **F2** 7 20N 28 44 E
Tonk, *India* ........... 80 **F6** 26 6N 75 54 E
Tonkawa, *U.S.A.* ...... 139 **G6** 36 44N 97 22W
Tonkin = Bac Phan, *Vietnam* ............ 76 **B5** 22 0N 105 0 E
Tonkin, G. of, *Asia* ..... 76 **B7** 20 0N 108 0 E
Tonlé Sap, *Cambodia* ... 76 **F4** 13 0N 104 0 E
Tonnay-Charente, *France* 24 **C3** 45 56N 0 55W
Tonneins, *France* ...... 24 **D4** 44 23N 0 19 E
Tonnerre, *France* ...... 23 **E10** 47 51N 3 59 E
Tönning, *Germany* ..... 26 **A4** 54 18N 8 57 E
Tono, *Japan* .......... 60 **E10** 39 19N 141 32 E
Tonopah, *U.S.A.* ...... 143 **G5** 38 4N 117 12W
Tonoshō, *Japan* ....... 62 **C6** 34 29N 134 11 E
Tonosí, *Panama* ....... 148 **E3** 7 20N 80 20W
Tønsberg, *Norway* ..... 14 **E4** 59 19N 10 25 E
Tonumea, *Tonga* ....... 121 **Q13** 20 30 S 174 30W
Tonzang, *Burma* ....... 78 **D4** 23 36N 93 42 E
Tonzi, *Burma* ......... 78 **C5** 24 39N 94 57 E
Tooele, *U.S.A.* ........ 142 **F7** 40 30N 112 20W
Toolondo, *Australia* .... 116 **D4** 36 58 S 141 58 E
Toompine, *Australia* .... 115 **D3** 27 15 S 144 19 E
Toongi, *Australia* ...... 117 **B8** 32 28 S 148 30 E
Toonpan, *Australia* ..... 114 **B4** 19 28 S 146 48 E
Toora, *Australia* ....... 117 **E7** 38 39 S 146 23 E
Toora-Khem, *Russia* .... 57 **D10** 52 28N 96 17 E
Toowoomba, *Australia* .. 115 **D5** 27 32 S 151 56 E
Top-ozero, *Russia* ...... 48 **A5** 65 35N 32 0 E
Topalu, *Romania* ....... 46 **E9** 44 31N 28 3 E
Topaz, *U.S.A.* ........ 144 **G7** 38 41N 119 30W
Topeka, *U.S.A.* ........ 138 **F7** 39 3N 95 40W
Topki, *Russia* .......... 56 **D9** 55 20N 85 35 E
Topl'a →, *Czech.* ...... 31 **C14** 48 45N 21 45 E
Topley, *Canada* ........ 130 **C3** 54 49N 126 18W
Toplica →, *Serbia, Yug.* 42 **D6** 43 15N 21 49 E
Toplița, *Romania* ...... 46 **C6** 46 55N 25 20 E
Topocalma, Pta., *Chile* . 158 **C1** 34 10 S 72 2W
Topock, *U.S.A.* ........ 145 **L12** 34 46N 114 29W
Topola, *Serbia, Yug.* ... 42 **C5** 44 17N 20 41 E
Topolčane, *Macedonia, Yug.* ..... 42 **F6** 41 14N 21 56 E
Topoľčany, *Czech.* ..... 31 **C11** 48 35N 18 12 E
Topoli, *Kazakhstan* ..... 53 **C14** 47 59N 51 38 E
Topolnitsa →, *Bulgaria* 43 **E9** 42 11N 24 18 E
Topolobampo, *Mexico* .. 146 **B3** 25 40N 109 4W
Topolovgrad, *Bulgaria* .. 43 **E11** 42 5N 26 20 E
Topolvătu Mare, *Romania* ........... 42 **B6** 45 46N 21 41 E
Toppenish, *U.S.A.* ..... 142 **C3** 46 27N 120 16W
Topusko, *Croatia* ...... 39 **C12** 45 18N 15 59 E
Toquepala, *Peru* ....... 156 **D3** 17 24 S 70 25W
Torá, *Spain* ........... 34 **D6** 41 49N 1 25 E
Tora Kit, *Sudan* ....... 95 **E3** 11 2N 32 36 E
Toraka Vestale, *Madag.* 105 **B7** 16 20 S 43 58 E
Torata, *Peru* .......... 156 **D3** 17 23 S 70 1W
Torbalı, *Turkey* ........ 88 **D2** 38 10N 27 21 E
Torbay, *Canada* ........ 129 **C9** 47 40N 52 42W
Torbay, *U.K.* .......... 17 **G4** 50 26N 3 31W
Tørdal, *Norway* ........ 14 **E2** 59 10N 8 45 E
Tordesillas, *Spain* ...... 36 **D6** 41 30N 5 0W
Tordoya, *Spain* ........ 36 **B2** 43 6N 8 36W
Töreboda, *Sweden* ..... 15 **F8** 58 41N 14 7 E
Torfajökull, *Iceland* .... 12 **E4** 63 54N 19 0W
Torgau, *Germany* ...... 26 **D8** 51 32N 13 0 E
Torgelow, *Germany* ..... 26 **B9** 53 40N 13 59 E
Torhout, *Belgium* ...... 21 **F2** 51 5N 3 7 E
Tori, *Ethiopia* ......... 95 **F3** 7 53N 33 35 E
Tori-Shima, *Japan* ..... 61 **J10** 30 29N 140 19 E
Torigni-sur-Vire, *France* 22 **C6** 49 3N 0 58W
Torija, *Spain* .......... 34 **E1** 40 44N 3 2W
Torin, *Mexico* ......... 146 **B2** 27 33N 110 15W
Toriñana, C., *Spain* .... 36 **B1** 43 3N 9 17W
Torino, *Italy* .......... 38 **C4** 45 4N 7 40 E
Torit, *Sudan* .......... 95 **G3** 4 27N 32 31 E
Torkovichi, *Russia* ..... 50 **B7** 58 51N 30 21 E
Tormac, *Romania* ...... 42 **B6** 45 30N 21 30 E
Tormes →, *Spain* ...... 36 **D4** 41 18N 6 29W
Tornado Mt., *Canada* ... 130 **D6** 49 55N 114 40W
Torne älv →, *Sweden* .. 12 **D18** 65 50N 24 12 E
Torneå = Tornio, *Finland* 12 **D18** 65 50N 24 12 E
Torneträsk, *Sweden* .... 12 **B15** 68 24N 19 15 E
Tornio, *Finland* ........ 12 **D18** 65 50N 24 12 E
Tornionjoki →, *Finland* 12 **D18** 65 50N 24 12 E
Tornquist, *Argentina* .... 158 **D3** 38 8 S 62 15W
Toro, *Baleares, Spain* .... 33 **B11** 39 59N 4 8 E
Toro, *Zamora, Spain* ... 36 **D5** 41 35N 5 24W
Torö, *Sweden* .......... 15 **F11** 58 48N 17 50 E
Toro, Cerro del, *Chile* .. 158 **B2** 29 10 S 69 50W
Toro Pk., *U.S.A.* ...... 145 **M10** 33 34N 116 24W
Törökszentmiklós, *Hungary* ............. 31 **D13** 47 11N 20 27 E
Toronías Kólpos, *Greece* 44 **D5** 40 5N 23 30 E
Toronto, *Australia* ..... 117 **B9** 33 0 S 151 30 E
Toronto, *Canada* ....... 128 **D4** 43 39N 79 20W
Toronto, *U.S.A.* ....... 136 **F4** 40 27N 80 36W
Toropets, *Russia* ....... 50 **C7** 56 30N 31 40 E
Tororo, *Uganda* ........ 106 **B3** 0 45N 34 12 E
Toros Dağları, *Turkey* .. 88 **E5** 37 0N 32 30 E
Torotoro, *Bolivia* ...... 157 **D4** 18 7 S 65 46W
Torpshammar, *Sweden* .. 14 **B10** 62 29N 16 20 E
Torquay, *Australia* ..... 116 **E6** 38 20 S 144 19 E
Torquay, *Canada* ....... 131 **D8** 49 9N 103 30W
Torquay, *U.K.* ......... 17 **G4** 50 27N 3 31W
Torquemada, *Spain* ..... 36 **C6** 42 2N 4 19W
Torralba de Calatrava, *Spain* .............. 37 **F7** 39 1N 3 44W
Torrance, *U.S.A.* ...... 145 **M8** 33 50N 118 19W
Torrão, *Portugal* ....... 37 **G2** 38 16N 8 11W
Torre Annunziata, *Italy* . 41 **B7** 40 45N 14 26 E
Tôrre de Moncorvo, *Portugal* ............ 36 **D3** 41 12N 7 8W
Torre del Greco, *Italy* ... 41 **B7** 40 47N 14 22 E
Torre del Mar, *Spain* ... 37 **J6** 36 44N 4 6W
Torre-Pacheco, *Spain* ... 35 **H4** 37 44N 0 57W
Torre Pellice, *Italy* ..... 38 **D4** 44 49N 7 13 E
Torreblanca, *Spain* ..... 34 **E5** 40 14N 0 12 E
Torrecampo, *Spain* ..... 37 **G6** 38 29N 4 41W
Torrecilla en Cameros, *Spain* .............. 34 **C2** 42 15N 2 38W
Torredembarra, *Spain* ... 34 **D6** 41 9N 1 24 E
Torredonjimeno, *Spain* . 37 **H7** 37 46N 3 57W
Torrejoncillo, *Spain* ..... 36 **F4** 39 54N 6 28W
Torrelaguna, *Spain* ..... 34 **E1** 40 50N 3 38W
Torrelavega, *Spain* ..... 36 **B6** 43 20N 4 5W
Torremaggiore, *Italy* .... 41 **A8** 41 42N 15 17 E
Torremolinos, *Spain* .... 37 **J6** 36 38N 4 30W
Torrens, L., *Australia* ... 116 **A2** 31 0 S 137 50 E
Torrens Cr. →, *Australia* 114 **C4** 22 23 S 145 9 E
Torrens Creek, *Australia* 114 **C4** 20 48 S 145 3 E
Torrente, *Spain* ........ 35 **F4** 39 27N 0 28W
Torrenueva, *Spain* ..... 35 **G1** 38 38N 3 22W
Torreón, *Mexico* ....... 146 **B4** 25 33N 103 25W
Torreperogil, *Spain* ..... 35 **G1** 38 2N 3 17W
Torres, *Mexico* ......... 146 **B2** 28 46N 110 46W
Torres, Is., *Vanuatu* .... 121 **C4** 13 15 S 166 37 E
Torres Novas, *Portugal* . 37 **F2** 39 27N 8 33W
Torres Strait, *Australia* .. 120 **E2** 9 50 S 142 20 E
Torres Vedras, *Portugal* . 37 **F1** 39 5N 9 15W
Torrevieja, *Spain* ....... 35 **H4** 37 59N 0 42W
Torrey, *U.S.A.* ........ 143 **G8** 38 18N 111 25W
Torridge →, *U.K.* ...... 17 **G3** 50 51N 4 10W
Torridon, L., *U.K.* ..... 18 **D3** 57 35N 5 50W
Torrijos, *Phil.* ......... 70 **E4** 13 19N 122 5 E
Torrijos, *Spain* ........ 36 **F6** 39 59N 4 18W
Torrington, Conn., *U.S.A.* ............ 137 **E11** 41 50N 73 9W
Torrington, *Wyo., U.S.A.* 138 **D2** 42 5N 104 8W
Torroella de Montgrí, *Spain* .............. 34 **C8** 42 2N 3 8 E
Torrox, *Spain* ......... 37 **J7** 36 46N 3 57W
Torsö, *Sweden* ......... 15 **F7** 58 48N 13 45 E
Tortola, *Virgin Is.* ..... 149 **C7** 18 19N 64 45W
Tórtoles de Esgueva, *Spain* .............. 36 **D6** 41 49N 4 2W
Tortona, *Italy* ......... 38 **D5** 44 53N 8 54 E
Tortoreto, *Italy* ........ 39 **F10** 42 50N 13 55 E
Tortorici, *Italy* ......... 41 **D7** 38 2N 14 48 E
Tortosa, *Spain* ......... 34 **E5** 40 49N 0 31 E
Tortosa, C., *Spain* ..... 34 **E5** 40 41N 0 52 E
Tortosendo, *Portugal* ... 36 **E3** 40 15N 7 31W
Tortue, I. de la, *Haiti* ... 149 **B5** 20 5N 72 57W
Tortum, *Turkey* ........ 89 **C9** 40 19N 41 35 E
Ţorūd, *Iran* ........... 85 **C7** 35 25N 55 5 E
Torugart, Pereval, *Kirghizia* ............ 55 **C7** 40 32N 75 24 E
Torul, *Turkey* .......... 89 **C8** 40 34N 39 18 E
Toruń, *Poland* ......... 47 **B5** 53 2N 18 39 E
Toruń □, *Poland* ...... 47 **B6** 53 20N 19 0 E
Torup, *Denmark* ....... 15 **G3** 57 5N 9 5 E
Torup, *Sweden* ........ 15 **H7** 56 57N 13 5 E
Tory I., *Ireland* ........ 19 **A3** 55 17N 8 12W
Torysa →, *Czech.* ..... 31 **C14** 48 39N 21 21 E
Torzhok, *Russia* ....... 50 **C9** 57 5N 34 55 E
Tosa, *Japan* ........... 62 **D5** 33 24N 133 23 E
Tosa-Shimizu, *Japan* .... 62 **E4** 32 52N 132 58 E
Tosa-Wan, *Japan* ...... 62 **D5** 33 15N 133 30 E
Tosa-yamada, *Japan* .... 62 **D5** 33 36N 133 38 E
Toscana, *Italy* ......... 38 **E8** 43 30N 11 5 E
Toscano, Arcipelago, *Italy* ................ 38 **F7** 42 30N 10 30 E
Tosno, *Russia* ......... 50 **B7** 59 38N 30 46 E
Tossa, *Spain* .......... 34 **D7** 41 43N 2 56 E
Tostado, *Argentina* ..... 158 **B3** 29 15 S 61 50W
Tostedt, *Germany* ...... 26 **B5** 53 17N 9 42 E
Tostón, Pta. de, *Canary Is.* ........... 33 **F5** 28 42N 14 2W
Tosu, *Japan* ........... 62 **D2** 33 22N 130 31 E
Tosya, *Turkey* ......... 88 **C6** 41 1N 34 2 E
Toszek, *Poland* ........ 47 **E5** 50 27N 18 32 E
Totana, *Spain* ......... 35 **H3** 37 45N 1 30W
Toten, *Norway* ......... 14 **D4** 60 37N 10 53 E
Toteng, *Botswana* ...... 104 **C3** 20 22 S 22 58 E
Tôtes, *France* ......... 22 **C8** 49 41N 1 3 E
Tótkomlós, *Hungary* .... 31 **E13** 46 24N 20 45 E
Totma, *Russia* ......... 51 **B13** 60 0N 42 40 E
Totnes, *U.K.* .......... 17 **G4** 50 26N 3 41W
Totness, *Surinam* ...... 153 **B6** 5 53N 56 19W
Totonicapán, *Guatemala* 148 **D1** 14 58N 91 12W
Totora, *Bolivia* ........ 157 **D4** 17 42 S 65 9W
Totoya, I., *Fiji* ........ 121 **B3** 18 57 S 179 50W
Totskoye, *Russia* ....... 54 **E3** 52 32N 52 45 E
Totten Glacier, *Antarctica* 7 **C8** 66 45 S 116 10 E
Tottenham, *Australia* ... 117 **B7** 32 14 S 147 21 E
Tottenham, *Canada* ..... 136 **B5** 44 1N 79 49W
Tottori, *Japan* ......... 62 **B6** 35 30N 134 15 E
Tottori □, *Japan* ...... 62 **B6** 35 30N 134 12 E
Touat, *Algeria* ......... 99 **C5** 27 27N 0 30 E
Touba, *Ivory C.* ....... 100 **D3** 8 22N 7 40W
Toubkal, Djebel, *Morocco* ............ 98 **B3** 31 0N 8 0W
Toucy, *France* ......... 23 **E10** 47 44N 3 15 E
Tougan, *Burkina Faso* .. 100 **C4** 13 11N 2 58W
Touggourt, *Algeria* ..... 99 **B6** 33 6N 6 4 E
Tougué, *Guinea* ........ 100 **C2** 11 25N 11 50W
Touho, *N. Cal.* ........ 121 **T19** 20 47 S 165 14 E
Toukmatine, *Algeria* .... 99 **D6** 24 49N 7 11 E
Toul, *France* .......... 23 **D12** 48 40N 5 53 E
Toulepleu, *Ivory C.* .... 100 **D3** 6 32N 8 24W
Toulon, *France* ........ 25 **E9** 43 10N 5 55 E
Toulon, *U.S.A.* ........ 140 **C7** 41 6N 89 52W
Toulouse, *France* ....... 24 **E5** 43 37N 1 27 E
Toummo, *Niger* ........ 96 **D2** 22 45N 14 8 E
Toummo Dhoba, *Niger* .. 96 **D2** 22 30N 14 31 E
Toumodi, *Ivory C.* ..... 100 **D3** 6 32N 5 4W
Tounassine, Hamada, *Algeria* ............. 98 **C3** 28 48N 5 0W
Toungoo, *Burma* ....... 78 **F6** 19 0N 96 30 E
Touques →, *France* .... 22 **C7** 49 22N 0 8 E
Touraine, *France* ....... 22 **E7** 47 20N 0 30 E
Tourane = Da Nang, *Vietnam* ............ 76 **D7** 16 4N 108 13 E
Tourcoing, *France* ...... 23 **B10** 50 42N 3 10 E
Tourine, *Mauritania* .... 98 **D2** 22 23N 11 50W
Tournai, *Belgium* ....... 21 **G2** 50 35N 3 25 E
Tournan-en-Brie, *France* 23 **D9** 48 44N 2 46 E
Tournay, *France* ....... 24 **E4** 43 13N 0 13 E
Tournon, *France* ....... 25 **C8** 45 4N 4 50 E
Tournon-St.-Martin, *France* ............. 22 **F7** 46 45N 0 58 E
Tournus, *France* ....... 25 **B8** 46 35N 4 54 E
Touros, *Brazil* ......... 154 **C4** 5 12 S 35 28W
Tours, *France* ......... 22 **E7** 47 22N 0 40 E
Touside, Pic, *Chad* ..... 97 **D3** 21 1N 16 29 E
Touwsrivier, *S. Africa* .. 104 **E3** 33 20 S 20 2 E
Tovar, *Venezuela* ...... 152 **B3** 8 20N 71 46W
Tovarkovskiy, *Russia* ... 51 **E11** 53 40N 38 14 E
Tovdal, *Norway* ........ 15 **F2** 58 47N 8 10 E
Tovdalselva →, *Norway* 15 **F2** 58 15N 8 5 E
Towada, *Japan* ........ 60 **D10** 40 37N 141 13 E
Towada-Ko, *Japan* ..... 60 **D10** 40 28N 140 55 E
Towamba, *Australia* .... 117 **D8** 37 6 S 149 43 E
Towanda, *Ill., U.S.A.* ... 141 **D8** 40 36N 88 53W
Towanda, *N.Y., U.S.A.* . 137 **E8** 41 46N 76 30W
Tower, *U.S.A.* ........ 138 **B8** 47 49N 92 17W
Towerhill Cr. →, *Australia* ............ 114 **C3** 22 28 S 144 35 E
Towner, *U.S.A.* ........ 138 **A4** 48 25N 100 26W
Townsend, *U.S.A.* ..... 142 **C8** 46 25N 111 32W
Townshend I., *Australia* . 114 **C5** 22 10 S 150 31 E
Townsville, *Australia* ... 114 **B4** 19 15 S 146 45 E
Towson, *U.S.A.* ....... 134 **F7** 39 26N 76 34W
Toya-Ko, *Japan* ....... 60 **C10** 42 35N 140 51 E
Toyah, *U.S.A.* ........ 139 **K3** 31 20N 103 48W
Toyahvale, *U.S.A.* ..... 139 **K3** 30 58N 103 45W
Toyama, *Japan* ........ 63 **A9** 36 40N 137 15 E
Toyama □, *Japan* ...... 63 **A9** 36 45N 137 30 E
Toyama-Wan, *Japan* .... 61 **F8** 37 0N 137 30 E
Tōyō, *Japan* ........... 62 **D6** 33 26N 134 16 E
Toyohashi, *Japan* ...... 63 **C9** 34 45N 137 25 E
Toyokawa, *Japan* ...... 63 **C9** 34 48N 137 27 E
Toyonaka, *Japan* ...... 63 **C7** 34 50N 135 28 E
Toyooka, *Japan* ........ 62 **B6** 35 35N 134 48 E
Toyota, *Japan* ......... 63 **B9** 35 3N 137 7 E
Toyoura, *Japan* ........ 62 **C2** 34 6N 130 57 E
Toytepa, *Uzbekistan* .... 55 **C4** 41 3N 69 20 E
Tozeur, *Tunisia* ........ 96 **B1** 33 56N 8 8 E
Tra On, *Vietnam* ....... 77 **H5** 9 58N 105 55 E
Trabancos →, *Spain* ... 36 **D5** 41 36N 5 15W
Traben Trarbach, *Germany* ........... 27 **F3** 49 57N 7 7 E
Trabzon, *Turkey* ....... 52 **F8** 41 0N 39 45 E
Trabzon □, *Turkey* .... 89 **C8** 41 10N 39 45 E

## X

Západoslovenský 287


Yiannitsa, *Greece* 44 D4 40 46N 22 24 E
Yibin, *China* 68 C5 28 45N 104 32 E
Yichang, *China* 69 B8 30 40N 111 20 E
Yicheng, *Henan, China* 69 B9 31 41N 112 12 E
Yicheng, *Shanxi, China* 66 G6 35 42N 111 40 E
Yichuan, *China* 66 F6 36 2N 110 10 E
Yichun, *Heilongjiang, China* 65 B7 47 44N 128 52 E
Yichun, *Jiangxi, China* 69 D10 27 48N 114 22 E
Yidhá, *Greece* 44 D4 40 35N 22 53 E
Yidu, *Hubei, China* 69 B8 30 25N 111 27 E
Yidu, *Shandong, China* 67 F10 36 43N 118 28 E
Yidun, *China* 68 B2 30 22N 99 21 E
Yihuang, *China* 69 D11 27 30N 116 12 E
Yijun, *China* 66 G5 35 28N 109 8 E
Yilan, *Taiwan* 69 E13 24 51N 121 44 E
Yıldızeli, *Turkey* 88 D7 39 51N 36 36 E
Yilehuli Shan, *China* 65 A7 51 20N 124 20 E
Yiliang, *Yunnan, China* 68 D5 27 38N 104 2 E
Yiliang, *Yunnan, China* 68 E4 24 56N 103 11 E
Yilong, *China* 68 B6 31 34N 106 23 E
Yimen, *China* 68 E4 24 40N 102 10 E
Yimianpo, *China* 67 B15 45 7N 128 2 E
Yinchuan, *China* 66 E4 38 30N 106 15 E
Yindarlgooda, L., *Australia* 113 F3 30 40 S 121 52 E
Ying He →, *China* 66 H9 32 30N 116 30 E
Ying Xian, *China* 66 E7 39 32N 113 10 E
Yingcheng, *China* 69 B9 30 56N 113 35 E
Yingde, *China* 69 E9 24 10N 113 25 E
Yingjiang, *China* 68 E1 24 41N 97 55 E
Yingjing, *China* 68 C4 29 41N 102 52 E
Yingkou, *China* 67 D12 40 37N 122 18 E
Yingshan, *Henan, China* 69 B9 31 35N 113 50 E
Yingshan, *Hubei, China* 69 B10 30 41N 115 32 E
Yingshan, *Sichuan, China* 68 B6 31 4N 106 35 E
Yingshang, *China* 69 A11 32 38N 116 12 E
Yining, *China* 64 B3 43 58N 81 10 E
Yinjiang, *China* 68 C7 28 1N 108 21 E
Yinnietharra, *Australia* 112 D2 24 39 S 116 12 E
Yiofiros →, *Greece* 32 D7 35 20N 25 6 E
Yioúra, *Notios Aiyaíon, Greece* 45 G6 37 32N 24 40 E
Yioúra, *Thessalía, Greece* 44 E6 39 23N 24 10 E
Yipinglang, *China* 68 E3 25 10N 101 52 E
Yirga Alem, *Ethiopia* 95 F4 6 48N 38 22 E
Yishan, *China* 68 E7 24 28N 108 38 E
Yishui, *China* 67 G10 35 47N 118 30 E
Yíthion, *Greece* 45 H4 36 46N 22 34 E
Yitiaoshan, *China* 66 F3 37 5N 104 2 E
Yitong, *China* 67 C13 43 13N 125 20 E
Yiwu, *China* 69 C13 29 20N 120 3 E
Yixing, *China* 69 B12 31 21N 119 48 E
Yiyang, *Henan, China* 66 G7 34 27N 112 10 E
Yiyang, *Hunan, China* 69 C9 28 35N 112 18 E
Yiyang, *Jiangxi, China* 69 C11 28 22N 117 20 E
Yizhang, *China* 69 E9 25 27N 112 57 E
Yizheng, *China* 69 A12 32 18N 119 10 E
Ylitornio, *Finland* 12 C17 66 19N 23 39 E
Ylivieska, *Finland* 12 D18 64 4N 24 28 E
Yngaren, *Sweden* 15 F10 58 50N 16 35 E
Ynykchanskiy, *Russia* 57 C14 60 15N 137 35 E
Yoakum, *U.S.A.* 139 L6 29 20N 97 20W
Yobuko, *Japan* 62 D1 33 32N 129 54 E
Yog Pt., *Phil.* 70 D5 14 6N 124 12 E
Yogan, *Togo* 101 D5 6 23N 1 30 E
Yogyakarta, *Indonesia* 75 D4 7 49 S 110 22 E
Yogyakarta □, *Indonesia* 75 D4 7 48 S 110 22 E
Yoho Nat. Park, *Canada* 130 C5 51 25N 116 30W
Yojoa, L. de, *Honduras* 148 D2 14 53N 88 0W
Yŏju, *S. Korea* 67 F14 37 20N 127 35 E
Yokadouma, *Cameroon* 102 B2 3 26N 14 55 E
Yōkaichiba, *Japan* 63 B12 35 42N 140 33 E
Yokkaichi, *Japan* 63 C8 34 55N 136 38 E
Yoko, *Cameroon* 101 D7 5 32N 12 20 E
Yokohama, *Japan* 63 B11 35 27N 139 28 E
Yokosuka, *Japan* 63 B11 35 20N 139 40 E
Yokote, *Japan* 60 E10 39 20N 140 30 E
Yola, *Nigeria* 101 D7 9 10N 12 29 E
Yolaina, Cordillera de, *Nic.* 148 D3 11 30N 84 0W
Yolombo, *Zaïre* 102 C4 1 36 S 23 12 E
Yombi, *Gabon* 102 C2 1 26 S 10 37 E
Yonago, *Japan* 62 B5 35 25N 133 19 E
Yonaguni-Jima, *Japan* 61 M1 24 27N 123 0 E
Yŏnan, *N. Korea* 67 F14 37 55N 126 11 E
Yonezawa, *Japan* 60 F10 37 57N 140 4 E
Yong Peng, *Malaysia* 77 L4 2 0N 103 3 E
Yong Sata, *Thailand* 77 J2 7 8N 99 41 E
Yongampo, *N. Korea* 67 E13 39 56N 124 23 E
Yong'an, *China* 69 E11 25 59N 117 25 E
Yongcheng, *China* 66 H9 33 55N 116 20 E
Yŏngchŏn, *S. Korea* 67 G15 35 58N 128 56 E
Yongchuan, *China* 68 C5 29 17N 105 55 E
Yongchun, *China* 69 E12 25 16N 118 20 E
Yongdeng, *China* 66 F2 36 38N 103 25 E
Yongding, *China* 69 E11 24 43N 116 45 E
Yŏngdŏk, *S. Korea* 67 F15 36 24N 129 22 E
Yŏngdŭngpo, *S. Korea* 67 F14 37 31N 126 54 E
Yongfeng, *China* 69 D10 27 20N 115 22 E
Yongfu, *China* 68 E7 24 59N 109 59 E
Yonghe, *China* 66 F6 36 46N 110 38 E
Yŏnghŭng, *N. Korea* 67 E14 39 31N 127 18 E
Yongji, *China* 66 G6 34 52N 110 28 E
Yŏngju, *S. Korea* 67 F15 36 50N 128 40 E
Yongkang, *Yunnan, China* 68 E2 24 9N 99 20 E
Yongkang, *Zhejiang, China* 69 C13 28 55N 120 2 E
Yongnian, *China* 66 F8 36 47N 114 29 E
Yongning, *Guangxi Zhuangzu, China* 68 F7 22 44N 108 28 E
Yongning, *Ningxia Huizu, China* 66 E4 38 15N 106 14 E
Yongping, *China* 68 E2 25 27N 99 38 E
Yongqing, *China* 66 E9 39 25N 116 28 E
Yongren, *China* 68 D3 26 4N 101 40 E
Yongshan, *China* 68 C4 28 11N 103 35 E
Yongsheng, *China* 68 D3 26 38N 100 46 E
Yongshun, *China* 68 C7 29 2N 109 51 E
Yongtai, *China* 69 E12 25 49N 118 58 E
Yŏngwŏl, *S. Korea* 67 F15 37 11N 128 28 E
Yongxin, *China* 69 D10 26 58N 114 15 E
Yongxing, *China* 69 D9 26 9N 113 8 E
Yongxiu, *China* 69 C10 29 2N 115 42 E
Yonibana, *S. Leone* 100 D2 8 30N 12 19W
Yonkers, *U.S.A.* 137 F11 40 57N 73 51W
Yonne □, *France* 23 E10 47 50N 3 40 E
Yonne →, *France* 23 D9 48 23N 2 58 E
York, *Australia* 113 F2 31 52 S 116 47 E
York, *U.K.* 16 D6 53 58N 1 7W
York, *Ala., U.S.A.* 135 J1 32 30N 88 18W
York, *Nebr., U.S.A.* 138 E6 40 55N 97 35W
York, *Pa., U.S.A.* 134 F7 39 57N 76 43W
York, C., *Australia* 114 A3 10 42 S 142 31 E
York, Kap, *Greenland* 6 B4 75 55N 66 25W
York Sd., *Australia* 112 B4 15 0 S 125 5 E
Yorke Pen., *Australia* 116 C2 34 50 S 137 40 E
Yorkshire Wolds, *U.K.* 16 D7 54 0N 0 30W
Yorkton, *Canada* 131 C8 51 11N 102 28W
Yorktown, *U.S.A.* 139 L6 29 0N 97 29W
Yorkville, *Calif., U.S.A.* 144 G3 38 52N 123 13W
Yorkville, *Ill., U.S.A.* 141 C8 41 38N 88 27W
Yornup, *Australia* 113 F2 34 2 S 116 10 E
Yoro, *Honduras* 148 C2 15 9N 87 7W
Yoron-Jima, *Japan* 61 L4 27 2N 128 26 E
Yos Sudarso, Pulau, *Indonesia* 73 C5 8 0 S 138 30 E
Yosemite National Park, *U.S.A.* 144 H7 38 0N 119 30W
Yosemite Village, *U.S.A.* 144 H7 37 45N 119 35W
Yoshii, *Japan* 62 D1 33 16N 129 46 E
Yoshimatsu, *Japan* 62 E2 32 0N 130 47 E
Yoshkar Ola, *Russia* 51 C15 56 38N 47 55 E
Yŏsu, *S. Korea* 67 G14 34 47N 127 45 E
Yotala, *Bolivia* 157 D4 19 10 S 65 17W
Yotvata, *Israel* 91 F4 29 55N 35 2 E
You Xian, *China* 69 D9 27 1N 113 17 E
Youbou, *Canada* 130 D4 48 53N 124 13W
Youghal, *Ireland* 19 E4 51 58N 7 51W
Youghal B., *Ireland* 19 E4 51 55N 7 50W
Youkounkoun, *Guinea* 100 C2 12 35N 13 11W
Young, *Australia* 117 C8 34 19 S 148 18 E
Young, *Canada* 131 C7 51 47N 105 45W
Young, *Uruguay* 158 C4 32 44 S 57 36W
Young Ra., *N.Z.* 119 E4 44 10 S 169 30 E
Younghusband, L., *Australia* 116 A2 30 50 S 136 5 E
Younghusband Pen., *Australia* 116 D3 36 0 S 139 25 E
Youngstown, *Canada* 131 C6 51 35N 111 10W
Youngstown, *N.Y., U.S.A.* 136 C5 43 16N 79 2W
Youngstown, *Ohio, U.S.A.* 136 E4 41 7N 80 41W
Youngsville, *U.S.A.* 136 E5 41 51N 79 21W
Youssoufia, *Morocco* 98 B3 32 16N 8 31W
Youxi, *China* 69 D12 26 10N 118 13 E
Youyang, *China* 68 C7 28 47N 108 42 E
Youyu, *China* 66 D7 40 10N 112 20 E
Yoweragabbie, *Australia* 113 E2 28 14 S 117 39 E
Yowrie, *Australia* 117 D8 36 17 S 149 46 E
Yozgat, *Turkey* 88 D6 39 51N 34 47 E
Yozgat □, *Turkey* 88 D6 39 30N 35 0 E
Ypané →, *Paraguay* 158 A4 23 29 S 57 19W
Yport, *France* 22 C7 49 45N 0 15 E
Ypres = Ieper, *Belgium* 21 G1 50 51N 2 53 E
Ypsilanti, *U.S.A.* 141 B13 42 18N 83 40W
Yreka, *U.S.A.* 142 F2 41 44N 122 40W
Ysabel Chan., *Papua N. G.* 120 B5 2 0 S 150 0 E
Ysleta, *U.S.A.* 143 L10 31 45N 106 24W
Yssingeaux, *France* 25 C8 45 9N 4 8 E
Ystad, *Sweden* 15 J7 55 26N 13 50 E
Ythan →, *U.K.* 18 D7 57 26N 2 0W
Ytterhogdal, *Sweden* 14 B8 62 12N 14 56 E
Ytyk-Kel, *Russia* 57 C14 62 30N 133 32 E
Yu Jiang →, *China* 65 D6 23 22N 110 3 E
Yu Shan, *Taiwan* 69 F13 23 30N 120 58 E
Yu Xian, *Hebei, China* 66 E8 39 50N 114 35 E
Yu Xian, *Henan, China* 66 G7 34 10N 113 28 E
Yu Xian, *Shanxi, China* 66 E7 38 5N 113 20 E
Yuan Jiang →, *Hunan, China* 69 C8 28 55N 111 50 E
Yuan Jiang →, *Yunnan, China* 68 F4 22 20N 103 59 E
Yuan'an, *China* 69 B8 31 3N 111 34 E
Yuanjiang, *Hunan, China* 69 C9 28 47N 112 21 E
Yuanjiang, *Yunnan, China* 68 F4 23 32N 102 0 E
Yuanli, *Taiwan* 69 E13 24 29N 120 39 E
Yuanlin, *Taiwan* 69 F13 23 58N 120 30 E
Yuanling, *China* 69 C8 28 29N 110 22 E
Yuanmou, *China* 68 E3 25 42N 101 53 E
Yuanqu, *China* 66 G6 35 18N 111 40 E
Yuanyang, *Henan, China* 66 G7 35 3N 113 58 E
Yuanyang, *Yunnan, China* 68 F4 23 10N 102 43 E
Yuat →, *Papua N. G.* 120 C2 4 10 S 143 52 E
Yuba →, *U.S.A.* 144 F5 39 8N 121 36W
Yuba City, *U.S.A.* 144 F5 39 12N 121 37W
Yūbari, *Japan* 60 C10 43 4N 141 59 E
Yūbetsu, *Japan* 60 B11 44 13N 143 50 E
Yucatán □, *Mexico* 147 C7 21 30N 86 30W
Yucatán, Canal de, *Caribbean* 148 B2 22 0N 86 30W
Yucatan Str. = Yucatán, Canal de, *Caribbean* 148 B2 22 0N 86 30W
Yucca, *U.S.A.* 145 L12 34 56N 114 6W
Yucca Valley, *U.S.A.* 145 L10 34 8N 116 30W
Yucheng, *China* 66 F9 36 55N 116 32 E
Yuci, *China* 66 F7 37 42N 112 46 E
Yudino, *Russia* 51 D16 55 51N 48 55 E
Yudino, *Russia* 56 D7 55 10N 67 55 E
Yudu, *China* 69 E10 25 59N 115 30 E
Yuendumu, *Australia* 112 D5 22 16 S 131 49 E
Yueqing, *China* 69 C13 28 9N 120 59 E
Yueqing Wan, *China* 69 C13 28 5N 121 20 E
Yuexi, *Anhui, China* 69 B11 30 50N 116 20 E
Yuexi, *Sichuan, China* 68 C4 28 37N 102 26 E
Yueyang, *China* 69 C9 29 21N 113 5 E
Yufu-Dake, *Japan* 62 D3 33 17N 131 33 E
Yugan, *China* 69 C11 28 43N 116 37 E
Yugoslavia ■, *Europe* 42 D5 44 0N 20 0 E
Yuhuan, *China* 69 C13 28 9N 121 12 E
Yujiang, *China* 69 C11 28 10N 116 43 E
Yukhnov, *Russia* 50 D9 54 44N 35 15 E
Yūki, *Japan* 63 A11 36 18N 139 53 E
Yukon →, *N. Amer.* 126 B3 62 50N 165 0W
Yukon Territory □, *Canada* 126 B6 63 0N 135 0W
Yüksekova, *Turkey* 89 E11 37 34N 44 16 E
Yukti, *Russia* 57 C11 63 26N 105 42 E
Yukuhashi, *Japan* 62 D2 33 44N 130 59 E
Yule →, *Australia* 112 D2 20 41 S 118 17 E
Yuli, *Nigeria* 101 D7 9 44N 10 12 E
Yulin, *Guangxi Zhuangzu, China* 69 F8 22 40N 110 8 E
Yulin, *Shaanxi, China* 66 E5 38 20N 109 30 E
Yuma, *Ariz., U.S.A.* 145 N12 32 45N 114 37W
Yuma, *Colo., U.S.A.* 138 E3 40 10N 102 43W
Yuma, B. de, *Dom. Rep.* 149 C6 18 20N 68 35W
Yumali, *Australia* 116 C3 35 32 S 139 45 E
Yumbe, *Uganda* 106 B3 3 28N 31 15 E
Yumbi, *Zaïre* 106 C2 1 12 S 26 15 E
Yumbo, *Colombia* 152 C2 3 35N 76 28W
Yumen, *China* 64 C4 39 50N 97 30 E
Yumurtalık, *Turkey* 88 E6 36 45N 35 43 E
Yun Ho →, *China* 67 E9 39 10N 117 10 E
Yun Xian, *Hubei, China* 69 A8 32 50N 110 46 E
Yun Xian, *Yunnan, China* 68 E3 24 27N 100 8 E
Yunak, *Turkey* 88 D4 38 49N 31 43 E
Yunan, *China* 69 F8 23 12N 111 30 E
Yuncheng, *Henan, China* 66 G8 35 36N 115 57 E
Yuncheng, *Shanxi, China* 66 G6 35 2N 111 0 E
Yundamindra, *Australia* 113 E3 29 15 S 122 6 E
Yunfu, *China* 69 F9 22 50N 112 5 E
Yungas, *Bolivia* 157 D4 17 0 S 66 0W
Yungay, *Chile* 158 D1 37 10 S 72 5W
Yungay, *Peru* 156 B2 9 2 S 77 45W
Yunhe, *China* 69 C12 28 8N 119 33 E
Yunlin, *Taiwan* 69 F13 23 42N 120 30 E
Yunling, *China* 68 D2 27 0N 99 20 E
Yunlong, *China* 68 E2 25 57N 99 13 E
Yunmeng, *China* 69 B9 31 2N 113 43 E
Yunnan □, *China* 68 E4 25 0N 102 0 E
Yunomae, *Japan* 62 E3 32 12N 130 59 E
Yunotso, *Japan* 62 B4 35 5N 132 21 E
Yunquera de Henares, *Spain* 34 E1 40 47N 3 11W
Yunta, *Australia* 116 B3 32 34 S 139 36 E
Yunxi, *China* 66 H6 33 0N 110 22 E
Yunxiao, *China* 69 F11 23 59N 117 18 E
Yunyang, *China* 68 B7 30 58N 108 54 E
Yuping, *China* 68 D7 27 13N 108 56 E
Yupukarri, *Guyana* 153 C6 3 45N 59 20W
Yupyongdong, *N. Korea* 67 D15 41 49N 128 53 E
Yuqing, *China* 68 D6 27 13N 107 53 E
Yur, *Russia* 57 D14 59 52N 137 41 E
Yurgao, *Russia* 56 D9 55 42N 84 51 E
Yuria, *Russia* 54 B4 59 22N 54 10 E
Yuribei, *Russia* 56 B8 71 8N 76 58 E
Yurimaguas, *Peru* 156 B2 5 55 S 76 7W
Yurya, *Russia* 51 B16 59 1N 49 13 E
Yuryev-Polskiy, *Russia* 51 C11 56 30N 39 40 E
Yuryevets, *Russia* 51 C13 57 25N 43 2 E
Yuryuzan, *Russia* 54 D6 54 57N 58 28 E
Yuscarán, *Honduras* 148 D2 13 58N 86 45W
Yushanzhen, *China* 68 C7 29 28N 108 22 E
Yushe, *China* 66 F7 37 4N 112 58 E
Yushu, *Jilin, China* 67 B14 44 43N 126 38 E
Yushu, *Qinghai, China* 64 C4 33 5N 96 55 E
Yutai, *China* 66 G9 35 0N 116 45 E
Yutian, *China* 67 E9 39 53N 117 45 E
Yuxi, *China* 68 E4 24 30N 102 35 E
Yuyao, *China* 69 B13 30 3N 121 10 E
Yuzawa, *Japan* 60 E10 39 10N 140 30 E
Yuzha, *Russia* 51 C13 56 34N 42 1 E
Yuzhno-Sakhalinsk, *Russia* 57 E15 46 58N 142 45 E
Yuzhno-Surkhanskoye Vdkhr., *Uzbekistan* 55 E3 37 53N 67 42 E
Yuzhno-Uralsk, *Russia* 54 D7 54 26N 61 15 E
Yuzhnyy Ural, *Russia* 54 E6 53 0N 58 0 E
Yvelines □, *France* 23 D8 48 40N 1 45 E
Yverdon, *Switz.* 28 C3 46 47N 6 39 E
Yvetot, *France* 22 C7 49 37N 0 44 E
Yvonand, *Switz.* 28 C3 46 48N 6 44 E


## Z


Zaalayskiy Khrebet, *Asia* 55 D6 39 20N 73 0 E
Zaamslag, *Neths.* 21 F3 51 19N 3 55 E
Zaan →, *Neths.* 20 D5 52 25N 4 52 E
Zaandam, *Neths.* 20 D5 52 26N 4 49 E
Zab, Monts du, *Algeria* 99 B6 34 55N 5 0 E
Žabalj, *Serbia, Yug.* 42 B5 45 21N 20 5 E
Žabari, *Serbia, Yug.* 42 C6 44 22N 21 15 E
Zabarjad, *Egypt* 94 C4 23 40N 36 12 E
Zabaykalskiy, *Russia* 57 E12 49 40N 117 25 E
Zabid, *Yemen* 86 D3 14 0N 43 10 E
Zabīd, W. →, *Yemen* 86 D3 14 7N 43 6 E
Ząbkowice Śląskie, *Poland* 47 E3 50 35N 16 50 E
Žabljak, *Montenegro, Yug.* 42 D4 43 18N 19 7 E
Zabłudów, *Poland* 47 B10 53 0N 23 19 E
Żabno, *Poland* 31 A13 50 9N 20 53 E
Zābol, *Iran* 85 D9 31 0N 61 32 E
Zābol □, *Afghan.* 79 B2 32 0N 67 0 E
Zābolī, *Iran* 85 E9 27 10N 61 35 E
Zabré, *Burkina Faso* 101 C4 11 12N 0 36W
Zabrze, *Poland* 47 E5 50 18N 18 50 E
Zacapa, *Guatemala* 148 D2 14 59N 89 31W
Zacapu, *Mexico* 146 D4 19 50N 101 43W
Zacatecas, *Mexico* 146 C4 22 49N 102 34W
Zacatecas □, *Mexico* 146 C4 23 30N 103 0W
Zacatecoluca, *El Salv.* 148 D2 13 29N 88 51W
Zacoalco, *Mexico* 146 C4 20 14N 103 33W
Zacualtipán, *Mexico* 147 C5 20 39N 98 36W
Zadar, *Croatia* 39 D12 44 8N 15 14 E
Zadawa, *Nigeria* 101 C7 11 33N 10 19 E
Zadetkyi Kyun, *Burma* 77 H2 10 0N 98 25 E
Zadonsk, *Russia* 51 E11 52 25N 38 56 E
Zafarqand, *Iran* 85 C7 33 11N 52 29 E
Zafora, *Greece* 45 H8 36 5N 26 24 E
Zafra, *Spain* 37 G4 38 26N 6 30W
Żagań, *Poland* 47 D2 51 39N 15 22 E
Zagazig, *Egypt* 94 H7 30 40N 31 30 E
Zāgheh, *Iran* 85 C6 33 30N 48 42 E
Zaghouan, *Tunisia* 96 A2 36 23N 10 10 E
Zaglivérion, *Greece* 44 D5 40 36N 23 15 E
Zaglou, *Algeria* 99 C4 27 17N 0 3W
Zagnanado, *Benin* 101 D5 7 18N 2 28 E
Zagorá, *Greece* 44 E5 39 27N 23 6 E
Zagora, *Morocco* 98 B3 30 22N 5 51W
Zagórów, *Poland* 47 C4 52 10N 17 54 E
Zagorsk = Sergiyev Posad, *Russia* 51 C11 56 20N 38 10 E
Zagórz, *Poland* 31 B15 49 30N 22 14 E
Zagreb, *Croatia* 39 C12 45 50N 16 0 E
Zāgros, Kuhhā-ye, *Iran* 85 C6 33 45N 48 5 E
Zagros Mts. = Zāgros, Kuhhā-ye, *Iran* 85 C6 33 45N 48 5 E
Žagubica, *Serbia, Yug.* 42 C6 44 15N 21 47 E
Zaguinaso, *Ivory C.* 100 C3 10 1N 6 14W
Zagyva →, *Hungary* 31 D13 47 5N 20 4 E
Zāhedān, *Fārs, Iran* 85 D7 28 46N 53 52 E
Zāhedān, *Sīstān va Balūchestān, Iran* 85 D9 29 30N 60 50 E
Zahirabad, *India* 82 F3 17 43N 77 37 E
Zahlah, *Lebanon* 91 B4 33 52N 35 50 E
Zahna, *Germany* 26 D8 51 54N 12 47 E
Zahrez Chergui, *Algeria* 99 A5 35 0N 3 30 E
Zahrez Rharbi, *Algeria* 99 B5 34 50N 2 55 E
Zailiyskiy Alatau, Khrebet, *Kazakhstan* 55 B8 43 5N 77 0 E
Zainsk, *Russia* 54 D3 55 18N 52 4 E
Zaire □, *Angola* 103 D2 7 0 S 14 0 E
Zaïre ■, *Africa* 103 C4 3 0 S 23 0 E
Zaïre →, *Africa* 103 D2 6 4 S 12 24 E
Zaječar, *Serbia, Yug.* 42 D7 43 53N 22 18 E
Zakamensk, *Russia* 57 D11 50 23N 103 17 E
Zakani, *Zaïre* 102 B4 2 33N 23 16 E
Zakataly, *Azerbaijan* 53 F12 41 38N 46 35 E
Zakavkazye, *Asia* 53 F11 42 0N 44 0 E
Zākhū, *Iraq* 84 B4 37 10N 42 50 E
Zákinthos, *Greece* 45 G2 37 47N 20 57 E
Zaklików, *Poland* 47 E9 50 46N 22 7 E
Zakopane, *Poland* 31 B12 49 18N 19 57 E
Zakroczym, *Poland* 47 C7 52 26N 20 38 E
Zákros, *Greece* 32 D8 35 6N 26 10 E
Zala, *Angola* 103 D2 7 52 S 13 42 E
Zala □, *Hungary* 31 E9 46 42N 16 50 E
Zala →, *Hungary* 31 E10 46 43N 17 16 E
Zalaegerszeg, *Hungary* 31 E9 46 53N 16 47 E
Zalakomár, *Hungary* 31 E10 46 33N 17 10 E
Zalalövö, *Hungary* 31 E9 46 51N 16 35 E
Zalamea de la Serena, *Spain* 37 G5 38 40N 5 38W
Zalamea la Real, *Spain* 37 H4 37 41N 6 38W
Zalău, *Romania* 46 B4 47 12N 23 3 E
Zalazna, *Russia* 54 B3 58 39N 52 31 E
Žalec, *Slovenia* 39 B12 46 16N 15 10 E
Zaleshchiki, *Ukraine* 52 B1 48 45N 25 45 E
Zalew Wislany, *Poland* 47 A6 54 20N 19 50 E
Zalewo, *Poland* 47 B6 53 50N 19 41 E
Zalīm, *Si. Arabia* 86 B3 22 43N 42 10 E
Zalingei, *Sudan* 97 F4 12 51N 23 29 E
Zaliv Vislinskil = Zalew Wislany, *Poland* 47 A6 54 20N 19 50 E
Zalṭan, Jabal, *Libya* 96 C3 28 46N 19 45 E
Zaltbommel, *Neths.* 20 E6 51 48N 5 15 E
Zambales □, *Phil.* 70 D3 15 20N 120 10 E
Zambales Mts., *Phil.* 70 D3 15 45N 120 5 E
Zambeke, *Zaïre* 106 B2 2 8N 25 17 E
Zambeze →, *Africa* 107 F4 18 35 S 36 20 E
Zambezi = Zambeze →, *Africa* 107 F4 18 35 S 36 20 E
Zambezi, *Zambia* 103 E4 13 30 S 23 15 E
Zambezia □, *Mozam.* 107 F4 16 15 S 37 30 E
Zambia ■, *Africa* 107 E2 15 0 S 28 0 E
Zamboanga, *Phil.* 71 H4 6 59N 122 3 E
Zamboanga del Norte □, *Phil.* 71 G4 8 0N 123 0 E
Zamboanga del Sur □, *Phil.* 71 H4 7 40N 123 0 E
Zamboanguita, *Phil.* 71 G4 9 6N 123 12 E
Zambrano, *Colombia* 152 B3 9 45N 74 49W
Zambrów, *Poland* 47 C9 52 59N 22 14 E
Zametchino, *Russia* 51 E13 53 30N 42 30 E
Zamora, *Ecuador* 152 D2 4 4 S 78 58W
Zamora, *Mexico* 146 C4 20 0N 102 21W
Zamora, *Spain* 36 D5 41 30N 5 45W
Zamora □, *Spain* 36 D5 41 30N 5 46W
Zamora-Chinchipe □, *Ecuador* 152 D2 4 15 S 78 50W
Zamość, *Poland* 47 E10 50 43N 23 15 E
Zamość □, *Poland* 47 E10 50 40N 23 10 E
Zamuro, Sierra del, *Venezuela* 153 C5 4 0N 62 30W
Zamzam, W. →, *Libya* 96 B2 31 0N 14 30 E
Zan, *Ghana* 101 D4 9 26N 0 17W
Zanaga, *Congo* 102 C2 2 48 S 13 48 E
Záncara →, *Spain* 35 F1 39 18N 3 18W
Zandijk, *Neths.* 20 D5 52 28N 4 49 E
Zandvoort, *Neths.* 20 D5 52 22N 4 32 E
Zanesville, *U.S.A.* 136 G2 39 56N 82 5W
Zangābād, *Iran* 84 B5 38 26N 46 44 E
Zangue →, *Mozam.* 107 F4 17 50 S 35 21 E
Zanjan, *Iran* 85 B6 36 40N 48 35 E
Zanjān □, *Iran* 85 B6 37 20N 49 30 E
Zannone, *Italy* 40 B6 40 58N 13 2 E
Zante = Zákinthos, *Greece* 45 G2 37 47N 20 57 E
Zanthus, *Australia* 113 F3 31 2 S 123 34 E
Zanzibar, *Tanzania* 106 D4 6 12 S 39 12 E
Zanzūr, *Libya* 96 B2 32 55N 13 1 E
Zaouiet El-Kala = Bordj Omar Driss, *Algeria* 99 C6 28 10N 6 40 E
Zaouiet Reggane, *Algeria* 99 C5 26 32N 0 3 E
Zaoyang, *China* 69 A9 32 10N 112 45 E
Zaozhuang, *China* 67 G9 34 50N 117 35 E
Zapadna Morava →, *Serbia, Yug.* 42 D6 43 38N 21 30 E
Zapadnaya Dvina, *Russia* 50 C8 56 15N 32 3 E
Zapadnaya Dvina →, *Belorussia* 50 C4 55 35N 28 10 E
Západné Beskydy, *Europe* 31 B12 49 30N 19 0 E
Zapadni Rodopi, *Bulgaria* 43 F8 41 50N 24 0 E
Západočeský □, *Czech.* 30 B6 49 35N 13 0 E
Západoslovenský □, *Czech.* 31 C10 48 30N 17 30 E

288 Zapala


Zapala, Argentina 160 A2 39 0 S 70 5W
Zapaleri, Cerro, Bolivia 158 A2 22 49 S 67 11W
Zapata, U.S.A. 139 M5 26 56N 99 17W
Zapatón →, Spain 37 G4 39 0N 6 49W
Zapiga, Chile 156 D4 19 40 S 69 55W
Zapolyarnyy, Russia 48 A5 69 26N 30 51 E
Zaporozhye, Ukraine 52 C6 47 50N 35 10 E
Zapponeta, Italy 41 A8 41 27N 15 57 E
Zara, Turkey 89 D7 39 58N 37 43 E
Zaragoza, Colombia 152 B3 7 30N 74 52W
Zaragoza, Coahuila, Mexico 146 B4 28 30N 101 0W
Zaragoza, Nuevo León, Mexico 147 C5 24 0N 99 46W
Zaragoza, Spain 34 D4 41 39N 0 53W
Zaragoza □, Spain 34 D4 41 35N 1 0W
Zarand, Kermān, Iran 85 D8 30 46N 56 34 E
Zarand, Markazī, Iran 85 C6 35 18N 50 25 E
Zărandului, Munţii, Romania 46 C3 46 14N 22 7 E
Zaranj, Afghan. 79 C1 30 55N 61 55 E
Zarasai, Lithuania 50 D5 55 40N 26 20 E
Zarate, Argentina 158 C4 34 7 S 59 0W
Zaraysk, Russia 51 D11 54 48N 38 53 E
Zaraza, Venezuela 153 B4 9 21N 65 19W
Zāreh, Iran 85 C6 35 7N 49 9 E
Zarembo I., U.S.A. 130 B2 56 20N 132 50W
Zaria, Nigeria 101 C6 11 0N 7 40 E
Zárkon, Greece 44 E4 39 38N 22 6 E
Zarneh, Iran 84 C5 33 55N 46 10 E
Zarós, Greece 32 D6 35 8N 24 54 E
Żarów, Poland 47 E3 50 56N 16 29 E
Zarqā' →, Jordan 91 C4 32 10N 35 37 E
Zarrīn, Iran 85 C7 32 46N 54 37 E
Zaruma, Ecuador 152 D2 3 40 S 79 38W
Żary, Poland 47 D2 51 37N 15 10 E
Zarza de Alange, Spain 37 G4 38 49N 6 13W
Zarza de Granadilla, Spain 36 E4 40 14N 6 3W
Zarzaïtine, Algeria 99 C6 28 15N 9 34 E
Zarzal, Colombia 152 C2 4 24N 76 4W
Zarzis, Tunisia 96 B2 33 31N 11 2 E
Zas, Spain 36 B2 43 4N 8 53W
Zashiversk, Russia 57 C15 67 25N 142 40 E
Zaskar →, India 81 B7 34 13N 77 20 E
Zaskar Mts., India 81 C7 33 15N 77 30 E
Zastron, S. Africa 104 E4 30 18 S 27 7 E
Žatec, Czech. 30 A6 50 20N 13 32 E
Zator, Poland 31 B12 49 59N 19 28 E
Zavala, Bos.-H., Yug. 42 E2 42 50N 17 59 E
Zavāreh, Iran 85 C7 33 29N 52 28 E
Zaventem, Belgium 21 G4 50 53N 4 28 E
Zavetnoye, Russia 53 C10 47 13N 43 50 E
Zavidovići, Bos.-H., Yug. 42 C3 44 27N 18 13 E
Zavitinsk, Russia 57 D13 50 10N 129 20 E
Zavodovski, I., Antarctica 7 B1 56 0 S 27 45W
Zavolzhsk, Russia 51 C13 57 30N 42 0 E
Zavolzhye, Russia 51 C13 56 37N 43 26 E
Zawadzkie, Poland 47 E5 50 37N 18 28 E
Zawichost, Poland 47 E8 50 48N 21 51 E
Zawidów, Poland 47 D2 51 1N 15 1 E
Zawiercie, Poland 47 E6 50 30N 19 24 E
Zāwiyat al Bayḑā, Libya 96 B4 32 30N 21 40 E
Zāwiyat Masūs, Libya 96 B4 31 35N 21 1 E
Zawyet Shammâs, Egypt 94 A2 31 30N 26 37 E
Zâwyet Um el Rakham, Egypt 94 A2 31 18N 27 1 E
Zâwyet Ungeîla, Egypt 94 A2 31 23N 26 42 E
Zāyā, Iraq 84 C5 33 33N 44 13 E
Zayarsk, Russia 57 D11 56 12N 102 55 E
Zaymah, Si. Arabia 86 B3 21 37N 40 6 E
Zaysan, Kazakhstan 56 E9 47 28N 84 52 E
Zaysan, Oz., Kazakhstan 56 E9 48 0N 83 0 E
Zayü, China 68 C1 28 48N 97 27 E
Zāzamt, W. →, Libya 96 B2 30 29N 14 30 E
Zazir, O. →, Algeria 99 D6 22 0N 5 40 E
Zázrivá, Czech. 31 B12 49 16N 19 7 E
Zbarazh, Ukraine 50 G4 49 43N 25 44 E
Zbąszyń, Poland 47 C2 52 14N 15 56 E
Zbąszynek, Poland 47 C2 52 16N 15 51 E
Zblewo, Poland 47 B5 53 56N 18 19 E
Zdolbunov, Ukraine 50 F5 50 30N 26 15 E
Ždrelo, Serbia, Yug. 42 C6 44 16N 21 28 E
Zduńska Wola, Poland 47 D5 51 37N 18 59 E
Zduny, Poland 47 D4 51 39N 17 21 E
Zearing, U.S.A. 140 B3 42 10N 93 20W
Zeballos, Canada 130 D3 49 59N 126 50W
Zebediela, S. Africa 105 C4 24 20 S 29 17 E
Zedelgem, Belgium 21 F2 51 8N 3 8 E
Zeebrugge, Belgium 21 F2 51 19N 3 12 E
Zeehan, Australia 114 G4 41 52 S 145 25 E
Zeeland, Neths. 21 E7 51 41N 5 40 E
Zeeland, U.S.A. 141 B10 42 49N 86 1W
Zeeland □, Neths. 21 F3 51 30N 3 50 E
Zeelst, Neths. 21 F6 51 25N 5 25 E
Zeerust, S. Africa 104 D4 25 31 S 26 4 E
Zefat, Israel 91 C4 32 58N 35 29 E
Zegdou, Algeria 98 C4 29 51N 4 45W
Zege, Ethiopia 95 E4 11 43N 37 18 E
Zegelsem, Belgium 21 G3 50 49N 3 43 E
Zégoua, Mali 100 C3 10 32N 5 35W
Zehdenick, Germany 26 C9 52 59N 13 20 E
Zeigler, U.S.A. 140 G7 37 55N 89 5W
Zeil, Mt., Australia 112 D5 23 30 S 132 23 E
Zeila, Somali Rep. 90 E3 11 21N 43 30 E
Zeist, Neths. 20 D6 52 5N 5 15 E
Zeitz, Germany 26 D8 51 3N 12 9 E
Zele, Belgium 21 F4 51 4N 4 2 E
Żelechów, Poland 47 D8 51 49N 21 54 E
Zelee, C., Solomon Is. 121 M11 9 44 S 161 34 E
Zelengora, Bos.-H., Yug. 42 D3 43 22N 18 30 E
Zelenika, Montenegro, Yug. 42 E3 42 27N 18 37 E
Zelenodolsk, Russia 51 D16 55 55N 48 30 E
Zelenograd, Russia 51 C10 56 1N 37 12 E
Zelenogradsk, Russia 50 D2 54 53N 20 29 E
Zelenokumsk, Russia 53 D10 44 24N 44 0 E
Zelënyy, Kazakhstan 53 B14 48 6N 50 45 E
Zeleznik, Serbia, Yug. 42 C5 44 43N 20 23 E
Zelhem, Neths. 20 D8 52 2N 6 21 E
Zell, Baden-W., Germany 27 H3 47 42N 7 50 E
Zell, Rhld-Pfz., Germany 27 E3 50 2N 7 11 E
Zell am See, Austria 30 D5 47 19N 12 47 E
Zella Mehlis, Germany 26 E6 50 40N 10 41 E
Zelów, Poland 47 D6 51 28N 19 14 E
Zelzate, Belgium 21 F3 51 13N 3 47 E
Zembra, I., Tunisia 96 A2 37 5N 10 56 E
Zémio, C.A.R. 102 A5 5 2N 25 5 E
Zemmora, Algeria 99 A5 35 44N 0 51 E
Zemmur, W. Sahara 98 C2 25 5N 12 0W
Zemoul, O. →, Algeria 98 C3 29 15N 7 0W
Zemst, Belgium 21 G4 50 59N 4 28 E
Zemun, Serbia, Yug. 42 C5 44 51N 20 25 E
Zendeh Jān, Afghan. 79 B1 34 21N 61 45 E
Zengbe, Cameroon 101 D7 5 46N 13 4 E
Zengcheng, China 69 F9 23 13N 113 52 E
Zenica, Bos.-H., Yug. 42 C2 44 10N 17 57 E
Zenina, Algeria 99 B5 34 30N 2 37 E
Zentsūji, Japan 62 C5 34 14N 133 47 E
Zenza do Itombe, Angola 103 D2 9 16 S 14 13 E
Žepče, Bos.-H., Yug. 42 C3 44 28N 18 2 E
Zeraf, Bahr ez →, Sudan 95 F3 9 42N 30 52 E
Zeravshan, Tajikistan 55 D4 39 10N 68 39 E
Zeravshanskiy, Khrebet, Tajikistan 55 D4 39 20N 69 0 E
Zerbst, Germany 26 D8 51 59N 12 8 E
Żerków, Poland 47 C4 52 4N 17 32 E
Zermatt, Switz. 28 D5 46 2N 7 46 E
Zernez, Switz. 29 C10 46 42N 10 7 E
Zernograd, Russia 53 C9 46 52N 40 19 E
Zerqani, Albania 44 C2 41 30N 20 20 E
Zestafoni, Georgia 53 E10 42 6N 43 0 E
Zetel, Germany 26 B3 53 25N 7 57 E
Zetten, Neths. 20 E7 51 56N 5 44 E
Zeulenroda, Germany 26 E7 50 39N 12 0 E
Zeven, Germany 26 B5 53 17N 9 19 E
Zevenaar, Neths. 20 E8 51 56N 6 5 E
Zevenbergen, Neths. 21 E5 51 38N 4 37 E
Zévio, Italy 38 C8 45 23N 11 10 E
Zeya, Russia 57 D13 53 48N 127 14 E
Zeya →, Russia 57 D13 51 42N 128 53 E
Zêzere →, Portugal 37 F2 39 28N 8 20W
Zghartā, Lebanon 91 A4 34 21N 35 53 E
Zgierz, Poland 47 D6 51 50N 19 27 E
Zgorzelec, Poland 47 D2 51 10N 15 0 E
Zhabinka, Belorussia 50 E4 52 13N 24 2 E
Zhailma, Kazakhstan 54 F7 51 37N 61 33 E
Zhalanash, Kazakhstan 55 B9 43 3N 78 38 E
Zhanadarya, Kazakhstan 55 A2 44 45N 64 40 E
Zhanatas, Kazakhstan 55 B4 43 35N 69 35 E
Zhangbei, China 66 D8 41 10N 114 45 E
Zhangguangcai Ling, China 67 B15 45 0N 129 0 E
Zhanghua, Taiwan 69 E13 24 6N 120 29 E
Zhangjiakou, China 66 D8 40 48N 114 55 E
Zhangping, China 69 E11 25 17N 117 23 E
Zhangpu, China 69 E11 24 8N 117 35 E
Zhangwu, China 67 C12 42 43N 123 52 E
Zhangye, China 64 C5 38 50N 100 23 E
Zhangzhou, China 69 E11 24 30N 117 35 E
Zhanhua, China 67 F10 37 40N 118 8 E
Zhanjiang, China 69 G8 21 15N 110 20 E
Zhanyi, China 68 E4 25 38N 103 48 E
Zhanyu, China 67 B12 44 30N 122 30 E
Zhao Xian, China 66 F8 37 43N 114 45 E
Zhao'an, China 69 F11 23 41N 117 10 E
Zhaocheng, China 66 F6 36 22N 111 38 E
Zhaojue, China 68 C4 28 1N 102 49 E
Zhaoping, China 69 E8 24 11N 110 48 E
Zhaoqing, China 69 F9 23 0N 112 20 E
Zhaotong, China 68 D4 27 20N 103 44 E
Zhaoyuan, Heilongjiang, China 67 B13 45 27N 125 0 E
Zhaoyuan, Shandong, China 67 F11 37 20N 120 23 E
Zharkol, Kazakhstan 54 G9 49 57N 64 5 E
Zharkovskiy, Russia 50 D8 55 56N 32 19 E
Zhashkov, Ukraine 52 B4 49 15N 30 5 E
Zhashui, China 66 H5 33 40N 109 8 E
Zhdanov = Mariupol, Ukraine 52 C7 47 5N 37 31 E
Zhecheng, China 66 G8 34 7N 115 20 E
Zhegao, China 69 B11 31 46N 117 45 E
Zhejiang □, China 69 C13 29 0N 120 0 E
Zheleznodorozhny, Russia 48 B9 62 35N 50 55 E
Zheleznogorsk, Russia 50 E9 52 22N 35 23 E
Zheleznogorsk-Ilimskiy, Russia 57 D11 56 34N 104 8 E
Zheltyye Vody, Ukraine 52 B5 48 21N 33 31 E
Zhen'an, China 66 H5 33 27N 109 9 E
Zhenfeng, China 68 E5 25 22N 105 40 E
Zheng'an, China 68 C6 28 32N 107 27 E
Zhengding, China 66 E8 38 8N 114 32 E
Zhenghe, China 69 D12 27 20N 118 50 E
Zhengyang, China 69 A10 32 37N 114 22 E
Zhengyangguan, China 69 A11 32 30N 116 29 E
Zhengzhou, China 66 G7 34 45N 113 34 E
Zhenhai, China 69 C13 29 59N 121 42 E
Zhenjiang, China 69 A12 32 11N 119 26 E
Zhenlai, China 67 B12 45 50N 123 5 E
Zhenning, China 68 D5 26 4N 105 45 E
Zhenping, Henan, China 66 H7 33 10N 112 16 E
Zhenping, Shaanxi, China 68 B7 31 59N 109 31 E
Zhenxiong, China 68 D5 27 27N 104 50 E
Zhenyuan, Gansu, China 66 G4 35 35N 107 30 E
Zhenyuan, Guizhou, China 68 D7 27 4N 108 21 E
Zherdevka, Russia 51 F12 51 56N 41 29 E
Zherong, China 69 D12 27 15N 119 52 E
Zhetykol, Ozero, Russia 54 F7 51 2N 60 54 E
Zhidan, China 66 F5 36 48N 108 48 E
Zhigansk, Russia 57 C13 66 48N 123 27 E
Zhigulevsk, Russia 51 E16 53 28N 49 30 E
Zhijiang, Hubei, China 69 B8 30 28N 111 45 E
Zhijiang, Hunan, China 68 D7 27 27N 109 42 E
Zhijin, China 68 D5 26 37N 105 45 E
Zhirnovsk, Russia 51 F14 50 57N 44 49 E
Zhitomir, Ukraine 50 F6 50 20N 28 40 E
Zhizdra, Russia 50 E9 53 45N 34 40 E
Zhlobin, Belorussia 50 E6 52 55N 30 0 E
Zhmerinka, Ukraine 52 B3 49 2N 28 2 E
Zhodino, Belorussia 50 D6 54 5N 28 17 E
Zhokhova, Ostrov, Russia 57 B16 76 4N 152 40 E
Zhong Xian, China 68 B7 30 21N 108 1 E
Zhongdian, China 68 D2 27 48N 99 42 E
Zhongdong, China 68 F6 22 48N 107 47 E
Zhongdu, China 68 E7 24 40N 109 40 E
Zhongning, China 66 F3 37 29N 105 40 E
Zhongshan, Guangdong, China 69 F9 22 26N 113 20 E
Zhongshan, Guangxi Zhuangzu, China 69 E8 24 29N 111 18 E
Zhongtiao Shan, China 66 G6 35 0N 111 10 E
Zhongwei, China 66 F3 37 30N 105 12 E
Zhongxiang, China 69 B9 31 12N 112 34 E
Zhongyang, China 66 F6 37 20N 111 11 E
Zhoucun, China 67 F9 36 47N 117 48 E
Zhouning, China 69 D12 27 12N 119 20 E
Zhoushan Dao, China 69 C14 28 5N 122 10 E
Zhouzhi, China 66 G5 34 10N 108 12 E
Zhovtnevoye, Ukraine 52 C5 46 54N 32 3 E
Zhuanghe, China 67 E12 39 40N 123 0 E
Zhuantobe, Kazakhstan 55 B9 43 43N 78 18 E
Zhucheng, China 67 G10 36 0N 119 27 E
Zhugqu, China 66 H3 33 40N 104 30 E
Zhuhai, China 69 F9 22 15N 113 30 E
Zhuji, China 69 C13 29 40N 120 10 E
Zhukovka, Russia 50 E8 53 35N 33 50 E
Zhumadian, China 66 H8 32 59N 114 2 E
Zhuo Xian, China 66 E8 39 28N 115 58 E
Zhuolu, China 66 D8 40 20N 115 12 E
Zhuozi, China 66 D7 41 0N 112 25 E
Zhupanovo, Russia 57 D16 53 40N 159 52 E
Zhushan, China 69 A8 32 15N 110 13 E
Zhuxi, China 68 A7 32 25N 109 40 E
Zhuzhou, China 69 D9 27 49N 113 12 E
Zi Shui →, China 69 C9 28 40N 112 40 E
Zīārān, Iran 85 B6 36 7N 50 32 E
Ziarat, Pakistan 80 D2 30 25N 67 49 E
Zibo, China 67 F10 36 47N 118 3 E
Zichang, China 66 F5 37 18N 109 40 E
Zichem, Belgium 21 F5 51 2N 4 59 E
Zidarovo, Bulgaria 43 E12 42 20N 27 24 E
Ziębice, Poland 47 E4 50 37N 17 2 E
Zielona Góra, Poland 47 D2 51 57N 15 31 E
Zielona Góra □, Poland 47 D2 51 57N 15 30 E
Zierikzee, Neths. 21 E3 51 40N 3 55 E
Ziesar, Germany 26 C8 52 16N 12 19 E
Zifta, Egypt 94 H7 30 43N 31 14 E
Zigazinskiy, Russia 54 E5 53 50N 57 20 E
Zigey, Chad 97 F3 14 43N 15 50 E
Zigong, China 68 C5 29 15N 104 48 E
Zigui, China 69 B8 31 0N 110 40 E
Ziguinchor, Senegal 100 C1 12 35N 16 20W
Zihuatanejo, Mexico 146 D4 17 38N 101 33W
Zijin, China 69 F10 23 33N 115 8 E
Zile, Turkey 88 C6 40 15N 35 52 E
Žilina, Czech. 31 B11 49 12N 18 42 E
Zillah, Libya 96 C3 28 30N 17 33 E
Zillertaler Alpen, Austria 30 D4 47 6N 11 45 E
Zima, Russia 57 D11 54 0N 102 5 E
Zimane, Adrar in, Algeria 99 D5 22 10N 4 30 E
Zimapán, Mexico 147 C5 20 54N 99 20W
Zimba, Zambia 107 F2 17 20 S 26 11 E
Zimbabwe, Zimbabwe 107 G3 20 16 S 30 54 E
Zimbabwe ■, Africa 107 F2 19 0 S 30 0 E
Zimnicea, Romania 46 F6 43 40N 25 22 E
Zimovniki, Russia 53 C10 47 10N 42 25 E
Zinal, Switz. 28 D5 46 8N 7 38 E
Zinder, Niger 97 F1 13 48N 9 0 E
Zinga, Tanzania 107 D4 9 16 S 38 49 E
Zingem, Belgium 21 G3 50 54N 3 40 E
Zingst, Germany 26 A8 54 24N 12 45 E
Ziniaré, Burkina Faso 101 C4 12 35N 1 18W
Zinkgruvan, Sweden 15 F9 58 50N 15 6 E
Zinnowitz, Germany 26 A9 54 5N 13 54 E
Zion, U.S.A. 141 B9 42 27N 87 50W
Zion Nat. Park, U.S.A. 143 H7 37 25N 112 50W
Zionsville, U.S.A. 141 E10 39 57N 86 16W
Zipaquirá, Colombia 152 C3 5 0N 74 0W
Zirc, Hungary 31 D10 47 17N 17 42 E
Žiri, Slovenia 39 B11 46 5N 14 5 E
Žirje, Croatia 39 E12 43 39N 15 42 E
Zirl, Austria 30 D4 47 17N 11 14 E
Ziros, Greece 32 D8 35 5N 26 8 E
Zisterdorf, Austria 31 C9 48 33N 16 45 E
Zitácuaro, Mexico 146 D4 19 28N 100 21W
Zitava →, Czech. 31 C11 48 14N 18 21 E
Žitište, Serbia, Yug. 42 B5 45 30N 20 32 E
Zítsa, Greece 44 E2 39 47N 20 40 E
Zittau, Germany 26 E10 50 54N 14 47 E
Zitundo, Mozam. 105 D5 26 48 S 32 47 E
Živinice, Bos.-H., Yug. 42 C3 44 27N 18 36 E
Ziway, L., Ethiopia 95 F4 8 0N 38 50 E
Zixi, China 69 D11 27 45N 117 4 E
Zixing, China 69 E9 25 59N 113 21 E
Ziyang, Shaanxi, China 66 H5 32 32N 108 31 E
Ziyang, Sichuan, China 68 B5 30 6N 104 40 E
Ziyun, China 68 E6 25 45N 106 5 E
Ziz, Oued →, Morocco 98 B4 31 40N 4 15W
Zizhixian, China 69 E8 25 0N 111 47 E
Zizhong, China 68 C5 29 48N 104 47 E
Zlarin, Croatia 39 E12 43 42N 15 49 E
Zlatar, Croatia 39 B13 46 5N 16 3 E
Zlatar, Serbia, Yug. 42 D4 43 25N 19 47 E
Zlataritsa, Bulgaria 43 D10 43 2N 25 55 E
Zlatibor, Serbia, Yug. 42 D4 43 45N 19 43 E
Zlatitsa, Bulgaria 43 E9 42 41N 24 7 E
Zlatna, Romania 46 C4 46 8N 23 11 E
Zlatograd, Bulgaria 43 F10 41 22N 25 7 E
Zlatoust, Russia 54 D6 55 10N 59 40 E
Zletovo, Macedonia, Yug. 42 F7 41 59N 22 17 E
Zlin = Gottwaldov, Czech. 31 B10 49 14N 17 40 E
Zlītan, Libya 96 B2 32 32N 14 35 E
Złocieniec, Poland 47 B3 53 30N 16 1 E
Złoczew, Poland 47 D5 51 24N 18 35 E
Zlot, Serbia, Yug. 42 C6 44 1N 21 58 E
Złotoryja, Poland 47 D2 51 8N 15 55 E
Złotów, Poland 47 B4 53 22N 17 2 E
Złoty Stok, Poland 47 E3 50 27N 16 53 E
Zmeinogorsk, Kazakhstan 56 D9 51 10N 82 13 E
Żmigród, Poland 47 D3 51 28N 16 53 E
Zmiyev, Ukraine 52 B7 49 39N 36 27 E
Znamenka, Ukraine 52 B5 48 45N 32 30 E
Znamensk, Russia 50 D2 54 37N 21 17 E
Żnin, Poland 47 C4 52 51N 17 44 E
Znojmo, Czech. 30 C9 48 50N 16 2 E
Zoar, S. Africa 104 E3 33 30 S 21 26 E
Zobeyrī, Iran 84 C5 34 10N 46 40 E
Zobia, Zaïre 106 B2 3 0N 25 59 E
Zoetermeer, Neths. 20 D5 52 3N 4 30 E
Zofingen, Switz. 28 B5 47 17N 7 56 E
Zogang, China 68 C1 29 55N 97 42 E
Zogno, Italy 38 C6 45 49N 9 41 E
Zogqên, China 68 A2 32 13N 98 47 E
Zolder, Belgium 21 F6 51 1N 5 19 E
Zollikofen, Switz. 28 C4 47 0N 7 28 E
Zollikon, Switz. 29 B7 47 21N 8 34 E
Zolochev, Ukraine 50 G4 49 45N 24 51 E
Zolotonosha, Ukraine 52 B5 49 39N 32 5 E
Zomba, Malawi 107 F4 15 22 S 35 19 E
Zomergem, Belgium 21 F3 51 7N 3 33 E
Zongo, Zaïre 102 B3 4 20N 18 35 E
Zonguldak, Turkey 52 F4 41 28N 31 50 E
Zonguldak □, Turkey 88 C4 41 20N 31 45 E
Zonhoven, Belgium 21 G6 50 59N 5 23 E
Zonqor Pt., Malta 32 D2 35 51N 14 34 E
Zonza, France 25 G13 41 45N 9 11 E
Zorgo, Burkina Faso 101 C4 12 15N 0 35W
Zorita, Spain 37 F5 39 17N 5 39W
Zorleni, Romania 46 C8 46 14N 27 44 E
Zornitsa, Bulgaria 43 E11 42 23N 26 58 E
Zorritos, Peru 156 A1 3 43 S 80 40W
Zory, Poland 31 A11 50 3N 18 44 E
Zorzor, Liberia 100 D3 7 46N 9 28W
Zossen, Germany 26 C9 52 13N 13 28 E
Zottegem, Belgium 21 G3 50 52N 3 48 E
Zou Xiang, China 66 G9 35 30N 116 58 E
Zouar, Chad 97 D3 20 30N 16 32 E
Zouérate, Mauritania 98 D2 22 44N 12 21W
Zousfana, O. →, Algeria 99 B4 31 28N 2 17W
Zoushan Dao, China 69 B14 30 5N 122 10 E
Zoutkamp, Neths. 20 B8 53 20N 6 18 E
Zrenjanin, Serbia, Yug. 42 B5 45 22N 20 23 E
Zuarungu, Ghana 101 C4 10 49N 0 46W
Zuba, Nigeria 101 D6 9 11N 7 12 E
Zubayr, Yemen 86 D3 15 3N 42 10 E
Zubia, Spain 37 H7 37 8N 3 33W
Zubtsov, Russia 50 C9 56 10N 34 34 E
Zudáñez, Bolivia 157 D5 19 6 S 64 44W
Zuénoula, Ivory C. 100 D3 7 34N 6 3W
Zuera, Spain 34 D4 41 51N 0 49W
Zuetina, Libya 96 B4 30 58N 20 7 E
Zufar, Oman 87 C6 17 40N 54 0 E
Zug, Switz. 29 B7 47 10N 8 31 E
Zug □, Switz. 29 B7 47 9N 8 35 E
Zugdidi, Georgia 53 E9 42 30N 41 55 E
Zugersee, Switz. 29 B7 47 7N 8 35 E
Zugspitze, Germany 27 H6 47 25N 10 59 E
Zuid-Holland □, Neths. 20 E5 52 0N 4 35 E
Zuidbeveland, Neths. 21 F3 51 30N 3 50 E
Zuidbroek, Neths. 20 B9 53 10N 6 52 E
Zuidelijk-Flevoland, Neths. 20 D6 52 22N 5 22 E
Zuidhorn, Neths. 20 B8 53 15N 6 23 E
Zuidlaardermeer, Neths. 20 B9 53 8N 6 42 E
Zuidlaren, Neths. 20 B9 53 6N 6 42 E
Zuidwolde, Neths. 20 C8 52 40N 6 26 E
Zújar, Spain 35 H2 37 34N 2 50W
Zújar →, Spain 37 F5 39 1N 5 47W
Zújar, Pantano del, Spain 37 G5 38 55N 5 35W
Zula, Ethiopia 95 D4 15 17N 39 40 E
Zulia □, Venezuela 152 B3 10 0N 72 10W
Zulpich, Germany 26 E2 50 41N 6 38 E
Zumaya, Spain 34 B2 43 19N 2 15W
Zumbo, Mozam. 107 F3 15 35 S 30 26 E
Zummo, Nigeria 101 D7 9 51N 12 59 E
Zumpango, Mexico 147 D5 19 48N 99 6W
Zundert, Neths. 21 F5 51 28N 4 39 E
Zungeru, Nigeria 101 D6 9 48N 6 8 E
Zunhua, China 67 D9 40 18N 117 58 E
Zuni, U.S.A. 143 J9 35 7N 108 57W
Zunyi, China 68 D6 27 42N 106 53 E
Zuoquan, China 66 F7 37 5N 113 22 E
Zuozhou, China 68 F6 22 42N 107 27 E
Županja, Croatia 42 B3 45 4N 18 43 E
Žur, Serbia, Yug. 42 E5 42 13N 20 34 E
Zura, Russia 54 C3 57 36N 53 24 E
Zurbātīyah, Iraq 84 C5 33 9N 46 3 E
Zürich, Switz. 29 B7 47 22N 8 32 E
Zürich □, Switz. 29 B7 47 26N 8 40 E
Zürichsee, Switz. 29 B7 47 18N 8 40 E
Zuromin, Poland 47 B6 53 4N 19 51 E
Zuru, Nigeria 101 C6 11 20N 5 11 E
Zurzach, Switz. 29 A6 47 35N 8 18 E
Žut, Croatia 39 E12 43 52N 15 17 E
Zutendaal, Belgium 21 G7 50 56N 5 35 E
Zutphen, Neths. 20 D8 52 9N 6 12 E
Zuwārah, Libya 96 B2 32 58N 12 1 E
Zuyevka, Russia 54 B2 58 27N 51 10 E
Zūzan, Iran 85 C8 34 22N 59 53 E
Žužemberk, Slovenia 39 C11 45 52N 14 56 E
Zvenigorodka, Ukraine 52 B4 49 4N 30 56 E
Zverinogolovskoye, Russia 54 D9 54 23N 64 40 E
Zvezdets, Bulgaria 43 E12 42 6N 27 26 E
Zvishavane, Zimbabwe 107 G3 20 17 S 30 2 E
Zvolen, Czech. 31 C12 48 33N 19 10 E
Zvonce, Serbia, Yug. 42 E7 42 57N 22 34 E
Zvornik, Bos.-H., Yug. 42 C4 44 26N 19 7 E
Zwaag, Neths. 20 C6 52 40N 5 4 E
Zwanenburg, Neths. 20 D5 52 23N 4 45 E
Zwarte Meer, Neths. 20 C7 52 38N 5 57 E
Zwarte Water, Neths. 20 C8 52 39N 6 7 E
Zwartemeer, Neths. 20 C10 52 43N 7 2 E
Zwartsluis, Neths. 20 C8 52 39N 6 4 E
Zwedru = Tchien, Liberia 100 D3 5 59N 8 15W
Zweibrücken, Germany 27 F3 49 15N 7 20 E
Zwenkau, Germany 26 D8 51 13N 12 19 E
Zwettl, Austria 30 C8 48 35N 15 9 E
Zwevegem, Belgium 21 G2 50 48N 3 20 E
Zwickau, Germany 26 E8 50 43N 12 30 E
Zwiesel, Germany 27 F9 49 1N 13 14 E
Zwijnaarde, Belgium 21 F3 51 0N 3 43 E
Zwijndrecht, Belgium 21 F4 51 13N 4 20 E
Zwijndrecht, Neths. 20 E5 51 50N 4 39 E
Zwischenahn, Germany 26 B4 53 12N 8 1 E
Zwoleń, Poland 47 D8 51 21N 21 36 E
Zwolle, Neths. 20 C8 52 31N 6 6 E
Zwolle, U.S.A. 139 K8 31 38N 93 38W
Żychlin, Poland 47 C6 52 15N 19 37 E
Zymoetz →, Canada 130 C3 54 33N 128 31W
Żyrardów, Poland 47 C7 52 3N 20 28 E
Zyrya, Azerbaijan 53 F14 40 20N 50 15 E
Zyryanka, Russia 57 C16 65 45N 150 51 E
Zyryanovsk, Kazakhstan 56 E9 49 43N 84 20 E
Żywiec, Poland 31 B12 49 42N 19 10 E
Zyyi, Cyprus 32 E12 34 43N 33 20 E

**NORTH AMERICA**

**ARCTIC OCEAN** 6

126-127

12

130-131

128-129

142-143  138-139  134-135

136-137

144-145  140-141

98-99

*ATLANTIC OCEAN*
**ATLANTIC OCEAN** 8-9

148-149

Tropic of Cancer

132

**PACIFIC OCEAN** 122-123

146-147

152-153

100-101

Equator

**AFRICA**

154-155

**SOUTH AMERICA**

156-157

Tropic of Capricorn

*PACIFIC OCEAN*

158-159

**KEY TO WORLD MAP PAGES**

160